LIVIA

LIVIA

FIRST LADY OF IMPERIAL ROME

ANTHONY A. BARRETT

Yale University Press
New Haven & London

Designed by Nancy Ovedovitz and set in Janson Oldstyle type by Keystone Typesetting, Inc., Orwigsburg, Pennsylvania.
Printed in the United States of America.

Library of Congress Cataloging-in-Publication Data
Barrett, Anthony, 1941–
Livia: first lady of Imperial Rome / Anthony A. Barrett.
p. cm.
Includes bibliographical references and index.
ISBN 0-300-09196-6 (alk. paper)
1. Livia, Empress, consort of Augustus, Emperor of Rome, ca. 58 B.C.–A.D. 29.
2. Empresses — Rome — Biography.
3. Rome — History — Augustus, 30 B.C.–A.D. 14. I. Title.
DG291.7.L5 B37 2002
937′.07′092 — dc21 2002003073

A catalogue record for this book is available from the British Library.

The paper in this book meets the guidelines for permanence and durability of the Committee on Production Guidelines for Book Longevity of the Council on Library Resources.

10 9 8 7 6 5 4 3 2 1

CONTENTS

ILLUSTRATIONS

FIGURES

PLANS

STEMMATA

PREFACE

If the general public has any impression of Livia, the wife of the first Roman emperor, Augustus, it is of the character created by the Welsh actress Siân Phillips in the highly acclaimed BBC-TV production of *I, Claudius*, first broadcast in 1976. This popular confusion between the historical and the fictional is hardly surprising, given Phillips' riveting performance. Cunning and sinister, her Livia devotes every waking hour to her consuming interests: plotting, scheming, conniving, and the cheerful eradication of an assorted variety of fellow citizens, be they strangers, friends, or even close family.

One of the burdens shouldered by the modern historian is that of correcting false impressions created by the popular media, particularly dangerous when a production is distinguished and the performances brilliant. This process usually involves the thankless task of demonstrating pedantically that, contrary to popular belief, truth is rarely stranger than fiction, and is usually far less exciting. For the historian of the ancient world the undertaking is difficult enough at the best of times, because the truth about any individual who lived some two thousand years ago must, by its very nature, be an elusive entity. But Livia poses a particular challenge. Robert Graves, whose two novels about the imperial family were the basis for the television series, might well have defended the integrity of his portrait by pleading that it rests on impeccable historical foundations, and that he took his lead from Rome's premier historian, Tacitus. But that argument has surprisingly little merit in this specific case. Livia achieves the near-impossible, for she forces us to shift our traditional allegiance and accept the authority not of the normally magisterial Tacitus but of ancient writers whose historical reliability is by and large seriously suspect: Dio, often naive and uncritical; Suetonius, incapable of resisting spicy anecdotes; and Seneca, invariably sycophantic or denigratory, whichever profited him most. On this one topic it is generally recognised that Tacitus was the weak brother, his portrait of Livia vitiated both by his deep-seated contempt for the Julio-Claudian family and by his unshakable conviction that the ambitious woman was evil incarnate.

The historical Livia was a much more complex individual than the cold-blooded schemer that Graves created for *I, Claudius* or that Tacitus created for his *Annals*. The simple fact that she survived intact and unscathed for more than sixty years at the very heart of Roman power—and, perhaps more remarkably, was revered and admired for many generations more after her death—is a testament to her adroit ability to win the support, sympathy and even affection of her contemporaries. Livia could thus be called Rome's first lady in the broad sense, in that no Roman woman before or after her succeeded in evoking a deeper or more long-lasting respect and devotion. She managed to live through a dramatic shift in the Roman constitutional system without creating clearly identifiable enemies—apart, of course, from Tacitus. Perhaps most impressively, she achieved this even though her status and position were never properly defined. Livia is the link between the two reigns that established the basic pattern of government for the Roman empire for the next four centuries. As the wife of Augustus, she was expected to embody the dignity and majesty of the newly created principate, yet at the same time remain a self-effacing and decorous symbol of domestic virtues. In this respect her role was very much that of a first lady in the more narrow American sense, that of someone who plays a public role but does not hold a public position, and indeed is liable to severe criticism should she presume to encroach into the sphere of a public position, and of someone whose domain is a private home but is traditionally expected to represent the domestic values and mores of the whole citizenry. Her position during the reign of the second emperor, her son Tiberius, was even more extraordinary, and presents the scholar with serious challenges. Women, with the possible exception of the Vestal Virgins, could not play a public role in the Roman state, no matter how much power and influence they might exercise informally behind the scenes. By her late husband's will, however, Livia was elevated to a status that brought her very close to an institutional position. Exactly what role he envisaged was not defined, and perhaps was incapable of precise definition—Augustus certainly never attempted it during his lifetime—because it would have been unaccompanied by the traditional powers of official magistrates. In any case, the question was moot, because it was a role, no matter how loosely defined, that Tiberius was unwilling to countenance for his mother. I shall argue that it was this ambiguity in Livia's position, a problem largely created by Augustus, that led to the well-documented tension between mother and son. Their inability to reach a mutually acceptable *modus vivendi* at the very least contributed to Tiberius' eventual decision to leave Rome and all its problems, and to spend much of the last decade of his reign in the less stressful surroundings of Capri.

Outside the field of portraiture and sculpture, Livia has been surprisingly neglected in the English-speaking world. The first biography was Joseph von Aschbach's *Livia: Gemahlin des Kaisers Augustus*, published in Vienna in 1864, and there have been two further German treatments since then. There have been no general studies in English, however, and relatively few articles devoted to her career, the notable exception being the work of Marleen Flory, who before her untimely death published a number of valuable pieces on Livia, especially on the symbolic aspects of her role within the principate. This book is the first biographical study of Livia in English, and it comes with all the usual limitations that afflict biographies, in that by its very nature it offers a lopsided and limited view of a historical period. That conceded, I take the position that noteworthy individuals do affect the course of history and that their influence can be felt for many generations. That is what makes them worth studying, apart from the perfectly legitimate consideration that they are inherently interesting.

I repeat a warning issued in other books in this series. Rumours abounded in antiquity—as they did about other women of the imperial family—that Livia was given to eliminating her opponents by poison. Much ink has been spilt in trying to establish the truth about such ancient poisoning cases, and, regrettably, it has been ink largely wasted. Even in a modern murder investigation, conducted by a professional police force, aided by forensic science and chemical analyses, and tried by a systematic court procedure, it is often impossible to reach a secure verdict where poisoning is suspected. To try to determine the truth in an age when the failure of a heart to burn on the funeral pyre was considered proof of poisoning is clearly futile. Poison was certainly widely used in antiquity, but common sense dictates that in any specific case the only prudent course is to settle for the Scottish verdict of Not Proven, and to rest content with that.

The format of this book is dictated by the nature of the material. The first part follows Livia's life and career and sets it out diachronically within its historical context. The second adopts a more thematic and analytical approach. The sources, both literary and material, are dealt with in an appendix, as are other topics whose analysis would interrupt the flow of the text. The material in the first part of the book will be familiar to those with specialist knowledge of the early period of Roman imperial history. For such individuals, the second part and the appendices are likely to be of more interest. The division into separate parts is not an ideal arrangement, but it offers the only workable solution to a problem imposed by the nature of the evidence. Information about Livia tends to come in spurts. It comes consistently enough to enable us to reconstruct a fairly coherent picture of her life and career, but there is an obvious and unavoidable imbalance in the degree of factual information available for any given period. Certain events, especially those associated with the death of Augustus and the accession of Tiberius, are recorded in a depth of detail not usually available in Roman history. At other times, in particular during the first part of her life, Livia can evade serious notice for years at a time. As a consequence, while we can gain a reasonable sense of her legal and constitutional status within broad chronological frameworks, the evolution of that status is far from clear, and any attempt to interlace it with specific events of her life is bound to fail. Hence the decision to separate the broader thematic discussions from the historical narrative.

A number of concessions have been made for the nonspecialist. Some of the more arcane historical problems are dealt with in the appendices, rather than in the text. Roman *praenomina* (given names) are provided in their full, rather than conventionally abbreviated, forms in the text, though not in the notes or appendices. Translation of Latin and Greek words or phrases that are not self-evident is regularly provided in the text, but, again, not necessarily in the appendices. Identifying markers, such as family relationships, are frequently repeated. Specialists will not need to be constantly reminded, for instance, that Octavia is Augustus' sister or that Drusus is Tiberius' son, but general readers may feel that they benefit from having their memories jogged.

Monetary values are expressed in sesterces. Monetary equivalence is a tricky issue, but, as a rough guide, in the early empire the annual pay for a legionary soldier in the ranks was 900 sesterces.

I have been fortunate in enjoying the help and support of a number of individuals and institutions. Duncan Fishwick guided me on some of the epigraphic problems and kindly made available to me material from his files. Susan Wood provided valuable assistance in the acquisition of plates, and Luigi Pedroni helped with the numismatic material. I am once again indebted to Tony Birley for permission to use his map of the Roman world, with minor adaptations. Michael Griffin aided me with computer problems and with reformatting my text. My friend Karl Sandor read through the finished manuscript and made several observations, invariably to the point and invaluable. Shirley Sullivan and Richard Talbert offered useful thoughts on the book's subtitle. I was assisted by the helpfulness of the staff at a number of institutions, particularly in the libraries of the University of British Columbia and of the Ashmolean Museum, Oxford (now the Sackler Library). I was aided in my work by a research grant from the Social Science and Humanities Research Council of Canada, to which I am pleased to express my gratitude. A special debt is owed the anonymous reader for Yale University Press, who offered sage guidance on the format and organization of the book. Any remaining faults are my own, but they are certainly fewer as a result of that advice. Also, I have benefitted from the industry and keen eye of Dan Heaton, my manuscript editor at the Press, who imposed order and consistency where both tended to be lacking. Finally, my family have once again not only endured the domestic clutter and distraction that such an undertaking invariably brings but have also taken on the task of proofreading with a brave show of cheerfulness.

The Roman World at the Time of the Death of Livia

Danube
MOESIA
HRACIA
PONTUS et
BITHYNIA
GALATIA
CAPPADOCIA
ASIA
Ephesus
LYCIA
CICILIA
thens
Antioch
SYRIA
CYPRUS
TA
JUDAEA
Alexandria
ARABIA
RENE
AEGYPTUS
Nile
Phasis
HIBERI
Artaxata
ARMENIA
Tigris
P A R T H I A
Euphrates
Ctesiphon
Seleucia

SIGNIFICANT EVENTS

63 BC	
September 23	Birth of Augustus
59/58 BC	
January 30	Birth of Livia
44 BC	
March 15	Assassination of Caesar
43 BC?	First marriage of Livia
42 BC	
Autumn	Death of Livia's father at Philippi
November 16	Birth of Tiberius
40 BC	Flight from Italy to Sicily, then Greece
39 BC	
Late summer?	Return to Rome
Autumn	Betrothal to Octavian (Augustus)
38 BC	
January 14	Birth of Drusus
January 17	Marriage to Octavian
36 BC	
September	Livia celebrates the battle of Naulochus

35 BC	Livia and Octavia granted special honours
33/32 BC	Death of Livia's first husband
31 BC	
September	Battle of Actium
	Cleopatra's supposed hope for Livia's intercession
27 BC	
January	The Augustan Settlement
27–24 BC	Livia possibly in Gaul and Spain
22–19 BC	Livia probably in the East
12 BC	
March	Death of Marcus Agrippa
11 BC	Death of Octavia
9 BC	
January 30	Dedication of Ara Pacis
September	Death of Drusus
Autumn?	Livia honoured by special privileges
	Banquet sponsored by Livia for Tiberius
7 BC	
January?	Dedication of Porticus Liviae
6 BC	Retirement of Tiberius to Rhodes
AD 2	Return of Tiberius to Rome
August 20	Death of Lucius Caesar
AD 4	
February 21	Death of Gaius Caesar
June 26	Adoption of Tiberius by Augustus
AD 7	Banishment of Postumus to Planasia
AD 14	
August 19	Death of Augustus
August 20?	Execution of Postumus ordered
September	Adoption of Livia into Julian *gens*
	Assumption of name Julia Augusta
AD 16	Participation of Livia in fighting fires

AD 19	
October 10	Death of Germanicus
AD 20	
May?	Trial of Piso
AD 22	Serious illness of Livia
AD 23	Death of Drusus Caesar
AD 29	Death of Livia
AD 41	Consecration of Livia

PART

I

THE LIFE OF LIVIA

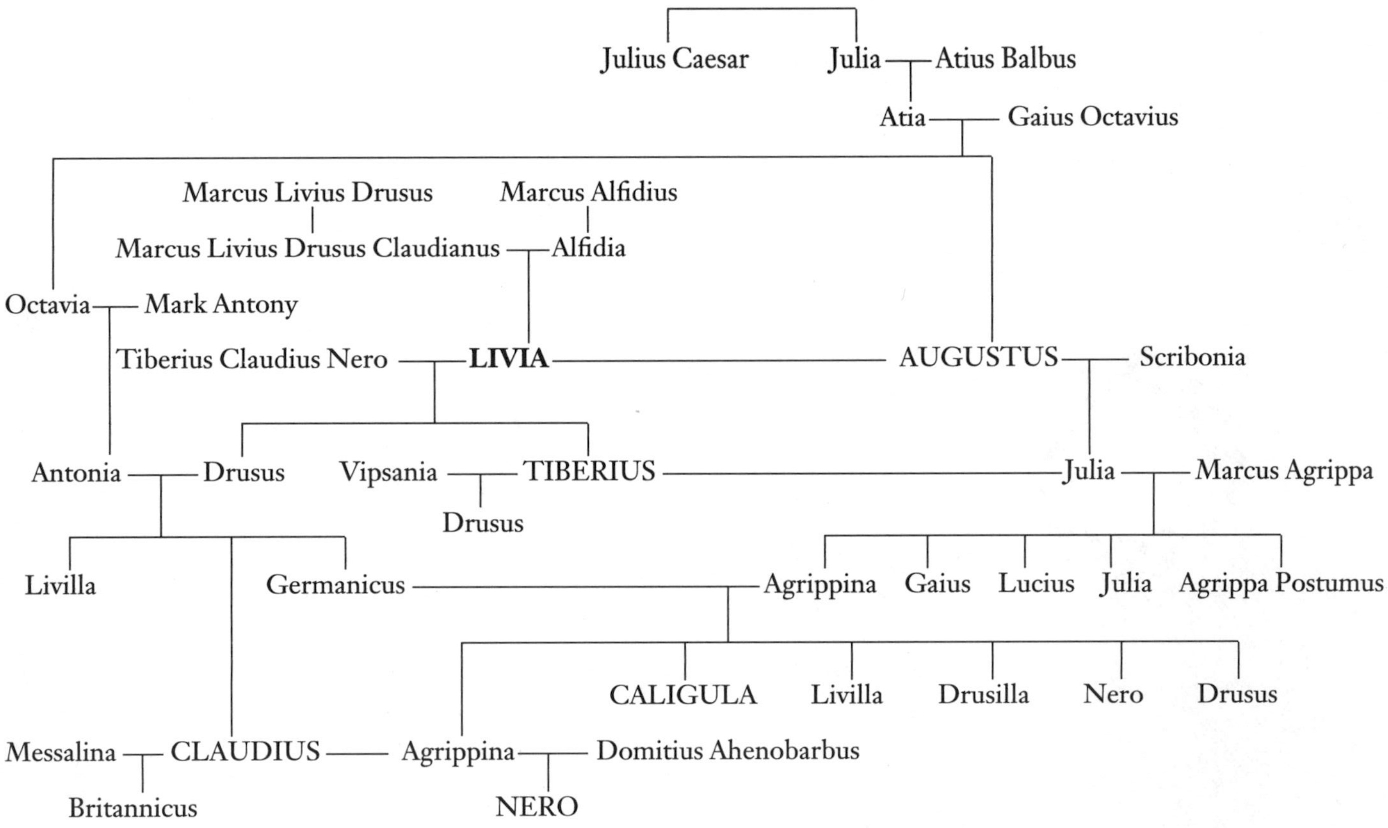

Stemma 1. Livia's significant family connections

I

FAMILY BACKGROUND

The expulsion of the last hated king from Rome, an event dated traditionally to 510 BC, ushered in a republican form of government that was to endure for more than four centuries and which was regarded by later Romans, especially those from the elite levels of society, with pride and an often naive nostalgia. At the outset, Roman society was characterised by a fundamental division between the patricians, who held a virtual monopoly over the organs of power, and the plebeians, who were essentially excluded from the process. Although the power and privileges of the patricians were eroded during the first two centuries of the republic, it is a mistake to think that the system became open and democratic in the modern sense. The removal of the barriers facing ambitious plebeians resulted in a modification of the aristocracy, not its abolition. The chief magistracies became the almost exclusive reserve of a small number of families, whether plebeian or patrician, and the historical record is dominated by a handful of prestigious families, such as the Cornelii or the Julii, who succeeded in keeping a tight grip on the key offices (the system is summarised in appendix 2). Anyone who broke into the closed system and reached the highest office, the consulship, despite lacking a consular ancestor was such a novelty that he was known as a "new man" *(novus homo)*. The popular assemblies, through which legislation had to be enacted and which might seem on the surface to have offered the masses scope to exercise an influence, in fact did little to upset the balance, because a complex voting procedure gave a distinct advantage to the wealthy.

The importance of family background as a virtual prerequisite to success in Roman society can not be overstated, and, as Tacitus acknowledges, few could have rivalled Livia's claim to family distinction.[1] On her father's side, she was descended by blood from one of the proudest and highest-flying of all the great Roman families, the Claudian. According to legend, the family's founder was Clausus, who supposedly helped Aeneas when the Trojan hero sought to establish himself in Italy.[2] In the historical record, the Claudii were in reality immigrants who did well, and their association with the city might be said to begin with the migration to Rome of the Sabine Attus Clausus and all his dependants in 503 BC. Co-opted into the patricians, Attus claimed the first Claudian consulship in 495. Subsequently his descendants would expect, almost as an entitlement, a consulship each generation. Suetonius records that they eventually boasted twenty-eight consulships, five dictatorships, seven censorships, six triumphs, and two ovations.[3] Their family history is a veritable parade of some of the giants of Rome's past. In 451, as a member of the Decemvirate (Commission of Ten Men), Appius Claudius was instrumental in giving Rome its first written legal code. One of his descendants was among the most distinguished and venerated figures of the old republic, and probably the first figure of Roman history to emerge as a clear and distinct personality—Appius Claudius Caecus, consul in 307 and 296. Even when aged and blind he was still consulted as an elder statesman, as on the celebrated occasion when in about 280 BC he addressed the Roman Senate, the senior deliberative and legislative body, made up of men who had held the important magistracies. In a speech passed down through the generations and still used as a school text when Livia came into the world, he persuaded his fellow senators to reject as dishonourable the peace terms offered by King Pyrrhus. Claudius Caudex led the Roman forces into Sicily at the outbreak of the First Punic War against Carthage in 264, and during the Second War, Gaius Claudius Nero defeated Hasdrubal in 207 as he made his way to join his brother Hannibal. This pattern of high office continued to the end of the republic.[4]

Like their modern counterparts, the important Roman families were often made up of more than one branch. Appius' two sons, Tiberius Claudius Nero and Publius Claudius Pulcher, were the founders of the two main subdivisions of the patrician Claudians, the Claudii Nerones and the Claudii Pulchri. Livia could claim descent from one and would marry into the other.[5] The Nerones apparently soon faded from view. Tiberius Claudius Nero was the last Neronian consul, in 202, until Livia's son, the future emperor Tiberius, was elected to the office in 13 BC. The Pulchri, on the other hand, went from strength to strength, and carved out a preeminent role in Roman political life.[6]

Amidst the paragons of public service and duty, however, tradition also ascribed to the patrician Claudii a motley collection of rogues and eccentrics, linked to the white sheep of the family by common possession of the notorious Claudian pride. Tacitus could speak of one of their descendants as marked *vetere ac insita Claudiae familiae superbia* (by the old inborn arrogance of the Claudian family); Livy speaks of a family that is *superbissima* and *crudelissima* (excessively haughty and excessively cruel) towards the plebeians, a sentiment echoed by Suetonius' description of them as *violentos ac contumaces* (violent and arrogant). Whether this reputation was deserved, or resulted from a hostile historical tradition, is perhaps not particularly relevant in the present context, because it was the *reputation* that would be bequeathed to Livia and the line of emperors that followed her.[7] Tradition has grafted onto the worthy if dull achievements of Appius Claudius, the decemvir and lawgiver, a luridly sinister role of would-be tyrant and insatiable defiler of women, the most noteworthy being Verginia, slain by her own father to save her from Appius' lust—and, of course, to save her father loss of face. Publius Claudius Pulcher, consul in 249, had contempt not only for man but also for the gods. He suffered a major defeat in a naval battle against the Carthaginians at Drepana, losing 93 of his 123 ships. His defeat was blamed by some writers on his outrageous behaviour when the auspices hinted strongly that his enterprise was headed for disaster. The sacred chickens refused to eat. He ignored the sign and, according to some, in a fit of pique dumped them into the sea, announcing, "If they won't eat, let them drink."[8] The stories seem endless. Appius Claudius Pulcher, father-in-law of Tiberius Gracchus, provoked the Salassi of Gaul into a costly war during his consulship in 143 and suffered a defeat and the loss of five thousand men. In a later engagement he redressed the balance by killing five thousand of the enemy. He assumed arrogantly that he was entitled to a triumph, the grand procession through Rome granted victorious generals who fulfilled a specific set of conditions, and he requested the necessary funds from the Senate. When his request was refused, he simply went ahead and staged the triumph at his own expense.[9] Suetonius tells a story, otherwise unknown and whose historicity cannot be determined, of a Claudius Drusus who set up his own crowned statue at Forum Appi and tried to use his clients to take over Italy.[10]

Tradition was even-handed in one respect, for the Claudian women were painted as no less arrogant than the males. Claudia, for instance, was the daughter of the distinguished statesman Appius Claudius Caecus and the sister of the Claudius Pulcher who lost his ships to the Carthaginians. When Claudia's carriage was blocked by a crowd of pedestrians, she lost her temper and prayed, loudly of course, for her brother to come back to life to lose another fleet of Romans. She was fined for her outburst. Another Claudia, the daughter of the pseudotriumphator Appius, joined him in his chariot during the triumphal parade. There was a danger that he would be hauled out, but she, as a Vestal Virgin with sacrosanctity, would be able to protect him from the intervention of the tribune. Arguably the most notorious Claudian woman of all time was still alive during Livia's youth. Clodia Metelli was famed for her profligacy and political power. Her numerous lovers almost certainly included the poet Catullus (he gave her the pseudonym Lesbia) and her brother, the demagogue Publius Clodius. She was berated by the orator Cicero for bringing shame on her distinguished Claudian ancestors.[11]

One of the descendants of this celebrated if eccentric family was Livia's father, Marcus Livius Drusus Claudianus. We have no knowledge of Marcus' biological parents, though he is described as a Claudius Pulcher by Suetonius (the only one actually to claim this), and his family seems to have had a connection with Pisaurum. This old colony, at the mouth of the Pisaurus in Umbria, was apparently a depressing place. Catullus, writing in the 50s, calls it *moribunda*, and Cicero describes it as a hotbed of discontent. Thus when Cicero at one point mockingly calls Marcus a Pisaurensis, it was clearly intended as a slur.[12] But Pisauran or not, Marcus was still a Claudian. Livia's mother Alfidia came from far less distinguished stock. She was the daughter of a Marcus Alfidius, a man of municipal rather than senatorial origins, and she may have attracted an eligible aristocrat like Marcus Livius Drusus through her family wealth.[13] She seems to have come from Fundi, a pleasant town on the Appian Way, in the coastal area of Latium near the Campanian border. Fundi was noted for its fine wine but was generally been viewed as a place for escape—many Romans had country villas in the vicinity. Suetonius twice alludes to Livia's connection to the town. He reports that some (wrongly) believed that Livia's son, the emperor Tiberius, had been born at Fundi because it was his grandmother's hometown. In another context, to illustrate one of the many vagaries of her great-grandson Caligula, Suetonius cites a letter to the Senate in which the emperor alleged that Livia had been of low birth because her maternal grandfather had been merely a decurion (town official) of Fundi. Caligula, of course, was much given to wicked jokes at his family's expense, and his charge should perhaps not be taken too seriously (see appendix 3).[14]

Livia's descent on her father's side from one of Rome's oldest and most prestigious families would have conferred enormous status on her. That status would have been enhanced by another link, no less important politically and originating in this case through adoption. An admirer of Livia's, the contemporary historian Valerius Maximus, describing the feud of Claudius Nero and Livius Salinator, censors of 204 BC, remarks that if they had realised that Livia's son would be descended from their blood, they would have ceased to be rivals. With this eloquent display of sycophancy Valerius testifies to the "dual line" of Livia. Her name, Livia Drusilla (see appendix 4), in itself gives no hint of a Claudian connection. Rather it reflects her family connection with a man who earned a secure if controversial place in Roman history. The Livii seem to have been an eminent Latin clan who received Roman citizenship in 338 following the Latin revolt.[15] Their most famous member emerged in the aftermath of the disintegration of the social order that followed the adoption by the Senate of violent emergency measures to counter the land resettlement schemes proposed in 133 BC by Tiberius Gracchus and subsequently by his brother Gaius. The republic was not to recover from the severe blows it suffered during this crisis, which brought martyrs' deaths to the Gracchi. The crisis also brought to the fore a distinction between the *optimates*, who represented the old senatorial class, with its traditional claim over the higher magistracies, and the *populares*, who sought to promote the initiative of the tribunes and the consuls to introduce legislation free of the heavy hand of the Senate.

Gaius Gracchus had included among his proposals a measure to extend the franchise to Rome's Latin allies, and a limited franchise to the Italians. In 91 BC the issue of the Italian franchise returned with a vengeance, and it was during this critical phase that Marcus Livius Drusus came into prominence, when as tribune of the plebeians he took up a number of causes, including agrarian reform and, most notably, a move to enfranchise all Italians living south of the river Po. He somehow succeeded in firing the imagination of the Italian communities to see him as the man to champion their rights. At the same time, however, he encountered considerable opposition in Rome. There were outbreaks of disorder, and Drusus was murdered by an unknown assailant. His death fomented widespread resentment and was the decisive element leading to the outbreak of armed revolt in the Social War. What he had sought through political action eventually came about through conflict, and by 89 the allies had been absorbed into the Roman state. Livia's family connection with the champion of the rights of the Italians must be seen as a major asset, especially in the later stages of the civil war that would end the republic, when warring factions competed for broad support.

As Drusus breathed his last he reputedly declared to his weeping entourage, *ecquandone similem mei civem habebit res public?*—when will the state have another citizen like me?[16] What precise qualities he had in mind in his final moments are not known, but his family, through adoption rather than bloodline, was to produce in Livia someone whose fame would far eclipse the tribune's. Livia's father, Marcus Livius Drusus Claudianus, was born a Claudius, as his name indicates, but was adopted into the Livian family. In the Roman fashion he assumed the *nomen* of the adopting *gens*, the Livii, and appended an adjectival form of his original gens, the Claudii.[17] With adoption he would have been expected to assume the *praenomen* of his adoptive father; the fact that he was a Marcus, combined with the absence of any prominent Livian other than the famous tribune with the *cognomen* Drusus, strongly suggests that this Drusus was the adoptive father.[18] From her link with the tribune Livia acquired her cognomen, Drusilla. It also gave her family the name Drusus, which some of her descendants opted to bear as a praenomen.

If Marcus was the adopted son of the tribune, he would have found himself in an advantageous position. On the death of his new father he could have inherited all or part of his estate. Diodorus Siculus called the tribune Marcus Livius Drusus the richest man in Rome, and his observation seems to be supported by other sources.[19] This wealth would have given an important boost to his son's career. Moreover, as we have seen, Marcus' inherited wealth might have been amplified by money from his wife's family. The Alfidii would have considered a lavish dowry a small price to pay for a connection with such a socially prominent Roman, a man described by Velleius Paterculus as *nobilissimus.*[20]

Livia's father steps onto the stage of Roman history in 59 BC, during a period of great political tension. The end of the struggle over the franchise in Italy did not mean an end to overseas conflicts. In 83 the general Sulla, flushed with his victories over king Mithridates, who ruled in the Black Sea area, returned to Italy at the head of his troops and after a period of turmoil and conflict was appointed dictator with special powers. He made it his mission to restore the supremacy of the Senate, retiring in 79. The Senate squandered their advantage. They offended the military commander Pompey, who, having undertaken a successful campaign in the East, on his return found the senators unwilling to ratify the measures he had undertaken. The Senate also offended the wealthy financier Crassus by restricting his financial dealings in Asia. The same body further alienated a new rising star, Julius Caesar, denying him the prospect of the consulship on his return from Spain in 60. In that year Caesar, Pompey, and Crassus found common cause and formed an compact often referred to casually by modern scholars (although not by the ancients) as the First Triumvirate, although the loose alliance did not have the formal status that the term might imply. Pompey married Caesar's daughter Julia to seal the agreement.

It is at this point that we find the first reference in the sources to Livia's father, Marcus. He was evidently an energetic opportunist, for he hitched his wagon to the triumvirate and was sent—or at least had reasonable expectations of being sent—on a mission to Alexandria in 59 BC to raise funds.[21] Marcus had perhaps just shortly before married Alfidia, and on January 30 of either 59 or 58 he became a father, with the birth of his daughter, Livia. The month and day of Livia's birth are established by inscriptions of the post-Julian period as *a.d.III Kal. Febr.*, the third day before the first of February, reckoned inclusively. This date is by convention given as January 30 in the modern calendar system, although there is in reality no truly satisfactory way of expressing it, because in the pre-Julian calendar January had only twenty-nine days.[22] The year is more problematic (see appendix 5). The place of birth is even more obscure; we have no direct hint of where it might have been. The absence of any boast in extant inscriptions from a town proudly claiming distinction as her birthplace, and the lack of speculation in the literary sources, suggest that she might have been born in Rome.

Livia's father is next heard of in 54, when he was prosecuted for improper legal practices *(de praevaricatione)* but acquitted through the efforts of Cicero—the kind of case, as Tacitus notes, that does not later arouse much interest.[23] In any event, the publicity does not seem to have impeded his career. By 50 he was praetor, or *iudex quaestionis* (president of a court), presiding over a case being tried under the Scantinian law, which covered prohibited sexual activity. Although there are grounds for suspecting that he might have been wealthy, through his adoptive father or his wife, he seems to have fallen into some financial difficulties at about this time, and we later find him trying to sell his gardens to Cicero. Marcus was a hard bargainer, but he met his match in the famous orator, who was determined to come out best in the deal.[24]

Meanwhile, the loose alliance of the powerful leaders had broken down. Crassus was killed by the Parthians at the Battle of Carrhae in 53. Pompey, a man of considerable integrity but little moral courage, was persuaded to lead the opposition to Caesar, and paid for the decision with his life, when he was assassinated as he disembarked in Egypt in September 48. Caesar was now preeminent. He was appointed dictator for two terms and, in 44, for life. He proved a vigorous and effective legislator, settling veterans, founding settlements (colonies), extending the franchise, reorganizing the corn dole, regulating traffic within the city of Rome, and, his most enduring measure, reforming the chaotic Roman calendar. But Caesar offended many in Rome by what was perceived to be his excessive ambition, rousing fears that he planned to make himself monarch. Although his person had apparently been declared sacrosanct, which made it a crime to harm him, in the end the privilege did him little good. A conspiracy was formed, led by Marcus Brutus and Gaius Cassius, and on the Ides of March, 44 BC, Caesar was assassinated.

It was probably not long after this pivotal moment in Roman history that a pivotal event took place in Livia's life also, her first marriage. Indeed, because nothing at all is known of Livia's early life apart from her birth, this is the first incident that the historian can infer. Her husband, Tiberius Claudius Nero, belonged to the less distinguished branch of the patrician Claudians. As we have seen, the last consulship the family could claim was in 202 BC. Very little has been passed down about Tiberius Nero's immediate forebears, although we know from a very fragmentary inscription that his father was also a Tiberius. The older Tiberius Nero served in 67 BC as legate of Pompey against the pirates, with command at the Straits of Gibraltar, and in 63 made a speech against the summary execution without trial of the associates of Catiline, who had been exposed by Cicero in a major conspiracy.[25] Their family names leave little doubt that Livia and her husband must have been related. How closely is far from clear, although some scholars assert with confidence that they were cousins.[26]

Tiberius Nero might have seemed a good marriage prospect. Cicero speaks of him having the qualities of an *adulescentis nobilis, ingeniosi, abstinentis* (a young man of noble family, of native talent, and moderation) and remarks that there was no one among the noble families he regarded more highly. (Of course, these warm testimonials appear in a letter of recommendation, a common repository of inflated praise.)[27] Tiberius Nero makes his own entry into history in 54 BC. In that year a Pompeian supporter, Aulus Gabinius, returned from Syria after a governorship that seems to have been marked by administrative incompetence and large-scale bribery, a common enough situation in many of the provinces of the late republic. Gabinius became the celebrity of the year, denounced by Cicero and hounded in a series of showy trials. Before his trial for extortion *(de repetundis)* there was a scramble for the high-profile role of prosecutor, and Tiberius Nero competed against Gaius Memmius and Mark Antony. The contest was keen and Cicero comments on Tiberius Nero's fine effort and the quality of his supporters. But Cicero anticipated that Memmius would win out, and was proved right. The outcome marked Tiberius Nero down in this first highly public incident as a worthy failure, a characterization that could probably be applied to his whole career.[28] In late 51 or early 50 he visited Asia, where he had a number of clients, and he called on Cicero during the latter's governorship of Cilicia. At this time the tortuous negotiations for the third marriage of Cicero's daughter Tullia were under way.

Tiberius Nero seems to have made a strong impression on his host, to judge from the warm letter of recommendation that Cicero wrote for him to Gaius Silius, propraetor of Bithynia and Pontus.[29] The young man declared an interest in Tullia and obtained her father's consent for the match. Messengers were despatched to Rome to give mother and daughter the happy news. Unfortunately, Tiberius' hostile *daemon* intervened—it seems that before he left, Cicero had told Tullia and her mother to arrange the negotiations in Rome themselves, and because he was going to be away for so long in his province, not to feel obliged to refer the issue to him. The messengers arrived in Rome just in time to miss Tullia's engagement party. Tiberius Nero would probably have been a better choice than his successful rival, the seedy Dolabella, a ruthless adherent of Caesar's and a man whose career was enlivened by dissipation and debts.[30]

Cicero had approved of Tiberius Nero as a potential prosecutor in the Gabinius case because of his stand against the power block represented by Caesar and Pompey (and Crassus). By 48 BC he was doubtless dismayed when his young champion displayed the often crass opportunism typical of the period. Putting his support behind Julius Caesar, Tiberius Nero signed up as his quaestor and commanded the fleet at Alexandria.[31] As a reward for his services he received a senior priesthood and in 46 was given responsibility for founding colonies at Caesar's behest in Narbonese Gaul, including Narbo and Arelate.[32] He might have seemed to the outside world to be on an upward trajectory, but cruel fate intervened. The Ides of March in 44 and the assassination of Caesar changed the destiny of many besides Caesar himself. Tiberius Nero had to make a career choice, and characteristically made the wrong one. Perhaps under the influence of Livia's father, he followed the course of many Caesarian supporters and jumped sides, hitching his wagon to the assassins' team, even proposing special honours for the killers.[33]

We do not know for certain when Tiberius Nero and Livia were married. The normal age of marriage for women at this period seems generally to have been in the late teens, but in upper-class families marriage at fifteen was probably the norm, and even earlier marriages were common in aristocratic circles, when there was a political advantage to the match. By this reckoning Livia, depending on her date of birth, might have reached a marriageable age in 46 or 45. But this earlier date may not have been possible if Tiberius Nero was serving in Gaul at that time. The birth of their first son in November 42 gives us a limit, and places the marriage probably in 43, when Livia was fifteen or sixteen. Her husband would likely have been in his late thirties.[34]

The marriage took place during the dramatic aftermath of Caesar's assassination. Two men competed to fill the vacuum left by his death. One was Caesar's lieutenant Mark Antony. The other was his great-nephew, Octavian, named his heir and adopted son in his will, the man destined to transform the character of the Roman state and to become Livia's second husband (fig. 26). He was born Gaius Octavius, on September 23, 63 BC, in Rome. Although malicious gossip claimed that his great-grandfather was a freedman and rope maker, the family, though not distinguished, was well-to-do. The Octavii originated from the Volscian town of Velitrae, two days' journey south of Rome. His father, also Gaius Octavius, was a prosperous banker, a member of the entrepreneurial middle class that largely constituted what is known as the equestrian order. By reaching the praetorship in 61 BC, he became the first of his family to move from that class into a senatorial career. The younger Octavius and his sister Octavia were the children of their father's second wife, Atia (another Octavia had been born to a first wife, Ancharia). Atia was the daughter of Atius Balbus, the son of Julius Caesar's sister, Julia, a family connection that proved useful indeed to her ambitious son. From 61 to late 59 Octavius' father was away from Italy, in Macedonia, where he served a term as governor. Not long after his return, when he might reasonably have been planning for a consulship, he died, leaving his son and two daughters to be brought up by Atia. She remarried some two or three years later.[35]

Through his link with Caesar, Octavius obtained some minor civil positions; then, because a career in Roman politics was difficult without some military background, he was chosen to join Caesar in an expedition to Africa in late 47 to deal with the remnants of Pompey's forces. But the young man was not in good health, and at his mother's insistence the plan was shelved. Ill health continued to dog him throughout his life. He seems to have been prone to nervous exhaustion and was particularly liable to sunstroke—he made it his lifetime practice to wear a hat when outdoors. Caesar returned from Thapsus in April 46, and for the remainder of the year he was active in promoting Octavius' prospects in Rome, even to the extent of allowing him to ride behind his own chariot in the triumph for the African war, which Octavius had missed. At the end of the year Caesar was off to Spain, where Pompey's elder son had gathered a large army. Once again Octavius was unable to leave with him. He fell dangerously ill, so ill that his life was feared for.[36] He recovered and followed Caesar, although he seems to have arrived in Spain too late to take part in the final battle of Munda, were the remnants of Pompey's supporters were finally crushed.[37]

In September 45, before he reentered Rome, Caesar stopped at one of his estates at Labici and wrote his will. His decision was a momentous one. He had been married several times and had a reputation among his soldiers as a sexual dynamo. But despite these promising attributes, he had produced only one child, a daughter Julia (Pompey's wife), to whom he was deeply attached. She died, leaving no surviving offspring. He now named Octavius as his chief heir and in a clause appended to the will adopted him. The will was deposited in the Temple of the Vestals, and its contents seem not to have been made known to the main beneficiary. Before the end of the year Caesar sent his heir to Apollonia on the coast of Macedonia to complete his education. Apollonia was not a great educational centre, and it was possibly hoped that Octavius would develop a closer familiarity with military matters from contact with the five legions stationed in the province.

Octavius had been in Apollonia for a few months only when a messenger arrived from his mother with the dramatic news that Caesar had been murdered. He decided to return to Italy at once with a few friends, including Marcus Agrippa. In Brundisium he learned from letters sent by his mother and stepfather that he had inherited most of Caesar's estate and, more significantly, had been adopted as his son. His family advised him to decline the adoption, perceptively anticipating the political firestorm that it would create. He did not follow their advice and proceeded to Rome. He now began to style himself Gaius Julius Caesar Octavianus, following the Roman custom of assuming the name of the adoptive parent with a form of the original gens appended.

The adoption fuelled Octavian's ambitions, and its importance to him is demonstrated by his desperate efforts to have it confirmed. The adoption of relatives or even of nonrelatives was a well-established tradition in Rome, and adopted sons and daughters naturally styled themselves henceforth as children of the adoptive, not the natural father. But testamentary adoption, which later played a significant part in Livia's own career, seems to have been in a dubious category of its own. The ancient evidence is not explicit, and the ancient jurists are silent on the matter, but it seems that adoption stipulated in a will was almost certainly not an adoption in the full sense of the word, but mainly a device to allow for the inheritance of property on condition that the adopted child assume the name of the legator (see chapter 8). This ambiguity explains why Octavian was determined at all costs to have the status of the adoption legally ratified. He attempted to do this soon after his arrival in Rome and took on as an ally in his campaign Antony, who pretended to be making every effort to have the appropriate law passed but was in fact doing everything he could to block it. When Octavian became consul, in May 43, one of his first measures was to have the proposed law presented to the popular assembly.[38] The symbolic importance of the adoption cannot be stressed enough. In practice he ignored the final element of his name, Octavianus, and preferred to use only Gaius Julius Caesar.[39] Although clearly an unfriendly source, Antony was not far off the mark when he said of him *et te, o puer, qui omnia nomini debes* (and you, lad, who owe everything to a name).[40] And more was to come. There is evidence that Caesar might have received divine honours even before his death. At all events, in 42 posthumous divine honours were granted him. Henceforth, Octavian could style himself not only as the son of Julius Caesar but as the son of *Divus* (the deified) Julius.[41]

The following years did in a sense vindicate his parents' reservations, for conflict arose between Octavian and Antony in their zeal to assume Caesar's mantle, a struggle that was punctuated by a series of pacts but was not resolved finally until the suicide of Antony in 30 BC following the decisive battle of Actium. Their first temporary rapprochement was reached in November 43, when the two joined a supporter of Antony's, Marcus Lepidus, to create the "Second" Triumvirate. This was a more formal arrangement than its predecessor and gave the trio almost absolute power for five years. It enabled them to eliminate their opponents, including Cicero, and to prosecute a campaign against the tyrannicides Brutus and Cassius, who were eventually defeated and induced to suicide at Philippi in Thrace in the autumn of 42.

The struggle between powerful and ambitious Roman political and military leaders in the last century of the republic inevitably embroiled the rest of the population, especially Romans of prominence, who, as is usually the case in a civil war, found it impossible to stand on the sidelines of the conflict. It also brought tragedy into Livia's life. Nothing explicit is known about her father Marcus' stand during the clashes between Caesar and Pompey or during the ascendancy of Caesar. Shackleton-Bailey has tentatively suggested that Marcus was a Caesarian, but whatever loyalty he might have felt certainly did not survive the dictator's death, when he emerges as a champion of the tyrannicides. In 43 we find him one of the sponsors of a senatorial decree to give command of two legions to the assassin Decimus Brutus. By the end of that year he had been proscribed by the triumvirs. He fled east to join Brutus and Cassius and shared with them their final defeat at Philippi. He personally survived, but afterwards reputedly died a courageous death. Refusing to ask for mercy, he committed suicide in his tent.[42]

We do not know what happened to Marcus Livius' property. Livia may have been his only natural child, but there are strong grounds for believing that in the absence of a natural son, Marcus before his death arranged in his will for the adoption of Marcus Livius Drusus Libo (consul in 15 BC). Libo's natural father, Lucius Scribonius Libo, later demonstrated powerful political connections.

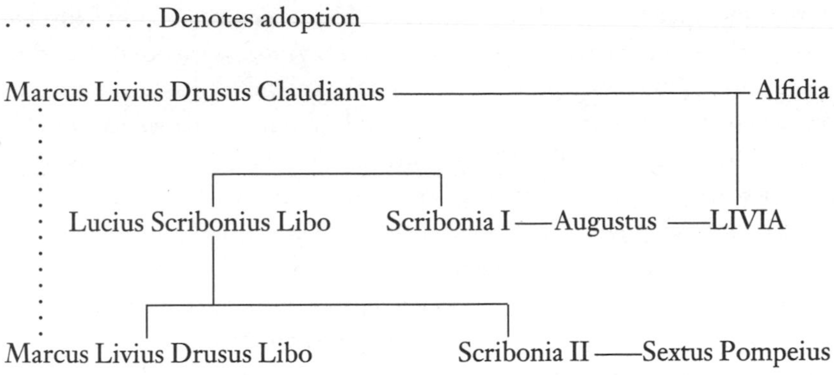

Stemma 2. Possible connections of Livia and Scribonia

Destined for a consulship in 34, Lucius was the brother of Scribonia, first wife of Octavian (see chapter 2), and father of a second Scribonia, who became the wife of Sextus Pompeius, the renegade son of Pompey. If the adoption of Marcus Libo did take place, it, like Octavian's, and like Livia's more than half a century later, would have been testamentary and would in time have resulted in the irony that Livia's stepbrother was the nephew of her husband Octavian's first wife (stemma 2). Marcus Libo would have inherited the bulk of his adoptive father's wealth. As a woman, Livia would have been limited by law (the Lex Voconia) to just less than half. But because the father was proscribed, there would in fact have been very little to collect.[43]

In the meantime, the conduct of Livia's husband, Tiberius Nero, highlighted the two dominant traits in his makeup: an inordinate opportunism and a penchant for guaranteeing that whatever opportunity he seized, it would be an injudicious choice. He did not follow Marcus in sticking to his principles to the bitter end. Once he recognised that the plight of the assassins was hopeless, he broke away from his father-in-law's position. The struggle for supremacy now clearly lay between Octavian and Marc Antony, and Tiberius Nero opted to back Antony. He was elected to the praetorship in 42, but following a dispute that arose among the triumvirs, he refused at the end of his term to leave office and stayed in place beyond his legally defined period.

Early in the same year, Livia became pregnant. It is said that she was very keen to bear a boy and used a method of determining the sex common among young women of the time: she took an egg from under a brooding hen and kept it warm against her breast. Whenever she had to yield it up, she passed it to her nurse under the folds of their dresses so as not to interrupt the warmth. A cock with a fine crest was hatched, a portent of a vigorous son.[44] Later in the year we have the first specific recorded evidence of her whereabouts. On November 16, 42, the first of her two sons, Tiberius (fig. 27), was born on the Palatine in Rome. Suetonius records both the date and the year, as well as the location in Rome, where it must be assumed that Tiberius Claudius Nero owned property on the highly fashionable Palatine Hill. Later a story arose that Livia, now aged sixteen or seventeen, was in Fundi at her mother's family home at the time of Tiberius' birth. Suetonius argues against this and also against those who place the birth in the following or preceding year. He notes that the correct date appears in both the *fasti* (the official calendars) and the *acta publica* (public gazette), and it is in fact vindicated in surviving inscriptions.[45]

After the successful campaign against Caesar's assassins at Philippi, the triumvirs had agreed on areas of command. Marcus Lepidus was restricted to Africa. Antony took the East, where he launched a campaign against the Parthians. Octavian commanded in the West. His task was to restore order in Italy and keep a check on Sextus Pompeius, the younger son of Pompey, who had set himself up with a large fleet in Sicily and had established a haven for fugitives from the triumvirs. Octavian also undertook the grim task of confiscating territory in Italy for the retiring veterans. Antony's brother Lucius Antonius, and Antony's wife, Fulvia, became the champions of the dispossessed Italians and sought to instigate an uprising against Octavian; Tiberius Nero joined the effort, and Livia and her son followed him to Perusia, the main centre of opposition. When Perusia fell in early 40, Tiberius Nero escaped with his family first to Praeneste and then to Naples, where he sought to instigate a slave uprising, helped by Gaius Velleius, the grandfather of the historian. That effort collapsed and the family had a hair-raising escape. As Octavian's forces broke into the city, the family decided to make a break for it. Velleius, by now old and infirm, was too weary and ran himself through with his own sword. Tiberius Nero and his family set out to make their way stealthily to a ship, avoiding the regular routes and going off into the wilds of the countryside. On the journey little Tiberius started to cry. There was panic that he might give them away. Livia snatched him from the nurse, and when he still did not settle down, one of her followers seized him from her and apparently saved the day. The ancient authors were quick to spot the irony of Livia fleeing the man she would eventually marry, with a son who would eventually succeed him.[46]

The family did in the end make their escape and went to Sicily. They perhaps hoped that family connections, through Marcus Libo, the brother-in-law of Sextus Pompeius, would stand them in good stead. But if this connection did exist, it did the couple little good, and their reception in Sicily must have been a considerable disappointment. Sextus Pompeius found Tiberius Nero something of an embarrassment and was reluctant even to grant him an audience. Also, perhaps to avoid unnecessary provocation, he ordered Tiberius Nero not to display the *fasces*, the rods of the office of praetorship, which he had illegally retained in his possession. Sextus' sister, perhaps motivated by personal rather than political concerns, was more welcoming, and even gave the little Tiberius a cloak with a clasp and some gold studs. These survived as celebrity items and were exhibited for tourists in the resort town of Baiae until Suetonius' day. But Tiberius Nero now fell foul of the complex and shifting tide of Roman politics. Octavian, faced with the prospect of a confrontation with Antony, sought to move closer to Sextus Pompeius. Tiberius Nero was obliged to pack his bags once again and go with his wife and infant son to join Antony in the East, where the Claudii Nerones seem to have acquired a large number of clients.[47] It might have been at this time that Tiberius Nero was proscribed. We certainly know that it happened at some point—Tacitus states so unequivocally, although without providing a date.[48] We cannot be sure why Livia followed her husband into exile, unless for the uncomplicated reason of personal affection. It was certainly expected that wives would either accompany proscribed husbands or stay at home and work on their behalf.[49] But they could not be compelled. By now it must have been apparent to Livia that her husband was not destined for greatness, and it perhaps says something for her strength of character that as a young mother of eighteen or so she seems to have put duty before personal convenience. The couple were able to get safe passage by joining a distant kin of Livia's, Lucius Scribonius Libo, who left Sicily to accompany Antony's mother, Julia, to Athens and allowed Tiberius Nero and his family to sail with him.[50] Antony was perhaps no more eager than Sextus to be lumbered with someone so tainted by failure, and he quickly despatched Tiberius Nero to Sparta, where the Claudii had long enjoyed patronage.

Sparta, perhaps because of its ties to the Claudians, offered the couple an extremely cordial welcome, in contrast to their earlier experiences. Livia was later able to acknowledge their support by rewarding the community for the loyalty it had shown her in times of trouble.[51] But Tiberius Nero was unable to break the habit of a lifetime. Once again they had to flee—the reasons are not known. This time it was by night, through a forest where a fire broke out. The family barely escaped. The event would have been especially memorable to Livia, who ended up with burning hair and a charred dress.[52]

In AD 40 Antony and Octavian settled their differences at the Peace of Brundisium, and the compact was sealed by the marriage of Antony and Octavian's sister, Octavia. A further, even shorter-lived compact, the Treaty of Misenum, was reached by the triumvirs and Sextus Pompeius in mid-39 BC. It promised an amnesty to those who had sided with Sextus. Livia and her husband were thus able to return to Rome at the same time as Mark Antony.[53] Livia's mood is not recorded, but it must have been sombre enough. Her father was dead, and she must by now have recognised that her husband's star had started to set even before it had properly risen.

2

MARRIAGE

In 39 Livia's harrowing experiences of restless exile came to an end when she returned with her husband to Rome. Her return would have far-reaching consequences not only for herself but for the entire Roman world, for it led to her lifelong association with a man who was to determine the shape of Rome's history for centuries to come. If there is such as a thing as the aphrodisiac of power, then Octavian might be said to have exercised an unmatched sexual attraction in the Rome of the time. He was still only in his early twenties, but an individual of remarkable achievement and obvious promise. Like Livia, he was married when they met, in a union that illustrated perfectly the all-important political dimension of marriage in the upper echelons of Roman society. Octavian's wife at the time was Scribonia. In 40 BC, in the complex play of Roman politics, it had been in his interest to move closer to Pompey's son Sextus Pompeius, whose fleets controlled the seas around Italy. (Octavian was particularly concerned about his own weakness in sea power.) One of Sextus' chief allies was Lucius Scribonius Libo, who was to attain the consulship in 34 BC, the first member of his family to reach the office. A consistent supporter of the Pompeian cause, Libo was an ambitious and able man, whose aspirations are marked by the marriages contracted by his female relatives. Sextus Pompeius married Libo's daughter, and, after negotiations conducted through Maecenas, Octavian married Libo's sister, Scribonia.[1] In the following year the alliance was cemented by the betrothal of Marcellus, Octavian's three-year-old nephew, to Pompeia, daughter of Sextus Pompeius, and thus Scribonia's niece.

Scribonia came from a powerful republican family, familiar to the inhabitants of Rome through a striking visible reminder. As people entered the Forum along the Via Sacra, they passed the monument set up by Scribonius Libo, the *Puteal Libonis* (also known as the *Puteal Scribonianum*), a large and handsome stone wellhead, alluded to in the literature and often depicted on coins. According to Suetonius, before Octavian came onto the scene, Scribonia had already been twice married, to two ex-consuls (see appendix 6). Her son by the second, Publius Cornelius Scipio, reached the consulship in 16 BC. For Scribonia to have produced this son (by a second marriage) early enough for him to become consul in 16, she would have needed to be some ten years older than Octavian, born in 63.

The marriage to Scribonia lasted only a year. She does not seem to have been endowed with what Tacitus calls Livia's "affability" *(comitas)*. Seneca describes her as a *gravis femina; gravis* applied to a man would mean something akin to "dignified," but in a woman could probably convey a quality closer to "severe." The only specific reference we have to shrewish behaviour is Mark Antony's claim that Octavian divorced Scribonia because she expressed her feelings very volubly over the influence of his mistress (possibly Livia). Octavian wrote that he was driven to distraction by her bitchy ways, a sentiment that has won over some modern scholars—Syme for instance calls her "morose," "tiresome," and "disagreeable." Perhaps, but she showed considerable character when her daughter by Octavian, Julia, was banished, and Scribonia quit Rome to share her exile (see chapter 4). Both Dio and Velleius agree that her gesture was voluntary and their testimony should probably be taken at face value, despite the modern theories that she might have been personally involved in the scandal that had brought Julia down. Moreover, she had the composure when in her eighties to try to talk her nephew Drusus Libo out of suicide when he was faced with the certain prospect of condemnation for treason early in Tiberius' reign. The image of Scribonia the shrew was almost certainly the end product of a propaganda effort designed to divert attention from the potentially scandalous circumstances of her divorce from Octavian. In the end, she could be said to have had the last laugh. She survived her younger last ex-husband, who died in AD 14, by two years at the least. (Seneca refers to her as alive in AD 16.)

The divorce took place in the latter part of 39, immediately after the birth of their daughter, Julia.[2] In reality, irrespective of Scribonia's charms, or lack of them, Octavian had decided on a new wife. The precise series of events by which this came about is difficult to disentangle. There is the usual problem of dealing with sources that may be incomplete, careless, or hostile. But we have the additional difficulty that these sources might have drawn much of their information on the marriage from material that was essentially fuel in a propaganda war, and thus already distorted at birth. The details have been much debated, and the basis for some of the assumptions in the following narrative are set out in appendix 7.

Livia cannot have reached Rome before late summer 39. She and her husband, Tiberius Nero, would probably have returned to their residence on the Palatine if it was still available to them. It may not have been. The Treaty of Misenum stipulated that those who had left Italy in fear for their safety would get their property back; those who, like Tiberius Nero, had been proscribed would recover only a quarter.[3] Livia might thus have found herself in considerably reduced circumstances. Where and when she and Octavian met we have no idea, and we cannot exclude the possible irony that she might have been introduced to him through her aunt by adoption, his then-wife, Scribonia. Dio is the only source to report on how the affair began. Octavian in 39 BC organised a lavish entertainment to celebrate the shaving of his beard (the event may have been his birthday, on September 23). Dio tells us that Octavian kept his chin smooth afterwards (although coins continue to show him bearded as late as 36). He clearly wanted to look his best because he "was *already (ede)* beginning to love Livia."[4]

For Livia, Octavian certainly represented a good catch. There are hints that in the eyes of contemporaries she quickly recognised his interest in her and turned it to her advantage. There is evidence that Octavian was already turning to Livia for help and advice well before they were married. Scribonia complained about her husband's mistress — almost certainly Livia — upset not by his infatuation, a situation that Roman wives generally learned to handle, but rather by her rival's *nimiam potentiam* (excessive power). *Potentia* is a term generally used of political rather than erotic power. Tacitus seems also to suggest that Livia may well have been active in encouraging Octavian's attentions, when he says that Octavian took her away from her husband *incertum an invitam* (it is not certain that she was reluctant).[5] But what did she have to offer him? We can certainly not dismiss the element of pure sexual attraction. Both Tacitus and Velleius speak of Livia's beauty, *forma*, although such descriptions of aristocratic Roman women tend to be formulaic, and beauty in a bride may have been as much a commonplace in ancient Rome as it is today (chapter 6). Tacitus asserted that Octavian was driven essentially by lust, *cupidine formae*, and a tradition that saw his interest as pure infatuation *(amore)* persisted down to the fourth century.[6]

But Livia had much more than sexual charms to offer. Certainly in his previous matches Octavian had always looked upon marriage as a means of furthering his career. He was betrothed first to Servilia, the daughter of Publius Servilius Isauricus, related by marriage to Brutus, Cassius, and Lepidus, in an engagement that was the product of a political alignment engineered by Cicero early in 43 BC. This first arrangement fell victim to the shifting political tides. When he became reconciled with Antony, to strengthen the new alliance he became engaged to Antony's stepdaughter Claudia, the child of Fulvia (see chapter 7) and her previous husband, Publius Clodius. The marriage was postponed because of his fiancée's youth, and the clash with Fulvia ended the arrangement. The marriage to Scribonia followed in 40 BC.[7] Octavian's ties to Scribonia would similarly have been weakened when the old problems between himself and Sextus Pompeius reasserted themselves. Velleius, in fact, explicitly places the divorce from Scribonia and the fresh outbreak of hostilities with Sextus in close sequence.

In fact, Livia would have seemed an ideal partner. Quite apart from any feelings of affection, she brought significant political benefits to the marriage. Octavian had considerable power. His desperate need now was for status. Although Antony's taunt of *ignobilitas* might have been overstated (Octavian's father had reached the praetorship, which would have given him a technical entrée into the *nobilitas*), Octavian was seen by the old nobility as something of a revolutionary parvenu, and this formidable obstacle had not yet been overcome even more than a quarter-century later, when, in 12 BC, some of the nobility declined to attend the funeral of his old friend and son-in-law Marcus Agrippa. Ancestry was a powerful element in making a marriage advantageous. As Tacitus observed in Livia's obituary notice, she could boast a lofty lineage *(nobilitatis . . . clarissimae)*, and Velleius describes her father as *nobilissimus*. Thus she would have helped Octavian to strengthen his ties with the old distinguished families. In fact, the union would have a double advantage. It would link Octavian with the powerful and prestigious Claudii. But beyond this the connection with Livius Drusus would resonate throughout Italy and help to strengthen Octavian's power base. It is worth noting that the names Drusus and Drusilla, both from the Livian side of the lineage, continued to be used by later generations of the family.[8]

If Livia has been correctly identified as the mistress who was the target of Scribonia's complaints, Octavian and Livia began an affair while he was still married to Scribonia. He waited for the birth of his daughter Julia, then immediately arranged a divorce.[9] Livia for her part secured a divorce from Tiberius Nero in turn, and it is likely that in late September or early October, 39 BC, Octavian and Livia became betrothed. They do not seem to have proceeded immediately to the marriage, probably because by early October, Livia was six months pregnant. Tacitus and Dio say that Octavian sought the guidance of the pontiffs on the problem that the pregnancy raised for her remarriage. Both historians present this consultation in sarcastic terms, perhaps reflecting Antony's propaganda. Tacitus says that the question was put, *per ludibrium* (in a farce), whether Livia, with a child conceived but not yet born, could legally wed. Dio provides the same question, and also records their answer: that if there was any doubt about the conception the marriage should be postponed, but if conception was confirmed, then the marriage could take place. Dio is sceptical about their finding this decision in the rules, but says that it was a moot point because they would have given the answer Octavian needed anyhow.[10]

Why go to the priests in the first place? This does not seem to be an issue on which sacred law would have had any say. It is noteworthy that when the emperor Claudius made known his intention to marry Agrippina, his niece, in a relationship considered incestuous, the pontiffs were not asked for a ruling; instead, dispensation was sought from the Senate. The German scholar Suerbaum has argued that the issue here was a simple one. If a woman at the time of divorce was not known to be pregnant, clearly a delay was essential before remarriage, in order to establish the absence of pregnancy, otherwise the paternity and consequent *potestas* over the child would be uncertain *(perturbatio partus)*. Tacitus seems to have got the approach to the pontiffs slightly wrong in stating that the issue was whether a pregnant woman could remarry. Dio had a better grasp of the problem, that it had to be determined whether a woman was pregnant after her divorce. There seems to be no explicit statement in Roman law about the period that should elapse after divorce and before remarriage, and it is not clear what the rule was. In the ancient Law of the Twelve Tables a child born eleven months after the *death* of the husband is deemed not to be his. In the republican period a widow was required to mourn her husband for ten months, and according to the third-century AD jurist Ulpian, a child born more than ten months after the husband's death could not be an heir. Later imperial legislation increased the period to one year. As for the consequences of divorce, the earliest rule belongs to AD 449, when the period is set at one year. When Augustus later passed his laws restricting the rights of inheritance, the widower had to remarry at once to escape their penalties. But because of her duty for mourning and to avoid perturbatio partus, the widow had to be exempted from the immediate application of this new legislation. Initially the Lex Julia allowed women to remain single for one year after the death of their husbands and six months after divorce. (Curiously, under the Lex Julia a perturbatio partus does not seem to be an issue after divorce.) The later Lex Papia Poppaea extended these periods to two years and eighteen months, respectively (on the laws, see chapter 7).[11]

The pontiffs' ruling removed the final obstacle, and Octavian could proceed to the betrothal.[12] But there was another bizarre twist to the event. In two places Tacitus retains a tradition that Livia was forcibly removed from Tiberius Nero, that she was *abducta Neroni uxor* (a wife abducted from Nero) and that Octavian *aufert marito* (carries off [Livia] from her husband). The cruel characterization of Octavian's conduct may, again, have originated in Mark Antony's propaganda. Tacitus and Suetonius refer to letters of Antony's which apparently survived the triumvir's disgrace and death. They are brimming with bitter invective against Octavian. The seeds of the story of Livia's abduction may have been sown by a claim made by Antony that Octavian carried off *(abductam)* the wife of an ex-consul (unnamed) from her husband's dining room before his very eyes and took her into the bedchamber, from where she returned with her hair in disorder and her ears glowing *(rubentibus auriculis)*. Was she Livia? Suetonius seems to relate the hasty marriage and the case of the unidentified consular wife as two separate events. Also, Livia's husband was not of consular rank. Some exaggeration may, of course, be expected in abusive attacks. It is also possible that this relatively minor error arose in the transmission of the anecdote. But Suetonius took the material directly from Antony's letters—it is hard to see why Antony would have given this misinformation, unless, as Flory argues, he obscured Livia's identity intentionally. The idea of the forced abduction was still in vogue during the reigns of Caligula and Claudius. When Caligula chose as his second bride Livia Orestilla, who at the time was betrothed to Gaius Calpurnius Piso, he made the witty comment that he was following the precedent of Romulus (the legendary founder of Rome) and Augustus, who both snatched their new brides away from their husbands. (Hersilia was married [to Hersilius] before she married Romulus.) Caligula got it only partly right. He tired of his new bride very soon—the most conservative figure is two months—in contrast to Octavian, who remained devoted to Livia for forty-one years. In the next reign the senator Vitellius contrasted Claudius, who wished to marry his niece Agrippina the Younger, with the earlier Caesars who had carried off their wives on a whim.[13] In fact, Tiberius Nero had always been prepared to bend in the political wind, even if he failed to benefit much from his compliance. Pliny describes him as Octavian's enemy *(hostis)*, and although this would not, strictly speaking, have been true after the amnesty, there would still have been an inevitable tension between the two men, whose mutual animosity went back to the time of Perusia. The marriage would have offered Tiberius Nero an ideal opportunity to bury his differences with the rising star of the state. Cicero described him as the kind of man who was excessively eager to show gratitude in return for a favour, and most of the ancient sources speak of him as the perfect model of the *mari complaisant*. This motive may well have been sweetened by another consideration. Octavian's divorce from Scribonia and marriage to Livia would cause a rift with Sextus Pompeius; this would be to the advantage of Antony, to whom Tiberius Nero might have had a residual loyalty. And we must also remember that he had received a personal snub from Sextus.

Suetonius says that Tiberius Nero *petenti Augusto concessit* (gave her up to Augustus at his request). In fact, both Dio and Velleius allude to what seems to have been an active, even eager, role for Tiberius Nero in the union, Velleius repeating the same information in two different sections, that he was the one who pledged Livia. Dio says that he officiated at the ceremony, giving away his wife as a father would give up his daughter.[14] It is possible that Antony's propaganda might have exaggerated his willingness to comply. But there were historical parallels for such behaviour. When the great orator Hortensius persuaded Cato Uticensis, a man known for his upright attachment to principle, to divorce his wife Marcia so that he could marry her, Phillipus, her father, refused to betroth her to her new partner unless Cato joined with him in the formal ceremony. They betrothed her jointly. Much later, Caligula compelled Memmius Regulus to betroth his ex-wife Lollia Paulina to him.[15]

Tiberius Nero's eagerness to please did cause one embarrassing moment, when he chose to attend the feast following the betrothal. Present at the event was one of the pretty slave boys, the *delicia*, who were trained in clever and naughty comments and appeared naked as a regular feature at social events of the fashionable. These slaves were selected for their talkativeness, and were particularly appealing if they were impudent and adept at risqué language. Seneca notes that they were trained by special tutors in the art of abuse and observes wryly that because their vulgarity was a matter of professional expertise, what they said was considered not offensive but smart *(nec has contumelias vocamus, sed argutias)*. The slave attending the betrothal feast seems to have lived up to expectations. When he saw Livia reclining next to Octavian, he told her that she was in the wrong place since her husband—as he pointed to Tiberius Nero—was in another part of the room. This would not have been a simple social gaffe, but a deliberately outrageous joke. The story may, of course, be apocryphal, but it does at the very least suggest that relations between Tiberius Nero and Octavian were cordial enough for the discarded husband to have attended the celebratory feast.[16] Some scholars associate this banquet with a notorious event from Octavian's past, the *cena dodekatheos* (Feast of the Twelve Gods), recorded only by Suetonius. At this infamous festivity Octavian and his guests appeared in the guise of gods and goddesses (he took the part of Apollo). Suetonius reports that Antony attacked the escapade in his letters, naming the guests (the list is not provided), and there was also an anonymous and ribald lampoon which suggests that Octavian produced a burlesque about "novel debaucheries of the gods" *(nova divorum . . . adulteria)* ending with Jupiter falling from his throne. According to Suetonius, the scandal became the subject of common gossip, which was all the more avid because there was a severe famine in the city, leading to the jocular comment that the gods had eaten all the grain. In 40 BC Sextus Pompeius had cut off the corn supply and there were popular disturbances; Octavian was even stoned. The Treaty of Misenum would have removed the root cause of these supply difficulties, but it would have taken a while for the problem to be totally alleviated, and there are reports of famine in the years 39, 38, and 36, any one of which might in fact have been the year of the banquet. Whatever the date, Livia would almost certainly have been one of the guests at this celebration.[17]

Following the betrothal it seems that Livia joined Octavian at his home on the Palatine. It is probably safe to assume that at this stage they were not yet married. There is, however, some confusion in the sources about the relationship of their wedding to the birth of Livia's second son, Drusus. The information in Suetonius and Dio that Drusus came into the world after the marriage may have resulted from a confusion between the betrothal and the wedding (see appendix 7). Antony seems to have been the source of this confusion, for he maliciously charged that the "wedding" was hasty *(festinatas Liviae nuptias)*, probably in allusion to a hasty *betrothal* in early October following their initial meeting in September.[18]

Early in 38 Drusus was born in Octavian's Palatine home *(intra Caesaris penates)*. The actual day can be deduced as January 14 (see appendix 7).[19] The marriage took place very soon afterwards, in a year that began with a number of compelling omens. The hut of Romulus was burnt down on the Palatine during a religious ritual. The statue of Virtus fell on its face. A rumour spread that the Magna Mater was angry with the Romans, causing panic. Purification rites were carried out, and people were reassured when four palm trees sprang up near her temple on the Palatine and in the Forum. Dio reports that in the midst of these dramatic occurrences Octavian and Livia married.[20] The *Fasti Verulani* record the date as January 17 (38 BC).[21] It seems that Octavian had simply waited a brief while for Livia to recover from delivering Drusus, then proceeded straight to the wedding.

Inevitably, these events led to considerable gossip about the true paternity of Drusus, and humorists coined a line in Greek, preserved in Suetonius and paraphrased by Dio, about some being lucky in having *trimena paidia* (children in three months). This became a proverbial saying, and seems to have been parodied by Caligula, who married his last wife, Caesonia, when she was close to the end of her term so that he could beget a *paidion triakonthemeron* (a thirty-day child). There was also a rumour that Octavian was Drusus' real father, a belief no doubt encouraged by his deep sorrow on the young man's death in 9 BC. This last particular ghost can surely be laid to rest. Livia must have conceived in late March or early April 39, before the Treaty of Misenum and the amnesty that brought her and her first husband back to Rome and into the company of Octavian.[22] It may have been to discourage such gossip that after the birth Octavian sent the infant Drusus to his father and made an entry in the record *(hypomnemata)* of the fact that it was Tiberius Nero who was the father. But it should be noted that it was normal for a man marrying a pregnant woman to send the child to the natural father.[23]

In the event Tiberius Nero does not seem to have made much, if any, political capital out of his compliance. When he died, some six years after the wedding, in 32 BC or the end of 33, he named Octavian in his will as guardian *(tutor)* to both his sons. In accordance with Roman tradition, his first son, Tiberius, now nine years old, delivered the funeral elegy. Tiberius Nero, Livia's first husband, thus quitted the scene, a tired failure, the brilliant hopes of his youth unrealised.[24]

The scandal provoked by the unusual marriage continued to haunt Octavian. A decade later (29–28 BC), while he was exercising the power of censor, someone brought before him a young man who had committed adultery with a married woman but then had afterwards married the woman in question. Octavian was in a major quandary, but he dealt with it prudently. He suggested that they forget the quarrels of the past and look to the future.[25]

3

IN THE SHADOWS

We hear relatively little about Livia in the first thirty years or so after her marriage to Octavian, a considerable period in any relationship, and one in which she and her husband passed from youth to middle age. There are a number of reasons for this general silence. To the extent that there was a "first lady" in Rome during these years, this role belonged not to Livia but to Octavian's sister, Octavia, who garnered the lion's share of the attention, almost all of it favourable. A second reason was Livia's own good political sense. She no doubt anticipated that during this formative period of the principate a powerful imperial woman who meddled where she had no business would attract attention to her misdeeds, actual and imagined. When after the death of Octavia she began to play a more prominent and public part in affairs, she had learned to handle her role with considerable skill. The publicity over her marriage to Octavian would have impressed on her the need to maintain a low profile, to project the image to the Romans of the wife as obedient helpmate who stays very much in the shadow of her husband. It is telling that the criticism voiced over the unusual circumstances of the marriage focussed not on her behaviour but on Octavian's. Her dignified demeanour seems to have made her immune to Antony's attacks.

In the period after her marriage Livia would presumably have lived for most of the time in Octavian's residence on the Palatine. But the first recorded event occurred outside Rome. She appears to have possessed a family estate not far from Veii at Primaporta, near the ninth milestone of the Via Flaminia, described by Suetonius as "hers," *Veientanum suum* (see chapter 9). How she came to own this property is not clear. We do not know how much of her father's assets she would have acquired after his death, given that he was proscribed. Her first husband, Tiberius Nero, would of course have returned her dowry on their divorce. At any rate this one estate seems to have remained in her family's hands. Here, about the time of her marriage, she was singled out for a dramatic and famous omen.[1] A tradition took hold that as Livia was returning to the villa, an eagle dropped a white chick with a laurel branch in its mouth into her lap. She rescued the small bird and raised it, and planted the sprig. (Pliny says that she did so on the instructions of the augurs [*haruspices*], as a religious obligation.) A great brood of white chicks was born, which in itself would have been considered remarkable, because there was a belief that white hens were sterile. From this event the villa was called *ad Gallinas*, and a grove of laurels sprang up, from which the *triumphatores* subsequently collected the sprigs that they carried in their hands and which made up their crowns during the celebration. It also became the tradition, probably begun by Augustus in 29 BC in his Actian triumph and continued by later Julio-Claudian emperors, for the celebrant to plant the cutting afterwards. Pliny testifies to seeing trees with labels identifying the individual triumphator who had planted them, and it was said that just before the death of one of these victorious generals, the shrub that he had planted would wither and die. The laurels and the brood of chicks survived for more than a century at least. According to Dio, the extinction of the Julio-Claudian line was foretold in Nero's last year, when the whole grove withered from the root up and all the hens died (Pliny mentions none of this). Julius Caesar had taken the laurel as his personal symbol, and a senatorial decree of 45 BC gave him the right to wear a laurel wreath in perpetuity. Octavian continued this association after the ad gallinas incident by taking a cutting from the grove for his triumph and replanting it, and at the time of the settlement in 27, laurel bushes were set by the doors of his house on the Palatine, after which they became important symbols on coins, altars, and other art.[2]

The story of the omen at Primaporta might well have been invented, or at least embellished, by Octavian, and it illustrates how from the beginning Livia was intended to play an important symbolic role in her new husband's career. Its appeal might be found at a number of levels. It would have reminded Romans of the sign that prophesied Caesar's ultimate victory over Pompey, when a kite dropped a sprig of laurel on one of the soldiers on the eve of their departure for the final campaign (49 BC). The portent clearly foretold the imminence of triumphant generals, and in Livia's case would have been appropriate at the time, because there would have been confidence that she and Octavian would have children. It would have been a perfect antidote to the mud thrown at them over their divorce and marriage, and would have told the world that their union met with the approval of the gods. In the event, they did not have living children, and Dio alone preserves an alternative interpretation: that Livia was to hold the emperor's power in her lap and dominate him in everything, a reading that reputedly pleased Livia but alarmed others.[3]

Apart from this striking airborne phenomenon, Livia tends to remain in the background in the thirties, eclipsed by her sister-in-law Octavia, to whom Octavian remained completely devoted throughout her life.[4] She had married Gaius Claudius Marcellus (consul in 50) some time before 54 and produced a son (Marcus Claudius Marcellus) and two daughters (Claudia Marcella Minor and Maior) from the marriage. Her husband Marcellus died in 40. A period of ten months of mourning should have followed, but protocol fell victim to pressing state needs. She was now called upon to render an important service to her brother. Fulvia, the wife of Antony, had also just died (see chapter 7). Antony could hardly be called inconsolable, for in the previous year he had met Cleopatra and begun his torrid love affair. But he did not have a wife. A special measure of the Senate was passed to allow Octavia to bypass the statutory period of mourning and to marry Antony later that year.[5] This was an important political marriage, intended to bring closer together Rome's two most prominent public figures. There was a general feeling that Octavia would be a powerful force for harmony, and their first months together augured well. The couple spent the winter of 39–38 in Athens along with their newborn daughter, Antonia Maior. Their second daughter, the famous Antonia Minor, followed soon after.[6] To all appearances the marriage was initially a happy one.

For all his diplomatic talents, Octavian's political difficulties continued to mount, and his rivalry with Antony simply refused to go away. The two men were saved from a direct clash only by the efforts in 37 BC of Octavia, a *chrema thaumaston gunaikos* (wonder of a woman), as she was called on the occasion (the phrase is almost certainly Octavian's). She prevailed on her brother and husband to agree to the Treaty of Tarentum, which extended the triumvirate for five years.[7] A further promising development came when Marcus Agrippa finally broke Sextus Pompeius' power at the Battle of Naulochus in September 36. (Sextus escaped to Asia Minor, where he was put to death by one of Antony's officers.) The news of Naulochus apparently reached Rome by divine agency, when a member of the praetorian guard had a sudden vision and proceeded to lay his sword at the feet of Capitoline Jupiter to signify that he had no further use for it. The public reaction was ecstatic and brought Livia briefly into the record once again, for among the honours voted was the right of Octavian and Livia and their children to hold a banquet in the Capitoline temple on the anniversary of the battle, and to celebrate a day of thanksgiving.[8]

Antony repaid his debt to Octavia with the same sensibility he had shown his previous wife, Fulvia. He returned with her to the East, but on reaching Corcyra despatched her to Italy, on the specious ground that he did not want to expose her to danger when he went on his campaign against the Parthians. The real reason, it was widely believed, was that he wanted her out of the way to clear the field for his affair with Cleopatra. He made no secret of this infatuation, and in 36 he acknowledged paternity of three of their children. In 35 he instructed Octavia (by letter) to return to Rome.[9] She did so but remained a model wife, staying in Antony's house and begging Octavian not to go to war for her sake. She continued to look after Antony's children, and presented herself as his wife until 32, when Antony formally divorced her and sent representatives to Rome to throw her out of his house, after which she chose to live in secluded retirement. Without the steadying influence of Octavia, the propaganda war between Octavian and Antony resumed its full vigour, catching Livia in its net. There were stories of dubious reliability circulating in Rome, always the best kind to besmirch a rival, and Octavian was happy to make use of them—lurid tales of Antony anointing Cleopatra's feet at a banquet, of leaving the platform while a distinguished orator was in midspeech to join Cleopatra at her litter, even of him reading her love letters while adjudicating legal disputes. Antony's defence was attack. One of his retorts, dating to about 33, came in a letter to Octavian, preserved by Suetonius. The text is difficult, and it is paraphrased here to convey Antony's meaning: "What has changed you? That I'm into the queen? Is she my wife? [No, but so what?] And have I just started or haven't I been doing it for nine years? And anyhow, is [Livia] Drusilla the only one you're into?" Antony's attack is not directed against Livia, of course, but by implication it might be seen as a verbal assault on her.[10]

It is against this background of vicious rivalry between Octavian and Antony that we should place a remarkable measure recorded by Dio in 35 BC. In that year, the historian tells us, Octavian returned to Rome from his campaigns in Illyria and was granted a triumph (deferred until 29). In addition he granted Livia and Octavia a form of protection against verbal insult similar to that of the tribunes, along with two other privileges, namely statues erected in their honour and the right to administer their own estates without a guardian. The constitutional significance of these honours is discussed in chapter 7. They are probably best seen in their historical context, as a response to the relentless indignities heaped on Octavia by her husband, rather than as a general measure designed to enhance Livia's status. Plutarch seems to have had a good insight into the workings of Octavian's mind in the period. He says that when Octavia sought permission from Octavian to join Antony in 35, he granted it, to give him a reasonable pretext for war if Antony resumed his old abusive ways. Antony could almost be guaranteed to perform on cue, and when Octavia was sent back from Athens to Rome that year, her public humiliation was palpable. Octavian could now move to denounce his opponent both in the Senate and before the people, contrasting his sister's noble conduct with Antony's scurrilous behaviour. Thus it was almost certainly Octavia rather than Livia who was at the top of Octavian's agenda in 35 when the special privileges were granted — and it is surely significant that in describing them Dio puts her name first.[11] Not that the protection of Livia would be without political value. Octavian knew that he was vulnerable through attacks on his wife — the insolent comments about his marriage were a prime example of this. But the primary reason for the addition of her name may well have been simply to create the fiction that Octavian was keeping the position of the triumvirs' wives equal.

Little specific information on Livia emerges during the next decade. Her first husband died in 33 or 32 without making any further political progress, placing his sons, Tiberius and Drusus, under Octavian's protection on his death.[12] At this early stage Octavian showed a willingness to bring the two lads within the dynastic scheme that he already seems to have been evolving, and he thus inadvertently inaugurated the process that ultimately led to Tiberius' succeeding him as emperor. Some time before March 32, Tiberius, aged ten, was betrothed to Vipsania. She was the barely-one-year-old daughter of Marcus Agrippa, Octavian's closest colleague and his commander at Naulochus, and Pomponia, whose father was Cicero's friend, the equestrian Atticus. Syme, who subscribes heavily to the principle of female intrigue, believes that the match was contrived by Livia, to bind the great general closer to her and to Octavian. Perhaps, but there is simply no evidence. This is not to suggest that Livia was above scheming, but Agrippa in fact probably had more to gain from the union, as Velleius observes. He was a novus homo, and through the link could anticipate grandchildren who would belong to the Claudian gens. If female machinations are to be sought, they might more likely be detected in what could be seen as Octavia's countermeasure, when Agrippa, after divorcing Pomponia, married Octavia's daughter Marcella, in 28 BC. It would not have escaped Octavia's attention that if her brother had started to visualise the principipate now, and as part of that vision saw succession from within his own line, then his daughter, Julia, would clearly be called upon to play a key role. The marriage of Marcus Agrippa and Marcella would in a sense remove a potential rival and clear the way for a union between Julia and Octavia's son Marcellus, which Livia might resent but could do little to prevent. Of course, it has to be stressed that all these family arrangements were made before Octavian's first settlement, and we must be alert to the danger of anachronistic thinking in introducing dynastic considerations prematurely.[13]

The rivalry between Octavian and Antony reached its climax in the naval battle at Actium on September 31. The surrender of Antony's fleet to Marcus Agrippa was followed by the suicides of Antony and Cleopatra. If we are to believe Dio's account, Livia played a role, albeit a minor and indirect one, in the immediate wake of the battle. Cleopatra, who had fallen into Octavian's hands, was convinced that he planned to take her back to Rome to be the chief spectacle in his triumph. She begged him to allow her to take her own life rather than face the humiliation. Cleopatra could not budge him and tried another tack. To put him off his guard, she pretended a change of heart and claimed that she was willing to sail to Rome. Her plan seems to have been a highly convoluted one, to create the impression that she was really hoping that he would relent, or that Livia would intercede for her. This expectation does not imply any special power or influence on Livia's part. Even if the anecdote is true in its details (and it does seem to involve a reading of Cleopatra's mind), the Egyptian queen did not actually expect Livia to intervene. The story is given a slightly different and more colourful twist by Plutarch. In his version, Cleopatra hid away some of her jewellery and gave a false accounting to Octavian. The discrepancy was pointed out by one of her stewards, Seleucus. Cleopatra had to be physically restrained from thrashing poor Seleucus and adroitly made a virtue out of necessity, saying that she had put some things aside not for herself but for Octavia and Livia, hoping through them to persuade Octavian to take a more gentle line. By this ingenious argument she supposedly convinced Octavian that she had given up any thoughts of suicide. Thus Plutarch and Dio seem to be in agreement that any faith that Cleopatra professed in Livia's assistance was nothing but a front, and indeed, she did shortly after take her own life. To the limited extent that this rather dubious anecdote might provide evidence for female power, Plutarch's version shows that in the eyes of the sources the putative influence was shared between Livia and Octavia. Of course, it could be argued that Cleopatra at the very least recognised that the notion of intervention from female members of the imperial family was not unfeasible. But there would be nothing remarkable in that. There were ample precedents for such intercessions in the republic, not least in Octavia's activities on behalf of Antony.[14]

In January, 27 BC, the history of the Roman world was transformed, and it is then that, by convention, the Roman republic is deemed to have ended and the empire to have begun. In that month Octavian handed over to the Senate the extraordinary powers that he had accumulated. They in return granted him a single large "province," embracing at its core Syria, most of Spain, and the Gallic provinces, for a ten-year period, open to renewal. He was granted other powers, nominally from the Senate and the Roman people, and received a new title, Augustus, which would be handed down to his successors. Augustus (as he is now called) had enough faith in his settlement and in the security of his own position to leave Rome later in the year for an extended absence, to settle matters in Gaul and Spain. This marked the beginning of a regimen, maintained for fifteen years, of spending extended periods in the provinces for three years, alternating the visits with two-year stays in Rome. Did Livia accompany him on these journeys? During the republic the traditional role of the governor's wife had been to see her husband off, look to his interests in his absence, and welcome him back on his return. This was not, however, a universal practice, and in the imperial period it became common for wives, along with the children, to go to the provinces when their husbands assumed the role of administrator, even when this meant that they might be in the vicinity of military action. Octavia, who had accompanied Antony to the East, provided an obvious precedent. The practice would be called into question during the next reign, after a number of highly publicised incidents centred around the conduct of governors' wives, which convinced many Romans that the presence of women was dangerous because it allowed them undue interference in matters of state.[15]

Livia on occasion certainly did venture outside Rome with Augustus. This is revealed in a senatorial debate that took place several decades later. When in AD 21 an unsuccessful attempt was made to force the wives of governors to stay at home, Drusus Caesar, son of Tiberius, spoke against the motion and cited Livia as a precedent, noting that she had gone with Augustus as a companion both to the West and to the East *(in occidentem atque orientem)*. Drusus, like any good politician, was using his material selectively, for Augustus was actually on record as believing that the legates of the imperial provinces should not spend time with their wives, and that if they did, it should be between campaigning seasons. That said, it is a fair assumption that he could not simply have made up this claim about a public figure with the high profile of Livia, still alive at the time of the speech. There must have been a basic truth in his assertion.[16] The sources record only two specific instances of Livia and Augustus having taken a journey together: when they went to Ticinum to receive the body of Livia's son Drusus in 9 BC, and when they took their last journey together to Campania in AD 14, just before Augustus' death. Neither of these trips took them outside Italy, and neither would qualify as one of the journeys "to the East and to the West." Clearly Livia must have journeyed with her husband on occasions not recorded in the literature. The trip that Augustus made in 27–24 BC to Gaul and Spain would be a good candidate. It is true that when he returned to Rome in 24, Livia and Octavia took part in the sacrificial ritual that celebrated the homecoming, but this would not preclude her having been with him. Certainly while in Spain he fell seriously ill and retired to Tarraco, where he spent some time recuperating. It is hard to believe that Livia would not have been at his side when his life was at serious risk. We face the recurring problem that in this period she seems to have been deliberately self-effacing, and successful in that effort. The silence of the sources about her possible presence in Spain need not be especially significant or surprising.[17]

After the settlement of 27 BC the issue of the succession dominated political thought for the remainder of Augustus' life. The position of the princeps was unprecedented, despite its veneer of republican respectability, and there was no theoretical mechanism by which his authority could be passed to a successor. To ease the process the princeps adopted the practice of associating his intended successors with him as partners in the chief powers of the principate, his proconsular power and the symbolically important tribunician *potestas*, the traditional authority of the plebeian tribunes. But by restoring openly what was in essence a monarchical principle, Augustus was bound to cause general offence, and particular offence to the old once-powerful families. Moreover, Livia bore no surviving children to him, a fact that was to have far-reaching impact on Rome's political history. The designation of an adopted, not natural, son, which probably made the policy somewhat easier for those same old families to accept, would conversely cause tensions within his own family. Only a natural son could be the undisputed successor, and family members excluded in the process of adoption would inevitably bear a grudge. This made the succession such a sensitive political issue, one that called on all of Augustus' tact and political acumen.

As early as in the immediate aftermath of Actium, Augustus seems to have given serious attention to the career of his nephew Marcus Claudius Marcellus, son of his sister Octavia, and by 25 BC he had decided on the betrothal of Marcellus, then seventeen, to his fourteen-year-old daughter, Julia. Marcellus' career was now promoted. What thoughts Livia had about these developments are not recorded, and in any case it is unlikely that she would have risked open opposition to Augustus, who was scrupulously careful to advance her son Tiberius also, although essentially as second string to Marcellus. In the event, when Augustus fell seriously ill in 23, he passed his authority on not to Marcellus, who probably was felt to lack the necessary judgement and maturity, but to his old comrade-in-arms Marcus Agrippa.[18]

Augustus was restored by his physician Antonius Musa, relying on a strict regimen of cold baths, and could look forward to many more years of active life. Agrippa would have been aware that his promotion at the time of the illness was no more than a stopgap. In an unhappy mood he departed for the East, established his headquarters in Lesbos, and from there governed Syria through legates. The problem resolved itself of its own accord. In the autumn of 23 Marcellus took ill, probably a victim of the same plague that had threatened Augustus' life. Despite the best efforts of Antonius Musa, he did not recover, and died in his twentieth year. This was the first major death for the imperial family and was treated in a style that later became familiar. After a grand funeral Marcellus was given a place in the mausoleum that Augustus was still in the process of constructing, where more than half a century later Livia herself would rest.

At this point Dio introduces a charge that she resorted to murder to clear the way for her own sons, bringing about the death of Marcellus because Augustus had openly given him priority. This is the kind of charge that routinely was made against Livia, often in contexts that make the allegation absurd. It is also the kind of charge that is impossible to refute. But it is worth noting that although Dio raises the issue, he is himself sceptical about the claim and notes that previous (unnamed) sources also were in disagreement over it. He also points out that in that year and the following one, Rome was suffering from plagues which took many lives.[19] In the very unlikely event that Livia was party to the death of Marcellus, it would have to be said that she made a serious miscalculation. Her sons garnered no political advantage from the death. Marcus Agrippa was the one to gain.

In September of the following year, 22 BC, Augustus set out on an extended tour of the eastern provinces, after summoning Agrippa back to take charge in Rome.[20] This eastern trip kept him away for three years, and on this occasion we can feel all but certain that he was accompanied by Livia.[21] We have the comment of her grandson Drusus about her visit to the East, and this was the only eastern trip that Augustus took after Actium. Moreover, there is the evidence of the special privileges granted during the journey both to Sparta and Samos, communities which particularly enjoyed Livia's favour. The couple went first to Sicily, where Augustus gave colonial status to Syracuse and various other cities and waited until the recall of Agrippa to Rome could be arranged. They seem to have spent the winter there. In the spring they proceeded to Greece. Augustus showed his regard for Sparta by awarding the city the island of Cythera, and he attended a banquet to mark the hospitality accorded to Livia some years earlier when she had passed through with her son and first husband.[22] Athens did not fare so well and was perhaps given a hint of the problems to come when the cult statue of Athena on the Acropolis turned 180 degrees and spat blood. The city lost Aegina and Eretria, supposedly, as some believed, because of Athenian support for Antony. It may have been in an attempt to try to win back the imperial favour that the Athenians at some point voted divine honours to Livia and to Julia.[23] It is also very likely that on this trip Livia visited the famous sanctuary at Delphi. While there she made a generous dedication, in the form of the letter epsilon inscribed in gold. (The exact significance of the letter is somewhat obscure.) Visitors to the site were later told that the inscription was the Epsilon of Livia; a less impressive version, in more modest bronze, was known as the Epsilon of the Athenians.[24]

The couple then passed over to Samos, and there they spent the winter of 21–20. Augustus had spent the winters after Actium there.[25] He had another good reason for choosing the island on this later occasion. The Samians had special ties with Livia, and her family had for long been their patrons (see chapter 10). In recognition of their steadfast loyalty, Augustus restored the colossal statues of Athena and Heracles, which Antony had removed to give to Cleopatra, to their rightful places in the famous Temple of Hera on the island.[26]

The following spring the imperial party were in Asia Minor. Apart from the cities attested in the record, there are others, like Pergamum and Ilium, where Augustus at some stage erected monuments and received honours, probably during this trip. He settled affairs in Bithynia, where Cyzicus lost its freedom because of a dispute in which some Romans had been put to death. They then travelled on to Syria, where Tyre and Sidon lost their freedom on the same grounds. It is likely that while Livia was in Syria, Salome and her brother Herod the Great came from Judaea to greet her, to mark the first stage in what would be a long and warm friendship (see chapter 10).[27] All in all, the year was a great success, crowned by two special achievements. Livia's son Tiberius was able to achieve a diplomatic coup by installing a pro-Roman figure on the throne of Armenia. More significantly, Augustus came to an agreement with

Rome's traditional enemy Parthia, and in a gesture heavy with symbolism succeeded in retrieving the standards lost to the Parthians at the disastrous battle of Carrhae in 53 BC.

In the winter of 20–19 the couple returned to spend the second winter in Samos.[28] On this occasion Augustus finally yielded to Livia's pleas to grant freedom to the island, a request he had previously declined. They were visited in Samos by embassies from far and wide, from the queen of Ethiopia and even from India, which sent gifts of tigers (which the Romans had not seen before), as well as a man born without arms (whom Strabo saw personally), huge snakes, a giant tortoise, and a partridge as large as a vulture.[29] Livia and Augustus seem to have remained on the island until as late as July of 19, at which point they began their return trip to Rome. They went first to Athens. A member of the Indian entourage named Zarmarus entertained the royal couple after he had been initiated into the rites of the mystery religion, presumably in nearby Eleusis. His initiation would have guaranteed him a happy afterlife, and he was clearly impatient to enjoy it. Wearing only a loincloth, he hurled himself into the fire. Augustus may well have been involved in the rites himself during this visit, already being an initiate. It has even been suggested that Livia might have used the opportunity to become initiated herself, an otherwise newsworthy event that might have been eclipsed by Zarmarus' fiery exit.[30] The poet Vergil met them in Athens. The celebrated author of the *Aeneid*, the great nationalistic paean to Augustus' achievements, was planning his own grand tour but was persuaded to return to Rome with the imperial party. He did not make it. He fell ill in Megara, and when the company finally reached Italy in September, he died, on the twentieth of the month, in Brundisium.[31] As Augustus and Livia travelled overland to Rome, one of the consuls, as well as leading senators, came out to meet them in Campania. The gesture was no doubt meant kindly but was not to the princeps' liking, and they managed to evade the deputation and eventually to enter Rome by night.[32]

While on his travels Augustus would have continued to be preoccupied with the old issue of what would happen after his death. He had clearly demonstrated at the time of his departure that he could not manage without Marcus Agrippa, married at the time to Marcella, Octavia's daughter. Agrippa now divorced her (her compensation was to be married to Iullus Antonius, the son of Antony and Fulvia), so as to be free in 21 to marry the widowed Julia. Plutarch says that this marriage came about through Octavia's machinations and that she prevailed upon Augustus to accept the idea. It is not clear what her motives would have been. If we are to believe Seneca we might see pure spite. He claimed that Octavia hated Livia after the death of Marcellus because the hopes of the imperial house passed now to Livia's sons. This could well be no more than speculation, and Seneca does not even hint at any specific action by Octavia against her supposed rival. The whole story sounds typically Senecan in its denigration of dead individuals who are easy targets. Once again, we are told nothing about Livia's reaction to the marriage. She might not have been able to object to the earlier marriage between Julia and Augustus' nephew Marcellus, but in 21 the situation was different. Her older son, Tiberius, who was not yet married, had been passed over in favour of an outsider to the family. But whatever his sense of obligation to his wife, Augustus probably felt that he had little choice in the matter. Agrippa's earlier reaction to having to take second place to Marcellus, a blood relative of Augustus, would have provided a good hint to Augustus of how his friend would have taken to playing second string to Tiberius. Agrippa was now a key figure in the governing of Rome. He was not a man to be provoked.[33]

If Livia had been entertaining hopes that this early stage of a preeminent role for either of her sons (and such a suggestion, while reasonable, is totally speculative), such hopes would have faded with the birth of two sons to Julia and Agrippa. Gaius Caesar was born in 20 BC, and, as if to confirm the line, a second son, Lucius Caesar, arrived in 17. Augustus was delighted, and soon after Lucius' birth signalled his ultimate intentions by adopting both boys. He thus might envisage himself as being "succeeded" by Agrippa, who would in turn be succeeded by either Gaius and Lucius, who were, in a sense, sons of both men. In late 16 BC Augustus set out on an extended trip to Gaul and Spain, where he established a number of veteran settlements. Livia may have accompanied him. Dio does report speculation that the emperor went away so as to be able to conduct his affair with Terentia, the wife of his close confidant Maecenas, in a place where it would not attract gossip. Even if the rumours were well founded, the implication need not necessarily follow that he had left Livia behind. Livia had a reputation as a *femme complaisante*, and Augustus may simply have wanted to get away from the prying eyes of the capital. Certainly at one stage Livia intervened with Augustus to argue for the grant of citizenship to a Gaul, and this trip provides the best context. Moreover, Seneca dates a famous incident to this trip, Livia's plea on behalf of the accused Gaius Cornelius Cinna. It could well be that Seneca misdated the Cinna episode, but he at any rate clearly believed that Livia had been in Gaul with her husband at the relevant time.[34] (These issues are treated in greater detail in chapter 7.)

Agrippa lived to see the birth of two other children, his daughters Julia and Agrippina. The first (born about 19 BC) is the namesake of her mother, and, in the historical tradition, cut from the same cloth; the second was to be somewhat eclipsed in the same tradition by her own daughter and namesake, the mother of the last Julio-Claudian emperor, Nero. Agrippa thus became the natural father of four of Augustus' grandchildren during his lifetime (a fifth would be born posthumously), and his stock rose higher with each event. He had served his princeps well, and could now take his final exit. In 13 he campaigned in the Balkans. At the end of the season he returned to Italy, where he fell ill, and in mid-March, 12 BC, he died. His body was brought to Rome, where it was given a magnificent burial, and the remains were deposited in the Mausoleum of Augustus, even though Agrippa had earlier booked himself another site in the Campus Martius.[35]

In the following year Octavia died. She is celebrated by the sources as a paragon of every human virtue, whose only possible failings had been the forgivable ones of excessive loyalty to an undeserving husband and excessive grief over the death of a possibly only marginally more deserving son.[36] As noted earlier, we should be cautious about Seneca's claim that Octavia nursed a hatred for Livia after the death of Marcellus. But there can be no doubt that her death was in a sense advantageous to Livia, for it removed one of the main contenders for the role of the premier woman in the state. Only Augustus' daughter Julia might now lay claim to a precedence of sorts, but she in fact became an agent in furthering Livia's ambitions, rather than an obstacle. Once her formal period of mourning was over, Julia would need another husband. Suetonius says that her father carefully considered several options, even from among the equestrians. Tiberius later claimed that Augustus pondered the idea of marrying her off to a political nonentity, someone noted for leading a retiring life and not involved in a political career. Among others he supposedly considered Gaius Proculeius, a close friend of the emperor and best known for the manner of his death rather than of his life: he committed suicide by what must have been a painful technique—swallowing gypsum. This drastic action was apparently not in response to the prospect of marriage to Julia but in despair over the unbearable pains in his stomach. In 11 BC, the year of Octavia's death, Augustus made his decision. He could hardly pass over one of Livia's sons again. They were the only real choices, given the practical options open to him. Both were married, and Drusus' wife was the daughter of Octavia, someone able already to produce offspring linked, at least indirectly, by blood to the princeps. Divorce in this case would not have been desirable. Augustus had already demonstrated his faith in Livia's other son, Tiberius, by appointing him to replace Agrippa in the Balkans. He was the inevitable candidate for Julia's next husband.

In perhaps 20 or 19 Tiberius had married Agrippa's daughter Vipsania, to whom he had long been betrothed. Their son Drusus was born in perhaps 14.[37] In 11 Vipsania was pregnant for a second time, but Tiberius was obliged to divorce her, although he seems to have been genuinely attached to her. Reputedly when they met after the divorce he followed her with such a forlorn and tearful gaze that precautions were taken that their paths would never cross again. He was now free to marry Julia. This marriage marks a milestone in Tiberius' career and in the ambitions that Livia would naturally have nursed for her son. Augustus was clearly prepared to place him in an advantageous position, and the process could be revoked only with difficulty.[38] It is inevitable that there should be speculation among modern scholars that Livia might have played a role in arranging the marriage. Gardthausen claimed that she brought it off in the teeth of vigorous opposition. Perhaps, but the suggestion belongs totally to the realm of speculation. If Livia did play some part in winning over Augustus, she did it so skilfully and unobtrusively that she has left no traces, and the sources are silent about any specific interference on this occasion. Nor can it be assumed that Augustus would have needed a great deal of persuading. No serious store should be placed in the claims in the sources that he held Tiberius in general contempt and was reduced to turning to him *faut de mieux*. Suetonius quotes passages from Augustus' correspondence that provide concrete evidence that the emperor in fact held his adopted son in high regard. Suetonius chose the extracts to show his appreciation of Tiberius' military and administrative skills, but his words clearly suggest a high degree of affection that seems to go beyond the merely formulaic. He addresses Tiberius as *iucundissime*, probably the equivalent in modern correspondence of "my very dear Tiberius." He reveals that when he has a challenging problem or is feeling particularly annoyed at something, he yearns for his Tiberius *(Tiberium meum desidero)*, and he notes that both he and Livia are tortured by the thought that her son might be overtaxing himself.[39]

Livia's other son, Drusus, although arguably his brother's match in military reputation and ability, seems to have been quite different from him in temperament. Where Tiberius was private, inhibited, uninterested in courting popularity, Drusus was affable, engaging, and well-liked, and there was a popular belief, probably naive, that he was committed to an eventual restoration of the republic. He had found a perfectly compatible wife in Antonia the Younger, a woman who commanded universal esteem and respect to the very end. They produced two sons, both of whom would loom large on the stage of human events: Germanicus, who became the most loved man in the Roman empire and whose early death threatened to erode Livia's popularity, and Claudius, whose physical limitations were an embarrassment to Livia and to other members of the imperial family, but who confounded them all by becoming an emperor of considerable acumen and ability. They also had a daughter, Livilla, who attained disrepute through her affair with the most loathed man in the early Roman empire, the notorious praetorian prefect Sejanus.[40]

Drusus dominated the landscape in 9 BC. The year seemed to start auspiciously for Livia. In 13 BC the Senate had voted to consecrate the Ara Pacis, one of the great monuments of Augustus' regime, as a memorial to his safe return from Spain and the pacification of Gaul. The dedication waited four years and finally took place in 9, on January 30, Livia's birthday, perhaps her fiftieth (figs. 20, 21). The honour was a profound one, but indirect and thus low-key, in keeping with Livia's public persona.[41] Her sons continued to achieve distinction on the battlefield. A decorated sword sheath of provincial workmanship has survived from this period. It represents a frontal Livia with the nodus hairstyle (see chapter 6), and shoulder locks carefully designed so as to flow along her shoulders above the drapery. She appears between two heads, almost certainly her sons, and the piece pictorially symbolises Livia at what must have been one of the most satisfying periods of her life.[42] To cap her sense of well-being, Tiberius, after signal victories over the Dalmatians and Pannonians, returned to Rome to celebrate an ovation. Following the usual practice after a triumph or ovation, a dinner was given for the Senate in the Capitoline temple, and tables were set out for the people in front of private houses. A separate banquet was arranged for the women. Its sponsors were Livia and Julia. Private tensions may already have arisen between Tiberius and Julia, but at least at the public level they were sedulously maintaining an outward image of marital harmony, and Livia was making her own contribution towards promoting that image.[43]

Similar festivities were planned to celebrate Drusus' victories. Presumably in his case Livia would have joined Antonia, Drusus' wife, in preparing the banquet, as she had joined Tiberius' wife on the earlier occasion. While Tiberius had been engaged in operations in Pannonia, Drusus had conducted a highly acclaimed campaign in Germany. By 9 BC he had succeeded in taking Roman arms as far as the river Elbe. So awesome were his achievements that greater powers felt the need to intervene. He was visited by the apparition of a giant barbarian woman, who told him — she conveniently spoke Latin — not to push his successes further. Something was clearly amiss in the divine timing. Suetonius implies that Drusus heeded the warning, but calamity befell him anyhow. In a riding accident Drusus' horse toppled over onto him and broke his thigh. He fell gravely ill. His deteriorating condition caused consternation throughout the Roman world, and it is even claimed that the enemy respected him so much that they declared a truce pending his recovery. (Similar claims were later made about his son Germanicus.) Tiberius had been campaigning in the Balkans at the time but had returned to Italy and was passing through Ticinum after the campaign when he heard that Drusus was sinking fast. Travelling the 290 km in a day and a night, a rate that Pliny thought impressive enough to record, he rushed to be with his brother. He reached him just before he died in September, 9 BC.

Drusus was universally liked, and his death at the age of twenty-nine could not seriously be seen as benefitting anyone. Nevertheless, it still managed to attract gossip and rumours. The death of a young prince of the imperial house would usually drag in the name of Livia as the prime suspect. In this instance such a scenario would have been totally implausible, and Augustus became the target of the innuendo instead. Tacitus reports that the tragedy evoked the same jaundiced reactions as would that of Germanicus, three decades later in the reign of Tiberius, that sons with "democratic" temperaments—*civilia ingenia*—did not please ruling fathers (Germanicus had been adopted by Tiberius). Suetonius has preserved a tradition that Augustus, suspecting Drusus of republicanism, recalled him from his province and, when he declined to obey, had him poisoned. Suetonius thought the suggestion nonsensical, and he is surely correct. Augustus had shown great affection for the young man and in the Senate had named him joint heir with Gaius and Lucius. He also delivered a warm eulogy after his death. Even Tiberius' grief was portrayed as two-faced. To illustrate Tiberius' hatred for the members of his own family, Suetonius claims that he had earlier produced a letter in which his younger brother discussed with him the possibility of compelling Augustus to restore the republic. But events seem to belie completely the notion of any serious fraternal strife. Tiberius' anguish was clearly genuine. His general deportment is of special interest, because of the light that it might throw on his and Livia's conduct later, at the funeral of Germanicus. According to Seneca, the troops were deeply distressed over the death and demanded Drusus' body. Tiberius maintained that discipline had to be observed in grieving as well as fighting, and that the funeral was to be conducted with the dignity demanded by the Roman tradition. He repressed his own tears and was able to dampen the enthusiasm for a vulgar show of public grief.[44]

Tiberius now set out with the body for Rome. Augustus went to Ticinum (Pavia) to meet the cortege, and because Seneca says that Livia accompanied the procession to Rome, it is probably safe to assume that she went with her husband. As she travelled, she was struck by the pyres that burned throughout the country and the crowds that came out to escort the funeral train. The event provides one of the few glimpses of Livia's private emotions. She was crushed by the death and sought comfort from the philosopher Areus (see chapter 6). On his advice, she uncharacteristically opened herself up to others. She put pictures of Drusus in public and private places and encouraged her acquaintances to talk about him. But she maintained a respectable level of grief, which elicited the admiration of Seneca. Tiberius may well have learned from his mother the appropriateness of self-restraint in the face of private anguish. It was an attitude that was later to arouse considerable resentment against both of them.[45]

During the funeral in Rome, Tiberius delivered a eulogy in the Forum and Augustus another in the Circus Maximus, where the emperor expressed the hope that Gaius and Lucius would emulate Drusus. The body was taken to the Campus Martius for cremation by the equestrians, and the funeral bier was surrounded by images of the Julian and the Claudian families. The ashes were deposited in Augustus' mausoleum. The title of Germanicus was posthumously bestowed on Drusus and his descendants, and he was given the further honour of statues, an arch, and a cenotaph on the banks of the Rhine. Augustus composed the verses that appeared on his tomb and also wrote a prose account of his life. No doubt less distinguished Romans, of varied literary talent, would have written their own contributions. The anonymous *Consolatio ad Liviam* represents itself as just such a composition, intended to offer comfort to Livia on this very occasion, although it was probably composed somewhat later (see appendix 1). Livia was indeed devastated, but as some form of compensation for her terrible private loss, she now, after some thirty years in the shadows, came into greater public prominence. The final chapter of Drusus' life seems to have opened up a new one in his mother's.[46]

4

THE PUBLIC FIGURE

The generous tribute that Augustus paid to Drusus at his funeral involved more than empty words strung together for the occasion. The emperor was genuinely attached to his stepson and earlier had publicly stated that Drusus was to be his joint heir. The fact that the funeral procession was accompanied by images of both Claudians and Julians was remarkable, for Drusus had never been adopted by Augustus. There are later parallels of a sort for the arrangement. Augustus' own funeral procession was accompanied by effigies of his own ancestors and of prominent Romans since the time of Romulus. Moreover, when the venerable Junia, half-sister of Cato Uticensis and mother of Marcus Brutus, the conspirator, died in AD 22, in her nineties, the effigies of twenty great families preceded her to her tomb.[1] But the very act of limiting the families to two in Drusus' case effectively made the honour both to him and, indirectly, to Livia all the greater, because it gave the Julian connection a special prominence. It might be seen as foreshadowing the even closer link that was to be established when Livia was adopted into the Julian line in Augustus' will.

For Livia the loss of her son would have been more a personal blow than an issue of state. She sought aid and guidance from the philosopher Areus and eventually came to terms with the death (see chapter 6). But while a mother's sense of bereavement is essentially a private matter, Drusus' death was at the same time considered a *public* sacrifice, and it brought her public recognition. To console Livia in her bereavement, the Senate voted statues for her, and she was granted the *ius trium liberorum*, the exemption from legal disabilities imposed on those who had borne fewer than three children (see chapter 7). We have no information about how many statues were commissioned, and it is to be acknowledged that no statue base has survived from the Augustan period recognizing her as the mother of Drusus, information that surely would have accompanied the statues voted in 9 BC. Moreover, the significance of the ius trium liberorum should probably not be given undue weight in her case. One of the main advantages it conferred, the right to handle property without a guardian, had already been granted her in 35. Dio notes that the Senate (and in his own day, the emperor) had the right to bestow this privilege on those whose failure to bear three children was involuntary. That principle would have applied in Livia's case. She had in fact given birth three times, but the child she shared with Augustus was premature and stillborn and thus did not legally qualify.[2] That said, it is noteworthy that both honours came in the same year as the dedication of the Ara Pacis, on her birthday. In addition, it is very possible that the decision to build a portico in her honour was taken in this same year. Up to this point Livia's role had been preeminently that of the dutiful wife. The events of 9 BC, as Flory has noted, mark her emergence into a much more public role.[3]

Now that Drusus was dead, Livia's maternal pride and hopes would have focussed entirely on her surviving son, Tiberius. He did not let her down. In the year following his brother's death, 8 BC, he took Drusus' place in command of the Rhine armies, joined by Augustus and by Gaius Caesar, who was introduced at this time to military service. Tiberius crossed the Rhine (Augustus stayed on the western side) and conducted a number of successful campaigns. He began to enjoy the marks of true recognition: an imperial salutation and a triumph (for the first time a full one), as well as a second consulship, to be held in 7 BC. The victorious Tiberius returned to Rome to assume his office and pledged himself to use the spoils of his campaigns for a worthy project. He would repair the Temple of Concord on the northwest side of the Forum in his own name and in that of his brother Drusus. Tiberius finally dedicated the restored building on January 16, AD 10. Having discharged this solemn responsibility, he went on to celebrate his triumph.[4]

Rome would have had a further reminder of Livia's special role as mother when she was joined by Tiberius in dedicating the great monument that bears her name, the Porticus Liviae (plan 3; see chapter 10). The dedication brought mother and son together in the first collaborative activity mentioned by the sources. Although this association with her son's recent achievements could have brought Livia nothing but pride and pleasure, we should not read too much into their joint role in the dedication. Augustus at this point was yet again in Gaul, and Tiberius had the task of deputizing for him at important events. The exact date is not known for certain, but Dio's narrative suggests very strongly that it took place in January, 7 BC. The seventeenth of the month, the anniversary of the wedding of Livia and Augustus, is a good candidate. After the dedication of the portico she gave a banquet to the women of the city, to match that given by Tiberius for the men. It is to be noted that two years earlier, on a similar occasion, Julia had joined Livia in giving a banquet. She was not involved in the present festivities. This may well be an early symptom of estrangement between Julia and Tiberius, but it could simply reflect the technicality that while Julia's presence on the earlier occasion as the wife of the victorious Tiberius was de rigeur, she had no proper part to play in a ceremony that belonged to Livia. Tiberius' duty was, after all, to represent Augustus in his role of princeps, not of father-in-law.[5] At some later date the portico received another component. Ovid in his *Fasti* records that on June 11 of an unspecified year Livia dedicated the *aedes* (shrine) to Concordia, to honour her husband (see appendix 8 and chapter 10). Flory draws attention to the different but parallel functions of the portico and the aedes that it housed. The Porticus Liviae was Augustus' work, though closely associated with Livia. The demolition of the luxury house whose site it occupied demonstrated his desire to restrain private luxury and promote public welfare in its place. The aedes was Livia's and stressed the idea of marital harmony, in a gesture in support of Augustus' marriage laws and his desire to revive family life, signalling that "the political unity of the state emanated from the domestic harmony of the imperial household." It can hardly be a coincidence that the dedication of the aedes occurs on the same day as the festivals of Matralia and Fortuna, both of which had their focus on the notion of marriage and women's lives.[6]

After his triumph and the dedication of the Temple of Concord and the Porticus Liviae, Tiberius returned to Germany, where he dealt with fresh disturbances with his usual competence and efficiency.[7] But the old problem of the succession now began to reassert itself. In 6 BC Augustus bestowed the tribunicia potestas on Tiberius for five years, but whatever self-confidence Livia's son might have derived from the grant would have been tempered by the situation of the princeps' adopted sons. Gaius was fourteen in 6 BC, Lucius eleven. Although it would almost certainly be an overstatement to say that the two boys were involved in some sort of political movement, their positions of privilege and luxury, not surprisingly, seem to have gone to their heads and turned them into insufferably arrogant youths. To make matters worse, their insolence was encouraged by hangers-on, eager to store up useful political credit. They may well have been egged on also by their mother, Julia, and she in her turn might have been encouraged by her own mother, Scribonia, still bearing a grudge against Livia. The situation grew worse when, in what seems like a fit of collective lunacy, the people elected Gaius to a consulship for the following year, an absurd gesture which would have installed a fourteen-year-old in an office that was steeped in ancient tradition and whose prestige Augustus was determined to maintain. The effort to promote Gaius' cause may well have been linked to demonstrations of popular support for Lucius when he turned up unattended at the theatre.[8] Although he might have been privately annoyed, Augustus certainly gave no overt signal that Gaius had behaved improperly. Gaius was granted a priesthood and the election was not really cancelled; it was merely postponed.[9]

At this stage a momentous event occurred in Tiberius' political career, one that must be classed as a blunder of epic proportions, mortifying both to Livia, who would naturally have been ambitious for her son, and to Augustus, who up to now had clearly seen him as someone who could potentially play a key role after his own death. Tiberius was offered an important commission in the East. He refused it and, astonishingly, sought permission to retire to the island of Rhodes, without his wife and with only a small retinue of close friends. The motives for this bizarre turn in Tiberius' thinking are unclear and are variously explained by the sources—antipathy towards Julia, a desire to leave the field clear for Gaius and Lucius, fear of Gaius and Lucius. The official reason given by Tiberius, according to Suetonius, was that he felt weary and simply needed a leave of absence. The truth behind Tiberius' action can probably not be recovered, and it may have come about through a complex combination of causes, some psychological, some political. Whatever Augustus' official intentions, Tiberius may well have harboured a sense, rightly or wrongly, that the emperor nurtured a deep-seated hope that it would be one of his adopted sons who would eventually succeed him, even though they had achieved little and were, if anything, showing every sign of being temperamentally unsuited for the task.

Tiberius' decision to leave Rome was a pivotal one, marking a turning point in his relations with Augustus and causing a breach that was to be healed only with the greatest difficulty and, apparently, with the repeated interventions of Livia. The emperor made no secret of his sense of betrayal and even declared openly in the Senate that he felt himself forsaken. In a desperate effort to demonstrate his loyalty, Tiberius opened his will and read it out to Livia and her husband. An imperial will could have political implications. Julius Caesar's did, because it contained Augustus' testamentary adoption. So did Tiberius' final will, invalidated after his death because it seemed to give Tiberius' grandson Gemellus a claim on the succession equal to Caligula's. Thus Tiberius might now have wanted to show that he harboured no feelings of resentment against Gaius and Lucius, and had named them as beneficiaries.[10]

The burden of trying to dissuade Tiberius from his foolhardy decision seems to have fallen on his mother. Livia begged him *(suppliciter)* to change his mind, but to no avail. His response was a petulant one—he went on a hunger strike for four days until he got his own way, an embarrassing stunt that can have done him no good in Augustus' eyes.[11] The blackmail worked, at least in the short term, and in this heavy atmosphere Tiberius made his exit. In Campania he was delayed by news that Augustus had fallen ill. The emperor had always been prone to nervous exhaustion, and his current ailment was probably aggravated by stress over recent events. When it was clear that he would survive, Tiberius continued his journey. On the way he sailed to the island of Paros, where he put pressure on the Parians to sell him the statue of Vesta, to be sent to Rome and placed in the Temple of Concord. He might have intended this as a pious gesture to Livia, often associated with Vesta. But he might also have wanted to convey a more overtly political message, a reminder to Livia not to fail her son. Once settled in Rhodes he moved into a quiet residence. He was based there for the next seven years, quietly attending the lectures of philosophers and debating with them, avoiding the attention of official visitors from Rome as much as possible.[12]

It was widely believed that at least a contributory factor in Tiberius' decision to get away from Rome was his antipathy towards his wife. It would be difficult to imagine a couple so ill-suited. Julia was a woman of considerable intelligence, with a good knowledge of literature and a love of well-informed and amusing company. But she was self-willed and held her own idiosyncratic views on what was socially acceptable. She outraged Augustus by her taste in friends and by her modish dress style. Augustus, who revered what were by his day considered old-fashioned traditions of morality and restraint, was out of touch with what proved to be a free-spirited daughter. He could not have helped the situation by persuading her to emulate the behaviour of Livia, and he scolded her about her acquaintances, her brazen language, her dress, even the fact that she was in the habit of removing grey hairs from her head. He tried unsuccessfully to keep her under a tight supervision and told the young men, even the most respectable, who visited her that they were not welcome in the emperor's home. Augustus' efforts to preserve his daughter's innocence were a failure, as they were bound to be. Julia had affairs from at least the time of her marriage to Agrippa—she is said to have advocated the safe interval offered by pregnancies, observing that she only "took on passengers when carrying freight."

Tiberius and Julia seem to have got along harmoniously at first, but their personalities were so different that it was inevitable that they would drift apart. The death of their infant child seems to have broken the last tie, and any fondness turned to contempt.[13] Matters came to a climax in 2 BC, when the revelation of Julia's promiscuous behaviour shattered the serenity of the *domus Augusta*. Seneca provides the fullest account. He reports in lurid terms that Julia, who had a legion of lovers, took to wandering the streets of the city seeking excitement, even prostituting herself with total strangers in the Forum at the statue of Marsyas. As a consequence many of her lovers were exiled (one was executed), and Julia herself was despatched to the small island of Pandateria, off the coast of Campania. A bill of divorce from Tiberius was sent to her in Augustus' name.[14] She did not face destitution, at least at the outset. The island had an imperial villa, and there was even a small operation to grow grapes (infested with field mice). But she was reputedly refused every comfort, even wine, and no visitors were allowed to land without making preliminary and exhaustive arrangements. By her father's will she was excluded from his mausoleum after her death. She had one champion, her mother, Scribonia, who had not remarried after her divorce from Octavian and now declared herself willing to accompany her daughter. Julia never returned to Rome.[15]

The literary sources put much emphasis on the moral facets of Julia's conduct, and Tacitus is struck by the extreme punishment dispensed to her. But there is a widespread scholarly view that the charges of sexual misbehaviour against members of the Julio-Claudian family were little more than diversionary tactics, intended to cover significant political transgressions, and that claims of sexual misconduct could be used to bring down dangerous claimants or their partisans.[16] The question can legitimately be raised whether Livia had any role in the scandal, and there has long been a suspicion among scholars that she was behind Julia's fall. Syme sees her prompting a reluctant Augustus to action by reminding him that Julia's behaviour was running counter to the tone of the moral reforms. He speculates that it was Livia who persuaded Augustus to launch an investigation into his daughter's conduct. Julia's temperament was such that it may have been difficult for Augustus and Livia to teach her by strict precept and example, and the tense situation that inevitably followed could have bred a certain resentment towards her stepmother. Perhaps, but we have no evidence of any serious political rift between the two women. Admittedly, it would not have helped that Livia was in a sense everything that Julia was not. Macrobius relates that Augustus confronted Julia with the wild behaviour of her friends and contrasted it with Livia's decorous conduct in public—but while such reprimands might well have irritated his daughter, they would hardly have provoked deep enmity between her and his wife. Julia's disgrace, following the earlier death of Octavia, did leave Livia in a unique position of power and prestige within the court, because there was now no female member of the imperial family to challenge her preeminent position. But if Livia's motive was to help Tiberius, it is difficult to see how she would have done so by engineering Julia's ruin. It could be argued that it was very much against Tiberius' interests for his wife to be brought down—she was Tiberius' link with the centre of power, as he doubtless realised when he wrote to Augustus from Rhodes and asked him to pardon her. The literary sources provide no information or even speculation on Livia's reaction to Julia's disgrace. This is an argument ex silentio, of course, but given the propensity of Tacitus in particular to tar Livia with every conceivable suspicion of malicious interference, even when the charge was absurd, the absence on this occasion of even a hint of her involvement in the scandal may well be significant.[17]

Inscriptional evidence, in fact, shows that Livia might have helped Julia when she went into exile, or at least at the stage when in AD 4 she was allowed to move from Pandateria to Rhegium, on the mainland. Such assistance would be in character, as Livia helped Julia's daughter, Julia the Younger, some years later when she was similarly sent into exile. The evidence for her support of the elder Julia is in the form of an inscription found in Rhegium that records the family of a Gaius Gelus, a freedman of Julia's. His father, Thiasus, is also identified as a freedman of Julia's, while his mother, also called Julia (after her mistress, of course), is identified as a freedwoman of Augusta's. The nomenclature of the mother shows that she must have been manumitted after AD 14, when Livia received the title Julia Augusta; thus the mother, and perhaps Thiasus, seem to have been seconded as slaves by Livia to Julia during her exile. What scant evidence we have suggests that Livia played her traditional conciliatory role, and Herbert-Brown even suggests that it might have been at this time that she dedicated the aedes to Concordia in her Portico, to advertise the fact that despite the departure of both Julia and Tiberius, there was still cohesion in the ruling family.[18]

The exile of Julia made Tiberius' position precarious, because it broke an important link between himself and Augustus at a time when relations between them had already soured. His sense of vulnerability would have increased in the following year, when his tribunicia potestas expired. At this point he underwent a change of heart and asked to be allowed to return. He no longer had any constitutional powers, and Gaius and Lucius were old enough that Tiberius would be less likely to be seen as a threat to any plans Augustus had formed for them. Tiberius' excuse for wanting to return was the desire to see his *necessitudines*, his close family, by which he presumably meant his mother and his son, Drusus. Augustus was not a forgiving person when wounded by personal slights from within his own family. He refused. Livia may well have supported Tiberius' request, but if she did, she was no more successful than her son. Suetonius claims that she managed to secure one concession from her husband, and only with the greatest difficulty: that as a front to conceal the fact that Tiberius was being kept out of Rome because of the emperor's displeasure, he would receive a form of commission *(legatio)* in the East.[19] If Livia did indeed intervene for her son in this matter, and we cannot be certain that she did, her intervention would have been natural in the circumstances, and we should not read deep political motives into her actions. It would be little more than what she frequently did for prominent Romans unrelated to her family. Tiberius had expressed a perfectly understandable desire to see his family, and Livia would have had a natural maternal instinct to want to protect the welfare of her only surviving son. Also, it is noteworthy that there were limits to what she could achieve. Augustus was prepared to offer no more than a compromise, and even then with some reluctance. Though willing to listen to Livia, he was in the end very much his own man.

In AD 2 Tiberius tried again to persuade Augustus to allow his return to Rome and once again, we are informed, Livia argued strenuously on his behalf *(impensissimis precibus)*. The emperor was still unwilling to give in to his wife's request, but he did indicate that he would be prepared to take directions on the matter from Gaius. Fortunately for Tiberius, Gaius was apparently prepared to be magnanimous and to support the older man's cause. That year, as Dio reports, the soothsayer Thrasyllus, a close confidant of Tiberius' in Rhodes, was looking out over the ocean when he espied an approaching ship. He predicted, accurately, the message it carried from Livia and Augustus: Tiberius could at last return to Rome. In reporting the prediction, Dio links Livia's name with Augustus' in playing a key role in the recall. It seems unlikely that she could claim much of the decision as hers, but her strenuous efforts on behalf of Tiberius in the recent past would explain why she received much of the credit. At last, Tiberius was recalled, but with the humiliating proviso that he drop completely out of public life. On reaching Rome he moved from his conspicuous house on the Carinae, on the southwest of the Esquiline, and relocated himself to the Garden of Maecenas, much farther away from the centre of the city. There he began to lead a life of quiet retirement.[20]

Tiberius had no doubt reconciled himself to retirement, and Livia might well have accepted that he had left the political scene for good had it not been for two major misfortunes that devastated the domus Augusta and necessitated a major rethinking of Augustus' dynastic intentions. Gaius had been given a command in the East in 1 BC, and after a three-year interval Lucius was given command of the armies of the Spanish provinces.[21] Both appointments were to end in tragedy. In the year when Tiberius was recalled, AD 2, Lucius Caesar fell ill at Massilia on his way to Spain and very quickly died, on August 20. Tiberius was allowed to compose a lyric poem, *Conquestio de Morte L. Caesaris*, to mark the occasion, in a gesture of family solidarity. He could not, however, have reasonably expected a serious change in his own status. Lucius, as the younger of the brothers, would have been essentially a junior partner to Gaius.[22] Two years later a further blow fell. Gaius had been sent to the East to deal with a rebellion in a traditional trouble spot, Armenia, the small mountainous country bordering Parthia east of the Euphrates. One of the rebels, Addon, persuaded him to come to the town of Artagira for a parley. The young Roman, with more courage than common sense, foolishly approached the walls of the town. In violation of the cease-fire he was struck by some sort of missile, presumably an arrow. The town was in the end taken and Gaius was honoured by being acclaimed as imperator. But the wound did not heal. Gaius' physical constitution had never been strong. He now grew weaker and started to behave so erratically that people suspected that his mind had been affected. He sought permission from Augustus to relinquish his command, expressing a desire to live quietly in Syria. Augustus prevailed upon him to return to Italy. Gaius set out on the return journey, taking a trading vessel as far as Limyra in Lycia. He stopped off there and got no farther. He died on February 21, AD 4.[23]

The opportune demise of the two princes inevitably aroused suspicions. Pliny speaks of the whispering campaign that followed *(incusatae liberorum mortes)*. Dio reports that Livia was suspected of causing both deaths, particularly because they followed Tiberius' return from Rhodes. Tacitus, once again in a blatant appeal to deep-seated prejudices, uses a familiar technique, saying that they died either by the simple working of fate or because the trickery of their stepmother, Livia, carried them off. He does not expand on this last suggestion, and offers no evidence, but succeeds in planting the seeds of suspicion. The idea seems implausible. Although some sort of plot was not logistically impossible, the complications of arranging poisoning at a great distance should arouse more than the usual scepticism about such charges. It would be stretching the record to the length of incredulity to suggest that Livia had been in league with Addon, especially given that Gaius exposed himself recklessly just before he was wounded, and that the effect of the wound was aggravated by his delicate physical condition. Moreover, there is no indication that anyone on the spot in the entourage of either Gaius or Lucius had any reason whatsoever at the time to suspect foul play by Livia. It is likely that the stories that arose later about Livia's secret plan to poison Germanicus at a distance (see chapter 8) have been grafted onto these earlier events. Suetonius at any rate voices no suspicions.[24]

The death of Lucius and then of Gaius would have left Augustus with one surviving male kin. Not long after the death of Marcus Agrippa in 12 BC a son had been born to Julia. In honour of his old friend Augustus arranged for him to be called Agrippa, dropping the Vipsanius, which his father had not used. He is thus called Marcus Agrippa in inscriptions. The familiar cognomen Postumus, found in some of the literary sources and conventionally attached to him, is not attested epigraphically.[25] Postumus was sixteen in AD 4—and, it seems, a highly immature and irresponsible sixteen, hardly ready for serious responsibilities. In the long term, there were women who might continue Augustus' line. One of these was Augustus' granddaughter, Agrippina the Elder, born to Julia in about 14 BC. Agrippina was to play an important role in the later story of Livia, and her personality ensured that the relationship would be prickly. She was a third-generation imperial woman, who had known no world other than one where she was a child of the imperial house. It showed. She was proud, touchy about her status, and intolerant of those who stood between her and what she saw as owed to her by destiny.[26] There was an ideal husband in the wings for Agrippina. Romans had a predilection for attributing to sons the qualities (or vices) of their fathers. Drusus, the son of Livia, had enjoyed immensely popular appeal. He had left two sons. The younger of these, Claudius, was ruled out because of his physical infirmities. The older, Germanicus, was a perfect candidate. Livia's grandson inherited the enormous popularity of his father. He seems to have combined this with perceived qualities of his own, for Suetonius describes him as handsome and courageous, universally admired for his broad compassion and his ability to win the affections of others. Tacitus saw him as the epitome of moral rectitude.[27]

Like his father, Germanicus was to safeguard his reputation with an early death, before he had been put properly to the test.[28] In fact, the early signs, for those willing to look closely, were not encouraging. Although his motives and intentions might have been unassailable, he could still make serious blunders. Tacitus has no choice but to criticise him on individual points of detail—the record would not allow otherwise—whether a mistake in military strategy in his German campaigns or a lack of judgement in giving in to the demands of the mutineers in the Rhine armies following Augustus' death. But these points of detail are not allowed to detract seriously from the overall enthusiastic portrait, one which survived him by several generations. The third-century record of the garrison at Dura Europus, the so-called *Feriale Duranum*, appears to include the celebration of Germanicus' birthday, a remarkable testimony to the durability of his reputation, showing that in the time of Severus Alexander he was still regarded as one of the great military leaders of the empire.[29]

At the time of Gaius' death Augustus had reached his sixty-fifth year and was not in robust health. He needed someone in place ready to share his burdens and to take over at once should it be necessary. Germanicus, probably only seventeen, was still too young to shoulder any major responsibility. Nevertheless, according to Tacitus, Augustus gave serious thought to adopting him, but was dissuaded by Livia, using what the historian in one place describes as *occultis artibus* (secret devices) and in another as her *precibus* (entreaties). Accordingly, he selected Tiberius instead. Suetonius makes an astute observation. He first cites previous authorities who suggest two possible, very unflattering, motives for Tiberius' adoption. Augustus either was worn out by Livia's appeals, or he thought that if Tiberius succeeded him the contrast with his own reign would be so marked that it would do great things for his own reputation. (An identical motive was ascribed later to Tiberius for his choice of Caligula as successor.) Suetonius adds his own observation that such speculation is nonsense, and sensibly refuses to believe that in such an important matter Augustus would not have given the issues the most careful thought. On the one hand Tiberius was distinguished in the field and a man of sober habits. On the other, his brooding personality had driven him to the disastrous gaffe of retiring from Rome in a huff. Balancing the merits and faults, Augustus decided that the former predominated. Suetonius does more than simply counter speculation with his own speculation. He quotes from a number of letters that demonstrate convincingly Augustus' faith in Tiberius' qualities. Thus while Livia may well have put some pressure on her husband, she clearly would not have been the deciding factor.[30]

Tiberius was the only man with sufficient experience and standing able to take on such a responsibility. Having made the decision to adopt him, Augustus knew that there could be no half-measures. He granted him the tribunicia potestas, probably for five years, although the period differs from source to source.[31] On June 26, AD 4, Augustus adopted Tiberius. Livia's son, forty-four years old, now became officially the son of her second husband.[32] Henceforth he is called Tiberius Julius Caesar and is clearly the man designated to succeed the emperor. As he had in the past, Augustus made provision for the possibility that Tiberius might not necessarily survive him. Agrippa Postumus had not given any evidence of being temperamentally suited for high office, but Augustus perhaps hoped that in the general way of things an unruly youth could mature into a responsible adult. Hence the emperor adopted Postumus on the same occasion. Moreover, Tiberius was obliged, before his own adoption, to adopt his nephew Germanicus, who would thereby become Tiberius' son and would legally have the same relationship to Tiberius as his natural son, Drusus. The marriage of Germanicus and Agrippina followed soon after, probably in the next year. There is no reason why the unconcealed manoeuvring on behalf of Germanicus should have upset Livia unnecessarily, despite the clear implications of Tacitus that it did. Germanicus, after all, was her grandson as much as was Drusus Caesar. The arrangement reinforced rather than weakened the likelihood of succession from her own line, as was to be demonstrated by events. The marriage would prove extremely fruitful. In time Agrippina bore Germanicus nine children, six of whom survived infancy. The first three were sons, great-grandsons of Livia: Nero, the eldest (not to be confused with his nephew Nero, the future emperor); Drusus (to be distinguished from the two more famous men of the same name: Drusus, son of Livia, and Drusus Caesar, son of Tiberius); and Gaius (destined to become emperor, and known more familiarly as Caligula). She also bore three surviving daughters, Drusilla and Livilla, and, most important, the younger Agrippina, mother of Livia's great-great-grandson, the emperor Nero.

The adoption of Tiberius in AD 4 would have been an occasion of joy and satisfaction for Livia, and would have helped to efface any lingering grief that still afflicted her over Drusus' death. If we are to believe Velleius, not only Livia but the whole Roman world reacted jubilantly to the new turn of events. Needless to say, his account should be treated with due caution. There was, he claims, something for everyone. Parents felt heartened about the future of their children, husbands felt secure about their wives, even property owners anticipated profits from their investments! Everyone looked forward to an era of peace and good order. A colourful exaggeration, of course, but there probably was considerable relief among Romans that the succession issue seemed at long last to be settled.[33]

Any possible role that Augustus might have dreamt of for Germanicus or Agrippa Postumus in some remote and distant future was largely academic. It is important to bear this point in mind when considering the last ten years of his life. Livia assumes a key role in the literary accounts of this period, especially towards the end, but that role remains clouded in obscurity and innuendo, and the claims made by Tacitus in particular about her contribution to the events of the decade have rightly been treated by scholars with considerable scepticism. Tacitus makes the charge that Augustus' public show of support for Tiberius was made at the open urging *(palam hortatu)* of Livia, in contrast to the secret campaign *(obscuris artibus)* she had waged earlier. This claim simply fails to convince. That Livia would have supported the adoption of Tiberius and made her pleasure known when it came about should occasion no surprise, or serious censure. But her efforts cannot have been the deciding factor. During Tiberius' quasi-exile in Rhodes, she had supposedly gone to great lengths on his behalf but had been able to wrest only limited concessions from a husband who clearly was resolved to make up his own mind on such matters. Also, the logic of Tacitus' account leaves much to be desired. Livia had supposedly promoted Tiberius' case by obscuris artibus. But Tiberius, along with his brother Drusus, had served openly, and with distinction, in the Roman armies. It is difficult to see how Livia could have been involved secretly, short of bribing the enemy armies to surrender in the field.[34]

In the immediate aftermath of the adoptions the ancient authors inevitably tend to focus on Tiberius and the campaigns he conducted in Germany and Illyricum, and they virtually ignore Agrippa Postumus, whose name was to be invoked later by sources hostile to Livia. A few details about Postumus emerge. In AD 5 he received the toga of manhood. The occasion was low-key, without any of the special honours granted Gaius and Lucius on the same occasion. It also seems to have been delayed. Postumus would have reached fourteen in AD 3, and under normal circumstances might reasonably have been expected to take the toga in that year. Something seems to be wrong. Augustus had certainly endured his share of problems with the young people in his own family. The pressures facing the younger relatives of any monarch are self-evident, given the sense of importance that precedes achievement, to say nothing of the opportunists attracted to the immature and malleable, and prepared to pander to their self-importance. As Velleius astutely remarks, *magnae fortunae comes adest adulatio* (sycophancy is the comrade of high position). These pressures must have been particularly intense in the period of the Augustan settlement, when no established standards had yet evolved for the royal children and grandchildren. Gaius and Lucius, the focus of Augustus' ambitions and hopes, caused him endless grief by their behaviour in public, clearly egged on by their supporters, and on at least one occasion Augustus felt constrained to clip their wings. Gaius' brave but distinctly foolhardy behaviour during the siege of Artagira is surely symptomatic of the same conceit. There is no reason to assume that Postumus would have been immune from the pressures that turned the heads of his siblings.[35]

Whatever traits of haughtiness Postumus might have displayed in his early youth, they were not serious enough to have entered the record, and the exact nature of his personal and possibly mental problems is far from clear.[36] The ancient sources speak of his brutish and violent behaviour. Some modern scholars have suggested that he might have been mad, but the language used of him seems to denote little more than an unmanageable temperament and antisocial tendencies.[37] For whatever reasons, eventually Augustus decided to remove him from the scene. The details of this expulsion are obscure. Suetonius provides the clearest statement, recording that Augustus removed Postumus *(abdicavit)* because of his wild character and sent him to Surrentum (Sorrento). The historian notes that Postumus grew less and less manageable and so was then sent to Planasia, a low-lying desolate island about sixteen kilometres south of Elba.[38]

Tacitus has no doubt about where the ultimate responsibility for Augustus' actions lay. Postumus had committed no crime. But Livia had so ensnared her elderly husband *(senem Augustum)* that he was induced to banish him to Planasia. Tacitus' technique here is patent. The use of the word *senem* is meant to suggest that Augustus was by now senile, even though the event occurred eight years before his death. Incapable of making his own rational decisions, he would thus be at the mercy of a scheming woman, just as later Agrippina the Younger reputedly "captivated her uncle" Claudius *(pellicit patruum)*. No reason is given for Livia's supposed manoeuvre—which as usual, according to Tacitus, was conducted behind the scenes—except the standard charge that her hatred of Postumus was motivated by a stepmother's loathing *(novercalibus odiis)*. Yet nothing in the rest of Tacitus' narrative sustains his assertion, and the historian himself admits that the general view of Romans towards the end of Augustus' reign was that Postumus was totally unsuited for the succession, because of both his youth and his generally insolent behaviour. Moreover, Augustus had made the strength of Tiberius' position so patently evident that Livia would hardly have considered Postumus a serious candidate. This seems to be confirmed in a remarkable passage of Tacitus which uncharacteristically reports public reservations about a potential role for Germanicus, supposedly Tiberius' rival. After reporting the popular view that Postumus could be ruled out, Tacitus says that people grumbled that with the accession of Tiberius they would have to put up with Livia's *impotentia*, and would have to obey two *adulescentes* (Germanicus and Drusus) who would oppress, then tear the state apart. Tacitus concedes that even the prospect of the reasonable Germanicus and Drusus being involved in state matters caused consternation. This surely offers some gauge of how far below the horizon Postumus was to be found.[39]

The precise reason for Postumus' removal to Sorrento, if it was not simply his personality, is not clear. The initial expulsion may have been provoked by nothing more serious than personal tension between him and his adoptive father. Whatever the initial reason, it soon became apparent that if Augustus had hoped that sending his adopted son out of Rome would solve the problem, he was mistaken. Dio places Postumus' formal exile to Planasia in AD 7. If, as Suetonius claims, he was sent first to Sorrento, what might have precipitated the change in the location and the more grave status of his banishment? We have some hints in the sources. Dio suggests that one of the reasons for Augustus' giving Germanicus preference over Postumus was that the latter spent most of his time fishing, and acquired the sobriquet of Neptune. Now this could point simply to irresponsibility and indolence, but the picture of Postumus as an ancient Izaak Walton serenely casting his line does not fit well with the very strong tradition of someone wild and reckless. His activities may well have had a political dimension. The choice of the nickname Neptune could allude to the naval victories of his father, Marcus Agrippa. The fishing story might well belong to the period after Postumus' relegation to Sorrento. This could have proved a risky spot to locate Postumus, because it lay just across the bay from the important naval base at Misenum that his father had established in 31 BC. The innocent fishing expeditions might have covered much more sinister activities.[40]

Augustus may well have concluded eventually that Postumus was too dangerous to be left in the benign surroundings of Sorrento. During Postumus' second, more serious phase of exile, on the island of Planasia, he was placed under a military guard, a good indication that he was considered genuinely dangerous rather than just a source of irritation and embarrassment. This final stage of banishment was a formal one, for Augustus confirmed the punishment by a senatorial decree and spoke in the Senate on the occasion about his adopted son's depraved character. Formal banishment enacted by a decree of the Senate would be intended to make a serious political statement and should have buried completely any thoughts that Postumus might have been considered a serious candidate in the succession.[41]

We cannot rule out the possibility that Postumus became involved, perhaps as a pawn, in some serious political intrigue, if not to oust Augustus then at the very least to ensure that he would be followed not by a son of Livia but by someone from the line of Julia. If Postumus was being encouraged to think of a possible role in the succession, it might reasonably be asked who was doing the urging. Although there is no explicit statement on the question in the sources, many scholars have accepted the notion that there existed a "Julian party," responsible for much of the "anti-Claudian" propaganda directed against Livia and Tiberius that is found in Tacitus in particular and possibly derived from the memoirs of Agrippina (appendix 1). The notion of Julian and Claudian factions within the imperial family has been called into serious question, on the grounds that division between the two gentes would have been largely annulled by the extensive network of adoption. But a split between those sympathetic to Augustus' first wife, Scribonia, and her daughter Julia on the one hand, and the supporters of Livia and her son on the other, is certainly a feasible scenario. That said, it is far from proved.[42]

A strong hint that Julia's supporters were involved in some sort of intrigue might be seen in yet another family scandal, this time involving her daughter of the same name, Julia the Younger. As confusing as the affair of Julia the Elder might have been, the details of the crisis that swept up her daughter are even more baffling, a situation aggravated by the loss of much of Dio's text for the period when it broke, in AD 8, the year following Postumus' exile.[43] Julia the Younger had been married to Lucius Aemilius Paullus, consul in AD 1, to whom she bore a daughter, Aemilia Lepida. Nothing much more is known about this Julia, except that she lived in some style in Rome. Tacitus tells us that she was found guilty of adultery (in AD 8) and sent into exile to the island of Trimerus, off the Apulian coast, where she remained for the rest of her days. It does not, however, seem likely that she could have been intriguing against Livia's interests, because she was supported in Trimerus by allowances from Livia for the next twenty years, until her death in 28. Tacitus adopts a cynical view of Livia's philanthropy, claiming that she hypocritically laboured to destroy Augustus' family while they flourished, then made a public display of her charity after they had been brought down. This is another good example of the historian's use of innuendo. He does not say that Livia had anything to do with the younger Julia's actual downfall but distorts her public display of charity into an insidious implication that she was somehow responsible. There is a serious logical gap in his argument. There might have been a political advantage for Livia in putting people off the scent during Augustus' lifetime, if she had indeed been responsible for Julia's ruin. But why keep it up for a further fourteen years after his death? The strength of the case, and of the feelings against Julia, can in fact be gauged from Augustus' personal resentment—he ordered that her residence in Rome should be demolished, and he refused to allow her ashes to be deposited in his mausoleum, just as he had refused her mother the same privilege. He reputedly would not allow a child born to her after the affair was exposed to live, or even to be acknowledged.[44]

There is one piece of evidence that Postumus seemed to hold Livia partly responsible for what had happened to him. Dio says that after Postumus was removed *(apekerychthe)*, his property was assigned to the military treasury, the *aerarium militare*. At some point he wrote to Augustus to complain about his ill-treatment on this precise matter, and Dio tells us that Postumus used to rebuke *(epekallei)* Augustus over being shut out of his inheritance. The Greek verb could mean that he simply reproached Augustus, or even that he brought an action against him, and the imperfect tense suggests that the charge was made on more than one occasion. In this same general context Dio says also that Postumus slandered Livia, and it looks very much as though he lumped her in with the complaints about his property.[45] Any claim launched by Postumus against Augustus (and Livia, indirectly) would have been a very weak one. If his father, Marcus Agrippa, had been aware before his death that his wife Julia was pregnant, he would certainly have made provision for a *tutor* (guardian) in his will; he probably would have appointed Augustus, adoptive father of Marcus Agrippa's other sons, Gaius and Lucius, and inheritor of the bulk of Marcus Agrippa's estate. If he assigned no guardian in the will, the *tutela* would fall to the nearest male relative, of which there is no record. If the decision fell to the praetor to decide guardianship, he probably would have appointed Augustus. Any property that Postumus inherited from his father would thereby have come under Augustus' administration. In any case, with the adoption of AD 4, Postumus was transferred into the *potestas* of Augustus and thereby lost all his private property, including whatever he might have inherited from his father. Like Tiberius, he would have retained control only over whatever allowance *(peculium)* his adoptive father approved. Postumus' complaint that he never received his inheritance might have been factually correct, but it would have had no strength in law. Thus Livia can hardly have played any kind of active or direct role in Postumus' loss of inheritance. Dio in any case argues that Postumus attacked Livia as stepmother, suggesting that he did not have specific charges to make against her.[46]

Whatever the intrigues in Rome, Livia's son was able to keep himself aloof and to play the role that suited him best, that of soldier. Tiberius conducted a brilliant series of campaigns in Pannonia for which a triumph was voted in AD 9. (This was postponed when Tiberius was despatched to Germany in the aftermath of the disastrous defeat of Quinctilius Varus, in which three legions were lost.) When the Pannonian triumph was voted, Augustus made his intentions crystal clear. Various suggestions were put forward for honorific titles, such as Pannonicus, Invictus, and Pius. The emperor, however, vetoed them all, declaring that Tiberius would have to be satisfied with the title that he would receive when he himself died. That title, of course, was Augustus.[47] It also appears that a law was later passed to make his imperium equal to that of Augustus throughout the empire, and in early 13 his tribunician power was renewed. His son Drusus Caesar received his first accelerated promotion, designated to proceed directly to the consulship in AD 15, skipping the praetorship that should have preceded this higher office.[48]

The virtual impregnability of Tiberius' position should be borne in mind in any attempt to understand the final months of Augustus' life. In the closing chapter of her husband's principate, Livia reemerges in the record to play a central and, according to one tradition, decidedly sinister role. This is perhaps the most convoluted period of her career, where rumour and reality seem to diverge most widely. To place the events in a comprehensible context, it is necessary to note one later detail out of its chronological sequence. As we shall see, after Augustus' death there was a rumour reported in some of the sources that Livia had murdered her husband. In the best forensic tradition, a motive would have to be unearthed to make the charge plausible, especially since sceptics could hardly have failed to notice that Augustus had never enjoyed robust health and was already in his seventy-sixth year. Death from natural causes could hardly be considered remarkable under such circumstances. The requisite motive would indeed be produced, and the kernel of the intricate thesis that evolved is found in a brief summary of Augustus' career by Pliny the Elder. Among the travails that afflicted the emperor, Pliny lists the *abdicatio* of Postumus after his adoption, Augustus' regret after the relegation, the suspicion that a certain Fabius betrayed his secrets, and the intrigues of Livia and Tiberius. Pliny's summary observations are clearly based on a more detailed source, which suggested that Augustus felt some remorse about Postumus. This simple and not improbable notion is developed by other sources into a far more complex scenario that creates an apparently plausible motive, because it could be claimed that Livia would have wanted to remove her husband before he could act on his change of heart. This reconstruction of the events is clearly reminiscent of the closing days of the reign of Claudius, when the emperor supposedly sought a rapprochement with his son Britannicus, to the disadvantage of his stepson Nero, and thereby inspired his wife Agrippina to despatch him with the poisoned mushroom (see appendix 1). But it is important to bear in mind that as Pliny reports the events he limits himself to the claim that Augustus regretted Postumus' exile, without further elaboration, and although Livia and her son supposedly engaged in intrigues of some unspecified nature, Pliny assigns no criminal action to either of them.

Pliny's "skeleton account" is to some degree validated by Plutarch. In his essay on "Talkativeness," Plutarch, in a very garbled passage, relates that a friend of Augustus named "Fulvius" heard the emperor lamenting the woes that had befallen his house—the deaths of Gaius and Lucius and the exile of "Postumius" on some false charge—which had obliged him to pass on the succession to Tiberius. He now regretted what had happened and intended *(bouleuomenos)* to recall his surviving grandson from exile. According to Plutarch's account, Fulvius passed this information on to his wife, and she in turn passed it on to Livia, who took Augustus to task for his careless talk. The emperor made his displeasure known to Fulvius, and he and his wife in consequence committed suicide. This last detail was perhaps inspired by the famous story of Arria, who achieved immortal fame in AD 42 when she died with her husband Caecina Paetus, who had been implicated in a conspiracy against Claudius. Plutarch's confused version of events does not inspire confidence, and in any case, although he gives Livia a more specific role than does Pliny, he follows Pliny in not attributing to Augustus any action, only supposed intentions.[49]

Dio's account is a much contracted one, but derived from a source that has added a very important wrinkle to the story and has Augustus taking action on his change of heart. Dio says that Livia was suspected of Augustus' death. She was afraid, people say *(hos phasi)*, because Augustus had secretly sailed to Planasia to see Postumus and seemed to be on the brink of seeking a reconciliation.[50] This bald and surely implausible story, involving a round trip of some five hundred kilometres, is given its fullest treatment in Tacitus, clearly drawing on the same source as Dio. He says that people thought that Livia had brought about Augustus' final illness, because a rumour entered into circulation that the emperor had gone to Planasia to visit Postumus, accompanied by a small group of intimates, including Paullus Fabius Maximus. Fabius, clearly Plutarch's "Fulvius," was a literary figure of some renown, a close friend of Ovid and Horace. He was also an intimate of Augustus, consul in 11 BC, governor of Asia, and legatus in Spain (3–2 BC). He would thus be a plausible participant in this mysterious expedition. Tacitus reports that the tears and signs of affection were enough to raise the hopes of Postumus that there was a prospect of his being recalled. (It is striking that Tacitus is ambiguous about the meeting's purpose and is too good a historian to bring himself to claim that Augustus had gone there to commit himself to Postumus' rehabilitation.) Fabius Maximus supposedly told the story to his wife, Marcia, and she in turn passed it to Livia. The text of the manuscript is corrupt at this point, but Tacitus seems to say that this indiscretion came to the knowledge of Augustus (reading the text as *gnarum id Caesari*). The subsequent death of Fabius, Tacitus says, may or may not have been suicide (the implication is that Augustus ordered it, as Plutarch suggests). Marcia was heard at the funeral reproaching herself as the cause of her husband's downfall (this presumably is how the story got out). After this detailed account Tacitus undercuts his own case when he goes on to say that Augustus died shortly afterwards, *utcumque se ea res habuit*. The force of this phrase is essentially "whatever the truth of the matter." It hardly inspires conviction.[51]

The story of the adventurous journey to Planasia and the tearful reconciliation has generally been greeted with scepticism by modern scholars. Jameson is an exception. She uses the Arval record to argue that Augustus did take the trip, noting that on May 14 there was a meeting of the brethren for the co-option of Drusus Caesar, the son of Tiberius, into their order. Fabius Maximus and Augustus were absent from the ceremony, and submitted their votes, in favour of the co-option, by absentee ballot. But is there anything remarkable in their absence? Clearly, the election of Tiberius' son was not in reality a particularly important occasion, for Tiberius himself failed to attend. Moreover, Syme notes that no fewer than five other arvals were absent from this meeting, and that there could be a host of explanations for Augustus' absence. Also, if the co-option was seen as an important family event, then it would surely have been the very worst time for Augustus to try to slip away unnoticed. The emperor was by this time in declining health, so weak that he even held audiences in the palace lying on a couch. In AD 12 he was so frail that he stopped his morning receptions for senators and asked their indulgence for his not joining them at public banquets. Yet we are supposed to assume that he made the arduous journey to Planasia, and that he did so without Livia realizing what he was up to. It is also important to observe that both Tacitus and Dio drew on a source claiming that Augustus was on the verge of making amends with Postumus. An actual reconciliation seems to be ruled out by the later sequence of events. Certainly he did nothing whatsoever on his return to strengthen Postumus' position or to weaken that of Tiberius. Finally, one might ask whether Augustus could ever have seriously considered recalling Postumus. He had put him under armed guard. There were plots to rescue him. His supporters published damaging letters about the emperor. It all seems implausible. Syme suggests that the details of the journey might have been added soon after Augustus' death, a "specimen of that corroborative detail which is all too apparent (and useful) in historical fictions." Syme bases his argument in part on aesthetic considerations. The episode as it appears in Tacitus is introduced in an inartistic fashion and appears to have been grafted on as an afterthought, introducing two names, those of Fabius Maximus and his wife, Marcia, that will not be mentioned again in the *Annals*. Moreover, neither Pliny nor Plutarch mentions Planasia. In Plutarch's confused account Fabius' role is merely to overhear Augustus expressing his unhappiness over the fate of Postumus.[52]

Making the situation even murkier, Suetonius alludes to a complicated plot hatched around Postumus. He provides only the briefest of details, but enough to establish that the ringleaders did not come from the top drawer of Roman society. There were two of them, otherwise unknown – Lucius Audasius, who had in his younger days been charged with forgery but was now old and decrepit, and Asinius Epicadus, half-Parthian by origin and presumably a freedman of the Asinian gens. They planned to rescue Postumus and Julia (specifically identified as the Elder) from their island prisons and whisk them away to the armies. We know nothing more of the plot or of the fate of the two unlikely ringleaders except that the whole thing was exposed before any harm could be done. It may well be that the plotters were ultimately responsible for the Planasia story, hoping to lay the foundation for a claim that Augustus intended Postumus as his successor. Julia certainly still had her followers in Rome. By the time of the plot she was no longer on Pandateria but in Rhegium, on the mainland of Italy. There had earlier been much popular agitation for her recall, to which Augustus had responded by asserting that fire would mix with water before he would relent. Nothing daunted, her supporters began to thrown firebrands into the sea. They were not completely successful, but in the end Augustus felt under so much pressure that he did make a modest compromise, and at some point after AD 4 moved her to Rhegium. Demands for her total recall continued. These Augustus resisted, ruefully wishing the same daughters or wives on the petitioners.[53] The plot described by Suetonius might then have been a last desperate effort to rescue her. In any case it seems to have come to nothing.

In addition to the supposed political intrigues in the period immediately before Augustus' death, there was no shortage of signs that the gods, too, were feeling distinctly uneasy, ranging from the usual comets and fires in the sky to more opaque portents, like a madman sitting on the chair dedicated to Julius Caesar and placing a crown on his own head, or an owl hooting on the roof of the Senate house.[54] But Augustus seems to have had no premonition that he had little time left when he set out from Rome in August 14. At that time Tiberius was obliged to leave the city for further service abroad, and he departed for Illyricum with a mandate to reorganise the province. Livia and Augustus joined him for the first part of the journey. This very public gesture is an affirmation of the emperor's faith in Tiberius – a very odd signal to send if only a few months earlier he had become reconciled to Postumus and had changed his mind about who would succeed him. The party went as far as Astura, and from there followed the unusual course of taking a ship by night to catch the favourable breeze. On the sea journey Augustus contracted an illness, which began with diarrhoea. They skirted the coast of Campania, spent four days in Augustus' villa at Capri to allow him to relax and recuperate, then sailed into the Gulf of Puteoli, where they were given an extravagant welcome from the passengers and crew of a ship that had just sailed in from Alexandria. They passed over to Naples, although Augustus was still weak and his diarrhoea was recurring. He managed to muster up the strength to watch a gymnastic performance. Then they continued their journey. At Beneventum the company broke up. Tiberius headed east. As Augustus began the return journey with Livia from Beneventum, his illness took a turn for the worse. Perhaps he had a sense that his end was near, as he made for an old family estate, in nearby Nola, where his father, Octavius, had died.[55]

Augustus was not to leave Nola alive. His condition quickly grew worse, and on August 19, 14, at the ninth hour, in Suetonius' precise report, he died.[56] According to Tacitus, as Augustus grew more sick, some people started to suspect *(suspectabant)* Livia of dirty deeds *(scelus)*. Dio is more specific, but is still cautious about the charge. He notes that Augustus used to gather figs from the tree with his own hands. She, *hos phasi* (as they say), cunningly smeared some of them with poison, ate the uncontaminated ones herself and offered the special ones to her husband. As can be seen in his handling of other events, Dio does seem to relish rumours of poisoning. He relates, for instance, that Vespasian died of fever in AD 79, but adds that some said that he was poisoned at a banquet. It was similarly said that Domitian murdered Titus in AD 81, although the written accounts agree that he died of natural causes. In the case of Augustus it may be possible to discern the origins of the rumour. Suetonius confirms that the emperor was fond of green figs from the second harvest (along with hand-made moist cheese, small fish, and coarse bread). Given Livia's interest in the cultivation of figs (she even had one named after her [see chapter 6]), she may well have had an orchard at Nola to which she would have given special attention during her stay. Dio in fact seems to have had little personal faith in the fig rumour, for he goes on to speak of Augustus' death as "from this or from some other cause." By its nature the fig story is unprovable yet impossible to refute. It falls in the grand tradition of such deaths, the best-known being the supposed despatch of Claudius by a poisoned mushroom. If Livia murdered Augustus, then her timing was oddly awry, for she had to go to considerable trouble to recall Tiberius, who was by then en route to Illyricum. Why not do the deed when he was still on the scene? It is perhaps worth bearing in mind that Livia had an interest in curative recipes (see chapter 6). It is possible that she would have inflicted one or more of her own concoctions on her husband. In the unlikely event that he was poisoned, alternative medicine might be a more plausible culprit than the murderer's toxin.[57]

From Beneventum, Tiberius headed for the east coast of Italy, where he took a boat to Illyricum. He had barely crossed over to the Dalmatian coast when an urgent letter from his mother caught up with him, recalling him to Nola. There are different versions of what happened next. Tacitus describes Augustus in his final hours holding a heavy conversation with his entourage about the qualifications of potential successors. Dio and Suetonius allow him a lighter agenda. They recount that he first asked for a mirror, combed his hair and straightened his sagging jaws. Then he invited the friends in. He gave them his final instructions, ending with his famous line of finding Rome a city of clay and leaving it a city of marble. In conclusion, he asked how they would rate his performance in the grand comedy of life. He seems to have taken a high score for granted, because just like a comic actor, he asked them to give him applause for a role well played. (The curious coincidence of the comic actors brought in during Claudius' last hours should be noted.) He then dismissed his friends and spoke to some visitors from Rome, asking about the health of Tiberius' granddaughter Julia, who was ill. The most serious discrepancy arises over the part that Tiberius might have played during the emperor's final hours. Dio preserves one tradition, which he says he found in most authorities, including the better ones, that the emperor died while his adopted son was still in Dalmatia, and that Livia for political reasons was determined to keep the death secret until he got back. Tacitus reflects a similar tradition, reporting uncertainty about whether Tiberius found Augustus dead or alive when he reached Nola. The house and the adjoining streets had been sealed off by Livia with guards, and optimistic bulletins were issued, until she was ready to release the news at a time dictated by her own needs. The story is reminiscent of Agrippina's arrangements after the death of Claudius. She was similarly accused of keeping the death secret and posting guards as Claudius lay dying (see appendix 1). The suspicions about Livia do not appear in the other extant accounts. Velleius reports that Tiberius rushed back and arrived earlier than expected, which perked up Augustus for a time. But before too long he began to fail, and died in Tiberius' arms, asking him to carry on with their joint work. Suetonius is even more emphatic about Tiberius' role. He says that Augustus detained Tiberius for a whole day in private conversation, which was the last serious business that he transacted. His final moments were spent with Livia. His mind wandered as he died—he thought that forty men were carrying him away—but at the last instant he kissed his wife, with an affectionate farewell, *Livia nostri coniugii memor vive, ac vale* (Livia, be mindful of our marriage, and good-bye), then slipped into the quiet death that he had always hoped for.[58]

That Livia might have kept the news of Augustus' death secret for a time is certainly plausible—there are all sorts of sound reasons why the announcement of a politically sensitive death might be postponed, although the similar delay after Claudius' death is disturbingly coincidental.[59] She also may well have put pickets around the house, but no sinister connotation need be placed on the action. The final hours of Augustus would doubtless have attracted the concerned and the curious, who in such situations follow a herd instinct to keep crowded vigils. After Agrippina the Younger had been shipwrecked near Baiae in AD 59, crowds of well-wishers streamed up to her house, carrying torches. The same would surely have happened in Nola, and some sort of control might have become necessary to give the dying emperor some peace. The house certainly became a place of pilgrimage afterwards, and was converted into some sort of shrine.[60] The romantic account of Augustus expiring in Tiberius' arms may be highly coloured, and Suetonius' claim that Augustus and Tiberius spent a whole day together sounds exaggerated, given that Augustus' health was fading so fast. But it is difficult to see how that whole sequence of events could simply have been invented if it did not have at least a basis of truth.

In any case, rumours surrounding the events at Augustus' deathbed were totally eclipsed by dramatic developments across the water. As an immediate consequence of the emperor's death, Postumus also lost his life: *primum facinus novi principatus fuit Postumi Agrippae caedes* (the first misdeed of the new principate was the slaying of Agrippa Postumus), as Tacitus words it. The events of this first and possibly murkiest episode of Tiberius' reign have been much debated, and it is probably now impossible to disentangle fact from rumour and innuendo, since there is considerable ambiguity in the ancient accounts of the incident.[61]

The general *outline* of the events is not particularly controversial. The officer commanding the guard at Planasia executed Postumus after he had received written instructions *(codicilli)* to carry out the deed. Postumus had no weapons other than his powerful physique, and he put up a valiant but ultimately futile struggle. A desperate attempt by a loyal slave, Clemens, to save him was frustrated when the would-be rescuer took a slow freight ship to

Planasia and arrived too late. After the execution, the officer then reported to Tiberius, presumably still at Nola, that the action had been carried out. He did so, as Tacitus describes it, *ut mos militiae* (in the military manner), presumably in the sense of a soldier reporting to his commander that his orders have been discharged.[62] Tiberius denied vehemently that he had given any such orders. According to Tacitus, he claimed that Augustus had sent the order, to be put into force immediately after his death, and insisted that the officer would have to give an account to the Senate.

Tacitus at this point adds a new wrinkle to the story, and gives a role to a figure not mentioned in any of the other sources in the context of this incident. The codicilli, he claims, had been sent to the tribune by Augustus' confidant Sallustius Crispus. This man was the great-nephew and adopted son of the historian Sallust. Although his family connections had opened up the opportunities for a brilliant senatorial career, Sallustius chose to fashion himself after Maecenas and seek real influence rather than the empty prominence of the Senate. He rose to the top through his energy and determination, which he managed to conceal from his contemporaries by pretending a casual or even apathetic attitude to life. He acquired considerable wealth, owning property in Rome, and among other landed estates he could list a copper mine in the Alps producing high-grade ore. More importantly, at least until his later years, he had the ear of both Augustus and Tiberius, as a man who bore the *imperatorum secreta* (secrets of the emperors).[63] When Sallustius learned that Tiberius wanted the whole matter brought before the Senate, he grew alarmed, afraid that he personally could end up being charged. He interceded with Livia, alerting her to the danger of making public the *arcana domus* (the inner secrets of the house), with all that would entail—details of the advice of friends, or of the special services carried out by the soldiers—and urged her to curb her son.[64]

Beyond this general framework the details are highly obscure, and, it seems, totally speculative. Tacitus says that Tiberius avoided raising the issue of Postumus' death in the Senate, and Suetonius observes that he simply let the matter fade away. There would thus have been no official source of information. Yet fairly detailed narratives have been passed down, which could have come only from eyewitness accounts. In particular one has to wonder how the supposed secret dealings between Livia and Sallustius could ever have become known. This uncertainty over the source and reliability of the information clearly makes it impossible to determine who was ultimately responsible for Postumus' death.

Suetonius summarises the problem nicely. He states that it was not known whether Augustus had left the written instructions, on the verge of his own death, to ensure a smooth succession, or whether Livia had dictated them *(dictasset)* in the name of Augustus, and, if the latter, whether Tiberius had known about them. Dio categorically insists that Tiberius was directly responsible but says that he encouraged the speculation, so that some blamed Augustus, some Livia, and some even said that the centurion had acted on his own initiative. Tacitus found Tiberius' claim that Augustus had left instructions for the execution hard to believe, and describes this defence as a posture *(simulabat)*, suggesting that the more likely scenario was that Tiberius and Livia hastily brought about the death, Tiberius driven by fear and she by *novercalibus odiis* (stepmotherly hatred). Velleius may have been aware of these speculations, for he is very cagey about Postumus' death. He insists that "he suffered an ultimate fate" *(habuit exitum)* in a way that was appropriate to his "madness" *(furor)*. Velleius may well have been deliberately ambiguous to avoid becoming enmeshed in a contentious and sensitive issue that might reflect badly on Tiberius.[65]

Scholars have generally been inclined to exonerate Livia, and only Gardthausen has held that Livia was totally responsible, without even Tiberius' complicity. Syme accuses Tacitus of supporting an imputation against Livia "which he surely knew to be false." The implication of Livia has been challenged by Charlesworth in particular. He sees it as emanating from the same tradition that had her poisoning Augustus. Certainly Pliny's brief summary imputes no criminal action against her. She seems on principle to have refrained from taking independent executive action. (The picket she set up around Augustus' house would be the only known counterexample.) At most, it is possible that she knew of such an order, but it seems highly unlikely that she initiated it.

Even if a meeting did actually take place between Sallustius and Livia, as Tacitus alleges, this need not mean that anything sinister had necessarily been underfoot. Sallustius may have wished simply to appeal to the wisdom and experience of Livia to counter the political naïveté of a son who had spent his career on military campaigns and had not yet become adept in the complexities of political intrigue. The suppression of information about the activities of the soldiers could just as easily have been meant to refer to Augustus' instructions as to Livia's, in a system where secrecy for the sake of secrecy was considered a vital element in the fabric of efficient government. If Livia had somehow been involved with Sallustius in carrying out Augustus' instructions, there would have had to be secret and dangerous communication between Rome and Nola, unless Sallustius was also with Augustus at the end (and Tacitus would surely have mentioned his presence).[66]

Tiberius seems largely exonerated by his own conduct. If he had been guilty, he would hardly have wanted an investigation by the Senate, and could simply have claimed that the execution was carried out on Augustus' orders or even have reported officially that Postumus had died from natural causes.[67] We can surely eliminate Dio's barely tenable suggestion that the guard might have executed Postumus on its own initiative, and the hardly more convincing notion that Sallustius Crispus similarly might have acted on his own initiative.[68] On balance, the most plausible suspect is Augustus, although plausibility is far different from conviction. Augustus might well have issued standing orders to the tribune to execute Postumus the moment news of his own death arrived. Sallustius could well have sent the announcement of the emperor's death in Tiberius' name (with or without his knowledge), which could account for the centurion's coming to Rome to make a report to Tiberius.[69] When he needed to, Augustus could behave quite ruthlessly against those who threatened him. He put to death Caesarion, the supposed son of Julius Caesar and Cleopatra, for purely political motives. He also could be harsh towards his own family. He swore that he would never recall the elder Julia from exile, refused to recognise the child of the younger Julia, and would not allow either Julia burial in his mausoleum. It was he who had set the armed guard over Postumus. Moreover, Augustus did make meticulous preparations for his own death. He left behind three or four *libelli*, with instructions for his funeral, the text of the *Res Gestae*, a summary of the Roman troops, fleets, provinces, client-kingdoms, direct and indirect taxes—including those in arrears—the funds in the public and in the imperial treasuries, and the imperial accounts. There was also a book of instructions for Tiberius, the Senate, and the people. Augustus went into considerable detail, with such particulars as the number of slaves it would be wise to free and the number of new citizens who should be enrolled. He was clearly a man determined not to leave any issues hanging in the balance, and the future of Postumus would have been an issue of prime importance.[70]

Postumus' death was the final blow for Julia the Elder. From this point on, she simply gave up and went into a slow decline, her despair aggravated by her destitution. She received no help from Tiberius, although he had earlier tried to win leniency for her from her father. According to Suetonius, Tiberius, once emperor, deprived her of her allowance, using the heartless argument that Augustus had not provided for it in his will. As we have seen, Livia might well have helped the exiled Julia at one point by giving her one of her slaves, and she certainly helped Julia's daughter when she was sent away from Rome. But she does not seem to have tried to intercede on this occasion. Julia died in late AD 14 from weakness and malnutrition.[71] The new reign had got off to a bloody start.

5

A NEW REIGN

The death of Augustus brought about a dramatic and inevitable change in Livia's situation. For the previous half-century or so her role had depended essentially on her personal bond with her husband. She was now the mother of a princeps whose notion of the principate differed greatly from his predecessor's and certainly from her own.

It is difficult to get a clear picture of the relationship that had developed between mother and son in the years before Tiberius came to power. Although the sources suggest that her husband had found Tiberius' personality tiresome and irritating, they give little insight into what Livia thought of her son. It might be suspected that she had favoured his brother, Drusus. Certainly, Drusus' death caused her, and Augustus, intense grief. But an early death will always be a catalyst for affection. There is no serious indication of any contest between Tiberius and his brother for their mother's regard. Suetonius claims some sibling antagonism, supposedly proved by Tiberius' making known a letter in which Drusus had revealed his republican sympathies. But Tiberius' reaction to his brother's death must surely belie any deep hostility. In the same general context Suetonius says that Tiberius showed his ill-will towards his *necessitudines* (close kin), but the examples he adduces to illustrate animosity towards Livia all belong to the period after the accession. That said, it must be conceded that there are no real signs of a close attachment, either. Livia did on occasion take up Tiberius' case, as when he was anxious to leave Rhodes, but she was in fact prepared to intervene for Romans of all classes and conditions.

Nor is there any recorded instance of any actual display of affection between them. This should not, however, occasion any surprise. Open displays of affection were not in their nature, and they both made clear their deep distaste for flaunting private feelings in public.

After Tiberius' accession, the sources paint a picture of deep antipathy between him and Livia, and there is no reason to doubt that there must have been considerable strain, given the ambiguity of her new status and a princeps who had firm ideas on the exclusion of women from affairs of state. These differences are considered in some detail in chapter 8, but it can be noted at the outset that whatever tensions may have existed between Tiberius and his mother, both were astute enough to appreciate that they were natural allies in the political battlefield of the early empire. Unlike Nero, who resorted to murder to rid himself of an interfering parent, Tiberius had the basic common sense to recognise that Livia was of great value to him. Suetonius notes that for all his effort at a public show of independence, he in fact at times sought from his mother the very guidance that he pretended to forswear, and, into the bargain, often followed her suggestions.[1]

Tiberius threw himself into action on Augustus' death. There was no serious rival hovering in the wings, but his situation was entirely without precedent, and he could clearly leave nothing to chance. Curiously, although the sources give Livia a prominent role in ensuring that Tiberius would be on the scene when Augustus died, and that the transmission of power would be a smooth one, they record no involvement by her in the immediate aftermath. That said, it seems inconceivable that she would not have been at her son's side, guiding and advising him, given that his own political experience was at this stage very limited. The public announcement of the old emperor's death carried with it the explicit statement that authority had devolved onto Tiberius. As an important symbolic gesture, it was he who passed on the watchword to the praetorian guard. He then sent letters to all the legionary commanders informing them of his accession. He also wrote to the Senate to tell them that he would be accompanying the body back to Rome. More importantly, he left the senators in no doubt about his own position, informing them that he intended, by virtue of his tribunician authority, to convene a meeting when he reached Rome. It was a diplomatic, yet emphatic, statement that henceforth he was in control.[2] With the transition smoothly under way, Augustus' body could be returned from Nola to Rome in a solemn procession, accompanied by Tiberius and almost certainly by Livia, although the sources, in their preoccupation with the new emperor, omit to mention her. The occasion can hardly have failed to remind both how more than twenty years earlier they had similarly accompanied Drusus' body to Rome. They would have reached the city in early September.[3]

When the Senate was convened, business was limited. The first item was the reading of the will. Augustus had made his last will on April 3, 13, when he was seventy-four, and had deposited it with the Vestal Virgins.[4] Drusus Caesar, Tiberius' son, now brought it into the Senate. After the witnesses examined the seals, it was read out to the senators by a freedman. Two heirs were instituted: Tiberius to two thirds of the estate, and Livia to one third. As heirs in the second grade (people who would inherit if the primary ones for any reason failed to do so) Augustus named Drusus Caesar to one-third of the estate and Germanicus and his sons to the other two-thirds. This must mean that Germanicus and his sons were to be the substitutes to Tiberius, and Drusus Caesar to Livia. The arrangement was advantageous to Germanicus, but it would be foolish to read any political significance into it. Drusus Caesar was still childless when the will was written, and his responsibilities were accordingly fewer. The third grade was made up of relatives and friends. To be named in this way brought them little practical benefit, because the chances of their inheriting were negligible. Their inclusion was really a declaration of *amicitia*, and they would almost certainly have been covered elsewhere in the will by individual legacies. Augustus explained that although he had taken in 1.4 billion sesterces from inheritances, he had spent it for the public good, along with what he had inherited from his father and from Caesar. Thus his actual estate would be considerably smaller than his income might have led people to expect. He left a number of legacies, in two groups. There were those given in bulk to the people and the army, to a total of about ninety million. Then there were individual bequests, the sums not recorded.[5]

Tiberius and Livia as his heirs would receive 150 million, a third of which would go to Livia. To enable her to inherit this substantial amount, special exemption from the financial disabilities suffered by women in inheritances had to be secured from the Senate (see chapter 9). This exemption, however, was to be the least remarkable of the arrangements made for her. By the terms of the will she was to be adopted by her late husband and entered into the Julian family. Moreover, just as Tiberius received the name of Augustus, she would receive the name Augusta, and be known henceforth as Julia Augusta. These extraordinary arrangements are discussed in detail in chapter 8.[6]

Once the will was settled, the arrangements for the funeral could go ahead. Tiberius was insistent that proper decorum should be observed. The Senate asked that members be allowed to act as pallbearers. The new emperor, who had an aversion to extravagant public gestures, declined their request. He also resisted the pressure to allow the body to be cremated in the Forum rather than in the Campus Martius, where Augustus' mausoleum had been built. He was particularly concerned about the risk of a repetition of the wild excesses following the cremation of Julius Caesar. To ensure public order, troops were lined up to guard the procession. Drusus and Tiberius delivered the funeral addresses. Then the body was placed on the pyre in the Campus Martius, to be lit by the centurions. An eagle was released and allowed to fly off, as if it were bearing his spirit to heaven. As it soared aloft, Numerius Atticus, a man of praetorian rank, swore that he saw the form of Augustus on its way to heaven, a claim supported by the Senate when later that year they declared Augustus a god. Numerius was rewarded by Livia with a million sesterces for his acute observation. At this point the chief mourners left, except for Livia. She displayed her devotion to the very end, remaining on the spot, along with the most prominent of the equestrians, for five days of mourning. She then gathered up Augustus' ashes and placed them in his mausoleum.[7]

The literary sources place much emphasis on the difficulties that soon arose between Tiberius and his mother. These differences were almost certainly philosophical, rather than personal, and caused by the impossible constitutional dilemma created by Augustus through his special arrangements for Livia (see chapter 8). In fact, the early years of the reign were dominated not by the Tiberius-Livia tensions but by the issue of Germanicus. In AD 12 he had general authority over the military districts on the Rhine frontier and command over the four legions stationed there. His wife, Agrippina, spent the summer in Antium, where Augustus owned a favourite villa, and on August 31 she bore her third son, Gaius.[8] She joined her husband in Germany, taking with her their new son, who was kitted out in a little soldier's uniform and boots and given the affectionate nickname of "little boots"—Caligula—a name that would later eclipse even that of his famous father. This domestic serenity was broken by the report of Augustus' death. The news caused considerable unrest among the northern legions, where severe conditions of service and unfulfilled commitments had already had an unsettling effect on morale, leading to scattered mutinies. Of considerable relevance to the story of Livia, the disaffection of the German legions is invested with a political flavour in the literary sources, which assert that the troops wanted Germanicus to usurp power. This idea is implausible, and difficult to reconcile with the trouble Germanicus later had in getting the soldiers to obey him. But once the notion had taken hold, it came to haunt Livia and Tiberius.[9]

Germanicus' handling of the mutiny seems to have been weak and incompetent, in contrast to the firm handling of a similar situation by Tiberius' son,

Drusus Caesar, who was sent to deal with military riots in Pannonia. Germanicus appealed unsuccessfully to the loyalty of the troops, and when he then dramatically threatened to kill himself was jokingly encouraged to go ahead. His final desperate move was to produce a bogus letter from Tiberius, supposedly offering to meet some of the concessions demanded. The gesture was backed up by bribes drawn from official funds. This bought a very brief respite. In the end only the theatrical gesture of his wife Agrippina resolved the crisis. Her threat to leave the camp with her children to seek the protection of neighbouring peoples shamed the mutinous troops into submission.[10]

Germanicus quickly set about removing the stain on his men by vigorous military actions. He would have felt a natural desire to pattern himself on his much-admired father, Drusus, by seeking to extend the Roman frontier as far as the Elbe. But his ambitions were not matched by a sound sense of strategy. His troops were forced to withdraw, and as they retreated hurriedly to the Rhine, Agrippina once again saved her husband's bacon. Tacitus tells us that the "great-spirited woman" *(femina ingens animi)* took on the duties of a commander *(munia ducis)* and met the retreating soldiers as they poured over the Rhine bridge at Vetera (Xanten). Although she was at an advanced stage of pregnancy (with her daughter and namesake, Agrippina the Younger), she came to their assistance by handing out clothing and supplying dressings for the wounded. Only later did they learn that her real contribution had been far more crucial. When news reached the military zone that the Romans had been trapped and that the Germans were teeming west, even threatening Gaul, panic broke out and there were frantic demands that the Vetera bridge be destroyed to stem the invasion. Agrippina stepped in to stop the demolition and saved the Roman troops from being trapped on the east bank of the river. At the same time she saved Germanicus' reputation from a fatal blow. Tacitus paints a vivid picture, derived from Pliny (probably from his work on the German wars), of the dramatic figure of Agrippina at the bridge, greeting the returning soldiers, praising them and expressing gratitude on behalf of the Romans for their sacrifices.[11] The whole incident infuriated Tiberius, who was deeply offended by the notion of women usurping the role of commanders or provincial legates *(duces* and *legatos)*.

Tacitus brings in the lengthy description of Germanicus' campaigns almost as a digression, to emphasise his loyal devotion to Tiberius in spite of the jealousy and hostility of the princeps and his mother. The historian insists that the mutual antipathy between Livia and her son was put aside in their common cause of opposition to Germanicus, who, he claims, felt harassed *(anxius)* by a hatred that was both unfair and irrational. The reason given for their enmity was the suspicion that Germanicus had inherited the republican tendencies of his father and wanted to see an end to the imperial system *(libertatem redditurus)*. Tacitus revives this theme later, when we learn of Germanicus' final illness and the resentment it ignited in Rome. He cites a belief that both father and son, Drusus and Germanicus, had been cut down because they desired to restore *libertas*. Germanicus no doubt did inherit his father's popularity, but nothing he did even hinted at an interest in restoring the republican system (and the same is true of Drusus). In fact, Germanicus' rapidly accelerated career suggests a privileged representative of the imperial system and not a champion of the old republic.[12]

The claims of hostility should be treated with caution. Although the special circumstances of Germanicus' popularity and the high regard in which he had been held by Augustus might have been a source of embarrassment for Tiberius, there is certainly no real evidence of personal animosities before his accession. Even after it Germanicus remained perfectly loyal to the new emperor, and Tiberius' conduct, certainly to all outward appearances, was proper and even positive. Both Livia and Tiberius had been devoted to Germanicus' father, and all the sources agree that there were close bonds of friendship between Germanicus and Tiberius' son, Drusus Caesar. Hence Tacitus is obliged to suggest that the hatred of Livia and Tiberius was concealed *(occultis odiis)*.[13] Is it plausible that Livia would have felt hostility towards Germanicus? Tacitus seems to contradict himself. He notes that Livia and Augustus had no children of their own, but thanks to Germanicus and his wife, Agrippina, had the consolation of sharing great-grandchildren. Moreover, Suetonius says that Germanicus was much loved by Augustus, to say nothing of the rest of his family *(omitto enim necessitudines reliquas)*, which implies very strongly that Livia had the same warm feelings towards him. Her treatment of Germanicus' children was exemplary. She assumed responsibility for looking after Caligula, and probably his sisters also, when Germanicus was dead and Agrippina in forced detention. Suetonius reports that when one of the children of Germanicus and Agrippina, a particularly loveable child, died in early boyhood, Livia dedicated a statue of him as Cupid in the temple of Venus on the Capitol. (Augustus had this statue or a replica placed in his bedroom and would kiss it when he entered the room.) Germanicus named two of his daughters, Livia Drusilla and Julia Livilla, after his grandmother. Tacitus relates that in AD 16, during a crucial part of his campaign in Germany, Germanicus had a dream that he was offering a sacrifice and his special vestments became spattered with blood. In the dream Livia then handed him another, more beautiful, robe. Germanicus was elated by the omen. We are not told what it actually portended, but Livia's role is clearly supportive. When Germanicus took the auspices, he found that they confirmed the message of the dream. So he called his men together and gave them a rousing speech to engage the enemy. This would have been an odd dream indeed if Germanicus' sleep was disturbed, as is claimed, by anxiety over Livia's supposed hatred for him.[14]

Germanicus conducted further campaigns in 16, moving his legions by boat down the Weser. A devastating storm scattered the vessels, and the survivors were cast up along the shoreline of the North Sea, some carried as far as Britain. Undaunted, he made further incursions into Germany, and Tacitus asserts that AD 16 closed with the morale of the Rhine legions at a peak and their commander fully convinced that with one further thrust he could advance the Roman boundary to the Elbe. Hope seems to have taken over reality, but in the event he was denied his final great opportunity to prove (or perhaps humiliate) himself. Tiberius recalled him to Rome, a gesture ascribed by some, surely unfairly, to jealousy and spite.[15] If Germanicus saw his recall from Germany as a private snub, he kept his thoughts to himself, and Tiberius went to every length to convey a public image of official approval. A posture of great military success was maintained, and on his arrival he was treated as a returning hero. On May 26, AD 17, he celebrated a magnificent triumph for his supposed victories.[16] The lavish triumph and the assurance of a consulship for the next year might not in themselves have been seen by Germanicus as adequate compensation for the loss of his German command. But Tiberius more than made up for any disappointment by offering him a responsibility that seemed perfectly suited to his diplomatic skills, a crucial mission in the East to deal with a number of problems, but primarily to mediate with Parthia over the controversial status of Armenia. Rome was resolved to ensure that this small mountainous country should remain in friendly control as a buffer state, and to foil Parthia's aim of controlling the territory. Velleius acclaimed the commission as a considerable distinction. Tacitus predictably saw it as a typical piece of Tiberian hypocrisy, designed to get Germanicus out of the way.

One of the problems that Germanicus would have to deal with was the status of the kingdom of Cappadocia, whose king, Archelaus III, had died in captivity in Rome not long before Germanicus' departure.[17] By AD 17 Archelaus had been in possession of Cappadocia for fifty years. There had been long-standing ill feeling between him and Tiberius. The emperor as a young man had responded to Archelaus' urgent appeal to act as his advocate, when an action was brought against the king by his own subjects. Archelaus clearly had an undeveloped sense of gratitude and gave Tiberius the cold shoulder when he was in Rhodes. Tacitus notes that this happened in the golden days of Gaius Caesar, who had been sent to settle affairs in the East, and Archelaus had clearly been given to understand that friendship with Tiberius could be dangerous. Once he became princeps, Tiberius had the satisfaction of getting his own back, but Dio makes it clear that the basic motive for his action was not in fact personal. Archelaus was accused of plotting rebellion. The precise indictment is unclear. He may have interfered in the confused affairs of Armenia, and Levick has suggested that his crime might have been that he helped a relative, Zeno, to the throne of Armenia without consulting Rome. Philostratus talks obscurely of intrigue between Archelaus and the governor of Cilicia. Whatever the basis of the charge, the incorporation of Cappadocia, an area of considerable military importance, was almost certainly a matter of state politics rather than private spite.

But how to get Archelaus to Rome? At this point Tacitus informs us that Tiberius turned to Livia to write to the king to entice him from his kingdom. She was quite frank in her letter to the king about Tiberius' anger, but she promised that if he came to Rome to make amends, he would receive clemency. Suetonius does not mention Livia in the context of Archelaus' being lured to Rome, but he does speak of Tiberius having recourse to *blanditias atque promissa* (blandishments and promises).

Archelaus took Livia at her word, but no sooner was he in Rome than he found himself brought before the Senate on what Tacitus describes as fictitious charges. He died in the city. It was not the charges that broke him but rather his old age—he was decrepit and suffered from gout. So frail was he that he could not sit straight; he was carried into the Senate and spoke from a litter. This physical weakness was aggravated by anxiety, for he had in the past been offended by anyone presumptuous enough to treat him as an equal, and straight humiliation was a novel experience. He seems to have suffered a nervous breakdown, creating the impression that he had lost his mind. Dio claims that during the trial he knew full well what he was doing and just pretended to be gaga. He would have been put to death, but one of the witnesses testified that Archelaus had declared that when he got back to Cappadocia he would show them that he was a man of muscle. This disclosure caused much mirth, and Tiberius saw that his execution was hardly necessary. Eventually he died, possibly a suicide. His kingdom was incorporated into the empire, a process that allowed for a reduction of the unpopular sales tax imposed by Augustus to finance his military treasury. Modern claims that Tiberius spared Archelaus' life because of the intercession of Livia cannot be substantiated by any ancient source, although a promise of support might be implied in the letter that she initially wrote to him. Nor is it clear that she was conscious that in corresponding with Archelaus she was laying the foundations for his ruin. Perkounig suggests that the whole incident has been distorted to associate Livia in a sordid affair for which Tiberius should bear the responsibility, just as Livia and Tiberius would later be associated in guilt in the death of Germanicus. Certainly, if she deliberately tricked Archelaus into coming to Rome, this would contradict Velleius' claim that those who associated with her only benefitted by her intervention. But Archelaus might have damned himself by his own conduct after his arrival, because Livia's letter did indicate to him that clemency would have to be preceded by contrition. Moreover, if one takes the broader view, it might be argued that Livia's conduct was directed towards the common good. Archelaus had fallen foul of Rome. He might have faced military action in Cappadocia, which could have proved disastrous for his people and his kingdom. Thus Livia's conduct would be seen as directed towards a constructive end. That said, the incident should serve to alert us to the danger of excessive naïveté in interpreting political affairs. It is clear that when political reality demanded it, Livia was prepared to place the interests of the state before any personal rapport she might have developed with a client-king.[18]

In autumn 17 Germanicus set out with a large retinue, including his wife, Agrippina, and his son Caligula. Technically, he was a functionary going to his *provincia*, but his journey to the East had all the atmosphere of a grand progress, as cities tried to outdo one another in the lavishness of their hospitality. On the island of Rhodes, Germanicus met the man who was to dominate the final months of his life, Gnaeus Calpurnius Piso. At about the same time as he had entrusted Germanicus with his eastern commission, Tiberius had appointed Piso, described by Tacitus as naturally violent *(ingenio violentum)*, as legate of Syria. The appointment was to have major consequences for both Tiberius and Livia. Piso belonged to a prominent Roman family. His father had been a bitter opponent of Julius Caesar, conducting a campaign against him in Africa, and after the dictator's death he had become an adherent of Brutus and Cassius. Following the amnesty he had refused to serve under Augustus until approached with a personal request to do so. He went on to hold the consulship in 23 BC and was entrusted with the accounts of the Roman armies and finances in the same year, when the emperor fell seriously ill and thought he was on the point of death.[19] Tacitus asserts that the younger Piso inherited the father's arrogance; he served in Spain and held the consulship with Tiberius in 7 BC, and at some point was governor of Africa, where Seneca claims that he acted with unwarranted brutality towards his own men.

Towards the end of his life Augustus supposedly held a discussion in which he pondered the names of potential successors. In some accounts Piso was included in the list, and it is implied that the emperor considered him a serious contender and bold enough to take on the responsibility if offered it. Certainly his stock was high enough for him to be co-opted not much later into the *sodales Augustales*, the priestly body charged with the cult of the deified Julius and Augustus.[20] Piso clearly felt, if Tacitus is to be credited, that his mission was to clip Germanicus' wings, and there were some who believed *(credidere quidam)* that he had received secret instructions to that effect. None of this is provable, of course, and even if true it does not mean that there was anything sinister afoot—Germanicus' conduct in Germany provided ample evidence of a tendency to recklessness, and it might have been felt that he would benefit from a steadying influence. We simply do not have enough information about his career to be sure why Tiberius thought Piso was the right man for the key position of legate of Syria at this particular time. His wife, Plancina, was a close friend of Livia's, but Tiberius' aversion to petticoat politics would have made him immune to any maternal pressure in such a matter. If Tacitus is correct that Piso, like his father, was the kind of man who could scarcely admit the superiority even of the princeps, his strength of will might have been a quality that was felt to be needed in the circumstances.

Whatever unfortunate family traits Piso might have inherited from his father, they were supposedly aggravated by the malign influence of his wife. Munatia Plancina was the daughter (or granddaughter) of Lucius Plancus, censor of 22 BC, and the sister of Lucius Munatius Plancus, who had held the consulship in AD 13. Judging from Livia's close ties to Plancina, Lucius Munatius may well have enjoyed the imperial patronage, and he was appointed to head a commission sent to help deal with the mutinies on the Rhine frontier in 14. Tacitus claims that Livia, inspired by the usual female spite to want to harass Agrippina, gave Plancina her own set of instructions, but he offers no clue about what, specifically, she was supposed to do. Perhaps Livia was anxious to avoid in Syria another theatrical performance like the episode at the bridge over the Rhine. Agrippina's gesture there may well have benefitted the distressed troops but would have been deeply offensive to conservative Romans, not least conservative Roman women, and would have been uncomfortably reminiscent of the worst aspects of the notorious Fulvia's behaviour (see chapter 7).[21]

On his journey to Syria, Piso stopped off in Athens, where he reputedly behaved with considerable rudeness, supposedly as a reproof of Germanicus for showing such deference to the riffraff that made up contemporary Athens, people who had supported Mark Antony against Augustus.[22] From there he took the fast route to Rhodes and then to Syria. Once in the province he reputedly pandered to the soldiers, bribing them and relaxing their good order (a claim difficult to reconcile with his reputation for brutal discipline in Africa). He also removed veteran officers and replaced them with men of his own choosing. Of course, after Germanicus' adventures in Germany, Tiberius might have considered it an important priority that Piso should keep the Syrian legions under his very tight control. Plancina also did her bit, and supposedly at Livia's direction used every opportunity to denigrate Agrippina, but at the same time she was prepared to imitate her earlier activities in Germany, taking part in the cavalry drills and the infantry exercises. She thus, as Tacitus observes, failed to observe the limits of female decorum *(decora feminis)*, although the historian omits to mention that the precedent had been set by Agrippina herself. Tacitus does not explicitly come out and say that this happened with the knowledge of Tiberius, but by stating that people increasingly believed the rumour that he knew, in his usual way he leaves an impression of Tiberius' culpability.[23]

Germanicus was supposedly aware of Piso's game but refused to let the awkward situation affect his performance. He dealt first with Armenia, where Zeno was installed—he was to last sixteen years in power. He then absorbed a number of old kingdoms into the empire, including Cappadocia, whose king Livia had helped remove.[24] With these tricky administrative issues settled, Germanicus returned to Syria. Late in 18 Germanicus and Piso had their first encounter in the province, at Cyrrhus, in the camp of the tenth legion. It was not a warm meeting. There was a clash over Piso's unwillingness to accept Germanicus' instructions, possibly because of a genuine misunderstanding over their respective authority.[25] In the winter of 18–19 Germanicus visited Egypt. He enjoyed a rapt reception at Alexandria, where he ordered a grain distribution to relieve a famine. He then took a cruise up the Nile, visiting the antiquities and the standard tourist destinations, such as the pyramids. The trip may have been quite innocent; indeed he owned estates there jointly with Livia (see chapter 9), which he may have wanted to visit. Moreover, in Alexandria, Germanicus went out of his way to demonstrate his loyalty to, and affection for, Tiberius and Livia, as revealed in two surviving papyri that preserve speeches to the people of Alexandria. In one he refers to the personal hardships caused by the prolonged absence from those close to him, including his "father and grandmother." In another he rejects any notion of special honours for himself but declares their appropriateness for Tiberius, the *soter* and *euergetes* (saviour and benefactor) of the world, and for Livia, whom

Germanicus again refers to as his grandmother *(mamme)*. But for all his declarations of loyalty, his actions were at the very least imprudent. Egypt was an imperial province different from all the others, in particular because of its importance as a source of grain. As a consequence, Augustus had banned visits by senators without express permission, a prohibition that was still in effect. When Germanicus returned to Alexandria, he found a stern rebuke awaiting him, along with a minor reprimand for dressing like a Greek. It is hardly likely that he had any designs on Egypt, but the episode does highlight Tiberius' concern—probably well-founded—about his adopted son's undeveloped sense of responsibility.[26]

When he got back to Syria, Germanicus discovered that Piso had rescinded the orders given to the legions and to the civilian communities. The tension now reached boiling point, and Piso recognised that the most diplomatic course would be for him to take his leave. In the meantime, Germanicus had fallen ill, and the discovery in his house of spells and curses, such as lead tablets carved with his name, along with other evidence of witchcraft, strengthened his suspicions that his illness was not natural. Piso was on the island of Cos when word was brought that his rival had breathed his last, on October 10, AD 19.

As Germanicus' condition had worsened, he had become increasingly convinced that he had been poisoned, and his dying wish was to ask his friends to make sure that Piso and Plancina would be brought to justice. He also asked them to exploit the high regard that Romans felt for his wife, Agrippina, while begging her to be more tactful and diplomatic. Tacitus cleverly relates Germanicus' conviction that he was dying *muliebri fraude* (through female treachery), presumably with reference to Plancina but deliberately ambiguous enough to associate Livia in the charge. That said, Germanicus also suggested in his final words that the notion of secret instructions given to Piso and Plancina was essentially a fiction: *fingentibus scelesta mandata . . . non credent homines* (people will not believe them if they pretend that there were wicked instructions).[27]

The funeral was conducted on a lavish scale in Antioch. The body was placed in public view, then cremated, and the fact that the heart could not be destroyed by the flames was taken as proof of poisoning, available for all the world to see. Finally, the ashes were collected for transportation to Rome.[28] When news began to filter to the city that Germanicus was ill, the gossip mill was sent into high gear. Tacitus claims that there was a widespread conviction that like his father, Drusus, he was paying the price for his republicanism, and suspicions were voiced about Piso's appointment to Syria and supposed secret discussions between Livia and Plancina. Suetonius also reports the general opinion *(creditur* and *opinio fuit)* that Tiberius had been in league with Piso to trick Germanicus. The usual appeal to rumour and mindreading confirms the suspicion that the speculation reflected in the sources over Tiberius and Livia's conduct and motives was based on little or no concrete evidence.[29]

When Rome was finally hit by the stunning news of Germanicus' death, there was near-hysteria in the city, and lavish posthumous honours were bestowed on him.[30] Passions rose even higher when the grieving Agrippina landed at Brundisium on Italy's east coast in early AD 20, clutching the urn containing Germanicus' ashes. As she proceeded along the Appian Way towards Rome, she was met by a stream of officials and ordinary people. Amidst pomp and ceremony the ashes were deposited in the Mausoleum of Augustus, and that night the Campus Martius was illuminated by blazing torches. There was an overwhelming outburst of emotion and sympathy for Agrippina. Livia, who had tried both publicly and privately to make her life a model of what was right and fitting, must have seen a cruel irony in the praise that Agrippina received as an "ornament to her country" *(decus patriae)*, and must have felt incensed to hear her described as "an unequaled example of old-fashioned virtues" *(unicum antiquitatis specimen)*. Politically, it was even more ominous when people acclaimed Agrippina as the last representative of the line of Augustus.[31]

Conspicuously absent from the public ceremonies were Tiberius and Livia. As often, Tacitus tries to put the worst possible complexion on their behaviour. He does concede that they probably felt it "undignified" *(inferius)*, but goes on to suggest that the paramount reason for their absence was that if they were seen in the act of mourning, it would be recognised for the hypocrisy that it was. Thus Tacitus, who regarded Tiberius as the master of deception, and his mother as a good match for him in this sphere, felt that they were afraid that their faces would give them away. Tacitus' conclusion runs into a serious obstacle. He concedes that he checked earlier historians and the official records *(diurna actorum scriptura)*, where the attendance of Germanicus' relatives was recorded by name, but was unable to find any evidence that Antonia, Germanicus' mother, played any role in the ceremony, nor could he find any clue for why she failed to attend. He admits that she might have been prevented by ill health but goes on to say, without any apparent basis for his suspicion, that he finds it "easier to believe" *(facilius crediderim)* that she was detained by Livia and Tiberius at the palace. Holding her there would confer some respectability on their absence by giving them the cover that they had stayed at home out of a sense of duty and respect for Drusus' widow. In fact, with the discovery of the *Tabula Siarensis*, which documents the posthumous honours voted to Germanicus, we now know that Tiberius was actively involved in selecting the tributes from among those proposed by the Senate, in consultation with his mother, his son Drusus, Agrippina, and Antonia. Thus Tiberius, Livia, and Antonia were not totally detached from the general process of honouring Germanicus.[32]

According to Tacitus, the people of Rome were struck by the comparison between Drusus' funeral in 9 BC and the rites arranged for Germanicus in AD 20. The absence of Livia and Tiberius from the ceremony aggravated the public displeasure, and there were rumblings that Germanicus had not even enjoyed the send-off that any respectable run-of-the-mill member of the nobility could rightly expect. But again, the *Tabula Siarensis*, with its wealth of honours for Germanicus, illustrates the general unfairness of the charge and shows that Tacitus' report of the official reaction to Germanicus' death is abbreviated and incomplete. His short account of the *honores* for the deceased hardly reflects what the Senate voted, such as the detailed sculptural montage for the arch to be erected in the Circus Flaminius, with the statue of Germanicus flanked by statues of his family. One of the specific complaints noted by Tacitus was the absence of panegyrics *(laudationes)*. The *Tabula* shows that such panegyrics in fact took place earlier, within the Senate, delivered on separate occasions both by Drusus Caesar and by Tiberius, and that the full text of both was to be inscribed in bronze. But Tacitus is surely right in his assertions of popular discontent. Tiberius felt obliged to issue a public statement in what proved to be a vain effort to defuse feelings. He declared that he shared the general sense of loss but believed that his response should be restrained (the Latin text is somewhat ambiguous at this point), because the same licence was not allowed ordinary people and rulers. The Roman world had endured in the past the destruction of armies, the deaths of generals, and the complete eradication of historic houses. Tiberius ended with the commonplace that their leaders were mortal, but the state was immortal. Although we cannot assume that the text as recorded by Tacitus is precisely accurate — there was a convention among ancient historians to invent plausible speeches — the thoughts are completely in character for Tiberius, who might well have felt that the public displays of mourning for Germanicus had turned into something of a circus. Tiberius later showed the same restraint during the funeral rites of his son Drusus, keeping his expression unmoved while those around him wept. He declared to the Senate on this later occasion that he found it easier to handle grief by an attitude of "business as usual," adding, significantly, that he recognised that he would be criticised for taking such a position. Also, Romans seemed to have forgotten that some years earlier Tiberius had expressly limited the mourning over his brother Drusus, on the grounds that "discipline had to be preserved" not only in warfare but also in grief. Livia, too, was commended for her dignity and restraint in dealing with the death of the elder Drusus, her son. But Tiberius' pronouncements about the need for a dignified response to Germanicus' death probably did little to win over the general public to him or his mother. Nor should this be surprising. Nearly two thousand years later the House of Windsor, mother and son, learned the cost of maintaining a reserve and dignity amidst fanatical displays of grief for a departed icon. It should finally be noted that a decade later Tiberius neglected to attend even his mother's funeral (see chapter 11).[33]

It appears that while Piso was lurking in Cos, it had devolved upon the senators in the province to appoint a new temporary legate, without the need to secure the authority of Germanicus (who perhaps had been too ill to take part). Their ultimate choice was Gnaeus Sentius Saturninus, who had been suffect consul in AD 4. To judge from a fragmentary inscription from Neopolis, Syria, dated between 21 and 30, where Sentius is described as *legatus Caesaris*, his position in Syria was confirmed by Tiberius, a detail that was to prove significant for Piso.[34] When news of Germanicus' death reached Cos, Piso received differing advice on his best next step. His son Marcus sensibly pressed him to return to Rome to face what would be inevitable unpopularity, but nothing more serious. Others with less foresight urged that he should exercise his authority as the true legate of Syria. These same men, as Tacitus relates their argument, reminded Piso that once he returned to Rome he would have no support. He had enjoyed the complicity of Livia and the backing of Tiberius. But that complicity could be acknowledged only in private. In public no one would put on a bigger show of distress over Germanicus than those who were secretly overjoyed by what had happened. This slur on Tiberius and Livia is contradicted, of course, by the earlier report that they in fact avoided a public display of grief. Piso chose to listen to the activists rather than to his son, and in doing so committed a literally fatal error. He set sail for the province but soon realised that he had seriously misread the situation in Syria, where he had anticipated that he would win the loyalty of the legions. In the event, the bulk of the army in Syria remained loyal to Sentius Saturninus. The beleaguered Piso was ultimately driven to find refuge in the fortress of Celendris in Cilicia, where after a brief siege he surrendered unconditionally. The only concession he secured was a safe passage to Rome, where he would now have to face far more serious consequences than the unpopularity that his son Marcus had predicted for him if he returned to Rome at the outset.[35]

Piso was full of self-confidence when he reached the city, early in AD 20. He threw a dinner party and gaily decorated his house.[36] But the euphoria was short-lived. The day after his arrival, charges were laid against him of murder, extortion, and treason, and Plancina was charged along with him. Until the 1990s evidence for the trial that followed consisted essentially of Tacitus' account, with brief notices in other sources. Recently discovered epigraphic material of major significance, consisting of bronze fragments found in various locations in Baetica in Roman Spain, has thrown new dramatic light on many of the issues raised in the trial. Although these sources vary in some small details, they represent the text of a summary of a senatorial decree (strictly speaking, several decrees), the *Senatus Consultum de Cn. Pisone Patre* (hereafter, the *Piso Decree*), enacted in connection with the trial, ending with a *subscriptio* of Tiberius in which he instructs that the document is to be posted in the major provincial centres and the army camps.[37]

Tiberius declined to hear the case himself *in camera* and remitted it to the Senate, where he presided over the proceedings. This arrangement, according to Tacitus, was to Piso's satisfaction, because he felt that the princeps had the integrity to discard rumours, and his confidence was boosted by what Tacitus calls Livia's guilty participation in the affair. This, of course, represents only Tacitus' conjecture of what was going on in Piso's mind — he makes no suggestion that Piso communicated any such thoughts to a third party.[38] The trial was convened in the portico of Apollo's temple on the Palatine. Piso made no progress on the more serious charges either in the Senate hearing or outside, where the public mood grew distinctly nasty. A lynch mob came up to the Palatine and collected outside the temple, baying for his blood. They hurled his statues down the Gemonian stairs, and Suetonius says that Piso himself came close to being torn to pieces.[39]

Tacitus notes that the *invidia* felt for Plancina was just as bitter, but that she enjoyed *maior gratia* (bigger support), and it was unclear how far Tiberius would be able to act against her. Plancina had insisted that she would stand by Piso. But as the trial progressed, she could see the writing on the wall and decided to look out for herself. She prevailed on Livia to intercede on her behalf and then began to dissociate her defence from Piso's.[40] At this stage Piso was ready to concede defeat, and only the urging of his sons convinced him to resume his defence. But he could sense the hostility of the Senate. After returning home, he wrote a few notes, which he handed to his freedman, then closed the door to his room. Next morning he was found with his throat cut. A sword lay on the floor. Conspiracy theorists denied suicide.[41]

Piso's last letter was read out in the Senate. In it he declared his loyalty to Tiberius and Livia, and begged that his sons not be made to suffer for their father's behaviour. The letter was perhaps most striking for what it omitted to say. As Tacitus laconically observes, *de Plancina nihil addidit* (he said not a word about Plancina). In his final hours Germanicus had demonstrated clearly his devotion to Agrippina, giving her fond if anxious farewells. The contrast between that scene of matrimonial bliss and tragedy and Piso's ultimate disdain for his wife is self-evident.[42]

The suicide of Piso did not bring an end to the trial. The Senate was instructed by Tiberius to reach findings on the case against Piso himself, his son Marcus, his wife, Plancina, and his chief lieutenants in Syria. The final resolution ensured that Piso's name would remain under a shadow. His statues were to be removed from public places, and his image was banned from funeral processions. Marcus was treated with understanding; part of the family property, although confiscated, was even returned to him as a generous gesture. The chief lieutenants were exiled and their property confiscated.[43] The treatment of Plancina is perhaps the most interesting. She spoke in her own defence to the Senate, although she may well have been obliged to stand at the entrance to deliver her speech. There are other examples of such personal appearances by women, although they are rare. Annia Rufilla, for instance, had on one occasion stood at the threshold of the Senate shouting abuse at one of the members yet was able to claim immunity because she held the portrait of the emperor as she did so.[44] In her speech Plancina was no doubt more restrained than Annia, but she did not mount a proper rebuttal. She would have found herself very vulnerable if she had been obliged to do so, for among other actions she had made her slaves available to Piso when he went into Syria, an action that would be difficult to defend. It was the intervention of Tiberius that saved her. He spoke on her behalf, and Tacitus describes his speech as a shameful performance, adding that it caused the emperor considerable embarrassment. In his defence he pleaded the intercession of his mother. The decree makes plain that Plancina was not in fact acquitted of the charges. Rather, the Senate acceded to Livia's wishes and decided to waive the penalty in her case.[45] (The issue is considered in chapter 8.) The proceedings wrapped up with a motion from Valerius Messalinus that the family of Germanicus be thanked for their efforts to ensure that he was avenged. Livia's name is included among those cited. The *Decree* sets out this *gratiarum actio* in some detail. In Livia's case it links the praise for her to that for Drusus, observing that they matched their devotion to the memory of Germanicus with their fairness in reserving judgement until the case was concluded. Unlike the other relatives of Germanicus, Drusus and Livia had been involved (in Livia's case indirectly) in the trial. The *actio* was perhaps intended to some degree to deflect the criticism that had been levelled against Livia and to argue that what had been perceived as bias was in fact the exercise of judicious balance. Again, when praising the moderation shown by Germanicus' children and his brother Claudius in their grief, the Senate gave full credit to the training *(discipulina)* that they had received from Tiberius and Drusus, and from Livia.[46]

The end of the trial did not bring an immediate end to the controversy. Tacitus observes, in perhaps his most insightful comment on the affair, that the Germanicus issue was a battleground of conflicting rumours *(vario rumore iactata)* and notes further that the frenzied speculation did not abate as time passed but perverted and confused the issues. Livia's conduct, Tacitus claims, was the object of savage but secret criticism, because she had consorted with the murderess of her grandson and had then rescued her from the Senate. The next step, it was feared, would be for her to turn the same poisons against Agrippina and her children. The expression used here is among the most powerful in the Tacitean corpus. Tiberius and Livia, it was believed, would seek to sate their hunger on the blood of a family reduced to calamity. As often on these occasions, the criticisms were supposedly made secretly, and thus were unprovable. That said, given the mood of the time, Livia's reputation must have suffered, at least in the short term, through her support of Plancina.[47] A hint of the strength of feelings may be found in the actual circumstances of the *Piso Decree*. In Tacitus' account the trial of Piso is followed by the ovation of Drusus, which had been voted earlier but postponed. The ovation is securely dated by the fasti to May 28, and the trial must have preceded that date. If Tacitus' sequence is chronologically correct, the decree must have been issued considerably later than the actual trial, for it is dated to December 10. The problem is far from settled, but the decision to promulgate the decree so long after the event might be evidence of anxiety about continuing unrest among the troops and throughout the provinces. That said, it is hard to imagine that it could have done much good. The self-serving nature of the document and its adherence to a strict party line would surely have been apparent even to the least cynical.[48] Although many of the inferences that Tacitus draws may arouse scepticism, the very decision to distribute the decree in a permanent medium outside Italy confirms his picture of the resentment stirred up by Germanicus' death.

Although Tacitus insists, not too convincingly, that Livia and Tiberius were racked by a seething hatred of Germanicus and his family, he concedes that relations between Germanicus and Drusus Caesar, brothers by adoption, had been strikingly amiable and harmonious *(egregie concordes)*. It comes as no surprise, then, that after their father's death, Germanicus' two eldest sons,

Nero and Drusus, were given a home by Drusus Caesar, who treated them as kindly as he would his own children. It is possible that the hand of Tiberius or Livia lay behind this gesture, as a public declaration that Livia's great-grandsons (and Tiberius' grandsons by adoption) would be accorded their due recognition when the issue of the succession came to the fore. In addition, Drusus Caesar had a personal cause to celebrate, in an otherwise gloomy year. His wife bore him twin sons. Tiberius was delighted by the happy event but did not allow his joy to cloud his judgement. Although his own bloodline now seemed assured, he remained punctilious in advancing the prospects of Germanicus' sons. But despite his efforts to be scrupulously fair, things began to go terribly wrong.

The blame for the domestic crisis that divided the imperial house in the twenties cannot be laid at the door of Tiberius or Livia. The distrust within the family was so deep that there would probably have been little prospect of reconciliation, and Agrippina, with her smouldering sense of injustice, did little to help. But this difficult situation was made immeasurably worse by the intrigues of the one man whose interests were best served by continued tension and infighting. Lucius Aelius Sejanus, later to become the most notorious figure of Tiberius' principate, had first entered the record while serving in an unspecified capacity in the retinue of Gaius Caesar. He became joint prefect of the praetorian guard with his father in AD 14 and sole prefect in 16 or 17. By that time he had the ear of Tiberius, playing on the emperor's insecurities during Germanicus' Rhine campaigns in the early days of his reign. Sejanus is given an active, if vague, role in the Piso affair, in arranging the suppression of incriminating documents.[49] He was clearly someone who could work well behind the scenes. Despite his very brief appearances in the public record, he had by AD 20 become the emperor's right-hand man, close enough to be described by Tiberius as the "partner of his labours" *(socius laborum)*. He had also built up a power base both in the army and in the Senate. He spread his net widely and reputedly sought to enlist Livia, among others, to further his cause.[50]

Livia was very conscious of the importance of staying in good health and seems to have reached her eighties unscathed. In AD 22, however, she received, perhaps for the first time, a clear and dangerous intimation of her mortality when she was brought down by a serious, unspecified, illness. Tiberius had left Rome for Campania in the previous year, pleading his own ill health. Tacitus is sceptical about his excuse but is less than helpful on what might have been the true reason. He cannot decide whether Tiberius wanted to prepare himself for a later, more protracted, absence from Rome or to allow his son Drusus

Caesar, who was to hold the consulship in 22, to get on with the job without his father's brooding presence. In any case, Livia's situation was precarious enough for her son to rush back to be at her side. This was a touching gesture, something of a speciality for Tiberius. Some thirty years earlier, in 9 BC, he had hastened to Germany from Ticinum to be at the sickbed of his brother Drusus, and he had also rushed from Illyricum to Nola in AD 14 to attend Augustus in his final hours.[51]

Ever the cynic, Tacitus claims that Tiberius' show of concern was a sham, that deep down he was furious with his mother because of her constant attempts to steal the limelight from him. He was particularly incensed over the recent dedication of a statue of Augustus during which she had tried to claim precedence (see chapter 8). To put on the proper public face, Tiberius suppressed his irritation, and her illness was officially treated as a matter of great communal concern. When she recovered, the Senate decreed *supplicia* (acts of thanksgiving) to the gods and *ludi magni* (great games), to be put on by the pontifices, the augurs, the quindecimviri (officials entrusted with the charge of the Sibylline books and the general supervision of the foreign cults), and the septemviri, whose historic role was the congenial one of managing the banquets. These four constituted the great priestly colleges, and to make the occasion especially grand they were to be assisted by the Sodales Augustales, a body that had been formed in AD 14 on the death of Augustus and charged with the cult of the two *divi*, Julius and Augustus. The fact that the celebrations were in honour of the mother of the emperor invested the occasion with a special solemnity, which brought out the worst pedantry in everyone involved. Lucius Apronius moved that the presidency of the games should fall to the Fetials, a quaint body whose functions had become largely obsolete and who were concerned with such formalities as declarations of war and conclusions of treaties. Apronius, who is ranked by Tacitus as a sycophant of the first order, was clearly keen to curry favour, but the actual nature of the flattery is rather elusive. In any case, the attempt backfired. Tiberius opposed the inclusion of the Fetials, giving a short lecture on the precedence and prerogatives of the priesthoods (the Fetials did not really make the grade). This hardly seemed consistent, for he included the "junior" Augustales. He justified their presence with the very best of reasons, their family connections. He could have added that Livia's status as priestess of Augustus (see chapter 8) would have made the participation of this particular college highly appropriate. The issue, in any case, is hardly likely to have aroused great passions.[52]

Between July 22 and July 23 Tiberius issued a dupondius, depicting on its obverse a draped bust of Salus, her hair parted in the centre and falling in waves at the side of the head, and identified by the legend SALUS AUGUSTA (fig. 4) The reverse carries no image, only Tiberius' names and titles. The date and the reference to Salus (Well-being) leave little doubt that the coin alludes to Livia's illness. But the allusion is indirect. Salus Augusta does not mean the well-being of (Julia) Augusta. Feminine abstractions, like Salus or Pietas, modified by the adjective Augusta, refer not to Livia but rather to the association of the personified abstraction with the Augustan house. In the case of Salus, this association had a long history. In 16 BC Augustan coins celebrate vows taken for the emperor's salus, and identify it with the salus of the *respublica*, and oaths were sworn by the *Salus Augusti*, where the genitive indicates that the *salus* belonged to Augustus specifically. There was a cult of Augustus' salus during his lifetime, and a priest is attested at Alabanda. Although Valerius Maximus calls Tiberius the Salus of the country, that emperor may have discouraged dedications to his personal Salus; instead, they are made to the broader Salus Augusta. Inscriptions of the Tiberian period at Nasium in Gallia Belgica speak of the perpetual Salus of the divine house *(pro perpetua salute divinae domus)*, and at Interamna there were dedications in AD 31 to Salus Augusta, along with Libertas Publica, the municipal *genius* and Tiberius' *providentia*, to celebrate the downfall of Sejanus. That said, the intention of the salus dupondius may be more nuanced. Although the legend does not refer overtly to Livia, and although the portrait technically is not hers, the head does have a human personality, and common sense dictates that in the year of her illness the coin would at the very least have been associated by the public with the emperor's mother.[53]

The equestrians were faced with a particularly knotty religious dilemma. They wanted to do their bit and to mark Livia's recovery by making an offering to equestrian Fortuna *(equestri Fortunae)*. But in what temple would they make it? There were many shrines to Fortuna in Rome, but none that alluded specifically to the equestrians. One had indeed been vowed in 180 BC and dedicated in 173 to honour the achievements of the Roman cavalry. It was apparently still visible in the Augustan period, for the architect Vitruvius, the emperor's contemporary, speaks of seeing it. By AD 22 it had clearly been demolished, and the equestrians had no choice but to select a site outside the capital. The pleasant resort town of Antium to the south of Rome offered an ideal alternative. It had close associations with the cult of Fortuna, and could even boast a temple to Fortuna Equestris. Moreover, it was the location of one of the most important imperial villas, the birthplace of Caligula, and later of Nero. As a favourite summer residence of Augustus, Antium would certainly have been well known to Livia.[54] It is noteworthy that in their accounts of the outpouring of regard and affection for Livia the sources say nothing of the ill will aroused earlier by the death of Germanicus. The public resentment seems to have been short-lived, perhaps assuaged to some degree by Piso's suicide. The affair clearly had no long-term impact on Livia's reputation.

There is some evidence that the Senate made an additional gesture to honour Livia in the year of her illness by drawing attention to her sons' *pietas*, a peculiarly Roman concept that embraced duty both to the gods and to the family. They voted for the erection of a structure to *Pietati Augustae*, long referred to by modern scholars as the Altar of Pietas Augusta. It was not completed for another twenty years, when its dedication was recorded in a Claudian inscription. The original stone is lost, but the text is preserved in a transcription, one of the many made by the itinerant and anonymous monk of Einsiedeln in the middle ages. Koeppel has pointed out that the notion of an Ara Pietatis was dreamt up by Mommsen in the nineteenth century, and since then its existence is simply taken for granted. In fact, we have no idea what the structure was or how large it was — it could have been something as small as a statue base or as large as a temple. The text records the dedication of the building, whatever it was, by Claudius in AD 43, though in fulfillment of a *senatus consultum* passed during the consulship of Decimus Haterius Agrippa and Gaius Sulpicius Galba — that is, more than twenty years earlier, in AD 22. The reason for the long delay between the original vote and the final dedication is puzzling. Tiberius left Rome within four years of the decree, and interest in the project might have fallen into abeyance for a time. It would be revived later by Claudius, who was keen to establish his own ancestral credentials and had arranged the consecration of Livia in the year immediately preceding the dedication.[55]

In 23 Sejanus further strengthened his position by concentrating the cohorts of the praetorian guard into one set of permanent barracks at the Porta Viminalis.[56] The main obstacle to his growing influence over the emperor was removed in September of the same year. Tiberius suffered a crushing personal blow when his son, Drusus Caesar, died. (It was revealed some years later that he may well have been poisoned by his wife, Livilla, who had become Sejanus' lover.) The emperor delivered a dignified speech in the Senate to mark the sad occasion and made it clear that he would now turn to Germanicus' sons, Nero and Drusus, to provide him with the support he would need to perform the duties required by his office. His mother, Livia, he pointed out, had reached *extremam senectutem* (extreme old age).[57] She was now eighty or eighty-one, and his thoughts were no doubt prompted by her serious illness in the previous year. There might also have been a quiet hint to Livia to yield to the conventional demands of years as advanced as hers, and to take more of a back seat (something of a vain hope). But she did not lack for honours. She was granted the privilege, whenever she entered the theatre, of taking her place with the Vestals. At one time men and women had been allowed to mix freely at the games. Augustus, who thought this promiscuity improper, had restricted women to the very highest seats. Only the Vestal Virgins were assigned decent seating, opposite the dais of the praetor. Caligula as emperor extended this entitlement, offering it to his grandmother Antonia and to his sisters. Claudius in turn granted it to his wife Messalina. There is also good reason to believe that Livia might at the same time have been offered the privilege of travelling in the *carpentum*, or covered carriage. Coins of AD 22 or 23 (dated by reference to Tiberius' twenty-fourth tribunician year) carry the device of the carpentum drawn by two mules, with its front and sides decorated with Victories and other figures (fig. 5). That these coins are associated with Livia's Vestal honours is strongly suggested by Dio's testimony that Messalina in 43 received the right to sit with the Vestals, and was at the same time allowed the use of the carpentum. The coin issue may, on the other hand, be related directly to Livia's illness, and the scene could relate to the procession of the supplicationes which the Senate decreed.[58] Also in AD 23 an honour came from farther afield, when with Tiberius' permission the cities of Asia decreed a temple to Tiberius, his mother, and the Senate (considered in some detail in chapter 8).[59]

These displays of family devotion would have helped to conceal a domestic atmosphere of increasing tension. Tiberius did go out of his way to treat Germanicus' boys with kindness and goodwill, and had their mother, Agrippina, reciprocated she might have been able to withstand the assault that Sejanus was preparing. In the event, her behaviour was the very opposite to what the situation demanded. Convinced, like her mother, Julia, that Tiberius was an unworthy *arriviste*, and embittered by the death of her husband and the exile of her mother and sister, she promoted the interests of her sons with a single-minded obsession. Sejanus was more than willing to encourage Agrippina on this suicidal course, and worked hard to isolate her, drawing on the help of Livia to bring this about. Clearly the prefect still thought Livia vigorous enough to be of use to him. She was supposedly urged through agents to go to Tiberius and persuade him that Agrippina was casting ambitious eyes on his position, which she had earmarked for one of her sons. Sejanus' task, Tacitus says, was made all the easier because Livia was antagonistic towards Agrippina, thus enabling Sejanus to exploit her *vetus odium* (old contempt). Livilla, Drusus' widow and Sejanus' mistress, helped her paramour. The *Piso*

Decree describes the bonds between Livilla and her grandmother as close. This could be an empty formula, but we do know that Livia provided a nurse from her own staff for Livilla. The young woman seems to have identified a way of winning Livia's support. She enlisted the aid of Julius Postumus, possibly the future prefect of Egypt in 47. He was supposedly known to Livia through his adulterous affair with her friend Mutilia Prisca, the wife of Livia's protégé Gaius Fufius Geminus, consul in AD 29. Julius is said to have worked hard to alienate Livia from Agrippina, and Tacitus observes that he was helped by the fact that she was herself *anxiam potentiae*, which could mean that she was desperate either to retain or to regain her influence, because Sejanus would by now have replaced her as Tiberius' closest advisor. Inevitably, Agrippina's ill-tempered zealotry would have created an atmosphere of rivalry in the imperial household. But we have no way of telling how successful Julius was, and there is no real evidence that Livia worked actively against her daughter-in-law. Her supposed intrigues may be little more than speculation.[60]

By now Livia was in her eighties and had been seriously ill. But she still remained involved, and that she was still a power in the land is suggested by a bizarre series of events dated to AD 24. In that year the praetor Plautius Silvanus entered in his modest way into the annals of history when he threw his wife out of their window to her death. He was charged before Tiberius. His answers to the emperor's questioning were rather fuzzy, and he claimed that he had been asleep at the time and unaware that his wife had committed suicide. Tiberius went to the house to examine the evidence on the spot and found signs of a struggle. He referred the case to the Senate. The case was a mysterious one, and it might be explained by the possibility that Silvanus was acting "under the influence." At any rate, his first wife, Numantina, was later charged with sending him crazy with drugs and spells (she was acquitted). As he awaited trial, Silvanus' grandmother Urgulania sent her grandson a dagger. Given Livia's close friendship with Urgulania, this was taken as tantamount to *monitu principis* (by guidance from the princeps), a clear sign that to the outside world Livia still carried much weight. The impression might have been reinforced by the prosecution and death (possibly suicide), about the same time, of Lucius Piso, who had shown contempt for Livia's potentia in acting against Urgulania some years earlier (see chapter 8). Silvanus attempted suicide but found that it was easier to finish off a wife than himself, and had to get help to do it properly.[61]

Meanwhile, within the imperial household the clashes between Tiberius and Agrippina grew, both in frequency and intensity. The emperor had by now endured enough of the strife and intrigue of palace life in Rome, and had come to the sober realization that it was time to take his leave. At some point in 26 he departed for Campania, and went from there to his villa on the island paradise of Capri. He was not destined to return to Rome, except for his own funeral. Why did he leave? The literary sources offer a wide range of suggestions.[62] There was the suspicion that Tiberius wanted a quiet spot to indulge in his acts of cruelty and lust. Another school of thought suggested that he left because of his appearance—he was by now totally bald, with an ulcerous face covered with plasters. The majority view of historians, according to Tacitus, ascribed the decision to leave to the relentless urging of Sejanus. The prefect kept bringing up the problems of life in the capital—the crowds, the endless petitioners—and stressed the pleasures of a quiet, peaceful life (but made no mention of Livia as an obstacle to a happy life). He also used the argument that Tiberius could rule from a distance, and would increase his popularity if Romans were not constantly reminded by his very presence that they were subject to his power. Tacitus does confront one obvious objection, that Tiberius stayed away from Rome after the prefect's fall. Of course, by then the aged emperor might simply have got used to the pleasure of being away from it all. All the main sources add another plausible reason: his desire to get away from his mother. Dio hedges a little, noting that it was chiefly because he found Livia such a handful even when she restricted herself to domestic matters that Tiberius removed himself to Capri. Tacitus records a common belief *(traditur)* that Tiberius could not stand his mother's uncontrollable passion for power *(matris impotentia)*. Suetonius is more specific. He reports that Tiberius was sorely put out that his mother had preserved letters of Augustus critical of him, and brooded over her behaviour, which seemed especially spiteful. Some thought, according to Suetonius, that this was the strongest of the reasons for his retirement.

It is clear that the sources are indulging in nothing more than speculation. In many ways the departure seems psychologically sound, the action of a man who found political life thoroughly distasteful yet who throughout his life had demonstrated an inability to resist the appeal of power. As an absentee emperor he could enjoy the best of both worlds. Tiberius no doubt was disgusted by the imperious behaviour of Agrippina, and the tension between the women of the house certainly may have influenced his decision. Syme points out that in the period before his departure Tiberius found himself in what he calls a nasty predicament, "being encompassed by no fewer than four widows"—Livia, Antonia, Agrippina, and Livilla (widow of Drusus).[63] All of this may simply have compounded his ongoing frustration over the insoluble problem that the complex constitutional situation of his mother had created, a problem that had dogged him since the beginning of his reign (see chapter 8).

Whatever motivated Tiberius' departure for Capri—and Livia personally was probably not the only cause—it is clear that little true affection remained between mother and son. They met on a single further occasion, and that was for only a few hours. History has not recorded where or when the meeting took place, or what was discussed. It certainly did not happen in Rome, which Tiberius never visited again. We do know that in 28 the emperor crossed from Capri to the mainland. Possibly during that visit he presided over the betrothal of Agrippina the Younger and her first husband, Gnaeus Domitius Ahenobarbus, parents of the future emperor Nero. Livia might well have been present in Campania, either specifically for the ceremony or to spend time at one of the imperial villas. But this is speculation.[64]

Tiberius had left behind a family rent by conflict. How closely involved Livia was in the internal wrangling is unclear. Intrigues there certainly were, but they seem mainly to have been instigated by Sejanus. The prefect's ultimate ambitions are a matter of some debate, but there can be no doubt that he would have seen Agrippina and her sons as their chief obstacle. His first efforts, once he had the field free to himself, seem to have been directed against Agrippina's sons. The oldest, Nero, suffered the common failing of young princes of the imperial house, an inability to hold his tongue. Sejanus bribed those close to him to egg him on. He made rash and injudicious statements, which were noted down and duly reported to Tiberius. At the same time the crafty prefect worked his way into the favour of Drusus, exploiting his resentment of his older brother, whom he saw as his mother's favourite.[65] Livia seems to have had little if any role in these family feuds. Nor in reality is there concrete evidence of a serious clash with Agrippina. To the contrary, Tacitus suggests very strongly that the presence of Livia in Rome to some degree protected Agrippina and her family.[66]

In the year following Tiberius' departure, AD 27, Sejanus finally made his move against his main target—Agrippina herself. He ordered his praetorians to keep watch over Agrippina and her son Nero and to make detailed reports on their activities. At some stage, probably in early 28, Agrippina was placed in a form of custody, possibly under house arrest. In another context Seneca remarks that she had a luxury villa at Herculaneum where she was once held under guard (the villa was later destroyed on the orders of Caligula).[67] Unfortunately, he does not indicate the date but it could well have been in AD 27. We do not know where Nero might have been, but he very possibly was subjected to similar restrictions. Livia was able to afford some limited degree of protection to Agrippina's family. Caligula, now aged fifteen, moved into his great-grandmother's home. The later role and wild reputation of Caligula have ensured that the ancient sources would take a lively curiosity in his whereabouts and record them in detail. But his younger sisters did not arouse the same interest. Thus if Livia took in his sisters Drusilla and Livilla also (Agrippina the Younger no doubt would have left home after her marriage in 28), it would not be remarkable for her gesture to go unmentioned. At any rate, we do know that after Livia's death, when Caligula was looked after by his other great-grandmother, Antonia, at least one of the sisters, Drusilla, lived with them (and reputedly engaged in incestuous underage sex with her brother). It is therefore a reasonable inference that Caligula and his two unmarried sisters had also lived together under Livia's roof.

Whatever Livia's personal feelings about the outspoken and headstrong Agrippina, a woman so different in temperament from herself, she clearly maintained a strong sense of family obligation. While Livia was still on the scene she could counter the influence of Sejanus, who, as Tacitus concedes, felt restrained by her presence from acting against his opponents in the imperial household. But Livia was not immortal. She had suffered a serious ailment in 22, and in 29 she fell ill again. This second illness proved to be fatal. It would prove in the end to be no less fatal for Agrippina and her oldest sons.

1 Denarius of Tiberius (enlarged). Numismatica Ars Classica, Zurich

2 Dupondius of Tiberius. Numismatica Ars Classica, Zurich

3 Dupondius of Tiberius. Numismatica Ars Classica, Zurich

4 Dupondius of Tiberius. Numismatica Ars Classica, Zurich

5 Sestertius of Tiberius. Numismatica Ars Classica, Zurich

6 Dupondius of Claudius. Numismatica Ars Classica, Zurich

7 Aureus of Nero (enlarged). Numismatica Ars Classica, Zurich

8 Denarius of Galba (enlarged). Numismatica Ars Classica, Zurich

9 Sestertius of Antoninus Pius. Numismatica Ars Classica, Zurich

10 Lead tessera (Tiberius). From Rostovtsev (1900)

11 Cameo, Tiberius and Livia. Soprintendenza Archeologica di Firenze

12 Head of Livia from Fayum. Ny Carlsberg Glyptothek, Copenhagen

13 Basalt head of Livia. Musée du Louvre, Paris

14 Head of Livia. Deutsches Archäologisches Institut, Rome. Inst. Neg. 78.1937

15 Head of Livia. Ny Carlsberg Glyptothek, Copenhagen

16 Giant head of Livia. From Aurigemma (1940)

17 Head of Livia. Musée Saint-Raymond, Toulouse

18 Bronze bust of Livia. Musée du Louvre, Paris

19 Sardonyx, Livia and Augustus. Kunsthistorisches Museum, Vienna

20 South frieze of Ara Pacis. Deutsches Archäologisches Institut, Rome. Inst. Neg. 72.2403

21 Detail of fig. 20. Deutsches Archäologisches Institut, Rome. Inst. Neg. 72.2403

22 Detail of statue of Livia as Ceres. Musée du Louvre, Paris

23 Statue of Livia as Ceres. Musée du Louvre, Paris

24 Statue of Livia as priestess. Monumenti, Musei e Galerie Pontificie, Città del Vatticano

25 Statue of Livia as priestess. Deutsches Archäologisches Institut, Rome. Inst. Neg. 67.1593

26 Head of Augustus. Ny Carlsberg Glyptothek, Copenhagen

27 Head of Tiberius. Ny Carlsberg Glyptothek, Copenhagen

28 Wall painting, Primaporta. From Antike Denkmäler (Berlin 1891)

29 Reconstruction of Mausoleum of Augustus. From Cordingley and Richmond (1927)

PART

II

LIVIAN THEMES

6

THE PRIVATE LIVIA

Livia was a prominent figure in Roman society for most of her long adult life. Yet we have surprisingly little direct information about Livia the person, as opposed to Livia the wife or mother of the princeps. To some extent this was doubtless her own doing. Although she was capable of considerable charm and affability, to the extent of earning a mild rebuke from Tacitus for displaying these qualities more than was traditionally expected in women of the old school, behind her public persona Livia maintained a deliberate reserve. She may not have been so inclined by nature, but she certainly was by circumstance. Seneca calls her a *feminam opinionis suae custodem diligentissimam* (woman who was the most diligent protector of her reputation). She felt obliged to conduct herself always in such a way that there could be no criticism of her, not only on major issues but also on trifling matters. She thus created a protective shell which few would manage to penetrate.[1]

The dearth of information cannot be attributed totally to Livia's conscious effort to discourage public curiosity. We are told almost nothing even about her external appearance, which she can hardly have kept concealed. The ancient literary sources generally did not trouble to give detailed descriptions of individual women, nor do women figure in the various physiognomic treatises that began to appear in the fourth century BC.[2] When ancient authorities do provide information about how prominent women looked, their reliability is highly suspect. Ovid in his exile poetry describes Livia as having the form of

Venus and the face of Juno. At the time she was in her seventies, and the description surely reflects the poet's desire to please rather than Livia's physical appeal. By implication Dio also suggests an attractive appearance, for he relates a story that Augustus was so besotted by Terentia, Maecenas' wife, that he made her enter a beauty contest with Livia (the outcome is not recorded). Both Tacitus and Velleius speak of Livia's *forma*, which without modification has a straightforward positive connotation, and means essentially "beauty." Velleius' general enthusiasm for Livia, of course, should make us wary of his testimony, and Tacitus often links physical beauty to spiritual corruption. But a more serious problem is that all such descriptions, whether friendly or hostile, of aristocratic Roman women tend to be formulaic.[3]

Potentially a more reliable source of information should be the contemporary depictions of Livia that appear in various media, especially coins and sculpture. The general importance of this evidence will be dealt with in some detail in appendix 1; here we shall limit ourselves specifically to what it tells us about her appearance. The first problem to be faced is that no portrait explicitly identified as Livia's appears on any of the imperial coins—that is, on coins minted in Rome or in "official" mints outside the capital for distribution throughout the empire. There are possible depictions of her seated, and identified by name, more than a decade after her death, but the image is on such a small scale that it offers no insight into her appearance (figs. 1, 6). There are abstract personifications on coins during her lifetime, portraits of such figures as "Salus," "Iustitia," and "Pietas," which might obliquely reflect Livia's appearance (figs. 2–4). We must be cautious. Abstract personifications such as Salus that are grammatically feminine and modified by the adjective Augusta are not a direct allusion to Livia's name Augusta and in a formal sense have nothing specifically to do with Livia. This would not, of course, preclude Livia's being identified informally with whatever virtue is depicted, just as the public might well have associated the abstract virtues represented with the virtues of Livia, or at least an idealised concept of Livia. Only the Salus issue has idiosyncratic personalised features. Certainly outside of Rome the Salus coin was used as a type for Livia's portrait, and although this does not prove that it was a precise record of her appearance, it is likely that it broadly reflected her features.[4]

Sculpture is a little more helpful, but while a large body of sculpted portraits have been assigned to Livia, the evidence they provide has to be treated with caution, because the facial features that are repeated as established elements of her iconography do not necessarily represent her appearance precisely, and only the broadest generalizations should be drawn. In early portraits Livia sports the nodus hairstyle, in which the hair rolls forward over the forehead and is then drawn back to form a distinctive topknot. This style was seen by Ovid as a useful corrective to a very round face.[5] Generally in the heads of this group the face is a regular oval with broad cheekbones. The eyes are large and the brow above them arches slightly. The nose is large and aquiline, while the curving mouth and the chin are very small. The portraits project an image well suited to Livia — one of ageless and elegant beauty, calm and dignified, perhaps strangely emotionless (figs. 12–13). The severity of the nodus style would be less appealing with age. Thus the hair in portraits of the Tiberian period generally has a centre parting, and falls from either side in waves (fig. 17). The head is still relatively youthful, given that Livia must have been now in her seventies, a tradition maintained by modern aging monarchs, whose images on stamps and coins tend to be frozen for several decades. It could be argued that the elusive issue of Livia's appearance is irrelevant in a political biography. But it has some historical importance. The sources suggest that Augustus was drawn to Livia initially by basic sexual attraction. Some knowledge of her physical appearance would help us place that claim in a proper context.

Whatever attributes Livia was granted by Nature she could enhance by Art. When it came to dress, Ovid attributes to Livia a surprisingly progressive attitude, that she was simply too busy to spend a lot of time on her appearance. The assertion has to be seen against the background of a large household and an enormous staff, whose task it would have been to pay attention to those details deemed unworthy of their mistress's time and effort.[6] The evidence for the wide range of functionaries operating within the household of Livia is dealt with in chapter 9. At this point we can limit ourselves to noting the surprising number of helpers devoted to Livia's personal appearance. Inevitably there were several *ornatrices* (dressers), as well as staff *a veste/ad vestem*, whose task it was to keep her clothes in good order. In addition, the *ab ornamentis* would have had responsibility for her ceremonial garments and accessories, along with a specialist who looked after those she wore as priestess of Augustus, a freedman *ab ornamentis sacerdotalibus*. Her *calciator* made her shoes. Augustus liked to boast that his clothes were made by his wife and sister. Perhaps, but they would have had help. Livia employed both *lanipendi* (wool weighers) and *sarcinatores / sarcinatrices* (sewing men / women). For her comfort she had an *unctrix* (masseuse). Perhaps most striking are the skilled craftsmen who would have been employed for the manufacture and maintenance of luxury items. Her *aurifex* (goldsmith) and *inaurator* (gilder) might have been occupied mainly with furniture, but the *margaritarius* (pearl setter) sounds like someone who would have been employed to work on her personal jewellery.[7]

Elizabeth Bartman has noted the absence of jewellery from the sculpted images of Livia, which she describes as "bordering on the ascetic." This, of course, may have been a deliberate fabrication of Livia's image in the sculptural prototypes that she allowed to be distributed. There was a tradition of Roman women making a sacrifice of luxury items for the good of the state, such as the women who donated their jewellery to help fund the war against Veii in the early republic. But it may be that Livia aimed for understated elegance, to be *simplex munditiis*, as Horace expressed the concept in his famous poem. This could explain why Augustus aroused amused disbelief among the senators when he held up Livia as an example of womanhood and, when pressed to explain, cited as evidence her appearance and dress and her *exodoi* (her public forays) as illustrations of moderation to be emulated.[8] Augustus had the evidence of his own eyes, and he admired her for avoiding extravagance. But the senators perhaps may have seen a kind of elegant *moderatio*, the appearance of simplicity that only the best dressmakers, coiffeurs, and jewellers can produce, using the finest and most expensive material.

Livia's energies would have been channelled mainly into her role as wife of Augustus and as mother of Tiberius. We know little of her private interests, or of how she tried to relax. Only one scrap of evidence survives for anything remotely approaching frivolity. She seems to have competed inanely with Julia, the granddaughter of Augustus, over the record for owning the smallest dwarf. This was settled honourably, as Julia owned the smallest male, at two feet, one palm (about sixty-seven centimetres), but Livia could boast the smallest female dwarf, Andromeda, height not recorded.[9] We might also detect perhaps a hint of a certain silliness when she was a young woman. The story of her trying to foretell her child's sex by means of a hen's egg is noted in chapter 1. After Tiberius' birth she seems to have consulted an astrologer *(mathematicus)*, Scribonius. He was able to forecast that her son would govern, but without the trappings of monarchical rule, an especially impressive performance, because he anticipated this before the principate had been established and before Livia had even met Augustus.[10] But this kind of behaviour should be viewed in the context of its age, and Livia was probably no more unsophisticated in such matters than the great mass of her contemporaries. Otherwise her interests are likely to have been more serious, and she seems to have been a literate and educated woman. At any rate, in one of his letters to her Augustus quotes frequently and extensively in Greek, presumably on the assumption that she would understand him. She did of course spend some time in the Greek world during the period of her first husband's exile, but she would at that time have moved mainly in a Latin-speaking milieu. It is more than likely that she learned the language through formal tuition.

Given her family background, we can assume that Livia would have been well educated as a child. Roman girls shared domestic tutors with their brothers before their marriage. There are many examples of the happy result of this practice. Pliny the Younger was flattered to find his young wife reading and memorizing his works, and setting his verses to music. Cornelia, the wife of Pompey, was educated in literature, music, and geometry, and enjoyed attending philosophical discussions. The existence of the highly educated woman, at least at a slightly later date, is confirmed by the caustic observations of the atrabilious Juvenal, who proclaims horror at females who speak with authority on literature, discuss ethical issues, quote lines of verse the rest of humanity has not even heard of, and even correct your mistakes of grammar.[11] Apart from Livia's knowledge of Greek, however, we have no concrete evidence of her intellectual pursuits, in contrast to her great-granddaughter Agrippina, whose memoirs survived and were read by Tacitus (see appendix 1). But we do have some testimony about Livia's intellectual sophistication. Philo was a contemporary and, though a resident of Alexandria, very familiar with Rome and the imperial house. For example, he met Caligula in person when he headed a delegation to Rome to represent the case of the Jews of his native town. In a speech that he attributes to Caligula's Jewish friend Herod Agrippa, he has Agrippa cite the precedent of Livia, whom he represents as a woman of great mental ability and untypical of her sex, for he contended that women were generally incapable of grasping mental concepts (whether this is Agrippa's or Philo's prejudice is not made clear). Agrippa supposedly attributed Livia's superiority in this sphere to her natural talents and to her education *(paideia)*. Livia was well disposed to the Jews and generous to the Temple, and we might expect some gilding of the lily. But Philo's characterization of her could clearly not have been absurdly wide of the mark, or the arguments attributed to Agrippa would have been discredited. The Corinthian poet Honestus describes Livia as fit company for the muses, a woman who saved the world by her wisdom. The inflated language traditional in such a dedicatory piece, however, means that it has little historical value. Apart from the uncertain case of Honestus, we have no other case of Livia's supporting any cultural or intellectual endeavour, although she was an active patron in many other areas. In this sphere she was eclipsed by Augustus' sister Octavia, who was a sponsor of the architect Vitruvius and to whom the Stoic philosopher Athenodorus of Tarsus dedicated a book of his work.[12]

Although Livia's interest in fostering artistic and cultural undertakings might have been limited, there was one field in which her enthusiasm seems to have been boundless: the issue of healthy living, both physical and psychological. Despite her general reserve in most other matters, she seems to have been willing, even eager, to impart her views on the issue of how to live a long and robust life. She was ahead of her time in her use of what would now be called a grief counsellor. When her son Drusus died in 9 BC, she was devastated. That she managed to handle the situation with dignity was due to no small extent to the counselling given her by the philosopher Areus (or Areius) Didymus of Alexandria. Areus was basically a Stoic but kept an open mind to other schools and ideas, the kind of eclectic pragmatist that the Romans found appealing. He was clearly a man of great charm, and at the time of Actium, Octavian described him as his mentor and companion. Octavian reputedly spared all the Alexandrians after the battle and stated publicly that he did so because of the fame of Alexander the Great, the beauty of the city, and his regard for one of its citizens, Areus. In the event Alexandria did not emerge totally unscathed, for Octavian followed up his generous gesture by visiting the corpse of Alexander, where he behaved like the worst kind of bad tourist, touching the nose and breaking it off.[13]

According to Seneca's account, to which the author undoubtedly added his own imaginative touches, Areus, in giving his advice to Livia, described himself as an *assiduus comes* (constant companion) of her husband and claimed to know not only their public pronouncements but also the *secretiores animorum vestrorum motus* (the deeper emotions of the two of you). He clearly knew his patient well, and in the event proved a highly effective consultant. He gently observed that Livia had been in the habit of repressing her feelings and of being constantly on guard in public. He encouraged her to open up when dealing with the subject of Drusus, to speak to her friends about the death of her son, and to listen to others when they praised him. She should also dwell on the positive side of things, particularly the happiness that he brought her when he was still alive. The advice may have the shallow ring of the popular psychology handed out in the modern media, but it worked. Seneca observed how well Livia coped with her loss by following this advice, in contrast to the morbidly obsessive Octavia, sister of Augustus, who never ceased to be preoccupied with thoughts of her dead son Marcellus.[14]

Livia lived a long and, by her own description, healthy life, with only one serious illness recorded, when she was already eighty. Her formula for her robust constitution seems to have been proper diet and the use of "natural" remedies. She clearly had the irritating habit of healthy people who insist on inflicting on others their philosophy of wholesome living. For history this has proved fortunate, because some of her dietary recommendations are recorded. In her early eighties she anticipated a trend that was to reemerge almost two thousand years later, attributing her vigorous condition to her daily tipple. She drank exclusively the wine of Pucinum. This was a very select vintage, grown on a stony hill in the Gulf of Trieste, not far from the source of the Timavo, where the sea breezes ripen enough grapes to fill a few amphorae. Pliny confirms its medicinal value, which he suspects might long have been recognised, even by the Greeks.[15]

It need not be thought that in following this regimen Livia had simply invented a formula for healthy living. In fact, she was echoing a nostrum that had become very trendy in her youth, and in doing so marked herself as an acolyte of one of the master-gurus of health-faddists, Asclepiades of Prousias. According to tradition, Asclepiades started as a poor professor of rhetoric before turning to medicine. During his career he acquired considerable fame (Pliny speaks of his *summa fama*) and provoked the animosity of other medical writers—he was still being attacked by Galen almost three hundred years after his death. The anger of his fellow healers is not hard to explain, because he turned ancient medicine on its head by distancing himself from dangerous pharmacological and surgical procedures, even describing traditional medicine as a "preparation for death." Instead, he placed emphasis on more humane and agreeable treatments—diet, passive exercise, massages, bathing, even rocking beds. Pliny felt that he mainly used guesswork but was successful because he had a smooth patter. How effective he was cannot be gauged now. He is said to have recovered a "corpse" from a funeral procession and then to have successfully treated it. But famous doctors in antiquity routinely restored the dead to life. Perhaps more impressive, and more alarming to the medical profession, was Asclepiades' pledge that by following his own prescriptions he could guarantee that he would never be ill, and that if he lapsed, he would retire from medicine. He was apparently never put to the test, and eventually died by accident, falling from a ladder.

It is not hard to believe that Asclepiades might have exercised an influence on Livia, especially in that Pliny remarks that he almost brought the whole human race round to his point of view, and Elizabeth Rawson argues that a case can be made that he was the most influential Greek thinker at work in Rome in the first century BC. Pliny notes a dilemma that has a strangely contemporary ring—whether wine is more harmful or helpful to the health. As the champion of the latter belief Pliny cites Asclepiades, who wrote a book on wine's benefits, based to some extent on the teaching of Cleophantus.

Asclepiades received a familiar nickname *oinodotes* (wine giver), although to avoid being cast as someone who encouraged inebriation, he did advocate abstinence under certain circumstances. As Pliny words it, Asclepiades stated that the benefits of wine were not surpassed by the power of the gods, and the historian, like Livia, seems to have been won over, conceding that wine drunk in moderation benefitted the sinews and stomach, and made one happy, and could even be usefully applied to sores. Livia might have become acquainted with Asclepiades' teaching while he was still alive (it is uncertain when he died), but in any case Pliny makes it clear that after his death his ideas took a firm hold on the population, and would still have been in circulation for many years after he made his ultimate precipitous descent from the ladder.[16]

Apart from her views on the benefits of fine wines, Livia was known for other health tips. Pliny adds his personal recommendation for one of her fads, a daily dose of *inula* (elecampane). The elecampane, with its broad yellow petals, is a common plant throughout Europe, and its root has long been a popular medicine. Because it is bitter and can cause stomach upset if eaten alone, it is usually ground up, or marinated in vinegar and water, then mixed with fruit or honey. It was supposedly useful for weak digestion. Horace describes its popularity among gluttons, who could overdo safely by using elecampane afterwards. Then, as now, celebrity endorsements helped; Pliny observes that the use of the plant was given a considerable boost by Livia's recommendation. In some modern quarters it is still promoted as an effective tonic and laxative.[17]

Livia's views on a healthy lifestyle seem to have been cherished by the devotees of natural cures, and the evidence for their abiding appeal is that her recipes were still used nearly four centuries later. Marcellus Empiricus of Bordeaux, who served as *magister officiorum* under Theodosius I (AD 379–95), composed his *De Medicamentis Liber* in the first decade of the fifth century. In some respects Marcellus resembles Asclepiades of Prousias in trying to teach people to do without doctors and surgery and essentially to cure themselves. He set out to collect all he could from such writers as Pliny and Scribonius Largus, whose entries he simply copied out in their entirety. He brought together a rich mix of popular remedies, charms, and herbal folklore, which in his preface he describes as "the uncomplicated and effective remedies of ordinary country dwellers." As a final colourful touch he added verses (either his own or someone else's) describing the contents of the work and ending with the hope that the reader will live a year for each line (seventy-eight of them).

This "extraordinary mixture of traditional remedies and conjuring" as Rose describes it, has preserved among other fascinating tit-bits the formula for toothpaste used by Livia's sister-in-law Octavia, as well as two recipes of Livia herself.[18] They are perhaps trivial in themselves, but they do offer an intriguing glimpse of a side of Livia not apparent in other sources. The first is for inflammation of the throat. Note the apothecary's use of coins as measures of weight.

> This medicine has proved beneficial to many:
>
> 2 denarii of each of the following:
> costus [an oriental aromatic plant]
> opium
> anis
> aromatic rush
> red cassia
> 1 denarius of coriander
> 1 victoriatus of amomum
> 2 denarii of seed of hazelwort
> 1 denarius of split alum
> 5 grains the size of chickpeas from the centre of oak-apple
> 2 denarii of saffron
> 1 victoriatus of saffron residue
> 1 victoriatus of myrrh
> 4 denarii of Greek birthwort
> 3 denarii of cinnamon
> 5 denarii of the ash of baked chicks of wild swallows
> 1 victoriatus of a grain of nard.
>
> All these ingredients, thoroughly ground up, are mixed with skimmed Attic honey. When there is a need to renew the medicine, a sufficient amount of the same honey is added and in that medium it is inserted into the jaws.
>
> Livia always had this ready on hand, stored in a glass vessel, for it is amazingly effective against quinsy and inflammation of the throat. [Marc. *De Med.* 15.6]

The second was intended to relieve nervous tension:

> Salve for chills, tiredness and nervous pain and tension, which when applied in winter prevents any part of the limbs from being chilled. Livia Augusta used this:
> Ingredients:
>
> 1 sextarius of marjoram
> 1 sextarius of rosemary

1 lb of fenugreek
1 congium of Falernian wine
5 lbs of Venafrian oil

Apart from the oil one should steep all the ingredients in the wine for three days, then on the fourth day mix in the oil and cook the medicine on a moderate coal, until the wine vanishes, and the next stage is to strain through two layers of linen and to add a half-pound of Pontic wax while the oil is warm. The medicine is stored in a clay or tin vessel. It is effective when rubbed gently into all the limbs. [Marc. *De Med.* 35.6]

These curiosities do provide a possible context for one of the charges levelled against Livia, which the scholarly world generally agrees was groundless: that of using poison to remove those who blocked her ambitions. The accusation is one that powerful women in competitive political situations throughout antiquity and the middle ages found difficult to refute, because poison has traditionally been considered the woman's weapon of choice. Because women took the primary responsibility for family well-being, they would have been the inevitable targets of suspicion if a person died of something brought on by gastric problems.[19] If Livia had insisted on inflicting her home cures on members of her family, it is not difficult to imagine that a malign reputation could have arisen after a death that was advantageous to her. One also should not discount the possibility that the combination of birthwort and ash of swallows did more harm than good, and that she might indeed have helped despatch some of her patients, despite the very best of intentions.

Allied to Livia's preoccupation with herbal remedies is her passionate interest and regular involvement in various aspects of horticulture. The most vivid illustration of this comes from her villa at Primaporta (see chapter 9). The highlight of the complex is the garden room, built and decorated around 20 BC in the form of a partially subterranean chamber nearly 12 metres long by 6 metres wide, perhaps a dining room intended for summer use. The most impressive feature of the room is the magnificent wall painting, unparalleled for its scale and detail (fig. 28). It creates an illusion of a pavilion within a magical garden, teeming with flowers and birds. Unusually for the Pompeian Second Style of painting, all structural supports have been dispensed with, even at the angles, although along the tops of the walls there is a rocky fringe, which conveys the impression of the mouth of a grotto. In the foreground stands a wicker fence. Behind that is a narrow grassy walk, set with small plants, bordered on its inner side by a low stone parapet. A small recess is set in the wall at intervals to accommodate a bush or tree. Behind it stands a rich tangled forest of carefully painted shrubs and trees, with various types of laurel predominating. The rich mass of foliage is framed at the top by a narrow band of sky. The painting is detailed and accurate, with flowers and fruit and birds perched on the branches or on the ground. The birds, of many species, range freely, with the exception of a single caged nightingale. Flowers and fruit of all seasons are mingled together.[20] This rich extravaganza belonged clearly to an owner who exulted in the richness and variety of nature.

But Livia's horticultural interests went beyond a mere feast for the eye—she had a direct and practical interest in produce. She developed a distinctive type of fig that bore her name, the Liviana, mentioned by agricultural writers and recommended by Columella and Athenaeus, and which may have contributed to the tradition that she eliminated Augustus by specially treated figs grown in their villa at Nola. They could well have been found on the estate, for Athenaeus describes them as grown near Rome, although they could not have been ripe at the time of Augustus' death because Columella places their ripening in the autumn.[21] In Egypt she gave her name to a class of papyrus. The top grade was called the Augustus, the third class the hieratic. Between them, in the second grade, was the Livia.[22] She probably cultivated the Pucine wine that she drank every day, and in Rome, Valerianus Cornelius considered it worthy of record that the single vine in the Portico of Livia (see chapter 9) provided shade and at the same time produced twelve amphorae of must each year.[23]

On her estate at Primaporta, Livia was said to be personally responsible for planting a laurel grove. It produced a low-growing shrub with crinkly leaves, quite rare, and was the source of the laurels carried by triumphatores in their processions.[24] This genus is distinct from another laurel to which Livia gave her name, originally called the royal laurel, then renamed the Augusta, with large leaves and berries and without a harsh taste. The form of this word is grammatically ambiguous, for it could simply be a feminine adjective agreeing with *laureus*, the "Augustus laurel." But it is worth noting that when Pliny introduces Livia a few paragraphs after describing the plant, he rather pedantically refers to her as Livia Drusilla *quae postea Augustam matrimonii nomen accepit* (who later received the name Augusta as a result of her marriage), a totally unnecessary clarification and explicable only in the context of how the laurel got its name.[25] Recent excavations at the villa have revealed perforated pots found mainly at the edge of the hill overlooking the Tiber. These were produced in a kiln from the villa itself, and offer good evidence for a laurel grove. They would have been used for the planting of laurels by the process known as layering, a form of propagation mentioned both by Cato and Pliny, the latter with specific reference to the Augusta laurel.[26]

From what we can glean about Livia's personality from the scant evidence available, the picture that emerges is not a remarkable one, and at first sight better suited to our modern notion of middle-class respectability than to an active if understated role at the very centre of Rome's political life. In reality, the very ordinariness of Livia as a private individual was one of her strongest assets. Romans had watched with alarm during the final years of the republic as women with powerful personalities asserted themselves on the political scene. Livia's dull normalcy was reassuring, and perfect for the times.

7

WIFE OF THE EMPEROR

By the early empire the image of women of past times was clouded by a nostalgic romanticism. The Roman woman was by tradition devoted to her husband, whom she would not think to cross, and she spent her time and energies on the efficient running of her household, a paragon of impeccable virtue, a perfect marriage partner. The realm of the woman was strictly the *domus*. A famous and familiar tomb inscription of the end of the second century BC expressed the most fulsome praise that could be bestowed on a deceased wife: *Domum servavit. Lanam fecit* (she kept house; she made wool). The qualities of this ideal wife were those of Amymone, wife of Marcus, as described in another inscription, *pulcherrima lanifica pia pudica frugi casta domiseda* (very beautiful, woolmaking, pious, modest, frugal, chaste, stay-at-home). The women of Augustus' domus, including Livia, were expected at least in their public personas to conform to this semimythical image. It was in this spirit that Augustus made it known that his simple clothes were all woven by his sister, wife, or daughter.[1] It cannot be an accident that those imperial women who were seen to embody such ideals—Antonia, Octavia, Livia—were in the long run honoured and rewarded. Those who contradicted them—both Julias, mother and daughter, both Agrippinas, mother and daughter—suffered the dire consequences of their wilfulness.

By Augustus' day the image of the Roman woman as a mere wife and mother was in practice becoming difficult to sustain, at least among the upper classes. The traditional form of Roman marriage, through which the bride was committed to the complete authority *(in manu)* of her husband, had become by the late republic little more than a vestige of a quaint past. Roman women had by then acquired the power to inherit, own, and bequeath property and had attained a level of independence still unmatched in many modern-day states. Their privileges were still in theory dependent on the authority of a man. A daughter was subject to the *potestas* (power) of her paterfamilias (the oldest surviving "head" of the household, usually her father, but possibly the paternal grandfather or even great-grandfather). On the death of the paterfamilias, authority passed technically to a guardian, *tutor*, usually the closest male relative. The activities of wealthy and prominent women in the late republic, however, show that this curb was more theoretical and apparent than real, and control could always be voided by a number of devices, such as an appeal to a magistrate. Even those formal restrictions were eventually removed by Augustus from those women who had borne three children.

The line between the independent woman and the ideal woman who excluded herself from involvement in political matters became increasingly less well defined. By the final century of the republic the aggressive political woman had become a familiar feature of the political landscape. As often as not, her ability to manipulate events came through her influence over her husband or lover. Chelidon, mistress of Verres, the notorious governor of Sicily (73–70 BC), for instance, was able to use her hold on the governor to control contracts and settle civil cases for a price. After Verres had reached a decision, a whisper in his ear was all that was needed for him to summon the parties back and alter his judgement.[2] One of the most celebrated of these powerfully corrupt women was the beautiful and aristocratic Sempronia, a well-read, witty woman of considerable intelligence, who appears in Sallust's account of the conspiracy of Catiline (63 BC). He asserts that Catiline won the adherence of several women whose extravagance had led them into debt, and he planned to use them for various nefarious activities. Sempronia turned her assets to bad purposes to cheat and to escape her debts, and even became involved in murder. She may also have been a victim of the paranoia noted earlier. When we look closely at Sallust's account of the conspiracy, we find that he does not in fact assign Sempronia any substantive role, nor is there any reference to her in other accounts of the conspiracy that have survived. No formal charges were made against her and there was no punishment—she simply fades from view. Her broadly defined image was intended to exploit fear of the damage that could arise when women became involved in public affairs. She illustrates yet another facet of the depiction of powerful women that reemerges in the accounts of Livia, especially in Tacitus: the use of innuendo in the absence of ascertainable facts.[3]

Throughout the republic, men tended to display an irrational anxiety about the threats they saw in growing female independence. Perhaps the most sinister characteristic of the ambitious woman was her ruthless willingness to murder her opponents, and her preferred method was supposedly poison. The first recorded case goes back as far as the great series of poison trials of 331 BC, when the deaths of a number of leading citizens were blamed on what Livy calls *muliebris fraus* (female treachery), an expression identical to the one used by Tacitus to explain the death in AD 19 of Germanicus, reputedly despatched by poison on the secret instructions of Livia.[4] Moreover, an incident in 180 BC is reminiscent of the claims made about Livia nearly two centuries later, as someone determined to clear the decks to make way for her son Tiberius. In that year the consul died, supposedly poisoned by his wife, Hostilia, to create a vacancy for her son.[5] There can be little doubt that such stories, handed down as popular lore from generation to generation, would have in turn influenced popular beliefs about the deaths of Augustus and Claudius, who, it was hinted, had similarly to make way for Livia's son Tiberius and Agrippina's son Nero.

If any precedent might have preoccupied Livia, especially in her early career, when she was attempting to mould an image fitting for the times, it would have been a negative one, provided by the most notorious woman of the late republic and, most important, a woman who clashed headlong with Octavian in the sensitive early stages of his career. Fulvia was the wife of Mark Antony, and his devoted supporter, no less loyal than Livia in support of her husband, although their styles were dramatically different. Fulvia's struggle on behalf of Antony, Octavian's archenemy, has secured her an unenviable place in history as a power-crazed termagant. While her husband was occupied in the East in 41, Fulvia made an appearance, along with Antony's children, before his old soldiers in Italy, urging them to remain true to their commander. When Antony's brother Lucius gathered his troops at Praeneste to launch an attack on Rome, Fulvia joined him there, and the legend became firmly established that she put on a sword, issued the watchword, gave a rousing speech to the soldiers, and held councils of war with senators and knights. This was the ultimate sin in a woman, interfering in the loyalty of the troops.

In the end Octavian prevailed and forced the surrender of Lucius and his armies at Perusia. The fall of the city led to a massive exodus of political refugees. Among them were two women, Livia and Fulvia. Livia joined her husband, Tiberius Claudius Nero, who escaped first to Praeneste and then to

Naples. Fulvia fled with her children to join Antony and his mother in Athens. Like Octavia later, she found that her dedicated service was not enough to earn her husband's gratitude. In fact, Antony blamed her for the setbacks in Italy. A broken woman, she fell ill at Sicyon on the Gulf of Corinth, where she died in mid-40 BC. Antony in the meantime had left Italy without even troubling himself to visit her sickbed.[6]

Fulvia's story contains many of the ingredients familiar in the profiles of ambitious women: avarice, cruelty, promiscuity, suborning of troops, and the ultimate ingratitude of the men for whom they made such sacrifices. She was at Perusia at the same time as Livia, and as wives of two of the triumvirs, they would almost certainly have met. In any case, Fulvia was at the height of her activities in the years immediately preceding Livia's first meeting with Octavian, and at the very least would have been known to her by reputation. Livia would have seen in Fulvia an object lesson for what was to be avoided at all costs by any woman who hoped to survive and prosper amidst the complex machinations of Roman political life.

In one respect Livia's career did resemble Fulvia's, in that it was shaped essentially by the needs of her husband, to fill a role that in a sense he created for her. To understand that role in Livia's case, we need to understand one very powerful principle that motivated Augustus throughout his career. The importance that he placed in the calling that he inherited in 44 BC cannot be overstressed. The notion that he and the house he created were destined by fate to carry out Rome's foreordained mission lay at the heart of his principate. Strictly speaking, the expression *domus Augusta* (house of Augustus) cannot be attested before Augustus' death and the accession of Tiberius (see appendix 9), but there can be little doubt that the concept of his domus occupying a special and indeed unique place within the state evolves much earlier. Suetonius speaks of Augustus' consciousness of the *domus suae maiestas* (the dignity of his house) in a context that suggests a fairly early stage of his reign, and Macrobius relates the anecdote of his claiming to have had two troublesome daughters, Julia and Rome. When Augustus received the title of Pater Patriae in 2 BC, Valerius Messala spoke on behalf of the Senate, declaring the hope that the occasion would bring good fortune and favour on "you and your house, Augustus Caesar" *(quod bonum, inquit, faustum sit tibi domuique tuae, Caesar Auguste)*.[7] The special place in the Augustan scheme enjoyed by the male members of this domus placed them in extremely sensitive positions. The position of the women in his house was even more challenging.[8]

In fashioning the image of the domus Augusta, the first princeps was anxious to project an image of modesty and simplicity, to stress that in spite of his extraordinary constitutional position, he and his family lived as ordinary Romans. Accordingly, his demeanour was deliberately self-effacing. His dinner parties were hospitable but not lavish. The private quarters of his home, though not as modest as he liked to pretend, were provided with very simple furniture. His couches and tables were still on public display in the time of Suetonius, who commented that they were not fine enough even for an ordinary Roman, let alone an emperor. Augustus wore simple clothes in the home, which were supposedly made by Livia or other women of his household. He slept on a simply furnished bed.[9] His own plain and unaffected lifestyle determined also how the imperial women should behave. His views on this subject were deeply conservative. He felt that it was the duty of the husband to ensure that his wife always conducted herself appropriately. He ended the custom of men and women sitting together at the games, requiring females (with the exception of the Vestals) to view from the upper seats only. His legates were expected to visit their wives only during the winter season. In his own domestic circle he insisted that the women should exhibit a traditional domesticity. He had been devoted to his mother and his sister, Octavia, and when they died he allowed them special honours. But at least in the case of Octavia, he kept the honours limited and even blocked some of the distinctions voted her by the Senate. Nor did he limit himself to matters of "lifestyle." He forbade the women of his family from saying anything that could not be said openly and recorded in the daybook of the imperial household.[10]

In the eyes of the world, Livia succeeded in carrying out her role of model wife to perfection. To some degree she owed her success to circumstances. It is instructive to compare her situation with that of other women of the imperial house. Julia (born 39 BC) summed up her own attitude perfectly when taken to task for her extravagant behaviour and told to conform more closely to Augustus' simple tastes. She responded that he could forget that he was Augustus, but she could not forget that she was Augustus' daughter.[11] Julia's daughter, the elder Agrippina (born 19 BC?), like her mother before her, saw for herself a key element in her grandfather's dynastic scheme. She was married to the popular Germanicus and had no doubt that in the fullness of time she would provide a princeps of Augustan blood. Not surprisingly, she became convinced that she had a fundamental role to play in Rome's future, and she bitterly resented Tiberius' elevation. Her daughter Agrippina the Younger (born AD 15?) was, as a child, indoctrinated by her mother to see herself as the destined transmitter of Augustus' blood, and her whole adult life was devoted to fulfilling her mother's frustrated mission. From birth these women would have known of no life other than one of dynastic entitlement. By contrast, Livia's background, although far from humble, was not exceptional for a woman of her class, and she did not enter her novel situation with inherited baggage. As a Claudian she may no doubt have been brought up to display a certain hauteur, but she would not have anticipated a special role in the state. As a member of a distinguished republican family, she would have hoped at most for a "good" marriage to a man who could aspire to property and prestige, perhaps at best able to exercise a marginal influence on events through a husband in a high but temporary magistracy. Powerful women who served their apprenticeships during the republic reached their eminence by their own inclinations, energies, and ambitions, not because they felt they had fallen heir to it.

However lofty Livia's station after 27 BC, her earlier life would have enabled her to maintain a proper perspective. She did not find herself in the position of an imperial wife who through her marriage finds herself overnight catapulted into an ambience of power and privilege. Whatever ambitions she may have entertained in her first husband, she was sadly disappointed. When she married for the second time, Octavian, for all his prominence, did not then occupy the undisputed place at the centre of the Roman world that was to come to him later. Livia thus had a decade or so of married life before she found herself married to a princeps, in a process that offered time for her to become acclimatised and to establish a style and timing appropriate to her situation. It must have helped that in their personal relations she and her husband seem to have been a devoted couple, whose marriage remained firm for more than half a century. For all his general cynicism, Suetonius concedes that after Augustus married Livia, he loved and esteemed her *unice et perservanter* (right to the end, with no rival). In his correspondence Augustus addressed his wife affectionately as *mea Livia*. The one shadow on their happiness would have been that they had no children together. Livia did conceive, but the baby was stillborn. Augustus knew that he could produce children, as did she, and Pliny cites them as an example of a couple who are sterile together but had children from other unions.[12] By the normal standards obtaining in Rome at the time they would have divorced — such a procedure would have involved no disgrace — and it is a testimony to the depth of their feelings that they stayed together.

In a sense, then, Livia was lucky. That said, she did suffer one disadvantage, in that when the principate was established, she found herself, as did all Romans, in an unparalleled situation, with no precedent to guide her. She was the first "first lady" — she had to establish the model to emulate, and later imperial wives would to no small degree be judged implicitly by comparison to her. Her success in masking her keen political instincts and subordinating them to an image of self-restraint and discretion was to a considerable degree her own achievement. In a famous passage of Suetonius, we are told that Caligula's favourite expression for his great-grandmother was *Ulixes stolatus* (Ulysses in a stola). The allusion appears in a section that supposedly illustrates Caligula's disdain for his relatives. But his allusion to Livia is surely a witty and ironical expression of admiration.[13] Ulysses is a familiar Homeric hero, who in the *Iliad* and *Odyssey* displays the usual heroic qualities of nerve and courage, but is above all *polymetis:* clever, crafty, ingenious, a man who will often sort his way through a crisis not by the usual heroic bravado but by outsmarting his opponents, whether the one-eyed giant Polyphemus, or the enchantress Circe, or the suitors for Penelope. Caligula implied that Livia had the clever, subtle kind of mind that one associates with Greeks rather than Romans, who were inclined to take a head-on approach to problems. But at the same time she manifested a particularly Roman quality. Rolfe, in the Loeb translation of Suetonius' *Life of Caligula*, rendered the phrase as "Ulysses in petticoats" to suggest a female version of the Homeric character. But this is to rob Caligula's sobriquet of much of its force. The stola was essentially the female equivalent of the toga worn by Roman men. A long woollen sleeveless dress, of heavy fabric, it was normally worn over a tunic. In shape it could be likened to a modern slip, but of much heavier material, so that it could hang in deep folds (figs. 20, 23, 24, 25). The mark of *matronae* married to Roman citizens, the stola is used by Cicero as a metaphor for a stable and respectable marriage. Along with the woollen bands that the matron wore in her hair to protect her from impurity, it was considered the *insigne pudoris* (the sign of purity) by Ovid, something, as he puts it, alien to the world of the philandering lover. Another contemporary of Livia's, Valerius Maximus, notes that if a matrona was called into court, her accuser could not physically touch her, in order that the stola might remain *inviolata manus alienae tactu* (unviolated by the touch of another's hand). Bartman may be right in suggesting that the existence of statues of Livia in a stola would have given Caligula's quip a special resonance, but that alone would not have inspired his bon mot. To Caligula's eyes, Livia was possessed of a sharp and clever mind. But she did not allow this quality to obtrude because she recognised that many Romans would not find it appealing; she cloaked it with all the sober dignity and propriety, the gravitas, that the Romans admired in themselves and saw represented in the stola.[14]

Livia's greatest skill perhaps lay in the recognition that the women of the imperial household were called to walk a fine line. She and other imperial women found themselves in a paradoxical position in that they were required to set an example of the traditional domestic woman yet were obliged by circumstances to play a public role outside the home—a reflection of the process by which the domestic and public domains of the domus Augusta were blurred.[15] Thus she was expected to display the grand dignity expected of a person very much in the public eye, combined with the old-fashioned modesty of a woman whose interests were confined to the domus. Paradoxically, she had less freedom of action than other upper-class women who had involved themselves in public life in support of their family and protégés. As wife of the princeps, Livia recognised that to enlist the support of her husband was in a sense to enlist the support of the state. That she managed to gain a reputation as a generous patron and protector and, at the same time, a woman who kept within her proper bounds, is testimony to her keen sensitivity. In many ways she succeeds in moving silently though Rome's history, and this is what she intended. Her general conduct gave reassurance to those who were distressed by the changing relationships that women like Fulvia had symbolised in the late republic. It is striking that court poets, who reflected the broad wishes of their patron, avoid reference to her. She is mentioned by the poet Horace, but only once, and even there she is not named directly but referred to allusively as *unico gaudens mulier marito* (a wife finding joy in her preeminent husband).[16] The single exception is Ovid, but most of his allusions come from his period of exile, when desperation may have got the better of discretion. The dignified behaviour of Livia's distinguished entourage was contrasted with the wild conduct of Julia's friends at public shows, which drove Augustus to remonstrate with his daughter (her response: when she was old, she too would have old friends). In a telling passage Seneca compares the conduct of Livia favourably with even the universally admired Octavia. After losing Marcellus, Octavia abandoned herself to her grief and became obsessed with the memory of her dead son. She would not permit anyone to mention his name in her presence and remained inconsolable, allowing herself to become totally secluded and maintaining the garb of mourning until her death. By contrast, Livia, similarly devastated by the death of Drusus, did not offend others by grieving excessively once the body had been committed to the tomb. When the grief was at its worst, she turned to the philosopher Areus for help. Seneca re-creates Areus' advice. Much of it, of course, may well have sprung from Seneca's imagination, but it is still valuable in showing how Livia was seen by Romans of Seneca's time. Areus says that Livia had been at great pains to ensure that no one would find anything in her to criticise, in major matters but also in the most insignificant trifles. He admired the fact that someone of her high station was often willing to bestow pardon on others but sought pardon for nothing in herself.[17]

Livia was not completely successful in evading the criticism of her contemporaries. We know that she attracted the censure of one of the leading Greek writers active in Augustan Rome. Timagenes of Alexandria was captured in 55 BC by Aulus Gabinius and taken back to Italy. He attained his freedom and gained a reputation as a teacher of rhetoric and as a prolific writer, composing a universal history down to the time of Julius Caesar. Initially he was friendly to Antony, but he switched his allegiance and came to enjoy the special favour of Augustus. His close relationship with the imperial house soured, and it was then that he made an unspecified attack on Livia. We should not read too much into his reported anomosity towards her. Seneca reports that he was a man who was inherently hostile to Rome and resented its success. He developed a particular aversion to the imperial family, and after the quarrel with Augustus destroyed the account he had written of his achievements by consigning it to the flames. He attacked not only Livia but also the emperor and the whole of the imperial family *(in totam domum)*. It is fair to conclude that his criticisms of Livia would have been made as a matter of course, given that she was the wife of the emperor, and Timagenes' unsympathetic views cannot be taken to represent a widely or even narrowly held opinion in the Rome of the time. Timagenes was banished from Augustus' house and went to live with another historian, Asinius Pollio. He eventually choked to death.[18] His attacks on Livia seem to have had no harmful effect on her reputation.

Perhaps most important, it was essential for Livia to present herself to the world as the model of chastity. Apart from the normal demands placed on the wife of a member of the Roman nobility, she faced a particular set of circumstances that were unique to her. One of the domestic priorities undertaken by Augustus was the enactment of a programme of social legislation. Parts of this may well have been begun before his eastern trip, perhaps as early as 28 BC, but the main body of the work was initiated in 18.[19] A proper understanding of the measures that he carried out under this general heading eludes us. The family name of Julius was attached to the laws, and thus they are difficult to distinguish from those enacted by Julius Caesar. But clearly in general terms the legislation was intended to restore traditional Roman gravitas, to stamp out corruption, to define the social orders, and to encourage the involvement of the upper classes in state affairs. The drop in the numbers of the upper classes was causing particular concern. The nobles were showing a general reluctance to marry and, when married, an unwillingness to have children. It was hoped that the new laws would to some degree counter this trend. The Lex Iulia de adulteriis coercendis, passed probably in 18 BC, made adultery a public crime and established a new criminal court for sexual offences. The Lex Iulia de maritandis ordinibus, passed about the same time, regulated the validity of marriages between social classes. The crucial factor here, of course, was not the regulation of morality but rather the legitimacy of children. Disabilities were imposed on the principle that it was the duty of men between twenty-five and sixty-five and women between twenty and fifty to marry. Those who refused to comply or who married and remained childless suffered penalties, the chief one being the right to inherit. The number of a man's children gave him precedence when he stood for office. Of particular relevance to Livia was the *ius trium liberorum*, under which a freeborn woman with three children was exempted from *tutela* (guardianship) and had a right of succession to the inheritance of her children. Livia was later granted this privilege despite having borne only two living children.

This social legislation created considerable resentment—Suetonius says that the equestrians staged demonstrations at theatres and at the games. It was amended in AD 9 and supplemented by the Lex Papia Poppaea, which seems to have removed the unfair distinctions between the childless and the unmarried and allowed divorced or widowed women a longer period before they remarried. Dio, apparently without a trace of irony, reports that this last piece of legislation was introduced by two consuls who were not only childless but unmarried, thus proving the need for the legislation.[20]

Livia's moral conduct would thus be dictated not only by the already unreal standards that were expected of a Roman matrona but also by the political imperative of her husband's social legislation. Because Augustus saw himself as a man on a crusade to restore what he considered to be old-fashioned morality, it was clearly essential that he have a wife whose reputation for virtue was unsullied and who could provide an exemplar in her own married life. In this Livia would not fail him. The skilful creation of an image of purity and marital fidelity was more than a vindication of her personal standards. It was very much a public statement of support for what her husband was trying to achieve. Tacitus, in his obituary notice that begins Book V of the *Annals*, observes that in the matter of the *sanctitas domus*, Livia's conduct was of the "old school" *(priscum ad morem)*. This is a profoundly interesting statement at more than one level. It tells us something about the way the Romans idealised their past. But it also says much about the clever way that Livia fashioned her own image. Her inner private life is a secret that she has taken with her to the tomb. She may well have been as pure as people believed. But for a woman who occupied the centre of attention in imperial Rome for as long as she did, to keep her moral reputation intact required more than mere proper conduct. Rumours and innuendo attached themselves to the powerful and prominent almost of their own volition. An unsullied name required the positive creation of a public image. Livia was despised by Tacitus, who does not hesitate to insinuate the darkest interpretations that can be placed on her conduct. Yet not even he hints at any kind of moral impropriety in the narrow sexual sense. Even though she abandoned her first husband, Tiberius Claudius, to begin an affair with her lover Octavian, she seems to have escaped any censure over her conduct. This is evidence not so much of moral probity as of political skill in managing an image skilfully and effectively. None of the ancient sources challenges the portrait of the moral paragon. Ovid extols her sexual purity in the most fulsome of terms. To him, Livia is the Vesta of chaste matrons, who has the morals of Juno and is an exemplar of pudicitia worthy of earlier and morally superior generations. Even after her husband is dead she keeps the marriage couch *(pulvinar)* pure. (She was, admittedly in her seventies.) Valerius Maximus, writing in the Tiberian period, can state that Pudicitia attends the couch of Livia. And the *Consolatio ad Liviam*, probably not a contemporary work but one at least that tries to reflect contemporary attitudes, speaks of her as worthy of those women who lived in a golden age, and as someone who kept her heart uncorrupted by the evil of her times. Horace's description is particularly interesting. His phrase *unico gaudens marito* is nicely ambiguous, for it states that Livia's husband was preeminent *(unicus)* but implies the other connotation of the word: that she had the moral superiority of an *univira*, a woman who has known only one husband, which in reality did not apply to Livia. Such remarks might, of course, be put down to cringing flattery, but it is striking that not a single source contradicts them. On this one issue, Livia did not hesitate to blow her own trumpet, and she herself asserted that she was able to influence Augustus to some degree because she was scrupulously chaste. She could do so in a way that might even suggest a light touch of humour. Thus when she came across some naked men who stood to be punished for being exposed to the imperial eyes, she asserted that to a chaste woman a naked man was no more a sex object than was a statue. Most strikingly, Dio is able to recount this story with no consciousness of irony.[21]

To reinforce this image of moral probity, an effort was clearly made to ensure that Livia's public activities should relate especially to the centrality of the family, such as the restoration of the temple of the Bona Dea or the dedication of her *aedes* to Concordia (see chapter 10). By her association with the religious rites of women she could promote her husband's moral legislation and help him to revive the old ideal of Roman womanhood, with its focus on the sanctity of marriage and the crucial place of the family in Roman life.[22] The role of Concordia in this process was important. *Concordia* could convey two notions, of harmony in both public and marital life. When Livia located her aedes to Concordia in her portico, she would have declared publicly that her own marriage was harmonious and that she wished to set an example for other wives to follow.[23]

Probably the first public declaration of the importance of the place of the Augustan family in the state comes in the form of the Ara Pacis, voted in 13 BC to commemorate the emperor's return from Gaul and Spain, and finally completed in 9 BC. It provides the perfect expression of Augustan ideology. The altar itself was decorated, but its reliefs are overshadowed by those on its surrounding rectangular precinct wall, with mythological panels on its east and west fronts, Roma and another female (Italy or Mother Earth?) on the east, and Mars and Aeneas on the west. On the north and south walls, long friezes portray a procession of religious officials intermingling with members of the Augustan house. The occasion depicted is the *supplicatio*, the celebration that followed Augustus' safe return, an event in which women and children were able to participate. There had been an earlier tradition of depicting ancestors within Roman houses, but public statues of women and children were rare, and Bartman characterises the inclusion of mortal women in a state ceremony as an "iconographic revolution."

There is not complete certainty about the identification of some of the family members depicted, but there seems to be little doubt that we have a grand dynastic portrait. Livia can probably be fairly securely identified as the first foreground figure on the frieze after Augustus, not because of any family likeness — the portraits generally are idealised — but because she and Augustus wear veils and laurel crowns (figs. 20, 21). Although the altar is dedicated to *Pax* (Peace), it cannot be said that Livia was ever closely associated with this particular concept. She is identified at Corinth as *Diana pacilucifera* (Diana bringing peace at dawn), but the inscription is securely dated to the Tiberian period, more than twenty years later than the Ara Pacis. The intention of the frieze is rather to present the family of Augustus and Livia symbolically, less in association with Pax than as examples of the virtues that Augustus was trying to promote through his marriage legislation. The prominence of children throughout the monument reinforces this idea. Thus Augustus and Livia appear as the symbolic father and mother of the Roman state. The depiction of Livia here constitutes the one exception to the rule of the prevailing modest coiffure in her likenesses during Augustus' lifetime (see chapter 6). Here she has the middle parting, and her hair falls in long waves to below her shoulders. The hairstyle, as Wood points out, gives a Livia a strong similarity to the goddess who appears on the east face. She, like Livia, is veiled and garlanded and has her hair parted in the middle. Similarly, Augustus is reminiscent of Aeneas on the west frieze.[24]

Livia was clearly expected to play an important role in the state as the emperor's consort, as a woman who embodied the values and qualities that he felt important. But did she have a role in her own right? Within the family circle, of course, she certainly did, and after her obligations to her husband, her first obligation would have been as materfamilias to the members of the domus Augusta. She certainly earned the esteem of her daughter-in-law, the venerable Antonia. We are told that after Drusus' death Antonia chose to live with Livia and resolved not to marry again, preferring the company of her mother-in-law over a second marriage.[25] Moreover, how seriously Livia took her family duties is illustrated by how conscientiously she met her obligations to her grandson, Antonia's son Claudius, whose physical handicaps and perceived mental limitations were considered an embarrassment to his family. As a child, Claudius lived for much of the time at his grandmother's home, presumably while Antonia accompanied Drusus on his military campaigns. Although Livia's attitude may fall far short of acceptable modern standards, it is only fair to observe that her intolerance was no worse than that shown by his own mother. Antonia, a woman universally admired, called him a *portentum . . . non absolutum a natura sed tantum incohatum* (a monster, only started and not finished by nature), and as a byword for stupidity she would call someone *stultiorem . . . filio suo Claudio* (more foolish than her own son Claudius). If we are to take Suetonius at his word, Livia was no different, treating her grandson with utmost contempt and rarely speaking to him, communicating with him through short letters or through messengers.[26] But after providing this broad characterisation of her attitude, Suetonius goes on to offer evidence for Augustus' opinions on Claudius, quoting extensively from his correspondence, and in the process furnishing a quite different picture of Livia's attitude. She, in fact, went to considerable trouble over his welfare, and it is little wonder that the *Piso Decree* praises her for the *discipulina* that she provided him.[27]

Suetonius has preserved extracts from three letters written by Augustus to his wife which show that Livia had assumed a general charge for Claudius. Augustus clearly wanted to evade any responsibilities in the matter, stressing in his letters that Claudius is Livia's grandson. The first extract indicates that Livia had asked her husband to speak to Tiberius about what should be done with Claudius at the games of Mars Ultor, celebrated in AD 12. Augustus felt that the family should come to a final decision about whether the young man was fit to be advanced. The letter shows clearly that Livia had made some specific request on behalf of her grandson and indicates that despite her supposed contempt for him, she was prepared to make an effort to help him towards some limited progress. Augustus was willing to go along with her suggestion that he be allowed to take part in the banquet of the priests, provided someone was there to make sure that he behaved himself. But the emperor drew the line at two other suggestions. He refused to allow Claudius to take a seat in the imperial box at the circus—he did not want to risk public embarrassment. He was also opposed to the idea of his taking part in the ceremonies in the Latin festival, either in Rome or on the Alban mount. It is interesting that he gives her leave, *if she should so wish*, to show that part of the letter to Antonia, Claudius' mother, who thus was recognised as having a legitimate interest but not the final responsibility in the matter. Livia also seems to have been concerned that there be proper supervision of Claudius during her absences, for in a second letter Augustus promises to invite him to dinner every day while she is away. Finally, in the third extract Augustus acknowledges that no matter how awkward his conversation in private, when it came to public speaking, Claudius could declaim splendidly. What is especially striking about this last passage is that its positive tone suggests strongly that it is just what Livia wanted to hear.[28]

Whatever his physical limitations, Claudius had a good mind. He took to writing history, with the active encouragement of the famous historian Livy. Among his projects was an account of events in Rome from the time of the death of Julius Caesar. The period was a political minefield, and he was persuaded by his mother and Livia to skip the civil-war phase and to start with the Augustan settlement. The advice was wise and well meant. The passions felt about the end of the republic had not yet calmed down, and Claudius' account, especially as coming from within the imperial family, was likely to rekindle some of the old resentments.[29] Livia's ongoing interest in Claudius' progress extended even to making the choice of his first wife. His bride, Plautia Urgulanilla, was the granddaughter of Livia's close friend Urgulania (see chapter 10), and the two women no doubt worked closely together to bring about the match.[30]

Livia's relationship with Claudius might in one sense be called neutral, in that, ironically, no one could have remotely imagined that he could play a role in the succession issue. Accordingly, it might be argued that there was no compelling reason why Livia should not have been willing to help his career. But she also seems to have concerned herself with those other members of the imperial family who might have been in a position to thwart the ambitions she entertained for Tiberius. The children of Julia would seem ideal candidates for this role. Yet Julia the Younger, who died in AD 28 after twenty years of exile, was sustained during this period of hardship by the charity of Livia. Tacitus is obliged to acknowledge her benevolence, although he insists that it was hypocritical, that she worked to bring down her "stepchildren" and then advertised her compassion to the world once they had been destroyed.[31] While Tacitus claims that she hated the same Julia's daughter, Agrippina the Elder, and used Piso's wife, Plancina, as a weapon against her, he admits that it was Livia who in her later years protected Agrippina from Sejanus, and that Livia's death opened up the field for a full-scale attack on her.[32] Livia seems to have involved herself with the well-being of Agrippina's children, as we might reasonably expect, for they were also her great-grandchildren. She took care of Caligula, and possibly two of his sisters, after his mother's removal from the scene, and seems to have treated them kindly (see chapter 5). Despite mischievous comments about Livia (he made similar comments about all his relatives), when it came to a more practical demonstration of his feelings, as in the honouring of her will, suppressed by his predecessor, Caligula demonstrated that he held his great-grandmother in high regard.[33]

Seneca called Livia a *maxima femina*.[34] But did she hold any real power outside the home? According to Dio, Livia believed that she did not, and claimed that her influence over Augustus lay in her willingness to concede whatever he wished, not meddling in his business, and pretending not to be aware of any of his sexual affairs.[35] Tacitus reflects this when he calls her an *uxor facilis* (accommodating wife). She clearly understood that to achieve any objective she had to avoid any overt conflict with her husband. It would do a disservice to Livia, however, to create the impression that she was successful simply because she yielded. She was a skilful tactician who knew how to manipulate people, often by identifying their weaknesses or ambitions, and she knew how to conceal her own feelings when the occasion demanded: *cum artibus mariti, simulatione filii bene composita* (well suited to the craft of her husband and the insincerity of her son) is how Tacitus morosely characterises that talent.[36] Augustus felt that he controlled her, and she doubtless was happy for him to think so. Dio has preserved an account of a telling exchange between Augustus and a group of senators. When they asked him to introduce legislation to control what was seen as the dissolute moral behaviour of Romans, he told them that there were aspects of human behaviour that could not be regulated. He advised them to do what he did, and have more control over their wives. When the senators heard this they were surprised, to say the least, and pressed Augustus with more questions to find out how he was able to control Livia. He confined himself to some general comments about dress and conduct in public, and seems to have been oblivious to his audience's scepticism.[37] What is especially revealing about this incident is that the senators were fully aware of the power of Livia's personality, but recognised that she conducted herself in such a way that Augustus obviously felt no threat whatsoever to his authority.

Augustus would have been sensitive to the need to draw a line between Livia's traditional and proper power within the domus and her role in matters of state. This would have been very difficult. Women in the past had sought to influence their husbands in family concerns. But with the emergence of the domus Augusta, family concerns and state concerns were now inextricably bound together. We know that Agrippina the Younger's transgression of this boundary in the Claudian period caused deep offence, and on his accession her son Nero, no doubt at the prompting of his tutor Seneca, promised that he would keep *discretam domum et rempublicam* (his house and the state separated). During Augustus' lifetime Livia certainly had a keen appreciation of where the line of demarcation lay, and her determination to observe it won the admiration of the next generation. Hence the poet of the *Consolatio* admired her because, as he worded it, she did not allow her powers to range over the Campus Martius or the Forum, but established her domus within the permitted limits: *nec vires errasse tuas campove forove / quamque licet citra constituisse domum*. The allusions are clear enough. The Campus Martius had been the traditional gathering place for the popular assembly, the *comitia centuriata*, and the name was in fact was used by contemporary writers figuratively to mean the elections themselves. The Forum was the centre of Roman legal life, and the scene also of many political events. It, similarly, has a figurative use, to denote state and legal affairs. Cicero uses the phrase *forum attingere* (to come in contact with the forum) to denote his entry into public life.[38] Livia thus was admired for maintaining traditional domesticity and not trying to play an unwarranted role in public affairs.

Although Livia did not intrude in matters that were strictly within Augustus' domain, her restraint naturally did not bar communication with her husband. Certainly, Augustus was prepared to listen to her. That their conversations were not casual matters and were taken seriously by him is demonstrated by the evidence of Suetonius that Augustus treated her just as he would an important official. When dealing with a significant item of business, he would write things out beforehand and read out to her from a notebook, because he could not be sure to get it just right if he spoke extemporaneously. Moreover, it says something about Livia that she filed all Augustus' written communications with her. After his death, during a dispute with her son, she angrily brought the letters from the shrine where they had been archived and read them out, complete with their criticisms of Tiberius' arrogance.[39] Despite Tacitus' claim that Livia controlled her husband, Augustus was willing to state publicly that he had decided not to follow her advice, as when he declined special status to the people of Samos (see chapter 10). Clearly, he would try to do so tactfully and diplomatically, expressing his regrets at having to refuse her request. On other issues he similarly reached his own decision but made sufficient concessions to Livia to satisfy her public dignity and perhaps Augustus' domestic serenity. On one occasion Livia interceded on behalf of a Gaul, requesting that he be granted citizenship. To Augustus the Roman citizenship was something almost sacred, not to be granted on a whim. He declined to honour the request. But he did make a major and telling concession. One of the great advantages of citizenship was the exemption from the tax *(tributum)* that tributary provincials had to pay. Augustus granted the man this exemption. When Livia apparently sought the recall of Tiberius from Rhodes after the Julia scandal, Augustus refused, but did concede him the title of *legatus* to conceal any lingering sense of disgrace. He was unwilling to promote Claudius to the degree that Livia wished, but he was willing to allow him some limited responsibilities. Thus he was clearly prepared to go out of his way to accede at least partially to his wife's requests. But on the essential issues he remained very much his own man, and on one occasion he made it clear that as an advisor she did not occupy the top spot in the hierarchy. In AD 2 Tiberius made a second request to return from exile. His mother is said to have argued intensively on his behalf but did not persuade her husband. He did, however, say that he would be willing to be guided by the advice he received from his grandson, and adopted son, Gaius.[40]

The most extensive account of any aspect of Livia's whole life and career relates to the advice she gave Augustus on how to deal with a supposed conspiracy by Cornelius Cinna, described in considerable detail by both Seneca and Dio (see appendix 10). Cinna was the grandson of Pompey the Great, and a man of limited natural intellect, if we are to believe Seneca *(stolidi ingenii virum)*. His offence is hard to determine, a difficulty complicated by the fact that Dio and Seneca differ on his name (Dio calls him Gnaeus; Seneca calls him Lucius) and on the date (Dio places the incident in AD 4, Seneca between 16 and 13 BC, while Augustus was in Gaul). Shotter suggests that the suspected conspiracy might have been related to some event during Tiberius' time of exile, because by a curious twist Cinna was not punished, but according to Dio was rewarded by the consulship, which he held in AD 5, the year after Tiberius' recall. The whole story is of less value for offering us an insight into Livia's mentality and her relationship with Augustus than might be expected from the degree of detail. The discussion supposedly took place at night, in private. Eavesdropping retainers would have needed formidable powers of memory to retain the particulars. As we have seen, Augustus did normally make extensive notes before any important discussion, which Livia retained. But in this case we are told that the exchange was unpremeditated.[41]

The plot involving Cornelius Cinna is absent from all the recorded lists of conspiracies against the emperor. The intrigue was apparently exposed in all its details, and Augustus was determined to punish Cinna. He summoned a council of his advisors, but before they met he consulted Livia. Seneca and Dio have the princeps pass a sleepless night, concerned about the young man's otherwise blameless record, his distinguished family, the fact that he had been proscribed by Mark Antony, and the question of whether his punishment would prevent new plots. Livia noticed his troubled state, and Seneca has her break in and ask if he would entertain advice from a woman *(muliebre consilium)*. Dio reflects the same idea, when he has Livia apologise for the fact that she, a woman, is about to express an idea that even his closest friends would not be bold enough to give voice to. She points out that nothing has been achieved by harsh treatment in the past, and to prove her point lists a succession of conspirators whose punishments were followed by further conspiracies—his friend Salvidienus Rufus, a man of humble origin whose only achievement noted in the record other than his consulship was that when he was tending his herds his head caught fire; Marcus Aemilius Lepidus, son of the triumvir, who headed a plot against Augustus soon after Actium; Varro Murena, brother or half-brother of Maecenas' wife Terentia, coconspirator of the otherwise unknown Faenius Caepio; and Egnatius Rufus, who in 19 seems to have intended to use his firefighting crew to spearhead a popular uprising.[42] With some men there was no hope—they were incurably depraved. But that said, in dealing with the others it was time to try *clementia*. Dio has Livia launch into a relatively long but well-observed psychological account of the strong sense of loyalty of those who are forgiven. She also shows a remarkably progressive attitude in speaking against the death penalty in a case like this, and in advocating rehabilitation. Cinna could do Augustus no harm, but the pardon would do the emperor's reputation a lot of good. Dio adds some further details, with Livia showing good common sense and demonstrating a shrewd understanding of political realities. She assured Augustus that opposition was inevitable to a figure of his importance. He was bound to displease some, and even those who had no axe to grind would aspire to his position. In the event, Augustus was relieved to receive her advice and cancelled the planned meeting of his consilium. Then he called in Cinna, and according to Seneca they spoke for two hours. Augustus rehearsed the favours he had bestowed on him and the benefits Cinna had received, and finished by offering friendship, an offer the other could hardly refuse. In fact, he became one of Augustus' most loyal followers and even received the consulship. On his death he bequeathed his estate in its entirety to the emperor. Livia's advice proved to be sound, and from then on, according to Seneca and Dio, there were no further plots against Augustus. They are mistaken in this, of course, in that they ignore the murky conspiracy of AD 6, which possibly involved Lucius Aemilius Paullus, husband of Augustus' granddaughter Julia.[43]

Even if we allow considerable exaggeration in the report of the Cinna case, there can be no doubt that Livia would have had some influence over Augustus' policies. But is there any evidence that he gave her a formal and institutional voice? It has been skilfully argued by Purcell that Livia's position in the state involved more than being a willing helpmeet of her husband in furthering his ethical and social aims. The principate was in itself an experiment, without precedent, evolved by Augustus with considerable skill and a canny knowledge of human nature. If there was to be further revolutionary change in the place of women in the governance of the Roman world, now might be seen to be the time. But on close examination it seems that while Augustus was prepared to allow his wife to assume something very close to an official role, he was careful to ensure that during his own lifetime her role was still securely defined by the traditional expectations of a woman's position within the domus.[44]

In the Cinna incident Dio has Livia point out that while Augustus is safe and sound she could continue *sharing in part of the rule (to meros archousa)*. Little faith should be placed in this striking assertion, for much of the Cinna episode has clearly been created from the imagination. Nor should we be influenced by allusions by the poets to Livia as *princeps*. Ovid calls Livia a *femina princeps*, but the expression appears in poems addressed to a woman, Ovid's wife, who was to look to Livia as her model and teacher. The *Consolatio* refers to her as *princeps* and as *Romana princeps*, but applies the term also to Drusus, her son, and uses Ovid's phrase, *femina princeps*, of Antonia. Clearly the word *princeps* could at this period still connote "prominent person" without necessarily implying any constitutional status.[45]

References to Livia's *potentia* are common throughout the literature, but they provide no insight into her constitutional position, for the term applies generally to extralegal power, generally when it is abused. Scribonia, for instance, complained about the potentia of Octavian's mistress, almost certainly

Livia, more than a decade before the Augustan settlement. When people were supposedly fearful of Livia's influence in the period before Augustus' death, they saw her as someone with *muliebri potentia*, implying the sinister influence of a woman exercising private pressure. Seneca speaks of mothers who exploit their sons with *muliebri impotentia* specifically because they are legally barred from exercising direct power themselves. To charge, then, that Livia enjoyed potentia tells us little, because in itself the word did not necessarily connote the formal exercise of power. More significantly, she did not exercise *potestas*, in the sense that the word usually conveyed in constitutional contexts—namely, the legal authority that was attached to a magistrate. In fact, at no point in Roman history did a woman have such authority. If Livia is indeed a "political woman" as Mommsen calls her, we must understand *political* in a very limited sense.[46]

There was a quality that Livia could lay claim to, a quality that was deeply embedded in the Roman political consciousness, that of *maiestas*.[47] In the broadest sense maiestas alludes to the dignity or honour of whatever individual, group, or institution it is attached to. Publius Scipio Africanus is said by Velleius to have possessed it, and Livy can refer to the maiestas of Roman matrons *(maiestas et pudor matronarum)*. But in the republic the concept is particularly associated with the Roman people, in the sense of the sovereign majesty of the state. Hence Cicero can talk of Gaul loyally defending the *maiestatem populi Romani*.[48] By a process that is complex and not fully understood, but all the same clearly inevitable, the "majesty" associated with the Roman people came to be embodied in the person of the princeps. Thus some ten years or so after the settlement of 27 BC, Horace could state that his modest verse could not do justice to Augustus' maiestas. Ovid, about a year after his exile in AD 8, can describe Augustus' maiestas as gentle. It is important to recognise that in the case of the princeps, maiestas was much more than simply the quality inherent in the offices he held. Thus when Augustus demanded two colleagues in the consulship, he met public resistance on the grounds that his maiestas would be diminished *(maiestatem eius imminui)* by having even one colleague. Also, Livy notes that in the early days of the republic it was confirmed that the people's maiestas was superior to the maiestas of consuls.[49] It was also inevitable that Augustus' maiestas would attach itself to members of his family. Hence we are told that he always addressed his troops by the formal expression, *milites* (soldiers), and insisted that his sons or stepsons do the same, believing that a more familiar term would not be appropriate to his own maiestas or that of his domus *(quam . . . aut sua domusque suae maiestas postularet)*. Tiberius was one of the most important beneficiaries of this development. After his adoption by Augustus nothing was spared to enhance his maiestas—*nihil ex eo tempore praetermissum est ad maiestatem eius augendum*. In fact, it soon became difficult to imagine that maiestas could repose in anyone outside the imperial family. Velleius states that when Tiberius was in Rhodes, he was treated with deference by the visiting officials, a deference that was remarkable for a private citizen, if indeed the maiestas he possessed was ever present in a private person *(si illa maiestas privata umquam fuit)*.[50]

Another beneficiary was Livia. The *Consolatio* words the concept indirectly, *non eadem vulgusque decent et lumina rerum* (the same things are not right for the ordinary people and for the world's glories). Ovid, in exile, becomes increasingly explicit. Livia alone, he says, is Augustus' equal and not overawed by his maiestas. Later the poet anticipates that his wife Fabia will feel overwhelmed and hardly able to speak when she comes into the presence of Livia. This, he feels, is not a serious problem, for Livia will recognise that Fabia stands in awe of her maiestas: *(sentiet illa / te maiestatem pertimuisse suam)*.[51] That Livia was conscious of sharing this very special quality is suggested by Tacitus' comment on the events of AD 20. When Germanicus' remains were returned to Rome, Livia and Tiberius held themselves aloof from the general lamentation, one explanation being that they thought that their involvement would be beneath their maiestas *(inferius maiestate sua rati)*.[52]

Violation of the maiestas of the emperor or his family *(maiestas laesa* or *minuta)* and the trials that ensued became one of the most hated aspects of the principate. The process by which this legal concept evolved is unclear and the subject of much controversy. It can certainly be traced back to at least 100 BC. Because the campaign against the Cimbri and Teutones had been conducted incompetently, a Lex Appuleia de Maiestate was passed, probably to punish incompetence rather than criminal action against the state. Sulla later passed a Lex Cornelia de Maiestate, designed to deter ambitious legionary commanders from taking their troops beyond the borders of their provinces. Caesar followed this with a Lex Julia de Maiestate, but unfortunately the offences covered by his law are not known. It might have been modified or perhaps even replaced by a Lex Julia passed under Augustus; at the very least the practical application of the preexisting law had to deal with the novel situation of the principate. Most important, because the state and the imperial domus were becoming more and more difficult to disentangle, Augustus' law covered not only attacks "committed against the Roman people and its security," as the the great legal code, the Digest, defines the term, but also attacks against the emperor and his family, and the punishments imposed became increasingly more stringent. Augustus initiated prosecutions for written libel under this law, and Tacitus cites the first case as that of Cassius Severus. Severus was sentenced in AD 8 or 12 (the sources are in disagreement), as a result of which he was exiled and his books burned. His case shows that women were also protected, for the prominent citizens whose defamation led to Severus' conviction are said to have included both men and women.[53]

In 35 BC we are told by Dio (the information appears in no other source) that Octavian granted his sister Octavia and his wife Livia security and protection against verbal insult *(adees kai anubriston)* similar to that provided for the tribunes *(ek tou homoiou tois demarchois)*, along with two other privileges: honorific statues and the right to administer their own estates without a guardian.[54] Dio seems to suggest that the privileges were granted by Octavian personally, but there must have been a formal grant. Whether it took the form of a lex or a senatus consultum or a tribunician edict, we cannot tell, nor can we be sure that the tribunician protection and the other distinctions were voted at the same time.

A year earlier, according to Dio, a formal law had granted Octavian protection against verbal and physical attacks and had stipulated that offenders would be liable to the same penalties as were applied in the case of the tribunes. This in turn might have had a precedent in similar privileges granted to Julius Caesar in 44 BC, although both of these supposed earlier grants have been much disputed.[55] Certainly, never before had such a status been enjoyed by a Roman woman. The grant of *sacrosanctitas* analogous to that of the tribunes was to give Livia and Octavia rights that lay at the very heart of the Roman system. Later emperors embraced the principle of tribunician privilege as a potent symbol of their office.

The legal and constitutional basis of the protection described by Dio is difficult to define. In the first place, it is not clear whether the reference to the tribunes is the historian's own gloss or whether his language reflects that of the enactment, in whatever form it appeared. If the latter, we cannot be sure from Dio's paraphrase whether the process involved detaching part of the tribune's authority. This seems very unlikely indeed. The grant of the powers of an office separated from the office itself had been recognised since 211 BC, and it was possible to separate office and powers to empower someone who was technically ineligible, as happened when the patrician Octavian received tribunician powers.[56] But Octavian was not dramatically ineligible, and he could, if necessary, have had himself adopted into a plebeian family. Nothing, however, could make a woman eligible, and it is more likely that the protection accorded Livia and Octavia was merely defined as analogous to that enjoyed by the tribunes. Even so, it is remarkable. Mommsen saw the measure as the extension of tribunician protection to the closest members of the emperor's family. But at this early stage there was no real concept of the principate, and it is doubtful that such a programme could have been in Octavian's mind in the mid-thirties. Purcell describes the arrangement as "traditional in flavour and nuance, in substance . . . revolutionary and novel." Its application to women, the wives of the triumvirs, is without precedent, and perhaps best seen as a specific response to the peculiar conditions of the period, with the primary intention being to protect Octavia rather than Livia (see chapter 3). It is difficult to know what the measure tells us about Livia's constitutional position. Nor is it clear whether the grant is to be regarded as an extension of the *maiestas populi Romani* to the wives (or wife and sister) of triumvirs. Resolution of this last question depends on the relationship between tribunician sacrosanctity and the *crimen maiestatis*, about which there is no unanimity.[57] Nor can the arrangement be explained satisfactorily as analogous to the privileges of the Vestal Virgins, as was first suggested by Willrich. As we shall see, the association between Livia and the Vestals seems to have developed gradually. Moreover, the Vestals received their immunity because of their virginity, and Vestal sanctity was as much an obligation as a privilege, for infractions could lead to punishment under the jurisdiction of the pontifex maximus, hardly a precedent that would have been sought after for Livia and Octavia.[58]

Although tribunician protection continued to be assumed by later emperors, the experiment was not to be repeated for the women. It was perhaps seen as coming too close to the admission of women into a formal role in Rome's governance, because it implies that a person who has a right to public protection must be fulfilling a public role. Different forms of protection evolved later. Women came to be included in the oath of allegiance sworn to the emperor, and the imperial family was after AD 8 protected by the law of maiestas when verbal insults were included. It may be that the legislation of 35 BC was an isolated but bold initiative by Octavian, one that may not have been received well and was not repeated. We do have one slightly bizarre instance of the protection of Livia's maiestas. On one occasion, noted earlier, not precisely defined and thus left to the imagination, she found herself in the presence of naked men. For the misfortune of being in the wrong place at the wrong time, they were condemned to death. Livia saved their lives by interceding on their behalf. In Octavia's case the only known instance of the apparent application of the law is in the case of a man condemned to the galleys for claiming that he was her son and that her real son, Marcellus, was a changeling.[59]

In practical terms, for Livia the most useful of the honours bestowed in 35 would have been the freedom from *tutela* (guardianship), because she was on course to becoming a very wealthy woman (see chapter 9). This privilege generally reflects the increasing independence of women in managing their property, a process that had been begun under the republic, when in theory the disposition of a woman's property was at the discretion of her *tutor* but in practice was very largely under her own control. Augustus' social legislation made the exemption formal for any woman who had borne three children. Livia was granted the *ius trium liberorum* in 9 BC, but this does not mean that Dio's testimony about 35 BC should be doubted. The Vestals had not been subject to the tutela and were similarly awarded the ius trium liberorum, in AD 9.[60]

It may well be that the award of the statues was meant to mark the receipt of the two other privileges. This honour did have precedents, but they were far from numerous. There were a few legendary examples, commemorating some special service rendered by women to the state. A public equestrian statue of Cloelia, a heroine of the sixth century BC, is described by Livy as an unprecedented honour for an unprecedented act.[61] The first concrete historical case is that of Cornelia, who received a statue honouring her, according to the report of Plutarch, as "the mother of the Gracchi." The information appears in the context of a report on a speech of 184 BC in which Cato the Elder condemned the erection of statues to women in the provinces. Pliny remarks that Cato was not effective, to the extent that there was a statue to Cornelia in Rome. But the very fact that Pliny mentions only this one example several generations after Cato's speech suggests that the honour was indeed rare, and there is no evidence of a public statue erected for a woman between Cornelia's and those of Livia and Octavia in 35 BC.[62] No known representations of Livia (or Octavia) can be assigned to this special grant, but they would almost certainly have been of the Marbury Hall type (see appendix 1, fig. 14), which comes closest to republican models. The earliest known evidence for a Livian statue comes a little later, from a group in the sanctuary of Demeter and Kore (Persephone) at Eleusis, dated perhaps to 31 BC. An inscription there records statues of her and Octavian (the actual figures are lost).[63]

Livia receives no mention in the *Res Gestae*, the great document in which Augustus recorded his achievements for publication after his death. Moreover, if she had enjoyed a formal institutional status during her husband's lifetime, we would expect it to be reflected in some of the traditional marks of distinction that the state bestowed on its official and semiofficial dignitaries. As an example, the birthdays of Tiberius, on November 16, of Germanicus, on May 24, and of Drusus Caesar, son of Tiberius, on October 7, are recorded in the *Feriale Cumanum*, a fragmentary calendar of festivals found at Cumae recording the honours paid to Augustus and the imperial house. Tiberius and his son

Drusus are named Caesars on the calendar, and the entry cannot have been made before AD 4, the date of Tiberius' adoption and his right to that cognomen. Augustus is not identified as Divus, and there is no reference to his death, which seems to place the calendar no later than AD 14. Thus there is evidence that the birthdays of the male members of the imperial family were being honoured in the latter part of Augustus' reign. There is no corresponding indication that this honour was bestowed on Livia, even though the parts of the calendars that would have covered her birthday have survived.[64] Livia, in fact, is not mentioned at all in any of the extant calendars until eight years after Augustus' death, when she dedicated a statue to him at the Theatre of Marcellus and caused a controversy by listing her name before Tiberius' (see chapter 8). There is no evidence that Livia's birthday was marked before AD 14, and the first extant recognition is, again, later than Augustus' death, in the record of the Arval Brethren in AD 27.[65]

Augustus did, of course, honour Livia indirectly on her birthday. The dedication of what was arguably the most important monument of his regime, the Ara Pacis, took place on the anniversary of her birth, perhaps her fiftieth, and was celebrated annually and entered accordingly in the calendars. The coincidence is an illustration of Augustus' adeptness in promoting his own image of himself, and, indirectly, acknowledging the regard in which Livia was held, without violating Roman tradition by honouring a woman publicly and officially. He seems to have demonstrated the same sleight of hand in timing the dedication of the altar to his Numen—carried out by Tiberius probably between AD 6 and 9—on January 17, the date of his wedding to Livia. As Fishwick has pointed out, the dedication of the altar to Augustus' Numen marked a radical step, far more significant than the cult of the emperor's *genius*, because it marked a recognition in Rome of a divine presence within the emperor. The altar probably stood on the Palatine and is presumably the one where Caligula carried out sacrifices on the day of his assassination. Once again Augustus sought to honour Livia indirectly, by timing a highly significant state event to coincide with the anniversary of one that had special significance for her (see appendix 11).[66]

It is striking that Livia is absent from her husband's official coinage.[67] This reticence cannot be attributed to a long Roman tradition that frowned upon the numismatic depiction of women. Any such tradition had been thoroughly violated by the time that Livia came to prominence. The first step had in fact been taken by Mark Antony. After the formation of the triumvirate in 43, Antony received Gaul (apart from Narbonensis) and placed his headquarters at Lugdunum, where his mint was established. Silver coins minted in the late forties BC in Lugdunum, some with Antony's name on the reverse, depict a winged bust. The type had appeared in earlier Roman coins, but in this case the figure has a nodus hairstyle, which seems to suggest a mortal woman, possibly Fulvia, Antony's wife. The type seems to be echoed in the Roman East. The Phrygian city of Eumenea was renamed Fulvia in honour of Antony's wife. Its bronze coins of the very late forties depict the same motif of a winged female bust with nodus. Also in the late forties, coins of the Roman mint depict the same Victory bust with nodus, although it may be that the Roman moneyer was inspired by the coins of Lugdunum without any deliberate intention of invoking the image of Fulvia. Indeed, there is far from general agreement on whether any of these busts is of a real woman, and if so, whether she is Fulvia, and the issue is complicated by uncertainty about the coins' dates. Wood has suggested that the winged Victory is probably best seen as a divine personification who subtly resembles a living woman, rather than as a deified portrait of that woman. If the bust is Fulvia's, it marks the first depiction of a historical female on a Roman coin and would represent a truly dramatic innovation, because even the triumvirs themselves had begun to appear on coins only in the mid-forties.[68]

Antony may or may not have put Fulvia on his coins. About the representations of Octavia, his second wife, there can be no serious doubt, even though she is nowhere identified by name. Some of the coins in question were struck in eastern mints under Antony's control and follow his marriage to Octavia in 40. On these the portrait of the woman with the nodus hairstyle is not winged, and in fact does not have any divine attributes. She is found in the company of mortal men, Antony and / or Octavian. Silver cistophori of Miletus and the aes coinage of Pergamum (dated before the mid-thirties) depict Octavia in a jugate position with Antony—that is, facing in the same direction with his head superimposed over hers, a type of portrait common in eastern ruling houses in the Hellenistic period. On silver cistophori of Pergamum, Antony's bust appears on the obverse, while on the reverse there is a small bust of Octavia rising above the sacred *cista* (basket).[69] Bronze tresses (three asses) minted in Rome show Octavia facing jugate portraits of the two important men in her life, her husband Antony and her brother Octavian. Other aes coins, sestertii, and dupondii show them facing, which is an innovation.[70] Gold aurei depict Antony on one side and Octavia on the other.[71]

Perhaps the most remarkable of Antony's coins in this context followed his breakup with Octavia and his open association with Cleopatra. He minted official denarii with his own bust on the obverse and Cleopatra's on the reverse and thus broke yet again with tradition, this time by portraying a foreign monarch, his consort, on Roman coins. But he went even further. Neither Fulvia (if indeed it is she who is depicted) nor Octavia was identified by name. The Cleopatra coins carry the legend *Cleopatrae reginae regum filiorum regum* (to Cleopatra queen of kings and of her sons-kings).[72]

Augustus did not follow the precedent established by Antony. Only one female portrait appears on his official coinage, that of his daughter Julia. Nor can even this one instance be called a true likeness. On denarii of 13 BC her bust appears in tiny scale between those of Gaius and Lucius, clearly celebrating her role in continuing the dynasty. Augustus' reluctance to portray his wife surely cannot have simply been a fear of being associated with an innovation of Antony's. The injunction was maintained to the end of the reign, more than forty years after Antony's death, and in any case some of the most striking portraits of Livia in local mints were struck in Alexandria. If there was any lingering sensitivity about the Roman coins depicting Cleopatra, it would have surely been felt in Egypt even more strongly than in Rome. Augustus' unwillingness to give Livia official recognition on his coinage doubtless arose from his conviction that such an honour would move her formally out of the domus into an unacceptable formal and public role in the state.

Only one official coin issue of Augustus has a potential Livian association. Precious metal coins that are generally assigned to the closing years of his reign depict a seated figure on their reverse. This motif reappears on the reverse of undated precious metal issues of his successor Tiberius (fig. 1), and some years later reappears on dupondii of Claudius, where there is no doubt about the identity, made clear by the legend DIVA AUGUSTA, balancing the radiate head of Divus Augustus, identified as such, on the other side (fig. 6).[73] Unfortunately, the identity of Livia is not confirmed on either the Augustan or the Tiberian coins, and there is no consistency in the depiction of the figure, which seems to speak against a representation of a statue of Livia. On the Augustan coins she is seated on a chair and holds a sceptre in her right hand, while on some of the Tiberian pieces the sceptre is replaced by an inverted spear. In her left she holds a branch or ears of wheat. On the Claudian pieces, which have a larger flan, she holds a torch in her right, and ears of wheat in her left. There is also the difficulty that we cannot be certain of a true Livian image even on the larger Claudian coins. As we shall see, she was closely associated in inscriptions and sculpture with the goddess Ceres (see also chapter 10). Claudius could well have adapted an established image of Ceres, identified as such by the ears of corn, to present Livia in this guise. Nor does the fact that contemporary provincial coins identify the same seated image as Livia's carry any special weight. Provincial mints regularly adopted and adapted the issues of the Roman mint and would not have hesitated to see nonexistent identifications or even create them. We have no way of telling what was in the minds of provincial engravers, or of those who commissioned their work. That said, the ubiquity of the type, with the clear identification of Livia, in the provincial mints indicates a widespread tendency to associate Livia with the image, apparently without official disapproval. Once again we seem to have a clever way in which Augustus sought to honour his wife without giving her an official institutional role, by using a type that would have suggested her without overtly depicting her. This stands in powerful contrast to the forceful and incontrovertible depiction of Agrippina the Younger on the coins of Claudius and on the early issues of her son Nero.

If Livia was to seek an institutional role within the state, there was one group of contemporary women who should in a sense provide a model. Up to this period, the institutional involvement of Roman women in public life was limited essentially to certain priestly offices, particularly to membership in the Vestal Virgins. There are good reasons to believe that the Vestals were one of the oldest religious organizations in Rome and their early standing was still noted in late antiquity by St Augustine.[74] Vesta was the goddess of the hearth. Her round temple near the Regia in the forum housed a sacred fire, and the community of Vestals (numbering six in the Augustan period) was charged with tending it.[75] A Vestal was required to stay chaste during her period of service, which was normally thirty years, after which she was then free to marry, although few seem to have exercised this option. While in service she did not stay under the authority of her paterfamilias but was responsible to the pontifex maximus, who could sentence her to death for violation of her chastity, although that penalty seems to have been imposed only rarely.[76]

The Vestal enjoyed several privileges. She possessed sacrosanctity, for example, which made her person inviolate. She also had the right to make a will without the consent of a tutor. Some of her entitlements were ancient. The freedom from tutelage, for instance, was guaranteed in the Twelve Tables. Others were more recent, such as the use of a lictor (see chapter 8), granted in 42 BC by members of the Second Triumvirate.[77] The Vestals' privileges were enhanced by Augustus, who held them in high regard. After the battle of Actium they headed the procession that greeted him on his return to the city. They carried out sacrifices on the anniversaries of the day of his return from Syria in 19 BC and to commemorate his return from Spain and Gaul in 13. They participated in the annual sacrifices at the anniversary of the dedication of the Ara Pacis, where they appear on an inner frieze.[78] Suetonius claims that Augustus once declared that if any of his granddaughters had been at the right age (Vestals were usually chosen between the ages of six and ten), he would have put them forward as candidates for the order. He never took the step, but he did increase the Vestal entitlements. Two specific examples are known. Vestals were given the exclusive right to watch shows from lower seats in the arena opposite the praetor's tribunal. Also, in AD 9 they received the privileges of women who had borne three children *(ius trium liberorum)*. Tiberius also increased their entitlements, and to encourage interest in the order and to raise its prestige he made an award of two million sesterces to a Cornelia on her becoming a Vestal in AD 23.[79]

After Caesar's death the triumvir Lepidus had seized the office of pontifex maximus, which he succeeded in holding on to until his death in 13 BC. The position was now open to Augustus, who was duly elected on March 6 of the following year, a spectacular occasion when more people came to Rome for an election than ever in its recorded history.[80] The pontifex maximus was traditionally required to live in an official house in the Forum next to the precinct of the Vestals. Julius Caesar had acceded to this requirement. Augustus was unwilling to move out of his house on the Palatine, but he devised a way to make part of his own house public property. Two months after the election, a statue and possibly a shrine or temple of Vesta were dedicated in his house on the Palatine (see appendix 12). The public hearth of the state was in a sense moved to the private hearth of the emperor. This act was of great symbolic importance, because it now could be said that the emperor's house and the state were in a sense synonymous.[81]

The cult of Vesta became increasingly important to Augustus as the domus of the emperor became increasingly identified with the state. Perhaps not surprisingly, there has been a general tendency to argue that Augustus used Livia's association with Vesta to reinforce his wife's image as a symbol of chastity and a fitting representative of the home of the princeps and, in a sense, the home of the nation. Had such a connection arisen in the public mind, then Augustus would surely have done nothing to discourage it. But there are some serious objections to the notion of a deliberate policy to create a special connection between Livia and Vesta.[82]

The claim that the cult of the Palatine Vesta might have been entrusted to her is little more than speculation. The only concrete evidence for her close association with the Vestal ritual is her restoration of the shrine of Bona Dea and Ovid's allusion to her carrying out sacrifices in the Vestals' company. She did involve herself in trying to extinguish two fires that threatened the temple of Vesta in the Forum Romanum; but her role there can be explained by her status as wife, on the first occasion, and mother, on the second, of the pontifex maximus. Ovid most strikingly calls her the "Vesta of chaste matrons." But this last expression postdates his exile in AD 8, after which his imagery had become generally extravagant, and his inflated expressions cannot be used to offer insight into official policy. In any case, Vesta is not the only divine figure drawn into an analogy with Livia, for Ovid compares her also with Venus and Juno.[83]

It is also important to note that an association with the Vestals was not the exclusive preserve of Livia. The grant of sacrosanctitas and exemption from tutela as early as 35 BC may well have made people associate Livia's new rights with the similar privileges of the Vestals, but these entitlements were also conferred on Octavia, and indeed it is generally argued that Octavia, not Livia, was intended as the main target of the benefactions. The sacrosanctitas bestowed in 35 is, in fact, the only "Vestal" privilege that Augustus granted his wife. She did indeed share with them the ius trium liberorum, but this privilege was granted to her in 9 BC to compensate for the death of Drusus. At the time this was still not a Vestal privilege, and they did do not seem to have acquired it until AD 9 and the passing of the Lex Papia Poppaea. Three other Vestal privileges are commonly linked to Livia, all after Augustus' death. She was granted a lictor, probably in AD 14. In 22 she may have been allowed the use of the *carpentum* (covered carriage), a privilege, albeit not an exclusive one, of the Vestals. In AD 23 she was granted the right to sit in the same lower seats in the theatre.[84] It should be noted, however, that these analogous distinctions are not so significant as they may seem at first sight. In the first place, the use of the lictor was almost certainly connected with Livia's role as priestess of the Divus Augustus, and in fact it seems that she was prohibited from employing one except in strict connection with her priestly duties. Nor were these privileges exclusively hers for long. Caligula allowed his sisters to occupy the special seats in the theatre. Indeed, Caligula conferred the rights and privileges of the Vestals en masse on his grandmother Antonia. Claudius granted his wife Messalina the special seating, as well the use of the carpentum.[85] Also, note that in any case these last entitlements were conferred on Livia not by Augustus but by Tiberius, who was resistant to the idea of her playing an institutional role. Hence when Claudius placed the cult of the deified Livia in the hands of the Vestals after her consecration, this should perhaps be seen not so much as a declaration of a special association of Livia but rather as a gesture appropriate to one of the women of the imperial family, all of whom were somehow seen as having an association with Vesta.[86]

Inscriptional evidence is similarly misleading if taken at face value. It is true that as early as the twenties BC Livia was included in the cult of Hestia, the Greek equivalent of Vesta, at Athens. But she shared the cult with Julia, Augustus' daughter, and they were served by the same priestess, documented by a theatre seat belonging to that priestess. Between 27 and 11 Livia, along with the Vestals, was thanked by the ambassadors of Mytilene. But being diplomats, they also passed on the same thanks to Augustus' sister Octavia, as well as to his children, relatives, and friends. At Lampsacus, Livia is given the cult name Hestia. But the inscription, as we can see from her name (Ioulia Sebaste), is at the earliest Tiberian and may be much later. Moreover, in the same inscription Livia also has the cult name *nean Demetera.* Demeter (Ceres) is in fact far more commonly identified with Livia than is Hestia, and the first record of a Livian statue is from the sanctuary at Eleusis, with its strong associations with Demeter. In her catalogue of cult names of Livia in the eastern provinces, Hahn notes that she is identified with nine goddesses other than Hestia on coins and inscriptions (quite apart from abstractions like Tyche and Pronoia). In addition to the obvious candidates, the list includes less common figures like Mnemosyne, Maia, and Isia.[87]

In any case, it can be noted that even the men of the Augustan house were associated with Vesta. Thus on the birthdays of Tiberius, Germanicus, and Drusus, son of Tiberius, special thanksgivings were offered to Vesta.[88] On his way to his Rhodian retirement Tiberius persuaded the Parians to part with the statue of Vesta and sent it to be placed in the Temple of Concord in Rome, which was associated in the public mind as a joint venture between Tiberius and his brother Drusus.

It is clear that while Augustus was happy to exploit Livia's standing and image to strengthen his own political position, and was willing to listen to her advice and to be influenced by it, he was punctilious during his own reign in keeping the boundaries of the domus and the respublica separate. He was not so willing to bequeath this important distinction to the next reign, and his apparent decision to elevate Livia's official position posthumously was to be the source of endless friction between her and her son, a problem not finally resolved until her death in 29.

8

MOTHER OF THE EMPEROR

In many respects Tiberius was eminently unsuited to the task he assumed in AD 14. Up to that point he had been trained primarily as a soldier, and even after being acknowledged unequivocally as Augustus' successor, and thus marked out for a future political role, he still continued to serve, with considerable distinction, with the troops on the frontiers, rather than in an administrative apprenticeship in Rome. Nor had he any taste, or instinct, for political life, which he viewed as inevitably corrupting. More than once he commented on the increasing perils facing any man the higher he climbed in the hierarchy of the state. The posture that Augustus adopted in 27 BC, that he was essentially an ordinary magistrate with extraordinary responsibilities, had been to no small degree an exercise in public relations. But that principle would have been genuinely in character for Tiberius, and it seems that, at least at the outset, he took it seriously and tried to see himself as an ordinary individual. Suetonius observes that, if anything, he behaved even less assertively than a private citizen *(civilem admodum inter initia ac paulo minus quam privatum egit)*. But this stance would have been difficult to maintain even for someone endowed with consummate political and diplomatic skills. Augustus had been just such a superb manager of people. Tiberius by contrast was "aloof and austere amid the grace and ease and smooth perfidy of fashionable society," as Syme describes him.[1]

It was inevitable that once he became princeps, tensions would arise between Tiberius and his mother. In the minds of many Romans she would have represented continuity after the death of Augustus in a way that her son was not able to do. It is noteworthy that in the earliest days of the reign it was to her that Sallustius Crispus reputedly expressed his concern over Tiberius' intention to refer all matters to the Senate, following the report of Agrippa Postumus' execution (see chapter 4). There are signs that such thinking was not limited to Sallustius. When Tiberius at his first meeting with the Senate behaved peremptorily with the obsequious Quintus Haterius, it was Livia who was called upon to calm the matter down. This kind of involvement would not have been viewed as a threat by Augustus, who had sought to find an informal role for women like his wife and sister in the state and was happy to listen to Livia's advice—and if necessary to reject it. But for Tiberius such a situation was difficult to accept, and he would have felt a natural reluctance to continue in his mother's shadow. Moreover, the idea of backroom politics was alien to his nature. His reaction to his mother is consistent with his vision of the principate, and his treatment of her is in line with his treatment of others he now had to deal with. Suetonius says that he avoided frequent meetings and long confidential conversations with Livia so as not to seem dominated by her. He may well be right, but one should not read anything dramatic or unusual into the situation. This principled stand would have been totally in character for Tiberius. Moreover, he was particularly averse to the intervention of women in matters he felt were properly the exclusive reserve of men. Hence his injunction against Livia's involving herself in "serious matters unsuited to a woman" *(maioribus nec feminae convenientibus negotiis)*. It is no surprise that, as Dio observes, Tiberius became very defensive about the part that Livia had played in his elevation to the principate and that he went to some effort to downplay her contribution. This had little to do with Tiberius' feelings for his mother. It tells us more about how Tiberius visualised the proper conduct of any princeps.[2]

In any case, the notion of mother-son conflict should not be pushed too far. To some extent the sources would have been instinctively inclined to exaggerate the differences between Tiberius and his mother, because they could not pick on a powerful wife—a Messalina or Agrippina the Younger—to denigrate as the sinister power behind the throne. The unavoidable difficulties that arose between Livia and Tiberius might have been expected to resolve themselves as his principate evolved and he became more experienced and self-confident. The fact that this did not happen probably has very little to do with their personalities or mutual feelings. Their situation was in fact irretrievably confounded by a fundamental complexity that would overtax the political skills and patience of both of them. In AD 14 Livia's quasi-legal status changed dramatically. The nature of the change was not spelled out precisely, and its consequent ambiguity laid the foundation for major confrontation between mother and son over their respective roles in the new order. Ultimately, they failed to reach a modus operandi, and the constitutional tension, if anything, grew more serious as the reign progressed. The problem was Augustus' doing, and it arose from his attempt after his death to grant Livia what he had denied her during his lifetime, a form of institutional status. In taking this action he bequeathed a problem to Tiberius that he himself had been unwilling to face and which his successor, as Augustus should have been able to anticipate, was temperamentally ill-suited to handle.[3]

The change in Livia's status was achieved in two stages. In his will Augustus specified that she was to be adopted, as his daughter, into the Julian gens. In addition, she was to assume the name Augusta *(nomen Augustum)*.[4] Despite its significance, Livia's adoption has attracted virtually no attention in the ancient literary authorities. It is of the type classed as testamentary, in that it was enacted in the adopter's will. This process is mentioned at times by ancient authors, but is never discussed by the jurists, and it is difficult to know what its strict legal consequences would have been. Known cases of individuals adopted by this means seem to betray a strange anomaly in the adoptee's filiation. He will be described as the son of his natural father, and not by the normal (for the Romans) designation as son of his adoptive father. Gnaeus Domitius Afer (consul AD 39), for instance, adopted in his will Titius Lucanus. Epigraphic evidence shows that Lucanus took the full name of his adoptive father but continued to call himself the son of Sextus *(Sexti filius)*. The famous Pliny the Younger was adopted by his uncle, the Elder Pliny, Gaius Plinius Secundus, but kept the filiation "son of Lucius." Scholars argue plausibly that because the original filiation is maintained, testamentary adoption is not real adoption, but rather a device to institute an heir on the condition that he take the testator's name. One must be cautious, however, about drawing inferences from such limited data, especially in a period where Roman nomenclature was undergoing considerable change.[5] In inscriptions dated clearly after AD 14, all from outside Rome, Livia is identified as the daughter of Marcus Drusus, but this may reflect the awkwardness of designating someone as the daughter of her husband. There is only one certain case of an inscription (from Velleia, dated to the Caligulan period) where she is identified as the daughter of Augustus. On the other hand the *Fasti Praenestini* record her dedicating a statue in Rome itself, in AD 22, to her father Augustus.[6] After the adoption, although Livia's freedmen took her new nomen Julius or Julia, they adopted the praenomen of her natural father, Marcus. This, however, may be a deliberate device to distinguish them from the slaves freed by Augustus.[7]

The issue of testamentary adoption is generally problematic at the best of times. It is especially complicated in Livia's case, for two primary reasons. Nothing is known about the testamentary adoption of females. Indeed, little is known even about conventional female adoption. Moreover, the principle of the adoption of a wife is especially problematic. Only one parallel has been suggested, from the so-called *Laudatio Turiae*, an inscription, dated to the Augustan period, in the form of an obituary addressed by a husband to his departed wife, Turia. The analogy is not persuasive. In one much-discussed passage the husband wishes that he had predeceased his wife *[super]stite te* and then wishes that he had adopted a daughter, or, as Wistrand has argued, had been survived by his wife in the role of a daughter *[f]ilia mihi supstituta*. Unfortunately, both the text and the general meaning of this segment of the *Laudatio* are so controversial that they cannot be used to provide a convincing precedent for Livia's new status.[8]

The dubious status of testamentary adoptions would not have presented an insuperable obstacle in Livia's case. Augustus took no chances when he came to write his will, leaving minute and almost comically detailed instructions on his funeral arrangements, on who should be allowed entry into his mausoleum, on the number of soldiers on active service, on the arrears in the treasury accounts, and more of the same. For good measure, he added the names of people who could provide the necessary information should further particulars be needed. We can therefore feel sure that he would have made meticulous and explicit provisions to ensure that Livia's adoption would be regularised. His task would have been made easier by the fact that he himself could provide the compelling precedent. He had in 44 BC been adopted by Julius Caesar in the late dictator's will. When he became consul in the following year, his top priority was to present to the popular assembly a law which he had been trying hard to enact for many months but had been blocked by the stalling tactics of Mark Antony. This *lex curiata* ratified his adoption and secured its legal basis. Appian notes that through the procedure Octavian, as he then was, acquired exactly the same legal status as would natural sons. There is no proof that Augustus made such an arrangement in AD 14, but it seems inconceivable that he would not have benefitted from his experience to ensure that Livia's adoption would be unimpeachable.[9]

The adoption could have been recognised by a *senatus consultum*, which would be passed on to the popular assembly to be enacted as a formal *lex*. We do at any rate have indirect evidence that the Senate was involved in the adoption process. To mark the fact that Livia had become Augustus' daughter, the senators voted for an Altar of Adoption (Ara Adoptionis). The gesture was not as dramatic as it may appear. Such an altar would been intended as a commemorative monument, not a place for worship, and altars in honour of the imperial family are a relatively common phenomenon. Their sponsors often looked on them as a harmless device to curry favour. In 28 the Senate sycophantically voted to honour Tiberius and Sejanus with an Ara Amicitiae and an Ara Clementiae, possibly never built. Altars were erected to celebrate the births of Agrippina's children. An Ara Ultionis, proposed to mark Germanicus' death, was turned down by Tiberius. He also rejected the Ara Adoptionis in AD 14, although there is no hint that he challenged the actual adoption provision in the will. Tiberius behaved as he did on other occasions, honouring to the wishes of his late adoptive father, but rejecting excessive reaction to those wishes.[10]

What could Augustus have intended in adopting his wife? There might have been several considerations. He had demonstrated from early in the principate a desire to be succeeded by someone from the domus Augusta. This determination sprang from a deep sense of his past, a feeling enhanced by his adoption by Caesar. That adoption had brought him his fair share of Caesar's political support. But it enabled him also to lay claim to a much greater legacy. Caesar belonged to a famous family, the Julians, whose name was invoked repeatedly by generations of his successors and attached for all time to the first ruling dynasty in Rome. When Caesar gave the funeral oration for his aunt Julia in 68 BC, he took the opportunity to remind his audience that the Julian gens had endured since the earliest days of the Roman people and could trace their descent from the goddess Venus, through her son Aeneas, and his son Julius, who had given the gens its name. The court poet Vergil converted this from a family tradition to a national myth in Rome's great epic, the *Aeneid*, in which the role to be played by Augustus and his family are laid out in prophecy.[11] The emphasis that Augustus placed on this legendary ancestry was later manifested in the decoration of the Forum of Augustus, which Zanker has described as a showplace of the Gens Iulia. Its centrepiece, the Temple of Mars Ultor, as Ovid noted, looked down upon the statue of Aeneas with his son and father, surrounded by the ancestors of the Julian house.[12] Denied a descendant of his own blood, Augustus was obliged eventually to adopt his stepson. Through his adoption Tiberius became a Julian. It will be remembered that the way had in a sense been prepared when Julian as well as Claudian images were carried in the funeral of Livia's Claudian son Drusus. When Livia was adopted into the

Julian house, Tiberius could claim Julian descent on both sides of his parentage, and his right to the principate would rest on stronger foundations. Thus the adoption of Livia, far from putting Tiberius in the shade, as some have argued, if anything strengthened his position.[13]

Livia's new status as a Julian would no doubt have helped to place Tiberius' principate on a surer footing. Yet its full impact would have been on Livia herself, and may have been intended primarily to provide the right conditions for Augustus' other, no less dramatic and far-reaching measure, the conferring on her of the name Augusta. Flory has aptly observed that if the emperor had granted her new name without a change in her gens, it would mean that the designation of Augustus or Augusta could pass to someone from any family. Livia Drusilla's transformation into Julia Augusta was a remarkable event. There was no precedent in Rome for the transfer of what was in effect an honorific title from a man to a woman.[14] Octavian had received the cognomen of Augustus, with its powerful religious associations, in 27 BC, in preference to the alternative Romulus. By AD 14 it had acquired the force of a title that marked the holder as princeps. This process may well have begun in the East. In AD 1 Augustus instructed the Parthian king to withdraw from Armenia and wrote to him as Phrataces, deliberately dropping the title of king. The Parthian rose to the occasion and wrote back haughtily, addressing the princeps simply as Caesar. The implication is that Augustus was thus a title, not a name, like Caesar, a title that belonged not to the individual but to his position.[15] This notion was reinforced by Augustus himself in AD 9 when the Senate sought to offer Tiberius various titles, such as Pannonicus, for his victories. The princeps observed that Tiberius would have to remain content with the one that he would assume after Augustus' death. Thus Ovid in the *Fasti* anticipates that when Tiberius takes on the burden of the world, it will be as *tanti cognominis heres* (inheritor of such a great cognomen).[16]

Even under normal circumstances the assumption of an honorific cognomen that had been granted by the Senate to a predecessor was unusual. Suetonius notes that among the honours originally decreed for Tiberius' brother Drusus, the Senate bestowed Germanicus on him and his descendants, implying that the latter would not have happened automatically, and may have been enacted because Drusus was dead and could not enjoy the honour himself. Later, after Claudius' successful campaign in Britain, the Senate in AD 43 made a similar gesture and bestowed on Claudius and his son the title of Britannicus. Dio claims that Tiberius did not allow the Senate to vote the title of Augustus to him. This injunction may have been purely legalistic, if he felt that it was part of his inheritance and did not need to be conferred by the Senate, and

Suetonius does indeed describe it as *hereditarium* (inherited). The Senate is unlikely to have raised any objection to the title in Tiberius' case, however it was technically acquired, because such a development had been anticipated since at least AD 9. Suetonius and Dio say, in fact, that in AD 14 Tiberius did not regularly name himself Augustus, although he did not object to others using it of him, either in speech or in writing, and he used it when addressing kings. Tiberius' hesitation must have had a very limited application. The title appears in official documents, letters to communities in the East and in the *Piso Decree* of AD 20, where the emperor, writing in the first person, alludes to himself as Augustus. It appears regularly on his coins from the beginning of the reign. If the claim of abstinence is serious, then it can refer only to Tiberius' more private communications.[17]

The fact that Tiberius acquired the legal right to the title of Augustus, whether or not he chose to use it, would not have been considered remarkable. But the same could not have been true of the transmission of the title not only to the successor of Augustus but also to his widow and adopted daughter. It is probably safe to assume that the Romans did not have an exact notion of what Augusta was meant to convey in AD 14. Precedents in the East would have been of little help. Even during Augustus' lifetime the feminine form Sebaste was applied to Livia, but it was used also of his daughter Julia and seems to have been intended there only as a general honorific.[18] The later force of Augusta seems to vary from reign to reign. Claudius made a point of not allowing it to be bestowed on his wife Messalina. Agrippina the Younger assumed it when she solidified her power (see appendix 13). Claudius posthumously bestowed the title on his mother, Antonia; she may already have received it during her lifetime under Caligula and may have refused to use it (see appendix 14). After studying the Augustae of the first two centuries, Temporini has argued that they had certain things in common — they were the props of the dynasty, and the title came to be intended for the mothers of emperors when the sons had succeeded.[19] Temporini may be correct that the concept evolved in this way. But we must avoid the temptation to project the later development in the meaning of a word back to its very beginning. Certainly Antonia, if she received the tile from Caligula, could not be seen as the mother of the emperor.

What were the consequences of the very first bestowal of the title Augusta, and what role did it presage for the Augusta? In 1864 Ashbach argued the extreme view — which unsurprisingly seems to have won no adherents — that the Augusta was the true ruler and that Tiberius was second to her. Mommsen's more moderate and more influential view, which he later discarded, was tentatively that while the bestowal of Augusta on Livia did not formally grant her joint rule with Tiberius, it did not exclude it. Mommsen's initial thesis has since been developed and refined by some scholars, on the principle that because the title of Augustus was limited to the princeps and his descendants and not allowed for private persons, the granting of the feminine equivalent, Augusta, must similarly suggest that Livia was no longer a *privata* and either was expected to have some share in governing or exploited the opening that Augustus' will inadvertently created.[20] To such scholars the term Augusta signified real political power. They see the senatorial behaviour in AD 14, when they competed to honour Livia in her new role as Julia Augusta, as a response to the new constitutional situation, in which Tiberius had a partner in the principate.

Other scholars have argued that the award of the name was intended to be purely honorary.[21] That certainly is how Tiberius sought to understand it, whatever Augustus' intentions. But if such was Augustus' intention, it is hard not to conclude that he behaved either naively or irresponsibly, and he was not generally subject to either of these failings. Although the notion of joint rule is surely an overstatement of his intentions, it is hard to believe that Augustus did not intend Livia to have some kind of formal constitutional role. He must have understood the emotive power of the title Augustus, and have been aware that its female equivalent would raise Livia to a level well beyond traditional honours. The fact that Augusta later became attached regularly to imperial women does not mitigate the impact that this unprecedented award of the title would have had in AD 14. It is surely telling that Augustus did not dare make Livia the Augusta during his lifetime. That reluctance was certainly not due to an obsessive possessiveness about the title—he was more than happy to declare publicly that Tiberius was earmarked to receive it. Of course, Tiberius could not be allowed to hold the title during the incumbent's lifetime. Similarly, giving Livia the name during his lifetime might have been felt to signal that she was some sort of coruler, at least at the symbolic level, in the manner of the Hellenistic rulers of the East. The fact that Agrippina the Younger managed to acquire it while Claudius was still alive is remarkable, but her ultimate fate and her reputation among succeeding generations show that Agrippina was willing to claim rights for which the Romans were quite unprepared.[22]

The key to the problem lies not so much in Livia's status after AD 14 as in Augustus' intentions. Unfortunately, for all that has been written on him, Augustus still remains something of an enigma—Syme was right to draw attention to the symbol that he used on his seal, the sphinx, the ultimate enigmatic icon.[23] And nowhere did he prove more of an enigma than in the arrangement made for his widow. In a sense he made it inevitable that after his death Livia would be seen in many quarters as someone who had been bequeathed a formal institutionalised position within the state. He was unwilling to proceed to the next logical step, to define what that position should be.

Ritter has recently argued with some vigour that Livia received no constitutional powers by her elevation to Augusta, because the position of the princeps rested not on his title of Augustus but on his specific powers, such as *imperium proconsulare* and the *tribunicia potestas*, which a woman could not possess. Livia was a powerful woman, but her power lay in her pragmatic effect on matters of state, not on her constitutional position. Ritter is technically correct, but Augustus may well have intended a constitutional status that would complement, not subsume, the official role of the magistrates. As Purcell observed, "there was a graded range of activities lying between the totally domestic and the completely public, not a sharply defined boundary." Augustus seems to have wished by his final gesture to his wife to move that boundary, but left it to the Senate and to Tiberius to define where it should lie. His action, inevitably, sowed seeds of confusion. The Senate and Livia understood his intentions to be directed to one end. Tiberius saw them quite differently. This placed the new emperor in an unenviable position. Tacitus paints his predicament in the darkest colours. He asserts that Tiberius rejected Livia's attempt to claim a share of his power, but at the same time he could not depose her because he had received that power from her as her gift *(donum)*. This is a very crude summation of Tiberius' dilemma. He was no Nero. He recognised the *pietas* due to his mother and he appreciated that she was entitled to certain distinctions. Moreover, Tiberius did not demand of his mother anything that he did not demand of himself. This is stated explicitly by Tacitus and is reflected in Dio's comment that Tiberius told his mother to conduct herself in a restrained manner. It was right and proper, he insisted, that she should imitate him.[24] Tiberius also had a respect, if not awe, for the figure of Augustus, whose wishes he could not easily countermand. But his sense of filial obligation could not move him to accept a form of constitutional arrangement that offended his very basic principles. We should also add to the formula the mundane observation that Tiberius was presented with this difficulty when his mother was in her seventies, and perhaps less willing to be as flexible and accommodating as when she was a young woman.[25]

Dio has Livia seek a substantial and formal role in the government of the state after Augustus' death. He says that she was not satisfied with the position of ruling as an equal partner *(ex isou archein)* but she sought precedence over Tiberius, and involved herself in government affairs *(pragmata)* as if "sole ruler" *(autarchousa)*. One sign of this, Dio informs us, was that she wrote and received official letters. Correspondence of Tiberius for a time supposedly bore her name as well as his, and communications were addressed to both alike. But we have no corroborating evidence to support Dio's claim, and in fact those examples of letters that have survived, written to the people of Cos and Gytheum, are in Tiberius' name only. We do know of a specific instance in which Tiberius exploited Livia's *amicitia* with Archelaus of Cappadocia (see chapter 5) to persuade her to write on his behalf, but this was the action of a willing servant of the princeps rather than a coregent, and probably involved a separate, independent letter. In any case, as Dio notes, the practice of joint letters lasted for a short time only. It may have involved only a small fraction of the total correspondence.[26]

Dio may well have been influenced by the conduct of Julia Domna in his own day. As a consequence, he could have developed an exaggerated view of Livia's political activism. Moreover, Goodyear suggests that in his depiction of Livia's exercise of power, Dio might well be working back from Agrippina the Younger. Although other sources recognise Livia's influence over her husband, Dio is the only one to give her a de facto share in the actual rule. In his version of the speech that she supposedly gave on behalf of Cinna in AD 4, she herself speaks of how even while Augustus is alive she has a share in ruling *(meros archousa)*. In fact, Dio seems to undercut his own thesis. He insists that Livia tried to exercise this autocratic power, except that she did not enter the Senate chamber, or the camps, or the public assemblies. But these in fact are the very places where power could be exercised. In one telling passage Dio describes measures passed by the Senate in honour of Augustus. He says that in reality they were carried by both Tiberius and Livia. The senators would pass their suggestions in writing to Tiberius, who then chose from them. Remarkably, Dio admits in his explanation that he added the name of Livia simply because of his general thesis that she was involved in public business. Thus he seems to have no formal evidence for his claim, but adds her anyhow, in a circular, though warped, argument. Suetonius sees the situation quite differently. He is very careful not to claim that Livia enjoyed or sought to enjoy an equal share in the rule *(partes aequas potentiae)*, a phrase that is reminiscent of Dio's *ex isou*. He states rather that Tiberius in his anger claimed it to be so, an assertion possibly made in a fit of pique and of little value in assessing Livia's constitutional role. Tacitus emphasises that after the death of Augustus, Livia had excessive influence, calling her a *mater impotens*, but as has been shown, this term did not necessarily connote the formal and legal exercise of power.[27]

Although the claims that Livia sought to share executive power are clearly exaggerated, this does not mean that Augustus did not intend to elevate her to some kind of public role. No matter how intensely scholars may debate the nature of Livia's status after AD 14, the Senate clearly had no doubts. Their response to the new order shows that in their view Livia now occupied a formal, no matter how ill-defined, position in the state. Tacitus reports that she received *multa . . . adulatio* (excessive adulation) from the members. There is nothing remarkable in that.[28] Far more significant, they voted that she should be given the title of *mater patriae* (mother of the nation), or of *parens patriae* (parent of the nation), a tribute by now associated, in its masculine form, exclusively with the person of the princeps.[29] The concept of *pater patriae*, familiar among the titulature of Roman emperors, goes back to the last century of the republic. The earliest extant evidence for the term is in connection with the great military figure Marius, who, Cicero said, should have received the title. The first recipient in the event was Cicero himself, after he had suppressed the famous conspiracy of Catiline, when in addition it was proposed that he should also receive the *corona civica*, the oak-wreath granted to a soldier for saving the life of a comrade in action. Suetonius and Appian record the title among the honours enjoyed by Caesar, on whose coins the legend *parens patriae* appears in 44 BC.[30] Augustus first declined the distinction when a delegation of senators went to his villa at Antium to offer it to him, and did the same afterwards at the theatre in Rome. Finally he yielded to the Senate's insistence, and formally assumed it on February 5, 2 BC. He made it clear that he considered this to be his most important attribute, and in his *Res Gestae* he emphasised that it had been bestowed by the Senate, equestrians, and people as a whole. Seneca sees the title as standing above any other given to a leader, even Augustus, and that it was intended to let the princeps know that he had been entrusted with *patria potestas* over the nation.[31] Augustus' hesitation in accepting explains why, even though the people repeatedly pressed it upon him, Tiberius consistently and characteristically refused the title. It is not found on his official Roman coinage (although it is found on coinage of Carthage and on non-Roman inscriptions). Contemporary writers avoided the expression but would use phrases that suggested it; Valerius Maximus, for instance, twice calls Tiberius *princeps parensque noster*.[32] Caligula declined the appellation of pater patriae when in March 37 the titles and powers of Augustus were assigned to him en bloc, and did not in fact assume it until September 21, 38, as we know from recently discovered Arval records.[33]

Whether a serious distinction was intended between parens patriae and mater patriae in Livia's case is not made clear. Some sort of difference between the two concepts is preserved in the earlier instances. Suetonius records that Caesar received the title pater patriae during his lifetime, but in a different context he notes that on the columns erected in the Forum to honour him after his death, the inscription *parenti patriae* was added.[34] *Parens patriae* did not catch on. As Flory notes, it was never a state title for emperors, as pater patriae was to become after 2 BC. It may be that in AD 14 it was used by the Senate to avoid mater patriae, which might have been taken to rival Augustus' title. Bauman argues the opposite, that *parens* as a common noun would have equated Livia with male rulers, while *mater* would have put her on a somewhat lower level.[35]

Whatever the precise form of the title, it is beyond doubt that the Senate voted for Livia a distinction intended by now only for the princeps himself, perhaps the clearest sign that the senators recognised that some form of public function had been intended by Augustus for his widow. It should not be considered remarkable, nor any evidence of serious dissension between himself and his mother, that Tiberius refused this honour for Livia. He fully understood its implication. Nor did his refusal mean that the title was not attached to her unofficially. The enthusiasm of the senators was echoed throughout the empire. A coin of Leptis Magna calls Livia mater patriae, and an issue of Romula designates her as *genetrix orbis*.[36] That said, until the time of Julia Domna, in the Severan period, no woman was officially recognised as mater patriae, not even the forceful and ambitious Agrippina the Younger.

In AD 14 the Senate did not limit itself to this innovation. Tacitus reports that in their enthusiasm a majority of the members wanted the phrase "son of Julia" to be added to Tiberius' official nomenclature, along with the regular formulaic phrase "son of Augustus." To do so would, again, have raised her in a sense to the status of the princeps himself, or in this case, the late princeps, and would have been an innovation at least as remarkable as the title of Augusta. Dio even seems to suggest that there was a proposal to bounce Augustus' name entirely, and to use the matronymic exclusively. Suetonius carelessly records the phrase as "son of Livia" (instead of "son of Julia"), but nothing should be read into this anachronism, for he is generally inconsistent in his use of Livian nomenclature, and on this issue is otherwise in general accord with Tacitus and Dio. Moreover, Tacitus probably took his material from the senatorial records, or from a source that used the records, for he provides the information in the context of the senatorial debates, while Suetonius sees it as a general element of the tense relations between Tiberius and his mother.[37]

The proposal to call Tiberius *Iuliae filius* is totally alien to Roman practice, and it might seem hard to believe that it was expected that the proposal could be accepted. Dio and Suetonius both report that Tiberius was annoyed by the suggestion, and some scholars have taken the measure to be provocative, a deliberate affront to Tiberius, perhaps intended to needle him. The senators might even have wanted to give him a gentle reminder that he came to power because Augustus had married his mother. Flory sees a possible analogy to 44 BC, when some senators voted for immoderate honours to deride Caesar.[38] But there is no need to see the gesture as a studied insult, and Tacitus certainly does not take it that way, for he places the offer in the context of senatorial *adulatio*. The mood of the Senate in general seems to have annoyed Tiberius by its sycophancy rather than its provocation.[39] The Senate's action doubtless reflected what they interpreted as the wish of Augustus rather than any desire to rile Tiberius. The matronymic, along with the title of Augusta and of mater patriae, would elevate Livia's status to something approximating that of her late husband. Not surprisingly, Tiberius turned down this proposal also.

Tiberius similarly turned his thumbs down on another measure that would have moved Livia's status yet closer to his and Augustus', the suggestion that the month of October be renamed Livius (along with the proposed renaming of September as Tiberius). It is likely that Roman months had originally been arranged by simple numbers and began gradually to acquire the names of gods. The Greeks after the time of Alexander had a tradition of naming months after individuals, who eventually came to include Roman generals. At Mytilene, for instance, it seems that a month was named after Pompey. This practice was eventually adopted in Rome also. The first authenticated case of an eponymous month in Rome belongs to 44 BC, when it was decreed that Quintilis should henceforth be called Iulius because Caesar was born in that month. Later, Sextilis was renamed Augustus, a choice made by the emperor on the grounds that his great achievements and first consulship belonged to it, rather than to September, the month of his birth. As the modern calendar demonstrates, both of these innovations have proved to be permanent. The intent of the motion for Tiberius and Livia was simply to link the two new holders of Augustus' name with their two predecessors. But Tiberius saw it differently, as the elevation of the princeps, and more important, his mother, to a station to which mortals should not aspire. He handled the situation deftly, and with considerable humour—he asked the Senate what they would do when the time came that there were thirteen Caesars.[40]

Tiberius was not adamantly opposed to all the honours directed towards Livia, and was clearly prepared to recognise that her preeminence as the widow of the former princeps and the mother of the incumbent deserved its proper recognition. During his reign, she was included with her son in the yearly vows for the safety of the ruler *(pro salute et incolumitate . . . Iuliae Augustae)* made by the Arval Brethren. This ritual had its origins in the practice of the consuls, who would offer *vota pro salute reipublicae* when entering office on January 1. According to Dio, annual public vows for Caesar's welfare were enacted in 44 BC, and similar vows were decreed for Octavian in 30 BC, and for emperors and their family after that. Although these vows for the imperial family no doubt continued to be made by the consuls, they were also added to the calendars of the priesthoods and are a standard feature of the Arval record.[41] Moreover, in line with a privilege enjoyed by male members of the domus Augusta, Livia's birthday was now officially celebrated in Rome. The earliest extant notice of her inclusion in the annual vows seems to belong to the Arval rites of AD 21, and her birthday celebrations to those of AD 27, but there is no reason to assume that both honours were not accorded in earlier years, where the record is incomplete. Outside Rome, birthday celebrations were registered at the Forum Clodii in AD 18, when honey, wine, and pastries were distributed.[42]

Tiberius, moreover, did not block what proved to be the most concrete manifestation of the willingness of Romans to see Livia in some form of official and public role. This arose from the consecration of Augustus. The Senate had assembled on September 17, AD 14, following the emperor's death, and it was probably on this occasion that the formal accession of Tiberius was confirmed. But the only item of business securely assigned to this date by the fasti was the consecration of his predecessor. Tiberius expressed no public opposition to this measure, and in some respects he must have found it satisfying. Despite his impatience about such honours when offered directly to him, the title of *Divi Filius* (son of a deified one) was an important but indirect means for him to strengthen the legitimacy of his accession. Augustus' worship was now ordained as a state cult, and he was voted the usual accoutrements of a god—that is, a temple and priesthood. The temple was a joint undertaking of Livia and Tiberius, in the sense that they would supply the funds (see chapter 9).

In the organization of the cult of Augustus the pattern of traditional Roman religion provided a model of sorts. Some of the individual Roman deities had personal *flamines*, who numbered fifteen by the late republic. They were not elected or co-opted, as were other priests, but chosen from a slate of candidates by the pontifex maximus. Three were considered senior *(maiores)*, the most important being the Flamen Dialis (Jupiter); the other two had responsibility for Mars and Quirinus. The Flamen Dialis's life was regulated by a number of quaint and cumbersome rules. To compensate for the inconvenience of not being allowed to touch a goat, and similar restrictive taboos, he enjoyed certain privileges, such as the right to a *sella curulis* and the *toga praetexta*, the garb and special chairs of higher magistrates, as well as a seat in the Senate and a lictor.[43]

Germanicus was appointed flamen of Divus Augustus. An immediate precedent was provided by Mark Antony, who was Julius Caesar's first flamen, and, if we are to believe Dio, selected by Caesar himself, in the capacity of pontifex maximus, to be his flamen during his lifetime. In the event, Antony was not inaugurated until after the Peace of Brundisium in October, 40 BC.[44] Germanicus' career does not seem to have been impeded by his appointment. On his death it was laid down that he could be succeeded only by another member of the Julio-Claudian house. It was a rule that proved impossible to maintain, for the office of Flamen Divi Augusti continued for two more centuries.[45]

In addition, a college of priests, the Sodales Augustales, was appointed to serve the cult of Divus Augustus. The most revolutionary innovation, however, was the role assigned to Livia. Before AD 14 we find her involved in activities that are associated with priesthoods, such as making offerings for Tiberius' safe return from Germany. The consecration of Divus Augustus took the process an important stage further, in that Livia was appointed *sacerdos* (priestess). This position was unprecedented. Outside the Vestal order, the major priesthoods at Rome were all held by men. Livia's relationship to the flamen and the sodales is not clear, and her closest model may have been the wife of the Flamen Dialis. This woman held the position of flaminica.[46] Like her husband, the flaminica was bound by a rigid set of prohibitions, aimed mainly at avoiding the exposure of her person to public view, even down to regulations against going up a ladder by too many rungs at a time. The precise rituals in which the flaminica was involved, according to Aulus Gellius, were the same as those of her husband. We hear very little of specific duties, although it is recorded that she, not her husband, sacrificed a ram on the *nundinae* (market days).[47] The parallelism should not be drawn too closely—Livia was certainly not bound by the arcane restrictions that must have bedeviled the life of the flaminica (and her husband).

Livia's appointment is little short of remarkable. It is not clear why, from the narrow point of ritual, her special office was needed, for the flamen and the Sodales Augustales were available to look after the cult of Augustus, and the Arval Brothers to carry out the appropriate sacrifices. It may be that the assignment represented the one concession Tiberius was willing to make in recognizing her right to a public role, choosing the one that would cause conservative Romans the least offence.[48] The appointment of Livia to a priesthood brought with it a concrete manifestation of her new place within the state. As a symbol of her new status, she was allowed a lictor.[49] The lictors were the attendants of magistrates, usually of the rank of freedmen, and their numbers varied according to the status of the official they served (consuls had twelve each in Livia's day). They went ahead of the magistrate when he was on the move, announcing his arrival and clearing bystanders from his path. The privilege was extended to the Vestals in 42 BC by members of the Second Triumvirate, supposedly because one of the Vestals on returning home from dinner was not recognised and was subjected to insulting behaviour. Dio states that Livia was granted a lictor, and in this claim seems to be flatly contradicted by Tacitus, who insists the opposite, that Tiberius refused his mother this privilege. Tacitus' claim may represent another example of his facility for presenting material about Livia that, while not strictly inaccurate, was intended to mislead. Dio makes his statement in the context of Livia's appointment as priestess and notes that she was granted the lictor *en tais hierourgiais* (in the exercise of her sacred offices). We might see a parallel in Agrippina's similarly being granted a pair of lictors strictly in her capacity as priestess of Claudius. Tiberius' injunction seems to have been against the general use of a lictor for other functions, an understandable concern, because the lictor was a symbol of office, and its general use would suggest to Tiberius a further violation of the important line between the state and the domus.[50]

Livia would have viewed her new role as one of great consequence. Ovid refers to her as "wife and priestess" *(coniunx sacerdos)*, while Velleius calls her "priestess and daughter of Augustus" *(sacerdotem ac filiam)*.[51] Her elevation to this novel duty may well be commemorated in a statue now in the Vatican, found in the basilica at Otricoli, apparently near a nude statue of Augustus. The archaeological context places it after Augustus' death, although she continues to sport the traditional nodus hairstyle. Her upturned gaze and outstretched raised hands suggest her priestly role (fig. 24).[52] A statue in the Louvre seems to combine Livia's priesthood of Augustus and her association with Ceres (fig. 22). Her veiled head is crowned with a floral wreath. In her left arm she holds a cornucopia, in her right, wheat and fruit, but much of this is modern restoration. In addition she has a very human attribute — the beaded woollen infula or band hanging from the floral crown inside the veil, generally taken to be an allusion to her role as priestess, for it is worn by women carrying out sacrifices.[53] But the most striking representation of the new Livia is on a sardonyx cameo in Vienna (fig. 19). Livia invokes the figure of Cybele, for she is enthroned, wears a turret crown, and holds a shield embossed with a lion. Thus she is presented as the protectress of the state. The foliage she holds includes wheat as well as poppies, thus suggesting simultaneously a reference to Ceres, goddess of rich abundance. The unique feature of the sardonyx, however, is that she is gazing at a bust of Augustus, whose radiate crown identifies him as a god.[54]

Tiberius must have felt himself beleaguered in dealing with the Senate in AD 14. The ghost of Augustus seemed to hover over the proceedings, and the Senate fell over itself in its zeal to implement what it saw as his posthumous wishes. Tiberius understood Augustus' intentions differently, or at least pretended to, and was determined to resist the dangerous tendencies he saw lurking in the measures the Senate proposed. He took the public position that Livia's role should reflect the status of women as it had been envisaged during the republic. Dio is surely right when he says that the emperor sought to restrict his mother's sphere to the domus. But defining this sphere now became a serious challenge, and at the outset Livia demonstrated that she did not share Tiberius' strictly conservative understanding of her role. The first recorded difference in outlook arose from a relatively innocuous incident, a celebration in honour of Augustus. In the festivities that followed Tiberius' ovatio in 9 BC, Livia and Julia together had invited the women to a banquet. Also on the dedication of the Porticus Liviae in 7 BC, Livia gave a party for women, while Augustus gave one for senators on the Capitol.[55] In AD 14, when Livia dedicated an image to Augustus in her house, she felt herself now entitled to break with tradition and to invite the senators and the equestrians, along with their wives, to mark the occasion. For a woman to host such an event, particularly on her own initiative, would have been a serious breach of protocol. Tiberius was tactful enough not to deny permission outright, but he insisted on observing the established proprieties. Livia was not allowed to proceed with the invitation until the Senate had given its formal approval, and even then she was not permitted to invite the men. Tiberius tactfully undertook to entertain them, and Livia was limited to carrying out the same function for the women.[56] The first potential crisis had passed over smoothly. Things would only get worse.

Tiberius' determined views on the proper role for women in general, and the proper constitutional role for Livia in particular, should not be taken, as they often are by the ancient sources, as a sign of personal animosity towards his mother. While reluctant to grant her a place in the governance of the state, he did not begrudge her the recognition her status demanded, as is demonstrated by the widespread homage to Livia recorded throughout the empire. In fact, on some occasions Tiberius actually shared that homage. Coins from eastern mints depict facing heads of Livia and Tiberius. At Smyrna a dedication to both of them has survived, with Livia specified as Tiberius' mother. At Tralles mother and son shared a priest.[57] Livia's divine status is widely attested in numerous inscriptions and coins in all quarters of the empire, and this process did not abate with the accession of Tiberius; in fact, it seems to have increased. The striking colossal statues of Livia, for instance, most familiar from examples at Leptis Magna, all belong to the period after Tiberius' accession.[58] Although this provincial veneration was certainly not orchestrated from Rome, it doubtless reflected what was locally perceived as the wish of the emperor. The persistence of such expressions of regard for Livia demonstrates that Tiberius made no consistent effort to try to suppress them. On the one occasion when we have evidence of his involvement in the resolutions, his response to the Gytheans to accord divine honours to the imperial family, he expressly allows Livia to make her own decision (see chapter 10). Tiberius did once decline to allow the worship of his mother, but that refusal must be seen in its context. In AD 25 a deputation came from Baetica in Spain to Rome. Citing the precedent of the Temple to Tiberius, Livia, and the Senate that had been given imperial sanction in Asia (see chapter 10), they sought permission to erect a shrine in honour of Tiberius and his mother. Tiberius refused the request, fully aware that he would appear inconsistent. As often happened when he was in a difficult corner, he was careful to spell out the precedent created by Augustus. His predecessor had allowed the city of Pergamum to build a temple to himself and to Rome, and Tiberius had consequently felt impelled to follow his example in Asia, especially in that the worship of his own person was to be linked with the worship of the Senate. But, as he argued, to yield that once was acceptable. If the process were to be repeated throughout the Roman world, the honour would become vulgar. In fact, he followed the pattern he had set down in Tarraconensis and Lusitania, which restricted divine honours to the consecrated members of the imperial house. Clearly, Tiberius' refusal on this occasion should be seen in the context of his general aversion to divine honours, especially when offered at the provincial rather than a merely local level; it should not be viewed as a deliberate attempt to deprive his mother of further distinction.[59]

The sheer number of the distinctions, divine and otherwise, that Tiberius allowed to be heaped on Livia in all quarters of the empire is clear evidence that he did not resent his mother's eminent stature. These distinctions were even extended to her family, for it is under Tiberius that we find honorific statues to her parents in such widely separated locations as Baetica in Spain, Marruvium in Italy, and Samos in the Aegean. Tacitus' claim that Tiberius behaved towards her as he did because he was consumed by envy *(anxius invidia)* is thus difficult to sustain.[60] But as fair-minded as Tiberius tried to be, the uncertainty about how to handle his mother's position in Rome constantly bedeviled him. In AD 16 an issue arose that illustrates perfectly how ambiguous her position was in her son's eyes. Dio reports under that year that Livia, as well as Tiberius, gave assistance to the victims of various fires. Her action would have been totally in keeping with her well-established tradition of a public display, whether genuinely heartfelt or not, of behaving generously to the unfortunate. But Livia's help came not only after the fire but during it. Suetonius reports that Tiberius took his mother to task for meddling in affairs unsuitable for a woman and was especially annoyed that she had played a role in a fire near the temple of Vesta, urging and encouraging people, as she had done when Augustus was alive. The allusion to Augustus' reign suggests that she might have been involved in helping to suppress the famous fire that broke out in the Basilica Aemiliana in 14 BC, when the flames threatened the temple of Vesta and the sacred relics were carried up to the Palatine to safety.[61] Certainly, during Augustus' life Livia had been involved in giving aid during fires herself, doubtless as a recognised duty, just as Agrippina the Younger later joined her husband Claudius in similar situations. Tiberius' annoyance seems at first sight uncharacteristically irrational. Her conduct could not reasonably be seen as a serious attempt to usurp his position, and she may well have found it offensive to be reprimanded for rendering such a worthy service. At the same time, Tiberius' sensitivity over the issue can be appreciated. In Rome the fire service was essentially a military operation, provided by the seven *cohortes vigilum*. After a serious conflagration in AD 6 Augustus created this unit of seven thousand vigiles, all freedmen, organised in seven cohorts, each commanded by a tribune, under the general command of a praefectus vigilum of equestrian rank appointed by the emperor. They could be asked from time to time to perform military duties, as in the arrest of Sejanus, when it would have been dangerous or impolitic to use the praetorians. There was also a serious potential for abuse. Tiberius would not have forgotten the conspiracy of Egnatius Rufus, who organised a private fire brigade in Rome and had the units at his disposal when he made his private bid for power around 20 BC. This sensitivity would be compounded by Tiberius' particular aversion to the idea of women being involved in military matters, as shown by his fury over Agrippina the Elder's defence of the bridge over the Rhine in AD 15.[62]

To illustrate the basic validity of his claim that Livia enjoyed an exalted status far above women of former days, Dio cites a custom that doubtless did cause Tiberius much unease, in that it gave her a formal, institutionalised role: the "salutation." Augustus was much given to these morning receptions, when people could come to the palace to greet him. His events were open affairs, which included ordinary citizens, and he was very affable when dealing with the requests of the participants. Hence his famous quip when a star-struck petitioner approached him nervously, that it was as if he was "giving a penny to an elephant." In addition to the "popular" salutations, regular appearance at a senatorial *salutatio* was expected of all members of the Senate. From 12 BC Augustus had dispensed with that ceremony on days when the Senate met, so that sessions should not be delayed, and in extreme old age he asked that the senatorial ritual be dropped altogether. Livia assumed the tradition of the salutatio, even reviving the senatorial gatherings, although in fairness it must be said that Augustus had not curtailed their visits out of deference but rather because he was too frail to take part. Livia's receptions, as Dio notes, were even entered in the public record, the *acta publica*. This contained items of public importance but also many items for which the border between private and public was not a sharp one, such as the birth of Livia's son Drusus.

It might have been argued by her defenders that Livia's willingness to engage in the salutations represented a selfless act of duty on her part rather than ambitious self-promotion. All the same, the activity was one that would have caused a Roman with traditional male views some concern. It is surely not coincidental that at the very time Agrippina received the title of Augusta, she also received the distinction of participating in the daily salutatio, so that when courtiers and clients paid their daily homage to the emperor, they would henceforth do the same to her. When Nero wanted to clip his mother's wings in 55, he made her move out of the palace into a private house once owned by Antonia, to prevent her from holding large salutations. Julia Domna, who under the Severans revived the notion that women could aspire to positions of power and influence, similarly made a point of receiving the Senate after she had been widowed.[63]

During Augustus' reign Livia had been a model of self-effacement. Now that the regime had changed, she did not take very long to make clear her conviction that as the Augusta she had certain quasi-legal entitlements. In AD 16 Lucius Calpurnius Piso, who later defended his brother Gnaeus in the famous trial in AD 20, managed to create a considerable stir. He was angered by the corruption of the judicial process and by the ruthlessness of the prosecutors. In disgust he finally announced that he would leave Rome forever and live out his days in some quiet backwater. Tiberius made every effort to dissuade him from leaving, and even called in members of the imperial family to help in the task. Piso was won over, and with a new sense of confidence proceeded to demonstrate his independence by summoning Plautia Urgulania to court to recover a sum of money. It was a bold act, because, as Tacitus puts it, he recognised that the friendship *(amicitia)* of Livia had raised Plautia above the law *(supra leges)*. Plautia may have enjoyed an additional degree of security if she was a Vestal Virgin—Tacitus' text seems to imply that she was, although his words are ambiguous. In any event, she refused Piso's summons and went to take refuge in the palace, where Livia championed her cause, even though Vestals were not exempt from giving testimony in court. Piso was not perturbed by Livia's *potentia*—he pursued Plautia there, and was prepared to remove her from the imperial quarters. Tiberius offered a compromise, calculating that it would not be a serious abuse of his power to promise to appear on Plautia's behalf in order to break the deadlock. He procrastinated on the way to court, telling his bodyguard to keep its distance while he broke off his journey to speak to the public. Tacitus implies that the delay was deliberate. Piso grew more and more impatient and increasingly insistent that Plautia turn up. But the tactic proved effective. Before Tiberius had arrived at the court, Livia paid the fine. Both Tiberius and Piso gained credit from the incident.[64]

The passage raises some interesting points. The notion that the amicitia of Livia had raised Urgulania above the law emerges as an issue, although it is not clear whether this was the belief of Piso or Tacitus' own gloss on events. *Amicitia* means more than just friendship—it implies reciprocal obligations. It is a very Roman concept, used in the political sphere of states or individuals who exploited their nexus of connections to advance their mutual interests. It is a word that helps to elevate Livia to the level of powerful men in the state. But if Livia felt that she had the right to protect friends from prosecution, then she would have put herself on a par with the emperor. Moreover, Tacitus states that the incident led Livia to complain that she personally *(se)*, not Urgulania the Vestal, was violated and humiliated *(violari et imminui)*. The wording here is striking, associated as it is with the language of offences against maiestas, which had been extended to cover members of the imperial family beyond the emperor.[65] This passage allows us considerable insight into Livia's own sense of her status. Her maiestas had not been violated by physical or verbal abuse. She had suffered only from Piso's determination to take her friend out of her house to court. No longer the self-effacing Livia of the previous reign, she let her indignation be known. The passage also shows that at this stage Tiberius was caught in the dilemma that Augustus had bequeathed him, and that he made every effort in the early part of his reign to resolve such issues in a diplomatic and nonconfrontational manner. He was therefore prepared to compromise and to indulge his mother up to a point. He took a considerable risk in doing so. There was nothing untoward in a man appearing for a client in a court case, nor for the head of a house to appear for a family member's client. But if the trial had gone ahead, the emperor's presence would have been interpreted as a clear signal to find on behalf of his mother's friend.

Urgulania did not learn to yield. She was later summoned as a witness in a case being tried before the Senate. She refused to appear, and a praetor was sent to her home to take her testimony. She might, however, have taken some comfort in the fate of her bête noire, Lucius Piso. He did not prosper. He faced prosecution for violation of maiestas in AD 24, possibly an act of revenge against the relatives and supporters of his late brother Gnaeus Calpurnius Piso, following his notorious trial. Before his case came up, Lucius died, either of natural causes or from suicide (*mors opportuna*, as Tacitus describes it).

The issue of Livia's maiestas arose again in the following year, AD 17. Appuleia Varilla, niece of Augustus' sister Octavia, was foolish enough to voice some outrageous indiscretions to companions who were equally indiscreet. She was found out and accused of insulting the Divus Augustus, as well as Tiberius and Livia, to which was added a charge of adultery, perhaps for security in view of the uncertainty of the law covering maiestas. In the event only the charge of adultery was proceeded with, under Augustus' Lex Julia de Adulteriis. On the other issues Tiberius instructed the senators that if she had made insulting comments against Augustus, which would have been tantamount to sacrilege, she should be punished. But he wanted no inquiry into comments made about himself. Tiberius was then asked about the attacks on his mother. After some thought he responded that no one should be made legally accountable for words uttered against Livia. He gave this as his own opinion, but represented it as her view also. This accords with Suetonius' comment that at the beginning of his reign Tiberius was an advocate of freedom of speech and thought, and prepared to tolerate verbal abuse of himself and his family. Bauman suggests the possibility that there was a formal cessation in maiestas proceedings at this point. If so, it was short-lived. The case was not carried forward, but the groundwork had clearly been laid for a legal response to insults against the emperor and against his family, and in time Tiberius proved unable to live up to his early high ideals. Dio notes that when eventually Tiberius pushed maiestas cases for slanderous attacks to the bitter end, these included attacks not only on Augustus but also on himself and his mother.[66]

The handling of the case of Appuleia is difficult to reconcile with the claim made by Tacitus that two years earlier, in AD 15, Tiberius was prepared to see a proceeding for verbal abuse go forward under the Lex Maiestas, because he had been irritated that verses were circulating taking him to task for his *saevitia* and *superbia* (cruelty and haughtiness) and claiming a rift between him and his mother *(discordem cum matre animum)*. The allusion is surprising, and seems to be contradicted by the verdict reached in the later case. Syme suggests that Tacitus has presented his information in the wrong order, and that such verses could not have not appeared so early in the reign. But the discord ridiculed in the lampoons need be based on little more than the charges made in the literary sources and attributed by those sources to the beginning of the reign, that Tiberius had refused certain honours for Livia out of personal antipathy. Also, Tacitus seems to have chosen his words carefully. The basis for Tiberius' reply when questioned by the praetor, that there was no reason that actions involving maiestas should not be proceeded with, was that the law should be followed. There is nothing in his response to indicate whether such actions involved attacks on himself or on the late Augustus. Tacitus adds, almost as an afterthought, that Tiberius had been annoyed by the satirical lampoons. But the association of that specific instance of annoyance with his position on the maiestas cases may well be Tacitus' own gloss.[67]

The discovery of new epigraphic material relating to the trial of Gnaeus Cornelius Piso in AD 20, following the death of Germanicus, has thrown important fresh light on many aspects of this period, including the unique status enjoyed by Livia. It appears from the *Piso Decree* that the Senate passed a separate *senatus consultum* in the case of Plancina, who faced *pluruma et gravissima crimina* (many very serious charges). These are not spelled out, probably intentionally, because, as Eck notes, the contrast between the punishment and the crime would have been made too self-evident.[68] Despite the discreet silence on this specific issue in the *Decree*, it is possible to reconstruct with some confidence the broad charges from Tacitus' narrative. In two instances it can be assumed that the indictments would have echoed those levelled against her husband. The *Decree* specifically notes that Germanicus testified against Piso (line 28). Tacitus provides the further detail that on his deathbed Germanicus in fact accused both Piso and Plancina of working against him. The *Decree* records also that Piso rejoiced at Germanicus' death (lines 62–80), and among other manifestations of this conduct it cites his sacrifices and visits to temples. Tacitus mentions these also, but he adds that Plancina's joy was even more shocking and demonstrated by the fact that she gave up the mourning garb that she had been wearing for her dead sister (we do not know, of course, how long previously her sister had died). This last was perhaps the weakest plank in the prosecution's case. Speaking at the opening of the trial, Tiberius made it clear that even if the alleged celebration had taken place, it would be morally reprehensible, but not criminal.[69] Much more serious charges were to follow. Plancina committed the cardinal sin of a woman meddling in military matters, and taking part in the army manoeuvres and suborning the soldiers' loyalty.[70] She received gifts from Vonones, the claimant to the Parthian throne and short-lived ruler of Armenia, at the time in question under Roman surveillance in Syria. Tacitus, perhaps reflecting the general view, claims that the gifts she accepted influenced Piso to support Vonones' cause.[71] The most serious, and probably irrefutable, charge was that Plancina had made her slaves available to Piso, to be joined up with his motley units of deserters and mercenaries in the ill-conceived effort to regain Syria by military force.[72] At any rate, whatever the precise indictments against her, the public seems to have been fully aware of them. In 33, with Livia dead for four years, Plancina died at her own hand after the very same charges had apparently been revived, charges which, according to Tacitus, were widely known *(haud ignotis)*.[73]

Plancina placed herself at the mercy of the emperor and the Senate. Her protection would ultimately rest upon Livia, but Livia could not address the Senate herself. That depressing duty fell upon Tiberius. The decree states that Tiberius spoke *saepe* and *accurate* (wisely and pointedly; line 111) in putting her case. Tiberius seems not to have addressed the legal question of the strength of the charges but to have made a special intercession on Plancina's behalf. The *Decree* uses the technical term *deprecari*, the same word used by Tacitus to describe Tiberius' intercession on behalf of Appuleia Varilla when he asked the Senate not to proceed against her on a maiestas charge in AD 17.[74] Tacitus describes Tiberius' speech as a shameful disgrace *(cum pudore et flagitio)*, in which he used his mother's request *(preces)* as his cover. In his account of Plancina's death thirteen years later, Tacitus levels the same charge, and in fact uses the same word, *preces*. Tacitus' version of events receives a strong endorsement from the *Piso Decree*, which explains (line 114) that Tiberius had received *iustissimas causas* (very just reasons) from Livia why she should have her way in this matter. Naturally enough, the decree does not echo Tacitus' thesis that Livia was asking the favour for Plancina for services against Agrippina.[75]

Even the language of the decree is striking and surprising. When Tiberius sought to intercede for Plancina, in accordance with his mother's wishes, the Senate declared its obligation to accede to the request of Livia, for *optume de r(e) p(ublica) merita* (having served the state excellently). The concept of *meritum* had been associated with women before this. Pliny illustrates its use from unspecified "Annals" that recorded the gratitude of the state for the Vestal Virgin, Gaia or Fufetia, who donated the Campus Martius to the Romans. But the actual formula used in the *Piso Decree* was one conventionally applied to men, and to men who had held office. Caesar uses the phrase *bene de republica meritum* of himself to describe the sterling qualities that convinced the decurions of a town that he should be allowed to enter. Cicero in a letter to Munatius Plancus at the end of 44 BC wrote that *de republica bene mereri* was the highest ideal his friend could aspire to (Plancus was to disappoint Cicero by throwing in his lot with Mark Antony).[76] The application of such a phrase to Livia in AD 20 was to accord recognition of signal public service to the state.

The decree notes that the Senate determined that they should acquiesce in Tiberius' requests for clemency on the basis that they were Livia's requests, which they were bound to honour. Livia was entitled to such respect, on two grounds (lines 115–19). The first argument was that she had benefitted the world. She had done so in her capacity as the mother of Tiberius, a sentiment expressed also in less formal documents. The *Consolatio* refers to her as "one woman who has given so many benefits through her two offspring" *(tot bona per partus quae dedit una duos)*.[77] Moreover, she had bestowed favours upon men of every rank. This is a familiar theme in all the literary sources, but it is striking to find it given a formal status in the decree. But even more remarkable is the pronouncement that Livia's wishes should be granted because she was entitled to a supreme influence *(plurumum posse)* in any request that she might put to the Senate, by right and deservedly *(iure et merito)*, even if in practice she chose to exercise that right sparingly. The phrase *iure et merito* does not have the strict juridical force it might seem at first sight to possess, and is in fact commonly used in Latin in a figurative sense, just as "rightfully" is used in English. It is found as early as Plautus, where one of his characters is said to find fault with himself *iure optimo merito*, and Juvenal in an obscure passage applies the phrase to people who, when they criticise moral humbugs, do so *iure ac merito*. Even in the political sphere the expression has a moral rather than a legal force, as when Cicero observes that the praetors, because of their loyal support in the Catiline crisis, deserve to be praised *merito ac iure*.[78] All the same, the expression is remarkable in a formal decree, and gives Livia an authority which would never have been given public and official sanction while Augustus was alive.

Conflict between Tiberius and his mother over her right to intervene in public issues plagued the two of them until Tiberius' departure for Capri. There were occasions when he had to admit essentially that he was beaten, that he could not prevent his mother's involvement in issues of governance. In these cases he could do little more than acquiesce, while disassociating himself as far as possible from what had transpired. Suetonius describes an incident, which he dates very vaguely to the period just before the departure for Capri, that nicely captures Tiberius' frustration. For much of the republican period judges were taken from the senatorial order, and traditionally their names, along with those of priests and other officials, had been made public by being posted in black letters on a white board, the *album*. The exclusive hold of the senatorials was broken by Gaius Gracchus when he selected the judges for his extortion court from the equestrian order. The issue became something of a political battleground in 70 BC when the Lex Aurelia established a balanced system by which the panels *(decuriae)* were made up of distinct socioeconomic divisions, the first consisting of senators, the second of equestrians, and the third taken from the *tribuni aerarii*, whose precise status is not clear. Modifications were introduced, and by the time of Tiberius' reign there were four panels, serving in both civil and criminal cases. In the early empire the decuriae consisted of about a thousand members each, all Roman citizens. Equestrians seem to have predominated, for with reference to the twenties AD both Tacitus and Suetonius allude loosely to the *decuriae equitum* (panels of equites). Membership was eagerly sought, and was limited initially under Augustus to citizens from Rome or Italy. By the end of the Julio-Claudian period the panels were opened up to provincials, but a strict rule was still maintained that a newly enfranchised citizen could not be appointed immediately (the qualifying period is not made clear).[79]

Suetonius records that Livia placed Tiberius in a difficult position when she sponsored the request of an unnamed individual to be empanelled, even though he had only recently acquired Roman citizenship. Livia was insistent, and Tiberius found himself on the horns of a dilemma, torn by the petition of the Augusta and by the time-honoured rule against accelerated elevation. His patience at trying to reach a diplomatic compromise seems by this stage to have been exhausted. With ill grace he allowed the appointment to go ahead but insisted that when it was gazetted, an entry should be added that he had acted under pressure from his mother. In the event, Livia was not assuaged and found it impossible to retain the poise and *comitas* of her more youthful days. The incident produced the one specific serious clash between Tiberius and his mother that is recorded in the sources. Suetonius claims that on hearing what had happened, Livia flew into a rage *(commota)*. She proceeded to a shrine where letters written to her by Augustus had been deposited. In Tiberius' presence she read out some of them, dredging up her late husband's views on Tiberius' sour nature and his intolerance. Tiberius was put out less by the opinions expressed by Augustus (he can hardly have been unaware of them) than by the fact that his mother had held on to the letters and used them so vindictively.[80]

At some point after the end of April, AD 22, Tiberius had hastened back to Rome on news of his mother's illness. Tacitus reports that at that time their relations were harmonious *(sincera adhuc inter matrem filiumque concordia)*, or that they were hypocritically keeping their mutual hatred well concealed *(sive occultis odiis)*. Bad feelings had supposedly arisen over an incident that occurred just before the illness. Tacitus explains that in AD 22, at some point before Tiberius' return, Livia, in dedicating an effigy *(effigies)* to Augustus at the Theatre of Marcellus, had put her son's name after her own in the inscription.[81] It was believed *(credebatur)* that Tiberius had felt that his dignity as princeps had been offended, although he had kept the insult to himself.[82] The essentials of this anecdote, in particular the order of the names, are confirmed by a notation in the *Fasti Praenestini* that on April 23 *sig(num) divo Augusto patri ad theatrum Marc(elli) Iulia Augusta et Ti. Augustus dedicaverunt* (Julia Augusta and Tiberius Augustus dedicated a statue to [their] father, the deified Augustus, by the Theatre of Marcellus).[83] Some also see an allusion to the statue in a contemporary coin, a sestertius minted in Tiberius' twenty-fourth tribunician year, in AD 22 or 23. On the reverse, Augustus, identified by the legend *Divus Augustus Pater*, wears a radiate crown and toga and sits on a throne, facing left, with his feet on a stool. He holds a branch in his right hand and a long sceptre in his left. In front of him, on the left, is an altar.[84]

The statue was dedicated in the names of both Livia and Tiberius, but because the emperor was absent from Rome, it is to be assumed that arrangements for the commemorative inscription were left to Livia. The entry in the fasti is almost certainly based on the dedication stone that she commissioned. It confirms the order of the names. That same sequence may be reflected in Dio's reference to Livia and Tiberius "making" a temple to Augustus in AD 14; Dio puts the names in that order. Dio's order may reflect the temple's dedicatory inscription, now lost, which could well have been the ultimate source for his entry. If so, it may have little significance for the Livia-Tiberius relationship, because the temple was finally completed only under Caligula in AD 37, and the word order could have reflected that emperor's choice rather than Livia's. The painted images recorded in the Gytheum decree are listed as those of Augustus, Livia, and then Tiberius, in that order, suggesting that the Gytheans gave Livia the place of honour after Augustus (see chapter 10).[85] If Tiberius was in fact offended in AD 22, his indignation was unwarranted. Livia was priestess of Augustus, and this office would justify her precedence. In any case, the most striking feature of the fasti inscription is the reference to *patri* after Augustus' name. The participation of Livia in a dedication to someone identified as a father may seem incongruous, but could in fact be a recognition of her adoption by her husband. Livia may have felt that on this occasion she had gone out of her way to observe strict protocol. For his part Tiberius clearly saw her action as an arrogation of rights properly his. Eight years after the death of Augustus and the opening of his will, the problem that he created had still not resolved itself.

With Tiberius' departure for Capri in AD 26 the stress over the constitutional issue abated. Livia was now in her eighties, and for the last three years of her life she almost disappears from the historical narrative, eclipsed by Sejanus and his efforts to exercise a de facto control over the affairs of state in Rome during the emperor's absence. Yet in the minds of the Romans she still enjoyed a status not normally associated with women. This was demonstrated after her death, when the Senate passed an extraordinary measure for an arch in her honour, in recognition of her acts of kindness and generosity. This vote was indeed an extraordinary gesture. As Dio notes, this was the first time that such a distinction had been bestowed on a woman, and indeed there is no known example of the Senate's ever again voting for an arch for a woman. The first to be set up to an individual man seems to be the one erected on the Via Sacra in 120 BC to Quintus Fabius Maximus for his victory over the Allobroges. The first recorded use of public funds voted for such a purpose was for the arch granted to Drusus on the Appian Way in 9 BC, as a posthumous honour. A grieving Senate voted for three arches for Germanicus after his death, and similarly, when Drusus Caesar, the son of Tiberius, died in AD 23, the Senate seems to have erected a memorial arch in his honour. Thus even in the case of men the grant of a posthumous arch financed from public funds in Rome was far from common. Livia's arch was never built, skilfully sidelined by Tiberius. But it did provide a final and dramatic opportunity for the senators to demonstrate that they had remained faithful to Augustus' intentions, when fifteen years earlier he had elevated her to the unprecedented position of the Augusta.[86]

9
WOMAN OF SUBSTANCE

Despite Livia's public image as a woman who lived soberly and unpretentiously, the evidence indicates that by the time of her death she had become one of the most wealthy women in Rome. The terms of her will, if correctly reported, seem to leave no doubt on this issue. In it she left a legacy of fifty million sesterces to her favourite, Galba.[1] Romans were restricted in the proportion of their estate that they could leave in individual legacies. The Lex Falcidia stipulated that at least one quarter of the whole inheritance had to be reserved for the heir(s) of the estate. This would mean that Livia's estate must have been worth at least sixty-eight million. But in fact Suetonius notes that Galba was only one of the legatees to receive bequests, albeit the most handsomely rewarded. The total value must have been considerably larger, though how much larger is a matter of speculation. Tiberius reduced Galba's bequest to 500,000, using the argument that the sum had not been written out and the numerical symbol was erroneous (see chapter 11). But it is significant that Tiberius did not argue that the amount violated the terms of the Lex Falcidia.[2]

It is unlikely that Livia could have owned much of this wealth before her marriage. She was the daughter of a proscribed Roman, and the wife of someone who had fled into exile. When she returned to Rome in 39 BC, she probably possessed very little, beyond perhaps a family estate near Veii (see chapter 3). This situation would have been transformed by her second marriage. She could not have benefitted by direct contributions from Augustus during his lifetime – Roman law prohibited gifts between husbands and wives. On his death, however, the financial benefits of her marriage were substantial indeed. Augustus in his will named Tiberius and Livia as his heirs. They were to receive 150 million sesterces, a third of which, 50 million, would go to Livia. The heirs were given a year's grace to pay out the bequests. This must mean that the cash in hand, which would obviously not represent the full value of the estate, was not sufficient to meet the demands of the legacies. These were made up of the gross amount of about 90 million to be paid to the army and the people, and a number of individual bequests whose amounts are not known.[3] In order for Livia to inherit her 50 million sesterces from her husband, special provisions had to be made for her, and Augustus in his will asked the Senate to allow him to leave her a sum that, strictly speaking, was prohibited by law. The capacity of women to inherit was restricted by two groups of legislation, the Lex Voconia of 169 BC and the Lex Iulia of 18 BC (amended by the Lex Papia Poppaea of AD 9). The latter restricted the right of women with fewer than three children to benefit from inheritances. The *ius trium liberorum* that Livia acquired on the death of her son Drusus in 9 BC protected her against this disability. But the Lex Voconia could have remained a problem. This law had been introduced in 169 at the behest of Cato the Censor. Its details are unclear, but it did contain a provision that a person whose property was valued in the census at 100,000 asses could not name a woman as heir, and it was presumably from this clause that Livia was given exemption.[4]

While Augustus was still alive, the indirect benefits of the marriage would have been enormous. Livia's position would have enabled her to create an extensive network of *amici*, and much of her wealth would have come in return for the favours she had shown to families. She would be rewarded by gifts, by legacies, and by being named heir. By tradition the Roman will was seen as a device for indicating friendship and esteem, and it was assumed that clients would bequeath their patrons a legacy. The potential benefits of this tradition are illustrated by the case of Augustus himself, who recorded in his will that he had received legacies worth 1.4 billion sesterces (and had spent them).[5] Augustus' prestige would have increased Livia's clientele and the potential for similar bequests for her. In this she benefitted from a special provision enacted sometime before AD 9 to allow certain women, doubtless including Livia, to inherit property worth more than 100,000 sesterces.[6] Unfortunately, we have no direct evidence for any legacies received by Livia in Rome. She owned a number of slaves who can be traced to distinguished Romans, but there is no way of telling whether they were inherited directly from the original owners. As an example, the name of one her freedmen, Timotheus Maronianus, indicates that he, like other slaves or former slaves similarly named, had once been owned by the poet Vergil (Publius Vergilius Maro). But Timotheus is recorded as the freedman of Livia as Julia Augusta, thus after Augustus' death, and had probably been bequeathed first to Augustus, who passed him on to Livia in his will.[7]

What direct evidence we have of Livia's legacies comes from outside Rome, especially Judaea. We know that she shared the five hundred talents that Herod the Great left Livia, his friends, and freedmen in his will. (Augustus received a thousand talents, but supposedly gave back most of it to Herod's sons.) As we shall see, some years later Herod's sister Salome on her death left Livia the major part of her estate. Both legacies could have included slaves. Tiberius at any rate later inherited from his mother a slave who had belonged to Herod or Salome.[8]

When Amyntas, king of Galatia, died in 25 BC, his kingdom was incorporated into the empire and Augustus received much of his personal property. Some of Amyntas' slaves may have been bequeathed to members of the imperial family. One has the name Marcus Livius Aug(ustae?) l(ibertus) Anteros Amyntianus—he possibly became a freedman of Livia's, while an Epinicius Caesar(is) ser(vus) Amyntianus became a slave of Augustus'. One must, however, be cautious in extracting information from the pattern of servile names. There are other inscriptions at Rome that mention individuals with the cognomen Amyntianus (or Amyntiana) without indication of any connection with the imperial family.[9]

Livia had lived a generally rootless existence with her first husband, passing from pillar to post as a wandering exile. When she returned to Rome and met Octavian, this wandering lifestyle changed. She moved into an established residence, and a very well-appointed one. Octavian had come to Rome in late summer 44 BC to claim his political inheritance after the death of Caesar. His first home, near the Forum Romanum, had belonged to the orator Gaius Licinius Calvus, probably best known through his friendship with the poet Catullus.[10] Calvus' property, though probably not humble, did not live up to Octavian's aspirations. In the late republic the choice residential district for the status-conscious was without question the Palatine hill. Octavian moved there and offered Livia a home in an area where she was to stay for the remainder of her long life. The Palatine, rising some forty metres to the south of the Forum Romanum, was closely associated with Rome's early history, especially in the southwest corner, where Livia resided. By tradition it contained Rome's oldest settlement, and in Vergil's *Aeneid* it was a place of veneration even before the founding of the city. The earliest private residence recorded there is that of Vitruvius Vaccus, which was destroyed in 330 BC. By the late republic Palatine residents could at one time or another rub shoulders with Cicero, the demagogue Clodius, and almost certainly Mark Antony. Octavian was born in the district, and Livia's first husband owned a Palatine residence, where she was certainly living in 42 BC, when her first son, Tiberius, was born there.[11]

We cannot be certain when Octavian obtained his Palatine address. We know from Suetonius that at some point he acquired (by what means remains unknown) the house of the celebrated orator Quintus Hortensius. This might have happened after his return from the battle of Philippi, in 42 BC, during a period of widespread proscriptions. It would have been into this fine residence that Livia moved (see appendix 15). In 36 BC their house was hit by a thunderbolt, and the priests declared this a divine sign that the god desired the site. Accordingly Octavian made that part of the house public property. He consecrated it to Apollo, whom he had adopted as his patron god as a consequence of his naval victory at Naulochus, and promised to build a temple with a portico, which he did in splendid style. This generous act was reciprocated. In return the public granted him another house at public expense.[12]

It was now politically opportune for Octavian to project an image of simple living. Suetonius describes his house as very modest, both in its size and in its decoration, with small colonnades of peperino (hard grey volcanic stone) and rooms without marble decorations or pavements. The same bedroom was used by Augustus in summer and winter, according to Suetonius, for more than forty years.[13] There is general agreement that the house is represented by remains on the south brow of the hill, south of the Domus Tiberiana, between the Scalae Caci and the Temple of Magna Mater on the west, and what is clearly identified as the Temple of Apollo to the east (plan 1). Livia spent the more than half-century of her marriage in the complex of public and private buildings that had this house at its core.

It was possible for a husband to bequeath to his widow the use of a house or part of a house until her own death, when it would revert to his heir.[14] It is likely then that on Augustus' death in AD 14, Livia moved from the main part of the imperial residence to her own quarters. The so-called Casa di Livia was discovered by Rosa in 1869 in the part of the Palatine behind the Domus Tiberiana, between the Temple of Magna Mater and the House of Augustus (plan 2). The Casa has a complicated history of construction and was decorated by an important series of paintings that are at a stage of development similar to those of the House of Augustus (Pompeian Second Style), and can be dated to about 25–20 BC. When the Roman authorities undertook conservation of the paintings, it was discovered that behind them there were

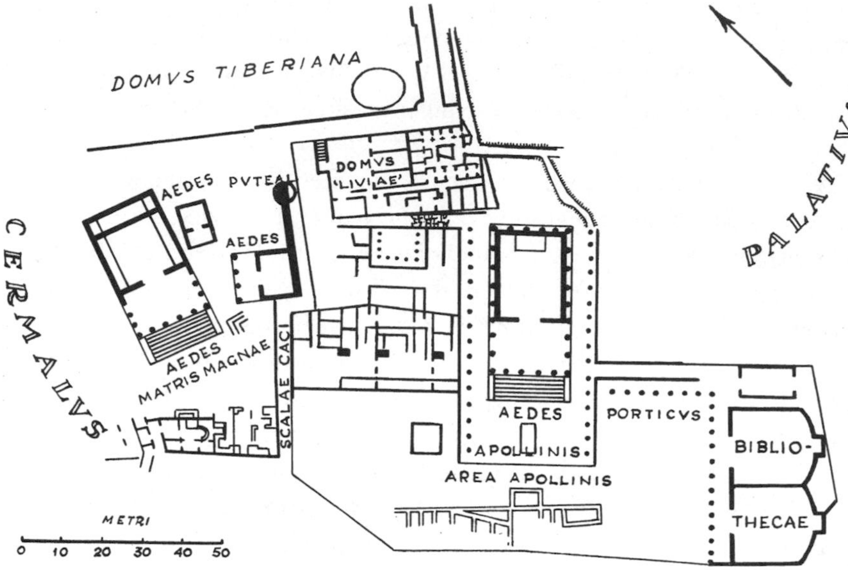

Plan 1. Augustus' Palatine residence. After Lugli, 1938 (Domus Liviae = Casa di Livia)

irregular reticulate-faced walls (a facing of bricks made up of a network of small blocks in diagonal lines), with doorways that had been blocked with masonry before the plaster was put down. Hence the building is earlier than the paintings and could have been erected in the mid-first century. The attribution to Livia is based on a lead pipe found in the excavations bearing the name of Iulia Augusta. This is strong evidence of her ownership, but not definitive proof.[15]

The house has a large lobby (atrium) onto which three halls open. The central larger hall has been called a *tablinum*, and the rooms at the side are designated as *alae* (wings), identified as right and left from the perspective of facing southeast. A room at the west corner has been called the *triclinium*. None of these labels is strictly valid, but because they have become established in the literature, they are retained for convenience. Beyond the tablinum was a yard flanked by a portico supported on heavy pillars. (The yard was later replaced by a number of small service rooms.) The main rooms of the house were underground. There is no evidence of windows, and there was perhaps a source of light through the ceiling. These lower rooms were reached by a stair and a ramp with a vaulted roof. Inside the atrium a stair led to a narrow corridor, along the southwest side of which was a series of small rooms.

There are traces of fine mosaic pavement throughout the house. The tri-

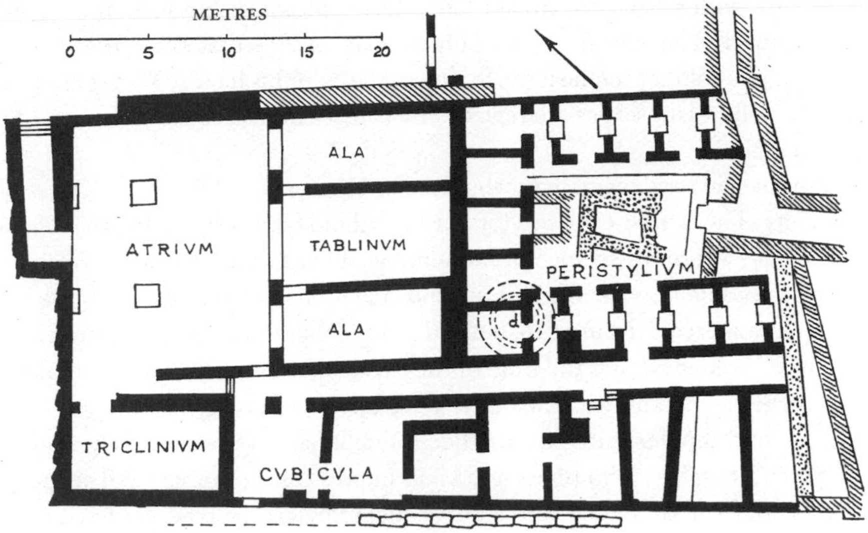

Plan 2. The "Casa di Livia." After Lugli, 1938

clinium was paved with white mosaic interspersed with irregular shapes of coloured marble and alabaster. More important are the paintings, conserved in the 1950s. It has been suggested that they and the stuccowork of the House of Livia, the House of Augustus, the Farnese Villa, and others, are the work of one main workshop, charged with commissions by Augustus and Marcus Agrippa. In the tablinum the most elaborate paintings are part of an architectural scheme with large central pictures, two of which survive, depicting Polyphemus and Galatea on the rear wall, and Argos and Io on the right. They are set in mainly closed structures with wall surfaces painted red. Narrow openings at the end of the long (right) wall and in the upper part of the scheme allow views onto further buildings which have small figures. There are typical features of the Second Style: elongated columns with vegetal sheaths around their shafts, grotesque creatures on the entablatures, chains of stylised floral ornaments, fanciful motifs such as a Gorgon head flanked by a pair of volute-tailed lion-griffins. The triclinium has a similar architectural scheme with pictures of rustic sanctuaries. The right ala depicts a repeating scene with a screen of columns linked by fruit garlands in front of orthostates, with a frieze portraying an idealised landscape with Greek and Egyptian elements interwoven, with boats, temples, statues, and animals (including a camel) in yellow monochrome. Ling calls this the "crowning achievement of monochrome painting," with a "ghostly, dream-like effect somewhat akin to that of Japanese prints." The left ala is basically similar, except that the garlands are omitted, the colour scheme is much richer, the columns have more vegetation, and the yellow landscapes are replaced by pairs of monsters facing in heraldic posture.[16]

Within her residence Livia would have been served by a large corps of retainers. The richest evidence for her household comes from the *Monumentum Liviae*, a form of sepulchral monument called a columbarium (dovecot), where the containers for ashes were deposited in the pigeonholes. The monumentum was excavated in 1726, but little of it, other than the inscriptions, has survived. Accounts from the time of the excavation indicate that it contained 550 niches, generally with two urns sunk into the floor of each niche. The inscriptions, supplemented from other columbaria, have been closely studied by Susan Treggiari, who offers us a vivid impression of the size and scope of Livia's domestic staff. The whole upper hierarchy can be reconstructed (menial jobs would tend not to have been identified), beginning with the *dispensator*, the steward of the household, chiefly involved with the expenditure of cash; the *arcarii* (keepers of the chest) and *tabularii* (accountants), whose task was aided by a slave *ad possessiones*, an office, it seems, unique to Livia's household, or at least not known elsewhere; and a *custos rationis patrimoni*, who would have looked after the accounts of her inheritance from Augustus. (It has been suggested that he was a member of Tiberius' rather than Livia's staff.) At the more personal level we find a surprising number of *ornatrices*, individuals devoted to her appearance; staff *a veste / ad vestem*, *ab ornamentis*, *ab ornamentis sacerdotalibus;* and a *calciator*, *lanipendi*, and *sarcinatores/-rices* (see chapter 6). For her comfort she had an *unctrix* (masseuse). She employed *pedisequi/-ae* (footmen / women) and a *puer a pedibus*, perhaps a head footman.[17] Livia seems to have been particularly attentive to her health, and her household contained many medical men for her own use and for that of her staff. Several *medici* are attested, as well as a *supra medicos*, or medical supervisor.[18] Finally, perhaps the most striking group are the skilled craftsmen who would have been employed for the manufacturing and maintaining of luxury items—her *aurifex* (goldsmith), *inaurator* (gilder), *margaritarius* (pearl setter), *colorator* (perhaps furniture polisher), *ab supellectile* (in charge of furniture), and *a tabulis* (in charge probably of pictures).[19]

A large household would also have its share of entertainers. Roman matrons liked to keep naked boys *(delicia)* in their company to amuse them. Dio describes an exchange between such a lad and Livia at a banquet shortly after her betrothal to Augustus (see chapter 2). One is attested for Livia, Gaius Julius Prosopas, whom she shared with her granddaughter Livilla. He died at the age of nine. Apart from this the only other entertainer recorded is a reader *(lector)*. Perhaps Livia felt that Augustus and Tiberius provided sufficient amusement. As we have seen (chapter 6), the imperial house considered it fashionable to own dwarfs, and Livia could boast the record for the smallest female.[20] It might just be argued, of course, that Livia maintained her Palatine residences as the wife or mother of the princeps and that a certain level of opulence had to be maintained, consonant with the dignity of the Roman state. This might have been at odds with an essentially personal frugality and modesty, but would be a burden she had no choice but to bear. There is evidence, however, that in addition to the Palatine residences, Livia seems to have owned property in the city, where she had blocks *(insulae)* with apartments and slaves who managed them.[21]

Although the possession of urban properties might have appealed to the basic capitalist instinct of wealthy Romans, the ownership of country estates was the ultimate goal of the aristocratic classes in the Roman world, as in other societies. Livia seems to have acquired a large number of rural properties during her lifetime in the form of land, homes, and commercial activities. We do not have a complete picture by any means—Josephus and Pliny are the only literary sources to make reference to her landed property, and most of our knowledge is based on papyri and inscriptions.

Some of Livia's holdings were spread throughout Italy. She had a fine home only a few kilometres from the city, near Veii, where the Via Tiberiana forks from the Via Flaminia (see chapter 3). The modern Primaporta was called Rubra or Saxa Rubra in antiquity, from the red colour of the surrounding earth. A track leads up from the road to the plateau on which Livia's villa stood in a delightful location. Cooled by a constant gentle breeze, it commands spectacular views, and the Alban Hills and the Appenines are visible in the distance. The best-known part of the complex is what might be called a pavilion, located at the westernmost edge of the plateau. Stairs lead down to a small vaulted vestibule, at the left of which an arched doorway opens into a large room with splendid wall paintings (fig. 28).[22] Suetonius refers to Livia *Veientanum suum revisenti* (revisiting her property at Veii) immediately after her marriage to Octavian. The fact that she was returning to her villa, described as suum (her own) at this time, suggests that she owned it before the marriage. There is general agreement that the *opus reticulatum* of the boundary walls of the villa and substructures belong to about 50 BC, and the estate may have come to Livia from her father, Marcus Livius Drusus Claudianus. His property was confiscated in the proscriptions at the end of 43. The villa might have passed to her earlier than that, possibly at her wedding to Tiberius Claudius Nero.[23]

Livia owned brickworks in Campania which were probably part of a great estate. Stamped tiles bearing the names of her household staff have been found at Herculaneum and Stabiae. She possessed estates on the island of Lipari just north of Sicily, where a Cornelius Manuetus is identified as the procurator of the Augustus and Augusta *(proc[urator] Aug[usti] et Aug[ustae])*. The term *procurator* is used for a number of quite distinct offices, one of which was the manager of the private imperial properties. Thus Livia and Tiberius presumably owned an estate there that they inherited jointly from Augustus. In the area of Tusculum she shared ownership of another estate with Tiberius. Because of the presence of house slaves on Capri, Willrich concluded that she had possessions there. A slave belonging to her is attested at Scolacium in Lucania.[24]

Outside Italy the record is even more impressive. One of the administrators of Livia's property would acquire considerable fame afterwards: Publius Afranius Burrus, who became the commander of the praetorian guard just before Nero's accession and played an important if shadowy role in the early years of his reign. Burrus was born in Vaison, and an inscription honouring him in that town records that for a time he was Livia's procurator in Gallia Narbonensis. She was by then Julia Augusta, indicating that Burrus held the office after Augustus' death in 14, although she may have acquired the property before that.[25] In Gaul, Livia owned land with copper deposits, which she would have been legally entitled to mine. In his general section on copper, Pliny the Elder indicates that the highest quality deposits of the mineral had by his time long been worked out. Of those remaining he ranked the best as the Sallustianum in the Alpine region of Haute Savoie, named after the Sallustius linked with the execution of Agrippa Postumus. Next was ranked the Livianum, found on Livia's estate in Gaul. Her deposits were all but exhausted by Pliny's day and were producing only a small output, but the fact that the product acquired a name of its own, *aes Livianum*, attests to its high quality. Davies tentatively suggests that Livia's mine was in the Rhône area at Chessy or St. Bel.[26]

Her holdings in Judaea were extensive. On Salome's death (c. AD 9–12), the major part of her estate, Jamnia on the coast and Phasaelis and Archelais with their palm groves in the Jordan Valley, passed under her will to Livia. Archelais in particular was noted for the size of its palm plantations and the high quality of its dates. Salome had been allowed to accept a bequest from Herod on his death, and Augustus may have given his permission on the understanding that she make an imperial disposition in turn. Livia's property would be administered by procurators resident in Jamnia. We know that the estate passed to Tiberius on Livia's death. It passed ultimately to Caligula, during whose reign it was the scene of violent disturbances between Greeks and Jews. The procurator in Caligula's day was Gaius Herennius Capito, who may have been appointed originally by Livia to that office.[27]

During Augustus' lifetime Livia acquired a large estate in the neighbourhood of Thyateira in Asia Minor, which still existed in the time of Caracalla. An *arke Leibiane* or *Liouiane* (Livian treasury) with its own procurator was still in use under that emperor and is mentioned in third century inscriptions. It presumably collected the rents of property which had belonged to Livia and had passed into imperial patrimony. Augustus inherited property from Lucius Sempronius Atratinus in AD 7. A freedman of Atratinus is recorded in Thyateira, and Shatzman concludes that Livia inherited the estate there from Augustus when he died in AD 14. The inscriptions refer to her as Leibia or Liouia rather than Ioulia Sebaste, but strict consistency in her nomenclature is not always maintained (see appendix 4). Huntsman notes that Tiberius took his first career steps representing the citizens of Thyateira (as well as Laodicea and Chios), who had suffered from an earthquake in 24 BC and were in Rome seeking help. He might have been discharging patronal obligations on behalf of clients. Other inscriptions at Thyateira mention Julia Augusta, but we cannot be certain that they do not refer to Julia Domna and the Severan period.[28]

In Egypt, Dio records that Cleopatra's land was confiscated after Actium. This would have enabled Augustus to acquire property there without incurring the unpopularity that would have followed widespread seizure of private holdings. It is generally assumed that it was these estates that were passed from Augustus to friends and family, although we cannot rule out the possibility that they might have been acquired on the open market.[29] Livia owned considerable property in Egypt, including papyrus marshes, grain lands, vineyards, vegetable farms, granaries, and olive and wine presses.[30] The earliest reference to her holdings dates to AD 5, when we hear of an estate owned jointly by Livia and Germanicus in the Arsinoite district (the modern Fayum). As seems to have happened frequently on estates in Egypt, a dispute broke out, in this case when a hired donkey driver stole some of the equipment and caused one of the donkeys to die. A petition referring to the incident has survived in which Callistratus, Livia's estate superintendent, writes to the senior police official *(epistates phulakiton)* of the area seeking redress for the lost equipment and the dead donkey, and even for the time lost for the other donkeys made idle by the misbehaviour. One piece of secondary information from this papyrus, provided that it has been restored correctly, is that the estate was large enough to have a donkey gaffer *(prostates ton onikon ktenon)*. It is possible that Germanicus' share was inherited from his father, Drusus, who might have held it in joint ownership with Livia.[31] Joint ownership with Germanicus is attested also at Bakkhias, where a labourer on one of the estates was similarly involved in some sort of petition to the *strategos* of the nome — the bad state of the papyrus prevents further details.[32] After Germanicus' death in AD 19, his share would have passed to his children. In fact, we find Livia and his children, or at least the sons, Nero, Drusus, and Caligula, in joint ownership of a long section of the papyrus marshes at Theadelphia, where they seem to have held a monopoly, and of grain lands at Philadelphia.[33] Also, there is a reference at Tebtynis to a treasury of their jointly held estate.[34] Livia seems to have continued to acquire properties in Egypt right to the end. In 28 or 29 she is recorded as owning lands for cultivating wheat and barley at Euhemeria, where a neighbouring farmer allowed his sheep and cattle onto the land, and they ate some of her grain.[35] There are also references to her Egyptian estates after her death.[36]

Livia's prominent position helped her acquire a considerable fortune, but it also imposed many obligations. Her generosity to individuals and to communities is noted in chapter 10. She would also have incurred many expenses relating to her own family, falling in the grey area between public and private liberality. Thus when Tiberius put on gladiatorial shows in honour of his father and of his grandfather Drusus, the cost was carried by Livia and Augustus.[37] Apart from the public honours voted for Divus Augustus, there would have been numerous gestures made by individual citizens in a private capacity. These included Livia, and at her own expense she established a private festival on the Palatine in Augustus' honour, probably beginning in AD 15. It was destined to continue for several centuries. Originally it lasted for three days, but this period seems later to have been extended, and at some point the festival became a public one, through an undated senatorial decree (see appendix 16).[38] By Caligula's day the event was not attracting the best people — Josephus seems to have viewed the assembled crowds essentially as riffraff, although he may just have been irritated that they were upset to hear of Caligula's assassination during the festivities in AD 41. There are hints that a low tone might have been set at the very outset. In AD 15 charges were brought against a knight, Falanius. It was claimed that he had allowed an actor and catamite by the name of Cassius to participate in the organised worship of Augustus that took place in the larger private homes in Rome. Tiberius took no action against Falanius, making the point that Cassius and other actors had taken part in Livia's Palatine celebrations, presumably the first ones, in that same year.[39]

When the Senate voted for Augustus' consecration, they approved a temple *(heroon)* to be erected in Rome. The responsibility for its construction was assumed by Livia and Tiberius. The building in question was presumably the Temple of Divus Augustus that stood in the depression between the Capitoline and the Palatine. If so, neither of its sponsors lived to see it completed. It reached an advanced stage under Tiberius, but he died before its dedication, and the honour (and excellent publicity) fell to his successor, Caligula, who carried out the dedication at the end of August 37. When finished, it was a splendid building, depicted on a sestertius of Caligula, where it is identified by the inscription DIVO AUGUSTO. It has a facade of six columns and various statue groups on its pediment. It was restored by Antonius Pius in 158–59, and it appears on his coins, now with a range of eight columns, in the Corinthian order (fig. 9).[40]

Probably separate from the temple eventually completed by Caligula is a second structure, mentioned by Pliny, who refers to a *templum* erected by Livia (with no mention of Tiberius) to Divus Augustus on the Palatine. Pliny visited the Palatine in person, where he saw an enormously heavy cinnamon root placed on a golden dish. Every year until the shrine was destroyed by fire (probably the major fire of AD 80) drops fell from the root and hardened into grains.[41] After Livia's own deification in AD 42, Claudius put her statue in the same temple and it was there that each January 17 (and also on other dates, such as Augustus' birthday), the Arvals sacrificed to her and to Divus Augustus. We have inscriptions alluding to servants attached to Divus Augustus' Palatine Temple, including one in service after Livia's own deification: *aeditus templi divi Augusti et divae Augustae quod est in Palatium* (the aeditus [steward] of the temple of Divus Augustus and Diva Augusta which is on the Palatine).[42]

10

FRIEND, PATRON, AND PROTECTOR

By Livia's time Romans were well acquainted with the phenomenon of women playing an influential, if indirect, role in public life. Their influence came not through military command or through political office—these were still very much male preserves—but through the exploitation of family connections in the complex personal process by which political business was often conducted in Rome.[1] Precedents of sorts could be cited from the earliest period of Roman history and tradition. The Sabine women, abducted by a subterfuge, interceded between their new Roman husbands and their former families and persuaded the two groups to form an alliance. Then there was the deputation of women in 491 BC, led by the wife and mother of Coriolanus, which is said to have persuaded the renegade commander against leading an army on Rome. In more recent times there was the example of Cornelia, mother of the Gracchi brothers. Gaius Gracchus introduced a law that would prevent a deposed magistrate from holding office again. It was aimed at a Marcus Octavius, who had been deprived of the tribunacy in 133 BC by Gaius' brother Tiberius. Cornelia interceded and succeeded in persuading Gaius to abandon his motion.[2]

There were certain limitations that could not be transgressed, and there had always been women who transgressed them, supposedly from sexual depravity or in the reckless pursuit of power. But provided the boundaries were respected, it was recognised that a woman could freely offer helpful and positive private advice to a male relative or exploit her influence with family friends. In the turbulent period of the triumvirate we find numerous instances of women being recruited to work on behalf of their husbands or sons. In 40 BC Sextus Pompeius despatched Antony's mother, Julia, to Athens to help him form an alliance with her son. (Livia and her husband sailed with him on the same ship.) Octavian responded by using Sextus' mother, Mucia, to make an approach on his behalf to Sextus. Antony's mother played a further role in the negotiations between Octavian and Antony that led to the peace of Brundisium, even applying a degree of maternal pressure on a reluctant Antony. Not long after, Mucia was sent at popular demand to urge Sextus Pompeius to conclude peace, and she was joined by his wife, Scribonia, in pressuring him to conclude the treaty of Misenum with Antony and Octavian in 39.[3]

Besides helping members of their own family, women could also properly intervene on behalf of those linked by a bond of *amicitia*. There are many instances of this kind of intercession in the late republic.[4] When Sextus Roscius sought refuge in Rome, under suspicion of murdering his father, he asked for the help of Caecilia Metella, who had been a friend of his father's. She chose Cicero to represent Roscius, which he did successfully in a case that had powerful political overtones. Cicero went out of his way to pay tribute to the way Metella met her obligations to her old friend's son.[5]

If there was one particular model for Livia to emulate, it would have to be Octavia, who through her diplomatic skills combined the qualities of the loyal wife with those of the devoted sister and mediated tirelessly between her husband Antony and her brother (see chapter 3).[6] But Octavia's activities were not limited to bridging the gap between husband and brother. Even before her marriage to Antony, she gained the reputation of someone who made positive use of her influence with Octavian. She is portrayed as the heroine of a bizarre episode dated to 43 BC. Among those proscribed by the triumvirs was a Titus Vinius. His wife, Tanusia, gave it out that he had been killed, and hid him in a chest at the house of one of their freedmen. This was a courageous gesture, for concealing a proscribed person was itself a capital offence. Tanusia now brought Octavia into the plan. She for her part supposedly engineered matters during a festival so that her brother would enter the theatre without the other two triumvirs. At the right moment, Tanusia dramatically produced the chest, as well as her husband. The ruse worked. Octavian, as his sister had anticipated, was so impressed by Tanusia's courage that he absolved both her and her husband. For good measure he even co-opted their freedman into the equestrian order. This is the first instance on record—even if that record is perhaps not totally reliable in all its details—of an admirable trait that can be observed later in Octavia, a willingness to intervene on behalf of worthy

Romans who found themselves at risk.[7] Even after her estrangement from Antony and her humiliating return to Rome, Octavia continued to work as a mediator. When her scurrilous husband's associates came to the city, she graciously welcomed them into her house and spoke to her brother on their behalf.[8] In addition, she was prepared to promote the careers of deserving people who had no link with politics. The architect Vitruvius, for instance, seems to have owed the continuation of his appointment under Augustus to Octavia's support, for which he thanks her in the preface to his famous treatise on architecture.[9]

Syme observed that under Augustus politics was managed "through a persuasive system of patronage and nepotism."[10] The emperor was expected to intervene on behalf of worthy citizens in need of help, and to assist them by such devices as access to office. He was also expected to show generosity on a lavish scale by bestowing his largesse on the Roman people or on the Roman army at large, and also on an individual basis on people of high or low rank facing personal crisis. Such blatant subsidies were an accepted part of Roman tradition. When an upper-class family got into difficulties, contributions were commonly made by the father's friends: Pliny the Younger made benefactions of this type. The princeps assumed this responsibility on a broad scale, as, for example, in the case of Quintus Hortensius, to whom Augustus gave a million sesterces to help raise his family and prevent his line from facing extinction.[11] Because they had the ear of the emperor, or simply because of the prestige of the family name, the emperor's close relatives were in a position to arrange similar help and support. Octavia's activities on behalf of her own and Antony's friends presaged a role that would become routine among women of the imperial family. They would look after not only their own relatives but also their extended nexus of contacts, from senatorials to foreign rulers.

As the wife of the princeps, Livia would be expected to be a generous patron, and there are numerous cases of individuals who were helped by her benefactions. It is to her credit that her amicitia did not limit itself to helping the upper classes. She extended her magnanimity to all orders. She gave financial help to the victims of fires. She was particularly attentive to the need to help families that had fallen on hard times. She paid the dowries of daughters when the relatives could not afford it, and assumed the obligation for the upbringing of children of respected but impoverished parents. Most of these individuals are now unknown, like the unnamed individual she tried to have empanelled as a juryman, or the Gaul for whom she sought Roman citizenship.[12] Broadly speaking, her interventions were seen to be directed to a positive end. According to Dio, she once astutely observed that people could be won over by good treatment and also by the good treatment they saw bestowed on others. He notes that she lived up to this worthy principle, and through her mediation saved the lives of many senators. Although it would be a mistake to argue a close causal connection, it is to be noted that after her death there was a surge in the number of treason trials. In his final comment in his history (apart from a brief envoi), Velleius states that no one felt Livia's *potentia* except for the alleviation of danger or for the promotion of rank. This is a sentiment echoed also in the *Consolatio*, that she had the power to harm but harmed no one, and no one had reason to fear her power *(nec nocuisse ulli et fortunam habuisse nocendi / nec quemquam nervos extimuisse tuos)*. Livia's altruism was recognised by a grateful Senate when she died, in the honours it tried to extract for her from a no less ungrateful son. Moreover, on at least one occasion her public spirit was proclaimed openly in an official document sent out to the Roman provinces. The *Piso Decree* speaks of her many great acts of generosity *(beneficia)* shown to men of all orders *(cuiusque ordinis homines)*.[13]

It is worthy of note that some of the people who enjoyed Livia's favour, or whose family enjoyed it, later rose to positions of considerable power, including the principate itself.[14] Sextus Afranius Burrus, the celebrated prefect of the praetorian guard who played a key role in the elevation and early reign of Nero, began his career as a procurator in her service.[15] The most prominent beneficiary was the future emperor Galba, who capped a distinguished military career with a brief reign as emperor in AD 68. According to Plutarch, Galba was related to Livia and owed his consulship to this family connection. We are provided with no further information on this connection, and it may well be that Plutarch confused Livia with Galba's stepmother, Livia Ocella, second wife of his father. At any rate, he was certainly highly regarded by Livia, who left him 50 million sesterces in her will, eventually paid out by Caligula. Her special favour seems to have encouraged a tradition that Galba had long been seen as a man earmarked for the principate.[16]

Galba's short-lived tenure of power was followed in January 69 by the even shorter-lived term of Marcus Salvius Otho, the old friend of the emperor Nero, and at one time husband of Nero's second wife, Poppaea. Here again there was a Livian connection, for Otho, grandfather of the emperor, had been raised in the home of Livia and reached the praetorship through her influence. The bond was obviously a close one, and the elder Otho seems to have been a childhood chum of Tiberius. At any rate his son Lucius Otho (father of the emperor) was on such warm terms with Tiberius that people thought Lucius was Tiberius' son.[17]

Not all of Livia's protégés, of course, attained such eminence. Quintus

Haterius, born about 63 BC, was a novus homo married to a daughter of Marcus Agrippa, when he assumed the suffect consulship in 5 BC. As an orator he was popular, but noted for his excessively fluent verbalism, and Augustus at one point expressed the opinion that he needed to be "cooled down" *(sufflaminandus)*.[18] Haterius was inclined to use his fluency to ingratiate himself with the important and powerful. When in AD 22 Tiberius sought the tribunicia potestas for his son Drusus Caesar from the Senate, Haterius' proposal that the Senate's resolution should be set up in the curia, inscribed in letters of gold, provoked mockery and the observation that he was a *senex foedissimae adulationis* (an old man given to disgusting flattery) who would gain nothing but *infamia* for his efforts.[19] He died in AD 26, the prophecy more or less proven true.

Haterius came to prominence early in Tiberius' reign. At the meeting of the Senate following the death of Augustus, the princeps designate displayed considerable hesitation about assuming authority. A number of senators spoke, including Mamercus Scaurus and Haterius. Scaurus ventured to hope that Tiberius' forbearance from using his tribunicia potestas to veto the motion of the consuls (who had sworn allegiance) meant that he would accede to the Senate's wishes. Scaurus' observation was received with nothing more damaging than a stony silence. Haterius, his natural obsequiousness fortified by his remote connection by marriage to the imperial family, asked in full rhetorical flow, *quo usque patieris, Caesar, non adesse caput* [as emended] *rei publicae?* (How long, Caesar, will you allow the state to be without a head?) Tiberius, who was contemptuous of the Senate's general lack of spine, took his irritation out on Haterius and turned his full invective on him. It seems that later he actually felt ashamed of his lack of self-control, if this was the occasion when he apologised to Haterius for speaking in language more blunt *(liberius)* than was proper for someone of his rank. The apology did not reassure the sycophantic senator, who was desperate to make amends and followed Tiberius to the palace to do so. At this point there ensued a scene of considerable chaos and even more embarrassment. Seeing Tiberius walking through the palace, Haterius threw himself down before the emperor and grabbed his knees, with such fervour that Tiberius fell flat on his back. The senator came very close to being despatched by the guards. Tiberius would not give him the time of day, and Haterius now had to turn to Livia for help. She perhaps was more willing than the unfortunate Haterius to see the humour in it all, and was at first inclined to brush the incident aside. But Haterius begged her to help, with increasing urgency. Finally she relented, and spoke to Tiberius on his behalf. This is the first recorded example of Livia's intervention under the new regime, and it is not clear how much should be read into it. We have no prior information on Haterius' relations with Livia, and Tacitus indicates no previous link. His approach to the emperor's mother may have been inspired by her general reputation for being helpful in such cases. The incident probably represents nothing more significant than Livia putting in a word for a silly but essentially harmless man.[20]

Livia continued to advance the careers of her friends in Rome, literally until her death in AD 29. The consul for that year was Gaius Fufius Geminus, possibly the son of the Gaius Fufius attested as suffect consul in 2 BC. According to Tacitus, Fufius the son owed his advancement to Livia's favour. After her death Tiberius criticised Fufius, attacking his *amicitiae muliebres* (friendships with women).[21] Fufius was married to Mutilia Prisca, who had earlier found herself caught up in one of the more sordid episodes of court politics (see chapter 5). On the death of Tiberius' son Drusus Caesar, Sejanus made serious efforts to isolate Agrippina, and part of this campaign involved working on Livia through agents to persuade Tiberius that Agrippina was scheming to replace him with one of her sons. The agent employed for this scheme was Julius Postumus, known to Livia through the adulterous affair he had conducted with her friend Mutilia.[22] We are unfortunately given no further information on this odd connection. Fufius and Mutilia were forced to commit suicide not long after Livia's death (see chapter 11).

Other female friends of Livia's are attested. There is Plancina, the wife of Calpurnius Piso, who supposedly acted against Germanicus and his wife in Syria as Livia's agent. Livia was loyal to her friend in the trial that followed, and secured the successful intercession of Tiberius. The death of Livia stripped Plancina of her protection; she was subjected to fresh charges in 33 and committed suicide (see chapter 11). The list would also include Marcia, the wife of Fabius Maximus. Fabius, a close friend of Augustus', was reputedly involved in Augustus' plan to seek a rapprochement with Agrippa Postumus. Marcia is said to have passed on the information to Livia but was afterwards smitten by conscience, and committed suicide. This Marcia is a rather shadowy figure. A far more distinct personality can be attached to another Marcia, also a friend of Livia's. This second Marcia was the recipient of a *Consolatio* from Seneca, probably at some time in the reign of Caligula (AD 37–41). From Seneca's account we can deduce that she had four children — two sons and two daughters — of whom only the daughters survived, and she was comforted by Seneca over the loss of one of her sons, Metilius. More important from a historical perspective, she was the daughter of the writer Cremutius Cordus. Cremutius composed a history of the civil war to the year 16 BC (and possibly beyond). He did not glorify Augustus, although he does not seem to have gone out of his way to criticise him, and he had good words for the tyrannicides, praising Brutus and calling Cassius the "last of the Romans." At the instigation of Sejanus he was charged, in AD 25, with treason, and committed suicide. His writings were burnt, but copies were preserved by his daughter, who was clearly a woman of some courage. They were republished under Caligula, when the memory of the earlier attempt to suppress them served to raise public interest.[23] Seneca speaks of a close friendship between Marcia and Livia *(quam familiariter coluisti)*. Marcia's influence is said to have helped Metilius secure an appointment to a priesthood, and it is probably safe to assume that she worked through Livia.[24] Livia's father had, of course, been an adherent of Brutus and Cassius; he had loyally followed them on their final campaign and died with them. While this might have provided a deep-seated psychological reason for Livia's willingness to support Marcia, whose family cannot have been especially popular, common family experience could hardly have been an overt reason and is unlikely to have been even a subconscious one. If a political motive is to be sought, it is more likely to have been Livia's urgent need to thwart the excessive influence of Sejanus over Tiberius.

Of all the female friends of Livia, none stands out so vividly as Plautia Urgulania. She was a member of a prominent Etruscan family who attained some distinction in the early empire. She was also the grandmother of Urgulanilla, the future wife of the emperor Claudius. Her son Plautius Silvanus, consul in 2 BC, may well have owed his office at least in part to Livia's friendship with his mother. Urgulania attained a certain notoriety two years after Tiberius' succession when she enlisted Livia's aid in taking a stand against the praetor Lucius Piso in AD 16 (see chapter 9).

Those who enjoyed Livia's patronage have not left any extant writings, and we are not given the opportunity to subject their public declarations of gratitude or loyalty to close scrutiny. But we do have a remarkable insight into the whole atmosphere of imperial patronage from the works of the poet Ovid. Admittedly we have no evidence that Ovid ever benefitted from Livia's support, but he clearly sought to do so, and he framed his efforts to win her backing in language that is extraordinarily fulsome. Ovid's early literary career saw him as the sophisticated observer of Rome's sexual mores and Roman institutions, and even the imperial family could be drawn in as targets for his clever and good-natured wit. In AD 8 he was banished to Tomi on the Black Sea in circumstances that are exceptionally murky but hint at political improprieties connected with the imperial family. From the time of his exile, his clever repartee was replaced by an often nauseating sycophancy, as he tried desperately to secure his recall.[25]

In the few references Ovid addresses to Livia before the exile, she appears as the model Roman wife, restoring the Bona Dea shrine or dedicating a temple to Concordia, and generally trying to emulate her husband in all respects, while providing a fine example of matronly virtue.[26] The picture is favourable, but moderate and reasonable. In the postexile period, Livia is assaulted by extravagant expressions of adulation. To communicate this adulation Ovid made extensive use of what we have seen as a time-honoured Roman tradition, employing a female relative as an intermediary, in this case his wife. Ovid's third wife, possibly called Fabia, was a kinswoman of the Fabius Maximus who reputedly accompanied Augustus to Planasia. Fabius' wife, the suicidal Marcia mentioned above, was a friend of both Fabia and Livia, and Ovid implies that the last two were also acquainted. The poet was clearly devoted to his wife. In the *Tristia* he suggests that if Homer had written about her she would have outclassed Penelope, the model wife of Odysseus, who patiently and dutifully awaited her husband's return. These qualities she derives from her own inner character, but also from the example that she is set by Livia, a woman she has regarded highly for many years and whom Ovid describes as a *femina princeps*. Livia is the only woman fit to be the wife of Augustus, and but for her the emperor would have remained unmarried.

In the slightly later *Ex Ponto*, by which time Ovid was feeling increasingly desperate, the tone is more dramatic. Fabia is still a model wife and a rival of Penelope, but Livia does more than just provide an example to her; Livia is now the universal exemplar of chastity for all time, with the beauty of Venus and the character of Juno, alone worthy of Augustus' couch. She is once again the femina princeps, but by now is also the most splendid thing in the universe, from the sun's rising to its setting (apart from Augustus, of course). She has to be approached at just the right time — she has weighty matters to deal with and those rare moments when she is idle allow her to snatch some brief time for herself.[27]

Ovid ascribes to Livia the divine qualities of Venus and Juno. He also associates her closely with Vesta, as the symbol of chastity. Thus in anticipating the triumph that Tiberius was to celebrate in October, AD 12, the poet pictures Livia carrying out sacrifices in the presence of the matrons and the Vestal Virgins, whose purity he emphasises. In the later *Ex Ponto* he expresses the idea in even stronger language, calling Livia the Vesta of chaste matrons *(pudicarum Vesta matrum)*.[28] These comparisons are harmless enough, but in other passages Livia's divine association becomes much more powerful. The worship of the imperial family was not officially sanctioned in Rome, but it is clear that on an informal and unofficial level people thought of the emperor in terms that came very close to the divine. The poets seem generally to have been reluctant to express the same feelings about Livia. In Vergil and Horace there are frequent laudatory allusions to Augustus, even to divine attributes that the poets observed in him. But Livia is mentioned only in passing by Horace, in a single innocuous context, and Vergil says nothing of her. By contrast Ovid throws restraint to the winds, and his special circumstances and desperate need for her intercession must surely lie behind the difference.

Ovid tells his wife that she must have the gods on her side, and to that end must light a fire on the altar, and offer incense and wine. Above all she must worship the *numen* (divine power) of Augustus and his pious son, and of the woman who shares his couch, Livia. The numen signifies the power residing in any person or thing, but tends to be associated with the power of a god, and by a natural process in Ovid's time it had become virtually synonymous with "god." To worship the numen of Livia is, strictly speaking, to worship the divine properties within her without technically acknowledging that she is divine, although one wonders how conscious the Romans were of the proper distinction. Elsewhere Ovid seems to drop even this reserve, and in another poem in the *ex Ponto* Livia is called worthy *(digna)* of Caesar, and offerings are made to them as true gods *(dis veris)*. This fulsome language, with its divine overtones, is not reserved exclusively for letters to his wife. In a poem to his bon vivant friend Cotta Maximus, Ovid speaks of receiving silver images of Augustus, Tiberius, and Livia and observes that their presence in the metal gives it numen. These statuettes are his most precious possessions, and he would suffer any torment rather than be deprived of them. In his eyes the three images are *praesentes deos*, to whom he offers prayers. In another piece, to the soldier-litterateur Pomponius Graecinus, he describes how he has set the effigies in a shrine, adding to them images of Tiberius' two sons, Drusus and Germanicus.[29]

The tone of these verse-epistles is echoed also in the section of the *Fasti* that Ovid reworked after going into exile. In his commentary on the festival held on January 24 in honour of Concordia, whose temple Tiberius restored and dedicated, Ovid calls Livia the consort of mighty Jupiter, hence drawing another association with Juno. But he introduces another clever touch. By the time that he wrote, or revised, this section of the *Fasti*, Livia had been adopted into the Julian line. Ovid refers to her not as *mater* but as *genetrix*, an epithet particularly associated with Venus, the mother of Aeneas and the mythical ancestress of the Julian line. He makes an even more remarkable statement in his section on the Carmentalia, celebrated on January 11. This festival commemorates the arrival in what later became Rome of the divine prophet Carmentis and her son, the future King Evander. The parallelism is striking. Evander, like Tiberius, was distinguished by his ancestry, especially on his mother's side. Carmentis, according to Ovid, prophesies that Augustus will be succeeded by his son and declares that one day Julia Augusta will be a new divinity, to be worshipped just as Carmentis is worshipped. Ovid proved to be prescient, although the consecration had to wait for more than a quarter-century and the accession of Claudius.[30] For all his efforts, in the end Ovid's petitions failed, and he died in lonely exile. This outcome might well reflect the cynicism of the age. Ovid's limited potential usefulness as an ally to Livia perhaps did not merit the serious effort that would have been needed to have him recalled. Moreover, Livia was not always successful in her appeals either to Tiberius or to Augustus, and she may have felt that his cause was just not winnable. His fulsome efforts may have served merely to alienate Tiberius further. And of course we do not know what transgression led to his exile in the first place. It could be that in Livia's eyes Ovid's earlier sins simply placed him beyond the pale.

The protective range of Livia's patronage extended even beyond the confines of the empire.[31] In the course of her long life she developed a nexus of friendships with rulers on the fringes of the Roman world. She seems to have had especially close ties with two areas, the Bosporus and Judaea. Polemo I was established by Mark Antony as king in Pontus, on the south coast of the Black Sea. This arrangement was confirmed by Augustus, and in about 19 BC the Romans helped Polemo seize the Cimmerian Bosporus in the Crimea area. The inhabitants were restive, but Polemo calmed things to some degree by his marriage in 14 BC to the Bosporan Dynamis, granddaughter of the old king Mithridates. The union had the full backing of Augustus.[32] Something went wrong—the details are not clear—and eventually Dynamis, with the help of Sarmatian warriors, expelled her husband. Despite her estrangement from the pro-Roman Polemo, Dynamis pursued a policy friendly to Rome, as her inscriptions demonstrate. She dedicated statues to Augustus, calling herself *philoromaios* (friend of Rome) and calling him *soter* and *euergetis* (saviour and benefactor). Moreover, she dedicated a statue of Livia in her native town of Phanagoria in 9–8 BC, once again calling herself philoromaios and honouring Livia as her euergetis.[33] The act that inspired the gesture is unknown, but it could be that Livia was helpful in persuading Augustus to recognise Dynamis' then-husband, Polemo, as king.

After his expulsion Polemo married a Pythodoris and continued fighting in the Bosporus. In 8 BC he lost his life there, and Pythodoris succeeded him, to become queen of Pontus. She refounded the cities of Sebaste (Cabeira) and Sebastia (Megalopolis), where she built a royal residence.[34] Pythodoris dedicated a statue of Livia, on this occasion at Hermonassa in the Bosporus, probably in 8–6 BC. In her dedication she uses the same familiar language to express her gratitude, calling her euergetis. We do not know when Pythodoris died. She may very well have outlived Livia; at any rate, one coin shows that she was still queen in AD 28.[35]

The daughter of Polemo and Pythodoris, Antonia Tryphaena, married the king of Thrace, Cotys. The uncle of Cotys, Rhescuporis, had designs on the throne and murdered his nephew at some point shortly before AD 19. Tryphaena took her three sons to Rome, where they stayed with Antonia and became friends of the future emperor Caligula (a friendship from which they later benefitted). Given that Antonia had apartments in Livia's house, it seems inevitable that Tryphaena would have made the acquaintance of Livia, who might well have championed her cause (see chapter 7).[36] Rhescuporis no doubt thought that he was now in an unassailable position, but he was lured to Rome, where Tryphaena, with the help of powerful patrons, possibly including Livia, had him charged with the murder of her husband. He was exiled to Alexandria and later killed "while attempting to escape." The whole of Thrace was temporarily placed under a Roman official, acting as regent for Tryphaena's children. She made her way eventually to the prosperous city of Cyzicus, where she settled down and became a benefactress of the city.[37] She held the position of priestess of Livia and dedicated a statue *(agalma)* to her patron in the Temple of Athena Polias in Cyzicus, as *Nikephoros* (bringer of victory). This epithet had earlier been granted to Athena for her help to Cyzicus during the siege of the city in the third Mithridatic war, and suggests that Livia was similarly seen as performing great, if unspecified, service to the city, although that service presumably had been delivered indirectly, through Tryphaena.[38] These dedications are surely more than simply an attempt by foreign rulers to curry favour with Livia. Their sponsors are all women who at one time or another had enlisted the aid of Rome, and almost certainly had benefitted from Livia's active intervention.

Another area where Livia clearly had strong connections was Judaea. Like other women of the imperial household, she formed close ties to the Jewish ruling family. She was a friend of Salome, sister of Herod the Great. This Salome, not to be confused with the infamous enemy of John the Baptist, seems to have perfected the arts of sinister intrigue that Tacitus unfairly ascribed to Livia. A bitter enemy of Herod's wife, Mariamme, Salome exploited her brother's natural suspicions and poisoned his mind against his wife. In the end Herod executed Mariamme, her two sons, her brother, her grandfather, and her mother. Livia and Salome might have met during the imperial visit to Syria in the late twenties BC. The two women became close confidantes, and Salome called on Livia's assistance at a time of great personal stress. Salome fell in love with the Nabataean Arab Syllaeus and needed Herod's permission to marry him. She tried to persuade Livia to intercede on her behalf. Herod had made no secret of his opposition to the match, given Syllaeus' refusal to convert to Judaism, and in fact had told his sister that he would consider her his bitterest enemy unless she gave up the idea. Livia had the good judgement to recognise that there was a danger of a serious rift in the Herodian family and joined others in urging Salome to give in. According to Josephus, it was Livia's advice, with all the prestige inherent in her role as the consort of the princeps, that persuaded Salome to accede to Herod's wishes, and, albeit reluctantly, agree to marry one of his friends, Alexas. Salome died a year or two before Augustus and demonstrated in a concrete way her regard for Livia, making her the heir to much of her estate (see chapter 9).[39]

These close political connections created the inevitable risk that Livia would be drawn inadvertently into political intrigues to which she was not a real party. Acme was a Jewish freedwoman of Livia's, much involved in Jewish issues. She became caught up in the dynastic machinations of Antipater against his father, Herod. Antipater forged a letter purportedly written by Salome to Livia, creating the impression that Salome had made abusive comments about Herod and his conduct in the Syllaeus affair. Antipater bribed Acme to pretend that she had found the letter among Livia's papers, and to send it to Herod. She was not the most astute of conspirators, and committed the elementary mistake of writing to Antipater to confirm to him that she had carried out his instructions, a communication that, unfortunately for both of them, came to light. Acme was put to death by Augustus, shortly before Antipater suffered the same fate at the hands of Herod, only five days before Herod's own death.[40]

In addition to her efforts for individual friends and protégés, Livia could also on occasion act on behalf of whole communities. The most tangible evidence of this practice is found in Aphrodisias on the west coast of Caria, in Asia. This city was to prove a most loyal supporter of Augustus and his descendants. It could boast a lavish *sebasteion* (sanctuary) to Aphrodite and the imperial family; its upper stories contained 180 relief panels flanked by columns. It is possible that the fragmentary remains of one the panels depicts Livia carrying out a sacrifice, perhaps in her capacity as priestess of Augustus.[41] The

Aphrodisians mounted important archives on the wall of their theatre, and so seriously did they seek to maintain their image that they included texts of any communications between the emperor and other cities that contained a favourable reference to Aphrodisias. One such document is in the form of a letter from Augustus to the people of the island of Samos, in response to their petition for free status. In turning down their petition (he eventually allowed it, in 20–19), Augustus explains that he is not disposed to grant freedom without good cause, and notes that he has allowed such a privilege to no community other than Aphrodisias (which explains why they had the text on display). His objection was not to the consequent loss of tribute, in that freedom would grant them exemption from taxes, but rather to the indiscriminate handing out of such entitlements.[42] Augustus clearly feels embarrassed at refusing the request. He notes that he is well disposed to the Samians, but even more remarkably he says that he would like to please his wife, who has been most energetic on their behalf. This reveals two aspects of Livia (Scribonia can be ruled out as the unnamed wife) and her relationship with her husband. It shows that she was prepared to act as the patron for a community and to intercede on its behalf with the emperor. It shows also that the level of collaboration between Augustus and Livia was so well established that he felt obliged to apologise in public when he was unable to accede to her requests. Unfortunately, this valuable evidence for relations between Augustus and his wife cannot be precisely dated (see appendix 17).

There is other evidence that Livia saw herself as a friend and patron of the Samians, in the form of two inscriptions discovered recently on the island. Both came originally from the Heraeum, the sanctuary of Hera, and record the dedication of statues of Livia to the goddess, one before 27 BC, the other after. Although married, she is in both cases called Drusilla. In public inscriptions Livia generally avoided her original cognomen after her marriage, but she may have continued to use it in private, and its use here might express her close personal ties with the Samians, also suggested by other inscriptions from the island honouring her parents.[43] She may well have stayed at Samos as a place of refuge with her first husband, Tiberius Claudius Nero, just as they had stayed at Sparta, which belonged to Tiberius' clientele. Livia, along with other members of the imperial family, also had strong personal links with the island of Lesbos, witnessed in coins and inscriptions. There is epigraphic evidence hinting that when ambassadors came from Mytilene some time shortly after 27 BC, Livia was of some assistance to them in their mission, although it is to be noted that in addition to recording their gratitude to Livia, they thank Octavia, Augustus' sister, as well as his children and his friends.[44]

A wealthy and powerful patron would give service not only by interceding with third parties on behalf of individuals or communities but also by the use of private wealth for communal welfare. There was much evidence of such activity on Livia's part in the physical reminders of her liberality scattered throughout Rome. Not all of these would be grandiose and showy—some, though valuable, were on a miniature scale. Pliny the Elder, who had a keen eye for such things and a good sense of anecdote, provides a history of just such a gift. Polycrates of Samos, we are told, had a passion for gems. This pleasure was offset by his obsession with the idea that he was so wealthy that he might provoke nemesis, so he decided to atone for his prosperity by making a major sacrifice. He put out in a boat and threw a ring with a splendid sardonyx stone into the water. The ring was swallowed by a huge fish *natus regi*, fit for a king, which appropriately ended up due course on the king's plate. Its reappearance seemed a bad omen for Polycrates, implying that Fortune had not been appeased. The gem eventually came into Livia's possession, possibly a gift from the grateful Samians. She decided on a more permanent home for it and donated it to the Temple of Concord, where it was set in a golden horn. Pliny expresses sensible reservations about its legendary provenance and also comments that even though splendid by normal standards, it would be ranked quite low in the context of such a grand collection.[45] In fact, the Temple of Concord seems to have been a kind of museum depository, with numerous dedications from Augustus and others, as well as the statue of Vesta that Tiberius had persuaded the Parians to part with when he stopped at the island on his way to his Rhodian exile.[46] Pliny also records that the largest mass of rock crystal he had ever seen was one dedicated on the Capitol by Livia—it weighed about seventy kilograms.[47]

Livia did not limit herself to gifts of objets d'art. She beautified Rome by involving herself in the construction or restoration of a number of important buildings.[48] Women are often associated with prestigious building projects in the Roman empire. One of the most impressive structures in the Forum of Pompeii, for example, is the one given to a workers' association by Eumachia, who advertises her name and her office on the building inscription, *sacerdos publica*.[49] Rome benefitted from similar largesse. Polla, the sister of Marcus Agrippa, began the construction of the Porticus Vipsaniae near the Aqua Virgo in the Campus Martius. It was completed by Augustus and used to house Agrippa's map of the world.[50] Polla also built a racecourse. Octavia, patron of the architect Vitruvius, was particularly associated with the beautification of the city. The most famous of the landmarks that she built, or that Augustus built in her name, were the Theatre of Marcellus, built to honour her son, and the nearby Porticus Octaviae.[51] Strabo expresses excitement over the new buildings of Augustan Rome, and he gives credit to Livia, among others. Her major contribution to the landscape of Rome, the Porticus Liviae, was strictly speaking not her gift, because Augustus paid for it, but some credit for the construction, and for the design, is clearly owed to Livia, and she certainly paid for the small shrine housed within the portico. The background of the portico is a colourful one. The site had at one time belonged to Vedius Pollio, an outrageously wealthy member of the equestrian class, descended from a freedman. He is not remembered for any noteworthy accomplishments but had somehow managed to become an intimate associate of Augustus. This close friendship was a source of embarrassment for the emperor, who was discomfited both by Vedius' great wealth and by his grim reputation for cruelty. In his home he maintained reservoirs with giant lampreys trained to eat men — he reputedly chose lampreys rather than savage land animals for the thrill of seeing people torn apart in an instant. If a slave was unfortunate enough to fall out of favour, he was at great risk of being tossed into the lamprey tank. On one occasion, according to Dio, while Augustus was dining at Vedius' home, one of the servants dropped and broke a crystal goblet. He was ordered into the tank but had the presence of mind to beg for mercy not from his master but from the emperor. Even Augustus was unable to secure a pardon, so he resorted to cunning. He asked Pollio to bring his valuable goblets, which he proceeded to break — thus putting his host in the position where he could not in fairness punish the slave without pitching the emperor into the tank to join him. Pollio had been taught a lesson, and to bring it home Augustus instructed him to put the tanks out of commission by filling them in.

Deep down, Pollio no doubt realised that he could never enjoy the emperor's true regard while he was alive, and he clearly made up his mind that the best time to secure it would be posthumously. When he died, in 15 BC, he left Augustus much of his estate, both in Rome and elsewhere, notably in Campania. In the city Pollio had an enormous house on the Esquiline Hill. Ovid describes it as so massive that it could have swallowed up the ground area of many a city. Augustus ordered that the house be razed, in part to atone for his earlier connections with Pollio and also to show his disapproval of private extravagance. There would have been the added bonus, mentioned by Dio, of guaranteeing that Pollio would leave no monument in Rome. Dio seems to imply that the razing of the structure took place almost immediately after the owner's death, although this does not necessarily tell us when work was begun on the portico that replaced it. At any rate, the new monument was not dedicated until 7 BC. Clearly embarrassed by the political support of a man whose abiding image was so negative, Augustus named it in honour not of Pollio but of Livia.[52]

The portico is an example of Augustus' general policy of creating public spaces in Rome, and it gave him an excellent opportunity to associate his wife Livia with a demonstration of his concern for the communal welfare. Two *cippi* (stone markers) in the area of S. Martino ai Monti, in the general area of Vedius' house, referring to the transfer of private to public land by Augustus, have been connected by Grimal to the conversion of Vedius' estate. Other than that possible link, no physical trace of the portico has survived. It is represented, however, on four adjoining fragments of the Severan Marble Plan, where its name, Porticus Liviae, is preserved, and if we assume that it was symmetrical, the overall design can be recovered (plan 3). Although it seems that Augustus financed the project, Livia may well have had a hand in its design. It was rectangular in shape, about 120 × 90 m, enclosing a garden, as we might expect in a building linked with Livia. It thus fits into the general category of portico and garden, a common feature of the later republic and early empire, both in Rome and in smaller towns. It was fronted internally by a double colonnade, behind which were open niches, themselves fronted by columns. The larger of these niches were rectangular, the smaller a mix of rectangular and semicircular. Pliny the Elder uses as his authority Valerianus Cornelius, who was particularly impressed by the way a single vine stock planted in the portico had spread to cover all the walkways and produced a dozen amphorae of wine, very much in keeping with Livia's close personal interest in horticulture. Ovid also reveals that the portico housed an art gallery, and Strabo describes the building (it is not clear whether he meant the gallery or the whole complex) as one of the great spectacles of Rome. The surrounding area seems to have been cleared of buildings. The very luxury of the project would in itself have had great propaganda value, for it would have drawn attention to the contrast between the private extravagance of Pollio and the fine building for the public sponsored on behalf of Livia. A century or so later Pliny the Younger was still meeting his smart friends there.[53]

More was to come. Ovid in his *Fasti* records that on June 11 of an unspecified year Livia dedicated a *magnifica aedes* to Concordia, to honour her husband. He follows this entry with an immediate reference to the Porticus Liviae, suggesting that the two structures are very closely related, but implying also that their dedication dates were different. Augustus, according to Dio and Suetonius, had taken responsibility for the financing of the portico, but Ovid makes it clear in this passage that it was Livia alone who dedicated and paid *(praestitit)* for the aedes. The term *aedes* is a fairly neutral one, and could refer to anything

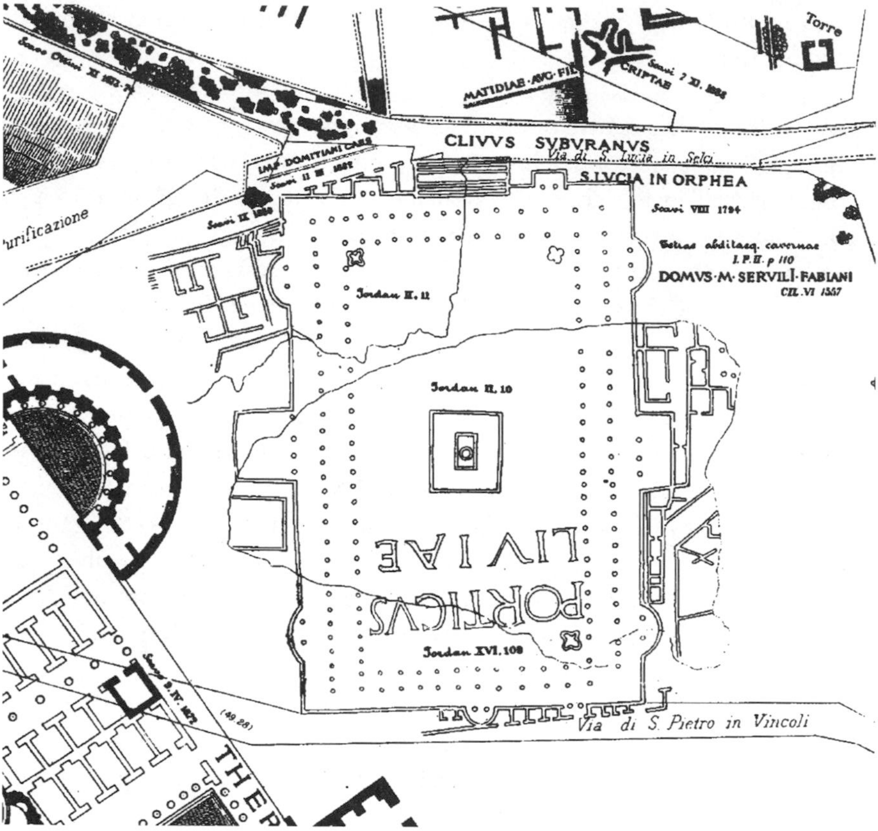

Plan 3. The Porticus Livia. After Lanciani (1893–1901)

from a small shrine to a larger temple. In the space within the portico on the Marble Plan there is a large square structure, with small features at its corners. It may well be Livia's building. Platner and Ashby objected that it was not suited to Ovid's description of *magnifica*. Coarelli, however, has noted the resemblance between the plan of this central structure and of the Ara Pacis. If its decoration also matched that of the earlier building, then Ovid's *magnifica* would be justified.[54]

Livia is associated with other buildings in Rome. A market, *macellum Liviae*, named after her, was restored by Valentinian, Valens, and Gratian (AD 364–78) and is recorded in the regionary catalogues under the sightly different name of *macellum Liviani*. Unfortunately, nothing more is known about the complex, although there have been many attempts to identify it in excavations.[55] There has also been speculation that Livia might somehow have been involved in the restoration of a shrine of Pudicitia Plebeia (Plebeian Chastity). The building was by tradition associated with a Verginia, who abandoned her patrician background to marry a plebeian, Lucius Volumnius, consul in 296 BC. Banned from the shrine of Patrician Chastity because of the marriage, she established a shrine in her husband's house on the Vicus Longus. Propertius in a poem written by 28 BC refers to temples to pudicitia, and Palmer takes this to mean that Augustus restored the two shrines, and links the restoration to Suetonius' use of the expression *de pudicitia* to describe Augustus' moral legislation. A man could not be involved in the cult of chastity, and accordingly a woman would have had to be called on to sponsor the restoration. Palmer bases Livia's supposed involvement on evidence that in the early fifth century there existed what was called a Basilica Libiana in the Vicus Longus, which he suggests was connected with the general provision of amenities and linked with Livia's restoration of the shrine of Pudicitia Plebeia there. But there are problems with the general theory, and also with Livia's supposed role. The most serious difficulty is the suggestion that Augustus' social legislation should be placed before 28 BC, the date of Propertius' poem, and thus even before the settlement. Also, Livia was patrician, and although Augustus was plebeian by birth, he had been enrolled as a patrician by the time of his marriage to Livia.[56]

Another contribution of Livia to the landscape of Rome was her restoration of the Temple of Bona Dea Subsaxana. The evidence for this work is found in the *Fasti* of Ovid, in his account of the celebration of Bona Dea held on May 1. Ovid locates the shrine of the goddess below the Saxum or Remoria (on the northeast Aventine), where Remus supposedly stood when he carried out the auguries for the founding of the city. He reveals that it was restored by Livia (it was later repaired yet again by Hadrian).[57] The cult was exclusive to females, and there were various explanations of its origins. The third-century AD authority Labeo cites the books of the pontiffs for evidence that Bona Dea was identical with Terra (Earth). Others link her with Faunus (either the Roman form of Pan or an early king of the Latins), as his wife or as his daughter. They claim variously that he committed incest with her (in the form of his daughter) or beat her to death (as his wife). Yet others associate her with Juno, Proserpina, or Hecate.[58] No doubt the secret nature of the rites account to a large degree for the great confusion about exactly who and what was being worshipped.

Ovid states that the Temple of Bona Dea was originally dedicated by a chaste Vestal of a distinguished family. In describing the rites, he calls their founder an inheritor of a famous name *(veteris nominis heres)*. Unfortunately, the manuscripts differ about the spelling of the name, either Clausorum or

Crassorum. If the former reading is accepted, the allusion to the Clausi would provide a pointed connection with Livia, for Clausus, according to legend, was the founder of the Claudians and was supposed to have helped Aeneas in establishing himself in Italy.[59] Thus Livia would be seen as restoring a temple that had been founded by an unknown ancestor (see appendix 18). It had fallen into disuse by the late republic, and, perhaps because of its disrepair, the December rites were carried out by the Vestals not in the temple but in the house of a magistrate with imperium. By restoring this building, as Ovid expresses it, Livia could imitate Augustus and follow him in every respect *(imitata maritum . . . et ex omni parte secuta)*. Thus Livia would have had a number of motives. At the simplest level she could show her generosity by repairing a public monument. She was able also to associate herself with something that in certain aspects symbolised chastity, through linking herself with the Vestal Virgins. Finally, she could be seen as a willing partner of her husband in helping to restore traditional Roman religious practices. Certainly Augustus was particularly proud of the large number of temples that he had refurbished, and no doubt delighted to see his wife involved in the same activity.[60]

Livia's gesture would have carried another powerful political message. The celebration of the Bona Dea ceremony had by her day become linked in the public mind with a notorious scandal involving another Claudian. A short time before Livia's birth, the disreputable demagogue Publius Clodius Pulcher, dressed in women's clothing, had made his way into the house of Julius Caesar, the pontifex maximus. Here the Vestal Virgins were performing December sacrifices to the goddess. Clodius' motives were not spiritual—he was lusting after Pompeia, Caesar's wife. Indeed, as a result of the scandal, Caesar had to divorce her, with a pronouncement later destined to become famous, that Caesar's wife had to be above suspicion.[61]

After he became pontifex maximus, Augustus' duties would have included the supervision of the Vestals, whose allowances and privileges he increased. The earlier scandal had taken place in the house of his adoptive father, Julius Caesar, in the official home of the pontifex on the Sacra Via. After assuming his priestly office, Augustus pointedly showed no interest in installing himself in that residence. He wanted to avoid any slur on his authority threatened by his own past association with Clodius—he had at one time been betrothed to Clodius' daughter Claudia. Thus Augustus would have been anxious to rehabilitate the good name of the cult. It is worth noting that the date of the celebration of Livia's restoration of the temple as provided by Ovid, May 1, would be appropriately removed from the month of December, indelibly associated with scandal. Thus Livia could in a sense atone for the behaviour of her kinsman Clodius.[62] Her association with the Bona Dea persisted into the next reign. An important inscription from Forum Clodii in Etruria, dated to AD 18, describes the honours to be paid to Augustus, Tiberius, and Livia on their birthdays. In Livia's case, wine and cakes were to be offered to the women who lived in the community near the shrine of the Bona Dea.[63]

Remains discovered at the fourth milestone on the Via Latina have been identified as those of a temple of Fortuna Muliebris. An inscription records its restoration by *Livia Drusi f(ilia) uxs[or Caesaris Augusti]* — Livia, daughter of Drusus and wife of Caesar Augustus — as well as a later restoration by Severus and Caracalla. This cult had been established early in the fifth century BC and was connected to the legend surrounding Coriolanus. He had been banished from the city for his supposedly tyrannical behaviour and placed himself at the service of the hostile Volscians, leading an army which threatened Rome. He was dissuaded only through the entreaties of his wife, Volumnia, and mother, Veturia, who had set out from Rome with a delegation of women. The temple to Fortuna Muliebris was established by the Senate to honour this event and the women who had taken part in it, supposedly at the very spot where Coriolanus had turned back. Dionysius of Halicarnassus, a contemporary of Livia's, indicates that the story of Coriolanus and the origin of the cult were very familiar to Romans in his (and Livia's) day. She could thus associate herself with women who had served the state, and who had served it by acting within the family, either as wives or as mothers, roles which Livia combined. It is striking that in the inscription she identifies herself by her father as well as by her husband, perhaps showing that her contribution was to be seen as an independent act, carried out in her own right.[64]

Her generosity is attested outside Rome and continued to the end of her life, and we see evidence for this in the aqueducts that she built with Tiberius in southern Etruria in Vicani Matrini.[65] Beyond the borders of Italy most of the information about her liberality relates to Herod and Judaea. Gifts were given to the Temple at Jerusalem. Herod travelled to Rome in about 16 BC to bring back his sons, who had been sent there to study. It is possible that after this visit he took home with him a donation that Livia, and probably Augustus, made to the rebuilt Temple in the form of gold vessels, destined to be melted down during the later Jewish War.[66] Another beneficiary was Caesarea. This city was one of Herod's greatest achievements, built to replace the old Phoenician settlement of Strato's Tower and to provide a major new port. It was an outstanding engineering feat, one which took some ten years to complete. On its inauguration (in either 12 or 10–9 BC), a festival was celebrated in Augustus' honour, with musical and athletic contests, along with beast and gladiatorial shows. Delegates from outside Herod's kingdom came. Augustus helped to defray expenses, and Josephus notes that Livia sent some of her best treasures from Rome, and that the total contribution was five hundred talents.[67]

Patronage and amicitia were at their heart reciprocal concepts, and Livia's generosity and support would be expected to bring her something in return. This return could take the form of simple material benefits—the extensive estates that she inherited from Salome, for instance (see chapter 9). She could also be honoured by statues or monuments, confirmed by the numerous dedicatory inscriptions that have survived. Often, however, the rewards could be less tangible, though no less important for that. These more abstract benefits, which continued after her death, would have constituted a recognition of Livia's importance and standing, a powerful element in the Roman consciousness.

We get glimpses from time to time in the fragmentary evidence of the expressions of respect for Livia that must have been frequent and familiar. In AD 13, for instance, Augustus received a deputation of envoys from Alexandria in the Roman library of the Temple of Apollo on the Palatine. We do not know the substance of the embassy's business—the papyrus that records the event is too fragmentary—but enough text has survived to show that one of the leaders of the deputation, Alexander, expressed the high regard in which the Alexandrians held Livia. The attestation may, of course, be largely formulaic, but even so, the very repetition of a formula represents a form of esteem and respect.[68]

Other communities celebrated festivals that honoured Livia. She was the patron of poetry competitions held in various parts of the Greek world. Such competitions are recorded in Corinth, where Gaius Cassius Flaccus Syracusius recited a poem dedicated to Livia at the Caesarea. More than a century after her death we hear of a triennial contest held in her honour in Egypt, also quite possibly artistic rather than athletic (see chapter 11). Nowhere were such contests more actively pursued than in Boeotia, the traditional home of the muses, and accordingly claiming a long association with music and poetry. In Chalcis in Boeotia, a festival, again almost certainly artistic, was held in Livia's honour, the Leibidea. But no Boeotian city prided itself more on its artistic heritage than Thespiae, famous for its nearby shrine of the muses. Mouseia—poetry festivals—were celebrated there, and inscriptions from the town mention Livia, one of them addressing her as the Muses' mother, Mnemosyne.[69] A possible competition piece has been preserved in the epigraphic record at Thespiae in the form of a poem by Honestus of Corinth. During the reign of

Tiberius this poet sought, perhaps successfully, the patronage of the imperial family. His poems are found inscribed on the statue bases of the Museion. One of them refers to an Augusta (Sebaste) who can boast of two Caesars, possibly Augustus and Tiberius, who are sceptred gods and twin lamps of peace. She is the proper company for the muses, and her wisdom saved the world.[70]

Not all cities, of course, could claim the artistic associations of Boeotia, but they could honour Livia in a number of other ways. One of these was by adopting her name. Among her links with the Herodian family, she may have been a friend of Herod the Great's son, Herod Antipas, who on the death of his father in about 4 BC was appointed tetrarch of Galilee and Peraea. Antipas was a close friend of Tiberius, who used him as an honest broker to mediate between the Romans and Parthians. Under Caligula he fell foul of the intrigues of his nephew, the emperor's favourite, Herod Agrippa. Among the strongholds of Antipas severely damaged during a rebellion in 4 BC were Sepphoris, the capital of Galilee, and Betharamphtha in Peraea. Antipas renamed the former Autocratoris (city of the emperor) in honour of Augustus (the change did not last long). Betheramphtha, on the east bank of the Jordan, was rebuilt as a major stronghold against the Nabataeans and was renamed in honour of Livia. The new name is given as Julias by Josephus, Livias by other sources. This suggests that the rebuilding might have taken place early in Antipas' reign and that he assigned the name of Livias from the start, but it was changed to Julias after the accession of Tiberius and the adoption of Livia into the Julian house. The original name might have taken too firm a hold to be replaced, and for that reason have continued in use. One of the administrative regions on the east side of the Jordan valley was still called Livias into the sixth century.[71]

The city of Augusta in Cilicia Pedias, mentioned by Pliny, was founded in AD 20, as indicated on its coins. Its name clearly derives from Livia's. The coins, carrying the legend *Augustanon*, bear the head of Livia until the Trajanic period. Its location is not known for certain, but it has been identified with Gübe, north of Adana.[72] Almost certainly one of the Bosporan rulers who had benefitted from Livia's friendship founded, or renamed, in honour of Livia the fortress city of Liviopolis on the southern shore of the Black Sea between Pharnaceia and Trapezusia.[73]

The most common expression of regard and respect for Livia comes in the form of divine honours, and she found fervent and enthusiastic worshippers throughout the empire. The tradition in the East of honouring Roman officials by revering them as gods had already become well established during the republic and was a continuation of the practice of venerating the Hellenistic rulers who had preceded them. Thus men like Titus Flamininus, Sulla, and Pompey had been treated as divine or quasi-divine figures, paving the way, as it were, for the widespread cult of the emperors.[74] As attention was increasingly focussed on the domus Augusta it was inevitable that similar honours would be accorded the women of the imperial family. Not only Livia but Octavia, Augustus' sister; Julia, his daughter; and Antonia, Livia's daughter-in-law, were much honoured, as indeed were the later imperial women, throughout both the eastern and, very quickly, the western provinces.[75] In Livia's case this process began during Augustus' lifetime and continued well after her death. Unfortunately, it is not always possible to date the evidence, especially in the East, where divine standing preceded Livia's official consecration in Rome. But it is clear that the process began early. Divine status is made explicit on a coin from Thessalonica dated 21–19 BC, and in the twenties BC Livia joined Julia as objects of a cult in Athens.[76] From at least that time on, the phenomenon manifested itself through the Roman world, and Livia is explicitly recognised as a goddess at numerous sites, both before and after her death. In the festivals at Corinth, for instance, the poems of Flaccus Syracusius are recited *eis thean Ioulian Sebasten* — to the goddess Julia Augusta. At Eresos on Lesbos, where she was worshipped as Livia Providentia (Pronoia), she had her own temple and a sanctuary.[77]

While attestations to Livia's divinity are more numerous in the East, probably the most visibly striking manifestations of the phenomenon are actually from the West, in the form of the huge statues familiar from Leptis Magna in Africa. One of the most arresting is a colossal (68 cm) head of Livia associated with the Temple of Augustus and Roma, in the Forum Vetus of Leptis (fig. 16).[78] Inscriptions in the temple and on two statue bases show that Livia appeared in a family group, set up at the same time, to judge from the inscriptions, which included Germanicus and Drusus, son of Tiberius, in chariots, along with their wives and mothers. Towering over the others were enormous heads of Augustus, Dea Roma, Tiberius, and Livia. The large statues were acrolithic — that is, the head, hands, and feet were made of marble attached to a frame of wood or metal covered with fabric. It is noteworthy that Livia in this grandiloquent form was distinguished from the other imperial women, and her likeness was grouped with the emperors and the personified Roma.

Another colossal statue from Leptis was found in fragments in the theatre. Now reconstructed, the figure is buxom and heavy, and stands just over three metres high. In the same theatre an inscription was found which, given its findspot, may be associated with this statue. It tells us that the proconsul Gaius

Rubellius Blandus (in office AD 35–36) dedicated the shrine to Ceres Augusta and was joined in making the dedication by a local woman, Suphunibal, perhaps a priestess of the cult or a wealthy patron, for she is described in the inscription as *ornatrix pa[triae]* (adorner of her country). It is possible, of course, that the statue is later than the dedication of the shrine.[79]

As Livia received divine honours, it was inevitable that she would come to be identified with existing deities. In her catalogue of cult names of Livia in the eastern provinces, Hahn records an identification with ten goddesses on coins and inscriptions.[80] Her associations with Vesta / Hestia are noted elsewhere, but two of the other more important identifications might usefully be noted here. First, Juno / Hera. Even in Rome, Livia is associated with this goddess by, for example, Ovid and Valerius Maximus, an inevitable comparison to balance Augustus' association with Jupiter. The connection is found throughout the empire. On coins of Tarsus, Eumenea, Pergamum, and Thessaly she is identified with Hera.[81] At Mylai (Thessaly), Aphrodisias, and Mytilene inscriptions assimilate her to that goddess, while at Assos she is called the "new Hera."[82] A similar assimilation seems to take place in the West, but the allusions in the western Latin inscriptions are ambiguous. At Falerii a dedication is recorded to the *genius* of Augustus and *Iunoni Liviae*, which in this case almost certainly conveys the notion of "to the Juno of Livia" rather than "to Livia Juno." From immediately after the battle of Actium, tributes were paid to Augustus' genius, the spirit with its own divine qualities that every Roman possessed, a useful device to avoid explicitly according divine honours to Augustus himself. The "Juno" of a woman, given the association of this goddess with childbirth, could be seen as the equivalent attendant spirit. Exactly the same grammatically ambiguous phrase, *Iunoni Liviae*, is found in inscriptions in Aeclanum, Zara in Dalmatia, and El Lehs in Africa.[83]

In Egypt, and perhaps elsewhere, Livia actively assumed the function of *Juno pronuba*, and her name is mentioned in marriage contracts as a goddess of marriage well into the mid-second century. These surviving contracts state that the document was concluded *epi Ioulias Sebastes* (in the presence of Julia Augusta), very likely before her statue (see chapter 11).[84]

Livia's most striking assimilation is with Ceres / Demeter, goddess of fruitfulness and abundance. In fact, the first known evidence for any Livian statue is from a group in the sanctuary of Demeter and Kore (Persephone) at Eleusis, recorded in an inscription dated perhaps to 31 BC (see appendix 1).[85] Livia's full identification as Ceres comes later, probably in the Tiberian period, although already under Augustus we get a close association between her and the abstraction Abundantia. Hence on Alexandrian coins of AD 10–11, Euthenia (the Greek equivalent of Abundantia) appears on the reverses of coins with Livia's portrait on the obverses.[86]

With the accession of Tiberius there is plentiful evidence for an assimilation of Livia and Ceres. Winkes has suggested that this identification was a spontaneous one in the provinces, perhaps meant as an alternative to the official designation of *mater patriae* that Tiberius refused to grant her (see chapter 8). Whatever the inspiration, this link with Ceres created an enduring association, one that would carry through and persist among later imperial women. Livia is often named in the epigraphic record as Ceres Augusta (or its Greek equivalent) in Asia and in Africa, and even in Malta, suggesting a large number of statues, now lost, in which she was given the goddess' attributes.[87] Of the surviving representations, one of the most striking is preserved on a cameo in Florence, almost certainly cut during her lifetime, depicting the jugate heads of Livia and her son (fig. 11). Tiberius wears a laurel crown, his mother, who bears a physical resemblance to him, a garland of poppies and ears of corn, held in place by a crescent diadem.[88]

Even in Rome the link between Livia and Ceres was recognised. A dupondius of Claudius depicts a draped seated female figure wearing a wreath of wheat and holding ears of wheat and a long torch (fig. 6). The figure is clearly meant to suggest Ceres, but the legend is that of the Deified Augusta, DIVA AUGUSTA. Moreover, the coin type suggests that the identification was an old one in Rome, for it is reminiscent of types of precious metal coins of Augustus that portray a similar seated female figure, holding a sceptre and a branch.[89]

When assimilated to Ceres, Livia often took on other attributes. In the fragmentary statue found in the theatre at Leptis Magna, she adopts various roles. She wears the poppy and wheat ears of Ceres, and also the turret crown of Cybele (this combination of the two is common). The turret crown can also be seen as an attribute of Tyche / Fortuna. Similarly, the striking representation of Livia on the Vienna sardonyx (fig. 19), where she gazes at the deified Augustus, reminds us of Cybele, with her turret crown and lion shield. But she holds wheat and poppies, symbols of Ceres. On the statue in the Louvre commemorating her priesthood, Livia's head bears a floral wreath and, if the restoration is correct, she carries a cornucopia and a bunch of wheat and fruit, all symbols of Ceres (fig. 22).

Such veneration, of course, tells us much about the social and religious life of the Roman empire, and the cult of Livia as an individual. But it should not be seen as having great political significance in Rome, where she did not receive divine recognition until after her death. There are only two recorded instances, in fact, of direct involvement of Rome in the issue of divine honours for Livia, although the incidents do not relate to honours in the city itself. Both occur during the reign of Tiberius.

Deeply opposed to the notion of veneration directed towards his own person, Tiberius after his accession declared that he would allow no sacred precinct to be set aside for him, or priests to be appointed, and no statue to be erected, unless the sponsors had obtained his permission. He added as an afterthought, "I won't grant it!" *(ouk epitrepso)*.[90] But for all his opposition to personal divine honours, he recognised the need to acknowledge the long-standing traditions outside Rome, as illustrated by the fascinating letter that he wrote to Gytheum, the port of Sparta, at a date now difficult to determine, but possibly in the spring or early summer of AD 15, less then a year after coming to power. His letter was in response to one sent by the town to Tiberius and his mother, laying out the honours that it was proposing in a forthcoming festival for Divus Augustus and his family, which included the commissioning of a set of statues (or painted images). In his carefully worded reply Tiberius approved the divine honours for Augustus, justifying them by his predecessor's contribution to the world, but he stated that he, Tiberius, would be satisfied with more modest tributes, on a human scale. Significantly, he added that he would leave it to his mother to send her own reply when she had received the communication. (Livia seems to have received a separate letter and was expected to make a separate response.) Tiberius' ambiguous language has been seen as a reflection of his supposed hypocrisy, and Rostovtsev has argued that he worded his refusal so vaguely that he left it open to the Gytheans essentially to ignore what he purported to be instructing. But his tone more likely reflects an effort to be particularly diplomatic, given that Sparta had long been part of the Claudian clientele and had offered hospitality to his mother and himself as an infant during their time of exile.

The festivities to which the Gytheans had alluded were laid out in a "sacred law" *(hieros nomos)* inscribed on a stone column in the town, with a copy held in the record office. Much of this inscription has survived. It enumerates the honours intended for Tiberius, which had presumably been toned down on receipt of his reply. That the townspeople did to some degree accede to his wishes is generally assumed, for it is unlikely that they would simply have ignored the imperial will, although there are in fact instances when communities went their own way in the teeth of imperial objections. Price notes that Thasos, whose divine honours Claudius had refused, had a priest of that same emperor. Clearly, local enthusiasm could make it difficult for some groups to accept a simple refusal. At any rate, as it stands, the festival could not have caused Tiberius serious offence. None of the living members of the imperial family in the document as recorded receives divine honours, and the sacrifices are made on their behalf, not to them. It is also possible that Tiberius' nomenclature had been much grander in the version originally sent for his approval.

Much of the "sacred law" is taken up with an account of the penalties to be suffered by the officials for financial incompetence or embezzlement, but it also provides a detailed account of the festival itself. The celebrations were to last for eight days. The initial five would be dedicated to members of the imperial house, the first to Divus Augustus, son of a god; the second to Tiberius Augustus, imperator and pater patriae (the relatively restrained language is to be noted); the third to Livia, the Tyche (Fortune) of the province and the city (representations of her in the turret crown of Tyche have been noted); the fourth to Aphrodite / Drusus; the fifth to Nike / Germanicus. The sixth was devoted to the legendary Titus Quinctius Flamininus, consul of 198 BC, revered by the Greeks as their liberator from Macedonian domination. Two further days honoured worthy locals. During the festival painted images *(graptas eikonas)* of Augustus, Livia, and Tiberius were placed in the theatre, where a burner was also set up so that officials could offer incense before the start of the performances. The procession was to make its way from the temple of Asclepius and Hygeia to the imperial temple, where a bull would be sacrificed for the well-being of the imperial family, both living and deified. Another sacrifice was to be carried out in the town square, and from there the procession would go to the theatre, where offerings of incense would be made before the imperial statues. The use of incense, as opposed to animals, might reflect the modesty advocated by Tiberius (as well as the frugality that loomed large in the town's deliberations). Moreover, the incense was to be burnt for the well-being of the imperial family, which fell far short of direct worship. The fact that Livia is honoured as Tyche suggests that her answer was different from Tiberius' and that she did not feel the need for a show of restraint and modesty, especially in a community where she was so highly revered.[91] It also suggests that Tiberius was not committed to blocking honours for Livia if they did not set awkward precedents for Rome or other parts of the empire.

Tiberius seems to have been equally flexible in other instances, as in his response to the request of the cities of Asia to establish his cult in the province. In 29 BC a temple to Rome and Augustus had been constructed in Pergamum. Some fifty years later a request for a second cult centre was to follow. In AD 22, two corrupt officials of Asia had been brought to justice. Gaius Silanus, governor of the province, had been convicted of extortion, and in the following year Lucilius Capito, procurator of the imperial estates in Asia, sustained a similar conviction. In gratitude for the way Tiberius had handled these cases, the cities of the province decreed a temple to him, his mother, Livia, and the Senate. Tiberius felt obliged to relax his embargo on such major initiatives and granted the request, recognising that the authorisation previously given by Augustus constituted a precedent of sorts. The matter did not stop there, however, for the cities fell into an unseemly dispute about which would have the honour of providing a home for the new temple. The wrangling went on for three years, at the end of which they agreed to submit the issue to the Senate, sending representatives to Rome to plead their cases. The sessions were contentious and the arguments ingenious, and Tiberius, who had a taste for pedantic disputations, made a point of attending. The Pergamenes shot themselves in the foot by parading the fact that they already possessed the Temple to Rome and Augustus. (They were told essentially not to be greedy.) Sardis produced a convoluted historical claim (which was taken quite seriously) that it had an ancient link with Etruria. Halicarnassus took a practical line: it could offer solid rock foundations and an earthquake-free environment. In the end, Smyrna won the day, with its claim of loyal service to Rome over two centuries. A special commissioner was appointed by the Senate to supervise the construction. Coins of Smyrna minted under Tiberius depict the three parties to the cult in a single issue. One side illustrates a simplified temple with four columns, enclosing Tiberius as pontifex. The other side carries a draped bust of a personified Senate (legend: *synkletos*) facing Livia (legend: *sebaste*).

Thus the only officially sanctioned temple to Livia during her lifetime was built in this wealthy and beautiful city, which was to boast the coveted title of *neocoros* (literally "temple warden"), bestowed on those cities that were homes to an imperial temple. The monument might well have remained a permanent reminder of the high regard in which the Roman world held Livia, and the gratitude felt for her services. Unfortunately, in the end Halicarnassus would have proved a better location. Symrna was virtually destroyed by earthquakes in the second century.[92]

It is difficult not to be cynical when analysing the expressions of public regard for officials who are in a position to bestow largesse and favours on a grand scale. Yet even though self-interest and ambition are bound to affect the record, it must surely be seen as remarkable that in the nearly seventy years during which Livia occupied a place close to the centre of power in Rome, there is hardly a hint of criticism that would seriously detract from her reputation for generosity and service. Velleius may well have been sycophantic and self-serving, but he seems to have come very close to the truth when he asserted that when people were affected by Livia's influence, they always came off for the better.[93]

II

DEATH AND REPUTATION

Laxatives and red wine had provided Livia with a healthy life, but they could not, of course, guarantee immortality. She had been seriously ill in AD 22. In 29, probably early in the year, she fell ill again, and finally passed away, at the age of eighty-six.[1] Tiberius did not attend his mother in her final illness, but because we have no idea how long it lasted, or whether its true seriousness had been appreciated, it would be dangerous to join Suetonius in ascribing unfilial motives.[2] That said, Tiberius' conduct certainly seems to conflict with his behaviour on previous similar occasions. During the illnesses of Augustus and of Drusus, his brother, he went to desperate efforts to be with them, and in AD 22 he hurried back to Rome to be at his mother's sickbed. Velleius proudly records that when on campaign, no soldier was too low in rank for Tiberius to take a personal responsibility for his well-being. We might expect some exaggeration from Velleius, but Suetonius does give some support to this rosy image in reporting an excellent example of Tiberius' high-minded sense of duty. Visiting a city on Rhodes, the emperor expressed a desire to visit all the sick people. This led to an embarrassing scene when overzealous attendants brought all the infirm they could find in the area to a public arcade and organised them according to their complaints. Tiberius was taken aback but went through with it, dutifully speaking to each individual in turn. Dio also comments on how punctilious he was in visiting friends when they were sick.[3]

Circumstances may have prevented Tiberius from getting to his mother's side in time to see her alive. But they could hardly have prevented him from going to her funeral. Indeed, the ceremony was actually postponed for a few days because, according to Suetonius, the emperor held out the prospect of coming over to attend. It was not to be, and nature in the end dictated the timetable. The body started to decompose, and the funeral had to go ahead, Tiberius or no Tiberius.[4] Tacitus implies that he was unwilling to give up the comforts of Capri to take the trouble to see his mother off, and that he simply wrote to say that the pressure of state affairs prevented his attendance. This might seem hypocritical, but it is at any rate quite in keeping with Tiberius' (and Livia's) aloofness during the funeral of Germanicus. Velleius is as loyal as ever. He skips over Livia's illness and funeral, simply observing that the loss of his mother added to Tiberius' other tribulations: *aegritudinem auxit amissa mater*. Tiberius did arrange in absentia for public rites, with the traditional procession of attendants wearing ancestral death masks. Dio, without specifying them, adds that he also ordered some other minor honours. Otherwise the funeral was extremely simple. Tiberius had always sought to model himself on Augustus, but in this case the contrast between the rites of Livia and of Octavia, Augustus' sister, in 11 BC, are painfully evident. Although Augustus did block some of the honours voted Octavia, he gave the funeral oration himself, with a second one delivered by Livia's son Drusus from the rostra in the forum. Moreover, Octavia's body lay in state in the Temple of Divus Julius and was carried in procession by her sons-in-law, Drusus and Lucius Domitius Ahenobarbus.[5] Hatzl has argued that the simple arrangements for Livia reflect Tiberius' own *modestia*. This may well be the case – he certainly did not approve of public demonstrations of emotion. But Hatzl claims further that the modest scale matched the wishes of Livia herself, and according to Suetonius the arrangements were made by Livia as she lay dying. This idea is more difficult to sustain – it is the same excuse that Tiberius used later to justify not granting her deification. Livia had never been averse to honours, and it is hard to believe that a funeral on the cheap would have been in her plans.[6]

Roman tradition called for the funeral address to be given by a young man of the family. In Livia's case the oration was given by her great-grandson Caligula, who had considerable oratorical skills. (As a child, he had delivered a speech to the people of Assos in Asia Minor.)[7] She was then laid to rest in the Mausoleum of Augustus (fig. 29).[8] The mausoleum was the first building begun by Augustus in the Campus Martius. It is dated by Suetonius to 28 BC (Augustus' sixth consulship) but had clearly not been completed by then, for Dio indicates that it was still in the process of construction in 23 BC when the remains of Marcellus were placed there. The building was intended to be impressive, and the flatness of the area, in the northern reaches of the campus between the via Flaminia and the Tiber, would have added to this impressiveness. It stood in a paved rectangular precinct, and the surrounding area was designed as a public park with trees, including a grove of black poplars and fine walks.[9] The mausoleum complex took the form of an earthen mound, rising from a concrete drum eighty-eight metres in diameter, faced with travertine limestone. There is no clear consensus on what stood above the base. Strabo suggests a single sloping knoll, planted with evergreen trees, rising to a point surmounted by a colossal bronze statue of Augustus. Modern reconstructions generally favour a stepped formation. Apart from the statue the structure seems to have been undecorated, its very simplicity probably intended for effect (unless the decorative elements were plundered in later years). The entrance was located to the south, and in front of the door stood two obelisks in red granite.[10] Augustus' *Res Gestae*, inscribed on tablets, stood somewhere outside the structure.

The base took the form of a central burial chamber surrounded by four concentric rings. The outer ring was broken into semicircular compartments, divided again by radial walls to create quarter-circles, the second into trapezoidal compartments. Neither the trapezoids nor the quarter-circles were accessible, and the purpose of the radial walls and divisions was presumably to support the mass of earth above. From the entrance a vaulted passage traversed two of the rings to a large inner circular ambulatory—perhaps for a ritual circuit of the burial chamber before the deposition of the remains. From the ambulatory one passed into a circular burial chamber, which had a large pier in the centre with a square niche, probably containing the ashes of Augustus, and possibly those of Livia (plan 4).

The mausoleum was the final resting place of the Julio-Claudian high and mighty and their associates. Marcellus was the first to gain admittance. He was followed by his rival Agrippa, and then by his mother, Octavia. (The gravestones of Octavia and Marcellus have survived.) Drusus the Elder and his son Germanicus followed. Augustus was joined there by Livia after her death, followed by Tiberius. On his accession Caligula brought the remains of Agrippina from her island of exile and rejoined her with her husband, Germanicus. He performed the same service for his brother Nero. (The ashes of his other brother could not be recovered.) Almost certainly Antonia would likewise have joined her husband, Drusus, in the mausoleum. Claudius followed. The mausoleum retained its cachet when the Julio-Claudian dynasty came to an end. As a special favour, Nerva's ashes were placed in it. Exclusion could be used as a weapon of disfavour, as when Augustus refused entry to the two Julias, his daughter and granddaughter. If Livia hoped for peace and quiet in

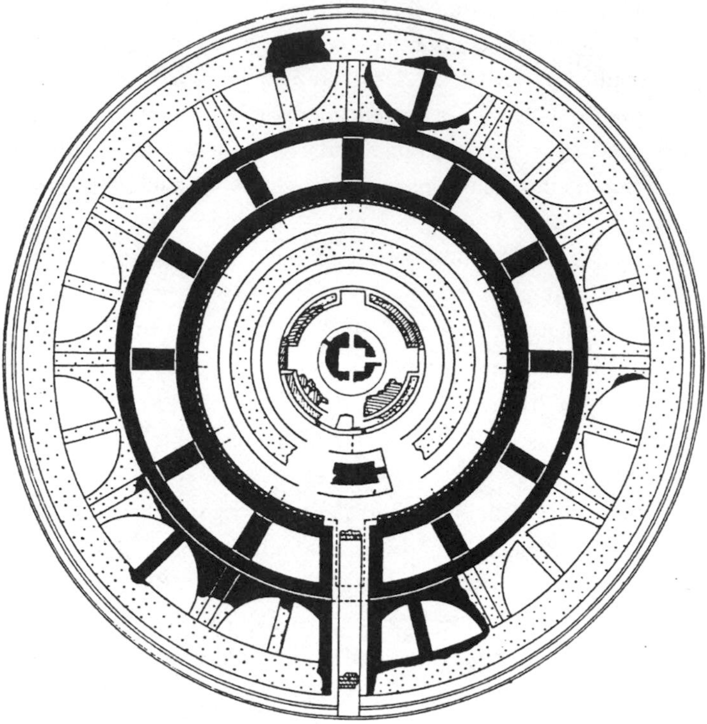

Plan 4. Mausoleum of Augustus. After Gatti (1938)

the next life, she would have been disappointed. The mausoleum, or at least its physical shell, has remained in continuous use, with functions ranging from a concert hall to a bullring.[11]

Although Livia's actual influence in her later years is legitimately questioned, there can be no doubting the high regard in which she was held right up to the end. Any unpopularity that she might have suffered in AD 19 as a consequence of the death of Germanicus and her support of Plancina in the subsequent trial seems to have been completely effaced by 29. The Senate responded to her death with striking generosity, but if we are to believe Tacitus, they faced an uphill battle against an almost totally unyielding Tiberius. He issued no coins to mark his mother's death. He did sanction some minor tributes, but they failed to satisfy the senators, who, according to Dio, went well beyond the emperor's instructions. They ordered an official period of mourning for a whole year for the women. During this time they were to don black clothing, wear their hair loose, and avoid any kind of adornment. Under pressure from Tiberius, the Senate conceded that this would not be a formal *iustitium*, during which all public business would have been suspended.[12] More dramatic was their vote for an arch in her honour, in recognition of her acts of kindness and generosity (see chapter 8). The arch, in common with the other unprecedented distinctions selected by the Senate, came to nothing. Tiberius did not oppose it head-on. As described by Dio, his method was much more devious (perhaps uncharacteristically so for Tiberius). Instead of annulling the senatorial decree, he promised to erect the arch at his own rather than public expense, but then never got around to building it. It is only fair to note that Tiberius took a very jaundiced view of all luxury building projects. Even the important Temple of Divus Augustus, constituted in AD 14, was not finished at the time of his death in 37 and had to be completed by Caligula.[13]

Most significant, the Senate moved to vote Livia divine honours. Her cult had been widespread throughout the empire during her lifetime (see chapter 10). The proposal of the Senate would have involved something much more dramatic, the official recognition of her divinity in Rome, with her own temple and her own priesthood. She would thus have become the first woman to be consecrated and worshipped officially as a goddess in Rome itself. Tiberius was adamant in refusing this honour, saying that it was not what she would have wished and that she had given specific instructions that it should not be allowed to happen. Although his reaction demonstrates a commendable restraint and common sense, it may not have met with popular approval. It is noteworthy that Velleius, Tiberius' ardent admirer, ends his history, apart from a very brief exordium, with the death of Livia, who, he says, in all details resembled the gods more than humans—*per omnia deis quam hominibus similior femina*. Some scholars have detected a modest reprimand of Tiberius in these words.[14]

We know of at least one contemporary Roman who got into hot water over the issue. Cotta Messalinus was a man noted for his generosity and his gluttony. (He invented a recipe for pickling the feet of geese.) According to Tacitus, he specialised in outrageous proposals, usually intended to ingratiate himself with the powers that be. It was he who had proposed after the suicide of Scribonius Libo, suspected of treason in AD 16, that his effigy should not be carried in the funeral of his descendants, and that they could not carry the cognomen Drusus. He also moved that governors of provinces be penalised for the misdeeds of their wives, and demanded a motion of the Senate condemning Agrippina and her son Nero. He was a protégé of Tiberius' and referred to him by the affectionate diminutive *Tiberiolus meus*. He also seems to have had a penchant for putting his foot in his mouth. After Livia's death he found himself in jeopardy on two grounds. He made snide comments about the sexual inclinations of Agrippina's surviving son, Caligula, who had been taken to Capri and placed under his grandfather's wing. Also, in AD 32, when dining with the priests on Livia's birthday, he made the witty comment that it seemed more like a *novendialis*, a feast for the dead held nine days after the funeral. Presumably the point of the joke was that a feast celebrating the birthday of a dead but undeified person was essentially a wake under another name.[15] Messalinus was charged before the Senate. The precise accusation is not specified. Bauman suggests that an alert accuser thought that Tiberius could be identified as the target of criticism implicit in the remark. At any rate, the case was so strong that Messalinus had to beg Tiberius' protection. The emperor obliged and wrote to the Senate noting Messalinus' past services and asking that a naughty witticism over dinner not be used as evidence of guilt. The incident was perhaps a trivial one in itself, but it does serve to show that the issue of divine honours for Livia was a sensitive one and could still strike a nerve three years after her death.

Livia's death may well have had an immediate impact on the contemporary political situation. Dio notes that during her life she had saved the lives of several senators. After her death there was a surge of treason trials. Between AD 15 and 28, thirty trials took place. In AD 30, six were charged; in 31, seven; in 32, eighteen; in 33, ten known by name and twenty anonymous. These figures might suggest a trend, but the relationship between cause and effect is unproved.[16] Suetonius levels the serious charge that Tiberius took action against Livia's close friends, even those who had been entrusted with her funeral arrangements, and condemned one of them, an equestrian, to the treadmill. Only one identifiable case is known, and the later fate of those of her supporters like Galba, whose careers are a matter of record, certainly proves that there was no general witch hunt.

Tacitus limits Tiberius' attacks in the immediate aftermath of Livia's death to a verbal assault on "feminine friendships," aimed at the consul Fufius. The emperor may have felt a personal antipathy for him beyond the mere fact that the consul had been a protégé of his mother's. Fufius seems to have combined a flair for ingratiating himself with elderly women and a clever talent for witticisms, which unfortunately he used to ridicule Tiberius, and which the emperor resented. By the following year, AD 30, Fufius had been charged with a violation of maiestas. He tried to make amends, even reading his will in the Senate to show that he had shared his estate between his children and the emperor. It did him no good. He was now criticised for being a coward as well as a traitor. He returned home and stabbed himself before the Senate could take a vote. He arranged beforehand for a report to be sent to them that he had died like a man. His wife, Mutilia Prisca, was also charged with some unspecified offence. She showed more style, reputedly managing to smuggle a dagger into the Curia, where she dramatically committed suicide before the assembled senators. Dio is our source for these events, and his account at this point survives only in epitomes. The version of John of Antioch (assuming that his "Mucia" is an error for "Mutilia") alleged that Tiberius also destroyed their two daughters because of the family's friendship with Livia. Tacitus reports that Fufius' aged mother, Vitia, made the mistake of mourning for her son, for which she also paid with her life.[17]

Another who ultimately suffered was Piso's widow and Livia's friend Plancina, who had emerged relatively unscathed from the turmoil of the celebrated trial that followed Germanicus' death. That respite proved temporary. The death of Livia in 29 removed her main support. Her hostility towards Agrippina continued to offer her a degree of protection for a time after that, according to Tacitus. Agrippina's death in 33 removed that last line of defence. Plancina was charged on counts that Tacitus describes as well known, perhaps implying that they were the old charges, on which she had never been given a formal acquittal. She took her own life, suffering a penalty that was *sera magis quam immerita*—postponed rather than undeserved.[18]

The main target of Sejanus and his backers after Livia's death would have been Agrippina and her sons. In the minds of the ordinary people there was a firm belief that Livia had continued to exercise a strong influence over events right up to the end. After her death, when the attacks on Sejanus' enemies were unchecked, a letter denouncing Agrippina and Nero was sent (from Capri) to Rome. The popular view was that the letter had been delivered much earlier but had been suppressed by Livia. Admittedly, the opinion of the public on this matter could hardly be called informed, and they seem to have based their inference on the simple fact that the letter was read out so soon after her death. But the anecdote itself does indicate that in the popular mind Livia could to the very end still have an impact on important decisions, and also that she had taken on a role as protector of Agrippina and her children, despite her supposed secret intentions to destroy Germanicus' family.[19] The chronology of what happened to Agrippina's family at this time is confused, and there are contradictory versions of what occurred. The basis for the sequence of events adopted here is laid out in the appendices.[20] What is clear is that after Livia's death Sejanus pulled no punches in his offensive. Formal charges were launched, coinciding with a frustrating lacuna in Tacitus' text and major gaps in Dio's account. Both Agrippina and Nero were proclaimed public enemies and banished, Nero to Pontia and Agrippina to Pandateria. Agrippina was a difficult and courageous prisoner. She lost an eye during a fracas with one of her guards and had to be force-fed after a hunger strike. Nero died in mysterious circumstances, shortly before Sejanus' own fall in late 31. Drusus, who had remained unscathed while Livia was alive but who was similarly arrested after her death, was starved to death in his prison in AD 33. He was survived by his mother for only a few months.[21]

Although Caligula made sarcastic comments about his great-grandmother Livia's relatively humble maternal origins, she was honoured during his reign, and the Arvals celebrated her birthday in 38 and 39, and probably in the other Caligulan years, for which the Arval record is lost.[22] His high regard for her is demonstrated by the belated execution of her will. Although Tiberius had not questioned the validity of Livia's will, which named him heir, he refused to honour the various individual legacies that she provided. Suetonius reports that one of her legatees was Galba, the future emperor, whose bequest, at 5 million sesterces, was the largest that she made. But there was a technical problem in the way the will was drawn up. It was written in figures and not spelled out verbally, presumably as $\overline{|D|}$. By claiming that it should be $\overline{D}$, Tiberius was able to reduce the sum to 500,000, and in the event did not pay even that amount.[23] Galba fared better under Caligula. On his accession in AD 37 the young emperor proved irresponsibly generous. Although he excluded Tiberius' natural grandson and heir from the late emperor's will on dubious legal grounds, even invalidating the will itself, all Tiberius' bequests were honoured, and the legacies earlier bequeathed by Livia but withheld by Tiberius were now, eight years later, finally paid. Whether Galba received his full amount or the drastically reduced figure is not stated.[24]

Livia's consecration would have to await Caligula's assassination in AD 41 and the accession of his uncle. For all his image as a scholar and harmless eccentric, Claudius had taken power efficiently and coolly, essentially by a military coup. He would doubtless have been keen to give himself respectability by emphasising the eminence of his own family line. The enhancement of his grandmother Livia's status would by necessity mean the enhancement of his own. Among his early measures, divine honours were voted to Livia on January 17, 42, the anniversary of her wedding to Augustus, and, if she was born in 59 BC, the one hundredth anniversary of her birth. At the circus games her image was to be carried in a chariot drawn by elephants. Her statue was set up in the Temple of Augustus that she had founded on the Palatine, and the Vestals were charged with the task of making the appropriate sacrifices. As a further manifestation of her divine status, it was ordered that women should use her name in taking oaths. In an extant fragment of the Arval chronicle for a year between 43 and 48, sacrifices to her and to Divus Augustus at the temple on the Palatine are recorded at the beginning of the year and on the anniversary of her consecration. Another fragment from between 50 and 54 records sacrifices to her and Divus Augustus on September 24 as part of the celebration of Augustus' birthday. Nor was this high regard limited to Rome. A dedication recorded in Egypt (Abydos?) on January 30, 49, seems to allude to a local celebration of her birthday. Bartman has noted that dynastic statuary groups including Livia become very popular during the Claudian period.[25] Moreover, she continued to be venerated under Nero, to judge from the frequency of the honours in the Arval record.[26] The fact that Seneca sought her out for praise during the reigns of the last three Julio-Claudian emperors suggests very strongly that at the official level she was continuously held in high esteem.

Livia enjoyed an abiding regard even after the Julio-Claudian dynasty had came to an end in AD 68. Galba saw the powerful propaganda effect of her image and issued several series of coins honouring her. She appears in the Arval record for Galba, Otho, and perhaps Vitellius.[27] Trajan reissued Tiberius' type with a reverse that depicts Livia, or at least strongly suggests her. A Trajanic inscription from an unknown colony, perhaps Trebula, securely dated by the names of consuls to AD 108, records that her birthday was still being observed then, with games and gladiatorial shows and a public banquet given to the local councillors *(decuriones)* and the *seviri Augustales*, the board responsible for the worship of Augustus.[28] Livia's and Augustus' birthdays were still being celebrated under Trajan at Pergamum. The complete calendar of the imperial choir in that city has survived. Its list of activities includes among the celebrations for imperial birthdays three-day events for Livia and Augustus.[29]

Livia's name was used in the marriage oath for more than a century after her death. The evidence for this comes from Egypt, in the form of marriage contracts preserved on papyri, and it may have been a custom observed throughout the empire, in places where the evidence has not survived. The most useful document in this context is a contract between Serapion and Thais, concluded in the reign of Hadrian in AD 127. It is almost complete and provides much interesting information on the dowry of Thais and the property brought into common stock by Serapion, as well as a prenuptial agreement about the disposition of the property in the event of a divorce (an extra sixty drachmae if Thais is pregnant at the time!). Most important for our purpose is the formula near the beginning of the text, *agathei tychei, epi Ioulias Sebastes*. Wilcken has pointed out the formula *agathei tychei* (for good luck) occurs in the body of the contract, not in its prescript, and that the following phrase, *epi Ioulias Sebastes*, does not, accordingly, allude to the location or the date. His conclusion, generally accepted, is that the phrase means something like "in the presence of Julia Augusta," in the sense of a general reference to her, or, more likely, because the contract is sworn before her statue (a common force of *epi* in oaths). Wilcken notes that the same reference to Livia occurs in other papyri of the first and second centuries, and, although the *agathei tychei* is missing, the context must surely be the same.[30]

Livia was still held in special honour in Egypt during the Antonine period. An edict of Marcus Petronius Honoratus, prefect of the province in 147–48, has survived on a fragment of papyrus from Oxyrhynchus. It records the particulars of a triennial contest held in honour of Livia and of another deified member of the imperial family, whose name is lost (Germanicus would be a good candidate). No further details about the contests have survived, and it is not known whether they were athletic or artistic. But it is clear that they were of considerable local interest. Some ten years later, Antoninus Pius depicted Livia along with Augustus on his coins of 157–59.[31]

Her cult seems to have lapsed by the end of the second century, if not before. Records of the garrison at Dura Europus on the Euphrates from the first quarter of the third century have survived on papyri. They include the observation of the birthdays of divi from Augustus to Caracalla, as well as of four divae, deified female members of the imperial family: Marciana, sister of Trajan; Matidia, niece of Trajan and mother-in-law of Hadrian; Faustina (which one is meant is not certain—either the wife of Antoninus Pius or the wife of Marcus Aurelius); and Maesa, grandmother of Severus Alexander. The list is not complete, for there are gaps in the papyri and some months are missing. But there is a complete record for January, and Livia's name does not appear there.[32]

Although her cult had lapsed by the time of Feriale Duranum, Livia's prestige seems to have persisted. Perhaps the most vivid demonstration of her lingering presence comes from Prudentius, the Christian poet born in the middle of the fourth century. In 384 the distinguished orator Symmachus had made an appeal to the Senate to tolerate pagan beliefs. The attempt was thwarted by Ambrose, bishop of Milan, but Symmachus published his appeal anyhow. Some twenty years later Prudentius, concerned about the unwillingness of the upper classes to abandon paganism, wrote a verse rebuttal of Symmachus (already dead by then). Prudentius illustrates the evils of paganism from various periods of Roman history but reserves some of his heaviest ammunition for Livia. He revives at length the old antipathy over her second marriage while she was pregnant by her first husband, and castigates the Romans for making a goddess of her along with the likes of Flora and Venus. Prudentius was deadly serious in his intentions, and he would not have wasted his time flogging a dead horse. The vehemence of his attack must have had a purpose. Clearly, in the dying days of ancient Rome, five centuries after Livia's own lifetime, her name was still a potent force among a broad section of the populace, and she remained a figure widely revered and admired.[33]

APPENDICES

APPENDIX 1: SOURCES

LITERARY SOURCES

The ancient literary sources present us with all the problems associated with any historical era, for written material cannot help but be tainted, to a greater or lesser degree, by the prejudices of its author. But the historian of classical antiquity faces additional difficulties generally spared researchers of more recent periods. The ancient texts are often fragmentary or incomplete, and, more seriously, employ a more flexible concept of objective truth than we now feel acceptable in a historical writer. For the Julio-Claudian period there are further hurdles to be overcome. The writers are inevitably preoccupied with the central figure of the emperor. This concentration can come at the expense of political analysis, a serious problem in itself. But it can create a further problem for the study of someone like Livia, in that secondary figures tend to be of interest primarily for what they tell us about the emperor. They rarely emerge as individuals in their own right, unless their public personas were vivid enough to enable them to carve out their own independent niche. Germanicus would be a prime example of this kind of rare exception. Consequently Livia, like most of her contemporaries, tends to move in and out of the historical narrative, temporarily dominating the scene when an emperor dies or a prince is intrigued against, but otherwise hovering in the background and making surprisingly little impression on the historical narrative.

One potential source of information on Livia should be the writings of the emperors themselves and of their family. In fact, surprisingly little overt use is made of this medium by the ancient authorities. Suetonius is happy to quote Augustus' correspondence and provides some insight into the emperor's relationship with Livia through the letters he wrote to her, presumably stored in the imperial archives. He also quotes from Augustus' will. But he was reluctant to use his more formal writings, and in fact is dismissive about imperial memoirs in general. It is not easy to understand why. Such personal reminiscences would have been self-serving, of course, but the ancient sources are generally more than happy to cite the self-serving views of rulers, if only to deride them.

Augustus, like many of the other Julio-Claudians, was an accomplished man of letters. He composed poetry and penned an unfinished play, as well as a number of scholarly works, of which he tired, passing them on to Tiberius to finish. He was also a historical writer of sorts. His most famous contribution in this sphere is his *Res Gestae*, the record of his achievements that he ordered to be set up outside his mausoleum and in the provinces. Whether this work should be classed as a memoir or public monument is perhaps moot for the present purpose, for Livia receives no mention in it. Augustus' *Commentaries* covered his career down to the Cantabrian War (27–24 BC), and Suetonius seems to make occasional use of them, as in his account of the emperor's family background. They must have contained allusions to Livia. Augustus committed to writing *(ut scribit)* his decision to divorce Scribonia because of her shrewish habits, and if this information was found in his *Commentaries*, we would have a likely context there for an appearance by Livia. Also, we would certainly expect Livia to have been featured in the biography of her son Drusus, which Augustus wrote after the young man's death in 9 BC.[1]

Tiberius left two sets of writings. Suetonius refers to the *Commentarii*, of an unspecified nature, and to his *Acta*, presumably an account of his political achievements. They were Domitian's favourite reading matter.[2] Apparently separate from these was his *Commentarius*, a brief and sketchy autobiographical narrative. This last doubtless had a great deal to say about Tiberius' mother, but none of the sources ever cites it, and Suetonius is in fact the only one even to indicate a knowledge of it.[3]

Claudius was a prolific writer. Suetonius refers to a contemporary history in forty-one books, which seems have covered the period from the settlement of Augustus down to his death (27 BC–AD 14). It would have dealt with the preceding civil wars, had Claudius not been frightened off this earlier period by his grandmother Livia and his mother, Antonia. The history doubtless contained much material of potential interest, but the sole reference to its contents is in Pliny the Elder, who cites Claudius on the qualities of an exotic tree resembling the cypress, with the information that it had powerful aromatic qualities and that the Parthians sprinkled it in their drink.[4] Claudius also wrote an autobiography in eight volumes, which would no doubt have contained information on Livia, who seems to have played a significant role in his early life. Suetonius scathingly describes the work as nonsense, although he admits that it had a certain literary charm. We know of only one apparent allusion to it: Nero stated that he had read in the *Commentarii* of Claudius that his predecessor had never forced anyone to undertake prosecutions.[5]

Probably the most familiar imperial memoirs, and potentially the most important in the present context, are those of Agrippina the Younger, now lost. We do know that they were available. Tacitus, under the year AD 26, cites information he found in her commentarii, where she left a record for later generations "of her own life and of the misfortunes of her family"—*quae Neronis principis mater vitam suam et casus suorum posteris memoravit*. The item in question involved the request of her mother, Agrippina the Elder, for permission from Tiberius to remarry. As further evidence of the neglect of imperial memoirs, Tacitus pointed out that this information had been overlooked by all other historians *(scriptores annalium)*. In fact, in the extant record only one other citation seems to originate from Agrippina's memoirs: Pliny the Elder records that Nero was delivered by a breach birth.[6]

It is far from certain when Agrippina put together the memoirs. When Tacitus alludes to her authorship he describes her as *mater Neronis*, but he may not necessarily mean that Nero was already born when she wrote them. (He was born, almost certainly, in 37.) Scholarly views on this question vary. Some have argued that Agrippina wrote them during Claudius' reign, when planning Nero's succession, and even used them as propaganda to balance Messalina's hostility. In this case the text would presumably have ended at the point when Agrippina became Claudius' wife. Most scholars, however, have Agrippina imitating Cicero, making use of her forced absence from political activities after 55 to engage in writing. Nor is there agreement on what they might have contained, or how influential they were. More than a century ago Stahr, without further elaboration, suggested that they contained attacks on Livia and Tiberius. Motzo has expanded on this suggestion and claims that they were the source for Tacitus' material on Agrippa Postumus, the involvement of Livia and Tiberius in his death, the story of Augustus' voyage to Planasia to visit Postumus, the story of Claudius Clemens and his impersonation of Postumus, and the death of Augustus, with its negative portrayal of

Livia. Motzo's thesis would thus make the memoirs the key source for the more controversial episodes in Livia's life. But at the other extreme Fabia has argued that Agrippina the Elder's petition to remarry is the only information borrowed by Tacitus from that particular source. In support of Fabia, Walker points out that Tacitus introduces the citation in a way that suggests that the memoirs were not used regularly by him.[7]

Consolatio ad Liviam

Although frequent passing reference is made to Livia in the literary sources, the only two surviving detailed accounts of her activities have to be treated with the utmost caution. One of those is the exhaustive description found in Seneca and Dio of the exchange between her and Augustus over how to handle the suspected conspirator Cornelius Cinna (see chapter 7). Livia's advice has the ring of a standard school exemplum, with a historical event lying only at the core of a highly elaborated rhetorical flight of fancy. The other example is more complex and at first sight potentially more valuable. The *Consolatio ad Liviam* was purportedly written to offer Livia consolation following the death of her son Drusus in 9 BC. It takes the form of a poem of 474 lines, composed in elegiac couplets, and is preserved in a number of late manuscripts, which ascribe it to Ovid. The manuscript text is highly corrupt, and it is often hard to distinguish between the errors of a careless copyist and the idiosyncracies of a mediocre poet.

Modern scholars universally agree that the poem is not what it represents itself to be—namely, a work written in or shortly after 9 BC. This view did not always prevail. In the late sixteenth century Scaliger was willing to accept it at face value. For some time his position held sway, but it was eventually demolished in the nineteenth century by Haupt, who went so far as to argue that the poem was confected during the Renaissance. Haupt's extreme position has not found favour, but his general principle of a later composition is now widely accepted, although there is no consensus on when it was written. The resemblances to Ovid suggest that it could not be earlier than he, on the assumption that it is hardly likely that Ovid would have imitated an unknown poetaster and have continued to do so after his exile. There are also resemblances between the *Consolatio* and Seneca's writings, dated after AD 43, but this may be because they share a common source.

The very strong likelihood that the *Consolatio* is not contemporaneous with the events it describes makes its value as a historical document questionable, because we do not know whether the author is drawing on personal observation. Richmond, for instance, observes that the poet might have made use of the historian Livy, who, we know, wrote on the death of Drusus and on his funeral in Rome.[8]

Contemporaries of Livia

Only a small portion of the contemporary accounts of the Julio-Claudian period have survived—no serious loss, according to Tacitus, who observes that records were falsified through cowardice when the emperors were still alive and infected with hatred after their deaths.[9] It is indeed the case that the writers active while Livia was on the scene are generally obsequious, or had a personal motive for winning her over specifically.

Velleius Paterculus

Velleius Paterculus was born in about 19 BC, of equestrian stock. Like his grandfather and father, he pursued a military career, serving first under Gaius Caesar and Tiberius, latterly as *legatus* in Germany and Pannonia. After this he moved up into the senatorial order, reaching the praetorship in AD 16. His *Historiae Romanae* is a compendium of Roman history from the legendary past, as far back as the Trojan War, down to AD 30, and is dedicated to his friend Marcus Vinicius to honour Marcus' consulship in that year. The earlier parts are missing and must have been summary indeed. He becomes more detailed as he reaches his own day, focussing very much on the figure of Tiberius.

Velleius' esteem for his old commander has won him many detractors. Summer, for instance, calls him an "obsequious royalist." Syme speaks of his "loyal fervour" and describes him as "voluble and unscrupulous." But his enthusiasm must be placed in its proper context. His coverage of Tiberius is limited to his successful period as an imperial prince and the earlier part of his reign, before things started to go awry. Although Velleius' account contrasts with the darker picture given by Tacitus, it is surely the case that Tacitus' impressions are coloured by the excesses that mark the later years. Velleius also can be subtly critical, as on the death of Livia, when he implies that she should have enjoyed consecration. He was an eyewitness to many of the events that involved Livia, and his admiration for her is patent.[10]

Valerius Maximus

Valerius Maximus published his volumes on memorable deeds and sayings *(Factorum ac Dictorum Memorabilium Libri IX)* in AD 31 and dedicated his work to Tiberius. He maintains an obsequious tone throughout, as in his description of Livia attended by Pudicitia.[11]

Philo Judaeus

Similarly, the Jewish writer Philo of Alexandria (30 BC–AD 45) much admired Livia and praised her for her intelligence and judgement. This is hardly surprising, for she had shown herself to be well disposed to the Jews and was a benefactress of the Temple at Jerusalem.

Ovid

The poet Ovid, born 43 BC, was a witty and impertinent observer of Roman life and morals, until his exile in AD 8 to Tomi on the Black Sea, for reasons still not understood and much debated. He had good reason to heap flattery on Livia, for his slender hope of recall depended entirely on regaining the favour of the imperial family. Before his exile he praised her as the model Roman wife and paragon of Roman virtue, a fairly conventional description and even echoed in Tacitus' obituary portrait. But after his exile Ovid's compliments become sickeningly fulsome, addressed to a goddess-in-the-making. His flattery was ultimately to no avail, for he remained in exile until his death, in about AD 17.

Seneca the Younger

Seneca's early career played out while Livia was still alive, but he wrote about her after her death. Born in Cordoba, Spain, towards the end of the first century BC, he was taken as a child to Rome. There he gained a reputation during the reigns of Caligula, Claudius, and Nero as a writer and a seducer of the imperial women. He died by suicide in AD 65. His writings cover a wide range—letters, essays, plays—and tend to be characterised by sycophantic flattery of the reigning emperor accompanied by denigration of his predecessor.

Livia appears in the works of Seneca three times. All three references come after her death; indeed, all are post-Tiberian. In each case her role is positive. This is surprising and uncharacteristic of Seneca. It may suggest genuine admiration on his part, but more likely it reflects the high regard in which Livia was held in the latter part of the Julio-Claudian era, a personage to be criticised at one's peril, while the lewd and adulterous Julia, as an example, was fair game and a safe target. In *De Ira* Livia's role is secondary. Seneca in describing rulers who have been able to control their anger relates that Timagenes the historian attacked Augustus and Livia and the rest of the imperial family but suffered no retribution, beyond being barred from the emperor's home (see chapter 7). Although Livia's role in this work is essentially incidental, she does at least by implication garner Seneca's admiration.[12]

In the *De Clementia* Seneca provides a detailed account of Livia's efforts to secure clemency for Cornelius Cinna. Although we can assume much rhetorical exaggeration, Vidén argues that if Seneca had wanted to persuade his pupil Nero to a sound philosophy of life, he would not have chosen examples that were incredible. In fact, the general image of Livia here comes very close to that found in Suetonius, of a woman who involved herself in her husband's business but did not control him. It is interesting that the disparaging term *muliebre consilium* (advice offered by a woman) is self-deprecatingly put by Livia into her own mouth.[13]

Livia's third appearance is in the *Consolatio ad Marciam*, as the *maxima femina* to be emulated by Marcia in dealing with her grief.[14] Seneca claims that after Drusus' death in 9 BC, Livia behaved with stateliness and moderation, unlike the traditionally impeccable Octavia, whom he describes as excessive in her behaviour and catty towards Livia. It is interesting here to contrast the inferences drawn from Seneca's description of Livia in the aftermath of Drusus' death, and her similar moderation following Germanicus', from which Tacitus draws the most negative conclusions.[15]

Pliny the Elder

The most important sources are not in fact contemporaries of Livia but come later. Pliny the Elder was born in AD 23 or 24, actually before Livia died, but he would have been too young to form a personal firsthand impression of her. After a varied and active life, he died during the eruption of Vesuvius in 79. Pliny was a diligent collector of facts and a prolific writer. His history of the German Wars in twenty books, as well as his annalistic history in thirty-one books, are both lost. His only surviving work, the extraordinary *Natural History*, comprises thirty-seven books. Pliny provides much information on Livia that reflects his encyclopedic approach to the world's varied wonders: details about her fertility, diet, drinking habits, and the size of her dwarf. But he also provides useful information of a more conventional historical nature, in which a relatively benign view of Livia emerges. The stories about the deaths of Gaius and Lucius distressed Augustus — but he was upset by the rumours, not by a belief in Livia's guilt. In his account of the death of Agrippa Postumus, Pliny attributes no responsibility to her, and limits his criticism to a reference to her *cogitationes* (intrigues) at the close of Augustus' life. This restraint does not reflect a bias in favour of imperial women and in fact is in telling contrast to Pliny's depiction of Agrippina the Younger, where his information is almost uniformly hostile, describing her as a misfortune for the whole world.[16]

Suetonius

Suetonius was born in about AD 70, probably in Africa. He held a number of imperial appointments under Trajan and Hadrian and was a productive writer, most famous for his *Lives of the Caesars*. He died in about 140. He had access to the imperial archives, and at his best can be the most impressive of the major authorities of the period on points of detail. Unfortunately, when he uses the material of others, he often lacks serious judgement, and he is unable to resist a lively anecdote.

Suetonius wrote biography, not history, and tended to handle his material by theme, not by chronological sequence. His subject was the lives of the emperors, and as a general principle he describes women only if they add something to the portrait of the emperor in question, usually in terms of the influence they had over them, or their place in their dynastic plans.[17] This does not imply that Suetonius was slighting towards the imperial women. Rather, he saw the literary advantage of focussing almost exclusively on his main subject. Generally speaking, Livia does not leap to the attention in Suetonius' writings. She emerges as someone who more or less kept within the bounds of what was suitable for a woman. As a consequence, Suetonius' depiction of her is far less savage than the one offered by Tacitus or even by the more restrained Dio. Suetonius says nothing of crimes or poisoning. The theme of cunning and hypocrisy that is so prevalent in Tacitus is perhaps reflected in only one place, Suetonius' report of Caligula's dictum that she was a *Ulixes stolatus*—Ulysses in a stola—in a context that is intended to illustrate Caligula's mischievous habit of denigrating his relatives and his facility for bon mots.[18] At worst, we are allowed a few glimpses of her ambition, her attempt to secure citizenship for a Gaul, her advancement of Otho's grandfather. Tiberius does express annoyance at Livia for claiming an equal share of the rule. But Suetonius' focus in this context is on Tiberius' view of things, such as his odium towards members of his own family and his conviction that women should not meddle in men's affairs. That the notion of her seeking an equal share in power is a rhetorical exaggeration is demonstrated by Tiberius' reaction to her engaging in the efforts to prevent the fires, something that in the past she had always done. Any criticism of Livia on the issue of her ambitions is at best muted and implied, rather than overt.[19]

Suetonius takes the position that Livia might have sought to sway Augustus from time to time but that her influence on political events was relatively slight. In a particularly telling passage he mentions the claims made by others that Augustus had been personally inclined not to adopt Tiberius but was won over by pressure from his wife. Suetonius emphatically states that in a matter of such great importance it is hardly credible that Augustus would not have given the issue very careful thought. He suggests that the princeps in fact weighed up the advantages and disadvantages of Tiberius very carefully and decided in the end that the advantages predominated. Livia's intercession, he suggests, was not the deciding factor. He backs up his claim by quoting letters from Augustus to Tiberius.[20]

Suetonius passes over opportunities to besmirch Livia's name. He reports the general opinion *(creditur* and *opinio fuit)* that Germanicus met his end through Tiberius' treachery, aided by Piso, but he does not associate Livia in the scandal. Often he follows the tradition that actually favours her. On the issue of whether she suppressed the news of Augustus' death to allow Tiberius time to return, Suetonius takes the unequivocal position that Tiberius reached the emperor's bedside before his death and that the two were able to hold a fairly lengthy conversation. This contrasts with Tacitus, who characteristically clouds the issue by raising doubts which he does not resolve, and Dio, who suggests that the most reliable authorities have Augustus dead before Tiberius' arrival. Suetonius makes no mention of a visit by Augustus to Agrippa Postumus or of any suspicion that Livia may have poisoned her husband. In only one place does he seem to take a Tacitean approach in characterizing Livia's actions. Suetonius reports the uncertainty about who wrote the letter that ordered the slaying of Agrippa Postumus. But the death of Agrippa was clearly an incident that left the ancient historians genuinely baffled, and Suetonius simply lays out the variants, without giving any opinion.[21]

Cassius Dio

Cassius Dio came from the province of Bithynia and held consulships in about AD 205 and in 229. He wrote a history in Greek, from the early kings down to the time of Severus Alexander (222–35). He was essentially an accumulator of information and gave little thought to broad synthesis or serious analysis. At times he claims acquaintance with several sources, but he rarely names them, and never with reference to Livia. He generally lacks serious critical judgement in assessing his material, and often fails to distinguish between the preposterous and the plausible, although he does in fact seem to go out of his way to suggest a sensible assessment of the various traditions about Livia.

Dio can in places be useful, in that he treats events in broad sequence, unlike

Suetonius, and thus provides the only extant annalistic account of Augustus' reign. Unfortunately, there are major gaps in his text, which are to some degree filled by Byzantine epitomes. This term is rather misleading, for the epitomators tend to excerpt rather than to summarise, and often simply omit significant events.

There is extensive material on Livia scattered throughout Dio's account, and he is our sole source for such important information as the grant of quasi-tribunician *sacrosanctitas* in 35 BC. His judgements on her are very much of a mixed bag. He depicts her as giving Augustus sound and moderate counsel on how to handle the Cinna conspiracy. Yet he claims that amidst the universal sadness, Tiberius and Livia were alone in their joy at Germanicus' death. He is also preoccupied more than any other of the extant sources with the notion that Livia saw herself as a coruler after the death of Augustus. Goodyear has suggested that Dio may have worked back from Agrippina the Younger in portraying an excessive desire for power on Livia's part. Moreover, it is possible that he was influenced by the reemergence of the powerful imperial women during the Severan period. He states as fact that Augustus sailed secretly to see Agrippa Postumus. He also repeats without comment the speculation that Livia was involved in the deaths of Gaius and Lucius. But he expresses scepticism over the claim that she brought about the death of Marcellus, the son of Octavia. Although he inclines towards the view that she postponed making public the news of Augustus' death, he concedes that there is a contrary tradition. He is our only source for the claim that Livia despatched Augustus by means of poisoned figs, but he demonstrates a noticeable ambivalence about the story. In none of these accounts does one detect the enthusiastic venom of Tacitus, but rather a general incuriosity.[22]

Dio made use of source material not found in Tacitus and other earlier extant writers. In the account of the debate over the conspiracy of Cornelius Cinna he echoes Seneca in a number of places. Both accounts clearly have elements in common. They use the same imagery, for instance, such as Livia's analogy between Augustus and the doctor who is forced to find a new cure when all else has failed. Because Seneca had a good reason for preserving the full form of the story, given that he was writing on the general topic of clemency, it might be expected that he would have been Dio's main source, and there certainly is evidence that Dio had read other works of Seneca, such as the *ad Polybium*. But Dio's version of the incident is in fact much longer, and it differs in a number of details, such as Cinna's name and the date of the incident. He clearly had access to a source independent of Seneca.[23]

Tacitus

Tacitus is the primary literary source for the Julio-Claudian period. His general qualities as a historian have already been treated in exhaustive detail and need not be entered into here. In particular his celebrated claim that he wrote impartially—*sine ira ac studio*—has been subjected to much scrutiny. It would be foolish to deny his bias against the imperial system, but unlike many other ancient writers he is not so naive as to accept as feasible every bit of nonsense passed down to him.

In assessing Tacitus' portrayal of Livia, we must note his general hostility towards ambitious women of the imperial family. There have been those who, like Wuilleumier and Bardon, have claimed that Tacitus was a misogynist, motivated by a basic hatred of females.[24] But he can surely be cleared of a general charge of misogyny, in the sense of an irrational and consistent hatred of women. He does recognise female qualities such as *constantia* and *fides*, and his women are at times capable of heroism.[25] The problem is not Tacitus' overall view of women but his view of a particular class of women, in a particular context. He was deeply offended by those women who were placed in positions of power and influence through their family connections and sought to use this power to manipulate the political process for their own ends, a process that in any case rightly belonged to the Senate and people and not to an autocrat or his relatives. For Tacitus, this corrupt use of power was manifested primarily in continuous manoeuvres to promote the interests of a potential successor, leading to inevitable factional feuds.

In the obituary notice that begins the fifth book of the *Annals*, Tacitus' assessment of Livia is commendably restrained. He depicts her as a woman of old-fashioned virtue and of impressive noble lineage. On the negative side he observes that she was more affable *(comis)* than women of the old school would have thought right, that she was a match for her husband's craftiness and her son's insincerity, and that she was a domineering mother *(mater impotens)*. This restrained tone is notably absent, however, from the allusions to Livia in the preceding narrative. Here Tacitus' hostility is blatant. He can scarcely mention her name without a touch of malice, and he creates a portrait of a scheming and ruthless manipulator that is glaringly at variance with the general picture that appears in the other historical authorities. As noted earlier, Suetonius' and Dio's criticisms of Livia are relatively measured; Suetonius in particular finds only vague gossip to use against her. Apart from an allusion to Augustus' distress over her intrigues, Pliny has nothing critical to say, while

Velleius, not surprisingly, and Seneca, somewhat remarkably, are unashamed admirers.[26]

This is not to suggest that Tacitus fabricated information. Rather, the problem is that where he has two sources and one is unfavourable, he either will follow the adverse account or will at the very least cloud the issue by raising it as a possibility. There would certainly have been a large body of anti-Tiberian (and anti-Livian) material for him to call upon. Tacitus himself alludes to the wide range of hostile charges made against Tiberius *cum omnia . . . conquirerent intenderentque* (when [writers] were collecting and exaggerating all sorts of things). The memoirs of the younger Agrippina were certainly known to him, and they are unlikely to have had many kind things to say about Livia. He knew of bitter letters denouncing Tiberius, sent to Augustus by Julia during her husband's stay in Rhodes.[27]

Apart from using information hostile to Livia, Tacitus was most skilful at presenting information that, while strictly accurate, created a damaging effect. Outside the early period of her marriage, it is probably fair to say that he never makes a substantial allusion to Livia that is not designed to arouse animosity, often by presenting the details in such a way that one cannot help drawing an unfavourable inference. Often he will avoid doing this explicitly, but will protect his historical integrity by citing public opinion or speculation. The trip to Planasia provides an excellent illustration of this technique. The story is implausible. Tacitus no doubt recognised it as implausible. He could defend himself by pointing out that he was presenting it only as a rumour. But in the end he would have been fully satisfied no doubt with the insinuation that he had deliberately planted.

Tacitus skilfully employs certain words that carry a powerfully negative connotation when characterising Livia. Thus he applies to her the term *potentia*, with its associations of unauthorised and improper power, often manifested by excessive influence. When Calpurnius Piso defies Livia and hauls her friend Urgulania into court, he does so *spreta potentia Augustae* (with Augusta's power thwarted), implying that her potentia was of such a malign nature that it was the duty of an intrepid official to stand up against it. When Sejanus uses Mutilia Prisca to stir up Livia's animosity towards Agrippina, Livia is described as *anum . . . natura potentiae anxiam*, a very powerful phrase suggesting not simply a love of power but a desperate innate desire for it *(natura . . . anxiam)*, and even more, an unhealthy unwillingness to give up that power even in old age *(anum)*.[28] Even more damning in its effect is the word *impotentia*, whose force is quite different from its English derivative, and conveys the sense of a lust for power that is completely out of control. Recording public opinion and the supposed anxiety about Tiberius taking over, Tacitus adds the problem of a mother driven by *muliebri impotentia* (a woman's passion for power), with the result that *serviendum feminae* (they would have to be slaves to a woman). Tiberius supposedly left Rome because his mother was desperate to share his rule, which Tacitus skilfully calls *dominatio*, implying an insatiable craving for a tyrannical form of control that was alien to Roman tradition, and echoing the supposed earlier concerns of the public. In his obituary notice Livia is described as a *mater impotens*, a cleverly ambiguous phrase because it can convey the notion of a woman desperate to control her son, but also a mother uncontrollable in advancing her son's ambitions.[29]

Tacitus suggests that as a woman Livia achieves her ends not by overt action but by devious underhand methods, usually involving intrigue. When Lucius and Gaius Caesar died he declined to commit himself about the cause, noting that it might have been simply the working of fate or it might have been the *dolus* (treacherous scheme) of Livia. Augustus was persuaded to promote the interests of Tiberius *obscuris . . . matris artibus* (by the murky devices of his mother), a convenient charge because by its nature it could not be refuted. When Livia helped Julia the Younger in her exile, it was part of a pattern of making a public show of concern for her stepdaughter's children while she worked to undermine them "in secret" *(per occultum)*. When word reached Rome of Germanicus' ill-health, Tacitus again used the shield of public opinion to express outrage over Livia's conduct and her secret conversations with Plancina *(secretos sermones)*. While Livia's conversations with her friends would naturally be expected to be private, the adjective *secretos* has an emotional impact, for it connotes intrigues, and especially devious and underhand intrigues. When Germanicus died in Syria, and Piso was considering his options, there were those who encouraged him to be bold, assuring him that Tiberius and Livia were making a loud show of grief for Germanicus *(iacantius)* but in their hearts were glad, and that he could count on Livia's secret complicity *(conscientia)*. Again Tacitus avoids making an explicit statement about someone's secret thought and protects himself by attributing what are in reality absurd, but prejudicial, statements to other parties.[30]

Perhaps the most vivid illustration of Tacitus' skill in arousing antipathy towards Livia is the way he applies the word *noverca* to her. The concept of stepmother had sinister connotations for the Romans as for other societies. Quintilian might have protested at the use of the stock evil stepmother in legal exercises *(declamationes)*, a stereotype he claimed belonged to the realm of fantasy, but in the popular mind the notion was firmly set, particularly in the association of stepmothers and poison, and stepmothers as the murderers of their stepchildren. So Ovid can describe how in the Iron Age the *terribiles novercae* mixed their dark poisons, and the boy in Horace's Epode who is carried into the witches' den so that they can use his body for a magic potion asks why they look at him "like a stepmother" *(ut noverca)*.[31] When Livia is first introduced, it is with the speculation that the deaths of Gaius and Lucius were caused by the *novercae Liviae dolus* (craftiness of their stepmother Livia). Quite apart from the unfairness of the stereotype, Livia was their stepmother only in a very technical sense, after Augustus' adoption of his grandchildren for political purposes. But the prejudicial damage of the word was deliberate. Similarly, in the speculation over the blame for the death of Agrippa Postumus, Tacitus suggests that it was likely caused by Tiberius and Livia, the latter from a stepmother's hate *(novercalibus odiis)*. Livia is said to be hostile towards Agrippina for exactly the same reason, novercalibus odiis. Here the stretch is even greater. Livia was in fact the stepmother of the elder Julia, Agrippina's mother. Finally, among the burdens that Augustus had to bear, Tacitus adds his wife, *gravis in rempublicam mater, gravis domui Caesarum noverca* (a stepmother who was a burden on the state, a burden to the house of the Caesars), a line of brilliant artistry. It shows the way in which state and domus had become intertwined. On the one hand she was mater reipublicae, standing as the counterpart to the pater patriae, whose obligations to and power over the state reflect a Roman man's position within his family. (It reminds the reader of the attempt to have Livia declared mater patriae on Augustus' death.) But in the purely domestic situation she was a noverca, and a gravis one at that, reminding us of the rumours about the deaths of Gaius, Lucius, and Agrippa Postumus. As a footnote, it might be added that Suetonius never calls Livia *noverca*.[32]

Livia's supposed intrigues against the rival members of the imperial family might be a legitimate theme, given that they would potentially have had serious consequences. But Tacitus continues his campaign of denigrating Livia after her son's accession. He speaks of the rift between Tiberius and his mother over the supposed struggle for power. This is mentioned in other sources, but we should be cautious about the weight and importance that Tacitus gives to the disagreement. As Syme has observed, the potentia of Livia and the effect on Tiberius barely correspond with the "sinister intimations" that Tacitus ascribes to them. He says at first that Tiberius held down Livia through envy *(anxius invidia)*. It is only later that the notion of discord arises, none of which is matched by what he says in Livia's obituary notice. Syme suggests that some of the incidents implying conflict may have been added after the obituary was written. Tacitus makes the plain statement that when Tiberius rushed back to Rome at the time of his mother's illness in AD 22 the *concordia* between the emperor and his mother was still *sincera*. Then he adds, almost as an afterthought, that the explanation could be that they were concealing their mutual antipathy—*sive occultis odiis*.[33]

The most dramatic Livian episodes in Tacitus' *Annals* belong to his account of the death of Augustus and its immediate aftermath, the execution of Agrippa Postumus and the succession of Tiberius. There are enough close parallels to make a case that Tacitus, Dio, and Suetonius had access to one or more common source for the events surrounding Tiberius' accession. The basic narrative is the same in Tacitus and Dio. It is also possible that Dio drew on Tacitus but had access also to other sources, possibly later than Tacitus.[34] Suetonius certainly drew from the same source as Tacitus (if not actually drawing on him directly), as is evidenced even by the similarity of their language. In describing the tribune in charge of the guard, for instance, Suetonius writes *tribunus . . . custos appositus*, Tacitus, *tribuno custodiae adposito*. Tiberius' response to the soldier who brings the information is described by Suetonius as *renuntianti tribuno . . . rationem respondit* and by Tacitus as *nuntianti centurioni . . . rationem . . . respondit*. We cannot now know what this source might have been, but the anti-Tiberian passages of the memoirs of Agrippina the Younger have been suggested as a candidate.[35] Although Tacitus may have used the same sources as Dio and Suetonius, he drew more fully from them, or supplemented them by other information or perhaps even by his own speculations.

Perhaps the most striking aspect of this part of the narrative is the way that Tacitus' portrayal of Livia's behaviour is echoed in the chronologically later account of Agrippina the Younger's role in the death of Claudius, separated by some forty years. The general parallels between Agrippina and Livia in the major sources are marked to a degree that raises suspicions. Both sons take power through the scheming of a mother, the removal by the mother of rival claimants, and possibly the poisoning of the incumbent emperor, her husband. In each case the mother tries to rule through her son but is rebuffed. Worn out by his mother's interference, Tiberius left Rome, and Nero threatened to leave for similar reasons. Livia's claim that she reminded Tiberius where he got his power from is echoed by Agrippina's assertion that she made Nero emperor and she could unmake him too. Both new emperors at the outset of their reigns seemed moderate, but after their mothers' deaths exercised evil tendencies without restraint. Interestingly, an explicit comparison between the two women is made only once by Tacitus, in an innocuous context, when Agrippina is said to have emulated Livia in providing the exact funeral arrangements that Augustus had enjoyed.[36]

To put this whole issue into perspective, some account must be given of

Claudius' death in October 54. The question of whether or not he was indeed murdered by his wife Agrippina is not important in this particular context. Much more important is that people believed she was guilty, and on this question there is almost complete unanimity among the ancient sources. There are only minor expressions of caution. Josephus twice notes tentative reservations, and Philostratus, in his life of Apollonius of Tyana, does the same. But these two are in a lonely minority, and the major sources express no doubt. Thus, quite apart from the question of actual guilt, it is clear that there was a strong tradition that Agrippina murdered Claudius. The notion that Livia had committed a similar crime was far less firmly established and reported as nothing more substantial than a rumour.[37]

It need cause no surprise that Claudius should have died when he did. He had always suffered from ill health, and the possibility of a natural cause of death, from, say, gastroenteritis and heart failure, cannot be ruled out.[38] The mere fact that a charge is made against Agrippina is not in itself significant, for such accusations tended to follow the deaths of prominent members of the Julio-Claudian family. There would have been no compelling motive for her to remove her husband. It is true that the longer the succession was delayed, the stronger would be the claim of the youthful Britannicus, Claudius' natural son. But we have to balance this with the fact that in 54 Nero, though Britannicus' senior, was himself still very young, probably only sixteen.

In the absence of a compelling motive, a tradition viciously hostile to Agrippina would have had no trouble concocting one. The sources agree that by 54 Agrippina's cunning plans were under suspicion and that there had been a reconciliation between Claudius and Britannicus. Suetonius and Dio give the initiative in this to Claudius. Tacitus, who generally sought to portray Claudius as a fool, the dupe of his wives and freedmen, gives the credit for smoking out Agrippina to the freedman Narcissus, who then became reconciled to Britannicus. Narcissus had been largely responsible for the execution of Britannicus' mother, Messalina, and believed that he had enough evidence similarly to undo Agrippina. Supposedly, he was so lacking in discretion that he revealed his plans to his friends, thereby conveniently offering his archenemy the chance to discover what he was up to.[39]

The opportunity for murder came about in October 54. Agrippina first made sure that Narcissus was off the scene, persuading him, according to Dio, to take the cure at the hot baths of Sinuessa in Campania.[40] The story of Claudius' subsequent death is familiar and famous. At a palace banquet, on the night of October 12, the emperor was served a poisoned mushroom. Tacitus and Dio provide the tradition that the poison was sprinkled on a particularly succulent sample, and Dio adds the further detail that Agrippina cunningly ate the rest herself.[41] The details of later events vary, and the sources note variant traditions. In the version reflected in both Suetonius and Tacitus, Claudius fell ill, then rallied, to be given a second dose, which finished him off. The news of the death was supposedly kept secret. The Senate was convened and the priests made their vows for the emperor's recovery, at the very time when his corpse was being wrapped up in warm coverlets to prevent the onset of rigor mortis. Otherwise, Agrippina blocked admission to the palace and gave out regular bulletins that maintained the fiction that there was hope for recovery. Tacitus and Suetonius provide the reason for the delay, which was to keep the news from the main body of the praetorians until the preparations for Nero's succession were completed.[42] Shortly after midday on October 13, 54, the emperor's death was reported, and the *Apocolocyntosis* indicates that the official report stated that he died happy, watching the performance of the comic actors brought in to entertain him.[43]

There is a solid core of fact in both successions—it is indisputable that each emperor had adopted a stepson as his heir and was succeeded by him. But beyond this, the common themes of the two deaths as they appear in the major sources should be viewed with caution. Each emperor regrets his decision and decides that he will restore the rightful heir. His wife gets wind of the scheme and decides to eliminate her husband before his plan can be implemented. The emperor dies but the event is kept secret until the stepson's position is secure. In each case the death is followed by the murder of a prominent Roman. There are disturbing resemblances of detail also. In the background hover the loyal retainers, who happen to be in the wrong place at the wrong time—Narcissus, the freedman of Claudius, and Clemens, the devoted slave of Agrippa. There is the powerful emotion of the reconciliation with the rival claimant, followed by the betrayal of the secret, by Narcissus and Marcia, both behaving indiscreetly. The means are strikingly similar, in that in each case the poison is introduced by a clever device intended to trick the emperor, on a succulent mushroom or on a fig still on the tree. Comic actors are brought in for Claudius' last hours, and Augustus likens himself to a comic actor in departing life's stage. There is the delay that follows each death, hard to explain if the emperor had been removed by a premeditated murder. In each case the wife barricades the house where the dead emperor lies and issues reassuring reports about his health until the political situation is right for her.[44]

While the general parallelism is striking, more remarkable are the verbal echoes evident in Tacitus' accounts of both incidents. Tacitus certainly can sometimes be an *imitator sui* in that he will use the same language to describe what he sees as similar events.[45] But there are no other episodes in Tacitus in which the verbal echoes and parallelism of incidents extend over so considerable a portion of continuous narrative. The actions of Livia and Agrippina are both described as *scelus*. Augustus and Claudius are both *exanimis*. Livia blocked the house *custodiis domum et viam saepserat*, and Agrippina did the same, *aditus custodiis clauserat*. The verbal parallels continue after the account of each death, and do so with powerful effect. Thus Tacitus follows the death of Claudius with a dramatic introduction to book 13 of the *Annals*, asserting that the first victim in the new regime of Nero was Marcus Junius Silanus, governor of Asia *(prima novo principatu mors Iunii Silani proconsulis)*, and thus echoes his claim at the beginning of Tiberius' reign that "the first misdeed of the new principate was the slaying of Agrippa Postumus" *(primum facinus novi principatus fuit Postumi Agrippae caedes)*. The link is reinforced by the sentence that immediately precedes the reference to Postumus' death. In reporting that Tiberius had taken power, Tacitus calls him Nero *(Neronem)*, although that name was no longer correct after his adoption by Augustus in AD 4. The deliberate anachronism is intended to insinuate that the accession of Tiberius is associated with the same infamy as Nero's. Also, Agrippina supposedly had Marcus Silanus killed *ignaro Nerone* (without Nero knowing), just as Tiberius claimed ignorance over the death of Agrippa.[46]

Which of these accounts influenced the other? The death of Claudius occurs later in Tacitus' narrative and might seem logically to have been inspired by the earlier incident. But as noted earlier, there can be no doubt that in the popular tradition the case against Agrippina is by far the stronger. Thus it seems very possible that Livia was depicted as a murderer on the analogy of Agrippina, and that the rumours about Augustus' death did not circulate until after AD 54.[47] This possibility is strengthened by the fact that Dio's reference to the poisoned fig is likely to have been inspired by the well-known story of Agrippina's poisoned mushroom. The notion that Livia murdered her husband, in the manner that would associate her with Agrippina, suits very well Tacitus' theme that in AD 14 power was in effect seized, not transmitted.

Goodyear suggests that Tacitus might not in fact have worked out the significance of the similarities. But they are likely to have been deliberate. Mellor describes the situation nicely: "Tacitus is content to use the rumours to besmirch by association Livia and Tiberius who, whatever their failings, never displayed the deranged malice of an Agrippina and a Nero. It is good literature but it can be irresponsible history."[48]

Livia is mentioned by other writers, but only incidentally. A list of literary citations follows. It will be noted that although there is no shortage of information, with the exception of the episodes relating to the marriage of Livia and Augustus, the death of Augustus and its immediate aftermath, and Livia's own death, relatively few of the references can be tied to precise dates.

Literary Citations

Anonymous, *Consolatio ad Liviam*

1–12:	Address to Livia.
13–20:	Drusus provides an *exemplum* through his military achievements.
21–40:	Livia anticipated a triumph but must prepare a funeral.
41–58:	Even Livia's virtues could not prevent the disaster.
59–74:	Despite his achievements, Augustus was not immune to grief, for Drusus' death was preceded by those of Marcellus, Agrippa, and Octavia.
75–84:	Drusus' great merits, matched by Antonia's.
85–94:	Tiberius is devastated by his brother's death.
95–118:	Livia's grief.
119–66:	Livia addresses Drusus.
167–78:	The return of Drusus' body to Rome.
179–98:	The people mourn and seek answers from the gods.
199–220:	The funeral.
221–52:	Mars and Tiber express their grief.
253–64:	The cremation.
265–70:	The immortality of Drusus' achievements.
271–82:	Germany will be punished.
283–98:	The temple to Castor and Pollux that Drusus would have dedicated with Tiberius.
299–328:	Antonia's grief.
329–40:	Drusus' departed ancestors will greet him.
341–78:	Livia has a duty to accept Fate and not to yield to grief.
379–92:	Livia has been blessed by her status, sons, and husband.
393–410:	Livia had time to cope with the news.
411–16:	Long life for Livia and Tiberius are wished for.
417–26:	Augustus and Tiberius have given their support, despite Livia's reluctance.
427–44:	No one can escape death.
445–70:	Drusus would not want Livia to grieve.
471–74:	Livia can draw comfort from Tiberius and Augustus.

Cornelius Nepos, *Atticus*

19.4: The granddaughter of Atticus was betrothed to the son of Livia.

Strabo

5.3.8: Livia and Octavia are credited with fine buildings in Rome, including the Porticus Liviae.

Horace, *Odes*

3.14.5–6: Livia carries out sacrifices to mark Augustus' return to Rome.

Ovid, *Tristia*

1.6.25–27: Ovid's wife's qualities might be derived from Livia, *femina princeps*, who was revered through the years.

2.161–4: Livia alone was worthy of Augustus. But for her he would have remained unmarried.

4.2.11–14: Livia makes offerings for the safe return of Tiberius in company with the matrons and the Vestals.

Ovid, *ex Ponto*

1.4.56: Livia is worthy of Caesar, and offerings are made to them as true gods *(dis veris)*.

2.2.69: Livia keeps the couch pure.

2.8.4: Ovid possesses a silver image of Livia.

2.8.29: Livia alone is equal *(par)* to Augustus.

2.8.45: Ovid prays for Livia's support and hopes that her family will prosper.

3.1.114–18: Ovid's wife must approach Livia, whose chastity overshadows that of previous ages. Livia has the beauty of Venus and the morals of Juno and alone is worthy of the celestial couch.

3.1.125–26: Livia is a *femina princeps* who proves the efficacy of Fortune.

3.1.139–45: Livia might be involved in major matters; she scarcely has time for her own person. Ovid's wife will approach the countenance of Juno.

3.1.163–64: Ovid's wife is asked to worship the *numen* of Augustus, his son (Tiberius), and his wife.

3.4.95–96: Livia is urged to prepare for Tiberius' triumph.

4.9.107: Beside the image of the Divus Augustus stands that of his priestess wife *(coniunxque sacerdos)*.

4.13.29: Livia is the Vesta of chaste matrons, and it is hard to tell whether she is more worthy of her father or of her son.

Ovid, *Fasti*

1.536: Ovid prophesies the deification of Livia.

1.640: Livia alone is worthy to share the couch of great Jove.

1.649: Livia, alone worthy of the bed of mighty Jove, established (?) *concordia.*

5.157–58: Livia restored the Bona Dea shrine to imitate her husband in all respects.

6.637: Livia dedicated a temple to Concordia.

Philo, *Legatio*

291: Livia was generous to the Temple in Jerusalem.

319–20: Livia gave golden bowls to the Temple. She was a woman of education and intellect.

Seneca, *De Ira*

3.23.4: Timagenes the historian said damaging things about Augustus and Livia.

Seneca, *De Clementia*

1.9: Livia advocates clemency towards Lucius Cinna.

Seneca, *Consolatio ad Marcium*

2–5: Livia, grief stricken over the death of Drusus, was advised by the philosopher Areus. Octavia hated Livia. Livia accompanied the corpse of Drusus to Rome.

Anonymous, *Apocolocyntosis*

9.5: Claudius ordered that Livia be made a goddess.

Honestus

SEG 13.348: Augusta has borne two sceptred sons. She is fit to accompany the learned muses, and her mind has preserved the whole world.

Velleius

2.75.2: Livia's family background, distinction, and marriages.

2.79.2: Tiberius Nero gave Livia to Octavian for marriage, which boded well for the state.

2.94.1: Tiberius Nero gave Livia to Octavian for marriage.

2.95.1: Livia bore Drusus in the house of the Caesars.

2.130.4–5: Tiberius grieved over the death of his mother, a preeminent woman. Her influence was always beneficial.

Valerius Maximus

4.3.3:	After the death of Drusus, Antonia went to live with Livia.
4.5.3:	The victorious Tiberius came to Ticinum to greet Augustus and Livia.
6.1.1:	Pudicitia attends the couch of Livia.

Columella, *de re Rustica*

5.10.11:	The Livian fig is recommended.
10.141:	The Livian fig ripens when Arcturus rises.

Pliny, *Natural History*

7.57:	Augustus and Livia are an example of an otherwise fertile couple who could not have children together.
7.75:	Livia owned the smallest dwarf, Andromeda.
7.150:	Among Augustus' misfortunes were the intrigues of his wife and Tiberius.
10.154:	Livia used an egg to determine the sex of her baby.
12.94:	Livia erected a temple to Augustus on the Palatine, containing a cinnamon root.
14.11:	The Porticus Liviae produced wine.
14.60:	Livia died at the age of 82 [*sic*], after drinking Pucine wine exclusively.
15.129:	The "Royal" laurel is now called the *Augusta*.
15.136–37:	An eagle dropped a chick with a laurel sprig in Livia's lap. The sprig grew into a laurel grove.
19.92:	Livia ate elecampane salad.
34.3–4:	Livia owned copper mines in Gaul.

Josephus, *Antiquities*

16.139:	Livia contributed to the celebrations for the founding of Caesarea.
17.10:	Livia dissuaded Salome from marriage to Syllaeus.
17.134–41:	A plot involving forged letters from Salome to Livia was exposed.
18.27:	Herod Antipas renamed Betheramphtha after Livia.

Josephus, *Jewish War*

1.566:	Livia advised Salome about her passion for Syllaeus.
1.641:	Antipater forged letters to Livia.
2.168:	Herod Antipas built the city of Julias.

5.562–63: Vessels sent to the Temple by Augustus and Livia were melted down.

Tacitus, *Annals*

1.3.3–4: Livia might have been involved in the deaths of Gaius and Lucius. She openly promoted Tiberius' claims and arranged the exile of Agrippa.

1.4.5: Livia had a female lack of control. People would have to obey a woman.

1.5: Some suspected Livia of causing Augustus' final illness; she had found out about his plans from Marcia. Livia concealed the death of Augustus until Tiberius could reach the scene.

1.6: Livia and Tiberius were responsible for the death of Agrippa. Livia was advised to dissuade Tiberius from revealing all the details.

1.8.1: Livia was Augustus' heir and was adopted into the Julian family and took the Julian name.

1.10.5: Octavian abducted Tiberius Nero's wife and consulted the pontiffs whether she could be legally married despite her pregnancy.

1.13.6: Livia saved Haterius.

1.14.1–4: The Senate voted honours for Livia but Tiberius out of envy insisted on restraint.

1.33.1: Germanicus was the grandson of Livia.

1.33.3: Livia had a stepmother's hatred for Agrippina.

1.71.3: Libellous poems spoke of stress between Tiberius and Livia.

1.72.4: Satirical verses claimed tension between Livia and Tiberius.

1.73.3: Actors took part in Livia's Palatine celebrations in honour of Augustus.

2.14.1: Germanicus dreamt of Livia.

2.34.2–3: Urgulania was protected against legal action by Livia.

2.42.3: Livia wrote to Archelaus, but only at the request of her son.

2.43.4: Livia instructed Plancina to undermine Agrippina.

2.50: Livia was verbally attacked by Appuleia Varilla, but Tiberius asked that no action be taken.

2.77.3: Piso enjoyed Livia's secret support.

2.82.1: Livia intrigued secretly with Plancina.

3.3: Livia and Tiberius abstained from mourning for Germanicus. They might have prevented Antonia from participating in the ceremonies.

3.15.1: Plancina acquired a pardon through Livia.
3.16.3: Piso declared that he had been loyal to Livia.
3.17.1–2: Tiberius pardoned Plancina through Livia's intercession. This caused much offence.
3.34.6: Livia accompanied Augustus to the East and the West.
3.64: Tiberius returned to Rome because of his mother's illness, and games were instituted. Livia had caused offence over the dedication of the Theatre of Marcellus. Games were decreed for her recovery.
3.71.1: The equestrians made vows for Livia's recovery.
4.8.3: Tiberius made reference to Livia's extreme old age.
4.12: Livia was drawn into Sejanus' intrigues against Agrippina.
4.15.3: Asia was given the right to build a temple to Livia, Tiberius, and the Senate.
4.16.4: Livia was granted the right to sit with the Vestals in the theatre.
4.21.1: Lucius Piso scorned Livia's *potentia*.
4.22.3: Plautius Silvanus committed suicide after a supposed hint by Livia.
4.37.1: Tiberius refused to allow a temple to be built in Spain for himself and his mother.
4.40.3: Tiberius cited Livia as an appropriate advisor to her granddaughter Livilla.
4.57.3: Tiberius could not reject his mother because he owed his power to her as her gift. She may have driven him to Capri.
4.71.6: Livia supported Julia the Younger in her exile.
5.1.1–4: Livia died in AD 29. Claudian by birth, she was adopted into the Livian and Julian houses. Her first husband was Tiberius Nero. Smitten by Livia's beauty, Octavian took her from her husband and brought her to his home, despite her pregnancy. After this she had no offspring. She had old-fashioned virtues. She was a demanding mother and an accommodating wife. She matched her husband's subtleties, her son's insincerity. Her funeral was simple. Her will for a long time was not executed. The funeral eulogy was delivered by Caligula.
5.2.1–2: Tiberius curtailed the tributes paid to Livia and refused her divine honours, claiming to act in accordance with her wishes. Tiberius attacked the consul Fufius, who had risen through Livia's favour.

5.3.1: The death of Livia removed a restraint on Tiberius, who was instinctively deferential towards his mother. It was believed that she had suppressed a letter from Tiberius denouncing Agrippina and her son.
6.5.3: Cotta Messalinus commented adversely on Livia's birthday celebration.
6.26.3: Plancina was protected by Livia.
6.51.3: While Livia was alive, Tiberius displayed a mixture of good and evil.
12.6.2: Vitellius told the Senate how they had heard from their fathers that women had been snatched from husbands on the whim of the Caesars.
12.69.4: Agrippina imitated Livia in arranging the funeral of Claudius.

Plutarch, *Antony*
83.4: Cleopatra hoped that Livia and Octavia would intercede for her.

Plutarch, *Galba*
3.2: Galba was related to Livia and owed his consulship to her.

Plutarch, *De garrulitate*
508A–B: Livia learned of Augustus' plans to recall Agrippa Postumus.

Plutarch, *Peri tou Ei tou en delphois*
385F: Livia dedicated the golden *E* at Delphi.

Athenaeus, *Deipnosphistae*
3.75: The highly recommended Livian fig grew near Rome.

Suetonius, *Augustus*
29.4: Augustus constructed the Porticus Liviae in his wife's name.
40.3: Livia asked Augustus to grant a Gaul citizenship.
62.2: Octavian divorced Scribonia and married the pregnant Livia. He remained devoted to her up to his death.
63.1: Livia bore Augustus no children. There was a conception followed by premature birth.
69.1–2: Mark Antony charged Octavian with a hasty marriage to Livia and later questioned his marital fidelity.
70.1: Augustus and entourage celebrated a banquet of the Twelve Gods.

71.1:	Livia reputedly provided Augustus with young girls.
73:	Livia made Augustus' clothes.
84.2:	Augustus wrote out beforehand what he would say to Livia.
99.1:	Augustus died in the arms of Livia, bidding her farewell.
101.2:	Augustus appointed Livia as chief legatee, with one-third of the estate.

Suetonius, *Tiberius*

4.3:	After returning from exile, Tiberius Nero gave up the pregnant Livia to Octavian.
6.1–3:	Livia endured many perils during her first husband's exile.
7.1:	Tiberius put on gladiatorial shows in honour of his father and of his grandfather Drusus at Livia and Augustus' expense.
10.2:	Livia begged Tiberius not to go to Rhodes.
12.1:	Livia secured a *legatio* for Tiberius while he was in Rhodes.
13.2:	Livia lobbied for Tiberius' return from Rhodes.
14.2:	Livia sought an omen for Tiberius' birth by hatching an egg.
21.2:	Livia begged Augustus to adopt Tiberius.
21.7:	Augustus and Livia were concerned for Tiberius' well-being.
28:	Tiberius was tolerant of verbal abuses against him and his family.
50.2–3:	Tiberius was angry at his mother's demands to share power, avoided meeting her, and avoided confidential conversations so that he would not seem to be guided by her advice — though in fact he did sometimes follow it. He refused her honorific titles and was annoyed when she helped during a fire.
51.1–2:	Tiberius appointed a man as juror at his mother's bidding. Livia read out letters of Augustus complaining to her about Tiberius. This may have been why he left Rome. Tiberius gave Livia a modest funeral. The decomposing body hastened the rite. Tiberius disregarded her will and punished her followers.

Suetonius, *Caligula*

7:	Livia dedicated a statue of her dead great-grandson.
10:	Caligula lived with Livia and gave her funeral eulogy.
14.2:	Livia's privileges were given also to Antonia.
16.3:	Caligula paid out Livia's bequests.
23.2:	Caligula referred to Livia as Ulixes Stolatus and claimed that she had a humble grandfather.

Suetonius, *Claudius*

1.1: Drusus was born within three months of the marriage of Livia and Octavian, and there was speculation that he was the latter's son. People joked about a "three-month child."

3.2–4.6: Augustus corresponded with Livia on family matters.

11.3: Claudius arranged divine honours for Livia and a chariot drawn by elephants in the circus.

41.2: Livia discouraged Claudius from writing on the civil war period.

Suetonius, *Galba*

1: An eagle dropped a chick with a laurel sprig in Livia's lap.

5.1: Livia bequeathed a legacy to Galba which Tiberius did not pay.

Suetonius, *Otho*

1.1: Otho's grandfather was reared by Livia.

Marcus Aurelius, *Meditations*

8.31: Livia and all the court of Augustus are dead.

Dio

48.15.2: Livia accompanied her husband out of Campania, then out of Sicily.

48.34.3: Augustus was beginning to fall in love with Livia.

48.44: Livia was six months pregnant when she married Octavian, who sought clearance from the pontiffs about the wedding. Tiberius Nero gave Livia in marriage just as a father would. At a party a slave boy confused Octavian and Tiberius Nero as husbands of Livia. When Drusus was born after the marriage Octavian returned the child to his natural father. People coined a proverb about the lucky having a child in three months.

48.52.3–4: An eagle dropped a chick with a laurel sprig in Livia's lap.

49.15.1 (cf. 49.18.6): Livia was granted the right to host a banquet in the Temple of Capitoline Jupiter (or Temple of Concord) on the anniversary of the battle on Naulochus.

49.38.1: Livia and Octavia were granted statues, the right to administer their own affairs without a guardian, and the same *sacrosanctitas* enjoyed by the tribunes.

51.13.3: After Actium, Cleopatra pretended to hope for Livia's intercession.

53.33.4:	Livia was suspected of causing the death of Marcellus.
54.7.2:	Augustus rewarded Sparta for its hospitality towards Livia.
54.16.4–5:	Augustus claimed to instruct Livia on matters of dress and deportment. The senators did not believe him.
54.19.3:	Augustus made Terentia and Livia compete in a beauty contest.
55.2.4:	Livia and Julia organised a feast for women for Tiberius' *ovatio*.
55.2.5:	On Drusus' death, Livia was granted statues and the *ius trium liberorum*.
55.8.2:	With Tiberius, Livia dedicated the Porticus Liviae and held a banquet for the women.
55.9.8:	Before departing for Rhodes, Tiberius opened his will in front of Augustus and Livia.
55.10a.10:	Livia was suspected of the deaths of Gaius and Lucius.
55.11.3:	Thrasyllus predicted that a ship would come to Rhodes with a message from Livia and Augustus.
55.14–22.2:	Livia counselled Augustus in the Cinna case.
55.32.2:	Agrippa Postumus spoke ill of Livia as a stepmother.
56.17.1:	When it came to the bestowing of honours on the dead Augustus, Livia played a full role as if she were sole ruler.
56.30.1–2:	Livia was suspected of murdering Augustus with poisoned figs because of his rapprochement with Agrippa.
56.31.1:	Some say that Livia postponed announcing the death of Augustus.
56.32.1:	Livia inherited one-third of Augustus' estate, more than she was allowed by law.
56.42.4:	Livia placed Augustus' bones in his mausoleum.
56.46:	Livia became a priestess of Divus Augustus, with a lictor. She gave money to a man who had seen Augustus' soul on the way to heaven. With Tiberius she built a temple to Augustus. She founded the Ludi Palatini.
56.47.1:	Tiberius and Livia were responsible for the decrees passed to honour Augustus on his death.
57.3.3:	Tiberius rejected the notion that he had received power from Livia, whom he hated.
57.3.6:	Some thought that Livia put Agrippa to death.
57.12.1–6:	Tiberius tried to keep Livia in check. Livia was in a position of unprecedented power for a woman. She received senators at her home. Tiberius' letters bore her name. Without any overt show

she exercised power. She sought to have precedence over Tiberius. Special honours were sought for Livia, which irritated Tiberius. Tiberius forbade her from celebrating at her house because of the expense. He removed Livia from public life, but she continued to be a nuisance. She was the main cause of his leaving Rome for Capri.

57.16.2: Livia helped the victims of fires.

57.18.6: Livia and Tiberius were pleased by Germanicus' death.

57.19.1: Tiberius prosecuted *maiestas* cases involving his mother.

58.2.1–6: Livia died at the age of eighty-six. Tiberius did not visit her when she was ill and took no measures other than arranging the funeral. He forbade deification. The Senate voted mourning by women for a year. The Senate voted an arch in Livia's honour, because she had reared the children of many and had helped to pay daughters' dowries. Some called her mother of the country. She was buried in the mausoleum. Tiberius did not pay her bequests. Livia claimed that for a chaste woman naked men had no appeal. Livia claimed that she exercised influence over Augustus by playing the role of the proper Roman wife. Tiberius did not build her arch because of the expense.

58.4.5–6: Tiberius destroyed Fufius Geminus and his family because of their friendship with Livia.

59.1.4: Tiberius did not pay out Livia's bequests.

59.2.3: Caligula finally paid out Livia's bequests.

60.2.5: Claudius lived for a long time with Livia.

60.5.2: Claudius consecrated Livia and entrusted her worship to the Vestals.

60.22.2: Messalina was granted some of Livia's privileges.

60.33.12: All Livia's privileges were bestowed on Agrippina the Younger.

63.29.3: On Nero's death, the laurels planted by Livia died.

Porphyry on Horace's *Odes*

4.4.28: Livia was pregnant when she joined Octavian.

Aurelius Victor, *Caesares*

1.7: Augustus was unlucky in his marriage.

5.17: With Nero's death, the laurel groves and white chickens died also.

Anonymous, *Epitome de Caesaribus*

1.23: Octavian married Livia from passion, with her husband essentially approving. Livia had two sons.

1.27: Some ascribe Augustus' death to Livia, because of his rapprochement with Agrippa Postumus, whom she had exiled.

Macrobius, *Satires*

5.2.6: The entourages of Livia and of Julia are contrasted.

3.20.1: Cloatius is cited on the Livian fig.

Prudentius, *Contra Symmachum*

1.251–70, 292: The worship of Livia as Juno is attacked, especially in light of her disgraceful marriage.

Marcellus Empiricus, *De Medicina*

15.6: Livia's recipe for a sore throat.

35.6: Livia's recipe for chills.

MATERIAL SOURCES

Portraits

Sculpture

Before Livia's time, Romans had been distinctly unenthusiastic about the notion of erecting statues to women. It comes as no surprise that in 194 BC the redoubtable Cato the Elder, always thoroughly reliable when we need to see Rome at her most reactionary, condemned the notion of women's statues in the provinces.[49] It was only with the emergence of the *domus Augusta* that this attitude changed, and the turning point can be seen as early as 35 BC, when statues of Livia and her sister-in-law Octavia received official sanction. As the wife of the first princeps, Livia became the first woman in Roman history to be honoured on a major scale by sculpted portraits.

It is now accepted that the surviving portraits of members of the imperial families go back to a limited number of types, probably produced under official supervision in Rome and distributed throughout the empire, to be copied locally. At the initial stage there could be firm control over the likenesses produced, but once the process of replication had begun, individual artists would no doubt add their own idiosyncratic variations to their commissioned works. There will never be unanimity about what constitutes a "type" in the case of any given individual, and the process of defining the prototypes on the basis of their replicas is charged with difficulties. The basic principle is simple enough. We assign to types those portraits that seem to share common features. But typology is not an exact science, and ultimately instinct and aesthetic sensibility will influence, or even be part of, scholarly judgement. The situation is further complicated by the inevitable idealization of revered figures like Livia. Her images showed a dogged reluctance to reflect Livia's increasing age. Also, given the prominence of Livia, artists outside of Rome might well have been influenced by the pervasive familiarity of her portraits when they undertook commissions to depict her contemporaries. Consequently, it may at times be difficult to distinguish Livia's image from those of other Julio-Claudian women, particularly Octavia and Julia the Elder.

It is rare indeed for any Roman sculpted portrait still to be accompanied by its identifying inscription. Only one possible Livian example is known, and as we shall see, it is much disputed. The identification of portraits of the male members of the imperial house, especially the emperors themselves, is much aided by comparison with their heads on imperial coins. This procedure can be of some limited use for the women, but in the case of Livia there is no indisputable representation on official coins. She is identified on provincial coins, but their value for precise portraiture is more limited.

The first scholar to attempt a systematic approach to the study of representations of Livia's portraits was Bernoulli, in 1886. Later generations have built on his work, and in recent years there has been much active scholarship of high quality in this field. In 1962 Gross produced an important and useful monograph on Livia's portraits, which was supplemented by the weighty contributions of Vagn Poulsen in 1973 and of Fittschen and Zanker in 1983. Bartman and Winkes have both recently published valuable catalogues and studies of Livia's portraits. Although not devoted exclusively to Livia, Rose's work on sculptural groups and Woods' on the portraits of Julio-Claudian women have made further very useful contributions to Livian iconography.

In light of the high calibre of recent contributions to the subject, I present just a brief summary of the current thinking on Livian typology here. Two broad principles can be applied to her portraits. One is simple, perhaps crude, but valid. There is a massive corpus of portraits of the early imperial period that share common features and can generally be taken to represent the same woman. Their sheer number precludes for practical purpose their assignment to any other person. The second principle is one already recognised by Bernoulli. Livia could be expected to be found in family groups, where often other members have been securely identified. A valuable illustration of this last point is provided by a group from Arsinoe, in the Fayum region of Egypt. Three marble busts have survived, two of which can be securely assigned to Augustus and Tiberius. The third is of a woman who so closely resembles Tiberius that she can hardly be anyone other than his mother (figs. 12, 26, 27). The head is a familiar one of the period (the Fayum type), and comparable replicas can similarly be attributed to Livia.[50]

There are two basic groups of Livian portraits.

The Nodus Group

Scholars are in broad agreement that this group is the first of the two, generally in vogue 38 BC–AD 14, although the temporal range is by no means rigid. It is named for the wide knot *(nodus)* created when the hair is rolled forward at the middle of the head, then drawn back to form a topknot. At the sides the hair is rolled back in plaits to behind the head, where it is bound in a bun. To soften its severity, short wisps may be allowed to appear on the forehead and temples, at the front of the ears, and at the back of the neck.

Within the nodus group different types have been identified. There is a general scholarly consensus about an early Marbury Hall type, named after the country house in Cheshire that once held a striking example. Here the nodus is broad and flat and the hair at the side is woven tightly into twisted braids. Winkes notes that this type is closest to Livia's portraits on Alexandrian coins (fig. 14). Close to this, most scholars (although not Bartman) recognise another major type, probably chronologically later than Marbury Hall, the Albani-Bonn type, named after two examples in the Villa Albani in Rome and the Akademisches Museum in Bonn. Here the nodus is larger and the hair around the face is thicker (fig. 13). The Marbury Hall and Albani-Bonn types tend to show Livia with a rather elongated oval face.[51]

The Fayum type is the most representative in terms of surviving examples. It broadens Livia's head and makes the lower part more triangular. The nose is strong, the lips small and very curved. The chin is small and firm. The details of the hair are reduced.[52] Wood notes that this type gives Livia a facial shape much closer to that of Augustus, with his characteristically Julian triangular face, and allows a fictitious resemblance of Augustus to his adoptive son Tiberius.

One group of nodus portraits is identified by some scholars as a separate type, the Zopftyp, in which two braids cover the sides of the heads, sometimes instead of, sometimes in addition to, the usual twisted plaits of hair that run along the same area. The earliest examples of the type are found on coins of Pergamum, where Livia is clearly identified by name, and it may represent a local creation in Asia Minor (fig. 15).[53]

The Centre-Parting Group.

The hair now has a centre parting and falls down at each side to frame the face in a series of waves (figs. 17, 21). The tresses at the back are drawn into a tight bun at the neck. There are no shoulder locks. (The head on the Ara Pacis [a representation of Livia, rather than a likeness] is a notable exception.) The centre-parting coiffure is widely adopted in portraits from AD 14. But the nodus style continues, for not all the sculptors would have had access to the new type, and many would simply have preferred the traditional old-fashioned style. The centre-parting group is a large one, and a wide range of varieties have been detected. It is less easy to categorise than its predecessor and there is much disagreement about precise types and precise dating, and general uncertainty in applying terms such as *type* or *group*. It seems unlikely that in her sixties Livia would have sat for a new type in the strict sense, and the sculptors may have adapted existing models. It is commonly referred to as the salus group or type, the name being derived from the portrait in the Salus Augusta dupondius of Tiberius (fig. 4).[54]

Among the earlier examples is a group sometimes classed as the Kiel type, in which the locks at the side of the centre parting bulge more heavily than the rest of the hair and rise to create almost a halo effect. The ends are drawn back into a bun that is split horizontally, a relic of the nodus style. Others, possibly of this early group but perhaps later, arrange the waves into a series of parallel bands.[55] These examples might be considered transitional, before what Winkes call the core group *(Kerngruppe)*. This last consists of the posthumous portraits that follow Livia's consecration under Claudius. The hair now waves back from the centre parting in parallel lines. The face is idealised and very regular, with wide cheeks and large, wide-set eyes.

Inscribed Bronze Busts

Two small bronze busts have survived from the town of Neuilly-le-Réal, which, if genuine, are a remarkable, indeed unique, find, for they represent a matched set of Livia and Augustus, identified by inscriptions. These read, *Caesari Augusto / Atespatus Crixi fi. v.s.l.m (votum solvit libens merito)* and *Liviae Augustae / Atespatus Crixi fil. v.s.l.m. . . .*, purporting to record that Atespatus, the son of Crixus, fulfilled the dedications, to Caesar Augustus and Livia Augusta (fig. 18).[56] The fortunate combination of a matched pair, identified by name, seems almost too good to be true, and indeed the absence of a proper archaeological context and the very fine state of preservation of these items have led some scholars to question their authenticity. Adding to this doubt is the oddity of the name, Livia Augusta, not otherwise known in any inscription.

The fact that this casual form is favoured by Suetonius is not reassuring, for Suetonius would have been an obvious literary source for a forger.[57] Balancing these doubts, however, it must be noted that there is no positive evidence indicating a forgery, and analysis conducted at the Louvre has revealed that the metallic content of the bronze is consistent with ancient pieces. Most modern scholars are willing to accept their genuineness.

The pieces are of inferior provincial workmanship, intended for the private ownership of someone of limited means, perhaps similar to the bronze statuette of Augustus as a boy, with the cognomen Thurinus, obtained by Suetonius.[58] Their provincial origin and modest workmanship would explain their "realism," because they would not have adhered to patterns of the official idealised portraits. Hence they show signs of aging, although their precise dates are difficult to determine. The absence of Divus in Augustus' name should mean that they were sculpted during Augustus' lifetime, but the presence of Augusta in Livia's would place them after his death. Livia's cheeks are drawn, she has bags under her eyes and deep folds from the sides of the nose to the outer edges of the lips. These features are matched by the lines on Augustus' forehead.

Livia's bust has a nodus hairstyle, of a variant that is not typical of sculpted heads but is found in more casual media. The nodus style is usually combined with small wisps of hair that fall behind the ears. The long shoulder locks on the Neuilly bust are unknown in other freestanding portraits securely identified as Livia's. This feature, again, might point to a provincial origin.

Other Media

It is safe to assume that Livia would have appeared in a wide range of media: on cups, lamps, and various items of domestic function. Most of these ephemeral items will now be lost, and among those that have survived it is likely that the image of Livia, often crudely executed, will not be recognised.

Gems

The most significant of this subgroup is represented by carved gems made from semiprecious stones. They would not have circulated widely but have remained in the private ownership of their well-to-do owners, allowing much more freedom in the subject matter.[59] This has produced some striking images. The most famous is probably the Grand Camée. There has been much debate about the meaning of the scene, but many accept that it represents the departure of Germanicus for his eastern mission, although the piece may have been engraved in the Claudian period. On this interpretation the seated central figure is Tiberius, who bestows the task on Germanicus, who faces him. Livia, seated by Tiberius, holds the poppies and corn ears of Ceres and dominates the centre of the composition.[60]

A striking gem in Vienna, made from gilded green glass, perhaps in imitation of carved stone, depicts a jugate pair of Augustus, wearing a laurel, and Livia, who has the nodus hairstyle.[61] Also in Vienna, a sardonyx depicts a diademed Livia as Cybele and priestess of Divus Augustus, holding a bust of Augustus and ears of corn, to create an allusion to Ceres also. She wears a stola and wisps of hair hang down the neck (fig. 19).[62] Livia is given the attributes of Ceres on a cameo in Florence, where she is portrayed jugate with Tiberius. He wears a laurel crown; his mother has a garland of poppies and ears of corn held in place by a crescent diadem. She wears a stola, the costume of a living woman. Her type is one that is generally dated early, further suggesting a living rather than posthumous portrait (fig. 11).[63]

A less expensive form of glass is represented by a number of flasks shaped like a female head. The hair is arranged in a severe style, with a nodus over the forehead and corkscrew curls falling from the bun at the back of the head. The flasks are meant to be seen in profile, for a seam runs down the centre of the face. The heads have been identified as those of Livia, perhaps as a personification of a goddess such as Hera.[64]

Tesserae

Token coinage, usually in the form of lead *jetons* (tesserae), but also in other metals or materials, was widely used in the Roman empire, sometimes by officials to regulate such activities as the distribution of grain or entry into the public games, and sometimes privately, presumably for business reasons. These tesserae often bore the portraits of the imperial family. Livia is depicted on a lead tessera in very poor condition now in the Terme Museum in Rome, with a female head on the obverse identified as Augusta. A carpentum appears on the reverse, drawn by two mules. This is clearly in imitation of the Tiberian carpentum sestertius of AD 22–33 (fig. 10). A lead example in Berlin depicts a bust of Livia, identified as Iulia Augusta, in the guise of Demeter, with a crown of grain.[65]

Gaming Counters

One fascinating subgroup of Livian portraits identified by inscriptions comprises those that appear on small game counters of bone or ivory. It is generally recognised that they originated in Alexandria, although the precise nature of the game is far from clear. It seems that it required counters numbered 1–15 and that the "fronts" had a series of pictures, such as sets of animals or

Egyptian landmarks or famous people, including rulers. Examples have been found with Livia's portrait for pieces numbered 2, 4, and possibly 6, thoughtfully provided in both Roman and Greek numerals.[66] An example of a Livian counter is preserved in the National Museum in Naples.[67] In the game it is numbered 4. The portrait is identified by the name (in Greek) LIBIA. It is unquestionably genuine, but of little value for determining Livia's portrait, as the quality of the carving is quite poor. The hair has the centre parting. A well-preserved example has survived in Knossos, from the Roman colony level, with the legend in Greek *Libia* and the number 2. The head has the nodus hairstyle, with thick shoulder locks. The carving is detailed, but the features are very heavy, and very stylised.[68] Another piece found in Oxyrhynchus in Egypt and now in Alexandria has been the object of some debate. The figure is identified, in Greek, as *Ioulia*, and is numbered 6, again in both Latin and Greek. The carving is better than in the earlier examples, and the face has more personality. It has full cheeks and lips, and a small chin. The hair is in the nodus style with the characteristic strands falling down the neck, thicker and longer than on most nodus types, but less so than on the Neuilly bronze. The head may be intended to be Julia's rather than Livia's, but as Alföldi-Rosenbaum points out, a later owner of the game would certainly have assumed the head to be that of Augustus' wife.[69]

Ceramic and Metalwork

Boschung has identified as Livia the profile bust of a woman on a first-century ceramic lamp found at Belo near Cádiz. She has a nodus hairstyle and faces the profile laureate bust of Augustus. Imperial portraits on lamps are very rare.[70] It has been suggested that Livia is depicted on one of the two splendid silver vessels known as the Boscoreale cups.[71] An Arretine drinking vessel from Vetera bears a diademed bust of a woman on a column facing left towards a man's bust on a column, identified by Lehner as Augustus and Livia.[72] Also from the Rhine area is another piece of provincial workmanship, a bronze plaque intended to decorate a sword sheath. It represents a frontal Livia with the nodus hairstyle and shoulder locks arranged to flow along her shoulders above the drapery. She appears between two young men, facing slightly towards her. The figure to the right bears a resemblance to known heads of Tiberius, and the other must represent Drusus. This item presumably belongs to the lifetime of Drusus, and is thus earlier than 9 BC.[73]

Paintings

We know that painted images of Livia and other members of the imperial family were carried at the festival at Gytheum (see chapter 10), and similar items for Livia and her grandsons are recorded at Ephesus.[74] She may have been honoured in the paintings that decorated the villa in Boscotrecase on the Bay of Naples, thought to have belonged to Marcus Agrippa, possibly commissioned shortly after his death by the widowed Julia.[75] Livia and Julia have been identified in the roundels inserted into the tops of elegant corner columns, possibly meant to replicate full-scale tondi. They have the nodus hairstyle and the long shoulder locks seen at Neuilly.

INSCRIPTIONS

Inscriptions are an important historical tool. They are particularly valuable for social history and for the reconstruction of the careers of prominent individuals. With some notable exceptions, the value of inscriptions for more narrowly political history may be limited. The majority involve dedications or other distinctions for the imperial family in the provinces, where the nomenclature does not always conform to official Roman practice (as in the striking example from Mytilene, where during the early phases of Augustus' reign Livia is called Julia). Moreover, they often reflect local interests and as such cannot be taken necessarily to reflect an official programme from Rome. There is a large corpus of inscriptions relating to Livia, their chief value being to show how highly she was regarded by the communities of the empire, and how consistently this was expressed, from the relatively early years of her marriage to beyond her death.

Frequent reference is made to the "Arval record." The cult centre of the Arval Brotherhood lay to the west of Rome, just outside the city limits, at the shrine of Dea Dia, but their rites were also carried out in the city. The college kept a record of its rituals inscribed on stone. These texts have survived in fragmentary sections from 21 BC to AD 304 and provide valuable information on the activities of the imperial family, who occupy a prominent place in the rituals.

The following is not meant to be an exhaustive catalogue. Nor does it offer any sophisticated epigraphical analysis. It is intended essentially as a checklist, and the basis for further study. Place names are given in either the ancient or modern form, whichever is the more familiar or the more conventional. Where the province is not named, a location in Italy should be assumed. The dating is added if internal content provides information not already obvious from material provided. Allusions to Divus Augustus or to Julia Augusta, for example, can normally be assumed to postdate Augustus' death. The list does not include the numerous sepulchral inscriptions for slaves, freedmen, and freedwomen who adopted Livia's name or identify her as their mistress.

Reference is generally limited to the most widely available source material. Abbreviations refer to the catalogues in the following works: H=Hahn (1992); M=Mikocki (1995); R=Rose (1997); B=Bartman (1999). Curved brackets (. . .) are used to fill out abbreviations. Square brackets [. . .] are used in the original text to indicate restorations. Square brackets are used in the translations only, to indicate where the translation is dependent on a major restoration.

Neo-Punic

Leptis Magna, Africa

Translation: Rose (1995), 182–84, Cat. 125; G. L. della Vida, "Due iscrizioni imperiali neo-puniche di Leptis Magna." *AfrIt* 6 (1935): 1–29.

Group portrait dedication to Rome and Augustus, Tiberius, Julia Augusta, Germanicus, Drusus Caesar, Agrippina the Elder, Livilla, Antonia and Vipsania Agrippina.

AD 23–31

B 57; R 125; Kokkinos (1992), 45

Bilingual (Latin and Greek)

IGR 4.1392, *CIL* 3.7107: Smyrna, Asia
Augustae Caesaris Augusti Matri (Latin)
Sebastei Kai[saros Sebastou metri (Greek)
Augusta, wife of Caesar Augustus, mother (of Tiberius)
B 64

IGR 1.1033, *CIL* 3.8: Cyrenae, Cyrene
Iuliae Augustae (Latin)
Ioulian Sebasten (Greek)
Julia Augusta
Tiberian
B 41

Latin

Arval Record, Rome

CIL 6.32340.17
Iulia[e Augustae
January 11, 21

AFA xxxiii*a*.7
Iuliae Augustae
January 4, 27

AFA xxxiii*a*.11
[Iulia Augusta]
January 4, 27

AFA xxxiv*e*.2
Iuliae A[ugustae]
January 30, 27

AFA xxxviii.3
[Iuliae Augusta]e
January 3, before 29

AFA xliii*c*.2
Iuliae Augustae
January 30, 38

AFA lv.10
Di[vae] Augustae
January 6–12, 43–48

AFA lv.16
Divae Aug(ustae)
January 17, 43–48

AFA lv.19
Divae Augusta]e
January 17, 43–48

AE (1969–70), no. 1 (Arval fragment)
Divae Au]g(ustae)
September 23, 43–48
Restoration uncertain.

AFA lxiii.6
Div[ae Augustae]
57

AFA lxvii*d*.18
Divae [Aug](ustae)
January 3, 57

AFA lxix.12
Divae Aug(ustae)
October 13, 58

AFA lxxi.45
Divae Aug(ustae)
January 3, 59

AFA lxxv.44
Divae Aug(ustae)
October 12, 59

AFA lxxvii.29
Divae Aug(ustae)
January 3, 60

AFA xc*d*.15
[Diva]e Aug(ustae)
January 3, 69

AFA xcii.52
Divae Aug(ustae)
January 30, 69

AFA xciii.80
Divae Aug(ustae)
March 14, 80

Fasti

EJ, p. 46 Fasti Verulani, Verulae
Augusta
January 17
Referring to an event of 38 BC.

EJ, p. 48 Fasti Praenestini, Praeneste
Iulia Augusta
April 23, AD 22

CIL 6.1178: Rome
ma]cello Liviae
market of Livia (on Esquiline)

ILS 4995 (EJ 125): Rome
aeditus templi divi Aug(usti) [e]t Divae Augustae
superintendent of the temple of Divus Augustus and Diva Augusta

CIL 11.3859: Rome
Dianae Augustae
Augusta Diana

CIL 6.883: Rome
Livia (D)rusi f. uxs[or
Livia, daughter of Drusus, wife (of Augustus)
Dedication of Temple to Fortuna Muliebris.

CIL 5.6416 (Codex Einsidlensis 326): Rome(?)
Livia[e] / Drusi f./uxori Caesaris Aug
Livia daughter of Drusus wife of Caesar Augustus
Long thought to belong to an arch at Pavia, but now see Rose, *JRA* 3 (1990), 163–69.
AD 7–8
B 18

CIL 15.7264: Rome, Palatine "Casa di Livia"
Iuliae Aug(ustae)
Julia Augusta
After AD 14

CIL 14.399: Ostia
Flaminicae / D[i]vae Aug(ustae)
Priestess of Goddess Augusta

CIL 9.787: Luceria
[Iuliae] / Augusta[e] / Divi Augu[sti
[Julia] Augusta wife of Divus Augustus
B 58

EJ 225; Smallwood (1967), 255: Teate Marrucinorum
C. Herennius . . . Capito . . . proc(urator) Iuliae Augustae
Gaius Herennius Capito, procurator of Julia Augusta
After AD 37

CIL 9.3304: Superaequum
L]iviae Drusi f(iliae) / Augusti / ma]tri Ti (berii) Caesaris et / [Drusi Germanici

Livia the daughter of Drusus, wife of Augustus, mother of Tiberius Caesar and [Drusus Germanicus]
After AD 4
B 22

CIL 15.7814: Tusculum
T]i(berii) Caesaris et Iuliae Augu[stae
of Tiberius Caesar and Julia Augusta
After AD 14

ILS 157: Interamna
saluti perpetuae Augustae
the perpetual health of Augusta
or the health of the perpetual Augusta
B 54; Gross (1962) 19 n. 32 (not Livia); see Hahn (1992), 96 n. 338

CIL 10.7489: Lipari, Sicily
procurator(i) Ti Caesar(is) / Aug(usti) et Iuliae August(ae)
the procurator of Tiberius Caesar Augustus and Julia Augusta

CIL 2.3320, 11.3322: Forum Cassi
[au]gusta Iuli[a]
Julia Augusta

CIL 11.1165: Velleia
[Iuli]ae Divi / A[ugusti] f(iliae) Augustae / matri Ti Caesaris / [Di]v[i Au]gusti f(ilii) / Aug[usti e]t Neronis / [C]lau[di] Dru[si]
[Julia] Augusta daughter of Divus Augustus, mother of Tiberius Caesar Augustus, son of Divus Augustus and Nero Claudius Drusus
Caligulan
B 76

ILS 123: Herculaneum
Divae Augustae
Diva Augusta
B 74

ILS 125: Marruvium
Alfidia M. f(ilia) mater Augustae
Alfidia, daughter of Marcus, mother of Augusta
After AD 14

ILS 122: Pompeii
Augustae Iulia[e] / Drusi f(iliae) / divi Augusti
To Julia Augusta, daughter of Drusus, wife of Divus Augustus

CIL 10.1023 (= 2340): Pompeii
Iunoni / Tyches Iuliae / Augustae
Julia Augusta, Juno, Fortune
M 61

CIL 6.29681: Trebula(?)
natali Iuliae August(ae)
on the birthday of Julia Augusta
AD 108

ILS 1.118 = *CIL* 14.3575: Tibur
Liviae Caesaris / Augusti
Livia the wife of Caesar Augustus
B 25

CIL 9.4514: Ager Amiternus
Augustae Iuliae / Drusi f(iliae) / Divi Augusti
Julia Augusta, daughter of Drusus, wife of Divus Augustus
B 29

AE 1927, no. 158: Cumae
Iuliae Augustae
(statues) of Julia Augusta
B 40; Rose 8

CIL 10.7340: Himera, Sicily
Iul(iae) Matri Imp(eratoris) Cae(saris)
Julia mother of Imperator Caesar

ILS 119 = *CIL* 10.7464): Haluntium, Sicily
Liviae Augusti / deae
Livia, wife of Augustus, goddess
Claudian
B 73

ILS 121 (EJ 126): Malta (Gaulos)
Cereri Iuliae Augustae / divi Augusti, matri / Ti. Caesaris Augusti / Lutatia . . . sacerdos Augustae / . . . consacravit

Lutatia the priestess of Augusta consecrated . . . to Julia Augusta Ceres wife of Divus Augustus mother of Tiberius Caesar Augustus
B 50; M 1

AE 1976, no. 185: Furcona
[Iuliae A]ugustae / [Drusi f(iliae) uxori Divi Au]gusti, Germanico / Caesari, Ti Augusi / [f(ilio)
[Julia] Augusta [daughter of Drusus, wife of Divus] Augustus and to Germanicus Caesar [son of] Tiberius Augustus
AD 14–19
B 49

ILS 154 (EJ 101): Forum Clodii, Etruria
natali Augustae
dedicatione statuarum Caesarum et Augustae
on the birthday of the Augusta
on the dedication of statues of the Caesars and the Augusta
AD 18
B 47; R 11 (with translation)

CIL 11.7552: Forum Clodii, Etruria
[Aug]ustae Iuliae / Drusi f(iliae)/[Divi] Augusti
Julia Augusta, daughter of Drusus wife of [Divus] Augustus
B 58

AE 1988, no. 422: Corfinum
[flaminica] Iulia(e) Augusta(e)
[priestess] of Julia Augusta

CIL 11.7416: Ager Viterbiensis, Etruria
Iuliae Drusi [f. Augustae] Ti. Caesaris [Aug(usti) et] Drusi Germani[ci matri]
Julia [Augusta] daughter of Drusus, mother of Tiberius Caesar [Augustus] and Drusus Germanicus

CIL 10.459: Buxentum, Lucania
Augustae Iulia(e) Drusi f. divi Augusti
Augusta Julia, daughter of Drusus, wife of Divus Augustus

CIL 10.8060: Herculaneum
Aug(usta)
Augusta
Attested by Bayardi (1755), 403 on a inscribed cornelian, now apparently lost

and clearly not the same as the cornelian from Herculaneum recorded by Pannuti (1983), no. 213; see Winkes (1995), no. 172.

CIL 10.1620: Puteoli
[Iu]lia August[a]
Julia Augusta

CIL 11.6709.33: Falerii
Liv[ia] Caesar[is
Livia wife of Caesar

CIL 11.7488: Falerii
Livi[a] Caesari[s]
Livia wife of Caesar
B 12; *M* 60

CIL 6.882a: Falerone
Augustae Iuliae Drusi f(filiae)
to Julia Augusta daughter of Drusus
B 46

CIL 9.1098: Aeclanum
Iononi Augustae
Juno Augusta or Augustan Juno
B 4

CIL 9.1155: Aeclanum
Divae Augustae
Goddess Augusta
Original lost, texts offer variants *Augustinae* and *Faustinae*.

CIL 9.1105: Aeclanum
Juliae Aug(ustae)
To Julia Augusta
B 28

Inscr. It. 10.3.1, no. 113: Polla
Insteia . . . sacerd(os) Iuliae / Augustae
Insteia priestess of Julia Augusta

Inscr. It. 10.5.1, no. 247: Brixia, Venetia
[P]ostumi[ae] . . . Paullae . . . sacerd(oti) Div[a]i August(ae)
To Postumia Paulla priestess of the Goddess Augusta

CIL 10.6309: Suara, Tarracina
C]aesari Divi Aug f. Augusto . . . Divae Augus[tae
Caesar Augustus son of Divus Augustus, Goddess Augusta

CIL 11.6172: Suara, Tarracina, Latium
Divae Augustae
Goddess Augusta

AE 1975, no. 403: Albengo / Albingaunum, Liguria
D[ivae Aug(ustae]
Goddess Augusta
Heavily restored.

AE 1982, no. 415: Gualdrasco, Transpadana
Divae Aug(ustae)
Goddess Augusta

AE 1988 no. 607: Collegno, Transpadana
[. . . divae Dru]sillae et divae Augu[stae
Goddess Drusilla and goddess Augusta
As restored, the worship of Drusilla, Caligula's sister, is linked with Livia's.

ILS 1321: Vasio, Narbonensis
proc[uratori] Augustae
to the procurator of Augusta
Dedication to Sextus Afranius Burrus, recorded as procurator of Livia.
After AD 51

ILS 6991: Vasio, Narbonensis
flam(inicae) / Iul(iae) Aug(ustae)
priestess of Julia Augusta

CIL 12.4249: Baeteris, Narbonensis
flaminica / Iuliae Augustae
priestess of Julia Augusta

CIL 12.1845: Vienne, Narbonensis
[Divae Augustae]
Deified Augusta
Preserved in a drawing of holes left after the removal of letters.
AD 42–45

ILS 112: Narbo, Narbonensis
imp(eratori) Caesari . . . Augusto . . . coniugi liberis gentique eius senatui / poluloque Romano et colonis incolisque
Imperator Caesar Augustus and his wife and children and family and the Senate and the Roman people and the colonists and inhabitants
AD 12–13

CIL 13.1366: Neuilly-le-Réal, Aquitania
Liviae Augustae
to Livia Augusta
On the base of inscribed bronze statues to Livia (with matching item for Augustus).
Fishwick (1987–92), II.1, 535

ILS 3208 (*CIL* 13.4769): Lugdunum, Lugdunensis
Mercurio Augusto et Maiae Augustae sacrum
Sacred to Mercury Augustus (or Augustan mercury) and Maia Augusta (or Augustan Maia)
M 103

AE 1980 no. 638: Lugdumum, Lugdunensis
[Augusta Iuli]a / [Drusi] f
Augusta Iulia daughter of Drusus
Massively restored.

CIL 2.3102: Segobriga, Tarraconsesis
Liviae [Drusi f. uxori Caesaris Aug(usti) matri Ti(berii) Caesaris] / aviae [Germanici et Drusi Iuliorum Tiberii) f.
Livia [daughter of Drusus, wife of Augustus mother of Tiberius Caesar] grandmother [of Germanicus and Drusus, Julii, sons of Tiberius]

AE 1966, no. 177: Santarem, Lusitania
flamen provinc(iae) Lusitaniae Divi Aug(usti) [et] Divae Augustae
Priest of Divus Augustus and Diva Augusta for the province of Lusitania
AD 48

AE 1915, no. 95, Emerita, Lusitania
[C]n. Cornelio . . . [fl]amini Iuliae Augustae
Cnaeus Cornelius priest of Julia Augusta
AD 14–29

CIL 2.473: Emerita?, Lusitania
flamen Divae Aug(ustae) provinciae Lusitan(iae)
Priest of Diva Augusta for the province of Lusitania
Soon (?) after AD 42

SC de Cn.Pisone Patre (Piso Decree) Various locations, Baetica
115, 133, 150
Iuliae Augustae
Julia Augusta
143
avia
grandmother (of Livilla)
December 10, AD 20

Tabula Siarensis I.7: Siarum, Baetica
Augusta mater eius
Augusta his [Tiberius'] mother
AD 19–20

CIL 2.1667: Tucci, Baetica
Alfidiae Mat(ri) Augustae (heavily restored)
Alfidia, mother of Augusta
After AD 14

CIL 2.2108: Arjona, Baetica
Iuliae Augustae
Julia Augusta

CIL 2.1571: Castro el Rio, Baetica
sacerdos div[ae / Augustae
Priest of Diva Augusta

CIL 2.2038: Anticaria, Baetica
Iuliae Aug(ustae) Drusi [fil(iae)] Div[i Aug] matri Tiberii / Caesaris Aug(usti) principis et conservatoris et Drusi / Germanici [g]en[etric]is orbis
Julia Augusta, mother of the world, daughter of Drusus wife of Divus [Augustus] mother of Tiberius Caesar Augustus princeps and conservator, and of Drusus Germanicus
B 31; EJ 123

ILS 6896 (= *CIL* 2.194): Olisipo, Lusitania
Flamini Germ(anici) Caesaris Fla / mini Iuliae Aug(ustae)
Priest of Germanicus Caesar, priest of Julia Augusta

AE 1976, no. 185: Mytilene, Lesbos, Asia
[Iuliae A]gustae / [Drusi f.uxor divi Au]gusti Germanico / Caesari Ti. Augusti / [f
[Julia] Augusta [daughter of Drusus, wife of Divus] Augustus (and) Germanicus Caesar [son of] Tiberius Augustus

AE 1904, no. 98: Ephesus, Asia
Liviae Caesaris Augusti
Livia wife of Caesar Augustus

ILS 8897, EJ 71: Ephesus, Asia
Liviae Casaris Augusti . . . patronis
their patrons (Augustus and) Livia the wife of Caesar Augustus
Inscription to Livia and Augustus from the gate of the agora, to identify statues.
4–3 BC
B 9; R 112

CIL 11.3196: Nepet, Africa
Cereri August(ae) / Matri Agr(orum)
Augusta Ceres, mother of the fields
AD 18
B 63

CIL 8.6987: Colonia Iulia Cirta, Africa
Divae Au(gustae) . . . flaminica Di[vae Augustae
Priestess of Diva [Augusta] to Diva Augusta . . . Claudian
B 71

AE 1948, no. 13: Leptis Magna, Africa
Divae Augu(stae)
Diva Augusta
AD 45–46
B 75

ILS 120 (EJ 127): El Lehs, Africa
Iunoni Liviae Augusti sacrum
Livia Juno (or the Juno of Livia), wife of Augustus
AD 3
B 27; M 62

AE 1948, no. 13: Leptis Magna, Africa
Divae Augu(stae)

Diva Augusta
After AD 29, probably after AD 42

IRT no. 269: Leptis Magna, Africa
Cereri Augustae sacrum
Sacred to Ceres Augusta
AD 35–36
M 2; Wood (1999), 121

AE 1914, no. 171: Thugga, Africa
Iulia Divi Augusti
Julia wife of Divus Augustus

CIL 3.12037: Gortyn, Crete, Cyrene
Iuliae (Aug(ustae)
Julia Augusta
B 51

Inscriptiones Creticae I.137, no. 55: Lebena, Crete, Cyrene
Iuliae Au[gustae / matr[i
Julia Augusta mother (of Tiberius)
B 56

ILS 7160: Salonae, Dalmatia
flamini / Iuliae Augustae
Priest of Julia Augusta

CIL 3.9972: Corinum, Dalmatia
Iuliae August(ae) divi / Augusti matri Ti. Cae / saris Aug(usti)
Julia Augusta wife of Divus Augustus mother of Tiberius Caesar Augustus

ILS 2.3089: Zara, Dalmatia
Iunoni Augustae
the Juno of Augusta (or Juno Augusta
B 26

CIL 3.651: Philippi, Macedonia
Sac(erdos) divae Aug(ustae)
Priestess of the goddess Augusta
H 51

AE 1991.1428a: Philippi, Macedonia
sacerdoti divae / Aug(ustae)

priestess of the Goddess Augusta
This and the next three belong to a base for statues for five women of whom at least four are priestesses of Livia.

AE 1991.1428b: Philippi, Macedonia
sacerd(oti) [divae Augustae)]
priestess of [the Goddess Augusta]

AE 1991.1428c: Philippi, Macedonia
Aug(ustae)
Augusta

AE 1991.1428d: Philippi, Macedonia
sacerd(oti) divae Aug(ustae)
priestess of the Goddess Augusta

AE 1941 no. 142: Antiocheia, Psidia
Deae Iul[iae / Au]gustae
Goddess Julia Augusta
H 50

EJ 130: Corinth, Achaea
[Dianae] Pacilucifer[rae Aug]ustae sacrum
Sacred to [Diana] Augusta, bringer of light and peace
B 39; H 69

Corinth 8.3 (1966), 33 no 55: Corinth, Achaea
Div]ae Aug[ustae av]ae / [Ti C]laudi Cae[saris / Aug]u[sti Germanici
[The goddess] Augusta [grandmother] of [Tiberius] Claudius Caesar [Augustus Germanicus
Claudian
B 72; H 53

Corinth 8.3 (1966), no. 55: Corinth, Achaea
div]ae Aug[ustae av]ae / Ti C[laudi Cae[saris / Aug]u[sti Germani]ci
[The goddess] Augusta [grandmother of Tiberius Claudius Augustus Germanicus
About AD 25
H 52

Corinth 8.3 (1966), no. 153: Corinth, Achaea
ad Iulia]m diva[m Au[gustam
to [Julia] Augusta, goddess

About AD 25
H 52

AE 1994.1757 (*CIL* 3.12105): Salamis, Cyprus
[Iulia Augusta Drusi f(ilia) c]oniuge div[i / Augusti matre Ti. Caesa]ris Aug(usti)
[Julia Augusta, daughter of Drusus] wife of Divus [Augustus, mother of Tinberius Caesar] Augustus
Heavily restored; earlier restorations assigned the inscriptions to Julia Domna.

R. Egger, *Carinthia* 156 (1966), 467, fig. 126: Magdalensberg, Noricum
Liv[i]ae Caeasaris Augu[st(i) uxori]
Livia wife of Caesar Augustus
One of three inscriptions, the other two honouring Julia the Elder and Younger.
10–9 BC
B 15

Greek

Miranda no. 40: Naples, Italy
kai Iouliai Sebaste[i
and Julia Augusta
Miranda (1990), 58–60, identifies Julia as the daughter of Titus; P. Hermann, *Gnomon* 66 (1994), 24, argues for Livia.

Lindos 2.2 *Inscriptions* (1941), 739, no. 387: Lindos, Rhodes, Asia
[Libi]as gunaikos / [Aut]okratoros / [Kaisaros] theou huiou / [Seabstou]
Livia the wife of Imperator [Caesar Augustus] son of a god
B 14

IGR 4.249: Assos, Asia
thean Leiouian Heran n[ean] / ten tou Sebastou the[ou gunaika
The goddess Livia, the new Hera, wife of the god Augustus
M 66

IGR 4.250: Assos, Asia
Euergetis tou Kosm[ou]
Benefactress of the world
Identified as Livia because of *IGR* 2.249
B 5; H 19

G. Bean, *Belleten* 29 (1965), 593, no. 3; Elaea, Asia
Leibian Sebasten
Livia Augusta
B 44; Rose 111

IGR 4.144: Cyzicus, Mysia, Asia
agalma tes metros autou / sebast[es Nei]ke[ph]orou
Statue of his (sc. Tiberius) mother, Augusta, Bringer of Victory
Dedicated by priestess Antonia Tryphaina
B 43; H 97; M 107; Price (1980), 63–64

SEG 33.1055, *AE* 1983, no. 910: Cyzicus, Mysia, Asia
[Liouian] thean Demeter[a
The goddess [Livia] Demeter
fragmentary inscription to Livia and Augustus
B 7; H 17; M 5

TAM 5.2.906: Thyateira, Asia
[thea]n Ioulian / [Se]basten
[The goddess] Julia Augusta
Possibly refers to Julia Domna.
B 68; H 37

IGR 4.1203: Thyateira, Asia
thean Ioulian Sebasten
The goddess Julia Augusta
Possibly refers to Julia Domna.
B 67; H 35

IGR 4.1193: Thyateira, Asia
thea[n Iou]lian / Se[b]asten
The goddess Julia Augusta
Possibly refers to Julia Domna.
B 66; H 36

ILS 8853: Thyateira, Asia
arches Leibianes
The Livian demesne
Also read as *arkes,* treasury.
cf. *CIG* 2.3484
Severan?

AE 1988.1025: Mahmudiye (near Troy), Asia
Autrokratori / Kaisari / theoi theou huioi / Sebastoi / Tiberioi Kaisari / Seabastoi / theoi Iulioi / Iulia Sebastei / Gaio kai Loukioi / Sextoi Appoleioi
Imperator Caesar Augustus, god, son of a god, Tiberius Caesar Augustus, the god Julius, Julia Augusta, Gaius and Lucius, Sextus Appuleius.
A Sextus Appuleius was consul in 29 BC; his son was consul in AD 14, and is probably the proconsul of the inscription.

IG 12 suppl. 50: Mytilene, Lesbos, Asia
Sebasten Her[en
Augusta Hera
B 62; H 76

IGR 4.39: Mytilene, Lesbos, Asia
tei te sug[kle]toi kai tais iereais tes Hes[ti] / as kai Iouliai tei gunaiki autou / kai Octaiai tei adelphei kai tois / teknois kai suggenensi kais phi / lois
(Thanks to) the Senate and the priestesses of Vesta and Julia his (Augustus) wife, and Octavia his sister and his children and relatives and friends
Soon after 27 BC; the name Julia may be a mistake.

SEG 15 (1958), no. 532: Brontados, Chios, Asia
[Sebast]es Theas Aphrodites Libias
[Augusta] Goddess Aphrodite Livia
H 23; M 124

IG 12 suppl. 124, 20: Eresos, Lesbos, Asia
[Lio]u[iai] Seb[astai / [Pro]noiai ta gunaiki to Sebasto theo Kaisaros
[Livia] Augusta Pronoia (Providentia), wife of the God Augustus Caesar
H 86; M 105

IGR 4.319: Pergamum, Mysia, Asia
Se[ba]sten Iou[lian Hera Ne]an Ba[sileian
Augusta Julia [New Hera] Queen (?)
H 74; M 64

AE 1969/70 no. 594: Elaea, Asia
Leibian Sebasten Deibon Kaisara
Livia Augusta Divus Caesar

MDAI(A) 75 (1960), 105 n. 12: Tigani, Samos, Asia
[D]rousil[l]an gunaika tou / [Autokrato]ros theou hiou Kaisaros dia / [ten pros t]en thean eusebeian Herei

(The people dedicated a statue) to Hera of Drusilla wife of the Imperator Caesar because of her piety towards the goddess
27 BC–AD 14
B 3; H 24

MDAI(A) 75 (1960), 104 n. 11: Heraeum, Samos, Asia
Drousillan Au[tokrato] / ros Kaisaros [theou uiou] / Sebastou gu[anaika Herei]
(The people dedicated a statue) [to Hera] of Drusilla, the wife of the Imperator Caesar Augustus, [son of a god]
27 BC–AD 14
B 20

IGR 4.982: Samos, Asia
Markon Libion Drouson, ton / patera Theas Ioulias Seba / stes
Marcus Livius Drusus, the father of the Goddess Julia Augusta
After AD 14
H 27

IGR 4.983: Samos, Asia
Alphidian ten metera Theas Iulias Seabst[e]s megiston agathon aitian gegonuian toi kosmoi
The mother of the Goddess Julia Augusta, Alfidia who has been been the cause of the greatest benefits to the world.

IGR 4.984: Samos, Asia
ten iereian tes Archegetidos Heras kai The / as Ioulias Sebastes Lollian Kointou thu / gatera
(the people honour) Lollia, daughter of Quintus, priestess of Archetis Hera and of the Goddess Julia Augusta
After AD 14
H 25

AE 1980, no. 870: Aphrodisias, Caria, Asia
Iouliai Sebastei
Julia Sebaste
Accompanies dedications to Augustus as Zeus Patroos and to Tiberius.

SEG 30 (1980), no. 1248: Aphrodisias, Caria, Asia
I]ouliai Sebaste[i
Julia Sebaste
Reynolds (1980), 79, no. 10

SEG 30 (1980), no. 1249: Aphrodisias, Caria, Asia
Io]ulian Sebaste[n
Julia Sebaste
Reynolds (1980), 82, no. 17
M 65

Reynolds (1982) Doc. 13: Aphrodisias, Cara, Asia
tei gunaika mou
My (Octavian / Augustus) wife
Dated disputed, see appendix 17

AE 1980, no. 877: Aphrodisias, Caria, Asia
[Io]ulian Sebaste[n] / Sebastou thugate[ra] / Heran
Julia Augusta, Hera, daughter of Augustus
Reynolds (1980), 79–80, 82, no. 17
Caligulan
B 70; H 77; R 104

Le Bas II.1611: Aphrodisias, Caria, Asia
[Th]ea Ioulia Sebaste
The Goddess Julia Augusta
H 28

CIG II.2815: Aphrodisias, Caria, Asia
Theas Ioulias, neas Demetros
The Goddess Julia, New Demeter
Possibly Julia Domna
H 31; M 3; Wood (1999), 112

IG 12.5, no. 628: Ioulis, Ceos, Asia
Leibian Autokratoros / Kaisaros gunaika
Livia wife of Imperator Kaisar
31–27 BC
B 2; R 71

IGR 4.584: Aezani, Asia
ton sebaston neon homobomion
the Augusti (Livia and Augustus) recently sharing an altar
Sebastes Pronoias
Augusta Pronoia (Providentia)
After AD 41
M 106

BCH 10 (1886), 516, no. 6: Tralles, Lydia
hiereus Tiberiou Kaisaros / kai Hekates Sebastes
the priest of Tiberius Caesar and Augusta Hecate
AD 4–14
H 71; M 55

IGR 4.1183: Apollonis, Asia
Thea[n Iouli]an S[eba]sten
The Goddess [Julia] Sebaste
May be Julia Domna.

SEG 37 (1987) no. 1007: Alexandreia Troas, Asia
Autokratori / Kaisari / Theoi Theou uiowi / Sebastoi / Tiberioi Kaisari / Sebastoi / Theoi Iulioi / Iouliai Sebastei / Gaioi kai Loukioi / Xestoi Ap-poloeioi
Imperator Caesar, God, son of a God; Tiberius Caesar Augustus, the God Julius, Julia Augusta, Gaius and Lucius, Sextus Appuleius

IGR 4.257: Assus, Asia
Aphroditei Juliai
Julia Aphrodite
The allusion to Augustus as Theos in the same inscription inclines it to Livia, but not conclusively.

IGR 4.180 (EJ 129): Lampsacus, Asia
Ioulian Sebasten / Hestian nean Deme / tra
Julia Augusta, new Hestia Demeter
B 55; H 60; M 4

SEG 4.515: Ephesus, Asia
Serbilia de Sekounda / tes Sebastes Demetros Karpo / phorou
Servilia Secunda (priestess of) Augusta Demeter Bringer of Produce
AD 19–23
B 45; H 63; M 6

Smallwood (1967) 380.viii.26: Ephesus, Asia
Iouliai Sebastei
Julia Augusta
Hymnodes of the deified Livia at Ephesus are entitled to same rights as those of Augustus.
After AD 42

AE 1993.1469: Ephesus, Asia
[... iereo]s [Tiberio]u K[aisaros] Sebastou kai Iouli[as] Sebastes
[priest] of Tiberius Caesar Augustus and Julia Augusta
AD 30/31
See Knibbe et al. (1963), no. 9, p. 117.

IGR 3.157: Ancyra, Asia
Iulias / Sebastes
(statue) of Julia Augusta
AD 19–20 (based on priests names)
B 30

AE 1940, no. 184: Attouda, Caria, Asia
Libian thean gu[naika Autokratoros] / Kaisaros theou [huiou theou Sebastou]
The goddess Livia wife of the god [Imperator] Caesar [Augustus, son of a god
AD 3–10
B 6; H 32

IG 3.460: Athens, Achaea
Sebaste Hugeia
Augusta Hygeia (= Salus)

IGR 1.821: Athens, Achaea
Ioulia Thea Autokratoros / Kaisaros Theou Sebastou
Julia, Goddess, [?] of Imperator Caesar Augustus, the god
May be for Julia the Elder.

IG 3.316: Athens, Achaea
Hiereas Hesti[as] kai Leibias kai Iulias
Priestess of Hestia, Livia and Julia

IG 3.381: Athens, Achaea
L[ei]bias
Livia
The text is not certain.

IG 2/3 3241: Athens, Achaea
[Lio]uian Seb[asten] ... ten eat[es euergetin]
Livia Augusta ... her [benefactress]
B 33; H 7

SEG 22 (1967), no. 152: Athens, Achaea
[Artemis] Boula[i]a Iulia Sebaste

[Artemis] Boulaia Julia Augusta
H 56; *M* 46

Hesperia 6 (1937), 464: Athens, Achaea.
Ioulian Sebasten Boulai[i]an Tiberiou Sebastou metera
Julia Augusta Boulaia mother of Tiberius Augustus

IG 2/3 3239: Athens, Achaea
Ioulian th[ean] / Seb[asten]
The goddess Julia Augusta
B 35; H 6

IG 2/3 3238 = *IG* 3.461 (EJ 128): Athens, Achaea
Ioulian thean Sebasten Pronoian
The goddess Julia Agusta Pronoia (Providentia)
B 36; H 5; *M* 104

IG 2/3 3240: Athens, Achaea
Sebast]ei Hygeiai
Augusta Hygeia
B 37; H 81

AE 1933, no. 2: Rhamnous, Attica, Achaea
Thea Leibia
The Goddess Livia
H 8
AD 45/46

AE 1971, no. 439: Eleusis, Achaea
Libian Drousillan [Au]tokratoros Kaisaros gunaika
Livia Drusilla wife of Imperator Caesar
Statue base of Livia accompanying one for Augustus.
31–27 BC
B 1; Rose 71

IG 4.1393: Epidauros, Achaea
Libian Kaisa / ros Sebastou / gunaika
Livia the wife of Caesar Augustus
B 10

IG 4.1394: Epidauros, Achaea
Leibia[n K]aisaros Sebastou / gunaika

Livia the wife of Caesar Augustus
B 11

SEG 23.472: Dodona, Achaea
Libian ten . . . / Kaisaros Se[bastou
Livia (the wife of) Caesar Augustus
B 8

IG 7.65: Megara, Achaea
Ioulian
Julia
B 59; H 9

IG 7.66: Megara, Achaea
Ioulian Thean Sebasten
The Goddess Julia Augusta
B 60

SEG 41 (1991), no. 328: Messenia, Achaea
l. 26 Tiberiou de Kaisaros
ll. 28–29 kai thean Leibian tan matera autou kai g[unaika theou sebastou kaisaros] / kai Antonian kai Libillan
Tiberius Caesar . . . and the Goddess Livia his mother and wife [of Divus Augustus Caesar] and Antonia and Livilla
AD 14

IG V.2.301: Tegea, Arcadia, Achaea
Theas Ioulias Sebastes (Ioulias added later)
The Goddess Julia Augusta
H 13

AE 1920, no. 1: Corinth, Achaea
Tiberion Kaisara Theou Sebastou hu(ion) Sebaston . . . Thean Ioulian Sebasten
Tiberius Caesar Augustus, son of Augustus the God . . . Goddess Julia Sebaste
The Goddess Julia Augusta
21–23 AD
H 11

Corinth 8.1, no. 19: Corinth, Achaea
eis thean I[o]ulian Sebasten
To the goddess Julia Augusta

AE 1928 no 50: Thespiae, Boiotia, Achaea
[Libian Autokratoros] / Kaisaros [Sebastou / gun[aika
[Livia] wife of [Imperator] Caesar [Augustus]
B 24; Rose 82

SEG 13, 348: Thespiae, Boeotia, Achaea
Sebaste
Augusta
From poem of Honestus.
Probably Livia rather than Julia; see Jones (1970), 249–55.
B 65; H 85

SEG 31 (1981), no. 514: Thespiae, Boiotia, Achaea
Sebasten Ioulian Mnemosunen
Sebaste Julia Mnemosyne
H 84; M 108

P. Jamot, *BCH* 26 (1902), no. 18: Thespiae, Boiotia, Achaea
Sebastes Ioulias
Julia Augusta
Probably Livia rather than Julia; see Jones (1970), 226.

BCH 3 (1879), 443: Chalcis, Boeotia, Achaea
en Chalkidi Leibidea
Contests in honour of Livia in Chalcis

SEG 24 (1969), no. 212: Eleusis, Attica, Achaea
Libian Driusillan / [Au]tokratoros Kaisaros / gunaika
Livia Drusilla wife of Imperator Caesar
Accompanies inscription to Octavian, perhaps 31 BC.

SEG 31 (1981), no. 409: Lebadeia, Boiotia, Achaea
Sebast[es Ioulias]
Augusta [Julia]

Kornemann (1929), no. 4: Gytheum, Laconia, Achaea
Epiphanestata / Thea Tyche tes Po / leos
Very present goddess Fortune of the city
Kornemann states that the goddess is "sicher Livia."
H 12

SEG 11.923 (EJ 102)
(a) ll. 3, 10, 35: Gytheum, Laconia, Achaea

Ioulias Seba]stes . . . Iulias Sebaste[s] / tes tou ethnos kai poleos hemon Tuches . . . Iulias tes Sebastes
(Statue of) [Julia] Augusta . . . of Julia Augusta the Fortune of our people and city . . . of Julia the Augusta . . . (b) l. 13: ten emen metera
My (Tiberius) mother
B 52; Rose 74; H 87; M 48

IG 12.8.65: Imbros, Asia
Ioulian Sebast[en Hygeian
Julia Augusta [Hygeia]
after AD 22/23
B 53; H80

SEG 24 (1969), no. 613: Mekes, Macedonia
Tiberiou Kaisa]ros kai Iulias Sebaston
[Tiberius Caesar] and Julia, Augusti
AD 21/22

IGR III 1507: Oinoanda, Lycia
ierasamenen theas Seb / astes
Priestess of the goddess Augusta
H 44

IGR III 540: Telmessus, Lycia
hiereia . . . theas Sebastes
Priestess of the goddess Augusta
H 45

IGR 3.720: Myra, Lycia
Ioulian thean Sebasten / gunaika theou Sebastou / Kaisaros metera de Tiberiou / theou Sebastou K[ai]saros
The goddess Julia Augusta wife of the god Augustus Caesar mother of the god Tiberius Augustus Caesar
B 61; H 43; Rose 102

IGR 3.721: Myra, Lycia
Tiberion Kaisara theon Sebaston theon Sebaston huion autok[r]ator
Tiberius Caesar Augustus Imperator, son of Augustus and Augusta

SEG 38 (1988) 914: Cnossus, Crete, Cyrene
Libia
Livia
On gaming counter, with portrait.

SEG 38.1887: Cyrenae, Cyrene
[Ioulian Sebasta]n Sebasto gunaika
[Julia Augusta] wife of Augustus

AE 1967 no. 491: Antioch, Galatia
Iul[ia Augusta]
Julia [Augusta]
Heavily restored; may be Severan, see Levick, *Anatolian Studies* 17 (1967), 101 n. 1.

Ditt. 533,25: Ankyra, Galatia
Kaisaros [Sebastou] kai Iulias Sebastes
Caesar Augustus and Julia Augusta

IGR 3.312: Apollonia Sozopolis, Galatia
[Theai Iouliai] or [Iouliai Sebastei]
[The goddess Julia] or [Julia Augusta]
Completely restored.
B 32; R 107; H 47

IGR 1.1150: Athribis, Egypt
Huper Tiberiou] Kaisaros Sebastou theou / huiou Autokratoros kai huper Ioulias Seba[stes neas / Isidos / metros autou] kai tou oikou auton
On behalf of [Tiberius] Caesar Augustus Imperator son of god and on behalf of Julia Augusta [the new Isis] and their house
B 38; H 82

IGR I. 1109: Pelusium, Egypt
Hyper Autokratoros Kaisaros Theou huiou Sebastou kai Leiouas Sebatou kai Gaiou Kaisaros kai Leukiou Kaisaros ton huion tou autokratoros kai Ioulias tes thugatros tou autokratoros
On behalf of Imperator Augustus son of Caesar the God and Livia, wife of Augustus, and Gaius Caesar and Lucius Caesar, the sons of the Imperator, and Julia, the daughter of the Imperator
4 BC

SEG 38.1678: Akoris, Egypt
Huper Tiberiou Kaisaros Sebastou kai Iul / ias Sebastes
On behalf of Tiberius Caesar Augustus and Julia Augusta
AD 29
B 69

ILS 8784: Thasos, Thrace
Leibian Drousillan ten tou Seabstou Kaisaris / gunaika thean euergetin
Livia Drusillan wife of Augustus Caesar goddess and benefactress
Dedication shared with Julia the Elder and Younger.
19–12 BC
H 4

IGR 1.835: Thasos, Thrace
Leibian Drou[sillan ten tou Sebastou Kaisaros] / gunaika thean euergetin
Livia Drusilla wife [of Augustus Caesar] goddess and benfactress
16–13 BC
B 23; R 95

IG 12.8.381: Thasos, Thrace
Leibian Drou[sill]an t[e]n tou Sebastou Kaisaros gunaikan Thean Euergetin / Ioulian Markou Ag[r]ippou Thugatera
Livia Drusilla the wife of Augustus Caesar goddess, benefactress; Julia daughter of Marcus Agrippa

IG 14.2414.40 (= *CIL* 10.8069.9): Naples
Libia
Livia
On gaming counter. May have originated in Egypt.

IGR 3.1086: Abila, Syria
Kyrion Sebaston
Lords Augusti (Tiberius and Livia)
H 96

IGR 3.1344: Gerasa, Syria
huper tes Sebaston soterias
For the welfare of the Augusti
Possibly AD 22, referring to Tiberius and Livia.

IG IX.2.333: Mylai, Thessaly
Iou / lias Heras Sebastes
Julia Hera Augusta
H 72; M 63

IGR 3.984: Salamis, Cyprus
Libian ten gunaika tou / [Au]tokratoros Kaisaros / [S]eb[a]stou

Livia, the wife of Imperator Caesar Augustus
B 19

JHS 9 (1988), 242, no. 61: Paleapaphus, Cyprus
Liouian thean nea[n Aphroditen]
The goddess Livia the new [Aphrodite]
B 16; H 49; M 123

IGR 1.902: Phanagoria, Pontus
[Lioui]a[n] ten tou Sebastou gunaik[a / basilissa] Dunamis philoromaios / [ten heau]tes euergetin
[Queen] Dynamis, friend of the Romans, (dedicated this statue) of [Livia] wife of Augustus, her benefactress
9–8 BC
B 17; H 92

SEG 39.695, 44.658: Hermonassa, Black Sea
[Puth]odoris Leiouian ten / heau[tes euergetin
Pythodoris [dedicated this statue of] Livia her own [benefactress]
Probably 8–6 BC
B 13; H53

PAPYRI

Much valuable historical material has been preserved in papyri unearthed in Egypt. The surviving documents provide an unparalleled insight into the details of commercial and social life, and contain the occasional item of political history, usually associated in some way with activities in the province. References to Livia in papyri consist of either expressions of gratitude, oaths in marriage contracts, or, most commonly, details of her commercial enterprises in the province.

P. Oxy 2435 verso, 45 AD 13 (EJ [1976] 379.1)
epai]non de kai Libias
praise(?) also of Livia

P. Oxy 2435 recto, AD 19 (EJ [1976] 379.2
dia to apestasthai patros kai mammes
because of my [Germanicus'] separation from my father and grandmother

P. Berol. SBA (1911), 796–97, 37–38: Alexandria, AD 19
tei metri autou, emei de / mammei
to his [Tiberius'] mother, my [Germanicus'] grandmother

P. NYU inv. 18.47 (= SB 9150): Arsinoite, AD 5
ousi]as Libias [kai] Germani[ikou Ka]isaros
[estate] of Livia and Germancius Caesar

P. Lond. II. 445: Bakkhias, AD 15/15
edaphon Ioulias Sebastes kai Germanicou Kaisaros
property of Julia Augusta and Germanicus Caesar

PSI 1028: Tebtynis, AD 15
thesaurou Libuias Sebastes
the treasury of Livia Augusta

P. Mich. inv. 735 (= SB 10536): Tebtynis, AD 25/6
thesaruou Ioulias Sebastes kai teknon Germanikou Kaisaris
the treasury of Julia Augusta and the children of Germanicus Caesar

P. Sorbonne inv. 2364: Philadelphia, AD 25/26
georgou Ioulias Sebastes kai teknon Germanicou Kaisaron
farmer of Julia Augusta and the children of Germanicus, Caesars

P. Med. 6: Theadelphia(?), Theoxenis, AD 26
biblou Iulias Sebastes kai tekno(n) Germanikou Kaisaros
the papyrus of Julia Augusta and the children of Germanicus Caesar

Pap. Ryl. 126: Euhemeria, AD 28/29
Ioulias Sebastes ousias
property of Julia Augusta

P. Mich. 560: Karanis AD 46
ousi]as Libianes
Livian [estate]
Might refer to an estate of Livia or Livilla.

P. Vindob. Tandem 10: Euhemeria, AD 54
proteron . . . Ioul[ia]s Sebastes
(an estate) previously of Julia Augusta

BGU 252, 2/3 (December 24, AD 98)
epi Ioul(*ias*) [*Sebastes*]
before Julia Augusta

P. Oxy. 17.2105, AD 147–48
timei theon Libias kai [. . .
in honour of the divine Livia and . . .

P. Oxy 3.496, AD 127
e[pi] Io]lias S[eba]stes
before Julia Augusta

P. Oxy 604, early second century
epi Ioulias Sebastes (published as restored)
before Julia Augusta

CPR 24.2, AD 136
. . .]i tes Ioulias Sebastes
before Julia Augusta

COINS

Coins are a useful tool of the historian of the ancient world, for they fulfilled a double function: they were units of currency or bullion and also a device by which the current ruler could project his image to the people at large and keep his policies and concerns in the public eye.

Apart from providing information on political issues, coins can often tell us much about the appearance of their subjects. This is particularly true of official issues—that is, coins produced in the imperial mint under the direct control of the central Roman authorities, although not necessarily in Rome itself, and intended for distribution throughout wide areas of the empire. Local coins, on the other hand, were intended for much more limited distribution, in either a province, a region, or a city. Their portraits tend to be far less individualised. Unfortunately, in the case of Livia there are no official coins on which a head is identified by her legend, although it is possible that one or more of the abstractions that appear on Tiberius' issues may be intended to represent her.

Official Coins

Augustus

RIC[2] 219–20
Aurei and denarii, 13–14
Obverse: Head of Augustus
Legend: Caesar Augustus Divi F. Pater Patriae
Reverse: Seated draped female figure holding a sceptre and a branch
Legend: Pontif Maxim

Tiberius

RIC[2] 25–30 (fig. 1)
Aurei and denarii, undated
Obverse: Head of Tiberius
Legend: Ti Caesar Divi Aug F Augustus
Reverse: Seated female figure holding a sceptre or spear and a branch
Legend: Pontifex Maximus
Probably associated with *RIC*[2] 23–24 with Divus Augustus on reverse.

RIC[2] 33–37
As, AD 15–16
Obverse: Head of Tiberius
Legend: TI CAESAR DIVI AUG F AUGUST / AUGUSTUS IMP VII
Reverse: Draped seated female figure, holding patera and sceptre between S and C
Legend: PONTIF MAXIM TRIBUN POTEST XVII

RIC[2] 71–73
As, undated
Obverse: Radiate head of Augustus, with star above and thunderbolt in front
Legend: DIVUS AUGUSTUS PATER
Reverse: Draped seated female figure holding patera and sceptre, between S and C
Legend: None
The seated female figure type is one of the most persistent and widespread features of aes coinage during Tiberius' principate. Local coinage at Hippo (*RPC* 711), Emerita (*RPC* 40), Caesaraugusta (*RPC* 341), and Italica (*RPC* 66–67) confidently identify the type as Julia Augusta; many scholars assume the same identification on official asses of Tiberius and suggest that the seated figure may represent Livia in her new capacity as priestess of Divus Augustus. There is less confidence that the same was intended in precious metal issues introduced under Augustus and copied by Tiberius. See Grant, *Aspects* (1950), 115; *Anniversary* (1950), 62; Sutherland (1951), 84, (1976), 109 n. 67; Wood (1998), 89.

RIC[2] 43 (fig. 2)
Dupondius, 22–23
Obverse: Veiled and diademed bust of Pietas
Legend: PIETAS
Reverse: No image

Legend: DRUSUS CAESAR TI AUGUSTI AUG TR POT ITER, round SC

Panormus depicts a similar head (*RPC* 642–43), which it simply identifies as Augus(ta); Gross (1962), 18–19; Fittschen-Zanker (1983), III.3–3, 3. Mikocki (1995), 25–28, 164, nos. 94, 95, accepts Pietas and Iustitia (see next) as portraits of Livia. Kokkinos (1992), 90–95, suggests that these two and the salus issue (below) depict Antonia Minor.

*RIC*² 46 (fig. 3)
Dupondius, 22–23
Obverse: Draped and diademed bust of Iustitia
Legend: IUSTITIA
Reverse: No image
Legend: TI CAESAR DIVI AUG F AUG TR POT XXIIII, round SC

*RIC*² 47 (fig. 4)
Dupondius, 22–34
Obverse: Draped bust of Salus, hair parted in centre
Legend: SALUS AUGUSTA
Reverse: No image
Legend: TI CAESAR DIVI AUG F AUG TR POT XXIIII, around SC

Gross (1962), 58, 62–66, notes that the salus type resembles local issues with Livia's head and so should be taken as having her features. Wood (1999), 109, notes that the arched nose, small mouth, and soft chin line are in contrast to the ideal features of Iustitia and Pietas.

See also Sutherland (1951), 96–97, 191–92; Weinstock (1971), 171–72; Torelli (1982), 66–70; Sutherland (1987), 51–52; Purcell (1986), 86, n. 45.

*RIC*² 50–51 (fig. 5)
Sestertius, 22–23
Obverse: Carpentum drawn by two mules, the sides decorated with victories and other figures
Legend: SPQR LIVIAE AUGUSTAE
Reverse: No image
Legend: TI CAESAR DIVI AUG F AUGUST P M TR POT XXIIII, round SC

The carpentum coins are dated on the reverse to Tiberius' twenty-fourth tribunician year, AD 22–23, and are presumably associated with Livia's illness. The scene may relate to the procession of the *supplicationes* decreed as a thanksgiving for her recovery. The coin could have another meaning. In 22 Livia received the right to sit with Vestal Virgins at public games. It is possible that at the same time she received another Vestal privilege, the right to be transported by the carpentum, and that the grant is alluded to in the coin. Carpentum types are generally posthumous, and it is argued by Grant, *Aspects* (1950), 123, that it is unlikely that Tiberius would have thus honored Livia in her lifetime. He notes that certain coins of Tiberius were issued some time after the date represented by the tribunician years, and he puts the carpentum type in that category, dating it shortly after Livia's death. See Sutherland (1951), 192–93; (1974), 151; Flory (1984), 321; Winkler (1995), 53–54; Winkes (1995), 24; Wood (1999), 82.

Claudius

*RIC*² 101 (fig. 6)
Dupondius, 41–50 (?)
Obverse: Radiate head of Augustus, between S and C
Legend: DIVUS AUGUSTUS
Reverse: Draped seated female figure with wreath of corn ears holding corn ears and long torch
Legend: DIVA AUGUSTA
This coin bears a certain resemblance to the Aurei and Denarii of Augustus depicting a seated female figure holding a sceptre and a branch. It may be that Claudius simply adopted a previously existing type and continued a tradition already established; see Sutherland (1951), 124–25, 131.

Nero

*RIC*² 44–45, 56–57 (fig. 7)
Aurei and denarii, dated 64/65, 65/66, respectively
Obverse: Head of Nero
Legend: NERO CAESAR AUGUSTUS
Reverse: Standing radiate male holding patera and sceptre, beside a standing veiled and draped female figure holding patera and cornucopia
Legend: AUGUSTUS AUGUSTA
Hahn (1994), 76 n. 85, suggests that the reverse might depict Nero and his wife, probably Poppaea.

Galba

*RIC*² 13–14, 36, 52 (fig. 8)
Aurei and Denarii, minted in Spain (Tarraco), April–late 68
Obverse: Head of Galba
Legend: GALB IMP / GALBA IMPERATOR / SER GALBA IMP CAESAR AUG P M TR

Reverse: Draped standing female holding patera, leaning on sceptre
Legend: DIVA AUGUSTA

RIC[2] 65–67
As, minted in Spain (Tarraco), April–late 68
Reverse: Draped standing female holding patera, leaning on a sceptre
Legend: DIVA AUGUSTA
Obverse: Galba riding
Legend: SER GALBA IMPERATOR / SERVIUS GALBA IMPERATOR

RIC[2] 331–38, 432–33
Sestertius
Obverse: Head of Galba, laureate or oak-wreathed
Reverse: IMP SER GALBA CAE AUG TR P / ser GALBA IMP AUGUSTUS
Reverse: Livia, seated holding patera and vertical sceptre between S and C
Legend: AUGUSTA
Kraay (1956), 58, says that Augusta is clearly Livia, but notes that the title Diva is omitted and that the type perhaps suggests Livia as the priestess of Divus Augustus.

Titus

RIC[2] 218–24
Dupondius
Draped and diademed bust (of Livia?)
Legend: Iustitia
Under Titus the Iustitia and Pietas coins were revived (*RIC* 2: 144, 145, nos. 218–24)

Trajan

RIC[2] 821: one of Trajan's "restored" issues, on which Trajan's legend was added to earlier dies and the coins reissued as an aureus with head of Tiberius on obverse and Livia (?) seated, facing right on reverse. Cf. *RIC*[2] 25–30
Hahn (1994), 76 n. 87

Antoninus Pius

RIC[2] 973–75, 978, 998, 1003–4 (fig. 9)
Sestertius, AD 157/58, 158/59

RIC[2] 988, 1013, 117, 1021

Dupondius, AD 157/58, 158/59

*RIC*² 1024–25
As, AD 158/59
Octastyle temple in which seated figures of Augustus and Livia appear

Local Coins

B = Bust or head of Livia / S = Seated image of Livia / v = veiled / p = holding patera / s = holding sceptre / c = holding earns of corn.

JA = jugate with Augustus / JT = jugate with Tiberius / FA = facing head of Augustus / FT = facing head of Tiberius / FS = facing head of personified Senate

/ = other side occupied by member of family / A = Augustus / DA = Augustus with Divine attributes / T = Tiberius / C = Claudius / N = Nero.
Greek legends in italics.

Augustus

Sparta *RPC* 1105: B
Chalcis *RPC* 1346: B / Hera, 1348: B / Hera
Thessalian League *RPC* 1427: B *Hera Leiouia* / DA
Thessalonica *RPC* 1563: B *Thea* or *Theou Libia*
Thrace: Rhoemetacles I *RPC* 1708–10: JA *Kaisaros Sebastou* / Rhoemetacles and Queen Pythodoris
Bithynia *RPC* 2097: JA Imp.Caesar Augustus Pontif / Max. tr. p./S
Methymna *RPC* 2338: B *Thea Libia* / A
Pergamum 2359: B *Libian Heran* / *Ioulian Aphroditen* Bust of Julia
Magnesia AD Sipylum *RPC* 2449/Gaius and Lucius Caesar: FA *Sebastoi*, 2450 B / A *Sebastoi*
Magnesia AD Maeandrum H 57: B Livia as Artemis?
Smyrna *RPC* 2464, 66: JA *Sebastoi*, 2467: Livia as Aphrodite, standing, holding sceptre and nike, leaning on column *Libian Zmurnaion Koronos*
Clazomenae *RPC* 2496: B *Thea Libia* / A *Seabstos Ktistes*
Nysa *RPC* 2663: JA
Ephesus *RPC* 2576, 2580: B, 2581–85, 2587, 2589–91, 2593–96, 2599–606, 2608–12: JA
Tralles 2647: Livia as Demeter holding corn and poppy *Kaisareon Libia* / A *Sabastos*, 2648: as 2647/head of Gaius Caesar *Gaios Kaisar*
Antioch AD Maeandrum *RPC* 2829: B / A *Kaisar Sebastos*
Eumenea *RPC* 3143: B *Hera Libia*

Alexandria *RPC* 5006: B: *Liouia Sebastos* / double cornucopia, 5008 (as 5006) / eagle, 5027: B / cornucopia *Patros Patridos*, 5042, 5046, 0554: B / oak wreath 5043, 5047, 5058, 5064, 5068 B / modius 5053, 5063: bust of Euthenia *Euthenia* 5055, 5065, 5072 B / Athena

Tiberius

Emerita *RPC* 38: B Salus Augusta, 39: B Salus Augusta / S Iulia Augusta, 40: B Iulia Augusta / T Ti Caesar Augustus Pox Max Imp

Italica *RPC* 66, 67: S with sceptre and pater Iulia Augusta / A Divus Augustus Pater

Romula *RPC* 73: B on globe Iulia Augusta Genetrix Orbis / A Divi Aug(usti)

Tarraco *RPC* 233: Facing heads of Drusus and Livia Drusus Caes Trib Pot Iul Augusta / T Ti Caes Aug Pont Max Trib Pot

Caesaraugusta *RPC* 341: S Iulia Augusta / T Ti Caesar Divi Augusti f Augustus

Gaul (city uncertain) *RPC* 538: B in diadem and veil in wreath of corn / A Divus Augustus Pater

Paestum *RPC* 604: Svsp / T

Panormus *RPC* 642–43: Bv Augus, 645: Ssp

Hippo *RPC* 711: Ssp Iul Aug / T Ti Caesar Divi Augusti f Augustus

Utica *RPC* 721–26: Svps / T Ti Caesar etc., 731–32: S / T Ti Caesar Divi f Aug Imp viii, 733–34 S

Carthage *RPC* 754–55: Svps / T Ti Caesar Imp PP

Paterna *RPC* 763–69: Svcs / T TiCae Divi Aug F Aug Imp viii cos iiii

Thapsus *RPC* 795: Ssc Cereri Augustae / T Ti Cae Divi Aug F Aug Imp vii, 796 Bv / as 795, 797 Sps / as 795

Oea *RPC* 833: B, between peacock and ear of corn, 835: B

Lepcis *RPC* 849: B Svsp Augusta Mater Patria / T Imp Caesar Au, 850: as 849/T Imp Ti Caes Aug COs iiii

Cnossus *RPC* 986: S Iulia Augus / A Divos Aug, 988: B Iulia Aug, 989: as 988/T Ti Caesar Aug

Corinth *RPC* 1149–50: S with sp or p or cs

Dium *RPC* 1506: Sps / T Ti Caesar Divi F Augustus

Edessa *RPC* 1525–27: B *Sebaste* / T *Ti Kai* or *Kaisar Sebastos*

Thessalonica *RPC* 1566: *Sebaste* Demeter in car, 1567–68: B *Sebaste* / T *Ti Kaisar Sebastos*, 1569: Sps *Sebaste* / as 1569, 1570–71: Bv *Sebaste* / as 1569

Amphipolis *RPC* 1634: Bv *Ioulia Sebaste Thea;* H 55 B (Livia or Artemis)

Byzantium *RPC* 1779: B *The Sebaste* / A *Theos Sebastos*

Sinope *RPC* 2126: S / A

Mytilene *RPC* 2345–6: B *Iou Thea Sebaste* / T *Ti Theos Sebastos*
Pergamum *RPC* 2368: Ssc *Thean . . . Menogenes* / TA *Sebastoi* 2369: FT *Sebastoi* / statue of Augustus in temple, *Theon Sebaston* H 62: Ss(and ähren) *Sebaste*
Magnesia AD Sipylum *RPC* 2453: B *Thean Sebasten* / bust of Senate *Sunkleton*
Smyrna *RPC* 2469: FS *Sebaste sunkletos* / statue in temple *Sebastos Tiberios*
Mastaura *RPC* 2673: FT *Sebastous*
Magnesia *RPC* 2699: B *Ioulia [Seb]ste*
Aphrodisias *RPC* 2840: B *Sebaste* *RPC* 2842: JT *Sebastoi*
Apollonia *RPC* 2865: B *Sebaste*
Cibyra *RPC* 2886: B *Sebaste* / Zeus, 2888: as 2886/T *Sebastos*
Sardis *RPC* 2991: Ssc *Sebaste* / togate Tiberius *Sebastos*
Tripolis *RPC* 3053: B *Sebaste*, 3054 JT *Sebaston Kaisara*
Aezani *RPC* 3071: B *Sebaste* / T *Kaisar*
Apamea *RPC* 3132: B *Sebaste*
Eumenea *RPC* 3148: B *Sebaste;* H
Eucarpia *RPC* 3160: B *Sebaste*
Cyprus *RPC* 3919–20: Sps Iulia Augusta / T Ti Caesar Augustus
Tarsus *RPC* 4005: Sc & poppies as Hera: *Sebastes Ioulias Heras Metr* / T *Tiberiou Kaisaros Sebastou*
Augusta *RPC* 4006–8, 4011: B 4009–10 *Iouliae Sebaste*
Mopsus *RPC* 4049: B *Thea Sebaste* / A *Theos Seb*[*astos*]
Judaea—Philip *RPC* 4949: B Ioulia Sebaste / *Karpophoros*, 4951: JT(?) *Sebas*[
Judaea—Procurators *RPC* 4959, 4961, 4963: *Ioulia*, 4964–66: *Ioulia* / *Tib Kaisar*, 4967: *Ioulia Kaisaros* / *Tiberiou Kaisaros*
Alexandria *RPC RPC* 5079–80, 5086: B
Unknown city *RPC* 5435: B *Sebaste*
Unknown city *RPC* 5447: B *Se*]*b* / T *Tib*

Claudius

Crete *RPC* 1030: B *Thea Sebasta* / C *Ti Klaudios Kaisar Germanikos Sebatos*
Thessalonica *RPC* 1577: B / C *Ti Klaudios Germanikos Sebatos*

Nero

Augusta (Syria) *RPC* 4013–14: B *Ioulia Sebaste* / veiled Tyche

Uncertain Emperor

Mysomakedones *RPC* 2568: Ss & branch *Sebaste* / cult statue of Artemis
Mallus *RPC* 4016: B / Athena

APPENDIX 2: THE ROMAN SYSTEM OF GOVERNMENT

Many of the institutions that evolved during the republic were maintained more or less intact through the imperial period. The following description applies to the years immediately after the Augustan settlement.

The chief deliberative and legislative body in Rome was the Senate, made up of about six hundred former magistrates of the rank of quaestor or above. A man (public offices were not open to women) could enter the quaestorship if he had reached at least his twenty-fifth year. Twenty quaestors were elected annually and were concerned with financial matters. The quaestorship might be followed by one of two offices, that of aedile, charged with certain aspects of municipal administration, or that of tribune, appointed originally to look out for the interests of the plebeians but by the Augustan period concerned chiefly with minor judicial matters. Alternatively, the quaestorship might lead directly to the next office in the hierarchy, the first major one, the praetorship (twelve elected annually, at least five years after the quaestorship). This involved responsibility for the administration of justice, and could in turn lead to one of the two consulships, the highly prestigious senior offices in the state. Strictly speaking, consular rank was attainable only after the candidate had reached the age of forty-two, but having an ex-consul in the family history made it possible to seek the office much sooner, possibly by thirty-two, and members of the imperial family achieved it at an even younger age. From 5 BC it was common for consuls to resign office during the year to make way for replacements (suffects). Technically, the Senate could not pass legislation in this period. For its decrees to have the force of a law *(lex)* they had to be passed by the popular assemblies, although the popular ratification tended to be something of a formality. Membership in the Senate was generally permanent, subject to the approval of the censor. This official maintained the citizen list and could expel senators on moral grounds or if they fell below the requisite property qualification.

Consuls and praetors exercised a special form of higher power, *imperium*. When their terms had expired, they would often be granted one of the "public" provinces, where they exercised their imperium in the capacity of their previous offices, as *propraetor* or *proconsul*. In the "imperial" provinces—generally those where the Roman legions were stationed—the governors *(legati Augusti)* and the legionary commanders *(legati legionis)* were appointed by the emperor, who thus effectively commanded the Roman armies. Accordingly, the high point of the soldier's career, the great military parade or "triumph" that followed a major victory in the field, became the prerogative of the imperial family. Lesser beings had to remain content with triumphal *insignia*. Egypt and some of the smaller provinces were governed by imperial appointees from the equestrian order (broadly, the commercial middle class) with the rank of prefect or (most common later) procurator. The latter term is used also for financial officers in the provinces, as well as for administrators of imperial estates.

Augustus acquired two of the privileges of the plebeian tribunes. Tribunician *sacrosanctitas* made any attack on his person sacrilegious. His tribunician *potestas* gave him a number of entitlements, including the right to convene the Senate and the popular assemblies, and to introduce or to veto legislation. This special authority was a symbolically important element of the principate, and emperors dated their reigns from the point when it was assumed.

APPENDIX 3: LIVIA'S MATERNAL ORIGINS

In the letter of Caligula to the Senate cited by Suetonius, in which the emperor charges that Livia's maternal grandfather was no more than a decurion of Fundi, the name of her grandfather is given as Aufidius Lurco. This slur on her birth is refuted by Suetonius. He knew that a good historian goes to the sources, and he reveals that the public records show that far from being a humble municipal functionary, Aufidius Lurco held important offices in Rome (Suet. *Tib.* 5, *Cal.* 23.2; Ollendorff [1926], 901). Unfortunately, for all his diligence at research, especially in family history, Suetonius might have got things wrong on this occasion. He may have confused Livia's grandfather with a senator and tribune of the plebs named Aufidius Lurco, who lived in Rome in the late republic and was probably the Marcus Aufidius Lurco mentioned by Pliny the Elder (Pliny *NH* 10.45; *RE* 2.2. [1986], 2293, no. 26 [E. Klebs]). This Aufidius made his mark on history by being the first to fatten peacocks for the market, making a nice profit from the trade. Unfortunately, inscriptions show that Livia's mother was not Aufidia but Alfidia, and Livia's maternal grandfather, if a Lurco, would thus be an Alfidius Lurco, quite unconnected with the Roman tribune and possible peacock rancher (*CIL* 2.1667 [Tucci, Baetica], *ILS* 125 [Marruvium], *IGR* 4.983 [Samos]). Some scholars argue that Aufidius and Alfidius are one and the same: see Broughton, *MRR* 2.529, 535, 647; Shackleton-Bailey (1965), 1.323. Huntsman (1997), 30, notes that a Marcus Alfidius without a cognomen is attested for the period: Asconius in his commentary on Cicero's *in Milonem* (55.8) notes that the Sextus Clodius who had Clodius' body taken into the Senate house was convicted by a prosecution conducted by Marcus Alfidius and Gaius Caesennius Philo. According to Asconius, he prosecuted Sextus Cloelius in 51 BC.

We cannot be completely certain that Livia's mother actually came from Fundi. Wiseman draws attention to the statues honouring Alfidia and her husband erected at Marruvium, a town originally settled by the Marsi. Livius Drusus, who probably adopted Livia's father, had been a friend of Quintus Poppaedius Silo, the leader of the Marsi during the Social War. It is suggested that her father might have continued the connection with the Marsi by marrying a woman from Marruvium. Wiseman has suggested that in the letter cited by Suetonius, Caligula might have impishly referred to Aufidius Luscus, an ex-scribe who had become praetor of Fundi in 37 BC and puffed himself up—to be much derided by Horace *Sat.* 1.5.34–36 for his pomposity; see *PIR*^{2} A528 (Stein); Wiseman (1965), 334, (1971), 57, 211; Perkounig (1995) 31–32. But Suetonius is consistent in his references to Fundi, and it is know that there were Alfidii from that town (*CIL* 10.6248), which has to remain the favourite for Livia's maternal origins.

APPENDIX 4: LIVIA'S NAME

By the imperial period Roman men allowed themselves considerable flexibility in their nomenclature. The naming of Roman women was even more varied. It seems that Livia was originally named by the feminine form of her *gens* (her father's gens by adoption, that is) and a feminine diminutive form of her father's *cognomen*, hence Livia Drusilla (*CIL* 6.13179). This name is used in Pliny, Suetonius, and Dio for Livia before she married Octavian (Nep. *Att.* 19.4; Pliny *NH* 15.136; Suet. *Aug.* 62.2, *Tib.* 4.3; Dio 48.15.3). In the literary sources relating to the period after this marriage, she is usually called Livia. The notion that the element Drusilla was dropped completely after her marriage to Octavian is not tenable (Ollendorff [1926], 900, Kienast [1990], 84; cf. Hahn [1994], 67 n. 13). An inscription from Eleusis dated before 27 (Octavian is not yet Augustus) refers to her as *Libian Drousillan* (*SEG* 24 [1969], 212); an inscription from Samos, possibly relating to her visit to the East (22–19 BC), calls her *Drousillan Autokratoros Kaisaros Sebastou gunaika* (Drusilla, wife of Imperator Caesar Augustus) (*MDAI[A]* 75 [1960] 104 n. 11); an inscription from Thasos dated 19–12 BC refers to *Leibia Drousilla Sabastou Kaisaros* (Livia Drusilla, wife of Augustus Caesar) (*ILS* 8784, EJ 77). Moreover, the name Drusilla can be attested in Rome, at least in private communications. Antony, for instance, uses it in a letter to Octavian (Suet. *Aug.* 69.2).

After her adoption in AD 14, she is officially called Julia Augusta. She is widely attested as such, but it sometimes is difficult to distinguish among her and Julia, daughter or granddaughter of Augustus, Julia daughter of Titus, and Julia Domna, wife of Septimius Severus. In the literature she is called Julia by Valerius Maximus 6.1.1, Augusta at Suet. *Claud.* 3, and throughout Tacitus, except in the more formal obituary, where she is Julia Augusta (Tac. *Ann.* 5.1.1). Similarly, Ovid *Fast.* 1.536 calls her Julia Augusta, presumably as a mark of respect. Suetonius inconsistently calls her Livia Augusta (Suet. *Cal.* 15.2, 23.2, *Galb.* 5.2, *Oth.* 1.1), as does Marcellus Empiricus in the early fifth century (Marc. *De Med.* 15.6).

APPENDIX 5: LIVIA'S BIRTHDATE

The year of Livia's birth must be calculated back from the information given by Dio and Tacitus for the year of her death, placed securely in AD 29 (Tac. *Ann.* 5.1.1; Dio 58.2.1). Dio adds the precise information that at the time of her death she had lived for eighty-six years, by which he means that she had completed eighty-six whole years; cf. 56.30.5 (Augustus), 58.28.5 (Tiberius), 60.34.3 (Claudius). Pliny the Elder says that Livia attributed her eighty-*two* years to her exclusive consumption of Pucine wine (Pliny *NH* 14.60), but we are not told that this remark was uttered in the year of her death (Nipperdey [1851–52] on Tac. *Ann.* 5.1.1 suggests emending Pliny's LXXXII to LXXXVI).

As we have seen, Livia's birthday was January 30, in the Julian system. When this is linked with Dio's evidence that she had passed her eighty-sixth birthday in AD 29, her year of birth could be either 59 or 58 BC, depending when in 29 she died. This uncertainty is not reflected in modern sources, which give the year 58 for her birth.

There are good grounds for allowing that she might have died before January 30. One of the *consules ordinarii* for AD 29 was Gaius Fufius Geminus, who was clearly in office when Livia died and was criticised, as consul and favourite of Livia, by Tiberius after her death (Tac. *Ann.* 5.2.2). Inscriptional evidence proves that Fufius and his colleague Lucius Rubellius Geminus had completed their terms by July 6 at the latest and been replaced by that year's suffects,

Lucius Nonius Asprenas and Aulus Plautius (*ILS* 6124; *CIL* 4.15555). Tacitus notes Livia's death as the very first item of AD 29. This is not in itself definitive, but enough of *Annals* 5 survives to show that the events of 29 as presented by Tacitus naturally follow, rather than precede, the announcement of Livia's passing. Thus a death before January 30, AD 29, is a serious possibility, with the consequence that Livia would already have reached her eighty-sixth birthday on January 30, AD 28, and thus have been born not in 58 BC, but in the previous year, 59.

(See Barrett [1999].)

APPENDIX 6: HUSBANDS OF SCRIBONIA

The identities of Scribonia's first two husbands have constituted the object of much scholarly debate, and the problem is considered by Syme to be "insoluble" (Syme [1939], 229; [1986], 246, Stemma XX). As we have seen, Suetonius reports that, before Octavian, Scribonia had been twice married, to two ex-consuls, and had borne children to one of them, whom we know to have been the second. This second husband was of the Scipionic line. One of their sons, Publius Cornelius Scipio, was consul in 16 BC. (His son in turn may have been the Scipio involved in a scandal later with Octavian's daughter, Julia.) Their daughter Cornelia, who died in the year of her brother's consulship, has achieved immortal fame through one of the most famous poems of Latin literature, the lament of the dead Cornelia for her husband Paullus Aemilius Lepidus (consul 34 BC) in the Fourth Book of Propertius' *Elegies* (4.16). The poet pays Cornelia a great compliment in saying that her death caused much grief to Octavian, who regarded her as a worthy sister to his daughter Julia. Syme argues for Publius Cornelius Scipio, consul of 35 BC, as the candidate for this second husband. If so, Suet. *Aug.* 62.2 made a slight mistake, or is misleading. Although he could be correct in stating that Scribonia's previous husbands both reached consular rank, the second could not have done so until after their divorce.

Scribonia's first husband may well have been Gnaeus Lentulus Marcellinus (consul 56 BC). An inscription refers to freedmen of Scribonia (after the marriage to Octavian) and her son Cornelius Marcellinus (*CIL* 6.26033: *Libertorum et familiae Scriboniae Caes. et Corneli Marcell. f. eius*). This indicates that she had a son from the first marriage, too, and that the young Marcellinus was still living in his mother's household after her marriage to Octavian. He may have died young and have been ignored by Suetonius.

APPENDIX 7: THE BIRTH OF DRUSUS

The birth of Drusus presents a historical problem. The marriage between Octavian and Livia took place on January 17, 38 BC (EJ, p. 46). Suet. *Claud.* 1.1 says that Livia married Octavian while pregnant and gave birth to Drusus *intra mensem tertium* (within three months); Dio 48.44.1 similarly says that Augustus married *(egemen)* Livia in her sixth month of pregnancy. The quips reported by Dio and Suetonius about the three-month pregnancy are consistent with these reports.

But the above statements cannot be reconciled with the evidence for the birth of Drusus. If Livia was six months pregnant when she married, this would logically mean that Drusus would have needed to be born by the end of March at the earliest. Suetonius informs us that Drusus and Mark Antony shared the same birthday, and that Claudius, when emperor, proclaimed that the birthday of his father, Drusus, would be marked with added intensity because it coincided with Antony's (Suet. *Claud.* 11.3; see also Dio 60.5.1). The *Fasti Verulani* put Antony's birthday, and thus by implication Drusus', on January 14 (EJ, p. 45), three days before the wedding.

A possible explanation is that Claudius might have officially placed the celebration of Drusus' birthday on a date different from the actual birth. Sumner makes the point that Dio's allusion to the grant of games to Drusus belongs to AD 41, yet the games could not have been held on January 14 of that year because Claudius did not succeed until close to the end of the month (Jos.

Ant. 19.77; Suet. *Cal.* 56.2; Dio 59.29.5–6; Barrett [1990], 169–70). Sumner's chronology is correct, but Dio in fact indicates only that the legislation was passed in 41—he does not actually say that the event was celebrated in that year. Sumner also makes the point that it would have been difficult for Livia to go through a wedding three days after the delivery. Difficult perhaps, but not impossible.

The notion of an alternate "official" birthday seems implausible. After nearly half a century Claudius would hardly have wanted to go out of his way to mark the official birthday of his father three days before the celebration of the marriage of his grandmother Livia and Octavian. Also, he would hardly have voluntarily chosen a day that was considered a *dies vitiosus* (cursed day) in the calendars because of the birthday of Antony. Moreover, celebration of Drusus' birthday caused some disruption, according to Dio, because Claudius had to move the established (unidentified) festivals on that day to another time to avoid a clash (Dio 60.5.1).

The concrete evidence of inscriptions and birthdates must, other things being equal, be considered more reliable than literary information that derives ultimately from gossip and propaganda. In the textual narrative I make the assumption that the confusion, perhaps deliberately fostered, between the wedding and the betrothal lies at the heart of the apparent contradiction. Octavian presumably was betrothed to Livia in early October, when she was six months pregnant, but made a point of delaying the actual marriage until Drusus was born. The liaison, scandalous in its own right, was presented by Antony in the most lurid terms available, presumably to deflect criticism of his own affair with Cleopatra.

References: Carcopino (1958), 73; Radke (1978), 211–13. Willrich (1911), 10, suggests that the marriage took place in the year 39 and that Drusus was born three months later; Sumner (1978), 424 n. 1, argues for March or April 38 as the birthdate; Hahn (1994), 34, puts it in March or July 38; Bleicken (1998), 209, places the birth in April; Gardthausen, I.2.1021; II.2.634; III.2706; and Ollendorff (1926), 902, between the end of March and the beginning of July 38.

APPENDIX 8: LIVIA'S *AEDES* AND THE TEMPLE OF CONCORD

In considering Livia's *aedes* to Concordia, it is important to keep two events distinct:

(a) Tiberius' pledge to restore the Temple of Concord, which took place about the time he participated with Livia in the dedication of the Porticus Liviae (in January, 7 BC), and
(b) Livia's dedication, at an unknown date, of the shrine (aedes) to Concordia within the portico.

It is probably inevitable that although two separate buildings were involved, the two dedications would come to be associated in the public mind, because both were made to Concordia. This connection seems to be reflected in Ovid. In a section of the *Fasti* not related to his account of the aedes inside the portico, Ovid describes the dedication of the Temple of Concord by Tiberius, on January 16 (AD 10). Because he calls Tiberius *dux venerande*, the lines must have been written after AD 14, at least four years after the temple's dedication. Ovid notes the republican precedent for the temple, which had come about as a result of partisan political tensions. Tiberius' gesture was far more noble—his restoration would come about from the spoils of the German wars. "You made a temple," Ovid says to Tiberius, "for the goddess you yourself worship" *(templaque fecisti, quam colis ipse, deae)*. In the final couplet the poet seems to allude to the other building, Livia's aedes, when he adds, almost as an afterthought, *hanc* (some mss *haec*) *tua constituit genetrix et rebus et ara* (*Fasti* 1.649). This is a difficult line to translate. *Constitutio* is the technical term by which a temple, altar, or the like was initially decreed. *Rebus* is unclear—it must mean something like "by her actions" (Frazer in the Loeb edition of *Fasti* translates as "by her life," hence "your mother set up [a shrine] for this goddess [sc. Concordia], by means of her [Livia's] actions and an altar." Ovid has already in an earlier section of the *Fasti* referred to the dedication of the aedes in the Porticus Liviae, and perhaps does not feel the need for any further explanation. In this later reference he speaks of an altar *(ara)*, not a shrine *(aedes)*, but that does not present an insuperable problem—presumably an altar would have been located inside the aedes. It is important to note, however, that there is a serious problem in the manuscripts. Some editors accept the reading *haec*, rather than *hanc*, a change of only one letter but one that completely alters the meaning of the passage. *Haec* would refer not to the goddess but to her temple, restored by Tiberius, and give Livia a role in the "constitutio" of that temple. Levick (1978) has shown that the controversial ideological associations of the temple would make it very difficult for any woman to be involved. Herbert-Brown (1984), 165 n. 72, accepts *hanc*, and her lead is followed here.

If Livia had no role in the restoration of the temple, why does Ovid tack on her name here? Herbert-Brown (1984), 167, suggests that in his description of the dedication of the portico by Livia and Tiberius in 7 BC, the poet had to be very careful about what he said of the dynastic problems. After AD 10, in a section of the *Fasti* that he revised in his exile, he can make up for that restraint by associating Livia with the harmony that the state now enjoys. There is no unanimity on the question. Simpson (1991), for instance, has argued that Ovid meant to indicate that Livia took part with Tiberius in the constitutio or ceremonial (re)inauguration of the temple, an occasion that would often involve the dedication of an altar. The insertion of Livia in this later passage of the *Fasti*, if she were not closely associated with Tiberius in the Temple to Concord, is, at the very least, awkward.

APPENDIX 9: THE *DOMUS AUGUSTA*

The first official recognition of the expression *domus Augusta* is in the text of the *senatus consultum* passed in December, AD 19, and preserved in the *Tabula Siarensis*. It stipulated that a marble arch honouring Germanicus should be put up, at public expense, near the statues of Divus Augustus and of the Domus Augusta that had previously been dedicated by Gaius Norbanus Flaccus in the Circus Flaminius: *ad eum locum in quo statuae Divo Augusto domuique Augus[tae iam dedicatae es]sent ab C(aio) Norbano Flacco* . . . Norbanus Flaccus' dedication no doubt occurred during his consulship, in the first half of AD 15, the year after Augustus' death, when Drusus, son of Tiberius, was his colleague (Tac. *Ann.* 1.55.1; Norbanus was still in office at the end of July when he was named in connection with the *ludi victoriae Caesaris: CIL* 6.37836). Flory (1996) believes that the group would have included Livia. The statues then were almost certainly voted by the Senate among the honours following the death of Augustus, and if the *Tabula* reflects the actual wording of the senatus consultum, the term *domus Augusta* was already in use by at least AD early 15. The first instance of the literary use of the exact term may be Ovid *Pont.* 2.2.74, written shortly before Augustus' death.

APPENDIX 10: THE CONSPIRACY OF CORNELIUS CINNA

Dio 55.14.1 gives Cinna the names Gaius Cornelius and describes him as the son of the daughter of Pompey the Great. Seneca *Clem.* 1.9.2 calls him Lucius (Cornelius) Cinna, grandson of Pompey the Great. Dio places the incident in AD 4. Seneca says that it occurred *cum annum quadragensimum transisset et in Gallia moraretur* (when [Augustus] had passed his fortieth year and was staying in Gaul). It is generally assumed that Seneca must be referring to Augustus' stay in Gaul from 16 to 13 BC. But there is an internal discrepancy. Augustus was born September 23, 63, and would have completed his fortieth year in 23 and have been in his late forties during this stay in Gaul.

Lucius Cornelius Cinna, praetor in 44 BC and an anti-Caesarean, was the husband of Pompey's daughter Pompeia (*RE* 4 [1900], 1287 [F. Münzer]). He had two sons:

(a) Lucius Cornelius Cinna junior, by an earlier wife (*PIR* C. 1338). This son was suffect consul in 32 BC and was not the grandson of Pompey; thus unless the sources are seriously confused, he could not be the conspirator.

(b) Gnaeus Cornelius Cinna Magnus, Lucius' son by Pompeia (*PIR* 1339; *RE* 4 [1900], 1288–89, and *Suppl.* 1 [1903], 328). This individual was a supporter of Antony and thus fits the description in Seneca (*Clem.* 1.9.11) of someone who was once an enemy *(prius hosti)*. Cinna is called an *adulescens* by Seneca (*Clem.* 1.9.3, 5), possibly applicable to him in 16–13 BC but

> impossible in AD 4. Nor was this Cinna consul in the year following this stay or indeed any of the stays in Gaul.

Fitzler and Seeck (1918), 370–71, find it impossible to reconcile the inconsistencies and point out that the conspiracy is not mentioned by Velleius, Livy, or Suetonius and that in his other reference to Cinna (*Ben.* 4.30.2), Seneca does not mention it. They suspect that the incident may be fictitious.

The general consensus is that Dio's account is the more reliable and taken from a source independent of Seneca, who may have confused Gnaeus with his father or his half-brother. Bauman (1967), 196, believes that Seneca was basically correct, in that Lucius was the conspirator, but that he distorted the events somewhat, which in turn misled Dio.

APPENDIX 11: THE CELEBRATION OF LIVIA'S MARRIAGE

An entry in one of the calendars, the *Fasti Verulani* (produced in the reign of Tiberius), seems to indicate that a festival was decreed by the Senate to mark Livia's marriage *(feriae ex s.c. quod eo die Augusta nupsit divo Aug[us]t[o])* on January 17. Livia is identified as Augusta and her husband as Divus Augustus, which seems to place the public celebration of the marriage in the post-Augustan period. But that later celebration has been called into question. In a different calendar, the *Fasti Praenestini*, there is a record of a dedication of some sort by Tiberius, presumably between AD 6 and 9, the period when the initial entries in this calendar seem to have been made. The record is fragmentary, but Mommsen's supplement, *n[umini Augusti ad aram q]uam dedicavit Ti. Caesar* ([sacrifices were carried out] to the Numen of Augustus at the altar that Tiberius dedicated), is generally accepted. The reference is followed by an entry in the same calendar, added probably soon after Augustus' death, revealing that the Senate decreed that the anniversary of the dedication of the altar was to be celebrated with a festival *(fe[riae ex s.c. q]u[od e.d. Ti. Caesar aram divo] Aug. patri dedicavit)*.

Degrassi (1963), 401 (see also Grether [1946], 235), suggests that the entry relating to the marriage in the *Fasti Verulani* was made in error, based on the erroneous belief that the festival established for the dedication of the altar had been established for the marriage.

APPENDIX 12: PALATINE VESTA

Calendars show that in 12 BC, on April 28, a dedication took place in Augustus' house on the Palatine (EJ, p. 48). The day and month are recorded also by Ovid (*Fast.* 4.949–50), who observes that on that date Vesta was received within the threshold of her kinsman *(cognati Vesta recepta est / limine)*.

The dedicator is not named by the calendars, but it is almost certainly Augustus. The *Fasti Caeretani* state that a *signum* was dedicated *in domo P(alatino)* (in the Palatine house). The *Fasti Praenestini* give the location as *in domu imp. Caesaris* (in the house of Imperator Caesar), but there is no real inconsistency in the two statements. Unfortunately, the stone of the latter is damaged, and we do not know what was dedicated. The text reveals only gaps connected by the word *et (eo di[. . .]a? et [. . .] Vestae)*. Mommsen on *CIL* 1, 226, 317, assumed the existence of an actual temple to Vesta on the Palatine, although there was no physical evidence for a specific structure, nor is it specifically mentioned in the literature. He restored the word *aedicula* before *et* (whatever the correct reading, it has disappeared completely except for its final *a*), and added *ara* after *et*, hence *aedicula et ara* (shrine and altar). Degrassi (1955), 146, decided that an *m* precedes *et* and restored *signum et ara* (statue and altar). Guarducci (1964) read *signum et aedis* (statue and temple), on which see Fishwick (1992). The issue has been much debated since; see Kolbe (1966–67); Weinstock (1971), 275–76; Radke (1981), 363; Fishwick (1987–92), 88 n. 37; (1993); Simpson (1991); McDaniell (1995), 81–83; Capelli, *LTUR* 5.128–29.

APPENDIX 13: THE TITLE AUGUSTA IN THE JULIO-CLAUDIAN PERIOD

It is possible that the much-revered Antonia was granted the title of Augusta by her grandson Caligula in 37. If so, the gesture would have been in keeping with a number of other revolutionary measures carried out by Caligula, such as the extraordinary privileges extended to his sisters and the consecration of one of them, Drusilla. In a sense Caligula's measure was less dramatic than it seems at first sight. Antonia could not represent a challenge to the emperor's authority. She was by Caligula's accession a very elderly woman and was to die within months (see appendix 14).

The title became a serious issue in the reign of Caligula's successor, Claudius. The birth of a son, Tiberius Claudius Caesar Germanicus (Britannicus), probably in 41, was a great occasion for Claudius, who delighted in displaying the infant in public to the applause of the masses or in showing him off to the praetorians. In gratitude to his wife, Messalina, he eagerly heaped distinctions on her. Her birthday, for instance, was officially celebrated, and statues were erected in public places. His generosity in this sphere was repeated later. After the British campaign in AD 43 she was granted the privileges — both enjoyed earlier by Livia — of occupying the front seats at the theatre and of using the carpentum, or covered carriage, on sacred occasions, a privilege previously limited to individuals like Vestals and priests. But this was as far as Claudius would go. Significantly he refused to allow Messalina to be granted the title of Augusta, offered by the Senate possibly when she produced a male heir. The emperor doubtless felt that such an award would have gone beyond honouring her merely as his consort and have elevated her to a quasi-constitutional position that was out of character with Roman tradition. Nor did he allow Britannicus the title of Augustus (Dio 60.12.4–5, 22.2; Suet. *Claud.* 17.3; note that Messalina is called Sebaste on coins of Nicaea [*RPC* 2033–34, 2038], Nicodemia [*RPC* 2074], and Aegae [*RPC* 2430], and Augusta at Sinope [*RPC* 2130]).

The first usurpation of the title of Augusta by the wife of a living emperor was by Agrippina (the Younger), wife of Claudius. She was much more skilled than her predecessor Messalina in laying claim to power. As a Julian and blood descendant of Augustus, she recognised that she could be a considerable political asset to Claudius. By the end of 49 she had married the emperor and betrothed her son Nero to his daughter Octavia. Her success was crowned in the following year, when she officially became Augusta (Tac. *Ann.* 12.26.1; Dio 60.33.2a; Levick [1990], 71). From then on her official name in coins and inscriptions was Iulia Augusta Agrippina, a change of great symbolic importance. It seemed to elevate her to the status of empress—not, of course, in the technical sense of a woman with authority to make legally binding decisions, but in the sense of a woman who could lay equal claim to the maiestas that the office of emperor conveyed. For the first time the portraits of the emperor and his consort appear on the same official coin of Rome: Claudius is depicted on the obverse, a draped bust of Agrippina, identified as Agrippina Augusta, on the reverse (*RIC*^{2} Claudius 80–81). An official silver coin of Ephesus, dated 50 or 51, similarly carries an obverse head of Claudius, and a reverse of Agrippina Augusta. Another Ephesian issue depicts jugate heads of Claudius and Agrippina Augusta (*RIC*^{2} Claudius, 117, 119, erroneously described). The heads of the emperor and his wife appearing together on the same face of a coin is a remarkable first for Roman official (as opposed to local) coinage. The jugate heads, a type first developed by Ptolemy II to celebrate his marriage to his sister Arsinoe, signal strikingly the official sanction of the role of Agrippina as Claudius' partner. After Agrippina, the application of the title to a woman was no longer considered revolutionary. Poppaea, the wife of Nero, became Augusta when her daughter Claudia was born at Antium in January 63, and Claudia received the title at the same time (Tac. *Ann.* 15.23; *AFA* lxxix.6–7, lxxxii.27; *ILS* 234; Griffin [1984], 103). Vitellius named his mother Augusta, and it became the regular title for the wife of the princeps from the accession of Domitian in 81 (Tac. *Hist.* 2.89.2).

APPENDIX 14: ANTONIA AS AUGUSTA

Suet. *Cal.* 15.2 claims that Caligula gave Antonia all the rights enjoyed by Livia; Dio 59.3.4 states that he gave Antonia the title of Augusta, made her priestess of Augustus, and granted her the privileges of the Vestal Virgins.

If Caligula offered Antonia such honours, she appears to have declined to use her new title during her lifetime. The *Fasti Ostienses*, recording her death on May 1, 37, describe her simply as Antonia. The first evidence for the application of the title of Augusta to Antonia in Rome is on an Arval fragment of January 31, 38, honouring her birthday in the year following her death (*AFA* xliii.7 [Smallwood 3.7]). The reference in Suet. *Claud.* 11.2 to *cognomen Augustae ab viva recusatum*, with Lipsius' emendation of the manuscript's *avia* to *viva*, suggests that Antonia had refused the distinction during her lifetime and that Claudius had the Senate bestow it on her after death. Unemended, reading *ab avia*, the text seems to suggest that Claudius' grandmother Livia had refused the honour, which clearly is nonsense. If Antonia declined the title during her lifetime, Caligula might have conferred it on her after her death (although Dio implies that he bestowed it at the very outset [*euthus*]). Claudius cancelled all Caligula's *acta* and may afterwards have reconfirmed the honour, as an act of piety towards his mother. The title appears in a fragmentary inscription from Corinth involving Tiberius (Gemellus) and Antonia Augusta, generally dated to the beginning of Caligula's reign, early 37 (Corinth 8.2.17; Kokkinos [1992], 46–47). Also, local coins of Corinth (*RPC* 1176–77) and of

Thessalonica (*RPC* 1573–74) of Caligula's reign call her Augusta / Sebaste, the only mints to do so. There is an undated coin of Tomi with the legend *Antonia Sebaste* (*RPC* 1833; see Kokkinos [1992], 87–89). The evidence of local coinage is of little value, if any, in deciding such questions. The coins of Thessalonica of the Claudian period do not give Antonia the title (*RPC* 1581–82, 1584–86). But Messalina is identified as Augusta / Sebaste on the local coins of Aegeae (*RPC* 2430), Nicaea (*RPC* 2033–34), Nicomedia (*RPC* 2074), and Sinope (*RPC* 2130), even though the title was officially withheld from her. On the question see Barrett (1996), 62, 268; Kokkinos (1992), 93.

APPENDIX 15: AUGUSTUS' PALATINE RESIDENCE

The assumption is made on page 177 that the modest residence excavated on the Palatine and identified as the house of Augustus is not the property that Suetonius claimed Octavian acquired from Hortensius (Suet. *Aug.* 72.1). It seems unlikely that Hortensius would have lived in a modest house (Claridge [1998], 128, suggests that he owned the "Casa di Livia"); he was noted for his collection of objets d'art, which included a sphinx that he had acquired in partial payment for the defence of the rascal Verres, and a painting of the Argonauts by Cydias for which he paid 144,000 sesterces. He built a special shrine in his villa at Tusculum to hold it (Pliny *NH* 34.48, 35.130). Moreover, soon after the initial acquisition, Octavian used agents to buy properties that were adjacent to his own (Vell. 2.81.3). This expansion probably embraced the house of Catulus, one of the finest on the Palatine, said by Pliny to surpass even the splendid *(magnifica)* house of Crassus (Pliny *NH* 17.2), and adjacent to a public portico with plantations of trees, donated by Catulus from the spoils of the campaigns against the Germanic Cimbri (Cic. *Dom.* 62). This house was used by the famous teacher Marcus Verrius Flaccus, who stimulated effort in his pupils by the offer of glittering prizes. Flaccus was employed by Augustus at 100,000 sesterces a year to teach his grandsons Gaius and Lucius, probably early in the last decade of the century. The instruction took place in the atrium of Catulus' house, identified at that time as part of the imperial palace (Suet. *Gram.* 17).

The surviving house was decorated probably not long after 30 BC, to judge from the painting style. This would fit a residence voted for in 36, after the lightning damage, and built on a modest scale, not suited to the neighbourhood but suited instead to Augustus' temperament. Suetonius may well have based his description of the simple residence on what had survived of it in his day, and may have mistakenly attributed it to Hortensius because he knew that Augustus had at one point acquired Hortensius' house. There is another complication. In AD 3 there was a serious fire on the Palatine. The Temple of Magna Mater to the west of the imperial palace was burnt down and rebuilt by Augustus. The imperial residence was also destroyed; at any rate, it was destroyed in the same year—whether in same fire is not known. Augustus' house was said to have been rebuilt at public expense after AD 3 (*RG* 19; Ovid *Fast.* 4.348; Val. Max. 1.8.11). But the surviving house was certainly not rebuilt after the early twenties—the paintings show us that. Moreover, Suetonius, *Aug.* 72.1, states that Augustus slept in the same room for more than forty years. This claim may exaggerate the emperor's true sleeping habits, but it does suggest continuous occupation of the same private residence for forty years, uninterrupted by the destruction in AD 3 and the replacement by a different residence. Otherwise the assertion would be self-evidently absurd. Nor need Augustus have named the forty-year figure—he may simply have made a general boast towards the end of his life, and Suetonius could have made the calculation.

It is likely, then, that the house that now survives was built for Augustus to take up residence after his return from Actium, in compensation for the land made over for the Temple of Apollo, and was in continuous occupation from then to the emperor's death, when it might have been abandoned. The fine residences of Hortensius and Catulus must have lain elsewhere in the imperial complex (Degrassi [1966–67]). The public aspects of the Roman house, particularly those at the upper end of the social scale, have been laid out in some detail by Wallace-Hadrill (1988). Also, Zanker (1988) 49–53, 67–68, 85–89, has observed that Augustus seems to have taken his lead from Hellenistic rulers, for at sites like Pergamum and Alexandria the structures adjacent to the palace served as a kind of showplace. The fine residences of Hortensius and Catulus could have formed the kernel of the public area. But where were they located? Ovid may provide a clue. The poet seems to give the shrine of Vesta that Augustus established in his home a prominent place in the landscape of the Palatine, seeing it as almost equal in importance to Apollo's temple, one unit in a tripartite arrangement (Ovid *Fast.* 4.949–51, *Met.* 15.864–65; see also Dio 54.27.3). The shrine could not lie to the west of the Temple of Apollo, for that was bounded by the Temple of Magna Mater. It may be that the public part of Augustus' residence, originally made up of the houses of Hortensius and Catulus, lay to the east, and was framed by the section that housed Vesta's shrine to the east. This part of the house was severely damaged and rebuilt in AD 3 at the time of the destruction and rebuilding of the Temple of Magna Mater, although not necessarily as part of the same event. This area to the east has been overlaid by later building. One might, however, note a room that has survived the Domitianic rebuilding, the Aula Isiaca, a large vaulted hall, with decoration in apparently Egyptianizing motifs. This building used to be assigned to Caligula, largely on account of the Egyptian themes, but is now generally recognised as dating to the Augustan period (R. Ling, *CR* 35 [1985], 218; *JRS* 89 [1999], 248; Iacopi [1997].

APPENDIX 16: LIVIA'S FESTIVAL ON THE PALATINE

The fourth-century calendar of Philocalaus and the fifth-century calendar of Silvius indicate that the Ludi Palatini began on January 17 (Grant [*Anniversary*, 1950], 156; Degrassi [1963], 239, 264). Although no ancient source mentions the connection, this date is significant as the anniversary of the wedding of Augustus and Livia in 38 BC.

Dio 56.46.5 states explicitly that the festival was established as a three-day event, and had been continued under every emperor down to his own day. Already by the reign of Caligula it had been extended. Dio 59.29.5–6 notes that Caligula added three extra days in the year of his death, AD 41. The assassins waited for five, and then struck on the last. This testimony seems to be corroborated by a contemporary source, Josephus (Jos. *Ant.* 19.77), who alludes to three extra days, although his text is so corrupt that his precise meaning eludes us (see Wiseman [1991], 56). Thus Dio and Josephus imply that the assassination took place on January 23. Suetonius says that it happened on January 24 (VIIII Kal. Febr.), although manuscript variants allow January 25 or 26. None of these dates matches January 23, six days after January 17. This might suggest that the games began originally on January 19. On the other hand, Degrassi suggests that the VIIII of Suetonius manuscripts might represent a confusion of XI for IX (numerals were notoriously prone to scribal errors). If he is right, Suetonius, Dio, and Josephus would be in harmony. Whether the six days instituted by Caligula remained in force after his day is not clear, but certainly by the fourth century the festival appears as a six-day event in the calendar of Philocalaus. The extension certainly seems to have occurred before the reign of Gordian III, whose birthday celebrations on January 20 seem to have interrupted the Palatine festival.

Dio asserts that initially the festival was a private one *(idian)* (Fishwick [1987–92] I.1, 163 n. 83). At some point the private celebration became a public festival, as recorded in the calendars of Silvius and Philocalaus. The date of this change is not known.

APPENDIX 17: DATE OF THE LETTER TO THE SAMIANS

The date of the document discussed on page 198 is uncertain. The text is in Greek, but the letter's author is called *Augustos* (*sic*), a rare transliteration at this period and possibly added later—thus it is not necessarily safe to assume that the name proves that the text was originally written after 27 BC. The document must precede 20–19, when the Samians did in fact receive their freedom, and can hardly be earlier than late 39, when Octavian began to adopt the *praenomen imperatoris* (that is, placed *imperator* before his other names). The document speaks of Aphrodisias having supported Octavian and having been taken by storm *en to polemo* (in the war). Reynolds (1982), no. 13, assumes that the reference is to the campaign waged by the renegade Labienus in 40–39 BC, and she suggests a date of 38 for the inscription, because the general allusion to the war without further specification would be confusing if the document were dated after the Actium campaign in 31. The Samians might also have sought in 38 BC to take advantage of the recent marriage of Octavian to Livia to make their request. Not everyone has accepted Reynolds' dating. It has been argued that to the Aphrodisians there would have been no confusion about the reference to the war of Labienus, and contexts have been suggested from immediately after Actium in 31 (Badian [1984]) to the late twenties (Bowersock [1984], 52); see also Millar and Segal (1984), 42, 58 n. 9; (1992), 431–32; Flory (1993), 303 n. 27. To this might be added the consideration that 38 seems very early in the marriage for Livia to have lobbied her husband so seriously that he feels obliged to explain publicly his refusal of the request. On this basis the request could belong to the trip to the East that Augustus and his wife took in 22 or 19. It is conceivable that the petition of the Samians was turned down in 21, but on the repeated urging of Livia was granted in the following year.

APPENDIX 18: THE CULT OF BONA DEA AND LIVIA

There is some uncertainty over the identity of the Vestal *veteris nominis heres*, associated by Ovid with the establishment of the cult of Bona Dea. If we are to read *Clausorum* in his text at *Fasti* 5.155, we have an allusion to an unknown legendary founder of the same gens as Livia, a situation which would suit the tone of Ovid's poem and give an excellent context to Livia's restoration of the goddess' temple. As Herbert-Brown (1984), 135 n. 15, has pointed out, however, the superior reading of the manuscripts is not *Clausorum* but *Crassorum* (of the Crassi). If this reading is correct, it will be difficult not to see a reference to Licinia Crassi, a Vestal of noble birth, who is mentioned by Cicero as dedicating *ara, aedicula et pulvinar sub Saxo* in 123 BC (Cic. *Dom.* 136; Herbert-Brown [1984], 135 n. 15). Licinia's Vestal office and the location of her dedication argue strongly for the identification of her as the benefactor of the shrine of Bona Dea, although it must be noted that Cicero does not specify to whom she actually dedicated her foundation.

The role of Licinia would, however, present a problem. It seems that her dedication in 123 BC was later declared invalid because of her personal impropriety. She was accused of incest and tried before the pontifices in 114 BC (Dio 26.87.3). Herbert-Brown (1984), 139–41, does point out that, in his allusion to Licinia, Cicero seems deliberately to have avoided giving precise details about her, and it may be that her connection with Bona Dea was relatively unfamiliar by Livia's day. That said, it is difficult to see why Ovid should have gone out of his way to remind the reader that a woman who had "known" no man *(virgineo nullum corpore passa virum)* was the very member of the family of the Crassi who, according to Dio, had entertained a host of lovers. Johnson (1997), 409, sees the allusion to Licinia as a "clumsy . . . act of historical revisionism."

APPENDIX 19: AGRIPPINA AND LIVIA IN AD 28–29

According to Tac. *Ann.* 5.3.1, the final attack on Agrippina the Elder and her son Nero was not made by Sejanus until after Livia's death—that is, in 29. Suet. *Cal.* 10.1, however, seems to contradict Tacitus, claiming that Caligula was taken to the home of Livia, still very much alive, after his mother, Agrippina, had been banished. Suetonius seems to gain some support from Pliny's account of the trial of Titius Sabinus, who had been an old friend of Germanicus and a frequent visitor to Agrippina's home (*PIR* T 202; *RE* 6 [1937], 1569 [A. Stein]). The reports of the soldiers on the headstrong and outspoken Nero had apparently been detailed enough to bring some sort of proceeding against the young man. As a result of what was disclosed there (we have no details), Sejanus began to investigate Sabinus. In early 28 Sabinus was convicted on the evidence of spies, who had kept him under surveillance by concealing themselves in his attic. He was executed and his body thrown down the Gemonian stairs (Tac. *Ann.* 4.68–70; Dio 58.1.1–3). When speaking of Sabinus' trial, Pliny *NH* 8.145 says that it came about *ex causa Neronis*—as a consequence of Nero's case. Because the trial of Sabinus belongs to 28, Nero must have been charged at least by that date and thus before Livia died. Velleius 2.130.4–5 is less specific, but he does strongly imply that Livia died after Agrippina and Nero had been brought down. The conflicting evidence has been the subject of much scholarly debate, and the most satisfactory explanation is probably that of Eckhard Meise, who argues that Sejanus' final attack was broken into two stages, the first before Livia's death in 29, when Agrippina and Nero were placed under house arrest on the mainland, and the second and more serious one when Livia was no longer on the scene and they could be banished to small islands. Admittedly, Suetonius does state that the children went to Livia's house after Agrippina had been banished *(ea relegata)*, but given that his narrative is very condensed at this point, events might well have been telescoped, and the phrase might have been used loosely not of the banishment proper but of her forced confinement in Herculaneum: Meise (1969), 240. Other modern treatments include Gardthausen, *RE* 10 (1918), 475; Gelzer, *RE* 10 (1918), 511; Charlesworth (1922), 260–61; Petersen, *PIR* I.217; Marsh (1931), 184–87; Rogers (1931), 160; (1935), 101; (1943), 57–59; Colin (1954), 389; Syme (1958), I.404–5; Koestermann (1963–68), on Tac. *Ann*. 5.3; Bauman (1992), 151.

ABBREVIATIONS

ANCIENT AUTHORS AND WORKS

AP	*Anthologia Palatina*
Apoc.	*Apocolocyntosis Divi Claudii*
App. *BC*	Appian, *Bella Civilia*
App. *Mith.*	Appian, *Bella Mithridatica*
Apul. *Apol.*	Apuleius, *Apologia*
Ath. *Deip.*	Athenaeus, *Deipnosphistae*
Aug. *Civ. Dei*	Augustine, *De Civitate Dei*
Aul. Gell. *NA*	Aulus Gellius, *Noctes Atticae*
Aur. Vict. *Caes.*	Aurelius Victor, *Caesares*
Bell. Afr.	*Bellum Africum*
Boethius, *Cons.*	Boethius, *De Consolatione Philosophiae*
Calp. Sic.	Calpurnius Siculus
Cato *De Agr.*	Cato, *De Agri Cultura*
Caes. *BC*	Caesar, *Bellum Civile*
Cic. *ad Att.*	Cicero, *ad Atticum*
Cic. *ad Fam.*	Cicero, *ad Familiares*
Cic. *ad Q. fr.*	Cicero, *ad Quintum Fratrem*
Cic. *Brut.*	Cicero, *Brutus*
Cic. *Cael.*	Cicero, *Pro Caelio*
Cic. *Cat.*	*In Catilinam*

Cic. *De Orat.*	Cicero, *De Oratore*
Cic. *De Rep.*	Cicero, *De Republica*
Cic.*Div.*	Cicero, *De Divinatione*
Cic. *Dom.*	Cicero, *De Domo Sua*
Cic. *Har. Resp.*	Cicero, *De Haruspicum Responso*
Cic. *Inv.*	Cicero, *De Inventione Rhetorica*
Cic. *Mil.*	Cicero, *Pro Milone*
Cic. *ND*	Cicero, *De Natura Deorum*
Cic. *Off.*	Cicero, *De Officiis*
Cic. *Phil.*	Cicero, *Orationes Philippicae*
Cic. *Pis.*	Cicero, *In Pisonem*
Cic. *Rab. Perd.*	Cicero, *Pro Rabirio Perduellonis Reo*
Cic. *Rosc.*	Cicero, *Pro Sexto Roscio*
Cic. *Sest.*	Cicero, *Pro Sestio*
Cic. *Tusc.*	Cicero, *Tusculanae Disputationes*
Cic. *Verr.*	Cicero, *in Verrem*
C. Th.	*Codex Theodosianus*
Col. *RR*	Columella, *De Re Rustica*
Cons. Liv.	*Consolatio ad Liviam*
Diod. Sic.	Diodorus Siculus
Dion. Hal.	Dionysius of Halicarnassus
Dem. *In Neaer.*	Demosthenses, *In Neaeram*
Donatus, *Vit. Verg.*	Donatus, *Vita Vergilii*
Eleg. in Maec.	*Elegia in Maecenatem*
Epit. de Caes.	*Epitome de Caesaribus* (anonymous)
Euseb. *Onom.*	Eusebius, *Onomasticon*
Eutrop.	Eutropius
Fast. Ant.	*Fasti* Antiates
Fast. Ost.	*Fasti* Ostienses
Front. *Aq.*	Frontinus, *de Aquaeductibus*
Gaius *Inst.*	Gaius, *Institutes*
Hor. *Epod.*	Horace, *Epodes*
Hor. *Odes*	Horace, *Odes*
Jer. *Chron.*	Saint Jerome, *Chronica*
Jos. *Ant.*	Josephus, *Antiquitates Judaicae*
Jos. *Ap.*	Josephus, *Contra Apionem*
Jos. *BJ*	Josephus, *de Bello Judaico*
Juv. *Sat.*	Juvenal, *Satires*
Lact. *Inst. Div.*	Lactantius, *Institutiones Divinae*

Livy *Per.*	Livy, *Periochae*
Lucan *BC*	Lucan, *Bellum Civile*
Lysias *In Diog.*	Lysias, *in Diogeiton*
Macrob. *Sat.*	Macrobius, *Saturnalia*
Marc. *De Med.*	Marcellus Empiricus, *De Medicina*
Marc. Aurel. *Med.*	Marcus Aurelius, *Meditations*
Martial, *Spect.*	Martial, *Liber de Spectaculis*
Nep. *Att.*	Nepos, *Atticus*
Nic. *Vit. Caes.*	Nicolaus Damascinus, *Vita Caesaris*
Obseq.	Obsequens
Ovid *AA*	Ovid, *Ars Amatoria*
Ovid *Fast.*	Ovid, *Fasti*
Ovid *Met.*	Ovid, *Metamorphoses*
Ovid *Pont.*	Ovid, *ex Ponto*
Ovid *Trist.*	Ovid, *Tristia*
Philo *Flacc.*	Philo, *Contra Flaccum*
Philo *Leg.*	Philo, *Legatio*
Philost. *Apoll.*	Philostratus, *Via Apollonii*
Phlegon, *Mir.*	Phlegon, *Miracula*
Plaut. *Most.*	Plautus, *Mostellaria*
Pliny *Ep.*	Pliny, *Epistulae*
Pliny *HN*	Pliny, *Historia Naturalis*
Pliny *Paneg.*	Pliny, *Panegyricus*
Plut. *Ant.*	Plutarch, *Antonius*
Plut. *Caes.*	Plutarch, *Caesar*
Plut. *Cat. Mai.*	Plutarch, *Cato Maior*
Plut. *Cat. Min.*	Plutarch, *Cato Minor*
Plut. *Cic.*	Plutarch, *Cicero*
Plut. *Cor.*	Plutarch, *Coriolanus*
Plut. *De garr.*	Plutarch, *De garrulitate*
Plut. *Gai. Gracc.*	Plutarch, *Gaius Gracchus*
Plut. *Galb.*	Plutarch, *Galba*
Plut. *Lucull.*	Plutarch, *Lucullus*
Plut. *Pomp.*	Plutarch, *Pompeius*
Plut. *Publ.*	Plutarch, *Publicola*
Plut. *QR*	Plutarch, *Quaestiones Romanae*
Plut. *Sull.*	Plutarch, *Sulla*
Plut. *Tib. Gracc.*	Plutarch, *Tiberius Gracchus*
Prop.	Propertius

Prud. *Con. Symm.*	Prudentius, *Contra Symmachum*
Ptol. *Geog.*	Ptolemy, *Geographia*
Quint. *Inst. Or.*	Quintilian, *Institutio Oratoria*
RG	*Res Gestae Divi Augusti*
Sall. *BC*	Sallust, *Bellum Civile*
Sall. *Cat.*	Sallust, *Catilina*
Schol. Juv. *Sat.*	Scholiast, on Juvenal's *Satires*
Sen. *Ben.*	Seneca, *De Beneficiis*
Sen. *Brev.*	Seneca, *De Brevitate Vitae*
Sen. *Clem.*	Seneca, *De Clementia*
Sen. *Cons. Helv.*	Seneca, *Consolatio ad Helviam*
Sen. *Cons. Liv.*	Seneca, *Consolatio ad Liviam*
Sen. *Cons. Marc.*	Seneca, *Consolatio ad Marciam*
Sen. *Cons. Polyb.*	Seneca, *Consolatio ad Polybium*
Sen. *Cons. Sap.*	Seenca, *De Constantia Sapientiae*
Sen. *Contr.*	Seneca, *Controversiae*
Sen. *Ep.*	Seneca, *Epistulae*
Sen. *Ira*	Seneca, *De Ira*
Sen. *QN*	Seneca, *Quaestiones Naturales*
Serv. on Verg. *Aen.*	Servius, on Vergil's *Aeneid*
SHA	*Historia Augusta*
Simplicius, *In cat.*	Simplicius, *In Categoria*
Stat. *Silv.*	Statius, *Silvae*
Suet. *Aug.*	Suetonius, *Augustus*
Suet. *Cal.*	Suetonius, *Caligula*
Suet. *Claud.*	Suetonius, *Claudius*
Suet. *Div. Jul.*	Suetonius, *Divus Julius*
Suet. *Dom.*	Suetonius, *Domitianus*
Suet. *Galb.*	Suetonius, *Galba*
Suet. *Gram.*	Suetonius, *De Grammaticis*
Suet. *Nero*	Suetonius, *Nero*
Suet. *Oth.*	Suetonius, *Otho*
Suet. *Tib.*	Suetonius, *Tiberius*
Suet. *Vesp.*	Suetonius, *Vespasianus*
Suet. *Vit.*	Suetonius, *Vitellius*
Sym. *Rel.*	Symmachus, *Relationes*
Tac. *Ag.*	Tacitus, *Agricola*
Tac. *Ann.*	Tacitus, *Annales*
Tac. *Dial.*	Tacitus (?), *Dialogus*

Tac. *Germ.*	Tacitus, *Germania*
Tac. *Hist.*	Tacitus, *Historiae*
Ulp. *Dig.*	Ulpian, *Digesta*
Ulp. *Reg.*	Ulpian, *Institutiones Regulae*
Val. Max.	Valerius Maximus
Varro, *LL*	Varro, *Lingua Latina*
Varro, *RR*	Varro, *Res Rusticae*
Vell.	Velleius Paterculus
Verg. *Aen.*	Vergil, *Aeneid*
Vitr. *Arch.*	Vitruvius, *De Architectura*
Zosim.	Zosimus

MODERN TITLES

AA	*Archäologischer Anzeiger*
AAAH	*Acta ad Archaeologiam et Artium Historiam Pertinentia*
AAntHung	*Acta Antiqua Academiae Scientiarum Hungaricae*
AC	*L'Antiquité Classique*
ACD	*Acta Classica Universitatis Scientiarum Debrecenensis*
AE	*L'Année Epigraphique*
AFA	*Acta Fratrum Arvalium*
AFLPer	*Annali della Facoltà di Lettere e Filosofia*
AfrIt	*Africa Italiana*
AHR	*American Historical Review*
AJA	*American Journal of Archaeology*
AJAH	*American Journal of Ancient History*
AJP	*American Journal of Philology*
Anc. Soc.	*Ancient Society*
ANRW	*Aufstieg und Niedergang der römischen Welt*
Arch. Class.	*Archeologia Classica*
BASP	*Bulletin of the American Society of Papyrologists*
BC	*Bulletino della Commisione Archaeologica Communale di Roma*
BCH	*Bulletin de Correspondence Hellénique*
BGU	*Berliner griechische Urkunden*
BICS	Bulletin of the Institute of Classical Studies
BJ	*Bonner Jahrbücher*
BMC	H. Mattingly, *A Catalogue of the Roman Coins in the British Museum* (London, 1923)

BMCR	*Bullettino del Museo della Civiltà romana*
BMCRR	H. A. Grueber, *Coins of the Roman Republic in the British Museum* (London, 1910, rpt. 1970)
BVAB	*Bulletin van de Vereeniging tot Bevordering de Kennis de Antieke Beschaving*
CAH	*Cambridge Ancient History* (Cambridge 1996), vol. 10
CB	*Classical Bulletin*
CIG	*Corpus Inscriptionum Graecarum*
CIL	*Corpus Inscriptionum Latinarum*
CJ	*Classical Journal*
C&M	*Classical et Mediaevalia*
Corinth	*Corinth: Results of Excavations conducted by the American School at Athens* (Cambridge, Mass., 1929–)
CP	*Classical Philology*
CPR	*Corpus Papyrorum Raineri*
CQ	*Classical Quarterly*
CR	*Classical Review*
CRAI	Comptes Rendues de l'Académie des Inscriptions et Belles-Lettres
CSCA	*California Studies in Classical Antiquity*
CT	*Les Cahiers de Tunisie*
CV	*Classical Views*
CW	*The Classical World*
DAW	*Denkschriften der Akademie der Wissenschaften*
Degrassi	A. Degrassi, *I fasti consolari dell'impero romano dal 30 avanti Cristo al 613 dopo Cristo* (Rome, 1952)
Ditt.[3]	W. Dittenberger, ed., *Sylloge Inscriptionum Graecarum*, 3d ed.
EClás	*Estudios Clásicos*
EJ	V. Ehrenberg and A. H. M. Jones, *Documents Illustrating the Reigns of Augustus and Tiberius* (Oxford, 1952)
EMC	*Échos du Monde Classique*
FGH	*Fragmente der Griechichsche Historiker*
FIR	*Fontes Iuris Romani*
FOS	M. T. Raepsaet-Charlier, *Prosopographie des femmes de l'ordre sénatorial* (Louvain, 1987)
FUR	*Forma Urbis Romae*
GNS	*Gazette Numismatique Suisse*

GR	*Greece and Rome*
GRBS	*Greek, Roman, and Byzantine Studies*
GS	Th. Mommsen, *Gesammelte Schriften* (Berlin, 1905–13)
HSCP	*Harvard Studies in Classical Philology*
HThR	*Harvard Theological Review*
IG	*Inscriptiones Graecae*
IGR	*Inscriptiones Graecae ad Res Romanas pertinentes*
IJCT	*International Journal of the Classical Tradition*
ILN	*Illustrated London News*
ILS	*Inscriptiones Latinae Selectae*
Inscr. Ital.	*Inscriptiones Italiae*
Inst.	*Institutiones*
IRT	*Inscriptions of Roman Tripolitania*
JDAI	*Jahrbuch des Deutschen Archäologischen Instituts*
JEA	*Journal of Egyptian Archaeology*
JNG	*Jahrbuch für Numismatik und Geldgeschichte*
JÖAI	*Jahrshefte des Österreichischen Archäologischen Instituts*
JRA	*Journal of Roman Archaeology*
JRS	*Journal of Roman Studies*
KölnJb	*Kölner Jahrbuch für Vor- und Frühgeschichte*
LEC	*Les Études Classiques*
LTUR	M. Steinby, *Lexon Topographicum Urbis Romae* (Rome, 1993)
MAAR	*Memoirs of the American Academy in Rome*
MDAI(A)	*Mitteilungen des Deutschen Archäologischen Instituts. Athenische Abteilung*
MDAI(R)	*Mitteilungen des Deutschen Archäologischen Instituts. Römische Abteilung*
MEFRA	*Mélanges de l'Ecole française de Rome, Antiquité*
MH	*Museum Helveticum*
MMAI	*Monuments et Mémoires publiés par l'Académie des Inscriptions et Belles-Lettres*
MRR	T. R. S. Broughton, *Magistrates of the Roman Republic* (New York, 1951, rpt. Chico, Calif., 1984)
NAC	*Numismatica e Antichità classiche*
NC	*Numismatic Chronicle*
NS	*Notizie degli Scavi*
NZ	*Numismatische Zeitschrift*

OCD	*Oxford Classical Dictionary*
ORF	*Oratorum Romanorum Fragmenta*
Pap. Ryl.	*Catalogue of the Greek Papyri in the John Rylands Library at Manchester*
P. Berol.	*Berlin Papyri*
P. Bour.	*Le Papyrus Bouriant*
PBSR	*Papers of the British School at Rome*
PCPhS	*Proceedings of the Cambridge Philological Society*
PIR	*Prosopographia Imperii Romani*
Piso Decree	*Senatus Consultum de Cn. Pisone Patre*
P. Lond.	*Greek Papyri in the British Museum*
P. Med.	*Papiri Milanesi*
P. Mich.	*Papyri in the University of Michigan Collection*
P. NYU	*Papyri in New York University*
P. Oxy.	*Oxyrhynchus Papyri*
PP	*La Parola del Passato*
PSI	*Papiri Greci e Latini*
P. Sorb.	*Papyrus de la Sorbonne*
P. Vindob.	*Papyrus Vindobonensis*
QAL	*Quaderni di Archeologia della Libia*
RA	*Revue Archéologique*
RAL	*Rendiconti dell'Accademia dei Lincei*
RBS	*Roman Brick Stamps*
RCCM	*Rivista di Cultura classica e medioevale*
RdA	*Rivista di Archeologia*
RE	*Paulys Real-Encyclopedie der classischen Altertumswissenschaft*
REA	*Revue des Études Anciennes*
REL	*Revue des Études Latines*
Rev. Hist.	*Revue Historique*
RH	*Revue Historique*
RhM	*Rheinisches Museum für Philologie*
RFIC	*Rivista di Filologia e di Istruzione Classica*
RIA	*Rivista dell'Instituto Nazionale di Archeologia*
RIDA	*Revue Internationale des Droits de l'Antiquité*
RIC^2	C. H. V. Sutherland and R. A. G. Carson, *The Roman Imperial Coinage* (London, 1984, 2d ed.)
RIL	Instituto Lombardo. Rendicanti. Classe di Lettere Morali e Storiche

RM	*Rheinisches Museum*
RN	*Revue Numismatique*
RPAA	*Rendiconti della Pontificia Accademia di Archeologia*
RPC	A. Burnett et al., *Roman Provincial Coinage* (London, 1991)
RPh	*Revue de Philologie*
RSA	*Rivista storica dell'Antichità*
SB	*Sammelbuch griechische Urkunden aus Ägypten*
SBA	*Sammelbuch griechischen Urkunden aus Ägypten*
SchNR	*Schweizerische numismatische Rundschau*
SEG	*Supplementum Epigraphicum Graecum*
Smallwood	E. M. Smallwood, *Documents Illustrating the Principates of Gaius, Claudius, and Nero* (Cambridge, 1967)
SO	*Symbolae Osloenses*
SR	Th. Mommsen, *Römisches Staatsrecht* (Lepizig, 1887, rpt. Graz, 1963)
StudClas	*Studii Clasice*
StudRom	*Studi Romani*
Syme *Papers A*	Syme, R. *Roman Papers* (Oxford, 1979–84) vols. 1–3
Syme *Papers B*	Syme, R. *Roman Papers* (Oxford, 1988) vols. 4, 5
Syme *Papers C*	Syme, R. *Roman Papers* (Oxford, 1991) vols. 6, 7
Tab. Heb.	*Tabula Hebana*
Tab. Siar.	*Tabula Siarensis*
TAM	*Tituli Asiae Minoris*
TAPA	*Transactions of the American Philological Association*
TZ	*Trierer Zeitschrift*
WS	*Wiener Studien*
Würz. Jhb	*Würzburger Jahrbücher*
YClS	*Yale Classical Studies*
ZÖG	*Zeitschrift für die Österreichen Gymnasien*
ZPE	*Zeitschrift für Papyrologie und Epigraphik*
ZSS	*Zeitschrift der Savigny-Stiftung*

NOTES

1. FAMILY BACKGROUND

1. Tac. *Ann.* 5.1.1.
2. Verg. *Aen.* 7.706.
3. Livy 2.16, see also Dion. Hal. 5.40.3, Suet. *Tib.* 1.1. On the consul of 495, see Wiseman (1979), 60–61.
4. Suet. *Tib.* 2.1 mistakenly calls Hasdrubal's opponent Tiberius.
5. Tac. *Ann.* 6.51; Suet. *Tib.* 3.1 (erroneously naming Publius as Appius). A plebeian branch of the family, the Claudii Marcelli, was descended, according to Cic. *De Orat.* 1.176, from a freedman of the patrician family.
6. Huntsman (1997), 41, argues that the eclipse of the Nerones may be more apparent than real, and simply reflect gaps in the sources. On the Pulchri during the triumvirate and Augustan periods: Wiseman (1970).
7. Tac. *Ann.* 1.4.3; cf. Livy 2.56.7; Suet. *Tib.* 2.4; Wiseman (1979), 113–39, attributes the hostile tradition to Valerius Antias, the annalist of the Sullan period; Alföldi (1965), 159–64, to Fabius Pictor; see also Ogilvie (1965), 217; Goodyear (1972), 121.
8. Livy *Per.* 19 (cf. 22.42.9); Cic. *ND* 2.7 (cf. *Div.* 1.29, 2.20, 71); Val. Max. 1.4.3, 8.1.4; Suet. *Tib.* 2.2.
9. Obseq. 21; Dio 22 fr. 74.1; Orosius 5.4.7; Livy *Per.* 53; Suet. *Tib.* 2.4; *RE* 3.2 (1899), 2848, no. 295 (F. Münzer).
10. Suet. *Tib.* 2.2; the name Clausius Russus is conjectured by Ihm (1901), 303–4. On the story: Premerstein (1937), 18; Taylor (1960), 137; Brunt (1988), 413. Taylor notes that the cognomen Drusus must be wrong, because it derived from Livia's ancestry. She suggests that the story was concocted by detractors of Appius the Censor (see also Mommsen [1864–69], 1.308–10).

11. Claudia, sister of Claudius Pulcher: Livy *Per.* 19; Suet. *Tib.* 2.3; Aul. Gell. *NA* 10.6; Val Max. 8.1.4; *RE* 3.2 (1899), 2885, no. 382 (F. Münzer). Claudia, daughter of Appius: Cic. *Cael.* 34; Suet. *Tib.* 2.4 (described as sister, not daughter); Val. Max. 5.4.6; *RE* 3.2 (1899), 2886, no. 384 (F. Münzer). Clodia: Cic. *Cael.* 14, 34.
12. Suet. *Tib.* 3.1 (Suetonius occasionally confuses the Claudii Pulchri and Nerones). Marcus: *ILS* 124; *IGR* 4.982; *RE* 13.1 (1926), 881–84 (F. Münzer), no. 19; Drumann-Groebe (1964), *Claudii*, no. 30; Willems (1878), I. 515, no. 308; Shackleton-Bailey (1991), 77, calls him a Pulcher. Münzer ("Claudianus," 1926), 882, claims that Livia's father was a Nero (and that Suetonius got it wrong); he suggests that there had been some earlier intermarriage between the Pulchri and Nerones, and thus the father had both ancestries. Huntsman (1997), 22, 39, 67, 69, supports the notion of Marcus being a Nero because it makes Livia's first marriage (to a Claudius Nero) more intelligible and is supported, he claims, by evidence of her property holdings (that evidence is very tenuous). If Marcus was in fact a Pulcher, there would be two known candidates for *his* father (and Livia's grandfather)—the consul of 92 BC, Gaius Claudius Pulcher (*RE* 3.2 [1899], 2856 no. 302 [F. Münzer]; Syme [1958], 424 n. 6) or Appius Claudius Pulcher, who held the office in 79 (*RE* 3.2 [1899], 2848–49 no. 296 [F. Münzer]). Pisaurum: Cic. *Sest.* 9; Catullus 81.3. Marcus' connection with Pisaurum: Cic. *ad Att.* 2.7.3.
13. *CIL* 2.1667 (Tucci, Baetica); *ILS* 125 (Marruvium); IGR 4.983 (Samos); see Syme (1939), 358 n. 1; Taylor (1960), 188–89; Linderski (1974), 465; Hurley (1993), 93–94; Huntsman (1997), 30. For marriage between senatorials and municipals: Taylor (1949), 39; Wiseman (1971), 53. For wealth as a possible attraction, Levick ("Tiberius," 1976), 13.
14. Suet. *Tib.* 5, *Cal.* 23.2; Ollendorff (1926), 901; Barrett (1990), 218–19.
15. Münzer ("Livius," 1926), 810; Huntsman (1997), 4–11.
16. Vell. 2.14.2.
17. Vell. 2.75.3, 94.1; Suet. *Tib.* 3.1; Tac. *Ann.* 5.1.1, 6.51.1.
18. But see Drumann-Grobe (1964), 2.158; Huntsman (1997), 3, 19–20. Note that Marcus was a *iudex quaestionis* presiding over cases under the Lex Scantina in 50 BC (*MRR* 248). If he did this as praetor *suo anno*, he would have to have been born in 89, two years after the famous tribune's murder. Livius Drusus might have adopted him as an infant: see Münzer ("Claudianus," 1926), 882. It is important to note, however, that there is no actual evidence that Livius Drusus the tribune was the adoptive father, as taken for granted in most modern sources. Huntsman (1997), 21, notes another candidate—Mamercus Aemilius Lepidus Livianus, consul in 77 (*RE* 1.1 [1893], 564 no. 80 [E. Klebs]); he was adopted by an Aemilius, but he could have adopted Livia's father before his own adoption.
19. Diod. Sic. 37.10.1; see also Dio 28.96.2.
20. Vell. 2.85.3.
21. Cic. *ad Att.* 2.7.3.
22. *AFA* xxxive.2 (AD 27); xliiic.2 (AD 38). With a different logic, Kienast (1990), 83, expresses Livia's birthday as January 28.
23. Cic. *ad Att.* 4.15.9, 16.5, 17.5; *ad Q.fr.* 2.16.3; Tac. *Dial.* 21.2.

24. Lex Scantinia: Cic. *ad Fam.* 8.14.4. Gardens: Cic. *ad Att.* 12.21.2, 22.3, 23.3, 25.2, 31.2, 33.1, 37.2, 38.2, 39.2, 41.3, 44.2, 13.26.1; Huntsman (1997), 43.
25. *CIL* 11.3517. Pirates: App. *Mith.* 95; Florus 1.41.9. Catilinarians: Sall. *Cat.* 50.4; App. *BC* 2.1.5.
26. The notion that Livia and her husband were cousins seems to be based on the assumption that Suetonius was in error in describing Livia's father as a Pulcher rather than a Nero: Willrich (1911), 8; Münzer ("Claudianus," 1926), 882; Ollendorff (1926), 901; Sirago (1979), 176; Winkes (1985), 56; Treggiari (1991), 129.
27. Cic. *ad Fam.* 13.64.
28. Cic. *ad Q. fr.* 3.1.15, 2.1; Gruen (1974), 322–24.
29. Cic. *ad Fam.* 13.64.
30. Cic. *ad Fam.* 3.12.2; *ad Att.* 6.6.1; Treggiari (1991), 127–34; Syme, *Papers C*, 239.
31. *Bell. Alex.* 25.3; Suet. *Tib.* 4.1; Dio 42.40.6.
32. On the possible colonies founded, see Christol and Goudineau (1987–88), 90–92.
33. Vell. 2.75.1; Suet. *Tib.* 4.1.
34. Age at marriage: Hopkins (1965, 1966); Weaver (1972), 182; Shaw (1987); Treggiari (1991), 399–402.
35. Suet. *Aug.* 2.
36. Priesthood and city prefecture: Cic. *Phil.* 2.71, 5.17; Caesar *BC* 3.99; Vell. 2.59.3; Nic. *Aug.* 5. Military posts: Nic. *Aug.* 9; Suet. *Aug.* 82.1.
37. Nic. *Aug.* 10; Vell. 2.59.3; Suet. *Aug.* 8 says nothing about Octavius' fighting in Spain; Dio 43.41.3 makes it sound as if he was there during the campaign.
38. App. *BC* 3.94; Dio 45.5.3–4; both claim that the main motivation was financial; Dio notes that Octavian would also benefit in other, unspecified, ways.
39. On coins of 43 BC he has started to call himself C. Caesar; Crawford (1974), no. 490.
40. Cic. *Phil.* 13.24.
41. Dio 47.18–19.3. Inscriptional evidence shows that Octavian was using the title after the Peace of Brundisium in 40 (Degrassi [1963], 1.87). Coins with the legend (Crawford [1974], nos. 525, 526) probably begin in the same year. Alföldi (1973) dates the coins to 43. See Weinstock (1971), 309 n. 12; Kienast (1982), 42; Pollini (1990), 346; Southern (1998), 219 n. 19.
42. Shackleton-Bailey (1960), 262 n. 2; Syme (1939), 199 n. 1, seems to incline towards Pompeian sympathies. Willems (1878), I. 515 n. 308, and Bruhns (1978), 47, suggest that there is no way to tell. Brutus: Cic. *ad Fam.* 11.19.1; cf. 11.14.2. Proscription and death: Dio 48.44.1; Vell. 2.71.3; see Hinard (1985), 485–86, no. 78.
43. On Marcus Libo: Weinribb (1968); Hallett (1984), 160 n. 8. Scheid ("Scribonia," 1975), 365–68, argues that Scribonia, wife of Octavian, was the daughter, not the sister, of L. Scribonius Libo, consul in 34 BC. On the penalties suffered by the proscribed: Hinard (1985).
44. Pliny *HN* 10.154; Suet. *Tib.* 14.2.
45. *ILS* 108; EJ, p. 54; Suet. *Tib.* 5 (date and year of birth), 73.1 (date of death: he died on March 16 in the seventy-eighth year of his life and in the twenty-third year of his reign); Tac. *Ann.* 6.50.5 (confirming March 16, 37, and the seventy-eighth year for death). Similarly Dio 58.28.5 reports that Tiberius had lived seventy-seven years,

four months, nine days. Dio had the day of death wrong as March 26 (cf. Dio 57.2.4).

46. Suet. *Tib.* 4.2; Vell. 2.75; Dio 48.15.3. Gaius Velleius: Vell. 2.76.1.
47. Rawson (1973), 226–27; (1977), 345; Bowersock (1984), 176–77. Huntsman (1997), 49, suggests that Tiberius Claudius went east before Octavian moved closer to Sextus Pompeius.
48. Tac. *Ann.* 6.51.1; Hinard (1985), no. 41.
49. App. *BC* 4.39–40 gives examples of wives who supported their husbands in time of exile. He notes also (*BC* 4.23) the case of a woman who added her husband's name to the proscription lists so that she could marry her lover.
50. App. *BC* 5.52; Dio 48.15.2.
51. Winkes (1985), 56; Huntsman (1997), 54: a Decius or Decimus Livius left a dedication at the Laconian port of Gytheum (*CIL* I^2 2650). He was presumably the client of a prominent Livian. On Sparta as a client of the Claudii: Carteledge and Spawforth (1989), 94.
52. Suet. *Tib.* 6.2–3; Dio 54.7.2.
53. Vell. 2.77.2–3; Tac. *Ann.* 5.1; Suet. *Tib.* 4.3. On early summer 39 for the Treaty of Misenum, see Gabba (1970), 118, citing Gardthausen (1896), I.220; middle of summer: Carcopino (1958), 69.

2. MARRIAGE

1. See Scheid ("Scribonia," 1975), 365–68, for the alternative theory that Scribonia was Libo's daughter.
2. Scribonia: Sen. *Ep.* 70.10; Suet. *Aug.* 62.2, 69.1; Dio 55.10.14; *PIR* S220, *PIR* C1395; *RE* 2 (1921), 891–92 (M. Fluss); Hallett (1984), 161 n. 9; Bauman (1992), 246 n. 45. Marriage to Octavian: App. *BC* 5.53; Dio 48.16.3; Leon (1951), Levick (1975); Syme (1986), 248. Character: Suet. *Aug.* 62.2; Syme (1939), 219, 229, 378. Son's consulship: Prop. 4.11.66. Mistress: Suet. *Aug.* 69.1; Sen. *Ep.* 1.70.10; Puteal Libonis: Lugli (1947), 46; Richardson (1992), 322–23. Sentia: *CIL* 6.31276. Age: Syme (1986), 256 n. 9. Julia's birth: Dio 48.34.3; Macrob. *Sat.* 2.5.2. Accompanies Julia: Vell. 2.100.5; Dio 55.10.14. Livia's *comitas:* Tac. *Ann.* 5.1.3.
3. App. *BC* 5.72; Dio 48.36.4; Hinard (1985), 253–55.
4. Dio 48.34.3; Carcopino (1958), 71. Coins: Crawford (1974), nos. 534.3 (38 BC), 538.1 (37 BC), 540.1 (36 BC).
5. Suet. *Aug.* 69.1; Tac. *Ann.* 5.1.2.
6. Vell. 2.75.3; Tac. *Ann.* 5.1.2; *Epit. de Caes.* 1.23. Bridal beauty: Catullus 61.186–88.
7. Plut. *Ant.* 20.1; Suet. *Aug.* 62.1 actually says *duxit uxorem* of Claudia, even though she was under age; Dio 46.56.3 implies that Octavian had done no more than agree to the union; Carter (1982), 182–83.
8. Vell. 2.75.3, 79.2; Tac. *Ann.* 5.1.1; Flory (1988), 345–46. Antony's taunt: Cic. *Phil.* 3.15; Ferrero (1911), 54–55; Kienast (1982), 44. Agrippa's funeral: Dio 54.29.6; Syme (1939), 132, 344, *Papers C*, 338–45.
9. Tac. *Ann.* 5.1; Suet. *Aug.* 69.1; Dio 48.34.3.
10. Tac. *Ann.* 1.10.5; Dio 48.44.1–2.

11. Claudius and Agrippina: Tac. *Ann.* 12.5. Perturbatio partus: Tab IV.4 (= Gell.3.16.2); Gaius *Inst.* 1.55: *item in potestate nostra sunt liberi nostri, quos iustis nuptiis procreavimus;* Digest 3.2.11; Ulp. *Reg.* 14; Ulpian *Dig.* 38, 16, 3.9.11; Justinian Codex 5,17,8,4b; Corbett (1930), 249–50; Humbert (1972), 127–30; Suerbaum (1980), 344.
12. The approach to the pontiffs may have been largely a public relations exercise. Bauman (1992), 95, speculates that when Aemilius Lepidus was allowed to retain his office as pontifex maximus after being deposed from the triumvirate in 36 (App. *BC* 5.131), it was in recognition of his service in this particular matter. Of the fifteen pontiffs at the time of the consultation by Octavian, we know the names of seven. The most prominent were not in Rome. Marcus Aemilius Lepidus was in Africa, Mark Antony was in Athens, Publius Ventidius Bassus, an Antonian, was in the East, dealing with the Parthians, and Gnaeus Domitius Calvinus was in Spain. Publius Sulpicius Rufus, a Caesarian, may have been in Rome. The other two known pontiffs were Octavian and Tiberius Nero. Thus the timing of the question could not have been better from Octavian's point of view; see Huntsman (1997), 63 n. 50.
13. Tac. *Ann.* 1.10.5, 5.1.2. Caligula: Suet. *Cal.* 25.1; Dio 59.8.7, who gives the bride's name as Cornelia Orestina Vitellius. Claudius and Agrippina: Tac. *Ann.* 12.6.2. Antonian propaganda: Tac. *Ann.* 4.34.5; Suet. *Aug.* 69.1, 70.1; Flory (1988); Charlesworth (1933), 172–77.
14. Vell. 2.79.2; 2.94.1; Pliny *HN* 7.150; Suet. *Tib.* 4.3; Dio 48.44.3; *Epit. de Caes.* 1.23; Levick ("Tiberius," 1976), 15; Schilling (1977), 214. Tiberius' motives: Cic. *ad Fam.* 13.641; Carcopino (1929), 225.
15. Marcia: Plut. *Cato Min.* 25.5. Lollia: Dio 59.12.1.
16. Dio 48.44.3. On the delicia: Sen. *Cons. Sap.* 11.3; Stat. *Silv.* 2.1.72, 5.5.66 (emended); Quint. *Inst. Or.* 1.2.7; on the form of the word see Slater (1974), 134.
17. App. *BC* 5.67–68; Suet. *Aug.* 70. On the dodekatheos: Pike (1919); Scott (1929), 140; Taylor (1931), 119; Eitrem (1932), 42–43; Weinrich (1924–37), 804; Tondriau (1949), 128–40; Carter (1982), 92 (late 39 or early 38); Flory (1988), 353–59; Pollini (1990), 345. Bauman (1992), 95–96, 124, notes that in 36 Octavian received the honour of an annual banquet in the temple of Capitoline Jupiter—an excellent context for Suetonius' description of Jupiter abandoning his seat.
18. Suet. *Aug.* 69.1; see also Tac. *Ann.* 5.1. Antony had every reason to know better, because he was probably in Rome at the time of the betrothal. A report given before the Senate by Antony and Octavian concerning a senatorial decree relating to the city of Aphrodisias is preserved in an inscription found in the city. The decree is dated to October 2, 39. Antony's name precedes Octavian's, and it would be natural to assume that he made the statement of their joint views because of his agreed responsibilities for Asia. If so, this would place him in Rome in early October: Reynolds (1982), 75.
19. Vell. 2.95.1; date: EJ, p. 45; Suet. *Claud.* 11.3; see also Dio 60.5.1.
20. Dio 48.43.4, 44.1; cf. *Epit. de Caes.* 1.23.
21. Calendar references to January 17: EJ, p. 46; Suerbaum (1980), 346; Degrassi (1963), 401; Herz (1975), 10, 13; (1978), 1149, 1151, 1153; Temporini (1979), 69 n.

339. The further information, that the day was marked by a public celebration with *feriae* decreed by the Senate, must be regarded with some suspicion (see appendix 11).

22. Suet. *Claud.* 1.1; Tac. *Ann.* 1.10.5; Dio 48.44.5; Carcopino (1958), 65–82; Winkes (1985), 61. Caligula: Dio 59.23.7.
23. Dio 48.44.5; Treggiari (1991), 467–68; Huntsman (1997), 73. Willrich (1911), 11, identifies the hypomnemata with the *Res Gestae*, Blumenthal (1913), 285, with the *acta diurna*, Bardon (1968), 24, with Augustus' *Commentarii* (see appendix 1). Hallett (1984), 324, speculates that Augustus in fact might have been quite happy to foster the impression that he was Drusus' father and that this paternity would explain his favouring Drusus; see also Kuttner (1995), 295 n. 38.
24. Suet. *Tib.* 6.4; Dio 48.44.5. The date of Tiberius Nero's death can be calculated from Tiberius' age at the time. Treggiari (1991), 468, speculates that the husband of a divorced wife might have had the privilege of deciding where a child of a divorced wife should be brought up.
25. Dio 54.16.6: the anecdote is told under 18 BC but clearly refers to the earlier date.

3. IN THE SHADOWS

1. Huntsman (1997), 39, points out that the Primaporta villa was in the territory of the Arnense and that the Claudii Nerones were assigned to the tribe Arnensis; see Taylor (1960), 204–5, 285; Ashby and Fell (1921), 145. Millar (1992), 25, states that Primaporta was Augustus' property. Pliny *HN* 15.137 describes it as *villa Caesarum*, but perhaps from the perspective of his own day.
2. Suet. *Galb.* 1; Pliny *HN* 15.136–37; Dio 48.52.3–4; 63.29.3; Aur. Vict. *Caes.* 5.17 (following Suetonius closely and adding little); Alföldi (1973); Flory (1989); Reeder (1996). Suetonius places the event just after the marriage, Pliny after the betrothal *(cum pacta esset)*. Dio dates it to the next year, 37 BC, among disturbing omens, but in a rather imprecise context. Donatus in Serv. on Verg. *Aen.* 6.230 may be referring to a continuity of this tradition by saying that triumphatores crowned themselves from the laurel that sprang up on the Palatium on the day of Augustus' birth (Syme, *Papers A*, 1264).
3. Dio 48.52.4. Caesar: Suet. *Div. Jul.* 45.2; Dio 41.39.2, 43.43.1. Sterility: Col. *RR* 8.2.7.
4. Octavian had two sisters, both of whom carried the name Octavia. The elder, born to the first wife of Octavian's father, Ancharia, married Sextus Appuleius (*ILS* 8783); her son Sextus became consul in 29 BC. Plut. *Ant.* 31.1 clearly confuses her with her half-sister. The more famous Octavia Minor was born in about 69 BC to Octavius senior's second wife, Atia, some six years before Octavian junior was himself born; Suet. *Aug.* 4.1. Plut. *Ant.* 57.3 implies that she was the same age as Cleopatra.
5. Dio 48.31.4; Plut. *Ant.* 31.3.
6. App. *BC* 5.76.
7. App. *BC* 5.93–95; Plut. *Ant.* 31.2, 33.3, 35.1–4; Dio 48.54.1–5; Singer (1947).
8. Dio 49.51.1; cf. Dio 49.18.6, which suggests that the banquet was to be held in the temple of Concord, not in the Capitoline temple.

9. Dio 49.33.4.
10. Plut. *Ant.* 58; Suet. *Aug.* 69.2.
11. Plut. *Ant.* 53.1, 54–55.1.
12. Huntsman (1997), 81–82, suggests that Tiberius Nero might have seen further service with Octavian.
13. Nep. *Att.* 19.4, 22.3; cf. Sen. *Ep.* 21.4; Vell. 2.96.1; Dio 48.44.5; Willrich (1911), 18; Syme (1939), 345; *Papers C,* 258; Levick ("Tiberius," 1976), 18, 27. Vipsania: *ILS* 165. Marcella: Bauman (1992), 102. Atticus died on March 31, 32; he was still alive at the time of Tiberius' betrothal.
14. Plut. *Ant.* 83.4; Dio 51.13.3. Aschbach (1864), 11, assumes Livia's presence in Egypt. This is not likely, but Herrmann (1960), 105, suggests that she might have joined Augustus when he was in Samos after Actium in 31–30 or 30–29.
15. Cic. *ad Att.* 4.1.4, 7.2.2; *ad Fam.* 14.5.
16. Tac. *Ann.* 3.34.6; Suet. *Aug.* 24.1; Marshall ("Women," 1975; *Tacitus,* 1975). The issue of Livia's presence in Augustus' travels has been complicated by Sen. *Cons. Marc.* 4.3: Areus in addressing Livia calls himself the *assiduus viri tui comes*—that is, the constant companion of Augustus. This is read as *assidua comes* by a number of scholars, presumably as a vocative referring to Livia, making *her* the constant companion of her husband. The reading has no manuscript authority and suits the context less well than *assiduus;* Willrich (1911), 15; Ollendorff (1926), 905; Winkes (1985), 60; Hahn (1994), 34; Perkounig (1995), 70.
17. Hor. *Odes* 3.14.5–6; Halfmann (1986), 137; Calhoon (1994), 68; Perkounig (1995), 71.
18. EJ, p. 36; Vell. 2.93.1–2; Pliny *HN* 7.149, 19.24; Tac. *Ann.* 1.3.1; Suet. *Aug.* 66.1, 3, *Tib.* 6.4; Dio 51.21.3, 53.1.2, 28.3–4, 30.1–5, 31.1–4; Syme (1939), 342, 344.
19. Marcellus' death: Vell 2.93.1; Prop. 3.18.1–10; Verg. *Aen.* 6.860–86; Dio 53.30.4. Livia's involvement: Dio 53.33.4.
20. Dio 64.6–10; Gardthausen (1896), I.2.810; Ollendorff (1926), 905; Magie (1950), 469–76; Halfmann (1986), 22–24, 158–61, map 7O.
21. Ollendorff (1926), 905; Gardthausen I.2.810; Willrich (1911), 15; Bosch (1935), 22, assume the journey. Hermann (1960), 105, n. 114; Hahn (1994), 34, n. 20, are more cautious. An epigram by Crinagoras (*AP* 9.224) supposedly spoken by a milk goat, tells of Augustus' taking the goat on the journey, so addicted was he to its milk. Remarkably, some scholars identify the goat with Livia and take this as proof that Livia went to the East with him: Willrich (1911), 15; Ollendorff (1926), 905; Winkes (1985), 59; contra: Hahn (1994), 69 n. 20.
22. Dio 54.7.2; Clauss (1989), 89.
23. *IG* 3.316; Ollendorff (1926), 905.
24. Plutarch, *Peri tou Ei tou en delphois* 385F.
25. Augustus had passed the winters of 31–30 and 30–29 on Samos after Actium. Suet. *Aug.* 17.2, 26.3; Dio 51.18.1; Orosius 6.19.21 (Asia); cf. App. *BC* 4.42; Mommsen (1883), 136.
26. Strabo 14, p. 637; Magie (1950), 1331 n. 4.
27. Willrich (1911), 16; Ollendorff (1926), 905; Hahn (1994), 68 n. 20.

28. *IGR* 4.976 refers to a monument erected by Augustus in Samos dated to the fifth year of his tribuncia potestas, so before summer 19 BC.
29. *RG* 31; Suet. *Aug.* 21.3; Florus 2.62; Dio 54.9.8; Strabo 15.4, 73; Eutropius 7.10.1; Orosius 6.21.19 (who places the events in Spain). On the embassies, see Rich (1990), 185.
30. Dio 54.9.10; Strabo 15.4, 79, calls him a stoic and gives his name as Zarmanochegas; Bowersock (1965), 78 n. 3; Clinton (1989), 1507–9; Wood (1999), 92–93.
31. Donatus, *Vit. Verg.* 35.
32. *RG* 12.1; Dio 54.10.4.
33. Sen. *Cons. Marc.* 2.4; Willrich (1911), 18–19; Dixon (1988), 178, points out that Octavia had daughters, but it was as the mother of a potential princeps that they supposedly vied.
34. Sen. *Clem.* 9; Dio 54.19.3; Ollendorff (1926), 905; Fischler (1989), 47; contra, Perkounig (1995), 70; Bauman (1992), 249 n. 78.
35. Suet. *Aug.* 64.1; Plut. *Ant.* 87.3; Dio 54.6.5; 8.5, 12.4, 18.1, 28; Sutherland (1951), 58; Balsdon (1962), 73–74; Levick (1966), 229; ("Retirement," 1972), 798; ("Tiberius," 1976), 29–30, 233 n. 26; Roddaz (1984), 311, 351–81.
36. Her death was the cause of great grief to her brother (*Cons. Liv.* 442; Sen. *Cons. Polyb.* 15.3).
37. Drusus was younger than Germanicus, whose birthdate was May 24, 15 BC, and who was born before Tiberius' divorce from Vipsania, in 12. Month and day, October 7: EJ, p. 53 (Feriale Cumanum); year: Mommsen *GS* IV.262 places it between 15 and 12; Rogers (1943), 91, and Levick (1966), 236–38, favour 13; Sumner (1967), 427–29, and Seager (1972), 25 n. 2, argue for 14.
38. Marriage: Livy *Per.* 140; Vell. 2.96.1; Suet. *Aug.* 63.2, *Tib.* 7.2–3; Tac. *Ann.* 1.12.6, 53.2, 4.40.9; Dio 54.31.2, 35.4. Proculeius: Pliny *HN* 36.183; Tac. *Ann.* 4.40.9; Suet. *Aug.* 63.2; Gardthausen (1896), I.1028; Willrich (1911); Hanslik (1957), 73; Seager (1972), 72; Levick ("Tiberius," 1976), 31–32; Bauman (1992), 103. Marriage to Vipsania: 20 or 19: Levick ("Tiberius," 1976), 27; Roddaz (1984), 317 n. 44, thinks it took place before the Julia-Marcellus marriage.
39. Tac. *Ann.* 1.10.7; Suet. *Tib.* 21.4–7; Birch, "Correspondence" (1981).
40. Vell. 2.97.3; Tac. *Ann.* 1.33.3, 2.82.3; Suet. *Claud.* 1.4.
41. *RG* 12.2; EJ 46; Ovid, *Fast.* 1.710; Fishwick (1987–92) I.2. On the coincidence of the constitutio of the Ara Pacis and Livia's birthday, see Herz (1975), 11, 136; (1978), 1153 n. 104; Syme, *Papers B*, 419; Barrett (1999).
42. Winkes (1995), 97 no. 20; Rose (1997), plate 10.
43. Dio 55.2.4. The chronology is uncertain—the ovation may have followed Drusus' death; see Rich (1990), 220. Capitoline: Ehlers (1939), 510.
44. *Cons. Liv.* 89–90; Livy *Per.* 142; Val. Max. 5.5.3; Sen. *Cons. Marc.* 3.1; *Cons. Polyb.* 15.5; Pliny *HN* 7.84; Tac. *Ann.* 2.82.3; Suet. *Tib.* 50.1, *Claud.* 1.3–4; Dio 55.2.1.
45. Sen. *Cons. Marc.* 3, *Cons. Polyb.* 15.5; Tac. *Ann.* 3.5.1; Dio 55.2.1.
46. Tac. *Ann.* 3.5.1; Suet. *Claud.* 1.5; Dio 55.2. Junia: Tac. *Ann.* 3.76. Augustus: Dio 56.34.2.

4. THE PUBLIC FIGURE

1. Tac. *Ann.* 3.5.1; Muretus' emendation of *Iuliorumque* to *Liviorumque* is unnecessary. Augustus: Dio 56.34.2; Junia: Tac. *Ann.* 3.76.2. Suet. *Claud.* 1.5 mentions Drusus as potential joint heir with Augustus' "sons"; Flower (1996), 242.
2. Suet. *Aug.* 63.1; Dio 55.2.5; Bartman (1999), 3–4; she is identified as mother of Drusus on a base from Velleia (*CIL* 11.1165), but this belongs to the Caligulan period.
3. Flory (1993), 299.
4. Vell. 2.97.4; Dio 55.6; Eutrop. 7.9; Orosius 6.21.24. Date of dedication: January 16, EJ, p. 45. Motives: Levick ("Retirement," 1972), 803–5, (1978), 217–33; Rich (1990), 226.
5. Dio 55.8.2; Suet. *Tib.* 20. Gaul: Dio 55.6.1, 8.3. Banquet: Dio 55.8.2.
6. Ovid *Fast.* 6.637–38; Flory (1984), 313–14, 324, 329. Flory notes that *concordia* is a common theme on tombstones: *CIL* 6.7579.6: *vixit mecum tam concorde; CIL* 6.23137.5: *sunt duo concordes; CIL* 6. 26926: *cum quo concordem vitam . . . vixit.*
7. Dio 55.8.3, 9.1.
8. Tac. *Ann.* 1.3.3; Dio 55.9.2.
9. Behaviour of Gaius and Lucius: Dio 55.9.1–3. The applause for Lucius noted by Suet. *Aug.* 56.2 might best be assigned to this context. Tiberius' tribunicia potestas: Vell. 2.99.1; Tac. *Ann.* 3.56.3; Suet. *Tib.* 9.3; Dio 55.9.4. Gaius' consulship: *RG* 14.1; *CIL* 6.3748. Sequence: Levick ("Retirement," 1972), 780–91. Imperium: Levick ("Retirement," 1972), 781–82, ("Tiberius," 1976), 36; Rich (1990), 228.
10. Tac. *Ann.* 1.53.2; Velleius 2.99.2; Suet. *Tib.* 10; Dio 55.9.5–8; Sattler (1959), 511; Levick ("Retirement," 1972). Huntsman (1997), 119, suggests that Tiberius was sent away rather than leaving on his own accord, for when he wanted to return, he (unsuccessfully) sought the permission of Augustus. But any major decision within the imperial family would require the permission of the princeps.
11. Velleius 2.99.1; Suet. *Tib.* 10.2; Dio 55.9.8; Levick ("Retirement," 1972), 790.
12. Vell. 2.99.4; Suet. *Tib.* 11.1, 12.2; Dio 55.9.6; Sattler (1969), 513–14; Levick ("Retirement," 1972), 793, 805; Rich (1990), 228–29.
13. Pliny *HN* 7.45; Vell. 2.100.3; Suet. *Aug.* 64.2; Macrob. *Sat.* 2.5. On Julia's witticisms: Richlin (1992), 65–91. Much of the information on Julia's character comes from the much later author Macrobius but is generally accepted by scholars: see Sattler (1969), 75. Julia and Tiberius: Tac. *Ann.* 6.51.3; Suet. *Tib.* 8.2–3; Macrob. *Sat.* 2.5.8; Bauman (1992), 112. For the date of the estrangement: Levick ("Tiberius," 1976), 37.
14. Suet. *Tib.* 11.4.
15. Sen. *Ben.* 6.32.1–2, *Clem.* 1.10.3; Pliny *HN* 21.9; Tac. *Ann.* 1.53.1–4; Suet. *Aug.* 65.2, 101.3, *Tib.* 50.1; Dio 55.10.12–14, 13.1, 56.32.4. The modern scholarship on the topic is massive: for material before 1970, see Meise (1969), 3–34; since 1970 see, inter alios, Levick ("Retirement," 1972; 1975; "Julia," 1976); Ferrill (1976); Shotter (1971), 1120–21; Corbett (1974), 91–92; Lacey (1980); Syme, *Papers A* 912–36; (1978), 192–98 (also [1939], 427); Raditsa (1980), 290–95; Raaflaub

(1990), 428–30; Bauman (1992), 108–19. Fate of lovers: Vell. 2.100.4; Tac. *Ann.* 1.10.4, 4.44.3; cf. Dio 55.10.15.

16. Sen. *Ben.* 6.32.1, *Brev.* 4.5; Vell. 2.100.4; Tac. *Ann.* 3.18.1: *qui domum Augusti violasset;* 1.53.1, 3.24.2, 6.51.3 (impudicitia); 4.44.3 (adultery); 3.24.3 (excessive punishment); Suet. *Aug.* 65.1; Dio 55.10.12. Lists of conspirators: Sen. *Clem.* 1.9.6; Suet. *Aug.* 19.1; Sen. *Brev.* 4.5 (the "Paulus" of Seneca's manuscript is clearly an error for Iullus, caused by confusion with the affair of Julia the Younger); Pliny *HN* 7.149; Suet. *Aug.* 19.2; Tac. *Ann.* 1.10.5, 3.24.4; Dio 55.10.15. For a discussion of Pliny's evidence see Tränkle (1969), 121–23; Swan (1971), 740–41; Ferrill (1976), 344–45; Till (1977), 137. Bauman (1967), 198–245, argues that there was no political conspiracy, but that Julia and her paramours were convicted of a form of treason.
17. Suet. *Tib.* 11.4; Macrob. *Sat.* 5.2.6; Blaze de Bury (1874); Gardthausen (1896), I.1101; Syme (1939), 427; *Papers A*, 925; Sattler (1969), 524–25; Winkes (1985), 63; Bauman (1992), 126; contra, Willrich (1911), 24; Groag (1919), 82.
18. Gaius Gelus: *AE* 1975 (1978), no. 289; (1995), no 367; Suet. *Aug.* 65.3, Tac. *Ann.* 1.53; Linderski (1988); Gardner (1988). Linderski, 187, says that it is possible that the servile Julia, Thiasus, and Gaius Gelus were all three slaves of Julia, that the two men were manumitted but not Julia, who on her mistress' death would have passed to Augustus' heirs and could then have been manumitted by Livia. Portico: Herbert-Brown (1984), 155; Ollendorff (1926), 911, assumed that Livia's aedes and portico were dedicated at the same time.
19. Suet. *Tib.* 11.5–12.1; Suetonius calls him *quasi legatus.*
20. Vell. 2.102.1; Tac. *Ann.* 3.48; Suet. *Tib.* 13, 15.1; Pliny *HN* 9.118; Dio 55.11.3.
21. *RG* 14; Ovid *AA* 1.194; Tac. *Ann.* 1.3.2; Dio 55.9.9–10; Bowersock (1984).
22. Vell. 2.102.3; Suet. *Tib.* 70.2; Dio 55.10a.9–10; EJ, p. 50, no. 68.
23. EJ, p. 39, 47, no. 69; Vell. 2.102; Dio 55.10a.4–9.
24. Pliny *HN* 7.149; Tac. *Ann.* 1.3.3; Suet. *Aug.* 65.1; Dio 55.10a.10; Ollendorff (1926), 912.
25. *CIL* 10.1240, 11.3305, 6.31275; Dio 54.29.5.
26. Tac. *Ann.* 6.25.3: *aequi impatiens, dominandi avida;* Mellor (1993), 76–77.
27. Tac. *Ann.* 1.33.1, 2.73.2–3; Suet. *Cal.* 3–6. Walker (1960), 232, notes the resemblances between Tacitus' depictions of Germanicus and of his own father-in-law Agricola.
28. Germanicus was born on May 24 (EJ, 49; Suet. *Cal.* 1.1). Tac. *Ann.* 2.73.2 states that at his death Germanicus had not progressed much beyond thirty years. Suet. *Cal.* 1.1 says that he died on October 10, AD 19: *annum agens quartum et tricesimum* (during his thirty-fourth year). Sumner (1967), 413, takes this to mean that he was past his thirty-third birthday, hence born in 15 BC; Levick (1966) argues that it means that Germanicus had passed his thirty-fourth year.
29. Tac. *Ann.* 1.78.2 *(male consulta)*, 2.8.2 *(erratum);* Mellor (1993), 75–76. For a recent analysis of Tacitus' depiction of Germanicus, see Pelling (1993). *Feriale Duranum* 12, reading *g[er]mani[c]ī cae[sa]ris;* Fink (1940), 136–38.
30. Tac. *Ann.* 1.3.3; 4.57.3; Suet. *Tib.* 21.4–7, *Cal.* 4. Velleius 2.103.2 says that Augustus did not have to think twice. A confused passage of Zonaras (Dio 55.13.1a)

seems to attribute Tiberius' success to Julia, who had been restored from banishment. Linderski (1988), 183, thinks that Zonaras' entry might contain a garbled allusion to a chronological link between Julia's recall to Rhegium and Tiberius' adoption.

31. Vell. 2.103.2 (period unspecified); Tac. *Ann.* 1.3.3; Suet. *Aug.* 65.1, *Tib.* 16.1 (five years); Dio 55.13.2 (ten years).
32. EJ, p. 49 (for the date); Tac. *Ann.* 1.3.3; Suet. *Aug.* 64.1, *Tib.* 15.2, *Cal.* 1.1, 4; Vell. 2.103.3 (June 27); Dio 55.13.2; Mommsen (1904), 4.272; Levick (1966), 232; Instinsky (1966); Birch ("Settlement," 1981).
33. Vell. 2.103.1, 4–5, 104.1; Suet. *Tib.* 21.3; Parsi (1963), 12; Instinsky (1966), 332; Seager (1972), 37–38; Woodman (1977), 136; contra, Sumner (1970), 269; Levick (1966), 229 n. 1.
34. Tac. *Ann.* 1.3.3.
35. Vell. 2.102.3. Toga: Dio 55.22.4; Pappano (1941), 32; Birch ("Settlement," 1981), 446–48. Birth: Levick (1966), 240 n. 4. Gardthausen (1896), II. 844 n. 1, argues that because Agrippa had not yet received the *toga virilis* when adopted by Augustus on June 26, AD 4, he must not yet have been fifteen years old.
36. The earliest hint of a more serious problem to come is in Velleius. After describing the campaign at the Volcaean marshes in Pannonia, fought in late AD 7, Velleius turns to the subject of Postumus, claiming that he had begun *qualis esset apparare* (to reveal what he was like) *iam ante biennium* (already two years before). Although this is surely not meant as a precise date, it does suggest that Postumus' behaviour started to cause real concern about late AD 5, more than a year after the adoption: Vell. 2.112.7; Woodman (1977), 170; Levick ("Tiberius," 1976), 57; cf. Hohl (1935), 350 n. 1.
37. Velleius 2.102.7; Tac. *Ann.* 1.3.4, 4.3; Suet. *Aug.* 65.1, 4; Dio 55.32.1–2. Drusus: Dio 57.14.9. Mad: Jerome (1912), 279; Charlesworth (1923), 148; H. von Hentig (1924), 20; Hammond (1933), 70; Hohl (1935), 350 n. 3. Sane: Pappano (1941); Norwood (1963), 152 ("a reckless temper"); Detweiler (1970), 290; Birch ("Settlement," 1981), 449 ("perhaps not overbright").
38. *Fast. Ost.*, *Inscr. Ital.* 13.i.183; Velleius 2.102.7; Suet. *Aug.* 65.1, 4 (Suetonius is the only one of our sources explicitly to recognise two stages in the banishment); Tac. *Ann.* 1.3.4, 2.39.1; Dio 55.32.2; Pliny *HN* 7.149–50.
39. Tac. *Ann.* 1.3.4, 1.6.3, 12.1.1, 3.1; Ollendorff (1926), 915. Criticism of Germanicus: Tac. *Ann.* 1.4.4; Detweiler (1970), 290. Tacitus was perhaps just reporting the claims that the Julian side made; *Epit. de Caes.* 1.27 claims that Livia banished Postumus *odio novercali*.
40. Vell. 2.112.7; Dio 55.32.2; J. Crook, *CR* 4 (1954), 153; Levick ("Abdication," 1972; "Tiberius," 1976); Jameson (1975); Birch ("Settlement," 1981), 451. The "Agrippa as" (*RIC*[2] Caligula 58) depicts the bust of Agrippa on the obverse and Neptune on the reverse; for a summary of the arguments about the date: Barrett (1990), 250–51.
41. Tac. *Ann.* 1.6.2; Suet. *Aug.* 65.4. Pappano (1941), 37, suggests that the exile was made permanent by a decree of the Senate to ensure against a personal change of heart on Augustus' part. Jameson (1975), 303, says that if Postumus had just been relegated, he would have been able to make a claim against Augustus' will. This

would not be so if he had a sentence of *aqua et igni interdictio* (a more severe form of banishment, literally "exclusion from water and fire") passed on him, which Jameson thinks was the force of the *senatus consultum*.

42. Charlesworth (1923), 153; Pappano (1941), 40. On the Julian–Claudian division: Levick (1975).
43. For modern treatments, see, inter alios, Meise (1969), 35–48, with bibliography; Levick ("Julia," 1976); Syme (1978), 206–14; (1986), 117–22; Raaflaub (1990), 430–31; Bauman (1992), 119–24.
44. Pliny *HN* 7.75; Tac. *Ann.* 3.24.2, 4.71.6–7; Suet. *Aug.* 64.1, 65.4, 72.3, 101.3; Schol. Juv. *Sat.* 6.158.
45. Inheritance: Dio 55.32.2.
46. Dio 54.29.5, 55.32.2; Jameson (1975); Levick ("Abdication," 1972), 695; ("Tiberius," 1976), 245, no. 71; *CIL* 5.3257: at least one slave, Sex. Vipsanius M. f. Clemens, did not pass to Augustus but seems to have remained Agrippa's property (to be distinguished from the Clemens the conspirator).
47. *RIC*[2] Augustus, 235–48, 469–71; Suet. *Tib.* 17.2.
48. Vell 2.121.1; Suet. *Tib.* 21.1; Dio 56.28.1.
49. Pliny *HN* 7.150; Plut. *De garr.* 508A–B. Arria: Pliny *Ep.* 3.16; Martial 1.13.
50. Dio 56.30.1–2; one of Dio's epitimators, Xiphilinus, makes the comment that he does not trust the story.
51. Tac. *Ann.* 1.5.1–3 (Haase [1848] reads *ignarum*, to suggest that Livia brought about Fabius' death to suppress information about the reconciliation); Dio 56.30.1.
52. *AFA* xxx; Dio 56.26.2–3; Gardthausen (1896) I.1252; (1918), 184; Domaszewski (1909), Ia 247; Jameson (1972), 320 (Scheid [*Arvales*, 1975], 87, reaches the same conclusion independently). Levick ("Tiberius," 1976), 65, is willing to meet the hostile tradition halfway and suggests that Augustus might have made the journey, but that it did not lead to any change in his dynastic plans. Rejecting the story completely: Charlesworth (1923), 149, 155; Willrich (1927), 75–76; Dessau (1930), 1, p. 477; Pappano (1941), 41; Syme (1958), 483, 693, 688, 693; (1986), 415; (1978), 149–51 (historical fictions); Koestermann (1961), 332–33; Seager (1972), 48; Goodyear (1972), 131.
53. Suet. *Aug.* 19.2. Julia's relocation: Tac. *Ann.* 1.53.1; Suet. *Aug.* 65.3; Dio 55.13.1. Confusion over the place of exile: Meise (1969), 29–30; Rogers (1931), 147. Two separate plots: Norwood (1963), 354, suggests a confusion between the two Julias. Pappano (1941), 41, links this plot with the later plot of Clemens. Jameson (1972), 311 n. 118, says that Epicadus was a freedman of the Pollio family. She says that his origins might suggest that he was a freedman of Asinius Pollio the triumphator (*PIR* 1241). His son was Asinius Pollio, described among those deemed *capaces imperii* by Augustus, marrying Vipsania, and later becoming a suitor for Agrippina and a bête noire of Tiberius. Zonaras 10.38 states that Agrippa Postumus was exiled with his mother. There is a problem in Suetonius' version of events. He talks about Julia and Postumus being rescued from the islands, but by this time Julia was no longer on Pandateria. The confusion could have resulted from a simple slip, because islands were the traditional place for banishment. There is no need to assume that Suetonius has confused mother and daughter, or conflated two plots, one to

rescue Julia, the other Postumus. Linderski (1988), n. 10, observes that there is some evidence that a detachment of the fleet was stationed near Rhegium.

54. Suet. *Aug.* 97.2–3; Dio 56.29.1.
55. Journey: Vell. 2.123.1; Suet. *Aug.* 97.3, *Tib.* 21.1; Dio 56.29.2: Ollendorff (1926), 915, places the supposed visit to Planasia during this journey. Father: Suet. *Aug.* 100.1
56. EJ, p. 40, 50; Suet. *Aug.* 100.1; Dio 56.30.5.
57. Suet. *Aug.* 76.1; Tac. *Ann.* 1.5.1; Dio 55.22.2; 56.30.1–3; *Epit. de Caes.* 1.28; Charlesworth (1923), 155–56; Questa (1959), 48; Gafforini (1996), 134–36. Vespasian: Dio 66.17.1. Titus: Dio 66.26.2.
58. Vell.2.123.1; Suet. *Aug.* 98.5–99.1, *Tib.* 21.1; Tac. *Ann.* 1.5.3–4, 13.2 *(supremis sermonibus);* Dio 56.30–31.1.
59. Levick ("Tiberius," 1976), 246 n. 1. Charlesworth (1927) notes that the death of King Ferdinand I of Roumania in 1927 was kept secret for political reasons.
60. Agrippina: Tac. *Ann.* 14.8.1. Shrine: Dio 56.46.3.
61. Velleius 2.112.7; Tac. *Ann.* 1.6.1, 2.39.1–2; Suet. *Tib.* 22; Dio 57.3.5–6; *Epit. de Caes.* 1.27; Charlesworth (1927), 55–57; Rogers (1931); Hohl (1935); Pappano (1941); Allen (1947); Martin (1955), 123–29, (1981), 162; Marsh (1959), 50–51; Questa (1959); Shotter (1965), 361; Lewis (1970); Detweiler (1970); Shotter (1971); Seager (1972), 49; Levick ("Abdication," 1972); ("Tiberius," 1976), 64–66, 245 n. 66; Shatzman (1974), 561–62; Jameson (1975); Birch ("Settlement," 1981), 455–56; Kehoe (1985), 247–54; Suerbaum (1990), 118; Sinclair (1995), 5–8; Watson (1995), 181–85; Gafforini (1996), 136–38; Woodman (1998). Shotter thinks that the purpose of Tacitus' account of the opening of the new reign is to illustrate Tiberius' character through his actions and to demonstrate the pressures that public opinion could place on a new ruler.
62. Suetonius and Tacitus agree that the report was sent to the tribune in Planasia. Suetonius states that the tribune then executed Postumus. Tacitus and Dio say that the blow was struck by a centurion. There need be no contradiction, if the centurion was simply acting on the tribune's instructions. Tacitus also has the centurion take the report to Tiberius. Perhaps more convincingly, Suetonius assigns that task to the tribune.
63. Tac. *Ann.* 3.30; Alps: Pliny *HN* 34.3. Rome: *CIL* 15.7508 (owned and probably inherited by his son); Syme, *Papers A*, 929.
64. Tac. *Ann.* 1.6.1–3, cf. 3.30.3.
65. Vell. 2.112.7. For the debate on Velleius' meaning, Woodman (1977), 177. In a careful analysis of Tacitus' account, Woodman (1998), 23–39, suggests that the "more likely scenario" was one proposed at the time, not a suggestion of Tacitus himself. Woodman argues that the sequence of Tacitus' narrative suggests that he did not in fact share the contemporary view, and considered Livia responsible.
66. Gardthausen (1918), 185; Charlesworth (1923), 156; Smith (1942), 16; Syme (1958), 306, 418; (1978), 149; Woodman (1998).
67. Detweiler (1970) argues that the ancient evidence seems to convict Tiberius; Marsh (1931), 50, and Hohl (1935) emphatically claim the contrary; Shotter (1971), 1120; (1965); Martin (1955), 123–29, (1981), 162.

68. Dio 57.3.5–6; Pappano (1941), 45; Jameson (1972), 314.
69. Charlesworth (1923), 156; Rogers (1935), 3; Hohl (1937), 323; Pappano (1941), 44; Norwood (1963), 163; Jameson (1972), 288; Seager (1972), 49–50; Levick ("Fortuna," 1972), 311; ("Tiberius," 1976), 65. The precise nature of the codicilli is not known. They might already have been on hand, left by Augustus, to be read when news of the emperor's death arrived. That would have been a highly risky procedure, because there would always be a risk that the instructions might come to light prematurely. Alternatively, they might have been signed by Augustus beforehand but kept in Rome ready for despatch when he died.
70. Suet. *Aug.* 65.3–4, 101.3; Dio 55.13.1. Arrangements in will: Tac. *Ann.* 1.11.4; Suet. *Aug.* 101; Dio 56.33.
71. Tac. *Ann.* 1.53.2; Suet. *Tib.* 50.1; Dio 57.18.1.

5. A NEW REIGN

1. Suet. *Tib.* 50.1–2.
2. Tac. *Ann.* 1.5.3, 7.3–5; Dio 57.2.1.
3. Tac. *Ann.* 1.7.4; Suet. *Aug.* 99.2; Dio 56.31.2–3.
4. Tac. *Ann.* 1.8.1; Suet. *Aug.* 101.2; Dio 56.32.1; Jos. *Ant.* 18.234. Julius Caesar also deposited his will with the Vestals: Suet. *Div. Jul.* 83.1. Dio 48.37.1 (see also 48.46.2) notes that the treaties negotiated between Sextus Pompeius and his opponents Octavian and Antony were stored in the same place. On the general practice, Vidal (1965), 555.
5. Tac. *Ann.* 1.8.1; Suet. *Aug.* 101.1, 3, *Tib.* 23; Dio 56.32.1, 4.
6. Vell. 2.75.3; Tac. *Ann.* 1.8.1; Suet. *Aug.* 101.2; Dio 56.46.1.
7. Tac. *Ann.* 1.8.5–6; Suet. *Aug.* 100.2–4; Dio 56.34.1–4, 42, 46.2.
8. Caligula: *Fasti Vallenses* and *Fasti Pighiani;* Suet. *Cal.* 8.1. On Antium as the birthplace of Caligula, see Barrett (1990), 6–7, 255 n. 10. Consulship: Suet. *Cal.* 1.1; Dio 56.27.5.
9. Vell. 2.125; Tac. *Ann.* 1.31–49; Suet. *Tib.* 25.2; Dio 57.5–6; Schove (1984), 4–6.
10. Tac. *Ann.* 1.40.3–44, 49.5–51.9; Suet. *Cal.* 48.1; Dio 57.5.6. On the different versions of the story, see Burian (1964), 25–29.
11. Tac. *Ann.* 1.69.3: *tradit C. Plinius, Germanorum bellorum scriptor . . .*
12. Tac. *Ann.* 1.33, 2.82.2; Suet. *Cal.* 3.
13. Tac. *Ann.* 1.33.1: *causae acriores quia iniquae*. Drusus and Germanicus: Tac. *Ann.* 2.43.6; see especially Shotter (1968).
14. Tac. *Ann.* 2.14.1; 5.1.2; Suet. *Cal.* 4, 7; Willrich (1911), 36; Ollendorff (1926), 920; Perkounig (1995), 179.
15. Tac. *Ann.* 2.26; Suet. *Tib.* 52.2.
16. Tac. *Ann.* 2.41.2–4; Eck et al. (1993), 13.
17. Velleius 2.129.2; Tac. *Ann.* 2.42.1. Archelaus: *PIR* A 1023; *RE* 2 (1895), 451–52 (U. Wilcken). Two other kings had recently died: Antiochus III of Commagene: *PIR* A 741; *RE* 1 (1894), 2490 (U. Wilcken); Philopator of Amanus: *PIR* P 282; Tac. *Ann.* 2.42.7; Jos. *Ant.* 18.53.
18. Tac. *Ann.* 2.42, 5.1.3; Suet. *Tib.* 8, 37.4; Philost. *Apoll.* 1.12; Dio 57.17.3–7. There

is a chronological problem. Dio 49.32.3 begins the reign in 36 BC. App. *BC* 5.7 implausibly places its beginning in 41 BC; see Magie (1950), 1286. Tacitus' fifty-year reign might be a mistake, or fifty could simply be an approximation. If Tacitus' fifty years is correct, it may refer to Tiberius' accession, in AD 14. Date of the defence: Levick (1971), 478–86, ("Tiberius," 1976), 20, says 26 BC; Bowersock (1965), 157–61, argues for about 18 BC. Zeno: Levick ("Tiberius," 1976), 140. Livia's supposed intercession: Hardy (1975), 25; Perkounig (1995), 160; Tiberius and Livia seem to have inherited a slave from Archelaus, *CIL* 6.4776: *Dardanus Ti. Caesaris Aug(usti) et Augustae ser(vus) Archelaianus* (see Chantraine [1976], 302, 354). Velleius' compliment: 2.130.5. Sales tax: Tac. *Ann.* 1.78, 2.42.6; Dio 55.25, 58.16.2.

19. *Bell. Afr.* 3.1, 18.1; Dio 53.30.2; *PIR* C 286; *RE* 3.1 (1897), 1391–92, no. 95 (O. Groag).
20. *Piso Decree* 83; Sen. *Ira* 1.18; Tac. *Ann.* 1.13.3, 2.43.2, 3.12.1, 13.1, 16.4; Strabo 2.5.33; *PIR* C 287; *RE* 3.1 (1897), 1379–82, no. 70 (O. Groag).
21. Plancina: *PIR* M 737; *RE* 16 (1933), 556–57 (R. Hanslik); *FOS* 562. Munatius Plancus: *CIL* 10.6087; Vell. 2.83; Tac. *Ann.* 1.39.2; *PIR* M 729; *RE* 16 (1933), 551–59 (R. Hanslik). Secret instructions to Plancina: Tac. *Ann.* 2.43.4. Senate approval: Tac. *Ann.* 3.12.2. On Piso's qualifications: Shotter ("Piso," 1974), 234–36. Plancina's role: Shotter ("Piso," 1974), 242.
22. Tac. *Ann.* 2.54.1.
23. Tac. *Ann.* 2.55.5. Bribes: *Piso Decree* 54–55.
24. Tac. *Ann.* 2.56; Suet. *Cal.* 1.2; Dio 57.17.7.
25. *Piso Decree* 34–35; Tac. *Ann.* 2.43.
26. Absence: *P. Oxy.* 2435.1; EJ 379 (1976), 1. Honours: *P. Berol.* (*SBA* 1911, 796–97), 34–38 (see Goodyear [1981], 459–60); Tac. *Ann.* 2.59–61; Suet. *Tib.* 52.2.
27. Tac. *Ann.* 2.71.2–3.
28. *Fast. Ant.* (EJ, p. 53), *Tab. Siar.* IIa.1; Pliny *HN* 11.187; Tac. *Ann.* 2.69–72; Suet. *Cal.* 1.2; Dio 57.18.9. Tac. *Ann.* 2.83.3 says that he died in the suburb of Epidaphne, a garbled version of Antioch epi Daphne.
29. Tac. *Ann.* 2.82.1–3; Suet. *Tib.* 52.3, *Cal.* 2; Dio 57.18.6. The denigration of Livia and Tiberius might have come from the memoirs of Agrippina the Younger: Goodyear (1981), 327 n. 4; Perkounig (1995), 185.
30. Tac. *Ann.* 2.73, 83; Suet. *Cal.* 5–6. Honours: *Tab. Heb.*: EJ 94a; *Tab. Siar.*: González (1984), 55–100; revision by W. D. Lebek, *ZPE* 67 (1987), 129–48; 86 (1991), 47–78; 87 (1991), 103–24; 90 (1992), 65–86; 95 (1993), 81–120. For the complete text: Crawford (1966), 1.507–43.
31. Tac. *Ann.* 3.1–2, 4. *Tab. Siar.* IIb. 11 dates the approval of the honours to December 16, AD 19, and presupposes Agrippina's presence in Rome. Tacitus may be incorrect in his date of January, AD 20, for Agrippina's return.
32. Tac. *Ann.* 3.3; *Tab. Siar.* I.6–7 (Tiberius is added on the basis of secure restoration); Woodman (1996), 91–93; Kokkinos (1992), 23–24, 38–39; Flower (1996), 250–51.
33. *Tab. Siar.* IIb. 12–13, 18–19; Tac. *Ann.* 3.5–6; Millar (1988), 17–18. Drusus, son of Livia: Sen. *Cons. Marc.* 3.2 (Livia), *Cons. Polyb.* 15.5 (Tiberius). Drusus Caesar, son of Tiberius: Sen. *Cons. Marc.* 15.3; Tac. *Ann.* 4.8.

34. *CIL* 3.6703; *Eph. Ep.* v.1336; Tac. *Ann.* 2.74.1.
35. Tac. *Ann.* 2.75–81.
36. Tac. *Ann.* 3.9.
37. See, in particular, Eck et al. (1996); Damon (1999); Griffin (1997).
38. Tac. *Ann.* 3.10.2.
39. *Piso Decree* 1; Tac. *Ann.* 3.14.4; Suet. *Cal.* 2. Tacitus writes that the mob assembled outside the *curia*, the term presumably used loosely of whatever building the Senate occupied when in session (see Woodman [1996], 162).
40. Tac. *Ann.* 3.15.1.
41. Tac. *Ann.* 3.15–16; Suet. *Tib.* 52.3; Dio 57.18.10.
42. Tac. *Ann.* 3.16.4; Pelling (1993), 83–84.
43. *Piso Decree* 6–11, 80–84, 121–23; EJ 39 (erasure); Tac. *Ann.* 3.17.4, 36.3.
44. *Piso Decree* 6–12; Tac. *Ann.* 3.17.1–2 (see Woodman [1996], 182–83). Rufilla: Tac. *Ann.* 3.36.3; Talbert (1984), 157.
45. *Piso Decree* 110–20; Tac. *Ann.* 3.17.1. Plancina and Agrippina: Tac. *Ann.* 6.26.3. Livia never entered the Senate: Dio 57.12.3.
46. *Piso Decree* 132, 150; Tac. *Ann.* 3.18.3. Claudius was inadvertently left out of the first draft, according to Tacitus, a claim given support by the awkward position of his name in the decree.
47. Tac. *Ann.* 3.17.1, 19.3.
48. EJ, pp. 41, 49; Tac. *Ann.* 3.11.1, 19.3. For useful summaries of both sides of the issue see Woodman (1996), 69–77; Griffin 87 (1997), 258–60; Barnes (1981).
49. Dio 57.19.6. Documents: Tac. *Ann.* 3.16.1.
50. Tac. *Ann.* 2.84.1, 4.2.4, 8.4; Suet. *Claud.* 27.1; Dio 57.19.7, cf. Dio 58.4.3.
51. Tac. *Ann.* 3.31.2.
52. Tac. *Ann.* 3.64.3. Apronius: Tac. *Ann.* 2.32.2; Woodman (1996), 448, notes the curious use of the word *supplicium*. *Supplicatio* can mean both "propitiation" and "thanksgiving"; *supplicium* strictly conveys only the former, while it is the latter that is needed in this context, because the events took place after Livia's recovery, not before.
53. *RIC*² Tiberius 47. The imperial coin had many imitators—*RPC* 1154 Corinth, 1567–68 (Thessalonika), 1779 (Byzantium), 2840 (Aphrodisias); it is copied in a lead tessera now in the Terme Museum (see appendix 1). Augustus: *RIC*² 356–57: *ob r(em) p(ublicam) cum salut(e) imp(eratoris) Caesar(is) August(i) cons(ervatam)*. Alabanda: EJ 114. Nasium: EJ 137. Interamna: *ILS* 157. Oaths: *Inst.* 2.23.1: *Divus Augustus . . . per ipsius Salutem rogatus*. Tiberius: Val. Max. 1.13 *praef.* (cf. Ovid *Trist.* 2.574); Grant (*Principate*, 1950), 114; Sutherland (1951), 96–97, 191–92; (1987), 51–52; Gross (1962), 18–19; Torelli (1982), 66–70; Weinstock (1971), 172; Fittschen-Zanker (1983), III.3–3, 3; Purcell (1986), 86 n. 45; Fishwick (1987–92), II.1, 465; Mikocki (1995), 164 no. 94, 166 no. 109, accepts Pietas and Iustitia as portraits of Livia. Kokkinos (1992), 90–95, suggests that all three are of Antonia Minor.
54. Vitr. *Arch.* 3.3.2; Livy 40.40.10, 42.10.5; Obseq. 53; Hor. *Odes* 1.35.1; Tac. *Ann.* 3.71.1. On Fortuna Equestris, Champeaux (1982), 155–57, 176. Antium: Suet. *Aug.* 58.2; Barrett (1990), 6–7, 255 n. 10; (1996), 46.

55. *ILS* 202 (= *CIL* 6.562); Ollendorff (1926), 921; Koeppel (1982), 453–55; Levick (1990), 46; Richardson (1992), 291. Torelli (1977–78), 179–83; (1982), 67, 70, asserts that the Ara Pietatis was not connected with Livia but related to the grant of tribunicia potestas of Drusus, which Tiberius obtained from the Senate in this year (Tac. *Ann.* 3.57.1). The event was marked by the usual senatorial flattery and included a request for a series of memorials, including *aras deum* (altars of the gods).
56. Tac. *Ann.* 4.2.1; Suet. *Tib.* 37.1; Dio 57.19.6.
57. Tac. *Ann.* 4.8.3; Syme *Papers A*, 1378.
58. *RIC*[2] 1.97, nos. 50–51; Tac. *Ann.* 4.16.4; Sutherland (1987), 52. Augustus: Suet. *Aug.* 44.3; Caligula: 59.3.4; Messalina: Dio 60.22.2; Willrich (1911), 40–41. Tac. *Ann.* 12.42.2 describes the carpentum as an honour reserved since antiquity for priests and for sacred objects. Livy 34.1 notes that the old veto on women driving in the city under the Lex Oppia applied only *nisi sacrorum publicorum causa veheretur*. See Clay (1982), 28–29, on the difference between a carpentum and a *tensa* (which carried divine figures).
59. Tac. *Ann.* 4.15.
60. Tac. *Ann.* 4.12.3–4 (the text and Tacitus' meaning are uncertain), 5.2.2; Hardy (1975), 35. Postumus: *PIR* P 482; *RE* 10 (1918), 482 (A. Stein). Livilla and Livia: *Piso Decree* 143; *CIL* 6. 4352: *Prima Augusti et Augustae L. nutrix Iuliae Germanici filiae* (cf. 3998);
61. Tac. *Ann.* 4.22. Lucius Piso: Tac. *Ann.* 4.21.1.
62. Tac. *Ann.* 3.31.2, 64.1, 4.57.3; Suet. *Tib.* 51.1; Dio 57.12.6.
63. Syme, *Papers A*, 943.
64. Tac. *Ann.* 3.29.3, 4.74–5; Suet. *Tib.* 52.1. On the date of the betrothal: Barrett (1996), 40. Ollendorff (1926), 921, speculates that Livia might have been behind the marriage and suggests that she might also have been behind the marriage of Nero, the oldest son of Germanicus, and Julia, daughter of Drusus, son of Tiberius. That last marriage took place probably in late 20.
65. Tac. *Ann.* 4.60.5–6.
66. Tac. *Ann.* 5.3.1.
67. Sen. *Ira* 3.21.5; Tac. *Ann.* 4.67.5; see Scott (1939), 462.

6. THE PRIVATE LIVIA

1. Sen. *Cons. Marc.* 4.4; Tac. *Ann.* 5.1.3.
2. Evans (1935); Barton (1994), 115–18; Bartman (1999), 26.
3. Ovid *Pont.* 3.1.117, 145; Vell. 2.75.3; Tac. *Ann.* 5.1.2; Dio 54.19.3. The same kind of cliché would be applied to Agrippina the elder. Dio twice (60.31.6, 61.14.2) calls Agrippina *kale* (beautiful). Tacitus, when comparing her on separate occasions (*Ann.* 12.64.4, 13.19.2; 14.9.1) to two contemporary women (Junia Silana and Domitia Lepida), claims that the women were well matched in their moral depravity and were equals in their *forma*, where the context requires that this word be understood in a positive sense of "beauty."
4. *RIC*[2] Tiberius 4; Fishwick (1987–92) II.1, 465. Local issues: *RPC* 1154 (Corinth),

1567–68 (Thessalonica), 1779 (Byzantium), 2840 (Aphrodisias); Gross (1962), 58, 62–66.

5. Ovid *AA* 3.139–40.
6. Ovid *Pont.* 3.1.142.
7. Ornatrices: *CIL* VI. 3993, 3994, 8944, 8958. A veste / ad vestem: *CIL* VI. 3985, 4041–40, 4251. Ab ornamentis: *CIL* VI. 3992. Ab ornamentis sacerdotalibus: *CIL* VI. 8955. Calciator: *CIL* VI. 3939. Lanipendi: *CIL* VI. 3973, 3977. Sarcinatores/-rices: *CIL* VI. 3988, 4028–31, 5357, 8903, 9038. Unctrix: *CIL* VI. 4045. Aurifex *CIL* VI. 3927, 3943–45, 3949. Inaurator: *CIL* VI. 3928. Margaritarius: *CIL* VI. 3981.
8. Livy 5.23; Hor. *Odes* 1.5.5; Dio 54.16.5; Bartman (1999), 44. Pliny *Paneg.* 83.7 praises Trajan's wife Plotina for her moderation in the number of her attendants.
9. Pliny *HN* 7.75.
10. Suet. *Tib.* 14.2. Augustus' letter: Suet. *Claud.* 4.2.
11. Pliny's wife: Pliny *Ep.* 4.19. Cornelia: Plut. *Pomp.* 55.1; Juv. *Sat.* 6.434–56.
12. Philo. *Leg.* 319–20; Gow and Page (1968), I.277; Jones (1970), 250–55. The identification of the Augusta in Honestus' poem is far from certain. Octavia: Plut. *Publ.* 17.5; Vitr. *Arch.* 1 *praef.* 2–3.
13. Plut. *Ant.* 80; Dio 51.16.3–5; *PIR* A1025; *RE* 2 (1895), 626 (H. von Arnim); Bowersock (1965), 33–34. Marc. Aur. *Med.* 8.31 cites Areus and Maecenas as prime examples of Augustus' friends.
14. Sen. *Cons. Marc.* 4.3. Suet. *Aug.* 89.1 speaks of the emperor's *contubernium* (close association) with Areus and with his sons Dionysius and Nicanor. Dio 51.16.1–4 says of Octavian that Areus *sunonti echreto* (he was in his company). Rawson (1985), 17, suggests that Areus might have come to Rome from Alexandria as a protégé of Caesar and might have taught Octavian before Caesar's death.
15. Pliny *HN* 3.127, 14.60, 17.31. Marchetti, "Del Sito dell'antico Castello Pucino e del vino che vi cresceva," *Archaeografo Triestino* 5 (1877–78), 431–50; 6 (1879–80), 58–59, places Castellum Pucinum in the neighbourhood of the small port of Duino, north of Trieste.
16. Cic. *de Orat.* 1.62 refers to a debate in which Asclepiades is mentioned as a great contemporary doctor. Cicero wrote in 55 BC, but the dramatic date of the passage is 91 BC. Pliny *HN* 7.124; 23.32, 37–40; 26.12–18 claims that Asclepiades was influential during the time of Pompey the Great (probably from the sixties to Pompey's death in 48). The nickname is provided by Anonymus Londinensis XXIV.30; Wellman (1896); Rawson (1982); Vallance (1990), 1–5 (1993), 694–95; Scarborough (1993).
17. Hor. *Sat.* 2.2.44, 2.8.51; Pliny *HN* 19.92.
18. Marcellus Burdigalensis, *De Medicamentis*, ed. M. Niedermann, trans. J. Kollesch and D. Niebel, *Corpus Medicorum Latinorum* 5 (Berlin: Akademie Verlag, 1968); Grimm (1865); Rouselle (1976); Rose "Superstition" *OCD* (1970); Brown (1981); Scarborough (1984), 224; Barton (1994), 144–45. Octavia's toothpaste: Marc. *De Med.* 13.1:2.
19. Bartman (1999); Wood (1999), 85.

20. Kellum (1994), 215; Ling (1991), 45, 135, 149–50.
21. Liviana: Pliny *HN* 15.70; Col. *RR* 5.10.11, 10.414; Cloatius in Macrob. *Sat.* 3.20.1; Ath. *Deip.* 3. 75.
22. Pliny *HN* 13.74.
23. Pliny *HN* 14.11.
24. Suet. *Galb.* 1; Pliny *HN* 15.136–37; Dio 48.52.3–4, 63.29.3. Pliny 15.136 says that the haruspices ordered the grove planted, but there is no real contradiction.
25. Pliny *HN* 15.129, 136; Reeder (1997), 95 n. 21.
26. Cato *De Agr.* 152 (133); Pliny *HN* 17.62; see Messineo (1984).

7. WIFE OF THE EMPEROR

1. *ILS* 8403. Amymone: *ILS* 8402; Suet. *Aug.* 73.
2. Cic. *Verr.* 2.1.120, 136–38; Hillard (1992), 42–46.
3. Sall. *BC* 24.3–25; Tac. *Ann.* 12.7.6; Balsdon (1962), 47–48; Syme *Papers A*, 1242–43; (1986), 198; Hillard (1992), 47.
4. Livy 8.18.6; Tac. *Ann.* 2.71.4. Tacitus also speaks of the imperial house being rent by *muliebres offensiones* (*Ann.* 1.33.5, 12.64.4).
5. Livy 40.37.5.
6. Vell. 2.74.3; Florus 2.16.2; Livy *Per.* 125; Martial 11.20; Plut. *Ant.* 10.3; App. *BC* 5.14, 55, 59; Dio 48.10.3–4, 28.3; Babcock (1965); Pomeroy (1975), 185, 189; Hallett (1977), 160–61; Dixon (1983), 109; Huzar (1986), 102; Delia (1991); Barrett (1996), 10–12.
7. Suet. *Aug.* 25.1, 58.2; Macrob. *Sat.* 2.5.3.
8. For general accounts, see Balsdon (1962); Pomeroy (1975); Hallett (1984); Gardner (1986); Bauman (1992).
9. Suet. *Aug.* 72–74.
10. Suet. *Aug.* 24.1, 44.2, 64.2; Dio 54.16.5. Funeral honours: Suet. *Aug.* 61.2; Dio 54.35.5; Flory (1984), 304.
11. Macrob. *Sat.* 2.5.8.
12. Pliny *HN* 7.57; Suet. *Aug.* 62.2, 63.1; Lacey (1996), 74. Correspondence: Suet. *Claud.* 4.1, 4.4, 4.6; one might compare similar expressions in Cicero *ad Fam.* 14.1.5: *mea Terentia;* 2.2 *mea lux;* 3.1: *mea Terentia.*
13. Suet. *Cal.* 23.2: *identidem appellans.* Syme *Papers A*, 1369, notes that the clever phrase is reminiscent of Caligula's expression "golden sheep" for Marcus Silanus (Tac. *Ann.* 13.1.1).
14. Suet. *Cal.* 23.2; Cic. *Phil.* 2.44; Ovid *AA* 1. 31–32; Val. Max. 2.1.5, 6.1 *praef.* Festus 112.26L. Caligula: Jos. *Ant.* 19.30; Sebesta (1994), 48–49; Bartman (1999), 42.
15. Fischler (1994), 122.
16. Hor. *Odes* 3.14.5; Syme (1939), 414.
17. Sen. *Cons. Marc.* 2.4–3.2, 4.4; Macrob. *Sat.* 5.2.6.
18. Sen. *Ep.* 91.13; Sen. *Ira* 3.23.4–6; *FGH* 88; *RE* 6A (1936), 1063–71; *PIR* T 156; Bowersock (1965), 109–10, 125–26.
19. Dio (54.10.5) states that in 19 BC Augustus was given the post of supervisor of

morals and (54.30.1) received the same office for another five-year term in 12 BC. Suet. *Aug.* 27.5 says that he was given the task for life, which seems to be contradicted by *RG* 6. The issue is much debated by scholars: see Rich (1990), 187.

20. Suet. *Aug.* 34.1; Dio 56.10.3. The differences between the Lex Julia and Papia Poppaea elude proper explanation. Sometimes the jurists cite what they call the Julian and Papian law, as if it were a single piece of legislation. The *ius trium liberorum* may well have been enacted at the later date.
21. *Cons. Liv.* 45–46, 343; Ovid *Pont.* 2.2.69, 3.1.115–16, 4.13.29; Hor. *Odes* 3.14.5 (cf. Flory [1984] 321); Val. Max. 6.1.1; Tac. *Ann.* 5.1.3; Dio 58.2.4, 5; Kunst (1998), 458.
22. Flory (1984), 322. On the marriage legislation: Frank (1975); Galinsky (1981).
23. Flory (1984), 313, has noted the significance of June 11, the dedication date of Livia's shrine to Concord. Ovid observes that June 11 was the *dies natalis* of the temple of Mater Matuta in Rome in the Forum Boarium and the day of the *Matralia*, a festival in her honour, and an occasion of importance to the family, with its emphasis on mothers and children (Ovid *Fast.* 6.479–807); Edwards (1993), 164–65.
24. Livy 3.7.7, 27.51.9; Simon (1967); Kleiner (1978); Pollini (1978), 75–172; Torelli (1982), 27–61; La Rocca (1983); Rose (1997), 15–17, 103–4; Bartman (1999), 86–92, plates 74, 75; Conlin (1992), 210–11; Wood (1999), 99–103, figs. 30–31, 53; Davies (2000), 111–14; Kleiner and Matheson (2000), 10–11, 46. The panels on the south frieze, where Livia appears, were reworked by Carradori, and we must accordingly be cautious about details.
25. Val. Max. 4.3.3.
26. Suet. *Claud.* 3.2; Dio 60.2.5.
27. *Piso Decree* 149–50.
28. Suet. *Claud.* 4.1–5. Technically, Claudius would have become *sui iuris* on the death of his father, and subject to a tutor only until his majority. Technically, Augustus was not his paterfamilias.
29. Suet. *Claud.* 41.2. Suetonius does not name Livia but refers to her as Claudius' grandmother *(avia)*. His maternal grandmother, Octavia, died a year before his birth (despite J. D. Rolfe's comment *ad loc.* in the Loeb translation); Syme, *Papers A*, 435.
30. Suet. *Claud.* 26.2.
31. Tac. *Ann.* 4.71.4; Phillips (1978), 75–76.
32. Tac. *Ann.* 5.3.1.
33. Suet. *Cal.* 10.1; 23.2. On Caligula and his relatives, Barrett (1990), 217–19.
34. Sen. *Cons. Marc.* 3.4; cf. Ovid *Pont.* 3.1.125.
35. Augustus' adulteries: *Eleg. in Maec.* 2.7–8; Suet. *Aug.* 69, 71.1 (with the rumour that Livia provided him with young women); Dio 54.16.3, 19.3, 19.6, 55.7.5.
36. Tac. *Ann.* 5.1.3; Dio 54.16.4–5, 58.2.5. See G. Williams (1958) on the traditional expectations that wives be obedient.
37. Dio 54.16.4.
38. *Cons. Liv.* 49–50; Lucan *BC* 1.180; Cic. *ad Fam.* 5.8.3.
39. Suet. *Aug.* 84.2, *Tib.* 51.1. Nero: Tac. *Ann.* 13.4.2.

40. Suet. *Aug.* 40.3, *Tib.* 12.1, 13.2.
41. Sen. *Clem.* 1.9; Dio 55.14–22.2; *PIR* C 1339; Speyer (1956); Millar (1964), 78–79; Bauman (1967), 196–97; Shotter (1971), 1118–19; ("Cinna," 1974); Manuwald (1979), 120–27; Giua (1981); Syme *Papers C*, 925, (1958), 404 n. 2; Raaflaub and Salmons (1990), 427–28.
42. Conspiracies: Suet. *Aug.* 19.1. Lepidus: Vell. 2.88; Dio 54.15.4; App. *BC* 4.50. Rufus: Dio 48.33.2. Murena and Caepio: Dio 54.3.4–7; Vell. 2.91.2. Egnatius: Dio 53.24.4–6; Vell 2.91.3–92.4.
43. On the conspiracy of AD 6: Suet. *Aug.* 19.1; Dio 55.27.2; Barrett (1996), 21, 256 n. 36.
44. Purcell (1986); see also Sirago (1979).
45. Ovid *Trist.* 1.6.25, *Pont.* 3.1.125. *Cons. Liv.*, Livia: 353, 365; Drusus: 285, 344; Antonia: 303. On the identification of Antonia in the *Consolatio* see the summary in Schoonhoven (1992), 24–25.
46. Dio 55.16.2. Potestas: Cic. *Tusc.* 1.30.74; *Phil.* 1.7.18; *Verr.* 2.4.5. Potentia: references to *(im)potentia* in the source are to actual power, not legal constitutional power; Sen. *Cons. Helv.* 14.2: *quia feminis honores non licet gerere;* Suet. *Aug.* 69.1: *nimia potentia* of Octavian's mistress (probably Livia); *Nero* 6.4: Agrippina's *potentia* while Messalina was alive; Tac. *Ann.* 12.57.2: Agrippina's *impotentia* as wife of Claudius; Suet. *Oth.* 2.2: Otho's *potentia* under Nero. Political: Mommsen *SR* II.664, 754, 1033.
47. On maiestas, see, inter alios, Kübler (1928); Drexler (1956); Burdeau (1964), 22; Bauman (1967), 228–29; Lear (1968), 49–72.
48. Cic. *Phil.* 3.13; Livy 34.2; Vell. 1.10.3.
49. Hor. *Epod.* 2.1.258–59: *sed neque parvum / carmen maiestas recipit tua;* Ovid *Trist.* 2.512: *maiestas adeo comis ubique tua est.* Two consuls: Suet. *Aug.* 37.
50. Vell. 2.99.4; Suet. *Aug.* 25.1, *Tib.* 15.2.
51. Ovid *Pont.* 2.8.30, 3.1.155–56; *Cons. Liv.* 347.
52. Tac. *Ann.* 3.3.1. For Tiberius' maiestas, see Ovid *Trist.* 4.9.68; Vell. 2.124.1; Tac. *Ann.* 1.47.2; 3.64.2.
53. Digest 48.4.1.1. See Allison (1962); Goodyear (1981), 141–50; Severus: Tac. *Ann.* 1.72.3; Jer. *Chron.* 176H: AD 8; Dio 56.27.1: AD 12.
54. Dio 49.38.1.
55. Octavian: Dio 44.5.3, 49.15.3–5, cf. App. *BC* 5.132.
56. Augustus had originally belonged to a plebeian family but was adlected to the patricians in accordance with the Lex Cassia by Julius Caesar: Suet. *Aug.* 2.1; Dio 45.2.7.
57. Mommsen (1899), 538–39, argues that the crimen maiestatis has its origins in the need to protect the maiestas of the tribunes. His view is not universally accepted; for a summary of the issues, Bauman (1967), 220–21.
58. Dio 44.5.3 (44), 49.15.5–6 (36), 49.38.1 (35). Ius trium liberorum: Dio 55.2.5; Mommsen *SR* II. 792 n. 2, 819; Sandels (1912), 12–13, 66–67; Bauman (1976), 217–20; Rheinhold (1988), ad loc.; Bauman (1981), 174–81; (1992), 93–98, 176; Scardigli (1982), 61–64; Purcell (1986), 85–87; Schrömbges (1986), 200; Flory (1993); Perkounig (1995), 55. Separation of powers of office: Siber (1952), 208, 214–18, 281. Analogy with Vestals: Willrich (1911), 54, followed by Hohl (1937).

Winkes (1985), 58, suggests that there was a deliberate ambiguity with reference both to the Vestals and to the tribunes.

59. Livia: Dio 58.2.4. Octavia: Val. Max. 9.15.2.
60. Dio 56.10.2.
61. Livy 2.13.11
62. *CIL* 6.10043: the bases have survived, possibly recut in the Augustan period; Plut. *Gai. Gracch.* 4.3. Pliny *HN* 34.31 says that the statue was to honour Cornelia not only as mother of the Gracchi but also as daughter of Scipio Africanus; see Flory (1993), 290, for a discussion and bibliography.
63. Suet. *Aug.* 93; Dio 51.4.1, 54.9.10; Rose (1997), 140–41 no. 71; Wood (1999), 92; Bartman (1999), 64. The emperor is still called Imperator Caesar (in the Greek form of the name) and not yet Augustus.
64. Tiberius: EJ, p. 54. Germanicus: EJ, p. 49. Drusus: EJ, p. 53; Degrassi (1963), 278.
65. Theatre of Marcellus: EJ, p. 48. Birthday: *AFA* xxxive.2; EJ, p. 46; Herz (1978), 1153. It is to be noted that AD 27 is the first year in the Arval record for which the section relating to the end of January has survived.
66. EJ, p. 46. Two famous early examples are known outside Rome, at Narbo (*ILS* 154) and Forum Clodii (*ILS* 154); Pippidi (1931), 100; Taylor (1937), 188–89; Fishwick (1987–92), 388; Wiseman (1991), 55.
67. See Kahrstedt (1910); Sutherland (1951), 53, 143; Kleiner (1992), 365–66.
68. Lugdunum: *RPC* 512–13. Eumenea: *RPC* 3139–40. Rome: Crawford nos. 494.40; 514.1; Kahrstedt (1910), 291–92; Kleiner (1992), 358–60; Woods (1999), 41; Bartman (1999), 37, 58. Earlier winged bust: Sydenham (1952), no. 747 (C. Valerius Flaccus, c. 82–81 BC).
69. Miletus: *BMCRR* 2.503, nos. 135–37. Pergamum, cistophori: *BMCRR* 2.502, nos. 133–34, pl. 114.1–2; Sydenham (1952), nos. 1197–98. Pergamum, aes: *BMCRR* 2.513, 516, 519, nos. 164–71.
70. *BMCRR* 2. 510–12, 515, 516, 518; Wood (1999), 50. The sestertii appear to depict on their reverses Antony and Octavia portrayed as Neptune and Amphitrite drawn in a carriage by sea creatures.
71. *BMCRR* 2, 1499; Sydenham (1952), no. 1196; Crawford (1974), no. 527/1, pl. 63: a unique aureus in Berlin. Obverse: head of Antony and inscription identifying him as triumvir; reverse: head of woman, without inscription. *BMCRR* 2, 507–8; Sydenham (1952), nos. 1200–1201; Crawford (1974), nos. 533/3a, b: aurei probably of 38–37 (later than the Berlin aureus). Obverse: head of Antony with inscriptions; reverse, an inscription describing further titles and a nodus head of Octavia, who is somewhat fleshier, perhaps because she had borne children, or possibly through assimilation to Antony. Recent discussion: Kleiner (1992), 362; Winkes (1995), 67–71; Wood (1999), 45.
72. *BMCRR* 2.525, nos. 179–82; Crawford (1974), no. 543, pl. 64. Cleopatra also appears on local issues: *BMC Ptolemies* 122–23; Kahrstedt (1910), 276–78, 292.
73. Augustus: *RIC*^{2} 219–220. Tiberius: *RIC*^{2} 25–30. Claudius: *RIC*^{2} 101.
74. Within the Roman empire it seems that only Rome had a temple to Vesta; *CIL* 6.2172, 14.2410 hints of a cult at Alba Longa (cf. Dion. Hal. 2.65), rejected by

McDaniel (1955); Aug. *Civ. Dei* 3.28: *nihil apud Romanos templo Vestae sanctius habebatur*.

75. On the ambiguity of the symbolic status of the Vestals: Beard (1980), (1993).
76. Cornell (1981), 28 nn. 5–7, claims only four historical cases.
77. *FIR* 37, 5.1. Lictor: Dio 47.19.4.
78. *RG* 10–12; Dio 51.19.2.
79. Suet. *Aug.* 31.3, 44.3; Dio 56.10.3. Hyginus 117 mentions land given to the Vestals, presumably by Augustus. Strictly speaking, the Vestals were chosen by lot from a list of twenty supplied by the pontifex maximus. Aul. Gell. *NA* 1.12 says that in his time (second century AD) anyone with correct social status could submit his daughter's name as a candidate; S. Price in *CAH*, 826–28. Cornelia: *PIR* C 1478; *FOS* 272; Tac. *Ann.* 4.16.4.
80. EJ, p. 47; *RG* 10.2; Livy *Per.* 117; Vell. 2.63.1; Ovid *Fast.* 3.415–28.
81. Weinstock (1971), 276–81.
82. On Livia and the Vestals, see especially Willrich (1911); Hohl (1939), and, among recent works, Bauman (1967), 217–18, (1981); Flory (1983), 320–21; Bartman (1999), 94–95.
83. Ovid *Fast.* 5.148–58, *Trist.* 4.2.11, *Pont.* 4.13.29. On the Palatine cult: Kienast (1982), 104, 196–97; C. Koch (1958), 1757. Fire: Dio 54.24.2, 57.16.2.
84. Seats: Tac. *Ann.* 4.16.4; Sutherland (1987), 51–53.
85. Antonia and Caligula's sisters: Dio 59.3.4. Antonia and Messalina: Dio 60.22.2.
86. Dio 60.5.2. It has been suggested that a relief depicting a Vestal banquet now in the Museo dei Conservatori in Rome was erected to honour Livia after her death: see Koeppel (1983), 114–16; Kampen (1991), 220–21, 222 fig. 3.
87. Athens: *IG* III 316; Grether (1946), 230 n. 43. T. Shear, *Hesperia* 50 (1981), 364, suggests that the Southwest Temple of the agora might have been dedicated to Livia. Mytileneans: *IGR* 4.39b. Lampsacus: *IGR* 4.180; Hahn (1992), 322–32. Mikocki (1995), who includes the abstractions, gives the total number as seventeen.
88. Tiberius: EJ, p. 54. Germanicus: EJ, p. 49. Drusus: EJ, p. 53.

8. MOTHER OF THE EMPEROR

1. Tac. *Ann.* 1.72.2; Suet. *Tib.* 26.1; Syme (1958), 425.
2. Tac. *Ann.* 1.6.3, 13.6, 1.14.3; Suet. *Tib.* 50.1–2, 3; Dio 57.3.3.
3. Tac. *Ann.* 5.1.3; Baldwin (1972), 94.
4. Vell. 2.75.3; Tac. *Ann.* 1.8.1; Suet. *Aug.* 101.2; Dio 56.46.1. Hoffsten (1939), 57 n. 37, says that Livia became Augusta when the title was conferred by the Senate. Tacitus uses *nomen* sometimes as an honorary name, sometimes as a simple title in association with an office. Tac. *Ann.* 1.9.2: *nomen imperatoris;* Tac. *Hist.* 1.62.2: *nomen Germanici;* Tac. *Ann.* 1.2.1: *triumviri nomine;* Tac. *Ann.* 12.4.1: *nomine censoris;* Tac. *Hist.* 5.9.2: *regium nomen;* Tac. *Hist.* 1.47.1, 2.90.2: *nomen Augusti;* 2.89.2: *Augustae nomine*.
5. Dio 45.5.4; von Premerstein (1923), 289; Schmitthenner (1952), 40–41; Weinribb (1968), 253–54; Syme, *Papers B* 159–70; Champlin (1991), 144–46; Perkounig

(1995), 123; Flory (1998), 134 n. 21; Kunst (1996); (1998), 470. Domitius: *ILS* 990; Pliny *Ep.* 8.18; Pliny: *ILS* 2927; Pliny *Ep.* 5.8.5.

6. Daughter of Marcus: *CIL* 6.882a; 2.2038, 3102; 5.6416.6; 11.7416, 7552. Daughter of Augustus: *CIL* 11.1165. A less certain example: Reynolds (1980), 82, no. 17.
7. *CIL* 6.3945,6. Treggiari (1975), 65 n. 11, for the suggestion that the filiation here was a distinguishing device.
8. *ILS* 8393, 52–53; Wistrand (1976), 64; Salomies (1992), 20 n. 1; Perkounig (1995), 122. Chatraine (1967), 221, argues that the adoption made it possible for Livia and Tiberius to inherit as joint Augusti, disputed by Weaver (1972), 63.
9. Augustus' will: Suet. *Aug.* 101. Lex curiata: App. *BC* 3.94.
10. Livia: Tac. *Ann.* 1.14.2; Goodyear (1972), 190. Agrippina: Suet. *Cal.* 8.1. Tiberius and Sejanus: Tac. *Ann.* 4.74.2. Germanicus: Tac. *Ann.* 3.18.2.
11. Verg. *Aen.* 1.288, 6.789; Serv. on Verg. *Aen.* 1.267, 2.166; Livy 1.30.1–2 (emended); Dion. Hal. 3.29.7; Tac. *Ann.* 11.24.2; Suet. *Div. Jul.* 6.1; Weinstock (1971), 5.
12. Ovid *Fast.* 5.563–64; Dio 55.10.6; Zanker (1988), 79–82, 113–14.
13. Ritter (1972), 323; Bauman (1992), 131; Perkounig (1995), 133, 136.
14. Flory (1998), 113, 117. Note that Suet. *Tib.* 26.2 calls Augustus a *nomen*.
15. Dio 55.10.20.
16. Ovid *Fast.* 1.615; Suet. *Tib.* 17.2.
17. Letters: EJ 102b, 318, etc.; *Piso Decree*, 174; Suet. *Tib.* 26.2; Dio 57.2.1; 57.8.1–2. Germanicus: Suet. *Claud.* 1.3. Britannicus: Dio 60.22.2; Scott (1932); Ritter (1972), 318–19. Flory (1998), 122, sees the influence of Hellenistic practice, and Ritter cites a Hellenistic precedent, noting that Ptolemy XII in his will made his son (Ptolemy XIII) and daughter (Cleopatra VII) his heirs, and they succeeded him as joint rulers. A copy of the will was sent to Rome (Caes. *BC* 3.108.6).
18. Ritter (1972), 316; *IGR* 3.940 (Palaepaphos, Cyprus): *I[ou]lian thean Sebasten, thugatera Autokratoro[s] Kaisaros* (Julia, goddess, Augusta, daughter of Imperator Caesar).
19. Tac. *Ann.* 12.26.1, 15.23.1; Dio 60.12.5; Temporini (1978), 23–36, 44; Perkounig (1995), 131; Flory (1998), 115.
20. Augustus' intentions: Aschbach (1864), 49; Mommsen, *SR* II.788 n. 4, 821–22; Gardthausen (1891), 46; Premerstein (1937), 269, 821; Willrich (1911), 56; Grether (1946), 233–34; Kornemann (1930), 35–36, 189; (1952), 205; (1960), 61; Gross (1962), 11; Königer (1966), 54; Pfister (1951), 20; Hatzl (1975), 23. Livia's exploitation of Augustus' will: Sandels (1912), 22, 76; Ollendorff (1926), 916; Ciaceri (1944), 58, 111.
21. Dessau (1926), 4; Ehrenberg (1946), 205; Grant (*Principate*, 1950), 126–28; Hardy (1972), 19.
22. Ritter (1972), 322–23; Flory (1998), 118.
23. Suet. *Aug.* 50; Syme (1939), 113.
24. Tac. *Ann.* 1.14.1; Dio 57.12.1.
25. Tac. *Ann.* 4.57.3; Ritter (1972), 313, 322 (also, Perkounig [1995], 130, 162); Purcell (1986), 87; Kunst (1998), 470.
26. Dio 57.12.2; Gytheum: EJ 102b; Cos: EJ 318; Ritter (1972), 328; Perkounig (1995), 151; Flory (1998), 115.

27. Tac. *Ann.* 5.1.3; Suet. *Tib.* 50.2; Dio 55.16.2, 56.47.1, 57.12.3; Goodyear (1972), 190.
28. Tac. *Ann.* 1.14.1; Suet. *Tib.* 50.2–3; Dio 57.12; Goodyear (1972), 190. On the honours bestowed on Livia: Schrömbges (1986), 191–221; Flory (1993), 302 n. 26; Kunst (1988), 451.
29. Tac. *Ann.* 1.14.1; Suet. *Tib.* 50.3; Dio 57.12.4, 58.2.3.
30. Cic. *Rab. Perd.* 27; *Pis.* 6; *Sest.* 121; Plut. *Cic.* 23.3; Aul. Gell. *NA* 5.6.15. Caesar: App. *BC* 2.106, 144; Crawford (1974), 491.
31. *RG* 35; *Fasti Praenestini*, EJ, p. 47; Sen. *Clem.* 1.14.2; Suet. *Aug.* 58.
32. Tac. *Ann.* 1.72.1 (under AD 15); Suet. *Tib.* 26.2, 67.2–4; Dio 57.2.1, 58.8.1 (under 14), 58.12.8 (under 31); Val. Max. 5.5.3, 9.11.4; Premerstein (1937), 166–75; Weinstock (1971), 200–205; Goodyear (1972), 138.
33. Scheid (1980), 225, lines 57–58.
34. Suet. *Div. Jul.* 76.1, 85; Juv. *Sat.* 8.243–44.
35. Bauman (1992), 250.4; Flory (1998), 121.
36. *RPC* 73 (Romula), 849–50 (Leptis).
37. Tac. *Ann.* 1.14.1; Suet. *Tib.* 50.2; Dio 57.12.4. The issue of Tacitus' use of senatorial records is hotly debated; for a summary of current views: Barnes (1998).
38. *IGR* 4.560 (restored) for an eastern parallel in an inscription from Aezani honouring Nero as natural son of Agrippina; Willrich (1911), 57; Kornemann (1952), 206; (1960), 66; Goodyear (1972), 190; Flory (1998), 120. Caesar: Dio 44.7.2–3, cf. 44.3.1–3; Ollendorff (1926), 916. Ritter (1972) sees Hellenistic influence.
39. Some have seen a parallel of the expansion of the names in Etruscan usage: Piganiol (1912), 163; Kornemann (1947), 206; (1960), 66.
40. Suet. *Tib.* 26.2. Dio 57.18.2 under AD 18 gives the month as November (Tiberius was born November 16); Scott (1931); Weinstock (1971), 154. Note that on a calendar from Cyprus between 21 and 12 BC a month beginning December 2 was named after Libaios, but the arrangement may have been only temporary (Scott [1931] 208; Grether [1946], 232). June: Macrob. *Sat.* 1.12.31; July: Dio 44.5.2; Macrob. *Sat.* 1.12.34; August: Suet. *Aug.* 31.2; Dio 55.6.6 (placing the event in 8 BC). Caligula renamed September as Germanicus: Suet. *Cal.* 15.2. Pompey: *IG* 12.2.59.18, restored as *menos Pom[peio]*. The actual numbering of the months Quintilis and Sextilis ("fifth" and "sixth"), our modern July and August, reflects the old Roman calendar, in which March was the first month.
41. *CIL* 6.32340.17; *AFA* xxxiii*a*.7; Dio 44.6.1, 50.1, 51.19.7; Weinstock (1971), 217–18.
42. Birthday: *AFA* xxxiv*e*.2; *ILS* 154.
43. Livy 1.20.2, 27.8.8; Plut. *QR* 113.
44. Cic. *Phil.* 2.110; Plut. *Ant.* 33.1; Dio 44.6.4; Weinstock (1971), 305–8.
45. *Tab. Heb.* (EJ 94a.50); Tac. *Ann.* 2.83.2. Germanicus was succeeded by Drusus Caesar, son of Tiberius, who was followed in turn by Germanicus' son Nero.
46. Wives of the other senior flamines may have held the same office: see Vanggaard (1988), 30–31.
47. Plut. *QR* 86 suggests that it was thought that the flaminica was priestess of Juno.

Aul. Gell. *NA* 10.15.26 *(eaedem ferme caerimoniae sunt)*; Serv. on Verg. *Aen.* 4.518; Macrob. *Sat.* 1.16.30.

48. EJ, p. 52; Vell. 2.75.3; 4.9.107; Tac. *Ann.* 1.10.8; Dio 56.46.1; Taylor (1931), 230; Grant (*Principate*, 1950), 119–20.
49. Taylor (1931), 230; Weber (1936), 92; Taeger (1960), 219; Ritter (1972), 324; Herz (1978); Fishwick (1987–92), 162–63. Gagé (1931), 15–20, argues that Livia was appointed to a domestic cult.
50. Tac. *Ann.* 1.14.2; Dio 56.46.2. Agrippina: Tac. *Ann.* 13.2.3; Sandels (1912), 30, Hoffsten (1939), 86; Weber (1936), 92; Ritter (1972), 324. Vestal privilege: Dio 47.19.4.
51. Ovid *Trist.* 4.2.11, *Pont.* 4.9.107; Vell. 2.75.3.
52. Fittschen-Zanker (1983), III.3.2.6; Winkes (1995), 39–41, 164–65; Rose (1997), 97–98, no. 25; Wood (1999), 114–15, fig. 37; Bartman (1999), 155–56, no. 22, dates it to the late republic.
53. Gross (1962), 106–7; Winkes (1995), 148–50, no. 74; De Kersauson (1986), 102–3, no. 45; Wood (1999), 115–16, fig. 38; Bartman (1999), no. 3, 146–47. On the infula see Small (1990), 224–28; Rose (1997), 77; Wood (1995), 478 nn. 79–84, suggests a broader significance, as a mark of sanctity.
54. Megow (1987), 254, no. B 15, pl. 9; Winkes (1995), 189, no. 113; Wood (1999), 119–20; Bartman (1999), 102, no. 110.
55. Dio 55.2.4, 8.2.
56. Dio 55.2.4, 8.2, 57.21.5; Willrich (1911), 59.
57. Pergamum: *RPC* 2369. Smyrna: *IGR* 4.1392, *CIL* 3.7107. Tralles: *BCH* 51 (1886), 516, no. 6; Bartman (1999), 108.
58. Kreikenbom (1992), 179–86.
59. Tac. *Ann.* 4.37; Fishwick (1987–92), I.1.158.
60. Tac. *Ann.* 1.14.2.
61. Suet. *Tib.* 50.2–3; Dio 54.24.2, 57.16.2; Agrippina: Dio 60.33.12.
62. Sejanus: Tac. *Ann.* 1.19.1, 69; Dio 58.9–13; Ritter (1972), 331; Perkounig (1995), 157.
63. Suet. *Aug.* 53.2–3; Dio 54.30.1, 56.26.2–3, 41.5, 57.12.2. Drusus: Dio 48.44.4. Nero: Tac. *Ann.* 13.18.3–5; Dio 61.33.1. Julia Domna: Dio 78.18.3; Ritter (1972), 329; Talbert (1984), 68; Kunst (1998), 455, 465–66.
64. Tac. *Ann.* 2.34; 4.21.1. Urgulania: *PIR* V 684; *RE* Suppl. 9 (1962), 1868–69 (R. Hanslik); *FOS* 619; see Syme (1939), 385; (1986), 375–76; Fischler (1989), 230.
65. Cic. Inv. 2.17.53: *maiestatem minuere.* Tac. *Ann.* 1.72.3: *maiestatem populi Romani minuisset.* Bauman (1992), 99, 135; Vidén (1993), 15; Fischler (1994).
66. Tac. *Ann.* 2.50.2; Suet. *Tib.* 28; Dio 57.19.1; Bauman (1967), 234; (1974), 77–78, 223; Goodyear (1981), 153.
67. Tac. *Ann.* 1.72.4; Syme (1958), 2.696.
68. Eck et al. (1996), 222.
69. Germanicus' claim: Tac. *Ann.* 2.71.2. Tiberius' statement: Tac. *Ann.* 3.12.2. Plancina's mourning: Tac. *Ann.* 2.75.2; Eck et al. (1996), 223.
70. Tac. *Ann.* 2.55.5.
71. Tac. *Ann.* 2.58.3.

72. Tac. *Ann.* 22.80.1.
73. Tac. *Ann.* 6.26.3.
74. *Piso Decree* 113; Tac. *Ann.* 2.50.3; cf. Quint. *Inst. Dr.* 5.13.5: *deprecatio . . . est sine ulla specie defensionis;* 7.4.18: *ubicunque iuris clementia est habet locum deprecatio.*
75. Tac. *Ann.* 3.17.1, 6.26.3.
76. *Piso Decree* 115; Eck et al. (1996), 228; Pliny *HN* 35.25; Flory (1993), 288; Cic. *ad Fam.* 10.5.2; *ad Att.* 10.4.5; Caes. *BC* 1.13, 3.39.
77. *Cons. Liv.* 82.
78. Plaut. *Most.* 3.2.23; Cic. *Cat.* 3.14; Juv. *Sat.* 2.34; Eck et al. (1996), 227.
79. Number and restriction to citizens: Pliny *HN* 33.30. predominance of equites: Tac. *Ann.* 3.30.2 (see also 14.20.7); Suet. *Tib.* 41; Galsterer (1996), 399–400.
80. Suet. *Tib.* 51.1. Wallace-Hadrill (1983), 94, suggests that Augustus' letters were kept in the imperial libraries. It was not unusual for correspondence to be kept in archives. Pliny *HN* 13.83 reports that he frequently saw documents in the hands of Cicero, Vergil, and Augustus, and that he had even seen documents in the hands of Tiberius and Gaius Gracchus written nearly two hundred years earlier and preserved in a private collection. Letters written in verse by Spurius Mummius were preserved by descendants (Cic. *ad Att.* 13.6.4). When charged with having won his wife Pudentilla by means of magic, the novelist Apuleius in his successful defence made use of letters of Pudentilla preserved by her son Pontianus and left by him to his archivist (Apul. *Apol.* 70.8, 78.6, 83.1, 84.5).
81. *RG* 21; *ILS* 5050.157; Pliny *HN* 8.65; Dio 54.26.1. This theatre was started by Julius Caesar, who acquired the land at the expense of the Temple of Pietas, for which he was much criticised. Augustus was obliged to buy up more land from private owners. After Marcellus' death in 23 BC, the theatre became a memorial to him. It was far enough advanced to house some of the celebrations of the secular games in 17 BC, but not dedicated until May 7, 13 BC. It appears on the Severan Marble Plan, between the Forum Holitorium and the Pons Fabricius.
82. Tac. *Ann.* 3.64.2.
83. EJ, p. 48; Degrassi (1963), 448. On April 23, AD 38, the Arvals sacrificed an ox before the simulacrum of Divus Augustus at the Theatre of Marcellus: AFA xliii. 25–26; Woodman (1981), 447. Torelli (1982), 69, argues that the statue was dedicated to commemorate the assumption of the toga virilis by Drusus, son of Tiberius, misdated according to Torelli to April 24. If we accept the sequence of events as provided by Tacitus, Tiberius could not have been present at the dedication ceremony, as the inscription implies he was.
84. *RIC*² Tiberius 49; Torelli (1982), 68, defining the Augustus side as the obverse.
85. Dio 56.46.3; see Degrassi (1963), 447. The incident has been seen by some scholars as a vindication of Tacitus' claim: Sandels (1912), 76; Ollendorff (1926), 50–58, 919; Hoffsten (1939), 15; Ciaceri (1944), 112; Kornemann (1947), 214; contra, Ritter (1972), 329. Mothers precede sons in grave inscriptions: *ILS* 1485, 1554. Gagé (1931), 16–17, says that Livia's claim to precedence was justified by her position as priestess of Augustus' cult and adoptive daughter of the divus. On the Gytheum decree, see Seyrig (1929), 91–92.
86. Dio 58.2.3–6; Kähler (1939), 378. Drusus, brother of Tiberius: Suet. *Claud.* 1.3;

Dio 55.2.3; *RIC*[2] Claudius: 69–72, 125–26. Germanicus: Tac. *Ann.* 2.83.2; González (1984), 58–69; Kleiner (1990), 511 n. 10. Drusus, son of Tiberius: Tac. *Ann.* 4.9.2 (Drusus received the same memorials as Germanicus). See Kleiner (1990), 512, for speculation that a posthumous arch was granted to Sabina, wife of Hadrian; arches honoured Livia outside Rome. At Ephesus, Augustus and Livia, along with Marcus Agrippa and Julia, were honoured on the south gate of the agora: *ILS* 8897, EJ 71. A supposed arch in honour of Livia on the Via Valeria is linked with a dedicatory inscription from Superaequum (*CIL* 9. 3304).

9. WOMAN OF SUBSTANCE

1. Thomas (1976), 192; Mratschek-Halfmann (1993), 45.
2. Suet. *Galb.* 5.2; Mratschek-Halfmann (1993), 279–80. Note, however, that Claudius' freedman Narcissus reputedly amassed a fortune of 400 million sesterces (Dio 60.34.4).
3. *RG* 17; Suet. *Aug.* 101.3, *Claud.* 4.7; the text of Suetonius gives as a limit of each legacy 20,000 sesterces *(vicena sestertia)*. This is a very small amount, and Suetonius, who had seen the will, states elsewhere that Claudius received 800,000 as a legacy, which was considered niggardly. Thus there are grounds for accepting the proposed emendation to *vicies*, which would allow a maximum of two million; Shatzman (1975), 368 n. 561; Millar (1992), 191; Champlin (1989); Mratschek-Halfmann (1993), 280.
4. Cic. *De Rep.* 3.10.17 says the Lex Voconia was unjust to women. Dio 55.2.5, 56.10.2, 32.1; Cato: *ORF* fr. 156–60; Steinwerter (1925), Astin (1978), 113–18; Bauman (1983), 176–78, (1992), 34. For the surviving terms of the Lex Voconia, see Thomas (1976), 487–88; Rogers (1947), 142, for individuals whose legacies to Augustus are known.
5. Suet. *Aug.* 101.3; E. Champlin (1989), 157, (1991), 11–17.
6. Dio 56.10.2 links the restriction to the Lex Voconia, but this is the only evidence that this Lex imposed such a constraint.
7. *CIL* 6.4173: Timotheus Maronianus; *CIL* 6.3952: Livia's slave Cascellianus, a legacy to the emperor from the distinguished lawyer Aulus Cascellius (*PIR* C 389); *CIL* 6.4124: Eros Maecilianus, freedman of Livia, perhaps from Marcus Maecilius Tullus, triumvir monetalis in the last decade BC; *CIL* 6.4358: *Pelops Scaplian(us) Ti Caesar(is) tabularius et Augustae*, owned jointly by Livia and Tiberius; *CIL* 6.9066: *Philadelphus Ti Caes(aris) Aug(usti) et Iuliae Aug(ustae) servus Scaplianus*, slave of Tiberius and Livia; *CIL* 6.5226: Servilia Scapula, slave of Tiberius and Livia and Quintus Ostorius Scapula, one of the first pair of praetorian prefects in 2 BC and grandfather of Ostorius Scapula, who later won fame for his command in Britain; see Stein (1942), 1672; *CIL* 6.4095: Anna Liviae Maecenatiana, *CIL* 6.4016: *Parmeno Liviae a purpur. Maecenatian(a)*, both acquired from Maecenas; *CIL* 6. 5223: *Castor Ti. Caesar(is) et August(ae) l. Agrippi(anus)*, acquired from Marcus Agrippa.
8. Jos. *Ant.* 17.146, 190; *AE* 1979, no. 33: *Idumaeus Ti. Caesaris maternus;* see Chantraine (1982), 132.
9. *CIL* 6. 4035: *M. Livius Aug(ustae?) Lib(ertus) Anterus Amyntian(us);* from the *Monu-*

mentum Liviae: CIL 6. 8894: *Epinicius Caesar(is) ser(vus) Amyntianus*. With no connections to the imperial family: *CIL* 6. 4715, 8738 (= *ILS* 7866), 10395: Strabo 12.8.4; Dio 53.26.3 Shatzman (1975), 361. Because Anteros was a *supellectile*, it may be that his job was to look after fine furniture and works of art, and Huntsman (1997), 164, suggests that Amyntas might have left a fine collection to Livia. Magie (1950), 1304 n. 3, is dubious about using inscriptional evidence to establish an inheritance from Amyntas.

10. Suet. *Aug*. 72.1; *LTUR* 1.129; Richardson (1992), 130.
11. Varro. *LL* 5.54. Vitruvius: Livy 8.19.4; Cic. *Dom*. 101. Octavian: Suet. *Aug*. 5; Tamm (1963), 28–45, 47 n. 23; Coarelli (1983) II.25, 31; Richardson (1992), 279–82.
12. Ovid *Fast*. 1. 951; Dio 49.15.5; Suet. *Aug*. 29.3; Vell. 2.81.3.
13. Suet. *Aug*. 72.1.
14. Digest 33.2.32.2; Treggiari (1991), 390.
15. *CIL* 15.7264.
16. Lugli (1970), 167–74; Coarelli (1985), 129–30; Carettoni (1987), 775; Richardson (1992), 73–74; Claridge (1998), 128; Macciocca, Iacopi: *LTUR* 2. 130–32. Paintings: Ling (1991), 37–38, 113, 142, 216. Bragantini (1982), 30–33, suggests that the Egyptian motifs of the House of Livia, the Aula Isiaca, and the Farnese Villa suggest a unified scheme. Kokkinos (1992), 149–53, believes that this house was shared by Livia and Antonia.
17. All references are to *CIL* 6: dispensator: 3965b, 3966, 3968, 4237; arcarii: 3937, 3938, 8722; tabularii: 4250; slave ad possessiones: 4015; custos rationis patrimoni: 3962; ornatrices: 3993, 3994, 8944, 8958; a veste / ad vestem: 3985, 4041–43, 4251; ab ornamentis: 3992; ab ornamentis sacerdotalibus: 8955; calciator: 3939; lanipendi: 3973, 3977; sarcinatores / -rices 3988, 4028–31, 5357, 8903, 9038; unctrix: 4045; pedisequi / -ae: 4002–6; puer a pedibus: 4001.
18. All references are to *CIL* 6: medici: 3983, 3985–87, 8901. 8903, 8904; supra medicos: 3982.
19. All references are to *CIL* 6: aurifex: 3927, 3943–45, 3949; inaurator: 3928; margaritarius: 3981; colorator: 3953; ab supellectile: 4035, 4036, 5358; a tabulis: 3970.
20. Pliny *HN* 7.75.
21. *CIL* 6.3973: *Helenus Liviae ad insulam*, and *CIL* 6. 3974: *Clerdo insularius;* he is not necessarily a slave of Livia, but his ashes (as well as Helenus') were deposited in the *Monumentum Livia;* see Garnsey (1976), 128.
22. Lugli (1923); Gabriel (1955); Blake (1947), 272; Calci (1994).
23. Suet. *Galb*. 1; Dio 48.44.1. Huntsman (1997) suggests that the imperial villa at Antium was Livia's.
24. Campania: *CIL* 10.8042, 41, 60; Willrich (1911), 73. Sicily: *CIL* 10.7489; Willrich (1911), 72. Tusculum: *CIL* 15.7814. Capri: *CIL* 6.8958: Juno Dorcas is a freedwoman of Livia, her *ornatrix;* she died in Rome but was born *a Caprensis*, cf. 8409, Willrich (1911), 73. Lucania: *AE* 1972, no. 147: *Pancarpus Liv(iae servus);* D'Arms (1970), 84 n. 55. L. Jacono, *NS* (1926), 230 n. 5, notes that a tile stamp at Ponza with the name *Augustae* may refer to Julia; similarly R. Paribeni, *NS* (1902), 630, believes that a slave of *Julia August(a* or *i)* in Puteoli may be Julia's.

25. *ILS* 259. Huntsman (1977), 159, argues that he may not have administered the same property for all three.
26. Pliny *HN* 34.3–4. Ulp. *Dig.* VI.I.13.5 states that occupants had the right to exploit the minerals beneath their land; Ollendorff (1926), 906; Davies (1935), 3 n. 7.
27. Jos. *Ant.* 18.31, *BJ* 2.167; cf. Pliny *HN* 13.44; Smallwood (1976), 158 n. 56; Paltiel (1991), 67; Mratschek-Halfmann (1993), 269. Procurator: *AE* 1941, 105; Fracarro (1940).
28. *IGR* 4.1204, 1213 (= *ILS* 8853); Suet. *Tib.* 8; Hermann *DAW* LXXVII 1 (1959) no. 12; Hirschfeld (1902), 303, disagrees; Willrich (1911), 72; Broughton (1934), 220; Jones (1971), 84; Crawford (1974), 39; Shatzman (1975), 362; Huntsman (1997), 158. Some scholars have read *arches* for *arkes*, suggesting an administrative unit rather than a treasury. Pflaum (1960–61), 579, no. 218, argues for a treasury of an official, Livius, unconnected with Livia.
29. Dio 51.5.5; Frank (1940), 6; Parassoglou (1978), 6; Crawford (1974), 41.
30. Willrich (1911), 73; Parassoglou (1978), 15–29; Crawford (1974), 39–40; Lewis (1974), 52–54; Rostovtzev (1979), 145; Mratschek-Halfmann (1993), 280.
31. *SB* 9150; see Wolfe (1952).
32. *P. Lond.* II.445.
33. Theadelphia: *P. Med.* 6. Philadelphia: *P. Sorb.* Inv. 2364.
34. *PSI* 1028, *SB* 10536.
35. *Pap. Ryl.* 126; the land belonged to Gaius Julius Alexandros, whose death is put between AD 26 and 28 (on the death: Parassoglou [1978], 17).
36. *P. Vindob.* 560: Euhemeria (AD 54); *P. Mich.* 560 (AD 46): *Libiane ousia* could have belonged to Livia or Livilla (see Parassoglou [1978], 19 n. 46); Huntsman (1997) notes another possible estate at Drymos Hieras Nesou (*P. Bour.* 42).
37. Suet. *Tib.* 7.1.
38. EJ p. 46; Tac. *Ann.* 1.73.3; Dio 56.46.5. Caligula: Jos. *Ant.* 19.77; Suet. *Cal.* 56.2; Dio 59.29.5; Barrett (1989), 169–71; Fishwick (1987–92), I.1.162. On the date of the decree: Degrassi (1963), 13.2, p. 161.
39. Jos. *Ant.* 19.75; Tac. *Ann.* 1.73.3. Tacitus says *solitum interesse*, which is problematic in AD 15 because the festival can have been held only once. Cassius may have participated in other festivals connected with Augustus. On Falanius: Syme (1970), 68, *Papers B*, 630–31.
40. Caligula: *RIC*^{2} 36. Antoninus: *RIC*^{2} 973; Dio 56.46.3; Richardson (1992), 45; Fishwick (1992). Tac. *Ann.* 6.45.2 says that Tiberius finished the temple. Suet. *Tib.* 47; *Cal.* 21 claims it was unfinished. Dio 57.10.2 mentions only Tiberius' name in connection with the temple. Richmond (1913) argues that Caligula's sestertius depicts the Temple of Apollo on the Palatine. Hill (1979), 207, suggests that the temple on Antoninus' coins represents the building as restored by Domitian, after the fire of 80.
41. Pliny *HN* 12.94; Rehak (1990). Torelli (1982), 73, identifies this shrine with the *sacrarium* mentioned at Suet. *Tib.* 51.1, but surely a smaller structure is involved. Boatwright (1991), 519 n. 26, believes that Pliny's temple is the same as the one mentioned by Dio 56.46.3. Fishwick (1992) suggests that a single temple was in-

volved, and that the temple on the "Palatine," broadly defined, was the Temple of Divus Augustus.

42. *AFA* lv, lvi; *ILS* 4992, *ILS* 4993. Aeditus: *ILS* 4995; Dio 60.5.2; Hänlein-Schäfer (1985), 113–28; Fishwick (1987–92) II.1.485; Winkes (1985), 68; *LTUR* 1.143–6: *Aedes Augusti*.

10. FRIEND, PATRON, AND PROTECTOR

1. On this, see especially Dixon (1981); Hillard (1992).
2. Sabines: Livy 1.13; Dion. Hal. 2.30. Coriolanus: Livy 2.33–35, 37–40; Dion. Hal. 6.92–94, 7.19, 21–67; Plut. *Cor.* 34–36. Cornelia: Plut. *Gai. Gracch.* 4.1; Fischler (1989), 23.
3. App. *BC* 5.52, 63, 69, 72; Dio 48.15.2, 16.2–3; Cluett (1998).
4. See Dixon (1981–82), 94–96, for these and other examples.
5. Cic. *Rosc.* 27.
6. Fischler (1994), 117–18; Hallett (1977), 170–71; Pomeroy (1975), 186; Champlin (1989), 80.
7. Dio 47.7.4–5; Vinius: *RE* 9A (1961), 123 (H. Gundel).
8. Plut. *Ant.* 35.2.
9. Vitr. *Arch.* 1 pr. 2
10. Syme (1939), 386.
11. Tac. *Ann.* 2.37.1; Edwards (1993), 185.
12. Cic. *Off.* 2.56; Pliny *Ep.* 2.4.2, 6.32.2; Dio 58.2.2. Gaul: Suet. *Aug.* 40.3. Jury: Suet. *Tib.* 51.1; Talbert (1984), 49 n. 15. Fires: Dio 57.16.2.
13. Vell. 2.130.5; *Cons. Liv.* 48; Dio 55.19.5, 58.2.3; Seibt (1969), 14; Martin (1981), 141; Perkounig (1995), 163–64; Flory (1998), 120.
14. Syme (1986), 169, 172.
15. *ILS* 1321.
16. Tac. *Ann.* 6.20.2; Suet. *Galb.* 4–5; Dio 57.19.4. Consulship: Plut. *Galb* 3.2; not mentioned by Suet. *Galb.* 6.1. Suet. *Galb.* 5.2 *paene ditatus* might suggest that Galba at best received a reduced amount of the legacy.
17. Tac. *Hist.* 2.50; Suet. *Oth.* 1; Syme (1986), 169; Saller (1982), 65.
18. Haterius: *PIR* H24; *RE* Suppl. 3 (1918), 889–90 (K. Gerth); Jer. *Chron.* 172H. Augustus: Sen. *Contr.* 4. *praef.* 7.
19. Tac. *Ann.* 3.57.2.
20. Tac. *Ann.* 1.13.6, 14.4–6. Suet. *Tib.* 27 says that the emperor fell on his back *supinus;* Tacitus, forward, *prociderat*. Apology: Suet. *Tib.* 29. Tacitus' text is corrupt; the "urgent appeals," in one reading of the manuscript, may be Livia's, but they suit Haterius better. Suetonius sees the episode as essentially humorous, Tacitus takes it more seriously.
21. Tac. *Ann.* 5.2.2. Father: EJ, p. 38.
22. Tac. *Ann.* 4.12.
23. Sen. *Cons. Marc.* 1; Tac. *Ann.* 4.34–35; Suet. *Aug.* 35.2, *Tib.* 61.3, *Cal.* 16.1; Dio 57.24.4.

24. Sen. *Cons. Marc.* 4.1, 24.3.
25. Ovid has been defended on the grounds that his references are ironical. For a summary and a balanced view: Johnson (1997).
26. Ovid *Fast.* 5.157–58, 6.637.
27. Ovid *Trist.* 1.6.25–27, 2.161–64; *Pont.* 1.4.56, 3.1.114–18, 125–28, 139–42. On the place of Livia in *Trist.* 1.6, see Hinds (1999), 139–41.
28. Ovid *Trist.* 4.2.11; *Pont.* 4.13.29. Syme (1978), 21–36, believes that the *Fasti* were written between AD 1 and 4, and revised in part after 14, 37–39; *Tristia* composed between AD 8–9 and 12, 39–44; *ex Ponto* I–III written in 12, published in 13, IV in 13–16.
29. Wife: Ovid *Pont.* 3.1.145–66. Images: Ovid *Pont.* 2.8.1–10, 51–52, 65–68, 4.9.105–8; see Scott (1931), 107, (1930), 43–69. Marcia: Ovid *Pont.* 1.2.126; Ovid also notes that she was highly regarded by Caesar's aunt Atia.
30. Ovid *Fast.* 1.461–586 (Carmentis), 649 (genetrix); Herbert-Brown (1984), 159.
31. Plut. *Gai. Gracch.* 19.2: Livia was not the first Roman woman to have such external connections. After Cornelia, the mother of the Gracchi, retired to Misenum, she maintained a lively contact with prominent individuals, and reigning kings exchanged gifts with her.
32. Dio 54.24.6; Paltiel (1991), 162.
33. Augustus: *IGR* 1.875, 901. Livia: *IGR* 1.902; Nawotka (1989), 326–28.
34. *RPC* 3803–7; Strabo 12.3.29, 8.16; Dio 49.25.4; Paltiel (1999), 138 n. 4.
35. *SEG* 39.695, Hahn (1992), 333 no. 91; Bartman (1999), 220 no. 13. Pythodoris married Archelaus, king of Cappadocia, after the death of Polemo, but the kingdoms of Pontus and Cappadocia were never united.
36. Val. Max. 4.3.3.
37. Tryphaena: *PIR* A 900; *RE* 1 (1894), 2641–42 (P. von Rohden).
38. *IGR* 4.144; Hahn (1992), 334, no. 97; Bartman (1999), 205, no. 43; Price (1984), 63–64. Athena: Plut. *Lucull.* 10; Magie (1950), 1208 n. 16.
39. Jos. *BJ* 1.566, *Ant.* 17.10. Date of Salome's death: Smallwood (1976), 156.
40. Jos. *Ant.* 17.134–41, 182, *BJ* 1.641, 661: Josephus' versions of the Acme-Antipater affair differs in some details in the *Antiquities* and the *Bellum*.
41. Smith (1897), 125–27.
42. Taxes: R. Bernhardt (1980).
43. Grant of freedom: Dio 54.9.7. Inscriptions: Herrmann (1960), 104–5, nos. 11, 12. Father: *IGR* 4.982. Mother: *IGR* 4.983. Priestess Lollia: *IGR* 4.984.
44. *IGR* 4.39: there may have been a later restoration of the inscription, for Livia is called Julia.
45. Pliny *HN* 37.3–4; the reading of the best MS, *Augustae*, with reference to Livia, is assumed in preference to *Augusti* (Augustus) of the inferior MSS.
46. Parian statue: Dio 55.9.6; Augustus dedicated four elephants made of obsidian (Pliny *HN* 36.196); statues of Apollo and Juno by Baton (Pliny *HN* 34.73); statue of Leto with the infants Apollo and Artemis by Euphranor (Pliny *HN* 34.77); statue of Asclepius and Hygeia by Niceratus (Pliny *HN* 34.80); statues of Ares and Hermes by Piston (Pliny *HN* 34.89); statues of Demeter, Zeus, and Athene by Sthennis (Pliny *HN* 34.90). The temple also contained a painting of Marsyas Bound by

Zeuxis (Pliny *HN* 35.66) and Nicias' painting of Father Bacchus (Pliny *HN* 35.131); see Becatti (1973–74); Kellum (1990), 278.

47. Pliny *HN* 37.27.
48. Eck, in Millar and Segal (1984), 139–42, notes that after 19 BC most public benefactions of the members of the senatorial order were outside Rome; in Rome such gestures were becoming the prerogative of the princeps and his family.
49. *CIL* 10.810.
50. Pliny *HN* 3.17; Martial 4.18.1; Dio 55.8.4.
51. Vitr. *Arch.* 1 pr. 2; Suet. *Aug.* 29.4; Dio 49.43.8; Livy *Per.* 138; Richardson (1976).
52. Ovid *Fast.* 6.640–48; Sen. *Clem.* 1.18.2, *Ira* 3.40; Suet. *Aug.* 29.4; Pliny *HN* 9.77; Tac. *Ann.* 1.10.5, 12.60.4; Dio 54.23.1–6; Syme, *Papers A*, 518–29; Edwards (1993), 164–65.
53. Suet. *Aug.* 29.3; Dio 55.8.2; Ovid *AA* 1.71–72; Pliny *HN* 14.11; Pliny *Ep.* 1.5.9; Strabo 5.3.8 (236); Grimal (1943), 155 n. 1; Boëthius and Ward-Perkins (1970), 327. Richardson (1976), 62, and (1978), 265–72, suggests that the land might have been donated by Augustus, but the building was paid for by Livia and Tiberius; Richardson (1992), 314; Flory (1984); Claridge (1998), 303; *FUR* pl. 18; Rodriguez pls. 7–9.
54. Ovid *Fast.* 6.637–38; Suet. *Aug.* 29.4; Dio 54.23.6; Flory (1984), 313–14, 329; Coarelli (1974), 206. Carettoni (1960), 69, tentatively suggests that the small structure is a fountain; see also Richardson (1992), 99–100, suggesting that the aedes and portico were "substantially identical."
55. *ILS* 5592; Coarelli (1974), 208; Richardson (1992), 241.
56. Propertius 2.6.25–26; Livy 10.23.1–10 (the cult had passed into disuse by Livy's time); Suet *Aug.* 34.1; Palmer (1974), 125–40. Palmer suggests that Julia might have been involved in the restoration of Pudicitia Patricia.
57. Ovid *Fast.* 148–58; *SHA Hadr.* 19.11; Wissowa (1899); Platner-Ashby (1929), 85; Coarelli (1985), 314; Richardson (1992), 59–60.
58. Propertius 4.9.23–74; Ovid *Fast.* 5.148–58 (pre-exile); Macrob. *Sat.* 1.12.21–22. Daughter: Macrob. *Sat.* 1.12.23–27. Husband: Sextus Clodius, Arnobius 5.18; Lact. *Div. Inst.* 1.22.11 (cf. Plut. *QR* 20). Theories on the origin of the cult are summarised by Herbert-Brown (1984), 132–33.
59. Verg. *Aen.* 7.706.
60. *RG* 19; Suet. *Aug.* 31; Dio 59.10.2–6; Hor. *Odes* 3.6.
61. Cic. *Dom.* 105, *Har. Resp.* 17.37.38, *ad Att.* 1.13.3; Plut. *Caes.* 9.
62. Vestals: Suet. *Aug.* 31.2. Caesar: Cic. *Har. Resp.* 3.4. Residence: Suet. *Div. Jul.* 46; Dio 54.27.3; Herbert-Brown (1984), 144.
63. EJ 101 (*ILS* 154): Rose (1997), 88–89.
64. *CIL* 6.883; Livy 2.40.1–12; Dion. Hal. 8.55–56; Val. Max. 1.8.4, cf. 5.2.1. Location: Ashby (1907), 79. Significance: Flory (1984), 318; Purcell (1986), 88; Wood (1999), 78–79. Filiation: Boatwright (1991), 520.
65. *CIL* 11.3322; Kornemann (1952), 209.
66. Visit: Jos. *Ant.* 16.6. Temple: Philo *Leg.* 157, 291. Philo *Leg.* 319 describes the bowls as a gift from Livia. Paltiel (1991), 84, prefers this account to the claim by Josephus (*BJ* 5.562–63) that they were donated jointly by Livia and Augustus.

67. Jos. *Ant.* 16.139. On the date see Smallwood (1981), 80 n. 62.
68. *P. Oxy.* 2435 verso, 45.
69. Corinth: *Corinth* 8.1, no. 19; 8.3, no. 153. Egypt: *P. Oxy* 17.2105. Chalcis, recording also *Caesarea* at Tanagra: *BCH* 3 (1879), 443. Thespiae: *AE* 1928, no. 50; *SEG* 13 (1956), 348; *SEG* 31 (1981) no. 514 (Mnemosyne); *BCH* 26 (1902), no. 18.
70. Jamot, *BCH* (1902), 153–55, no. 4; Gow and Page (1968), I. 277 (also II.309); Jones (1970), 249–55. Cichorius (1922), 356–57, argues for Antonia, and Caligula and Gemellus, her grandsons, both of whom were in line for the succession; see also Bowersock (1965), 141; D'Arms (1970), 85–86; Temporini (1978), 28–29; Kokkinos (1992), 42, 88–89, 92–93 (but Kokkinos suggests Germanicus and Drusus, or Caligula and Claudius).
71. Jos. *Ant.* 18.27, *BJ* 2.168. Josephus gives the name consistently as Julias: Jos. *Ant.* 20.159, *BJ* 2.252, 4.438. Livias: Pliny *HN* 13.44; Ptol. *Geog.* 5.16.9; Euseb. *Onom.* (Larson and Parthey), 112–13; Jones (1937), 275; Smallwood (1981), 118–19.
72. *RPC* 4006–11, 4013–14. Trajan: *BMC* 8; Pliny *HN* 5.93; Magie (1950), 1355 n. 14; Gough (1956); Jones (1971), 204, 438 n. 22.
73. Pliny *HN* 6.11; Pliny provides no information other than that Liviopolis did not stand on a river.
74. Taylor (1931), 35–57.
75. Livia's divine honours: Scott (1930), 57, 64–65; Ollendorff (1926), 907–23; Taylor (1933), 270–83; Grether (1946), 22–52; Grant (*Principate*, 1950), 108–29; Flory (1984), 320; Fishwick (1987–92); Hahn (1992); Mikocki (1995).
76. Thessalonica *RPC* 1563. Athens: *IG* 3.316.
77. *IG* 12 (Suppl.), 124, 18–24; Price (1984), 249, no. 5; Mikocki (1995), 105.
78. Gross (1962), 106–9; Fittschen-Zanker (1983), III.2.6; Kreikenbom (1992), 179 Cat. III.36; Winkes (1995), 181, no. 105; Rose (1997), no. 125, 182–84; Wood (1999), 110–12, fig. 35; Bartman (1999), 179, no. 72, 208. Aurigemma (1940), 21–27, argued that the group must belong to the lifetime of Germanicus; Trillmich (1988) deduces from the inscriptions on the bases that the group could not be earlier than 23 BC, Drusus' last year, and that it contained posthumous honours to both Drusus and Germanicus.
79. *IRT* no. 269; Fittschen-Zanker (1983), III.4.9; Sande (1985), 154–58; Kreikenbom (1995), 180–81, Cat. III.39; Winkes (1995), 184–85; Mikocki (1995), 156, no. 37, pl. 14; Rose (1997), 182–84; Wood (1999), 121–23, fig 43; Bartman (1999), no. 74, 179–80.
80. Hahn (1992), 322–32.
81. Tarsus: *RPC* 4005. Eumenea: *RPC* 3143. Pergamum: *RPC* 2359. Thessalian League: *RPC* 1427. Rome: Val. Max. 6.1.1; Ovid *Fast.* 1.650; *Cons. Liv.* 380. Association of Jupiter with Augustus: Alföldi (1970), 220–21.
82. Mylai: *IG* 9.2.333. Aphrodisias: *AE* 1980, no. 877. Mytilene: *IG* 12 Suppl. 50. Assos: *IGR* 4.249.
83. Falerii: *ILS* 116 (*CIL* 11.3076). Aeclanum: *CIL* 9.1098. Zara: *ILS* 2.3089. El Lehs: *ILS* 120 (EJ 127). The difficulty arises from the syntactical ambiguity of the form *Liviae*, whose case could be dative (to Livia) or genitive (of Livia).

84. Wilcken (1909); Flory (1984), 319–20.
85. Suet. *Aug.* 93; Dio 51.4.1, 54.9.10; Rose (1997), 140–41, cat. 71; Wood (1999), 92; Bartman (1999), 64.
86. Alexandria: *RPC* 5053, 5063.
87. Ephesus: *SEG* 4.515. Nepet, Africa: *CIL* 11.3196. Malta: *ILS* 121. Lampsacus: *IGR* 4.180. Aphrodisias: *CIG* 2.2815. The last two could be Julia Domna; Winkes (1988), 560–61; Mikocki (1995), 18–21, 141, 151–58; Wood (1999), 112–13.
88. The portrait type is one that is generally dated early: Winkes (1995), 103, no. 128; Mikocki (1995), 157, no. 40; Megow (1987), 179–80, no. A49; Wood (1999), 113, fig. 36.
89. Augustus: *RIC*[2] 219–20. Claudius: *RIC*[2] 101; Sutherland (1951), 124–25, 131.
90. Suet. *Tib.* 26.1; Dio 57.9.1; Charlesworth (1939).
91. *SEG* 11.922–23 (EJ 102): the letter of Tiberius is restored to indicate his sixteenth tribunician year (which lasted from July AD 14 to the following July), when he was already pontifex maximus—that is, after March 10, 15. Rose (1997), 269 n. 3, prefers a date closer to AD 17 and Germanicus' triumph; Sandels (1912), 41–44; Grether (1946), 238–40; Magie (1950), 502, 1360; Seyrig (1929), 92–102, 102; Kornemann (1929), (1952), 210, (1960), 106; Grether (1946), 240; Ritter (1972), 327; Price (1984), 60–61, 72, 103, 106, 109, 188, 210–11, 226; Winkes (1985), 67; Fishwick (1987–92), I.1.158–59; Mikocki (1995), 158, no. 48; Bartman (1999), 119 n. 77, 207, no. 52; Rose (1997), 142–44, no. 74. Thasos: Price (1984), 72 (cf. Veyne [1962], 62). Hypocrisy: Rostovtzev (1930), 23–24. Diplomacy: Charlesworth (1939), 3. Painted images: Blanck (1968).
92. *RPC* 2469; Tac. *Ann.* 3.68, 4.15, 37, 55–56, 51.20.7, 59.28.1; Magie (1950), 501, 1361; Price (1984), 64, 66, 185, 258, no. 45.
93. Vell. 2.130.5.

11. DEATH AND REPUTATION

1. Tac. *Ann.* 5.1.1; Dio 58.2.1 (Xiphilinus); Zonaras' summary is slightly different.
2. Suet. *Tib.* 51.2; Dio 58.2.1.
3. Vell. 2.114.1; Suet. *Tib.* 11.2; Dio 57.11.7.
4. Suet. *Tib.* 51.2; Dio 58.2.1.
5. Dio 58.35.4–5.
6. Suet. *Tib.* 51.2; Willrich (1911), 43; Hatzl (1975), 57; Flower (1996), 254.
7. *IGR* 4.251 (Assos); Suet. *Cal.* 53; Dio 59.19.4; Barrett (1990), 48.
8. Vell. 2.130.5; Tac. *Ann.* 5.1.4, 2.1; Dio 58.2.1, 2.
9. Strabo 5.3.8 (236); Suet. *Aug.* 100.4; Dio 53.30.5.
10. Pliny *HN* 36.69–74: the obelisks are not included in Pliny's account of the obelisks of Rome and perhaps were added later—they are first mentioned in the fourth century.
11. Marcellus: Dio 53.30.5, Octavia: Dio 54.35. Drusus: Suet. *Claud.* 1.4; Dio 55.2; 56.10; Aur. Vict. *Caes.* 12.12. Julias: Suet. *Aug.* 101.3; Cordingley and Richmond (1927); Boëthius and Ward-Perkins (1970), 197; Kokkinos (1992), 28; Richardson

(1992), 247–49; von Hesberg (1994); Claridge (1998), 181–84; von Hesberg, *LTUR* 3.234–37; Macciocca, *LTUR* 3.237–39.

12. Tac. *Ann.* 5.2.1; Dio 58.2.2.
13. Dio 58.2.3–6. On Caligula's completion of the Temple of Augustus, see Barrett (1990), 69–71.
14. Vell. 2.130.5 (see Woodman [1977], ad loc.); Tac. *Ann.* 5.2.2; Dio 58.2.1; Suet. *Tib.* 51.2.
15. Tac. *Ann.* 6.5.1; M. Aurelius Cotta Maximus Messalinus: *PIR* A 1488; *RE* 2.2 (1896), 2490–91 (P. von Rohden); Tac. *Ann.* 2.32.2, 4.20.4, 5.3.4. Gluttony: Persius 2.72; Pliny *HN* 10.52. Generosity: Ovid *Pont.* passim; Bauman (1974), 103.
16. Dio 58.2.3; Seibt (1969), 14; Perkounig (1995), 163–64.
17. Tac. *Ann.* 5.2.2, 6.10.1; Suet. *Tib.* 51; Dio 58.4.5–7.
18. Tac. *Ann.* 6.26.3.
19. Tac. *Ann.* 5.3.1; Martin (1981), 141.
20. Pliny *HN* 8.145; Tac. *Ann.* 5.3.1; Suet. *Cal.* 10.1. Martin (1981), 141, expresses serious doubts about any true role for Livia in holding back Sejanus from Agrippina, which he thinks is belied by the narrative of events between 23 and 29. He suggests that what influence Livia still possessed after 23 must have been confined to narrow family matters.
21. Suet. *Tib.* 53.2, *Cal.* 10.1.
22. *AFA* xliii*c*.2.
23. Tac. *Ann.* 5.1.4; Suet. *Tib.* 51.2, *Galb.* 5.2; Dio 58.2.3, 59.1.4, cf. Dio 59.2.4. Willrich (1911), 79.1, doubts that Galba was initially left such a large sum; see Perkounig (1995), 169 n. 945.
24. Dio 59.1.4, 2.4.
25. *Apoc.* 9.5; Suet. *Claud.* 11.2; Dio 60.5.2; *AFA* liv, lv; Torelli (1982), 74; Winkes (1985), 68; Bartman (1999), 131; *AE* 1969–70, 1 (43–48); *AFA* lix (50–54). Anniversary of birth: Grant (1950, *Anniversary*), 70. Abydos: *IGR* 1.1161; Snyder (1940), 234. Fishwick (1992) argues that the "Palatine" temple is in fact the Temple to Divus Augustus completed by Caligula.
26. *AFA* lxiii (57), lxvii (58), lxix (58), lxxi (59), lxxv (59), lxxvii (60).
27. Galba: *AFA* xc (69). Otho: *AFA* xcii (69). Vitellius?: *AFA* xciii (69).
28. Trajan: *RIC*[2] 821. Trebula (?): *CIL* 6.29681. Consuls Appius Annius Gallus and Marcus Atilius Bradua: Fishwick (1987–92) II.1, 576, 613.19. Taylor (1914), 240, identifies the colony as Trebula Suffenatium in Latium. The inscription apparently mentions both Augustales and seviri Augustales. On the difference, if any, see Taylor (1914).
29. *IGR* 4.353; Fishwick (1987–92) II.1, 569; Price (1984), 61, 118, 191; Bartman (1999), 140 n. 46. In the Asian calendar Livia's birthday fell on September 21.
30. *P. Oxy.* III.496 (AD 127). Other examples: *BGU* 252, 2/3 (December 24, AD 98): *epi Ioul(ias)* [*Sebastes*]; *CPR* 24.2 (AD 136); [. . .]*i tes Ioulias Sebastes; P. Oxy* III.604 (second century); Wilcken (1909); Grether (1946), 242; Temporini (1978), 69.
31. *P. Oxy.* 17.2105; Antoninus Pius: *RIC*[2] 973, 988, 998, 1003, 1013, 1017, 1024.
32. Fink et al. (1940), 187–90; Grether (1926), 251; Hahn (1992), 82 n. 124; Bartman

(1999), 140 n. 46. Oliver (1949), 36, suggests that Vespasian might have dropped Livia from the list of divi.

33. Sym. *Rel.* III; Prud. *Con. Symm.* 245–70.

APPENDIX 1. SOURCES

1. Suet. *Aug.* 2.3, 62.2, 85, *Claud.* 1.6; Blumenthal (1913); Bardon (1956), 99–100; (1968), 23–25.
2. Suet. *Dom.* 20.
3. Suet. *Tib.* 61.1: *quem de vita sua summatim breviterque composuit.*
4. Pliny *HN* 12.78; Suet. *Claud.* 41.2; Momigliano (1932), 317.
5. Suet. *Claud.* 41.3: *composuit et de vita sua octo volumina magis inepte quam ineleganter.* Nero: Tac. *Ann.* 13.43.4; Durry, in Latte (1956).
6. Pliny *HN* 7.46; in his preface Pliny also lists Agrippina as one of sources for book 7; Tac. *Ann.* 4.53.3.
7. Stahr (1867), 194; Raffay (1884); Fabia (1893), 331; Motzo (1927), 52; Paratore (1952), 41–42; Bardon (1956), 172; Syme (1958), 277; Kornemann (1960), 95; Walker (1960), 139; Balsdon (1962), 121; Michel (1966), 124; Wilkes (1972), 181; Hatzl (1975), 37; Clarke (1975), 50; Griffin (1984), 23, 28; Duret (1986), 3283; Syme (1986), 140; Wood (1988), 424; Eck (1993), 22, 52.
8. Scaliger (1572), 528; Haupt (1875), 315–57. Among recent theories: Herrmann (1951), AD 63, by Petronius; Shrijvers (1988), AD 20; Richmond (1982), 2780, some time before Tiberius' death in AD 37. Schoonhover (1992) argues that it was composed after the death of Claudius in the brief period before Britannicus died, to make the case for a Claudian succession; Kokkinos (1992), 99, suggests Ovid as author.
9. Tac. *Ann.* 1.2–3.
10. Summers (1920), 139, 147; Dihle (1955); Syme (1958), 367; Hellegouarc'h (1964); Sumner (1970). Woodman (1977), 28–56, for a well-argued defence of Velleius. Eck et al. (1996), 227, suggests that Velleius' final encomium about no one having suffered from her comes from the speech at Livia's funeral, which would have taken place shortly before Velleius' death.
11. Maslakov (1984), for a recent survey of Valerius Maximus.
12. Sen. *Ira* 3.23.4.
13. Sen. *Clem.* 1.9; Vidén (1993), 133.
14. Sen. *Cons. Marc.* 6.4.
15. Sen. *Ben.* 6.32, *Brev.* 4.
16. Pliny *HN* 7.45, 149, 33.63, 35.201.
17. Wallace-Hadrill (1983), 12–13.
18. Suet. *Cal.* 23.2; Vidén (1993), 89.
19. Suet. *Aug.* 40.3, *Tib.* 21.2–3, 50.2–3, *Oth.* 1.1.
20. Suet. *Tib.* 21.4–7.
21. Suet. *Tib.* 22.1, 52.3.
22. Goodyear (1972), 190. Sacrosanctitas: Dio 49.38.1. Gaius and Lucius: Dio

55.10a.10. Marcellus: Dio 53.33.4. Death announcement: Dio 56.31.1–2. Figs: Dio 56.30.1–2. Germanicus: Dio 57.18.6.

23. On the relationship between Dio's and Seneca's accounts: Adler (1909), 198; Smith (1951), 183. On Dio's general debt to Seneca: Giancotti (1956), 30.
24. Wuilleumier (1949), 79–80; Bardon (1962), 283; Syme (1958), 535; Riposati (1973). The issues are clearly set out in Wallace (1991).
25. Baldwin (1972), 84.
26. Exceptions are the later Aurelius Victor, *De Caesaribus*, and the anonymous *epitome de Caesaribus*, where the information seems to derive from Tacitus.
27. Tac. *Ann.* 1.53.5, 4.11.4. See Willrich (1911), 3; Harrer (1920), 57–69; Gafforini (1996), 129–34.
28. Piso: Tac. *Ann.* 4.21.1. Prisca: Tac. *Ann.* 4.12.4.
29. Accession: Tac. *Ann.* 1.4.5. Departure from Rome: Tac. *Ann.* 4.57.3. Obituary: Tac. *Ann.* 5.1.3 (see Vidén [1993], 17).
30. Gaius and Lucius: Tac. *Ann.* 1.3.3. Tiberius: Tac. *Ann.* 1.3.3. Julia: Tac. *Ann.* 4.71.4. Plancina: Tac. *Ann.* 2.82.1. Piso: Tac. *Ann.* 2.77.3.
31. Hor. *Epod.* 5.9; Ovid *Met.* 1.147; Quint. *Inst. Or.* 2.10.4–5; Gray-Fow (1988), 741–57; Vidén (1993); Watson (1995); Barrett (2001); Kleiner and Matheson (2000), 131.
32. Tac. *Ann.* 1.3.3, 6.3, 10.5, 33.3. Suet. *Galb.* 4.1 uses *noverca* of Livia Ocellina, the stepmother of Galba, but in a totally neutral context. Galinsky (1996), 78, suggests that Tacitus might be playing on the alternative meaning of *gravis*, pregnant, thus alluding to her scandalous wedding.
33. Tac. *Ann.* 1.14.2. Discord: Tac. *Ann.* 1.72.4. Illness: Tac. *Ann.* 3.64.1; Syme (1958), 308, 483 n. 4.
34. Syme (1958), 273. Marsh (1931), 278, feels that the discrepancies between Tacitus and Dio are so marked that they must have used different sources and that Tacitus had a different authority for the machinations in the palace.
35. Tac. *Ann.* 1.6.3; Suet. *Tib.* 22; Motzo (1927), 38; Martin (1981), 109.
36. Walker (1960), 70; Griffin (1984), 39. Nero's threat: Suet. *Nero* 34.1. Funeral: Tac. *Ann.* 12.69.4. Mother's claim to have made son emperor: Dio 57.12.3; 61.7.1–3.
37. Guilt: *Apoc.* 1–6; *Octavia* 31, 44, 64, 102, 164–65; Pliny *HN* 22.92; Juv. *Sat.* 5.146–48, 6.620–23 (with scholiast); Tac. *Ann.* 12.66–67; Martial 1.20; Suet. *Claud.* 44.2–46; *Nero* 33.1, 39.3; Dio 60.34.2–6, 35; Aur. Vict. *Caes.* 4.13; *Epit. de Caes.* 4.10; Orosius 7.6.18; Zosim. I.6.3. Reservations: Philost. *Apoll.* 5.32: *hos phasi* (so they say); Jos. *Ant.* 20.148: *logos ên para tinōn* (it was reported by some), 151: *kathaper ên logos* (according to report).
38. Illness: *Apoc.* 6–7; Suet. *Nero* 7.2; Dio 60.33.9. Death by natural causes: inter alios, Ferrero (1911), 450; Pack (1943); Bagnani (1946).
39. Tac. *Ann.* 12.65, 66.3; Suet. *Claud.* 43; Dio 60.34.1; Paratore (1952), 57; Barrett (1996), 138–39.
40. *Apoc.* 13; Tac. *Ann.* 12.66.1; Dio 60.34.4.
41. Suet. *Nero* 33.1; Dio 60.34.3, 35.4.
42. *Apoc.* 1, 3; Tac. *Ann.* 12.68.3; Suet. *Claud.* 45; Suet. *Nero* 8.1. See Pack (1943).
43. *Apoc.* 4.

44. Livia's role reflecting Agrippina's: Charlesworth (1923), (1927); Willrich (1927), 76–78; Martin (1955); Goodyear (1972), 125–29; Martin (1981), 109–10; Griffin (1984), 39; but see also Syme, (1958), 483, *Papers A*, 1036.
45. As an example, when a potential rival is eliminated, Tacitus seeks to emphasise that he was blameless. Drusus, the son of Tiberius, whom Sejanus supposedly got rid of with the help of Drusus' wife, Livilla, was *nullius ante flagitii compertum* (Tac. *Ann.* 4.11.1). This phrase clearly echoes Tacitus' description of Agrippa Postumus as *nullius tamen flagitii compertum* (Tac. *Ann.* 1.3.4).
46. Nero: Tac. *Ann.* 13.1.1. Tiberius: Tac. *Ann.* 1.5.6, 6.1; Benario (1975), 136; Mellor (1993), 118; Morford (1990), 1082, 1601. Tac. *Hist.* 2.64.2 notes the murder of Dolabella on the instructions of Vitellius, *magna cum invidia novi principatus.*
47. Two possible external influences on the account of Tiberius' succession have been suggested: first, the story of Tanaquil, who kept the death of Tarquinius Priscus secret until her son Servius Tullius could establish his position: Livy 1.41.5; Aur. Vict. *Caes.* 4.13; Charlesworth (1927); Martin (1981), 109–10; Goodyear (1972), 128; and second, the delay in the announcement of Trajan's death so that Hadrian's adoption could be established: *SHA Hadrian* 4; Dio 69.1.2–3; Syme (1958), 481–83; Syme, *Papers C*, 169; Koestermann (1963–68), 220. For reservations about the suggestions, see Goodyear (1972), 127–28.
48. Charlesworth (1927); Willrich (1927), 74–78; Hohl (1935); Weber (1936), 33–36; Martin (1955), 125 (arguing that the facts derive from Nero's accession but that the linguistic similarities derive from Tiberius' accession); Questa (1959); Koestermann (1961), 334–35; Timpe (1962), 29–33; Goodyear (1972), 126–27; Martin (1981), 253; Mellor (1993), 44; Barnes (1998), 140–41.
49. Pliny *HN* 34.31.
50. Ny Carlsberg Glyptothek, no. 615; Poulsen (1973), 65–71, no. 34; Gross (1962), 87–91, pls. 15–16; Winkes (1965), 114, no. 41; Rose (1997), 188–89, no. 129, pls. 237–40; Bartman (1999), 174–75, no. 64–65, pls. 161–62; Wood (1999), 93, pls. 22–23. Recent contributions: Kleiner (2000).
51. Poulsen (1968), 21, puts the Albani-Bonn first in the sequence; Winkes (1995), 32, 63, considers the Marbury Hall the earliest; Fittschen-Zanker (1983), III.1–2; Wood (1999), 94–95; Bartman (1999), 144–45.
52. Bartman (1999), 76, dates the Fayum type to the decade after Actium, against the prevailing view that would link it with adoption of Tiberius in AD 4.
53. Fittschen-Zanker (1983), III.4a–e; Winkes (1995), 35–38; Wood (1999), 95–96; Bartman (1999), 221, no. 2 (= Winkes, no. 2), 222, no. 7 (= Winkes, no. 40), considers two of the examples assigned to this type as not of Livia.
54. *RIC*² 47; Bartman (1999), 115, suggests that the Salus dupondius might have been inspired by the known sculptures, rather than the other way around.
55. Bartman (1999), 116, 182, no. 81 (Kiel), 156, no. 24 (Paestum); Winkes (1995), 46, 48; Rose (1997), 98, no. 26, pl. 95. Rose and Winkes consider the Paestum example post-Tiberian; Wood (1999), 118.
56. *CIL* 13.1366; Paris, Musée du Louvre, br. 22, inv. no. 3235: 21 cm. total height. Gross (1962), 85–86 (suspicious); Fittschen-Zanker (1983), 3.2.1, no. 1 (genuine); Fishwick (1976), 535, 545, pl. XCIX (genuine); De Kersauson (1986), 94–97, nos.

41–42 (genuine); Winkes (1995), 37–38, 146, no. 73 (genuine); Bartman (1999), 194–95, nos. 114, 189 (highly suspicious, perhaps eighteenth-century); Wood (1999), 105–6, nos. 32–33 (genuine).

57. Suet. *Cal.* 15.2, 23.2; Suet. *Galb.* 5.2; Suet. *Oth.* 1.1.
58. Suet. *Aug.* 7.1. Déjardins (1968), 3, 215–17, suggests that they are household spirits *(Lares)* meant to be kept in a domestic *lararium.* But Fishwick (1987–92), n. 363, notes that the inscriptions are in the dative, not the usual nominative (Latin) or accusative (Greek), and argues that the statues were dedicated in honour of Augustus and Livia. See also De Kersauson (1986), 94–97.
59. Bartman (1999), 12; Wood (1999), 91.
60. Paris, Bibliothèque de France, Cabinet des Médailles 264; Jucker (1977); Megow (1987), 202–7, no. A85; Mikocki (1995), 21, 157–58, no. 8; Winkes (1995), 49, 145, no. 71; Wood (1999), 137–38, 308–10.
61. Vienna, Kunsthistorisches Museum XII 1083; Winkes (1995), 188 no. 111; Bartman (1999), 12, 193, no. 109, pl. 8.
62. Vienna, Kunsthistorisches Museum IXA 95; Winkes (1995), 189, no. 113; Bartman (1999), 193, no. 110, pl. 79; Wood (1999), 119–20, pl. 41.
63. Winkes (1995), 103, no. 28; Mikocki (1995), 157, no. 40; Megow (1987), 179–80, no. A49; Wood (1999), 113, pl. 36.
64. Matheson (1980), 59–60; Stern (1992).
65. Rome: Rostovtsev (1900) III, p. 35, fig. 8; (*Bleitesserae,* 1905), 26, pl. 1; Winkes (1995), 164, no. 87. Berlin: Mikocki (1995), 152, no. 8; Grant (*Principate,* 1950), 111 (legend: *A Vitellius Cur*[*avit*] on reverse). Winkes (1995), 192, no. 120, notes another uninscribed (bronze) tessera in private ownership, possibly depicting Livia.
66. Rostovtsev ("Interpretation," 1905), 111, reads the legend LIV as *L(oco) IV,* on a bone counter from El Djem depicting an amphitheatre.
67. Naples Museo Nazionale, inv. no. 77129. *IG* 14.2414.40 (= *CIL* 10.8069.9); Rostovtsev (1904), pls. 3–4; Rosenbaum (1980), 32–33, nos. 9, 9.2; Winkes (1995), 140, no. 63.
68. *SEG* 38 (1988), 914; Warren (1987–88), 88–89, pls. 12, 13.
69. Alexandria, Graeco-Roman Museum, inv. no. 23869; Grimm (1973); Rosenbaum (1980), 31–32, no. 8, pl. 9.1. Winkes (1995), 81, no. 1, considers it Livian.
70. Boschung (1989), 121, no. 56. The subject was previously identified as Agrippina the Elder by Dardaigne (1981).
71. Héron de Villefosee (1899), 128; Kuttner (1995), 31. The cups are now lost.
72. Lehner (1912), 430–35, pl. 8. The vase is signed by the potter "Chrysippus."
73. Bonn, Rheinisches Landesmuseum 4320; Curtius (1935), 264; Kuttner (1995), 173–74; Winkes (1995), 97, no. 20; Rose (1997), pl. 10; Bartman (1999), 82–83, pl. 67; Wood (1999), 106–7. Identification as Livia is now generally accepted. Dressel (1894) hovers between Livia and Julia (with Gaius and Lucius); Kuttner maintains that Livia displays aspects of Venus Genetrix.
74. Ephesus: *SEG* 4.515. Gytheum: EJ 102.
75. New York, Metropolitan Museum, 20.192.1; Anderson (1987), 127–35; Kleiner and Matheson (1996), 35–36, pl. 6; Winkes (1995), 198, no. 134 (Livia), 221, no. 269 (Julia); Wood (1999), 107; Bartman (1999), 12.

BIBLIOGRAPHY

Abbott, F. F., and A. C. Johnson. (1926). *Municipal Administration in the Roman Empire*. New York.

Ackroyd, B. "Porticus Iulia or Porticus Liviae: The Reading of Dio 56.27.5." *Athenaeum* 80 (1992): 196–99.

Adler, M. "Die Veschwörung des Cn. Cornelius Cinna bei Seneca und Cassius Dio." *ZÖG* 60 (1909): 193–208.

Alföldi, A. (1965). *Early Rome and the Latins*. Ann Arbor.

——. (1970). *Die monarchische Repräsentation im römischen Kaiserreiche*. Darmstadt.

Alföldi-Rosenbaum, E. "Ruler Portraits on Roman Game Counters from Alexandria." In *Eikones. Studien zum griechischen und römischen Bildnis Hans Jucker zum Sechzigsten Geburtstag Gewidmet* (Bern, 1980: *Antike Kunst Beiheft* 12): 29–39.

Alföldy, G. (1973). *Flamines Provinciae Hispaniae Citerioris*. Madrid.

Allen, W. "The Political Atmosphere of the Reign of Tiberius." *TAPA* 72 (1941): 1–25.

——. "The Death of Agrippa Postumus." *TAPA* 78 (1947): 131–39.

——. "Imperial Table Manners in Tacitus' *Annals*." *Latomus* 21 (1962): 374–76.

Allison, J. E., and J. D. Cloud. "The Lex Julia Maiestatis." *Latomus* 21 (1962): 711–31.

Allmer, A. *Revue épigraphique du midi de la France* 2 (1884–89): nos. 513, 75–77, 138–39, 231–33.

Anderson, M. L. "The Portrait Medallions of the Imperial Villa at Boscotrecase." *AJA* 91 (1987): 127–35.

Andreae, B. "Wandmalerei augusteicher Zeit." In M. Hofter (ed.), *Kaiser Augustus und die verlorene Republik* (Mainz am Rhein, 1988): 283–86.

Antike Denkmäler (1891). Kaiserlich Deutsches Archäologisches Institut, Rome, vol. 1.

Archer, L. J., S. Fischler, and M. Wyke (eds.). (1994). *Women in Ancient Societies*. Rome.

Arthur, M. B. " 'Liberated' Women: The Classical Era." In R. Bridenthal and C. Koonz (eds.), *Becoming Visible: Women in European History* (Boston, 1977): 60–89.
Aschbach, J. (1864). *Livia. Gemahlin des Kaisers Augustus. Eine historisch-archäologische Abhandlung*. Vienna.
Ashby, T. "The Classical Topography of the Roman Campagna." *PBSR* 4 (1907): 1–160.
Ashby, T., and R. A. L. Fell. "The Via Flaminia." *JRS* 11 (1921): 125–90.
Astin, A. E. (1978). *Cato the Censor*. Oxford.
Aurigemma, S. "Sculture del Foro Vecchio di Leptis Magna raffiguranti la Dea Roma e principi della casa dei Giulio-Claudi." *AfrIt* 8 (1940): 1–92.
Baar, M. (1990). *Das Bild des Kaisers Tiberius bei Tacitus, Sueton und Cassius Dio*. Stuttgart.
Babcock, C. "The Early Career of Fulvia." *AJP* 86 (1965): 1–32.
Babelon, E. (1897). *Catalogue des Camées Antiques et Modernes de la Bibliothèque Nationale*. Paris.
Badian, E. "Notes on Some Documents from Aphrodisias Concerning Octavian." *GRBS* 25 (1984): 157–70.
Baldwin, B. "Women in Tacitus." *Prudentia* 4 (1972): 83–101.
———. (1983). *Suetonius*. Amsterdam.
Balsdon, J. P. V. D. (1934). *The Emperor Gaius* (Oxford).
———. (1962). *Roman Women: Their History and Habits* (London).
Bang, M. "Das gewöhnliche Älter der Mädchen bei der Verlobung und Verheiratung." In L. Friedländer (ed.), *Darstellungen aus der Sittensgeschichte Roms* 4 (1922): 133–41.
Bardon, H. (1956). *La Littérature latine inconnue*. Vol. 2, *L'Époque impériale*. Paris.
———. "Points de vue sur Tacite." *RCCM* 4 (1962): 282–93.
———. (1986). *Les Empereurs et les lettres latines d'Augustus à Hadrien*. Paris, 2d ed.
Barini, C. C. "La tradizione superstite e alcuni giudizi dei moderni su Livia." *RAL* (1922): 25.
Barnes, T. "Julia's Child." *Phoenix* 35 (1981): 362–63.
———. "Tacitus and the *Senatus Consultum de Cn. Pisone Patre*." *Phoenix* 52 (1998): 125–48.
Barrett, A. A. "Gaius' Policy in the Bosporus." *TAPA* 107 (1977): 1–9.
———. "Polemo II of Pontus and M. Antonius Polemo." *Historia* 27 (1978): 437–48.
———. (1990). *Caligula: The Corruption of Power*. London and New Haven.
———. "Claudius' British Victory Arch in Rome." *Britannia* 22 (1991): 1–19.
———. (1996). *Agrippina: Sex, Power, and Politics in the Early Empire*. New Haven.
———. "The Year of Livia's Birth." *Classical Quarterly* 49 (1999): 630–32.
———. "Tacitus, Livia, and the Evil Stepmother." *RhM* 144 (2001), 171–75.
Bartels, H. (1963). *Studien zum Frauenporträt der augusteischen Zeit, Fulvia, Octavia, Livia, Julia*. Munich.
Bartman, E. (1999). *Portraits of Livia: Imaging the Imperial Woman in Augustan Rome*. Cambridge.
Barton, T. (1994). *Power and Knowledge: Astrology, Physiognomics, and Medicine Under the Roman Empire*. Ann Arbor.
Bastet, F. L. "Die grosse Kamee in Den Haag." *BVAB* 43 (1968): 2–22.

Bauman, R. A. (1967). *The Crimen Maiestatis in the Roman Republic and Augustan Principate*. Johannesburg.
——. (1974). *Impietas in Principem*. Munich.
——. "Tribunician Sacrosanctity in 44, 36, and 35 BC." *RhM* 124 (1981): 166–83.
——. (1992). *Women and Politics in Ancient Rome*. London.
Bayardi, O. (1755). *Catalogo degli antichi monumenti di Ercolano*. Naples.
Beard, M. "The Sexual Status of Vestal Virgins." *JRS* 70 (1980): 12–27.
——. "Re-reading (Vestal) Virginity." In R. Hawley (ed.), *Women in Antiquity: New Assessments* (London, 1995): 166–77.
Becatti, G. "Opera d'arte greca nella Roma di Tiberio." *Arch. Class.* 25–26 (1973–74): 18–53.
Becker, K. (1950). "Studien zur Opposition gegen den römischen Prinzipat." Diss. Tübingen.
Benario, H. W. "*Imperium* and *Capaces Imperii* in Tacitus." *AJP* 93 (1972): 14–26.
——. (1975). *An Introduction to Tacitus*. Athens, Georgia.
Bengston, H. (1967). *Grundriss der römischen Geschichte mit Quellenkunde*. Vol. 1. Munich.
Béranger, J. "L'Hérédité du Principat: Note sur la transmission du pouvoir impérial aux deux premiers siècles." *REL* 17 (1939): 171–87.
——. "Remarques sur la Concordia dans la propagande monétaire impériale et la nature du principat." *Festschrift Altheim* (1969): 470–91.
Bergener, A. (1965). "Die führende Senatorenschicht im frühen Prinzipat (14–68 n. Chr.)." Diss. Bonn.
Bernhardt, R. "Die Immunitas der Freistädte." *Historia* 29 (1980): 190–207.
Bernouilli, J. (1886). *Römische Ikonographie. Die Bilnisse der römischen Kaiser und ihrer Angehörigen*. Vol. 2, *Das jülisch-claudische Kaiserhaus*. Berlin.
Besnier, R. (1847–48). *Les Affranchis impériaux à Rome, de 41 à 54 P.C.* Paris.
Best, E. E. "Cicero, Livy, and Educated Roman Women." *CJ* 65 (1970): 199–204.
Bianchi-Bandinelli, R., et al. (1966). *The Buried City: Excavations at Leptis Magna* (trans. B. Ridgway). London.
Birch, R. A. "The Correspondence of Augustus: Some Notes on Suetonius, *Tiberius* 21.4–7." *CQ* 31 (1981): 155–61.
——. "The Settlement of 26 June AD 4 and Its Aftermath." *CQ* 31 (1981): 443–56.
Birt, Th. (1932). *Frauen der Antike*. Leipzig.
Blanck, H. "Porträt-Gemälde als Ehrendenkmäler." *BJ* 168 (1968): 1–12.
Blaze de Bury, H. "L'Impératrice Livie et la fille d'Auguste." *Revue des deux mondes* 44 (1874): 591–637.
Bleicken, J. (1998). *Augustus. Eine Biographie*. Berlin.
Bloomer, W. M. (1992). *Valerius Maximus and the Rhetoric of the New Nobility*. Chapel Hill.
Blumenthal, F. "Die Autobiographie des Augustus." *WS* 35 (1913): 113–30, 267–88; 36 (1914): 84–103.
Boatwright, M. T. "The Imperial Women of the Early Second Century A.C." *AJP* 112 (1991): 513–40.

Boëthius, A., and J. B. Ward-Perkins. (1970). *Etruscan and Roman Architecture*. London.
Bömer, F. (1958). *P. Ovidius Naso. Die Fasten*. Heidelberg.
Bonamente, G. (1987). *Germanico: La persona, la personalità, il personaggio. Atti del Convegno, Macerata-Perugia, 9–11 maggio 1986*. Facoltà di Lettere e Filosofia Università Macerata, 39, Rome.
Boschung, D. "Die Bildnistypen des Iulisch-claudischen Kaiserfamilie." *JRA* 6 (1993): 39–79.
Boulvert, G. (1970). *Les Esclaves et les affranchis impériaux sous le Haut-Empire romain: Rôle politique et administratif*. Aix en Provence, 1964.
———. (1974). *Domestique et fonctionnaire sous le Haut-Empire romain: La condition de l'affranchi et de l'esclave du prince*. Paris.
Bouvrie, S. D. "Augustus' Legislation on Morals: Which Morals and What Aims." *SO* 59 (1984): 93–113.
Bowersock, G. (1965). *Augustus and the Greek World*. Oxford.
———. "Augustus and the East: The Problem of the Succession." In Millar and Segal (1984): 169–88.
———. Review of Reynolds (1982). *Gnomon* 56 (1984): 48–53.
Braccesi, L. "Pesaro romana, moribunda e felix." *SO* 2–3 (1982–83): 77–98.
Bragantini, I., and M. de Vos (1982). *Museo Nazionale Romano. Le pitture II.1. Le decorazioni della villa romana dell Farnesina*. Rome.
Brisson, J.-P. "Achaicus ignis: Horace, Odes I, 15 et IV.6." *REL* 71 (1993): 161–78.
Broughton, T. R. S. "Roman Landholding in Asia Minor." *TAPA* 65 (1934): 207–39.
Brown, P. (1981). *The Cult of the Saints*. Chicago.
Bruhns, H. (1978). *Caesar und die römische Oberschicht in den Jahren 49–44 v. Chr.* Göttingen.
Brunt, P. "The Lex Valeria Cornelia." *JRS* 51 (1961): 71–83.
———. "Lex de Imperio Vespasiani." *JRS* 67 (1977): 95–116.
———. (1988). *The Fall of the Roman Republic and Related Essays*. Oxford.
Burdeau, F. "L'Empereur d'après les Panegyriques Latins." In F. Burdeau, N. Charbonnel, and M. Humbert (eds.), *Aspects de l'empire Romaine* (Paris, 1964).
Calci, C., and Messineo, G. (1984). *La Villa di Livia a Prima Porta*. Rome: *Lavori e studi di archaeologia* 2.
Calhoon, C. G. (1994). "Livia the Poisoner: Genesis of an Historical Myth." Diss. California, Irvine.
Cameron A., and A. Kuhrt (eds.). (1983). *Images of Women in Antiquity*. London.
Carandini, A. (1988). *Schiavi in Italia*. Rome.
Carcopino, J. "Le Marriage d'Octave et de Livie et la naissance de Drusus." *Rev. Hist.* 161 (1929): 225–36.
———. (1958). *Passion et politique chez les Césars*. Paris.
Carettoni, G., et al. (1960). *La Pianta marmorea di Roma antica: Forma urbis Romae*. Rome.
———. "The House of Augustus." *ILN* 255, no. 6790 (1969): 24–25.
———. "La X Regione: Palatium." In *L'Urbs. Espace Urbain et Histoire* (Rome, 1987): 771–79.

Carteledge, P., and A. Spawforth (1989). *Hellenistic and Roman Sparta*. London.

Carter, J. M. (1982). *Suetonius: Divus Augustus*. Bristol.

Castagnoli, F. "Note sulla topographia del Palatino e del Foro Romano." *Arch. Class.* 16 (1964): 173–99.

Champeaux, J. (1982). *Fortuna. Recherches sur le culte de la Fortuna à Rome et dans le monde romain*. Rome.

Champlin, E. "The Testament of Augustus." *RM* 132 (1989): 154–65.

——. (1991). *Final Judgments: Duty and Emotion in Roman Wills, 200 B.C.–A.D. 250*. Berkeley.

Chantraine, H. (1967). *Freigelassene und Sklaven im Dienst der römischen Kaiser. Studien zu ihrer Nomenklatur*. Wiesbaden.

——. "Zu AE 1979, 33." *ZPE* 49 (1982): 132.

Charlesworth, M. P. "The Banishment of the Elder Agrippina." *CP* 17 (1922): 260–61.

——. "Tiberius and the Death of Augustus." *AJP* 44 (1923): 145–57.

——. "Livia and Tanaquil." *CR* 41 (1927): 55–57.

——. "Some Fragments of the Propaganda of Mark Antony." *CQ* 27 (1933): 172–77.

——. "The Refusal of Divine Honours, an Augustan Formula." *PBSR* 15 (1939): 1–10.

Chastagnol, A. "Les Femmes dans l'ordre senatorial: Titulature et rang social à Rome." *RH* 103 (1979): 3–28.

Christ, K. "Tacitus und der Principat." *Historia* 27 (1978): 449–87.

Christol, M., and C. Goudineau, "Nîmes et les Volques Arécomiques au 1er siècle avant J.-C." *Gallia* 45 (1987–88): 87–103.

Ciaceri, E. (1944). *Tiberio, succesore di Augusto*. Rome, 2d ed.

Cichorius, C. (1922). *Römische Studien*. Leipzig.

Claridge, A. (1998). *Rome*. Oxford.

Clark, G. "Roman Women." In I. McAuslan and P. Walcot (eds.), *Women in Antiquity* (Oxford, 1996): 36–55.

Clauss, M. (1983). *Sparta, Eine Einführung in seine Geschichte und Zivilisation*. Munich.

Clay, C. L. "Die Münzprägung des Kaisars Nero in Rom und Lugdunum. Teil 1: Die Edelmetallprägung der Jahre 54 bis 64 n. Chr." *NZ* 96 (1982): 7–52.

Clinton, K. "The Eleusinian Mysteries: Roman Inititates and Benefactors, Second Century B.C. to A.D. 267." *ANRW* 18.2 (1989): 1499–1539.

Cluett, R. G. "Roman Women and Triumviral Politics." *CV* 42 (1998): 67–84.

Coarelli, F. (1974). *Guida Archeologica di Roma*. Rome.

——. (1981). *Dintorni di Roma*. Rome.

——. (1983). *Il Foro Romano*. Rome.

——. (1984). *Lazio*. Rome.

——. (1985). *Roma*. Rome, 3d ed.

Colakis, M. "Ovid as praeceptor amoris in Epistulae ex Ponto 3.1." *CJ* 82 (1987): 210–15.

Conlin, D. A. "The Reconstruction of Antonia Minor on the Ara Pacis." *JRA* 5 (1992): 209–17.

Corbett, J. H. "The Succession Policy of Augustus." *Latomus* 33 (1974): 87–97.

Corbett, P. E. (1930). *The Roman Law of Marriage*. Oxford.

Cordingley, R. A., and I. A. Richmond. "The Mausoleum of Augustus." *PBSR* 10 (1927): 23–35.

Corsaro, F. "Sulla relegatio di Ovidio." *Orpheus* 15 (1968): 5–49.

Cousin, J. "Rhétorique et psychologie chez Tacite." *REL* 29 (1951): 228–47.

Crawford, D. J. "Imperial Estates." In Finley (1976): 35–70.

Crawford, M. H. (1974). *Roman Republican Coinage*. Cambridge.

—— (ed.). (1996). *Roman Statutes*. London.

Crook, J. (1955). *Concilium Principis*. Cambridge.

Curtius, L. "Ikonographische Beiträge zum Porträt der römischen Republik und der Julisch-Claudischen Familie." *MDAI(R)* 50 (1935): 260–320.

Damon C., and S. Takács. *The Senatus Consultum de Cn. Pisone Patre*. Special issue, *AJP* 120 (1999).

Dardaigne, S. "Portraits impériaux sur une lampe de Belo." *Mélanges de la casa de Velazquez* 17 (1981): 517–19.

D'Arms, J. H. (1970). *Romans on the Bay of Naples*. Cambridge, Mass.

——. (1981). *Commerce and Social Standing in Ancient Rome*. Cambridge, Mass.

Davies, O. (1935). *Roman Mines in Europe*. Oxford.

Davies, P. J. E. (2000). *Death and the Emperor: Roman Imperial Funerary Monuments, from Augustus to Marcus Aurelius*. Cambridge.

Degrassi, A. "Esistette sul Palatino un Tempio di Vesta?" *MDAI(R)* 62 (1955): 144–54.

——. (1963). *Inscriptiones Italiae*. Rome: vol. 13.2.

Degrassi, N. "La Dimora di Augusto sul Palatino e la Base di Sorrento." *RPAA* 39 (1966–67): 77–126.

De Kersauson, K. (1986). *Catalogue des portraits romains*. Vol. 1, *Portraits de la République et d'époque Julio-Claudienne*. Paris.

Delia, D. "Fulvia Reconsidered." In S. Pomeroy (ed.), *Women's History and Ancient History* (Chapel Hill, 1991): 197–217.

Demougin, S. (1988). *L'Ordre Equestre sous les Julio-Claudiens*. Rome: Collection de l'École Français de Rome No. 108.

D'Ercé, F. "La Mort de Germanicus et les poisons de Caligula." *Janus* 56 (1969): 123–48.

De Serviez, J. R. (1752). *The Roman Empresses*. London.

Desjardins, E. E. A. (1885). *Géographie historique et administrative de la Gaule romaine*. Paris.

Dessau, H. (1924–26). *Geschichte der römischen Kaiserzeit*. Vol. 2.1. Berlin.

Dettenhofer, M. H. (ed.) (1994). *Reine Männersache. Frauen in Männerdomänen der antiken Welt*. Cologne.

Detweiler, R. "Historical Perspectives on the Death of Agrippa Postumus." *CJ* 65 (1970): 289–95.

Devillers, O. (1994). *L'Art de la persuasion dans les Annales de Tacite*. Collection *Latomus* 223.

Dixon, S. "A Family Business: Women's Role in Patronage and Politics at Rome, 80–44 B.C." *C&M* 34 (1981–82): 91–112.

——. (1988). *The Roman Mother*. London.

Dobbins, J. "Chronology, Decoration, and Urban Design at Pompeii." *AJA* 98 (1994): 648–49.

Domaszewski, A. von (1885). *Die Fahnen im römischen Heere*. Vienna.

——. (1909). *Geschichte der römischen Kaiser*. Vol. 2. Leipzig, 2d ed.

——. (1967). *Die Rangordnung des römischen Heeres*. Cologne-Graz, 2d ed.

Domenicucci, P. "La caratterizazione astrale delle apoteosi di Romolo ed Ersilìa nelle Metamorfosi di Ovidio." In I. Gallo and L. Nicastri (eds.), *Cultura, poesia, ideologia nell'opera di Ovido* (Salerno, 1991): 221–28.

Dorey, T. A. "Adultery and Propaganda in the Early Roman Empire." *University of Birmingham Historical Journal* 8 (1962): 1–6.

Downey, G. (1961). *A History of Antioch in Syria from Seleucus to the Arab Conquest*. Princeton.

Dressel, H. "Beschlag eine römischen Schwertscheide." *BJ* 95 (1894): 61–66.

Drexler, H. "Maiestas." *Aevum* 30 (1956): 195–212.

Drumann, W. (1964). *Geschichte Roms* (rev. P. Groebe). Rpt. Hildesheim.

Dudley, D. R. (1968). *The World of Tacitus*. London.

Duff, A. M. (1928). *Freedmen in the Early Roman Empire*. Oxford.

Duret, L. "Dans l'ombre des plus grands. II. Poètes et prosateurs mal connus de la latinité d'argent." *ANRW* 2.32.5 (1986): 3152–346.

Durry, M. "Le Mariage des filles impubères à Rome." *REL* 47 (1970): 17–24.

Duruy, V. (1885). *Geschichte des römischen Kaiserreichs*. Vol. 1. Leipzig.

Eck, W. "Senatorial Self-Presentation: Developments in the Augustan Period." In Millar and Segal (1984): 129–67.

——. (1993). *Agrippina, die Stadtgründerin Köhns:* Eine Frau in der frühkaiserzeitlichen Politik. Cologne.

Eck, W., A. Caballos, and F. Fernandez. (1996). *Das Senatus Consulto de Cn. Pisone Patre*. Munich.

Edwards, C. (1993). *The Politics of Immorality in Ancient Rome*. Cambridge.

Ehlers, W. "Triumphus." *RE* 7A (1939): 493–511.

Ehrenberg, V. (1946). *Aspects of the Ancient World: Essays and Reviews*. Oxford.

Eitrem, S. "Zur Apotheose." *SO* 10 (1932): 31–56.

Espérandieu, E. (1929). *Inscriptions Latines de Gaule*. Paris.

Esser, A. (1958). *Cäsar und die julisch-claudischen Kaiser im biologisch-ärztlichen Blickfeld*. Leiden.

Evans, E. "Roman Descriptions of Personal Appearances in History and Biography." *HSCP* 46 (1935): 43–84.

——. (1969). *Physiognomics in the Ancient World* Philadelphia.

Evans, J. K. (1991). *War, Women, and Children in Ancient Rome*. London.

Fabia, Ph. (1893). *Les Sources de Tacite dans les Histoires et les Annales*. Paris.

Fabbrini, L. "Livia Drusilla." *Enciclopedia dell'Arte Antica* (1961): 4.663–67.

Fau, G. (1978). *L'Empancipation féminine dans la Rome antique*. Paris.

Favro, D. (1996). *The Urban Image of Augustan Rome*. Cambridge.

Felletti Maj, B. M. (1953). *Museo Nazionale Romano*. Vol. 1, *Rittratti*. Rome.

Ferrero, G. (1911). *The Women of the Caesars*. London.

Ferrill, A. "Augustus and His Daughter: A Modern Myth." In *Studies in Latin Literature and Roman History* 2. Collection *Latomus* 168 (1980): 332–66.

Fink, R. O., A. S. Hoey, and W. F. Snyder, "The *Feriale Duranum*." *YClS* 7 (1940): 11–222.

Finley, M. (ed.). (1976). *Studies in Roman Property*. Cambridge.

Fischler, S. (1989). "The Public Position of Women in the Imperial Household in the Julio-Claudian Period." Diss. Oxford.

——. "Social Stereotypes and Historical Analysis: The Case of the Imperial Women at Rome." In Archer, Fischler, and Wyke (1994): 115–33.

Fishwick, D. "Prudentius and the Cult of Divus Augustus." *Historia* 39 (1990): 475–86.

——. "Ovid and Divus Augustus." *CP* 86 (1991): 36–41.

——. (1987–92). *The Imperial Cult in the Roman West: Studies in the Ruler Cult of the Western Provinces of the Roman Empire*. Vols. 1–2. Leiden.

——. "A Temple of Vesta on the Palatine?" *Mélanges Tadeusz Kotula* (Breslau, 1993): 51–57.

Fittschen, K. "Zur Panzerstatue in Cherchel." *JDAI* 91 (1976): 175–210.

Fittschen, K., and P. Zanker. (1983). *Katalog der römischen Porträts in den Capitolinischen Museen und den anderen kommunalen Sammlungen der Stadt Rom*. Mainz.

Fitzler, K., and O. Seeck. "Iulius Augustus." *RE* 10 (1918): 275–381.

Flaig, Egon. "Loyalität ist keine Gefälligkeit. Zum Majestätsprozess gegen C. Silius 24 n Chr." *Klio* 75 (1993): 289–98.

Flory, M. "*Sic Exempla Parantur:* Livia's Shrine to Concordia and the Porticus Liviae." *Historia* 33 (1984): 309–30.

——. "*Abducta Neroni Uxor:* The Historiographical Tradition on the Marriage of Octavian and Livia." *TAPA* 118 (1988): 343–59.

——. "Octavian and the Omen of the *gallina alba*." *CJ* 84 (1988–89): 343–56.

——. "Livia and the History of Public Honorific Statues for Women in Rome." *TAPA* 123 (1993): 287–308.

——. "Dynastic Ideology, the *Domus Augusta*, and Imperial Women: A Lost Statuary Group in the Circus Flaminius." *TAPA* 126 (1996): 287–306.

——. "The Meaning of *Augusta* in the Julio-Claudian Period." *AJAH* (1998): 113–38.

Flower, H. I. (1996). *Ancestor Masks and Aristocratic Power in Roman Culture*. Oxford.

Foley, H. P. (1981). *Reflections of Women in Antiquity*. New York.

Forbis, E. P. "Women's Public Image in Italian Honorary Inscriptions." *AJP* 111 (1990): 493–512.

Förschner, G. (1987). *Die Münzen der Römischen Kaiser in Alexandrien*. Frankfurt.

Forsyth, P. Y. "A Treason Case of A.D. 37." *Phoenix* 23 (1969): 204–7.

Fracarro, P. "C. Herrenius Capito di Teate: Procurator di Livia, di Tiberio e di Gaio." *Athenaeum* 18 (1940): 136–44.

Frank, R. I. "Augustus' Legislation on Marriage and Children." *CSCA* 8 (1975): 41–52.

Frank, T. "Livy's Deference to Livia." *AJP* (1998): 223–24.

Freyburger, G. "La Supplication d'action de grâces sous le Haut-Empire." *ANRW* 16.2 (1978): 1418–39.

Freyer-Schauenburg, B. "Die Kieler Livia." *BJ* 182 (1982): 209–24.

Friedrich, W.-H. "Eine Denkform bie Tacitus." In *Festschrift E. Kapp* (Hamburg, 1958): 135–44.

Fuchs, M. (1989). *Il teatro e il ciclo statuario giulio-claudio*. Rome.

Furneaux, H. (1896). *The Annals of Tacitus*. Oxford, 2d ed.

Gabba, E. (ed.) (1970). *Appian: Bellorum Civilium Liber V*. Florence.

Gabriel, M. M. (1955). *Livia's Garden Room at Prima Porta*. New York.

Gafforini, C. "Livia Drusilla tra storia e letteratura." *RIL* 130 (1996): 121–44.

Gagé, J. "Divus Augustus. L'Idée dynastique chez les empereurs julio-claudiens." *RA* 55 (1934): 11–341.

Galinsky, K. "Augustus' Legislation on Morals and Marriage." *Philologus* 125 (1981): 126–44.

———. (1996). *Augustan Culture: An Interpretative Introduction*. Princeton.

Galsterer, H. "The Administration of Justice." *Cambridge Ancient History* (Cambridge, 1996, 2d ed.): 397–413.

Gardner, J. F. (1986). *Women in Roman Law and Society*. London.

———. "Julia's Freedman: Questions of Law and Status." *BICS* 35 (1988): 94–100.

———. (1998). *Family and Familia in Roman Law and Life*. Oxford.

Gardner, P. "A New Portrait of Livia." *JRS* 12 (1922): 32–34.

Gardthausen, V. (1891). *Augustus und seine Zeit*. Leipzig, rpt. Darmstadt, 1964.

———. "Agrippa Julius Caesar." *RE* 10 (1918): 183–85.

Garlick, B., S. Dixon, and P. Allen (eds.). (1992). *Stereotypes of Women in Power: Historical Perspectives and Revisionist Views*. New York.

Garnsey, P. (1970). *Social Status and Legal Privilege in the Roman Empire*. Oxford.

———. "Urban Property Development." In Finley (1976): 123–36.

Garnsey, P., and R. Saller (1987). *The Roman Empire: Economy, Society, and Culture*. London.

Garzetti, A. (1974). *From Tiberius to the Antonines* (trans. J. R. Foster). London.

Gatti, G. "Nuove osservazioni sul Mausoleo di Augusto." *L'Urbe* 8.16 (1938): 1–17.

Ghedini, F. "Il dolore per la morte di Druso maggiore nel vaso d'onice di Saint Maurice d'Agaune." *RdA* 11 (1987): 68–74.

Giancotti, F. "La consolazione di Seneca a Polibio in Cassio Dione, LXI, 10.2." *RFIC* 34 (1956): 30–44.

Giua, M. A. "Clemenza del sovrano e monarchia illuminata in Cassio Dione, 55.14–22." *Athenaeum* 59 (1981): 317–37.

González, J. "Tabula Siarensis, Fortunales Siarenses, et Municipium Civium Romanorum." *ZPE* 55 (1984): 55–100.

González, J., and J. Arce (eds.). (1988). *Estudios sobre la Tabula Siarensis*. Madrid.

Goodyear, F. R. D. (1972). *The Annals of Tacitus, Volume I*. Cambridge.

———. (1981). *The Annals of Tacitus, Volume II*. Cambridge.

Gough, M. "Augusta Ciliciae." *Anatolian Studies* 6 (1956): 168–70.

Gow, A. S. F., and D. L. Page. (1968). *The Greek Anthology II: The Garland of Philip*. Cambridge.

Grant, M. (1946). *From Imperium to Auctoritas: A Historical Study of Aes Coinage in the Roman Empire, 49 B.C.–A.D. 14*. Cambridge.

———. (1950). *Aspects of the Principate of Tiberius: Historical Comments on the Colonial Coinage Issued Outside Spain*. New York.

———. (1950). *Roman Anniversary Issues*. Cambridge.

———. "The Pattern of Official Coinage in the Early Principate." In *Essays in Roman Coinage Presented to H. Mattingly* (Oxford, 1956): 96–112.

———. (1958). *Roman History from Coins*. Cambridge.

Gratwick, A. S. "Free or Not So Free? Wives and Daughters in the Late Roman Republic." In E. M. Craik (ed.), *Marriage and Property* (Aberdeen, 1984): 30–53.

Gray-Fow, M. J. G. "The Wicked Stepmother in Roman History and Literature: An Evaluation." *Latomus* 47 (1988): 741–57.

Grether, G. "Livia and the Roman Imperial Cult." *AJP* (1946): 222–52.

Griffin, M. "The Senate's Story." *JRS* 87 (1997): 249–63.

Grimal, P. (1943). *Les Jardins Romains*. Paris.

Grimm, G. "Zum Bildnis der Iulia Augusti." *MDAI(R)* 80 (1973): 279–82.

Grimm, J. "Über Marcellus Burdigalensis." *Kleinere Schriften* (Berlin, 1865): 121–25.

Groag, E. "Studien zur Kaisergeschichte III. Der Sturtz der Iulia." *WS* 41 (1919): 74–88.

Gross, H. W. (1962). *Iulia Augusta*. Göttingen.

Gruen, E. (1974). *The Last Generation of the Roman Republic*. Berkeley.

Guarducci, M. "Vesta sul Palatino." *MDAI(R)* 71 (1964): 158–69.

———. "Enea e Vesta." *MDAI(R)* 78 (1971): 73–118.

Guarino, A. "Il Coup de foudre di Ottaviano." *Labeo* 27 (1981): 335–37.

Haase, F. "Tacitea." *Phililogus* 3 (1848): 152–59.

Hahn, U. (1994). *Die Frauen des Römischen Kaiserhauses und ihre Ehrungen im Griechischen Osten anhand Epigraphischer und Numismatischer Zeugnisse von Livia bis Sabina*. Saarbrücken.

Halfmann, D. (1986). *Itinera Principum*. Stuttgart.

Hall, J. "Livy's Tanaquil and the Image of Assertive Etruscan Women in Latin Historical Literature of the Early Empire." *Augustan Age* IV (1985): 31–38.

Hall, M. D. "Eine reine Männerwelt? Frauen um das römische Heer." In Dettenhofer (1994): 207–8.

Hallett, J. P. "Perusinae Glandes and the Changing Image of Augustus." *AJAH* 2 (1977): 151–71.

———. (1984). *Fathers and Daughters in Roman Society*. Princeton.

———. "Women as Same and Other in Classical Roman Elite." *Helios* 16 (1989): 59–78.

Hammond, M. (1933). *The Augustan Principate*. Cambridge, Mass.

———. "Octavius (Octavia)." *RE* 17.2 (1937): 1859–68.

Hänlein-Schäfer, H. (1985). *Veneratio Augusti. Eine Studie zu den Tempeln des ersten römischen Kaisers*. Rome.

Hanslik, R. "Proculeius." *RE* 23.1 (1957): 72–74.

———. "Urgulania." *RE* Suppl. 9 (1962): 1868–69.

Hanson, J. A. (1959). *Roman Theater-Temples*. Princeton.

Hardy, L. E. (1976). "The Imperial Women in Tacitus' 'Annales.'" Diss. Indiana.

Harkness, A. G. "Age at Marriage and at Death in the Roman Empire." *TAPA* 27 (1986): 35–72.

Harrer, G. A. "Tacitus and Tiberius." *AJP* 41 (1920): 57–68.

Hatzl, Ch. (1975). "Die politische Roll der Frauen um Tiberius." Diss. Innsbruck.

Haupt, M. (1875). *Opuscula*. Vol. 1. Leipzig.

Hawley, R., and B. Levick (eds.). (1995). *Women in Antiquity: New Assessments*. London.
Hellegouarc'h, J. "Les Buts de l'oeuvre de Velleius Paterculus." *Latomus* 33 (1964): 669–84.
Hemelrijk, E. A. (1999). *Matrona Docta: Educated Women in the Roman Elite from Cornelia to Julia Domna*. London.
Hentig, H. von (1924). *Über den Cäsarenwahnsinn, die Krankheit des Kaisers Tiberius*. Munich.
Herbert-Brown, G. (1984). *Ovid and the Fasti: An Historical Study*. Oxford.
Heron de Villefosse, P. "Le Trésor de Boscoreale." *MMAI* 5 (1899): 1–129.
Herrmann, C. (1964). *Le Rôle judiciare et politique des femmes sous la république romaine*. Brussels.
Herrmann, L. (1951). *L'Age d'argent doré*. Paris.
Herrmann, P. "Inschriften aus dem Heraion von Samos." *MDAI(A)* 75 (1960): 68–183.
———. (1968). *Der römische Kaisereid*. Göttingen.
Herz, P. (1975). "Untersuchungen zum Festkalender der römischen Kaiserzeit nach datierten Weih- und Ehreninschriften." Diss. Mainz.
———. "Kaiserfeste der Prinzipatszeit." *ANRW* II.16.2 (1978): 1135–1200.
———. "Die Arvalakten des Jahres 38 n. Chr. Eine Quelle der Geschichte Kaiser Caligulas." *BJ* 181 (1981): 89–110.
Hesberg, H. von, and S. Panciera (1994). *Das Mausoleum des Augustus. Der Bau und seine Inschriften*. Munich.
Heuss, A. (1964). *Römische Geschichte*. Brunswick, 2d ed.
Hill, P. V. "Buildings and Monuments of Rome on Flavian Coins." *NAC* 8 (1979): 207.
Hillard, T. "Republican Politics, Women, and the Evidence." *Helios* 16 (1989): 165–82.
———. "On the Stage, Behind the Curtain: Images of Politically Active Women in the Late Roman Republic." In Garlick, Dixon, and Allen (1992): 37–64.
Hinard, F. (1985). *Les Proscriptions de la Rome républicaine*. Rome.
Hinds, S. "First Among Women: Ovid, *Tristia* 1.6, and the Traditions of the 'Exemplary' Catalogue." In S. M. Braund and R. Mayer (eds.), *Amor: Roma, Love, and Latin Literature* (Cambridge, 1999): 123–42.
Hirschfeld, O. "Der Grundbesitz der römischen Kaiser in den ersten drei Jahrhunderten." *Klio* 2 (1902): 284–315.
———. (1905). *Die kaiserlichen Verwaltungsbeamten bis auf Diocletian*. Berlin.
Hoffsten, R. B. (1939). "Roman Women of Rank of the Early Empire." Diss. Pennsylvania.
Hohl, E. (1931). *Die römische Kaiserzeit*. Berlin.
———. "Primum Facinus Novi Principatus." *Hermes* 70 (1935): 350–55.
———. "Zu den Testamenten des Augustus." *Klio* 12 (1937): 323–42.
———. "Besass Cäsar Tribunengewalt?" *Klio* 14 (1939): 61–75.
Hopkins, M. K. "The Age of Roman Girls at Marriage." *Population Studies* 18 (1965): 309–27.
———. "On the Probable Age Structure of the Roman Population." *Population Studies* 20 (1966): 245–64.
Humbert, M. (1972). *Le Remariage à Rome. Etude d'histoire juridique et sociale*. Milan.
Huntsman, E. (1997). "The Family and Property of Livia Drusilla." Diss. Pennsylvania.

Hurley, D. W. (1993). *An Historical and Historiographical Commentary on Suetonius' Life of C. Caligula*. Atlanta.
Huzar, E. G. "Mark Antony: Marriages vs. Careers." *CJ* 81 (1986): 97–111.
Iacopi, I. (1997). *Palatino: Aula Isiaca. La Decorazione Pittorica dell'Aula Isiaca*. Milan.
Ihm, M. "Suetoniana." *Hermes* 36 (1901): 287–304.
Instinsky, H. U. "Augustus und die Adoption des Tiberius" *Hermes* 94 (1966): 324–43.
Jameson, S. "Augustus and Agrippa Postumus." *Historia* 24 (1975): 287–314.
Jerome, T. S. "The Tacitean Tiberius." *CP* 7 (1912): 265–82.
Johnson, P. J. "Ovid's Livia in Exile." *CW* 90 (1997): 403–20.
Jones, A. H. M. "The Aerarium and the Fiscus." *JRS* 40 (1950): 22–29.
———. (1960). *Studies in Roman Government and Law*. Oxford.
———. (1971). *The Cities of the Eastern Roman Provinces*. Oxford, 2d. ed.
Jones, C. P. "A Leading Family of Roman Thespiae." *HSCP* 74 (1970): 222–55.
Jucker, H. "Der Grosse Pariser Kameo." *JDAI* 91 (1977): 211–50.
———. "Zum Carpentum-Sesterz der Agrippina Major." In *Forschungen und Funde: Festschrift Bernhard Neutsch* (Innsbruck, 1980): 205–17.
Kähler, H. "Triumphbogen (Ehrenbogen)." *RE* 7A1 (1939): 373–493.
———. (1959). *Die Augustusstaue von Primaporta*. Cologne.
Kahrstedt, V. "Frauen auf antiken Münzen." *Klio* 10 (1910): 261–314.
Kampen, N. B. "Between Public and Private: Women as Historical Subjects in Roman Art." In Pomeroy (1991): 218–48.
Kaplan, M. "*Agrippina semper atrox:* A Study in Tacitus' Characterization of Women." *Studies in Latin Literature and Roman History* 1. Collection *Latomus* 164 (1979): 410–17.
Kaser, M. (1965). *Roman Private Law* (trans. R. Dannenbring). Durban.
Kaspar, D. "Neues zum Grand Camée de France." *GNS* 25 (1975): 61–68.
Kehoe, D. "Tacitus and Sallustius Crispus." *CJ* 80 (1985): 247–54.
Kellum, B. A. "The City Adorned: Programmatic Display at the *Aedes Concordiae Augustae*." In Raaflaub and Toher (1990): 276–96.
———. "The Construction of Landscape in Augustan Rome: The Garden Room at the Villa ad Gallinas." *Art Bulletin* 76 (1994): 211–24.
Kienast, D. (1982). *Augustus: Prinzeps und Monarch*. Darmstadt.
———. "Der heilige Senat. Senatskult und 'kaiserlicher' Senat." *Chiron* 15 (1985): 253–82.
———. (1990). *Römische Kaisertabelle*. Darmstadt.
Kleiner, D. "The Great Friezes of the Ara Pacis Augustae: Greek Sources, Roman Derivatives, and Augustan Social Policy." *MEFRA* 90 (1978): 753–85.
———. "Politics and Gender in the Pictorial Propaganda of Antony and Octavian." *EMC* 36 (1992): 357–67.
———. "Livia Drusilla and the Remarkable Power of Elite Women in Imperial Rome." *IJCT* 6 (2000): 563–69.
Kleiner, D., and S. B. Matheson (1996). *I, Claudia: Women in Ancient Rome*. New Haven.
———. (2000). *I, Claudia II: Women in Roman Art and Society*. Austin.
Kleiner, F. (1985). *The Arch of Nero in Rome*. Rome.
———. "An Extraordinary Posthumous Honor for Livia." *Athenaeum* 78 (1990): 508–14.

Knibbe, D., H. Engelmann, and B. Iplikçioglu, "Neue Inschriften aus Ephesos." *JÖAI* 62 (1993): 113–22.
Koch, C. "Vesta." *RE* 8A2 (1958): 1717–75.
Koeppel, G. "Die 'Ara Pietas Augustae': Ein Geisterbau." *MDAI(R)* 89 (1982): 453–55.
———. "Die historischen Reliefs der römischen Kaiserzeit I: Stadtrömische Denkmäler unbekannter Bauzugenhörigkeit aus augusteischer und julisch-claudischer Zeit." *BJ* 183 (1983): 61–144.
Koestermann, E. "Der Eingang der Annalen des Tacitus." *Historia* 10 (1961): 330–55.
———. (1963–68). *Cornelius Tacitus, Annalen*. Heidelberg.
Kokkinos, Nikos. (1992). *Antonia Augusta: Portrait of a Great Roman Lady*. London.
Kolbe, G. "Noch einmal Vesta auf dem Palatin." *MDAI(R)* 73–74 (1966–67): 94–104.
Königer, H. (1966). *Gestalt und Welt der Frau bei Tacitus*. Erlangen-Nurenberg.
Kornemann, E. (1929). *Neue Dokumente zum lakonischen Kaiserkult. Breslau, Abhandlungen der schlesischen Gesellschaft für vaterländische Cultur*, Heft 1.
———. (1930). *Doppelprinzipat und Reichsteilung im Imperium Romanum*. Leipzig-Berlin.
———. (1952). *Grosse Frauen des Altertums*. Leipzig, 4th ed.
———. (1960). *Tiberius*. Stuttgart.
———. (1963). *Römische Geschichte* (rev. H. Bengston). Stuttgart, 5th ed.
Kraay, C. (1956). *The Aes Coinage of Galba*. New York.
Krause, C., et al. (1985). *Domus Tiberiana: Nuove Richerche, Studi di Restauro*. Zurich.
Krause, K. "Hostia." *RE* suppl. 5 (1931): 236–82.
Kreikenbom, D. (1992). *Griechische und römische Kolossalporträts bis zum späten ersten Jahrhundert n. Chr.* Berlin.
Kromayer, J. "Forschungen zur Geschichte des zweiten Triumvirats." *Hermes* 29 (1894): 561–62.
Kübler, B. "Maiestas." *RE* 14.1 (1928): 542–59.
Kuhoff, W. "Zur Titulatur der römischen Kaiserinnen während der Prinzipatszeit." *Klio* 75 (1993): 244–56.
Kunst, C. "Adoption und Testamentadoption in der Späten Römischen Republik." *Klio* (1996): 87–104.
———. "Zur sozialen Funktion der Domus. Der Haushalt der Kaiserin Livia nach dem Tode des Augustus." In P. Kneissl and P. V. Losemann (eds.), *Imperium Romanum* (Stuttgart, 1998): 450–71.
Kuttner, A. L. (1995). *Dynasty and Empire in the Age of Augustus: The Case of the Boscoreale Cups*. Berkeley.
Labaste, H. "Comme Plutarque, Tacite aurait-il menti?" *Humanités* (Paris): *Cl. de Lettres* 7 (1930): 92–95.
Lacey, W. K. "2 B.C. and Julia's Adultery." *Antichthon* 14 (1980): 127–42.
———. (1996). *Augustus and the Principate*. Leeds.
Lackeit, C. "Iulius (Iulia)." *RE* 10, no. 556 (1918): 909–14.
Lahusen, G. (1983). *Untersuchungen zur Ehrenstatue in Rom*. Rome.
Laistner, M. L. W. (1963). *The Greater Roman Historians*. Berkeley.
Lanciani, R. A. (1893–1901). *Forma Urbis Romae*. Milan.

La Rocca, E. (1983). *Ara Pacis Augustae*. Rome.
Latte K., et al. (1956). *Histoire et historiens dans l'antiquité*. Geneva.
Lear, F. S. (1965). *Treason in Roman and Germanic Law*. Austin.
Le Bas, Ph., and W. H. Waddington. (1870). *Inscriptions Grecques et Latines receuillies en Asie Mineure* (Paris, rpt. New York, 1972).
Lehman, G. "Das Ende der römischen Herrschaft über das 'westelbische' Germanien: Von der Varus-Katastrophe zur Abberufung des Germanicus Caesar 16/17 n. Chr." *ZPE* 86 (1991): 79–96.
Lehner, H. "Zwei Trinkgefässe aus Vetera: II Der Trinkbecher des Chrysippus." *BJ* 122 (1912): 430–35.
Leipoldt, J. (1954). *Die Frau in der antiken Welt und im Urchristentum*. Leipzig.
Leo, F. (1901). *Die griechisch-römische Biographie nach ihrer literarischen Form*. Leipzig.
Leon, E. F. "Scribonia and Her Daughters." *TAPA* 82 (1951): 168–75.
Lesuisse, L. "L'Aspect héréditaire de la succession impériale sous les Julio-Claudiens." *LEC* 30 (1962): 32–50.
Levick, B. "Drusus Caesar and the Adoptions of A.D. 4." *Latomus* 25 (1966): 227–44.
——. "The Beginning of Tiberius' Career." *CQ* 21 (1971): 478–86.
——. "Abdication and Agrippa Postumus." *Historia* 21 (1972): 674–97.
——. "Atrox Fortuna." *CR* 22 (1972): 309–11.
——. "Tiberius' Retirement to Rhodes in 6 B.C." *Latomus* 31 (1972): 779–813.
——. "Julians and Claudians." *GR* 22 (1975): 29–38.
——. "The Fall of Julia the Younger." *Latomus* 35 (1976): 301–39.
——. (1976). *Tiberius the Politician*. London.
——. "Concordia at Rome." In *Scripta Nummaria Romana: Essays Presented to Humphrey Sutherland* (London, 1978): 228.
——. "The SC from Larinum." *JRS* 73 (1983): 97.
——. " 'Caesar omnia habet': Property and Politics Under the Principate." *Entretiens Hardt* 33 (1987): 187–218.
Lewis, J. D. "Primum facinus novi principatus." In B. F. Harris (ed.), *Auckland Classical Essays* (Auckland, 1970): 165–85.
Lewis, M. W. H. (1955). *The Official Priests of Rome Under the Julio-Claudians*. Rome.
Lewis, N. "Notationes Legentis." *BASP* 11 (1972): 44–59.
Lewis, R. G. "Some Mothers." *Athenaeum* 66 (1988): 198–200.
Liebeschutz, W. (1979). *Continuity and Changes in Roman Religion*. Oxford.
Linderski, J. "The Mother of Livia Augusta and the Aufidii Lurcones of the Republic." *Historia* 23 (1974): 463–80.
——. "Julia in Regium." *ZPE* 72 (1988): 181–200.
Ling, R. (1991). *Roman Painting*. Cambridge.
Luce, T. J., and A. J. Woodman (1993). *Tacitus and the Tacitean Tradition*. Princeton.
Lugli, G. "Note topografiche intorno all antiche ville suburbane." *BC* 51 (1923): 3–62.
——. (1938). *I Monumenti Antichi di Roma e Suburbio*. Rome.
——. (1946). *Roma Antica*. Rome.
——. (1947). *Monumenti minori del Foro Romano*. Rome.
——. (1970). *Itinerario di Roma Antica*. Milan.
MacMullen, R. "Women in Public in the Roman Empire." *Historia* 29 (1980): 208–18.

——. "Women's Power in the Principate." *Klio* 68 (1986): 434–43.

Magie, D. (1950). *Roman Rule in Asia Minor*. Princeton.

Manuwald, B. (1979). *Cassius Dio und Augustus: Philologsiche Untersuchungen zu den Büchern 45–6 des dionischen Geschichtswerkes*. Wiesbaden: *Palingenesia* 14.

Marino, P. A. "Woman: Poorly Inferior or Richly Superior?" *CB* 48 (1971): 17–21.

Marsh, F. B. "Roman Parties in the Reign of Tiberius." *AHR* 31 (1926): 65–68.

——. "Tacitus and the Aristocratic Tradition." *CP* 21 (1926): 289–310.

——. (1931). *The Reign of Tiberius*. Oxford.

Marshall, A. J. "Roman Women and the Provinces." *Anc. Soc.* 6 (1975): 109–27.

——. "Tacitus and the Governor's Lady: A Note on Annals iii.33–34." *GR* 22 (1975): 11–18.

Martha, J. "Inscriptions du Vallon des Muses." *BCH* 3 (1879): 441–48.

Martin, R. H. "Tacitus and the Death of Augustus." *CQ* 5 (1955): 123–28.

——. (1981). *Tacitus*. London.

Martin, R. H., and Woodman, A. J. (1989). *Tacitus: Annals Book IV*. Cambridge.

Maslakov, G. "Valerius Maximus and Roman Historiography." *ANRW* II.32 (1984): 437–96.

Matheson, S. B. (1980). *Ancient Glass in the Yale University Art Gallery*. New Haven.

McDaniel, M. J. (1995). "Augustus, the Vestals, and the *Signum Imperii*." Diss. North Carolina.

McDonnell, M. "Divorce Initiated by Women." *AJAH* 8 (1983): 54–80.

Megow, W. R. (1973). *Kameen von Augustus bis Alexander Severus*. Rome.

Meise, E. (1969). *Untersuchungen zur Geschichte der Julisch-Claudischen Dynastie*. Munich.

Mellor, R. (1993). *Tacitus*. London.

Mendell, C. W. (1957). *Tacitus: The Man and His Work*. New Haven.

Messineo, G. "Ollae Perforatae." *Xenia* 8 (1984): 65–82.

Michel, A. (1966). *Tacite et le destin de l'empire*. Paris.

Mikocki, T. (1995). *Sub specie deae: Les Impératrices et princesses romaines assimilés à des déesses. Etude iconologique*. Rome.

Millar, F. (1964). *A Study of Cassius Dio*. Oxford.

——. "Imperial Ideology in the *Tabula Siarensis*." In González and Arce (1988): 11–19.

——. (1992). *The Emperor in the Roman World*. London, 2d ed.

——. "Ovid and the *domus Augusta*: Rome Seen from Tomoi." *JRS* 83 (1993): 1–17.

——. (1993). *The Roman Near East, 31 BC–AD 337*. Cambridge, Mass.

Millar, F., and E. Segal (eds.). (1984). *Caesar Augustus: Seven Aspects*. Oxford.

Miranda, E. (1990). *Iscrizioni greche d'Italia. Napoli I*. Rome.

Mommsen, Th. "Die Familie des Germanicus." *Hermes* (1878): 245–65.

——. (1864–79). *Römische Forschungen*. Berlin.

——. (1883). *Res Gestae Divi Augusti*. Berlin, 2d ed.

——. (1899). *Römisches Strafrecht*. Berlin.

——. "Bruchstücke der Saliarischen Priesterliste." *Hermes* 38 (1903): 125–29.

——. (1904). *Gesammelte Schriften*. Berlin, rpt. Berlin, 1965.

——. (1996). *History of Rome Under the Emperors* (trans. C. Krojz). London.

Montero, S. "Livia y la divinación inductiva." *Polis* 6 (1994): 225–67.
Morford, M. "The Training of Three Roman Emperors." *Phoenix* 22 (1968): 57–72.
Morkholm, O. (1991). *Early Hellenistic Coinage*. Cambridge.
Motzo, B. R. "I commentari di Agrippina madre di Nerone." In *Studi de Storia e Filologia*, vol. 1 (Cagliari, 1927).
Mratschek-Halfmann, S. (1993). *Divites et Praepotentes. Reichtum und soziale Stellung in der Literatur der Prinzipatszeit*. Historia Einzelschriften no. 70, Stuttgart.
Mullens, H. G. "The Women of the Caesars." *GR* 11 (1941–42): 59–67.
Münzer, F. "Claudius." *RE* 3.2 (1899): 2885–86.
———. "Clodia." *RE* 4 (1900): 105–7.
———. "Fulvia." *RE* 7 (1900): 281–84.
———. "Servilia." *RE* 2A (1923): 1817–21.
———. "Livius." *RE* 13.1 (1926): 810.
———. "M. Livius Drusus Claudianus." *RE* 13.1 (1926): 881–84.
Nawotka, K. "The Attitude Towards Rome in the Political Propaganda of the Bosphoran Monarchs." *Latomus* 48 (1989): 326–28.
Nenci, G. "Sei decreti inediti da Entella." *Atti della Scuola Normale Superiore de Pisa* 10 (1980): 1271–75.
Nipperdey, K. (1851–52). *Cornelius Tacitus*. Leipzig.
Norwood, F. "The Riddle of Ovid's *relegatio*." *CP* 58 (1963): 150–63.
Oberleitner, W. (1985). *Geschnittene Steine: Die Prunkkameen der Wiener Antikensammlung*. Vienna, Cologne, and Graz.
Ogilvie, R. M. (1965). *A Commentary on Livy, Books 1–5*. Oxford.
Oliver, J. H. "The Divi of the Hadrianic Period." *HThR* 42 (1949): 35–40.
———. "On the Edict of Germanicus Declining Divine Acclamations." *RSA* 1 (1971): 229–30.
Oliver, J. H., and R. E. A. Palmer. "The Text of the Tabula Hebana." *AJP* 75 (1954): 225–49.
Ollendorff, L. "Livia Drusilla." *RE* 13 (1926): 900–927.
Paladini, M. L. "La Morte di Agrippa Postumo e la Congiurra di Clemente." *Acme* 7 (1954): 313–29.
Palmer, R. E. A. "Roman Shrines of Female Chastity from the Caste Struggle to the Papacy of Innocent I." *RSA* 4 (1974): 113–59.
Paltiel, E. (1991). *Vassals and Rebels in the Roman Empire*. Brussels.
Pannuti, V. (1983). *Museo archeologico nazionale Napoli: Catalogo della collezione glittica*. Vol. 1. Rome.
Pappano, A. E. "Agrippa Postumus." *CP* 36 (1941): 30–45.
Parassoglou, G. (1978). *Imperial Estates in Roman Egypt. American Studies in Papyrology*, vol. 18: Amsterdam.
Paribeni, R. (1876). *Il ritratto nell'era antica*. Milan.
Parker, E. R. "The Education of Heirs in the Julio-Claudian Family." *AJP* 67 (1946): 29–50.
Parsi, B. (1963). *Désignation et investiture de l'empereur romain*. Paris.
Pearce, T. "The Role of the Wife as Custos in Ancient Rome." *Eranos* 72 (1985): 16–33.

Pelham, H. F. (1911). *Essays.* Oxford.
Pelling, C. "Tacitus and Germanicus." In Luce and Woodman (1993): 59–85.
Perkounig, C.-M. (1995). *Livia Drusilla-Iulia Augusta.* Vienna.
Peter, C. (1867). *Geschichte Roms.* Halle.
Pfister, K. (1941). *Der Untergang der antiken Welt.* Leipzig.
——. (1951). *Die Frauen der Cäsaren.* Berlin.
Pflaum, H. G. (1950). *Les Procurateurs équestres sous le Haut-Empire romain.* Paris.
——. (1960–61). *Les Carrières procuratoriennes équestres sous le Haut-Empire romain.* Paris.
Phillips, J. E. "Roman Mothers and the Lives of Their Adult Daughters." *Helios* 6 (1978): 75–76.
Piganiol, A. "Observations sur une loi de l'empereur Claude." *Mélanges Cagnat* (Paris, 1912): 153–67.
Pike, J. B. "Cenat Adulteria in Suetonius." *CJ* 15 (1919): 372–73.
Pippidi, D. M. "Le 'Numen Augusti.'" *REL* 9 (1931): 83–111.
Pistor, H. H. (1965). "Prinzeps und Patriziat in der Zeit von Augustus bis Commodus." Diss. Freiburg.
Platner, S. B., and T. Ashby (1929). *A Topographical Dictionary of Ancient Rome.* Rome, rpt. 1965.
Pollini, J. (1978). "Studies in Augustan 'Historical' Reliefs." Diss. California, Berkeley.
——. "Man or God: Divine Assimilation and Imitation in the Late Republic and Early Principate." In Raaflaub and Toher (1990): 334–57.
Pomeroy, S. (1975). *Goddesses, Whores, Wives, and Slaves: Women in Classical Antiquity.* New York.
——. "The Relationship of the Married Woman to Her Blood Relatives in Rome." *Anc. Soc.* 7 (1976): 215–27.
—— (ed.). (1991). *Women's History and Ancient History.* Chapel Hill.
Pommeray, L. (1937). *Etudes sur l'infamie en droit romain.* Paris.
Poulsen, F. (1928). *Porträtstudien in norditalienischen Provinzmuseen.* Copenhagen.
Poulsen, V. (1973). *Les Portraits Romains.* Vol. 1, *République et dynastie Julienne.* Copenhagen.
Premerstein, A. von (1937). *Von Werden und Wesen des Principats.* Munich.
Prévost, M. H. (1949). *Les Adoptions politiques à Rome sous la république et le principat.* Paris.
Price, S. (1984). *Rituals and Power: The Roman Imperial Cult in Asia Minor.* Cambridge.
Purcell, N. "Livia and the Womanhood of Rome." *PCPhS* 32 (1986): 78–105.
Questa, C. "La morte di Augusto secondo Cassio Dione." *PP* 14 (1959): 41–53.
——. (1960). *Studi sulle fonti degli Annales di Tacito.* Rome.
Raaflaub, K. A., and L. J. Samons II. "Opposition to Augustus." In Raaflaub and Toher (1990): 417–54.
Raaflaub, K. A., and M. Toher (eds.). (1990). *Between Republic and Empire.* Berkeley.
Raditsa, L. F. "Augustus' Legislation Concerning Marriage, Procreation, Love Affairs, and Adultery." *ANRW* 2.13 (1980) 278–339.
Radke, G. "Der Geburtstag des alteren Drusus." *Würz. Jhb.* 4 (1978): 211–13.
——. "Die drei penates und Vesta in Rom." *ANRW* 2.17.1 (1981): 343–73.

Raepsaet-Charlier, M.-Th. "Ordre sénatorial et divorce sous le Haut-Empire: Un chapitre de l'histoire des mentalités." *ACD* 17–18 (1981–82): 161–73.

———. "Epouses et familles de magistrats dans les provinces romaines aux deux premiers siècles de l'empire." *Historia* 31 (1982): 64–69.

Raffay, R. (1884). *Die Memoiren der Kaiserin Agrippina*. Vienna.

Randour, M. J. (1954). *Figures de femmes romaines dans les Annales de Tacite*. Louvain.

Ranke, L. (1883). *Weltgeschichte*. Leipzig.

Rantz, B. "Les Droits de la femme romaine tels qu'on peut les apercevoir dans le pro Caecina de Ciceron." *RIDA* 29 (1982): 56–69.

Rapke, T. T. "Tiberius, Piso, and Germanicus." *AC* 25 (1982): 61–69.

Rawson, B. (1985). *Intellectual Life in the Late Roman Republic*. London.

——— (ed.). (1986). *The Family in Ancient Rome: New Perspectives*. London.

Rawson, E. "The Eastern Clientelae of Clodius and the Claudii." *Historia* 22 (1972): 219–39.

———. "More on the *Clientelae* of the Patrician Claudii." *Historia* 26 (1977): 340–57.

———. "The Life and Death of Asclepiades of Bithynia." *CQ* 32 (1982): 358–70.

Reeder, J. C. "The Statue of Augustus from Prima Porta and the Underground Complex." *Studies in Latin Literature and Roman History*, Collection *Latomus* 8 (1996).

———. "The Statue of Augustus from Prima Porta, the Underground Complex, and the Omen of the Gallina Alba." *AJP* 118 (1997): 89–118.

Rehak, P. "Livia's Dedication in the the Temple of Divus Augustus on the Palatine." *Latomus* 49 (1990): 117–25.

Reinhold, M. (1933). *Marcus Agrippa: A Biography*. New York.

———. (1988). *An Historical Commentary on Cassius Dio's Roman History Books 49–52 (36–29 B.C.)*. American Philological Association Monographs, no. 34: Atlanta.

Reinhold, M., and P. M. Swan. "Cassius Dio's Assessment of Augustus." In Raaflaub and Toher (1990): 155–73.

Reynolds, J. M. "The Origins and Beginning of Imperial Cult at Aphrodisias." *PCPhS* 26 (1980): 70–84.

———. "New Evidence for the Imperial Cult in Julio-Claudian Aphrodisias." *ZPE* 43 (1981): 317–27.

———. (1982). *Aphrodisias and Rome*. London.

Reynolds, J. M., and J. B. Ward-Perkins. (1959). *The Inscriptions of Roman Tripolitania*. Rome.

Rich, J. W. (1990). *Cassius Dio: The Augustan Settlement (Roman History 53–55.9)*. Warminster.

Richardson, L. "Evolution of the Porticus Octaviae." *AJA* 80 (1976): 57–64.

———. "Concordia and Concordia Augusti." *PP* 33 (1978): 260–72.

———. (1992). *A New Topographical Dictionary of Ancient Rome*. Baltimore.

Richlin, A. "Julia's Jokes, Gallia Placidia, and the Roman Use of Women as Political Icons." In Garlick, Dixon, and Allen (1992): 65–91.

Richmond, J. "Doubtful Works Ascribed to Ovid." *ANRW* 2.31.4 (1981): 2744–83.

Richmond, O. L. "The Temples of Apollo and Divus Augustus on Coins." In *Essays Presented to William Ridgeway* (Cambridge, 1913): 198–212.

Richter, G. (1968). *Engraved Gems of the Greeks, Romans, and Etruscans*. London.

Riposati, B. "Profili di donne nella storia di Tacito." *Aevum* 45 (1971): 25–45.

Ritter. H.-W. "Livia's Erhebung zur Augusta." *Chiron* 2 (1972): 313–38.

Rizzo, G. E. "Base di Augusto." *BC* 60 (1932): 7–109.

Rockwell, K. A. "Vedius and Livia (Tac. *Ann.* 1.10)." *CP* 66 (1971): 110.

Roddaz, J. M. (1984). *Marcus Agrippa*. Rome.

Rodriguez Almeida, E. (1981). *Forma Urbis Marmorea: Aggiornamento generale*. Rome.

Rogers, R. S. "The Conspiracy of Agrippina." *TAPA* 62 (1931): 141–68.

——. (1935). *Criminal Trials and Criminal Legislation Under Tiberius*. Middletown, Conn.

——. (1943). *Studies in the Reign of Tiberius*. Baltimore.

——. "The Roman Emperors as Heirs and Legatees." *TAPA* 78 (1947): 140–58.

Rose, C. B. (1993). *Dynastic Commemoration and Imperial Portraiture in the Julio-Claudian Period*. Cambridge.

Rose, H. J. (1960). *A Handbook of Latin Literature*. New York.

Rostovtsev, M. "Livia und Julia." *Strena Heligania* (Leipzig, 1900): 262–64.

——. (1905). *Römische Bleitesserae*. *Klio*. Beiheft 3: Lepizig.

——. "Interpretation des tessères en os." *RA* (1905): 110–24.

——. (1922). *A Large Estate in Egypt*. New York, rpt. 1979.

——. (1957). *Social and Economic History of the Roman Empire*. Oxford, 2d ed.

——. "L'Empereur Tibère et le culte impérial." *RH* 163 (1970): 1–26.

Rostovtsev, M., and M. Prou (1900). *Catalogue des Plombs de l'Antiquité, du Moyen Age et des Temps Modernes*. Paris.

Rousselle, A. "Du sanctuaire au thaumaturge: La Guérison en Gaule au IVe siècle." *Annales* 31 (1976): 1085–107.

Rumack, B., and E. Salzman. (1978). *Mushroom Poisoning: Diagnosis and Treatment*. West Palm Beach, Fla.

Rutland, L. W. (1975). "Fortuna Ludens: The Relationship Between Public and Private Imperial Fortune in Tacitus." Diss. Minnesota.

——. "Women as Makers of Kings in Tacitus' *Annals*." *CW* 72 (1978): 15–29.

Ryberg, I. S. "Tacitus' Art of Innuendo." *TAPA* 73 (1942): 383–404.

Sage, M. "Tacitus and the Accession of Tiberius." *Anc. Soc.* 13–14 (1982–83): 292–321.

——. "Tacitus' Historical Works: A Survey and Appraisal." *ANRW* 2.33.2 (1990): 851–1030.

Saletti, C. (1968). *Il ciclo statuario dell Basilica di Velleia*. Milan.

Saller, R. (1982). *Personal Patronage Under the Empire*. Cambridge.

——. "*Familia, domus*, and the Roman Conception of the Family." *Phoenix* 38 (1984): 336–55.

Salomies, O. (1992). *Adoptive and Polyonymous Nomenclature in the Roman Empire*. Helsinki.

Salvatore, A. "L'Immoralité des femmes et la décadence de l'empire selon Tacite." *LEC* 22 (1954): 254–69.

Salway, P. (1981). *Roman Britain*. Oxford.

Salzmann, D. (1990). *Antike Portäts im Römisch-Germanischen Museum Köln*. Cologne.

Sande, S. "Römische Frauenporträts mit Mauerkrone." *AAAH* 5 (1985): 151–245.

Sandels, F. (1912). "Die Stellung der kaiserlichen Frauen aus dem Julisch-Claudischen Hause." Diss. Giessen.

Santoro L'Hoir, F. (1992). *The Rhetoric of Gender Terms*. Leiden.

———. "Tacitus and Women's Usurpation of Power." *CW* 88 (1994): 5–24.

Saria, B. "Pucinum." *RE* 23.2 (1959): 1938.

Sasel, J. "Huldingung norischer Stämme am Magdalensberg in Kärnten. Ein Klärungsversuch." *Historia* 16 (1967): 70–74.

———. "Julia und Tiberius: Beiträge zur römischen Innenpolitik zwischen den Jahren 12 vor und 2 nach Chr." In W. Schmitthenner (ed.), *Augustus* (Darmstadt, 1969): 486–530.

Scaliger, J. (1572). *Publii Virgilii Maronis Appendix*. Leiden.

Scarborough, J. "Roman Medicine to Galen." *ANRW* II.37.1 (1993): 26–29.

——— (ed.). (1984). *Symposium on Byzantine Medicine. Dumbarton Oaks Papers*, no. 38. Washington, D.C.

Scardigli, B. "La sacrosanctitas tribunicia di Ottava e Livia." *Atti della Facoltà di Lettere e Filologia della Università di Siena, Perugia* 3 (1982): 61–64.

Scheid, J. (1975). *Les Frères Arvales. Recruitement et origine sociale sous les empereurs julio-claudiens*. Paris.

———. "Scribonia Caesaris et les Julio-Claudiens. Problèmes de vocabulaire de parenté." *MEFRA* 87 (1975): 349–75.

———. (1990). *Romulus et ses Frères. Le Collège des Frères Arvales, Modèle du Culte Public dans la Rome des Empereurs*. Rome.

Scheid, J., and H. Broise. "Deux nouveaux fragments des Actes des Frères Arvales de l'année 38 ap J.C." *MEFRA* 92 (1980): 215–48.

Scheider, K. Th. (1942). "Zusammensetzung des römischen Senates von Tiberius bis Nero." Diss. Zurich.

Schiller, H. (1872). *Geschichte des römischen Kaiserreichs unter der Regierung des Nero*. Berlin.

Schilling, R. (1977). *Histoire Naturelle* 7. Paris.

Schmidt, J. "Physiognomik." *RE* 20.1 (1941): 1064–74.

Schmidt, W. (1908). *Geburtstag in Altertum*. Giessen.

Schmitthenner, W. (1952). *Oktavian und das Testament Caesars: Eine Untersuchung zu den Politischen Anfängen des Augustus*. Munich.

Scholtz, B. I. (1992). *Untersuchungen zur Tracht der römischen Principats*.

Schoonhoven, H. (1992). *The Pseudo-Ovidian ad Liviam de morte Drusi*. Groningen.

Schove, D. J. (1984). *Chronology of Eclipses and Comets, AD 1–1000*. Woodbridge, Suffolk.

Schrijvers, P. H. "A propos de la datation de la *Consolatio ad Liviam*." *Mnemosyne* 41 (1988): 381–84.

Schrömbges, P. (1986). *Tiberius und die Res Publica Romana. Untersuchungen zur Institutionalisierung des frühen römischen Principats*. Bonn.

Schuller, W. (1987). *Frauen in der römischen Geschichte*. Constance.

Schulz, F. (1951). *Classical Roman Law*. Oxford.

Schürenberg, D. (1975). "Stellung und Bedeutung der Frau in der Geschichtsschreibung des Tacitus." Diss. Marburg.

Schwartz, D. R. (1990). *Agrippa I: The Last King of Judaea*. Tübingen.

———. (1992). *Studies in the Jewish Background of Christianity*. Tübingen.

Scott, K. "Octavian and Antony's *De Sua Ebrietate*." *CP* 24 (1929): 133–41.
———. "Emperor Worship in Ovid." *TAPA* 61 (1930): 43–69.
———. "Greek and Roman Honorific Months." *YClS* 2 (1931): 199–278.
———. "Tiberius' Refusal of the Title 'Augustus.'" *CP* 27 (1932): 43–50.
———. "The Political Propaganda of 44–30 B.C." *MAAR* 11 (1933): 39–40.
———. "Notes on the Destruction of Two Roman Villas." *AJP* 60 (1939): 459–62.
Seager, R. (1972). *Tiberius*. London.
Sebesta, J., and L. Bonfante (eds.). (1994). *The World of Roman Costume*. Madison, Wis.
Seibt, W. (1969). "Die Majestätsprozesse vor dem Senatsgericht unter Tiberius." Diss. Vienna.
Setälä, P. (1977). *Private Domini in Roman Brickstamps*. Helsinki.
Seyrig, H. "Inscriptions de Gythion." *RA* 29 (1929): 84–106.
Shackleton-Bailey, D. R. "The Roman Nobility in the Second Civil War." *CQ* 10 (1960): 253–70.
———. (1965). *Cicero's Letters to Atticus*. Cambridge.
———. (1991). *Two Studies in Roman Nomenclature*. Atlanta, 2d ed.
Shatzman, I. "Tacitean Rumours." *Latomus* 33 (1974): 547–78.
———. *Senatorial Wealth and Roman Politics*. Collection *Latomus* 142 (1975).
Shaw, B. D. "The Age of Roman Girls at Marriage." *JRS* 77 (1987): 30–46.
Shotter, D. C. A. "Three Problems in Tacitus' *Annals* I." *Mnemosyne* 18 (1965): 361–65.
———. "Tacitus, Tiberius, and Germanicus." *Historia* 17 (1968): 194–214.
———. "Julians, Claudians, and the Accession of Tiberius." *Latomus* 30 (1971): 1120–21.
———. "The Trial of M. Scribonius Libo Drusus." *Historia* 21 (1972): 88–98.
———. "Cn. Cornelius Cinna Magnus and the Adoption of Tiberius." *Latomus* 33 (1974): 306–13.
———. "Cnaeus Calpurnius Piso, Legate of Syria." *Historia* 23 (1974): 229–45.
———. (1989). *Tacitus, Annals IV.* Warminster.
Siber, H. (1952). *Römisches Verfassungsrecht in geschichtlicher Entwicklung*. Lahr.
Sievers, G. R. (1870). *Studien zur Geschichte der Römischen Kaiser*. Berlin.
Simon, E. (1967). *Ara Pacis Augustae*. Greenwich, Conn.
Simpson, C. J. "Livia and the Constitution of the Aedes Concordiae. The Evidence of Ovid, Fasti 637 ff." *Historia* 40 (1991): 449–55.
Sinclair, P. (1995). *Tacitus the Sententious Historian*. University Park, Penn.
Singer, M. W. "Octavia's Mediation at Tarentum." *CJ* 43 (1947): 173–77.
Sirago, V. A. "Livia Drusilla. Una nuova condizione femminile." *Invigilata Lucernis* 1 (1979): 171–207.
Sirks, A. J. B. "A Favour to Rich Freedwomen *(libertinae)* in A.D. 51." *RIDA* 27 (1980): 283–94.
Slater, W. J. "Pueri, Turba Minuta." *BICS* 21 (1974): 133–40.
Small, A. "A New Head of Antonia Minor and Its Significance." *MDAI(R)* 97 (1990): 217–34.
Smallwood, E. M. (1967). *Documents Illustrating the Principates of Gaius, Claudius, and Nero*. Cambridge.
———. (1981). *The Jews Under Roman Rule*. Leiden, 2d ed.
Smilda, H. C. (1896). "Suetonii Tranquilli vita Divi Claudii." Diss. Groningen.

Smith, C. E. (1942). *Tiberius and the Roman Empire*. Baton Rouge.
Smith, H. R. W. "Problems Historical and Numismatic in the Reign of Augustus." *University of California Publications in Classical Archaeology* 2.4 (1951): 133–230.
Smith, R. R. R. "The Imperial Reliefs from the Sebasteion at Aphrodisias." *JRS* 77 (1987): 88–138.
Snyder, W. F. "Public Anniversaries." *YClS* 7 (1940): 223–317.
Southern, P. (1998). *Augustus*. London.
Späth, T. " 'Frauenmacht' in der frühen römischen Kaiserzeit." In Dettenhofer (1994): 159–206.
Spengel, A. "Zur Geschichte des Kaisers Tiberius." *Stizungsberichte der K.B. Akademie des Wissenschaften zu München* (1903): 5–11.
Speyer, W. "Zur Verschwörung des Cn. Cornelius Cinna." *RhM* 99 (1956): 277–84.
Stahr, A. (1865). *Römische Kaiserfrauen*. Berlin.
Starr, C. G. (1960). *The Roman Imperial Navy*. Cambridge, 2d ed.
Steidle, W. (1951). *Sueton und die antike Biographie*. *Zetemata* 1: Munich.
Stein, A. (1927). *Der römische Ritterstand*. Munich.
——. "Ostorius." *RE* 18, no. 5 (1942): 1671–72.
——. (1950). *Die Präfekten von Ägypten*. Bern.
Steinby, E. M. (ed). (1993). *Lexicon Topographicum Urbis Romae* I. Rome.
Steinwenter, A. "Lex Voconia." *RE* 12 (1925) 2418–30.
Stern, M. E. "A Glass Head Flask Featuring Livia as Hera?" *Kotinos: Festschrift für E. Simon* (Mainz, 1992): 394–99.
Stewart, Z. "Sejanus, Gaetulicus, and Seneca." *AJP* 74 (1953): 70–85.
Strong, E. (1923–26). *La Scultura Romana*. Florence.
Stuart, M. "How Were Imperial Portraits Distributed Throughout the Empire?" *AJA* 43 (1939): 601–17.
Stumpf, G. R. (1991). *Numismatische Studien zur Chrolonolgie der römischen Statthalter in Kleinasien*. Saarbrücken.
Suerbaum, W. "Merkwürdige Geburtstage." *Chiron* 10 (1980): 337–55.
——. "Zweiundvierzig Jahre Tacitus-Forschung: Systematische Gesamtbibliographie zu Tacitus' Annalen 1939–1980." *ANRW* 2.33.2 (1990): 1032–476.
Sulze, H. "Die unteridischen Räume der Villa der Livia in Prima Porta." *MDAI(R)* 47 (1932): 174–92.
Summers, W. C. (1920). *The Silver Age of Latin Literature*. London.
Sumner, G. V. "Germanicus and Drusus Caesar." *Latomus* 26 (1967): 413–35.
——. "The Truth About Velleius Paterculus: Prologomena." *HSCP* 74 (1970): 257–97.
Sutherland, H. C. V. (1951). *Coinage in Roman Imperial Policy, 31 B.C.–A.D. 68*. London.
——. (1976). *The Emperor and the Coinage: Julio-Claudian Studies*. London.
——. (1987). *Roman History and Coinage, 44 BC–AD 69*. Oxford.
Sydenham, E. A. (1952). *The Coinage of the Roman Republic*. London.
Syme, R. (1939). *Roman Revolution*. Oxford.
——. (1958). *Tacitus*. Oxford.
——. (1970). *Ten Studies in Tacitus*. Oxford.

——. (1978). *History in Ovid*. Oxford.
——. (1986). *The Augustan Aristocracy*. Oxford.
Taeger, F. (1960). *Charisma. Studien zur Geschichte des antiken Herrscherkultes* 2. Stuttgart.
Talbert, R. J. A. (1984). *The Senate of Imperial Rome*. Princeton.
Tamm, B. (1963). *Auditorium and Palatium*. Stockholm.
Taubenschlag, R. "Die materna potestas in gräko-ägyptischen Recht." *ZSS* 49 (1929): 115–28.
Taylor, L. R. "Augustales, Seviri Augustales, and Seviri: A Chronological Study." *TAPA* 45 (1914): 231–53.
——. "Tiberius' Refusals of Divine Honours." *TAPA* 60 (1929): 87–101.
——. (1931). *The Divinity of the Roman Emperor*. Middletown, Conn.
——. "Tiberius' *Ovatio* and the *Ara Numinis Augusti*." *AJP* 58 (1937): 185–93.
——. (1949). *Party Politics in the Age of Caesar*. Berkeley.
——. (1960). *Voting Districts of the Roman Republic*. Rome.
Taylor, L. R., and A. B. West. "The Euryclids in Latin Inscriptions from Corinth." *AJA* 30 (1926): 389–400.
Temporini, H. (1978). *Die Frauen am Hofe Trajans. Ein Beitrag zur Stellung der Augustae im Principat*. Berlin and New York.
Thibault, C. J. (1964). *The Mystery of Ovid's Exile*. Berkeley.
Thomas, J. A. C. (1976). *Textbook of Roman Law*. New York.
Thornton, M. K., and R. L. Thornton. "Manpower Needs for the Public Works Programs of the Julio-Claudian Emperors." *Journal of Economic History* 43 (1983): 373–78.
Till, R. "Plinius über Augustus (nat. hist. 7.147–150)." *Würz. Jbb.* 3 (1977): 127–37.
Timpe, D. (1962). *Untersuchungen zur Kontinuität des frühen Prinzipats*. Wiesbaden.
——. (1968). *Der Triumph des Germanicus. Untersuchungen zu den Feldzügen der Jahre 14–16 n. Chr. in Germanien*. Bonn.
Tondriau, J. L. "Romains de la République assimilés à des Divinités." *SO* 27 (1949): 128–40.
Torelli, M. "Trebulla Mutuesca: Iscrizioni corrette ed inedite." *RAL* 18 (1963): 230–84.
——. "La valetudo atrox di Livia del 22 d. C., l'Ara Pietatis Augustae e i calendari." *AFLPer* 15 (1977–78): 179–83.
——. (1982). *Typology and Structure of Roman Historical Reliefs*. Ann Arbor.
Tränkle, H. "Augustus bei Tacitus, Cassius Dio, und dem älteren Plinius." *WS* 82 (1969): 108–30.
Treggiari, S. (1969). *Roman Freedmen During the Late Republic*. Oxford.
——. "Jobs in the Household of Livia." *PBSR* 43 (1975): 48–77.
——. "Jobs for Women." *AJAH* 1 (1976): 76–104.
——. (1991). *Roman Marriage*. Oxford.
Trillmich, W. (1978). *Familienpropaganda der Kaiser Caligula und Claudius. Agrippina Maior und Antonia Augusta auf Münzen*. Berlin.
——. "Julia Agrippina als Schwester des Caligula und Mutter der Nero." *Hefte des Archäologischen Seminars der Universität Bern* 9 (1983): 21–38.

———. "Der Germanicus-Bogen in Rom und das Monument für Germanicus und Drusus in Leptis Magna." In González and Arce (1988): 51–60.
Vallance, J. T. (1990). *The Lost Theory of Asclepiades of Bithynia*. Oxford.
———. "The Medical System of Asclepiades of Bithynia." *ANRW* II.37.1 (1993): 693–727.
Van Berchem, D. (1939). *Les Distributions de blé et d'argent à la plèbe romaine sous l'Empire*. Geneva.
Van Bremen, R. "Women and Wealth." In A. Cameron and A. Kuhrt (eds.), *Images of Women in Antiquity* (London, 1983): 231–33.
Vanggaard, J. H. (1988). *The Flamen: A Study in the History and Sociology of Roman Religion*. Copenhagen.
Veyne, P. "Les Honneurs posthumes de Flavia Domitilla et les dédicaces grecques et latines." *Latomus* 21 (1962): 49–98.
Vidal, H. "Le Dépôt in aede." *RD* 43 (1965): 545–87.
Vidén, G. (1993). *Women in Roman Literature. Studia Graeca et Latina Gotheburgensia* 57: Gotheburg.
Villers, R. "La Dévolution du principat dans la famille d'Auguste." *REL* 28 (1950): 235–51.
Visscher, F. de. "La Politique dynastique sous le règne de Tibère." *Synteleia V. Arangio-Ruiz* (Naples, 1964): 54–65.
Vittoria de la Torre, C. "Los nombres de Livia." *EClás* 34 (1992): 55–61.
Walker, B. (1952). *The Annals of Tacitus: A Study in the Writing of History*. Manchester.
Wallace, K. G., "Women in Tacitus." *ANRW* 2.33.5 (1991): 3556–74.
Wallace-Hadrill, A. (1983). *Suetonius*. London.
———. "Image and Authority in the Coinage of Augustus." *JRS* 76 (1986): 66–87.
———. "Time for Augustus: Ovid, Augustus, and the *Fasti*." In M. Whitby (ed.), *Homo Viator: Classical Essays for John Bramble* (1987): 221–30.
———. "The Social Structure of the Roman House." *PBSR* 56 (1988): 43–98.
———. (1989). *Patronage in Ancient Society*. London.
Wardle, D. "Cluvius Rufus and Suetonius." *Hermes* 120 (1992): 466–82.
Warren, P. M. "Knossos: Stratigraphical Museum Excavation, 1978–82. Part IV." *Archaeological Reports* 34 (1987–88): 86–104.
Watson, A. (1967). *The Law of Persons in the Later Republic*. Oxford.
Watson, P. (1995). *Ancient Stepmothers: Myth, Misogyny, and Reality*. Leiden.
Weaver, P. R. C. "Freedmen Procurators in the Imperial Administration." *Historia* 14 (1965): 460–69.
———. "Social Mobility in the Early Roman Empire: The Evidence of the Imperial Freedmen and Slaves." *Past and Present* 37 (1967): 3–20 = *Studies in Ancient Society*, ed. M. I. Finley (London, 1974): 121–40.
———. (1972). *Familia Caesaris: A Social Study of the Emperors' Freedmen and Slaves*. Cambridge.
———. "Dated Inscriptions of Imperial Freedmen and Slaves." In M. Clauss et al. (eds.), *Epigraphische Studien* (Cologne, 1976): 215–27.
Weber, W. (1936). *Princeps, Studien zur Geschichte des Augustus*. Stuttgart.

Weinribb, E. "The Family Connections of M. Livius Drusus Libo." *HSCP* 72 (1968): 247–78.
Weinrich, O. "Zwölfgötter." In W. H. Roscher (ed.), *Ausführliche Lexikon der Griechischen und römischen Mythologie* (Leipzig and Berlin, 1924–37): 6.764–848.
Weinstock, S. (1971). *Divus Julius*. Oxford.
Wellmann, M. "Asclepiades." *RE* 2.2 (1896): 1632–33.
Wessner, P. (1967). *Scholia in Iuvenalem Vetustiora*. Rpt. Stuttgart.
Wester, M. (1944). *Les Personnages et le monde féminin dans les Annales de Tacite*. Paris.
Westermann, W. L. (1955). *The Slave Systems of Greek and Roman Antiquity*. Philadelphia.
Wilcken, U. "Ehepatrone im römischen Kaiserhaus." *ZSS* 30 (1909): 504–7.
Wilkes, J. "Julio-Claudian Historians." *CW* 65 (1972): 177–203.
Willems, P. (1878). *Le Sénat de la république romaine*. Paris.
Willenbücher, H. (1914). *Der Kaiser Claudius*. Mainz.
Williams, G. "Some Aspects of Roman Marriage Ceremonies and Ideas." *JRS* 48 (1958): 16–29.
Willrich, H. (1911). *Livia*. Leipzig and Berlin.
——. "Augustus bei Tacitus." *Hermes* 62 (1927): 54–78.
Winkes, R. "Der Kameo Marlborough, ein Urbild der Livia." *AA* (1982): 131–38.
——. "Leben und Ehrungen der Livia. Ein Beitrag zur Entwicklung des römischen Herrscherkultes von der Zeit des Triumvirats bis Claudius." *Archeologia* 36 (1985): 55–68.
——. "Bildnistypen der Livia." *Rittrati ufficiale e ritratto privato: Atti della II Conferenza Internazionale sul Ritratto Romano* (Rome: Consiglio Nazionale delle Ricerche, *Quaderni de la Ricerca Scientifica* 116, 1988): 555–61.
——. (1995). *Livia, Octavia, Julia*. Louvain-la-Neuve and Providence.
——. "Livia: Portrait and Propaganda." In Kleiner and Matheson (2000), 29–42.
Winkler, L. (1995). *Salus: Vom Staatskult zur politischen Idee, eine archäologische Untersuchung*. Heidelberg.
Wiseman, T. P. "The Mother of Livia Augusta." *Historia* 14 (1965): 333–34.
——. "Pulcher Claudius." *HSCP* 74 (1970): 207–21.
——. (1971). *New Men in the Roman Senate*. Oxford.
——. "Legendary Genealogies in Late-Republican Rome." *GR* 21 (1974): 153–64.
——. (1979). *Clio's Cosmetics: Three Studies in Greco-Roman Literature*. Leicester.
——. "Calpurnius Siculus and the Claudian Civil War." *JRS* 72 (1982): 57–67.
——. (1991). *Death of an Emperor*. Exeter.
Wissowa, G. "Bona Dea." *RE* 3.1 (1899): 686–94.
——. (1912). *Religion und Kultus der Römer*. Munich, 2d ed.
Wistrand, E. (1976). *The So-Called Laudatio Turiae*. Lund.
Wittrich, H. (1972). "Die Taciteischen Darstellungen vom Sterben historischer Persönlichkeiten." Diss. Vienna.
Wolfe, E. R. "Transportation in Augustan Egypt." *TAPA* 83 (1952): 80–99.
Wood, S. "Agrippina the Elder in Julio-Claudian Art and Propaganda." *AJA* 92 (1988): 409–26.

——. "Diva Drusilla Panthea and the Sisters of Caligula." *AJA* 99 (1995): 457–82.
——. (1999). *Imperial Women: A Study in Public Images, 40 BC–AD 68*. Leiden.
Woodman, A. J. (1977). *Velleius Paterculus: The Tiberian Narrative*. Cambridge.
——. (1998). *Tacitus Reviewed*. Oxford.
Woodman, A. J., and R. H. Martin. (1996). *The Annals of Tacitus: Book 3*. Cambridge.
Wuilleumier, P. (1949). *Tacite, l'homme et l'oeuvre*. Paris.
——. "L'Empoisonnement de Claude." *REL* 53 (1975): 3–4.
Zanker, P. (1988). *The Power of Images in the Age of Augustus*. Ann Arbor.
Zinserling, G. "Der Augustus von Primaporta als offiziöses Denkmal." *AAntHung* 16 (1967): 327–29.
——. "Die Programmatik der Kunstpolitik des Augustus." *Klio* 67 (1985): 74–80.
Zuleta, F. De (1967–69). *The Institutes of Gaius*. Oxford.
Zwierlein-Diel, E. "Der Divus-Augustus-Kameo in Köln." *KölnJb* 17 (1980): 36–37.

INDEX

The lists of inscriptions, papyri and coins found on pages 267–302 are not indexed. Citations in the literary sources are likewise not indexed, unless the author had a direct relationship with Livia. The literary citations are listed on pages 247–58.

Items in the endnotes already indexed through the text are not listed separately.

Emperors and the better-known members of their families are listed in their familiar forms; otherwise Roman names are listed alphabetically by *nomen*, if the *nomen* is known, and by *cognomen* in the absence of a known *nomen*.

Buildings and districts of Rome are listed under "Rome."

Handbook of College and University Administration

Handbook of College and University Administration

ACADEMIC

Asa S. Knowles editor-in-chief

President, Northeastern University

McGraw-Hill Book Company

New York St. Louis San Francisco Düsseldorf London
Mexico Panama Sydney Toronto

HANDBOOK OF COLLEGE AND UNIVERSITY ADMINISTRATION: ACADEMIC

Library of Congress Catalog Card Number 73-77957

35194

1234567890 QBQB 7543210

To my wife Edna

Contributors

HENRY E. ALLEN *One-time Professor of Religion and College President, Coordinator of Student Religious Activities, University of Minnesota, Minneapolis*
(RELIGIOUS ACTIVITIES IN STATE AND INDEPENDENT COLLEGES AND UNIVERSITIES)

HUGH D. ALLEN *Vice-president, College Relations, Beloit College, Beloit, Wisc.*
(FIELD EXPERIENCE AS AN INTEGRAL PART OF EDUCATION)

PETER H. ARMACOST *President, Ottawa University, Ottawa, Kansas*
(STUDENT PERSONNEL ADMINISTRATION POLICIES)

DAVID F. BARTZ *Bell System Educational Communications Coordinator, American Telephone and Telegraph Company, Detroit, Mich.*
(INSTRUCTIONAL COMMUNICATIONS SYSTEMS)

RICHARD W. BISHOP *Assistant to the President, Northeastern University, Boston*
(THE MILITARY AND THE COLLEGE STUDENT)

CLYDE BLAKELEY *Theatre Arts, University of Maryland, Baltimore*
(THEATERS)

PAUL A. BLOLAND *Dean of Students and Associate Professor of Education, University of Southern California, Los Angeles*
(STUDENT ACTIVITIES)

WILLIAM J. BOWERS *Director of Research, The Russell B. Stearns Study, Northeastern University, Boston*
(DISCIPLINARY ADMINISTRATION—TRADITIONAL AND NEW)

RALPH A. BURNS *Former Director of Evaluation, Commission on Institutions of Higher Education, New England Association of Colleges and Secondary Schools, Inc., Boston*
(ACCREDITATION)

PORTER BUTTS *Director of Wisconsin Union and Professor of Social Education, University of Wisconsin, Madison*
(COLLEGE UNIONS—FACILITIES AND ADMINISTRATION)

HAROLD G. CLARK *Dean of the Division of Continuing Education, Brigham Young University, Provo, Utah*
(CORRESPONDENCE STUDY PROGRAMS)

JAMES J. COSTELLO *University Counsel, University of Illinois, Urbana*
(FACULTY RELATIONS)

JOHN A. CURRY *Associate Dean of Admissions, Northeastern University, Boston*
(COMMUNICATIONS WITHIN THE LARGE ADMISSIONS DEPARTMENT)

ALBERT S. DAVIS, JR. *Resident Counsel, Research Corporation, New York*
(ACADEMIC INVENTIONS, PATENTS, AND LICENSES)

JOHN M. DAWSON *Director of Libraries, University of Delaware, Newark*
(LIBRARY COLLECTIONS AND SERVICES; LIBRARY ORGANIZATION AND ADMINISTRATION)

WILLIAM DEMINOFF *Associate Director, Committee on Institutional Cooperation of the Big Ten Universities and The University of Chicago, Purdue University, Lafayette, Ind.*
(INTERINSTITUTIONAL COOPERATION)

EDWARD J. DONNELLY *Director, Division of Instructional Media, Northeastern University, Boston*
(AUDIOVISUAL MEDIA SERVICES)

PAUL L. DRESSEL *Assistant Provost and Director of Institutional Research, Michigan State University, East Lansing*
(EVALUATION OF THE ENVIRONMENT, THE PROCESS, AND THE RESULTS OF HIGHER EDUCATION)

J. GARBER DRUSHAL *President, The College of Wooster, Wooster, Ohio*
(SELF-DIRECTED STUDY)

JOHN P. EDDY *Dean of Students, Johnston State College, Johnston, Vt.*
(THE CHAPLAINCY AT CHURCH-RELATED AND OTHER COLLEGES)

NORMAN L. EPSTEIN *General Counsel, The California State Colleges, Los Angeles*
(THE SOCIAL FRATERNITY IN RELATION TO THE UNIVERSITY)

MARTIN W. ESSIGMANN *Dean of Research, Northeastern University, Boston*
(RESEARCH)

GILBERT C. GARLAND *Dean of Admissions, Northeastern University, Boston*
(ADMISSIONS—FRESHMAN CLASS QUOTA; ADMISSIONS—PUBLIC RELATIONS)

THOMAS GARVER *Director, Newport Harbor Art Museum, Balboa, California, former Assistant Director, Rose Art Museum, Brandeis University, Waltham, Mass.*
(MUSEUMS)

JAMES E. GILBERT *Associate Dean of University Administration, Northeastern University, Boston*
(INSTRUCTIONAL SERVICES)

DOROTHY C. GOODWIN *Assistant Provost and Director of Institutional Research, University of Connecticut, Storrs*
(WORKLOAD ASSIGNMENTS)

L. P. GREENHILL *Assistant Vice-president for Resident Instruction and Director of University Division of Instructional Services, The Pennsylvania State University, University Park*
(LEARNING RESOURCE CENTERS)

WARREN T. GRINNAN *Campus Center Manager and Lecturer, Restaurant and Hotel Management Program, University of Massachusetts, Amherst*
(FACULTY CLUBS)

MYRON D. HAGER *Director of Admissions, Westbrook Junior College, Portland, Me.*
(THE PRACTICE OF ADMISSIONS IN THE JUNIOR COLLEGE)

ERVIN L. HARLACHER *President, Brookdale Community College, Lincroft, N.J.*
(SERVICE PROGRAMS OF COMMUNITY JUNIOR COLLEGES)

CHARLES W. HAVICE *Professor of Philosophy and Religion and Dean of Chapel, Northeastern University, Boston*
(RELIGIOUS ORGANIZATIONS AND PROGRAMS ON THE CAMPUS; SUMMARY OF BASIC INFORMATION FOR CHIEF ADMINISTRATORS CONCERNING THE RELIGIOUS AFFAIRS PROGRAMS)

GENE R. HAWES *Consultant, Columbia University Press, New York*
(UNIVERSITY PRESS)

C. ADDISON HICKMAN *Vandeveer Professor of Economics, Southern Illinois University, Carbondale; and President, American Association for Higher Education, 1968–1969*
(FACULTY ROLE IN GOVERNANCE)

JOHN C. HOY *Vice Chancellor—Student Affairs, University of California at Irvine*

(THE MECHANICS OF ADMISSIONS; ADMISSIONS—STUDENT SELECTION, EVALUATION OF CREDENTIALS, USE OF THE PREDICTIVE FORMULA AS AN ADMISSIONS TOOL; PLANS FOR THE ADMISSION OF NEW FIRST-YEAR STUDENTS; ADMISSION OF THE TRANSFER STUDENT TO UPPER-CLASS STANDING)

THOMAS E. HULBERT *Associate Professor and Associate Director, Office of Educational Resources, Northeastern University, Boston*
(INSTRUCTIONAL SERVICES)

F. DON JAMES *President, Central Connecticut State College, New Britain*
(ACADEMIC ORGANIZATION; FACULTY ORGANIZATION AND ADMINISTRATION)

ROY J. JOHNSTON *Director of Division of Instructional Communications, Northeastern University, Boston*
(INSTRUCTIONAL TELEVISION SERVICES)

ROBERT J. KATES, JR. *Assistant Director, Northeastern Regional Office, College Entrance Examination Board, New York*
(FINANCIAL AID)

ISRAEL KATZ *Dean, The Center for Continuing Education, Northeastern University, Boston*
(HIGHER CONTINUING EDUCATION)

ALVIN KENT *Director, Office of Educational Resources, Northeastern University, Boston*
(PROGRAMMED LEARNING SERVICES)

WALTER J. KENWORTHY *Dean of the College, Wheaton College, Norton, Mass.*
(INSTRUCTION)

ASA S. KNOWLES, Editor-in-Chief
(FACULTY PERSONNEL POLICIES AND REGULATIONS; ORIENTATION OF NEW FACULTY; CAMPUS UNREST)

JOHN C. LIVINGSTON *Professor of Government, Sacramento State College, Sacramento, Calif.*
(COLLECTIVE NEGOTIATIONS)

JAMES W. LONG *Director, Division of Physical Education, Oregon State University, Corvallis*
(ATHLETICS ADMINISTRATION)

EDWARD C. MC GUIRE *Dean of Students, Rutgers, The State University, Newark, N.J.*
(FRATERNITIES AND SORORITIES)

JAMES P. MC INTYRE *Vice-president for Student Affairs, Boston, College, Boston*
(GOVERNING THE STUDENT COMMUNITY)

ERNEST E. MC MAHON *Dean, University Extension Division, Director of the Institute of Management and Labor Relations, and Professor of Adult Education, Rutgers, The State University, New Brunswick, N.J.*
(ADULT EDUCATION DEGREE PROGRAMS; COOPERATIVE AND GENERAL EXTENSION PROGRAMS)

EDMUND J. MC TERNAN *Dean, School of Allied Health Professions, State University of New York, Stony Brook, N.Y.*
(CLINICAL INSTRUCTION IN AFFILIATED OR COOPERATING INSTITUTIONS)

EDWARD MALTZMAN *Director of Educational Research, Commercial Electronics Division, Sylvania Electric Products, Inc., Bedford, Mass.*
(LEARNING LABORATORIES AND INDEPENDENT-STUDY SERVICES)

THURSTON E. MANNING *Vice-president for Academic Affairs, University of Colorado, Boulder*
(ACADEMIC POLICIES AND STANDARDS)

WILLARD MARCY *Vice-president, Patents, Research Corporation, New York*
(ACADEMIC INVENTIONS, PATENTS, AND LICENSES)

JULIUS J. MARKE *Law Librarian and Professor of Law, New York University, New York*
(COPYRIGHT)

ELLSWORTH MASON *Director of Library Services, Hofstra University, Hempstead, N.Y.*
(LIBRARY ASSOCIATIONS; THE LIBRARY BUILDING; THE FUTURE LIBRARY)

PAUL E. MATTE *Director of the Student Health Service, University of Arizona, Tucson, and Member of the Arizona Bar*
(HEALTH SERVICES)

LEWIS B. MAYHEW *Professor of Education, Stanford University, Stanford, Calif.*
(CURRICULUM CONSTRUCTION AND PLANNING; THE SUPERIOR STUDENT)

RICHARD E. MEYER *Assistant to the Dean of Continuing Education, University of Washington, Seattle*
(CONFERENCE AND CONTINUING EDUCATION CENTERS)

FRANK NOFFKE *Director, College Union, California State College at Long Beach*
(COLLEGE UNIONS—PROGRAMS AND SERVICES)

MAURICE S. OSBORNE, JR. *Director of Student Health Services, Tufts School of Medicine and Dental Medicine, Boston*
(HEALTH PROGRAMS AND THE COLLEGIATE COMMUNITY)

RICHARD R. PERRY *Associate Executive Vice-president for Institutional Research and Administrative Planning, The University of Toledo, Toledo, Ohio*
(THE OFFICE OF ADMISSIONS—ROLE OF THE ADMINISTRATOR; ADMISSIONS DEPARTMENT COSTS AND BUDGETING; ADMISSIONS RESEARCH AND FOLLOW-UP STUDIES)

JOHN F. POTTS *President, Voorhees College, Denmark, South Carolina*
(BLACK STUDENT AFFAIRS)

IVAN PUTMAN, JR. *Acting University Dean, International Studies and World Affairs, State University of New York, Albany*
(INTERNATIONAL STUDENTS)

ALBERT L. QUINAN *Associate Bursar, Northeastern University, Boston*
(VETERANS AFFAIRS)

KENNETH G. RYDER *Vice-president for University Administration, Northeastern University, Boston*
(FACULTY RIGHTS AND RESPONSIBILITIES)

RICHARD G. SALEM *Research Associate, The Russell B. Stearns Study, Northeastern University, Boston*
(DISCIPLINARY ADMINISTRATION—TRADITIONAL AND NEW)

STANLEY F. SALWAK *President, Aroostook State College, Presque Isle, Me., former Director, Committee on Institutional Cooperation of the Big Ten Universities and The University of Chicago, Purdue University, Lafayette, Ind.*
(INTERINSTITUTIONAL COOPERATION)

LLOYD W. SCHRAM *Dean of Continuing Education, University of Washington, Seattle*
(CONFERENCE AND CONTINUING EDUCATION CENTERS)

HAROLD W. SEE *Vice-president for Research and Planning, University of Bridgeport, Bridgeport, Conn.*
(ACADEMIC FREEDOM AND TENURE)

ROBERT H. SHAFFER *Professor of Education and former Dean of Students, Indiana University, Bloomington*
(ORIENTATION OF NEW STUDENTS)

ROSEMARY SHIELDS *University Representative, International Business Machines Corporation, Cambridge, Mass.*
(REGISTRATION, SCHEDULING, AND STUDENT RECORDS)

JUSTIN C. SMITH *Professor of Law, Texas Tech University, Lubbock*
(LEGAL PROBLEMS IN SPONSORSHIP OF EXCHANGE PROGRAMS)

CHESTER W. STOREY *Assistant to the President, Northeastern University, Boston*
(CAMPUS UNREST)

CLARENCE H. THOMPSON *Dean of University College and Professor of Adult Education, Drake University, Des Moines, Iowa*
(ADMISSION AND COUNSELING OF ADULT STUDENTS)

PATRICIA ANN THRASH *Associate Dean of Students and Associate Professor of Education, Northwestern University, Evanston, Ill.*
(ADMINISTRATIVE CONCERNS OF WOMEN DEANS)

B. ALDEN THRESHER *Director of Admissions Emeritus, Massachusetts Institute of Technology, Cambridge, Mass.*
(ADMISSIONS IN PERSPECTIVE)

EDWARD A. TOMLINSON *Associate Professor of Law, University of Maryland Law School, Baltimore*
(COLLEGES AND UNIVERSITIES AND DISCRIMINATION)

PHILIP A. TRIPP *Vice-president for Student Development, Georgetown University, Washington, D.C.*
(ORGANIZATION FOR STUDENT PERSONNEL ADMINISTRATION)

HARVEY VETSTEIN *Assistant Professor of English and Faculty Adviser to Student Publications, Northeastern University, Boston*
(STUDENT PUBLICATIONS)

JOY WINKIE VIOLA *Editorial Assistant to the President, Northeastern University, Boston*
(BLACK STUDENT AFFAIRS)

WOLF VON OTTERSTEDT *(deceased), former Consultant on Higher Education Law, Eugene, Oregon*
(STUDENT RELATIONS)

LOUIS VRETTOS *Dean of Instruction and Director of Suburban Campus, Northeastern University, Boston*
(EDUCATIONAL ASSISTANCE PROGRAMS)

EVERETT WALTERS *Senior Vice-president and Dean of Faculties, Boston University, Boston*
(PROFESSIONAL EDUCATION; GRADUATE EDUCATION; DEGREES, DIPLOMAS, AND ACADEMIC COSTUME)

WARREN D. WELLS *Registrar, Massachusetts Institute of Technology, Cambridge, Mass.*
(ACADEMIC CALENDARS)

EUGENE S. WILSON *Dean of Admissions, Amherst College, Amherst, Mass.*
(ADMISSIONS—PUBLIC RELATIONS; ADMISSIONS—INTERNAL LIAISON WITH ADMINISTRATION, FACULTY, STUDENT, AND ALUMNI GROUPS; SPECIAL PROBLEMS OF ADMISSIONS)

ROY L. WOOLDRIDGE *Vice-president and Dean of Cooperative Education, Northeastern University, Boston*
(COOPERATIVE EDUCATION)

GEORGE YOUNG *Dean of Student Affairs, Broward Junior College, Fort Lauderdale, Florida*
(COUNSELING AND TESTING)

Preface

In 1966 the McGraw-Hill Book Company made a survey to determine the possible interest of college and university administrators in a handbook of administration. Their inquiry was prompted by the growing size and complexity of higher education, with new influences resulting in new administrative problems and policy considerations. Educator response to the survey strongly indicated that a handbook was indeed needed. Subsequently, I was invited to become the Editor-in-Chief.

As John Stecklein, Director, Bureau of Institutional Research, University of Minnesota, and author of the chapter on "Institutional Research" in the companion volume on general administration of this Handbook, states:

> There is little doubt that the business of higher education has become too complicated to "run by the seat of the pants." . . . The sheer magnitude of the increases in numbers [of students] and finances has made the operation of colleges and universities much more complex and harder to understand. Because of the increased magnitude of the enterprise, and because of the markedly more conspicuous allocation of resources, individuals and boards responsible for the conduct of the enterprises have become increasingly concerned about efficient operation and effective utilization of resources. The administrators running the enterprise have been forced to adopt management science techniques to assist them in understanding a multitude of bewildering problems.

During the past decade the administration of higher education has been undergoing significant changes involving greater participation of students and faculty and greater sharing of administrative responsibilities. This has introduced many new concepts and, to a certain degree, a restructuring of the administrative organizations of our colleges and universities. Insofar as possible, this Handbook deals with administration in terms of new ideas and concepts which are fast becoming established practices on campuses of U.S. colleges and universities.

The Handbook recognizes that there is a wide spectrum of administrative responsibilities in today's colleges and universities. It further recognizes that information must be presented so as to give the top administrator an overall view of the operating and administrative problems for which he has general responsibility, as well as provide those who are immediately responsible for various operations with an indication as to what is considered good administrative practice. Newly appointed officers, deans, directors, and department heads will find the Handbook of particular value in terms of gaining insight into and perspective on the administrative problems of higher education. Experienced administrators will find that the Handbook will be helpful in ascertaining the efficiency and adequacy of their own system of administration. As such, the Handbook is a checklist of principles and information.

The chapters contained in the Handbook have been written either from the "how to do it" point of view or in such a way as to provide information essential to reaching administrative judgments. Controversial topics, for which there may be no universally agreed upon method of operation—such as student unrest, black student affairs, and employee unionization—also are discussed, in order to assist those endeavoring to establish their own institutional policies.

The approach has been that of making the Handbook universally applicable to institutions of all sizes and types. Where the characteristics of an institution would affect the administration of specific areas, special chapters have been written, i.e., the admissions program and community service responsibilities of junior colleges as opposed to those of a four-year or graduate school.

The entire Handbook is presented in two volumes. Each volume contains a grouping of chapters in related areas of administration. One volume, *General*, covers areas of administration that are primarily the responsibility of officers of general administration. The other volume, *Academic*, covers administrative areas that are primarily the responsibility of the officers concerned with academic programs, standards, policies, and academic personnel administration, as well as areas that relate to the administration of academic affairs. For example, the sections "Student Personnel Administration" and "Health Programs and the Collegiate Community" are contained in the *Academic Volume* because in most institutions the academic administrators and faculty have a major role in determining student personnel policies, and health administration is usually the responsibility of the chief officer of student personnel administration.

The two volumes encompass 200 chapters. Over 160 contributing authors have been carefully selected for their expertise in administration and their knowledge of the subject matter. Some authors have been assigned two or more chapters on related subjects. The Editor-in-Chief and his staff also have assumed authorship responsibilities for certain chapters.

An undertaking of this immense scope and detail can only be accomplished with the cooperation and assistance of others. Special acknowledgments must be made to certain of these individuals who have contributed so much to the preparation of Handbook materials.

The Honorable Byron K. Elliott, Chairman of the Board of Northeastern University, encouraged the Editor-in-Chief to undertake the organization and preparation of the Handbook, recognizing the importance of this undertaking to the welfare of higher education.

The following served as consultants and advisors on entire sections of the Handbook or on several related chapters contained in particular sections:

STUDENT PERSONNEL ADMINISTRATION: Peter H. Armacost, President, Ottawa University, Ottawa, Kansas; Christopher Kennedy, Associate Dean of Students, Northeastern University; Gilbert G. MacDonald, Vice-president for Student Affairs, Northeastern University; Edward W. Robinson, Dean of Men, Northeastern University

PLANNING, SPACE REQUIREMENTS, AND INSTITUTIONAL RESEARCH: Loring Thompson, Vice-president and Dean of Planning, Northeastern University

PHYSICAL PLANT ADMINISTRATION: Cecil A. Roberts, former Director of Buildings and Grounds, Harvard University, Cambridge, Mass., and Consultant, Construction and Building Management; Edward S. Parsons, former Vice-president—Business, Northeastern University; George B. LeBeau, Superintendent of Buildings and Grounds, Northeastern University

ADMISSIONS: John A. Curry, Associate Dean of Admissions, Northeastern University

NONACADEMIC PERSONNEL ADMINISTRATION: William D. Poore, Director, Personnel Services, University of Missouri, Columbia, Missouri

LEARNING RESOURCES—LIBRARY AND INSTRUCTIONAL RESOURCES: James E. Gilbert, Associate Dean of University Administration, Northeastern University; Thomas E. Hulbert, Associate Director, Office of Educational Resources, Northeastern University; Roland H. Moody, Director of University Libraries, Northeastern University

BUSINESS AND FINANCIAL ADMINISTRATION: Lincoln C. Bateson, Vice-president—Business, Northeastern University; Edward M. Parsons, former Vice-president—Business, Northeastern University; Daniel J. Roberts, Jr., Vice-president for Finance, Northeastern University

RELIGION ON THE CAMPUS: Charles W. Havice, Dean of Chapel, Northeastern University

PUBLIC RELATIONS, DEVELOPMENT, AND ALUMNI RELATIONS: Kenneth W. Ballou, Dean of University College, Northeastern University; Jack R. Bohlen, former Vice-president for Development, Northeastern University; Rudolf O. Oberg, Director of Alumni Relations, Northeastern University

The following persons at Northeastern University served as readers and advisors on the content of specific chapters:

Richard I. Carter, Director, Computation Center; Ronald W. Clifford, Director of Purchasing; Charles M. Devlin, Associate Director of Alumni Relations; Edith E. Emery, Dean of Women; Walter H. Floyd, Manager of Bookstore; William F. King, Associate Dean of Faculty; Robert W. McLean, Food Services Manager; Rudolph M. Morris, Associate Dean of University Administration; Edmund J. Mullen, Associate University Registrar; Philip W. Pendleton, Director of Testing and Counseling Center; Eugene M. Reppucci, Jr., Assistant to the President; Norman Rosenblatt; Associate Dean of

Faculty; Kenneth G. Ryder, Vice-president and Dean of Administration; Donald J. Taylor, Assistant to Vice-president—Business; Donald K. Tucker, Director of Career Information Center; William C. White, former Executive Vice-president and Provost; Roy L. Wooldridge, Vice-president and Dean of Cooperative Education.

The following persons outside Northeastern University also served as readers and advisors on the content of specific chapters:

James E. Bray, Secretary-Treasurer Chi Psi Fraternity, Ann Arbor, Michigan; Norman Grimm, Director of Food Services, Brandeis University, Waltham, Mass.; Francis A. Hunt, Director of Public Relations, Veterans Administration, Boston, Mass.

A debt of gratitude is due to officers of companies and organizations who gave advice and designated staff to prepare materials for the Handbook:

Francis M. Mead, Vice-president—Marketing, New England Telephone and Telegraph Company, Boston, Mass.; Alvin C. Zises, President, Bankers Leasing Corporation, Boston, Mass.; Frank R. Farwell, President, Liberty Mutual Insurance Company, Boston, Mass.

The following persons performed special work, research, checking, and typing: Salvatore A. Amico, Nancy Abreu, Geraldine Murphy, Jane North. Eleanor M. Jones prepared the illustrations for the chapter on Degrees, Diplomas, and Academic Costume.

Richard Bishop, Assistant to the President, has assisted the Editor-in-Chief by maintaining visual wall-size control charts essential to the coordination of such an extensive undertaking, showing titles of chapters, authors, progress of manuscripts, galleys, and page proof. He has assisted also in editing and rewriting the contents of several chapters, as well as in proofreading.

Chester Storey and Joy Winkie Viola, serving in the capacity of Editorial Assistants to the President of Northeastern, have aided the Editor-in-Chief by preparing and typing chapters, revising several chapters and also assisting in proofreading of galleys and page proof as well as the preparation of indexes.

Elizabeth H. Howkins, Secretary to the President, has assisted the Editor-in-Chief by controlling and coordinating outlines, manuscripts, galleys, and page proof contained in both volumes. She has also typed outlines of chapters and chapters prepared by the Editor-in-Chief, performed extensive editorial work, and assumed major responsibility for proofreading as well as for the preparation of indexes of both volumes.

The preparation of this Handbook began over four years ago and has been for the Editor-in-Chief a part-time project. In order to minimize the interference with responsibilities as a University President, it has been necessary to perform many of the duties of Editor-in-Chief on weekends and during evening, holiday, and vacation periods. This has meant sacrificing time which might otherwise have been devoted to my family. Without their helpful understanding, it would have been impossible to have fulfilled the assignment as Editor-in-Chief of this Handbook.

Asa S. Knowles EDITOR-IN-CHIEF

Contents

section three Admissions

section four Learning Resources—Library and Instructional Resources

section five Adult Education

section six Academic Personnel Administration

section seven Student Personnel Administration

section eight Athletics Administration

section nine Health Programs and the Collegiate Community

section ten Religion on the Campus

section eleven Campus Community Facilities and Enterprises

Contents of Companion Volume on General Administration

section four Planning, Space Requirements, and Institutional Research

section five Public Relations, Development, and Alumni Relations

section six Nonacademic Personnel Administration

section seven Physical Plant Administration

section eight Business and Financial Administration

Section One

Legal Aspects of Academic Administration

Chapter 1

Legal Aspects of Academic Administration— Introductory Statement

Administrators of all types of institutions of higher learning are confronted with a wide variety of complex legal problems and questions. The chapters contained in this volume of the *Handbook* are intended to provide administrators with information about laws, regulations, and court decisions which relate particularly to the academic administration of colleges and universities. The chapters dealing with the legal aspects of general administration are presented in Volume 1, *General.*

The discussion of legal aspects has been divided between Volumes 1 and 2 for the benefit of those whose primary interests are such that they would wish to purchase only one volume of the handbook. Within each volume, readers will find it helpful to consult related chapters, i.e., those concerned with the legal aspects of student relations also will find it advisable to review the chapter on discrimination.

The legal aspects discussed in Volume 1 include taxes; real property; campus security and safety; conduct of enterprises; agriculture; mergers; tort liability and insurance; employee relations and unions; fund raising, contracts, and other related considerations.

Recent trends stemming from problems of student unrest have resulted in a whole new body of law relating to the academic community. It is not intended that the chapters on the legal aspects of academic administration will answer all legal questions but rather that they will provide a guide for administrators as to when to seek legal advice and assistance.

Chapter 2

Student Relations

WOLF VON OTTERSTEDT *

Consultant on Higher Education Law, Eugene, Oregon

DUE PROCESS AND STUDENT DISCIPLINE

During the last 10 years, college administrators and their legal counsel have become increasingly aware of administrative and legal problems caused by student unrest on the campuses of American colleges and universities. The student revolt in the academic world has found expression in student demonstrations, riots, violence, and an overall demand for greater student participation in the administration of colleges and universities in a context of pressures which are directed at the heart and founda-

* *Deceased* September 6,1969.

tion of academic life as it has existed since the time of the beginning of this nation. Activities stemming from student unrest affect the academic community as well as the immediate local environment and the nation at large. They appear to be caused by a general dissatisfaction of the present generation of students with the "establishment." The impact of student pressures is no longer limited to reforms and change of the academic community itself.

The striking change which has taken place during the last decade, and which has gradually and dramatically increased in its intensity, is not primarily a result of any rules and regulations relating to academic achievement or conduct in the academic environment. It has, rather, been occasioned by student expression, actions, and demonstrations directed at problems originating not within the academic community but in the nation at large and in its social and economic milieu. If one were to single out the principal causes of unrest, one might refer to such problems as the war in Vietnam, the recruiting activities of governmental agencies for personnel in sensitive areas of national defense, corporations holding government contracts with such agencies as the Department of Defense and the Atomic Energy Commission, unrest stemming from the Black Power movement, and the expressed desire on the part of other extremist student organizations to take over the administration of the university in an obvious attempt to convert the educational institution into an instrument of political activism.

A statement which perhaps typifies the attitude of the revolting student groups was made by Mark Rudd, the leader of the Columbia University chapter of Students for a Democratic Society (SDS), who said:

"If we win, we will take control of your world, your corporation, your university, and attempt to mold a world in which we and other people can live as human beings. Your power is directly threatened since we will have to destroy that power before we take over."

The recent assassinations of Dr. Martin Luther King and Senator Robert F. Kennedy have only accentuated the tensions already existing. Some of the multi-universities, such as Columbia, the University of California, the University of Michigan, Wayne State University in Detroit, and the University of Colorado, to name a few, have borne the greatest brunt of the attack thus far. Without exception, it can be stated that the SDS, the Friends of SNCC, campus CORE chapters, the various Black Power movements such as the Student Afro-American Society, the Student Mobilization Committee, SSOS, SCAL, and other groups of the New Left, have been in large part responsible for initiating a revolutionary approach to change rather than following the democratic process under law within the spirit of the Constitution.

American colleges and universities are singularly ill-prepared for and particularly vulnerable to violence. Universities and colleges in this country are dedicated by nature and definition to the free interchange of ideas and doctrines, and it has thus far been assumed that the members of all groups in the academic community will have the same respect for contrary opinions and views that they demand for themselves. It appears clear that the aim of the leaders of the revolution is to transform the American college and university from an institution of liberal learning and education into an instrument for social revolution. The use of revolutionary tactics in universities and colleges in order to bring about social, economic, and political changes has its roots in European and particularly Latin American countries.

In view of the fact that student unrest, or, if you will, the student revolt, has taken the form of destruction of property, has resulted in danger to the safety of the individual and, in many instances, in disruption of the academic community, it is frequently difficult to decide when and to what extent the administration of the university is able to cope with the problem and when civil authorities must be called in to restore law and order. Society will not long tolerate the succession of incidents where neither campus discipline nor criminal prosecution is applied to disruptive student conduct. The potential consequences of institutional nonfeasance were pointedly reflected in a resolution introduced in the Michigan Legislature in May, 1968, and signed by 60 members of both parties, calling upon college officials to "maintain order and discipline and to expel students who seize control of school buildings," and warning that the Legislature will "hereafter look with favor" on the idea of reducing the appropriations of schools where disorderly demonstrations occur.

Case Law and Student Discipline

As a direct consequence of the developments over the last 10 years, an ever-increasing body of case law has developed and voluminous articles have been written in an attempt to define what, within the framework of the Constitution, should and must be the relationship between the student and the university or college.

In drawing the line between "academic freedom" and anarchy, the courts have been called upon to interpret the Constitution, particularly the due-process clause of the Fourteenth Amendment, the right of free speech, freedom of assembly under the First Amendment, the Fourth and Sixth Amendments, and the Civil Rights Act, 42 U.S.C.A., Sec. 1983.

Historically, the relationship between the student and the university was based upon the doctrine of *in loco parentis*. As has been pointed out by Dr. James A. Perkins, former president of Cornell University, Professor William Van Alstyne, then associate professor of law at Ohio State University, and Warren A. Seavey, professor of law emeritus of the Harvard Law School, it was completely unrealistic to view the university-student relationship in 1968 in the light of the doctrine of *in loco parentis*. Dr. Perkins pointed out that some 77 years ago a decision was handed down by the Illinois Supreme Court involving the dismissal of a student from a state university on the grounds that by voluntarily entering the university he necessarily surrenders his individual rights as a citizen. The Illinois court commented that in the way a student spends his time, behaves himself, chooses his recreation, and the places he visits, "in all these matters, and many others, he must yield obedience to those who, for the time being, are his masters."

Most college students today are at least agewise, if not mentally, mature and emancipated beyond the point where one can even pretend to assume that a parent-child relationship exists between the university and the student. Thus, the relationship between the student and the university must be based upon other grounds. Among those advanced have been the theory of contract or implied contract, the theory of consent or implied consent to the rules and regulations of the university at the time of matriculation or admission, and the trust or fiduciary theory. All these must be viewed within the framework of the due-process clause and the First Amendment of the Constitution.

Historically, the courts have been extremely reluctant to interfere with university and college disciplinary matters under the broad application of the doctrine of *in loco parentis*. (42 *Texas L. Rev.* 344; 70 *Harvard L. Rev.* 1406; 72 *Yale L. Jour.* 1362; 38 *Notre Dame Lawyer* 174; 58 *A.L.R.* 2d 903.) The scarcity of case law prior to *Dixon v. Alabama* is attributable to the fact that the courts dismissed the problem under the theory of *in loco parentis* and made it clear that they would not interfere with the administration of university and college disciplinary matters with possibly two exceptions, dating back to an old English case in 1723 and a Pennsylvania case in 1887. (*The King v. Chancellor of the University of Cambridge*, 2 Raym. Ld. 1334, 92 English Rep. 370 (K.B. 1723), and *Commonwealth ex. rel. Hill v. McCauley*, 3 Pa. County Ct. 77, 1887.)

The status of the law prior to *Dixon v. Alabama*, 294 F. 2d 150 (1961), was such that a clash was inevitable between those school administrators who advocated broad sweeping powers of discipline over students and the students—aided and abetted by lawyers, law professors, the American Civil Liberties Union, and the American Association of University Professors (AAUP)—who advocated that disciplinary procedures for students should be patterned after judicial proceedings. In the process, legal scholars in the field, like Dr. Van Alstyne and Professor Seavey, went overboard in trying to analogize a student disciplinary proceeding to a full-dress criminal proceeding with its attendant constitutional safeguards for the accused.

When the Illinois Supreme Court in 1956 decided *Bluett v. Board of Trustees of University of Illinois*, 134 N.E. 2d 635, which upheld the dismissal without a hearing of a student for cheating, Professor Seavey felt compelled to make the following comment:

> "It is shocking that the officials of a state educational institution, which can function properly only if our freedoms are preserved, should not understand the elementary principles of fair play. It is equally shocking that a court supports them in denying to a student the protection given to a pickpocket. . . .
>
> "On the other hand, if a professor is dropped under similar circumstances, not only is he given protection by the courts, but the associations of professors apply all their effective extralegal pressures against the offending institution, even though the latter may not have violated its contract. These same professors, so careful in protecting the interests of their fellows, are in fact fiduciaries for their students and should be the first to afford to their students every protection." *

In an article published by Michael T. Johnson on "Constitutional Rights of College Students," appearing in 42 *Texas L. Rev.* 344 (1964), the same trend in attempting to correlate due-process rights of the college student under the due-process clause of the Constitution to a full-dress criminal proceeding, going way beyond the actual requirements of the *Dixon* case, is apparent, and the most recent cases do not support the conclusions drawn by Mr. Johnson, although the article is well written and deserves attention.

Case Law in State-supported and Public Colleges and Universities

It should be pointed out that major case law in the area of student discipline and due process has developed primarily in state-supported and public universities and colleges. So that there may be no mistake on the part of the private college administrator, the due-process clause of the Fourteenth Amendment is expanding constantly. "State action" may become applicable in almost any given situation or if federal support to private institutions increases to the point where the courts will be diluting the distinction between public and private schools in the due-process area.

On the other hand, it should be recognized that the courts are still making a distinction between the rights of students in public and private universities. In *Greene v. Howard University*, 271 F.S. 609 (D.D.C., 1967), Judge Holtzoff was faced with the question of whether the relations between a university and its students and between the university and its faculty are subject to judicial control and, specifically, whether the termination by the university of the status of a student or, incidentally, of a member of the faculty is subject in whole or in part to judicial review.

The background was set by a series of disorders which took place on the campus of Howard University involving, in one instance, the head of the Selective Service System of the United States who had been invited to make a speech at the university. A group of students created such a disturbance as to make it impossible for him to address the audience. On another occasion, the university authorities were about to conduct a hearing on charges of misconduct against a student when a group composed of some students and some members of the faculty created such a commotion and uproar as to render it impracticable for the hearing to proceed. Threatening utterances were heard on the campus. Several fires took place. The university authorities concluded, after careful and thorough investigation, that the student plaintiffs as well as the plaintiff faculty members actively participated in creating this chaos and disorder. Accordingly, in an effort to bar a continuation and repetition of such disruptive incidents, the university, in June 1967, sent a form letter to each of the students involved, notifying them that they would not be permitted to return to the institution for the next academic year. Any reference to action taken against faculty members is omitted because this subject is covered in Chapter 3 of this section.

Federal District Judge Holtzoff concluded that the student plaintiffs had no constitutional, statutory, or contractual right to a notice of charges and a hearing before they could be expelled or their connection with the university could be otherwise severed, and that it was entirely within the discretion of the university authorities to grant or withhold a hearing. At least in the Howard University case the court felt that attendance at Howard University is a *privilege* and that the university reserves the right to deny admission to or require the dismissal of any student at any time for any reason deemed sufficient by the university. The judge concluded by saying:

"It would be a sad blow to institutions of higher learning and to the development of independent thought and culture if the courts were to step in and control and direct the administration of discipline and the selection of members of the faculty in universities and colleges. An entering wedge seemingly innocuous at first blush, may lead step-by-step to a serious external domination of universities and colleges and a consequent damper and hindrance to their intellectual development and growth."

Just how long this distinction between public and private colleges and universities is going to be recognized by the courts, in the light of the "state action" concept of the Fourteenth Amendment, is difficult to foretell. Professor Van Alstyne, in his article published in 10 *U.C.L.A. L. Rev.* 368 (1963), may well be correct in stating, "Nevertheless, just as the perimeter of due process has expanded, so the perimeter of 'state action' has also expanded." Therefore, the college administrator and his legal counsel, even at private institutions, should take a long hard look at the development of the cases over the last 10 years and give serious consideration to the requirements of due process as outlined in *Dixon v. Alabama* and the cases following through 1968.

Scope of Problem of Student Unrest as Reflected by Statistical Data

The scope of the problem of student unrest has been reflected by statistical data compiled by universities and colleges and by selected national organizations concerned with the legal problems of higher education. It will be helpful to examine some, if not all, of the statistical data for the simple purpose of demonstrating that no institution of higher learning in the United States is immune from student action which can be disruptive to the main purpose of a college or university, which is to provide the best possible post-high school education to as many young people as possible.

The National Student Association, in a poll taken during a two-month period during 1967, shows that 14,567 students took part in 71 demonstrations on 62 campuses in October and November of 1967. It can, of course, be argued that the participants represented only 2.7 percent of the combined undergraduate enrollment of the schools canvassed.

The National Association of College and University Attorneys (NACUA) mailed out questionnaires to member institutional attorneys and received 123 replies. Generally speaking, the campuses of 78, or 63.4 percent of those reporting, have had student demonstrations, 52 of which, or 66.5 percent, have been peaceful and orderly. The remaining institutions, 26 in number, or 33.3 percent, have had disruptive or otherwise disorderly demonstrations. In 16 of the 26 institutions referred to, or 61.5 percent, civil disobedience was encouraged by the SDS; and in 13 instances the institutions were required to call in civil authorities. In 12 cases, personal injury and property damage were involved. In 13 cases, the institutions were compelled to initiate criminal and/or civil proceedings. The above figures cannot really give or indicate an accurate picture of the magnitude of disruptive conduct on the part of students. It should be kept in mind that NACUA received replies from only 123 of the approximately 2,132 colleges and universities that exist, not counting community colleges and new four-year degree-granting institutions established since 1965. (For some more up-to-date statistics, see *College and University Business,* p. 38, August, 1968; *The Politics of Protest,* a report by Jerome H. Skolnick to Dr. Milton J. Eisenhower, Ballantine Books, Inc., 1969, published in arrangement with Simon and Schuster, Inc.; and U.S. Riot Commission Report, 1968, New York Times Company, Bantam Books, Inc.)

Student Rights as Outlined in Significant Cases

On the basis of the foregoing, let us turn to an examination of the requirements outlined in *Dixon v. Alabama; Knight v. State Board of Higher Education,* 200 F.S. 174 (1961); *Due v. Florida A. & M.,* 223 F.S. 396 (1963); *Goldberg v. Regents of University of California; Madera v. Board of Education,* 267 F.S. 356; *Zanders v. Louisiana State Board of Education,* 281 F.S. 747 (1968); and *Buttny v. Smiley,* 281 F.S. 280 (D. Colo., 1968). In the *Dixon* case, Judge Rives, speaking for the court, laid down the following guidelines relative to student discipline at tax-supported or public institutions:

1. The student should be given notice that he is charged with certain misconduct. He should be told the nature of the charge, the reasons for the hearing, and the circumstances or acts which support the bringing of the charges.
2. The student should be given the names of the witnesses against him and either an oral or written report of the facts which each would testify to.
3. The student should be given the opportunity to present to the hearing body his own defense and to produce it either orally or in writing.
4. If the hearing is not before a board of education, the findings of the hearing and adjudicatory body should be presented in a report open to the student's inspection.

It is interesting to note that, as far back as 1901, in *Koblitz v. Western Reserve University,* 21 Ohio C.C.R. 144, the Ohio court stated:

> "Custom, again, has established a rule. That rule is so uniform that it has become a rule of law; and, if the plaintiff had a contract with the university, he agreed to abide by that rule of law, and that rule of law is this: That in determining whether a student has been guilty of improper conduct that will tend to demoralize the school, it is not necessary that the professors should go through the formality of a trial. *They should give the student whose conduct is being investigated every fair opportunity of showing his innocence.* They should be careful in receiving evidence against him; they should weigh it; determine whether it comes from a source freighted with prejudice; determine the likelihood, by all surrounding circumstances, as to who is right, and then act upon it as jurors, with calmness, consideration and fair minds. When they have done this and reached a conclusion, they have done all that the law requires of them to do." [Emphasis supplied.]

In addition to the above requirement, question has been raised concerning additional safeguards and rights of students:

1. Should students or administrators, or even lawyers, appear as witnesses and sit on the hearing board in view of the fact that any one or more of them might have brought the charges and thus serve, simultaneously, in a double capacity as decision makers and as prosecutors?

In part, this question was answered in *Buttny v. Smiley,* and the court fully approved of the procedure adopted by the University of Colorado and its able legal counsel. (See also *Wasson v. Trowbridge,* 382 F. 2d 807 (1967); *Jones v. State Board of Educa-*

tion, 279 F.S. 190 (1968); and *Wright v. Texas Southern University,* 277 F.S. 110 (1967).

2. Should cross-examination under oath be a requirement and should the hearing board consider statements of witnesses who are not available for cross-examination?

3. Should the hearing board permit the taking of evidence "improperly" acquired during a search of the student's room under the search-and-seizure clause?

On the question of search and seizure, see *People v. Kelly,* 16 Cal. Rptr. 177 (1961); and 16 *Stan. L. Rev.* 318 (1964); also *People v. Overton,* 283 N.Y.S. 2d 22 (N.Y. Ct. App., July 7, 1967).

4. Is there a requirement that the student accused of misconduct and facing sanction, including suspension or dismissal, be entitled to legal counsel at the hearing?

In *Barker v. Hardway,* president of Bluefield State College in West Virginia, 283 F.S. 228 (D. W. Va., April 10, 1968), Judge Christie, following the rationale of *Dixon v. Alabama, Buttny v. Smiley, Zanders v. Louisiana State Board of Education,* and *Goldberg v. Regents of the University of California,* concluded that all the requirements of the due-process clause of the Fourteenth Amendment had been complied with regarding notice, opportunity for hearing, and production of evidence against the student involved. Of the ten students accused who had requested a hearing before the Faculty Committee on Student Affairs, four appeared and received hearings. The other six appeared, but refused to submit to hearings unless represented by counsel, standing on the due-process clause of the Fourteenth Amendment. Judge Christie points out that there is no universal application to all situations and that the hearing committee had none of the attributes of a judicial body, since its only function was to get information and to make recommendations which had no binding effect on the president, faculty, or Board of Education. As was explained in *Dixon v. Alabama,* student disciplinary hearings *need not be full-dress judicial hearings,* and the courts have repeatedly negated such a concept. The court simply refused to expand the guarantees of the Sixth Amendment of the Constitution relating to right of counsel to anything other than criminal or semicriminal proceedings. In *Wasson v. Trowbridge,* 382 F.S. 807 (2d Cir. 1967), the court expressly declined to grant right to counsel under the facts and circumstances of that case, and in the *Madera* and *Zanders* cases the court avoided a definitive ruling on the point. (See also 58 A.L.R. 2d 909–912.)

Judge Christie reiterates the position that enrollment in a school does not mean that the student is required to surrender any of his constitutional rights, but, by the same token, this does not give him the right to abuse and harass the administrator or the institution or to engage in conduct detrimental to its well-being or which may tend to deprive other students of their right to a peaceful atmosphere in which to pursue their ambition for an education.

It is not known with certainty just exactly how far the courts will go in extending the constitutional rights of the student under the due-process clause beyond the criteria enumerated in the *Dixon* case. One of the best recent opinions in this area was written by Justice William E. Miller, chief judge of the U.S. District Court, Nashville Division, in *Jones v. State Board of Education of and for the State of Tennessee,* 279 F.S. 190. This was an injunction proceeding brought initially as a class action on behalf of 70 students threatened with expulsion from Tennessee A. & I. State University. However, the case eventually narrowed itself down to three principal contestants, and the court ruled that since the case applied only to the three plaintiffs and possibly three other persons, totaling six, a class action could not be maintained. Thus the court rejected the students' contention that the class was so numerous that joinder of all others would be imperative. Without resorting to detail or segregating the charges against each individual, the accused students were charged with misconduct in the cafeteria and with boycotting registration at the university for the fall quarter of 1967. One was charged with being arrested by the Nashville Metropolitan Police Department on a charge of disorderly conduct, with the promotion of unrest on the campus by distributing literature designed for the purpose of disrupting the function of the university, with inciting riot, and with disrupting fellow students in the pursuit of their studies. One was charged with a morals charge, with the display of a disrespectful attitude toward the university authorities during a meeting of the student body, with participation in a rock-throwing incident, with unauthorized entry of a building on the university campus, and generally with continuous disrespect for the authority of the university officials, contrary to the provisions of the *Student Handbook* published by Tennessee A. & I. Each of the three offenders was charged respectively with one or more of the above violations and no useful purpose would be served in reciting the specific charges against each one of the three students.

The Faculty Advisory Committee held the hearings on the charges. The court in the person of Mr. Justice Miller found that, while a state school must comply with the elementary principle of procedural fair play, it is not necessary that it adopt all the formalities of a court of law. It went on to say that the court of law will not interfere with this function when, as in the case cited, the university proceeds in a manner which is found to be *fundamentally fair and reasonable.* It is interesting to note how far the Faculty Advisory Committee went in giving the students all the latitude possible and in providing them with an opportunity to defend themselves against the charges made:

1. Notice of charges, with appropriate specificity, was properly given in each instance.
2. Hearings were held with appropriate advance notice.
3. Legal counsel was made available to plaintiffs in the hearings.
4. The students were given an opportunity to testify, to ask questions of their accusers, and to present witnesses and other evidence in their own behalf. The witnesses were not under oath and the judge indicated that the formal rules of evidence were not invoked as they might be in a civil or criminal court proceeding.
5. Transcripts were made of the proceedings before the Faculty Advisory Committee, and the court found that the charges preferred against the students were actually more detailed than many indictments presented in courts of law and that the plaintiffs understood fully the charges against them.
6. Plaintiffs' counsel was given an opportunity to cross-examine witnesses. It is implied from the judge's opinion that the hearing accorded to the accused students went way beyond the basic requirements established in the *Dixon* case.

In answer to the contention of the students that a fair hearing was denied because of commingling of prosecutorial and adjudicatory functions (two members of the Faculty Advisory Committee testified against the plaintiffs), the court held that there is no violation of procedural due process when a member of a disciplinary body sits on a case after he has shared with others the facts of a particular incident. The court also rejected the contention of the students that the Faculty Advisory Committee acted with bias or prejudice. The court held that there was substantial evidence in the transcript of the hearings to support the findings of the Faculty Advisory Committee against each of the three plaintiffs.

Against the contention of the students that the regulations of the university *Student Handbook* were unconstitutionally vague, the court observed that in comparing the legal principles applicable in the loyalty-oath cases, which were based on state statutes, the students were not attacking a state statute but rather a student regulation found in a university handbook. Accordingly the court ruled that university regulations for students, because of the very nature of the institution and its goals and purposes, should not be tested by the same requirements of specificity that are applied to state statutes.

Speaking parenthetically about the common assertion by students regarding vagueness or specificity of a particular student conduct rule, Tom Cunningham, the chief counsel of the University of California, observed that the militant student elements who most loudly denounced the former standard of conduct at the University of California for its vagueness bitterly attacked the revision of the same rules for specificity.

Judge Miller also ruled on the contention of the students that the Faculty Advisory Committee had deprived them of the equal protection of the law because not all students involved were treated alike. His answer was that the equal-protection clause of the Fourteenth Amendment is intended to secure the full and equal benefit of all laws and proceedings for the security of persons and property and to subject all persons to like punishment, pains, penalties, taxes, licenses, and exactions of every kind and to no other. He found that there was no violation of equal protection of the law when a statute or regulation, or the application or enforcement of either of them, makes a classification that is reasonable rather than arbitrary. The record simply did not support the students' position that they were arbitrarily and invidiously discriminated against by the Faculty Advisory Committee.

As to the contention by the students that they were disciplined because they retained counsel, the court commented that this is totally without merit because other students who retained the same counsel as plaintiffs were permitted to continue at the university.

Finally, with regard to the First Amendment freedoms, the judge observed that the students' conduct, as shown by the evidence at the hearings, involved a clear departure from the exercise of free speech and that the action taken was in no way an attempt to suppress the plaintiffs' political views but rather an effort by the Faculty Advisory Committee to control and regulate conduct obstructing the educational functions of the university. He underscored this ruling by a citation from Mr. Justice Holmes in *Schenck v. United States*, 249 U.S. 47, as follows: "The most stringent protection of free speech would not protect a man in falsely shouting fire in a theatre and causing a panic."

The two latest cases on student discipline and due process, *Barker v. Hardway*, 283 F.S. 228, previously mentioned, and *Wright v. Texas Southern University*, 392 F. 2d 728 (1968), came to the same conclusion.

Colleges and universities have the right to enact rules and regulations concerning student conduct, whether this right be granted by the legislature, the charter, or the Constitution, and whether the school is private or public. A frequent argument has been made that the rules and regulations of a particular institution are too vague to give the student notice and warning of the type of conduct which will expose him to disciplinary proceedings. In the *Goldberg* case, the California court held that the Board of Regents has the implied powers to enact rules and regulations concerning discipline and that a general statement of rules of conduct is sufficient. However, the careful administrator and his university attorney, after reviewing the formidable array of case law which has built up in the last few years, would do well to reexamine the student discipline procedures of his institution.

Suggested Standards of Punishable Conduct

The governing body of the college or university should, not only in order to protect itself but also to give the student clear and unambiguous warning, establish a standard of punishable conduct which might include, among others, the following (taken almost verbatim from the University of California Conduct Code):

1. Dishonesty, such as cheating, plagiarism, or knowingly furnishing false information to the university or its staff.
2. Forgery, alteration, or misuse of university documents, records, or identification.
3. Obstruction or disruption of teaching, research, administration, disciplinary procedures, or other university activities, including its public service functions, or of other authorized activities on university premises.
4. Physical abuse of any person at any university-owned or controlled functions or conduct which threatens or endangers the health or safety of any such person.

5. Theft of or damage to the property of the state, of a member of the university community, or of a campus visitor.

6. Unauthorized entry into or use of university facilities.

7. Violation of university policies or of campus regulations, including campus regulations concerning the registration of student organizations, the use of university facilities, or the time, place, and manner of public expression.

8. Use, possession, or distribution of narcotics or dangerous drugs, such as marijuana and LSD, and all drugs termed addictive by the State Board of Pharmacy, the use of which is prohibited by the laws of the state involved.

9. Violation of rules governing residence in university-owned or controlled property.

10. Disorderly conduct or lewd, indecent, or obscene conduct or expression on university-owned or controlled property or at university-sponsored or supervised functions.

11. Failure to comply with directions issued by university officials in the course of the performance of their duties.

12. Conduct which adversely affects the student's suitability as a member of the academic community and disrupts the ordinary function of education.

13. Violation of federal, state, and local laws involving conduct on or off campus which represents a continuing threat to the university community.

It should be made clear that the First Amendment rights, including the right of free speech, are guaranteed to all students and do not come under the scope of university rules and regulations. On the other hand, students should be warned that the right of free speech does not include a right to engage in disruptive physical action or any conduct which interferes with the ordinary processes of administering a college or university engaged in providing the student with the education he is seeking to obtain.

Suggested Standards for Disciplinary Hearings

As far as setting up standards for disciplinary hearings is concerned, in accordance with the cases, it might be useful to adhere to the following guidelines:

1. The notice should contain a statement of the specific charges and grounds which, if proven, would justify expulsion or other disciplinary action under the rules and regulations of the governing board. By its nature, a charge of misconduct, as opposed to a failure to meet the scholastic standards of a university, depends upon the collection of the facts concerning the charge of misconduct, easily colored by the points of view of the witnesses. This is not to imply that a full-dress judicial hearing, with the right to cross-examine witnesses, is required. A hearing must provide the board or the administrative authority of the university to which the hearing procedure is delegated with an opportunity to hear both sides in detail in order to protect the rights of all involved. The full-dress judicial hearing would not only be extremely cumbersome to administer but would be detrimental to the university's educational atmosphere and impractical to carry out. Nevertheless, the rudiments of adversary proceedings may be preserved without encroaching upon the interest of the university.

2. The student should be given the names of the witnesses against him and an oral or written report of the facts to which each witness testifies.

3. The student should be given the opportunity to present to the board or the university, or at least to an administrative official of the university, his own defense against the charges and to produce either oral testimony or written affidavits of witnesses in his behalf.

4. A transcript, not necessarily in detail, should be kept by the hearing body, which may consist of faculty, students, or administrative officers, or any combination thereof, as determined by the administration, in order to perpetuate the testimony for possible appeal.

5. Some system of appeal from the initial hearing to the chief administrative officer of the university or the governing board might be considered.

6. Whether or not the hearing is open to the public or closed is a matter for policy

determination. The composition of the hearing body is also a question of policy. A review of 90 institutions reveals that the student disciplinary body is composed as follows: students, faculty, staff, 45; faculty alone, 16; students alone, 19; two separate committees, one student and one faculty, 10.

7. There is no absolute requirement that the accused student be represented by legal counsel. A review of the above-mentioned 90 institutions reveals that in 34 instances students were not represented by counsel, student or otherwise, and in 31 instances they were represented by counsel. In most cases, the university's position was presented by the office of the dean of students, but in the University of Colorado case, the chief counsel for the University of Colorado represented the Board of Regents and was also the hearings officer. However, he did not act in an adversary capacity. He functioned largely as an adviser on procedural matters to the committee. He made no argument to the University Disciplinary Committee and made no argument whatsoever to the Administrative Council or to the Regents in connection with the appellate proceedings, and the United States District Court for Colorado rejected the argument of plaintiffs that the university counsel acted as judge and prosecutor simultaneously.

(Examples of recently developed student conduct programs, including a code of student conduct and student remedies, may be found in readily available versions of the student conduct codes of the University of California at Berkeley and the University of Oregon at Eugene. The student conduct code of the University of Oregon, as revised in July, 1967, is an example of what in this author's opinion would satisfy the legal requirements of the *Dixon* case and in effect goes far beyond them, as was observed in *Jones v. Tennessee.*)

The courts are not at all unanimous on the exact relationship between the student and the university and on whether or not the legal basis is founded in contract, revocable privilege, trust or fiduciary relationship, or the inherent power to maintain discipline at publicly supported institutions. There is no reason why a college or university should not be able to meet the criteria prescribed by the courts, which basically amount to fair play and an opportunity to be heard, without adhering to the rigid standards of the due-process clause in the First, Fourth, Sixth, and Fourteenth Amendments of the United States Constitution or their equivalent in the state constitutions as they apply to criminal cases. To force a college or university to adopt a judicial system in the administration of student discipline, as has been advocated by some, would be an impossible task; but, if the governing boards fail for any reason to meet the criteria prescribed by the courts, they will be relinquishing their responsibilities to the civil authorities and judicial process.

Civil Disobedience and University Tactical Policy Objectives

No discussion of the maintenance of student discipline and rules and regulations relating thereto would be complete without a consideration of the alternative in cases of violent demonstrations, riots, or disruptive conduct resulting in academic penalty, and without also giving consideration to a bitter fact of life, namely the absolute necessity for the administrator to call upon the law enforcement agencies at the proper time and for the proper reason. Recent events at Columbia University are an example of what not to do in a situation which demands immediate attention because of the force and violence involved, which, in this instance, resulted in complete disruption of the function of the university.

The entire academic world is now aware of the goals and aims of certain student organizations such as the SDS and of the fact that it is not possible to negotiate with them. This is a fact of life which the administrator must face, and he must face it immediately and by prompt action. If he does not, events similar to those that occurred at Columbia University will take place all over the country.

This does not mean that in every instance of a demonstration or sit-in the police should be called, but if the administrator has knowledge of the principal instigators of the riot or demonstration and if he is fully aware of the fact that no amount of negotiation will bring about a desired and satisfactory result, then there is no recourse but to call in the law-enforcement authorities at the earliest possible moment in order to avoid damage to property and injury to persons.

Earl F. Morris, president of the American Bar Association, recently speaking on "American Society and the Rebirth of Civil Obedience," commented as follows:

> "The concept of civil disobedience has been distorted in these times to justify violence and anarchy. As an example, I refer to the students at a southern university who completely stopped the operations of the school by invading the administration building and camping there, demanding that charges be dropped against students who had allegedly participated in a previous disturbance; at this same school, a year before, students attacked a classroom building, knocked down campus policemen, ripped out a door, in order to disrupt a disciplinary committee meeting that had been called to hear charges against a student.
>
> "These people misdirect and misrepresent the philosophy of dissent and the doctrine of civil disobedience. They are not attempting to change a law or influence government policy; they are expressing, in a violent manner, their distaste with 'the way things are being run'; they are using civil disobedience as a pressure technique and as an almost instinctive response to any grievance, real or imagined. This is not genuine civil disobedience; it is the wanton, reckless use of 'muscle,' without order, without logic, without intelligence.
>
> "I seriously question whether many of those who perpetuate violence, if not upon persons or property then certainly upon the concept of peaceful, lawful dissent and protest, recognize that an essential concomitant to civil disobedience is the actor's willingness to accept the punishment that follows his breaking the law. . . . Many of those who engage in civil disobedience today seem to be demanding for themselves the unlimited right to disobey laws. . . .
>
> "In tolerating, and often encouraging, certain forms of civil disobedience throughout our history, we have wittingly walked a necessarily fine line between individual liberty and anarchy, because of the belief that the freedom of each person to say and do what he feels is right is paramount. But we must not allow freedom to become license, and the right to say and read and hear what one wants does not bear with it the right to ignore the rules completely—even in the name of the 'higher law.'
>
> "In our society, the rule of law serves as a basis for all social action. . . . Perhaps the most significant application of the rule of law—and surely the most timely in our present context—is the concept that each of us must comply with the law if we are to have an ordered society in which rights and responsibilities are concomitants. An ordered society cannot survive—and ours, strong as it is, will not survive—if each individual may determine which laws he will obey, and may with impunity flout those which he finds distasteful. . . .
>
> "Whatever the attempted rationalizations to justify civil disobedience, whatever the claims for its necessity throughout our history, we have reached a point in the life of our nation when there arises an imperative need for the full acceptance of the rule of law as an essential doctrine and for a rebirth of civil obedience."

It has been suggested by William L. Steude, director of student-community relations at the University of Michigan, that, in dealing with disorders which confront the campus with physical disruption, the tactical policy objectives might be outlined thus:

1. To retain general community support within the university, both faculty and student, for actions taken by the administration
2. To separate the militant from the moderate elements if a physical confrontation should be necessary
3. To retain the initiative and, if possible, some measure of control over the extent and manner of participation by law-enforcement officials

If the administration of the college or university fails to establish adequate rules and regulations governing student discipline and does not provide a hearings procedure which meets the minimum requirements of "due process," one can expect that there will be a continuing trend toward incidents involving the courts in cases where disciplinary action is taken against students. The students seem to feel that a legal solution may be more favorable to their interest, and they also appear to hope that court action will incidentally have the effect of compelling university administrators to change the status quo.

Student Legal Action Against Universities

As far as legal remedies are concerned, a review of the cases indicates that the student may take action against the college or university in a number of different ways. In most states, the writ of mandamus or its equivalent is available against both private and public institutions. This remedy, however, is restricted to those cases where it can be shown to the court that the governing authority has clearly abused its discretion or has failed to perform some statutory duty imposed upon it by law. It must be conceded that most of the cases do involve public universities; but there are some instances where mandamus was employed against private institutions. (See *Barone v. Adams,* 240 N.Y.S. 2d 390 (1963); reversed in 248 N.Y.S. 2d 72 (1964), involving Hofstra College.)

Other possible remedies may be injunction or specific performance of the contract existing between the student and the university. The choice of remedies and the success thereof depends upon the legal theory upon which the student relies in bringing action against the university. As has been previously noted, the various legal theories involved may be based on the now outmoded doctrine of *in loco parentis,* or on contract, trust, status, or the invasion of statutory or constitutional rights. Whether or not the action or suit is brought in federal or state court depends upon the jurisdictional requirements in a given case. A review and analysis of student remedies seeking court relief for disciplinary action taken against them was prepared in 1968 by a third-year law student at Cornell University Law School. The article makes a significant contribution to the important dialogue which is now taking place on the campuses of this country and among lawyers concerning the matter of the rights of the student as opposed to those of the institution in disciplinary matters. (See Stephen R. Knapp, *The College Counsel,* vol. 3, no. 1, p. 16, National Association of College and University Attorneys, 1968.)

There has been an attempt, thus far unsuccessful and justifiably so, on the part of some students to claim the constitutional right of double jeopardy as provided for in the Fifth Amendment of the United States Constitution and the constitutions of probably all the states in the union. In the author's opinion, this argument is not legally supportable because the double jeopardy clause applies only to criminal prosecutions for violations of state or federal statutes, and no authority whatsoever has been uncovered which would even indicate that the question of double jeopardy has any bearing in those situations where the student is not only convicted in a court for violation of statute but, as a consequence, is also suspended or dismissed from an educational institution pursuant to its rules and regulations of student conduct.

Summing up the foregoing discussion of student discipline in the courts, we must recognize that the courts are reluctant to interfere in the disciplinary problems of educational institutions and have no desire to usurp the function of the administrator. On the other hand, if certain minimal requirements of due process, as outlined above, are not met by the educational institution, the court will step in and respond to the student's request for redress of grievances. That the courts do not consider a student disciplinary proceeding as a criminal adversary proceeding is made perfectly clear in *Madera v. Board of Education,* 267 F.S. 356; reversed by the Federal Circuit Court in

386 F.S. 2d 778; but see *Tinker v. Des Moines Ind. Community School Dist. et al.* (No. 21—October Term 1968, Supreme Court of the United States; opinion dated Feb. 24, 1969).

ADMISSION REQUIREMENTS, ACADEMIC STANDARDS, AND STUDENT CONTRACTS

Requirements for admission and matriculation to colleges and universities are governed exclusively by the appropriate governing boards or institutional administrations. Public universities and colleges derive this authority usually from a general grant by the legislature of any given state, and private institutions derive it from the inherent power to set standards of admission. The institutions have the almost unqualified right to deny admission to those students who do not meet the academic requirements. Occasionally the registrar or admissions officer of a college or university will encounter a situation where it may be deemed advisable to deny admission to a student on grounds of defect in moral character. In those instances, the standards for determining who is to be excluded should be reasonable and reasonably applied, that is to say without discrimination in any particular case. Very few cases can be found where courts have attempted to interfere with the rights of educational institutions to set admission standards; and as indicated previously, the courts have taken jurisdiction only in those cases where enrollment of the student is terminated for disciplinary reasons or in cases of discrimination based on race, color, creed, or national origin, as covered in Chapter 4 in this section.

It may be presumed and taken for granted that publicly supported colleges and universities have the right to make a distinction in the requirements for admission, tuition, and fees depending upon whether or not the student applying for admission is a resident or nonresident. Residency requirements in public colleges and universities are left to constitutional or legislative mandate or general legislative authority delegating that power to the governing board of the state college or university. (See *Newman v. Graham*, 349 P. 2d 716 (1960) and the latest reported case of *American Commuters Association, Inc. v. Levitt*, 279 F.S. 40 (N.Y. Dist. Ct. 1967).)

The courts have been fairly consistent in upholding classification of in-state students as opposed to nonresident students for tuition purposes. In 1964 the Colorado Supreme Court held that the classification prescribed in the Colorado statutes is not unreasonable nor is it in violation of any of the clauses of the state constitution or the United States Constitution (*Landwehr v. Regents of University of Colorado*, 396 P. 2d 451 (Sup. Ct. Colo., November 9, 1964)). The Colorado Supreme Court ruled that neither the equal-protection nor due-process clause of the Fourteenth Amendment, the power of Congress to regulate commerce among the states, the privileges and immunities clause, or the civil rights clause of the Colorado constitution were applicable if the classification prescribed is reasonable. The classification of students applying for admission to a tax-supported institution into resident and nonresident groups is a matter of legislative determination according to the court. With appropriate delegation to the governing body of the institution by the legislature, the same type of classification would be held reasonable.

In *Cobbs v. State Board of Education* (Dist. Ct. 3d Jud. Dist. Idaho, in and for County of Ada, Civil Case no. 36600, January 16, 1967), the judge concluded his opinion by saying, "The nonresident tuition policy is within their discretion [the Regents of the University of Idaho] and cannot be said to be a spending of public money for the private benefit of nonresidents of Idaho, as a matter of law." A good discussion of the case may be found in M. M. Chambers, *The Colleges and the Courts, 1962–1966*, Interstate Printers and Publishers, Inc., Danville, Ill., 1967, pp. 16ff.

In a fairly recent case involving the State University of Iowa, the principal question before the court involved a determination of whether the plaintiff was being deprived of certain constitutional rights because he was charged a nonresident rather than a resident tuition fee while attending the College of Law at the university. Prior to the time he entered the University of Iowa Law School in September, 1961, he had resided in Illinois. Since his enrollment at Iowa, he had been continuously attending the university and was at the time of the decision 22 years of age. Then, in August, 1964, he married a girl who had lived in Iowa all of her life. During his entire school tenure, he was charged with a nonresident tuition fee. His contention was that he was now a resident and citizen of Iowa and that the school regulations on tuition fees discriminated as between a male student whose wife is a resident of Iowa and a female nonresident student whose husband is a resident of Iowa. The court ruled:

> "The regulation classifying students as residents or nonresidents for tuition payment purposes is *not arbitrary or unreasonable and bears a rational relation to Iowa's object and purpose of financing, operating and maintaining its educational institutions.*" [Emphasis supplied. *Clarke v. Redeker,* 259 F. Supp. 117 (D. Iowa, September 15, 1966).]

Some words of caution may be in order, since a very few limited instances have been recorded in which the courts have been called upon to rule on questions involving admission, readmission, academic achievement, and scholarship. In *Kolbeck v. Kramer,* 202 A. 2d 889 (Sup. Ct. N.J., July 23, 1964), a suit was brought to compel Rutgers University, which is now a state university, to admit the plaintiff as a student. He had been accepted by admission but refused to submit to medical tests because of his religious beliefs. He further refused to sign a statement that he was a member of the Christian Science faith. He claimed that the tests were against his religious beliefs and that he was not a member of an organized religious sect. The court ruled in favor of the plaintiff, recognizing that Rutgers University is a political subdivision of the state of New Jersey and that the statute generally requires pupils to undergo physical examinations, vaccinations, diphtheria immunizations, polio immunizations, and tuberculosis tests. The court's opinion was generally based upon the protection of the rights of the individual provided by the First Amendment to the Constitution within the protection of the Fourteenth Amendment thereof. Even though the court ordered the university to admit the plaintiff, the case has now become moot since the student disavowed his intent to pursue his application to Rutgers. (*Kolbeck v. Kramer,* 214 A. 2d 408 (Sup. Ct. N.J., November 22, 1965).)

As a matter of practice, most institutions by rule or regulation provide for an exemption of compliance with such requirements as vaccination and immunization on the condition that the student and his parents assume full responsibility for any consequences which might ensue as a result of failure to comply with the health requirements.

A general statement concerning the attitude of the courts regarding admission was made in *State ex rel. Stallard v. White,* 42 Am. R. 496 (1882) as follows:

> "The admission of students in a public educational institution is one thing, and the government and control of students after they are admitted, and have become subject to the jurisdiction of the institution, is quite another thing.
>
> "The first rests upon well-established rules, either prescribed by law or sanctioned by usage, from which the right to admission is to be determined. The latter rests largely in the discretion of the officers in charge, the regulations prescribed for that purpose being subject to modification or change from time to time as supposed emergencies may arise.
>
> "Having in view the various statutes in force in this State touching educational affairs, and the decisions of this court as well as of other courts bearing on the general

subject, we think it may be safely said that every inhabitant of this State of suitable age, and of reasonably good moral character, not afflicted with any contagious or loathsome disease, and not incapacitated by some mental or physical infirmity, is entitled to admission as a student in the Purdue University.

"This right of admission may not be enforced when there is not sufficient room in the university, and may be postponed until the applicant has made some proficiency in merely preliminary studies; but it is a right which the trustees are not authorized to materially abridge, and which they cannot as an abstract proposition rightfully deny."

In another early case, *Brown v. the Board of Education of the City of Cleveland,* 6 Ohio N.P. 411 (1899), concerning a student who had been dropped from a normal school for not being adapted to the profession of teaching, the lower Ohio court ordered the student readmitted. In that case, the court commented as follows:

"There is a marked distinction to be drawn between matters of discretion as to the manner of performing official duties, and the right of pupils to be admitted into schools and to be excluded therefrom. *Courts will not attempt to interfere with rules established by the board of education where the same are reasonable and do not deprive a pupil of any right.*" [Emphasis supplied.]

In *Lesser v. The Board of Education of the City of New York,* 239 N.Y.S. 2d 776 (1963), the court commented concerning the arbitrariness, unfairness, and unreasonable conduct of the school administrators as follows:

"Courts may not interfere with the administrative discretion exercised by agencies which are vested with the administration and control of educational institutions, unless the circumstances disclosed by the record leave no scope for the use of that discretion in the matter under scrutiny.

"If the Board of Higher Education performs its discretion fairly and not arbitrarily, the court may not substitute its judgment for that of the Board.

"More particularly, a court should refrain from interpreting its views within those delicate areas of school administration which relate to the eligibility of applicants and the determination of marking standards, unless a clear abuse of statutory authority or a practice of discrimination or gross error has been shown.

"The determination as to what factors should enter into the standards set for college admission was within the exclusive province of the college authorities. *The judicial task ends when it is found that the applicant has received from the college authorities uniform treatment under reasonable regulations fairly administered.*" [Emphasis supplied.]

Within the last two years, a few cases have been decided concerning the reasonableness of action taken by colleges and universities in the area of admissions and academic achievement.

In *Woody v. Burns,* 188 S. 2d 56 (Dist. Ct. App. Fla., July 21, 1966), suit was brought by a student against an order of the college prohibiting him from being admitted to the College of Architecture and Fine Arts. It appears that the student was prevented from registering when he voluntarily disclosed that during the preceding trimester he had not taken the Art 207 course as he had been instructed to do by his department head and student adviser, who had refused to accept a Pensacola Junior College course as a substitute for the required 207 course. For this offense, Woody was charged with altering a basic record of the University, a course-assignment card, without prior permission from the professor involved. The student took his case to the president of the University of Florida and then the matter was appealed to the Board of Regents. The Board affirmed the decision of the president to deny Woody admission to the College of Architecture and Fine Arts *without prejudice to apply for enrollment in the other colleges of the University.* This decision was affirmed by the State Board of Education.

Then Woody applied for a court order. The trial court denied his application but, on review by the Court of Appeals, the ruling of the trial court was reversed, stating as follows:

"This record presents an incongruous situation wherein the University . . . says this student's conduct is not acceptable to the faculty members of one college but that the same conduct does not make him ineligible for acceptance by other colleges of the University complex. We are not aware of the delegation by the legislature or the State Board of Higher Education or the Board of Regents to the faculty members of any college of the higher education system of this state to arbitrarily or capriciously decide who they desire to teach, and should such delegation be attempted it would amount to creating a hierarchy contrary to all of the fundamental concepts of a democratic society. This is not to say that those charged with the responsibility of operating our universities are not responsible for establishing basic standards of conduct and enforcing same on the campuses of our state-supported colleges and universities. On the contrary it is their duty to take affirmative action to exclude from the student body those individuals not conforming to the established standards. *However the manner of enforcement must be by a duly authorized body in accordance with procedures which permit the student an opportunity to vindicate himself, if he can and so desires.*" [Emphasis supplied.]

In a case specifically related to a private college, already mentioned above, *Greene v. Howard University,* 271 F. Supp. 609 (D.D.C., August 28, 1967), a suit was brought by students whose status was such that they were terminated at the end of the term. The Howard University catalog stated that the university reserved the right to deny admission to and to require withdrawal of any student at any time for any reason deemed sufficient by the university. The court denied the plaintiffs' request for readmittance. In commenting upon the rule of the courts in the area of admission and academic achievements and proficiency, the following was stated:

"It would be a sad blow to the institutions of higher learning and to the development of independent thought and culture if the courts were to step in and control and direct the administration of discipline and the selection of members of the faculty in universities and colleges."

It should be kept in mind that the above case in fact arose from some disciplinary disturbances during the preceding term. As such, it should be considered in the light of both student discipline and the right of colleges and universities to admit or deny admission to a student.

In *Cornette v. Aldridge,* 408 S.W. 2d 935, West Texas State University had suspended a student because he violated the conditions of probation after a hearing before a faculty committee. Under appropriate statutory power to make rules and regulations concerning student conduct, the Board of Regents of the university adopted rules and regulations concerning student conduct. The principal issue in the case was whether or not the trial court in ruling against West Texas State University substituted its discretion for the statutory discretion vested in officials of the school *if such officials acted unreasonably, arbitrarily, and capriciously by indefinitely suspending the student and if the trial court had the authority to order such officials to perform a discretionary function in a particular manner.* The appellate court took the position that an indefinite suspension from an institution of higher learning does not leave a mark on one's record as bad as a conviction of a felony and that the courts will not interfere in the exercise of discretion by school districts in matters confided by law to their judgment, unless there is a clear abuse of the discretion or a violation of law. Acting reasonably within the powers conferred, it is the province of the board of education to determine what things are detrimental to the successful management, good order, and discipline of the schools and the rules required to produce these conditions.

In the court's own words:

"Under the authorities heretofore cited and those of courts of last resort from other jurisdictions of like import announcing the broad discretion vested in school officials concerning the operation of public schools, we hold the officials did not act unreasonable, arbitrary and capricious, but to the contrary showed considerable restraint in dealing with this student who was obviously unmindful of the rules of the university seeking to give him an education and prepare him for useful citizenship."

In November, 1966, an unreported case was tried in the District Court of Boulder, Colorado, involving a student at the University of Colorado. The student, Jacalyn Dieffenderfer, was given a failing grade for disciplinary reasons (she was accused of letting another student copy from her examination paper). The court held that her grade could not be changed by court action and that the University of Colorado has discretion in matters of scholarship.

In *Connelly v. the University of Vermont and State Agricultural College,* 244 F.S. 156 (1965), the court, in reviewing decisions on the subject, held that school authorities have absolute discretion in determining whether a student has been delinquent in his studies and placed the burden on the student of showing that his dismissal was motivated by bad faith, arbitrariness, or capriciousness. As was also said in *Eddie v. Columbia University,* 168 N.Y.S. 2d 643 (1957), "The court may not substitute its own opinion as to the merits of a doctoral dissertation."

The appellate court, however, did rule that the student was entitled to a hearing on the limited issue of whether the university had acted arbitrarily, capriciously, or in bad faith in dismissing him.

Examination privileges at public schools came under scrutiny in *Goldwyn v. Allen,* 281 N.Y.S. 2d 899 (Sup. Ct. N.Y., June 23, 1967). The court concluded that the Department of Education had deprived the infant petitioner of her rights by imposing sanctions predicated solely on the letter of the acting principal, without a hearing to ascertain the truth of the charges during which she might defend herself with the assistance of counsel.

The question of recourse to the courts and a case of denial of conferral of a B.A. degree was raised in *Blank v. Board of Higher Education of City of New York,* 273 N.Y.S. 2d 796 (Sup. Ct. N.Y., September 28, 1966). The court invoked the doctrine of estoppel and waiver in a situation where a B.A. degree was withheld by Brooklyn College because the student had failed to take two psychology courses "in attendance."

On the other hand, in *University of Miami v. Militana,* 184 So. 2d 701 (Dist. Ct. App. Fla., April 20, 1966), the court refused to intercede when a medical student on probation was dismissed for academic failure, pointing out, however, that the operation of a private college or university is touched with eleemosynary characteristics and that even though the public has a great interest in seeing these institutions encouraged and supported, they are operated as private businesses.

In establishing scholarship and academic regulations, the university should keep in mind that such standards may not be applied retroactively, as evidenced in *Schoppelrei v. Franklin University,* 228 N.E. 2d 334 (Ct. App. Ohio, July 25, 1967).

The right of the student to a transcript of his academic records may be limited either by contract or by rule and regulation of the governing body. In Oregon, for instance, the public colleges and institutions have the right to withhold the furnishing of transcripts under the administrative rules and regulations of the Oregon State System of Higher Education in those cases where the student owes the state university money.

No hard and fast rule can be drawn concerning the probability of judicial interference where admission standards and scholarship achievement are concerned. The cases are scattered; they are not uniform. The administrator and his counsel should carefully review state statutes and rules and regulations of the governing board concerning admission requirements and scholarships, and they should be sure that the school's catalog includes adequate notice to the student so that he may be fully apprised of the academic requirements and admission standards.

Since the relationship between the university and the minor student is in large part based on contract, the question inevitably arises whether or not the student can be held legally responsible for dormitory room and board, student loans, tuition, fees, and other obligations incurred by him during his time of attendance at the university.

As a general rule, a person under 21 years of age is not liable on any contract he wishes to disaffirm. However, there are certain exceptions to this common law rule relating to the student's emancipation from infancy for reasons other than reaching age 21. An excellent dissertation on "Minors and Contracts with Universities" was given by Edmund McIlhenny in the *Report of Fourth Annual Conference, National Association of College and University Attorneys* in 1964. Here again, the relationship between the student and the university depends entirely upon the applicable law of the state and the manner in which the administration handles contractual obligations which, in many instances, includes involvement of parents or guardians as cosigners to any contractual obligations. In Oregon, for instance, it is fairly well established that the expenses of a college education are "necessaries," as held in *Jackson v. Short,* 165 Or. 625 (1941). For discussion of the minor and the contract of enrollment and the question of whether or not a college education is a "necessary," see Blackwell, *College Law,* p. 101; Chambers, *The Colleges and the Courts Since 1950,* p. 3; Blackwell, "Can a Minor Bind Himself for His College Education?" *College and University Business,* December, 1961, and December, 1967.

Without going to the statutes and case law in the 50 states, there are certain precautions and protective measures the administrator can adopt in order to assure himself that the contractual obligations by the student and the university will be honored and upheld as valid in a court of law. Note may be taken of a comprehensive examination of a college education as a legal necessary in 18 *Vand. L. Rev.* 1400 (1965) and 6 *J. Fam. L.* 230 (1966). Taking the State of Oregon as an example, the courts, it seems, uphold contractual obligations in connection with attendance at a state university as a "necessary." Consideration might be given to obtaining the cosignature of parents or guardians.

With particular reference to student loans, it is definitely advisable to obtain cosignatures of either parents or other guarantors if a minor is involved. In the Oregon State System of Higher Education this has become almost universal practice with regard to any student loans regardless of the source of funds for the loans, which may be either under the National Defense Education Act, under the State Scholarship Commission, or from private sources available to the universities and colleges under the Oregon State System of Higher Education. Comment on this subject may be found in Thomas E. Blackwell's articles in the September, 1959 issue of *College and University Business* (p. 30) and in the December, 1961 issue of the same publication (p. 32).

In some states, like Oregon, specific statutory provision is made for enforcing loan obligations against persons under 21. O.R.S. 348.060 reads as follows:

"348.060 Loan obligation enforceable against person under 21. (1) Notwithstanding any other provision of law, any written obligation made by any person less than 21 years of age to repay or secure payment of a loan made in compliance with O.R.S. 348.040 to 348.080, or which forms part of the transaction of making such a loan, shall be as valid and binding as if the student were, at the time of making and executing the obligation, 21 years of age.

"(2) Any obligation made in compliance with O.R.S. 348.040 to 348.080 may be enforced in any action or proceeding by or against such student in his name and shall be valid, in so far as the issue of age is concerned, without the consent of the parent or guardian of the student. The student may not disaffirm the obligation because of age nor may any student interpose in any action or proceeding arising out of the loan the defense that he is or was, at the time of making or executing the obligation, a minor." [Same provision in O.R.S. 348.610.]

In connection with the subject of student loans, the colleges and universities under the Oregon State System of Higher Education require the cosignature of spouse for any student loan, and the student loan officers are instructed to record social security numbers of all students making loans.

As a further precautionary measure as far as collection of delinquent student loans is concerned, the loan officers at the Oregon institutions are required to obtain a power of attorney from the student borrower which has the effect of authorizing the college or university to institute suit or action in an Oregon court in case of delinquency. This device can be very helpful because a great percentage of students graduating from our universities and colleges move to other states and it is extremely difficult for the student loan officers to keep track of former students' whereabouts. Some question has been raised by the Office of Education about the propriety of requiring the execution of such a power of attorney for loans under the National Defense Education Act of 1958 or the Health Professions Assistance Act of 1963, both as amended. Thus far no ruling has been obtained and, to the best of this author's knowledge, the validity of the power of attorney has not been tested in any of the Oregon courts.

In conclusion and as a caveat to the administrator, it must be kept in mind that the area of student contracts, admissions, and academic achievements, insofar as they are based on contract and state law, should be referred to legal counsel for the university.

STUDENT RECORDS

Probably every college and university in this country has developed some guidelines or rules concerning the development, maintenance, and use of student records which are essential to faculty and administrators of the university. As the foreword to the *Administrative Manual of the University of Oregon,* the statement of policies and practices relating to development and utilization of student records, says:

> "Higher education today is concerned with the full development of the student and his potentialities. It is realized that individuals differ in ability, background, interests, social maturity, emotional maturity, and goals. To plan educational opportunities to meet the needs of individual students and to counsel effectively with them, the University must accumulate data and keep records. . . ."

Student records maintained by the institutions include admission and registration records, academic records, disciplinary records, personnel records, counseling records, records of relationships with parents, organization membership records, placement-service registration files, and health service records, to name some of the more important ones.

Educators generally are convinced that it is not only advisable but also imperative to the educational process to maintain and assert the confidentiality of student records in certain sensitive areas. These would categorically include student discipline records, counseling records, organization membership records, health service records and, to some degree, records relating to the academic achievement of the student.

The American Council on Education on July 7, 1967, published the following statement on confidentiality of student records:

> "In the summer of 1966, the House Un-American Activities Committee issued subpoenas to obtain from two leading universities the membership lists of campus organizations known to oppose the present policies of the United States in southeast Asia. The institutions in question complied. Thus far, the information obtained by the Committee has not been publicly released.

"Although educational institutions, like others, have an obligation to cooperate with committees of the Congress, they also have an obligation to protect their students from unwarranted intrusion into their lives and from hurtful or threatening interference in the exploration of ideas and their consequences that education entails. The American Council on Education therefore urges that colleges and universities adopt clear policies on the confidentiality of students' records, giving due attention to the educational significance their decisions may have.

"For educational reasons, our colleges typically favor the forming by students of organizations for political activity and the consideration of politically relevant ideas. For instance, space is regularly provided such groups for offices and meetings. In such circumstances, it seems only appropriate for students to expect their institutions to resist intimidation and harassment. Where particular persons are suspected of violating the law or are thought to possess information of value to an investigatory body, they can be directly approached in properly authorized ways. There is no need to press the college or university into the doubtful role of informant.

"The maintenance of student records of all kinds, but especially those bearing on matters of belief and affiliation, inevitably creates a highly personal and confidential relationship. The mutual trust that this relationship implies is deeply involved in the educational process. Colleges acquire from students and other sources a great deal of private information about their enrollees for the basic purpose of facilitating their development as educated persons. This purpose is contravened when the material is made available to investigatory bodies without the student's permission. Thus, although a student may not require that his record be withdrawn, improperly altered, or destroyed, he may appropriately expect his institution to release information about him only with his knowledge and consent. Without that consent, only irresistible legal compulsion justifies a college's indicating anything more about a student than his name, dates of registered attendance, the nature of any degrees granted, and the dates on which degrees were conferred.

"The educational concept of a confidential relationship between the student and his college or university is supported here by the legal principles of freedom of association and the right of privacy. Like other citizens, students are entitled to engage in lawful assembly; if they are to learn true respect for the Constitution, they must learn from their own experience that that entitlement is never abridged without serious reflection, due cause, and profound reluctance. Similarly, at a time when every individual's privacy is subject to serious erosion, each new invasion should be strongly resisted. Except in the most extreme instances, a student's college or university should never be a source of information about his beliefs or his associations unless he has given clear consent to its serving this function.

"Finally, requests for information about a student's beliefs and associations inevitably imply the spectre of reprisals. To the extent that they do, they put at hazard the intellectual freedom of the college and the university. This dampening of free inquiry and expression may affect faculty members and administrative officers as well as students. It is therefore in the interests of the entire academic community to protect vigilantly its traditions of free debate and investigation by safeguarding students and and their records from pressures that may curtail their liberties. America cannot afford a recurrence of the incursions made on intellectual freedom in the 1950s.

"In the light of these considerations, the American Council on Education offers four recommendations to institutions of higher learning:

"1. Mindful of the principle that student records should be held in a relationship of confidentiality between the student and the institution, each college and university should formulate and firmly implement clear policies to protect the confidential nature of student records. Such policies should reflect a full understanding of the intimate connections between this relationship and the historic traditions of freedom of association, of the right of privacy, and of intellectual liberty.

"2. When demands which challenge the fundamental principle of confidentiality are made for information about students' beliefs or associations, no response, beyond the reaffirmation of the principle, should be made without consultation with attorneys. Counsel for the institution should be asked not merely to advise a prudent course, but to prepare every legal basis for resistance.

"3. Institutional policy should pay proper respect to the interests of research and scholarship to insure that the freedom of inquiry is not abridged. Neither investigators seeking generalizable knowledge about the educational enterprise, historians examining the background of a deceased alumnus who became a publicly significant figure, nor other legitimate scholars should be unduly restricted in their pursuits. The confidentiality of the individual student's record is paramount, however. When there is any doubt about its being safeguarded, the person's consent to its use should be formally obtained, and the same general principles should be applied to the preservation of records as are recommended here with respect to the maintenance of records.

"4. Colleges and universities should discontinue the maintenance of membership lists of student organizations, especially those related to matters of political belief or action. If rosters of this kind do not exist, they cannot be subpoenaed, and the institution is therefore freed of some major elements of conflict and from the risks of contempt proceedings or a suit. To communicate with a campus group, the institution needs only to know its officers, not its entire membership. Whatever may be the advantages of more comprehensive listings, they must be considered, in the determination of policy, against the disadvantages and dangers outlined here. In addition, it must be remembered that the surrender of membership rosters to investigative bodies carries no guarantee that they will not be reproduced and fall eventually into unfortunate hands. The use of blacklists, limited neither in time nor by honor, is a practice to which no college or university wishes to be, even inadvertently, an accessory."

From the student's point of view, confidentiality of his records has become a platform in the "Student Bill of Rights," a draft of which was adopted by a committee of educators in 1967 and endorsed by the AAUP. The complete text of the draft of the "Student Bill of Rights" is reprinted in an article entitled "Administrator's Handbook," which appeared in the July, 1968, issue of *College and University Business*. (See also Section 7, Chapter 2, in this volume.) The section in the "Student Bill of Rights" relating to student records reads as follows:

"Institutions should have a carefully considered policy as to the information which should be part of a student's permanent educational record and as to the conditions of its disclosure. To minimize the risk of improper disclosure, academic and disciplinary records should be separate, and the conditions of access to each should be set forth in an explicit policy statement. Transcripts of academic records should contain only information about academic status. Information from disciplinary or counseling files should not be available to unauthorized persons on campus or to any person off campus without the express consent of the student involved, except under legal compulsion or in cases where the safety of persons or property is involved. No records should be kept which reflect the political activities or beliefs of students. Provisions should also be made for periodic routine destruction of noncurrent disciplinary records. Administrative staff and faculty members should respect confidential information about students which they acquire in the course of their work."

Private institutions which are not subject to legislative control in the area of maintenance of student records have great latitude in developing policies and guidelines for the maintenance and development of student records with which the courts will not interfere. For this reason, this chapter will, of necessity, be largely limited in application to public colleges and universities, because the legal status of the student record depends entirely upon the applicable statutes and cases in any particular state. It is here that you are likely to find a clash between the law on public records and the policy of the university or college administration regarding the maintenance and access to student records.

Harold L. Cross, an attorney and newspaperman, whose principal concern is access to information by the press, published *The People's Right to Know: Legal access to public records and proceedings* in 1953. He broke down the subject matter into four basic issues:

1. Is the record public?
2. If it is public, is it open to inspection?
3. If it is open to inspection, to whom is it open for inspection?
4. To what extent will the court enforce the right of inspection?

In the 1959 supplement of Mr. Cross's original publication, he took the position that even where the courts recognize the important distinction between the admissibility of evidence and the right to know, they tend to give it only lip service. He points out that there is a new emphasis and greater insistence on the right of privacy as evidenced by the above statement of the proposed "Student Bill of Rights."

One of the most recent cases on the question of the right to inspect public records is *MacEwan v. Holm*, 226 Or. 27 (1961) in which the Oregon statute is discussed in detail. Traditionally, the courts have used a very narrow definition of what is a public record or writing. For example, in 76 C.J.S., Records, paragraph 1, it is said:

"A public record is one required by law to be kept, or necessary to be kept in the discharge of a duty imposed by law, or directed by law to serve as a memorial and evidence of something written, said, or done, or a written memorial made by a public officer authorized to perform that function, or a writing filed in a public office."

In the *MacEwan* case, the Oregon court shifted from this traditional concept to a much more liberal approach, in view of the broad Oregon statute on public records which contains the following definition:

"192.005(5) 'Public Record' means a document, book, paper, photograph, file, sound recording or other material, such as court files, mortgage and deed records, regardless of physical form or characteristics, made, received, filed or recorded in pursuance of law *or in connection with the transaction of public business, whether or not confidential or restricted in use.*" [Emphasis supplied.]

In the same statute, "public writing" is defined as meaning a written act or record of an act of a sovereign authority, official body or tribunal, or public officer of the state of Oregon, whether legislative, judicial or executive.

The status of Oregon law as it relates to student records is used here merely to point out that the situation differs from state to state and that no categorical conclusion can be drawn without specific reference to local statutes and case law. The states having statutes on public records are in the minority, with the balance relying upon the common law to determine the status of public records. Suffice it to say that the statutes of the state of Oregon and the *MacEwan* case, above referred to, have placed the state of Oregon in the category of a very liberal approach, aligning it with the rationale used by Mr. Cross in giving expression to *The People's Right to Know.*

In a recent opinion of the attorney general of the state of Oregon, dated August 6, 1968, the question of confidentiality of student records at state-supported institutions of higher learning is discussed in some detail. The opinion points out that public records under Oregon statutes are confidential only in those instances where specific statutory exemption is provided. Such exemption is provided for adoption records, juvenile court records, conciliation-service records, civil service records, crime records of the state police, and records kept by state hospitals and public institutions under the Oregon State Board of Control. No such exception is made for student records at state-supported institutions of higher learning.

The traditional restrictive definition of public records appears to be favored in the Texas cases as, for instance, *Morris v. Rousos*, 397 S.W. 2d 504 (1965), and *Morris v. Smiley*, 378 S.W. 2d 149 (Tex. Civ. App. 1964). Some confusion exists in the state of California, as is evidenced by *People v. Russel*, 29 Cal. Rptr. 562 (1963), where the court affirmed the forgery conviction of a person who had attempted to obtain the college transcript of a former student. The court stated that negligent handling of student transcripts could be a violation of a student's right of privacy and commented as follows:

> ". . . the fraud here injures the public because it has been determined that the best interests of society are served by not opening to the general public the grades achieved by individuals. . . .
>
> ". . . These sections [referring to the California statutes] do not make public every state record apart from those specifically rendered confidential by statute. There remains a category of records in which the public as a whole has no interest.
>
> "A person who attended a public school might be injured by the promiscuous circulation of his school records. There is certainly a reasonable basis for the college authorities to restrict the circulation of this information."

The view of the California court is supported in 50 *Cal. L. Rev.* 79 (1962).

Without possible further court determination or amendment of the Oregon statute, student records will remain public records, open to inspection, subject to the restrictions of the statute, and, of course, subject to the statutes which make certain communications confidential, such as the relationship between husband and wife, attorney and client, physician and patient, nurse and patient, and certified psychologist and his client. (O.R.S. 44.040.) Thus, even in Oregon, and in other states which have taken a liberal approach, student records are protected to a limited extent, at least insofar as they relate to the student health service and counseling by professional psychologists. This, then, leaves open a wide spectrum of student records which will presumably be open to public inspection, including disciplinary records, records of academic achievement, records of association with organizations, counseling records, personnel records, and many others.

A helpful discussion of the confidential nature of student records may be found in two papers presented before the NACUA: one by Robert B. Meigs, legal counsel of Cornell University, in June, 1962; and one by Burnell Waldrep, counsel for the University of Texas, in June, 1965.

No discussion of access to and confidentiality of student records would be complete without at least a brief reference to the legal remedies available to the student in case of improper disclosure of records as well as a discussion of the administrator's protection from possible exposure to legal liability for libel, slander, or violation of the student's right of privacy. The law is fairly clear that, in the event of refusal of a public officer to disclose a public record, mandamus is the appropriate remedy. This remedy was used in the *MacEwan* case. With regard to the right of privacy, it is unlikely that reasonable acts of university officials regarding student records could successfully be attacked, particularly where the administrator is protected by statute or an opinion of the attorney general. As far as defenses to libel or slander actions are concerned, the first defense is the truth. The second is what is termed a "qualified privilege" for statements or writings "fairly made by a person in the discharge of some public or private duty, whether legal or moral, or in the conduct of his own affairs, in matters where his interest is concerned." (See *Prosser on Torts,* 3d Ed. (1964), page 805, quoting Baron Parke.) Both defenses, however, may be lost if malice can be shown.

Frequent contacts with college administrators in the nine institutions under the control of the Oregon State System of Higher Education would seem to warrant a brief comment on the responsibility of college administrators and faculty to respond to (1) court processes in the form of subpoenas for the production of documents, or (2) requests, formal or otherwise, from federal or state governmental agencies, for information contained in student records. When a subpoena is issued by a court of proper jurisdiction and the custodian of the records has been served according to statute, requiring him to appear before a judicial tribunal with the records demanded, he has no choice but to respond to the order of the court at the risk of being held in contempt of court. Whether or not the evidence he is requested to produce will be admissible and will be published or disclosed depends upon the ruling of the court and thus the administrator is relieved of any further responsibility.

Some of the federal and state agencies have subpoena powers and, when the administrator or faculty member is served with documents requiring the production of records, he ought to discuss compliance with such demands with university legal counsel in order to determine the legal propriety of the subpoena.

At the beginning of this discussion on confidentiality of student records, the statement of the American Council on Education of 1967 was quoted in full. This statement, as previously noted, was prompted by the issuance of subpoenas by the House Un-American Activities Committee to obtain from certain universities the membership lists of campus organizations known to oppose the present policies of the United States in Southeast Asia. There are no doubt many instances when a representative from a federal or state agency will contact an administrator or faculty member in order to obtain information relating to a particular student or even faculty member. Here again, it is imperative that the rights and obligations of the administrator and staff member be reviewed with university counsel before any records are disclosed.

Hopefully, the foregoing discussion of student records has made it amply clear that the present status of the law is by no means uniform, and that the facts on disclosure and confidentiality of student records depend upon which side of the fence one is on and on the law in any particular jurisdiction. There is moral justification for the stand taken by the American Council on Education and supported by most college and university administrators and faculty members as well as by the students, but this moral justification is not always supported by the law in a given jurisdiction.

STUDENT PUBLICATIONS, LIBEL, DEFAMATION, AND FREEDOM OF SPEECH

Most American colleges and universities print a student newspaper or are involved otherwise in the publication of books, magazines, law reviews, articles, and other varieties of written material. There are two principal areas of legal concern for the administrator in handling student publications.

First, there is the possibility of risk of and exposure to libel and slander actions as a result of material published in the student publication which might involve not only the writer of the article but also the student publications board, the university administration and, in fact, the governing board of the university, whether it be a private or public institution. Many of the states now have tort claims acts, such as the one enacted in Oregon in 1967 (Chapter 627, Oregon Laws 1967), which deprives the state universities and colleges of any governmental immunity from suit. It has been suggested by some that student publications should be incorporated as a separate legal entity under the appropriate statutory provisions in any given state for the incorporation of nonprofit organizations. In most cases, the relationship between the student publications board or the editor of the student newspaper and the university is not exactly clear in legal terms, but it seems clear that in many situations state funds are used to promote and maintain student publications.

Secondly, the administrator is confronted with the guarantees of both the state and federal constitutions, entitling the citizen to freedom of speech and assembly when it comes to the censorship of publications. (U.S. Constitution, Amend. I; Oregon Constitution, Art. I, Sec. 8.)

Returning then to the exposure of the student, staff, and university administration for libelous statements made in student publications, it might be useful to briefly point out that a libel is a malicious publication, expressed in writing, intending to damage the reputation of a person or persons and to expose him to public hatred, contempt, and ridicule. Whether or not the writing has that consequence is determined by viewing the writing as a whole and by asking the question whether or not the average reasonable man would conclude that the writing would tend to have such an effect. Writings may be actionable per se or per quod. If the words are actionable per se, malice and damage are presumed. Imputations adversely affecting a person in his occupation, profession, or employment would constitute a libel per se.

The student newspaper of the University of Oregon, the *Oregon Daily Emerald,* has had a number of experiences with threatened libel suits. Also, a situation arose on the campus of the University of Oregon involving Student Projects, Inc., a separate nonprofit corporation organized under the laws of the state of Oregon, which prepared and published a course survey bulletin. The survey contained evaluations of courses offered at the University of Oregon as well as ratings or student evaluations of the faculty members giving the courses. A professor, through his attorney, charged that the written description of the students' evaluation of him and of the course which he taught was defamatory, false, and inaccurate and that the statement was a gross distortion of the actual grading of the course and of the evaluation of the professor made by the students. No suit was actually filed, but Student Projects, Inc. made a retraction, pursuant to Oregon statute.

What to one person may be freedom of speech may to another result in damage to his reputation and character. This is not to advocate that strict censorship regulations should be maintained in the area of student publications, but the administration should make very sure that the students participating in preparing written material for student publications are fully aware of the risk involved in printing material which can be construed as being libelous, and it is imperative that facts reported in a student publication be verified to ascertain the truth thereof.

There are a number of defenses to an action for libel. One stems from the fact that consent to the publication of a libel by the plaintiff precludes an action for defamation or libel. Also, truth of the defamatory statement is a complete defense in an action for libel. Qualified privilege may be a defense in an action for libel if the communication is made in good faith on any subject matter in which the person communicating has an interest or in reference to which he has a duty. This may be true even though it contains matter which, without this privilege, would be actionable, and although the duty is not a legal one but only a moral or social duty.

Essential elements of qualified privilege are (1) good faith in making the statement; (2) a common interest to be upheld; (3) a statement limited in its scope to this purpose; (4) a proper occasion; and (5) publication in a proper manner to proper parties only.

The defense of fair comment and criticism has also been recognized by the Oregon courts as well as in courts of other states. A person has a privilege to give his opinion on matters of sufficient general interest. However, the statement made must be a statement of opinion and not a statement of fact. To give a few examples, in Oregon a high school football coach was deemed to be a public figure, and therefore critical, defamatory remarks made about him by a member of the school board were held to come under the privilege. In a case decided in Missouri, it was held that a law school in that state was a public institution and consequently matters pertaining to it were of public interest. For this reason, criticism of a dismissed professor by some members of the faculty, who called him "unfit to teach," was protected as fair comment.

In *McNayr v. Kelly,* 184 S. 2d 428, it was held that the defamatory publication made in connection with the performance of duties and responsibilities of office of executive officials of government are *absolutely* privileged.

Turning now to the question of the right to free speech under state and federal constitutions, let us review briefly two very recent cases in Alabama and New Jersey. In *Avins v. Rutgers State University of New Jersey,* 385 F.S. 151 (3d Cir. N.J., November 2, 1967), suit was brought for injunctive and declaratory relief against the state university. The plaintiff alleged that he submitted to the editor for publication an article which reviewed the legislative history of the Civil Rights Act of 1875 as it pertained to school desegregation and which concluded that, in the light shed by the congressional debates, the United States Supreme Court had erred in *Brown v. Board of Education,* 347 U.S. 483 (1954), in holding that "although these sources cast some light, it is not enough to resolve the problem with which we are faced. At best, they are inconclusive." The article was rejected by the editor with a letter indicating "that approaching the problem from the point of view of legislative history alone is insufficient." The plaintiff asserted that the editor had adopted a discriminatory policy of accepting only articles reflecting a "liberal" jurisprudential outlook in constitutional law, an outlook which, he said, rejects the primacy of legislative history and the original intent of the framers of a constitutional provision. The Court of Appeals affirmed the dismissal of the case by saying the following:

". . . The right to freedom of speech does not open every avenue to one who desires to use a particular outlet for expression. . . . 'True, if a man is to speak or preach he must have some place from which to do it. This does not mean, however, that he may seize a particular radio station for his forum.' . . . Thus one who claims that his constitutional right to freedom of speech has been abridged must show that he has a right to use the particular medium through which he seeks to speak. This the plaintiff has wholly failed to do . . . he does not have the right, constitutional or otherwise, to commandeer the press and columns of the Rutgers Law Review for the publication of the article, at the expense of the subscribers to the Review and the New Jersey taxpayers, to the exclusion of other articles deemed by the editors to be more suitable for publication. On the contrary, the acceptance or rejection of articles submitted for publication in a law school review necessarily involves the exercise of editorial judgment and this is no wise lessened by the fact that the law review is supported, at least in part by the State."

The second case is *Dickey v. Alabama State Board of Education,* 273 F.S. 613 (D. Ala., September 8, 1967). This was an action by a student who had been expelled and suspended from the state college. It appears that he was the editor of the student newspaper. He was an outstanding scholar and was editor in chief of the college literary magazine. He was also the copy editor of the college's annual student yearbook and editor in chief of the student handbook. He was a member of a national honorary journalism fraternity. His expulsion was brought about by the invocation of a ruling of the college precluding editorial criticism of the Governor or the state Legislature. The court ruled in the student's favor and held as follows:

"It is basic in our law in this country that the privilege to communicate concerning a matter of public interest is embraced in the First Amendment right relating to freedom of speech and is constitutionally protected against infringement by state officials. . . . Boards of education, presidents of colleges and faculty advisers are not excepted from the rule that protects students against unreasonable rules and regulations. This Court recognizes that the establishment of an educational program requires certain rules and regulations necessary for maintaining an orderly program and operating the institution in a manner conducive to learning. However the school and school officials have always been bound by the requirement that the rules and regulations must be reasonable. . . . A state cannot force a college student to forfeit his constitutionally protected right of freedom of expression as a condition to his attending a state-supported institution."

The *Dickey* case is one of the latest court expressions on the subject of censorship by boards of education, presidents of colleges, and faculty advisers, and the right of free speech of the student which is protected against unreasonable restrictions under the

First Amendment of the United States Constitution, as well as most, if not all, of the state constitutions.

For a comment on the hazard of libel, see Thomas E. Blackwell, *College Law*, page 189.

A recent incident at the University of Oregon involved the privilege of the student editor of the *Oregon Daily Emerald* in not identifying the sources of her news story. In 1966, Miss Annette Buchanan, editor of the *Oregon Daily Emerald*, published a story on the use of marijuana by students, implying that the background information for her news story was based upon interviews with marijuana users on the campus. The use of marijuana is a crime in the state of Oregon and one of the circuit judges of Lane County, after appropriate grand jury investigation, ordered Miss Buchanan to reveal the names of the persons to whom she talked concerning the use of marijuana on the campus to the Lane County Grand Jury or be in contempt of court, with a possible maximum penalty of six months in jail and a $300 fine. Miss Buchanan refused to reveal the names in court or to the jury, asserting that it would be a breach of fiduciary relationship. She was convicted of the contempt of court charges and fined $300, which fine was suspended. The case was appealed to the Supreme Court of the State of Oregon in *State v. Buchanan*, 86 Adv. Shts., no. 2, p. 81 (Sup. Ct. Or., February 7, 1968). On appeal, the Oregon Supreme Court held that it would be difficult to rationalize a rule that would create special constitutional rights for those possessing credentials as newsgatherers which would not conflict with the equal-privileges and equal-protection concepts also found in the Constitution. Quoting from the court:

"Freedom of the press is a right which belongs to the public; it is not the private preserve of those who possess the implements of publishing. . . .

"We hold that there is no constitutional reason for creating a qualified right for some, but not others, to withhold evidence as an aid to newsgathering. We do not hold that the Constitution forbids the legislative enactment of reasonable privileges to withhold evidence. That question is not before us. We hold merely that nothing in this state or federal constitution compels the courts, in the absence of statute, to recognize such a privilege."

To the best of the author's knowledge, the case has not been appealed to the Supreme Court of the United States and the contempt conviction, with accompanying finding, was upheld.

REGULATION OF CAMPUS ACTIVITIES

The scope of campus activities is so broad that it would be difficult to cover all areas of concern to the administrator in the space allotted, but it would be useful to touch upon at least some of the problems which have received particular scrutiny of the courts, among them guest speakers on campus, fraternities and sororities and their relationship to the institution, control of nonstudents on campus, and the use of institutional property.

Speakers and Guest Entertainers

In 1957, William F. Buckley, editor of the *National Review*, a conservative magazine, began the sponsorship of periodic forums, making use of the facilities and space at Hunter College, one of the municipal colleges of the City of New York. Parenthetically, it should be said that in 1954 a predecessor organization had commenced sponsorship of these periodic forums, using space in one of the college's buildings leased for the purpose of holding the forums. Mr. Buckley and Mr. Rusher, editor and publisher of the *National Review* respectively, took over the series of forums in 1957, using the same space and continuing in the same manner until the spring of 1961, at which time the dean of administration of Hunter College advised Mr. Buckley that the college did not intend to renew the contract of lease, giving as reason the fact that the forum sponsored by Mr. Buckley was "a political group representing a distinct point of view of its own." This statement of the dean was then reaffirmed in an exchange of correspondence which resulted in a four-point statement by the president on April 24, 1961, in which he said in part that the college's facilities were not available to "groups in presenting a distinct position . . . opposed by substantial parts of the public" because the college must avoid giving the appearance of favoring such groups over those opposed to them, that petitioner's forum was such a group and, accordingly, was not eligible for use of the college's facilities. On June 15, 1961, the president of Hunter College stated that it was his duty to preserve "the college's dedication to impartiality . . . and . . . neutrality in the context of political, religious, economic, and social forces."

Mr. Buckley and Mr. Rusher then filed an action in the Supreme Court, Special Term, New York County, the result of which is reported in *Buckley v. Meng*, 224 N.Y.S. 2d (1962). The New York court referred to a prior decision, *Ellis v. Allen*, 165 N.Y.S. 2d 624, by citing the following rule:

> "School authorities may not deny to one organization the use of school buildings and permit such use to other organizations in the same category, all factors being reasonably equal. . . . If they open the door they must treat alike all organizations in the same category."

Unfortunately for Mr. Buckley, the case was dismissed not on the merits, but because he failed to plead in his petition that there was discrimination in that Hunter College had opened the door to other organizations. This the New York court felt was a fatal defect in the pleadings. The court however felt constrained to comment that while it may not take judicial notice to limit the defects in the pleading and proof, it may do so to assist in the exercise of discretion. The court concluded by saying:

> "One cannot so much as glance at the daily papers without knowing that Buckley is a controversial figure, and the wish to discriminate against him is evident. Indeed, as has been said, that is all that has been pleaded or proven here. The very memoranda and statements of policy of respondents point clearly to respondents' desire to avoid controversy with other groups by keeping petitioner out of Hunter College. This is so, even though these statements may not be taken to prove the actual discrimination itself. The public interest requires that petitioner have an opportunity to assemble the proper evidence and to come into court with a proper petition and proper proof; respondents' refusal to disclose information as to other lessees will avail not in the face of appropriate examinative procedures. To this end, the dismissal herein is without prejudice to any steps petitioner may take to re-plead and reprove in a new proceeding."

It did not take long to raise the same question again, this time properly pleaded in *Egan v. Moore*, 245 N.Y.S. 2d 622, when Herbert Aptheker, a conceded member of the Communist Party, was invited to lecture at the University of Buffalo by the student association as part of a series of lectures on political thought from fascism to communism. The speakers selected for the series were chosen after consultation as being articulate spokesmen for the ideology with which they were identified. A few days before Dr. Aptheker was scheduled to present his lecture, an attempt was made to compel the board of trustees of the university to cancel his appearance. The chairman of the board of trustees, after consultation with all other members of the board, denied this request and, as a result, the lawsuit was filed.

Justice Reynolds of the Supreme Court of New York wrote the opinion and conceded that the Communist Party is a continuing conspiracy against our government. He took notice of the fact that the trustees contended that allowing avowed Communists to preach their ideology at a tax-supported university cloaks their activities with a mantle of academic and intellectual integrity which makes their subversive propaganda more acceptable to impressionable young people, but, on the other hand, the court points out that the tradition of our great society has been to allow universities in the name of academic freedom to explore and expose their students to controversial issues without government interference. Quoting from *Sweezy v. New Hampshire,* 354 U.S. 234: "Teachers and students must always remain free to inquire, to study and to evaluate, to gain new maturity and understanding; otherwise our civilization will stagnate and die."

The court observed that there is no legislation directly governing the situation and felt compelled to overrule the decision of the board of trustees, saying:

> "Here there is no contention that Dr. Aptheker advocates, has advocated or will advocate at the lecture in question the forcible overthrow of our Government as any more than an abstract doctrine. The courts without express legislative action cannot find such abstract advocacy to be against the law of this State."

The entire problem of appearance of guest speakers and entertainers came under close scrutiny in New York in *East Meadow Community Concerts Association v. Board of Education of Union Free School District No. 3,* 272 N.Y.S. 2d 341. The plaintiff in that case was a nonprofit educational and cultural association which had, during 10 years prior to the filing of the lawsuit, been permitted by the defendant school board to present concerts in the auditorium of a high school in East Meadow on Long Island. The concert association had scheduled a concert for March 12, 1966, which was to feature Pete Seeger as a performing artist. In December, 1965, the school board withdrew the previously granted permission for the March 12 concert on the grounds that Seeger had given a concert in Moscow and because some of the songs he sings are critical of American policy in Vietnam and that, furthermore, Pete Seeger was a "highly controversial figure" whose presence might provoke a disturbance with consequent damage to school property. The remedy sought by the plaintiff concerts association was an injunction with a twofold purpose; that is, (1) declaring the board's action to be unconstitutional; and (2) enjoining the board from interfering with the presentation of the scheduled concert in the school auditorium.

It may be taken for granted that the state is not under a duty to make school buildings available for public gatherings, but, *if it elects to do so,* it is required, by constitutional provision (U.S. Constitution, Amend. XIV; N.Y. Constitution, Art. I, sec. 11) to grant the use of such facilities "in a reasonable and nondiscriminatory manner, equally applicable to all and administered with equality to all." (See *Brown v. State of Louisiana,* 383 U.S. 131, 134.) The school board had concededly allowed a number of organizations, including the concerts association, to use the school auditorium for nonacademic purposes for many years.

The court in ruling for the concerts association stated in part as follows:

> ". . . the board must not unconstitutionally discriminate against the plaintiff.
>
> ". . . The expression of controversial and unpopular views, it is hardly necessary to observe, is precisely what is protected by both the Federal and State Constitutions. . . . As the Appellate Division noted in the Rockwell case, where the threat of public disorder and violence was far greater than that alleged in the present case, 'there is no power in government under our Constitution to exercise prior restraint of the expression of views, unless it is demonstrable on a record that such expression will immediately and irreparably create injury to the public weal—not that such expression, without itself being unlawful, will incite criminal acts in others.' . . . Consequently, if there were no danger of immediate and irreparable injury to the public weal, the de-

fendant's refusal to permit Seeger to appear at the March 12 concert would be an unlawful restriction of the constitutional right of free speech and expression."

A recent case dealing with speaker bans, either pursuant to statute or rule and regulation of the governing board, is *Dickson v. Sitterson,* 280 F.S. 486, again involving appearances by Frank Wilkinson and Herbert Aptheker. The North Carolina statute specifically provided that no college or university receiving state funds should permit any person to use the facilities of the college or university for speaking purposes where the speaker (1) is a known member of the Communist Party; (2) is known to advocate the overthrow of the Constitution of the United States or the state of North Carolina; or (3) has pleaded the Fifth Amendment of the Constitution in refusing to answer any questions before any duly constituted legislative committee, any judicial tribunal, or any executive or administrative board of the United States or any state. The statute authorizes the Board of Trustees of the University of North Carolina to enforce the statute by appropriate regulation or policy statement.

By specific resolution of February 7, 1966, the Executive Committee of the Board of Trustees of the University of North Carolina adopted a resolution denying the use of the university facilities for speaking purposes for the scheduled appearance of Herbert Aptheker and Frank Wilkinson. The court took full notice of the fact that Aptheker had been a member of the Communist Party of the United States since 1939 and alluded to other various close connections of Aptheker with Iron Curtain countries, making particular reference to Aptheker's relationship with the North Vietnamese Government. The court also noted that Mr. Wilkinson had pleaded the Fifth Amendment in refusing to answer any questions with respect to Communist or subversive connections or activities before a duly constituted legislative committee.

The three-judge court affirmed the position that the state is under no obligation to provide a sanctuary for the Communist Party or a platform for propagandizing its creed, and that beyond question boards of trustees of state-supported colleges and universities have every right to promulgate and enforce rules and regulations *consistent with constitutional principles* governing the appearance of all guest speakers.

Nevertheless, the court ruled that the North Carolina statute and the procedures and regulations adopted by the board of trustees are facially unconstitutional because of vagueness and therefore in violation of the First and Fourteenth Amendments of the Constitution.

In essence, the court analogized its reasons to the loyalty oath cases and made the following statement which will serve as a useful guideline to legislators and college administrators alike:

"The statement of policy and the procedures and regulations adopted by the Board of Trustees suffer from the same infirmities. In order to withstand constitutional attack, they must impose a purely ministerial duty upon the person charged with approving or disapproving an invitation to a speaker falling within the statutory classifications, or *contain standards sufficiently detailed to define the bounds of discretion.* Neither criterion has been met with respect to the procedures and regulations in question."

The conclusion drawn from the case law in the area of regulation of guest speakers and performers by universities is fairly obvious. While the public institution has the right to control the use of campus facilities and has the right to formulate rules and regulations pertaining thereto, the governing board may not unconstitutionally discriminate. Therefore, the university administration has one of two alternatives open. One is to prohibit appearance of all guest speakers and performers, and the other is to grant permission to all for their appearance and for the presentation of views or artistic performances, setting up standards and classifications which meet the requirements of the due-process clause and the First Amendment. Only in cases where there is "*clear and present danger*" of injury to persons or property can there be justification for the unequal treatment of guest speakers and performers on university-owned premises. (*Brooks v. Auburn University, etc.*, 296 F.S. 188 (Ala.).)

Fraternities and Sororities

At the risk of duplication, a brief discussion of the relationship between the university administration and sororities and fraternities or other student social organizations might be useful. (See Chapter 5 in this section.) A fairly comprehensive review is presented in 10 A.L.R. 3d 389, which discusses the validity of statutes in the various states authorizing school authorities to forbid or limit membership of students in fraternities and sororities and imposing or authorizing the imposition of the penalty of suspension or expulsion for any violation. Most of the cases deal with statutes prohibiting membership in fraternities, sororities, or secret orders and other organizations at the high school level.

The Mississippi statute prohibiting membership in secret orders, chapters, fraternities, sororities, societies, and organizations of whatever name was broad enough, however, to prohibit such membership at the University of Mississippi and in all other educational institutions supported in whole or in part by the state. This statute was held valid under the Fourteenth Amendment in *Waugh v. Board of Trustees of University of Mississippi*, 237 U.S. 589.

A Louisiana statute, granting the parish school board the power and authority to abolish fraternities and sororities, was upheld under the Fourteenth Amendment against the same conditions. See *Hughes v. Caddo Parish School Board*, 323 U.S. 685. A similar result was reached by the appellate court of California in *Bradford v. Board of Education*, 18 Cal. App. 19.

A comparable statute in Illinois was upheld in *Sutton v. Board of Education*, 306 Ill. 507, 138 N.E. 131, and in a split decision the same was true of a Michigan statute, *Steel v. Sexton*, 253 Michigan 32, 234 N.W. 438.

The latest case upholding such a statute was *Burkitt v. School District*, 195 Or. 471, 246 P. 2d 566. All of the cases rely upon the Supreme Court decision in the *Waugh* case above cited.

As far as private colleges are concerned, which derive no aid whatsoever from the state, a rule of the administration of Wheaton College outlawing student membership in secret societies was upheld in the early case of *People ex rel. Pratt v. Wheaton College* (1866).

Generally speaking, the statutes either controlling or prohibiting membership in secret societies, fraternities, and sororities are based upon the strong conviction of many people that fraternities and sororities are inimical to the best interests of the pupils and the schools because they tend to engender an undemocratic spirit of caste, to promote cliques, and to foster a contempt for school authority. Thus, the basis of the power to enact prohibitory statutes is derived from the legislature's control of educational institutions maintained at public expense.

With only a very few exceptions, as pointed out in the A.L.R. article, the cases and statutes are limited to pupils in elementary, secondary, and high schools.

Many universities and colleges have enacted, through their governing boards, rules and regulations concerning fraternities and sororities because they practice discrimination in their membership based upon color, creed, race, or national origin.

In March, 1967, for instance, the Oregon State Board of Higher Education enacted the following policy relating to fraternity and sorority membership:

"1. Membership in Oregon State University and University of Oregon fraternities and sororities shall not be dependent upon criteria based on race, color, or religion.

"2. Members including both pledges and initiates shall be selected by the active student membership of the local chapter from students who have satisfactorily met fraternity and sorority affiliation standards of the Universities, and shall not be subject to approval or veto by any outside individual or agency, including, specifically, local alumni, national officers, or members and alumni of other chapters. This principle does not deny the local chapter the right to counsel with and seek advice on membership matters from national officers or others, but the ultimate selection must rest with the chapter's student membership.

"3. Should it be determined, after a review of all evidence, that a local chapter of a national fraternity or sorority is not in fact operating within the principles announced herein, the Universities will withdraw recognition of the chapter."

In the fairly recent case of *Webb v. State University of New York*, 125 F.S. 910, the opinion being delivered by Justice Augustus N. Hand, a resolution of the State University of New York in 1953, effecting a ban on social organizations having a direct or indirect affiliation with any national or other organization outside the particular unit of the State University where such social organization was located, was enacted. The social organizations involved were Sigma Tau Gamma, Delta Kappa, Inc., Phi Sigma Epsilon, Alumni Association of Iota of Alpha Kappa Kappa, Inc., Pi Kappa Sigma, Delta Sigma Epsilon, Alpha Sigma Tau, and Theta Sigma Upsilon. They charged that the resolution was adopted without due process of law, that it encroached on their freedom of assembly, that it denied them equal protection of the law, and that it adversely affected existing contract rights. Relying upon the *Waugh* case, cited above, involving Mississippi University, the court denied that the fraternities and sororities involved were deprived of any civil rights under 42 U.S.C.A., sec. 1983, and the action was dismissed because the resolution of the Board of Trustees did not encroach on any constitutional rights.

The problem of hazing during Hell Week of fraternities was judicially reviewed in *People ex rel. State of New York v. Robert Lenti*, 260 N.Y.S. 2d 284 (1965). The State of New York deals with this subject in its penal code, section 1030, which reads as follows: "It shall be unlawful for any person to engage in or aid or abet what is commonly called hazing . . . and whoever participates in the same shall be deemed guilty of a misdemeanor."

This was a criminal prosecution for hazing and third degree assault, involving both members of the fraternity and the pledges who were subjected to hazing practice. The court held that the statute was vague and ambiguous in that the term "hazing" was not sufficiently informative to warn an individual in advance of the criminal implications involved, and that it was inherently defective because it led to subjective interpretation and arbitrary enforcement. The result was a dismissal of all charges.

Nevertheless, Judge Dowsey minced no words in condemning the practice of hazing and let it be known that he was shocked by the conduct of the defendants and the members of the fraternities and that their conduct and the treatment of their contemporaries could only be characterized as sadistic, barbaric, and immoral. He felt that this practice and custom is one which a mature society should not allow its young people to engage in, since it has no educational value or significance but, on the contrary, is shameful, degrading, and despicable.

For these reasons, the judge took the extraordinary step of recommending a revised statute for submission to the New York legislature which would properly define "hazing" and "aiding and abetting" and the participants. The judge also pointed out that it should be immaterial where the hazing practices conducted during Hell Week occur; that is, whether they occur on or off the school premises.

Problems Relating to Use of School and Public Property and Control of Nonstudents

Much of the area of student discipline is covered in Section 7, Chapter 2, but it may nevertheless, at the risk of overlap, be useful to examine some of the existing case law which relates to public demonstrations either on the campus or off the campus. Many of the cases in this area have racial overtones, but some guidelines can be developed which may be helpful to both the legislator and the public administrator.

Student demonstrations in the light of the First Amendment freedoms of speech and assembly are discussed in *Hammond v. South Carolina State College*, 272 F.S. 947 (1967). In March, 1960, the Board of Trustees of South Carolina State College passed the following resolution: "Be It Resolved that hereafter any student at South Carolina State College who shall engage in any public demonstrations without prior approval of the College administration shall be summarily expelled." The *College Handbook* contained certain rules relating to demonstrations on the campus without the approval of the office of the president, and these were challenged by a number of students of the school.

From the conclusions of other cases covered above, the court held that the right to peaceable assembly is not to be restricted except upon the showing of "a clear and present danger of riot, disorder, or immediate threat to public safety, peace, or order."

Thus, the particular resolution of the trustees was on its face held to be a prior restraint on the right to freedom of speech and the right to assemble. Ironically, the students were charged under the wrong rule, as the court points out on page 950 of the case, and while sustaining the position of the students and finding their suspension to be unlawful under the particular rule applied, the court commented that this did not mean that the school may not institute proper disciplinary proceedings against the students for poor deportment and violation of disciplinary regulations.

The case again points out the need for specific and accurate charges.

In *Adderley v. the State of Florida*, 87 S. Ct. 242, a number of students of Florida A. & M. University in Tallahassee had gone from the university to the jail of Leon County, Florida, to demonstrate at the jail and protest the arrest of other protesting students the day before and perhaps to protest more generally against state and local policies and practices of racial segregation, including segregation within the jail. Arrests were made under applicable Florida statute on trespass and the conviction of the accused student demonstrators was upheld by the Supreme Court, stating on page 247 of the case that "the United States Constitution does not forbid a State to control the use of its own property for its own lawful nondiscriminatory purposes."

It is difficult to foretell how long this decision will stand in view of the fact that a dissent was filed by Justices Douglas, Brennan, and Fortas and the Chief Justice of the Supreme Court, thus making it a 5-4 decision.

In *Cameron v. Johnson*, 262 F.S. 873 (1966), a number of persons were arrested for blocking the sidewalks and entrances and interfering with the free use of the courthouse of Forrest County, Mississippi. The persons arrested filed a declaratory judgment and injunction proceeding to prevent criminal prosecution under the applicable Mississippi statute prohibiting unlawful picketing of state buildings, courthouses, public streets, and sidewalks. The majority of the court concluded that the statute was not so broad, vague, or indefinite and did contain sufficiently ascertainable standards of conduct, and that therefore injunctive and declaratory relief was not justified. In a concurring opinion, Judge Cox observed:

> "These plaintiffs well understood that which was proscribed thereby [the Mississippi statute] and defiantly persisted in ignoring the request of the sheriff that they desist from walking so close together and that they picket in a lawful fashion. . . . Consequently, no more than a reasonable degree of certainty can be demanded. Nor is it unfair to require that one who deliberately goes perilously close to an area of proscribed conduct shall take the risk that he may cross the line."

Judge Rives, the third member of the three-judge Federal District Court, filed a long dissent and pointed in detail to the actual facts involved and came to the conclusion that on the basis of the facts the statute was applied unconstitutionally, since the picketing was peaceful. Judge Rives refers to *Cox v. State of Louisiana*, 379 U.S. 536 (1965) where the Supreme Court was called upon to consider the constitutionality of a statute forbidding the obstruction of public passages.

Depending upon the particular fact situation involved, the judges are not always consistent in evaluating the standard of vagueness, but one may assume that appropriate limited discretion, under properly drawn statutes or ordinances, concerning the time, place, duration, or manner of use of streets or public property for peaceable assembly may be vested in administrative officials provided that such limited discretion is exercised with *uniformity of method of treatment upon the facts in each given situation and free from improper or inappropriate considerations and from unfair discrimination.*

The North Carolina statute which prohibits knowing, willful, and unlawful interruption and disturbance of public schools was upheld in *State v. Wiggins*, 158 S.E. 2d 37 (1967). The violators involved were nonstudents charged with picketing, resulting in disorder in the classrooms and hallways of the school building in front of Southwestern High School in Bertie County, North Carolina. Here is another case demonstrating the limitations afforded by the First and Fourteenth Amendments when the violator involved steps over the line by willfully disturbing the operation of a school.

Many of the large universities are experiencing considerable difficulty with nonstudents who attempt to interfere with the administration and the academic life on campus by various means such as distributing inflammatory pamphlets, entering school buildings and school-owned grounds without authorization, or committing other acts which are likely to interfere with the peaceful conduct of the activities of the campus.

A California statute directly on this point came under attack in *People v. Agnello*, 66 Cal. Rptr. 571 (March 4, 1968). The California statute is quite specific and was helpful to the school administration of the University of California, recognizing that in many states school authorities have to rely upon general trespass statutes which, in many cases, are wholly inadequate to justify prosecution of a nonstudent. There follows the exact language of the California statute involved:

"(a) In any case in which a person who is not a student or officer or employee of a state college or state university, and who is not required by his employment to be on the campus or any other facility owned, operated or controlled by the governing board of any such state college or state university, enters such campus or facility, and it reasonably appears to the chief administrative officer of such campus or facility or to an officer or employee designated by him to maintain order on such campus or facility that such person is committing any act likely to interfere with the peaceful conduct of the activities of such campus or facility or has entered such campus or facility for the purpose of committing any such act, the chief administrative officer or officer or employee designated by him to maintain order on such campus or facility may direct such person to leave such campus or facility, and if such person fails to do so, he is guilty of a misdemeanor.

"(b) As used in this section:

"(1) 'State university' means the University of California, and includes any affiliated institution thereof and any campus or facility owned, operated or controlled by the Regents of the University of California.

"(2) 'State college' means any California state college administered by the Trustees of the California State Colleges.

"(3) 'Chief administrative officer' means the president of a state college or the officer designated by the Regents of the University of California or pursuant to authority granted by the Regents of the University of California to administer and be the officer in charge of a campus or other facility owned, operated or controlled by the Regents of the University of California."

The California court concluded that the statute was clear and understandable in its terms, definite enough to withstand the attack of vagueness, and in terminology clear enough to put all persons on notice of the proscribed conduct.

Having reviewed many of the trespass statutes including those in the State of Oregon (O.R.S. 164.452, 164.410, 164.480, and 166.060) as well as rules and regulations promulgated by the governing boards of many of the universities in the general area of trespass on school or other public or private property and on vagrancy and disorderly conduct, the author feels that action should be taken by many legislatures and governing bodies having the authority to enact rules and regulations to afford themselves proper protection in those situations where nonstudents become a disruptive influence to the academic life on campus. The large campuses are particularly vulnerable because many of the student action groups of the so-called "New Left" are led by nonstudents inciting certain factions of the student population to conduct inimical to and disruptive of the goal of higher education, which is to provide a peaceful atmosphere for the useful educational process including a free and open exchange of ideas and knowledge.

Concerning the enforcement of social regulations and the "parietal rule," the reader is invited to see *Jones v. Vassar College,* 290 N.Y.S. 2d 283 (N.Y.), April, 1969.

A brief note on traffic regulations at state-supported colleges and universities. Spacewise, the use of the automobile by the student as well as the faculty and visitors has become a formidable logistics problem and consequently many of the states have found it necessary either to enact traffic regulations or to give the governing boards authority to do so. The most recent cases in the area are *Cornette v. Aldridge,* 408 S.W. 2d 935 (Texas 1966), *Cohen v. Mississippi State University of Agriculture and Applied Science,* 256 F.S. 954 (1966), and the as yet unreported case of *Risner v. Arizona Board of Regents* in the Superior Court of the State of Arizona for the County of Pima, case no. 104466. Here again, watch for the pitfalls of possible vagueness of the statute or the regulations, unconstitutional delegation of authority by the legislature to the governing board, and the legal soundness of the contractual relationship between the student and the university.

The legal problems of higher education are discussed, reviewed, and researched by the National Association of College and University Attorneys, whose headquarters are at Northwestern University, Evanston, Illinois, and a report is made annually of all papers and articles presented during the conferences. In addition thereto, NACUA publishes periodically *The College Counsel,* copies of which may be obtained from the association at the national office, 625 Grove Street, Evanston, Ill. 60201.

Late decisions and cases on legal problems relating to higher education are also published in *The Education Court Digest* by the Judicial Digest Institute, 1860 Broadway, N.Y., N.Y. 10023, and the *NOLPE Newsletter,* published by the National Organization on Legal Problems of Education, 825 Western Avenue, Topeka, Kan. 66606.

A helpful and up-to-date case law review is now being published by T. E. Blackwell on an annual subscription basis, and information can be obtained by contacting him at 535 Ocean Avenue, Santa Monica, Cal. 90402.

BIBLIOGRAPHY

Burnside v. Byars, 363 F.S. 744 (Miss. 5th Cir. Ct. 1966).
Camara v. Municipal Court, 387 U.S. 523; 18 L. Ed. 2d 930 (1967); 87 S. Ct. 1727.
Carr v. St. John's University, New York, 231 N.Y.S. 2d 410 (1962).
In Re Carter, 137 S.E. 2d 150 (1964).
Clarke v. Redeker, 259 F.S. 117 (D. Iowa, Sept. 1966).
Davis v. Firment, 269 F.S. 524 (La. Dist. Ct. 1967).
Dehaan v. Brandeis University, 150 F.S. 626 (D. Mass. 1957).
In Re Jacalyn Dieffenderfer, unreported case in Dist. Ct., Boulder, Colo., no. 1966.

Esteban v. Central Missouri State College, 277 F.S. 649 (D. Mo. 1967).
Holden v. Pioneer Broadcasting Co., et al., 365 P. 2d 845.
In Re Kinchloe, 157 S.E. 2d 833 (1967).
Knight v. State Board of Education, 200 F.S. 174 (1961).
Kolbeck v. Kramer, 270 A. 2d 889 (Super. Ct. of N.J., July 1964).
Marshall v. Oliver, 87 S. Ct. 319 (1966).
Moore v. Troy State University, 284 F.S. 725 (D. Ala. 1968).
Morris v. Nowotny, 323 S.W. 2d 301 (Tex. 1959).
New York Higher Education Assistance Corporation v. Mallare, 276 N.Y.S. 2d 326 (S. Ct. of N.Y., App. Div., Jan. 1967).
Palacias v. Corbett, 172 S.W. 777 (Tex. Civ. App. 1915).
Pare v. Donovan, 281 N.Y.S. 2d 884 (N.Y. Super. Ct. 1967).
Robinson v. University of Miami, 100 So. 2d 442 (D.C. App. 1958).
Rothman v. Michigan, unreported case, January 15, 1968.
Schoppelrei v. Franklin University, 228 N.E. 2d 334 (Ct. of App. Ohio, July 25, 1967).
Shelton College v. State Board of Education, 226 Atl. 2d 612 (S. Ct. N.J. Feb. 6, 1967).
Sigma Chi Fraternity, etc., v. Regents of University of Colorado, 258 F.S. 515 (U.S. D. Colo., Aug., 1966).
State v. Fry, 230 N.E. 2d 363 (C.P. Sept. 1, 1967).
State ex rel. Sherman v. Hyman; State ex rel. Avakin v. Hyman, 180 Tenn. 99; 171 S.W. 2d 822; certiorari denied, 319 U.S. 748 (1943).
State Bank of Albany v. United States, 389 F. 2d 85 (Circuit Court of Appeals, 1968).
Steier v. New York State Education Comrs., 161 F.S. 549 (E.D. N.Y. 1958); 271 F. 2d 13 (C.A. 2 1959).

Chapter 3

Faculty Relations

JAMES J. COSTELLO

University Counsel, University of Illinois, Urbana, Illinois

A persistent aim of American higher education is the establishment and maintenance of ideal faculty relations at public and private institutions. The national presence of more than two thousand mutually independent colleges and universities attests to the hard fact that "ideal" faculty relations will differ among institutions and will vary with such diverse factors as size, age, prestige, resources, mission, affiliation, and composition of the governing board as well as the special characteristics of the students, faculty, and administrators. Physical location alone will result in substantial differences in the applicable law.

At one institution, for example, antecedents of current faculty relations may be lost in antiquity except as they hover in a kind of institutional common law which everybody knows but no one writes down. The flexibility of this arrangement will appeal to the administrator, but is probably illusory. In faculty relations adjustments he will find that the sole precedent quoted to him from the distant past goes against his own view, while he will be permitted to utilize the products of modern analysis and experience to reverse an established but antiquated treatment only when he finds it totally unacceptable to do so.

At another institution, the faculty may only yesterday have given its unanimous approval to lengthy rules and regulations drafted with exquisite specificity. Their certainty comforts institutional counsel, but not the administrator who, tomorrow, may be called upon to resolve the one faculty relations circumstance which all failed to anticipate, whereupon the entire new code will be denigrated.

Obviously there is no single pattern of faculty relations that fits all institutions equally or that eliminates the considerable need for the exercise of sound administrative discretion. Institutional style and the historical relationships between the component parts of an academic community are factors which may either dictate preservation of the status quo or require immediate action for substantial change.

It seems to be the consensus of institutional counsel that, absent valid reasons to the contrary, the promulgation of detailed regulations defining all aspects of the legal relations between an institution and its faculty is the preferred method of ensuring fairness and protection against allegations of arbitrary or capricious administrative action. This is especially the case in an era of national mobility of faculty which increases the potential for misunderstanding and disenchantment. It is unnecessary to admonish even fledgling administrators that no system will have utility unless it is developed with full faculty participation and consensus and unless it is applied by men of good will.

How the administrator identifies and implements the appropriate "ideal" for faculty relations at his particular institution is beyond the scope of this chapter, which is limited to the legal aspects of the subject. Fortunately the courts have displayed more national uniformity in this area than have the institutions of higher education. What is intended is an overview of certain legal principles which have special relevance to the field and which may stimulate the administrator to make inquiries of institutional counsel concerning the application of these principles to his special circumstances.

To professional colleagues: It is acknowledged that statements of legal principles are here outrageously oversimplified and that exceptions to general rules are ignored. The chapter is not designed to enable administrators to pass a bar examination. To nonlawyer administrators: Any review, formulation, or modification of regulations defining faculty relations which fails to involve institutional counsel at an early stage will be assured of eventual disaster as certainly as will the failure to arrange faculty participation and consultation. In the area of faculty relations the fact of litigation is often as divisive as its ultimate disposition.

NATURE OF THE RELATIONSHIP

The appointment of a faculty member is universally regarded by the courts as a nonassignable employment agreement, voluntarily entered into by an individual as the employee and an institution as the employer, governed by the law of contracts. As with any other contract, the employment of faculty involves an offer and an acceptance (written or oral) upon ascertainable terms and conditions (expressed and implied), with enforceable rights and duties on both sides.

Faculty appointments are textbook examples of the proposition that all facts and circumstances must be weighed in determining whether, in the eyes of the law, a specific contractual arrangement constitutes the individual an employee, an independent contractor, or a joint adventurer. Some of the distinguishing characteristics of each are found in faculty engagements at most institutions, but what the relationship is, in fact, will depend upon the predominance of those elements which the law regards as determinative of a particular status. To date the courts have declined to view the faculty contract as anything other than an employment arrangement. No change in this judicial attitude is imminent, yet a contractual undertaking for the degree of "independence" claimed as essential to academic freedom by some academicians could alter the legal character of the relationship, with possible side effects neither anticipated nor desired.

The principal criterion used by courts for determining a contract to be one of employment is the right of the employer to supervise and control the details and method of the employee's performance of the work. The work need not actually be supervised and controlled so long as the prerogative to do so exists. The special nature of faculty services in teaching and research not only does not adapt them to close administrative supervision or control, but the prospect of involvements of this nature would persuade most administrators to take up other pursuits. One must search hard to find the institution, if it exists, where administrators regulate and restrict the teaching and research methods of individual faculty, even though the power to do so is inherent in the employer-employee relationship. When there is a right to control the work, courts will generally hold the transaction to be one of employment, notwithstanding the presence of agreed conditions which would otherwise indicate a different status.

Where all of the circumstances of the transaction indicate the parties intend that the individual is to render services which will produce a given result, without being controlled in any way concerning the method of accomplishing it, the law says the individual is an independent contractor and not an employee. The courts are not bound by the parties' characterization of the arrangement but will look through the form of the contract to its substance. The distinguishing factor between the status of an employee and an independent contractor is that the latter is free to execute the work without being legally subject to institutional orders with respect to the details thereof. Such normal employer-employee features as retirement benefits, sabbatical leaves, tenure, paid vacations, and coverage under workmen's compensation laws would tend to disappear if the courts were to find the usual faculty appointment to be an independent contractor relationship.

A joint adventure is a special association of persons for the purpose of carrying out a special project or enterprise in which they combine their property, money, effects, skill, and knowledge. The history of the organizational form of higher education in this country suggests that few institutions are likely to undergo the restructuring which would be necessary to amalgamate governing boards, administrators, and faculty into a kind of massive educational partnership. Nevertheless, the definition of the joint adventure status describes a de facto situation which prevails at many well-run institutions blessed with enlightened governing boards which have had the wisdom to employ perceptive administrators and dedicated faculty, each respecting the authority and function of the others.

In discussions of faculty relations in higher education, "collective bargaining," "shared authority" and "academic freedom" appear as recurring themes. Frequently overlooked are the legal implications of accomplishing the objectives of each, however described. Collective bargaining in traditional patterns presupposes the existence and continuation of an employer-employee relationship. Shared authority by faculty in institutional decisions (policy or otherwise) is also consistent with an employment arrangement, although it may imply faculty participation in institutional decisions unrelated to educational policy or its implementation. It is possible to have complete compatibility between the status of the faculty member as an employee and the concept of academic freedom in the meaning of that term as a protection against an institution's legally enforceable but "unwarranted" exercise of its right as an employer to control the details of the individual's work.

As long as courts continue to regard faculty appointments as employment contracts under which the institution may direct the work, then, in the absence of controlling statutes, the existence and extent of collective bargaining, the limits of shared authority, and the definition of unwarranted restraints on the individual's freedom in the area of his scholarly interest will be matters for negotiation. Mutual agreements as to collective bargaining and shared authority should have considerable specificity since they will usually modify long-standing conditions of the employment relationship but will not destroy it. The state of academic freedom at an institution, on the other hand, will more likely be dependent upon joint attitudes and practices than upon a detailed set of expressed conditions. It can thrive on a general statement of principles. In this respect academic freedom is distinguished from tenure, which is worrisome in the absence of statute or express agreement but does guard against unwarranted restraints through limiting the power of arbitrary discharge.

The legal danger in establishing a minutely drawn contractual provision on academic freedom is that the logical extension of freedom is obvious. If a court should find the institution has thereby relinquished its right to supervise and control the individual's performance of the work and, instead, has contracted with a former employee to teach a course in his own way to produce a given educational result, the individual may become an independent contractor even though the parties specify that the agreement is one of employment. This would provide the absolute in academic freedom, however defined, but it would cost the former faculty member most of his fringe benefits, his tenure, and whatever expectations he may have had concerning collective bargaining and shared authority.

Judges in the higher courts have increased the frequency of their collateral references to and discussions of the nature of "academic freedom" in the American educational system. This could signal that an authoritative judicial definition of the term and its application as the law of the land is on the way. Whatever that definition may be, the courts currently regard the legal status of a faculty member as an institutional employee and not as an independent entrepreneur.

FORMATION OF THE CONTRACT

All contracts result from an offer by one authorized party and its acceptance by another. If, instead of accepting the tendered offer in accordance with its terms, the recipient attempts to qualify his acceptance or modify the arrangement, he is deemed to have made a counter offer, which has the effect of revoking the original offer. The original offerer may then accept or reject the counter offer or, in turn, make a new counter offer, which may or may not be different from his previously rejected offer. These simple guidelines do not appear to be unduly complex or beyond the comprehension of educators. Yet, in the labyrinth of faculty recruitment, it is often difficult to ascertain with certainty the precise moment of commitment when an offer (or counter offer) is met by an acceptance, thereby forming the employment contract. The fault, of course, lies with the system and not with the individuals.

Although faculty recruitment is a permanent process with seasonal commitment peaks, many institutional governing boards cannot delegate or have not delegated their authority to bind the institution on the engagement of faculty. The fact of academic life at most institutions is that negotiations for potential faculty appointments are initiated at the level of the department or the discipline and then processed through various channels for further recommendation and approval. Except for public institutions in some states, most institutional boards have the legal power to delegate to subordinate officers the authority to engage necessary staff, but many have declined to do so whether or not restricted by law. The legitimate concerns of a governing board in retaining the important function of faculty appointments are recognized and respected, but its position on the matter needs full and clear internal and external exposition.

During periods of intense competition in the academic marketplace, the ability to provide prompt reaction in negotiations can be the touchstone to success. The prerequisite of specific governing board action before a faculty appointment becomes binding may not only get in the way of effective staffing but can lead to confusion or disappointment on the part of the prospective faculty member.

An administrator from one institution may have authority only to enter into preliminary negotiations subject to board approval, while his counterpart from another institution may be in a position to advise the prospect that he is authorized to tender a firm offer. If the first administrator has not been specific in identifying his restricted authority or if the prospect assumes that the board approval is a mere formality, the prospect may be in for a surprise if he commits himself to the first institution, especially if it is a public one. Under the legal principles of agency and estoppel, an institution may be bound by the acts of its administrative officer if the governing board knowingly permits him to assume apparent authority or if the board holds him out to the academic community as possessing it. However, the courts rarely apply these doctrines against public bodies, and the prospect is not entitled to assume that the recruiter from the public institution has the power of commitment, even if the recruiter assures him he will be employed.

There is no acceptable substitute for a clear and specific definition, widely publicized, of who may bind the institution on faculty appointments. If approvals by "higher authority" are by custom and practice consistently described as, and are in fact, *pro forma* at an institution which has neglected to establish precise delegations or retentions of authority, eventual litigation is a certainty.

An employment contract need not be in writing except as may be required by a local statute of frauds, and there are wide variations in the practices of institutions with respect to what matters are to be incorporated into the written document. The desirability of a complete statement of all the terms has been expressed earlier in this chapter.

The parties are presumed to contract with reference to existing law and all relevant law is considered to be a part of the agreement, as if fully incorporated, except where the parties legally can and specifically do disclaim such intention. In this connection, the same contract form may have different legal results, depending upon the public or private character of the institution using it. For example, tenure rights do not normally exist apart from contract, but some jurisdictions have legislation on tenure status at public institutions. The tenure provisions would be deemed incorporated into the public institution's contract, but not in the one at the private institution.

In the absence of expressed contrary intention of the parties, the law implies certain terms and conditions from the mere existence of the contractual relationship. These include an implied agreement by the employee that he will be faithful and honest, and that he will not betray the interests of the institution. While the concept of "institutional loyalty" is implicit in the acceptance of a faculty appointment, its judicial definition may vary from jurisdiction to jurisdiction.

When a faculty member is originally engaged for a specified period and thereafter continues with the institution by mutual consent but without the formality of a new contract, the presumption is that his employment is continued or renewed on the same terms and conditions as the original arrangement. However, if the original employment was for a longer period than one year, the implied renewal will normally extend the contract only on a year-to-year basis.

TENURE

"Tenure" is generally descriptive of the protection afforded a faculty member against arbitrary, capricious, or summary dismissal. It is a matter of express contract or statute, and the courts will not usually read tenure into the faculty employment arrangement by implication. In the case of public institutions, a tenure statute may be included in the law of the jurisdiction, which is also a part of the employment contract. Most tenure rules, regulations, and statutes contain hearing procedures and identify substantive grounds for dismissal for cause.

Since tenure is contractual, wide variations between standards for tenure at various institutions are inevitable. Favorable permanent tenure provisions are said to be a significant factor in attracting and retaining faculty of high caliber, since tenure guarantees that dismissals will occur only after fair hearings and for acceptable causes, thereby safeguarding academic freedom.

Most tenure arrangements involve an initial probationary period (usually not more than seven years), after which decision is made concerning the granting of "permanent" or "indefinite" tenure. If this is obtained, the faculty member can thereafter be dismissed only for cause and, customarily, after hearing.

Academicians and administrators alike are divided on the question of whether it is better to have tenure regulations expressed in great detail or to rely on vague traditions. The decision will be influenced by institutional history, experience, and other related factors, not the least of which should be the disposition of the governing board and the faculty. The principal argument for relying on tradition is that it permits flexibility in dealing with the equities of a specific case.

Recent litigation in the field of higher education includes a large number of tenure questions, a circumstance which suggests that there may be value in an explicit definition of the legal relationships of the institutional tenure. If it is true that tenure is a significant factor in faculty recruitment, that fact would also encourage specificity and formal adoption of tenure regulations.

COLLECTIVE BARGAINING

Whatever may be said for or against the utility and propriety of collective bargaining on the terms and conditions of employment of faculty members at institutions of higher education, it is on the near horizon of many colleges and universities not already experiencing it. Collective bargaining is regarded by some as ineffective unless it is reinforced by strike and lockout sanctions—techniques foreign to an academic community which is engaged in the education of students, research, and public service (all preferably on an uninterrupted basis), not profit making. Others view the procedure as a way to achieve more "shared authority" in the conduct of institutional affairs. Still others are persuaded that it is the only effective device for improving employment conditions at some institutions, especially in the lower faculty ranks.

Administrators are assumed to have the ability to adjust competitive intercampus, interdisciplinary, intercollege, interdepartment, or interfaculty demands (economic and otherwise) to the mutual satisfaction or dissatisfaction of all. When put on public display in the visibility of the bargaining table, their quantum of skill in this regard may be impaired, particularly if some segments of the faculty are still "bargaining" noncollectively.

Collective bargaining looks toward a binding labor agreement, and the early involvement of institutional counsel is a necessity, at least until adequate experience is accumulated. Otherwise, the initial negotiations may result in consequences not anticipated on such matters as exclusive representation, determination of the bargaining unit, and "no-strike and no-lockout" undertakings.

The current federal law on the subject excludes public colleges and universities from the jurisdiction of the National Labor Relations Board. By practice, the board has in the past also declined to assert jurisdiction over a nonprofit private educational institution when the activities involved are noncommercial in nature and intimately connected with the charitable and educational purposes and activities of the institution (except, possibly, where the activity is fully supported by federal funds and substantially benefits private industry). Accordingly, existing federal legislation and practice supports the generalization that faculty in both public and private institutions currently have no right under federal law to force the institution to recognize an exclusive bargaining agent or to bargain collectively.

State legislation on the subject has been sparse, but there is a definable trend towards the enactment of public-employee collective bargaining laws which considerably erode the traditional exemption of educational institutions. To the extent that the state labor law is applicable to all personnel at an institution, there is a duty to bargain collectively with faculty in accordance with its terms. Even without enabling legislation, if a governing board, in the exercise of its discretion, determines that collective bargaining is an appropriate method for resolving the terms and conditions of faculty employment, its decision to do so will probably be upheld. Generally, the right to strike is not recognized in the public area, and public employees are not bound by the prohibitions of the state anti-injunction statutes.

UNCONSTITUTIONAL OR ILLEGAL CONDITIONS (LOYALTY OATHS AND RELATED MATTERS)

Parties to a contract ordinarily have the inherent right to agree to whatever terms have their mutual assent. However, this principle yields to the doctrine that the public welfare is best served by denying enforcement of agreements to do what the law seeks to prevent. A contract condition which is unenforceable because it requires the performance of an illegal act is said to be severable if the condition was not the essential purpose of the agreement and the validity of the other stipulations would not be affected. Contract conditions violating federal or state constitutions have been prominently displayed in the field of faculty appointments at public institutions, specifically in the "loyalty oath" and related cases.

During the post-World War II period, legislatures in many states required all employees of public institutions to attest to their loyalty or to disclaim subversion. The objectives of such legislation are still appropriate and legally supportable, but the statutes enacted to accomplish them were generally not in proper form. Private institutions were not directly involved because their action is not usually regarded as the "state action" against which the Constitution protects and because the oath requirements were limited to public employment. Such matters may become of increasing concern to private institutions if legislatures continue to enact laws applicable both to state institutions and to all institutions within the state entitled to the benefits of tax exemption. Additionally, private institutions considering assimilation into a state system or participation in state funding will want to assess whatever restrictive conditions may thereby be imposed upon their faculties.

In a series of cases over the past several years, the United States Supreme Court has reviewed and found unconstitutional many of the state statutes which required employees of public institutions to take "negative" or "disclaimer" loyalty oaths, either as a condition for initial employment or for continued employment. Such negative oaths customarily required an assertion that the taker was not or had not been a member of a subversive organization (variously defined) or would not advocate the "alteration" of the form of government. Unconstitutionality was based either on grounds of vagueness and overbreadth or on the ground that the statutes violated the First Amendment by prohibiting public employment on account of mere membership in an organization, without regard to specific intent to further its illegal aims.

The cases emphasize that statutory vagueness in the regulation of speech is unacceptable, particularly in the academic area, because the classroom is the "marketplace of ideas" and "when one must guess what conduct or utterance may lose him his position, one necessarily will 'steer far wider of the unlawful zone.'" The First

Amendment will not tolerate laws that "cast a pall of orthodoxy over the classroom" or have a "chilling effect upon the exercise of vital First Amendment rights." The loyalty oath "must not be so vague and broad as to make men of common intelligence speculate at their peril on its meaning." Nevertheless, the opinions of the Supreme Court in these negative loyalty-oath cases consistently restate the legitimacy of a state's interest in protecting its educational system from subversion so long as the legislation directed to that purpose is sufficiently clear and specific.

In a 1967 loyalty-oath case the United States Supreme Court also reversed an earlier position and found a statute making Communist Party membership prima facie evidence of disqualification for public employment to be an unconstitutional abridgement of freedom of association, the reason being that there was no provision for rebuttal through proof of nonactive membership or the absence of intent to further the organization's unlawful aims. "Mere knowing membership without a specific intent to further the unlawful aims of an organization is not a constitutionally adequate basis for exclusion" from a faculty position at a state university.

The Supreme Court took cognizance of the state's interest in protecting its educational system from subversion, but found that the statutes and regulations suffered from impermissible "overbreadth" in that they barred employment both for association which legitimately could be proscribed and for association which could not be proscribed consistently with First Amendment rights. Public employment, including academic employment, may not be conditioned upon surrender of constitutional rights which could not be abridged by direct governmental action.

The high rate of attrition on negative loyalty oaths (expected to continue in most jurisdictions where the statutes so far have escaped recent judicial scrutiny) suggests the probable demise of attempts to legislate new negative oath requirements that are narrowly drawn with the precision and clarity necessary to correct the deficiencies identified by the Supreme Court. On the other hand, in 1968 the United States Supreme Court affirmed, without opinion, two decisions of lower federal courts sustaining "positive" loyalty oaths. These pledged the taker to uphold the laws and constitutions of the state and the United States and, in one case, to subscribe to professional standards of competency and dedication.

Constitutional issues apart from loyalty oaths may also arise in connection with the discharge of an employee of a public institution. In June, 1968, for example, the United States Supreme Court handed down a decision which would seem to apply equally to institutions of higher education. In this case a teacher had written a "letter to the editors" criticizing his board of education and superintendent of schools for their handling of past proposals to raise new revenue for the schools. The board of education, after a full hearing, had found that publication of the letter was "detrimental to the efficient operation and administration of the schools of the district" and that the "interests of the school required his dismissal." The court ruled that, in the absence of proof of false statements knowingly or recklessly made, the teacher's right to speak on issues of public importance was constitutionally protected and the letter could not furnish the basis for his dismissal. The questions of vagueness and overbreadth of the standards for dismissal were not involved in the case.

The Supreme Court denied any attempt to set up a general standard against which all critical statements by public employees concerning their superiors could be judged. Instead, it noted that the problem was "to arrive at a balance between the interest of the teacher, as a citizen, in commenting upon matters of public concern and the interest of the State, as an employer, in promoting the efficiency of the public services it performs through its employees."

The court indicated some guidelines for analysis and evaluation in striking a balance between these conflicting claims and narrowly limited its decision to the case before it. However, the opinion poses enough unanswered questions that public institutions may want to reappraise the wisdom of continuing to rely on implied contract conditions that require an employee to be loyal to his employer and to refrain from insubordination. Attempts to state these conditions expressly in the contract will presumably have to avoid the vices of vagueness and overbreadth described in the "unconstitutional condition" loyalty-oath cases. Again, the private institutions would appear to be unaffected. Their action is not normally state action, and their faculties are private employees performing a private act, at least in the eyes of the law.

TERMINATION AND DISMISSAL

Upon certain occurrences, such as the death or disability of an employee, employment contracts automatically terminate without consequences beyond those expressly stated in the agreement. The relationship may also be concluded upon the occurrence of any event which the parties have stipulated, such as the failure of the institution to receive a grant upon which the employment was conditioned. However, an arbitrary dismissal before the expiration of the contract term will subject the institution to liability unless the right to discharge without cause is specifically reserved.

Even without a contract specification, an employee may be dismissed at any time for good cause. Tenure regulations will usually restrict the definition of "good cause" which justifies the dismissal of an academic employee, and they will also establish dismissal procedures which must be scrupulously followed. In the event that no hearing or review procedures have been provided in connection with a faculty dismissal for cause, some form of notice and opportunity to be heard is desirable and, especially in the case of public institutions, may be a necessity.

Without a contrary definition of "good cause," the term will ordinarily justify dismissal of an employee for conduct inconsistent with the employment relationship, such as incompetency, insubordination, disloyalty, misconduct, dishonesty, assertion of adverse interests, and material breach of an express or implied condition of the contract. Usual waiver and estoppel principles may prevent dismissal by an institution which, after knowledge of the faculty member's breach, continues to accept his services without reasonable cause for delaying discharge proceedings.

Except in unusual circumstances, the courts will require the parties to deal with a breach of the employment contract in terms of damages and will not enforce specific performance of the arrangement. Judicial orders to "reinstate" a faculty member discharged in contravention of contractual procedures only mean that the procedures must be observed before the substantive validity of the dismissal will be considered. The institution always has the option to dismiss without cause and pay the damages resulting as a natural and legal consequence of a wrongful discharge. These would include, as a minimum, the agreed salary to the end of the period and any amounts payable by reason of the tenure provisions, less appropriate offsets.

Administrators in the unhappy situation of initiating an early termination of a faculty appointment without cause should also discuss with institutional counsel the question of potential special damages when a negotiated settlement cannot be accomplished. It is never safe to assume that the extent of damage is limited to the salary for the unexpired term.

A faculty member who abandons his contract without cause during the stipulated period is, in theory, liable in damages for the loss sustained by the institution, including any increased costs to obtain equivalent services for the balance of the term. Few, if any, reported cases on this point exist in the field of higher education, nor are many expected to appear.

CONCLUSION

As indicated earlier, the purpose of this chapter is to identify rather than resolve legal concerns in faculty relations. The mood of the times encourages challenge to the old order in faculty relations as elsewhere in higher education. Recently, national attention has focused on the legal aspects of student relations. The doctrine of *in loco parentis* has now been largely discarded, the theory of the student's contractual relationship is being seriously debated, and the courts are struggling to clarify the status of the student as a citizen. In the field of faculty relations no such doctrinal change is yet apparent. The courts continue to regard the relationship as essentially one of employment although, as suggested, at some point the status of the faculty member as an entrepreneur may be before the courts.

Traditionally and by practice, the judiciary has been reluctant to intervene and mandate the processes, functions, and policies of higher education unless and until persuaded that some supervening and legally protected individual right has been compromised by capricious or arbitrary institutional action or by a misuse of institutional power. This is reflected in a 1968 Federal District Court order which stated: "If it is true, as well it may be, that man is in a race between education and catastrophe, it is imperative that educational institutions not be limited in the performance of their lawful missions by unwarranted judicial interference." Nevertheless, to be a plaintiff in litigation against an educational institution is no longer generally regarded as bad form, if it ever was that in fact, and the volume of formal actions in the courts can be expected to increase.

It is considerably less important to prevail in litigation than it is to identify and correct imprecise internal arrangements which invite the filing of the suit. If the faculty contract is a conglomerate of bits and pieces of federal and state statutes, unpublished or invisible rules and regulations, and poorly defined customs and practices, the litigation so deplored can hardly be termed unjustified. Administrators, in tandem with institutional counsel, have the means of correcting the condition through providing clarity and specificity in the contract terms.

Chapter 4

Colleges and Universities and Discrimination

EDWARD A. TOMLINSON

Associate Professor of Law, University of Maryland Law School, Baltimore, Maryland

INTRODUCTION

What Is Discrimination? Discrimination carries today the meaning of any unfavorable treatment which assigns a minority group an unequal and inferior place in society. The Negro and other minority groups have suffered centuries of discrimination in this country. While these groups have not yet obtained their rightful place of full equality in American life, this country has developed a national commitment to eradicate discrimination. The civil rights movement has fostered this commitment and has become a major force in shaping American law and society. This chapter emphasizes the law's coercive function in the achieving of this goal. There are serious limitations, however, to the role of the law in shaping popular attitudes and institutions. The passage of laws does not eliminate personal prejudices. An equally strong force is the voluntary efforts of decent people to refrain from making invidious distinctions based on a person's race, religion, sex, or national origin, even in situations where the law at present does not require them to do so. Further, the discussion in this chapter of what the law does require should not be taken as a complete or final statement. A single chapter cannot present in any detail what federal law or the law of the 50 states requires. For the details the interested reader must go to larger treatises or to the federal or state agencies which have the responsibility for enforcing and interpreting the law on discrimination. The reader of this chapter must also realize that the law on discrimination remains in a state of flux and may change very rapidly. Change may come not only from the courts but also from the legislatures as additional states adopt antidiscrimination statutes modeled on those discussed in this chapter.

THE FEDERAL CONSTITUTION

The Thirteenth, Fourteenth, and Fifteenth Amendments These amendments, enacted immediately after the Civil War, respectively abolished the institution of Negro slavery, granted all persons born or naturalized in the United States national citizenship and citizenship in the state in which they resided, and conferred on Negroes the right to vote. In addition, section 1 of the Fourteenth Amendment provides that no state shall "deprive any person of life, liberty, or property, without due process of law; nor deny to any person within its jurisdiction the equal protection of the laws." The original, pervasive purpose of these amendments was to protect and further the Negro race.[1] At an early date, however, the Supreme Court interpreted section 1 not to apply to the acts of private persons but only to "state action" (i.e., legislation or the conduct of public officers) which deprived a person of due process of law or equal protection of the laws. Thus, these clauses were held not to prohibit privately owned hotels, theaters, or railroads from refusing to serve Negro customers.[2] In the eighty-odd years since the adoption of this interpretation, the courts have wrestled with the question of whether a state or local government has become sufficiently involved in a discriminatory practice for that practice to be considered "state action" and therefore to be struck down under the Fourteenth Amendment.

State Colleges and Universities and the Negro The equal protection clause proscribes all state-imposed discriminations against the Negro which seek to assign him an in-

[1] *Slaughter-house Cases,* 16 Wall. 36 (1873).
[2] *The Civil Rights Cases,* 109 U.S. 3 (1883).

ferior, unequal place in society.[3] The regents, trustees, or curators of state institutions of higher learning are clearly state officers subject to the commands of that clause. The same is true of the subordinate officials or employees to whom the regents delegate the daily operation of the institution. Colleges and universities operated by a county or municipality are also subject to the equal protection clause, because counties and municipalities derive their governmental powers from the state. Their actions are "state action" and their educational institutions are considered state institutions for the purpose of applying the U.S. Constitution.[4] Under the doctrine announced by the Supreme Court in its 1896 decision of *Plessy v. Ferguson*,[5] a state educational system did not violate the equal protection clause if it afforded whites and Negroes substantially equal facilities, even though these facilities were segregated by race. This "separate but equal" doctrine was overturned in 1954 by the Supreme Court's school desegregation decision.[6] The Court there viewed separate educational facilities as inherently unequal and as depriving Negroes of the equal protection of the laws. Segregated facilities were held unconstitutional because they stamped the Negro as a member of an inferior race and deprived him of the opportunities for education and advancement offered the white majority. Under this decision, state colleges and universities cannot close their doors to Negroes but must admit them on at least as favorable a basis as they do white applicants. The Negro must also be accorded equal treatment once he is admitted.[7] He must enjoy, on the same basis as a white student, all the rights and privileges of students, including participation in school athletics and access to school dormitories and housing.

Discrimination Based on Race, National Origin, Religion, or Sex The benefits of the equal protection clause have not been limited to Negroes but have been extended to other racial and ethnic groups. The Supreme Court has consistently repudiated "distinctions between citizens solely because of their ancestry" as being "odious to a free people whose institutions are founded upon the doctrine of equality."[8] Distinctions based on a person's race or national origin are thus constitutionally suspect. Courts have employed the equal protection clause to declare unconstitutional state action singling out for unfavorable treatment a variety of minority groups, including Chinese,[9] Mexican-Americans,[10] and resident aliens.[11] The equal protection clause also shields a person from discrimination based on his religion. The state cannot deny access to its facilities to a person simply because it does not like his religious beliefs.[12] The First Amendment's guarantee of the free exercise of religion may require even more. The state (including a state university) must take reasonable steps to accommodate individuals whose religious beliefs prevent them from engaging in certain conduct or working on certain days.[13]

Discrimination based on sex poses a more difficult problem. There is not much constitutional law in this area yet, but future decades may witness a movement for women's rights comparable to the present movement for Negro rights. The Texas Court of Civil Appeals has upheld the male-only admissions policy of Texas A & M against a challenge based on the equal protection clause. The state of Texas did not unconstitutionally discriminate against females because it operated, in addition to Texas

[3] *Strauder v. West Virginia*, 100 U.S. 303 (1880).
[4] *Avery v. Midland County, Texas*, 390 U.S. 474 (1968).
[5] 163 U.S. 537 (1896).
[6] *Brown v. Board of Education*, 347 U.S. 483 (1954).
[7] *McLaurin v. Oklahoma State Regents*, 339 U.S. 637 (1950).
[8] *Hirabayshi v. United States*, 320 U.S. 81 (1943).
[9] *Yick Wo v. Hopkins*, 118 U.S. 356 (1886).
[10] *Hernandez v. Texas*, 347 U.S. 475 (1954).
[11] *Truax v. Raich*, 239 U.S. 33 (1915).
[12] *Niemotko v. Maryland*, 340 U.S. 268 (1951).
[13] *Sherbert v. Verner*, 374 U.S. 398 (1963).

A & M, 16 coeducational and one all-female institution of higher learning.[14] Courts in the future may not be so generous in upholding state-imposed segregation by sex. However, a coeducational state college or university seems to have wide leeway in making distinctions based on sex in the regulation of campus life.[15] A state has even more flexibility in making distinctions and according different treatment to different groups when a person's race, ancestry, or beliefs are not the basis for the distinction. A state college or university supported by state funds may discriminate against non-resident applicants in favor of its own residents. The courts only demand that there be a rational basis for this type of distinction.

Private Colleges and Universities There is no clear answer at present to the question of whether the equal protection clause prohibits discrimination by colleges and universities that are privately operated and endowed. As mentioned previously, that clause only applies to the action of the state. In recent years, however, "state action" has proved to be an expansive concept. The Supreme Court has often found that the state has become so involved in the activities of private persons that any discrimination by the latter must be attributed to the state. If such is the case, the discrimination by the private party becomes state action in violation of the equal protection clause. Thus, the Supreme Court has held that a private restaurant operating on property leased from the state in a state-owned building could not constitutionally exclude Negro customers.[16] The leasehold arrangement made the state a participant in the discriminatory practice of the private party and thus rendered it unconstitutional. State and federal governments are likewise deeply involved in private education. State governments have an overriding concern for the education of all their citizens and rightly insist that private colleges and universities obtain state accreditation. Benefits conferred on private educational institutions by the states also include tax exemptions, public services, loans and scholarships for students, and direct financial aid. Federal funds under the National Defense Education Act, the Higher Education Facilities Act, and other major congressional statutes are becoming more and more available for the support of private higher education. Governmental involvement is so significant that few colleges and universities remain sufficiently private to permit them to discriminate. Of course, in dealing with private schools the courts must sift the facts and weigh the circumstances in each case to determine whether the state has become sufficiently involved to be considered a participant in any discrimination by the private school. Very likely the most significant factor to weigh is the amount of direct financial aid to the school. The Federal Court of Appeals for the Fourth Circuit emphasized this factor in a case involving a private hospital. The court held that a private hospital which received federal funds to cover 17.2 percent of the cost of slightly over $7,000,000 in construction projects could not constitutionally exclude or segregate Negro patients and physicians.[17]

STATUTES AND EXECUTIVE ORDERS

State Statutes Many states in the North and West have enacted civil rights acts which prohibit discrimination in employment, public accommodations, housing, and education based on a person's race, religion, national origin, or (in some of the statutes) sex. Discrimination by private businesses and institutions is the major target of these statutes, although they normally also proscribe discrimination by agencies of state and local governments. The most important feature of the great majority of state antidiscrimination laws is the establishment of a commission charged with the administra-

[14] *Heaton v. Bristol*, 317 S.W. 2d 86 (1958).
[15] Cf. *Goesaert v. Cleary*, 335 U.S. 464 (1948).
[16] *Burton v. Wilmington Parking Authority*, 365 U.S. 715 (1961).
[17] *Simkins v. Moses H. Cone Memorial Hospital*, 323 F. 2d 959 (4th Cir. 1964).

tion and enforcement of the law. While details vary from state to state, the general pattern is for the commission to receive individual complaints of discrimination and investigate to determine whether there has been a violation of the law. A commission occasionally may investigate on its own initiative to determine if the law is being obeyed. When the commission discovers instances of discrimination, it has the authority to secure compliance with the law through negotiation, public hearings and, as a last resort, a judicially enforceable cease and desist order against the offending party. Statutes of this type which force private persons to refrain in their business or professional affairs from certain types of discrimination have been consistently upheld by state courts. These statutes are also valid under the U.S. Constitution. The Supreme Court has upheld the state's power to pass legislation to protect its residents from discriminatory treatment by private persons.[18] Another type of statute is found in many southern states. These statutes, premised on the now discredited "separate but equal" doctrine of *Plessy v. Ferguson,* require segregation of the races in many areas of life. Public and private schools are often included. *Brown v. Board of Education,*[19] the Supreme Court's school desegregation decision, rendered these statutes unconstitutional. While the *Brown* decision only ordered an end to segregation in the public schools, it made clear that any state-imposed segregation is unconstitutional. Subsequent Supreme Court decisions have held that a state cannot require private businesses or institutions to operate on a discriminatory or segregated basis.[20]

Local Ordinances and Executive Orders A growing number of counties and municipalities have enacted antidiscrimination ordinances which may affect colleges and universities. Also, a number of state governors have issued by executive order codes of fair practices which prohibit discrimination by state agencies and in state-financed programs.

Federal Statutes The 1960s have witnessed the enactment of major federal legislation prohibiting discrimination in public accommodations, employment, and housing. These statutes are based on Congress's power to regulate commerce and are clearly valid.[21] These federal laws generally defer to state commissions for enforcement in states which have antidiscrimination statutes of comparable coverage. Federal court actions by aggrieved persons, following efforts by federal officials at conciliation and persuasion, are the means of enforcement in states where there are no such statutes or where a state commission proves unable or unwilling to eliminate the discriminatory practice.

Admission and Treatment of Students *State Law.* At least 14 states have provisions in their antidiscrimination statutes which specifically prohibit discrimination by colleges and universities against students. See the Appendix. Seven of these states (Indiana, Massachusetts, Minnesota, New Jersey, New York, Pennsylvania, and Washington) have comprehensive statutes, often referred to as fair educational practices acts, which cover all public and most private institutions and which are commission-enforced. In the remaining seven states (Alaska, Hawaii, Idaho, Illinois, Montana, Nevada, and Wyoming), the statutes apply only to state institutions of higher learning or to private ones receiving substantial funds or assistance from the state. In addition, there are executive orders proscribing discrimination by educational institutions. California and New Jersey, for instance, have codes of fair practices which require that private schools licensed by the state comply with the state's policy of nondiscrimination in order to participate in any state program or to be eligible to receive any form of state assistance. These schools must not discriminate in student admissions or other practices on the basis of race, creed, color, national origin, ancestry and (in New Jersey

[18] *Railway Mail Association v. Corsi,* 326 U.S. 88 (1945).
[19] 347 U.S. 483 (1954).
[20] *Peterson v. City of Greenville,* 373 U.S. 244 (1963); *Gayle v. Browder,* 352 U.S. 903 (1956).
[21] *Heart of Atlanta Motel v. United States,* 379 U.S. 241 (1964).

only) age, sex, or liability for service in the Armed Forces of the United States. Codes of fair practices in other states which proscribe in general terms any discrimination by the state and in state-financed programs would presumably require that state schools and schools receiving state aid not discriminate in admissions and other areas.

Fair educational practices acts in four states (Massachusetts, Minnesota, New Jersey, and Washington) contain exemptions for schools which are "distinctly private." This phrase has not yet received an authoritative interpretation. An intermediate appellate court in New Jersey has construed the term "distinctly private" to exempt an out-of-state college which was subject to no external control scholastically and which was not in any way supervised by reason of a contribution of public money.[22] This interpretation of the statutory exemption seems to be too broad. The "distinctly private" exemption is intended to protect the associational rights of the members of social organizations. Education today is vital for an individual's advancement in life and thus involves much more than purely personal social relations. A criterion more consistent with the purpose of the exemption would be whether the college or university presents itself to the community as primarily an educational institution. There is judicial authority, in addition, that a school or other facility which publicly advertises or solicits applications from the public generally is not "distinctly private" and free to discriminate.[23] Under this interpretation, very few colleges or universities would qualify for the exemption.

A college or university covered by one of these statutes normally may not discriminate against a student in any facet of university life. The student is entitled to the "full enjoyment" or "full advantages" of the institution's facilities free of any discrimination. However, the Massachusetts and New York fair educational practices acts seemingly are directed only at discriminatory admissions policies. The general Civil Rights Act in New York makes up for this omission by declaring that all persons shall be entitled on a nondiscriminatory basis to the full and equal accommodations, advantages, facilities, and privileges of educational institutions covered by the Fair Educational Practices Act.

Inquiries during the admission process on an applicant's race, color, creed, religion, or national origin pose a special problem. Statutes in both Massachusetts and Minnesota prohibit any educational institution from making any oral or written inquiry concerning the race, religion, creed, color, or national origin of a person seeking admission. A religious or denominational institution, however, may inquire into the religious affiliation of an applicant. Antidiscrimination commissions in other states may have adopted a similar policy by regulation. Although these provisions may be necessary to prevent a college or university from subtly concealing the discriminatory rejection of an applicant, very few educational institutions today entertain any such discriminatory purpose. Often they wish to identify minority group applicants to extend to them special help or preferential treatment. In states other than Massachusetts and Minnesota, an inquiry by an admissions officer should not be considered an unlawful discriminatory practice when it is clearly motivated by this latter purpose.

Federal Law. Title IV of the Civil Rights Act of 1964[24] is designed to overcome the difficulties individuals have sometimes encountered in enforcing their constitutional right to nondiscriminatory treatment in public education. Under Title IV, the Attorney General of the United States, when he receives a meritorious complaint that an individual has been denied admission to or not been permitted to continue in attendance at a public college by reason of race, color, religion, or national origin, may,

[22] *Howard Savings Institute v. Trustees of Amherst College,* 61 N.J. Super. 119, 160 A. 2d 177 (1960), affirmed on other grounds 34 N.J. 494, 170 A. 2d 39 (1961).

[23] *McKaine v. Drake Business School,* 107 Misc. 241, 176 N.Y. Supp. 33 (1st Dept. 1919); *Clover Hill Swimming Club v. Goldsboro,* 47 N.J. 25, 219 A. 2d 161 (1966).

[24] 42 U.S.C. sec. 2000c(b) (1964).

when certain conditions have been met, institute a legal action on behalf of the injured party to obtain redress. Title VI of the same act has a broader impact and affects all colleges and universities which receive federal financial assistance for research, construction of facilities, student loans and scholarships, or any other purpose. The statute provides that "No person in the United States shall, on the grounds of race, color, or national origin, be excluded from participation in, be denied the benefits of, or be subjected to discrimination under any program or activity receiving Federal financial assistance."[25] The Department of Health, Education, and Welfare has issued regulations implementing this section which require a wide variety of assurances of nondiscrimination from educational institutions receiving financial assistance from the federal government.[26] Noncompliance results in the termination of the federal funds. The regulations require that applications for federal funds contain assurances that the institution will not discriminate on the basis of race, color, or national origin in admission practices or in any other practices relating to the treatment of students. Even if the federal funds support only one department or project, the assurances with respect to the nondiscriminatory admission and treatment of students must apply to the entire institution unless the applicant establishes to the satisfaction of the department that discriminatory practices in the remainder of the institution will in no way affect its practices in the program for which federal funds are sought or the beneficiaries or participants in the federally funded programs.[27]

Employment *Federal Statutes.* Title VII of the Civil Rights Act of 1964 makes it an unlawful employment practice for an "employer"

> (1) to fail or refuse to hire or to discharge any individual, or otherwise to discriminate against any individual with respect to his compensation, terms, conditions, or privileges of employment, because of such individual's race, color, religion, sex, or national origin; or (2) to limit, segregate, or classify his employees in any way which would deprive or tend to deprive any individual of employment opportunities or otherwise adversely affect his status as an employee, because of such individual's race, color, religion, sex, or national origin.[28]

The statute defines the term "employer" as a "person engaged in an industry affecting commerce who has 25 or more employees for each working day in each of 20 or more calendar weeks in the current or preceding calendar year." The term "employer," however, does not include "the United States, a corporation wholly owned by the Government of the United States, an Indian tribe, or a State or political subdivision."[29] A subsequent section of Title VII provides an exemption "to an employer with respect to the employment of aliens outside any State, . . . or to an educational institution with respect to the employment of individuals to perform work connected with the educational activities of such institution."[30] The combined effect of these provisions is that Title VII covers all private colleges and universities with respect to their employment of individuals to perform other than educational activities but does not cover at all colleges and universities operated by federal, state, or local governments. No definition of the exempted "educational activities" appears in the statute, but it was clearly intended to exempt the employment of faculty and deans. Title VII does cover, however, the employment by a private educational institution of maintenance men, kitchen workers, campus policemen, dormitory housemothers, secretaries, and like person-

[25] 42 U.S.C. sec. 2000d (1964).
[26] 45 C.F.R. 80.1–80.13.
[27] 45 C.F.R. 80.4(d).
[28] 42 U.S.C. sec. 2000e-2(a) (1964).
[29] 42 U.S.C. sec. 2000e(b) (1964).
[30] 42 U.S.C. sec. 2000(e)-1 (1964).

nel.[31] Private institutions with foreign facilities must comply with Title VII in the employment of United States citizens at these facilities but receive an exemption from Title VII with respect to the employment of aliens for work at these facilities. Title VII further provides that a covered employer may hire and employ an employee based on his religion, sex, or national origin "in those certain instances where religion, sex, or national origin is a bona fide occupational qualification reasonably necessary to the normal operation of that particular business or enterprise."[32] The question of what is a bona fide occupational classification has provoked much controversy and uncertainty. There is authority that an educational institution operated or supported by a particular religion may under this provision employ only those of that religion.[33] Religion may be a bona fide occupational qualification because the institution wants to maintain a religious atmosphere. However, under Title VII race or color may never be a bona fide occupational qualification.

Title VII establishes an Equal Employment Opportunity Commission (EEOC) to interpret and implement its prohibitions on discrimination in employment. The EEOC has statutory authority to require employers covered by the title to keep records, file reports, and post notices. These requirements are complex and can only be summarized here. Employers must retain all personnel records for six months after they are made or after disposition of the personnel action involved (whichever occurs later), or until any charge of discrimination to which the records are relevant has been disposed of. Employers must also display where employees and job applicants can see it a poster issued by the EEOC which summarizes the provisions of the law. Employers with 100 or more employees covered by the provisions on unfair employment practices must in addition submit either to the federal EEOC or to a state or local antidiscrimination commission annual reports on the race, color, sex, and (in the case of certain minority groups) the national origin of their employees. Employers should acquire this information by visual surveys of the work force or by postemployment record keeping. Direct inquiry as to the racial or ethnic identity of an employee is discouraged.[34] While neither Title VII nor EEOC regulations expressly prohibit preemployment inquiries concerning a job applicant's race, color, religion, or national origin, the commission has stated that it looks upon them with extreme disfavor and that such inquiries may, unless required by a state fair employment practices program or otherwise explained, constitute evidence of discrimination.[35]

State Statutes. Thirty-seven states and the District of Columbia have enacted fair employment practices (FEP) laws prohibiting discrimination in employment because of race, color, creed, national origin, or (in some states) sex. Provisions vary in detail from state to state, but most statutes exempt nonprofit educational institutions altogether or contain an exemption with respect to their employment of faculty or deans similar to that found in Title VII of the federal statute. However, these exemptions have been interpreted narrowly. The New York Court of Appeals has held that an exemption for nonprofit educational institutions was limited to private schools and that a municipally operated college was covered by the New York Fair Employment Practices Act in the same manner as other government agencies.[36] Under most of these statutes, preemployment inquiries on a job applicant's race, color, religion, national origin, or (in some states) sex are unlawful. State antidiscrimination commissions have drafted elaborate guidelines on what preemployment inquiries are lawful.

[31] Equal Employment Opportunity Commission, General Counsel's Opinion of March 3, 1966, and Opinion Letter of April 13, 1966.

[32] 42 U.S.C. sec. 2000e-2(e) (1964).

[33] Equal Employment Opportunity Commission, Opinion Letter of October 18, 1965.

[34] Employer Information Report EEO-1.

[35] CCH *Employment Practices Guide*, 16,901 (statement issued on January 13, 1966, and amended on May 27, 1968).

[36] *Board of Higher Education v. Carter*, 14 N.Y. 2d 138, 199 N.E. 2d 144 (1964).

Government Contracts. State and federal governments often enter into contracts with colleges and universities. Executive Order 11246, signed by President Johnson in 1965, basically requires that most contracts with the federal government contain a provision that during the performance of the contract the contractor will not discriminate against any employee or applicant for employment because of race, color, religion, sex, or national origin and that he will take affirmative action to ensure that there is no such discrimination against employees in recruitment, promotion, transfer, demotion, layoff, compensation, or other aspects of the employment relationship. The contractor must also insert these antidiscrimination provisions in his contract with his immediate subcontractor. Most northern and western states have statutes or executive orders requiring similar provisions in state public works contracts. In addition, state and federal governments may have a constitutional obligation to ensure that the recipients of governmental funds or contracts do not discriminate.[37]

Age and Sex Discrimination. The federal Age Discrimination in Employment Act of 1967 [38] makes it unlawful for an employer to discriminate on account of age against any individual between 40 and 65. The act defines the unlawful employer practices in language similar to that in the Civil Rights Act of 1964. "Employer" is defined to exclude all government-operated colleges and universities but to cover most private ones with respect to all their employees. The prohibition of discrimination based on age does not apply where age is a bona fide occupational qualification. Twenty-six states have similar laws. The federal Equal Pay Act of 1963 [39] requires employers to pay all their employees covered by the Fair Labor Standards Act equal pay for equal work regardless of sex. Thirty-five states and the District of Columbia have similar statutes.

Housing The equal protection clause requires all public and most private colleges and universities (certainly those receiving government aid) to assign students on a nondiscriminatory basis to any living accommodations operated or controlled by the school. There would seem to be no unlawful discrimination by the school, however, when it simply recognizes the preferences (discriminatory or otherwise) of individual students for roommates when two or more students must share a single dormitory room.[40] In this area the school may rightly concern itself with the individual student's privacy and with the need for harmony and order in crowded dormitories. The equal protection clause also proscribes any discrimination in the operation of an office which obtains off-campus housing for students. Certainly the school cannot deny this service to Negroes or other minority groups or maintain lists of available landlords on a segregated basis, and there is doubt whether it may even list landlords who refuse to give assurances that they will not discriminate. The attorney general of California, in dealing with an analogous situation, has ruled that a state redevelopment agency which maintains a list of landlords interested in renting property to persons displaced by urban renewal cannot confer on landlords who discriminate against minority groups the benefit of inclusion on the list.[41] Furthermore, statutes now make it unlawful for most private persons to discriminate in selling or renting living accommodations. The Supreme Court recently interpreted the federal Civil Rights Act of 1866, which was enacted during Reconstruction, to prohibit any person from discriminating against a Negro in the purchasing, selling, or leasing of property.[42] Title VII on fair housing in the federal Civil Rights Act of 1968 [43] protects not only Negroes but other minority

[37] *Ethridge v. Rhodes,* 268 F. Supp. 83 (S.D. Ohio 1967).
[38] Pub. L. 90-202 (December 7, 1967).
[39] 29 U.S.C. sec. 201ff (1964).
[40] See *Toles v. Katzenbach,* 385 F. 2d 109 (9th Cir. 1967).
[41] 34 Ops. Att'y Gen. Cal. 1 (1959).
[42] *Jones v. Alfred H. Mayer Co.,* 391 U.S. (1968).
[43] Pub. L. 90-284 (April 11, 1968).

groups against discrimination in housing. Title VIII, however, does not cover an owner who sells or rents a single family house without the services of a broker or agent or who sells or rents rooms or units in a dwelling containing living quarters occupied by no more than four families or individuals living independently of each other if the owner occupies one of these living quarters as his residence. A housing office should deal only with landlords or property owners who obey these laws or it may face a charge of participating in an unlawful housing practice. The antidiscrimination provisions in these statutes also apply directly to any college or university when it supplies dormitory or housing accommodations to its students or employees. This would be true whether or not the institution's doing so amounts to "state action" subject to the equal protection clause. There are also an increasing number of state and local fair housing laws which may affect educational institutions.

Job Placement Both Title VII of the federal Civil Rights Act of 1964 [44] and most state laws on fair employment practice prohibit discrimination by employment agencies. Basically, these statutes prohibit an agency from discriminating against an applicant for employment by refusing to list, classify, or refer him for employment on the grounds of his race, religion, or ethnic background. The definitions of employment agencies found in these statutes are broad enough to cover placement offices of educational institutions. Both the New York and Pennsylvania commissions specifically held this in interpreting their respective statutes.[45] Title VII covers private employment agencies but exempts any agency of a state or political subdivision thereof which does not receive federal assistance. However, the latter agencies are generally covered by the state laws or by codes of fair practices for state agencies. In addition, the equal protection clause would seem to prohibit a placement office at a college or university supported or aided by public funds from discriminating against job applicants or from honoring discriminatory requests by employers.

SPECIAL TOPICS

Religious or Denominational Educational Institutions Discrimination by church-related or religiously oriented colleges or universities poses a special problem. The free exercise clause in the First Amendment to the Constitution protects churches and religious associations from governmental interference in selecting their members and in managing their internal affairs.[46] One of the most important duties of any church is the religious education of its members. To fulfill this responsibility, churches have established many colleges and universities. These institutions may believe that they can maintain a proper religious atmosphere only by restricting admission to members of the church. Although there is no direct judicial authority on the point, it would seem that the free exercise clause permits these institutions to admit only applicants who share the common religious faith or to favor such applicants over those who do not. If this is so, then no federal or state civil rights act can constitutionally compel such an institution to refrain from discrimination against applicants who are not of the same faith. There is of course a broad spectrum of church-related institutions of higher learning in this country. This spectrum extends from seminaries for the training of future clergy to large universities offering programs in the liberal arts, sciences, and professions scarcely distinguishable from those offered at secular institutions. In the latter case, the university may lose its distinctive religious basis and no longer be protected by the free exercise clause. This would certainly be true once the univer-

[44] 42 U.S.C. sec. 2000e(c) (1964).

[45] 1952 N.Y. SCAD Report of Progress 29; Pennsylvania Legal Rulings, CCH Employment Practices Guide 27,251.

[46] *Kedroff v. St. Nicholas Cathedral*, 344 U.S. 94 (1952); *Watson v. Jones*, 13 Wall. 679 (1871).

sity accepts substantial state or federal financial assistance, because then any religious discrimination practiced by it would be prohibited "state action."

The fair educational practices acts of five states recognize the free exercise claims of church-related institutions and grant exemptions to educational institutions operated, supervised, or controlled by a religion or denominational organization which certifies itself as a religious or denominational educational institution. Massachusetts and Minnesota only permit such institutions to favor members of their own faith, while New Jersey and Washington exempt them altogether from the antidiscrimination provisions of the act. This latter exemption seems too broad, because normally there is nothing in the religious nature of the institution which requires racial or ethnic discrimination. The New York statute takes a middle ground and permits a religious or denominational educational institution to favor applicants of its own faith or make any selection of applicants calculated to promote its religious principles. This middle ground adequately protects the institution's claim to the free exercise of religion and at the same time proscribes all racial or ethnic discrimination by it that does not have a religious basis. State laws prohibiting discrimination in employment also generally recognize the special nature of religious institutions and either exempt them altogether or permit them to select employees in any way calculated to promote their religious principles. Title VII of the federal act, however, contains a much narrower exemption which permits religious corporations and associations to discriminate on the basis of religion in employing individuals to carry on "religious activities."[47] Under state and federal laws a person's religion is in addition often a bona fide occupational qualification.

Preferential Treatment for Minority Groups In recent years many colleges and universities have actively recruited minority groups, particularly Negroes, and have adjusted their admission standards to favor such groups. Often these adjustments merely recognize that many standard admissions tests do not validly measure the ability of those from culturally deprived backgrounds.[48] Institutions often go further and grant outright preferential treatment to Negro applicants. These institutions are making a racial classification in their admissions policy and are in effect discriminating against the white majority. To determine whether this practice is legal, an administrator must first investigate the law of his state. Some state statutes are worded in a manner that seems to prohibit the practice (e.g., an Indiana statute provides that no college or university supported wholly or in part by state funds shall *approve* or *deny* the admission of a student on the basis of race, creed, or color).[49] State antidiscrimination commissions may also have ruled one way or another on the question. The courts have not yet determined whether this practice violates the federal equal protection clause. The stronger argument seems to be that it does not. There is a long history in this country of discrimination against the Negro and other minorities; the clause's primary purpose of protecting these groups from unfavorable treatment based solely on race has not yet been accomplished. Preferential treatment serves to eradicate the effect of past injustice. Furthermore, the poverty and lack of education of many Negroes today itself provides a rational if not compelling basis for preferential treatment for the Negro. The equal protection clause should not be interpreted to prohibit state action which favors a disadvantaged group in order to alleviate social ills and further actual equality. The history of the Fourteenth Amendment discussed earlier supports this interpretation. There is also judicial support for such an interpretation in the numerous decisions upholding the efforts of local school boards in the North and West to eliminate racial imbalance or de facto segregation in the public elemen-

[47] 42 U.S.C. sec. 2000e-1 (1964).

[48] Note, "Legal Implications of the Use of Standardized Ability Tests in Employment and Education," 68 *Colum. L. Rev.* 691 (1968).

[49] Ind. Stat. Ann. 28-5160 (Supp. 1968).

tary and secondary schools.[50] These school boards also drew distinctions based on race and singled out for special treatment the disadvantaged Negro in the ghetto schools. In addition, a prestigious federal Court of Appeals has held in a related context that a redevelopment agency responsible for the relocation of persons displaced by urban renewal must make special efforts to assist Negroes and Puerto Ricans who face a generally closed housing market. The following comment by the court is also applicable to college or university admissions:

> What we have said may require classification by race. That is something which the Constitution usually forbids, not because it is inevitably an impermissible classification, but because it is one which usually has been drawn for the purpose of maintaining racial inequality. When it is drawn for the purpose of achieving equality it will be allowed, and to the extent it is necessary to avoid unequal treatment by race, it will be required.[51]

These considerations may also influence judges and state officials to interpret state antidiscrimination statutes to permit preferential treatment for minority groups.

Discrimination by Student Groups The United States Constitution and state civil rights statutes operate jointly to prohibit most public and private colleges and universities from discriminating on the basis of race, color, religion, or national origin in the admission and treatment of students. Student groups at such institutions may also be subject to these prohibitions, depending on the closeness of their ties to the institution. Some student groups operate quite autonomously off campus, while colleges and universities actively promote or control others. Many student organizations are officially recognized, which normally means that they are entitled to certain rights, benefits, and advantages and subject to a degree of control and discipline. The significance of recognition to the student group varies greatly depending on the scope of its activities and the policy of the school. Because of the great variety of factual situations, there can be no categorical answer to the questions of whether student groups may discriminate and whether the school may recognize or otherwise assist a student group which does discriminate. Certainly a science club and a campus publication which receive substantial benefits from the use of school laboratories and printing presses must be open to all students on a nondiscriminatory basis, and the school must refuse to so assist any student group that does discriminate. Otherwise, the assistance rendered by the school makes it an unlawful participant in the discrimination practiced by the student group. On the other hand, a student political or social club which does not ask for any substantial assistance and which operates autonomously should be permitted to discriminate just as any private club is permitted to do. The limited use by these groups of school property or facilities to express their views or carry on their activities should not normally make the school a participant in the discrimination.

Fraternities and Sororities. Fraternities and sororities have often maintained restrictive membership policies. The attorney general of California has ruled that whether or not a fraternity or sorority may discriminate depends on the facts in each particular case as to the extent to which the school assists and becomes involved in the operation of the fraternity system.[52] The attorney general did make clear, however, that fraternities and sororities may not discriminate when the school goes so far as to supply them with land and houses on campus, to maintain strict control and regulation over them, and to furnish them with other administrative and financial assistance. In such a case the school has an obligation to make sure that they do not discriminate. It

[50] The cases are collected in Emerson, Haber, and Dorsen, *Political and Civil Rights in the United States* 1346–1402 (3d ed., 1967). See also *Tometz v. Board of Education,* 39 Ill. 2d 593, 237 N.E. 2d 498 (1968); *Hobson v. Hansen,* 209 F. Supp. 409 (D.D.C. 1967).

[51] *Norwalk CORE v. Norwalk Redevelopment Agency,* 395 F. 2d 920 (2d Cir. 1968).

[52] 32 Ops. Att'y Gen. Cal. 264 (1959).

is also clear that even in situations where there is no such obligation the school may act voluntarily to withdraw the advantages and benefits of official recognition from a fraternity or sorority which at a full and fair hearing has been found to discriminate. In *Webb v. State University of New York*,[53] the court upheld the State University's policy of permitting no social organization on campus which had an affiliation with a national organization or which barred students from membership on account of race, color, religion, creed, or national origin. The more recent decision of *Sigma Chi Fraternity v. Regents of the University of Colorado* [54] upheld the Board of Regents' action against the local chapter of Sigma Chi fraternity. The Regents had adopted a policy of placing on probation a fraternity, social organization, or other student group whose constitution, rituals, or government compelled it to deny membership to any person because of race, color, or religion. The court held that this limited regulation did not abridge the student's freedom of association.

Charitable Trusts and Scholarships Donors to colleges and universities often place restrictions on the use of their gifts. A donor may specify that the money should be devoted to scholarships or to the construction of new facilities. The college or university administers these funds as a trustee. Occasionally a donor has a discriminatory purpose and seeks to impose it upon the school. The *Girard College* case [55] prevents a publicly supported college or university from accepting or administering discriminatory provisions attached to trust funds. Stephen Girard, when he died in 1831, left several million dollars to the city of Philadelphia as trustee to establish and maintain a school for "poor white male orphans, between the ages of six and ten years." In 1954, two Negro boys brought suit to compel the trustee to admit them to the school. The Supreme Court held in their favor on the ground that the city's administration of the "white only" restriction in Girard's will was discriminatory "state action" forbidden by the Fourteenth Amendment.[56] Girard, in founding the school, had designated a government trustee to operate it on a segregated basis. The equal protection clause forbids any such discrimination by an organ of state or local government. The founder of a school, however, more often selects private trustees. Discrimination practiced by private trustees in operating a private school may not always constitute "state action" covered by the equal protection clause and may therefore be legal in some cases. Private trustees and administrators may nevertheless find very embarrassing and harmful to the school an outdated provision in the trust instrument which restricts admission to white students. These institutions cannot receive federal financial aid and may have difficulty in attracting high-caliber students and faculty. In this situation the school should seek judicial relief from the discriminatory provision. Courts apply the equitable doctrines of cy pres and deviation to relieve a charitable institution of a restrictive condition imposed by the founder when the condition frustrates the founder's primary charitable purpose of establishing a first-rate educational institution. Rice University obtained a court order authorizing it to depart from the provision in its original trust and charter, which limited admission to white students.[57] Sweet Briar Institute also obtained relief from a provision in the will of its founder which restricted enrollment to "white girls and young women." The court based its decision on the grounds that the discriminatory provision was unenforceable.[58] The attorney general of a state normally has the responsibility for enforcing charitable trusts, but the court held that his enforcing of a discriminatory

[53] 125 F. Supp. 910 (N.D. N.Y. 1954).
[54] 258 F. Supp. 515 (D. Colo. 1966).
[55] *Pennsylvania v. Board of Directors of City Trusts of the City of Philadelphia*, 353 U.S. 570 (1958).
[56] For the subsequent history of the Girard College controversy, see *Commonwealth of Pennsylvania v. Brown*, 392 F. 2d 120 (3d Cir. 1968).
[57] *Coffee v. William Marsh Rice University*, 408 S.W. 2d 269 (Tex. Civ. App. 1966).
[58] *Sweet Briar Institute v. Button*, 12 Race Rel. L. Rep. 1189 (W.D. Va. 1967).

provision would constitute "state action" prohibited by the equal protection clause.

Scholarships restricted to whites, Negroes, Indians, or any other group pose a different problem. The founders of Girard College, Rice University, and Sweet Briar Institute sought to maintain segregated institutions. A fully integrated institution, on the other hand, may classify some of its scholarships by race in order to ensure that disadvantaged groups receive sufficient financial aid. Statutes in some states provide for special scholarships for Indians, and many colleges and universities have special scholarships for Negroes. Although there is no judicial authority on this problem, it appears unlikely that a court will interfere with an institution's scholarship program unless that program is discriminatory in the sense of excluding or treating unfavorably an identifiable minority group. Trouble does arise, however, when a donor specifies that his money shall be used for scholarships for white students only or Protestants only. In today's world the donor's preference may well indicate a discriminatory intent. A college or university, particularly one supported by public funds, should be very reluctant to administer such a scholarship. Once again the school may obtain judicial relief from the discriminatory provision. When Amherst College received a testamentary gift of $50,000 to be used as a scholarship loan fund for "American born, Protestant, Gentile Boys," the college announced that it could not accept the gift unless the religious restriction was deleted. The court held that the testator's primary purpose was to benefit Amherst College and that this could only be accomplished by striking the discriminatory provision.[59]

APPENDIX: STATE STATUTES PROHIBITING DISCRIMINATION BY COLLEGES AND UNIVERSITIES AGAINST STUDENTS AS OF LATE 1967

State	*Coverage of the statute*	*Types of discrimination prohibited*
Alaska	University of Alaska	Sex, color, or nationality
Hawaii	University of Hawaii	Sex, color, or nationality
Idaho	Educational institutions wholly or partially supported by public funds or schools of special instruction	Race, creed, color, sex, or national origin
Illinois	Officers or employees of state educational institutions	Race, color, religion, or national origin
Indiana *	All places where an education may be acquired	Race, creed, color, or national ancestry
Massachusetts *	Any college or university which accepts applications for admission from the public generally and which is not in its nature distinctly private †	Race, religion, creed, color, or national origin
Minnesota *	Any public or private educational institution †	Race, color, creed, religion, or national origin
Montana	Educational institutions wholly or partially supported by public funds or schools of special instruction	Race, color, or creed
Nevada	University of Nevada	Sex, race, or color
New Jersey *	Any college and university and any educational institution under the supervision of the state which is not in its nature distinctly private †	Race, creed, color, national origin, or ancestry

[59] *Howard Savings Institute v. Peep,* 34 N.J. 494, 170 A. 2d 39 (1961).

State	*Coverage of the statute*	*Types of discrimination prohibited*
New York *	Any educational institution of postsecondary grade subject to visitation by the state Board of Regents or the commissioner of education †	Race, color, or national origin
Pennsylvania *	Any college, university, or educational institution under the supervision of the Commonwealth which is not distinctly private	Race, creed, or color
Washington *	Any educational institution which is not distinctly private †	Race, creed, color, or national origin
Wyoming	University of Wyoming	Sex, race, or color

* States with Fair Educational Practices Acts.
† Statute contains an exemption for religious or denominational educational institutions.

BIBLIOGRAPHY

Bittker: "The Case of the Checker-board Ordinance: An Experiment in Race Relations," 71 *Yale L.J.* 1387 (1962; discusses problems posed by racial classifications).

Bonfield: "The Substance of American Fair Employment Practices Legislation," 61 *Nw. U.L. Rev.* 907; 62 *Nw. U.L. Rev.* 19 (1967).

Bureau of National Affairs: *Labor Relations Expediter* (weekly supplements).

Clark: "Charitable Trusts, The Fourteenth Amendment and the Will of Stephen Girard," 66 *Yale L.J.* 979 (1957).

Commerce Clearing House: *Employment Practices Guide* (weekly supplements).

Dorsen: "Racial Discrimination in 'Private' Schools," *Wm. & Mary L. Rev.* 39 (1967).

Emerson, Haber, and Dorsen: *Political and Civil Rights in the United States*, 3d ed., 1967.

Kaplan: "Equal Justice in an Unequal World: Equality for the Negro—The Problem of Special Treatment," 61 *Nw. U.L. Rev.* 363 (1966).

Nelkin: "Cy Pres and the Fourteenth Amendment: A Discriminating Look at Very Private Schools and not so Charitable Trusts," 56 *Geo. L.J.* 272 (1967).

Note: "Constitutionality of Restricted Scholarships," 33 *N.Y.U. L. Rev.* 604 (1958).

———: "State Universities and the Discriminatory Fraternity: A Constitutional Analysis," 8 *U.C.L.A. L. Rev.* 169 (1961).

Power: "The Racially Discriminatory Charitable Trust: A Suggested Treatment," 9 *St. Louis L.J.* 478 (1965).

Sovern: *Legal Restraints on Racial Discrimination in Employment*, Twentieth Century Fund, New York, 1966.

Van Alstyne: "Discrimination in State University Housing Programs: Policy and Constitutional Consideration," 13 *Stan. L. Rev.* 60 (1960).

Chapter 5

The Social Fraternity in Relation to the University

NORMAN L. EPSTEIN

General Counsel, The California State College, Los Angeles, California

This chapter examines the legal aspects of the university in its relationship to the social fraternity.[1]

Webster's *Third New International Dictionary* defines "fraternity" (in the sense used here) as "a group of people associated or formally organized for a common purpose, interest, or pleasure: as . . . c: a national or local men's student organization formed chiefly for social purposes having secret rites and a name consisting of usually three Greek letters; . . . ."[2]

It is in the sense of this definition that this chapter discusses the college fraternity. Of course, our context embraces the social sorority as well as the fraternity.[3]

[1] The remarks in this chapter reflect Mr. Epstein's personal views; they do not necessarily represent the views of the Trustees, the Chancellor, or the California State Colleges.

[2] By permission. From *Webster's Third New International Dictionary* © 1966 by G. & C. Merriam Co., publishers of the Merriam-Webster Dictionaries.

[3] The term "fraternity" used in relation to high school or college social organizations is generally so understood. See *Bradford v. Board of Education*, 18 Cal. App. 2d 19, 28; 82 Pac. 1124 (1912).

THE GENERAL RELATIONSHIP

While in theory the fraternity may exist independently of the educational institution, in point of practice and practical effect, it is unable to do so with any viability.[4]

Typically, the university exercises its authority through the medium of "recognition" —a term which connotes the system through which a student organization, including the social fraternity, is accorded privileges and status denied to others. These embrace not only the use of college facilities and the attention of student personnel professionals but, of perhaps greater significance, permission to represent an official relationship to the institution.

The articulation of this principle is particularly well stated in a recent California trial court decision, *Acacia Fraternity, Inc., v. Regents of the University of California.*[5] The case arose out of a petition by a fraternity and sorority to enjoin the University of California and the California State Colleges from enforcing their respective regulations against discrimination based on race, religion, or national origin in the selection of members. In his opinion denying a preliminary injunction, Judge Stevens Fargo said:

> The power of the defendant authorities over the plaintiff organizations rests upon the furnishing by the defendants to the plaintiffs of benefits by way of facilities or services. But for such benefits the plaintiffs or those similarly situated might conduct their affairs with entire freedom from any control by the defendants. While plaintiffs argue that they receive no such benefits, the contrary is apparent. Without attempting a full list, the defendants furnish to plaintiffs and like organizations on their campuses the inestimable value of identification with the university or college of an undergraduate social fraternity; coordination of student activities; use of physical properties of the campuses; monitoring grade information, an important feature of a fraternity's control over its members; furnishing of faculty assistance in respect to fraternal affairs; coordination of rushing and orientation programs, and many others. The mere fact that these plaintiffs bring this action to enforce their recognition by the defendant authorities is in itself proof that they value the benefits accompanying such official recognition of their status and participation in the school programs. If the required certificate is not filed, the only threat by the defendant authorities is of withdrawal of recognition of such fraternal orders as shall not allow freedom of choice to their own members.[6]

The modern view rationalizes the relationship between the university and the social fraternity as fundamentally of the same order as the relationship between the university and other recognized student organizations. That is, the social fraternity is viewed as an extension of the educational process itself. It is for this reason that the university channels a portion of its resources, in terms of professional talent, support functions, and the use of its name, to these organizations.

AUTHORITY OF THE UNIVERSITY TO RESTRICT OR PROHIBIT FRATERNITIES, AND TO BAR DISCRIMINATORY PRACTICES

There is no question now, and there probably has never been any in terms of the reported decisions, as to the power of a university, whether public or private, to altogether refuse to recognize fraternities. In the earliest reported case, *People ex rel.*

[4] See, e.g., *Baird's Manual of American College Fraternities,* 17th ed., George Banta Company, Inc., Menasha, Wis., 1963, pp. 29–30.

[5] Unreported; Superior Court of California, Los Angeles, no. SW C 5042.

[6] Subsequent to the decision, the fraternity plaintiffs complied with the university and state college regulations and their suit was dismissed with prejudice.

Pratt v. Wheaton College,[7] the court affirmed the power of a private institution to suspend students who belonged to a social fraternity in violation of college rules.

Waugh v. Board of Trustees[8] has been regarded since its pronouncement as the leading case in the area. In it, the United States Supreme Court considered a rule, adopted by the governing authority of the University of Mississippi, barring attendance at the university of students who subsequent to promulgation of the rule remained members of social fraternities. After noting the broad power of the Legislature over institutions maintained by public funds, the Court held that the rule under consideration was subject to no Fourteenth Amendment infirmity. Instead:

> . . . whether such membership [in a social fraternity] makes against discipline was for the state of Mississippi to determine. It is to be remarked that the university was established by the state and is under the control of the state, and the enactment of the statute may have been induced by the opinion that membership in the prohibited societies divided the attention of students, and distracted from that singleness of purpose which the state desired to exist in its public educational institutions.

No reported decision has been found since *Waugh* involving a flat prohibition of social fraternities at the college level. Prohibitions at the grade school level are common and have been uniformly upheld.[9]

The notion that social fraternities detract from "that singleness of purpose which the state desired to exist in its public educational institutions" appears to be of questionable validity now, whatever its application might have been in 1914, when *Waugh* was decided.[10] The more recent cases have cited and relied upon *Waugh* and similar authorities, but their language has seldom been so sweeping, nor have their factual contexts involved university action as drastic as flat prohibition of all fraternities, let alone disbarment of fraternity members from attendance at the university. In light of the recent freedom of association cases,[11] it is seriously questioned whether a public university could today bar *attendance* on account of a student's membership in a social fraternity or, for that matter, in any secret society.

But there is no doubt that the university may decline to *recognize* social fraternities (as well as other student organizations) which discriminate in the selection of their members on the basis of race, religion, or national origin or which are otherwise inconsistent with reasonable objectives of the institution. The leading authorities are the two State University of New York (SUNY) cases, *Webb v. State University of New York*[12] and *Beta Sigma Rho, Inc. v. Moore.*[13] Each arose out of a policy of SUNY barring social fraternities with national affiliations.

Both the federal court and the New York State court, in reviewing the university policy, concluded that it was a valid exercise of the state's authority and involved no violation of constitutional rights. This was held to be true both in the case of fraternities on the campus at the time the rule was announced and, in the *Beta Sigma Rho*

[7] 40 Ill. 186, 187–188 (1866). See also *State ex rel. Stallard v. White,* 82 Ind. 278, 284–285, 286, 288; 42 Am. R. 496 (1882).

[8] 237 U.S. 589, 595–597, 35 S. Ct. 720, 722–723 (1914).

[9] The cases are collected in 10 A.L.R. 3d 389 (1966). A 1953 compilation lists 24 states having laws prohibiting social fraternities at the grade school level. (*States with Anti-fraternity and Anti-sorority Laws,* the State Legislative Counsel Compilation by the State Legislative Counsel of Oklahoma [March 24, 1953].)

[10] This aspect of the case has been questioned virtually since the decision was announced. See, e.g., "College Fraternities and the Law," *Law Notes,* vol. 19, pp. 166–169, December, 1915.

[11] See particularly *N.A.A.C.P. v. Alabama,* 357 U.S. 449, 78 S. Ct. 1163 (1958); *Bates v. City of Little Rock,* 361 U.S. 516, 80 S. Ct. 412 (1960); *Louisiana v. N.A.A.C.P.,* 366 U.S. 293, 81 S. Ct. 1333 (1961); *Gibson v. Florida Legislative Investigation Commission,* 372 U.S. 539, 83 S. Ct. 889 (1963).

[12] 125 F. Supp. 910, 911–912 (D.C. N.D. N.Y., 1954), app. den. 348 U.S. 867, 75 S. Ct. 113 (1954).

[13] 46 Misc. 2d 1030, 261 N.Y.S. 2d 658 (1965).

case, fraternities which came into the system by reason of the merger of what had been an independent institution into SUNY.

In *Sigma Chi Fraternity v. Regents of the University of Colorado,*[14] a three-judge federal court reached a similar conclusion in connection with action by the Regents of the University of Colorado. This case was an indirect product of the well-publicized action of Sigma Chi in suspending the charter of its chapter at Stanford University. The university concluded that the suspension had occurred on account of the intention of the Stanford chapter to pledge a Negro in violation of "an unwritten tradition or practice of the national Sigma Chi Fraternity." As a result, it placed the Colorado chapter on probation "with immediate loss of the privilege of rushing and pledging." Sigma Chi sought to enjoin the action. The court discussed the freedom of association cases (cited in footnote 11) and concluded that "It is clear from an examination of these cases that the right of association is not, as plaintiffs have contended, an absolute right but is always subject to evaluation in relation to the interest which the state seeks to advance."

After discussing *Waugh, Webb,* and other cases, the court held that "the particular relationship before us renders the plaintiffs susceptible to regulation of the kind here questioned" and upheld the university's action.[15] *Acacia Fraternity v. Regents of the University of California,* discussed earlier, is a trial court holding to the same effect.

The line of decisions beginning with *McLauren v. Oklahoma State Regents,*[16] including *Brown v. Board of Education,*[17] and continuing to the present, strongly suggests that the university not only may deny recognition to social fraternities and other student organizations which discriminate on the basis of race, religion, or national origin but, at least if it is a public institution, that it is constitutionally compelled to do so.[18]

Thus, it would appear that no violation of the Fourteenth Amendment or the Bill of Rights provisions implicit in it is involved in university action barring recognition to all social fraternities or to some social fraternities, so long as the selection is based on reasonable criteria such as nondiscrimination or local control. The fact that university action of this character may incidentally result in some financial hardship to individuals or groups has been regarded as constitutionally insignificant.[19]

The remaining constitutional issue concerns procedure. In *Webb,* the Second Circuit held that due process did not require notice or hearing to any of the fraternities affected prior to promulgation of the SUNY systemwide rule banning national fraternities.[20] In the *Sigma Chi* case, an action against a particular fraternity for violating an already established rule, the court devoted considerable attention to procedure.[21] It held "fundamental fairness" to be the standard, and concluded that it had been satis-

[14] 258 F. Supp. 515, 525–529 (D.C. D. Colo. 1966).

[15] *Ibid.,* p. 527.

[16] 339 U.S. 637, 70 S. Ct. 139 (1949).

[17] 347 U.S. 483, 74 S. Ct. 686 (1954).

[18] See *Sigma Chi Fraternity v. Regents of the University of Colorado,* 258 F. Supp. 515, 527 (D.C. D. Colo. 1966); Horowitz, "Discriminatory Fraternities at State Universities: A Violation of the Fourteenth Amendment? 25 *So. Cal. L. Rev.* 289 (1952) (a particularly perceptive article, considering that it was written two years prior to the decision in *Brown*); Epstein, "The State University, the Social Fraternity and 'State Action'," *Report of the Fifth Annual Conderence,* National Association of College and University Attorneys, p. 25, June 24–25, 1965; and 32 Ops. Cal. Att'y. Gen. 264 (1959; a particularly able summary of the case law through 1958).

[19] *Beta Sigma Rho v. Moore,* federal courts in *Webb v. State University of New York, Sigma Chi Fraternity v. Regents of the University of Colorado,* and the California court in *Acacia Fraternity, Inc. v. Regents of the University of California* (all of which have been cited above) among others, have all applied *Pyeatte v. Board of Regents of the University of Oklahoma,* 102 F. Supp. 407 (D.C. W.D. Okla. 1951) aff'd. 342 U.S. 936, 72 S. Ct. 567 (1952) to that effect.

[20] Compare the result under statutes similar to the Federal Administrative Procedure Act which do require certain kinds of notice and a public hearing on regulations of this character.

[21] 258 F. Supp. 515, 528–529 (D.C. D. Colo. 1966).

fied by procedure which had afforded (1) adequate notice of the opposing claims; (2) a reasonable opportunity to prepare and meet them; (3) an orderly hearing in which to do so, adapted to the nature of the case; and (4) a fair and impartial decision.

If the rationale of recognition is that the student organization is an extension of the educational process and the university chooses this means, among others, as a channel for its resources, then it would seem that even less formality may be necessary should the university choose to deny recognition. In the absence of a claim of invidious discrimination among fraternities, it is possible that a court would hold that the university may grant or withhold recognition from social fraternities simply on the basis of its own good judgment in the allocation of its resources.

RESTRICTIONS ON THE USE OF THE PROPERTY

There would appear to be no doubt but that the university may impose any reasonable restriction on the use of its own land by a fraternity pursuant to a lease arrangement or, as a condition of university recognition, to the use by a local chapter even of its own property.

There are several cases which have challenged the compatibility of a fraternity house to a residential environment. Where these questions have arisen, reported decisions have held the two to be incompatible. Thus, in *Mu Chapter Building Foundation v. Henry*,[22] the court held the maintenance and operation of a fraternity house to violate the provisions of a covenant which limited use of that and adjacent property to "residential purposes." The court emphasized that the fraternity house involved far more than mere lodging and residence, but was likely to be used as well for "exuberant and hilarious behavior." An annotation on the covenant issue may be found in 7 A.L.R. 2d 436 (1949).

In *Hannan v. Harper*,[23] the court held the operation of a fraternity house in a duplex to constitute a constructive eviction against a family which occupied another unit of the duplex. And in *In re Jennings Estate*,[24] the court held that a fraternity house constituted a "multiple dwelling" within the definition of a zoning ordinance which restricted use of residences to single families, and hence that it violated the ordinance.

ELIGIBILITY FOR TAX EXEMPTION

Federal Income Tax

This brief section is not an appropriate vehicle to discuss in any detail the complicated questions of federal income tax pertinent to college fraternities and their operations. Instead, the following comments are offered as a general guide.

As is usually the case in questions of charities and quasicharitable entities where deduction problems are encountered, there are two basic exemption provisions to be considered: section 170(a)(1) of the *Internal Revenue Code*, which authorizes a contributor to deduct contributions to organizations described in section 170(c); and section 501(c), which exempts organizations themselves from the payment of income tax. Insofar as is pertinent here, the latter is considerably broader than the former.

In order to qualify for exemption, the transfer must be a "charitable contribution." There are a number of requisites to the attainment of that status. The most critical for these purposes is section 170(c)(2)(B) which requires that the contributee be "organized and operated exclusively for religious, charitable, scientific, literary, or educational purposes or for the prevention of cruelty to children or animals." As a general

[22] (Ga. 1949) 51 S.E. 2d 841.
[23] 189 Wis. 588, 208 N.W. 255, 259, 45 A.L.R. 1119 (1926).
[24] 330 Pa. 154, 198 A. 621 (1938).

rule, "college fraternities are not exempt organizations but are primarily social clubs." As a result, contributions to them are not deductible.[25] Thus, while contributions to a fund which is to be used primarily to provide scholarships to students of a fraternity may qualify for the exemption as an "educational" purpose, it must be clear that that is the real purpose rather than mere window dressing to cover an arrangement not entitled to an exemption. *Phinney v. Dougherty*[26] illustrates the point. In that case, deductibility to the "Texas Beta Students Aid Fund" was claimed. The fund was incorporated to aid students of a particular chapter of a particular fraternity. A Treasury letter had been issued to the effect that contributions would be deductible. However, when it appeared that substantially all of the funds of the contributee entity were used for the acquisition and maintenance of a chapter house, the Treasury withdrew the exemption letter. On appeal, Treasury's decision was upheld on the ground that education was not the primary function of the fund.[27]

Exemption from the *payment* of income tax is authorized in section 501 of the *Internal Revenue Code* for organizations falling within the categories of subdivision (c) of that section. There are two pertinent paragraphs of subdivision (c). The first, numbered (3), insofar as is pertinent here, extends the exemption to entities "organized and operated exclusively for religious, charitable, scientific, testing for public safety, literary or educational purposes, or for the prevention of cruelty to children or animals . . ." where certain other requirements are also met. As the *Phinney* case indicates, the test under this subdivision is very largely the same as that used under section 170 with respect to deductibility. As a result, fraternities are not entitled to an exemption from the payment of income tax under *this* provision. They are, however, entitled to an exemption from the payment of tax under section 501(c)(7), relating to "clubs organized and operated exclusively for pleasure, recreation and other nonprofitable purposes, no part of the net earnings of which inures to the benefit of any private shareholder."[28]

Property Tax

There has been considerable litigation over the application to the fraternity house of state constitutional and statutory property-tax exemptions for eleemosynary purposes. Of course, each situation must be examined in light of the particular constitutional and statutory language and the case law of the jurisdiction where the question arises.

In general, the courts have held that exemptions of this character do not apply to fraternity houses. The cases up to 1959 are collected in 66 A.L.R. 2d 904. Typical of these authorities is a more recent decision, *Cornell University v. Board of Assessors,*[29] in which the New York court held that the operation of a fraternity house was not "exclusively" for educational purposes and hence not entitled to an exemption from property tax. This decision was reached even though, under the facts of the case, the property was owned by the university and leased to the fraternity. But under some circumstances, it can be done. *Alford v. Emory University*[30] is such a case. Here, an exemption was claimed under a Georgia law which extended it to property used "exclusively [for the] benefit of . . . educational . . . institutions." In this case, the land and the fraternity houses were owned by Emory University. Their occupancy was restricted to Emory students and the use by fraternities was permissive

[25] I.T. 1427, C.B. 1–2, p. 187; G.C.M. 5952, C.B. viii–1, p. 172.

[26] 307 F. 2d 357 (5th Cir., 1962).

[27] 307 F. 2d 370, 361. See also Rev. Rul. 60–367, 1960–2 *Cum. Bull.* 73.

[28] See Rev. Rul. 64–118, 1964–1 *Cum. Bull.* (Part 1) 182; I.T. 1427, C.B. 1–2, p. 187; and Rev. Rul. 68–222, I.R.S. 1968–19, 10.

[29] 24 A.D. 2d 526, 260 N.Y.S. 2d 197 (1965).

[30] 216 Ga. 391, 116 S.E. 2d 596 (1960).

and cancelable by the university at any time. No rent was charged, although interest payments were made on loans made to the fraternities for construction of the facilities. The right to use was not inheritable and was assignable only on university consent. The houses were built by the university and located in the heart of the campus. Of particular significance, they were considered a part of the university dormitory system, "an integral part of the operation of the college."

An instructive and candid discussion of this case by the attorney who won it may be found in "Tax Exemption for Fraternities in Private Colleges," by Henry L. Bowden.[31]

[31] *Report of the Fourth Annual Conference,* National Association of College and University Attorneys, p. 84, June 24–26, 1964.

Chapter 6

Legal Problems in Sponsorship of Exchange Programs

JUSTIN C. SMITH

Professor of Law, Texas Tech University, Lubbock, Texas

The legal problems associated with the university sponsorship of exchange programs are by no means insurmountable. The establishment of an exchange visitor program is basically the same as the sponsorship of any other university activity. However, there are several points which should be kept in mind. First, exchange programs are intended to benefit both the host institution and the visiting alien, not merely to solve a university's staffing problems. Second, the institution should establish an administrative office to assure the federal government that its program will conform to the goals announced in the Mutual Educational and Cultural Exchange Act of 1961[1] Third, the Department of State requires that each sponsor identify some member of the administrative family[2] to execute documents and to make such reports as are required from time to time.

VISA AND IMMIGRATION PROBLEMS

Establishing an Exchange Visitor Program

Once an institution has determined that it is feasible to establish an exchange program, the first problem which will confront it is to obtain State Department recognition for its program. An institution desiring to sponsor aliens as students—(F) visa holders—must submit an application for approval to the District Director of the Immigration and Naturalization Service which has jurisdiction where the institution is located.[3] The appropriate form is I-17 and the filing fee is generally waived in the case of an educational institution.[4] The decision relating to the approval or disapproval of an application is made by the District Director after consultation with the Office of Education and the petitioning institution, which is notified directly.

An application for recognition as a sponsor of an exchange visitor program is made on form DSP-37 to the Secretary of State.[5] The prefix to the sponsor's designation indicates the type of institution. For example: P-1 relates to programs sponsored by educational institutions and institutions devoted to scientific and technological research. Hospitals and related centers are designated by the prefix P-2. The designation P-3 relates to programs sponsored by nonprofit associations, foundations, and institutions.[6] An institution can apply for and receive more than one program designation.[7]

Length of Stay

Heretofore, there were only informal statements with respect to the maximum length of stay of an exchange visitor as opposed to an alien student.[8] However, guidelines have now been published[9] which specify that scholars who are not degree candidates and whose primary duty is teaching are allowed a maximum of two years, while nondegree candidates primarily engaged in research are allowed a maximum of three

[1] Mutual Educational and Cultural Exchange Act of 1961; Public Law 87-256, 87th Congress, H.R. 8666, September 21, 1961.

[2] For a detailed discussion of exchange visitor programs and the necessity for the appointment of a responsible officer, see *General Instructions for Sponsors of Designated Exchange-visitor Programs*, Department of State, Bureau of Educational and Cultural Affairs, Facilitative Services Staff, Washington, September, 1965; available from the above-mentioned office.

[3] See appended instructions to "Petition for Approval of School for Attendance by Nonimmigrant Students," form I-17 (rev. 7-11-67).

[4] *Ibid.*

[5] See "Exchange Visitor Program Application," form DSP-37.

[6] Federal Registers of February 2, 1963 (28 F.R. 1630) and February 28, 1964 (29 F.R. 2783); Code of Federal Regulations, Title 22—Foreign Relations, chap. 1—Department of State, part 63, chap. I.

[7] Two or more designations are used here to segregate various types of programs. For example: an academic program is distinguished from an in-service training program for nursing personnel.

[8] It is to be noted that many alien students enter the United States under a "Certificate of Eligibility" (for nonimmigrant F-1 student status), and after completing their undergraduate degree programs they either effect a change to resident alien status or continue their status as exchange visitors.

[9] See *Limits on the Stay of Aliens in the United States in Nonimmigrant Exchange-visitor Status* (undated, 2 pages) and *Special Notice for Hospitals*, Department of State, Bureau of Educational and Cultural Affairs, Facilitative Services Staff, August, 1965 (1 page).

years. Students who are full-time degree candidates may be allowed up to 18 months for practical training if such training is approved by the university sponsor.

Types of Visas

Since both the student and exchange visitor will enter the country as nonimmigrants, thought should be given to the type of symbol which appears on the nonimmigrant visa.[10] These symbols are as follows: temporary visitor for business (B1), temporary visitor for pleasure (B2), student (F), temporary worker performing services unavailable in the United States (H2), and exchange visitor (J).[11] Where a student has been selected by his own government to study in the United States, the "official visitor" is classified by the symbol (J).

American consuls abroad ordinarily issue to the spouses and children of principal exchange visitors exchange-visitor visas. The principal exchange visitor is given a (J-1) visa, while the spouse and children are given (J-2) visas. If the wife will be working to advance her own career, a (J-1) visa would be appropriate.

Two-year Requirement of (J) Visa

It is to be remembered that an alien who has entered the United States as an exchange visitor is ineligible to apply for immigration or permanent resident alien status until he has physically resided abroad in the country of his nationality or last residence for at least two years following his departure from the United States.[12] Under certain conditions the Attorney General may grant a waiver of this requirement upon the favorable recommendation of a United States government agency and the Secretary of State.

Waiver Petitions Details for the petition for waiver of the two-year requirement are to be found in 22 CFR, section 63.6–63.7.[13]

The Position of the Council on International Educational and Cultural Affairs A detailed statement of official concern relative to "any possible future use of Exchange Visitor Programs as channels for immigration" and the position of the Council on International Educational and Cultural Affairs is to be found in a recent issue of the *Foreign Affairs Manual Circular*.[14] This publication goes into considerable detail with respect to the evolution of interagency policy on the return of participants in exchange-visitor programs. The criterion apparently being employed by the member agency Exchange Visitor Waiver Review Board or Waiver Review Office is set forth as follows:

a. The services of the individual must be needed in a highly important program or activity of national or international significance in the areas of interest of the department or agency concerned. . . .

b. A direct relationship must exist between the individual and the program or activity involved, so that loss of his services would necessitate discontinuance of the program, . . .

c. The individual must possess unusual and outstanding qualifications, training, and experience, . . . capability to make original and significant contributions to the program.

[10] The responsible officer is well advised when interviewing a foreign faculty appointee to ask to see the appointee's passport in order that he may check on the date and manner of entry.

[11] An excellent discussion of our immigration laws is to be found in a publication of the United States Department of Justice Immigration and Naturalization Service; *United States Immigration Laws General Information*, M-50 (rev. 1966), available from Superintendent of Documents, U.S. Government Printing Office, Washington, D.C. (price, 15¢).

[12] For a detailed discussion of the two-year requirement see Department of State, Subject: "The Return of Participants in Exchange Visitors Programs," *Foreign Affairs Manual Circular*, no. 292, March 24, 1965.

[13] See footnote 6.

[14] See footnote 12.

Waiver requests based on the exceptional hardship provision of section 212(e) are made by the alien directly to the nearest district office of the Immigration and Naturalization Service which has sole jurisdiction in such cases.[15]

Effecting Change of Status

Sooner or later the institution will receive a request to file an application for change of status on behalf of a nonimmigrant alien.[16] Prior to the enactment of the Immigration and Nationality Act of 1962,[17] there was no specific procedure for such change of status.

The Immigration and Nationality Act of 1962 for the first time made statutory provision for such nonimmigrants in the United States, enabling them to adjust their status to that of aliens lawfully admitted for the purpose of permanent residence. It relieved them of the necessity of having to leave the country and obtain an immigration visa at an American consulate office abroad.

In applying for change of status, the nonimmigrant of course is subject to deportation should his request for change of status not receive favorable consideration.[18]

(H-1) Visas

In the event that an exchange-visitor visa appears inappropriate for an alien, such as a foreign scholar for example, he may enter the United States under an (H-1) visa.[19] Under the (H) classification the person enters with no intention of abandoning his residence in a foreign country. An (H-1) is an alien who possesses distinguished merit or ability and who is coming temporarily to the United States to perform temporary service of an exceptional nature requiring such merit or ability. The petition, form I-129B,[20] requires a full description of the person's education, technical training, specialized experience, or exceptional ability.

TAX PROBLEMS

Scholarships and Fellowships

The Education and Cultural Exchange Act of 1961 did not alter the tax treatment accorded foreign visitors. Foreign scholars are treated the same as U.S. citizens with respect to stipends awarded as scholarships and fellowships.[21] Any student is wholly exempt from income-tax withholding on any sum provided him by an institution of higher learning solely for the purpose of pursuing his degree; e.g., a scholarship.[22] Aliens who qualify may claim an exemption of $300 per month for up to 36 months for

[15] See footnote 12; also Department of State Bureau of Educational and Cultural Affairs, sec. 212(e) of the Immigration and Nationality Act as amended: *Determination of Secretary of State Regarding Foreign Residence of Exchange Visitors* (undated, 1 page).

[16] Under certain circumstances a nonimmigrant may change his status to that of an alien. This may either lawfully admit him for permanent residence or it may place him in another nonimmigrant classification.

[17] Immigration and Nationality Act as amended by Public Law 89-236, 89th Congress, H.R. 2580, October 3, 1965.

[18] The responsible officer will undoubtedly find it prudent to inform the nonimmigrant alien of this fact in writing, with a carbon copy to the alien's department head or immediate superior.

[19] Institutions are well advised to utilize (H-1) entry provisions of the immigration laws where the visiting faculty member will be in the United States for a relatively short period of time; e.g., to attend a conference and give a series of lectures.

[20] Considerable time should be allotted in order that the supporting documents necessary under an (H-1) petition may be obtained from abroad. Copies of papers and reprints of articles are excellent supporting documents in the case of (H-1) petitions.

[21] Internal Revenue Code (1954 Code, subtitle A, chap. 1B, part III, sec. 117, *Scholarships and Fellowship Grants*).

[22] *Ibid.*, (b)(1).

postdoctoral fellowships providing they have not made this claim before.[23] There would appear to be no distinction between a foreign scholar and a citizen of the United States as regards travel and other allowable expenses. The matter of scholarships and fellowships is treated under section V of *Information Guide* no. 7.[24]

Resident versus Nonresident

Some confusion arises when one attempts to distinguish between the resident and nonresident foreign scholar. There is an excellent treatment of this topic in section VI [25] of the *Information Guide* referred to above. Additionally, it is helpful to remember that residency is established, first, by the nature of the visa which the scholar holds and, second, by the nature of the work which he has undertaken. If his visa suggests that he is merely a temporary sojourner, such as an (H-1) visa entrant, it is clear that he cannot qualify for treatment as a resident alien. *Information Guide* no. 7 sets up the criterion of whether or not the individual is here for an "extended period." In defining what is meant by "extended period," the booklet says:

> The precise length of an extended period is not set by statutory law. However, an alien who lives continuously in the United States for longer than two years is considered to have been here for an extended period. . . . [A]n alien who lives continuously in the United States for longer than two years, and whose stay is characterized by the establishment of a home temporarily in the United States, is presumed a resident alien. . . .[26]

Tax Treaty Status

With regard to exemptions, *Information Guide* no. 7 distinguishes broadly between two groups: (1) those aliens who receive their income from foreign employers and (2) those aliens who are entitled to tax treaty benefits.[27] In the latter case the language varies considerably. A "short period of time" is defined anywhere from 90 to 183 days; hence, the appropriate treaty must be consulted in each case.

Sailing Permit

Under certain circumstances departing aliens may be entitled to a refund of tax withholding during the course of their stay in the United States. Information concerning filing for such refunds may be obtained from the nearest District Director of Internal Revenue. In virtually all cases departing aliens will find it necessary to obtain a "certificate of compliance," or "sailing permit," as it is popularly known, before leaving the United States. Consultation with the nearest District Director of Internal Revenue approximately one month before departure is advisable.[28]

CONCLUSION

Those responsible for alien students and faculty will find the various federal agencies involved in administering these exchanges most helpful. Consultation with an appropriate officer will strain out a majority of the routine problems which arise as a result of an institution's involvement in this area. It cannot be stressed too strongly that the success or failure of a university's program oftentimes hinges on the institution's delegation of responsibility to a particular office within the university.

[23] *Ibid.*, (b)(2).
[24] U.S. Treasury Department–Internal Revenue Service, Office of International Operations, *Information Guide* no. 7, Sept. 24, 1962.
[25] *Ibid.*, sec. VI 15.
[26] *Ibid.*, sec. VI 15.
[27] *Ibid.*, sec. X 21.
[28] *Ibid.*, sec. VIII 16.

Chapter 7

Health Services

PAUL J. MATTE

Director of the Student Health Service, University of Arizona, Tucson, Arizona, and Member of the Arizona Bar

I. GENERAL PRINCIPLES

1. Nature of Health Services

Operation of the medical service on the college campus presents administrative and legal problems of greater complexity than are involved in the provision of any other service. Medical services are subject to a number of controls and policy considerations which are largely extramural to the college or university. Procedures and channels of authority and responsibility which serve well in the administration of other service units may prove inadequate for the health service.

Good medical care is expensive, and budgetary requirements of the health service may often seem excessive when compared to the costs of operating other components of the college or university. A poorly operated health service can consume assets needed elsewhere at a rate represented by no other department, with the notorious exception of a school of medicine.

2. Quality of Care

The law makes no distinction between persons in terms of needs and quality of medical care. The day is long past when inadequate or poor-quality medical care could with legal and moral impunity be furnished the college student simply because such limited care was inherent in his status as a student.

Today the law and the constituency of the institution require that medical care provided to the student shall meet the standard of care available in the community at large. The dependent status of the majority of students brings their medical care under greater scrutiny than that care which is available to the general public, with the result that public and parental expectations often exceed the standards required by law.

The purpose in operating a health service is the provision of necessary medical care to defined members of the campus community; not the avoidance of litigation. But such principles as have evolved to define adequacy of medical care have been hammered out in lawsuits where liability of the provider of services has been the basic issue. Where rules exist they have been laid down by courts after the fact of administrative or medical-professional inadequacy.

3. Basic Concepts

Two themes run through this chapter. The first is the legal concept of the standard of care, encompassing the legal requirement that anything done medically must be done well. The second theme is organization of the health service in legal form and under organizational control adequate to avoid inefficiency and administrative errors which may lead to litigation or to departmental insolvency. Subsequent sections deal with these matters in detail. For standards of care, see part V, 1*b*, below. For organization see part II.

4. Initial Considerations

Organization of the health service should begin with consultation with personnel experienced in problems of medical administration. Ideally this will be done by the health service director. Administrative decision should be reached early on the following matters:

a. The standard and scope of medical care. This includes the degree of responsibility for student care assumed by the institution.

b. Eligibility for services. Health examination and payment of health fee should be required of all eligible persons.

c. Care of employees injured while on campus.

d. Facilities and staffing required to provide defined services.

e. Adequate financing. This includes realistic fees and automatic or optional coinsurance for care beyond that provided by the health service.

f. Organizational control of the health service.

g. Relations with the outside medical community. This includes referrals, use of facilities, and arrangements for care of students injured or acutely ill off campus.

h. Relations with other departments of the college or university, including medical school.

i. Responsibility for safety of physical facilities on campus.

All these matters have legal dimensions. There is a tendency to focus on issues of financing or potential liability and impaired public relations. Although important, such considerations cannot serve as primary determinants. Organization in terms of student needs and institutional capabilities will reduce relational and legal problems to a minimum.

II. ORGANIZATION OF HEALTH SERVICES

1. Determinants

Medicolegal adequacy of the health service depends on the size and character of the institution. Major determinants include residential or nonresidential student body; urban or isolated location; availability of private physicians and hospitals; the socioeconomic characteristics of the student population; and the presence or absence of a medical school.

In response to these factors the health service will vary in scope and complexity from a simple first aid station staffed by a nurse to a complete outpatient clinic with its own fully accredited hospital.

2. Junior Colleges

In this chapter the term "college" is used generically to include the larger concept of the university and the lesser concept of the junior college. The character and responsibilities of the junior college are in a process of change throughout the country. Where the junior college is organized to provide the first two years of a four-year program and is part of a state college system, the principles of this chapter should be followed so far as they apply. If the junior college falls under the aegis of a board of education and follows secondary school patterns of organization, charges no fees, and assumes little or no responsibility for the student outside the classroom, the extent of medical facilities depends on local custom.

3. Medical Records

Professional and legal standards require adequate recording of medical care and of medical data acquired in the course of treatment. Records must be filed in form suitable for immediate retrieval when the patient presents himself for medical attention. Medical confidentiality must be maintained. Unauthorized persons must not have access to individual records.

Health service records differ from those of private clinics in that access to them may be required in the course of administrative or academic management of the student. Among the circumstances which may call for such access are exemption from courses or regulations, withdrawal from school, and modification of curricular requirements when required by illness or disability.

The smallest health service requires clerical personnel to maintain necessary files and to effect, under medical supervision, necessary communication with other departments.

A common error of the small institution with a minimal health service is consolidation of student health records with academic data in the administrative offices of the university. This is a breach of medical confidentiality and is improper in medical and legal terms. (See part V, 2, below.)

III. TYPES OF SERVICES

1. The First Aid Station

The first aid station is the simplest and least costly of health services and is staffed by one or more registered nurses under the supervision of a physician employed part-time or on a volunteer basis. It is described in detail because it forms the nucleus of the health service. Its basic requirements and potential liability are common to health services of whatever size. Such a facility is adequate for the small college provided there is ready access to outside medical facilities and that students live at home.

The first aid station should be centrally located and must have a telephone, a medically qualified person in attendance at specified hours, and adequate emergency supplies and equipment.

Records include at minimum an *emergency log* of the format used in hospital emergency rooms and a folder for each student, filed alphabetically or by registration number, in which is filed such health data as the institution requires for admission plus any medical correspondence. *Accident report forms* for the recording of medical and circumstantial data including disposition of the patient should be maintained in duplicate; one copy filed in the student's folder. A summary report should be furnished at least monthly to a designated administrative officer. In case of serious injury, a copy of the original report should be sent immediately to the appropriate dean or personnel administrator.

Such records meet medical and legal requirements and permit response to inquiries from insurance companies or student request for transmittal of medical data to draft boards, attorneys, or outside physicians. Kept properly, they are adequate response to court order or *subpoena duces tecum,* which requires the responsible party to appear in court and to bring the records with him. Since personal injury, especially vehicular, is likely to result in lawsuit, requests for medical data concerning emergency care are common in student health services.

First aid includes treatment only to the degree necessary to permit transfer to definitive medical care and in theory can be given by anyone. However, when an organized facility exists for this purpose, it must be equipped for such emergencies as can be reasonably anticipated and must be operated by medically qualified personnel.

The common error of first aid personnel is undertaking under pressure from patients treatment for which the staff and service are neither equipped nor qualified. The first aid station is properly limited to the application of dressings to superficial wounds, the arrest of hemorrhage, the treatment of shock, the management of seizures, the application of emergency splints, and the provision of cardiac and respiratory assistance.

On order of a physician a specially trained nurse may give routine advice in the management of common minor problems of the student and arrange for referral of more serious problems to outside physicians.

Medication should not be furnished to patients. The dispensing of drugs requires license as a pharmacist or physician, or a physician's order. Even proprietaries require diagnosis of a sort, a function for which the registered nurse is not legally qualified. A locked kit of emergency medications for use on telephone order of a physician can be provided for use in acute situations. The supervising physician is responsible for purchase, security, and administration.

Space and equipment must be adequate for anticipated emergencies. Oxygen with equipment for its administration should be available. Personnel, including registered nurses, should be trained in resuscitative procedures and in external cardiac massage. For cardiac emergencies and major toxicity or trauma, a respirator or resuscitative unit is essential. The AMBU® respirator * is inexpensive and adequate for first aid purposes. Rescue units of fire departments can provide technical advice as to equipment and costs. Early contact with local units should be made for necessary assistance in severe emergency.

Routine procedures for referral of patients to physicians or outside facilities for adequate follow-up care are essential. Failure to provide adequate follow-up care to patients whose treatment has been undertaken constitutes the tort of *abandonment,* and is a potent source of liability. Lists of physicians and hospitals who have agreed to care for ill or injured students should be available and kept up to date. Prior arrangement for necessary transportation or ambulance service must be made. Notation should be made in the emergency log of the person assuming charge of the patient, and in serious or potentially serious cases, telephone follow-up should ensure that the patient has arrived at his destination and log entry should be made of this fact. This ensures that the institution has been relieved of immediate responsibility for the care of the patient.

Where a first aid station represents the limit of college facilities, it should be clearly defined and recognized as such to avoid liability for "holding out" services and facilities not available. Statement of the extent of services should be included in brochures or catalogs.

* Obtainable from Air-Shields, Inc., Hatboro, Pa.

2. Limited Outpatient Service

This is suitable for the institution of moderate size located within emergency distance of an urban community but whose resident students find it impractical to obtain medical care for minor problems because of time lost from classes or lack of necessary transportation.

The limited outpatient service resembles the private medical office or small clinic staffed by general physicians, often with part-time consultant services. Equipment, staffing, and standards of care should equal or exceed those of the local community within the limits of services provided. Physicians may be present for only a few hours daily. During their absence, the service functions as a first aid station, with immediate availability of telephone advice or orders. Under these circumstances the unit becomes a limited emergency department and will be forced to care for student problems which are not true emergencies. Limited standing orders permit care of minor problems by nursing personnel. The legal problems of emergency care by nurses are discussed in part VII, 4, below.

Diagnostic laboratory facilities are essential to the outpatient clinic. Often the part-time services of a local technician can be obtained, under supervision of the parent laboratory. Mail-order laboratories should be avoided unless a reputable service is regularly used by local physicians. Where transportation problems exist, a small X-ray unit capable of handling extremities and chests should be available for immediate diagnosis in order that proper disposition of the patient can be determined without delay which might aggravate the problem and prove a source of injury and subsequent liability.

Records required are those described for the first aid station, plus a record of student visits. This should include at minimum diagnosis, treatment, and disposition. These should be filed in the student's folder with laboratory or X-ray reports. The emergency log should be restricted to actual emergencies and patients seen outside of regular clinic hours.

Because a corporate entity cannot in legal theory practice a profession, a physician must be in charge as director of student health or university physician, full- or part-time.

3. Infirmaries and Inpatient Units

Infirmary. The residential college requires a specialized domiciliary facility for students too ill to go to class or requiring rest and supervision which cannot be provided in the dormitory. The simplest of these units is the *infirmary,* so designated to make clear that no pretense at hospital-type care is made. The infirmary will serve also for isolation of the milder contagious diseases of adolescence in students whose illness permits continued enrollment for the current term.

As a rule, students should not be retained in the campus infirmary or hospital whose illness is such as to require dropping out of school. Once this decision has been reached or the outcome has become apparent, the student should be transferred to private medical care and the direct responsibility of the institution should be terminated.

Infirmary care should be limited to problems which would result in the student being put to bed for a few days under parental supervision if he were living at home.

A specialized facility is not necessarily required. A dormitory unit can be set aside for the purpose, provided that sufficient isolation to prevent the spread of contagious disease can be had. Meals can be brought in from the student union or a college dining facility; students nearing discharge and not contagious may be permitted to go out for meals. Part-time attendance at important classes or examinations is permissible under similar circumstances.

Once responsibility for medical care, however limited, has been assumed, the infirmary must be prepared to cope with any medical problem which may foreseeably arise,[1] and for this reason it should be located adjacent to the first aid station or outpatient service. Registered nurses on 24-hour duty are required. Local custom may make LPNs (licensed practical nurses) or trained nursing aides adequate for certain shifts. A registered nurse should be in charge under supervision of a physician. Daily visits by a physician are required.

Patients under care in an unlicensed medical-care facility must be able to leave the building unaided in case of fire or other disaster. Design should include access by disabled persons. This is a requirement of federal funding and often a matter of state law.

Adequate medical records of bed patients are required. Forms are familiar to nurses and physicians. Records should be transferred to the student's medical file at the outpatient unit on his discharge from the infirmary.

The facilities of an infirmary correspond to those of a convalescent home, for which standards local or state health departments should be consulted.

The major legal and medical problems of the infirmary result from constant pressure to attempt, usually on grounds of indigency or economy, the care of persons too ill for adequate treatment by limited facilities and staff. The expanded infirmary exists in constant danger of failing to do properly that which is undertaken, a basic criterion of negligence. Careful medical screening of patients admitted to the expanded infirmary is imperative.

Licensed limited hospital. The infirmary which is forced to exceed its limitations should be converted to a licensed limited hospital as soon as practical. Conformity with established standards is required. Medicare has resulted in convergence of state and federal standards of licensure or approval. State licensing agencies are concerned primarily with standards of construction, equipment, and safety; federal agencies with standards of operation and facilities for professional care.

Federal regulations set out conditions for participation of hospitals in Medicare[2] and furnish a practical guide to the organization of an approved medical facility. The requirements are reasonable and should be within the capabilities of any institution which undertakes the care of student patients with a closed staff of physicians under institutional control. It is ordinarily not necessary, to qualify for licensure, that the student health hospital provide facilities for pediatrics, maternity cases, or major surgery, as is required of the community general hospital.

State regulations and health department officials should be consulted prior to construction or expansion for definition of facilities and services meeting standards for limited licensure.

4. Accredited Hospital

The requirements for full accreditation are beyond the scope of this chapter.[3] Standards are set by a composite board including representatives of the AMA, the American Hospital Association, the American College of Physicians, and the American College of Surgeons. Standards are more restrictive than present federal requirements for care of Medicare patients, particularly for staff organization, medical record keeping, and required facilities. Accreditation is a prerequisite for approved internship and

[1] Liability for reasonably foreseeable consequences of an act or situation under control of the defendant is basic to the law of negligence. Medically, the concept is inherent in the duty owed to the patient by the physician or hospital once care has been assumed and is expressed in terms of the standard of care. See B. Shartel and Marcus L. Plant, *The Law of Medical Practice,* Charles C Thomas, Springfield, Ill., 1959, pp. 116–128, 183–191.

[2] "Conditions of Participation, Federal Health Insurance for the Aged," Code of Federal Regulations, Title 20, chap. III, part 405, found in HIR-10 (6/67) HEW. See also H. M. Somers and Anne Ramsey Somers, *Medicare and the Hospitals, Issues and Prospects,* Brookings Institution, Washington, D.C., 1967, pp. 83–84.

[3] See *Hospital Accreditation References,* American Hospital Association (rev. ed.), Chicago, 1965.

residency programs and for participation in certain specialized federal programs of medical care.

There would seem to be little advantage in obtaining accreditation for a health service hospital provided there is compliance with Medicare and state standards. Accreditation requires services whose cost is usually not justified by the requirements of student health services limited to student care.

5. Health Service as Component of Medical School

Experienced health directors are divided on the merits of this system. So also are deans of medical schools.

The medical school is properly more oriented to teaching than to service. Problems may arise in the use of student doctors to treat student patients. Lines of responsibility for student care may remain unclear, while joint staff appointments are subject to a certain ambiguity. Bed costs per day are higher in a teaching hospital than in a facility geared specifically to care of the not-very-ill student, and bed shortages within the teaching hospital may lead to resentment at the requirement of treating students who require only domiciliary care.

The advantages of the system are administrative convenience and avoidance of duplication of medical facilities.

If the health service is to be operated by a school of medicine, *the best compromise* is the provision within the medical school hospital of a special ward, service, or clinic under the supervision of a physician charged with responsibility for student health and appointed both in that capacity and as a member of the medical school staff. Ideally, the health service should be funded separately and retain some degree of organizational autonomy.

6. Contract with Private Physician or Clinic

Here physical facilities are provided on campus and staffed by the contracting clinic, or students are required to go to the clinic location in the local community. Necessary administrative personnel are hired by the college. Records should be segregated from those of private patients, for reasons previously stated. If care is provided at the local clinic, a secretary should be hired for the handling of correspondence and communication with the parent institution.

The system is adequate for the small- to moderate-sized residential college which is convenient to adequate facilities. The responsibilities of the institution are limited to selection of a competent agency, to contractual provision of such services as are necessary to maintain the health of the student population, and to adequate financing.

Insulation from liability is incomplete. The organization which makes a specific physician available to its personnel is required to take care that the selected professional is competent. Opposing this is a doctrine that in certain circumstances the physician may be regarded as an independent contractor, for whose uncontrolled actions the organization is not liable.

Negotiation involves a prepaid medical program with the individual or clinic, based on the estimated number of student visits per year and the services to be rendered. Health fees are set accordingly. Separate hospital and accident insurance should be provided, by inclusion in health fees or by requirement of mandatory purchase, with exemption of students adequately insured by parental plans. Negotiation should not be undertaken without the assistance of an attorney experienced in such matters. The problems are complex and serious errors are easily made.

The difficulties are negotiation of a contract satisfactory to students, college, and clinic; lack of orientation of clinic personnel to student and institutional problems; and lack of administrative control by the institution.

For the college unwilling or unable to undertake the operation of a medical service, the arrangement is an adequate alternative.

IV. LEGAL FACTORS IN ORGANIZATION AND CONTROL

1. Corporate Medical Practice by Colleges

The legal structure of the college is that of a corporate entity deriving power and authority from the state. The state institution is defined as a public corporation when specifically incorporated. Otherwise it operates as a de facto corporation under authority of the state. The private college is a private corporation chartered by the appropriate body or commission of the state. The charter of the public corporation may be changed by legislative action, while the charter of the private corporation is a contract without reserved power and cannot be altered except with the consent of the corporation.

The public corporation is normally exempt from taxes; the private institution is exempt only for such activities as bear a direct relationship to its educative function. The corporation, public or private, has only such powers as are conferred by statute plus such implied or incidental power as is required to accomplish the purposes for which the charter has been granted.

The governing body is the board of regents of state colleges. Junior colleges are usually governed by the board of education or board of directors for junior colleges. The board of trustees or directors is the corresponding body for the private institution.

The statement is commonly made that a corporate body may not legally practice one of the so-called "learned professions."

> In dealing with the corporate practice of medicine we are faced by two facts which are exceedingly difficult to reconcile. The first is that courts have said over and over again that the corporate practice of medicine, dentistry and the like is illegal. The second is that, with the knowledge and acquiescence of all concerned, there are corporations in every state of the Union which are hiring physicians to practice medicine and which are furnishing, through physicians, a considerable portion of the medical care of the American people.[4]

The extent to which corporations, including colleges in every state, are engaged in the provision of medical care leaves no doubt that despite theoretical considerations, medical care may be provided by an organization.

It must be done, however, in accordance with well-established principles and precedents. Those most relevant to the operation of university health services involve delegation of authority and lay control of professional activity. In the college situation, the board of trustees or regents finds itself in the position of the governing board of any hospital, public or private.

The powers and duties of the board in this respect are determined by hospital law. Only the board can determine who shall administer, who shall practice in the facility, and who shall be admitted as a patient. Only the board has the right to set standards and to promulgate rules and regulations. With this power goes responsibility for ensuring that the health service discharges its functions and purposes.[5]

2. Delegation of Authority

Delegation of authority for professional acts is the mechanism which insulates the institution from the practice of medicine. Responsibility, however, cannot be delegated.

[4] A. W. Willcox, "Hospitals and the Corporate Practice of Medicine," *Cornell Law Quarterly*, vol. 45, no. 3, p. 486, Spring, 1960.

[5] Adapted from J. F. Horty, "Survey of Hospital Law," in *Readings in Hospital Law*, American Hospital Association, Chicago, 1965, pp. 1–2.

. . . To operate the hospital most efficiently, it is necessary that much of the board's authority be delegated to the administrator, to the medical staff, and to the officers and committees of the board.

. . . [T]here is a limit to the power of the board to delegate authority. The authority to delegate is implied by the business necessity of managing the corporation. There is a crucial difference between delegation of authority and abdication of authority by the board. A delegation of authority is, by definition, limited in time, scope, or purpose. What constitutes permissible delegation and what constitutes abdication is, of course, a question of fact.

The board may permit the formulation of rules and regulations by the administrator or his subordinates or by committees of the hospital, subject to review and approval by the board. . . .

Perhaps the most important specific management duties peculiar to hospitals include: (*a*) determining hospital policies in accordance with community health needs, (*b*) maintaining proper professional standards in the hospital, (*c*) assuming general responsibility for adequate patient care throughout the institution, and (*d*) providing for adequate financing of hospital operation and expansion.[6]

3. Autonomy of Professional Staff

The degree of control permitted the governing body has been stated as follows:

It is of first importance, of course, that professional acts and professional judgments be free from lay control. But it is also essential, if hospitals are to continue as centers of organized medical care, that their governing boards have authority to exercise the kinds of control over personnel . . . without which the boards cannot discharge their responsibility to make the various services available when they are needed. The reconciliation of professional freedom with organizational control, though troublesome at times, presents basically no different problem from the employment of professional personnel in any large organization, public or private, which is managed by laymen.[7]

The prohibition of practice by an unlicensed individual carries with it, as a necessary corollary, a prohibition of control by a layman of the professional judgments or professional acts of a physician . . . But this implied prohibition can extend no further than those aspects of medical practice for which licensure is required—namely, its professional aspects . . .[8]

The medical staff organization and bylaws are the means by which distinctions between administrative and professional acts are determined. The requirements of staff organization are not legally specific. However, patterns are well established in hospital practice.[9] Health service bylaws may be patterned on those of a local hospital. In addition to delineation of control, staff bylaws delegate necessary authority in areas purely professional. Even if the health service consists of a first aid station supervised by a lone physician, a statement of organization, responsibility, and services available should be spelled out in a document patterned on relevant portions of hospital staff bylaws. Necessary mechanisms of implementation are as follows:

. . . [T]he staff should adopt its own bylaws establishing the pattern of staff organization and fixing rules for its internal management. The staff bylaws should be approved by the hospital's governing body and should, if legally possible, be made a part of the [institution's] own bylaws. This is best accomplished by a rather precise provision to that effect. Further, the medical staff bylaws should affirm that responsibility for the patient rests with the Board of Trustees and that it is the policy of the board to delegate

[6] *Ibid.*, pp. 4–5.

[7] Willcox, *op. cit.*, p. 434. See also Charles U. Letourneau, *The Hospital Medical Staff*, Starling Publications, Chicago, 1964, pp. 40–60, 92–96.

[8] *Ibid.*, p. 445.

[9] For model medical staff bylaws, see *Hospital Accreditation References* rev. ed., American Hospital Association, Chicago, 1965, pp. 187–205.

supervision of the quality of the care to the appropriate bodies of the medical staff so far as it is legally permissible to do so . . .

The medical staff bylaws should determine the procedure for amendment of the bylaws. If they have been properly approved and adopted by the governing board, the board and the medical staff are both legally bound by the procedure agreed upon. This affords some protection to members of the medical staff against arbitrary and capricious action by the board in regard to medical staff privileges.[10]

4. Recruiting and Retaining Medical Staff

Recruiting and retaining a competent medical staff has become increasingly difficult for academic and other institutions in recent years with the possible exception of schools of medicine. Nevertheless, to meet the required standards of care, the health service must be provided with sufficient personnel for medical duties once undertaken.

The medical and legal hazards of staffing inadequate to meet patient demands are well recognized. It is no defense to a charge of professional negligence that the practitioner was overworked and underpaid. Only an emergency situation, clearly recognizable as such, will excuse work below ordinary professional standards. A high turnover rate of professional personnel is a potent source of organizational incompetence and potential liability.

The legal obligation of the institution for the selection and utilization of competent personnel includes provision of sufficient salary, status, and benefits to recruit and retain competent medical personnel in numbers sufficient to meet patient needs.

Conditions of employment and available benefits should be made an official policy determination of the governing body of the college.

5. Qualifications and Licensure of Staff Physicians

Only the Board of Medical Examiners can grant a license to practice medicine. Where licensure of physicians employed by state institutions is less restrictive than that required for private practice, the college is not thereby excused from ensuring that the professional competence and moral character of the physician meet local standards. The employment of a medical impostor can prove embarrassing and legally hazardous.

Application for appointment should include evidence of a medical degree, approved internship, and current licensure, plus a curriculum vitae or resume of previous education and employment. Gaps in continuity of professional employment should be explained. Letters of recommendation from previous employers or associates should be required.

Failure to investigate the background of a physician-candidate for medical employment is inexcusable negligence. The local medical society has access to sources of information, and the AMA maintains a file of physicians known to have practiced in the United States. Direct contact with the candidate's former community is essential to evaluate personal traits which might make employment as health service physician undesirable. Similar precautions should be followed for nurses, technicians, social workers, and clinical psychologists.

V. LEGAL MATTERS INTRINSIC TO THE HEALTH SERVICE

1. Liability for Malpractice

a. Malpractice may be defined as failure of the physician to perform properly the duty which results from a professional relationship to the patient, with the result that injury occurs. For negligent acts which do not result in injury, the result of patient

[10] A. F. Southwick, "Legal Aspects of Medical Staff Function," in *Readings in Hospital Law*, American Hospital Association, Chicago, 1965, p. 155. See also Letourneau, *op. cit.*, pp. 40–60.

dissatisfaction may still be a lawsuit whose defense will prove time-consuming and expensive to the physician.

b. The standard of care required of the physician is measured by the usual conduct of a reasonably prudent practitioner under the same circumstances. The standard is determined by comparing the act alleged to have been done negligently with its usual performance by competent physicians of the same or a similar locale and under the same circumstances as those in which the act took place. Expert testimony is required unless the act is so outrageous or the result so unwarranted that its negligent character falls within the common knowledge of the layman. Failure to meet the standard of care includes nonperformance of a medical act required by the situation.[11]

c. Institutional standards of care have come increasingly to be recognized in the law. For hospitalized patients these are likely to be national, or at least regional, rather than local. The facilities and care of emergency services are likely to be measured against those of other similar institutions of the community or similar communities.

In addition to malfeasance, liability for operation of an emergency service is likely to result from failure to meet public expectations. The leading case in this area is *Wilmington General Hospital v. Manlove,* 174 A.2d 135 (1961), in which the Supreme Court of Delaware held that although a hospital is not required by law to establish an emergency department, if it does so it is holding itself out as offering emergency care to those who require it. It thereby undertakes a duty to accept any emergency patient brought to it, provided there exists a true emergency. Recent cases have held that once a patient is brought into the emergency department, the hospital assumes the duty to provide reasonable care.[12] [*New Biloxi Hospital v. Frazier,* 146 So.2d 882 (1962); *Methodist Hospital v. Ball,* 362 SW.2d 475 (1962)]

The extent to which these decisions become applicable will depend on the location of the service, its accessibility to the general public, and the services it holds itself out to provide. As a rule, the emergency department cannot turn away bona fide emergency cases because of administrative ineligibility and must be prepared to give at minimum initial care to any case which can be reasonably expected to arrive at its door. On the usual college campus, this will afford few limits. For equipment necessary to adequate initial emergency care, see part III, 1, above.

d. Respondeat superior means "let the master answer"—for the negligence of his servants. On this basis the college is liable for the malpractice or negligence of its physicians or other employees of the health service. The doctrines of charitable and sovereign immunity afford little protection, even in those jurisdictions where they still survive. Health fees are normally involved in student medical care, and the doctrine of sovereign immunity affords no protection to suit against the practitioner himself.[13]

The likelihood of lawsuit can be minimized by the employment of personnel who are interested, tolerant, and adept in the management of student problems. Breakdown of interpersonal relations is the recognized major catalyst of the suit for malpractice. Maintenance of adequate standards, equipment, and facilities, with limitation of services to available equipment and staff, are obvious factors in reduction of patient injury and thus litigation. Curiously, injury itself is less likely to lead to lawsuit than mishandling of student or parental dissatisfactions with medical care.[14]

[11] Allan H. McCoid, "The Care Required of Medical Practitioners," *Vanderbilt Law Review,* vol. 12, pp. 549–632, 1959.

[12] R. P. Bergen, "Legal Aspects of Emergency Departments," in *Emergency Department: A Handbook for the Medical Staff,* American Medical Association, Chicago, 1966, pp. 106–113.

[13] For principles of liability equally applicable to private institutions, see *Legal Aspects of PHS Medical Care,* U.S. Public Health Service Publication no. 1468, 1966.

[14] R. Blum, *The Management of the Doctor-Patient Relationship,* McGraw-Hill Book Company, New York, 1960, pp. 252–253; "Professional Liability and the Physician," Committee of Medicolegal Problems, *Journal of the American Medical Association,* vol. 183, no. 8, pp. 695–704, 1963.

e. Malpractice insurance must cover both professional personnel and the medical installation itself. A blanket liability policy should contain a specific clause affording protection against suit for malpractice, not only against the institution but against the individual practitioner involved. The language should provide for legal defense and for indemnification of any liability. A clause specifying that settlement shall not be made without consent of the defendant should be included. This is important to the physician, whose professional reputation is involved. Care should be taken that the carrier understands clearly the nature and extent of the medical facility and the conditions of practice therein. Statement to this effect should be incorporated in the policy contract in order to avoid the possibility of a basis for subsequent disclaimer of contractual responsibility.

A second basis for disclaimer is failure of the insured to give timely notice to the insurer of threatened suit or incident likely to result in a claim of negligence. Adequate and routine "incident reports" should be forwarded to an officer of the college charged with responsibility for their evaluation and, where indicated, notification of the insurer or his agent.

The advice of experts is highly desirable. Malpractice claims in excess of one million dollars have become common.

This brief summary by no means exhausts the complexities of the law of malpractice and is intended only for general orientation to the subject.

2. Confidentiality of Records and Reports

a. The American College Health Association has recently revised policy guidelines with respect to confidentiality.[15] The issues are complex and the reference document should be read carefully.

b. Legal issues resulting from breach of confidentiality include defamation, invasion of privacy, interference with beneficial relationships, and medical malpractice, all legally compensable should injury occur. In some jurisdictions breach of professional confidence is cause for revocation of licensure.

c. Basic Principles

(1) Health records are medical data and subject to the legal restrictions thereof. They are not administrative data.

(2) Administrative access to medical data is limited to general information sufficient only to meet the problem involved.

(3) Access to medical data is limited to individuals or offices requiring it to function in the interest of the student or, rarely, in the interest of the general community.

(4) Data acquired in the course of the doctor-patient relationship cannot be used for disciplinary purposes.

(5) Release of information from medical records requires either:

(*a*) Administrative necessity

(*b*) Court order or action of law

(*c*) Potential hazard to the individual, other persons, or the community

(*d*) Permission of the individual concerned

(6) Release of information in one context does not permit release in other contexts.

(7) There is no obligation on the part of the institution to release medical data to the press or to private, federal, or state investigative or employment agencies unless release is requested by the individual concerned or is obviously in his interest.

(8) Parents are entitled to only such data as is essential to meet their responsibilities to the student.

[15] *Ethical and Professional Relationships: A Supplement to Recommended Standards and Practices for a College Health Program*, rev. ed., American College Health Association, Evanston, Ill., 1969.

(9) Record files must be so managed as to ensure that confidentiality is maintained and that unauthorized persons do not gain access.

(10) Medical data should not be incorporated in central data banks.

d. Privileged and Confidential Communications

(1) A *privileged communication* between physician and patient is information which cannot be introduced as evidence in judicial proceedings without permission of the individual concerned.

(2) *Confidential communications* include any information transmitted in the course of the doctor-patient relationship. Absent waiver of privilege or action of law, release of such information constitutes unprofessional conduct. Waiver of privilege or action of law permits release of only such information as is required by the judicial situation. Release of data unnecessary to these purposes is a breach of confidentiality which may be actionable.

3. Liability tor Administrative Error

Liability may result from administrative error of the health service or the parent institution. Errors of omission are a fertile source of liability. There may be failure to provide medical coverage of an athletic contest involving substantial risk of injury, with the result that preventable injury occurs from lack of immediate treatment; or the institution may require participation in physical education of a student whose file contains a record of definite medical data prohibiting strenuous exercise. Remote field trips may be lacking in emergency medical supplies or emergency transportation for the injured. Duty rosters for professional personnel may fail to make provision for foreseeable emergencies. At the individual-patient level are such occurrences as administration of medication to a student whose record clearly indicates allergy to it and failure to notify of examination or test results indicating serious disease or need for further treatment.

The possibilities are limitless and can be minimized only by sufficient staffing to meet demands on the medical facility and by adequate delineation of responsibility, the granting of sufficient authority to perform or cause performance of required duties, and adequate channels of communication between the medical service and other departments of the university.

Routine accident and injury reports (part III, 1, above) are essential to the correction of environmental hazards. They must be read by someone with sufficient authority to ensure appropriate action. Failure to correct a hazard in the face of documentary evidence of its existence is negligence for which liability can be guaranteed should preventable injury occur.

4. Student Discipline, Regulations, and Violations of Law

a. Police work is not a health service function. The first barrier is medical confidentiality: health service personnel cannot ethically report to other departments matters learned in the course of the doctor-patient relationship. The second barrier is loss of student confidence, with impaired utility of the health service to both students and college. Students most in need of professional advice will avoid the health service if disciplinary action may result from nonmedical aspects of their medical or psychiatric problems. Under such circumstances, minor problems tend to evolve into major ones whose satisfactory resolution by deans and college officials becomes difficult if not impossible.

b. Enforcement of health regulations. The nondisciplinary character of the health service does not prevent the use of administrative sanctions to enforce health service regulations. Admission requirements can be enforced by refusing or terminating eligibility for nonemergency use of the health service or by encumbrance of registration in the same manner that the business office enforces collection of fees or the library ensures return of books. The health service may also enforce necessary order upon its premises and impose medically required restrictions on patients and visitors. The rare cases in which use of force is required are best handled by the campus security department.

c. Refusal of medical care. Treatment cannot be forced upon the student who refuses it. Consent obtained by threat of administrative sanction is likely to prove invalid in case of subsequent litigation.

(1) Where there is reasonable belief of *substantial hazard* to the student or to others, as in the case of serious or contagious disease, college regulations may properly require as a condition of continued enrollment that the student receive private medical care or remove himself from the campus environment until resolution of the problem.

(2) *If the student is a minor,* the parent or guardian should be advised of the situation, and authority to treat the student should be requested.

(3) *If the parents cannot be reached,* a health service physician or other university official may grant permission to treat under the doctrine of *in loco parentis.* In such cases, the emergency should be apparent, and only such treatment as is essential should be given. Although in theory liability may result, the possibility of successful litigation is remote. In doubtful cases, a court order should be obtained. The granting of such an order permits treatment; refusal relieves the health service of further legal, though not necessarily moral, responsibility. For further discussion of these problems, policy statements of the American College Health Association should be consulted.[16]

(4) *If the parents refuse permission,* a health service physician should explain the serious nature of the problem, state institutional policy, and make it clear that the health service and the college can assume no further responsibility in the matter. If possible, the conversation should be witnessed and a written release from responsibility obtained in standard form.[17] In absence of the parent, the signature of the student should be obtained. If this is refused, the facts should be noted over the signature of the physician and a witness.

(5) *Students over 21 years of age* require neither parental approval of refusal of treatment nor parental permission for treatment. There is no legal requirement of notification, but public relations factors make it advisable that parents be notified of the general nature of the problem in the case of students who occupy college housing and remain subject to regulation in social terms.

(6) In the absence of a health- or life-threatening situation which justifies either consent by an official *in loco parentis,* the assumption of implied consent, or request for a court order, if the student refuses medical care and parental permission cannot be obtained, the responsibility of the health service and the college is limited to making known the necessity of further medical care and where this can be obtained. When possible, such advice should be witnessed and reduced to writing.

In all such cases, an appropriate college official should be advised of the situation, and assistance should be obtained for resolution in terms of institutional policy. Consultation with the college's legal adviser may be indicated. It is obvious that the official may and must be provided with sufficient medical data to permit him to handle the problem.

For consent to treatment of cooperative minors, see part VI, below.

d. Violations of law are handled in accordance with medical ethics and the moral and legal responsibility of the practitioner concerned. Breach of confidentiality of the doctor-patient relationship is required and justified only in the case of major crimes, recognized hazard to other persons, or offenses specifically reportable by law.

Difficult questions arise in matters of drug abuse, particularly on psychiatric ser-

[16] *Ibid.*

[17] *Medicolegal Forms with Legal Analysis,* American Medical Association, 1961, p. 37.

vices, where such information is most likely to be obtained. Policy statements of the American College Health Association should be consulted.[18]

State law commonly requires reporting of cases of intentionally inflicted wounds, felonious assault, and rape which come under treatment in emergency rooms or the physician's office. Local statutes should be consulted and reporting procedures made routine and a matter of record.

The health service should avoid involvement in police problems and matters of student discipline. Close liaison with the campus security department should be maintained, and police matters should be reported promptly to that office. Ideally, health service liaison with local law-enforcement officials should be through the campus police, who can do much to protect the interests of the immature student.

5. Eligibility for Health Service Care

Eligibility for health services should be limited to persons paying allocated health fees and complying with routine admission health requirements of medical history, physical examination, chest X-ray, and required immunizations. Basic health data is essential to the avoidance of liability from improper treatment or management of chronic or preexisting disease.

The legal problems of undefined eligibility for health services are (*a*) failure of compliance with admission health requirements with resulting inadequate medical records and basic data, (*b*) the furnishing of medical care to persons who do not fall within the corporate responsibility of the institution, and (*c*) "loophole utilization" by persons of undetermined age whose very identity is a matter of doubt.

The college should clearly define student categories in terms of eligibility for health services and provide eligible persons with identification without which, as a matter of institutional policy, nonemergency treatment is not to be given.

In no case, however, may the health service refuse necessary emergency care to persons who present themselves in need of it. Care of ineligible persons should be limited to that necessary to permit referral to a private facility. Procedures should provide for collection of customary fees for emergency service. Units approved under Medicare regulations are eligible for compensation under Title XVIII of the Social Security Act for services rendered to persons eligible under the law.

6. Vehicular Accidents

Vehicular accident cases require care which is likely to exceed the facilities of the average health service, and they involve the near certainty of subsequent litigation and court appearance of health service personnel. Litigation of vehicular accident cases includes a search for liability wherever this may be found, with the result that the treatment rendered by the student health service is certain to come under legal scrutiny.

For these reasons, a majority of health services limit the care of vehicular accident cases to treatment necessary to permit transportation elsewhere for subsequent care. Local police and ambulance departments should be advised of institutional policy in this area and encouraged to take accident victims to the nearest community hospital unless the condition of the victim warrants resort to the nearest facility, however inadequate this may prove.

The so-called "emergency doctrine," requiring only such care as normal facilities permit, will usually excuse liability for inadequate treatment under these circumstances. Where the university emergency service is of substantial adequacy, policy exceptions can be made for single-vehicle accidents occurring on campus and for accidents involving college transportation, where involvement of the institution in any

[18] "Policy Statement on Drugs," adopted by the Executive Committee of the American College Health Association, Oct. 19, 1967.

resulting litigation is practically assured, or where public relations factors outweigh other considerations.

7. Dispensing of Medicines

Dispensing of medicines by student health services requires compliance with state and federal law. The relevant statutes are Title 26 of the United States Code, controlling narcotic prescriptions; Title 21 of the United States Code, Food and Drugs, amended 1965 to control hallucinogens, psychotherapeutic agents, barbiturates, and combinations thereof; the State Pharmacy Act; and the State Drug Control Act, if such exists.

The health service of any size should if possible organize a pharmacy in accordance with local law. This will normally require the employment of a full-time registered pharmacist. Smaller institutions should obtain the services of a part-time pharmacist to ensure proper organization and compliance with law.

Institutions which do not employ a pharmacist may dispense medicines only through a licensed physician or his direct agent, and only to those who can be considered his patients. Savings of funds may well prove illusory in view of enhanced liability.

Colleges with ready access to a private pharmacy can often arrange discount rates for students, reducing the necessity for dispensing in the health service to a minimum.

The dispensing of medications by a registered nurse in the absence of the physician or pharmacist is, strictly speaking, not legal, but it is commonly done. The justification is that of necessity. This should be real. Such an arrangement requires a physician's order in each case and the dispensing of medication only in case of authentic need and in quantity only sufficient to meet the situation until the physician or pharmacist becomes available.[19]

Written standing orders may permit the nurse to provide simple medications to students who appear after hours with minimal, readily recognized, common problems. The physician in charge retains responsibility for any error. Such orders should be kept to the irreducible minimum. Difficulties arise from the fact that a registered nurse is not legally qualified to make a medical diagnosis because she is not a physician, and she is not legally authorized to dispense medication without supervision because she is not a registered pharmacist.

Public relations will be improved and legal problems minimized if pharmaceutical aspects of the student health service are organized in consultation with the pharmaceutical association of the state or local community.

8. Religious Objections to Medical Treatment

Only in rare circumstances may the college force medical care upon the unwilling student (part V, 4, above).

a. Admission Health Requirements. When religious beliefs prohibit medical care, the items at issue are normally the admission physical examination and medical history, the chest X-ray or tuberculin skin test, and vaccination against smallpox. The basic question is whether the student refusing to comply may be denied admission to the college.

Courts have recognized the obligation of a school or college to protect students from contagious disease in others and have usually upheld the right to establish and enforce reasonable requirements of examination.

The private college may impose whatever reasonable requirements it sees fit. Subject to limitations of liability, it may waive these in particular cases.

The public institution may set requirements which neither discriminate between potential students nor infringe personal rights, including the right of attendance at a

[19] See Wm. E. Hassan, Jr., "The Small Hospital, Nursing Homes, and Part-time Pharmacists," in *Hospital Pharmacy*, 2d ed., Lea & Febiger, Philadelphia, 1967, pp. 358–369.

public institution. Admission health examination and chest X-ray have generally been considered reasonable and nondiscriminatory. Compulsory smallpox vaccination, on the other hand, is arguably an infringement of personal rights in view of the present rarity of the disease and the division of medical opinion on the subject.

A distinction between treatment and required medical examination, chest X-ray, and vaccination has been recognized by Christian Science practitioners confronted by statutes requiring health examination as a prerequisite to teaching, food handling, and other health-related employment. Although exemptions are almost routinely requested, it is generally agreed that submission to required tests and examinations does no special violence to the precepts of Christian Science and may therefore be enforced as a requirement of admission to the state or private college.[20]

b. Emergency Medical Care. Difficult questions arise with respect to responsibility of the college for the acutely ill or injured student with religious objections to medical care. There is no completely satisfactory solution to this problem. The college with substantial custody of the student and standing *in loco parentis* is on safer legal and moral ground in providing necessary medical treatment than in running the risk of serious disability or death from lack of treatment. Where parents are available, the institution may return the student to their custody and terminate the responsibility of the institution.

Documents requesting exemption usually include a waiver of responsibility for the consequences of refusal of medical care. Such waivers offer little protection to the institution after serious injury has resulted from failure to provide treatment. On the other hand, courts are unlikely to find liability for successful administration of medical care in a life-threatening situation even though this be in violation of religious precepts.

For the above reasons it is reasonable to conclude that Christian Scientists and other religious objectors to medical care should not be exempt from admission health requirements nor denied necessary emergency care for serious illness or injury regardless of recorded waiver of responsibility or statement of intent to refuse medical treatment.

Jehovah's Witnesses are likely to refuse blood transfusions required by an emergency situation. In a majority of health services this problem does not arise, since cases of this severity are usually referred to private care. Although the constitutional issues have by no means been resolved, the best solution appears to be request for a court order permitting necessary treatment. Granting the request permits treatment. The refusal relieves the institution of further legal responsibility except that for the provision of alternate remedies, however ineffective.

VI. CONSENT TO TREATMENT

1. Treatment without Consent

Treatment without consent of the patient may result in liability for malpractice or for assault and battery. As a rule there is implied consent of the individual who voluntarily submits to treatment, provided he is legally qualified to give consent. Parental consent to routine necessary services which carry no substantial hazard can be implied from enrollment in the college and delegation to it of a significant degree of responsibility for control of the minor student. *Written consent* of the parent or guardian should routinely be obtained for elective, cosmetic, or potentially hazardous medical or surgical procedures except in an emergency where this is impractical or delay may prove hazardous to the patient.[21] In such cases there is implied consent

[20] A pamphlet called *Legal Rights and Obligations of Christian Scientists* is published by the Christian Science Committee on Publication of each state with reference to the law of that state.

[21] *Mediocolegal Forms, op. cit.*, p. 33.

of the patient or guardian.[22] A documented effort to reach the parent should be made before implied consent is assumed.

2. In Loco Parentis

In loco parentis has come recently under fire as a result of student activism, particularly in areas of social control.[23] However, it retains validity in emergency situations when parents cannot be reached. The extent of the authority of the college under the *in loco parentis* doctrine is in direct relationship to the degree of responsibility imposed on the college for the personal, nonacademic welfare of the student.

3. Responsibility for Consent

Responsibility for consent to outside hospital admission or treatment of serious injury or life-threatening illness may and should be assumed by a designated college official, normally a dean of students or vice-president for student personnel. Because of potential conflict of interest, the treating health service physician should not be so designated. Responsibility may properly be placed in a well-functioning campus security office routinely involved in cases of student catastrophe. Similar procedures apply to the adult student whose condition renders him incapable of consent. Here the *emergency doctrine* will furnish implied consent for such treatment as is reasonably necessary. Although litigation is not unknown in such cases, the possibility of liability is remote.

4. Informed Consent

Informed consent to elective procedures has received recent emphasis in the law of malpractice, and the case and journal literature has become substantial.[24] The patient or his parent must be given sufficient information, including potential hazard or anticipated results, to render the consent valid.

5. Signed Consent Form

A signed consent form should be obtained from the appropriate party in all cases of minor surgical procedures of a nonemergency nature. Verbal consent obtained by telephone is adequate when properly witnessed and recorded.

6. Blanket Consent Forms

Blanket consent forms included in health examination or registration forms should be avoided. They are unnecessary for routine care of minor illness and completely inadequate in case of serious injury or illness, where the generality of the forms and the requirement of informed consent are likely to render such consent invalid. In addition they furnish an opportunity for blanket denial of consent which is certain to be exercised by a small minority of parents, complicating any emergency situation which may later arise.

7. Emancipated Minors

Emancipated minors are defined by statute or case law, which varies from state to state. Local counsel should be consulted for definition and accurate data should be

[22] Alternatively this may be stated in the legal terms that in a true emergency situation, consent is not required.

[23] The leading case is *Goldberg v. Regents of the University of California,* 57 Cal.Rptr. 463 (1967), *rehearing denied* April 26, 1967; see also Robert Callis, "Educational Aspects of *In Loco Parentis,*" *Journal of College Student Personnel,* vol. 8, no. 4, pp. 231–233, July, 1967; Clarence J. Baaken, "Legal Aspects of *In Loco Parentis,*" *ibid.,* pp. 234–236; John H. Wilms, "Medical Aspects of *In Loco Parentis,*" *ibid.,* pp. 237–238. For judicial response to parents' demands for social control, see *Jones v. Vassar College,* 299 N.Y.S.2d 283 (1969).

[24] *Medicolegal Forms, op. cit.,* pp. 15–22.

made available to the health service and administrators who may be concerned with questions of consent. The emancipated minor may consent to his own medical care or that of his dependents on an adult basis. In a few jurisdictions, case law has specifically dealt with the issue of whether a minor person of "sufficient maturity" and freedom from parental control may consent to medical procedures, and decisions have been in the affirmative.[25]

VII. MISCELLANEOUS SOURCES OF LIABILITY

1. Interference with Beneficial Relationships

In addition to defamation, or damage to reputation, there is a poorly defined body of law protecting from wilful or negligent interference such "interests" as family relations, contractual or economic interests, and employment. Interference with *prospective advantage* such as future employment and, in rare cases, marriage may also be actionable if causation and damages can be proved. Malicious intent is generally though not uniformly required.

Liability may result on this basis from inappropriate action of any department of the college. Where the college includes a cross section of the population, litigation on this basis is not uncommon. The most common claim involves loss of employment.

Health service records may include data on general health, treatment for venereal or other disease, pregnancy, psychiatric treatment, or information on personal affairs which may prove a potent weapon against the student and his interests in such matters as parental disapproval of a marriage, divorce proceedings, child-custody suits, property settlements, alimony payments, and the like. Breach of confidentiality or deliberate misuse of personal data is less likely to arise from medical personnel than from clerical personnel in other departments who may have access to information transmitted in the course of necessary administrative action.

The best corrective is careful supervision of clerical employees in departments whose administrative responsibilities require handling, however limited, of medical or disciplinary data. Health service personnel should be alerted to the hard fact that not every inquiry which may be received from personnel employed in other offices of the college will be motivated by administrative necessity. Under certain circumstances an acknowledgment of the mere fact that a student is under treatment will provide the confirmatory information to other data which may be used to his detriment.

Health service communication with other departments must conform to the principles of confidentiality described in part V, 2, above. Medical recommendations for academic or administrative action by other departments should be stated only in terms of "medical reasons."

Student records in routine clinical use should be maintained free of potentially defamatory data. Where such data must be recorded for administrative or medicolegal reasons, they should be kept in locked confidential files of controlled and limited access, keyed to the student's health record by the notation "information filed elsewhere." The health service should be authorized to refuse inquiries for specific medical data from faculty members and administrators, however highly placed, who have no official need of such information.

2. False Imprisonment

False imprisonment is the unlawful detention or restraint of a person for any length of time. As a compensable tort in the college situation it is most likely to occur from well-intended efforts to retain the student in hospital against his will or to convey him

[25] Ohio and Michigan. *Lacey v. Laird,* 166 Ohio St. 12, 139 N.W. 2d 25 (1956); *Bishop v. Shirley,* 237 Mich. 76, 211 N.W. 75. A recent California statute authorizes certain minors to consent to their own treatment [C.C. 346 and C.C. 347 (1968)].

by threat or actual force to the health service for treatment thought necessary.[26] It is not false imprisonment to require admission of the protesting student to the infirmary or hospital on the basis of parental request or permission. A telephone call will usually resolve the problem when the student is a minor. Transportation of the uncooperative student to the health service is best handled by campus security officers whose professional expertise should include knowledge of legal limitations in this area.

Release of the uncooperative student from hospital or infirmary should follow normal hospital practice. Hospital personnel have no authority to retain forcibly under medical care the patient who is determined and able to leave. Subject to the considerations of part V, 4, above, the student-patient is free to seek other medical care or none at all.

Continued enrollment of the student who neglects treatment of potentially serious illness or injury is a matter for local policy determined by the nature of the student population and the college. Necessity for action is based on recommendation of the physician, but any resulting administrative action should come from offices other than the health service.

Without legal action permitting or requiring detention, adult students must be permitted to leave the infirmary or hospital. Usual hospital practice requires a release of responsibility for discharge against advice,[27] and a statement of refusal of treatment.[28] If signature is refused, the fact should be noted on the form over signature of the physician and a witness.

3. Detention or Commitment of Acutely Disturbed Students

This is a complex area in the law, with constitutional dimensions.[29] Statutory and case law varies from state to state and the requirement of strict adherence to statute is notable in reported cases. Every forcible detention or commitment of a patient presumed mentally ill is a potential lawsuit. The advice of local counsel should be obtained before rather than after the fact of necessary emergency detention.

The so-called "common-law right of restraint" permits any person to restrain, by force if necessary, the individual who poses an immediate and obvious threat of damage to himself or to others. If litigation ensues, the issues are usually those of good faith, reasonableness, and validity of the assumed emergency. The physician must balance apparent necessity with the possibility of lawsuit. Liability may also arise from failure to protect the individual or others from his destructive impulses.

The safest course to be followed in cases of apparent necessity is imposition of minimal restraint for the shortest possible time until the disturbed individual can safely be transferred to other care, through appropriate judicial proceedings if necessary.

A majority of apparently disturbed students will revert to normal self-control within a day or so under adequate treatment and will be able to return to school with or without psychiatric treatment. The residential college should provide suitable facilities for such short-term care as is necessary and should avoid early and frantic recourse to detention in public facilities or to emergency orders for commitment. Such action may permanently impair the professional career of a student whose self-limited problem required no more than a day or two of rest in a hospital environment.

Commitment procedures or request for emergency detention in public facilities will prove necessary for a small number of students with acute or preexisting psychosis for whom no private care is available and for whom no family member can be found to

[26] See Shartel and Plant, *op. cit.*, pp. 22–34.
[27] *Medicolegal Forms, op. cit.*, p. 5.
[28] *Medicolegal Forms, op. cit.*, p. 37.
[29] Shartel and Plant, *op. cit.*, pp. 22–34.

assume custody. Commitment or detention procedures should observe the letter of the law and should not be entered into hastily. A college official unassociated with the health service should be designated to sign necessary legal forms. A campus security officer of sufficient training, responsibility, and authority may properly be assigned this function. While litigation is common, the likelihood of liability for considered well-intended action in this area is remote. Because of conflicts of interest, professional attitudes, and student confidence, the college psychiatrist or other health service personnel should not sign requests for detention or commitment.

4. Emergency Care by Registered Nurse

Professional licensing and definitions of medical and nursing practice remain the prerogative of the states. The scope of medical practice is in theory unlimited and thus generally consistent from state to state. The practice of nursing includes certain medical acts, permissible to physicians, which have been carved out of medical practice as appropriate for delegation to the professional nurse. The extent of this delegation is determined by statute, regulation, and case law, with the result that the medical acts which may be performed by the registered nurse remain variable and unclear.[30]

In general, diagnosis and the ordering of medical treatment are reserved to physicians and may not be performed independently by a nurse except in an emergency situation. The difficulty lies in defining an emergency. Costs and availability of physicians make it impossible for the average health service to provide instant physician care, day and night, for every person who appears with a self-defined emergency. During hours when formal clinics are closed, the patient will be seen first by a registered nurse.

The responsibility which she may be permitted to assume will depend on local custom, her experience and training, the urgency of the situation, nursing board regulations, opinions of the attorney general, and such statute and case law as may have dealt with the subject. Since anyone may give first aid in an emergency, the issue of front-line emergency care by the health service nurse boils down to the management of minor problems which are emergencies only in the eyes of the patients. The basic question is how much the nurse may do without calling the on-call physician for orders or attendance upon the patient.

Physicians and counsel familiar with local custom and the medical law of the jurisdiction should be consulted before rather than after the fact of emergency treatment, and appropriate rules should be laid down. Local hospitals will furnish a precedent of sorts, as will industrial plants which furnish medical services and operate on a 24-hour basis.[31]

In the absence of restrictive rulings or regulations, carefully written standing orders permit the specially trained nurse to give minimal care for simple problems without a physician present provided that a supervising physician is available by telephone for necessary advice in any case which in the opinion of the nurse exceeds her competence.

Health service policy may properly provide that students with medical problems which do not in fact constitute an emergency requiring the immediate services of a physician may be given interim advice and told to return the following day when full facilities are available. The need for competent and well-trained personnel here is

[30] See N. Hershey, *Toward a Better Definition of Nursing,* Health Law Center, University of Pittsburgh, 1965; and B. Anderson, "The Legal Scope of Nursing Practice," in *The Best of Law and Medicine,* American Medical Association, Chicago, 1968, pp. 121–122.

[31] *Burns v. Bakelite Corporation,* 17 N.J. Super. 441 (1952), 86 A. 2d 289, is the leading case on corporate liability for diagnosis by a registered nurse. See also C. Letourneau, "Liability of the Physician for Negligent Acts of Others," *Hospital Management,* vol. 98, pp. 52–54, December, 1964.

obvious, since the college and the physician share liability for any error. For dispensing of medications by nurses see part V, 7, above.

VIII. WORKMEN'S COMPENSATION

Acts vary from state to state. As a rule, there is imposition on the employer of liability without fault for injury incurred in the scope of employment, with compensatory immunity from suits for simple negligence. Liability is insured at rates determined by claim experience and related to job hazard. It is financially in the interest of the employer to minimize the number of claims, the extent of injury, and the cost of treatment. Insurance is required through an industrial commission or, in some jurisdictions, alternatively through private carrier.

1. Hazards within the Health Service

These hazards relate to laboratory accidents, physical violence to employees from patients, radiation from maladjusted X-ray equipment, exposure to infection, and physical hazards of the premises. Compensable injuries vary from state to state in relation to difficulties of proof, variable definitions of "accidental injury," and the requirement in some jurisdictions of physical "impact" as a condition of compensation. For employees of the college, the primary function of the health service is accurate reporting of such injuries as are brought to the service and appear or are stated to have occurred on the job.

2. Students Employed by the College

Students working part-time for the college should be treated administratively as employees for injuries incurred on the job. Students compensated for teaching or work on grant-funded projects will usually fall under workmen's compensation. The safest rule is to submit a report to the industrial commission in standard form for any injury or illness which appears related to the employment of the student or staff member.

Ineligible claimants will be promptly rejected, and the health service will be so notified. As a matter of legal propriety, claim forms describing the accident should report the circumstances not as a fact of independent observation, which rarely will be the case, but as a statement made by the injured party.

3. Health Service Treatment of Employees

This treatment is not a requirement but a matter of policy. If health service care is provided for injured employees, treatment should be limited to minor injuries requiring a minimum of visits. Cases with a potential of chronicity or prolonged treatment subject the health service to the risk of accumulating a load of patients for whose medical care it has no direct responsibility. However, under no circumstances should the health service refuse initial emergency treatment to an injured employee on the ground that he is not a student.

4. Billing and Income Tax Liability

Care provided injured employees should be billed to the industrial commission. Established fee schedules are common, providing payment for initial visit and report, cost of necessary medication, and for necessary follow-up visits. Ordinarily, payment cannot be made to the college or the health service; an individual physician must sign vouchers and receive payment for the health service. Funds thus received represent under I.R.S. regulations taxable income to the physician signing the voucher. The director or assistant director should be designated to sign all industrial forms and statements. Tax liability is relieved when the physician files with his income tax return I.R.S. form 1099 indicating institutional rather than personal receipt of payment.

As a rule health services lacking complete facilities should limit their service to initial treatment and referral to an outside physician for follow-up care. Such referral terminates the medical responsibility of the college for the case.

IX. LEGAL ASPECTS OF HEALTH SERVICE FINANCING

1. Funding the Health Service

For patterns of financing see Section 9, Chapter 7. Funding must be adequate to permit the service to meet demands upon it and to maintain an adequate standard of care (part V, 1*b*, above). Usual sources include student fees, legislative appropriation, and allocation of general college funds. Legal problems are most likely to arise when funding comes largely from student fees. Commonly maintenance of facilities and grounds is provided from general funds, with use of student fees for salaries, expendable equipment, drugs, and supplies.

2. Allocation and Conservation of Resources

The health service funded by student fees is essentially a prepaid medical plan serving within stated limits a defined population. In this context the college and its board of trustees constitute a corporation engaged in the provision of medical care (part IV, 1, above). As a result the college becomes a constructive trustee of funds collected from students for the purpose of providing them with medical care. Corporate responsibilities include the expenditure of funds for purposes for which their collection has been authorized. Other responsibilities include conservation of resources, the collection of lawful debts, and the avoidance and defense of liability claims which might deplete the resources of the service. These are not theoretical considerations. Student activists have become well aware of the legal implications of disbursement of student fees. Requests for audit and accounting are not uncommon.

3. Permissible Expenditures of Student Funds

Permissible expenditures of funds derived from student fees include the provision of medical care and the meeting of administrative costs incident to such care. Questionable areas include services provided the college as a whole in such matters as processing for registration, withdrawal from school, or screening for admission or readmission to the college. Costs of services required by the student as an individual may properly be allocated to health service funds.

Medical services to the college as a whole, such as medical attendance at public gatherings, extraordinary services to varsity athletes, examinations for staff employment, emergency care to staff and faculty, and the furnishing of medical services or supplies to other departments for research or specialized teaching programs are open to question. No fast rules can be stated. The mere presence of a medical facility on the campus does not guarantee free medical care to all persons within the boundaries, although opinions to the contrary can be anticipated. *Eligibility* for services should be determined early and clearly stated. Care of ineligible persons other than those presenting true emergencies can seriously deplete funds available for student care. (See part V, 5, above.)

4. Contract Services to Other Departments

When the health service is the only medical facility on campus, limited services in the interest of the college may be furnished at cost to other departments provided that staff time and resources are not occupied to the extent that there is interference with student care. Costs of such services should be borne by the department concerned and appropriately budgeted. Prior agreement on costs and extent of services should be reached and recorded in memorandum form. This is essential when large sums are involved, as in medical support of athletic programs and care of students exposed to special environmental hazard.

5. Business Management

Proper resource allocation requires accurate data. The gap between solvency and bankruptcy is never very wide in provision of medical care. Normal business practices of purchasing, inventory, accounting, audit, and cost analysis should be followed. A facility meeting the medical needs of more than 5,000 students will require a business manager.

Financial records should be maintained under supervision of the business office of the college, following normal procedure for other service departments. Where charges are made for certain services, accounts should be handled through central offices, with responsibility for collection or administrative enforcement of payment removed from the health service. Collection efforts are destructive to the "image" of the health service and may catalyze litigation.

Health service employees handling substantial funds should be bonded.

6. Purchasing Procedures

Normal procedures of the college should be followed, including annual bid purchase of drugs and supplies for which a continuing need can be anticipated.

Emergency purchase of urgently needed drugs and supplies must be permitted apart from routine procedures. Blanket purchase orders within determined limits and for monthly voucher may be processed to drug and supply houses through normal channels to permit purchase of items required for emergency use.

Narcotics and control of prescription drugs require purchasing procedures determined by state and federal law (part V, 7, above). Federal regulations provide for designation and licensure of one official of the college to purchase narcotic drugs for use in teaching or research. Normally this is a member of the purchasing department rather than the health service. However, requests for a health service physician to "lend his license" for the purchase of drugs for teaching or research use in other departments are common. These should be rejected as legally hazardous, since the physician thus assumes responsibility for utilization over which he has no effective control. Accident or improper use by unqualified persons may result in prosecution under state or federal statutes or in a civil claim for negligence. Unsupervised use of prescription drugs is a recognized problem of departments of athletics.

7. Health and Accident Insurance

Misunderstanding of the degree of responsibility for student care assumed by the college is common, particularly for injuries which occur in scheduled classes or college-sponsored activities. Although the college is not liable in the absence of negligence, parents are likely to assume and argue that the college is responsible for any medical bills which result. The student who requires private medical care or hospitalization for injury or sudden illness exceeding the facilities of the health service can become a major problem to himself and others if he is without funds, available parents, and adequate insurance.

The accident statistics of the 18-to-25 age group leave unarguable the advisability of health and accident insurance for every student. For foreign and out-of-state students, insurance should be a requirement of registration.

Compulsory health and accident insurance is the best solution for student and college. Where insurance is "automatic," premiums form part of health fees, often with provision for refund of premium on proof of equivalent coverage. This is most easily accomplished in the private college. College-sponsored plans require careful tailoring to student needs and should be designed to supplement care available at the health service. The services of a broker experienced in this field are advisable.

Optional health and accident insurance should afford every student a documented opportunity to buy it. Ideally, registration packets should include a "waiver form" to be signed by the student and, where possible, his parent or guardian. The form should provide for acknowledgment of the offer of insurance, indication of acceptance or refusal, and certification of understanding that the financial responsibility of the college is limited to routine health service care with referral to outside care at the personal expense of students whose illness exceeds the limitations of the health service. A similar policy statement should be included in catalogs or college bulletins.

8. Ambulance Service

Unless local commercial service is entirely lacking, the college or its health service should not attempt to operate an ambulance service. Liability and danger to patients are inherent in inadequate services. Trained personnel are almost impossible to retain, and 24-hour staffing would normally be required. Health services which have attempted the operation of ambulances uniformly report excessive costs and abuse by immature students who demand service for trivialities.

Ambulances serving a student population must anticipate calls to vehicular accidents. Federal and state standards for ambulance services have been imposed as a result of the Highway Safety Act of 1966.[32] Required are levels of training, staffing, and equipment which are likely to exceed the resources of the average health service.

These factors combine to make prohibitive the costs of providing ambulance service without charge to a limited population. Fees adequate to make the enterprise self-sufficient are unlikely to find acceptance on the college campus.

9. Faculty and Dependent Care

Responsibility for services for faculty members and families or for dependents of married students should be assumed only after thorough consideration of the problems involved. More is involved than problems of eligibility and adequate fees. (See part V, 5, and part IX, 3, above.)

Traditionally, the function of the college health service has been to maintain the student in a sufficient state of health to permit him to graduate. The health service is oriented to handle student problems and organized to provide medical care to adolescents. Extension of responsibility to include patients ranging from infants to the aged will inevitably alter the character of the health service to the detriment of the student, whose orientation to "his" health center forms an important part of his adjustment to college and his educative experience.

Broad-spectrum medical care requires a clinic and hospital complex, comparable to such facilities in the general community, for which few health services possess the potentiality in terms of funds or staff. Whether funded from payroll deductions, coinsurance, or contribution from general funds as a fringe benefit, faculty medical care constitutes a prepaid medical plan contractually bound to provide facilities adequate at minimum to cope with the initial management of any medical problem which may arise at any age. If such a plan is instituted, it should be organized in careful consultation with experts in the field of prepaid hospital and clinic services. Required will be pediatric services, major surgery, and pre- and postpartum care, if not actual delivery services.

If faculty care is undertaken it should be instituted on a limited basis. The emergency department of the health service considering such expansion will normally be

[32] Public Law 89-564, September 9, 1966. Requirements for ambulance services are contained in *Highway Safety Programs Standards*, U.S. Government Printing Office, 1967, p. 40. Specific implementation is left to the states.

equipped with adequate facilities to handle any true emergency problem brought to it. The major change required will be formalization of fees for services and provision for an increased load of patient-defined minor emergencies at irregular hours. Care must be taken that staffing remains adequate and that interference with student care does not occur.

Arrangement should be made for collection for services from any faculty medical plan or other insurance carried by the faculty member.

Medical services to dependents of students should be assumed with caution and such dependents should remain of limited eligibility until experience is gained. Normally this will include wives and children of regularly enrolled students, most commonly at graduate level. These patients form part of the student subculture. Apart from space requirements and the necessity of 24-hour service for pediatric and obstetrical emergencies, such care, if adequately funded by realistic fees or insurance coverage, need not prove disruptive to the health service.

10. Medicare and Medicaid

Medicare and Medicaid may appear irrelevant to the college health service. The college must anticipate, however, that projected extension of these programs will cause a significant part of the general student population to become eligible for medical care under governmental programs as survivors or dependents of eligible persons.

The legal problems which may result from such eligibility remain speculative, but some impact on the present funding of health services in both private and public institutions can be anticipated, particularly with respect to mandatory health fees. Colleges in a position to do so should bring the problem to the attention of appropriate committees of the state legislature when implementing legislation is under consideration for passage or revision.

The safest course which the college can legally pursue under current law is initial organization of the health service in terms of qualification for federal funds for care of eligible patients. As discussed in part IV above, federal regulation in this area, implemented by state licensure, provides the best single guide to adequate standards of organization and care presently available.

In addition, internal accounting, cost analysis, and charges for service should be established which will permit billing of the intermediate carrier of the state for care rendered to eligible persons on an emergency basis or under extension of the law.

GENERAL REFERENCES

American Hospital Association: *Readings in Hospital Law*, Chicago, 1965.

Conditions of Participation: Federal Health Insurance for the Aged, HIR-10, U.S. Department of Health, Education, and Welfare, 1967.

Hassan, William E., Jr.: *Hospital Pharmacy*, 2d ed., Lea & Febiger, Philadelphia, 1967.

Legal Aspects of PHS Medical Care, U.S. Public Health Service Publication no. 1468, 1966.

Letourneau, Charles U.: *The Hospital Medical Staff*, Starling Publications, Chicago, 1964.

Shartel, Burke, and Marcus L. Plant: *The Law of Medical Practice*, Charles C Thomas, Publisher, Springfield, Ill., 1959.

Stetler, C. Joseph, and Alan M. Moritz: *Doctor and Patient and the Law*, The C. V. Mosby Co., St. Louis, 1962.

Chapter **8**

Academic Inventions, Patents, and Licenses

WILLARD MARCY

Vice-president, Patents; Research Corporation, New York, New York

ALBERT S. DAVIS, JR.

Resident Counsel, Research Corporation, New York, New York

WHAT INVENTIONS, PATENTS, AND LICENSES ARE

In the widest sense, an *invention* is any creation or first realization of a new thing or a new interrelation between things. A *patentable* invention is, under United States laws, much more narrowly defined. First, with certain limited exceptions, it is what is created by the inventor; not merely what he may have discovered to be existing. Second, the invention must lie within certain categories—it must be a process, machine, manufacture, or composition of matter, or an improvement thereof, or a certain type of plant or design. The significance of this is that many forms of even creative invention do not fall within the scope of the patent law. For example, a business scheme—e.g., the operation of a particular type of specialty shop serving a particular need within the business setup of a major department store—cannot be patented.

A United States *patent* covering an invention, though it is hedged about with more conditions than almost any other form of government-created property, is essentially a very simple thing. It is the right, granted by the government, to exclude anyone or everyone else from making something or doing something for a period of 17 years from the date on which the patent issues.

This right to exclude (i.e., the patent) is transferable in part or whole. Permission to use an invention covered by the patent can be given to others, usually in a formal manner through the issuance of a *license.* The complete transfer of ownership, in whole or part, is called an *assignment;* an assignment may well be on conditions which to all intents and purposes make it a license. A license, however, is the usual means by which income is derived from the development and commercial use of a patent by someone other than the inventor.

INVENTIONS IN UNIVERSITIES AND COLLEGES

Educational institutions have two major objectives: teaching students from the existing store of knowledge and increasing this store through further research and study.

Individual staff members have the implicit obligation to advance either or both of these objectives, whether in the arts or the sciences. Thus employment by a university or college carries with it the tacit understanding that the staff member is being paid to teach and to do research and conduct studies.

Since teaching involves the study and interpretation of accumulated knowledge, discoveries and inventions seldom result from teachings per se, except in the rare cases where unusually perceptive insight leads the way to new concepts. Such concepts are usually theoretical and very seldom lead directly to practical (that is, patentable) inventions.

Research, on the other hand, is invariably undertaken to increase knowledge and develop improved means of using existing knowledge. In carrying out research, new discoveries and new or improved devices are frequently made and better methods of use are developed. Most of these will not result in patentable inventions; if patentable, they may not be marketable. The remainder, a small minority, will be of widespread benefit to the public. These should be made as widely available as possible, using every means available. Patenting and licensing is one of the most practical and effective means of accomplishing this.

Inventions made in universities and colleges result from research sponsored in various ways, as outlined below.

Institution-sponsored Research In this case the institution provides assistance, including salary, additional personnel, equipment, supplies, office space, and library facilities, in meeting its basic obligations to stimulate original thinking and the development of new ideas; while the faculty and staff doing research in such a favorable environment produce innovative ideas. Thus both the institution and the staff members owe a great deal to each other and both should benefit from the public application and use of the resulting inventions.

Government-sponsored Research Frequently the government provides major financial support for scientific research and thus has a major interest, in addition to the previously mentioned interests of the institution and the staff inventor, in the utilization of inventions resulting therefrom.

Industry-sponsored Research Industry-sponsored research is similar to government-sponsored research except that it is usually considerably more oriented toward a specific goal. Industry sponsors research more to obtain profitable new products or processes than to increase the store of knowledge. Profitable new products or processes, however, would not be profitable if they were not developed and used for the benefit of the public. Although industry-sponsored research at academic institutions is usually performed with the institution's facilities, the research may also be done in the industrial plant or laboratory by or under the supervision of institutional staff members.

OBLIGATIONS SUSTAINED BY AN INVENTOR AND HIS SPONSOR

Moral Obligations Whenever an invention is made—whether on the inventor's own time and entirely as a matter of abstract thinking; or with the use of substantial university facilities, time, materials, and personnel; or as the result of money given, with various strings attached, to the faculty member in his individual or faculty status by the government or an industrial sponsor—the inventor is under moral compulsion to enlighten at least the scholarly world. The academic community has historically accepted this as an obligation of its commitment to inquire into the nature of the physical universe, just as much in the case of results which may be physically embodied and put to practical use as with those whose immediate nature and use are entirely a matter of further speculative inquiry. This benefiting of the community is perhaps seen at its emotional height in the communication of information of medical and therapeutic significance, but it is no less real where the emotion is harder to justify.

Proprietary Obligations The ownership of property rights to university and college inventions depends on the circumstances, financial and otherwise, leading to the invention. Determination and allocation of the product of these rights rests on mutual trust and confidence. Where the development and use of ownership rights can best be developed into a viable commercial venture through patenting and licensing, the institution and the staff member have a mutual obligation to enter into a program for so doing.

As a general practice no assertion of property rights is made by the institution where it provides no specific support of the work leading to the invention and where the exploitation of the invention is solely an obligation of the staff member.

When institutional funds or facilities have been used, the institution has an interest in and obligation with respect to the acquiring of property rights to inventions, usually through the exercise of a right of first refusal.

When inventions result from research supported by grants or contracts with the institution, the institution is obligated to abide by the terms of the grant or contract and to assure the contracting agency that the inventor will also observe these terms. This applies to both government and industrial grants and contracts. The institution usually assumes ownership of patent rights in these cases.

Obligation on Use of Income The institution, as a matter of academic practice, usually shares with the inventors any income produced from patenting and licensing inventions. The basis for distribution varies with the magnitudes and types of contributions made by the institution and the granting agency, if any; the technical area of the invention; and the effect on the public welfare. These factors are complex and require separate evaluation in each case.

The institution's share of income should be treated as an unplanned windfall adjunct to its normal income. Its use by the institution is most often in the furtherance of scientific research, frequently in the department of the inventor's discipline. Such income is also frequently used to fulfill unusual, one-time needs of the institution as a whole.

Obligation to Control Use of Invention in the Public Interest Ownership of patent rights by the institution may be desirable to afford a measure of control in the public interest over the products of the invention, with or without income production. This feature is most often encountered with inventions in the pharmaceutical or medical instrument field.

Other Substantial Reasons for Controlling the Use of Inventions Although generally of rare occurrence and not directly related to production of income or licensing to manufacture, some reasons for patenting can best be illustrated through the hypothetical examples given below:

1. A basic invention is made on campus. It has genuine commercial appeal in a highly competitive industry. As soon as publication is made, a dozen firms set out to "improve" the invention, and to secure the patent rights on these improvements. If the university does not patent, these improvement patents will give their owners effective control of the unpatented basic invention, perhaps in disregard of the public interest.

2. An economic monopoly is in a position to take undue advantage of its position, price-, profit-, and qualitywise. A campus inventor discovers a process which lies squarely in the center of the monopoly's field. If he fails to patent it, thus in effect dedicating it to the entire world, the monopoly may continue unchecked until excess brings it down. A valid and significant "outside" patent owned and controlled by a public-minded institution can hold such a monopoly in check.

3. A new product requires scientific control to prevent its abuse. It is not govern-

mentally controlled, or at least not sufficiently so controlled, to prevent its abuse by the public or at the public's expense. The emotional and legislative climate are not yet at a point which would permit legislative action toward control. By patenting and proper licensing, the university through which the product was invented can assert this control without legislation.

4. A patent is not usually seen as an inducer of secondary creative invention, but actually it often acts as such. The patent excludes the world, or at least the unlicensed world. The unlicensed world thereupon proceeds to conduct research, hopefully resulting in creative invention, so that it may avoid the claims of the existing patent.

METHODS OF PROTECTING OWNERSHIP OF INVENTIVE IDEAS

The diverse obligations of disclosure, income production, protection of the university and public, and observation of the provisions of a government or industrially sponsored contract can be met in a number of ways.

Secrecy is not an attractive alternative. Secrecy might serve the purposes of an industrial sponsor in a limited number of cases or of the government in a greater number, but it would run clearly counter to the basic idea of complete disclosure for the good of the community and the advancement of human knowledge and its utilization. While the common law gives the inventor the right to make and use his invention and to do so exclusively provided he does not disclose it to the public, it does not protect him against fair imitation or independent invention by another. This right not to have a secret stolen can be transferred, but in the case of something which must be sold to the public in order to make use of it (e.g., a radio), secrecy is impossible, and in these days of multiple analogous research efforts even a process which can be hidden is a highly fragile form of property.

The disclosure of an invention in a publication can be copyrighted, but a *copyright* protects only literary exposition and plot lines, not the inventive content itself. Provided the literary form is not copied, the copyrighting of an article gives the inventor-author no protection against use of the intelligence it communicates.

A federal *trademark* can be secured by devising a mark, using it on goods or in connection with a service in interstate commerce, and registering it. (State trademarks are available as well, but the types of marks that can be protected are somewhat limited.) Since the federal trademark cannot be registered until it has actually been used in commerce, the protection which the trademark system can give to a university inventor's brainchild, even if that brainchild is the mark itself, is highly limited.

The tendency, therefore, is to protect by obtaining a *patent*, simply because it best meets the needs and obligations which the invention lays upon the university and staff inventor.

PATENTING AND LICENSING UNIVERSITY INVENTIONS

The patenting and licensing of university inventions is undertaken by or on behalf of the owner of the patent rights. This may be done by the inventor himself, the institution, an organization acting for the inventor or the institution, or by the sponsor of the original research.

Patenting and licensing is time-consuming, frequently expensive, and susceptible to major legal, financial, and entrepreneurial hazards. Therefore, the inexperienced individual inventor is at a distinct disadvantage if he handles a licensing program on his own, especially if it is done as a part-time venture while teaching and doing further research.

Institutions with little experience or no real interest in developing a commercial venture are vulnerable to these same hazards and would be well advised to entrust patenting and licensing to an experienced individual or organization.

Government granting agencies will frequently handle patenting and licensing programs covering inventions arising in the course of their sponsorship. However, government policy is for the most part to license such inventions royalty-free and nonexclusively to anyone wishing a license. This policy is inhibitory in many cases and does not generally lead to an effective and widespread distribution of the fruits of the invention. In addition, no royalty income is obtainable for use by the institution and as a reward to the inventor.

Industrial sponsors will undertake patenting and licensing at their expense, will wish to have the right of first refusal, or will request the institution to undertake patenting, reserving the right to a nonexclusive license. In any case, an industrial sponsor will normally agree to paying a royalty to the institution.

Patenting and licensing programs can be undertaken on behalf of the institution using a number of methods. Patent lawyers and commercial patent brokers can be engaged. Usually the services provided by such individuals are limited in scope and frequently provide little more than patent filing and prosecution or an introduction to potential licensees. Negotiating licenses, defending validity, and policing for infringement are still the responsibility of the institution.

Some universities develop patents and licenses through separate, nonprofit foundations associated with and oriented exclusively toward the particular institution. Some foundations, such as the Wisconsin Alumni Research Foundation, have been quite successful in certain instances, but again they generally lack scope and freedom of action because they do not have a wide enough base of inventions and also because they are usually bound by academic regulations.

Two major nonprofit organizations have been active in patenting and licensing for a large number of institutions. Both have existed for many years and have broad experience in all areas of patenting and licensing. These are Research Corporation and Battelle Development Corporation.

Patent assistance agreements with Research Corporation provide that the institution may submit for evaluation such staff inventions as it wishes. If this evaluation is favorable, Research Corporation will accept title to the invention and proceed to obtain patents and negotiate licenses with industrial concerns, all at no cost to the institution or the inventor. Any resulting royalty income is apportioned between the institution, the inventor, and Research Corporation. All normal costs for these services are paid out of Research's share. Any income remaining after these expenses have been met is used in support of the foundation's grants programs for the support of academic research and the advancement of science.

The agreements with Battelle Development Corporation provide for the same services. In special instances Battelle may provide funds of its own for further development of promising but inadequately defined inventions. However, the Battelle agreements usually provide for the recouping of any expenses for these services before the division of royalty income, and Battelle does not normally use any of its share of the income for grants programs at other academic or scientific institutions.

A taxpaying, wholly owned subsidiary of the University of Illinois Research Foundation, University Patents, Inc., has recently expanded and now makes its patenting and licensing activities available to both educational institutions and industrial concerns.

THE CONCEPT OF THE PATENT

Essentially, there are two explanations of a patent's worth. The first is derived from the provision in the Constitution which states that the copyright and patent powers of Congress are intended "to promote the progress of science and useful arts." This provision implies that public policy requires the making of inventions and their disclosure to the public, and that it is proper to reward the inventor, or to coax him, with a limited monopoly. The theory has interesting results when one contemplates the government, which issued the patent through one agency, contending in the Court of Claims through another agency that the patent is invalid and should not be recognized.

The other explanation resides in the theory of contracts. The government invites one to invent and disclose. In exchange for the disclosure, it bargains to give the inventor a limited monopoly. This theory is more attractive, because the patent system lays great stress on the adequacy of the patent's teaching, that is, its disclosure. The theory breaks down, however, before the spectacle of the government contending for the invalidity of a patent, knowing that the disclosure cannot be recalled. It is as though one party only were able to renounce a contract at will while keeping the benefit which it itself had decided was sufficient consideration.

The important thing is not to decide which theory is correct, if either, but to recognize the fact that the government *does* award a monopoly and that not all monopolies are necessarily contrary to the public interest. However, it must be recognized that monopolies, at least when they are made apparent and attacked for whatever reason, are generally abhorrent to the American public, and thus patent monopolies have been hedged about with conditions as to their granting, their use, and their effective assertion more than any other form of legal monopoly. In spite of this, the patent monopoly is an extremely useful, effective, and practical means for the development of inventions for the public benefit.

By way of initial restriction, only creative inventions are recognized for patenting, and only certain forms of creative invention will qualify within that restriction. Then, certain tests of value and newness for creative inventions so limited are applied.

The courts do not quite know what is meant by the words "*patentable* invention"—one government treatise has, indeed, said that the phrase is not capable of definition. Various catch phrases such as "flash of genius" have been used by the courts and overruled, withdrawn, or hopefully legislated away. For present purposes it is sufficient to recognize that invention requires unusual nonroutine results at least, and involves as well the question of whether the invention was obvious by reconstructed contemporary judgment.

To be patentable an invention must be useful. Twenty years ago this meant that it was what the inventor said it was, that it could clearly be used for something other than an illegal or immoral purpose, and that in achieving its purpose it did not become worthless because of some other self-defeating characteristic. Today it means, at least in pharmaceutical and increasingly in chemical cases, that at a minimum some arguable, genuine, actual usefulness must be shown. The tides of this battle shift to and fro, but it is probable that over the next 20 years this tendency will increase and that the Patent Office may eventually demand a substantiated assertion of commercial usefulness. This will, in the view of various theoreticians, tend to decrease the number of unused patents, reduce the filing of speculative patent applications, cut down the number of patents which do not possess a firm showing of utility, and help to prevent violations of the antitrust laws accomplished through the use of multiple patents. It may also be expected to decrease research in some areas because, while actual utility is being achieved and proven, especially actual commercial utility, others will be happily imitating the work and negating the full value of the patent monopoly if and when it is granted.

An invention must also be new to be patentable. This is in essence simply an inquiry as to whether or not there is something in the prior art which is so close to the claimed patentable invention that the difference is without significance.

In general, processes, machines, new compositions of matter, manufactured products, asexually reproduced plants, and certain specific designs can be patented.

Patenting an invention is subject to statutory bars. An applicant cannot get a patent on his invention if it: (1) was known or used by others in the United States, or patented, or described in any printed publication, anywhere in the world before he made his invention; or (2) was patented, or described in a printed publication anywhere in the world, or in public use or on sale in the United States more than one year before he files his patent application. There are also several other less commonly invoked statutory bars.

The construction of these statutory bars through the judicial interpretation of legislative action shows the courts' tendency to expand and proliferate the obstacles to obtaining a valid and enforceable patent. For example, although the statutory words "printed publication" are fairly straightforward, it has been held that they may mean a typewritten doctoral thesis, one cataloged copy of which exists on the shelves of a university library.

A patent cannot be granted if the invention would have been obvious at the time it was made to a person having ordinary skill in the art. This is difficult to determine in an absolute sense since an expert speaking as an expert must speculate as to what this hypothetical nonexpert person would have found obvious.

Theories, ideas, plans of action, and discoveries of scientific laws and principles are also defined as unpatentable. So the patent monopoly itself is hedged about with these and a number of other restrictions. The patent application procedures, moreover, and the process of prosecution in the Patent Office are highly artificial and formal and are directed toward narrowing down the scope of the claims allowed while making more precise the "disclosure," which represents the price of granting the monopoly.

It is a paradox that in this situation the inventor, no matter what the intrinsic, stimulative, or scientific value of his patented invention may be, is left to his own devices and to the mercies of time in realizing the monetary value of his invention. The United States does not extend the life of patents by statute; if the inventor was a poor businessman, if the economic world was not ready for him until his patent expired, or if others refused to use his invention without conspiracy, he is not recompensed no matter how much he taught and regardless of the scientific or innovative merit of his work.

Yet, despite all these problems, the patent is a useful economic tool when employed in connection with good inventions of real substance. Witness Polaroid, Xerox, and the thousands of little corporations whose bread and butter are protected against large competitors by a bread-and-butter patent. The individual inventor is now, for the most part, replaced by the inventor who works within a corporation; but the corporation which employs him now spends millions on his research. It has no wish to contribute this seed money to the well-being and profit of its competitors by failure to patent.

Almost a decade of review of the United States patent system is culminating today in various proposals for legislative changes to the patent laws. To a large extent, these seem to be directed toward encouraging conformity with foreign statutory patent law, so that there may be the beginnings of what has been called "an international patent system." Considerable thought is also being given to streamlining and making more efficient many present Patent Office practices. Although substantial reforms are expected, the patent system has been too effective over the years to justify a truly radical change or its abandonment in favor of a different system.

PATENT PROSECUTION STEPS

Structure of Patent Application A characteristic patent application consists of several parts:

Title and inventor's name

Abstract of the invention

Specification describing the invention, its usefulness, and its operability, with one or more specific examples

Claims describing and claiming for the inventor the exact subject matter of the invention

Oath, petition, and power of attorney

Drawings, if needed, to show clearly the features of the invention

Since the drafting of a patent application is a highly technical matter, it should be done by an expert patent attorney, although this is not a requirement of the Patent Office. However, it is essential that the inventor review the application before filing to ensure that the actual invention is properly and adequately described. If more than one inventor is involved, all inventors must execute the application.

Prosecution of Patent The filing of a patent application in the United States Patent Office initiates a complex series of operations culminating in the final granting of or refusal to grant a patent. The steps in the series can be characterized by thinking of them as a debate between a patent examiner and the inventor or, due to the complexity of such practice, the inventor's attorney acting for him. It is the inventor's task to convince the examiner that the invention is patentable. The debate takes place in major part through correspondence, but it may also include telephone conversations and personal interviews.

If the examiner is finally convinced of the patentable merits of the invention, he will allow a patent to issue.

If, however, he is not convinced, he issues a final rejection. The inventor may appeal this rejection, first, by last-ditch discussion with the examiner himself, and, if this is unavailing, then by taking his case to the Patent Office Board of Appeals. Further appeal may be taken if necessary outside the Patent Office to the Court of Customs and Patent Appeals, or, alternatively, to the Federal District Court for the District of Columbia. Actions in the Court of Customs and Patent Appeals can be reviewed by the United States Supreme Court if it chooses to hear such a case—which it seldom does. Actions in the District Court can be appealed to the Court of Appeals for the District of Columbia, from which a similar discretionary review lies in the Supreme Court.

Interferences If two or more inventors file nearly simultaneous applications covering the same invention, under the present Patent Office rules, the application filed first is processed, and, if found patentable, is allowed to issue. The second inventor then can move to have an interference declared in order to determine prior inventorship between the two parties. This is resolved by a presentation of evidence before a Patent Office Board of Interference made up of patent examiners. Appeals are available up through the courts.

Written, witnessed, dated, and signed laboratory records are vital to corroborate the testimony of the inventor in interference proceedings.

Continuations in Part Frequently the inventor will continue research, leading to the establishment of an additional aspect to the invention, including part of it but new in itself. Provided the original disclosure is broad enough in scope to cover part of and link with the new information, this new aspect can be filed upon through submission of a continuation-in-part patent application having the first application's date as to that part of the first invention incorporated in it.

Reissues Issued patents, under certain circumstances, can be reissued to correct a failure of the patent to reflect the disclosed invention. This does not extend the life of the original patent; that is only infrequently done by special legislation.

Foreign Patents Patenting and licensing in countries other than the United States present numerous problems and risks in addition to those inherent in patenting and licensing in the United States. Each country has its own definition of patentable inventions and most countries, unlike the United States, have tax or working requirements for maintaining patents in force. Enforcing foreign patents against infringers can also be at least as difficult and costly as it is to enforce those granted by the United States.

SELECTION OF LICENSEES

A licensing program can be undertaken as soon as a patent application has been filed, although the claims in the issued patent comprise the property licensed. The extent and scope of these rights obviously can be determined only after the patent issues.

Method of Licensing The first step in licensing is to determine how the invention is to be licensed, weighing many important factors. These include the extent of the need for the product or process; the number of competing products or processes already being marketed and the strengths and weaknesses of each; the likelihood of early obsolescence of the invention being licensed; and the pros and cons of providing nonexclusive or exclusive licenses. Other important factors to be considered are the impact of antitrust and restraint-of-trade laws, the licensing methods customary in the industry, the manner in which the licensed invention is likely to be marketed, and the best ways to encourage the licensee to put forth maximum effort in producing salable products as quickly as possible and marketing them as widely as possible.

Analyses should be made of the effects to be expected from different methods of licensing. These effects should be related to the total effort to be expended by the licensee, to the benefit of the public, and to the amount of royalty income to the licensor.

It is usually not possible to maximize all of these factors simultaneously, and some compromise must be accepted. For example, it may be desirable to accept a lower royalty income in order to obtain a wider public distribution through a lower selling price of the product. Or, it may be necessary to extend the exclusivity period in order to encourage a licensee to do the necessary testing work to obtain clearance from a government agency without the danger of a competitor riding into the marketplace on the licensee's coattails.

Searching Out Potential Licensees With the method of licensing in mind, the second step is to search out a suitable licensee (or licensees in the case of nonexclusive licenses). There are a large number of methods available for doing this, but perhaps the most effective way is to establish a working file of companies with which person-to-person contact has been established. Such a file can be developed only after an extended period of time, but it will save time and produce more satisfactory licensees than any other single method.

There are a number of reference publications listing industrial corporations and their product lines, addresses, and major executives. *Thomas' Register of American Manufacturers* and *Poor's Register of Corporations, Directors and Executives* are the most comprehensive and useful.

Trade associations are frequently good sources of information on individual companies, their interests, and their executives, but such information is better obtained by personal contact with the association director and his staff than through correspondence.

The federal, state, and local governments all maintain information on corporate interests, usually in their departments of commerce. Several government agencies have special divisions set up to seek new ventures, primarily for small business enterprises.

Published corporate annual reports usually provide very good general information on both present products and possible future marketing objectives.

A large number of corporations now employ corporate planners whose duties include the searching out of possible new products. Direct contact with such individuals as well as with corporate vice-presidents or directors of research and development will lead to an understanding of the capabilities of specific concerns.

By studying the type and scope of information published in technical and scientific periodicals and at technical society meetings, comprehensive knowledge of the interests of specific companies can be obtained.

Adequate and current financial information can usually be obtained from Dun and Bradstreet reports. Many market survey firms and consultants are available to make comprehensive studies of specific markets.

Evaluation of Potential Licensees With product interests, marketing methods, financial strength, production facilities, and other available information at hand, the strengths and weaknesses of each possible licensee can be evaluated. The most attractive licensees can then be considered in view of the previously determined optimum licensing method. Usually several licensees will emerge as strong candidates.

Size alone should not be regarded as the dominant factor in selecting a licensee. A large concern often has large capital investments or other major vested interests in a competing product already being marketed and thus might not be willing to put forth as much initiative, effort, and capital as a smaller firm wishing to get into a sizable existing market with a new product. On the other hand, only a large, well-established firm can afford the technical manpower and the major expenditure necessary for some development and testing programs, as for example in the drug field.

Considerable weight should also be given to the personalities and capabilities of the company executives and managers, their business reputations and apparent entrepreneurship. Any new venture invariably brings to light unsuspected problems and pitfalls that only creative thinking, good business sense, and production and marketing know-how can solve.

In the final analysis the ultimate selection of a licensee depends on whether a mutually satisfactory license can be negotiated, and this, in turn, depends on the individual negotiators. There are many factors that must be considered by both sides during the course of negotiations; these are oftentimes evaluated intuitively on the spot. The worth of the license is determined in major part by the skill of the negotiators.

Foreign Licensing Licensing in foreign countries requires a knowledge of foreign patent and antitrust laws as well as an understanding of the marketplace. Since these factors vary considerably from country to country, the wise licensor will want to work through native representatives. Whenever possible negotiations should be carried on in the language of the country and a team approach should be used, especially in eastern European countries.

United States-based companies with extensive foreign operations often can be induced to develop the foreign markets under license. In this case the legal, tax, and business problems are usually handled by the licensee. Frequently the licensee will also agree to share the foreign patenting and any litigation expenses.

NEGOTIATION OF LICENSES

The art of license negotiation is composed of proportionate parts of persuasion and concession. The licensor must state and show unequivocally that the invention contains at least the seeds of sound commercialism; that there are lively expectations of the issuance of a patent; and that there is the likelihood of sufficient profits to justify the commitment of corporate money and effort. The licensor must concede that the invention itself will quite likely need improvement; that the market must be developed and the product readied and distributed to it; and that the license is a contract mutually agreed upon.

The licensee must state and show his firm desire, intention, and ability to develop and exploit the market; his financial and entrepreneurial strength; and his willingness to undertake with imaginative thinking the necessary development of the invention itself. He must concede that many difficulties and weaknesses must be overcome, and he must be willing to cooperate with the inventor and licensor in solving these problems.

Patent rights are intellectual property and their worth is determined by law in a wholly artificial way; they often exist only by sufferance of litigation. For these reasons they are fragile and can be destroyed by placing unrealistic values on them or by overvigorous and inflexible bargaining. In such cases a prospective licensee may decide to infringe and take his chances on a lawsuit, or he may decide not to commit money and effort at all.

Expertise in license negotiations requires a thorough knowledge of the strengths and weaknesses of the patent rights to be licensed, the ability to forcefully present the strengths and concede the weaknesses as necessary, and an instinctive understanding and realistic appraisal of the value to be placed on the patent rights by the market. Philosophically, license negotiators should endeavor to "agree; take a little, leave a little."

License Content It is impossible to cover completely the entire list of specific matters to be considered in dealing with the licensing of an invention and its corresponding patent rights; indeed the list changes radically from case to case. The sources given in the bibliography contain some helpful check lists, and many other pertinent articles and books are available. It will be more useful simply to suggest here the broader areas that should be studied and considered and to give a few examples showing how expansion of these areas can be made.

Basic to the concluding of any agreement, generally, are the answers to these questions:

1. Precisely what is to be turned over to the licensee (what present and future inventions, patent applications, and patents in what countries)?
2. What may the licensee do with them?
3. What must the licensee do with them?
4. What must the licensee pay for this, and when?
5. What assurance is there that the licensee will perform his various duties?
6. What happens if either the licensor or licensee defaults?
7. What happens if the licensee's rights are interfered with (e.g., by an infringer)?
8. Under what conditions should either party be allowed to terminate the deal?

It is easy to construct models for illustration of the answering of such questions; the answers themselves are much more difficult. A few of the problems encountered frequently by any licensor in answering these questions are developed below.

Inventions Licensed. Usually the licensee will want a license under the original invention and closely related modifications of it and also under any improvements, since the commercial payout may often be in the improvements and having patents both on the original invention and the improvements gives two layers of protected exclusivity. Can the licensor, if the inventor is a faculty member, safely agree to add them to the license? Suppose the inventor goes to another institution or to an industrial competitor of the licensee? Suppose he is simply a coinventor of the improvement with an outsider? Suppose he makes the improvement invention entirely on his own time, or that the university policy does not require assignment, or he makes the invention under a government-funded contract requiring a royalty-free license to the government, or under a contract sponsored by an industrial competitor? Or suppose that the improvement invention which (by the terms of a license with a 2 percent royalty rate) must be added to the licensed matter would, if separately negotiated, easily support a 5 percent royalty rate? To summarize:

1. The licensee has a good deal of merit on his side in asking that the license include improvements.

2. The licensor's principal realistic worry is whether he will be able to deliver at all, or without heavy cost.

3. The licensor's other realistic worry is whether the royalty for the original invention will be out of line for the improvement.

The licensor should remember that the addition of improvements to the license is an excellent way of keeping the licensee satisfied with the deal over a period of years. If the licensor feels that exclusivity or the simple inertial forces of a long and close relationship might create too much academic dependence on a particular industrial firm, the forethought remedy might well be a limited exclusivity, by time or product, or a breakout clause and a decision to use it.

Exclusivity. The principal questions are aptness for an academic milieu, justification as to a particular licensee and a particular invention, and escape. The aptness argument is a matter of basic academic philosophy: is it proper for an educational and research institution to turn any of its intellectual output over to a single firm for the 17-year life of the patent or longer? This question does not involve the thought that industry-sponsored research or patenting research results are bad per se, but inquires, rather, "What economic and social uses can *and will* be made of the results of the research?" Some inventions require some exclusivity in their initial use to justify a commercial licensee's investment of money and effort, as a speculation, to bring them to the market. Not every invention does require this; very often such considerations as getting in on the ground floor, the ability to control the first development of know-how plus licensee-created patentable early improvements, and the momentum of being first on the market make exclusivity inappropriate even where initial work under the license is expensive. Exceedingly few significant inventions require exclusivity for the life of a patent in order to secure an adequately interested and royalty-producing licensee.

Royalty Rates and Bases. Usually these result from the application of agreed percentages to agreed values, usually a product's net selling price. This is determined by subtracting from the gross sales price those elements which do not generate profit (e.g., prepaid outbound freight billed at net). This serves well for patents on simple products and processes. Determination of the percentage to be applied results from the weighing of many complex factors such as the novelty of the invention, the readiness of the market, the degree of patentability, the economic strength of the prospective licensee, the cost of reduction to commercial practice, and many others. As much of this information as is reasonably possible should be secured for use as a basis for mutual discussion. Since the list of factors is very long and their quantitative accuracy is not very great, the final figures agreed upon cannot be the result of mathematical manipulation but rather must result from a series of compromises.

Royalty rates are frequently either a regular percentage or percentile range, or they may sometimes be related to a fraction of the additional profits or the production savings derived from the invention. Often the basic question will be, "What is this industry accustomed to paying for this kind of invention?" If a royalty-rate pattern has previously been established in an industry, it is usually quite difficult to change.

A cents-per-unit royalty perhaps derived from a percentile is often adopted to make it easier to report, pay, and audit. A paid-up royalty is a percentage of an informed estimate of the total worth of an invention during the life of a patent. Many other variations on these means of determining royalties have been used.

Due Diligence. Some assurances must be given by the licensee that he will not shelve the patented product or process to favor himself or a third party and that he will spend enough and do enough to get the invention broadly and quickly used. Although industry does not ordinarily shelve inventions, inventors and licensors often feel that it often pays less single-minded, whole-souled, open-pursed attention to them than they deserve. This apparent less-than-desired effort by an industrial licensee often results from the economic situation that the licensee usually produces and markets many interdependent products, all of which he must develop as effectively and expeditiously as possible. The due diligence requirement ensures that the licensee will get the invention industrially and commercially started and then pushed along as a regular part of the product line, thus assuring development in the public interest.

There are three ways frequently used to encourage diligence on the part of the licensee. The first is a simple agreement by the licensee that he will be "diligent" or "duly diligent" in working the invention. In practice such a clause is substantially unenforceable, because of its vagueness and because courts interpret the words to mean "duly diligent in the light of all the circumstances affecting the invention, including the licensee's business affairs in full."

A better way is to include a requirement to perform particular things which, when done, constitute the framework of diligence. The due-diligence clause then provides a specific objective standard. The licensor may well add minimal required expenditures for at least certain steps; the licensee, however, should be allowed a way out if the task is harder than anticipated or is complicated by forces beyond his control.

A minimum royalty requirement alone can serve as an effective tool for securing due diligence, but its effectiveness is debatable. If the licensee really wishes to shelve the invention, no minimum royalty which a licensor could in reason expect to negotiate will prevent it. The licensor usually considers a minimum royalty as either a partial repayment for his research and patenting expenses or an amount sufficient to discourage the licensee from continuing if he loses interest in developing the invention. Where the license cannot be canceled by the licensee or can only be canceled on what amounts to a penalty, the effect of a high minimum royalty can be effective in forcing at least a genuine attempt to develop and try to market the invention.

Infringement Provisions. The usual academic invention has no intrinsic value to the originating institution apart from the value of the patent, since normally academic inventors generate little or no commercially valuable know-how, trade secrets, or other marketable but unpatentable commercially useful knowledge. When litigated, patents are notoriously fragile. However, to remain valuable, patents must be protected from infringement, and institutions holding patents should be prepared to sue infringers. The licensee should not be entrusted with the sole decision to sue since he is usually less timid about a patent suit than the patentee. If the patent should be held invalid, the licensee would still have his know-how, at least part of his first-in-the-field impact, product recognition and acceptance, more easily controllable sources of supply, production facilities, and any improvement patents of his own. The licensor would not.

Since the litigative risk to the licensor's position is great, negotiations leading to license provisions designed to suppress infringement should at a minimum take cognizance of these factors:

1. Clear infringement or exceedingly strong reason to suspect it should be apparent.
2. A clear threat of real economic or market-position damage to the licensee should be established.
3. The effective decision to sue for infringement should at least be a joint decision between the licensor and the licensee. Provision should be made to allow for appeal or arbitration.
4. Provision must be made for current financing and eventual responsibility for litigation expenses, for distribution of damage awards, and for intervention by other licensees.

INFRINGEMENT AND OTHER POST-ISSUE LITIGATION

A sardonic observer of the American patent system has said that a patent is nothing but an invitation to commence a lawsuit. Possession of any form of property of course involves its protection—in our society we use the courts to do this. The distinction as to patents is their peculiarly fragile nature as property.

The major source of conflict is the third-party infringer who arrogates to himself the use of the invention and refuses to recognize the patent. This usually happens either because of lack of knowledge or an honest conviction that the patent is invalid; there are, of course, some companies which recognize even court-tested patents only after they themselves are sued. A suit for infringement may be commenced by the patent owner in the federal district court where jurisdiction over the particular defendant can be obtained (a government contractor can be sued by suing the government in the Court of Claims). Such litigation is highly specialized and should be entrusted only to specialist law firms. It is also lengthy and extremely expensive. In an infringement suit the four major issues before the court are: (1) Should the patent have been issued? (2) Has the defendant actually infringed it? (3) Has the patent owner so misused the patent that relief should be denied? and (4) What relief (including damages and injunction) should be granted?

The first of these amounts to a trial *de novo* of exactly what the Patent Office was supposed to determine, except that the defendants will almost always refer the court to a number of examples of prior art which were not found by the Patent Officer examiner. The court will accord these more adverse weight than those references considered in the Patent Office; it will also tend to view the question of obviousness more critically than the Patent Office. A particularly expensive and time-consuming aspect of such trials is the taking of depositions from those who have any pertinent knowledge of the invention and the prosecution of the patent application. Similar to this is the formal discovery in which whole banks of files of documents bearing on the invention and patent application are examined by both the plaintiffs and the defendants.

In current practice it is often charged that the patent was obtained by fraud (usually argued as a suppression or misrepresentation of prior art and pertinent facts before the Patent Office) and that the patent has been misused. Where the patent has been obtained or licensed in violation of the antitrust statutes as construed, this procedure rests on the consideration that an infringement suit is one in equity, demanding what amounts to conscience-of-the-court relief. If the patent holder has behaved inequitably, then, whether or not validity and infringement are proved, the court may find against the patent owner.

One unusual limitation on patents as property is that the assertion of them as being infringed, even inferentially stated, permits the accused party to sue the patent owner for a declaratory judgment that the patents are invalid, or not infringed, or unenforceable as misused. In a quarrelsome, cutthroat, or litigious industry, this can make licensing quite difficult.

Other areas of litigation may involve a private or public suit against the patent holder for violation of the antitrust laws, suits relating to the establishment of the ownership of patent rights, damage suits for breach of a license, actions against trade associations for boycotting, suit brought by an outside inventor for stealing his invention, actions asserting that use of an invention according to its teachings resulted in injury or damage, and suits for infringement by a third party against a licensee together with a licensor who supplied detailed drawings or the like to the licensee.

Another area of legal though not litigious concern is the tax treatment to be accorded an inventor and his institution with respect to royalty income, since proper tax planning can secure capital-gains status for such income.

It should be obvious that the institution which is really concerned with patent matters, or the organization which regularly does patenting and licensing, must seek continuous close cooperation of the highest order from skilled legal counsel.

WHAT RECOGNITION OF PATENTING AND LICENSING IMPLIES TO THE INSTITUTIONAL ADMINISTRATOR

After deciding that an invention is to be patented and licensed, the institutional administrator must undertake complex and often formidable actions in bringing the invention successfully into widespread public use. A list of the major and most common problems needing solution will indicate the scope of the necessary activity.

Needed Expertise

Expertise is required to:

1. Determine the extent of useful patentability
2. Determine the extent of commercial usefulness
3. Seek out and develop industrial contacts
4. Develop and negotiate fair, reasonable, and lawful licensing terms
5. Develop and negotiate acceptance of contractual agreements adequately and fairly protecting the institution, the inventor, and the licensee
6. Determine how to undertake the defense of the patent against possible infringers
7. Make informed and expert risk decision of an entrepreneurial nature

Recognition of Costs Recognition of the costs involved in patenting and licensing is required. Such costs include:

1. Evaluation of the invention as to patentability (patent search by patent counsel)
2. Evaluation of the invention as to technical feasibility and commercial usefulness (a limited-scope technical and market survey)
3. Preparation and filing of a patent application
4. Prosecution of the application, including appeals where necessary
5. Interference proceedings where necessary
6. Seeking out prospective licensees and negotiating licenses
7. Defending the validity of the patent in the courts
8. Defending the patent against infringers (includes court litigation)

Resolution of Campus Problems It is necessary to consider and resolve local campus problems such as:

1. Any negative feeling among staff members and departments arising from privileges accorded to individual inventors
2. Determining when, how much, and in what manner recognition of inventiveness should be made
3. Determining the scope, type, and extent of public announcements of staff inventions
4. Weighing and evaluating pressures on the institutional administration brought by government and industrial grantors and contractors as well as by the staff inventor himself

Need for Administrative and Clerical Staff A clerical staff to handle the extensive volume of correspondence, record keeping, and reports must be set up and administered.

Administrative Time Appreciable amounts of administrative time must be allotted for carrying out the patenting and licensing function.

INSTITUTIONAL PATENT POLICY

Since the making of inventions and discoveries is not predictable and may occur at any time whether research is being undertaken or not, a prudent university or college administration will want to develop a patent and copyright policy with which to guide itself when problems arise. Development of this policy is best undertaken through a joint effort of the administration and faculty. The institution's governing body should then provide a thoughtful and thorough review of the policy before approval, any recommended changes being considered and discussed by both the administration and faculty before final official action.

The functions of the administration in setting the policy are to clearly establish the need for it, develop a favorable atmosphere for its consideration, obtain and make available detailed data on alternative policies, and provide for the administrative duties necessary to the consideration of alternative policies.

The functions of faculty members in establishing the policy are to recognize the need for a patent policy, cooperate with the administration in setting up a faculty committee to consider alternative policies, recommend to the administration a reasonable policy recognizing the equities of all parties, and review and reconsider improvements to the policy suggested by the administration and the institutional governing body.

The drafting of the policy can be done by a responsible officer of the administration, by a respected faculty member, by a faculty committee, by a joint faculty-administration committee, or by a combination of these. The policy so drafted should be submitted to general counsel before submission to the top officer of the institution and the governing body. Initial drafting of the patent policy by an outside attorney is usually not recommended, but examination of the policy by the university counsel and consultation with any possible outside licensing group before its approval and publication are essential.

Although sufficient time and opportunity should be allowed for every faculty member to have a chance to present his viewpoint for consideration, deliberations on the policy should not be allowed to drag.

The patent policy should include:

Recognition of the rights of the inventor
Recognition of the rights of the institution
Recognition of the rights of sponsors
Prescription of one or more mechanisms for carrying out the policy
Setting of size and type of awards to faculty inventors
Specification of faculty-institution patent agreement
Arrangements for other staff and student inventors

The policy should be short, concise, and as flexible as possible, and should set general guidelines rather than spell out too specifically methods for handling all contingencies.

The patent policy should be implemented by administrative officers on recommendation of a patent committee made up of faculty members. Membership on the patent committee should be for a specified time and appointments should be staggered to provide continuity. Representation on this committee should include the arts as well as the sciences and engineering. The committee should hold regularly scheduled, well-publicized meetings several times during the academic year.

BIBLIOGRAPHY

Thomas' Register of American Manufacturers, Thomas Publishing Company, Inc., New York (annual editions).

Poor's Register of Corporations, Directors and Executives, Standard & Poor's Corporation, New York (annual editions).

Calvert, R. (ed.): *Encyclopedia of Patent Practice and Management,* Reinhold Book Corporation, New York, 1964.

Davis, A. S., Jr.: "Putting Patents to Work," *Journal of the Patent Office Society,* vol. 36, no. 10, p. 713, October, 1954.

Eckstrom, L. J.: *Licensing in Foreign and Domestic Operations,* Foreign Operations Service, Inc., Essex, Conn., 1964 (supplemented).
Smith, A. M.: *Patent Law Cases, Comments and Material,* Overbeck, 1964.

APPENDIXES

University Patent Policy

[*Note: The form shown here serves to stimulate recognition and consideration of special problems on particular campuses and also to serve as a model for use.*]

The University is concerned with discovery, reason, and knowledge, and their application to the problems of mankind. To the extent that the results of this application are patentable, patents upon them are perfectly proper if it is kept in mind that patents are simply by-products, not ends in themselves.

1. This policy applies to all members of the faculty, graduate and undergraduate students, and employees ("university personnel").

2. Matters of policy relating to the operation of this Patent Policy shall be handled by the University Patent Committee. The University Patent Committee shall be composed of three (3) permanent members of the faculty, to be appointed from time to time by the Faculty Senate.

3. Administrative matters relating to the operation of this Patent Policy shall be handled by the Patent Officer, who shall be appointed by and be an employee of the University. He shall be Secretary of the University Patent Committee.

4. All University personnel who have reason to believe that they have made a patentable invention shall report that belief in writing at once to the Patent Officer, with a full description of the invention and any matters relevant to it. Subject to reference, by way of appeal, to the University Patent Committee at the request of the inventor, the Patent Officer shall finally decide how the invention shall be handled under the following paragraphs:

a. Subject to paragraph *4b:*

(1) Any invention made with only a nominal use of materials, supplies, facilities, and services of the University and without any substantial use by a member of the faculty of the services of graduate or undergraduate students of the University shall belong to the inventor.

(2) Any invention made with more than a nominal use of materials, supplies, facilities, or services of the University or with a substantial use by a member of the faculty of the services of graduate or undergraduate students of the University shall belong to the University.

b. Any invention made by University personnel with funds controlled by or derived from an extra-University contract or otherwise subject to such a contract shall be subject to that contract's terms respecting ownership of patents.

5. A copy of each contract calling for research, investigation or development by the University or University personnel shall, before commitment thereto by the University or University personnel, be submitted to the Patent Officer for review; if it is thereafter executed, a copy of it as executed shall be furnished to him. A similar procedure shall be followed on all contract amendments.

6. All inventions falling within paragraph 4*a*(2) shall be submitted by the Patent Officer to ________________, a nonprofit corporation skilled in licensing patents in the public interest, for evaluation as to patentability and the prospects of commercial use under the University's contract with ________________ dated ________, 19___, a copy of which shall be available to University personnel at the University's business office. Should ________________ elect to accept the invention and patent rights therein under that contract for patenting and licensing, the inventor shall assign the invention and patent rights thereon to ________________ for that purpose, and shall receive fifteen (15%) per centum of the gross sum of money received by________________ from its licensing of the invention and patent rights. Should ________________ decline to accept the invention and patent rights thereon, all rights thereto shall revert to the inventor.

7. All inventions falling within paragraph 4*a*(1) may, at the inventor's option, be submitted by him to ________________, through the Patent Officer, for such evaluation, patenting, and licensing, but upon such financial terms as may be agreed upon by inventor and ________________.

8. All inventions falling within paragraph 4*b* shall, to the extent such action is not precluded by the terms of the pertinent contract, be handled pursuant to paragraph 6.

9. The University Patent Committee shall, as a portion of its activities:

a. In cases of coinventorship, determine the division of the fifteen (15%) per centum share

b. In unusual cases, confer with ________________ as to whether a higher percentage than fifteen (15%) per centum should apply, subject however to express consent thereto by ________________ and the University.

Specimen Patent Assistance Agreement Between Research Corporation and Educational and Scientific Institutions

THIS AGREEMENT, made this _____ day of _________, 19___, between ________________, a ___________ corporation with offices at ___________, ___________, hereinafter called "UNIVERSITY," and RESEARCH CORPORATION, a New York nonprofit corporation with offices at 405 Lexington Avenue, New York, New York 10017, hereinafter called "RESEARCH":

WITNESSETH THAT:

A. WHEREAS, UNIVERSITY believes that patentable inventions may be made by members of its faculty, its associates, students or employees; and

B. WHEREAS, RESEARCH has had broad experience in the evaluation of inventions for patentability and commercial and scientific utility, in seeking patents thereon, and in introducing them into use in the useful arts and manufactures and for scientific purposes; and

C. WHEREAS, UNIVERSITY desires that inventions referred to in Paragraph *A* be evaluated, patented and introduced into use in an effective manner and with due regard for the public interest; and

D. WHEREAS, UNIVERSITY further desires that any net income from these inventions be used to provide means for the advancement and extension of technical and scientific investigation, research, experimentation and education; and

E. WHEREAS, RESEARCH is a corporation organized for the purpose of providing means for the advancement and extension of technical and scientific investigation, research and experimentation, no part of the net earnings of which inures to the benefit of any private shareholder or individual; and

F. WHEREAS, RESEARCH is prepared to evaluate such inventions, to obtain patents on them, and to introduce them into use through its ownership of any patent applications filed and patents issued on them, and issuing licenses to third parties;

NOW, THEREFORE, in consideration of the mutual covenants and undertakings herein contained, the parties DO AGREE AS FOLLOWS:

I. *UNIVERSITY's Duties:* UNIVERSITY agrees to:

(1) Recommend to members of its faculty, its associates, students and employees, in such cases as UNIVERSITY may in its discretion determine, that they assign to RESEARCH inventions which they have made, any patent applications filed on them, and any patents issuing on them.

(2) Afford to RESEARCH to a reasonable extent, upon request, the advice and assistance of such members of UNIVERSITY's faculty, associates, students and employees, in seeking patents upon such inventions, without charge therefor.

(3) Advise RESEARCH of any commitments UNIVERSITY has made to any third party for licenses or other rights under such inventions, patent applications or patents.

II. *RESEARCH's Duties:* RESEARCH agrees at its own sole cost and expense to:

(1) Evaluate all such inventions, report thereon to UNIVERSITY, and accept assignment of those of such inventions, under the terms of this agreement, as it may determine in its discretion should be made the subject of patent applications.

(2) File United States patent applications thereupon, and prosecute the same in good faith with the intention of securing issuance of patents.

(3) File corresponding foreign patent applications thereupon, and prosecute the same in good faith with the intention of securing issuance of patents thereon, and maintain such patents and cause them to be worked, all to the extent that it may in its discretion determine.

(4) Attempt to introduce such inventions, patent applications and patents so assigned, into public use, and to secure a reasonable revenue therefrom in such manner as its considered judgment best dictates, primarily by issuing licenses thereunder.

(5) Issue to each inventor so assigning to it a letter-agreement, substantially in the form attached hereto as Exhibit A, entitling him to participation hereunder. [See note.]

(6) Pay to each such inventor (or coinventors), his (or their) heirs, assigns and personal representatives, not later than March 15 in each year a fixed percentage (to be determined by UNIVERSITY in each case and communicated by it to RESEARCH) not exceeding a total of fifteen (15%) per centum, of all moneys received by it against the preceding calendar year by reason of RESEARCH's ownership of such inventions, patent applications and patents, as he (or they) shall be entitled to under the pertinent letter-agreement, or letter-agreements issued under Article II, paragraph 5, hereof, and furnish to him (or them) simultaneously a report showing the computation thereof. [See note.]

(7) Pay to UNIVERSITY, its successors and assigns, not later than March 15 in each year, fifty (50%) per centum of the sum remaining of all moneys received by it against the preceding calendar year by reason of its ownership of all such inventions, patent applications and patents, following subtraction of (*a*) all payments made to inventors pursuant to Article II, paragraph 6, of this agreement, and (*b*) retention by RESEARCH of any amounts needed to reimburse it for Special Expenses. "Special Expenses" shall mean RESEARCH's expenses for litigating in courts of record to obtain, or assert or defend the validity or scope of, any patent, it being agreed that the expenses of such litigation shall not be so charged as Special Expenses unless UNIVERSITY shall have given its prior assent to the incurring of such expenses as such Special Expenses. The remaining fifty (50%) per centum shall be retained by RESEARCH for the general purposes of its charter. [See note.]

(8) Furnish simultaneously to UNIVERSITY a report showing (*a*) activities during the preceding calendar year in connection with each such invention, and (*b*) the computation of payments made under Article II, paragraphs 6 and 7, of this agreement. [See note.]

(9) Maintain at its offices, in usual form, books of record, ledgers and accounts relating to its activities under this agreement, all of which shall be open to examination by UNIVERSITY or its nominees, during usual business hours. [See note.]

(10) Assign to UNIVERSITY or its nominee or nominees, upon any termination of this agreement, all inventions assigned to RESEARCH hereunder, all patent applications filed and patents issued thereon and all right to damages for infringements taking place after such termination, but subject to (*a*) any letter-agreements which RESEARCH may have entered into with inventors with respect thereto under Article II, paragraph 5, of this agreement; and (*b*) to any licenses, grants, working rights, agreements or other contracts with respect thereto theretofore made by RESEARCH. [See note.]

(11) Continue as licensor, grantor or contracting party as to licenses, grants, working rights, agreements or other contracts to which the inventions, patent applications and patents assigned pursuant to Article II, paragraph 10, of this agreement are subject at the time of such assignment, and to continue to report upon and make division of royalties under Article II, paragraphs 6, 7, 8 and 9 of this agreement, with respect thereto. [See note.]

(12) Issue to any third party any license required by any contract between UNIVERSITY and such third party, entered into prior to acceptance, as to any invention acquired by it under Article II, paragraph 1, of this agreement, and as to patent applications filed and patents issued thereon.

III. *UNIVERSITY's Reserved Rights:*

(1) UNIVERSITY reserves the right to terminate this agreement upon ninety (90) days written notice to RESEARCH at any time.

(2) UNIVERSITY reserves the right to advise RESEARCH that UNIVERSITY desires that a particular inventor or coinventors be paid more than fifteen (15%) per centum of the moneys received by RESEARCH with respect to his (or their) invention. Upon such request RESEARCH and UNIVERSITY shall confer in good faith to determine a policy and appropriate action, if any, with respect thereto.

IV. *RESEARCH's Reserved Rights:* RESEARCH reserves the right to:

(1) Terminate this agreement upon ninety (90) days written notice to UNIVERSITY.

(2) Give written notice to UNIVERSITY of its intention to abandon any patent application or foreign patent subject to this agreement, or not to proceed further with the introduction into public use of any invention, patent application or patent subject to this agreement, and, unless UNIVERSITY shall, within sixty (60) days after such notice, require the assignment of such invention, patent application, or patent to UNIVERSITY or its nominee, to abandon or take no further action as to such invention, patent application, or patent.

(3) Receive for the general purposes of its charter thirty (30%) per centum of the amount remaining, from all money received by its assignee or assignees under Article II, paragraph 10, of this agreement by reason of such assignee's or assignees' ownership and/or management of any inventions, patent applications or patents so assigned or thereafter filed or issued thereon, following subtraction and retention therefrom by such assignee or assignees of any amounts needed to reimburse it or them for such expenses as RESEARCH and such assignee or assignees may have previously agreed upon in writing for litigation in courts of record to obtain, or to assert or defend the validity or scope of, any patent.

V. *General:* The parties agree that:

(1) Any controversy or claim arising out of or relating to this agreement or the breach thereof, shall be settled by arbitration, in accordance with the Rules, then obtaining, of the American Arbitration Association, and judgment upon the award rendered may be entered in the highest court of the forum, state or federal, having jurisdiction.

(2) This agreement is entered into for the express benefit of, and shall be binding upon, all members of the faculty, associates, students and employees of the UNIVERSITY, their heirs, assigns and personal representatives, who shall accept in writing any letter-agreement issued by RESEARCH pursuant to Article II, paragraph 5, hereof. [See note.]

IN WITNESS WHEREOF, the parties hereto have caused this agreement to be signed and their corporate seals to be hereunto affixed, all by their corporate officers thereunto duly authorized, and as of the day and year first above written.

Attest:	RESEARCH CORPORATION
______________________________	By ______________________
Assistant Secretary	Vice President
Attest:	______________ UNIVERSITY
______________________________	By ______________________
(title; seal)	(title)

EXHIBIT *A*
[See note.]

Name and Address
of Inventor

Dear Sir:

In accordance with the agreement between Research Corporation and ______________ University dated ______________, under which Research Corporation acquires ownership of inventions made by members of the University's faculty, its associates, students and employees, with the patent rights thereon, and introduces them into public use, the University has advised us that your invention described as ______________________________ is to be taken care of by us under that agreement, in furtherance of the University's regular patent policy.

The specific terms of the agreement with University are available to you through University. Briefly, they provide that inventions, patent applications and ensuing patents shall be assigned to Research Corporation by the inventor, and that the patent filing and prosecution, and introduction into use, is to be undertaken by us at our expense. From any income that may be derived from the patent, before deduction of any expenses, the agreement provides that there shall be paid by us to the inventor, his heirs, assigns, and personal representatives, a percentage of that income which is established in each case by the University. In the case of your invention the University has informed us that this figure should be ______ per centum. Payments of this amount and reports as to the progress of the invention will be made to you on March 15 of each year.

You might be interested in knowing that the balance of any income is, in general, divided equally between the University and Research Corporation. The amount remaining with Research Corporation after payment of its expenses is used for the general purposes of our charter for the support of technical and scientific investigation and research in educational institutions through our grants-in-aid programs. A copy of our Annual Report, descriptive of Research Corporation's activities, is enclosed for your information.

There is attached to this letter in duplicate a form of assignment, and if you have no further questions concerning the matter, it would be appreciated if you would:

(1) sign and date the enclosed copy of this letter and return it to us; and

(2) sign the enclosed form of assignment, swear to it before a notary public, and return one copy to us, retaining the other copy for your personal files.

Thank you very much for your cooperation.

Very truly yours,
RESEARCH CORPORATION
by: ________________
Vice President

Accepted
Date:
Place:

[*Note:* The full form shown above is useful where university policy provides that the inventor shall receive a set percentage of gross royalties direct from the patent licensing organization. Where (*a*) the inventor is to receive no share, (*b*) his share is to be paid him by the University, or (*c*) his share normally would exceed that which the patent licensing organization would agree to, the following changes may be made:

Delete: in Article II, paragraphs (5)–(11); in Article V, paragraph (2); Exhibit A.

Insert in Article II: Paragraphs (5)–(9) below.

Change: in Article II, number of paragraph (12), to (10); in Article IV, paragraph (3), internal reference "10" to "8"; in Article V, paragraph (1), delete "1."]

(5) Pay to UNIVERSITY, its successors and assigns, not later than March 15 in each year, fifty-seven and one-half (57.5%) per centum of the sum remaining of all moneys received by it against the preceding calendar year by reason of its ownership of all such inventions, patent applications and patents, following subtraction and retention by RESEARCH of any amounts needed to reimburse it for such expenses of litigation in courts of record to obtain, or to assert or defend the validity or scope of, any patent, it being agreed that the expenses of such litigation shall not be so charged as Special Expenses unless UNIVERSITY shall have given its prior assent to the incurring of such expenses as such Special Expenses. The remaining forty-two and one-half (42.5%) per centum shall be retained by RESEARCH for the general purposes of its charter.

(6) Furnish simultaneously to UNIVERSITY a report showing (*a*) activities during the preceding calendar year in connection with each such invention, and (*b*) the computation of payments made under Article II, paragraph 5, of this agreement.

(7) Maintain at its offices, in usual form, books of record, ledgers and accounts re-

lating to its activities under this agreement, all of which shall be open to examination by UNIVERSITY or its nominees, during usual business hours.

(8) Assign to UNIVERSITY or its nominee or nominees, upon any termination of this agreement, all inventions assigned to RESEARCH hereunder, all patent applications filed and patents issued thereon and all right to damages for infringements taking place after such termination, but subject to any licenses, grants, working rights, agreements or other contracts with respect thereto theretofore made by RESEARCH.

(9) Continue as licensor, grantor or contracting party as to licenses, grants, working rights, agreements or other contracts to which the inventions, patent applications and patents assigned pursuant to Article II, paragraph 8, of this agreement are subject at the time of such assignment, and to continue to report upon and make division of royalties under Article II, paragraphs 5 and 6, of this agreement, with respect thereto.

Chapter 9

Copyright

JULIUS J. MARKE

**Law Librarian and Professor of Law, New York University,
New York, New York**

COPYRIGHT REVISION

The current copyright law was enacted in 1909. The significant changes since 1909 in the technology of communicating printed matter, visual images, and recorded sounds as well as the emerging technology in information storage and retrieval have caused great concern among consumers and proprietors of copyright works. How should a copyright law be modernized to respond to these new methods for the reproduction and dissemination of copyrighted works? The Copyright Office was directed by Congress to study the situation and recommend changes in the copyright law reflecting these developments. After years of study, bills were introduced in Congress to revise the copyright law based on these studies. Since 1964, many hearings have been held and reports issued on what is now recognized as a highly controversial copyright revision bill. The contending parties have been unable to reach a consensus on such topics as the extension of copyright-infringement liabilities to community-antenna television and computer data storage and retrieval systems, and the provision that juke-box operators pay royalties for the first time. As a result, Congress decided to reconsider the proposed revision in the 91st Congress and to extend expiring copyrights until December 31, 1969. Congress is also considering the establishment of a National Commission on New Technological Uses of Copyrighted Works to study and compile data on the reproduction and use of copyrighted works of authorship in automatic systems of storing, processing, retrieving, and transferring information and by various forms of machine reproduction. The reports issued by this commission will be highly significant in the revision of copyright law.

SCOPE OF COPYRIGHT PROTECTION

A copyright protects authors of literary, dramatic, musical, artistic, and other intellectual works by conferring on them the exclusive right to reproduce, multiply, publish, sell, or distribute their works. It also denies to others the right to transform or revise such works by means of dramatization, translation, musical arrangement, or the like. With certain exceptions, only the author of a copyrighted work may perform or record it. These exceptions generally pertain to musical compositions where the exclusive privilege governs only if the performance is in public and for profit. Then again, "compulsory license" provisions of the federal copyright statute permit recordings of musical works upon payment of prescribed royalties provided the copyright owner had authorized an initial recording.

DISTINCTION BETWEEN STATUTORY AND COMMON-LAW COPYRIGHT

Copyright protection arises from both statutory and common law. Common-law copyright protects unpublished works. Until the author of a work authorizes its publication, the common law or state law automatically grants him "the exclusive right of first publication." An author may preserve his common-law rights by restricting or limiting circulation of copies of his work to certain persons for a specific purpose—such as for criticism or use in a classroom. Once a manuscript is published, it is dedicated to the public unless it bears a proper copyright notice. An author who publishes his work without first obtaining statutory copyright protection loses his exclusive rights therein, and his work may be published by anyone for profit or otherwise. The sale or distribution of copies of a work is deemed a general publication under copyright law. "Publication," therefore, is the act of making a book public. Statutory copyright is based on laws enacted by Congress. It is a form of monopolistic privilege granting exclusive publication rights to authors in their works for a specific period of time. Strict compliance with all the conditions prescribed by the law of copyrights must be observed to procure its protection.

WHO CAN ASSERT COPYRIGHT PROTECTION?

Copyright protection can only be claimed by the author or those authorized by him to assert this right. Possession of a manuscript by itself, therefore, is not sufficient for this purpose. Private letters, for example, unless dedicated to the public, may not be published by the addressee or owner. Each work must be separately copyrighted. Works made for hire are copyrightable by the employer and not the author-employee.

ADMINISTRATIVE REQUIREMENTS TO SECURE STATUTORY COPYRIGHT

Statutory copyright may be secured for a published work by producing the work in printed or otherwise processed form bearing a proper copyright notice and by filing an appropriate registration form. Various forms are used for different types of registration—for example, form A is used for books and form D for dramatic or musical works. These may be obtained by writing to the Register of Copyrights, Copyright Office, Washington, D.C. 20025. Directions for filling out the forms are printed on the forms. A fee must be paid, and two copies of the published work must be furnished for registration. A copyright need not be registered with the Copyright Office to be valid. Copyright is obtained when the work is published with the correct copyright notice in the correct position. However, until the copyright is registered, the copyright owner is not permitted to go into court to protect his rights against infringement and the Copyright Office will not accept an application for copyright renewal.

Statutory copyright for an unpublished work may be secured by registering a claim in the Copyright Office. This involves filing an appropriate application form and depositing one complete copy of the manuscript with the Copyright Office.

COPYRIGHT NOTICE

A copyright notice in a publication printed in book form must appear upon the title page or page immediately following. Copyright notices for periodicals must appear upon the title page, upon the first page of text, or under the title heading. Similarly, for a musical work, the notice must appear upon the title page or upon the first page of music. The Copyright Office recommends that the form of notice should consist of the following three elements:

1. The word "Copyright," the abbreviation "Copr.," or the symbol ©. (Use of the symbol © may result in securing copyright in countries which are members of the Universal Copyright Convention.)
2. The name of the copyright owner.
3. The year date of publication. (If the work has previously been registered as unpublished, the year date of such registration should be given, since the copyright term began on that date.)

These three elements should appear as follows:

© John Author 1970

Maps, works of art, models or designs for works of art, reproductions of works of art, drawings or plastic works of a scientific or technical character, photographs, prints and pictorial illustrations, and prints or labels used for articles of merchandise are permitted to bear a special form of copyright notice. The symbol ©, accompanied by the initials, monogram, mark, or symbol of the copyright owner will be sufficient if the owner's name appears upon some accessible portion of the work.

DURATION, RENEWAL, AND EXTENSION OF COPYRIGHT

Section 24 of the copyright law (U.S. Code, Title 17, sec. 24) now provides that statutory copyright endures for 28 years from the date of first publication (not from the date of registration). Proprietors of such copyright may renew and extend it for an additional term of 28 years provided application is made to the Copyright Office within one year of the expiration of the original term of copyright. If the author of the work is not living, the widow, widower, or children of the author may apply for renewal. If they are not living then, the author's executors or next of kin may similarly apply.

The proposed revision of the copyright law would change the present term of copyright to a basic term of the life of the author plus 50 years. A term of 75 years from publication with a maximum limit of 100 years from creation would apply to anonymous works, pseudonymous works, and works made for hire. Common-law copyright protection would be abolished for unpublished works, and they would be brought under statutory protection with the same applicable statutory term. Subsisting copyrights would last for 28 years from the date they were secured with a right to renew this term for a second term of 47 years. Subsisting renewal copyrights are extended automatically until 75 years elapse after first publication or registration. In anticipation of the enactment of a revised copyright law, Congress has extended expiring copyrights to December 31, 1969. This has been the fourth extension since 1962.

ASSIGNMENT OF STATUTORY COPYRIGHT

A copyright may be assigned, transferred, granted, or mortgaged by an instrument in writing signed by the proprietor of the copyright. It may also be bequeathed by will (U.S. Code, Title 17, sec. 28). To be effective, an assignment or transfer of copyright must be recorded in the Copyright Office within three calendar months after its execution in the United States and six months after its execution abroad (U.S. Code, Title 17, sec. 30). A copyright holder may also transfer or assign his expectancy of renewal right arising at the expiration of the original 28-year copyright grant. It should be noted, however, that the author must be alive on the first day of the 28th year of the copyright to effectuate the renewal in the name of the assignee, as the renewal can only be made in the name of the author "or his widow or children if he be dead." The assignee is not entitled to make such an application. Thus, if the author does not survive, only his statutory beneficiaries are entitled to the copyright renewal and the assignee loses all his rights under the assignment.

ELEMENTS OF COPYRIGHTABILITY

Copyright protection does not extend to words and short phrases such as names, titles, and slogans. Neither does it extend to ideas, plots, dramatic situations, plans, methods, systems, or devices. Rather, it is limited to the tangible, visually perceptible arrangement of words the author uses to express his ideas. Thus, themes, plots, or ideas may be freely borrowed, as a copyright does not give an exclusive right to the art disclosed. In this sense a copyright is distinguishable from a patent, which gives an inventor an exclusive right to the idea or art disclosed therein. Similarly, works consisting entirely of information that is common property containing no original authorship, such as standard calendars or schedules or public events, are not copyrightable even though expressed in otherwise copyrightable form.

A work must be original to be copyrightable. The author must have created it by his own skill, labor, and judgment. Direct copying or surreptitious imitation of the work of another defeats copyright. Originality of the wording is the important test as to whether a work is copyrightable, and novelty or uniqueness by themselves are not sufficient. By the same token, therefore, neither is literary skill significant in obtaining copyright protection.

If the original text of a work is in the public domain or dedicated to the public, it cannot be copyrighted. Nor can copyright subsist in any publication of the United States government (U.S. Code, Title 17, sec. 8). However, compilations or abridgements, adaptations, arrangements, dramatizations, translations, or other versions of works in the public domain, copyrighted works (with permission of copyright owner), or works republished with new matter are copyrightable as new works (U.S. Code, Title 17, sec. 7). If the new version retains some of the publication which is in the public domain, it is copyrightable only as to the new matter which is the result of the author's original contribution. If there still is subsisting copyright in the work republished with new matter, the subsisting copyright is neither affected nor extended by the new version.

INFRINGEMENT OF COPYRIGHT AND FAIR USE

Infringement of another's copyright can subject the infringer to an injunction action or to an action for damages (loss of profits, etc.) suffered by the copyright owner. Statutory penalties are also imposed for copyright infringement (U.S. Code, Title 17, sec. 101). The infringer also becomes responsible for full court costs and a reasonable attorney's fee as part of the costs (U.S. Code, Title 19, sec. 116).

Infringement of a copyright occurs when there is an appropriation to an injurious extent of a substantial or material portion of the copyrighted work without permission of the copyright holder. The whole work or a large portion thereof need not be copied. The test is one of quality and value as well as quantity. In addition, the courts will consider how far the copied matter will tend to supersede the original or interfere with its sale.

The courts have recognized, however, that under some circumstances and for certain purposes authors, compilers, or publishers may use portions of a copyrighted work in their own publications without the permission of the copyright owner, even though they eventually compete with the copyrighted work. Known as the doctrine of "fair use," it has been applied particularly with reference to works in the arts and sciences. In a sense, the fair use of copyrighted material is the privilege of others than the owner to use the copyrighted material in a reasonable manner without his consent in order—in the words of the Constitution—"to promote the progress of science and useful arts."

The doctrine of fair use is a judicial rule of public policy. Initially enunciated by Mr. Justice Story in the 1841 case of *Folsom v. Marsh* (9 F. Cas. 342, 343), it is an equitable principle under which every case is decided on its own facts. Interestingly, there is no reference to the fair-use doctrine in the existing 1909 copyright law. As a result, the courts have evolved criteria which, although not decisive, do provide some guidelines for determining when a taking is fair use. The proposed revision of the copyright law (sec. 107) provides that

> The fair use of a copyrighted work, including such use by reproduction in copies or phonorecords or by another means specified (in the law), for purposes such as criticism, comment, news reporting, teaching, scholarship, or research is not an infringement of copyright. In determining whether the use made of a work in any particular case is a fair use, the factors to be considered shall include:
>
> 1. The purpose and character of the use
> 2. The nature of the copyrighted work
> 3. The amount and substantiality of the portion used in relation to the copyrighted work as a whole
> 4. The effect of the use upon the potential market for or value of the copyrighted work

Copyright experts unanimously agree that this provision correctly restates the present status of the judicial doctrine of fair use as defined and applied by the courts. The report of the House Committee on H.R. 2512 (H.R. Rep. no. 83, 90th Cong., 1st Sess., 1967), however, recognizes that "the endless variety of situations and combinations of circumstances that can arise in particular cases precludes the formulation of exact rules in the statute." (p. 32.) The report illustrates some educational uses of copyrighted materials that would be permitted under the fair-use doctrine (pp. 32–37). Actually, the layman-teacher or librarian would have difficulty in applying these criteria to a contemplated use of copyrighted material. Even lawyers would have reservations about predicting how a court would consider such use. A criticism often made by educators and librarians is that by reason of these vague criteria, they are prevented by uncertainty from doing things that they are legally entitled to do and that would improve the quality of their teaching or library service. As a result, the scope and limits of fair use are considered the most troublesome issues in the field of copyright law today, particularly with reference to the nonprofit use of copyrighted materials in computer data storage and retrieval systems. To be absolutely sure of avoiding an infringement suit, permission must be obtained in advance, from the copyright owner, to use extracts from the copyrighted work. But the necessity of procuring such a license, of course, defeats the very purpose of the fair-use doctrine.

PERMISSION TO REPRINT

Permission to reprint copyrighted material should be sought whenever use does not fall clearly under the principles of fair use. Use of copyrighted material without authorization is not permissible. An unsuccessful search for the copyright owner is not a defense to an action for infringement. Usually the publisher of a work has authority to grant permission or is able to refer requests to the proper person. In the event that the copyright holder cannot be located, the Copyright Office, for a small fee, will conduct a search. Full acknowledgment should be given to the copyrighted source.

MANUFACTURING REQUIREMENTS

The copyright law now requires that English-language books and periodicals be manufactured in the United States in order to be protected for the full copyright term. Known as the "manufacturing clause," it is now subject to many exceptions and limitations. Affected in the main by this clause are the works, manufactured abroad, of American authors. Ad interim copyright protection for these works can be obtained for a period of five years by a special registration. If, after five years, another edition of the work is not printed and published in the United States, then copyright protection is lost. This is a highly controversial clause and the proposed copyright revision substantially changes it by narrowing its scope and preventing it from causing technical forfeitures of protection. It should be noted that the clause does not presently apply to motion pictures, to musical or dramatic compositions, or to works for which copyright protection is claimed under the Universal Copyright Convention.

UNIVERSAL COPYRIGHT CONVENTION

The United States belongs to the Universal Copyright Convention (1955), along with all the major countries of the world except the Soviet Union and China. If the published copies of a work originating in a signatory country bear the symbol ©, accompanied by the name of the author and the year of first publication, and appears in the book in such manner that reasonable notice of the copyright claim is given, the other UCC nation members will recognize that the technical formalities have been observed to obtain copyright protection in the country involved. Each signatory to the UCC protects the published and unpublished works of the citizens of other signatory nations even though its own technical requirements for copyright protection may not have been met.

Section Two

Academic Affairs Administration

Chapter 1

Academic Policies and Standards

THURSTON E. MANNING

Vice-president for Academic Affairs, University of Colorado, Boulder, Colorado

ACADEMIC POLICIES

The word "policy" has a flexible use in administrative understanding. On the one hand, it may mean a statement principally expressive of an attitude (e.g., "As a matter of policy, deans should be selected from the faculty"). On the other hand, it may express a sharp and precise rule (e.g., "The University's vacation policy for employees permits one day of vacation for every twelve days of full service"). It is used in still another sense in the aphorism "Every administrative decision makes policy."

In the present chapter "policy" is (1) a *written* statement that (2) provides a *guide* for the *actions* of individuals (3) within an *organization*. Since our concern here is with academic policies, the organization affected is a college or university; and the individuals whose actions are to be guided are those associated with academic affairs—faculty members, students, and others in their roles associated with the activities of learning and teaching.

In some cases it is convenient to think of academic policies as setting academic standards—those guides to selection that indicate the preferred nature of certain possible choices. For example, a policy on admitting students that required those admitted to be in the upper half of their respective secondary school classes could be regarded as "setting a standard" for admission. In the present discussion there will be some examples of such "policies that set standards," but this aspect of the policies will probably be so evident that we will not set them apart for separate discussion.

Because the purpose of policies is to guide behavior, the general approach of this discussion will be to emphasize the need for such precision in statements of policy that they give *explicit* guidance for operational decisions. This does not mean that policy statements should not provide scope for administrative discretion; it does mean, however, that the bounds of discretion should be well defined, and the identity of the persons who must exercise discretion should be clear. A corollary is that policies no longer useful in the operation of the institution should be removed either by replacement or repeal. Experience has shown that imprecise and obsolete (but still formally active) policies can lead to confusion that unnecessarily complicates the activities of an institution.

DETERMINING ACADEMIC POLICIES: ROLE OF THE BOARD OF CONTROL

An institution of higher education in the United States is legally the board of control, almost without exception. The board may be styled a Board of Trustees, Board of Regents, or Panel of Overseers; it may derive its authority from a charter, a statute, or from special provision in a state constitution. But regardless of the details pertinent to a particular institution, it is the board that represents the ultimate and inclusive authority within the institution, and in a true sense all policies of the institution are policies adopted by the board, either explicitly or implicitly.

In general, boards of control today are lay boards; that is, their members are predominately (and often exclusively) persons who are not especially experienced or trained in academic affairs. As a consequence, it has become common for boards to delegate to groups or individuals within the institutions authority to formulate policies affecting the academic affairs of the institution. In many cases this delegation of authority is complete; that is, explicit endorsement by the board is not required before the policy becomes operative. In other cases, the board will delegate responsibility for formulating or revising a policy, but it will also require that the statement be reviewed and possibly modified by the board before the policy can be effective. Whatever the attitude of an individual board may be (and the attitudes of different boards may be quite different), it is essential that the board indicate fully and explicitly whatever full or partial delegation of authority it wishes to make. An appropriate place for such indications is in the bylaws of the institution.

It may be helpful to give examples of such clear statements, drawn from the bylaws of one institution:

"The college faculty shall decide matters of educational policy, including requirements for the admission of students, for the continuance of students in the academic program, and for the award of earned degrees." (Complete delegation.)

"The college faculty shall have jurisdiction over matters of academic dishonesty, under such policies and procedures as may be approved by the Board of Trustees." (Partial delegation.)

In those areas in which the board has chosen to exercise its authority in fixing policies directly, members of the administration and of the faculty may still play important and necessary roles in providing staff assistance to the board. It is not common for members of the board themselves to prepare proposed policy statements for board consideration. Rather, the common pattern is for the board to request draft policies from the president or the faculty. The importance of this staff assignment in structuring the policies of the institution should not be underestimated, particularly in matters of academic policies in which the board will not usually have expert opinion within its own membership.

While groups are often loath to delegate responsibility, the board should be sure that those areas of policy that it has not delegated or has delegated conditionally are areas in which the board really does wish to exercise its discretion, and that it has within itself the necessary knowledge to exercise this discretion wisely. For the board to insist on review and approval and then to issue its approval pro forma is to clutter up its agenda and to divert the attention and energies of the board from the business that only it can conduct. Further, the board will by this activity have always present the possibility of unwise board interference; it is a rare board that has not from time to time found a member whose personal interests have projected the board into random tampering in areas of policy which have, in fact, been fully delegated years before but retained for pro forma ratification.

In formulating its bylaws to provide for the delegation of policy-making authority, the board should be certain to obtain competent legal advice. In some jurisdictions there may be statutory requirements of formal board action for certain activities, or such provisions may have been written into the institution's original charter. These extrainstitutional constraints may limit the possibility of the board's delegating certain policy responsibilities.

Since the board of control is a deliberative body, the process by which it arrives at policies should depend upon staff preparation of proposed policies. The board, if concerned about a policy matter, should request the president (or, if more appropriate, some other officer or committee) to draft a proposed statement; in its request the board may wish to identify certain elements of the policy it particularly wishes to have considered. The staff assignment should be finished early enough to permit circulation of the proposed statement to members of the board (and possibly others associated with the institution) for consideration before the meeting at which the board as a whole will consider the policy. The staff document should provide comment on the effects of the proposed policy, and it should deal with the reasons for departing from any part of the board's instructions in the preparation of the statement. The board can then consider the proposed policy and adopt or reject it; or, as a result of its discussion, it may wish to request additional staff work. It is usually a mistake for the board to attempt in its meeting to make changes in the draft proposal unless these changes are minor.

In those cases in which the policy under consideration is of great interest to groups within the institution (for example, a new policy on faculty tenure), the board is well advised to permit well-identified groups and individuals who are members of the institution to direct to the board written statements of their views. In some cases the board may even wish to allow oral presentations during a meeting of the board; however, this practice requires much time—an element usually in short supply at board meetings—and should be reserved for policy considerations of exceptional importance.

In later discussions of specific policies will be found suggestions of policies that should be explicitly considered by the board.

DETERMINING ACADEMIC POLICIES: ROLE OF THE FACULTY

Once the board of control has specified those parts of policy that are the domain of the faculty, it is possible for the faculty to consider policy matters fruitfully.

Details of faculty organization are subject to considerable (and justified) variation. For the present discussion we restrict consideration to certain general principles:

First, since faculties comprise many individuals, their formal actions are legislative in character. Like any deliberative body, a faculty will succeed in formulating reasonable policies only if it places initial reliance on preliminary drafting and consideration by staff—in the case of most faculties, the staff represented by faculty committees. Drafts of proposed policies as submitted can be accepted, rejected, or modified by the faculty during its meetings (although these modifications should be minor to avoid confusion). A faculty should also give careful thought to employing the deans as "staff for the faculty"; a policy statement prepared by a good dean may be available much faster than a committee report and may be at least as satisfactory.

Second, the faculty should be careful to avoid pro forma approvals of committee proposals. Unless the faculty as a whole is competent to consider and act upon the policies brought before it, it should itself delegate authority to its committees or to administrative officers. Retention of unnecessary authority to approve consumes the time and energy of the faculty in its meetings. More seriously, it provides an opportunity for mischief should an individual member wish to use the faculty meeting as a forum to express personal prejudice under the guise of reasonable discussion. More than one faculty that has retained a policy calling for explicit faculty approval of degree candidates (such approval being pro forma upon receipt of the registrar's list) has been embarrassed by having to hear one or two individuals voice personal complaints about the presence on the list of some particular student. The basic principle is just that suggested for boards of control: delegate fully unless the parent body has the knowledge, time, and experience to provide detailed consideration.

Third, just as it is important for a faculty to delegate authority for policies that require a special expertise available to only a small part of the faculty, so it is important in those universities having several college or school faculties that the whole faculty not be required to consider policies affecting only one of the constituent faculties. Nor should the general faculty impose policies not appropriate to all parts of the institution. For example, the effect of class attendance in a school of law, in which the measure of success is student performance on final examinations, is quite different from its effect in a college of music, where much of the instruction is given in individual lessons. For the general faculty to set a policy on class attendance applying equally in such diverse situations would be to impose unwise restraints that would invite flagrant violations of the policy.

Fourth, a faculty should establish a mechanism by which review of its policies can be carried out regularly. The mechanism may appropriately require examination of policies by the committees of the faculty, but it should also permit individual members of the faculty to raise questions regarding existing or proposed policies.

DETERMINING ACADEMIC POLICIES: ROLE OF THE ADMINISTRATIVE OFFICERS

It is clear from the discussion above that administrative officers can play important roles in the formulation of academic policies. As staff for the board of control, they exert initiating influence on the content and expression of policies. The academic officers, as members of the faculty, not only have many of the same responsibilities as other members of the faculty but, because in many cases their special experience is pertinent, their advice and recommendations can appropriately influence the consideration of policies within the faculty.

The administrative officers also have an obligation to inform the board and the faculty of existing policies and to draw attention to policies that are obsolete and to areas in which policy is ill defined. The preparation and publication of handbooks and other summaries of policy is an obligation of the administrative staff, and it is an obligation that, when conscientiously fulfilled, is of great help in adjusting policy to the continuing needs of the institution.

A special duty of the officers is to recognize that when a policy allows for individual decisions those decisions may, in fact, establish a pattern that should be formally considered as a modification of policy. Individual decision is really exercised only when the decision maker exercises discretion. If he has in fact formulated clear rules for his decisions, he has implicitly added to his "guides for behavior," and the additions should be considered by the body that set the basic policy. For example, if faculty policy on the admission of students states that "the admissions officer may admit at his discretion any student in the upper half of his secondary school graduating class" but the admissions officer himself has consistently been refusing admission to students in the second quarter of their respective classes, then the officer has really modified the policy. He should, in these circumstances, return to the faculty with the proposal that his more restrictive policy be adopted.

DETERMINING ACADEMIC POLICIES: ROLE OF STUDENTS

While it is an old saw that "Institutions of higher education were founded on the premise that the faculty knows more than the students," it is also true that the policies of the institution so strongly affect the students that serious thought should be given to the question of whether a student voice in policy formulation is desirable. In recent years the students themselves have raised this question with increasing force, and it is now evident that complete disregard of the interest of students in academic policy making can no longer be sustained, even if it were demonstrated to be desirable. In fact, however, there are strong reasons for desiring effective student participation in academic policy considerations.

For one thing, students (and in many institutions, only students) are the most constant observers of the educational process of the institution. It is from them that the other members of the university or college community discover that classes at 7:30 A.M. are frequently not attended. It is from the students that faculty members find out that five courses taken at one time constitute so heavy a load that one of them is deliberately chosen as "easy to get a C in without much work outside of class."

For another, those institutions that have encouraged student participation in policy considerations have discovered that the students provide a most useful stimulus to changes in the academic life of the institution. Such a stimulus may arise because the students—unlike members of the faculty or administrative staff—have a minimum of personal concern with the status quo.

A third reason (which might be considered as an academic policy justification) is that student participation in academic policy formulation can help students to become aware of the difficulties of the learning and teaching processes and of the constraints under which the institution and its members must do their work. This can have the effect of increasing student sympathy for the life of the university and of encouraging student cooperation with learning.

However, one of the principal problems that must be resolved in providing for student participation is the determination of an appropriate mechanism. The students of a university are not a group with a stable membership—over one-fourth of the undergraduates are new each year. Further, student government is often structured after a pattern that falsely assumes student homogeneity, and the nominal student leaders may in fact have little support, if the number of votes cast for electing them is an indication. The problem of identifying true representatives of the student body is most acute in the large universities, where to all the matters indicated above is added the diversity of student interests and backgrounds characteristic of different professional and graduate schools.

To deal effectively with the diversity of the student body, many institutions have sought with some success to provide for student participation in the process of educational policy formation by turning attention to student groups oriented to the smaller units of the faculty organization—the subject matter departments and professional schools. These student groups, sometimes elected and sometimes appointed, can, because of their attachment to clear elements in the faculty, express student opinion at a point before faculty opinion is solidified and so can be quite effective in representing student interest. Further, because of the common subject matter interests, the student and faculty groups have a common ground on which to stand during their discussions; this common ground also frequently means that the members of the student and faculty groups know one another well outside of the context of their academic policy discussions. At the moment, the principal disadvantage of such a mechanism for student participation is its lack of obvious visibility.

In addition to such student groups based on subject matter division, many institutions have provided for a general student committee or panel, paralleling in a sense the activities of the general faculty committee charged with academic or educational policy matters. The student committee sometimes meets together with the faculty committee and sometimes by itself. Its purpose is to provide for student views on general matters (such as degree requirements and the academic calendar).

In some institutions, especially those that are small and of single purpose (such as the liberal arts colleges), it has proved helpful to incorporate student members into the usual faculty committees. When this is done, care should be taken that the student members, like the faculty members, are regarded as *individual* members, not as student "representatives." The comprehension of the work of the committee is destroyed when some members must be spokesmen for a large group while others speak only from their individual viewpoints.

DETERMINING ACADEMIC POLICIES: ROLE OF EXTRAINSTITUTIONAL INFLUENCES

While there is general understanding that the academic life of an institution of higher education is the primary responsibility of the internal organization—principally the faculty—it is naive to expect that this internal organization can exist in isolation from external influences. What these influences are, and to what extent they must be explicitly considered, will depend upon the characteristics of individual institutions. Here we can only draw attention to some of these influences and suggest how they may be incorporated effectively into the policy considerations of the institution.

General restrictions upon the institution imposed by parent groups (as in colleges having affiliations with religious groups) or legal restrictions (as in public institutions) should be remembered and injected into policy considerations by the president and other administrative officers. Such restrictions may refer to the obligatory teaching of certain subjects. Or the restrictions may, especially for public institutions in states having strong coordinating boards, prohibit the offering of certain subjects or courses. Sometimes these external restrictions are imposed through an *ex post facto* review required for approval of curriculum changes already approved within the internal policy mechanism. But again, regardless of the form of the restriction, the administrative officers are the appropriate group to be aware of it and to express the restriction within the internal policy procedures of the institution.

Restrictions on the free formation of academic policy are also imposed externally by accrediting organizations. In the cases of professional degree accreditations, these restrictions are often quite explicit and may include the specification of courses that must be offered or of the amount of time that must be devoted to study to qualify for the professional degree. In other cases (such as the accreditation provided by the regional associations), the restrictions may be much more general—perhaps requiring only the existence of certain groups that have explicit responsibility for the work of the institution. It is probably wisest to place with those most closely associated with the external group the responsibility for incorporating these external influences into the internal considerations. Thus, the chemistry department should raise internally any policy questions associated with American Chemical Society accreditation; the department of education (or school of education) should be responsible for knowing about and reflecting the requirements of the National Council on the Accreditation of Teacher Education; the president (or other institutional representative) should play this role with respect to the regional associations.

Of course, a basic question of academic policy that should be considered within the institution (although to some it may be "unthinkable"), is whether to continue the external relationships that restrict the institution's academic policies. Many institutions have concluded that their educational roles do not require certain accreditations and have consequently formulated their policies without reference to these requirements. Other institutions have concluded that their associations with religious groups require too high a price in terms of freedom of academic policy, and they have therefore broken historic ties. Obviously such actions can have the most serious effects upon an institution, and undertaking them requires the most careful and wide-ranging consideration possible. A more complete discussion of the subject may be found in Chapter 5, "External Forces in Higher Education," Section 3 of the companion volume.

A PATTERN OF DELEGATION

Anyone examining the range of institutions of higher education in the United States would conclude that variety is the only common characteristic. There is no single typical institution. Instead, colleges and universities range in size from a few hundred to tens of thousands of students; they range in educational mission from single-purpose liberal arts colleges to "multiversities" which embrace not only the arts and sciences but also schools directed at training professionals, and which regard the extension of knowledge through research as important to their task as the transmission of knowledge through teaching. In the face of this variety it is obvious that one single organizational pattern to provide for consideration of academic policies is not possible. What is suggested here is an outline pattern that could be adapted to various kinds of institutions of higher education. Those within an institution who understand its purpose and the external constraints under which it lives must consider the following rough pattern as suggestive and adaptable. If any general rule is possible it is this: the larger the institution, the more delegation to lower levels is necessary to ensure consideration of policies by those most knowledgeable of the effects of policy.

Because the *board of control* does not usually have within itself persons having extensive experience in academic affairs, it is well advised to delegate full responsibility for academic policy to the faculty and academic administrative officers. The board should retain supervisory powers by requiring regular reports of the academic life of the institution and by reserving to itself the approval of those policies that clearly enlarge or constrict the academic program—for example, the creation or dropping of degrees. By making the faculty responsible for the policies related to the admission, continuance, and graduation of students as well as the curricula and courses of study, the board does not abdicate its responsibility for the institution. Rather, by freeing itself from the details of these academic activities, the board opens up opportunity and time for general oversight of the institution, for those matters of detail for which board members are especially well qualified, and for placing responsibility for academic policies squarely on those who have the knowledge, experience, and time for dealing with them.

The *faculty*, in turn, should delegate to its subdivisions (departments and schools) responsibility for those academic affairs that affect only the subdivisions. The faculty should reserve for its committees and for itself supervision of those matters that affect more than one subdivision or for which uniformity throughout the institution is desirable. For example, the department should be responsible for the designation of faculty members to teach individual courses or sections; but the faculty should determine the requirements for graduation with a liberal arts degree. In its academic policy activities the faculty should make extensive use of its committees, as suggested earlier.

The *academic administrative officers* should have their policy-making and implementing activities clearly indicated by delegation from the board of control and the faculty. For the board, the officers should provide regular reports telling what the academic policies are, how they might be changed, and what the effects of current or contemplated policies seem to be on the activities of the institution. For the faculty, the officers should serve in a staff capacity, proposing new policies to meet changing conditions and assisting in the detailed drafting of policies. The experience of the officers in observing the effects of policies can be of the greatest assistance to the faculty in changing academic policies and in providing the discretion necessary to adapt policies to the individual needs of students and faculty members.

The *students* can effectively participate in academic policy determinations through association with the working groups of the faculty and the officers. While these associations have always occurred, there is advantage, especially in large institutions which may seem impersonal, to formalizing the student participation in academic policy formulation.

As suggested earlier, the *extrainstitutional influences*, whatever their character, should be represented by the awareness of the officers of the institution of them and by placing on the officers the responsibility to reflect these influences at the appropriate point in the policy-making process. This suggestion relies on the ability of the officers to move freely throughout the policy-making organization, working within the institution with both faculty and board and outside the institution with those groups who have rights to participate in the academic life of the institution.

While the variety of institutions of higher education makes these suggestions very general, each institution would benefit by considering whether its pattern conforms to these broad statements and whether its policy making might be improved by changes suggested in outline above.

SOME POLICY SUGGESTIONS

In this section are collected a number of guidelines for policies related to academic activities. In general these suggestions reflect policies in reasonably widespread use throughout the United States, although probably no one institution follows all the suggestions here. In each suggestion are provided some comments about the appropriate group within the institution which could reasonably have responsibility for this area of policy. As was true for the suggested pattern of delegation (discussed above), these comments can be only general, and individual institutions must provide details appropriate to their individual circumstances.

Course Requirements for Earned Degrees The policies specifying the number of courses and the distribution of those courses among all those in the institution are usually regarded as matters for faculty determination. In many institutions the board explicitly delegates full authority for setting these policies to the faculty. In fixing these educational policies, the faculty must recognize the constraints placed upon it by generally accepted procedures enforced implicitly by the regional accrediting agencies and explicitly by some of the professional accrediting procedures. However, there is still a broad range of discretion that faculties must exercise, and a comparison of these requirements (which include such matters as number of hours for degrees, "general education" for the undergraduate degrees, and major and minor requirements in areas of specialization) as published by several institutions in their catalogs will convince the skeptic of the variety in American higher education. In those institutions in which the board has elected to retain the right of approval, any action by the board to reverse the faculty-adopted policy is generally regarded as board interference in the right of the faculty to set those policies directly affected by the professional expertise of the faculty. Unless the board has within itself a similar expertise, it is well advised to delegate policy formulation in this area to the faculty. The administrative officers frequently have ministerial duties in implementing these policies; for example, the registrar is usually charged with reviewing individual student records to be certain that each student has constructed his program in agreement with the faculty policy.

Requirements for Advanced Degrees Policies setting degree requirements for advanced degrees, as for first degrees, should be determined by the faculty. In the case of advanced degrees it is common to require the passing of examinations and the writing of essays or dissertations in addition to the successful completion of course work. While this practice is universal for earned doctorates, a number of universities provide requirements for earned master's degrees that do not necessarily require the submission of a master's essay. The policies setting forth the degree requirements should carefully state the times at which the various requirements are to be satisfied. Failure to include this provision has led, in the experience of many institutions, to long delays in completing the degree—particularly in the case of earned doctorates. A not uncommon practice is to provide a maximum interval of seven years from the time of first accepting the degree candidate to his completing the requirements.

Approval of New Courses and Curricula Policies respecting new courses and curricula are matters for faculty consideration. Most faculties receive proposals for new courses and curricula from the interested department or from groups of faculty members. The proposals are then examined by a curriculum or educational policy committee of the faculty and the committee recommendations are referred to the entire faculty for detailed action. It is appropriate for the faculty to establish a policy outlining this procedure and also, possibly, providing general guides to the kinds of curricular proposals that the faculty wishes to see developed. In obtaining information about the proposed courses the faculty committee should inquire into any special qualifications of students taking the courses—for example, whether the students must have taken other courses as prerequisites.

The faculty should also have a mechanism for dropping courses or curricula and should exercise this responsibility as carefully as it does that for approving additions. The academic administrative officers can be of special help in noting whether approved courses have been dropped de facto by simply not being offered. The temporary absence of a qualified teacher is often good reason for omitting a course for a limited time. However, once it becomes clear that the normal mechanisms of faculty recruitment and assignment will not provide for an approved course or curriculum, the question of its abolition should be considered through the procedures specified in the faculty policy on course approvals.

All policies on new courses and curricula are matters for faculty action. The administrative officers should be careful to keep the board informed of the curricular developments, since these developments will influence other parts of the institution and since, in many institutions, it is possible for the curriculum to develop in directions not contemplated by the board of control. In some circumstances the board of control itself may feel obliged to pass upon basic issues of curricular policy such as, for example, a proposal that a university establish a new professional school. Except for such unusual cases, however, the board does well to leave matters of courses and curricula to the faculty.

Graduation with Honors The determination of policies respecting the award of earned degrees with honors (cum laude, magna cum laude, summa cum laude, or their English equivalents) should reside in the faculty. There is no standard pattern to guide the faculty policy of a given institution. In some institutions the Latin gradations are awarded on the basis of high grades throughout the student's course of study. In other institutions there may be special courses or examinations that must be passed. Whatever the decision of the individual faculty, it should provide a policy telling explicitly the criteria that will be used and, in those cases in which judgment is to be exercised, the identity of the faculty group that will make the final determination of honors. In its consideration of policy the faculty should carefully provide for students who transfer to the degree-awarding institution after having begun their studies elsewhere.

Grade Requirements for Continuance and Graduation Most institutions require at least some work above the "pass" level to continue a student in good standing in the institution and to graduate him. The fixing of this policy is a matter for the faculty. It is common for these policies to assign numerical values to letter grades in order to facilitate "grade averaging." In fixing its policy, the faculty should bear in mind that some institutions have found a more satisfactory policy in requiring a certain number of courses to be completed with a grade of, say, C or better and so avoiding the necessity of computing a grade average. The faculty should also recognize that cumulative averaging can work to the disadvantage of a student whose academic performance improves over time, since he may be unfairly penalized in the cumulative average for poor initial performance. Similarly, a cumulative average may permit a student who has established a very good record in his early years to coast and work at less than his full potential near the end of his course of study.

Requirements for Admission of Students It is appropriate for the faculty to specify policies for admitting students, and these policies often deal with the standard of the school from which the student comes (secondary schools as well as colleges are accredited by the regional associations) and his performance there (as shown by his academic record and possibly by the standardized examinations provided by the College Entrance Examination Board, the American College Testing Service, and, in some states, by the state university). Experience has shown, however, that the officer responsible for admitting students, whether new or transfer, must have some flexibility to provide for individual cases. Perhaps the most embarrassing situation an admissions officer can face is to be forced, by a rigid policy of admitting only students in the upper half of their secondary school classes, to refuse admission to a student ranking 12th out of 20 in a highly selective secondary school all of whose graduates succeed in colleges of high reputations.

It is clear that the principles mentioned above should also apply to the admission of graduate students and of those transferring from other institutions before completing a degree. The comments provided on transfer credits (below) also have some pertinence here.

Transfer Credits The amount of credit toward his degree that should be allowed a student transferring to an institution after having begun his work elsewhere can be a vexing problem. The faculty is well advised to provide very general guidelines (for example, specifying that the final quarter of the total credits must be earned at the new institution), but to leave the detailed evaluation to the registrar or admissions officer. A reasonable general policy statement may direct that transfer credits be evaluated on the basis of comparison with courses within the evaluating institution.

When the credits have been earned in an institution that is not accredited, it is common practice to make the evaluation and establish the transfer credit contingent upon the student's successful completion of an academic year's work in the new institution. Such a policy avoids both placing the student at a disadvantage and being unduly critical of the nonaccredited institution. Since the regional accrediting associations usually require that at least one class pass through an institution before accreditation will be entertained, it is important not to have a policy on transfer credits from nonaccredited institutions that penalizes newly established institutions which may be of very high quality.

Unusual Ways of Earning Course Credits Since the requirements for earned degrees are commonly stated in terms of credits accumulated by the successful completion of courses, it is common practice to provide such credits by noncourse experiences judged by the faculty to be educational in nature although they do not involve normal class attendance. The faculty should, if it wishes to provide such credits toward graduation, develop explicit policies specifying these experiences and the ways in which they can be validated. Guided by these policy statements, the administrative officers (or perhaps designated members of the faculty) can provide certification of credits toward graduation for these unusual activities. Among these activities is independent study which is validated by an examination or series of examinations. The study may have taken place at another institution, perhaps outside the United States, or it may have taken place in a secondary school—in which case the validating examination is frequently that administered through the Advanced Placement Program of the College Entrance Examination Board. Another experience that some institutions will credit toward an earned degree is gainful employment related in some way to the course of study pursued by the student. In institutions in which a cooperative work-study plan has been highly developed, there may be a policy requiring that a certain number of credits toward graduation be earned through the work experience. In such circumstances, the faculty has really provided for two kinds of credit as requirements for the degree: that earned through the academic program and that earned through the work experience.

Study-abroad Programs A number of American institutions provide special programs outside the United States through which students may study and earn academic credit. When an American institution has established this program it will usually provide credits in terms of its own curriculum, and another institution may evaluate these credits on an ordinary transfer-credit basis. In some cases in which a student has studied on his own in a university outside the United States it may be difficult to meet the usual transfer-credit criteria. But if the faculty has provided for credit by examination (as it may do for other forms of independent study), a reasonable evaluation is possible.

Student and Faculty Work-load Measures American institutions generally award first degrees for the successful completion of a number of credit hours or courses, and even graduate degrees usually require such accumulation of credits in addition to other requirements. The faculty should have specified the degree requirements (see "Course Requirements for Earned Degrees," above), but there are often policy questions regarding the amount of work a student must undertake during any given term to be counted as a full-time student. These questions affect not only the time required for the completion of degree requirements but will in many institutions affect the tuition charge, eligibility for extramural activities, and permission to reside within the institution's housing system. Fixing the amount of credit toward graduation for a course should be a faculty matter; however, the determination of whether or not an individual is to be considered a full-time student should be delegated to the organizational unit directly affected. The central administrative officers will have an important role in policy coordination, to be sure that the policies established by the operational units are reasonably consistent. (Consider the turmoil that would result if all the "full-time" football players required eight years to complete a four-year course of study!)

The measures of student load (in terms of credit hours or courses) are often used also to determine faculty work load. While this is a convenient practice, the policies on faculty work load should recognize that student credit hours are devised primarily to fix the *student's* obligation, and that there should be a well-established conversion formula to translate such measures into measures of *faculty* obligation. In setting the policy on faculty work load, the faculty, administrative officers, and board should collaborate through a mechanism of mutual referral, with final adoption of policy by the board after general agreement has been reached. The adoption of measures and amounts of faculty work load affect not only the educational program (for which the faculty has primary responsibility) but also the financial health of the institution and the work loads of the nonfaculty employees.

FOR FURTHER READING

Information on the academic policies of individual institutions is available directly from the institutions themselves. The pertinent information is to be found in the catalogs (frequently called "bulletins") and in various compilations for internal use (such as faculty handbooks). Catalogs are freely available from individual institutions upon request to the secretary or admissions office. Internal documents like handbooks may not be always available for wide distribution; however, a request to the chief academic officer (dean or vice-president for academic affairs) will provide information about availability.

The following books are standard references on practices and organization in higher education. Each contains much information about academic policies and also extensive references to articles and other books:

Anderson, A.: *Policies and Practices in Higher Education,* Harper and Brothers, New York, 1961.

Corson, John J.: *Governance of Colleges and Universities,* McGraw-Hill Book Company, New York, 1960.

Millett, John D.: *The Academic Community: An Essay on Organization,* McGraw-Hill Book Company, New York, 1962.

Chapter 2

Instruction

WALTER J. KENWORTHY

Dean of the College, Wheaton College, Norton, Massachusetts

ADMINISTRATION OF INSTRUCTION

General Aims and Procedures

Every college administers its educational program to provide the students with high-quality instruction aimed to fulfill its educational purpose. Defining educational purpose is a first step, because any college which has not done so can have no coherent program and its administrative structure will be chaotic. College teachers must communicate to students the basic knowledge, intellectual procedures, and the mechanical skills characteristic of scholarly pursuits. Ideally they are communicated with enthusiasm and clarity by teachers who like to work with students and are enthusiastic about their disciplines. The academic administrator selects teachers who can develop these traits, assists them in their development, and provides these teachers with the physical and service facilities that they need. Administrative officers should be concerned with the quality of each instructor's teaching, should have good information about that quality, and should communicate this to him in a manner which will help him develop well as a teacher.

A faculty member must not be distracted by having to carry out nonprofessional duties. He must be provided with his own office, properly furnished; with secretarial services; and with freedom from all clerical duties.

Classrooms furnished for specialized types of teaching must be available as required, as must all types of audio or visual aids, data processing, computer equipment, and the assistance of people skilled in operating these aids. No support to teaching is more important than the library, and the librarian must be a well-trained individual, sensitive to teaching needs and able to assist faculty members in developing library facilities. Finally, a faculty member needs accurate class lists, a simple method of registering grades, and access to information and advice about students with difficulties.

Roles of Administrators

In this chapter, descriptive phrases rather than titles of administrative officers are used because titles are so varied. (Where there is only one variant, the common title is used.) The most common titles are quoted in parentheses after the descriptive phrase. The phrases used are those found in the *1967–1968 Administrative Compensation Survey* sponsored by the College and University Personnel Association, which, while designed to be a salary study, gives good, concise descriptions of the responsibilities of major officers.

Those Evaluating Teaching The president (chancellor) selects the highest administrative officers and reviews their functions. In small institutions he is the most important officer involved in individual faculty appointments and the granting of tenure. In larger institutions he limits his role to developing the policy governing such appointments. In institutions of all sizes, he reviews all operational policies and corrects operational weaknesses.

The chief academic officer (provost, academic vice-president, dean of the college, dean of faculty) reviews and, in a large institution, approves individual faculty appointments, appoints and supervises the educational administrative officers, reviews and approves administrative policies in all educational areas, and assists department chairmen in evaluating and advising faculty members. He has responsibility for the development of the curriculum and is well informed on faculty and student opinion on educational matters.

The chief advising officer (dean, academic dean, associate or assistant dean of the college) organizes the academic advising system, selects and trains faculty members to carry on the academic advising program, advises those students with special problems, provides faculty members with information about students, and assists the registrar with students who have registration problems. He concerns himself with all the educational problems of individual students and is the officer who implements institutional policy in individual cases.

The department chairman is the most important officer concerned with the administration of instruction. He initiates each search for new faculty members, acts as the major line of communication between the chief academic officer and the members of the department, obtains a departmental evaluation of faculty members being considered for reappointment, evaluates his colleagues and is best informed about their activities, works with the registrar on the classroom needs of the department, has a close relationship with the students majoring in his department, and deals first with teaching problems in his department.

Those Supporting Teaching The registrar (recorder) is the principal record-keeping officer of the institution. He registers students for courses, enforces the academic requirements for degrees, certifies students for academic honors, requests grades from faculty members and records such grades when they are received, notifies the advising office of academic deficiencies, and prepares an agenda listing students who do not meet the standards of the institution for consideration by appropriate officers and committees. He prepares directories and lists of properly registered students, implements and enforces calendar provisions, assigns class hours, classrooms, and final examination schedules, deals with requests for changes in any of these, and inspects and maintains classroom equipment and facilities.

The librarian has an understanding of and sympathy for instructional needs. He must be able to discuss library holdings and facilities with individual faculty members and fix firm priorities relating teaching needs to the budget. Even in a small college it is useful to have a person in charge of audiovisual aid equipment. The supervisor of the audiovisual aid equipment assigns the equipment, arranges for it to be moved as needed, looks after the maintenance of the equipment, and demonstrates its use to the faculty. He relieves faculty members of all responsibility for the equipment except that of describing what they need and specifying when it will be used. The director of computer services schedules the use of the computer facility, sees to its maintenance, and instructs faculty members and students in its use. He assists and advises them on the incorporation of machine data processing and computer use in their teaching.

DEVELOPING AND IMPROVING INSTRUCTION

Information about Instructional Quality

Most administrative officers hear a great deal about the quality of teaching from students, faculty, and other administrative officers. Evaluation of this information appears to be difficult because it consists of subjective statements obtained from very small samples. Opinions about bad teaching are uniform and widespread, and the same is true of opinions about excellent teaching. However, it seems to be more difficult to be well informed about instruction which one would classify as satisfactory or good. Complete objectivity in grading the performance of teachers is not possible, and different groups emphasize different things about a teacher. Faculty colleagues are impressed by scholarly credentials and are the primary source of pressure to distribute punishments or rewards on the basis of scholarly publications. If such an emphasis is contrary to the aims of the institution, administrative officers must stress this contradiction to others and to themselves whenever the performance of a teacher is discussed. Popularity with students may depend upon traits in a teacher which are in conflict with the aims of the institution. A faculty member with high standards, an ability to communicate with others, strong scholarly credentials, and an interest in students and their problems will be a successful and popular teacher. Good teachers are not likely to be unpopular, but some individuals who are not good teachers can be well received by students. Showmanship, friendliness, or exciting political opinions can make an inadequate teacher popular. Students prefer demanding teachers and dislike those who are easy. When students complain that a teacher is too easy, it is an indication of an acute teaching problem.

Advising Officers Faculty advisers are uneven sources of information. They are reluctant to be critical of colleagues except those who are very poor teachers. The chief advising officer is a good source of information obtained from students. He confers with various types of students, not only those who are in academic difficulty. He develops good relationships with many students, and they will speak freely to him. Students who have encountered poor teaching will also come to him for help. His position and interest in the success of the students makes him less reluctant than faculty advisers to pass on what he learns about teaching.

Senior Faculty Members Senior faculty members must be encouraged to participate in the evaluation of their colleagues and provide evaluations of them. It is well to consult all senior faculty members (professors and associate professors) in a department regularly in order to create a tradition that the evaluation of their junior colleagues is one of their duties. The chief academic officer should have periodic group meetings with them to discuss teacher evaluation in general. Specific information and evaluations from senior faculty members should be transmitted through the department chairman. Although it is a sensitive subject with most faculty members, the chairman must establish a policy of visiting classrooms. If such a policy is instituted early, problems are usually minimized. All senior faculty members should be involved in visiting the classes of their junior colleagues. It is better for administrative officers such as the president and chief academic officer to avoid visits to classrooms. They are more likely to be thought of as judges than as—like senior colleagues—sources of constructive criticism.

Student Opinion The chief academic officer must have direct contact with students through a student committee selected to express all the educational concerns of students. Additional information can be obtained from questionnaires distributed to students. These should not originate from administrative officers nor should they be returned directly to administrative officers. The most acceptable kind of questionnaire is one which is designed by students and returned only to the faculty member who is being evaluated. It is of no use to an administrative officer as a source of information, but it allows the students to tell a faculty member what they consider to be the strength and weakness of his teaching. These surveys are useful to new instructors but rarely tell experienced teachers anything they do not know already. Frequently student organizations set up questionnaire systems which they use to compile an annual report on instructors, but such evaluation books rarely are based on good questioning or sampling techniques and are of less use to an administrative officer than his other sources of student opinion.

Curriculum Improvement

Both administrative officers and the faculty share the responsibility for continuous improvement of the curriculum, individual courses, and individual teachers. New ideas for the curriculum come primarily from the faculty. The administrator should press for continuous review of the curriculum and course offerings and encourage those who suggest and develop new ideas.

Radical Curriculum Revision Continuous curriculum review is better for a college than periodic review, and a habit of continuous review must be developed in the faculty. In contrast to continuous small revisions, major reviews held at intervals of several years cause some faculty members to develop defensive attitudes toward the existing curriculum. Moreover, extensive revisions of the curriculum create procedural problems which can be avoided when an evolving curriculum is adopted.

A thorough review may be necessary because the curriculum has not been reviewed continuously, but machinery which will generate continuous review in the future must then be set up. The review should be undertaken by a faculty committee which includes only those administrative officers whose responsibilities require that they participate. In the selection of the committee membership, those who lack interest in the total curriculum or are overly concerned with purely procedural or formal matters should not be included. Specific deadlines should be set for reports, and the areas that the committee is to review should be outlined with precision and clarity. The committee should be urged to study what is being done at other institutions, and the committee's report must contain a device for a continuous review of the curriculum by the faculty in the future.

Continuous Curriculum Revision Continuous curriculum evaluation begins within the departments, and an active department is constantly adding and dropping courses and changing its major requirements to allow for changes in the characteristics of the student body and in the interests of the faculty. Once approved by the department, a curriculum change is reviewed by a faculty committee. The amount of authority entrusted to such committees will vary with the type of college and the attitude of its faculty. It can range from full authority to approve new courses and new degree programs to authority only to make recommendations to the whole faculty. The authority granted is also determined by the size of the agenda at faculty meetings and the faculty's attitude toward the amount of work it does. Sometimes the faculty feels that its committees are too powerful, and at other times it may find that too many small items are coming before the whole faculty. Constant revision of the committee's authority is probably a healthy sign of faculty interest in the curriculum.

A curriculum committee must publicize its agenda well because the primary role of a committee is to explore everything with thoroughness before taking action or making recommendations. All persons who are interested in the question before the committee must be consulted. In its continuous review of the curriculum, a curriculum committee must take note of those departments which rarely change their program or offerings and inquire into the reasons. The committee should also review the validity of all distribution requirements each year. Administrative officers should participate as very active members of a curriculum committee, but they must take care that they are not the sole source of its ideas. Care must also be taken to prevent routine business from occupying the committee to the exclusion of broader questions.

Student participation in curriculum innovation and evaluation is desirable. Such participation can be arranged through student membership on the curriculum committee or through a student committee which considers the curriculum. A combination of both which works well is to have a student academic-affairs committee which considers all things related to the educational program and which designates two of its members to sit on the faculty curriculum committee.

While administrative officers, particularly the president and chief academic officer, originate as few programs as possible, they encourage course program review. They require such review of departments, discuss new ideas sympathetically with faculty members, and talk with committees and individuals constantly about instructional improvements. They also keep the faculty informed about what takes place at other institutions.

Implementing Curriculum Change Once a new program has been developed, it must be implemented as quickly as possible. The disruptive effects of new programs are invariably overestimated, and it is more disruptive to teaching to have two sets of requirements operating simultaneously. The chief academic officer or the officer in charge of advising should circulate information on any curriculum change to the faculty and the student body as quickly as possible. The registrar should revise the registration information and have it approved by the chief academic officer as promptly as possible.

Course Improvement

As with curriculum revision, course improvement is the responsibility of the individual faculty member, the department, and a faculty committee. Where the revision involves a single course, the committee's role is primarily one of reviewing and maintaining standards. The committee is not qualified to devise new courses which are needed. Its review causes an instructor to consider his course carefully, organize his course fully, and deal with the weak points in his program.

By continuous discussion, the chief academic officer ensures that individual faculty members evaluate the content of their courses continuously, change their offerings to alternate years when they are not heavily enrolled, and drop courses which are no longer of interest to the students. He does these things by checking enrollments, making suggestions to individual faculty members, and praising those who do evaluate their courses, particularly those who admit readily that certain programs are not working and should be abandoned. He watches for redundancy in the course offerings and calls it to the attention of the curriculum committee when he finds it.

The chief academic officer plays both positive and negative roles in course improvement. He implements the curriculum committee's actions by insisting that every course stay within the limits approved by the committee, and he requires an instructor to bring his course back to the committee for review if it differs significantly from what has been approved. He shows interest in the content of all courses and encourages instructors to review them by being an interested listener and making concrete, constructive suggestions whenever an instructor wants to review the nature of his course.

Colleagues also aid course improvement by encouraging the discussion of courses. Departments should be expected to hold regular meetings for the review and evaluation of their course offerings.

The Development of Teaching

Faculty Selection and Review The most important decision influencing the quality of instruction is the selection of teachers. Colleges appoint their teachers for one-, two-, or three-year periods until six or seven years have elapsed. If retained beyond that time, the instructor is given a permanent appointment in accordance with the practice recommended by the American Association of University Professors (see *Bulletin of the AAUP*, vol. 27, pp. 40–46, February, 1941; and vol. 49, p. 373, December, 1963). Every teacher is evaluated several times before he receives a permanent appointment.

Every new faculty appointment should be made with the assumption that it is a permanent appointment. No administrator can project faculty needs six years into the future. A calculated system of long-term rotating appointments generates morale problems and reduces the quality of the people appointed. Those appointed to substitute for sabbatical years are the only proper exceptions, and it is undesirable to retain them beyond one year. Tenure decisions must be made forcibly and objectively, comparing the individual to those available outside the institution for the same appointments. Although all appointments are made with the hope that the individual will qualify for tenure, some will not fulfill this promise. Decisions on the retention of faculty members should be made as early as possible. Unsatisfactory teachers or scholars will demonstrate their deficiencies by the end of their second year and should be informed of a negative decision at that time. Postponing the decision prevents the person to be dropped from finding a permanent place for himself in another institution while he is still young.

A faculty member whose appointment term is ending should be evaluated in the fall prior to reappointment. The department chairman should consult all the tenured members of the individual's department and present the departmental evaluation to the chief academic officer. This statement should express any divergence of opinion among the members of the department. It can be made verbally or in writing and may be added to the faculty member's personnel file. When all departmental evaluations of faculty to be reappointed have been received, the chief academic officer organizes them into a set of recommendations for the next year and presents them to the president, who decides which individuals are to be reappointed. Those who are not reappointed should be notified in December of their last year. Anyone who is not to receive a permanent appointment when due should be notified in September of his last year.

Teaching Improvement Faculty members must be encouraged to have frequent meetings with their students and have frank discussions of their courses. They can do this by talking with students after class, holding departmental teas for students, and encouraging students to invite faculty members to lunch and dinner. If a friendly atmosphere is created, many teaching problems will be overcome by the faculty member who receives advice directly from his students.

The department chairman should know more than anyone about the teaching skills of every faculty member. He talks with students when he advises them on their course programs, and he must be sensitive to the signs which indicate teaching problems within his department.

Direct action by the chief academic officer to improve teaching is confined to problem cases. These frequently reach the point where they must be resolved by dropping the teacher in question from the faculty, although in a few cases the chief academic officer may be able to assist a teacher where a senior colleague has failed. The chief academic officer can be more helpful by stating general principles to groups, and he should conduct a series of group meetings for new faculty members at the beginning of the year to orient them to the operation of the college and, with the help of some senior colleagues, to suggest teaching techniques which might be helpful.

THE SUPPORT OF INSTRUCTION

Good college teaching must be supported by many services such as the academic counseling program, the staff which provides equipment and services needed for the classroom, the evaluation and reward system for the academic progress of the student, and the system of instructional record keeping.

Academic Counseling

Who is to be counseled, who is to do the counseling, and what types of counseling are to be provided will differ in every institution; and a college decides these questions in accordance with its institutional aims and objectives. One type of college will provide only instruction in the scholarly disciplines and take no responsibility for assisting students with their academic or personal problems while another will assist students with all types of problems. The former college offers its students few services beyond advising them in course selection and warning them of their academic failures, while the latter provides services such as psychiatric counseling and remedial reading programs.

The basic advising system teaches beginning students the mechanics of course selection, explains the nature of the educational program, and helps them determine which courses are relevant to their interests. Advanced students are shown the mechanics of selecting a concentration program, are advised on which concentration program fits their interests, have interdepartmental programs explained to them, and have the opportunity to discuss independent research and off-campus programs with an adviser. The transfer student is a special type of advanced student who must be shown the mechanics of registration at his new institution and must receive full advising as to the selection of a concentration program. Preprofessional students have specialized needs in addition to the selection of programs which meets the degree requirements. Remedial features of advising deal with problems connected with the student's ability to organize his work, study skills in which he is deficient, emotional problems which interfere with his college work, and academic disciplinary problems.

Advising of New Students The advising of new students begins before they reach the campus. Materials should be sent to them during the summer and they should select a preliminary course program and return it before fall registration. They do not have an opportunity to see an adviser and this selection is not binding, but it does force them to review the program and requirements. This preliminary selection is used by the adviser as a basis for discussion when he sees the student. The advisers should not make choices for the students but should discuss the choices that the students have already made.

Most colleges have the faculty advise beginning students, and few are satisfied with the results. In the usual program, each available faculty member is assigned approximately ten freshmen students and advises them during their freshman and sophomore years. Two or three briefing meetings are conducted for the advisers by the chief advising officer to explain registration and the curriculum. Despite these efforts, students complain that advisers do not know the curriculum and advisers complain that they serve no function other than that of a clerk who signs cards.

Advising by a full-time staff is an alternative to using members of the faculty. It has the advantage of using individuals who like the work and are familiar with the curriculum, but its disadvantages are its expense and the fact that it cuts off contact with the faculty. Another possibility is an intermediate arrangement in which faculty members who have shown themselves to be particularly interested and skilled in this work are selected for a two-year term and are compensated by relief from some of their teaching assignments. In both of these last two systems, the individual counsels a fairly large number of students.

When the curriculum is rigidly prescribed, each counselor is able to advise 20 new students each year. At course selection time each student should be encouraged to arrange his own program as far as possible. His contact with his adviser can be limited to group discussion sessions unless the student specifically requests an individual appointment. In a curriculum which allows a fairly free selection of courses, the adviser must have an extended conference with each student. The student should be encouraged to draw up his own program as a basis for this discussion, but each student will require an appointment before registering. In a rigidly defined curriculum, advisers to sophomores will devote relatively little time to each student. However, a freely elected sophomore curriculum will involve extended individual appointments and discussions. A free curriculum requires a large number of thoroughly briefed advisers. Briefing of advisers should be done by the chief advising officer and his full-time staff. Briefing of advisers at registration time must include a description of general curriculum, a list of those courses which are not open to everyone together with the reasons for their restriction, and a list of those courses which are to be preferred by certain categories of students.

The advising of new students should be limited to a single day and, if possible, confined to a single classroom building. The chief advising officer and his staff should be on hand to assist advisers. All parts of the procedure of registration should be set up in the same place so as to make it unnecessary for students to travel around the campus in search of people.

Transfer students need special assistance because they are unaccustomed to the procedures of their new college. Their advising falls heavily on the department chairmen or their representatives. The staff of the chief advising officer should assist with the general problems of transfer students and should see them first. They should be briefed as a group on general registration procedures, after which they will have individual appointments with departmental representatives to plan their major programs. As with freshmen, transfer students should be asked to make course selections during the summer to make them familiar with the course offerings and requirements.

Preprofessional Advising Prelaw, premedical, and predental students, students preparing for elementary and secondary school teaching, and students oriented toward graduate schools all must meet certain special requirements in addition to the regular degree requirements. Students who are entering a specialized undergraduate professional program such as engineering, business administration, or nursing will have many requirements specified by the curriculum and should be advised by faculty members who teach in their program and understand their curriculum.

Prelaw students will usually find that normal distribution and concentration requirements fulfill the admission requirements of law schools. Unlike medical schools, law schools generally do not require that specific courses be part of an applicant's undergraduate program. However, courses in history, government, English composition, mathematics, philosophy, a modern language, science, and art or music are recommended for applicants by most law schools. In addition, the student must take the law school aptitude test and must apply to take this test at a proper testing date. A faculty member or member of the advising staff should be designated as the prelaw adviser. He can be well versed in the admission requirements of individual law schools, can maintain a list of prelaw students for advising purposes, and can notify all students of the aptitude test dates and application dates.

Admission requirements of medical schools are highly varied. The basic requirements common to all schools are the completion as an undergraduate of a year of English, including composition and literature; a year of mathematics; a year of physics; two years of chemistry (including organic chemistry); a year of biology (dealing with both plants and animals); and a year of a modern foreign language. Many medical schools require some courses in addition to this basic list. It is best to designate several members of the faculty or advising staff, preferably from the science departments, as premedical advisers. Students will require advice on which medical school to select, which school is most likely to accept them, how to apply, and when and under what circumstances they must take the medical aptitude test. Premedical advising should begin when students enter as freshmen. The academic advising office must compile a list of premedical students as early as possible and revise this list as students change their objectives. Medical school applications must be submitted during the student's junior year, and he must obtain his faculty recommendations at that time. Although some medical schools will urge that a committee evaluate all premedical students and submit one composite recommendation for each student, all schools will accept individual recommendations from faculty members. Requirements for individual medical colleges may be found in the *Guide to American Medical Colleges* published annually by the Association of American Medical Schools.

The basic courses required for dental school admission are the same as those required by medical schools but, again, individual schools have additional requirements. Since the needs of premedical and predental students are very similar, the same individuals may be designated to advise both groups of students.

Graduate school admission is determined largely by the individual graduate school departments, and advice for graduate school admission should come from someone in the student's major department. Advising on a concentration program can be combined readily with advising students about graduate work, and this is recommended. Books which students and advisers will find useful in selecting graduate schools are *An Assessment of Quality in Graduate Education* and *Graduate Degree Programs.* These may be purchased from the American Council on Education, 1 Dupont Circle, N.W., Washington, D.C. 20036.

Students planning to enter careers in elementary or secondary school teaching will find it necessary to meet state requirements in education. Most colleges have a department of education responsible for teaching those courses which meet the requirements. The members of the education department are best qualified to discuss the state requirements with the students, and a member of the department should be designated as the adviser to students who plan to teach at the elementary or secondary level.

Special Problem Advising Students rarely request academic career counseling. In most cases, those careers which require specialized training are open only to those who hold degrees from specialized undergraduate schools, and career advising is a part of the general advising program. Placement officers can provide literature listing career opportunities for people who have had certain types of training and listing the requirements for certain types of employment. Placement officers must be discouraged from undertaking course advising because few are qualified to advise on academic programs.

Helping the student with his academic problems is a major aspect of advising. These will arise from poor work habits, skill deficiencies, emotional problems, and problems of discipline. Most academic problems result from the students' inability to organize materials and define priorities. College work comes as a shock to some students because their high school experience has been carefully supervised. In secondary school they received short-term assignments, were closely supervised, and were surrounded by less able fellow students. They are shocked to find themselves with long-term assignments, disinterest on the part of the instructor as to whether or not they complete their work, and a student peer group which consists entirely of able individuals. Typically the student who has trouble initially can be helped sufficiently by an adviser who tells him how to organize material, clarifies the nature of his problems to him, and listens sympathetically. In dealing with such difficulties, the adviser should discuss the student's work with him course by course, pointing out that his failure has been mostly a failure to schedule his time and organize his work. The adviser can give him a few hints about how to determine priorities, extract material effectively from books, and take good notes in class. If the student has few skills in these directions and needs additional help, student tutors are effective. The advising office should keep a list of suitable tutors who have been recommended by departments. Although it is useful for the advising office to suggest a standard tutorial fee, financial and other arrangements should be left entirely to the tutor and the student who needs assistance. Faculty members and students who work as teaching assistants should not be permitted to tutor students.

Reading deficiencies require specialized assistance. Except with students who have been accepted as a part of a program designed to remedy such deficiencies, these will be rare among students accepted by highly selective colleges. Specialists, who may be part-time, will be needed if the college is to undertake remedies in this area. The specialist should be part of the staff of the academic advising officer, and those who do the advising should identify individuals with reading problems and assign them to the specialist for assistance.

Language aphasia is a rare disorder which makes it impossible for a student to learn a foreign language. A student afflicted with it can perform well otherwise and may have no difficulty in entering college. It can be diagnosed by proper psychological testing but cannot be eliminated. The college must either grant the student an exception to the foreign-language requirements or refuse to grant him a degree. The academic advising officer should make faculty members aware of the existence and nature of aphasia before any decision is made. He should also know enough about this disorder to be able to recognize the possibility of its existence.

Large numbers of students have to be counseled because they think that they lack mathematical aptitude. This is rarely true in a selective college. Students having difficulty with mathematics courses should be treated with firmness and encouragement by both their instructors and advisers. Part of the problem may be poor teaching. Younger mathematics instructors may preserve the integrity of their mathematical explanations by presenting them at a level which is understandable only to a student of unusually high mathematical aptitude. A large number of failures in a class may be an indication of such instructional problems, and the chief academic officer should discuss these problems with the instructor. A mathematics department must have an unusually good chairman who can explain to young mathematicians how elementary mathematical concepts can be taught with sufficient integrity to those who are not mathematicians and still be understood.

Problems with writing almost always have to do with style. Students make few grammatical errors or errors in punctuation. When unsatisfactory, their work tends to be disorganized, verbose, and laden with clichés. Most students were once thought to need remedial work in writing, but the emphasis has changed and colleges today no longer require that large numbers of students study composition. The advising program must be organized to identify those whose tests or classroom writing show that they need more work. If the lack of writing skill is a problem of only a minority of the students at a given college, the solution may lie in having a specialized staff teach this skill on a noncredit basis. Many English literature scholars prefer not to teach writing skills to students.

In highly selective colleges, most course failures are due to emotional difficulties. Frequently the student's emotional confusion arises from ambivalent feelings about being in college. Most students can resolve their problems during a period of self-evaluation and discussions with the help of their advisers. When such problems are acute, serious academic failure results and it is best to drop the student from college. The committee which reviews academic failure should try to evaluate the student in terms of whether he will continue to fail. If, in their opinion, this is the case, he should be dropped from college and urged to work for a year. Most students who have been dropped in this manner can return to college after a year away and perform well. When parents consult the advising office staff, the staff should suggest that the problem be left to the student. Parental pressure on the student to return to school too early or to enter another college is likely to intensify his emotional problems.

Students with serious emotional disorders should be referred to a consulting psychiatrist retained by the college. He can decide whether or not the disorder will interfere with the student's academic performance. Psychiatrists privately retained by the student or his parents will frequently appeal to the college to allow the student to stay in order to remove him from his home environment. Retaining a student for this reason rarely serves the best interests of the student and is disruptive to other students.

Problems involving intellectual honesty are infrequent but continuous and are dealt with by the academic advising office. The college must have clearly defined standards of honesty in written work and these should be stated to new students in writing before they register. The students should subscribe to these by signing a statement. Faculty members should not dispose of cases of suspected dishonesty but should be required to turn such cases over to the chief advising officer. The determination of whether or not dishonesty has occurred and of the extent of the dishonesty should be made by a joint faculty-student board of which the chief advising officer is a member. The board should receive written evidence from the instructor and an oral statement from the student. The board's procedures must be stated clearly in printed material circulated to all students. These procedures must be designed to protect a student's rights following the 1967 recommendations of the American Association of University Professors (see *Bulletin of the AAUP*, vol. 53, pp. 365–368). However it is important for the board to avoid pseudolegal procedures which magnify the issue and add nothing to protect the student. While he should receive the best possible advice from people he chooses, the student should be his own advocate. Documentary evidence should be used as much as possible, and the student should be given ample opportunity to question the validity of such evidence. No one should play the role of prosecutor, and decisions should be made on the basis of documents and the student's statements. Since dishonesty undermines the basis of the evaluation system, the appropriate penalties are either failure for the piece of work involved, failure in the course, or dismissal from the college, depending upon the extent of the dishonesty. The decision as to which penalty should be imposed should be left to the board, but it is necessary to have every board decision reviewed by the president or the chief academic officer for procedural errors or inconsistent penalties.

Poor class attendance and misbehavior in class are the other disciplinary problems in the educational area. The faculty member should deal with classroom behavior himself, but he should be assured of full administrative support and action when necessary. As more institutions liberalize their attendance rules, failure to attend class becomes less a disciplinary problem than a faculty morale problem. Poor attendance may result from either a teaching failure or from the personal problems of the student. Most students who are performing poorly will be found to have poor attendance records. The rarer case in which a student with poor class attendance is performing well indicates poor instruction. Faculty members whose courses are characterized by poor attendance should be counseled by the chief academic officer and urged to discuss classroom problems with their students. At colleges where attendance is required, daily reports of absence should be sent to the registrar. The registrar should notify the chief advising officer when a student is absent beyond the acceptable limit, and the latter officer should deal with the case. Nothing should be required of the faculty member involved beyond sending the absence report to the registrar.

Equipment and Services

Many materials and services are needed to assist classroom instruction. In the use of such classroom aids the instructional staff must determine needs and priorities, analyze the effectiveness of supporting materials and services, and make the policy decisions concerning them.

The assignment and equipping of classrooms are among the registrar's functions. He will know which rooms are furnished for certain specific uses and which are equipped with projection facilities and other special equipment. He has responsibility for selecting the initial furniture for the rooms, for the maintenance of the rooms and their furniture, and for administering the maintenance budget for classrooms. Requests for rooms equipped in special ways are made by department chairmen and assigned by the registrar.

While library operation is a specialized activity requiring a considerable amount of special training, the library exists to support classroom work and policies with respect to its functions should be made by those who teach. A library committee of the faculty should review and make library policy. To give them a close relationship to the teaching operation, the librarian and his staff must be assigned to the educational division of the administration. The librarian is responsible for maintaining the integrity of the library budget, but he is dependent upon the faculty for recommending purchases and should consult the library committee to determine the relative size of allocations to different disciplines. The librarian should report to the faculty which collections have been neglected and which are reasonably complete. The department chairman, after consulting his department, should recommend the library materials that are needed for his discipline. The librarian must advise the chairman and exercise control over the recommended purchases to avoid purchasing materials in the wrong form or acquiring large numbers of duplicate copies. The librarian must encourage all departments to develop balanced collections in their areas and to avoid patternless purchasing. Even in a small college, faculty members must be encouraged, both by the librarian and by the chief academic officer, to see that the library collections are useful for faculty research as well as classroom use.

Individuals or individual departments should not be permitted to purchase audiovisual equipment specifically for the use of one teacher or one department. All equipment should be supervised by a single individual who acts as stockroom clerk and maintenance manager and instructs people in its use. Coordination of use and maintenance of the equipment eliminates costly duplication and prevents highly paid faculty members from concerning themselves with maintenance problems. All types of cameras, projectors, tapes and recorders, and television equipment should be administered in this way. The equipment should be set up to make movement from room to room easy. A faculty member should only have to telephone and specify his needs in order to have the equipment set up for him. The audiovisual-aids coordinator should provide trained operators, preferably students, who can operate the equipment in any manner required by the faculty member. Certain rooms should be permanently equipped with audiovisual aids and should be assigned by the registrar on the basis of heavy use of the equipment, but such permanently located equipment should also be the responsibility of the audiovisual-aids coordinator.

A language laboratory requires that a technician be on hand to assist in its operation during all class hours. This should not be part of the regular audiovisual-aids coordinator's area except where the two responsibilities may be combined in a small institution. All purchases, maintenance, and procedural instructions for the use of the language laboratory should be the responsibility of the language laboratory coordinator. However, policy decisions about the use of the language laboratories must not be left to the supervisor. Either the supervisor or the chief academic officer should work with a policy-determining committee chosen from the language departments.

The computer facility on campus, whether it is a remote terminal connected to an off-campus computer or a complete computer facility, requires supervision by a single individual who is well trained in computer use. He must be responsible for the purchase of equipment, the maintenance of the equipment, and for instructing others in its use. Initially a faculty member may be supervisor of the computer services on a part-time basis, but the use of the facility is likely to become heavy in a short time and a full-time person, with faculty rank and qualifications, will be needed.

Scientific equipment must be supervised by the individual science departments. The department chairman or secretary should process the purchase of the equipment and see to its maintenance. Procurement of the equipment should be subject to review by the college purchasing agent to be certain that the vendor chosen will give the college the best possible financial arrangement. The purchasing agent should work carefully with the departments, acting as an adviser, and he should avoid arbitrarily changing the vendor recommended by the department. The same principles should be applied to maintenance and maintenance contracts. Some scientific equipment which cannot be purchased must be constructed at the college, and other equipment is more easily maintained there. A well-equipped workshop which is shared by all the science departments is necessary for simple machine, carpentry, and electronics work. It should be under the direction of a well-qualified electronics maintenance man who is able to do general carpentry and metal work. Faculty members must be permitted to use shop equipment, but the shop supervisor should be responsible for maintenance, replacement, and the scheduling and supervision of the use of the equipment. Except in very large institutions, a separate stockroom for each science department is undesirable. A stockroom clerk should do all ordering and issuing of scientific equipment and supplies. A single stockroom makes deliveries easy, allows bulk buying, and permits a large inventory of commonly used items to be maintained. One aim of stockroom operation is to have all standard items available to professors when needed. No professor should have to plan his use of standard types of laboratory glassware, chemicals, or electrical equipment far in advance.

Most institutions will have galleries, special practice rooms, and staging facilities available for artistic use. It may be desirable to employ specialized individuals such as gallery directors to supervise and operate these facilities. Directors of these facilities should report to the chairman of the department concerned, and that department should determine the policies which affect these facilities.

Many colleges find it desirable to allow their students to undertake part of their study away from the campus. Special administrative arrangements are needed for special courses given jointly with other institutions, facilities shared by several colleges and universities, students working in museums or government agencies, and students engaged in field work. Only the more common types of study away from the campus are discussed because such facilities are so diverse that the administration of their programs cannot be briefly described. Permitting students to take courses for credit at neighboring institutions is a common practice. A simple agreement may be drawn up among the institutions concerned and students may then make arrangements for courses at any of the cooperating institutions through their own registrars. Programs of study abroad, particularly junior-year-abroad programs, are very popular. It is not necessary for a college to sponsor its own program because arrangements can be made for students to participate in other colleges' programs. A list of current programs with full descriptions may be found in *Undergraduate Study Abroad,* published by the Institute for International Education, 809 United Nations Plaza, New York, N.Y. 10017.

Facilities shared by several institutions, such as computer centers, urban studies institutes, or astronomical observatories, require directors to supervise them. The director reports to a committee composed of representatives of the member institutions who set policy and review operations.

Many major museums and laboratories now appoint undergraduate students for summer work. One officer should be designated at the college to obtain publications and information and be well informed about such opportunities. He should send regular notices to the department chairmen describing such opportunities. It is the department chairman's responsibility to call them to the attention of students.

Field trips to such places as mental hospitals, museums, or interesting geological or biological localities are a part of effective instruction. The institution should provide all the necessities for such trips. The department chairman must request funds in his budget for the number of trips expected. It is best to use rented or college-owned transportation rather than private automobiles for field trips because the liability incurred by the institution when private cars are used more than outweighs any saving in cost which results.

It is desirable to obtain a general agreement which permits reciprocal library use by students in a given area. Librarians are increasingly restricting the use of college libraries and the chief educational officer must discourage restrictiveness and take measures to provide enough space for all individuals who need to use the library.

Evaluating and Rewarding Academic Progress

Grading systems are designed to provide incentive, reward achievement, and assist in identifying students with problems. Various types of grading, reward, and warning systems are available. All combine grading, reward, and warning together, although different systems differ in the aspects they emphasize.

Nongraded Systems Systems which replace grades with written evaluations are used successfully in several colleges. At specified times, the instructor submits a written evaluation of a specified maximum length of each student's progress. When this system is used, evaluations by each instructor should be required twice a term; once after approximately six weeks and again at the end of the semester, quarter, or trimester. The evaluation should be written out on a form provided by the registrar. This form should have complete instructions at the top of the page, specifying to the instructor what characteristics of the student are to be evaluated. Comments should be requested on the student's writing ability, the quality of his class participation, his ability to comprehend the subject matter, and his problems. For laboratory courses, each college must determine whether or not separate laboratory and recitation evaluations will be more useful in the files than single course evaluations. The written evaluation system's principal disadvantages are mechanical. Each student's record becomes a large notebook which must be consulted every time the student is counseled or recommended. A brief evaluation of the contents of this notebook must be produced for graduate schools and employers. The usual method is to have this brief evaluation made by a committee of faculty and administrative officers at the time of graduation or earlier if required, and this is a time-consuming and expensive process.

Confidential Grading This may be used separately or in combination with the written evaluation system. Under this system, grades are recorded for purposes of outside evaluation but are not available to the student or faculty. Grades are submitted by the faculty for every student, just as in the grading systems described below, and recorded by the registrar on a regular transcript. This may be sent to persons outside the institution but is never used for any purpose within the institution.

Evaluation by Special Examination In a system which evaluates the student's performance entirely by examination, teaching is separated from evaluation. It is usual to apply such a system to only a part of the student body, particularly to those who are pursuing honors programs, and to limit it to upperclass students. Freshmen and sophomores, therefore, are graded in the usual manner, and those who perform at a certain level are permitted to elect a program leading to an honors degree. Students who elect honors are not graded during their junior and senior years, and the level of honors awarded is based upon an examination or series of examinations which may be oral, written, or both. The examinations may be given by a faculty committee with members drawn from the whole faculty or solely from the student's major department. Frequently examiners are obtained from outside the college. An examination type of evaluation system need not be restricted to upperclass or honors students. The student can be examined at the end of the freshman and sophomore years as well as at the end of senior year, or he may be examined more frequently; but a high frequency of examinations will probably preclude the use of outside examiners. When outside examiners are used, the system operates best when relatively few levels of grades (such as honors, pass, and fail) are used. It is difficult for an outside examiner, whose time is limited, to distinguish many levels of performance. While this system deemphasizes grading during the semester, it has the disadvantage of overemphasizing the examination.

Grading, Honors, and Probation Systems

Two- and Three-level Systems Any of the above systems may be combined with a standard grading system. Standard grading can be used for the early years, with a written evaluation, confidential grading, or examination system being used during the upperclass years. The simplest grading system is one which merely indicates whether or not the student has achieved a satisfactory level of performance by marking the student pass or fail. This system may be extended to three levels, designating also those students who have distinguished themselves academically as honor students. Pass-fail grading or the three-level system of honors, pass, and fail are commonly combined with a multilevel grading system. There are two common practices. In the systems most commonly used in undergraduate colleges, an advanced student will be graded only pass or fail in courses outside his area of concentration. In the other system, the instructor determines whether or not his course is to be graded according to a multilevel system or on a pass and fail basis, and once he has adopted it, pass-fail grading applies to all students in the course. This system is common in graduate school. Graduate schools, professional schools, and others requiring grade records of the students for admission purposes have shown themselves to be receptive to any type of grading system provided an explanatory note is enclosed with each transcript. Consequently, the needs of other institutions should not be considered in deciding which grading or reward system is to be adopted.

Letter Grading A system of letter grades, A through E, is the type most frequently used. Its popularity probably results from its rough correspondence to the number of subjective categories which psychological studies have shown an individual to be capable of distinguishing. When this system is used, definitions for each letter grade should be written for the catalog and for enclosure with each transcript. These may be the short descriptive phrases such as "A = excellent, B = good, C = satisfactory, D = passing (but unsatisfactory), E = failing," or they may be much longer phrases. The set of definitions to be used should be approved by the faculty. The two most common variations of the letter grade system are the inclusion of two levels of failure, represented by E and F, and the use of + and −. In one use of E and F levels, E permits the student to take a reexamination which may change his grade to D, while F indicates a failure without the privilege of reexamination. Another system uses E to designate a level of failure which permits a student in a year-long course to continue in the course at the end of one term while F is used to designate those failing students who are required to drop out of the course at the end of one term.

In the other common variation of the letter grading system, recording + and − produces a 13-level grading system (+ and − are rarely used for the failing level). This system often proves to be unsatisfactory in practice because the faculty use only six levels with any frequency and these letter grades will not conform to those used by other colleges. When the recording of + and − is the practice at a college, the grading patterns should be reviewed annually to see if very few As or Ds are awarded (B+ and C− tend to take on the roles of A and D).

Numerical Grading A few colleges use numerical grading systems based upon 100. These suggest a precision which does not exist because neither the faculty member nor his examinations are able to distinguish the 100 categories specified. In practice, this lack of precision is understood by those who use the grades and they tend to group the students into categories of tens.

The grading systems selected should be designed solely to support the needs of the educational programs, and decisions about grading systems must never be based upon what is required of the system by those outside the college. For the benefit of those outside, the system should be clear and not lend itself to misinterpretation. This clarity will be enhanced if a statement of the percentage of grades awarded at each level is enclosed with each transcript.

There are many types of awards which recognize high overall performance. The educational aim of these honors should be determined by considerations similar to those used to select a grading system. Relatively few types of honors awarded at relatively few levels will deemphasize rewards, while large numbers of honors in which there are many categories of awards will emphasize the necessity for rewards. The former system is suitable for a highly motivated student body, while the latter may be useful for the opposite type.

Short-term Honors There are honors of two sorts given on the basis of short-term performance. One is inclusion of the student's name on the Dean's List at the end of a semester upon attainment of a specified grade average. A Dean's List student receives a letter from the chief academic officer, his attainment is noted on his record by the registrar, and his name is posted on a list released to the campus newspaper and sent to the student's hometown newspaper. Special prizes for excellence in specific areas —based upon high performance in particular courses, on special examinations, or on the writing of special papers—are customary at many colleges. Recognition for these awards is usually given at a college assembly by the award of a book or certificate.

Graduation Honors Two types of awards based upon the student's entire performance customarily are made at graduation. Degrees granted with distinction (sometimes called "Latin honors"), cum laude, magna cum laude, and summa cum laude, are based primarily on the student's grade average. Degrees with honors are granted for extra work at the honors level, most often in the student's concentration area. Most colleges grant both distinction and honors. Degrees with honors should be granted only if the student attains a minimum grade level, but the award emphasizes attainments other than grades: usually performance within the student's major department and performance on an individual research project. An honors examination which emphasizes the student's research project or other extra work is also required. When possible, special courses or a special section of a regular course should be set up for students who are likely to receive honors. Some colleges provide honors students with special types of teaching throughout their junior and senior years. Three levels of honors, designated as "Honors," "High Honors," and "Highest Honors," are usual. Both Latin distinctions and honors are recorded on the student's official transcript and diploma.

Honor Societies Election to national honor societies is another form of recognition extended to students for outstanding academic achievement. Some of the organizations, such as the well-known Phi Beta Kappa, elect students majoring in any of the traditional liberal arts disciplines. Others, such as The Society of the Sigma Xi, restrict their membership to a general area such as science. The largest number are more narrowly professional and limit election to those who major in specific disciplines. Election of a student to one of these societies is the prerogative of the local campus chapter, which consists of the faculty members and students previously elected. New members elected by campus chapters must meet certain qualifications set by the national organization, but chapters are free to elect or not to elect anyone who meets these qualifications. College officers have no control over the elections and other activities of these organizations beyond that exercised over campus organizations generally. New chapters are organized by consultation between the college and the national office of the honor society. After the college meets the qualifications set by the national office, the chapter is installed. National honor societies are too numerous to list in a handbook of this type, but a list which includes addresses of the national offices may be found in the *World Almanac* (pages 341–343 of the 1970 edition).

Probation and Warning The faculty usually designates a grade average which a student must achieve for graduation, and those students who do not have that average in a given year are not in good academic standing. Students not in good standing are either dismissed for academic failure, placed on academic probation, warned, or refused registration unless a specific requirement is completed.

A student is dismissed when it is evident that he is wasting his time and money by remaining in college. Students in selective colleges fail most often because of emotional difficulties rather than because they lack ability. Dismissal helps a student face his difficulties and resolve them, and every student dismissed should have the right to be considered for readmission at a later time. Readmission should be determined by whether or not a student has resolved his problems.

Students who perform below the level required for graduation but are not dismissed are placed on academic probation. This may carry with it educational and social restrictions such as mandatory attendance in class or the requirement of special permission to leave the campus. Many colleges, however, no longer attach penalties to academic probation.

Warning is given to those who meet graduation standards but show other signs of unsatisfactory performance. In such a case, a warning letter is sent to the student and his parents stating his academic difficulty. Registration is refused to students whose difficulties arise from a single problem. The student is not permitted to reregister until he has resolved the problem. He may be required to change his major area of study, transfer to a different program, or complete a certain requirement in a summer session or by examination before the next academic year. These restrictions are most useful for those students who want to concentrate in a field in which they are not qualified or who have difficulty with a distribution requirement and procrastinate in meeting it.

Recommendations for the dismissal of students, placing them on academic probation, giving them warning, and refusing registration to them should be made by the chief academic officer and the chief advising officer within general policy guidelines and confirmed by a faculty committee. The review procedure begins when the registrar prepares the list of those not meeting requirements. This list is sent to the chief advising officer, who recommends the actions he considers to be appropriate for each student. These recommendations are then reviewed by the chief academic officer and presented to the proper faculty committee.

Administration of the Grading System The registrar is in charge of student records and he should assemble, store, and disseminate all grading information. The chief academic officer and the chief advising officer work closely with the registrar, but they must not duplicate any of his services. The registrar should send an accurate class list for each course to each instructor at the end of each grading period. This list may be on cards, but a printed list is more convenient for the instructor. Such a list can be produced easily by standard punch-card data processing equipment. The instructor records the grades on the list and returns it promptly to the registrar. It is best to fix a limit of two days after the examination of a course for grades in that course to be returned. The chief academic officer should assist the registrar by calling those members of the faculty whose grade sheets are late.

In determining procedures for the dissemination of grading information, the registrar should consult the chief academic officer and the chief advising officer. Grade records must go promptly to the students, and it is recommended that the registrar use punch-card data processing methods which can prepare completely addressed grade summaries for the students. A college without machine data processing can use cards with built-in carbon copies for the recording of grades by the instructor. When these have been returned to the registrar, the original is kept for the registrar's record and the carbon copy sent to the student immediately, thereby providing prompt notification.

The registrar must also be prompt in providing the chief academic officer and the advising officer with grade averages for the distribution of awards and for the identification of students not in good academic standing. Grade averaging must be done quickly, and it can be done most rapidly and least expensively by a computer. Registrars should compare the cost of having grade averages calculated on a commercial computer with that of having it done by hand. The form in which the grade averages are listed should be determined by the chief academic officer and the chief advising officer in consultation with the registrar.

Other Instructional Records Instructional records which are required by a college are grades, attendance records, records of honors and prizes, records of place in class and grade average, records of probation, dismissal, and disciplining, records of conferences and discussions of academic difficulties, records of a student's status with respect to completing degree requirements, class lists, grade lists, room use lists, and correspondence concerning students and their academic status. The registrar is the scheduling and record-keeping officer who maintains most of these records. He assembles, records, files, and distributes grades, attendance records, honors and prizes, grade averages and placement in class, notations of probation, dismissal, and discipline, degree-requirement status reports, class lists, grade lists, room use lists, and faculty teaching loads. In addition, he sends official certification of the degree status and good standing of students to government agencies and others requesting them. His procedures are circumscribed by rules laid down by the faculty and administrative principles laid down by the chief academic officer. It is his responsibility to devise the administrative system by which all of these records are obtained, stored with maximum safety, and disseminated to those who need them, and decisions as to the manner in which these three functions are to be carried out are entirely his. His records must be useful to others and their form should be reviewed by the chief academic officer. Data provided by the registrar must be presented in the form needed by those who use them and must never have to be rearranged or reworked by another office.

The chief advising officer keeps records of discussions of probation, dismissal, and discipline; conferences with students; discussions of their academic difficulties; and correspondence concerning students. The admission office should set up a file folder of admission credentials for each student. When the student is admitted, this folder should be transferred to the advising office. The admission office records will include applications, correspondence, transcripts, and letters of recommendation concerning the student's admission. All correspondence with or about the student and notes of each conference with the student are added to this folder. Notes made by the advising office on student conferences should be limited to the topics discussed and the options offered to the student. Advising officers must avoid the temptation to write out evaluations of the student after conferences. Those who read such evaluations take them seriously and even a one-hour appointment is insufficient for a worthwhile judgment of the student. At graduation, this folder is removed from the advising office and placed in a permanent file.

Other officers will find it necessary to keep records of students, but these officers are not likely to be involved in instruction. Medical records should be designed by the college physician entirely for his own use, and there is no reason for him to consult anyone about the form of these records. If the college physician thinks that any of his records should be retained after the student has been graduated, these can be added to the student's permanent file upon graduation.

The student personnel officer (dean of students, dean of men, dean of women, assistant dean for student affairs) keeps a set of records involving the student's personal difficulties, rooming assignments, and disciplinary problems. If the college is small (500 to 3,000 students), it is recommended that these records be made a part of the regular folder stored in the advising office and that this folder be available to both advising officers and student personnel officers. Knowledge of personal and disciplinary problems is of use to the academic adviser, and knowledge of academic achievements and difficulties is of use to the student personnel officers.

It is a general rule that the records kept by the registrar are needed by many college officers, and the transmission of information is an important function of the registrar. Those records kept by other offices noted above are for use within the offices of origin and are distributed to others only when specifically requested for a sound reason.

Information Needs The president and the chief academic officer will occasionally discuss individual cases with faculty members, students, or parents of students. In most cases, individual discussions are initiated because of dissatisfaction with the answers received at some lower administrative level. Both officers must have access to the advising office records, but neither officer receives them on a regular basis. They require summary material rather than individual material. The kind and amount of data sent to the president depends upon the size of the college and the scope of his responsibilities. In a small college he receives material on and concerns himself with all the details of educational policy which in larger universities must be left to groups of academic officers. The president's needs should be met in a large university by regular reports at specified intervals from the chief academic officer describing the state of the curriculum, the faculty, and the student body. In a college of 3,000 students or less, these reports will be informal and the president will also inform himself by serving on important faculty committees and receiving the agendas and minutes of their meetings. He should also receive grade distribution reports and statistics on academic failure from the registrar.

The chief academic officer is a member of the committees charged with the development of educational policy, with maintaining academic standards, and with any other educational matters. Membership on these committees keeps him well informed on the development of educational policy. His other information needs depend upon the size of the institution. In a college of 500 or less, there is no chief academic officer in the true sense and his function is performed by the president and the chief advising officer. In a college of 800 or more, he is as little concerned with the details of individual student performance as is the president, although he has access to individual student files as noted above. At regular intervals, the registrar and the admission officer provide him with statistical reports on grade distribution, numbers leaving college, the reasons for their departure, and the quality of the entering class. He should also receive from the chief student-personnel officer general statistical information on the frequency of personal and disciplinary problems among the students. His office should maintain a file on each faculty member containing a resume of his background, all correspondence with him, records of his achievements, copies of his publications, and the terms of his present appointment. This file is available to the president's office when requested. In addition, the chief academic officer requests reports of department chairmen each time an instructor's appointment is being considered.

The chief advising officer receives summary data on the performance of students as well as individual data from the registrar. The registrar sends him a grade record for every student at the end of every grading period, and this is incorporated into the student's file, preferably in the form of the student's most recent transcript. The registrar also sends the advising officer a degree status report for each student at the end of each term. These materials are also distributed to each individual adviser, and this distribution should be directly from the registrar's office and not through the chief advising officer. The student's file in the advising office is never duplicated and sent to another office. If another officer needs material from it, he should obtain the file itself from the chief advising officer.

The chief student-personnel officer is served best by sharing the student files with the chief advising officer, thus making it unnecessary for the registrar to send him separate grade information. In a large institution, one with 2,000 or more students, it may not be possible to place the student-personnel staff near enough to the advising staff for them to share files. If such sharing is not possible, the student-personnel officer must be sent duplicates of all of the records on file in the student advising office including correspondence about students, notes about conferences with students, admission information, and grade records. This is the only case in which these records may be duplicated and distributed.

It is chiefly the registrar who provides information to other offices. His own needs are usually met by the grade reports he receives from the faculty, the student information he receives from the admission office, and the statements of financial standing received from the business office.

The admission officer needs specific information on students only for special studies. The registrar should send him summaries of achievement levels of students arranged according to class. Psychiatrists on the college physician's staff need access to certain academic records. They should be provided by the chief advising officer for specific students when requested. The college physician notifies the advising officer, the student-personnel officer, and the physical education department of any special disabilities which individual students have. The registrar notifies the business office of changes in the status of students in college, changes of address, and changes involving the naming of another person to be financially responsible for the student. The financial-aid officer should receive grade records of all students on financial aid as well as statistics about the performance of students so that financial-aid planning may be carried out effectively.

Members of the faculty will be interested in summaries of the achievements of students and in the grade distributions. Those who are advisers will need grade records of and degree status information on their students. As noted, these should be provided by the registrar directly. When a faculty member needs details of academic or personal problems, he should call the appropriate officer and receive this information from that officer but he should not be permitted to review the student's file. Students' files in the advising office consist of notes to be used by that office and they may not be understood by others.

Requests from those outside the college will be primarily for transcripts of individual students, special information about the emotional stability and honesty of students, and certification that a given student is enrolled in good standing. The first and last of these should be provided by the registrar. Recommendations and statements of the student's stability and honesty should be prepared jointly by the chief advising officer and the student-personnel officer. They can be prepared in either office on the basis of the common file on the student.

ADDITIONAL READING

Burns, Gerald P.: *Administrators in Higher Education: Their Functions and Coordination,* Harper & Row, Publishers, Incorporated, New York, 1962.

Dennis, Lawrence E., and Joseph F. Kaufman (ed.): *The College and the Student,* American Council on Education, Washington, 1966.

Eddy, Edward D., Jr.: *The College Influence on Student Character,* American Council on Education, Washington, 1959.

Williams, Robert L.: *The Administration of Academic Affairs in Higher Education,* University of Michigan Press, Ann Arbor, Mich., 1965.

Administration of Higher Education: An Annotated Bibliography, U.S. Department of Health, Education and Welfare, OE-53002, 1960.

Chapter 3

Curriculum Construction and Planning

LEWIS B. MAYHEW

Professor of Education, Stanford University, Stanford, California

INTRODUCTION

Overview

The curriculum should be one of the most important concerns of academic administration for it is the principal vehicle for the achievement of one of the three missions of colleges or universities, namely, the teaching or transmission of culture. The other two missions are research and service. Unfortunately academic administrators such as department or division heads or chairmen; deans and their assistants and associates; directors of academic service activities such as libraries, testing service or guidance; and presidents frequently become so preoccupied with other administrative matters that curriculum growth and development is left to chance. Ideally academic deans and department or division chairmen should devote about a third of their professional time to the curriculum or matters directly related to the curriculum. This would include meetings of curriculum committees, periodic review of course listings, conversations with faculty about their courses and teaching, preparation of college catalogs, conduct of workshops and special meetings on curricular matters, and study of new curricular developments in higher education (or that part of higher education of direct concern to a particular administrator). Such an allocation of time is not easy to accomplish because budget, personnel, public relations, and spatial problems demand time as well. However, the ideal should be kept in mind when making choices for the use of professional time.

Terms Although individual institutions may develop specialized terminology for curricular matters (e.g., "no-preference students," "man and —— courses," "final warning," "activity credits"), there are a number of relevant terms in quite general use. Some of these are defined below.

Curriculum. The organized body of information, principles, and theory comprising what the college or university teaches in formal courses, seminars, tutorials, or independent study.

Course. The principal curricular subdivision of a curricular program, usually extending over a term, quarter, semester, or year. Courses are assumed to be organized in response to a definite logic as well as to what is psychologically consistent with student learning.

Prerequisites. Stipulated prior experiences judged to be necessary before a student has a reasonable chance to survive the demands of a course or curricular program. Generally these are most significant in the sciences, mathematics, and foreign languages, but they are used throughout a curriculum.

Credit-hour System. An academic accounting system which assigns a numerical value to a term, quarter, or semester course according to the number of times a course meets each week. Thus a three-hour course in theory meets three times a week. In actual practice the index need not reflect actual meeting time (e.g., a three-hour science course may meet six hours including laboratory work, and a three-hour seminar may meet only one hour a week).

Honor or Quality Points. A numerical ratio designed to reveal the relationship between the credit-hour value of a course and student achievement level. The most commonly used ratio is A = 4, B = 3, C = 2, D = 1, F = 0. A student who registered for a three-hour course and received a grade of A would have earned 12 honor or quality points. To obtain ratio of academic terms, quarters, or semesters, the total number of quality points is divided by the total number of credits for which students registered.

Degree Requirements. Those courses, credit hours, or honor-point averages which students must obtain before a degree or certificate is granted. A common pattern is to require certain specific basic courses, selected courses from among a specified list, a total number of credit hours (120–130 for a school organized into semesters, 180–200 for a school organized into terms or quarters), and a specific quality-point average (generally a 2 or C, with a 2.5 or C+ to B– for work in a major).

Elective System. The system of curricular organization which allows students to select, frequently under guidance, those courses which appear most relevant to them for their own purposes. The concept was first elaborated by President Charles Eliot of Harvard in opposition to the previously prescribed curriculum.

Distribution Requirements. A system which is intended to ensure some balance in a student's program by requiring him to take a specified number of courses from each of the major fields of knowledge. Frequently these fields are science and mathematics, social science, and the humanities.

General Education. That portion of a college program designed to affect the non-vocational life of the student such as his role as an individual, family member, and citizen. Frequently the term suggests some prescribed course, including courses of an integrated character.

Upper and Lower Division. The system which divides a four-year bachelor's into the first two years—lower division—and the last two years—upper division. Frequently the terms are meaningless, but some institutions formalize the transition from lower to upper division by such things as changes of advisers, a specified number of credit hours, or a specified honor-point average. A few institutions offer only upper-division work, and junior or community colleges offer just lower-division work.

College Catalog. An official bulletin of the college or university which lists courses offered, degree requirements, and other pertinent information. The catalog is usually considered contractual in nature in that a student may receive a degree by complying with the regulations listed in the catalog at the time he matriculated. However, courts have not been consistent in upholding this contractual character.

Matriculation. The act of enrolling in a program leading to a degree, whether it be a two-year, four-year, or advanced degree. Generally matriculation is equivalent to being accepted as a candidate, although in some graduate and professional schools, this is not the case.

Class Schedule. A supplementary document to the catalog, published each term, quarter, or semester, which lists the days, hours, rooms, and instructors for each course. This does not have the contractual character of a catalog.

Comprehensive Examination. An examination covering one quarter, term, or semester of work and which is basic to all or a portion of the student's grade for the work which the examination covers. Frequently broad comprehensive examinations are given at the end of the junior year covering the college experience to that date. Passing these is a degree requirement. Increasingly, one comprehensive examination is given at the end of lower-division work and another in the last year of the upper division.

Degrees. Titles conferred on the completion of specified academic programs. While there are many specialized degrees, the most common are:

Associate of Arts or Science, representing two years of work including some general education courses

Bachelor of Arts or Sciences, representing four years of college work

Master of Arts or Sciences, representing generally one to two years of work beyond the bachelor's degree

Ph.D., representing generally three to four years beyond the bachelor's degree

At one time there were significant distinctions between a degree in arts and a degree in science, but these are no longer very meaningful.

Common Curricular Faults College curricula frequently seem ineffective, out of balance, or without logic. These malfunctions are brought on by any or all of several phenomena.

Proliferation. The tendency for college courses to multiply as a result of faculty interests, developing research frontiers, public relations demands, or student pressures. It results in expensive and out-of-balance programs and is the greatest single curricular problem of administration.

Too Many Discrete Courses. A tendency to adjust the credit-hour value of courses and degree requirements so that students must register for and pass five or six courses each term if they are to graduate on time. A more desirable load would be no more than three courses, but faculty pressures make this a difficult principle to maintain.

Lack of Relevance of Prerequisites. A tendency to stipulate certain required courses as necessary for enrollment when it can be clearly shown that the course in question really assumes no prior knowledge. A sensible rule would be to minimize the number of prerequisites except when the need is well established.

Lack of Congruence with the Psychosocial Needs of Students. Students are in a developmental process which entails quite definite needs. Frequently, however, curricular requirements are out of phase with these needs. For example, freshmen and sophomores want to know more about themselves. A beginning psychology course which emphasized only the animal or infant experimentation would be ineffective. It may be that required physical education is also irrelevant to the needs of late adolescents.

Lack of Vocational Relevance. Rightly or wrongly, most students view college as preparation for a vocation. A program which does not let students feel that they are moving toward a vocational goal is likely to be rejected. If the institution requires general education, it should also allow students to take some vocational courses as well as the required courses during their freshman year.

Misleading Course and Program Descriptions. Frequently college catalogs claim more for programs than can be fulfilled. Also, frequently course descriptions are not clear, so that students are led to enroll for what turns out to be irrelevant to their needs. A common, almost dishonest practice is to list courses which have not been offered recently or to list courses offered only in alternate years. In the latter case, a student's entire program may be jeopardized because he cannot register for an alternate-year course.

Rigidity of Program Requirements. It is possible to insist upon so many prescribed courses that students have no time to explore elective courses. This frequently happens in Catholic colleges with heavy philosophy and theology requirements. It also happens in engineering and in teacher education in states having heavy certification requirements.

Failure to Conform to Student Motivation. Especially in universities, the research interests of faculties determine the content of courses, and their content may well be irrelevant for students. A sociology department which rejects concern for actual human problems is irrelevant to the student who wishes to enter counseling and who believes sociology should contribute to his ability to work with people.

Excessive Costs. As a general rule, small classes cost more than do large classes. One outcome of the proliferation of courses is increased cost of instruction. Now an institution cannot eliminate all small classes, but it can keep the number of them within limits. To illustrate, history classes which are taught in large lecture situations will cost between $6 to $8 per student credit hour. Music courses may cost as much as $250 to $300 per student credit hour.

Excessive Faculty Loads. College-level courses should reflect recent scholarship. Yet a system which may expect faculty members to teach three or four different courses in a semester precludes this and results in a lecture-textbook kind of teaching. Probably no faculty member can keep abreast of more than two different courses each year if he is to do an excellent job of college teaching.

Creating New Curricular Programs

In view of the rapid expansion of knowledge and the increase in size of institutions as the proportion of youth attending college grows, all institutions must continuously add new elements to the curriculum. Hopefully, obsolete elements will also be removed, or else the curriculum becomes too unwieldy and out of balance. While growth is relatively easy to accomplish—just allow a faculty its head—orderly growth is a much more difficult task.

Sources of New Curricular Programs First it should be recognized that the forces, pressures, or initatives for creating new programs are varied, and the relative importance of each must be weighed carefully.

Expansion of Scholarly Fields As the frontiers of research in the various disciplines are extended, the need for new subspecialties arises. This need is especially acute in graduate and professional schools but is also relevant in the undergraduate college. Thus psychology subdivides into social psychology, mathematical psychology, and the like. Institutions which wish to remain in the mainstream of intellectual life must add some of these new fields—but not too many. It is quite possible for institutions to bankrupt themselves just keeping abreast of too many important new scholarly developments. Probably each institution should allow those fields in which it has considerable strength to expand and subdivide, leaving to others fields in which they are not likely to be able to attract needed resources.

Interests of Faculty Relatedly, the interests of faculty are a potent source of pressure for new curricula. The young assistant professor just out of graduate school quite logically would like to teach the subject of his thesis. And this is not a bad idea.

Conventional Wisdom There is a generally agreed upon body of information which people almost without thinking assume is essential for an educated person to master. For a long time conventional wisdom held that the main intellectual strands of the Western tradition comprised the parameters of this body of information. Increasingly, however, the conventional wisdom says that non-Western materials should also be included. Currently, in international problems, non-Western traditions are accepted by the conventional wisdom as being of value, although actual practice may not implement the conception. The conventional wisdom is for the most part codified in college catalogs, which resemble each other to a high degree. Indeed, one of the more frequently used techniques for building the curriculum of a new institution is to collect catalogs of other, similar institutions to ensure that conventionally accepted courses are included. Accrediting agencies are in a very real sense instrumentalities for enforcing the conventional wisdom. A good example would be the insistence of regional accrediting agencies that accredited institutions offer a certain complement of general education.

Fads Closely related to the conventional wisdom are fads and fashions in the college curriculum. During the period of 1955–1965, a number of these can be identified: special programs for honors students; accelerated courses; tutorials; terms, semesters, or years abroad; precollege reading programs; mandatory leaves of absence; and modification of the academic calendar would all be illustrative. Some of these fads are likely to become part of the conventional wisdom and will be put into effect by a majority of institutions; but many of them will experience only a brief flowering and then will disappear from practical significance, although they may very well last in college catalogs for some time to come. There is a great deal of "monkey see—monkey do" in curriculum development, with institutions adopting programs which have been successful elsewhere without considering whether or not the program would be successful at the adopting institution. Currently there is a great deal of interest in the interdisciplinary courses, with virtually all institutions claiming to be moving toward such entities. It is labeled a fad, however, since few institutions have faced up to the difficult problems of staffing and finance which make interdisciplinary programs work.

Needs of Society In the final analysis, colleges and universities are creatures of society designed to provide the services which society wants, and institutions keep reasonably alert as to what the society seems to be expecting. An institution may do this by noting what prospective employers look for in new recruits. It may conduct polls to find out what constituencies expect. It may study the literature of social criticism to see what the emerging demands of society are. And, of course, colleges and universities do respond to those fields in which society invests considerable money. Good examples of institutional response to the needs of society would be the burgeoning number of programs in computer science founded by junior colleges across the country; the attempts on the part of medical schools to create new deliverers of primary medical service; or the concentration of heavy resources in the biological and life sciences. This latter seems to have intensified just since the passage of Medicare, which holds out the promise of good health care for the entire people.

Demands of Students Although students have not been quite as effective in articulating their demands with respect to the curriculum, student demands are accommodated. If students simply do not take certain courses, eventually these courses are taken out of the curriculum. Recently, students have organized free-university kinds of courses, and some institutions have tried to create similar courses within the formal structure. Students, for the most part, come to college expecting some sort of vocational preparation, and their demands for early exposure to vocational work are probably partly responsible for the fact that general education requirements are sometimes modified to allow such vocational work in the freshman year. Historically, of course, student demands have resulted in major modifications of the college curriculum. Intercollegiate athletics, libraries, music and theater, and, of course, the fraternity system all resulted from student dissatisfaction with the way things were done. Ultimately, institutions adopted the students' ideas and institutionalized them. In the late 1960s a number of institutions have explored ways in which students can have a regular place in policy-making councils. While all institutions perhaps need not follow this route, all should make some regular and sustained attempts to find out what students believe they need.

Demands of External Agencies This appears to be one of the most potent determiners of the curriculum. Junior colleges shape their curricula in the light of what four-year institutions, which receive their transfer students, seem to want; and four-year institutions increasingly look to the expectations of graduate schools. But all institutions look to other agencies as well. The various professional associations which engage in accreditation, such as the American Chemical Society, exercise a profound influence over curriculum structure. The already-mentioned regional accrediting associations are responsible for much of the interest in general education. State certifying agencies of course also have an influence. Given sanction through legal means, these external agencies have tried to exercise reasonable restraint in the demands they placed on institutions. The mischief is frequently done by faculties which overinterpret what a given external agency really wishes. Over the years, departments of education have been sorely criticized for a proliferation of requirements which were defended on the ground that they were needed for state certification. A comparison with actual state certification requirements suggests that generally these courses were much less important than faculties of professional education departments claimed they were.

Expectations Regarding Graduate Schools As graduate education becomes increasingly important, institutions more and more look to graduate programs to determine the content of the undergraduate program. A number of prestigious liberal arts colleges have become in fact nothing more than preparatory institutions for graduate schools; and a larger number of liberal arts colleges, while not sending a large number of students to graduate school, still use the graduate ideal as the determinant for their own curricula.

Administrative Interests Although faculty power seems to be increasing, the interests and the influence of administrators is still probably central in curriculum development. As one thinks back over major curricular innovations, they typically seem to be associated with the names of college or university presidents. Robert M. Hutchins developed a particular brand of general education at the College of the University of Chicago, as did John Hanna at Michigan State University. The new graduate curricula developed in the last part of the nineteenth century seem forever related to the names of major university presidents. Thus it is no accident that one state university having a president from an Italian background should create a major center for Italian studies.

Availability of Funds Although this is seen most clearly at the graduate level, there are a number of examples of undergraduate colleges responding curricularly simply to the availability of financing. In the early 1950s, the Ford Foundation was interested in supporting experiments in general education in Arkansas. Virtually all institutions in that state, therefore, mounted major new general education developments. The interest waned almost coincidentally with the termination of the Ford grants. In the late 1960s, federal interest in sea-grant universities has led even midcontinental institutions to move into curricular programs in ocean or maritime studies.

Institutional Uniquenesses The very fact that Goddard College tries to exemplify a Deweyan philosophy of education suggests the sorts of courses it would provide, and these will be different from those developed at St. John's College in Maryland. If one knows something about the history and tradition of a given institution, one can reasonably predict what sort of courses and programs will and will not be acceptable to it.

APPROACHES TO CURRICULUM CONSTRUCTION

Techniques of Curricular Study

The curriculum ought to be one of the central responsibilities of college faculties and academic administration, for it is the vehicle through which the institution seeks to make its most significant impact on the lives of students. It is the organized total of courses, programs, sequences, and their directly related activities which are generally codified in the college catalog.

Self-study Perhaps the most widely used technique of curricular study, other than the administrative review process by which new courses each year are added to the aggregate, is a self-study. Whether it be mounted in response to the requirements of an accrediting association, to the offer of philanthropic dollars, or to an internal feeling of a need for change, the self-study provides an opportunity to talk about the curriculum. The general pattern is to divide a portion of a faculty into a number of committees of which the curriculum committee is one and the committee on objectives or purposes and goals is another. Those committees meet, talk, and circulate reports which eventually are bound and become the self-study report.

Ad Hoc Committee A modification of the full self-study technique is the use of a few ad hoc committees charged with preparing recommendations, specifically focused on the curriculum, for later consideration by the full faculty. Members of each committee prepare position papers which are then debated and finally reconciled by a steering committee. Through this process gradually emerge broad policy statements which the college can endorse.

Outside Consultant A less often utilized approach, but one which is appealing in its directness and simplicity, is the use of an outside consultant. In one institution the president had been able to develop the physical plant and the financial structure but had been unable to stimulate the faculty to look at the curriculum. He invited in a consultant who spent much time with departments and divisions and then suggested the composition of the curriculum and the ways by which the faculty might prepare itself to offer the curriculum. Here, of course, the validity of the study rests with the wisdom of the consultant, and the effectiveness of any change rests with the amount of faculty respect he can command.

Board Committees Another device is to use the board of trustees, organized into working committees, to recommend curricular structure. This scheme possesses the obvious advantage of appropriate power but also the clear danger that a faculty will be suspicious of whatever a board suggests. Further, a board committee, regardless of the dedication of its members, simply cannot spend the enormous amount of time which conversation about a curriculum entails.

Panels of Experts Another unique form of curricular analysis makes a different use of a panel of experts. First, a staff officer prepares a profile of the college and its supporting community. This is submitted to a panel of professors from other colleges with the request that they recommend what courses and programs should be offered. The reasoning is that the experts, not affected by local community pressures, would be able to make a more objective appraisal of what really should comprise the curriculum.

Product Analyses W. W. Charters attempted to base the curriculum of Stephens College on the needs of college-educated women. He asked several hundred women to keep diaries of their activities. Then he classified and codified these into nice clusters of activities which became the structure for the curriculum. The courses developed were intended to speak to the actual behavior of women.

Needs of Society Similarly, looking to the needs of people, the role and scope study of the Florida higher education system sought through economic and social analysis to identify the kinds of vocations the state of Florida needed. This information was then used to indicate the broad division of curricular responsibility for each of the state's public institutions.

Informed Faculty A more sophisticated approach to curriculum study is represented by a recent Columbia University study of general education. A distinguished sociologist was granted released time to look at general education as it was offered in several similar institutions, the problems which his own college had faced in the past, and the changed conditions of higher education throughout the nation. In the light of all this, he made a series of recommendations which then became the subject of faculty debate. Generally such monumental studies have provided more guidance for other institutions than for the campus which sponsored the study. For example, the Harvard report *General Education in a Free Society* made the concept of general education respectable but did not substantially affect the Harvard curriculum.

The history of the Harvard report underscores the most widely used device for curriculum construction; i.e., a study of what is being done elsewhere. A dean of a new college first collects catalogs of colleges which he regards as similar to his own and then constructs his curriculum based upon normative averages. Or, a new course or program is described at a conference or in a journal article and immediately adopted by other similar (and dissimilar) institutions. Although the United States does not maintain a ministry of education, curricular practice is remarkably uniform, largely, one suspects, because of the propensity of colleges to emulate each other.

Contemporary practice thus suggests that discussion, political activity, judgment of experts, emulation, and search for social needs are the prevailing methods of curricular analysis and development.

Curricular Theory

Several significant attempts have been made to develop a theory of curriculum although, generally, these have not been used as a basis for curricular analysis. Perhaps the most widely quoted are the insights of Alfred North Whitehead, who emphasizes the rhythm of education and its cyclic quality. He sees the states of romance, precision, and generalization following one another throughout life and setting the form and substance of each level of education. For those who continue beyond secondary school, the college or university course represents a period of generalization, and the spirit of generalization should dominate the university. Courses should assume familiarity with details and should not bore students by forcing them to go over specifics which they already have studied. But this does not suggest a prescribed curriculum for everyone. Whitehead sees at least three curricula—literary, scientific, and technical—and, by implication, subdivisions of these.

John Henry Cardinal Newman also has things to say about the curriculum. But aside from arguing that theology has a key place in a curriculum, that a university should contain all branches of knowledge, and that students should not take too many subjects, his theories are of scant help to one who would build a curriculum. Indeed at one point he suggests that if he had a choice between a university which stressed a wide range of subjects for all students and one which did absolutely nothing save allow students to live together, he would opt for the latter.

A more recent formulation is that by Ralph W. Tyler, who argues that the objectives of education are value choices beyond which one cannot go. They are conditioned by such things as the needs of society, needs of individuals, and the laws of learning. If a college develops a set of objectives which differ radically from those of another institution, there is really no way of validating one set against the other. Once objectives are stated, however, there is a clear way of converting them into curricular form. First, they must be specified into descriptions of actual behavior, then realistic learning experiences which will produce the desired behavior must be identified, and finally these experiences must be consolidated into patterns or courses.

It is really to perfecting the engineering of the curriculum that several other contemporary theories address themselves. Paul L. Dressel, who stands in direct continuation of Tyler's emphasis on behavioral outcomes, sees 10 problems which must be solved if a curriculum is to be viable:

1. The gap between liberal and vocational education must be bridged.
2. Course and credit-hour structure must be loosened.
3. Common experiences must be provided.
4. Continuity, sequence, and integrity should be ensured.
5. Fewer blocs of subjects should be the rule.
6. Courses should be more infused with psychologically sound learning devices.
7. Values should be considered.
8. Preoccupation with the West should be combined with non-Western emphases.
9. Better learning facilities should be created.
10. Costs should be considered.

As a tool to solve these problems, he uses a set of conservative limiting principles, such as a fixed proportion of work to be taken in common by all students to establish curricular limits. Then, within those limits, he would have the faculty, following a Tyler sort of analysis, decide what the content of courses should be.

Earl McGrath ends up with a similar set of limiting principles through a somewhat different mode of analysis. McGrath, looking at desirable, commonly accepted outcomes of undergraduate education, finds that achievement of those outcomes bears little relationship to the number of specific courses a department offers, although the number of courses is related to the cost of education. Hence, for economic reasons, he arrives at the concept of a limited curriculum the content of which can be changed as conditions change but the size of which must remain constant.

There are other less engineering-styled theories of curriculum. Father Robert J. Henle, S.J., identifies five different approaches to reality, each of which must be given curricular statement. The humanistic approach deals with concrete reality. The philosophical approach is an activity of pure reflective intelligence working upon actual experience. Science also is a reflection of pure intelligence, but it acts upon interrelationships of facts. Theology, of course, deals not with experience but with data accepted from God. Mathematics is also a discipline of pure intelligence which develops a purely intellectual world of intelligible entities applicable to the physical world. To order these into a curriculum requires a theory of knowledge based upon personal experience with ways of knowing. To select from among the five approaches and to balance the effort, Father Henle suggests several principles:

Subjects should reveal the ultimate meaning and explanation of human life and reality.
Courses should provide students with personal experience appropriate to each approach to reality.
Courses should relate the student to his own environment and prepare him to live in his own culture.
Courses should be chosen for inclusion in the curriculum because of the magnitude of their possible impact on students and because of the likelihood that they will produce personal insights at basic points.

Father Henle, with his Roman Catholic orientation, has a secular counterpart in Philip H. Phenix. For Phenix, the basis of human nature is that human beings discover, create, and express meanings. And meanings possess various dimensions. The first dimension is that of experience which refers to the inner life, the life of the mind. Then, there is rule, logic, or principle which allows for categories of things. A third dimension is selective elaboration, which allows an unlimited combination of meanings. And the last dimension is expression or communication.

Meanings also can be divided into realms, which, in turn, become the structure of the formal curriculum. The first realm is symbolics, which comprises language and mathematics. The second, empirics, includes natural science. Then, esthetics contains the arts, synnoetics embraces personal knowledge, ethics includes moral meanings, and synoptics, the sixth realm, involves meanings that are comprehensively integrative. Since the available knowledge is so great in each of these realms of meaning, the prime task of the curriculum builder is to select from the richness that which should comprise the curricular content.

There also are other, more casual theories of curriculum building. The first really abdicates responsibility for the content of the undergraduate curriculum by tailoring courses to fit the requirements of the graduate school, or, in the case of junior colleges, to fit the demands of four-year institutions. This method assumes that the end of education is professional competence, and that the responsibility for preparing people for such roles rests with the specialized schools and departments. The undergraduate years simply provide students with the skills and knowledge which will make work easier at the next stage. Were this rationale not so widely accepted, it would almost be a caricature to mention it seriously. Nevertheless, hundreds of liberal arts colleges are courting financial ruin by following just such a theory.

The second such theory is a more thoughtful approach based upon Deweyan pragmatism, which holds that there is really no finite body of information. Rather, knowledge emerges and evolves as individuals seek to accommodate their conception of reality. Therefore, there should be no formal curriculum. Rather, there should be students and faculty in close proximity. The most eloquent contemporary spokesman for this approach is Harold Taylor, and its most visible manifestation is the idea of the free university.

Any systematic theory of curriculum probably will result in a better educational program than will growth without theory. The very act of thinking through the content of education in terms of a set of presuppositions and premises forces conscious choice. Whether one translates abstract objectives into behavior or selects from specified bodies of knowledge or even tries to intuit what students really want when they express a desire for a given experience, the results will probably be a clearer, more effective education. Hence, in one respect one could argue that once a theory has been adopted, whether by chance or temperament, the biggest curricular problem has been solved.

Barriers to Curricular Construction

Putting a curriculum into effect requires the solution of other theoretical problems and also of some quite serious practical ones. First among these is the problem of criteria. How does a liberal arts college with limited resources decide which subject should be taught from among the enormous variety of subjects that could be taught? Basing curricula upon the demands of a graduate school, the interests of individual faculty, the drawing power of courses, or the existence of attractive text material seems to be a denial that a curriculum can possess an internal logic and consistency. Although each of these elements must be considered realistically, they are not rational criteria for curriculum building.

Allied with the problem of criteria is the matter of setting limits on a curriculum in the face of the increase in knowledge. How does one decide what to drop when, for example, an infusion of non-Western material must be added to the curriculum? Or, how close to the frontiers of an expanding subject should undergraduate courses be kept? The significance of this problem can be judged by the fact that some people are arguing that physics is moving so rapidly as a field that no college which is not part of a graduate school should even attempt to teach it.

Then, there is the political problem. Given the premises of academic freedom, professorial privilege, the pedagogical importance of a professor's enthusiasm for a subject, and departmental power over course offerings, how does a theoretical curriculum actually become a reality? In a few recently created institutions some effort was made to develop a theoretical curriculum before the faculty was appointed. But as quickly as the first professors arrived, the theoretical idea was modified.

Related to the political problem is that of administration. The two sources of official academic power are the central administration and the faculty. Although the central administration is in the position to visualize a curricular total, the faculty is generally given responsibility for curricular decisions. The arrangement of a system which utilizes departmental thinking, a collegewide committee structure, and the knowledge of administrators is a problem for which no ideal solution has yet been found.

While these and kindred problems cannot be solved in the absolute, a start can be made, as starts have been made for other equally complicated human activities, by accumulating information. Just as the natural sciences rest upon detailed observation of nature, so should an educational theory be derived from an observation of specifics. Until now, college faculties have not really possessed much knowledge about many factors which impinge on a curriculum. The idea of institutional research is really not very old. Now, with a concept of institutional research, with improved techniques of social research, and with improved information systems, it would seem possible to obtain a great deal of information as to how the curriculum actually is working.

TECHNIQUES AND MECHANISMS FOR CURRICULAR CHANGE

Personal Involvement

Perhaps the most important element in effecting changed practice on the part of individual professors is to contrive to have them become personally involved in a movement which makes explicit to them the importance of teaching, the fact that others are concerned, and the fact that change is possible.

The Danforth Foundation has for 11 years conducted workshops on liberal education. It invites each of 25 colleges to send a delegation of four faculty members to a two-and-a-half- or three-week workshop. During the workshop, individuals may participate in seminars dealing with broad educational questions, and the delegations work as teams on projects having significance for their own institutions. At the end of the experience the team is asked to report in writing on its plans and then to report the progress of the new attempt during the following year to a representative of the foundation.

Obstacles to Involvement

This concept of contriving underscores the basic dilemma in college or university government. There is strong desire for a collegial form of government in which decisions are arrived at by consensus. Yet, in practice there is, and very likely must be, a hierarchical form of government in which one element of the community is labeled "administration" and the other "faculty." Within American higher education the faculty has been inclined to be conservative with respect to educational and instructional matters. The subjects taught are normally conservative subjects, keeping and recording important cultural elements for the future. The division of college faculties into departments based on subject matter categories also contributes to conservatism. The administration, on the other hand, is the dynamic element. It is the administrative officer who is charged with exercising educational leadership. It is typically the administrative officer who hears of innovations being practiced elsewhere and seeks to have them adopted on his own campus. It is the central administration which must take a look at the total mission of the institution and then marshal the energies of the faculty to achieve that mission. Thus, the administration is the natural agent of change, and it is the administration which is expected to contrive those situations which will involve faculty. It is the administration which must make the strongest effort to keep channels of communication unclogged. It is the administration which must seek to develop a consistent philosophy of education which can govern practice and establish parameters for programs.

Emerging Change Agents

In just the past four or five years a new administrative subspecialty has begun to grow upon the campuses of the nation's colleges and universities. The following description will serve to catalog a few of the forms it takes. Florida Presbyterian College lodges in the academic vice-president responsibility for being the principal change agent. He views himself as a catalyst operating in an intensely political environment, with his principal responsibility to facilitate innovation and change in the educational process. The University of South Florida created positions for a director of institutional research and a director of educational resources, both of whom were responsible for stimulating changes in educational practice. In addition, the University of South Florida sensed a responsibility for effecting changed instruction in a number of the state junior colleges. With outside financial support, the university has organized activities designed to improve instruction both in the university and in a cluster of junior colleges.

The University of Michigan has created a center for the improvement of instruction and has staffed it with a number of psychologists, each of whom represents a different psychological subspecialty. This center is assigned the mission of advising, consulting, and assisting the university faculty in the improvement of instruction. The University of Tennessee created a learning resource center after a university committee realized a need for several different functions. There was need for continuous research regarding teaching, for dissemination of information about teaching to professors whose time normally was spent becoming more proficient in their disciplines, and for stimulating faculty experimentation with new educational approaches.

Guidelines for Administration

In the light of this premise regarding the role of administration, several guidelines can be suggested. First, an administration seeking to stimulate innovation or change should have a clear notion of the nature of academic government. One such theory emphasizes four points: (1) that administrative authority, regardless of form and/or legal structure, consists of what is willingly delegated to it by personnel within the organization, (2) that the primary body within this organization of governments is the faculty, which functions responsibly through representative channels and designated institutional officers, (3) that the faculty is interested in assuming and coordinating leadership and can be educated for such leadership and cooperation, and (4) that the end result of such a process is the maintenance and enhancement of a productive morale—a condition or attitude in which individuals in representative groups make reasonable subordination of their personal objectives to the overall objectives of the institution. The factors essential to such a condition or attitude are feelings of mutual respect; a sense of common task; a recognition of the role of politics, debate, understanding, and due process; and the understanding that the basis of good government is ultimately the quality, character, and policy that exists in and between the persons and groups within the government.

Uses of Rewards

The manipulation of rewards, prerogatives, and perquisites is an important device for the exercise of administrative leadership. Greater use of individual independent study can be encouraged by paying a professor extra to offer such a course. Providing a faculty member with paid periods of leisure during the summer, to allow him to prepare for an innovation, is likely to be more productive than expecting him to make the preparation on top of an already full schedule of teaching and scholarship. In this connection the catalogs of American colleges and universities are full of descriptions of programs for superior students or programs for independent study which are not operational. They are not operational primarily because they were created as overloads on faculty members without commensurate remuneration. A faculty member may direct independent study of students for several years because he is interested and enthusiastic about the idea, but unless this effort is rewarded in some way, he is likely ultimately to devote his time and energy toward increasing his own stature, his own earnings, or his own personal freedom.

There are, of course, numerous minor rewards which can encourage faculty to be innovative or at least intellectually alert. The provision for adequate clerical services, authorization of reasonable travel funds, institutional purchase of journal article reprints, and institutional recognition of notable achievements are all illustrative. Even such a small thing as an administrative officer going to a faculty member's office rather than calling the faculty member to the central administrative building can develop rapport which can be a potent tool to stimulate faculty motivation to change.

Faculty Responsibility

The administrator who is willing to make faculty members truly responsible for the consequences of decisions about their own affairs also illustrates good administrative practice. During the time when the state of Michigan was experiencing a severe financial crisis, the faculty members in one college of one of the tax-supported universities in that state were given the largest salary increases in the history of the institution. The dean of this college gave his faculty the choice of devising ways to accommodate increased enrollment with no additional staff but with increases in average faculty salaries or to keep the student ratio as it had been by adding necessary staff members with only nominal changes in salary. The faculty, under this stimulus, responded creatively and discovered that adding five persons to each laboratory section did not really spoil the whole concept of a laboratory experience in a natural science course.

Communication

Communication is essential and sound, effective communication is a primary responsibility of college administration. Initial communications with faculty members take place at the point of employment and proceed through various individual conferences over the years of the professor's service. But these are not enough. There should be a variety of written communications between the central administration, the faculty, the board of trustees, students, and even parents. There might be voluntary faculty meetings in which no decisions are made but matters of a controversial nature could be discussed. The administration could well use social activities as a way of communicating. The point being made here is that innovation and change are most likely to come about in an open society in which most people know most of the things important to them personally and to the group of which they are a part.

Use of Power Figures

Even a strong, imaginative college administration cannot operate without fully recognizing the enormous elements of power which do exist among college faculties. Normally, there will be a limited number of professors whom everyone respects and judges to possess controlling influence. To engineer change, the administration should make full use of such people, not only because it is politically wise but because it is a way by which the broadest hearing can be given to innovative ideas.

Significance of Need

Innovation and change are not likely to come about unless the need for them is clearly perceived. A number of the more successful innovations are clearly traceable to the simple fact that a need had become painfully apparent. At Oxford College the majority of students were seriously in need of remedial work in language and mathematics. The faculty was quite aware of these deficiencies in basic academic skills, but it did not possess the time to rectify them through orthodox ways. When programmed textbooks and multimedia approaches to instruction became available and the faculty was shown the relevance of these new devices to remedial work, an innovation was quickly accepted.

The significance of this point cannot be overemphasized. Until the events at the University of California at Berkeley in 1964 dramatized a need for a reappraisal of undergraduate education in major universities, the primrose path of increased emphasis on research and upper-division and graduate work was being followed by most institutions having pretensions of major academic stature. The events at Berkeley and a few other institutions indicated that the time was ripe, that the need was present for a renaissance in undergraduate education.

Encouraging Motivation

Related to this matter of seeking innovation where need for innovation is present is the principle of providing ad hoc assistance for professors as they develop their own ideas. At the University of Michigan a Wolverine fund of $25,000 can be dispersed in quite small grants to help faculty members solve a particularly vexing problem. This is not long-term assistance, but assistance given on an ad hoc basis for an immediate problem.

Sociological Stranger

The use of the "sociological stranger" is increasingly seen as being of considerable importance. The sociological stranger is one who is a part of an institution yet is apart from it. One of the earliest expressions of this concept was made at Stephens College in Columbia, Missouri. The dean of education at the University of Illinois, who then became the first director of research at Ohio State University, W. W. Charters, was designated as director of research on a part-time basis at Stephens. He went onto the campus several times during a year to consult with individual faculty members, listen to their problems, suggest experiments, or point out things to which the institution should give attention. Then, by establishing deadlines, he would create motivation for action when he departed the campus. On his return to the campus he would check back to find out what had happened. By having reasonably high status, he reported directly to the president; but having no administrative responsibility, he could fire no one; and by being a person with great personal integrity, he could look at the institution more objectively than could the people who were there day after day. This role requires something more than just a one- or two-day visit of a consultant, although consultants' services can be of value. The role of the sociological stranger requires that the person who plays it be familiar enough with the institution to identify areas of need, sense readiness for innovation, and be able to tap the resources to bring it about. An institution making use of this device should consider contracting with someone for a period of at least four or five years. A first visit of several months on the campus would help the stranger know and be known. Visits of about five days' duration three or four times a year should then suffice.

Use of Information

The next guideline, in one sense, is simply an extension of the need for communication. But in another sense, it is a completely different point. A vast amount of information is becoming available about higher education and its practices. There is the outpouring of research, either in book, article, or more fugitive form, from centers for the study of higher education. There are increasing numbers of professors of higher education who are directing doctoral studies focusing on the college enterprise. Increasingly members of some of the disciplines are doing research on higher education. Many institutional research offices are producing information, as are such paraeducational agencies as the Educational Testing Service and the College Entrance Examination Board. This literature is approaching flood stage, but much of it has relevance for an individual faculty member seeking to innovate. The question arises, however, as to how the relevant information can be brought to his attention. One of the important missions which the centers for the improvement of instruction described earlier see for themselves is the dissemination of information. Generally they publish a news bulletin, letter to the faculty, or brochure which describes what is going on at the local campus or elsewhere which might be of relevance for the deans and faculty on that campus.

Self-studies

One of the more important tools for motivating an institution for change is the institutional self-study. Part of the regeneration of the University of Kentucky came from a massive self-study which then became the basis for an equally massive academic master plan. Stanford University shifted its character from that of a strong regional university appealing to bright, wealthy, underachieving students to a university of international stature primarily as a result of the findings of a self-study. Stephens College, of its own volition, undertook a self-study when its administration believed the time had come to minimize the traditions of an earlier era. That self-study was used to loosen up the soil of academia so that a new president could have a reasonable chance of exercising academic leadership.

A last guideline is simply a restatement of the aphorism that nothing succeeds like success. The faculty at Oxford College looked more readily on multimedia devices when it was demonstrated that student deficiencies in academic skills could be rectified by using automated self-instructional devices.

Principles

Out of these broad guidelines it is possible to derive several principles which may combine one or more of the guidelines. These principles are advanced with the intent that they could become categories in an emerging theory of engineering for change.

The first principle is that vigorous, strong, and even, occasionally, ruthless administrative power is necessary. If an institution lodges too much power in the hands of the faculty, the institution becomes moribund. Innovation just doesn't take place. When the administration is too strong, the sheer rapidity of change can shake the institution to pieces. An institution can only assimilate so much change in a given time. If one accepts the reality of this construct, that is, one power valence in the hands of faculty and another in the hands of administration, then it is possible to seek ways by which these two forces can be brought into positions of creative tension. Out of this creative tension could come innovation, but it must be tempered by a knowledge of what innovations the institutions can stand.

The second principle is that all human beings, including faculty members, are sufficiently venal so that it is possible to purchase interest or to purchase loyalty. Through financial incentives, through incentives of free time, through incentives of perquisites, it is possible to move faculty members from a preoccupation with limited disciplinary concerns to some interest in pedagogy and the broader problems of education.

The third principle is that leadership for innovation and change can be exercised by almost anyone who begins to make the motions of a leader. A person doesn't really need to have a high-sounding title in order to exercise considerable leadership.

The fourth principle is that improvement requires time. One can speculate that college professors don't teach better than they do because they are inclined to impose on themselves, or have imposed upon them, impossible time schedules. The faculty work load is improving, yet, in junior colleges and a fair number of liberal arts colleges, teaching loads extend from 12 to 15 hours a week divided into four or five courses. These loads may require three different preparations in any given semester, and perhaps six, seven, or eight different preparations over a two-year period, particularly if the institution follows the practice of offering some courses every other year. Given the present rapid rate of increase of knowledge, few college professors are sufficiently intelligent or cosmopolitan to teach five or six different courses at the college level over a two-year period.

Repeatedly in this discussion have been mentioned financial considerations. This leads to still another principle which is that innovation is likely to be encouraged if the institution develops a sufficiently refined system of cost accounting so that actual costs of instruction, as presently performed, can be revealed. If instructors could be shown the high cost to themselves personally of the small, inefficient courses taught by lecture techniques, one can speculate that changes in the curriculum would come about quickly. If cost accounting could show economies from the use of independent study, from television, or from some of the other innovations which have been discussed, faculties would likely be more willing to consider them.

The sixth and last principle is based on an assumption that many faculty people are threatened and insecure individuals. Change is threatening, and an insecure person reacts defensively to threats. In some way or other, the officer or agency for change must build into the planning provision for alleviating faculty anxiety and insecurity.

LONG-RANGE CURRICULAR BUDGET MAKING AND PLANNING

Need for Long-range Planning

In the past, much curricular planning has been on an ad hoc basis. This fact is probably involved in the unbalanced proliferation of courses. Increasingly it becomes apparent that for sound institutional development some long-range plans should be attempted. One device which has proved quite effective in several different institutions has been for the president (or central administration) to make his own initial long-range plan for the academic program and then to turn this plan over to the faculty for discussion and debate with the injunction that the faculty should come up with a plan for at least five years of curricular development. This faculty plan then becomes the blueprint for development. As a general rule an institution can plan with reasonable precision for a five-year period but with only broad guidelines for a ten-year period.

Forecast for Personnel

As a companion report to the academic long-range plan, there should be a plan for personnel which outlines the expected number of retirements each year, the anticipated replacements, and some indication of the academic specialties which must be covered. Personnel planning can never be a precise thing, but the very reduction of personnel needs to writing should facilitate rational thinking about the institution's future.

Forecast for Financing

Although institutions will probably continue to operate on annual budgets, there is need for budgetary forecasting to go along with program and personnel planning. Such a forecast should indicate clearly assumptions regarding sources of income, changes in tuition, faculty salaries, the cost of services, and the like. This financial planning should be tied closely to program planning so that decisions about the new program can be made in the light of the best available financial forecast. It is just possible that the recently popularized cost benefit analysis may prove to be of value for colleges and universities. This system of program budgeting has been tried out in some industries and by the U.S. Defense Department. At present a number of efforts are being made to apply the principles of program budgeting to colleges and universities, but as yet there is no viable model which institutions can follow.

There seem to be two major approaches to fiscal forecasting and budget making, and each may have some validity in some circumstances. The more frequently used device is for central administration to ask operating units to make budget request in support of programs they have planned. This generally results in requests for more funds than are available. Central administration then must reconcile the demands from a number of units. Occasionally, however, it may be well for the process to be reversed, so that the central administration allocates lump sums of money to each operating unit, assigns educational missions, and then allows freedom for the operating unit to achieve its mission by expending its funds in whatever way it wishes. Several institutions using this technique occasionally have achieved quite substantial economies by making responsive departments face up to the financial facts of life.

Chapter **4**

Evaluation of the Environment, the Process, and the Results of Higher Education

PAUL L. DRESSEL

Assistant Provost and Director of Institutional Research,
Michigan State University, East Lansing, Michigan

INTRODUCTION

Evaluation in its basic meaning of making judgments about the worth of an act or experience is inevitably involved in every phase of the operation of an institution of higher education, for every decision or resource allocation involves—wittingly or unwittingly—some choice among values. Evaluation in this decision-making interpretation is not only essential and inevitable in all phases of the operation of the university, but it is also evident that an institution of higher education which exists primarily to inculcate in its students competency in making wise judgments should itself evidence this behavior. Thus evaluation, in its broadest sense, is coextensive with the operations and goals of the university. However, evaluation in this section will be interpreted in a somewhat more restricted sense, emphasizing primarily the goals, the environment, the process, and the results of the efforts of an institution of higher education.

An educational institution offers an environment (physical, social, and psychological) in which learning takes place. The institution provides educational processes or experiences (courses, instruction, social activities, community involvement, recreational and cultural events), all of which presumably are to promote learning. The institution must also have broad purposes and a statement of desired objectives or student competencies which define the nature of the impact it purports to have on students and, through them, on society. Finally, the institution, to justify its existence, must evaluate its effectiveness in producing the desired results and its efficiency in utilizing resources to do so.

The environment of an urban university may be effectively restricted to the facilities provided for instruction and to the social and psychological characteristics of the formal educational process provided in classes, offices, library, and laboratories. The environment of a residence institution comprehends residence halls, food services, recreational facilities, and the social and cultural opportunities of a large city. The residence institution is not, however, despite tradition and mythology, inevitably a better learning environment than the former. Indeed, the more diverse and rich the environment, the greater the possibility of interference and conflict between it and the central goals of learning. Confusion, incoherence, and disillusionment may result as the student expends vast energy coping with a multiplicity of uncoordinated and unrelated aspects of his environment without perceiving any undergirding or unifying goals.

The educational process which takes place in a complex environment may also disintegrate into a number of unrelated experiences. The malcontent and the activist student reportedly (and understandably) see no relationship between logic, political science, or scholarly objectivity and their immediate concerns. The vocation-oriented or even the grade-oriented student may attain some sense of unity by restricting his experience to his course work and to those accomplishments to which the faculty quite obviously give priority. Even in the formal academic program of courses and instruction the student may find that departmental isolation and competition coupled with the myopic concentration of each instructor on his own course focus attention on knowledge and discrete content rather than on pervasive goals and competencies. When unifying concepts and principles are nonexistent or at least not apparent, the process of education breaks down into a series of unrelated and well-nigh purposeless experiences rather than presenting a challenging sequence of steps by which the student rises to new levels of competency and to increased self-confidence in their utilization.

Especially is this true when an institution lacks an ongoing evaluation program which focuses the attention of both students and faculty on long-term pervasive goals and makes continually evident to both that their conjoint effectiveness as students and faculty in an institution of learning must ever be judged by the nature and extent of the learning which takes place. Thus the continuing evaluation of the effects of an institution on its students provides in itself a process and an environmental quality which models the rational, reflective, self-critical, flexible, and, withal, compassionate behavior which we hope will be evident in our graduates. What the institution is must communicate constantly and unambiguously to students what we want them to become.

SELECTION, CLASSIFICATION, AND PLACEMENT OF STUDENTS

Recruiting The selection, the classification, and the placement of students are preceded in almost all institutions by some form of recruitment. Recruitment may be carried on by full-time workers who participate in high school-college day programs and visit students and their parents in their homes. Prospects are sought upon the basis of athletic prowess, grades, activities records, and sometimes on no other basis than that the parents can pay the bills. Recruitment, whether carried on by full-time paid workers, by alumni, by athletic coaches, or by correspondence directed to National Merit Scholarship winners, involves blandishment, equivocation, and, at times, actual misrepresentation. Both the full-time recruiter and the football coach ultimately justify their salaries by their recruiting activities, and hence they sometimes promise more than an institution can or should deliver. Recruiters also have been known to force major changes in an institutional curriculum on the grounds that, without such change, it would be impossible to get students. Sometimes, too, especially with athletes, there are sub-rosa agreements with regard to financial support by the alumni recruiters which ultimately reflect discredit on the institution.

Despite widespread recruiting, even by publicly supported institutions, the recruiting process has not been studied in any depth. Some private, high-cost institutions must engage in recruiting in order to exist; some do so to maintain their quality. Other institutions engage in recruiting because they wish to change their image—that is, they wish to attract a different type of student than they have had in the past. This may promote such diverse goals as raising the intellectual quality of the student body, upgrading the athletic program, improving the band, orchestra, or any other special aspect of the program. Still other institutions engage in extensive recruiting simply because their administrators are enchanted with large numbers and somehow believe that having more students than other institutions will make them better than other institutions. Recruiting can be an expensive enterprise, with the costs varying from a few dollars per student recruited in those situations where recruiting is done largely by mail or by volunteers to several hundred dollars per student recruited when recruiting is done as a professional, full-time specialty.

The distinction between students who enrolled only because of recruitment activity and those who would have enrolled in any case is not easily made. It is of particular importance to take note of the length of time that students remain in college when the recruitment costs are high. When many students who were recruited transfer after one year or drop out of college it may be taken as an indication that there is something basically wrong with the recruitment process. When only a small percentage of the students continue through to a degree, recruitment costs are increased by the large turnover. Rather than relating total recruiting expenditures to numbers of students recruited, it is more appropriate to divide total recruiting expenditures by the total student years produced by recruiting (sum of the products of student by years enrolled in the college). This can only be done finally after a lapse of four years, but a similar approach can be used for lesser periods. Comparison of the effectiveness of individual recruiters may also be facilitated by relating each salary plus expenses to the student years of attendance which result. As with all attempts to quantify, some caution must be observed. Rigid application of such a procedure would encourage recruiters to concentrate their efforts on students already favorable to the institution rather than to seek new prospects and develop new territories.

Selection From those students who apply for admission to an institution must be selected those who are formally admitted to the institution. Selection, however, is a gradual or cumulative process rather than a decision made at a moment in time. The recruitment process involves some selection. The image of an institution which students, parents, and high school guidance people have determines in great measure which individuals apply to an institution. Many initial contacts with an institution are informal (made by personal visit or by telephone) and lack of enthusiasm or even active discouragement of the student at that point may eliminate the necessity of formal action on an application for admission. Institutions which admit almost all applicants may attempt to make a case for selectivity on the basis of these "informal rejections." Since these contacts are often purely informational and exploratory, the case is a dubious one; in fact, one may suspect that, for institutions which seek recourse to such evidence, it was, in many cases, the institution rather than the inquirer who was rejected.

After students are admitted there is still further selection because some of those admitted fail to appear. Indeed, in certain types of institutions, those who fail to appear may run as high as 50 percent or more of those admitted, and they may be more able than the students who actually appear. Presumably, most of the "no shows" make multiple applications but attain admission into a more selective institution which they preferred. Selection does not cease when the student appears on campus. One highly regarded private institution has had a history of eliminating 30 percent of its freshman class by the end of the first year. Public institutions with very coarse admissions screens may, in effect, become selective institutions by the elimination which occurs within the first year or two. Indeed, whatever the care and the criteria used in the admissions process, there is so much chance of error that, were it not for the costs, selection by trial might be preferable to ensure that each individual with any reasonable chance of success has the opportunity to prove himself. Institutional practices vary with regard to time of admission. In some cases admission is no longer confined to a particular time interval but has become a year-round operation. Individuals with excellent credentials may be admitted (tentatively) perhaps by the end of their junior year in high school or at whatever subsequent date they apply during the following year. This is especially common in large state universities which attempt to take care of all qualified students. More selective institutions may hold off, since they wish to select the cream of those applying. The problem of admission date is complicated by financial aid and scholarship awards, by testing dates and score reporting, and by competition among institutions for the most outstanding students. Although admission can be and usually is separated from decisions on assistance, students qualifying for assistance will withhold acceptance until all offers are in. Thus some uniformity in application deadlines and award announcements has become important in some groups of institutions. With increasing pressures on graduate schools, some departments have developed the policy of accepting only students to whom an award can be made. This policy is a composite result of federal research and fellowships and selectivity. Graduate students of the quality desired will obtain assistance somewhere, so that admission without award would be productive only with lower-quality students.

Most institutions admit at least four types of students: first-time freshmen, transfers, specials, and graduate students. Special students are usually nondegree students and, as the designation suggests, constitute a group about which little can be said. Occasionally the "special" designation is used as the equivalent of a probationary admission for an individual who somehow does not meet the usual admission standards.

Most of the emphasis in admission selection of regular students is placed upon cognitive evidence: previous grades, high school ranks, test scores, and patterns of courses. The latter appears to offer some evidence of student interest, but when an institution specifies a certain pattern of courses for admission or when a secondary school indicates a certain pattern as preparation for college, the goal of college attendance may outweigh any personal preference that the student might have. High school grades or ranks generally have given somewhat higher correlation with college grades than have any other types of data. Various types of academic aptitude tests and achievement tests, however, run a close second, and the combination of (1) grades or ranks which depend upon the particular school in which they were attained and (2) test scores which are independent of the variations in schools will be somewhat better than either taken alone.

One may anticipate that the correlation of grades, ranks, or test scores with first-term grades will be someplace in the interval from .4 to .55, and that a combination may occasionally raise the correlation as high as .70. Although Bloom, working with a selected group of schools associated with the Educational Records Bureau, found that, by a progressive adjustment of high school grades for differences in high schools and college grades for differences in colleges, a somewhat higher correlation might be achieved, other studies have cast considerable doubt both on the utility and the generality of that finding. The expectation is that, regardless of the combination of cognitive evidence used, no more than 50 percent of the variation in first-term college grades will be accounted for. Some students will do better than predicted; others will do far worse. Some students who are admitted fail despite the selection process, and some persons not admitted would have succeeded.

On the whole, course patterns have not shown any significant relationship to success in college, although there are some obvious connections. The student with no mathematics in high school is obviously in difficulty if he attempts engineering or a college major in mathematics. The student with all of her work in secretarial or business courses may, despite high grades, have difficulty in college. For transfer students, undoubtedly the best evidence is the record made in the previous institution. It is quite common to find that transfers suffer a slump their first term after transferring, and a rather higher mortality occurs among transfer students than among the native students at similar levels. Hence, an institution may find it worthwhile to establish some differential in the prior performance of transfers or to require some kind of test demonstrating competency equal or superior to that of native students at the same class level. For graduate students, the undergraduate record plays very much the same role as the high school record of the new freshmen. Here again the disparity in standards among disciplines and among colleges leads many institutions to require the Graduate Record Examination, the Miller Analogies Test, or some other test or battery of tests as a supplement to grades in making decisions about admission.

Affective factors, such as biographical background, interests, values, and personality, have been much studied with a view to improving the selection process. Insofar as prediction of grades is concerned, the weight of the evidence is that assessment in this area adds very little. One of the problems, of course, is that college grades either take little account of affective factors or they take account of them in a very unsystematic way, depending upon the idiosyncrasies of individual instructors. Another factor may well be that other factors in selection result in a sufficiently close matching between the affective characteristics of an individual and those prevalent in an institution that the resulting spread and mix is tolerable, both to the institution and to the individuals. However, individuals with atypical values, interests, or personalities are often among those who change their curricula and whose academic performance is markedly lower than predicted. Often too, they are among those who drop out during the freshman year but whose academic performance is satisfactory. Some colleges require an interview, and experienced admissions personnel often insist that from an interview they can make rather accurate assessments in the affective domain. Research evidence casts considerable discredit on the interview as a selective procedure, but it may prove satisfactory in those cases where the institution desires the kind of students that favorably impress its admissions officer. Psychophysical factors such as athletic prowess, artistic talent, musical skill, and social competency may also be taken into account in the admissions process, especially where some balance in these factors is considered essential to a stimulating environment. At the present time there is considerable concern that colleges make entirely too much of cognitive qualifications and pay too little attention to the creative area.

Three possibilities must be considered in selection in respect to the psychophysical domain. First, within the specified range of cognitive ability an institution may well wish to diversify its talent so as to have individuals with athletic ability, individuals with artistic skills, etc., and thereby build a community in which a wide range of cultural activities can be conducted at a fairly high level to the advantage of all. Secondly, an institution may decide to accept a somewhat lower cognitive standing when this is balanced by unusual talent in the physical, social, or arts area. Here the risk to be faced is that these individuals may not have the interests or the ability to maintain necessary scholastic standards in required courses in science, language, etc. Conceivably, talent in art or music may result in sufficiently high grades in these fields that these can counterbalance less-than-satisfactory grades in some other fields. This leads to the third possibility that an institution desiring to include in its student body individuals with a high degree of creative ability, athletic prowess, artistic talent, and the like may have to adjust its curriculum and its requirements to suit these individuals. In effect, the music major in many institutions is already so demanding that it is a vocational rather than a liberal arts experience.

An institution which wishes to evaluate the effectiveness of its recruiting and admissions should collect data on each of the following points:

Contacts made with prospective applicants
Applications filed
Admissions granted
Initial enrollments
Continuing enrollments: 1 year
2 years
3 years
4 years
Degree recipients

Only then can the costs and effectiveness of the earlier stages of this sequence be critically examined. The conclusion might be reached that more effort expended at later stages would pay greater dividends than increased effort at the earlier ones. The most selective institutions graduate only 85 to 90 percent of those initially enrolling, and less selective ones may graduate 30 percent or less. Some of the reasons for this will become evident in the subsequent discussion.

Classification (Majors, Programs) The classification of a student into an appropriate major or curriculum may or may not be part of the selection process. At the graduate level it almost inevitably is, for applications are for specific programs and admissions are by schools or departments. In complex institutions with a number of specialized undergraduate programs, differences in required course patterns may result in selection and classification being, at least in part, combined. The student may be told that, because of his lack of adequate work in mathematics or science, admission to engineering is impossible—at least until certain deficiencies are removed. In many cases, however, the problem of classification is separable from the problem of admission in the sense that the student is qualified for any of several majors or curricula and is himself seeking for some kind of evidence to assist his choice.

Classification can be conducted on a probabilistic or mechanical basis employing objective data or it can be based upon a clinical and individual approach. Using a technique of regression analysis, a number of variables may be combined to predict the average grades that a student would make in each of several fields. A different set of regression weightings would be determined for each field, but the same basic variables would be used throughout. Presumably, then, the predicted grade averages would provide an indication of those fields in which the student would be most likely to do the best work. This may differentiate effectively among such broad fields as the sciences, social sciences, and humanities. However, since verbal ability or general academic aptitude play such a significant role in success in all college fields, it is to be expected that a few variables will be the determining factors in prediction in all fields and that the differences in predictions will be relatively small. There may, moreover, be a few curricular areas where courses are relatively easy and grading is relatively generous, so that almost all students might be predicted to make satisfactory grade averages in these areas and many individuals might find that their highest predicted performance would be in one of these areas. Such information is practically useless and possibly dangerous, for it may encourage ill-advised choices. Although systems of comparative prediction have been worked out in a number of universities, the use of this approach for actual determination of the field appropriate to an individual is quite inappropriate. The results, however, may be very useful in providing individual counseling as to groups of fields generally appropriate or inappropriate.

The term "differential prediction" is often used to describe a situation wherein comparative prediction has been used. Strictly speaking, differential prediction would involve prediction of the differences in performance in fields. This ideally would involve different test batteries for the several fields or the use of an unusually comprehensive and unwieldy composite covering all fields but containing information irrelevant to many. As already indicated, the actual difference in grade-point averages for groups of students with the same general level and pattern of ability may be very small. Indeed, the amount of distinctiveness in the programs may be limited to a very few courses in which, however, success is essential and special abilities are required. Thus in differential prediction one becomes concerned with the study of abilities or aptitudes which may not make a major contribution to overall prediction of the grade-point average but may contribute to successful performance in a few requirements or courses which are distinctive to a particular field. One difficulty with attempting to set up a differential predictive model is that students seldom, if ever, complete the requirements for a number of different fields. Thus, in practice, there exists no basis for predicting the difference in performance of an individual in two or more different fields.

Another model which may be used for classification is that of the multiple-discriminant function. The comparative or differential prediction requires quantifiable data and proceeds on a regression model set up to predict success in one or more different fields. The multiple-discriminant function model takes into account a wide range of information, some of which involves only classification into categories, and attempts to determine whether there are distinctive subgroups of individuals characterized by a distinctive array of traits. It then sets up a weighted combination of these which maximizes the spatial separation of these groups. The information on a given individual may then be utilized to determine his location in reference to these various subgroups. Thus the individual is placed with those persons whom he is most like in respect to whatever characteristics have been used in the original analysis. The multiple-discriminant function approach may provide usable information where the regression approach does not. Thus an individual might have predicted grade averages in physics and in engineering which are essentially identical, but he might be found by a multiple-discriminant function approach to be much more like majors in physics than majors in engineering. Several studies have indicated that there are indeed differences in student groups enrolled in the pure and in the applied sciences.

Finally, there is, of course, the classification approach which is based on specific requirements. To enter engineering requires a certain number of units in specific mathematics and science courses. If the student does not have them he will not be accepted in the engineering curriculum. It may be further argued that, since students do not pay the full cost of their education, the institution cannot afford to subsidize the extra time in school that would be required for a student to make up deficiencies. There is often the further interpretation that the student who has not taken such courses in the secondary school has, in some way, betrayed a lack of motivation or commitment and therefore should be discouraged. The inequity of such an approach is most obvious when one recognizes the vast range of competencies among students who have completed requirements. When requirements are general in nature—that is to say, when they are not specific prerequisites to further study in the same field—classification on the basis of such requirements should be viewed with suspicion and, at the very minimum, alternative bases for a decision should be provided. For instance, if in a certain field two years of high school mathematics are required but no further mathematics is to be taken in college, the significance of that requirement is dubious. In other cases, however, where the student must continue in the same field—mathematics, foreign language, etc.—the mere presence on his record of the units required cannot be taken as satisfactory evidence of his ability to proceed with curricular requirements in that particular classification. Further testing will be necessary. We shall return to this point under the discussion of placement.

A second approach to classification is the clinical or individual approach. In fact, as we have already noted, the data resulting from comparative prediction have been, in most cases, used as part of a counseling process with individuals rather than as a definitive basis for stating to a person that he can or cannot enter a particular field. The multiple-discriminant function approach can similarly be used. In fact, the multiple-discriminant function analysis corresponds more closely to counseling procedures than does the prediction approach in the sense that the counselor is interested in having an individual consider a wide range of interests, personality traits, and physical competencies as well as intelligence, and then exploring the relationship of these to a number of possible fields of work. Some counselors utilize a rather directive approach in analyzing aptitudes and interests relative to curricular and vocational possibilities and suggest specific possibilities to an individual. Others urge that individuals engage in a self-examination in depth and perhaps in an exploration of curricular or vocational possibilities in order to reach their own conclusions. Frequently, the counseling approach will encourage an individual to try out a possibility for a semester or a year to determine the extent of his interest and the adequacy of his ability for the field. One difficulty with this in college is that so many of the fields require a firm basis in the basic arts and sciences and the courses which are distinctively characteristic of the special curriculum are not available in the freshman and sophomore years.

The counseling approach to classification may also put remedial work in a more appropriate light. People continually find that new developments require of them knowledge or competencies which they have not developed. Whether or not a student has had mathematics in high school, whether or not he has heretofore been interested in it, the issue to be faced, if he seriously wants to consider a field requiring mathematics, is whether he is willing to take the time and apply himself to the extent required to develop these competencies. The problem is really the assessment of where the student is relative to where he wants to be at the completion of college and where he must be if he is to meet the standards set for the completion of a particular program. If an individual and flexible approach is possible, there is no undergraduate program that an able student could not finish in four years, whatever his status with regard to specific requirements at the time of entrance. The catch, of course, is on the adjective "able."

Finally, the clinical or individual approach can be expedited by curriculum requirements which place a great deal of emphasis on general education and orientation. Thus a program in which the first year or two is made up largely of core course requirements coupled with the possibility of orientation to the various special curricula makes it possible, in effect, for all students to have a period of exploration. Ideally, the general education courses should open up for the student some of the possibilities implicit in the more specialized curricula and thus simultaneously provide a basis for specialized work as well as some experience helpful in making a choice. One difficulty is that the student with definite vocational concerns may be irritated or at least unchallenged by the general education requirements, and he may therefore disappear. Too often, also, this period does not provide opportunity for exploration, so that the student at the end of a year or two has progressed no further than he was at the time of admission insofar as knowing what he wishes to specialize in in college or do after college. Students interested in the sciences and technical fields can, of course, keep open a wide range of possibilities by concentrating on mathematics and science in the first year or two.

In the American conception of education as an opportunity for individual development, minimal attention is given to economic and social needs in the classification process. Students may be informed that there are shortages in certain areas and possibly oversupplies in others, but the student is seldom overtly pressured to choose on this basis. There is even a definite antipathy in American higher education to tying undergraduate financial aid to a vocational field, although this has been done to some extent—as, for example, in the forgiving of some portion of a loan to teachers who engage actively in a teaching career after graduation. At the graduate level, the preponderance of support for study in scientific and technical fields has generated demands for equal assistance in other fields. Promotional material dramatizing needs and increased salaries in response to needs are no doubt effective in motivating choice. Ultimately, though, there exists a belief in this country that a person well educated in any field can adapt to demands and find a suitable niche.

Placement (in Course or Class Levels) Subsequent to selection and classification there may still be a problem of placement. For example, students enter college with and without chemistry from high school. Chemistry courses in high school vary greatly in their quality; some courses are very poor, others are the equivalent of college courses. The mere fact of having had chemistry is not an adequate basis for placement of the student in a chemistry sequence. Testing may indicate that some students should be placed in the second or third quarter of a freshman chemistry sequence or occasionally at an even more advanced level. It may also be found desirable to section the first term of chemistry to distinguish not only between those who have had no chemistry and those who have had chemistry but also to recognize those who have superior ability in mathematics and in sciences other than chemistry.

Foreign language and mathematics involve similar problems perhaps of even greater intensity because these fields may be pursued for three or four years in the secondary school. Development of local placement tests is expensive and time-consuming. Unless expert assistance is available, they may be of poor quality. Furthermore, the task is never done, for frequent revision is essential for security and for maintaining a proper relationship between the test and the course which will usually change somewhat from year to year. Tests available from the Educational Testing Service may be satisfactory, but their adoption by a faculty is more frequently a matter of expediency than of conviction. The Advanced Placement Tests of the College Entrance Examination Board are usually taken only by students who have had special programs in secondary school. Most institutions which accept large numbers of students from a variety of secondary schools will find that a locally developed testing program (which may include some commercially available instruments) is required to appropriately classify students.

Experience in one institution indicates that students with two years of study of a foreign language may vary in competency from a level suggesting practically no experience up to a level approximating that of two years of study in college. In mathematics it is not unusual to find entering freshmen who can take relatively advanced undergraduate mathematics. In disciplines which are highly sequential, the task of placement may involve quite comprehensive testing to determine whether knowledge and skills basic to continuation in advanced courses is present. In fields which are not so highly cumulative or sequential, vocabulary level, wide reading, and excellent reading ability may be more significant indicators of the appropriate level at which an individual can function. With adults and with transfer students, where the concern in placement is largely that of determining the appropriate class level (freshman, sophomore, etc.) of the individual rather than placement in particular course sequences, the problem is even more complicated. How does one evaluate the educational level of an intelligent adult who has read widely, traveled extensively, and held responsible positions in higher education? In higher education we have tended to be past-oriented in our evaluation, and we emphasize knowledge of specifics even though we know that these do not long remain with individuals. We do not have adequate equivalency examinations which measure whether one has the insight, the power, and the ability to learn—qualities which hopefully remain after specifics have fled.

Recognition and Reward Once the student is admitted, classified, and appropriately placed in an educational program, the next stage of student evaluation involves continuing appraisal, recognition, and suitable reward for progress or lack of it. The most prevalent form of continuing appraisal is that of course grades. Course grades involve a highly subjective appraisal by faculty members, although this is not always recognized. Indeed, some faculty members operate on the assumption that they have in mind a definite standard of performance against which an individual's performance is appraised and assigned a grade. Other faculty members quite frankly admit that a grade is a highly subjective appraisal which inevitably, and perhaps appropriately, incorporates affective elements. The difficulty with grades is not only that they are subjective and that they may be unfair because they involve professorial bias but also that, in the combination of pressure by students and the desire of most faculty members for some reasonable degree of objectivity, factual information is overemphasized. Application and judgment inevitably involve values and their appraisal becomes more time-consuming and more subjective than testing of knowledge. Thus the student demand for some degree of objectivity forces the instructor toward emphasis on factual knowledge which, in turn, forces the students to emphasize memorization and rote recall while objecting violently that, because of the grading system, they are unable to give attention to the really important things in college. The elimination of grades, as demanded by many students and some faculty members, is no solution to the problem. Maintenance of quality requires standards, and completely individualized standards are synonymous with no standards. If completion of a course or a degree is to have any significance, then judgments must be made about student performance. It would be a confession of complete inadequacy and total lack of standards for an institution to turn this judgment over to the students themselves. The real deficiency in student evaluation is not so much in grades as in our compartmentalization of knowledge into courses and the resultant tendency to lose sight of the major and pervasive goals of a college education. Comprehensive examinations constitute one attempt to do this, but comprehensive examinations, like grades, can be too easily past-oriented—assessing what the student has done and what he knows rather than providing continuing feedback to students and faculty as to what the student is now able to do as a result of his past experience.

Presently, proposals for pass-fail systems of grading are popular. This is a recurring and passing fad. Neither able students nor faculty are long satisfied with a mere indication of pass covering 85 to 95 percent of the reports. They are concerned with excellence in higher education, and excellence both deserves and requires recognition. If there is no recognition for superior performance in academic areas, students will tend to settle for the mediocre performance that achieves the passing standard and seek for other areas of activity where rewards are forthcoming, just as faculty members, finding that the lack of adequate appraisal of teaching results in very limited recognition of good teaching, gravitate to research where tangible evidence of publication brings reward. In the recognition of outstanding students it is, of course, possible to offer rewards other than grades. The privilege of enrolling in honors programs or in independent study is, in some institutions, reserved to outstanding students, although there are educators who argue that all students can benefit from this experience. Honors are often awarded, too, on a routine basis to those demonstrating outstanding performance in grades. Grades themselves are not highly visible so that honors societies and the granting of degrees with various levels of honor (cum laude, grade 3–3.49; magna cum laude, grade 3.50–3.99; summa cum laude, grade 4) becomes a more public way of appraising and rewarding outstanding performance. It is unfortunate that, in some institutions, admission to an honors college or an honors program is based entirely upon grades and provides certain privileges without any obligations for a distinctive pattern of study. Admission to an honors program really should be an opportunity-oriented and tentative recognition which says, in effect, that the student appears to have the ability to do a different and unusual quality of work. The actual attainment of honors should be based upon fulfillment of some set of obligations involved in accepting that opportunity.

A major weakness of most systems of recognition and reward is that they overemphasize competition, faculty judgments, and public approbation. This is perhaps necessary, recognizing the nature of the human animal, and it may also be essential to demonstrate the concern of the faculty and the institution for excellence. However, education fails unless it also inculcates in the individual a respect for excellence, a motivation to attain it to the best of his ability, and some capacity for assessing his own success. A responsible, self-reliant individual must be willing and able to evaluate himself and not seek solely for the approbation of others.

EVALUATION OF INSTRUCTION

Discussions of instruction seem frequently to assume implicitly that instruction can be separated from other aspects of the educational experience. One reason for this is found in the failure to make a distinction between what we shall call for convenience "teaching" and the broader concept of instruction. Teaching, narrowly conceived, refers to the activities of the teacher in direct scheduled contacts with students. The difficulty with this limited construction is that it focuses on teacher activities and teacher characteristics and ignores the student learning which may or may not ensue. The term "instruction" as usually interpreted is broader than the term "teaching," for it includes the total array of stimuli and opportunities for response which are provided by the instructional staff.

A significant result of this distinction is that evaluation or planning of instruction must start from some accepted statement of the responsibilities of instruction. The *first* function or obligation of instruction is that of motivating the student. It is not unreasonable to assume that a student coming to a college has some basic motivation for self-improvement, but it is too much to assume that this basic motivation provides adequate stimulus for involvement in depth in each and every course which the student may be required to take by virtue of selection of a certain curriculum. The student must be helped to see the relevance of each course in terms of his ultimate goals. The *second* function of instruction is that of demonstrating to the student just what in the way of new knowledge, behavior, or reactions is expected of him. This obligation requires some supervision or guidance of the student's efforts in trying to acquire these reactions. Talking is not enough. A *third* function of instruction is to provide extensive and meaningful materials upon which the student can practice. It is not sufficient to assume that either a demonstration or the actual supervision of a student in one experience with a new bit of behavior will yield mastery. It is hardly much better to suggest to the student that he needs more practice and then to leave it to him to select the materials and proceed on his own. The *fourth* function of instruction is that of providing the student with satisfaction by indicating that he is making progress. Doing so involves pointing out to the student what is good about what has been accomplished, although it is sometimes necessary also to point out the weak and inadequate aspects of the performance, else the route to improvement is uncertain. The *fifth* function of instruction is that of organizing the work so that the sequential cumulative aspect of it is readily apparent to the student and so that current learning is related to past and future study. The learning of isolated facts or skills must be interspersed with activities which give some indication of how these facts and skills fit together. The *sixth* function of instruction is that of providing the student with high standards of performance and with means for judging the extent to which his performance meets these standards. If this function is to provide an incentive for continued learning and increased mastery, it must proceed on some basis other than the common testing practices which merely punctuate various phases of learning by the insertion of an A or F. The real evil of grades is that they may encourage the student to settle for satisfactory grades rather than to strive for high-quality performance.

If these six functions are accepted as descriptive of the obligations of instruction, it becomes clear that an attempt to evaluate instruction could proceed by examination of the extent to which these functions are fulfilled. It could likewise proceed by inquiry regarding the extent to which these functions have resulted in significant learning or change in the student. One approach involves an examination or evaluation of the process; the other involves attention to the results. Both are necessary, and they supplement each other because one cannot interpret findings about results without extensive knowledge of the process, and detailed study of the process is a waste of effort unless one also knows whether the process is effective. To put the matter another way, the quality of instruction must ultimately be measured by the amount and quality of learning which ensues; but if we are to understand why certain experiences and certain instructors are more effective than others, we will need to understand the nature of the instructional and learning processes involved so that this understanding can be adapted and utilized by others. It should be evident that systematic evaluation of instruction is essential. There are at least three identifiable reasons why this is so. The first is that it is required for the recognition and reward of good instruction; for faculty members, like students, are motivated by tangible recognition as much as or more than by personal satisfaction. The second is to provide knowledge and understanding which will make it possible to improve instruction and the learning by students which is the reason for providing instruction. The third, which represents an interest on the part of psychological and educational researchers who are primarily interested in the nature of learning and the facilitation of it, involves research on instruction, altogether apart from whether this research will be used to improve the process or not. In fact, however, such research is of little consequence unless it does contribute to improvement. Thus all three reasons ultimately condense into one: the improvement of the educational process.

Student Evaluation Undoubtedly the most common systematic approach to the evaluation of instruction is through student evaluation. Programs of student evaluation, as developed and approved by the faculty, tend to be sporadic. Student evaluation questionnaires are readily prepared but, whatever the extent of involvement of faculty and the utilization of empirical modes of study, most questionnaires have a short life. For convenience, an objective checklist is most desirable, but to find a set of items which is acceptable to all faculty members is almost impossible. A common contention is that a checklist just doesn't communicate anything to an individual faculty member, and that the only useful item is a written statement by the student. Such statements are difficult to summarize and are not likely to be utilized by anyone other than the faculty member himself, if even by him. This is, undoubtedly, one reason why some faculty members prefer that pattern.

The question is repeatedly raised as to whether student evaluation is a valid indication of good teaching. The answer is by no means a simple "yes" or "no," although the negative judgment is unhesitatingly given by many professors. Good teaching is basically facilitation of the learning process. Accordingly, it is desirable that every teacher learn what his students think about the experience provided in the course. This includes not only an appraisal of what the teacher does but also an appraisal of the assignments, the examinations, the textbook used, and other relevant considerations. Furthermore, student appraisal should be, in some sense, self-appraisal, for the student must be brought to realize that he, too, has some responsibility in connection with learning. He ought to know what the objectives of the course really are. He should try to see the relationships of the various activities in which he engages to the achievement of these purposes. If the student does not know what the objectives of the course are, then the teacher may reasonably ask himself whether he adequately presented them, and he may also ask whether the course experiences are appropriate to the objectives. The student should be led to engage in similar reflections.

A low student rating does not necessarily mean that the teacher is doing a poor job. It is, however, relevant to know what students think about a teacher and about a course, for when students appraise an experience as being poor they are unlikely to attain the optimal benefit from it.

Students respond more frankly to a third person than to the instructor or a rating scale. There is something about recording a reaction on a sheet of paper which leads a student to be, on the one hand, charitable and, on the other hand, hesitant about being overly critical—perhaps for fear that his response will be traced back to him. Thus systematic interviewing of students may be a very revealing way to evaluate teaching. Student appraisal may be directed to the course or to the instructor. Teachers will often be more receptive to student appraisal of a course than they will to appraisal of their teaching. Comments on teaching become very personal and make the teacher defensive, so that he may become incapable of profiting from the comments. In large, multiple-section courses in which certain uniform policies are employed, student comments on the course may be appropriate because much of the student reaction is to matters not fully determined by the individual teacher. Student evaluation should be primarily directed to those things which the student directly experiences. There are better ways to judge the scholarship of a professor than by asking a freshman or sophomore to make that judgment, but even a freshman can render his judgment on such first-hand experiences and observations as the clarity of the lectures, the amount of individual assistance provided by the faculty member, the appropriateness and reasonableness of the assignments, etc.

The evidence is not completely consistent, but it does not appear that grades of students have great impact on their ratings. The instructor who insists that only A and B student reactions are appropriate ignores both his obligation to other student levels and the fact that he gives the grades. The instructor has an obligation to all students: majors and nonmajors; honors students and failures; freshmen and seniors. If any significant portion of any of these groups in his classes finds some element unsatisfactory (e.g., lectures incoherent, etc.), then the knowledge is worth having. The value of student ratings is not to be argued on the grounds that they reveal the truth about the teaching or the course, for truth here at least is relative. The value lies in making evident the students' judgments of an instructor or course, and any procedure which does that is valid for that purpose.

It will be unusual to find an instructor who is rated poorly in all respects by all students or rated uniformly high in all respects by all students. This provides the possibility, first, that by noting those points on which a person is rated uniformly high it may be possible to modify his instructional assignment to take account of his strengths. This might be in reference to the type of instruction (lecture, discussion, seminar, etc.) which he carries on or to the students (low ability, honors, nonmajors, etc.) with whom he works. By noting weaknesses, the individual himself may find ways to make improvements. In many cases the deficiency lies in lack of communication. An instructor may insist that he has explained objectives when most of his students insist that he has not. It may be that the instructor has not adequately explained the objectives, or it may be that he failed to communicate to students the importance of understanding the objectives.

In recent years student governments and other student organizations have instituted programs of student evaluation of instruction. Usually the results have been published with the avowed intent of assisting students to select their instructors and courses. Other motivations also exist, although they are not always made explicit. The students want a voice in personnel actions; especially they would like to get rid of the incompetent. Such student-run programs are especially subject to serious weaknesses. The quality of the instruments, the inadequacy of sampling, and often an inherent bias in the approach make the results dubious. It is doubtful that the publication of such results accomplishes anything in the improvement of instruction, and they may actually have a deleterious effect, particularly when certain professors, who are by no means regarded by their colleagues as good teachers, are rated high because they have captured the students' imagination for reasons quite unrelated to the quality of their teaching. Some students do not seem to perceive the difference between titillation and teaching.

Peer and Administrative Evaluation Peer and administrative evaluations of instruction are also made, whether or not they are formally structured. The departmental associates of any person develop, through their contacts with him and with his students, some conception of the quality of his teaching. Departmental chairmen and deans likewise make appraisals. These informal appraisals are based on very inadequate evidence, they are seldom recorded and hence cannot be contested, but they do influence decisions. The complaints of a few students in the absence of other information can irretrievably damn the teacher. The professor who talks glibly and interminably about his teaching and his "experiments" may convince administrators and peers even though he only confuses the students. The misguided or incompetent teacher argues that, since his peers have no intimate contact with his teaching and cannot, therefore, demonstrate its inadequacy, they must accept it as satisfactory—innocent until proven guilty. The argument is appealing and is admirably buttressed by a perverted concept of academic freedom which bars intruders from the classroom.

Peer and administrative evaluation may be directed to courses, in which case emphasis is on the quality and value of a course and on its contribution to the individual student and total program. If only one person is teaching a course, it may be difficult to separate the quality of instruction from the course itself, but when several teachers are involved the course may be appraised apart from the individual assigned to teach it. Course appraisal is then more focused on content, on requirements, on relation to other courses, and on the specified instructional pattern (lecture, seminar, laboratory, etc.).

Peer and administrative evaluation of the individual is usually related to decisions with regard to promotion, tenure, and salary; but it may also be concerned with improvement of instruction and with the career development of individuals. Peer and administrative evaluation may thus proceed by the collection and the utilization of a wide range of evidence including student evaluations. A rather limited but systematic conception of peer evaluation involves visits to classes by colleagues or administrators, reviews of teaching plans and tests, and conferences with each instructor. Every new junior member of a faculty should be visited by the department chairman or another senior member of the department faculty who can assist him in adjusting to a new institution and student body as well as point out any obvious errors or flaws in his approach. The visits also provide first-hand information on the quality of instruction.

Administrative evaluation at any level above the department chairman must, except in very small institutions, depend upon the judgments of others closer to the scene. It is desirable that not only the judgments but the evidence upon which they are based be available to the dean or other administrator. Otherwise, he can only rubberstamp a judgment or invite difficulty by questioning the summary judgment rendered by chairmen and peers. The remoteness from evidence results in overvaluing of the occasional student complaint brought to the dean's office. At another extreme, in some universities deans have had to be satisfied with checking faculty teaching assignments to be sure that the individual has actually done some teaching!

It is desirable to have some formalization of the administrative evaluation by developing report forms and requiring that these be completed and returned along with some recommendations when significant decisions are to be made with regard to an individual. Thus if a person is to be reappointed for another term, to be promoted, or to be given tenure, it is desirable that the department chairman and senior members of a department review carefully the performance of the individual, render some judgment, and record this and some substantiating evidence in some fashion that can be readily reviewed by the dean or other administrative officers who must pass on the recommendations. Evaluation at these critical points, however, is necessarily a broad evaluation of the total area of faculty performance rather than that of instruction only. We shall return to this broader problem of evaluation of faculty efforts shortly.

Self-evaluation Self-evaluation is essential to improvement. Until an individual confronts his weak points and deficiencies and attempts to do something about them, evaluation will be resented and rejected. Thus student ratings, colleague comments, classroom recordings, or video tapes all can and should be used by the instructor to appraise his own performance and obtain clues for improvement. This does not negate the possibility, however, that an insightful colleague, an observer, or even a student may make specific suggestions for improvement that will be very helpful. The only justification for teaching is in the learning that it promotes, and therefore the evaluation of teaching is useful only if it improves teaching and thereby improves learning. It is no doubt true that teaching could be improved by eliminating the incompetent teachers, but the supply of qualified teachers is limited and the number of really excellent teachers is small. Improvement must be the goal.

Another way to evaluate instruction is by measuring the achievement of students. Yet one can readily imagine the teacher so demanding and so unreasonable that students, despite a very high level of achievement, refuse further contact with that teacher's field. There is more than one type of objective of concern in education, and in some respects affective outcomes may be of more importance than cognitive ones. Nevertheless, if there are a number of sections of a course, if abilities are reasonably matched, and if the students of a given teacher regularly excel or regularly fall below the mean performance of the entire group, some judgments may reasonably be made about the capabilities of this person. However, this requires common examinations, and experience indicates that the teacher whose students fall below the mean commonly denounces the examination as being invalid and unfair relative to what he is trying to accomplish. Unless the teacher is a participant in the process and committed to acceptance and use of the results, improvement is unlikely to follow.

Pitfalls of Ratings All modes of evaluation of instruction involve some problems. There is always the question of validity. Whether or not student ratings, for example, really tell how good or poor an instructor is may be less significant than finding out what students think. Yet ultimately someone does have to make a judgment as to whether certain evidence is valid, whether the issue is that of changing a pattern or determining whether a person remains at an institution. There is also the problem of reliability. Would the technique used reveal the same kind of information upon repeated use? Would two or more different persons seeing the same evidence make the same kind of judgment with regard to it? There is no question but that reliability and validity are important, but overconcern with them can eliminate any possibility of evaluation of instruction. Subjectivity and the presence of personal bias or prejudice are ever-present concerns in appraisal of instruction. Despite the raising of these objections to any systematic form of evaluation, it is probable that these drawbacks operate to a far greater extent than faculty members realize even in the unsystematic, sporadic type of evaluations which are usually made. Another problem is that of a halo effect. To the extent that some one facet of teaching or of personality is predominant, so far may any attempt to make judgments about various aspects of that person's teaching be overshadowed by an appraisal based upon this one factor. In this particular era, for example, an instructor who speaks critically of the administration, institutional or national, or shows marked sympathy with prevalent student concerns may widely be regarded by students as a good teacher when he is, at most, a "good guy" from a very limited point of view.

EVALUATION OF THE FACULTY

A program of evaluation of instruction can only be developed in the broader context of a complete program of faculty appraisal. This broader conception becomes especially relevant when cognizance is taken of the extent to which undergraduate education is being extended to include experiences in research, in foreign travel and study, in community service, in supervised employment, and in community living and governance. In effect the range of experiences open to the undergraduate is coextensive with the range of functions usually ascribed to the faculty. Only by complete appraisal of faculty effectiveness over all these functions can wise decisions be made in allocating faculty resources to their appropriate role in the education of the undergraduate.

Evaluation of the faculty may be pursued as an evaluation of the faculty as a whole or an evaluation of individual faculty members. In evaluating the faculty as a whole, one is concerned with the variety of competencies available in the faculty and with the complementariness and the balance of the faculty as a whole. Likewise, it is important to assess the extent to which the faculty is dynamic, alert, and adaptive. Does the spirit of inquiry pervade the campus? Is there a real sense of commitment to the institution and to some accepted set of educational values? Is there a willingness to innovate, to take action, and to improve the program, the institution, and the community? Do the faculty insist upon excellence but, at the same time, exhibit compassion, recognizing their own and others' frailties in meeting high standards?

It is commonplace in assessing the faculty to look at certain critical statistics—age, rank, tenure, degrees, areas of specialization, sources of degrees, years of service, and the like. Each of these has some obvious implications in extreme cases, and there are no generally accepted norms or standards with regard to them. Though some individuals have suggested that the ideal would be to have a faculty so good that all its members have professorial rank and tenure, one may wonder what the future holds for an institution in which this is true. The institution that prides itself on having a very young faculty may do well to consider what this young faculty will be in 20 or 25 years. An institution which prides itself not only on the number of disciplines provided but on the number of subspecialties within those disciplines may suddenly find that courses are proliferating and education is fragmenting.

Evaluation of the faculty as individuals requires knowing something of the interests and competencies of the individual, something of the activities and functions carried out by the individual, and it requires continual attention to the collection of data on the activity and productivity of each person. The appraisal of faculty as individuals requires the identification of several areas of faculty competence and activity. The first might be designated as that of scholarship and advanced study. Scholarship can be differentiated from research on the grounds that the latter is commonly limited to the pursuit of new knowledge and the publication thereof. Scholarship includes an integrative type of activity which could be labeled research and certainly is not inferior to it, but it is also much more related to the instructional function. Curriculum revision requires that our best minds be continually examining the implications of rapidly increasing knowledge for the organization of more effective and more efficient curricula. Related to scholarship in this sense is the matter of advanced study. The day is past when an individual who has completed his doctorate can be regarded as having terminated his period of formal study. The person who does not engage in continuing study is soon a period piece.

A second type of professional competence is that of research. Research is a significant function, and one cannot condone involvement of a faculty member in graduate instruction unless that faculty member himself is engaged in significant research. A person cannot long remain an outstanding teacher with undergraduates without engaging in scholarly activity; but research, in the more restricted sense in which it is used here, is hardly necessary for undergraduate instruction. Certainly there is no evidence for the oft-repeated contention that the person who is a good researcher is automatically a good teacher. It should be noted that evaluation of research presents most of the problems of evaluating instruction. The assumption is too readily made that all research which is published is satisfactory simply because no one with knowledge of the field takes the time or makes the effort to determine how worthwhile the research is. Thus pointless research is encouraged, subsidized, and lauded while quality performance of other functions yielding less apparent results may go unnoted.

Activity in professional associations is one means not only of advancing the career of the individual but of advancing the profession and the discipline. In many fields, too, the research findings and the knowledge of the scholar have immediate relevance to problems which communities, government, business, and industry are facing. In a university which accepts a service obligation and where a professor is regarded as truly a member of a profession in the fullest meaning of that term, there is some obligation to make available his special competencies for the improvement of society. The person who does so should be recognized for it and it may be noted that such activity ultimately redounds to the benefit of instruction by making it more current and more practical.

Classroom teaching and instruction have already been discussed as major activities of a faculty member. It should be noted that this includes not only behavior in the classroom but also curriculum planning and evaluation, the planning and—possibly, where several people are involved—supervision of instruction, the evaluation of student progress, and the continuing evaluation and improvement of the instructional process itself.

Another area of faculty activity which receives too little attention and, like instruction, is often handled very poorly is that of the academic advising of students. Academic advising at the undergraduate level suffers because few faculty members have any conception of what undergraduate education is all about. The horizon of each professor is limited by the fences around his discipline, and the large number of courses impedes discussion and understanding of the curricular offerings even within the discipline. The problems of the undergraduate student often are much less with his major than with the planning of a total program which provides liberal education combined with sufficient vocational orientation that the student is capable of doing something when he finishes his degree. A good adviser must know his institutional resources in depth, must know and understand its regulations, and should have sufficient authority to deviate from specified regulations when this is advisable.

Public service, another area of professional activity, is frequently identified as a major function of colleges and universities. If so, there must be a willingness on the part of the faculty member to engage in public service—with or without pay, as appropriate. The faculty member gains from this experience, the public benefits therefrom, and, because of it, instruction can be more realistic. Public service is, then, in a sense, a professional responsibility. If we accept it as such, then it must be recognized as a function for which time will be assigned and which will be evaluated. The relevance of this function to instruction is particularly evident in those institutions which recommend or require off-campus service experiences for students.

One of the results of the loyalty of faculty members to their discipline and their professional field is that they may show little commitment to the institution with which they are currently affiliated. They may view the institution as only a means to their own ends and become critical or even abusive of any policy or administrative action which narrows their range of freedom or conflicts with their own views. There is a need for faculty members who think otherwise but who, nevertheless, are able to empathize with others and place the good of the institution, the community, and of higher education generally in proper perspective and so strive for those changes most beneficial to all concerned rather than demanding freedom to go their own way.

If evaluation of faculty efforts is to be carried on on this broad base, it is essential that the interests and competencies of faculty members be determined, that they be assigned loads which take advantage of their interests and competencies, and that there be recurring surveys of just what these loads are and of how well the activities are performed. Thus the program really becomes one of careful selection and of trying to find the best possible correspondence between the interests and competencies of the individual on one hand and the needs of the institution on the other. Continuing appraisal of the persons joining the staff, with emphasis in the initial periods on assisting the individual to find his particular niche and to develop in it, is required. Finally, the individual must be rewarded as he develops and performs meritoriously or be counseled into other activity more appropriate to his talents.

EVALUATION OF ADMINISTRATION

There has been a great deal written about problems of administration in higher education, but too much of it constitutes reminiscing by presidents which makes no significant contribution to the development of a science or even an art of administration. Much of the study of administration in business, industry, government, and even in elementary and secondary education is quite irrelevant to higher education. The difficulty is that there is no simple answer as to what constitutes the administration. Usually there is a governing board which is responsible for the operation of the institution. In recent years there may even have been several governing boards with a division of responsibilities. Though presidents are selected by the governing boards and, in turn, usually propose for board approval all of the administrative officers who work under them, much of the business of the university, instruction and research, must be carried on by faculty members organized into disciplinary or professional education groups. Faculty members are the authorities in their particular fields. They are and must be accorded a great deal of autonomy in the development of their programs. However, the often-expressed faculty view that the institution really should be run by the faculty, that the administrative officers should carry out the policies determined by the faculty, and that the major role of a governing board and the top echelon of administrative officers is that of seeing that the resources which the faculty wish are made available to them must be regarded as unreasonable and impractical. The challenge of governance in a democracy is certainly highlighted in the modern university where the supporting clientele feel that they should have much to say about how it is run, where the immediate governing boards know that legally they have the responsibility for running the institution, where presidents and other administrative officers are viewed as responsible for making decisions, but where, increasingly, the faculty, student body, and even the various classes of nonacademic personnel, through bargaining associations, are increasingly demanding a role in policy determination. If the university cannot solve this problem, there is little hope for democracy.

There are no accepted sets of categories for talking about patterns of governance in higher education. There exist still a few institutions (and in the past there have been many) in which the president operates as a dictator, often as a paternalistic one. This is most likely to be the case in a small institution where the president can be cognizant of everything that goes on, although even in the small institution the obligations of a president sometimes keep him away from the campus so much that this becomes impossible. History suggests that some of the most progressive developments of higher education are due largely to the powerful personalities of presidents who effectively dominated their institutions for a period of years. But this was in a period when institutions were isolated, when professional associations were less powerful, and research was incidental or ignored.

An institution may operate as a bureaucracy. There is some tendency, as institutions get larger, to formalize the organizational pattern, to write down rules, regulations, and policies and, as a result, to develop a pattern where each unit and individual is more interested in preserving his personal prerogatives and the responsibilities of his immediate office than he is in forwarding the purposes of the university. Another pattern of administration which has been described is that of collegiality, presumably a pattern in which a group consensus is achieved. In many respects collegiality might be the ideal pattern of administration—one based upon discussion, goodwill, mutual respect, and embodying many of the characteristics of the New England town meeting. Some small institutions may approximate this pattern and departments in larger institutions may effectively utilize it. Unfortunately, collegiality often degenerates into an oligarchy which retains some of the appearances of the ideal but actually results in domination by a small group. A fourth pattern of administration, one seen by some faculty members as ideal, is that of anarchy (more tactfully labeled a situation of laissez faire)—a pattern in which each individual is free to go his own way, to teach what he wants when he wants, and in general to do as he pleases. Some prestigious departments in universities appear to achieve this state.

These categories of administration are useful only in suggesting different approaches to decision making. The ideal really must be one which draws in some measure upon all, preserving some prerogatives and initiative for administrators while providing for faculty involvement in decision making and a high degree of freedom on the part of the faculty in pursuing their own assignments and commitments. Communication is one of the major problems in administration. Administrators, faced with many problems, are naturally desirous of solving a problem once their attention has been focused upon it. The result is that too often decisions are made before faculty members are alerted to the problem. Faculty members are under less pressure for prompt action, usually represent a multiplicity of views, and like to discuss any issue at great length. Yet a synthesis of opinion is sometimes very difficult to achieve in this way, and there is good reason to believe that, except for those decisions which the faculty see as their prerogatives (curriculum, instruction, etc.) or matters which affect deeply each individual faculty member, such as promotion and tenure policies, the major concern is that the faculty voice be heard and that there be assurance that the individual concerns of faculty members are understood before a decision is reached.

One of the problems of administration in higher education is that it ought to provide to its students a model of the judgmental decision-making process which it is trying to inculcate in those students. In fact, higher education does not often provide this model, for administration proceeds by some combination of expediency, opportunism, and competition. The tendency of too many administrators is to take the route which presents the least difficulty, stirs up the fewest people, and involves the least threat. Thus it is very difficult for colleges and universities to face up to moral issues. If a governor threatens an institution's appropriations because it denies admission to his daughter, the daughter will be admitted. Indeed, the likelihood is that the daughter will be admitted immediately in order to avoid even the possibility of the threat. Sons or daughters of prominent alumni, especially those making large gifts to the institution, are in a different admissions category than other students. Institutions also reach decisions on the basis of opportunism. When money becomes available for a new program or even when interest is displayed in a new program, institutions rush in without considering whether this is an appropriate expansion of activity. Finally, despite increasing evidence of cooperation among institutions, competition still plays a very significant role. The fads that one observes in curriculum and in instruction occur largely because each institution is concerned about the publicity given others and fears that status will be lost if it does not follow suit or trump. The university supposedly is committed to seeking the truth without regard to consequences; but when it comes to reaching major decisions, most institutions are quite unable to make a decision on sound educational grounds and then face up to the consequences, whatever these may be. Expediency, opportunism, and competition have played such a significant role in higher education developments in the past century that, despite the high respect which a college education is accorded in this country, the motivations and the operations of higher education are viewed with some distrust.

Statements of goals often have little meaning because they are written to impress rather than to give direction. More detailed statements of goals and long-term plans based upon these are very often rejected by faculty and administration alike because they are unwilling to see their aspirations eliminated by the adoption of realistic goals and plans. The result is that carefully developed statements of policy and procedure which give the appearance of effective planning and administration are so ambiguous that they can be read or perverted to suit the pressures of the moment.

Administration, of course, is increasingly complicated. The students who once paid for an education and willingly left it to the faculty to determine what that education might be now demand a voice in it, and since colleges and universities will do almost anything to avoid bad publicity, even when created by only a few persons, students will have more voice. The faculty, too, demand more of a role in the operation of institutions while at the same time demonstrating increasingly that their loyalties are not at all to the institutions. The public, while on one hand pressing institutions always to expand their services and the range of educational programs, increasingly express doubts about the necessity of the funds required and the efficiency with which they are used. Thus administrators are caught in a complex of pressures which make truly creative administration and long-term planning nearly impossible. It is surprising that colleges operate as well as they do despite external concerns and criticisms.

The evaluation of administration really is an evaluation of the processes utilized in an institution to set goals, develop plans, and work out policies and procedures for the attainment of these goals and plans. The quality of the communications system and the mode of involvement of the various groups concerned with the institution in the decision-making process are instrumental to this broad concern. In turn, the way in which an administrator deals with people, his availability to people, the clarity of his communications, oral and written, and his sensitivity to the concerns of the individual and of the various groups with which he must deal are significant aspects of his administrative activity. Just as a faculty member can and should know how students react to his teaching, so the administrator ought, from time to time, to solicit in some objective fashion reactions from those with whom he works. This might be in terms of a prepared questionnaire or checklist filled out anonymously by the faculty. Many presidents would avoid major difficulties with their boards if from time to time they reviewed with the board some of the administrative issues of the preceding several months and their own role in them and then requested evaluation by the board. One thing any administrator can be sure of—that is that his administrative effectiveness is being evaluated. As with teaching, if that evaluation is less laudatory than the administrator believes appropriate—that is, even if he questions the validity of negative criticism—he nevertheless has a problem, and he should know about it. The administrator who does not seek and accept evaluation of his own activity is on dubious ground when he insists that his faculty undergo such evaluation.

INSTITUTIONAL APPRAISAL, INTERNAL AND EXTERNAL

Each of the previous sections on evaluation involves appraisal of some phase of an institution's operations, but only those that are most commonly evaluated and perhaps most in need of continuing systematic evaluation have been touched. Study of any one aspect of an institution, pursued to its fullest ramifications, leads ultimately to appraisal of the integrity and effectiveness of the institution as a whole. The appraisal of institutions of higher education usually involves an examination of the operations rather than the results, although it seems obvious that the efficiency and the effectiveness of an institution must be judged by the degree to which it accomplishes its purposes, aims, and objectives. Ideally, every institution should engage in continuing appraisal, but it is also appropriate that, from time to time, an institution undergo a thorough restudy in depth. This may be done by asking a group of educators or a consulting firm to undertake a survey of the total institution or some part of it. It may be done on a self-study basis by the utilization of faculty members, administrators, trustees, students, alumni, and others directly concerned with the institution. It may also, and perhaps more commonly, be done by some combination of outside consultants and individuals immediately concerned with the operation of the institution. Either of the last two patterns is likely to be more effective and perhaps less expensive, at least in direct cash outlay, than a survey or study conducted entirely by outsiders. Participation in the study process often is essential to the ultimate acceptance of recommendations. Even though the involvement of individuals connected with an institution may increase the subjectivity and increase the threat to vested interests, individuals from outside an institution, no matter how experienced, may not sense the unique elements in that institution. Commercial consulting firms may have fixed views about operations and organizational patterns, and these may be inappropriate to the particular situation. When the self-study is locally organized, outside consultants may effectively be used, and their recommendations may help to overcome some of the more sensitive problems which those directly affiliated with an institution cannot effectively tackle. However, when major weaknesses in the business or administrative operations exist, an independent analysis by outside consultants may be necessary. An institutional appraisal can hardly be made without some clarification of the aims and objectives of the institution. Usually there are many different statements of aims and objectives, and many different sources contribute to them. Statements by presidents or board members and statements included in catalogs, committee reports, board minutes, the charter or enabling act, and other sources will throw light on why an institution was organized and what it purports to do. Not infrequently there are different points of view in the administration, the faculty, the student body, and the supporting clientele as to what an institution is or should become. The board and supporting clientele may view an institution as primarily a community college providing some transfer general education but committed heavily to the provision of vocational education of various types and duration; whereas the president and faculty may hope for baccalaureate degree status and elimination of the vocational elements. Likewise, a former teachers college, supposedly still committed primarily to undergraduate education, may be moving without fanfare toward becoming a graduate institution.

The major purposes of higher education are perhaps everywhere the same: collection and organization of the cultural heritage (a museum, library, and scholarly function), augmentation of the cultural heritage (a research function), and dissemination of the cultural heritage (an instructional and service function). The true university will have all three purposes, whereas liberal arts colleges and community colleges or technical institutes are more likely to concentrate on the dissemination or instructional function. However, there is a hierarchical organization in American higher education which places graduate and professional education at the top and freshman or sophomore work and terminal technical education at the bottom. Expediency, opportunism, and competition characterize the effort of institutions to move up this ladder. The attempt to achieve excellence at any level requires an able faculty and an administration with ambition and enthusiasm who aspire to move to a still higher level. Thus it is desirable to clarify initially what the purposes of the institution really are.

Objectives arise out of purposes, but they attempt to spell out in more concrete terms the institution's hopes for the students that it accepts. Objectives should be stated as desired qualities of students or as student behavior; unfortunately, these statements tend to become highly verbose and abstract. By espousing God, family, and democracy, they may make an emotional appeal but provide little guidance to the educational program. What is needed is a limited and succinct statement of the competencies which the institution expects to produce in its students; these should be so specific that it is feasible to determine whether students have obtained these competencies in some reasonable measure before degrees are granted to them. Much time can be wasted on discussion of purposes and objectives because everyone expresses his ideals and his hopes rather than realistic goals appropriate to the clientele which the institution serves and the financial level at which it operates. It may be necessary to let agreement on objectives and purposes grow out of the study rather than to try to make them preface it.

In defining the scope of a study, one may divide the operations of an institution into such areas as instruction, curriculum, administration, finances, student life, and faculty. These are interrelated, and it is not possible to pursue one very far without involving others. Certainly instruction and curriculum can hardly be separated, and these immediately raise problems of administrative organization and finance; yet it is possible to regard one or more of these categories as defining the major emphasis of the study. The curricular area has often been studied in recent years. Student life has also attracted considerable study because of widespread student unrest.

Organization for Self-study Whatever the scope of the study, certain problems must be faced with regard to the respective roles of faculty, administration, trustees, students, alumni, and others. Here several factors are to be weighed. First, the more groups involved the more difficulty there may be arranging work sessions and the slower the project is likely to move. Second, the more groups that are involved the greater may be the tendency to divide the self-study into parts corresponding to the a priori roles of the various groups. Thus administrators may be asked to study the administrative organization, trustees to study some of the problems of financial support, etc. When those most intimately involved with a problem are assigned to study it their report may defend the status quo rather than probe it. Third, the greater the range of individuals involved in study of a particular problem the greater will be the difficulty in getting down to specifics.

A study should be so organized that those who will be asked ultimately to approve changes are made aware of that prospect well beforehand. Institutional appraisal is perhaps most successful if it is conducted in such a way that it promotes a readiness to make the changes which emanate from that appraisal. Internally conducted studies usually proceed through a number of committees. A coordinating committee or council, including all committee chairmen and the study coordinator, is appropriate. The study coordinator could be chairman of this council, although he probably has greater freedom if he is not. Under this council there will be committees or task forces assigned to particular areas or problems. The council and director should have assistance to coordinate the activities, handle paper work, gather facts, etc. An institution which is attempting to reshape its destiny through self-study may reasonably expect to spend as much as 1 percent of its annual budget for such a study, although much of the cost is usually hidden in additional hours of time given to the self-study. Many self-studies are focused on some limited problem and find no necessity for such widespread involvement. A curriculum study involving a look at general education requirements may be largely a faculty enterprise, although administrators and students will surely be involved.

Self-study, especially when done as a requirement for accreditation, may be quite perfunctory, amounting to little more than a spring housecleaning. Things are tidied up and imperfections retouched—the operation looks cleaner and neater but nothing is really changed. The study is historical and descriptive rather than analytical and prescriptive. Yet, even in this case, comparisons with characteristics of accredited institutions may have some impact. For example, the need for improvement of salaries, retirement programs, and library appropriations may become evident.

Financial Records, Budgeting, and Costs The financial procedures and records, the auditing, budgeting, and purchasing aspects of the business side of an institution are poorly understood by most faculty. There is a tendency in a self-study to reserve this area for those most closely involved with it. This not only eliminates an opportunity to generate, on the part of the faculty, increased insight into and understanding of an important area, but it may even encourage some suspicion and doubt about the academic orientation of the business operation. In any faculty there surely are a few individuals in economics, business, or other areas who can contribute to a look in depth at the institution's business operations. One or two board members should be involved and probably, in most institutions, an outside consultant.

One of the problems with the business aspect of an educational institution is the lack of relationship between income and expenditures—other than the necessity that income at least equal expenditures. Income sources are primarily from student tuition and fees, the government, endowment, and gifts. Some of these are restricted and must be handled as separate funds, although they actually support, in part, the instructional and research functions. Income channeled into the educational and general fund is spent on instruction, research, service, and supporting activities with no regard to source. Since individuals may contribute to all of these functions, it is difficult to relate income sources to functions, although it is readily possible to relate income to objective categories of expenditures such as salaries, services, and equipment. The outputs of an educational institution are not readily interpretable in numbers or in dollars. Faculties produce and students earn credit hours, but the credit hour is not an indication of accomplishment. Even if one accepts the credit hour or number of degrees as an objective indication of output, research and service are not so easily quantified. The outputs of a college involve effects on students, effects on the public generally, effects on the social structure and the economy, and effects on the individuals who operate the institution. In view of the importance of the faculty and the environment, the latter may be as important as any other outcome. Because of the difficulties in defining outcomes and because of the involvement of most individuals in several different functions and outcomes, programs, in the sense used in program budgeting, are not easily specified nor used as bases for assigning expenditures. Likewise, cost-benefit analysis (a most attractive combination of concepts) suffers from the fact that the most tangible benefit of education is the increased income of those who receive the education. Not surprisingly, then, study of the financial and business operations has little connection with educational outcomes other perhaps than examining the percentage of the educational and general budget which is expended on instruction, on administration, or the library. Cost studies to determine the cost of producing a student credit hour at various levels in various fields can be made but, because of the lack of uniform practices (e.g., where such items as faculty retirement benefits are assigned), the problems in apportioning certain expenditures (e.g., the proportion of library expenditures to be assigned to a given course or department), and the unquantifiable nature of quality, cost studies have very limited utility for comparison purposes. Even within an institution, the meaning of great differences in the cost of a credit hour in various fields is not easily determined. Costs may be high in some professional or technical field because of the faculty-to-student ratio required, because of the laboratory time and equipment required, or simply because one department is a mature department of national standing with largely tenured senior faculty while another one is a rather new department staffed heavily with individuals in the lower ranks.

MEASURES OF QUALITY

What determines the quality of an institution? The answer is not easily provided, for quality, goodness, or excellence can have various meanings. Furthermore, almost any college is sufficiently complicated that it is unlikely to be of equal quality in all aspects. Much depends upon the point of view and the values of the person who makes the judgment. The Cartter report,[1] assessing quality in graduate education, emphasized the judgment of department chairmen, of senior scholars, and of junior scholars in each of the various disciplines. Quality here, then, is a matter of subjective judgments by individuals of the strength of the graduate work and research in a department. Presumably, on this basis the quality of an institution would be determined by the number of its departments which receive high rating. Another survey, conducted by Dr. Earl McGrath, has emphasized the dynamic, innovative characteristics of an institution. Here institutions like Antioch College, Stephens College, and Michigan State University receive attention because of the large number of innovative ideas appearing in these institutions over a period of time. Innovation is not in itself a criterion of quality, but lack of innovation surely characterizes an institution as moss rather than ivy covered. If one turns to the annual AAUP report on salary, quality is found by noting those institutions that receive A or A+ ratings in salaries. Yet the location, the purposes, and the affiliations of an institution cannot be ignored in looking at the salary structure. Commitment (institutional or doctrinal) should never be accepted as substituting for quality, and neither should it be taken as an excuse for inadequate salaries. Nevertheless, some denominationally related colleges do have faculties of quality committed to service to their institutions despite grossly inadequate salary scales.

Thus it is with each of the particular measures of quality that we consider—every one fails if pushed too far. This is why regional accrediting associations, which a few years ago emphasized quantitative requirements, now have generally dropped these in favor of an overall integrative assessment of how well an institution accomplishes the goals which it sets for itself. A baccalaureate level institution which has no Ph.D.s on its faculty would be one of dubious quality, but there exists no minimum level or percentage determining quality. Indeed, the Ph.D. is not always interested in undergraduate instruction. The publications and the professional activities of the faculty also provide some index of quality, but a somewhat different point of view (as to the nature and number of publications) must be taken in a university than in a community college or baccalaureate degree institution. The lack of professional activities on the part

[1] Allan M. Cartter, *An Assessment of Quality in Graduate Education,* American Council on Education, Washington, 1966.

of faculty members may be a sign of isolation and provinciality in a college, but participation may be overdone. One recurring complaint in universities is that too many of the faculty are oriented primarily to their professions and professional organizations rather than to the institutions.

The quality of students admitted or the performance of graduating seniors is often used as the basis for determining the quality of an institution. The two are closely related, for the most potent determiner of the level of performance of the graduates of an institution is the quality of the students admitted. One cannot compare the Graduate Record Examination performances of seniors in two institutions and decide that one is better or worse than the other without detailed knowledge of the intelligence and accomplishments of the students admitted in the first place. Moreover, especially in a democratic society, it seems inappropriate to judge the quality of an institution by its restrictive admissions. Excellence must, rather, be determined in relation to the accomplishment of goals and purposes. A community college which admits any high school graduate may be a very good institution.

Library holdings have been another criterion of excellence. But the fact that a liberal arts college possesses the minimum number of volumes recommended by the Association of College and Research Libraries means little until one knows just what volumes are present. A library which is a literary morgue holding the collections of deceased ministers may exceed the recommended number and yet be inadequate. Furthermore, the library holdings might be twice the minimum number but be nonfunctional because of lack of utilization by students and faculty. A similar point holds with regard to the seating capacity of the library. If the library seats only the minimum of 25 percent of the full-time equivalent students but is fully occupied most of the day, the situation may be much better than in a larger library with row after row of unoccupied seats. Furthermore, knowledge of the kind of usage is essential to appraisal. When library facilities accommodate mainly students who are studying textbooks rather than actually using library facilities, some doubts as to the role of the library in the institution are appropriate. It is commonly suggested that the library appropriation should be at least 5 percent of the educational and general budget. In an institution changing its character from a junior college to a senior college or from a baccalaureate institution to a graduate-level institution, a considerably larger percentage may be necessary over a period of time. In large, complicated institutions with a wide range of research and service functions and often with departmental libraries supplied by departmental funds not recorded in the library expenditures, a much lower figure may be appropriate.

The quality and utilization of space and facilities certainly require attention in evaluating any institution, but the wide application of any square-foot ratio per student (such as .83 assignable square feet per weekly student hour for classroom space or per faculty member or 120 square feet per full-time equivalent person for faculty office space) is far less important than learning just how well the facilities are utilized and how well they serve the purposes of the institution. The unusual experience of finding a science laboratory equipped very largely with instruments and equipment made by the students, accompanied by an unusually high level of enthusiasm and of understanding of scientific principles and methodology, raises some doubts as to the validity of evaluating a science program by looking at the newness of the laboratories and the equipment in them.

Appraisal of the curriculum may take place on the basis of individual reviewing of the disciplines to determine whether an adequate array of offerings is provided. This may lead to such criticisms as "inadequate offerings in physics and mathematics for majors in these fields"—a comment quite correct but equally inappropriate to the women's college which neither had nor anticipated having majors in these fields. The quality of maintenance in an institution may be considered as one aspect of its operations. Spotless floors may be hygienic and esthetically attractive, but they may lead one to wonder about maintenance costs and also about the institution as a place in which to live and work. On the other hand, grimy science laboratories and odoriferous lavatories may, with some assurance, be taken as not only evidence of inadequate maintenance but also of ineffective instruction and administration.

The style of governance in an institution also indicates something about institutional quality. The institution dominated by the president or by a coterie of top-level administrative officers is hardly appropriate to the twentieth century. It cannot, in these days, hold a strong self-respecting faculty, and it exhibits an atrocious example for students of democracy in action. Against this must be weighed the other extreme in which a simple request for an opinion addressed to a dean is forwarded to all department chairmen for a vote by the departmental faculties before a reply is forthcoming. Between these two extremes there is a wide range of styles of involvement of students, faculty, administration, boards, etc., in the governance of an institution. Thus no standard can be imposed, but some evidence of involvement, of effectiveness, and of resulting morale can surely be found.

Using the Results The preceding section has made evident the dilemma of the individuals or groups who would appraise an institution. It is easy to say that the appraisal should be based on institutional effectiveness and should avoid comparisons with other institutions, but criteria of institutional effectiveness are many, complex, and fallible and one often does require some sort of external standard in order to make some judgment. It is useful to know how the library appropriation compares with that in other institutions, and it is also useful to know something about the faculty salary level in comparison with that in other institutions, but the problem remains that knowing each of these does not in itself tell whether the local situation is satisfactory. Presumably it is if the institution effectively performs its task, but the outputs of higher education are so many and varied that no institution ever successfully appraises its overall effectiveness. More time and money devoted to appraisal would help but, to a very considerable extent, the difficulty resides in lack of clarity in specifying outputs and the lack of instruments or means to assess them.

How, then, can one combine and use the diverse evidence accumulated in institutional appraisal? The answer is that one must seek for relationships among the many types of data examined and one must propose alternatives and select among them by imposing some values upon these. If the evidence shows that salaries are inadequate and if there is also high faculty turnover, a lack of Ph.D.s, and dissatisfaction among students as to the quality of instruction, then a course of action may become reasonably evident. If it is found that an unusually low percentage of the budget is being expended on instruction, that there appear to be an unduly large number of administrative officials as compared with other institutions of the same size, and that the business office employs archaic and inefficient procedures, then the composite of these may add up to reasonably acceptable recommendations. However, the soundness of recommendations does not ensure their acceptance. If, in the situations suggested above, the evidence and tentative conclusions were kept secret until final recommendations were made, dissension rather than orderly change might ensue. If, on the other hand, findings were widely disseminated and extensively discussed, readiness for the change might be promoted.

There is always some question in connection with a self-study as to whether it should be conducted under the auspices of existing committees or by a separate group. The question is not easily answered, but it is worthwhile to note that, in most cases, self-study in an institution must be concurrent with continuing operations. For this reason, it is probably unwise to charge standing committees with the study assignment. It is too easy for them to put off from day to day the probing in depth into the problems of the institution because of the routine which comes before them, and the members may lack the vision for the task of review and innovation. On the other hand, if the study is conducted by an ad hoc group, then the decision must be reached as to whether the recommendations which emanate from the study group must be processed through the existing committee structure. The answer is not clear. The study might recommend a complete reorganization of the faculty structure and an entire new set of committees. In this case, it would seem hardly appropriate for the existing set of committees to pass on the recommendations; rather, a general faculty acceptance, supported by the approval of the president and action by the board, would seem to be adequate. The source of a self-study group's assignment is an important concern. If it is appointed by the president, the report is directed to the president. If it is set up by action of the faculty, the report is to the faculty. Even so, someone must sort out the recommendations and send them to the appropriate spots. A recommendation for clarifying the functions of the treasurer of the board and the vice-president for finance is properly forwarded to the board. Clarification of the assignments of existing committees may well be forwarded to those committees for study as well as to the president. Here again much difficulty may be avoided if these items, in their formative stage, are discussed with the respective groups.

One of the problems of using the results of a self-study is that of attaining and maintaining proper balance. The problem is partly an economic one. An institution has limited resources and, while these may be augmented by a fund-raising campaign, the new income level still constitutes limited resources. Within these limited resources the institution has problems of allocation. If percentage of Ph.D.s and high faculty salaries are taken as major criteria of excellence, then money may be devoted to this end, but student services, library holdings, maintenance, and other aspects of the institution may suffer. In fact, the effort to pay high salaries may result in inadequate clerical service, so that the institution pays high salaries to professors for doing clerical work. Concern with improving the quality of the student body could lead to allotment of more money to the hiring of recruiters and to expansion of the admissions operation, but it might, at the same time, lead to empty residence hall space and difficulties in debt retirement.

One difficulty in this preservation of balance is that self-studies are too often past- and present- rather than future-oriented. To oversimplify the problem of goodness or excellence, one might summarize by saying that *the good institution, in a certain sense, is one that knows what it is trying to do and knows where it is going.* An institutional self-study which focuses on the solution of current problems without taking into account possible changes in the character of the institution, either as a result of external pressures or announced intent on the part of the institution, may bring about changes which impede forward movement. Institutional self-evaluation should encourage orderly change in reference to possible future developments and, at the same time, create flexibility so that further changes may be made as those anticipated developments occur or are, with reason, supplanted by others.

PERIODIC VERSUS CONTINUOUS SELF-EVALUATION

Many colleges and universities in recent years have accepted the necessity of an institutional research office charged with continuous study of the institutional operations. In large institutions such an office, charged with overviewing the data system of the institution, with developing organized patterns of data collection and dissemination, with making studies for faculty committees and administrators, with initiating studies designed to point up problem areas, and with facilitating the long-term planning of the institution, is a necessity. In smaller institutions a full-time director of institutional research may be financially unfeasible, but certainly the major functions of institutional research must be performed, and someone must be assigned responsibility for coordinating these and seeing that the administration and faculty committees are provided with current and relevant evidence of the institutional operation as a basis for decision making and planning. However, such an office does not take care of all aspects of institutional appraisal. For one thing, such an office will develop a series of somewhat routine but continuing responsibilities which take up much of the time available. The demands of faculty committees and administrative offices may utilize all the residual resources. Such an office, once established, becomes part of the existing bureaucracy of the institution, comes to have its own vested interests, and is unlikely to endanger these by critical examination of the activities or policies of major administrative offices or powerful faculty committees. Furthermore, its whole approach will be so inextricably interwoven with the existing pattern of operation in an institution that it is unlikely to have the time to take a creative look at major new and needed directions of development of the institution and may have great difficulty in attempting to do so. From time to time, then, such continuous self-evaluation needs to be supported by special institutional committees or full-scale institutional self-evaluation projects which, by the charge given them, the resources supplied, and the prospect of utilizing outside consultants, are in a position to give a critical look at the institution which is not possible to an ongoing element in the institution. Of course, a unit or individual involved in the continuous self-evaluation of an institution can contribute immeasurably in terms of data, general familiarity with the institution, and technical know-how to those charged with the periodic appraisal. In fact, the director or coordinator of institutional research or a member of his staff could well be a key person in such self-appraisal, either as a member of the committee or as a staff officer to it. The point can be made in another way. Any attempt to carry on a complete self-appraisal of an institution in a situation in which there has been no continuing data collection and study will inevitably mean that the people assigned the appraisal task will spend most of their time, for six months to a year, in gathering necessary background data to define what the institution's problems are and where it is at the moment.

REFERENCES

Bloom, Benjamin S., and Frank R. Peters: *The Use of Academic Prediction Scales for Counseling and Selecting College Entrants,* The Free Press of Glencoe, New York, 1961.

Cartter, Allan M.: *An Assessment of Quality in Graduate Education,* American Council on Education, Washington, 1966.

Dressel, Paul L., and associates: *Evaluation in Higher Education,* Houghton Mifflin Company, Boston, 1961.

Gage, N. L. (ed.): *Handbook of Research on Teaching,* Rand McNally & Company, Chicago, 1963.

Harris, Seymour E.: *Higher Education: Resources and Finance,* McGraw-Hill Book Company, New York, 1962.

Hungate, Thad L.: *Management in Higher Education,* Teachers College Press, Columbia University, New York, 1964.

Lavin, David E.: *The Prediction of Academic Performance,* Russell Sage Foundation, New York, 1965.

McGrath, Earl J.: *Cooperative Long-range Planning in Liberal Arts Colleges,* Teachers College Press, Columbia University, New York, 1964.

Meeth, Richard L. (ed.): *Selected Issues in Higher Education,* Teachers College Press, Columbia University, New York, 1965.

Chapter 5

Self-directed Study

J. GARBER DRUSHAL

President, The College of Wooster, Wooster, Ohio

In the recent literature of innovation, the term "independent study" has been used to describe a method which has been prominent in the college and university catalogs since 1924. The term has come to represent many types of educational procedures partly because of the rather broad concept inherent in the words themselves and, perhaps more importantly, because there seems to have been a greater need for an all-inclusive philosophy than for a description of the technique. At the outset some delimitation may be useful.

WHAT CONSTITUTES INDEPENDENT STUDY

Independent study is a program of self-directed study designed to enhance a student's sense of responsibility, self-reliance, and perception. It may be implemented by a variety of pedagogical methods. Formal classroom experiences are replaced by individual or small group meetings with the faculty. Instruction is carried out through informal discussions, seminars, colloquia, supervised reading, etc.

First, a procedure may fall properly in this class if a student is freed from a prescribed area of subject matter. His topic and direction of endeavor may differ from those of all contemporary and former students in a particular department. However, an independent-study project does not involve the graduate requirement of being a new contribution to knowledge. It need only be new to the learner.

Secondly, the technique may be said to be independent when the student finds his own pace, his own rate of progress. Deadlines and targets may be necessary for the academic necessities of the registrar's office, but the student's opportunity to schedule his own use of time is important to the concept of independence. Inasmuch as the rate of achievement is controlled by the student, to that degree the procedure is independent.

A third provision involves independence from the teacher. Here the degree of freedom varies from complete uninvolvement of the instructor to regular tutorial sessions with differing levels of guidance. Some programs permit the student to go off on his own, submitting his material for evaluation to a committee or teacher who has not seen him prior to the completion of the project. Some of the strong tutorial-type programs involve a great amount of one-to-one teacher-student time. This feature of any program will be affected by the ability of the student, the ability and inclination of the teacher, and by the character of the institutional program.

Finally, the program must provide a measurable way for the student to move toward graduation. There must be some evaluation in terms of grades, acceptance for credit, or assignment of credit-hour or course values. As Rhett[1] pointedly observes, "The classroom is also the basis for the system of academic accounting. . . ." The same slide rule cannot be used for work done in other systems. Hence careful consideration will need to be given to the description of the unit of work and the identification of mileposts on the road to commencement whether they be grades, courses, hours, or committee certificates.

In independent study, therefore, each of these four characteristics—free choice of subject matter, pace control, freedom from teacher control, and eligibility for credit—must be present to some degree.

Programs which involve the elimination of class attendance requirements are more generally accepted. These have certain virtues, but they should not be mistaken for independent study if the pace must match that of those who do attend class and if the content is prescribed by the teacher. Further, the same examinations are often used. Such a program of freer classroom and course management may have virtues, but it should not be confused with independent study.

The administrator, be he department head, dean, or tutor, should evaluate the work of such a program on his own campus in terms of students, teachers, and the institution as a whole. The remainder of this chapter will consider the objectives and the problems for each of these groups.

THE STUDENT, THE TEACHER, AND THE INSTITUTION

The Student

To be valid, an academic program must provide opportunities for student achievement. Independent study has certain goals in terms of the participants which must be considered in relation to values which do not accrue under other types of time investments.

Values of Independent Study Independent study provides for more breadth of learning. A student may cross departmental lines. Outside his own specialty or depart-

[1] Leigh C. Rhett, "IS and the Campus Crisis," *Saturday Review*, July 16, 1966.

mental course boundaries, there are no restrictions on the outreach of the inquiring mind and the adaptation of this inquiry to the student's graduation requirement.

Certain learning skills which may not be used in class programs either because the teacher neither inspires nor permits them or because the student can get by without them may become important in independent study. Research methods in both social and physical sciences seldom find application in the average course-classroom procedure. Creative designs used in fine arts and other subdivisions of the humanities can be important parts of a self-designed study. Students usually go through the 124 course credits without experience in these learning devices. Independent study can orient the student's outlook in an important way and create a life style otherwise absent from his academic experience.

The pace of independent study similarly provides a unique opportunity for self-evaluation and development by the student. He must ask himself frequently, "How am I doing?"

Perhaps a major goal in independent study relates to the opportunities for developing intellectual diversity. Current attitudes on campuses reflect the belief on the part of many young people that they are forced into a mold in all really important experiences. A program which says "find a direction, determine a pace, move out" has an important effect on student attitudes, which in turn reveal the strengths and weaknesses of the other formal parts of their academic experience.

It should be noted here that independent study is often mistakenly viewed as only for the intellectually elite. Rogge and Gallagher[2] and others have shown that the so-called "gifted student" is not the only person to profit by the experience of learning more on his own. Motivation is an important factor. Even the so-called C student need not be deprived of an opportunity to express his intellectual curiosity even though this may differ in quality or quantity from that of other students.[3]

The Problems Encountered Independent study creates problems for students. Those who procrastinate in other areas of life will do so here, sometimes with disastrous results. Yet the student may learn something very important from such an adjustment to pace, even in failure.

It is disturbing to some students to try to move forward without frequent checkpoints which indicate degrees of success or failure. They feel directionless without frequent mileposts.

Related to the problem of guidance is the reliance on evaluation. Some believe that grades should be established at regular intervals. Fear of failure at a final evaluation should be recognized as a real roadblock. Yet independent study can be the very device which frees the student from the strictures of living from grade to grade. Some means of success assurance may need to be a part of the reinforcement offered by the faculty adviser.

The Teacher

Not all teachers are superior lecturers. Not all scientists are superior laboratory instructors. Similarly, not all faculty members have developed the skills which enable students to turn to them for counseling as they proceed through an independent project. Further, not all teachers have an attitude which accepts students' work when all of its dimensions are not prescribed by a teacher.

Guidelines for Faculty and Administrators Teachers should certainly try to help students learn to direct themselves. Success along these lines is both a goal and a reward. At the same time, the teacher learns to draw out the student, to help him over roads not heretofore traveled, and to make sure that unsuspected talents are being utilized.

[2] W. Rogge and J. J. Gallagher, "The Gifted," *Review of Educational Research,* February, 1966.

[3] See the description of the Hiram College program for an evaluation of these factors. Charles L. Adams, *Hispania,* pp. 483–487, September, 1967.

Some administrators believe that an independent-study program will automatically free the teacher for other activities, by making possible a general reduction of his teaching load. Such a result does not necessarily follow. This occurs only in those completely independent types of programs where an administrator handles the scheduling and the reading of results.

The mistaken view that all types of independent study lead to reduced teaching loads necessitates a discussion of certain other problems for the teacher. The administrator must not only be aware of these but should plan to protect the faculty members' time from their own zeal.

Many of the better teachers often find themselves in the hands of possessive students. These learners fear independence. Consequently, they involve the adviser and others in as many facets of their projects as possible. It is difficult but necessary for a teacher to draw a sharp line between reasonable student relationships and total possession by the insecure. When the uncertainties of these students dominate, anti-independent-study attitudes develop and the whole program suffers.

A further complication for the teacher may be his feeling of inadequacy as an adviser to a student whose project goes far afield from his own area of specialization. To become a specialist in all possible areas of study is of course impossible. Fortunately, this is not necessary for the student's effective progress. Since there must be sufficient checking for credit approval, some expertise is essential. It is not often that a department completely lacks this resource. The possibility should not discourage the faculty or the administration.

Some teachers will find control of the student's rate of work a problem. They have made out so many syllabi which have the tests all scheduled, term papers due on specified dates, and book list completion dates fixed that they become nervous when they see 10 students on as many different schedules. It takes a special combination of skill and attitude for the teacher to ride easy with this kind of program.

Even so, the teacher has the continuing responsibility in all areas, no less in independent study, to prevent educational disaster for the student. That point at which the guidance of the teacher can prevent the collapse is not easy to identify. One clue certainly can be seen in the case of the student who has taken a project so broad in scope as to be unachievable. This person certainly needs help. A project calling for "A Critique of the Major Philosophers of the Seventeenth, Eighteenth, and Nineteenth Centuries" should be curtailed before the student gets started. In the other direction, the student whose work is unlikely to fit within the restrictions of the academic calendar needs someone to alert him to that. Some teacher or administrator needs to be in sufficient touch with the student to be able to provide these safeguards. He is not forcing him into a schedule but making clear the relationship of his progress to the demands of time limits, graduation requirements, or other goals.

These obligations of the teacher are not necessarily time-consuming but may become so. It is the responsibility of the administrator to make sure that no one faculty member draws all the problem cases.

One other responsibility of the administrator is to see that the faculty member has adequate opportunity to keep his own batteries recharged. Some kind of sabbatical or research-leave program is imperative if any kind of independent study by students is to have a clear-cut and measurable relationship to contemporary needs. Even those we sometimes identify as "less brilliant students" may very likely, in the challenge of independence, move into areas which will necessitate the expansion of the mind of the teacher. Some provision must be made for the teachers to have time for their own independent study so that they may set an inspiring example. Here it is the administration's responsibility to permit teachers to keep up to date. Students without the fences of prescription of course content learn much about ideas and the educational processes surrounding them. The teacher who does not vary from his long-established syllabi and class notes is soon identified. He may need to be forced out into the bright light of new study himself. Otherwise, he will find that students are passing him by.

The teacher on a campus where independent study is a basic part of the student experience has therefore a unique challenge. His opportunities and benefits and problems are different from those of the classroom. With an understanding and committed administration, an academic climate can develop that will have unique rewards for both student and teacher.

The Institution

Institutional goals are basically the responsibility of the administration. However these may be determined, objectives must be kept fresh and effective by the administrator, especially those involved with the employment of teachers and those associated with the development of both faculty and curriculum.

Independent study can make an important contribution to institutional goals in three ways.

First, it commits the college or university to a freer curriculum, one which gives breadth to the student in ways not otherwise achieved. To be vital there must be institutional commitment to this breadth all along the organizational chart.

Secondly, the presence of a lively independent-study program on a campus makes possible other forms of educational thrust. What Kean[4] calls the "dynamics of dialogue" certainly is more likely to occur where the by-products of independent study are present.

Finally, the interdepartmental course development in recent years has a precursor in the work of students who cut through traditional boundaries by means of their independent work. The current vogue for the elimination of "distribution requirements" is less disruptive where faculty members and students have experienced the enrichments of independent study free from strictures of specific structures.

Problems in Administration It is almost a truism today that any committee report suggesting new programs to a faculty must include some use of the term "independent study." The administration should insist on a clear definition of what is meant by the developers of the new programs and more particularly the extent to which the proposed new procedures can contribute to some inherently new experience for the campus. Faculty meetings may often be carried away by the popular concept of the term and fail to consider its complete implications. Further, the administrator bears the responsibility for the clear working out of the faculty load and the solution of financial problems posed by the new program. The argument that it will look good in the committee report because "everyone is doing it" must be more than a cliché.

There are other difficulties to be anticipated. It must be remembered that the abilities of superior teachers may vary widely, and individual faculty may respond quite differently to good independent-study programs. The administrator may need to provide some departmental guidance to enable all teachers to reach their maximum effectiveness in terms of their varied talents.

Scheduling is often complicated because the traditionalists tend always to claim priority for the "regularly scheduled courses." In some way they believe that "these courses have first demand on the student's time." How many credits a given project may contribute toward those required for final degree certification gets involved here. The administrator must be sure the guidelines are clear to avoid confusion all along the way.

Of course the problem of major concern to the administration is the cost of any new program. Theoretical reports can be educationally sound and economically disastrous. The administrator is responsible for preventing this impasse.

[4]Robert Kean, *Dialogue on Education,* The Bobbs-Merrill Company, Inc., Indianapolis, 1967, p. 77.

Independent-study programs increase in cost as the direct tutorial responsibility of the teacher increases. The tutorial-type programs are the most expensive. At the College of Wooster, eight tutorial independent-study students are the equivalent of a three-hour course in teaching load. Hence, the instructional budget is increased by about 22 percent by the existence of the program. The teaching load needs to be calculated in terms of the demand on the teacher's time, and in this way a cost figure is arrived at.

Other factors of cost grow out of increased demands upon the laboratory and library budgets. It takes more space and often more sophisticated instrumentation to make possible experiments beyond the standard course programs and in addition to the scheduled laboratory spaces. All departments make greater demands upon the library. Rereading books from old outside-reading lists as an independent-study project hardly puts a student out on the new frontiers of learning in any program.

These costs—laboratory and library—will increase under almost any system of independent study regardless of the degree of faculty involvement.

There are only two ways by which any kind of independent-study program can save money: (1) by reducing the student-teacher contacts and subsequent teacher responsibility for evaluation to a point almost at zero so the teacher may spend his time doing other things for other and more students or for himself; (2) by structuring the independent-study program in such a way that it is almost a complete off-campus venture, utilizing some other facilities on some other campus—hopefully with consent!—and freeing the space-time demands on campus for other student functions. If these two approaches can be adopted, money can be saved. If not, the college simply plans to take it out in sweatshop demands on the teachers.

An independent-study program highlights all of the weaknesses of a campus and curriculum. With correct adaptation and direction it will, however, enable the students in spite of their problems to rise to more than they envisioned as their best.

CONCLUSION

The administrator who must provide the financial support must be convinced of the educational excellence of an independent-study program.

It is worth the cost. Students often rise above what they thought they could do and achieve more than they had hoped when they began their college careers.

Independent study is not only for the intellectually elite. It has results for students at all levels of academic ability. It is worth the cost to bring each student to his best self. It is probably true that some kind of independent study takes him more quickly and sometimes unexpectedly into "real life," no matter where he started. Granting different starting points and different growing rates, bringing students to their best selves through this experience is rewarding to all concerned. It is this challenge which makes such a program of vital concern to both administrators and to teachers, and so rewarding to the life of the student.

Chapter 6

Field Experience as an Integral Part of Education

HUGH D. ALLEN

Vice President, College Relations, Beloit College, Beloit, Wisconsin

This chapter considers *field experience*—as distinguished from *field work*—directly related to academic disciplines. It deals with the work and service carried out on a paid or volunteer basis during free hours and terms away from campus. It shows a relationship to the cooperative education movement (see Chapter 15 in this section) but is concerned largely with opportunities for expanding the scope of colleges and universities involved in general undergraduate education.

THE QUEST FOR MEANING AND RELEVANCE

Colleges and universities today are confronted by the strange paradox of the perpetual student and the dropout. In between are the turned-off, the hostile, the alienated, the walking wounded. Also in between, in numbers disproportionate to the words written about them, are students with varying degrees of enthusiasm and zeal pursuing educational objectives in a more or less traditional manner.

Whatever his condition—eager, indifferent, or alienated—today's student often is troubled by the delay in gaining rights of passage to the meaningful responsibility that lies beyond the long-extended pursuit of academic excellence. Disillusioned by social problems, the issues of war and peace, and by the adult establishment generally, he may become convinced that education as he experiences it has little relevance to the achievement of his life goals. The forms of his revolt and defection are well known. He seeks something real, tangible, and challenging to push against. College administrators too often fail to see the connection between education and direct confrontation with work, social change, and human suffering. The result is ingrown hostility and haggling over matters unworthy either of bright students or enlightened members of the establishment.

While the familiar signs of students in various stages of rebellion are manifest, there is the equally distressing phenomenon of students so snugly sheltered within the ivory tower that they may reject any confrontation with harsh reality. The result too often is a "Peter Pan complex" or what psychiatrist Lawrence Kubie calls "aging children" and "erudite adolescents."

College administrators seem to be more preoccupied with the protection and sheltering of students than with fostering opportunities for growth through the assumption of adult responsibility. Most recently we have witnessed the tug of war or worse over privileges and self-determination in matters that would seem trivial if we were really to try enlisting *ourselves and our students* in affairs of social, economic, and political urgency. Yet, in all too many cases, we are having to be dragged into the mainstream by students' concern rather than by our own sensitivity to institutional responsibility.

Field experience offers no panacea for either chronic student unrest or indifference. Indeed, any such suggestion would be presumptuous. However, comprehensive and sophisticated programs designed to bring deep involvement in the adult world through work and service are helping many students find new outlets for their concern, their compassion, their intelligence, and their energies with attendant gains in maturity and self-esteem.

It is the purpose of this chapter not to draw models for emulation but to describe a wide range of possibilities and to suggest ways in which college administrators may effect changes toward a greater realization of human potential.

DEVELOPING PROGRAMS IN WORK AND SERVICE

Part-time employment and community-service projects are about as old as education itself. The changes that are taking place come from deeper analyses of social, political, and economic problems and from a greater investment in professional leadership on the part of institutions. Breaking the duration of field experience into two arbitrary divisions, *part-time* and *full-time,* will show some of the possibilities for comprehensive institutional involvement.

Part-time Work and Service College students giving baskets at Thanksgiving time and collecting purses for the poor were a part of the surface treatment given to social problems for all too many years. Today both public and private agencies are going deeper into the causes of poverty, unemployment, and ill health, and they are desperately in need of help.

Almost as time-honored as charity is the giving of time by the sociologist, the psychologist, and other faculty members as "interested laymen" in community affairs. Also common has been the paid consultant role, and certainly the involvement of presidents and deans in local service clubs has been a hallmark of town-gown relationships.

Today, nothing short of complete institutional involvement in the community will suffice if we are to play the role worthy of our heritage. One of our problems is that our students either are getting into action ahead of us or are clinging to the ivy along with administrators and professors, hopeful that the whole mess will go away.

We need to find ways to apply our enormous reservoirs of manpower and know-how toward a better assessment of community needs and to channel our own and our students' efforts toward meaningful and strategic involvement in the business community, in social service agencies, and in city hall.

Under federal, state, and municipal auspices, community action programs exist in almost every college community. Students are needed as office workers, as researchers, as writers, and as liaison persons with local agencies, churches, YMCAs, YWCAs, Boys' Clubs, Red Cross, service clubs, hospitals, special schools, and others. These agencies in turn need youth workers, tutors, recreation leaders, and office helpers.

Faculty members, their wives, and students are combining forces to establish centers for cooperation with community action programs, with councils of social agencies, and with their many organizations. These centers are developing programs on their own for tutoring, literacy training, and special education. Task forces to assist in community improvement radiate from such centers with amazing results *if the institution and its leaders provide the continuity and effort.*

State, regional, and city planning commissions are finally being established and, with a very late start, are struggling with ecological problems in an unprecedented way. The college community now can get off the critics' bench and go to work on matters of air and water pollution, transportation, housing, and land use. Surveys, schematic concepts, and even second guessing now can become useful. Proposals and constructive criticism are even welcome. Opportunities for paid and volunteer services are growing.

Legislation for civil rights, equal employment opportunity, and fair housing has created federal and local commissions. These commissions and their agents seek cool and intelligent heads for studies and surveys.

There is much to be said for the development of deep institutional roots in the community. These roots often are firmly established in an intellectual and cultural sense but severely lacking in terms of economic, political, and social relevance. A far better system of part-time placement and counseling than most schools have had in the past is called for. Haphazard and opportunistic placement can and should give way to a more careful matching of student and job. This means counseling and planning. There is little doubt that much of the negative attitude toward business and industry, government agencies, and social service organizations is due to mismatching and lack of communication between student, employer, and school placement officers. The implications for college staffing and placement systems are outlined in the concluding portion of this chapter.

Full-time Work and Service Any consideration of student involvement in full-time work and service must take into account the fact that most schools use an academic calendar that provides for a summer vacation as the only departure from the academic quarter or semester sequence, especially on the undergraduate level.

A small but increasing number of schools are providing other interims for volunteer or required terms of work and service. Whatever the institutional situation may be, there is great opportunity for meaningful student experience, especially if the institution is willing to invest in leadership that can assist in negotiation and in guidance.

Consider the impact on enterprises of all kinds that even a small college can have if it harnesses its student manpower under official off-campus programs of work and service and if it ensures continuity through a calendar that places regular contingents in the field. And consider the opportunities its students have for translating academic principles to action, for testing-out of career interests, and for developing the personal ability to cope with conditions of living and managing in totally different environments.

Following is a statement from a report by the author of this chapter to the faculty of his institution * which during the past four years has placed some 150 students per term on a continuous, year-around basis:

> Our students have assisted physicians, research scientists, teachers, city planners, social workers, midwives, publishers, camp managers and business executives. They have sold books, clothing, tickets, and sundry merchandise. They have served as naturalists and guides; they have interviewed mental patients and people on welfare rolls. They have worked with animals, serviced vehicles and sailed ships. They have taught and supervised children under many trying circumstances. They have been trainees in advertising departments, insurance companies and banks. They have operated computers, calculators, typewriters and oil drilling rigs. They have experienced at close range the inner workings of great research institutions, newspapers, hotels, factories, hospitals, ranches, federal agencies and department stores.
>
> They have been involved in strikes, blackouts and breakdowns. They have felt the responsibility of being depended upon, trusted and respected for something other than academic prowess. This aggregate experience, coupled with diversity in geographic exploration, has given a new flavor to the academic pursuit. There are many indications that a taste of meaningful responsibility and even hardship have cleared some misconceptions, raised some sights and reduced some conflicts of self-understanding and self-esteem and even have helped make some important decisions.

Summer employment opportunities tend to be stereotyped. There is nothing particularly wrong with resorts, camps, construction projects, and routine office jobs, but often good talent is wasted and attendant boredom sets in through lack of challenge. Parental influence is all too operative, providing little boost to self-esteem.

Even so, a vigorous program of summer placement on the part of the college can unearth a wide selection of work and service opportunities. Skillful counseling and referral can mean well-utilized talent and worthwhile experience.

National and international service organizations provide an array of inner-city, work-camp, and conservation projects spread all over the world. An excellent list of projects published annually may be secured by writing the Commission on Youth Service Projects, 475 Riverside Drive, Room 832, New York, N.Y. 10027. These projects, many of which have been used as models for Peace Corps and VISTA programs, call for dedication, stamina, and personal commitment. They provide an understanding of cultural differences and a reality test for classroom abstractions. Most significantly, they foster an expression of manhood and womanhood that often comes as a delayed puberty rite for youth too long held in comfortable but debilitating provincial surroundings. A few colleges are working through social agencies to provide mobile units as resources in teaching, tutoring, and manual labor. Others have "adopted" disadvantaged communities where they send supplies and manpower.

Business and industry are constantly at the doors of college placement offices, seeking graduates. With a little encouragement, they come up with an amazing number of summer internships and training programs. They want to make them good, and they want to make them fit academic interests as well as career goals.

Government agencies too are concerned with training on national, state, and local levels. Planning agencies, legislative offices, parks and forests, commissions and departments will work directly with institutions of higher education to effect sound and appropriate placement. Again, haphazard applications and chance opportunities are a poor substitute for a thorough placement process.

Cooperative education, discussed by Roy Wooldridge in Chapter 15, offers a model

* Beloit College. Full description of the Beloit plan is available to readers. Address Director of Field Placement, Beloit College, Beloit, Wis. 53511.

well worth emulating by colleges that seek a broader, more comprehensive approach to work and service. Many colleges already have adopted calendars that provide for year-around placement and have made provision for staffing a placement office. Some have made field experience an integral part of the academic program, either granting credit, requiring a regular number of off-campus terms, or both. Among the smaller colleges, Antioch, with its students alternating terms off and on campus, has been followed by schools such as Goddard, Bennington, Beloit, Kalamazoo, Alderson-Broaddus, Elmira, and Wilmington, each with its own variation on the theme. Among larger universities committed to the idea are Northeastern, Drexel, and South Florida. More than one hundred colleges and universities now have some form of cooperative education.

INSTITUTIONAL CHANGE

Many faculty members tend to write off "work" as vocational training and service as do-goodism. They often scorn administrators' relationships to business institutions and to public agencies as money grubbing and public relations. And not without some justification. We have been all too solicitous of both public and private sectors, treating them as benefactors who must be pleased by all kinds of public relations gimmicks. We are far less expert in effecting meaningful relationships through the involvement of students and faculty in common community tasks. As a matter of fact, until very recently we have screened the campus so well that there has not been significant interaction. Certainly there has been little to suggest that the campus and the outside world really *need* each other in the true sense of the word.

Now the screen is being thrust aside, and we often look pretty naked and insignificant. Not that we lack intellectual lustre, but that somehow our purpose is lacking in consequence. Our students see and feel this shortcoming even more deeply than the public. And they are not amused.

Change in institutional commitment seldom takes place effectively through administrative fiat. Its success depends upon deeply rooted faculty and student concern and action. There is growing evidence that on every campus there are faculty members ready to break out of the tradition that says education takes place only in the classroom. There are even some who will give time and effort toward the development of creative programs of experience through direct confrontation with adult responsibility and with the task of ministering to human suffering. Students may be counted on to be ready and waiting.

The president and academic dean must give high priority to institutional outreach through work and service if they expect faculty to buy it as an integral part of education. Selecting a key group of faculty and students to examine existing efforts toward outreach, to assess untapped possibilities, and to explore some of the programs being carried out in other colleges is a good first step. Leadership, task orientation, and timetable are imperatives for such a committee. Nothing would seem to promise success so well as the actual involvement of top administrators, including a business officer who can think creatively and give the reality test to ideas that may be generated.

Early on the agenda of an investigating group should be meetings with leaders of the business, government, and social-service agencies in an effort to identify places where help is needed and where cooperation and supervision can most benefit the student.

If institutional leaders believe that their outreach may lead to regional, national, and international scope, they should seek sources of expert help. Colleges and universities engaged in cooperative programs of wide diversity are listed, along with descriptions of their programs, in a publication that may be secured by writing the Executive Secretary, Cooperative Education Association, Office of Industrial Coordination, Drexel Institute of Technology, Philadelphia, Pa. 19104.

Institutions involved in comprehensive programs will gladly share their experience and will welcome visits by interested committees of faculty, students, and administrators. Leaders in existing programs like nothing better than to spread the gospel by meeting with advocates of new ideas on renewed campuses.

A thorough investigation of need on the part of students and community may reveal the worth of coordinated management on the part of the institution. It also may conclude that provision for academic credit on an elective or required basis is advisable. As a matter of fact, programs that have been "built in" on a required basis under professional direction appear to be thriving, whereas more casual programs tend to encounter problems of poor continuity and lack of leadership. Colleges willing to pay the price in leadership, counseling, and placement resources have seen the gain in applications for admission and in the retention of students.

Faculty action in the form of "enabling legislation," based upon the conviction that direct experience adds a dimension of maturity and responsibility to the educational process, is urgently needed if an institution is to launch a successful program of work and service.

Once an institution has accepted the idea of outside involvement as a part of its academic plan, it has to face the question of staffing and financing. Meaningful work and service do not just happen through the release of students for off-campus time. Stereotyped jobs and projects, seasonal limitations, parental influence, and hometown convenience are limitations that can best be transcended by systematic, imaginative placement procedures.

"Placement" is a function known in many institutions only as the process through which graduates may go as they look beyond commencement. If a placement office exists, it may well provide the core for an expanded function of field involvement for undergraduates. In any event, a person and a headquarters must be established as the launching pad for students who are eager to play a vital part in the work of the world even as they develop the insights and knowledge that come through classroom participation.

Persons charged with implementing the program must be educators with deep understanding of students, their needs, and their problems. They must understand the economic, political, and cultural realities of the community outside the college walls. The diversity of student intelligence, motivation, and ambition calls for counseling of a most uncommon quality as well as for powers of persuasion and perception in dealing with leaders in business, government, and social service.

A single "catalyst" of this kind, with adequate clerical help, can make a solid contribution to any student body if he is allowed to give full time to the enterprise and if he has faculty recognition and respect. Institutions seeking to provide individual counseling and placement on a year-around basis should allow a ratio of one counselor for every 50 to 100 students, depending on the frequency and repetition of placement and on the geographic spread of their cooperating agencies.

There would seem to be some evidence that year-around quarter or trimester calendars, allowing for blocks of on- and off-campus experience on the part of students and making possible the rotation of students on work and service assignments, can be managed by liberal arts colleges. Such calendars also make possible full utilization of plant and accommodation of many more students.

The cost for such programs, whether it be $10,000 or $100,000, ultimately should be seen as part of the annual operating budget, the justification being enrichment of education, the attraction for students, and the retention of many whose "slumps" may turn into exciting new experience. But seed money for starting such programs can and should be within easy reach of an enterprising development officer. Individuals, businesses, foundations, and the federal government are open to appeals that speak relevantly to the needs of the youth in our colleges.

CONCLUSION

It seems certain that the quest for meaning and relevance in education is not a phase likely to go away. The long and arduous academic route of the young now stretches from very early childhood well into the twenties and beyond. Society seems to defer its demand for youth's services to a time when somehow, as "educated" men and women, they are ready and obligated to shoulder adult responsibilities. During the years of academic preparation, while students learn their lessons so well, it seems that they are seldom asked to contribute in any way that might seriously affect the crying needs that they see about them. So they may either immerse themselves more deeply in their academic pursuits and wait for that magic day when they are thrust forth to conquer the world, or they may throw off the academic straitjacket entirely and enter the world of work or nonwork.

Greater than the need to keep the academic enterprise under taut discipline is the obligation to consider constructive outlets for the competence, compassion, and leadership that abound on our campuses. The institutions outside academe are ambivalent about such manpower, but a place is available on a more than routine basis if we are willing to make it part of our business to relate honestly, openly, and creatively to business, government, social service, and the professions. This can be done without coercion and exploitation of students and without paternalistic self-interest if we are willing to broaden our concept of what goes into education and if we are willing to pay the price.

Colleges and universities that openly embrace the challenge of facilitating an earlier confrontation with work and service, either as an intermittent adventure or as a continuous process, seem to be reaping great reward in terms of higher motivation and seriousness of purpose on the campus. Certainly there is much to recommend a comprehensive program designed to test and challenge the worth of any academic community.

Finally, the institution must recognize the implications of projecting its commitment and responsibility into a far-flung classroom that is complex, dangerous, and wonderful. It is not a task for the unadventuresome nor the fainthearted. It can be frustrating. It can be risky. It never can be static.

RESOURCES FOR INFORMATION ON WORK AND SERVICE OPPORTUNITIES

Department of Community Service
The United Christian Missionary Society
222 South Downey Avenue
Indianapolis, Ind. 46207

Council of the Southern Mountains
Berea, Ky.

American Camping Association
Bradford Woods
Martinsville, Ind.

National Society for Crippled Children and Adults, Inc.
2023 West Ogden Avenue
Chicago, Ill.

U.S. Forest Service
Department of Agriculture
Washington, D.C.

U.S. National Park Service
Department of Interior
Washington, D.C.
Unitarian Universalist Service Committee
78 Beacon Street
Boston, Mass. 19102
Evangelical United Brethren
Voluntary Service Committee
601 West Riverview Avenue
Dayton, Ohio
Lutheran Church in America
Board of College Education and Church Vocations
231 Madison Avenue
New York, N.Y. 10016
American Friends Service Committee
160 N. 15th Street
Philadelphia, Pa. 19102
The Methodist Church
Box 871
Nashville, Tenn. 37202
Presbyterian Service and Study Projects
United Presbyterian Church, U.S.A.
Room 1206, 475 Riverside Drive
New York, N.Y. 10027
Committee on Voluntary Service
Episcopal Church Center
815 Second Avenue
New York, N.Y. 10017
National Council, YMCA
291 Broadway
New York, N.Y.
National Council, YWCA
53d Street and Lexington Avenue
New York, N.Y.
American Youth Foundation
Hampton Avenue
St. Louis, Mo.
Boys' Clubs of America
771 First Avenue
New York, N.Y. 10017
National Council of Churches
475 Riverside Drive
New York, N.Y. 10027
The Commission on Youth Service Projects
Room 832, 475 Riverside Drive
New York, N.Y. 10027
United Church of Christ Headquarters
287 Park Avenue South
New York, N.Y. 10010

Pamphlets

The Quiet Revolution, Office of Economic Opportunity, Washington, D.C.
Voluntary Help Wanted, Office of Economic Opportunity, Washington, D.C.
Vocations for Social Change (monthly listings), Vocations for Social Change, Inc., 2010 B Street, Hayward, Calif.
Invest Yourself, The Commission on Youth Service Projects, 475 Riverside Drive, Room 832, New York, N.Y.
Summer Service Opportunities, United Church of Christ, Pottstown, Pa.

Action Jobs, Summer, National Federation of Settlements and Neighborhood Centers, 232 Madison Avenue, New York, N.Y.

Summer Employment Directory of the U.S., National Directory Service, Box 32065, Cincinnati, Ohio.

Books

Friedenberg, E.: *The Vanishing Adolescent,* Beacon Press, Boston, 1962.

Kubie, Lawrence: *Neurotic Distortions of the Creative Process,* Farrar, Straus & Co., New York, 1961.

Musgrove, F.: *Youth and the Social Order,* Indiana University Press, Bloomington, Ind., 1965.

Chapter **7**

The Superior Student

LEWIS B. MAYHEW

Professor of Education, Stanford University, Stanford, California

Specific academic concern for the unique educational problems of the superior student or the especially talented individual is a recent development in American higher education. ,Historically it was assumed that the admissions processes channeled able high school graduates into colleges where they were provided with an appropriate educational challenge. However, in the 1950s several events transpired to suggest the fallaciousness of such an assumption. A study of general education revealed that freshmen in three Ivy League institutions were frequently bored with their studies, in part because the work duplicated studies already mastered in preparatory schools. After Sputnik, the American people discovered that the nation was underproducing scientists and engineers. Potentially high-level scientific and technical workers were staying away from college or dropping out because their interests were not stimulated. Assessment studies, such as Dael Wolfle's *American's Resources of Specialized Talent,* Byron Hollingshead's *Who Should Go to College?* and Ralph F. Berdie's *After High School, What?* showed that a sizable number of individuals of superior ability were not being educated to their maximum ability: some because they did not wish to be, some because they could not get the education they wanted, and some because they were never effectively identified by school authorities.

Those in higher education discussed several courses of action: (1) a search for additional funds for able but impecunious students; (2) the development of special secondary school programs for superior students, ranging from offerings of single courses to the development of complete secondary schools modeled after the Bronx High School of Science in New York City; (3) an attempt to persuade colleges to identify superior students and provide programs and services for them; and (4) the development of special admissions programs which would allow the intellectually mature to accelerate their educational progress. In considering these courses of action, it became necessary to examine the conflicting theories on the educational needs of academically superior students. One such theory is that the mission of the school is to force the student to make his own identifications and achieve his own development through the trial and error of independent study. This theory suggests that the best thing an institution can do for the superior student is to leave him alone. The other theory, which, in principle at least, has come to prevail, holds that the superior student is one who is likely to make the most demands on the teacher and therefore requires more and better teaching time than other students. Teachers are seen as the activating factors in the development of potential abilities.

MAJOR THEORETICAL STUDIES

The response to the challenge of meeting the needs of superior students took several different forms. One was an increased interest in research dealing with giftedness, creativity, and special talents.

E. Paul Torrance and his associates at the University of Minnesota conducted some longitudinal and cross-cultural studies.[1] They discovered that some children judged at first grade as being highly creative never reached their potential, while others in different schools continued to expand. The implication was that schools and colleges can do something to aid the superior, talented, or especially endowed student.

Another line of inquiry was opened by Donald W. MacKinnon and associates, at the University of California at Berkeley, who studied mature individuals identified as being especially creative. The case studies indicated that creative persons reveal characteristic score patterns on commonly used tests, such as the Strong Vocational Interest Blank, and demonstrate certain consistent personality tendencies, such as an enhancement of the feminine side of their nature. Of particular significance for administrators was the finding that creativity is not highly correlated with high intelligence or high academic aptitude as measured by currently available tests of verbal intelligence. While creative people do not score low, their selection for appropriate educational experiences demands something other than conventional aptitude testing. Studies were made by Abraham H. Maslow and Rollo May which identify self-actualizing individuals as potentially deserving of special treatment in education. Largely through the interest of Joseph Cohen, the Inter-University Committee on the Superior Student was formed, and with funds from the Rockefeller Foundation, this Committee developed a newsletter and visited selected institutions to disseminate ideas and develop close liaison with educators.

Sidney L. Pressey at Ohio State University demonstrated by his work that bright students can successfully terminate their secondary school experience early. The Ford Foundation sponsored a series of programs which clearly demonstrated that students exposed to early acceleration into college out-achieved students of the same ability who remained in high school for four years. Furthermore, the former experienced greater physical and emotional health. The Advanced Placement Program of the College Entrance Examination Board helped high schools develop college-level

[1] E. Paul Torrance, "Must Creative Development Be Left to Chance?" in John Curtis Gowan (ed.), *Creativity: Its Educational Implications*, John Wiley & Sons, Inc., New York, 1967.

courses and techniques of assessment so that high schools could certify that some students had completed college-level courses and could be granted college credit.

PIONEER PROGRAMS

The early Swarthmore College tutorial program became a model for other institutions. In this program approximately half of the junior class is allowed to take the last two years of college work in the form of tutorials featuring large amounts of independent reading. Then these students are examined by a panel of outside examiners who seek to determine whether the students have the general competency expected of college-trained individuals. Although this plan has always been expensive, it has apparently maintained the interest and enthusiasm of students throughout the years.

Harvard College made provision for superior students to do honors work within those departments offering a major. Such work could involve bringing talented students into early research contact with professors, independent study, or an especially arranged major sequence. While the strong disposition at Harvard was to keep honors work restricted to departments, the faculty gradually tolerated an expansion of honors concepts into interdisciplinary seminars.

Of special interest in the 1940s at Michigan State University was the development of a comprehensive program of general education with explicit provisions for superior students. Out of this program evolved a separate Honors College with its own director who reported to the vice-president for academic affairs and later to the provost when that office was created. Students were selected for the Honors College on the basis of academic performance during their freshman year rather than on the basis of aptitude testing. Students were provided certain amenities, such as a special room in the library and early registration, and were encouraged to work out curricula tailored to their own needs as determined by the student and a counselor. Departments were encouraged to create specially designed courses for honors students which were open either to students of the Honors College or to precocious students not so enrolled. In practice, Honors College students were frequently faced with regulations; but in theory students were entitled to select programs most consistent with their own needs. The students were generally of two types: those who had an intense interest in a single subject and were allowed to spend most of their years following it and those who were dilettantes having so many interests that they sampled course work lightly throughout the institution.

During the late 1950s and early 1960s, programs for superior and gifted students spread throughout the country. Some institutions reemphasized the possibility of graduating with honors. Others created special honors courses and stipulated on the diploma that the student had completed honors work. Interdisciplinary seminars seemed a particularly popular device. In the sciences particularly, students were encouraged to work with professors on research projects, and some institutions arranged for the publication of undergraduate research efforts. A few institutions adopted a policy of early admissions; Shimer College in western Illinois was one such example. Generally, however, college faculties opposed early admissions, as did a number of high school principals. Each feared that early passage through school would cause deterioration of the intellectual tone of the student body. A typical pattern was for a college to announce an honors program in its catalog and to designate some courses as of honors level, but to make no specific provisions for such a program.

GUIDELINES FOR PROGRAMMING OF SUPERIOR STUDENTS

Out of such efforts has emerged what might be called the superior wisdom for dealing with superior students.

1. Early identification is essential. This requires close articulation with secondary schools.

2. Programs should begin immediately upon admission to college and university.

3. Honors programs should be continuous. They should not represent the spasmodic dedication of particular faculty members or administrators. Programs should be institutionalized and budgeted for.

4. Honors programs should relate to collegewide requirements as well as to needs in major areas of concentration.

5. Programs should be varied and flexible and feature special courses, ability sections, honors seminars, colloquia, and independent study.

6. Honors programs should be highly visible in the hope that they will provide standards and models of excellence for the total institution. A pass-fail system of grading might be one way of accomplishing this.

7. Materials and techniques appropriate to superior students should be used, such as small groups or classes using primary sources and original documents, the elimination of lecturing, predigestion of materials by faculty, greatly increased use of independent study, emphasis on continuous counseling, the making of appropriate sex differentiations and differentiations between creative and formally cognitive styles of superiority.

8. A specially selected faculty seems essential.

9. When possible, collegewide regulations and requirements should be set aside so that superior students can continue their education in a style consistent with their developmental needs.

10. Evaluation of the honors program by faculty and student honors committees should be continuous.

11. Superior students should be used in teaching and research. Even freshmen can serve in this capacity.

12. Superior students should be used in counseling and orientation, not only for the insights they provide but to symbolize the emphasis placed on superior students.

13. A closer articulation between honors programs and graduate schools should be initiated and maintained so that students selecting a somewhat asymmetrical program will not be penalized.

Program Evaluation

Much of the material about existing programs for superior students is descriptive rather than evaluative, but there is information which suggests that colleges are failing to serve the needs of these students. The tenor of all of the papers in *The Creative College Student: An Unmet Challenge*, edited by Paul Heist (Jossey-Bass, San Francisco, 1968), is that creative students tend to drop out of college more frequently than do less creative ones and are highly critical of the course experiences and teaching. They find that requirements stifle their interests, that courses are somewhat irrelevant, and that they themselves are restive under restrictions to the free expression of their own particular talents. Thus, the administrator who would create a viable program for superior students should listen carefully to the dissatisfactions expressed by creative individuals.

Selection of Superior Students

There is evidence that orthodox methods of measuring aptitudes are predictive only of college grades, and that college grades are predictive of subsequent grades and not necessarily of creative or superior performance in life. Also, nonintellective predictors of specific kinds of performance have not produced satisfactory results. It is possible, using a combination of prior academic record and academic aptitude tests, to select a verbally superior group of students. Whether or not these are the ones institutions should single out for increased attention is moot. At this point the best suggestion is to obtain as many different subjective impressions of a student's potential as possible. These impressions should be the basis for selection, whether formed while the student is in high school or after he has enrolled in college.

Nature of Program

Beyond the question of selection, there is the issue of whether or not highly talented individuals should be segregated from the rest of their contemporaries. One point of view holds that some segregation is necessary so that superior students can exploit their potential; another point of view holds that superior students must live in a real world with a heterogeneous population. There are those who feel that the superior student operates as a kind of leavening in classrooms, thereby helping to teach the larger majority. To remove these students would be to do a disservice to them and to all the other students enrolled.

A further concern is the way in which institutions handle superior students with special talents. Most honors programs seem to emphasize a highly verbal, cognitive approach. Courses are disciplinary in nature. These penalize the superior student talented in music, theater, or plastic arts. There is evidence that students having talents in the arts are discouraged from exploiting these talents in high school, are penalized in the admissions process, and then are forced to take academic-style courses in college rather than practice-style courses which seem necessary for the flowering of this form of creative talent. An institution interested in superior individuals should wish to develop superiority in all fields. However, because of the way admissions procedures operate, students superior in academic courses are likely to receive the advantage. Directors of admissions in highly selective institutions, for example, testify to the difficulty of recruiting students talented in music or theater arts who, in addition to these talents, must demonstrate a high degree of competency in more orthodox academic pursuits.

Importance of Rewards

If honors programs or programs for the superior student are simply more of what students would ordinarily experience in a course, students are not going to be particularly attracted. It is common to require students identified as superior to do extra work and to meet higher standards for grades. In view of the high premium set on good grades as a prerequisite for graduate or professional school admission, many students are simply not willing to embark on such a program. In order to attract students, honors programs must have a definite and visible payoff. An honors program distinctly different from other programs seems to attract students. It is for this reason that the tutorials at Swarthmore College and the Honors College at Michigan State University succeed. Rewards come through allowing students a lot of personal freedom, allowing them to spend time off campus and to select individually tailored programs while other students must face requirements. The opportunity for early registration, special library privileges, increased grade-point value for work taken, and special designations on diplomas also attract superior students.

Relatedly, there must be a reward for faculty who are asked to work with honors students. Faculty seem to believe that honors work does require additional time and they want recognition for this. Perhaps they feel that the reason so many honors programs are listed in catalogs but in fact are inoperative is that the institution inaugurated the program and maintained it for the first few years on the enthusiasms and interests of a small number of faculty. Interest and enthusiasm will sustain a faculty member for some time, but if working with honors programs is added to an existing work schedule, enthusiasm quickly wanes. It can be advanced almost as an axiom that unless an institution budgets professorial time to be spent on honors students, an honors program will not work. Perhaps professors asked to work on honors courses should have their teaching, advising, and counseling loads cut in half. A professor offering interdisciplinary honors work might be provided with a collapsed sabbatical leave pattern so that he may follow several years of honors work with time off in which to reestablish interest in his departmental specialty.

Assignment of Administrative Responsibility

No consistent and comprehensive program for any special type of student can be maintained unless someone is given administrative responsibility for it. In large institutions this officer could be a vice provost or director of an honors program. In smaller institutions, a director or an associate dean might be given the responsibility. Inertia can be overcome by a counterforce of good leadership. However, faculty time, administrative time, and special provisions cost money. As a rule, an institution should not involve itself in special honors programs unless verbal provision is accompanied by financial provision.

Conclusion

The development of programs for superior students is still primitive. However, several elements have some demonstrated validity. The first of these is acceleration. Virtually all available evidence suggests that acceleration for some students is wise and healthy. Accelerated students tend to achieve professional leadership and make more frequent contributions at an earlier age than do those pursuing a slower course. Yet faculties resist acceleration.

Secondly, it seems clear that superior students should pursue independent study and, when required to take formal courses, should be restricted to a few at a time.

Thirdly, evidence suggests that all undergraduate college students, and especially the superior ones, need to develop a sense of personal identity and to learn how to expand and utilize their impulse life. Honors programs should feature opportunities for questioning and for experiencing, understanding, and expressing emotion. It could almost be argued that superior students during the freshman year should be guided into literature, art, or philosophy rather than disciplinary courses. Their own academic facility is such that when they find the need for more disciplinary experiences, they will be able to accelerate work in those areas and gain the necessary disciplinary confidence.

ADDITIONAL READINGS

Cohen, Joseph (ed.): *The Superior Student in American Higher Education,* McGraw-Hill Book Company, New York, 1966.

Cohen, Joseph (ed.): "Proceedings of the Southern Honors Symposium," Tulane University, New Orleans, La., April 21–22, 1967 (unpublished).

Rett, Leigh: "Independent Study and the Campus Crisis," *Saturday Review,* July 16, 1966.

then a letdown over the Christmas vacation. This leads to the anticlimactic January lame-duck period. The more terms there are in an academic year, the more problem there is with this rise and fall of momentum.

A general final-exam period and any associated review or reading period is part of the pace and intensity consideration. They should be weighed against class time, as part of the overall consumption of time for education during the year.

SOCIAL FACTORS

Summer is the accepted time for vacations throughout society. Students find jobs available and special programs geared to their interests. Faculty members, too, are accustomed to using this period for their own interests and vacations. Many students do attend summer sessions, of course, but often at a different pace and at a different college than during the regular year. To ask or expect students to undertake regular academic programs during the summer is probably not feasible at this time. The obvious exception to this is the cooperative program which regularly is on a year-round basis but does have the compensation of alternate terms in a work situation. Labor Day is the accepted end of summer, and starting the academic year before this holiday will bring protests.

The other major vacation is at Christmas, when again people have come to expect a break of two weeks or more. Most of the major holidays are observed by colleges as one day off, but these should be accounted for when determining the length of a term.

Articulation with other colleges and with high schools is a factor to take into consideration. Intercollegiate athletics calls for some degree of coordination between colleges, and the growing practice of cross registration between colleges is facilitated by similar calendars.

ADMINISTRATIVE FACTORS

The academic calendar is directly related to the degree of space utilization possible. Involved here are decisions on whether to operate on a five- or six-day week, a nine- or twelve-month academic year, or with or without evening classes. Such decisions involve much more than efficiency since they strongly influence the style of a campus and affect the morale of a most valuable and costly part of a college, the faculty. An analysis of year-round proposals of either the trimester or four-quarter type of system shows that, to greatly increase the use of facilities, it would be necessary for a college to require all or some whole classes of its students to attend in the summer term and to have equal size groups entering each term. An American Council on Education report[1] points out:

> Granting the urgency of maximum utilization of educational resources, this consideration should not result in false or misplaced economies which stand in the way of improving education. . . . So important is the end in view, both to the individual and to our free society, that true economy dictates the choice of the most effective rather than the least expensive means.

There are inevitable administrative expenses associated with starting and ending a term. Thus, efficiency argues for fewer terms per year. There is extra work involved for the faculty at the start and end of terms, so that the faculty would probably also like to have as few terms as possible.

[1] Nathan M. Pusey et al., *The Price of Excellence,* American Council on Education, Problems and Policies Committee, Washington, October, 1960.

The calendar should allow some time for plant maintenance and renovation, which are constantly required by shifts in emphasis in academic and research fields. Such activities have customarily been concentrated in the summer period, when major portions of the school may be freed for this purpose.

The timing of commencement exercises is determined by college tradition and the need to allow a time lag after the end of the term in which to check student records for successful completion. Some colleges have found it advisable, for reasons of student attendance, among others, to hold commencement as a ceremony immediately after the close of the term and before the students' records have been reviewed. The degrees are then awarded and distributed subsequent to the commencement exercise. A more common practice is to have degree candidates finish their last term early.

TYPES OF CALENDARS

A semester system is the most prevalent calendar, being used currently by about four-fifths [2] of the colleges in the country. This calendar is generally composed of two regular terms of 15 weeks of classes each, extending from mid- or late September to early June. The summer session normally is outside the regular-term academic pattern, is composed of sessions of varying length, caters to a different clientele, has a different and limited array of course offerings, and is taught by a fraction of the regular staff. A survey [3] of 76 colleges on a semester calendar found the length of a semester to be 15 weeks in 40 percent of the cases; 70 percent of the semesters were in the range of 14½ to 15½ weeks of actual class time. In addition to the 30 weeks of classes, a typical college year encompasses time for registration and final exams and time for breaks including three days at Thanksgiving, approximately two weeks at Christmas, a week between terms, a one-week spring vacation, and the recognized holidays.

The lame-duck session is one of the most undesirable features of this type of calendar. Unfortunately, the fixed calendar constraints of Labor Day and Christmas do not allow enough time for a full semester between them. There are 16 to 16½ weeks between Labor Day and Christmas, which leaves 14 to 15 weeks available for a term after deducting holidays. When further allowance is made for freshman orientation, registration, and the final exam period, the resulting net time available for classes is inadequate for a semester. A few colleges have recently modified their semester calendars to eliminate the lame-duck session by starting their first semester before Labor Day, in late August, and completing the final exam period for this term before Christmas. Another possibility is to move the terms in the other direction, so that the first term would start in mid-October and end in early February and the second term would end in mid-June. The latter would put a two-week Christmas vacation in the middle of the first term, where it might be less disturbing than in its present location just before the end of the first term. Some colleges have found it helpful to regularize their spring vacation by having it occur in the middle of the spring semester, without regard to Easter.

The next most popular academic calendar is the quarter system, which is composed of three regular terms per year with about 10 weeks of class time per term and which encompasses a school year with about the same overall length (typically 37 or 38 weeks) and with similar beginning and ending dates as under a semester system. The fourth quarter is most often a summer-session period outside of the regular program and with a different emphasis. Generally, the student takes four to six courses concurrently, similar to the programs of the semester system. This calendar does have

[2] *Report of Length of Sessions in Colleges in 1960 and 1956,* American Council on Education, Office of Statistical Information and Research, Washington, 1960, p. 10.

[3] Paul S. Dwyer et al., *Report of the University Calendar Study Committee,* The University of Michigan Press, Ann Arbor, Mich., June, 1958, p. 69.

the advantage of convenient timing, since it is generally arranged so that Christmas and spring vacations fall between terms.

Some people feel that the semester is a more favorable time length for the preparation of term papers, for extensive reading in connection with courses, for the maturing process, and for student interest to be built. Others feel that more frequent class meetings under the quarter system favor education and help maintain student interest. It is easier to allow time for a reading period at the end of each semester than it is to allow one at the end of each quarter. Some also maintain that it is easier to arrange sequential course offerings under a semester plan than under a quarter plan. Some contend that there are fewer examination periods per year in a semester system, which is advantageous to students, and that there is less time devoted to examinations. This point may be debated, since the number of examinations throughout the year may be varied under either system and now varies from course to course within any college. Final exams are also variable, since some courses may not require finals and the length of a final exam may be controlled. Some maintain that frequent exams under a quarter system interfere with the calm perusal of the subject matter, while others maintain that frequent exams stimulate better student performance. This is a matter of opinion and is best left to the instructor's judgment.

The quarter system requires the expenditure of more time for starting and closing terms. From an operational point of view, the semester plan is easier and more efficient. All the standard administrative procedures of registration, scheduling of classes and rooms, examinations, and the processing of grades and records are carried out twice during the academic year rather than the three times called for under the quarter system. More time, pressure, and work are involved in operating under a quarter plan for much of the academic administration. This greater amount of work might be offset to some extent by having each student take fewer courses per quarter. The faculty would have a greater load also, since they would participate in advising students for an additional registration and in an additional examination and grading period under the quarter plan. Administrative costs would be higher under the quarter plan, but the main institutional costs, such as faculty salaries and overhead, would be the same for both systems.

Under a quarter plan the additional term per year permits readier evaluation of student progress and more frequent student counseling. A quarter system allows greater flexibility in planning a program of studies or at least more changes, since students wishing to change their programs may do so more readily and frequently. On the other hand, the confusion attending the dropping and adding of courses during the early part of a term occurs less frequently under the semester system. Articulation with secondary schools, junior colleges, and other universities is better under the semester plan, which seems to be particularly significant for teacher education and evening programs. Arguments are advanced on both sides as to which calendar system favors faculty research and leaves of absence. This seems to depend more on the faculty load and administration policy within a particular college than on the calendar plan prevailing.

Cooperative programs most often use a quarter system, but with the fourth quarter being fully utilized as part of their regular year-round operation. The alternate terms at work afford both the students and the faculty a break in the academic routine. Very often cooperative programs are only a part of a college's total program and operate under the calendar arrangement which has been adopted to meet the overall goals of the college. Thus, many cooperative programs for groups of students in particular fields function satisfactorily under a semester calendar, with the summer also being fully utilized. Some cooperative programs cover the student's whole undergraduate curriculum, which generally results in an extension of the total time to five years, some others only cover two years. Proposed new federal programs for further developing cooperative education will create new interest and may lead to a wider use of this approach.

Some critics contend that under the quarter system courses go at too rapid a pace in the short 10-week terms, to the detriment of learning and contemplative thinking. Most institutions with experience in the quarter system have programs with four or five courses taken concurrently, each containing less material than a semester course. A variation of the quarter system, often called the 3-3-3 plan, has been adopted by some colleges recently as a rebuttal to the above argument. This plan operates with the same three terms per year as in the quarter system, but a student may only take three courses in each term and they must cover the same material as semester courses. In comparison with the semester system, the three-term, three-course calendar reduces the subdivision of student attention, the aim of which is to focus student effort and to make independent work more feasible by reducing the multiplicity of demands upon the student's time.

Another academic calendar variation, referred to as the 4-1-4 plan,[4] has been adopted by a number of colleges in the last few years. Under this plan the first term, which is about two weeks shorter than a regular semester, starts in early September and ends as the Christmas vacation begins. During this term each student takes four courses which have the same coverage as semester courses. The second term is a four-week "interim" or "winter term" in January, during which students concentrate on a single course. The third term, which starts in February, is set up in the same way as the first. The principal advantages of this plan are the elimination of the lame-duck session, the establishment of a period designed to encourage independent study and curricular experimentation, and the provision of a break or change of pace in the middle of the school year. Students are actually undertaking a large variety of activities in the interim term, not only in different colleges but within a single college. Some of these activities are intensive study in classes ranging from the standard to the esoteric, faculty-guided individual study or projects, off-campus work and research including study abroad, and in some cases a concentration by all students on some phase of a general topic or problem. There is an informality about this period that encourages students and faculty to work in different ways and that often results in a closer relationship between students and teachers than there can be during the regular school year. Not only do faculty present new material in the interim term, but students may propose individual study projects and ask for guidance for group study of a topic which they wish to pursue.

Some colleges have tried a 4-4-1 arrangement with the short term in May. This has the advantage of allowing students who are going off campus to extend this study into the summer. It has not been a very popular arrangement since it comes at the end of the year, when students are often weary of school work. The opportunity to provide a break or chance to do something different between two standard terms is also missing. To date, the 4-1-4 calendar plan has been most popular with moderately small colleges, under 4,000 in enrollment. Whether it is feasible in or will ever be tried by larger colleges is a question for the future.

A few universities have tried a trimester calendar in recent years, a type of year-round academic system composed of three 15-week terms. It was devised to cope with the increasing pressure of more students and to provide for accelerating the education of students who contemplate an extended period of graduate study. A year-round system is a way of trading time for space and enables a college to handle more students in the same physical facilities. These experiments with a trimester plan have not proved very successful so far, due to the unpopularity of summer attendance and of

[4] "A Calendar to Meet a Curriculum: Why St. Olaf Adopted a Four-one-four Year," *College Management*, vol. 1, no. 3, p. 24, September, 1966.

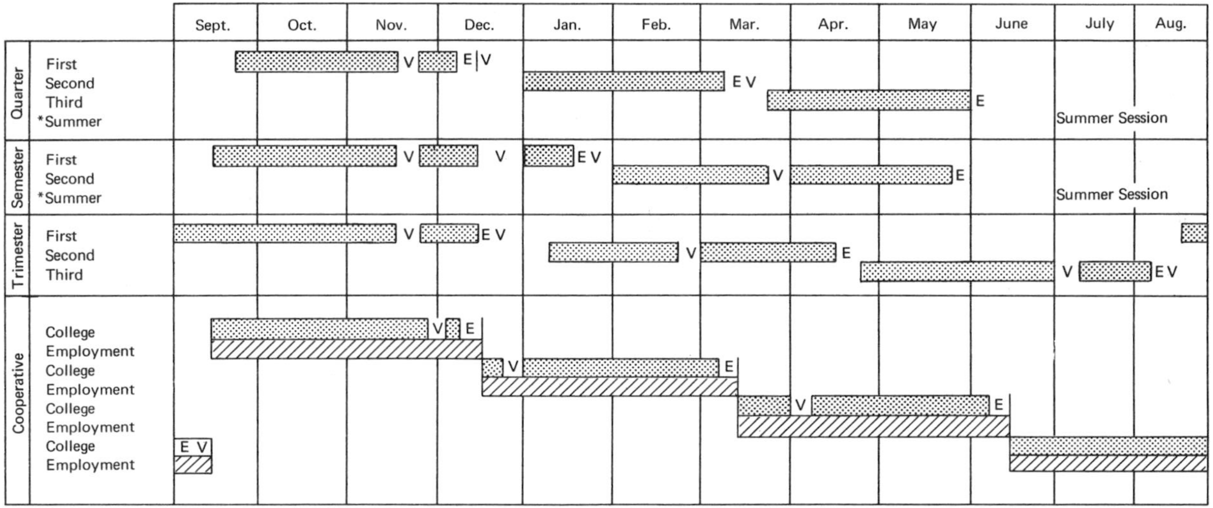

Fig. 1 *Academic calendars.*

Quarter .... *Three regular terms plus a summer session which may be of the same length as the regular term or which may be of shorter duration (see page 2-105).*

Semester.............. *Two regular terms plus a summer session of specified length (see page 2-105).*

Trimester............. *Three regular terms per year. Students are required to study in two of these terms only (see page 2-107).*

Cooperative .... *Alternating periods of employment and study on a year-round basis (see page 2-106).*

attending college the year-round. Its success would require a change in attitude on the part of many people and its adoption by many colleges. Such conditions depend, in part, on still greater increases in enrollment pressure.

CALENDAR CHANGE

A major academic calendar change is difficult and expensive to bring about and should not be undertaken lightly. As well as affecting the routine of everyone at the college, such an action includes the direct costs of the time of the many people who must plan and implement it, of the printing of a multitude of revised forms and publications, and of the extra communication and publicity to all interested parties. A careful appraisal of the work and cost involved for the advantages sought by a calendar change is vital in order to judge its worth.

Detailed planning should be carried out, based on a clear statement of the main objectives of the change and of the existing features to be retained. The particular calendar arrangement may affect the operating expenses of a college not only in terms of the academic budget but also with regard to the costs of dormitory operation, food service, maintenance, and construction.

A key factor in determining the calendar to use is faculty and student morale. The academic calendar determines to a major extent the schedule of each faculty member with regard to teaching, research, study opportunities, and his personal life as well. The personal schedule of each student with regard to study, work, vacations, and family relations is also affected. Since the individual's schedule is important to him, the calendar is a sensitive issue. The timing of faculty appointments, the cost of instruction, and the relation of the program of course offerings desired to faculty appointments all should be considered with respect to a calendar change. Particular groups such as part-time, cooperative, nondegree, evening, and extension students all have their own peculiar time problems. The best calendar pattern is that which enjoys the most enthusiastic backing of faculty and students.

Various curricular and pedagogical questions need to be considered in relation to a change. What should be the length of a class period, the number of class hours per week and term, the number of weeks per term? Should the calendar accommodate students progressing at a faster or slower rate than the usual four years for a bachelor's degree? Should students be allowed or encouraged to study on a year-round basis? Should students be restricted in the number of courses which they take concurrently? How many courses are required for a degree? Should there be a reading period, and how long should it be?

If the length of the term is changed, the system of credit units may have to be changed (e.g., from semester hours to quarter units). For the sake of uniformity and clarity, it is desirable that unique types of units not be devised but rather that one of the accepted varieties be adapted. A change in credit units will affect degree requirements, the relative weights of courses, tuition schedules, grade-point averages, and other similar items. The coverage in courses may have to change, and curricula may need wholesale revision. A review may be needed in order to ascertain which courses should be offered more than once a year.

The length of the final examination period may need to be modified in relation to the fraction of the term which it consumes and to the length of the school year which is desired. The length of the examination period must also be weighed against considerations of the pace or exam frequency for the student and the availability of exam facilities and proctors.

Other items which need attention include articulation with interacting institutions, holidays, the break between terms, the timing and frequency of special events, board and room charges, and revised course and classroom schedules.

This is not meant to imply that calendar changes pose insurmountable problems. A survey[5] shows that in the last two years over two hundred colleges have made fairly extensive calendar changes.

BIBLIOGRAPHY

Committee on Utilization of College Teaching Resources: *Better Utilization of College Teaching Resources,* Fund for the Advancement of Education, New York, May, 1959.

Dushane, Graham, et al.: *Interim Report on the Semester and Quarter Systems,* Committee of Educational Inquiry, Stanford University, Palo Alto, Calif., May, 1955.

Easton, Elmer C.: *Year-around Operation of Colleges,* Rutgers, The State University, New Brunswick, N.J. Engineering Research Bulletin no. 41, 1958.

Jones, Putnam F., et al.: *Report of Committee on a Trimester Calendar,* The University of Pittsburgh, Pittsburgh, Pa., April, 1958.

McCune, Shannon, et al.: *The New College Plan,* University of Massachusetts, Amherst, Mass., 1958.

Morrison, Donald H.: "An Educational Program for Dartmouth," *Dartmouth Alumni Magazine,* April, 1957.

"One-course Campus," *College Management,* vol. 2, no. 5, May, 1967.

Wells, W. D., et al.: *The University Calendar,* American Association of Collegiate Registrars and Admissions Officers, University Calendar Committee, 1961.

[5] American Association of Collegiate Registrars and Admissions Officers, "Report of Committee on Academic Calendars," *Newsletter,* vol. 10, no. 1, p. 8, Summer, 1967.

Chapter 9

Registration, Scheduling, and Student Records

ROSEMARY SHIELDS

University Representative, International Business Machines Corporation, Cambridge, Massachusetts

ROLE OF A REGISTRAR

Student Record Keeping The registrar is the keeper of students' academic records with full responsibility for the generation, storage, and use of these records. His relationship with the various segments of the academic community is illustrated in Figure 1.

The registrar is not a data processing director, nor can he be replaced by one. Responsibility for the contents and use of records is not the same as responsibility for the manipulation of the data contained therein. In any case, effective use of these records depends upon keeping these functions separate, since the skills required of a good data processing director are quite different from those required of a good registrar.

While the primary role of the registrar is operational rather than academic or policy making, he must be involved in policy-making decisions in light of his knowledge of what is and is not feasible under given sets of conditions. The registrar is in a position to see the whole student academic picture from probation reports and space-utilization information to course-enrollment forecasts for next semester's master schedule.

The functions for which the registrar usually is responsible are a necessary part of any academic institution, regardless of size or objectives. While in some cases a dif-

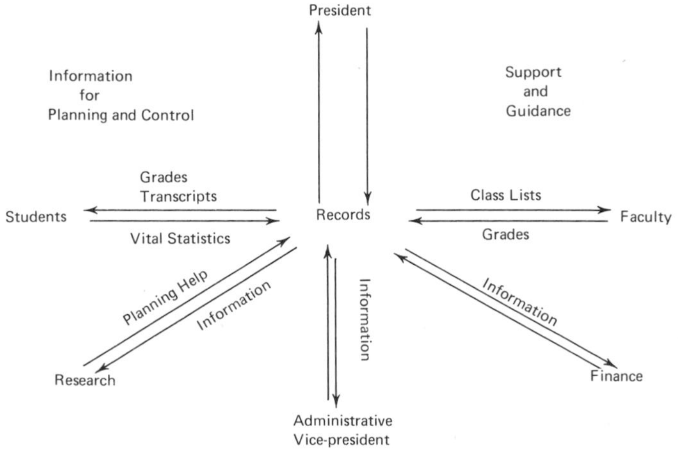

Fig. 1 *Information flow.*

ferent official may be responsible for one or another individual function, they logically fall under the registrar's primary goal—development, care, and utilization of academic records.

Scheduling and Sectioning This function includes the development of a master schedule of courses to be offered during a particular academic period, the instructors for each course, the times and places of class meetings, sectioning—in which the actual assignment of students to individual classes is made—and examination scheduling.

Registration This encompasses the period just prior to the opening of classes when students confirm their presence for the upcoming academic term, receive their individual class schedules, and make whatever course adjustments are necessary, desirable, and possible. The actual selection of courses prior to the receipt of individual schedules may take place during the actual registration period or it may be separated in time by a few days or months in a preregistration course advisement and selection period.

Report and Transcript Production The registrar is responsible for issuing transcripts to any student or former student requesting them. These official copies of the student's academic record may be requested throughout the lifetime of the individual, thus necessitating careful preservation of the primary records. The registrar is not just a record archivist, however. In addition, he should issue reports to the president, academic deans, and other administrators on the status of such developments as student enrollment and academic achievement.

Data Recording and Storage This phase of responsibility involves the development and care of student academic information; i.e., the legal evidence of the period in which the student was enrolled and the work he accomplished while he was there. In a small college, however, the registrar may keep all the records including those pertaining to activities, athletics, health, housing, finances, and alumni.

The minimum student record contains vital statistics such as name, home address, parents' names, birthdate; a record of what academic work was accomplished and when it was done; and records of any academic actions such as transfers, periods of study abroad, or withdrawals. Thus the registrar is responsible for the continuing process of building the basic student record, adding the record of courses taken and the grades received each semester.

Evaluation The registrar is in the position of having full knowledge of his institution's academic standards. Standards will vary from institution to institution and from college to college within a given institution. Cognizant of this, the registrar can advise the faculty on standards as they prevail in other institutions and other colleges within the home institution, and therefore he can be of great assistance as a member of the academic standards planning and policy-making committees.

Public Services and Publications As the registrar is in constant contact with students, faculty, and administration, he frequently is called upon to explain the school's academic policies to the public. This can include anything from university information counter service to production of the yearly course catalog.

VARIABLES IN OPERATIONS

Organization A registrar's office organization is as unique as a fingerprint. It is determined by the scope of his responsibilities and the size of the student body. Large and small operations are outlined in Figures 2 and 3. Variations can be deduced from these.

Among institutions of comparable size and complexity, one cannot safely generalize about the organizational structure. In one institution, the registrar may exercise authority over a complex structure of subregistrars who in turn control scheduling, student records, catalog production, etc.; whereas in an apparently similar school the registrar controls only the registration, with separate offices controlling student records

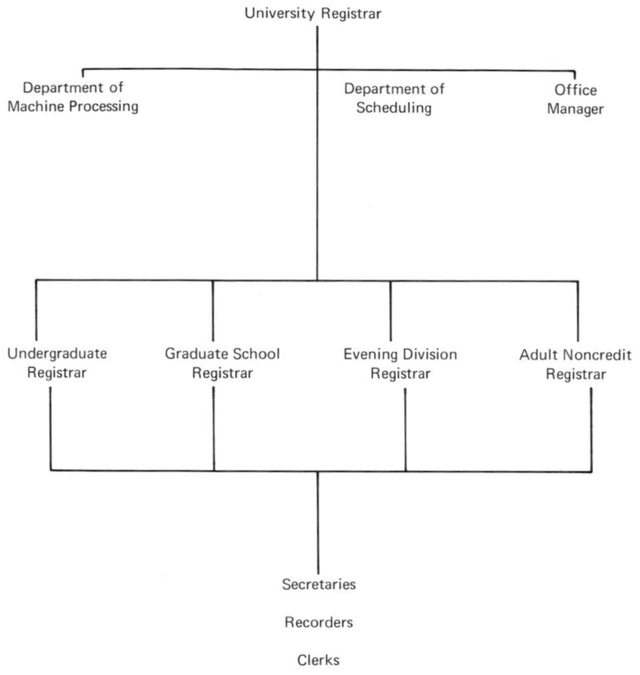

Fig. 2 *University.*

and scheduling. On the small end of the scale, one is likely to find the registrar cast in the role of chief administrative assistant to the president with a variety of responsibilities ranging from the seven categories discussed above to housing and equipment inventory.

What the registrar does is strongly influenced by his immediate circumstances—such as the existence of a separate admissions operation as opposed to a combined admissions-registration office. If the admissions operation is separate, the registrar must establish lines of communications with the admissions office to facilitate student record development, to reach agreement on such questions as student enrollment, and to establish effective freshman counseling, orientation, and registration procedures. In a combined admissions-registration situation, the head officer must be concerned with all the functions normally performed by a separate admissions office. The advantages lie in the potential for a truly integrated student records system. The dis-

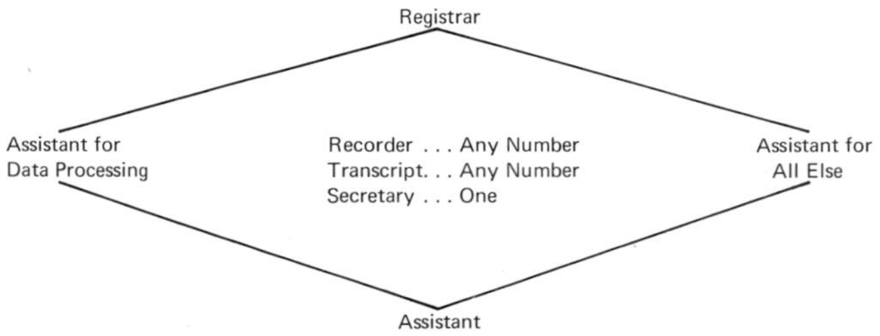

Fig. 3 *Small college.*

advantages lie in the complexity and quantity of the work involved. Some of the additional concerns of an admissions-registration officer are the collection and collation of admissions data, admissions profiles and other reports such as financial-aid statements, interviewing, school recruiting, informing applicants of admission decisions, and entrance examinations.

Calendar The design of the academic year affects the registrar in many ways. Notable are the number of times the registration cycle must be experienced, the mode of calculating and recording grades, and the balancing of enrollments for each academic period. The preceding chapter on academic calendars discusses this topic at length.

Student Population Procedures will vary in accordance with the number of students involved. While registration is a necessary function regardless of size, the impact of 15,000 students is vastly different from that of 500 students. Such differences necessitate qualitative differences in approach. Merely adding more clerks and ordering more forms will not be sufficient. Indeed, it was this fact more than any other which hastened the development of administrative computer usage in the large midwestern universities in the early 1960s. Other developments which attempted to ease the bottleneck were preregistration and computer sectioning.

Registration is basically the same function regardless of institutional size, but the methodology can be vastly different. In a large university, such questions may arise as: How much freedom of choice do technical students exercise? Are graduate students registered separately? How are part-time students to be registered—are records to be in the central registrar's office? Are branch campuses involved, and if so, do the students register separately or on the main campus? Is ROTC required of men students and how are selective-service problems to be handled?

Intercollege Cooperative Information Sharing A detailed discussion of this topic appears in the chapter on interinstitutional cooperation. Suffice it to say that this type of program is becoming increasingly necessary for small liberal arts schools which want to retain their unique atmosphere and still attract good teachers and good students. Problems have arisen, however, out of the varying concepts of an adequate information base, methods of reporting, and transcript formats. The American Association of Collegiate Registrars and Admissions Officers (AACRAO) has attempted to provide guidance by issuing such publications as *Data and Definitions* and *An Adequate Record and Transcript Guide.* The most definitive work, however, is to be found in the report of the National Science Foundation—NSF 67—15—entitled *Systems for Measuring and Reporting the Resources and Activities of Colleges and Universities.*

Use of Data Processing Out of the increased cooperative sharing of information and the accelerated demand and financial necessity to make all academic enterprises more productive has come a second major trend—the use of mechanical and electronic machines to facilitate information processing. Initially, the basic justification came in such areas as volume handling, increased efficiency, and error control of routine clerical tasks. Registrars found data processing useful in the production of class lists, grade reports, and transcript updates. Gradually some pioneers like Purdue University began to use it for more sophisticated problems such as class scheduling, examination scheduling, and space-utilization studies. This, in turn, has led to the concept of a total academic information system in which operating and planning personnel can obtain the type of information they need when they need it. Examples of this are the concepts of demand reporting and exception reporting. These supplement but do not replace the more familiar periodic reports.

Information systems are discussed in detail in Chapter 8 of Section 3 in the companion volume on general administration. In this connection, however, it is well to point out that on all levels it becomes increasingly necessary that the registrar have some knowledge of data processing and what it can and cannot do to facilitate his operation.

BASIC OPERATIONS

Decision Charts The following charts are an elaboration of the seven major functions described earlier. No attempt is made to be exhaustive, because the ways of performing these functions are as numerous as the schools which need them. Nor is any attempt made to say which circumstances require which solution. These charts are designed merely to point out some of the major decision areas now in use and some of their implications.

The master decision chart (Figure 4) depicts the general time flow through the registration cycle. Two points need to be kept in mind:

1. Registration cycles overlap so that, depending on the academic calendar, at all times there may be activities going on pertaining to as many as four separate cycles. This necessitates careful office management procedures to avoid the confusing of files and data.

2. This chart does not give a complete picture of the functions of a registrar. That would require the portrayal of report and transcript production, data recording and storage, and public liaison and publication duties.

Scheduling and Sectioning As stated earlier in the discussion of operational responsibilities, scheduling students into classes consists of two major parts—building the master schedule of classes and sectioning, the actual assigning of individual students to specific class times.

Master Schedules. The master schedule is the list of all the courses being offered for a particular term. It includes the time, place of meeting, and instructor responsible for each course. On the basis of student course choice, it is then adjusted in four major phases: (1) updating of scheduling files, (2) preparation of current action forms, (3) collection of current course data material, and (4) production of the master schedule. Certain variables in the process include course additions and deletions, number of sections, class size limits, faculty availability and teaching fields, course prerequisites, requirements for specific majors, availability of teaching equipment, and relation of class sizes to the capabilities of existing physical facilities.

This process is further complicated by the ongoing dispute between the faculty and

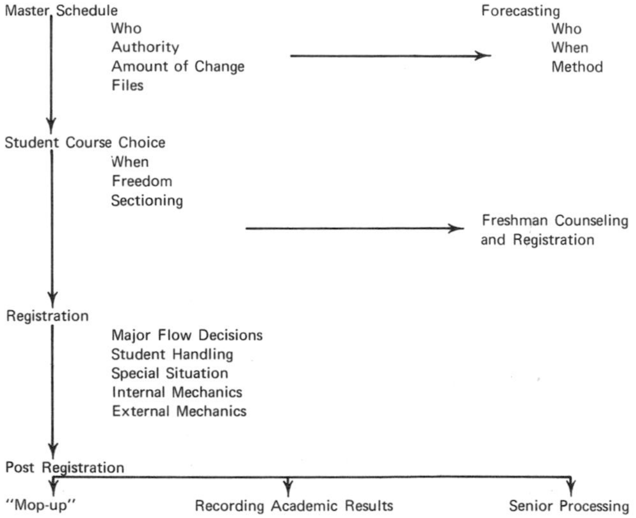

Fig. 4 *Master decision chart.*

the scheduling officer over who should have the responsibility and authority for establishing class hours and locations. If the former, the faculty is happy, but the scheduling officer is limited to suggestions and is unable to develop effective facilities-utilization patterns. If the latter, the scheduling officer has the chance to develop a good utilization pattern, but the faculty is likely to be unhappy with the loss of this authority and with the full scheduling of the less popular class times.

The minimum information needed to build a master schedule is knowledge of what instructors will be available to teach what courses, what class and laboratory space exists, and the vital characteristics of each room—such as size, location, equipment, etc. Within the above framework, the following technique is most common: the basic course and section information files are updated to reflect changes, additions, and deletions for the coming semester. At this time, the scheduling officer determines that (1) enrollment figures are not being padded so that extra sections at unpopular hours can be dropped and (2) that the department-requested time distribution of courses is evenly spread and not grouped around midmorning weekday classes. Parenthetically, it should be mentioned that the examination schedule is also produced as a part of this procedure.

After this preliminary preparation, the actual scheduling begins. There are several parameters which the scheduling officer must keep in mind in all scheduling procedures. Courses must be relatively conflict-free for anticipated student request groupings. Faculty assigned to particular courses should not have conflicts. The recitation, lecture, and laboratory requirements for particular courses must be met.

The requirements for department majors are developed first, with sufficient sections of university-required courses scattered throughout to prevent conflicts between departmental and university requirements. Then, strictly elective course schedules are developed at the hours and locations left, with consideration being given to (1) predictable conflicts, (2) time distributions for courses in the same department, (3) faculty preferences, and (4) physical facilities available. After the initial master schedule is finished, extensive reviews are conducted in which departments may request necessary changes. The final result is seen in the course selection booklet from which the student will select his courses.

Student Course Choice. There are four areas of decision in student course selection. Two—when to have it and how to develop student schedules—are essentially procedural in nature, with the advantages and disadvantages stemming from time,

TABLE 1 Master Schedule Building

Decision	Alternatives	Implications	Requirements
Who	Schedule office	Usually more central control	Strong central organization
	Committee	Usually departmental control	Willingness to accept what department decides
Authority ...	Department	Satisfied departments and inefficient space utilization	Surplus space and faculty
	Central	Opportunities for optimum space utilization	Strong administration
Amount of change	Evolution	Minimum immediate headaches; less chance for strong change	
	Radical	High risks; results can be worth the risk	
Files	Detailed	Large staff—central control	
	Minimal	Less staff—department control	

TABLE 2 Student Course Choice

Decision	Alternatives	Implications	Advantages/disadvantages
Freedom of course	Track	Vocationally oriented school in which a student is expected to work towards a specific career objective.	Makes forecasting much easier but limits the exploration possibilities open to a student.
	Elective	Liberal arts attitude of education can be found at some schools. Places great deal of emphasis on individual student and requires highly competent advisers.	Can foster dilettantism in immature students while at same time fostering deeper educational exploration in others. More costly in faculty and forecasting difficulty. Preregistration would be helpful in prediction.
Freedom of section	Allowed	Students have ability to design their time schedules to suit personal needs. Gives them stronger sense of control over their education.	Students are pleased but it makes effective space utilization impossible.
	Not allowed	Students select courses but not sections or branches. For the most part they resent this, particularly if Professor A is a better teacher than Professor B.	This is only way to make maximum facilities use possible. It is worth noting that upperclass courses usually will have only one section anyway.
Date of preregistration		Usually held some time during the semester prior to the one being planned. Can be done by mail, in a one-day advisers' period, or over a period of several weeks. Remote terminals similar to a typewriter can be used to request courses.	Gives some indication of what the course demand will be, as well as giving the student a chance to think about his choices. The number of changes at registration is usually high but evenly spread.
	No preregistration	Course selection is done immediately prior to the opening of classes during formal preregistration. Advising is also done at this time.	Students choose their courses at a time when they know what they need. Does not permit prediction of fads and the hiring of additional teachers or adjustments to the master schedule.
Method............	Hand	Student schedules are developed by pulling cards from a tub file of class cards. When a class is full a decision is made to expand or open a new section. Conflicts are resolved by consultation with department heads and scheduling office.	Permits greater flexibility in section choice since the decisions can be made in different ways for each case. Conversely, it is so time-consuming that effective space utilization is impossible.
	Computer	The master schedule is fed into the computer along with student course requests. An analysis of conflicts is produced and the master schedule adjusted. Student schedules and class lists are the final output.	This method is less flexible in handling student section requests, but it permits more effective space utilization and provides information useful for planning.

TABLE 3 Postregistration

Phase	Process	Description	Purpose	Destination
"Mop-up".............	Dropping or adding courses	Provide procedures to permit students to change courses.	To adjust errors in mechanics or judgment.	
		Update student master record to reflect changes.	To keep student master file up to date.	
		Produce list of all changes since registration.	To inform faculty and administration of the current student status and to keep a record of how many changes there are in order to judge the efficiency of the registration system.	Faculty and academic deans
	Withdrawals	Provide procedure for officially separating the students from the college. Problems which arise include how to reflect withdrawal in the student record, what regulations a student must fulfill before he can leave in good standing, what will be the status of his record after he leaves.	To permit orderly, voluntary withdrawal with maximum protection to the student and minimum disruption to the college.	Faculty and academic deans
	Late registration	Impose regulations and fines (usually) on those who fail to register during the official registration period. Questions include how late students may be permitted to register and how fines should be assessed.	To discourage and yet permit late registration.	Faculty and academic deans
	Enrollment analysis	Produce a variety of enrollment-distribution reports. The analyses can range from relatively simple geographical analyses to highly sophisticated analyses of the student body.	To help administration and institutional research evaluate the composition of the current student body.	President, academic deans, institutional research

TABLE 3 (Continued)

Phase	Process	Description	Purpose	Destination
Recording academic results	Grade reporting	Send grade cards or lists to instructors (or they may use their class cards) so that they may record the grades on them. These records are sent back to the registrar.	To ensure accurate grade reporting without student intervention.	Faculty
	Grade checking	Check out illogical, duplicate, or missing grades with the instructor before the grades are posted.	To eliminate later work by checking the input before it is processed.	Faculty
	QPA (quality point average) calculation	Compute current QPA if university is on that system.	To establish overall measure of students' academic work.	
	Record posting	Post current grades and updated QPA to the student's record.	To update the student record so that any transcript requests may be filled with current information.	
	Grade reports	Check in individual record of grades and new QPA.	To inform those authorized of the grades of individual students.	Students, parents, advisers
	Grade lists	Produce various lists of grades.	To inform different groups how their members are doing.	Fraternities, sororities, dormitories, etc.
	Grade analysis	Analyze grades with respect to particular areas of interest.	To evaluate results of different programs. To aid in planning for the future.	President, institutional research
	Honor lists, scholarship and loan lists	Produce special versions of grade lists.	To highlight and reward the superior student.	Honor societies, scholarships and loan office
Senior processing ...	Degree audit	Check on students to make sure they are fulfilling their requirements for graduation.	To prevent disappointments just prior to graduation.	Academic deans

TABLE 3 (Continued)

Phase	Process	Description	Purpose	Destination
	Graduation preparation	Ensure that diplomas are correctly ordered. (Not always the registrar's responsibility.)	To ensure smooth graduation procedures.	
	Certification	Fill out certification forms for various accrediting agencies, such as the National Teachers' Association. Best procedure occurs when the student transcript can serve as certification document.	To give recognition to those who have fulfilled requirements for their profession.	Accrediting agencies
	Transcript production	Produce an official copy of the student's academic record. Problems include: 1. Confidential nature of student records (the rule of thumb here is that only the student may authorize distribution of his transcript unless the request is from an agency that can subpoena it). 2. Legal and moral responsibility for student academic records means that there must be provision for file security and backup in case of loss. 3. Cost—should a college refuse transcripts unless a fee is paid, or should it bill afterwards? Should the first transcript be free? 4. How should the transcript be produced—in the form of a photocopy, computer printout, hand copy, etc.?		

money, facilities, and personnel costs. Two other areas—freedom of choice with regard to course section and instructor—are related directly to the way the institution views the student. The lines are blurred in the area of methodology of sectioning and section choice, because the method can affect what amount of freedom is possible.

Scheduling Examinations. Final examinations must be scheduled in such a manner that most students will have evenly spaced schedules with no two examinations at the same time. Most colleges set up guidelines for the maximum number of examinations to be given in 48 hours and the minimum amount of time between the last class and the first examination.

Forecasting. One of the important peripheral tasks frequently performed by the registrar is forecasting. Each term or year, usually, he submits a report to the president predicting the enrollment in the different major study plans offered by the school. He bases his projections only in part on past figures. A large part is shrewd speculation based on his observations of developments in the nation at large as well as in his own community. Many things can affect these projections—from the opening of an explosive new field in science, such as laser research, to the acquisition of a famous scholar who attracts many students to the school and to his field.

Registration Registration is the overall process by which students choose courses, are sectioned, and confirm their individual schedules. In one system, registration may be accomplished in one specific period just prior to the start of classes. A second system divides the process into a preregistration period, in which students select courses from a master schedule listing, and a registration period where they receive and may attempt to change their actual schedule for that academic period. There are as many ways to undertake this process as there are schools, but most lie within the framework of the "two-part" system or the "all-at-once" system.

It is worth noting that in the future it may well be possible for a student to register for a learning resource-center course by punching his identification badge, the name of the course, and the name of his adviser into a data-collection machine. He will then use the resource center for most of his work (it will be open 24 hours a day, with graduate students on call for discussion), with periodic tutorial and small group sessions with his adviser arranged at their mutual convenience. The same initial input will update his record and calculate fees. In this situation the registrar will be able to design and implement other education administration systems.

Freshman Counseling and Registration. This is a special situation, since not only do incoming freshmen need to have records established—this is also true for transfers and graduate students—but they need very careful guidance and orientation into the choices open to them. This means above all time and competent staff for schools on the semester calendar. The two most common ways of handling the problem are:

1. By holding weekend orientation and testing sessions for small groups of freshmen. The advantage of this system is the time it allows both advisers and the registrar to counsel, test, and register the students. The students, in turn, have a chance to meet department members, choose a dormitory, and become acquainted with the campus before the rush of opening. The disadvantage lies in its very advantage—time. Faculty, who are necessary components, frequently balk at such intrusions upon their summer. The expense of staff, data processing time (if used), housing, and food for each weekend the freshmen are there can also be a factor.

2. By having a freshman week—the week prior to registration—during which the whole freshman class is counseled and registered. The advantage lies in the saving of time and money. The disadvantage is in the pressure exerted on students to make a choice fairly quickly and in the lack of planning information available for the adjustment of course sections.

An interesting innovation by one university provides for the counseling and registration of freshmen by mail. The college works with the student and his high school counselor to develop the range of choices which coincides with his abilities and interests. The university cites as advantages of the system the lack of pressure, the close ties which are established between the high school and the university, and the care with which the student makes his choices under the supervision of people who know him. (See "Orientation of New Students," Chapter 7 of Section 7.)

Postregistration. After the students are duly settled in their classes, three major phases complete the registration cycle: (1) a "mop-up" campaign with assessment of results, (2) recording of the results of student work, and (3) helping the seniors in their effort to graduate.

Data Handling

Report and Transcript Production. Before discussing the nature of records to be kept by the registrar, it would be well to examine the information he is usually called upon to produce. These considerations hold regardless of who requests the report, because the best service is intelligent service, and a meaningless or redundant report or one based on faulty or inadequate data is much worse than no report at all. The following questions should be kept in mind when considering the production of a particular report:

1. What kind of information is wanted?
2. Could this information be more easily obtained elsewhere?
3. What purpose is it to serve?
4. Who is to use it?
5. When is it to be produced?
6. How often is it needed?
7. How crucial is the information? What will happen if it is not available?
8. Is the report to be periodic—produced routinely at a specific time—or will it be produced only when certain conditions actually exist, such as a student taking too many hours? Is it a one-time report tailored to fit a special need?
9. Are the necessary data available in the necessary format?
10. If not, can they be obtained?
11. What guarantee is there that the data are valid or meaningful? For example, students will sometimes deliberately falsify psychological tests as a protest against the "system."

The foregoing questions may seem somewhat esoteric when applied to such traditional and essential reports as class lists, grade reports, and transcripts. They are intended, however, to highlight the considerations which the registrar should keep in mind for his own self-interest when he is increasingly bombarded with requests for information from internal groups such as institutional research offices or external academic groups and government agencies.

To place some general questions into perspective, let us consider some reports actually being produced in at least one college or university today. Given below is a chart showing reports, when produced, to whom directed, and functions served. No outside agency reports are alluded to here because by their very nature they are one-time reports and are therefore exceedingly variable as to their requirements. Exceptions to this statement would be the annual October government enrollment-statistics report and the fairly standard certification request. Indeed, under the urging of common sense and AACRAO, many transcripts are now being designed to be directly photocopied for certification. Formerly, much additional work was required in the registrar's office each time a certification form requiring manual filing came in.

Data Recording and Storage. The prime responsibility of the registrar is the care of records relating to the student's academic career. This usually entails student record files and in addition may include such files as facilities information files and curriculum files (actually the basis for the catalog).

TABLE 4 Reports

Subject of report	*When report is issued*
Enrollment forecasting	Annually
Faculty utilization	Annually
Class rosters	Registration
Selective service rating	Registration
Bookstore lists	Registration
Drop-add lists	Postregistration
Student directory	Postregistration
Curriculum transfers	Postregistration
Enrollment analyses	Postregistration
Geographical	
Parents' addresses	
Summary by class and college	
Field of concentration	
New students—alpha	
New students—married	
New students—entrance status	
Evening division	
Veterans	
Dropout analysis by major	Postregistration
Probation	Postregistration
Withdrawals	Postregistration
Transfer	Postregistration
Graduation list	Postregistration
Graduation deficiency	Postregistration
Grade reports	Postregistration
Missing grades	
Academic action	
Student individual reports	
Honor lists	
Permanent record	
Grade distribution	
Grade point	
Fraternity–sorority	
Residence hall	
Loan	
Scholarship	
Student status	Weekly

Master Student Data. However, for the registrar, "good data" means one primary thing—accurate *student* records, and it is with these that we shall be predominantly concerned. Good student records have always been of greatest concern to the registrar, for the transcript is based on the records—and the transcript is the currency of the academic "bank account" which the student has been building since entering school. Just as with any bank, it is the registrar's legal and moral obligation to respond immediately to any legitimate request for "funds."

Thus, in a climate of increasing cooperative use of records and continuing education for all men, the availability, credibility, and comprehensibility of these records is of the utmost importance. It thus becomes necessary to inquire as to the standards for judging the quality of the records; the systems which generate, store, and use them; and the nature of a satisfactory academic records system.

The AACRAO guide published in 1966, entitled *An Adequate Permanent Record and Transcript Guide,* states that a good academic records system should include:

(*a*) A permanent record form carefully planned to meet all the needs for and uses of academic evidence, (*b*) provision for a filing and storage system for both preliminary and permanent records, and (*c*) the reflection of a complete understanding and full appreciation on the part of the admissions-records-registration staff of the aims and purposes of the system.

In other words, the student's academic record must be based on an integrated academic records system which is thoroughly up to date in its security, storage, and accessibility methods and is clearly and accurately stated in the official transcript or school-authorized copy.

What then is involved in the design of an adequate student records system? Regardless of whether one is planning a full-scale teleprocessing system to accommodate 20,000 students or working with the records of 200, there are certain basic student functions which dictate what must be in the files.

First, there are two main types of student record files which may be kept separate or brought together in one student master file. These are the *personnel file* and the *academic record file*. The latter is the one which primarily concerns the registrar, but the first may also be under his jurisdiction.

The Master Student Data List (Table 5) gives some indication of what might be included in a total student record. But for a more limited guide to the minimum needed in an academic student record, refer to the AACRAO's permanent record and transcript

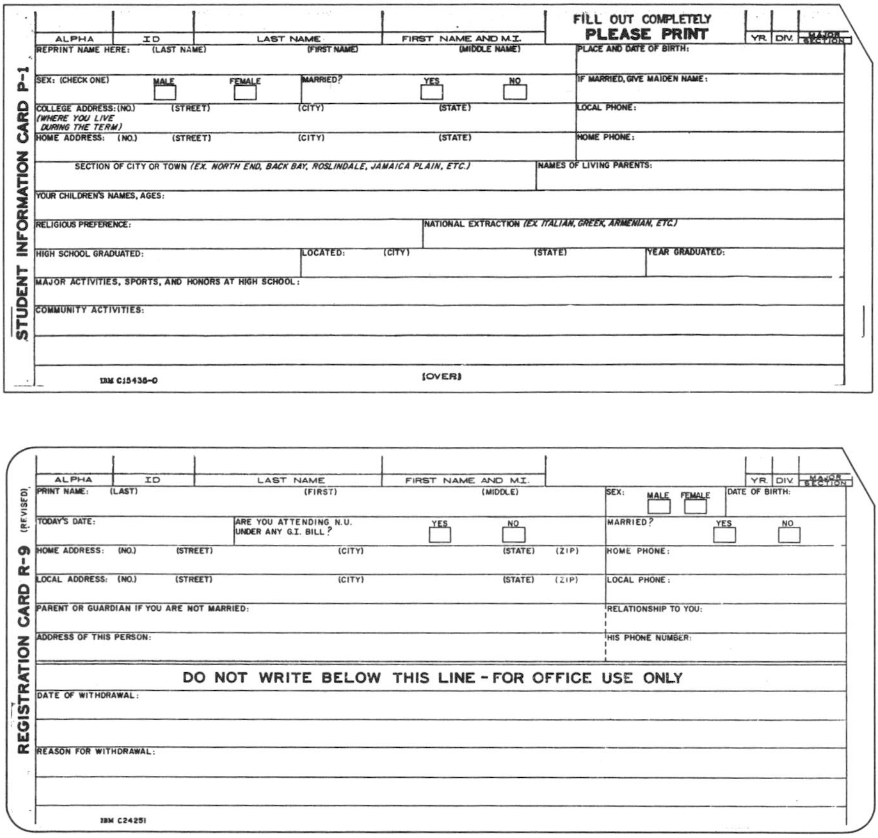

STUDENT INFORMATION CARD P-1

ALPHA | ID | LAST NAME | FIRST NAME AND M.I. | FILL OUT COMPLETELY PLEASE PRINT | YR. | DIV. | MAJOR SECTION

REPRINT NAME HERE: (LAST NAME) (FIRST NAME) (MIDDLE NAME) | PLACE AND DATE OF BIRTH:

SEX: (CHECK ONE) MALE ☐ FEMALE ☐ MARRIED? YES ☐ NO ☐ | IF MARRIED, GIVE MAIDEN NAME:

COLLEGE ADDRESS: (NO.) (WHERE YOU LIVE DURING THE TERM) (STREET) (CITY) (STATE) | LOCAL PHONE:

HOME ADDRESS: (NO.) (STREET) (CITY) (STATE) | HOME PHONE:

SECTION OF CITY OR TOWN (EX. NORTH END, BACK BAY, ROSLINDALE, JAMAICA PLAIN, ETC.) | NAMES OF LIVING PARENTS:

YOUR CHILDREN'S NAMES, AGES:

RELIGIOUS PREFERENCE: | NATIONAL EXTRACTION (EX. ITALIAN, GREEK, ARMENIAN, ETC.)

HIGH SCHOOL GRADUATED: | LOCATED: (CITY) (STATE) | YEAR GRADUATED:

MAJOR ACTIVITIES, SPORTS, AND HONORS AT HIGH SCHOOL:

COMMUNITY ACTIVITIES:

IBM C15436-0 (OVER)

REGISTRATION CARD R-9 (REVISED)

ALPHA | ID | LAST NAME | FIRST NAME AND M.I. | YR. | DIV. | MAJOR SECTION

PRINT NAME: (LAST) (FIRST) (MIDDLE) | SEX: MALE ☐ FEMALE ☐ | DATE OF BIRTH:

TODAY'S DATE: | ARE YOU ATTENDING N.U. UNDER ANY G.I. BILL? YES ☐ NO ☐ | MARRIED? YES ☐ NO ☐

HOME ADDRESS: (NO.) (STREET) (CITY) (STATE) (ZIP) | HOME PHONE:

LOCAL ADDRESS: (NO.) (STREET) (CITY) (STATE) (ZIP) | LOCAL PHONE:

PARENT OR GUARDIAN IF YOU ARE NOT MARRIED: | RELATIONSHIP TO YOU:

ADDRESS OF THIS PERSON: | HIS PHONE NUMBER:

DO NOT WRITE BELOW THIS LINE - FOR OFFICE USE ONLY

DATE OF WITHDRAWAL:

REASON FOR WITHDRAWAL:

IBM C24251

Fig. 5 *Sample student information card registration forms.*

NORTHEASTERN UNIVERSITY
BOSTON, MASSACHUSETTS

I.D. NUMBER

MR.
MISS.
MRS

STUDENT'S NAME: ______ FIRST NAME / MIDDLE NAME / LAST NAME

COLLEGE OF

MAJOR

HOME ADDRESS:

BORN

COURSE NUMBER	TITLE	QUARTER HOURS	GR	COURSE NUMBER	TITLE	QUARTER HOURS	GR	COURSE NUMBER	TITLE	QUARTER HOURS	GR	COURSE NUMBER	TITLE	QUARTER HOURS	GR

GRADUATED FROM ______

DATE GRADUATED ______

REGISTERED ON ______

OTHER COLLEGES ATTENDED ______

R-61

SCALE OF MARKS
A – SUPERIOR ATTAINMENT.
B – GOOD ATTAINMENT.
C – SATISFACTORY ATTAINMENT.
D – POOR ATTAINMENT.
F – FAILURE.
I – INCOMPLETE.
F-D– ORIGINAL F CLEARED BY COND. EXAM.
F-F– CONDITION EXAM. ALSO F
WF– WITHDREW FROM COURSE, FAILING
ONE QH = THREE-FOURTHS SEM. HR. TWELVE-WEEK QUARTER CALENDAR.
IN COMPUTING NUMERICAL AVERAGE: A IS RECKONED AS 4, B AS 3, C AS 2, D AS 1, F AS 0, F-D AS 1, AND F-F AS 0.

FACULTY ACTION

DEGREE:

DATE:

ENTITLED TO AN HONORABLE DISMISSAL

ISSUED REGISTRAR

Fig. 6 *Sample undergraduate permanent record form.*

guide. No attempt shall be made here to reproduce its very detailed discussion of the minimum information necessary for a good student academic record except to quote these summary points:

I. Identification of the institution
 A. Name
 B. Address
II. Identification of the student
 C. Full name and sex
 D. Date and place of birth
 E. Home or current address
III. Basis of admission
 F. By secondary school graduation
  1. Name and location of school
  2. Date of graduation
 G. Other
  1. Individual approval
  2. Examination
  3. Other
 H. Transfer from other college or university
  1. Name and location
  2. Designation of transfer credit
IV. The record of work taken
 I. Curriculum or major subject
 J. Dates of attendance
 K. Department, catalog number, and descriptive title of each course (including field of practice teaching and level of instruction)
 L. Amount of credit granted for each course
 M. Grade for each course
V. Termination status and verification of the record
 N. Statement of graduation
 O. Status at time of last attendance
  1. Good standing
  2. Probation
  3. Suspension
  4. Dismissal
 P. Signature of proper official
 Q. College or university seal
VI. Institutional policies—pertinent regulations and definitions of terms
 R. Length of term
 S. Definition of credit unit
 T. Adequate column headings
 U. Clear designation of types of credit
 V. Explanation of the grading system
VII. Supplemental information for graduate schools
 W. Honors and awards
 X. Examination results
 Y. Waiver of requirements
 Z. Title of dissertation and/or thesis

Other considerations, which must be kept in mind both during the planning of a student academic records system and during the operation of its functions, are:

1. *Backup.* Since, unlike the bank account referred to earlier, there is no way to reimburse the student in case of loss of his records through any cause (such as fire, for example), it is imperative that there be exact duplicates stored in a physical location separate from that of the primary records.

Another aspect of backup needs lies in the necessity of having such data as student schedules available at all times for access in case of emergency, even during peak processing periods.

2. *Safety.* This means not only safety from the aforementioned destruction of records but also safety from tampering and forgery. This involves provisions to ensure computer file security and, if terminals are being used as input-output devices, to prevent unauthorized access to codes and records.

3. *Convenience.* Is the permanent record in a form which meets most certification requirements (full descriptive title, etc.) and which is easily updated and converted to transcript form?

4. *Systems Management.* Are there adequate error safeguards in the record creation and updating system?

5. *Legal.* What are the laws regarding the release of information in the state? Can one be sued by a student for releasing information without his consent? Should one give FBI investigators full access to the files?

TABLE 5 Master Student Data List

Student number and/or social security number
Name
Home address and area code
In/out of state code
Home phone number
Parents'/guardian's name
Parents'/guardian's address and area code
Birth date
Sex
Marital status
Military status
Selective-service class and number
Health
Religion
Graduate/undergraduate
Admission year and term
Admission date
Class
College name and code
Curriculum name and code
Application date
Application status—application fee, all information in, accepted, early notification, rejected, refused offer, matriculation fee, pending, check stop
High school name and code
High school address
High school courses and grades
High school rank in class and converted rank
High school rating factor
High school graduation date
College testing service scores
Achievement scores
Previous institution
Previous terms attended (advanced standing students)
Previous curriculum name and code (advanced standing students)
Previous courses, credits and grades
Previous cumulative credits, grade-point average
Predictions
Adviser number
Aptitude and interest test scores
Placement-test scores
Probability percentages of grade achievement
Activities, honors, awards at high school or previous college
Financial plans—loan, scholarship, work
Home and community environment
Parents' occupations, income, education, degrees
Siblings' ages, sex, occupations, education, degrees
Hobbies, interests
College name and code
Curriculum name and code
Courses, credits and grades
Cumulative credits, grade-point average
Current standing
Action codes
Expected graduation date
Institutions
Colleges
Curriculums
Degrees and dates received (graduate students)
Date of admission
College
Curriculum
Degree sought
Expected date of receiving degree
Campus residence and address
Campus telephone number
Roommate(s)
Scholarship, fellowship, assistantship—number, amount restriction codes, number previously received, total amount received, code for means to pay or credit student

TABLE 5 (Continued)

Loan-number, amount, restriction codes, interest rate, repayment frequency, number of payments, start date, remainder amount, balance due, interest paid to date, delinquency codes, number of delinquencies, code for means to pay or credit student, number received previously, total amount, loans repaid code
Current billing fees—tuition, laboratory, music
 Charges—housing, board, activities, insurance, athletics, etc.
 Other charges—parking, library, breakage, telephone
 Other credits—dormitory assistant
Student employment
Fraternity/sorority
Organizations—total number, codes, offices held
Honor groups—academic, nonacademic, total number codes

Other Files. Other files which the registrar needs access to and which he normally controls are the facilities information file and the curriculum information file.

Briefly these would contain the following types of information:

1. Course Information. Including title, number, description, credit, breakdown of lecture, recitation and labs, majors for which the course is a requirement
2. Summary Enrollment Information. Total enrollment in a specific course for each past term, the number of sections during that term, and the average enrollment per section
3. Section History Information. Giving the actual history of the enrollment for a particular section
4. Term and Course Distribution Information. Essentially the information on required and suggested courses for majors in given fields which appears in the catalog in the introduction to each major field
5. Room Data Information. Room number and building; classification (general-purpose classroom, teaching laboratory, or specialized classroom facility); seating capacity; type of seating; amount of blackboard space; audiovisual facilities available in the room; other pertinent facts regarding the physical or instructional features of a particular facility
6. Final Examination Schedule Room Information. Size and nature of the facilities
7. Faculty Information. Includes specialties, times available to teach, alternate possibilities in case of emergency need, research schedules, load limitation figures

This information is used not only for master schedule and examination schedule building but also in projecting future personnel, physical facilities, and financial requirements.

Format of Files. The form in which data is stored affects its accessibility. For example, suppose student records are recorded in a combination of card and tape files. Reference to a particular taped student record would be difficult because it would mean reading through the whole tape file until the desired record was found. Therefore, instead of tapes, the paper backup would be used for researching individual students. On the other hand, it would be a simple matter for the registrar to produce reports pertaining to many or all of the students in his files because a program could be written which would take the information from the tape, make any calculations wanted, and produce the desired report. To do this manually would be a time-consuming, almost impossible task.

Another problem arises when a report requiring information from several files is needed—such as admissions, dean's, bursar's, and registrar's files. Since these files were set up by different departments without cross consultation, there are discrepancies in the way the information is stored. For example, the registrar's permanent student file may be on tape and have the student's name in this format—last (12 positions), first (10 positions), and middle initial. The registrar's course file has the student name as one field 15 characters in length, with the last name and first initial constituting the one field. The dean's file may not be in machinable format and may give the first name, middle initial, and last name in that order. Any reference by name to these three files would be impossible by machine, even if the dean's files were in machinable form.

Under such a system such a report would be exceedingly difficult if not impossible to obtain. On the other hand, such files are relatively easy to set up and maintain and are adequate for most routine purposes of the department using them.

Public Liaison and Publication Activities

General Information Services. To the general public the registrar's office is the information bureau for the academic community. Thus, office personnel should be prepared either to answer or route a wide variety of questions ranging from college history to research budgets.

Counter Service. Students, parents, and the public in general expect to find copies of the catalog and informative brochures in the registrar's office. In small colleges, this office sometimes serves as a message routing center and college post office.

Selective Service Liaison. Since the registrar has student records, he is frequently asked to serve as selective service liaison with the students. This involves informing students about current regulations, dates for examinations, etc., and answering selective service requests for information about students. (See Chapter 17 in this section.)

Veterans Administration. This is similar to selective service liaison, except that the questions concern not deferments from military services but rather financial aid as a result of previous military service. (See Chapter 15 in Section 7.)

Foreign Student Affairs. The concerns here include travel permits, student visas, passports, foreign credit evaluation, and—since the State Department has been phasing out of this area—exchange-student arrangements, to name just a few. (See Chapter 14 in Section 7.)

Civic Affairs. As an extension of his general information function, the registrar is often called upon to represent the college at civic functions.

Catalog Production. The registrar has course files and information on department major requirements and university requirements; it is logical that he should sometimes be called upon to compile the annual catalog.

Student Directory. The student directory is produced after the late-registration period is over and the full student body is known. This is an alphabetic list which gives local address, telephone number, and sometimes class.

Education and Professional Services. This covers a broad spectrum but would include such activities as serving on faculty policy-making committees, activities in support of his profession, and making records accessible to those who wish research information.

Chapter 10

Interinstitutional Cooperation

STANLEY F. SALWAK

President, Aroostook State College, Presque Isle, Maine, Formerly Director, Committee on Institutional Cooperation of the Big Ten Universities and The University of Chicago, Purdue University, Lafayette, Indiana

WILLIAM DEMINOFF

Associate Director, Committee on Institutional Cooperation of the Big Ten Universities and The University of Chicago, Purdue University, Lafayette, Indiana

INTRODUCTION

Interinstitutional cooperation can be defined as any arrangement, formal or informal, entered into by two or more colleges or universities for purposes of sharing resources or of conducting joint planning and execution of programs for their mutual benefit. Such cooperation can take place in any area of instruction, research, institutional administration, or public service activity. It is directed principally toward the accomplishment of objectives acknowledged to be desirable but beyond the ready capability of any single institution to mount, maintain, or realize on its own. The concept also encompasses the programs of cooperative assistance entered into by strong, established institutions for the benefit of "developing" colleges and universities. And it includes as well the programs conducted by institutions of higher learning in conjunction with such facilities as national research laboratories, oceanographic institutes, independent libraries and museums, and similar resources.

Cooperation in higher education is hardly a new phenomenon. Since the end of World War II, there has been an increasing number of arrangements for resource sharing and interchanges of various kinds. These have included interlibrary programs, faculty and student exchanges. sharing of research facilities, information exchanges on instructional and administrative processes, and many others. In their earlier phases, these have been informal arrangements, generally involving a small number of neighboring institutions. But since the late 1950s these rather fragmentary efforts have been supplanted in many instances by a much more organized form of cooperative activity.

Today there are literally hundreds of such groupings, ranging from two-institution arrangements to loosely federated or fully chartered combinations of many institutions. A count by the U.S. Office of Education as of 1965–66 shows a total of 1,017 consortia, with another 245 planned.[1] However, it must be noted that the word "consortium" is used in the USOE tally to cover *all* cooperative arrangements, from a simple interlibrary program between two institutions to a formally organized combination of 10 or more institutions working jointly in many areas of institutional operation. For the purposes of this handbook, it seems wise to reserve the term "consortium" for the associations having some form of structured organization (of which there are only about 30) and to use "cooperative arrangement" for the limited-purpose and less formal types of interchange. This is not to imply any value judgment as between the two kinds of activity. The differentiation is made solely for purposes of rough classification in a field marked by great diversity of plan, purpose, and practice.

REASONS FOR COOPERATION

The current thrusts toward cooperative activity are a reflection of certain all-too-familiar problems marking American higher education today. The general impetus is, of course, the growing pressure on colleges and universities to create, communicate, and apply new knowledge, to spread the opportunities and benefits of such a process among

[1] *A Guide to Higher Education Consortiums: 1965–66*, U.S. Office of Education, 1967, Explanatory Note.

the populace at large, *and* to do so within available wherewithal. The individual institution finds that this pressure manifests itself in "an almost resistless tide of surging enrollments, increasing costs, threats to balance and quality, and proliferating demands for services." This statement from a report of the Committee on Institutional Cooperation (CIC) of the Big Ten Universities and The University of Chicago refers primarily to the situation at large universities. But it is not a very different condition at the smaller institutions. The enrollment factor may be less pressing, but as the Associated Colleges of the Midwest reports for its 10 private-college members, there is a need "to obtain some of the advantages of expanded resources while preserving the values of small size."

For both the university groups and for the liberal arts colleges (and indeed for other types of institutions), the constant prompting toward joint effort is thus the need for enhancement of quality through resource improvement and augmentation, whether of facilities or personnel. There is also the expectation of some cost reduction through curtailment of duplication in offerings and programs.

PURPOSES OF COOPERATIVE ACTIVITY

In any discussion of purposes and objectives, it must be noted that cooperative arrangements in higher education may take place (1) among institutions relatively equal to each other in strength of general resources, and (2) among institutions of unequal strength in which the stronger seek to assist the weaker.

In the first instance, cooperation proceeds on the assumption that equal institutions, no matter how strong, cannot be equal in every possible respect. Hence there is room for reciprocity or complementarity in various areas.

In the second instance, the strong, established institutions extend their own resources to help the weaker or developing ones, thus cooperating in the general upgrading of higher education while at the same time deriving knowledge about developing educational processes which the resulting interchange affords.

Cooperation among Equals Among institutional "equals," the complementary process can function in several areas. Thus, university A offers a program in Scandinavian languages while nearby university B does not. But B offers astronautics and A does not. Under a reciprocating arrangement, both A and B augment their curricular resources by making these offerings available to each other. Similarly, A may have a poet in residence while B has a visiting Nobel laureate in science. A student-exchange arrangement helps to make each accessible to the students of both institutions.

Then, too, A has a nuclear accelerator and B does not, but B has a controlled-environment laboratory and A does not. Here again, barring unusual impediments, arrangements can be made to reciprocate rather than duplicate. Each institution thus gains the benefit of both facilities and effects some economies in the process.

For another example, we can have, let us say, four institutions within relatively short distances of each other. All are interested in having available certain library materials for specialized types of research. The cost is high; the uses are important but limited. The answer may well then be: centralize. The four institutions acquire one complete collection by cooperative purchase, maintain it by joint agreement at a central place, and make the holdings available to all.

These are only a few examples of the kinds of purposes pursued by cooperating equals. The complementary approach underlies much of this effort and is therefore evident in the detailed listing below of the specific purposes prompting two or more institutions toward such cooperation. Each of these aims is intended to assist the participating institutions in (1) maximizing instructional, research or administrative efforts, (2) curtailing duplication wherever possible, (3) effecting some savings on costs, or (4) guiding the general planning process for the development of new programs. These purposes thus include:

1. Augmenting research and library facilities by pooling and sharing
2. Expanding opportunities through centralized efforts—e.g., cooperative courses, joint study-abroad offerings, and summer institutes in certain specialized subject-matter areas marked by low enrollments or scarcity of teaching personnel
3. Increasing availability of courses, programs, resources, and facilities by fostering intercampus exchanges of students and faculty members
4. Promotion of greater economy and efficiency through joint programs in institutional administration (calendar standardization, cooperative admissions and financial-aid procedures, joint purchasing, interinstitutional data processing, etc.)
5. Establishing a strong interinstitutional base for seeking foundation or government funding of new projects, for engaging in joint fund raising (private institutions), and for influencing public policy in higher education
6. Utilization of the interinstitutional base for broad-scale experimentation and innovation
7. Provision of a concerted approach to major social, environmental, and economic problems (urban affairs, the disadvantaged, water and air pollution, international assistance, etc.)
8. Promotion of continuing information exchanges on all the above

Assistance to Developing Institutions Of major importance today are the cooperative arrangements by which strong institutions assist weaker or developing institutions, particularly the many Negro colleges and universities in the American South. Congress has given some impetus to this form of cooperation by appropriating support funds under Title III (Strengthening of Developing Institutions) of the Higher Education Act of 1965. The large private foundations (Carnegie, Ford, Rockefeller, etc.) have made substantial grants in support of such activities, as have many of the smaller foundations and certain other organizations.

The need for such assistance programs is self-evident. As Hugh M. Gloster, dean of faculty of Hampton Institute, points out:

> In four years . . . the predominantly Negro colleges have the difficult job of trying to help young people overcome handicaps that reach three and a half centuries into the past. In this formidable task [these] colleges are handicapped not only by limited funds but also by cultural isolation. Moreover, during the past few years these colleges have had the additional burden of being judged by national norms and of having to compete on equal terms with all other American colleges. By gaining access to the administrative, instructional, and investigative resources of large universities, predominantly Negro colleges, which enroll more than half of America's 200,000 Negro college students, can more effectively prepare individuals for successful life and work in an integrated society.[2]

The principal purposes served by such cooperative assistance are generally similar to those listed previously for equal institutions. The difference is that emphasis is shifted from the complementary process to one in which direct resource assistance is given by a strong to a weaker institution.

In general, then, the aim is to enhance the quality of instructional, research, and administrative programs at the developing institutions through exchanges of students and personnel, opening of the stronger institution's graduate resources to students of the developing school, establishment of seminars and workshops as means of improving course content of curricular programs offered at the developing institutions, assistance in improving administrative procedures, provision for independent study and research

[2] Hugh M. Gloster, "Cooperative Programs and the Predominantly Negro College: A Dean's View," in Lawrence C. Howard (ed.), *Interinstitutional Cooperation in Higher Education,* Institute of Human Relations, The University of Wisconsin Press, Madison, Wis., 1967, p. 68.

at the stronger institutions by faculty members of the developing schools, assistance with remedial programs, cultural exchanges and activities, etc.

TYPES OF INTERINSTITUTIONAL ARRANGEMENTS AND GROUPINGS

As mentioned earlier, there are literally hundreds of arrangements for cooperative activity in higher education. Among these, there is considerable variation in organization, objectives, and programs conducted.

Limited-purpose, Minimally Structured Types First, there are the hundreds upon hundreds of single- or limited-purpose and minimally structured joint programs involving groups of two or three (or more) neighboring institutions. Thus, George Washington University and Virginia Polytechnic Institute have a joint urban studies program; Alaska Methodist University and the University of Puget Sound have cooperative summer sessions; the University of Idaho and Washington State University have cooperative courses; the University of Detroit and Niagara University share a preengineering program; Colorado Women's College, Loretto Heights College, Regis College, and the University of Denver cooperate in an advanced practice-teaching program; the University of Kansas, the University of Nebraska, and the University of Colorado (with the University of Bordeaux), jointly run a junior-year program at Bordeaux; Yale University and the University of Connecticut share an animal diseases program; and there are many, many others.[3]

The fields in which such minimal but productive cooperation takes place are legion. And they are generally those in which pooling and sharing can lead to a reduction in costs as well as to better educational results through maximizing of available resources. Thus, there are current programs in the pooling of library resources, joint seminars and colloquia, coordinated graduate and undergraduate courses, combined lecture series, computer facilities sharing, international programs, teacher-training and educational administration programs, urban studies, fieldwork in various scientific curricula, water resources research and marine studies, archaeological fieldwork and research, joint law offerings, combined programs in the various health sciences, work-study programs, and programs in forestry, labor and industrial relations, etc. Included also are the information sharing and cooperative procedures undertaken bilaterally or multilaterally in the business and administrative operations of the participating institutions.

Multipurpose and/or Structured Types Second, there are the groupings interested in broader sets of objectives and/or in more structured means of coordinating joint efforts—especially those launched by a rather large number of institutions. There are usually two aspects or phases of this type of development:

1. The grouping may be in a beginning stage of operation in which project activity is minimal, the principal effort being exploratory interinstitutional conferences of faculty and administrative people on matters of mutual concern. Assuming that the grouping is interested in multipurpose functions, it will usually utilize the services of a part-time faculty "coordinator" to foster plans, identify objectives, maintain communications, and move ideas along toward definitive consideration. Financial support for operations is invariably and understandably minimal, and statements of purpose or degree of commitment are (perhaps intentionally) general.

2. If, on the other hand, the grouping has traversed the latter stage and finds that its program development activities are expanding *and* there is an avowed commitment to a more organized effort, then the coordinating function is supplanted by a full-time staff operation. The coordinator is replaced by an executive director, headquarters space is

[3] These and the succeeding examples are culled from *A Guide to Higher Education Consortiums*, *op. cit.*

provided, a budget is agreed upon and funded (usually through annual membership fees levied on the participating institutions), articles of agreement are drawn, and a formal board of control is instituted. Invariably, all of this eventuates in corporate or chartered status for the grouping as a nonprofit, tax-exempt educational organization. And at this juncture, it may seek and receive funds from various sources and disburse them in terms of program objectives and corporate procedures.

Geographical Distribution of Institutions in Multipurpose Groups. The institutions in such groupings may be located *within a single city or metropolitan area* (Consortium of Universities of the Washington, D.C., Metropolitan Area; Atlanta University Center Corporation; Higher Education Coordinating Council of St. Louis; Claremont Colleges in California; etc.), *in a particular area of a single state* (Five Colleges, Inc., in Massachusetts; Associated Mid-Florida Colleges; Piedmont University Center of North Carolina, Inc.; Associated Colleges of Central Kansas; College Center of the Finger Lakes in New York State; Dayton-Miami Valley Consortium in Ohio; etc.), *in a contiguous interstate region* (Kansas City Regional Council for Higher Education; Mississippi Valley College Association; etc.), or *in a widely dispersed interstate region* (Committee on Institutional Cooperation of the Big Ten Universities and The University of Chicago; Mid-America State Universities Association; Mid-Appalachia College Council, Inc.; Associated Colleges of the Midwest; Associated Midwest Universities; Associated Western Universities, Inc.; Central States College Association; Great Lakes Colleges Association; etc.).

Types of Institutions in Multipurpose Groups. Besides the geographical classification, there are other ways of categorizing the groupings. Thus, there are the *large-university groups* (Committee on Institutional Cooperation or Mid-America State Universities Association); *private liberal arts colleges* (Great Lakes Colleges Association); *church-related colleges* (Central States College Association or Associated Christian Colleges of Oregon); and *heterogeneous combinations* including public and private, secular and church-related, college and university (Dayton-Miami Valley Consortium of Ohio; Higher Education Coordinating Council of St. Louis; etc.).

Examples of Structured Multipurpose Groups. To give some idea of the types of operations conducted by various multipurpose groups, below are listed a number of examples with brief details as to their programs. This list is far from exhaustive and is intended simply to be illustrative of the kinds of activity found in such groups.

Associated Colleges of the Midwest, Inc. (ACM). Ten private liberal arts colleges in four states: Beloit (Wis.), Carleton (Minn.), Coe (Iowa), Cornell College (Iowa), Grinnell (Iowa), Knox (Ill.), Lawrence (Wis.), Monmouth (Ill.), Ripon (Wis.), and St. Olaf (Minn.). Programs: pooling of library resources; joint fund raising and certain administrative procedures (purchasing, standardized admissions and financial-aid procedures, etc.); nuclear energy instruction program in cooperation with Argonne National Laboratory; faculty sharing; experimentation in language instruction; operation of a wilderness field station for summer programs in botany, zoology, geology, and limnology; international activities (non-Western studies, field studies in anthropology, biology, economics, sociology, etc., in Central America); student teaching program in Chicago public schools; and instruction in urban sociology and education.

Central States College Association (CSCA). Nine liberal arts colleges and three universities, all church-related, in six states: Alma (Mich.), Augustana (Ill.), Carroll (Wis.), Gustavus Adolphus (Minn.), Illinois Wesleyan University, Luther (Iowa), MacMurray (Ill.), Manchester (Ind.), Millikin University (Ill.), Mundelein (Ill.), Saint John's University (Minn.), and Simpson (Iowa). Programs: cooperative philosophy curriculum taught at 12 high schools by CSCA faculty members to help students form values "in an age of rapid change dominated by science and technology"; undergraduate field work in marine biology, geography, geology, sociology, and psychology; nuclear instruction program in cooperation with Argonne National Laboratory; extensive study-abroad opportunities; cooperation in calendar standardization; faculty sharing; student exchange in which basic costs to student stay constant when he "travels" and credit earned on any of the twelve campuses is applied in same way as that earned at home institution.

Committee on Institutional Cooperation (CIC). Nine large public universities and two private universities in seven states: University of Chicago, University of Illinois, Indiana University, University of Iowa, University of Michigan, Michigan State University, University of Minnesota, Northwestern University, Ohio State University, Purdue University, and University of Wisconsin. Programs: CIC Traveling Scholar Program (qualified graduate students may visit neighboring CIC campuses for one semester's or two quarters' work in specialized areas; student pays home-university fees only and earned credit is automatically transferred from host to home university); Biometeorology Graduate Training Program; language institutes (Far Eastern, South Asian, Slavic) and Spanish program in Mexico; instructional resource studies and interchange; course-content improvement projects; geology field camp and geography field laboratories and seminars; advanced research training project in dentistry; international programs, including studies of institution building overseas; interuniversity conferences on the disadvantaged; university computer studies; project development in comparative literature, music education, educational testing, continuing education in health sciences, water resources, library facilities, study-abroad programs, oceanography, cartography, and other areas; regular meetings of graduate deans, liberal arts deans, summer session directors, etc.; and various administrative studies conducted by staff.

Great Lakes Colleges Association (GLCA). Nine liberal arts colleges and three universities, all private, in three states: Albion (Mich.), Antioch (Ohio), Denison University (Ohio), DePauw University (Ind.), Earlham (Ind.), Hope (Mich.), Kalamazoo (Mich)., Kenyon (Ohio), Oberlin (Ohio), Ohio Wesleyan University, Wabash (Ind.), Wooster (Ohio). Programs: faculty development and student exchange activities; cooperation in calendar uniformity and admissions procedures; non-Western studies programs, including a number of overseas arrangements in Africa and Asia; overseas centers in Beirut, Tokyo, Bogota, etc.; summer program in marine biology in conjunction with the University of California at Santa Barbara; studies of role and nature of the arts and humanities in the inner city; urban studies summer program in conjunction with large-city school systems, etc.; campus language centers; various course-content and instructional improvement projects; college teaching intern program.

Mid-America State Universities Association (MASUA). Nine public universities in six states: University of Colorado, Colorado State University, Iowa State University, University of Kansas, Kansas State University, University of Missouri, University of Nebraska, University of Oklahoma, Oklahoma State University. Programs: traveling scholar exchange; reciprocity programs in professional fields, providing opportunities to residents of states where certain programs are unavailable (e.g., Kansas State accepts Missouri students in space science and technology, Missouri accepts Kansas students in dentistry, Kansas State and Iowa State accept Nebraska students in veterinary medicine, Missouri at Columbia accepts Nebraska and Kansas students in forestry, etc.); cooperative international programs (agricultural development in Colombia; assistance in engineering at National Engineering University, Lima, Peru, and at Assuit University, Egypt); joint development of curricula in Oriental languages and computer sciences; coordination of regional medical program; cooperative planning in graduate education; conferences of research administrators, graduate deans, directors of international programs, department chairmen in physics, chemistry, geology, speech, mathematics, etc., deans of engineering, registrars, business officers, directors of computing centers, and others.

Five Colleges, Inc. Four private colleges and a state university located in the Connecticut Valley of Massachusetts: Amherst, Smith, Mt. Holyoke, and Hampshire Colleges and the University of Massachusetts. Organization began as the Four-College Cooperation Program for operation of Hampshire Inter-Library Center and student exchange in certain courses unavailable on home campuses. Association expanded to include the new Hampshire College generated out of Four-College cooperation. Programs: student and faculty interchange; cooperative courses and Ph.D. program; Five-College radio station (WFCR-FM); publication of *Massachusetts Review*, professional quarterly of the arts, literature, and public affairs; overseas study programs; calendar cooperation; school-college relations committee; computer-center cooperation, etc.

College Center of the Finger Lakes. Seven private colleges, one private university, and one community college in the Finger Lakes area of New York State: Alfred University, Cazenovia College, Corning Community College, Elmira College, Hartwick College, Hobart and William Smith Colleges, Ithaca College, Keuka College, Wells College. Programs: Corning Graduate Center for interchange in various curricular programs (includes participation of Syracuse University and State University of New York (SUNY) at Buffalo; Syracuse offers business administration program, SUNY at Buffalo an engineering science program, Alfred an English program, and Elmira and Alfred a program in professional education—all at the master's level; the center also offers continuing education seminars for area business executives and other programs); program for enhancement of educational research capabilities through personnel training seminars and other activities; aquatics program; non-Western studies and overseas arrangements; research grants-in-aid program; visiting-scholars program (poets, philosophers, sociologists, artists, etc.); library cooperation; student seminars; conferences of various kinds (guidance counselors, advisers for premedical students; etc.).

Other groupings with multipurpose objectives are the Kansas City Regional Council for Higher Education, the Dayton-Miami Valley Consortium in Ohio, the Piedmont University Center of North Carolina, the Atlanta University Center Corporation, the Higher Education Coordinating Council of St. Louis, etc.

The Claremont Colleges. Perhaps the most cohesively organized group is The Claremont Colleges, consisting of the Claremont Graduate School and University Center, Pomona College, Scripps College, Claremont Men's College, Harvey Mudd College, and Pitzer College. This grouping, which combines the qualities and values of the small residential college with the broad facilities of a university, has been described as a "cluster" institution similar to England's Oxford and Cambridge. The central coordinating institution is the Claremont Graduate School and University Center, which provides all the graduate studies offered within the group; it plans and provides the joint facilities used by the undergraduate colleges and initiates new member colleges on lands set aside for this purpose when needed. An administrative council of the presidents of the component institutions supervises the planning of academic programs and administration of the common facilities supported by joint budgets. The member institutions are otherwise independent and have their own curricula, faculties, students, endowment, etc. By agreement, however, they restrict enrollment and maintain relatively separate curricular emphases: Pomona College maintains a coeducational undergraduate program in the general arts and sciences; Scripps, a program for women in the arts and sciences with emphasis on the humanities; Claremont Men's College, arts and sciences; Harvey Mudd, a coeducational program with emphasis on the physical sciences and engineering; and Pitzer College, a program for women in arts and sciences with emphasis on the social and behavioral sciences. Under the Claremont arrangement, a student takes the majority of his courses in his own college, but a wide range of offerings is available in the neighboring colleges at no additional cost.

Limited-purpose but Structured Groups While most if not all of the groupings described in the preceding section are multipurpose in function, there are others which concentrate their efforts either within one major area or within a small number of related areas. These groups, unlike those mentioned under "Limited-purpose, Minimally Structured Types," are fully organized, staffed, and funded, with defined objectives in a fairly large area of operation. Thus, the Associated Universities, Inc. (AUI)—Columbia, Cornell, Harvard, Johns Hopkins, MIT, the University of Pennsylvania, Princeton, Rochester, and Yale—has as its purpose the establishment and operation of large-scale research facilities, under governmental and other funds, for the benefit of the higher education community in general. AUI operates the Brookhaven National Laboratory for research in nuclear physics and the National Radio Astronomy Laboratory, and it is making explorations for the establishment of comprehensive interuniversity information systems as well as working in other developmental areas.

Another grouping—The Associated Midwest Universities,* a consortium of 33 institutions—is established for the purpose of facilitating research and education in the nuclear field at the Argonne National Laboratory under funds from the U.S. Atomic Energy Commission. Under similar auspices, the Associated Western Universities conducts joint activities in nuclear science and engineering, but it is also making plans for a more wide-ranging multipurpose program.

Other groups working in limited-purpose areas are: the Midwest Consortium for International Activities; Associated Universities for International Education, Inc.; the Consortium of Colleges and Universities of the Adlai Stevenson Institute of International Affairs; The Center for Research Libraries, a national interinstitutional facility in Chicago which began as the Midwest Inter-Library Center for pooling, joint purchase, and centralized cataloging, etc., of infrequently used research materials; The University Communications Council, or EDUCOM, whose more than 40 institutional members throughout the country collaborate in efforts they make to utilize the communications sciences; Five Associated Libraries (of Cornell, the State University of New York at Buffalo, the State University of New York at Binghamton, the University of Rochester, and Syracuse University) aimed at coordinating long-range development of the member libraries; and others. There are also groups like The Association for Graduate Education and Research in North Texas (TAGER) which confine their activities to advanced areas of instruction and research.

Interstate Compact Groups Third, there are also cooperative institutions within the interstate compact groups: i.e., the Southern Regional Education Board (SREB) comprising 15 states, the Western Interstate Commission for Higher Education (WICHE) comprising 13 states, and the New England Board of Higher Education (NEBHE) comprising six states. These groups are not, strictly speaking, interinstitutional associations so much as they are instruments of government serving broad educational objectives for purposes of general social and economic improvement of a geographical region. Thus, the compact groups are managed by boards of control appointed by state governors, and the sources of their operational funds are appropriations made by state legislatures.

Within this framework, there is considerable cooperation among the various institutions of higher education coming under the compact's jurisdiction. This may take the form of reciprocal student exchanges in specialized or professional fields, of the sharing of certain instructional and research resources, and of the joint conducting of data-gathering and research activities for concerted planning of regional educational facilities. All three of the compact groups mentioned above cooperate in the development of graduate education in their regions as well as on problems of administrative efficiency, financing, etc.

Cooperative Assistance: Developing Institutions Increasingly, arrangements are being made between one or more established institutions and various developing in-

* Now merged into the Argonne Universities Association.

stitutions. Funding for such cooperative assistance programs comes from the federal government, private foundations, and other sources. Thus, Brown University has a continuing program with Tougaloo College in Mississippi; Cornell University with Hampton Institute; the University of Michigan with Tuskegee; the University of Wisconsin with North Carolina College and others; etc.

Under Title III of the Higher Education Act of 1965, 42 grants were made in 1968 for support of such programs. Institutions involved included the following: Southern Union State Junior College (Ala.) with Auburn and Yale; Henderson State College (Ark.) with Indiana University; the Clinton (Iowa) Community College with the University of Iowa; Warren Wilson College (N.C.) with the University of North Carolina at Chapel Hill and Duke; Voorhees College (S.C.) with the University of South Carolina; Morris Harvey College (W.Va.) with Ohio State University; Virginia State College with Northeastern University and Virginia Polytechnic Institute; Highline College (Wash.) with the University of Wisconsin and Eastern Washington State College; and many others.

There are also arrangements such as the Indiana-Washington-Wisconsin Program for Graduate Study in Business for Negroes, the Harvard-Yale-Columbia Intensive Summer Studies Program, the Harvard Law School Program for outstanding Negro college students considering law careers, etc. Also, a recent grant of the Carnegie Corporation of New York to the Southern Regional Education Board has made possible an assistance program for public junior colleges seeking to meet the needs of Negro students.

FOUNDING AND ORGANIZATION OF STRUCTURED GROUPS

Source of Initiative The structured consortia discussed in this chapter are generally begun through initiative of the presidents of the participating institutions. But this might be characterized as "ultimate" initiative, since there are invariably other spurs to action preceding that stage. There is, for instance, always some form of interinstitutional cooperation—informal and haphazard though it may be—already occurring among institutions contemplating a more organized approach. The impetus toward such an approach might also come at national or sectional educational conclaves where faculty groups intermingle and discuss possible cooperative projects. The result among faculty members from contiguous institutions may then be the initiation of resolves on the home campuses and a filtering up of departmental discussions to the end that interpresidential consideration begins.

There are of course other modes of initiation—in which executive action, for instance, anticipates tendencies at the faculty level. In general, however, there is no "magic moment" when the collective shout goes up for cooperation. As mentioned above, a number of interchanges usually occur before an official framework is provided. These might include some research arrangements, interlibrary programs, and faculty and student exchanges of one kind or another. These become the footpaths to more organized routes of cooperative effort.

Voluntary Nature of Agreements In initiating an interinstitutional grouping of "equals," the institutions involved usually insist on one commanding principle—that their own interests be enhanced in some way by such cooperation. Otherwise, there is seen a blurring of the fundamental role of the individual institution and a possible undermining of its mission as an autonomous organism for academic advancement. Hence, too, the participating institutions of the consortia operate strictly on a voluntary basis. Thus, as the 1965–66 annual report of the Committee on Institutional Cooperation notes:

Participation in a specific project is always on the highest feasible level of interest, there being no requirement that all eleven universities [of the CIC] must agree to participate before a program is launched. The voluntary nature of the CIC also insures that each university's status as an independent and autonomous institution will in no way be compromised.

For the public institutions—like those in CIC, Mid-America State Universities Association (MASUA), and Associated Western Universities (AWU)—some legislative action might be needed for certain projects or programs, but this would be very minimal. Thus, the CIC sought and received needed legislative agreement in some states to permit its Traveling Scholar Program to operate on a reciprocal, home-university fee basis. On the other hand, MASUA has programs which provide professional education at member institutions for residents of states where such instruction is unavailable, and these arrangements are established by contract or other agreement instead of legislation.

Project development on a voluntary basis is thus seen as a means of gaining flexibility and "the highest feasible level of interest." This approach is pursued for good and valid reasons: among proud institutions which value independence as a means of sustaining integrity and quality, a compulsory arrangement might breed inaction on the one hand or burdensome entanglements on the other. The voluntary approach is thus seen as both liberating and protective.

Membership The institutional participants in the various groups discussed here are not generally "elected" to membership through any kind of admission requirements. Rather, there is a process of natural selection which governs their formation. Generally, there is some common orientation which brings them together. Indeed the "pact" under which they finally organize as cooperative groups usually has its roots in various joint meetings under subsections of national or sectional conferences on higher education. Other kinds of conferences also give rise to consortium activity Thus, the CIC had its beginnings in the semiannual meetings of the Big Ten presidents. The agendas for these meetings are heavy with academic problems, many of which call for joint response. In 1958, therefore, the chief executives formally agreed on the establishment of an association to develop policy and foster cooperative programs. The Big Ten conference was thus the natural framework encompassing the CIC. And since The University of Chicago has always been intimately associated with Big Ten activities, it subsequently joined also.

The same principle of "natural selection" holds for such groups as the Central States College Association (CSCA), the Associated Colleges of the Midwest (ACM), and the Great Lakes Colleges Association (GLCA). The first has an ecumenical base, comprising 12 distinguished church-related (Protestant and Catholic) liberal arts colleges. The difference between the other two groupings is simply geographical: the ACM institutions are north and west in the Midwest; the GLCA is south and east in the same region.

In many consortia, there is this regional or area framework simply because geographical contiguity determines certain common interests and expectations. And hence the regional association is seen as helping in establishing concerted "interfaces," instead of fragmented efforts, between the educational community, the federal government, and other major sectors of society.

The regional consortia discussed here generally have institutional members similar to some extent in size of enrollment—but, more important, also in general structure and orientation. CIC embraces the major comprehensive universities of the Midwest, nine of these public and two private; MASUA encompasses both large and small public universities; AWU the same, with the addition of public technological colleges; and the liberal arts colleges follow a self-evident orientation. Some of these, like the CIC and the liberal arts groups, remain fixed in membership. Others, like MASUA and AWU, are expanding. Many are incorporated in order to receive and administer funds and to strike a note of permanence in their activities. The CIC, on the other hand, is not yet incorporated—but as one of the oldest and strongest groups in the country (in an admittedly still-young field of endeavor) it strikes the note of permanence, too.

Form of Agreement In most cases, the consortia in this category are incorporated as nonprofit, tax-exempt educational organizations. Many are chartered as such upon beginning operation; others reach this status after passing through intermediate stages. Incorporation is sought principally to permit the organization to receive and administer funds for project development. The boards of control are usually the presidents of the member institutions; but such boards may also be composed of vice-presidents or other officials or of a combination of faculty members and administrators from the member campuses.

In some instances, the consortium is begun as an informal association providing simply for exploratory conferences of faculty and administrative people on matters of mutual concern. But once these discussions eventuate in proposals for a more structured approach to project development, articles of agreement may be drawn up to establish the nature of control and representation, limits of commitment, operating procedures, etc. Then, as project activity continues to increase, this preliminary accord is supplanted by formal incorporation.

Although no firm generalizations can be drawn from what is still a nascent process, it is interesting to note that MASUA operated under articles of agreement from 1961 to 1964, with incorporation effected in the latter year and establishment of a central office in 1966. MASUA's continuing conference activities plus its current programs in

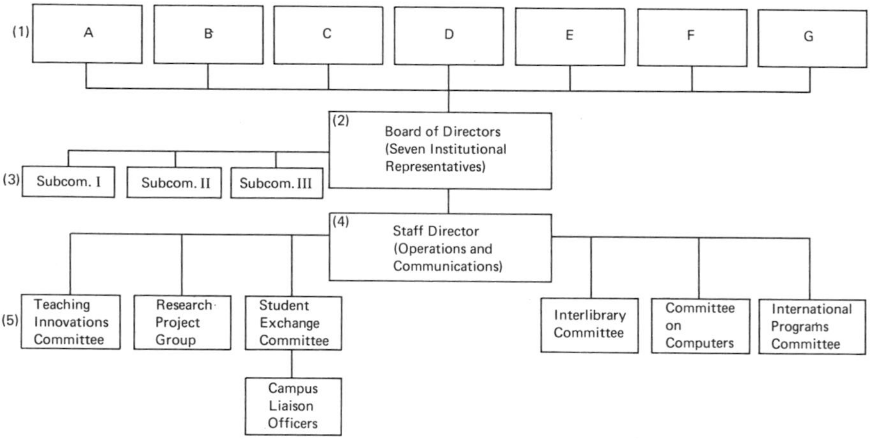

Fig. 1 *Sample organizational chart of a multipurpose interinstitutional consortium. (1) A–G: The member institutions. (2) The board of control; one representative from each member institution. (3) Subcommittees of the board; members drawn from the board itself; function is to advise on policy formation in major areas. (4) Staff director coordinates operational and communications activities; also advises on policy formation; total number of personnel in staff office varies with size and purposes of consortium. (5) The operational committees; members drawn from faculty and administrative personnel of the participating institutions; each committee has direct liaison with applicable campus offices or resources (i.e., libraries, computer centers, deans' or directors' offices, etc.). Committees listed here are illustrative only.*

a number of important areas thus reflect a five-year development toward a "mature" phase of consortium operation.

In the case of the CIC, which has been operating successfully since 1958, the member universities have conducted their cooperative affairs without charter, formal articles of agreement, or indeed any written document at all. The CIC simply acts according to a tacit agreement of the presidents and in terms of procedures and policies developed in CIC deliberations over the years.

Financing As mentioned above, most of the groupings in this category are incorporated as nonprofit, tax-exempt educational organizations. The CIC is an exception in that it is unincorporated, but it nevertheless operates largely in the same manner as its counterparts. The only difference is that, while the incorporated groups may receive and disburse funds from the central office, money for a CIC project is generally assigned to one of the universities participating in the activity and acting as project headquarters. Staff funds are administered by the business office of Purdue University, where the CIC is based, and are accounted for in the same manner as any regular departmental account at Purdue.

The staff operations of most of these groupings are supported through membership fees paid by the participating institutions. In some cases, establishment of a cooperative organization is made possible through grants awarded by major private foundations. This may take the form of support for the initial or pilot phase of the group's work or of catalyzing funds granted to assist interuniversity faculty meetings for the development of particular projects. Thus, the Carnegie Corporation of New York provided the CIC with its very effective Seed Grant Fund, used to support exploratory interuniversity faculty meetings by defraying the travel, lodging, and other expenses involved.

Moneys for structured projects and programs are derived from federal agencies, private foundations, and the participating institutions. There are also some legislative authorizations which help to facilitate the participation of a consortium's public institutions in reciprocity programs conducted on an interstate basis. The CIC's Traveling Scholar Program is an example. One association (ACM) has a small endowment and some investment income in addition to the kinds of funding described above.

Types of Interchange Most of the consortia discussed in this chapter work, by and large, in the entire spectrum of college and university activity. Hence the interchanges in which they participate may involve students, faculty, facilities, programs, and services—to a greater or lesser degree in each instance, depending upon the individual consortium.

The CIC's Traveling Scholar Program, now in its fifth year of operation, is a strong example of successfully operative student exchanges. Under it, a graduate student from one campus may visit a neighboring member institution for a semester or two quarters to take advantage of a special library collection, laboratory facility, unique course offering, or the lecture hall of a faculty member who is especially distinguished in his field—in other words, any major resource that is not available on his own campus. Red tape is cut to a minimum. While on his visit, the student continues to be registered at his home university, pays its fees only, and receives full academic credit for work taken at the host institution. CSCA is launching a similar program on the undergraduate level, and MASUA has instituted a graduate program on the CIC model. Some of the consortia (CSCA, ACM) also effect arrangements with facilities like the Argonne National Laboratory to enable students to work with mature scientists on "live" projects and earn academic credit while doing so.

Faculty interchange within these consortia takes the form of actual exchanges as well as the gathering together of faculty talents at summer language institutes, study-abroad programs, research at great private libraries like the Newberry of Chicago, and other instructional and research programs which are too specialized to be conducted as part of the regular program of each of the institutions. The scarcity of competent scholar-teachers in the newer fields makes this "nucleating" approach particularly attractive.

There is also a facilities exchange in the sense that certain resources are made readily available to faculty members and students of the participating institutions. A good example of the way in which such facility interchange can be integrated into the development of new subject-matter areas lies in the CIC's biometeorology program. An interdisciplinary curriculum, the program involves the study of the effects of weather and climate—or the general environment—on plants, animals, and man. Requiring a wide variety of specialized environmental laboratories and field facilities, the CIC project enables graduate students in the specialty to take work at several of the 11 member institutions. They study under distinguished scientists in various fields and use special facilities which could not be duplicated by other universities without capital outlays running in the many millions of dollars. The sharing concept may lead, as a result, to the establishment and strengthening of such new subject-matter areas—a process that might otherwise be impracticable if attempted unilaterally on the various campuses.

Other programs and services are also available under the consortia's auspices. These may include such things as art conservation facilities; television, radio, and other communications resources; data processing facilities; special library services; etc.

Functional Areas of Cooperation As mentioned earlier, the consortia work—actually or potentially—in almost all areas of college or university purview. While concentrating most heavily on the academic area, they enter the administrative area as well.

In the academic context, they strive for augmentation of resources in the traditional fields and for strength and quality in the newer fields, particularly those highly specialized, low-enrollment areas characterized by a scarcity of competent scholar-teachers to work in them. Language programs, especially of the "exotic" type, are amenable to such approaches, as are newer scientific fields. Certain areas of the humanities and social sciences, professional fields, continuing education programs, non-Western studies, and a number of interdisciplinary curricula are also served well by cooperative activity. Such programs are all generally in evidence in one or more of the groupings discussed in this chapter.

In the administrative area, problems of calendar uniformity and scheduling (principally among the college consortia), certain aspects of business management, sharing of information on salaries and benefits, pooling of library resources, coordination of admission and fellowship applications (e.g., ACM's "single application method" for students applying to these colleges), data processing and communications procedures, exchange of information on summer programs, coordination of study-abroad programs, administration of honors programs, etc.—all these are considered as developmental areas among these cooperatives. In almost all of the consortia, therefore, the boards of representatives maintain liaison with deans and other administrative officials having responsibility in such areas.

There are also joint efforts in research areas, particularly those in which there is need for large, complex kinds of apparatus and equipment.

In addition, these consortia have contracts with various agencies of the federal government as well as with private foundations for conducting major activities in a great variety of areas of instructional development, research, and public service. These include international projects of assistance to developing countries—e.g., programs related to the building or strengthening of educational institutions abroad, teacher training, evaluation of technical assistance projects in overseas settings, faculty and student exchanges, etc.

Inevitably, too, there is interaction with the nearer community, particularly the urban settings now undergoing immense pressures and tensions. Attention is also given to problems of water resources development, environmental health, etc. In all such activities, the institutions conducting them strive to make certain that the public-service function will lead to substantial academic benefits appropriate to the fundamental role of the college or university as an institution of higher learning.

Advantages First, there is the spur to innovation and experimentation. Cooperative groupings provide a means by which large numbers of institutions may monitor developments in the broad policy areas such as research and instruction in various fields, international education, the general commitments needed to anticipate future needs in higher education, the means of coordinating developments in the field of data processing and information retrieval, etc. Inevitably, this kind of interuniversity consideration of common problems and challenges affects planning on the individual campuses and leads to at least some profitable accommodations in program.

Making available the individual strengths of the member institutions to students throughout the consortium is another major benefit. In this connection, the consortium can provide a bridge between the older curricula and new subject-matter areas. As the boundaries between the traditional and the new fields are blurred by the growth of knowledge, institutions of higher learning have been faced with the need to develop new patterns and relationships to deal with cross-disciplinary subject matter. The complexity of such programs, the diversity of needed facilities, and the high degree of specialization among faculty members make the interinstitutional approach almost uniquely suited to such efforts.

The consortium concept permits greater flexibility in the testing out of certain innovative ideas. Departmental "vested interests" are less at stake when a program is conducted as a pilot effort under cooperative auspices. If the program works, there is a gain in the curricular increments accruing to a participating department. If the program fails, it does not significantly alter the proponents' viability within their own departments or universities. Most important, the cooperative associations rely on their own faculty members for the development of ideas and projects—rather than on outside specialists or consultants. This provides an indigenous quality to any joint activities which facilitates the general acceptance of strong proposals. But certainly without the consortium, many a good faculty idea would die aborning.

Increasingly, too, agencies of the federal government are looking to interinstitutional cooperation as the instrumentality not only for pursuing certain complex project objectives but also for guidance on substantive and procedural relations between such agencies and their academic constituencies. Most recently, the dialogues with various cooperative educational groups by the Assistant Secretary for Education, Dr. Paul A. Miller, in regard to implementation of the International Education Act of 1966 (when funding is at last available) have given clear evidence of the policy and program guidance expected of cooperating colleges and universities. The literature describing programs of the U.S. Office of Education, the National Science Foundation, and other agencies also gives due emphasis to the increasing importance of interinstitutional groups in fulfilling certain objectives of the federal effort in instruction, research, and general public service.

Not the least of the benefits of the consortia has been their provision of opportunity for exchange of information and coordination of programs. The consortium—from its board of directors to its newest faculty group—is an arena for the productive comparison of experience and the talking out of problems and issues on a regular basis. It is also a means for linking together high-level administrative groups—such as arts and science deans, graduate deans, etc.—on an interuniversity basis for the shaping of profitable common policies, the coordination of major efforts (as in study-abroad programs), and the launching of cooperative surveys and studies intrinsic to orderly development within such offices.

Principal Problems and Challenges The foremost and continuing problem associated with consortium activity is communication. Thus, while the voluntary nature of the groupings described here leads to a desirable sense of flexibility regarding cooperative ventures, there is as a result a need for continual and complete intercommunication among constituencies on several levels of responsibility. Lapses in the process lead to misunderstandings which in turn undermine and compromise the strength of the commitment proffered by the individual institutions considering joint programs.

A lack of clarity in spelling out objectives, failures of interpretation, poor reporting systems, failure to inform key personnel, inadequate publicizing of programs—these and other defects of communication are prime means of weakening the cooperative structure. It is for this reason that the consortia depend heavily upon the directors of their central staff offices. A burden must be laid somewhere to ensure that the lines of interconnection and intercommunication will be kept strong and effective. Each of these consortia therefore has full-time, experienced administrators—drawn from the academic milieu—to do the necessary work of communication and coordination. In a sense, such persons constitute a new kind of educational personnel—that is, practitioners whose loyalties are tied to several institutions, who must promote advancement along a multi-institutional front, and who must be adept at catalyzing, communicating, interpreting, harmonizing.

But ultimately, of course, it is the representatives of the participating institutions, the board members of the consortium, who have the most difficult assignment. As Eldon Johnson, former president of the Great Lakes Colleges Association and an astute observer of the higher educational scene, has stated, "I think it safe to say that the association which sets itself off with distinction will be the one which better solves the perpetual problem of how to keep informed all those responsible for the policy and affected by the policy."[4] But the policy itself is the crux of the matter.

This then is the consortium board member's challenge. The responses to the challenge are being worked out in the yearly labors of the representatives serving the groupings discussed here, all of which enjoy an acknowledged degree of success. It is premature to try to describe any grand policy lines being fashioned in such deliberations. And perhaps the nature of the cooperative's mission is such as to preclude any settled state in the first place, particularly since the consortium's work is always on the innovative frontier. Certainly for present board members—as well as for future ones—there are still the immense problems of attempting to work productively among a mass of relationships which are not only intricate and often sensitive but also steadily growing in number and complexity.

The successes of the consortia described here would tend to indicate that the problem is at least in the process of being confronted. But consortium activity is still in a fairly nascent stage. And hovering over it are the behemoth concerns and pressures of an ever-expanding effort in education. There are thus no illusions about the current phase of cooperative policy making: it is a trail-breaking phase, with all of the difficulties that this pioneering term implies. The developmental task faced by the representatives affects two loyalties—one relating to their own institutions and the other to the consortium. In theory, the two are one because the net effect of long-range cooperative effort is a series of gains for the participating institution. In practice, the representative must strike for what he considers to be the right balance in making recommendations for action to his institution. At times, then, the cooperative group might seem to be moving tentatively rather than forthrightly. Yet it must be remembered that the representatives must cope with a host of relationships and interests within their own institutions before commitments can be made. Much therefore depends upon the kind of authority vested in the institutional representatives—individually and collectively. The measure of success of a consortium then becomes the number of substantive programs it establishes under such authority. We emphasize the word substantive, for the really meaningful program reflects the fact that the representatives

[4] Eldon L. Johnson, "College Federations: Requisites of Success," *Journal of Higher Education*, vol. 37, no. 1, January, 1966.

have confronted the hard problems of consensus, have determined that such a project is better undertaken in common than singly, have some assurances that it will work, and are willing to live with their overall recommendations and decisions.

It is understandable, then, that the institutional representatives are often wariest of programs smacking of "grand expectations" and "supreme designs." While some boldness of vision and experimentation is vital to the process, there is nothing which chills the cooperative effort so thoroughly as the highly touted project whose limits are but dimly seen. There is good evidence that the more modest pilot program or feasibility study generally leads to more effective accomplishments than the broad design. Once again, generalizations are risky. But it seems better to have cooperative projects moved upwards, through several stages of consideration and acceptance, than to have a broad framework or pattern imposed on a large interinstitutional constituency. The problem for the board member is thus to discriminate between the workable project which is but one element in an eventual mosaic as against the persuasively projected large concept offered as a comprehensive solution and covering a broad area. This is not to say that broad designs are inevitably unproductive. Obviously, some programs cannot be undertaken in any other way. But in general a period of experimentation, or the building up from a small to a larger program, can accomplish more than years of protracted and possibly fruitless effort to achieve a large pattern of operation.

CHECKLIST OF ITEMS TO BE INCLUDED IN AGREEMENTS AMONG INSTITUTIONS ESTABLISHING INTERINSTITUTIONAL RELATIONSHIPS

Institutions entering into cooperative arrangements generally formulate articles of agreement[5] which include specifications or statements regarding the following items:

1. Name of consortium or grouping
2. Address of staff or headquarters office
3. Purpose of organization
4. Membership (names of founding institutions plus conditions under which other institutions may join)
5. Control or governance (form of governance, number of board representatives, requirements regarding appointment, statement of voting powers, term of office, method of electing officers of board, frequency of meetings, bylaws, maintenance of records, etc.)
6. Staff organization and functions (organization chart, job titles and descriptions, etc.)
7. Budget
   a. Operating funds usually come from annual membership fee paid by the participating institutions.
   b. Program funds may be supplied by the member institutions but generally are sought from federal agencies and private foundations.
8. Means or system of reporting, record keeping, publicity, and intercampus communication with respect to cooperative operations
9. General mode of operation (initiation and development of projects, means of coordination and liaison, etc.)

SELECTED BIBLIOGRAPHY

Bunnell, Kevin P., and Eldon L. Johnson: "Interinstitutional Cooperation," in Samuel Baskin (ed.), *Higher Education: Some Newer Developments,* McGraw-Hill Book Company, New York, 1965.

[5] Note: If association is to be incorporated, see applicable U.S., state, and other statutes for nonprofit organizations.

Howard, Lawrence C. (ed.): *Interinstitutional Cooperation in Higher Education,* Institute of Human Relations, The University of Wisconsin Press, Madison, Wis., 1967.
Moore, Raymond S.: *A Guide to Higher Education Consortiums: 1965–66,* U.S. Office of Education, 1967. (Superintendent of Documents Catalog no. FS 5.250:50051.)
Perkins, James A.: "From Autonomy to Systems," part III in *The University in Transition,* Princeton University Press, Princeton, N.J., 1966.
Wells, Herman B.: "A Case Study on Interinstitutional Cooperation," *Educational Record,* pp. 355–362, Fall 1967, American Council on Education, Washington, D.C.
Wilson, Logan (ed.): *Emerging Patterns in American Higher Education,* American Council on Education, Washington, D.C., 1965, parts 4 and 5.

Chapter 11

Research

MARTIN W. ESSIGMANN

Dean of Research, Northeastern University, Boston, Massachusetts

INTRODUCTION AND DEFINITIONS

The purposes of research in a college or university are twofold: to advance or produce new knowledge and to train students—especially at the graduate level. It is doubtful that research activities that meet neither purpose are appropriate for a university to undertake. A healthy research program has as a major advantage: that of attracting good faculty and good students.

Support for sponsored research can be awarded to individuals on the faculty for specific projects, to an operating division of the university, or to the university as a whole for use at its discretion. The award may be a grant or a contract, grants being employed where considerable freedom is intended, and contracts where the research will be of a directed nature. Usually, a grant requires some form of cost sharing, while a contract allows for full reimbursement of all expenses including indirect costs, or overhead.

The federal government has formulated rather detailed rules for administering research supported through public funds. These rules are incorporated in the *Armed Services Procurement Regulations* [1]* (ASPR), and include the official interpretation of the terms *organized research, departmental research,* and *other institutional activities.* These terms are of paramount importance in determining the allowable distribution of costs within the cost-accounting structure of the university. In essence, *organized research* is defined as those research activities that are separately budgeted and accounted for. *Departmental research* means research activities that are not separately budgeted and accounted for. *Other institutional activities* includes all other activities (except research and instruction) that contribute to those direct or indirect costs that are allowable under the regulations.

There are various meanings of the term "research." In science, it means basic research to discover new truths. In engineering, medicine, and pharmacy, it usually means the application of these truths to new problems. Care needs to be given to distinguish between applied research and routine testing, which is generally accepted as having little justification in the academic program. In the nonscience liberal arts areas, research includes scholarly work such as reading to formulate new instructional plans or programs; and similarly, in education, it may involve the application of scientific methodologies to studies aimed toward the promotion of good teaching.

The proper ratio of basic to applied research for a university is an important factor in its planned development. It is determined by whether the university desires to project as its image that of the scholarly academy or that of the institute of technology. If neither, then a ratio of 1:1 is generally the target.

The research staff will usually include professors who both teach and do research, research associates and research assistants who normally do not teach, and support personnel including technicians, computer programmers, and secretaries. In addition, students may participate in the research program either on a paid or unpaid basis. Each project (usually a unit operated under a separate contract or grant) is commonly under the direction of a professor who is designated as the *principal investigator* (or P.I.). *Research associates* are the backbone of the research project. They usually concentrate their efforts on the research, with little if any emphasis placed on teaching. Normally their formal education through course work has been completed. On the other hand, *research assistants* are considered to be in training and may teach as part of their apprenticeship.

In order to begin research, assuming none (or very little) exists, it is first necessary to decide that a research program will be established and to recognize that this will entail an initial monetary outlay for staff and facilities. This embryo staff undertakes the search for support by writing and submitting unsolicited (or in some cases solicited) proposals to the various agencies likely to provide support. When the research topic

* Bracketed numbers refer to the references at the end of the chapter.

proposed happens to coincide with the interests of one of these agencies, there usually results an attempt to arrive at a mutually acceptable work statement and budget through negotiation. In the process of negotiation, technical matters are handled by the proposed principal investigator and administrative matters by the proper administrative officers (such as the office of research administration, if one exists).

POLICIES RELATED TO RESEARCH ADMINISTRATION

Policies of importance are those related to the *type of research conducted*, to the *disciplines* imposed upon the research staff [2], and to the *protection* of the university. Since the requirements of research differ significantly from those of the university's normal day-by-day operations, including teaching, these policies will in most cases need to be separately established and administered.

Type of Research Sponsored research is favored over unsponsored research for the obvious financial reasons; however, it is not uncommon for the sponsor to impose limitations such as denial of publication rights and patent restrictions. In addition, the research will probably be of the applied or hardware-oriented type with but little freedom for the investigator to change his methods or objectives. Organized (or separately budgeted) research is generally more efficiently conducted than is the fragmented research administered under an operating unit such as an instructional department. However, the latter offers definite advantages from the standpoints of faculty morale and overall instructional effectiveness. Classified research is seldom justified, and then only where the needs of national security and the desire of the university to fulfill a public responsibility dictate its pursuance. The financial resources of the university determine the ratio of numbers of tenured research faculty to total research staff. If this ratio is excessive, a sudden cutback in support could result in disaster due to the need to divert other funds to cover the research commitments.

Disciplines The policies covering the disciplines of research personnel are different from those governing the teaching staff. The very nature of research as a creative activity precludes its segmentation in a way comparable to class schedules and its control by routine procedures. However, recently established government rules require substantiation by an authorized university official of charges made for time spent on research. These so-called "time and effort" reports are also required to substantiate the effort of those persons whose salaries are used to satisfy cost sharing requirements.

While considerable flexibility is shown in the case of the faculty, the requirements are more stringent with respect to nonprofessional personnel. Time and attendance records are required on a regular basis. Sometimes this is daily, but more often it is at intervals corresponding to the pay period (e.g., weekly, bimonthly, etc.).

The salaries and wages paid to the research staff represent one of the most sensitive areas in research administration. It is a cardinal principle that premium salaries, based only on the fact that the employee is performing research, not be paid. On the other hand, it is necessary to recognize that in some instances higher pay is justified, as when a researcher's freedom to consult is restricted because of his research responsibilities. Also, especially in positions of leadership, the research workers may be required to present better academic credentials than their teaching counterparts.

Recognizing that the professional-level research staff cannot effectively produce results on a "nine to five" basis, the assignment should be made in such a way as to indicate the fraction (either full or part time) of the man's full professional effort that he is expected to devote to his research. With due regard to the limits determined by his need to supervise subordinates, he should be free to select his hours within reason.

Protection of University Rights The most important policies governing university and faculty rights are those which pertain to the freedom to publish and to obtain patents based on research results.

The mechanics of patenting and copyrighting are covered fully in Section 1, Chapters 8 and 9. Government contracts contain limitations on the patenting of inventions made on work covered by the contract. Generally speaking, these reserve all "rights, title and interest in and to each Subject Invention (made by the contractor), subject to the reservation of a nonexclusive and royalty free license to the contractor."

Industrial sponsors are generally more flexible as to the possibilities of negotiating terms. When the sponsor is investing large sums of money in support of a faculty member's efforts to develop new products or processes, it is only reasonable that the sponsor should be the one to profit. Otherwise, reasonable rights to publish information and to profit from patents can usually be negotiated on a case-by-case basis. As a general policy, the university should not allow faculty members to enter into agreements of any type with sponsors that involve overly restrictive patent limitations.

Graduate students who are paid for working on research under sponsored contracts and grants and who use the results of their work in their dissertations are usually treated in the same way as faculty in the determination of their rights to patents based on their theses. When the graduate student is employed by an industrial organization on work that is not under the direct control of the university, the employer may want to reserve the patent rights. Figure 1 shows a sample agreement that has been found useful in preventing misunderstandings in this connection.

1. In accordance with regulations established by the University Committee on Patents which were approved by the Executive Council on November 17, 1960, the undersigned hereby waives any and all patent rights for any invention that may result from research in the conduct of his thesis undertaken as a Graduate Student at his place of employment.

____

Name of Industrial Organization

Signed: ____________________

Graduate Student

2. The undersigned, in the capacity of University Thesis Supervisor, hereby waives any and all patent rights for any invention that may result from the research in the conduct of the above student's thesis.

Signed: ____________________

University Thesis Supervisor

3. The ________________ Corporation hereby agrees to permit ________________, an employee of the Company, to carry on research in its laboratories in connection with his thesis, with the understanding that any and all patent rights for any invention that may result from this research shall be wholly the property of the Corporation.

Signed: ____________________

For the Corporation

4. Northeastern University agrees to permit ________________, a Graduate Student, to carry on research incident to his thesis at the plant of the ________________ Corporation and hereby waives any and all claim to any patent rights for any invention that might result from this research. The completed thesis, however, will become the property of Northeastern University when it is submitted as part of the requirement for the degree of ________________

Signed for the University

Date: ____________________, President

Fig. 1 *Sample form of agreement concerning possible patent rights arising from research carried on at an industrial plant.*

The university should see that all research agreements allow free dissemination of research results through oral or written presentations wherever this does not affect the security of a nation or otherwise act unduly to the sponsor's disadvantage.

SOURCES OF FINANCIAL SUPPORT FOR RESEARCH

Financial support for research can be arranged through internal budgeting of the institution's own funds or through grants and contracts from outside agencies [3].

Support for Research Projects

When the institution's own funds are concerned, this may be handled through the establishment of a central research fund to which all departments have access or through a line item in each department's annual budget, depending upon which is more convenient. In either case, it is important to segregate the accounts from other institutional or departmental funds in order to exercise fiscal control and to prevent the diversion of research funds to other purposes.

At one university, the mechanism employed is called the "basic research fund." A sum of money is added to the fund each year primarily to be used as "seed" money. Awards cannot be used for faculty salaries, but wages of the support staff such as student assistants, computer programmers, etc., are allowable. In a common variation of the plan, a standing universitywide committee evaluates faculty proposals submitted at regular intervals and makes the awards on the basis of competitive merit.

"Released time" is another means of providing university support for research, and it is commonly employed when an expansion of graduate participation is being encouraged. On the assumption that a full professional load is equivalent to 12 class hours per week (a commonly accepted figure), a 6-hour teaching load is consistent with one-half released time for research. Funds for released time, and in some cases for related expenses, are provided through line items in the department's annual budget or through a grant from a central research fund.

In some universities, the sabbatical leave is used to provide university support for research.

The use of released time and sabbatical leaves is not limited to university-supported research but may also be applied where grants and contracts are concerned.

Some schools have a policy of providing each new faculty member, especially the younger man whose training has just been completed, with a modest sum, commonly $5,000, with which to initiate his research. In addition, he will be given half the usual full teaching load.

The largest fraction of university research support is provided by the federal government. Some of this comes from agencies that fall under the Department of Defense (DOD), the Department of Health, Education and Welfare (HEW), and the Atomic Energy Commission (AEC). Most of the remainder comes from the National Science Foundation (NSF) and the National Aeronautics and Space Administration (NASA). Each of these sources has established its own procedures and requirements for obtaining support and administering the resulting research projects. This proliferation of requirements which must be met is a chief source of trouble to the research administrator.

Agencies falling under the Department of Defense that are major sources of university research support are the Air Force Cambridge Research Laboratories (AFCRL), Advanced Research Project Agencies (ARPA), the Office of Naval Research (ONR), the Army Research Office (ARO), and the Air Force Office of Scientific Research (AFOSR). The AFCRL and ARPA commonly employ the contract as an instrument for funding research. The ARO and AFOSR commonly employ the grant, and ONR uses both. The contract is used when the agency has some special need that can be met by the university research faculty. A request for procurement (RFP) is prepared by the agency, and proposals are solicited from qualified institutions. The best proposal received, provided it is otherwise acceptable, is awarded the contract. Quite often the aspect of competition is eliminated and the award is made on a sole-source basis to an institution because of its unique qualifications.

Support of university research by industry is rather spotty, with some universities being able to obtain very little while others get the major part of their total support from industrial sources. The variations are strongly influenced both by geographical location and by discipline. Most universities today have adopted conflict-of-interest policies that ensure the maintenance of the integrity of the company-consulting practice, including the fair reimbursement of the university for the use of its facilities.

One such policy, based upon a joint statement by the American Council on Education and the American Association of University Professors,* is reproduced below:

RESOLVED THAT: the following be University Policy for prevention of conflicts of interest in government-sponsored research.

1. The University fully endorses the principles set forth in the joint statement on conflicts of interest by the American Council on Education and the American Association of University Professors.

2. At the beginning of each academic year, a copy of the joint ACE-AAUP statement will be sent to every member of the administration and of the research and teaching faculty and staff.

3. Faculty and staff members are required to report in writing to their Department Chairman all pertinent professional activities outside the University. The report, which should provide adequate detail with respect to nature, extent, and duration, must be made prior to the commencement of the activities. A duplicate file of this information will be maintained in the Office of Research Administration.

4. The Department Chairmen, the Dean of Research, and the Dean of Faculty are available for advance consultation relating to potential conflict situations. The University expects faculty and staff members to seek advice from these sources. Legal guidance is available for problems not otherwise resolvable.

5. That a statement of the conflict of interest policy of the University as outlined in parts 1–4 of this resolution be incorporated in the Faculty Handbook.

Industrial support is usually provided through a fixed-price type of contract rather than the cost-reimbursement type used by the government. Industrial support is less likely to provide continuity of work than is government support. Under the latter, the repeated renewal of contracts is common and more or less automatic. Title to equipment remains with the sponsor in the case of the usual government contracts but often passes to the university in the case of industrial support.

There are numerous private or nongovernmental public foundations [4] that provide support for research. Most of these provide only partial support through "grants in aid," which usually do not allow for indirect costs (overhead) and are usually not renewable —at least not as readily as are government grants and contracts. They seldom allow for reimbursement for faculty salaries; however, where needed, the wages of an assistant may be allowed. Nearly always they allow for the purchase of supplies and equipment.

Table 1 identifies some of the private foundations which support university faculty in their research and gives some of their requirements. Included is an order-of-magnitude estimate of the average grant.

* "On Preventing Conflicts of Interest in Government-Sponsored Research at Universities," American Council on Education, 1 Dupont Circle, N.W., Washington, D.C. 20036. The AAUP article is reproduced in an appendix to this chapter.

TABLE 1 Private Foundations Providing Research Support

Name	Field of interest	Limits of support	Application deadlines	Address inquiries to:
American Philosophical Society	All fields of learning	Average, $1,000	Six weeks in advance of first Friday in February, April, June, October, and December	American Philosophical Society 104 South Fifth Street Philadelphia, Pa. 19106
Ford Foundation	All critical national problems	Open	Open	Ford Foundation 477 Madison Avenue New York, N.Y. 10022
Kresge Foundation	Research facilities	Open	Open	Kresge Foundation 211 Fort Street West Detroit, Mich. 48226
The Rockefeller Foundation	Urban problems, civil rights, cultural development	Open	Open	The Rockefeller Foundation 111 West 50th Street New York, N.Y. 10020
American Council of Learned Societies	All fields of humanities	Grants in aid not in excess of $2,000; fellowships to $8,500	September 30, October 15, November 2, and February 15, depending upon the program	American Council of Learned Societies 345 East 46th Street New York, N.Y. 10017
Resources for the Future, Inc.	Regional and urban problems	Open	Open	Resources for the Future, Inc. 1755 Massachusetts Avenue, N.W. Washington, D.C. 20036
Social Science Research Council	Social sciences (also other areas of interest)	Open	November 1 February 1	Social Science Research Council Fellowships and Grants 230 Park Avenue New York, N.Y. 10017
Carnegie Corporation of New York	Higher education	Open	Open	Carnegie Corporation of New York 589 Fifth Avenue New York, N.Y. 10017
The Geological Society of America, Inc.	Geology	Open	February 15	The Geological Society of America, Inc. 231 East 46th Street New York, N.Y. 10017

TABLE 1 (Continued)

Name	Field of interest	Limits of support	Application deadlines	Address inquiries to:
National Safety Council	Accident prevention	Not to exceed $1,000	March 1, July 1, or December 1	Research Department National Safety Council 425 Michigan Avenue Chicago, Ill. 60611
American Cancer Society	Cancer	Open	January 1, May 1, or September 1	Research Department American Cancer Society, Inc. 219 East 42nd Street New York, N.Y. 10017
American Heart Association	Cardiovascular function and disease	Not in excess of $15,000	November 1	Research Department American Heart Association 44 East 23rd Street New York, N.Y. 10010
Life Insurance Medical Research Fund	Medical research	Not in excess of $15,000	September 15	Life Insurance Medical Research Fund 1030 East Lancaster Avenue Rosemont, Pa. 19101
The John A. Hartford Foundation, Inc.	Medical research	Open	Open	The John A. Hartford Foundation, Inc. 405 Lexington Avenue New York, N.Y. 10017
The Pharmaceutical Manufacturers Association Foundation, Inc.	Pharmacology	Open	Open	Pharmaceutical Manufacturers Association Foundation, Inc. 1155 Fifteenth Street, N.W. Washington, D.C. 20005
Foundations' Fund for Research in Psychiatry	Problems of mental and emotional illness	Open	Open	Foundations' Fund for Research in Psychiatry 100 York Street New Haven, Conn. 06511
The Population Council	Demography	Open	Open	The Population Council 230 Park Avenue New York, N.Y. 10017
Planned Parenthood—World Population	Human reproduction	Open	Open	Planned Parenthood—World Population 515 Madison Avenue New York, N.Y. 10022

TABLE 1 (Continued)

Name	Field of interest	Limits of support	Application deadlines	Address inquiries to:
Research Corporation: A Foundation	Science	Open	Open	Research Corporation: A Foundation 405 Lexington Avenue New York, N.Y. 10017
The Society of Sigma Xi	Any field of science	$100 to $2,000	February 1, May 1, or November 1	Sigma Xi National Headquarters 51 Prospect Street New Haven, Conn. 06511 Attn: Committee on Grants in Aid of Research
The Petroleum Research Fund	Petroleum	Open	September 1, December 1, or March 1	The Petroleum Research Fund American Chemical Society 1155 16th Street, N.W. Washington, D.C. 20036

Support of Research Facilities

As research becomes more and more sophisticated, the cost of the facilities, including such major pieces of equipment as cyclotrons, telescopes for radio astronomy, etc., can make up the major part of the total project cost. Where this is the case, separate proposals covering the costs of initial procurement and of operation of the facilities may be involved.

Several federal agencies have programs providing support for facilities to be used for general institutional research. Typical of these are the NSF, the National Institutes of Health (NIH), and the Office of Education. Both NASA and DOD have limited programs which provide facilities for research in areas in which these agencies have some special interest.

The NSF's grants for the *Graduate Science Facilities Program* provide up to 50 percent of the cost of planning, construction, and furnishing of buildings for scientific research and for research training in the sciences. This program also allows for similar support of the renovation of existing facilities. Funds for general-purpose laboratory apparatus pertinent to the project to be housed may be allowed up to 15 percent of the cost of construction and fixed furnishings (blinds, storage racks, fire protective equipment, etc.). In preparing the proposal, the format prescribed in the most recent NSF program booklet should be followed.

The NIH and Office of Education facilities programs differ in detail from that of the NSF, so that the multiple submission of proposals requires the preparation of separate proposals. The Office of Education, for instance, provides up to one-third of the cost. It is not unusual for NASA or DOD to provide the full cost for facilities which they support.

ROUTINES OF RESEARCH ADMINISTRATION

Once university research has reached the point where a number of departments are involved, it usually becomes evident that a central administrative unit is needed. Typical of such a unit is what is commonly called an "Office for Research Administration" (ORA). Senior personnel involved in operating such a unit perform as research coordinators, although they may have titles such as "Dean of Research" or "Director of Research." Other personnel are provided to fulfill specific functions such as those related to purchasing, security, inventory control, technical and secretarial services, etc.

Of prime importance to the administration of research in a university is a manual of information for principal investigators. It should describe the local ground rules governing the acquisition of research support and the rules governing the operation of the research program (including the procurement of personnel) once support is secured.

Figure 2 shows the outline followed by one typical manual.

Proposal Preparation Most of the government agencies have prepared brochures that describe their preferred procedures for making research proposals and, while considerable flexibility is allowed as to the details, it is advisable to follow their outlines closely—if only as a convenience to the proposal reviewer. Some agencies which have prepared such brochures are the NSF, NASA, ONR, and AFOSR. A perusal of these brochures will indicate strong similarities among the agencies. The material to be discussed below will assume that a proposal is being prepared for a typical agency.

Sometimes a single proposal is prepared and transmitted broadside to several agencies. When this is done, it is important that the unique requirements of all agencies be covered in the master proposal. The following summarizes some characteristics of a good proposal [5].

1. A carefully prepared *abstract or summary* is most important.

2. Sufficient local *background information* should be given to provide pertinent information about the competence of the principal investigator and the university to conduct the proposed research.

3. A carefully prepared *statement of the proposed research* should be included. It must be both specific, so that the reviewer can follow in his mind's eye the procedures the proposer intends to follow, and broad, so that the researcher will be free to deviate from courses of action that prove unfruitful.

4. Somewhere in the early portion of the proposal the *relevance of related work by others* should be presented. The proposer's competence to undertake work in the field probably will be judged by many reviewers by his familiarity with the field as demonstrated by his proposal. Mention should be made, at least by reference and inclusion in the bibliography, to all related research that has implications affecting the proposed work. Failure to include this will probably be interpreted as ignorance of the work.

5. While the *budget estimate* is of great importance in the overall proposal, it ought not be made a matter of great concern to the principal investigator since it is usually

Title Page
Table of Contents
Foreword
I. The Office of Research Administration
II. The Principal Investigator—General
A. Recruitment of Personnel
B. Change in Status of Personnel
C. Vacation Arrangements
D. Arrangements for Research Space
E. Costs Not Reimbursable from Grant Funds
F. Research Reporting and Administrative Approvals
G. Copies of Research Reports for Principal Investigators
H. Typing and Other Services
III. Preparation and Submission of Unsolicited Research Proposals
IV. Initiation of Solicited Contract Projects
V. Miscellaneous Details Related to Research Administration
A. Acceptance of Award and the Beginning of Research
B. Purchasing Procedures
C. Receiving Procedures
D. Inventory and Property Accountability
E. Security and Classified Work
F. Accountability for Time Worked on Research
G. Travel Regulations
H. Procedures for Processing Co-op Work Schedules
I. Patent Policy
J. Radiological Safety
K. Other Policies Pertinent to Research Administration

APPENDICES

Appendix I: Senate Statement
Appendix II: Official Statements Pertaining to the Appointment of Personnel
Appendix III: Graduate Student Financial Aid
Appendix IV: Procedures for the Control of Government Property
Appendix V: University Travel Regulations
Appendix VI: Patent Policy
Appendix VII: Miscellaneous University Regulations Pertinent to Research Administration

Fig. 2 *Sample outline for manual of information for principal investigators.*

given serious attention by financial specialists. Budgets for grant proposals differ from those for contract proposals in that the law requires that the university make a cost sharing contribution toward grant-supported research.

Related to the matter of mandatory cost sharing is the charging for faculty salaries. Many schools do not charge for academic-year salaries. Other schools may follow this practice to a lesser extent to meet the demands of the cost sharing requirement. A common practice is for the faculty member to divide his time equally between teaching and research, with the agency being charged for one-eighth of the full academic-year salary.

Salaries and wages paid to persons working on the grant or contract research are always classified as direct costs, as are travel expenses and expenditures for equipment and material. Other costs, such as computer charges, publication costs, and fringe benefits, may or may not be direct costs depending upon the practice of the university as established in the determination of its overhead rate.

Figure 3 shows a typical grant budget sheet prepared according to the current established policy of the NSF.* The overhead costs (or the indirect costs) are obtained by multiplying the total of all salaries and wages by 60 percent, assumed here to be the applicable audited overhead rate.

In the example, fringe benefits include retirement-fund payments at 5 percent of total faculty salary charges and social security payments at 4.2 percent (up to $6,000 per year). Other costs which might have been included would be appropriate shares of major medical insurance and other similar benefit plans.

When computer charges are included as direct costs, it is necessary to provide a listing of established hourly rates charged for the main computer and its ancillary equipment. Records must be maintained to justify charges made against the resulting grant

	Cost to	
	NSF	*Grantee*
Salaries:		
1. Dr. John Doe, principal investigator		
Academic-year salary (½ time, 9 months)	$ 4,500	$4,500
Summer salary (full time, 2 months)	4,000	–
2. *X*, research assistant	3,600	–
3. *Y*, technician (¼ time)	2,000	–
4. Secretarial assistance	500	–
Overhead:		
(Audited rate = 60 percent of salaries and wages)	8,760	2,700
Equipment and materials:		
Blackman Model DR-2 spectrophotometer	4,000	–
Expendable supplies	1,000	–
Computer costs:		
10 hours at $200 per hour, CDC-3300	2,000	–
Publication expenses:		
10 pages at $60 per page	600	–
Travel:		
Washington meeting of APS	200	–
Fringe benefits:		
TIAA	425	225
Social Security	340	189
Totals	$31,925	$7,614

Fig. 3 *Sample budget sheet for NSF proposal.*

* From "Important Notice to Presidents of Universities, etc.," Office of the Director, National Science Foundation, September 22, 1965.

or contract funds if an award is received. In cost sharing, the same degree of cost accounting must be maintained for the contributed part as for the supported part.

6. The proposal should include a description of all other sources of research support held by the principal investigator. It should identify all other agencies to which the subject proposal is being submitted. If there are other pending proposals in the name of the principal investigator, these also should be identified.

7. The proposal should be covered by a title page which identifies the proposal by title, by name of principal investigator, and by identification of the submitting institution. It should be signed by the principal investigator, the president of the university (or a designee who is authorized to commit the institution financially), and by the appropriate academic officers. It should be dated.

8. Where the amount of supported research represents a significant fraction of the total institutional budget, it becomes important to assess the financial and academic impact of a particular proposal on the university's overall program. The president of one institution makes use of the responses prepared in fulfillment of the following quoted statement in making this assessment:

> Each proposal is to be accompanied by a signed statement from the dean of the college containing his recommendations and specific statements of the impact of the proposal on:
>
> *a.* The overall development plan of the college or department concerned
>
> *b.* Additional laboratory or other space requirements (including remodeling and special services)
>
> *c.* Additional research equipment required at university expense
>
> *d.* Future teaching loads in the department, and how they are to be handled
>
> *e.* Compatibility of new staff to be hired (if any) with present faculty structure (especially salaries)
>
> *f.* Housing and office furnishings required

If, after his assessment, he is convinced that the proposed research will be to the advantage of the overall program, he signs the proposal.

9. The agency brochures describe the proper methods for transmitting proposals, and it is important that these instructions be followed so that the distribution within the agency can be expedited. This usually includes the assignment by the agency of an identification number to each proposal. This number should be used in future communications related to the proposal.

Contract and Grant Negotiation It usually takes several weeks for the necessary reviews to be made. If the reviews are not good, the proposal will be turned down by a polite letter from the agency, usually with the offer to discuss the reasons for denial should this be desired. Sometimes the proposal will be accepted as presented and a grant or contract will be made. More commonly, however, some revisions will be requested in the scope of the work or in the budget. This begins a period of negotiation which should involve three-way participation of the agency, the faculty member, and the university research coordinator. It is considered prudent to avoid unnecessary delay in this negotiation.

During the proposal preparation period and any ensuing period of negotiation, the university administration should be able to guarantee that in all aspects the undertaking of the project will be in the best interests of the university, be these interests financial or academic. This can be best handled by a senior member of the office of research administration.

The usual instrument used between the federal government and a university is a so-called "cost-reimbursement contract." An NSF grant (with cost sharing) was assumed in the discussion of the preparation of the budget estimate in the preceding section.

For a contract, the two columns of costs would be combined in one since there would be no cost sharing.

In rare cases, a fixed-price contract may be offered instead of a cost-reimbursement contract. In the cost-reimbursement case, a later adjustment of the overhead rate ensures a no-profit no-loss program. In the fixed-price case, the contractor may make or lose money. In the first case, the government retains title to nonexpendable material; while in the second case, it automatically becomes the property of the contractor.

Cost-reimbursement research and development contracts with educational institutions are generally administered through a "basic agreement" which serves as a master document applicable to all contracts with a given agency. It covers such items as allowable costs, examination of records, terminations, patents, rights in technical data, security, labor restrictions, overtime, negotiation of overhead rates, property accountability, travel restrictions, etc.

The grant instrument is a comparatively simple document with a minimum of restrictions.

Common to both are certain administrative requirements of fundamental importance. Prior approval is required for foreign travel with respect to maximum per-diem limitations and restrictions on first-class accommodations. Under cost-reimbursement contracts, title to residual property purchased remains with the government; with grants, however, it usually remains with the institution.

The choice of instrument, grant or contract, is usually the prerogative of the sponsor. Obviously, from the standpoint of academic freedom, the grant is preferred. However, from a financial standpoint, the contract would appear preferable since a grant by law now requires cost sharing.

Financial Aspects of Contract and Grant Negotiation Once the grant or contract terms have been negotiated to the point of joint agreement among the sponsor's technical and administrative representatives and the faculty member and his research coordinator, the president can make the necessary acknowledgment of this agreement by either signing the contract document or accepting by letter the grant award. The orderly processes of performing the research (by the faculty member) and of monitoring the work (by the research coordinator) can now begin. *The Handbook for Principal Investigators* (previously introduced in this section) and the *Armed Services Procurement Regulations* (ASPR) serve as guides in these processes.

The integrity of the system is ensured through the use of government-employed auditors who regularly check on the procedures followed at institutions performing work for the government. The ASPR provides the guidelines within which the auditors work.

The auditors also participate in the determination of the *overhead rate.* This is the factor by which total salaries and wages are multiplied to obtain the indirect costs chargeable under cost-reimbursement-type contracts.

More complete information is included in circular no. A-21 (revised) entitled "Principles for Determining Costs Applicable to Research and Development under Grants and Contracts with Educational Institutions." *

It is necessary in the beginning that certain of the terms used be defined. *Indirect costs* include (1) general administration and general expenses, (2) research administration expenses, (3) departmental administration expenses, (4) operation and maintenance expenses of the physical plant including equipment and building use charges, and (5) library expenses. *Direct costs* will include (1) salaries and wages, (2) fringe benefits, (3) matériel (i.e., equipment and supplies) costs, (4) travel expenses, (5) publication costs, and (6) computer costs.

* Available from the Superintendent of Documents, U.S. Government Printing Office, Washington, D.C. 20402 as part of *A Guide for Educational Institutions.* (Price: 35 cents)

Organized research is research that is separately budgeted and accounted for. *Departmental research* is all other research; and, insofar as the overhead determination is concerned, it is considered as part of the *instructional costs.* All costs not covered by the *organized research* and *instructional* categories are classified as under *other institutional activities.* Typical of these latter costs are those related to bookstores, dining halls, athletics, etc. These cost types (namely organized, departmental, and other) are often referred to as *direct-cost objectives.*

The process called *apportionment* is used to separate total indirect costs into two groups, one related to *instruction and research* and the other to *other institutional activities.* The process called *allocation* is used to separate instruction and research costs into two groups, one giving the costs of *organized research* and the other the costs of *instruction* including those of *departmental research.*

The first step in the determination of the overhead rate is to determine the total cost of each *indirect-cost* component (i.e., those identified as 1 through 5 in the preceding) for some period of time such as the prior fiscal year. Each component cost should then be reduced by amounts which reflect the fair share chargeable to any other indirect-cost components (e.g., some of the building and equipment use charge is properly chargeable to the library and to general administration and general expenses). The

Indirect costs		Direct-cost objectives		
		Organized research	Instruction	Other activities
1. General administration and expenses				
Total	$1,000,000			
Less portion due to other indirect costs	200,000			
To be apportioned	$ 800,000	$160,000	$ 320,000	$320,000
Apportionment ratios (based on personnel count): 1:2:2				
2. Research administration				
Total	$ 200,000	$200,000	–	–
3. Departmental administration				
Total	$ 600,000	$200,000	$ 400,000	–
4. Operation and maintenance (includes building and equipment use charge)				
Total	$1,000,000			
Less portion due to other indirect costs	300,000			
To be apportioned	$ 700,000	$ 70,000	$ 350,000	$280,000
Apportionment ratios (based on areas): 1:5:4				
5. Library				
Total	$ 300,000	$100,000	$ 200,000	–
Total indirect costs after apportionment and allocation to direct cost objectives	...	$730,000	$1,270,000	$600,000

Total salaries and wages for personnel on organized research projects: $1,400,000

$$\text{Overhead rate} = \frac{730{,}000}{1{,}400{,}000} \times 100 = 52.2\%$$

Fig. 4 *Sample calculation of overhead rate (simplified case, for illustration only).*

remainder is then apportioned and allocated among the three direct-cost objectives; namely, *organized research, instruction,* and *other institutional activities.* Decisions regarding the apportionment, allocation, or other division of costs should be made on some reasonable and justifiable basis such as the relative numbers of teachers, research workers, and students served or on the basis of space allotments. In this simplified example, the overhead rate would be given by the ratio of the total indirect costs allocated organized research to the total salaries and wages paid to all personnel employed in the organized research activity.

It will be seen that when the overhead costs are determined, in the case of a particular contract or grant, by multiplying the total salaries and wages for that contract or grant by the overhead rate, the fair share or properly prorated overhead cost is charged to the funds of that contract or grant.

Figure 4 shows a much simplified example of an overhead-rate determination. It is included to provide some insight into the philosophy behind the determination.

Under ASPR, overhead is never paid on salaries paid consultants or on the premium portion of overtime compensation. This is reasonable since the additional indirect expense in both cases is inconsequential. In the example given, fringe benefits are treated as direct costs. In practice, the opposite is often the case.

Where the total volume of government-sponsored research is less than $500,000 per year, a short form of overhead-rate determination is allowed. The procedure is described in circular no. A-21.

In cases where organized research is conducted in several locations, say at remote field sites as well as on the main campus, a single overhead rate may not fairly represent the actual costs. In these cases, ASPR allows for the determination of separate rates that apply to the off-campus locations.

Many of the fine details behind the apportionment of costs depend upon arbitrary decisions, but consistency in applying the results is a cardinal requirement. For example, if fringe benefits are considered as indirect costs in the overhead-rate determination, they must not be treated as direct costs in billing the government for costs incurred under a contract or grant. The same holds true for computer costs, travel, publications, etc.

In the case of contracts, the overhead rate determined in the way described is considered to be a provisional rate for the succeeding year. If experience shows the rate to be low or high, a retroactive adjustment is made. In the case of grants, however, the overhead rate is generally considered a fixed rate not subject to a retroactive adjustment.

The ASPR are rather specific with respect to the accounting of time and effort in the case of personnel related to organized research. One convenient method is to use a monthly proration report, such as that shown in Figure 5.

Department of Physics — Month of February, 1968

	Fraction of full professional effort						
	Sponsored research project						
Name	9841	9842	3641	Departmental research	Instruction	Other	Signature
John Doe	½	—	—	—	½	—	
James Doe	—	¼	—	¼	½	—	

Fig. 5 *Sample proration sheet.*

A very recent revision of circular A-21 has eliminated the requirement that professional staff members, for whom salary and time allocations are stipulated in the research agreement, must regularly submit time and effort reports. Any significant deviations from the stipulated amounts must be reconciled, however, in the annual and/or final fiscal reports.

Special regulations pertain with respect to the use of consultants who are already full-time employees of the institution. No extra compensation is allowed under normal circumstances. Exceptions can be made, however, where consulting is across department lines or where it involves remote locations and is performed in addition to a full departmental load. In all exceptional cases, the consulting arrangement must be specifically provided for in the research agreement or subsequently approved in writing by the sponsoring agency.

NORTHEASTERN UNIVERSITY № 9732

REQUEST FOR RESEARCH MATERIALS

PURCHASE ORDER No.__________

CONTRACT or GRANT No.__________

DATE__________

1. White-Office of Research Administration
2. Pink-Principal Investigator

MATERIAL OR EQUIPMENT

Quantity	Catalog No.	Item	Unit Price	Total

EXPENDABLE / NON EXPENDABLE

Suggested Supplier:

Delivery Information:

Use to be Made of Equipment:

Signed__________ Requester

Approved__________ Principal Investigator

Accounting Information

Account No. Inventory No.

Estimated Cost:

Actual Cost:

Remarks:

Fig. 6 *Sample form for purchase of research materials.*

When a professional divides his time between two or more objectives, his compensation for each shall be at the same basic salary rate. This applies also to the determination of compensation for summer or vacation periods. The NSF requires as a matter of policy that any compensation over and above that of the academic-year salary shall not exceed two-ninths of the academic-year salary. While some of the other agencies are more generous, all agencies oppose the payment of premium amounts for services on sponsored research.

The purchasing of matériel, both equipment and expendable supplies, is handled by a division of the office of research administration. Figure 6 shows a form found convenient in initiating a purchase. The principal investigator or his designee transmits the completed form to the ORA, where the necessary purchase order in standard university style is issued. When the matériel is received, the person who made the request checks the shipment for completeness. If complete, a signed copy of the packing slip is sent to the ORA indicating approval for releasing payment to the supplier. The completed form then serves as a permanent record of the transaction. In the case of government contracts, all such records must be kept for 10 years. The form described contains all the information usually required in a routine audit.

Property Accountability and Controls Government regulations require the preparation and subsequent agency approval of written procedures for the control of government property. The outline in Figure 2 includes such a document as an appendix.

Items which may well be covered in the property control document are:

1. Procedures for purchasing, receiving, and making payment for matériel.
2. Identification of government property by decal or other means.
3. Records. Stock cards are required for all nonexpendable matériel, be it plant equipment, minor equipment, or special tooling. Figure 7 shows a typical stock card.
4. Procedures for maintenance and repair.
5. Procedures for taking inventory. Government regulations require that inventories be made annually.
6. Procedures for disposing of government-owned property.

When the amount of government-owned equipment and facilities at an institution becomes large and a number of different contracts are involved, it is common for a facilities contract to be established to provide a master account and thus simplify the control procedures.

Security Administration Most universities, especially those with strong science orientations, eventually find themselves involved in classified research. The level of involvement may range from very slight, where contracts become classified simply to

AF No.　　　　Class

Desc.

Model No.　　　　Serial No.

Mfr.

Mfr.'s Address

Date Rec'd:　　　　Cost: $

Acq. Ref.　　　　Location:

Contract No.

Northeastern University, Boston, Mass. 02115

Fig. 7 *Sample stock card for property control.*

allow the faculty concerned to visit government installations, to complete involvement with secret projects on campus. The government defines the work as classified by making its DD form DD254 a part of the contract instrument and through it indicating the level of clearance required (i.e., "secret," "confidential," etc.).

Quite commonly the reason for classification is to provide access to restricted test areas such as missile sites so that, even though unclassified experiments are being conducted, the project personnel can come and go at their convenience. Sometimes the reason is to make it possible for the sponsor to use university personnel as consultants on related but classified problems.

Security aspects of classified research and development projects performed by universities are controlled by the same regulations that are applied to industry. These regulations are contained in the *Industrial Security Manual for Safeguarding Classified Information* (ISM).*

Each university under the security system is assigned to a local military unit which serves as its cognizant security office. Periodic inspections by representatives of this office ensure compliance with the regulations of the ISM.

A university becomes a part of the security system by executing a secrecy agreement with one of the government agencies, such as the Army or Air Force. Members of the governing body of the university must either obtain personal clearances or formal action must be executed that will prevent uncleared members of the governing body from gaining access to classified information.

Once the secrecy agreement is made, the university is required to designate one of its employees as the *security officer,* and to prepare a security manual which will establish local ground rules for protecting classified information that are within the limits prescribed by the ISM. Clearances for individuals are then initiated through the submission of the required number of copies of the Personnel Security Questionnaire (DD Form 48), a set of fingerprints, and a statement concerning membership in certain suspect organizations (DD Form 48-1).

Positive action on a personal clearance request does not automatically make security information available to the applicant. A "need to know" has to be established by a responsible government agent such as the contracting officer or contract monitor. This may be accomplished through the DD Form 254 attached to the contract with which the applicant is concerned.

Security is considered a very serious matter by the federal government and heavy penalties are provided for willful violation of the regulations.

Research Reporting The reporting requirements imposed by the sponsors of supported research vary widely, with more stringent requirements for contracts than for grants.

Contracts usually require the submission of quarterly reports to provide information concerning the status of and future plans for the technical details of the research and the staffing as well as updated fiscal information concerning residual funds. The dates when these reports should be submitted are usually stated in the contract document. These reports need not be pretentious since they are for limited internal distribution and use.

Scientific reports are prepared at those times during the conduct of the contract research when sufficient technical information has been amassed to justify its publication. The contract document provides the distribution list for scientific reports, and this usually includes in excess of a hundred names. In addition, the author may have scientific colleagues to whom he will want to send copies. In all cases, the government sponsor will reserve the right to review the report before it is distributed. This

* Available as attachment to DD Form 441 from the Superintendent of Documents, U.S. Government Printing Office, Washington, D.C. 20402.

is to prevent the release of questionable results, to protect proprietary rights in the case of patentable items, and to ensure that classified information is not involved.

Publication in the technical press is accepted as partially fulfilling the reporting requirements. Contracts usually reserve for the sponsor the right to review the manuscript; however, this is not the case for grants. In the case of oral presentations, contracts require the prior approval of the paper abstract. The cost of publication (i.e., "page costs") can be significant in the case of some fields of applied science. If such costs are not included under overhead, it is advisable to include a realistic estimate for these charges in the budget estimate.

In addition to information copies of reprints of published papers, grant research usually requires the submission of short annual and/or semiannual reports on the current status of the work. These should involve information covering technical details, personnel, and financial status.

Both contracts and grants require the submission of final technical reports. In the case of contracts, a report in considerable detail is expected and its distribution is usually extensive. In the case of grants, the requirements are minimal.

Both contracts and grants require formal financial reports from the university's business officer. Special forms are usually provided for this purpose, but this is not the case for the administrative and technical reports.

In addition to the aforementioned reports to the research sponsor, it is important that certain reports be prepared for the use of the university administrative officers. Figure 8 shows a portion of a typical monthly listing of research projects.

TYPES OF ADMINISTRATIVE ORGANIZATIONS [6]

All research administration was initially centered in the department. With the volume of university research growing at approximately 17 percent per year, more and more universities are now turning to centralized coordinating offices. In some cases, the change has seen the creation of such separate entities as government-owned research centers, university-affiliated research foundations and parks, or research institutes. More common, however, has been the establishment of an office for research administration within the academic framework of the university.

The trend to create separate entities has led to the development of three distinctly different types of organizations. Some universities have set up autonomous groups (e.g., incorporated research institutes or research foundations) designed primarily to provide administrative housekeeping services for heterogeneous assortments of applied research projects. These institutes or foundations, by virtue of being separately incorporated, have fiscal autonomy from the parent university but share the senior professorial staff of the university. In addition, they have full-time professional employees who fill the technical and administrative needs of the research. This latter group, while usually sharing in the employee benefits provided by the university, lack the security that is inherent in the standard university faculty appointment.

The second type of organization is that of a center to provide research in some specialized field such as electronics, water resources, computer sciences, etc. It may incorporate many of the features of the first type; however, protection of the fiscal soundness of the university is not the primary objective.

The third type, which may involve characteristics common to the first two, is intended to provide facilities of an interdisciplinary nature. It brings together the faculty and staff with different but related interests to work on broad problems such as those of urban living, space sciences, rehabilitation, etc.

Below will be discussed some of the important considerations involved in the administration of organized research.

Identification	Title	Sponsor	Dates	Allotment for period given
BIOLOGY: (60.7K)*				
Barkley–8081	Haemaglutination Substances (Lectins) from Seeds, Transformation of Organic Compounds by Algae	Warner-Lambert	1 Apr. 1966 31 Mar. 1967	$ 2,000
Gabliks–8213 DADA17–68–C–8060	Studies of Biologically Active Agents	AMRDC	1 Jan. 1968 31 Dec. 1969	37,392
Gainor–9963 CA–07703–04	Nature of Proteinases Associated with Plant Tumors	HEW(NIH)	1 Jan. 1967 30 Sept. 1968	23,286 3,000 (NU)
Moyer–8151	Evolution of Detrimental Genes in a Population of Fruit Flies	American Philosophical Society	Apr. 1967 Mar. 1968	1,400
Pearincott–9201	A Comparative Study of Experimental Arteriosclerosis in the Mongolian Gerbil, *Meriones Unguiculations*, and the Amphibian, *Rana Pipiens*	BRF	May 1967	1,676
BIOPHYSICS AND BIOMEDICAL ENGINEERING: (72K)*				
Fine–8260 DA–49–193–MD–2436	Biological Effects of Laser Radiation	AMRDC	1 June 1963 30 Sept. 1968	350,918
COLLEGE OF BUSINESS: (20.2K)*				
Walls–9692 1 R21 HM00638–01	Estimating Hospital Debt Capacity	HEW	1 Apr. 1968 31 Mar. 1969	20,231

Fig. 8 *Sample monthly listing of research activities issued by the Office of Research Administration (asterisks indicate average annual rate).*

The Research Coordinator The central coordinating office for organized research may be headed by a person designated by any of several titles such as "Dean of Research," "Vice-president for Research," "Director of Research," "Director of Research Administration," etc. He usually has some background in scientific research and a bent towards administration and management. The National Council of University Research Administrators (NCURA) is composed of several hundred such persons who meet annually for the interchange of information on common problems. A similar group is encompassed by the Engineering Colleges Research Council (ECRC) of the American Society for Engineering Education.

The research coordinator maintains communication between the faculty, the university administration, and the appropriate funding agencies. He accomplishes this through periodic visits to the agency offices, through attendance at meetings of groups such as the NCURA and ECRC, through the conduct of meetings on campus of the graduate and research faculty, through the conduct of surveys of faculty research activities, and in general through his service as a central clearing agency for proposals and requests requiring university approval. In order to fulfill these functions effectively, he should be a member of all university planning committees involving the graduate faculty. He should monitor the planning of future research programs and ensure that these are properly coordinated with graduate instruction.

The research coordinator usually supervises the operations of the office of research administration. In addition to overseeing the administrative details described above, he is also responsible for promoting the research programs of the faculty. He can accomplish this by conducting surveys to determine faculty interests and by providing information pertaining to support sources. He should take the initiative in arranging conferences among faculty and administrators to discuss research policies. He is in a unique position to evaluate the impact and effectiveness of the research program, a factor which can make him a valuable member of the academic administration team.

The research coordinator plays a leading role in establishing communications between the graduate faculty and the financial and academic administrative officers. A recent study * has included in its recommendations the statement that ". . . one form, which we believe could be widely useful, is a joint committee or board, made up of representatives of the administration, the faculty engaged in research, and supporting staff." Among other things, this board would review research proposals to ensure that they are consistent with the long-range academic aspirations of the university for its growth and development and that they are financially sound.

Separately Incorporated Nonprofit Research Foundation This type of organization is probably the most highly organized of all. Some examples are the Illinois Institute of Technology Research Institute and the Research Foundation of the State University of New York. Most laboratories operated by universities for the federal government fall in this category; for example, the Lincoln Laboratory of the Massachusetts Institute of Technology and the Jet Propulsion Laboratory of the California Institute of Technology. In addition to serving as instruments to facilitate the handling of the routines of research administration, they provide specialized personnel and facilities for the conduct of the research per se.

The foundation is usually managed by a board of directors drawn from among the top administrative officers of the university, the faculty, and alumni. Sometimes there is representation by one or more members from outside the university community. Usually the senior research coordinator and the president are permanent members, but the other members are subject to periodic replacement or reappointment.

* See *Federal Support of Basic Research in Institutions of Higher Learning,* A Report by the National Academy of Sciences—National Research Council, 1964, p. 7.

A research foundation may be either weak or strong depending upon the dictates of its founders. Where its main purpose is to provide administrative flexibility, it will probably be weak. Where its purposes include facilitating the conduct of research, the exploitation of inventions made by the faculty, the solicitation of funds, and the provision of services and facilities otherwise unavailable for research by the faculty, it will be a strong force acting in the development of the university. This latter type may also establish and maintain scholarships, fellowships, and professorships. It may purchase, or acquire by gift, property and facilities. It may employ faculty and students as consultants. Most important of all, it may bestow the fruits of its research endeavors, or the earnings of its investments, upon the parent university at the pleasure of the board of directors who, happily, are de facto representatives of the university.

There are two reasons given for the establishment of research foundations. The first, and probably most common, is to provide a device to circumvent restrictive state statutory controls over funds at state universities. It is common practice at state universities to have all items of income, such as tuition, go into a central fund, with all items of expense, such as instructional costs, operated by a budget out of the central fund. Obviously, if the items of income include sums derived from research contracts and grants, they cannot appropriately be handled in this fashion. The second reason sometimes given is to provide a mechanism which would protect the financial resources of the university should it suddenly be necessary to cut back on expenditures in a given area due to a reduction in or cancellation of research support. There seems to be general agreement that separately incorporated research foundations are difficult to justify in the case of private universities, there being other ways of mitigating the second reason, as will be seen.

Research Center This type of organization, which can be used very effectively to administer large-scale research in a single area of concentration, is exemplified by the Research Laboratory for Electronics at the Massachusetts Institute of Technology. By appropriately categorizing faculty and research staff appointments, it is possible to avoid the consequences underlying the second reason given above.

Research centers exist primarily to provide centralized administrative and managerial services and functions such as personnel, purchasing, property control, and reporting. The faculty rather than a board of directors has top authority and control over the academic features of the program. The use of graduate students as research assistants and of professors as principal investigators is greatly facilitated under these conditions. This, along with the efficiency involved inherently in sharing costs, provides strong reasons for the center being a common type of organization.

Interdisciplinary Research Center The distinguishing characteristic of this type of organization is the heterogeneous nature of its controlling interests. It is usually headed by a committee made up of representatives of these interests. The major advantages just cited for the research center hold here, and in addition there is the flexibility allowed with regard to interdisciplinary graduate programs leading to terminal degrees.

Not to be overlooked in the selection of this type of organization is its effect in obtaining funds. There is currently a definite bias toward favoring the development of interdisciplinary projects. In some cases, several government agencies have banded together to provide joint support for research centers of both types.

Other Types of Research Operations There are several additional schemes for operating research programs. Many universities administer research through the separate departments in a totally decentralized manner. In these instances the department head or his executive officer acts as the research coordinator. The university's financial or business office provides most of the administrative and managerial services and functions.

Another scheme involves the concept of the *research park*. The academician does not generally hold this scheme in the high esteem that the others command. Usually the nature of the park is such that graduate students and faculty are involved more as part-time workers or consultants than as the main research personnel. Quite often, parks go beyond the category of nonprofit institutions and enter the not-for-profit or profit-making realm.

Occasionally the research takes such form that off-campus *field stations* are involved. These can become a part of any of the several types of overall organizations that have been discussed.

Probably the oldest of the various forms of research organization is the *experiment station*. This goes back to the days of the land-grant college. The term has fallen into disuse, but the functions of the experiment station can be considered to be covered by any of the previously described types of organization.

THE REVIEW AND EVALUATION OF RESEARCH PROGRAMS

It is common today to relate the major objective of the university's research (and graduate) programs to the attainment of excellence in selected areas of endeavor.

The task is complicated because basic research inherently involves certain protected faculty prerogatives. Basic research cannot be regimented as can course teaching. The best ideas of a researcher often come at the least probable times. This requirement for freedom and the high cost of research makes the process of review and evaluation of research results a most important one, lest good money be wasted on poor work. A precise evaluation, say one based on an input-output analysis, is difficult to accomplish because intangible considerations such as faculty tenure, rights to promotion, and opportunity to consult and publish are involved in the assessment. Three basic questions can be asked for which the answers can either be readily obtained or estimated. These are: (1) How long after a project is begun should results be looked for? (2) What are the tangible indicators of successful research results? and (3) What is the impact of the project on the overall program of the university?

The answer to the first question depends upon several initial conditions. In the case of the new Ph.D. holder, the work may be a continuation of his dissertation research and results may be expected immediately. In other cases, it may take from six months to two years for a promising approach to be formulated. Most government agencies recognize this and allow the principal investigator considerable freedom to change his method of attack, or even the complete approach, during the course of his investigations.

Publications in recognized professional journals are generally considered to be the best indicators of research effectiveness, especially when a review of the paper by the man's peers is a part of the process. Oral presentations at meetings, especially when they are made by invitation, are similarly accepted as evidence of superior attainment. Of importance also are patents (in the case of the applied fields) and the number of times that a researcher's publications are cited by others in their writings. In less direct ways, the researcher can be rated by the number and quality of the graduate students he attracts and the ease with which his research support is renewed.

Concerning the impact of research on the overall university program, the effect may be felt in many areas and to varying extents depending upon the project and the circumstances involved. It may have a significant effect on fund raising—either through alumni giving, through industrial subscriptions, or through foundation grants. It will certainly play a large part in attracting good faculty and good students to the university as a whole.

A factor defining quantitatively the effectiveness of research in the university complex would be extremely handy to have available when decisions concerning the future of specific graduate programs need to be made. The difficulties of arriving at a universal figure of merit are obvious due to the nature of the variables involved, and to the best of the author's knowledge none has been found. Furthermore, it may be folly to suggest that one might exist, since this would be in a certain sense tantamount to establishing a universal standard for excellence.

On the other hand, certain approximations to the universal criterion can be postulated. One such factor has been called the *Direct Cost Return Factor* (DCRF). It is useful in evaluating graduate programs in different areas from the standpoint of comparative direct incremental costs when a high degree of cost sharing is involved. The factor can be expressed as

$$\text{DCRF} = \frac{D_a + I_a + \Sigma T}{D_a + D_u}$$

where D_a = Total direct costs charged to agency as cost sharing
I_a = Indirect cost (overhead) charged to agency
ΣT = Sum of all other determinable income items, prorated and credited to program
D_u = Total direct costs charged to university

A DCRF of unity represents the situation where the income to the university for a given project or program just balances the out-of-pocket additional direct costs incurred because the project or program is undertaken. It must be recognized that this does not represent a break-even point in the true sense. It can, however, be used as a basis for comparison for program-planning purposes.

CHANGING PATTERNS IN RESEARCH ADMINISTRATION

Research administration follows patterns controlled by changing conditions in the external world of politics [7]. The effective conduct of research depends upon timely response to these changing patterns. The more important of these trends will be discussed below.

The part played by Congress is basic to the existence of organized research. Out of its annual budgetary deliberations come statements of principles relative to appropriations. These statements often have as great an effect on the conduct of the research program as do the scientific and technological considerations. For example, the enabling legislation in many instances has included requirements aimed toward a more uniform geographical distribution of funds rather than usefulness of research results and productivity.

Until the 1940s, support for organized research in the university was sparse. In the early fifties, the trend swung towards project support and the support of individuals. Now, in the late sixties, the trend has reversed and departmental grants, institutional programs to develop excellence, block grants, etc., are gaining popularity.

Trends Away from Project Support Four of the more important programs providing institutional support are the NSF's University Science Development Program and its Departmental Science Program; the DOD's THEMIS Program; and the NIH's Health Sciences Advancement Award Program. The NSF's programs provide three-year support in amounts up to \$6,000,000 and \$600,000, respectively. Both are aimed toward the development of excellence in graduate study and research where its promise already exists. The THEMIS Program is scaled toward the university not yet very active in research related to DOD's fields of interest and provides awards of about

$250,000 per year. The Health Sciences Advancement Award Program is limited to schools that have reached a minimum level and show great promise of attaining a higher level of achievement in health sciences activities. Grants are nonrenewable, for no longer than a five-year period, and generally in the range of $1 to $3 million.

One way in which institutional programs are realized is through interdisciplinary projects involving several different departments within the university. The THEMIS Program, for one, encourages this kind of participation. It is a consequence of natural evolution that interdisciplinary programs in many instances have bred new disciplines, as exemplified by the field of biomedical engineering. Project administration of interdisciplinary programs involves added complications over those for a single discipline. New dimensions are added when the research budget requires coordination of more than one departmental budget. What usually results is the establishment of an administrative unit for the interdisciplinary program that reports to the university's central office for research administration.

Just as there is a trend toward interdisciplinary support, there is a growing tendency toward the sharing of facilities and faculties among institutions through the formation of consortia. This may involve the joint ownership of libraries, computer centers, seagoing vessels, etc. This trend is evidenced by recent action by federal agencies where support for major facilities has been requested. In some cases, federal contract centers have been formally established to fulfill this function. Typical examples are the Associated Universities Association, which manages the Argonne National Laboratories, and the Institute for Defense Analyses.

Mention also should be made of the growing importance of the "research initiation grant." As employed by the NSF, this type of grant does not require the depth of review normally accorded the project grant, and it is made only to teaching faculty members who have held the doctorate for not longer than four years. The awards are small, usually not in excess of $20,000, and for a period of two years. Their purpose is to help the young, inexperienced faculty member attain the professional background required for regular grant support.

Step Funding In its usual form, step funding is accomplished through an award sufficient to provide for full support during the first year, two-thirds support during the second year, and one-third support during the third year. If the research is to be continued, the grants for the second and succeeding years are for one year. The money allotted is so budgeted that the one, two-thirds, one-third pattern is reestablished during each of the succeeding years. Thus, should it be necessary to summarily terminate the research, a tapering-off schedule can be worked out which will allow, statistically at least, any doctoral candidates involved to complete their dissertation research. At the present writing, step funding is a standard practice with THEMIS and a growing one with NASA grants.

Cost Sharing The sharing by the university in the total costs incurred under government grants became mandatory by congressional legislation in 1965. While the law itself did not specifically define the minimum acceptable level of cost sharing, statements by the agencies concerned have since established guidelines. Generally the minimum is 5 percent, with some agencies, notably the NSF, expecting more.

Mandatory cost sharing has two important side effects. First, where the university is devoting a significant amount of money to the support of a given research project, it is going to be more critical concerning the overall values involved. In this sense, it will deter the building up of research empires. Second, should there be a sudden cutback in outside support, the impact on the operating budget of the institution is softened.

In the case of the NSF, the established practice is to require cost sharing to the extent of one-half of the academic-year salaries for all faculty involved. Full reimbursement for summer salaries for time worked is allowed provided the equivalent of a one-month vacation is excluded. While this is the formally defined practice, in actuality several of the divisions within NSF have more stringent ground rules. In these cases, the final extent of cost sharing in a particular instance is a matter of negotiation. It is not unusual that cost sharing to the extent of full academic-year salaries for the professorial staff is the result.

Grant Administration Grant administration is being affected in several ways by the changing policies of Congress and the support agencies. There has been a tendency towards tightening up on administrative procedures. In the case of the NIH a voluminous document* has been issued to provide administrative guidance.

Until recently, grantees, as opposed to contractors, were denied access to surplus property through the excess personal property program of the federal government. The NSF and HEW have now established procedures whereby requisitions for such equipment and facilities can be processed.

In the beginning days of organized research, most of its support was provided by the federal government. Recent actions by Congress have stressed the need for cost sharing, matching funds from nonfederal sources, etc. Some states are seriously considering the funding of university research from their own funds. A good example is the state of Connecticut, which established the Connecticut Research Commission in 1965. Currently funded at $2,500,000 for the biennial period, the commission acts much like NSF in its operations.

Some new federal programs, for example NSF's Sea Grant Program, require that a significant fraction of the funding come from nonfederal sources. Where this funding is obtained locally, say through the state or municipality, many of the arguments for a uniform geographical distribution of scientific activities can be dispelled. It is true, of course, that there is a strong selling job regarding the importance of research to society to be done before generous appropriations can be expected from these new sources. Inherent is the careful assessment of local and regional economic and social needs versus those of national and international significance. A recent study [8] by Sapolsky describes the present status of programs designed to stimulate state and municipal participation in scientific endeavors.

Today the major emphasis in the day-to-day activities of the university office of research administration is being placed on management activities, with an eye to improving the status of the office on the campus. The reasons are:

1. The rapid expansion of the number of support sources, each with its own distinctive set of operating rules and reporting requirements
2. The growing popularity of interdisciplinary and interinstitutional programs
3. The greater involvement of the teacher-researcher in the program
4. The maturing of those campus systems affecting faculty rights and privileges such as tenure, sabbatical leaves, etc.
5. The greater involvement of graduate students with the attendant problems of meshing the requirements of their doctoral theses with the requirements of the research sponsor

Classified Research At the time of this writing, there is a definite trend toward a reduction in the amount of classified research appropriately performed by a university. The reasons pro and con are many [9], with most of the arguments against its continuation based upon emotional reaction to the war in southeast Asia. There seems to be general agreement, however, that a limited amount of classified research can offer advantages that outweigh the disadvantages as far as the faculty is concerned. It makes possible a better informed faculty and provides a testing ground from which the ap-

* *Grants for Research Projects, Guide to Operating Procedures,* U.S. Public Health Service.

plied scientists and engineers can gain needed experience. This is all in addition to the valuable service provided in maintaining the welfare and security of the country and its people.

Deescalation of Support Over the past decade, research support has been increasing at a rate of approximately 17 percent per year. This is during a period when the gross national product has been following a trend of about half this value. It now appears that research support will begin to decrease if the present attitude on the part of Congress should persist.

Should this be so, a general belt-tightening across the board will be sought, with the beneficial results that programs of marginal value will be eliminated and efficiency will be improved. There is danger, however, that research of a basic nature may be stopped and that this will have deleterious effects on future applied research and development.

LIMITATIONS, PITFALLS, AND HAZARDS

Fortunately, in recent years there has been no cutback of serious consequence in federal support of research. The possibility of one happening exists, however, and several times minor cutbacks have been experienced. Notable among these was one which took place at the close of the Korean conflict and just prior to the onset of the space race. The prudent administration will be prepared to cope with the exigencies of such a cutback should one occur.

The best hedge against large-scale cutbacks is careful and cautious program planning at the departmental and institutional level. Graduate programs at the project level should match the university's overall objectives. Any necessary budget adjustments will then be more palatable.

By keeping that fraction of faculty time which is budgeted against contract and grant funds at a low figure, the impact of a cutback on the financial condition of the institution can be lessened. Obviously, this approach can be justified only where the subject of the research is closely related to the academic objectives of the university, since the academic program will probably be making up the difference between the budgeted fraction for faculty time and the actual fraction representing time released for research purposes. It follows that hardware- or service-oriented programs are to be avoided in such circumstances, because a sudden termination involves the awkward consequences of requiring the sudden dismissal of the supporting technical staff along with the cancellation of equipment orders.

Caution must be exercised in filling faculty positions where dependence is placed upon outside support for research. New positions and vacancies should be reserved for the able teacher-researcher for whom it can be expected that replacement support will be readily available.

Required cost sharing has become a way of life with sponsored research. Without it, the university administrator could with impunity expand the volume of supported research on the campus. With it, however, there is the need to carefully weigh the academic advantages of each acquisition of a research program and to compare the result with the net cost of the program. In this respect, cost sharing can be credited with adding a healthy aspect to the process of university planning and development.

In some instances the requirement for cost sharing is satisfied through the acceptance of less than the audited overhead rate. Care should be taken, however, that this is not overdone since the integrity of the financial structure of the entire university is imperilled if this practice is extended to include service-oriented programs of little academic value.

Judgments based on incremental cost arguments are sometimes justified where programs of high academic merit are concerned; however, there is an easily recognized fallacy in carrying the notion too far. A thoughtful long-range analysis covering the tangible and intangible elements involved should be made before reaching a final decision in such instances.

In considering whether or not a new program should be undertaken, attention should be given to the prospects for continued support. Factors involved include the probable future availability of the proposed research staff, the long-range program of the sponsor, the nature of the problem, the evolution of the field in which the problem falls, and the political climate of the times.

The university will eventually develop some means for providing seed money to support the initial investigations of experienced researchers in new areas or of the novice in his beginnings. The mechanism employed may take many forms, as was discussed earlier in this chapter; however, regardless of the type, it should not be a "prize-paper" or "popularity" contest judged by university administrators. It should involve the same degrees of discipline regarding research progress reporting and financial accountability as are required of sponsored research.

A recent study * attempted to identify the major problems faced by the universities as seen by their research administrators. Some of the results of the survey are tabulated below:

Insufficient research space and/or equipment	39%
Finding qualified research manpower	30
Obtaining adequate funding	28
Lack of continuity in funding	15
Adjusting to new federal cost-sharing policy	13
Relationships between research and teaching	12
Inadequate cost reimbursement	7
Lack of uniformity in federal agency policies	7
Red tape in government contract work	6
Allowing staff time for research	5
Imbalances in research support	3
Excessive time for proposal preparation	3
Other problem areas	14

The percentages indicate the number of times in a total of 164 returns that the given problem area was cited in the survey.

APPENDIX: ON PREVENTING CONFLICTS OF INTEREST IN GOVERNMENT-SPONSORED RESEARCH AT UNIVERSITIES [10]

The following is a joint statement prepared by the Council of the American Association of University Professors and the American Council on Education.

The increasingly necessary and complex relationships among universities, Government, and industry call for more intensive attention to standards of procedure and conduct in Government-sponsored research. The clarification and application of such standards must be designed to serve the purposes and needs of the projects and the public interest involved in them and to protect the integrity of the cooperating institutions as agencies of higher education.

The Government and institutions of higher education, as the contracting parties, have an obligation to see that adequate standards and procedures are developed and applied;

* *Industrial Research*, p. 34, April, 1966.

to inform one another of their respective requirements; and to assure that all individuals participating in their respective behalfs are informed of and apply the standards and procedures that are so developed.

Consulting relationships between university staff members and industry serve the interests of research and education in the university. Likewise, the transfer of technical knowledge and skill from the university to industry contributes to technological advance. Such relationships are desirable, but certain potential hazards should be recognized.

A. CONFLICT SITUATIONS

1. *Favoring of outside interests.* When a university staff member (administrator, faculty member, professional staff member, or employee) undertaking or engaging in Government-sponsored work has a significant financial interest in, or a consulting arrangement with, a private business concern, it is important to avoid actual or apparent conflicts of interest between his Government-sponsored university research obligations and his outside interests and other obligations. Situations in or from which conflicts of interest may arise are the:

a. Undertaking or orientation of the staff member's university research to serve the research or other needs of the private firm without disclosure of such undertaking or orientation to the university and to the sponsoring agency;

b. Purchase of major equipment, instruments, materials, or other items for university research from the private firm in which the staff member has the interest without disclosure of such interest;

c. Transmission to the private firm or other use for personal gain of Government-sponsored work products, results, materials, records, or information that are not made generally available. (This would not necessarily preclude appropriate licensing arrangements for inventions, or consulting on the basis of Government-sponsored research results where there is significant additional work by the staff member independent of his Government-sponsored research);

d. Use for personal gain or other unauthorized use of privileged information acquired in connection with the staff member's Government-sponsored activities. (The term "privileged information" includes, but is not limited to, medical, personnel, or security records of individuals; anticipated material requirements or price actions; possible new sites for Government operations; and knowledge of forthcoming programs or of selection of contractors or subcontractors in advance of official announcements);

e. Negotiation or influence upon the negotiation of contracts relating to the staff members' Government-sponsored research between the university and private organizations with which he has consulting or other significant relationships;

f. Acceptance of gratuities or special favors from private organizations with which the university does or may conduct business in connection with a Government-sponsored research project, or extension of gratuities or special favors to employees of the sponsoring Government agency, under circumstances which might reasonably be interpreted as an attempt to influence the recipients in the conduct of their duties.

2. *Distribution of effort.* There are competing demands on the energies of a faculty member (for example, research, teaching, committee work, outside consulting). The way in which he divides his effort among these various functions does not raise ethical questions unless the Government agency supporting his research is misled in its understanding of the amount of intellectual effort he is actually devoting to the research in question. A system of precise time accounting is incompatible with the inherent character of the work of a faculty member, since the various functions he performs are closely interrelated and do not conform to any meaningful division of a standard work week. On the other hand, if the research agreement contemplates that a staff member will devote a certain fraction of his effort to the Government-sponsored research, or he agrees to assume responsibility in relation to such research, a demonstrable relationship between the indicated effort or responsibility and the actual extent of his involvement is to be expected. Each university, therefore, should—through joint consultation of administration and faculty—develop procedures to assure that proposals are responsibly made and complied with.

3. *Consulting for Government agencies or their contractors.* When the staff member engaged in Government-sponsored research also serves as a consultant to a Federal agency, his conduct is subject to the provisions of the Conflict of Interest Statutes (18 U.S.C. 202–209 as amended) and the President's memorandum of May 2, 1963, *Preventing Conflicts of Interest on the Part of Special Government Employees.* When he consults for one or more Government contractors, or prospective contractors, in the same technical field as his research project, care must be taken to avoid giving advice that may be of questionable objectivity because of its possible bearing on his other interests. In undertaking and performing consulting services, he should make full disclosure of such interests to the university and to the contractor insofar as they may appear to relate to the work at the university or for the contractor. Conflict of interest problems could arise, for example, in the participation of a staff member of the university in an evaluation for the Government agency or its contractor of some technical aspect of the work of another organization with which he has a consulting or employment relationship or a significant financial interest, or in an evaluation of a competitor to such other organization.

B. UNIVERSITY RESPONSIBILITY

Each university participating in Government-sponsored research should make known to the sponsoring Government agencies:

1. The steps it is taking to assure an understanding on the part of the university administration and staff members of the possible conflicts of interest or other problems that may develop in the foregoing types of situations, and

2. The organizational and administrative actions it has taken or is taking to avoid such problems, including:

a. Accounting procedures to be used to assure that Government funds are expended for the purposes for which they have been provided, and that all services which are required in return for these funds are supplied;

b. Procedures that enable it to be aware of the outside professional work of staff members participating in Government-sponsored research, if such outside work relates in any way to the Government-sponsored research;

c. The formulation of standards to guide the individual university staff members in governing their conduct in relation to outside interests that might raise questions of conflicts of interest; and

d. The provision within the university of an informed source of advice and guidance to its staff members for advance consultation on questions they wish to raise concerning the problems that may or do develop as a result of their outside financial or consulting interests, as they relate to their participation in Government-sponsored university research. The university may wish to discuss such problems with the contracting officer or other appropriate Government official in those cases that appear to raise questions regarding conflicts of interest.

The above process of disclosure and consultation is the obligation assumed by the university when it accepts Government funds for research. The process must, of course, be carried out in a manner that does not infringe on the legitimate freedoms and flexibility of action of the university and its staff members that have traditionally characterized a university. It is desirable that standards and procedures of the kind discussed be formulated and administered by members of the university community themselves, through their joint initiative and responsibility, for it is they who are the best judges of the conditions which can most effectively stimulate the search for knowledge and preserve the requirements of academic freedom. Experience indicates that such standards and procedures should be developed and specified by joint administrative-faculty action.

SELECTED REFERENCES AND BIBLIOGRAPHY

1. *Armed Services Procurement Regulations* (ASPR), available from Superintendent of Documents, U.S. Government Printing Office, Washington, D.C. 20402.
2. Hill, K., et al.: *The Management of Scientists,* Beacon Press, Boston, 1964, pp. 87–99.

3. *National Patterns of R & D Resources, 1953–1968,* National Science Foundation bulletin no. 67–7.
4. *Grant Data Quarterly, Selected Overview of Grant Support,* in four parts, available from Academic Media, Inc., 10835 Santa Monica Boulevard, Los Angeles, Calif. 90025.
5. Allen, E. M.: "Why Are Research Grant Applications Disapproved?" *Science,* vol. 132, no. 3439, pp. 1532–1534, Nov. 25, 1960.
6. *Industrial Research,* a monthly controlled-circulation magazine published by Industrial Research Inc., Beverly Shores, Ind. The April issues for the years 1963–1968 have been primarily concerned with university research. They provide much useful supplementary information pertinent to this chapter.
7. Roback, Herbert: "Congress and the Science Budget," *Science,* vol. 160, no. 3831, pp. 964–971, May 31, 1968.
8. Sapolsky, Harvey M.: "Science Advice for State and Local Government," *Science,* vol. 160, no. 3825, pp. 280–284, April 19, 1968.
9. Strickland, S., and T. Vallance: "Classified Research: To Be or Not to Be Involved?" *Educational Record,* pp. 224–235, Summer, 1967.
10. Strickland, Stephen: *Sponsored Research in American Universities and Colleges,* American Council on Education, 1968.

Chapter 12

Professional Education

EVERETT WALTERS

Senior Vice-president and Dean of Faculties, Boston University, Boston, Massachusetts

In reviewing its professional degree programs as well as in contemplating new ones, the university administration should answer the following questions:

1. Has institution determined genuine need for existing or proposed program?
2. Has long-range program budget been developed, including faculty costs, fellowship costs if graduate programs, new facilities' costs, and so forth?
3. Has proper consideration been given to competitive factors involved in entering new programs?
4. If program is predominantly undergraduate, can it compete in quality with programs which offer both undergraduate and graduate courses in a particular field?
5. Can an adequate faculty be obtained for a new professional program such as dentistry, pharmacy, nursing, or law?
6. Does the college have specialized faculty to provide professional education and meet standards of accrediting agencies?

7. Can accreditation and licensing requirements be met? And how met during initial period of organization of program?

As an aid in helping to answer these questions and others like them, this chapter has been prepared.

The preparation of men and women for practice of the various professions has increasingly become a major feature of higher education in the United States. What for many years had been learned by self-education or apprenticeship has now become almost entirely formalized in schools and colleges of the universities. This development has constituted recognition of the fact that many of the professions possess a body of knowledge which can be applied to the uses of man by an educated group of practitioners.

Because of the difficulty of determining which occupations (or vocations) may be properly designated as professions, this chapter attempts to deal only with those whose training is part of the university or is closely related. Not included are the officers of the military services, the foreign service, or students in independent schools such as music conservatories or art institutes. The preparation of scientists, social scientists, humanists, and others who obtain the major part of their specialized education in the graduate schools of the universities and are awarded master's and doctoral degrees (Ph.D., Ed.D., etc.) is discussed at length in another chapter.

In the interest of simplification, this chapter will set forth, first, a discussion of the undergraduate or first professional degree and, second, professional education at the graduate level.

THE RISE OF PROFESSIONAL EDUCATION

The colleges of the colonial and post-Revolutionary periods to some extent provided professional education inasmuch as one of their chief purposes was to prepare clergymen. Typical of these were Harvard, Yale, and William and Mary. For the early part of the nineteenth century most colleges continued, along with the preparation of teachers, to train "lettered gentlemen." Although most lawyers and doctors during the early years of the republic were trained by the apprenticeship method, there were a few university law schools: the University of Maryland (founded in 1816), Harvard (1817), Yale (1824), and Virginia (1826). So too there were a few schools of medicine, chiefly at King's College, later Columbia (1772), and Harvard (1782). There were a number of proprietary schools for professional preparation.

In the post-Civil War years there was a steady increase in the number of professional schools, namely, proprietary, independent (nonprofit), and university related. The latter type especially grew rapidly as a result of the land-grant influence, the founding of institutes of technology, the accumulation of technical knowledge which demanded organization, and the requirements of an expanding industrial society. At the state universities, particularly the Midwestern and Western land-grant institutions, courses in engineering, education, agriculture, and other subjects were greatly increased in numbers and in time became so administratively complex as to require organization as schools or colleges. Other universities and colleges, private and public, followed these developments to varying extents. This university movement tended to blur the traditional distinction between profession and vocation and also between the older learned professions and the new. For years it had been popular to speak of the vocations of theology, law, and medicine as the "learned professions," now others began to lay claim to this designation.

Unfortunately, the rapid evolution of education for the professions was accompanied by low standards. Teachers were usually poorly prepared or incompetent while buildings and facilities were maintained in wretched condition. Since many institutions were operated for profit or with only minimal support from state funds, almost every applicant for admission was accepted and few students were dismissed for academic failure.

To correct these deficiencies and to upgrade the level of instruction in the late nineteenth century and the early twentieth century, several developments occurred. First, the schools formed associations to set standards and refused to admit to membership those schools whose practices did not conform to these standards. Association publications and meetings did much to raise and maintain professional educational standards. In recent years every field of professional education has come to have a national association.

Second, to ensure the standards of these professional schools, accreditation was undertaken. The accrediting agency was either a division of the professional association or an independent organization. In the former instance, a council or board is formed as the accrediting arm. In engineering education, for example, there is the Engineers' Council for Professional Development; and in dental education there is the Council on Dental Education of the American Dental Association.

A third means of raising standards was the professionwide study or survey. Most famous was the report of Dr. Abraham Flexner on medical education in the United States and Canada made in 1910 for the Carnegie Foundation for the Advancement of Teaching. Dr. Flexner's survey revealed so many shocking conditions and practices in a number of medical schools that many of them were forced to close their doors and others drastically reformed their entire practices and procedures.

PROGRAMS IN PROFESSIONAL EDUCATION

In general, each profession has developed its own patterns for professional education. Usually the accrediting council or board of the professional association established minimal standards such as admissions requirements, the balance between science and other courses, and the number of clinic hours with patients. Since there is considerable latitude, variations do exist, especially among the powerful universities, which demand much higher standards. Furthermore, standards of performance and level of professional development frequently change. There is, for example, a growing stress on requiring additional courses in the liberal arts and sciences (general education) before embarking on the professional course sequences. Also, in the allied health professions including nursing, there has developed a growing requirement for extensive course preparation in the basic life sciences.

No standard plan exists for all professional education, although there have been definable trends. Thus, most plans are now expanded to incorporate more preprofessional courses as well as additional professional courses. In optometry, for example, the one year preoptometry requirement has been extended to two and additional professional courses have been added. Only a few law and medical schools accept applicants without bachelor's degrees; decades ago almost every law school and medical school accepted students with three years of undergraduate preparation and without degrees. In the latter instance, some universities would grant the bachelor's degree after one year of professional school education.

Perhaps the clearest definable direction is that professional education will soon call for a bachelor's degree as a basic requirement for admission and that the professional program will be a one- or two-year master's somewhat like the present M.B.A. or M.S.W.

The basic plans for professional programs leading to the first professional degree are listed in Table 1. Sources of information for curricula and degree requirements may be obtained from the professional schools themselves, the accrediting agency of the professional association, or from one of the volumes listed in the bibliography of this article.

TABLE 1 Summary of Education Program Leading to the First Professional Degree [a]

Professional field	Years of liberal arts and sciences (General education)	Years of professional curriculum	Most commonly awarded first professional degree [b]
Four-year Programs			
Agriculture	...	4	Bachelor of Science in Agriculture
Business Administration	2	2	Bachelor of Science in Business Administration or Bachelor of Business Administration
Education	2	2	Bachelor of Science in Education
Engineering [c]	1 to 1½	3 to 2½	Bachelor of Science in Civil Engineering, in Electrical Engineering, etc.
Fine Arts	...	4	Bachelor of Fine Arts
Forestry	...	4	Bachelor of Science in Forestry
Home Economics	...	4	Bachelor of Science in Home Economics
Journalism	2	2	Bachelor of Arts (or Science) in Journalism
Landscape Architecture	...	4	Bachelor of Landscape Architecture
Music	...	4	Bachelor of Music
Nursing	1 to 1½	3 to 2½	Bachelor of Science in Nursing
Occupational Therapy	...	4	Bachelor of Science in Occupational Therapy
Physical Therapy	...	4	Bachelor of Science in Physical Therapy
Five-year Programs			
Architecture	1 to 1½	4 to 3½	Bachelor of Architecture
Pharmacy [d]	2	3	Bachelor of Science in Pharmacy
Library Science	4	1	Master of Library Science
Public Health	4	1	Master of Public Health
Six-year Programs			
Dentistry	2	4	Doctor of Dental Surgery or Doctor of Dental Medicine
Hospital Administration	4	2	Master of Hospital Administration
Law	3	3	Bachelor of Law or Doctor of Jurisprudence
Optometry	2	4	Doctor of Optometry
Pharmacy	2	2	Doctor of Pharmacy
Social Work [e]	4	2	Master of Social Work
Veterinary Medicine	2	4	Doctor of Veterinary Medicine
Seven-year Programs			
Medicine [f]	3	4	Doctor of Medicine
Theology [g]	4	3	Bachelor of Divinity

[a] Based on Walter C. Eells and Harold A. Haswell, *Academic Degrees,* U.S. Office of Education, 1960.

[b] Certain variations.

[c] Professional engineering education is undergoing drastic changes. See *Goals of Engineering Education: Final Report of the Goals Committee,* American Society for Engineering Education, January, 1968.

PROFESSIONAL EDUCATION AT THE GRADUATE LEVEL

During the past 40 years there has been a steady growth of graduate education in the professional fields. This has developed because of the demand for research persons, teachers, and specialists in the professions as well as a desire to heighten the prestige of the individual profession and to give it individuality. In education, the Doctor of Education (Ed.D.) was first launched at the Harvard Graduate School of Education in 1922 and was quickly copied at universities across the nation. In business, the Doctor of Business Administration (D.B.A.) was inaugurated in 1953 at Harvard Business School. And dozens of master's degrees were similarly established, some of them designated as the Master of Education (M.Ed.) and Master of Dental Science (M.D.Sc.). At some institutions these master's degrees are identical to the first professional degree.

Programs leading to master's degrees normally demand from one to three years of advanced course work and independent study and research. The long-established requirement for a thesis has now been generally abandoned. In a number of fields such as education, nursing, and engineering, master's degrees are popular because they reward the holder with salary increments and an appreciable amount of professional-academic prestige. These degrees are usually especially designated (i.e., "professional master's"), as the M.Ed. and M.D.Sc., mentioned above.

The constant upgrading of professional standards and the desire of the practitioners to keep abreast of developments in their field and to seek advancement have also led to a demand for recognition of graduate work that goes beyond the master's degree but not so far as a doctorate. Consequently, many universities now offer the Certificate of Advanced Graduate Study (C.A.G.S.). To acquire the C.A.G.S., a candidate must hold a master's degree and be formally accepted to pursue a planned program of study consisting usually of not less than 30 semester credits beyond the master's degree.

At the doctoral level, graduate professional degrees are also often specifically designated, such as the Doctor of Public Administration, the Doctor of Sacred Theology, the Doctor of Social Work, and the Doctor of Musical Arts. In other instances, the doctoral degree is the Ph.D. regardless of the specific professional field. Although institutional tradition and practice have dictated the choice of degree, the usual mark of differentiation is that in the Ph.D. emphasis is upon research. In truth, however, the distinction between the Ph.D. and the Ed.D. in the field of education is not entirely clear.

At universities where all graduate education is administered by a universitywide graduate school, professional graduate study is under the control and supervision of that school. Where it is not, it is under the professional school. At Ohio State University, for example, only the Ph.D. is given for both professional and research study and is handled administratively by the Graduate School; at Indiana University the Ed.D. and the D.B.A. are administered by the School of Education and the School of Business, respectively. In both instances, instruction is conducted by the departments of the professional schools, although students are usually permitted and encouraged to enroll in courses outside their particular professional school. Admis-

---

[d] Colleges of pharmacy vary in the organization of their curricula: some institutions require five years on an integrated program while others require one or two years of preprofessional education prior to admission.

[e] Certain universities award a Bachelor of Arts degree with a major in social work.

[f] Preprofessional work varies from two to four years of undergraduate work; preference is given to applicants with four and with a bachelor's degree. The normal professional program is four years, but there are special six-year combined undergraduate-professional programs as at Northwestern University and Boston University. For a convenient summary, see Allan M. Cartter (ed.), *American Universities and Colleges*, American Council on Education, Washington, D.C., 1964, pp. 111–117.

[g] The Master of Theology has recently been accepted as a first professional degree. There are no accrediting agencies for Catholic seminaries or rabbinical seminaries.

sions, degree requirements, and standards of performance are established by either the graduate school or by the professional school as the case may be.

In today's dynamic situation in the professions, in order to keep up with the growth of knowledge, practitioners increasingly require postdoctoral courses of study. Medical schools, for example, cognizant of the need for acquainting doctors with the latest developments in medicine, now offer regular refresher courses. Some foundations and government programs have established "Career Investigator" awards to support competent people while they conduct research. Though professional schools up to now, exclusive of those in the medical sciences, have offered little postdoctoral work, as our knowledge increases and our technology grows more complex they will undoubtedly be called upon to offer more through special programs, refresher courses, and research fellowships.

INTERDISCIPLINARY PROGRAMS

More than other schools, the professional schools are confronted by two compelling but antithetical needs: (1) the need for increasing specialization and fragmentation of the professions into narrower fields; and (2) the consequent necessity to achieve integration of different special knowledge. They have attempted to solve the dilemma through a number of means, the most common being new methods of instruction. Team teaching in medical, nursing, and social work schools brings to the student a battery of experts attacking a central problem. For example, the School of Medicine at Case Western Reserve University has reorganized its curriculum so that the student (working with many different specialists at the same time) studies organ systems rather than disciplines. Increasing reliance on case, problems, project, research, or clinical methods is further evidence of the need professional educators feel for greater integration of the disciplines.

The problem, however, is far from being solved. Most of the professional schools still do little to integrate their specialties with other disciplines. The principal difficulty is, of course, the time available for producing a skilled practitioner, and the answer to the need for a concerted approach to human problems which overlap the disciplines seems to lie in the formation of special institutes such as the Law-Medicine Institute of Boston University, which offers a broad interdisciplinary program of training research and consultation, or similar boards or clinics where specialists may meet to mount a common attack on all the ramifications of a problem or issue.

INTERINSTITUTIONAL COOPERATION

The high cost of technology's hardware and the shortage (and cost) of competent teachers and researchers seem to point the way toward more cooperation among the professional schools. Already, as at the Massachusetts Institute of Technology, it is common practice for a number of New England schools to "plug in" to another school's computer or for more than one school to use the part-time services of a specialist. Increasingly, arrangements are made between schools to enable students to take courses in institutions other than their own; this is especially true in narrow or exotic specialties. Schools are also beginning to pool their talents in the form of special institutes or boards which are designed to cope with special problems that overlap different professions and which, while performing a teaching and research function, also offer a service to the community.

Interinstitutional cooperation has already been established on geographical bases. In the southeastern part of the United States, the Southern Regional Education Board is an effective regional organization which saves state funds and human effort by preventing duplication of professional degree programs. A similar organization is the Western Interstate Commission for Higher Education. Through WICHE, as this association is familiarly known, a qualified University of Montana graduate, seeking to obtain a law degree, attends the University of Colorado Law School and pays only the tuition required of him at Montana. Boards of regents in several states are now planning studies of cooperation among colleges and universities both public and private.

Despite the administrative difficulties involved, it is imperative for university officers to explore constantly the benefits of interinstitutional cooperation among professional schools on a local, state, or regional basis.

LICENSING REQUIREMENTS

In those professions which involve the health or safety of the public, graduates must successfully undergo examinations for licensing before being permitted to practice. The examining and licensing is done by the states, although they are usually guided and coordinated in their efforts by the national professional and accrediting associations (see Table 2 for a list of these accrediting agencies).

The practice of dentistry, law, nursing, optometry, physical therapy, or veterinary medicine requires state examination after graduation from an approved school. In some professions, such as architecture, landscape architecture, medicine, and pharmacy, a student must also serve a period of internship after his formal schooling before he can be accepted as a candidate for state examination. Teaching in the public schools requires "certification" rather than examination and licensing; the certification is based upon the candidate's completion of certain courses in his schooling. In engineering one may be licensed, but this is not obligatory for the practice of the profession.

The tendency is to increase the number of professions which are so regulated by state law and licensing procedures; for example, a number of states have followed New York in requiring that clinical psychologists pass an examination and be licensed to practice. There is, moreover, increasing pressure from within occupational or trade associations for state licensing as these occupations seek higher standards and greater prestige; the intensive efforts of morticians is a case in point. If the past is any indication of the future, as licensing requirements are extended so as to, in effect, create new professions, the universities and professional schools will respond by offering programs to satisfy the state requirements.

TABLE 2 Professional Accrediting Associations *

Architecture	National Architectural Accrediting Board 521 18th Street, N.W. Washington, D.C.
Art	Committee on Admissions and Accreditations National Association of Schools of Arts 50 Astor Place New York, N.Y.
Business Administration	American Association of Collegiate Schools of Business 101 North Skinker Road Station 24 St. Louis, Mo.
Dentistry	Council on Dental Education American Dental Association 222 East Superior Street Chicago, Ill.
Education	National Council for Accreditation of Teacher Education Mills Building Washington, D.C.

* Includes only those recognized by the National Commission on Accrediting. Some professional fields, such as agriculture and home economics, have professional associations but do not accredit schools.

Engineering	Education and Accreditation Committee Engineers' Council for Professional Development 345 East 47th Street New York, N.Y.
Forestry	Society of American Foresters Mills Building Washington, D.C.
Journalism	Accrediting Committee American Council on Education for Journalism 215 Fisk Hall Northwestern University Evanston, Ill.
Landscape Architecture	Committee on Education American Society of Landscape Architects 2000 K Street, N.W. Washington, D.C.
Law *	Council of Section of Legal Education and Admissions to the Bar American Bar Association 1155 East 60th Street Chicago, Ill.
Library Science	Committee on Accreditation, American Library Association 50 East Huron Street Chicago, Ill.
Medicine	Council on Medical Education and Hospitals American Medical Association 535 N. Dearborn Street Chicago, Ill.
Music	National Association of Schools of Music Knox College Galesburg, Ill.
Nursing	Department of Baccalaureate and Higher Degree Programs National League for Nursing 10 Columbus Circle New York, N.Y.
Optometry	Council on Optometric Education American Optometric Association 2808 Clark Avenue Cleveland, Ohio
Pharmacy	American Council on Pharmaceutical Education 77 West Washington Street Chicago, Ill.
Public Health	Director of Professional Education American Public Health Association 1790 Broadway New York, N.Y.
Social Work	Council on Social Work Education 345 East 46th Street New York, N.Y.
Theology	American Association of Theological Schools Third National Building Dayton, Ohio
Veterinary Medicine	Director of Professional Relations American Veterinary Medical Association 600 South Michigan Avenue Chicago, Ill.

* While the American Bar Association accredits law schools, the standards for membership in the Association of American Law Schools are more exacting; hence there are accredited law schools which are not members of the latter association.

POLICIES GOVERNING CONDUCT OF PROFESSIONAL EDUCATION

Organization Most professional schools today are semiautonomous or autonomous units within a university. The semiautonomous school is administratively related to a group of similar schools; e.g., schools of medicine, nursing, and public health may be component parts of a medical center—and the dean of that center is generally responsible to a special administrative officer other than the president or vice-president of the university. Autonomy, on the other hand, means that while a school has control of its curriculum, students, and faculty in most matters and has some influence on university policy, its chief administrative officer is responsible directly to the central administration of the university. In this way both freedom and status are achieved.

In either arrangement there are, of course, practical difficulties, especially on matters of public relations and fund raising. A profession by its very nature exerts influence in particular quarters and rightfully seeks recognition and funds on the basis of its own strengths; however, the university must be careful that its central functions and those of the professional schools do not overlap, or that the efforts of a particular school do not weaken or damage those of the university as a whole.

The older professions, especially law and medicine, place considerable emphasis on autonomy; while architecture, nursing, and teaching, which in many schools are organized as departments, place less. The trend, however, in all of the professions is toward autonomy as opposed to independence or semiautonomy. Most accrediting agencies imply or state their preference for autonomy, while several associations, such as the American Association of Collegiate Schools of Business and the Association of American Law Schools, will not admit schools to membership unless they are autonomous.

The faculty of semiautonomous and autonomous schools are generally responsible for determining the curricula, though they are guided by the standards of the accrediting associations. These standards, while precise as to the length of curricula, are general in other respects, indicating, with few exceptions, only the necessary areas or proportions of study. In addition to their role in the governance of the school, faculty in the semiautonomous and autonomous schools also serve on all-university committees and as representatives on such university governing bodies as faculty senates.

More specific information regarding the faculty's role in governance, as well as such information as teaching load and faculty qualifications, can be obtained from the professional accrediting associations.

Financing Although there are no precise or trustworthy figures available, most university administrators consider professional education programs to be among the most expensive. And their cost is increasing steadily. The attempts to elevate faculty salaries to points comparable with those of practitioners, the clinical and demonstration methods of teaching, and the supervision of off-campus internships are some of the reasons for the high costs. On the other hand, professional school administrators, particularly those in law and medicine, argue that the universities are starving them, and that cost accounting procedures would demonstrate that their total services to a university actually make their schools far less expensive than they appear to be.

Professional schools have raised notable amounts of money themselves from private philanthropy and public revenues, but their costs continue to rise. Their future would seem to depend upon funds drawn from the widest possible base, and that base will probably continue to be the federal government. As Algo D. Henderson points out, despite the generosity of private sources, in a recent year the percentage of the total income received by all institutions from private philanthropy was 6.45 while the amount from student fees has been 55 percent for private and 18 percent for public institutions.[1]

[1] Algo D. Henderson, *Policies and Practices in Higher Education*, Harper & Row, Publishers, Incorporated, New York, 1960, p. 287.

In view of the increasing importance of federal grants as a source of funds, professional schools should be careful that they do not allow their programs to be unduly affected without sufficient planning. Growth through grant-funded new programs is tempting, but the professional administrator should be aware that such grants rarely pay the total cost to the university of such programs, and if the grant is suspended or discontinued, the university might find it much more difficult to phase out the program than it was to begin it. Rapid growth and proliferation through grants can damage a school or an entire university. Graduate programs, in particular, are expensive, usually requiring additional special facilities, fellowships, and additional high-salaried faculty.

It is therefore essential that the university devise a detailed plan for dealing with grant requests, especially when they involve new programs. Such requests should be carefully considered by a committee consisting of the chief academic officer, the chief business officer, and the chief planning officer of the university. And, of course, there should be a constant emphasis on planning both within the professional school and the university as a whole, in order that available funds do not become the tail that wags the dog.

PROFESSIONAL STANDARDS AND ETHICS

A concern with ethics, second only to the necessary skills of a profession, has evolved because the trust of the public is essential to practice and because historically professional figures have seen themselves as "gentlemen," with the ideals of "noblesse oblige," of service, and of dedication.[2] Most professions have developed codes of ethics designed to protect the practitioner, the profession, and the public.

Most professional schools are concerned with teaching professional ethics to their students, and in some institutions they are now required to take formal courses in ethics in the school or college of liberal arts. Not only do methods differ among the professions, but the degree of emphasis varies with the profession. William J. McGlothlin makes a useful distinction in this respect between what he calls the "facilitating" professions—architecture, business administration, engineering, and veterinary medicine—and the "helping" professions—law, medicine, nursing, psychology, social work, and teaching.[3] The former, as one might expect, are less concerned with a specific code of ethics (and business administration has established no code); while the latter have all put a great deal of emphasis upon such codes. However, there is little uniformity in methods of instruction in ethics, and generally the feeling is that schools do not do enough, preferring to concentrate upon professional competence rather than upon ethics, relying too much upon the example of faculty and practitioner, and failing to discharge their responsibilities as the teachers of ethical standards.

PROBLEMS OF THE FUTURE

William J. McGlothlin lists five principal problems with which the professional schools must cope in the future.[4]

1. Growing demands for professional services and shortages of practitioners will require the universities and the professions to attract and recruit more students. There will have to be a reexamination of current standards in some of the professions; e.g., it appears unlikely that the minimum future need for social workers can be met if the profession continues to insist upon a master's degree as the minimum standard for employ-

[2] A. M. Carr-Saunders and P. A. Wilson, *The Professions*, Clarendon Press, Oxford, 1933, p. 422.

[3] William J. McGlothlin, *Patterns of Professional Education*, G. P. Putnam's Sons, New York, 1960, p. 218.

[4] William J. McGlothlin, *The Professional Schools*, The Center for Applied Research in Education, Inc., New York, 1964, pp. 96ff.

ment. Moreover, the professions must recognize, and the universities must assist them to do so, that they will have to reserve their practitioners for the top jobs and to delegate many of their present functions to ancillary personnel.

2. The knowledge explosion, plus the necessity for increased public service, will require a further agglomeration of specialists. The schools will have to recognize that the day of the self-directed, self-employed practitioner is probably coming to an end, and that they consequently will have to allow for this in their training methods.

3. The professional schools will have to join, and even take the lead, in furthering a sense of social responsibility. There will have to be more emphasis on problem solving and public service, so that the professions may become even more the instruments of social progress.

4. The professional schools must place a greater emphasis on education for research and teaching in the professions. Since the schools grew largely out of the demands for trained practitioners, there has been an understandable delay in preparing persons to train the practitioners. More recently schools have recognized the problem, but there is still no conscious effort in some of the professions to train such persons differently. There must also be a recognition of the necessity for upgrading the income and the status of the teachers and researchers to a level comparable with that of the practitioners.

5. The financing of professional education remains a thorny problem. In addition to an unceasing quest for funds, the schools must be inventive in seeking new, less costly, and more efficient methods of instruction and training.

BIBLIOGRAPHY

Blauch, Lloyd (ed.): *Accreditation in Higher Education,* U.S. Government Printing Office, 1959.

———: *Education for the Professions,* U.S. Government Printing Office, 1955.

Brickman, William W.: "Education for the Professions," *School and Society,* vol. 75, pp. 262–267, April 26, 1952.

Cogan, Morris: "Toward a Definition of Profession," *Harvard Educational Review,* vol. 23, pp. 33–50, Winter, 1953.

Dressel, Paul, et al.: *The Liberal Arts as Viewed by Faculty Members in Professional Schools,* Teachers College Press, Columbia University, New York, 1959.

Gilb, Corinne L.: *Hidden Hierarchies,* Harper & Row, Publishers, Incorporated, New York, 1966.

Henry, Nelson B. (ed.): *Education for the Professions,* National Society for the Study of Education, Sixty-first Yearbook, University of Chicago Press, Chicago, 1962.

Lynn, Kenneth S. (ed.): *The Professions in America,* Houghton Mifflin Company, Boston, 1965.

McGlothlin, William J.: *Patterns of Professional Education,* G. P. Putnam's Sons, New York, 1960.

———: *The Professional Schools,* The Center for Applied Research in Education, Inc., New York, 1964.

McGrath, Earl J.: *Liberal Education in the Professions,* Columbia University Press, New York, 1959.

Mosher, Frederick C.: *The Professions, Professional Education and the Public Service,* Center for Research and Development in Higher Education, University of California, Berkeley, 1968.

Symposium on Continuing Education in the Professions, October 25, 1961: *Continuing Education in the Professions,* Department of University Extensions, University of British Columbia, British Columbia, Canada, 1961.

Towle, Charlotte: *The Learner in Education for the Professions,* University of Chicago Press, Chicago, 1954.

The Professions

Architecture

Association of Collegiate Schools of Architecture: *Architecture and the University,* Conference Proceedings, Princeton University, December, 1953, Princeton University Press, Princeton, N.J., 1954.

Bannister, Turpin C. (ed.): *The Architect at Midcentury: Evolution and Achievement,* Reinhold Book Corporation, New York, 1954.

Business Administration

Gordon, Robert A., and James E. Howell: *Higher Education for Business,* Columbia University Press, New York, 1959.

Pierson, Frank C.: *The Education of American Businessmen,* McGraw-Hill Book Company, New York, 1959.

Senkier, Robert J.: *Revising a Business Curriculum: The Columbia Experience,* Columbia University Press, New York, 1961.

Dentistry

Gardner, Alvin F.: "Education of Dental Students," *Journal of Dental Education,* vol. 29, pp. 364–368, December, 1965.

Nedelsky, Leo: "Some Educational Principles in Designing a Dental Curriculum," *Journal of Dental Education,* vol. 25, pp. 213–219, September, 1961.

Education

Beggs, Walter: *The Education of Teachers,* The Center for Applied Research in Education, Inc., New York, 1965.

Engineering

Estrin, H. A. (ed.): *Higher Education in Engineering and Science,* McGraw-Hill Book Company, New York, 1963.

Law

Association of American Law Schools Special Committee on the Law School Administration: *Anatomy of Modern Legal Education,* West Publishing Company, St. Paul, Minn., 1961.

Carvers, D. F.: *Legal Education in the United States,* Harvard Law School, Cambridge, Mass., 1960.

Library Science

Leigh, Robert E. (ed.): *Major Problems in the Education of Librarians,* Columbia University Press, New York, 1954.

Survey of Library Education Programs, Fall 1964, U.S. Office of Education, 1965.

Medicine

Cope, Oliver, and Jerrold Zacharias: *Medical Education Reconsidered,* Report of the Endicott House Summer Study on Medical Education, J. B. Lippincott Company, Philadelphia, 1965.

Deitrick, John E., and Robert Berson: *Medical Schools in the United States at Mid-Century,* McGraw-Hill Book Company, New York, 1953.

Evans, Lester J.: *The Crisis in Medical Education,* The University of Michigan Press, Ann Arbor, Mich., 1964.

Nursing

Davis, Fred (ed.): *The Nursing Profession,* John Wiley & Sons, Inc., New York, 1966.

Guinee, Kathleen K.: *The Aims and Methods of Nursing Education,* The Macmillan Company, New York, 1966.

Social Work

Boehm, Werner W. (director): *Social Work Curriculum Study,* Council on Social Work Education, New York, 1959 (13 volumes).

Hollis, Ernest V., and Alice L. Taylor: *Social Work Education in the United States,* Columbia University Press, New York, 1951.

Theology

Niebuhr, H. Richard, Daniel Williams, and James Gustafson: *The Advancement of Theological Education,* Harper & Brothers, New York, 1957.

Van Dusen, Henry: "Ministers in the Making," *Education for Professional Responsibility,* Report of Proceedings of Inter-professions Conference on Education for Professional Responsibility, Carnegie Press, Carnegie Institute of Technology, Pittsburgh, Pa., 1948, pp. 60–66.

Veterinary Medicine

Blood, Benjamin D.: "The Veterinary Medical Profession in the Americas: Its Educational Program," *Journal of the American Veterinary Medical Association,* vol. 126, no. 938, May, 1955.

Hogan, William A.: "Education in Veterinary Medicine," in Lloyd E. Blauch (ed.), *Education for the Professions,* U.S. Government Printing Office, 1955.

Chapter 13

Graduate Education

EVERETT WALTERS

Senior Vice-president and Dean of Faculties, Boston University, Boston, Massachusetts

Serious administrative consideration must be given to proposals for new graduate programs as well as to existing programs of this high level. The questions to be studied may be summarized as follows:

1. In what fields should the university (or college) offer graduate work?

2. Does the university have the financial and physical resources to conduct graduate programs without impairing the quality of undergraduate programs?

3. Has long-range projection of the university's future been developed to determine future financial obligations resulting from the offering of graduate programs, including extra costs for faculty having lighter teaching loads, recruitment of research-oriented faculty members, fellowships, and added facilities?

4. What faculties or committees will approve the graduate programs and recommend the degrees to be offered?

5. What changes in the academic organization are essential if graduate programs are to be offered?

6. Is there competition with other institutions in the local, state or regional area? Is interinstitutional cooperation possible?

7. How will the requirements of accreditation be met if accreditation is demanded by state or regional educational associations?

Graduate education in the United States may be said to have begun in 1861, when Yale awarded the first Ph.D. degrees. Earlier graduate study consisted of informal work beyond the baccalaureate. The American Ph.D., an adaptation of the doctorate awarded by the great German universities, developed steadily during the latter part of the nineteenth century, especially after the founding of Johns Hopkins University, the University of Chicago, and Clark University primarily as graduate-study institutions. By 1900, the Ph.D. degree had become well established in higher education. In recent years it has been widely imitated in other countries.

The master's degree, older than the doctorate, became transformed in the late nineteenth century from a degree given to a college graduate after three years and on payment of a fee to a degree representing one or two years of advanced study beyond the baccalaureate and culminating in a master's thesis. During the twentieth century it has become a degree awarded for postbaccalaureate work in subject-matter areas ranging from the traditional arts and sciences to such fields as business, agriculture, social work, physical therapy, dentistry, and education.

Since 1950 the graduate schools have become increasingly the nation's source of college teachers, research scholars, and scientists as well as persons trained to seek solutions to the vast array of problems brought about by the complexities of modern society. The demand for persons with graduate training in agriculture, business, industry, government, and social organization has mounted steadily each year. Since research both pure and applied is an integral part of graduate education, graduate faculty and students now perform a considerable portion of the research required by government, business, and industry. Graduate students and their advisers work on such wide-ranging research problems as the control of spacecraft, interpersonal and mass communication, oceanography, linguistics, food chemistry, cytogenetics, and chemical thermodynamics.

A discussion of professional education at the graduate level—e.g., the master's degree in dentistry or the doctorate in business—appears in the preceding chapter.

THE DOCTOR OF PHILOSOPHY

The Ph.D. possesses a unique status in higher education. It is the union card for teachers in virtually every college and university, and it is increasingly required for certain leadership positions in government agencies and the research divisions of industrial and business organizations. Traditionally, the degree has represented a research degree—"the badge of the proved investigator"—although many holders of the degree do not continue research endeavors.

Requirements for the Ph.D. generally include the following: approximately three years of advanced (postbaccalaureate) course work and independent study; facility in one or more foreign languages; the passing of a comprehensive or general examination of the student's subject-matter field; and a dissertation including a defense. Most graduate schools also require at least one academic year in residence, the passing of a qualifying examination at the end of the first year of graduate work, and completion of all degree requirements within a given period of time after admission to candidacy (i.e., the passing of the comprehensive examination). Few students are able to complete the degree in the minimum three-year period, and in recent years the average time taken has been well over five years. In some areas, especially in the humanities and social sciences, a period of more than seven years is not uncommon. Plans to "speed up the Ph.D." have been instituted at many graduate schools; they call for full financial support for the student, full calendar-year registration, credit for graduate courses taken during undergraduate years, and less pretentious dissertations. Many well-established graduate schools recommend that students planning doctoral work should not take a master's degree. Yale no longer awards the master's degree except in terminal degree programs such as the Master of Arts in Teaching (M.A.T.).

THE OTHER DOCTORATES

The so-called "other doctorates" were created during the present century to meet the needs of developing professional schools such as those in education, business, music, fine arts, social work, and pharmacy. Following the general pattern of university development, graduate courses in these professional areas offered first the master's degree and then the doctorate. Typical are the Doctor of Education, Doctor of Business Administration, Doctor of Musical Arts, Doctor of Architecture, Doctor of Engineering, Doctor of Fine Arts, Doctor of Library Science, Doctor of Public Health, Doctor of Religious Education, and Doctor of Nursing Science.

Differences between the Ph.D. and the other doctorates are not always easy to determine. Depending on the individual university, the chief differences are the foreign language requirement, the nature of the research, and the dissertation. A former graduate dean made this observation:

> The research for the Ph.D. has traditionally been pure or fundamental, whereas that in the professional fields has tended to be applied. Theoretically, the student in economics might concern himself with a research problem in economic theory or history, but a candidate for a business degree would investigate the application of economic or management principles to a particular business situation—in one sense, a case study. A student might do research in the history or theory of music for the Ph.D., but if he wished, say, to create a sonata or perform a significant type of music, he would do so in the pattern of the Doctor of Music. Again, in education, the Ph.D. candidate might do his research in the history or philosophy of education, but for the Ed.D. degree he would make a practical study of an educational problem, perhaps by surveying a school system or a national or regional curricular pattern, or would draw up a testing program.[1]

Such distinctions, of course, do not always hold. They are easier to make in the areas of business and music but much more difficult in the field of education.

THE MASTER'S DEGREE

Programs for study at the master's level have steadily grown in popularity. In 1965–1966, universities and a number of colleges awarded 112,195 master's degrees, approximately 14 percent of all degrees awarded that year.

The master's degree is especially popular among teachers in the schools because its

[1] John W. Ashton, "Other Doctorates," in Everett Walters (ed.), *Graduate Education Today*, American Council on Education, Washington, 1965, pp. 65–66.

possession means a salary increment. It is taken either in a subject-matter field, such as chemistry or English, or in education. In the former it is usually the Master of Arts (M.A.) or the Master of Science (M.S.) and in the latter a Master of Education (M.Ed.). The master's degree has also been the highest degree held by many college teachers, and it is usually the M.A. or the M.S.

In recent years there have been attempts to "rehabilitate" the master's degree as a degree for college teachers (rather than the Ph.D.), so that the Ph.D. might be reserved for university teachers and researchers. Several moves to establish a specially designed master's degree, such as the Master of Philosophy (M.Phil.), for four-year and junior college teachers have met with some success.[2] Two other trends toward recognizing the need for specific programs for training college teachers have been the establishment of the Candidacy of Philosophy degree at the University of Michigan and the Master of Philosophy at Yale. Both these programs also attempt to solve the age-old problem of the "A.B.D."s ("All But Dissertation")—that is, those individuals who have satisfied all the requirements for the doctorate except the dissertation. Those institutions which support these degrees maintain that they are satisfactory for teacher preparation because only the research part of the doctorate is lacking.[3] As this writer has pointed out in several articles, such a contention does not appear valid in that the programs in question require nothing specific in the way of preparation for the future teacher.

Another degree, the Doctor of Arts, has been proposed on several occasions for college teachers and has received considerable attention. At this writing no institution has announced work leading to this degree.[4]

ADMINISTRATIVE PATTERNS IN GRADUATE EDUCATION

Graduate education is organized administratively in several patterns. In the older and more traditional institutions, the graduate school or graduate division represents the arts and sciences; professional graduate work is offered by the individual professional school. Such patterns exist at Harvard, Columbia, Yale, Syracuse, Indiana, and Boston. But the majority of universities have the "umbrella" or universitywide graduate school which administers all graduate study, both the arts and sciences as well as the professional areas. Typical of this type are Illinois, Wisconsin, and the University of California at Los Angeles. There are numerous variations of these two patterns: at New York University, for example, the Ph.D. is granted by the Graduate School of Arts and Sciences, the School of Business Administration, the School of Education, and the School of Engineering and Science—and the latter two also offer professional graduate degrees. Many graduate schools administer a number of different doctoral degree programs.

GENERAL POLICIES FOR CONDUCTING GRADUATE PROGRAMS

Administration

The most common organization for the administration of graduate study is that of a dean, a graduate faculty, a graduate council, committees, and departmental committees.

[2] See Everett Walters, "Trends Toward a Degree for College Teachers," *Educational Review*, Spring, 1967.

[3] See Stephen Spurr, "The Candidate's Degree," *Educational Record*, Spring, 1967; and John Perry Miller, "The Master of Philosophy: A New Degree Is Born," *Ventures*, Spring, 1966.

[4] See Mary Wortham, "The Case for a Doctor of Arts Degree: A View from Junior College Faculty," *AAUP Bulletin*, December, 1967.

The Graduate Dean Administratively, the graduate dean (or the dean of the professional school) is responsible to the provost or the vice-president for academic affairs. He is the academic leader, responsible for setting and maintaining the standards of graduate education. Depending on the size of the school, he should have associate or assistant deans; one of these associates might be concerned with the administration of research. The dean presides at council meetings and at meetings of the graduate faculty, if held, and serves as chairman of the executive committee.

The graduate dean holds an anomalous position in higher education. One dean pointed out that

> . . . the dean of some other school, generally an undergraduate school rather than the dean of the graduate school, has the means and the responsibility. Some dean who has a budget supervises the graduate dean's departments in the recruiting of teaching staff. . . . This must be the procedure because the graduate dean seldom has a budget or authority to appoint.[5]

So too the graduate dean usually does not have the authority to recommend promotions, salary increases, or departmental budgets. Thus all too often he is neglected in that decision making which affects graduate education. Whatever influence he has usually stems from his own personality, politics, and propagandistic methods.

The Graduate Faculty Membership should be based upon such criteria as broad educational background, possession of the doctor's degree (or equivalent) and considerable teaching and research experience. It is highly desirable that graduate faculty members have published the results of their research. They should have attained professorial rank in their department of instruction, preferably full or associate professorships.

The Graduate Council Members of the graduate faculty should elect representatives to the graduate council from the various areas or departments authorized to offer graduate work. The council should meet frequently, preferably monthly during the academic year. It does the following:

1. Determines general policies and regulations for graduate programs, general admission requirements, foreign language requirements, procedure for conducting the general examinations, and regulations for preparation of dissertations
2. Formally recommends to the president and the trustees those candidates to be awarded graduate degrees
3. Recommends new degrees and new degree programs to the president and the trustees

Committees The most important committee is the executive committee, which assists the dean in interpreting and administering academic policies and regulations and proposes new ones to the council, approves curricula as submitted by departments, and assists in the preparation of bulletins and other publications. Other committees may be selected for special purposes such as new degree programs and new degrees.

Departmental Graduate Committees Such committees are organized to oversee special problems within the department. These include processing of applications for admission within the general policies established by the graduate council, recommendation of department members for membership in the graduate faculty, setting up regulations for programs of study to ensure proper depth and breadth, and recommending changes in curricula and degree requirements; e.g., modification of language requirement for the doctorate.

Despite any number of organizational diagrams or administrative directives, the quality of graduate education rests with the individual graduate adviser. It is he who

[5] Roy F. Nichols, "Administering Graduate Education," in Everett Walters (ed.), *Graduate Education Today*, American Council on Education, Washington, 1965, p. 106.

plans his advisee's program of studies, courses and seminars to be taken, the foreign languages which will be required, the time for both qualifying and general examinations, and, above all, the nature and scope of the dissertation. It is in this latter role that the adviser inculcates in his advisee the spirit and discipline of research as well as the traditions of graduate work in his subject. His personality and personal standards and ethics are immeasurably important quantities in this relationship. Perhaps the most difficult requirement of his role is the courage to say "no" to the unprepared student or to the student obviously unable to write an acceptable dissertation. It is in the adviser-advisee relationship that the traditional high standards of graduate education are maintained. For a graduate faculty member it is a mark of high academic achievement to have served as a graduate adviser successfully.

Degree Programs: General Requirements and Regulations

It is extremely important that there be clearly understood policies concerning the general requirements and regulations for doctoral and master's degree programs. Suggested policies for the Ph.D. might be as follows:

Admission Prerequisites should include high attainment in undergraduate work with an overall average of B and/or a satisfactory score on the Graduate Record Examination, letters of recommendation from major undergraduate teachers and, if applicable, special tests or, in the case of candidates in the field of fine arts, a portfolio of art work. These criteria and any others which indicate potential for independent study, research ability, and intellectual skill would apply.

Residence Requirement A full academic year or its equivalent spent full time at the university should be required.

Course Requirements Course requirements should include three academic years of advanced course work (including independent study) and seminar participation and research beyond the bachelor's degree. Credit for work in courses which permit undergraduate enrollment should be given only under certain circumstances; more extensive research and reading assignments should be required of the graduate student and only grades B or better should be accepted.

Qualifying Examination This is an examination to determine if a student should be permitted to begin doctoral studies; special emphasis is placed upon capacity for research. It should be taken early in a doctoral program.

Foreign Language Except in unusual instances, a student working toward the doctorate should demonstrate by examination his ability to read at least one modern foreign language. This examination should be prepared by the subject-matter department in conjunction with the department of languages and it should be administered by the graduate school.

General or Comprehensive Examination This is one of the two most important aspects of the doctoral degree, the test of a student's knowledge and skills in his general subject-matter area of concentration (such as, for example, political science, chemistry, or biology). It should be both written and oral, and reasonably formidable. Often a student offers a specific number of divisions or categories within a general area. The examining committee consists of the adviser as chairman, at least four other graduate faculty members of the department, and preferably a faculty member from another area. Successful completion of this examination admits the student to official status as "candidate for the Ph.D."

Dissertation Another vital aspect of the degree, the dissertation, is a written work which indicates the candidate's ability to pursue independent research and to interpret the results of this research. The dissertation is defended by the student before a committee of at least three graduate faculty members from his subject-matter area and one from another area.

General Policies to Be Established for the Doctorate

1. A time limitation for obtaining the degree, preferably not more than five years after admission to candidacy.

2. Limitation of transfer credit; i.e., the master's degree from a reputable institution to count as one year of the three required postbaccalaureate years.

3. Dissertation requirements. Rigid requirements for the physical appearance, format, and composition of the dissertation should be clearly set forth and made available to all candidates. Copies of the dissertation and the dissertation abstract should be microfilmed by Microfilm Abstracts, Inc.

Suggested Policies for Master's Degrees (Policies for professional master's degrees are described in the preceding chapter.)

1. Admission requirements as for Ph.D., although many graduate schools will accept less than a B average for master's candidates.

2. Academic requirements. Because of the wide range of master's degrees it is impossible to make specific suggestions. In certain areas either the professional accrediting organization or tradition have pretty well established requirements. Some areas hold to a thesis for the master's, others do not; some require general examinations, others do not. A few subject-matter areas require competency in one or more foreign languages. Credit for work in courses which permit undergraduate enrollment should be given only under limited circumstances; more extensive research and reading assignments should be required of the graduate student and only grades of B or better should be accepted.

3. Credits earned toward a master's degree, either in courses at the institution or at another recognized institution, should be valid only for a seven-year period unless a specific extension is granted.

Graduate Faculty

In view of the nature of graduate instruction and research, it is advisable to establish policies such as the following specifically pertaining to graduate faculty members:

1. Teaching loads, especially classroom instruction, should be considerably lighter than those of undergraduate teachers. The prestigious graduate schools maintain a six-hour load or, *mirabile dictu*, an even lighter one.

2. Leaves of absence, with or without pay, should be permitted whenever possible. In this connection it should be noted that the concept of the sabbatical leave is fading in popularity and is being replaced by the attitude that leave should be granted as frequently as possible. On the other hand, the proverbial "nonresident" distinguished professor performs a disservice to his university because he is not available for the instruction and guidance of graduate students.

3. A grants-in-aid program to encourage research, especially for the not-yet-established faculty members, is extremely beneficial. Funds should be available for travel to meetings of learned societies and to libraries, for manuscript typing, and for microfilming of manuscripts and similar purposes.

GRADUATE STUDENTS

As indicated earlier, there is a great demand for holders of the Ph.D., other doctorates, and master's degrees. The number of persons entering graduate schools has increased enormously. Total graduate school enrollment has skyrocketed from 106,119 in 1940 to 705,000 in 1966–1967.

This dramatic increase has necessitated changes in the treatment of graduate students. No longer is it possible to maintain the casual and somewhat aloof attitude of earlier decades. These changes include:

Fellowships and Assistantships

Virtually every graduate student expects to receive full or partial financial support. Such support usually takes the form of:

1. Fellowships which include remission of tuition and fees and a stipend to cover the living expenses of the student and his family, if any. Fellowships range in value up to $6,000 per year. With a few exceptions, fellows perform no services.

2. Assistantships for teaching and research duties. Stipends for graduate assistants range widely from graduate school to graduate school and often from department to department within a graduate school. They usually offer remission of tuition and pay modest stipends. Assistants teach or assist faculty members to perform their research. Teaching assistants, or T.A.s as they are commonly called, in the last 15 years have carried the bulk of freshman teaching duties at large universities. Assistantship funds usually are included on the regular university budget as an instruction expense or appear as an expense on a faculty member's grant or contract.

3. National Fellowship Programs. The federal government sponsors the largest fellowship programs; the most important of these are:

1. The National Defense Education Act (NDEA) Title IV, which grants three-year awards to doctoral students in both newly established graduate programs and well-established programs
2. The National Science Fellowships, primarily in the sciences
3. The National Aeronautics and Space Administration Fellowships for students in space-related sciences and technology
4. The Atomic Energy Fellowships
5. The National Institutes of Health Fellowships in health-related areas

The two largest foundation-sponsored fellowship programs are the well known Woodrow Wilson National Fellowship Program (Princeton, New Jersey) and the Danforth Foundation (St. Louis, Missouri).

Information about these and similar programs may be found in *Fellowships in the Arts and Sciences,* published annually by the American Council on Education, or by writing to the federal agencies or the foundations. Information about specific institutional fellowships is issued by the individual graduate schools.

Fellowships are generally considered to be nontaxable stipends if the holder is working toward a degree. If the holder is not a degree candidate, the exemption is limited to amounts received at a rate not in excess of $300 a month. On the other hand, graduate assistants must pay income tax on their stipends.

Federally financed loans, available through the National Defense Education Act of 1958, are awarded by the student financial aid office of the university.

Graduate Student Organizations

Since the late 1950s there has been a marked trend toward graduate student organizations such as a graduate student council or an association of graduate students.

These councils or associations are primarily organized to create a "professional" spirit among the students, to act as spokesmen for the graduate students—especially as opposed to the undergraduate government organizations—and to conduct a limited number of social functions. Certain graduate student councils publish sophisticated guides for their members, replete with judgments about courses, faculty members, the university administration, housing, newspapers, and local restaurants and bistros.

Graduate Student Housing

Facilities for housing and feeding graduate students have become increasingly desirable as the number of graduate students has grown. These students prefer modern apartments and rooms with good food, all at reasonable prices. Since a large percentage of students are married, they must be provided for. Understandably, such housing facilities should have only the most sophisticated regulations. At those institutions which have large graduate residence halls experience has shown that there should be ample facilities for social affairs and for meetings.

MINIMUM STANDARDS FOR NEW PH.D. PROGRAMS

The Council of Graduate Schools in the United States has set forth a list of standards which should be regarded as minimal for any institution contemplating a new doctoral program. These standards are herewith summarized:

Administration

1. The firm commitment of the president and the governing board to support Ph.D. work is needed, as is their awareness of the costs of a quality program. The institution should not be interested in a program primarily for prestige or for financial support from federal agencies.
2. The faculty not only of the involved department but the faculty in general should be enthusiastic about the program. The former should have already been engaged in research and the latter should recognize and accept the necessity of lighter teaching loads for graduate advisers.
3. The institution should have a suitable organization for the administration of graduate work, including a dean or other administrative officer, a graduate faculty, and a graduate council. These units are necessary for the maintenance of the standards of graduate work.
4. The institution should have experience in educating graduate students; i.e., it should have established graduate courses and facilities for research.

Faculty

The institution should have a faculty actively engaged in research independent of the graduate program and before students are admitted to the program.

Library

Doctoral candidates must have access to an adequate research library, a library which represents adequacy in depth and in breadth. The institution should not depend upon the library resources of a neighboring university but ought to possess the basic research materials itself.

Facilities

Laboratory facilities, equipment and library study space must be adequate for independent study, and funds should be available to maintain these facilities.

An Adequate Student Body

Sufficient university-financed teaching assistantships and fellowships should be available to assure a student body large enough to justify graduate courses and seminars and to establish a stimulating body of students. The bulk of these students should be full-time day students.

Any university contemplating a new doctoral program is advised to consult the Council of Graduate Students, Washington, D.C. 20036. Information about existing and proposed programs is available, as is the assignment of knowledgeable consultants. The latter would, of course, supplement the recommendations of the university committees which previously had examined proposed degree programs.

INTERINSTITUTIONAL COOPERATION OF GRADUATE PROGRAMS

The ever-increasing cost of supporting graduate educational programs has stimulated interest in cooperative programs by universities in certain geographical areas or in educational associations. Such cooperation ranges from the most informal arrangements whereby students from one institution are permitted to attend classes and seminars at another without credit and without financial commitments to tightly drawn agreements which require carefully integrated programs of studies, interinstitutional seminars, examinations, and dissertation reading committees.

Two well-established interinstitutional cooperative programs are the Committee on Institutional Cooperation (C.I.C.) of the Big Ten Universities and the University of Chicago in the Midwest. Under the C.I.C. Visiting Scholars Program, graduate students at any one of the 11 institutions may, with departmental endorsement, spend one or two quarters at another, paying tuition and receiving credit at the home university while taking advantage of special facilities or programs not otherwise available.

ACCREDITATION

In recent years several regional accrediting associations have required that new doctoral programs be approved before association recognition will be given. Usually the accrediting association appoints a committee of well-known scholars to examine, by means of a site visit, the ability of an institution to offer a new doctorate. The recommendations of these committees form the basis for preliminary accreditation by the association. Later, usually after the graduation of five or more students, a second committee recommends permanent accreditation.

All the regional associations soon will be engaged in the accrediting of graduate programs, especially as the federal and local governments grant larger sums of money for both general institutional and specific purposes.[6]

TRENDS IN GRADUATE EDUCATION

An ever-increasing demand for holders of doctorates and master's degrees is certain to bring about larger graduate enrollments in the years to come. One estimate made by Allan M. Cartter and Robert Farrell holds for a sixfold expansion, much greater than for undergraduates.[7] This estimate predicts that about 75,000 doctorates will be awarded annually by the year 2000. These predictions and those of other statisticians clearly indicate that the last three decades of this century will witness significant growth in enrollment.

Another trend will be the increasing degree of prestige of certain graduate schools. Allan M. Cartter's *An Assessment of Quality in Graduate Education*[8] emphasizes the sharp competition among graduate schools. Related to this trend, it seems to the author, is the fact that the number of readily recognized "prestige" institutions will be extended to 60 or 70. A nation as large as ours with such a heavy commitment to higher education can easily support this large a number.

A third trend will be that the less prestigious graduate schools will continue to expand as they have since the advent of the NDEA Title IV Graduate Fellowship Pro-

[6] A statement of procedures and criteria for the accreditation graduate programs may be obtained from the North Central Association of Colleges and Secondary Schools, Commission on Colleges and Universities, 5454 South Shore Drive, Chicago, Ill.

[7] Allan M. Cartter and Robert Farrell, "Higher Education in the Last Third of a Century," *Educational Record*, p. 124, Spring, 1965.

[8] Washington, 1966.

gram. A quick survey of the *Guide to Graduate Study* reveals that 59 universities offered their first Ph.D. programs soon after 1959, the founding date of the Title IV Program. Typical are Clarkson College of Technology, Clemson University, Kent State (Ohio), Bowling Green, Arizona State, Atlanta, Ball State, Kentucky, Rhode Island, South Dakota, Wesleyan, and Texas Christian. One small eastern university has 22 doctoral programs, 14 of them begun since 1959. In keeping with patterns established several decades ago, thousands of graduate students will attend these graduate schools because of their easy accessibility. For many students, especially those who are married or who have heavy family obligations, the local graduate school is the only one they could possibly attend. Even if offered a plush graduate fellowship, they simply could not afford to accept it. Furthermore, the universities themselves have learned that they are obligated to offer doctoral work if they wish to attract bright young Ph.D.s to their faculties and if they wish to have adequate numbers of graduate students to teach freshman subjects.

A fourth major trend is the establishment of cooperative graduate programs. It is only natural that this movement will expand, especially in certain large metropolitan areas and in states with highly organized systems of higher education like New York or in closely related geographical areas like the mountain states. The graduate study exchange of the Consortium of Universities in Washington, D.C. and others like it will expand and flourish; so too will cooperative programs in the several regional associations such as the Western Intercollegiate Compact of Higher Education and the New England Board of Higher Education. The reasons for such cooperative programs are obvious: the high cost of certain graduate fields of study, the need to avoid duplication of course offerings, and the pooling of efforts to gain program strength.

Unquestionably a number of well-established and well-endowed independent undergraduate colleges will set up selected graduate programs at least to the master's level. The trend toward this has already begun in certain areas where these colleges find themselves faced with the problem of attracting and retaining good faculty members and of offering sufficient challenges to their very bright and highly motivated students. Several New England colleges are actively planning for modest graduate programs, some of which they would conduct themselves and others which they would manage in conjunction with well-established graduate schools with doctoral programs. Although most ranking graduate schools emphasize "straight through to the doctorate" programs, they do seem quite willing to consider accepting superior students with master's degrees.

A sixth significant direction is the thoroughgoing reappraisal of traditional degree requirements and of course content. Over a century ago James Russell Lowell observed that "new occasions teach new duties"; here the new occasions result from the breathtaking sweep of present-day change. The traditional language requirement in some fields of study has no significance whatsoever for the Ph.D.; indeed, it serves only as a ridiculous hurdle erected anachronistically as a great gesture to past culture. The effort to speed up the doctorate has been most commendable and should be encouraged in every area. There is no logic whatsoever in awarding doctoral degrees to persons in their late thirties. So too, traditional requirements for certain master's degrees are out of date by three decades. The built-in conservatism of graduate faculty members cautions against change or innovation. Similarly, graduate faculty members have been slow to reexamine their courses, to change and to update them. While the computer and other research tools have found ready acceptance in some areas (at budget-breaking annual rentals, as any administrator will testify), they are not at all used in others.

Closely related to this development will be a growing willingness to use interdisciplinary approaches—the historian accepting sociological approaches and the biologist accepting certain engineering principles. Such interdisciplinary approaches will be customary in area study programs such as African and Sino-Russian studies. And most certainly the burgeoning urban studies centers at the large metropolitan universities will inevitably involve graduate interdisciplinary arrangements.

And as knowledge becomes more extensive and specialization becomes more and more cultivated, it appears quite obvious that postdoctoral programs will continue to expand. Many important departments at large universities have been inundated with postdoctorals, have become accustomed to them, and have come to use them. Indeed such are the numbers of postdoctorals that one wonders whether or not the old specter of the "super Ph.D." will be revived.

It is widely believed that the recently launched quest of teaching assistants for more prestige, especially in the form of faculty benefits, will be successful and that these young people will soon be acknowledged as junior members of our teaching staffs. The ever-increasing demand for college teachers—at least for the next decade—will place teaching assistants in crucial positions as seminar leaders, section or quiz masters, and laboratory instructors. These "T.A.s," as they have widely come to be known, should have much more recognition in higher stipends, faculty club privileges, health-related benefits, and even parking privileges.

And these T.A.s should have a benefit which few graduate schools are now willing to extend, the preparation for college teaching. The regrettable state of college-teacher preparation has been clearly described in a recent study of a number of so-called "more successful programs for the recruitment and training of college teachers." This study by Frank Koen and Stanford C. Ericksen discloses that, despite recognition of the need for training programs for teaching assistants, virtually nothing has been done to remedy the situation.[9] Included in the study are programs at 42 of the country's important graduate schools. Training programs at these graduate schools are conducted, almost without exception, by the subject-matter departments. Such programs generally consist of the provision of individual supervision, "brown bag" (informal) weekly meetings, and some help on the construction of course outlines and reading lists. There is "at least an occasional brush with the problems of evaluating student achievement. 'Methods' courses per se appear to be a universal anathema."

A desirable innovation would be the recognition of a new degree for college teachers. This should be a specially designed degree for teachers at undergraduate, junior, and community colleges. The University of Tennessee Master of Arts in College Teaching, for example, requires 60 quarter hours, 15 more than the 45 required for the M.A. or M.S. Of these 15 additional hours, 12 must be in the student's subject-matter field. Most of the departments have reorganized their master's offerings to fit the new program; the science departments call for some research, some research design, and some methodology. All candidates for the M.A.C.T. are required to take a continuing one-credit, three-quarter graduate seminar in college teaching during their first year of residence. Included in this seminar are such basic considerations as testing and measurement, new teaching techniques, basic learning theory, a critical review of traditional teaching methods, and study of the influence of federal agencies and private foundations. Field trips are periodically scheduled to nearby two-year and four-year colleges.

By means of a teaching internship, supervised instructional experience is an integral part of the degree program. All M.A.C.T. students are required to serve six quarters (two academic years) as part-time teaching interns either in their subject-matter department at the university or at an institution in the surrounding area. Careful supervision is provided. The degree is offered in chemistry, English, physics, psychology, biology, economics, German, history, political science, Romance languages, and sociol-

[9] Koen and Ericksen, *An Analysis of the Specific Features Which Characterize the More Successful Programs for the Recruitment and Training of College Teachers*, Center for Research on Learning and Teaching, The University of Michigan Press, Ann Arbor, Mich., 1967.

ogy. It is possible for those who have earned M.A.C.T.s to work toward the Ph.D. Although it is much too early to judge the Tennessee M.A.C.T., it does appear to be well designed and executed.

Finally, in thinking ahead toward the future of graduate education, it seems obvious that the federal government will enact a comprehensive and all-inclusive measure of legislation which will ensure a basic and continuing place for graduate education. Such legislation would guarantee a continuing investment in human beings at the highest level of education. There have, of course, been pleas of a kind for such legislation, but none of them have called for a thoroughgoing program. Possible suggestions would include the following:

1. A graduate fellowship program to replace the present conflicting hodgepodge of programs including the NDEA, NSF, NASA, and ACE. Such fellowships would provide adequate stipends including allowances for dependents and for travel. Selection of fellows would be on a basis similar to the present NDEA plan, but with adequate safeguards to ensure that the awards go only to highly qualified persons. Each fellowship would be tenable on an annual 11-month basis and would expressly provide for a reasonable dissertation period.

2. Institutional grants for the education of these fellows. These grants would specifically include the cost of education and allowances for research, travel expenses, and unusual institutional expenses. The grants also would provide for funds for the general support of graduate education; i.e., monies that would be available on a continuing and permanent basis for the maintenance of high-quality graduate faculty and adequate research facilities.

BIBLIOGRAPHY

Berelson, Bernard: *Graduate Education in the United States,* McGraw-Hill Book Company, New York, 1960.

Carmichael, Oliver C.: *Graduate Education: A Critique and a Program,* Harper & Brothers, New York, 1961.

McGrath, Earl J.: *Are Liberal Arts Colleges Becoming Professional Schools?,* Columbia University Press, New York, 1958.

McGrath, Earl J.: *The Graduate School and Decline of Liberal Education,* Teachers College Press, Columbia University, New York, 1959.

Walters, Everett (ed.): *Graduate Education Today,* American Council on Education, Washington, 1965.

Full explanation of the varieties and requirements of the master's degree appear in the preceding chapters on graduate and professional education.

Doctor's Degrees By contrast to the master's, the stature of doctoral degrees has remained uniform and remarkably uncluttered. They fall into two principal types, the research degree and the professional degree. The Doctor of Philosophy, the Ph.D., is generally regarded as the former type and the Doctor of Education, the Doctor of Pharmacy, and the Doctor of Business Administration are considered professional degrees. The difference, however, is not always clear-cut.

Full explanation of the types and requirements of the doctorate appear in Chapters 12 and 13 of this section.

Most Commonly Awarded Earned Degrees

A.A.	Associate in Arts
A.M.	Master of Arts
A.Mus.D.	Doctor of Musical Arts
B.A.	Bachelor of Arts
B.B.A.	Bachelor of Business Administration
B.Ch.E.	Bachelor of Chemical Engineering
B.D.	Bachelor of Divinity
B.F.A.	Bachelor of Fine Arts
B.Mus.	Bachelor of Music
B.S.	Bachelor of Science
B.S.E.E.	Bachelor of Science in Electrical Engineering
B.S.M.E.	Bachelor of Science in Mechanical Engineering
B.Pharm.	Bachelor of Pharmacy
D.Arch.	Doctor of Architecture
D.B.A.	Doctor of Business Administration
D.C.L.	Doctor of Civil Law
D.Comp.L.	Doctor of Comparative Law
D.D.S.	Doctor of Dental Science or Doctor of Dental Surgery
D.Ed.	Doctor of Education
D.Eng.	Doctor of Engineering
D.Eng.Sc.	Doctor of Engineering Science
D.F.	Doctor of Forestry
D.F.A.	Doctor of Fine Arts
D.For.	Doctor of Forestry
D.H.L.	Doctor of Hebrew Literature or Doctor of Hebrew Letters
D.L.S.	Doctor of Library Science
D.M.A.	Doctor of Musical Arts
D.M.L.	Doctor of Modern Languages
D.M.S.	Doctor of Medieval Studies
D.M.Sc.	Doctor of Medical Science
D.Mus.	Doctor of Music
D.Mus.A.	Doctor of Musical Arts
D.Mus.Ed.	Doctor of Music Education
D.N.Sc.	Doctor of Nursing Science
D.P.A.	Doctor of Public Administration
D.P.H.	Doctor of Public Health
D.Phys.Ed.	Doctor of Physical Education
D.R.E.	Doctor of Religious Education
D.S.M.	Doctor of Sacred Music
D.S.S.	Doctor of Social Science
D.S.W.	Doctor of Social Work
D.Sc.	Doctor of Science
D.V.M.	Doctor of Veterinary Medicine
Ed.D.	Doctor of Education
Ed.R.D.	Doctor of Religious Education
Eng.D.	Doctor of Engineering

Eng.Sc.D.	Doctor of Science in Engineering
J.C.D.	Doctor of Canon Law
J.S.D.	Doctor of the Science of Law
LL.B.	Bachelor of Laws
M.A.	Master of Arts
M.A.T.	Master of Arts in Teaching
M.B.A.	Master of Business Administration
M.D.	Doctor of Medicine
M.E.	Master of Education or Master of Engineering or Mechanical Engineer
M.Ed.	Master of Education
M.F.A.	Master of Fine Arts
M.M.	Master of Music
M.P.A.	Master of Public Administration
M.P.H.	Master of Public Health
M.S.	Master of Science
M.S.W.	Master of Social Work
M.S. in Ed.	Master of Science in Education
M.Sc.	Master of Science
Med.Sc.D.	Doctor of Medical Science
Mus.A.D.	Doctor of Musical Arts
Pharm.D.	Doctor of Pharmacy
Ph.D.	Doctor of Philosophy
S.B.	Bachelor of Science
S.J.D.	Doctor of the Science of Law
S.M.D.	Doctor of Sacred Music
S.T.B.	Bachelor of Sacred Theology
S.T.D.	Doctor of Sacred Theology
S.T.M.	Master of Sacred Theology
Sc.D.	Doctor of Science
Th.D.	Doctor of Theology

Honorary Degrees Honorary degrees have been awarded by American colleges and universities since early colonial times. In 1692, Harvard, only 50 years after its founding, awarded the first such degree and thus began what has become a recognized function of degree-granting institutions of higher learning. From the beginning honorary degrees were granted to recognize the achievements of persons in the particular field of their interest. Clergymen, teachers, and political leaders as well as many others have been so recognized. For some time the M.D. was given to recognize physicians who had distinguished themselves professionally but who had not gained their medical education at a medical school. In certain cases the degree was awarded simply to give medical school faculty members an established degree.

In the past honorary degrees were awarded at the bachelor's, master's and doctor's level, but in recent years the doctorate has become the most commonly used. Commencement time, and to a lesser extent other academic exercises, have become occasions for colleges and universities to single out persons who have made contributions to society in almost every area of activity: politics, public service, education, scholarship, poetry, music, drama, business, health, and science to name a few. Frequently those honored reflect dominant political, social, or economic trends or events of contemporary concern. In the 1940s and 1950s, military and international political figures were conspicuous on June commencement platforms; while in the mid-1960s civil rights leaders predominated. A common practice is to award the commencement speaker an honorary degree; similarly newly elected college or university presidents without earned doctorates are accorded such recognition either by their alma maters or by other institutions. Certain institutions in recent years have established the practice of awarding certificates of service, usually to persons associated with the awarding institution. These certificates recognize meritorious service without the distinction of contribution to society that is associated with the honorary doctorate.

Regrettably, over the years the practice of awarding honorary degrees has been greatly abused. In far too many instances during the latter part of the nineteenth century and the early decades of the twentieth, degrees were awarded to woo, flatter, or reward wealthy donors of buildings and athletic facilities or to give academic respectability to professors, presidents, and educational leaders. Soon after Yale granted the first earned Ph.D., it became widely awarded as an honorary degree. In the 1870s more honorary Ph.D.s were awarded than earned. Other honorary doctorates were the Litt.D., LL.D., L.H.D., Mus.D., D.D., and Sc.D. Protests against the abuse of granting honorary degrees began as early as 1867 when Daniel C. Gilman, later to found Johns Hopkins University, declared "If a man is made a doctor of laws the public has a right to know whether it means he has fought a battle, or is on the right side in politics, or is the donor to the extent of five thousand dollars and upwards." [6]

Opposition to the honorary Ph.D. was by far the most vigorous. University and college presidents, the newly founded scholarly associations, the U.S. Bureau of Education, the influential *Educational Review,* and the short-lived Convention of Graduate Clubs all denounced this flagrant abuse of the Ph.D. and created such scorn for it that the practice declined rapidly by 1900. Since that time only a few honorary Ph.D.s have been awarded.[7]

The number of honorary degrees given has increased as higher education has expanded. Almost 200 varieties of such degrees were awarded to approximately 50,000 recipients from 1870 to 1939. Since 1900 the honorary doctorate has come to predominate while the honorary bachelor's and master's have declined to a minor percentage of degrees awarded annually. Several institutions do continue the awarding of the honorary master's to trustees and full professors if they do not possess earned master's degrees. Another discernible trend is that while most awards are made to academic, professional, and political figures, the number of leaders in business, industry, journalism, and the fine arts so honored has increased considerably.

In the last four decades there has been a movement against the promiscuous and wide-scale conferring of honorary degrees. The reaction to the abuses of the past culminated during the 1920s and 1930s and brought about more sensible practices. Sensational as well as well-balanced popular magazine articles aided in bringing about the change. Typical titles of these articles are illuminating: "The American Peerage," "The Roll of Honor," "Degree Racket," "Degrees of Honor," "Honorary Degrees Go Hollywood," and "Doctors of Industry." Most educational leaders now believe that the abuses of the past must be avoided and that only persons worthy of distinction who have made meritorious contributions should be rewarded. Rarely are persons so recognized because they make large financial contributions. Useful guidelines for selecting potential recipients are listed later in this article.

THE AUTHORITY AND PROCEDURES FOR CONFERRING EARNED DEGREES

In most states institutions of higher learning are compelled by state law to have formal approval to grant academic degrees. Certain states formerly required incorporation of the trustees for this purpose. More recently such authority is granted by a state board of education, board of regents, or a similar agency which examines the credentials of an institution in much the same manner as an accrediting association.

Governing boards of colleges and universities usually delegate control of their insti-

[6] Quoted in Stephen Edward Epler, *Honorary Degrees: A Survey of Their Use and Abuse,* American Council on Public Affairs, Washington, 1943, p. 61.

[7] *Ibid.,* pp. 60–69.

tutions' academic curricula to their faculties. The latter in turn prescribe the courses and specific programs which must be pursued by those who wish to qualify for specific degrees. Faculties thus are expected by the governing boards to recommend the candidates upon whom degrees are to be conferred. Faculties may refuse to recommend particular candidates who have failed to meet part of the program or requirements or who appear to be of immoral character or unsound mind. Most institutions in their bulletins set forth quite precisely the requirements for the degrees they offer.

Specific procedures should be established for the conferring of degrees. These might be as follows:

1. Ensure that all degree requirements are clearly and succinctly stated in bulletins, new degree announcements, and other widely used publications. Students should be requested periodically to review their degree program to determine if they are making satisfactory progress.

2. Set up in the registrar's office or in a records office an accurate and efficient record-keeping system for all students, degree candidates or not. Records today are usually maintained in an electronic computer system.

3. Maintain check-off system so that at the proper time student records will indicate completion of degree requirements. Prepare list of candidates for degrees at the next commencement.

4. Call faculty meeting to vote degrees, i.e., recommend to the president and trustees that those candidates who have fulfilled all the requirements should receive the degrees.

5. Have trustees meet to approve the conferring of degrees.

6. Award degrees at commencement.

Special consideration should be given to these matters in connection with the foregoing procedure:

1. In general, degrees should be awarded only at commencement. To do otherwise will tend to lessen the academic prestige of the degree, since mailing diplomas during the year creates an impression of the institution as a "diploma mill." Some graduate and professional schools make a practice of furnishing students with letters certifying completion of all requirements and indicating the awarding of a degree at the next commencement.

2. It is preferable to require that all candidates attend commencement exercises, but a well-defined and reasonable plan should be set up to provide for the awarding of degrees *in absentia*. In this instance, the diplomas may be obtained from the office of the registrar or may be mailed.

3. Most colleges and small universities conduct one commencement a year, but large and complex institutions have as many as four each year, one at the end of each quarter.

4. It has been a long-established practice to charge a commencement fee, usually sufficient to cover the cost of the diploma itself, hoods if degree recipients are to keep them, and some expenses of the exercises. More recently the practice is changing and commencement fees are absorbed into the institution's all-inclusive fee. Candidates normally bear the expense of renting caps and gowns.

POLICIES AND PROCEDURES RELATING TO HONORARY DEGREES

All colleges and universities should have explicit policies and procedures to be followed in the awarding of honorary degrees. As was pointed out in the historical section of this article, the widespread abuse of this type of degree in the past makes it imperative that reasonable and defensible policies and practices be established.

1. The basic policy should provide for the types of persons to be recognized with honorary degrees; e.g., prominent alumni, important women leaders, businessmen, pro-

fessional persons, civic leaders, national leaders in public affairs, statesmen, prominent educators, and distinguished persons in the arts, sciences, and the humanities. At any one commencement it is advisable to plan for a balanced group of six to eight recipients, although the number may vary either way. Some institutions also believe it prudent to maintain representation of the major religious faiths and to recognize academic fields in which the institution offers degree programs. Finally, if the commencement speaker is of distinction—and he should be—he should be awarded an honorary degree.

2. Supplementing the basic policy should be a statement that prohibits the awarding of honorary degrees (*a*) on a quid pro quo basis (i.e., no such degree will be conferred upon a person solely on the basis of donations of any kind which he may have made to the institution); (*b*) to certain persons merely to obtain publicity; (*c*) to administrators and faculty members of the institution.

3. Whether or not trustees should receive honorary degrees should be carefully investigated. Despite the continuing practice at certain colleges and universities to award honorary master's degrees to trustees, it appears to this writer to be an unwise practice. Certainly under no circumstance should an earned doctorate be awarded as an honorary degree.

4. As set forth earlier, the authority to confer degrees rests in the hands of the trustees. Yet it is good policy to have recommendations made by a joint trustee-faculty committee. Such a committee itself proposes names of candidates and it screens names suggested by members of the university community.

5. The joint committee may find it helpful to maintain a roster of approved candidates. Such a roster of 50 or more persons can be extremely useful and may help to ensure that the list of recipients at any commencement will be balanced (it is always difficult to avoid conflicts in the availability of persons designated to receive degrees). Obviously such a list must be held in strictest confidence.

6. Institutions which follow the practice of awarding honorary degrees normally prepare a formal citation either to be read at the awarding of the honorary degree or to be printed in the program. These citations must be prepared with great care and restraint as to phrasing. Most institutions today follow a fairly rigid pattern. No longer are long and flowery citations regarded as being in acceptable academic taste; in fact, if any trend is apparent in citation writing, it is toward brevity. There is some variation in presentation procedure. Some citations are written in the second person rather than the third, with the citation addressed to the recipient directly rather than to the attending audience. Another variation is to have the citation written in two parts, one of which is read by the representative of the college or university who presents the candidate to the president, who then reads the degree.

Who prepares honorary degree citations? Response to a survey by officials at Pace College shows a common pattern of procedure with certain variations. In almost all cases, the president exercises final approval and contributes through his personal editing. In fact, the survey indicated that at 10 of the colleges that replied, the president personally writes the honorary degree citations, while five colleges reported that writing was assigned to individual faculty members best qualified through their knowledge of the background of the honorary degree recipient. In other colleges and universities, the writing assignment is handled by the director of public relations, chairman of the honorary degrees committee, director of publications, dean of faculty, or secretary of the college.

7. Honorary degrees should not be conferred *in absentia*. If a candidate cannot attend commencement on a specific date he should be asked to return at a future exercise.

Commonly Awarded Honorary Degrees

Most popular among honorary degrees are:

1. Doctor of Laws (LL.D.), first conferred in 1773, is the most popular honorary doc-

torate now awarded. Despite a wide variety of recipients in the past (clergymen, aviators, bankers, sportsmen, and scholars), it is now regarded as the most appropriate award for a person distinguished in general service to the state, to learning, and to mankind.

2. Doctor of Letters (Litt.D.), first awarded in 1892, is considered to be appropriate as a reward for scholarly work of a somewhat restricted nature. It is usually conferred upon scholars in particular disciplines.

3. Doctor of Science (Sc.D.), first conferred in 1884, unfortunately also is awarded as an earned doctorate at several prominent universities including the Massachusetts Institute of Technology. Despite this confusion, it is an increasingly popular award for persons who have made distinguished contributions and performed services in the sciences.

4. Doctor of Humane Letters (L.H.D.), first awarded in the 1880s, is the honorary doctorate usually given to persons who have distinguished themselves in the humanities.

ACADEMIC COSTUME

American academic costume (also referred to as academic "dress" or "regalia") had its origins in the ancient European universities. Apparently it was devised to distinguish academic persons such as doctors, licentiates, masters, and bachelors from other parts of the population. Gowns probably were a necessity because of unheated buildings, and hoods were needed to cover the heads of medieval scholars. Most universities issued strict regulations concerning the design and use of academic dress.

As they were founded, American colleges and universities inevitably adopted the gown, hood, and cap from their European antecedents. Although some common standards and practices were observed, no uniform code or system existed until late in the nineteenth century. On May 16, 1895, representatives from a number of leading colleges and universities met at Columbia University and agreed to establish a uniform code of academic dress. Then in 1902 an Intercollegiate Bureau of Academic Costume was chartered by the Regents of the University of the State of New York to serve as an arbiter on matters of academic dress. These developments led to a high degree of uniformity in the design and use of academic costume. In 1932, at the instigation of the American Council on Education, a committee was organized to review the 1895 code and recommend revisions. The resultant revised code was nationally accepted and became the uniform code until 1959, when a new council committee revised the 1932 code. The council's Academic Costume Code is herewith reprinted in full:

Gowns

Pattern. Gowns recommended for use in the colleges and universities of this country have the following characteristics. The gown for the bachelor's degree has pointed sleeves. It is designed to be worn closed. The gown for the master's degree has an oblong sleeve, open at the wrist, like the others. The sleeve base hangs down in the traditional manner. The rear part of its oblong shape is square cut and the front part has an arc cut away. The gown is so designed and supplied with fasteners that it may be worn open or closed. The gown for the doctor's degree has bell-shaped sleeves. It is so designed and supplied with fasteners that it may be worn open or closed.

Material. Cotton poplin or similar material for the bachelor's and master's degree, and rayon or silk ribbed material for the doctor's degree. As a means of adaptation to climate, the material of the gowns may vary from very light to very heavy, provided that the material, color, and pattern follow the prescribed rules.

Color. Black is recommended. (For permissible exceptions, see below.) *

* In recent years many colleges and universities have adopted institutional colors for their gowns.

Fig. 1 *Academic gowns. Doctoral gown: The velvet panels and sleeve bars are in the distinctive color representing the field of learning and immediately identify the doctor's degree. Master's gown: The official master's gown is identified by the sleeve which drapes freely to the wrist, with back end extending down below the knee in crescent shape. Bachelor's gown: The distinguishing feature of the bachelor's gown is the official pointed sleeve, lavish in its drape and fullness.*

Trimmings. None for the bachelor's or master's degrees. For the doctor's degree, the gown to be faced down the front with black velvet with three bars of the same across the sleeves; or these facings and crossbars may be of velvet of the color distinctive of the subject to which the degree pertains, thus agreeing in color with the binding or edging of the hood appropriate to the particular doctor's degree in every instance.

In some instances American makers of academic costumes have divided the velvet trimming of the doctor's gown in such a fashion as to suggest in the same garment two or more doctor's degrees. Good precedent directs that only a single degree from a single institution should ever be indicated by a single garment.

Hoods *

Pattern As usually followed by the colleges and universities of this country, but with observation of the following specifications:

Material The same as that of the gown in all cases.

Color Black in all cases.

Length The length of the hood worn for the bachelor's degree to be three feet, for the master's degree three and one-half feet, and for the doctor's degree, four feet; while that worn for the doctor's degree only shall have panels at the sides.

Linings The hoods to be lined with the official color or colors of the college or university conferring the degree; more than one color is shown by division of the field color in a variety of ways such as chevron or chevrons, equal division, etc. The various academic costume companies have in their files complete data on the approved colors for various institutions.

* Several institutions including Columbia have recently adopted a new-type doctoral hood which lies flat on the wearer's back. The chevron showing the university colors is thus clearly revealed.

Trimmings The binding of edging of the hood to be of velvet or velveteen, in widths two inches, three inches, and five inches for the bachelor's, master's and doctor's degrees, respectively; while the color should be distinctive of the subject to which the degree pertains (see Figure 3). For example, the trimming for the degree of Master of Science in Agriculture should be maize, representing agriculture, rather than golden yellow, representing science. No academic hood should ever have its border divided to represent more than a single degree.

Caps *

Material Cotton poplin, broadcloth, rayon, or silk, to match gown, or, for the doctor's degree only, velvet.

Form Mortarboards are generally recommended, although soft square-topped caps are permissible for women.

Color Black.

Tassel A long tassel to be fastened to the middle point of the top of the cap only and to lie as it will thereon; to be black or the color appropriate to the subject, except that the doctor's cap may have its tassel of gold thread.

Other Apparel

It is recommended that institutions require that graduates wear shoes and other articles of visible apparel of dark colors that harmonize with the academic costume. Flowers and decorative jewelry should not be worn on the academic gown.

Some Permissible Exceptions †

1. Members of the governing body of a college or university, and they only, whatever their degrees may be, are counted entitled to wear doctors' gowns (with black velvet), but their hoods may be only those of degrees actually held by the wearers or those especially prescribed for them by the institutions.
2. In some colleges and universities, it is customary for the president, chancellor, or chief officer to wear a costume similar to that used by the head of a foreign university. This practice should be strictly limited.

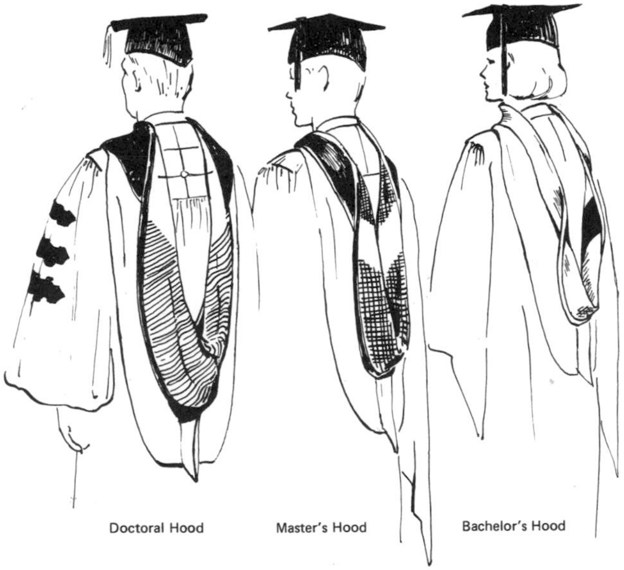

Fig. 2 *Academic hoods.*

* Soft velvet tam-type doctoral caps, four or six sided with gold thread tassels, have become popular, especially as they complement the new colored gowns.

† Reprinted with permission of the American Council on Education.

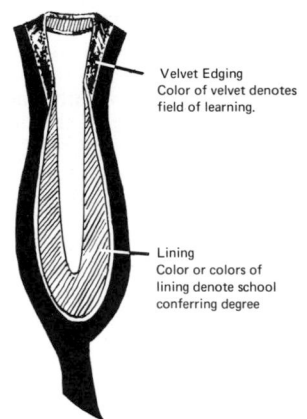

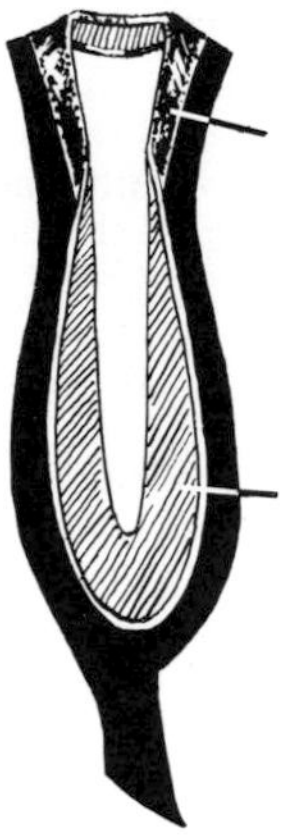
Velvet Edging
Color of velvet denotes
field of learning.
Lining
Color or colors of
lining denote school
conferring degree

Distinguishing Features of Academic Hoods

	Length	Width of Velvet Edging
Doctoral Hood	4 Feet	5 Inches
Master's Hood	3 1/2 Feet	3 Inches
Bachelor's Hood	3 Feet	2 Inches

Fig. 3 *Official degree colors. The following is a list of colors established by the Intercollegiate Code to represent the different departments of learning:*

Maize	*Agriculture*
Lilac	*Dentistry*
Copper	*Economics*
Light blue	*Education*
Orange	*Engineering*
Brown	*Fine Arts, Architecture*
Russet	*Forestry*
Maroon	*Home Economics*
Peacock blue	*Public Administration*
Crimson	*Journalism*
Purple	*Law*
Lemon	*Library Science*
Green	*Medicine*
Pink	*Music*
Apricot	*Nursing*
Silver gray	*Oratory (Speech)*
White	*Arts, Letters, and Humanities*
Olive green	*Pharmacy*
Dark blue	*Philosophy*
Sage green	*Physical Education*
Salmon pink	*Public Health*
Gold yellow	*Science*
Citron	*Social Work*
Gray	*Veterinary Science*
Scarlet	*Theology or Divinity*
Sapphire blue	*Business Administration*

3. The chief marshal may wear a specially designed costume approved by his institution.
4. It is customary in many large institutions for the hood to be dispensed with by those receiving bachelor's degrees.
5. Persons who hold degrees from foreign universities may wear the entire appropriate academic costume, including cap, gown, and hood.
6. Members of religious orders and similar societies may suitably wear their customary habits. The same principle applies to persons wearing military uniforms or clad in special attire required by a civil office.
7. It is recommended that collegiate institutions that award degrees, diplomas, or certificates below the baccalaureate level use caps and gowns of a light color; e.g., light blue for teacher-training and light gray for other types of institutions.

DIPLOMAS

Earlier in this chapter it was mentioned that recipients of all degrees are given formally worded documents known as diplomas. Because they were formerly embossed on parchment, diplomas have often been called "sheepskins." However, the scarcity of genuine parchment and its excessively high cost has caused most institutions to turn to an imitation parchment, such as Crane's or Parsons' parchment, for their diplomas.

Printing on these diplomas is usually done by letterpress, thermography, or engraving and the engrossing is done by hand or by machine. Although most institutions prefer to use a single ink, usually black, some institutions have chosen to add color to their diplomas. Excellent examples are those of St. Xavier College, the University of Washington, and Shawnee University.

Diploma sizes vary greatly. The larger diplomas are normally given for professional degrees such as law, pharmacy, and medicine and are designed to be displayed in offices or places of business. The smaller diplomas are usually given in cases where display is not necessary.

Who signs diplomas? This also varies from college to college. Diplomas may be signed by the president, chairman of the board of trustees or corporation, secretary of the corporation, the chancellor, the registrar, or one of many other college or university officers. As brevity is the trend in degree citations, so too is the trend toward fewer signatures evident on the diploma. Today, the president of the institution is the most common signatory of diplomas.

Diploma holders may be of leather, imitation leather, plastic, or cardboard. It should be mentioned here that there are many excellent imitation leather holders which are inexpensive and attractive.

Diploma Storage and Handling It is important that one officer be designated as responsible for all diplomas and that they should be stored in a secure area. If at all feasible, sample diplomas from each year of graduation should be kept on file; this is particularly important if duplicates are issued to replace those lost or destroyed.

Although one person may have the sole responsibility as "guardian of the sheepskin," it is not always possible for this person to be the only one handling the degrees. As few personnel as possible should be allowed to handle diplomas. This is done for two reasons: first, of course, to prevent soiling and, secondly, to eliminate the possibility of pilferage. Diplomas which are found to be unusable for one reason or another should be destroyed as quickly as possible. Sample diplomas appear in Figures 4 through 9.

BIBLIOGRAPHY

Cartter, Allan M. (ed.): *American Universities and Colleges,* 9th ed., American Council on Education, Washington, 1964.

Eells, Walter Crosby, and Harold A. Haswell: *Academic Degrees,* U.S. Office of Education Bulletin no. 28, 1960.

Epler, Stephen Edward: *Honorary Degrees: A Survey of Their Use and Abuse,* American Council on Public Affairs, Washington, 1943.
Whaley, W. Gordon: "American Academic Degrees," *The Educational Record,* Fall, 1966.

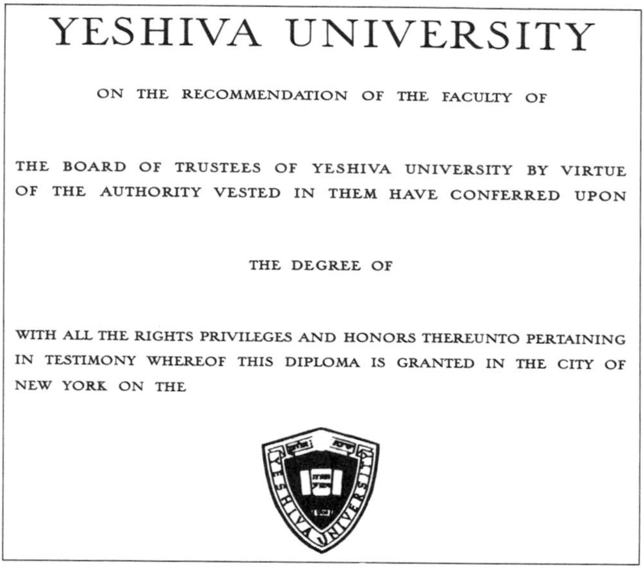

YESHIVA UNIVERSITY

ON THE RECOMMENDATION OF THE FACULTY OF

THE BOARD OF TRUSTEES OF YESHIVA UNIVERSITY BY VIRTUE OF THE AUTHORITY VESTED IN THEM HAVE CONFERRED UPON

THE DEGREE OF

WITH ALL THE RIGHTS PRIVILEGES AND HONORS THEREUNTO PERTAINING IN TESTIMONY WHEREOF THIS DIPLOMA IS GRANTED IN THE CITY OF NEW YORK ON THE

Fig. 4 *Yeshiva University, undeclared degree. The design is contemporary and may be used at any level of achievement.*

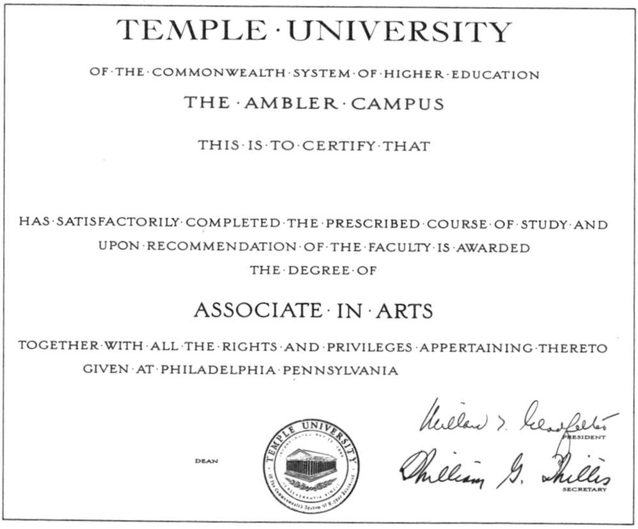

TEMPLE · UNIVERSITY

OF · THE · COMMONWEALTH · SYSTEM · OF · HIGHER · EDUCATION

THE · AMBLER · CAMPUS

THIS · IS · TO · CERTIFY · THAT

HAS · SATISFACTORILY · COMPLETED · THE · PRESCRIBED · COURSE · OF · STUDY · AND UPON · RECOMMENDATION · OF · THE · FACULTY · IS · AWARDED THE · DEGREE · OF

ASSOCIATE · IN · ARTS

TOGETHER · WITH · ALL · THE · RIGHTS · AND · PRIVILEGES · APPERTAINING · THERETO GIVEN · AT · PHILADELPHIA · PENNSYLVANIA

DEAN

PRESIDENT

SECRETARY

Fig. 5 *Temple University, Associate in Arts degree. Contemporary design. Partial pre-printing of signatures.*

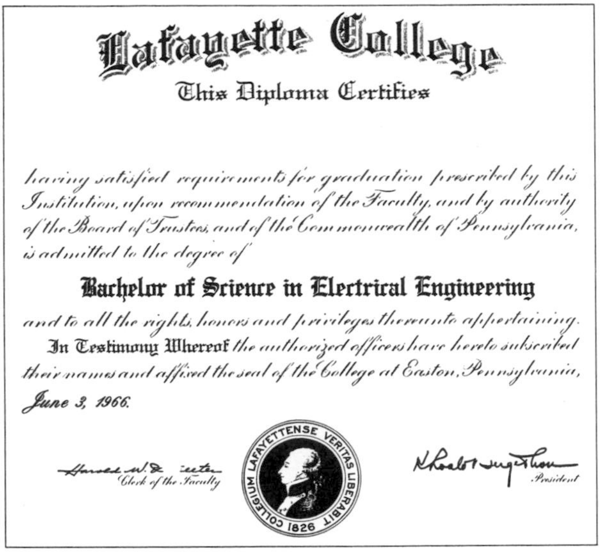

Lafayette College

This Diploma Certifies

having satisfied requirements for graduation prescribed by this Institution, upon recommendation of the Faculty, and by authority of the Board of Trustees, and of the Commonwealth of Pennsylvania, is admitted to the degree of

Bachelor of Science in Electrical Engineering

and to all the rights, honors and privileges thereunto appertaining.

In Testimony Whereof the authorized officers have hereto subscribed their names and affixed the seal of the College at Easton, Pennsylvania, June 3, 1966.

COLLEGIUM LAFAYETTENSE VERITAS LIBERABIT 1826

Clerk of the Faculty

President

Fig. 6 *Lafayette College, baccalaureate degree with specification. Traditional design. The seal is an excellent example of fine line engraving.*

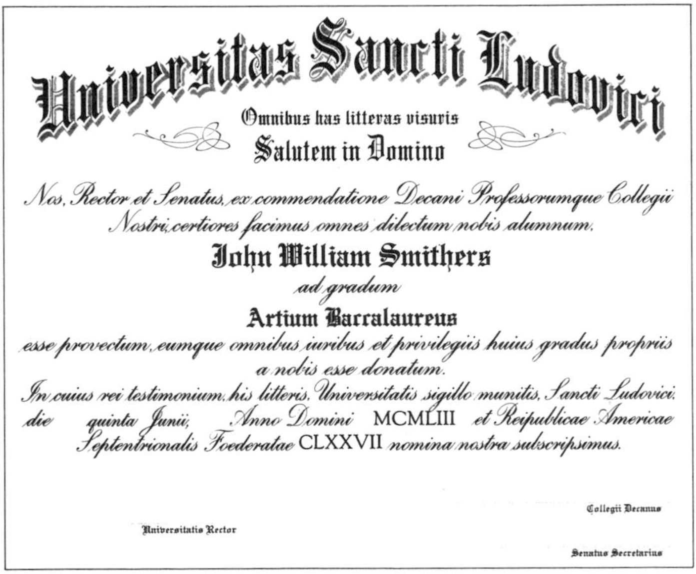

Universitas Sancti Ludovici

Omnibus has litteras visuris

Salutem in Domino

Nos, Rector et Senatus, ex commendatione Decani Professorumque Collegii Nostri, certiores facimus omnes dilectum nobis alumnum,

John William Smithers

ad gradum

Artium Baccalaureus

esse provectum, eumque omnibus iuribus et privilegiis huius gradus propriis a nobis esse donatum.

In cuius rei testimonium, his litteris, Universitatis sigillo munitis, Sancti Ludovici die quinta Junii, Anno Domini MCMLIII et Reipublicae Americae Septentrionalis Foederatae CLXXVII nomina nostra subscripsimus.

Collegii Decanus

Universitatis Rector

Senatus Secretarius

Fig. 7 *Baccalaureate degree printed in Latin. Traditional design.*

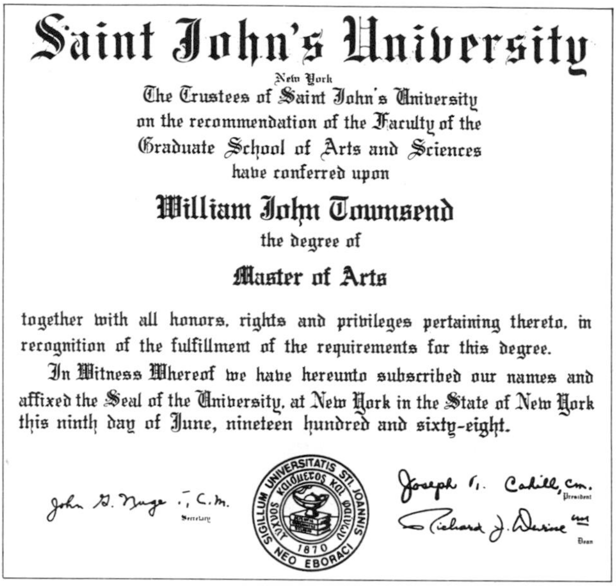

Saint John's University

New York

The Trustees of Saint John's University
on the recommendation of the Faculty of the
Graduate School of Arts and Sciences
have conferred upon

William John Townsend

the degree of

Master of Arts

together with all honors, rights and privileges pertaining thereto, in recognition of the fulfillment of the requirements for this degree.

In Witness Whereof we have hereunto subscribed our names and affixed the Seal of the University, at New York in the State of New York this ninth day of June, nineteen hundred and sixty-eight.

Secretary

SIGILLUM UNIVERSITATIS STI. JOANNIS NEO EBORACI 1870

Joseph T. Cahill, C.M.
President

Richard J. Devine C.M.
Dean

Fig. 8 *Saint John's University, Master of Arts degree. Each signature has been pre-printed in this diploma of traditional design.*

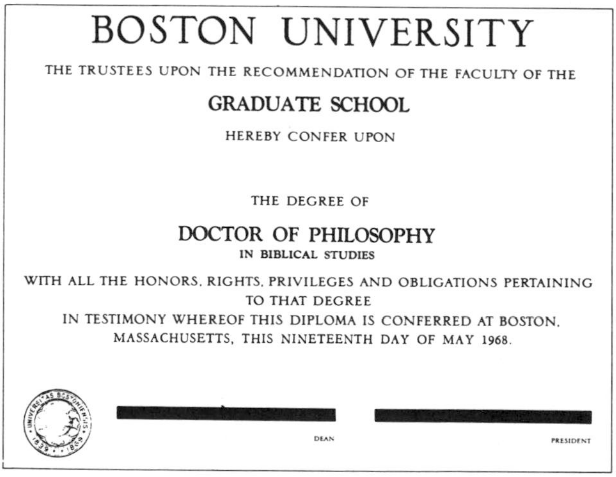

BOSTON UNIVERSITY

THE TRUSTEES UPON THE RECOMMENDATION OF THE FACULTY OF THE

GRADUATE SCHOOL

HEREBY CONFER UPON

THE DEGREE OF

DOCTOR OF PHILOSOPHY

IN BIBLICAL STUDIES

WITH ALL THE HONORS, RIGHTS, PRIVILEGES AND OBLIGATIONS PERTAINING
TO THAT DEGREE
IN TESTIMONY WHEREOF THIS DIPLOMA IS CONFERRED AT BOSTON,
MASSACHUSETTS, THIS NINETEENTH DAY OF MAY 1968.

[redacted]
DEAN

[redacted]
PRESIDENT

Fig. 9 *Boston University, Doctor of Philosophy degree. Contemporary design.*

Chapter **15**

Cooperative Education

ROY L. WOOLDRIDGE

Vice-president and Dean of Cooperative Education, Northeastern University, Boston, Massachusetts

BACKGROUND INFORMATION

The National Commission for Cooperative Education adheres to the following definition of cooperative education:

> It is that educational plan which integrates classroom experience and practical work experience in industrial, business, government, or service-type work situations. The work experience constitutes a regular and essential element in the educative process and some minimum amount of work experience (at least two different periods of work, totaling at least 16 weeks) and minimum standards of performance are included in the requirements of the institution for a degree. In addition, there must be liaison between the administration of the institution and the employing firm. The essential criteria are that the work experience be considered an integral part of the educational process, and that the institution take a definite responsibility for this integration.[1]

It is called "cooperative education" because it is dependent upon the cooperation of employers and educators in combining to form a superior total educational program for the students. This program has an interrelated work and study content, carefully planned and supervised to produce optimum educational results for each student involved.

Basic Observations

This system of education is based on two observations regarding students in the United States:

1. Every profession for which students are preparing contains certain knowledge elements that cannot be taught in the classroom. These elements can only be learned by students through direct, on-the-job experience, working with professionals who are already in the field. In some advanced professions, this requirement is met by the intern principle.

2. Most of the students in this country must find employment on a part-time basis while they are in school and during their vacation periods in order to earn part of the cost of their education. In almost all cases, jobs have no relation to ultimate career aims and, therefore, do not contribute substantially to the educational program of the students.

Work-study cooperative education, on the other hand, satisfies the dual desire of providing income-producing jobs and at the same time extending and amplifying the learning process of students. Under a cooperative program, the educational institution designs an academic calendar which allows the insertion of work periods at appropriate intervals in the curriculum. The institution assumes the responsibility for finding positions which are related to the students' professional objectives and which thus provide work experience that enhances knowledge associated with educational aims. These jobs are regular, paying positions, producing income by which students can finance their education.

In general, a key operative factor in the cooperative plan is a faculty coordinator. His responsibility is to find employers in his students' fields of interest and to bring such employers into a cooperative relationship with the institution. A cooperating employer must be willing to provide work to be shared by two students, one of whom works on the job while the other attends college. At the end of a specified period of time, the two students change places. This keeps the job continuously filled, while each of the two students assigned to it is enabled to spend half his time in college. The length of the period of alternation varies in different institutions, as does the total

[1] James W. Wilson and Edward H. Lyons, *Work-Study College Programs*, Harper & Brothers, New York, 1961, p. 19.

amount of work experience required and the point in the student's curriculum at which it starts.

The two-man-team principle is generally observed in cooperative programs, but it is not universally followed nor is it considered a fundamental principle of the cooperative system. Some institutions have arranged their programs so that all their students go to work at the same time, with all returning to college at one time. Even those institutions that use the two-man-team arrangement have found it desirable in certain instances to provide only one co-op student for a given job providing the job assignment can be handled in such a way as to permit the student to return to college for the regular class period. The essential feature of cooperative education is not the pairing of students but alternation between periods of employment, regulated by the college, and periods of classroom work at the college.

Description of Programs

Most, although not all, cooperative programs require five years for a bachelor's degree rather than the four-year conventional pattern. This lengthening of the curriculum is necessary to satisfy the academic requirements of various accrediting agencies. The cooperative student in completing his degree requirements must accumulate the same number of credit hours in the classroom setting as the conventional student. The work phase of the program is supplementary to the academic work and does not replace any part of it. In most cases, the first year on campus is a normal academic year from September to June, followed by four years on the alternating cycle of work and study.

In some programs, such as those at Drexel Institute, the University of Cincinnati, the University of Detroit, and Antioch College as well as Northeastern University, all students in certain colleges of the institutions are included in the program, and the faculty coordinators must find employment opportunities for a wide cross section of students. In others, such as those at Georgia Institute of Technology, the University of Tennessee, the University of South Florida, and Northwestern University, the program is optional; therefore, only part of the student body participates in the work-study alternation. Frequently, when an optional program is in existence, the institution will also exercise some selectivity, and not all students who elect the program will be allowed to participate. In most cases, this selectivity is based on academic performance, and the student must maintain a certain designated quality point average to qualify for and remain in the cooperative program.

Rensselaer Polytechnic Institute, Cornell University, and Massachusetts Institute of Technology operate highly selective programs wherein the student not only must meet certain academic requirements but must also be selected by one of the participating companies following a series of personal interviews. Under this system, the cooperative program is set up on a contractual basis between the company and the educational institution.

Another variation is found at such schools as Keuka College, Bennington College, and Goddard College, wherein all the students are assigned to work at the same time and an alternating pattern is not utilized. Frequently, this work period is scheduled between semesters in the winter and is considered part of the requirements for a degree.

Finally, there are programs such as one at Berea College in which the entire student body is employed on campus jobs by the institution. Under this system, the students provide a useful work force for the college and at the same time earn financial credits which are used to reduce tuition charges.

Methods of Application

Cooperative education is thought of by some as exclusively identified with engineering disciplines. This misconception stems from the fact that it began in an engineering school and has enjoyed its greatest growth in technical education. Since 1946, however, there has been a marked and rapid proliferation of cooperative education into other areas such as business administration, education, and liberal arts.

The extension of cooperative education into many professional fields reflects acceptance by educators of the idea that work experience should be part of the student's total education. Even the generalist in liberal arts can enhance his education through periods of guided employment in the world beyond the campus. Such productive employment under realistic competitive conditions in a real-life, adult-dominated environment will provide the student with insights that will enrich his educational experience. Obviously the learning process in a variety of off-campus conditions will vary from student to student, according to the maturity and judgment of the individual. His education will be enhanced and his responsiveness heightened to the extent that the faculty of the institution will recognize the possibilities for learning and capitalize on these in their counseling and classroom presentations.

For the students who are vocationally oriented and who have a clear idea of their ultimate career choice, the job assignments will provide sequences of work with increasing responsibility in the fields for which they are preparing. This frequently means that the job assignments will be with a minimum number of employers. Indeed the most effective development may be brought about if the student remains with one employer all through the program.

For students who do not have clear vocational objectives and who are seeking to orient themselves to a work view, a series of job assignments can be arranged to provide breadth of experience. In such situations, however, the student will frequently be placed in starting positions with several employers and will not normally achieve much increase in responsibility as he samples different fields of work. There is less integration of work and study in this type of program, and the value to the student is more dependent on his initiative and perception. As a rule, even such a variegated work experience helps the student to define a career objective.

SPECIAL ADMINISTRATIVE PROBLEMS

One of the problems facing each institution in the installation of the cooperative program is the willingness of the faculty to accept the philosophy of education upon which it is based. Simply stated, cooperative education is based on the principle that well-educated individuals can be best developed through a pattern which dips them into the reality of the world beyond the boundaries of the campus. Through these controlled and structured experiences the students bring an enrichment to the classroom which enhances their total development. This is a difficult concept for many faculty members to accept. Traditionally, in this country, higher education has been designed on the classic formula of separating the student from the distractions of life during his formative years and allowing full concentration on academic pursuits. In the cloistered atmosphere of the community of scholars, the student, in dialogue with the faculty and fellow students, searches for truth and knowledge.

Administrative and Faculty Acceptance

In every institution where the cooperative program is to be successfully installed, there must be one or two individuals, either teaching faculty or administrators, who are willing to accept this philosophy of education. Not only must they accept it, but they must also develop a strong conviction that this educational plan will best serve the students in achieving their objectives. These individuals then become the leaders who spearhead the investigation and development of the cooperative education program.

In order to proceed beyond this initial stage, there must be an openmindedness among at least a majority of the rest of the faculty and administration. If not, the program will never get beyond the exploratory stage. This openmindedness involves a willingness to consider the possibility of major changes in the institution as a result of the adoption of cooperative programs. The academic calendar, the mechanics of operation, and the curricula must all be designed in terms of what is best for the cooperative students. These needs must have primary consideration, and the possibilities of alternate curricula on a conventional pattern must be incidental. If the cooperative feature is treated merely as a secondary objective, the plan will not thrive. Not only the administration but also the entire faculty of the institution must believe in cooperative education and collaborate in making it work. Many academic subjects are sequential, and advanced courses necessarily build on prerequisite elementary courses. The faculty must arrange the curricula so that a cooperative student who is away from the campus on alternate terms can pursue a logically organized sequence of courses.

Calendar Design

One of the great strengths of cooperative education is its flexibility in the method of operation. The basic concept of integrating work experience in an educational curriculum can be applied in many different ways. The calendar and schedule can be designed to fit the needs of the particular local community and the students to be served.

Regardless of the system to be used, the purpose of the calendar is to allow the alternation between study and work of a dual student body. Through this pattern the employer has year-around coverage of job assignments. On campus, the course sequences must be set in such a manner that progress toward the degree is achieved in a logical manner. This usually means frequent repetition of courses.

The most common calendar to be found among existing cooperative institutions is the quarter system. The 52-week calendar year is divided into four 13-week quarters. Another frequent calendar is a modification of the semester system. In this case, three 16-week semesters with four weeks of vacation distributed throughout the year make up the 52 weeks. In all cases, the complete year-around operation of the educational plan is envisioned in the design. This means that the conventional summer vacation commonly found in academic calendars does not exist.

There are certain areas of administration that are complicated by the alternating pattern of a cooperative program calendar. Student housing is one of these areas, since allowance must be made for some students living in university residences during their work periods as well as during academic periods. This makes scheduling of room assignments an unusually difficult task. Also, there are potential problems in housing students in a dormitory who are not involved with academic subjects and thus free to disturb others.

The student activities and athletic programs are directly affected by the calendar. Almost all student clubs and organizations must be conducted in duplicate with a set of officers and programs in each division of the student body. For intercollegiate athletics, the assignment of student athletes to a division must be made with a careful consideration of location and the duration of the active season of the sport. For some teams where the season covers both school and work periods, potential members must be placed on job assignments in the vicinity of the institution to allow attendance at practice sessions as well as participation in games.

The Reserve Officers' Training Corps is another area affected by a cooperative program calendar. Not only must course sequences be carefully planned to allow cooperative students the opportunity to participate, but the scheduling of summer camp must be handled on a very special basis. Since cooperative students do not have the usual summer vacations during their upperclass years, ROTC camp must be scheduled for the summer following their graduation. This means that commissions for cooperative students are not awarded at commencement in June but held over pending successful completion of summer camp.

Contracts for the hiring of faculty in a cooperative institution are complicated. Since the institution operates on a year-around basis, adequate coverage must be planned for the summer session. This usually means that some faculty will be hired on a longer-than-normal contract year. A salary adjustment must be made to maintain their wages on a competitive basis with colleagues on standard contracts. Some extra faculty must be engaged in the summer for courses which will not be covered by regular faculty.

A final complication due to the calendar appears in the general tightness of the schedule and the pressure on both the faculty and the administration to gets things done in an efficient and businesslike manner. There is not much opportunity for a leisurely approach to commitments and responsibilities. From a housekeeping point of view, the scheduling of maintenance, repair work, and remodeling is a problem due to intensive use of all facilities.

Establishment of Coordination Staff

The key to the success of cooperative education in meeting the cyclical variations of employment lies in the caliber of the faculty coordinators who are responsible for the operation of the program. It is imperative that a centralized staff of faculty coordinators be engaged to implement the cooperative plan if it is to grow to be a substantial part of the institution's program. Only if cooperative education is to be optional and limited to a very small percentage of the student body can the teaching faculty operate the program as a part-load arrangement. Building a strong and effective staff of faculty coordinators is the most effective way of reducing variations in the employment market. Through their knowledge of various companies, through their friendships with personnel directors, department managers, or owners of businesses, through their ability to maintain a balanced program between stable employment opportunities and those less stable but still offering good experience, employment can be held to a high level.

If an institution is to begin a modest program with less than 200 students and one faculty coordinator, the following table represents estimated costs for the establishment

TABLE 1 Estimated Costs for Establishment of Cooperative Education Program *

Expense item	1st year		2d year		3d year	
Salaries:						
Director	$15,000		$16,000		$17,000	
Secretary	5,000		5,300		5,600	
Social Security, etc.	2,000		2,130		2,260	
		$22,000		$23,430		$24,860
Office expenses:						
Supplies	$ 2,900		$ 400		$ 400	
Postage	100		100		100	
Telephone	1,000		1,000		1,000	
Travel	2,000		2,000		2,000	
Publications	2,000		2,000		2,000	
Conferences	1,000		1,000		1,000	
		$ 9,000		$ 6,500		$ 6,500
Training and development:						
Living expenses at training center	$ 2,400		$ –		$ –	
Faculty travel	1,000		1,000		–	
		$ 3,400		$ 1,000		$ –
Total		$34,400		$30,930		$31,360

* Figures compiled in 1969; to be adjusted to cost-of-living fluctuations.

of this department over the first three years. Salary figures would vary according to local economic conditions. It is assumed that after the initial three-year period, the income from additional students who can be accommodated under the dual calendar would offset the cost of operation.

Fiscal Policies

Generally, a sizable cooperative program creates a favorable financial situation for several reasons. The dual student body allows a more efficient use of both physical facilities and faculty. More students can be accommodated and, therefore, income is increased. The community service aspect of establishing cooperative arrangements with employers gives the university fund raisers an opening for soliciting financial support. Many of the service departments, such as library, admissions, student activities, student accounts, etc., do not have to be expanded in proportion to the larger student body.

Despite these advantages there are some fiscal problems which result from the alternating calendar. The income to the university is distributed throughout the year at the beginning of each school session. This sets up a different pattern of income than is normally found in a conventional institution and must be carefully planned for in plotting a flow-of-funds chart. At times it is necessary to use short-term loans to carry the institution through periods of expense until the income period is reached.

ADOPTION OF THE COOPERATIVE PROGRAM

The initial step in the consideration of the cooperative program usually involves requesting consulting aid. There are two main sources that provide consulting service: The National Commission for Cooperative Education in New York City and the Center for Cooperative Education at Northeastern University in Boston, Massachusetts. Both these organizations have received partial support from Ford Foundation grants.

During the first consulting visit there is usually a discussion of the cooperative program with the president and administrators of the institution. A thorough examination is made of the advantages and disadvantages, the various methods and forms of cooperative education, and the role the program can play in the development of the institution and its goals.

Following this meeting, if the reaction is favorable, the cooperative plan is presented to larger segments of the university community. In some cases this involves a presentation to a board of trustees or committees of the board, to faculty committees, departmental committees, or the entire faculty at a general meeting. All interested parties are given an opportunity to hear about the program, read available literature, and receive answers to their questions.

Consulting aid is also available to follow up with specific planning of the program, assuming a positive action by the faculty and administration. This aid involves assisting in the calendar design and in the formulation of appropriate policies and procedures. The selection and training of a faculty coordinator often requires considerable consultation, and even after the inauguration of the program the new coordinator will need some assistance in finding solutions to various problems.

Establishment of Planning Committee

After the initial exploration of the program, it is customary for the college or university to establish a planning committee of faculty and administrators. This committee is charged with the responsibility for proposing preliminary policy and curriculum changes, planning the transition, and setting target dates for the accomplishment of the objectives.

Policy Decisions

Some of the preliminary policy decisions involve the following questions about various aspects of a cooperative program:

Institutional Calendar Should the program be designed to lead to a bachelor's degree in five years or four years? Will the basic pattern be a quarter system, a semester system, or some special-length term? Should students spend the first year entirely on campus before beginning the alternating pattern? Should there be a full-time-on-campus senior year? Does the calendar allow a perfect alternation of students so that potential employers have continuous coverage of job assignments? How can transfer students be integrated into the program?

Student Participation Is the program to be optional or mandatory? If optional, should the institution be selective in choosing students to participate? Can cooperative education be offered in all colleges or divisions of the institution? Should it be limited to professional programs? What are the economics of various size programs? How many students are needed to ensure financial success?

Objectives of the Program Should the program seek to provide students with in-depth exposure through a series of experiences with a minimum number of employers? Is it better to plan a variety of experiences with different employers? What kinds of employers should be contacted and what are their expectations? How wide a geographic distribution of assignments should be sought? Should cooperative assignments be realistic jobs or observer positions?

Coordination Staff Should the program be coordinated by faculty members on a part-load basis, or is it better to have a central coordination staff devoting full time to the coordination? Should these coordinators have faculty rank? What place in the institution's administration does the director of the program hold? To whom does he report and on what committees does he serve?

Rules and Regulations How can the cooperative program be made a degree requirement? Should academic credit be given for work periods? What procedure is to be followed when students fail on assignments? Is there a procedure to be followed for students to appeal unfavorable decisions? What types of reports are required from the employers and students? Are the rules firm but fair in allowing an orderly administration of the program? Is there sufficient flexibility to allow for the unusual cases?

The planning committee also has the responsibility for determining the changes in curriculum that are necessary for the integration of the cooperative program. This means the planning of proper course sequences so that the cooperative students can proceed in a sound manner toward their degree. Decisions must be made on the repetition of courses and the methods of covering these courses by appropriate faculty assignments. Generally, the cooperative program does not entail any changes in the basic curriculum. Students on the program should study the same academic subjects as students pursuing the same major in a conventional program.

If the cooperative program is to be introduced into an existing institution, then the committee must give some thought to the transition phase. Will the program be offered to students already enrolled? If so, how can their curriculum be changed to allow completion of degree requirements? Also, enrolled students must be allowed to complete their program in a conventional manner if they decide to do so. If the program is to be offered only to new entrants, how can they be phased into the existing structure of the institution? These and other related questions must be answered by the planning committee.

Finally, after all other decisions have been made, the committee must establish target dates for the installation of the program. If possible, a full year of planning is recommended before beginning the program. Sufficient time is needed for announcing the program, hiring and training the coordinator, publishing the necessary materials, contacting the employers to determine their needs, and interviewing and counseling the students.

Hiring and Training of Coordinators

The basic question, as with many positions, is whether to look for a candidate with experience in the field or to appoint a person already with the institution and have him trained to handle the job. Since cooperative education is a relatively new field, there are not many people with experience available on the market. However, both the National Commission for Cooperative Education and the Northeastern University Center for Cooperative Education occasionally have résumés from coordinators seeking new positions.

The most common pattern in the establishment of new cooperative programs has been to appoint someone from within the institution. This has the advantage of making the coordinator a person who is thoroughly familiar with the institution and its channels of authority and communication. Also, if a member of the teaching faculty is chosen, he will probably already have the acceptance and respect of his faculty colleagues. If no one is available on the current staff, then frequently the institution will turn to an alumnus. Again, the advantage is the familiarity with the institution and its goals.

In any event, the training of the individual is best accomplished with consulting aid which is now available through the Center for Cooperative Education at Northeastern University. Individual and workshop sessions are scheduled throughout the year, and many new coordinators have received successful training. It has also been helpful to have the new coordinator visit several existing cooperative education institutions as part of his training program.

Preparation of Publications

Once the preliminary planning has been done and the coordinator hired, it is necessary to prepare the publications announcing the program. The first item would normally be a general announcement about the installation of the cooperative program, its objectives, and its time schedule. This brochure would be used broadly in the community to bring the program to the attention of a wide audience.

An attractive booklet designed for high school students and guidance counselors should be prepared presenting the program from the standpoint of a prospective student. It should be written so that it is easily understandable on that level, and generous use of pictures and illustrations has been found to be effective. A sufficient quantity should be ordered to allow a free distribution to any and all interested parties.

A similar booklet must be produced explaining the cooperative program from the potential employers' viewpoint. Again, the booklet must be written to suit the anticipated audience. This means that one booklet cannot be produced to cover both the students and the employers. The employer booklet must be brief, to the point, informative, and free of pictures and illustrations.

It must be borne in mind that the cooperative program must be mentioned in appropriate places in revisions of the catalog and other standard institutional publications.

Contacts with Employers

It is necessary to bring the cooperative program to the attention of the business community, since this is the source of job assignments for the students in the program. Generally, an enthusiastic response can be anticipated since cooperative education enjoys a favorable reputation with employers across the country.

Often, the initial announcement can be made at a luncheon conference on campus, with the college or university president serving as host. In some cases this luncheon has been followed up by afternoon conference sessions on the details of the cooperative program.

It is also the job of the faculty coordinator to make personal visits to solicit cooperative assignments. This can be done on a general exploratory basis to establish relationships, or it can be very specifically planned to meet the particular needs of certain students in the program.

Finally, it has been useful in some cases to use local service clubs and organizations to announce the cooperative program. Sometimes this involves sending mailings to members and at other times sending a guest speaker to luncheon and dinner meetings. Such organizations as chambers of commerce, Rotary clubs, and Kiwanis clubs have been used to serve this purpose.

Contacts with Schools

It is also important that appropriate information be distributed to high school counselors and principals so that they may understand the nature of the program and its advantages in referring students. In many instances, the initial announcement can be made at a luncheon meeting or conference on campus. It has been found profitable to have annual meetings of this type in order to keep the program in front of the guidance counselors and principals.

For coverage over a wide geographic area, the admissions staff of the college or university should be thoroughly acquainted with the program so that they can carry the story during their recruiting visits. Frequently it has been found that employers in remote areas will cooperate with the admissions staff in bringing the program to the attention of local school authorities. Naturally, their motivation is to attract students to the cooperative program who may accept assignments with their companies during their work periods.

FINANCING THE PROGRAM

Earlier in this chapter there was some discussion of fiscal policies and the estimated costs of staffing the coordination department. In addition to these costs, some funds will be needed for additional faculty to cover the year-around operation of the academic program.

Consulting Service

Funds are needed to purchase consulting aid. Sample annual costs are as follows, assuming 30 days of consulting time per year (20 days at the college or university and 10 days in the consultant's office):

TABLE 2 Estimated Annual Cost of Consulting Service

Expense item	Cost	
Fees:		
Consultant 30 days at $100 per day	$3,000	
		$3,000
Travel:		
20 days × $25 expenses per day	$ 500	
6 trips at estimated airline fare of $250	1,500	
		$2,000
Total		$5,000

Source of Funds

It is obvious that presidents of colleges and universities that are installing cooperative programs should use their contacts at various foundations to seek financial support. In recent years, several major foundations have been interested in giving total or partial support for cooperative education programs. In most cases the support has included the direct costs of establishing the coordination staff and the cost of consulting services. The hiring of extra faculty has been left to the institution to provide as its own contribution.

At times there is sufficient interest in the program on the part of local businesses and industries to support a fund-raising program to provide the start-up costs. This is particularly true if they can see a recruiting advantage in the establishment of the program. The danger is that programs supported in this manner are often dependent upon continued retention of graduates by the employers. Companies and business firms become disenchanted and dissatisfied if they do not attract and hold the best students and graduates. It is extremely difficult for the educational institution to promise success to the employer from this standpoint.

Recently the federal government, through the Office of Education in the Department of Health, Education, and Welfare, has given some financial aid for the installation of cooperative programs in developing institutions under Title III of the Higher Education Act of 1965. Information concerning application procedures can be obtained by contacting the Director of the Division of College Support in the U.S. Office of Education.

In October, 1968, the Higher Education Amendments of 1968 were signed into law by President Lyndon B. Johnson. Title IV D of this act authorizes grants to institutions of higher education to expand and strengthen student programs which alternate periods of full-time study and full-time employment. At the time of writing, the application guidelines are being developed by the staff of the U.S. Office of Education. It is suggested that interested parties contact the Director of the Division of College Support for information about application procedures.

BIBLIOGRAPHY

Leuba, Clarence: *Effective Learning and Cooperative Education,* paper read before Cooperative Education Division of the American Society for Engineering Education, 1964, National Commission for Cooperative Education, New York, 1964.

Knowles, Asa S.: *A College President Looks at Co-operative Education,* paper read before Co-operative Education Division of the American Society for Engineering Education, 1964, National Commission for Cooperative Education, New York, 1964.

Park, Clyde W.: *Ambassador to Industry, The Idea and Life of Herman Schneider,* The Bobbs-Merrill Company, Inc., Indianapolis, 1943.

Seaverns, Charles F., Jr.: *A Manual for Coordinators of Cooperative Education,* Center for Co-operative Education, Boston, 1966.

Wilson, James W., and Edward H. Lyons: *Work-Study College Programs,* Harper & Brothers, New York, 1961.

Wooldridge, Roy L.: *Analysis of Student Employment in a Cooperative Education Program,* Center for Cooperative Education, Northeastern University, Boston, 1964 (revised 1966 and 1968).

———: *Student Employment and Cooperative Education—Its Growth and Stability,* National Commission for Cooperative Education, New York, 1964.

———: *Cooperative Education and the Community Colleges in New Jersey,* National Commission for Cooperative Education, New York, 1966 (Supplementary Report Prepared for the Governor's Committee on New Jersey Higher Education).

Hand in Hand, Fifty Years of Industry-aided Selective Cooperative Education, 1908–1958, The Hand in Hand Book Committee, Alfred L. Dowden, Chairman, Gordon & Company, Medford, Mass., 1958.

Chapter 16

Accreditation

RALPH A. BURNS

Former Director of Evaluation, Commission on Institutions of Higher Education, New England Association of Colleges and Secondary Schools, Inc., Boston, Massachusetts

Voluntary accreditation of educational institutions is a uniquely American device to promote and uphold high standards of quality in education. The United States has no national control over education. Governance of our colleges and universities remains in the hands and heads of our institutional leaders, who have formed a voluntary association for mutual guidance and protection. This association does not control but acts as a catalyst for the preservation and improvement of the standards of our institutions of higher learning.

The voluntary self-regulation of colleges and universities is described by the United States Office of Education in this manner:

> The voluntary accrediting organizations, regional and nationwide, have no legal control over institutions of higher education. They merely promulgate standards of quality or criteria of institutional excellence and approve or admit to membership the institutions that meet those standards or criteria. The only power that the accrediting organizations have is that of giving publicity to the lists of institutions they have accredited. Inclusion on the approved list of a nationally recognized accrediting organization is generally accepted as the most significant available indication of institutional quality.

Accreditation in higher education, therefore, is the recognition by a voluntary association composed of its peers that the quality of a degree-granting institution's operation meets certain standards preconceived by the association. Such recognition is called "institutional" or "general" accreditation.

There is, however, another type of accreditation, generally designated as "program" or "professional" accreditation. The basic principles or criteria underlying each form are similar. In this latter case, the recognition is by a voluntary specialized association that establishes standards for the programs offered by its peers. This type of accreditation is characteristic of professional, semiprofessional, and many other specialized programs both at the undergraduate and graduate levels.

The primary purpose of all accreditation, whether it be general or professional, is that of raising the general level of higher education. This is a goal to which all subscribe. Accreditation benefits the public by providing it with a basis by which it can measure an institution's integrity and general competence in providing higher education within the confines of its own objectives. To the student, accreditation affords a guarantee of the level of education he is receiving and the acceptability of his undergraduate education as a basis for advanced study. Here, it should be noted that some graduate schools will not accept a student into their programs if he has not completed his undergraduate studies at an accredited institution.

Failure to receive accreditation or loss of accreditation can cost a school the services of good faculty, most of whom would not agree to teach in an institution where the level of education is beneath that required for accreditation. Even the federal government will not approve the appropriation of funds to an institution lacking appropriate accreditation credentials. From this it can be seen that accreditation, or the pursuit of it, is the backbone of high standards of education.

RESPONSIBILITY FOR ACCREDITATION

The responsibility for accreditation of educational institutions in the United States has been assumed by two major agencies which have arisen from associations formed by institutions of higher education on their own initiative. These agencies are officially approved by appropriate authorities (federal and state governments, foundations, and peer groups) to perform the function known as accreditation. One group of these agencies is regional in scope and organization and has six subdivisions; the other major agency is national. The former encompasses the entire institution; the latter, specialized programs of study within the institution. Both agencies have similar objectives.

The regional agencies, the states served by each, and their headquarters for higher education, listed alphabetically, are as follows:

Middle States Association of Colleges and Secondary Schools
Canal Zone, Delaware, District of Columbia, Maryland, New Jersey, New York, Pennsylvania, Puerto Rico, Virgin Islands
F. Taylor Jones, Executive Secretary
Commission on Institutions of Higher Education
225 Broadway
New York, N.Y. 10007

New England Association of Colleges and Secondary Schools
Connecticut, Maine, Massachusetts, New Hampshire, Rhode Island, Vermont
Robert Ramsey, Director of Evaluation
Commission on Institutions of Higher Education
50 Beacon Street
Boston, Mass. 02108

North Central Association of Colleges and Secondary Schools
Arizona, Arkansas, Colorado, Illinois, Indiana, Iowa, Kansas, Michigan, Minnesota, Missouri, Nebraska, New Mexico, North Dakota, Ohio, Oklahoma, South Dakota, West Virginia, Wisconsin, Wyoming
Norman Burns, Secretary
Commission on Colleges and Universities
5454 South Shore Drive
Chicago, Ill. 60615

Northwest Association of Secondary and Higher Schools
Alaska, Idaho, Montana, Nevada, Oregon, Utah, Washington
James F. Bemis, Executive Director
Commission on Higher Schools
3917 Fifteenth Avenue, N.E.
Seattle, Wash. 98105

Southern Association of Colleges and Schools
Alabama, Florida, Georgia, Kentucky, Louisiana, Mississippi, North Carolina, South Carolina, Tennessee, Texas, Virginia

Charles B. Vail, Acting Executive Secretary
Commission on Colleges and Universities
795 Peachtree Street, N.E.
Atlanta, Ga. 30308
Western Association of Schools and Colleges
California, Guam, Hawaii
Accrediting Commission for Senior Colleges and Universities
Francis H. Herrick, Secretary
In care of Mills College
Oakland, Calif. 94613
Accrediting Commission for Junior Colleges
Henry T. Tyler, Secretary
In care of Modesto Junior College
Modesto, Calif. 95350

General institutional accreditation is performed by these voluntary regional accrediting agencies. The United States is divided into six regions, as mentioned above, each of which has organized a voluntary educational association in which membership means accreditation. These associations accredit not only degree-granting institutions but also secondary schools, public and independent. These regional agencies accredit only nonprofit public and private educational institutions. They do not attempt to accredit proprietary institutions.

Recently the requirement that an institution must be a nonprofit corporation in order to be eligible to apply for regional accreditation has been challenged by court action. The Marjorie Webster Junior College, a proprietary institution located in the District of Columbia, brought suit against the Middle States Association of Colleges and Secondary Schools. The plaintiff invoked the antitrust laws of the United States mainly under the provisions of Section 3 of the Sherman Antitrust Act, and Section 16 of the Clayton Act.

Judgment in this case was in favor of the plaintiff. An injunction was issued by the Court prohibiting the defendant from excluding the plaintiff from eligibility for accreditation due to its proprietary character. The Middle States Association appealed the decision. The United States Court of Appeals for the District of Columbia Circuit has granted a temporary stay on the injunction to provide time for the defendant to prepare arguments for the appeal.

Commissions are formed by the associations to implement the accrediting process. In general, there is a commission for higher education and one for secondary education in each association. There are, however, some regional associations which vary from this organizational pattern. For instance, the New England Association has three commissions—one for higher education, one for independent secondary schools, and one for public secondary schools. In the Western Association, there are two commissions of higher education (one for the junior colleges and one for four-year colleges and universities) and one for the secondary schools. It should be pointed out, further, that the Southern Association also accredits or approves elementary schools and has a separate commission for this purpose. The number of members forming a commission varies from region to region; otherwise, two commissions, higher and secondary, are the rule.

It is the commission for higher education that is authorized by its association to establish the standards, policies, and procedures which are used in the accrediting process. In some cases, like the Middle States Association, it is the commission alone which makes the final decision on whether an institution is accredited; but in general the commissions only recommend accreditation to their executive committees and member delegates who finalize the accrediting action. Accreditation is the main business of the Commission on Institutions of Higher Education and the other commissions.

ELIGIBILITY FOR REGIONAL ACCREDITATION

In general, eligibility for consideration of an institution for regional accreditation rests on six basic requirements, as follows:

1. An institution should already have a charter and/or formal authority from the appropriate governmental agency to award the associate or higher degree.

2. The institution should be a nonprofit organization with a governing board representing the public interest.

3. Ordinarily, it should offer at least two years of higher education at the undergraduate level or at least one year at the graduate level.

4. Normally, it should have been in existence long enough to have graduated two classes.

5. It should require for admission the completion of not less than an appropriate secondary school curriculum or satisfactory evidence of equivalent educational achievement.

6. Its principal educational programs should rest upon a base of liberal studies required of all or most students.

Institutions which have branches in two or more of the designated regions are eligible in each region but can be accredited only through interregional action. The guidelines for such action are described by the following six regulations established jointly by the regional associations involved:

1. When important parts of an institution are located in the areas of two or more regional associations, the accreditation of the institution is the joint responsibility of all the commissions concerned, acting as though they had merged for this purpose.

2. The executive secretary of the commission in whose area the principal headquarters of the institution are located arranges and directs the evaluation, normally using his commission's materials and procedures, drawing upon the others for help.

3. The chairman of the evaluation team proposes a recommendation for action by the cooperating commissions. The executive secretary of the directing commission forwards it to the other commissions before action is taken by any of them. If time permits, he solicits comments on the proposal before any cooperating commission meets and tries to frame a revised recommendation, if that seems desirable.

4. No commission's action on an interregional accreditation is final until all the commissions involved have taken identical action.

5. If the action of any one commission varies in a minor way from the action of another in an interregional accreditation, the executive secretaries of the regions concerned attempt to find a compromise on behalf of the commissions involved.

6. When the action on accreditation has been completed, the executive secretary of the directing commission notifies the institution officially on behalf of all the commissions concerned.

THE NATIONAL COMMISSION ON ACCREDITING

The National Commission on Accrediting is responsible for professional or program accreditation. The accrediting action is taken by specialized agencies representative of the programs involved after the agency has been formally approved by the National Commission. The National Commission on Accrediting maintains a headquarters at 1785 Massachusetts Avenue, N.W., Washington, D.C. The specialized agencies, both professional and otherwise, have their own headquarters which are used to implement their programs. A detailed alphabetical list of agencies as of May, 1968, follows:

Architecture (professional schools)
National Architectural Accrediting Board
Harlan McClure, Secretary, NAAB

521 Eighteenth Street, N.W.
Washington, D.C. 20006
Art (institutions offering professional preparation)
National Association of Schools of Art
James R. Shipley, Chairman
Committee on Admissions and Accreditation, NASA
In care of Department of Art
University of Illinois
Champaign, Ill. 61822
Business (bachelor's and master's degree programs)
American Association of Collegiate Schools of Business
Cyril C. Ling, Executive Secretary, AACSB
101 North Skinker Road, Station 24
St. Louis, Mo. 63130
Chemistry (institutions offering undergraduate professional programs)
American Chemical Society
John H. Howard, Secretary
Committee on Professional Training, ACS
343 State Street
Rochester, N.Y. 14650
Cytotechnology (undergraduate programs)
American Medical Association, in cooperation with the American Society of Clinical Pathology
C. H. William Ruhe, Secretary
Council on Medical Education, AMA
535 North Dearborn Street
Chicago, Ill. 60610
Dental Hygiene (professional programs)
American Dental Association
Reginald Sullens, Secretary
Council on Dental Education, ADA
211 East Chicago Avenue
Chicago, Ill. 60611
Dentistry (programs leading to D.D.S. or D.M.D. degrees)
American Dental Association
Reginald Sullens (see Dental Hygiene)
Engineering (first professional degree curricula)
Engineers' Council for Professional Development
W. Scott Hill, Executive Secretary, ECPD
345 East 47th Street
New York, N.Y. 10017
Forestry (professional schools)
Society of American Foresters
John R. Meyering
Director of Professional Development, SAF
1010 Sixteenth Street, N.W.
Washington, D.C. 20036
Journalism (undergraduate professional programs)
American Council on Education for Journalism
Baskett Mosse, Executive Secretary
Accrediting Committee, ACEJ
563 Essex Court
Deerfield, Ill. 60201
Landscape Architecture (professional schools)
American Society of Landscape Architects
Frederick A. Cuthbert, Chairman
Committee on Education, ASLA
2065 Floral Hill Drive
Eugene, Ore. 97403

Law (professional schools)
American Bar Association
John G. Hervey, Adviser
Council of Section of Legal Education and Admissions to the Bar, ABA
Liberty Bank Building
Oklahoma City, Okla. 73102
Association of American Law Schools
Michael H. Cardozo, Executive Director, AALS
1521 New Hampshire Avenue, N.W.
Washington, D.C. 20036
Librarianship (schools offering five-year master's degree programs)
American Library Association
Lester Asheim, Director
Office for Library Education, ALA
50 East Huron Street
Chicago, Ill. 60611
Medical Record Librarianship (professional schools)
American Medical Association, in collaboration with the American Association of Medical Record Librarians
C. H. William Ruhe, Secretary
Council on Medical Education, AMA
535 North Dearborn Street
Chicago, Ill. 60610
Medical Record Technicians (associate degree programs)
American Medical Association, in cooperation with the Medical Record Library
C. H. William Ruhe (see Medical Record Librarianship)
Medical Technology (professional schools)
American Medical Association, in collaboration with the Board of Schools of Medical Technology (ASCP-ASMT)
C. H. William Ruhe (see Medical Record Librarianship)
Medicine (programs leading to M.D. degree)
Liaison Committee on Medical Education representing the Council on Medical Education of the American Medical Association and the Executive Council of the Association of American Medical Colleges (Note: Inquiries regarding accreditation of programs in medicine should be addressed in even-numbered years to the AMA Council and in odd-numbered years to the AAMC.).
C. H. William Ruhe, Secretary (see Medical Record Librarianship)
or
Robert E. Berson, Executive Director
Association of American Medical Colleges
1346 Connecticut Avenue, N.W.
Washington, D.C. 20036 (office address)
2530 Ridge Avenue
Evanston, Ill. 60201 (mail address)
Music (institutions granting degrees in music)
National Association of Schools of Music
David A. Ledet, Executive Secretary, NASM
1501 New Hampshire Avenue, N.W.
Washington, D.C. 20036
Nursing (bachelor's and master's degree programs)
National League for Nursing, Inc.
Mary A. Dineen, Director
Department of Baccalaureate and Higher Degree Programs, NLN
10 Columbus Circle
New York, N.Y. 10019
Occupational Therapy (professional schools)
American Medical Association, in collaboration with the American Occupational Therapy Association
C. H. William Ruhe (see Medical Record Librarianship)

Optometry (professional schools)
American Optometric Association
Charles Seger, Chairman
Council on Optometric Education, AOA
1407 Garden Street
San Luis Obispo, Calif. 93401
Osteopathy (programs leading to D.O. degree)
American Osteopathic Association
Lawrence W. Mills, Secretary
Bureau of Professional Education, AOA
212 East Ohio Street
Chicago, Ill. 60611
Pharmacy (professional schools)
American Council on Pharmaceutical Education
Fred T. Mahaffey, Secretary, ACPE
77 West Washington Street
Chicago, Ill. 60602
Physical Therapy (professional schools)
American Medical Association, in collaboration with the American Physical Therapy Association
C. H. William Ruhe (see Medical Record Librarianship)
Podiatry (professional)
Dr. Abe Rubin, D.S.C., Executive Director
Council on Education, American Podiatry Association
3301 Sixteenth Street, N.W.
Washington, D.C. 20010
Psychology (institutions offering doctoral programs in clinical or counseling psychology)
American Psychological Association
C. Alan Boneau, Administrative Officer for Educational Affairs
Education and Training Board, APA
1200 Seventeenth Street, N.W.
Washington, D.C. 20036
Public Health (graduate professional schools)
American Public Health Association
James L. Troupin
Director of Professional Education, APHA
1790 Broadway
New York, N.Y. 10019
Social Work (graduate professional schools)
Council on Social Work Education
Kurt Reichert, Director
Division of Educational Standards and Accreditation
345 East 46th Street
New York, N.Y. 10017
Speech Pathology and Audiology (master's degree programs)
American Speech and Hearing Association
Earl Schubert, Chairman
Education and Training Board, ASHA
9030 Old Georgetown Road, N.W.
Washington, D.C. 20014
Teacher Education (institutions offering bachelor's and higher degree programs)
National Council for Accreditation of Teacher Education
Rolf W. Larson, Director, NCATE
1750 Pennsylvania Avenue, N.W.
Washington, D.C. 20006
Theology (graduate professional schools)
American Association of Theological Schools in the United States and Canada
Jesse H. Ziegler, Executive Director, AATS

534 Third National Building
Dayton, Ohio 45402

Veterinary Medicine (schools offering D.M.V. or V.M.D. degree programs)
American Veterinary Medical Association
Ronald J. Kolar, Director
Department of Education & Licensure, AVMA
600 South Michigan Avenue
Chicago, Ill. 60605

X Ray Technology (technical, associate degree, and undergraduate programs)
American Medical Association, in cooperation with the American College of Radiology
C. H. William Ruhe (see Medical Record Librarianship)

A recent addition to this list of professional agencies is

Community Health Education (institutions offering master's degree programs)
American Public Health Association
James L. Troupin (see Public Health)

The following four groups are Auxiliary Accrediting Associations:

Dental Assisting (professional programs)
American Dental Association
Reginald Sullens (see Dental Hygiene)

Dental Technology (professional programs)
American Dental Association
Reginald Sullens (see Dental Hygiene)

Engineering Technology (two-year programs)
Engineers' Council for Professional Development
W. Scott Hill (see Engineering)

Nursing (technical nurse programs)
National League for Nursing
Gerald J. Griffin, Director
Department of Associate Degree Programs, NLN
10 Columbus Circle
New York, N.Y. 10019

The National Commission on Accrediting is an independent educational agency supported by the colleges and universities of the United States to improve the operation and effectiveness of accreditation in higher education. It is concerned with program accreditation in junior colleges, technical institutes, colleges and universities, and professional schools; but its purview does not extend to the accreditation of other types of institutions.

Membership in the National Commission on Accrediting consists of two types: constituent and institutional. Constituent members are represented by seven voluntary associations, as follows:

American Association of Junior Colleges
Association of American Colleges
Association of American Universities
Association of State Colleges and Universities
Association of State Universities and Land-grant Colleges
Association of Urban Universities
State Universities Association

Any college or university belonging to one of the above constituent associations is eligible for institutional membership. At present, over 1,270 colleges and universities are institutional members of the National Commission on Accrediting.

Each of the seven associations named appoints six representatives to the Board of

Commissioners, which is the governing body of the National Commission. These representatives are presidents or chief administrative officers of colleges and universities belonging to the associations. This 42-member Board of Commissioners establishes a commission at its annual meetings, based upon the recommendations of an executive committee and ad hoc committees. Policies are carried out by a commission staff consisting of an executive director and an assistant director.

The constitution of the National Commission on Accrediting stipulates that the commission shall:

1. Study and investigate present accrediting practices with a view to establishing satisfactory standards, procedures, and principles of accrediting; to correct abuses; and to support the freedom and integrity of member institutions
2. Define the accrediting responsibility of the several agencies
3. Prepare and distribute a list of accrediting agencies whose policies and procedures are acceptable to the commission
4. Coordinate the activities of the approved accrediting agencies in order to avoid duplication and overlapping of functions and to reduce costs
5. Cooperate with foundations, agencies of government, and educational organizations with respect to matters of joint interest in the field of accrediting
6. Establish, promote, or direct research programs for the purpose of improving methods and techniques of accrediting
7. Collect and publish information of higher education pertinent to accrediting
8. Establish a method or procedure whereby member institutions may present grievances with respect to actions of accrediting agencies
9. Study, review, and make recommendations with respect to state and federal legislation and rulings involving accrediting as well as the legal status and powers of accrediting agencies

The National Commission on Accrediting establishes the general criteria upon which each agency approved by the commission must base its policies and procedures for accreditation.

LIAISON BETWEEN THE REGIONAL AND NATIONAL AGENCIES FOR ACCREDITATION

The Federation of Regional Accrediting Commissions of Higher Education is the coordinating organization between the National Commission on Accrediting and the regional associations. The chairman of the Federation of Regional Accrediting Commissions of Higher Education is a member (ex officio) of the National Commission on Accrediting board, and the executive secretary of the National Commission on Accrediting is a member (ex officio) of the Council of the Federation.

The federation issues a semiannual directory (February and September) which lists institutions of higher education accredited by the six regional accrediting associations and endorsed and recognized for national accreditation by the federation. The directory also lists institutions designated as "correspondents" and "recognized candidates for accreditation" of these associations.

The primary purpose of the federation is the development of a series of policy papers common to all the regional commissions on higher education. The policy papers which have been agreeable up to this time to the members of the federation council will be found in the Appendix.

"Eligibility for Consideration for Accreditation"

"Relations between the Federation of Regional Accrediting Commissions of Higher Education and the National Commission on Accrediting"

"The Relationship between General and Professional or Specialized Accrediting Agencies"

"The Accreditation of Educational Institutions Conducted by Religious Communities for Their Own Members"
"Evaluation and Accreditation of Graduate Work"
"Code of Good Practice in Accrediting in Higher Education"
"Collegiate Programs on Military Bases"
"External Budget Control"
"General Education Requirements in Technical, Specialized, and Professional Programs"
"Institutional Integrity"
"Inter-regional Accreditation"
"Undergraduate Study Abroad Programs"
"Substantive Change"
"The Evaluation of Graduate Work"

Example of Liaison Practice

The National Commission on Accrediting considers that the most desirable and proper means for ensuring quality education at the associate degree level for the purpose of eligibility for federal funds is through the medium of institutional accreditation conducted by regional accrediting associations, under an arrangement where specialized accrediting associations (such as the National League for Nursing, Inc., and Engineers' Council for Professional Development) would furnish the regional associations with guidelines for the assessment of associate degree programs, would provide lists of qualified specialists in the profession to serve as members of regional accrediting teams at the associate degree level, and would, in turn, receive relevant team reports from the regional associations, along with notification of the regional association's decision regarding its award of reasonable assurance or accreditation to the institution.

The Accreditation of Postsecondary Non-degree-granting Vocational Institutions

Regional Commitments The regional associations, acting on the recommendation of the Federation of Regional Accrediting Commissions of Higher Education, have assumed the responsibility for the accreditation of postsecondary non-degree-granting vocational institutions operating under public auspices. Up to this time only two regionals, the New England and the Southern associations, have developed procedures by which these institutions may be accredited as members. The private not-for-profit and proprietary institutions of this type have an opportunity to gain accredited status through the National Association of Trade and Technical Schools, the National Home Study Council, or the Accrediting Commission of Business Schools. These accrediting agencies are on the approved list of the United States Commissioner of Education.

The Executive Committee of the New England Association of Colleges and Secondary Schools, Inc., voted that an ad hoc committee be authorized to formulate standards, policies, and procedures pertaining to all matters involved in the accreditation of publicly controlled vocational high schools and postsecondary institutions, and that this committee implement a program of accreditation beginning in the school year 1968–1969. Upon recommendation by this ad hoc committee, the New England Association would offer membership to those institutions recommended by vocational directors in the six New England states.

This program has been implemented and on December 6, 1968, the association accredited for five years its first block of schools to the number of 34, located in Connecticut and Massachusetts. During this five-year period each institution will be evaluated by a visiting committee on the basis of the following standards devised by the ad hoc committee:

1. *Philosophy and Objectives.* The school shall have a clearly stated educational

philosophy which shall be supported by definitely stated objectives designed to serve the individual students and advance the dignity and relevance of vocational-technical occupations.

2. *Program of Studies.* The school shall have a carefully planned program of studies consistent with its stated philosophy and the needs of business and industry. There shall be visible evidence of coordination between laboratory courses and related theory. The program of studies shall also consider both immediate employment and further education.

3. *Guidance Service.* The school shall have an organized, coordinated guidance service to aid students in meeting educational, vocational, and personal problems. Counseling shall include the provision of career information and placement services to both graduates and undergraduates.

4. *The Library.* The school shall have library services with appropriate centers for resource material for every aspect of the school program. There shall be an adequate collection of books and periodicals, auditory and visual aids, and other resource material. The facilities shall be effectively used in the educational program.

5. *The School Staff.* The school shall have a staff well qualified in character, health, personality; and staff members shall exhibit evidence of professional competency and state certification in their assigned areas of instruction. The staff shall be sufficient in number, adequately paid, and shall be continually motivated by the dignity of vocational-technical education.

6. *Records.* An adequate system of student records and permanent files shall be safely maintained. These should include cumulative records of attendance, progress in school, and level of vocational attainment. There shall be an adequate reporting of grades, and student records concerning previous educational and vocational training shall be available for educational and placement purposes.

7. *Administration.* Each school shall be supervised by a full-time, responsible administrative employee who, although accountable to higher authority, shall be the responsible head and professional leader of the school.

8. *Plant and Equipment.* The plant and equipment shall include the place or places used for the instruction of theory and skills. The plant shall be consistent with the vocational or technical objectives of the school, and the facilities shall be operated to assure the safety and health of both students and faculty. The equipment used for the purpose of instructing vocational skills must be sufficient in quantity and appropriate in quality and must be of recent design.

9. *School and Community Relations.* School and community relations are of such importance in the development of a good secondary school that an appropriate program for promoting effective relations between school and community shall be maintained and constantly improved.

10. *Financial Support.* Financial support of the school shall be adequate to sustain the educational program—including activities—consistent with the philosophy and objectives of the school and with the standards of the New England Association of Colleges and Secondary Schools.

11. *School Atmosphere.* The school shall have an appropriate intellectual atmosphere which indicates that an effective educational program prevails.

National Commitment The National Commission on Accrediting, cooperating with the Federation of Regional Accrediting Commissions of Higher Education, is being expanded to include a Council on Technical-Vocational Accreditation to its traditional Council on Specialized Professional Accrediting.

Procedure for Eligibility Determination to Be Employed for Associate Degree Nursing Programs [1]

Purpose The general purpose of this procedure is to enable the National Commission on Accrediting to implement a policy which affords junior colleges and four-year

[1] Quoted from an official letter (7/7/67) from Frank Dickey, Executive Secretary of the National Commission on Accrediting, to all accrediting associations recognized by NCA.

institutions having associate degree programs in nursing, but no four-year programs in the same field, a satisfactory degree of freedom of choice regarding eligibility for federal funding while also stimulating the colleges toward quality programs development. Arising out of this policy is a conceived system of optional eligibility determination machinery at the associate degree collegiate level.

Procedures The National League for Nursing will seek recognition from the National Commission on Accrediting by:

1. submitting its accreditation guidelines, criteria, and procedures relative to associate degree programs to the National Commission on Accrediting for review and approval; and

2. providing the National Commission on Accrediting with a "letter of intent" stating that the League agrees, in principle, to participate in this optional system of eligibility determination at the associate degree level; and that it will

   a. furnish the regional accrediting associations with appropriate guidelines which will be used in the examination of associate degree programs, and

   b. furnish the regional associations with lists of specialists who are qualified to serve on regional association accrediting teams and from which lists of representatives will be selected.

The regional accrediting associations will agree to engage in this system of eligibility determination by filing a "letter of intent" with the Federation of Regional Accrediting Commissions of Higher Education. Also, the regional associations will issue statements indicating their willingness to

1. utilize guidelines submitted to them by the National League for Nursing, and

2. appoint, as members of the regional accrediting teams, personnel from the lists of specialists provided by the National League for Nursing, whenever relevant programs form a part of the institution to be examined.

Following an on-site examination, the regional accrediting association will transmit a single report to the Commissioner of Education including relevant findings and recommendations concerning the nursing program. The report shall indicate that, through the institutional accrediting process, special attention—utilizing professional association guidelines and representation—has been given the nursing program. In addition, the report shall recommend to the Commissioner of Education whether or not the quality of the institution and the nursing program, in particular, is considered to be equivalent to institutions and nursing programs designated as holding reasonable assurance of accreditation.

It is anticipated that in by far the majority of cases recommendations by the regional accrediting associations concerning the overall quality of the institution will coincide with the recommendations of the specialists on the team concerning the quality of the nursing program. In those few cases where the regional accrediting association is willing to certify to the overall quality of the institutions but the professional specialists have reservations regarding the quality of the nursing program, it is anticipated that every effort will be made to resolve those differences between members of the visiting team and officials of the applicant institution.

The Commissioner of Education shall establish an advisory committee to advise him on all matters relating to institutional eligibility and accreditation. In those extremely few instances where despite efforts at resolution the overall institutional report conflicts with the assessment of the nursing program, such cases with all relevant information will be referred to this committee for decision.

It is anticipated by the National Commission on Accrediting that some institutions, for their own individual purposes or for purposes of seeking eligibility for federal funds, may choose to seek specialized accreditation of associate degree level programs in nursing. Such a choice is the recognized prerogative of each institution.

THE RELATIONSHIP BETWEEN GENERAL AND PROFESSIONAL OR SPECIALIZED ACCREDITING AGENCIES

The regional or general accrediting agencies and the National Commission on Accrediting have a common philosophy concerning the integrity of the educational institution and of the accreditation process. The membership of the general accrediting agencies and the National Commission on Accrediting is institutional and virtually identical. Their orientation also is institutional; they represent and serve whole institutions rather than particular schools or programs. They insist that an institution must control its own educational programs and facilities. This is a basic principle of general accreditation and one of the principal reasons for the creation of the National Commission.

The activities of the general associations and of the National Commission are complementary, the general associations working directly with educational institutions; the National Commission with agencies of special interest on behalf of the educational institutions as well as with the general associations.

The general associations and the National Commission have a common attitude toward the specialized accrediting agencies. They favor and support efforts of the specialized agencies to improve professional education and to base it firmly upon general education.

A policy paper of the Federation of the Commission on Higher Education describing the approval of this relationship between the National Commission follows:

Basic Principles The following principles are assumed as axiomatic:

1. Each institution of higher education must be free to decide for itself whether or not to seek accreditation by any particular agency.

2. A general (regional) accrediting agency in granting accreditation accredits an institution as a whole, and therefore cannot omit from its evaluation any area of the program of the institution. However, the general accreditation of the institution as a whole is not and should not be interpreted as being equivalent to specialized accreditation of each of the several parts or programs of the institution.

3. The general accrediting agencies draw upon the experience of the professional accrediting agencies in establishing standards of excellence in the specialized fields and for assistance in evaluating them, and in turn, aid the professional agencies in the appraisal of supporting and related areas and of institutional control and management. Appropriate assistance on the part of the professional agencies might include suggesting evaluators for the general agency to serve it and to report to it alone, providing a panel of nominees from which the general agency might choose its evaluators, providing information concerning its standards and criteria, and the like; and on the part of the general agency, providing information concerning the organization, overall governance and administration of the institution, the quality of supporting programs, and the like.

4. A general and a professional accrediting agency collaborate in evaluating a specialized program whenever the program or the institution is accredited by both, or desires accreditation by both, or invites both to participate in the evaluation.

In the contrary case, the general accrediting agency may nevertheless receive unofficially appropriate assistance (see item 3 above) from the specialized agency, but the latter is not officially involved.

Institutional Freedom An institution is free to determine the accrediting agencies with which it will deal, whether general or professional. The existence of a professional accrediting agency recognized by the National Commission on Accrediting implies that a determination has been made on behalf of the institutions of higher education (which constitute the membership of the National Commission) that a social need exists for accreditation in that particular field.

Nevertheless, an institution may choose not to avail itself of such accreditation for any one or more of a number of valid reasons. It may disagree with the conclusion of the National Commission, may have reservations concerning the standards or the nature of the evaluation of the accrediting agency, or may not accept the appropriateness of the agency's standards, point of view, or emphasis for it, or may feel that the cost is disproportionate to the value of accreditation, or may just want to be independent.

What the institution must not do, however, is to interpret its general accreditation as validating a specialized program in the same manner and to the same extent as specialized accreditation.

If in such a case the specialized agency wishes to attempt to convince the institution that it should seek specialized accreditation, it is of course free to do so, but the general agency should take no position whatsoever on this point.

General Accreditation of Specialized Institutions

It is entirely in order for a general accrediting agency to evaluate a specialized institution if such an institution is otherwise eligible for evaluation. Such an evaluation should be no less searching, though perhaps based on more general criteria, than an evaluation conducted separately by, or jointly with, a specialized agency. The validity of general accreditation for a specialized institution is to be found in the meaning of accreditation set forth by the general agency, not in terms of the standards and criteria of the specialized agency. Normally, general accreditation testifies to the worthiness of the objectives of an institution; the adequacy of its organization, program and resources, both material and human; and to the existence of evidence of the accomplishment of institutional objectives in reasonable measure. Moreover, the criteria of eligibility provide that the programs, however specialized, must rest upon a base of liberal studies required of all or most students.

Example The two-year technical institute provides an excellent example of the general accreditation of a specialized institution. The standards which follow are taken directly from the files of the Commission on Higher Education of the New England Association.

A two-year specialized institution should meet all of the following criteria before being visited by a full-scale accreditation team:

1. It should have a financial base adequate to insure continuity of operation.
2. Its entrance qualifications should be such as to assure that the typical student will be of collegiate level.
3. Its instruction should also be at the collegiate level.
4. It should have an adequate general education program of approximately one fourth of its total program, or fifteen units.[2]
5. It should offer an Associate Degree.[3]
6. It should have been in operation for a minimum of three years.
7. It should submit evidence regarding the extent to which its institutional objectives are being achieved.

INSTITUTIONAL AFFILIATES OR ASSOCIATES AND MEMBERS IN REGIONAL ASSOCIATIONS

The regional associations have established a series of steps preliminary to accreditation. These steps perform two functions: firstly, they provide guidance by the association to assist the institution in preparing for eventual accreditation and, second, they give the regional association the authority to write a letter of "Reasonable Assurance" to any agency of the federal government or organizations dispersing aid funds. This letter of "Reasonable Assurance" is an official statement that the institution

[2] This criterion may be interpreted to mean that the institution shall require that any candidate for the Associate Degree must have completed general education courses to the extent indicated. These need not have been taken in the institution being visited, but should have been taken in an accredited institution with verification on an official transcript.

[3] This criterion should be interpreted to mean that the institution will demonstrate that it annually grants such degrees.

named is proceeding toward accreditation in an appropriate manner. In each of the six regional associations, the same terminology is used to define these preliminary steps by which institutions are designated as affiliates of the association. The first or beginning step is called "correspondent."

Correspondent Status

"Correspondent" is a status of affiliation or association for an institution still in the planning stage which may not be operational for a period of several years. Each regional association has different requirements which must be met to attain this status, but in general each includes certain basic principles such as those prescribed by the Standards for Membership. In the Middle States, North Central, Southern, and Northwest regions, both old and new institutions may apply for correspondent status, but in the Western region only new institutions may apply and in New England only paper institutions may apply.

A sample of the criteria used by the New England Association of Colleges and Secondary Schools illustrates the requirements generally used by the regional associations for election to the correspondent category:

1. The institution must have been given, by the appropriate legal agency, the authority to grant degrees.
2. The institution must be a nonprofit organization (as evidenced by a letter from the federal government certifying tax-exempt status).
3. The institution's board of trustees must be independent of the school administration and governed by the public interest.
4. The institution must offer at least a two-year program, meeting the normal undergraduate standards.
5. The institution's principal educational programs must rest upon a base of liberal studies required of all students.
6. The institution must own or have a long-term lease on land adequate not only for its founding but also for development.
7. The institution must give evidence of financial capability with the current capacity to
    a. build educational facilities appropriate to its functions,
    b. pay salaries for an adequate staff, and
    c. maintain at least two years of operation.
8. At least a year prior to the opening, the institution must provide the commission with an accurate timetable, showing concretely the several stages of the development of the plans in respect to the
    a. physical plant,
    b. administrative staff,
    c. faculty appointments, and
    d. program of studies.

Recognition of Candidacy for Accreditation (R.C.A.)

The second stage of affiliation or association begins after the institution has been actually operating for at least a year. The common name for this category is "recognition of candidacy for accreditation." Both old and new institutions may apply for this status in the Middle States, New England, North Central, and Western regions, but only new institutions may apply in the Southern and Northwest regions.

The regional accrediting associations acknowledge the importance to a considerable number of institutions, old and new, of attaining an affiliation with the association to assist them in preparation for accreditation. The Commissions on Institutions of Higher Education, therefore, have established a category called "recognition of candidacy for accreditation." This category is by no means to be confused with membership in the association. It is a temporary status. Acceptance as a recognized candidate for accreditation attests that the Commission on Institutions of Higher Education considers the institution to be offering its students, on at least a minimally satisfactory level, the educational opportunity implied by its objectives. In the commission's view, the institution's organizational structure and staffing are acceptable for its stage of development if its sponsors are committed to supplying its needs and are able to do so, if its governing board is functioning properly, and if its academic and financial plans are well designed. Candidacy is *not* accreditation; it indicates that an institution is progressing steadily and properly toward accreditation. Names of institutions in this category are published by the association at intervals, and the institutions are entitled to announce their status in conformity with the official list.

The conditions for recognition in this category are as follows:[4]

1. Any unaccredited institution, old or new, authorized to grant degrees, may be considered for recognition under the following provisions:
   a. One class must be enrolled, and normally one year of operation must be completed; and
   b. the institution must be developing in accordance with the general standards of the New England Association of Colleges and Secondary Schools.
2. Such an institution would be required:
   a. to provide a preliminary statement of purpose and organizational structure, and
   b. to undergo a preliminary visit by representatives of the commission, in the course of which information would be sought on educational objectives, control and management, administrative organization, faculty and curriculum, admission policies, physical plant, financial prospects for general stability and long-range planning, and the degree to which progress toward accreditation is being made.

Membership

The third stage, membership, means regional association accreditation. As pointed out earlier, lists of members are published either annually or on some other interim time schedule.

Membership is attained in general by each institution's first making a formal application for membership to the regional association covering the local geographical area.

At this point the Commission on Higher Education makes a preliminary survey of the institution and either approves or denies the request. If approved, the Commission on Institutions of Higher Education through its office of evaluation provides the institution with a set of guidelines which act as a framework for a self-study. This self-study generally takes about one academic year and upon its completion is returned to the evaluation office together with a catalog and other descriptive material. During this period of self-study, the Commission on Institutions of Higher Education has selected a visiting committee of a size sufficient to accomplish its mission. These committees are made up of administrators and qualified faculty personnel from comparable member institutions. They number anywhere from three to ten or twelve, depending on the need. A chairman is appointed by the office of evaluation.

By mutual agreement a date is set for the committee to make an on-site visit of the institution. The self-study and other materials are placed in the hands of the committee members in ample time prior to the visit for their analysis.

The on-site visit lasts at least two or three days; longer in some instances. It consists largely of dialogues with administrators, faculty, and students together with observations of facilities, activities, and classroom methods. The committee members make their judgment of the quality of the institution in reference to a set of standards com-

[4] From procedure standards prepared by Office of Evaluation of the Commission on Higher Education of the New England Association of Colleges and Secondary Schools, Inc.

piled by the Commission on Higher Education. In all cases the final judgment is an answer to the general question: How well is the institution meeting its goals as stated in the catalog? Each institution is appraised on this basis.

The chairman of the visiting committee collates the report of the members and in turn meets with the full commission to discuss the results of the visit.

The commission recommends membership or not (the Middle States Association gives final authority to the commission); and later the executive committee approves or disapproves, with the general assembly of delegates having final jurisdiction.

Standards for Membership—NEACSS The basic ingredients of membership standards established by the Regional Commissions on Higher Education are the presence in the program of studies of a balanced requirement of the three great areas of learning—the humanities, the social studies, and the natural sciences, including mathematics.

The standards are couched in general terms because they are qualitative in nature. Quantitative standards cannot be used due to the wide range of institutions involved in membership in the regional associations. The range proceeds from the two-year technical institute to the complex university. Quantitative criteria are not effective also because these do not often measure the overall quality of the institution.

To illustrate the type of standards used by regional associations, there follow those currently in use by the New England Association. While there are some variations in form and expression among the several regional associations, the basic principles of all are compatible and embodied herein.

NEW ENGLAND ASSOCIATION OF COLLEGES AND SECONDARY SCHOOLS, INC.

STANDARDS FOR MEMBERSHIP INSTITUTIONS OF HIGHER EDUCATION

The New England Association of Colleges and Secondary Schools, Inc. is a voluntary, self-governing organization of educational institutions, the purpose of which is to develop and maintain sound educational standards. Admission to, and renewal of membership in, the New England Association denotes formal accreditation. It signifies that a school or college has been carefully evaluated and has been found to follow basic educational policies, practices, and standards comparable to those of the other member institutions.

Member institutions of higher education include public and private senior colleges and universities, junior colleges, professional schools, and specialized institutions of collegiate level.

Membership as an institution of higher education is open only to a post-secondary, degree-granting institution which offers at least two years of academic work of college grade. In general, application by a new institution will not be considered until two years after graduation of its first class. An institution is elected to membership by vote of the delegates of member institutions at an annual meeting of the Association. The institution is nominated by the Executive Committee after a visiting committee examines the institution and reports to the Commission on Institutions of Higher Education, which in turn reports to the Executive Committee recommending action.

To be accepted for membership, an institution of higher education should base its program of studies upon general education, derived from courses in the humanities, the social sciences, and the natural sciences, and should provide opportunity for laboratory experience in the sciences.* The program should provide for the orderly development of subject matter and should promote the intellectual growth of the students; and the resources and facilities of the institution should be adequate for the program.

The standards of evaluation are qualitative and are applied to an institution as a whole. Aside from the general purposes and objectives of the institution, the areas of

* In certain types of specialized institutions, the requirement of laboratory experience in the sciences may be waived by vote of the Commission, if circumstances warrant its exclusion.

major concern in the evaluation of an institution of higher education are: organization and control, program, faculty, students, facilities and resources. In applying for membership, an institution is asked to submit detailed information bearing on all these areas. In reaching its decision, the Commission takes into account the nature and purposes of the individual institution and makes a qualitative rather than quantitative judgment as to whether the institution is functioning effectively as a whole in fulfilling its objectives, as well as whether those objectives are appropriate in the realm of higher education.

A. Organization and Control. The non-profit character of the institution should be clear beyond any doubt. Responsibilities for the operation of the institution should be allocated in a well-defined and reasonable fashion among the governing board, the administration, and the faculty.

The governing board should represent the public interest and should have general control over and responsibility for the institution. It should provide counsel, and accept counsel, in determining the purposes, objectives, and overall structure, and assure the support necessary to effective functioning.

An institution should have administrative staff competent to carry out its stated purposes. The administration should oversee the total program, and have power to insure that it is conducted well.

The faculty should have clearly-defined responsibility in developing and conducting the educational program and in maintaining the standards and conditions which pertain directly to the curriculum within the limits of the general purposes established by the governing board.

B. Program. Each program of studies should insure an adequate cultural background and a degree of concentration in one field; there should be breadth to give some awareness of the extent and range of human knowledge, and penetration into a particular area of inquiry to afford some mastery of the subject. Terminal programs and curricula in technical, specialized, or professional fields must exhibit in appropriate regard the three major areas of knowledge: i.e., the humanities, the natural sciences, and the social sciences.

The program of study and the requirements for graduation should be clearly stated, and students should be held to the accomplishment of a defined amount and quality of work. The institution should present evidence that its students are qualified for transfer to other institutions of recognized standing and that its graduates are well prepared for continued study.

C. Faculty. The faculty and the quality of its instructional program are the main strengths of an institution of higher education. The professional qualifications of the faculty, the conditions of employment and service, and the effectiveness of teaching are paramount considerations in determining acceptability for membership.

In general, a substantial majority of the faculty members should hold full-time teaching positions on the staff and should have a major personal commitment to the institution. Their preparation and qualifications must be suited to their instructional assignments. Those in the conventional academic fields should hold degrees or present evidence of scholarship or creative achievement appropriate to their positions. Those in the professional or technical fields should have preparation, experience, and attainments comparable to the qualifications of their academic counterparts.

Teaching loads and schedules will vary from field to field and from institution to institution, but should in all cases allow time for adequate preparation and continuing professional growth.

The governing board and the administration should give active support to the development of an instructional staff of high quality. The Association will study carefully the institution's practices in matters of appointment, tenure, and academic freedom.

D. Students. The Association expects of its members an orderly and ethical program of admission based on systematic appraisal of the intellectual competence of prospective students. The visiting committee will look for evidence that the students have a genuine concern for intellectual matters and a serious attitude toward their academic work.

Careful consideration will be given to quality in the counseling program, the medical and health services, and the extracurricular activities of students.

E. Facilities and Resources. The quality of the library and the degree to which the library is used by students and faculty are particularly important. The library should be professionally staffed and should be strong enough to support all parts of the curriculum. The faculty and library staff should cooperate in developing the collection as an integral part of the teaching program.

Classrooms and laboratories should be of adequate size, properly equipped for teaching safely and effectively the courses taught in them, and maintained in good order. Residence accommodations, food service, student centers, and athletic facilities should meet acceptable standards.

The institution should present evidence of a sound financial structure. Because the resources of institutions of higher education vary widely, standards of acceptability cannot be defined quantitatively in terms of endowment funds, instructional space per student, per capita expenditures for institution or library books, salary schedules, or other specific measures. These resources should be appropriate to the institution insofar as is possible. But it should be remembered that it is the spirit and the intellectual life that matter most in the quality of an institution of higher education.

Procedures Used by the Regional Associations

Procedures for implementing accreditation vary with each regional association. Each, however, utilizes two actions in common:

1. A self-survey by the institution
2. A visit to the institution by an official committee representing the Commission on Higher Education

A brief questionnaire submitted to the secretaries of the six regional associations elicited the information shown in Table 1.

Accreditation Standards of the Several Agencies of the National Commission on Accrediting

These specialized standards, mainly quantitative, are under constant review by the several agencies; and changes occur at frequent intervals. Therefore, an accurate statement of the definitive criteria used by each agency may be obtained by request from an institution to the national headquarters [5] of the specialized program.

Accreditation Procedures of the Several Agencies of the National Commission on Accrediting

By and large, the specialized types of accreditation use the same general procedures as those followed by the regional agencies:

1. A self-survey is required of the institution's specialized program.
2. A committee is appointed composed of personnel from member institutions and sometimes staff, or a combination of both.
3. The committee studies the substance of the self-survey and visits the institution for an on-site investigation.
4. The findings of the visiting committee are reported to the appropriate authorities for final action by the agency.

GLOSSARY (APPROVED DEFINITIONS USED IN ACCREDITATION)

Branch. A degree-granting division or unit of an institution located in a geographical setting separated from the parent institution and legally authorized for a stated purpose

[5] See page 2-238 for title and address.

TABLE 1 Procedures Used by the Regional Associations

Question	Western Association	Northwest Association	North Central Association	Middle States Association	Southern Association	New England Association
Who selects committee?	Executive secretary	Chairman by higher commission; members by executive secretary	Central office	Executive secretary	Commission staff	Director of evaluation
Size of committee	3–12	7–16	Varies according to degree level	Varies	Varies according to complexity of institution	3–12
Nature of committee	Faculty of major disciplines, chairman from administration	Academic areas; administration, student personnel services	Generalists representing the humanities, natural sciences, social sciences, and administration	–	Organization; librarian; student personnel; business officer; academicians	Administration, faculty
Length of visit (days)	2–3	2–4	2–4	3	3	3
Preliminary visit prior to committee visit?	Often	Yes	No	Always	Yes	No
Are evaluators paid? If yes, how much?	No	No	No	Yes – $50	Yes – expenses plus $100 for chairman; $50 for others	Yes
Are all expenses for visit borne by the institution?	No – commission pays	Yes	Yes – drawn from examination fee	Yes – reimbursed through commission	Yes	Yes
Do you have an application fee or visiting fee?	Yes – fees for visit	Yes – $50	$1,400 for junior colleges and 4-year baccalaureate programs; $2,000 for graduate master's programs; and $2,600 for Ph.D. programs.	No	No	Yes – same as annual dues
Annual membership dues	$200–$350; vary with size of institution	$200–$600; vary with size of institution	$200–$600; vary with degree level	$250–$600; vary with size of institution	$400–$1,300; vary with size of institution	$500–$750; vary with size of institution

in relation to the parent institution and the area served. It has planned programs leading to undergraduate, graduate, or professional degrees which are granted by, or in the name of, the parent institution.

Candidate for accreditation. See *Recognized candidate for accreditation.*

Community or junior college. A collegiate institution that offers at least two years of higher education but does not offer baccalaureate degrees.

Correspondence. A course offered through the mail which can be accomplished at home without the instructor in attendance.

Correspondent. The classification given to a collegiate institution, not necessarily yet in operation, which has indicated its intent to work toward accreditation and which, having provided evidence of sound planning and the resources to implement these plans, appears to have the potential for attaining this goal within a reasonable time. Correspondent status is not accreditation nor does it assure or even imply eventual accreditation.

Criteria. See *Standards or criteria for accreditation.*

Eligibility. Indication by the federal government that an institution qualifies for consideration as a participant in federal funding programs.

General or regional accreditation. An expression of confidence by a regional association that an institution's own goals are soundly conceived, that its purposes are being accomplished, and that the institution is so organized, staffed, and supported that it should continue to merit such confidence for a specified number of years. It indicates that each constituent or related unit has been examined and has been found to be achieving its own particular purposes satisfactorily, although not necessarily all on the same level of quality.

Interregional accreditation. Accreditation by two or more regional associations of an institution that conducts a substantial part of its work in more than one regional territory.

Junior college. See *Community or junior college.*

Off-campus location. Supplemental and special educational programs that are integral parts of an institution and serve to help achieve institutional objectives and responsibilities to constituents. Such locations are usually identified as branches or centers.

Probationary accreditation. A term used by some associations to indicate that an accredited institution has certain deficiencies which must be corrected within a specified period of time in order for it to remain accredited.

Professional recognition. See *Specialized or professional recognition.*

Reaffirmation of accreditation. The renewal of accreditation of member institutions through reevaluation at periodic intervals.

Reasonable assurance. An indication by a regional association that an unaccredited institution appears to have the potential and to be making appropriate progress which, if continued, will result in its meeting accreditation requirements on a normal schedule.

Recognized candidate for accreditation. The classification given to a fully operative collegiate institution which, as attested to by a higher education commission of a regional accrediting agency, appears to be offering students, on at least a minimally satisfactory level, the educational opportunities implied by its objectives. In the commission's view the institution's organization, structure, and staffing are acceptable for its stage of development; its sponsors are committed to supplying its needs and are able to do so; its governing board is functioning properly; and its academic and financial plans are well designed. Candidacy is not accreditation. It indicates that an institution is progressing steadily and properly toward accreditation but does not assure or even imply eventual accreditation.

Regional accreditation. See *General or regional accreditation.*

Self-evaluation or self-study. An analysis of a collegiate institution's total educational effectiveness made by its own faculty and administration. It is a comprehensive review of the reasons for an institution's existence and of the relevance of all its activities to its fundamental purposes.

Self-study. See *Self-evaluation or self-study.*

Senior colleges and universities. Institutions that grant at least the baccalaureate degree.

Specialized or professional recognition. Assurance by one of the recognized professional accrediting agencies that the purposes and accomplishments of professional programs offered by an institution meet the needs of society and of the profession.

Standards or criteria for accreditation. The criteria, developed by the membership of a recognized accrediting association, by which institutions are accredited and admitted to membership in the association.

Substantive change. Any change which appears to modify the nature and scope of the institution, which affords instruction at a more advanced level, or which adds one or more new geographic locations for instruction.

APPENDIX

Policy Statement on Eligibility for Consideration for Accreditation

To be eligible for consideration for accreditation:

1. An institution should already have a charter and/or formal authority from the appropriate governmental agency to award a certificate or the associate or higher degree.
2. The institution should be a non-profit organization with a governing board representing the public interest.
3. Ordinarily it should offer at least two years of higher education at the undergraduate level or at least one year at the graduate level.
4. Normally it should have been in existence long enough to have graduated at least one class.
5. It should require for admission the completion of not less than an appropriate secondary school curriculum or satisfactory evidence of equivalent educational achievement.
6. Its principal educational programs should rest upon a base of liberal studies required of all or most students.

Adopted March 4, 1964.

Relations between the Federation of Regional Accrediting Commissions of Higher Education and the National Commission on Accrediting

The regional or general accrediting agencies and the National Commission on Accrediting have a common philosophy concerning the integrity of the educational institution and of the accreditation process. The membership of the general accrediting agencies and the N.C.A. is institutional and virtually identical. Their orientation also is institutional: they represent and serve whole institutions rather than particular schools or programs. They insist that an institution must control its own educational programs and facilities, a basic principle of general accreditation, and one of the principal reasons for the creation of the National Commission.

The activities of the general associations and of the National Commission are complementary, the general associations working directly with educational institutions, the National Commission with agencies of special interest on behalf of the educational institutions, as well as with the general associations.

The general associations and the National Commission have a common attitude toward the specialized accrediting agencies. They favor and support efforts of the specialized agencies to improve professional education and to base it firmly upon general education. They seek opportunities to work with the specialized agencies in every way calculated to benefit higher education without impairing any institution's control of its own educational programs.

Therefore the plans and operations of the National Commission and of the Federation of Regional Accrediting Commissions of Higher Education need to be closely coordinated. Regular participation of the officers of each in the deliberations of the other, and the routine exchange of minutes, reports, and other communications should be their established practice.

Adopted by the National Commission, April 18, 1963.

Adopted by the Federation, October 12, 1964.

The Relationship between General and Professional or Specialized Accrediting Agencies

Basic Principles. The following principles are assumed as axiomatic:

A. Each institution of higher education must be free to decide for itself whether or not to seek accreditation by any particular agency.

B. A general (regional) accrediting agency in granting accreditation accredits an institution as a whole, and therefore cannot omit from its evaluation any area of the program of the institution.

However, the general accreditation of the institution as a whole is not and should not be interpreted as being equivalent to specialized accreditation of each of the several parts or programs of the institution.

C. The general accrediting agencies draw upon the experience of the professional accrediting agencies in establishing standards of excellence in the specialized fields and for assistance in evaluating them, and in turn aid the professional agencies in the appraisal of supporting and related areas and of institutional control and management. Appropriate assistance on the part of the professional agencies might include suggesting evaluators for the general agency to serve it and to report to it alone; providing a panel of nominees from which the general agency might choose its evaluators; providing information concerning its standards and criteria; and the like; and on the part of the general agency, providing information concerning the organization, over-all governance and administration of the institution, the quality of supporting programs, and the like.

D. A general and a professional accrediting agency collaborate in evaluating a specialized program whenever the program or the institution is accredited by both, or desires accreditation by both, or invites both to participate in the evaluation.

In the contrary case, the general accrediting agency may nevertheless receive unofficially appropriate assistance (cf. *C* above) from the specialized agency, but the latter is not officially involved.

Institutional Freedom. An institution is free to determine the accrediting agencies with which it will deal, whether general or professional. The existence of a professional accrediting agency recognized by the National Commission on Accrediting implies that a determination has been made on behalf of the institutions of higher education (which constitute the membership of the National Commission) that a social need exists for accreditation in that particular field.

Nevertheless, an institution may choose not to avail itself of such accreditation for any one or more of a number of valid reasons. It may disagree with the conclusion of the National Commission, may have reservations concerning the standards or the nature of the evaluation of the accrediting agency, or may not accept the appropriateness of the agency's standards, point of view, or emphasis for it, or may feel that the cost is disproportionate to the value of accreditation, or may just want to be independent.

What the institution must not do, however, is to interpret its general accreditation as validating a specialized program in the same manner and to the same extent as specialized accreditation.

If in such a case the specialized agency wishes to attempt to convince the institution that it should seek specialized accreditation, it is of course free to do so, but the general agency should take no position whatsoever on this point.

General Accreditation of Specialized Institutions. It is entirely in order for a general accrediting agency to evaluate a specialized institution, if such an institution is otherwise eligible for evaluation. Such an evaluation should be no less searching, though perhaps based on more general criteria, than an evaluation conducted separately by or jointly with a specialized agency. The validity of general accreditation for a specialized institution is to be found in the meaning of accreditation set forth by the general agency, not in terms of the standards and criteria of the specialized agency. Normally general accreditation testifies to the worthiness of the objectives of an institution, the adequacy of its organization, program and resources, both material and human, and to the existence of evidence of the accomplishment of institutional objectives in reasonable measure. Moreover, the criteria of eligibility provide that the programs, however specialized, must rest upon a base of liberal studies required of all or most students.

Adopted October 14, 1964.

The Accreditation of Educational Institutions Conducted by Religious Communities for Their Own Members

Colleges, seminaries, and schools of theology, including those which are conducted by particular religious communities solely for their own members, are eligible for accreditation through the regional accreditation agencies who welcome inquiries from them.

Accreditation criteria for church-related institutions, as for others, emphasize clarity of objectives, adequacy of programs and resources for attaining them, and evidence of success in doing so. Accreditation is an expression of confidence on the part of competent, representatitve observers that an educational institution has defined its purposes and educational aims precisely, has obtained the resources and established the conditions under which, in the judgment of experienced colleagues, it should be able to achieve them and to continue to do so under varying circumstances, and appears in fact to be accomplishing them in substantial measure.

The institution itself always has a major part in the accrediting process. Its first responsibility is to express its educational objectives for its students in such exact, realistic, and appropriate terms that its entire program and every aspect of its work can be assessed in their light. Basically, this assessment must be made by the institution's faculty, administration, and trustees, with the guidance of the regional association as to material and procedures. The Commission on Institutions of Higher Education then appoints a group of visitors to review the findings of the institution's staff and trustees, to conduct an evaluation, and to make an appropriate recommendation to the regional Commission.

Accreditation should therefore be viewed as a constructive process through which an institution clarifies its insights, gains increased perspective, and increases its effectiveness. Thinking of accreditation simply as conformity with quantitative standards impairs its usefulness as an educational tool.

The visiting evaluation teams have lay and religious members. The team members do not necessarily all come from the same region, nor need they be drawn from similar institutions.

When a religious community conducts a closely integrated educational program in two or more stages—in a minor and a major seminary, for example—they are evaluated and accredited as one, even if they are at different locations. Closely related units whose campuses are within different regional associations may be accredited by the two associations acting as one.

Since the regional associations deal with each institution on its own terms, a school of theology is expected to justify itself as a professional school, and also as a graduate school if it offers graduate degrees. As a professional school it must prepare clergymen for religious, intellectual, and cultural leadership and also for the practical duties implied by their calling and stipulated by their superiors. If a school of theology confers graduate as well as professional degrees or diplomas it must also achieve the level of expectation common to recognized graduate schools in such matters as specialized programs of advanced study, research, faculty productivity, and extensive library resources.

The first criterion of excellence in a junior or senior college curriculum is breadth and depth of liberal education. Philosophy may have a principal place in the curriculum of such a college, and theology will focus and motivate it. In addition the course of study should open to the student something of the great reaches and variety of human thought and experience, past and present, and require more detailed and comprehensive work in some one area of the humanities, science, or social studies.

A second criterion for a college curriculum is the precision with which it is designed to provide the content and emphases the religious community wants. The institution's educational objectives must therefore be pinpointed explicitly, and a program boldly created to give them effect. Consultation with other colleges and recommendations of educational associations and conferences are useful, but never are substitutes for a faculty's own responsible devising of the means by which its particular objectives, which may differ in some degree even from those of a college of another community, can best be achieved.

Laboratories, studios, and whatever other special facilities and equipment the curriculum requires must of course be provided. Laboratories in particular are critically important. They are expensive to construct and supply, but a liberal education without a substantial introduction to science is clearly inadequate today.

There can be no rule or formula to prescribe what either a college or a seminary library should contain, for each library must fully meet the needs and feed the minds of its own students and faculty. The size of the collection required has little relation to the number of students, for the basic reference and general holdings of books and periodicals have to be available for even the fewest users. Obviously the proportionate cost of the library rises sharply as the number of students decreases.

The limited enrollment such institutions sometimes have is not in itself a barrier to accreditation, but a very small student body unavoidably produces certain problems. A primary one, especially in a religious community, is that of maintaining a numerous and varied enough faculty to provoke continuous and many sided professional discussion among its members, present them continuously with new interests and points of view, and excite their scholarly activity; to generate, in short, an intellectual climate which favors the vigorous scholarship and stimulating teaching which ought to be among the high rewards of academic life.

Another problem with a very small student body and faculty is to provide enough courses to give the curriculum proportion and adaptability to the individual. Another is to foster, when the students are few and homogeneous, the interaction and competition among them which is as important educationally as personal instruction is.

As a result a religious community which wants its own college of high quality must be prepared for greater per-student costs than a larger institution would face. It is especially important that the members of a small faculty should have superior training in a diversity of graduate schools, and should hold graduate degrees, including a substantial proportion of doctorates, in the subjects they teach.

In summary, it is possible for a religious community to develop a good college or seminary of its own only if it understands how much is entailed and is able and willing to meet the cost in personnel and money.

There are also other possibilities which a religious community should consider. It can send its younger members to already established colleges, even those which are open to lay people, meanwhile, if it chooses, beginning the long process of selecting and preparing instructors for the college it will ultimately establish for itself. If the community sends its student members elsewhere it may want to maintain a house of studies there for their temporary residence instead of transporting them back and forth. Another possibility is to ask an established college to set up, staff, and administer an institutional branch to meet the community's educational needs—to buy instruction, in effect, from an already existing college which may or may not belong to the congregation which needs the services. Another course is for the community to have its own junior college, where per capita human and financial costs are lower, joining with others for its upper level work. Even communities which are distant from established institutions usually ought not attempt to provide more than junior college work unless they are large enough and strong enough financially to maintain a faculty, student body, and library comparable to those of any first class liberal arts college.

When colleges with similar purposes are near each other, possible advantages and economies through academic and business cooperation should constantly be sought.

One other approach which deserves serious thought is for a community to associate itself with an existing college as a partner, in an agreement under which its own thoroughly trained members will provide part of the instruction, thereby adding the community's own flavor to the program, carrying its own share of the academic responsibility for religious formation, and at the same time stimulating the community's own intellectual progress.

When such a cooperative project is feasible it should not result in simply an extension center under the auspices of the established college, but in a single faculty whose members are drawn both from the established college and from the community where the branch is located, a faculty whose members teach at both the branch and the center. Integration of the faculty gives every instructor the advantage of working in a larger academic context, of associating professionally with many colleagues whose backgrounds are different from his, of participating continuously in the full responsibilities of an organized faculty, and of facing different types of students.

Needless to say it is implied that the community which enters an academic affiliation will engage to select its potential instructors from among its ablest members, and will afford them the opportunity for complete academic training. They must qualify on their own merits for membership in the common faculty. They must have the necessary freedom to travel or to reside at times at the central institution in order to do part of their teaching there. The cooperating communities will of course prorate administrative and other general costs.

A community's choice among the various ways in which it may educate its members should rest on their relative educational effectiveness, for nothing more closely affects its welfare than the formation of its future members and leaders.

Adopted October 14, 1964.

Evaluation and Accreditation of Graduate Work

A Statement by a Joint Committee,* representing the
National Commission on Accrediting
Federation of Regional Accrediting Commissions of
Higher Education
Council of Graduate Schools in the United States

1. It is the conviction of the Joint Committee on Evaluation and Accreditation of Graduate Work that no group should undertake to accredit institutions with respect to their programs of graduate education unless it is responsible to an organization of the institutions themselves.

2. The Joint Committee identifies two kinds of accreditation, i.e.,
   A. General accreditation, which is accreditation of a total institution as evidenced by admission to membership in a regional association, and is understood to be an expression of confidence by the member institutions of a regional association in an institution's purpose, resources, and performance, and
   B. Special (i.e., programmatic) accreditation, which is accreditation of a professional school or program within a particular college or university, and may be granted by a national organization representing a single professional area, such as architecture, law, medicine, psychology, or social work primarily in order to assure that the purposes and accomplishments of the professional program meet the need of society and of the profession.

3. In the opinion of the Joint Committee, the review and appraisal of graduate programs and work should be included as part of the over-all evaluation and general accreditation of a college or university and should be done only by a regional association.

* The membership of the Committee included Gustave O. Arlt, Frank G. Dickey, Philip G. Hoffman, Milton C. Kloetzel, Asa S. Knowles, Walter C. Langsam, Joseph L. McCarthy, Albert E. Meder, Jr., J. Boyd Page.

4. It is the conviction of the Joint Committee that special accreditation of particular graduate programs in a college or university should, in general, be avoided because it tends to force narrowness and conformity in graduate student experience and to retard graduate program evolution. In certain professional fields, however, special accreditation may be appropriate, but only provided it is conducted in those fields and by those organizations approved by the National Commission on Accrediting.

5. In the opinion of the Joint Committee, the granting of general accreditation should take cognizance of, but need not require, special accreditation of individual programs.

6. Representatives of the several organizations concerned with general and special accreditation are encouraged by the Joint Committee to collaborate, especially by coordinating campus visitations.

7. The regional associations are urged by the Joint Committee to work toward further agreement in policies and procedures concerning general accreditation of colleges and universities.

8. The Joint Committee does encourage the Council of Graduate Schools to work toward the further development and dissemination of general statements describing the characteristics of programs of good quality leading to graduate degrees.

Approved by the Council of Graduate Schools, December 2, 1965.
Approved by the National Commission, April 1, 1966.
Approved by the Federation, April 21, 1966.

Policy Statement on Code of Good Practice in Accrediting in Higher Education

This statement and the following five policy statements, all by the Federation of Regional Accrediting Commissions of Higher Education, were adopted October 1966.

Any organization conducting accrediting activities in higher education should follow the guidelines of the Code of Good Practice. Under this Code, the organization agrees

(*a*) to evaluate or visit an institution or program of study only on the express invitation of the president or, when the action is initiated by the organization with respect to an institution already accredited by the organization, with the specific authorization of the president of the institution or his officially designated representative;

(*b*) to permit the withdrawal of a request for initial accreditation at any time (even after evaluation) prior to final action;

(*c*) to recognize the right of an institution or program to be appraised in the light of its own stated purposes so long as those purposes demonstrably fall within the definitions of general purpose established by the organization;

(*d*) to rely upon the regional accreditation for evaluations of general quality of an institution;

(*e*) to state criteria for accreditation in terms that are manifestly relevant to the quality of an institution or program, respecting institutional freedom in other matters;

(*f*) to use relevant qualitative and quantitative information in its evaluation process;

(*g*) to consider a program or programs of study at an institution, including its administration and financing, not on the basis of a single predetermined pattern but rather in relationship to the operation and goals of the entire institution;

(*h*) to assist and stimulate improvement of the educational effectiveness of an institution, and to this end to be prepared to provide consultative assistance;

(*i*) to encourage sound educational experimentation and permit innovations;

(*j*) so to design questionnaires and forms as not only to obtain information for the visiting examiners but also so far as possible to stimulate an institution to evaluate itself;

(*k*) to conduct any evaluation visit to an institution by experienced and qualified examiners under conditions that assure impartial and objective judgment;

(*l*) to follow the principle that there shall be adequate representation in an evaluation from the staffs of other institutions offering programs of study in the fields to be accredited;

(*m*) to avoid appointment of visitors who may not be acceptable to an institution;

(*n*) to cooperate with other accrediting agencies so far as possible in scheduling joint visits when an institution so requests;

(*o*) to provide for adequate consultation during the visit between the team of visitors and the faculty and staff of an institution, including the president or his designated representative;

(*p*) to provide adequate opportunity for inclusion of students in the interviewing process during accrediting visits;

(*q*) to provide the president of an institution being evaluated an opportunity to read the factual part of the report prepared by the visiting team, and to comment on its accuracy before the agency takes action on it;

(*r*) to regard the text of the evaluation report as confidential between an institution and the accrediting agency, with the exception that it may be made available to other recognized accrediting agencies by which the institution has been accredited or whose accreditation it is seeking;

(*s*) except as provided in (*r*) to permit an institution to make such disposition of evaluation reports as it desires;

(*t*) to consider decisions relative to accreditation only after receipt of the comments of the president, as provided in (*q*), and when the chairman of the visiting team is present or the views of the evaluation team are otherwise adequately represented;

(*u*) to refrain from conditioning accreditation upon payment of fees for purposes other than membership dues or actual evaluation costs;

(*v*) to notify an institution as quickly as possible regarding any accreditation decision;

(*w*) to revoke accreditation only after advance notice has been given to the president of an institution that such action is contemplated, and the reasons therefor, sufficient to permit timely rejoinder.

Policy Statement on Collegiate Programs on Military Bases

The military, like other segments of our population, is very much aware of the critical shortage of well educated manpower. Advances in science and modern technology have affected the soldier just as they have the other sectors of our society. While the technological aspect of the military has gained in significance and complexity, the military is equally aware of the need for extended knowledge in the arts, the social sciences, and the humanities.

Collegiate programs by higher institutions on military bases for service personnel are not new. A number of such programs are now under way. Many of the colleges and universities involved are departing from the practice of providing courses on military bases which merely repeat the regular day courses of the campus. Courses designed for the young undergraduate, or for the professional preparation in an academic discipline, may not adequately meet the needs or capitalize on the experiences of military personnel. The usual fixed requirements of residence and other methods of accumulating credits may neglect to consider the nature of the military person as an undergraduate or graduate student. The regime under which he must perform his duties and pursue his studies can be quite different from that of the typical students on campus. Thus, there is a need for adapting campus offerings to a somewhat different clientele. It is highly desirable, wherever possible, for higher institutions to provide opportunities which will enable military personnel to engage in collegiate study. Colleges and universities that have military bases within their service area should feel a sense of obligation to those individuals of the military who wish to work toward a degree or broaden their base of general education or improve technical competence through organized academic studies.

Providing college opportunities for interested personnel on military bases is a dual responsibility. There are certain guides and requisites which may provide incentive and direction for officers of the military in positions of responsibility on base. There are also certain helpful guides that might provide direction for those responsible for such services on the college campus. Successful programs in such situations will not be realized unless there is mutual understanding, a sharing of responsibilities and a marshalling of resources essential for such offerings.

Guides and Obligations of the Military

A. The military should not hesitate to initiate negotiations for the purpose of providing collegiate programs on base.

When higher educational opportunities are not being provided and when personnel on base express an interest in furthering their collegiate study, officials on base should not hesitate to initiate the action necessary for securing such programs. The leadership should first assess and identify the types of programs and services desired before approaching a nearby college or university. Before approaching a college or university, it is always helpful to know precisely what is desired, the approximate number of students involved and the resources which the base might be able to provide.

B. A joint meeting of both college and base leadership should come early in the deliberations.

After there is an understanding of the educational needs of base personnel there should be a joint exploration and planning session of base and college representatives. Such a meeting should define the need, identify essential resources, describe the general nature of the programs desired, then spell out specific responsibilities. There are agreements to be reached. Such agreements should result in a written understanding which can guide both personnel of the base and campus in the future.

C. The military will have a responsibility for supplying certain essential resources.

In addition to identifying programs desired, the number of persons to be involved, and the costs, the military should expect to provide certain essential ingredients for the success of such programs on base. Space for a library as well as certain basic library materials will be a requisite. There will need to be suitable and adequate classrooms. If courses requiring laboratory experiments are contemplated, the military will be expected to provide both space and certain basic laboratory equipment. Few institutions will have sufficient funds for initiating such programs, so the military in most instances will be expected to provide certain initial funds for starting such programs and supplying essential space and equipment.

D. The military must give full support and backing to the program once it is initiated.

No program will succeed without the continuing interest of the post commander and his staff. A collegiate program will also need the attention of an educational officer who is a qualified educator and is given time and staff to manage the program. The educational officer will need the full support of all base officials. The success of such programs will be highly dependent upon the experience, leadership, and resourcefulness of such an individual.

E. It would be helpful to such programs if there were greater uniformity of policy and practice between the various branches of the military.

It has been noted that differences exist in both policy and practice between the various branches of the service. There is a need for greater uniformity in the sponsorship of such programs. Administrative organization could have greater communality. Tuition support could be more comparable. A common formula for financial support would strengthen services. A basis for such a formula could well be a full-time equivalent enrollment served. Certainly common agreement on what constitutes adequate classroom space would facilitate such efforts on the part of participating higher institutions. The element of uniformity of commitment on the part of the various branches could do much to bring greater comparability of program and services from base to base.

Guides and Responsibilities of the College and University

A. Programs offered should relate to the purposes and adhere to the academic standards of the college or university.

Provisions should be made for students to work toward certain of the degree programs offered by the institutions. Degree requirements should be just as demanding as those for students on the campus.

Course offerings might be more flexible than those required of the less mature campus student. Thus the educational goal of the base student might be given greater consideration within the general degree requirements of the college or university without depreciation of standards. Higher institutions should be very hesitant to offer programs not recognized in their accreditation and certainly should refrain from attempting to offer work unrelated to either their mission or resources. This should not mean that colleges should not feel obligated to give service or cultural courses without credit when such experiences can be of personal worth or upgrade competencies required of the military person in his own work.

B. The organization and administration of base programs should take into consideration the uniqueness of such situations.

The college staff member assigned the responsibility of representing the college in its base effort must recognize the uniqueness of the situation. He must realize the first demand upon the base personnel is a military commitment. The time and arrangements for such individuals must fit into this demand. The planning for and scheduling of courses should recognize the time and scheduled demands of the military mission. Organization and administration practices need not duplicate nor conform to campus routines. Being flexible and innovative to meet unique conditions of the military need not mean any depreciation or departure from recognized collegiate requirements. Collegiate level standards should be maintained. When the higher institution is reviewed for accreditation purposes, this aspect of its efforts should be visited and appraised.

C. Student personnel policies and services should be such as to facilitate the success of a program on a military base.

Admission requirements should recognize collegiate level studies and degree requirements. Registration procedures should take into consideration the conditions under which the military work. Guidance and counselling services should be provided when needed. There may need to be special provisions made for program advising and counselling so students may know requirements as well as make adjustments in terms of their own educational goals. Some adjustments may need to be made in regard to the residence requirements and substitution of courses in the transfer of credits for degree purposes. Provisions should be made for the mature students to quality for advanced placement or credit by examination just as is provided on most campuses for the abler students.

D. Both faculty and instruction should be of recognized collegiate quality.

The participating higher institution must maintain collegiate level quality in its faculty on base. The quality of instruction should be comparable to that on campus. The same degree of concern for teaching tools and learning resources should exist on base as exists on the home campus. Comparable library resources should be available or accessible. There may need to be special provisions made for the completion of course work when students are called from the base during alerts or emergencies. Regardless of departures from campus practice, grades should not be given until students meet all the requirements of a course.

Policy Statement on External Budget Control

The governing board of an institution must control the institution's budget, which is the expression of the institution's plans in financial terms. Unless the governing board has control of the budget it cannot complete its planning function or ensure the implementation of its plans.

When an institution depends for its support on an external agency—state, church, or other public or private agency—the external agency will determine the amount of support it will provide and may appropriately indicate in broad terms the categories for which support is provided and the amounts. The external agency should not, through line items control or other means, determine in detail how the funds are to be spent. This is a function of the governing board and the institution's officers.

Once funds have been allocated, the normal expectation should be that the amount of funds will not be reduced. If subsequent developments necessitate reduction of the allocation, the governing board and the institution's officers should determine how and where the reductions are to be made.

If an external agency has a responsibility for pre-auditing or post-auditing it should check only on such matters as arithmetic accuracy, authenticity of signatures, consistency with the provisions of the budget, and legality; it should not question the appropriateness of a particular expenditure.

Policy Statement on General Education Requirements in Technical, Specialized, and Professional Programs

Degree requirements in any institution should ensure for its graduates a cultural background in the humanities, the social studies, and the natural sciences, and also an appropriate level of mastery in one area of inquiry or skill or preparation for attaining such mastery in further studies.

Undergraduate programs in technical, specialized, and professional fields should include or make provision for humanistic, social, and scientific studies equal to at least a quarter of the usual program, exclusive of courses preparatory to the major or only marginally related to the cultural fields. Post-baccalaureate degree requirements should either include such studies or expect their completion before admission. The quality and status of instruction in the general fields and in the major areas should be comparable.

Policy Statement on Institutional Integrity

By academic tradition and by philosophical principle an institution of higher learning is committed to the pursuit of truth and to its communication to others.

To carry out this essential commitment calls for institutional integrity in the way a college or university manages its affairs—specifies its goals, selects and retains its faculty, admits students, establishes curricula, determines programs of research, fixes its fields of service.

The maintenance and exercise of such institutional integrity postulates and requires appropriate autonomy and freedom.

Put positively this is the freedom to examine data, to question assumptions, to be guided by evidence, to teach what one knows—to be a learner and a scholar. Put negatively this is a freedom from unwarranted harassment which hinders or prevents a college or university from getting on with its essential work.

A college or university must be managed well and remain solvent, but it is not a business nor an industry. It must be concerned with the needs of its community and state and country, but an institution of higher learning is not a political party nor a social service. It must be morally responsible, but even when church related, it is not a religion nor a church.

A college or university is an institution of higher learning. Those within it have as a first concern evidence and truth rather than particular judgments of institutional benefactors, concerns of churchmen, public opinion, social pressure, or political proscription.

Relating to this general concern and corresponding to intellectual and academic freedom are correlative responsibilities. On the part of trustees and administrators there is the obligation to protect faculty and students from inappropriate pressures or destructive harassments.

On the part of the faculty there is the obligation to distinguish personal conviction from proven conclusions and to present relevant data fairly to students because this same freedom asserts their rights to know the facts.

On the part of students there is the obligation to sift and to question, to be actively involved in the life of the institution but involved as learners at appropriate levels. The determination and exercise of proper responsibilities will be related to the students' status as undergraduate, professional, or graduate students.

Intellectual freedom does not rule out commitment; rather it makes it possible and personal. Freedom does not require neutrality on the part of the individual nor the educational institution—certainly not toward the task of inquiry and learning, nor toward the value systems which may guide them as persons or as schools.

Hence institutions may hold to a particular political, social, or religious philosophy as may individual faculty members or students. But to be true to what they profess academically, individuals and institutions must remain intellectually free and allow others the same freedom to pursue truth and to distinguish the pursuit of it from a commitment to it.

All concerned with the good of colleges and universities will seek for ways to support their institutional integrity and the exercise of their appropriate autonomy and freedom. In particular, the Federation and the regional commissions, which have a particular responsibility to look at an institution in its totality, will always give serious attention to this aspect and quality of institutional life so necessary for its well-being and vitality.

Policy Statement on Inter-regional Accreditation

1. When important parts of an institution are located in the area of two or more regional associations, the accreditation of the institution is the joint responsibility of all the commissions concerned, acting as if they had merged for this purpose.

2. The executive secretary of the commission in whose area the principal headquarters of the institution are will arrange and direct the evaluation, normally using his commission's materials and procedures, drawing upon the others for help.

3. The chairman of the evaluation team will propose a recommendation for action by the cooperating commissions. The executive secretary of the directing commission will forward it to the other commissions before action is taken by any of them. If time permits, he will solicit comments on the proposal before any cooperating commission meets, and try to frame a revised recommendation, if that seems desirable.

4. No commission's action on an inter-regional accreditation will be final until all the associations involved have completed identical action.

5. If the action of any one commission varies from the action of another, the executive secretaries of the regions concerned will seek agreement on behalf of the commissions involved. They will have the authority and responsibility to do so in case of minor variations, recommending actions by the appropriate commissions or associations, if necessary.

6. When the action on accreditation has been completed, the executive secretary of the directing commission will notify the institution officially, on behalf of all the commissions concerned.

7. The executive secretary of the directing commission will be responsible for any follow-up activities or reports which may be ordered, as the agent of the cooperating commissions.

8. When the accreditation action has been completed, the institution as a whole shall become a member of each of the cooperating associations, and each association shall bill the unit in its area for dues in accordance with its regular practice. The institution shall designate its representatives in each of the cooperating associations, if it is customary in that association to do so.

9. The names of institutions which are accredited by common action shall appear in the Federation directory under each state in which an accredited branch is located, in a uniform manner.

Policy Statement on Undergraduate Study Abroad Programs

This statement by the Federation of Regional Accrediting Commissions of Higher Education was adopted March 1967.

Study abroad is increasingly accepted as an important phase of many undergraduate programs in American colleges and universities. Carefully planned and administered, opportunities for foreign study can add significant dimensions to a student's educational experience. At the same time, the great diversity of programs poses serious problems for their evaluation and control.

As guidelines for institutions which conduct programs of foreign study or whose students participate in such programs, the Federation of Regional Accrediting Commissions of Higher Education suggests that undergraduate study abroad programs should

1. be clearly relevant to the purpose and objectives of the sponsoring or participating institutions;

2. be designed to provide educational experiences integrally related to the institution's undergraduate curriculum but otherwise unavailable;
3. be limited to carefully selected students;
4. have rigidly specified language proficiency requirements when appropriate to the program and place of study;
5. include extensive preliminary orientation for intended participants;
6. so far as conditions permit, be staffed and directed under the same policies as the home institution—continuity of administrative direction is especially important;
7. provide counselling and supervisory services at the foreign center equal to those on the home campus, with special attention to problems peculiar to the location and nature of the program;
8. include clearly defined criteria and policies for judging performance and assigning credit in accordance with prevailing standards and practices at the home institution;
9. stipulate that students will ordinarily not receive credit for foreign study undertaken without prior planning or approval;
10. include provisions for regular follow-up studies on the individual and institutional benefits derived from such programs.

Cooperative arrangements are encouraged among American institutions seeking to provide foreign study opportunities for their students. Travel programs *per se*, or commercially sponsored "study-travel programs," will not normally be countenanced for degree credit by the regional accrediting commissions, nor will they accredit independent foreign study programs unrelated to specific college or university curricula.

The Federation suggests the following publications:

Undergraduate Study Abroad: U. S. College-Sponsored Programs. New York: Institute of International Education, 1965. The introductory essay by Stephen A. Freeman is especially significant.

Abrams, Irwin and Hatch, W. R. "Study Abroad," *New Dimensions in Higher Education,* Number 6, U. S. Office of Education, 1960.

"Guidelines for the Review of Undergraduate College and University Study Abroad Programs." The University of the State of New York, State Education Department. Division of Higher Education, Albany, New York 12224.

A Guide to Institutional Self-Study and Evaluation of Educational Programs Abroad. New York: Council on Student Travel, 1965.

Policy Statement on Substantive Change

This statement by the Federation of Regional Accrediting Commissions of Higher Education and the following statement were adopted April 1968.

A substantive change is one which appears to modify the nature and scope of the institution, which affords instruction at a more advanced level,* or which adds one or more new geographic locations for instruction. When an institution commits itself to a substantive change, it is the responsibility of the institution to notify the commission on institutions of higher education of its region. During the change the institution should take the steps necessary to assure an orderly transition consistent with the regulations of the commission. At a time deemed appropriate by the commission the institution must seek the approval of the commission. An accrediting action taken as a result of substantive change is to be interpreted as accreditation of the institution as a whole including the change, not as accreditation of that part of the institution which was changed.

The Evaluation of Graduate Work

Mature Institutions. The evaluation of graduate work carried on in institutions with well-established programs of graduate study should be included as part of the general evaluation of the institution whenever a comprehensive evaluation is made.

* See FRACHE statement on The Evaluation of Graduate Work.

Developing Institutions. Cognizance should be taken by the regional association of the extension of the work of an accredited institution to a higher degree level.* The institution should provide the association with a report indicating the rationale for the program; the financial, faculty, library, and laboratory resources available for its support; evidence of strength in supporting fields; requirements for admission and graduation; number of students involved; and the administrative arrangements.

The report should be followed by a review by the association of the adequacy of the new program and of its impact on other aspects of the institution's work.

In a developing institution a continuing check should be made on further extensions into new subject matter areas at the new level until such time as the institution has developed the means for effective quality control of programs at the new level.

* This is a type of substantive change. See FRACHE Policy Statement on Substantive Change.

Chapter 17

The Military and the College Student

RICHARD W. BISHOP

Assistant to the President, Northeastern University, Boston, Massachusetts

THE MILITARY AND THE COLLEGE STUDENT

Legal Obligation In November, 1969, Section 5(a)2 of the Military Selective Service Act of 1967 was repealed. This section required that the President, after designating the prime age group for induction, had to select those for induction on the basis of "oldest first" within the prime group. By repealing this section of the Act, Congress restored to the President the discretionary authority to determine the relative order of selection for induction within specific age groups. With the prohibition removed, the President exercised his authority and immediately instituted a random selection system which he deemed to be "fair and just" within the scope of the law. It should be noted that repeal of this one section of the Selective Service Act did not drastically change the entire Act, only the method of selection for induction within the prime age group.

Basically, the Selective Service Act of 1967 is the same as that adopted by Congress in 1940. Registration with a local board at age 18 is mandatory for every male citizen of the U.S., every male alien admitted to the U.S. for permanent residence, and every male alien who has remained in the U.S. in a status other than that of a permanent resident for a period or periods totaling one year. Technically, an individual becomes draftable at age 19, and his chances of being drafted after that depend on four variables: (1) the size of the draft calls, (2) the supply of nondeferred men in his local board area, (3) the status of the individual as a deferred or nondeferred person, and (4) the position of the individual within the random sequence.

When a call is placed by the Secretary of Defense for a specific number of men, the order of induction is as follows: (1) individuals age 19 or over who have failed to register, keep their draft boards informed of their whereabouts, or otherwise have become delinquent; (2) volunteers under 26 years of age, in the order in which they volunteered; and (3) nonvolunteers, not in a deferred status, 19 years of age, according to their position in the national random selection sequence.

The National Random Selection Process The purpose of the "lottery" system is to establish for the 19- to 20-year-old age group, and those older if in a deferred status, one year of maximum exposure to the draft. After that one year, those not inducted will be placed in a lower order for call.

The selection process may best be explained in the following manner. Near the end of each year, a drawing is held at Selective Service Headquarters in Washington. Closed capsules, each containing a month and day, are drawn in random fashion. The order in which these capsules are drawn determines the relative position in the national random sequence of registrants who turned 19 years of age on any date during that year, including February 29. If, for example, June 8 was drawn first, all men born on that date would be number one in the national random sequence. If September 14 was drawn last, all men with that birthday would be number 366. Following this drawing, a second drawing is made of the 26 letters of the alphabet, placing them in a random fashion. If the letter *M* was drawn first, all men whose last name begins with that letter would be the first to be inducted when their birth date number appeared at the top of the induction list.

Once the drawing is completed, each local board assigns numbers to its registrants who are in I-A or who become I-A in accordance with the national sequence. It is feasible for one local board to fill its quota of draftees by using only a few numbers in the national sequence while another board may have to use many more numbers to meet its quota. For example, one board might meet its quota by going no higher than number 122, while other boards may have to go as high as 240. Therefore, it is possible that a registrant holding 122 and a registrant holding 240 will be called for induction at the same time.

Deferments The law guarantees deferment, if requested, to any individual who is a full-time undergraduate student in any accredited college as long as he is making satisfactory progress toward a degree. In a four-year institution, this would mean completion of 25 percent of the total requirements during each academic year. In colleges which operate on the five-year cooperative plan of education, i.e., where alternating periods of study and employment related to study begin in the sophomore year and continue for a four-year period, defining satisfactory progress is more difficult. In these institutions, the student's scholastic advancement is usually determined by his progress in the term, quarter, or semester in which he is enrolled. If a student is allowed to repeat a term because of poor achievement, his local draft board should be notified. It is then the decision of the board whether or not he will be reclassified. Students pursuing a full-time course of study which does not lead to a baccalaureate degree may be considered for a II-A deferment by their local board. Transfer students may be considered for a II-S or II-A deferment, depending upon the educational program in which they enroll, provided that they continue to make normal progress, in accordance with the regulations, toward the completion of their programs. The law specifies that student deferment ends when the individual receives a degree or at age 24 at the latest, although even a 24-year-old will be allowed to finish an academic year. When the deferment ends, the individual is immediately placed in the I-A pool. For example, if his birthday is drawn as number 90, and he is now deferred for college, but loses his college deferment in June of next year, he will be number 90 in the national random sequence in use next year regardless of the position of his birth date in next year's drawing.

Graduate students and those pursuing part-time undergraduate programs do not fare as well under the new law. No deferments will be given for graduate students except in the fields of medicine, dentistry, allied health fields, theology, and in a few technical courses listed as essential to the United States.[1] Students pursuing a program of part-time study will not generally be deferred; however, the local selective service board has the right to judge each case on its individual merits.[2]

Alternatives Following Graduation The man who holds a low number (1 to 122) in the national random sequence is virtually assured of being called for the draft assuming that he is mentally, physically, and morally qualified to serve. Those in the middle third of the numbering sequence (123 to 244) fare a little better depending on the size of draft calls and the availability of personnel in their local board area. Individuals in the final third of the numbering sequence (245 to 366) will have few worries barring a national emergency and are free to make plans accordingly. What then are the alternatives for the men in the first two categories? The man with the low number has few choices. If his number has been reached while he is in a deferred status he will be inducted as soon as appeals, examinations, and so forth, are concluded even though the year may end. There is no way he can gain an advantage by delaying his actual induction through time required for personal appearance, appeals, examination, and other processing if his random sequence number has been reached. On the other hand, if his

[1] Interpretation of the "essential courses" is presently being considered at both the state and national levels.

[2] Generally, a student is required to carry 12 semester hours of credit in order to maintain his deferment.

number has not yet been reached, graduate school will offer a one-year delay in his induction. If called while he is in graduate school, the low number man will be allowed to complete only that academic year in which he is presently enrolled before induction takes place. Therefore, it would appear to be unwise to enter graduate school, particularly if the individual is planning advanced study in science or engineering. A two-year hiatus caused by the draft could result in technical obsolescence and necessitate repetition of the first year of graduate study. For the student in non-technical programs whose number is called while he is in school, the loss of time may not be quite as serious; however, the anxiety which he may feel after his number has been called might not be worth the delay in induction. Employment in industry is not a viable alternative for the low-number registrant either. Although nothing has yet been published, it is predicted that occupational deferments will tighten up considerably in the near future. Companies which once were willing to hire a man in whom they were interested, regardless of his draft status, will now be more selective with the knowledge that there is a large pool of individuals who are not going to face induction.

The low number registrant is really left with two alternatives: (1) wait to be drafted, or (2) enlist in a program of his choosing. There are advantages to enlisting and completing a military program immediately after college. One argument in favor of immediate commitment to the military is that it provides the individual with time to do some serious soul searching about his future and about his chosen area of graduate study. Another is that by enlisting, the individual has a choice of branch of service and type of training he wishes to receive.

For the man in the middle third of the numbering sequence, the decision to move in any given direction is more difficult. It is not truly feasible to suggest that he adopt one course of action as opposed to another. He should, of course, stay in close touch with his draft board in order that he be apprised of his relative position in the order of induction. Beyond that, his military status is a one-year gamble.

Commissioned or Enlisted Service The author has seen both sides of this coin, having served on active duty initially as an enlisted man and later serving as a commissioned officer. He would urge very strongly that any college graduate faced with a military obligation who has the opportunity for a commission give it serious consideration. This is not, however, *the* answer for every young man facing military service. One thing is certain—when his number is called, the individual is going to have to be available for service for a period of six years at the minimum. He may see as little as four months of active duty with the remainder being served in the reserves; he may serve as a draftee without choice of branch of service or type of training for a period of two years of active duty and four years of reserves; or, as a volunteer, he may serve the entire six year period in active service. Whatever his choice, short-, medium-, or long-term active duty, the graduate should bring to his military obligation the same attitude he would bring to a position in business. With the proper attitude, service in the armed forces can be an enriching educational experience—with an indifferent attitude, it can and will be a wasteful, drab, and tedious time in life.

Conclusion The uncertainty which faces two-thirds of the nation's qualified male population and the number of military programs available for the college graduate suggest that a military service advisory office become a part of today's campus. This may not and probably will not be a full-time staff position. The author suggests that the office of student personnel is probably best equipped to handle such a service, and that the assistant dean of students or the assistant dean of men be named as the individual responsible for such information.

It would be the function of the military service advisory office to (1) gather together all the information available concerning the various programs offered by the uniformed armed services and information concerning nonmilitary government activity in lieu of military service, (2) establish a liaison with the local armed service representatives—

not to become a campus recruiter for them, but to be able to take advantage of their background and knowledge to clarify points in individual cases, (3) make known the fact that such an advisory office exists in the institution and that its purpose is to truly serve the needs of the students on campus, and (4) present the facts objectively to each student who takes advantage of the services of such an office.

The table which begins on page 2-274 presents some of the wide variety of choices which are available to the college graduate.

THE RESERVE OFFICERS' TRAINING CORPS (ROTC)

Introduction The concept of citizen soldiering is an integral part of American history. From the days of the "Infamous Militia Act" of 1792 to the present, this nation has followed a policy of civilian control of its military force. The establishment of military science courses at a nonprofessional military institution began in 1819 with the founding of Norwich University in Northfield, Vermont. Although its founder was a military man, its purpose was to provide officers who would be "identified in views, in feelings, and in interests, with the great body of the community."

With the passage of the Morrill Land-grant College Act in 1862, another alternative for the training of military officers became available. Civilian educational institutions could now train a qualified officer corps while providing a hedge against a military clique loyal only to itself and not to the nation. The act however, was vague, leaving each college a great deal of latitude with regard to the conduct of the program. The War Department also showed little enthusiasm for the training. A series of supplementary acts followed which established a better relationship between the War Department and the land-grant colleges, but it was not until 1916, when the National Defense Act was passed, that the ROTC system as we know it today was established. Essentially, the act established the Reserve Officers' Training Corps, outlined a program of instruction, and authorized the appointment of those who successfully completed the program as second lieutenants in the Organized Reserve Corps. This program remained basically unchanged until 1964, when the ROTC Vitalization Act was signed. This act, which updates the ROTC program, called for additional financial assistance, scholarships, and uniform allowances. The added financial assistance is in the form of fees, tuition, and books for selected students participating in a four-year senior-division ROTC program. The act also provided for a new two-year program for students who were unable to participate in ROTC during their first two years of college or junior college. The scholarship program and the two- and four-year senior division programs will be examined in detail later in this chapter.

Purpose and Mission Stated in its broadest possible terms, the purpose and mission of the Reserve Officers' Training Corps program has varied little from its spiritual inception in 1819. The purpose then, as it tends to be today, was to provide civilian-oriented, college-educated officers for limited active service in the armed services. Additional purposes as listed by the various branches of the armed services include:

Army: To develop college-educated officers for the Active Army and Reserve components
To supplement the number of officers turned out annually by West Point and other commissioning programs
To provide a source of regular or career Army officers

Navy: To train young men who wish to serve their country in time of emergency as reserve officers of the Navy or Marine Corps
To educate and train well-qualified young men for careers as commissioned officers of the regular Navy and Marine Corps

Air Force: To commission career-minded officers to meet Air Force requirements through its educational programs on college campuses

TABLE 1 Summary of Service Opportunities by Branch of Service *

Program	Age limits	Active duty	Reserve obligation	Special information
Draft	$18\frac{1}{2}$–26	2 years	3 years ready 1 year standby	Must report whenever called; has little if any choice as to branch of service or type of training
Volunteering for the draft	17–25	2 years	3 years ready 1 year standby	
ARMY:				
Regular Army	17–34	3 years 4 years 5 years 6 years	2 years ready, 1 year standby 2 years standby 1 year standby No further obligation	*Graduate Specialist Program:* Qualification by examination for choice of classroom program before enlistment *Choose-it-yourself system:* Qualification by examination for vocational training *Combat Arms Program:* Choose combat arms – get choice of location for overseas tour of duty
Army Enlisted Reserve	17–26	2 years	3 years ready 1 year standby	
Army Reserve	17–26	4 months minimum	Remainder of 6-year obligation in ready reserve	Length of service (active) depends on the specialty for which the individual enlists
	26–35	4 months minimum	Remainder of 3-year obligation in ready reserve	Same as above
Army National Guard	17–26 26–35	4 months minimum	Same as Army Reserve	Same as Army Reserve
United States Military Academy (West Point)	17–22	4 years	2 years ready	Entrance is largely by Congressional appointment and examinations. Requirements are rigid. Applicants should be interested in a military career
Women's Army Corps	18–35	3 years		Applicants must receive parental consent if under 21 years of age

Army Reserve Officers' Training Corps (ROTC)	14–28	6 months	6½ years ready 1 year standby	Attendance at a college or university having an ROTC unit or available host unit for cross-enrollment. Graduate may not be commissioned until age 18. (See pages 2-279 to 2-291 for a discussion of ROTC.)
		2 years nonscholarship reserve appointments	3 years standby 1 year standby	
		3 years nonscholarship regular army appointments	2 years ready 1 year standby	
	17–25	4 years scholarship cadets	2 years standby	
Army National Guard–College Commission Plan	18–28			Attendance at college or university which does not have an ROTC unit
Army Officer Candidate School (OCS)	18½–28	2 years, 10 months	About 3 years ready, 1 year standby	College graduates only. Program guarantees entrance to OCS after 16 weeks training. High school graduates may apply after entering service, but entrance is not assured
Direct appointment	21–27 (regular) 18–39 (reserve)	Varies	Depends on amount of active duty time	Limited to individuals possessing certain professional and technical specialties. Must hold doctoral, master's, or baccalaureate degree with practical experience
Warrant Officer Flight Training	18–30	3 years, 11 months	About 2 years ready	
NAVY:				
Regular Navy Enlistment	17–30	3 years 4 years 6 years	2 years ready, 1 year standby 1 year ready, 1 year standby No further obligation	Special training is available for high school, vocational school, or junior college graduates
Naval Reserve Enlistment	17–26	2 years	3 years ready 1 year standby	May delay active duty one year after enlisting
U.S. Naval Academy (Annapolis)	17–22			Same as U.S. Military Academy
Naval Reserve Officers Training Corps (regular)	17–21	4 years	1 year ready 1 year standby	Career oriented. See parts of this chapter mentioned above on ROTC

° Reprinted with permission from *Changing Times*, The Kiplinger Magazine, June, 1966; and *It's Your Choice*, U.S. Government Printing Office, May, 1965.

TABLE 1 (Continued)

Program	Age limits	Active duty	Reserve obligation	Special information
Naval Reserve Officers Training Corps (contract)	17–21	3 years	2 years ready 1 year standby	See parts of this chapter mentioned above on ROTC
Navy Enlisted Scientific Education Program (NESEP)	21–25	4 years	1 year ready 1 year standby	Open only to enlisted personnel who are petty officers on active duty. Provides 4 years college education in systems engineering and general scientific and engineering fields
Navy Officer Candidate School (OCS)	19–27½ (varies for some specialties)	3 years, 4 months	2 years ready 1 year standby	Open only to college graduates
Naval Reserve Officer Candidate (ROC)	17–27½	3 years	2 years ready 1 year standby	Must be a member of the Naval Reserve. Must have completed three years of college. Two 8-week summer training cruises
Naval Aviation Reserve Officer Candidate (AVROC)	17–26½ (pilot training)	3½ years plus 1 year of training	1½ years standby	Similar to ROC program with a longer training period following graduation
	17–27½ (aviation observer training)	3½ years plus 1 year of training	Same	
Naval Aviation Officer Candidate (AOC)	19–26	5 years (including 18 months of training)	1 year standby	College degree required
Naval Aviation Officer Candidate (NAOC)	19–27½	5 years (including 12–18 months of training)	1 year standby	College degree required
Naval Officer Candidate Airman (OCAN)	18–25	4½ years	1½ years standby	Must have at least two years of college
AIR FORCE:				
Regular Air Force Enlistment	17–28	4 years	2 years ready	Must attain a qualifying score in electronics (general, administrative, or mechanical)
Air Force Reserve Non-prior Service	17–28	4 months minimum	Remainder of 6-year obligation in ready reserve	Length of active duty is determined by specialty for which trained

Air National Guard	17–35	4 months minimum	Remainder of 6-year obligation in ready reserve	Length of active duty is determined by specialty for which trained
U.S. Air Force Academy	17–22	4 years	1 year ready	Same as U.S. Military Academy
Air Force Reserve Officer Training Corps (AFROTC)	14–24	4 years (nonflying) 5 years (flying)	2 years ready 1 year ready	See parts of this chapter mentioned above on ROTC
Air Force Officer Training School (OTS)	20½–29½	4 years (nonflying) 5 years (flying)	2 years ready 1 year ready	College degree required
Airman Education and Commissioning Program (AECP)	18–30	4 years		Must have completed two years of college. Air Force pays for completion of college program
MARINE CORPS:				
Regular Marine Corps Enlistment	17–28	3 years 4 years 6 years	2 years ready 1 year standby 1 year ready 1 year standby No further obligation	Assignments are in accordance with the needs of the service, based on education, skills, prior training, physical capabilities, and personal preferences
Marine Corps Enlisted Reserve	17–32			Reserved for veterans of the USMC
Marine Corps Reserve Training Program	17–26	6 months	5½ years ready	
Marine Corps Officer Candidate Course	20–27 (ground) 20–26 (aviation)	3 years	2 years ready 1 year standby	Open to college seniors or graduates
Marine Platoon Leaders Class	17–27 (ground) 17–26 (aviation)	3 years 3½ years	2 years ready, 1 year standby 2 years ready, 1 year standby	College degree required. Open to college freshmen, sophomores, and juniors. Requires summer training sessions
Marine Aviation Cadet	17–26	4½ years	1 year ready 1 year standby	Must have at least two years of college or 60 semester hours of credit
COAST GUARD:				
Regular Coast Guard Enlistment	17–26	4 years	1 year ready 1 year standby	Designed for career-minded individuals

TABLE 1 (Continued)

Program	Age limits	Active duty	Reserve obligation	Special information
Coast Guard 6-month Reserve	17–26	5 months minimum	Remainder of 6-year obligation in ready	Applicants must be single
		6 months minimum	Remainder of 6-year obligation in ready	Applicants must be single
		2 years	2 years ready, 2 years with no special training	Applicants preselected to attend specialized training schools after recruit training
Coast Guard Reserve	17–26	6–12 months	Remainder of 6-year obligation in ready	R.L. Program
Coast Guard Reserve	17–26	2 years	3 years ready 1 year standby	2X6 Program
U.S. Coast Guard Academy	17–22			Same as other military academies
Coast Guard Officer Candidate School (OCS)	21–26	3 years	2 years ready 1 year standby	College senior or graduate

For additional information, individual inquiries may be directed to:

Army: Army Careers
U.S. Continental Army Command
Fort Monroe, Virginia

Navy: Chief of Naval Personnel (PERS–B 61)
Department of the Navy
Washington 25, D.C.

Air Force: Headquarters USAF Recruiting Service
Attn: Director of Advertising & Publicity
Wright-Patterson Air Force Base, Ohio

Marine Corps: Commandant, United States Marine Corps
Code D.P.
Washington 25, D.C.

Coast Guard: Commandant (P.T.P.)
U.S. Coast Guard Headquarters
Washington 25, D.C.

Because of the changing nature of war and the increasing commitments of the United States abroad, there is a trend away from the "reserve" aspect of the ROTC and greater emphasis is being placed on developing the career-oriented officer. Although sufficient data is not yet available to accurately predict where this trend will lead, it is safe to assume that the role of the career ROTC officer will become much more important in the future.

Types of ROTC Programs *Army.* Traditionally, Army ROTC cadets have undergone a four-year training program which consists of two years of a basic course—compulsory at some schools, elective at others—and an advanced program which is elective at all colleges.

During the first two years of the program, cadets receive training in basic military subjects, military history, weapons, equipment, and leadership techniques. Class time is approximately three hours per week, consisting of two hours of drill and one hour of classroom work. The advanced course is normally taken during the junior and senior years. This course is open only to those who apply for it; however, application is definitely not synonymous with acceptance under today's ROTC standards. Actually, only 15 to 20 percent of those students who enter the ROTC program in their freshman year receive their second lieutenant's bars through the program. The Department of the Army has, in recent years, placed increased emphasis on academic achievement, not to the exclusion of military knowledge but as a complement to it. Today's Army officer brings to his military career a broad background of knowledge which enables him to perform many of his duties more effectively and efficiently. Instruction in the advanced course includes military tactics, logistics, administration, teaching methods, leadership techniques, and the exercise of command. Class time in the advanced course comprises three hours of classroom work and two hours of drill.

A variation of the normal four-year ROTC program is the opportunity to be commissioned by taking only the two-year advanced course. This program, authorized in 1964 under the ROTC Vitalization Act, extends the advantages of ROTC to junior college graduates, to transfer students from schools that do not offer ROTC, and to students in four-year colleges who were unable to take the basic course during their first two years. To a limited degree, this program is also available to graduate students who have two years remaining in their educational program. The future of this graduate school arrangement is very uncertain because of changes in the Selective Service Act which practically eliminated graduate deferments and because of the extended deferment privilege which it would offer to otherwise nondeferable students.

Instruction in the two-year program consists of a basic six-week summer training period prior to the start of the junior year which takes the place of the traditional two-year basic course. When a student with two years of college has been selected for the program and has successfully completed the summer training period, he is then eligible to apply for the ROTC advanced course in his junior and senior years.

The six-week advanced-course summer camp normally is attended between the junior and senior years of college, but, depending upon the circumstances, it can be scheduled following graduation. Institutions which operate on other than the standard four-year curriculum such as colleges operating under the cooperative plan of education must arrange with the Department of the Army for summer camp training. Northeastern University, for instance, because of its cooperative plan of education, would not find it possible to allow members of the cadet corps to attend the advanced course summer camp at the normal time. Through an arrangement with the Department of the Army, the Northeastern cadets attend the summer camp immediately following commencement exercises in the spring.

Two additional programs which should be mentioned in connection with Army ROTC are (1) the flight instruction program and (2) the distinguished military graduate program. Flight training is offered at some ROTC colleges and is usually given during the second year of the advanced course. This training is an extracurricular activity conducted by an FAA-approved flying school at an airfield near the institution. All costs of this program, including flight instruction, textbooks, navigational equipment, flight clothing, insurance, and transportation to and from the flying school, are paid by the Army. The instruction consists of 35 hours of ground instruction and more than 36 hours of flight training. Students who take this training must agree to participate, if selected, in the Army aviation program upon entering the service. On completion of the Army aviation training, the newly commissioned officer must serve on active duty for three years. Application for this program may be made through the professor of military science (PMS) of the institution.

The distinguished military graduate program permits ROTC students who have compiled outstanding academic and military leadership records to apply for a Regular Army commission upon graduation. At the end of the junior and prior to the advanced course summer camp, approximately one-third of the ROTC students may be designated as potential distinguished military students. Students are nominated by a selection board and approved by the institution. The student who maintains high standards throughout the camp period and during the senior year may qualify for designation as a distinguished military graduate and for appointment to a Regular Army commission.

Prior to 1955, Army ROTC programs were branch oriented. That is, schools offered ROTC programs which led to a commission in a specific branch of the Army; i.e., Signal Corps, Engineers, Artillery, etc. Since 1955, however, when the option was presented to the institutions, most schools have found it advantageous to switch their programs to one of general military science. This allows the student to select a branch which may be more closely allied with his major area of study and also provides an opportunity to postpone the major decision of a branch choice until each branch has been carefully examined.

The modified curriculum represents another element of flexibility which has been introduced into the ROTC program. Since its inception in 1961, a number of different curricula have been proposed and tested. Each case involves the substitution of a certain number of hours of selected academic subjects for the traditional military science courses. In some cases, the academic subjects would be selected from the standard course offerings of the institution. In other cases, such as the plan developed at Ohio State University, the courses, each a selected academic subject, would be oriented toward military concepts.

Navy. The original NROTC was established in 1926 to offer the naval science courses necessary to qualify college students for commissions in the Naval Reserve. In 1946, the mission was altered slightly to incorporate a new program, the regular NROTC. It was established to produce well-trained and educated junior officers to supplement the output of the Naval Academy. The original NROTC concept remained as a reserve officer procurement program and is now referred to as the "contract NROTC program."

Regular NROTC. Candidates for the regular NROTC program enter national competition in November of the year preceding enrollment. High school seniors, college freshmen, and college sophomores may compete. Application to and acceptance at the college or university of his choice is the responsibility of the candidate. Subsequently, successful candidates are nominated by the chief of naval personnel to the college of their choice. Final selection is determined by the institution concerned. Regular NROTC students are appointed midshipman, USNR, and are sponsored by the Navy which provides tuition, cost of textbooks, laboratory fees, and a subsistence allowance during the time that the candidate is in college.

Once he is accepted into the regular NROTC program, each midshipman is obligated to attend three at-sea summer training sessions and to serve a minimum of four years of active duty following his commissioning as an ensign, USN, or a second lieutenant,

USMC. In addition to completing the naval science curriculum, the midshipman is required to complete one year of college mathematics and one year of physics—these to be taken before the end of the sophomore year. English requirements are normally fulfilled by meeting the standards of the institution.

Contract NROTC. Four-year Program. Students entering their first year of college may apply for the four-year contract NROTC program any time prior to registration. Selections are made by the professor of naval science (PNS) prior to registration on the basis of aptitude, personal interviews, and the meeting of required physical qualifications. Contract students in the four-year program are required to complete all naval science courses and one at-sea training session of approximately six weeks' duration which is normally given between the junior and senior years. Contract students in this program are under no obligation to the Navy until the beginning of their junior year in college, at which time, as required by Section 2104, Title 10, U.S. Code, they must enlist in the USNR for a period of six years if they wish to continue in the program.

Two-year Program. Applicants for the two-year contract program apply during the spring of their sophomore year. Selection is made by the Bureau of Naval Personnel based upon nationwide competition. Selected candidates for the two-year program attend a special six-week training course during the summer between their sophomore and junior years. Upon successful completion of the summer training they are enrolled in the two-year program at the beginning of their junior year. Contract students in the two-year program complete the naval science or marine option courses prescribed for the junior and senior year and attend the at-sea or field training session which the four-year students attend.

After graduation and commissioning as an ensign, USNR, or as a second lieutenant, USMCR, graduates of the contract program must serve three years of active duty.

The naval science curriculum consists of essential naval subjects, basic military drill, practical instruction in such subjects as naval weapons, navigation, and naval engineering, and an introduction to the naval way of life through summer training at sea or in the field. Naval science courses normally require three hours a week of classroom work per term and two hours of leadership laboratory or drill.

NROTC students, like those in the Army program, have the opportunity to participate in a flight indoctrination program and, upon successful completion, to enter naval aviation.

The Navy, like the other two branches of the service which offer ROTC programs, is constantly reviewing its curriculum with the following objectives:

1. To broaden and improve intellectual and academic content
2. To move all material of an orientation and indoctrinational nature and all material that primarily involves memory work into the "laboratory" periods
3. To have more NROTC courses taught by civilian faculty members
4. To tailor these NROTC courses offered by civilian faculty members so that these courses will be appropriate for all students

Air Force. Although it was not to become a separate service for another year, the Air Force in 1946 had already established its own ROTC units on 78 college campuses. It was not until 1949 that Army and Air Force ROTC units were separated at the institutional level, however. In both cases, the emphasis was on "reserve" training. Today, the Air Force program, unlike that of the Army, is designed as a procurement program geared to the production of career-minded officers.

When the Air Force became a separate service, there was a brief period when the concept of specialized training was the basis for the curriculum. In 1952, a new curriculum was presented and has evolved over the years into today's broader, less specialized curriculum which is designed to produce "well-rounded junior grade officers who possess high growth potential."

The AFROTC program is divided into a basic and an advanced course. During the basic course in the freshman and sophomore years, the program focuses on world military systems and the existence and scope of world military power with present and future implications. Class time in the basic course normally consists of three hours per week in the classroom. Entrance into the advanced course is competitive. During the junior year of the advanced program, which is known as the "professional officer course," the nature of war and the development of aerospace power are studied. In the senior year, the course deals with the meaning of professionalism, professional responsibility, the military justice system, leadership—its functions and practice, management principles and functions, and problem solving. In the advanced course, class time is divided into two hours of classroom work and one hour of leadership laboratory or drill.

The ROTC Vitalization Act of 1964 authorized a two-year program of study for the Air Force in addition to the traditional four-year course. As a basic requirement, applicants must have two years of academic study remaining. Other qualifications include a written examination, selection by an interview board of Air Force officers, and completion of the six-week field-training course which is actually the first two years of the basic program. After selection, the cadets complete the final two years of instruction on campus in the professional officer course. Upon admittance to the POC, cadets are required to enlist in the Air Force Reserve.

In addition to the regular AFROTC curriculum, a flight-instruction program is available to those who wish to become pilots. This program is similar to that of the Army and Navy ROTC programs except that ground instruction is given in the classroom by Air Force personnel.

The officer who receives his commission through AFROTC has an active-duty obligation of four years. Those applying for pilot or navigator training have a five-year obligation.

Extracurricular Activities Attendant to the ROTC programs are a number of extracurricular activities. These include Scabbard and Blade, an honor fraternity for Army advanced-course cadets; and the Pershing Rifles, an Army group for those who wish to pursue military training over and above that offered in the formal program. Other Army extracurricular activities include intercollegiate rifle, drill, and band competitions and a coed auxiliary organization which functions in a manner similar to Angel Flight (see below). The Arnold Air Society is a national professional service organization of the Air Force ROTC cadet corps which exists to promote the interests and ideals of the Air Force. In addition, there is a coed program allied with the Arnold Air Society known as Angel Flight. These girls assist the members of the Arnold Air Society as hostesses in university, civic, and AFROTC functions. They also carry out their own program of professional and service projects.

The extracurricular activities associated with ROTC programs receive the full support of the armed services and should be recognized by the institutions as an integral part of the ROTC program.

Pay, Allowances, and Benefits Cadets in the Army, Air Force, and Navy contract ROTC programs receive approximately the same benefits. Textbooks for military courses, uniforms, and equipment are provided by the service concerned, normally at little or no cost to the individual or institution. Advanced-course students receive a monthly subsistence allowance during their upperclass years in addition to the benefits offered in the basic program. The subsistence rates for ROTC cadets in the advanced corps have increased substantially since the late 1930s; however these increments have not been commensurate with increases in general college expenses and the cost of living. Pay for members of the active military is being brought into line with comparable civilian occupations and consideration should be given to raising the subsistence allowance for students enrolled in the various ROTC programs.

Cadets participating in summer training activities receive travel pay to and from the training site and are also reimbursed for their period of training to compensate for funds that could have been earned through summer employment. This reimbursement varies among the services but the base is always greater than the regular monthly subsistence allowance.

ROTC Scholarships One of the major changes brought about by the ROTC Vitalization Act of 1964 was the establishment of a scholarship program. Although not explicitly stated, the purpose of this part of the act seems to be to bring into the Army and Air Force programs students who are as highly motivated and as career-oriented as those enrolled in the regular Navy ROTC program. The act established two-year and four-year scholarships which pay for tuition, textbooks, laboratory fees, uniforms, and a monthly subsistence allowance. Recently, a one-year scholarship has become available for seniors enrolled in ROTC. This award provides benefits similar to those of the two- and four-year scholarship. Students enrolled in ROTC in colleges operating on the cooperative plan of education receive the full tuition scholarship for a five-year period. The two-year scholarship applies to each of the three years of their advanced ROTC course, and the one-year award covers the last three terms in which they are enrolled prior to graduation.

To be eligible for the Army Scholarship Program or the Air Force Financial Assistance Grant Program, the applicant must:

1. Be at least 17 years of age prior to the date on which the scholarship will become effective
2. Be able to complete all requirements for a commission and a college degree at not more than 25 years of age on June 30 of the year in which he becomes eligible for appointment as an officer
3. For the Army program, agree to enlist in a reserve component for a period of time necessary to complete the requirements for a commission, or, in the Air Force, enlist for a period of eight years or until he is commissioned as a second lieutenant
4. Be enrolled in or acceptable for enrollment in one of the colleges or universities which offer the four-year ROTC program
5. Agree to complete the requirements for a commission, to accept either a regular or reserve commission, whichever is offered, and to serve on active duty for a period of at least four years (five if accepting a regular commission) after being commissioned; or, if pilot or navigator qualified, to serve for five years on active duty after receiving the rating of pilot or navigator

As an additional requirement, the Army program insists that the candidate must agree that, if a regular Army commission is offered and accepted and this commission is terminated prior to the sixth anniversary of his date of rank (date commissioned), he will accept an appointment in a reserve component of the Army until the sixth anniversary of his date of rank.

Air Force special requirements include the following:

1. All first-year grant recipients must agree to enter a flight training program at the time they are called to active duty, provided that they have remained fully qualified.
2. All applicants are required to take the Air Force Officer Qualification Test.

Selection of students to receive four-year scholarships will be based on:

a. Results of the C.E.E.B. Scholastic Aptitude Test (S.A.T.)
b. High school academic record
c. Participation in extracurricular athletic and nonathletic activities
d. Personal observation
e. Physical examination
f. Interview

Recipients of financial assistance grants for AFROTC are also selected on the basis of qualifying scores received on the Air Force Officer Qualification Test and they must, by the end of their first year of college, achieve a 2.5 (4 = A) cumulative grade average based on all college studies.

Applicants for two-year scholarships, in addition to meeting the requirements listed above, must complete the basic course of ROTC study, be accepted into the advanced course, have at least two years of academic study remaining, and receive an acceptable rating from an interview board composed of institution officials and military personnel.

Selection is based on the applicant's college record, personal observation, and such other criteria as may be established by the professor of military science (PMS) or the professor of aerospace studies (PAS).

Students interested in applying for the two-year scholarship program should contact the PMS or PAS of their institution. Those interested in the four-year program may write to the Army headquarters in their area or to:

Air Force ROTC
Attn: ARTO–O/TA
Maxwell Air Force Base
Alabama 36112

The ROTC scholarship program is still in its infancy. It is a subject which invariably comes under scrutiny at any ROTC advisory committee. There are a number of avenues open for the program. Feasible alternatives include:

1. Availability of scholarship aid to students enrolled in the two-year program
2. One- and three-year scholarship awards
3. Annual scholarship awards which may be renewable at the discretion of the PMS or PAS.

ROTC AND THE COLLEGE AND UNIVERSITY

Many of the subjects which will be discussed in this section vary so greatly in terms of application and practice that they must of necessity be discussed in general terms.

Before applying for an ROTC unit, college administrators must ask some searching questions. Among them are:

1. Why bring ROTC to the campus at all?
2. What will be the cost of such a program to the institution?
3. Are facilities available to house a unit (i.e., classrooms, offices, area for drill, storage facilities, etc.)?
4. What does the service concerned require of the institution, and can the institution meet these requirements?
5. Is the overall climate of this campus such that an ROTC program will be successful?
6. What will be the attitude of the students and faculty to a unit on campus?
7. What type of ROTC program is best for this campus—Army, Navy, Air Force, or multiple-service?
8. Is the socioeconomic status of the student population such that ROTC will be attractive to the student body?
9. Are the objectives of ROTC consistent with the objectives and philosophy of this institution?

This is merely a sampling of the questions which should be answered. Undoubtedly they will, or should, cause others to be raised in the minds of university officials who will be responsible for the ROTC program. If serious consideration is being given to ROTC on campus, each question should be answered in a completely objective manner. Neither current world situations nor personal feelings should be allowed to cloud judgment or bring about a subjective evaluation as to the desirability of an ROTC unit.

ROTC: Advantages and Disadvantages There are, of course, certain advantages and disadvantages which accrue by hosting an ROTC unit. Some of the advantages include the following:

1. ROTC provides an opportunity for male students to fulfill their military obligation, after they complete the program, as officers in the armed services.

2. ROTC provides a leadership opportunity for male students which is not usually developed through standard college course work.

3. During their upperclass years, ROTC cadets receive a monthly compensation for participating in the program. The money received is sufficient to defray almost all the tuition charges in a low-cost public institution or a major portion of the costs of some private colleges and universities.

4. ROTC officers are the products of a civilian-oriented, civilian-controlled institution. This is an advantage to the institution and the nation in that it precludes the formation of a military clique trained wholly by and for the military.

5. ROTC is advantageous because it offers an opportunity for the institution to make a material contribution to the national welfare.

There are other advantages to having ROTC on campus. Many of them may be classified as intangible and many would be classified as advantages only to those who are favorably disposed toward ROTC.

Disadvantages of the ROTC program include:

1. The costs to the institution, which cannot always be accurately measured

2. A potential negative attitude on the part of some administrators, faculty, staff, and students which can create problems

3. Attendant problems related to scheduling ROTC courses along with regular academic programs

4. To the student, the academic overload created by participation in ROTC. This factor normally diminishes as the student progresses in the program.

There is no question that other disadvantages can be cited; however, they are not necessarily applicable to all institutions and therefore are not considered here.

Procedure for Obtaining an ROTC Unit The general procedure for obtaining an ROTC unit is similar for each of the three services. In each case, it is necessary to send a letter of intent to the service concerned expressing an interest in obtaining a unit. This letter, which has no specific format, should be addressed to one of the following:

The Adjutant General
Department of the Army
Washington, D.C. 20315

Chief of Naval Personnel
Attn: "C"
Department of the Navy
Washington, D.C. 20315

Commandant
AFROTC
Maxwell Air Force Base
Alabama 36112

After receipt of the letter, a formal application for the establishment of an ROTC unit will be sent to the institution. A sample of the form used by each service is included in the Appendix. Once this form has been completed and forwarded through channels, an evaluation procedure begins. This evaluation terminates in a report to the service secretary concerned and determines the final outcome of the application.

In evaluating any institution for the purpose of establishing a unit, the following factors are considered:

1. *Male Enrollment and Growth Potential.* Can the population support the program in terms of production requirements? What is the projected long-range enrollment and will the production rates increase, decrease, or remain stable? (Although production rates are frequently mentioned, it should be understood that the armed services are also looking for exceptionally high quality in their officer personnel.)

2. *Geographic Distribution.* What other institutions in this area already host ROTC units?

3. *Collocation with ROTC Units of Other Services.*

4. *Cross Enrollment.* Can the applying institution serve as a host school for other colleges in the area which do not have ROTC? Are the calendars (academic) compatible? Is there a host college in the area which could cross enroll students from the applying institution?

5. *Accreditation.* Is the applying institution fully accredited?

6. *Admissions Standards.* Are the admissions standards comparable to those of other institutions offering ROTC?

7. *Degrees Granted in Areas of Special Interest to the Armed Services.*

8. *Orientation of the Institution toward National Service Based on Past Experience.*

9. *Anticipated Faculty and Student Support of ROTC.*

10. *Amount of Academic Credit Anticipated To Be Given.* The amount of academic credit given for ROTC varies, ranging from zero to approximately 30 percent of the total credits required for graduation. The amount of credit given reflects the image which ROTC has on a particular campus and can be important in the recruitment of candidates for the program.

11. *Facilities to Be Made Available for an ROTC Unit.*

Following an examination of the application, arrangements will be made by the armed service concerned for a visit to the campus to see facilities and talk with institution officials concerning the program to be offered. Formal notification of receipt of an ROTC unit will usually be sent to the institution shortly after this visit has been completed.

It should be noted here that at the present time and for the foreseeable future, there are no plans to increase the number of units for any of the three services. The first major expansion of any of the programs in over a decade took place between 1967 and 1969, when the Army added 30 new units, bringing its total to 277. Officials of the Air Force (175 units) and the Navy (54 units) are not planning any comparable expansion in their programs.

Institutional Responsibilities in the Administration of the ROTC Program It is required by the agreement between the institution and the armed service concerned that the Department of Military, Naval, or Aerospace Science be an integral academic and administrative department of the institution. The secretary of the service concerned will prescribe the course of instruction for the ROTC curriculum and will also provide the instructors and supporting literature for conducting the courses. It is the responsibility of the institution to appoint an officer of the institution as military property custodian who will be empowered to receive, stock, and account for government property, to provide facilities for the conduct of the ROTC program, including classroom and administrative facilities, and to grant appropriate academic credit (see paragraph 10 above) for ROTC courses.

Requisites for a Successful ROTC Program It is not feasible to compile a list of dos and don'ts which will guarantee a successful ROTC program on the college campus. Clearly, once an institution has applied for and received an ROTC unit it assumes a responsibility to assure the success of the program. The following suggestions may be useful in developing a strong ROTC program:

1. Promote ROTC by including the PAS, PMS, or PNS and the ROTC faculty in institutional functions.

2. Develop an effective interaction between ROTC and institutional faculty members by encouraging a free exchange of ideas.

3. Demand a high-caliber instructional staff of ROTC faculty (screen instructors with the assistance of the commanding officer to ensure getting the best officers possible).

4. Encourage members of the ROTC staff to continue their education by providing educational benefits such as free tuition, etc.

5. Promote ROTC through admissions and public relations programs emphasizing the benefits to be derived from participation in ROTC.

6. Extend academic rank to other members of the ROTC instructional staff in addition to the commanding officer.

7. Insist on high academic standards from the ROTC staff and reward high standards by granting appropriate academic credit.

8. Support the rights of ROTC protagonists and antagonists to speak their minds—this can assist in developing an effective dialogue and understanding between the two groups.

9. Extend financial as well as verbal support of an ROTC recruitment program in high schools in order to familiarize incoming students with the ROTC.

10. Send to each incoming male student a letter informing him of the availability of ROTC at the institution. Even though it may be a form letter, its tone and its source (e.g., president, vice-president, etc.) will serve as an indication of the support given the program by the institution. In the case of regular NROTC students and ROTC scholarship award recipients, a letter of congratulations from the institution would be well received.

The Place of ROTC in the Organization of the Institution Military personnel are constantly concerned about following the "chain of command." So too, at the college or university there is a chain of command that must be followed. The ROTC program, academic in nature (as opposed to administrative), should be considered as another academic department, responsible to that person concerned with the administration of academic programs. This may be a vice-president for academic programs, dean of academic administration, dean of faculty, or an equivalent officer. His responsibilities with regard to ROTC will include:

1. Assisting the PMS, PAS, or PNS in the preparation of the annual ROTC budget to be funded by the institution.

2. Assisting in planning and conducting functions which concern both the ROTC and the institution. For example, a visit to the campus by a high-ranking officer for the purpose of addressing or inspecting the cadets may be preceded by a luncheon at which certain university officials should be present. Who should and who can attend are two questions which the institutional "liaison officer" should be able to answer.

3. Answering questions concerning academic requirements of the institution for members of the ROTC faculty.

4. Acting as a buffer between the ROTC and other faculties when conflicts arise.

Cost of the ROTC Program Institutional costs of the ROTC program may be classified as direct or indirect and will depend to a great extent on the degree to which the institution wishes to support the ROTC program. Direct costs may include the following:

1. Compensation of the assistant military property custodian.

2. Compensation of secretarial and clerical personnel which the institution may provide.

3. Financial support of student activities directly related to the ROTC program (i.e., Angel Flight uniforms, transportation for student organizations to and from events, etc.).

4. Full or partial scholarship aid, as may be determined by the institution. This is in addition to any type of scholarship aid provided under the ROTC Vitalization Act.

5. Furnishing of a bond to cover the value of all government property except uni-

forms issued to the institution. This bond may be waived in cases where institutional assets are large enough to cover any liability.

6. Cost of equipment (i.e., desks, chairs, filing cabinets, etc.) which the institution may have to supply.

Indirect costs include the following:

1. Facilities which must be given over to the conduct of the ROTC program constitute a major expense for the majority of institutions. Facilities consist of classrooms, office space, an area for drill (if required), and other facilities as may be requested by the service concerned. Unfortunately, ROTC is often relegated to some of the less desirable areas on campus. This is not to say that facilities for the program should be among the most modern, attractive, or centrally located; it is to say that the location of ROTC away from the mainstream of college or university activity in an area which is not particularly desirable is hardly evidence of support on the part of the institution's administrators.

2. Perhaps the most intangible of the ROTC costs is time—the time devoted by the administrative official who is delegated as the military property custodian and the time of other institution administrators who become involved with the ROTC program in the course of their day-to-day work. At first glance, this may appear to be an insignificant cost; however, most university officials find it otherwise.

A sample budget for one Army ROTC program is presented below. This budget, from a large urban institution, may give the reader some indication of the direct costs which can be incurred by an institution. This particular program is voluntary and enrolls approximately 1,100 cadets.

TABLE 2 Sample Budget for ROTC—Institutional Costs

Salaries *	$16,600
Postage and telephone	250
Printed and other supplies	1,000
Books and periodicals	100
Subscriptions	100
Travel, operational	100
Capital equipment	500
Capital equipment maintenance	200
Student activities	1,400
Conferences (on campus) †	800
Social Security	1,100
Retirement	400
Total	$22,550

* Assistant military property custodian, secretarial, and part-time assistants.
† Inspection teams, visitations by dignitaries, etc.

Curriculum Development in ROTC One criticism which has been leveled at ROTC concerns the total program. Some critics point out that this is nothing more than a job training program for the various branches of the military, and that the colleges and universities of this country should not be used as on-the-job training sites for the government. Another, and perhaps the most severe of the criticisms of the ROTC programs, concerns the curriculum. Basically, this criticism is directed at specific military courses within the program, a feeling that the courses are "Mickey Mouse," simple, not of college caliber, and that they should be deleted from the campus schedule and relegated to a place in the summer camp training program. Still another criticism has centered around the instructors themselves—that they are not of the caliber of the regular faculty of the institution, and that the courses which they teach, in many cases, could be better taught by civilian instructors.

In reviewing ROTC, its problems and its progress, it becomes readily apparent that some of the criticism, those charges leveled by responsible educators, are completely valid. It is also readily apparent that the criticism meted out by dissident groups has little if any validity—theirs is merely part of a national movement to eliminate the military from the campus. The criticism of the military ROTC as an on-the-job training program for the United States government falls into this latter category. As long as there is a need for military preparedness, a need to "watch out for the other guy," there will be a need for military leadership. And the profession of military leadership is as honorable a profession to those who serve as is the profession of medicine, law, education, or engineering—all of which are areas prepared for in college. For this reason, and because the colleges bring a civilian-oriented type of education to bear on those it is preparing, the ROTC program belongs as an integral part of the campus scene. Secondly, if ROTC is classified as an academic department within the college or university, then it may well have some courses in its curriculum which are "Mickey Mouse"—each institution, if the faculty and administrators are honest with themselves, will prove to have some of these courses in its own curricula. The armed services are extremely cognizant of the fact that these courses exist and that they should be eliminated from the campus program. ROTC personnel at the national level are constantly studying the curriculum with an eye to modifying and streamlining the program to meet the needs of today's officer personnel. For example, a new Army ROTC program, known as "track C," is presently being conducted in 11 schools across the country. Its purpose is to bring a more academically oriented program to the cadet; to eliminate the "mechanics" of ROTC by relegating them to the summer camp training period. The new curriculum may be taught wholly by military personnel, wholly by civilian instructors, by a combination of the two, or by civilian and military instructors working in concert. This latter team-teaching approach is a particularly effective method and brings to bear both civilian and military expertise. From this new curriculum may emerge a program which can be instituted on all campuses hosting Army ROTC.

The military instructor is, in all probability, as well qualified as are the majority of his civilian counterparts. Officers selected for ROTC teaching assignments have been carefully screened before being assigned to the college campus. Although many of them do not possess the terminal degree expected of the civilian instructors, it may be because they have been gaining equivalent on-the-job experience serving in many different capacities throughout the world. Also, it should be remembered that ROTC instructors have immediate access to a wide range of teaching tools, including the most sophisticated of visual aids and highly refined lesson plans.

Just as the curriculum is changing, so too are the instructors. In order to better prepare the officers who would teach the new "track C" program previously mentioned, the Army designated 17 junior officers who were sent back to college for study leading to the master's degree. This was done in order that the officers would be better prepared to work with their civilian counterparts in the institutions where the program was to be taught.

ROTC curriculum and instructor development will continue to be of primary concern to the military. Colleges and universities can and should be helpful. The appointment of a standing faculty committee to assist in the development of new "tracks" and to encourage the free exchange of ideas between civilian and ROTC faculty members is one of the ways in which ROTC and the academic community can work together for the benefit of both.

New Developments in ROTC Curricula Recently, criticism from student and non-student leftist organizations has been directed at the ROTC. At most affected institutions this anti-ROTC sentiment has followed three paths: (1) eliminate credit for all ROTC courses; (2) once this is accomplished, demand immediate abolition of ROTC; or, (3) demand a gradual "phasing-out" of ROTC over a four-year period to meet the commitments already made to the existing classes. Although this movement has not been particularly successful to date, it has caused the Department of Defense to move more rapidly in liberalizing the ROTC curricula of the three armed services concerned.

Under the Army concept, the PMS is given sufficient latitude to develop a program suitable for the students of his particular campus. Officials in the Department of the Army feel that in view of the differences which exist between institutions, a single standard curriculum is neither feasible nor desirable. It is, however, desirable to have common elements within the curriculum. This commonality will be provided through a core of military subjects which must be taught at all institutions. Additional subjects will be drawn from the academic core program as follows:

Core area	*Examples*
Mathematics and natural sciences	Mathematics, Computer Sciences, Natural Sciences, Biology
Social sciences	Anthropology, Economics, Government or Political Science, History, Psychology, Sociology
Humanities	Foreign Languages, Philosophy
Applied sciences and professions	Management, Urban Studies, Communication Studies, Accountancy, Budgeting

When developing the military portion of the ROTC curriculum, the PMS must weigh carefully the situation on his particular campus. If the school concerned does not grant academic credit for military courses, the PMS must consider the fact that the student will have to carry the military instruction as an overload. In such cases, it may be desirable to keep the military instruction to the minimum and limit it to the reduced minimum core (180 hours). If, however, the institution wishes, and has traditionally supported a more detailed and expanded military course of study, the PMS may adjust the core of military subjects accordingly.

The Department of the Army policy also provides that such features as drill, weapons instruction, and other technical military courses may be conducted at a nearby military base or armory if the institution desires; also that ROTC cadets will not be required to wear uniforms if there is any objection to this aspect of the program. The granting of credit for courses taught by military personnel and academic titles of ROTC officers beyond that of the PMS will also be open to negotiation.

In essence, the new program allows each institution to negotiate separately with the Department of the Army for the type of program it desires for its campus.

Navy officials are also instituting changes in their ROTC program. While not as sweeping and liberal as those of the Army, these changes do, in fact, liberalize the curriculum of the Navy and allow greater authority to the individual professors of naval science.

In the Navy program, an effort has been made to lighten the burden of professional naval subjects during the freshman and sophomore years, and to place the major emphasis on the study of professional naval subjects during the junior and senior years. Courses in history, political science, calculus, physics, chemistry, and computer science, formerly taught by Navy faculty, will now be acceptable if taught by civilian faculty members.

While the Air Force program has been changed, it is difficult to determine whether the program has been truly liberalized. As in the preceding two programs, responsibility for curriculum changes rests with the professor of aerospace studies; however, his freedom to make final decisions does not appear to be as well defined or as far reaching as that of his Army and Navy counterparts. Also, the course substitution package offered by the new Air Force program is difficult to interpret as liberal because goals and "learning outcomes" are established by the Air Force and not by the civilian faculties who are to teach the courses.

Conclusion It is impossible for the military academies to provide the tremendous numbers of officers required to staff the military establishment—an establishment required to protect and preserve our constitutional rights and privileges. No other single institution is better equipped to perform this function than the college or university. The concept of these institutions educating young men to become military officers is in the best time-tested tradition of civilian control of the military forces of our nation. Without this control and without the civilian influence of the college campus, the future of this free society would certainly be tenuous.

The appendix follows on page 2-292.

APPLICATION AND AGREEMENT FOR ESTABLISHMENT OF ARMY RESERVE OFFICERS' TRAINING CORPS UNIT
(AR 145-350)

Form Approved
Budget Bureau Number 49-R342

SUBJECT: Application for the Establishment of Army Reserve Officers' Training Corps Unit

THRU : (1) Commanding General, ____________ United States Army, ____________

(2) Commanding General, United States Continental Army Command, Fort Monroe, Virginia 23351

TO : The Adjutant General, Department of the Army, Washington, D. C. 20315

APPLICATION

By direction of the governing authorities of ____________ *(Name of Institution)*

I, ____________ *(Name)*, ____________ *(Title)*

hereby submit application for the establishment of a unit in the senior division of the Army Reserve Officers' Training Corps at this institution under the provisions of section 2102, Title 10, United States Code. Attached hereto is a catalog and a statement of particulars with reference to this institution.

AGREEMENT

1. Contingent upon the acceptance of the above application and conditioned upon the fulfillment of all promises enumerated in paragraph 2 following, the Secretary of the Army agrees as follows:

a. To establish and maintain a senior division unit of the Army Reserve Officers' Training Corps at the institution named in the foregoing application.

b. To assign such military personnel as he may deem necessary for the proper administration and conduct of the Army Reserve Officers' Training Corps program at this institution and to pay the statutory compensation to such personnel from Department of the Army appropriations.

c. To provide for use in the Army Reserve Officers' Training Corps program such available Government property as may be authorized by law and applicable tables of allowances, and to pay at the expense of the Government costs of transportation, drayage, packing, crating, handling and normal maintenance of such property, exclusive of costs including utilities, involved in the storage of such property at the institution.

d. To pay at the expense of the Government, subject to law and regulations, retainer pay at a prescribed rate to enrolled members of the Army Reserve Officers' Training Corps admitted to advanced training.

e. To issue at the expense of the Government uniform clothing for enrolled members of the Army Reserve Officers' Training Corps, except that monetary allowances, at the prescribed rate or rates, may be paid in lieu of uniform clothing.

f. In providing financial assistance to specially selected members under the provisions of section 2107 of Title 10, United States Code, to arrange accounting procedures with the appropriate fiscal officer of the institution.

2. Contingent upon the acceptance of this application by the Secretary of the Army and conditioned upon the fulfillment of the promises enumerated in paragraph 1 above, the governing authorities of this institution agree as follows:

a. To establish a Department of Military Science as an integral academic and administrative department of the institution and to adopt as part of its curriculum ☐ (1) a four-year course of military instruction; ☐ (2) a two-year course of advanced training of military instruction; or ☐ (3) both of the above, which the Secretary of the Army will prescribe and conduct.

b. To require each student enrolled in any Army Reserve Officers' Training Corps course to devote the number of hours to military instruction prescribed by the Secretary of the Army.

c. To make available to the Department of Military Science the necessary classrooms, administrative offices, office equipment, storage space, and other required facilities in a fair and equitable manner in comparison with other departments of the institution.

d. To grant appropriate academic credit applicable toward graduation for successful completion of courses offered by the Department of Military Science.

e. To arrange for the scheduling of military classes to make it equally convenient for students to participate in Army Reserve Officers' Training Corps as in other courses at the same educational level, and to include a representative of the Department of Military Science designated by the Professor of Military Science on all faculty committees whose recommendations would directly affect the Department of Military Science.

f. To appoint an officer of the institution as military property custodian who will be empowered to requisition, receive, stock and account for Government property issued to the institution and otherwise to transact matters pertaining thereto, for and in behalf of the institution, or to comply with provisions of the supplement to this agreement *(DA Form 918a)*, if application is made for and the Army accepts responsibility for all Government property provided for military instruction at this institution.

g. To conform to the regulations of the Secretary of the Army relating to issue, care, use, safekeeping, turn-in and accounting for such Government property as may be issued to the institution.

h. To comply with the provisions of law and regulations of the Secretary of the Army pertaining to the furnishing of a bond to cover the value of all Government property issued to the institution, except uniforms, expended articles, and supplies expended in operation, maintenance and instruction.

i. To produce a minimum of twenty-five officers each year.

j. To maintain an enrollment of one hundred in the basic course, when the basic course is maintained.

3. It is mutually understood and agreed as follows:

a. That this agreement shall become effective when the authorities of this institution have been notified officially that the Secretary of the Army has approved the establishment of an Army Reserve Officers' Training Corps unit on the date specified.

b. That this agreement may be terminated upon giving one academic year's notice of such intent by either party hereto.

c. That no Army officer shall be assigned to the Department of Military Science without prior approval of the authorities of this institution, and no Army officer will be continued on duty after the authorities have requested his relief for cause.

d. That the Secretary of the Army shall have the right at any time to relieve from duty any officer, warrant officer, or enlisted man of the Army assigned to the institution.

4. The authorities of this institution understand that the law requires that no unit may be established or maintained at an institution unless the senior commissioned officer assigned to the institution is given the rank of professor.

5. This agreement supersedes all existing agreements between the Department of the Army and the institution pertaining to this matter.

FOR THE INSTITUTION

TYPED NAME AND TITLE	SIGNATURE	DATE

FOR THE SECRETARY OF THE ARMY

TYPED NAME AND TITLE	SIGNATURE	DATE

DA FORM 1 JAN 65 **918** REPLACES EDITION OF 1 AUG 64, WHICH IS OBSOLETE.

Fig. 1 *Application and agreement for establishment of Army Reserve Officers' Training Corps unit.*

The Following Agreement and Information is to be Considered as Part of this Contract:

AGREEMENT REGARDING FACILITIES TO BE PROVIDED FOR THE USE OF THE ARMY RESERVE OFFICERS' TRAINING CORPS PROGRAM, WITHOUT EXPENSE TO THE DEPARTMENT OF THE ARMY

The authorities of the above-named institution agree that the facilities specified below shall be furnished for the use of the Army ROTC program, without expense to the Department of the Army *(phrases such as "as needed", "as required", etc., will not be used in describing the following)*:

1. OFFICES

NO. OF ROOMS	SIZE	BUILDING IN WHICH LOCATED	EXCLUSIVE OR JOINT USE[1]
	' x '		
	' x '		
	' x '		
	' x '		

[1] *Specify whether for exclusive use of Army Department or joint use with Air or Naval Science or other Departments.*

NOTE: Minimum of eight (8), seven (7) of which contain a minimum floor area of two hundred square feet each; one of which contains a minimum floor area of three hundred square feet.

2. STORAGE ROOMS

a. FOR STORAGE OF CLOTHING, SUPPLIES, SMALL ARTICLES OF EQUIPMENT, ETC.

NO. OF ROOMS	SIZE	BUILDING IN WHICH LOCATED	EXCLUSIVE OR JOINT USE
	' x '		
	' x '		
	' x '		
	' x '		

b. FOR STORAGE OF LARGE ITEMS OF EQUIPMENT, TRAINING AIDS, MOTOR VEHICLES, ETC. *(Describe)*

NOTE: Storage rooms, particularly for clothing and small articles of equipment, must be adequately lighted and ventilated and be provided with shelving, cabinets, and locked arms racks. Windows must be securely barred and doors reinforced and fitted with cylinder locks. For small storage a minimum floor area of one thousand (1000) square feet, and possessing two entrances is required; minimum requirement for large storage is four thousand (4000) square feet.

3a. CLASSROOMS

ROOM AND BUILDING	SEATING CAPACITY	EXCLUSIVE OR JOINT USE

NOTE: Classroom must be adequately lighted and ventilated and provided with standard equipment. If joint use is specified, rooms must be available for Army ROTC classes when scheduled. Minimum requirement - five classrooms, three of which have a normal capacity of thirty five students and two which have a normal capacity of fifty students.

b. ASSEMBLY HALL

SEATING CAPACITY	☐ IS ☐ IS NOT PROVIDED WITH PROJECTION EQUIPMENT FOR ☐ 35 MM ☐ 16 MM FILM	WILL BE AVAILABLE FOR ARMY ROTC CLASSES AS FOLLOWS:

NOTE: Assembly hall should be of adequate size for assembly of entire unit. (Normal size unit - 300)

4a. SIZE OF GYM OR OTHER INDOOR DRILL AREA ' x '	b. WILL BE AVAILABLE FOR ARMY ROTC CLASSES AS FOLLOWS:

NOTE: Minimum requirement of 7,000 square feet.

5a. SIZE OF OUTDOOR DRILL AREA YDS x YDS	b. LOCATION WITH RESPECT TO OFFICES AND STOREROOMS	c. WILL BE AVAILABLE FOR ARMY ROTC CLASSES AS FOLLOWS:

NOTE: Minimum requirement of 20,000 square yards.

6. INDOOR TARGET RANGE

a. NO. OF FIRING POINTS	b. WILL BE UNDER JURISDICTION OF

NOTE: Minimum requirement of five (5) firing points.

7. SPECIFY HEALTH-SERVICE OR DISPENSARY FACILITIES AND PERSONNEL WHICH WILL BE AVAILABLE ANNUALLY FOR MILITARY TYPE PHYSICAL EXAMINATIONS OF ARMY ROTC STUDENTS

8. ADDITIONAL FACILITIES SUCH AS JANITORIAL SERVICE, CLERICAL SERVICE, AND ANY OTHERS, AS SPECIFIED BELOW

9. Plan of campus, showing relative location of facilities to be provided for the Army ROTC Program *(Attach additional sheet)*.

AN ORIGINAL AND FIVE (5) COPIES OF THE APPLICATION AND AGREEMENT FOR ESTABLISHMENT OF ARMY ROTC UNIT WILL BE MADE. ONE (1) COPY WILL BE KEPT BY THE INSTITUTION AND THE ORIGINAL AND FOUR (4) WILL BE FORWARDED AS FOLLOWS:

1. To The Commanding General, First U.S. Army, Governors Island, New York, N. Y. 10004, from those located in:
CONN, MASS, N. J., R. I., MAINE, N. H., N. Y., VT

2. To The Commanding General, Second U.S. Army, Fort George G. Meade, Maryland 20755, from those located in:
DEL, KY, OHIO, VA, D. C., MD, PA, W. VA

3. To The Commanding General, Third U.S. Army, Fort McPherson, Ga 30330, from those located in:
ALA, GA, N. C., TENN, FLA, MISS, S. C.

4. To The Commanding General, Fourth U.S. Army, Fort Sam Houston, Texas 78234, from those located in:
ARK, LA, N. M., OKLA, TEXAS

5. To The Commanding General, Fifth U.S. Army, 1660 East Hyde Park Blvd, Chicago, Illinois 60615, from those located in:
COLO, IOWA, MINN, N. DAK, WYO, ILL, KANS, MO, S. DAK, IND, MICH, NEBR, WIS

6. To The Commanding General, Sixth U.S. Army, Presidio of San Francisco, California 94129, from those located in:
ARIZ, IDAHO, NEV, UTAH, CALIF, MONT, OREG, WASH

Page 2 of 3 Pages

Fig. 1 *(Continued)*

DATA PERTAINING TO INSTITUTION

NAME OF INSTITUTION	COMPLETE MAILING ADDRESS

1. IF ARMY ROTC TRAINING IS TO BE CONDUCTED AT ANY AUXILIARY OR SUB-CAMPUS OR AT ANY LOCATION OTHER THAN THAT STATED ABOVE, EXPLAIN FULLY:

2. TYPE OF INSTITUTION *(Check appropriate box)*

☐ STATE COLLEGE *(Land-Grant)* ☐ STATE *(Other)* ☐ MUNICIPAL

☐ STATE UNIVERSITY *(Land-Grant)* ☐ STATE UNIVERSITY *(Non-Land-Grant)* ☐ OTHER PUBLIC

☐ DENOMINATIONAL *(Specify)* ________ ☐ OTHER *(Specify)* ________

3. LIST AGENCIES WHICH ACCREDIT THE VARIOUS COURSES GIVEN BY INSTITUTION

a. REGIONAL

b. PROFESSIONAL

c. OTHER

4a. OFFICIAL DESIGNATION OF GOVERNING BODY	*b.* NO. OF MEMBERS	5. OFFICIAL DESIGNATION OF HEAD OF INSTITUTION

6. ANNUAL RATE *(based on 2 semesters or 3 quarters)* OF TUTITION AND GENERAL FEES FOR BOTH RESIDENT AND NON-RESIDENT STUDENTS:

7. THIS INSTITUTION ☐ HAS ☐ DOES NOT HAVE A COOPERATIVE "BINARY" ARRANGEMENT WHEREBY AT THE END OF THE JUNIOR YEAR STUDENTS TRANSFER TO ANOTHER INSTITUTION AT WHICH, AFTER AN ADDITIONAL TWO YEARS' WORK THEY RECEIVE A DEGREE. INDICATE NAMES OF INSTITUTIONS WITH WHICH THIS ARRANGEMENT EXISTS:

8. THIS INSTITUTION OPERATES ON A ☐ NORMAL ☐ ACCELERATED SCHEDULE. THE ACADEMIC YEAR CONSISTS OF ☐ 2 SEMESTERS ☐ 3 QUARTERS ☐ OTHER *(Specify)* ________ THERE ☐ IS ☐ IS NOT A SUMMER SESSION. THE TOTAL DURATION OF THE ACADEMIC YEAR, EXCLUSIVE OF VACATION PERIODS AND EXAMINATIONS, IS ______ WEEKS.

9. THIS INSTITUTION CONFERS EARNED DEGREES AS FOLLOWS: *(Place an "X" in proper column)*

	BACHELOR'S	MASTER'S	DOCTOR'S
ARTS AND SCIENCES			
ENGINEERING			
BUSINESS ADMINISTRATION			
EDUCATION			

10. SPECIFY THE TYPE OR TYPES OF SCREENING OR COLLEGE APTITUDE TESTS ADMINISTERED TO ALL ENTERING FRESHMEN

11. EXTENT TO WHICH ALL ENTERING MALE FRESHMEN ARE PHYSICALLY EXAMINED

12. THIS INSTITUTION PARTICIPATED IN THE FOLLOWING ☐ ARMY ☐ ARMY AIR FORCES ☐ NAVY ☐ OTHER *(Specify)* ________ TRAINING PROGRAMS DURING WORLD WAR II:

13. INDICATE THE STATUS TO BE ACCORDED THE ARMY ROTC UNIT WITHIN THE INSTITUTIONAL ORGANIZATION *(school, department, etc.)*

14. IS IT CONTEMPLATED THAT A BAND WILL BE AVAILABLE FOR ROTC CEREMONIES? ☐ YES ☐ NO *(State whether institutional or ROTC).*

15. MALE ENROLLMENT *(Include only full-time, regular, undergraduate, day students.)*

TOTAL MALE ENROLLMENT	FRESHMAN ENROLLMENT	SOPHOMORE ENROLLMENT	JUNIOR ENROLLMENT	SENIOR ENROLLMENT

16. REMARKS

Page 3 of 3 Pages

Fig. 1 *(Continued)*

APPLICATION AND AGREEMENT FOR THE ESTABLISHMENT OF A SENIOR AIR FORCE RESERVE OFFICERS' TRAINING CORPS UNIT

(AFR 45-48)

SUBJECT: Application for the Establishment of A Senior Air Force Reserve Officers' Training Corps Unit

TO: Commandant, AFROTC, Maxwell Air Force Base, Alabama 36112

Commander, Air University, Maxwell Air Force Base, Alabama 36112

Chief of Staff, United States Air Force, Washington, D.C. 20330

Secretary of the Air Force, Washington, D.C. 20330

APPLICATION

By direction of the governing authorities of ______________________________

(Name of Institution)

I, ______________________________, ______________________________

(Name) *(Title)*

hereby submit application for the establishment of a senior Air Force Reserve Officers' Training Corps Unit under the provisions of Section 2102, Title 10, United States Code, as amended.

AGREEMENT

1. Contingent upon the acceptance of this application and upon the initial and continuing fulfillment of all the conditions enumerated in paragraph 2 following, the Secretary of the Air Force agrees as follows:

a. To establish and maintain a Senior Air Force Reserve Officers' Training Corps Unit at the Institution named in the foregoing application.

b. To assign such Air Force personnel as he may deem necessary for the proper administration and conduct of the program at the above named Institution, and to pay the statutory compensation of such personnel.

c. To pay, subject to law and regulations, subsistence allowance at the prescribed rate to cadets who are members of the Professional Officer Course (POC), and those cadets who are selected for the Financial Assistance Program.

d. To pay authorized expenses of cadets who are selected for the Financial Assistance Program, to include tuition, fees, books, and laboratory expenses, where applicable.

☐ e. To pay to the Institution commutation in lieu of issue uniforms, at currently prescribed rates, in behalf of General Military Course (GMC) and/or Professional Officer Corps (POC) cadets, if that procedure is elected by the institution.

☐ f. To assume custodial responsibility for authorized items of uniform clothing issued to the professor of Aerospace studies under the issue-in-kind uniform system and to pay all costs incident to the transportation, packing, crating, alteration and disposition of such uniforms if the issue-in-kind uniform system is elected by the Institution.

g. To assume custodial responsibility for all items of Air Force equipment issued to the professor of Aerospace studies as authorized by applicable Tables of Allowances, and to pay all costs incident to the transportation, packing, crating, and normal maintenance of such property.

h. To insure that assigned Air Force members are available for faculty and administrative committees on the same basis as other faculty members.

2. Contingent upon the acceptance of this application and upon the fulfillment of the conditions enumerated in paragraph 1 above, the governing authorities of this Institution agree as follows:

a. To establish a Department of Aerospace Studies as an integral academic and administrative department of the institution. The Secretary of the Air Force will prescribe the course content, conduct of the courses, and provide the support literature for the following curriculum(s) which the institution adopts:

☐ (1) A four-year course of Aerospace Education covering the General Military Course (GMC) and the Professional Officer Course (POC): or,

☐ (2) A two-year course of Aerospace Education covering the Professional Officer Course; or

☐ (3) Both of the above.

☐ (4) If a four-year program is maintained, enrollment in the first two years, known as the General Military Course, will be compulsory.

b. To require each student enrolled in any of the programs to devote the number of class hours to Aerospace Education prescribed by the Secretary of the Air Force.

c. To grant appropriate academic credit applicable toward graduation for the successful completion of courses offered by the Department of Aerospace Studies.

d. To arrange for the scheduling of Aerospace Studies classes to make it equally convenient for students to participate in the academic offerings of the Air Force Reserve Officers' Training Corps program as in other courses at the same educational level.

e. To confer the rank of Professor on the Senior Air Force Officer assigned to the AFROTC Detachment, as is required by law, and the rank of Associate or Assistant Professor on all other officer personnel assigned to the Detachment.

f. To make available to the Department of Aerospace Studies the necessary classrooms, administrative offices, storage space, government vehicle parking areas, staff parking areas and other required facilities in the same manner and at the same level as is provided to other Departments of the Institution. Parking space for government vehicles will be provided without charge.

g. To provide adequate secretarial, janitorial, and telephone services to the Department of Aerospace Studies on the same basis as is provided to other Departments within the Institution.

h. To elect the uniform commutation in lieu of uniform system for the GMC ☐, POC ☐, and to assume responsibility for the procurement, receipt, storage, maintenance, issue and disposition of uniform items by appointing a civilian institutional official empowered to perform the administrative and custodial function incident to these uniforms.

i. To elect the issue-in-kind uniform system for the GMC ☐, POC ☐, and to provide a separate storage facility for issue-in-kind uniforms where both issue-in-kind and commutation systems are elected.

AF FORM MAR 67 1268 PREVIOUS EDITION OF THIS FORM IS OBSOLETE.

Fig. 2 *Application and agreement for the establishment of a Senior Air Force Reserve Officers' Training Corps unit.*

j. To conform to the applicable regulations of the Secretary of the Air Force pertaining to the administration and operation of the Air Force ROTC Program.

k. That the institution is accredited to award baccalaureate degrees by.

____

(Name of accreditation agency)

3. It is mutually understood and agreed:

a. That this agreement shall become effective when the authorities of the Institution have been notified officially that the Secretary of the Air Force has approved the establishment of the Air Force Reserve Officers' Training Corps Unit, or Units, cited herein and, on the date specified.

b. That this agreement may be terminated at the completion of any school year by either party, by giving at least one year's notice, or sooner by mutual agreement.

c. That no Air Force Officer will be assigned to the Department of Aerospace Studies without the prior approval of the authorities of the Institution, and no Air Force member will be continued on assignment after the authorities have requested his relief.

d. That the Secretary of the Air Force shall have the right at any time to relieve any Air Force member assigned to the Institution.

e. That AFROTC or other equivalent peacetime programs will be the officer candidate program conducted in colleges and universities during a national emergency.

4. When preferred, Institutions may use the terminology "Air Force Aerospace Studies" rather than "Aerospace Studies" as titles of the department and Professor and Associate or Assistant Professor as titles for Air Force Officer faculty members.

5. For good and valid mutual consideration, and as a condition precedent to acceptance and continuance of this agreement, the Institution warrants and represents that it does not, and will not, discriminate in any way with respect to the admission or subsequent treatment of students on the basis of race, color, or national origin. It is further mutually agreed that a violation of this covenant, as determined by the Secretary or his designee, may be regarded as a breach of this agreement, justifying termination thereof, at no cost to the government, by the Secretary or his designee.

6. This agreement supersedes all existing agreements between the Secretary of the Air Force and the Institution pertaining to the establishment of an Air Force Reserve Officers' Training Corps Unit.

FOR THE INSTITUTION		
TYPED NAME AND GRADE	SIGNATURE	DATE

FOR THE SECRETARY OF THE AIR FORCE		
TYPED NAME AND GRADE	SIGNATURE	DATE

AF FORM MAR. 67 1268 B-29528

Fig. 2 *(Continued)*

____
(Date)

To: Chief of Naval Personnel,
Washington 25, D.C.

Subject: Application for Establishment of a Unit of the Naval Reserve Officers Training Corps.

1. By direction of the governing authorities of __________________, application is hereby submitted for the establishment of a unit of the Naval Reserve Officers Training Corps at this institution.

2. Should this application be accepted by the Secretary of the Navy, this institution hereby agrees to the establishment and maintenance of a four-year course of Naval training for its physically fit male students under a Department of Naval Science, staffed with Naval Personnel. This course, equal in standing with major courses in other departments, will comprise instruction in Naval Science carrying the same weight toward a degree as the same number of hours in any other subject in the university's curriculum. Students who successfully meet the course requirements outlined in the *Naval Reserve Officers Training Corps Regulations* including approximately twenty-four (24) semester or equivalent quarter hours of Naval Science, will be considered for the appropriate degree.

3. The institution will provide space for classrooms, offices, equipment, and drill for a normal size unit of 300 in accordance with the following minimum requirements:

Classrooms (5), three of which have a normal capacity of 35 students; one of which has a normal capacity of fifty students; one of which with a capacity of 35 students, contains a minimum floor area of 1,000 square feet for use as a navigation workroom.

Offices (8), seven of which contain a minimum floor area of two hundred square feet each; one of which contains a minimum floor area of three hundred square feet.

Clothing and Textbook Storage and Issue Space, one room having a minimum floor area of one thousand square feet, and possessing two entrances.

Armory, heavily reinforced floor area of approximately four thousand square feet, on which will be placed heavy ordnance equipment, permanent installations. This area should have at least a twenty foot ceiling clearance, and flooring capable of carrying a load of one thousand pounds per square foot.

Auditorium, of adequate size for assembly of entire unit, available for use at various times. Usage to be determined in advance in keeping with standard procedure in effect at the institution.

Drill Field, any readily accessible, level, grass-covered, unobstructed area, with a minimum of eight thousand square yards.

Swimming Pool, available for naval student personnel.

4. It is understood that for normal operation an annual initial enrollment in the Naval Science course of eighty physically fit students of the freshman class, citizens of the United States, over 17 years of age, is required to maintain a Naval Reserve Officers Training Corps Unit.

5. This institution also agrees to promote and further the objects for which the Naval Reserve Officers Training Corps is established and to conform to the regulations of the Navy Department relating to the operation of the unit and to the care, use, safekeeping and accounting for such Government property as may be issued for use by the unit.

____
(President)

____
(Name of Institution)

Fig. 3 *Form of application for establishment of an NROTC Unit.*

BIBLIOGRAPHY

Books

Harwood, Michael: *The Student's Guide to Military Service,* Appleton-Century-Crofts, Inc., New York, 1965.

Lyons, Gene M., and John W. Masland: *Education and Military Leadership,* Princeton University Press, Princeton, N.J., 1959.

MacCloskey, Monro: *Reserve Officers' Training Corps: Campus Pathways to Service Commissions,* Richards Rosen Press, Inc., New York, 1965.

Masland, John W., and Laurence I. Radway: *Soldiers and Scholars,* Princeton University Press, Princeton, N.J., 1957.

Tax, Sol (ed.): *The Draft: A Handbook of Facts and Alternatives,* The University of Chicago Press, Chicago, Ill., 1966.

Theses, Addresses, Magazine Articles

Brown, Melvin C.: *Army ROTC in the Sixties,* U.S. Army War College, Carlisle Barracks, Pennsylvania, Student Thesis, AWC Log #61-2-20, 10 February 1961.

Conference on the Role of Colleges and Universities in ROTC Programs, Mershon National Security Program, Ohio State University, Columbus, Ohio, June, 1960.

(C) Department of Defense, Report: *Nationwide ROTC Conference,* Washington, D.C., 15–17 November 1967.

Department of the Army, *Strength in Reserve—A Bibliographic Survey of the United States Army Reserve,* Headquarters, Department of the Army, Washington, D.C. 20315, DA Pam 140-3, April, 1968.

U.S. News and World Report, "20 Questions About the Draft Answered," vol. 63, no. 2, pp. 36–37, July 10, 1967.

Chapter 18

Clinical Instruction in Affiliated or Cooperating Institutions

EDMUND J. MC TERNAN

Dean, School of Allied Health Professions, State University of New York Health Sciences Center, Stony Brook, New York

From the standpoint of the college or university, the administration of clinical instruction relates primarily to educational programs in the health sciences. "Clinical instruction" refers to that portion of the formal curricular program which takes place in the setting where professional services are actually rendered. This kind of instruction differs from fieldwork and from cooperative work experience. In clinical instruction, students are taken, for a portion of their carefully planned instructional program, to the real-life setting in which their fully qualified counterparts are at work.

The term "clinical setting" is used here to denote any place in which actual services are rendered and where student instruction is taking place.

Many of the principles which apply to education conducted by an educational institution at an off-campus clinical setting may also be found useful in considering the converse situation, wherein students in educational programs conducted by clinical institutions are sent to a college or university for supplemental academic instruction. In this discussion, this kind of arrangement will be referred to as "academic affiliation."

THE NEED FOR CLINICAL INSTRUCTION

A recent U.S. Public Health Service publication included the following career groupings which ordinarily require a clinical component in the educational program.[1] (The *primary title* is given; several alternate titles may be included in the source list from which this list has been drawn.)

Health Administrator
Clinical Laboratory Scientist
Clinical Laboratory Technologist
Clinical Laboratory Technician
Clinical Laboratory Aide
Dental Hygienist
Dental Assistant
Dietician
Dietary Technician
Health Educator
Health Education Aide
Medical Librarian
Medical Record Librarian
Medical Record Technician
Chemist (Clinical Chemist)
Microbiologist
Nutritionist
Nurse
Practical Nurse
Occupational Therapist
Orthotist
Prosthetist
Pharmacist (Hospital)
Physical Therapist
Physical Therapy Assistant
Radiologic Technologist
Clinical Social Worker
Clinical Social Work Assistant
Corrective Therapist
Educational Therapist
Manual Arts Therapist
Music Therapist
Recreation Therapist (Therapeutic)
Audiologist
Speech Pathologist
Vision Care Technician
Physician's Associate
Physician's Assistant
Extracorporeal Circulation Specialist
Inhalation Therapist or Technician
Emergency Technician

TYPES OF CLINICAL INSTRUCTION

The nature of clinical instruction varies considerably from one discipline to another, but the essential factor lies in its real-life aspect as contrasted to a simulated or otherwise contrived situation. The student must be involved in the actual work load of the clinical facility, under direct supervision of an instructor. Activity involving real people or specimens but not actually part of the patient-care program is not clinical experience but rather a form of laboratory exercise.

Several health professions require particular mention at this point:

[1] Pennel, M., and Associates: *Health Resources Statistics: 1968*, U.S. Public Health Service Publication no. 1509–68, 1969.

Medical Technology

The medical technology student must receive one year of instruction in an approved hospital laboratory school in a program of didactic and clinical instruction according to a curriculum specified by the American Society of Clinical Pathologists (ASCP) if the student is to be eligible for admission to the registration examinations in medical technology supervised by that society. Recently, there has been willingness to consider approval of some schools conducted on a basis which varies from the basic plan, including an organization based on the cooperative plan of education, provided there is assurance that equivalent standards are being satisfied. The society also specifies qualifications and maintains registries for several specialty groups in medical technology, as follows: histologic technique; clinical chemistry; microbiology; blood banking; exfoliative cytology; and nuclear medical technology.

An assistant-level category of worker also exists in the clinical laboratory structure known as the "certified laboratory assistant." An approval board for this group also exists, with specified educational content, which is essentially based on a one-year training program in an approved laboratory. Some junior colleges have established programs to prepare personnel for this level, but the essential training is vocational in nature. A few programs have been established at an intermediate level, called "clinical laboratory technician," and there is currently discussion among pathologists and technologists about giving official approval to this group.

The American Medical Association requires that an acceptable school of medical technology be under the direction of a physician who is certified in clinical pathology and acceptable to the AMA's Council on Medical Education. The actual responsibility for the training program rests with this physician; and his daily attendance, devoting sufficient time to supervise laboratory work and training, is required. The ratio of qualified medical technologists (ASCP registered, with one year or more experience) to students in laboratory practice is set at 1 to 2, with one of the technologists being held responsible for supervising the teaching program. This individual is supposed to have a baccalaureate degree with at least three years of experience in practice. Approved schools should have a minimum of 50,000 lab tests per year, distributed to provide adequate technical training in the various divisions of laboratory practice. The equivalent of laboratory services required for a 100-bed hospital with 3,000 admissions per year is suggested.[2]

Physical Therapy

Essentials of an Acceptable School of Physical Therapy, published by the American Medical Association, requires that each school of physical therapy designate a department or departments of physical therapy in institutions or agencies "with sufficient patient loads, qualified physical therapy personnel, and adequate equipment to provide the type and amount of experience" needed by the student. These departments must be under the direction of a physician or physicians with qualifications acceptable to the Council on Medical Education of the AMA but must not be in the physician's private office. At present, 600 clock hours of clinical experience are required, and the approving authority recommends that 8 semester hours of credit be assigned for this experience.[3]

The American Physical Therapy Association has very recently approved a category of worker to be known as the "physical therapy assistant." These people will be prepared at the junior-college level and will require a large segment of clinical experience in their programs.

[2] American Medical Association: *Essentials of an Acceptable School of Medical Technology*, AMA, Chicago, 1962.

[3] American Medical Association: *Essentials of an Acceptable School of Physical Therapy*, AMA, Chicago, 1955.

Occupational Therapy

In occupational therapy, the program director must be a registered Occupational Therapist with qualifications acceptable to the American Medical Association's Council on Medical Education and to the American Occupational Therapy Association. Among the requirements for such approval are five years of clinical and administrative experience and an academic degree. A clinical experience segment of six months' full-time duration is required for approval of a program in occupational therapy, and this, too, must be under the direction of a competent occupational therapist. Half of this six-month period must be primarily concerned with psychiatric patients and half with patients with physical disability. Programs in occupational therapy must be in accredited colleges or medical schools and must satisfy the minimal requirements for a baccalaureate degree.[4]

Several curricula have been developed for the preparation of an occupational therapy assistant, ranging from brief on-the-job training programs through associate degree curricula. The American Occupational Therapy Association currently has this topic under study, and it is probable that recommended standards will be published for the preparation of occupational therapy assistants in the near future.

Other Specialties

The preceding pages have detailed the general criteria required for clinical experience in some of the more populous allied health professions. Medicine, osteopathy, dentistry, public health, podiatry, optometry, and chiropractic have been omitted from discussion because these programs are strictly limited to separate professional schools—each of which would require, even in initial stages, administrative considerations far more detailed than it is possible to outline here.

The American Medical Association, through its Council on Medical Education and in cooperation with the various specialty organizations, is involved in the accreditation of nine different kinds of health-related professions including those discussed above. The American Dental Association conducts similar activity for the dental-related groups, and the American Nurses Association is concerned with accreditation of programs for professional and practical nurses. Programs approved by the AMA in cooperation with other professional organizations are as follows:

Allied health occupations	*Collaborating organization(s)*
Certified laboratory assistant	American Society of Clinical Pathologists and American Society of Medical Technologists
Cytotechnologist	American Society of Clinical Pathologists and American Society of Medical Technologists
Medical technologist	American Society of Clinical Pathologists and American Society of Medical Technologists
Inhalation therapy technician	American Association for Inhalation Therapy, American Society of Anesthesiologists, and American College of Chest Physicians
Medical record technician	American Association of Medical Record Librarians
Medical record librarian	American Association of Medical Record Librarians
Physical therapist	American Physical Therapy Association
Occupational therapist	American Occupational Therapy Association
Radiologic technologist	American College of Radiology and American Society of Radiologic Technologists
Radiation therapy technologist	American College of Radiology and American Society of Radiologic Technologists

[4] American Medical Association: *Essentials of an Accredited Curriculum in Occupational Therapy*, AMA, Chicago, 1965.

Supervision of the AMA approval programs is the responsibility of its Department of Allied Medical Professions and Services. The following is a selected list of approval programs in the health field which are *not* conducted through the offices of the AMA:

Title of program	*Cooperating organization*
Dietician; dietetic internships	American Dietetic Association
Hospital administration	Association of University Programs in Hospital Administration
Nurse anesthetists	American Association of Nurse Anesthetists
Pharmacy	American Council on Pharmaceutical Education
Public health	American Public Health Association
Social work	Council on Social Work Education

While no institution should permit any outside agency to dictate policy contrary to its own best judgments, the conduct of a program which produces graduates who cannot gain recognition or employment is meaningless. Programs in the field of health should be entered into only when the "essentials" dictated for accreditation are consistent with university and clinical affiliate policy and philosophy. Development of a quality program, which requires clinical experience in a university or college which lacks facilities to conduct this portion of the program, absolutely dictates a carefully developed, educationally sound, and well integrated clinical affiliation. (For further, more detailed information, see Chapter 16 in this section.)

CLINICAL INSTRUCTION AND THE COLLEGE OR UNIVERSITY OFFERING HEALTH PROGRAMS AND HAVING NO HOSPITAL OR MEDICAL SCHOOL

Many new educational centers for the preparation of health manpower are coming into existence. Increasingly, universities, colleges, or junior colleges which do not conduct medical schools and which maintain no clinical facilities of their own are becoming involved in this area of education. To meet the demands placed upon them by the need for clinical education, these institutions must enter into affiliation agreements with suitable clinical facilities, usually in close geographic proximity.

When a program is suggested in the health field, it is always safe practice to locate the most appropriate related professional society and to ask that society to suggest suitable individuals or committees of its membership which may be approached for consultation. The county medical society (or, if appropriate to the goals and local situation, the local osteopathic society) can usually assist in identifying the proper organization to be contacted. Much future embarrassment may be avoided by taking this step at an early date. This will lead not only to appropriate professional participation but also to the identification of institutions which have the most suitable clinical facilities.

Once identification of the desired clinical affiliate is determined, an approach may be made to determine the degree of interest in entering into an affiliate relationship. Appropriate procedure absolutely requires that initial official contact is made with the chief administrative officer of the potential affiliate. Care must be taken to apprise the chief administrative officer of the institution of this interest early both for public relation reasons and to avoid needless effort if there is no official interest in the program on the part of the clinical facility.

Many factors must be taken into consideration in developing an affiliate relationship between an institution of higher education and a patient-care facility. Consideration must be given to the university—with its special concerns, its faculty and students; and to the clinical group—the hospital; the hospital's staff (both medical and allied groups) which has a primary commitment to care for today's patients; and finally, but most importantly, to the patients themselves.

There are legal and moral obligations which require the hospital to see that nothing—not even educational programs—detract from the quality of care the patient receives or infringe upon his rights to comfort, privacy, protection of property, and a sense of confidence in those caring for him. The patient should not be required to pay an inordinate share of the cost of preparing health manpower.

The best interests of the student are served when the affiliation provides a productive and real exposure to the full spectrum of professional functioning, including understanding of the responsibilities the professional person assumes with regard to the patient and to society in entering his chosen field.

The interests of the service staff of a patient-care institution which participates in an affiliation arrangement are served essentially in two ways; first, through assuring them that the program concerned meets or exceeds the educational standards set by the appropriate professional society or by state licensing laws. In the absence of these criteria (as, for example, in new programs for which no standards have been set), high standards should be assured through the active participation of a blue-ribbon professional advisory panel. Secondly, their more basic interests are served by structuring the program so that it does not markedly increase the workday or work load placed upon the staff nor detract seriously from the attention the staff is free to devote to professional practice.

It is a good idea to involve faculty in direct patient care on a part-time basis, such as one half-day per week, in order to keep their skills current and their professional identification strong.

Careful analysis of the costs of clinical education will certainly show that students cannot be expected to defray them unaided and that costs incurred by the clinical center in a quality program will usually exceed the value of the very limited volume of actual student services rendered. The hospital or other clinical facility will frequently feel its own responsibility to its future staffing needs by making some contribution to these costs in ways other than those which will increase the costs charged to today's patients. In some programs there will be no surplus costs other than those already borne by the university or college; but in others a considerable surplus of costs may be incurred, costs for which the hospital may legitimately ask reimbursement. It may be necessary for the college or university to enter into a financial contract to reimburse the hospital for any additional costs which may accrue to it as the result of affiliation.

Good practice would seem to dictate an honest effort to assess the cost of the educational program in the clinical setting. The following questions could serve as a basis for such an assessment.

1. Are the students rendering any actual patient-care services the loss of which would require the addition of extra-pay staff time?

2. Are paid staff personnel spending time in student supervision which is thus lost to the total volume of patient-care services available on the unit?

3. Are hospital supplies—either directly charged to a specific patient or to the overall costs of patient care—being consumed for student instruction?

4. Are school supplies being utilized in patient care, thus reducing the amount of these supplies which must be acquired by the hospital and charged to patient care?

Of course, administrative and overhead costs are not included here. Any estimated additional costs for administrative expenses to the hospital should be added to the total costs. The value of space used for the teaching program can be included on any basis agreed upon by both institutions. It is usually considered fair to base this merely on the cost of heat, light, other utilities, and maintenance—unless the hospital sees the education solely as a source of revenue to which it has no commitment. In this latter case, it may seem fit to add a rental rate for use of instructional space.

A final area in which educational and patient-care interests often conflict is the scheduling of educational activity in the clinical setting. If the decision is made to integrate student educational activities into the service program of a patient unit, the different kinds of calendars honored by hospital and educational institution may create problems. It is difficult to "change gears" for periods when students will not be present. Judicious planning can overcome much of this problem. The values which derive from actual integration of the students' clinical education into the patient-care program far outweigh these problems which must be considered in planning. Some educators insist on almost total separation of the teaching faculty from the service staff, but this creates an artificial situation in which the student never feels a part of ongoing patient care and hence feels no responsibility for it. While the goals of education and patient care sometimes seem to conflict, the long-range objectives are actually identical.

Special Problems of the Cooperative School

Universities, colleges, and junior colleges organized on the cooperative plan of education have some unique problems to face in working out the administrative aspects of an affiliation plan. The essential nature of the cooperative plan is that it divides the student body (usually excepting the freshman class) into two groups which alternate with each other in work and study periods. For the university and for the clinical affiliate, this means that the same educational experience must be repeated twice for each class. For example, when group *A* is out on work assignment, group *B* is receiving on-campus instruction. That same instruction must be repeated for group *A* when it returns to school and group *B* replaces it in the work situation. To provide this repetition economically requires a total entering class of greater size than usual—for all instruction must be repeated twice and hence the cost is doubled. The limiting factor on many health career programs is the limited availability of clinical experience or supervision. Medical technologists, for example, must be prepared on a ratio of two students to each instructor in the clinical program; respiratory therapy students cannot exceed five per registered therapist-instructor. Other health programs have thus far been unsuccessful in attracting large numbers of students (for example, medical records or medical library science).

One possible solution to this problem is to keep all students in one section—hence the entire group is out in job assignments for one period and in academic work in the next. This proves undesirable in most cases because of the fluctuation in the faculty's work load and the variation of student impact (and adjustment to this impact) in the clinical setting. Another solution often tried is to admit all students in the fall quarter one year and the summer or winter the next, keeping them all in one section. Thus all students in one year are either "in" or "out" together, but the years alternate, so that second-year students are all "in" when third-year people are all "out," etc. Solutions to this special problem may tax the imagination and ingenuity of the faculty, but some solution which preserves the values of both co-op and clinical experience is usually possible.

Office and Conference Facilities

The integration of the instructional and service staffs has been urged as the most effective means towards deriving the greatest educational benefits from the clinical portion of the program. It has been suggested that clinicians participate in the formal teaching program—not only in the clinical setting but in the academic one—on a regular part-time basis, and that the academicians return to a clinical role part-time on a regular basis to keep current professionally and to maintain their identity with the specialty field. In both these situations the participants should feel comfortable and "at home." Facilities such as lockers and use of dressing rooms for the faculty personnel in the clinical area must be provided. Clinicians in part-time teaching should have an academic "home base" too, even if it is only one drawer in a desk available for their use as needed. The teaching program as a whole should have a focus in the clinical setting in the form of conference and office or desk space, the former available at least by reservation and the latter accessible to the faculty on a full-time basis.

Interinstitutional Administrative Committees

The educational program must be clearly the responsibility of one institution. In the case of a clinical affiliation, the program is obviously a responsibility of the educational institution. Both institutions—educational and clinical—should feel a responsibility for it, but control must clearly rest with the university, college, or junior college. In the case of an academic affiliation, the control rests with the hospital—and students come to the academic setting under the terms of the contract agreement.

In both cases, communication must be facile in order to make possible constant evaluation of the program, the reception and consideration of suggested improvements from all parties concerned, and the integration of revisions. This calls for communication at all levels.

Administrative policy should be determined by a conference committee consisting of the senior academic representative concerned with the program and a representative of university administration on the one hand and the senior clinician concerned and a representative of the clinical institution on the other. It is here that decisions which will constitute the affiliation agreement should be determined. When an affiliation is being developed, this committee might meet frequently; whereas in an established situation, one meeting per year might suffice.

The second level would be concerned with the daily operational policies and procedures of the program, within the content of the affiliation agreement. It is suggested that continuity be provided by the service on this committee of the educational director and the clinical department head from the Committee on Administrative Policy. In addition, there might be one or several representatives of faculty and clinicians who are involved in the program.

The third level would be intended to assure integration of student viewpoints in the program; ideally, this would be achieved through service of elected representatives of the student body on the operational committee just outlined. If some reason seems to preclude this, a separate student advisory committee might be formed.

Chairmanship of the operational committee might be handled in different ways; one method that has been used with success is to rotate the chairmanship between the academic and clinical chiefs on a six-month or annual basis. Educators and clinicians alike often decry the seemingly excessive numbers of committee meetings to which they are subjected; however, human nature seems to be such that many important communications will be overlooked unless a reasonable number of meetings—as brief as possible—are scheduled to provide a scheduled opportunity for discussion of matters of importance.

ACADEMIC CONSIDERATIONS

Control of Curricula

In most health programs the freedom enjoyed by the individual institution in constructing curricula is somewhat curtailed by professional standards and the essentials which are prescribed for many of the career entities. Medical technologists are expected to possess a certain set of skills and competencies—and the curriculum developed to prepare these technologists must include preparation in the areas essential to develop these abilities. When two institutions join forces to prepare specialists, as in a clinical affiliation situation, questions and conflicts often arise as to the appropriate curriculum content.

Efforts to negotiate any serious differences are always desirable. It is sound policy to assure that communications relative to curricular decisions be shared with the affiliate, both for public relations and effective coordination purposes.

Admission and Recruitment of Students

A vigorous recruitment effort is incumbent upon all who have a serious concern for the health care of mankind.

The educational institution has an immediate purpose for encouraging recruitment efforts to its health curricula—it must fill the available seats with qualified students. The clinical institutions, however, have a more vital, long-range purpose: to maintain the quality and efficiency of patient care, which will be adversely affected as long as the supply of qualified health specialists is inadequate. These different reasons place the educational and clinical institutions in a vital partnership for recruitment efforts.

One way in which the university or college aids the clinical facility is through its response to the needs which develop for new kinds of highly qualified health manpower—by the development and conducting of new kinds of educational programs for health manpower. In the course of its general recruitment effort, the university supports the recruitment of health-programs students: it includes information about health careers and curricula in its publications; it publicizes these programs in high school and other locations where university recruiters work; and it tests and counsels potential students as well as students already enrolled. The field of health is so broad and its needs are so great that there is a place for everyone; very often the university alone has the counseling capabilities to help a student find his niche in his field.

The hospital is the place where many career goals first begin to form, and there must be at least enough counseling service available there to put the prospect in touch with the counselor in the affiliated university. Many health careers, especially some of the newer ones, are obscure or unknown to the general public. Hospitals can also assist in the recruitment effort by lending personnel and equipment to contribute to university recruitment programs.

There does not seem to be any real hope of filling the positions needed in health care by reliance on those high-school graduates who can be lured into the field. Imaginative approaches are needed to many other potential recruit pools: the disadvantaged (economically, socially, and educationally); the vocationally displaced worker seeking a second career at the midpoint of his working life; the housewife returning to the labor force after years of child rearing; early retirees; and returning military servicemen. Attracting and graduating recruits from these groups often forces adaptation of the curriculum offerings and of procedures employed to methods more appropriate to and consistent with the needs of these older students.

Admission of these applicants for education also calls for special administrative considerations. Traditional admission standards for recent high school graduates are inappropriate and wasteful of good talent when applied to the special groups we have cited. When a university has the foresight and imagination to experiment with other admission standards, the clinical affiliate must often work even more closely and cooperatively to ensure success of the program.

In the academic affiliation, potential conflicts lie in the fact that the admission criteria of the clinical sponsor may not coincide with those of the affiliated academic institution. Usually, it is better to adapt admission standards so that the criteria of both institutions are met. If this proves impossible, flexibility must be expected of the university as well as of the hospital. If the affiliation calls for the university or college to confer a degree as well as the hospital certificate upon the graduates, lowering of standards for this special group is not an appropriate step; in this case, decision must be made and included in the affiliation agreement as to management of students who are failing the academic program.

Generally, the best course is for the clinical program sponsor to choose carefully the content and level of academic instruction desired and to terminate students who do not achieve minimal success in the total program. In the case of an academic affiliation arrangement, good practice would suggest that the university have an opportunity to review the candidates scheduled for acceptance before final notification is sent to the applicant.

UTILIZING FACULTY

Clinical Faculty

An attempt has been made earlier in this chapter to state a strong case for actual integration of clinical and academic faculty to the greatest extent possible. Medical schools have long recognized the validity of this argument and have developed a sophisticated mechanism for the recognition in the teaching program of participants who are primarily practitioners by building a "clinical faculty." This mechanism is appropriate for any educational program which employs clinical instruction.

A special clinical faculty category is established by the educational institution to which persons may be appointed who regularly and routinely participate in the teaching program but who are primarily concerned with the service functions of the clinical setting (i.e., practitioners). Generally, this faculty category has all the hierarchy structure of the general faculty (from full professor down to the lowest levels), with the prefix "clinical" ahead of the rank assigned. Appointment is made to a rank consistent with experience and professional stature as well as academic background. Clinical faculty ordinarily are welcome to participate in meetings and discussions but do not have the privilege of the vote. Reward factors for service on the clinical faculty vary from merely the title, through stipend arrangements and part-time salary plans, to a regular salary system. University fringe benefits do not usually apply to the clinical faculty except where the clinical facility is university owned. Generally, the clinical faculty member remains primarily the employee of the hospital or other clinical facility (or is self-employed), and draws his fringe benefits accordingly.[5]

Conversely, academicians who travel to the clinical setting on a regular and routine basis and who participate in patient care incidentally to student supervision (as we have suggested) on a full-scale, part-time basis may receive an associate appointment to the clinical staff. In both cases, the dual appointment confers some status within each institution and assists the individual in recognizing his responsibility to both participant institutions. The integration which has been recommended should not extend to the wholesale and meaningless conferring of faculty or service-staff titles on any and all who bear any relationship to the program, however tangentially, and who make no contribution to the teaching or service program.

An old legal doctrine of "charitable immunity," which held that a patient could not bring suit for injuries received by him at the hands of hospital personnel, has been ruled invalid in all but two states. Any student and any faculty member who goes into the clinical setting is open to (and increasingly liable to encounter) litigation as the result of real or alleged direct or indirect injuries sustained by a patient. No academic institution should permit any of its students or faculty to set foot in a patient-care setting until the university's insurance program has been extended to include a rider protecting both students and faculty against such legal actions. In a rider form, this coverage is relatively inexpensive in terms of the protection it provides, whereas individual policies of this type are quite costly. This coverage should, of course, also extend to cover the university in case of suit under the doctrine of *respondeat superior* (literally, "let

[5] Knowles, Asa S.: *Memorandum: Ranks of Clinical Instructor and Clinical Professor,* August 9, 1968 (unpublished).

the master answer for the acts of the servant"). If, for some reason, liability insurance coverage of faculty and students is not adopted by the university, consideration should be given to requiring direct purchase of such coverage—certainly by faculty, but preferably also by students.

Granting Credit for Clinical Instruction

Occasionally, a university or college faculty balks at the thought of granting academic credit for educational experiences gained in the clinical setting. It is submitted that this objection is without foundation where the following criteria are met:

1. The clinical instruction must be truly a learning experience; not simply exposure to a stated number of hours of service. Clinical instruction must be conducted according to a set plan, to meet stated and measurable educational goals.
2. Clinical instruction must be under the overall control of a regular faculty member who is responsible for supervising and directing the experience.
3. All clinical instruction should be conducted by faculty appointees, either regular or clinical faculty members, who meet at appropriate times to evaluate and develop the course, review goals and methods, and to evaluate student progress.
4. A record must be kept of each student's clinical experience, and participating faculty must submit a grade for each student at appropriate intervals. Evaluation conferences with each student are also recommended.
5. In general, individual student activity outside the clinical setting but related to the clinical experience should be included in the syllabus. This may include, for instance, seminar participation and the preparation of individual oral and/or written reports on the materials studied in the clinical setting.

Indeed, it is submitted that the best educational practice requires that academic credit be given for clinical instruction in order to encourage equal standards, educational focus, and thoughtful evaluation of both student and program.

Credit allowed is not, of course, equated on a one-to-one basis with classroom instruction. Usually, required hours should correspond in roughly the same ratio as laboratory hours correspond to lecture hours in the university setting (two or three lab hours to one lecture hour). This may, however, go as high as twice the lab hours (four to six lab hours per one lecture hour) if the concentration of clinical material, because of the nature of the specialty, is light or if the nature of the specialty requires gaps (such as travel time, etc.) between patient exposures.

Granting Degrees and Certificates

Generally, university- or college-based curricula will be planned so that the terminal reward for successful completion of the entire program (both academic and clinical) is both qualification for an academic degree and professional qualification for admission to a certification examination. Often the academic institution will present both a certificate and a degree to the graduate. A true academic affiliation qualifies the student for a degree from the educational affiliate at the same time that qualification for the professional or technical certificate is achieved. This affiliation is different in kind from contractual arrangements by which hospital or similar schools purchase part-time instruction for their students according to a curriculum plan over which the university has no control.

The involvement of two institutions complicates almost exponentially the problems which any single institution would encounter in offering a program to prepare qualified health personnel. However, there is little question that our society will see to it that the following recommendation of the National Commission on Community Health Services, that "Every effort should be made by educational institutions, operating agencies, and professional occupational groups to identify and carrying out their individual and mutual responsibilities"[6] will be adopted in all phases of education for health manpower.

ROLE OF COLLEGE OR UNIVERSITY DEAN OR COORDINATOR

Recently, a special study committee at Northeastern University, working under support from the Commonwealth Fund, examined the structure of health occupation programs in that and related institutions in an attempt to identify an ideal organizational structure. Perhaps the single most obvious point which emerged from the first year of study of the question was the need for an individual within the university or college to serve as the focal point for coordination, stimulation, and integration of programs in this field. In the past, each specialty has stimulated and developed its own educational program; however, there has been, until recently, no one who was recognized as having expertise in the broad field of education for health professions and essentially no coordination or cross-disciplinary communication between curriculum planners for these various fields. As a result, there has been overlap and duplication in education.

In recent years, several leaders in the field of education have recognized the values that would result from an integrated and coordinated program in the health-related disciplines and a number of universities have established colleges, schools, or divisions for this purpose. By 1966, Dean Darrel J. Mase of the University of Florida's College of Health Related Professions had identified 13 of these units, and under his leadership a new national organization, the Association of Schools of Allied Health Professions, had come into being with those 13 institutions as charter members. By 1968, the association had 18 institutional members, with estimates predicting close to 50 in two additional years' time. The importance of this concept is attested to by an associate membership (composed of other schools and organizations interested in education for the allied health professions) of close to 100 and an individual membership roster of close to 500. A permanent Washington office has been established with the aid of the Kellogg Foundation, and other institutions interested in this field can turn to the staff there for expert advice. The headquarters is at Suite 300, 1 Dupont Circle, N.W., in Washington, D.C., 20036.

THE AFFILIATION AGREEMENT

Whether the affiliation is a clinical one to serve a program conducted by a university, college, or junior college or an academic one to strengthen the content of a program conducted by a hospital or clinic, the following points should receive consideration and be included (or specifically excluded) from the agreement as considered appropriate by the participating institutions:

1. Dates covered by the agreement	Is the affiliation to continue indefinitely, or does this agreement cover a stated period of time? If indefinite, will it be reviewed at stated intervals? If so, when? If indefinite, how can it be terminated, and what notice of termination is required? If dated, how may it be terminated before the expiration of the agreed length of time?

[6] Task Force on Health Manpower, National Commission on Community Health Services: *Health Manpower: Action to Meet Community Needs*, Public Affairs Press, Washington, 1967.

2. Schedules	When will the first group get to the clinical center? What dates, or portions of the year, will students be there? What dates, or portions of the year, will no students be in the clinical setting? What holidays or vacation periods are excluded? What will the typical weekly schedule of student assignments be? What hours of the day will be included in assignments?
3. Facilities	What facilities will be provided for student/faculty use in clinical settings? What facilities will be provided for students at the academic base (if an academic affiliation)?
4. Academic considerations	What credit will be given for the clinical program (for academic program if an academic affiliation)? Grades: Who has responsibility for determining grades? How are they determined and submitted? When, and to whom? Academic failure and probation: details; what steps will be taken in case of clinical/academic failures? Where will academic instruction take place (if an academic affiliation)?
5. Student considerations	Has affiliating institution any recruitment responsibilities to sponsoring institution? What is application process? What are selection criteria? Does affiliate have option to accept/reject given student(s)? Does academic institution have any voice in accepting students in academic affiliations? How many students will be involved each year, semester, or quarter? Each week? How many in each group? What is status of students in university and/or clinical setting? What regulations govern students? What facilities and/or privileges are available to student in each setting? What provisions will be made for dormitories, meals, laundry, uniforms, library services, and extracurricular and cocurricular activities?
6. Faculty and staff considerations	What will be responsibilities of academic faculty? Of clinical facility staff? How many and which members of the

	academic faculty will be sent to the clinical setting? On what schedule? How will the clinical staff be involved? Will there be any direct payment and/or fringe benefits to faculty at the clinical setting? To the staff at the academic institution? Are clinical/faculty appointments to be made? If so, under what conditions? Will extra compensation be made direct to staff by the university? If so, what sort?
7. Fiscal considerations: student payments	Do university students make any added payment for clinical services? Do clinical students make any added payment for academic instruction/fees? What payments will be made to clinical institution by academic institution (or vice versa) for services. Precisely what services? When will payment be made? Who will provide any needed texts, supplies, uniforms, transportation?
8. Communications	How should official communications regarding affiliation be referred from one institution to other? What committees will be constituted to coordinate this affiliation? What are the responsibilities and privileges of each committee? How will committee membership be constituted? How will chairmanship be determined?

It will be of immeasurable assistance to employ legal counsel in arriving at an affiliation agreement. One should remember that any agreement constitutes a legal contract; the difficulty in a verbal contract is in reaching later agreement on what was agreed to; the difficulty in a nonlegal agreement lies primarily in indefinite or hazy wording. Often institutions find it sufficient to develop the agreement between the two administrators involved, with each signing two copies and retaining one for later reference, if needed. The avoidance of word-of-mouth agreements is urged as a means to the avoidance of future misunderstandings and detrimental public relations stemming from the failure of memory or from misunderstanding.

Section Three

Admissions

Chapter 1

Admissions in Perspective

B. ALDEN THRESHER

Director of Admissions Emeritus, Massachusetts Institute of Technology, Cambridge, Massachusetts

THE NATURE OF THE ADMISSIONS FUNCTION

It is natural, and perhaps fatally easy, for the college or university administrator to regard admissions as merely one of a number of administrative functions concerned with the various aspects of student personnel. The very word "admissions" calls up the image of a gatekeeper who opens a gate for some, but not all. This simplistic notion leaves out a host of questions: Who does, or might, or should seek admission? Be admitted? How can or should the institution communicate with or seek to influence prospective students? Should it remain passive or search them out? If the latter, then by what means? How does such activity affect the shape and objectives of the educational process? How does it affect students? Does it contribute to the public welfare? Should college teachers play a part in this process? How do their predilections and habits of thought influence it? What is the significance of selection at admission, and what should be the criteria?

Merely to suggest the range of such questions is to make it apparent that the admissions function, broadly conceived, is deeply involved not only with the entire educational process, its philosophy and objectives, but also with the values and aspirations of the surrounding society. This is clearly more than just an administrative detail of university management.

The admissions function constitutes a major conduit or taproot between the college and the society that generates and sustains it. Properly to perform this function imposes the obligation to hold out and make known the institution's offer of educational opportunities in ways which speak to the needs and aspirations of the segment of youth which constitute its natural clientele. In the complex university this may be a very wide segment of youth. Its needs and aspirations, however, are seldom fully and consciously articulated or realized. So an important educational task is to sense and often to anticipate these needs by giving form to educational programs that help to define as well as to meet them. All this is at the farthest remove from the nineteenth-century concept of a conventional "college course," tradition-bound, static, and complete, with an annual batch of students poured, as it might be, into a hopper. In the next few years postsecondary education in unprecedented variety, in novel and still-to-be-invented forms, will need to be made available to youth. Decisions about how and to what extent a given college or university is to participate in this pioneering process lie close to the heart of its educational policy. A well-conducted admissions operation, reaching out to and in close touch with potential students, their parents, and secondary schools can contribute much to the wisdom of these decisions as well as to effective educational guidance of students.

All colleges and universities are "affected with a public interest" regardless of whether they are operated by independent boards of trustees or more specifically under government auspices. All arise out of and depend upon the society that contains them. The subsidy implicit in freedom from taxes is a reminder to "independent" institutions of the obligations imposed by their membership in and dependence upon the general polity. The so-called "admissions" function, then, as broadly conceived, is central because it deals with a major part of the metabolic interchange between the college and the enveloping society.

ACCESS TO EDUCATION

Of the two million boys and girls who graduate from high schools each year in the United States, more than half distribute themselves among some 2,300 colleges, universities, junior colleges, and technical institutes. This "great sorting" is a social process of great complexity, not fully understood by the students themselves, by their parents and advisers, or by the educators, including admissions officers, who participate in it. Popular opinion pictures the screening processes of college admission as largely intellectual in character. So they are, in part, but in a larger sense they are sociological. The sorting process, taken in its entirety, is a product of an immense number of individual choices and decisions made by millions of people, under the influence in part of calculations and estimates projected a generation into the future and in part of beliefs, opinions, whims, ancient loyalties, and areas of ignorance scarcely amenable to rational estimate. It is important to note that most of the decisions involved occur outside college admissions offices, not in them. In the main it is students who select colleges, not the reverse. The increasing degree of selectivity being exercised by many colleges is a minor factor compared with the range of choice exercised by the student. Access to higher education is essentially a social process deeply involved with the society's entire cultural pattern and system of values. Often the key decision *not* to enter college is made almost unconsciously because the student's environment has not led him to believe that higher education has anything to offer him.

The entire process of admission to college is conditioned by historical circumstances that have caused a sharp break to occur at the end of the secondary school years. We now see this break, in one sense, as artificial and arbitrary. Education in the current perspective is coming to be thought of as a seamless web, a continuous cradle-to-grave affair. Even the span of formal education—roughly from nursery school through graduate or professional school—is but a part of the whole. We have learned to appreciate both the determinative importance of preschool experience for infants and the continuity of growth and development made possible by adult education. So the location of the school-to-college breaking point, with the major reshuffling among students and institutions that occurs at this stage, is essentially arbitrary. It is a healthy sign that this sharp boundary line is beginning to be eroded, on the one hand by college-level courses in secondary schools and on the other by courses in college designed to pick up the student at his existing level and move him forward. But the boundary line remains an important one because the four undergraduate years impose a heavy cost on the student and his parents. By contrast, elementary and secondary education are available free of cost, and postgraduate study is heavily subsidized.

The simplest schematization of "the great sorting" would treat it as a matter of the supply of and demand for students—a convenient though greatly oversimplified concept. On the one hand is the American society sending forward its annual crop of young people. Facing these young people stands a system of higher education more varied in its origins, more diversified in its auspices and management, more chaotic in its atomized separation, covering a wider range of "standards," and possessing, perhaps, more vitality than any in the world. This is the "supply" side of the educational process.[1] The ways in which these youth are drawn back after varying lengths of time into the social complex of the economy constitute the "demand" side. Considerations from the demand side, such as employability, economic productivity, manpower distribution, and social mobility constantly reflect back to the supply side of the equation. The interaction of these social complexes generates powerful forces. The admissions process acts as a kind of hinge point through which many of these stresses are transmitted. So the procedures connected with admissions, viewed in their full significance, are much more than a series of administrative rules and customs. Through them are conducted social stresses, the study of which can tell much about the processes of the society that contains them.

In recent years there has been a radical shift in viewpoint with regard to the broad social problem of access to higher education—that is, the supply side of the equation. This shift in turn has led to a changed view of the admissions function. Inspection of admissions credentials had been thought of traditionally as belonging to the more routinized aspect of education, and it therefore seemed natural in many colleges to put admissions under the direction of the registrar, to be looked after as a detail of academic accounting. Only in recent years have the social complexities involved in access to higher education come to be realized in anything like their full significance. The academic-records aspect, though not negligible, has been dwarfed by comparison.[2]

[1] The convention of speaking of the "supply" of students coming out of the general population and the "demand" for students by colleges is adopted here arbitrarily. At the postgraduate stage, the "supply" is the annual crop emerging from the undergraduate course and the "demand" arises from employers. The British "Robbins Report," with equal propriety, adopts the converse convention: it speaks throughout of the "demand" for education (on the part of students) and the "supply" of education (by the colleges). As in any market situation, demand and supply are opposite aspects of the same set of transactions. *Higher Education; Report of the Committee Appointed by the Prime Minister under the Chairmanship of Lord Robbins*, H. M. Stationery Office, London, 1963, chap. 6, (335 pp.).

[2] Of 811 admissions officers, 18 percent were found to have the title of "Registrar" and 8 percent a title combining "Registrar" with "Admissions Officer" in some form. Jane Zech Hauser and Paul F. Lazarsfeld, *The Admissions Officer in the American College: An occupation under change*, College Entrance Examination Board, New York, 1963.

The more recent concept of the "search for talent," useful as a step in the evolution of thought,[3] has yielded in turn to repeated demonstrations that talent must be nurtured and encouraged at every stage if it is to survive and blossom—that talent, in fact, comes closer to being something produced than something stumbled upon and uncovered. This concept is broadly true, though here and there a nugget of pure genius turns up against all the odds. Access to education in Europe has always been organized traditionally along lines that implied a "pool of ability" manpower theory. It is significant that the British "Robbins Report" explicity disavowed this doctrine in 1963 and recognized the wide elasticity of the supply of able students, given the necessary conditions.[4] To be sure, not all children are equally bright. There is a genetic factor of great importance. But we simply do not know how to separate the genetic from the environmental component. We do know that intelligence, within far wider limits than anyone had suspected, can be increased by a favorable early environment or stunted by a bad one. This is a conclusion of the first importance for a society like ours, already pressing hard against the limits of its educated manpower and desperately in need of more.

Repeated experiments have shown that culturally disadvantaged children in surroundings of poverty could, by enriched programs and skillful guidance, be carried far beyond the expectations conventionally held about them.[5]

Many of the teen-agers who participated in these programs underwent a true revolution of identity—they acquired a self-concept that gave them status, hope, and a respected place in a scheme of things they could begin to understand. Little enough is known, still, about the nature of these powerful psychosocial forces. But it is clearly in this area that we must look for the energies needed to bring about broad and fruitful access to higher education. The machinery of selection, recruiting, tests, classification, and the like remains useful and significant. But the true "nuclear" forces of the personality, which have begun to be tapped in these efforts with deprived children, lie at the root of the really basic problems of admission to college. In the light of these developments, what used to pass for "recruiting" by colleges which sent emissaries to high schools is seen in current perspective as a relatively minor effort to rearrange the educational destinations of such students as had managed to reach this level without having had their growth pinched off by the combination of unfavorable environment and poor education.

There is a kind of continued tension between the two major forces that keep the wheels of education turning. On the one hand, a large majority of college students would admit quite frankly that the hope of a better job and a chance to rise in the world are their chief motives in seeking higher education. Confucius wrote, 2,500 years ago, that it is difficult to find anyone who will study for three years without thinking of money. But it is not so simple. Education undertaken solely with a remote, practical end in view can be insufferably dull. It needs to be illuminated at every stage, if only fitfully, by the inherent interest that characterizes the pursuit of knowledge. Education is "autotelic"—a self-rewarding occupation. This quality is most clearly apparent in young children, but it persists in greater or less degree throughout the lives of most people. There is a deep delight in learning that is a profoundly human characteristic. We are constantly in danger of overestimating the purely economic motive. Perhaps we can say of many people that economic motives lure them into college and the un-

[3] See, for example, "The Search for Talent," *College Admissions*, no. 7, College Entrance Examination Board, New York, 1960 (131 pp.).

[4] Cited in note 1. This report and the discussions of it provide a useful case study of the forces at work in these situations. For a penetrating criticism of the report, see Martin Trow, "A Question of Size and Shape," *Universities Quarterly*, p. 136, London, March 1964.

[5] Henry T. Hillson and Florence C. Myers, *The Demonstration Guidance Project, 1957–1962*, Board of Education, New York, 1963. This outlines the follow-up in senior high school of the original experimental groups in Junior High School 43.

suspected delights of education keep them there. We see constantly at work the interplay of both motives—the practical and immediate on the one hand, and on the other the importance and fascination of completely disinterested learning, uncontaminated by self-interest or even by practical usefulness.

Curricula in the so-called "liberal arts" colleges are heavily infused with subjects having an occupational or professional cast, while schools devoted to professional fields, whether engineering, business, or journalism, find it important that their graduates become immersed in the liberal arts at first hand. It is a curious anomaly that we have been so long in recognizing that both of these elements are essential to education—we have persisted in treating them as mutually exclusive. As Alfred North Whitehead put it: "The antithesis between a technical and a liberal education is fallacious. There can be no adequate technical education which is not liberal, and no liberal education which is not technical, that is no education which does not impart both technique and intellectual vision." [6]

The college, in exhibiting its wares, need not feel ashamed that some programs, even at the undergraduate level, tend toward some definable, useful niche in society. Such an objective, even though it may turn out to be mistaken in its aim, imparts to the student an impulse and direction and a certain sturdy self-respect which is hard to reproduce in an atmosphere of completely neutral cognition. So it is only natural that the great majority of college undergraduates today should be in programs that have definable occupational objectives or at least occupational tendencies. Thus the demand side of the talent equation feeds back continually into the supply, shifting its direction and emphasis. This feedback sometimes follows too closely the ephemeral fluctuations in the job markets. But, basically, the job market in its broad tendencies must be followed.

Another complicated set of social forces comes into play here: social mobility and the desire for it, parental ambition, customary levels of aspiration, regional and ethnic groupings with special objectives. Such influences impinge on the admissions process, affecting the demand for education, the direction it takes, and the way it affects individual colleges.

These, then, are some of the social complexities with which the problem of college admissions is entangled. In an earlier era, preoccupation with the academic hurdles erected to control entrance led to almost complete neglect of the deeper, social forces which in reality determined who entered college. Contemporary admissions problems usually present themselves to the admissions committee or the admissions officer in terms of the recruiting-cum-selection complex. Detailed academic qualifications in terms of subject-matter definitions have receded in importance; considerations of aptitude and achievement as measured by marks and tests have come to the fore. But, with this evolution, there is still a general neglect of the deeper cultural and social forces at work. To understand this job, the admissions officer or the faculty member concerned with admissions needs some understanding of the place of his efforts in this social process.

SCARCITY AND SELECTION

The most conspicuous feature of higher education in the world today is the universal and growing shortage of facilities in relation to the demand for education.[7] Every nation in the world is seeking to multiply and enlarge its universities. Some, espe-

[6] *The Aims of Education and Other Essays,* The Macmillan Company, New York, 1929, p. 74 (247 pp.).

[7] Frank Bowles, *Access to Higher Education,* Unesco and the International Association of Universities, New York, 1963 (212 pp.). This is a unique and classic study of the problem in a worldwide context.

cially among the developing countries, are doing this in an atmosphere of total emergency and crash programs. In many others, cost, apathy, habit, and the vested interests and inertia of an ancient establishment impose such a lag that the gap between demand and supply, instead of shrinking, widens from year to year. The unslaked thirst for education is building up, in entire populations, pressures that may well topple governments in the years ahead.

In many nations the running disparity between the demand for and supply of education has led to drastic, even heroic, screening measures. These may consist of examinations or other hurdles that are intellectual in form but do not effectively identify the ablest. They may be based, for example, on an obsolete syllabus; they may reward rote memory, the reflection of received opinion, or persistence in taking tests rather than intellectual power. In some countries expensive secondary-school systems with room for only small numbers effectively throttle the flow of students into universities. Such hurdles reduce numbers without ensuring that those showing the greatest promise will be chosen for admission. Populations have often shown remarkable patience with situations involving unreasonable or misdirected selectivity, perhaps because they have regarded universities with awe born of ignorance. There are signs that this patience may be running out.

For most colleges in the United States recruiting and selection go on concurrently, one or the other being more emphasized as conditions change. It is a kind of paradox that many of the most selective colleges carry on the most vigorous recruiting. The naive view that selection and recruiting are alternatives—that one recruits when he needs more students and selects when he needs fewer—is so oversimplified as to be quite misleading. Every college, however low its standards, will refuse some applicants, and, conversely, even the most sought-after college will bestir itself to attract candidates whom it regards as exceptional.

But these are practical, surface phenomena. The selection principle raises deeper social and educational issues about which most people have strong views but little real knowledge. Each college is busy selecting among applicants—some very vigorously select a minority of applicants in, others rather loosely select a minority out. In every case concepts are entertained of comparative merit, worth, or promise. We don't know how far these are valid or absolute or how far they reflect predispositions and prejudices built into us by the culture in which we are embedded or by the subculture in which we grew up. Least of all can we be sure whether these very unconscious and unrecognized predispositions may not be shutting off, perversely and tragically, types of talent that we simply have not learned to recognize or to encourage. One has only to read at random in the field of biography to realize that the history of education is strewn with unrecognized talent. All admissions officers and admissions committees share in this general ignorance.

The college justifies its selectivity on two main grounds. First, it says, the intellectual issues and processes with which we are concerned are esoteric and subtle. They can be dealt with adequately only by students of more than average intellectual power and stature; we have assembled a faculty of great distinction whose efforts would be wasted on the mediocre. This argument is especially persuasive in the natural sciences, where a student without the necessary aptitude and preparation, particularly in mathematics, quickly sinks without a trace.

Second, argues the college, we are going to be judged, in the last analysis, by the broad effectiveness of our graduates in the context of society. We are entitled to pick the people who seem most likely to contribute the most value and who will have the maximum impact on the life of their time.

These are defensible arguments, but they nevertheless often serve as rationalizations for a kind of insensate avarice. "We want the best and only the best, we are never satisfied, we regret that every class, no matter how able and promising, still has a bottom third." Much of the vital work of the world is done by people who are intelligent but not in any special sense "intellectual." They find their chief satisfaction and outlet in action, not in thought. A major purpose of education is to bring into the lives and work of such people the illumination of rational thought, to introduce them to the "life of reason," not for its own sake but for what they can accomplish with its help.

In the broad context of the general welfare, the overwhelming obligation of higher education is to provide education for all those capable of realizing its benefits and to send these individuals back in multiplied vigor into the general polity. Seen in this wide context, the selection versus rejection problem is converted into one of differentiation, classification, multiple characterization. No doubt it will become more apparent in the years to come how far it is necessary or desirable to differentiate higher education into environments of widely different kinds with reference to such characteristics as degrees of intellectual sophistication, practical versus theoretical bent, or social involvement versus detachment. It may even be possible to find out how to "fit" each student into a college with an atmosphere—social, moral, intellectual—whose tone evokes from him the most active response. All this remains at the borderline of human knowledge, though enough experimentation has been carried on to suggest that some progress can be made.

It is realistic to view the admissions process as the result of a series of social forces, often blind, seldom fully understood, interacting in complex ways. Reason enters into this process, but only fitfully and partially. Devices such as school grades and marks, clumsy at best, do serve a helpful purpose. Tests, after a half century of development, have proved to be useful adjuncts in the general classification process. But they are easily misused; and critics who want to abolish tests forget that it is usually some obvious misuse, or in some cases some secondary effect of this valuable device, and not testing itself that leads to trouble.

If the individual college sees its fundamental public obligation for providing education chiefly in the guise of a right to select ever more rigorously, the result must be defensible on some grounds broader than a competitive, avaricious impulse to reach out for more and better. Leaving aside the delicate question whether college A deserves better students or whether it has done anything to earn them (except for high-pressure recruiting), there remain many other unanswered questions. Do the "best" colleges indeed attract the best (or most) students? Are some colleges merely marshaling yards for switching groups of students from particular secondary schools with particular clienteles, reshuffling and sorting them, and moving them on into various postgraduate destinations? May this traffic-interchange function overshadow the educational process itself, so that the institution becomes a kind of large-scale broker in talent rather than a generator of education in its own right? Has the college that congratulates itself on getting "a better class of students" simply exchanged its natural clientele for one artificially induced or constructed? To ask questions of this kind is to present a series of caricatures, necessarily exaggerated, yet pointing to tendencies that are to some extent present and operative in the contemporary scene.

LEVELS OF ANALYSIS

It is useful to consider three viewpoints, or, more properly, three levels of analysis from which the general problem of access to education in the United States can be viewed. The first viewpoint is that of the individual student, or Level One; the second that of the individual college, or Level Two. The third, or Level Three, presents a conspectus of the system as a whole, including the competitive and cooperative relationship among all colleges in the matter of the entrance and exit of students.

These are not merely three viewpoints chosen at random; they are organically related in a hierarchy of degrees of complexity. They can properly be regarded not only as three modes of discourse but, even more appropriately, as three levels of analysis at progressively higher degrees of complexity. The subject matter remains the same, but the purview of the discussion broadens and the intricacy of the analysis increases from level to level.

Level One is clearly the simplest. The student thinks at this level, and guidance counselors, parents, teachers, and other advisers seeking to help him usually fall into this level of discussion quite unconsciously.

The individual student is so intent on gaining admission to some college he regards as suitable that he accepts the existing situation quite as it is. He has neither time nor inclination for critical analysis. The system, with all its inherent chaos and unreason, is nevertheless a built-in part of his problem, and he has to cope with it as it is. The extensive literature on "how to get into college," much of it very good and very useful, is pitched to this situation. It is uncritical in the sense of accepting the educational world as it is and helping the student get his bearings in it.

Level Two concerns only the single college, but the problems of a single college are manifold and difficult, with many conflicts of principle and difficult choices, so that Level Two is a higher plane of complexity. Most of the professional literature on admissions is written, again quite unconsciously, on this level. The existence of other colleges is ignored, except as they may appear as competitors or, rarely, as models. The inevitable article that the admissions officer writes at intervals for the alumni magazine is pure Level Two discourse. The dominant criterion against which everything is judged is the interest, or supposed interest, of the single college, its image and aggrandizement. The unspoken assumption is that what is good for college X is good for the United States.

The individual college has a struggle and its own set of problems to cope with, financial and otherwise. It is intent on getting more students, or better students (by its own quite uncertain definition), or some combination of the two. Its standards of excellence in selecting students are a complex mixture of values derived from the faculty, the administration, the alumni, the community, the coaching staff, and the surrounding culture. In this way, the college is as intent on its own problem and as self-centered as is the harassed student. Both are running a maze whose exits and goals are partly hidden from them. Seldom indeed is a serious effort made to get a bird's-eye view of the process with the general welfare as the ultimate criterion. Yet to make a serious effort in this direction is a first duty of any admissions officer or admissions committee seeking a broad perspective on its task.

The tacit presupposition is that the college seeks, and should have, more students or "better" students or both. Such questions as whether the college deserves more or better students, or whether some of its students might better, in their own interest and in the public interest, go to college elsewhere, lie outside the purview of this body of thought. The typical admissions committee, like the faculty and the administration it represents, is, in the candid phrase of one such committee, "greedy" for talent.[8] Colleges are generally quite willing to tell the applicant, "You are not good enough for us." Few ever say "We are not good enough for you."

Level Three is the "systems" view of the entire process, and so is of a still higher degree of complexity. Discussion at this level involves the interaction of all the colleges and universities with each other and with secondary schools as they appraise and deliver their annual crop of students coming forward out of the society; it involves not only the "manpower" demands of the economy in a narrow sense but also the demands of the entire polity for an increasingly literate population, an increasingly knowl-

[8] See *Admissions to Harvard College: A report by the special committee on college admission policy*, Harvard University Press, Cambridge, Mass., 1960 (56 pp.).

edgeable electorate, and a citizenry with a depth of cultural awareness that would scarcely have been thought of a generation ago. At Level Three it is permissible, at least, to query whether what college X thinks is good for it is indeed good for the United States and in the public interest. At this level questions arise about how students distribute themselves among colleges and whether the existing distribution is in the public interest.

THE STUDENT: INCENTIVES AND CHOICE

At Level One, that of the individual student, the "system" with its constituent structure of schools and colleges is taken for granted as it stands. Whatever its defects, injustices, or illogicalities, it is there; the student has to deal with it if he is to find and enter a college. The extensive literature[9] on the theme of "choosing a college" or "how to get into college" has special importance for students in the United States, who have open to them a bewildering variety of educational opportunities. Yet, in any broad sense, it has to be uncritical, accepting the complexities and idiosyncrasies of higher education in the United States as "given." Matters of history, evolution, change, or reform are beyond its scope, as are normative views of what higher education "ought" to be. It is ad hoc, and its end is served once the student gets into a college. He is then assumed to have solved his educational problem, at least passably.

However complex the social forces that condition the problem of access to college, they must all come to a focus in the mind and intention of the individual student. He, in the last analysis, must decide whether he wants to go to college; and for this decision, whether it is yes or no, he usually produces some colorable reason or rationalization. If the decision is yes, he then has to decide where he wants to go, make some estimate about where he probably can go, and make and implement a series of subsidiary decisions. If, alas, a parent or a counselor makes these decisions for him, the student still has to live with the consequences. On him alone rests the responsibility for making some kind of adjustment to the college environment; he alone can provide the continuing drive and energy necessary to get an education. The world of admissions at Level One shows, in the student's conception, no tendency to change. It is part of his existential environment, scarcely thought of as subject to growth, evolution, or reform. It is "given." His problem is merely to cope with it.

The incentives that propel students into higher education and keep them there involve a tension between two polar opposites. There are, at one extreme, a few "natural students" for whom the urge to know is overmastering, who need no other incentive. At the other extreme is the much larger group impelled by practical considerations to "hire themselves educated." For these, a degree is the goal, and what pleasure and interest can be got along the way is only a small extra. The great bulk lie between these extremes, the useful and the poetic. Without some spark of response to the inherent interest of the subject, study becomes so intolerably dull that few could continue it; some vestige of interest in learning is always present in those who stick to a course while, to help them over the dull stretches, there is the shining hope of a degree and a job.

Of these dual forces, it seems clear that at the stage of admission to college the prudential is the more powerful. In our culture, it is a psychological necessity for most students to have at least a tentative occupational goal of some kind by the time they enter college. This need is apparent from the large majority who enter four-year programs nominally directed at such fields as business, journalism, nursing, engi-

[9] See, for example, two of the best books, E. A. Wilson and C. A. Bucher, *College Ahead! A Guide for High School Students and Their Parents*, Harcourt, Brace & World, Inc., New York, 1961 (180 pp.); and Frank Bowles, *How to Get into College*, E. P. Dutton & Co., Inc., 1960 (185 pp.).

neering, or medicine. Even the minority who enter a nominally undifferentiated "liberal arts" course include a substantial group whose actual orientation is vocational, as expressed for example by a chemistry or economics major. At the same time, the proportion of genuine liberal arts studies included in the nominally vocational courses is steadily rising. The undifferentiated liberal arts programs tend to attract a larger proportion of "natural students," for whom eventual graduate study is a natural sequel, and also a larger proportion of those sufficiently well-to-do to be able to extend the exploratory period preceding an occupational commitment. For these fortunate few, the undergraduate years of "moratorium" can be a ripening period of great value. These contrasting motives, seen against the backdrop of innate cultural predisposition, are the key factors in the decision to continue education past the secondary level, and to a large extent they are also the key to the choice of a college.

College admission as conducted in the United States can have one unfortunate effect on the student at Level One: he becomes so caught up in the processes of choice, selection, comparison, and competitive differences among colleges that he often loses sight of the main issue, the educational process itself. He is encouraged to think of education as something favorable that will be done to him, or in his behalf. Attainment of membership among the happy few seems a final goal rather than a beginning. So the task of guidance, from whatever source, is to emphasize to the student the central importance of his own initiative. He must learn to see the college as an incidental aid and supplement to his own effort, not as the source from which all enlightenment streams down. College, to change the metaphor, is a crutch, not a stretcher. Having grasped this concept, the student is still faced with the necessity of making a choice and the tactical problem of implementing it.

In a wholly rational world, the student would look to the stated purpose of a college to determine whether it might meet his needs. Up to a certain point, catalog information will serve him as a useful guide to a college's curricular orientation. But to draw up a general statement of a college's purpose is a task, deceptively simple in appearance, which has defeated most authors of catalog prose.[10] Such statements are likely to have little practical bearing on the processes involved in "the great sorting." Naive efforts to state in simple, straightforward terms the objectives of a school or college are seldom successful. Education is, above all, an open-ended process. A great many things, fortunately, happen to college students that neither they nor anyone else had planned or contemplated. This fact lends a certain air of unreality to any statement about the college's purpose.

In a century the chief locus of the problem of access to higher education has shifted from remote rural regions to the heart of the great metropolitan areas. It has been well said that today's frontier lies in the cities. A Puerto Rican girl in New York or a Negro boy in South Chicago can be in fact as isolated from educational opportunity as were many farm boys a century ago. Their counterparts, of course, still exist in rural areas today, but the immense forces of urbanization have produced a far more dangerous and explosive social configuration, confined within a small space and ready to be touched off by the slighest spark.[11]

These perilous forces are at the heart of the college admissions problem in the United States. Compared with them, the problem of the middle-class boy or girl trying to decide where to go to college is relatively mild. Yet this problem, too, is worthy of attention, because so much of the effectiveness of education depends on environmental influences of a subtle, almost invisible kind. The student tends to be thrown back

[10] See William C. Fels, "The College Describes Itself," *College Board Review*, no. 38, pp. 30–32, Spring, 1959. This masterpeice of gentle satire should be read by anyone who expects to write admissions literature.

[11] See especially James B. Conant, *Slums and Suburbs: A commentary on schools in metropolitan areas*, McGraw-Hill Book Company, New York, 1961 (147 pp.).

on the somewhat nebulous concept of "prestige" for lack of anything more tangible or more specifically related to the quality of the educational process. Accustomed to a commercial culture in which brand names play a large part, he carries this point of view over into education.

The fashionable current hypothesis is that the best-known and most prestigious colleges are in some not very clearly defined way "better." In its crassest form, this is simply the widely held belief that a degree from such a college will give preference in employment or social esteem. At one remove from this is the hypothesis that in such institutions the faculty is abler, the facilities are superior, the student body is more highly selected, and the quality of the educational process to which the student is exposed is consequently better. Within certain limits, this may well be the case. But this view overlooks the possibility, first, that applicant pressure, in the current scarcity conditions, is not a safe measure of a college's real excellence, since none of these institutions is nearly as good as it ought to be, could be, and eventually will be; second, that many if not most other colleges, now less sought after, could be radically improved if the processes of educational innovation and experiment were systematically pursued, followed up, and acted upon.[12]

The considerable recent literature of differentiation among colleges with reference to their social, intellectual, and psychological atmospheres[13] has great theoretical interest and even some immediate utility in placing the student in an environment suited to his needs. It has by no means displaced the purely intuitive differentiation, based on hearsay and gossip, which is still the main reliance of many students and some guidance counselors. As indicated below, the more theoretical approach raises as many questions as it answers. How far will these techniques "freeze" colleges in particular stereotypes? Is the best education one in which all students tend to resemble each other in values and viewpoint? Is the small "specialty" college more comfortable but less truly educational than a large institution in which contrasting subcultures coexist and interact?

It seems certain that we have underestimated the extent to which education is itself a phenomenon of acquiring customs, values, systems of belief, and habits of thought in addition to the nominal content of learning itself. The "cultural shock" for a student from an alien environment (either a poverty environment or a foreign culture) can defeat even a youngster of outstanding intellectual gifts unless pains are taken to introduce him gradually to ways he does not know and "signals" he does not recognize or understand.

These are the kinds of problems that present themselves to the student seeking higher education. The forces briefly sketched above may be hidden from him or only partly visible to him. He senses simply a confused world of education that he does not understand, in which he is usually forced to exercise choices and make decisions for which he is ill equipped. A student may not know what information he needs, how to get the information he wants, or how to use the information he has.[14] The guid-

[12] Nevitt Sanford's compendium *The American College* reflects in a number of passages recurring doubts about the effectiveness of many current educational practices. John Wiley & Sons, Inc., New York, 1962, note 27 (1,084 pp.).

[13] This literature ranges from the impressionistic but useful sketches of David Boroff through the penetrating sociological comparisons of different colleges by Everett C. Hughes (for example: "How Colleges Differ," in "Planning College Policy for the Critical Decade Ahead," *College Admissions,* no. 5, pp. 16–22, College Entrance Examination Board, New York, 1958, 116 pp.) to the more rigorous psychological characterizations by C. R. Pace (for example: "Five College Environments," *College Board Review,* no. 41, pp. 24–28, Spring 1960). Among the classics in this general area are David Riesman's *Constraint and Variety in American Education* (Doubleday & Company, Inc., Garden City, N.Y., 1958, 174 pp.); and Nevitt Sanford, ed., *ibid.,* note 26.

[14] This elegant formulation of the nub of the student's problem is taken from Martin Katz, *Decisions and Values: A rationale for secondary school guidance,* College Entrance Examination Board, New York, 1963, p. 25 (67 pp.).

ance counselor needs to contribute what enlightenment he can, and the admissions officer has an obligation to look beyond the competitive advancement of the interests of his own college and to serve a broader function as trustee of the student's long-term interests and welfare.

ADMISSIONS AND THE FACULTY

The ways in which a college or university organizes itself internally to deal with admissions reflect its attitudes about the meaning and purpose of the admissions function in the life of the institution, the attitudes referred to above as constituting the Level Two view. In these organizational expedients there are not only responses to current opinion and alignments but also many fossilized traces of conditions long past.

The admissions function, broadly conceived, concerns the deep roots by means of which higher education in general and the individual college in particular tap and draw sustenance from the general population. Few college people concerned with admissions realize how deep these roots are. The invincibly "collegiocentric" posture so characteristic of most colleges largely inhibits attention to the social roots of the educational enterprise. The college thinks of itself as a little community carrying on certain activities and striving toward certain objectives. Obviously there must be an input of students. The faculty, keenly aware that there are numerous young people who are poorly adapted to the routines and seemingly impervious to the influences that the faculty conceive as constituting education, early develop a bias in favor of those with whom they feel most comfortable. Identify and exclude those "unable to profit" from education—this is the simple and obvious prescription. Thus the recruiting and selection processes come to favor particular subcultures and particular temperaments, personality types, and styles of behavior, with a bias toward the student who exhibits eagerness tempered by a generous admixture of docility. The teacher has a deep personal need to feel that he is handing on something both wanted and appreciated. So recruiting and selection, to the extent that they are under faculty influence, are generally slanted, often quite unconsciously, in favor of those whose early background and schooling have already carried them some way toward education, who exhibit the cultural traits with which educators feel most at home. Conversely, those standing in the greatest need of education, including some with great native ability, are often excluded. One is reminded of the merchant who complained that the bank would let him have a loan only if he could prove that he did not really need a loan.

In the kind of admissions activity spontaneously developed by most colleges, a heavy weighting exists in favor of adapting the student body (by suitable recruiting and selection) to the processes of the college. Up to a point this kind of adapting is necessary and proper; whether it is a principle that should operate to the exclusion of the converse—adapting the processes of the college to the student body—is more doubtful. The point is that most colleges take the former view automatically and exclusively. Education, in this view, is defined as what the college has long been doing. Those who do not respond to these influences are thus, by definition, ineducable.

There are encouraging signs that higher education may be beginning to adapt its processes to the student instead of choosing students to fit preexisting processes. But the internal organization of admissions, as well as the curriculum itself, still reflects the traditional thinking. In its reliance on concepts of "processing"—of subjecting many individuals to what is essentially uniform treatment—higher education, like education at lower levels, has disregarded or suppressed its greatest asset: the inherent diversity of talents with which nature has endowed individuals. Nature, as Emile Duclaux remarked, loves diversity, but education aims at repressing it.

Because the faculty thinks in terms of particular disciplines and bodies of subject matter, its natural impulse is to lay down rather minute specifications about prerequisites for admission. To the degree that the teacher can be relieved of the burden of working through an elementary introduction to his subject, he can spend time on the more recondite aspects that interest him most and can bring the student closer to the cutting edge of new research and new knowledge, where the excitement lies. It is easier and a great deal more fun to teach people who are already three parts educated. Thus the hope recurs in faculty discussion that the student will have at least a "decent" elementary grounding, or a "respectable" foundation. Such words have the ring of modest reasonableness. They are supposed to imply that one is willing to settle for the barest minimum, but that nevertheless there are limits; one cannot teach an ape or a complete barbarian. The definition of what is "decent" or "reasonable" may, of course, include anything one wishes—from spelling to an acquaintance with *Hamlet;* from arithmetic to the second law of thermodynamics. The phrase "college preparation" embodies the quite unconscious arrogance—indeed an innocent arrogance—of generations of college teachers immersed in this thinking.

There is a kind of *reductio ad absurdum* lurking behind all such reasoning which tends to admit to education those who need it least and to exclude those for whom the "value added" by education would be greatest. It is obviously essential to exclude those so unprepared that they cannot benefit from instruction at the going level; yet this tendency, if left unchecked, can focus the educational process on a small and indefinitely diminishing fraction of students.

Thus the impelling force behind the institution of faculty committees on admissions has been the solicitude of faculties for specific regulations about the subject matter that students were expected to have mastered. A great deal of faculty debate has been concerned with the minutiae of these regulations. The profound sociological implications of admission to higher education and its attendant problems are quite generally ignored. To require a year of calculus as a prerequisite for admission may look like real progress to the mathematics department, which sees the one student who comes in with the added head start. It does not see the many candidates of equal or greater ultimate promise who will be automatically excluded by a provision of this kind. It is largely as a result of this type of thinking that, in about one quarter of American colleges,[15] the vestigial connection between the admissions function and that of the registrar is retained by combining both in a single individual or placing one under the other. This organizational form is a kind of fossilized relic of the viewpoint that was dominant at the turn of the century and that grew out of faculty solicitude for minute specifications; it became important to record and keep track of the extent to which each student met or fell short of the specifications.

The viewpoint of the earlier faculty committees was of a piece with the entire "credits" approach to educational record keeping which has come to be characteristic of American higher education. The registrar is of necessity a central figure in this conception, so that, to the extent that it pervaded admissions practice, the registrar seemed the logical functionary to supervise admissions. The idea of small, interchangeable units of learning, redeemable at par, certified much as were the coins stamped by medieval goldsmiths, has been irresistibly practical and convenient, particularly in an educational environment characterized by a wide variety of colleges and universities. The concept is congenial to the characteristic American idea of interchangeable parts in industry. Yet in using this procedure most educators have felt somewhat uneasily that it partakes of the "fallacy of misplaced concreteness."

DILEMMAS OF SELECTION

As a practical matter the main burden of negotiation about admission falls on the admission staff and the high school. At its lowest and least imaginative level, exchange between high school counselors and admissions people constitutes a kind of broker-

[15] See Jane Zech Hauser and Paul F. Lazarsfeld, *op. cit.*

age operation. At this level, the job is one of negotiation: the high school counselor tries to make the best possible bargain on behalf of his "client" for admission to a strong college. In an independent school, the student is quite literally a client, and in the eyes of status-conscious parents, a school's reputation may, to an embarrassing degree, depend on its success in getting its graduates into the particular colleges favored by its parent group. This objective is often only remotely related to the genuine educational worth of the processes carried on in these colleges or their suitability for the students concerned.

The counselor, if tempted to "oversell" a candidate, knows that he is always subject to the risk that another year the college will be more wary of his recommendations. The admissions officer in turn has a recruiting problem—or thinks he has. He is looking for the strongest students, or those who in his scheme of values are deemed more "desirable." In such an atmosphere of negotiation it is very easy to fall into a predominantly bargaining habit of thought, losing sight of the fact that both parties to the transaction are in a deeper sense obligated to act as trustees of the student's welfare and to serve in a fiduciary capacity, giving him the benefit of whatever special skill and experience they can muster. What the student or his parents want, or think they want, may not represent the wisest educational solution. But they have a right to choose. Solutions cannot be imposed on them. It is a task of persuasion and diplomacy to carry them, perhaps, some distance but not all the way toward what seems the best solution. There are no certainties; guidance, like politics, remains the art of the possible.

In recent years, faculty admissions committees in many colleges, abandoning the earlier preoccupation with details, have assumed policy-making functions of a much broader scope, particularly in institutions which have become highly selective. These committees often raise far-reaching questions of general policy—questions so broad as to be unanswerable in any definitive sense because they involve profound philosophical issues about the aims of education, its functions in society, and the adaptability of various human types to those versions of the educational process to which different colleges are committed. Sometimes special ad hoc committees have been set up to deal with these issues, and there is a considerable polemical literature in which individual faculty members wrestle with questions of educational policy.[16]

This more recent current of thought represents an almost complete reversal of the earlier emphasis in which admissions committees laid down detailed specifications about subjects of study. Two converging forces have brought about this reversal. One of these forces is the spread of the comprehensive high school, the general improvement of secondary education, and the consequent greatly improved articulation between secondary and higher education. A student having possible college attendance in mind is much more likely to be guided into a reasonably appropriate program and less likely to fall into one that is unacceptable to colleges than was the case a generation ago. Specific subject matter requirements persist, but in diminishing degree, and they are more rational in the sense of fitting broad curricular objectives instead of reflecting arbitrary selections of "units" made at the whim of individual colleges.

The second force is the view of the more selective colleges that subject matter requirements serve only as minimum qualifications. Nearly all candidates meet these requirements because the others have been scared away at earlier stages; so the really difficult policy decisions involve selection from a group already "qualified." The grounds on which the final decision is based may seem arbitrary and capricious to one observer, while to another they may seem natural reflections of values deeply

[16] An admirable example of determined faculty effort to wrestle with some of the insoluble dilemmas is *Admission to Harvard College*, cited in note 8. See also pp. 52–73 of the "Annual Report of the Admission and Scholarship Committee," in *Report of the President of Harvard College, 1959–60,* for the late Dean Wilbur Bender's discussion of some of these problems.

and sincerely held. In any case there are few guidelines, and the scope for disputation is vast. This is the area of "invisible" or "ambiguous" admissions requirements.[17] So it comes about that in selective colleges committees frequently find themselves trapped in prolonged sessions dealing with individual cases; relatively trivial differences among candidates turn the scales. Such decisions are basically ignorant decisions and may reflect whims and prejudices of individuals simply because no hard evidence is at hand. Schools complain of the difficulty of predicting admission decisions and hence of advising students.[18] The late Irwin Lorge summed up the situation by saying that selection for college admission is made tolerable only by its inaccuracy.

A great deal of soul searching goes on about the kind of selection that should occur in these situations. Admissions officers look for "interesting," "creative," or "original" candidates. They are, not unnaturally, drawn toward youngsters who have shown intellectual curiosity, exceptional energy, or initiative; who have pushed some unusual project to successful completion; or who have demonstrated marked qualities of leadership. It is quite probable that many of these individuals will show exceptional achievement during their mature years, at least in the qualities and activities that our society values. But there are two defects in this kind of selection.

First, the criteria in all this selection are based on limited values and objectives. The college will benefit through the splendor of its reputation as a place from which leaders come. But is this kind of gain good for the system as a whole? Perhaps these human focuses of imagination and energy would be more broadly effective and influential if they were scattered more widely among more diverse student bodies. Perhaps, in the wider view, the obligation to provide an education must, at some point, begin to outweigh the privilege of choosing whom one will seek out to educate. Nobody ever seems to question the usual Level Two approach, which simply assumes that this obligation does not exist, which pictures the college ranging the jungle, seeking whom it may devour and richly entitled to whatever student material it can pounce upon regardless of the effect on other colleges. Centers of excellence are, indeed, essential. But not if they are artificially constructed by depriving others; not if tighter selection is, in effect, made a substitute for education by assembling a group that will perform well under even the most dull and unimaginative tutelage. Excellence should be a product of the educational process and experience, not a product of exclusion that may do more harm than good.

The second defect is that all the factors that enter into "ambiguous" selection imply that we know a promising student when we see one. But our decisions are ignorant. Even if we set as a criterion merely the applicant's ability to shine in our existing academic environment, we miss the mark in many cases.[19] How much wider of the mark would we be if our students had access to the full range of nurture, stimulus, and excitement that a truly imaginative university environment would be capable of providing? As A. N. Whitehead said, only certain kinds of excellence are possible in particular historic epochs. It is entirely conceivable that some of the human types whom we reject as a matter of course would, under a different concept of life and its purpose, turn out to be most needed.

The moral for admissions policy seems to be this: as a practical matter some floor has to be put under the level of preparation and apparent intellectual aptitude in order to avoid tragic misfits. Even if the educational process is all wrong, we cannot change it overnight. But above this floor, a good argument can be made for something

[17] See particularly Henry S. Dyer, "Ambiguity in Selective Admissions," *Journal of the Association of College Admissions Counselors,* p. 15ff, Fall, 1963.

[18] See Mary E. Chase, "The Admissions Counselor—Guide or Gambler?" *College Board Review,* no. 27, pp. 25–28, Fall, 1955.

[19] See Joshua A. Fishman and Ann K. Pasanella, "College Admission Selection Studies," *Review of Educational Research,* vol. 30, no. 4, pp. 298–310, October, 1960 (see especially the bibliography.

like a random choice of applicants. Then each college will be more nearly carrying its fair share of the load of providing education. It will in time come to be judged by the "value added" to its alumni, and it will have the satisfaction of knowing that its achievement is inherent and earned, not adventitiously and artificially gained through the shunting of a super-select group into its gates.

In other words, we need to entertain the possibility that our society is not infallible in its characteristic judgments and values. Should our criteria for access to higher education turn out, in a longer perspective, to be limited and provincial, one way to mitigate their harmful impact would be by increasing the randomness of the selection process.

It is a basic principle of evolution, as well as of human affairs, that diversity is a chief source of progress.[20] Because we cannot begin to imagine all the kinds of diversity that might help us, we need to imitate nature by permitting random processes to play their unpredictable part. It has been well said that the universe is not only stranger than we imagine—it is stranger than we *can* imagine. The same is undoubtedly true of the depth and variety of ability concealed in human personality. The worst way to get at the truth is to start with the assumption that you have it already. For generations the universities of the Old World have assumed that they knew how to select students. They tested their assumptions by pointing to the leaders the system produced. This argument had two fatal flaws: first, there was virtually no other source of leaders against which to measure the success of the system, and second, the real test of selection is the quality of the rejects. As the saying goes, the doctor can bury his mistakes. The university system has been able to render its mistakes invisible by condemning them to noneducation and hence, for the most part, to nonperformance—a perfect example of the self-fulfilling prophecy. We say to a candidate, or to a social group, "You are not able enough to benefit from education." We accordingly deprive him of education, he accomplishes little, and we can then point to the wisdom of our decision.

The interest of some faculties in broad questions of admissions policy is a development of great significance. The sagacious admissions officer will do everything in his power to involve the faculty in admissions problems, confront them with admissions quandaries and dilemmas, and give them a sense of participation in a difficult and vital area. Committees (the chairmen of which should be drawn from the faculty) are only one means to this end. School visits, the reading of admissions folders, participation in interviews, and admissions research are all possible avenues to the end of letting the faculty know at first hand how complex admissions problems are. Faculties so involved are less likely to limit their activity to painting word pictures of the ideal student with the suggestion that the class be limited to these types.

MODELS OF STUDENT DISTRIBUTION

To represent the "system" behavior of the entire college admission process, one can distinguish a number of oversimplified models, each an extreme case of how such a system might operate. Granted that what actually happens is a mixture of all these, such caricatures help to clarify the problem by sorting out the kinds of forces that seem to be operating. Some of the more obvious models would be the following.

Since in this country 80 percent of college students attend colleges within their state of residence, it is probably safe to conclude that geographic propinquity is the strongest single force leading to choice of a college. Though the strongest, it is by no means the only force because, depending on the populousness of a state and the complexity of its education system, much scope remains for the exercise of other influences

[20] I am indebted to Henry B. Phillips for his original thought along these lines. See his paper "On the Nature of Progress," *American Scientist*, vol. 33, no. 4, pp. 253–259, Autumn, 1945.

as well. State boundaries are of course arbitrary. In a large and populous state with a wide variety of colleges, students can stay near home and still find wide opportunity to follow educational preferences based on reasons other than propinquity. In other states the range of opportunity may be restricted to a handful of institutions of limited variety in type or quality. Though here the incentive to go farther afield is greater, to do so is expensive, so that many will find themselves in colleges less well adapted to their needs and preferences. The recent marked tendency of state institutions to discriminate against out-of-state applicants as places become scarcer is increasing the validity of this model and increasing the provinciality of the educational opportunities available in each of the 50 states. With the vast growth of community colleges, we can confidently predict that higher education will remain for the most part a local business.[21]

Logically next on the list of models, but numerically much less important, is the opposite kind of situation, in which students seek out the most distant opportunities in order to maximize the benefits of geographical diversification. This tendency, pressed to its utmost, brings an increase in interregional and international study, with all the educational benefits of intercultural experience. Such cosmopolitan exposure, despite its undisputed value, can affect only a small minority of students. In terms of numbers of students involved, it represents a far weaker force for college selection than does propinquity.

Quite different in principle is a third model in which the strongest institutions attract the ablest students. This concept is simplistic in that it leaves unanswered a tangle of questions about which are the strongest institutions and which the ablest students. In complex universities different undergraduate schools may properly have widely differing "standards," and it is in any case an oversimplified abstraction to measure the varieties of effective human talent on a single, unidimensional scale. There may be, too, some divergence between true excellence in a college and the sort of prestigious reputation that can attract applicants. One must allow for the inevitable human tendency to want what others seem to be running after; fads and fashions come to play a part. Yet, despite such limitations, objective support for this model can be found. A. W. Astin and John L. Holland have shown that there is a strong tendency for "high endowment" private institutions to attract abler students than "low endowment" private institutions, and a somewhat less pronounced tendency for "high budget" public institutions to attract abler students than "low budget" institutions.

The fourth model is one in which students distribute themselves into categories separated by clearly defined educational and vocational objectives. This is a model of commanding significance. Between 20 and 25 percent of all undergraduate degrees in the United States go to students preparing for teaching below the college level. About 16 percent are in business administration, 10 percent in engineering, 6 percent in fine arts, 3 percent in agriculture, and 3 percent in home economics. These six fields account for more than 60 percent of all undergraduate degrees granted in this country.[22] The remaining 40 percent might be thought of as "liberal arts" and hence nonvocational

[21] It is important to judge the student's motives more by what he does than what he says. The fact that about 80 percent of students attend colleges within their own state is in sharp contrast to a study that shows 52.9 percent of college males explaining their choice of a college because it was a "good college," while 18 percent explained their choice as "close to home." See John L. Holland, "Student Explanations of College Choice and Their Relation to College Popularity, College Productivity, and Sex Differences," *College and University*, vol. 33, no. 3, pp. 313–320, Spring, 1958. There is ample evidence that for most students few colleges other than those nearby come into consideration. See for example David Riesman, "College Subcultures and College Outcomes," in *Selection and Educational Differentiation*, pp. 1–14, Center for the Study of Higher Education, Berkeley, Calif., 1959 (187 pp.).

[22] John D. Millett, *The Academic Community*, McGraw-Hill Book Company, Inc., New York, 1962, p. 125 (265 pp.).

degrees. In fact, however, vocational objectives are likely to be concealed in many majors in the so-called "liberal arts" colleges, particularly in natural sciences, social sciences, mathematics, and languages. It is only with the help of these concealed vocational objectives that many small liberal arts colleges manage to compete with the larger and better-financed state institutions, many of which have curricula that are overtly and unashamedly vocational. Public institutions are freer from the kind of inhibition that caused the economics department of one leading women's college to be dissuaded from offering a course in accounting because this would be a "useful" subject. This model represents a central mode in our current mores and reflects the widespread habit of looking on education as a means, not an end. It fits the upward-striving youth, seeking to better himself, willing to "hire himself educated," and uncritical of the means for accomplishing this. He may be limited in the breadth of his horizons, not necessarily interested in "ideas," but driving with intense energy toward a degree as a key to professional advancement. It is to be expected that a society in the midst of a vast expansion of education will place a high value on such considerations.

A fifth possible model is one in which the "atmosphere" of a college plays a large part in determining the student's choice. Traditionally, information about the social, intellectual, and psychological climate of various colleges has been spread in covert, informal, and unorganized ways by hearsay, rumor, and personal report. Only in the last few years has the college as a study in social psychology become a popular field of research. Behavioral scientists more recently have sought to define the "press," the loose congeries of impressions and pressures that constitute the student's environment in a college. They have worked out categories of "press," using student questionnaires to search out attitudes, backgrounds, values, tastes, habits, and beliefs. This is a reasonable procedure, since it is clear that an important, if not the chief, determinant of the press upon the individual is the kind of student who populates the college. The chief college influence on students, in other words, is exerted by or mediated through their peer groups. To treat the college itself as a field of sociological and anthropological study has been a novel idea, somewhat frightening to both administrators and members of the more traditional disciplines.

Such efforts to relate student types to types of colleges raise difficult questions of methodology as well as a broader range of issues which would still be present even if the methodologies were unexceptionable. One possible use of such material is to try to fit students into the particular environments they will find congenial, stimulating, adapted to their needs, or calculated to serve their purposes. This effort would accord with the proposals of David Riesman and others that some kind of "consumers' report" be available for different colleges so that the prospective student can know in advance what he is buying. To the extent that such a device prevents the student from getting into a college he is not up to (an unlikely contingency) or from getting into a college not up to him (which is much more probable), it could be useful. The net result might be an intensification of "typing," so that the student seeking a college looks for a student environment that most nearly fits his own subculture, origins, values, and attitudes. Any such tendency would reduce the variety of the social "mix" that is an indispensable ingredient in all education. The invincible propensity of most human beings to associate with others as nearly like themselves as possible is a contra-educational force of great power. It is only partly offset by the innate adventurousness of a minority who are stimulated by people different from themselves. Only the more intrepid succeed in overcoming this pull toward security, which represents the basic need for roots, stability, and an environment that is comprehensible and predictable.

OPTIMUM DISTRIBUTION

Two major questions arise in studying the "great sorting" of students among colleges. The first question that pioneer studies like those of Pace and Astin[23] seek to answer is, essentially, "What is happening?" The objective is description and analysis. At least a start has been made toward answering this question. But if the ultimate object is to study not merely college admissions as a system but "college admissions and the public interest," there arises the much more difficult problem of trying to decide what the sorting *ought* to be. This normative purpose has been little thought about beyond repeating the ideal prescription that each student ought to have as much education as he can digest and use.

We shall have to begin to clarify ideas beyond this stage. For example, given the present assortment of 2,300 colleges, universities, and junior colleges, what is the optimum way of distributing students among them, taking the long-run public interest as the criterion? Does the present scheme of things, representing an intricate mix of all the models sketched above, approximate the ideal of the classical assumptions about free enterprise? Would it be better, for example, to change the structure of the institutions by encouraging them to merge or to subdivide than to try to change the distribution of students?

The need for innovation and experiment to strengthen the educational process everywhere and to increase its vitality is overwhelmingly great. If competitive recruiting can be a means to this end, let us by all means have it. What we seem to lack now, and what gives rise to doubts about competitive recruiting, is evidence of a direct coupling between advances in educational quality and recruiting appeal. The student himself, to say nothing of his parents and advisers, scarcely realizes the extent to which his real need is not just to learn but to acquire the habit and technique of learning and the appetite to go on with it indefinitely. In the public consciousness, education associates itself still, to a large extent, with the concept of a fixed corpus of knowledge that must be mastered, and the further concept of this mastering as instrumental—as the key to prescribed preferment and lifetime competency. A degree or a certificate is something negotiable and tangible to wave at a potential employer, but the "half-life" of the corpus of knowledge it represents may be dangerously short.

It would be unrealistic to hope for neat or definitive answers to large questions of this kind. Higher education in the United States is too complex and vast to lend itself to more than a modicum of central, purposeful control. Though mutual emulation tends toward some degree of uniformity and governmental policy can exert salutary influence in some general directions, there is, in a certain large sense, nobody "in charge." Even governmental policies, weighted with the power of financial resources, constitute only one of many forces acting. Many aspects of change, of amelioration, must remain in the hands of the thousands of individuals whose decisions, decentralized and seemingly unrelated, will collectively determine the ponderous movements of the national rudder.

It is for this reason that educators collectively, though primarily concerned with their local decisions, need the habit of looking at the system as a whole. An infusion of thinking at Level Three in the training and the habitual practice of all concerned with college admissions can do much to broaden their perspective. A step forward for many of these people would be the mere realization that such a concept as Level Three thinking exists and that it involves criteria different from those to which they are accustomed. This realization could influence their day-to-day task as they grope,

[23] See A. W. Astin, "Productivity of Undergraduate Institutions," *Science*, pp. 129–135, April 13, 1962. See also "Undergraduate Institutions and the Production of Scientists," *Science*, pp. 334–338, July 26, 1963; and "The Distribution of 'Wealth' in Higher Education," *College and University*, vol. 37, no. 2, pp. 113–125, Winter, 1962.

according to their lights, toward the fulfillment of their annual quotas of students.

The study of college admissions as a system will inevitably merge, as time goes on, into the broader study of higher education in its totality as a system. A decade ago we were startled by the high proportion of able high school students who failed to continue their education. This proportion is decreasing rapidly, partly through increased financial aid, partly through a heightened public consciousness of the importance of education. In one respect our concept of higher education remains primitive. We speak of "going on to college," a simple idea, inherited from nineteenth-century practice. But just over the horizon we can sense two important changes in this oversimplified view.

As the first of these changes we shall see important new departures in the teaching and learning process at the undergraduate level. Undoubtedly more will be learned faster, but, more important, what is learned will have increased relevance to the process of lifelong education, to cultivating the habit of learning and the appetite for it. For the first time, we shall educate for coping with a changing environment. College faculties will be relieved of much of the expository labor of education so that they may devote more time to their unique and indispensable function of interacting with students—needling, stimulating, questioning, browbeating, and encouraging. This interchange, which is the essence of education, can be greatly strengthened if the student has full and convenient recourse to film, television, records, tape, and similar aids to exposition. These will free the teacher's time for more important personal interaction and will bring the student to a higher level of preparation to take his part in this dialogue.

The leading objective of public policy will be rapidly shifting from getting people into college to the more difficult and subtle one of making college a truly educational experience in the contemporary meaning of the term. We need a general *aggiornamento* of higher education. Beyond this, we need means of coupling the forces of innovation and experiment to the forces that influence the distribution of students among institutions.

The second, and concurrent, development will be the evolution of a much richer variety of institutions and organized forms. The four-year college course, a legacy of the nineteenth century, even with all its recent revisions, retains a rigidity of concept, content, and method. Even its calendar is rigid. The pressure of increasing numbers has created such a massive emergency problem that it diverts energy and attention from innovation and reform. Indeed, the temptation has been to accept the pressure for admission to college as evidence that the product is already so appealing to the customers that it stands in little need of improvement. The public habit of brand loyalty and the mindless reliance on degrees as status symbols have retarded the needed development of flexible forms of post-high school education. The possibilities of interfusing liberal studies with programs of vocational utility have been incompletely explored.

The large number of college students who need a change of pace and an interruption of study are poorly served by our existing procedures. Many able youngsters are "action oriented." For them a prolonged period of purely intellectual study becomes frustrating. A year or two in a job, or in exploring several jobs, can give many of them a completely new view of life and send them back to college refreshed, with an appetite for study. Our habit of regarding a four-year course as a norm and ideal does great harm to such youngsters. They are likely to be tagged as "dropouts" or "failures," with permanent injury to the self-confidence they need and should retain. Flexibility of timing will have to be included among the major aspects of educational reform.

All these things will come to pass, some of them sooner than we now dare hope. In the meantime the year-to-year work of recruiting, selection, and guidance will go on. To bring these processes into the central stream of education by increasing the student's awareness of the options open to him, with all their values and implications, will become a major preoccupation of those concerned with admissions and will inevitably involve faculties to a much greater extent than now. The concept of education in the light of the public interest must include the guidance process as an integral part of education, and admissions are a part of the guidance function. College teachers, it is to be hoped, will aspire to reach whatever students come before them and be less insistent that unless they can teach the most promising they would rather not teach at all. When this day comes, admissions committees, at the same time, may admit that they cannot always spot the winners, that the race is not always to the swift, and that the eager student sometimes outpaces the bright one. They may even grow more willing than now to accept with humility the duty of doing as much as they can for whatever students present themselves, in the assurance that, among those who look least impressive to begin with, unsuspected talent will come to light.

SUGGESTED READINGS

Selection and Admission

Anastasi, Ann (ed.): *Testing Problems in Perspective,* American Council on Education, Washington, 1965.

Astin, A. W.: *Who Goes Where to College,* Science Research Associates, Inc., Chicago, 1965.

Brown, Nicholas C. (ed.): *Higher Education: Incentives and Obstacles,* American Council on Education, Washington, 1960 (165 pp.).

Duggan, John M., and Paul H. Hazlett, Jr.: *Predicting College Grades,* College Entrance Examination Board, New York, 1961 (71 pp.).

Dyer, Henry S.: "The Past, Present and Future of Admissions Research," *College Board Review,* vol. 42, pp. 21–25, Fall, 1960.

———: "Ambiguity in Selective Admissions," *Journal of the Association of College Admissions Counselors,* p. 15ff., Fall, 1963.

Fels, William C.: "The College Describes Itself," *College Board Review,* no. 31, pp. 30–32, Spring 1959.

Fishman, Joshua A.: "Unsolved Criterion Problems in the Selection of College Students," *Harvard Educational Review,* vol. 28, no. 4, pp. 340–349, Fall, 1958.

——— and Ann K. Pasanella: "College Admission-Selection Studies," *Review of Educational Research,* vol. 30, no. 4, pp. 298–310, October, 1960 (extensive bibliography).

Gallagher, J. Roswell: "The Role of the Emotions in Academic Success," *College Admissions,* no. 1, pp. 106–108, 1954.

Goslin, David A.: *The Search for Ability: Standardized Testing in Social Perspective,* Russell Sage Foundation, New York, 1963.

Hauser, J. Z., and P. E. Lazarsfeld: *The Admissions Officer,* Bureau of Applied Social Research, Columbia University, New York, College Entrance Examination Board, Columbia University Press, New York, 1964.

Katz, Martin: *Decisions and Values,* College Entrance Examination Board, New York, 1963, p. 25.

Morrison, Wilma: *The School Record: Its use and abuse in college admissions,* College Entrance Examination Board, New York, 1961 (15 pp.).

Severinghaus, Leslie R.: "A Philosophy for College Admissions," *Journal of the Association of College Admissions Counselors,* vol. 8, pp. 5–8, Winter, 1963 (this debate is continued in the Spring issue by Eugene S. Wilson and B. Alden Thresher).

Stouffer, Samuel A.: "Social Forces that Produce the 'Great Sorting,'" *College Admissions,* no. 2, pp. 1–7.

Thresher, B. Alden: *College Admissions and the Public Interest,* College Entrance Examination Board, New York, 1966.

Ward, Lewis B.: "The Interview as an Assessment Technique," *College Admissions,* no. 2, pp. 62–71.

Watts, Charles H.: "The Cliché Expert Experiences College," *Brown Alumni Weekly,* pp. 8–10, February, 1957.

Foreign Education

Access to Higher Education, vol. 1, Unesco and International Association of Universities, 1963 (distributed by Columbia University Press, New York, 212 pp.).

Fortier-Ortiz, Adolfo: "Problems of University Admissions in Latin America: A report to the trustees of the college entrance examination board," College Entrance Examination Board, New York, 1963 (36 pp.).

Harbison, Frederick, and Charles A. Myers: "Education, Manpower, and Economic Growth," McGraw-Hill Book Company, Inc., New York, 1964 (229 pp.).
Higher Education, Report of the committee appointed by the Prime Minister under the chairmanship of Lord Robbins, H.M. Stationery Office, London, 1963 (the "Robbins Report").
Kaulfers, Walter V.: "Pitfalls in Comparing Foreign Schools with Ours," *Educational Record,* pp. 275–281, July, 1963.
Sasnett, Martina T. (ed.): *A Guide to the Admission and Placement of Foreign Students,* Institute of International Education, New York, 1962.
Trow, Martin: "A Question of Size and Shape," *Universities Quarterly,* p. 136, London, March, 1964.

Guidance Manuals

Bowles, Frank H.: *How to Get into College,* rev. ed., E. P. Dutton & Co., Inc., New York, 1960 (185 pp.).
Lass, Abraham H.: *How to Prepare for College,* Pocket Books, Inc., New York, 1962 (466 pp.).
Sulkin, Sidney: *Complete Planning for College,* McGraw-Hill Book Company, Inc., 1962 (268 pp.).
Wilson, Eugene S., and Charles A. Bucher: *College Ahead!* rev. ed., Harcourt Brace & World, Inc., New York, 1961 (186 pp.).
Wing, Cliff W. Jr.: *On Selecting a College and Seeking Admission,* reprinted from "American Universities and Colleges," American Council on Education, Washington, 1964.

Background Reading

Berelson, Bernard: *Graduate Education in the United States,* McGraw-Hill Book Company, Inc., New York, 1960.
Blocker, Clyde E., Robert H. Plummer, and Richard S. Richardson: *The Two-year College: A social synthesis,* Prentice-Hall, Inc., Englewood Cliffs, N.J., 1965.
Clark, Burton R.: *The Open-door College: A Case Study,* McGraw-Hill Book Company, Inc., New York, 1960.
Coleman, James S.: "Style and Substance in American High Schools," *College Admissions,* no. 6, pp. 9–21, 1956.
———: *The Adolescent Society,* The Free Press of Glencoe, New York, 1961.
Conant, James B.: *The American High School Today,* McGraw-Hill Book Company, Inc., New York, 1959.
———: *Slums and Suburbs,* McGraw-Hill Book Company, Inc., New York, 1962.
Cremin, Lawrence A.: *The Transformation of the Schools,* Alfred A. Knopf, Inc., New York, 1961 (387 pp.).
Farnsworth, Dana L.: "Some Non-academic Causes of Success and Failure in College Students," *College Admissions,* no. 2, pp. 72–76.
Funkenstein, David H.: *The Student and Mental Health,* Riverside Press, Cambridge, Mass., 1959.
Getzels, Jacob W., and Philip W. Jackson: *Creativity and Intelligence,* John Wiley & Sons, Inc., New York, 1962.
Hughes, Everett C.: "How Colleges Differ," *College Admissions,* no. 5, pp. 16–30.
Hunt, J. McV.: *Intelligence and Experience,* The Ronald Press Company, New York, 1961.
Medsker, Leland L.: *The Junior College: Progress and Prospect,* McGraw-Hill Book Company, Inc., New York, 1960 (367 pp.).
Pace, C. Robert: "Five College Environments," *College Board Review,* vol. 41, pp. 24–28, Spring, 1960.
Reisman, David: *Constraint and Variety in American Education,* Doubleday & Company, Inc., Garden City, N.Y., 1958.
Rudolph, Frederick: *The American College and University: A History,* Alfred A. Knopf, Inc., New York, 1962.
Sanford, Nevitt (ed.): *The American College,* John Wiley & Sons, Inc., New York, 1962.
Schmidt, George P.: *The Liberal Arts College,* Rutgers University Press, New Brunswick, N.J., 1957.
Spindler, George D. (ed.): *Education and Culture: Anthropological Approaches,* Holt, Rinehart and Winston, Inc., New York, 1963 (571 pp.).
Whitehead, Alfred North: *The Aims of Education,* The Macmillan Co., New York, 1929 (paperback, New American Library, 1961).

Periodicals

College Admissions, College Entrance Examination Board, New York, vols. 1–10, 1954–1963 (proceedings of annual colloquium; Publications Order Office, Box 592, Princeton, N.J.).
College Board Review, College Entrance Examination Board, New York (quarterly).

College and University, Journal of the American Association of Collegiate Registrars and Admissions Officers (quarterly; 1501 New Hampshire Ave., Washington, D.C. 20036).

Daedalus, Journal of the American Academy of Arts and Sciences; see especially "Education in the Age of Science," Winter, 1959, and "Excellence and Leadership in a Democracy," Fall, 1961.

Educational Record, American Council on Education (quarterly; 1785 Massachusetts Avenue, Washington, D.C. 20036).

The Independent School Bulletin, National Association of Independent Schools (quarterly; 4 Liberty Square, Boston, Mass. 02109).

Journal of the Association of College Admissions Counselors (quarterly; 610 Church Street, Evanston, Ill.).

Directories

Association of College Admissions Counselors: *A Handbook for the Counselors of College Bound Students,* 1967–1969, Evanston, Ill., 1967.

Cass, James, and Max Birnbaum: *Comparative Guide to American Colleges for Students, Parents and Counselors,* Harper & Row, Publishers, Incorporated, New York, 1964.

College Handbook, 1967–69, College Entrance Examination Board, New York (revised biennially).

Hawes, Gene R.: *The New American Guide to Colleges,* 2d ed., The New American Library of World Literature, Inc., New York, 1962 (349 pp.).

Lovejoy, Clarence E.: *Complete Guide to American Colleges and Universities,* Simon and Schuster, Inc., New York (335 pp.; revised frequently).

Manual of Freshman Class Profiles, 1967–69, College Entrance Examination Board, New York (revised biennially; Publications Order Office, Box 592, Princeton, N.J.).

Patterson, *American Education,* Educational Directories, Inc., Mt. Prospect, Ill. (768 pp., revised frequently).

Sargent, F. Porter: *Handbook of Private Schools,* F. Porter Sargent, Boston (revised frequently).

———: *Junior Colleges and Specialized Schools and Colleges,* F. Porter Sargent, Boston (1,277 pp.; revised frequently).

Chapter 2

Admissions— Freshman Class Quota

GILBERT C. GARLAND

Dean of Admissions, Northeastern University, Boston, Massachusetts

INTRODUCTION

One of the chief responsibilities of admissions personnel relates to the enrollment of a freshman class which, as nearly as possible, will equal a predetermined size. It should appear obvious that the institution's total budget is prepared in part on the assumption that a certain number of freshmen will arrive to register. The enrollment of a significantly smaller number of new students than originally planned would have serious budgetary implications. It is equally true that the arrival of significantly more new students than originally planned would seriously affect staffing plans, classroom-laboratory arrangements, and student residence preparations. The close control of freshman class size, therefore, logically is a matter of vital concern to admissions personnel and, in fact, to the entire administrative and faculty staff.

Important to the determination and control of class size are those admission statistics which relate to the number of inquiries and applications for admission received during past academic years. Inquiries received reflect the extent of interest on the part of secondary school students in a particular college—whether such inquiries represent actual visits to campus, telephone calls, or personal letters. Applications for admission provide still more accurate evidence of student interest.

In planning the freshman class size, it is important, also, to determine how many freshmen will constitute a section. This decision is normally a matter of institutional policy, and section sizes for freshmen may vary from twenty to thirty or more. Both class size and section size must be predetermined in order that admissions personnel may plan an intelligent recruitment program. The multiple applications problem alone, to be discussed later, demands that freshman class target goals be somewhat flexible, for it is virtually impossible to recruit and enroll students in any arithmetically exact number.

TRANSFER CLASS QUOTA

The attitude of the college toward students who seek to enter from other colleges with advanced standing will have a direct bearing upon the enrollment of transfer students. It is true that some colleges welcome such students as a means of filling class vacancies created by normal upperclass attrition. Other colleges are less enthusiastic about students who wish to transfer credits from other institutions. With the expansion of two-year junior and community colleges and in line with our democratic goal of providing an education to large numbers of students who are not necessarily ready for college at seventeen or eighteen, the four-year institution has a genuine responsibility to open its doors to those students who have demonstrated their ability to handle a university program.

The processing of transfer students properly requires close liaison between admissions personnel and the academic faculties. Insofar as the evaluation of college transcripts is concerned, the determination of allowable transfer credits may be handled by an admissions counselor or an academic dean. The number of transfer students to be admitted to certain areas of study may well be a joint decision on the part of academic planning officers and admissions personnel. In any event, determination of class size should account for the number of "new" students, whether they be classified as freshmen or transfers.

It is essential to the admissions task that accurate statistics be maintained and updated on a frequent and regular basis (see Figure 1), with provision for weekly comparison with the previous year's experience (see Figure 2). In addition, checks must be made against the reports of previous years as a safeguard. The comparative admissions report, transmitted regularly to the president and other administrative officers, should include such categories as the following:

Number of applications
Number of withdrawals
Number of rejects
Number of acceptances
Number of tuition deposits
Number of residence applications
Number of residence deposits

The institution which has a data processing center as a part of its facilities is in a favorable position to provide excellent reporting and statistical services to the department of admissions. It has been clearly demonstrated, whether in the small college or the large university, that reporting, research, and control methods and services are greatly improved with the use of computer techniques. The department of admissions, in its internal control of numbers and in its research services provided to secondary schools, offers unlimited opportunities for the application of data processing services.

The entire area of enrollment control and enrollment prediction requires constant study of admissions experience in previous years. Because of all the factors which

ADMISSIONS DEPARTMENT WEEKLY REPORT

SEC	QUOTA	COLLEGE		ACTIVE	PNDG	ACPD	DEPOSITS
23	782	ENGINEERING	MALE	1962	549	1413	215
			FEMALE	20	3	17	1
			TOTAL	1982	552	1430	216
15	540	BUS ADMIN	MALE	1386	555	831	121
			FEMALE	86	33	53	8
			TOTAL	1472	588	884	129
3	105	LIBERAL ARTS MATH-PHY	MALE	353	125	228	25
			FEMALE	126	40	86	7
			TOTAL	479	165	314	32
6	198	BIO SCI	MALE	483	196	287	28
			FEMALE	227	75	152	24
			TOTAL	710	271	439	52
13	429	NON-SCI	MALE	867	347	520	42
			FEMALE	835	212	623	77
			TOTAL	1702	559	1143	119
22	732	TOTAL	MALE	1703	668	1035	95
			FEMALE	1188	327	861	108
			TOTAL	2891	995	1896	203
1	35	EDUCATION SCIENCE	MALE	103	47	56	7
			FEMALE	61	18	43	6
			TOTAL	164	65	99	13
7	231	NON-SCI	MALE	213	94	119	12
			FEMALE	762	212	550	62
			TOTAL	975	306	669	74
8	266	TOTAL	MALE	316	141	175	19
			FEMALE	823	230	593	68
			TOTAL	1139	371	768	87
3	90	PHARMACY	MALE	141	42	99	16
			FEMALE	53	3	50	10
			TOTAL	194	45	149	26
2	66	CRIM JUSTICE	MALE	130	50	80	17
			FEMALE	10	6	4	2
			TOTAL	140	56	84	19
3	90	NURSING ASSOC	MALE	0	0	0	0
			FEMALE	142	44	98	14
			TOTAL	142	44	98	14
4	120	B S	MALE	1	1	0	0
			FEMALE	265	73	192	29
			TOTAL	266	74	192	29
7	210	TOTAL	MALE	1	1	0	0
			FEMALE	407	117	290	43
			TOTAL	408	118	290	43

SEC	QUOTA	COLLEGE		ACTIVE	PNDG	ACPD	DEPOSITS
4	120	BOSTON-BOUVE PHY ED	MALE	122	69	53	3
			FEMALE	116	47	69	8
			TOTAL	238	116	122	11
2	60	RECREATIO	MALE	10	3	7	0
			FEMALE	41	6	35	0
			TOTAL	51	9	42	0
2	64	PHY THER	MALE	18	10	8	1
			FEMALE	196	79	117	11
			TOTAL	214	89	125	12
8	244	TOTAL	MALE	150	82	68	4
			FEMALE	353	132	221	19
			TOTAL	503	214	289	23
88	2930	BOSTON TOTAL	MALE	5789	2088	3701	487
			FEMALE	2940	851	2089	259
			TOTAL	8729	2939	5790	746
		BURLINGTON CAMPUS					
3	105	ENGINEERING	MALE	135	40	95	14
			FEMALE	1	1	0	0
			TOTAL	136	41	95	14
4	140	BUS ADMIN	MALE	170	64	106	19
			FEMALE	2	0	2	0
			TOTAL	172	64	108	19
2	60	LIBERAL ARTS NON-SCI	MALE	66	25	41	3
			FEMALE	15	4	11	2
			TOTAL	81	29	52	5
1	35	EDUCATION NON-SCI	MALE	26	6	20	1
			FEMALE	43	11	32	3
			TOTAL	69	17	52	4
		CRIM JUSTICE	MALE	22	10	12	3
			FEMALE	2	0	2	1
			TOTAL	24	10	14	4
10	340	BURL TOTAL	MALE	419	145	274	40
			FEMALE	63	16	47	6
			TOTAL	482	161	321	46
98	3270	GRAND TOTAL	MALE	6208	2233	3975	527
			FEMALE	3003	867	2136	265
			TOTAL	9211	3100	6111	792

Fig. 1 *Admissions department weekly report.*

ADMISSIONS DEPARTMENT WEEKLY REPORT — WEEK ENDING MARCH 15,1968 — PAGE 3

DORMITORY REPORT

FRESHMEN

INTERESTED IN DORM
ACCEPTANCE PENDING

MALE	1056
FEMALE	498
TOTAL	1554

INTERESTED+ACCEPTED
DORM NOT PAID

MALE	1868
FEMALE	1079
TOTAL	2947

QUOTA	ACCEPTED+PAID DORM	
922	MALE	274
715	FEMALE	165
1637	TOTAL	439

COMPARATIVE ADMISSIONS REPORT

	APPLICATIONS			WITHDRAWALS			REJECTS			PENDING			ACCEPTANCES			DEPOSITS		
	LAST YEAR	THIS YEAR	PCT	LAST YEAR	THIS YEAR	PCT	LAST YEAR	THIS YEAR	PCT	LAST YEAR	THIS YEAR	PCT	LAST YEAR	THIS YEAR	PCT	LAST YEAR	THIS YEAR	PCT
ENGINEERING	2519	2611	3	62	20	-67	572	473	-17	631	593	-6	1254	1525	21	187	230	22
BUS ADMIN	2003	2259	12	37	6	-83	671	609	-9	456	652	42	839	992	18	139	148	6
LIBERAL ARTS	3170	3619	14	109	45	-58	825	602	-27	854	1024	19	1382	1948	40	157	208	32
EDUCATION	1168	1504	28	43	19	-55	327	277	-15	318	388	22	480	820	70	55	91	65
PHARMACY	231	243	5	9	8	-11	56	41	-26	52	45	-13	114	149	30	20	26	30
CRIM JUST	87	224	157	1	2	100	25	58	132	28	66	135	33	98	196	9	23	155
NURSING	470	479	1	42	11	-73	84	60	-28	96	118	22	248	290	16	49	43	-12
BOSTON BOUVE	676	668	-1	20	15	-25	238	150	-36	204	214	4	214	289	35	34	23	-32
TOTAL	10324	11607	12	323	126	-60	2798	2270	-18	2639	3100	17	4564	6111	33	650	792	21

(INCLUDES 3561 GIRLS)

Fig. 2 *Comparative admissions report.*

bear upon the important period of transition from school to college and the competitive nature of college entrance today, admissions personnel should rely upon carefully thought out and sophisticated methods of control. The age of subjective judgment, intuition, and pure guesswork has long since passed.

CAREER TRENDS AND APPLICATIONS

Closely related to a realistic establishment of quotas by fields of study is an awareness of career trends among young adults, both at the regional and national level, for such trends will have a direct effect upon the realization of quota targets. A decline, for example, in the number of students who have expressed interest in such careers as nursing or engineering must be recognized in the early stages of planning for a new class.

A useful planning tool is the annual "Statistics of Attendance in American Universities and Colleges," which appears in *School and Society.*[1]

This report provides a picture of national enrollment trends in various fields of study, and it also gives information of interest by sex, enrollments in public institutions versus private institutions, a study of part-time versus full-time college population, and many other points of information important to planning class composition. Publications of the College Entrance Examination Board, the Association of College Admissions Counselors, and other professional agencies are helpful, also, in calling attention to national trends which may affect the local institutions.

Class quotas are unquestionably affected by national trends which reflect changes in the proportion of secondary school students going on to college. It is important, for example, to appreciate that, in 1940, 15 percent of our young adults were in college. It is projected that, by 1970, 50 percent will be continuing their education at the college level. A look at the projected number of high school graduates in one of the most populous states, Massachusetts, depicts the evident trend as students born in the 1950–1954 period plan ahead for college (see Table 1). Such growth may be offset in part

TABLE 1 Graduates from Massachusetts High Schools

Year	*Number*
1958	42,857
1959	–
1960	54,745
1961	–
1962	54,109
1963	54,287
1964	69,578
1965	76,945
1966	78,406
1967	76,184
1968	75,260
1969	79,220
1970	82,823
1971	84,385
1972	89,013
1973	91,439

* State of Massachusetts high school graduate figures for the years 1958–1973, from Massachusetts State Department of Education, *Pupil Projections,* ED-RS, 1M-3-64, publication 272

[1] *School and Society,* Society for the Advancement of Education, 1860 Broadway, New York, N.Y. 10023.

by international tensions, economic pressures, available financial aid, and other factors. Implicit in any enrollment planning, however, should be an awareness and careful study of all factors which have a direct bearing upon the college entrance plans of young adults.

ADMISSIONS PROJECTION FIGURES

Certainly the most important part of the entire admissions operation is the *individual* counseling which trained professionals, concerned with young people as people, perform.

Yet there is no doubt that a large measure, if not the entire measure, of any college's success in matriculating a strong, diversified, well-rounded freshman group can be correlated with that college's ability to project enrollment figures for the coming year. If these statistics of acceptances projected to reach a desired quota figure vary widely from the actual situation in the spring of the year, then the admissions department cannot possibly enroll as strong a class and the entire concept of attaining a quality class is weakened.

At most universities the quota, or number of freshman students to be entered in any year, is set by the president of the school in conjunction with the dean of admissions and the deans of the various colleges. This quota is a reflection of the philosophy prevailing at the school in any given year. As an example, it may be decided that a particular program—let us say physical therapy—ought to be enlarged because (1) statistics reveal increased interest on the part of high school seniors, (2) physical facilities at the school have been expended, and/or (3) the quality of applications is extremely high.

After the quota has been set in the fall of the year, the admissions office begins to calculate the number of students who must be offered acceptance in order to reach the quota figure for each college and, of course, for the entire incoming class. Perhaps admissions officers should be more careful about the kind of information they release to the general public in this regard. For instance, we probably scare many applicants away when we tell counselors, parents, and students that "Central University accepts only 3,000 students of every 12,000 that apply." Almost all universities actually accept about 100 percent over the 3,000 in order to obtain the 3,000 students. In other words, if the application pool is 12,000 and the quota is 3,000, the "needed" acceptances may run to 6,000; certainly a very different picture than that which is seen by the public.

In order to calculate the total number of needed acceptances, the admissions director finds the total number of acceptances granted for entry into a particular college in the past year. Assuming that there are no unusual factors to be taken into consideration in this given year (e.g., a much smaller application pool, an attempt to change admissions standards), he plots his calculations as follows:

College (program)	Quota	Total acceptances last year	Ultimate acceptances
Liberal Arts (math-physics)	3 sections of 35 each (105)	223 accepted withdrawals 109 deposits 332	305% × quota or 320

Fig. 3 *Calculation of required acceptances for attaining a given quota.*

By dividing the number of deposits (109) into the total number of acceptances (332), he finds the percentage of deposits. He then multiplies this percentage factor by the given quota (105) and finds that he must accept 320 students to attain his goal of 105.

Next he makes the same calculation for all the colleges and all the programs of each college. After checking these statistics against figures of the two previous years to note trends, he releases his estimates to the staff, which then knows what needs to be done in order to reach the desired goals. (See Figure 3.)

Yet two very important considerations must be kept in mind as the year develops. First, and more importantly, the projected goals *must be reached* by a certain date, in the case of most colleges by April 1.

If the goal is not attained by this date, then it is almost impossible to find well-qualified students in April, May, June, and July, and the college may be forced to accept substandard applicants in order to fulfill its fiscal responsibilities. When the reply date arrives on April 1, and when the students who have been accepted but have decided to go elsewhere do not pay the required deposit, then the impact is slight as this event has been figured

Then, too, by setting the date of April 1 as the date for completion of acceptance, the admissions director also adds to group involvement; in the author's opinion the most important single factor in attaining the quota goals. It is the admissions team which obtains a class, not the dean or director.

As a second major consideration, the admissions officer must constantly reflect on his projections. At Northeastern University the admissions director spends one hour a week every week checking projections against developing factors such as a diminishing applications pool or excessive rejection rates. In addition, summer shrinkage must be figured before it occurs and mailings must be made during the summer to assure that nothing is occurring to negate the predictions made.

In conclusion, the director must not become defensive about his figures. There is the natural tendency to "do or die with my projections." If he is observant of trends, if he recognizes his awesome responsibility, if he is flexible in terms of that responsibility, if he checks on his calculations frequently—then he has the exciting satisfaction of knowing that he has added quality to his university.

CONTROL OF DORMITORY QUOTA

Those colleges and universities which provide residence facilities must be careful that the number of new dormitory students will neither exceed nor be less than the number of available spaces. Necessary to effective planning is institutional policy with reference to those students who live within commuting distances but who, for one reason or another, prefer to live in dormitories. In general, a strict policy which prevents local area students from living on campus is unwise. Many such students need the experience of dormitory life and, in fact, may choose to enter another college if residence on campus is denied them. Dormitory construction which provides some flexibility in the availability of rooms is highly desirable since, however careful the planning may be, it will not be possible to determine precisely the number of resident students who will appear to register.

DEPOSITS

It is common practice among all colleges and universities to require a deposit as concrete evidence of a student's intention to enroll. This is generally agreed to be an important control device. It is usually nonreturnable and may vary in amount from $50 to $100 or more. Two such deposits are frequently required: one is applied to tuition costs and one to the costs of residence. Normally, such deposits are required on May 1, commonly referred to as the "candidates' reply date," a date agreed upon by most colleges which are members of the College Entrance Examination Board. A few institutions require deposits one month after notice of acceptance has been sent to the applicant. This practice, however, is generally frowned upon since it imposes a financial hardship in certain cases and forces students to make college decisions before they have heard from all those institutions to which they have applied. Extension of time for payment of the deposit(s) is generally favored as a practice by those colleges whose reply date falls earlier than May 1.

It should be emphasized that there are those who believe that deadline dates were created to be ignored. For this reason, the department of admissions should establish procedures designed to remind accepted students that they failed to submit deposits as requested.

It should be recognized that the policy of requiring deposits, as logical as it may be, still is a source of public relations problems. Despite careful and conspicuous statements in college catalogs and other literature to the effect that the deposit is not returnable, the director of admissions can expect a number of refund requests. It is important, therefore, that there be a clearly defined policy to enable him to handle such requests effectively. The institution may favor a refund policy in cases of proven financial hardship, entrance into military service, or illness. A referral form for use between admissions and the financial office of the college, through which refund action can be recommended or disapproved, can be an effective instrument (see Figure 4).

DEPARTMENT OF ADMISSIONS
MEMORANDUM

____
DATE

TO: Professor Roberts, Comptroller

FROM: Dean Garland

SUBJECT: Request for Return of Deposit(s)

ADMISSIONS DEPARTMENT RECOMMENDATION:

____

____

____

____

____

GCG

Fig. 4 *Referral form.*

It is common practice for students to apply for admission to a number of colleges so that acceptance by at least one institution is assured. Secondary school counselors generally encourage students to apply to no more than three to five colleges, although in some instances applications may be submitted to seven or eight. It is possible, therefore, that the names of accepted students will appear in common on the prefreshman rosters of several colleges.

Colleges which boast a remarkable control over the number of new students who appear to register and which consistently are able to report maximum enrollments on target point to a weekly study of admission activity and a constant follow-up of prefreshman plans through the late spring and summer months. A final declaration of intention to enroll with an enclosed return postal card, mailed in the late spring, is an effective device to ensure that the candidate has not changed his mind after having paid his deposits (see Figure 5). At the same time the university ascertains whether any

June 5, 1968

Dear Student,

We want to thank you for submitting your deposit(s) to us. Prior to mailing our registration information to entering freshmen, we are conducting a final survey in order to verify your intention to enroll this fall.

Will you kindly fill out the attached postal card and return it to us as soon as possible.

Gilbert C. Garland
Dean of Admissions

PLEASE REPLY PROMPTLY DATE____________________

☐ I plan to register at the Suburban Campus of Northeastern University on Wednesday, September 11, 1968.

☐ My plans have changed and I do not intend to register at Northeastern University this fall.

I have been accepted to:

____________________ ____________________
Program of Studies Major Field

Fig. 5 *Declaration of intention card.*

accepted student now has plans to change his major. He can then be called for counseling concerning this matter. In the early summer appropriate registration information of the sort usually sent to accepted freshmen, is, therefore, mailed to a roster of students which is as completely accurate as possible (see Figure 6).

Dear Entering Freshman:

This information is sent to all those students who have indicated their intentions to enroll at Northeastern this fall. If there has been any sudden change in your plans, we would appreciate your notifying us to this effect as promptly as possible.

Freshman Registration at the University will take place on Tuesday, September 10, 1968, at 8:45 a.m. At this time you are expected to report to the main campus, in front of Richards Hall, for complete registration information. The Orientation Period for all freshmen extends from Registration Day on Tuesday through the remainder of the week. Attendance at all registration sessions is required.

During the second week of August you will receive the following bills dated for August 26, 1968 payment. It will facilitate your busy orientation period if you will endeavor to make your payment by mail for the first term promptly.

$365.00 Tuition for Quarter 1 (This assumes that the $100 tuition deposit has previously been paid.)

25.00 Health Services fee – required of all students.

329.00 For students who live in dormitories. This includes board and room for Orientation Week and **Term 1**- (Assumes that the $100 residence deposit has previously been paid.)

12.50 Student Center Fee

10.00 Infirmary Fee (Required of all students who live in dormitories.)

10.00 ROTC deposit (Required for all students who plan to enroll in the ROTC program.)

Special tuition arrangements apply to students who are recipients of scholarship aid.

The following payments are to be made in person: The Bursar's Office, located on the second floor of Richards Hall, is open every weekday from 8:30 a.m. to 4:30 p.m. during the month of August. Students visiting the University prior to registration are urged to make the following applicable deposit or fee payments at the Cashier's Office:

$1.00 Locker deposit for all students desiring lockers.

$ .25 Parking permit for students who plan to commute and use University parking areas.
15.00 Laboratory deposit card for students planning to enroll in chemistry laboratory course.

Students who wish to make payments by mail prior to registration should make checks payable to Northeastern University and mail to Bursar, 249 Richards Hall, Northeastern University, 360 Huntington Avenue, Boston, Massachusetts 02115. Enclose appropriate bills so that your account can be credited properly.

Fig. 6 *Registration information for entering freshmen.*

For your convenience in making plans for the continuation of your studies after Quarter 1, you will find below the expenses you will need to have in mind:

$465.00	Tuition for Quarter 2	Due December 9, 1968
396.00	Board and Room for Quarter 2 (if applicable)	Due December 9, 1968
10.00	Infirmary Fee (if applicable)	Due December 9, 1968
12.50	Student Center fee	Due December 9, 1968
465.00	Tuition for Quarter 3	Due March 17, 1969
396.00	Board and Room for Quarter 3 (if applicable)	Due March 17, 1969
10.00	Infirmary Fee (if applicable)	Due March 17, 1969
12.50	Student Center fee	Due March 17, 1969

Purchase of Textbooks: The Orientation Schedule which you will receive on September 10 indicates when your textbooks and other supplies may be purchased from the University Bookstore. For your guidance approximate costs will be as follows:

For students in	Engineering	$50 - 75
	Business Adm.	50 - 55
	Liberal Arts	45 - 55
	Education	45 - 55
	Criminal Justice	45 - 55
	Pharmacy	
	Boston - Bouvé	55 - 60
	Nursing	

All purchases made at the Bookstore must be paid for either by check made payable to the Northeastern University Bookstore or by cash.

All required supplies, including Gym equipment (approximately $10), may be purchased at the Bookstore. Students who find it possible to do so are encouraged to purchase books and supplies prior to registration, thus avoiding waiting at the counter. Such purchases may be made on or after Monday, August 26.

SPECIAL INFORMATION: All freshmen must have completed registration steps and purchased their books and supplies so they may start classes on Tuesday, September 17.

Students receiving financial aid from outside sources (i.e. local awards, industrial scholarships, loans, etc.) should contact the Office of the Bursar either prior to or during registration.

On or before August 12, all students who plan to reside in dormitories will receive definite notice of their room assignments.

You are reminded that your Health Questionnaire must be returned to the University Health Services prior to registration.

If you have other questions not anwsered in this communication, you will find that Admissions Counselors, the Dean of Freshmen, and student guides will be glad to assist you during Registration. Please bring with you a pen to be used in filling out necessary forms. We are looking forward to greeting you.

Gilbert C. Garland
Dean of Admissions

Fig. 6 (*Continued*)

Chapter 3

Admissions—Public Relations

GILBERT C. GARLAND

Dean of Admissions, Northeastern University, Boston, Massachusetts

EUGENE S. WILSON

Dean of Admission, Amherst College, Amherst, Massachusetts

INTRODUCTION

There can be no question that public relations is one of the chief areas of responsibility for any dean or director of admissions. The very nature of admissions counseling requires a keen sense of interpersonal relationships as one speaks to students, parents, alumni groups, and faculty. To the person with whom he communicates, the admissions counselor *is* the institution he represents. It is important, therefore, that he be knowledgeable, skilled in the art of communication, and sensitive to the pulse of the many publics he serves.

As the counselor presents his college to various groups, but particularly to students, he should realize that there is no single track to the promotion of interest in his college or university. Most counselors today use a wide variety of approaches and methods of communication in helping these groups gain a better knowledge of their colleges.

THE COLLEGE CATALOG AND OTHER INFORMATIONAL LITERATURE

The typical college catalog has long been considered a factual publication of interest to upperclass students but a somewhat uninspiring piece of reading material for those still in secondary school. A specially designed catalog for freshmen, however, has proved very effective in helping students to bridge the gap between high school and college. Such a publication, attractively prepared, can provide both verbal and pictorial information which will be important to the entering freshman. It may include copy related to entrance requirements, financial aid, student activities, and programs of study. Equally important, it may provide information related to educational and career interests, and in so doing it will serve effectively as a guidance tool. (See Figure 1.) The young adult who is interested in the study of biology, for example, will find helpful copy devoted to the nature of the curriculum, the types of employment in which he might ultimately be engaged, and a statement of current placement opportunities in the field. The development of a freshman catalog should not be undertaken with the thought of cost saving for this is unlikely to occur. It is an acknowledged fact, however, that professional associations and acknowledged educational leaders have long been critical of the typical college catalog as it appears on the shelves of most libraries today. Missing are such important facts as how courses are taught and graded, what criteria are employed in assessing applicants, how students fare academically, and what enterprises graduates enter.

Sandwiched between catalogs and sometimes on a special shelf are the college view books and/or college yearbooks. The former always show happy teachers and happy students engaged in the joyful pursuit of learning. Rarely is the hard work and the drudgery of learning hinted at. As harbingers of the realities of college life, they are often misleading and inaccurate. College administrators who are contemplating the publication of a new view book or the revision of an old one should visit the local high school guidance office and inspect the current crop of promotional literature.

The most important and the most helpful communication from college to counselor is the annual college profile or report on the freshman class. This profile, usually issued in September or early October, presents statistical data that enable counselors to give students some estimate of their chances for admission.

Counselors are pretty well agreed that profiles should include all or most of the following information:

1. Number of applications filed, number of applicants accepted, and number who actually enroll.

2. In three vertical columns headed "applied," "accepted," and "enrolled," a distribution by regular intervals of results on the College Board tests or the American College Tests.

3. Three columns with headings indicating quartile, quintile, or decile standings of applicants.

4. Percentage distribution according to public and independent schools.

5. In the case of colleges with national representation, a listing by states of applicants' geographical origin.

6. A description of the new class's academic and occupational interests. Though interests change during four years of college, figures of this sort tell counselors what kinds of aspirations freshmen take to college.

7. Brief statistics on the academic performance of the previous year's freshman

class. These should include class averages by quartiles, number of dropouts, and types of dropouts (i.e., academic, disciplinary, or voluntary).

8. Some brief account of number of freshmen granted financial aid and size of awards.

9. Comments on changes in course offerings, grading practices, new physical plant, etc.

10. Information on qualities most desired in students and factors that influence the decisions of admissions committee.

Prescription Pharmacy Laboratory

PHARMACEUTICAL SCIENCES LABORATORIES

THE COLLEGE OF PHARMACY is housed in the new Mugar Life Sciences Building on the Main Campus of the University, where the services of all other divisions of the University are available to the students. This wing, completed in the fall of 1963, was built and equipped at a cost of $2,250,000 and is considered to be one of the finest physical facilities devoted to pharmaceutical education.

Four floors of the five-story wing contain staff offices, classrooms, animal quarters, storerooms, and fully equipped laboratories for undergraduate instruction in General and Physical Pharmacy, Manufacturing Pharmacy, Prescription Pharmacy, Pharmacy Administration, Medicinal Chemistry, Pharmacognosy, and Pharmacology.

In addition, specially designed laboratories are available to graduate students and faculty in the aforementioned areas of instruction. Also, a modern and well-equipped radio-isotope laboratory is available for instruction and research in radiological health.

Scene in the Pharmacology Laboratory.

Fig. 1 *Example of catalog which supplies career information, from Northeastern University Freshman Catalog.*

they effectively meet the needs of students, parents, and visiting counselors. Those colleges which have adopted admissions conferences have found it possible to devote greater attention to the individual applicant as he seeks a personal interview.

The guided tour is a particularly effective method of helping interested students to appreciate the physical aspects of the campus. With carefully selected, enrolled students serving as guides, visitors are able to inspect classrooms, laboratories, and other facilities. Together, the admissions conference and the guided tour have proved to be highly successful means of orienting interested students to the college or university scene. In this regard, the college should give careful thought to the publication of a campus guide for the convenience of visitors.

THE COLLEGE OPEN HOUSE AS A PROMOTIONAL DEVICE

The familiar open-house type of program, thoughtfully structured, can serve as an excellent guidance and promotional tool in that visiting students and school counselors may speak directly with teaching faculty and departmental heads, receiving thereby an in-depth appreciation of educational opportunities and facilities. In a large college or university, the open-house program may be devoted to a particular area of study, such as engineering, or it may embrace all areas of study offered by the institution. Such a program provides a unique opportunity for the several faculties of the college to cooperate in planning efforts and to bring them more directly in contact with a secondary school audience. (See Figure 2.)

COLLEGE DAY-NIGHT PROGRAMS

During the late spring, summer, and early fall, admissions personnel may expect to receive many requests to participate in school-sponsored college-day or college-night programs. Such events may be jointly sponsored by a number of secondary schools in a given geographical area or they may be sponsored by a single school. They are viewed with mixed emotions by admissions personnel, for some are well organized and conducted while others can best be described as confusing or even chaotic Again, some have a distinctly commercial flavor while others are soundly based in the best student personnel tradition. In any event, the properly conducted college day-night program may have real recruitment-promotional possibilities which should not be ignored.

OTHER STUDENT PROMOTIONAL PROGRAMS

In attempting to attract qualified students, the college's news or press bureau may provide a strong assist to admissions personnel by releasing hometown news stories about enrolled students or local students who intend to enroll. Press releases may concern on-campus functions, visits of admissions personnel to area secondary schools, facilities under construction, ground-breaking and dedication exercises, and new programs of instruction. Closely related to such news stories are the activities of the college's public relations personnel. As institutional programs, both on and off campus, are planned, it is important to keep in mind the needs and interests of the college-bound, young adult audience. The dynamic, forward-looking institution will prosper as it recognizes and implements its role of service to the local and broader community and as it makes those services known to and appreciated by its several publics.

For suggested readings see page 3-23.

Northeastern University

College of Business Administration
College of Education
College of Engineering
College of Liberal Arts
College of Nursing
College of Pharmacy
Boston-Bouvé College
Physical Therapy
Physical Education
Recreation

EXHIBITS — DEMONSTRATIONS
CAMPUS TOURS
ADMISSIONS CONFERENCES
PROVIDED HOURLY
THROUGHOUT THE DAY.

Program

This Open House Program is planned to give interested students, parents, and guidance counselors an opportunity to become better acquainted with the new facilities and programs of study at Northeastern University.

You are cordially invited to inspect at your leisure the laboratories and classrooms of all our colleges and to visit other areas especially designed to meet the academic and extracurricular activity needs of Northeastern students.

The Cafeteria and Snack Bar in the new addition to the Ell Student Center will be available for the convenience of guests.

Fig. 2 *Open House invitation sent to all applicants and to area guidance counselors, from Northeastern University Department of Admissions.*

Chapter 4

Admissions—Internal Liaison with Administration, Faculty, Student, and Alumni Groups

EUGENE S. WILSON

Dean of Admission, Amherst College, Amherst, Massachusetts

ROLE OF THE ADMISSIONS OFFICER IN LONG-RANGE PLANNING AND DECISION MAKING

The admissions officer, because of his extensive knowledge of developments in feeder institutions, secondary schools, and junior colleges, can contribute important information to committees of faculty and administration which are concerned with the future of the institution. These committees are involved, for instance, with the size of the college, finances and costs, financial aid, orientation, curriculum, counseling and guidance, and research.

The admissions officer need not be an active member of any or all of these committees, but there are times when the information and experience of an admissions officer can contribute to sound planning and decisions.

For example, several years ago the engineering faculty of a large university, impressed by the number of applications for engineering, voted without consulting the admissions officer to require calculus and proficiency in a foreign language of all accepted candidates. When the dean of the engineering faculty informed the admissions officer of the new requirements, the admissions officer said, "Under this new requirement you will have 33 percent fewer students; which third of your faculty are you planning to drop?" The dean was skeptical until the punch cards for freshmen were run through the sorter, and then he discovered that 34 percent of his new class had not met his faculty's new requirements. When the dean reported this information back to his faculty, it rescinded its recently voted demands and decided to continue with the old requirements.

REPORTING TO THE PRESIDENT AND OTHER ADMINISTRATIVE OFFICERS

An admissions officer serves without tenure at the pleasure of the president who appointed him and the board of trustees. The admissions officer should make an annual report to the president, with copies for administrative officers and the faculty. This report should give important statistics on the applicant group, the admitted group, and the matriculated group. Trends and developments in feeder schools should be noted in the report. Recommendations for changes in admission practices, procedures in curriculum development, and in care of students should be presented in this annual report.

PARTICIPATION IN MEETINGS OF ACADEMIC FACULTIES

The admissions officer should have faculty status, including voting rights and a comparable pay scale. He should be expected to attend faculty meetings so that he may offer his special knowledge if needed and so that he can be fully aware of developments in his own institution—developments he must often interpret to applicants, parents, and the counselors in feeder schools. The admissions officer must be the kind of individual who can be trusted with confidential information of the sort which often comes out in faculty meetings.

NEED TO KEEP ABREAST OF CURRICULUM DEVELOPMENTS, PARTICULARLY THOSE WHICH AFFECT THE FRESHMAN YEAR

The admissions officer, through his conversations with applicants and secondary school counselors, gathers information on curricular developments in feeder institutions—developments which often have special meaning to the college curriculum committee.

New secondary school programs have been introduced in the last 10 years in languages, mathematics, social studies, physics, chemistry, and biology. New honors and advanced placement programs have been initiated in many public and private schools, and now independent-study programs are gaining popular attention in the schools of the nation. The admissions officer should interpret these curricular changes and developments to appropriate college faculty committees so that articulation between schools and colleges may have order and sequence. Able students will shun colleges whose curriculums require repetitive learning experiences or curriculums which fail to capitalize on the advanced academic work and learning experiences now offered in many secondary schools.

USE OF ALUMNI AND UNDERGRADUATES IN STUDENT RECRUITMENT

The two strongest aids to the admissions officer in the recruitment of students are the alumni and the undergraduates.

The cooperation of undergraduates is encouraged in the following ways:

1. Freshmen give the admissions office names of qualified and interested students in the senior classes of their secondary schools.
2. Undergraduates communicate with their secondary school teachers and counselors about the advantages of their own college.
3. Undergraduates act as hosts to applicants from their old school.
4. Undergraduates follow up applicants from their old school when they are given the names of candidates by the admissions office.

Alumni recruitment should be directed by the admissions office and can be successful if the following program is introduced:

1. Alumni recruiters must be given monthly bulletins with up-to-date information on all aspects of admissions and college life.
2. Alumni recruitment should be coordinated through a special committee of alumni, and state or regional directors under the special committee.
3. Alumni recruiters should be encouraged to visit the campus as often as possible.
4. Admissions staff should meet with regional groups of alumni recruiters whenever travel plans make this possible.
5. Alumni recruiters must be aware of their role—they are talent scouts, and as such they may make recommendations to the admissions committee which, however, makes the final decisions.
6. Alumni recruiters must be kept informed of the action taken on their prospects by the admissions committee.
7. All alumni should be kept informed on the admissions situation by occasional articles and reports in the alumni magazine. The more competitive the admissions situation, the greater the chance of a misunderstanding between the admissions committee and the alumni.
8. Children of alumni and faculty should be given an opportunity to receive special counseling from the admissions staff on college selection at the end of grade eleven. If the child of an alumnus or faculty member is not qualified, the sooner this information is relayed to the candidate and family the less chance there is for serious misunderstanding.
9. The admissions officer should take advantage of every chance to speak to alumni at meetings about the admission situation.

For suggested readings see page 3-23.

Chapter 5

Special Problems of Admissions

EUGENE S. WILSON

Dean of Admission, Amherst College, Amherst, Massachusetts

WHO SELECTS FOR ADMISSIONS

What control on admissions decisions can or should be exercised by the trustees, the president, the faculty, alumni, politicians (in the case of state universities), or coaches? Since the answer to this question will determine much in the admission process, the answer should be made after very careful thought and should be known and understood by all members of the college family.

Our discussions over the years with admissions officers in all kinds of colleges and universities convince us that there is only one satisfactory answer to this question—the admissions committee must bear the responsibility for acceptances and rejections. Any other policy will not only undermine the confidence of the admissions staff but will in time bring injury, misunderstanding, and recriminations to the parties in a position to make exceptions.

Influential individuals who have special reasons for wanting to see applicants admitted should be encouraged and required to acquaint the admissions committee with their reasons for sponsoring these applicants, confident that the admissions committee, aware of the total needs of the college and the academic ability of the candidate, will make decisions in the best interests of the college. Students who are clearly unqualified academically should be rejected regardless of sponsorship. Time and again colleges have discovered, after accepting a heavily sponsored student and then dismissing him for academic insufficiencies, that not only have they injured the student but the important sponsor also has turned against the college for admitting the very student he so heartily recommended.

WHICH TESTS FOR ADMISSIONS

Should applicants be required to take tests given by the College Entrance Examination Board (CEEB), the American College Testing Program (ACT), or the State Testing Agency? There is no one right answer to this question; the answer will be uncovered after a study of the advantages and disadvantages of each testing program with a quick glance at which tests competing institutions require.

The one guideline should be: Don't establish firm requirements which shut out qualified candidates. For example, a college in a state which operates a strong testing program, a state where both ACT and CEEB are active, might announce its willingness to accept from applicants any one of these three programs, leaving the choice to the individual candidate. The same approach should control the establishment of deadlines for tests. If a college needs candidates there is no reason to announce firm deadlines. Competitive colleges usually stipulate a fixed deadline for tests, but almost all of these colleges will make exceptions for good reasons, as when an unusual candidate appears at the gate after the deadline.

INTERVIEWS ON CAMPUS

The rush to college has brought an interview crisis to many college admission centers. The interview on campus may provide data for assessment, but it also offers counseling to potential applicants and an opportunity for a college to present its case to the public. The number of individual interviews granted will be determined by the space, time, and personnel available. Most colleges try to accommodate all the visitors to the admissions office and, when under undue pressure, invite faculty members to help with the interviewing. Sometimes a peak period can be handled by shortening the interview from the standard thirty minutes to fifteen or by arranging group meetings. When group meetings are used, admissions counselors as a rule remain available to students and parents for special questioning after the group sessions.

A typical program for group meetings might be as follows:

1. Presentation of information about the college
2. Presentation of information about admission procedures
3. Question period

Inasmuch as 60 to 95 percent of the strongest candidates will visit a college, the admissions staff must be prepared to:

1. Give prompt attention to all requests for interviews
2. Afford courteous treatment to drop-ins who call without appointments
3. Afford honest, considerate, sensitive counseling to all candidates and their parents

CAMPUS GUIDES

Proper attention to the needs of visitors requires a student guide service during the hours the admissions office is open. Some colleges use volunteer guides; others pay their guides as part of a student employment program. Some colleges have guide services on Saturday afternoons and Sundays when the admissions office is closed.

Whatever program for guide service is adopted, information on this service should be broadcast to the college community. Guides should have some orientation and preparation for their work, and this orientation should include the reading of the history of the college.

ENFORCEMENT OF CONFERENCE REGULATIONS WITH REFERENCE TO THE ADMISSION OF ATHLETES

The admissions staff should be familiar with the regulations governing the admission of athletes in the conference in which the college operates The admissions committee should adhere strictly to the conference regulations and not permit itself to be swayed by the eager recommendations of coaches. As a rule the coaches will be the first to spot violations in other institutions, but occasionally the admissions office can uncover such irregularities. This information should be given to the president of the institution for special handling.

QUESTIONNAIRES SEEKING INFORMATION ABOUT COLLEGES

The admissions officer and other administrative officers are flooded with questionnaires from all kinds of individuals and organizations, questionnaires seeking information on admissions statistics. The temptation is to heave these in the wastepaper basket, but it is suggested that all questionnaires be completed and returned promptly on the grounds that if a college itself does not complete the questionnaires, the individual or sponsoring organization will, and it is far better to have a college present itself as it wishes to be presented rather than have some outside agency prepare informational data for public distribution.

For suggested readings see page 3-23.

Chapter 6

The Mechanics of Admissions

JOHN C. HOY

Vice Chancellor—Student Affairs, University of California at Irvine, Irvine, California

INTRODUCTION

B. Alden Thresher, Dean Emeritus of Admissions at M.I.T., has described the annual college admissions process in the United States as "the great sorting." Clearly the procedures for handling the multiple applications of more than two million students must be partner to systematic and "mechanical" processes. However, "mechanical" approaches need not be construed as impersonal. Indeed, an accurate, efficient, well-balanced system of processing, formulating, and reporting information about human beings can increase the degree of individualized and equitable attention each candidate for college receives prior to the actual determination of the decision to accept or reject his application. Present computer hardware permits a far more extensive process of evaluation than colleges presently use. Technology is far ahead of the admissions procedures and systems of virtually all colleges in the United States, and during the next decade college personnel will increasingly discover more complete and humanistic ways to use this technology if they choose to do so.

USE OF DATA PROCESSING AND COMPUTER PROGRAMMING

The example given here is but one of the many formats used by admissions offices across the country. The approach in this instance is to ready a docket for committee use in the decision-making process, and the final decision on a candidate is based on the judgment of responsible individuals who can fill in the gaps by reason of their experience and the availability of additional non-computer based information. The system is tailored to the priorities given to the process by the particular institution involved. (See Figure 1.) The following list explains the code used in entering information on the form shown in Figure 1.

Line 1
  Name, City and State
Line 2
  School
Line 3 (coded information)
  Rank–Class = e.g., 10 in a class of 100
  %ile = 90%
  E.D. = Early decision applicant
  Alum = Son of an alumnus
  Parent = Parental status – living, deceased, divorced
  Sport = Interest in athletics
  Major I = First choice of major
  Major II = Second choice of major
  Career = Career preference
  G.D.R. = Guidance director rating
  S = Guidance director rating as a *student*
  P = Guidance director rating as a *person*
  O = Guidance director rating *overall*
  T.R. = Teacher recommendation rating
  Interview = Interview with staff or alumnus
  A = Academic rating
  P = Personal rating
  E = Extracurricular rating
  A = Intellectual curiosity rating
  % D = Overall interview rating
  SAT Scores = Scholastic Aptitude Test
  V = Verbal [576 = 58]
  M = Math [623 = 62]
Line 4
  ACH Scores = CEEB Achievement Test
  Code & Score = Title and score of test
  Read = Staff reader or evaluator of actual full application
  % A = Academic percentile rating
  % NA = Nonacademic percentile rating
  Cum %ile = Average overall rating
  CSS Need = College Scholarship Service need evaluation
  Wes Need = Wesleyan need evaluation

DEAN

WESLEYAN UNIVERSITY

ADMISSIONS—CANDIDATE REPORT

STUDENT NAME	CITY & STATE
Line #1	
SCHOOL NAME	
Line #2	

RANK	CLASS	% ILE	E.D.	ALUM	$ $	RACE	PARENT	SPORT	MAJOR I	MAJOR II	CAREER	G.D.R. S.	P.	O.	TR	TR	AR	INTERVIEW A	P	E	A	%D	S.A.T. SCORES DATE	V	M	V	M
Line #3																											

ACH SCORES CODE & SCORE	CODE & SCORE	CODE & SCORE	CODE & SCORE	CODE & SCORE		READ	% A	% NA	READ	% A	% NA	READ	% A	% NA	READ	% A	% NA	READ	% A	% NA	CUM % ILE	CSS NEED	WES NEED
Line #4																							

STUDENT NAME	CITY & STATE
MICHAEL L BRIGGS	SEYMOUR MASS
SCHOOL NAME	
MEMORIAL H S	

RANK	CLASS	% ILE	E.D.	ALUM	$ $	RACE	PARENT	SPORT	MAJOR I	MAJOR II	CAREER	G.D.R. S.	P.	O.	TR	TR	AR	INTERVIEW A	P	E	A	%D	S.A.T. SCORES DATE	V	M	V	M
168	271	60					1	0	20	64	30	4	4	4	4	0		2	2	3	2	84	7	74	77		

ACH SCORES CODE & SCORE	CODE & SCORE	CODE & SCORE	CODE & SCORE	CODE & SCORE		READ	% A	% NA	READ	% A	% NA	READ	% A	% NA	READ	% A	% NA	READ	% A	% NA	CUM % ILE	CSS NEED	WES NEED
A 60	H 72	Q 60				1	82	83	2	82	82												

STUDENT NAME	CITY & STATE
RICHARD C OHERN	RIVER N J
SCHOOL NAME	
RIVER SR H S	

RANK	CLASS	% ILE	E.D.	ALUM	$ $	RACE	PARENT	SPORT	MAJOR I	MAJOR II	CAREER	G.D.R. S.	P.	O.	TR	TR	AR	INTERVIEW A	P	E	A	%D	S.A.T. SCORES DATE	V	M	V	M
6	384	5	1	1	1		1	9	73	79	73	5	5	5	3	0		3	2	1		85	7	73	75		

ACH SCORES CODE & SCORE	CODE & SCORE	CODE & SCORE	CODE & SCORE	CODE & SCORE		READ	% A	% NA	READ	% A	% NA	READ	% A	% NA	READ	% A	% NA	READ	% A	% NA	CUM % ILE	CSS NEED	WES NEED
A 71	Q 79					1	91	84	2	89	83								87	79		1530	

STUDENT NAME	CITY & STATE
VICTOR M BARNET	MIDDLEVILLE VA
SCHOOL NAME	
CITY H S	

RANK	CLASS	% ILE	E.D.	ALUM	$ $	RACE	PARENT	SPORT	MAJOR I	MAJOR II	CAREER	G.D.R. S.	P.	O.	TR	TR	AR	INTERVIEW A	P	E	A	%D	S.A.T. SCORES DATE	V	M	V	M
17	114	10	1	1	1		1	0	60	65	60	4	4	4	3	2			3	4	2	76	7	48	68	46	64

ACH SCORES CODE & SCORE	CODE & SCORE	CODE & SCORE	CODE & SCORE	CODE & SCORE		READ	% A	% NA	READ	% A	% NA	READ	% A	% NA	READ	% A	% NA	READ	% A	% NA	CUM % ILE	CSS NEED	WES NEED
A 52	E 42	Q 65	A 57	E 45		5	75	81	1	71	75	2	71	78	4	65	75					2000	

Fig. 1 *Wesleyan University Candidate Report sheet enables Admissions Committee to look at any category as a group. See explanation of abbreviations in text.*

It is possible to gather quickly and accurately, through standard data processing approaches, a wide variety of significant information.

For example, if the admissions staff wish to review all alumni sons as a group, or all the candidates from Iowa, or all the tentative physics majors as a group, printed "dockets" can be prepared in this fashion.

School groups, test-score averages, career preferences, athletic interest, or scholarship awards can be pulled together in the same fashion.

Each admissions office will, of course, wish to design its own format and approach to information retrieval, but in each instance the result should be better-informed decision making.

An interesting new development is the use of the computer to aid students in selecting colleges which meet their particular requirements.

This system, so far used experimentally in certain areas of the country, will soon spread nationally, because of the interest of such organizations as the College Board and the Association of College Admissions Counselors, as well as various private, profit-making guidance organizations.

First, the student fills out a questionnaire covering at least three hundred factors of concern to students and counselors. Then, on the basis of the student's answers, information about him is punched on a card which is fed to the computer. The computer then prints out a suggested list of colleges which fulfill the requirements of the student. As a variation, through terminals located in guidance offices of participating schools the student can type coded questions for the computer, which has stored in it hundreds of thousands of pieces of information about various colleges and universities.

Although it is still too early to make accurate assessments of this system, it can be said that if the system is properly utilized, it offers the advantage of allowing the counselor to use his time more economically. Counselors simply cannot have at their fingertips all the information that a student may require about colleges and universities. As the student narrows his choices by use of the computer, rather than function as an information giver, the counselor can spend more time in actual counseling. However, counselors must make sure that realistic questions are being asked of the computer by the student. Otherwise, decisions will be based on faulty premises. Also, the sponsors of computer systems must make certain that computer information about colleges is current.

As a by-product research surveys will be conducted by colleges to evaluate student answers to computer questionnaires. This should give college administrators insight into factors of vital concern to applicants.

Professional admissions organizations, secondary school guidance counselors, and the public in general will watch developments in this area with great interest.

DEVELOPMENT AND SUPERVISION OF ADMISSIONS PROCEDURES

The Application Process Each institution develops procedures designed to gather the kind of information it requires and to process such data in an accurate and efficient manner.

The following forms are chosen as representative of those used at a number of institutions. Depending on the complexity of criteria used, some forms may be added and others eliminated.

The Candidate's Autobiographical Form (Figure 2)
The Secondary School Report (Figure 3)
Teacher Recommendation Form (Figure 4)
The Interview Form (Figure 5)

Information from these forms can be collated and evaluated through data processing, as described earlier.

The "Laundry List" or Checklist (Figure 6) In order that applications may be completed on time, it is essential that candidates be informed whether all necessary information is complete or whether parts of the applications are missing.

A checklist is usually sufficient for this purpose and helpful to the candidate as well as essential for accurate staff programming.

THE UNIVERSITY OF CHICAGO
OFFICE OF ADMISSIONS AND AID
CHICAGO, ILLINOIS 60637

APPLICATION FOR ADMISSION TO THE COLLEGE

Class of 1973

NAME Mr. / Mrs. / Miss ....
First *Middle* *Last*

HOME ADDRESS ....
Street and Number *Telephone*

....
City *State and Zip Code*

MAILING ADDRESS ....
Street and Number *Telephone*

....
City *State and Zip Code*

INSTRUCTIONS

To be considered for admission each candidate must submit:

1. *The Application for Admission to the College.* This form, including the inclosed cards, is to be completed carefully by the candidate and sent to the Director of Admissions and Aid, The University of Chicago, Chicago, Illinois 60637. Please use ink or typewriter.

NOTE.—*The inclosed cards are an important part of your application.*

2. *Secondary-School Transcript and Recommendation Request Card.* This form, inclosed herewith, should be filled in and returned with this application to the Director of Admissions and Aid.

3. *Scores on the Scholastic Aptitude Test of the College Entrance Examination Board.* Applications for these tests may be secured from secondary-school counselors or directly from the Educational Testing Service, Box 592, Princeton, New Jersey, 08540, or, for residents of states west of the Rocky Mountains, Box 1025, Berkeley, California, 94701.

4. *Application Fee.* A check or money order payable to the order of The University of Chicago should be sent with the inclosed fee slip directly to the Bursar in the envelope provided. No receipt will be returned. The application fee is not refundable.

Important: If you are applying for transfer from another college or university, check here, and a supplementary information sheet for transfer candidates will be sent to you. ☐

1. Do you wish to be a candidate for Early Decision? ☐ Yes ☐ No

NOTE.—Admission decisions will be granted early to qualified candidates who apply to the University of Chicago as the college of their single choice after their junior year of secondary school, but who do not plan to matriculate at the University until after graduation. Application for Early Decision should be filed after May 15, but before October 15. Early Decisions are announced in mid-November of the candidate's senior year. Consult the *Announcements* of the College or your school counselor for information.

2. Do you wish to be considered for financial aid? ☐ Yes ☐ No

If you answer "Yes" an application for financial aid will be sent to you.

3. List in chronological order *all* schools attended, beginning with the ninth grade of high school. Please make this information complete. If a diploma is pending, please indicate when it will be awarded.

NAME OF SCHOOL AND ADDRESS	DATES OF ATTENDANCE (MONTH-YEAR) From	To	DIPLOMA AND DATE

4. Indicate month and year you have taken or plan to take the Scholastic Aptitude Test ....
The Committee on Admissions asks that applicants take this test in November, December, or January of their senior year. Junior year scores are acceptable.

Fig. 2 *Admissions application form, The University of Chicago, Chicago, Illinois.*

5. If you are a resident of the Chicago area, do you plan to live at home during your first year? ☐ Yes ☐ No

6. Do you plan to attend summer school before entering the College? ☐ Yes ☐ No

If "Yes," where? ....

(Courses taken in college prior to the freshman year will not receive credit toward the Bachelor's degree. They may, however, be helpful in obtaining advanced standing.)

7. How did you first become interested in the College? ....

....

....

8. Have you ever applied before for admission to the University of Chicago? ☐ Yes ☐ No

If "Yes," when? ....

9. Do you have friends or relatives currently at the University? ☐ Yes ☐ No

If "Yes," give their names and positions ....

....

10. To what other colleges have you applied or do you intend to apply? Be sure to indicate any decision that you have received.

College	Decision
....	....
....	....
....	....

11. How many hours a week do you usually study? During school hours .... After school hours ....

12. Have you ever been placed on probation or dismissed from any school? ☐ Yes ☐ No

If "Yes," explain the circumstances here. Please be specific ....

....

....

....

13. Have you read the *Announcements* of the College of the University of Chicago? ☐ Yes ☐ No

14. In what field do you plan to specialize while in the College? .... Undecided ☐

Fig. 2 (*Continued*)

PERSONAL HISTORY

15. Date of birth..Place of birth..

What is your height..Weight..

16. Citizenship..Draft classification..

If you are not a citizen of the United States, what type of visa do you have?..

....

17. If you are married, give the full name of your husband or wife..

....

18. Give father's full name..Is he living?..

Place of birth..Age..

Occupation (If deceased, what was his occupation?)..

College(s) attended..

Degree(s) and year..

19. Give mother's full name..Is she living?..

Place of birth..Age..

If she is employed, what is her occupation?..

College(s) attended..

Degree(s) and year..

20. Give names and ages of your brothers..

Give names and ages of your sisters..

Are any attending colleges? If so, where?..

21. Have any members of your family been associated with the University of Chicago? If so, please state their names, their relationship to you, and their connection with the University..

....

....

22. If only one of your parents, or if any person other than your parents is responsible for you, please give the following information concerning the person to whom first-year grades and other official College communications should be sent.

Name..Relationship to you..

Address..
Street and Number *City* *State and Zip Code*

Fig. 2 (*Continued*)

23. Rate as excellent, good, fair, or poor:

Your general health..

Eyesight........................Hearing........................

Is your speech normal?..

Do you have any physical handicaps that interfere with your studies or extracurricular activities?..

If so, please explain..

....

....

....

SPACE FOR

SIGNED

PHOTOGRAPH

24. Have you ever had a serious illness or a hospitalization that interrupted a school term?........................

If so, please describe it and give dates..

....

....

25. Are you at present receiving medical care of any sort?..............If so, explain........................

....

EMPLOYMENT

26. List all jobs you have held. Include full- and part-time employment and military service.

Firm or Organization and Location	Kind of Work	Inclusive Dates

27. Do you expect to work part-time during the coming academic year? If so, check the appropriate box below.
☐ One or two hours a day ☐ More than two hours a day

Fig. 2 (*Continued*)

INTERESTS AND ACTIVITIES

28. List in order of preference a few books and authors *other than required school readings* that have especially interested you.

29. List in order of preference the magazines or newspapers that you read regularly.

30. List in the order of their importance to you school and community activities in which you have participated and positions or offices that you have held. Indicate the appropriate school year (e.g., 9, 10, 11, or 12).

Fig. 2 *(Continued)*

31. In what activities do you intend to participate in college?

32. If you have received honors or other evidences of high scholarship, citizenship, creative talent, or athletic ability, please list them.

33. Do you have any personal interests that you pursue in your spare time?

34. How did you spend the last two summers?

STATEMENT AND ESSAY

35. Discuss briefly the major influences (people, home life, specific experiences) that have helped to determine your educational objectives and the particular kind of college education you seek.

Fig. 2 *(Continued)*

36. Since the Writing Sample of the College Entrance Examination Board, previously required of all applicants, is no longer available, the Committee on Admissions requests that you fulfil (*a*) or (*b*) below.

a. Please write an essay, not to exceed 500 words, on *one* of the following subjects: 1) The idea of success in America; 2) The importance of knowledge for its own sake; 3) The relevance of the scientific method to the study of the Humanities.

b. Please submit with your application a paper of about 500 words written for one of your junior or senior classes

Date..Candidate's signature..

Parent's or guardian's signature..

(*Signature required if the candidate is under twenty-one.*)

Relationship to candidate..

PLEASE DO NOT USE THE SPACE BELOW

HS2 HS3 HS4 C:Less/1 C:1 C:1+ C:2 C:2+

Reg. ☐ Sch. ☐

Transcripts....................	Disch....................
Recommendations....................	H. Clear....................
App. Fee....................	CSS Form....................
Interview req....................	F.A....................
Interview rec'd....................	Deposit....................
Ph....................	Supp. t/c....................
C.R....................	Cert....................

Register....................

0:1 0:2 0:3

1. .... WN....................
2. .... FN....................
3. ....

68 Apr 15M

Fig. 2 (*Continued*)

Please Complete and Return This Form as Soon as Possible

WESLEYAN UNIVERSITY

SECONDARY SCHOOL REPORT

PART II

Name of Candidate ....
(Please print or type) Last First Middle

Candidate's Address ....
Street Address City State Zip

School ....
Official Name Street Address City State Zip

School Telephone Number ....
Area Code

To the Candidate:

After you have filled in the four lines above, give this form to your principal, headmaster, or college adviser.

To the Principal or College Adviser:

This student is applying for admission to Wesleyan University in 1968. A full and candid report from his school is essential if he is to be given fair consideration. We therefore ask for careful ratings of and comments about his character and ability by a school official who knows him well. An inadequate report may damage the candidate's chances for admission.

Deadlines: Please file this report as soon as possible after you receive it and in any case not later than January 1, 1968. Retain the Mid-Year School Report form to report grades, rank and additional comment for the current school year through the first senior term. The Mid-Year School Report should also reach us by February 10, 1968. Late filing of either of these reports will make careful consideration more difficult.

Rank in Class: It is essential to include in your report a statement of the candidate's rank in class and how it is determined. If this rank is not given, the processing of the application will be delayed and he may not receive full consideration with our other candidates.

The Transcript: A transcript form is included on the back page for your convenience. However, you may send us any legible transcript form which your school currently uses. The transcript should provide at least the following information:

a. Courses taken, year taken, and grades.
b. Courses failed or repeated.
c. Courses currently in progress.
d. Indication of honors, accelerated, and Advanced Placement courses or sections.
e. A brief explanation of your grading system.
f. Test results, such as IQ, NMSQT, CEEB, and Reading.
g. Numerical rank in class. (Please explain which course grades, which school terms, and what course weighting—if any—are considered in the computation of the class rank.)

Mailing Instructions: Please return the completed form to Director of Admissions, Wesleyan University, Middletown, Connecticut 06457

Thank you for your assistance.

ROBERT L. KIRKPATRICK, JR.
DIRECTOR OF ADMISSIONS

As of May 1, 1967, 71 colleges were planning to use this school report form. Space is too limited to list the colleges here, but a list of colleges using the form is available on request.

Questions A1 through C1 of this form are designed so that secondary schools may send similar or duplicated descriptions of a candidate to any of the colleges using this form. We hope this possibility will be helpful to you and will welcome any comment you may have about this experiment, which is now in its fifth year.

Fig. 3 *Candidate submits this part of application to his guidance counselor, who forwards it to Wesleyan.*

A. Intellectual Ability and Achievement

1. How would you rate the candidate as to academic ability and motivation?

	1 Poor	2 Below Average	3	4 Average	5	6 Above Average	7	8 Excellent	9 Truly Superlative
Ability:									
Motivation:									

2. How well does the candidate express himself in:

	1	2	3	4	5	6	7	8	9
(a) Writing?									
(b) Speech?									

3. This candidate ranks { ☐ exactly / ☐ approximately } .... from the top, in a { ☐ class / ☐ college preparatory group }

numbering .... students. This rank covers the period from .... (month year) through .... (month year)

(If precise rank is not available, please indicate approximate rank to the nearest tenth from the top: ....)

Approximately .... per cent of the graduating class expects to attend four-year colleges.

4. Is his record with you a true index of his ability, or have outside circumstances interfered with his academic achievement? (For example: illness, excessive involvement in extracurricular activities, term-time employment, difficult home situation, an overshadowing brother or sister, etc.) If not a true index, please explain in the "Summary and Recommendation" on the opposite page.

B. Character and Personality

1. In making the following ratings, please keep in mind that they will be used to compare this student with other very capable students. Please make them as realistically as you can in comparison with your college preparatory students. We recognize that you may not be able to rate with the precision implied by "top 2 or 3 per cent"; the figures are rough guides only.

	No basis for judgment	Below Average	Average	Good	Excellent (top 10% but not 2 or 3%)	Truly outstanding (top 2 or 3%)		
a.							Energy and Initiative	a.
b.							Independence	b.
c.							Originality	c.
d.							Leadership	d.
e.							Self-confidence	e.
f.							Warmth of Personality	f.
g.							Sense of Humor	g.
h.							Concern for Others	h.
i.							Reaction to Criticism	i.
j.							Reaction to Setbacks	j.
k.							Respect Accorded by Classmates	k.
l.							Respect Accorded by Faculty	l.

2. Has applicant a respected status among fellow students?

The main factors contributing to the respect accorded him seem to be:

☐ superiority in studies ☐ success in athletics ☐ leadership in activities

☐ accomplishment in activities ☐ interest in other students ☐ personality

The main factors contributing to his not being respected seem to be:

☐ superiority in studies ☐ lack of interest in other people ☐ manners, personal habits

☐ conceit ☐ not well known ☐ other (specify)

3. Do you have unqualified confidence in the candidate's integrity? Yes ☐ No ☐
If your confidence is qualified in any way, please explain under "Summary and Recommendation."

4. Has the candidate experienced any physical or emotional disability which affected his performance in school or is likely to do so in college? (If so, please explain fully under "Summary and Recommendation.")
Yes ☐ No ☐

Fig. 3 *(Continued)*

C. Summary and Recommendation

1. Please write a summary appraisal of the candidate, assessing his personal and academic qualities and his promise as a Wesleyan University student. We are particularly interested in evidence about character, relative maturity, independence, his values and the things he is enthusiastic about, and any special talent or quality he possesses. We would like to know about both strong and weak points. Your description of him will become a part of his permanent confidential college file and, if he is admitted, will help us in advising him. Please feel free to insert an additional sheet or to write a separate letter if the space below seems inadequate.

2. I recommend this candidate for admission to Wesleyan University

	not recommended	without enthusiasm	fairly strongly	strongly	enthusiastically
for academic promise:	☐	☐	☐	☐	☐
for character and personal promise:	☐	☐	☐	☐	☐
Overall recommendation:	☐	☐	☐	☐	☐

Signed .... Length of time acquainted with candidate ....

Please Print Name .... Position .... Date ....

Fig. 3 *(Continued)*

Secondary-School Record

Name, in full .... Birth Date ....
Last Name First Name Middle Name

Home Address ....
Number and Street City State Zip

Name of Parent or Guardian .... School accredited by

Entered .... Was graduated / Will be graduated / Withdrew .... Month Year ....
Name of School

....
Month Year Location of School

Class periods are .... minutes, ... times a week, ... weeks a year. Passing mark is .... College recommending mark ....

1. List your complete marking system, highest to lowest: .... Honor marks ....

2. List other secondary schools attended: ....

Are all failing marks for each year listed? ☐ yes ☐ no

CLASS RECORD

Check (√) all subjects where no marks are given.
Star (*) all subjects in progress.

Subject	Grade → / Year → 19	1st Sem 9		1st Sem 10		1st Sem 11		1st Sem 12		Extra		Standard Exams	Units or Cred.
English													
Lang.													
Math.													
Science	Check Special Lab Periods: Yes / No												
Soc. Studies													
Other Subjects													

Notes

Any course designed to prepare students for the College Board Advanced Placement tests should bear the symbol (A.P.)—e.g. Math V (A.P.)
Use extra column for extra school year.
Use exams column for special exams, as Regents, *etc.*

TEST RECORD

	Name and Form of Test	Year Given	Score	%-ile Gr. Level	Basis*
Mental Ability					
Reading					
Achievement					
Others					

ADDITIONAL INFORMATION

*Give available interpretation of tests on an enclosure

Date .... Signature .... Title ....

Permission to use this form granted by the National Association of Secondary-School Principles of the NEA, 1201 Sixteenth Street, N. W., Washington 6, D. C.

Fig. 3 (*Continued*)

WESLEYAN UNIVERSITY

MIDDLETOWN, CONNECTICUT

TEACHER RECOMMENDATION

In Support of Application for Admission

....

Name of Applicant

The above-named student is making application for admission to Wesleyan University and we will appreciate any information you can give us which would aid us in judging his fitness for admission and in dealing sympathetically and understandingly with him after admission.

Whatever you have to say concerning the applicant will be treated as strictly confidential. We shall be most grateful for your frank and full appraisal.

ROBERT L. KIRKPATRICK, JR.
DIRECTOR OF ADMISSIONS

If you are not familiar with Wesleyan . . .

The University — "Wesleyan is a small university of liberal arts and science, independent and nondenominational, committed to helping young men of outstanding character grow in knowledge and wisdom, and in service to their fellow men." This characterization of Wesleyan was written by Past President Victor L. Butterfield in his *Faith of a Liberal College* and is perhaps the most succinct statement of the broad aims of the college.

The small size of the college (1,300 undergraduate students, 200 graduate students and 220 faculty) has helped to encourage extraordinarily close relationships between students and faculty. Wesleyan is noted for curriculum experiments and approaches to independent study which provide the student with the means and opportunity to educate himself. More than a third of the undergraduate classes at Wesleyan are tutorials in which one student and one faculty member work out a special program of study between them. As you know, a liberal arts college is built around the idea that an intensive general education is the best preparation for a satisfying and worthwhile personal and public life. We feel the various programs and departments must be as flexible as possible to give the student a wide range of choices.

The Program — Among the optional undergraduate programs are:

The College Plan, established in 1959, to capitalize on the imagination and energies of students by freeing them from traditional academic requirements and encouraging a more independent and resourceful approach to their studies. It relieves the student of regular classroom schedules, periodic testing and grades but it demands a great deal of reading and writing. The College Plan subjects the student's work to a close criticism by his tutors.

Students who prefer the College Plan to the traditional major may apply for admission to it at the end of the Freshman year. The two independent colleges now established are: The College of Letters, organized around the study of Western literature and The College of Social Studies, which offers a broad program in economics, government, history and philosophy.

The Honors College, a program for seniors of high academic standing who are accepted as candidates for degrees with honors. Each candidate chooses a faculty member to guide him on his own independent research or writing project, such as a long-range original laboratory experiment, the writing of a novel or analysis of the thought of an influential philosopher. Since it is a major undertaking, the student is allowed to reduce some part of his regular academic program. His thesis is usually defended orally before a committee of the faculty.

Humanities and the Integrated Program was organized to provide freshmen with a broad orientation in liberal studies. All freshmen are required to take one or the other. Members of the faculty from every department of the College have participated in these programs which include reading of major works of literature, philosophy, social thought, and religion. Independent study projects, frequent critical papers and workshops in the fine arts are elements of the programs.

The Student — Wesleyan students come from a wide variety of racial, religious, economic, cultural and geographic backgrounds, but have a common desire for a rigorous and demanding academic program. They enjoy hard work, are anxious to contribute something of themselves to the community, and have a desire to develop to the fullest of their abilities. Students at Wesleyan are considered mature and responsible individuals as is most notably reflected in a powerful and extensive student government. Even the honor system, which has been in existence since 1893, is entirely administered by the student body.

Although the college is small and relationships between faculty and student are more intimate and informal than is frequently possible at the college level, both the academic program and the organization of a student's social and personal life requires maturity and self sufficiency. Students must be reasonably able to sustain themselves without close supervision or close direction from adults.

Fig. 4 *Teacher Recommendation form to be forwarded to Wesleyan.*

DIRECTIONS

Please indicate, by a check-mark in the appropriate place opposite each question, the description which you think best fits the applicant. By checking on the line between the descriptive phrases, you may indicate tendencies of varying degrees. Space is provided under each question in which you are encouraged to comment upon your rating. (Specific illustrations in regard to any of your answers would be of real value to us.)

If you dislike this type of questionnaire, please do not hesitate to put your statement in any form you choose.

How long have you known this applicant? ....

What subject did you teach this applicant? ....

Note any other capacity in which you have known applicant (adviser, family-friend, etc.) ....

....

NOTE: A very favorable answer is usually at the right-hand end of the scale, but in some questions it is not in this position.

How easily does student learn?	Learns slowly and with difficulty.	Learns fairly readily.	Learns quickly and with great ease.

COMMENTS:

No opportunity to observe ☐

What standards does student set for himself?	Tends to be slipshod and careless.	Holds self to average set of standards.	Sets unusually high standards for himself.

COMMENTS:

No opportunity to observe ☐

Does student get things done?	Needs prodding.	Does tasks of his own accord.	Finds and does extra work.

COMMENTS:

No opportunity to observe ☐

What creative capacities does student have?	No originality; is plodder; can only imitate.	Average amount of originality.	Great originality and imagination; very talented.

COMMENTS:

No opportunity to observe ☐

Has student genuine sense of integrity?	Cannot be relied on; dishonest in small things.	Usually meets any situation squarely and honestly.	Has integrity of highest order.

COMMENTS:

No opportunity to observe ☐

Has student good emotional control?	Easily over-excited; responds over quickly to emotional stimulus.	Usually well-balanced with good emotional control.	Appears to repress emotional response of any kind; stolid and unresponsive.

COMMENTS:

No opportunity to observe ☐

Has student well-balanced sense of his own worth?			
(a)	Aggressive; demands unreasonable amount of the time of others.	Ambitious, not too self-assertive.	Inclined to be too timid and retiring.
(b)	Sees no faults or lacks in his own work; expects over-praise.	Knows pretty well where his work is strong or weak. Likes to earn praise, but not dependent upon it.	Always underestimates own work; cannot accept even earned praise.

COMMENTS:

No opportunity to observe ☐

Fig. 4 *(Continued)*

If this student's intended line of study is known to you, does it seem reasonable? ....

If not reasonable, please comment ....

In what respect does this student need help in his development? ....

....

....

How would this student react to an environment in which a substantial number of students were equal or superior to him in terms of intellectual ability and accomplishment? ....

....

....

....

....

From your teaching experience with this student and with other students who have successfully prepared for college, would you rate him (underscore) (1) within the group but below the average (2) top half (3) top quarter (4) top 10%?

What strengths are not brought out by this questionnaire?

....

Or weaknesses? ....

....

PLEASE ANSWER ONLY IN CASES WHERE APPLICABLE

If in your judgment this student is a *truly exceptional* applicant to college would you rate him:

Possibly the most capable student in .... years of teaching	Among the few most capable students in .... years of teaching	Among the most capable students in recent classes
☐	☐	☐

Fig. 4 *(Continued)*

Are there any special circumstances the college should know in deciding on admission and in dealing wisely and sympathetically with him if admitted? (Examples: long illnesses, troubling divorce or dissension between parents, over-indulgent parents, dominating relatives, serious emotional difficulty, etc.)

Do you know the program at Wesleyan University (underscore) very well? Somewhat? Very little?

Considering this student's ability, interests, and personality do you recommend admission to Wesleyan University (underscore) Strongly? Moderately? Doubtfully?

We would appreciate knowing it if you have an opinion about a kind of college that might be better suited to his needs and interests.

....

....

Signature ....

Teacher of ....

School Address ....

.... Zip

Date ....

Note

The very great volume of our correspondence prohibits the acknowledgment of your thoughtful comments concerning this applicant. The admissions staff, however, would like to thank you for completing this important form. We have found Teacher References to be of unusual value.

Fig. 4 *(Continued)*

PER CENT OF DESIRABILITY

85-90 = 1 STAR LETTER
91-100 = 2 STAR LETTER

WESLEYAN UNIVERSITY, MIDDLETOWN, CONN.

NAME and ADDRESS

HIGH SCHOOL

ADDRESS

School Counselor or Head

NICK NAME

Interview Situation

Remarks:

Average	Rank in Class	Scholarship? yes maybe no

College Board Scores

Junior Year V M

Senior Year V M

PSAT ENG.

Other Tests

NMSQT —

Alumni, Undergrad, others interested

Career plans

Outstanding talents or accomplishments:

EXCELLENT RAPPORT ☐ GOOD RAPPORT ☐ FAIR ☐ A BIT TENSE ☐ UNSATISFACTORY ☐

OTHER COLLEGES—

RATING: 1 - 6

As A Scholar ☐
As A Person ☐
Extracurricular ☐
Physical Vigor ☐
General Vitality ☐

Interviewer ....

Date ....

Place ....

Fig. 5 *Interview form used at Wesleyan University.*

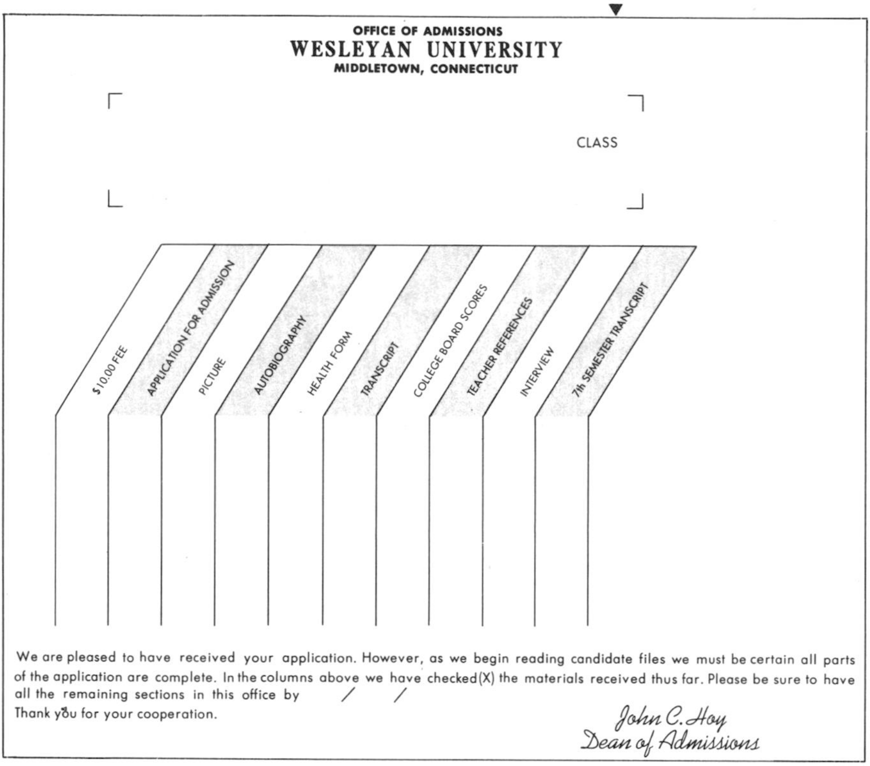
OFFICE OF ADMISSIONS
WESLEYAN UNIVERSITY
MIDDLETOWN, CONNECTICUT

CLASS

$10.00 FEE
APPLICATION FOR ADMISSION
PICTURE
AUTOBIOGRAPHY
HEALTH FORM
TRANSCRIPT
COLLEGE BOARD SCORES
TEACHER REFERENCES
INTERVIEW
7th SEMESTER TRANSCRIPT

We are pleased to have received your application. However, as we begin reading candidate files we must be certain all parts of the application are complete. In the columns above we have checked(X) the materials received thus far. Please be sure to have all the remaining sections in this office by / /
Thank you for your cooperation.

John C. Hoy
Dean of Admissions

Fig. 6 *Candidate is notified of items missing for completion of credential file.*

The Application File By utilizing the admissions folder, much information can be entered by the admissions staff as it reviews a candidate's credentials, thus avoiding the time-wasting task of repeatedly searching through the file for important data or, as is often the case, double checking on phone calls and opinions on the candidate.

Filing Systems and Office Organization Because of the enormous volume of mail encountered in each "admissions year," a key area of concern is the discrimination between correspondence which is essential and that which is perfunctory. Clerical staff should have a clear-cut routine and responsibility should be so delegated that staff time can be devoted to important decision-making roles.

The kind of approach which seems most successful emphasizes the various phases of admissions work and gives clerical staff specific responsibility in line with the office system of the organization. One schematized approach is shown in Figure 7.

At various times during the year some clerical staff will be overburdened. An atmosphere of cooperation and familiarity with all phases of the organization permits clerical staff to shift from one sort of work to another at peak load periods. For example, September and October are heavy inquiry periods, November is a key time for interviews and alumni organization, December and January are heavy applications-processing months, and April and May are notification months.

In general, an office manager can plan ahead for these cyclical changes in emphasis and foresee difficulties in work load.

Increasingly, corporations like IBM have undertaken a systems analysis approach to admissions office organization and are willing to develop programs suited to the in-

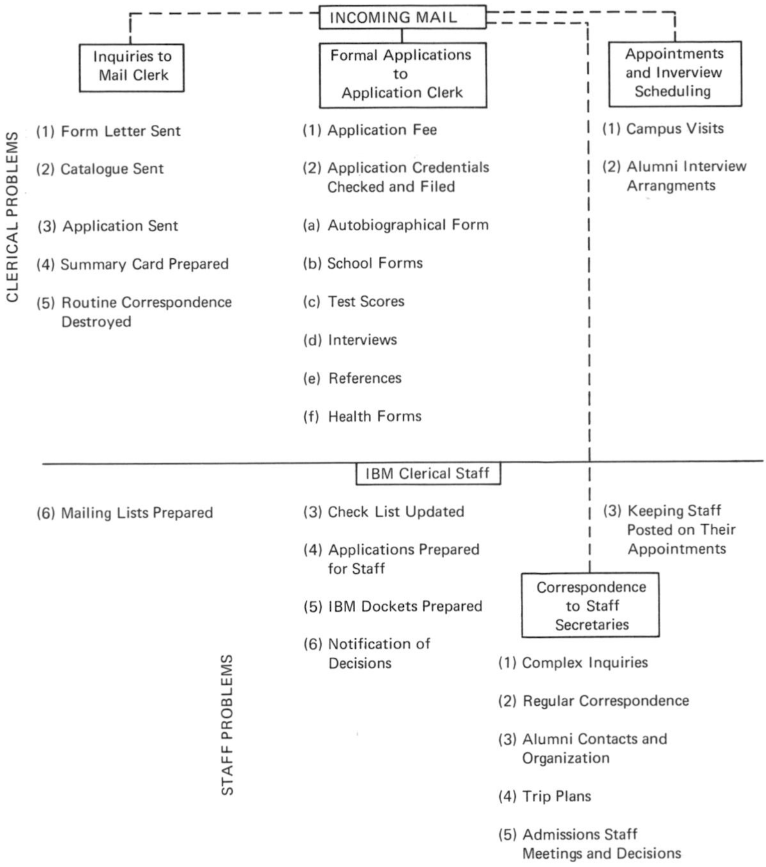

Fig. 7

dividual approach pursued by an institution. No single approach can or should be recommended for every college, but shared experience indicates that data processing is flexible enough to encompass an extraordinary variety of tasks and emphases.

SECURITY CONTROLS AND THE CONFIDENTIAL NATURE OF ADMISSIONS INFORMATION

A number of legal cases in recent years have emphasized all too clearly the absolute necessity for admissions offices to operate according to the highest professional principles in support of the confidentiality of their applications and procedures.

Confidential information from secondary school counselors, references, and professional reports must be secure and used in a manner which is above reproach.

All professional and secretarial staff need to understand the importance of confidentiality in the admissions office, and clerical workers must not be placed in a position where the mechanics of processing routine information place them in a compromising situation. The best procedure to assure security and confidentiality will center on the awareness of the office manager or person in charge of processing. No file on a student should be removed from the admissions office and all files should be covered by an interoffice check-out system. No file should be available to persons other than those officially involved in the admissions operation. If information is to be interpreted to faculty or other interested individuals, this should be done by a competent staff person with full consideration for the confidentiality of the applicant.

THE DEVELOPMENT OF THE ADMISSIONS TIMETABLE

The admissions calendar is of interest and importance to three distinct groups of people who are involved in the admissions process.

1. Candidates and school counselors
2. The admissions staff and clerical personnel
3. Alumni co-workers who serve as liaison personnel with schools and candidates

Each group must operate under the same guidelines. However, the timetable in the admissions office will usually be more flexible and subject to adjustment than the publicly announced calendar. An admissions calendar for the year 1966–1967 at Wesleyan University is shown below.

May 1–September 15, 1966	Group interviews on campus for prospective students.
September 15, 1966–January 15, 1967	Admissions staff field trips announced in advance to alumni, schools and candidates. Group sessions, alumni meetings, and individual interviews.
September 15, 1966–May 15, 1967	Individual interviews on campus or with an alumnus *by appointment.*
November 5, 1966	Deadline for December College Board registration.
November 30, 1966	*Deadline for submitting early-decision application for admission and financial aid* (for those schools which offer this plan). Candidates to be notified of the decision by January 15, 1967.
December 3, 1966	College Board Examination date.
December 10, 1966	Deadline for January College Board registration.
January 7, 1967	College Board Examination date.
March 1, 1967	*Deadline for submitting application for admission and financial aid.* Candidates for financial aid should file the College Scholarship Service (CSS) form by February 1 in order to ensure adequate time for processing and mailing.
March 15, 1967	Deadline for completing interview requirement (schools differ here).
April 17, 1967	Candidates and schools committee personnel are notified of decision concerning admission to Wesleyan and financial aid.
May 1, 1967	Candidates' reply date. Successful candidates are required to notify the university by this date of their decision to accept or reject offer of admission.
May 15, 1967	Waiting list candidates are generally notified of the disposition of their applications.

In addition to the general calendar, it is best to arrange a tentative schedule of all staff visits in advance and to publicize this schedule. The following calendar was widely distributed by one college in August to alumni and counselors in order that plans might be generally known in each region. (See Figure 8.) Alumni, counselors, and candidates clearly appreciate such advance planning.

Of course each institution will make up its own timetable based on its basic plan of admissions operation. For example, the college operating under rolling admissions, whereby the candidate is accepted as soon as the admissions committee feels he is

Tentative Admissions Calendar—Visitations

STATE/CITY	LOCAL SCHOOLS COMMITTEE CHAIRMAN	DATES	OFFICER
California			
Los Angeles	Bruce C. Corwin	Jan.	RLK
San Francisco			RLK
Colorado			
Denver	W. Donald Friedman	Oct. 11-13	PLC
Colorado Springs			
Connecticut			
Fairfield Co.	David P. Jones— Westport	Oct. 2 & 3	EIMcD
Hartford	Steven Humphrey— Hartford		
State		Oct. and Nov.	Staff
Delaware			
Wilmington	Richard Sanger	Oct. 25	BCN
District of Columbia	Robert Chase— Alexandria, Va.	Sept. 25 & 26 Dec. 20	BCN JCH–BCN
Hawaii	William Claybaugh— Kailua, Hawaii	Jan.	RLK
Illinois			
Chicago	John Williams— Chicago	Oct. 9 & 10 Dec. 28	RLK–PLC JCH–RLK
Indiana			
Indianapolis	John E. Burns— Indianapolis	Nov. 27 & 28	PLC
Iowa	James A. Thomas— Des Moines	Nov. 6-8	BCN
Louisiana			
New Orleans	William Cunningham— New Orleans		
Maine			
Maryland			
Baltimore	Robert Dalsemer	Oct. 26	BCN
Massachusetts		Sept. 27-29	PLC
Boston	Frank Kilburn—Boston	Dec. 6-7	EIMcD
Springfield	Donald Emerson	Dec. 20	PLC–RLK
Michigan			
Detroit	Pell Hollingshead— Detroit	Oct & Nov	David Nichols
Minnesota			
Minneapolis	John S. White— Minneapolis		
Missouri			
St. Louis	George Jenkins	Oct. 10 & 11 Dec. 27	BCN–FMS JCH–RLK

STATE/CITY	LOCAL SCHOOLS COMMITTEE CHAIRMAN	DATES	OFFICER
New Hampshire	David Nixon— New Boston		
New Jersey			
Northern	Pete Fellows— W. Caldwell	Sept. 27-29 Dec. 20	BCN–FMS EIMcD–FMS
Southern	Robert Bowman— Haddonfield		
New York			
NYC		Oct. 26-27	JCH
Long Island	Clifford Hordlow— Westbury	Oct. 18-24	BCN
Long Island		Dec. 21	BCN–FMS
Buffalo	Robert Gillette— Buffalo	Nov. 27-28	BCN
Rochester	Thomas Robinson— E. Rochester	Nov. 29-30	BCN
Westchester Co.	Jonathan L. Rosner— Hartsdale	Sept. 25 & 26 Dec. 21	RLK RLK–EIMcD
Albany	Richard Adams	Dec. 1	BCN
Ohio			
Cleveland	Don Fitzgerald— Hudson	Oct. 4 Dec. 29	PLC–BCN JCH–RLK
Cincinnati	James Sailer— Cincinnati	Nov. 29	PLC
Pennsylvania			
Philadelphia	Morris Gelblum— Rydal	Oct. 2 & 3 Dec. 21	RLK–PLC JCH–PLC
Pittsburg	E. Bruce Butler— Pittsburgh	Oct. 26	RLK
Rhode Island			
Providence	Lee Hayes—Bristol		
Tennessee			
Memphis	George Smith—	Oct. 12 & 13	BCN–FSM
Texas			
Dallas		Nov. 9 & 10	BCN
Vermont			
Virginia			
D.C. Area	Robert Chase— Alexandria	Sept. 25 & 26	BCN
Richmond			
Norfolk		Oct. 27	BCN
Wisconsin			
Milwaukee	Jeffrey Williamson— Madison	Oct. 9	BCN
New England Prep Schools		Oct. 30-31 Nov. 1-3	RLK–PLC JCH–EIMcD

Fig. 8 *Sample of Admissions Calendar. Note that heavy visiting and promoting is done during fall of each year. From Wesleyan University.*

qualified, might notify the candidate in the fall of his senior year. Basic plans of operation will be discussed in another chapter.

For suggested readings see page 3-23.

Chapter 7

Admissions—Student Selection, Evaluation of Credentials, Use of the Predictive Formula as an Admissions Tool

JOHN C. HOY

Vice Chancellor—Student Affairs, University of California at Irvine,
Irvine, California

COMMITTEE OF ADMISSIONS COUNSELORS VERSUS FACULTY COMMITTEE

The professional staff of admissions offices should offer a high level of expertise and academic training to be fully capable of making decisions appropriate to their institution. When the admissions staff is not fully responsive to the needs of an institution's faculty, questions arise as to the extent of the involvement of the faculty committee on admissions.

Though many approaches can be designed to meet institutional needs, the approach outlined in Figure 1 has worked well for single-purpose as well as highly complex institutions.

The admissions policy committee should be the vehicle for review, development, and discussion of admissions problems. Actual implementation of policy should be under the direction of a competent, well-informed, and dedicated staff.

Because of the time-consuming nature of actual admissions fieldwork, correspondence, interviewing, and decision making, these activities do not lend themselves to part-time or secondary faculty involvement. However, the best judgment which faculty can offer should be utilized by a policy committee with powers of review.

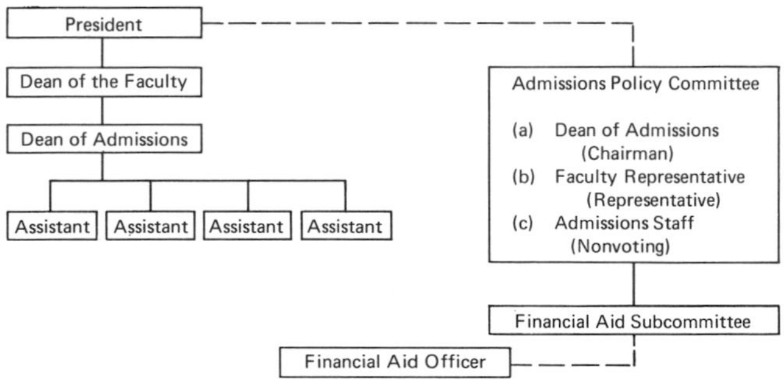

Fig. 1 *Organization chart.*

THE HUMAN EQUATION VERSUS THE STATISTICAL EQUATION

Each institution must seriously weigh the relevance of particular criteria of admission for the specific academic programs available. It must also consider the weight which will be given to nonacademic criteria, in line with the general philosophy and purposes of the institution as it attempts to serve society.

During the last decade, test scores have come under increasing scrutiny and most colleges have attempted to limit the indiscriminate use of tests in the selection of young people for college. Continued heavy reliance on secondary school grades and rank remains the key factor in admission decisions.

In addition, the College Entrance Examination Board (475 Riverside Drive, New York, N.Y.) and the American College Testing Program (Iowa City, Iowa) have developed systematic approaches to the development of "prediction formulas" which are now available to any institution or any academic program using tests in the admissions process. Hundreds of colleges have now established minimum acceptable grade-point averages; that is, they have worked out formulas which weigh the various factors appropriate to the prediction of academic success in their programs. Depending on the specific nature of a collegiate or technical curriculum, some factors will prove more significant than others. For example, verbal aptitude may be given more weight than mathematical aptitude, interviews more than teacher ratings, and class rank more than achievement-test results.

Colleges should be careful to avoid excessive use of formulas, for no perfect formula exists and the potential for college success is an elusive, if not unpredictable, dimension when the individual and not his "statistical" summary is reviewed.

THE FACTORS OF RANK IN CLASS, SCHOOL RECORD, TEST SCORES, RECOMMENDATIONS

By developing a prediction formula, colleges can place relative weight on each of the various criteria used in evaluating a candidate. In refining each criterion, it is possible to develop an equitable balance and, depending on actual policy considerations, to arrive at a reasonable and fair decision-making process. The following outline is illustrative:

1. Class rank
   a. Rank in total graduating class.
   b. Rank in college preparatory program.
   c. Rank in advanced placement courses.
   d. Weighted class rank.
   e. Rank in verbal courses (i.e., English, history, social studies, and languages).
   f. Rank in mathematics and sciences.
2. Test scores
   a. Relative weight to be given to verbal score.
   b. Relative weight to be given to mathematics score.
   c. Relative weight to be given to individual achievement tests or the average of three achievement tests.
   d. Development of a test-result formula, e.g., 2 (verbal aptitude) + 1 (mathematical aptitude) + 3 (achievement-test scores).
3. School record
   a. Weight given to a five-course academic program (i.e., years of English, mathematics, science, social science, and languages) if this is deemed advisable. For example, a program devoting four years to each of these areas would be given a higher rating than a less demanding sequence.
   b. Track in the school program.
   c. Quality of school based on past experience of the college or university.
   d. Work of the National Registration Office at the University of Chicago indicates that excellent predictions of college success can be made by rating schools strong, average, or weak and relating school quality to school competitiveness.
4. Recommendations
   a. Guidance counselor's or principal's recommendation or rating.
   b. Teacher's recommendation or rating.
   c. Alumnus' recommendation or rating.
   d. Interviewer's recommendation or rating.

By using the above criteria, a complex system which offers the fairest possible rating of factors for each candidate can be developed for an individual admissions office. The weights to be given each criterion are matters of institutional policy, and it is now possible to develop statistically the most relevant formula for each admissions program.

IDENTIFICATION OF CARNEGIE UNITS

In the last decade the Carnegie unit has lost significance because of the variety of and complexity of secondary school programs. In general, it is wise to apply less simplistic measures of a candidate's school program, as described above.

IDENTIFICATION OF SPECIAL SECONDARY SCHOOL COURSES

Admissions staff members must be familiar with the variety of course offerings of hundreds of schools and be continually curious about innovations in secondary school programs. For example, relatively new courses such as PSSC Physics, Chem-Bond Chemistry, AP English, and MLA French all require admissions and placement attention. Because of the complexity of such offerings, it is better, in making admissions decisions, to emphasize the placement value of such programs as determined by the interested department than to use a complex scale weighing individual programs against others.

EQUIVALENCY DIPLOMAS AND CREDIT FOR NONTRADITIONAL COURSE WORK

It is highly likely that admissions counselors will deal with many applicants who do not offer the traditional Carnegie-unit courses nor the testing results from one of the major services—the Educational Testing Service or the American College Testing Program.

Many students who have dropped out of high school return to their state department of education in the hope of gaining an equivalency diploma. In most states the applicant gains this diploma by completing 15–16 Carnegie units as he prepares himself for the college curriculum of his choice.

Within the last few years many states, such as Massachusetts, have adopted the General Educational Development Test method as an alternative to the acquisition of the equivalency diploma. Under this procedure the applicant must attain a certain standard score on a series of examinations which test his development in verbal and mathematical areas. He need not have even attended high school prior to completing the examination. If a college decides not to accept this method, it, nevertheless, will find the tests helpful in providing some indication of ability.

Most universities will accept home study courses if these are, in turn, honored by the high school. Yet candidates in this category may have health problems which would affect admission.

Colleges vary in their willingness to grant credit for adult education courses. It is fair to say that most universities will give credit for these courses if they are satisfied with the overall credentials of the candidate.

High-school-level university extension courses are offered two or three times a week at many universities. Most universities will give credit for these courses, although obviously a three- or four-month course, two nights a week is not a strong substitute for a full year of a high school course.

In terms of testing, many universities offer their own battery in lieu of one of the two major batteries—CEEB or ACTP—when they are dealing with a late applicant in whom they are interested or with the nontraditional student. Tests which correlate highly with these aptitude tests—for instance the School College Ability Test with the Scholastic Aptitude Test—would be substituted.

In 1967 the College Entrance Examination Board introduced the College Level Examination Program (CLEP). The intent of this program is to enable certain nontraditional students to receive college credit for past personal experience or for previous independent study other than the usual academic work.

It is anticipated that this new program will be most useful for the part-time adult student population, but it is also a convenience to the many colleges that are currently offering freshman and transfer credit to adults interested in day colleges who successfully complete the subject level tests.

In summary, universities appear to be willing to deal with the nontraditional applicant in nontraditional ways. As more states offer varying approaches to the granting of diplomas and as organizations such as CEEB introduce programs like CLEP, universities will have to study existing policies in the light of new research information.

OBTAINING HEALTH CLEARANCE (PHYSICAL AND EMOTIONAL)

Most but not all colleges inquire as to a candidate's emotional and physical health. The question is a controversial one. If a campus has limited medical and counseling facilities, it seems more important to screen out candidates who will require extensive follow-up medical attention. This, of course, is done for the candidate's protection. However, with rapid expansion of medical facilities on American campuses, institutions increasingly have ignored the past medical and emotional histories of candidates in the decision-making process, preferring to solicit complete information after the admissions decision has been made.

The middle-of-the-road position has been to inquire about any current disabilities a candidate may have and to point out the extent of the facilities available on the specific campus which will be of service to a student who is handicapped.

The public must be made increasingly aware that campuses vary greatly and, further, the public should have confidence that whatever information is provided is interpreted with the highest professional standards and with the best interests of the candidate in mind.

Questions of policy concerning medical and emotional problems should be delineated by the admissions policy group in consultation with the college physician and psychiatrist.

All information which comes into the hands of an admissions office on individual candidates must be treated with extreme confidence and preferably should be sent directly to the college physician, who should be responsible for making well-informed decisions on such questions as might arise. (See Figure 2.)

PRELIMINARY EVALUATION OF CREDENTIALS

Colleges have increasingly found it advisable to assist candidates by attempting a preliminary assessment of a candidate's chances of gaining admission. The following guideline may be helpful in this area:

1. Preliminary evaluations should only be given by authorized admissions office personnel.
2. The tentative nature of such preliminary evaluations must be made explicit.
3. If a commitment for admission is made, an official letter of intent should follow in order that the candidate and the college may be protected.
4. Early letters of rejection should be encouraged so that students are informed of negative decisions in time to make alternate plans.

SPECIAL PROBLEMS OF ADMISSION OF CULTURALLY AND ECONOMICALLY DISADVANTAGED STUDENTS

American institutions of higher education have come to recognize during the past decade that deserving students from minority and disadvantaged socioeconomic groups have, in the past, been deliberately overlooked. Indeed, the opening of college doors to such students may be one of the major revolutions in higher education during the 1970s, for the task has only begun and the results of "talent search" programs to date are extremely modest when the enormity of the task is fully realized.

Traditional criteria for college admission cannot be applied in the traditional way with socioeconomically disadvantaged students. Several points are worthy of emphasis:

1. Most of these students come from our weakest and most neglected secondary schools.

DEPARTMENT OF ADMISSIONS
MEMORANDUM

TO: Dr. George M. Lane, University Physician, 135F

FROM: Department of Admissions

SUBJECT: Health Referral of Applicant for Admission

Student:

Address:

College for which applying:

The above named student has indicated in (his, her) application for admission the following health disability:

This student, who has been advised that admission to the University requires full health clearance, will arrange to have forwarded to your office an official report.

________________ Date

________________ Admissions Counselor

HEALTH DEPARTMENT ACTION

☐ Full Clearance ☐ Rejected

COMMENT

________________ Date

________________ University Physician

AD 27 (2/7)
2M

Fig. 2 *Health Department informs Admissions when family doctor has forwarded necessary information and Health Department has granted clearance. From Northeastern University, Department of Admissions.*

2. Because of poor teaching, insufficient books and materials, and family background, their test scores and school records will not compare well with those of typical candidates.

3. In evaluating these students it is necessary to rely on recommendations and evaluations from people who may know the candidates from nonacademic situations.

4. Standard extracurricular activities and culturally advantageous experiences are limited in the situations from which these candidates come, and hence they should be evaluated on the basis of the experiences available to them and the limitations under which they have had to labor. Therefore, work experience, settlement-house programs, neighborhood service enterprises, family background and difficulties, all take on enormous significance.

5. Students with this kind of background should not be admitted unless a college is prepared to provide new educational services such as the following:

a. Compensatory summer programs prior to college entrance for enrichment and remedial purposes.

b. Reduced course load in the freshman year (or beyond, if necessary) with possible extension of the four-year program to five or six years.

c. Special counseling facilities staffed by knowledgeable personnel.

d. Special curricular offerings and extracurricular programs which encourage students to have pride in their own cultural background as well as to gain insight into the society of which they have been a so-called "disadvantaged" part.

e. Emphasis on summer and term-time job placement which is aimed at providing educationally relevant experience.

f. In the case of minority-group students, an emphasis on the employment of faculty and staff of similar background.

The recruitment of such students is extremely complex and cannot be a casual side effort in the admissions operation. Knowledgeable staff are necessary, and liaison with counselors in the schools and in the community at large takes on increased significance, as does the need for continued feedback and cooperation.

Also, emphasis should be placed on working with the students' families in relation to financial-aid counseling, emotional support, and the interpretation of the college experience to parents who will have had minimal educational benefits themselves.

If such extra effort seems excessive, it nevertheless is clear that those institutions which have engaged in such complete programs have had unusual success. Those that have pursued a casual approach have fostered failure and bitterness and have been of no service in solving a major national problem.

SPECIAL PROBLEMS OF ADMISSION OF FOREIGN STUDENTS

Approximately one hundred thousand foreign students from virtually every nation in the world now attend American colleges and universities. Each such student represents a special situation for the admissions office. In larger universities, one staff member is designated as foreign-student admissions officer or as half-time admissions officer and half-time adviser. In smaller institutions, a member of the faculty frequently serves as consultant to the admissions office on foreign-student admissions.

In either case, three organizations have proven extremely helpful to admissions staffs across the nation with regard to foreign students. They are:

The National Association of Foreign Student Advisers
1860 Nineteenth Street, N.W.
Washington, D.C. 20009

The Institute for International Education
809 United Nations Plaza
New York, N.Y. 10017
The Association of Collegiate Registrars and Admissions Officers
c/o Mr. John Vlandis
University of Connecticut
Storrs, Conn.

These organizations offer guidelines and publications concerned with the educational systems of all nations and they also provide interpretative information.

In the case of The Institute for International Education (I.I.E.), direct referrals of candidates are available as well as information on other agencies serving students and colleges interested in international exchange. I.I.E. also maintains field representatives in many nations and works through the American Embassy in others.

In addition, the African Scholarship Program of American Universities (866 United Nations Plaza, New York, N.Y. 10017) and the Latin American Scholarship Program of American Universities (75 Mount Auburn Street, Cambridge, Mass. 02138) offer referral and information services of extremely high quality.

It is now possible to receive test information on candidates through prior arrangement with Educational Testing Service, Princeton, N.J. 08540, which administers its Test of English as a Foreign Language (T.O.E.F.L.) to foreign students in many nations each year. The results are sent directly to the college.

CHILDREN OF ALUMNI

One of the most controversial problems in college admissions is the applicant who is the son or daughter of an alumnus or alumna. In recent years many institutions have publicly stated that all alumni children will be treated like any other candidates. However, alumni erroneously believe that some special privilege should be granted their children, especially if the parent has been "loyal and active."

Each college must search its own conscience in this area, but it should clearly have a consistent policy. In any event, children of alumni should receive cordial and full attention, and where a negative decision is made the practice of tactfully making the parent an early partner to such notification by special letter often proves the better part of valor. The best interest of the candidate should be, as in all cases, the primary concern, and the use of a modicum of tact usually permits a college to pursue a policy which leaves its integrity *intact.*

For suggested readings see page 3-23.

Chapter **8**

Plans for the Admission of New First-year Students

JOHN C. HOY

Vice Chancellor—Student Affairs, University of California at Irvine, Irvine, California

OPEN-DOOR POLICY

Increasingly, public junior and community colleges have pursued open-door admission policies. Under such an approach all students who successfully complete secondary school are permitted to enroll in programs for which their high school preparation is designed.

The revolution in the college-attendance patterns of Americans is in large part to be attributed to the community college and the access to higher education which has become available to all who qualify. This trend is clearly going to assure an accelerated social and technological revolution in the decades to come.

An open-door admissions policy is not as simple as it may seem, for it requires an intense effort in several key areas:

1. Prediction of class size based on high school graduating classes and the intent of the graduates with respect to community enrollment

2. Projections for future class size, faculty appointments, program planning
3. Emphasis on placement and guidance so that appropriate programs are selected
4. Emphasis on flexibility so that students may, without severe penalty, shift their interests and programs

As these points make abundantly clear, the open-door policy is one which creates unusual and demanding problems for the admissions staff of the institution that adopts it, and the counseling function takes on enormous significance.

REGULAR ADMISSION (WITHOUT CONDITION)

Under regular or "normal" procedures, candidates apply before a specific deadline and know that decisions will be announced on a specific date, for example: applications may be completed by February 1; decisions may be announced by April 15; candidates' acceptances may be received by May 1.

Under such a timetable, which is actually used by the majority of American colleges, candidates are fully aware of the various planning stages necessary, and generally students will apply to several colleges realizing that the timetable may vary but taking steps to assure that their plans are appropriate.

When students are accepted under such a procedure, they usually are required to honor this acceptance with a deposit on tuition or room to assure their place in the entering class. Their acceptance is then unconditional and the student need only appear for orientation on the designated day before the opening of the term.

ROLLING ADMISSION

When an admissions office makes decisions on candidates as applications are received and notifies students of their acceptance, rejection, or waiting-list position within two to four weeks, it is making rolling admissions.

Such an approach is most advisable for the following kinds of institutions:

1. Colleges which have clear-cut criteria for admission, criteria which do not require comparisons of all candidates before individual selections are made
2. Colleges which have developed reliable methods of predicting the number of candidates who will respond positively to acceptance
3. Colleges that maintain close liaison with secondary school counselors who will keep them informed as to the intentions of admitted candidates

The procedure of rolling admission should be undertaken when an institution is convinced that announcement of admission on this basis serves the best interest of the institution and its candidate group.

EARLY ADMISSION

Following a series of experiments in admitting secondary school juniors to freshman classes on a fairly extensive basis, most colleges now expect students to complete high school before entrance. Three basic factors have been responsible for the decline in the early admission experiment:

1. In the last decade, secondary school curricula have been improved and enriched.
2. High school students can now attend college summer sessions and in many cases take courses on college campuses while they are still in secondary school.
3. Colleges have begun to realize that the social maturity of freshmen is highly significant in predicting academic success.

As early admission has declined, early acceptance has increased. Under this procedure, secondary school juniors or first-term seniors are informed of their college acceptance on the basis of their first three years of secondary school work. By means of early planning and strong credentials, students may apply to the college of their choice and be considered in a primary group which receives an early indication of its acceptability. By this means, multiple applications are reduced and students can spend their senior year without concern for the hectic problems of college entrance.

Increasingly, colleges are joining together in presenting the early-acceptance option to candidates. An outline of the procedures involved is presented in a statement from an actual application (see Figure 1).

ADMISSION ON CONDITION

A number of candidates are admitted on the condition that they will attend a regular or special summer session, do creditable work (usually on a level of grade C or better) and then be admitted to unconditional status at the beginning of the regular term.

Such a procedure permits an admissions office to give a student a trial period in which to prove himself worthy of bona fide degree candidacy. The admissions office is in a position to guide the student in terms of those areas needing remedial attention and to place the burden of performance in college courses squarely on the student who, after all, is the only person who can ultimately demonstrate his ability to handle the academic program.

Many students have found that this early second chance has salutary effects on their approach to the college experience and that it enables them to gain considerable personal and academic confidence before the regular freshmen arrive.

WESLEYAN UNIVERSITY

Middletown, Connecticut

General Instructions

(Please read carefully before completing the application)

APPLICATION — The application is in two parts. Part I is to be completed and submitted by the candidate. Part II should be given to your secondary school authorities for completion and forwarding. The deadline for submitting applications is March 1 for all candidates, both scholarship and non-scholarship applicants. More consideration can be given to applications received before February 1.

TEACHER REFERENCES — Two personal reference forms to be given to teachers who know you well and can offer perceptive evaluation concerning your readiness for college.

HEALTH QUESTIONNAIRE — To be completed by your parents or guardian.

COLLEGE BOARD EXAMINATIONS — It is required that all candidates take the College Entrance Board Scholastic Aptitude Tests. Candidates must also take the English Composition Achievement Test and two other Achievement Tests in subjects of their own choice. The Writing Sample may be submitted as an *additional* test if the candidate so desires. It is required that all candidates complete the entire battery of examinations not later than January of the senior year.

PERSONAL INTERVIEW — A personal interview at Wesleyan with a representative of the Admissions Office is strongly encouraged for all candidates. In some cases it is impracticable for a candidate residing at a considerable distance from Middletown to visit the campus. At the discretion of the Admissions Committee, it is possible that an appointment can be arranged with an alumnus living in the applicant's immediate area.

SCHOLARSHIP AID — All candidates for scholarship aid must submit the Parents' Confidential Statement of the College Scholarship Service directly to the service in Princeton, New Jersey. Forms may be obtained from your school guidance office. No other scholarship forms are necessary. All forms must be sent to C.S.S. *by February 1.*

PHOTOGRAPHS — Two photographs, 2″ x 3″, must be submitted with this application. These will be used in a freshman Directory, and therefore should *not* be informal snapshots.

APPLICATION FEE — An application fee of *Ten Dollars* ($10.00) must be submitted with this application. This fee is not refundable. Checks or money orders should be made payable to Wesleyan University. Your cancelled check will serve as an acknowledgment of the receipt of your application.

Fig. 1 *Early decision application, from Wesleyan University.*

Early Decision Program

For the past several years the Committee on Admissions has made early decisions on those applicants who, after looking critically at their various college choices, have decided Wesleyan is their first choice.

To help reduce the multiple application problem, the Committee evaluates such candidates after November 30 and informs them of their status prior to January 15. Amherst, Bowdoin, Dartmouth, Williams and others subscribe to the following procedures for Early Decision applications.

1. The student's application, and request for Early Decision, must be received by November 30.
2. All other forms and credentials (i.e., transcripts, school reports, junior year College Board test results, and recommendations) must be completed by December 20. Action on applications not completed by December 20 will be postponed until the spring.
3. While we are willing to work with an applicant on a "single application" basis, *the Early Decision program in no way is intended to prohibit applications to other colleges.*
4. A firm decision on the amount of financial aid award, within a range of $200, as determined by an evaluation of the College Scholarship Service form, is made and announced concurrently with the decision on admission.
5. The Early Decision program is *not* limited to a predetermined portion of the entering class.
6. The decision rendered by the Committee will be one of the two as follows:
   a. A firm offer of admission and, if applied for, financial aid.
   b. A "hold" status indicating that a decision will be made later together with all the other candidates applying for admission under normal procedures.
7. Should the decision be positive, the Committee requests that all applications at other colleges be withdrawn since Wesleyan is definitely the college preference and admission has been granted. The other alternate decision allows, of course, an applicant to pursue his other applications.
8. Carbon copies of the decision letters are sent to the Guidance Counselors so that appropriate advisement may continue.
9. Early acceptance of an applicant does not relieve him of the requirement to take and report senior year College Board scores, and is contingent on the successful completion of his senior year in good standing.

Request for Early Decision

To: Committee on Admissions, Wesleyan University Date ....

From: ....
(Print Full Name)

After carefully considering my college applications I have decided that Wesleyan University is definitely my first choice.
Please consider this note as my formal request for an early decision.

....
Signature

....
Address

....
Zip

....
• *Secondary School*

Fig. 1 *(Continued)*

ADMISSION TO HONORS PROGRAMS: THE RECOGNITION OF INDIVIDUAL DIFFERENCES AMONG STUDENTS

With the significant growth of innovative and enriched programs in secondary schools has come increased recognition of the need for colleges to expand offerings for students with varying interests and capabilities.

Honors programs attempt to facilitate the following approaches:

1. Increased flexibility in course selection
2. The development of experimental and imaginative approaches to first- and second-year work of a departmental or interdisciplinary nature
3. Early intellectual orientation to the academic community
4. Reemphasis and highlighting of the importance of quality teaching in the underclass years
5. Offering of opportunities for upper-level or independent-study programs for exceptional students in the first year

As secondary school preparation improves, colleges such as Michigan State have acknowledged the importance of making available the best resources of the academic community to the precocious, promising, or highly motivated student.

Honors programs also permit a college to attract particularly promising students who view the special opportunities as a key factor in their college choice.

ADVANCED PLACEMENT: THE USE OF ADVANCED PLACEMENT TESTS IN GRANTING CREDIT AND PLACEMENT

Highly motivated students have the opportunity of taking special secondary school courses designed to be the equivalent of college-level work or to pursue programs of reading and study which culminate in sitting for the Advanced Placement Tests of the College Entrance Examination Board.

Advanced Placement Tests are individually read and graded by college examiners, and students are awarded grades from 5 (high) to 1 (low) on the papers they have written. As a general rule, colleges have granted credit for work graded 3 or higher and have in addition placed students who wished to pursue the subjects in which they had been tested in upper-level courses. Indeed, on the basis of Advanced Placement Test results, some colleges grant sophomore standing. For example, Harvard University grants sophomore standing to students who receive a grade of 3 or higher on three or more tests. Students so placed have gone on to do extremely well, and most colleges have viewed the Advanced Placement Program as a significant approach to permitting the acceleration and/or accurate placement of students in college programs.

Undoubtedly the Advanced Placement Program will continue to grow in significance and to expand as a precursor to unusual developments in secondary school–college cooperation and understanding.

For suggested readings see page 3-23.

Chapter 9

Admission of the Transfer Student to Upper-class Standing

JOHN C. HOY

Vice Chancellor—Student Affairs, University of California at Irvine, Irvine, California

CLOSE LIAISON WITH COLLEGES FROM WHICH STUDENTS TRANSFER

Unfortunately most student transfers are accomplished in isolated patterns with only a modest degree of cooperation between institutions. However, the dramatic development of the junior- and community-college movement indicates the absolute necessity for clearer lines of communication between institutions in this era of educational mobility.

Colleges should wisely pursue admission programs which enlist the recommendation and advice which is available at the original institution, so that the student accepted for transfer will receive the benefit of better guidance, placement, and adjustment resources than is presently the case.

THE DEAN'S CLEARANCE FORM

One essential procedure is the use of a form or a required letter from the original institution concerning a student's overall record. Such a form or letter should inquire into the following areas:

1. Academic performance
2. Reasons for transfer
3. Physical and emotional health and stability
4. Record of citizenship

If any question arises concerning a candidate's qualifications, it is well to write or call the dean's office of the original institution. By means of careful clearance pursued in this fashion it is possible to assure that transfer candidates add something to the new campus and that they are making a change which is educationally sound. All too often students elect to transfer in an attempt to avoid problems rather than face them. The grass looks greener elsewhere, and this attitude often leads to a change that is less than healthy for the moderately confused college freshman or sophomore. (See Figure 1.)

DETERMINATION OF MINIMUM GRADE-POINT AVERAGE FOR TRANSFER ELIGIBILITY

Some colleges require a C or 2.0/4.0 grade-point average for transfer. Others, feeling that they already have their fair share of C students, require a minimum of a B average in the hope of not adding just another student but a solid student.

Because of the variety in standards among American colleges, it is virtually impossible to establish equations for transfer acceptability, and it is best under these circumstances to measure candidates on the basis of a wide variety of criteria once the minimum average has been established.

EVALUATION OF COLLEGE TRANSCRIPTS

One method of evaluating college records from unfamiliar institutions is to request that a current catalog be submitted by the candidate and then to refer student records deemed minimally acceptable to the department of intended major for review. (See Figure 2.)

If a candidate is minimally acceptable, has a clearance letter from his former dean, and is viewed favorably by the major department, chances are that the transfer of the student can be facilitated. If, on the other hand, the minimally qualified candidate is not seen as desirable by the major department and is given modest support by his former dean, transfer acceptance should be denied in the belief that the student will do better to improve his record and overall pattern at the college he presently attends before taking on the obligations and challenges of a new community.

In the final analysis, a successful college record generally can be viewed as sound enough to warrant consideration at even the most selective colleges. The record of *carefully selected* transfer students is generally excellent and the record of the minimally qualified minimal.

DETERMINATION OF TRANSFER-STUDENT POLICY

By means of admitting qualified transfer students, colleges can often strengthen various aspects of the academic community in ways which had not been possible at the time of freshman entrance. For example, transfer priority can be given in the sciences, in business programs, in minority-group representation, or in geographic diversity. Such dimensions should be considered before policy guidelines are determined.

NORTHEASTERN UNIVERSITY

BOSTON, MASSACHUSETTS 02115

DEPARTMENT OF ADMISSIONS Date____________

TO: THE DEAN OF STUDENTS____________

FROM: Gilbert C. Garland, Dean of Admissions

has applied for admission to Northeastern University as a transfer student. Your assistance in determining his eligibility will be appreciated. Any information you may provide will be used in strict confidence. A self-addressed envelope is enclosed for your convenience.

When was this student in attendance?____________

Is he (she) entitled to honorable dismissal?_____Was he (she) ever on social_______, disciplinary_______, academic_______probation? Remarks:____________

____

Was there ever any question of his (her) conduct? On campus?_______Off Campus?_______

Remarks:____________

____

Would this student be readmitted to your college?_______If under certain conditions, please explain. ____________

____

Do you recommend this student for transfer to Northeastern University? _______

(For officials of two-year, junior colleges and community colleges.) Please indicate curriculum in which student was enrolled: _____Transfer; _____Terminal.

Any further comments you may wish to make will be appreciated. ____________

____

____

____

Signed____________

Date____________ Title____________

AD 63 (6/7)
15C

Fig. 1 *Student is cleared by previous institution attended prior to acceptance action. From Northeastern University.*

Once priorities and procedures are established, it is well to publish a candid and complete appraisal of the policy for all candidates and to make it available to deans at two- and four-year colleges. (See Figure 3.) It should be stressed that transfer candidates and college officials are vastly more experienced than secondary school students and counselors and that it is best to err on the side of completeness and the frank discussion of policy than to offer false optimism or an inadequate statement.

EVALUATION OF TRANSFER CREDIT

TO: Dean of the College of ____________________ Date____________

FROM: Admissions Counselor,____________________

SUBJECT: Referral of Transcript (s) for Evaluation

Name of Student________________________________

Major Field of Study____________________________

Special Comment________________________________

____

____

- -

The above student has applied for admission as a transfer student seeking advanced credit. Where two transcripts are presented, please indicate amount of credit from each.

For study at________________________: Sem. Hrs.__________(Qtr. Hrs.)__________

For study at________________________: Sem. Hrs.__________(Qtr. Hrs.)__________

Total Credit Granted: Sem. Hrs.__________(Qtr. Hrs.)__________

This evaluation is based upon credit for Northeastern's Quarters________through________.

(Please indicate on back side specific courses for which credit is granted.)

Granting of credit is conditional upon successful completion of semester in which student is enrolled.

Student may register for Quarter______________.

Special condition, if any________________________________

____

____

____

____

____

____

____

____

Date of Evaluation________________ ________________________
Dean (Assistant) of the College

OVER

AD 64
2M

Fig. 2 *Department head informs Admissions of amount of credits which can be transferred. From Northeastern University, Department of Admissions.*

PROBLEMS OF ADMISSION FROM NONACCREDITED COLLEGES

With the extraordinary increase in the number of new colleges, it is natural that students in nonaccredited or yet-to-be accredited institutions should be deeply concerned with their reception at accredited institutions.

ABOUT NORTHEASTERN UNIVERSITY

Northeastern University offers students the opportunity to gain actual working experience in their chosen field of study under the five-year Co-operative Plan of Education. By alternating periods of academic study and on-the-job training, this program emphasizes the values of experience related to a specific field of study.

This program is not recommended for those having previous work experience, or for those who have had to delay their college education several years.

Students may enroll in one of the Basic (undergraduate) Colleges of the University: Boston-Bouvé College, College of Business Administration, College of Criminal Justice, College of Education, College of Engineering, College of Liberal Arts, College of Nursing and College of Pharmacy.

PLAN OF ADMISSION

A student wishing to transfer into the Basic Colleges of Northeastern University may request advanced standing as an upperclassman on the basis of acceptable credits earned in an accredited two or four-year institution or a technical institute.

It is possible that a student whose educational objective has changed may be admitted as a freshman with partial credit. Electives are not available in the freshman year and transfer students admitted as freshmen may not elect upper-class courses. Even if partial credit is granted, five years is still required to complete the program.

BASIC REQUIREMENTS

1. Only a candidate who presents satisfactory college records can be considered for advanced credit. No credit is given for the lowest passing mark.

   Graduates (2.5 index) of approved Engineering Technology curricula (except chemical) will start quarter 5 in the fall with the opportunity to complete requirements for the Bachelor of Science degree in three years.

2. Credit is given for those courses which are the equivalent of required subjects offered in the particular college at Northeastern. Credit may also be given for elective courses.
3. Candidates must be in good standing and eligible to continue in the institution they are currently attending.
4. Evidence of honorable dismissal and satisfactory health are required. Appropriate forms will be sent.
5. Special student status is not possible in any of the Basic Colleges of Northeastern.

APPLICATION PROCEDURE

An applicant for advanced standing is required to:

1. Complete an application for admission no later than *May 1* of the year of intended entrance. Transfer students are admitted only in September.
2. Submit a transcript of his high school record.
3. Request that an official college transcript of his completed courses be sent and a list of courses which will be completed prior to the end of the academic year.
4. After the student has forwarded his credentials, he may obtain an interview with an admissions counselor by writing or calling the office for an appointment. The Admissions Office is open on Monday through Friday from 9:00 a.m. to 4:00 p.m. and on Saturday morning from 9:00 a.m. to 11:30 a.m.

Note: Transfer students are not required to take College Board Tests.

All records must be received by the Department of Admissions no later than June 15 of the year of intended entrance.

Upon receipt of all items required, the candidate will be notified of the action taken.

FINANCIAL AID

A number of scholarships, loans and grants are available to qualified transfer students.

Candidates must submit an application to the Office of Financial Aid and file a Parents' Confidential Statement with the College Scholarship Service, Box 176, Princeton, New Jersey, no later than May 1.

Requests for further information should be obtained from the Office of Financial Aid.

Fig. 3 *Application information concerning transfer for students who inquire. From Northeastern University, Department of Admissions.*

The best procedure in face of these for the most part positive changes in the evolution of American higher education is simply to encourage a supportive position among the more established institutions.

Students should, in any event, be selected on the basis of their personal credentials. When letters of acceptance are sent to unaccredited two-year colleges, the accepting institution may be well advised to stress the significance it attaches to accreditation. It may also mention the fact that, in the absence of accreditation, students have been given the benefit of the doubt.

In a period of transition, accredited institutions can maintain their own standards in an atmosphere of support and encouragement without applying a rigid standard which penalizes the individual student.

FINANCIAL AID TO TRANSFER STUDENTS

In outlining their policies on the admission of transfer students, colleges should clearly state the facts concerning financial aid resources. If an institution has no funds for transfer candidates, such a situation should be clearly defined. If particular limitations prevail, these should be described.

During the past decade, colleges have found that transfer students are very worthy recipients of financial aid. However, strict adherence to the highest standards of financial aid administration are required so that institutional skirts will be clean if it should appear that students are changing campuses because of "better financial aid arrangements." College Scholarship Service procedures are sufficient to this purpose, and guidelines are available from the College Scholarship Service on the interpretation of complex procedures in this area.

Increasingly colleges will find that financial aid policy will need to be linked to the transfer admission problem. As we see more rather than less educational mobility, institutions will have to be prepared to handle the financial problems of such students equitably.

THE EMERGING COMMUNITY COLLEGES

Throughout this discussion special attention has been paid to the two-year college. The evolution of the transfer phenomenon in American higher education is inextricably linked to the further development of community colleges. It has been seriously suggested that the future pattern of our educational system may be linked to a trend within four-year institutions toward upper-class work only, with well-integrated programs leading to graduate and professional schools. In either case, the evaluation of the two-year college and its student has yet to receive the full consideration it deserves. In the process of developing the procedures for transfer in this area, it is essential that a degree of flexibility and appreciation of the role of the two-year college emerge as a part of admissions policy. Very frequently students mature rapidly in the community-college setting. Colleges should be willing to go beyond the paper record in their evaluations. If a premature and fixed pattern is established without thoughtful attention to the exceptional service these institutions perform, all colleges may stand to lose.

Further, a pattern of visitation by admissions officers to community colleges will undoubtedly assist in broadening the necessary communications between the more established and the newly emerging colleges. Where close liaison has been developed, both types of institutions have benefited.

For suggested readings see page 3-23.

Chapter 10

The Practice of Admissions in the Junior College

MYRON D. HAGER

Director of Admissions, Westbrook Junior College, Portland, Maine

INTRODUCTION

The admissions operation in the junior college is in many respects identical to that in the senior college.

In both the two-year and four-year colleges, individual adaptations of standard admissions policies and procedures must be made to conform to institutional peculiarities. At both levels, the very large institution may feel the need to automate much of the mechanical work while the comparatively small independent college tends toward a more intimate hand operation. The total mechanics of catalog distribution, processing of applications, interviewing of candidates, admissions decision making, and the several other duties allotted to the college admissions office have become rather standardized in the ordinary college set up, whether four-year or two.

In the overall pattern of American higher education, there are commonly understood differences between the two-year and the four-year colleges that are more than quantitative. It is true that in some sections of the country more than others, in some types of junior college more than others, and for some junior college students more than others, the two-year college experience turns out to be simply the first half of the

to resist the setting up of such requirements as college admissions tests, for example, which make no claim of testing the kinds of abilities required to succeed in his technical curriculum. Unless his career curriculum includes considerable liberal arts content he should strongly urge his administration to avoid the temptation to require for admission unrelated high school "college prep" subjects simply because such requirements tend to "raise the standards" of the curriculum and of the college.

In his assessment of the admissions qualifications of the marginal applicant to the career program, the admissions person must make a special effort to find signs of promise wherever they may be found; for example, an unusual hobby in a related activity, or the counselor's description of unusual character or leadership qualities which give strength to the applicant's professions of determination. Whether the admissions officer's knowledge of the psychology of motivation comes from a research-degree background or from his experience in carefully playing his hunches, he must use all his resources and gather extended evidence in an effort to assess the strength of the applicant's motivation because, in technical studies particularly, strong motivation can overcome almost any degree of "academic disability." In fact, for success in technical fields of study, the junior college admissions officer must deal with the reality that the less "academically qualified" candidate is in some instances the better candidate for admission.

THE JUNIOR COLLEGE PROVIDES THE OPPORTUNITY FOR GROWING UP

Not all humans develop physically, emotionally, or intellectually at the same rate. The junior college offers an opportunity to catch up for the student who, in one or more of these aspects of maturity, is "trailing behind the norm."

Frequently the slow-developing student has strong academic goals and plans that include not only the bachelor's degree but professional schooling as well. Standing in the way at the point of high school graduation is an uneven achievement record and perhaps "below-standard" college admissions test results. This student is often the junior college success story.

As opposed to the capable and highly developed student for whose success no college can take very much credit, the slowly developing student needs preferential treatment for proper development. The *small* college can offer such special treatment, particularly the small junior college with its modified program where indicated and its attention to the individual.

The junior college admissions officer, then, does well to provide some means for special recognition of the slow developer. Where class rank is an important admission criterion, for example, he must not be content with the ratio as it stands, but he must analyze it: the four-year high school record that starts weak and ends strong may result in the same class rank as the record that starts strong and drops off in the last two years. Other factors being constant, the improving record clearly offers the better prognosis.

If his summing up of the objective criteria includes the computation of a high school point average of some kind, the junior college admissions officer should in some way add weight to the later years as compared with the earlier, thus giving preference in his weighted summary to the student who may have been slower than others in showing academic results.

In the area of personality and social development, the junior college offers in the second year the unique opportunity for the student to carry organizational responsibilities which he does not have until the fourth year in the senior college or university. The students tell us that these junior college responsibilities have often had a maturing effect that has enabled them to make better choices after transfer to the senior college.

These reports give the junior college admissions counselor the encouragement he needs in order to give extra and favorable attention where possible, not only to the late academic bloomer but also to the social wallflower who seems to show evidence of the capacity to develop.

Such evidence of hidden potential comes frequently, of course, from the secondary school counselor. The junior college admissions officer should take special pains to develop close relationships with school counselors, through school visits and frequent telephoning as well as correspondence, if he expects to give adequate attention to the special characteristics of this kind of junior college candidate.

THE JUNIOR COLLEGE SPECIALIZES IN ATTENTION TO THE INDIVIDUAL

A professed attribute of every small college, its ability to give close attention to the needs of the individual student, is a universally claimed characteristic of the junior college. Perhaps all the foregoing functions of the junior college depend on this one. Senior colleges of moderate size probably vary considerably in their efforts and success in this area, but certainly no two-year college (with the possible exception of the "juniorversities" of the West) can be considered to be truly offering the "two-year opportunity" unless it shows results in this effort.

The place to begin giving attention to the individual is in the admissions office. If the prospective student cannot sense, in his dealings with admissions, that someone is interested in him as an individual with his own peculiar personal and educational successes and failures, how is he to believe that the institution will be concerned about him?

The personal note in reply to the applicant's opening inquiry, the letter that really answers his question instead of routinely enclosing another brochure, the friendly interview, the decision and notification procedure that is designed in consideration of *his* welfare and not only that of the college, and the friendly and personalized transition of the accepted student from the admissions office into the custody of the deans—all are opportunities for the junior college admissions officer to affirm his institution's interest in the individual. Some of these steps deserve further mention.

The interview is a frequently misused admissions technique. Some colleges can so structure and conduct a student interview that they feel its results can be used with confidence as an important factor in the admissions decision, but reports of the unreliability of the interview as a screening device are legion.

Whether or not the junior college admissions officer has confidence in his ability to measure the candidate's eligibility for admission in an interview, he would do well, if he cares to convince anyone that his institution is concerned for the individual, to give the interview a different emphasis. What matters tremendously here is the attitude of the interviewer toward the interview. Whether he talks or listens, whether he explains or questions, whether the session is long or short, all is really of little importance if he can do one thing: get across to the interviewee the fact that *his* (the student's) questions, *his* concerns, *his* plans, and *his* welfare are the interviewer's concerns of the moment.

This attitude on the part of the interviewer does several things to the interview. First of all, it takes the formidable challenge out of it. Few interviewers are qualified to employ the interview as a reliable test of anything, and if they mistakenly *feel* they are, they certainly do not belong in the junior college admissions office. Rather than being a test or a challenge, the initial interview should aim toward achieving rapport, toward removing tension, toward setting the stage so that the student feels comfortable enough to learn something from the interview.

What he should get out of the interview, primarily, is information. The interview, in the junior college admissions office, more than anything else, should be a two-way information session. What characteristic techniques an interviewer may have for stimulating questions and for handing out information he feels to be pertinent is immaterial as long as his attitude is the proper one and he can get it across to the candidate. There probably is not an experienced admissions interviewer in the business who has not been surprised occasionally by a student's report of "the interviewer's negative and unconcerned attitude" during the interview. Having the proper feeling for the interview is one thing, but one must never let up on the effort to make it show through and get it over the desk and across the carpet.

In the matter of the admissions calendar, there is opportunity for the junior college to show that it is trying to lessen the tension the applicant goes through during the admissions process. The withholding of an admissions decision after it has been made seems to be a peculiar kind of torture. As long as no demand for early commitment by the student to the college is made, there is no reason why the college cannot advise each student individually of the admissions decision as soon as it is made without regard to any agreed-on date among the colleges. This "rolling decision" or "rolling admission" procedure, when it can result in rather prompt notification of the candidate, is the only humane procedure, and every junior college which professes to be concerned about the welfare of the individual student should practice it. When this procedure is effectively carried out, probably no formalized "early decision" plan that insists on set dates of single application and notification is necessary or even helpful.

The most frequently abused step in the college admissions process occurs at the point referred to above at which the accepted candidate is asked to commit himself to the college. The practice of resorting to a sizable, early, nonrefundable deposit to "nail down" the student is not characteristic of either the four-year or of the two-year college but, because so many of the independent junior colleges resort to this practice, it has regrettably come to be thought of in some areas as an opportunistic practice common among junior colleges.

Whether a college does or does not require a deposit from a candidate before he has had a chance to get the results of his other applications (or before the candidates reply date, May 1) is a question of whether the college is concerned primarily about its own planning problems at the expense of the student or whether the college is concerned for the welfare of the student. It is a mockery for the junior college, which insists that it is concerned for the individual, to insist on a penalty payment from that individual who wishes only to wait a reasonable time (until May 1) to hear from other colleges before committing himself to any one. Junior colleges which continue to ignore the student's right to make his college choice by a reasonable date without penalty can hardly convince anyone that in other, more important, matters they are seriously concerned with students' rights.

Junior college admissions offices, adapting as they must to institutional characteristics, will discover other admissions procedures and emphases to support the recognized functions of the two-year colleges. The one thing certain about junior college admissions practice is that, if the two-year college accepts for itself special duties and functions in the pattern of American higher education, the admissions officers in these colleges must go beyond the routine and continually search for manners and means of adapting their admissions procedures to these specialized junior college functions.

Students entering two-year colleges must not only be qualified, but they must have some understanding of why they are there and what is expected of them and of the colleges. The junior college admissions office has the responsibility for careful evaluation of the parties involved—the student and the college—and for bringing the two together into a relationship which has the best possible chance, within the understood functions of the junior college, of being a meaningful and satisfying experience for both.

For suggested readings see page 3-23.

Chapter 11

The Office of Admissions—Role of the Administrator

RICHARD R. PERRY

Associate Executive Vice President for Institutional Research and Administrative Planning, The University of Toledo, Toledo, Ohio

The administration and organization of higher education have been the subjects of inquiry for better than 300 years in the course of the development of colleges and universities in the United States. Both have received increasing attention in this century, and such attention has intensified considerably since 1950. A search of an annotated bibliography provided by Eells and Hollis indicates that about 75 percent of the publications in this area have been developed since 1955. The largest number, which focus most directly on administration, have appeared in the last decade.[1]

The admissions office has received its share of attention in the literature concerning higher education. This attention has increased in recent years. With so much

[1] Walter Crosby Eells and Ernest V. Hollis, *Administration of Higher Education: An annotated bibliography*, U.S. Office of Education Bulletin 53002, no. 70, 1960.

concern of colleges and universities focused upon the kinds of students who are to enter classes, and with colleges and universities evidencing an increasing interest in meeting their obligations to these students, the importance of the college office responsible for the selection of entering classes increases. And, as the responsibility of an office increases, so does the amount of scrutiny fixed on this office.

Significant attention is given to the admissions office in recent writings on higher education. Burns[2] devotes an entire chapter, prepared by Kastner, to the subject of the registrar and director of admissions. Millett[3] indicates the importance of the admissions program to an institution when he establishes that the quality of a college or university depends in the first instance upon the quality of student input. Upholding the quality of student input is the function of an admissions program. Millett points out further that the admissions function has become a specialized service in which a large amount of talent is devoted exclusively to the achievement of important institutional goals. Ayers and Russell[4] carry forward an extensive discussion of the office of admissions in a study of internal structure in higher education, and they describe some of the problems which face it in the rearrangement of organizational structure in institutions of higher education.

The most recent studies of substance which have focused on the admissions office were done by Hauser and Lazarsfeld of the Bureau of Applied Social Research at Columbia University and by this author at the University of Toledo. Both studies bear the title *The Admissions Officer*. The Hauser and Lazarsfeld study establishes the concept that the admissions officer is a specialist who brings unique skills to the responsibilities of his office. These skills result in a singular efficacy for the admissions process.[5] The Perry study suggests a necessity for the admissions officer to be more of a generalist in terms of the competence necessary to discharge the responsibilities of the admissions function.[6]

HISTORICAL ORIGINS OF THE OFFICE

An informative and interesting account of the development of the admissions office is found in the writings of William H. Smerling. His account indicates that this university office has its origin, as do many educational offices, in the medieval university organization. The title given the person holding the office was "major beadle."[7]

There is evidence from other authors that the admissions office is derived from the ancient office of the archivist, which undoubtedly was the forerunner of the registrar.[8] Cambridge University is cited as having had a registrar in 1506, and as having required, by 1544, that all students wishing to attend present themselves to this office. Although Harvard was founded in 1636, it was not until almost 200 years later, according to Smerling, that one finds any evidence of the office of the registrar being identified as part of the administrative structure.

A rapid rise in the number of registrars between 1880 and 1900 is reported, and

[2] Gerald P. Burns, *Administrators in Higher Education*, Harper & Brothers, New York, 1962, pp. 185–205.

[3] John D. Millett, *The Academic Community*, McGraw-Hill Book Company, Inc., New York, 1962, pp. 214–215.

[4] Archie Ayers and John H. Russell, *Internal Structure: Organization and administration of institutions of higher education*, U.S. Office of Education Bulletin OE-53012, no. 9, 1962.

[5] J. Z. Hauser and P. F. Lazarsfeld, *The Admissions Officer*, Bureau of Applied Social Research, Columbia University Press, New York, 1964, pp. II-6–II-8.

[6] Richard R. Perry, *The Admissions Officer*, University of Toledo, Toledo, Ohio, 1964, pp. 50–51.

[7] William H. Smerling, "The Registrar: Changing Aspects," *College and University*, vol. 35, no. 2, pp. 180–186, Winter, 1960.

[8] E. E. Lindsey and E. O. Holland, *College and University Administration*, The Macmillan Company, New York, 1930, p. 6.

McGrath[9] indicates that this increase was necessary because of the concurrent adoption, by many colleges, of the elective system. Fewer than five colleges reported registrars up to 1880; however, by 1890 fifteen colleges had reported registrars and, by 1930, fifty-nine reported registrars.[10] The literature dealing with the history of the admissions office indicates that it grew in a rather haphazard manner and with little attention to professional development in the office. It was the outgrowth of the ineptness of inexperienced clerks and the vagaries of medieval pomp and circumstance which attached themselves to institutions of higher education. However, over the centuries it has grown to such stature that it can be said to rank as one of the major college administrative offices.[11]

If one quarrels with the use of the title "Registrar" when discussing the admissions office, it might be well to settle for the idea that the administrative official charged with the admission of students has historically in hundreds of colleges throughout the United States been known as "the registrar." Specialization in the field of admissions is relatively new to the scene of American higher education, having developed generally since World War II.

CHANNELS OF AUTHORITY AND REPORTING

The office of admissions is in a unique position in the organizational structure of institutions of higher education because it has two channels of authority through which it must report and to which it is accountable. This is true also of the office of the registrar, or the office of admissions and records in those institutions which have combined the operations of admissions and registration.

The first channel of authority for the admissions office is that created for it by the faculty of the institution. It is the faculty of an institution which is charged generally by the board of trustees with the responsibility for establishing the standards of admission which are to be applied by the institution. Thus, this channel of authority must be recognized and kept open without fail by the office of admissions. The office of admissions can keep its channel of communication open to the general policy-making authority of the faculty by various means. One is to have the office of admissions supply the committee on admissions, which is generally composed of faculty members, with periodic reports concerning the results of admissions-office operations. A second means of communication with the faculty is the involving of members of the faculty in the operational admissions decisions. The extent to which faculty are involved in admissions decisions may vary. The faculty members of an admissions committee may be asked to read the admission files of all candidates, making recommendations for admissions as they see fit. On the other hand, they may look at sample files cases of applicants only, letting the admissions office know which kinds of students they are interested in having and, concomitantly, keeping themselves informed about the types of students available to the institution under its current admissions policy. In keeping the lines of communication open to the faculty, which is the authority behind admissions policy, the admissions office is recognizing its role of being that office which interprets the admissions policy of the institution, formulated by the faculty, to the general public, schools, and candidates and in turn being that office which implements the general admissions policy of the faculty operationally.

The admissions office must recognize the absolute importance of this channel of

[9] Earl J. McGrath, *The Evolution of Administrative Offices and Institutions of Higher Education in the United States, 1860–1933,* doctoral dissertation, University of Chicago, Chicago, 1936.

[10] B. H. Jarman, "The Registrar in Institutions Accredited by the Association of American Universities," *College and University,* vol. 23, no. 2, pp. 96–113, October, 1947.

[11] Edith D. Cockins, "The Registrar: A Present-day Appraisal," *Bulletin of the American Association of Collegiate Registrars,* vol. 7, no. 2, pp. 205–229, 1932.

faculty authority and the necessity for the admissions office to communicate with faculty about necessary changes in the institution's admissions policy. No other office on the campus should be more informed about the need for changes in admissions policy than the office of admissions. It is the professional staff of the office of admissions which is in daily contact with hundreds of secondary schools and professional counselors and should be in the best position to keep faculty informed about the kinds of students the institution should be admitting. This responsibility requires a particularly well-qualified admissions staff; otherwise recommendations for changes in admissions policy which emanate from the admissions office will not be received with respect by the faculty nor will they receive the attention necessary for implementation.

The second channel of authority and reporting for the admissions office is the formal administrative structure of the institution. An effective way of determining to which superior administrative office in an institution the admissions office reports is to determine to which office the annual report of the admissions office is presented. Perry found that 50 percent of the directors of admissions reported directly to the president of the institution. In other instances the admissions office reported next most frequently to the office of the provost, the vice-president for academic affairs, or the dean of a college; and then next most frequently to the vice-president for student affairs or the dean of students. In some instances admissions officers reported to the ranking financial officer of their institutions or to the officer in charge of development.

The question of to whom the person responsible for the admissions office is to report will naturally be settled by individual institutions. However, it is well for any institution to consider the nature of the function being performed when deciding where the admissions office shall be placed in an administrative organization. Is the admissions office to be considered part of student personnel administration, as indicated by Ayers, Russell and Tripp,[12] or shall it be considered part of the academic administration as suggested by Kastner?[13] The answers to these questions will be different on different campuses; however, any such answer needs to contend with at least a brief analysis of the importance which is attached to the function being located in an administrative structure.

Experienced and perceptive educators are increasingly aware that size and complexity in institutions of higher education have tended to produce an ennui in leadership among faculty where the basic administrative policy of an institution is concerned. This inability on the part of the faculty to exercise leadership results directly from the increasing complexity and expanding activity in higher education, which seem to place the total, complex operational thrust of the university or college beyond the mastery and understanding of the individual faculty member or even that of the faculty as a group.[14]

The ability of the admissions officer to contribute to the leadership of the university from his extensive knowledge of students who seek admission and of the contribution these students can make toward improving the intellectual climate of the institution can be effective only to the extent that the admissions office is directly involved in the central administrative policy formulation of the university. This necessity has been recognized. One college president has stated, "The admissions officer is at the very center of the campus authority structure."[15]

An understanding of this relationship of centrality for the admissions office in the

[12] Archie R. Ayers, John H. Russell, and Philip A. Tripp, *Student Services Administration in Higher Education,* U.S. Office of Education Bulletin, no. 16, 1966, p. 3.

[13] Elwood Kastner in Gerald P. Burns (Ed.), *Administrators in Higher Education,* Harper & Row, Publishers, Incorporated, New York, 1962, p. 200.

[14] Ross Mooney, "Leadership in the University," *Harvard Educational Review,* vol. 33, no. 1, p. 51, Winter, 1963.

[15] Val H. Wilson, "Who Wields the Power: Administrators and campus authority structure," *ACAC Journal,* vol. 9, no. 2, p. 27, Fall, 1963.

institution's power structure is voiced by Millett, who indicates that "the quality of a college or university depends in the first instance upon the quality of its student input."[16] No more cogent statement of the importance of the admissions office and the necessity of bringing the understanding of that function to bear on the policy decisions of the university is likely to be made.

If one is willing to accept judgments offered by knowledgeable college presidents that the admissions office occupies a central position in the authority structure of an institution and that it is responsible for a most important resource necessary for sustaining and improving the academic climate of an institution, then an enigma is identified. For many admissions offices this enigma lies in the fact that they bear the responsibility for one of the most important activities of a university and yet they are often unable to participate equally and directly in basic administrative decisions affecting the responsibility which the office must meet.

It seems that a solution is to have college administrative authority reexamine the worthiness of having contributions of their experienced admission officers present in the regular and routine deliberations through which general university policy is formulated.

The arguments for placing the admissions office within the administrative structure of an institution can lead to the conclusion that, since the major responsibility of the office is in sustaining and improving the academic climate on the campus, it should be located administratively in the academic segment of university administration.

There are numerous arguments for placing the office of admissions under a vice-president or a dean; but if the institution values the importance of the office to the educational objectives of the campus it will honor that valuation by having it report to the office of the president. No other office of the university or college has the opportunity to create the total impact of change in an institution that is available through the office of admissions. The quality of the students recruited for the institution will in large measure determine the academic reputation of the institution. Although an institution may seek an outstanding faculty, that faculty will not stay without a student body willing and able to accept the level of academic challenge that it can offer. Institutional budgets are founded, both in public and private colleges, on the assumption that the office of admission will meet enrollment quotas and in doing so provide a student body with as little potential for attrition as possible. Such responsibility calls for outstanding leadership and direct access to the office of the president, for the office of admissions serves the total institution.

SUPERVISION OF FACULTY AND CLERICAL EFFORTS

The admissions office, with its responsibility of reporting to the faculty and of working closely with members of the faculty, must develop reasonable procedures to effectively use the talents of faculty in the admissions process. The most notable procedures followed are those which involve faculty in the admissions committee which reviews credentials offered by candidates for admission. While faculty are often eager to take on this kind of responsibility, the admissions office may find that it must adopt one of two practices in making credentials available to faculty for review. Either the faculty member will be asked to review admission files in the office of admissions only, in order to protect the confidential nature of the information in the candidate's file, or the admissions office will have to operate a close check and follow-up system on files which it makes available to faculty members in their own offices. No more distressing situation can develop than to have a candidate inquire about the status of his application only to find that the file has been given to a faculty member of the admissions committee

[16] John D. Millett, *op. cit.*, p. 214.

for review who has subsequently taken the file to his office and now is unable to produce it because it has been mislaid.

Whether the policy is to have the faculty of the admissions committee review all cases or only marginal cases, the admissions office is responsible for the security of every admissions folder and it should keep track of its whereabouts. A good procedure to be followed in ensuring the security of files and fixing the responsibility for their location where faculty are involved in the review of such files is to request faculty who remove files from the admissions office to sign for the files. A far better procedure is to have the admissions office so located that a nearby conference room is available for meetings that the admissions committee holds in order to review credentials. If it is necessary for individuals to review files, private office space should be available in the admissions office complex for this purpose. A general recommendation is that no admissions folder be removed from the admissions or registrar's office.

Modern data processing procedures available through the use of either machine tabulating or computer equipment make it possible to provide members of the admissions committee with as much information in printout form, with suitable coding of recommendations, as one can find in the original data located in the admission folder. Thus original documents can be retained secure in the admissions office and printouts of information can be given to faculty who review these credentials.

A second area of faculty involvement which requires careful coordination is the use of faculty in advising students about the academic programs of the institution. Many offices of admissions invite members of the faculty to represent the institution at college day or college night programs to which the institution has been invited to send representatives. Many faculty members are willing to accept a limited number of such assignments. The admissions office must see to it that the faculty member is fully informed of the admissions policy of the institution and that the faculty member is made fully aware of the requirements for admission to programs outside of his own discipline in order that the faculty can serve the total interests of the institution with confidence.

It is well for an admissions office which makes use of faculty to assist in its recruiting program to have those who will be involved identified early in the fall of the year and called together for a number of orientation sessions. During these sessions the admissions office can cover an agenda of details which the faculty member will have to familiarize himself with in order to serve satisfactorily. Some of the items to be covered in such orientation sessions are:

1. A short history of the institution
2. The educational objectives of the institution and their meaning for the student
3. The accreditation of the educational program of the institution
4. Requirements for admission to all educational programs of the institution
5. Composition of the student body
6. Cost of attending the institution
7. Financial aid available to students
8. The institution's academic calendar
9. Residence hall regulations
10. The student activity program of the institution

Individual institutions will want to add to the above list, but it is comprehensive enough to be used as an agenda for orientation sessions involving faculty who will recruit students for the institution.

The supervision of clerical personnel in the admissions office will vary, naturally, with the size of the institution and the functions for which the office is responsible. The smaller college which has as its staff only a director of admissions and perhaps one or two clerical workers will find that such supervision is a matter of direct contact and communication between the director of the office and the clerical staff. However, as the admissions office increases its staff, in terms of professional admissions counselors and supporting clerical staff, the job of direct supervision is one which cannot be undertaken solely by the administrative head of the office. Large admissions office staffs which serve complex universities are quite likely to have a director or executive dean and several associate or assistant directors or deans. Specialization is the keynote in such offices, with a professional administrator in charge of each of the following: entering freshmen, transfer students, foreign students, graduate students, and students being admitted to the professional colleges or schools of the university. Each of these professional associates in the office will in turn be developing his own clerical staff which will report directly to him, just as he is responsible to the executive head of the office. In general the direct supervision of clerical personnel should be left in the hands of an experienced senior administrative assistant who can act as an office or section manager, seeing to it that correspondence is kept up-to-date and that all admissions files and records are processed according to the procedures established for the office. The orientation of new clerical employees to their responsibilities is a matter best left to the administrative assistant and the associate professional in the office who will be directing the work of the clerical staff, leaving the executive administrative head of the office free of these details.

PROBLEMS OF RECRUITMENT OF ADMISSIONS FACULTY PERSONNEL

A number of problems present themselves in the selection of faculty who are to be involved in the admissions process. The most important problem is the identification of those faculty members who are seriously enough interested in the admissions function to devote sufficient time to their responsibility in this area. If the admissions office is interested in having something more than a casual involvement of faculty in its functions, it will be placing a considerable work load on faculty. Reading hundreds of candidates' folders, visiting high schools, and making appearances before secondary school student groups is demanding. A satisfactory way of compensating faculty for this demanding involvement in the admissions processes of the institution is to arrange with the academic administration to have reduced teaching loads established for those faculty who accept the responsibility of reviewing candidates credentials or performing other regular professional services in the admissions office. In those instances where members of the admissions committee are teaching faculty, they may be compensated for their admissions responsibilities by a one-quarter reduction in their teaching loads. The same holds true for that member of the faculty who, though not a member of the admissions committee, is asked to involve himself in any substantial number of visits to secondary schools.

A most effective way to identify faculty who are interested in the admissions process is to meet with the top-level members of the academic administration of the institution, explaining to them the need for involvement of faculty in this process and encouraging the administration to identify for the admissions office those members of the faculty that it would recommend for such involvement. It is then the responsibility of the admissions office to contact the faculty members and talk extensively with them, explaining the responsibilities of the function.

An additional problem to be reckoned with in the recruitment of faculty for involvement in the admissions process is that of involving those faculty who have had experience of reasonable length at the institution. It is unwise, and indeed probably an imposition, to involve a new member of the faculty in the admissions process during his first year or two of service to the institution. Admissions decisions cannot be made as effectively by persons who are completely new to an institution as they can by those who have had some experience. Any admissions decision must be made within the context of the objectives and overall purpose of the college or university. To effect admissions decisions without this knowledge, gained by institutional experience, is possible and can be an efficient procedure; but it is unlikely that it will be effective in terms of either the needs of the students who are applying for admission or the educational objectives of the college or university. Those involved in the admissions process should have had some experience at the institution before effecting decisions or playing major roles in the admissions process because of the tendency of new faculty to bring with them the imprint of educational objectives and procedures in force at the institutions which they have left. This is not to reject out of hand the benefits which can be derived from the infusion of new ideas and the experiences of individuals who have operated in different contexts, but it is to say that the tendency to imprint procedures of one institution with the benefits of those procedures in another institution requires careful testing and evaluation of the possible outcomes of such change before decisions are finalized.

PROFESSIONAL AND PERSONAL QUALIFICATIONS OF THE ADMISSIONS COUNSELOR

Personal Qualifications The admissions counselor who is a junior staff member of the admissions office should be professionally qualified as a counselor if the institution identifies his position with that title. This means that the professional preparation of the admissions counselor should include a graduate degree in the field of educational counseling. It is unfair to the student and to secondary schools with which the institution works to identify personnel in an admissions office as counselors unless they can demonstrate that they have completed a professional program in the field of counseling. One of the significant dilemmas in the admission of students to college is that the great majority of admissions staff personnel bear the title "Admissions Counselor" and yet are not professionally prepared in the field of counseling. No professional counselor-educator in the field of higher education is likely to agree that a person who is not professionally prepared can do what is implied in the job title "Admissions Counselor." Compounding this dilemma is the fact that most secondary school counselors who guide high school students on their way into college are better prepared professionally in the field of counseling than are many of the admissions counselors who visit secondary schools seeking to "counsel" students concerning admission to their respective colleges or universities.

An indication of the characteristics which are thought desirable in a person to be employed as assistant in the office of admissions or as an admissions counselor, since the latter is often the more prevalent job title, is found in the listing in Table 1.

TABLE 1 Characteristics Considered Important in Hiring an Assistant *

Four Groups of Characteristics

1. Friendliness	83%
2. Poise	77%
3. Educational beliefs	70%
4. Familiarity with high school	43%
5. Experience in guidance	37%
6. Teaching experience	17%
7. Training in psychology	14%
8. Statistical training	13%
9. Alumnus	8%

* J. Z. Hauser and P. F. Lazarsfeld, *The Admissions Officer*, Bureau of Applied Social Research, Columbia University Press, New York, 1964, p. IV-9.

Another way of looking at the personal qualifications of the admissions officer or the admissions counselor who aspires to such a position is to look at those qualities in the individual which are considered important in evaluating the effectiveness of the office of which they are in charge. Table 2 shows a ranking of criteria judged important, by directors of admissions, for the purpose of evaluating the effectiveness of an admissions office. While the criteria are to be applied in evaluating the effectiveness of an office, it is apparent that they apply with equal rigor to the individual in charge of the office and to those junior assistants directly involved in the success of the office.

These personal qualities suggested as criteria for measuring the effectiveness of the office reflect the interest of the admissions office in gaining friends for the institution and in acquiring the professional respect of fellow educators and admissions officers, in exercising leadership, and in maintaining high academic standards. Along with these goes a concern for the integrity and ethical fiber of the admissions officer. His willingness to work long hours and, importantly, his concern for the influence of his moral character upon students and faculty support the view that those personal qualifications which represent the highest academic and moral issues should be given serious consideration in the selection of those who serve the admissions office.

Professional Qualifications Competence in professional skills is the result of achievements in a formalized educational program. The studied opinions of practitioners in a field of endeavor are a reasonable source from which to gain an idea of the areas of study which might be helpful to the future admissions officer.

TABLE 2 Criteria of Effectiveness for the Admissions Officer *

Rank	*Item*
1.	Facility in making friends for the institution
2.	Respect accorded him by other educators, including other deans or directors of admissions
3.	Leadership in maintaining high academic standards for the institution
4.	Continued improvement in the academic quality of the student body
5.	Willingness to work long hours
6.	Influence of his moral character upon students and faculty
7.	General intellectual leadership in the college and community
8.	Performance as a public speaker
9.	The graduation of a high percentage of the entering class
10.	Ability to produce favorable publicity
11.	Ability to maintain a balanced budget
12.	Continuing growth of the institution's enrollment

* Richard R. Perry, *The Admissions Officer,* University of Toledo, Toledo, Ohio, 1964, p. 41.

Kastner has indicated that the work of the admissions office is a career in itself and that this career requires a definite preparation and specific abilities. Kastner outlines 15 specific areas which would be helpful as fields of study in preparation for the admissions officer's position.[17]

The opinions of the admissions officers reported in the Perry study indicate a ranking of possible areas of course work. (See Table 3.)

In establishing this ranking for course work areas, the admissions officers seem to indicate a need for graduate work which will sharpen competence in human relations and interpersonal dimensions. There is strong reason to suspect that course work at the graduate level for the admissions officer should be concentrated in the field of student personnel administration. There is hardly a course or area of study suggested

[17] Gerald P. Burns, *op. cit.*, pp. 201–203.

TABLE 3 Ranking of Graduate Course Work Helpful to the Admissions Officer *

1.	Guidance and counseling
2.	Personnel administration
3.	Human relations
4.	Psychology
5.	Philosophy of education
6.5	Humanities
6.5	Public relations
8.	Educational planning
9.	Curriculum and higher education
10.	Administrative theory and practice
11.	Statistical methods
12.	Educational business management
13.	History of education
14.	Research techniques
15.	Educational facilities
16.	Group dynamics
17.	Journalism
18.	Educational finance

* Richard R. Perry, *The Admissions Officer*, University of Toledo, Toledo, Ohio, 1964, pp. 42–43.

in the top 15 which is not included in some way or other in student personnel-administration programs.[18]

The Hauser and Lazarsfeld study discloses (see Table 4) the experiences and attitudes of admissions officers toward available course work which may be relevant to their responsibilities.

One should note the similarity in the information offered in Table 4 and that in Table 3, as comparisons are made between the ranking of importance of course work in Table 3 with those courses taken and considered valuable in Table 4. Courses identified in

TABLE 4 Experiences and Attitudes of Admissions Officers Concerning Course Work *

Course subject	Percent who took course	Percent who considered course valuable	Percent who planned to take course
History of education	74	26	3
Measurement and statistics	68	73	16
Experimental methods	30	21	8
Teaching methods	70	14	1
Clinical psychology	19	22	6
Educational administration	54	54	13
Sociology	67	33	3
Guidance	56	66	12
Adolescent psychology	64	52	4

* J. Z. Hauser and P. F. Lazarsfeld, *The Admissions Officer*, Bureau of Applied Social Research, Columbia University Press, New York, 1964, p. II-11.

[18] Thomas A. Emmett, *Current Professional Degree Training Programs for College and University Student Personnel Administrators and Workers Based upon Course Work, Practicum and Internship in Student Personnel Work in Higher Education as a Major Field of Study*, Studies in Higher Education for College and University Student Personnel Workers, no. 2, University of Detroit, Detroit, Mich., Autumn, 1962.

Table 4 which represent study in what can be classified as the student personnel-administration area were not only taken by more of the respondents but were considered to be valuable by more of the respondents than other types of courses identified. Information in these two studies supports the contention that course work in the general area of student personnel administration is of significant value in developing the professional qualifications of an admissions officer.

In addition to the formal education qualifications represented by areas of course work, it is interesting to note the level of degrees earned by admissions officers. The level of degree possessed by those in a profession is one indication of the level of competence demanded of them as they seek to enter and advance in the profession. The Perry study discloses that of all the directors of admissions who held a master's degree, each considered that his present level of professional preparation was inadequate. This study suggests that, increasingly, it is considered desirable for persons in charge of admissions to hold a doctorate.

A concern for competence is one which centers in skills and particular kinds of knowledge which need to be present to accomplish particular tasks. Perhaps the concern for each institution needs to begin with an identification of what the institution expects the admissions office to accomplish. Skills and knowledge must be related to the objective the office is to achieve.

Competence may grow out of graduate programs in guidance and counseling, statistical methods, research techniques, and administration; but to hold that only studies of this kind can qualify a person for admissions work would be to limit unnecessarily the consideration of competence to the area of formalized course work. Some competence is gained by demonstrated successful experience in carefully prescribed disciplines. However, it is suggested that the qualifications of an admissions officer need to be greater than those that may be gained from course work alone. The business of the admissions office is education; indeed it is higher education. The admissions officer has a specific responsibility for riveting the attention of the academic community to its central and most important commitment—the education of an enlightened citizenry. This challenge seems to require qualifications beyond the ordinary level.

IN-SERVICE TRAINING TECHNIQUES AND PROFESSIONAL IMPROVEMENT

Fortunately, a number of professional organizations provide varied in-service experiences at the state, regional, and national levels for admissions office personnel interested in in-service experiences. Conferences and national meetings scheduled by the American Association of Collegiate Registrars and Admissions Officers, the Association of College Admissions Counselors, the College Entrance Examination Board, the American College Testing Program, and the American Personnel Guidance Association all contain information and experiences which provide valuable in-service results. Participation in these formal meetings yields beneficial results for both the admissions officer and the assistant professionals of the office. However, the inexperienced counselor should especially try to participate in the growing number of summer institutes for admissions office personnel. The College Entrance Examination Board began sponsoring such institutes in the summer of 1959, beginning with a single institute at Harvard College, and while that institute has continued each summer since, the College Entrance Examination Board has expanded the number of such institutes to include those held at the University of Virginia, the University of Chicago, Tulane University, Duke University, Stanford University, Washington University, and Interlochen, Michigan, in cooperation with the University of Michigan. While the purpose of these institutes has been to bring the inexperienced admissions person into contact with the issues, techniques, challenges, and problems of admissions work, many experienced admissions officers have found them to be of significant help in keeping them up to date with their respective fields. The Ohio Association of College Admissions Counselors sponsored a successful summer institute at Mt. Union College during August, 1967. Other institutes have been held at Siena College, in 1966, and at John Carroll University in the summer of 1967.

The professional admissions officer will also want to continue his formal education. The majority of admissions officers, as shown in the Hauser and Lazarsfeld and the Perry studies, are persons who have earned less than the doctorate. Participation in formal study toward the doctoral degree should be given serious consideration by each admissions officer. Such study can be accomplished during summer months and, where convenient, in part-time doctoral programs at major universities. The selection of a major field of study at the doctoral level is, of course, a matter of individual choice; but it should be noted that there is no particular pressure for the selection of one major field of study over another. While the weight of evidence seems to point to the popularity of doctorates in student personnel administration, many competent admissions officers who have made significant contributions to the profession have done their doctoral work in other fields.

An admissions staff has many opportunities on its own campus for in-service training and the upgrading of the professional qualifications of its members. Drive-in conferences for the college counselors of secondary schools in the immediate area will yield beneficial results for inexperienced personnel. Regular meetings which center on acquainting staff with the latest developments in the field under the guidance of an experienced admissions officer will be helpful. The admissions office should make ready use of experienced admissions personnel from other colleges and universities nearby on a consulting basis in order to benefit from their professional experience. The American Association of Collegiate Registrars and Admissions Officers, the Association of College Admissions Counselors, the National Association of Foreign Student Advisors, and the College Entrance Examination Board all provide consulting services to individual colleges or to the staffs of groups of colleges.

In-service training of the admissions staff must be looked upon as the continuing responsibility to keep the entire staff of the office, from the senior professional officer to the newest clerical member, aware of the newest developments in the field of college admissions.

THE DEPARTMENTAL FACULTY MEETING AS AN EDUCATIONAL EXPERIENCE FOR THE CAREER ADMISSIONS OFFICER

Departmental meetings of the faculty can be valuable experiences in the education of the career admissions officer. Their value is in the communication which can be established between the faculty and the professional admissions staff on matters of academic policy which affect the quality of students admitted to the university and the performance of those students in academic programs after admission. Most important for the admissions staff is the benefit of establishing a close liaison with departmental faculty so as to achieve an understanding of the objectives of academic programs directed by the departmental faculty. It is important for admissions staff to be aware of and to understand significant changes in a department's curriculum in order that the admissions staff can give the most up-to-date information to the students and counselors of secondary schools. Without participating in departmental faculty meetings—unless strong communication is developed in a different fashion between the admissions staff and the faculty—the admissions office will find its knowledge of the institution's programs inadequate.

By meeting regularly with departmental faculty, the admissions officer can develop a thorough knowledge of the academic climate and the general educational objectives of the campus he serves. He cannot operate administratively in an academic vacuum. The interchange of ideas between departmental faculty and the professional staff of the admissions office serves also as a testing procedure for the implementation of proposed changes in admissions policy. Departmental faculty meetings can inform the admissions office of what a faculty would like to have done to satisfy the growth needs of the department. In turn, the admissions office can keep the departmental faculty informed of fluctuations in secondary school graduation rates which will affect the number of applicants for department programs. The chief value to the admissions officer of the departmental faculty meeting is the opportunity it gives him to become better informed about the academic programs of the institution.

For suggested readings see page 3-23.

Chapter 12

Admissions Department Costs and Budgeting

RICHARD R. PERRY

Associate Executive Vice President for Institutional Research and Administrative Planning, The University of Toledo, Toledo, Ohio

INTRODUCTION

The greater portion of the administrative responsibility of the admissions office centers in its contact with students and its cooperation with the academic programs of the institution. There is, nevertheless, an important administrative responsibility involved in seeing to the efficient administration of the budget for the office. It has been said that everything costs money. This is as true of the operation of the office of admissions as it is of any department of a university. The responsibility for developing and gaining approval of a budget which will enable the office to successfully serve the institution belongs to the executive head of the department.

Shown in Figures 1 and 2 are summary and detail forms used at the University of Toledo in the preparation of departmental budget requests. Included are budget categories which must be justified and provided for each department. Satisfactory explanation is required for each item or action requested.

FORM 28–FI 1–68

1968–69 EXPENDITURE BUDGET REQUEST
INSTRUCTIONAL A N D GENERAL
T H E U N I V E R S I T Y O F T O L E D O

NOTE: ROUND ALL AMOUNTS TO THE NEAREST DOLLAR, OMITTING ALL CENTS.

COLLEGE	DEPARTMENT	ACCOUNT

ACCT. NO.	ACCOUNT NAME	1967–68 BUDGET	DEPARTMENT REQUEST	RECOMMENDED BY DEAN	AMOUNT APPROVED
	SALARIES				
111	–ADMINIS. PROF. AND TECH.				
112	–SECRETARIAL, CLERICAL AND FISCAL				
121	–FULL TIME FACULTY				
122	–FACULTY SUMMER SESSION				
123	–PART TIME FACULTY				
124	–PART TIME FACULTY – SUMMER SESSION				
125	–GRADUATE ASSISTANTS				
141	–MAINTENANCE AND SAFETY				
151	–PART TIME – STUDENT				
152	–PART TIME – NON–STUDENT				
184	EMPLOYMENT CONTRACTORS				
191	HONORARIA				
221	RETIREMENT – ACADEMIC				
222	RETIREMENT – NON–ACADEMIC				
231	WORKMEN'S COMPENSATION				
241	GROUP INSURANCE				
256	FEES WAIVED – GRADUATE ASSISTANTS				
	SUPPLIES				
311	–OFFICE SUPPLIES				
312	–OFFICE EQUIPMENT REPAIRS				
313	–OFFICE EQUIPMENT RENTALS				
321	–INSTRUCTIONAL SUPPLIES				
322	–INSTRUCTIONAL EQUIPMENT REPAIRS				
323	–INSTRUCTIONAL EQUIPMENT RENTALS				
392	–OTHER				
411	TRAVEL – CONFERENCES, COMMITTEES, ETC.				
461	ENTERTAINMENT – LOCAL				
511	SUBSCRIPTIONS				
521	DUES				
531	PRINTING				
541	ADVERTISING				
551	TELEPHONE AND TELEGRAPH				
571	POSTAGE				
642	ROOM RENTAL				
941	CAPITAL OUTLAY – OFFICE EQUIPMENT				
942	CAPITAL OUTLAY – INSTRUCTIONAL EQUIPMENT				
	TOTALS	$	$	$	$

APPROVED (DEPARTMENT HEAD)	APPROVED (DEAN OR DIRECTOR)

FI 71 168 2M

Fig. 1 *Summary budget form used at the University of Toledo.*

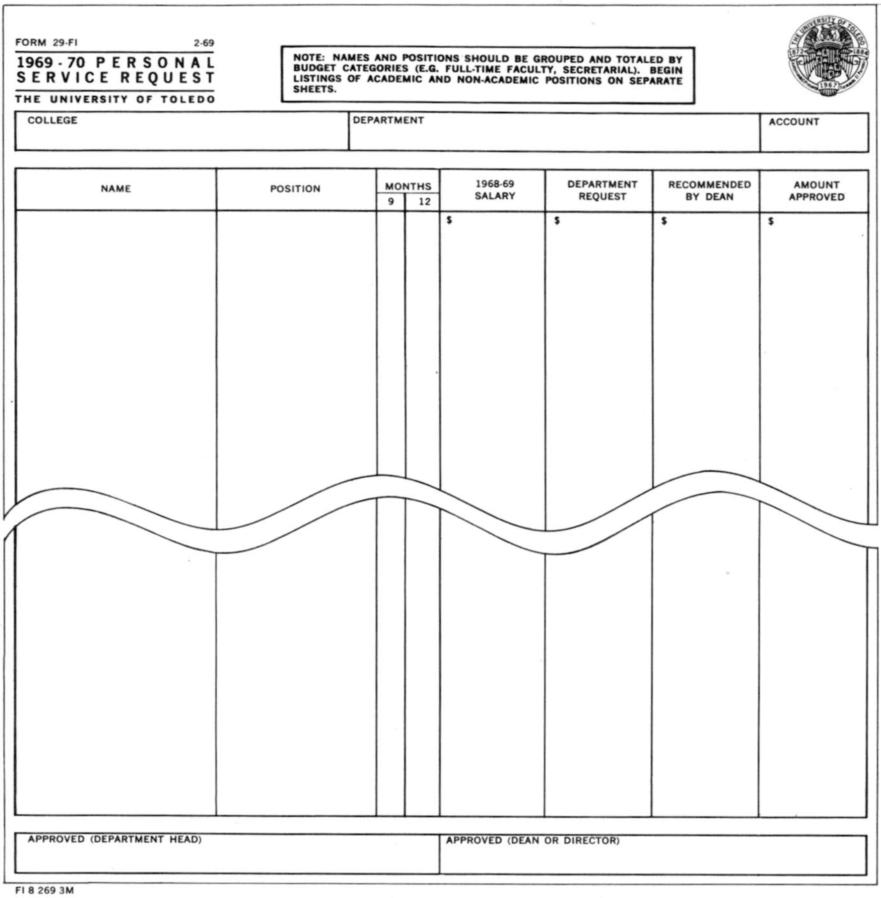
FORM 29-FI 2-69

1969-70 PERSONAL SERVICE REQUEST

THE UNIVERSITY OF TOLEDO

NOTE: NAMES AND POSITIONS SHOULD BE GROUPED AND TOTALED BY BUDGET CATEGORIES (E.G. FULL-TIME FACULTY, SECRETARIAL). BEGIN LISTINGS OF ACADEMIC AND NON-ACADEMIC POSITIONS ON SEPARATE SHEETS.

COLLEGE	DEPARTMENT	ACCOUNT

NAME	POSITION	MONTHS 9	MONTHS 12	1968-69 SALARY	DEPARTMENT REQUEST	RECOMMENDED BY DEAN	AMOUNT APPROVED
				$	$	$	$

APPROVED (DEPARTMENT HEAD)	APPROVED (DEAN OR DIRECTOR)

FI 8 269 3M

Fig. 2 *Budget request form used at the University of Toledo.*

While other budget matters are important, it is likely that those which will demand considerable time and thought before the department head arrives at his recommendations to the administration for the next year are those affecting salaries for administrative and clerical staff.

ADMINISTRATIVE SALARY RECOMMENDATIONS

Administrative salary recommendations require that the performance record of each staff member be reviewed carefully. An executive administrator who, as a matter of policy, treats each member of his staff equally on the ground that differences in performance cannot be determined is identifying himself as ineffective and irresponsible.

Criterion areas which need to be considered in the review of a professional staff member's performance are:

Performance What has been the effectiveness of the individual in meeting the responsibilities of his special assignment in the office? Have crises developed as a result of his performance? Have serious lapses in communication between the institution and prospective students or the faculty developed as a result of his actions? Has the number of candidates for admission attributed to the individual's work come up to the institution's expectations?

Innovation What useful changes in admissions procedures or contacts with students can be attributed to him? Are his recommendations for change thoughtfully prepared and comprehensively presented? Have past recommendations by this staff member been accepted, successfully implemented, and proven to be of benefit to the operation of the office and the institution?

Education What has the staff member done to improve his knowledge of higher education and the role of the admissions office? Has he participated in formal course work leading to a higher degree? Has he taken advantage of opportunities to attend summer institutes? Has he participated where possible in the meetings of professional organizations?

Personal Image Do students and counselors in the schools have a positive reaction to him and hence to the college? Do faculty and administration also have a positive reaction toward this member of the staff?

Does the institution have a general salary-increase policy for administrative personnel? How will the requested salary compare with what is paid in the institution for positions of comparable responsibility that are staffed by persons of comparable qualification?

The above may be taken into consideration as salary recommendations for professional staff are considered. However, the responsible administrator must also provide in his budget for additional administrative staff if necessary, and he must be prepared to justify such additions. This justification will generally depend on:

1. Changes in institutional policy which may necessitate more extensive recruiting in secondary schools and in entirely new geographic areas.
2. Inauguration of special educational programs which may also require additional administrative staff, as the difficulty involved in recruiting students with special talents is considerably greater and more demanding than making contacts for the usual programs.

Attention must be directed also to salaries to be requested for the purpose of filling staff vacancies. Decisions must be reached as to whether the replacement should be an experienced and well-qualified professional or whether the position should be filled by someone of less experience at a lower salary than that which was paid the person who left the position. The practice of paying new persons salaries nearly equal to or greater than those received by staff members with reasonably long tenure is foolhardy unless, of course, new members of the staff are of clearly superior qualification.

Recommendations for clerical personnel also depend on whether the institution has a set policy for across-the-board-increases with additional sums available for merit increases. Criteria generally applied in reviewing nonacademic staff for merit increases are:

1. Competence in performing assigned tasks
2. Reliability on the job in terms of absenteeism
3. Loyalty to the organization and the institution
4. The extent to which the employee has improved in job skills
5. Continued evidence of a sound moral character

Much of the success and efficiency of the admission office rests firmly in the hands of a competent, cheerful, and courteous clerical staff. An admissions office operates properly only with the wholehearted support of the clerical staff. Its interests should receive full attention in budget salary recommendations.

COSTS OF TRAVEL

Costs of travel can be accurately estimated for realistic budgeting by making a few elementary calculations in regard to proposed expenditures. Following the steps outlined in Figure 3 will permit the executive officer to arrive at some realistic totals for travel.

1. $\frac{\text{No. of high schools to visit}}{\text{Schools per day}}$ (Per diem allowance × staff) *	______
2. Reimbursement per mile × miles in personal car + anticipated tolls = mileage charge	______
3. Rental autos: no. of days + mileage = leased charges	______
4. Public transportation (air, rail, bus, other): these can be accurately estimated in advance by planning travel six months to a year in advance	______
5. Travel for conferences and meetings not directly related to recruiting in schools: follow guidelines above and add registration fees to get off-campus conference and meeting costs	______
6. Entertainment of university guests; explain purpose	______

* If no per diem limits are imposed, average of last three years' per diem can be used as guideline.

Fig. 3 *Form for estimate of travel costs by admissions department, University of Toledo.*

COSTS OF PROMOTIONAL LITERATURE

Costs of promotional literature are often included in the admissions budget. Therefore, it is necessary for the office to keep a record of the number of catalogs, view books, and small brochures distributed by the office. These materials, designed to offer information and attract the attention of candidates, are important to the success of the recruiting program. Their cost can be determined with accuracy by submitting proposed copy to a printer for firm quotations. Printers' quotations should be part of the supporting document accompanying budget requests. The standard form shown in Figure 4 may be useful as a model for this purpose.

The admissions office should not limit its consideration of promotional material to catalogs, booklets, and pamphlets. Imaginative and innovative admissions offices have made good use of filmstrips and long-playing records detailing the characteristics of their colleges. The filmstrips and long-playing records used by the University of Toledo were developed, principally, under the direction of Guidance Associates of Pleasantville, N.Y. Also, the admissions offices of colleges in Ohio belonging to the Ohio College Association produced during the 1965–1967 period a series of half-hour public-service TV programs on video tape. These programs focused specifically on admissions policies, procedures, and the educational programs of Ohio colleges. The entire series of 55 programs was used by 15 commercial and educational television stations during this period. Other colleges have developed the use of audio tapes of admissions information which can be placed on file in the offices of guidance counselors in high schools or in high school libraries. Thus, the preparation of this portion of the budget must provide for the possibilities of these new media.

FORM 24–PO 2–66

REQUEST FOR PUBLICATIONS ESTIMATE

THE UNIVERSITY OF TOLEDO

THE UNIVERSITY RETAINS THE RIGHT OF FREE ACCESS TO AND USE FOR OTHER REPRODUCTIVE PURPOSES OF ALL PREPARATORY MATERIALS INCLUDING GRAPHIC NEGATIVES AND POSITIVES AND/OR ENGRAVING REPRODUCTIONS AS WELL AS ORIGINAL ART AND OTHER GRAPHIC PRESENTATIONS.

FROM **Publications Office, Room 224 University Hall** **Telephone: (Area 419) 531-5711 Ext. 255 or 525**	DATE April 13, 1967
BY Thomas Durnford, Publications Manager	ESTIMATES MUST BE RECEIVED BY 4:30 P.M. ON: Apr. 19, 1967
ITEM The University of Toledo Time Schedule	PUBLICATIONS JOB NUMBER AR-52-467-15M

DESCRIPTION

QUANTITY 15,000 (15M)	FINISHED SIZE 5 1/2" x 8 1/2"	METHOD Offset
COVER [X] SELF [ ] SEPARATE — NUMBER OF COLORS 1	TEXT NUMBER OF PAGES 64 — NUMBER OF COLORS 1	STYLE (FORM WORK ONLY)

ADDITIONAL INFORMATION

NOTE: Cover to have one halftone, 3" x 8 1/2"

SPECIFICATIONS

STOCK
60#, Hamilton Offset, Vellum Finish, Yellow, Book Weight.

INK
Black

ART AND/OR COPY
Furnished, camera ready and/or keylined.

BINDING
Saddle Stitched

NOTE: COMPREHENSIVES AND/OR FINISHED ARTWORK MAY BE EXAMINED IN THE PUBLICATIONS OFFICE

ADDITIONAL INFORMATION

NOTE: Art will be ready by April 20, 1967 (a.m.)

DELIVERY JOB MUST BE DELIVERED ON: May 4, 1967 SURE!

TO: (F.O.B.) The University of Toledo
Office of the Registrar
Room 121, University Hall, Toledo, Ohio
ATTN: Mrs. Alina Markowski

DELIVER 12 COPIES TO THE PUBLICATIONS OFFICE

PROPOSED PRICE (BIDDER MUST COMPLETE ALL ITEMS – INCOMPLETE BIDS CANNOT BE CONSIDERED)

PROPOSED PRICE TO INCLUDE:

Proof: Silverprints, folded, stapled and trimmed.

Packing: In cartons in even amounts and labeled.

PREPARATORY	$
PRESS	
STOCK	
BINDERY	
TOTAL	$
PRICE PER ADDITIONAL M AT THE SAME TIME	$

ADDITIONALS PREPARATORY (FOR ITEMS WHICH MAY BE INCLUDED AFTER REQUEST FOR ESTIMATE DATE ABOVE) ITEM(S): $

TOTAL FOR ADDITIONALS $

RERUN PRICES (PLATES STANDING)

PRICE PER M BASED ON: 5M	$
PRICE PER M BASED ON:	$ (none)

COMPANY	SUBMITTED BY	DATE

PO 2 266

Fig. 4 *Request for printer's quotations on prices for promotional literature. University of Toledo.*

ON-CAMPUS CONFERENCES

On-campus conferences can represent a sizable amount in any admissions budget. Major expense categories for such conferences may be identified as in Figure 5.

The budget should include expenses which may be charged against the admissions office for the entertainment of university guests. These guests may be visiting groups of secondary school students, visiting secondary school counselors, or other persons to whom the institution will want to extend the privileges of its courtesy. The simple calculation suggested in Figure 5 can be an aid in the budgeting process for this item.

	Expense	Income	Institutional subsidy
1. Announcement printing	______		
2. Announcement mailing	______		
3. Meals	______		
4. Speaker honorarium	______		
5. Speaker travel	______		
6. Facility rental	______		
7. Other	______		
8. Reimbursement of secondary school counselors' travel	______		
9. Registration fees		______	
Total			

Fig. 5 *Major expense categories for on-campus conferences, University of Toledo.*

CAPITAL EXPENSES

Capital expenses need to be justified and described in the budget request just as do all other items. Each institution may provide different procedures for such justifications. Some which are complex will require that all capital expense items be channeled for the purposes of budget review through the office of purchasing or property control. The reasoning behind such a procedure, in the complex institution, is to make it possible for the institution to review requests for capital expense items identified with office operations in order that the requests for such items can be checked against existing inventories of university equipment. Theoretically, this will prevent the authorization of purchases for capital items which other offices have returned to central stores. In those cases where these budget requests are not channeled through central purchasing and are left as budget request items in the operating department budget, there may also be the requirement that the request for office equipment and other general capital expense items be verified by central property control or purchasing on the basis of obsolescence or effective life of the item. If these procedures are not requirements in the smaller institution, it is helpful to at least require explicit justification of each capital item in the budget request with supporting documents indicating the condition of equipment which needs to be replaced. Similar justification must be

	Cost
1. Dorm rooms (no. of days × rental × guests)	______
2. Meals (no. of meals × guests)	______
3. Reimbursement of travel	______
Total	

Fig. 6 *Budget estimate sheet for entertainment of university guests, University of Toledo.*

provided for new items of a capital nature which are required for the office. These are items generally related to the expansion of the services of the office or to the adoption of new office procedures which require changes in equipment.

MAILING COSTS

Mailing costs can be projected for budget requests with reasonable accuracy. It is much easier to project these costs if the institution has a central mail service which can keep account of the mailing costs for each office authorized to use university mail services. Monthly reports of such costs, as well as yearly totals, can be provided from the mail service office. These can be used to develop a ratio of mailing costs to numbers of students admitted and registered. Those persons preparing the admissions office budget must be astute enough to anticipate increases in mailing costs of as much as 20 to 25 percent in one year without any increase in the volume of mail. This occurred in the year 1967–1968 as a result of increased postal rates placed in effect by the U.S. Postal Service. Provisions must be made for bulk mailing, catalogs, and other book-like materials sent by the admissions office to the secondary schools and other sources of candidates.

OFFICE FORMS

Office forms are items of general office expense which can be accurately estimated if firm quotations have been received from form companies for the type and quantity needed. Unless the budget request is for a reprinting of office forms which do not require substantial changes, the budget requests for these items should be accompanied by firm quotations from office form companies. The admissions office, like any administrative office, should be ever alert to the possibility of reducing the number and complexity of the forms used in its operation. The standard variety of forms found in an admissions office may represent those used separately for:

1. Entering freshmen
2. Transfer students
3. Readmitted students
4. Foreign students
5. Financial aid
6. Evaluation of credit
7. Recommendations

The special characteristics of particular institutions will call for additions to the above list, but in terms of the general utility of forms the above represent those which might be found in any admissions office. Many of the above can be combined into one form. For example, the application for admission can be designed so that it serves all entering students, whether they be freshmen, transfers, readmitted students, or foreign students.

Visual aids are often expensive, but they are of great importance to the success of student recruiting. The use of view booklets, slide photographs, still photos, drawings of new buildings planned for the campus, views of educational programs in action, the use of filmstrips, and film and video presentations must be accurately projected. At this point in the preparation of the department's budget, careful attention must be given to communication with the publications office or university editor's office in order that the admissions office can make known its need for visual aids for its recruiting program so explicitly that no duplication of budget requests can be expected. It is quite possible that the office of public relations or the institution's news service will be engaged in the production of visual aids to be used in the institution's development program. These same aids can be used effectively by the admissions office without encumbering the admissions budget.

INCOME FROM APPLICATION FEES

Income from application fees represents a sizable percentage of the admissions office budget in institutions of higher education. To be sure, there are many which do not charge an application fee, but the trend has been toward an increasing number of institutions making an application fee charge of candidates. The reasons for the application fee are understandable and justify its existence. The evaluation of student credits, the careful reading of recommendations, the significant amount of clerical attention which must be given a candidate's file in order that all necessary correspondence can be kept up to date, and the time and talent of the admission office staff which is committed to interviewing students and parents clearly demonstrate that a useful and necessary service is being performed for candidates. The operational principle that charges should be made where service is performed represents the guiding warrant for the application fee.

Difficult as it may be, it is necessary that the office adopt a policy that no application will be processed unless payment is made or an authorized waiver of the application fee is presented. A daily journal of applications and fees received must be kept within the office of admissions if that office is expected to be the receiving point for application fees. The keeping of a journal of receipts in the office may be a satisfactory procedure for the smaller institution which receives relatively small numbers of applications, but such procedures are too cumbersome when the daily volume of applications mounts rapidly. An effective method of accounting to the office of finance and of acknowledging receipt of the application to the candidate is to incorporate notification forms in the application itself. Such a design is found in the application for undergraduate admission used at the University of Toledo (see Figure 7).

The top part of the form, when stamped with a receipt stamp from the office of admissions, is forwarded to the office of the bursar, where it serves as the official record that the application fee has been paid. These forms are transmitted daily to the office of the bursar, which compares the total number of such receipted forms with the total application-fee income. The office of the bursar then becomes the official source of verification that the application fee has been paid. The office of the bursar furnishes the office of admissions on request with a total of the number of such fees received up to a given date.

The bottom part of the form, when receipted, is placed in the mail to the candidate as his receipt from the office of admissions, acknowledging the fact that his application has been received and is being processed.

The procedures indicated above are suitable for the recording of and accounting for application fees received by an office of admissions. However, it is entirely possible for application fees to be received by the office of finance, with a transmittal of their receipt being made from that office to the office of admissions. This procedure ensures that the office of finance has complete internal control over the collection of fees. For several reasons it may not be appropriate to have applications for admission filed through the office of finance. However, that office can place a member or members of its staff in the office of admissions for the purpose of recording and accounting for the receipt of application fees. Such separation of the collection of fees from the professional services of the admissions office is desirable if it is at all possible.

Accounting practices of institutions vary, but usually receipts represented by application fees will be placed in the general fund of the institution and not allocated directly to the office of admissions. The application fee charged should not be directly related to the total budgetary requirements of the admissions office. The fee should represent the minimal and reasonable charge required to meet the basic costs of processing the application.

THE UNIVERSITY OF TOLEDO
OFFICE OF THE BURSAR
TOLEDO, OHIO 43606

APPLICANT, PLEASE COMPLETE

RECEIPT

NAME____________________

ADDRESS____________________

CITY AND STATE____________________ (Zip Code)

SOCIAL SECURITY NUMBER

FINANCE RECORD

FORM 33-AR 4-67

PLEASE PRINT WITH BALL POINT PEN — DO NOT DETACH

THE UNIVERSITY OF TOLEDO
OFFICE OF THE BURSAR
TOLEDO, OHIO 43606

Non-Profit Organization
U. S. POSTAGE
PAID
Toledo, Ohio
Permit No. 1610

TO:

[redacted]

(STUDENT RECEIPT)

FORM 33-AR 4-67

Fig. 7 *Forms for accounting of receipt of application used by University of Toledo.*

MEMBERSHIPS IN PROFESSIONAL SOCIETIES

Memberships in professional societies are authorized generally as institutional memberships with the staff of the admissions office designated to represent the institution in the professional society. Information about the costs of such memberships is easily obtained and these costs can be identified explicitly in the budget request. Justification for such memberships should rest principally on the benefit which can be derived by the institution and not principally on the benefit which can be achieved for the individual representing the institution.

BUDGET DEVELOPMENT AND APPROVAL

Budget development and approval is accomplished throughout the entire year's operation and not concentrated within the space of a few weeks or even a few months. To be sure, the budget may be reviewed by the institution's chief administrators and budget review meetings may be held by them, together with the head of the admissions office, during the late winter and early spring. But the detail work involved in developing the budget for the office and gaining approval for it continues throughout the year. Each record of publications distributed, of conferences held, of travel, of school visitation, of participation in conferences, of the academic achievements of the entering freshman class, and, finally, the reports received from secondary schools evaluating the visits of admissions staff—all of these contribute to the overall impression of the job done by the office and offer evidence of progress.

It must be remembered that the purpose of the office is to serve the institution and that the institution must, in turn, supply the resources with which the office is to do the job. One may expect budget requests to be reduced, but it should be made clear to the administration that when necessary cuts are made in budget requests, each cut will cause some objective to remain unrealized. This last point must be established as valid for the budget review; otherwise one must consider that the item to be reduced or cut entirely from the budget did not belong in the budget in the first place.

FISCAL ACCOUNTING AND A MONTHLY FLOW CHART

Fiscal accounting and a monthly flow chart are valuable procedures for the office to have available to it as means for keeping an accurate record of the expenditure of its funds. These data related to the current and past rate of expenditure by the office at any point in time should be provided for admissions as a service by the institution's office of finance. Monthly or biweekly budget reports from the office of finance detailing the appropriated amounts, the amounts expended, the amount encumbered, and the unencumbered balance for each account of the admissions budget is expected. The admissions office is, in turn, responsible for executing the plan of the year's activities and operations in such fashion that there will be no need for supplementary budget requests toward the end of the operating year unless such supplementary requests represent newly identified and institutionally approved objectives for the admissions office.

Such items as salaries, retirement contributions, and fringe benefits for staff of the office will represent uniform expenditures monthly throughout the year, providing all staff are on 12-month contracts. Items for publication, travel, and conferences as well as those for entertainment of university guests and office expenditures are likely to be unequally distributed throughout the year. If the fiscal affairs of an institution are likely to be critical at any point in the budget year, it is well that sufficient communication exist between the operating departments such as admissions and the office of finance in order that some expenditures can be planned for times in the budget year when assets are greater.

The office of finance has been identified as that office which should supply requisite information on fiscal accounting and the monthly flow charting of expenditures. It is ineffective and uneconomical to have each operating department of the institution trying to maintain its own fiscal accounting and its own monthly chart of expenditures when modern accounting procedures can supply that information for all operating departments in a uniform and understandable fashion.

Budgets for an admissions office may vary from less than $25,000 to more than $1,000,000, depending on the size of the institution and the responsibilities assigned to the office. Whether the budget is large or small in terms of dollars, the responsibility for the development of a detailed, intelligently presented, and effectively executed budget cannot be escaped.

For suggested readings see page 3-23.

Chapter 13

Admissions Research and Follow-up Studies

RICHARD R. PERRY

Associate Executive Vice President for Institutional Research and Administrative Planning, The University of Toledo, Toledo, Ohio

INTRODUCTION

Valuable service can be given a college or university by an admissions office if that office will involve itself in a continuous program of operations research. Research is described as operations research because it focuses on the results of the administrative operations of the admissions office and how those administrative operations contribute to the success of the educational program of the institution. This research is a requisite also in order that constant evaluation of the effectiveness of the operation of the office can be available.

In general, the operations research activities can be classified into four areas. The first is *administrative research.* Such research centers on management information type data which can provide evaluation of the cost effectiveness of the operation of the admissions office. The other three categories of research are *predictive research, directive research,* and *illuminative research.* Trow, in describing the last three research categories, indicates that predictive research "is the considerable body of research that attempts to develop predictors of academic achievement for use by admission offices." Directive research is described as that "which intervenes directly into educational practice with statements of what ought to be done on the basis of its findings." Illuminative research is that which "aims to explore and illuminate the nature of educational institutions and processes—to show the connections among student characteristics, organizational patterns and policies and educational consequences."[1]

ADMINISTRATIVE OPERATIONS RESEARCH

Administrative operations research can produce studies related generally to the cost effectiveness of the office in terms of keeping the expenses of the admissions office in line with the growth of the total financial resources of the institution. Each unnecessary dollar increase in administrative budgets represents a dollar loss to the educational program resources of an institution. One helpful, continuous operations research project which should be undertaken by every admissions office is the analysis of the cost of the office in relation to the results of its efforts. Such research could provide answers to questions such as:

1. What is the cost of processing an application for admission?
2. What is the cost of recruiting an applicant?
3. What is the cost of enrolling an accepted candidate?
4. How do the costs of the admissions office compare to the institution's total operating budget now, a year ago, three years ago, and five years ago?

Additional operations research efforts could be directed at constant revision of the admissions information system in order that:

1. The professional staff could be released from routine activities to concentrate its efforts on providing greater individual attention to the candidate
2. Difficulties in the collection of data necessary to complete applications could be identified and the time lag between decisions on applications and the notification of candidates concerning their admission could be reduced
3. Duplicate clerical work could be eliminated
4. Continuous evaluation of the admissions policies of the institution could take place

Administrative operations research which represents an ongoing effort by the admissions office in the above areas should provide useful information to better serve the institution.

GEOGRAPHICAL STUDIES

Geographical studies of the composition of the entering class are important to the college because they provide information on one aspect of the diversity represented in the student body of the college. Information identifying the geographical origin of entering students is readily obtained from questions supplied on the application for admission and usually is limited to identifying the students' nationalities, home states, and residences. Many public colleges are required also to identify the counties in which students reside. For the public institution, these data are necessary to demonstrate the institution's service effectiveness to the entire state, which assists in the support of the institution. Data processing facilities make it possible to elaborate on the study of the geographical origin of entering students by making it possible to categorize the qualities of students by geographical area. Characteristics of the class in terms of test scores, secondary school grade achievement, leadership potential, participation in extracurricular activities, and many other criteria of interest to the selection of a class

[1] Martin A. Trow, "Social Research and Educational Policy," in *Research in Higher Education*, College Entrance Examination Board, New York, 1965, p. 53.

can be identified by geographical area. Table 1 illustrates a simplified report on the geographical distribution of an entering class. The general format of this report can be expanded to include a summation of any quantifiable set of characteristics for a class. The same general format can be used to identify characteristics of entering students by high schools within states. The report on the geographical source and quality of entering freshmen by college can be modified to include a listing of the high schools within the state with the totals for each state broken down into separate categories representing various criteria.

TABLE 1 Geographical Source and Quality of Entering Freshmen by College *

	Arts and sciences		Business administration		Education		Engineering		Total students and av. score	
	Men	Women	Men	Women	Men	Women	Men	Women	Men	Women
Alabama										
High School 1..........	4	0	4	0	2	6	1	0	11	6
Scholastic Aptitude Test (verbal).........	575		600		585	640	710		588	640
Scholastic Aptitude Test (mathematical)................	625		580		550	525	690		600	525
High school grade point average........	3.0		2.9		3.4	3.8	3.6		3.1	3.8
High School 2..........	10	4	7	1	15	20	8	1	40	26
Scholastic Aptitude Test (verbal).........	550	590	525	540	505	560	540	720	526	570
Scholastic Aptitude Test (mathematical)................	570	520	530	625	515	540	645	750	557	548
High school grade point average........	2.8	3.4	2.7	3.6	2.7	3.5	3.7	4.0	2.7	3.6

* Format may be continued for each state and, if desired, it may be altered to include high schools by county and city.

ENROLLMENT APPLICATION EXPERIENCE INFORMATION

Enrollment application experience information is of particular importance to the operation of the admissions office. Considerable time and money is spent in contacting hundreds of high schools and thousands of possible candidates for admission. It is necessary for the office to have explicit objective data concerning the results of all expenditures in terms of the number of applications derived from particular areas and individual schools as well as the numbers accepted and actually registered. An adaptation of Table 1 is shown in Table 2. Such a listing of the application-accepted registration experience compiled at the end of each registration for a new academic period will show what the experience has been with any particular geographic area or any particular high school. Totals can be obtained for any category or geographic area.

PREDICTIVE RESEARCH

Predictive research has been a popular activity with increasing numbers of admissions offices, particularly since the emphasis on selective admissions gained so much attention in the 1950s. The overarching objective of predictive research in the college or university is to provide an entering freshman class which will have the best possible

TABLE 2 Application-Accepted Registration Experience

	Arts and sciences			Business administration			Education			Engineering			Total		
	Applied	Accepted	Registered	Applied	Accepted	Registered	Applied	Accepted	Registered	Applied	Accepted	Registered	Applied	Accepted	Registered
Alabama															
High School 1	9	4	4	10	6	4	16	11	8	4	4	1	39	25	17
Percent	...	33	100	...	60	67	...	63	73	...	100	25	...	64	68
High School 2	25	20	14	15	11	8	61	53	35	19	10	9	120	94	66
Percent	...	80	70	...	73	73	...	87	66	...	53	90	...	78	70

chance of earning the highest grade-point averages and will show a very low attrition rate. In order that this may be done, sophisticated statistical techniques have been applied to the predictive factors thought to represent the best base from which to achieve a high level of academic achievement. The statistical procedures necessary to accomplish a prediction equation for an individual institution are readily available in standard texts on statistics and need not be repeated at length here. Procedure is relatively clear. The admissions office which makes use of a prediction equation must obtain test scores and records of academic achievement from secondary schools, and it must also obtain figures on grades earned in college by those students who will be used in developing a prediction equation. All data necessary are readily available. Of great help to the admissions office, which may not be staffed for the development of its own prediction equation, are the research services available from the College Entrance Examination Board, the Educational Testing Service, and the American College Testing Program. Both the College Entrance Examination Board and the American College Testing Program provide validity study services for the member colleges of their organizations. These services can provide prediction equations and expectancy tables for individual colleges. Examples are shown in Figure 1 and Table 3.

Interviews as well as recommendations from counselors and secondary school principals are valuable additions to the information that may help to predict which candidates will have the best chances for success. The multiple-prediction system described in basic statistics and known as "multiple prediction," "multiple correlation," or

---

$$\text{Predicted grade point average} = (\underline{0.4924} \times \text{HS avg.}) + (\underline{0.0008} \times \text{SAT verbal score}) + (\underline{0.0019} \times \text{SAT math score}) - 0.4430$$

The underlined numbers in the equation are the optimal combining weights used as the multipliers of the appropriate measures in order to obtain the most accurate possible estimate of a student's first-semester-freshman grade average. The use of this equation for the computation of a predicted grade average is illustrated, using the scores indicated, below:

Variable	*Score*	*Multiplier*	*Product*
High school average	2.10	0.4924	1.0340
SAT (verbal)	450	0.0008	0.3600
SAT (math)	610	0.0019	1.1590
		Constant	−0.4430
		Sum (predicted grade)	2.1100
			= 2.11 or 2.1

Fig. 1 *A multiple-variable prediction equation. (Reproduced by permission of Educational Testing Service.)*

"multiple regression" still remains the single best procedure to use in predicting for great numbers of applications. Modern data processing techniques make it possible for the required data on each candidate to be coded in such fashion as to permit the predicted grade-point average for every candidate to be computed quickly.

TABLE 3 Chances in 100 That Candidates with a Given Predicted Grade Will Earn at Least the Indicated Grade*

Predicted grade	Chances in 100 that candidates will earn grade shown									
	0.84	1.16	1.49	1.81	2.13	2.45	2.77	3.09	3.41	3.73
3.73	99	99	99	99	99	99	94	87	70	50
3.41	99	99	99	99	99	94	87	70	50	30
3.09	99	99	99	99	94	87	70	50	30	13
2.77	99	99	99	94	87	70	50	30	13	6
2.45	99	99	94	87	70	50	30	13	6	1
2.13	99	94	87	70	50	30	13	6	1	1
1.81	94	87	70	50	30	13	6	1	1	1
1.49	87	70	50	30	13	6	1	1	1	1
1.16	70	50	30	13	6	1	1	1	1	1
0.84	50	30	13	6	1	1	1	1	1	1

* Permission received from Educational Testing Service to reproduce.

Interest in the prediction of academic success has held the spotlight in admissions circles for the last decade. However, the admissions office must engage itself in predictive research which makes use of factors other than intellective indices of students' past records in school and performances on tests. A review of research which makes use of multiple correlation or multiple regression in the analysis of predictors of academic success based on intellective factors with achieved criterion levels indicates that the median correlation achieved by these measures was .56, with 50 percent of the cases falling between .50 and .66.[2] Other research which has made use of several predictors has been able to improve these correlations to about .65.[3] Anyone seriously interested in the significant research being done currently with other than intellective predictors is urged to study carefully data offered by Lavin in his comprehensive review of research on the subject.[4] This review covers the four broad major categories of performance determination: intelligence and ability factors, personality characteristics, sociological determinants, and the sociopsychological factors.

A comprehensive systems approach to the research efforts of an office of admissions is described by Glover.[5] The admissions information and research system described here stems from the project through which the Cooperative Admissions Information System was developed and operated, from 1965 through 1967, for 12 women's colleges in the Northeast; a system which was implemented through the data processing facilities of the University of Massachusetts.

Predictive research by the office of admissions is not limited to the utilization of intellective factors such as test scores and grade-point averages, and it should be

[2] Joseph Paul Gieusti, "High School Average as a Predictor of College Success: A survey of the literature," in *College and University*, vol. 39, no. 2, p. 207, Winter, 1964.

[3] See the numerous studies listed in *Dissertation Abstracts*, beginning with vol. 15 and continuing through vol. 17, 1955–1957, and the numerous articles appearing in the *College Board Review*.

[4] David E. Lavin, *The Prediction of Academic Performance,* Russel Sage Foundation, New York, 1965.

[5] *Cooperative Admissions Information System,* College Entrance Examination Board and International Business Machines Corporation, 1967.

noted that predictive research which relies on data assessing nonintellective factors can be as readily pursued as that which concentrates on intellective factors. The present concern of institutions of higher education with the necessity of providing for a more complete cultural mix of students on their campuses requires that predictive research by the office of admissions expand beyond the limitations of intellective factors.

DIRECTIVE RESEARCH

Directive research may seem to be the most difficult for the admissions office to pursue, since the outcome of such research ultimately will change institutional policy. An admissions office should not shrink from the possibility of presenting conclusive research findings which can be interpreted as telling the institution what it *should do.* Admittedly the results of directive research move the impact of such activity from a position of seeking to describe what is to that of making use of research to move an institution into new directions.

Directive research may, for example, influence educational programs and faculty policy when an admissions office, in its presentation of the profile of the entering freshman class over a period of years, indicates with that profile a graphing of the distribution of grades in freshman courses. The results can be startling, for if the academic profile of entering freshman classes over a period of five years demonstrates continuous improvement in the quality of the entering classes and yet the distribution of grades remains relatively stable, then admissions office research in this area should direct an appropriate faculty committee to evaluate the possible reasons for such an occurrence. An example of such research results is shown in Figure 2.

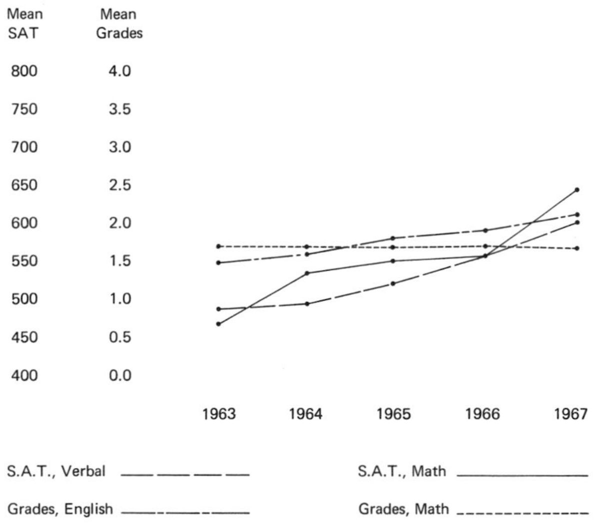

Fig. 2 *Entering freshmen.*

One of the reasons for an admissions office to direct a faculty committee to evaluate reasons for such occurrences is the inevitable questioning which arises from knowledgeable college counselors of secondary schools. These counselors, familiar with the fact that the quality of candidates being accepted from their schools has improved, wonder why these better-qualified candidates do not earn appreciably higher grades than their predecessors did. One ready explanation is that as the general quality of the class rises, so does the competition for grades. However this leads to some question about whether the grading standards applied in departments are "floating standards."

A completely different kind of research can be undertaken by an office of admissions to change the direction of an institution. A college or university may find that since it has emphasized achievement in academic fields, its extracurricular, student activity, or individual enrichment programs have suffered considerably. Such programs often emphasize creative effort of a sort quite different from that which is demanded in regular classes. Since the college has been using prediction variables which were successful in producing high academic achievement, it might be well to identify other variables which would be capable of improving prediction in activities other than purely academic pursuits.[6] Such research has been done and an example of its results is shown in Table 4.

TABLE 4 The Relation of College Outcomes to Nonacademic Accomplishment in High School (the Percentage of Students with Each Collegiate Outcome)*

Area of achievement in high school and college outcome	Number of high school achievements							
	Men				Women			
	0	1–2	3–4	5+	0	1–2	3–4	5+
Leadership								
2 or more leadership achievements	4.1	7.0	13.3	22.9	6.9	9.7	16.0	24.9
GPA below C	20.1	16.2	15.5	11.8	13.4	9.0	9.9	8.8
No longer enrolled	26.4	21.0	16.9	14.4	17.0	12.7	13.5	14.7
Art								
2 or more art achievements	3.7	20.6	34.4	52.8	1.8	10.9	28.4	46.7
GPA below C	16.3	12.4	25.5	16.7	8.4	13.2	11.4	10.0
No longer enrolled	19.3	23.4	22.2	27.8	13.1	14.0	20.5	26.7
Science								
1 or more science achievements	5.3	17.8	29.6	35.6	2.5	6.8	17.3	19.0
GPA below C	19.9	14.2	14.3	13.7	9.6	11.9	2.5	0.0
No longer enrolled	21.3	20.9	15.3	12.3	14.6	12.5	11.1	9.5
Music								
1 or more music achievements	1.7	10.7	25.6	38.1	1.4	8.1	18.9	35.9
GPA below C	16.6	14.8	15.3	15.8	12.0	9.1	8.9	7.4
No longer enrolled	21.7	18.0	17.9	16.3	16.4	13.1	13.2	12.0
Writing								
2 or more writing achievements	1.9	8.5	15.8	34.6	3.7	8.7	26.4	47.2
GPA below C	17.2	13.9	13.8	11.5	11.2	8.1	9.6	11.1
No longer enrolled	21.6	18.9	13.8	15.4	14.6	14.0	13.0	11.1
Speech and drama								
2 or more speech and drama achievements	1.6	6.6	13.4	52.5	2.3	6.0	12.5	26.0
GPA below C	16.9	14.0	18.0	10.7	10.9	8.9	9.7	9.4
No longer enrolled	22.6	18.2	20.3	14.7	13.5	13.9	14.7	15.6

* Permission received from American College Testing Program to reproduce.

[6] Leonard L. Baird and James M. Richards, Jr., "The Effects of Selecting College Students by Various Kinds of High School Achievement," ACT Research Report no. 23, American College Testing Program, Iowa City, Iowa, February, 1968, p. 11.

The outcome of such research, done in the spring of 1966 with students at 14 two-year colleges and 41 four-year undergraduate colleges, indicates that it is possible to predict the nonclassroom achievement of college students by making use of the nonacademic achievement records of such students during their high school years. For example, Table 4 indicates that while only 3.7 percent of male students with no art achievements in high school had two or more achievements in art in college, 52.8 percent of male students with five or more achievements in art in high school had two or more achievements in art in college. The percentages in each row of Table 4 confirm that high school nonacademic achievement forecasts college nonacademic achievement.[7] This research for the admissions office from data compiled by it could direct a college toward revision of criteria applicable in the admissions process in order to select for the campus a student body which could significantly change the image and thrust of the college.

ILLUMINATIVE RESEARCH

Illuminative research which seeks to explore the nature of an educational institution and its processes may be referred to also as descriptive research, for it seeks to describe as explicitly as possible the nature of the institution. The work of C. R. Pace and George G. Stern which resulted in the College Characteristics Index (CCI) represents the development of research techniques which, when applied by an admissions office to its own institution, can result in a certain descriptive analysis of the college or university. The CCI measures the needs and press of a college climate in terms of the activities, policies, procedures, attitudes, and impressions characteristic of various types of undergraduate colleges.[8] The application of the CCI to students at a particular institution can result in a profile of the institution in terms of the intellectual and nonintellectual climate evident on the campus. An example of such a profile is shown in Table 5. Similar profiles can be achieved for many categories of students on a campus whether they represent colleges, divisions of enrollment, sex, year of entrance, or major field of study.

Another procedure which will yield a different picture of the campus is the administration of the College and University Environment Scales (CUES) developed by C. Robert Pace. This instrument describes the atmosphere or environment of the campus as seen by the student. Campus environments are measured in terms of five dimensions. These are Practicality, Community, Awareness, Propriety, and Scholarship.[9] Theoretically a college could, once its environmental profile had been established, administer the CUES test to prospective candidates for admission and, by matching the profiles of individual candidates or of the class as a whole, anticipate difficulties which might arise as a result of great discrepancies between how the campus is and how the entering freshman class thinks it is.

SUMMATION

A summation of admissions research and follow-up studies must establish that the primary function of such activity by the admissions office is to provide the institution with accurate data and its careful analysis so that the institution's educational program can proceed with utmost effectiveness. An additional important purpose is to assist in meeting the educational needs of students attracted to the institution. It is question-

[7] *Ibid.*, pp. 10–12.

[8] George G. Stern, "The Intellectual Climate in Colleges," *Harvard Educational Review*, vol. 33, no. 1, p. 6, Capital City Press, Montpelier, Vt., Winter, 1963.

[9] C. Robert Pace, *College and University Environment Scales Manual*, National Testing Service, Princeton, N.J., 1963.

TABLE 5 CCI Profile

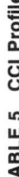

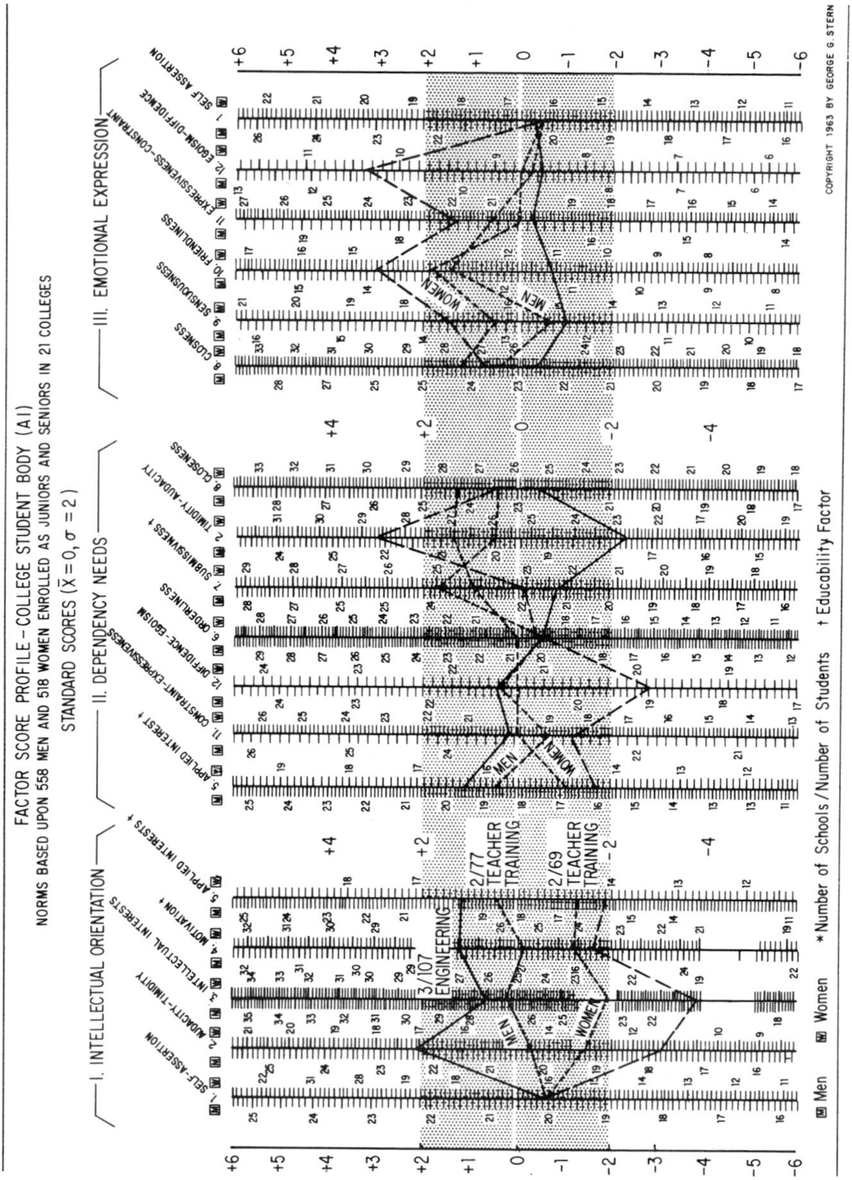

able whether admissions offices in general have within their professional staffs the research competence necessary to carry on all of the extensive study of the institution, its faculty, and its student body which can be generated from data resulting from the admission process. Additionally, the administrative demands placed on the admissions office in discharging its responsibility of selecting the best qualified class possible leave it little time for extensive research activity. Therefore, it is well for the admissions office to cooperate with and to seek the total assistance of the institution's office of institutional research to accomplish most of the analysis of data available from admissions records.

For suggested readings see page 3-23.

Chapter 14

Communications within the Large Admissions Department

JOHN A. CURRY

Associate Dean of Admissions, Northeastern University, Boston, Massachusetts

As an admissions office grows in size and, consequently, counselors assume more diversified roles, it becomes imperative that lines of communication within the department remain open. To make sure of this, many universities have developed written guidelines in the areas of departmental philosophy and policy. If this is done, then both veteran and new counselors as well as the secretarial staff have access to a source of information as they perform their various responsibilities, and the admissions department is assured of ongoing communication despite changes in philosophy, policy, or personnel.

ADMISSIONS HANDBOOK

With this thought in mind, some large admissions offices have recently developed an admissions handbook organized, perhaps, in an 8½- by 11-in. looseleaf notebook so that philosophy, policy, and/or procedures can be referred to quickly by the counseling and secretarial staff. Then too, this organization allows for flexibility, as a policy can be added or deleted without disturbing the entire framework.

A handbook of this type can be divided into certain key areas of consideration: administration, public relations, business procedures, personnel, and student policies. Within each area can be written a series of statements concerned with philosophy, where applicable, and the mechanics of a situation where this is necessary.

Although each admissions office will have certain matters worth including that are unique to its own operation, the listing below includes many of the items which could become part of each section:

1. Administration
   - Departmental organization chart
   - Current job specifications (see Appendix 1)
   - Working schedules
   - Office regulations
   - Special emergency operating policies
2. Public relations
   - Communications with the public
     - Promotion of students (see Appendix 2)
     - Interview procedures
     - Policy concerning walk-ins
     - Registration—freshman and transfer students
     - Group conferences
   - Communications with guidance personnel
     - Regular mailings
     - Requests from counselors to visit college
     - Requests to visit secondary schools
     - Professional associations
   - Communications with alumni
     - Alumni conferences
     - Admissions cases
   - Recruitment
   - Communications with outside agencies
3. Business procedures
   - Recording processes
   - Preparation of folders (see Appendix 3)
   - Security
   - Handling of folder materials
   - Rescinding certificates
   - Health clearances
4. Personnel
   - Statements affecting staff—benefits, responsibilities (see Appendix 4)
5. Student policies
   - Financial aid
   - Housing
   - Health clearance procedures
   - Physically handicapped
   - Emotionally disturbed
   - Testing
   - Equivalency diplomas and nontraditional work

Adult education
USAFI course credit
G.E.D. tests
Correspondence courses
University extension courses
Federal forms processing
Evening school credit
Reentries (see Appendix 5)
Transfer policies
Extension of deposit dates
Return of deposits
Advanced placement
Granting of partial credit

STAFF MEMORANDUM

It is true, of course, that such a flexible handbook does not substitute for other important means of communication which are as vital to internal efficiency. The staff memorandum, an extremely effective means of disseminating information of the factual type, can be very useful in maintaining internal communications. Through this device, the administrator can report short briefs which do not affect existing policy and news briefs that concern all. It is important to remember that irritating personal situations such as difficulties involving one counselor or a secretary are better handled through personal discussion than through the "If the shoe fits, put it on" type of memorandum which reaches all department members but whose message is generally lost on the offender.

WEEKLY STAFF MEETING

The weekly staff meeting is almost a necessity in these days of constant change. There exists the temptation to use this occasion as an opportunity to dish out trivia which could just as easily be given in a memorandum.

This meeting, normally an hour in length, can be used in so many more productive ways, for example:

1. To develop policy on matters pertinent to admissions and, in the process, involve all members of the staff who wish to contribute
2. To discuss procedural implementation of a policy idea so that, again, all staff members are involved
3. To communicate with guest speakers who can add to the professional development of staff personnel; i.e., deans of various colleges, curriculum committee members, community officials, students, admissions officers from other campuses
4. To provide the setting for new interdepartmental workshops; i.e., in programmed instruction as a counseling tool, recruiting of disadvantaged students, financial aid counseling, etc.
5. To discuss the results of research activity
6. To evaluate the effectiveness of current policies and procedures
7. To discuss new and meaningful developments in the admissions field and within the university

Without question the lines of communication existent in a department determine the effectiveness of the total operation. If the handbook proposed herein is developed internally by the department members and is used intelligently by all staff members in conjunction with the other methods of communication described, then certainly the department is making a solid effort to alleviate the complex communication problems evident in all large departments today.

APPENDIXES: SAMPLE PAGES FROM AN ADMISSIONS HANDBOOK USED AT NORTHEASTERN UNIVERSITY

1. Current Job Specifications—Secretaries

Secretarial Staff

Secretary to the Associate Dean of Admissions

1. Administers the secretarial needs of the Associate Dean of Admissions
2. Assumes responsibility for training new personnel on the secretarial staff
3. Orders capital equipment and advises the Dean of capital equipment needs
4. Maintains inventories of office supplies, form letters, and promotional literature
5. Serves as a consultant to other members of the secretarial staff
6. Arranges secretarial office coverage including Saturday morning coverage
7. Assumes responsibility for purchasing office supplies
8. Assists in arranging special group visits to the campus
9. Assumes responsibility for maintaining staff attendance records
10. Assists the Dean in screening new staff personnel

Secretary Stenographer

1. Assumes responsibility for Advanced Standing Transfer Students
2. Processes applications of Advanced Standing Students and Evening part-time programs
3. Assumes responsibility for general typing of form letters and certificates of acceptance
4. Provides typing and/or stenographic services for members of the counseling staff
5. Assists in the preparation of special rosters
6. Assists call director

2. Promotion of Applicants

Without a question we are very much dependent on our Mailing Service to place our promotional materials into the hands of potential applicants. Our liaison officer takes the responsibility of periodically checking this system to ensure that our literature reaches the general public.

At present, the following system is in effect:

1. The inquiry is received and our mail secretary forwards the name to Office Services.

2. At this point a postcard is sent to the student, letting him know that there may be a two-week delay before he receives materials. (This is done so that the student will not request a *second* catalog immediately, thus preventing duplication.)

3. A label is forwarded to the Mailing House and the student then receives *Adventures in Education, Co-opportunities*, and an application with a direction sheet.

If we exhaust our supply of catalogs, the student is so notified and his name is placed on a waiting list. He still will receive other publications.

3. Preparation of Folders

Each day all applications received by mail are given to the application secretary who checks them for unanswered or incorrectly answered items, application fee, etc. Applications without fees are kept in a marked folder on the application secretary's desk. If application fee is not received within a few days, the application is returned with a form letter asking applicant to resubmit it with fee. For the application to be processed, the application fee check is clipped to the front of each individual application and if necessary a note indicating any incomplete item (i.e., college boards, parents signature, etc.). Applications are alphabetized and placed in a folder bearing day's date. The following morning a control card is punched for each application. From this card, four cards are duplicated—the application fee card which is taken to the Bursar's Office with the application fee, the tuition deposit card, the dormitory deposit card, and the financial aid scholastic rating card. The control cards are stamped with the application receipt date and then filed with the existing active control cards. The financial aid cards are taken to the payroll department and a strip of twelve name and address labels is made for each card. Although the labels may be made within a day, it may also be a week or more before they are made.

The individual folder for each application is made as soon as correspondence, transcripts, and college boards have been looked up. During the busiest season there may be several days' folders waiting to be made up. When the folder is made, a receipt card is sent to the applicant. In cases where items on application are unanswered, a duplication is sent with request to complete item(s) checked in red. This is noted on original application. When the duplicate application is returned, it is stapled to the back of the original. If college board letter or Dean's form is sent, this is also noted on the application. If applicant checks Burlington campus and indicated major not offered, there is a card sent telling him that the application has been processed for Boston campus and this is noted on the application. If the applicant asks for dormitory space at Burlington, a card is sent advising him that his application is being processed for Boston because there are no facilities at Burlington. All new folders with transcripts are given to counselors. After a counselor has seen the transcript, he initials it. The others are placed in file until transcript arrives.

4. Tuition Scholarships

Full-time Faculty, General and Academic Administrators

The University grants full-tuition scholarships to members of the above groups to the extent of two courses per term or quarter in any of its Colleges, the Graduate Division, or the Center for Continuing Education, provided they are qualified for admission and that prior approval of the enrollment in such courses is given by their Dean or Department Head.

In courses offered by the Center for Continuing Education, the Center for Reading Improvement, and other special noncredit programs where there are sufficient paid enrollments to justify the offering of the courses, full tuition is waived.

The University grants full-tuition scholarships to spouses of members of the above group to the extent of one undergraduate or graduate course per term or quarter. Additional courses taken concurrently must be paid for at the regular rate.

The University grants full-tuition scholarships to the dependent children of members of the above group who qualify for admission to one of the programs of any of its Colleges leading to a degree. This policy is extended to the dependent children of any member of the above group who dies or retires after having served Northeastern University for fifteen years or more. When requested, special situations involving children whose parent served less than fifteen years shall be considered by the Executive Council of the University. Authority is granted to the Council to approve or disapprove awards based on special situations.

Dependent children of members of this group who enroll in special part-time programs will be charged one-half of the standard tuition for the program.

5. Reentry Cases

The following applies to those formerly enrolled Northeastern students who wish to reenter as first-quarter freshmen. (Upperclassmen, or those eligible to reenroll in quarters 2 or 3 of the freshman year, are not processed by Admissions, but report to their respective academic deans.)

1. Student should be referred to the Office of the Dean of Freshmen, where he is issued a Petition to Reenter form.

2. The completed Petition to Reenter, with the Dean's recommendation for admissions action, is forwarded to Admissions for appropriate processing. Normally, the Petition is attached to the complete folder of the student when it is forwarded.

3. The formerly enrolled Northeastern student who, following his enrollment here, attended another college and seeks to enroll as a transfer student with advanced standing credit, need not be referred to the Dean of Freshmen.

The admissions counselor is ethically bound to honor the recommendation of the Dean of Freshmen, and therefore would act upon the case accordingly. He may, however, discuss the case with the Dean if he feels he is in possession of extenuating information which might result in different recommendation action.

Section Four

Learning Resources—Library and Instructional Resources

Chapter 1

Library Collections and Services

JOHN M. DAWSON

Director of Libraries, University of Delaware, Newark, Delaware

A library is a collection of books, journals, microfilms and other materials systematically collected and organized for use. "The primary purpose of any library is to serve the reading, reference and research needs of its users."[1]

THE FUNCTION OF THE LIBRARY IN THE ACADEMIC COMMUNITY

The basic function of the library in the academic community is to provide the materials necessary to support and to supplement the teaching-learning program of the institution at all levels and to provide, where appropriate, the materials for graduate and faculty

[1] Association of College and Research Libraries, *Statement on Service to Library Users*, American Library Association, 1966.

research. The library has the responsibility, in conjunction with the faculty, to teach skill in the use of the library. This oft-neglected function has been called, by at least one writer, one of the liberal arts. The library is or should be an active and not a passive element in the academic process, and the academic administrator should encourage his faculty to teach its students, as an integral part of their subject courses, how to use books and libraries. Another function of the academic library is to encourage students to read beyond the requirements of the curriculum for their own edification, enjoyment, and satisfaction, in the hope that when formal education is at an end these students will have developed the necessary skills and habits to continue their education.

LIBRARY COLLECTIONS

Factors which govern the size, scope, and character of library collections and of current acquisitions are the character of the institution (community college, technical institute, four-year college, university, etc.); the nature of the curriculum (noncredit make-up courses, general education, technical courses, honors courses, graduate and professional work); research programs; size of student body; scope of service (to local community, state, industry); and accessibility of other collections, either belonging to the same institution or to others.

The breadth of a community-college curriculum may require as extensive a collection as that of a four-year liberal arts collection. Majors and honors work in a variety of fields require extensive collections of some depth. Collections of even greater depth are required for the special areas of professional and graduate study, and universities offering doctoral work in a number of fields require very large collections. The libraries of technical institutes require not only the materials for applied sciences but should also contain a broad selection of materials in general studies. In all libraries materials must be provided for the professional reading of the faculty and staff.

Components of Library Collections Today's libraries are no longer simply collections of books and periodicals. They contain, in addition, maps, government documents, microforms (microfilm, microfiche, microcards, and microprint); films (including filmstrips, film loops, and motion-picture films); recordings; audio tapes; video tapes; museum objects; and special collections for the handicapped, such as braille books and talking books.

The modern academic library is sometimes called a learning center. This is particularly appropriate in the junior or community college and the four-year college where the library is likely to embrace almost all forms of communication media with the appropriate equipment. This pattern is somewhat less usual in the university, where problems of size, complexity, geography, and administrative convenience frequently separate from the library the audiovisual and museum functions.

Special Collections Special collections in libraries vary in size and character. Most often they are of local history, both of the institution and the community. Even the smallest library may well acquire books of exceptional value—"rare books." In addition there will be books which, for one reason or another, are subject to a high incidence of theft and which require special protection.

Special Materials for the Handicapped The modern academic library will acquire and own special materials for the handicapped. Unfortunately, large-print books exist for only a few titles, and while there are more recordings, these too are in short supply. Braille books for the blind are expensive but can be borrowed from the Library of Congress, usually through the state library agency. So far very little has been done in local production of tape recordings of books, but this is a project which could well involve the energies of service fraternities and sororities to produce useful materials for students who are sightless or whose vision is seriously impaired.

STANDARDS FOR LIBRARIES

Each regional accrediting association has minimum standards to be used in the evaluation of libraries in the accrediting process, but these usually do not give quantitative criteria. More useful to the academic administrator are the standards of the American Library Association. These standards are prepared by the Committee on Standards of the Association of College and Research Libraries (a division of the American Library Association).

Standards for Junior College Libraries These standards are "designed to provide a guide for the evaluation of libraries in American two-year colleges." Junior colleges, as defined by the standards, include junior colleges which are primarily concerned with the liberal arts; community colleges serving a wide range of educational objectives; and technical institutes.

The standards cover functions, structure and government, budget, staff, the library collection, building, quality of service and evaluation, and interlibrary cooperation. The full text of these standards can be found in *The American Library and Book Trade Annual, 1961* (R. R. Bowker Company, New York, 1960).[2]

Standards for Four-year College Libraries "These standards are designed to provide a guide for the evaluation of libraries in American colleges and universities which emphasize four-year undergraduate instruction and may or may not have graduate programs leading to a master's degree. They are not applicable, however, to junior college libraries nor to libraries of academic institutions stressing advanced research." These standards cover the same topics as those for junior college libraries (see above) and the complete text may be found in *The American Library and Book Trade Annual, 1961*.

Standards for University Libraries Standards for university libraries are now being prepared by the Committee on Standards. The diversity of size, scope, and objectives of universities has been a major obstacle to the framing of concise standards. It is expected that the committee will produce standards for university libraries as useful as those for college and junior college libraries.

Two articles in recent years have suggested standards for the size of book collections of university libraries. In 1966 Robert B. Downs, Dean of Libraries of the University of Illinois, suggested that "it seems doubtful that high-level doctoral work in a variety of fields can be carried on with less than half a million volumes and with annual expenditures of under $200,000."[3] Verner W. Clapp and Robert T. Jordan of the Council on Library Resources suggest a formula for size and composition of book collections based on number of students, number of honors students, number of faculty, number of fields of undergraduate majors, number of master's programs, and number of doctoral programs.[4] While neither of these suggestions has official sanction, they could be used as minimal measuring sticks until The American Library Association's standards are promulgated.

TWENTY-FIVE MOST IMPORTANT SELECTION AIDS[5]

American Institute of Physics: *Check List of Books for an Undergraduate Physics Library*, The Institute, New York, 1962.

[2] For those involved in establishing new junior college libraries, a most useful article is "Guidelines for Establishing Junior College Libraries," *College and Research Libraries*, vol. 24, pp. 501–505, November, 1963.

[3] "Doctoral Programs and Library Resources," *College and Research Libraries*, vol. 27, pp. 123–129, March, 1966.

[4] "Quantitative Criteria for Adequacy of Academic Library Collections," *College and Research Libraries*, vol. 26, pp. 371–380, September, 1965.

[5] Collected by Roland H. Moody, Director, University Libraries, Northeastern University, Boston.

Bertalan, Frank J.: *Books for Junior Colleges; a List of 4,000 Books, Periodicals, Films, and Filmstrips,* American Library Association, Chicago, 1954.
Books Abroad, University of Oklahoma Press, Norman, Okla. (quarterly, 1927–).
Books for College Libraries, American Library Association, Chicago, 1967.
British Book News: a Guide to Book Selection, British Council, London (monthly, 1940–).
Choice: Books for College Libraries, Olin Library, Wesleyan University, Middletown, Conn. (monthly, except bimonthly July–August, 1964–).
Committee on College and Adult Reading List of the National Council of Teachers of English: *The College and Adult Reading List of Books in Literature and the Fine Arts,* Washington Square Press, Pocket Books, Inc., New York, 1962.
Committee on College Reading: *Good Reading,* 19th ed., New American Library, New York, 1964.
Harvard University: *A Short Bibliography of History,* Graduate History Club, Harvard University, Cambridge, Mass., 1959.
Harvard University: *Harvard List of Books in Psychology,* 3d ed., Harvard University, Cambridge, Mass., 1964.
Harvard University Library, Lamont Library: *Catalogue,* Harvard University Press, Cambridge, Mass., 1953.
Hawkins, R. R.: *Scientific, Medical and Technical Books Published in the United States of America,* rev. ed., R. R. Bowker Company, New York, 1958.
International Economics Selections Bibliography, Department of Economics, University of Pittsburgh, Pittsburgh, Pa. (quarterly).
Kuhn, Warren B.: *The Julian Street Library: a Preliminary List of Titles,* R. R. Bowker Company, New York, 1966.
Massachusetts Institute of Technology Science Library New Book List, Massachusetts Institute of Technology, Cambridge, Mass. (monthly).
New Technical Books, Science Division, New York Public Library, New York (bimonthly, 1951–).
New York Times Book Review, The New York Times, New York (weekly, 1896–).
Paperbound Book Guide for Colleges, R. R. Bowker Company, New York (annually, 1964–).
Publishers' Weekly, R. R. Bowker Company, New York (weekly, 1872–).
Saturday Review, New York (weekly, 1924–). Book reviews.
Scholarly Books in America, University of Chicago, Chicago (quarterly, 1959–).
A Selective Bibliography in Science and Engineering, compiled by Northeastern University, G. K. Hall & Company, Boston, 1964.
Southern Association of Colleges and Secondary Schools, Commission on Colleges and Universities: *The Classified List of Reference Books and Periodicals for College Libraries,* 3d ed., The Association, Atlanta, Ga., 1955.
Syllabus: a Select List of In-print Books on the History of Art and Archaeology, Worldwide Books, New York (semiannually, 1966–).
Winchell, Constance M.: *Guide to Reference Books,* 8th ed., American Library Association, Chicago, 1967.

Chapter 2

Library Associations

ELLSWORTH MASON

Director of Library Services, Hofstra University, Hempstead, New York

A number of national and international library associations have been established over the years to promote the development of libraries and librarianship. Each association serves a special purpose, but all are uniformly dedicated—within the confines of their individual purposes—to the improvement and extension of library services to a variety of specialized publics, the continuing development and coordination of library resources, and the promotion of innovations in library services and techniques.

These associations also serve to promote librarianship as a profession by increasing the competence of their members through the exchange of information relative to various professional practices.

The following is a list of these library associations: [1]

NATIONAL ASSOCIATIONS

American Association of Law Libraries
53 West Jackson Boulevard
Chicago, Ill. 60604
(312) 939-4764

[1] For full information about officers, committee structure, and changes in address, consult *The Bowker Annual of Library and Book Trade Information.*

American Association of School Librarians
50 East Huron Street
Chicago, Ill. 60611
(312) 944-6780

American Association of State Libraries
50 East Huron Street
Chicago, Ill. 60611
(312) 944-6780

American Society for Information Science
2000 P Street N.W.
Washington, D.C. 20036
(202) 332-6365

American Library Association
50 East Huron Street
Chicago, Ill. 60611
(312) 944-6780

* American Theological Library Association

Association of College and Research Libraries
50 East Huron Street
Chicago, Ill. 60611
(312) 944-6780

* Association of Jewish Libraries

Association of Research Libraries
1755 Massachusetts Avenue N.W.
Washington, D.C. 20036
(202) 462-2618

Canadian Library Association
63 Sparks Street
Ottawa 4, Ont.
(613) 232-9625

Catholic Library Association
461 West Lancaster Avenue
Haverford, Pa. 19041
(215) MIdway 9-5250-1

* Council of National Library Association

Educational Film Library Association
250 West 57 Street
New York, N.Y. 10019
(212) CIrcle 6-4467

* Library Public Relations Council

Lutheran Church Library Association
122 West Franklin Avenue
Minneapolis, Minn. 55404
(612) 332-2571

Medical Library Association
919 North Michigan Avenue
Chicago, Ill. 60611
(312) 642-3724

* Music Library Association

* Society of American Archivists

Special Libraries Association
235 Park Avenue, South
New York, N.Y. 10003
(212) 777-8136

* Theatre Library Association

* The address changes when officers change.

REGIONAL ASSOCIATIONS

* Atlantic Provinces Library Association
  (New Brunswick, Newfoundland, Nova Scotia, Prince Edward Island)
* Mountain Plains Library Association
  (Colorado, Kansas, Nebraska, North Dakota, South Dakota, Utah, Wyoming)
* New England Library Association
  (Connecticut, Maine, Massachusetts, New Hampshire, Rhode Island, Vermont)
* Pacific Northwest Library Association
  (Idaho, Montana, Oregon, Washington, British Columbia)
* Southeastern Library Association
  (Alabama, Florida, Georgia, Kentucky, Mississippi, North Carolina, Tennessee, Virginia)
* Southwestern Library Association
  (Arizona, Arkansas, Louisiana, New Mexico, Oklahoma, Texas)

STATE AND PROVINCIAL ASSOCIATIONS *

Alabama Library Association
Alaska Library Association
Alberta Library Association
Arizona Library Association
Arkansas Library Association
British Columbia Library Association
California Library Association
Colorado Library Association
Connecticut Library Association
Delaware Library Association
District of Columbia Library Association
Florida Library Association
Georgia Library Association
Hawaii Library Association
Idaho Library Association
Illinois Library Association
Indiana Library Association
Iowa Library Association
Kansas Library Association
Kentucky Library Association
Louisiana Library Association
Maine Library Association
Manitoba Library Association
Maryland Library Association
Massachusetts Library Association
Michigan Library Association
Minnesota Library Association
Mississippi Library Association
Missouri Library Association
Montana Library Association
Nebraska Library Association
Nevada Library Association
New Hampshire Library Association
New Jersey Library Association
New Mexico Library Association
New York Library Association
North Carolina Library Association
North Dakota Library Association
Ohio Library Association
Oklahoma Library Association

* The address changes when officers change.

Ontario Library Association
Oregon Library Association
Pennsylvania Library Association
Puerto Rico Library Association
Quebec Library Association
Rhode Island Library Association
Saskatchewan Library Association
South Carolina Library Association
South Dakota Library Association
Tennessee Library Association
Texas Library Association
Utah Library Association
Vermont Library Association
Virginia Library Association
Washington Library Association
West Virginia Library Association
Wisconsin Library Association
Wyoming Library Association

Chapter 3

Library Organization and Administration

JOHN M. DAWSON

Director of Libraries, University of Delaware, Newark, Delaware

STAFF

The Librarian The librarian should be responsible directly to the president or to the chief academic officer. He should rank with the deans and other top administrative officers, for the library serves the entire institution and has direct relations with virtually every department. The librarian should be a member of the deans' council and should serve on the curriculum planning committee and on other campuswide committees.

The librarian is responsible for selecting, training, organizing, and supervising the library staff; for preparing the library budget and supervising library expenditures; for developing (in collaboration with the faculty) and implementing the library's acquisitions policies; for the custody of the library's collections; and for providing library services to students, faculty, and staff.

The role of the professional librarian is to provide the bibliographical expertise requisite for a sound program of acquisition and cataloging, to provide a collection adequate in number and appropriate to the aims of the institution, properly cataloged and organized for use; to mediate between the collections and the readers; to teach the use of libraries and bibliographic tools both in formal classes and in one-to-one encounters with students at all levels; and to plan, organize, and supervise the work of the nonprofessional staff and student assistants.

The Professional Library Staff This staff is the nucleus around which the rest of the library staff is built. (A professional librarian has, as a minimum, a baccalaureate degree in a subject field and a degree from a library school—preferably one accredited by the American Library Association.) The professional staff should be conscious of the library's role in the institution, aware of the special needs of students and faculty, and alert to curricular developments. Their work should be at a high level and they should be accorded faculty status, including retirement, vacations, sabbatical leaves, etc., on the same basis as faculty. Professional librarians in many institutions have faculty titles as well as full faculty status.

The Nonprofessional Staff The nonprofessional staff (clerks, typists, and so forth) is necessary to perform the subprofessional work in the library. In smaller libraries the professional staff should probably outnumber the nonprofessionals in a ratio of five to three, but in the larger university library a ratio of two clerical to one professional is not uncommon. Student assistants should also be used to supplement the full-time staff in whatever capacities their talents and training permit, but they should not be used as substitutes for full-time staff.

Organization of Staff The library staff is usually organized into specialized departments. The more common are order, cataloging, circulation, reference, and chief librarian's office. In the larger libraries these departments may be subdivided into many departments and there may be an assistant chief librarian in charge of reader's services departments and another in charge of the technical departments (acquisitions, cataloging, etc.). In the smaller library the functions of these departments must be performed by one or two librarians.

The Faculty Library Committee This committee should be advisory only and should be composed of representatives from various instructional fields who have an understanding of and an interest in the growth and development of the library's collections and services. The members of the committee should interpret to their colleagues the library's policies and should, in turn, transmit to the librarian suggestions and comments from the faculty. The librarian should always be a full voting member of the committee. A student library committee may be appointed or elected to provide a similar link to the student body, or student representatives may be appointed to a joint faculty-student library committee.

BOOK SELECTION AND ACQUISITION

Book Selection Book selection is the joint task of the faculty and the professional library staff. Faculty should be encouraged to suggest books and other materials to be acquired, not only in their special fields but in general. The library staff should participate in selection in all fields, but with particular attention to general bibliography, interdisciplinary materials, and areas of general interest which the faculty ignore. In smaller institutions faculty are likely to be much aware of book selection and participate in it gladly, but in larger institutions, particularly with research-oriented faculty, there is a tendency to select only in narrow fields, so that a major part of selection devolves on the library staff. In the larger university libraries there is an increasing tendency to place blanket orders for certain kinds of books so that they are received automatically as published. This reduces the necessity for selection and ordering. In the larger universities with the objective of wide inclusiveness, this method may be highly satisfactory, but it has the danger of adding to the library material of doubtful value. This method of acquisition should be used with care.

Acquisition of Books The acquisition of books requires the use of a variety of avenues. The use of book jobbers will, in general, be less expensive in that orders for a variety of books may be placed with one jobber, who will ship (hopefully!) in bulk with consolidated invoices. Discounts vary, and promises of large discounts should be followed carefully to see that the actual invoices reflect the promises. Some publishers encourage direct purchases; others prefer to supply only through jobbers. A good librarian is alert to the various modes of obtaining books and will seek to obtain the best possible service at the lowest possible cost.

In general, institutions should avoid placing their current book purchases with jobbers through annual bids, for, once let, the service or the discounts or both may prove to be less than satisfactory.

Out-of-print books can only be sought through the antiquarian book trade, and finding out-of-print books wanted for the library demands on the part of the librarian a vast knowledge of this highly specialized market.

A useful list for libraries in new colleges is *An Opening Day Collection,* a listing of some books recommended as the minimum collection any college library should have on the day the college opens classes. This was compiled by the editors of *Choice* in 1967 and is available for $5 a copy from their editorial offices in Middletown, Conn. A more extensive list is *Books for College Libraries,* whose self-explanatory subtitle reads, "a selected list of approximately 53,400 titles based on the initial selection made for the University of California New Campuses Program and selected with the assistance of college teachers, librarians and other advisers" (American Library Association, Chicago, 1967). Brief scholarly annotations of current books, written by specialists, appear in *Choice,* a monthly journal (11 issues a year) published by the Association of College and Research Libraries. There are many scholarly journals, too numerous to mention, with excellent reviews which are useful as book selection aids. See Twenty-five Most Important Selection Aids on page 4-5.

CATALOGING AND CLASSIFICATION

Only when a collection of books is *organized for use* does it become a library. The means for organizing book collections are classification and cataloging.

Classification is the arrangement of books on the shelf so that books on a given subject are together, books on related subjects nearby, books less related farther away, and so on, all according to some system. The most widely used systems in American libraries are the Dewey Decimal Classification and the Library of Congress Classification.[1] Neither system is perfect and each has its partisans. In recent years a large number of academic libraries have chosen the Library of Congress Classification at their founding or, having used the Dewey Decimal Classification, have decided to change to the Library of Congress Classification.

The Dewey Decimal Classification will be familiar to most entering students because it is widely used in school libraries and it has mnemonic features which are said to be useful. On the other hand, as collections grow, the classification numbers tend to become long and cumbersome; because there are only ten main classes, some major fields must be crowded into subordinate schedules; and Dewey Decimal Classification numbers are not printed on all the Library of Congress printed cards, as are Library of Congress numbers.

The Library of Congress Classification is well suited for academic libraries, large or small; it is kept up to date by the Library of Congress; it is flexible and readily expandable as collections grow and as new subject fields emerge; for libraries which fully utilize Library of Congress printed cards it is economical; its notation is short and simple. Finally, should a national network of libraries develop, there are likely to be substantial advantages to using the Library of Congress Classification. Disadvantages are that few new students will be familiar with it, and its schedules are difficult to obtain because the Library of Congress has not kept the schedules in print.

Subject Cataloging Subject cataloging is related to classification. By using a schedule of subject headings ("descriptors"), the reader can go to the catalog and find books on a particular subject or some aspect of it.

Descriptive Cataloging Entering books in a catalog according to some accepted (but, regrettably, not widely understood) scheme, together with a brief bibliographic description of the book, is descriptive cataloging. This apparently simple task is in truth rather complex. The "author" of a book may be a person or persons whose name or names are complex; each must be distinguished from the other; and an author may be an organization, government, association, or other body.[2]

The Card Catalog The card catalog has been standard in American libraries for over half a century; in some libraries today book catalogs, printed in some instances by computer, either supplement or replace the card catalog. Each form has its virtues and its drawbacks. Either form may be arranged as a dictionary catalog, with author, title, and subject entries all arranged in a simple alphabet; or the catalogs may be divided into a separate subject catalog and an author-title catalog. There are numerous variations as to what is included in each.

Methods of cataloging and classification, once adopted and applied to collections, are difficult and expensive to change; decisions on the methods to adopt should be carefully considered. Cost is but one factor and should be outweighed by ease of use and comprehension by students and faculty.

[1] For full treatment of cataloging and classification, see Margaret Mann, *Introduction to Cataloging and the Classification of Books*, 2d, ed., American Library Association, Chicago, 1943. While intended for library-school students, certain chapters of this book will also be useful to the college administrator who desires a good understanding of cataloging and classification.

[2] See Mann, *op. cit.*, pp. 119–128.

CIRCULATION

The charging out of books for use outside the library—or inside, when stacks are closed—is the circulation function. In an academic library the system of charging out books should provide information on what books have been loaned out, to whom, and when they are due to be returned. There are various manual systems in use, and in recent years charging systems using data-processing or computing equipment have been developed.[3]

Policies and regulations governing the use of books should be as liberal as possible while still ensuring equitable access to all materials by all members of the academic community. In practice, loan periods vary from two weeks to an entire semester for books, while periodicals may be loaned for briefer periods or not at all. Loan periods for records, films, and other audiovisual materials are usually limited to between two weeks and one month. The tendency is to extend loan periods of materials whenever possible.

Reserve Books Reserve books are books whose loan periods are restricted so that all members of a class may use them during a limited time. There is a wide variety of loan periods for reserve books—two-hour, one-day, three-day, etc.—depending on length of assignment, number of students, number of copies of books in the library, etc. The availability of a wide range of paperback books (not now so inexpensive as could be wished) should diminish the reserved book stock.

REFERENCE

The function of the reference staff is to assist the reader in finding the materials needed to serve his purpose. Frequently this requires extensive use of diagnostic techniques to determine the true question in the reader's mind. Then the reference librarian must direct the reader to the sources, providing such assistance as the reader's knowledge and competence—or lack thereof—may demand. This is a sensitive and delicate area in which the librarian is a teacher in the truest sense, leading the reader to define his question or problem and then leading him to find the sources which will answer the question or lead to the solution of the problem. In most instances the mission is not to provide the answer, but to lead the reader into finding it; there are, of course, many circumstances which require only producing an answer as promptly as possible.

The reference collection consists of those books which assist the reference librarian in this service: encyclopedias, dictionaries, handbooks, bibliographies, guidebooks, etc. The standard American bibliography of general reference books is Constance Winchell's *Guide to Reference Books*, 8th ed. (American Library Association, Chicago, 1967).

ORGANIZATION OF COLLECTIONS

Open Stacks or Closed Stacks Open stacks are stacks open to any reader in which he may browse at will; such stacks are usually self-service stacks, although some larger libraries will also page books from the stacks. In a closed-stack system only selected readers (faculty, graduate students, honors students) are normally admitted to the stacks; others must find the call number of the book desired through the catalog and present this to a staff member who will then have the book secured from the stacks by a page. The educational advantage lies almost wholly with open stacks in which

[3] See Fry and Associates, *Study of Circulation Systems*, Library Technology Project of the American Library Association, Chicago, 1961.

the reader may browse at will, selecting, inspecting, and rejecting *at the shelves.* There is, inevitably, some disorder: misplaced books, and books in use in the stacks and thus temporarily "lost." While closed stacks do, to a great extent, alleviate these difficulties, the system interposes a formidable barrier between the reader and the books. Many large university libraries have achieved a compromise by having an open-stack library for undergraduates and restricted-access stacks for their research collections.

Centralization versus Decentralization Centralized collections are less expensive in that fewer personnel are required to staff the public desks, the interdisciplinary reader has access in one collection to all materials needed, and duplication of books is reduced. However, it is claimed that decentralized collections place the materials near those who use them, the smaller specialized library is easier to use, the relations between librarian and user are more intimate, and service is more direct and more personal.

Joint Use of Collections Joint use of collections by adjacent or nearby institutions permits the development of more adequate collections for all, which might not otherwise be possible. The Joint University Libraries in Nashville and the Honnold Library of the Claremont Colleges are examples of this. Research materials may be pooled in or purchased by a "clearinghouse" library for use by its members. The Center for Research Libraries in Chicago is an example of both on a nationwide scale; the Smith–Mt. Holyoke–University of Massachusetts–Amherst libraries have a common storage for less-used materials.

Interlibrary Loans Libraries have, for many years, been cooperating to advance scholarship and learning by lending books, journals, and other materials to each other. Interlibrary loans are voluminous and libraries have adopted a uniform code governing interlibrary loan transactions.[4] Interlibrary loans are intended only to give access to the unusual materials occasionally needed by scholars and are not intended to be nor should they be used as a substitute for adequate local collections. The borrowing library is responsible for paying costs of transportation both ways and for the replacement of books lost or damaged in transit. Because of the heavy use of periodicals, many libraries will no longer lend journals but will make and send photocopies of periodical articles at a nominal cost.

Interpreting Library Services The librarian must interpret the library to the community both on and off the campus. On campus, he must interpret the library to the administration, the faculty, and the students by personal contacts, reports, news stories in all media of communication, displays, and, most of all, by developing a helpful, cheerful attitude on the part of all staff.

The Library Handbook A library handbook is an excellent means of interpreting the library to its users. The handbook should be imaginatively designed and attractively printed. It should contain a general statement of library policies and regulations, explanation of the catalog and classification used, diagrams locating collections and and facilities, an explanation of how to use the library, a list of special features and services, and a list of the more useful indexes and reference books.

Use of the Library by the Noncollege Community The use of the library by the noncollege community should be permitted so long as it does not interfere with the use by the campus community. Even when circumstances make it necessary to restrict use by outsiders, arrangements should be made for use by exceptional high school students or adults working on a definite problem requiring use of the library's resources. Too, books should, when possible, be loaned to public libraries on interlibrary loan.

[4] "General Interlibrary Loan Code, 1952," *College and Research Libraries*, vol. 13, pp. 350–358, October, 1952; or in *American Library Annual and Book Trade Almanac, 1959*, R. R. Bowker Company, New York, 1958.

LIBRARY FINANCE

The Library Budget The library budget should normally be about 5 percent or more of the educational and general budget. This will not be adequate for the library in a new or developing institution which must acquire books and other materials at a rate beyond that of established libraries.

While division of the library budget will vary to some extent according to local conditions, a generally accepted rule of thumb is 60 percent for salaries and wages and 40 percent for books, periodicals, binding, supplies, equipment, travel, etc. The "Standards for College Libraries" and "Standards for Junior College Libraries" cited in Chapter 1 of this section should be consulted.

The budget should be administered by the librarian. He may, in certain instances, wish to consult with the faculty library committee on the allocation of book funds. When book funds are allocated to instructional departments, a substantial percentage should be reserved to the librarian for the purchase of reference, general, and interdisciplinary works.

Analyses of library operations have not reached the stage where meaningful program budgeting is feasible. Some multicampus institutions (e.g., the California State Colleges) have adopted formula budgeting; when applied to libraries, this has had but mixed success.

Library cost analyses are rare and, because of the infinite differences between institutions, have not been altogether meaningful. There is room for much development in this area.

Federal Funds Federal funds are available for library purchases under Title III of the Higher Education Act of 1965 (Public Law 89–329) and for audiovisual material and equipment under Title IV. Funds are available for medical school libraries under the Medical Library Assistance Act (Public Law 89–291). Guidelines for funds for acquisitions under Title III of the Higher Education Act are issued each year by the Office of Education.

Friends of the Library Friends of the library groups may be useful in securing additional funds for the library, usually for the acquisition of books. Members may also donate useful and valuable books. The president of the institution should involve himself in founding such a group so as to bring in wealthy and influential citizens, and the librarian must actively promote activities for the "Friends" if the effort is to be successful. Friends should be a link with the community as well as a fund-raising organization.

Reports and Evaluation The librarian should each year prepare a written report to the president which should touch on the highlights of library development and activity, problems that have arisen, and the general state of the library. This report should be succinct and avoid pettiness. Following the narrative portion should be the statistics on library growth and use. The librarian should use his report as an evaluative tool. The librarian's annual report should be widely distributed on and off campus.

It is salutary, from time to time, to have faculty committees or experienced library consultants evaluate the library. Experienced professional librarians who serve as consultants can take an unbiased look at library operations and from their knowledge and experience recommend changes to improve services or methods. The American Library Association will, on request, suggest library consultants.

Sources of Information Two books which are useful in any consideration of academic libraries are Guy R. Lyle, *The Administration of the College Library,* 3d ed. (H. W. Wilson Company, New York, 1961); and Louis Round Wilson and Maurice F. Tauber, *The University Library,* 2d ed. (Columbia University Press, New York, 1956). These give an overview of their respective fields and both have useful and extensive bibliographies.

The best summary of the amount and effect of reading by college students is still Harvie S. Branscomb's *Teaching With Books: A Study of College Libraries* (American Library Association, Chicago, 1940). An early work on ways of making the library a truly effective teaching instrument is B. Lamar Johnson's *Vitalizing a College Library* (American Library Association, Chicago, 1939), in which the author, who was simultaneously dean and librarian of Stephens College, describes how he merged teaching and the library. This concept has again been revived in the "library-college" movement; the chapters in *The Library College* (Drexel Press, Philadelphia, 1966) are most useful for the administrator who wishes to promote an active library program. These three books should be read by every college and university administrator.

Two periodicals which contain articles on academic libraries are *College and University Libraries,* published bimonthly by the Association of College and Research Libraries, and *The Library-College Journal,* published quarterly by the Library-College Associates.

Much useful information on libraries and publishing appears each year in *The Bowker Annual of Library and Book Trade Information* (R. R. Bowker Company, New York). The Office of Education of the United States Department of Health, Education, and Welfare collects and proposes to publish each year library statistics of colleges and universities. When published, this will give statistics on growth of libraries, expenditures, salaries, and similar useful information.

Chapter **4**

The Library Building

ELLSWORTH MASON

Director of Library Services, Hofstra University, Hempstead, New York

INTRODUCTION

Many academic libraries have been built in the past 20 years, but only a few of them are very good. Sometimes the architect is the source of failure, but more often the client has demanded unreasonable results from a poverty budget or has imposed an impossible timetable on the planning. Most bad library buildings have resulted from the inability of the client, through ignorance and bad planning procedures, to state clearly to the architect what he wants in a building and why he wants it and to conduct negotiations with the architect to their conclusion in successful plans. Even today it is astonishing how poorly understood are the elements of good library planning, despite well-documented examples of totally good planning methods that have led to good library buildings.

THE PLANNING COMMITTEE

The first step in planning a library building, and one of the most important, is the appointment of a local planning committee and the establishment of proper organizational arrangements for negotiating on plans with the architects. If a power struggle develops within this committee, decisions are thrown back to the architects. Architects cannot produce a good library building, whose problems are multifold and sensitive, without constant, informed review of their planning by the clients. The role of each member of the committee must therefore be carefully spelled out in writing to the entire committee.

The librarian is a key member of the committee because so much of the planning involves library technicalities, which are extremely complex and sophisticated at present. Without a strong librarian, it is impossible to achieve a totally successful library building. He must be released from half of his administrative load, by additions to his staff, while he is planning the building. The librarian's special function should be to project, with his staff, the building implications inherent in their future operations and to work more closely with the library building consultant than other committee members can. He should draft the library building program for review by the committee. Most important, he must be the one responsible for the exacting, detailed review of each set of plans and the variation in the plans that go on for more than a year.

If the librarian is weak or unable to learn with the guidance of a library building consultant the new skills and ideas necessary to manage the planning details, the committee must use the consultant for this crucially important function. In such a situation, the consultant must be involved much more constantly in the planning than otherwise would be necessary.

The coordinator of buildings, if there is one, should represent on the committee a specialized knowledge of construction problems and campus planning. He should not be allowed to control the design of the building.

The administration need not be represented directly on the committee but should receive a flow of information through frequent reports, submitted at specified stages in the planning process. The trustees should not participate in the committee, but the chairman of the committee should be invited to all meetings of the administration or trustees that concern the library building. Lack of coordination between these two levels of operation has undone many library buildings.

The faculty members of this committee must have a proven interest in the library's welfare and be of high standing among their faculty peers. They should form a two-way information channel, to discuss with the faculty and report back to the committee, throughout the planning. They should concern themselves particularly with those aspects of the building pertinent to student and faculty use.

When the administration has appointed a strong committee, has defined in writing each member's function, and has issued instructions for periodic reporting to the administration and trustees, the committee should be empowered as the *only* body on campus to negotiate plans with the architects. Impatient pleas to the administration, however reasonable they seem, must be referred to the committee as the center for negotiations, since the administration cannot possibly be informed enough to make unilateral decisions. All local differences must be settled locally and multilaterally through the committee. More buildings are damaged, and some in a major way, by architects who have access to the administration behind the committee's back than by any other factor.

THE CONSULTANT

Immediately after this committee is appointed, a library building consultant should be appointed. He should serve as a guide in planning and a constant reviewer of planning documents throughout the planning process. It is a waste of money to hire him for only a few days, because the problems which occur constantly during the development of drawings are shifting, remarkably varied, and totally unpredictable. Merely to detect them requires a background of experience which cannot be developed on campus even under the best conditions.

The consultant will charge about $150 to $250 per day, plus expenses. If he is good, he will save the institution at least 10 times his total cost in actual savings on the final cost of the building. In addition, he will speed up the planning process, ease the way for the architect to achieve his peak performance, and maximize the usefulness of the building, with consequent savings in the cost of running the library when completed. The consultant must be hired by the client, even if the architect has hired his own building consultant, since he must represent the client's interests in negotiations with the architect.

The consultant should be brought on campus as soon as possible. He will need a day or two to get the feeling of the physical plant and the educational dynamics and trend of the institution. He will discuss possibilities of site, outline the proper sequence of planning steps, indicate sources of information, discuss the future of the entire library system, predict implications of nonbook media—including the computer—for the local situation, suggest library buildings to be inspected, suggest architects for consideration, describe what negotiations with the architect involve, and warn against pitfalls. In general he will focus in the minds of the committee a vague and chaotic situation and start the committee along the preliminary steps that must be taken before the building program can be written.

The consultant should be intimately involved in developing and reviewing the program. He should review every version of preliminary plans well into working drawings and review final working drawings. Much consultation can be done by mail or by phone, but the consultant should be present at every meeting in which the weight of his experience and expertise is needed to establish confidence in the proceedings of the planning committee. It is especially important for him to participate in meetings with the architects at which the general concept of the building is presented and at subsequent meetings until the direction of the planning is definitely agreed upon. Subsequent to bid drawings, he should be consulted on the special problems involved in planning stack bid documents, and if the consultant has aesthetic skills, he should be used to review presentations of the interior design as they develop.

SOURCES OF INFORMATION

As soon as possible, the committee should begin to read significant literature on library buildings. The literature of this field is vast, repetitive, and extremely uneven in quality. Fortunately, a few key books on planning academic libraries provide an excellent foundation for neophytes. The most important is Keyes D. Metcalf's *Planning Academic and Research Library Buildings* (McGraw-Hill Book Company, New York, 1965), a massive and extremely thorough treatise on every conceivable building problem, which should be studied and kept at hand for reference during the entire planning process. This book contains a useful annotated bibliography. A much shorter and simpler introduction to the subject is Ralph E. Ellsworth's *Planning the College and University Library Building* ([Boulder, Colo.], 1968). A summary, organized review of the most important literature up to 1960 is contained in Ralph E.

Ellsworth, "Buildings," in Ralph R. Shaw (ed.), *The State of the Library Art*, vol. 3, part 1 (Rutgers Graduate School of Library Service, New Brunswick, N.J., 1960).

The Educational Facilities Laboratories in New York City are a source of information about new problems in library buildings, especially those involving the use of nonbook media, and can recommend consultants for most aspects of library planning. The Library Administration Division of the American Library Association in Chicago has a small collection of library building programs and library floor plans available on interlibrary loan.

STUDY OF LIBRARY BUILDINGS

All information about three-dimensional facilities requires solidification by observation and, after reading about library buildings, the next step is to visit a number of libraries at similar colleges or universities. They should be selected carefully, with advice. A study of bad buildings wastes time and is confusing. The librarian and at least two members of the planning committee should visit together, so that future reference to these libraries will have a common basis of understanding.

This study visit should aim at observing meticulously many aspects of the library and gathering information about sizes, shapes, and brands of furniture and equipment and the names of consultants, architects, or other good specialists. Traffic patterns and acoustics should be observed, and the function of each of the library elements should be carefully analyzed. Much of the best information about the virtues and shortcomings of the building will come from the library's department heads. In addition to a study of details, the committee should pay special attention to the site, the building's exterior and interior design, its lighting, and its temperature comfort level.

By this time, the committee will have a good deal of information about architects who have designed successful libraries—and the architect should be chosen on no other basis. At least two of his libraries must be visited and studied before he is hired. It must be understood that an architect is not one man but a firm, with various levels of talent on its staff. The university must make sure that the staff that has planned successful libraries in the past, or a strong core of it, will be used on its job. Frequently this is not the case.

BASIC DECISIONS

The architect can advise on the site location, but he should not begin thinking about the nature of the building until the library building program is completely finished and handed to him in a dozen mimeographed copies. Before the program can be started, the administration must make the following series of basic decisions, which must be firm, enlightened, and stated in writing: (1) the time period, stated in years, for which the library is intended to serve, *after* it is open; (2) the maximum student enrollment, broken into significant segments, during that time period; (3) the percentage of that enrollment which the library plans to seat at one time; and (4) the maximum book collection to be housed during the life of the building. These statistics must not be drawn out of a hat but should be developed responsibly with the aid of those on campus most informed about these various factors.

The budget is *not* a basic decision that should be made in advance. The library building program should emerge intelligently from the quantities stated above and must estimate accurately the net area required. This can be converted by formula to gross area. It then will be apparent how much the building is likely to cost; and the budget can be set. Obviously, no loaves-and-fishes act can produce money when not enough exists, but intelligent basic decisions can now be made about revising the library planning, whereas they cannot be made before the program is developed.

If the size of the building is reduced, accurate estimates will indicate how many years sooner it will have to be expanded, and provisions for easy expansion or alternate arrangements can be made. Recent experience indicates that very many libraries are serving far too short a time after they are occupied. States that, by policy, prevent library buildings or additions from being planned for more than 5 years ahead are wasting about 20 percent of the cost of the construction. It would be far more economical to build half as many each year and project them for 10 years.

WRITING THE PROGRAM

The library building program should emerge from an outline of the building units to be included in the library that has been worked out with the library building consultant. Ideally, first drafts of the specifications of the units should be written locally, revised by the consultant, reviewed locally, and then fully outfitted with detailed lists of furniture and equipment and accurate square footage estimates for each unit by the consultant. The process of writing the program for a building of 200,000 gross square feet will take about 3 or 4 months and no less than 3 months for smaller academic libraries.

PROBLEM AREAS

Three areas of the building are particularly difficult to plan—the main floor, the technical processes areas, and special-collections areas. The main floor requires a larger area than can be conveniently massed with the rest of the building's requirements because so much of the library's operation must be close to the main card catalog. One solution is to have a large main floor which becomes a podium or platform for a tower of considerably smaller dimensions. The podium may consist of one to three stories depending upon the size of the project; on a sloping site it may be cantilevered, producing a design which is both artistic and functional.

Most libraries built in the past 10 years quickly overran their technical processes areas (basically ordering, cataloging, and subordinate mechanical activities). The surge of acquisitions that has marked recent years still is escalating, and it is especially difficult to predict with any degree of accuracy a maximum acquisitions figure for rapidly growing universities (among which are all the new ones). Ideally, the technical processes should be close to the card catalog, their basic tool, but great accelerations in acquisitions can drive them from such proximity to some other part of the library building even when they are properly located to begin with.

In such a case, an official catalog, comprising a single main entry card for each book, is developed. If the technical processes are removed from proper proximity to the catalog, they may as well move out of the library building, and the future of technical processes will probably involve placing them in a separate building, much cheaper to construct than library square footage and planned for easy and cheap expansion. They can then generate their own expansion needs in their own building. It should be close to the library, and will have to be connected to the main card catalog by telephone, with an assistant on duty to answer questions directly from the catalog.

No totally satisfactory rare-books library, or special collections department in a general library, has yet been built. The problems of ultraviolet-light control from windows and fluorescent lights, temperature and humidity control, air filtration, fire prevention, the hazards of electrical and water systems, and exhibition cases have never been satisfactorily solved in one library. The way is open for any library willing to undertake the study required to solve these problems before planning the first totally successful special collections facility.

SUBJECT ORGANIZATION

Library organizational arrangements based on subject specialties are capable of a wide range of solutions, especially in larger universities. The solutions, which must answer sensitively actual needs of the instructional program, vary with each institution, but a few generalizations can be made from recent experiences with these problems. The practice of establishing separate subject areas for the humanities, social sciences, and sciences within a central library has largely been discontinued because of numerous difficulties found to exist in systems presently established. Separate departmental libraries within the buildings occupied by the corresponding faculty have given way, with the overlapping of disciplines, to the combination of similar disciplines into divisional libraries or larger group libraries. Physical facilities for both departmental and divisional libraries, when they are parts of larger office and classroom buildings, have been badly planned almost without exception, because their planning has been largely in uninformed hands, more concerned with faculty office and classroom problems.

The tendency to establish separate undergraduate libraries, either as separate buildings or as a separate part of a general library, continues, but such libraries are now aimed at only the two lower college classes. Use of a library by juniors and seniors tends to be the same kind of use made by research graduate students or even faculty members, and their needs are the same.

A study at the University of Wisconsin revealed that the use by undergraduates of a central library varies directly with the distance of their living facilities from the library. This study indicates the need, on large campuses, to have centrally assigned books in branches of the general library nearer the dormitories.

TOWERS

In the past few years, tower library buildings have returned to the scene after years of exile. Buildings of this type already built or under construction at Brown, Hofstra, the University of Massachusetts, and Notre Dame show clearly that the disadvantages long attributed to the tower structure have been exaggerated and that its possibilities for the solution of contemporary library problems are just beginning to be realized.

MECHANICAL FACILITIES

Security can be obtained by posting guards at exits controlled by turnstiles. This system is not aesthetically pleasing and not entirely effective, but it is better than nothing. In recent years, universities have installed electronic detecting systems at exits. Such systems should be investigated before the building is planned, since conduits have to be poured into the structure to provide for them.

Interior communications provided by loudspeaker systems are an anathema in libraries. Interconnected internal telephones and chime-signal systems or radio-signal devices that summon individuals to telephones are preferred. Recently some libraries have experimented with soft background music, with varied results.

Vertical movement of books should be supplied by key-summoned staff elevators, *not* freight elevators, wherever the building requires them. Enough should be supplied so that long staff waiting is not required. Mechanical book-conveyor systems from the stacks and mechanical book return systems to the stacks have long been used. Book lifts of the automatic dumbwaiter type should not be used, because they require double loading of books into and out of the lift. Instead, books should be placed on book trucks and wheeled directly to their reshelving locations.

Fire authorities sometimes urge the installation of sprinkler systems throughout the library for fire prevention. Since water is more destructive to books than fire and since students set off sprinkler heads when they are low enough, this provision should be resisted in favor of a heat- or smoke-sensing detection system. This should be wired directly to the local campus security control office or to the local fire department so that response to a fire is immediate.

Lighting in most library buildings is quite bad because very few architects understand the basic principles of good lighting, and they override the advice of their electrical engineers. Electrical engineers themselves are often not well informed about illumination engineering, which is no longer taught in most engineering schools. Consequently, the university must inform itself, by empirical evidence, about the kind of lighting fixtures that produce well-diffused, good *quality* lighting. Footcandle readings are meaningless unless the lighting fixtures diffuse well and are free of both direct and reflected glare. This condition can be achieved by fixtures with a translucent, diffusing lens with a low surface brightness. Mockups of all fixtures and lenses proposed for a building must be made in order to experience directly the results in terms of vision comfort. A good lighting consultant should be used to review the lighting system proposed in any library building.

Temperature discomfort in buildings is common today, and a careful study must be made during the drawing stage of the temperature zones planned for the building and the location of the temperature controls. Interior rooms should, ideally, have their own separate controls. Peripheral heat as well as a central heating system must be provided in humid climates, especially on window walls which tend to encourage convection currents that act as drafts. Fin-tube units do not temper the air as well as fan-coil units or induction units. If the latter are used, they should be selected to put out the desired tempering capacity at medium speed or velocity in order to keep their noise level within reasonable limits, although it is highly desirable to plan a background noise from the ventilation facilities to mask normal noise of movement and conversation in a library and the ballast noise of fluorescent lights. A ventilation engineer should be used to review the ventilation system and its plan of controls before plans are let out for bid.

Since the future probably will require much more use of portable electrical machines for nonbook media and may require the location of electronic carrels at unpredictable places in the library, and since the use of computer consoles around the library may also be required, a premium is placed on providing in the building the greatest possible electrical flexibility. It should be possible, with a minimum of alteration, to tap electricity anywhere on the peripheral walls of a floor. Under-floor ducts should be poured into the building, probably of the flat duct type, 6 inches wide on 6-foot centers in at least one direction. It should be possible to run cables from floor to floor through vertical ducts, and one outlet should lead out of the building to connect with remote central production units.

PLANNING STANDARDS

Seating: 30 percent of the student body at one time for resident campuses.

Shelving: 250 books per standard double-face section of 7 shelves. One double-face section will average 18 sq ft in stacks on 4 ft 6 in. centers.

Ceilings: 8 ft minimum, 8 ft 6 in. preferable. Over 9 ft 6 in. should be avoided except for special effects.

Lighting: 70 to 80 footcandles of *good quality* light for all reading and work areas.

Air conditioning: 75°F temperature, 35 percent humidity in general; 70°F, 50 percent humidity in rare-book areas.

Filtration: 85 percent effective filtration of dust. In polluted atmospheres, activated charcoal filters must be added. 95 percent filtration of dust plus activated charcoal filters for rare books.

Floor load: 150 lb per sq ft live load throughout.

Column spacing: If stacks fall between columns, they require clear space that is a multiple of 3 ft (for the stacks) *plus* 6 in. (4 in. for two end uprights and 2 in. to allow for irregularities in pouring).

TIMETABLE

Haste is the worst enemy of successful buildings, and the following is a reasonable timetable for the planning of a library:

Reading literature—1 month.
Visiting libraries—1 month.
Writing the program—3 months.
Developing final preliminary drawings—6 to 7 months.
Developing working drawings—4 to 5 months.
Calling bids—1 month.
Contracting and setting up machinery—1 month.

This is a total of 17 to 19 months from the beginning to the time of breaking ground in earnest. It will take about a year and a half to build a library of 150 to 200,000 square feet, 2 years for 500,000 square feet, 3 years for a million square feet.

COSTS

While the distribution of structural costs varies greatly, some rule-of-thumb generalizations about library building costs can be made. In a university, assuming no cost for the site, the following can be used as general distributions of the total project costs:

Building costs	75 percent
Furniture and equipment, including stacks	15 to 16 percent
Architects' fees (for a 2- to 4-million-dollar building)	6 to 7½ percent
Administrative costs (legal, surveying, consultants, supervision, etc.)	3 to 4 percent

The building costs can be broken down as follows:

Structural (not including walls, unless load bearing)	18 to 25 percent
Mechanical (total)	33 percent
Electrical	8 to 10 percent
Air conditioning	20 percent
Plumbing	3 percent
Other (outer walls, interiors, finishes)	17 to 25 percent

These estimates are for high-quality construction and equipment, good lighting, and a well-designed interior.

Library costs in 1968 tended to run about $35 per square foot for the building, without furniture and equipment. These costs are larger than for other buildings because if the library is to be flexible and convertible to library uses not predictable at the time it is built, all floors must be able to withstand 150 pounds per square foot live load to hold the weight of books.

It is possible to cut costs by using central, tier-built, self-supporting stack cores, but a library of this nature is forbidding in feeling and adds considerably to staff costs because it is difficult to use. It is possible to hold materials costs down by using simple materials and inexpensive finishes. Usually, the lighting is skimped in an attempt to reduce the costs of libraries, cheap furniture is bought, and the interior design of the building is dispensed with. These sacrifices in the feeling of the building's interior inhibit use of the library and its collections by the students and faculty, and this is a staggering waste of the potential of a very large investment as well as contrary to the central intention of a learning institution.

The largest factors in variations of a building's costs are likely to be the bidding competition among contractors, which can send prices up or down unpredictably, and the costs of labor delays during construction. Especially if it is necessary to have a building finished by a specified date, it can cost as much as 10 percent more than contracted costs, if the client has to pay premium wages for overtime, standby labor, etc., to finish the building on time. Penalty clauses in contracts are nearly impossible to invoke successfully, and in the case of a time bind, it often pays to contract with a company other than the low bidder if its performance record indicates that it will deliver the building on time.

REVIEWING FIRMS

In recent years, the practice of using reviewing architects and engineers during the entire planning and construction process has developed as a way of insuring the lowest possible costs for the building's requirements. Such a firm, if good, can save far more than its costs in the price of the building. However, it is necessary to recognize that many of the changes they may recommend may have to be rejected if the architectural excellence of the building and the feeling of its interior are to be achieved at a high level. It is recommended that they should be used with discretion.

Chapter **5**

The Future Library

ELLSWORTH MASON

Director of Library Services, Hofstra University, Hempstead, New York

At a meeting of a select group of technicians, architects, and librarians held in June, 1967,[1] the participants agreed that it seemed impossible to look further ahead than ten years and that, within that period, no radical changes from what we now know would be likely to occur. Within the life of this edition of this handbook, the following developments, or substantial movements in their direction, can be expected.

INTERCONNECTIONS BETWEEN LIBRARIES

The greatest change will be organizational, reshaping relations between libraries and changing their nature somewhat. Interconnections between libraries on various bases—similarities, geographical proximity, etc.—have begun with the increasing exchange of materials on a permanent or a loan basis. This process ultimately will turn libraries into more central pumping stations for materials, able to soar above the physical limitations of their buildings and their geographical isolation to serve a far wider range of patrons and to be served by a far wider range of libraries than at present. Ultimately, the nation should be served by three equivalents of the Library of Congress (a new one to be developed in the South and one on the West Coast), each with massive holdings. Their contents would be distributed to substations, such as the New York Public Library, as screening and distributing points. The New York

[1] Summarized in *The Impact of Technology on the Library Building*, Educational Facilities Laboratories, New York, 1967.

Public Library would in turn be connected to smaller stations with more local responsibilities. The interconnections will make it easier to define the collection which should develop at any given library for its level of responsibility and the services which should be expanded to facilitate the interlibrary process. The end result will be a decrease in the rate of growth of collections, except for the larger, more important levels of the system which will grow faster, and an increase in growth of staff.

NONBOOK MEDIA

Much of this process will be facilitated by facsimile reproduction and, indeed, the impact of the photocopying machine on library use has been greater than that of any other mechanical development in recent times. The future should bring even greater reductions in costs, with machines coined for 2½-cent tokens and actual machine and material costs (excluding the labor of copying) as low as 1 cent or 1½ cents per sheet. The production of small, portable, electrostatic facsimile machines should make them standard equipment for any research scholar.

The increase in the use of nonbook media in the library building will be greatly accelerated by small, transistorized units for playing cartridge tapes, which ultimately will replace larger tapes and discs as the common listening material. Students will own their machines or obtain at charging desks in libraries machines to use anywhere and to take home. Smaller colleges will issue these machines to their students as standard equipment at the beginning of the year. Nonbook materials will be cataloged and shelved beside books in open-shelf libraries, and they will be specially packaged, when necessary, to stand on the shelves.

The release in the near future of a great range of important documentary material in tape cassettes, coupled with a coin-operated machine that will generate additional copies of the tape cassette will accelerate the growth of this medium. Filmstrip viewers, slide projectors, and 8-mm film projectors are already small enough to serve in the same way. Television-tape players are small enough to be located conveniently around a library building in multiples. The use of scientific slides and samples with small microscopes will be common in libraries.

While the miniaturization of the machines has made unnecessary the use of dial access, many libraries will prefer, for local reasons, the use of electronic carrels. If they are used at all, a minimum requirement should be their use in dormitory areas—lounges or rooms—as well as in library areas. They will be located in classroom buildings, especially on larger campuses, for specialized uses, although small portable equipment will undoubtedly carry the day. The use of compressed-time tape players to reproduce daily lectures of outstanding professors will be common.

The computer is now capable of performing wild and wonderful tasks at incredible expense, and the expense is not decreasing with new generations of computers, but increasing. In the library, nearly every process done by hand can be done by computer, but in no operation are economies clearly assured. There have been in recent years a series of retreats in prominent libraries from computerized projects launched with great publicity, and the field will be mixed until it becomes clear that the economics of computerization in libraries is not marginal but clearly advantageous. Occasionally, as in the need for multiple-center charging systems with central charge records, only the computer can do the job, and the premium must be paid.

The future should see, economics aside, more use of the computer in circulation, bookkeeping, ordering, and serials procedures. The generation of catalogs for complex materials—such as maps—by computer will be more common; however, conversion of large card catalogs to computerized form still faces very long-range problems of programming and machine capacity. The very near future should see a large increase in the retrieval of small-unit highly used specialized data in the physical and life sciences, brief references such as law citations, and bibliographical information from subject-specialized areas of limited size.

The use in libraries of computer cards and tapes to manipulate statistical data of great importance, such as census data, will increase. Information retrieval, which is now possible to some degree for specialized materials such as NASA reports, will develop slowly and not make an impact until real-time access to a massive range of material is possible for a large number of consoles simultaneously. Sometime in the undefined future, full texts of highly used materials will be published and available only in the computer.

Microforms will have a larger impact on the nature of the library than will the computer, but lack of coordination and lack of a focal point in the microform industry seem to prevent it from responding to the real need for standardization and easy convertibility from one form to another. The acquisition of larger quantities of microforms will change the nature of the stack arrangements in libraries (to accommodate the smaller sizes) and bring about a need for new forms of packaging and a great increase in the number of seating spaces required for microform readers. As rear-projection readers come into use in large numbers, the illumination intensity in those areas of the library where they are located must be lowered to keep from bleaching out the images on them. Great advances in miniaturization will not greatly change the use of the library.

While it is not necessary to use teaching machines for programmed instruction in the library building, the tendency to locate them there is increasing. As they become increasingly tied into the computer, the noise factor will make their location in the library a greater problem.

The use of nonbook media, machines, and teaching devices has been overemphasized in recent years to cover up inadequate support of the library budget, especially in newly developed institutions which never have attempted to absorb from the beginning the very large expenditures required by library staffs and book acquisitions needed to give even token support to a basic curriculum. This widespread weakness is compounded when a scattering of machines is used to cover up extreme poverty in books and staff at the very time when ever-larger book collections, increased purchases from expanding publications, and more and better services are demanded by any college or university that aspires to at least the intellectual challenge of our best high schools and prep schools. It is clear that the use of nonbook media and machines cannot be a substitute for building library book collections. Staff and services lag even behind the building of collections in the face of rapidly increasing expectations by students, spurred on by more demanding curricula. There is no easy choice between books or machines; the brute fact for administrators is that both books and machines will be necessary on a much greater scale in the future. Libraries are expensive, and they will grow continually more expensive unless the entire academic enterprise cools down, which is inconceivable.

Chapter 6

Instructional Services

JAMES E. GILBERT

Associate Dean of University Administration, Northeastern University, Boston, Massachusetts

THOMAS E. HULBERT

Associate Professor and Associate Director, Office of Educational Resources, Northeastern University, Boston, Massachusetts

INTRODUCTION

Objectives of This Chapter This chapter will attempt to meet five objectives. Each of these objectives sets the stage for material to follow both in this chapter and in other chapters concerned with the administration of instructional resources. The first objective specifies the challenge—a definition of the problem and a description of the setting in which the instructional resources and services can be profitably discussed. The second objective deals with meeting this challenge by providing an administrative rationale or "set of glasses" for looking at and implementing instructional services in a college or university. Objective three presents a model for the solution of instructional problems, that is, a model providing data which more nearly optimize the decision processes concerning the administration of instructional services.

Objective four discusses questions of organization to implement the model in a practical, realistic, and meaningful manner. Personnel, administrative hierarchies, and lines of authority and responsibility will be discussed in relation to the perceptual orientation defined by objectives one and two. This objective is concerned with making the system work in the real world of academe. The final objective of this chapter functions as a transactional agent in bridging the gap between the model given in this chapter and each of the instructional services discussed in the following chapters. This chapter will integrate those chapters comprising the isolated areas of instructional services which tend to speak to specific administrative considerations peculiar to their own area of specialization. The basic conceptual orientation of the authors is an involvement with a dynamic process rather than a static content. It is hoped that the reader will be mindful that the process is undergoing both acute and chronic changes which demand a flexible and energetic application of the ideas expressed in these chapters.

The Challenge—Defining the Problem The role of the university has been undergoing a revolutionary change, and it is in the midst of making adjustments to accommodate that change. The rapid explosion of knowledge not only has contributed to that change but has also become a real parameter of the problem itself. It is difficult for the teacher now, and will be even more so in the future, to disseminate information as a primary function of the instructional process. Since more knowledge is available and easier to obtain, the university student of this era is undergoing a change.

The post-1960 university student is more informed, more highly skilled, and more demanding in his educational expectations. Couple this changing student with an ever-increasing number of students of diverse and unique backgrounds to whom higher education is now available, and yet another constraint upon higher education has been established.

This increase in the number of students who can overcome fiscal, academic, and environmental barriers to higher education (some at the expense of the university itself) tends to multiply the already difficult problem of shrinking faculty and staff and inadequate facilities on many college and university campuses. A typical solution to this problem of course is financial, but this too is a parameter. If one increases the student population in order to increase income, this overtaxes the facilities and the academic program to an even greater extent. Seeking federal or foundation research monies presents the danger of disrupting the delicate balance between instruction and research. Soliciting dedicated gifts hamstrings the administration to the development of facilities for which individuals wish to donate funds rather than the priority items required by the university. Wooing legislatures is fraught with the difficulties of whim, fad, and influence. The interactive effects of each of these variables then define some of the areas of higher education that demand attention and require solution.

Although the above problems are merely a sample of those besetting higher education, they are dynamic enough to necessitate instructional services. From the point of view of instructional technology, all the capabilities of an institution as well as all of the forces acting upon it focus in one area—the learning of the student.

It is not inappropriate nor is it a nonsequitur to restate that individual students learn. No one learns for them. Further, students are quite capable of learning by themselves—they participate every day in the process. Given the learning or instructional objective, motivation, materials, and time, students are quite capable of changing their own behavior to attain specified goals. The role of the educational institution may be viewed as providing a mechanism to make certain that such learning experiences are efficient and meaningful. The institution must do for the student what the student is unable to do for himself—that is, specify those learning activities that are the most profitable in terms of time and effort. Each program of the university or college can be tested against this basic criterion. This does not imply the exclusion of other objectives of the institution, but it certainly is a primary objective and, from observation, very rarely utilized by students, faculty, or administration.

Present-day instructional systems are inadequate to meet the institutional, student, and faculty demands placed upon them. Recent research, however, has made possible the development of newer, more adequate components of instructional systems that hold great promise for education. These developments are presently sophisticated enough to contribute materially to the solution of many instructional problems. Such solutions are especially effective when faculty is intimately involved in the development of such systems and ultimately is the implementer of the resulting instructional innovations.

The application of instructional technology and innovation incorporated into the instructional services concept will result in major changes in the administration, organization, and physical facilities of educational institutions and will effect major modifications in instructional methods as well as instructor and student roles. Such modifications and changes must not only be planned but must also be within the scope and objectives of the institution itself. If the latter is not accomplished, such developments merely become part of the problem. Socrates once wrote: "Give us the tools to learn, and we will give you progress." We now have some tools.

Meeting the Challenge—An Attempt at Solution The administrative imperative is change. Things must be done differently. Traditional solutions are not adequate to meet the problems of this day or the constraints within which these problems occur. Unfortunately, there is no other alternative—change must take place. Such a demand may be made on the administration in any field of endeavor—industry, business, government, religion, and education. When the system changes, the establishment must change; the rules are different, the game is not the same. Administration must not only be flexible to change, but the change must be timely. The majority of change on the part of the educational establishment is post hoc. Education tends to "react to" rather than cause change. It is interesting that an institution which represents the greatest potential for change seems itself to be one of those most resistant to change. This must be altered.

Change and the influence of change in an educational institution create problems. Any time the status quo is threatened, myriads of problems (administrative, logistical, fiscal, psychological, etc.) arise. Some of these problems will be instructional in nature and will come within the framework of the instructional systems concept.

One way to react to such change and to the problems it creates is to adopt a problem-solution approach. The process then becomes one of analysis and synthesis—analysis of the problem and synthesis of the solution. Here, one is concerned with identifying the instructional problems, defining the problems, and designing alternative solutions to solve the problems. In the area of instructional services, it is very easy to fall into the trap of having an arsenal of solutions which force one to search frantically for instructional problems to solve. In order to accomplish the former task, administrators must become more analytical and systematic than they have been in the past.

Certainly, there are advantages and disadvantages to any system purporting to accomplish what a systematic approach professes to do. Some of the many will be enumerated here. The reader should realize that these advantages and disadvantages could be expanded into longer lists. Some of them will be treated briefly in this chapter.

A well-defined goal or objective is crucial for the utilization of instructional services to produce ultimately solutions to instructional problems. One needs not only to know in what direction he is headed but also how he is to get there. Another necessary task is to define when and under what circumstances one will be able to ascertain when the objective has been reached. Any mystery as to the objective or its accomplishment will disappear and both faculty and students will know what is to be learned and when such learning has taken place. Any instructional system designed will provide information that will define the "real world" way in which the system will operate. Because of this, administrative and management considerations are to be taken into account prior to implementation. Detailed planning of the solution to the instructional problem is guaranteed and includes all relevant variables and parameters. Because of the closed-loop feedback features of the design procedure, the system may be continuously monitored and modified. Such data also permit evaluation of the efficiency and effectiveness of the solution in terms of cost, performance, and time criteria. All developed instructional systems are tested before use and permit easy integration of other similarly designed systems with little if any disruption of organizing activity.

Unfortunately, disadvantages do exist. There is a general reluctance on the part of individuals to change their perception. Changing a perception is a difficult task even when one is conscious of the problem, but it is even more difficult when such a mechanism operates on an unconscious basis. Resistance to change will always be a problem. Another problem, perhaps unique to education, concerns the resistance to a rigid and systematic formal structure as applied to analysis of the instruction/learning process. Such resistance does exist and severely limits the effectiveness of any instructional systems developed. Time as a factor represents another disadvantage of significance. Instructional systems development time limits the kinds of instructional problems that are soluble utilizing these techniques. Hastily implemented instructional services usually fail to produce desired results. Fiscal considerations in terms of personnel, facilities, and equipment are also relevant and must be listed in the disadvantage column. Even though such costs amortize over a period of time, they can still be hazardous. Quite often, these techniques, although superior to traditional ones, cannot be used because they are incompatible with ongoing methodologies. In an isolated situation they are the methods of choice, but when integration is desired, difficulties arise. The implementation of designed systems often creates bothersome administrative problems in the areas of media, copyrights, tuition, accreditation, registration, storage, and teaching load. The last disadvantage is perhaps the simplest but most significant—hard work. The dictum "if the student fails, the teacher fails" is a hard taskmaster. The expenditure of time, effort, and creativity required to do the job at times becomes almost intolerable.

Creative teaching involves a number of simply stated elements. The teaching goal is to facilitate the learning of the student, to make a change in specific learning behavior more efficient and economical. The creative aspect enters into the picture by determining ways in which the instructor can achieve the teaching objective in spite of the constraints placed upon him by the existing educational system. It is the responsibility of the administrator to do all he can to provide the required tools, techniques, and methods to assist the instructor. The instructional systems model set forth in this chapter and the instructional services outlined in succeeding chapters will help him attain this goal.

INSTRUCTIONAL PROBLEMS, SYSTEMS ANALYSIS, AND DECISION MAKING

The framework for the construction of a decision model, definitions of instructional problems, systems analysis as applied to instruction, and the decision-making process will be the subjects of this section. Instructional problems can be defined as those situations where a student is not achieving the objectives of a learning unit at a satisfactory level. This definition presumes that the unit or course has defined objectives for which performance criteria can be developed. The definition is student-centered since the ultimate criterion for achievement of the objective is a demonstrable change in student behavior. Instructional problems can be conceived and developed in a systematic manner by cooperatively working with faculties or by allowing the instructional services organization to provide an independent solution. Practical experience indicates a combination of both methods to be the most productive approach. The sensitivity of instructional resources personnel and faculty to potential problems and their knowledge of the emerging instructional technologies provides the groundwork for the approach.

Turning to systems analysis, one is faced with a complex term—one which is defined differently by almost every author writing on the subject. Further, the term is found in the vocabularies of most professors in fields ranging from engineering to medicine to computers and more recently to the area of education and, even more specifically, instruction.

In order to evolve the concept of systems analysis for incorporation into the instructional systems model, let us first define the elements of a system. Nadler[1] defines the term relative to the design of work systems as follows: "work systems . . . involve any level of the whole complex of physical (mechanical, electrical, chemical) and human activities required to process material or information to the desired state of product or service." By changing the emphasis of the physical to equipment or material such as teaching machines, projectors, films, slides, and models and the human activities to the processing of information, a definition for systems as applied to instruction can be established.

Analysis needs little explanation except to again emphasize the quantification of parameters and variables that are required to reach near-optimum solutions. The analysis assigns values and ranges of values to all parts of the model before a decision is reached.

Combining the above into a definition of instructional-systems analysis, one would derive the following:

Instructional systems analysis is the involvement and interaction of any level of the complex of media and equipment (physical) and instructor and learner (human) activities required to process information to the desired state of performance as determined by the objectives to be attained.

Turning to the above definition (or conceptualization), one can readily see the requirement for a decision-making process to be employed when analyzing instructional systems. Decision making has been portrayed by a number of persons in various disciplines as a step-by-step process. Examples of the steps in this process are summarized in Table 1.

Similarities are apparent in all cases and the "model" adopted by any administrator is dependent on style of leadership and administration. The important point to be recognized is that the process can be modeled and that the output of the process is a decision selected from among a number of alternatives.

Thus far, three concepts have been established relative to the instructional process,

[1] Nadler, G., *Work Design*, Richard D. Irwin, Inc., Homewood, Ill., 1963.

TABLE 1 Comparison of Decision-making Process

Griffith's study	Litchfield's minor proposition	Drucker's model
Recognizing a problem and the need to prepare to make a decision	Definition of the issue	Defining the problem
Preparing for clarification of the problem	Analysis of the existing situation	Analyzing the problem
Initiating work in preparation	Calculation and delineation of alternatives	Developing alternatives and solution
Organizing and judging facts, opinions, and situations	Deliberation	Finding the best solution
Selecting alternatives	Choice	Making the decision effective
Deciding and acting		

namely the identification of an instructional problem, the definition of instructional systems analysis, and an outline of the decision-making process. Prior to construction of the model, a review of the development of a systematic approach to problem solving is appropriate in order to place the process in proper perspective.

The roots of decision making can be traced to F. W. Taylor (circa 1880), who is the father of scientific management. Taylor organizes the approach to management in a series of steps culminating in a decision or an answer to a problem, but always with the qualification that there is no one best way. Constraints, parameters, and variables are dynamic, not static; and as these change, so do the feasible solutions or decisions.

As the industrial development matured, attention was focused on the evolution of a product or process design. Theoreticians organized their thinking around the development of a process similar to that of general decision making originated by Taylor. Let us examine the steps to successful product design as hypothesized by experts in the field. Table 2 summarizes these steps. Again, striking similarities are noted among these techniques as well as a close resemblance to the steps of the decision-making process in Table 1. If one were to identify the two most important steps of the product-design process, the steps relative to problem identification and the generation of alternative solutions would be foremost. The problem formulation step identifies the real problem to be solved and brings it down to the hard core of practical reality.

The generation of alternatives is the creative phase of the process, and recent think-

TABLE 2 Comparison of the Design Processes

Scientific method	Krick design process	Dewey think process	Decision theory
State problem	Problem formulation	Perplexity	States of nature
Form hypothesis	Problem analysis	Analysis and clarification by observation and reflection	
Observe and experiment	Search for alternative decisions	Consideration of different solutions	
Interpret data		Verification of solution	
Draw conclusions	Decision phase		Prediction of state
	Specification of a solution		Outcomes

ing has shed significant but controversial light on the subject. Experts are divided on the question of whether creativity can be taught or is an innate quality. Regardless of the position, this phase certainly is the key to effective problem solution. With this brief background on decision making and product design, let us evolve a rationale for instructional systems design and instructional problem solution.

If the learner is substituted for the product, then instructional systems design is learner centered and directed (as opposed to product centered and directed) and is process rather than content oriented. The dynamics of the situation do not mitigate the necessity for establishing limits on all parameters, variables, and constraints of the system under development. In following this format, one is able to evaluate the changes in the technology and/or the objectives of the problem under study.

Problem definition must be precise and all limitations must be specified. This enables the creative phase of alternative solution generation to be productive and unobstructed. The way in which this step is approached is dependent on the organizational structure existing in the university. (This will be discussed in a later section of this chapter.)

The output of the design then becomes a solution or a decision and can be implemented into the total university or academic system. It is important to note that the components or modifications of the solution can be fed back into the system at any point for reevaluation and redesign.

The product or solution then is specified by the instructional process, and through the integration of the learner with the system, a resulting change in behavior is evaluated against the criteria established in the model.

The last step before the development of the instructional resources system model itself is a brief review of curriculum development, the apparent forerunner to instructional systems analysis. The beginning of modern curriculum development can be traced back to the roots of our modern system of education. One might say that the major emphasis of curricular development techniques and philosophies through World War II was on content. Emphasis was placed on a course outline, lesson plan, and syllabus and not the learner or the learning process.

The launching of the Sputnik rocket caused a decisive change in educational philosophy and attitudes in the United States. This revolution, coupled with rapid advances in technology, the sciences, and in the understanding of human behavior, marked the beginning of the instructional systems approach to the total educational process.

This total impact has been recognized at all levels of education with substantial increase in federal and private foundation support for the development of analytical solutions to the instructional problems faced by institutions of learning. Monies have been allocated and granted for the study of systems from complex to basic, and from practical to theoretical.

The examples analyzed by the model developed in the next section of the chapter are geared toward the solution of specific instructional problems, not toward the total spectrum of education and all its ills. With few modifications, this model will deal with the more broadly based problems and their solutions.

DEVELOPMENT OF INSTRUCTIONAL SYSTEMS MODEL

Steps in the Model Development A number of instructional systems models, quite similar to decision-making and product-design processes, have been developed. For the purpose of this chapter, however, the systems cycle developed by a task force concerned with the systems approach to education and training (a task group under the aegis of Project ARISTOTLE[2]) surveyed the field and evolved the following

[2] *Eight Steps in the Design of an Education and Training System,* Task Group on Systems Approach to Educational and Training, Project ARISTOTLE, Washington, D.C., 1967.

approach to the solution of instructional problems. The steps of this approach follow. Modifications and comments have been added.

1. Determination of instructional requirement or need
2. Definition of instructional objectives (in behavioral terms)
3. Identification of constraints
4. Generation of alternative solutions
5. Selection of solution
6. Implementation of solution
7. Evaluation of solution
8. Evaluation of feedback from solution and selection of appropriate modifications

The first step in determining the need is the identification of the instructional problem. It includes the statement of the problem which initiates the consideration of educational technology as a potential solution. One must be cautious that the actual need is not identified as a subproblem of the system. The latter relates to the "brush-fire fighting" concept where the major issue is never identified and faced realistically. Secondly, one must analyze the need with a critical eye to ascertain whether too much has been assumed on too few verified facts. At this step, it is important to place the need at the proper stratum within the total system. Care should be exercised in targeting the statement of the need before embarking on the next phase of the cycle.

The second step converts the need to a set of terminal objectives. In this statement of objectives, one determines and specifies the terminal capacity of students (learners) after the successful completion of the learning experience(s), subterminal objectives. The terminal objectives, in measurable terms, are the observable acts which guide the instructor in assuming the achievement of the objectives and specifying the environmental conditions in which the behavior must be demonstrated. Obviously, the problems of this step are twofold—one must first test the conditions in the light of the stated need, and, second, state the objective in behavioral terms.

The third step of the cycle is the identification of constraints. This entails specifying the limiting conditions which must be observed in order to satisfy the attainment of the instructional objective. Here, one is faced with the parameter imposed by the establishment in terms of manpower, facilities, equipment, money, media, etc. Caution must be exercised in separating facts from assumptions, constraints from variables, intuition from bias, and need from pressures. Provision for constraints must be included within the framework of the instructional system, and the analyst should work around these constraints.

Next, realistic alternatives are generated that have potential to meet the instructional need. Here, the creative ability of the faculty member, the instructional systems analyst, and the instructional media specialist is tested by the evolution of candidate systems which could possibly achieve the objectives. The goal is to generate a number of qualified solutions meeting the stated objectives and constraints. Such alternative solutions are the best possible alternatives and are listed in priority order.

Quantitative evaluation is then the next step of the process of selecting a feasible solution. Evaluation, where possible, in terms of objectives and constraints, is carried out to select the "most desirable" alternative. Quotation marks are used to emphasize the dynamics of this cycle since the solution is valid only under the defined objectives and constraints. It must be admitted that the optimum solution very rarely, if ever, can be identified. Changes in either the objectives or constraints require reassessment of the system. The analyst must assume the consideration of all vital selection criteria with an objective scoring system which is not biased to effect the answer. Since all variables, parameters, and constraints are not quantifiable in precise terms, the employment of a balance between analysis and judgment is required. Since the constraints have been defined, care must be exercised not to penalize solutions because of their potential problems.

Implementation is the adoption of the "most desirable" alternative to meet the specified objective(s). Administrators are fully aware of the pitfalls and problems encountered when making the transition from an idea to an ongoing system. Care should be taken during this phase of the cycle in order to assure that the implemented alternative is not penalized by the implementation process itself. The way the proposed solution is actually "tested" should not bias the test itself either positively or negatively.

Evaluation of the trial system is the next step of the cycle. This phase determines the conformance or discrepancy between or among all of the objectives initially specified and the performance actually attained. Conventional and innovative methods of testing and evaluation are employed at this time. The depth of analysis is highly dependent on the impact of the changed system. If the "most desirable" alternative does not meet the stated objectives within the specified constraints or cannot be modified to do so, the "next most desirable alternative" is subjected to examination.

Finally, feedback for purposes of reevaluation of an adopted system is needed. This step involves the process of modifying the learning system to correct the deficiencies in meeting the objectives.

These eight steps can be depicted and summarized in the schematic diagram below (Figure 1).

To illustrate the first three steps of the systems cycle, let us examine an instructional problem from an area familiar to most administrators. It is from the field of physical education or recreation and is only illustrative and not designed to demonstrate a "typical instructional problem" nor to provide a prototype model of the process for general application.

An Illustration for an Instructional Problem

You have just reported to work in a new middle-class suburban community college and have been asked to accomplish the following task: students will play one set of tennis with minimum competency observing the proper and appropriate strategies, rules, and customs of the game, given the proper space and equipment.

You will have thirty-five (35) freshmen students (15 men and 20 women) with no previous instruction in tennis, and no instructional assistance. You will meet the students one hour a day, three days a week for four weeks (12 instructional periods). You will have any equipment and media you require but only enough money for *testing* the objective (tennis court fees).

Essentially, you must provide instruction in tennis without a tennis court or other outdoor facility. The *only* other space you have available is a standard gymnasium with one windowless wall and a classroom (capacity 15 students, one instructor).

Following are the first three steps of the systems cycle stated in terms of the above problem:

Need. To provide instruction in tennis without a tennis court or any other outdoor facility.

Objective. Students will play one set of tennis with minimum competency observing the proper and appropriate strategies, rules, and customs of the game, given the proper space and equipment.

Constraints.	LOCATION	Middle-class suburban community.
	STUDENTS	35 college freshmen (15 men and 20 women).
	TIME	One hour per day, three days per week for four weeks.
	STAFF	One instructor.
	SPACE	Standard gymnasium with one windowless wall plus one classroom.

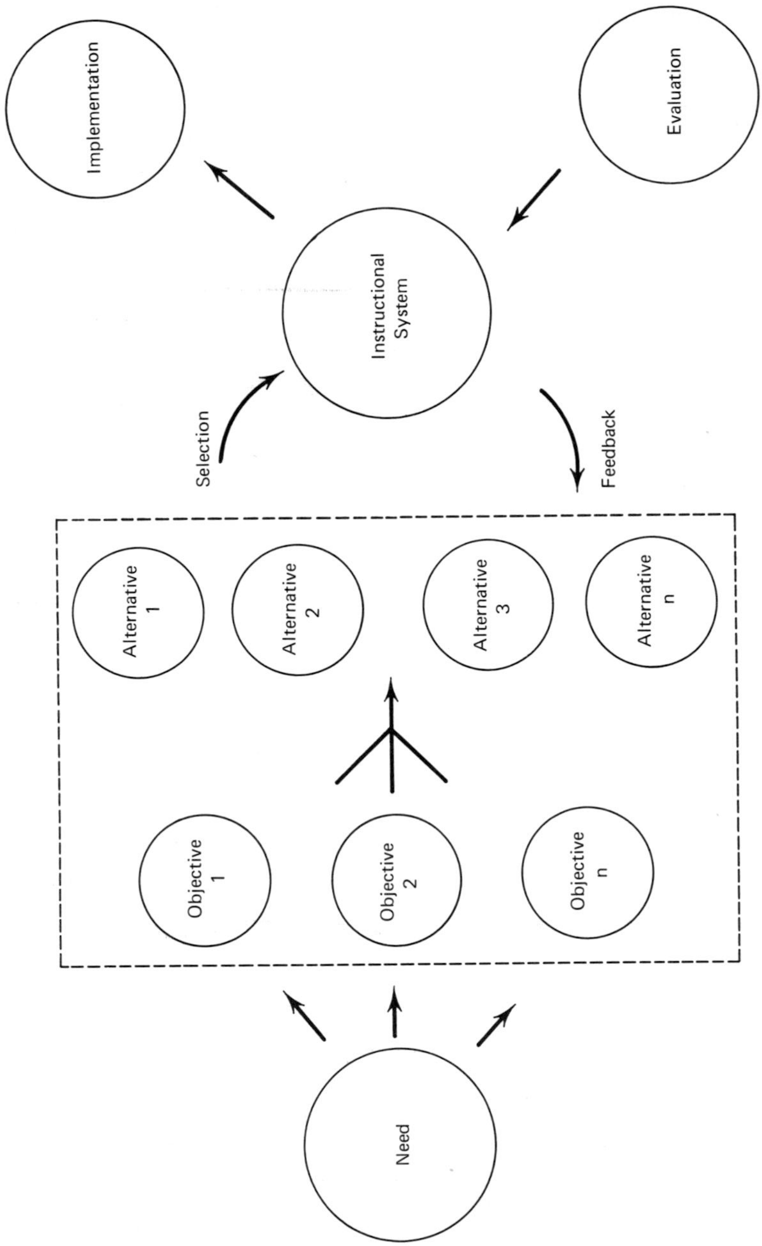

Fig. 1 *The systems cycle*

EQUIPMENT There will be no constraints.
MONEY Fees for testing the objectives.

Alternatives. These can be generated from the viewpoints presented in the succeeding chapters of the instructional services section; however, examples might include:

1. Videotaping of performance for student assessment.
2. Programmed learning material for learning rules, strategies, and customs.
3. Films, filmstrips, and slides showing professional tennis players and their style.
4. Utilization of printed media in an independent study setting combined with audiotape.

These examples are not intended to meet the total objective but represent examples of some of the learning experiences that could be transformed into an instructional module to help achieve the specified behavioral objective.

Selection, Implementation, Evaluation, and Feedback. These steps would be based on the alternative selected and will not be illustrated since the specification of alternatives is not inclusive enough to develop these steps.

Another Systems Model For comparison purposes, the following model (Figure 2) is presented to illustrate procedures for the analysis of instruction and implementation of new media in college learning developed at Michigan State University.[3] This model was demonstrated and evaluated in a project completed in 1967.[4]

Figure 2 defines the problem specifically in instructional and curriculum terminology and is more detailed than the eight steps of ARISTOTLE. A summary table (Table 3) compares the two models step by step.

TABLE 3 Comparison of ARISTOTLE Systems Cycle and MSU Instructional Systems Development Flowchart

ARISTOTLE systems cycle	*MSU procedures for instructional systems development*
1. Need	1*
2. Objectives	2, 3, 4
3. Constraints	5, 6
4. Alternatives	7
5. Selection	8, 9
6. Implementation	10, 11
7. Evaluation	12, 13, 14, 15
8. Feedback	16

* Refers to numbered steps in Figure 2.

One can readily see the close similarity between the two cycles. It is apparent that the cycle is a closed-loop system with feedback at several stages, thus allowing for developmental or administrative changes to occur to keep the subsystem in harmony with the total system.

The latter model defines the roles and the responsibilities of the various specialists in the system. This concept can be referred to in a later portion of this chapter when the alternate organizational structures to implement the model are discussed. The choice of model to adopt is dependent on two dominant factors—the total system or

[3] Paul L. Dressel, et al., *A Procedural and Cost Analysis Study of Media in Instructional Systems Development,* Michigan State University, 1965, ERIC document number ED 011 050.

[4] John Barson, *Final Report: Instructional Systems Development: A Demonstration and Evaluation Project,* Michigan State University, 1967, Contract no. OE-5-16-025.

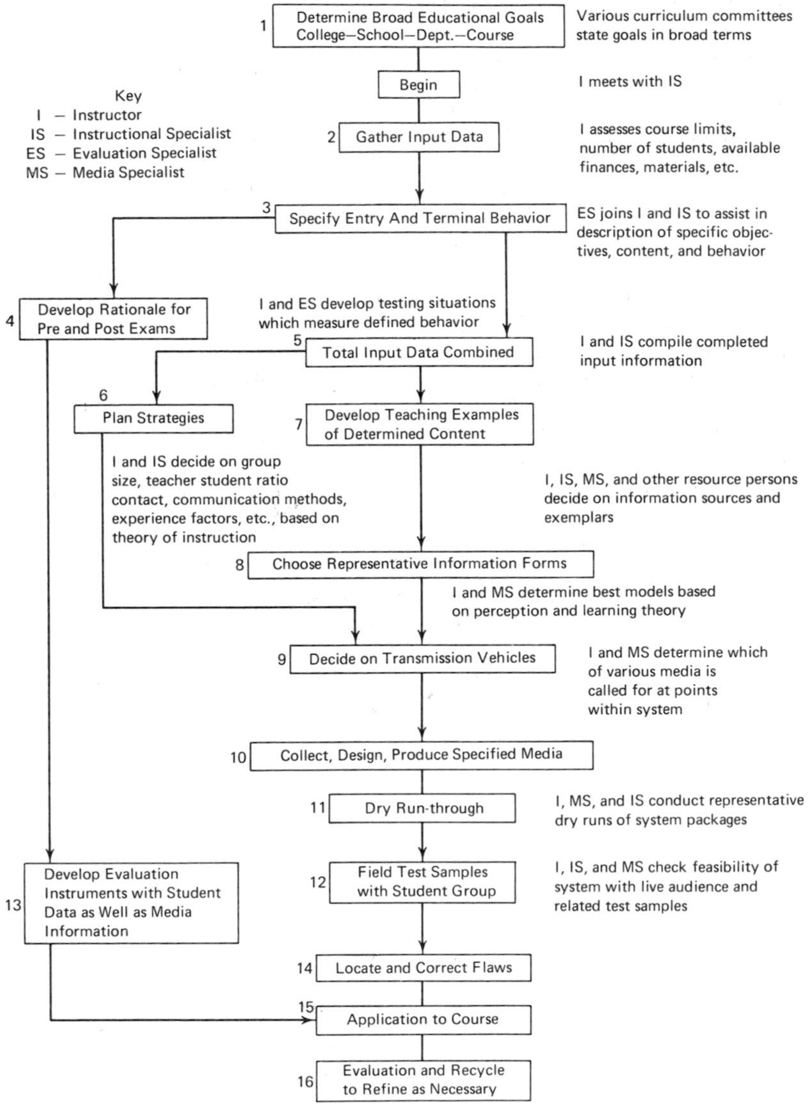

Fig. 2 *A flowchart of procedures for analysis of instruction and implementation of new media of communications. (Note: Information feedback loops have been deleted from this illustration.)*

concept into which this subsystem is to be implemented and the organizational concept adopted. The administration determines the environment or system for the concept, and the organizational alternatives will be discussed in the following paragraphs.

ORGANIZING TO IMPLEMENT THE MODEL

At this point, we have a rationale for the necessity of instructional problem solution, a rationale for the system-analysis approach to arriving at alternative solutions to instructional problems, and an instructional systems model. A scheme for managing the implementation of the model will now be developed. Such implementation should integrate the total instructional services package into the university or college milieu.

Models and Services Up to this point, much has been said concerning an instructional systems model and very little concerning instructional services. The instructional systems model is concerned with the overall process of solving specified instructional problems—a process, a "how to," a method in which all relevant variables in the real world in which the system must exist are specified. Services, on the other hand, are concerned with the raw material that composes the alternative solutions specified by the systems model. Services may be, in one sense, likened to content (where the model is the process). Services, then, are made up of hardware and software components (equipment and media) that are manipulated by an instructor either directly (as in the classroom) or indirectly (as by a computer) to facilitate the learning of the student.

The relationship between the instructional systems model and instructional services is one of process to content; of who, what, when, where, why, to how; of prescription to medication. The model defines which of the instructional services will be used when and in what configuration.

Objectives and Functions The objectives and functions of the organizational unit developed to implement the model are perhaps more important than the actual organizational structure itself. These objectives should represent the total effort of the instructional services organization and stem directly from the problem defined earlier. The objectives listed below are independent one from another and cover the total range of services of the kind of activity germane to this chapter. Objectives, therefore, may be excluded to meet the specific requirements of a university or college.

1. To facilitate the learning of students and assist the faculty in providing efficient and effective instruction through the use of instructional innovation and technology.
2. To apply research findings from behavioral science, education, and academic subject-matter areas, and industry, to the instructional process and to conduct those basic research activities as are necessary to support this effort.
3. To maintain contact with the state of the art, relevant activities, and research concerning instructional innovation and technology.
4. To provide the setting for more adequate implementation of instructional innovation and technology by improving the interrelationship of all levels of the educational establishment, including government and industry.
5. To assist the university administration in the establishment of plans, policies, and facilities where instructional innovation and technology would be relevant.
6. To develop academic programs and courses relating to instructional innovation and technology.

The following 14 functions relate to the objectives and assist in defining the objectives in operational terms. All functions are relevant to either stated or implied instructional technology (e.g., programmed learning, computer-based learning, simulation, instructional games, films, tape/slide presentations, instructional television, etc.).

1. Determine, analyze, and evaluate instructional problems, identifying require-

ments and specifying and designing instructional systems to meet such requirements utilizing known methods and techniques.

2. Develop, produce, and evaluate instructional systems and processes.
3. Provide tested instructional facilities, services, and media.
4. Collect, process, store, and disseminate relevant media, data, information, and devices to requesting individuals or organizations.
5. Relate identified research data to ongoing or developing instructional problems or systems.
6. Adopt results of prior research or proven applications to the solution of instructional problems.
7. Identify basic research needs germane to instructional innovations and technology and carry out necessary investigation.
8. Inform the university faculty and staff of the existing and potential capabilities of instructional innovation and technology.
9. Provide courses, workshops, and seminars on instructional innovation and technology for infra- and extra-university individuals or organizations.
10. Recommend policies, plans, and facilities to the university administration concerning the utilization of instructional innovations and technology.
11. Participate in the activities of professional societies and organizations germane to instructional innovation and technology.
12. Implement, under auspices of relevant university colleges, departments, and faculty, degree-oriented undergraduate and graduate instructional systems curricula.
13. Provide consultation services to the total educational establishment concerning instructional innovation and technology.
14. Represent the university on committees, task groups, or projects directed toward the interface of education, government, and industry and relevant to instructional innovation and technology.

Components of Instructional Services Regardless of the actual objectives, functions, and structure of an instructional services organization, the following five operations must be represented in one form or another.

Instructional Systems:

ANALYSIS The identification and definition of the problem, specification of the objective, and analysis of learning tasks.

PROGRAMMING The development of instructional strategies, identification of the sequence of learning experiences, and the specification of appropriate instructional media.

PRODUCTION The production of instructional system packages in the form best suited to realize the specified objectives under given constraints.

UTILIZATION The implementation of the instructional system into the existing curriculum. Evaluation and monitoring of the system on a continuing basis.

MEDIA The acquisition, storage, and retrieval of existing instructional media (films, slides, tapes, programs, textbooks, games, simulations, models, etc.).

Most of the instructional services now available in the typical college or university may be grouped under these media (curriculum laboratories, libraries, information centers); utilization (television distribution systems, audiovisual centers, remote-access information retrieval systems); and production (audio and video production facilities, programmed-learning writing center, visual and graphic production centers) components. These components are, of course, modules and may be integrated into the instructional services organization as required.

Two Organizational Formats The interface of these components with the university or college at large can be effected through three areas of effort; academic, service, and research. The academic area can contribute by providing service courses for undergraduate teacher education, graduate programs in educational technology, and in-service training of university faculty. The service element was described previously and will be somewhat elaborated upon in the chapters following. Research, by supporting an instructional technology research and development group, meets both intra- and extra-university demands.

This type of organization would allow the instructional services component to have an academic base, for example in the college of education, and at the same time the service element could function free from any affiliation with any one college or department. It is suggested that the instructional services organization report to a dean of faculty, vice president, provost, or president directly. In this way the organization does not become "captured by" or "dedicated to" any one special interest in the college or university. In some of the larger universities such instructional services are considered a part of educational resources and are combined with the library and university reproduction services.

Considering the organization of the instructional services component, two organizational models will be presented. The first represents a specialist organizational structure where functions are assigned in terms of the type of media being utilized to solve the instructional problems. In this type of organization the analysis, programming, production, and utilization functions are bound to media and any integrated "multimedia" solution must be coordinated between organizational elements. The types of solutions that are generated by such an organization tend to be of high quality but directed toward the speciality involved. Many alternative solutions are proposed, but in a narrow area of specialization. An advantage of the system is that projects usually have the total commitment of the organizational element assigned to the development of the instructional system. This organization would appear as outlined in Figure 3.

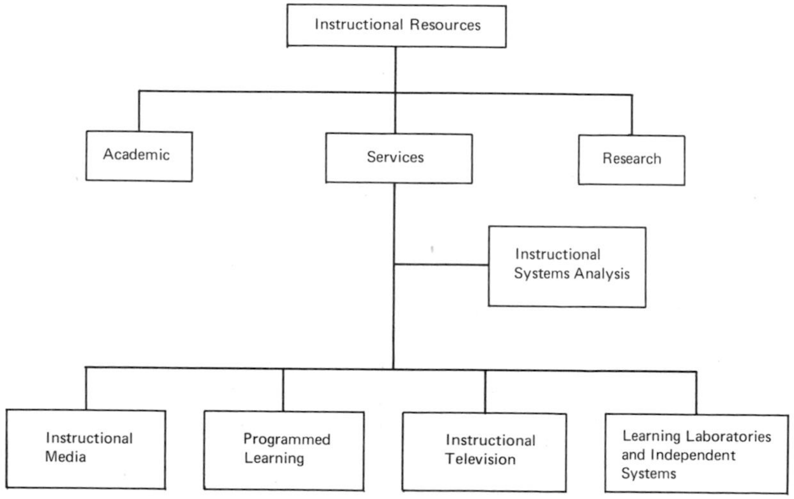

Fig. 3 *Specialist instructional resources organization.*

The instructional systems analysis group identifies specific instructional problems, determines precise requirements, and evaluates the effectiveness of the total learning experience as well as the instructional system developed and its implementation. The instructional media unit administers a resource center of instructional materials and equipment for the faculty and disseminates information on educational innovation and technology to students, faculty, and staff. Programmed learning, as an organizational element, develops and administers self-instructional materials for credit courses, noncredit courses, remedial work, and enrichment purposes. The component charged with instructional television and radio provides television and radio broadcast facilities as well as other instructional communications facilities (graphic writing systems, amplified telephone systems, etc.). This group also produces the instructional media that are broadcast on the systems. Audiovisual media production is located in this unit as is a graphic artist. Learning laboratories and independent study systems develop, implement, and test independent learning systems for learning laboratories from simple audiovisual programs to computer-based learning systems to remote-access information-retrieval systems.

The second organizational model represents one based on a functional structure where administrative personnel are generalists rather than specialists. If such personnel have a speciality, it is in the broad area of the functional organization (e.g., analysis, programming, production, utilization). The obvious advantage of this organizational format is that the emphasis is on the integration of all instructional technology independent of speciality areas. No one organizational element is responsible for an entire instructional system. Each instructional module developed has a guaranteed multispecialist series of inputs. The disadvantage of course is that unless a particular project is followed very closely it tends to get lost in passing from one element to the next. This type of organization would appear as outlined in Figure 4.

The media element is essentially a support unit for the other three units and is concerned with the administration of a resource center of instructional materials available to the faculty. It disseminates information on educational innovation and technology to students, faculty, and staff. Such a function could be provided by the university or college library, which is an educational resource itself and could be considered (and administered) as an instructional service.

The programming element carries out two primary tasks, the first being the identification and definition of a problem and the specification of the objectives of the instructional system to be developed. The second task concerns the development of strategies, sequences of learning experiences, and specification of alternative instructional media.

Production concerns the development of instructional systems packages in the most

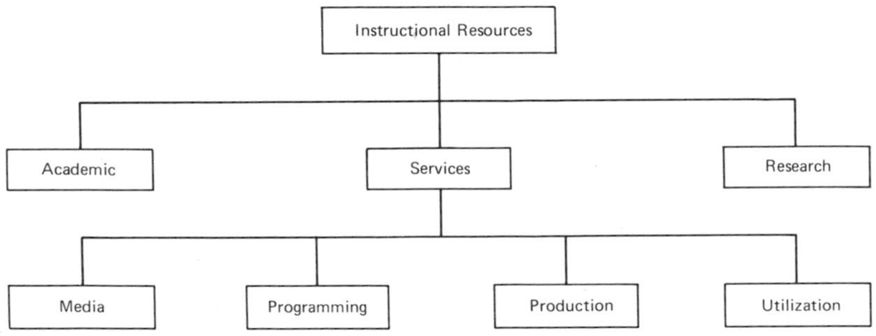

Fig. 4 *Generalist instructional resources organization.*

appropriate modules for realization of the instructional objectives. Here the actual videotapes, films, programs, and computer routines are put together to meet the prescriptions arrived at by the programming group.

Utilization must meet the requirements of implementing the instructional system developed by the production unit into the university or college curriculum. The system is monitored and evaluated and, if required, revised or redeveloped by the programming element.

Integration of the Model and the Organizational Format An instructional systems analyst in the programming group locates and identifies an instructional problem in an academic department. This may result from the perceptiveness of the analyst, or the analyst's assistance might have been requested by the instructor. After the objectives have been specified and the constraints under which the instructional system will be implemented have been listed, a behavioral analysis is completed using the talents of the programming group and the instructor. Utilizing the data generated by the behavioral analysis, instructional content is specified and conventional as well as innovative instructional strategies are identified.

Acting as a project coordinator, the analyst calls together individuals from programming, production, and implementation with the instructor to generate alternative solutions that will meet the objectives within the specified constraints, utilizing the specified instructional prescriptions. Once these alternatives have been listed and a priority order has been established, the production group initiates the development of the media required. The instructor is a crucial part of this procedure regardless of the types of media utilized.

The analyst, again acting as project coordinator, assures adequate rapport between the instructor and implementation personnel. Here plans are laid in order to make the instructional system operational. At this time training programs must be planned and developed to train the faculty, graduate assistants, and even the students themselves to use the system properly. Evaluation and feedback monitoring systems are also specified and instruments and procedures to carry out this phase are developed. Actual use of the instructional packages produced is supervised by the implementation unit, the instructional systems analyst, and the instructor.

SUMMARY

In this chapter the authors have established the setting or rationale for administering the instructional services subsystem in higher education. The scope of these functions will vary depending on the overall administrative model within the university or college structure. This chapter evaluates some of the alternative approaches one may take to organize the function or strengthen its capabilities within the structure.

We must emphasize that *learning is a process* and that the organization to implement this must be established accordingly. The basis for this chapter has been a systems model or systematic approach to instructional problem solving. Once the prescription is decided with the appropriate parameters and constraints, the system can be implemented in a number of alternative ways. Implementation is, indeed, the most difficult. If the instructional services model and concept are consistent within the total administrative framework, the implementation phase produces tangible data to mitigate operational hangups.

Succeeding chapters will discuss specific instructional techniques and services to augment student learning. From these chapters, administrators can adapt the general framework to the specific problem. Technology and its development far outstrip the ability to develop instructional modules to exploit the capability. The challenge and the dynamics of the process therefore are to create the environment and organization for efficient and effective implementation.

Chapter 7

Audiovisual Media Services

EDWARD J. DONNELLY

Director, Division of Instructional Media, Office of Educational Resources, Northeastern University, Boston, Massachusetts

The truly effective instructor is the one who possesses a variety of skills in communicating with his students. He is master of a full range of communication techniques evolving out of an up-to-date technology of teaching and learning.

HISTORY AND DEVELOPMENT

The first quarter of the twentieth century was a rather crucial period in the audiovisual movement, initially referred to as visual instruction. Prior to the turn of the century it was generally agreed that the role of the student in the learning process should be one of passive listening. John Dewey was one of the first in the United States to promulgate the notion that perhaps there were more efficient and effective ways to implement the teaching-learning process. In a sense he was only echoing the words of earlier European educators like Froebel, Herbart, Pestalozzi, and Rousseau.

Films were the first modern audiovisual medium introduced into the classroom. At first theatrical films were applied to classroom needs. Later, industrial, government, and welfare films found their way into the academic environment. Educators became aware of the outstanding success of training films developed and used during World War II. Indeed, the increasing use of instructional films gave considerable impetus to the more general use of audiovisual instruction. The development of the audiovisual movement and its ultimate acceptance is shown by the mass of data concerning the general aspects of the communications process as well as the theoretical rationale supporting the use of specific audiovisual materials. Thirty years of educational research have clearly indicated that audiovisual instruction can significantly improve the teaching-learning process—that is, if appropriate procedures govern the selection, utilization, and follow-up of materials.

WHY USE AUDIOVISUAL MEDIA?

Audiovisual media have certain characteristics which can make learning experiences more meaningful. The following six characteristics (by no means definitive) are often presented as the most significant ones:

1. *Audiovisual media focus attention on the material to be learned.* By the focusing of high-intensity lighting, by the compelling sound of the spoken word, and by the involvement of more than one sense at a time, the learner's attention is better controlled. Consider how an image on a screen, with or without sound, can automatically focus the attention of almost everybody within a large auditorium.

2. *Audiovisual media add concreteness and realism to the learning process.* Learning theorists and psychologists generally agree that we learn a great deal of what we know by performing a particular activity. Whether tying knots or learning to swim, interacting with the instructional material—responding in some mode—generally results in greater learning. When the instructional process depends, as it does in many instances, on vicarious experience, learning can become highly effective through the use of visualization and sound reproduction. For example, TV's action scenes of the war in Vietnam, a visual experience in the middle of the nation's living rooms, have had more of an impact than the thousands of stories written about the agonies of war.

3. *Audiovisual media bring remote events into the classroom.* During recent years students in many universities throughout the world have witnessed such events as the orbiting Apollo spaceship and the explorations of the undersea world of Jacques Yves Cousteau.

4. *Audiovisual media are able to show relationships among ideas, events, and things.* Consider the advantages of using time-lapse photography to illustrate the growth sequence of a plant.

5. *Audiovisual media stimulate interest by providing memorable experiences.* Recalling a sigificant or memorable event in one's life most often evokes a visual image. If most people "see a picture" when asked to recollect something from the past, the implications are obvious for didactic purposes.

6. *Audiovisual media are available for continued and repeated study.* Through the use of films and tapes, the learning experience can be repeated for different groups or can be adapted to individualized or independent study.

WHAT ARE SOME OBJECTIVES OF AN INSTRUCTIONAL MEDIA SERVICE?

The following objectives can be utilized as a set of guidelines or principles for setting up an instructional media service:

1. To maintain a constant contact with the faculty concerning instructional problems and the application of instructional media
2. To provide consultation, assistance, instruction, and services concerning the selection and application of instructional media
3. To facilitate the teaching-learning process through the competent application of instructional media
4. To contribute to the development of courses and programs in all areas of educational technology
5. To maintain an awareness of all relevant research technology and activity concerning the application of instructional media

WHAT ARE SOME OF THE MOST WIDELY USED AUDIOVISUAL MEDIA?

Audiovisual media currently being used in most institutions of higher education tend to fall into the following categories: still projection, motion-picture projection, record players, tape recorders, and sound systems.

Still Projection Still projection equipment refers to slide projectors, filmstrip projectors, overhead and opaque projectors. The oldest of the slide projectors is the lantern slide projector, sometimes called a 3¼- by 4-inch slide projector. Current models still use the basic elements of the original projector: horizontal straight-line projection, lamp, reflector, condensing lens, objective lens, and a slide carrier. The first slides used for this projector were usually etched on glass. Although glass slides are still used, along with slides made from drawings on cellophane and acetate, the most popular slide is the photographic slide. Recent innovations by Polaroid Corporation facilitate the production of 3¼- by 4-inch slides within 60 seconds. The lantern slide projector provides ease of operation and flexibility of application and techniques. Its major disadvantages are its relatively large size in comparison to other slide projectors and a limitation on the number and variety of commercially available slides.

The most popular slide projector currently being used in the classroom is the 2- by 2-inch carrousel type projector. It uses the same basic horizontal straight-line projection system as the 3½- by 4-inch slide projector. It is relatively compact and extremely easy to use. An abundance of commercially prepared slides in virtually all areas of the curriculum are available. The only equipment needed to produce the slides that are used in the 2- by 2-inch projector is a 35-mm camera. Consequently, instructor-produced or university-produced slides afford an unlimited source and variety of materials. Also, this slide projector has a remote-control feature that allows the instructor to control his presentation from the front of the classroom.

Filmstrip projectors often accommodate both filmstrips and individual 2- by 2-inch slides. The projection system is similar to the ones already noted. The filmstrip itself is a continuous strip of 35-mm film or slides arranged in a meaningful sequence. Its advantages are similar to those of the 2- by 2-inch slide projector. Research indicates that the teaching-learning process is enhanced when filmstrips are used with other media and teaching techniques.

The overhead projector is one of the newer developments in projection devices. The optical elements of this projector are similar to the ones already discussed. The only major difference is that the light rays are projected vertically before being reflected from a mirror located in the head of the projector. It can project transparent materials with dimensions up to $8\frac{1}{2}$ by 11 inches. The size of the transparent materials being used as well as the construction of the projector makes it possible to use overlay material on the original transparency. Among the advantages of the overhead projector are: (1) The projector is usually placed in front of the room, thus allowing the instructor to face the class at all times. (2) The brilliant light source, concentrated at a short distance, makes it possible to use the projector under normal lighting conditions. (3) The instructor can easily maintain complete control of the material; thus, no projectionist is needed. (4) Because the aperture or stage, as it is called, is in a horizontal position and exposed, the instructor can easily point out specific parts of the transparency.

Almost as old as the lantern slide projector is the opaque projector. The opaque projector is used to project an image of materials or object surfaces that are not transparent. It differs from most other types of projection equipment that shows only transparent materials. A reflected light system is used rather than the direct light system used in other projectors. The greatest value of the opaque projector is its ability to project a wide variety of materials prepared or collected by students or instructors, such as pictures from textbooks, written materials, postcards, flat pictures of all kinds, photographs, and small objects. The major disadvantages of this projector are its relatively large size and weight and the need to darken the room during projection.

Motion Picture Projection The popularity of motion picture projection continues to increase. Considerable research carried out since the end of World War II by the armed services and other investigators clearly identifies the advantages of motion projection: Creative responses are stimulated, factual information can be taught and retained, affective or attitudinal changes can result, and films that provide opportunities for students to respond during the presentation bring about increased learning.

Although 16-mm motion picture projection is the most popular film medium, the rise of 8-mm or super 8-mm film is steadily finding a place in the teaching-learning process. The use of short film clips in sealed cartridges for continuous-loop operation has many applications. The compactness, light weight, and ease of operation of the film loop projector allows the instructor or the student learning independently to stop the projector at strategic moments in order to practice a skill or simply interact with the subject matter.

The motion picture itself is a strip of clear, transparent cellulose-acetate. A coating of emulsion with light-sensitive chemicals on one side of the film permits the recording of pictures or frames. These pictures or frames are passed through the motion picture projector at the speed of 24 frames per second, the same speed as the film passed through the camera. Thus, it is possible to recreate action. Techniques such as slow-motion and time-lapse photography make it possible to show events otherwise not readily observed. For example, it is possible with time-lapse photography to compress the growth, flowering, and withering of a plant.

Record Players Sound also ranks as a vital component in the technology of instruction. Record players have always retained their popularity because of the variety of commercially available material as well as the variety of applicable classroom uses. Besides the many uses for background purposes, records also have brought to the classroom the contributions of countless resource persons in all areas of human endeavor. Research points out that the teaching-learning process is enhanced when records are used as part of a larger teaching strategy—that is, as a supplemental aid.

Tape Recorders The tape recorder as a complement to the record player has many applications in higher education: language laboratories, programmed instruction, counselor education, self-evaluation for students and instructors, individualized and independent study through taped lectures and exercises, and electronic learning situations. Another significant application of the tape recorder is in the area of information storage and retrieval systems.

Sound Systems Although never really fulfilling its predicted value for classroom instruction, the radio is still a worthwhile audio aid. Many institutions of higher learning maintain or are establishing their own radio stations. Not only can prerecorded material be used for instruction, but other programs planned and produced by the students may be used as well.

Tele-Lecture is a comparatively recent audio innovation. By means of voice amplification equipment connected to regular telephone wires, practically any resource throughout the world can be brought to the classroom. The only requisites are an available telephone and a willing conversationalist. The expert is able to disseminate his ideas directly with a minimum of inconvenience; he need travel no further than the nearest telephone. Communication is two-way, allowing students to discuss issues with the lecturer. By use of Tele-Lecture it is possible to arrange a panel presentation or discussion by several speakers from different parts of the country.

HOW DO YOU ORGANIZE AN AUDIOVISUAL MEDIA SERVICE?

An institution of higher learning should provide for at least one expert in audiovisual media. He can either work alone or, if the institution is large enough, function as director of a complete audiovisual media service. The director's support would consist of both professional and clerical personnel. The number of personnel would depend on faculty demand as well as the size of the student body. As an adjunct to audiovisual services, materials centers or learning resource centers are being developed in many colleges and universities throughout the country. In terms of this concept, the role of the audiovisual media specialist will continue to expand, ultimately to be integrated into a more comprehensive organizational context.

The structure of an audiovisual media service can be described in terms of four general areas: audiovisual media storage and distribution service, instructional technology information center, instructional media demonstration laboratory, and production services. The four general areas are shown in Figure 1.

The audiovisual media storage and distribution service component is responsible for (1) ordering, scheduling, delivering, and operating the various audiovisual media materials and equipment; (2) providing assistance and consultation in the evaluation of commercially available audiovisual media; (3) training groups and individuals in the technology of audiovisual media; (4) maintaining an up-to-date, comprehensive collection of source books for commercially available materials such as films, film loops, filmstrips, slides, audio tapes, and transparencies; and (5) providing audio and visual preview facilities.

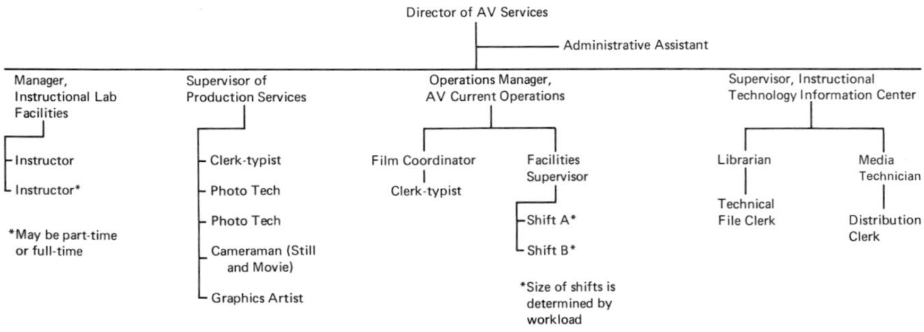

Fig. 1 *Audiovisual organization structure.*

The instructional technology information center serves as a research and demonstration center concerned with educational technology state of the art. Such a central source of information should be made available to students and faculty as well as to community groups. The types of materials would include source files on new products, shelved collections of instructional media and devices, and research reports and journals on instructional innovation and technology. The center would assume responsibility for publishing periodic information bulletins and providing a liaison service through correspondence, conventions, and exchange visits with all groups in the field of instructional technology and innovation.

The instructional media demonstration laboratory would be designed to train small groups of faculty and students in the proper methods of operating audiovisual equipment and the preparation of instructional materials. A representative collection of audiovisual equipment should be constantly housed in the facility: 16-mm and 8-mm motion picture projectors, film loop projectors, overhead and opaque projectors, slide and other transparency production equipment, 2- by 2-inch and 3½- by 4-inch slide projectors, record players, and video and audio tape recorders.

The production or media preparation service is responsible for providing the facilities as well as personnel necessary to enable instructors to prepare instructional materials. These materials should include such basic media as slides, transparencies, tapes, photographs, and film.

Although requests for audiovisual information and services will be expressed in a variety of ways, personnel within each of the four basic areas noted above must be aware that each request reflects an instructional need. By encouraging faculty members to discuss the objectives they expect to achieve through the application of audiovisual technology, the service personnel will be in a much better position to recommend equipment and media appropriate to the task.

Quantitative standards for audiovisual personnel, equipment, and materials in programs of higher education have been adopted by the Department of Audiovisual Instruction of the National Education Association.[1]

Figure 2 represents the materials guidelines for higher education.

Considerable difficulty arises when one attempts to determine quantitative guidelines for every type of audiovisual material. To be successful, an audiovisual media service should be equipped to make a wide variety of materials available to participating faculty. Selection by faculty, of course, should be based on a careful analysis of the instructional problem as well as availability of materials. The following list indicates what materials may be used to augment those included in the guidelines for higher education: 8-mm films, 2- by 2-inch slides, 3¼- by 4-inch slides, transparencies and transparency masters, study prints, maps, globes, dioramas, games, and simulations.

The National Education Association's statement on the materials budget is as follows:[2]

To provide for a well-rounded materials program, it is recommended that the basic complement of films, filmstrips, and recordings be considered capital equipment and be purchased with such funds. To provide for the ongoing materials program, including maintenance and replacement but not expansion, no less than 1 percent of the

[1] *Quantitative Standards for Audiovisual Personnel, Equipment and Materials (in Elementary, Secondary, and Higher Education)*, developed by Dr. Gene Faris and Dr. Mendel Sherman, Audiovisual Center, Indiana University, as part of a study conducted under the auspices of the United States Office of Education, National Defense Education Act, Title VII, Part B program. Adopted by the Department of Audiovisual Instruction, NEA, at the Board of Directors Meeting in Washington, D.C., on October 30, 1965, and The Association of Chief State School Audiovisual Officers at the Executive Board Meeting in Chicago on December 14, 1965. Published by Department of Audiovisual Instruction, National Education Association, 1201 Sixteenth St., N.W., Washington, D.C. 20036.

[2] *Ibid.*

Material	Basic	Advanced
16-mm films	500 college-level titles plus 2 per instructor over 500. In addition, teacher-education institutions should have the basic film collection recommended for elementary and secondary schools (1,000) or an average of 3 film rentals per instructor per course	1,000 college-level titles plus 3 per instructor over 500 plus elementary and secondary basic collection in teacher-education institutions or an average of 5 film rentals per instructor per course
Filmstrips	200 titles with duplicates as needed	3,000 titles with duplicates as needed
Recordings—tape and disc but not electronic lab materials	1,000	2,000

Fig. 2 *Materials guidelines (higher education).*

average per pupil cost in the school unit should be spent per year per student. The 1 percent amount would include film rentals if no basic film collection is started and subscription television (i.e., MPATI), but would not include salaries, building construction or remodeling, CCTV installations, or electronic learning centers.

To provide for an advanced materials program, the 1 percent should be increased to 1.5 percent.

Figure 3 represents equipment guidelines for higher education. Budget statements should be based on the existing prices of specific models preferred.

It is extremely difficult to suggest budget figures for an audiovisual media service. Initial investment costs would be determined by projected faculty requirements. Annual operational costs must be carefully controlled. However, for purposes of providing some insight and guidance, the following approximate budget figures are presented. These figures are based on a typical university of approximately 15,000 students and are based upon the staff as presented in the organization chart in Figure 1.

Audiovisual personnel.........	22–35 persons (number of part-time dispatch workers determined after review of such factors as size of campus, amount and type of equipment, and class schedules)	
	Annual salary cost (1969–1970)	$137,000
Audiovisual materials and equipment......................	Equipment and facility replacement costs	25,000
	Media rental, purchase, and media development supplies	17,000
Total audiovisual media budget..........		$179,000

HOW DO YOU SET UP A DISTRIBUTION SYSTEM?

The audiovisual media service must publicize what is available as well as guarantee convenient access to all services. The catalog is the first step in any system for publicizing materials. A comprehensive annotated catalog should be revised and distributed each year. Figure 4 illustrates the kind of brief annotated catalog that can be of considerable value to instructors. As noted from the annotations, various media (FS =

Equipment	Basic	Advanced
16-mm sound projector	1 per 12 teaching stations (multipurpose institution)	1 per 8 teaching stations
	1 per 8 teaching stations (single-purpose institution)	1 per 5 teaching stations
8-mm projector	1 to 3 sound projectors per institution	1 per 10 teaching stations
	Significant changes are occurring in the 8-mm medium which do not at present justify quantitative guidelines. Because of the important contributions of these films to individual and small group learning, however, conservative quantities have been suggested. As equipment and materials become more stabilized and as sources expand, schools should increase the quantities beyond the amounts suggested in these guidelines.	
2- by 2-inch slide projector (automatic)	1 per 10 teaching stations	1 per 6 teaching stations
Filmstrip or combination filmstrip-slide projector	1 per 10 teaching stations	1 per 5 teaching stations
Sound filmstrip projector	1 per 15 teaching stations	1 per 10 teaching stations
$3\frac{1}{4}$- by 4-inch projector (overhead)	2 per institution	1 per building
$3\frac{1}{4}$- by 4-inch projector (auditorium)	1 per auditorium	1 per auditorium plus arc or similar power
Filmstrip viewer	5 to 10 at each filmstrip depository	10 to 20 at each filmstrip depository
	It is assumed that viewers will be available for individual use at the depositories. As this activity increases, additional viewers should be secured.	
Overhead projector (10- by 10-inch) classroom type	1 per 4 teaching stations	1 per teaching station
Overhead projector (10- by 10-inch) auditorium type	Appropriate number for large group instructional areas	
	An auditorium model overhead merely implies that the machine utilized has sufficient light output and optical capabilities to project a satisfactory image in an auditorium-type situation.	
Opaque	3 to 6 per institution	8 to 12 per institution
TV receivers	1 per each 24 viewers where programs available (or projection TV is needed)	1 per teaching station but no more than 24 viewers per set
Record players	1 per 25 teaching stations	1 per 15 teaching stations
Tape recorders	1 per 5 teaching stations	1 per 2 teaching stations
Projection carts	1 per 3 to 6 pieces of equipment	1 per 2 to 4 pieces of equipment
Light control	Every classroom should have adequate light control. "Adequate" means that light can be controlled to the extent that all types of projected media can be utilized effectively.	
Video tape recorders	1 per institution	1 per TV production unit
Closed-circuit TV	1 studio per institution capable of distribution of programming to each teaching station	
	Many institutions may desire portable closed-circuit units for specialized use. Where this is the case, the portable units should be secured in addition to the basic recommendations noted above.	
Radio receivers (AM–FM)	3 available in central location	Equivalent of 1 per classroom building

Fig. 3 *Equipment guidelines (higher education).*

Equipment	Basic	Advanced
Projection screens..................	1 per teaching station (at least 70- by 70-inch) with provision for keystone elimination plus 1 portable screen per building. Suitable screen for auditorium—large- or small-group use.	
Electronic learning lab............	1 lab per institution	As programs dictate
Local production equipment.....	Dry mount press and tacking iron Paper cutter Transparency production equipment 16-mm camera 8-mm camera 35-mm camera Rapid-process camera Equipped darkroom Spirit duplicator Primary typewriter Copy camera Light box Film rewind Film splicer Tape splicer	Add to basic list: Slide reproducer Second type of transparency producer Mechanical lettering

Fig. 3 *(Continued)*

filmstrip; S, 2 × 2 = slides; video tape, and films) are integrated within the catalog by subject area. An instructor can quickly determine the variety and extent of materials available for his immediate use. Such a catalog should be kept constantly up to date by periodic supplements.

Specific listings for broad subject matter areas should also be developed. A news bulletin prepared on a regular basis will serve as an additional vehicle to acquaint members of the instructional staff with new materials, equipment, techniques, services, and the availability of any preview materials. Figure 5 presents an example of a typical newsletter.

Ordering Procedures and order forms for audiovisual services are determined by unique local conditions. Some machine scheduling processes have been established in selected institutions. The following guidelines are designed for ready-made or individually tailored forms:

1. Writing must be minimized.
2. Care should be taken to eliminate all superfluous data.
3. Ample space should be provided to allow the instructor to place the entire request on one form.
4. A carbon copy for the instructor's record should be provided. Figure 6 presents an example of a typical order form. It is recommended that this procedure of providing a carbon copy of the order be carried out regardless of how the order is placed; i.e., by phone, note, etc. The carbon copy helps assure the instructor that his request has been completely understood; thus, errors in fulfilling requests are minimized.
5. The form should be carefully designed so as to minimize the amount of time necessary to record the order.

Scheduling This is the most crucial part of the entire ordering-scheduling-delivery system. The system breaks down when instructors are not kept up to date concerning the status or disposition of their requests. Theoretically, a scheduling system has the following basic essentials: reservation and confirmation. Requests for "in house" or institution-owned materials present little problem in terms of reservation and con-

UNDERSTANDING OUR DEEP FRONTIER: OCEANOGRAPHY SERIES (8 filmstrips) FS, color

Part I – Physical Oceanography
Part II – Chemical Oceanography
Part III – Biological Oceanography
Part IV – Ecological Oceanography
Part V – Ocean Engineering
Part VI – Marine Resources
Part VII – Air-Sea Interaction
Part VIII – A Career in Oceanography

THE UNIVERSE 26 min., b&w

Explores the solar system. Uses animation, live photography and special effects to show scenes of the moon, the earth's sister planets, the rings of Saturn, the gaseous geysers of the sun, and other galaxies.

THE UNIVERSE S, 2 × 2, color

A pictorial study of the stars, the planets, comets and the sun. Life Series.

THE WINGED WORLD Video Tape, 60 min., b&w

A generalized study of but a fraction of the 8,600 some odd species of birds, as well as their ecological background. Done in the Walt Disney Nature Series tradition certain species, such as the stork and albatross are dealt with in detail. In general the emphasis is placed on evolution from reptiles, bird intelligence vs. bird instinct, competition, courtship ritual and migration. Sequences of J. Goodall's studies on birds as tool users are shown, etc.

THE WONDERS OF LIFE ON EARTH S, 2 × 2, color

This set of slides deals with the various forms of living things both animal and plant. The set takes the viewer from the primitive, through the process of evolution, to the present. Published by Life.

WORLD IN A MARSH 22 min., color

A film depicting the birth, death and rebirth cycle of inhabitants of a marsh. Includes close-up scenes of animals and flowers and their methods of adapting to the marsh.

THE WORLD WE LIVE IN S, 2 × 2, color

Included in this large series are excellent views of the earth complete from its inception to the development of the pageant of life. Included are slides covering all areas of the planet earth from the rain forests of the Tropics to the frozen Arctic wastes, also slides of other planets and the universe. Pub. by Life.

Fig. 4 *Sample page from an annotated catalog.*

firmation. However, materials and/or equipment that must be rented from outside agencies do present some uncertainty. The typical practice in requesting materials and/or equipment from other agencies is to provide the instructor with a copy of the transaction, indicating that the request has been initiated and that he will be notified as soon as confirmation is received. There are occasions when confirmation is not received but the materials are. Therefore, it is desirable, particularly from a public relations point of vew, to keep instructors continually and fully informed until the materials are received. Specially prepared forms can be used to maintain adequately multiphase communications between the instructor and the audiovisual center. It should also be noted that salesmen from the communications industry as well as other specialists can be called on to help devise a system of ordering and scheduling that will be appropriate for a unique environment.

Distribution The last process is delivery and pick up. Late delivery, a haphazard

INSTRUCTIONAL MEDIA
Published by the Special Projects Group

Bulletin Number 3, Volume 2
November 1968

The Division of Instructional Media (DIM) is an instructional services division of the Office of Educational Resources. Facilities include storage and distribution of audiovisual equipment, acquisition and storage of instructional materials and an instructional materials information center. Its primary aim is to work with faculty in the task of improving instruction by means of instructional media (hardward and/or software).

New Hardware

In recent months, the Division of Instructional Media has acquired several pieces of equipment. One of the more unusual applications of this equipment is the use of two *Super 8 Movie Cameras* by the Northeastern University Laboratory School for Roxbury High School dropouts. Students are experimenting in the writing, acting, directing, and editing of their own films. Problems depicting a conflict in the student's everyday life are determined and selected by the students, as are alternative solutions. The student not only becomes aware of the differences in personal values but also gets an opportunity to examine his own values. These films will be used next spring on an experimental basis in selected public school sessions as well as in Problems in Democracy classes.

In addition to the cameras, several new projectors have been added to DIM. The *Kodak Ektagraphic MFS-8 Projector* allows films to be projected one frame at a time, with an indefinite viewing time for any single frame, in slow motion or at normal speed. Therefore, aside from its ability to project Kodak Super 8 movies, it can also be used for motion analysis and programmed instruction. With the *Cinema Sound Model 850 with Multi-Media Control* (by Creatron Services, Inc.) faculty can produce synchronized slide-tape programs. The machine allows the operator to mix media, that is, combine slides, movies and even live action with a programmed audio tape. Four additional *Sony Portable Videotape Recorders* are being put to good use primarily by the Department of Instruction, the Department of Drama and Speech, the Department of Women's Physical Education, and the athletic coaching staff.

The Instructional Materials Information Center (IMIC) in 406 DG has recently acquired a *Microfilm and Microfiche Reader*. This will make available for general use the microfiche collection from the Educational Resources Information Centers (ERIC), a network of the United States Office of Education. There are nineteen ERIC Clearinghouses, each one specializing in a separate area of interest to education. Microfiche reproductions of documents on any of these nineteen areas are available.

Fig. 5 *Example of a newsletter.*

manner in setting up equipment, or faulty media can result in a devastating end to a request for services. While local situations will dictate variations in the type of distribution system employed, the use of some full-time staff members, rather than a staff made up only of part-time students, is needed to assure reliable delivery. Satellite storage centers located in strategic sections of larger universities will facilitate a distribution system.

A normally hectic situation suddenly becomes critical when an audiovisual center overextends its staff distribution capabilities. The result is invariably a compounding of otherwise simple problems. To provide for this contingency, it is useful, particularly when part-time help is used, to keep a status report on the availability of staff members to assist during emergencies.

HOW DO YOU SET UP A PRODUCTION SERVICE?

Many universities have established convenient facilities for the preparation of a variety of instructional materials, including photographs, slides, filmstrips, overhead projection materials, drawings, illustrations, cartoons, charts, maps, graphs, displays

OFFICE OF EDUCATIONAL RESOURCES
DIVISION OF INSTRUCTIONAL MEDIA

MEMO

EQUIPMENT REQUEST

INSTRUCTOR: ____________________
COURSE: ____________________
DATE PREFERRED ____________________
ALTERNATE DATE: ____________________
CLASS ROOM #: ____________________
TIME TO BE SHOWN: from __________ to __________

ALL EQUIPMENT IS RESERVED ON A FIRST-COME-FIRST-SERVED BASIS. IT IS SUGGESTED THAT YOU ORDER AT LEAST 24 HOURS BEFORE THE CLASS FOR WHICH IT IS NEEDED.

16mm projector	( )	tape recorder	( )
8mm projector	( )	P.A. System	( )
overhead	( )	screen	( )
opaque	( )	filmstrip	( )
carousel (2 X 2 slides)	( )	phonograph	( ) mono ( ) stereo ( )
3 1/4 X 4 polaroid slides	( )		

FILMS ORDERED FROM OUTSIDE SOURCES ARE NOT SUBJECT TO UNIVERSITY CONTROL. PLEASE ALLOW ENOUGH TIME AS POSSIBLE TO INSURE THAT WE WILL BE ABLE TO PLACE YOUR ORDER. USUALLY 14 TO 21 DAYS IS SUFFICIENT.

FILM TITLE	SOURCE OF RENTAL
__________	__________
__________	__________
__________	__________

OFFICE USE ONLY

DISPOSITION OF REQUEST

( ) The above equipment is available on the date preferred. ( ) Alternate date

( ) The above material is not available on either dates requested and is NOT reserved for your use.

Fig. 6 *Sample order form. Instructor retains third copy; second copy is used to inform instructors of the disposition of their request.*

and exhibits, set and costume design, lettering, animation, models, and motion pictures. Production staff for this kind of operation should include a director, a secretary, a photographer, and an artist. The quantity and variety of materials produced will be dictated by the needs of faculty members and utilization patterns. Instructors often prefer to produce their own material for the following reasons:

1. There is a sense of immediacy in up-to-date instructor-produced material.
2. Commercially prepared materials sometimes are not available. This is especially true when instructors are involved in innovative approaches.
3. Instructor-produced materials often reflect local environment and problems. Hence, they are better adapted to unique situations.

Instructors are increasingly developing their own media in consultation with audiovisual media specialists for large-group instruction, individualized instruction, independent study, multimedia presentation techniques, and public relations presentations. A production unit, therefore, should have the minimum capability of producing the following kinds of materials:

1. 2- by 2-inch color slides
2. 3¼- by 4-inch Polaroid slides

3. Audio tapes
4. Overhead transparencies
5. Filmstrips
6. Motion pictures (16-mm and 8-mm cartridge)
7. Photographic enlargements
8. Printed material produced by duplicating machines
9. Laminated material

Some specific areas must be clearly designated to enable a staff to produce the foregoing materials. For example, special space must be provided for producing audio tapes. A darkroom must be provided for the photographic processes. An editing room must be set up for motion picture production. A general or multipurpose area should be set up to accommodate the production of other materials listed. As seen in Figure 7, the general workbench area provides the flexibility needed to produce a host of materials. Ample bench space is provided for drawing boards, slide selection, laying material out, and for general operational work. In addition to serving as workbenches, storage is permitted underneath. A bench for binding, mounting, and laminating is close to a sink. Other benches with a Polaroid camera and other mounted cameras for preparing slides as well as a Repronar to produce filmstrips are placed near the refrigerator. Ample space is provided for storage of supplies by utilization of floor-to-ceiling shelving. Other features of the multipurpose room are also seen in Figure 7.

Audiovisual media have been an accepted part of the teaching-learning process in higher education for a considerable period of time. However, recent technological breakthroughs as well as some exciting innovations have increased the opportunities to creatively apply audiovisual media. The application of audiovisual media to a total system of teaching-learning experiences will continue to provide the effective instructor with a variety of skills in communicating with his students.

ADDITIONAL READINGS

Allen, William H.: "Audiovisual Communication," in Chester W. Harris (ed.), *Encyclopedia of Educational Research,* 3d ed., The Macmillan Company, New York, 1960, pp. 115–137.

American Educational Research Association (a department of the National Education Association): "Instructional Materials," *Review of Educational Research,* pp. 115–212, April, 1962.

Brown, James N., and Kenneth D. Norberg: *Administering Educational Media,* McGraw-Hill Book Company, New York, 1965.

Ely, Donald P.: "The Changing Role of the Audiovisual Process in Education: A Definition and a Glossary of Related Terms," *Audiovisual Communication Review,* January–February, 1963.

Erickson, Carlton W.: *Administering Instructional Media Programs,* The Macmillan Company, New York, 1968.

deKeffer, Robert E.: *Audiovisual Instruction,* Center for Applied Research in Education, Inc., New York, 1965.

Department of Audiovisual Instruction, National Education Association: *Quantitative Standards for Audiovisual Personnel, Equipment, and Materials (in Elementary, Secondary, and Higher Education),* Washington, 1966.

Green, Alan C. (ed.): *Educational Facilities with New Media,* The Department of Audiovisual Instruction of the NEA, Washington, 1966 (prepared under a contract with the U.S. Office of Education).

Hoban, Charles F., Jr., and van Ormer, Edward B.: *Instructional Film Research 1918–1950,* Technical Report SDC 269-7-19, U.S. Department of the Army and U.S. Department of the Navy, Special Devices Center, Port Washington, N.Y., 1950.

Kinne, W. S., Jr.: *Space for Audio-Visual Large Group Instruction,* University of Wisconsin Press, Madison, Wis., 1963.

Koppes, Waine F., Alan C. Green, and M. C. Gassman: *Design Criteria for Learning Spaces: Seating, Lighting, Acoustics,* Office of Facilities, The University of the State of New York, Albany, 1964.

Fulton, W. R.: *Criteria Relating to Educational Media Problems in Colleges and Universities.* These criteria were developed pursuant to a contract with the United States Office of Education, Department of Health, Education, and Welfare, under the provisions of Title VII, Public Law 85–864. Printed and distributed by the Department of Audiovisual Instruction of the NEA

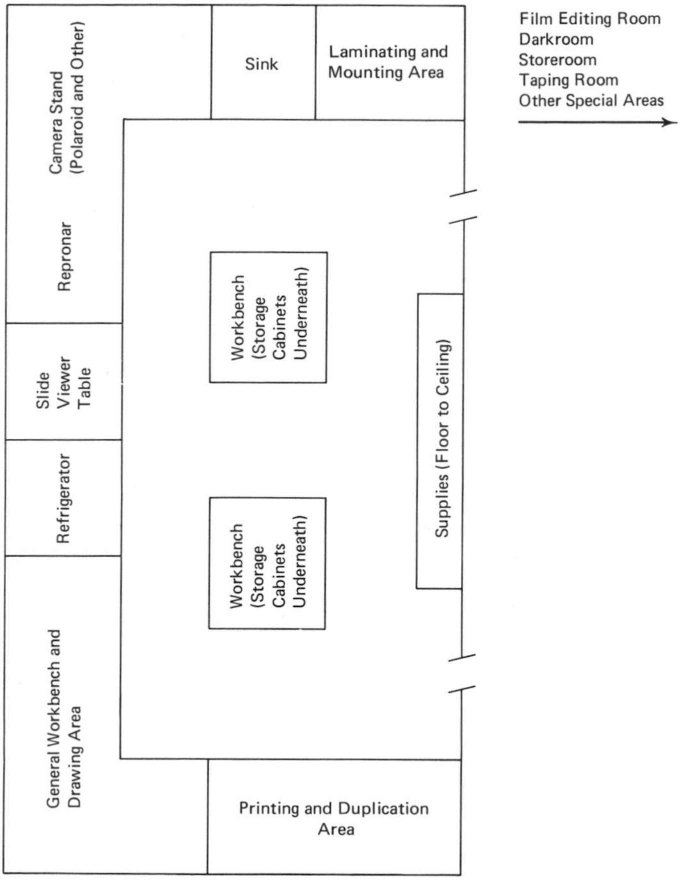

Fig. 7 *A typical multipurpose working area.*

without use of government funds as a service to the teaching profession, 1966 (mimeographed).

———: *Evaluative Checklist: An Instrument for Self-Evaluating an Educational Media Program in Colleges and Universities,* Department of Audiovisual Instruction, National Education Association, Washington, 1966.

Meierhenry, Wesley C. (ed.): *Media and Educational Innovation,* University of Nebraska Press, Lincoln, Neb., 1966 (In cooperation with the U.S. Office of Education under Title VII, Part B).

National Audio-Visual Association, Inc.: *Audio-Visual Equipment Directory,* Fairfax, Va. (issued annually).

National Information Center for Educational Media: *Index to 16-mm Educational Films,* McGraw-Hill Book Company, New York, 1967.

———: *Index to 35-mm Educational Filmstrips,* McGraw-Hill Book Company, New York, 1968.

Pula, Fred: *Application and Operation of Audiovisual Equipment in Education,* John Wiley & Sons, Inc., New York, 1968.

Saettler, Paul: *A History of Instructional Technology,* McGraw-Hill Book Company, New York, 1968.

Society for the Study of Education: *Audio-Visual Materials of Instruction,* 48th Yearbook, University of Chicago Press, Chicago, 1949 (Part I).

Wendt, Paul R.: "Audiovisual Instruction" (no. 14 of the "What Research Says to the Teacher" series), National Education Association, Department of Classroom Teachers, Washington, 1966.

Wittich, Walter Arno, and Charles F. Schuller: *Audio-Visual Materials, Their Nature and Use,* 3d ed., Harper and Row, Publishers, Incorporated, New York, 1967.

Chapter 8

Instructional Television Services

ROY J. JOHNSTON

Director, Division of Instructional Communications, Northeastern University, Boston, Massachusetts

WHAT IS INSTRUCTIONAL TELEVISION?

On May 12, 1953, KUHT-TV, owned and operated by the University of Houston, inaugurated noncommercial or educational telecasting in the United States. The following decade witnessed educational television leaping and stumbling along pathways bordered by vacillating program emphases of formal instruction, cultural and informational presentations, and "educational" entertainment. A general concept slowly evolved that broadcast television should serve home viewers in the informal areas of culture and information, and that formal instruction should become the purview of the more flexible and less expensive medium of closed-circuit television. Some notable exceptions to this general concept exist, for example, the Midwest

Program of Airborne Television Instruction, the Chicago Junior College of the Air, and the Alabama Educational Television Network. However, the National Association of Educational Broadcasters gave formal recognition to the concept outlined above in 1963 by establishing two semiautonomous television divisions within their organization. These are the Educational Television Stations Division, for membership by noncommercial broadcast stations; and the Instructional Division, for membership by closed-circuit and instructional television fixed-service operations.

The recent report (January, 1967) issued by the Carnegie Commission on Educational Television states:

> ". . . the Commission believes that instructional television must be regarded as an element in the total educational process. The question must be asked whether, in a given educational context, television has a role of its own to play in relation both to a set of educational objectives and to the full battery of educational tools available. If television contributes to the quality of education, or makes possible a greater quantity of education, it will take its place as a tool of education, but it is in those terms that it should be approached and ultimately judged."[1]

Instructional television, therefore, defined in terms of its own evolution and in Carnegie Commission phraseology, is an educational tool utilizing the various hardwares of closed-circuit television.

WHY USE INSTRUCTIONAL TELEVISION?

An instructional television operation can be a source of imaginative and creative instruction and can support a faculty with advantages not previously possible, or it can be an expensive luxury accomplishing little beyond the exhibition of a desire for progressive educational methods.

A distillation of the voluminous reports on the evaluation of television as an instructional medium can be expressed in two sentences: (*a*) learning can be accomplished as effectively by televised instruction as by conventional teaching methods; and (*b*) television is capable of providing the best possible instruction for the greatest number of students. For the economically minded, it can be stated that, within certain parameters of enrollment, academic disciplines, and geographical locations, instructional television can alleviate instructional costs.

Proper use of the illustrative techniques of television can provide a more direct instructive impact than can a conventional lecture or textbook. This is accomplished through the direct pictorial interpretation of fact or theory, utilizing static and dynamic visualizations. Each student has a vocabulary peculiar to his experience and to the sensory reactions and knowledge acquired through such experience. Each student, through his vocabulary, practices an individual translation to thought of the words he hears. Each student's translation from word to thought differs from the translation of a person of divergent experience. The verbal or printed communication of knowledge from the teacher to the student requires a translation from the instructive vocabulary to the learning vocabulary with a consequent loss of impact. Pictures provide stronger and more direct stimuli to personal thought and understanding than do words. Communication by speech is a learned skill; seeing and the thought stimuli provoked by sight begin shortly after birth and comprise the base of experience on which sensory reaction and knowledge are built. Through the use of visual media, a consistency of instruction is built into the instructional system and thus a higher reliability of the instructional message is available to shape the learning of the student.

[1] Carnegie Commission on Educational Television, *Public Television, A Program for Action*, Bantam Books, Inc., New York, January, 1967, p. 82.

More specifically, television as an instructional tool makes possible multiplication, magnification, the nullification of distance and time factors, and the storage of accomplished and tested instruction.

Multiplication means the exact reproduction of an instructive situation with transmission to an unlimited number of points of exhibition. Magnification is the enlargement of an instructive procedure to proportions which make possible profitable exhibition for an unlimited number of students, i.e., the magnification and distribution of "live" surgical techniques and the magnification of minute reactions, especially in circumstances where normal observation would be difficult. Through television, the "super lecturer" or "master teacher" is available in a number of places simultaneously without the expense of time or travel. The storage of accomplished, tested, and validated instruction provides the release of faculty for individual student/teacher activity, for research, and for self-observation and evaluation, as well as providing immediate retrieval, eventual review and revision of instructional media, and easier scheduling.

DOES INSTRUCTIONAL TELEVISION SAVE MONEY?

Within logical limitations, it is possible to achieve fiscal economies through instruction by television; but such limitations should be understood thoroughly in their application to individual situations. A sophisticated installation can be profitable only if it can be justified by the number of students served or if it makes possible an instructional mode not possible in any other way. A loose but effective measurement is the comparison of the cost of televised instruction per student-hour with a similar student-hour cost of instruction by conventional methods. Such costs will vary in proportion to the number of students, the disciplines involved, the instructor level required, and the type of instruction; i.e., laboratory, lecture hall, etc. Experiments are currently being conducted on the desirability of distributing televised lectures into dormitories in an effort to eliminate classroom space problems, thus providing another dimension to the most effective new data bank.

Through the utilization of television, it is possible for the small college or university to offer instruction which could be economically prohibitive otherwise because of instructor or equipment cost. Courses in such relatively expensive areas as ichthyology, oceanography, nuclear radiation, etc., can be made available on videotape at schools and colleges where lack of facilities would normally negate such course offerings.

THE QUALITY QUESTION

Television, however, is not the long-awaited panacea for all educational ills and should be approached with proper administrative caution. Beyond the basic questions of profitable use and academic desirability lie the profound considerations of quality. Today's university students are a part of a generation completely conditioned by a smooth and expensive commercial television product. They are able critics of productions which are presented in a haphazard, ineffectual manner.

To have acceptable stature, instructional television must compare well with the commercial product; it cannot afford to be justifiably dubbed as a second-class effort. Too often, instructional television places cameras in a poorly lighted classroom situation, using them only to magnify and multiply the mediocrity which has existed in that classroom for generations. To properly utilize those peculiar characteristics of television which can improve a learning situation, it is not necessary to provide commercially competitive equipment, but it is imperative that the production of instructional presentations be entrusted to persons knowledgeable in the capabilities and limitations of television production.

ADMINISTRATIVE CONSIDERATIONS

Television, a complex tool for the possible development of excellent instruction, can be only as good as its component parts and only if properly used by good craftsmen.

The key to an efficient, inspirational, and practical ITV operation is cooperation; cooperation among a progressive administration, a dedicated and sincerely curious faculty, and an educationally aware and technically knowledgeable ITV staff. The administration must be oriented to the desirability of a union between instruction and available instructional technologies and must be willing to support the expense of good equipment and good staff as a guarantee of quality. It must be understood by all concerned that a record of excellent classroom instruction does not automatically qualify a faculty member as a good television instructor, and that the introduction of media-oriented instruction can be traumatic to the able instructor and to the inept instructor alike. Administration must be agreeable to accepting the expertise of persons not educationally experienced to act as mediator in the inevitable clashes between the academic temperament and the technician's desire for perfection and to encourage by recognition the difficult accomplishments produced through the cooperative efforts of academician and technician.

Faculty members to be involved in an ITV situation must be dedicated to high standards of instruction and must be aware that the instructional world has burst the walls of the cloistered classroom and has advanced beyond the advantages of the printing press. They must embrace a curiosity concerning the advantages available to education through technology and must present an open mind to modes of instruction previously foreign to the academic experience.

The staff of a good ITV center must be aware that education presents an opportunity for technical knowledge to assume proportions of value in instructional and cultural situations otherwise impossible of achievement. A good staff member must be imbued with the concept of service and, equally with the faculty, must possess a curiosity that makes possible the conception and application of new techniques of instruction. Above all, a good staff must be practicing diplomats in the world of emerging instructional technology.

The end product of an ITV operation is superior instruction which, in turn, has been made possible by the organization and integration of above-average ideas, talents, people, and equipment. Audiovisual instruction suffered through a long period of academic disrepute because it became a haven for the opportunist, for the intellectually lazy, and for the academically inept. Instructional television is faced with similar disrepute because it also offers equal haven for the opportunist and because, through improper use of its peculiar abilities, it is accepted as instructional television when it is simply televised instruction multiplying the often prevalent ills of the instructional process.

The previously mentioned component parts which comprise the total tool of instructional television must be carefully chosen and carefully assembled to produce a quality product.

THE RIGHTS OF TEACHERS

In the utilization of instructional television, teachers' rights become a necessary area for administrative consideration. Such problems as program content control, revision control, program withdrawal date, distribution control, teachers' compensation and residual rights require definitive solution prior to production.

Historically, course content is an academic responsibility not to be relegated to administrators. In television production, course content should remain the responsibility of the individual instructor or of a specialist or group assigned such responsibility, but there should be sufficient latitude to allow production personnel an opportunity for improving content presentation through pertinent visualization.

With few exceptions, recorded instructional material becomes outdated, and a decision must be made to revise the content or to withdraw the program from distribution. It is important that the clear responsibility for such a decision shall be given either to the individual teacher concerned or to a curriculum committee. It has, in fact, proved desirable to have such decisions made in advance of production by formulating a revision schedule or by predetermining the period of time for which a program should be distributed.

It is sometimes difficult to determine in advance the areas of distribution which may be desirable for any lecture or course series. It is flattering for an individual or an institution to discover that his or its product is desired for distribution by outside agencies, but serious disagreements can arise concerning the rights of the individual and the rights of the institution if previous agreements have not been reached.

The matter of distribution control exerts a direct influence on the problem of teachers' compensation and on the residual rights of teachers. If the lecture or course series is to be used only within the originating institution, compensation agreements can be relatively simple; but paid distribution to outside agencies raises complex questions.

For instructional programs to be distributed within the originating institution, it has become widespread practice to provide the instructor with released time for preparation. The range of released time is an exercise of the complexity of the production, of the program length, etc. If the program is recorded for continuing use, further provision is commonly made for future released time for purposes of revision. In a survey of compensation practices in 1963,[2] Fred S. Seibert states:

> About 18 percent of the replying colleges and universities report that they assign a teacher full time to the production of television programs. One institution reports a formula under which one television course equals a full load. Others report that a full load consists of two television courses. Over 60 percent of elementary and secondary schools indicate a similar full-time assignment.

If the program or course series enjoys paid distribution to outside agencies, it is necessary to agree as to the disposition of such income. Certain institutions extend the regulations which cover authorship rights in university publications to apply to "talent" rights in productions supported by the institution. Other institutions make an initial payment to the instructor in return for which he waives all future rights in the production. In some instances, an agreement is made between the "talent" and the institution as to the percentages of future income to be assigned to each.

EQUIPMENT

Hardware is one essential consideration of any television operation and should be selected after cautious consideration of the desired use and product. The most important advice which can be followed by an academic administrator approaching the bewildering vastness of television equipment is to seek the counsel of a qualified expert. Insofar as possible, such counsel should be selected on the basis of neutral interests. The sales staffs of television equipment manufacturers or service companies are eager to supply counsel—and their own equipment. Given the constraints of desired use and budget, a qualified expert can determine the most efficient installation. He can make decisions on questions ranging from studio size through camera types, control equipment, telecine equipment, videotape recorders, and lighting instruments to anticipated maintenance needs and costs. Instructional television originating com-

[2] Fred S. Siebert, *Copyrights, Clearances, and Rights of Teachers in the New Educational Media,* American Council on Education, Washington, 1965.

plexes can range in cost from $2,000 to $500,000 and must be meticulously tailored to the desired needs if waste is to be avoided.

Another hardware facet requiring careful analysis is the system of transmission to be used to carry the television signal from its originating point to the classroom. A number of such systems exist, differing widely in sophistication and expense. They include land lines or cable transmission, point-to-point (microwave) transmission, 2,500-megahertz or Instructional Television Fixed Service (ITFS) systems, community antenna television systems, broadcast transmission, and even airborne television.

The simplest of the foregoing systems, but not necessarily the most inexpensive, is the land-line or cable transmission, which carries the signal directly from the point of origination to the classroom receiver. Intrastate, it is legally permissible for an institution to install and maintain its own cables for instructional purposes; interstate, it is required that the facilities of a public carrier be used. The decision to use telephone lines or to install self-owned equipment is dependent on individual factors of utility fees, distance, location, property rights, etc.

Point-to-point transmission, often referred to as microwave transmission, is line-of-sight transmission employing a microwave transmitter at the point of origination with a microwave receiver at the point of distribution (microwaves are so named because of their extremely high frequency and corresponding wavelength range of from 50 cm to 1 mm). Microwave transmission is most often used as long-distance linkage rather than as a system of short-distance distribution.

Instructional Television Fixed Service systems (2,500-megahertz transmission) operate in the 2,500- to 2,690-megahertz frequency range (microwave range) and have been designated by the Federal Communications Commission for use by educational institutions (FCC Rules and Regulations, Section 74.90). The frequency range has been divided by the FCC into 31 channels in 8 groupings (7 groups of 4 channels, 1 group of 3 channels). An applicant for use of ITFS channels must submit to the FCC the intended program for use and the plan for construction of the system. The FCC grants approval to an applicant on the basis of public interest. ITFS distance range is dependent on topography and rarely exceeds a 20-mile radius. The ITFS system differs from straight microwave systems insofar as the pattern of transmission in ITFS allows multiple reception from a single transmitter rather than single reception.

Community antenna television (CATV) systems can be used for the transmission and distribution of instructional television signals in areas where CATV exists.

Broadcast transmission of instructional television is accomplished by both noncommercial and commercial television stations on VHF (very high frequency, channels 2 to 13) and UHF (ultrahigh frequency, channels 14 to 82). Such transmission is generally unsatisfactory for instructional use because of the single-program channel constraint and because commercial stations must be primarily involved with profit considerations and noncommercial or ETV (educational television) stations are basically concerned with cultural or informational programming as differentiated from formal credit-earning instruction.

The Midwest Program on Airborne Television Instruction (MPATI) utilizes an aircraft cruising at an altitude of 30,000 feet while broadcasting instructional programs on UHF frequencies. The airborne television system could hardly be considered as the solution for instructional television at a single institution of higher education.

Combinations of the above systems are possible and often desirable. ITFS systems can be interconnected by microwave transmission, with distribution of both types of systems being accomplished by cable installations. Universities which are dispersed geographically in extensive complexes can utilize ITFS systems in individual complexes while interconnecting the complexes by microwave transmission.

Attention should be given to the future. As concretely as possible, plans for expansion of an ITV system should be formulated before the original investment and installation is begun. Television equipment does not lend itself to inexpensive alteration, and a burgeoning university quickly can discover that its faculty has embraced television's capabilities beyond all proportion to the original facilities.

A third important hardware consideration in the overall ITV operation is the television receiver. As in home reception, an improperly installed or improperly adjusted receiver in a classroom can defeat the most carefully produced television presentation. It is necessary at the outset of planning to determine such factors as the desired distribution of color or monochrome pictures, the numbers of students viewing one receiver, the locations of receivers, the maintenance of classroom equipment, etc. The picture to be viewed is the final product of all planning and preparation, and if the quality of the picture is diminished by poor exhibition, the entire effort is wasted.

THE SOFTWARE QUESTION

Another vital component of the television tool is personnel involved in the production of the programs to be distributed via ITV. A common error made by administrators is the deliberate division of the total staff into segments of competence and capability. No other medium of instruction relies as heavily for quality on the interaction and interdependence of a team of experts: the administrator, the educator, the technician, the producer, the director, the artist and, depending on the scope and complexity of the operation, a number of other persons to be selected as much for their ability to cooperate and interact with others as for their competence in their respective fields. From the beginnings of organization, personnel should be impressed with their importance as integral members of a functioning team.

In our past educational experiences, certain instructors stand out as clearly as lighthouses on a misty coast of learning. Rarely do we stop to analyze the reasons for such prominence, but when doing so we are most often confounded by our inability to pinpoint any one factor. The elusive and intangible quality which causes students to seek the classes of one instructor rather than another could be classified as academic "ham" and often denotes the superior television instructor. This does not mean, however, that the instructor who is thoroughly knowledgeable in his discipline but lacks a certain personal flamboyancy cannot become, through training and desire, a good television instructor; it means that while some instructors are "naturals," others must work at teaching in the unfamiliar atmosphere which a busy television studio presents.

Perhaps the greatest advantage which instructional television offers the educative process is the exposure of the greatest possible number of students to the best available instructor in a given discipline. It is, therefore, of prime importance that instructors be auditioned, that the decision to assign an instructor to instructional television be the joint decision of academic and technical responsibility. A television camera provides an intimacy between teacher and student which exceeds that found in conventional instructional situations; weaknesses in instruction are magnified, content presentation is concentrated, and interruptions become intolerable. The instructor appearing on the television screen must also be capable of accepting and assimilating criticism which he would not ordinarily receive in the cloistered classroom.

In watching standard television fare on a commercial network, the lay viewer is often amazed by the length and number of credits which pass in review at the conclusion of a program. How is it possible for so many unseen persons to contribute to one program of thirty minutes' length? Television, any kind of television, is a team effort, and all the unseen members of the team contribute in a highly specialized fashion to the support of the person or persons actually appearing on the screen. In instructional television, the constraints of budget usually prohibit the employment of great numbers of specialists; this fact does not preclude, however, the accomplishment of the same tasks which are necessary for the quality production of a commercial program. Instructional television production teams have to work harder, do more with less, for less, than do their commercial counterparts. The quality of instructional presentations are an exercise of the knowledge and experience of the production teams. The talents and capabilities of the commercial producer and the commercial director are often combined in one person in the instructional field. The relationship between the instructor, or instructional expert, and the production expert determines the quality of instructional presentations. If possible, the producer/director of an instructional television operation should have at least an M.A. degree to encourage the faculty members with whom he is associated to have confidence in him. Too often, the traditionalists among a faculty tend to regard the "technician" as a purveyor of "gimmicks," a person without academic stature or appreciation. The possession of a degree equivalent to that of the instructional expert can ameliorate the path of cooperation for the production specialist.

As previously mentioned, the number of members of an instructional television team is generally determined more by the available funds than by the actual need. Without certain personnel, however, it is impossible to produce an acceptable product. The producer/director must have available the skills and talents of good equipment technicians, of a good artist, of capable cameramen, audio operators, telecine operators, etc. Many of the necessary positions can be filled by intelligent students or other persons of ability not previously trained in production techniques, but much grief can be avoided by the employment of a fully qualified technician and a trained artist.

It is especially advantageous to have one engineer or technician responsible for the design, the installation, and the operation of an ITV facility. This person need not be a graduate engineer, but he should have complete familiarity with the rapidly changing manufacture of instructional television equipment. He should be capable of organizing and supervising an expanding technical staff; should be able to train the technicians needed for operation, maintenance, and repair; and should have an active sympathy for the problems of production. The actual number of technicians needed will depend upon programming, scheduling, expansion, etc., and can best be decided by the technical supervisor.

Television is a visual medium, and to attempt the production of good instructional television without an artist is similar to attempting the production of dairy products without a source of milk. The basic qualification for a television artist is that he be an artist, not a commercial illustrator, but an artist—one who is talented and trained in the exercise of imagination and ingenuity. The visual products supplied by the artist should provide an aesthetic base for the vicarious experiences of learning as well as literal illustration of the factual materials of instruction. A good artist will be able to familiarize himself with such technical aspects of television production as gray scale values, acceptable contrasts, etc.; whereas a technical master of illustration can rarely produce the inspirational art work so necessary to excellent instruction. The use of art students as assistants can relieve the artist of much of the tedious work of printing, mechanical reproduction, etc.

As previously stated, the whole of television is but a tool in the instructional process, a complex tool to be wielded by expert craftsmen. Organization of the total effort should include, with the instruction specialists and the production specialists, an expert in program systems analysis whose responsibility it would be to analyze the educational needs of the departments scheduled to participate in the ITV effort and to recommend the most efficient uses of the medium. An educational psychologist should also be an integral member of the team for the purpose of testing and evaluating the results of the instructional methods as well as for advising on methods to be employed.

As with any venture, planning and time are two of the most important elements contributing to success in the field of instructional television. The design of facilities, the purchase of equipment, the employment of personnel, and the scheduling of installation and production should all flow smoothly into a point where the insertion of instructional television into the educative processes of an institution can be accomplished without a ripple of dislocation.

MINIMUM EQUIPMENT AND STAFF

For the institution which wishes to aid instruction through the use of television for simple magnification or for the self-evaluation of instructor or student, it is possible to accomplish such limited objectives with the new models of vidicon cameras and ½-inch videotape recorders at a minimal expense.

The industry has developed thoroughly portable configurations of cameras and recorders which can be purchased for $1,300, for example: camera with tripod, pan head, cables, and microphone—$350; portable ½-inch videotape recorder/playback—$725; 18-inch (diagonal measure of screen) monitor/TV receiver—$225. If a viewfinder for the camera is desired, it can be purchased for $175 (1969 prices).

With such equipment, consignment to the audiovisual media area of the institution for assignment and maintenance would eliminate the necessity for staff members responsible for television activity.

From this minimum of equipment and expense it is possible to assemble more sophisticated equipment for any purpose up to fully equipped studio production.

The minimum cost for equipping a studio for simple production is as follows: two vidicon camera chains complete with controls, viewfinders, cables, etc.—approximately $25,000; a six-position switcher with fader—$1,200; a multiplexer with film and slide projectors which will make possible the integration of 16-mm film and 35-mm slides into a studio production—$12,000; one 1-inch videotape recorder/playback—$2,800; studio lighting sufficient for simple production—$2,000, for a total of $53,800. To this cost should be added 20 percent, or $10,600, for such technical items as test equipment, microphones, audio consoles, etc. This brings the final expenditure to $64,400. The figures quoted are for monochrome television and do not include distribution items such as classroom monitors or receivers at $250 each or cable connections and classroom junction boxes at approximately $80 per classroom.

If use of 2,500-megahertz distribution is desired, each receiving point should be estimated at approximately $2,200 for receiver equipment and each transmitter should be figured at $10,000.

To equip a studio to the point where it is possible to produce live or videotaped programs equivalent to those produced by commercial operations, a minimum expenditure of $200,000 should be budgeted. Northeastern University is currently completing installation of a three-camera studio feeding a two-channel 2,500-megahertz system with five reception points at an approximate cost of $300,000 for 800 separate pieces of equipment including color-capable transmitters, projectors, a multiplexer, and videotape recorders.

Staff members and expense can range from the previously mentioned assignment of responsibility to the audiovisual media section to a highly trained and capable production group including directors, writers, artist, and technicians whose salaries will be dictated by such factors as geographical location, sophistication of equipment used, experience necessary, and excellence of production desired.

For a small two-camera studio, the minimum staff should include a capable and experienced person to direct the total effort; at least one producer/director with a background conducive to working with faculty; an artist familiar with such constraints of production as linearity and resolution requirements, contrast and gray-scale factors, etc.; and a technician capable of installing and maintaining the standard of equipment desired. To these basic staff people must be added full- or part-time cameramen, audio operators, floormen, set builders, writers, etc.

Equipment and staff considerations are not a function of the size of the institution but of the desired capability of the television operation. It is impossible to list with any degree of accuracy the equipment and staff needed for a general configuration; the only reliable guide in planning is consultation with an experienced and responsible person who understands the objectives of the institution involved. A request to the National Association of Educational Broadcasters, at the address below, will supply a list of qualified consultants and of exemplary installations which can be visited:

National Association of Educational Broadcasters
1346 Connecticut Avenue N.W.
Washington, D.C. 20036

FROM DESIRE TO ACTUALITY: A CHECKLIST
(A Partial List of Necessary Considerations)

Why Television for Instruction? Decide what instructional problems you want television to solve.

Decide how television can accomplish your instructional objectives better than any alternative method.

Who Will Use Television? Consult with faculty, staff, students, and administration to determine needs and attitudes.

Decide who constitutes "talent" for ITV.

Decide on "type" of use: enrichment, total instruction, magnification, and/or mass instruction.

Staff Procure an experienced and capable director as soon as you decide to use television.

Make available to the director sufficient monies to allow immediate hiring of a qualified technician.

Space Considerations Decide on space needs and locations for studios, shops, storage, etc.

Define classrooms, auditoriums, and other areas as instructional areas.

Consider equipment security problems.

Consider humidity- and temperature-control problems, noise problems, and electrical supply problems.

Budget Considerations Match the sophistication of your equipment to your instructional needs and to available monies.

Decide whether your organization can support the capital expenditure required or if you should seek outside support.

Estimate the cost of continuing operation (supplies, staff, amortization of equipment, expansion) and be sure you can afford the continuing expense. (Historically, instructional television has been plagued by administrators who, having provided a capital expenditure, have for various reasons failed to provide continuing support.)

Equipment Decide the extent of production desired (classroom, studio, simple multiplication of presentation, integration of films), and procure the proper equipment for satisfactory work.

Decide on the process of distribution: cable, microwave, 2,500-megahertz, "bicycled" video tape.

Give responsibility for decisions concerning equipment to a person qualified to write bid specifications.

Obtain specific warranties for equipment.

Obtain educational discounts wherever possible.

Decide how and by whom installation is to be accomplished.

Confirm with manufacturer or representative the processes for major servicing and repair.

Set deadlines for delivery and installation of equipment.

ASSOCIATIONS CONCERNED WITH ITV

A number of organizations are dedicated to the advancement and improvement of educational and instructional television. Among these are:

National Association of Educational Broadcasters
1346 Connecticut Avenue N.W.
Washington, D.C. 20036

The NAEB serves the professional needs of noncommercial radio and television. Its members represent over four hundred radio and television stations, production centers, and closed-circuit instructional television operations. *The NAEB Directory and Yearbook of 1968* lists the following services of the organization: workshops, seminars, regional and national conferences, consultant services, and numerous radio and television publications. The NAEB also operates a radio tape network and television-program library service for its members, administers government-financed projects, and maintains liaison with national educational organizations in other countries. The NAEB maintains an active personnel placement service.

Association for Professional Broadcasting Education
1812 K Street N.W.
Washington, D.C. 20036

The APBE is concerned with improving the educational training of people studying for careers in broadcasting.

Educational Media Council
1346 Connecticut Avenue N.W.
Washington, D.C. 20036

The EMC lists its objectives as (1) providing a forum for the discussion of significant educational problems relating to the improvement of instruction, (2) stimulating needed research and development in the media and related areas, (3) disseminating information to the nation's educational community about research developments and effective applications of media, and (4) developing projects and studies in the educational media area which, by their nature and scope, are beyond the abilities or resources of individual organizations.

National Great Plains Instructional Television Library
Lincoln, Neb. 68508

Recorded ITV courses are continually being produced privately for independent use in school systems at all levels throughout the country. The NGPITL constantly searches for and arranges national distribution of the best quality courses produced by any agency. An annual catalog describing the content, course level, production agency, etc., of available material is issued from NGPITL headquarters in Lincoln.

University of the Air
Michigan State University
Continuing Education Service
East Lansing, Mich.

The *National Compendium of Televised Education* is an annual publication edited by Dr. Lawrence E. McKune and published by the University of the Air at Michigan State University. The Compendium lists the activities in instructional television of over 2,500 educational organizations. Dr. McKune states ". . . the Compendium presumes value in substance and in fact as a source of information not available otherwise to those who are charged with the responsibility for rational development and substantive use of new media—particularly of television."[3]

Midwest Educational Television, Inc.
1640 Como Avenue
St. Paul, Minn. 55108

MET coordinates the distribution of programs produced by the member stations of the organization.

National Center for School and College Television
Box A
Bloomington, Ind. 47402

The NCSCT distributes instructional materials and programs on a national basis to stations and closed-circuit installations.

Western Radio and Television Association
633 Battery Street, Suite 654
San Francisco, Calif. 94111

The WRTA provides services to West Coast organizations similar to those provided nationally by NAEB.

[3] Lawrence E. McKune, *Compendium of Televised Education*, vol. 13, Michigan State University, September, 1966, Foreword, p. i.

Chapter 9

Instructional Communications Systems

DAVID F. BARTZ

Bell System Educational Communications Coordinator, American Telephone and Telegraph Company, Detroit, Michigan

The previous eight chapters have presented pertinent data, administrative techniques, and selected references on the very comprehensive subject of learning resources and instructional services. Some of the chapters developed, to a degree, guidelines and parameters for the physical communications systems required to serve these methods of instruction. The purpose of this chapter is to draw together and develop, in more detail and under one heading, a comprehensive guide to administrating the communications systems that make possible and economically feasible many of these learning resources and instructional aids.

WHAT IS INSTRUCTIONAL COMMUNICATIONS?

Instructional communications differs from administrative communications in that instructional communications should be considered as a part of the educational process —that is, a communication device or service that the student can use to help him learn.

Both administrative and instructional communications have as their end objective the fullfillment of the basic goals of any educational system—the development and advancement of the learning process. But, while administrative communications is generally supportive in nature, i.e., involved in "running the school" by registering students, record keeping, and the myriad of communications activities that are needed to meet the logistic requirements of a college or university, educational communications, on the other hand, is utilized *by the student.*

A relationship between instructional and administrative communications is apparent when we consider that each might utilize the same physical plant distribution and/or switching systems. For this reason it is important (especially if the administration of each system is under separate control) that the short- and long-range objectives of each area be considered before any decision affecting basic service is made. For example, if three schools were planning to share facilities for administrative and/or research purposes, care should be taken to explore potential instructional uses such as "sharing the professor" type programs with amplified telephone calls (Tele-Lecture) between the participating schools. Without this type of planning, it would be difficult to derive *full* value from any communications facility leased or purchased.

To develop instructional communications in more detail, it is helpful to divide the discussion into three parts, as follows:

1. Group Applications
2. Individual Applications
3. Educational Network Concepts

Again, as in the division of administrative and instructional communications, these three areas are closely interrelated and no strict and unbending dividing lines can be established. For example, a student in a carrel listening to a taped instructional lesson is involved in an individual application of instructional communication, but introduce a loudspeaker on the carrel telephone line and place this speaker in a classroom, and the same basic facility is now serving a group application. The section dealing with educational network concepts will include a discussion of library services related to communications.

GROUP APPLICATIONS

Application of modern communications techniques to the group learning process can vary from the relatively simple amplified telephone connection to the more complex closed-circuit television. The decision as to which instructional aid to use in a given situation must be determined by the course instructor, but his decision will be guided by what facilities are available and the amount and quality of professional backing he has to produce the required programs.

Tele-Lecture Services

Tele-Lecture is a medium that uses amplified telephone communication between a speaker at one location and one or more groups of people at other locations. The communication is two-way—so participants may question the speaker. He, in turn, may key his presentation to the responses of his audience, or he may initiate a general discussion. Visual material can be used. The speaker can send a set of this material to each location before the discussion begins.

For a teacher or guest speaker, Tele-Lecture can be as easy as picking up the telephone already on his own desk and dialing a number. It enables a specialized teacher (for example, in drama or theatrical productions) to be available to a large number of groups at widely scattered locations. Tele-Lectures have originated from homes, offices, the White House, from hospital beds, and—when the lecturer was detained by traffic—from a public telephone.

Several colleges and universities have made Tele-Lecture a permanent part of their teaching program. They have established Tele-Lecture centers which are available for a variety of course subjects and projects. Other colleges have worked together to present Tele-Lectures on a regional basis, and some educators are working toward the establishment of a national and international clearinghouse for Tele-Lecture resources. Tele-Lecture is also being used in conjunction with FM radio. The lectures, as received by telephone, are recorded and broadcast over university stations so that they can be heard by the student and community audience.

In the experience of those who regularly present Tele-Lectures, the first step in organizing a successful program is to appoint a Tele-Lecture coordinator. The coordinator, usually a member of the audiovisual department of the school, is responsible for all phases of the program and assists professors in setting up their Tele-Lecture classes.

Institutions using Tele-Lecture as a somewhat regular part of these courses have found permanent amplification equipment or at least a permanent termination of the institution's basic telephone service in the classroom a real aid in arranging for Tele-Lectures. This termination can also be used for any other instructional aid that involves telephone service.

Telewriting Services

Telewriting adds another whole dimension to Tele-Lecture. With telewriting, a speaker's handwriting may be transmitted and projected on a screen or television receiver at remote locations as he or an associate is writing or drawing. If needed, telewriting can also be arranged so that all locations in the network can communicate with one another. And if a teacher is working with a class of his own while participating in Tele-Lecture to another location, the writing or drawings can be projected on a screen for his own class too.

Recent advances now permit the tape recording of telewriting (and the audio or Tele-

Lecture portion) on standard, dual-track audio tapes. This innovation permits important or unique classes to be retained for editing or improvement or for re-use by students at a later time.

As in Tele-Lecture, the regular telephone network is capable of carrying telewriting signals and, if the terminal equipment is available, the cost for each Tele-Lecture/telewriting class is relatively low when compared to the cost of the same program on a live basis for an individual class.

Television

Production of instructional television (ITV) programs of the quality necessary to be acceptable for use in a modern educational institution is no simple task. Professor Johnson has related in detail some of the problems and challenges that await those educators willing to try.

Once produced and recorded on videotape (live ITV can have a significant role when used with the companion service of audio "talk-back," which will be discussed in another section of this chapter), the instructional TV program awaits replay before a live class. At this point the videotape is no different than a movie film (except for the fact that it generally would have cost far *more to produce* and, without a distribution system permitting direct pickup on a TV receiver, it would be *more costly to show*, requiring a videotape player in addition to a TV receiver at each location desiring to see the program). What will make it different is creativity in the design of the communications network used to distribute the program.

A distribution system within a single building (generally privately owned) between campus buildings, between satellite campuses, or on a network basis between several schools is the medium that establishes ITV as an instructional aid that offers curative promise for some of today's educational ills.

How Many Channels? Early in the design stages of an ITV distribution system, after determination of what buildings, building areas, campuses, etc., are to be connected by the system, the question of "how many channels" will be paramount. And paramount it should be—too few channels and the distribution system becomes an expensive substitute for messenger or mail service, too many channels and excessive costs will decrease the overall economic value of the system. Before attempting to answer the "channels" question, it is necessary to consider usage-oriented considerations such as:

1. Will all programs be scheduled? (e.g., Physical Education 101 at 9 A.M.—Monday–Wednesday–Friday)
2. Can the classroom instructor ask for specific programs as supplements to the regular course?
3. Will remote locations have facilities for videotape recording, permitting replay at will?
4. Will live telecasts be made?
5. How many total courses and course hours will be involved in the use of ITV?

Chances are that, to a degree, all of these questions will have at least a partly affirmative answer. It will therefore be necessary to place time values on each of the areas to determine the number of channels that will be required.

What about "Live" Instructional Television? Live television has almost become a thing of the past in commercial broadcasting except for sports programs or when events of overriding national concern or interest are involved.[1] The reasons for this are simple: videotape recording permits editing and replay at a time more convenient to the viewers. For the most part, the same considerations affect ITV, with one exception:

[1] Carnegie Commission on Educational Television, *Public Television, A Program for Action*, Bantam Books, Inc., New York, Jan., 1967, p. 54.

when the course being taught can benefit from two-way conversations with the TV instructor.

This system is referred to as "talk-back" and permits the live lecture or lab session to have the added advantages of questions and answers between instructor and student. Consideration should be given in the design stage of a distribution system to the desirability of providing two-way voice communications with all classroom locations. Regular telephone service connections to the classroom can be modified to permit talk-back service.

What Type of Closed-circuit Facilities? Frequently, there is no single facility or method of acquisition (lease or purchase) that meets all of the objectives for an ITV system. Distribution can be provided by a number of methods:

1. Cable transmission
2. Microwave
3. 2,500-megahertz (ITFS)
4. Broadcast transmission (generally not acceptable for ITV)

It is very possible that the final distribution system will utilize two or more of these basic methods or a combination that will take advantage of a distribution system that has been installed for another purpose, for example, a community antenna system (CATV) which, incidentally, is basically multiple-channel cable transmission. No formulas exist that can be used to determine the mix except that, as the objectives of the system are determined (including growth objectives), the economies of the various facilities will dictate, in part, the final configuration.

It will be helpful to think of distribution facilities required to fill the following needs:

Intrabuilding. Each building to be connected to the system will require a distribution facility within that building, receiving or originating or a combination of both. The only method practical is cable service. Local distribution facilities can be (1) purchased and installed by the institution or (2) leased from the common carrier (if connected to interbuilding service) or private companies specializing in the lease of this type of facility. As a general rule, most institutions find ownership of intrabuilding services most practical. In some cases, the use of a combination of privately owned and leased services might be the most suitable means of providing intrabuilding service.

Interbuilding. Choice of interbuilding facilities becomes more complicated. Major factors influencing the decision will be property lines, intervening streets, and total distance between buildings. If all buildings to be connected are located on the institution property, the problems of private ownership will be reduced. In any case, a complete comparison of all costs (including negotiations for right-of-way, right-of-way payments, maintenance, etc.) for private ownership should be compared to the lease charges of the common carrier.

Satellite Campuses and Network Connections. Many of the same basic criteria used to determine type and method of providing interbuilding services will be used to determine the service method for satellite campuses and network connections to other institutions. Additional complications will be encountered in acquiring property rights if line-of-sight microwave distribution is the best apparent method of private ownership. Again, the local common carriers should be called upon to supply a proposal for the needed facilities to ensure that the most economical choice is made.

Audiovisual Retrieval for Group Instruction

Preparation of audio and video tapes for sequentialized instruction or general enrichment is a costly process, and to restrict their use to individual or independent study purposes will tend to keep the cost per student high. Extending these tapes to groups of students in classroom situations can provide an effective means of achieving maximum dollar value and, at the same time, provide the classroom instructor with yet another instructional service to complement the course.

A classroom equipped with a telephone line and appropriate speakers can be used by the instructor for Tele-Lecture, direct retrieval of audio tapes from the learning laboratory and, if ITV is available, to request specific TV programs (and also to command stop, start, and replay). Video control today is most economically feasible on a manual basis but, through new developments, direct control will become more feasible. The Carnegie Commission states: "In its consideration of technological advances, the Commission has dealt at times with matters of considerable significance to instructional television. The most important of these are the low cost storage devices, whether by television or by motion picture techniques. The outstanding characteristics of such devices are that they promise to return to the classroom the flexibility that the present use of open circuit broadcasting denies it. The teacher can select the program, play it at the moment of his own choosing, replay it at will in whole or in part, interrupt it for his own comments—in sum, fit the program to the needs of his own classroom as he understands them."

The Group or Classroom Carrel The group or classroom carrel should have available the same basic facilities as the individual carrel, but it is possible to achieve design economies in the classroom by taking advantage of engineering techniques that will take into account anticipated usage.

The individual study carrel is frequently, if not always, engineered to permit maximum use of all locations. For example, a system of 50 carrels will be designed to permit all 50 carrels simultaneous access to the available resources. However, if the same system were extended to 50 classrooms, then the probability of all 50 classrooms simultaneously using the retrieval capabilities would be extremely remote. It is on this probability theory that engineers efficiently design classroom systems which require less equipment to provide access and which, therefore, can be provided at lower cost than the individual-access arrangements.

The concept of probable access (the standard basis for the design of almost all telephonic switchgear) also introduces the possibility of establishing "mini" carrels throughout the campus and community by interconnecting the basic telephone system to the learning laboratory.

INDIVIDUAL APPLICATIONS

Audio-video Retrieval

As the learning laboratory expands from the individual student carrel (and group location) to the dormitory, off-campus housing locations, and the community itself, a number of new and complex factors must be considered. This is particularly true because in most instances this growth will mean a tie-in with the basic campus telephone service (especially if dormitory Centrex service is available) and possibly to the local telephone exchange service as well.

Dormitory Access Providing Centrex telephone stations in dormitory rooms is becoming increasingly common. Initially, dormitory-room telephone service was installed to provide the student with easy access to the outside world. The dormitory telephone also became helpful to the student and teacher as an alternative to face-to-face meeting in the instructor's office. Now a new and instructionally oriented use is being made of the dormitory telephone—access to the learning laboratory.

The benefits to the institution that can extend the resources of its learning laboratory to the resident locations of the students are numerous. Among them are:

1. Increased use of the taped or recorded material, which becomes available 24 hours a day

2. An increase in the number of study carrels without capital outlay, since every telephone becomes a "mini" (part-time) carrel

3. Reduction in traffic (vehicle and pedestrian) on the campus and in the learning laboratory

4. The complementing of continuing education courses by permitting "at home" attendance of lectures

The method used by students to access the desired tape has a great deal to do with the total cost of extending the learning laboratory beyond its building confines. Some schools have installed special telephones with direct-wire connections to the campus learning laboratory. This method is one of the simplest and, in some cases, the least expensive, but it has the specific disadvantage of requiring the *special* telephone location. Although this might not be the ultimate way of remote-access, it should not be overlooked as a starter arrangement to provide experience for the students and to develop faculty confidence in this instructional aid.

Use of the existing dial telephone in the dormitory or the off-campus residence locations will require more effort in the area of equipment specifications and in the administration of the day-to-day use of the system.

Access Techniques Some techniques of access and comments on the value of each are given below:

The Media Staff Technique. Students and faculty gain access to the recording wanted by selecting a tape out of a catalog of subjects, dialing the learning laboratory (information resource center or multimedia library) and asking the staff at the center to play the desired tape.

This technique, the simplest and least expensive method of extending the resources of the learning laboratory, was also one of the first techniques to be used in education. The University of Wisconsin has for several years offered this service to doctors in that state on a charge-free basis by using inward WATS telephone service. (Inward WATS is flat-rate incoming long-distance service.) The technique does not require rigid predetermination of tape demand; consequently tape playout equipment is kept to a minimum.

Two main disadvantages exist with this technique:

1. It requires an attendant.

2. It permits only one person to listen to a given tape at a time, requiring duplicate (or multiple) copies of tapes in cases of high tape demand.

The Direct-access Technique. Individuals, in this case, gain access to the information wanted by dialing direct the number of the tape that has been selected from the catalog of subjects.

This technique involves an arrangement whereby each tape in the catalog has its own playout device and telephone access line associated with it. Only one person at a time may listen to the tape. It is easy to see that a system built exclusively around this technique would be extremely costly. If used for tapes that have low-volume demand and are of longer duration, in conjunction with one or more of the other techniques, direct access can be economically feasible.

The Scheduled-access Technique. This method enables a number of individuals to gain access to information on a program schedule basis by dialing the learning laboratory at a specified time of the day. This technique offers the most economical method of dial access to the laboratory. Thirty or more students may listen to the same tape (only one audio playout device is required) at the same time. The instructor can assign students times to call the tape (each class could be offered, for example, three access times, 9:30 A.M., 2:30 P.M., and 8:30 P.M.). In this manner, a class or several sections of one course can listen to the tape with a minimum of equipment dedication. Those students missing the assigned time can call for the tape later, as described in the media staff technique (above).

The Random-access Technique. By this method a number of individuals can gain access to information. One individual or many individuals may listen to any tape out of the catalog of subjects at any time by simply dailing the tape code number at the laboratory.

The random-access method, although offering the greatest flexibility, can also be the most expensive in terms of dollars per student use. Low-demand tape must be afforded the same playout facilities as high-demand tape. As the number of "online" tapes (tapes available by dialing) increases, total costs for equipment will increase with a multiplier effect.

The Special-arrangement Technique. Depending on the goals and objectives of the institution, almost any combination of the preceding techniques can be designed into a single medium or multimedia arrangement. Such an arrangement is potentially the most desirable in terms of satisfying instructional objectives while minimizing costs.

Computer-aided Instruction (CAI)

The use of the modern computer as an instructional aid is, as Dr. Edward Maltzman points out (Chapter 11, "Learning Laboratories and Independent-study Services"), one of today's most exciting topics for discussion. The value of the computer as a tutorial aid to learning has been established, and students across the country are beginning to reap the rewards of this newest technique.

Three developments incorporated in the modern computers have made their use practical as an instructional aid:

Multiprogramming. This makes it possible to store more than one program, ready for near-instantaneous use, and allows shifts from program to program to be made with high-speed efficiency.

Multiprocessing. This makes it possible to do several jobs "simultaneously."

Multiple Access. This provides many in and out "doors" to the computer.

The multiple-access development makes possible and practicable classroom or individual study carrel access to a remotely located computer. Coupled with the computer's ability to be multiprogrammed and to multiprocess input and output, not only can we have remote terminals but numerous students can have near-simultaneous attention from one computer.

Without the remote-access communications capabilities of the computer, it seems that there could be little use of computers as an instructional aid. Subordinate only to the software itself, the communications terminal (input/output devices) and the communications link are of prime importance to a productive CAI program.

Terminal Gear Input/output (I/O) devices range from relatively low-speed punched card transmission terminals to high-speed magnetic tape terminals. For CAI, terminal-gear requirements are most often met with these devices:

Touch-Tone Telephones.[2] When the computer is equipped with an audio-response unit, a student can use a keyboard-only device. For example, a student using Touch-Tone telephones in the classroom, study carrel, dormitory room, or even from a distant campus could call the computer (just as in dialing a regular telephone call) and, using a guide outline, in one instance, answer a series of sequentialized questions by means of the telephone's pushbuttons. The computer can evaluate the answers and then reinforce or advance as the student's individual requirements dictate. Another example of keyboard input-voice output would be the use of the computer by the student as a highly efficient slide rule in the solution of routine problems which otherwise would be relatively mechanical in nature and would consume much time. The result is error-

[2] Trademark of Bell System. Similar phones are provided by other telephone companies and manufacturers.

free calculations that will permit the students to do more problems and get more practice in setting them up.

Teletypewriters. Alphabetic and numeric input is accomplished by use of the keyboard and output is by means of a printing mechanism. This device will generally meet most of the requirements of a computer-assisted instruction program and is well suited for the task. Its typewriter characteristics are familiar to students and the printing mechanism provides a retainable (hard) copy of the work performed, useful to the student for reference during the exercise or for the instructor's use later.

These devices can be leased or purchased, used on private-line or telephone-exchange service, and are compatible with almost all computer systems.

Visual Display Terminals. Visual display terminals, also known as cathode ray tubes (CRTs), provide visual presentation of information stored within a computer system. Transmission from the terminal is accomplished by a keyboard similar to that of a teletypewriter and output is on a visual display screen similar to a television screen. The main advantage is generally considered to be the speed with which the readout by the operator can be accomplished. The screen itself is filled with information from the computer almost instantly and can be retained until read or longer (but not indefinitely). It can then be erased and the screen is ready for the next output sequence. If review of material presented is required, a teleprinter can be used to record the transmitted material or the computer can be readdressed and the information re-presented.

Graphic presentations from the computer can be displayed on the CRT. Some CRT devices permit entering or altering graphic presentation by use of a light pen attached to the terminal. This feature has many advantages when the CAI application can benefit from the presentation of graphics in much the same way as Tele-Lecture presentations can benefit from telewriting transmission.

Connection of Terminal to Computer Space will not permit a complete discussion of all the facilities that can be used to connect the terminal to the computer. Many of the same considerations that must be weighed in ITV distribution are also applicable to CAI systems, that is, the number of buildings, distance, volume of circuits required, etc.

Generally, all CAI applications will be requirements, in a sense, for real-time access to the computer. The speed of the real-time access will be governed by the speed of the student in entry and reading of output from the computer.

A single terminal can be used for access to more than one computer. For example, student A might want access to the institution's own computer for a given course, but student B, using the terminal next, might be assigned a CAI exercise with the distant computer of another institution or private computer utility. For this reason, to ensure maximum use of the terminal gear, all possible course applications should be completely analyzed before a decision is made on a communications facility. Cost and flexibility both must be considered.

A more extensive discussion of the specific facilities (telephone exchange, broadband, Telpak, etc.) that can be utilized for the connection of CAI terminals to the computer is presented in Chapter 10 of Section 7 in the companion volume.

Shared-time Computer Use Any new instructional aid will generally encounter obstacles in its introductory stage that tend to minimize its total effectiveness. Costs and faculty understanding are two of these obstacles. In addition, development of software (the program) is a major consideration.

Timesharing might offer a means to overcome or at least reduce the impact of these barriers. The potential of sharing a computer with another institution or a computer utility can substantially reduce the cost of an initial CAI project and, at the same time, serve to acquaint the academic community with the values of CAI as a tutorial aid.

In some instances even the software problem can be minimized by the use of shared-time computer facilities. It might be possible to utilize another institution's program intact and, in the process, gain a better understanding of program techniques.

EDUCATIONAL NETWORK CONCEPTS

The concept of a network implies sharing. An educational network, more specifically an instructional network, to meet the context of this chapter, means the sharing of instructional resources. Simply, it is the application of hardware (communication links) to increase the total usefulness of the instructional software.

Replies to a July 1966 questionnaire sent out by the EDUNET Task Force on Information Networks to EDUCOM institutional representatives are helpful in establishing goals for any such network. "The reasons given for wanting a network terminal were varied. They included, among others, the desire to obtain more effective communications with other universities; to use specialized teaching talent at other institutions; to have access to specialized library resources; to share computer facilities; to interconnect with planned or existing internal networks and statewide networks; to have a means of studying file organization, executive routines, interface problems, systems compatibility, query constraints and other important problems in the information sciences; and to be able to introduce locally generated information into a national distribution system." These varied reasons for interest in the network concept can be categorized into objectives to fill the needs of:

1. Administration
2. Instruction (including library services)
3. Institutional research (including clinical services)
4. Professional services to educators

The design and implementation of a communications network to meet all of the above needs is complex and will require complete interaction between administrator and educator to ensure optimum standards of design. It will be necessary to gather and analyze the facts and relate them to the objectives in order to determine the specifications for:

1. Distribution. In addition to deciding upon the institutions which will be on the network, including the number and location of buildings at each institution, it is necessary to establish the patterns of communications, that is, which locations will receive and from whom and which location can transmit and to whom. A combination of distribution patterns will evolve that will include transmitting and receiving from one to one, one to many, many to one, and many to many.

2. Volume. If the network under consideration is to be a multimedia system, then all volumes of anticipated use must be calculated. This can range from voice communications for Tele-Lecture, to data transmission for CAI, to ITV program distribution. Maximum day use and peak hour demand must be calculated.

3. Urgency. Must all uses of the network be on a real-time basis—that is, in effect, live transmission? Would the addition of videotape recorders at specific locations permit "off-hour" transmission of video tapes for replay later? In effect, priorities are established for all uses to be included in the network.

4. Language. Language is related to transmission in two ways. First, the physical form of transmission and receiving, that is, what types of terminal gear will be required (teleprinters, voice, visual display tubes, etc.), and, secondly, the "code" that will be used to store and transmit the information. The first area, physical form, will be of great interest to the instructor and the instructional resource people and will determine the "code" information for the programmers.

5. Accuracy. In addition to consideration of "error rates" of the transmission and receiving facilities the overall quality required will have to be determined. For ex-

ample, if the network is to carry voice services for audio retrieval, what frequencies will be required to utilize all course applications? As the quality increases, so does the cost.

It follows that the objectives and specifications determined for the above must now be related to costs. This will generally require the laying out of several alternative communications systems. It is easy to see that the counsel of a qualified expert in the field of telecommunications is a necessity for the proper design of any communication system or network.

Network Concepts Applied to Library Services

The use of communications techniques to extend and increase the value of the basic catalyst of education, the instructor, has been discussed. The use of library services as an additional support for instructional aids will depend on the configuration of the services rendered by the library. "*Library-type resources* (books, periodicals, reports, etc.). This is *the* basic formal information resource. It is largely underexploited, probably from habit and the staid image of libraries. Both data processing requirements and the network idea are forcing and will demand, for self-preservation, a definite move from passive to a more active role."[3]

The "move" referred to in the EDUNET conference need not be delayed until an extensive educational network is developed but can begin with a more or less simple improvement in library communications. Several cooperative library groups are now using teleprinters (frequently service is being provided by common carriers through the use of teletypewriter exchange service or TWX) to extend the resources of each member library. Cooperative lending arrangements are greatly facilitated by the use of two-way written communications. Introduce low-cost facsimile transmission devices into such a cooperative arrangement and the actual pages of a book, etc., can be transmitted within minutes.

An illustration of the use of teleprinters and communications to combine the resources of a group of libraries can be found in a description of a system in operation in the state of Virginia today. The University of Virginia has an excellent library. In addition there are the libraries of several other institutions, including Virginia Polytechnic Institute, the College of William and Mary, the Virginia Military Institution, the Virginia Institute of Marine Science, Old Dominion College, the Medical College of Virginia, and the Virginia Institute for Scientific Research. Each of the libraries is linked with the others by means of common-carrier teletypewriter exchange service, making the facilities of all readily available to any one of them.

The University of Virginia Library is additionally equipped with a teletypewriter used as an I/O device to a computer in which all the library volumes will be recorded, ready for immediate reference by other Virginia libraries. Depending on their length, inquiries may be received as page copy and on eight-channel punched paper tape on the teletypewriter, which operates automatically and does not need to be attended most of the time. The paper tape so produced can be fed directly into the computer and its output, also produced on the same eight-channel tape, can be used to transmit the answer back to the inquiring location automatically.

These facilities can be used in many ways, such as arranging for interlibrary loans of books, films, and other materials; confirming research efforts, helping to find alternate sources for needed material, speeding up orders for photo duplicating, providing copies of loan and other transactions for the record, and for general administrative purposes. This means of "instant" communication among libraries makes in-

[3] G. W. Brown et al. (eds.), *EDUNET—Report of the Summer Study on Information Networks Conducted by the Interuniversity Communications Council (EDUCOM)*, John Wiley & Sons, Inc., New York, 1967, pp. 37–60.

formation more broadly available to Virginia industries, many of which have teletypewriters of their own and, through the library, to any organization or any citizen of the state.

In addition to this intrastate service, the University library has access, via teletypewriter exchange service, to libraries all over the country and to the many thousands of business, government, and private organizations listed in the teletypewriter exchange-service directory. Under Virginia's program, even a small college library can now reach out and get information almost anywhere and get it in the form of an accurate printout.

Multimedia Libraries

Today's library is still basically a depository for printed material. To increase the quality of today's facility it is common practice to build a new floor, establish an annex, or in some other way increase the physical capacity to store printed material. In view of the information explosion a natural question is: "How big can libraries get?"

Sharing of materials is a partial answer, but this alone will not be enough to meet ever-mounting demands. Libraries will have to become multimedia service centers linked together in networks that will permit retrieval of information in multiple form; high-speed facsimile, video tapes, audio tapes, films (conventional and microfilms), in addition to the standard printed material. The evolution of a national knowledge network will link together local information centers with state, regional, and national information centers. Specialized materials available in industry or technical libraries will also be interconnected. The information available from this network will be extended to students and teachers at almost any location through modern communications technology, adding a valuable new dimension to education.

SELECTED READINGS

Brown, G. W. et al. (eds.): *EDUNET—Report of the Summer Study on Information Networks Conducted by the Interuniversity Communications Council (EDUCOM)*, John Wiley & Sons, Inc., New York, 1967.

Bushnell, D. D., and D. W. Allen (eds.): *The Computer in American Education*, John Wiley & Sons, Inc., New York, 1967.

Gentle, Edgar C., Jr. (ed.): *Data Communications in Business—An Introduction*, Publishers Service Co., New York, 1966.

Lecklider, J. C. R.: *Libraries of the Future*, The M.I.T. Press, Cambridge, Mass., 1966.

Chapter **10**

Programmed Learning Services

ALVIN KENT

Director, Office of Educational Resources, Northeastern University, Boston, Massachusetts

INTRODUCTION

Of all the media being considered at the college level, programmed learning is the one which at first appears to require the least administrative involvement and support. However, a programmed learning service supported by both the administration and faculty can frequently represent the cornerstone of a more systematic approach to dealing with instructional problems.

In this chapter we will examine the rationale for establishing a programmed learning service, discuss the advantages that accrue to both faculty and staff from an organized effort in this area, describe the operational ramifications for such a service and, finally, develop the guidelines for its administration at the university or college level. A brief review of programmed learning covering some definitions, its history, a few outstanding characteristics, and the general state of the art will provide common ground for the discussion to follow.

OVERVIEW OF PROGRAMMED LEARNING

What Is Programmed Learning? In any general definition of programmed learning, it should be noted first that we are concerned with matching instruction to individual learning capabilities. To support this approach to learning, the programmer must employ a variety of highly specialized though not really unfamiliar techniques in preparing and presenting the teaching materials. These techniques are designed to keep learning within prescribed, manageable, and, above all, observable limits. Through constant response feedback and the continued use of criterion measures like unit tests, progress checks, and pre- and post-tests, the method also provides for determination of subject-matter mastery at every stage of the learning experience.

History Programmed learning evolved principally out of the work of three men: Pressey, Skinner, and Crowder. B. F. Skinner of Harvard is widely thought of as the progenitor of this new method, but actually Dr. Sidney L. Pressey of Ohio State University is credited with being the first to develop, back in the 1920s, a modern teaching machine. Unfortunately, the economic depression of the thirties overshadowed any interest the public may have had in improving education, and Pressey, discouraged in spite of positive findings, abandoned this line of research.

The teaching-machine concept lay dormant until 1954, when Dr. Skinner of Harvard published a journal article reporting the events leading up to his development of a teaching machine and a revolutionary approach to learning which he called programmed instruction. With the rising furor over Sputnik's sinister implications concerning U.S. education, Skinner's teaching machine and the methodology underlying the development of programs caught on. The public, ripe for acceptance of educational innovation, reacted with fired imagination.

Three Programming Methods Skinner advocated the use of a teaching device which required the student to construct or write his response. In Skinner's program, which features the *linear* method, the student studies a small bit of material at each step. After he responds to this material by answering a question, filling in a blank, or solving a problem, he immediately compares what he did with the correct response.

Next came Norman A. Crowder, a former researcher for the USAF. He introduced a different version of programmed learning, once again to a receptive educational community. Crowder's program and a specially designed teaching machine featured a *branching* capability. After the student reads a segment of material, he is required to answer a multiple-choice question. If his choice exhibits a lack of understanding, he is automatically branched to a remedial sequence before progressing to new material. While Skinner advocated the strict limitation of error in learning, Crowder allowed, even encouraged, a much higher rate of error in his programs. The best programs developed today combine a judicious blend of both branching and linear techniques.

Pressey's teach-test devices and his approach to programming, the *adjunct* or auto-elucidatory method, was regarded with renewed interest. The adjunct program features a combination of narrative text as it originally appeared in conventional sources and, following immediately after, a set of multiple-choice questions designed to explicate those portions of the material known to cause difficulty.

When all the excitement over novel devices died down, programmers realized that the format used to present the instructional material could in itself constitute a kind of teaching machine. These came to be known as programmed texts. Most programmed material fits quite readily into a programmed text format, and although there are notable exceptions, that is how the majority of our programs are produced today.

What Functions Are Built into Programs? Whether we are talking about a teaching device or a programmed text, we have to consider four functions. First, the instructional vehicle must control the presentation of material. The student reads, sees, or hears the

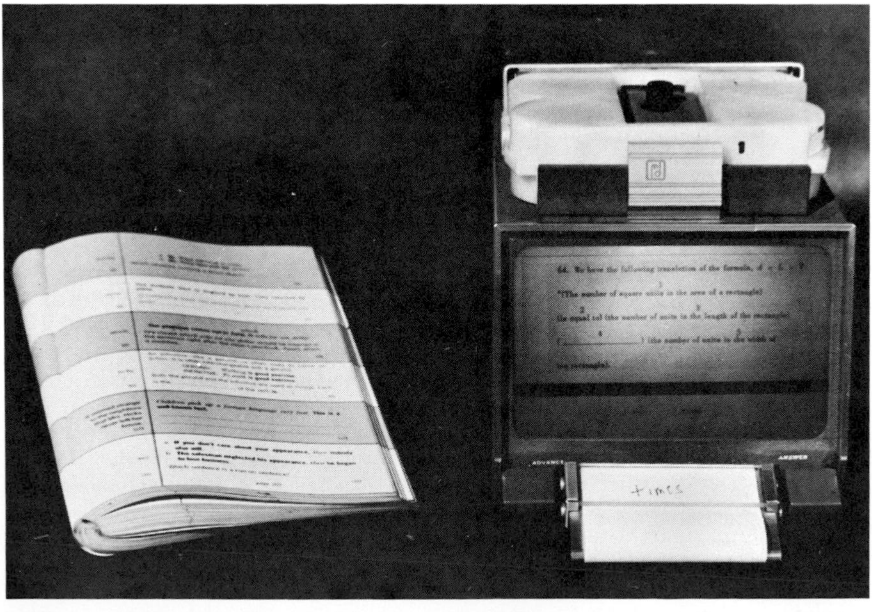

Fig. 1 *Example of a program in printed text and in a teaching machine.*

material in accordance with a prearranged plan. Secondly, the program must control the behavior of the student. He is required to respond to the material, and provisions must be made to guarantee appropriate and correct responses. A third function is the creation and maintenance of the student's motivation. Essentially, this function is assigned to the facility which allows the response to be confirmed. Often this is spoken of as reinforcing the response, but researchers have cautioned that the relationship between knowledge of results and psychological reinforcement is not always demonstrable. Finally, the programmed text must function economically. In a word, the student must learn effectively and at the same time efficiently.

How Does Programmed Learning Work? Programs actually do exemplify a number of significant concepts of learning agreed upon by psychologists and educators. A student generally learns more effectively when the stimulus and response occur close in time, when he receives immediate knowledge of results, when he is able to study at a rate which best suits his individual capabilities, and, as a matter of fact, when he simply has numerous opportunities to interact with and to respond to the subject matter.

Materials that have been programmed exhibit many of the following features which are known generally to promote learning:

1. Specification of the learning goal
2. Analysis of the material into small, manageable steps toward that goal
3. Careful sequencing with respect to the internal logic and complexity of the subject matter
4. Techniques to assure mastery of old steps before the introduction of new steps
5. Revisions of the material based on student tryouts

Programming as a Process Originally, programs were expected to conform to a limited number of acceptable formats. The emphasis has since been shifted from product to *process*. Material is considered programmed not on the basis of what it *looks like* but in terms of its development according to the following set of criteria:

1. An extensive and systematic behavioral analysis of the material to be learned—a breakdown, as it were, of what the student is to do
2. Development of a teaching strategy or learning prescription that is closely tied to this analysis (regardless of its appearance)
3. Modifications of this teaching strategy based on validation procedures and empirical feedback—in other words, revisions of the instructional sequences on the basis of student tryouts

The programmer is, furthermore, expected to provide concrete evidence that these criteria have been met.

CURRENT VIEWS OF PROGRAMMED LEARNING

What Are Some of the Advantages? Programmed learning, when it is systematically developed and effectively administered, contributes a number of singular advantages to most instructional situations. For example, because of the attention paid to planning, preparation, and testing, programs become vehicles which promote quality control over instruction. Each student experiences equal treatment within a framework of continuous evaluation.

Programs facilitate continual activity for the student. Each student selects his own pace for learning, so that slow and fast learners do not interfere with each other's abilities. Different instructional tracks and strategically placed diagnostic sequences are used to shift the student to appropriate learning levels. Ultimately, concern for individual differences results in the development of instructional vehicles that can be depended upon to guarantee a minimum level of achievement for a maximum number of students.

One of the by-products of programmed learning is, almost invariably, a more efficient use of the instructional time. Students are known to complete courses using programs in one-half to three-quarters the usual time, with proficiency levels equal to or even exceeding those achieved through conventional means.

What Are Some of the Developmental Lags? Programmed learning has emerged from its infancy. However, while representing advancements over 1954 that are truly significant, the state of the art reveals a number of areas in which the lag is significant too. We still lack definitive criteria, standards, and guidelines concerning the development and use of programmed materials. Research in this field has too often turned out to be inept or to deal with inappropriate analyses. Provisions for training programmers do not even come close to matching the demand for professional personnel. Hardly any consideration, let alone acknowledgment, has been given to the need for training teachers to use programmed learning. Finally, we find that not enough attention has been given to the unique administrative problems that are generated through the use of programmed learning.

What Do Programs Promise? Whatever deficiencies and shortcomings still persist, we know that the methods used in programmed learning are based on sound, accepted, and tested psychological theory. Further, these methods have the support of much empirical research. The many plus factors inherent in programmed learning are available to the college and university administrator who hopes to help his faculty deal more effectively with the burgeoning demands of education. The following discussion will describe the vital concerns and the critical details involved in organizing a programmed learning service on the college campus.

PROGRAMMED LEARNING AND HIGHER EDUCATION

Rationale On virtually every college campus, whether large or small, the same kinds of instructional problems exist. They differ only in degree. Programmed learning is recognized as one of the possible solutions to dealing with many of these problems, which include instructor shortages, difficulty in reaching large groups of students, upgrading the quality of instruction, broadening the curriculum to cope with the tremendous increases in knowledge, curtailing the high rate of attrition, implementing creative teaching, and others. On the one hand, mass media can be and are being improved to cope with the same problems. On the other hand, programs can perform a function which is beyond the capability of mass media except at a minimal level. Programs have the potential to attend to individual needs.

The Focus on Individual Needs Much has been said and written about programmed learning and individual needs. Admittedly, until the computer becomes the exclusive mediator of programs, the satisfaction of individual learning needs will fall vastly short of the ideal. However, the techniques used to develop programs in their present form, as well as many of the features built into the vehicle itself, represent significant strides in shifting the instructional considerations away from the teacher while focusing insistently on the learner. Such learner orientation has, of course, spilled over to other areas of education. We now find this view very clearly expressed in the systems approach, where the integration of men, machines, and technology represents an optimal plan for meeting the needs of individual learners. Indeed, programmed learning itself, because of its feedback capability and modification procedures, has been described as a miniscule systems approach.[1]

How Are Programs Utilized to Meet Academic Needs? The uses to which programmed learning materials have been put are infinitely varied. At the college and university

[1] See Gabriel D. Ofeish, *Programmed Instruction: A Guide for Management*, American Management Association, New York, 1965.

level, however, utilization is generally described in terms of four principal categories or needs: remedial, enrichment, supplementary, and independent study. We will see that supplementary and independent-study needs originate almost exclusively within the domain of the instructor, while remedial and enrichment needs are generated both through the interaction of the instructor (or administrator) and student and by the student himself.

The following outline and discussion summarize the function of programmed learning materials with respect to each of the four needs:

1. Remedial
   a. Academic standardization
   b. Prerequisite skills
   c. Course skills
2. Enrichment
   a. Course-related instruction
   b. Course-unrelated instruction
3. Supplementary
   a. Course and curriculum extension
   b. Course and curriculum support
4. Independent study
   a. Classroom "lecture" material (including instructor)
   b. Autoinstructional credit courses
      (1) Individual
      (2) Group

Remedial Needs Entering freshmen generally have varying academic backgrounds, each individual being a product of the conservative or progressive orientation of his home community's school system. For example, some school systems do not adequately treat the concepts of modern mathematics. Rather than build a regular course into the curriculum to ensure standardization, specific areas of deficiency are diagnosed for each student and appropriate programmed learning units in modern mathematics are made available on an individual basis.

Students who encounter difficulty in their regular courses will find that programmed materials provide remedial instruction on two levels, prerequisite skills and course skills. Through the use of diagnostic measures, a student determines whether the source of his problem is actually the advanced materials he is studying or his deficiency in the skills which are, in fact, prerequisite to learning the material.

Enrichment Needs When students seek out programmed learning for enrichment purposes, the materials fit into one of two categories. They are intended either to prepare the student for a course he intends to take in the future or else simply to provide him with knowledge and skills in a subject-matter area that interests him. One student may decide to use a program in French to prepare him for taking the course during the following year, while another student may study the subject because he likes to learn as many different languages as possible.

Supplementary Needs Programs provide for supplementary needs in two ways. When insufficient time requires an instructor to exclude altogether certain areas of the subject matter, he can assign programmed units to perform, literally, as his surrogate. In this way he does actually extend curriculum coverage. While the learning of this additional material is wholly independent of class time, the instructor is still able to maintain control of the student's experience by including in any of his evaluations proficiency measures related to the content of the program.

When time does permit coverage of the subject matter in class, the instructor can use programmed units, once again as homework assignments, to *support* his presentation. The program can be used to provide the student with an introduction to the subject matter, or, by following the lecture, with in-depth coverage or even a review of the class discussion.

Independent Study Needs Assigning programmed learning for independent study is also a function delegated exclusively to the instructor. In one version of independent study, the instructor substitutes programmed learning for most of his lecture. The program becomes the primary vehicle of instruction. The instructor remains present during the entire classroom session, identifying and attending to each student's specific study needs as they are manifested in the students' use of the program as well as occasionally delivering, when appropriate, ad hoc or scheduled short presentations. In a sense, he functions as a tutor to each student. To maintain the classroom schedule and still preserve the advantage of self-pacing, students keep the program with them and use it, as they would a text, between sessions. Through the constant use of quick-scoring unit tests, the instructor continues to evaluate each student's performance. When deficiencies become evident, he prescribes review pathways, either in the program or in supplementary material; or, when administratively manageable, he discusses the problem directly with the student.

An alternate approach to independent study for the most part excludes the instructor's classroom involvement. Students may still be scheduled to use their programs—as well as other materials—in group lessons, or they may be permitted to use the program on an individual basis. In either case, a subject-matter consultant—the instructor—is available to the student only intermittently or through remote channels such as written and telephoned requests for assistance. The student operates within a framework of periodic evaluation, which is also used to prescribe remedial measures when necessary. A final evaluation entitles the student to regular course credit when he gives evidence of satisfactory proficiency.

What Are Some Objectives of a Programmed Learning Service? These four categories of study needs provide the focal point for organizing any programmed learning service at the higher education level. The following statement of objectives for such a service is generated out of direct consideration of those needs:

1. To assist the faculty in solving instructional problems
2. To promote the most effective utilization of autoinstructional materials and techniques

Concomitant with such an organization's existence is the pursuit of two additional objectives:

1. To sustain interest in programmed learning among all members of the educational community—including its own faculty
2. To produce empirical evidence as well as to disseminate the results of all appropriate research for guiding the development and application of programmed materials and techniques

If a programmed learning service is expected to achieve these four objectives, the organization that is established must be geared to carry out a number of significant functions. Next, we will turn our attention to the requirements and steps involved in establishing such a service.

ORGANIZING A PROGRAMMED LEARNING SERVICE

To provide an institution of higher learning with facilities and service for developing and administering programmed learning media, it is convenient to consider three groups: the program-development group, the program-implementation group, and the program-utilization group.

Figure 2 illustrates how three such groups can be organized. While other representations are certainly feasible, the discussion that follows is based on this organizational chart.

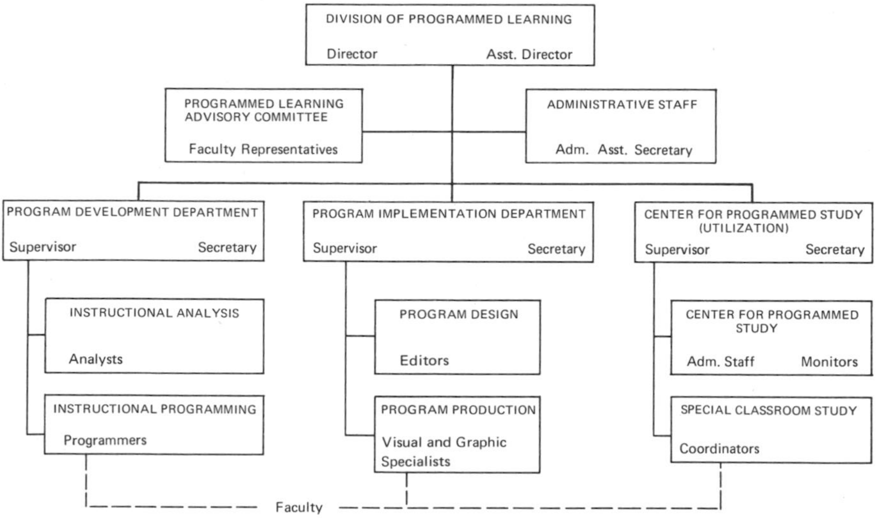

Fig. 2 *Organization chart of a division of programmed learning identifying elements and personnel. Such an organization may function as an autonomous unit, part of an instructional resources service organization, or attached to a particular college or school.*

The Program-development Group This group collaborates with members of the faculty from various departments and colleges in (1) developing new programs, and (2) adapting commercially available programs to better meet the needs of students.

For any given project, the faculty member, together with a member of the program development group, is an equal partner in a team of instructional designers. On rare occasions, the programmer is able to function as his own subject-matter expert, and on even rarer occasions the faculty member is able to function as his own programmer.

Development Group Personnel The program development group is made up of personnel whose backgrounds and experience are associated either directly or indirectly with learning psychology, educational psychology, curriculum planning, industrial training, systems analysis, or commercial programming. Additional experience or training in a particular discipline may qualify certain programmers to concentrate their major effort with faculty in related subject-matter areas. For example, a programmer with a strong background in mathematics or the sciences may specialize in dealing with engineering faculty. At a university, the effectiveness of the service benefits greatly when each programmer, on the basis of his background, is assigned as the liaison between the organization and a specific college or group of related colleges. This approach enables qualified personnel to become thoroughly familiar with the instructional problems and needs prevailing in each area.

What Are the Elements of Program Development? After the instructional problem has been identified and analyzed and the decision has been reached to develop new programmed materials, the programmer and subject-matter expert continue working in joint sessions during the initial phases of development. In a later phase, the programmer may write the material himself or train the faculty member to do the writing while he functions as editor. Finally, the programmer may carry out the validation procedures almost independently, calling on his collaborator only for special counsel.

All together, there are four distinct stages involved in the development of an instructional program. These stages may be summarized as follows:

1. Identifying and defining the problem
2. Analyzing the subject matter in terms of behavior and content
3. Producing the program
4. Field testing the finished product

The third stage very clearly evolves from the first and second stages, but all three are tied into a number of interrelated activities. The fourth stage, on the other hand, cannot be initiated until all phases of one, two, and three are complete.

Developing programs according to the procedure just described requires that the group perform the following functions on a routine basis:

1. Consult with faculty on instructional matters.
2. Apply known principles of learning and strategies of teaching to instructional design
3. Integrate appropriate technology into the solution of all instructional problems
4. Supervise the efforts of faculty and other subject-matter experts in the production of programmed learning materials

How Are Programs Adapted? Adapting programmed material originally developed for other student groups represents a task which is both time consuming and well worth doing. Commercially available programs abound on a wide variety of topics and at many different levels. If a suitable program is located, the time, effort, and cost involved in adapting the material for one's own student population is infinitely less than undertaking the initial development of a program. The problem lies in finding programs which have been proven effective and which come close to matching the needs of your students.

Where it is possible to select a program that has been developed for a population similar to yours and which is based on instructional objectives and content comparable to your own curriculum requirements, the next step is to tailor the given material into an even closer match through modification and supplements. The staff can bring to bear a wide variety of adaptive techniques: supplementary programmed units, supplementary text materials, keyed textbook references, simulation exercises, extended practice and review sequences, diagnostic measures, achievement-test batteries, progress checks, and so forth. For example, a commercially available paper-and-pencil program on arithmetic for nurses was upgraded with simulation exercises that required students to practice preparing drugs and solutions using a doctor's order form, placebos, and actual pharmaceutical equipment. A lengthy algebra program was converted into a series of modular units through the use of a carefully constructed diagnostic entry examination. Additional tests, progress checks, vocabulary exercises, and supplementary vocabulary tests were all used to adapt a commercially available text/tape language program to the needs of first-year college students.

The adaptation of a commercially available program also follows from the analysis of an instructional problem. In this case, the faculty member and program-development staff member, working conjointly, are fortunate to locate an existing suitable program. As with developing programs, adapting programs involves four stages:

1. Identifying and defining the problem
2. Evaluating the selected program by inspection
3. Adapting the program to better meet the needs of students
4. Field testing the finished product

Although the purposes of the first and second stages here differ from those in the development of programs, all three stages are actually comparable since the evaluation process requires a careful analysis of the existing program's objectives and content. The fourth stage for the adaptation of programs can be considered identical in all respects with that of the fourth stage for the development of programs.

The adaptation of programs requires that the program-development group add the routine performance of the following two functions to the first four:

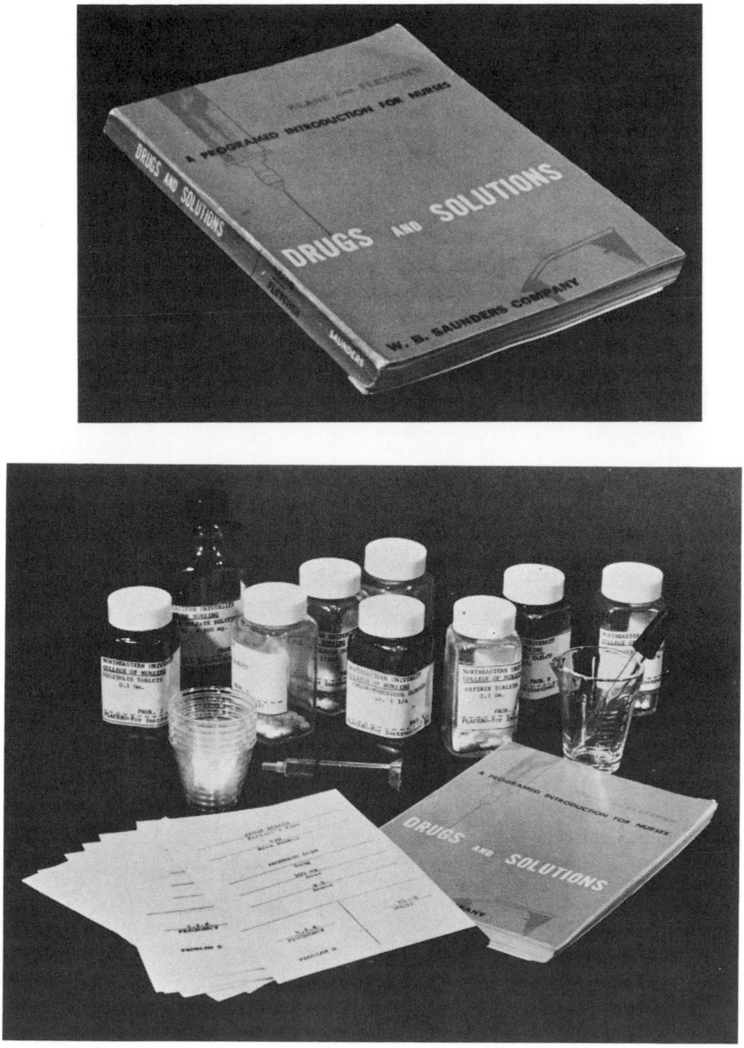

Fig. 3 *The upper photograph represents a program in its original form. The lower photograph shows the necessary changes needed in the program to achieve the stated objective.*

5. Assist subject-matter experts in selecting commercially available programmed learning materials

6. Devise techniques for adapting commercially available programmed materials to specific needs of students

The Program-development Process The procedures followed by the program-development group in developing or adapting programmed materials are charted in Figure 4. Each step presupposes that the subject-matter expert and behavioral specialist are either engaged in active collaboration with one another or pursuing individually the consequences of a mutual decision.

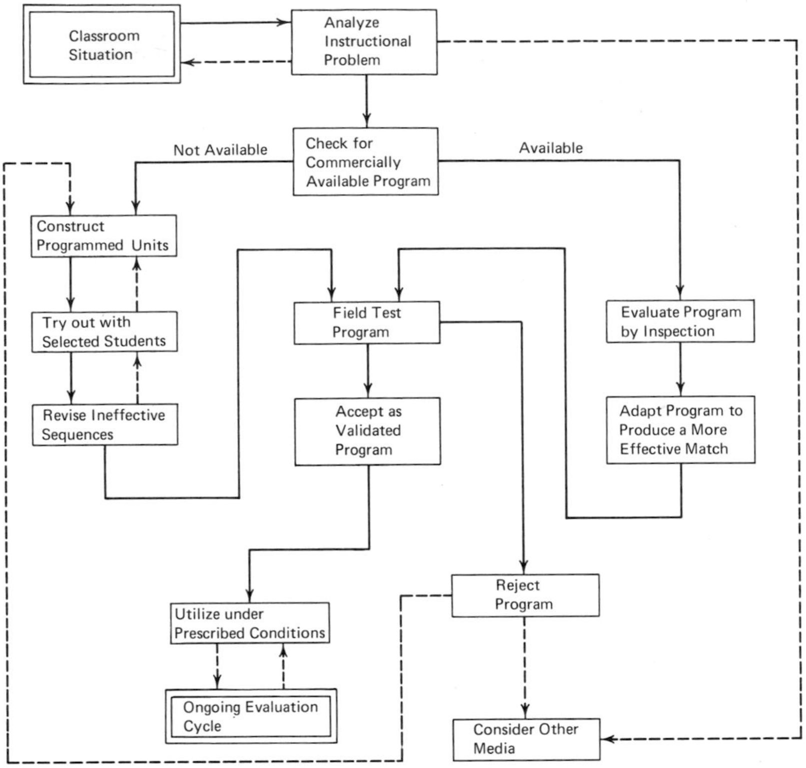

Fig. 4 *Chart of program development procedures.*

We begin by assuming that each problem brought to the attention of the development group is associated in some way with a classroom situation. Generally, a faculty member brings the instructional problem to the group, as represented by the solid arrow in Figure 4, but there are occasions when the behavioral specialist, through observation, identifies a problem where none was thought to exist. This contingency is represented by the broken arrow leading back from the analysis step to the classroom situation. Both the program-development staff member and the instructor analyze the instructional problem. If the use of programmed instruction is warranted, checking for commercially available programs becomes the next step. Should an analysis of the instructional problem rule out the use of programs as an appropriate solution, the instructor is then advised to follow an alternate route (the broken arrow in Figure 4) leading to the consideration of some other more appropriate instructional medium.

When a commercially available program is located, the collaborating members, operating literally as an instructional design team, next evaluate the program by inspection, methodically comparing its record of development, pedagogical features, and content structure with established standards as well as specific requirements. If acceptable, gaps in the program are identified and adaptation techniques are applied to produce a more effective match with students' needs.

Should any material located prove unsuitable, the alternate route as shown in Figure 4 would lead directly to rejection of the program. At this juncture, the instructor is also in a position to consider other media or perhaps to follow the route that would initiate the development of original programmed material.

When adaptation has been undertaken and completed, the new package is then field tested among a relatively large group of representative students. The purpose of the field test is to determine whether the program is actually effective and could be used with additional classes, or whether it is ineffective and should be rejected as unsuitable for further use among the instructor's students. If successful, the program is accepted as a validated medium of instruction. Students assigned to or interested in the material will then be advised to use the program under study conditions which are known to produce maximum results.

If the check for a commercially available program turns up nothing, the subject-matter expert and the programmer proceed through the steps involved in developing a program. Construction of programmed units, tryouts with selected students, and revision of ineffective sequences are depicted serially but represent steps taken in either direction (as indicated with solid and broken arrows in Figure 4). Construction, tryouts, and revisions can function only as interdependent phases in the development of programmed units.

When these phases have been completed, the next step is to field test the developed material among a relatively large group of representative students. If all or, more probably, parts of the program are found to be ineffective, rejection of this material generally leads back to redesign, construction, tryouts, and revisions. Final acceptance as a validated program, one that reliably produces a satisfactory proficiency level among the instructor's students, qualifies the material to be utilized more widely under prescribed conditions.

After reaching this phase, as illustrated in Figure 4, both developed and adapted programs continue to undergo periodic evaluation. Such a review procedure is necessary to guarantee that rapidly changing academic needs will be met with upgraded programmed materials.

Within the process we have just described, two additional functions can now be observed. The aforementioned list of six will be extended by the following:

7. Develop and refine evaluation techniques
8. Evaluate the effectiveness of all programmed learning materials developed or adapted under supervision of the service organization

The Program-implementation Group This group provides support in designing and preparing the formats recommended for developed and adapted materials. In consultation with programmers and subject-matter experts, qualified personnel will fabricate programmed material and teaching-machine formats as well as modified formats for adapted programs. They will select or devise prescribed audiovisual materials, construct simulation exercises, and plan and execute the development of supplementary subject-matter guides, word lists, keyed references, and other related materials. Although a great many of the tasks in which this group engages seem to be clerical in nature, a considerable degree of creative effort is involved.

The Program-utilization Group The third group is assigned the responsibility of administering the finished product to students whose use of programs results from the needs described earlier. A study center is recommended to provide this utilization service.

Philosophy of Independent Study Some research and extensive experience indicate that programmed materials produce much more efficient and effective results when students, at any level, use them under supervised conditions rather than in remote and isolated surroundings, as, for example, at home or in the dormitories. There is no reason why independent study—of which programmed learning is a part—cannot be pursued in a structured environment. In fact, if the environment is geared to attend to students' study needs, the independent study situation cannot help but benefit. Moreover, one of the basic features of independent study, self-pacing, is in no way impaired when the student is required to use programmed material in a monitored study center.

What Is the Ideal Configuration of a Study Center? A study center designed to administer programmed learning should be centrally located. If possible, this facility should also be situated in or near a location which normally accommodates long hours of student self-study, as, for example, the library. The center, too, should be available to students for many hours during each day and on weekends as well. It should exist, however, as a separate facility, no matter where the location, and should depend for its supervision on personnel drawn from the programmed learning service organization.

Such a facility should contain separate areas for (1) study, (2) administration, (3) counseling, and (4) large class groups. A moderate-sized installation would be expected to accommodate 25 to 30 students each hour, and by remaining open from early morning to late evening, it could make available to students as many as 3,000 study/space hours each week.

1. The *study area* is best furnished with individual carrels, some of which should be enclosed with acoustical insulators to provide a suitable environment for studying language programs or any other instruction involving audio tapes. A limited number of carrels can even provide for conversion to a small group-study space. Each carrel need be equipped with no more than an electrical outlet to accommodate the variety of powered devices which could be used to mediate instructions: a tape playback, a slide projector, a single concept cartridge film projector, a TV monitor or portable videotape recorder and playback system, or an automatic teaching machine. A more

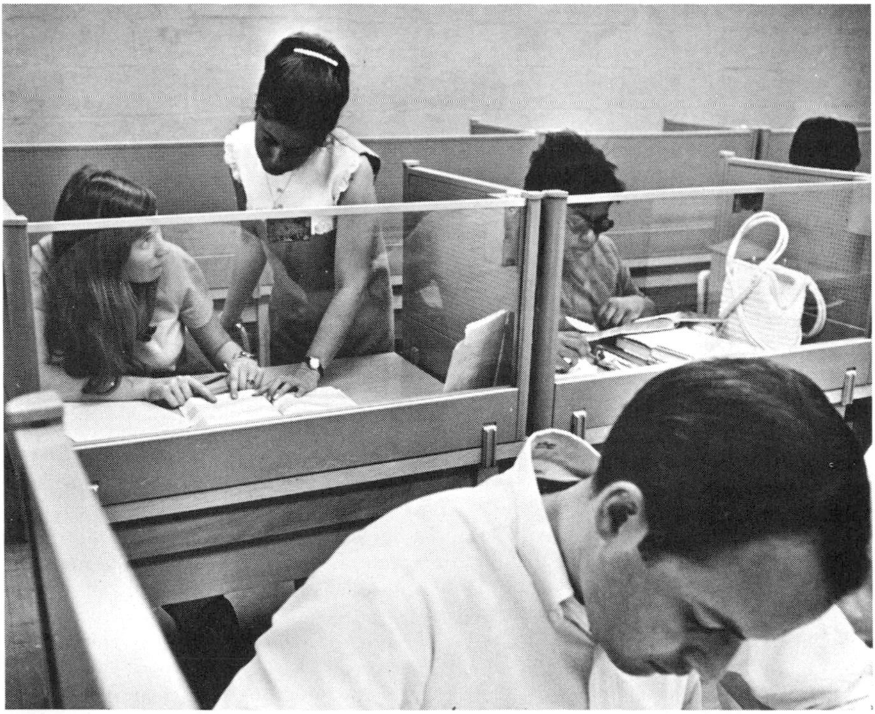

Fig. 5 *A programmed learning study center providing individual student carrels.*

sophisticated installation could, of course, make all of these media available through a centralized, remote, dial-access system.

2. The *administrative area* is designed to facilitate scheduling of students, processing of programmed materials for use by students, test distribution and scoring, and record keeping. Computerizing each of these functions represents a feasible and, when the load is large enough, desirable approach. However, conventional administrative techniques are suitable in most instances. The anticipated peak-traffic flows should guide consideration of the physical space allocated for administration.

3. The *counseling area,* if possible, should afford the privacy of a detached space or separate room. The area is used to orient students coming into the facility for the first time, to acquaint the student with the administrative aspects of the program he intends to study, and to discuss with him subject-matter deficiencies that are disclosed either through his test score and progress records or through his complaints of difficulty with specific portions of the program.

4. The *large subject-matter group area* will accommodate regularly scheduled classes assigned to use the same program under the study center's supervision. Such a sporadic activity is probably best carried out in a multipurpose space.

Study Center Personnel The center should have a full-time supervisor whose professional background and training involve some of the aspects of education or counseling. When the center provides a day and evening schedule, the responsibility for running the center is best divided between the supervisor and a full-time assistant. The remainder of the personnel needs can be satisfied adequately through the use of graduate assistants, who are assigned the specific counseling tasks, and part-time student workers, who can handle, routinely, the clerical tasks as well as, occasionally, some counseling tasks.

Although the operation of the center is relatively autonomous, the efforts of the personnel are guided by the team originally responsible for the program. Each of the personnel should be encouraged to depend on and confer with the program-development group for solutions to pedagogical problems and with the instructor for solutions to subject-matter problems.

What Are the Functions of a Study Center? The center's primary responsibility is to administer programs placed under its supervision by members of the program-development group, who have acted directly in response to faculty- and student-related needs. In its operation, the center would supplement this responsibility by surveying from its vantage point the subject-matter needs and interests of students and by communicating the results to the program-development group and the appropriate instructor.

The techniques applied by persons other than subject-matter experts when counseling with students on their difficulties with portions of the program are predicated on the assumption that a high percentage of these contingencies results from sources other than actual lack of understanding of the subject matter. For example, merely accompanying the student over a careful review of material reported as difficult may turn out to be the solution to a careless first reading. The low percentage of problems actually resulting from content sources are, of course, turned over to the subject-matter expert. Identifying the source of the problem and applying the appropriate solution are the principal functions of center personnel.

The functions of the center can be based on one of a variety of plans to provide service to students. These plans may be summarized as follows:

1. All materials are made available free of charge to all students.
2. There is no charge to full-time students or any student assigned a programmed course; a moderate fee is charged to all others.
3. All students are required to pay a moderate fee.
4. Students buy the programs they use and are furnished with the peripheral materials free of charge.

For plans one, two, and three, it is assumed that the program is treated in a way which leaves it reusable.

Finally, the center is expected to set up guidelines for instructors who elect to administer directly in their classrooms programs developed or adapted by the development group.

ADMINISTRATIVE CONSIDERATIONS

Besides the eight operational functions enumerated above, a programmed learning service organization would be expected to perform the following:

1. Conduct courses, workshops, and institutes pertaining to the development and utilization of programs
2. Provide consultant services to the educational community
3. Conduct research and surveys in all areas of programmed learning
4. Assist the administration in formulating policies and plans to govern the role and rights of faculty in developing and utilizing programmed materials

A service organization of this kind must be able to depend on administrative counsel and subject-matter expertise. We recommend the establishment of an advisory panel (see Figure 2) drawn from the administrative body of the institution, for example, college deans in the case of a university or department heads in the case of a college. Members of a consultant panel, responsible for subject-matter support, should be officially assigned from individual departments.

What Are Some of the Financial Aspects? The major portion of financial support for such an organization, if it is to remain viable as a service, should come from institutional funds. Research funds are not to be discouraged, but this source of support should not be allowed to predominate.

A moderate-sized programmed learning service can be established for an estimated $100,000. This amount would include the costs involved in the conversion of existing plant space and the addition of capital equipment (approximately $15,000) as well as operating expenses such as salaries, production, purchasing student work materials, and collecting a library of programs. Geographical location and future price trends would obviously have an effect on the proposed estimate.

Space allocations would provide for 900 square feet of office area devoted to program development and implementation and 1,500 square feet devoted to program utilization. To accommodate program utilization, the 1,500 square feet would be divided into a study area, an administrative control area, a library area and, for the multiple copies of programs, a storage area, all of these comprising the units of a center for programmed study. The study area would consist of 25 to 30 independent study carrels, each with an electrical power source for plugging in a tape recorder/playback, a slide or film-loop projector, or even a teaching machine. Initially, the purchase of such powered devices would be kept at a minimum. The administrative control area would provide for counseling activity and ample record-keeping facilities. While a substantial investment would be made to establish the core of a library of programs and the necessary shelving, upgrading the collection would be carried on over a period of years. Equipping the space devoted to program development and implementation would require the purchase of regular office furniture and devices. Provision should be made as well for a small conference area.

The personnel required to staff a moderate-sized service would consist of director, division secretary, supervisor of program development (who would combine instructional analysis with a programming function), one assistant programmer, supervisor of program implementation, supervisor of the center for programmed study, one administrative assistant for the center, three graduate assistants for the center, and the equivalent of three full-time monitors for the center (drawn possibly from part-time student help). During the initial stages, the range of a supervisor's responsibilities would necessarily overlap with subordinate staff functions. More definitive lines of responsibility would be drawn only after the organization had grown and more personnel had been added to the staff.

The estimate does not include costs involved in the time that a faculty member invests in developing or adapting a program. It is assumed that this will either be absorbed by the particular college department or charged to an additional budget allocation for the programmed learning service.

The cost of producing programs ranges from $500 to $1,500 per instructional hour, depending on the complexity of the material; the cost of adapting programs is, of course, a fraction of these amounts. The primary source of this cost is the expert's investment of time. To encourage faculty involvement and to create a more efficient approach to development, we recommend released time from teaching loads. Faculty members collaborating with the program-development group on their own time become involved in interminably prolonged projects and frequently, because of sheer impatience and frustration, abort the activity long before it can be brought to fruition.

Authorship Rights Each institution must establish for its faculty members' participation in the development of programs a policy governing publishing rights and remuneration. We strongly recommend that the issue be resolved before the organization engages in any operational activity with the faculty. Guidelines for formulating this policy can generally be found in the institution's existing policy for copyrights and patents.

Should the Service Be Independent Finally, the status of such a service organization has to be considered. The advantages of an independent service must be weighed against the disadvantages. Providing an institution-wide service from an administrative, hence independent, base will result in more equitable considerations and, probably, greater efficiency. However, when dealing with an innovative area such as programmed learning, it is difficult to assess the loss in political effectiveness stemming from the absence of a college-based source of academic strength. Rather than as an independent organization, such a service may prosper as a department in a college, as, for example, the college of education.

The same status considerations must be extended to the organization's personnel. Their concern is primarily with instruction, but their positions in an independent service will probably be administrative. Here, too, the issue of credentials, administrative or academic, must be resolved.

SUMMARY

We have seen that organizing a programmed learning service requires a vigorous commitment from both the faculty and the administration. The teaching staff must, of course, be willing to acknowledge the need for improving instruction. The administrative staff must be willing to tolerate, give credence to, and even encourage the demands for revolutionizing existing teaching methods and for redesigning the curriculum that generally follow endorsement of innovative practices.

To make such an organization work, many professors will have to give up their biases regarding innovative approaches to learning. The administration, for its part, has to accept the consequences and the implications of a commitment to innovation. For example, there will be an increase in requests for released time to develop programmed materials. And since new and untried methods frequently produce negative results before the skill is perfected, the administration must adopt a more tolerant attitude toward failure. The faculty will have to feel secure in the knowledge that the status of any collaborative member will be unaffected by any adverse contingencies.

A programmed learning service opens up new frontiers in education. The administration should be willing to accept the challenge of these frontiers even before taking the first step.

SUGGESTED ADDITIONAL SOURCES OF INFORMATION AND READINGS

Center for Programmed Instruction, The: *The Use of Programmed Instruction in U.S. Schools,* U.S. Government Printing Office, 1963.

Coulson, John E. (ed.): *Programmed Learning and Computer-Based Instruction,* John Wiley & Sons, Inc., New York, 1962.

DeCecco, John P. (ed.): *Educational Technology: Readings in Programmed Instruction,* Bantam Books, Inc., New York, 1964.

Finn, James D., and Donald G. Perrin: *Teaching Machines and Programmed Learning,* U.S. Government Printing Office, 1962.

Glaser, Robert (ed.): *Teaching Machines and Programmed Learning II,* National Education Association, Washington, 1965.

Hendershot, Carl H. (ed.): *Programmed Learning: A Bibliography of Programs and Presentation Devices,* Carl H. Hendershot, Michigan, 1964 (updated biannually).

Jacobs, Paul I., Milton W. Maier, and Lawrence M. Stolurow: *A Guide to Evaluation of Self-Instructional Programs,* Holt, Rinehart and Winston, Inc., New York, 1966.

Lumsdaine, A. A., and Robert Glaser (eds.): *Teaching Machines and Programmed Learning: A Source Book,* National Educational Association, Washington, 1960.

Margulies, Stuart, and Eligen (eds.): *Applied Programmed Instruction,* John Wiley & Sons, Inc., New York, 1962.

Meirhenry, Wesley C., and Gabriel Ofeish (eds.): *Trends in Programmed Instruction,* National Education Association and National Society for Programmed Instruction, Washington, 1964.

Northeastern University: *Programmed Instruction Guide,* Entelek, Inc., Newburyport, Massachusetts, 1967.

Ofeish, Gabriel D.: *Programmed Instruction: A Guide for Management,* American Management Association, New York, 1965.

Rummler, G. A., J. P. Yaney, and A. W. Shrader (eds.): *Managing the Instructional Efforts,* The University of Michigan Press, Ann Arbor, Mich., 1967.

Schramm, Wilbur: *The Research on Programmed Instruction: An Annoted Bibliography,* U.S. Government Printing Office, 1964.

Skinner, B. F.: *The Technology of Teaching,* Appleton-Century-Crofts, Inc., New York, 1968.

Taber, Julian, Robert Glaser, and Halmuth Schaefer: *Learning and Programmed Instruction,* Addison-Wesley Publishing Company, Inc., Reading, Mass., 1965.

Chapter 11

Learning Laboratories and Independent-study Services

EDWARD MALTZMAN

Director of Educational Research, Commercial Electronics Division, Sylvania Electric Products, Inc., Bedford, Massachusetts

DEFINING THE LABORATORY FOR LEARNING AND INDEPENDENT STUDY

There are valid and urgent reasons underlying the present movement towards laboratories for learning and for independent study. One set of reasons has to do with such general problems as the knowledge explosion, the population explosion, the shortage of teachers, the lack of facilities, and the need to learn more faster. Another set of reasons relates more immediately to basic functions and problems in education proper, namely, that education needs to be made more efficient and that technologies are at hand for making education more efficient. The learning laboratory—independent-study movement appears to hold considerable promise for fulfilling the challenges and goals inherent in both sets of reasons.

To give a precise and detailed definition of a learning laboratory, however, is not an easy thing to do, and no such definition will be attempted in these discussions. Instead, it is hoped that the present work will assist in the formulation of a number of definitions, or rather, of implementations, each appropriate to a particular set of needs and circumstances.

"Learning laboratory" implies a facility especially designed for accommodating the needs of individual students for the purposes of study, learning, and the performance of educational tasks. It will have a logistical plan of operation in which the functions of the laboratory, institution, faculty, administration, and students are clearly set forth and coordinated. It will contain the types of furnishings, equipment, materials, and supplies appropriate to its plan, to its successful utilization on the part of individual students according to their needs, and to the objectives of instruction.

"Independent-study services" implies a set of procedures within the laboratory with extensions into the total educational complex to enable the laboratory, institution, faculty, administration, and students to carry out their various functions and responsibilities with respect to instruction and learning needs efficiently and effectively. Included in such services are the use of the laboratory by the student at predetermined times or at his own convenience; the availability of equipment and materials for students to proceed at their own rate of study-learning speed; the availability of instructional assistance to students requiring special help; and the availability of guidance and direction to students seeking more rapid advancement.

Learning laboratories may be designed in a variety of shapes and contexts to implement a number of educational purposes and functions. Laboratories may deal with:

1. All types of audiovisual media such as microforms, slides, films, tapes, transparencies, and TV, or with selected media
2. All types of equipment, from single-concept film projectors and multiple-choice teaching devices to complex, computerized instruction systems, or with selected presentational or interactive types of equipment.
3. Varied types of response behavior such as multiple choice, verbal, written, manipulative, or with selected responses, as in the language laboratory
4. Automated, nonautomatic, manual, or self-service procedures
5. A single subject area or multiple subject areas
6. Main-line instruction (laboratory instruction rather than classroom instruction), supplementary instruction, enrichment, remedial instruction, or combinations of instructional modes
7. Different kinds of learning (rote, drill, discrimination, and conceptual)

In brief, the concept of the learning laboratory is flexible and not rigid, lending itself to many kinds of implementation. What will constitute a valid solution for one instructional problem may be entirely inappropriate for another. The "best" laboratory will be one that fulfills the needs, objectives, and strategies of the faculty and students of a particular educational institution efficiently and at reasonable cost.

The lasting value of such a laboratory need not be affected by changes which will come with advancing technology. Changes occur in educational institutions as well, and it is more than likely that a laboratory that does its job well today will be more immediately affected by changes in the institution itself than by sudden radical changes in technology. By that time, the laboratory will have amortized itself several times over.

INDIVIDUALIZING INSTRUCTION IN AN INSTITUTION OF HIGHER LEARNING

Historically, our educational processes have been content-centered and group-oriented. Study activities have been left to highly unstructured and individualistic student efforts. Learning is the responsibility of the student and, in this context, relationships between instruction and learning have not been tightly knit. For some time it has been generally recognized that the instructional and learning phases in education can no longer be equated in the sense that what is provided or intended in the one necessarily achieves the desired result in the other. Instruction can no longer be considered merely as the presentation of materials or information or the provision of "learning experiences" or "opportunities for learning," no matter how elaborate, ingenious, or well intentioned these may be.

On the other hand, learning can no longer be considered simply as an automatic function of exposure to presentations, information, or learning experiences. Nor can learning or the lack of learning be attributed simply to inherent student capabilities. A considerable body of research has shown that relationships do exist between instruction and learning (Skinner[1]); and that learning is a function of a complex variety of conditions, external and internal (Gagne[2]). If we recognize the present meager and incomplete state of our knowledge of such relationships and conditions, we must be aware also that very little of what has been learned and gleaned from research has been brought to bear on educational processes and practices. A notable exception to this is a recent book by Briggs et al.[3]

New developments, such as the reworking of subject matter in new conceptual organizations, programmed instruction, and interactive logic-computer systems, have been making inroads in education. Significantly, these as well as the other developments have as their goals and objectives greater student involvement and interest, individualizing of instruction, and the facilitation of learning. These goals represent no new objectives in education but new ways of realizing such objectives. They are receiving new emphasis and greater implementation in today's efforts to individualize instruction; they involve changes in procedures and environments which operate to affect students' study and learning behaviors.

The learning laboratory and independent study movement represents a departure from the traditional lockstep, single-trial classroom process. What this change implies for education can be highlighted by comparing briefly the potentials of implementing certain desirable and necessary educational processes in the classroom and in the laboratory. In the traditional classroom context it is quite impossible for the teacher to accomplish all of the following meaningful activities: present material most advantageously for each student, involve each student in the material, see that students respond appropriately to the unfolding material, and provide adequate and sufficient reinforcement and feedback to each student. All of these activities correlate highly

[1] Skinner, B. F., *The Technology of Teaching*, Appleton-Century-Crofts, New York, 1968.

[2] Gagne, Robert M., *The Conditions of Learning*, Holt, Rinehart and Winston, Inc., New York, 1965.

[3] Briggs, Campeau, Gagne, and May, *Instructional Media*, American Institute for Research, Palo Alto, Calif., 1967.

with classroom achievement. In the laboratory contexts, any or all of these functions can be taken into account operationally as a matter of course. Instructional materials can be student tested for maximum learning efficiency; the student can become involved in the material on an individual basis; materials and equipment can be designed to elicit, accept, evaluate, and record student responses at each learning step; and reinforcement, feedback, and knowledge of results can be provided to students almost instantaneously.

Individualizing instruction, though not a new concept, represents an innovative advance because of the changes involved in its instruction-learner relationships. It would indeed be of little value to use the learning laboratory with its new media and technology merely to preserve outmoded methodology.

GENERAL LEARNING LABORATORIES

This section will deal with laboratory implementations which fall within a class we may designate as general learning laboratories. These are designed for handling materials and processes common to many subject areas, in audio and/or visual presentational or tutorial (interactive) modes. Highly specialized functions, such as would be required in a science laboratory course, would not usually be accommodated by the general learning-laboratory concept.

Student Study Centers

The original student study center must have been the library. Although the word "library" literally means a collection of books, the librarian has long recognized that many forms of stored information and data should be considered part of the library domain.

With the vast amount of information that must be made available to students today, the role of the library as a lender of material which the student takes away with him for study at home or in the dormitory room is being deemphasized; more and more material must be restricted for use only in the library itself. To facilitate this, the library table has sprouted wings or dividers so that the student can study and do what was formerly known as "homework" right in the library. This naturally led to the evolution of the "study carrel" which began to be installed in "reading" rooms.

Modern libraries or institutions of higher learning often provide large rooms filled with study carrels, sometimes having enough carrels for a quarter or more of the student body simultaneously. Here the library has become the nucleus for student study and is often given a name like "Learning Resource Center." Books, films, tapes, and other learning materials are checked out by each student for use in the carrels. Equipment needed to play records and tapes and to view the films and slides may also be checked out.

In the library reading room–study center described above, all material and equipment is filed, checked out, and otherwise handled by conventional library procedures, and therefore it does not introduce anything basically new for the librarian to cope with. Such a setup frequently lends itself well to research work and individualized study. Equipment for listening and viewing is conventional and individual, thereby posing no larger problems of operation and maintenance than those of traditional library services. Among the difficulties encountered here, however, are the following:

1. Multiple simultaneous usage, which requires multiple copies of material (and multiple listening and viewing equipment)

2. Wear and tear on materials due to individual, uncontrolled, and possibly careless handling by the user

3. Inefficient use due to "dead time" when the material is held but not being used by the person who has checked it out

4. Loss or destruction of material because it is physically entrusted to the user

Such a center can well begin to serve the independent study needs of the smaller school or college, while institutions with large student populations will require other forms of laboratory designs.

Dial-access Learning Systems

Automating the Study Center If we take the student study center as described above and provide for the remote, automatic accessing of audiovisual materials, we immediately solve the four problems listed at the end of the previous section, as well as increasing our capability to deal with larger numbers of students. In such a system, the study booths or carrels are equipped in such a way that audiovisual materials can be looked at or listened to simply by dialing an index number. A telephone-type switching network makes it possible for any or all carrels to be connected to the same or different information sources; hence, fewer working copies of the material are needed.

Wear and tear is minimized because the tapes and films are operated on heavy-duty studio machines, and the less frequent handling is done by a responsible staff.

Dead time is eliminated—as soon as one user is finished, the material is immediately available for another user, and often the material can be used simultaneously by all who desire it.

Because the material is kept in the hands of the staff, loss is almost impossible, and destruction is unlikely.

Substitute for Some Classes Although lectures can be printed and thereafter made a reading assignment, the live lecture has remained a large part of the classroom routine. New facilities, however, make possible new procedures. Colleges are now learning that lectures can be effective as well as efficient by recording them on audio tape and video tape (or film) and, instead of using class time, making these recorded lectures available on call in the study carrels of a dial-access system. The gains, listed below, are significant and worthwhile.

1. Gains to the instructor:
   a. He need give his lecture only once (although he may want to spend some of the time saved in editing and rerecording his lecture for better impact).
   b. He knows for certain that all classes get the same lecture, without omissions.
   c. If the instructor should fall ill or be called away, the lecture will still be available as scheduled.
   d. The time saved by not duplicating lectures live can be devoted to other more scholarly activity or to conferences with students.
2. Gains to the student:
   a. He knows that the lecture he gets contains all necessary material without accidental omission.
   b. He can replay it as often as necessary to better understand difficult points and for review and study.
   c. He can get the lecture at a time of his own choosing, when he is most receptive and alert.
3. Gains to the institution:
   a. The lecturer has time for other activities.
   b. Usage of class and lecture rooms is more efficient.
   c. Temporary or permanent absence of a professor does not disrupt the lecture schedule.
   d. Guest lecturers and VIPs become economically feasible because their appearances can be replayed.

Once a school has established a lecture retrieval system, means for expanding its use become more apparent. Time-consuming, expensive, unreliable, or dangerous experiments, field trips, etc., can be filmed or video taped, edited to save time lapses, and made available for study in the carrels. New material can be dictated or audio taped and made available immediately without waiting for printing and distribution. Through the use of recently available equipment, such media can be compressed to provide even more efficient mediation.

The Carrel as the Student's Prime Study Area There is much to be said, psychologically, for establishing the study carrel as *the* place where the student does all or most of his outside-of-class work. If the study carrel is big enough and is located in a suitable environment, it is conceivable that good results can be obtained by having students assigned to specified carrels which they will use to retrieve lectures, films, and other audio-visual resources on call. Where it is possible to provide carrels on a one-for-each-student basis, students can be encouraged to do all their work within them and an annual carrel rental can be charged (as at Oklahoma Christian College). Such carrels can be centrally located in group study areas in the library, student union, and other places. On large campuses, they are being installed in dormitories and in other decentralized locations near the students' living quarters and student gathering areas.

Multimedia Information and Data Retrieval Systems As the study carrel becomes more sophisticated in its facilities and capabilities, it begins to approach a remote-controlled library. Through more recent telephonic techniques, the student can call for and get not only recorded lectures, films, and programs of all sorts, but also data, drawings, texts, and other printed matter by means of a high-resolution microfiche reader and, with the help of the librarian, a direct view of book pages. Right now a DAIRS (Dial Access Information Retrieval System) carrel can bring to the user audio material stored on audio tapes and video material (with accompanying audio) stored on video tapes and films. It can also serve to distribute live radio and TV programs, local broadcasts and closed-circuit TV from the local studio. When the study carrel is equipped with a standard "touch-calling" button system, it may be interconnected on a time-sharing basis with a suitable centrally located computer, enabling the student to do mathematical computations.

Computer-based Learning

The use of the computer to provide effective learning experiences without the constant, direct supervision of the live teacher is one of today's most exciting topics for discussion among educators. The vast capabilities of the computer for rapidly processing data, storing data, resuming instruction where it had ceased, and printing out an analysis in any desired format provides individualized, tailored-to-fit-the-student instruction.

What CBL Can Do The attraction of CBL (computer-based learning) is that it can do for the student so many of the things that an expert, individual tutor can do.

1. It can pretest the student and from the results determine what course objectives he already has mastered and delete those from the presentation.

2. CBL can evaluate the student's progress and provide for (*a*) appropriate branching so that objectives easily mastered can be abridged, (*b*) additional work on objectives not easily mastered, (*c*) remediation where the teaching program has erred, and (*d*) drill work tailored to the student's capabilities and the demands of the instructional system.

3. It can determine when the student has met the criteria of successful instruction and therefore assure that anyone who completes the program has reached at least a minimum level of acceptable performance on the terminal course objectives.

4. Should the instructional system consistently fail as measured in terms of student progress, the computer can indicate this to the instructor so that the system may be altered and alternative pathways may be provided for the student.

Computer-based learning advocates will say that almost anything is possible, and the few things which appear to be impossible today (such as recognizing oral and graphic patterns) are the subject of continuing research. This research has as its goal not only the achievement of these capabilities but also the development of innovative ways to circumvent such technical difficulties. Although complex and expensive, the hardware is available. What is really lacking is the software—the heart of the CBL system.

The Software Problem The real problem is providing adequate software for use with the hardware. Except for a few educators who are also well trained in the use and programming of computers, today's teachers must rely on the specialist for the CBL programs that are used by the students. The software problem is being attacked in several ways:

1. CBL systems' manufacturers recognize that they must encourage software production.
2. Large school systems (e.g., Philadelphia, New York) are setting up staffs of teachers and computer specialists to produce courses.
3. Smaller school systems are setting up regional centers for investigating CBL and determining whether it is feasible to produce or buy courses.
4. Government-funded production of general curricula usable by large numbers of educational institutions is being investigated.

The Teacher's Role Everyone recognizes that no form of technology will eliminate the teacher, but technology will and should affect the role of the teacher. Instead of being a presenter, demonstrator, recorder, disciplinarian, tester, and the like, the faculty member will be an instructional systems analyst and developer as well as a manager of the instructional-learning transaction. The instructor will select appropriate media packages for use in DAIRS, CBL, and programmed learning machines. He will spend more time in individual tutoring of his students and in moderating group discussions. Faculty will specialize more in given areas of the instructional process—some as producers of software, some as counselors, and some as supervisors. Faculties will be enlarged by nonteaching personnel: librarians, technicians, programmers, and media specialists. In brief, the teacher will become more the educational professional, the guide and mentor of educational processes, and a more active developer of the human potential of students. It must be remembered that the majority of the systems employed in independent-study and learning laboratories do *not* come packaged with contagious human excitement. This must be added by the teacher. The instructor's role is primarily one of the facilitation of learning by the most advantageous manipulation of the student learning experience and the instructional media.

Other Independent-study Learning Laboratory Equipment and Media

The classroom itself is a learning laboratory, whether it is of the conventional type or contains many automated media facilities. Those institutions which cannot yet take advantage of DAIRS and CBL can assist the teaching process by some relatively inexpensive teaching aids. Some of these are mentioned below:

Programmed Software The use of programmed instructional material, whether it is a programmed text or programmed audiovisual device, facilitates learning.

Responsive Learning Devices Earlier responsive learning devices were called teaching machines and were little more than automated page turners for programmed texts. Newer machines deserve a new term, and "responsive learning device" is one such general term. No learning device is better than the software available, hence those who are tempted to utilize these devices should ask themselves certain very pertinent questions about the software:

1. Is software available that will meet the instructional requirements of the cur-

riculum or course objectives as well as integrate with the unique student-population characteristics of the institution?

2. Is the available software professionally well prepared and adequately tested?
3. Can the software be edited, amended, and updated by the faculty?
4. Can software be produced quickly and at reasonable cost by the instructor or in accordance with the instructor's teaching plan?
5. Is the locally prepared software easily and economically compatible with the responsive learning device used?

The student-response characteristics of the device are also important and affect its usefulness. The following are pertinent questions:

1. How does the student respond?
   a. Multiple-choice push button, dial, light pen.
   b. Pressure-sensitive display.
   c. Constructed (graphic) response (written or typed).
   d. Constructed oral response.
2. How does the student's response affect the program?
   a. Program proceeds only when correct response is made.
   b. Program provides alternative branching.
   c. Program provides remedial information when an incorrect response is made.
   d. Error signal is given when student doesn't respond or makes consistently incorrect responses.
3. How is the student's performance evaluated?
   a. No evaluation is made.
   b. Number of responses made to complete the program are counted.
   c. Response time and/or total time to complete the program is recorded.
   d. Record of student's actual responses for each question is made.

Many responsive learning devices are incorporating ingenious ways of providing meaningful response modes for the student which affect the presentation of the curriculum material to fit better the needs and interests of the student.

Learning Laboratory Instructional Devices There are available other devices and systems which may be incorporated in the learning laboratory concept. Some of them are described below.

Presentation Devices. There are devices for playing three or four tapes at once from which each student can receive a segment of his choice (or as assigned) by setting a switch on his receiver. Wired equipment is lowest in cost and simplest to maintain, but it must either be installed with permanent wiring or with loose wiring carefully laid out on floor and tables. Similar equipment that is wireless is also available. Wireless systems overcome the above objections and are portable. Means can be provided for recording a lecture and playing it back whenever desired.

Student-response Systems. In student-response systems, or what might better be called instructor-feedback systems, each student is given a control box by means of which he can select one of three, four or five responses. These responses are tabulated into cumulative readings for the class as a whole and are displayed by percentage meters at the teacher's console. Provision is generally made for scoring each student on a cumulative basis and for marking each student's answers to each question.

Multimedia Systems. The systems described above may be integrated in many ways with various audiovisual devices, together with programming tracks, so that projectors and sound sources can be automatically operated in conjunction with student-response devices if desired. Although excellent results have been reported for multimedia systems, there are few programs readily available and the cost and complexity of producing a program locally is considerable.

SPECIFIC LEARNING LABORATORIES

Although the trend will continue strong toward learning laboratories which can accommodate material on any subject, there are certain curriculum requirements that can best be met adequately when the learning laboratory can perform certain unique functions. Where the need for such special features is great enough, locating such a learning laboratory in the department area where it will be used seems justified. Some of these specific types of laboratories are treated below:

Language Laboratories

Language laboratories have unique functions that are designed to facilitate the learning of foreign languages. They present material to the student that provides a sample of the correct pronunciation of foreign-language words and phrases, they enable the student to identify and imitate the pronunciation, and to evaluate his response and compare it with the sample, and they permit independent drill with provision for the instructor to monitor student performance and comment when necessary. To accomplish these functions, language laboratories are characterized by the presence of several or all of the following features:

Teacher's console:

1. Several tape decks.
2. Record player.
3. Headset with boom microphone.
4. Banks of switches which permit:
   a. The connection of any program source to any student.
   b. Intercommunication between teacher and one or more students or between selected students.
   c. Monitoring by teacher of any student position.
   d. Remote control of student's tape deck.

Student positions:

1. Headset with boom microphone.
2. Tape deck which can rerecord the master program on one track and the student's response on a second track and play back both tracks together so that the student can compare his response with the master. The student can erase the response track and try again.
3. Facilities and circuitry so that the student can hear his own voice through headphones at the instant he is speaking (audio-active), automatically repeated a few seconds later (variable-response loop), and repeated at will from a recording.

Some dial-access systems, wireless classrooms, and other types of general learning-laboratory equipment also contain one or more of the features described above and can therefore frequently act as language laboratories. It should also be noted that many language laboratories are being used as general learning laboratories.

Automated Science Laboratories

Various science laboratories and laboratory-type carrels have been developed by which the student can independently perform scientific experiments. These experiments often consist of arranging or hooking blocked modules together in experiments that can be repeated many times without exhausting the consumable supplies. Subjects available include electronics, chemistry, physics, and biology.

Video Trainers

The development of low-cost "video trainers" which consist of a TV camera, microphone, TV receiver, and videotape recorder have several applications utilizing the videotape recording capability as well as the "instant replay" feature of such equipment. Multi-audio track capability allows the teacher to comment as students perform. The student then can replay the tape, first observing and hearing the event as it happened and then seeing the event but hearing the instructor's commentary. When similar equipment is automated and installed in a "performance carrel" or small studio, playing a musical instrument, public speaking, skill training, counseling, practice teaching, and acting techniques can be tried, recorded, evaluated, and perfected with only a minimum of supervision. Wherever performing arts and skills are important, video-trainer installations can be most valuable.

Automated Planetariums

Like other educational equipment, the planetarium can be automated within multimedia systems. Lectures can be recorded and cue tracks devised which will cause the various projectors involved to properly position themselves and operate in accordance with an instructional plan and its learning objectives.

ORGANIZATION AND ADMINISTRATION OF STUDENT LEARNING FACILITIES AND PROGRAMS

The learning-laboratory development, while gaining in momentum, is still largely in its infancy. Nevertheless, from its brief history thus far, a number of guidelines emerge which can be of invaluable assistance in planning and organizing a learning laboratory for maximum utilization. Effective organization as well as economical operation can only follow and be based on a thorough and comprehensive understanding of the overall objectives to be achieved.

Will the Laboratory Serve a Single Discipline or Multiple Disciplines?

A laboratory may be required to meet the needs of a single instructional department and a single academic subject area. Frequently, however, the requirement may be for a single laboratory to be utilized by several departments and their corresponding subject areas. Data for planning should include the number of instructional departments interested as well as the instructional-learning objectives of each.

What Instructional Modes Will Be Involved?

Here, the concerns are for whether students receive audio information only, visual information only, or both audio and visual information. For lecture-listening functions, a laboratory equipped with appropriate audio capabilities will suffice. However, if lectures are to include illustrations or demonstrations, then some form of audiovisual or video supplement is called for.

What Will the Laboratory Be Used For?

Laboratories can fulfill a number of educational purposes. In one case, the purpose may be to have the students receive their main-line instruction in the laboratory instead of in the classroom. In this context, teachers may plan for meetings with individual students as required or as desired and for periodic classroom meetings for seminar and discussion sessions. In other contexts, purposes may include, among others, use of the laboratory for student drill work, making up missed classroom lectures, reviewing material, testing, and providing supplementary instruction.

How Will the Laboratory Be Used?

Laboratory planning necessarily must call for considered provisioning and balancing of two major procedures, lockstep and individual access. In using the laboratory for providing main-line instruction, a lockstep procedure would perhaps be most desirable.

However, there may also be requirements for simultaneous use of the laboratory for providing individual student access to individual programs, as well as for subdividing the laboratory for use by more than one group in lockstep procedure. Flexibility for such multiple usage is readily available.

What Kinds of Student Participation-interaction Activities Are To Be Implemented?

Student participation activities constitute one of the most important areas of consideration in laboratory planning. In presentational-type audiovisual laboratories in which students listen and observe, participation activities and involvement with instruction can be greatly increased by incorporating various forms of workbook (pencil and paper) implementations. Instructional materials may also be designed to provide feedback at question points. Interactive-type laboratories will have built-in participation functions in addition to workbook implementations.

The considerations for planning and organizing listed thus far are by no means complete. Before going on to others, it will be wise perhaps to pause at this point to indicate that the initially obtained data may appear to be all but impossible to organize. Indeed, it will not be possible to incorporate every objective, function, and procedure touched upon or suggested in these discussions into a single laboratory without making it so complex as to be utterly unwieldy. Compromises between objectives will have to be made. Common functions and procedures will have to be agreed upon.

Still to be considered are such factors as number of students, space, number of audio and visual program sources, instructional material and programs (referred to as "software"), personnel, and production.

How Many Students Will the Laboratory Serve?

Space requirements for a laboratory will depend on the number of students to be served and the kinds of facilities provided. In some cases, for example, in small colleges or individual departments or schools in large universities, it may be desirable for each student to have his own study area or carrel. In other cases, carrels are used by many students on a time-sharing or first come, first served basis. Finding favor also is the placing of carrels in dormitories, libraries, and other areas to facilitate student access.

How Many Program Sources Will Be Required?

Students receiving instruction in lockstep utilize one program source. A student receiving a program on an individual basis utilizes one program source. For other students to receive the same program at or near the same time, also on an individual basis, would require additional sources as well as additional copies of the instructional program. Audio and visual program-source requirements, therefore, will depend on the number of individual programs of instruction made available to students in lockstep as well as on an individual-access basis. In a DAIRS system, key programs may be scheduled on a time-clock basis, making them automatically available for student use at various times during the day or week.

How Will Instructional Materials and Programs Be Obtained?

Instructional materials and programs, the software, constitute the very heart of the learning laboratory. For laboratory use, software must be prepared in advance on films, tapes, video and graphic recordings, slides, and other media forms. The important thing is that enough good-quality software be available to meet the general and specific needs of instruction and students. Software may be obtained in several ways: from commercial software producers, from publishers, and from university and library exchange programs. Software may also be generated within the university by the faculty. Internal software generation requires appropriate production facilities and services. Depending on the circumstances, these may be incorporated in the laboratory functions or, because of the special activities and skills involved, they may best be handled by a production or resources center. Keeping ahead with software will for some time represent a major challenge.

What Are the Interface Requirements?

Interfacing arrangements will be required with individuals and organizations both within and outside the immediate school environment for every operational and servicing aspect involved. To cite some illustrations, there may be requirements for (1) providing training or other assistance to the faculty to implement their present instructional methodologies for learning-laboratory techniques and independent-study procedures, (2) providing assistance in developing student scheduling procedures and in handling student administrative matters, and (3) providing all the services and functions of a materials resource and production center, should such services not be available otherwise.

How Much Technology Will Be Appropriate?

A good deal of technology offers a wide variety of presentation and mediating-interactive-mode devices and systems for education today. The right mix for a laboratory will depend upon the particular circumstances and objectives. The effectiveness of a laboratory will depend on how well it implements the objectives of instruction and learning and not merely on how much technology is involved.

The more objectives call for mediating-interactive modes of implementation, the more physical technology will be involved. The caution here is not with the technology but with the human and software resources which are also involved in successful implementation. This applies to presentational-mode and nonautomated approaches as well. Sufficient technology is available today to meet the laboratory objectives of most institutions of higher learning. A major consideration will be to see that the physical technology does not exceed the institution's capability to deal with the software technology component.

Equipment in the laboratory should not be viewed in isolation, as a collection of "things" or "boxes" which have some value, but rather in the context of the system of which it is a part. In this way, it can be determined how each of the constituent parts interacts with every other, what functions each must fulfill, and how well each part contributes to the system.

How Much Staffing Will Be Required?

The number and kinds of people required to staff and service a laboratory is a most important consideration and will depend on the type and scope of activities involved. Many types of laboratory operations can be performed by students, such as checking out pieces of equipment and materials, placing programs on tape decks in the control switching center, and the like. Laboratories with multiple program and switching sources will require trained technicians to maintain the system. Assistance to faculty in developing materials will require programming or instructional technology specialists. As a general case, every laboratory organization should have provisions for familiarizing the faculty with laboratory equipment and techniques and for training the faculty to use them. Each of the considerations entering into the determination of laboratory organization will, of course, have its own imperatives for personnel on a part-time, full-time, professional, or nonprofessional basis.

What Types of Services for Independent Study Will Be Required?

The total facilities of the laboratory should be readily available to students and faculty according to their needs. This means that equipment must be in working order, that materials and programs must be available by check-out or call-up means, and so on.

The success of a learning laboratory will depend to a very large extent on how well it implements certain other necessary services of a more personalized educational nature. These services include especially detecting the student experiencing difficulty in his work and getting him to the assistance he needs with as little delay as possible. Services of this nature must be considered the combined responsibility of the laboratory and the instructional faculty.

Taking into consideration all the elements which may go into the makeup of a learning laboratory, it is quite obvious that the laboratory director's job may be quite complex. In any laboratory for learning and independent study, the director's job is enormously important and one of leadership. A great deal of care should be taken in selecting a director. What are the qualities for a laboratory director? A list of desirable qualities is easy to compile. Finding a person who meets them all is something else. The laboratory director should be a capable administrator, have a technical-engineering orientation, be knowledgeable in technological developments, be familiar with educational procedures and processes, have a broad interest in subject matter and curriculum development, be a philosopher of education and have high educational goals, be able to deal with statistics, be a specialist in learning theory and creative in educational technology, and be an experienced practitioner in human relations.

One person with all these qualities may not be available and may not even exist. Many persons with mixtures of these qualities do exist. A few of these will also be aware of the qualities they do not have but will have the desire and creativity to do something about them.

SUGGESTED READINGS

Audiovisual Instruction, Department of Audiovisual Instruction, National Education Association, Washington, October, 1967.

Beggs, David W. III, and Edward G. Buffie: *Independent Study: Bold New Adventure,* Indiana University Press, Bloomington, Ind., 1965.

Brown, James W., and K. D. Norberg: *Administering Educational Media,* McGraw-Hill Book Company, New York, 1965.

Brown, James W., and James W. Thornton, Jr. (eds.): *New Media in Higher Education,* Association for Higher Education and the Division of Audiovisual Instructional Service, National Education Association, Washington, 1963.

Cay, Ronald F.: *Curriculum: Design for Learning,* The Bobbs-Merrill Company, Inc., Indianapolis, Ind., 1966.

Coombs, Philip A.: *The World Educational Crises. A System Analysis,* Oxford University Press, Fair Lawn, N.J., 1968.

Cohen, Joseph W. (ed.): *The Superior Student in American Higher Education,* McGraw-Hill Book Company, New York, 1966.

Silvern, Leonard C.: *Systems Engineering of Education I: The Evolution of Systems Thinking in Education,* Education and Training Consultants Co., Los Angeles, California, 1968.

deKieffer, Robert E.: *Audiovisual Instruction,* The Center for Applied Research in Education, Inc., New York, 1965.

Doll, Ronald C.: *Curriculum Improvement: Decision-Making and Process,* Allyn and Bacon, Inc., Boston, 1964.

New Approaches to Individualizing Instruction, Educational Testing Services, Princeton, N.J., 1965.

Eye, Glen G., and Lanore A. Netzor: *Supervision of Instruction—A Phase of Administration,* Harper & Row Publishers, Incorporated, New York, 1965.

Gage, N. L. (ed.): *Handbook of Research on Teaching,* A project of the American Educational Research Association, National Educational Association, Rand McNally & Company, Chicago, 1963.

Journal of Educational Research, vol. 56, no. 6, Reading Section, February 1966.
Lee, Calvin B. T. (ed.): *Improving College Teaching*, American Council on Education, Washington, 1967.
Loughary, John W., *Man-Machine Systems in Education*, Harper and Row Publishers, Incorporated, New York, 1966.
Miles, Mathew B.: *Innovation in Education*, New York: Teachers College Press, Columbia University, New York, 1964.
Schuller, C. F., and W. A. Wittich: *Audiovisual Materials. Their Nature and Use*, Harper and Row Publishers, Incorporated, New York, 1967.
Skinner, B. F.: *The Technology of Teaching*, Appleton-Century-Crofts, Inc., New York, 1968.
Saettler, Paul: *A History of Instructional Technology*, McGraw-Hill Book Company, New York, 1968.
DeBernardis, Àmo, et al.: *Planning Schools for New Media*, U.S. Department of Health, Education & Welfare, Office of Education, OE-21021, 1962.
Spectrum of Electronic Teaching Aids in Education, School Planning Lab, School of Education, Stanford University Press, Stanford, Calif., 1965. (Out of print but available from the ERIC Document Reproduction Service.)
The Impact of Technology on the Library Building, Educational Facilities Laboratories, Inc., New York, 1967. (Out of print but available from the ERIC Document Reproduction Service.)
Ellsworth, Ralph E., and Hobart D. Wagener: *The School Library Facilities for Independent Study in the Secondary School*, Educational Facilities Laboratories, Inc., New York, 1963.

Chapter 12

Learning Resource Centers

LESLIE P. GREENHILL

Assistant Vice-president for Resident Instruction and Director, University Division of Instructional Services, The Pennsylvania State University, University Park, Pennsylvania

THE LEARNING RESOURCE CENTER AND THE INSTITUTION

Many colleges and universities are feeling the pressures of increasing enrollments of students and the need to teach these students to higher levels of attainment in circumstances where knowledge is expanding at an ever-increasing rate.

Many institutions are responding to these pressures by adopting new methods of instruction—methods involving the teaching of large groups of students by using live television, videotape courses, motion pictures, and team teaching, and by using methods involving the self-instruction of learners through programmed instruction, computer-assisted instruction, cartridge-loading projectors, and audio-tutorial laboratories.

There has also been much developmental work in recent years on the planning and construction of special teaching auditoriums and other facilities for learning.

The federal government has recognized these developing trends in higher education and is providing matching funds through various agencies for the acquisition of many kinds of instructional equipment and for the construction of new instructional facilities. Institutions are also budgeting for their shares of matching funds and are providing increasing amounts of money from their regular financial resources for the purchase of new instructional equipment.

Another important area of concern to administrators is the encouraging of faculty members to take advantage of these new developments, which can lead to improvements in learning, to the expansion of learning opportunities for more students, and to the development of independent study habits.

In fact, one of the greatest barriers to the introduction of new instructional technology has been the fact that relatively few college teachers have been interested in using such new methods. There may be several reasons for this:

1. College teachers tend to teach in the way that they were taught, and thus traditional methods are perpetuated.

2. People are usually "down on what they are not up on." In other words, unfamiliarity with modern developments in instructional media leads people to reject them, or even unconsciously to fear technological unemployment.

3. College teachers receive little formal training in the use of media and other new methods of instruction.

4. Supporting services to assist the faculty in introducing and evaluating new instructional methods are generally lacking, and faculty members often lack the technical knowledge for successfully using new technologies in teaching.

As a result of all these developments and needs, many colleges and universities are finding it desirable and, indeed, essential to establish special organizations to provide a variety of supporting services to faculty members in order to assist them with their teaching responsibilities. In some institutions such organizations are known as "The Office of Instructional Resources," "The Learning Resource Center," or "The Division of Instructional Services."

In the past, many institutions have had limited services of this type. Some institutions have film libraries and projection services and perhaps a photographic laboratory which can produce slides and simple films. Television and language laboratories may have been added in recent years. However, such resources are often located in several different administrative units of the university and their efforts are relatively uncoordinated. Furthermore, in the past the emphasis has often been on equipment per se rather than on the identification, analysis, and solution of instructional problems.

The new types of organizations now emerging provide a well-coordinated variety of instructional services, with a primary emphasis on the identification of instructional objectives and needs and a secondary emphasis on the means of achieving them through the use of new instructional equipment and materials and other services.

In some institutions, such organizations have been developed by bringing together existing, scattered services into one organization and giving it a new direction and the necessary budgetary support to provide a well-coordinated service.

In other instances the organization has been newly created, without any antecedents. In still other institutions, these services may be offshoots of regular academic departments, some of whose members may have an interest in instructional developments.

The size of the instructional services organization may range from two to three people to thirty, forty, or more full-time professional staff members, depending on the size of the institution and the variety and volume of services required.

In establishing such an organization, careful thought should be given to its location within the administrative structure of the university. Since the learning resource center will be expected to serve all of the academic departments (as the library does), many institutions have found it most effective to attach this organization to the officer of the college or university who is responsible for the general coordination of the instructional program of the institution, i.e., the vice-president for academic affairs, the provost, or the dean of the faculty.

OBJECTIVE AND FUNCTIONS OF THE LEARNING RESOURCE CENTER

The overall objective of a learning resource center may be defined as *the improvement of teaching and learning* within a college or university. In order to achieve this objective, a variety of services can be provided for the faculty. The extent of these services will depend on the size and needs of each institution. This section will describe briefly the nature and scope of some of these services.

Instructional Research Research is put first because, as in most endeavors, it constitutes the best foundation for advancement. The instructional services organization can have staff members who are expert in research design and evaluation and who also have expertise in the basic principles of learning. Such individuals can be of assistance to faculty members in conducting research to evaluate the effectiveness of instructional innovations and in designing questionnaires and other procedures to obtain systematic reactions of students, faculty, and others to such developments.

Course Development The concept of "empirical course development" is one that merits attention. This is sometimes referred to as the "systems approach" to teaching and learning. In its simplest form it involves a series of steps which an experienced educational psychologist can assist faculty members to follow, as outlined below:

1. Develop detailed instructional or course objectives for each lesson and express them in terms of desired behavior. That is, describe what the students should be able to do as a result of studying this course or lesson.
2. Construct tests which will enable the teacher to determine the extent to which the learners are achieving the desired goals.
3. Select appropriate course content. Most teachers begin with course content and only vaguely spell out objectives.
4. Select methods of presentation and appropriate activities for the learners. Here, one should consider a wide range of possibilities and employ those which appear to be most satisfactory on the basis of known learning principles and related considerations (e.g., size and location of groups, costs, availability of faculty, etc.).
5. Teach the lesson or course to a sample group of learners and give the tests previously developed.
6. On the basis of test performance, identify weaknesses and revise the methods and/or content. Repeat the process, making successive revisions.
7. In some circumstances, as when the basic course materials are recorded on videotape, it may be possible to conduct a well-controlled experiment in which the revised versions are compared with the original in order to determine whether actual improvement has been achieved.

The clear definition of course objectives can lead to significant improvements in course content and structure.

Production of Instructional Materials The previous discussion of course development emphasizes the need for an institution to have, in a well-coordinated center, the facilities, equipment, and staff for producing a wide range of instructional materials.

These may include films (16-mm and 8-mm), instructional television (including videotapes), audio tapes (for use in language laboratories or audio-tutorial methods in other disciplines), color and black-and-white slides, transparencies (with overlays) for the overhead projector, charts and other graphics, programmed instructional materials, and so forth.

These services can be useful for supporting both the teaching programs of the institution and its research functions. For example, the film production services could include equipment and experienced personnel for high-speed and time-lapse photography and for cinemicrography for the production of research films.

Library Services Library services provided by an instructional services center could be of several kinds. The first would be an information center or library of reference books, journals, and research reports dealing with instructional media and methodologies. These constitute a valuable resource for the academic staff of the institution as well as for the professional staff of the center.

A second library service would be for nonprint instructional materials of various kinds which require special handling and the use of special equipment. These services may include special storage for films, audio and video tapes, and the like.

A third library service could be for the provision of special instructional equipment used by faculty members, e.g., film projectors, videotape and audio-tape machines, overhead and slide projectors. An accompanying operator service would be available whenever needed. This latter service would become decentralized as it became increasingly practical to have classrooms and teaching auditoriums permanently equipped, so that such instructional equipment would always be available at the point of use. It should be noted that much equipment of this type is now designed so that it can easily be operated by the teacher rather than requiring a specialist.

Design of Instructional Facilities The staff of an instructional services center should keep abreast of new developments in instructional equipment and be available to work with those designing new classrooms and teaching auditoriums to ensure that proper attention is given to such functional requirements as good acoustics, adequate ventilation, appropriate lighting for students' work areas and chalkboards as well as for television and projection, arrangement of seats for good visibility of display areas, facilities for various kinds of projectors and television, and adequate areas for the storage of instructional materials.

Many of these essential requirements are overlooked in the design of classrooms, which frequently have poor acoustics, inadequate ventilation, no control of lighting, seating arrangements that do not give every student an unobstructed view, and little or no provision for projection equipment.

Evaluation of Learning An important aspect of teaching is the evaluation of students' performances. It is necessary to know whether students are meeting required standards and whether the instruction is satisfactory. Furthermore, the kinds of examinations that are given determine, to a large extent, the kinds of learning that take place.

Many teachers, because they have had no training in testing, are satisfied with one particular kind of examination, such as the essay test or the objective test, each of which has its advantages and disadvantages when used for certain purposes. Teachers rarely analyze tests for reliability or for the ability to discriminate between the better and the poorer learners.

There is a wide variety of testing procedures that can be used to assess various kinds of learning, and a professional testing staff can assist the faculty in many ways to improve the examinations they use. Test-scoring and test-analysis services can also be provided, and assistance can be given in the development of new kinds of tests.

Faculty Development Services Very few college faculty members have received any formal training in modern instructional methods, in the use of new media and equipment, or in the development and analysis of examinations. An important function of an instructional resources center is to work with faculty members individually and in groups to provide them with training and experience in the use of this emerging technology. Demonstrations and short-term seminars are very useful, as is the recording on videotape and playback of demonstration lessons given by individual faculty members.

Assistance in the Preparation of Grant Applications With the growing availability of federal and other funds for the support of instructional research, equipment, and facilities at the college and university level, and with the increasing complexity of regulations, it is very useful for an institution to have someone who is familiar with the ininstitution's instructional needs, who can keep abreast of new sources of funds, and who can work with the faculty and administration in preparing proposals to obtain such financial support. This kind of service logically falls within the scope of a learning resources center.

The above types of services are simply examples of what might be done; others can be developed as the need arises. The fact is that such support is essential if new methods of instruction are to be introduced and used successfully.

STAFF AND FACILITIES OF THE LEARNING RESOURCE CENTER

Staff A learning resource center that seeks to provide the kinds of instructional services that have been described above is only as good as the professional staff that it is able to bring together.

In order to focus the efforts of the center on the right objective—namely, the improvement of teaching and learning—it is proposed that the director of the center be an individual with training and experience in learning principles and with an interest in the application of new methods and media in college teaching. Such individuals most frequently come from departments of educational psychology or from institutions that have advanced programs in instructional media.

The director should be backed up by an appropriate staff of professional people who have the necessary technical backgrounds. These may include individuals who have experience in instructional television, instructional film production, photography, instructional graphics, and the like. Unfortunately, most college-level training programs that prepare such people give them an orientation for positions in industry, rather than for college-level instruction, and the commercial needs and the requirements for teaching and learning are often quite different.

Professional organizations such as the National Association of Educational Broadcasters, the Division of Educational Technology of the National Education Association, and the University Film Producers Association have placement services that can be helpful in finding suitable staff members. Such individuals should have appropriate academic backgrounds, including at least a baccalaureate degree, frequently a master's degree, and in some instances a doctorate. They should be given appropriate ranks and titles in accordance with their professional status.

Although teaching duties are not ordinarily considered to be the responsibility of instructional services organizations, the staff members may, in many instances, be given joint appointments in academic departments or they may at least have part-time teaching opportunities, as they often have much to contribute to the academic programs of an institution.

In many instances it is appropriate and desirable to use students as part-time assistants in learning resource centers. Such students may be majors in various fields of communication, and they, therefore, value the opportunity for some supervised on-the-job experience. Most institutions find it better to select students and pay them for this part-time work than to take all comers as a part of the credit requirements for a course.

Facilities Many learning resource organizations in the past have been designated as audiovisual services with limited responsibilities, and they have been housed in spaces in basements, temporary buildings, or other makeshift areas which are totally inadequate.

The trend today is toward the construction of specially designed facilities in new buildings. Such facilities provide proper studios, control rooms, laboratories, work areas, and offices which are planned to meet the specialized needs of an instructional services center.

Such a building can bring scattered services together in one location which should be conveniently accessible to faculty members and which can function with maximum efficiency.

Equipment It is essential also to provide such an organization with adequate, up-to-date equipment and with the means of keeping it in good operating condition. Such equipment may be obtained as part of new construction funds, by institutional budgeting, and/or from matching fund grants. There should be budgetary provision for adding to the equipment inventory as new needs develop.

ADMINISTRATION OF THE LEARNING RESOURCE CENTER

Organization It has been suggested earlier that in most institutions it is appropriate to have the learning resource center under the administrative officer who is responsible for the coordination of the instructional programs of the institution. Thus, the director would report to the dean of the faculty or the vice-president for academic affairs.

It is essential to make the various services of the organization as readily available as possible to the faculty. Consequently, as the center grows in size, it will probably be desirable to designate subunits which have specific areas of responsibility—e.g., instructional television services, photographic services, examination services, etc.,—and to have a qualified individual responsible for each subunit. This usually improves the efficiency of the operation and aids in the recruitment, training, and supervision of staff specialists. Clerical staff and technicians will also be needed.

Budgeting If an instructional services agency is to function effectively, it should have appropriate financial support for salaries, wages, supplies, and the like.

In the past, some universities have budgeted such organizations on a self-financing basis. Under this plan the units charge to academic departments the complete costs for all services, and income is expected to equal expenditures. Funds may be put into the budgets of academic departments to pay for such services.

Experience has shown that this method of budgeting has severe disadvantages. First, it tends to inhibit the use of the services by faculty members. Second, the funds in departmental budgets gradually get diverted for other needs.

At the other extreme, the instructional services center may be fully budgeted for all services and not make any charges at all to academic departments. This works very well for some services and certainly encourages maximum use of them. On the other hand, in the case of services which make use of relatively expensive materials (e.g., films, slides, etc.), it may lead faculty members to request materials they really do not need, and much unnecessary expense can be incurred. This may be offset by some system of job approvals signed by appropriate administrative officers.

A third procedure involves the partial budgeting or subsidy of the services center and the passing on to departments of a certain part of the costs. For example, at The Pennsylvania State University, the Division of Instructional Services makes no charge to academic departments for the professional labor involved in any services rendered, but it does charge for the actual materials used. In general, these charges are modest and departments can readily afford them. This system provides an automatic control on job requests which might otherwise result in excessive expenditures for materials and other out-of-pocket expenses. Money received for material charges to departments may be credited to the materials budget in order to purchase more materials.

Modest, regular budgets for new equipment are desirable, and these can be supplemented by nonrecurring or "one-shot" allocations of funds periodically for purchase of special new equipment. Sometimes such allocations can be used as matching funds for federal grants.

Incentives to the Faculty It is desirable in most institutions to provide some kinds of incentives to the faculty to encourage the exploration of innovations in teaching. It is often not sufficient simply to have the services available and to publicize them regularly.

One type of helpful incentive is a small grants program operated by the university. This could provide grants of a few hundred dollars to faculty members to underwrite the costs of travel to special workshops or institutes which relate to their individual teaching functions. Such grants may also underwrite the cost of constructing special equipment or the out-of-pocket costs of materials for films or transparencies to be used in some new way.

The Pennsylvania State University has a small grants program of this sort, called The Central Fund for the Improvement of Teaching, which has stimulated the introduction of a number of teaching innovations by individual faculty members.

The redevelopment of courses on a large scale or the planning and videotaping of such courses requires a large investment of time and effort on the part of a faculty member or group of faculty members as well as appropriate supporting services if it is to be done well.

It is highly desirable, therefore, for an institution to have some way of providing funds for "released time" so that a faculty member can be released from other duties and can work full time for a designated period on course development projects. Additional funds may also be needed for the preparation of new instructional materials for the course.

Since such special funds are often in short supply in institutions, this would be an area in which the federal government could play an important role in improving college-level instruction by providing matching funds for worthwhile course development projects.

SELECTED BIBLIOGRAPHY

Baskin, S. (ed.): *Higher Education: Some Newer Developments,* McGraw-Hill Book Company, New York, 1965.

Brown, J. W., and J. W. Thornton: *New Media in Higher Education,* National Education Association, Washington, 1963.

Schueler, H., and G. S. Lesser: *Teacher Education and the New Media,* American Association of Colleges of Teacher Education, Washington, 1967.

Thornton, J. Ward, and J. W. Brown: *New Media and College Teaching,* National Education Association, Washington, 1968.

Audiovisual Instruction, published monthly by the Division of Educational Technology, National Education Association, Washington.

Audio Visual Communications Review, published bimonthly by the Division of Educational Technology, National Education Association, Washington.

Educational Broadcasting Review, published bimonthly by the National Association of Educational Broadcasters, Washington.

Section Five

Adult Education

Chapter 1

Adult Education—Introductory Statement

Adult education is an all-encompassing term which can denote everything from citizenship classes to agricultural demonstrations to full-credit, degree-oriented, formal course work. For the purposes of this handbook, the presentation is confined to those elements of adult education which regularly involve institutions of higher learning. These are the organization and administration of part-time evening degree programs; the admission and counseling of those enrolled in degree-credit courses who may or may not be interested in the pursuit of a degree program; higher continuing education—illustrating the relationship of short-term institutes, workshops, and state-of-the-art courses to the overall adult education spectrum; cooperative extension and general extension programs, correspondence study—or home study, as some prefer to term it; the adult education programs of community colleges; and, finally, special mention is made of the varied educational assistance programs operative in the field of adult learning.

Adult education, in all its diverse facets, has only recently begun to come into its own. Problems of academic standards, administrative responsibility, and the determination of community needs are being resolved, with the result that adult education is one of the fastest-growing dimensions in higher education today. College administrators need to keep themselves informed of the developments in this field as more and more institutions take on new or expanded responsibilities in the field of adult education.

Chapter 2

Adult Education Degree Programs

ERNEST E. MC MAHON

Dean, University Extension Division, Director of the Institute of Management and Labor Relations, and Professor of Adult Education, Rutgers, The State University, New Brunswick, New Jersey

INTRODUCTION

Management of adult education degree programs is one of the least understood areas of college and university administration. The major reason is that although the units or divisions which offer the programs usually are referred to as evening colleges, there is no prototype of an evening college. The term itself is confusing within the academic community because of the lack of a generally accepted concept of *an* evening college. Each university has its own concept, and the notions differ.

There are, of course, common elements. The programs are designed for adult, part-time students. Most of the courses are credit courses. The students may earn degrees, although many of them are not interested in credit or degrees. Most of the instruction is given at night. Few of the evening colleges have regularly assigned faculty members. Control of curriculum generally rests with a day college. In short, the evening college is not like the other colleges of the university.

Fortunately, what a specific evening college may be and how it is organized may have little to do with the scope of its educational program, its academic standards, or its service to the constituent community.

The problems of starting or appraising an evening college revolve around the basic issues of educational purpose, academic standards, administrative relationships, and faculty organization. The reason there is no standard notion of how to organize and conduct degree programs for the adult student is that there are differences among universities with respect to those four basic issues and the most desirable methods of resolving them.

EDUCATIONAL PURPOSE

The first decision to be made is with respect to purpose. Is the program for adults intended to provide a conventional curriculum leading to a degree, or is it intended to provide a general program of adult education with emphasis on community needs? The two purposes are not mutually exclusive, but they are difficult to combine. A clear understanding of the differences between them will make it easier to determine administrative policies and practices.

Adult Education Services

Much of the confusion which surrounds the evening degree program activities stems from the attempt of the evening college to meet the demands of the two dissimilar kinds of education, namely, traditional academic instruction and nontraditional adult education. The attempts to combine two such antithetical ideas result in the ambiguity which marks the evening college.

In the academic tradition, courses offer credit toward a degree, and students must qualify for admission by means of various credentials. In the field of adult education, the evening college may offer courses which do not provide credit and, also, may enroll in the credit courses students who do not qualify for formal admission and who do not seek credit. It is the imposition of the adult education activities upon the traditional degree curricula which blurs the picture of the evening college for so many administrators and faculty members.

Administrator's Checklist 1

Because the academic tradition and the adult education movement are so dissimilar, there is difficulty in attempting to resolve their conflicting purposes by theoretical discussions. A step-by-step analysis of a specific university's objectives, made by answering specific questions, may result in clarity as to what kind of program is really wanted. Once that decision is made, the other issues may be approached systematically.

The following checklist of questions may be helpful:

	Yes	*No*
1. Do we want to allow part-time students to earn a degree?	____	____
2. Is our evening degree program to be similar to our existing daytime degree programs?	____	____
3. Do we want comparable standards for day and evening degree programs?	____	____
4. Do we want to provide general adult education services as well as degree opportunities?	____	____
5. If so, will we provide adult education through the degree program?	____	____
6. If not, will we organize a separate adult education agency?	____	____

If the administrator wants to understand better or to evaluate an existing evening degree program, the above six questions may be modified in the manner suggested by the following examples:

	Yes	*No*
1. Do we want to continue to allow part-time students to earn degrees?	____	____
2. Should we continue (expand, review) general adult education services?	____	____
3. Do our present day and evening programs have comparable standards?	____	____

Additional modifications are obvious. The questions lead, also, to elaboration of the extent or the nature of the similarity or difference in standards, to consideration of the kinds of adult education services, and to clarification of the way in which they are provided. If the decision is to establish or continue a degree-granting program for adults, the question of standards is inevitable.

ACADEMIC STANDARDS

The usual approach to the subject of the academic standards of the evening program is to compare them with those of the day college in an effort to establish a condition of similarity or even of identity, but it is better to make a direct approach to analysis of what is involved in providing an educational program of excellence for the evening student. In other words, what special aspects of the evening program may have some effect on how its quality should be determined?

It is well to keep in mind that *opinions* as to standards are sometimes as important as the actual realities of the situation. For example, what faculty members *think* of the evening college may be the significant test of its acceptance both within the parent institution and outside. Therefore, practices should conform to the pattern, although not necessarily to the substance, of those of the rest of the university. Particular attention needs to be given to the five points of control of standards: admissions, course content, curriculum requirements, retention of students, and degree requirements.

Administrator's Checklist 2

Just as the philosophical issue of purpose must be resolved by a step-by-step analysis which keeps degree-granting concepts clearly distinguished from adult education notions, so the issue of standards can be most effectively approached by a similar question-and-answer examination. It is assumed that most administrators and faculty members will want to have comparable standards (question 3 in preceding checklist) for any curricula leading to a degree within their institutions. The question which has to be answered is how much identity is sought, how realistic identity is as an ideal, and where differences can be justified educationally.

The following checklist of questions may be helpful:

	Yes	*No*
1. Is there such a thing as identity between two sections of the same course?	___	___
2. Is a high school record which is 10 years old as much of an indication of academic potential as a record completed in the present year?	___	___
3. Are the educational needs of a mature, employed person necessarily the same as those of a teen-ager?	___	___
4. Do admission requirements need to be the same for day and evening students, qualitatively and quantitatively?	___	___
5. Should all adult, part-time students be required to meet the evening college's admission requirements?	___	___
6. Should all adult students be required to do satisfactory academic work to be allowed to continue?	___	___

Other questions may be added to the list, but the above can be used effectively either in planning for a proposed adult education degree program or evaluating an existing one. They do, however, need brief explanatory statements because most of the day-to-day difficulties of the evening college revolve around the answers to those particular questions.

Identity As indicated above, a common approach to establishing adequate evening college standards is to attempt to construct something which is identical to the day college. Yet, different instructors and different students create nonidentity for any two sections of the same course, whether day or evening. The search, if the preceding sentence is accurately stated, should be for valid standards which will recognize differences but which will be recognized as adequate by the participating faculty.

Entrance Credentials The admissions director may establish a pattern of reliability for the high school records of young people coming directly from high school to college. However, when an adult has worked for some years, has assumed family obligations, has developed a record of leadership in community affairs, or has been frustrated by the lack of a college degree, the motivation which was lacking in high school may be replaced by a new drive, and the third-quarter student may become a late bloomer. The best example is the performance of veterans under the GI Bill of Rights after World War II.

Faculties can recognize such differences. What a faculty cannot understand is the complete absence of admission requirements. In other words, the faculty member is puzzled when the evening college requires degree candidates to meet the day college requirements but will admit noncredit students to the same classes without requiring them to submit their high school records or to meet other entrance criteria. It is then inferred that the evening standards must be low because the noncredit student, who has not qualified for admission, may enter the course and, indeed, may pass it.

One solution is to agree upon realistic entrance requirements for the adult students and then to require *all* of them to meet those requirements by going through a standard admissions procedure. Too often, the admissions test for the adult education student is his ability to pay the tuition.

Retention of Students Most evening colleges require their degree-candidate students to maintain satisfactory academic records, but the adult education (nondegree) students are permitted to reenroll regardless of failures. Faculty members who have failed those students and then find them continuing in class for a second or even a third semester form low opinions of the evening standards.

Regardless of the policies and procedures which are adopted, there will be faculty members who remain convinced that all part-time or evening study is inferior. Their opinions may not be subject to change. However, the need is to establish policies and procedures which will lead the faculty to recognize the evening work as acceptable rather than to reject it as unsatisfactory.

ADMINISTRATIVE RELATIONSHIPS

A major reason for the duality of procedures for degree and nondegree students is the locus of responsibility and authority. Frequently, a faculty controls the requirements for the degree students, but the evening college dean or director has complete jurisdiction over the enrollment of the adult education students. Consequently, he may put them into classes without imposing any sort of admissions qualifications.

The practice frequently is based upon budgetary necessity. Evening degree programs historically have been self-supporting in terms of meeting direct costs such as those of instruction, administration, supplies and equipment, printing and publications, and postage. Some have been charged for use of the plant, and others have paid an overhead to the institution. The only source of funds to meet such costs has been fee income, and the balancing factor frequently has been the nondegree student. His recruitment and enrollment have been the evening dean's equivalent of endowment income.

College or Division Regardless of the evening administrator's authority to enroll noncredit students, there is a fundamental question of administrative relationship which varies from institution to institution. Although the adult degree units are commonly referred to as evening colleges, some of them are divisions of day colleges. An example is the School of General Studies of Brooklyn College. The entire institution is a college, and the evening program is a division within that college.

Nomenclature Unfortunately, the names of the units do not help to distinguish them as to type, purpose, or organization. In contrast to the Brooklyn College situation, there are so-called "evening divisions" which provide adult education degree programs for two or more different colleges of the institution. The School of General Studies at Columbia University is an autonomous college with its own legislative faculty, in contrast to the similarly named unit at nearby Brooklyn College. Another common name is "university college," which again indicates no similarity among those so designated. "Evening college" and "evening division" are common names. "Division of continuing education" is becoming popular for both evening colleges and extension divisions. Other evening colleges are named for individuals, such as Millard Fillmore College of the State University of New York at Buffalo.

What an individual evening college is has to be determined in accordance with the institution's total administrative structure; it is not a concomitant of the evening college's name. Where the unit is operated as a division of one or more day colleges, there may be more control by the day units and the evening director may report directly to a day dean. On the other hand, the opposite condition may exist.

Autonomy Autonomy need not imply lack of cooperation. Regardless of the amount of freedom which the evening college dean has technically, his relationship to the day

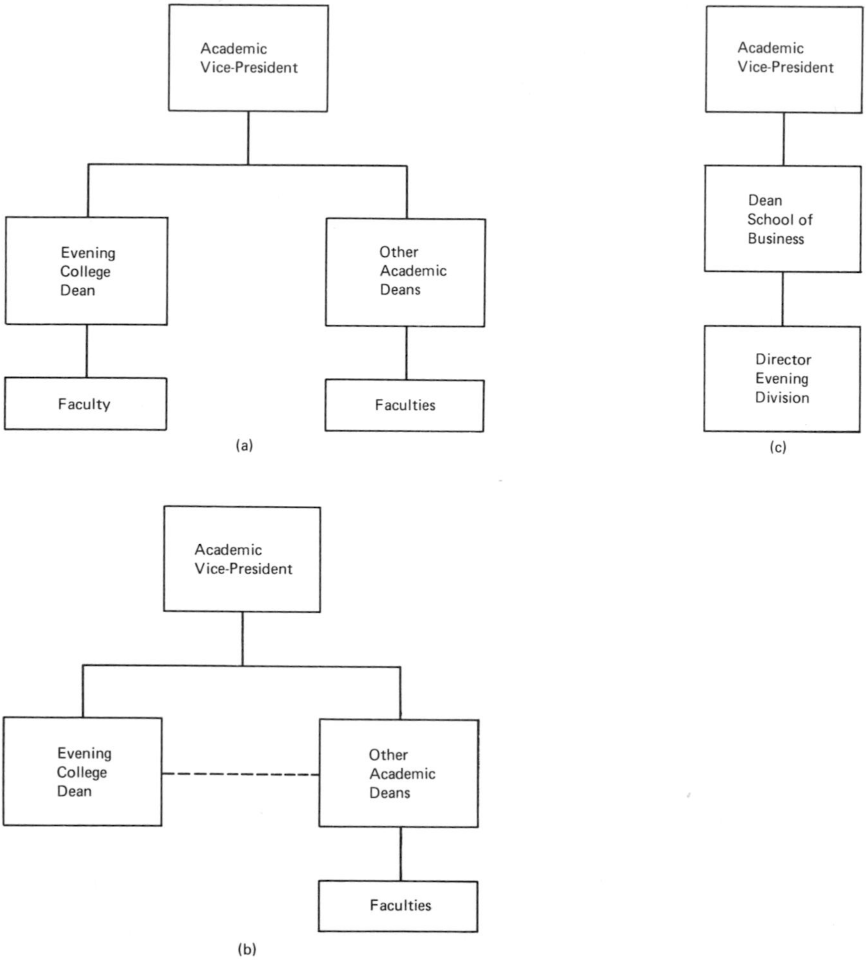

Fig. 1 *Three prevailing evening college organizations: (a) with autonomous evening faculty; (b) without evening college faculty; (c) evening college as division of day or resident college.*

deans may be one of close cooperation or one of remote aloofness. It may be speculated that many factors, including the general institutional attitude toward the evening college, affect the actual working relationship, and autonomy is only one of them.

Administrator's Checklist 3

The way the adult education degree program fits into the day-to-day operating mechanism of the institution may be determined or modified by the answers to certain questions which affect the status of the evening dean or director and, through his status, the institutional concept of the evening college as an educational unit as distinguished from a service unit. One of the basic problems which runs like a thread through all of the issues affecting the evening college is whether it is truly an educational unit like the other colleges or whether it is essentially an auxiliary service like the dining halls.

The following checklist of questions may be helpful in assessing the place of the adult education degree program in the institution's administrative hierarchy:

	Yes	*No*
1. Does the chief administrator of the evening program report to the same administrator as do the deans of the colleges?	____	____
2. If not, does the evening college administrator report to a college dean?	____	____
3. Is the budget for the evening program prepared and submitted in the same manner as the budgets of the colleges?	____	____
4. Are there charges to the evening division for overhead and building use which are not levied on the day colleges?	____	____
5. Is the evening division represented on the university senate or other major governing body?	____	____
6. Does the evening division have jurisdiction over the admission and retention of its students?	____	____

Fiscal controls and administrative relationships have much to do not only with the operational practices of the evening division but also with the dean or director's attitude toward changes in those practices. Status also may be a factor in recruiting the kind of person who can perform the necessary administrative role.

THE EVENING FACULTY

Further confusion with respect to adult education degree programs results from the use of the word "faculty" to mean two different things. "Faculty" means the legislative group of professors who determine curricula and other academic matters; "faculty" also means the group of individuals who carry on instruction, the teachers who meet with the students. In day colleges, the groups consist of the same individuals. In evening colleges, most of the instruction is by part-time teachers, men and women from the community at large, and they usually have no part in the academic legislative process.

Because of the difference, it is necessary to specify which faculty is meant when the term is used in connection with evening instruction. There are degree programs for part-time students which have their own legislative faculties of regularly appointed university faculty members with a primary responsibility for the evening courses. Two such faculties are those of the School of General Studies at Columbia and of University College at Rutgers.

A few other institutions have regularly appointed evening teachers, but there is not a separate legislative organization for them. An example is the City University of New York.

In other cases there is a division of the teaching load on the basis of a joint appointment or released time. The joint appointment provides for sharing of the salary between the evening college and another college of the university. The percentage of sharing is related to the percentage of teaching load performed in the respective colleges. When released time is involved, the faculty member may be assigned to an evening class without budgetary reimbursement; in other words, the other college concerned would actually contribute such faculty member's time to the program of the evening college.

Part-time Faculty

The most common practice, however, is the employment on a course-by-course and semester-to-semester basis of qualified men and women from the community at large. Even where an organized evening faculty exists, much of the instruction is given by part-time appointees. Essentially, they are business and professional persons who enjoy teaching.

The part-time teacher may also be a member of the regular faculty who teaches an evening course as an overload for extra compensation. Such an appointment must be distinguished from the joint appointment or other arrangement for the sharing of regular faculty time. The overload teacher may come from within the institution or from a neighboring institution. On an overload basis, a faculty member usually has the same status as the nonfaculty part-time teacher.

Remuneration The part-time teachers are the philanthropists of the adult education degree programs. They are paid at a rate which is about one-half that of the regular faculty. A nationwide survey of part-time stipends paid by member institutions of the Association of University Evening Colleges indicated a median salary of $12 per class hour, which amounts to less than $4,500 per year for a normal teaching load of 12 hours per semester.[1] There is no indication that the rates have changed significantly since that study was made. With most evening colleges on a self-sustaining financial basis, the payment of professional salaries to the evening teachers could terminate the programs.

In addition to low remuneration, part-time faculty do not receive tenure. Usually their appointments are subject to immediate cancellation if sufficient enrollment does not materialize. They generally do not receive academic rank regardless of qualifications or length of service. They do not hold membership in an organized faculty; in other words, they have no voice in the decisions about the program which they make possible.

Selection Where an organized evening faculty exists, the selection and appointment of part-time teachers is a responsibility of the appropriate departments. In some other institutions, the day departments take an active part in the selection of the evening teachers. In many evening colleges, however, the evening dean or director is the actual recruiter of part-time teachers, although his nominees then may be subject to approval by the departmental chairmen.

Utilization Regardless of full-time faculty appointments and regardless of the nature of faculty organization, adult education degree programs will continue to utilize part-time teachers. The limited scheduling possibilities alone are enough to require some part-time teachers. The general shortage of full-time teachers is another factor. The availability of outstandingly qualified experts in some areas is another.

The problems are the integration of such part-time teachers into the institution and their orientation with respect to standards, educational objectives, and the like. Effective coordination of their efforts requires a close working relationship with the full-time faculty on a departmental basis at least. The attainment of a close working

[1] Roger DeCrow, *Administrative Practices in University Evening Colleges,* Center for the Study of Liberal Education for Adults, Chicago, 1962, pp. 42–43.

relationship is not likely unless there are full-time faculty members with a primary responsibility for the quality of the evening program.

Sample Regulations Because of the rather complex relationships between an evening college and faculty members of other colleges within the institution, many universities have adopted regulations or policy statements which set forth the responsibilities and jurisdictions of the faculties or make provision for the appointment of part-time instructors.

At Columbia University, where the School of General Studies has a legislative faculty of university appointees, the statutes make the following provision for appointment of part-time teachers:

> *Appointments.* Persons not otherwise in the service of the University may be appointed, upon proposal of the Department concerned and upon nomination of the Faculty, by the President, subject to confirmation by the Trustees, to give instruction in the School of General Studies. Persons in the service of the University may similarly be designated to give instruction in the School of General Studies with additional compensation, or they may be assigned by their departments to give such instruction without additional compensation.

At Northeastern University full-time faculty and department heads are paid extra compensation to serve as consultants and advisers on new programs, faculty appointments, and academic standards of the part-time and evening programs. These consultants, meeting jointly, may serve as a legislative body on certain matters. They provide liaison with full-time faculty in their respective departments and disciplines and introduce new programs and courses for approval of appropriate college faculties or the Faculty Senate, if appropriate.

Administrator's Checklist 4

There are several ways of arranging the relationship of full-time faculty to the evening program and to the part-time teachers. The ways will vary according to the institutional situation. The following questions, however, may be helpful in developing effective professional relationships:

	Yes	*No*
1. Does an organized faculty of the institution take legislative action with respect to evening curricula, courses, and other academic matters?	___	___
2. Does that faculty include professorial personnel specifically appointed for evening teaching?	___	___
3. Are there evening teachers with the same institutional status as to salary, rank, tenure, and fringe benefits as day faculty members?	___	___
4. Are part-time teachers recruited and selected by full-time faculty members?	___	___
5. Do part-time teachers participate in departmental meetings?	___	___
6. Is the quality of evening instruction a designated responsibility of full-time faculty members?	___	___

The underlying assumption is that the faculty—not the organizational structure—determine the educational quality of the enterprise. A related assumption is that something which is everybody's job becomes nobody's job. Hence, it is concluded that an adult education degree program requires the appointment of some full-time faculty members with the quality of that evening program as their primary institutional responsibility. How they are appointed or organized is not the significant factor; the primary responsibility is the significant factor.

HISTORICAL DEVELOPMENT

The evolution of the evening college has had much to do with its problems of organization and intrainstitutional relationships. Many of the older evening colleges grew out of extension teaching programs which were organized in the first two decades of the present century, largely in urban institutions. Consequently, the organizational structure and the faculty relationships were more typical of university extension than of the liberal arts college or professional school.

Thirty years later, the extension structure of a relatively autonomous administration without a legislative faculty was a convenient expedient during the rapid and extensive growth of the evening college movement which occurred immediately after World War II, when the GI influx exceeded the physical capacity of the day programs and many new evening colleges were established. Through the use of part-time teachers, it was possible for an institution to keep its buildings open at night and provide, on a self-sustaining fiscal basis, degree programs for the veterans.

Thus, the extension teaching nature of many of the early evening colleges was replicated in the newer ones, and vague or nonexistent faculty relationships became common.

SPECIAL CHARACTERISTICS OF THE EVENING PROGRAM

The salient characteristic of the adult education degree program is its part-time students. The fact that classes are held in the evening stems in a sort of accidental way from the availability of physical plant and of students. The college buildings are in use for day students during the hours in which the employed adult is occupied. Where buildings and students have been available, part-time college education has been carried on in the daytime. So, actually, the adult education degree program should be considered in terms of educational opportunities for part-time, adult students rather than in the context of evening versus day.

Another characteristic of such programs is the irregularity of the students' schedules. When the college experience is predicated on a four-year sequence which begins with elementary courses and moves through advanced courses, there are patterns of scheduling and of teaching load which become rather rigid. In contrast, the adult degree candidate takes fewer courses per year and requires seven or eight years to earn the degree. It is possible, then, to complete advanced courses in some disciplines before beginning elementary courses in others. It is possible, too, that the adult student may be motivated for personal reasons to want to complete his major subject, whether it be chemistry or accounting, before he takes all of the courses of the general education requirement.

The institution, however, may find it desirable to insist upon completion of required courses, such as English composition and freshman mathematics, early in the degree program or to insist on early completion of general education requirements. A practical reason for such insistence is the usefulness of the skills or subject matter in work for other courses. Another practical reason is avoidance of the embarrassment which occurs when a part-time student has completed his major requirements for a degree and then cannot pass a freshman course.

TYPES OF PROGRAMS AND SERVICES

The variation among evening colleges has been mentioned. Not only do they provide courses, but they may also offer workshops and conferences. They may provide daytime classes. Further, a single evening college may provide students with courses otherwise available only from several different day colleges of the institution. The problem for each institution is to decide what kinds of services will be provided for the part-time student and what the limits of the evening program will be.

Curricula Leading to Degrees

The standard function of the evening college—and in most institutions its major role—is the provision of undergraduate degree curricula. The enrollments of baccalaureate candidates have been both the backbone and the major social contribution of the evening colleges.

In addition, many evening colleges offer graduate work leading to the master's degree, especially in business administration and in education. To date, the graduate schools have resisted pressures for doctorates earned on a part-time basis.

The main question for the university administrator is not what kinds of programs shall be offered on a part-time basis but who shall administer them. He has several choices. The evening college may administer *all* part-time programs. Or it may administer only the programs through the master's degree. Or it may administer only undergraduate programs, with administration of graduate work for part-time adult students remaining with the graduate and professional schools.

It is possible, too, that the evening college may exercise much control over academic aspects of some of the programs and little or none over some of the others. The relationship to graduate programs may be solely administrative in terms of registration, fee collection, and scheduling, whereas the relationship to the undergraduate courses may be much more extensive.

Nondegree Services

If the primary function is the provision of adult degree programs, then nondegree services become almost a contradiction. Yet, in the drive to be all things to all people, the evening college in most cases provides nondegree or noncredit services. Because credit is only valuable as a counting device in the process of earning a degree, the terms "nondegree" and "noncredit" are probably synonymous. "Noncredit," as a term, is itself confusing. Evening colleges have at least four commonly accepted categories of noncredit students: (1) a student who does not want credit, (2) a student who cannot qualify for credit; i.e., cannot meet the admission requirements to become a degree candidate, (3) a student in a course for which no credit is given, and (4) a student who intends to apply for credit but who has not yet matriculated.[2] Some evening colleges have all four kinds of noncredit students; a few have none. Most have two or more. The presence of such students in large numbers is one of the characteristics of the adult program which makes it markedly different from the programs of the day colleges.

There are several ways in which educational opportunities are made available to the nondegree or noncredit student. The most common is the enrollment in credit courses of students who are not candidates for degrees. Another common method is the provision of courses which do not carry credit, although in most institutions such courses are generally few in number.

Conferences and Workshops In addition to regular semester-length courses, either credit or noncredit, some of the adult degree colleges offer conferences or workshops or provide lecture series on a noncredit basis. Such a practice is more common where the evening college serves the function of an extension division as well as the part-time degree function.

Nature of Nondegree Service The enrollment of noncredit students in the credit courses of a degree program usually is intended to facilitate the personal growth and

[2] Ernest E. McMahon, *The Emerging Evening College*, Bureau of Publications, Teachers College Press, Columbia University, New York, 1960, p. 69.

development of the individuals. The same reason is advanced for the offering of non-credit courses.

On the other hand, the conferences or workshops frequently are developed in co-operation with a business, industry, or trade association for the in-service training of employees or members. The same thing is true of short training courses, many of which are given in the plants of the participating companies.

Sponsorship of noncredit educational services thus falls into two main categories. There is the opportunity for individuals to enroll in courses provided and offered solely by the university, and there are the special programs which are cosponsored with a client agency.

Correspondence Study

Correspondence study is offered by only a few evening colleges. It is primarily a service of the extension divisions of state universities, and it is described in the chapter on correspondence study.

Special Degree Programs

Because of the experience and maturity of the adult student, concern has been expressed over whether or not there is any actual need for him to follow a curriculum similar to that designed for young students right out of secondary school. It is argued that the adult has learned much by experience and that, where appropriate, such experience should be credited toward the degree requirements.

The arrangements to recognize experience utilize proficiency examinations, independent study, and special seminars. The plans shorten the length of time required to earn the degree, and they reduce the amount of time that has to be spent in class or on campus. Frequently they are built around brief, intensive residential periods with intervening time for independent study.

Some of the special degree programs lead to the institution's conventional degree; others lead to a special degree such as Bachelor of Liberal Studies. The first special program was established at Brooklyn College. Others are in existence at Goddard College, Johns Hopkins, the University of Oklahoma, Queens College (New York City), and Syracuse University.

Special Programs for Women

Approximately a hundred colleges and universities have special adult education programs for mature women.[3] Not all of them are degree programs, and not all of them are conducted by evening colleges. Their purposes, however, are similar. They provide instruction or counseling to retread educationally the woman whose career was interrupted by homemaking. Many of the courses are given in the daytime so that the women may attend classes while husbands are at work and children are in school. Some of them are specialized, like the Mathematics Retraining program at Rutgers. Radcliffe offers postgraduate opportunities for advanced study. Other programs offer counseling which directs their clients to available educational opportunities.

Daytime Courses

Courses for women are not the only daytime educational programs for adults. The School of General Studies at Columbia has always had large daytime enrollments. University College of Syracuse has given daytime courses. The University of California's Extension Center at San Francisco has developed an extensive group of daytime courses. The determining factors have been the availability of students and facilities.

[3] U.S. Department of Labor, *Continuing Education Programs for Women*, 1966.

As leisure time increases, it is possible that the number of daytime college classes for adults will increase. There were late-afternoon classes for veterans immediately after World War II. Before the five-day week made the long weekend universally popular, there were many Saturday classes, especially for teachers.

In addition, there are late-afternoon classes in those colleges which do not organize a separate administrative agency for the adult degree candidate. There are urban institutions, such as New York University, which schedule classes in some of their colleges from early morning until late in the evening and enroll the part-time as well as the full-time students in a single program.

Consequently, despite the common use of "evening college" as a descriptive term for an institution offering part-time degree study, there are many adult degree students who may not be evening students. Again, the part-time characteristic is the significant one rather than the accident of evening attendance.

Branch Campuses

Another dimension has come to the adult education degree program with the proliferation of branch campuses. An earlier pattern involved a few courses at various off-campus locations. The development of the past two decades has been in the direction of fully developed and sometimes fully staffed centers. Because these evening programs frequently have been started in available high school buildings, they have been evening programs with large numbers of adult degree candidates although the basic reason for establishment may have been to serve those just out of high school. Because they were evening and off-campus operations involving part-time students, many institutions assigned their administration to the evening college dean.

The development of branch campuses has aggravated some of the problems of control and of faculty jurisdiction and has, also, created a rather fluid situation for many institutions because the controls have changed. Wisconsin, for example, began a series of branches of the University of Wisconsin as activities of the extension division and then removed the off-campus units from extension, placing them under a chancellor. Other institutions have made similar changes as the branches have grown in size, acquired permanent daytime facilities, and developed their own faculties and programs.

THE EVENING STUDENT

A willingness to give up time which for other adults is leisure and, except for those under employer tuition-refund plans, a willingness to spend their own money for education are the universal characteristics of the evening student population. Otherwise, they are a heterogeneous group in terms of age, educational background, work experience, and personal goals. The mixture of degree programs and adult education objectives further complicates the situation.

Motivation is high and has a practical value in that it may help offset weaknesses in preparation.

Mobility is a problem because degree candidates often have to transfer from one evening college to another as a result of job relocation. Consequently, the more flexible an adult degree program, the better it is for more of the adult population.

Adult degree students reside in a single geographic area, but they may be the most cosmopolitan student group within a university. Part-time students come from home or place of business and, therefore, live and work within a commuting radius of the university. However, their upbringing and prior education may have taken place anywhere, and thus they may provide a national or even international student body for an otherwise provincial institution.

Academic Handicaps

Much attention is given to the negative aspects of part-time study. The complaints focus on fatigue, competition of job and family responsibilities, and lack of library time. Careful limitation of course loads, extended library hours, the maximum use of paperbacks, and an insistence on high-quality academic performance will overcome the handicaps.

Recruitment

The two factors which limit an institution's recruitment potential are the total population within the geographic area and the transportation network, both roads and common carriers, which will enable members of that population to attend classes and to get home afterward. Although city locations have had an advantage in the past because of population and transportation facilities, the increasing parking problems and the threat of unrest is raising interest in suburban branches, especially when limited-access highways are available.

Surveys of evening students have indicated that word of mouth is the most common source of new students. Fellow employees and other acquaintances tell about programs and their reaction to them. Thus, a satisfied customer appears to be an asset.

Promotional Efforts Evening colleges are promotion-minded organizations. Their need for advertising is real. They are serving a population which does not have access to guidance counselors. Half of their students never attended college nor planned to and, therefore, are not fully aware of educational opportunities. Many of their potential students have come from other geographic areas and do not know of the evening programs in the area. The educational programs vary, and information about the variation must be published so that the adults may know which institution offers what to whom.

Word of mouth has been mentioned as the most effective method of recruitment. Direct mail, posters on bulletin boards in places of employment, newspaper advertising including the use of special Sunday supplements, catalogs, visits to personnel offices and to high schools, and spot announcements on radio and television are in common use.

Because most evening colleges have small administrative staffs, it may be advisable to utilize an advertising agency whenever newspaper or other mass-media advertising is planned. The evening college is not likely to have an advertising expert, and the cost of the advertisement is the same because the agency fee reimburses the professional.

Supporting Services

The services which bring the institution and the student together generally are provided by the evening college for its own students, although there is a trend toward bringing the evening student into the workings of the central apparatus of the university. Such services are counseling, both academic and personal; student life with respect to extracurricular activities and discipline; registration and admissions; and placement.

Because of the differences in entrance procedures and course scheduling, it is advisable to have separate personnel handling both the admission and registration of the part-time student. The personnel may be stationed within a central admissions or registrar's office, but specialization of function is urged.

FACILITIES

Except for office space for the evening college staff themselves, adult degree programs generally utilize the same physical plant used by the day students. When conferences and workshops are part of the program, obviously there must be a conference center unless all such activities are conducted off-campus in hotels or motels.

A few evening colleges have some classroom facilities of their own, and many of them rent space, especially in downtown locations. The current trend, however, appears to be one of on-campus location which, of course, includes the branch campus. A major reason for the campus trend is the availability of library and laboratory facilities.

ORGANIZATIONS

The major organizations to which adult education degree-granting institutions belong are the following:

Association of University Evening Colleges. The secretary-treasurer is Dr. Howell W. McGee, University of Oklahoma, Norman, Okla. 73069.

National University Extension Association. The executive director is Robert J. Pitchell, 1820 Massachusetts Avenue, N.W., Washington, D.C. 20036.

For associate degree programs, in addition to the above, a third organization is the American Association of Junior Colleges. Its executive director is Edmund W. Gleazer, Jr., 1315 Sixteenth Street, N.W., Washington, D.C. 20036.

BIBLIOGRAPHY

DeCrow, Roger: *Administrative Practices in University Evening Colleges,* Center for the Study of Liberal Education for Adults, Chicago, 1962.

Dyer, P. John: *Ivory Towers in the Market Place,* The Bobbs-Merrill Company, Inc., Indianapolis, 1956.

Gordon, Morton: *Daytime School for Adults,* Center for the Study of Liberal Education for Adults, Boston, 1967.

Gowin, D. Bob: *An Experimental Study of Part-time College Faculty,* University of Bridgeport, Bridgeport, Conn., 1958.

Liveright, Alexander A., and Roger DeCrow: *New Directions to Degree Programs Especially for Adults,* Center for the Study of Liberal Education for Adults, Chicago, 1963.

McMahon, Ernest E.: *The Emerging Evening College,* Bureau of Publications, Teachers College Press, Columbia University, New York, 1960.

Stern, Milton R.: *People, Programs, and Persuasion,* Center for the Study of Liberal Education for Adults, Chicago, 1961.

Thornton, James W., Jr.: *The Community Junior College,* 2d ed., John Wiley & Sons, Inc., New York, 1966, chap. 16.

U.S. Department of Labor: *Continuing Education Programs for Women,* 1966.

Chapter 3

Admission and Counseling of Adult Students

CLARENCE H. THOMPSON

Dean of University College and Center for Continuing Education and Professor of Adult Education, Drake University, Des Moines, Iowa

ADMISSION OF PART-TIME AND ADULT STUDENTS

Part-time adult students have problems and create concerns for the institution that differ significantly from those associated with full-time youthful students. Adults have different motivations. They are more likely to place their preoccupation with job and home responsibilities ahead of their academic work. Also the adult student's aspirations for a better job and his desire to satisfy his employer, especially one who pays all or part of his educational costs, are more evident and immediate than those of the full-time student. The recognition of these differences should be reflected in the admission policies and practices affecting the part-time adult student.

Admission Policies and Practices

Admission practices of colleges and universities enrolling considerable numbers of adult students into programs leading to degrees fall generally into three categories. These are referred to here as (1) "One University—One Policy," (2) "Open-door Policy," and (3) "Deferred Matriculation Policy." Variations and modifications of these three policies are also practiced by some institutions.

One Institution—One Policy Many colleges have a single admission policy administered by a dean or director of admissions. With this policy, any full- or part-time student who is planning to work for credit or toward an undergraduate degree fills out the appropriate forms, requests transcripts from his high school and any institutions of higher learning he has attended, and pays the required fees. If the adult student has no evidence of completion of one of the standard tests, such as the SAT or ACT, or in the event that he has been out of school for a number of years, he may be required to sit for one or more tests of aptitude, interest, personality, or ability before a decision to grant or deny admission is reached. Normally, the test scores and the high school record, together with transcripts of any work completed subsequent to high school graduation, are considered in arriving at the decision. Cases that do not clearly fall within the "accept" or "reject" categories established by an institution are usually reviewed by an admissions committee prior to decision.

Open-door Policy In the peak post-World War II period of the returning veteran, many institutions followed a permissive policy of admission for the high school graduate 21 or older with GI benefits. In the case of the mature veteran who seemed to have a goal and a definite idea of what he wanted, it was not uncommon for the institution to approach his part-time enrollment with the attitude of "What night can you come?" Concern for his ability to do satisfactory work toward a degree frequently became evident only after he began to have problems. There are still institutions that follow a modified version of this policy.

Records of high school and any subsequent academic work are analyzed by institutions which follow a modified "open-door policy," but more stress is placed upon evidence of ability to do satisfactory work by completing college-level courses with passing grades. This is particularly relevant for the adult who has been out of school for several years. Differences in motivation, seriousness of purpose, additional responsibilities, and maturity tend to improve his chances of academic success. The policy of accepting the enrollment of any adult (variously defined as over 19, over 21, or mature) in any class or course from which his background will enable him to benefit is rather widely practiced. This pattern, however, is more common for "special" or "nonmatriculated" students. In the case of those in this category who want eventually to complete a degree program, most evening colleges or extension divisions will require that matriculation be accomplished relatively early in the program.

Deferred Matriculation Policy This system involves the minimum requirements as far as entering upon a course of study is concerned. Ordinarily, furnishing evidence of high school completion or equivalency will suffice. This approach is predicated upon the assumption that the best predictor of academic success is evidence of having attained satisfactory results in the completion of college-level courses.

Many of the larger urban universities use some variation of this policy in their part-time adult admissions. The applicant furnishes evidence of high school completion, is interviewed by an admissions counselor, and is assisted in the registration process by an adviser from the broad discipline of his choice, i.e., a student planning to study in the business curriculum would be advised by faculty teaching in the area of business. Provided he maintains a C (2.0) or better average, he may continue as a nonmatriculated student until he reaches a specified number of hours, at which time he must apply for matriculation. This point will vary from 10 semester hours to 60 semester hours, with a preponderance of colleges using 30 semester hours as the maximum which can be earned by a part-time student without qualifying for acceptance (matriculation) to degree candidacy. Because of the diversity of the part-time adult student body in terms of background, age, interests, needs, etc.; because of full-time commitments to their jobs, families, and communities; and because of the variety of individual goals such as job advancement, retraining for new careers, or personal enrichment, the deferred matriculation policy offers adults an opportunity to prove themselves capable of pursuing a degree program without sacrificing the academic respectability of the institution.

Admission of Special or Nonmatriculated Adult Students

Many adult part-time students, at least initially, do not plan on working for a degree. They are motivated to enroll in a single course, in a series of related courses, or even to work for a certificate. For some, there is interest or curiosity in a subject such as music appreciation, painting, foreign affairs, etc. For others, a discovered need may be the propellant that brings them to the continuing education facility in search of a skill or further knowledge or understanding with which to overcome their deficiency. Many students seek specific, job-related courses in the hope of achieving earlier promotion, better positions, or a complete shift in career emphasis. Another group is represented by the housewife who wishes to study real estate in order to work part-time in this field, or by the graduate engineer who takes courses in data processing to broaden his understanding of certain management functions. Finally, there are those adults who initially use part-time education for social purposes; that is, to make new acquaintances and to fill otherwise lonely leisure hours with stimulating and satisfying activities.

Adults who approach part-time higher education from one of these points of reference frequently consider the necessity of completing the formal admission process prior to enrollment as an unnecessary harassment. In fact, if carried to the extreme, a person might be expected to sit through entrance examinations in order to enroll for a non-credit course.

The majority of colleges and universities maintaining adult divisions permit non-credit enrollments on a "special" or "nonmatriculated" basis. The student who "enters" on this basis and later decides to pursue a formal program will need to meet the requirements for admission or matriculation before being accepted into the program.

Responsibility for Admission of Part-time and Adult Students

In some institutions the admission of part-time and adult students is the responsibility of a single central admissions office for the entire university. In others, this function is fulfilled by a separate office, such as a university college admissions office.

Single versus Separate Admissions Office Advocates of a central admissions office for the processing of all admissions to an institution maintain that this system gives better control. Another commonly expressed opinion is that all persons who work toward the same degree should meet the identical requirements and standards for enrollment, and that a single office can better see to this. In 1953, Neuffer [4] [1] found that 65 percent of the reporting institutions in the Association of University Evening Colleges (AUEC) used the same requirements for admission for both full-time and part-time students. Eight years later, DeCrow [1] found that only 50 percent of the reporting AUEC institutions used the same requirements for admission to both evening and day programs.

Whether the admissions office is a single central office of the institution or whether a separate office is maintained for part-time adults does not in itself determine whether or not the same admission requirements are used for all students. However, DeCrow's study indicates that at least 50 percent of the colleges have different admission requirements for part-time evening students. These differences, he states, "all suggest that gaining admission to the evening program is easier, or at least, less formalistic and tedious than entering the day program." He also noted that 65 percent of the schools required some type of entrance examination for the part-time group. These differences in process for admitting the part-time adult student, it is suggested, offer partial justification for a separate, adult-oriented admissions office within the overall administrative framework of the university college or evening division.

Arguments for separate, specialized admission facilities usually center around the following four points:

1. Access to the facility during convenient hours in the evening and on Saturday is made possible for the employed adult. A single central office usually maintains regular daytime working hours.

2. A concern for and understanding of the particular problems of adult students is more readily shown. Administrators whose knowledge and understanding of adult students is a major thrust of their professions are better able to deal with students fairly, realistically, and with the best interests of both the student and the institution in mind than are the "day-oriented" admission personnel who need to shift philosophical gears each time they deal with part-time adult students who do not fit the youth-centered mold of the full-time day student.

3. The differing processes of admission established for adult part-time students are more easily administered. These include such matters as testing, evaluation of experience, and deferred matriculation.

4. The organizational or functional structure of the administrative unit responsible for the adult programs is simplified. The dean of university college or a vice-president for continuing education can exercise best his administrative, supervisory, and philosophical responsibilities for the effectiveness and quality of the adult programs when all of the units which admit, advise, counsel, and service the operation are responsible to and report to him.

Staffing the Part-time and Adult Admissions Office The size of the staff necessary to appropriately administer the part-time adult student programs will depend upon the size and the nature of the university of which it is a part as well as on the organizational structure within which it operates. The functions to be fulfilled by the assignment of subordinate members of the dean's staff include the admission, advisement,[2] counseling, and registration of part-time adult students. Also, testing is a service that is

[1] Bracketed numbers refer to the references at the end of the chapter.

[2] Advisement is the function of advising students about courses to take, requirements of a specific program, proper sequence of courses and satisfying of prerequisites. This function can be performed by a member of the faculty, an administrator, or a counselor. Counseling, on the other hand, should properly be performed by a trained professional. Counseling deals with problems and the search for solutions thereto with the counselee or student. Sometimes "counseling" is incorrectly used to cover any situation where the student confers with a member of the university family.

needed in the admission process. This latter may be an integral part of the administrative setup of the adult division or it may fall under the testing and counseling service of the university. If the latter, then close coordination must exist. Some schools use the number-two man in the testing center to work closely with the adult-division staff.

Admission of Part-time Graduate Students By and large, the admission of graduate students to degree candidacy, whether full-time or part-time, is the responsibility of the graduate school or division. There being little identifiable difference between part-time and full-time graduate students, other than the number of hours carried at one time, the process of admission usually is similar if not identical for both. In addition to an acceptable baccalaureate degree together with appropriate grades, the candidate normally must perform adequately on one or more of the testing devices, such as the Miller Analogies Test, the Graduate Record Examination, etc. It is also common practice to permit qualified graduates to enroll in classes on a nondegree basis. This permits the non-degree-seeking individual the opportunity to enroll in a course having some special interest. Many schools, however, will not count toward the higher degree requirements work completed before formal acceptance to candidacy.

Admission of Transfer Students

In today's mobile society the problems associated with adult students who have attended other institutions of higher learning are nearly as numerous as those related to the admission of first-time adult students.

Admission from Other Colleges and Universities In general, colleges accepting students with advanced-standing credits from other institutions of college rank take into consideration most of the following:

That the college is accredited.

That an official transcript is furnished from each institution attended indicating courses, credits, and grades.

That satisfactory scholarship was maintained at the former institution. (This is interpreted as at least a C average, 2.0 or better on a 4.0 scale.)

A statement of honorable dismissal from the college attended.

The secondary school record.

Satisfactory test scores on the ACT, SAT, or other specified instrument.

In recognizing credit by transfer from other institutions, ordinarily credit for courses in which the candidate received grades lower than C (on a scale of A, B, C, D, F) is not accepted.

Admission from Area Schools, Community and Junior Colleges The considerations of the preceding paragraph apply also to junior and community colleges as recipients of transfer students. Recently there has been a dramatic increase in the number of post-secondary area schools, community colleges, and junior colleges, and in the area they serve. Massachusetts, Iowa, and other states have developed comprehensive state-wide coverage by the establishment of area schools or community colleges for each region of the state. Tuition is often lower in the junior and community colleges than in the senior institutions. In view of the rising costs affecting all of higher education, including dormitory living expenses, more and more full-time students stay at home and attend schools in their geographic area. Thus more students than ever before are applying for admission and transfer to senior institutions after one or two years at junior colleges, bringing about more problems of evaluation and acceptance of advanced-standing credit from the newer community colleges. New elements of concern for the four-year colleges and the universities have therefore developed.

The specialized vocational aspects of some of the area-school programs make difficult the decisions of what, if any, credits should be accepted for transfer to a baccalaureate degree program. Some of the junior-college programs have been designed to be terminal. A part of the dilemma involved in the evaluation of this group affects especially the adult part-time student who subsequently, perhaps years later, decides upon the desirability of further education and a higher degree. Misguidance at the secondary-school level may encourage capable students to engage in programs below their ability levels. There are also the technically oriented programs of the community colleges or technical institutes that do not logically lead to the upper-division courses of the baccalaureate degree program. For example, a student who completed an associate degree in an engineering technology program may find that his preparation is inadequate to continue in the field of engineering, at least without repeating a significant number of courses.

There would appear to be serious concern in academia about the baccalaureate degree which in effect adds the equivalent of another associate degree to the one already completed; i.e., the adding of two years of basic business subjects (for which the student might otherwise qualify for an associate degree) to an already earned associate degree in engineering technology. The analogy of fitting half an orange to half an apple to make a piece of fruit illustrates the obvious.

Not all of these problems are unique to evening colleges. Administrators of adult programs should, therefore, be aware of the policies regarding transfer students that are practiced by the full-time admissions department.

Other Considerations in Admitting Transfer Students There are numerous other problems encountered in the acceptance of transfer students and in the determination of the amount of advanced-standing credit to be allowed to apply to the program at the accepting institution. Some of the more troublesome of these problems involve the evaluation of work completed at nonaccredited institutions, at foreign universities, or at several different institutions and transcripts showing low grades, time lapse since work was completed, or changes of major or degree objectives.

A sizable number of institutions fail to grant credit for any work taken at a nonaccredited institution. Some schools accept only limited hours of credit provided the work was of similar level and was completed with a B or better grade. Others permit students to take examinations for credit or for placement in subjects completed in this manner.

Since European and other foreign universities do not operate on the semester-hour basis, it is difficult to equate portions of their programs to the American university system of classroom minutes and credit hours. One reliable source of help in this matter is the American Council on Education, which will offer meaningful suggestions in terms of equivalent credit when asked about a specific individual case.

In evaluating the transcripts of a student who has attended several institutions, the problem of what advanced-standing credits to allow is compounded by the possibility that courses from different institutions with different titles may, in fact, be identical. In addition, due to the differing requirements of institutions, it might be difficult to find room within the new program for all those courses that cannot be substituted for the required courses. This naturally depends upon the hours of elective subjects permitted. These problems also pertain, perhaps even more emphatically, to the student who makes a change in his major or degree objective. It is especially a problem when a student who has taken a variety of courses—in, for instance, the liberal arts—tries to apply a conglomeration of electives to a more restrictive degree program such as engineering.

The problem of time lapse since completion of previous work is handled differently by different schools. On the one hand an arbitrary 5-, 8-, or 10-year limit in using hours toward a degree may be in effect. At the opposite end of the scale are some few institutions that will count any work that has previously been satisfactorily completed. Still others will allow credit for hours earned in the recent past but will require testing for credit in order to count work over 10 years old.

Low grades present two kinds of problems for personnel dealing with admission of adult part-time students. One has to do with the acceptance of credit toward advanced standing. For example, should a student who received a D in the first semester of a full-year course—in, for example, a language or accounting—receive credit for the full year's work if he received a C or better in the final semester? What if the semester grades were reversed? The second problem of serious concern to the admissions staff has to do with the second chance. If a student has been placed on academic probation or has been dismissed for academic reasons, should a university college permit him to enroll for a part-time load? Some colleges say "no." Some say "only after a semester (or a year) of nonattendance." A third group feel that nearly any student should receive a second (or third) opportunity to prove himself and that through part-time study he will have the best chance for success.

Many of these problems may be resolved at least in part by the wise use of testing for equivalency, for credit, or for placement. There is increasing evidence of a trend in this direction.

Admission of Students to Advanced Standing by Testing

Many colleges and universities have procedures whereby adult students may qualify for advanced-standing credit by taking and passing examinations.

College Examinations for Credit Perhaps the most common situation involves the student who has had the equivalent of a course but, due to the period of time that has elapsed since its completion or because of the standing of the institution at which it was taken, cannot get credit for it. In this case the student may petition for credit by examination. If a satisfactory grade is achieved, then credit is allowed for the course. Sometimes a grade of B is required. A number of schools will allow an adult student to petition for credit by examination in any course, whether or not he has had a similar course. There is ordinarily a fee of from $10 to $25 for taking the examination. In addition, a few of these schools will charge the tuition rate for the course if the examination is passed for credit. In this latter case, the only advantage to the student is the avoidance of class attendance and the routine assignments.

Examinations for Placement There are also situations where an adult student, by virtue of experience or independent study, can "pass out" of a subject or a required level of a subject. One of the more common examples of this is in the area of foreign language. A student may possess sufficient background and knowledge to move directly into a higher-level language course. He should be encouraged to take a placement examination and, if he successfully "passes out" of the first-year course, he may have the opportunity of taking a course more appropriate to his ability or his interests.

Other Qualifying Examinations Some state departments of education have moved to the granting of credit to adult students who take and pass certain qualifying examinations. One example of this trend is in New York State where certain prerequisite teacher-education courses may be skipped by the experienced adult who is able to demonstrate his proficiency by passing a course-content test. The examination, developed by the state, is administered by the institutions granting the credit.

The College-level Examination Program The newest and seemingly most hopeful of the methods of testing for either placement or college credit is the College-level Examination Program (CLEP) developed by the College Entrance Examination Board. In the words of the descriptive brochure [11]:

> The Program has five major objectives: to provide a national program of examinations that can be used to evaluate nontraditional college-level education, specifically including independent study and correspondence work; to stimulate colleges and universities to become more aware of the need for and the possibilities and problems of credit by examination; to enable colleges and universities to develop appropriate

procedures for the placement, accreditation, and admission of transfer students; to provide colleges and universities with a means by which to evaluate their programs and their students' achievement; to assist adults who wish to continue their education in order to meet licensing requirements or qualify for higher positions.

The program consists of two series of examinations, general and subject examinations. The general examinations measure achievement in five areas of the liberal arts: English composition, humanities, mathematics, natural science, and social science—history. Given as a battery, they are used for determining the educational background of persons with one or two years of college. The general examinations lend themselves particularly to providing information for use in the admission and placement of part-time adult students into college programs. The subject examinations, of which there are currently 30 with additional ones under construction, are essentially end-of-course examinations to test the competence commonly expected of college students in undergraduate courses in the subject. The subject examinations lend themselves to credit by examination or placement, both of which are desirable in programs for part-time adult students.

The College-level Examination Program offers exciting possibilities for interesting older adults in continuing their education by assisting institutions through the use of a nationally administered program of college-level examinations to recognize and reward the educational achievement which they attained outside the regular classroom setting. This should prove a boon to institutions having special degree programs for adults and especially those which include segments of independent study in their degree programs.

Testing as a Part of the Admission Process Admission departments frequently require testing as a part of the process of admission to degree candidacy. This may be at the beginning stages of the adult student's exposure to college or it may be a part of the matriculation process. Different institutions use a variety of instruments, including the American College Testing program (ACT), the Scholastic Aptitude Test (SAT) of the College Boards, the Ohio State Scholastic Aptitude Test, the College Qualification Test (CQT), and the Test of Adult College Aptitude (TACA). The last one, TACA, requires further comment. Tests for admission which involve norms based on youthful students are inappropriate for adults who have been out of school several years. TACA, developed by King M. Wientge and Philip H. DuBois, was normed on the adult population of evening college students attending University College at Washington University in St. Louis, and it has shown promise as a measure of adult learning. It has the unique feature of including biographical information items [6].

One further use of testing is fairly common. At some schools it is a part of the admission process. Other institutions, however, use tests in a diagnostic manner. Students wishing to enroll in, for example, freshman English or beginning mathematics are given a diagnostic examination. Persons scoring below the "cut-off score" will instead be encouraged to enroll in remedial or developmental noncredit courses in the subject.

Admission Records and Forms

The purpose of the forms and records used in the admission process is to collect personal data, high school records, transcripts of academic work attempted, and test data in a systematic sequence. When properly assembled, these data enable the admissions committee to make appropriate judgments on admission. Forms vary with each institution but in general require the same types of information for all students.

A first-time adult college student completes the application-for-admission form (Figure 1) and forwards the scholastic-standing form (Figure 2) to the high school from which he graduated. A transfer student, in addition, requests a transcript from each institution he has previously attended. He also forwards a personal-reference blank (Figure 3) to the dean of students at each of these institutions.

Promotion of Admissions

To promote or not to promote is really not the question. Promotion takes place. What must be decided is how: that is, by what means, and what image the institution wishes to project. If you believe in the product you are offering, promotion is essential.

FOR OFFICE USE ONLY	DRAKE UNIVERSITY	I AM APPLYING FOR
Receipt No.	DES MOINES, IOWA 50311	...... Fall 1968
Date		...... Spring 1969
Application Fee	APPLICATION FOR ADMISSION	...... Summer 1968
Prepayment		......Both Summer & Fall 1968

Mr.
Miss
Name Mrs. .... Sex .... Telephone ....
(Please print in ink or type) Last First Middle or Maiden
Home Address ....
Street and Number or R.F.D. Number Town or City State or Country Zip Code
Mailing address if different ....
Place of Birth ....Date of birth............................ Age.....
Town or City and State or Country Month, Day, Year
....
Name of Parent or Guardian Street City State
Are you married?.............. If married woman, give maiden name....................... Social Security No..................

BE SURE to answer all questions completely, sign in indicated places, and enclose the $10.00 application fee. THIS APPLICATION CANNOT BE PROCESSED IF INCOMPLETE IN ANY WAY . . . **but will be returned to you for further information.** Make check payable to "Drake University." Mail or give the application and check to: Admissions Coordinator, Drake University, Des Moines, Iowa 50311

COLLEGE AND FIELD OF STUDY (MAJOR)

I plan to enroll as a:

.......Full-Time student
(Ten semester hours or more)

.......Part-Time student

.......Day classes

.......Saturday classes

.......On-campus evening classes

.......Off-campus evening classes

(Indicate One)

.... College of Business Administration Major ....
.... College of Education Elementary Major, Secondary Major ....
.... College of Fine Arts Art, Music, Theatre Arts, Speech ....
.... School of Journalism Major ....
.... College of Liberal Arts Major ....
.... College of Pharmacy ....
.... Divinity School ....
.... Law School ....
.... Graduate Division ....
(For application write Dean of Graduate Division)

EDUCATION & EXPERIENCE

Fill in the table below to make a complete chronological history of your education, work experience and military service, beginning with the high school from which you were graduated. If you leave chronological gaps, explain them on a separate sheet. You **must** list each school you have attended. Failure to do this can result in your dismissal.

High School, College, Firm, or Establishment (Including Drake University)		Period of Attendance or Work	Degree, If Any, and Date
High School:................	....	19.... to 19....	....
....	....	19.... to 19....	....
....	....	19.... to 19....	....
....	....	19.... to 19....	....
....	....	19.... to 19....	....
....	....	19.... to 19....	....

Date of previous enrollment at Drake University ....
I am presently enrolled in a college or university yes.... no.... ....
(Name of the institution)
Give date when you took, or will take the ACT test ....and/or SAT test............................
......**ACT** ......**SAT Check here if you have requested that your ACT or SAT test score report be sent directly to Drake University from the national test headquarters. We require either ACT or SAT.**

In order to determine your qualifications for admission, the Registrar must be supplied with transcripts of your records in institutions you have previously attended. READ THE FOLLOWING STATEMENTS AND CHECK THE ONE THAT APPLIES TO YOU:

...... I HAVE NEVER ENROLLED IN ANY COLLEGE OR UNIVERSITY.
(Ask your high school counselor or principal to complete the enclosed white form and return it to the Registrar, Drake University, together with an official transcript of your high school record).

...... I HAVE BEEN ENROLLED IN A COLLEGE OR UNIVERSITY BUT HAVE COMPLETED LESS THAN 30 SEMESTER HOURS (ONE YEAR) OF WORK.
(Ask your high school counselor or principal to complete the enclosed white form and return it to the Registrar, Drake University, together with an official transcript of your high school record. Also, ask each college or university you have attended to send an ORIGINAL transcript of your college record to the Registrar. Also, ask the dean of the last college you attended to complete the enclosed blue personal reference form and return it to the Registrar.)

......I HAVE COMPLETED 30 OR MORE SEMESTER HOURS (ONE YEAR) OF WORK IN A COLLEGE OR UNIVERSITY.
(Ask each college or university you have attended to send an ORIGINAL transcript of your college record to the Registrar, Drake University; also ask the dean of the last college you attended to complete the enclosed blue personal reference form and return it to the Registrar).

Page 1

Fig. 1 *Application for admission, Drake University.*

ADDITIONAL INFORMATION

Have you ever been dismissed from, or placed on probation in any school or college? ....

If so, give college and circumstances ....

....

If transferring from another college, did you leave the last college attended in good standing? ....

If you enter for the summer session, will you return next fall? ....

Do you plan to complete a degree program at Drake University?.................. If not, what are your plans?..................

....

Have you ever discontinued your study or work because of physical illness or nervous disturbances?..............If so, explain:

....

Any physical limitations? ....

....

Have you made, or will you make, application for financial aid?.....................What date?...................................

Have your parent's submitted the confidential financial statement?....................What date?...............................

List here honors and special recognition you have received in high school:...

....

....

If there are any comments you wish to make, please write them here...

....

....

Do you sing or play a musical instrument?......................Which instrument?...

Applicant's Certificate: To the best of my knowledge, I have no physical, mental or social handicap that would disqualify me for full and normal participation in regular activities, and the statements I have made on this application are correct.

DATE.. ....
Applicant's Signature

RESIDENCE INFORMATION

1. If you are an unmarried man or woman younger than 21 in your first year at Drake University, you will be REQUIRED to live in a University student residence (unless you plan to live with your family or blood relatives or you will be a part-time student). If this paragraph describes your circumstances please mark the "yes" and complete the student residence agreement on pages 3 and 4. yes .... no ....
2. If you are not required to live in a University student residence and plan to live with your family or blood relatives in or near Des Moines, please discard pages 3 and 4 and provide the following information.

   Name of relative.. Relationship......................

   Address ....

3. If you are not a freshman but are an unmarried woman younger than 21 and are not now a member of a sorority represented at Drake University, and do not plan to live with your family or blood relatives, you will be REQUIRED to live in a University student residence. If this paragraph describes your circumstances please mark the "yes" and complete the student residence agreement on pages 3 and 4. (Men may live in approved off-campus housing after the freshman year.) yes .... no ....
4. If you are not required to live in a University student residence but wish to do so if a reservation is available, please mark the "yes" and complete the student residence agreement on pages 3 and 4. yes .... no ....
5. If you are not required to live in a University residence and plan to live elsewhere, please discard pages 3 and 4 and provide the following information:

   Address while attending Drake (if known)..

   ....
   (Off-campus housing must be approved by the Director of Student Residences)

APPLICATION FEE

Your application for admission (pages 1 and 2) must be accompanied by a $10 fee. Your application will be returned if the $10 fee does not accompany it. (Former Drake students, summer (only) students, and those taking less than 10 hours per semester do not pay the $10.) THIS FEE IS NOT REFUNDABLE.

When completed, please mail or give this application with the $10 fee to: Admissions Coordinator, Drake University, Des Moines, Iowa 50311.

All admissions to the University will be subject to the finding by the University Student Health Services that you are physically and mentally fit to carry on a normal college program.

Page 2

Fig. 1 *(Continued)*

Since each potential applicant for admission to the part-time adult programs of a college or university cannot be identified in advance, promotion must be aimed at the community at large from which these students come. To some extent the image that your institution has created in its various communities will determine the kinds of students that come or are sent. There is a tendency on the part of some administrators to assume that most of the persons who want to come, or at least those for whom the institution feels some responsibility, already know all that is necessary to get started. This is an unfortunate fallacy.

Colleagues from member institutions of the Association of University Evening Colleges have suggested many of the following methods of promotion which are used by their schools. The list is not intended to be all-inclusive. The most common method of promotion is the printed schedule of offerings for the semester or for the school year. Information is included about admission, registration, costs, and other "administrivia." These schedules are mailed to former students, to business and industry, and are furnished to YMCAs, YWCAs, libraries, and churches. Posters with tear-off postage-paid cards are distributed to appropriate organizations, industries, offices, and

APPLICATION FOR ADMISSION
PART II

Scholastic Standing and Certificate of Recommendation

Please MAIL completed application to the Registrar
Drake University
Des Moines, Iowa

DO NOT send by the applicant

IMPORTANT
Key to grading system
Symbol Num. Gr.

This is to certify that..
Name in full—Last First Middle

of..
Number and street (or R. F. D.) Town or City State

withdrew before graduation
was graduated from the
will be graduated

........................High School of........................ on........................
Name Location Date

Entered this school........................ 19........

(Rank) (estimated rank) mark out one ....from top in class of ....members.

Note: THE RANK OR ESTIMATED RANK IS ESSENTIAL. IT IS USED IN DETERMINING ELIGIBILITY FOR ADMISSION AND FOR SCHOLARSHIPS.

SUBJECTS	Year studied 1, 2, 3, 4	No. weeks studied	Periods per week	Mark 1st sem.	Mark 2nd sem.	Units
ENGLISH						
First year						
Second year						
Third year						
Fourth year						
FOREIGN LANGUAGE						
French						
German						
Latin						
Spanish						
SOCIAL STUDIES						
United States history						
World history						
Civics						
Economics						
Sociology						
MATHEMATICS						
Algebra—first year						
Algebra—third sem.						
Plane geometry						
Trigonometry						

SUBJECTS	Year studied 1, 2, 3, 4	No. weeks studied	Periods per week	Mark 1st sem.	Mark 2nd sem.	Units
SCIENCE						
Agriculture						
General Science						
Biology						
Botany						
Chemistry						
Physics						
Physiography						
Physiology						
Zoology						
PRACTICAL ARTS (Industrial, Commercial, Home Economics)						
FINE ARTS						
OTHER SUBJECTS						

To Whom It May Concern: The above is a complete and correct statement relative to the high school record of the student named.

Note: This report is not complete unless the form on the back of this page is filled out.

.... Date

.... Signature of Superintendent, Principal or Registrar

Fig. 2 *Application for admission, part II, Drake University.*

DRAKE UNIVERSITY

Des Moines 11, Iowa

(TO BE FURNISHED BY THE HIGH SCHOOL OFFICERS)

A. **Test Record of Applicant.** Test information is wanted on all applicants and is especially important when the applicant ranks in lower half of the graduating class.

Name of Test	Date Given	Point Score	Percentile Score	Kind of Norm (See footnote)*

*National, local, twelfth grade, college freshman, etc.

B. Counselor's statement

1. PERSONALITY RATING SCALE. Please give your frank opinion as to the student's qualifications by putting an X over each rating that best describes the student.

ACHIEVEMENT Relation of achievement to ability.	Highly motivated; works to capacity	Works to capacity in areas of special interest	Achievement below capacity, satisfied with average record	Happy-go-lucky attitude, achievement irregular	Indifferent; achievement far below capacity
COOPERATION Consider willingness to work with people in various capacities, loyalty.	Outstanding	Usually willing	When convenient	Indifferent	Unwilling
RELIABILITY Consider dependability, willingness, consistent industry.	Scrupulous and punctual in fulfilling obligations	Makes considerable effort to be dependable	Usually fulfills obligations	Wants to be dependable but finds excuses, lazy	Undependable; fulfills obligations only under pressure
EMOTIONAL STABILITY Consider way he reacts in various situations when stress is likely.	Unusual balance	Well balanced	Fairly well balanced	Easily depressed or elated	Unresponsive
PERSONALITY Consider relationships with other students.	Sought out	Well liked	Accepted	Tolerated	Rejected by others

2. Has the applicant been involved in any disciplinary situation? If so, explain:

3. General Comments: Are there factors, favorable or unfavorable which should be considered in processing this application. If so please comment:

Please Check One:

.... This student is recommended.

.... This student is not recommended.

.... This student is recommended with following reservations: ....

....

Signed.. ....

Name Position Date

Fig. 2 *(Continued)*

the like where adults congregate. Newspapers, both of urban communities and of small towns, contribute to promotion by using stories, pictures, and features of a newsworthy nature. Human-interest releases are more plentiful for adult students since there are more different sets of circumstances to write about. Papers of the minority groups should not be overlooked in the process. Newspaper advertisements offer opportunities to reach more people. Also, a newspaper will be more willing to give you free coverage if a paid ad is inserted occasionally. Several of the urban universities use the Sunday supplement to advantage. This offers the institution an occasion to tell its story in an effective way and to get it into the homes of the readership of the paper.

Radio and television spot announcements also can be effective. Many stations are willing and eager to work with universities in the development of programming which can include the continuing education story by using panels or a discussion format.

PERSONAL REFERENCE BLANK
DRAKE UNIVERSITY, DES MOINES, IOWA

To the applicant for admission:

Each applicant for admission to Drake University who has attended another college or university must submit this reference blank to the Dean of Students, Dean of Men, or Dean of Women at the school from which the applicant is transferring. The blank is to be mailed by the dean directly to Drake University

By signing the following blank, the student gives permission to the dean to release to Drake University pertinent confidential information.

Signature of Student..

To the Dean:

Drake University will appreciate your cooperation in answering the following questions concerning the above-named student who is an applicant for admission to Drake.

Has this student been subject to college censure for non-academic reasons at any time?

........Yes ....No. If yes, please explain.

Is this student eligible to return in good standing to your school?

........Yes ....No. If no, please explain.

Are you aware of any problem (health, personality, etc.) with which Drake University should be acquainted if it is to be of maximum assistance to this student?

........Yes ....No. If so, please specify.

Please check the statement that best indicates your attitude:

........Recommend admission.

........Recommend admission with reservations.

........Do not recommend admission.

Please use the reverse side of this sheet if additional space is needed for your replies. Thank you.

Name.. Date..

Title.. College..

Fig. 3 *Personal reference blank, Drake University.*

Of course, the adult educator should be willing to speak to community groups, service clubs, associations, and similar organizations. Brochures aimed at special-interest groups are also effective; i.e., putting together courses in the language, literature, history, and government of a particular country or area, such as Russian studies. The alumni magazine is another medium for promoting new ideas and concepts pertaining to adult education. Sponsoring a booth or exhibit at the annual Career Day of the institution is another way of spreading the concept of continuing education. Use of the telephone, especially for follow-up of inquiries, brings a sense of personal interest to the timid or reticent person who needs a push. Another source of potential students is frequently overlooked. Many colleges invite school counselors and guidance workers to visit the institution in order that they may be briefed and become familiar with the programs available for high school graduates. Yet there are many students who complete high school but do not go on to college. One group of counselors to whom I suggested the possibility that some of these students might want to consider part-time evening education was shocked that no one had mentioned this to them before.

No doubt one of the best sources of promotion is the satisfied student. This force can be utilized through orientation sessions, through the use of evening-student newspapers, and through information letters in August and December, to mention a few. One caution needs to be suggested. The appearance of whatever promotion is undertaken is most important. This will have a lasting effect upon the image of the institution in the communities it serves. As the late Ralph Kendall, then president of AUEC, said, "Your printed promotional material is the image you create of your operation."

COUNSELING PART-TIME AND ADULT STUDENTS

Counseling is a most important and too often neglected area of concern for the part-time and adult student. The extreme view of "if he wants a degree he should be treated as any other freshman and do what he is told at our convenience," on the one hand, is as wrong as "since he is older, he knows what he wants and therefore needs no counseling" is on the other. Neither position concerns itself with the student's individuality as a person nor with the concept that as an adult he is different from the youthful day student and should therefore be treated differently.

Nature of the Adult Student

An adult is different from a youth in his role, ranging from dependence at the one extreme to independence at the other. In fact, there are five differences between the adult and youth which have important implications for higher education and for adult counseling [5]. First, an adult's self-concept is different from that of the youth when he comes into a learning situation. Second, an adult comes into a learning situation with a body of experience. Third, adults enter into a learning situation with a different set of developmental tasks. Fourth, an adult enters into a learning situation with the aim of making immediate use of his learning to solve immediate life problems. Fifth, the adult enters into the learning situation voluntarily.

Most counselors will agree that:

> adults have problems; . . . they need help in identifying their problems and in their search for solutions to their problems. Adults, more so than youth, are reluctant to admit a need for help. They are more likely to work out their own problems, or conversely, to let their problems work on them. They tend to rationalize and give the socially acceptable answer rather than expose their doubts and feelings of inadequacy. All this points up the fact that in many respects adult students are in fact different from their youthful daytime counterpart. They need the help of counselors who understand the differing nature of the adult student [5].

Adult Counseling Service

Adult and part-time students pay tuition for that portion of the academic services they use. They do not receive, comparatively, a fair share of student services. Institutions that have adequate counseling services for adults are still in the minority. Most schools have advisers to assist the student in the selection of courses. Many have testing and remedial services. As a part of the admission process, an applicant will receive some guidance as to academic goals and programs. But this is not enough.

There is a need for counselors who can deal with the full spectrum of educational, vocational or professional, and personal problems of adult students. These services, to be effective, must be available when the student can take advantage of them, such as at night and on Saturday. There should be a staff large enough to handle the volume of counseling sessions without lengthy delays for appointments. The best time for assisting a person in reaching a solution for a problem is at the point of frustration which motivates him to seek help.

Community-oriented Counseling Services

Several universities in urban areas are organized to render service to members of the community. In most cases a nominal fee is charged. Two examples are University College at Syracuse University and the Portland (Oregon) Counseling Center for Adults. Varying in detail, they fill a need for adult-level counseling and testing services and provide depth interviews and extended counseling at reasonable cost. The major function is to provide vocational, educational, and personal counseling [7].

Training Staff for Adult Counseling

A few universities have elaborate counseling facilities including psychological, psychometric, and psychiatric services available to adult students. It is evident that staff engaged to function in the area of counseling should have the educational and experiential skills and competencies of the profession. In addition, staff working with adults should be familiar with the writings of Malcolm S. Knowles, Cyril O. Houle, and other adult educators. The counselor of adults should become proficient in dealing with the problems of adults.

Institutions with essentially no adult counseling services can establish such facilities with a minimal financial investment by using part-time personnel and key institutional personnel on an overload basis. Utilizing the physical facilities of the regular counseling service of the institution at night and under the direction of a member of the department, high school counselors, personnel of other institutions, psychologists, and part-time teaching faculty can be utilized to get an adult counseling program inaugurated. A series of orientation and training sessions should be conducted jointly by the counseling department personnel and by the adult administrative staff to ensure basic understanding of adult academic programs and of institutional policies. Depending upon the size of the adult student body, a beginning can be made with one part-time counselor per evening. As the reputation and utilization of these services expand, either full-time or additional part-time personnel can be added.

By making use of appropriate adult counseling services the quality of the adult programs can be ensured and enhanced. The identification and alleviation of problems, together with the upgrading of the qualified student and the referral, probation, or weeding out of the unqualified student is a responsibility of institutions of higher learning. The college that fails to take seriously this responsibility toward its part-time and adult students deserves the disdain of students and educators alike.

SUGGESTED READINGS AND SOURCES OF INFORMATION

1. DeCrow, Roger: *Administrative Practices in University Evening Colleges,* Center for the Study of Liberal Education for Adults, Chicago, 1962, pp. 19–27.
2. Farmer, Martha L. (ed.): *Student Personnel Services for Adults in Higher Education,* The Scarecrow Press, Inc., Metuchen, N.J., 1967.
3. McMahon, Ernest E.: *The Emerging Evening College,* Teachers College Press, Columbia University, New York, 1960.
4. Neuffer, Frank R.: *Administrative Policies and Practices of Evening Colleges,* Center for the Study of Liberal Education for Adults, Chicago, 1953, pp. 12–17.
5. Thompson, Clarence H. (ed.): *Counseling the Adult Student,* Proceedings of a Pre-Convention Workshop conducted in Dallas, Tex., Mar. 17–18, 1967.
6. Thompson, Clarence H. (ed.): *College Personnel Services for the Adult,* Proceedings of a Pre-Convention Workshop conducted in Detroit, Mich., Apr. 5–6, 1968.
7. Association of University Evening Colleges: *Proceedings of Twenty-third Annual Meeting,* Cleveland, Ohio, 1961, pp. 63–69, 119–121.
8. Association of University Evening Colleges: *Proceedings of Twenty-fifth Annual Meeting,* Boston, 1963, pp. 165–167.
9. Association of University Evening Colleges: *Proceedings of Twenty-seventh Annual Meeting,* Dallas, Tex., 1965, pp. 51–53.
10. Association of University Evening Colleges: *Proceedings of Twenty-eighth Annual Meeting,* Buffalo, N.Y., 1966, pp. 74–79.
11. College Entrance Examination Board: *College-level Examination Program: Description and Uses,* College Entrance Examination Board, New York, 1967.

Chapter **4**

Higher Continuing Education

ISRAEL KATZ

Dean, The Center for Continuing Education, Northeastern University, Boston, Massachusetts

Although the term "continuing education" is applied to a wide variety of adult educational opportunities, it is used increasingly by urban universities that have formal adult degree programs to designate noncredit seminars, workshops, institutes, short courses, and other public services.

These are learning situations in which a businessman may find a solution to a knotty distribution problem. A married woman, whose children have grown and gone off to school, prepares for a fascinating and remunerative career. A plant manager learns a better way to improve production. A lawyer, highly competent, discusses with colleagues how to interpret recent Supreme Court rulings. A housewife who never finished high school studies the elements of music listening. A nurse learns more about the proper dispensing of drugs. An engineer or scientist keeps up with the latest advances in his field.

People like these and many others who vary considerably in education, age, interests, and ability have turned to their urban university to meet their needs for new knowledge. And the university, through its continuing education program, has helped them inquire into their conditions and develop insights necessary to further their self-development.

CONTINUING EDUCATION IN THE URBAN INSTITUTION

Through continuing education, urban institutions serve individuals, professionals, industries, businesses, minority groups, hospitals, government agencies, trade associations, and local communities in a variety of educational, research, and service roles.

Such a service-oriented program must present a wide array of subject matter in a variety of formats to a broad spectrum of talents. Though it does not grant academic credit or confer degrees, it must meet the student's immediate developmental needs. Here is a list of those needs:

1. *Stretching* further the competences of alert, up-to-date professionals
2. *Bridging* the gap between the theoretical and increasingly liberal preparations of recent graduates and what they need to know to become productive in a creative sense on a specific assignment in a particular business or industrial organization
3. *Updating* the knowledge and skills of individuals who have slipped behind
4. *Retreading* or retraining individuals whose specialties have obsolesced
5. *Upgrading* the competence of individuals who have been inadequately prepared
6. *Familiarizing* support personnel with professional concepts and terminology so that they may communicate effectively with the practitioners

Since topics for course material are chosen to provide immediate solutions to perplexing problems for individuals and groups, some of them are dropped or replaced as new knowledge develops or technological advances are made. Here is a representative listing of subjects offered:

Courses and Workshops for Employees of Business and Industry

Organization Design
Conducting Business in the Ghetto
Problems of Acquisitions and Mergers
Proposal Management
Purchasing and Inventory Control
Early Identification of Management Talent
Management of Government Property
Advanced Technologies for Business Managers
Product Planning and Timing
Management of Business Growth and Technological Change
Advanced Financial Management
Basic Business Information Systems
Labor Relations for Owner-Managers
Public Speaking for the Small Business Administrator
Supervisory Management Training
Industrial Dynamics
Executive Development Seminars
Introduction to Data Processing—Selected Supervisors
Applied Operations Research

Courses for Scientific Personnel

Physiology for Engineers
Space Environment
Digital Communication System Analysis
High-vacuum Technology
Stability and Optimization of Nonlinear Systems
Advanced Infrared Systems Engineering
Guidance and Control of Ballistic Launch Vehicles
Electron Microscopy in the Biological Sciences
Digital Logic Design
Cryogenic Engineering
Special Topics in Artificial Intelligence
Oceanographic Instrumentation
Infrared Systems Engineering
Polymer Bulk Properties and Processing Theory
Hardened Antenna Design

Workshops in Community and Social Services

Institute on Chemical Dependency (Drugs and Alcohol)
Workshop in Sensitivity Training for Dynamic Leadership
Workshop in Nursing Home Administration
Study Group on Development of Training Materials for Training Staff
Fundamentals of Public Works Construction
Urban Redevelopment
Child Development Techniques for Social Worker Aides
Real Estate Acquisition and Redevelopment
Puerto Rican Spanish for Community Communication

Courses for Adult Women

Career Horizons for Women
Human Relations Field Work
Workshop in Arts and Crafts
Fundamentals of Stock Market Investments
Color in Interior Design and Decorating
Environment: The Land We Use
Islamic Religious History and Culture
Nonfiction Writers' Workshop
Jazz: Evolution and Essence
Philosophies in Conflict
Rock Gardens in the Northeast
Preparing for Life in the Last Third of the 20th Century

Courses for Health Care Workers

Program for Updating Medical Laboratory Technicians
Program for Updating Dental Assistants
New Techniques in Radiologic Technology

Programs for Self-employed Specialists

Annual Labor-Management Conference
Annual State Tax Forum
Annual Federal Tax Forum
C.P.A. Comprehensive Review Course
Community Pharmacy Management
Recent Changes in Copyright Law
Impact of Medicare on Nursing Home Administration

By far the greatest potential market for continuing education, albeit not the most attractive financially, consists of providing noncredit course work, seminars, and workshops to culturally stimulated as well as culturally hungry adults. Such educational programs are similar to extension programs, but they cater mainly to heterogeneous groups of students with extreme variations of background and capability.

FORMAT

There seems to be no "best method" for conducting a program. However, an idealized setting for continuing education, to which other formats may be compared, is a reasonably unhurried round-table learning experience led by an appropriate expert, where all participants have an opportunity to contribute actively to the work and deliberations of the group and have adequate time to prepare between sessions. Here are the principal patterns that have been adapted to continuing education:

Short Courses Short courses are the most popular across the country and seem to be the pattern that many programs settle on after other means have been tried. They are intensive sessions, lasting from a few days to several weeks, of instruction by experts drawn from academic institutions, the professions, or industry. Short courses, when properly promoted, have the advantage of attracting people nationally, and some selectivity can be exercised in accepting participants.

Stretch-out Courses These courses, given on a two-hour-per-week basis over a period of a semester, are gradually gaining in popularity because students can reflect on the subject matter between classes, prepare assignments, and do required reading. Moreover, stretch-out courses are generally conducted during late-afternoon or evening hours and do not require individuals to be absent from work.

In-plant Courses Such courses are popular when the instructor can be drawn from the same company or from a nearby educational institution. With few exceptions, however, in-plant courses tend to be on a somewhat lower scholastic level than courses open to all qualified students. They cater to upgrading rather than updating and competence stretching, even though those purposes also may be objectives. In-plant courses have the advantage that instruction can be given during working hours to keep students and management happy or to concentrate on specific company needs or proprietary matters. When the subject is advanced, however, in-plant courses usually suffer from being "loaded" with people who cannot even comprehend most of the lectures let alone benefit from the course work, in an attempt to obtain management approval through higher attendance figures.

In-plant courses are not usually popular with regular college faculty because considerable study of a company's specific needs is required to develop a course that can help employees cope with their company's difficult problems. Yet, it is precisely that kind of study and contact which may increase a teacher's effectiveness in a regular classroom setting. Some college faculty members may pass off in-plant courses as personal consulting activity and drum up in-plant courses for themselves. Doing so has its hazards! College instructors moonlighting on the side in teaching roles find themselves quickly in a conflict-of-interest situation. More teaching does not seem to be a particularly sound consulting activity for a full-time instructor who may already be committed to a full teaching load.

Residential Courses These are extremely intensive short courses given to small groups of students. They may be used to teach a particular technique—as, for example, the applications of electronmicroscopy in biological investigations—which can be discussed at length while still allowing enough time for each student to work individually on the microscopes and in the specimen preparation laboratory. Instruction in residential courses is particularly attractive to regular college teachers if conducted during school vacation periods.

Extended Residential Programs Such programs are ambitious patterns in which business or industrial organizations conduct or sponsor a variety of updating courses for their managers and key professional personnel, inviting noted authorities to lecture and to lead workshops. In general, emphasis is placed upon the functional areas of management, new technologies, and markets affecting the company's future; but the employees may also be familiarized with new policies having business, political, and social implications. With few exceptions, such programs incorporate features as follows:

1. Participants are separated from their regular job responsibilities and concerns for periods ranging from a few weeks to three months.

2. Participants are separated from their families, but provision is made for their occasional weekend visits home plus an occasional weekend visit by the spouse to the educational facility—all at company expense.

3. Attendance is open mainly to ranking company employees whose responsibilities fall within well-defined limits.

4. There is cross-functional representation in all classes and workshops. Particular emphasis is placed on the presence of at least one representative from the company's top administration and from the departments of engineering, manufacturing, marketing, plant and community relations, labor and personnel relations, and legal operations in each session.

5. Lectures dwell usually on generalized subject matter, on new ideas affecting all aspects of business administration and the application of business principles to practice; but the discussions that follow are based on case studies into which the company's provocative problems are woven.

6. Sessions are conducted throughout the day, with an afternoon break for recreation. Evening hours are reserved for socializing, dinner, distinguished lectures, preparation of assignments, and group discussions of designated materials.

7. Sessions may be held Saturday mornings and Sunday evenings—the remainder of the weekend being free.

8. Considerable camaraderie and socializing develops. Some employees may be evaluated by their managers who are also in attendance. While educational institutions may rate the participants in terms of course performance based upon attendance and quizzes, they should not fall prey to requests by company management to comment or report on the professional merits or growth potential of participants because doing so not only may seriously inhibit the students, but also may expose the educators to legal liabilities.

9. Results of the class and workshop discussions may stimulate experiments in management and influence evolving company policies.

Care must be taken to ensure diversified enrollment of personnel from organizations in entirely dissociated industries to prevent, consistent with federal antitrust regulations, even the appearance of collusion among employees of competitors. Where a trade association sponsors an educational program for employees of its members, detailed records of all sessions and persons who participated therein should be maintained. The subject matter and discussions must exclude such topics as specific pricing policies and arrangements, specific customers or groups thereof, specific product lines and related markets, and personalities or operating practices of particular companies. Under no circumstances should employees of well-known competitors be allowed to caucus privately even during social hours. Literature from any company even remotely associated with the program should not be distributed at any time.

One popular variation of the extended residential program is a pattern of an initial two-week residential period followed by a single week of residence per month over a 9- to 12-month period. This format does not interrupt the participant's job as much as would several months of continued absence.

Although continuing education is most effective when the courses and workshops are led by part-time faculty consisting of experts who earn their livelihoods through professional practice, consulting, or research in the fields concerned, it is extremely difficult to conduct extended residential programs, particularly on a repeat basis, without a nucleus of full-time instructors. Such personnel should, however, be recognized as experts in their own right and be granted full academic status. They should be measured not only in terms of their performance as instructors and conference leaders but also in terms of their research, publications, and administrative accomplishments. Moreover, such people should also be permitted to consult in their fields provided that a conflict of interest does not develop between their responsibilities to the program and personal benefits accruing through extracurricular activities.

Remote Classes Remote classes, in which lectures or demonstrations are transmitted via television, blackboard-by-wire, or other electronic means, will grow in popularity because they can cater to the masses. While audiovisual media are powerful educational tools, particularly in academic courses, they are not ideal for conducting continuing education programs. Not now, at least. The disadvantages are lack of student-and-teacher interactions, the inability of some teachers to project effectively before cameras, and the high cost of production (approximately $50,000[1] for a 24-hour TV course). These factors could change in the future, making remote classes practical and effective.

Midcareer Programs These programs, which consist of intensive full-time commitments of a year or more by executives or high-level professionals to study at a university as special or graduate students, have been adopted by some of the larger industrial organizations as a means for updating key personnel. In most cases, a special program is designed for each student, who may also be assigned individually to a noted professor for guidance in course selections. Sometimes, the adviser follows up the progress of

[1] All cost estimates in this chapter are based upon 1969–70 cost estimates.

the student after leaving the program to assess the merits of the midcareer period at the university and provide additional guidance. A full year's commitment to study by an executive or professional can be very expensive, sometimes representing a total outlay of $50,000 or more per student; but the expectation is that such students will help educate others upon their return to duty.

Each sponsoring business or industry must evaluate the benefits derived from a midcareer program in terms of its own criteria and objectives, but the scheme hardly seems to be the way to come to grips with the crucial need for *continual* continuing education of large numbers of "working level" people.

Instructors from educational institutions and industry alike regard an invitation to lecture in a midcareer program as an important form of recognition because they may come in contact with leaders from industry or the professions. They find their executive students stimulating even though the subject matter taught is comparatively dull.

MARKET ANALYSIS

Prompt Returns: Measurable Enrichment, Preferably Income from Educational Investments

In theory, every professional person who has completed what he considers to be his formal education or who is in the process of a career change is a prospective student. Yet, in practice, it is largely the motivated or driven individuals who commit themselves to a regimen of continuing education provided it is given at no personal expense, at convenient times, in suitable places, and under personally advantageous circumstances. Therefore, programs must meet demanding requirements of personal benefit and convenience as well as the economic enhancement of business, commercial, industrial, or professional activities if employers are expected to underwrite their employees' participation.

Serving Local Needs

While it is commonplace to design programs that draw students regionally or even nationally, with few exceptions less than 50 percent of the enrollments will come from beyond the local community. In fact, it is unlikely that on a sustained basis more than 5 percent of the students will be drawn from beyond a distance which represents approximately 90 minutes of round-trip commuting time. In densely populated areas, where traffic and parking may be problems, this maximum allowable commuting time may be cut to 60 minutes per round trip, representing a travel radius of no more than 15 miles. Thus, with the exception of a few unusual offerings, mainly infrequent residential short courses given in country-club settings or in-plant courses serving private groups, the majority of students for almost any program will be drawn from the local population. For that reason, any course, workshop, or seminar that does not first and foremost serve a local need is unlikely to fill satisfactorily. Even universities in isolated locations must cater to the special needs of professionals in nearby cities if their programs are to fill properly.

Importance of Population: Percent of Professional People in Area

Experience further indicates that the average number of persons who are presently motivated to undertake continuing education is 4 percent of those eligible in any local area on a nationwide basis and not more than 9 percent of those eligible in highly progressive metropolitan centers. For example, if 5,000 practicing engineers were located within a 15-mile radius of an advanced technology-based industrial center and an additional 8,000 engineers were located at reasonable commuting times beyond that distance, the maximum number of engineers who would probably undertake continuing education at any given time would be:

$$E = 0.09 \times 5{,}000 + 0.05 \times 0.09 \times 8{,}000 = 450 + 36 = 486 \text{ individuals}$$

With an average of 15 students per course, it would be possible to run about 32 courses per term or about 64 courses per year. Professionals from almost any other field will react similarly, but there will be approximately half as many students. Some courses might have as many as 25 students and a few less than 10. It seems a wise business practice to run a few new key courses that do not fill well at, or slightly below, the break-even point if the confidence of the market is to be established or maintained and if attendance in such emerging-knowledge courses is to be strengthened. Commercial educational operations may not be able to afford such experiments or to devote much effort to determining local needs, but some universities have sufficient flexibility to incubate potential producers—in fact, it is a university's responsibility to assist in the economic development of its locale by providing education in new and speculative fields, even at a temporary economic disadvantage, so as to create new competences and business opportunities. In this connection, it is well to bear in mind that trail blazing is a rough business which does not always elicit massive support.

Appraising the Market

Experience reveals that to formulate a new program of continuing studies in any field, it is advisable to meet with several leading local professionals in that field to assess local receptivity to continuing education as well as to discuss a few possible offerings and obtain suggestions as to authorities residing within commuting distances who can participate as teachers and attract students. It is then essential to meet with the suggested instructors, either individually or in a small group, to pinpoint one or more offerings and develop promotional strategy.

Here is a checklist of procedures for analyzing the professional market:

1. Define the geographic area to be served.
2. Become intimate with the economic history of that area, with particular attention to the reasons for changes in economic patterns over the years, and find out which resources of the region have not been effectively tapped.
3. List the professions, businesses, and companies in the area by industries or product lines.
4. Obtain breakdowns from the principal professional groups and trade associations of the number of professional people working in each profession, industry, or product line.
5. Pinpoint key individuals in the area to be interviewed regularly for spotting economic developmental trends and related educational needs. It helps if these individuals can be instrumental in "motivating" students to take courses. Concentrate on company presidents, managers, training directors, and officers of professional societies.
6. Explore possibilities for new industries, businesses, products, professions, or ventures that could utilize local manpower, material, and natural resources.
7. Keep records of local employment advertisements for professional personnel and tight specialties.
8. Become knowledgeable of local contract and proposal activities and the continually shifting needs for people with special competences.
9. Present objectives of continuing education to key professional, business, and industrial groups to obtain recommendations for programs and estimates of probable enrollments. Establish an educational advisory council of community leaders representing such groups and have them to lunch annually for such presentations, but always also have a speaker of prominence as well as sympathetic representatives of the faculty on hand who can contribute ideas for enhancing the local economy.

In the long run, the sources of ideas for courses, workshops, and seminars, in the order of reliability to assess local needs and interests, are:

1. Instructors currently or recently involved in programs
2. Students currently enrolled in the programs
3. Regular college faculty having liaison or advisory relationships to the programs
4. Remarks of professionals at social functions
5. Managers of professionals during visits to industrial plants or businesses
6. Telephoned suggestions by professionals
7. Classified advertisements for professional personnel
8. Inquiries about specific topics by prospective students
9. Advisory committee drawn from industry and professions
10. Industrial training and educational directors
11. Announcements of programs offered by other institutions
12. Professional society surveys

It is helpful when administrators of continuing educational programs are familiar with the local industrial mix and with advances in knowledge pertinent to the economic development of their region.

The means of evaluating the market for cultural programs differ markedly from the methods necessary to assess vocationally related educational needs in the same geographic area. Where local educational institutions offer credit extension programs, there is virtual certainty that a market exists among the local population for similar programs on a noncredit basis.

In those places where local collegiate institutions do not offer extension programs, administrators of continuing education are advised to review offerings of similar institutions at other locations and solicit outlines for such course work from faculty members of local institutions who may express an interest in participating in culturally oriented continuing education. A group of offerings will evoke some positive response from the local community and serve as a nucleus for further expanding the program.

In locations devoid of institutions of higher learning and remote from centers of education, the chances for operating a sustained program of continuing education are poor because students and faculty are generally unwilling to travel for periods exceeding an hour to and from classes. Furthermore, most educational institutions are content to serve only the students that come to their facilities and are reluctant to operate distant branches.

Attitudes of Industrial Management

A variety of attitudes is encountered. The prevailing official position of company executives, as well as of professionals and for the most part of training directors and personnel administrators, is enlightened encouragement of continuing education. Most industrial managers also support full-tuition refunds if courses are job-related and if classes can be given after working hours or late in the afternoon. Many professionals, especially those in private practice, are willing to give up a day—usually Wednesday—or an occasional weekend to attend a seminar or intensive course, but they resist attending week-long short courses. Most businessmen and industrial managers take an extremely dim view of continued employee attendance at courses that cut into working time.

In general, a friendly attitude is fostered by keeping local professionals and industrial managers informed about programs and plans for continuing studies. This kind of communication means regular visits with the executives, managers, or training directors of at least one industrial or business organization each week the year-round. Feedback from such contacts has been helpful, not so much in terms of new ideas for program development but as a barometer of local acceptance. Moreover, people who pay the tuitions want to see who represents the recipients thereof. Obviously, the representative had better be a good one: he must speak from knowledge and strength. Otherwise, it is better not to have anyone making such rounds.

The initial reluctance of some executives to have their key people teach competitors' employees can be completely reversed by indicating the prestige benefits that may accrue by having their own people acknowledged as leaders in their fields. Some companies open their laboratories and auditoriums for lab-related courses, involving considerable expense as well as complicated negotiations with their security people, even though only a small number of their own people may be taking the course.

Unfortunately, such encouraging attitudes are not universal. A few employers have no interest in continuing education for themselves or their employees. Such employers may stop tuition refunds for continuing education when some of their employees who have taken courses leave for higher-paying jobs. A few companies will give tuition refunds only for academic credit programs, although the number of such firms is decreasing.

ADMINISTRATION OF INSTRUCTION

A single individual, knowledgeable in the subject field and supported by an efficient secretary, can develop and conduct up to 100 courses, seminars, or workshops per year of which about 50 percent are entirely new in the program and the others are continually updated. Once in the swing of such a large program, about 40 clock hours of combined time are required by an administrator and secretary to survey community needs for a particular new offering. This work involves discussing the matter with advising faculty, finding and interviewing a well-qualified instructor and helping him develop a course outline, preparing promotional material and arranging for its printing, selecting a strategic mailing list of prospective students, negotiating a contract with the instructor and following through on related approvals, examining course registrations and interviewing questionable registrants, answering written and telephoned questions from prospective students or their wives, arranging for text and other instructional material, and scheduling classrooms. An additional average of 20 clock hours of combined time is required to update a previously run course, plan the program, and attend to a myriad of administrative details such as recording student attendance and monitoring facilities, collecting and recording student performance data, discussing problems with instructors or students and taking remedial action as indicated, assuring the collection of tuitions and fees, notifying students by phone in advance and arranging for make-up classes in the event of extremely adverse weather conditions or if an instructor must inadvertently miss a class.

The addition of a subordinate administrator professionally trained in some discipline of interest may double the volume of operations yet add only about 80 percent to the direct administrative expense. Extra benefits provided by a second administrator are that there can be more informed coverage at the office when one of the administrators is on the road, there can be greater flexibility in the performance of duties by having the administrators spell one another when conflicting commitments occur, and a greater breadth of topics can be covered if the professional qualifications of the administrators are complementary.

A second full-time, nonteaching subordinate administrator may be of advantage when a program in a given discipline, as in business, has achieved notable acceptance. Substantial specialization by each administrator within that discipline would be possible; the two may assume responsibility for different aspects of arrangements for unusual programs, they may be excused from routine duties at the office to concentrate on some particularly time-consuming assignment, and they may take responsibility for specific parts of the routine workload. Of course, a third administrator and second secretary would add about $16,000 to the costs of administration, which would be justified only by proportionate expansions of program offerings and enrollments.

While it is desirable that administrators be qualified to teach in their own programs, and they may wish to do so on occasion, inordinate amounts of teaching may seriously degrade the efficiency of the total operation because of their inattention to business detail and preoccupation with teaching. Continuing education should be taught almost exclusively by part-time or adjunct faculty.

Because of its interdisciplinary content, breadth, depth, and range of levels as well as scope transcending the curricula usually found in institutions of higher learning, continuing education should be organized as an independent division of such institutions reporting to top levels of administration. Programs in continuing education cannot tolerate meddling on the part of uninformed or hostile faculty in the regular departments of a university, although the cooperation of regular faculty, through service as advisers or participation as teachers when qualified, should be encouraged. Well-established criteria for the control of content as well as quality, or rigid criteria of accreditation and hence restriction of students lacking formal academic credentials, will surely destroy any program of continuing education, however well conceived and administered. The fundamental idea behind continuing education should be to motivate virtually everyone, but particularly professionals, to commit themselves to a lifetime regimen of continuing studies rather than to erect presumably "well-intentioned" hurdles to keep such people from participating.

Academic Tasks and Rank for Administrators

Administrators should have senior academic ranks and hopefully joint appointments in pertinent academic departments to strengthen their entrée to the market and provide a tie between continuing educational activities in a given field and interested regular faculty. Although they will seldom teach, administrators should be recognized as able teachers in their own right; but it is crucial to the success of the program that they be promotion-motivated rather than research-minded. The most important function of the administrator is to "sell" his programs to the community, students, managers, instructors, and regular faculty alike. For that reason the most effective administrator may not meet the stringent requirements for appointment, promotion, or tenure that prevail for regular teaching faculty, but it would be shortsighted indeed to overlook the qualities that such people bring to continuing education and deny them the privileges of faculty status and tenure that they deserve. Without appropriate recognition, it is doubtful that the required people can be attracted to such administrative positions and retained as career personnel.

Promotion of Programs

Word-of-mouth advertising is a valuable amplifier of enrollments in established programs, but without appropriate formal promotion, even the best educational program will fail to attract students.

Announcements of a particular course or seminar, very modestly priced, given in cooperation with a professional society and distributed to its members, usually yield between 4- and 25-percent response. Such programs are usually financially unattractive even if the speakers are volunteers; but they constitute a form of public service, so that a limited number of such offerings are a good form of promotion. All other announcements mailed broadly to a selected potential clientele will yield between 2- and 4-percent return. Reinforcements by spot advertisements in the public press and professional periodicals usually pay for themselves and serve to remind committed students to send in their registration forms. Advertisements alone seldom fill classes. Nationally distributed announcements or listings of offerings are effective only for intensive short courses or full-time seminars; they have little effect on the response from the local market.

Promotional costs of recruiting a single student range between $5 and $25, depending upon the demand for the course work offered. The average cost of promotion is in the neighborhood of $10 per student. Four thousand printed, single-page folders announcing a course or seminar cost approximately $250 and involve an additional mailing cost of about $300, not counting labor to address and stuff envelopes. The yield from such mailings will usually range between 40 and 160 responses, provided there is a market for the program, acuity in mailing, appropriate timing, and appeal in the announcement.

Massive mailings of well-conceived announcements or bulletins covering up to 60 courses will cost about 80 cents per bulletin as mailed. For 10,000 bulletins, printed and mailed at a combined cost of $8,000, the yield may be up to 800 registrants for a unit cost of about $10 per student. All mailings should be first-class and must contain an application form and instructions for registering. Applications received by mail must be acknowledged promptly and indication must be given as to acceptance of the student in the program. If an application must be rejected, the potential student should be so informed by personal letter, the reasons for rejection should be indicated, and an alternative course or program should be suggested.

Promotional material should contain information as follows:

1. Concise name and number of course or program—the name must accurately identify the nature of the course or program.
2. General description of the course, seminar, workshop, program, etc., indicating its objectives and level.
3. Concise and accurate, but detailed, topical outline of the program.
4. Names and affiliations of the instructors and the topics each instructor will cover. A short biographical note about the instructor helps.
5. Precise scheduling of the course as to day of week, time of day, starting date, and length of course, as well as location in terms of city, state, address of campus, building, and room number. Include a map to facility from several readily accessible points or roads.
6. Description of living arrangements for residential programs. A map of the campus or facility helps if residences are separated from classrooms.
7. Tuition, fees, and living expenses where applicable. Description of special transportation available if required.
8. Credits granted for work done or type of certificate awarded for completion.
9. Description of preparation or background deemed necessary to benefit from program.
10. Source which may be contacted for answers to questions concerning program. Give phone number, including area code, of informed source.
11. Instructions for applying to course as well as how and when to pay for it.
12. Indication of whether instructional materials will be furnished, how much they will cost, and where to pay for them. If a text is to be used, give the name, author, edition, and publisher of the book. Indicate its price in hard-cover as well as paperback form.
13. Indication of counseling services, library facilities, and laboratories that are available as learning aids.
14. Statement concerning the career benefits that may be derived from the program.

Costs

The complete costs of operations are difficult to estimate because so many expense factors are highly variable and yet dependent upon the specific requirements and arrangements associated with particular programs.

Table 1 illustrates the typical effect of classroom enrollment on the per-student cost of operations and how such costs may be used to determine the tuition charge. The costs are based on actual and estimated expenses associated with several comparable 12-week nonresidential stretch-out courses, given two hours per week, for which the instructor's stipends were about $600. Administrative costs per course are taken arbitrarily at 50 percent of the direct stipend. Promotional costs are essentially identical and taken at $150 prorated from a 40-course offering promoted at a total expense of $6,000. Texts plus supplies per student are taken at an average value of $15. Where costs other than instructor's stipend are unknown, the probable total cost will be about three times the stipend. Thus, the probable "break-even tuition" will be equal to

TABLE 1 Typical Cost per Student as a Function of Class Size

Cost item	Cost per student with number of students shown					
	5	10	15	20	25	50
Promotion	$ 30.00	$ 15.00	$10.00	$ 7.50	$ 6.00	$ 3.00
Instruction	120.00	60.00	45.00	30.00	24.00	12.00
Administration	60.00	30.00	22.50	15.00	12.00	6.00
General	15.00	15.00	15.00	15.00	15.00	15.00
Total cost per student	$225.00	$120.00	$92.50	$67.50	$57.00	$36.00

In any comprehensive program where some poorly populated courses are carried by well-populated courses, the tuition charges should fall between two and three times the expected cost per student. Thus, if the target attendance is 20 students to permit good student participation, using the above figures for 20 students the tuition should be between $135 and $200. The lower value might be used if it is expected that junior people will be attracted to the course, whereas the higher value should be quoted if senior-level personnel are anticipated in order to reflect the higher costs of plush facilities or greater ability to pay. For residential courses, the typical cost factors, given in percent of total costs as a function of student enrollment, are given in Table 2.

TABLE 2 Cost Factors as a Function of Enrollment

Cost item	Cost factor (percent of total costs) for enrollment shown		
	25	50	100
Instruction	20	13	8
Administration	10	7	5
Facilities	5	4	2
Promotion	20	15	10
General expense	3	4	4
Recreation	1	2	3
Texts and supplies	15	20	23
Lodging	15	20	24
Meals	10	14	20
Transportation	1	1	1
Total	100	100	100

These cost factors for residential short courses, given as percentages of total costs and as a function of student enrollment, are based upon five years' experience involving hundreds of residential short courses. It will be noticed that the cost per student generally decreases with increased enrollments and that the percentage costs for texts, lodging, and meals increase with enrollment because these items of cost do not vary rapidly with enrollment.

three times the anticipated instructor's stipend divided by the expected enrollment. The actual tuition should be at least twice that amount or whatever higher amount is felt to be appropriate to help carry less popular offerings. Another approach to actual tuition determination is to divide three times the instructor's stipend by 10, so that at least 10 students are required to break even.

Tuitions for residential short courses must be consistent with tuitions for similar courses offered by other institutions. A quick rule of thumb is to set tuition at about three times the total cost expected divided by the number of students anticipated. If the resulting tuition figure is significantly lower or higher than tuition for comparable courses given by other institutions, it may be in order to review the cost figure. It is, however, not necessary to become unduly alarmed by a higher figure because most institutions do not know their costs and consequently do not charge appropriate tuitions.

Table 3 provides an analysis of typical 1968 costs for high-quality full-time residential courses as a function of days for a group of 25 participants on a per-student basis. Costs in every category can be cut by as much as 50 percent by drastic reductions of quality.

TABLE 3 Analysis of Typical Costs on per-student Basis of Full-time Residential Program for 25 Participants

Cost item	Cost per student for program lasting number of days shown					Cost per student of two-day optional instruction-free weekend
	1	2	3	4	5	
Instruction	$ 16	$ 32	$ 55	$ 75	$100	$ 0
Administration	12	20	28	36	40	10
Facilities (classrooms)	6	12	18	24	30	0
Promotion	10	15	18	20	22	5
General expense	5	10	15	20	25	5
Recreation	0	3	5	10	15	15
Instructional materials	15	20	25	30	30	0
Lodging	0	8	16	24	32	16
Meals	11	25	35	43	50	12
Refreshments	3	6	9	12	15	6
Transportation	0	0	5	5	10	10
Gross cost	$ 78	$151	$229	$299	$369	$ 79
Suggested net at 25% of gross cost	20	38	57	75	92	20
Suggested tuition per person	100	190	285	375	460	100

Instruction costs reflect honoraria paid to usual evening-session lecturers for the three-, four-, and five-day courses. The 25 percent net fee is recommended to cover costs of executive administration and future program developments.

Instructor Selection

The prime objective in instructor selection is to choose individuals who can lead groups of adults in exploring means to inquire into their needs for further development and who are able to provide them with learning experiences that help meet those needs. As a practical measure, it is essential to instructor selection that those needs be predicted beforehand and that the educational program be defined as to content and level. The instructor must be expert in the pertinent subject matter and must share the chores of program structuring. Other important factors in selection are the instructor's willingness, availability, and reliability to do the job required. Program administrators must assess these qualities in advance and monitor them informally while the instructor's course is in progress. Such monitoring, however, is not accomplished by popping in on a session but rather by listening to student comments. Moreover, commonly accepted pedagogical techniques are not necessarily applicable to teaching sharp and aggressive professionals, some of whom are well qualified to be instructors, nor can they always be used to teach culturally deprived adults. Here the acid test of a teacher's skills is in the results and not the means.

The expertise of prospective instructors is best determined beforehand by interviewing them as well as talking about them with proven faculty, students, and leaders in pertinent professions or industries who will identify individuals knowledgeable in a subject area and able to teach. Another technique is to invite a prospective instructor as a seminar speaker. A suggested procedure for enlisting the services of qualified instructors is as follows:

1. Negotiate with only one individual or group (for courses requiring several instructors) at a time.

2. Explain everything the prospective instructor needs to know at the outset, covering such details as:

a. Why he was contacted and who recommended him.

b. Objectives of the program and how it will meet the needs.

c. Format and content of proposed course: Be flexible but realistic, and let him make suggestions.

d. Stipend policy and payment procedure: Establish a firm price schedule (about $25 per hour for lecture courses and $50 to $100 for one-shot seminars) and stick to it. Do not look for bargains in instructors and do not discriminate among instructors or subjects. If a prospective instructor is not worth the established stipend, he should not have been contacted. If a subject does not merit an instructor who deserves the established stipend, it should not be in the program.

e. Policy concerning selection of students, mix of students anticipated, and student performance evaluation requirements: Instructors must not set policy for student acceptance because doing so would produce almost as many policies as instructors. If an instructor wishes to know beforehand who has signed up for his course so that he can better slant his presentations, let him see the students' applications giving their backgrounds. He will discover, however, that an actual encounter with a class is the most reliable means of ascertaining student qualifications for absorption of specific course material.

3. Arrive at an immediate decision as to whether he is the instructor required. Do not pursue the matter any further if there is doubt.

4. Obtain an immediate decision as to whether he will give the course. If a qualified prospective instructor seems anxious to give a course, it is a very good sign. Drop indifferent or very difficult candidates. Some prospective instructors need to be "sold." Since it takes about a week of full-time administrative work to "wrap up" a new course, it is better to concentrate on cooperative or at least tractable candidates.

5. Secure a brief but detailed outline of a proposed course during the initial interview. A comprehensive outline and description of the course should be obtained from a proposed instructor within two weeks after the first interview. Once an instructor is involved in a program and his course is going well, he will update the course voluntarily and continually.

It seems a foregone conclusion that the majority of instructors for continuing education will be drawn from among experts in the professions and industry, with the remainder mainly from regular faculties of local educational institutions. All these teachers will have had considerable exposure to practice in their fields and experience in presenting their thoughts to groups. Since relations between regular full-time college faculty and part-time adjunct faculty are often delicate, the able administrator will recognize this situation where it occurs and intermix teaching personnel with discretion. Here are the factors that seem to encourage regular college faculty participation in continuing education:

1. A sympathetic attitude on the part of department heads or deans toward continuing education, particularly as exemplified by their creation of a continuing educational activity
2. Extra compensation for teaching at the same rate as adjunct faculty
3. Exposure to latest developments in their fields through research or consulting
4. Stimulating students drawn from among practicing professionals
5. Recognition by administration and colleagues that participation requires expert knowledge of latest developments in their field
6. Contacts with professionals that may lead to consulting opportunities or at least to recognition by the professional community
7. Esteem of regular undergraduate and graduate students who may recognize requirements for special competence to teach professionals

On the other side of the coin, here are some factors that tend to discourage the participation of regular college faculty:

1. Disproportionate effort and time that must be devoted to the preparation and continued adjustment of fast-changing subject matter
2. Lack of textbooks or other professional literature to supplement lectures at the frontiers of knowledge
3. Adverse attitudes towards continuing education on the part of the teacher, a dean, a department head, or colleagues
4. Assignment of continuing education courses as part of the regular teaching load without extra or adequate compensation
5. Higher priority or preference for after-hours graduate-program teaching
6. Interference with research, consulting, recreation, or family responsibilities
7. Lack of familiarity with applied aspects of their subject, particularly as it relates to the changing needs of local industry
8. Preoccupation with other matters or responsibilities
9. Reluctance to confront a class of adult practicing professionals
10. Generally poor compensation in comparison with consulting income
11. Lack of familiarity with the purposes and scope of continuing education

Whereas participation in continuing education by regular faculty might be "more of the same" or might constitute a "busman's holiday," it may be a welcome diversion or challenge for instructors from industry. Experts from industry are often torn by several conflicting considerations, but the overriding motive favoring their participation seems to be recognition by their peers, employers, and students coupled with a genuine desire to be of service to their profession. Several factors that favor the participation of people from the professions or industry as instructors in continuing education may be listed as follows:

1. Further learning of subject through teaching
2. Desire to teach as an aid in preparing a paper or writing a book
3. Opportunity to bounce new ideas off others in their field
4. Added income when compensation is significant
5. Appointment as adjunct professor during term of teaching
6. Encouragement by employer and recognition of such teaching as an important form of self-development

In like manner, the factors that may inhibit participation of professional or industrial people as teachers in continuing education are:

1. Lack of self-confidence in ability to teach

2. Demands of business travel
3. Time and effort required to prepare subject matter and correct homework
4. Employer's expectation of casual overtime
5. Fear of compromising classified or proprietary information
6. Employer's disapproval of teaching by employees, especially if doing so might add to competence of competitors
7. Red tape in obtaining clearance from employer to teach
8. No compensation or low compensation
9. Interference with recreation or family and community commitments
10. Modesty or reluctance to appear in role of teacher

Obviously each instructor, whether from academe, the professions, or industry, must weigh the merits of participation as a personal matter. It helps, however, to put some "english" on an instructor's contemplations by stressing the positive aspects of participation in terms of wholesome self-interest as well as professional development. Administrators and managers can help fill the need for qualified instructors by encouraging people who can teach to do so. Professionals as students also can play a decisive role in attracting instructors by identifying the people who have a pertinent subject to teach and by cooperating with instructors to make continuing education mutually profitable and enjoyable.

Employers will usually reimburse employees for continuing studies when they feel that immediate and meaningful benefits accrue to them. They feel much the same way about employees who teach. It takes ingenuity to convince employers that they have experts among their employees who ought to teach certain courses open to any qualified student. The most persuasive approach for achieving an employer's acquiescence is to ask him, "Who do you think will get the contracts when the customer discovers that his people are teaching the most advanced and pertinent courses in the industry?"

Program Structuring

Prospective instructors should prepare the tentative outlines for proposed courses. In reviewing and adjusting this outline, a number of factors must be considered and reconciled:

1. Objectives of the proposed program and the needs to be met
2. Relationships to the total pertinent field of knowledge, particularly to current offerings in the field at undergraduate and graduate levels
3. Prior knowledge required by students to benefit from the program
4. Topics to be covered in time available
5. Follow-on course possibilities
6. Relationships to peripheral areas of knowledge
7. Probable sources and backgrounds of prospective students
8. Requirements for demonstrations and laboratory sessions, if any
9. Methods to be used for evaluating student performance
10. Probable impact on local industry or profession
11. Related courses that should be taken concurrently
12. Overlap with other courses or programs
13. Level at which course is to be given
14. Desired size of class
15. Need for instructor team effort
16. Text or notes to supplement instruction
17. Outside preparation requirements

In structuring a sequence of courses, a team should be assembled by a key person from the profession, industry, or faculty who may be relied upon to serve in both a teaching and advisory capacity. The team will generally formulate a long-range program which, although starting with common core courses, may branch into several specialties. Members of a team will usually divide the work of instruction among themselves, adding other individuals of reputation for instruction in special areas. It is also particularly beneficial to obtain the counsel of persons from local branches of pertinent professional societies, who may not only provide information concerning special needs for continuing education in that field but also assist in promoting the programs.

In giving interrelated courses, not only is it advisable to schedule at least two such courses on the same day in tandem to reduce travel time and confine course work to one day or evening each week, but also it is advantageous to integrate some of the contents of such courses so that they reinforce each other, thereby compressing the time necessary to cover the combined subject matter. Sometimes it is possible to telescope three courses into two this way and accelerate the rate of knowledge transfer to the students.

Student Selection and Motivation

Accurate descriptions of courses, workshops, or seminars, accompanied by outlines of topics to be covered, generally attract only serious and qualified students. Requirements for at least the basic academic degree in the field of interest or some related field or, alternatively, proof of professional activity in the field or related areas further help assemble competent classes in advanced studies. It must be realized, however, that some individuals without formal preparation or what seem to be the appropriate academic degrees can also benefit. Lack of adequate student preparation is seldom a problem; it can be readily detected by interview at the time of registration. Payment for a course in advance invariably eliminates all unqualified would-be registrants, but it may also radically reduce enrollments of qualified students. Failure to pay tuition once a student is committed to taking a course is virtually unheard of.

Several guides for student selection are:

1. Students should be admitted to job-related courses, or to courses in peripheral areas bearing upon their work, even if the courses are not in the same area as their formal preparations.

2. Students should be encouraged to take the first course in a sequence unless they can demonstrate competence to benefit by entering the sequence at an advanced level. Actual performance of related work on the job is a better guide than prerequisite courses.

3. Students should be permitted to withdraw early from a course, without penalty, if they find themselves unable to cope with the subject matter or find the course to be at a lower level than expected. Students can usually be transferred to other courses; few students are lost by changing to their proper levels.

The most effective forms of continuing education are those learning opportunities that provide professionals with new, advanced, highly applicable, and frequently speculative knowledge and techniques that stretch their competences and enhance their competitive positions without disrupting their working routines or family and community responsibilities. Table 4 lists the factors that motivate or impede commitments to continuing education. They are given in the order of importance as determined by the questioning of over 1,200 students participating in continuing educational programs.

Measurement

Accurate measurement of program effectiveness is essential to the enhancement of continuing education and its further development. Testing the student at the completion of a course might be an indicator of his immediate ability to reproduce some of the knowledge gained, though such tests hardly measure the true impact of a learning experience on a student's intellectual stimulation and growth.

TABLE 4 Factors Motivating and Impeding Participation in Continuing Education as Determined by Questioning 1,200 Seemingly Well-motivated People

Motivators	*Alleged impediments*
Challenge of job	Complacency
Drive to succeed	Business travel
Availability of learning opportunities	Paid overtime
Tuition refund by employer	Community commitments
Course content and correct level	Need for casual overtime work
Convenience of classroom to work	Lack of credits
Outstanding reputation of instructor	Indifference of employer
Previous worthwhile experience with continuing education	Distance of work from class
Convenient schedule of courses	Traffic
Credit or recognition by certificate	Parking difficulties
Self-confidence of student to benefit	Cost to student
Adequate preparation of student	Marginal facilities
Stimulating mix of students in class	Outside assignments
College environment	Inadequate preparation of student
Proper tuition charge	Lack of self-confidence
Timely announcement of courses	High cost of course to employer
Size of classes	Faulty publicity
Assignment to program by employer	Poor quality of instruction
Related proposal activity in area	Poor match of courses to job needs
Relation of subject matter to job	Difficulties in registration
Reputation of sponsoring organization	Lack of personal goals
Availability of pertinent text	Job dissatisfaction
Fear of obsolescence	Family problems
Knowledge of own field by student	Laziness
Casual atmosphere of class	Poor health
Availability of reference library	
Clear goals of a coherent program	

Student responses to a questionnaire about a course distributed at its completion can provide feedback useful to the instructor or administrator in extending its good features while correcting unfavorable aspects in subsequent repetitions.

Undoubtedly, the most reliable measures of program effectiveness are to be found in the long-range consequences of enduring student participation in continuing education. Here are several extremely general measures that seem to constitute reliable indicators of total program effectiveness and acceptance:

1. Growth in enrollments
2. Return enrollments by individual students
3. Willingness of employers to pay continually increasing tuitions
4. Growth of in-plant course business and return engagements
5. Increase in participation by instructors with national reputations
6. Growth in net return from total program
7. Growth in course offerings
8. Rate of progress of students in their professions as compared with similarly trained professionals who are nonparticipants in continuing education
9. Contributions of students through on-the-job activities to the economic development of their local community as determined by their contributions in attracting new business or their responsibility for developments as well as for an increase in the number of professionals moving into the area
10. Gradual shift from company-operated, closed educational programs to centralized continuing education open to all qualified students
11. Desire of regular college faculty to identify with programs

12. Requests from other educational centers for help in getting started in continuing education operations

An additional approach might be taken by using evaluations based upon measurable factors, obtainable as matters of record, expressible in numerical form and free of bias, so as to collect reproducible data and avoid the need for calibrating the evaluators. Such measures of effectiveness can be designed to test performance factors such as the following:

1. Increased capacity to handle difficult assignments
2. Ability to contribute creatively, especially in speculative areas of work—as in research, development, or unusual service
3. Increased professional activity leading to the development of new cultural, scientific, or business opportunities
4. Recognition of growing expertise by colleagues, managers, customers, and competitors
5. Productivity in terms of ideas, developments, or business results
6. Ability to promote relations with recipients of their services, management, vendors, and colleagues

In evaluating the effectiveness of a particular form of continuing education for employed professionals, it is also necessary to consider the probable effects of environment as it may influence the benefits of education on an individual's performance. Typical of such factors are items such as the following:

1. Opportunity to learn on the job
2. Pertinence of specific, complex courses to work on the job
3. Opportunities on the job for creative contribution
4. Availability of reference sources on the job
5. Attitudes of management toward innovation
6. Support of innovative developments on company or contract funds
7. Pressure of contractual commitments
8. Adequacy of support services for creative effort
9. Inhibiting factors or policies
10. Physical conditions of environment
11. Travel requirements or restrictions
12. Professional climate and general morale

Representative of specific measures that may be applied when evaluating the effectiveness of continuing education on the personal development of professionals are items such as:

1. Number of ideas submitted in written form for exploration
2. Number of such ideas actually funded
3. Dollar value of funded ideas
4. Number of ideas brought to successful completion
5. Number of papers presented or published
6. Number of speaking invitations received
7. Number of formal requests for consultations
8. Number of people supervised
9. Number of projects completed during year
10. Dollar value of projects completed during year
11. Number of courses taught during year
12. Number of business-visit reports submitted
13. Number of written letters of commendation received
14. Number of written complaints received
15. Salary increments received

SPECIFIC SUGGESTIONS

On the basis of experiences gained in administering various continuing studies programs, specific suggestions on scheduling, location, policy, and operations may be offered.

Scheduling

Residential programs catering to either open or closed groups that draw students regionally or nationally should operate on schedules that thoughtfully reflect considerations as follows:

1. Maximum educational effectiveness is achieved with sessions lasting from 9 A.M. to 4 P.M.
2. No instructor should lead a session for more than two hours during a given day. One-hour sessions are preferable.
3. Not more than five different instructors should be involved in sessions during a given day.
4. The last day of program, or of a given week in a multiweek program, should terminate with lunch. Certificates for attendance may be awarded after lunch, even at the dining table.
5. Saturday and Sunday sessions should be avoided, with the exception of programs specifically planned for weekends. Occasional evening sessions or workshops with distinguished leaders are permissible.
6. A half-hour break every three hours. Coffee breaks at 10:30 A.M. and 3 P.M. are popular.
7. Adequate time for socializing, with provision for refreshments or a snack.
8. Not more than two hours of preparation to be assigned per day.
9. Availability of instructors for informal discussions, as at dinner.
10. Deemphasis of frills such as cookouts, picnics, sports events, etc.
11. Provision for use of recreational facilities during off hours.
12. Travel time requirements as well as arrival and departure arrangements.
13. Provisions for signing in, registration, and arrangements for personal matters or travel.
14. Overlap with other groups in residence.
15. Parking facilities for students arriving in own vehicles.
16. Residential arrangements for families.
17. Events for accompanying family members.
18. Capacity of kitchen and dining facilities.
19. Prudent costs of ancillary services to students. Acceptance of tips by service employees should be discouraged.
20. Provision of services in event of unusual needs or emergencies, including medical and security emergencies.
21. Dates of the program should be carefully selected to coincide with the available time of students and faculty yet without conflicting with legal or religious holidays, vacation periods, or other crucial events.

Programs operated on a stretch-out or in-plant basis should be conducted between 4 and 9:15 P.M., Mondays through Thursdays, scheduled to suit the instructor's availability. The premium times are 5 to 7 P.M. and 7:15 to 9:15 P.M. This arrangement makes it possible for some students to take two courses during a given evening and allows time for classrooms to empty and refill. The 7:15-to-9:15 period is most popular with students and instructors alike.

Schedules of courses should correspond generally to the local high school calendar or to that of an evening graduate school, if such programs exist in the area.

At least 15 minutes should be allowed between classes. Some courses can be started at 4 P.M., but since their students are required to leave work about an hour in advance, such early courses should cater primarily to executive-level people.

Location

Commuting students should not be expected to travel more than 30 minutes each way to class or to fight heavy traffic. About 70 percent of the students will be drawn from a 10-mile radius. Few students will travel more than 15 miles.

Adequate parking or public transportation should be available. Since few students will leave the campus before the next shift arrives, twice the normal parking area is required.

Premium classroom space on campus should be used in preference to high school settings. Classrooms should be equipped with adult seating, adequate writing surface and blackboard space, and adequate lighting and ventilation.

A good food facility should exist in the vicinity, preferably a cafeteria serving meals at reasonable prices.

Policy

Programs should be clearly related to local community, business, or industrial needs and should not be competitive with other successful programs already available in the area. Tuitions for continuing education should be comparable with those for graduate work, but they should reflect the need for income to carry developing or free programs to the financially deprived.

Courses should make students stretch their competences and in no sense should level be compromised if the majority of the students can cope with the subject matter. Where grades are given, they should be limited to "passed" or "not passed." Needs for assessing student performance must be discussed with the instructor, but he should determine the means to be employed. Uninvited auditors of classes should not be tolerated, and when they are detected they should be asked either to register or to leave.

Instructors should be permitted to conduct classes as they see fit within the framework of good taste and pedagogy. Classes should not normally be visited to appraise instructor performance. Formal feedback about instructor performance is unnecessary, if not detrimental. Informal reports will suffice. Word of mouth endorsement of a given course among students will be measurable in subsequent popularity. Cancelled classes should be made up at the convenience of the class.

A liberal policy should be developed for accommodating substitute lecturers recommended by a reliable instructor to avoid canceling a class session. Students welcome such changes, and qualified substitutes are an excellent source for new instructor talent as well as new courses.

Criticism of a program should be handled judiciously. Student comments must be weighed critically. Where criticism of an instructor is indicated, the instructor should be confronted privately with the criticism and given an opportunity for corrective action.

Operations

Commuting students should not be expected to devote more than one evening a week to class attendance, although some will come twice a week. Enrollments will suffer seriously if most students cannot take the courses they need during the same evening.

Accurate attendance records are important, but a liberal policy should prevail on absences. Up to 25 percent absence from class may be unavoidable. Students with faulty attendance records should not be penalized if they make earnest efforts to absorb the work and contribute to class discussions. Lateness is an incurable feature of adult education. Zealous efforts to correct late arrivals will eliminate both the problem and the program.

Audiovisual aids, as well as an operator, should be available on one or more weeks' notice at a preset time. Instructors should be responsible for making their own arrangements through an assigned assistant. Administrative helpers coming in contact with both the students and instructors must be intelligent and cooperative. Some students act superior. Matters become very difficult when the staff also does so.

Classes should be kept at optimal size. Survey courses may be large, but established in-depth courses and workshops should not have less than 10 or more than 30 students. Seminars are very flexible; some can accommodate 100 students with ease. Residential programs should be limited to 25 students or less, as the specific situation may dictate.

Sequences of courses require long-range commitments by students. Such programs should not be started unless a market analysis demonstrates appropriate and sustained demand over the long haul.

Instructors may be plagued by requirements for business travel. Provisions for making up missed sessions must be available, and students should be informed that the risk of some cancelled sessions is characteristic of continuing education. Students should be informed well in advance of any anticipated cancellations and make-up sessions, or they should be phoned at work if a class must be postponed on short notice.

Instructional materials, including texts, should be furnished as part of the tuition to increase efficiency and conserve time. Since some employers will balk at paying for books to the extent of prohibiting employees from enrolling in courses, provisions for deleting the cost of books from the tuition may be helpful where this matter appears to be a problem.

TRENDS AND GOALS

Continuing education will play a vital role in all learned professions, and an educational institution determined to stay abreast of realistic developments must become deeply involved in serving its community's continuing educational needs in meaningful ways.

Continuing education, however, faces an uphill struggle for recognition as an activity that merits substantial investment, enlightened management, and the participation of top-notch teaching talent. Given the necessary encouragement and provided professionals as well as able teachers respond favorably to it, continuing education will become a decisive factor in the nation's continued economic growth as well as its preeminence in science, industry, agriculture, commerce, the arts, and social development.

Television and new electronic learning aids will provide most of the necessary continuing education on a massive scale. The adult population will depend on such mass media as a means for acquiring most of their new knowledge. Once established and adequately supported, a considerable amount of continuing education can be dispensed through mass media on a national scale.

Continuing education also will play an enlarged role in connection with community efforts to alleviate poverty; develop economic opportunities for the underprivileged; provide better housing, health care, transportation, business and vocational skills, recreation, and public services as well as to cope with problems of chemical dependence, drug abuse, and crime.

Educational institutions whose administrative personnel and teaching staffs have not been deeply involved in the affairs of core communities are advised to avoid educational operations therein until such time that they have acquired an understanding of the forces at play and developed abilities to cope with them.

Continuing education in the core communities will be characterized by the following developments:

Programs will leapfrog fundamentals and dwell specifically on highly applied aspects of subject matter with a view toward prompt utilization of the knowledge gained for purposes of earning a livelihood or being of practical service in the community.

Education will be brought to the community in facilities furnished and controlled by the community.

Programs will be taught by experts, with increasing involvement of resident professionals as they become qualified to teach.

Learning readiness of the students will be accelerated by their realization that the solution of urban problems is critically related to their own constructive involvement in community affairs as informed adults.

RESOURCE ORGANIZATIONS

American Association of Volunteer Services Coordinators
1700 18th Street
Washington, D.C. 20009

American Council on Education (ACE)
1785 Massachusetts Avenue
Washington, D.C. 20036

Adult Education Association (AEA) branch of NEA
National Education Association
1225 19th Street
Washington, D.C. 20036

Academy for Educational Development, Inc.
505 Symes Building
820 16th Street
Denver, Colo. 80202

American Society for Engineering Education (ASEE)
2100 Pennsylvania Avenue, N.W.
Washington, D.C. 20037

Center for the Study of Liberal Education for Adults (CSLEA)
4819 Greenwood Avenue
Chicago, Ill. 60615

Engineers Joint Council (EJC)
345 East 47th Street
New York, N.Y. 10017

Harvard University Study Project of Technology and Society
61 Kirkland Street
Cambridge, Mass. 02138

National Health Council
Division of Continuing Education
1790 Broadway
New York, N.Y. 10019

National Science Foundation
Office of Economic and Manpower Studies
1800 G Street, N.W.
Washington, D.C. 20550

National University Extension Association (NUEA)
1820 Massachusetts Avenue, N.W.
Washington, D.C. 20036

SUGGESTED READING

Adult Education Association of the United States of America: *Conducting Workshops and Institutes: Step by Step Help on Every Phase of the Workshop Method,* ITS Leadership Pamphlet no. 9, 1956.

Adult Education Association of the United States of America: *Federal Support for Adult Education: A Directory of Programs and Services,* 1966.

Adult Education Association of the United States of America: *How to Use Role Playing and Other Tools for Learning,* ITS Pamphlet no. 6, 1956.
Aker, G. F.: *Adult Education: Procedures, Methods, and Techniques: A Classified and Annotated Bibliography, 1953–1963,* Library of Continuing Education, Syracuse University, Syracuse, N.Y., 1965.
American Society for Engineering Education: Monographs nos. 1 and 2 in the Continuing Engineering Studies Series, 2100 Pennsylvania Avenue, N.W., Washington, D.C. 20037.
Beals, Albert: *Aspects of Post-collegiate Education,* American Association for Adult Education, 1935.
Bell, Wendell, R. J. Hill, and C. R. Wright: *Public Leadership: A Critical Review with Special Reference to Adult Education,* Chandler Press, San Francisco, 1961.
Bryson, Lyman: *Adult Education,* American Book Company, New York, 1936.
Burns, Norman, and C. O. House (eds.): *The Community Responsibility of Institutions of Higher Learning,* University of Chicago Press, Chicago, 1948.
Clark, B. R.: *Adult Education in Transition: A Study of Institutional Insecurity,* University of California Press, Berkeley, Calif., 1956.
Crane, C. E.: *Continuing Education Centers in the United States: A Critical Analysis of Selected University Continuing Education Centers in the United States,* University Microfilms, 1959.
Debatin, F. M.: *Administration of Adult Education,* American Book Company, New York, 1938.
Dees, Norman: *Approaches to Adult Teaching,* Pergamon Press, New York, 1965.
Gardner, John W.: "Education as a Way of Life," *Science* (Journal of the American Association for the Advancement of Science), May 7, 1965.
Hewitt, Dorothy, and Kirtley F. Mather: *Adult Education: A Dynamic for Democracy,* Appleton-Century-Crofts, Inc., New York, 1937.
Johnstone, J. W., and Ramon J. Rivera: *Volunteers for Learning: A Study of the Educational Pursuits of American Adults,* Aldine Publishing Co., Chicago, 1965.
Joint Advisory Committee Report on Continuing Engineering Studies, Engineers' Council for Professional Development, 345 East 47th Street, New York, N.Y. 10017.
Katz, I.: "Philosophy and Education in the Space Age," *Annals of the New York Academy of Sciences,* vol. 140, art. 1, December, 1966.
Kempfer, Homer: *Adult Education,* McGraw-Hill Book Company, New York, 1955.
Kidd, J. R.: *Financing Continuing Education,* Scarecrow Press, Metuchen, N.J., 1962.
Kilpatrick, W. H.: *Education and the Social Crisis; a Proposed Program,* Liveright Publishing Corporation, New York, 1932.
Knowles, M. S.: *The Adult Education Movement in the United States,* Holt, Rinehart and Winston, Inc., New York, 1962.
Lanning, F. W., and W. A. Many: *Basic Education for the Disadvantaged Adult: Theory and Practice,* Houghton Mifflin Company, Boston, 1966.
Peers, Robert: *Adult Education: A Comparative Study,* Humanities Press, New York, 1958.
Peffer, Nathaniel: *Educational Experiments in Industry,* The Macmillan Company, New York, 1932.
Sheats, P. H., Clarence D. Jayne, and R. B. Spence: *Adult Education: The Community Approach,* The Dryden Press, Inc., New York, 1953.
UNESCO: *Adult Education: International Directory,* New York, 1966.
Ziegler, Jerome M.: "Continuing Education in the University," *Daedalus* (the journal of the American Academy of Arts and Sciences), Fall, 1964.

Chapter **5**

Cooperative and General Extension Programs

ERNEST E. MC MAHON

Dean, University Extension Division, Director of the Institute of Management and Labor Relations, and Professor of Adult Education, Rutgers, The State University, New Brunswick, New Jersey

INTRODUCTION

The term "extension" may best be understood literally. It means the extension of the university's educational resources to those who are not regularly enrolled students. The resources may be faculty, facilities, or aids such as books or films.

There are two main streams of extension: (1) the Cooperative Extension Service in agriculture, home economics, and 4-H Club work, and (2) the other extension services, commonly known as general or university extension. General extension may be conducted by any type of university; cooperative extension is linked to the land-grant colleges.

THE EXTENSION CONCEPT

The notion of university extension began to take root in America during the nineteenth century as a part of the developing interest in a variety of forms of adult education. Activity by individual faculty members and institutions occurred as early as 1830, and the American Society for Extension Teaching, which continued for a decade, was organized in 1890.

General extension received a major impetus when President Van Hise, in his inaugural address at the University of Wisconsin in 1906, said, "I shall never be content until the beneficent influence of the University reaches every family in the state."[1] Because of his support and the fact that Wisconsin has the longest history of uninterrupted service among university extension divisions, there is frequent reference to university extension as "the Wisconsin idea."

By 1915, there were enough general extension divisions in the United States for the organization of the National University Extension Association (NUEA) to be formed. The 22 institutions which met in Madison, Wisconsin, to found NUEA consisted of 5 private and 17 public institutions.

[1] Merle Curti and Vernon Carstensen, *The University of Wisconsin,* The University of Wisconsin Press, Madison, Wis., 1949, pp. 88–89.

The Smith-Lever Act

Although there had been earlier extension service in agriculture—just as forerunners of university extension had preceded formal organization—the Cooperative Extension Service (CES) came into existence with the passage of the Smith-Lever Act by Congress in 1914.

Popularly, the underlying idea of cooperative extension often is attributed to Seaman A. Knapp and his successful demonstrations of control of the cotton boll weevil in 1903, although there had been agricultural field agents as early as 1887. The subsequent federal legislation brought extension into existence for rural America on a national scale with emphasis on the production of food and fiber and on the improvement of rural life.

COOPERATIVE EXTENSION

The Smith-Lever Act provides that there shall be extension service in agriculture and home economics administered by the land-grant college in each state, and there are now 51 state and territorial services. In addition to the activities in agriculture and home economics, there is an extensive program of youth work through the 4-H Clubs.

The Meaning of Cooperative

"Cooperative" does not mean cooperation with the clients. The term indicates the tripartite nature of the sponsorship and support of this particular kind of extension. The federal government, the states through the land-grant colleges, and the county, city, or other local governments participate in a cooperative undertaking which includes both financial support and a role in policy making. The amount of support and degree of control varies from state to state, but the basic arrangement of the three-way partnership is the foundation.

Obviously, there is strength in the relationship. The resources and continuity of the federal partner supplement the grass-roots interest and support of the county partner. Further, the service's own representatives, going out from the college or stationed in the counties, are accessible and can concentrate on individual state problems.

U.S. Department of Agriculture The federal partner is the United States Department of Agriculture, which exercises a supervisory role over the entire enterprise. State directors of the CES are appointed with the concurrence of the USDA. Each participating land-grant college executes a memorandum of agreement with the USDA. Congressional appropriations are made to the USDA for distribution to the several states, although the distribution of most funds is made by formula.

The strong federal participation does not imply a monolithic, regimented control by Washington. Policies are developed in cooperation with the field through organizations such as the Extension Committee on Organization and Policy, known as ECOP, a committee of the National Association of State Universities and Land-Grant Colleges.

Also, the USDA adds its vast research, demonstration, and publications activities as a major contribution to the work of cooperative extension. In contrast, university extension has no counterpart source of continuing national coordination and assistance.

The State Each of the land-grant colleges receives appropriations from its own state government for the particular state's support of the extension service. The land-grant relationship has brought together the extension service, resident instruction, and research because the college of agriculture, the experiment station, and the CES have usually worked from one campus (most frequently under a single dean with total responsibility for all three), have shared resources, and often have shared faculty on joint appointment. The result has been a cohesive working relationship which has tended to make the total educational resource available to the field worker and his client.

The County The third partner is usually county government, and this partnership is real, also, because a county does not have to take part in cooperative extension, despite the interest of the federal and state governments. An example is Hudson County in New Jersey, which has never taken part.

County governments provide funds largely through the provision of office space, secretarial staff, and operating expenses, although they may pay fractions of the professional staff salaries. In addition to the official participation of a county through its governing board, there are also advisory committees for the three branches of CES.

The Structure

Cooperative extension, which is often described as the world's largest adult education activity, reaches several million adults and young people a year through meetings, visits, and telephone calls. In addition, educational information reaches another large audience through publications, radio, and television. The service's capability in large measure is a function of its distribution of manpower.

Agents Known to millions of Americans in the cities and suburbs as well as on the farm are the county-stationed agents of CES. The agricultural agent usually is known as the "county agent." There is a county home economist who used to be known as the "home demonstration agent" when her duties primarily consisted of going into the farm home and showing the farmer's wife a better way to make jelly or to do the family sewing. There may also be a third agent in the county, a 4-H agent.

A county staff is not limited to three persons. Each of the agents may have assistants. Frequently, there are both men and women 4-H agents. There may be assistant agricultural agents because of the special production interests of a given locality such as forestry, horticulture, or poultry; or there may be assistant home economists.

The agents have their offices in the county, in the county office complex, or in some other central location. They live in the county, and they spend their time working with the people in the county. The result is a close identification of the agents with the community which they serve.

The visibility of the county agents has led many people, especially those concerned with bringing the university's resources to bear effectively on the problems of urban society, to seek the development of a corps of urban agents. Valuable as urban agents may be, there is another resource of cooperative extension which appears to be its major source of strength.

Specialists Serving as a back-up to the county staff is a corps of specialists. Most of them are located at the college of agriculture, where they conduct research and prepare informational materials. They may be veterinarians, nutritionists, child-care specialists, marketing specialists, or any of a variety of experts who can help solve problems brought back to them by the field workers in the counties.

Many of the most significant advances in agricultural production and home economics have been the results of the work of these specialists, who have found the cures to animal diseases, better ways to process foods for market, or better ways to increase crop production. Not only has the extension specialist a research potential in himself but he also has the additional resources of the experimental station and the college faculty. In addition, he is available to go out into the county with the agent and to demonstrate the application of a recommended method or material. Further, he can prepare instructional material for widespread distribution.

Other extension activities, including university extension, are built on a staff of field workers, but they do not have the counterpart of the specialist of CES. Where university extension has a few specialists, they usually are committed to instruction and to program development for income-producing courses or conferences and are not available as resource people for the field.

Regional Organization All specialists are not located on the campus. A specialist such as a forester may be assigned to part of a state and may be stationed in one of the county offices within the region. Such an arrangement, in effect, moves him from the campus to a point nearer the demand. The county where he is stationed has no special claim on him.

Another variation is the designation of a county agent as a regional specialist, so that he continues to be responsible for agricultural extension in his employing county but, in addition, is available on call to the agents in nearby counties. For example, one county agent may be a poultry specialist, and his neighboring agent may be a horticulturist. Under a rigid application of county assignment, they should not cross the boundaries. Under a less rigid interpretation, they are expected to.

Information Services Usually unheralded and unsung is the communications unit of the CES. The service has always taken literally its responsibility for dissemination of useful information. Consequently, through bulletins and pamphlets, columns or feature stories in the local newspapers, and radio and television broadcasts, the CES has continued to inform its clientele of practices, prices, and procedures.

The spreading of information and its preparation is a responsibility of every staff member, but there are within CES information specialists who can translate the research report into guidelines for the farmer or who can help the county agent with his weekly column. Other extension services prepare and distribute little that is comparable to the flood of information which cooperative extension makes available to every person in the state, rural or urban.

The Scope

Cooperative extension asserts a responsibility for meeting educational needs in the following nine areas: efficiency in agricultural production; marketing, distribution, and utilization of farm products; conservation, wise use, and development of natural resources; management on the farm and in the home; family living; youth development; leadership development; community improvement and resource development; and public affairs. The areas were set forth in *A Statement of Scope and Responsibility, the Cooperative Extension Service Today,* a document nationally known as "The Scope Report," issued by ECOP in 1958 and amplified in a 1959 task-force report, *A Guide to Extension Programs for the Future.*

Agriculture Although the spotlight has been on the work of cooperative extension in the areas of agricultural production, marketing, and farm management, the agricultural agents have been concerned with the suburban lawn, the city dweller's foundation plantings, the pollution of air and water, and a variety of nonrural services related to agriculture.

Home Economics As the farm population has decreased and the urban and suburban areas have developed, the home economists have moved from a rural family emphasis toward a more general concern with such problems as family stability, consumer competence, family housing, family health, and community resource development as outlined in *Focus,* a report of the Home Economics Subcommittee of ECOP. Participation in efforts to aid low-income urban families is becoming a major activity in many urban areas.

Youth Work 4-H is the youth development arm of the CES. Its concern is with four age groups: boys and girls from 10 to 13, from 13 through high school, the years immediately after formal schooling ends, and young married couples. The early emphasis is on project activities with a gradual change toward group action, community service, and recreational or cultural activities as the age of the members increases.

The county 4-H agent, however, is an adult educator rather than a youth educator because the 4-H program functions through volunteer leaders. The recruitment, training, and support of those leaders is the main task of the 4-H agent who, like his agricultural and home-economics colleagues, is moving into the inner city.

Projects include not only agricultural activities such as livestock raising and tractor driving but also more general activities such as automotive instruction, conservation, and photography.

Changing Emphasis

The Cooperative Extension Service prides itself on its adaptability to change, on its gear shifting during and after two World Wars, on its ability to keep abreast of the scientific and technological advances on the farm and in the home. Its main thrust today is to make the necessary changes to move effectively into the cities and other poverty pockets of the nation to provide educational services for nonrural and nonfarm families within the wide-ranging limits of the Scope Report.

GENERAL OR UNIVERSITY EXTENSION

"General extension" is the term used by the National Association of State Universities and Land-Grant Colleges (NASULGC) to describe those extension activities which are not carried on by CES. "University extension" has been the term commonly used, as evidenced by the associational name, the National University Extension Association.

Whereas cooperative extension is an activity of the land-grant colleges, university extension is not a function solely of publicly supported institutions of higher education. General extension programs are maintained by several private universities as well as by state universities and other public institutions. Indeed, about one-fifth of the members of NUEA are private institutions such as the University of Chicago, New York University, Syracuse University, and the University of Southern California.

In addition, many of the evening-class, off-campus, and noncredit activities of the nation's evening colleges are extension programs in nature although not by designation. Thus, the contribution of the private sector to university extension is a substantial one.

Institutional Nature

University extension is an institutional activity as distinguished from cooperative extension, which has the national guidance and participation of the USDA and the extramural participation of the county governments. General extension has no central unifying force such as the USDA nor, as a general practice, the official involvement of local governments. There have been many cases of state, county, or municipal governments providing support of various kinds for general extension programs, such as branch-campus centers, but such developments have been particular arrangements and not part of any national pattern.

Consequently, university extension varies widely in the breadth and nature of services, in organization, and in financing. Although the implementation of the Scope Report is not identical among states, there is a common structure and there are common concerns for CES. General extension divisions have no such similarity.

The Structure of General Extension

A common element of university extension organization is centralization. Even where regionalization has occurred, there is likely to be strong home-office direction. The common pattern has been the development of a central office staff under a dean or director without counterparts of the county agents. Extension field men have traditionally traveled from the home office, a time-consuming way of working despite the time savings brought about by throughways and airplanes.

Whereas cooperative extension has been organized along the three functional lines of agriculture, home economics, and youth work, university extension has had no single form. Its organization may be in broad areas such as credit classes, audiovisual instruction, and community development, or it may be by specialized services such as management training, labor education, or technical institutes.

The NUEA structure reflects the major interests of its members by the existence of five major operating divisions: audiovisual communications, community development, conferences and institutes, correspondence study, and evening college and class instruction. A sixth division in the field of teacher education is under consideration. Other specialized activities are served through committees. However, the member institutions do not necessarily provide educational services in all of the areas represented in the structure of the national organization.

Regional Organization As general extension has expanded its services and as parent institutions have become multicampus, a regional expansion of university extension has been taking place. Examples are Pennsylvania State University with a system of regional offices and the University of California with extension offices on each of the university's several campuses.

Regionalization has resulted from efforts to utilize personnel more effectively by locating them where the programs take place, to develop closer local ties by establishing a community identification for the extension worker in place of a traveling-salesman image, and to encourage the development of activities for specific local needs. Another major force has been the establishment of branch campuses of the parent institution. It is common practice to create a local extension office as part of the branch-campus structure.

Statewide System A third form of regionalization has occurred when a state has coordinated the extension activities of two or more public institutions. The end result is a pattern similar to that which results when a single university, such as the University of California, has a number of campuses throughout the state, but the organizational structure and operating problems are different.

An example is the statewide extension system of Oregon. That state's seven public universities and colleges offer their general extension services through a single administrative body, the Division of Continuing Education of the Oregon State System of Higher Education.[2] Essentially, the division calls upon the several colleges in accordance with their capabilities and their location.

Intramural Relationships In addition to variations in internal organization among university extension divisions, there are problems of relationship to other parts of the university. A general extension division extends the resources and services of several schools and colleges of a university, but the division also may have competitors within its own institution.

For example, if "general extension" is a term applied to all extension work outside of CES, there may be jurisdictional difficulties when the university has a university extension division, an engineering extension service conducted by the college of engineering, and a management development program conducted by the school of business administration. Perplexing questions can arise when one of the services offers an educational program which attracts the clients of one of the others. Which service, in the situation indicated above, might lay sole claim to a one-day conference on "Cost Controls in the Construction Industry"?

If there are no problems of competing extension services, there may be questions of the extension division's relationship to the several schools and colleges with respect to conferences, workshops, or evening courses within the subject-matter domains of the various colleges. If there is a public demand for computer science courses and the university's department of computer science will not participate, should the extension division refuse to offer the courses or should extension go ahead and meet the need?

[2] James W. Sherburne, "Oregon's Statewide Extension System," *The NUEA Spectator,* vol. 31, no. 3, February–March, 1966, pp. 18–21.

Further, should extension rely on instructors from industry or other universities, or should extension hire a full-time computer expert who will have no official connection with the university department of computer science? Such problems arise in connection with old and well-established academic fields as well as in newly developing ones.

The problem is the appropriateness of offering educational programs by extension without the participation of the faculty members who constitute the institution's body of experts in the subject matter of the programs. Such activity provides an educational service but does not, literally, extend the existing faculty resources to another group of persons. Instead, a nonuniversity resource may be utilized.

The basic need of the university extension division, therefore, is the development of effective cooperation with the schools and colleges whose resources it seeks to extend. Such cooperation requires a respect by extension, despite its autonomy, for the professional concerns of the various faculties, especially within the professional schools. It may well be that extension should refuse to meet certain requests, as a matter of institutional policy, if the appropriate professional school refuses to provide the necessary support. Obviously, the philosophic question which must be answered is whether the mission of extension to meet legitimate educational needs has priority over the considered professional judgment of a competent faculty. The decision may become the responsibility of the institution's chief administrator, who may have to act as the arbitrator.

Administrative Emphasis An extension division is an administratively oriented operation. Although it is an instructional unit of the institution—providing educational services to an adult, nonresident population—it usually has no organized faculty and is not a degree-granting division in its own right. Thus, an extension division is not directly comparable to a school or college despite the fact that it may have an equivalence to the colleges of the university in its hierarchical status.

Scope

General extension has already been defined as the agent for all extension services except those in agriculture and home economics. The scope, therefore, is as broad as the university's capabilities and intent. Whatever areas of scholarship are represented on the university's faculty become appropriate and possible areas of extension instruction.

Difficulties occasionally arise about the level of content or application rather than about broad subject-matter areas. A college of engineering, for example, may be interested in continuing education for the professional engineer but disinterested in or openly opposed to the training of technicians. Further, if technicians are trained, are they for industry as aides for engineers or does the university train repairmen for television sets and oil burners? If the school of business is opposed to the training of foremen although interested in the development of middle and upper management, what is the institutional decision with respect to extension programs for foremen?

A practical solution is the practice of identifying the professional school, such as engineering or business administration, in the sponsorship of only those programs acceptable to the school concerned. However, other programs, such as those for technicians or foremen, are offered by the university as a recognized educational service under the sole sponsorship of university extension. In such cases, faculty members of the professional schools may serve as professional resources, but the professional school is not listed as an official participant in the offering of the course or conference.

Pioneering A special problem of university extension arises in the many educational areas in which the parent institution may have no organized department or curriculum. For example, the university offers no instruction in studio art; yet there are requests for extension classes in painting and sculpture. The extension division can easily staff such classes with well-known professional artists who are experienced teachers. Another example may be hypothesized in the field of computer science. The university may have no department nor any instructional computer. Again, the extension division may recruit instructors from industry and may borrow or rent computer time. Although the educational program, in either of the above cases, is not an extension of the university's resources beyond capitalizing on the organizing skill of an extension staff member, should the service be denied?

Some persons tend to criticize extension for offering such instruction because there is no faculty base within the university from which to extend in the literal sense. Others argue that the organization of such instruction is a highly desirable and valuable service. Historically, when such instruction has led to the ultimate founding of a department of art, or a school of fine arts, or a department or center of computer science, the action of extension has been cited as pioneering, as showing the way for ultimate establishment of the discipline within the university.

Changing Emphasis

Much of early university extension was off-campus credit course work or specialized noncredit instruction for individual plants or companies. Although there is still a substantial volume of such instruction, there has been a growth in conference activities, both one-day and residential, both on and off campus. In recent years, community development has become an extension function. General extension, also, is shifting from an earlier concern with remedial instruction for the nonprofessional to a growing concern with the continuing education of the professional.

CONTRASTS BETWEEN THE TWO EXTENSIONS

Although much that has been stated above has indicated obvious differences between cooperative and general extension, there are some points of difference which should be specifically emphasized to help develop a clearer understanding of the total extension situation. Those familiar with cooperative extension frequently have trouble understanding why university extension cannot meet certain types of requests or why university extension seems to be so income-oriented. Similarly, those familiar only with university extension often fail to understand the goals and policies of cooperative extension. Exploration of some of the significant differences in terms of specific contrast may help both to clarify them and to facilitate cooperation between the two types of extension.

Administration

There are significant administrative differences between CES and general extension. Cooperative extension is related to one college, the college of agriculture, and at most to two when the university also has a college of home economics. General extension may be operationally related to a dozen colleges, but it does not have the close relationship with any of the dozen which CES has with its one.

Credit Cooperative extension does not engage in programs which offer college credit. General extension, on the other hand, may provide credit courses. A few university extension divisions stress the noncredit aspects of their activities, but many of them have a large component of evening and off-campus classes for credit. Historically, extension courses for teachers have been a major element of extension service. In recent years, graduate work in engineering has become an increasingly important element.

The offering of credit complicates the administrative involvement for general extension because credit generally is offered by the faculty of a school or college. The extension division performs administrative services in connection with registration, fee collection, and other arrangements, but academic control remains with the faculty which grants the credit. In contrast, noncredit activities are extension controlled.

The difference leaves the cooperative extension director freer in meeting needs because all of his programs are under his jurisdiction as noncredit activities.

Methodology

The types of services and program also vary between the two extensions. Cooperative extension does not offer courses. It may provide group instruction through lectures or conferences, but such instruction is not on an organized course basis.

The basic method of cooperative extension, since the days of the earliest agents, has been the demonstration of a practice or procedure, to be followed by instruction after the success of the demonstration. Much of the county agent's service to the farmer or to the individual homeowner is individual instruction, akin to consultation. The early work of the home demonstration agent, also, was highly individualized.

In addition, the CES has utilized publications, films, radio, and television extensively.

In contrast, university extension has made wide use of regularly organized classes. The credit programs, of course, have consisted almost entirely of semester- or quarter-length courses. Many of the noncredit offerings have also been organized on a term-length or short-course basis.

General extension, too, has made considerable use of correspondence instruction, both credit and noncredit, whereas the use of correspondence instruction within cooperative extension has been limited.

Conferences and institutes of a residential or on-campus nature have been a major method for university extension, but it has lacked the resources for the sort of informational publications which have poured from CES.

Extension Budgets

As stated earlier, cooperative extension receives its funds from three sources: federal, state, and county appropriations. Although, legally, cooperative extension can charge for reimbursement for direct expenditures—not staff salaries or related support—for programs, the common practice is to provide services without charge.

In contrast, university extension is essentially a self-supporting activity; it relies on fee income. Even in public institutions, general extension may be self-supporting. In only a few instances does subsidy reach a 50-percent level as compared with cooperative extension's 100-percent level.

Self-support, it must be pointed out, in extension terminology means the production of sufficient fee income to pay for the administration, instruction, and operating costs of the program; the term is not used commonly to include such items as physical plant and university overhead.

Frequently, certain extension activities are heavily subsidized while other work of the same extension division receives no subsidy. The distinction may be based on ability of the participants to pay or on a belief in the social urgency of specific undertakings. For example, there is a common acceptance of charges for credit courses, for advanced or refresher instruction for professionals, and for business and industrial training. There is a general willingness to subsidize community-service activities, art and library services such as traveling collections, and world affairs study.

The fiscal policies have an impact on extension. Service is limited in many instances to those clients who can afford to meet the costs of the service, with the result that obvious educational needs go unmet. A facet of this limitation is that university extension personnel are not available for an appreciable amount of free service or advice; their time is required for the development and administration of the fee-producing activities.

Cooperative extension does not have the same problem. Its income is appropriated and is expended in accordance with an annual work plan. Although CES, like any other educational unit, could always utilize more funds than it receives, its personnel are not concerned with income production and, therefore, have more flexibility.

Another aspect of the pressure on the income-producing elements of general extension is the knowledge that failure of extension to meet income estimates will, obviously, require diversion of funds from other sections of the university's educational budget.

Title I Funds for community-service activities under Title I of the Higher Education Act are available to both of the extension services and also to institutions without extension services on a project basis in accordance with the several state plans. The emphasis on community service and the annual funding provisions of the act limit its value as a long-range factor in extension budgeting, and its availability to all institutions is in sharp contrast with the land-grant college relationship of the Smith-Lever Act.

Faculty Relationships

The final point of special contrast between the two extension services is in the area of faculty relationships. The noncredit feature of cooperative extension enables CES to be largely self-sufficient; whenever university extension engages in credit instruction, it becomes dependent upon the particular faculty involved.

Further, CES is *the* extension service in agriculture and home economics, and most of its staff members are products of curricula in agriculture or home economics. University extension, because of its multiple representation, does not enjoy such a direct relationship. The general extension staff member, regardless of educational background, may develop programs in several fields of study; his role is that of catalyst rather than expert in many cases. Consequently, the participating faculty members may tend to look upon him as a nonexpert. Such a relationship gives rise to difficulties in program organization and direction.

Staffing The faculty relationship is affected, also, by the staffing situation. Cooperative extension, with its specialists, has built-in academic resources. University extension, without such resources, must look to the resident faculties or to the outside.

Because faculty members are committed to their teaching and research responsibilities, the extension teaching in many institutions becomes an extra duty, undertaken for extra compensation within limitations of policy or endurance. As a result, much extension teaching is carried on by persons from outside the university, just as evening college teaching is often a task of part-time teachers. Without implication that the instruction is better or worse under the circumstances, there is an unfortunate outcome in that the extension program in those cases comes to be thought of as something apart from the primary educational tasks of the faculty.

An example of a special arrangement to cope with the situation is at Michigan State University, where the continuing education budget provides for faculty positions in several of the schools and colleges. The colleges, in return, owe an equivalent amount of total faculty time to the continuing education service for its courses and conferences, largely those in the Kellogg Center at East Lansing.

There are cases, also, of extension professorships; that is, full-time appointments for extension teaching. There seems to be general agreement that it is desirable for such appointments to be related to the appropriate faculties rather than set apart.

CURRENT ISSUES

Two issues currently highlight the roles and the relationship of cooperative and general extension. Those issues are urban extension and merger.

The Urban Scene

As urbanization increases in America, pressures upon the universities increase. The problems are not only those of the ghetto and the inner city but also those of air and water pollution, traffic congestion and mass transportation, housing, and citizen participation. The pressures come from those persons and groups who believe that the university can make a significant contribution toward the solution of the problems in the same way that, through extension, the university has contributed to America's improvement in the production of food and fiber and to the continuing education of professional people.

Both extension services are interested in the problem. Both have contributions to make. Cooperative extension has an advantage with a subsidized staff and with commitments in such areas as family living and youth development. Whether the background of essentially rural experience can be effectively redirected is its challenge. General extension has had, in some institutions, a major role in community development. Its major liability is its fee dependency, because urban extension does not appear to contain the seeds of self-support.

The history of the two extensions is not one of cooperation. Can they join forces now within the city?

Philosophical Issue Even more basic than the operational relationship between cooperative extension and university extension in the city is the issue of the university's role in social change. Each institution must answer for itself whether its extension effort is to include a broadened educational service, such as basic and vocational education and direct intervention in community affairs, or whether it is to concentrate solely on the kind of instruction, such as leadership training and research, for which universities have been responsible in the past. Either approach may mean a high degree of community involvement, but the level of activity and the nature of the work will be entirely different in the two situations.

Merger

In the institutions which house both extension services, there has been concern about the increasing possibility of duplication of services—in suburban and rural areas as well as in the city. Years ago, the overlap between the two was a minimum risk. Today, the situation has changed as both services move into the urban areas, as the food industry becomes more highly mechanized and organized, and as farms become factory sites. Shall university extension train managers, accountants, and salespeople in all businesses except the food industry, and shall cooperative extension provide management, accounting, and customer-relations training for the food industry through duplicate departments? Shall community developers in university extension recruit a home-economics staff separate from the home economists already on location in CES? Or shall the two services cooperate to help each other and thereby help their publics most effectively?

The need for a single extension service can be debated. Universities consist of several colleges, and no one suggests the desirability of merging all of the colleges into one. Indeed, there is a growing movement toward more and smaller colleges within universities. Cannot one extension service provide instruction or advice for another, as the liberal arts faculty may provide instruction in English and mathematics for the engineers and the agricultural students?

There have been mergers. Although the basic structure of cooperative extension remains unchanged in its relationship to the USDA and county governments, the two services have been brought together administratively in a few situations, under a single vice-president or other administrator, to effect coordination of their services. The most widely publicized merger organizations are those at the University of Missouri, Utah State, the University of Nebraska, West Virginia University, and the Uni-

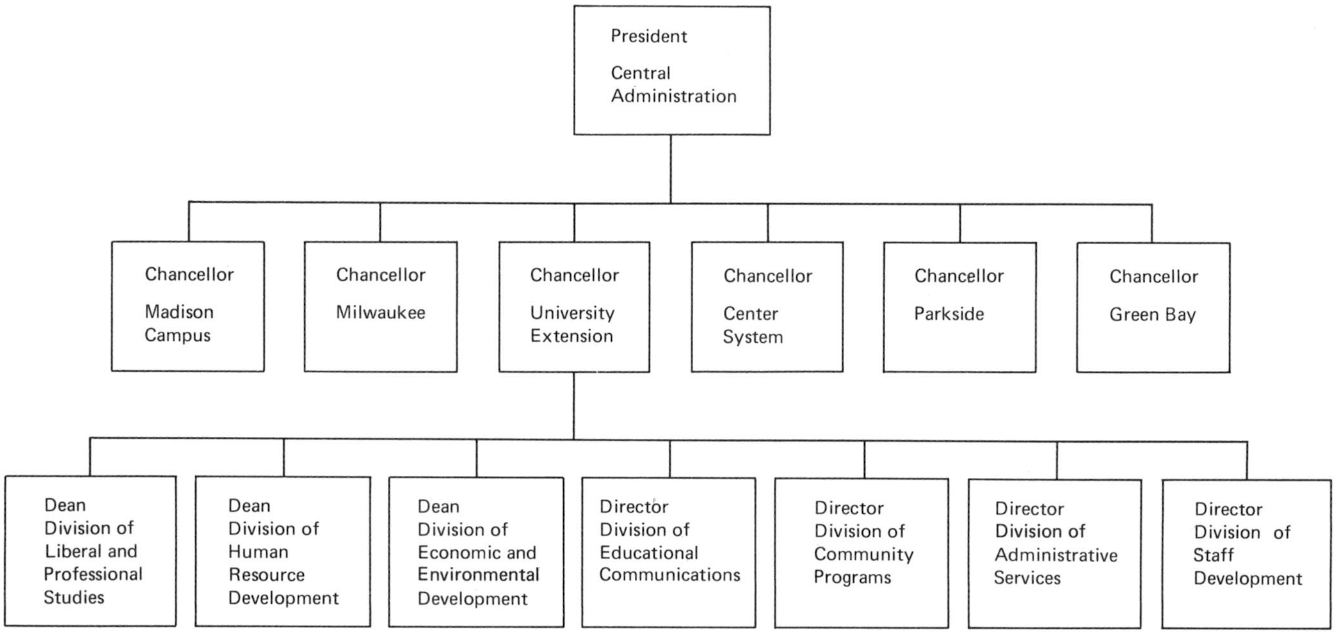

Fig. 1 *Typical extension organization plan. Activities of the Cooperative Extension Service and of General Extension are assigned to appropriate divisions. For example, 4-H and Youth Work is under Human Resource Development, and Agriculture Agents are under Community Programs. This chart is adapted from University Extension Makes a Difference in Wisconsin, a report of progress issued by Chancellor Donald R. McNeil in November, 1967.*

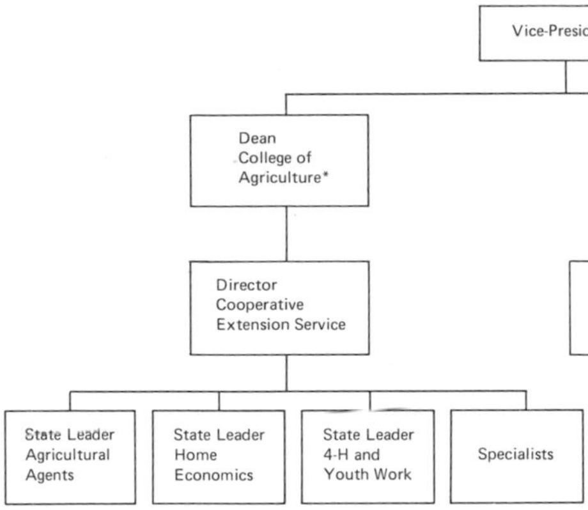

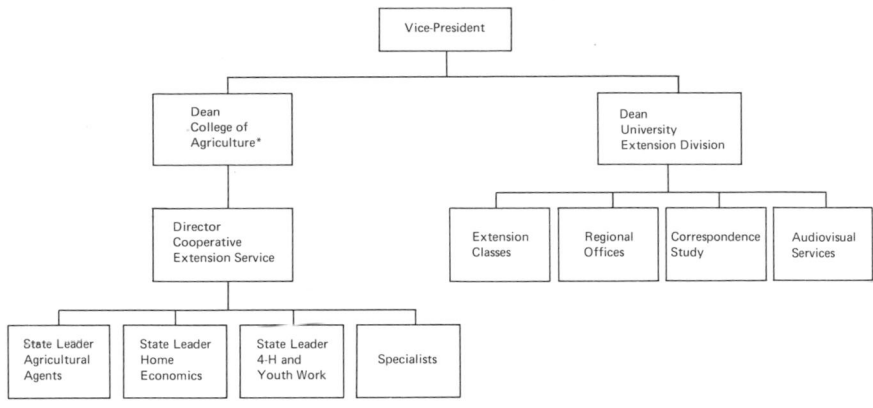

*May also serve as Director of Cooperative Extension Service.

Fig. 2 *Typical extension organization plan—separate extension services. This chart is representative of the traditional type of dual extension organization.*

versity of Wisconsin. Committed to increasing collaboration but not merger are the two extension services at Rutgers, The State University, which are self-coordinated through a joint committee on cooperation made up of staff members of the two agencies plus a representative of the Urban Studies Center.

CURRENT TRENDS

Among the current trends which appear to promise continuity are the proliferation of off-campus or regional extension centers and offices, the construction of residential facilities for extension conferences, and an increase in the number and kind of continuing education programs for professionals.

Residential Centers

The residential centers, such as the Kellogg Centers at several universities, the Adirondack Centers of Syracuse, and Arden House—to cite a few among the forty or fifty now in existence—make extension education more available on a year-round basis because residential programs used to be possible only when the institution's dormitories were vacant. They also make possible a greater involvement of university faculty members because of convenient location on or near the campus.

SPONSORSHIP

Because extension derives its name from the carrying forth of the university's basic educational resources, it is appropriate to close with guidelines for cooperative educational programs conducted jointly with outside organizations. In 1951, the National University Extension Association adopted the following principles for joint sponsorship of activities:

1. The university will sponsor a program only when the educational service cannot be given better by a nonuniversity agency.

2. University sponsorship or cooperation will always involve related colleges, schools, or departments.

3. Sponsorship will be accorded only to educational programs.
4. The university must play an active role in the planning and not merely provide facilities and prestige for a "canned" program.
5. The university will participate in the financial arrangements for the activity and normally will collect all income and make all disbursements.

ADDITIONAL INFORMATION

For further information about university extension, write to the National University Extension Association, National Center for Higher Education, 1 Dupont Circle, N.W., Washington, D.C. 20036. For further information about cooperative extension, telephone your county agricultural agent or write your state land-grant college.

EXTENSION BUDGETS

Budgets for extension services contain the traditional items included in most university and college budgets, and such items are discussed in detail in the section on financial administration.

However, the need for many general extension activities to be entirely or largely self-supporting has led to some interesting fiscal-management procedures, such as the following:

A. Total extension income is allocated:

50%	for instruction
20%	to parent institution for overhead
20%	for promotion and advertising
10%	for administration of program
100%	

B. Estimate of anticipated income agreed upon (by negotiation)...... *X*
Return to parent institution... *Y*
Available to extension .... *X–Y*
(Extension retains *all* funds except *Y*, including contract overhead and other nontuition income.)

C. Multiple-budget systems:

Account no. 1 – Staff salaries and basic operating funds

Account no. 2 – Revolving fund for food service, lodging, text materials and other items for which a direct, nontuition charge is levied

Account no. 3 – Revolving instructional account to cover direct teaching costs when program exceeds limits set in Account no. 1 above

BIBLIOGRAPHY

Kearl, Bryant E., and O. B. Copeland (eds.): *A Guide to Extension Programs for the Future,* The Agricultural Extension Service, North Carolina State College, Raleigh, N.C., 1959.
Knowles, Malcolm S. (ed.): *Handbook of Adult Education in the United States,* Adult Education Association of the U.S.A., Chicago, 1960, chaps. 17 and 18.
Petersen, Renee, and William Petersen: *University Adult Education,* Harper & Brothers, New York, 1960.
Sanders, H. C. (ed.): *The Cooperative Extension Service,* Prentice-Hall, Inc., Englewood Cliffs, N.J., 1966.
Shannon, Theodore J., and Clarence A. Schoenfeld: *University Extension,* The Center for Applied Research in Education, New York, 1965.
Tyler, Ralph W.: *An Evaluation of General Extension Work by Land-grant Institutions,* a paper presented before the American Association of Land-Grant Colleges and State Universities, at Kansas City, Mo., Nov. 14, 1961.
Watts, Lowell H. (ed.): *A People and a Spirit,* a report of the Joint USDA-NASULGC Extension Study Committee, Colorado State University, Fort Collins, Colo., 1968.

Chapter 6

Correspondence Study Programs

HAROLD GLEN CLARK

Dean of the Division of Continuing Education, Brigham Young University, Provo, Utah

INTRODUCTION

Correspondence study with individual tutorial instruction as its basic premise presents a challenge to administration. This is heightened by the recent development of a multitude of educational devices and techniques, some of which may be utilized in correspondence study under computer control.[1] In so doing, the concern of administration goes beyond the use of only the written word, the chief medium employed back in 1892 by Dr. William Rainey Harper, the father of university teaching by mail.

Dr. Harper became the president of the new University of Chicago just before the turn of the century. Twelve years before this he had taught extensively by correspondence as a professor of Biblical literature at Yale. In his first year as president, he incorporated correspondence study as an integral part of the University of Chicago. In that first year, 39 courses were offered by 23 instructors, and 82 correspondence students were enrolled. When President Harper died in 1906, there were 297 courses, 113 instructors, and 1,587 students in what was termed the "Home Study Department."

The real challenge in Dr. Harper's day was not the use of computers but the very validity of correspondence instruction as an intellectual function and whether or not the privileges of the university should be extended in that manner. Dr. Harper's firm belief in the correspondence-study system and the quality of his administration were his two great legacies to university correspondence study. He gave the correspondence-study program excellence and respectability and strove to make it consonant with the purpose of all education, as indicated by these two Harperisms:

> Whatever a *dead teacher* may accomplish in the classroom, he can do nothing by correspondence.
>
> If a student is lacking in earnestness, ambition, appreciation, aliveness, he can do nothing by correspondence. Either he will acquire these qualities and succeed, or he will remain as he was at the beginning and fail.[2]

Dr. Harper insisted that teaching by mail is in principle the same as any other kind of teaching and should not be separated from other forms. This insistence on sound teaching and learning in correspondence study was continued by President Van Hise of the University of Wisconsin when a correspondence teaching department was established there in 1906. By 1928, 149 colleges and universities reported established correspondence departments.[3] Studies of the last few years indicate that progress is being made in establishing this basic principle of the integration of correspondence teaching into the regular university curriculum but that it is still necessary for administrators to emphasize this principle of integration if they would build a sound correspondence-study program.[4]

For over 60 years these two great universities, Chicago and Wisconsin, forged ahead with sound programs of teaching by mail. Scores of others followed suit with well-

[1] Charles A. Wedemeyer (ed.), *The Brandenburg Memorial Essays on Correspondence Instruction*, vol. II, The University of Wisconsin, University Extension, Madison, Wis., 1966, pp. 69–73.

[2] Walton S. Bittner and Harvey F. Mallory, *University Teaching by Mail*, The Macmillan Company, New York, 1933, p. 23.

[3] *Ibid.*, pp. 18–22.

[4] Wedemeyer, *op. cit.*, p. 79.

developed correspondence-instruction departments. In the same period, hundreds of commercial correspondence-study schools—some false, others with integrity—appeared. Large business concerns, churches, labor unions, and the federal government have utilized this important medium for varied educational purposes.

The basic components involved in correspondence administration, which Dr. Harper took into account in setting up his pioneer program, seem as valid today as then. These components are reflected in the National University Extension Association's *Criteria and Standards and Guide to Self-evaluation*[5] for correspondence departments in universities as follows:

Philosophy
Instruction
Staff
Student services
Administration

The National University Extension Association (NUEA) might have added research and evaluation, for the spirit of review and examination is an important administrative function and concern of the alert chairman of correspondence study. The five constituent parts of a correspondence program in the instrument of evaluation developed and approved by the NUEA, plus the elements of self-evaluation and research, will be treated in the above order. Credit is given the NUEA's *Criteria and Standards and Guide to Self-evaluation* for many of the suggestions in this paper.

PHILOSOPHY

Correspondence study is individual-centered. It is essentially tutorial instruction by mail and other means and, in the last decade, instruction through means which supplement the printed word. The values of independent study and the place of such a study system in the basic philosophy of education of the university need to be made clear. A philosophy of correspondence education expresses the basic belief of the school in the dignity of the individual and in the opportunity for him to improve himself regardless of status or geographic location. The institution should indicate its commitment to individual differences and needs since the design and conduct of the correspondence program seeks to meet individual differences and needs.

A basic philosophy of education should express the position of the university with respect to professional competence, ethical practice, and responsible conduct on the part of all involved in the correspondence-study program. The university should state its intentions with respect to the evaluation of the achievement of its correspondence students, and the accreditation of that achievement, in terms and practices consistent with the best practices of other universities.

A published statement of university correspondence-study purposes and goals has its advantages, as it permits the administrator to more objectively relate that stated philosophy to what is being done in his correspondence department. This philosophy clearly stated, continually reviewed and improved, and consistently supported by all concerned is the basis of the correspondence-instruction program.[6]

Failure to arrive at a written statement of philosophy of necessity deprives organization and administration of the goal-directedness it furnishes. But a verbal agreement on goals by administration and staff is better than no goals at all; meantime the administrator should certainly work toward the time when this agreement may be put in writing.

[5] *Criteria and Standards and Guide to Self-evaluation,* National University Extension Association, Division of Correspondence Instruction, 900 Silver Spring Ave., Silver Spring, Md.
[6] *Ibid.*

The aimlessness which sometimes characterizes the university correspondence program, "its open-endedness, opportunistic service approach, and its cafeteria offerings of whatever the public demands,"[7] is in part due to the absence of a statement indicating *why* the program was organized, for *whom,* and *what* interests correspondence study is intended to serve. Its student body seems never quite definable. Perhaps it shouldn't be. If so, then the statement of philosophy should take this into account.

Perhaps the first and most important decision an administration must make, as it hammers out its philosophy, is just to what extent it wishes to make correspondence instruction an integral part of the total educational system of the university. Task committees from the various disciplines of the university may be assigned to work on a statement of beliefs and purposes. Added to this can be the engagement of a recognized educator of professional standing in the field of correspondence education from another university to assist the committees.

Whatever the philosophy and its form turn out to be, a continuing self-evaluation of it should be made. A sampling of student, faculty, and public opinion, along with an analysis of complaints and inquiries, is one method of determining the extent to which the philosophy is understood and accepted.[8] Ripley S. Sims, in a thoughtful treatise on *The Search for Purpose in Correspondence Education,*[9] objectively compares precepts with practices and then suggests that the "why" of correspondence study determines the practices and procedures of the program.

The criteria and standards set up by the NUEA Correspondence Division are a fruitful source of suggestions on philosophy.[10]

INSTRUCTION

The quality of learning by correspondence study is directly dependent upon the quality of instruction. The best instruction in the parent institution is the standard for teaching by correspondence.

Instruction then becomes a joint administrative responsibility of the department of correspondence and the academic department furnishing the teacher and the subject. The goal in correspondence-study subject content and teaching should be to make it equal to or better than that on the resident campus, both in scope and depth. Certainly the instruction should be adequate to achieve the purposes for which the course is being offered.

The administrator keeps abreast of what is happening in methods of instruction. Newer theories appear to stress the following:

The importance of the learner in the development of program and methodology.

Learner participation in setting learning goals.

The needs and experience of the learner relative to the learning process and to lesson plans.

The creation of a favorable climate in which the learner may find acceptance and recognition.

Learner participation in the evaluation of outcomes.[11]

The administration and supervision of this kind of instruction as a joint responsi-

[7] Paul H. Sheats, in Malcolm S. Knowles (ed.), *Handbook of Adult Education in the United States,* Adult Education Association of the U.S.A., Chicago, 1960, p. 554.

[8] Charles A. Wedemeyer, *The Brigham Young University Home Study Self-evaluation Report,* Adult Education and Extension Services, Brigham Young University, Provo, Utah, 1963, p. 18.

[9] Wedemeyer, *The Brandenburg Memorial Essays on Correspondence Instruction,* vol. II, pp. 86–88.

[10] *Criteria and Standards and Guide to Self-evaluation, op. cit.*

[11] Sheats, *op. cit.,* p. 559.

bility is an important key to a successful correspondence program. This key is sometimes dull with disuse or misuse.

Too often supervision and administration take the form of hiring clerks and supervisors efficient in the mechanics of clearing faculty, duplicating study guides, processing the lessons between teacher and student, and recording grades. These are important functions, but not high-priority duties in the supervision of instruction.

A correspondence department becomes more than a mill, receiving and grinding out study guides, when an administrator or his assistants who are trained in teaching conceive it their duty to set up and keep oiled the machinery which encourages and rewards excellence in teaching. The administrator sets up an atmosphere in which the teacher takes pride in being a teacher, a teacher who shuns shoddiness both in himself and in his students. Both teacher and student, at the end of a correspondence-course experience, feel that real help has been given and received and that learning has taken place.

While course content is primarily the responsibility of academic departments, the correspondence administrator has the obligation to specifically set up the means whereby this responsibility may be exercised. Excellent forms and procedures have been formulated by universities to assure that this integration takes place and to facilitate it. Both administrator and academic officer are kept informed. Frequent and personal contact with department heads and college deans is part of the price an administrator must pay for integration. Through such contacts, standards can be set cooperatively to do the following:

Base instruction procedures on current knowledge of how students learn.

Study and use various types of student motivation. Silent print without the classroom teacher can be very dull.

Work for variety in instruction with respect to the use of textbooks, library references, audiovisual techniques, and other educational media.

Set up and follow well-designed study guides.

Acquire promptness in the return of lessons.

Make students continuously aware of their progress.

Provide well-designed examinations administered with integrity.

Strive to award credit equal to residence credit.

Any one of these functions tests the best in skills and performance in educational administration. One can readily see that an educator-administrator must be acquainted with curriculum, be sensitive to good teaching methods, and be knowledgeable with respect to how to establish, apply, and reward high educational standards. The already busy chairmen and deans of academic departments often expect these standards to be maintained without too much of their time being spent on supervision.

It soon becomes apparent, then, that sound instructional methods and materials and a qualified faculty that performs remain primary concerns of the administrator of the correspondence-study program. At the same time, he must remember that the responsibility for the teachers and subject disciplines belongs to the academic departments and not to him. He does not have original jurisdiction unless it is delegated to him.

Some do well in this job of integrated administration. Teachers come through with correspondence outlines and quality teaching that upgrade the whole standard for resident teaching. Indeed, some teachers have said, "This is the first time I have known my subject so well. I am happy that I have prepared this outline for correspondence study. It has helped me tremendously in my lecture classes." Not infrequently, correspondence-study guides are used in resident teaching.

Correspondence credit should be accepted as equal in value to resident credit when standards in correspondence-instruction content, teaching, examining, and grading equal or excel the standards in campus classrooms. Practices vary in just how much correspondence credit will be accepted toward the baccalaureate degree. A common figure is 25 semester hours. Generally, no correspondence credit may be applied toward a graduate degree. In time this situation should change. The marginality accorded correspondence credit might be blamed in part on correspondence administrators operating substandard programs. Accrediting associations and/or the hierarchy of the university itself must also share this blame. At any rate, until all agencies concerned unite in their support of sound correspondence-study instruction, it will be viewed as instruction of uncertain quality in a low-priority program in the university.

There has been enough analysis and research, beginning back in the 1930s,[12] to establish the effectiveness and validity of sound correspondence instruction. The administrator can strengthen his confidence in the system by reading George F. Aker's classified and annotated bibliography of studies in procedures, methods, and techniques in correspondence-study programs from 1953 to 1963.[13] These valuable summaries of research made by scholars and administrators in the field define correspondence study, indicate how instruction may be effective, clarify its roles, and point up both its significance and its problems.

The challenges to the administration of correspondence instruction are made plain when the chief correspondence officer studies and works with scholars and specialists in the field.

He must listen to and work with subject-matter specialists.

He must assess the impact of the new educational media on correspondence study.[14] He must assist in the recruitment of teachers. He must have a part in the extremely difficult task of assessing the quality of study outlines and the effectiveness of correspondence teaching.

He must deal with persistent unresolved problems of correspondence education such as effective counseling and admission to correspondence study. He must help decide what courses to insert in the correspondence-study catalog and in the regular university catalog; what courses, if any, form a common core; what courses will enrich the gifted, the average, and the slow learners.[15]

He must be concerned with dropouts. He may be cheered by the fact that resident instruction has its unresolved problems also—they too have their dropouts. However, correspondence study should not use this as an excuse nor should it be proud of correspondence's mortality rate of enrollees who never finish a course, which goes as high as 50 to 60 percent. This record cannot be shrugged off on the grounds that the initiative required in independent study "separates the men from the boys." The good administrator is challenged to do something about low completion rates. Wedemeyer, in *The Brandenburg Memorial Essays*, points out the change correspondence instruction is undergoing, the tremendous growth in research and experimentation now taking place, and the new subject matter being offered to new client groups on new levels. All of this represents a distinct trend toward improved acceptance, recognition, and accreditation of correspondence education,[16] brought about largely through effective administration.

The correspondence-study administrator must know, everlastingly, that his task is to relate correspondence study closely with resident academic departments and the services on campus such as the library, the bookstore, curriculum-development laboratories, educational media, and counseling. This ability to relate will always be a

[12] Bittner and Mallory, *op. cit.*, pp. 317–331.

[13] George F. Aker, *Adult Education: Procedures, Methods and Techniques*, The Library of Continuing Education, Syracuse, N.Y., 1965, p. 26.

[14] Peter H. Rosse and Bruce J. Biddle, *The New Media and Education*, Aldine Publishing Co., Chicago, 1966, p. 340.

[15] Wedemeyer, *Brandenburg Memorial Essays on Correspondence Instruction*, vol. II, pp. 80–86.

[16] *Ibid.*, pp. 3–16.

basic ingredient of good administration even though the correspondence-study department may reach a point where it employs its own full-time faculty.

STAFF

Staffing a correspondence-study department calls for special executive skills and decisions which materially affect the capacity of that department to perform and get results.

The appointment of the chief officer in the correspondence-study department is a number-one decision. Is it to be a position of responsibility, decision making, and authority in matters of strategic importance? If it is, this calls for a man of special talents. Is he to be an individual worthy of a relatively free hand in the employment of subordinates, in recommending budgets, and in improving instruction? If so, then experience and skill in these functions may be desirable. On the other hand, if he is to be a competent manager of office detail with the dean or his assistant handling the weightier functions, then an individual skilled in office management can do the job.

A glance at those representing correspondence-study departments at the annual National University Extension professional meetings reveals varied arrangements, all the way from the office manager to the stronger executive type. University correspondence-study programs have had substantial growth, using either of these types of organization. Regardless of the organizational structure of the department, it is well to keep in mind Wedemeyer's observation that "the quality of any program will be directly related to the level of ability, experience, and sense of dedication of the staff responsible for its operation."[17] The dean or the other chief administrative officer responsible for the appointment should recognize and meet his responsibility to provide competent administrative, supervisory, and teaching personnel if he wishes to develop a superior university correspondence-study program.

The chief administrative officer of the correspondence-study department—regardless of where he is in the organizational structure—should have academic and/or administrative rank and salary commensurate with his qualifications. His duties require interrelations with the university, the colleges, the departments, and the general administration. He is linked with the office of admissions. He works with deans and department chairmen in the selection of faculty, in determining their compensation for correspondence work, in the preparation of study outlines, and in setting and maintaining standards in scope and in content of the courses taught. In other words, this individual officer must possess the professional and personal qualifications established by the parent institution for persons in equivalent academic or staff responsibility and should be paid an equivalent salary. One has but to turn to a fully developed correspondence-study program such as the Wisconsin system to see the importance of a strong officer who performs the administrative function.

As the correspondence-study program enlarges, special methods and developments can make the problems of administration easier as, for example, when the chief officer is permitted to employ his own teachers in a separate teaching staff and when field services are added. Most universities do not yet have the larger resources or make the special appropriations to correspondence-study work needed for this larger organizational structure. Whether the university correspondence-study program is or is not moving in the direction of more independence, there will always be the continuing responsibility of its administration to make and keep the program an integral part of the academic responsibility of the parent institution.

The executive head of correspondence study maintains a planned program of in-service education for his teachers and employs special staff members such as coun-

[17] Wedemeyer, *The Brigham Young University Home Study Self-Evaluation Report*, p. 51.

selors, editors, and other personnel which the unique character of the correspondence-study program demands.

The clerical and other staff members, directed by an office manager, should be competent, trained, and should work under conditions which encourage efficiency and the feeling that their work is important to the success of the correspondence program.

The question of who has responsibility for, and authority over, various aspects of the correspondence-study program must be answered candidly if the program is to be of high quality. Existing correspondence-study systems can well be reviewed continuously. What responsibilities and authorities does the academic vice-president possess with respect to the program? the dean? the director of correspondence study? Should any business officer of the university exercise educational authority? Is the chief officer in the correspondence-study department encumbered with routine? Is he able to do more than keep up with current office work? Is he able to keep abreast of new developments by visiting other institutions? Does he make surveys, institute research, and experiment with new projects? Who should handle the custodial duties of money and enrollments, student records and examinations, recording lessons and grades, typing, multilithing?

The organization chart of one correspondence division of 5,000 students follows the general structure indicated in Figure 1.

This shows that the duties of overall administration are centered in a chairman. Curriculum development, counseling, promotion publicity, in-service training, and policy matters with regard to faculty and office personnel usually fall under the jurisdiction of the chairman and/or his associate. In larger organizations, assignments may be even more specialized. The person working under the chairman, often referred to

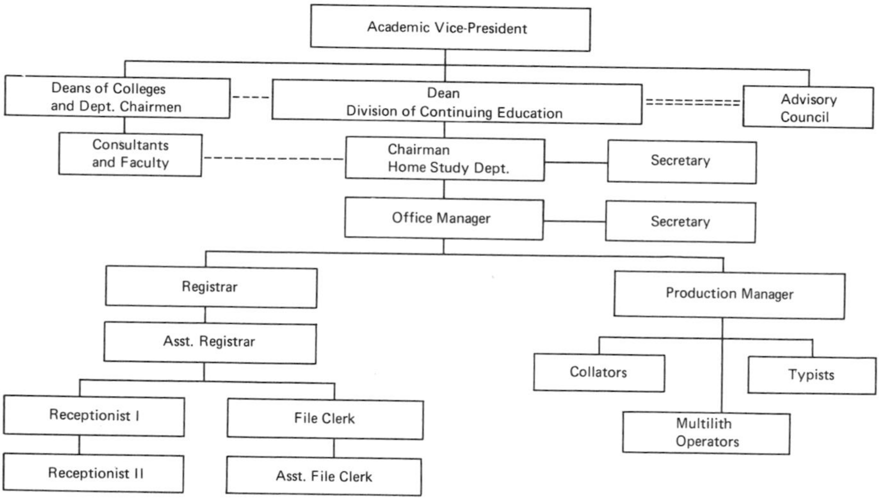

Dotted lines (---) indicate that final approval of teachers and courses is obtained through academic channels of the university. Dotted lines (===) show the advisory council as advisory only.

Fig. 1 *Organization and administration of Department of Home Study, Brigham Young University 1968–69.*

as the office manager, is concerned with the functions of registering and the production and distribution of lesson outlines, textbooks, and catalogs.

If the department stocks and sells textbooks used in correspondence study or does its own printing, these functions would enlarge the organizational structure. Curriculum assistants and sometimes special representatives from each college are added where the volume of teaching warrants such. Larger institutions may also employ and directly supervise full-time teachers.

The Advisory Council, shown in Figure 1, is appointed by the Academic Vice-President upon recommendation of the Dean of the Division of Continuing Education. This council of five advises with the Dean and the Chairman of the Department of Home Study on matters of university policy and in particular on universitywide problems and standards affecting faculty teaching. The dotted line from the Dean of the Division of Continuing Education to other deans and their department heads is indicative of the approval channel followed. The Dean of Continuing Education and his Department of Correspondence Chairmen recommend, but the dean and department chairmen in the various colleges put the final stamp of approval on the teacher and the course outline to be taught. In practice, much of the detail leading up to final academic approval is handled directly between teacher and correspondence-department chairman as shown by the dotted lines in Figure 1.

The development of a well-prepared set of desired qualifications for teachers of correspondence courses and for each member of the office for which the chief officer in correspondence study is responsible is an administrative duty. A statement of tasks and standards for each position in the office operation is strategic to the functions of pre-service and in-service training, salary schedules, and pay increases.

When training meetings with faculty and staff result in helpful lessons returned with reasonable speed and courteous treatment, a favorable image is provided that is contagious. It has obvious relationship to increases in enrollments. One course which satisfies the enrollee leads to additional enrollments at the same institution or results in the satisfied customer telling his friends about the excellent service. This usually results in increased volume, and increased volume means lower unit costs. When a staff increases its efficiency, through in-service education to handle increased volume without increasing overhead costs, the total picture in the department points toward a success situation financially and academically.

Quality educational service to larger numbers of correspondence-study students can become the rule in American universities. When it does, correspondence study will come nearer being accorded the place it deserves in the hierarchy of every American university. Malcolm Knowles envisions the future when "the size of the adult student body would grow to be twice the size of the youth student body in numbers." [18] Industry, government, and other agencies are increasingly interested in the continued education of their employees. Quality correspondence-study services may some day be looked upon as a condition of the survival of both the institution and its personnel. It is not difficult to see that the university under these circumstances will be willing more and more to design and pay for facilities, curriculum, and trained personnel to serve this larger clientele for correspondence study.

STUDENT SERVICES

One of the criticisms leveled at correspondence study is the lack of adequate student services. This includes library resources; counseling services; adequate supplemental teaching aids and supplies; ready access to transcripts and certification records; and

[18] Malcolm S. Knowles, *The Adult Education Movement in the United States*, Holt, Rinehart and Winston, Inc., New York, 1962, p. 277.

recognition of student achievement. This criticism is not without some justification.

Library services are too often inadequate. This inadequacy, along with other inadequate student services, is part of the reason why almost no graduate credit is offered through correspondence study. The job of knowing the criteria of a sound student-services program and doing something about it rests squarely on the shoulders of the chief administrative officer of the correspondence-study program. The standard here, as in other areas of operation, requires that these services be as nearly comparable to residence opportunity as time and distance factors permit.

Dr. Harper, in administering correspondence instruction in the 1890s, felt that student services should not be restricted to the classroom student. This key point in the extension movement needs to be emphasized repeatedly[19] to keep correspondence study from moving in the direction of the simple scheme of having any good clerk ship printed materials through the mail. Adjusting to the needs of a student *in absentia* is a difficult task. When a chairman of a correspondence-study department sets his mind to this function and enlists the resources of his staff in performing it, excuses and barriers fall and adequate student services appear. Varied and regular facilities and services for students which aid them in their learning are a built-in aspect of a superior correspondence-study program.

Correspondence-study students should be authorized to use the university library, directly or by mail, through the regular or special procedures or through both. Whatever books may be needed to complete a course in a satisfactory manner should be made available. The services available should be clearly described to the student through the correspondence-study catalog. The adequacy of these services and just how much they are used should be the concern of the chairman of the correspondence-study department. Textbooks need to be periodically reviewed and kept up to date, with new books or editions added as needed. The faculty should be made aware of the need for certain services and their part in furnishing these to the students.

Unreasonably long periods of waiting to receive needed books should signal the chairman to do something about the situation. Loan periods and renewal privileges need careful attention.

When a teacher writes a course, he should be able to tell his students what university library services may be expected. Someone in the correspondence-study department must establish a checking system to review, with the library, holdings for the course and the need for additional copies of books and pamphlets. Such a system of continuous review helps determine the most needed references.[20]

Where there is a concentration of off-campus students, branches of county and city libraries can usually be enlisted to serve them. When needed, consideration can be given to the purchase of a special library collection for a particular course. The books are then placed in the most available library for use in that course by correspondence students.

The use of disk recordings, maps, graphs, and charts to supplement the printed page has not yet come into its own. They are often expensive to produce, inventory, and send through the mail. These materials are not a substitute for teaching but are a part of effective correspondence teaching. They are used at their best when they clarify, fortify, enrich, and facilitate learning.

The correspondence-study chairman has the practical job of seeing that the aids support the content and that the expense of preparing and circulating them is within budgetary bounds. Some programs send enriching and supportive visual-aid materials on a loan basis. The director of correspondence study needs to adopt a method of keeping informed in this fast-moving area. This function can be assigned to an au-

[19] Bittner and Mallory, *op. cit.*, p. 19.

[20] Wedemeyer, *The Brigham Young University Home Study Self-evaluation Report*, p. 81.

diovisual coordinator if the program is large enough. New low-priced tape recorders, for example, have possibilities. The coordinator can work with faculty in the preparation of tailor-made audiovisual materials. The director of correspondence study must take the initiative in seeing that writers and teachers of correspondence-study courses are aware of campus curriculum laboratories and new education media and utilize them to advantage.

Counseling services provided for correspondence students in universities leave much to be desired. An analysis of the problems a university correspondence-study student faces as he enrolls includes the following: making an appropriate choice of courses, improving his study ability, making enough of his time available, and meeting the requirement of course prerequisites. A secretary-clerk can handle many problems dealing with routine policies, rules, and regulations. This, however, is a poor substitute for a definite counseling service which gives students information and help on university policies that seriously affect course offerings. A survey of the critical educational problems that occur forms the basis for counseling needs. A good counselor may also be employed to examine catalogs and flyers, evaluate their guidance values, and recommend changes that will make the catalog a better counseling tool. He can research these and other problems and determine better techniques for their solution.

A *record-transcript-certification* service can make significant materials and data readily available to the student. This is a distinct and useful service. These records may serve for advancement on the job, evaluation for graduation, and/or for transfer and certification purposes. Cooperative action on the part of the chairman of the department of correspondence study with the centralized or decentralized system of the university admissions and records office requires definite administrative action. Whatever system of record-transcript-certification the correspondence-study department uses, it should be integrated with the practices of the resident university admissions and records office.

The correspondence-study records system, counseling services, library services, and the educational media facilities should reflect the basic philosophy of the university and constitute an integral part of its total operation.

The dean and the chairman of the correspondence-study department have the obligation and privilege not only of implanting the educational philosophy of the university, but also of magnifying it in the correspondence-study program. They provide the leadership required to conduct a program which, because of its scope and quality, will command recognition, financial support, and accreditation equal to or better than those of the other academic departments of the university.

ADMINISTRATION

Financial support of correspondence study is an inherent responsibility of dean and chairman. First, they must jointly see that ways and means are devised to bring about interest and understanding of the full possibilities of a university correspondence-study program on the part of all agencies of the university. Following this, they formulate the financial needs of such a program. Third, they point out to the top echelon the benefits and sell them on the need to provide adequate financial support for the approved program.

J. R. Kidd has a thoughtful book, titled *Financing Continuing Education,*[21] which is worth the time of all interested in financing correspondence study. In it he asks the question, "Where does the money come from?" His approach to various ways and means of financing tends to provoke the administrator to seek new and different means of financial support. He includes the following as main sources of financial support:

[21] J. R. Kidd, *Financing Continuing Education,* The Scarecrow Press, Inc., New York, 1962, pp. 77–78.

Fees (paid as tuition or membership)
Taxes
Philanthropy (including foundation grants)
Sale of services
Voluntary services

The conclusion is that there is no best way of financing. Kidd hopes that this observation will challenge creativity and ingenuity and "stimulate exploration of new approaches rather than engender either satisfaction or resignation with present practices."[22]

The costs of correspondence education must be anticipated and provided for. Sound cost accounting of staff, faculty, office-management requirements, and catalog needs and analyses of the production costs of study outlines provide half the solution to the financial problem.

Budgeting patterns differ widely from institution to institution. They differ because salary and honorarium scales differ. They differ because tuition rates differ. They differ too because universities differ in amounts of cash appropriation, space, utilities, and other benefits provided. Some of these come as subsidies to the correspondence department. In general, the lion's share of income for the department comes from student fees. On the expense side of the ledger, the larger items are payments for salaries and honorariums to staff and faculty.

The budget for one university[23] with a correspondence-department student body of over 5,000 was as follows:

TABLE 1 Correspondence Department Budget

Income:		
Tuition and fees	$153,001.08	
Sales income (texts, tapes, and manuals)	18,962.70	
Budget allocation from university	13,620.00	
Total income		$185,583.78
Expenditures:		
Inventory purchases (textbooks)	$17,823.11	
Faculty honorariums	72,064.28	
Staff wages and payroll taxes	25,481.85	
Office expense:		
Travel	500.00	
Supplies	6,110.21	
Telephone	795.75	
Maintenance and miscellaneous	433.41	
Printing	2,200.00	
Postage	5,500.00	
Promotion (circulars, catalogs)	20,842.20	
Special contracts	25.00	
Capital and operating equipment	1,050.00	
Administrative overhead	10,000.00	
Utilities	1,800.00	
Total expenditures		$164,625.81

It can be seen from this budget that 80 percent or more of the income is derived from tuition and fees and that approximately 60 percent of the expenditures are for staff and faculty wages. These and other amounts in any university budget, to be properly understood, must be interpreted in the light of the philosophy of the institution,

[22] *Ibid.*, p. 78.
[23] *Calculated Home Study Budget*, Brigham Young University, Provo, Utah, 1968.

the geographic location of the clientele of the correspondence department, the department's pay scale, and many other variables.

Where does the money come from becomes a meaningful and objective question when the necessary spending requirements are carefully established budgetwise. The answers to this question are not always ready answers. Certainly, how university governing boards, their administrative officers, and their clientele feel about correspondence education, and how they define and assess its purposes, greatly influence the approach used to foot the bill for the correspondence study program. The author of *Financing Continuing Education* indicates how attitudes of people toward continuing education programs are markedly affected by notions such as the following "facts or folklore." [24]

The adult student should always pay for what he gets.

The adult student values only what he pays for.

No taxpayer will "stand for" paying for the education of some other adult.

Correspondence study is of less worth than other forms of education.

Special safeguards and financial controls are required for correspondence education.

The "market place" or "cafeteria" approach is most favorable for correspondence education.

Social utility rather than individual and economic benefits should apply in the financing of correspondence education.

Correspondence study may deal with subjects that are controversial, and tax funds should not be used for such purposes.

Correspondence study is investment.

(Semantic liberties have been taken in reporting Kidd's nine notions. For example, the term "correspondence education" was used in place of Kidd's "continuing education." It is assumed that this is not objectionable.)

The directions to an administrator responsible for the financial support of correspondence study are summarized as follows:

1. Find out how much revenue is needed.
2. Discover the ability of prospective students to pay. Who are the clients and to what extent can they be expected to support the program through fees?
3. Indicate the forms of financing that can be found. In addition to fees, are there other sources?
4. Answer the question of just how the chosen form or forms of financing affect the quality and integrity of the program.[25]

The first step moves along more readily for the neophyte in correspondence-study administration if a careful study of the operational costs of comparable programs of other institutions is made. His cost analysis of the particular program to be established could then be compared to the study he has made. The second and third steps would involve where and how the needed revenue is to be obtained. Over a dozen years ago, Morton [26] discovered that out of 46 major universities, 37 used fees to raise more than 50 percent of their extension budgets. Twenty-two of these universities raised 71 percent or more of their budgets from fees. The heavy dependency on fees suggests that this practice needs careful weighing.

If the philosophy and structure under which the administrator works call for complete support from fees, Kidd has suggested that the chairman of the department of correspondence not resign himself to his fate but follow steps three and four, which chal-

[24] *Ibid.*, pp. 19–48.

[25] *Ibid.*, p. 50.

[26] John R. Morton, *University Extension in the United States*, University of Alabama Press, University, Ala., 1953, p. 98.

lenge him to think of additional sources of support. Some excellent continuing education programs in the country five years ago appear to have operated on annual budgets given to them in amounts ranging from $2,500 to $75,000.[27] This is not an endorsement of these figures but a statement of fact.

Fees are generally charged on a quarter- or semester-hour basis and are above $10 an hour.[28] Refund policies range all the way from no refunds up to a fair charge for services already rendered the person asking for a refund. Fairness would dictate a policy moving in the direction of assisting the student in dropping a class for which he is not suited and to do so at no great financial loss to him or the correspondence-study department.

One of the virtues of correspondence study is an individualized instruction program with latitude as to when the lessons may be completed. In the last five years, government grants and contracts have been a source of income for services rendered. But a program built on subsidies from the government or any one source may be seasonal and shifting. A regular student body, enrolled annually, paying a fair fee supplemented by the general budget of the university and expanding in accordance with need and demand is a great financial asset. It seems sound administration to have reasonable fees coming in which pay a majority of the costs and to have special grants for special needs. Correspondence education is so important in the life of the nation and covers such an inexhaustible range of interests and people that its support should not be confined to one agency, authority, or source.

Great foundations in this country have provided funds for experimental educational projects and programs in correspondence study. Carnegie, Rockefeller, Kellogg, and others are likely sources. In 1960, an estimated 8.2 billion philanthropic dollars were dispensed in the United States, 16 percent of which went to education.[29] These dollars are more likely to increase than to decrease.

Faculty salaries make the heaviest drain on the correspondence-study budget. However, faculty services are strategic, and good administration calls for paying teachers a fair wage as soon as possible after services are rendered. It is poor fiscal policy to have outstanding or carryover debts to faculty for services rendered. It is not too difficult for teachers to be late with lessons when delay in pay is the order of the day in the correspondence-study office.

Faculty compensation for teaching correspondence courses varies widely. Palmer, in an unpublished survey[30] based on 40 questionnaires returned from universities in this country in 1967, found a variety of practices. For example, payments made by 21 institutions administered on a semester-hour basis ranged all the way from $10 to $250 per semester hour, with a median payment of $75. Fourteen universities indicated that the "decision of the department as to what is just" was the basis. Three indicated that honorariums for writing a course were based on the equivalent salary the faculty member would have received from teaching on campus. Another used an established schedule of $50 per credit hour for all teachers, while another paid a flat rate of $15 for each lesson in the outline.

The same survey showed a wide range of fees paid for correcting correspondence lessons. Twenty-five institutions paid from 30 cents to $3 a lesson to their faculties for this service. Others paid from $7 to $20 per credit hour; another paid a set percentage of the enrollment fee; while some paid from $7 to $30 per course. More per hour was paid to others if the lessons were returned within a specified time.

[27] *Ibid.*, p. 100.
[28] Mack Palmer, unpublished survey (1967) of 40 universities in the United States, Brigham Young University Home Study Department, Provo, Utah.
[29] Kidd, *op. cit.*, p. 87.
[30] Palmer, *op. cit.* (Also appendix of this chapter.)

Common figures appeared to be $75 per semester hour for constructing a correspondence course and $1.25 for correcting a lesson.

Sound personnel administration points to differentiation in fees paid for faculty services. Correspondence divisions which move in the direction of a compensation system which differentiates between the pay scale of the instructor and that of the professor are going in the right direction. While the same payment schedule for all correspondence teachers is administratively convenient, this convenience may not add to the effort to improve the quality of professional instruction in the long run. The regular university instructional programs appear to improve the quality of their teaching through differentiation in pay. Differentiation would seem to be an important consideration for correspondence teaching as well.

Provision for adequate facilities is an administrative obligation. The handling of incoming and outgoing mail, storage, addressing, mailing, and recording are routines requiring special physical work-flow arrangements in order to simplify and speed up procedures. Proper facilities actually reduce costs over a period of time.

Promotion and publicity are strategic functions of the department of correspondence. It must know its clientele, distinguish their needs, and focus attention on providing effective assistance for them.[31] Schoenfeld, in the *Brandenburg Memorial Essays*, gives 10 excellent steps for promoting correspondence programs. He regards correspondence study as unusually well suited to the demands of space-age education, yet feels that the promotion of correspondence education is one of the neglected areas of administration. Hundreds of thousands of potential users, eager and able to profit from study by mail, never have its benefits brought forcefully to their attention.[32] Schoenfeld would follow in progression these steps:

Know the organization represented.
Recognize the mission to be performed.
Define exactly what you want to communicate.
Identify your publics and determine the media to be used.
Estimate costs and make budget.
Mate the encodes with the decodes.
Make a campaign plan.
Have a built-in plan to measure results.[33]

He suggests that by cooperating with the regular public-relations channels of the university, a correspondence-study department has much to gain from a planned program of public information. There are vast resources that have not been tapped for building a total plan of administering and financing a correspondence-study program.

Office management is a clearly defined function of good correspondence administration. The chairman of a correspondence-study program cannot regard it lightly. He should have the responsibility and authority to define the procedures concerned with the enrollment, progress in, and successful completion of a correspondence-study course by a student. The maintenance of effective communication on the management level through proper feedback and democratic approaches is essential. The modern use of the correspondence medium requires a modern record system and the effective management of that system in cooperation with the central records office of the university. This cooperation and integration avoids duplications and confusions and maintains university policies and standards. Correspondence-study record-keeping should be comparable to or better than the record-keeping by other academic departments of the university.

[31] Morton, *op. cit.*, p. 138.
[32] Wedemeyer, *The Brandenburg Memorial Essays on Correspondence Instruction*, vol. II, pp. 109–118.
[33] *Ibid.*, pp. 110–118.

The National University Extension Association and other national educational record-keeping agencies ask for information annually. Record-keeping should be so organized that the reporting of these statistics by the dean or director of the continuing education program is facilitated.

SELF-EVALUATION AND RESEARCH

The NUEA Correspondence Division has prepared an excellent instrument for self-evaluation which any correspondence department may use to advantage.[34] To paraphrase the introductory statement in this evaluation booklet, "The unexamined correspondence-study program is not worth conducting."

Brigham Young University made an effort to apply this instrument in 1962–63.[35] Thirty-two suggestions were made as a result of the study. Twenty-five were acted upon and the other seven have been progressively pursued. The following five steps seemed important in the achievement of results from the self-evaluation study:[36]

1. The right start. The top administration and the faculty must be involved from the start.

2. The use of a well-prepared instrument of evaluation. Take time and use professional help to build this, before beginning.

3. Simplicity in organization, administration, and commitment. Simple, definite instructions, reasonable deadlines, and a dedicated beginning with the highest echelon are important.

4. The use of an outside professional evaluator. Weight and seriousness of purpose, increased validity to the study, and attention to unexamined areas are the benefits of this step.

5. Follow-through. The "what shall we do now," "who will do it and when" questions must be asked and answered if the purposes of self-evaluation are to be fulfilled.

The results of this study leave a clear impression that the roles of the dean and the chairman of the correspondence-study department are to be stimulus and catalyst in the initiation and completion of a successful self-evaluation.

Each component part of correspondence study may benefit from a periodic self-survey. Though the philosophy of correspondence study, for example, may be well conceived and full of promise, the extent to which it is understood or accepted and actually achieved cannot be ascertained without inquiry and sampling. This is also true of staff, student services, and every phase of administration. There must be examination, probing, and analysis. Investigations marked by candor usually result in healthy affirmations and new and stronger approaches to program development.

Research provides the basis for administrative decisions. Correspondence-study departments are not noted for their emphasis on research. Gayle Childs, reviewing this aspect of correspondence administration,[37] places the responsibility on administration for not giving this practice high priority in terms of financial support or personal assignment. Lack of research is evidenced by the wide divergence in teaching practices, policies, and administrative rules and regulations. Granted that diversity has its place, Childs points out that all the diversity cannot be explained on the basis of need for variation. As an example, he points out that recent research shows that the time taken to complete a correspondence-study course has no practical effect on grades received. This research, if thoroughly confirmed, would materially affect the chair-

[34] *NUEA Criteria and Standards and Guide to Self-Evaluation, op. cit.*

[35] *The Brigham Young University Home Study Self-Evaluation Report,* Division of Continuing Education, Brigham Young University, Provo, Utah, 1963.

[36] Wedemeyer, *The Brandenburg Memorial Essays on Correspondence Instruction,* vol. II, pp. 123–124.

[37] *Ibid.,* pp. 126–140.

man's decision about how much time students should be granted to complete a course.

Administrative rules, regulations, and attitudes now in effect need testing through demonstrative research to permit correspondence-study administrators to move away from procedures based on happenstance. Completion rates, comparative achievement of correspondence and television students, programmed instruction, teaching methods, an analysis of those making catalog requests—all represent areas likely to yield fruitful research.

Programs in operation in different universities, examined and observed as to structure, administration, procedure, and achievements, can be enlightening, build insights, and break down provinciality. A Carnegie grant to study nine large but differing university extension programs was made in 1959–60.[38] The survey included the correspondence-study departments in each instance. The dean of each of these institutions presented, in symposium fashion, the history, objectives, geographical setting, programs, methods of operation, finances, relationships with other institutions, and expectations of the future with respect to operation. The symposium, designed to "inspire and instruct the entire staff of the Continuing Education services of The Pennsylvania State University," inspired and instructed the deans themselves.

A resourceful staff is developed largely through professional improvement and study. The push of immediate administrative detail so often crowds out this long-range administrative function. Participation in the workshops and the regional and central meetings of the correspondence-study division of the National University Extension Association keeps a staff creative and progressive. The Adult Education Library at Syracuse University provides excellent bibliographies and reading lists for those interested in this field.

Private and other types of correspondence schools have practices and procedures that bear investigation and observation. The National Home Study Council, an accrediting agency for private home study schools, listed 102 accredited private home study schools in its 1968 directory. Many of these are commercial, including the International Correspondence Schools, which began about 1890 in Pennsylvania.[39] The Council estimates that approximately 1¾ million Americans, mostly adults, are engaged in private home study courses at any given time during the year, and 3½ million are enrolled annually in all types of correspondence study. There are more new students annually enrolling in home study courses than new students enrolling in colleges and universities in this country.[40]

Churches, some agencies of the federal government, labor unions, and corporations use the correspondence media for purposes peculiar to each institution. Deans and chairmen of correspondence-study departments, alive to the needs of these groups, may render them specific services and learn much as they try to adapt the university program to specific institutional needs. A classic example of cooperative educational effort with government is the program of the United States Armed Forces Institute.

The USAFI, as it is known, was established in 1942 in Madison, Wisconsin,[41] to provide a variety of services, including correspondence courses, to the military and civilian personnel in the Armed Forces. Through this institute, the United States government makes contracts with colleges and universities to furnish courses to members of the Armed Forces at high school and college levels in both academic and technical areas.

A minimum enrollment fee covering cost of course materials and administrative

[38] *Symposium: General University Extension*, Pennsylvania State University, University Park, Pa., 1959–1960.

[39] Sheats, *op. cit.*, p. 16.

[40] *The Accreditation of Private Home Study Schools*, National Home Study Council, Washington (pamphlet).

[41] Knowles, *op. cit.*, p. 99.

charges is assessed and the serviceman enrolls in accordance with USAFI rules, making application through his education or commanding officer. The university is reimbursed by the government on the basis of lessons completed. The student pays the university the minimum fee for a course in accordance with the contract made between the government and the institution. The university receives the current enrollment fee of $8 for each course, regardless of length or hours of credit, plus the agreed-upon contract price per lesson.

For more than 25 years, this service has been offered by USAFI, which publishes and distributes annually a schedule [42] of the colleges and universities offering correspondence instruction to military personnel. Responsibility for course instruction, content, number of lessons, and fees rests with the contracting institution. Contracts are negotiated annually, terminating June 30 of each year. Universities interested in affiliating with USAFI may make application by writing directly to USAFI, Madison, Wisconsin.

Service to USAFI is a distinct and worthy personal service to men and women engaged in the defense of the country and a social service to the Armed Forces of the United States of America. The lesson completion rate is not over 25 percent. The remuneration to the institution may not be as high as that found in serving other groups. Bradt, in his study,[43] points up some of the reasons for failure to complete USAFI courses: lack of time, failure to master the mechanics of studying and completing lessons and changes of plans. However, some 50 colleges and universities [44] provided this service in 1967 and apparently found it worth their time and resources.

Judged on the basis of its services to the Armed Forces for over a quarter of a century, USAFI is a successful, bona fide correspondence-study program, fulfilling the wider educational interests and obligations of the university and, in part, the educational needs of the Armed Forces. The educational service is unique, requiring adaptation of regular administrative procedures to armed services conditions and requirements. This program has demonstrated that a correspondence-study chairman can build a pattern of joint cooperative action between a public or a private university and the federal government in the vital field of correspondence education.

The total enrollment in all courses offered by USAFI was 277,691 from June, 1967, through May, 1968.

SUMMARY

The first step in the sound administration of university correspondence education requires a definite search for purpose in correspondence-study education.

Tutorial or independent instruction in the second half of this century has assumed an increasingly important role in society, not only because of technical advances in information processing, computers, and the development of new media, but also because of the need for men and women in all walks of life to keep informed. This progress challenges the alertness of deans and department chairmen in continuing education.

The knowledgeable administrator, both dean and chairman, recognizes and avoids separation of correspondence study from the total academic program of the university and the ongoing purposes of the institution in which it has its setting.

Correspondence study is based on valid assumptions and has proven its worth. It calls for wise, firm, creative leadership at this point in its history in order to further

[42] *Correspondence Lessons, USAFI,* Department of Defense, United States Armed Forces Institute, Madison, Wis.

[43] Kenneth H. Bradt, *Why Service Personnel Fail to Complete USAFI Courses,* Research Division, Office of Armed Forces Information and Education, Washington, August, 1954.

[44] *Correspondence Lessons, USAFI, op. cit.*

improve instruction, staff, and course materials and to take it into new and more varied fields of service.

Progress is also dependent on how the dean and chairman come to grips with the weighty problems of financial support. This problem throws the spotlight on the depth of belief in the place of correspondence study in the hierarchy of the university. Leadership in correspondence study must meet its responsibility head-on to assist in developing a plan to provide adequate finances. In so doing, many sources of financial support need to be uncovered, evaluated, and used.

The chairman of the correspondence-study department must have the necessary ability and flair to actively promote correspondence education. This skill is a part of sound administrative technique. Instruments of self-evaluation and research may be effective tools in his hand to ensure progress, sound expansion, and a solid foundation for the correspondence-study program.

Administrative provincialism can be avoided by staff attendance at professional meetings, exchanging information with sister institutions, and by an understanding and appreciation of other ongoing correspondence-study programs, including private correspondence-study programs.

The trend in correspondence study is toward increased usefulness, new client groups, and the wider application of the correspondence method to dropouts and the deprived. Superior administration is the key to acceptance, recognition, and desirable change in correspondence study.

SELECTED BIBLIOGRAPHY

Erdos, Renée F.: *Teaching by Correspondence,* Longmans, Green & Co., Ltd., London, 1967.

The chief value of this book is the practical experience it contains and its readiness for use by administrators and teachers interested in modern techniques of teaching and administering correspondence.

Holmberg, Börje: *Correspondence Education,* Hermods–NKI, Malmö, Sweden, 1967.

Dr. Holmberg gives practical help in constructing correspondence courses as well as many useful, down-to-earth applications, methods, and problems.

Mager, Robert F.: *Preparing Instructional Objectives,* Fearon Publishers, 2165 Park Boulevard, Palo Alto, Calif., 1962.

The need for specific objectives, stressed by Dr. Mager, will be of interest to those preparing correspondence outlines which communicate certain skills and knowledge to their students.

Tough, Allen M.: *Learning Without a Teacher,* Educational Research, Ser. no. 3, The Ontario Institute for Studies in Education, 10 Bloor Street, West, Ontario 5, Canada, 1967.

Professor Tough supports the hypothesis that self-teachers can and do perform successfully several of the tasks of a professional teacher. Self-teachers obtain assistance from a variety of sources and individuals. These sources are identified by the author.

University of Texas: *Report of the Conference on Newer Media in Correspondence Study,* prepared in cooperation with the U.S. Department of Health, Education and Welfare, U.S. Office of Education, 1962.

The guidelines to the present and future use of newer media in correspondence study developed in this study are especially helpful.

Wedemeyer, Charles A.: *Correspondence Education—Manual of Training Conference Materials,* University Extension, University of Wisconsin, Madison, Wis. (In manuscript only, publication date probably 1970.)

This manual will be helpful in training administrators of correspondence in the techniques of correspondence instruction through well-defined steps. This will be an excellent reference for the neophyte as well as for the experienced administrator who wants to organize a correspondence program.

APPENDIX

QUESTIONNAIRE ON PRACTICES AND POLICIES OF CORRESPONDENCE STUDY

SUMMARY OF RESPONSES RECEIVED FROM FORTY MEMBER INSTITUTIONS OF THE NATIONAL UNIVERSITY EXTENSION ASSOCIATION TO A QUESTIONNAIRE ON THE PRACTICES AND POLICIES OF THEIR CORRESPONDENCE DEPARTMENTS, 1967.

1. How do you motivate students to complete their courses?
   36, form letters, cards, and personal letters of encouragement; others, miscellaneous answers.
2. If a student does not submit lessons, how often is he contacted during the period of his enrollment?
   Over half contacted the student once or twice; others, more than twice or irregularly.
3. Do you offer a formal counseling service to students?
   10, yes; 30, no.
4. Should graduate credit be offered?
   20, yes; 9, no; 6, no answer; 5, other answers.
5. If your program is offered to prisoners in penal institutions, how much is your tuition to them?
   2, charge no tuition; 32, three-fourths of the full tuition; others, offer varied forms.
6. Do you have high school students presently enrolled for college credit courses?
   17, yes; 23, no.
7. Do you have a program for placing advanced high school students in college correspondence courses?
   8, yes; 32, no.
8. At what time of the year do you begin negotiations with faculty members to write new courses?
   1, October; 38, no specific period; 1, no answer.
9. How often are correspondence courses rewritten?
   9, one year to three years; 17, four to five years; others, more than five years or when textbooks go out of print.
10. Are special conferences or in-service training programs held for correspondence instructors?
    13, yes; 25, no; 2, no answer.
11. If you have special conferences, how often are they held?
    2, once a month or once a year; 7, irregularly; the rest, on an irregular basis.
12. Who determines the amount of honorarium payment made for writing a course?
    20, correspondence department decision; 14, university decision; the remainder, other types including joint department-university decision.
13. How much is the honorarium?
    No pattern of response; range from $5 a course to $475 per semester hour.
14. On what basis is the honorarium payment made?
    1, equivalent salary for teaching on campus; 14, what correspondence department thought was just; 14, variety of responses, "best possible amount," etc.; 11, no response.
15. How much do correspondence instructors receive for correcting lessons?
    No set pattern; range from 30 cents to $3 per lesson; some paid on semester-hour basis.
16. How is faculty promptness in returning corrected lessons encouraged?
    11, pay bonus for on-time lessons; others, make personal appeal for cooperation.
17. How much time are instructors given to correct lessons before follow-up is made?
    1, two days; 24, five to fourteen days; others, fifteen or more days.

18. What steps are taken with respect to consistently delinquent instructors?
    29, explain problem to academic department chairman and let him handle it; 6, dismiss him and employ someone else; 5, other means.
19. When an instructor is replaced, how does this affect the use of the old syllabus?
    36, no effect; others, effects changes or revisions.
20. Is the correspondence department financially self sustaining?
    29, yes; 10, receives some university appropriation; 1, no answer.
21. Do you anticipate an increase in the currently published tuition rate?
    13, yes; 26, no; 1, no answer.
22. Are bad checks received as tuition a problem?
    30, minor; 10, no problem.
23. Are catalogs distributed free to the student?
    38, yes; 2, no answer.
24. How much do you spend annually for promotion through certain media?
    30, less than $3,000; 5, $3,000 to $10,000; 5, no answer (some included cost of catalog, others did not).
25. What percentage of the annual budget is this promotion cost?
    21, less than 2%; 8, 2 to 5%; 3, more than 5%; 8, no response.
26. Check the advertising media used and percentage of the advertising budget it represents.
    14, direct mail (100%); 12, direct mail (1 to 95%); 5, newspaper media (50%); the remainder, other media, radio, magazines (less than 25%).
27. Do you have representatives in foreign countries registering students for correspondence courses?
    38, no; 1, yes; 1, no response.
28. Who prints or reproduces the course syllabi?
    24, own mimeograph department; 1, own multilith department; 10, university press; 5, miscellaneous.
29. Do you copyright all courses?
    5, yes; 35, no.
30. Do you carry a programmed-learning course?
    7, yes; 33, no.
31. Have you implemented IBM lesson correction?
    7, yes; 33, no.
32. Do you offer courses with teaching machines?
    40, no; 0, yes.
33. How often does your department conduct a complete self-evaluation study?
    4, every year; 4, every two years; 2, every five years; 4, held irregularly; 4, continuous process or once a month; 5, never conduct one; 17, no response.
34. What is your course completion rate?
    1, 25%; 9, 46 to 55%; 10, 56 to 65%; 15, 66 to 90%; 5, no response.
35. How many pages in an average correspondence-study lesson?
    25, one to several pages; 12, eight or more pages; 3, varied.
36. Does each lesson in the average course syllabus contain a statement of the lesson objective so labeled?
    22, has objective labeled; 13, not labeled; 2, no objective; 3, no response.
37. Is the average syllabus "discussion type" material?
    34, yes; 1, no; 4, depends on course or teachers; 1, no response.
38. Are there established requirements for lesson assignments (e.g., a lesson must have at least five questions, but not more than 10)?
    2, yes; 37, no; 1, no response.
39. If the answer above is "yes," what is the criterion?
    1, each assignment is equivalent of two class periods on campus; 1, must fill objectives of the assignment; 38, no response.
40. Are new would-be authors of course outlines given special instructions before beginning their work?
    39, yes; 1, no.

41. If "yes," what do these special instructions include?
    2, each is given a guide for authors; 34, a correspondence department staff member meets author personally; 1, course is written by competent writer from material supplied by the instructors; 3, no response.

Questionnaire conducted by
MACK PALMER, *chairman, Home Study Department, Brigham Young University, Provo, Utah.*

Chapter 7

Service Programs of Community Junior Colleges *

ERVIN L. HARLACHER

President, Brookdale Community College,
Lincroft, New Jersey

* This material has been extracted from the following:
Ervin L. Harlacher, *Effective Junior College Programs of Community Services: Rationale, Guidelines, Practices*, Junior College Leadership Program, Occasional Report no. 10, School of Education, University of California, Los Angeles, Calif., 1967.
Ervin L. Harlacher, *The Community Dimension of the Community College*, Report to the American Association of Community Colleges, November, 1967.

The community college is a junior college claiming community services as a major function or purpose. While the community college serves its community through its regular programs and activities, it also provides, in cooperation with other community groups and agencies, special programs of community services—i.e., educational, cultural, and recreational—which are provided the community above and beyond regularly scheduled day and evening classes. The community college emphasizes community programs for all age groups, including elementary and secondary school children, and for citizens from widely divergent social, economic, and educational backgrounds. Effective programs of community services are built upon a solid foundation of citizen participation, college-community interaction, and a thorough understanding of the community.

BASIC PROGRAM OF COMMUNITY SERVICES

Community-service programs generally fall into four categories.

1. Community Use of Facilities and Services Making college facilities and services available to the community, when such use does not interfere with regularly scheduled programs, helps fulfill an urgent community need for available space and services, guarantees fuller use of college facilities, and serves to acquaint area residents with the community college. Included in this category are the provision of physical facilities and services for meetings and events (social, recreational, cultural), food services, cosponsorship of community events and activities, community use of library facilities, and campus tours.

2. Community Educational Services Educational programs, which utilize the special skills of the college staff and outside experts, are geared to specific age and interest groups within the community district: children, parents, senior citizens, businessmen, professional men, and those in government services such as policemen, game wardens, public utilities workers, community planners, and so forth. Not all community college educational programs consist of formalized classroom instruction; many are conducted in off-campus locations such as business establishments, empty stores, hotels, and public schools. Campus radio and television facilities are utilized for both credit and noncredit courses. Many programs are geared to human-resources development—retraining programs, basic education programs, short-term occupational and basic skills programs for the disadvantaged, and increased-leisure programs for senior citizens. Faculty consulting services, community counseling, provision of a speakers' bureau, and student programs for the community—all are examples of educational services provided by community colleges.

3. Community Development It is in the area of community development that the community college has its best opportunity to integrate with the community. This can be accomplished through leadership and advisory assistance by college personnel; research and planning, studies, surveys, and polls; workshops, institutes, and conferences; and organization of community councils and other needed community agencies and groups. While the community college makes available its resources of knowledge and skills, decision making must be left to the citizens.

4. Cultural and Recreational Activities Included here are such events as lecture and fine-arts series, conferences, film series, concerts, recitals, cultural tours and field trips (art exhibits, historical-site visits, field trips to explore the sciences and arts), physical activities (skills classes, tournaments, track-and-field events, weight conditioning, special events, free-time activities), science services (planetariums, science museums, lectures, fairs), festivals, community performing groups (choral groups, orchestras, theater groups). Through these programs the community college can contribute greatly to the cultural development of the area and can help raise community standards of entertainment and recreation.

EFFECTIVE ADMINISTRATION AND SUPERVISION OF COMMUNITY COLLEGE PROGRAMS

Involving Community in Planning and Development Involving the community—groups, individuals, leaders—in the planning and development of the program of community services can be highly effective. Not only do community groups provide valuable suggestions for program development, but they can also be counted on to promote community interest and support. When planning short courses, for example, community involvement is imperative if the college proposes to meet the specific needs of requesting groups. Their help makes possible the tailoring of services to specific needs and interests.

Citizen advisory committees serve a unique function in planning and helping to promote programs. Such a committee might be made up of chamber-of-commerce members, school superintendents, radio and newspaper editors, businessmen, representatives of service groups, and members of bankers' and merchants' associations. The help of advisory committees is particularly useful in the cosponsorship of community events.

Holding social events in connection with certain cultural activities and organizing patrons' groups are also effective procedures for the maintenance of cooperative relationships between the college and various community groups.

Maintaining Effective Internal and External Communications One of the most pressing problems facing community colleges is how to keep all segments of the community aware of the services available. There is little purpose in having community-service programs unless the community is made aware of their existence. For this reason it is important to utilize every one of the available news media: newspapers, magazines, radio, television.

In view of the importance of conducting a well-planned and well-executed public-information service, it is advisable to employ a full-time information officer with the special skills and knowledge necessary to promote the community-service programs and to help interpret these programs to the community. His job will involve the development and maintenance of good relationships with the community press, the making of arrangements for direct coverage of events, and the issuing of special publications designed to appeal to specific audiences.

Providing adequate time in which to plan publicity campaigns is an important factor in making events successful. If publicity for a function is handled at the last minute, attendance may be disappointing. In this connection, time should be provided in which to follow up on initial publicity. Continuous coverage is more effective than a "one shot" campaign. When programs are geared to special audiences, publicity should be directed toward that special audience rather than toward the whole community. Direct-mail campaigns and the issuing of personal invitations to interested community leaders are recommended procedures, as are the use of portable displays which can be set up in shopping centers and public buildings and "quick change" signs for the campus.

Although the primary responsibility for publicity resides with the college, community groups can be counted on to promote community interest. A good community-service program opens up avenues of direct public contact, and many citizens will become ambassadors of community college programs.

Within the college, channels of communication between the community-services office and other college offices involved, such as the plant service department, should be clear-cut so that confusion and duplication of effort can be avoided.

Involving Faculty and Students in Planning and Development The services of students and faculty can be utilized effectively in planning campus tours, career days, business-education days, and musical events, for example. Many successful programs have been developed with the help of entire art, music, and science departments. Both students and faculty should be encouraged to take an active part in programs. Also, staff members who belong to community organizations should be encouraged to involve their organizations in the use of college resources—facilities, faculty, and students.

Coordinating Services with Other Community Groups In order to avoid unnecessary duplication of services, community colleges should recognize the need for cooperation with other community, regional, and even statewide agencies, i.e., public schools, four-year colleges and universities, recreation districts, state and governmental agencies, museums, art galleries, libraries, neighboring community colleges. For instance, a community recreational committee might make a survey of all recreational offerings in the community and then make recommendations for a community college program based upon actual need.

Encouraging College Staff to Participate in Community Affairs Many opportunities are available for college personnel to participate in community leadership and cultural affairs. When college personnel serve as consultants and provide leadership to community groups, they are perhaps most effective when serving as catalysts rather than when assuming aggressive roles. In order to do this, college personnel should provide leadership from a neutral ground.

Providing Effective Planning and Research So that programs and events do not grow indiscriminately, long-range planning is suggested. Timing is very important if programs are to be successful. Busy executives, for example, must be given adequate notice of programs planned for them so that they can arrange to clear their calendars. Checking with the college master calendar of events and consulting with community groups will help assure that programs geared to the same audiences do not conflict. Parking facilities, registration fees, ticket sales, and course content must be considered. Involving interested citizens in the planning of events and then later obtaining the evaluation of services from participants through research studies and polls will help greatly in assuring that offerings are well received and meet real needs in the community.

Establishing High Standards for Public Performance Obtain well-known people to conduct lecture series, top artists for fine-arts series, and qualified instructors for short courses and recreational programs. The community wishes to be entertained and/or informed but not bored to death. Making sure that speakers are well prepared, holding orientation sessions for performers, and previewing as many offerings as possible will help to maintain a high level of quality.

Defining Program Purposes and Objectives Before organizing and administering a program, its philosophy and objectives must be stated. Although it is difficult to determine the distribution of program emphasis for differing communities, it is probably unwise to stress any one facet. Generally, community college administrators seem to feel that too many college-type short courses should be avoided and that programs should be geared to widely differing audiences. Before establishing citizens' committees, their precise functions should be determined.

Identifying Community Needs and Interests Community needs and interests must first be identified if the community-services program is to reach every segment of the community. Community groups are very helpful in discovering these needs. Utilize community advisory councils in the planning and promotion of programs and encourage cosponsorship of services and activities. Community surveys are helpful in this regard. Also, the community should be encouraged to request specific services.

Providing Effective Administration and Supervision It is important to centralize leadership in a single administrator who has been relieved of all other duties so that he may devote his full time and energies to developing and administering community programs. This administrator should be free to spend time in off-campus fieldwork, working with community groups and spotting areas in which community programs are needed. He will help oversee the activities of community groups set up to represent every segment of the community, and he will coordinate his activities with those of the business office and financial office of the college. The centralization of administrative responsibility is necessary to avoid duplication of efforts and confusion of functions. When authority for a program is divided, some jobs may never get done, since each party thinks the other has taken care of them.

In addition to an administrator, the community-services department might include full-time assistants for community education, a public-information officer, qualified, enthusiastic staff coordinators with freedom and authority to develop their activities, and clerical assistants. A full-time auditorium manager, professional managers for the radio and television stations, and a recreational coordinator might also be members of the staff of the community-services department. All programs should be staffed with competent instructors, full-time and part-time.

Supervision of the use of college facilities is best performed by college staff members whenever facilities are used for either college-sponsored programs or cosponsored programs and events. Requiring staff members to be present at all functions taking place on the campus assures that the events run smoothly and that college rules are adhered to. This supervision need not be obtrusive. Citizen advisory committees should also be adequately supervised.

Establishing and Adhering to Written Policies, Regulations, and Procedures Many administrative problems can be avoided by establishing and adhering to written policies, regulations, and procedures regarding all community services and particularly for the use of all facilities. These policies should be reviewed periodically. Meeting with groups using the facilities to make sure that all rules and regulations are fully understood will help eliminate unnecessary misunderstandings and violational acts on the part of all parties. However, maintaining some flexibility in meeting community needs is advisable.

Utilizing Community Facilities and Resources In addition to encouraging the use of college facilities by community groups, the college resources can be taken to the community. Offering courses throughout the entire college district through the use of extension centers, portable and mobile units, churches, public schools, business establishments, and other community facilities helps acquaint many individuals, who might not come to the campus or be aware of the community college offerings, with the college and its services.

Securing Board, Administration, and Faculty Support In order to have wholly successful programs, it is necessary to orient board, administration, and faculty to the community-services program. Without this support, credit programs may take precedence in facilities and funds. One way to establish community-services programs as a major function of the college is to have the community programs director report directly to the president. Also, if faculty members are compensated for their part in the programs, they are more apt to be enthusiastic about participating. In this connection, it is important to establish and adhere to policies regarding the reimbursement of faculty members for their services.

Obtaining Essential Resources Where and how to obtain funds for community programs is a problem facing most community-services administrators. The solution lies in part in the financial structure of the district. To a large extent, the ability of the administrator to organize available resources will mean the success or failure of the programs.

Some community colleges have secured funds from federal programs for community development and human resources training. A few have benefited from Title I of the Higher Education Act of 1965. Very little state aid is available to community colleges. California permits a local district maintaining a community college to increase its maximum tax rate by 5 percent per $100 of assessed valuation for community-services purposes. This system, however, is unique to California.

Many programs are self-supporting. For this reason, it is important to develop effective means of selling tickets, and a college box office should be organized.

The importance of encouraging community groups to make use of the community college facilities cannot be overemphasized as a factor in helping to gain community support. Very often a bond or tax-increase election has been carried because persons on advisory committees have actively supported community college programs and and have helped sell them to the community.

CHECKLIST FOR PROGRAMS OF COMMUNITY COLLEGES

The effective administration and supervision of the program of community services involves:

I. Securing community college support

A. Involve community in planning and development

1. Utilize personnel of appropriate community groups in planning and promotion of program
2. Engage community advisory committees in planning of program
3. Obtain cosponsorship of services and activities by local groups
4. Actively involve a large number of community people and groups in program
5. Secure active participation and support of community leaders
6. Organize community advisory council as means of identifying community needs and interests
7. Develop and maintain cooperative, friendly relationships with community groups
8. Arrange for community cultural groups to affiliate with college

B. Maintain effective internal and external communication

1. Establish regular information service to keep citizens of college-district community informed on college matters
2. Provide adequate time to plan publicity campaigns
3. Use a wide variety of media to communicate with public and reach all segments of college-district community
4. Direct publicity and publications toward specific publics in community
5. Utilize extensive direct-mail publicity
6. Arrange for direct coverage of college events by area press
7. Develop and maintain personal relationship with area press
8. Prepare brochures regarding activities and services and distribute throughout community
9. Issue personal invitations to community leaders to attend events
10. Keep public fully informed of services available from college
11. Establish citizens' committees as an aid in presenting programs to community
12. Clarify channels of communications between community-services office and other college departments involved in providing services

C. Involve faculty and students in planning and development

1. Encourage active participation of faculty and students in program
2. Organize student-faculty planning committee
3. Provide opportunity for faculty to help plan program informally and through study and advisory committees

D. Coordinate services with other community groups

1. Coordinate program with other community and regional groups to avoid unnecessary duplication of services
2. Maintain close liaison with public school personnel of college district

3. Encourage communitywide coordination of cultural and recreational activities

E. Encourage college staff to participate in community affairs

1. Encourage college personnel to participate in community activities
2. Make college personnel available to community as consultants
3. Provide leadership in organizing needed community groups and solving community problems

F. Orient faculty and staff to community-service function

1. Interpret community-service function to college faculty and staff on continuous basis

II. Determining nature and scope of program

A. Provide effective planning and research

1. Ensure long-range planning of program
2. Plan carefully all details of each individual service or activity
3. Begin planning of individual services and activities at early date
4. Consider carefully timing of services or activities
5. Encourage staff experimentation and innovation in developing program
6. Invite community groups to utilize college facilities and resources
7. Preplan advisory committee meetings carefully
8. Obtain evaluation of services and activities from participants
9. Conduct appropriate research studies, including surveys and polls

B. Establish high standards for public performance

1. Select known, quality artists and lecturers
2. Determine and adhere to standards for public performance

C. Tailor services to specific needs and interests

1. Tailor program and individual services to meet needs and interests of specific groups in district community

D. Define program purposes and objectives

1. Determine objectives and philosophy of program and individual services
2. Emphasize educational aspects of program
3. Present diversified and balanced program
4. Define specific functions of citizens' advisory committees

E. Identify community needs and interests

1. Make community survey to determine specific needs and interests of district community
2. Base each decision to provide a service or activity on analysis of community needs and interests
3. Hold conferences and informal discussions with community people for purposes of determining community needs and interests
4. Encourage community at large to express its desires and needs for specific services

III. Organizing and administering program

A. Provide effective administration and supervision

1. Establish community-services division as major administrative area
2. Obtain full-time community-services administrator to provide leadership and assume overall responsibility for program
3. Provide adequate staff to organize and implement program
4. Select enthusiastic, well-qualified staff supervisors for program
5. Employ qualified public-information officer
6. Provide supervisors with sufficient time and authority to plan and coordinate activities
7. Assure staff supervisors of freedom and authority to develop their activities
8. Obtain adequate clerical assistance

9. Select membership of citizens' advisory committees carefully on basis of purposes of committee
10. Provide expert staff help for citizens' advisory groups
11. Provide overall coordination of events cosponsored by community groups

B. Establish and adhere to written policies, regulations, and procedures
1. Establish written policies, regulations, and procedures for all aspects of program
2. Apply policies and regulations uniformly
3. Review policies, regulations, and procedures periodically to see if they are still effective
4. Maintain flexibility in accommodating community needs
5. Require that all instructions and requirements for use of college facilities be in writing
6. Arrange meeting with representatives of groups using college facilities for detailed, joint planning
7. Require college supervisor to be present during time facility is being used by community group

C. Utilize community facilities and resources
1. Offer services and activities at off-campus locations
2. Utilize qualified consultants in developing program when need arises

D. Secure board, administration, and faculty support
1. Secure understanding and support of board of trustees for program
2. Elicit support and cooperation of administration and faculty
3. Obtain support of board, administration, and faculty for community service as a major function

E. Obtain essential resources
1. Secure essential financial support for program
2. Provide adequate facilities and equipment for program

SELECTED REFERENCES

Ashby, Sir Eric: "Higher Education in Tomorrow's World," *University of Michigan Sesquicentennial,* Apr. 26–29, 1967.
Commins, Saxe, and Robert N. Linscott (eds.): *The Social Philosophers,* Random House, Inc., New York, 1947, pp. 115–183.
Gould, Samuel B.: "Whose Goals for Higher Education," remarks prepared for delivery before 50th annual meeting, American Council on Education, Washington, D.C., Oct. 12, 1967.
Harlacher, Ervin L.: "What's Past is Prologue," chap. IV in *The Community Dimension of the Community College, Report to the American Association of Junior Colleges,* November, 1967.
Harlacher, Ervin L.: "California's Community Renaissance," *Junior College Journal,* vol. 34, May, 1960.
Hutchins, Robert M.: *The Conflict in Education,* Harper & Brothers, New York, 1953, p. 97.
Jones, Bertis L.: *The History of Community Development in American Universities With Particular Reference to Four Selected Institutions,* unpublished Ed.D. dissertation, University of California, Los Angeles, Calif., 1961, pp. 329–332.
Littlewood, Joan: "A Laboratory of Fun," *New Scientist,* vol. 22, pp. 432–433.
Moberly, Sir Walter: *The Crisis in the University,* S.C.M. Press, London, 1949, p. 63.
Mousolite, Peter S.: "The Edge of the Chair," remarks presented to National Conference on Vocational and Technical Education, Chicago, May 16, 1967.
Price, Cedric: "Potteries Thinkbelt," *New Society,* June 2, 1966.
Seay, Maurice F., and Ferris N. Crawford: *The Community School and Community Self-Improvement,* Clair L. Taylor, Superintendent of Public Instruction, Lansing, Mich., 1954, p. 144.
Thornton, James W., Jr.: *The Community Junior College,* John Wiley & Sons, Inc., New York, 1960, p. 66.

Chapter 8

Educational Assistance Programs

LOUIS VRETTOS

Dean of Instruction and Director of Suburban Campus,
Northeastern University, Boston, Massachusetts

INTRODUCTION

The growing number of educational assistance programs being established in parts of the United States is of great significance to institutions of higher learning which are conducting adult and continuing education programs.

Established by business and industry to reimburse employees for attending u graduate and graduate institutions, these programs have given a dynamic new i to adult education across the nation.

These programs are beneficial to both the company and the employee. The benefits by helping to develop employees who enhance their value and effectiveness, while the employee takes courses which may be useful in his present position or in the position for which he expects to qualify, or courses which are required for him to remain on his present job.

Motivation is thus extremely high in this age of intense company and personal competition, both on the part of the employer and the employee.

TYPES OF PROGRAMS

The type of program which is reimbursable varies from company to company. Courses in most cases must be approved prior to registration and they must be job related. They may be credit or noncredit, and their applicability to the job is usually evaluated on an individual basis by the training director or the immediate supervisor.

Some examples of typical programs and courses are as follows:

1. Unit courses selected to directly improve performance
2. Degree programs in which the employee's major field of study lies within the scope of the company's educational policy
3. Specific professional or technical career training for the benefit of the company
4. Courses or programs required by the company
5. General career-related programs devoted to employee self-improvement
6. Correspondence, extension, or home-study programs (usually approved on an individual basis and dependent upon the availability of programs at the local colleges)

The institution itself is also of major importance and subject to the following criteria:

1. It must be accredited
2. It must be approved by the company
3. It must be of "recognized standing"
4. It must be approved by the company's education committee

ELIGIBILITY

Assistance programs are generally available to all full-time employees of a company. In a few cases, participation is restricted to certain classes of employees, usually excluding clerical or production workers. Most companies require at least a 3-month period of employment prior to the beginning of a course, although eligibility may range from 12 months of service to immediate eligibility upon acceptance of employment.

Many companies have education committees for the purpose of approving institutions and employee applications. They are generally composed of a representative of top management, an official who has a function in development and training, and a representative of an operating department. In cases where companies do not have such committees, approval of educational institutions and employee applications may become the responsibility of the general manager, personnel director, training director, or immediate supervisor.

REIMBURSEMENT

Nearly all educational assistance programs require the submission of application forms prior to registration. Some firms have a definite policy which requires forms to be submitted 2 weeks prior to the opening of the course, while others state that employees must submit written requests for approval prior to enrollment.

Grade Requirements Grade requirements will also vary from company to company. Some reimburse employees with the provision that they complete the course with a

C average or better. Company policies sometimes detail requirements; i.e., a C shall be 2.0 where an A equals 4.0, or a 1.0 where an A equals 3.0. If percentage grades are given, a minimum of 75 percent must be achieved for the company to reimburse the employee. Many companies refuse future requests if an employee has a history of failure or low grades. Most indicate that the employee must receive a passing grade.

Amount of Reimbursement If an employee is pursuing a course at the specific request of the company, all charges for tuition, books, and applicable fees are paid by the company. The stipulation is often found here that the employee must satisfactorily complete the course for reimbursement. Some companies will reimburse employees for total cost of tuition, registration, laboratory, and other required fees and for textbooks as well.

Few, if any, companies will cover incidental and transportation expenses.

Most companies will reimburse for tuition and laboratory fees only, but with a maximum amount for each term. They also often stipulate a school-year maximum.

Employees receiving scholarships, grants, or other outside financial aid which does not fully cover tuition and fees will be reimbursed for the difference between the aid and the actual charges up to the maximum prescribed by company policy.

Method of Reimbursement The usual method of reimbursement requires the submission of evidence of successful course or program completion. A few companies advance sums for tuition, but employees must repay the company if they fail the course. Still another group of employers requires an agreement of obligated service by the employee upon completion of a course or program, and certain portions of the cost are absorbed by the company at stated intervals of service. The percentage of tuition reimbursement varies from company to company. Fifty and 75 percent are common increments in educational assistance programs. In some rare instances reimbursement is based upon grades; i.e., A equals 100 percent, B equals 75 percent, and C equals 50 percent.

SELECTION

Selection is generally based on the submission of an application for educational assistance. Because companies consider their programs to be business expenses, the only limiting factor is the actual budgeted amount. In most cases, budget requirements are regularly reviewed and suitable adjustments made; there have been very few recent significant exclusions from educational assistance benefits because of budget limitations.

Selection for advanced-study programs, usually at the graduate level and in certain special categories (i.e., state-of-the-art courses), frequently follows the same procedure as that described for undergraduate and special courses. Some companies do require an additional review by a special screening and selection committee.

RELEASED TIME

In almost all companies, employees must avail themselves of educational opportunities outside of working hours. In a few, however, released-time programs have been established to allow some employees to take courses during working hours. This has been done mainly to encourage career development among professional and technical employees. For example, one company grants a maximum of 156 hours per year as "paid academic time off" which must be spent attending degree-required (and committee-approved) university classes. Eligibility for these full-time programs is normally determined on an individual basis, and a normal maximum is one full academic year.

A recent survey of 24 companies, most of them dealing in technical and professional services, indicated that 18 of them did allow employees to take courses during working hours. Nine of these had provision for making up the time.

SPECIAL PROGRAMS

A few firms have special programs which are separate from educational assistance programs, whereby a few carefully selected employees are granted awards for full-time residence at various universities. These programs are generally on the doctoral level and virtually always culminate in the doctoral degree.

Another program has emerged recently which is of direct interest to many employers. This program recognizes the need for updating through state-of-the-art courses which are generally noncredit and often ungraded. Administration of these courses often rests with the college or university's center for or division of continuing education. A more complete discussion of the function of continuing education appears in Chapter 4 of this section.

Still another type of program is that of in-plant training. Courses offered here are generally noncredit and are geared specifically to the needs of the company. Participating organizations range from supermarkets to research and development groups. Normally, in-plant training can be divided into the general areas of management development and skill improvement. Problems connected with this type of program include the method of candidate selection, reluctance of an employee's immediate supervisor to release him, and the type of material to be presented.

A 1968 research report from the National Industrial Conference Board[1] cites still another special type of program now being company sponsored—the fellowship plan. Run strictly on the graduate level, companies provide fellowships for students to attend colleges or universities on a full-time basis to pursue the master's or doctoral degree.

Requirements in the majority of the 60 companies surveyed (10 of them Canadian) are as follows:

1. *Eligibility*—restricted to graduate students in particular departments of participating universities
2. *Universities and courses*—fellowships placed in particular departments of designated universities
3. *Duration of fellowships*—one year, with most companies permitting from one to four annual renewals
4. *Annual allowances for fellows*—a minimum of $1,500 to a maximum determined by tuition expenses, marital status, and company affiliation
5. *Grants for universities*—annual supplemental grants ranging from $250 to $4,200

No plan requires agreement to future employment as a fellowship condition. A fellow creating an invention must assign patent rights to the company only if he is an employee; otherwise the patent policy of the university applies.

APPLICATION

Application forms are fairly similar in information requested. They include name, date, job location, job title, name of institution, course name, course number, credit hours, tuition cost, additional fees, type of instruction, type of program, comments, and approval spaces. Several different application forms have been included as an appendix to this chapter.

[1] *Combating Knowledge Obsolescence, I. Company Fellowship Plans,* Studies in Personnel Policy, no. 209, National Industrial Conference Board, Inc., New York, 1968.

LIAISON

Communication between the educational institution and the company is extremely desirable, especially if the institution intends to react to the needs of business and industry. Direct communication includes the following:

1. Establishment of an industrial advisory committee
2. Selection of institution and company liaison officers
3. Cooperative planning and execution of an employee-needs survey
4. Establishment of a method for complete dissemination of institutional literature and information
5. Systematically scheduled meetings of liaison officers
6. Provisions for distribution of statements of company needs and suggestions to appropriate institution officials

The establishment of an industrial advisory committee or council is a first step in ensuring the free flow of information between company and institution. This group of key industrial and business representatives should meet with university personnel on a regular basis. Its membership could be composed of technical management, industrial relations personnel, and top-management officials. Experience with such an organization indicates the establishment of a mutual respect and receptivity between business and university. Equally important is the establishment and maintenance of individual contacts between the university and the various firms in its service area. Conferences held on a continuing basis serve to assure industry of the university's willingness to cooperate in solving problems and also assist the university in its planning and program development.

SUMMARY

Educational assistance policies vary considerably, but they do so along easily identifiable paths. Eligibility in most cases is accorded a permanent employee, depending on his job classification. Courses must generally be approved prior to registration, and they must be job-related. The courses may be credit or noncredit, and their applicability to the job is usually evaluated on an individual basis.

Procedures for obtaining educational assistance are fairly consistent, although the amount of time allowed and the amount of reimbursement vary. A few companies pay the employee in advance, others on receipt of bills; in still other cases, reimbursement takes the form of a partial refund and a partial loan which may be repaid through continuous service to the company.

The results of educational assistance programs should be evaluated periodically. The results of in-plant programs should be analyzed and the employee's performance studied. The same scrutiny should be applied to employee-subsidized educational activities outside the company. In any case, employee educational activities should be correlated with job performance.

There seems to be some lack of communication between the business organization and the educational institution. This can be improved considerably by cooperative efforts and liaison between the two areas. Industry and education must cooperate in helping the employee plan his development for the benefit of all three parties concerned.

APPENDIX

Figures 1 through 5 illustrate some of the application forms used in connection with educational assistance programs.

GM 1257 - 11-64
Printed in U.S.A.

GENERAL MOTORS CORPORATION
Enrollment and Refund Application
TUITION REFUND PLAN FOR SALARIED EMPLOYES

THIS APPLICATION IS FOR ONE SEMESTER ONLY AND MUST BE SUBMITTED PRIOR TO EACH ENROLLMENT

NAME ______ *(last)* ______ *(first)* ______ *(initial)* ______ *DATE* ______

DIVISION ______ *PLANT* ______ *DEPARTMENT* ______

POSITION OR JOB TITLE ______

I wish to take the following course(s) under the provisions of the General Motors Tuition Refund Plan beginning ______ *(date)* ______ *and ending* ______ *(date)* ______ *at* ______ *(name of institution)*

COURSE NAME	COURSE NO.	CREDIT HOURS	TUITION COST	COMPULSORY FEES

TYPE OF INSTITUTION (please check)

- ☐ *Graduate School*
- ☐ *Undergraduate School*
- ☐ *Secondary School*
- ☐ *Other* ______

TYPE OF PROGRAM

- ☐ *Special Course(s) - not leading to a degree*
- ☐ *Course(s) leading to a degree*

If a candidate for a degree, please complete:

Degree sought ______

No. of Credit Hours Completed ______

No. of Additional Credit Hours Required ______

State briefly how you believe the above course(s) may relate to your working skills and their enhancement ______

Are you eligible for any benefits resulting from service in the Armed Forces or any other scholarship aid?

______ *No* ______ *Yes, Amounting to* ______

______
APPLICANT

APPROVALS

______
Supervisor

______

______

______
Personnel Department

______

THIS SECTION TO BE FILLED IN AFTER COURSE IS COMPLETED

ATTACH EVIDENCE OF SATISFACTORY COMPLETION

REFUND AUTHORIZED ______ $ ______

______
Personnel Department Date

______
Date

______
Date

Fig. 1 *General Motors Corporation, enrollment and refund application.*

PAGE	FILE CODE
4 OF 4	36 1003 110
REVISES ISSUE DATED	EFFECTIVE DATE
Sept. 1, 1968	Apr. 18, 1969

GENERAL POLICIES AND PROCEDURES

EDUCATIONAL ASSISTANCE PROGRAM - NON-EXEMPT SALARIED EMPLOYEES

RAYTHEON

10-0225 (12/68)

APPLICATION FOR EDUCATIONAL ASSISTANCE

APPLICANT'S NAME (LAST) (FIRST) (INITIAL)	EMPLOYEE NO.	DEPT. NO.	EXT.	LOCATION	DIVISION

DATE HIRED	PAYROLL 1. EXEMPT 2. NON-EXEMPT	JOB TITLE

PREVIOUS EDUCATION

COLLEGE OR UNIVERSITY ATTENDED	MAJOR FIELD	MINOR FIELD	CERTIFICATE OR DEGREE		CREDIT HOURS COMPLETED
			TITLE (INITIALS)	YEAR RECEIVED	

COURSES APPLIED FOR

CATALOG TITLE OF COURSE	CATALOG NUMBER	COURSE LEVEL (X)		REASON FOR TAKING COURSE(X)			COURSE DATES		COSTS		
		UNDER GRADUATE	GRADUATE	REQUIRED FOR DEGREE-NON JOB RELATED	DIRECTLY JOB RELATED	INFUNCTIONAL AREA OF EMPLOYMENT	BEGINS (MO./YR.)	ENDS (MO./YR.)	TUITION	LAB	TOTAL
									$	$	$
									$	$	$
									$	$	$
									$	$	$

COLLEGE OR UNIVERSITY TO BE ATTENDED	SCHOOL OR DIVISION OF	TERM 1. QUARTER 2. SEMESTER	QUARTER OR SEMESTER COST	$

TYPE OF PROGRAM IN WHICH REGISTERED

1. UNIT COURSE 2. DEGREE	IF IN DEGREE PROGRAM, FURNISH THE FOLLOWING INFORMATION	DEGREE SOUGHT (INITIALS)	EXPECTED GRADUATION DATE	MAJOR FIELD

NOTE: AN EMPLOYEE IS INELIGIBLE FOR EDUCATIONAL ASSISTANCE WHILE HE IS ENTITLED TO OR RECEIVING SCHOLARSHIP AID OR VETERANS ASSISTANCE UNLESS SUCH AID OR ASSISTANCE IS LESS THAN THE TUITION AND LAB CHARGES FOR THE QUARTER OR SEMESTER. IN THIS CASE THE EMPLOYEE MAY APPLY FOR THE DIFFERENCE.

ARE YOU PRESENTLY RECEIVING OR ENTITLED TO RECEIVE ASSISTANCE UNDER SCHOLARSHIP, GRANT, OR FROM ANY PUBLIC LAWS COVERING VETERANS?

1. YES 2. NO	IF YES, FURNISH THE FOLLOWING INFORMATION	NAME OF SCHOLARSHIP/ GRANT/ PUBLIC LAW	SPONSORING AGENCY	MAXIMUM ALLOWANCE AVAILABLE FOR THIS QUARTER/ SEMESTER
				$

REMARKS:

APPLICANT'S SIGNATURE DATE

APPROVAL SIGNATURES

SUPERVISOR	DATE	LAB / OPERATION / PLANT INDUSTRIAL RELATIONS REPRESENTATIVE	DATE
DEPARTMENT MANAGER	DATE	DIVISION INDUSTRIAL RELATIONS REPRESENTATIVE	DATE

Fig. 2 *Raytheon, application for educational assistance program.*

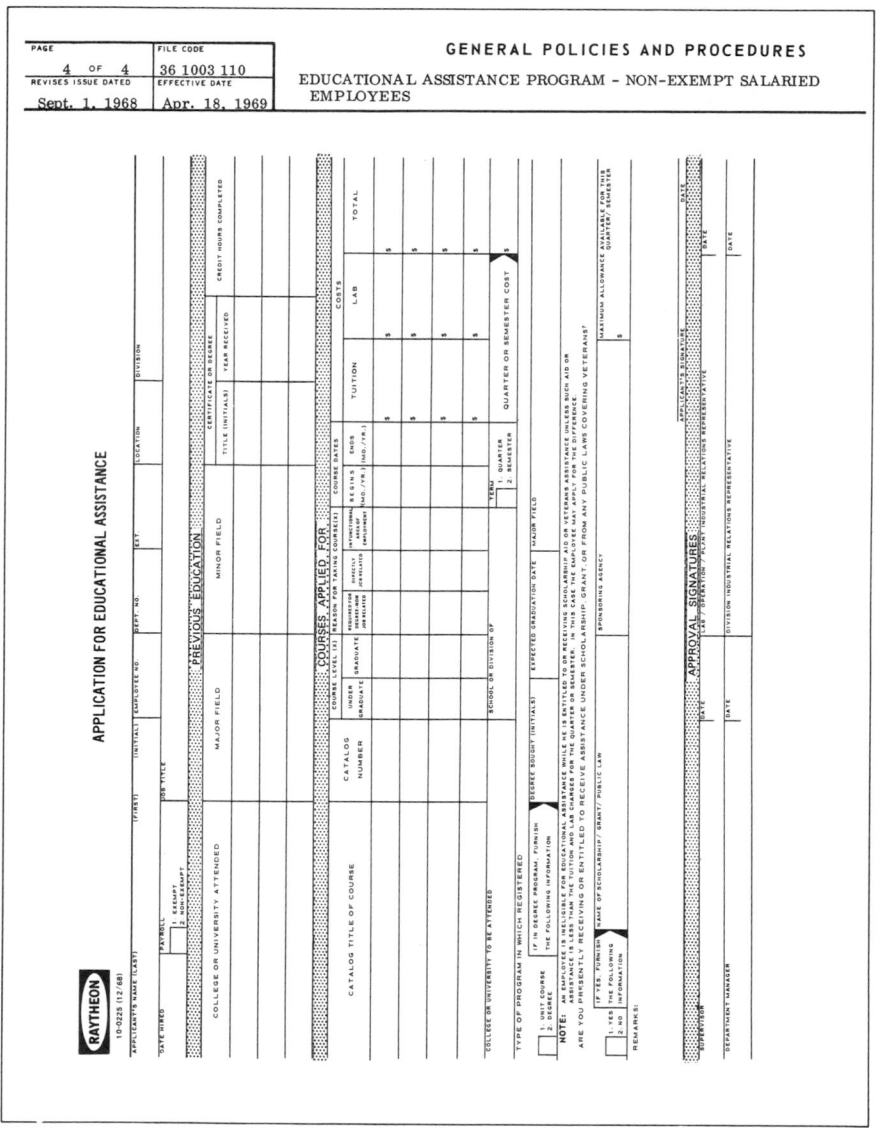

NEW ENGLAND DEACONESS HOSPITAL
BOSTON, MASSACHUSETTS

TUITION PAYMENT APPLICATION FOR FULL-TIME EMPLOYEES

PURPOSE

The New England Deaconess Hospital offers full tuition payment of credit courses within a degree curriculum to:

1. Help improve direct or indirect patient care
2. Assist employees in their professional growth
3. Encourage all employees to secure advanced education

ELIGIBILITY

Free tuition payments for degree courses are offered from the date of employment to all who plan to work full time at the New England Deaconess Hospital. As these courses are to be taken in off-duty hours, every effort will be made to arrange shift assignments around class schedules.

AMOUNT OF TUITION

Full tuition payment will be made for all approved courses with 6 credits constituting a normal course load.

REFUNDS

Each employee will be responsible for refunding tuition payments if:

1. A course is not completed
2. Change if full-time employment status occurs during the semester.

PROCEDURE

The steps below should be followed in applying for tuition payment:

1. Obtain an application from your department head or the Personnel Office and fill it out
2. Submit it to your department head at least 2 weeks before the time for registration
3. Pick up your voucher from the Personnel Office when notified for presentation at school
4. On satisfactory completion of course, submit evidence to Personnel Department

Fig. 3 *New England Deaconess Hospital, application for shared tuition payment.*

	COURSE NUMBER	TITLE OF COURSE	CREDIT HOURS	COURSE BEGINS/ENDS	TUITION FEE	NAME OF SCHOOL
1.	______	______	______	______	______	______
2.	______	______	______	______	______	______
3.	______	______	______	______	______	______

Reason for Application______________________________

Date__________________ Signature______________________________

Approval/Disapproval by Department Head______________________________

Date__________________ Signature______________________________

Approval/Disapproval of Administrative Officer_ ______________________

Date__________________ Signature______________________________

Voucher Issue Date_______ Signature of Applicant______________________

9/68

Fig. 3 *(Continued)*

HARVARD TRUST COMPANY

EDUCATIONAL INCENTIVE PROGRAM APPLICATION

(Please Print)

Date ____________________

TO: ____________________ Supervisor's Name ____________________ Title

FROM: ____________________ Employee's Name

I am planning to enroll in the course(s) indicated below and wish to request partial tuition reimbursement consideration under the Harvard Trust Company's Educational Incentive Program:

	Course 1	Course 2	Course 3
Name of Educational Institution			
Name of Course			
Duration of Course			
Credits			
Full Tuition Cost			

Approval Immediate Supervisor ____________________ Signature ____________________ Date

Approval Division Head ____________________ Signature ____________________ Date

I understand that to be eligible for such consideration I must have been a full-time employee of the Bank for at least 12 months and that the course(s) taken must be pertinent to and realistically related to my career in the Bank. I further understand that before receiving such reimbursement, I must certify that I am not receiving any scholarship, Veteran's Administration or other similar financial aid for the course(s) entailed and that I must complete the approved course(s) with a passing mark while still in the employ of the Bank. It is also agreed that should any reimbursement paid under the policy be judged "taxable income" that such reimbursement will be subject to payroll withholdings as required by law.

____________________ Signature

(The Division Head is requested to forward this form to the Personnel Department for coordination and record.)

Distribution: Original to Personnel Dept. through Supervisor
1-copy returned to employee through Supervisor

FORM CM 251

Fig. 4 *Harvard Trust Company, educational incentive program application.*

Shipley Company

Application for Educational Aid

Name of School____________________

Courses Start ____________

End____________

Approved, Subject to Receiving C Grade or Better ______ ______

Courses	Estimated Cost	Grades Received	Actual Cost
Other (Books, etc.)			
Total			Total

Amount of Aid Received Since Last July 1st $________

Remarks____________________

Applicant________ Date________

Amount Approved for Payment $________

Remarks____________________

Payment of $________

Approved by ________ ________

Fig. 5 *Shipley Company, application for educational aid.*

Section Six

Academic Personnel Administration

Chapter 1

Academic Organization

F. DON JAMES

President, Central Connecticut State College, New Britain, Connecticut

OFFICERS OF ACADEMIC ADMINISTRATION

That the excellence and strength of an institution directly corresponds to the combined excellence and strength of the officers of academic administration cannot be disputed. Strong though its faculty may be, powerful though its faculty voice may be, an institution cannot continue that strength nor build upon it without a strong academic administration. The formulation and implementation of policies and procedures as well as the implementation of policies and procedures set up by the faculty are the responsibilities of the administrator. As he fulfills his responsibilities well, the faculty find opened the channels for the fulfillment of their own responsibilities and opportunities. If he does not fulfill his functions properly nor with imagination, initiative, and enthusiasm, then his office becomes an impediment to the functioning of those under his jurisdiction and to the fulfillment of their own responsibilities and potential.

The academic administrator must maintain a sensitivity toward all areas that influence his administration. He certainly must have a keen understanding of and an empathy with the three major elements of an academic institution, namely faculty, students, and administration. He must also be very much aware of outside influences and their impact on his area of jurisdiction, this being especially true in the publicly assisted colleges and universities. He must be a jack-of-all-trades and above all must be able to work with and give leadership to all the persons under his jurisdiction.

The academic administrator is one who in most cases was educated and trained to serve as a faculty member and to carry the scholarly responsibilities of teaching and research. Thus, usually the academic administrator is one with full academic credentials as a faculty member. He is appointed by a superior academic officer and usually by the president to his position, often upon the advice and recommendation of a special advisory selection committee from the faculty. His appointment usually is not for a fixed term but is always subject to continuation by the president. Tenure in an administrative post is nonexistent, though an academic administrator may carry tenure as a faculty member.

To define the particular role and responsibilities of officers of academic administration, one must go to each institution of higher education; though there are, of course, similarities in roles from one institution to another. It is difficult to equate administrative officers of various institutions except in general terms. This is perhaps due to the individual nature of institutions, but it is also due to the nature of academic administration in which the man who fills the post usually plays a part in the determination of the responsibilities of that position within the general framework of the scope of the office. Thus the following definitions are in general only, with a great deal of flexibility and difference to be found in the definition of each office within each particular institution.

President

The president is the chief administrative officer of the institution which he serves. Thus he also serves as the chief academic administrator, though his responsibilities include all aspects of the life of the institution as well. The qualifications expected for this office are many, and one has only to look at several statements of qualifications circulated by presidential search committees to realize how diverse are the specific qualifications that they often include. The following are examples of such requirements:

1. Qualities of absolute integrity and the highest character.
2. An earned terminal degree with some training in college administration as well as teaching experience.
3. Administrative experience and demonstrated ability as an executive.
4. A pleasing and strong personality with demonstrated talent in the field of public and community relations.
5. Ability and experience as a public speaker.
6. Abilities of outstanding leadership and the ability to delegate authority with forcefulness and tact.
7. The kind of personality that inspires confidence and willingness on the part of others to work as members of a team.
8. The knowledge of when and how to call in expert assistance when needed to resolve any problem related to the welfare of the institution.
9. Considerable training in at least one of the disciplines or subject matter areas offered by the institution that might qualify the candidate for a professorship in the university.

10. The qualities of a firm, fair, and diplomatic disciplinarian. The candidate should have an understanding of the unique opportunities and functions of an urban university, an understanding which carries with it the recognition of the significant role that the president and the university must play in identifying with the needs of modern urbanized society.

11. The candidate should be forward looking and innovative in a practical fashion, and he should be willing to support and develop a strong college of arts and sciences.

12. The candidate should have some knowledge of finance and budgeting.

Above all, the president must be able to appreciate the purposes and strengths of his institution, to provide the leadership to give it new direction and motivation, and to alter its weaknesses.

Vice-president for Academic Affairs—Provost

The administrative officer responsible for all the academic affairs of an institution and who reports directly and only to the president is the vice-president for academic affairs and/or provost. He thus serves as the chief educational officer for the institution and has within his purview the entire educational concern including all academic programs and academic personnel. He also, in most institutions, serves as second in command to the president. Though the title varies, in general the terms "provost" and "vice-president for academic affairs" refer to the same office. An institution that has several vice-presidents will often use the title "vice-president for academic affairs" to distinguish this office from that of the vice-president for business affairs, vice-president for research, or other vice-presidents. The dual title of "vice-president for academic affairs and provost" is not uncommon. The title "provost" is often used where the organization does not include vice-presidential titles.

The vice-president for academic affairs and/or provost ordinarily has under his jurisdiction all the academic deans, the chief admissions officer, the registrar, the chief librarian, the chief research officer unless he is at the vice-presidential level, and all other academic officers. All faculty appointments and academic administrative appointments should be channelled to the vice-president for academic affairs and/or provost before going to the president. He approves all college and departmental budgets and academic expenditures.

The academic vice-president is the chief academic officer for handling the educational responsibility of the institution. He should encourage and promote new programs, improvement of existing programs, and educational change and innovation, and he should give leadership and guidance in all of the academic areas in the institution.

In institutions where student personnel administration and student activities do not fall under a vice-presidential position, they usually come within the purview of the academic vice-president.

Dean of Faculty

In an institution which is less complex in its organization, the chief academic administrative officer directly responsible to the president is the dean of faculty or dean of the college. This position then carries similar responsibilities to those described above for the vice-president for academic affairs and/or provost. Those reporting directly to the dean of faculty or dean of the college—besides the admissions officer, registrar, and chief librarian—would include the department chairman.

Dean of a College or School

As distinguished from the title used above in an independent college, the title "dean" used here refers to the chief academic administrator of a college or school which is a part of a larger institution such as a university.

The dean of a college is without question one of the key administrators in any academic institution. The president and the vice-president for academic affairs must rely heavily on the academic dean not only to handle all the administrative details of the college but to foster and nurture the growth in academic excellence of the college.

The scope of the responsibilities of the academic dean is extremely broad and indeed covers all the major concerns of the college and its faculty. His responsibilities include:

1. Faculty personnel recommendations, including recommendations of persons for initial appointments, for promotions, and recommendations concerning salary increments and compensations
2. Assignment of teaching loads, academic advisory responsibilities, and special assignments
3. Orientation of new faculty
4. Annual evaluation of faculty performance
5. Promotion of faculty professional activities
6. Presiding at and conducting faculty meetings
7. Approval of all part-time faculty appointments, including assignments and rate of compensation
8. General supervision over the academic advising of students within the college and the handling of student requests for exceptions to the academic standards and rules
9. Curricular and course planning, including the planning and promoting of improvements within the curricula of the college, the compilation of the descriptions of courses and programs, the preparation and approval of catalog statements on general and specific requirements, the maintenance of the standards of instruction, and the compilation of information for accreditation
10. Budgetary control and supervision of academic departments, including faculty and staff salaries, equipment and supplies for classes and laboratories, office supplies and equipment, travel, special faculty expense items, etc.
11. Space utilization of the academic plant occupied by his college, including the maintenance of records of floor plans for buildings, the inventories of equipment in laboratories and offices, the assignment of space to the departments in his college, the preparation and implementation of a master schedule for the use of facilities, and the development of plans for remodeling, redecorating, and the building of new facilities
12. Textbook adoptions, including the maintenance of an official list of texts for all courses in the college and the notification to the bookstore of the adoptions of texts and enrollment by courses
13. Committee appointments, including the recommendation of faculty committees necessary to handle and advise on the academic and administrative matters of the college, the recommendation of personnel for the established committees, and involvement in the appropriate committee meetings
14. Participation in professional activities and ceremonial functions, including representing the college in the appropriate professional organizations, attending the various functions and ceremonies within the college itself, and representing the college at special functions, both within and outside the institution
15. Institutional research, including the conducting of inquiries into academic affairs, the completion and reporting of statistics and class enrollment, and the promotion and conduct of research on academic matters
16. Approval of publications for faculty, including faculty handbooks on policies, procedures, and general information; handbook for students; literature promoting enrollments in particular programs and departments; announcements and brochures on the college; and the portion of the institutional catalog dealing with the college
17. Nonacademic personnel administration (if the institution does not have a separate personnel director) including the recommending of appointments, the approval of the classification of positions, the approval of salary schedules and payrolls, the assignment of the staff, the approval of policies on vacations, overtime, sick leave, etc., and the approval of part-time help

Even though this list of responsibilities of the academic dean may seem exhausting, it is not exhaustive. Thus, it is easy to see that the qualifications for a person to fill the position of academic dean include outstanding leadership ability and a willingness to work long and hard to accomplish objectives, good health, outgoing personal qualities, earnestness of purpose, and concern for the feelings and rights of others. Prerequisite even to these necessary qualifications is a record of academic achievement, usually including the attainment of a doctoral degree and indications of scholarly ability, if the dean is to carry the respect of the faculty over which he presides.

Dean or Director of Professional School

All the responsibilities and qualifications enumerated for the dean of a college or school apply equally to the position of dean or director of a professional school or college. A college of engineering, for example, has most of the same concerns as a college of arts and sciences or a general college, though usually in differing proportions. The dean of a professional college or school must also build up a working relationship and maintain a liaison with the profession akin to his college. A college of business administration, for example, can do a more effective educational job when it maintains a close liaison with business and industry. The dean can play an important role in interpreting the academic program of the professional college to the profession and in bringing the benefits and experience of the profession itself into the academic environment of his college.

Dean or Director of a Graduate School

Unlike the dean of a college or school or a professional college or school, the dean or director of a graduate school does not have a faculty assigned under his jurisdiction, nor does he have the responsibility for assigning teaching loads, for review of departmental budgets, for space utilization, etc. He should be involved in these matters in many instances through consultation with the deans of the colleges or schools, but he does not carry the same authority over such matters. His academic jurisdiction becomes far broader than that of the dean of the college or school, for his academic concerns embrace all academic departments of the institution that are involved in graduate work. Thus, his responsibility is more uniquely institution-wide than is that of the dean of a college or school.

Though in comparison with the dean of a school or college the graduate dean must rely more on persuasive power than on real authority in matters of faculty assignments, teaching loads, salary increments, tenure, promotions, etc., his position does command a great many responsibilities, including the following:

1. Curriculum and course planning for graduate programs, including preparation and approval of catalog statements on the general and specific requirements of graduate programs
2. Presiding at and conducting graduate faculty meetings
3. The promotion of the professional activities of faculty, especially in the area of research
4. Consultant to undergraduate deans concerning recommendations for appointments, promotions, and salary increments for faculty involved in graduate teaching
5. Consultant to undergraduate deans in matters of evaluation of the performance of faculty involved in graduate teaching
6. The maintenance of standards of graduate instruction by the faculty and graduate achievement by the students
7. Committee appointments, including the recommending of faculty committees needed to handle the matters pertaining to the graduate school, the recommendation of personnel for the committees, and the involvement in apppropriate committee meetings

8. Participation in professional activities and representation of the graduate division of the institution in the appropriate organizations
9. Institutional research into the academic capabilities of departments for graduate instruction and graduate programs
10. Liaison with all areas of the undergraduate programs of the institution and involvement in their relationship with the graduate division

Certainly, the qualifications for the person to fill the position of graduate dean are no less than those for any other academic dean. If anything, an additional quality of having interests and capabilities as broad as the entire institution itself is required.

Dean or Director of Extension Division or Evening College

The dean or director of the extension division or evening college has responsibilities and problems unique to his area of jurisdiction that certainly differ from those of the dean of a college, professional school, or graduate school. He must be both a leader and innovator of programs and course offerings to the students of his division and he must also be responsive to their wishes with regard to programs and courses.

His responsibilities and concerns include:

1. Staffing of all course offerings. Such staff almost always consists of part-time faculty with fixed rates of compensation for the number of hours taught.
2. Planning of courses and special programs to meet the requests and needs of the constituency of his division.
3. Budget preparation and supervison. Unlike the dean of the college, professional school, or graduate division, the dean of the extension division or evening college must base his budget on both income from fees for courses taken and on expenditures. Many institutions follow the general policy that the evening division must be self-supporting or must operate with a fixed subsidy from the parent institution.
4. Maintenance of liaison with all academic departments of the institution offering courses in the extension division.
5. Supervision of student registration for extension division and courses.
6. Encouraging the development of both credit and noncredit offerings as a part of continuing education for adults.

With the growing expansion of knowledge and with the rapidly changing technology of our society, the dean of an extension division or evening college has a particular opportunity in providing the kinds of programs and offerings that will enable adults to keep pace with these changes in their own professional involvement. Certainly the dean of the extension division needs to be extremely sensitive to the kinds of programs and offerings that both meet this need of the public at large and yet fall within the purview and scope of the parent institution.

Dean or Director of Summer Session

In many institutions where a summer session separate from the regular academic year program is conducted, the position of dean or director of summer session has been established. This position entails the full administrative responsibility of handling the preparation and planning and actual operation of the summer session programs. The dean or director of summer session has responsibilities not unlike those of the dean or director of an evening college or division of university extension. He normally employs faculty, on a part-time basis only, to teach one or two courses during the summer session. These faculty are drawn both from the institution itself and from outside the institution. He must operate the budget of the summer session and, like the evening college dean or director, be concerned both with income from students attending the summer session classes and with expenditures. Many institutions place the summer session on a self-operating basis with no funds coming from the general budget of the institution.

The dean of the summer session must work closely with all the academic departments on campus in setting up the offering of the particular courses and handling the staffing of these courses. He must be an administrator who can use a great deal of initiative and imagination in providing opportunities in the summer session both for the student who wants to accelerate his regular academic program by going to school the year round and also for the student who comes back in the summer for refresher or self-improvement courses. He must be sensitive to all the needs of the so-called "typical" college student as well as the needs of adults from all walks of life. He must be concerned not just with the academic program but also with the physical arrangements of housing, meal service, special programs, etc. With the current general trend toward greatly expanded summer-session enrollments and increasingly complex course and program offerings, the position of dean or director of summer session has already become in many institutions ar. extremely important academic administrative post.

Dean or Director of Divisions, Bureaus, Centers, Special Programs

As institutions of higher education have expanded in their involvements and in programs apart from the traditional disciplines, many have found it necessary to establish administrative posts over these special areas in order to make them fully operative and effective. This is especially true in the public-assisted colleges and universities which have an obligation and responsibility to provide special kinds of services and programs to meet special needs. Examples are numerous and would include such areas as a bureau of government research, division of allied health sciences, center for international and area studies, special programs for the disadvantaged, etc. Such special areas under a dean or director should operate under their own budgetary provisions as a part of the total budget of the institution, and thus the responsibilities of the dean or director involve both program and budget considerations. Perhaps some of the primary qualifications for many such administrative posts would be initiative and imagination, since often these are new and nontraditional programs.

Vice-president, Dean, Director, or Coordinator of Research

Those institutions with large or expanding research programs and with heavy commitments in graduate programs have definite need of an administrator who is responsible for the research interests of the entire institution. According to the size and complexity of the institution and its own organizational framework, this position may be known as "coordinator," "director," "dean," or even "vice-president" of research. This administrative officer, like the graduate dean, does not have his own faculty with which to deal, but he must have the broad interests of the entire institution within his concern. His is a leadership role in planning and supervising the research commitments of the institution and in encouraging and supporting the research interests of the individual faculty members. He may be in the position of an assistant to the graduate dean, an academic administrator on the level of authority with an academic dean, or he may rank as high as the vice-presidential level.

His responsibilities are many and diverse according to the particular institution, but they can include the following:

1. Overall administrative responsibility for all the research involvements of the institution
2. Involvement in the general budget of the institution as far as the financial commitments to research are concerned
3. Encouraging, promoting, and supporting the research interests of the individual faculty members
4. Administration of outside research monies including federal, state, and private funds that come into the institution
5. Administration of all research proposals, grant applications, and requests

ORGANIZATION FOR ACADEMIC ADMINISTRATION

Development of Organization Plan

As institutions change in nature and scope and as they grow in size and complexity, it is imperative that an organizational plan be developed and be subjected to continual scrutiny and modification. In a very small, single-purpose institution, the president can serve in many functions and have every major segment of the institution reporting directly to him. As size and complexity enter into the picture, neither the president nor his administrative officers can function properly unless areas of responsibility and lines of authority are clearly spelled out for all persons within the institution. The larger colleges and the multipurpose institutions certainly cannot operate without confusion, misunderstanding, and lack of direction unless the organizational structure is well planned and clearly delineated.

The following steps are necessary in the development of an organization plan:

1. Define the major academic areas of the institution and the personnel serving in each area. These areas would normally be the departments.

2. Determine the groupings of several areas and the officers needed to administer this segment of the institution. These groupings would normally become divisions, colleges, or schools of the institution.

3. Determine the higher administrative offices that are necessary to give effective leadership to the institution and to effect coordination and coherence among the several segments.

Most institutions of any size have already followed such procedures in the development of their organization plans. However, a review of such procedures in modification of organizational structure is important. The development and modification of an organizational plan, with the above three factors as the basic premises on which to work, should facilitate an organizational structure for an institution that spreads the responsibility and authority in manageable proportions that can be handled by the administrative officers and that clearly defines the lines of authority and relationships within the institution.

Periodic modification of the organizational structure of institutions is of great importance, with the span of time between such organizational changes being determined by the rate of growth and modification of the scope and purpose of the institution. Examples of such modifications are the splitting of departments as they grow larger and more complex; the splitting of divisions, colleges, or schools as they grow larger and more complex; the addition of new departments or colleges as the institution moves into new areas, the changing of divisions into colleges as the organizational structure moves from a college to a university organization, and the regrouping of existing colleges and departments into more comprehensive units, such as "umbrella" divisions.

Organization and Size of Institution

It is necessary for even a so-called "single-purpose" institution to modify its organizational structure as it grows in size. It is mandatory for a multipurpose institution to make such modifications as it grows, if for no other reason than to have the institution divided into manageable units. As a group, the public institutions perhaps offer the best example of such organizational change because of their very rapid growth over the past decade. A typical example would be a small liberal arts college that, as it grows in size, must add one or more assistant deans of a college, must begin to modify its departmental structure, must then establish several divisions headed by deans or directors, and must change the position of the dean of the college to the dean of the faculty or academic vice-president, and so on. It is said that faculties and boards of trustees often feel that the administrative structure of an institution, as it grows in size, becomes much too large in numbers and much too complex in nature, while the administrators of that same institution know that they are too few to handle all the administrative affairs and matters that need attention. Certainly with the kinds of services and opportunities provided by institutions of higher education in this nation, the growth in size of an institution must be accompanied by the growth and modification of the administrative structure.

Organization and Scope of Operation

Recognizing that the size of an institution affects its organizational structure, it can be said even more emphatically that the scope of operation of an institution directly affects the structure of its organization. When an institution moves from a single-purpose to a multipurpose institution it, obviously, must change its organizational structure to accommodate this change in its scope of operation. Less obviously, but equally important, a structural change must take place in the organization of a multipurpose institution as it modifies and expands its scope of operation. A typical example of the former is the teachers' college which modifies its scope and purpose by establishing a liberal arts program as distinguished from its teacher education program and perhaps expands on into professional programs as well. A typical example of the latter is the multipurpose institution with several colleges and professional schools that creates a larger "umbrella," perhaps a division or school, to join together administratively all the segments of the institution pertaining to one major area, such as allied health professions, marine sciences, environmental sciences, and so on.

Geographical expansion of an institution also requires modification of the organizational structure. When a single-campus institution expands into a multicampus institution, the organizational structure must be modified not only to handle the additional administrative responsibilities but also to keep clearly defined the relationships between the campuses and the lines of authority to the top administrative officers. Extension divisions, adult education centers, evening colleges, and the like require additional modifications to the organizational structure as they come into being and grow. Perhaps the prime examples of multicampus and multipurpose institutions which have experienced modifications of organizational structure are the University of California and the State University of New York.

Organization Charts of Academic Administration

Figures 1 to 3 are sample charts of academic administration for three types of institutions. While these charts are typical, modifications of all kinds could be found in the organizational charts of academic institutions in our nation.

Organization and Control of Academic Service Department

A discussion of the organization of academic administration could not possibly be complete without concern for the organization and control of all the supporting areas of an educational institution. Perhaps some of the most frequent and irritating problems on a college or university campus exist because of a lack of understanding or a failure to appreciate the relationships of the supporting areas to the academic areas and a failure to recognize the lines and channels of authority. The example of the faculty member who acts as if he were the immediate superior of a staff member in the janitorial or maintenance department is not unusual, and the problems resulting from such misunderstandings are all too commonplace on most campuses. It is important that lines of authority within the several areas of an educational institution, including academic and business administration, student personnel and services, public relations, community service, etc., be carefully delineated and observed. Crossing of areas of authority should not take place except under prescribed procedures that should be

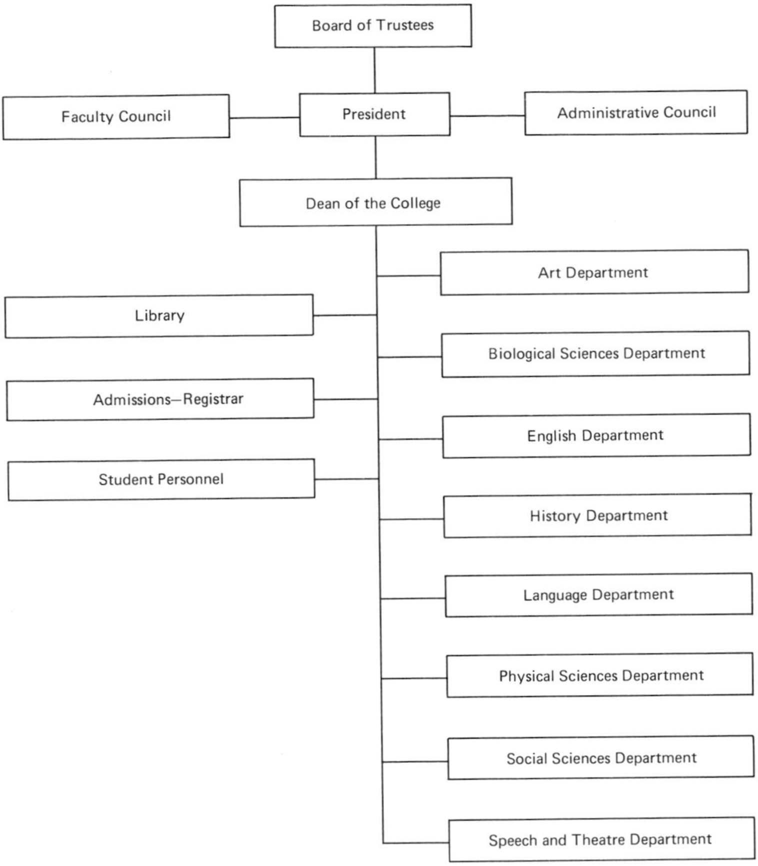

Fig. 1 *Small, single-purpose college.*

established for routing requests, suggestions, and complaints from one area to another. For example, it is important that requests for remodeling or repairing from a faculty member be routed through his department chairman and dean and not directly from him to the buildings and grounds department. To keep a person within one of the supporting departments or areas of an institution from serving a multitude of "bosses," these organizational relationships must be clearly defined and followed.

One of the complexities of an organizational chart for an institution is the definition of lines of authority for those areas that are most closely related to but do not fall within the teaching and academic functions of the institution. Such areas are the departments or offices of audiovisual aids, radio and television, international student advisers, placement, etc. According to the complexity of the institution and the traditional relationships between such nonacademic but closely related offices, these are placed within the organizational structure. For example, the audiovisual services of an institution might fall under the academic vice-president or the vice-president for public relations and development. The placement officer might report directly to the academic vice-president or to the head administrative officer for student affairs. Numerous other examples could be mentioned.

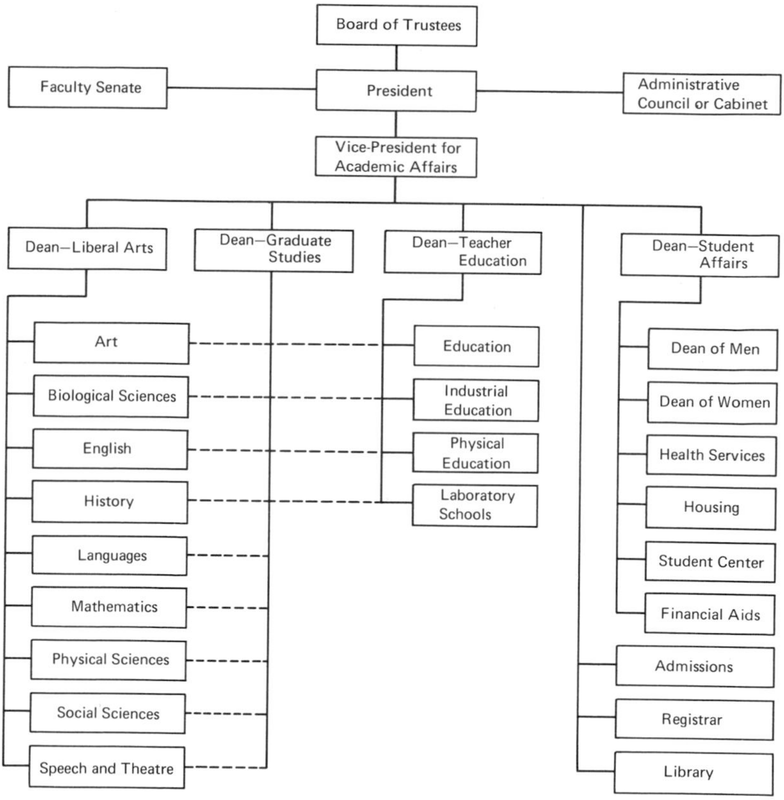

Fig. 2 *Multipurpose college.*

Lines of divided authority or dual reporting are sometimes built into organizational structures. This arrangement is exemplified, for instance, by a chief of security who reports both to the chief student affairs official and to the chief business affairs official. Such dual reporting, however, can present very serious problems in administrative organization and can be effective only when close agreement can be easily achieved between the two officers holding such divided responsibility.

Institutional Organization Charts

Some examples of institutional organization charts depicting the relationships between the service and academic areas of an institution appear as Figures 4 to 6. These charts are simplified examples which, in practice, would obviously carry institutional deviations and modifications.

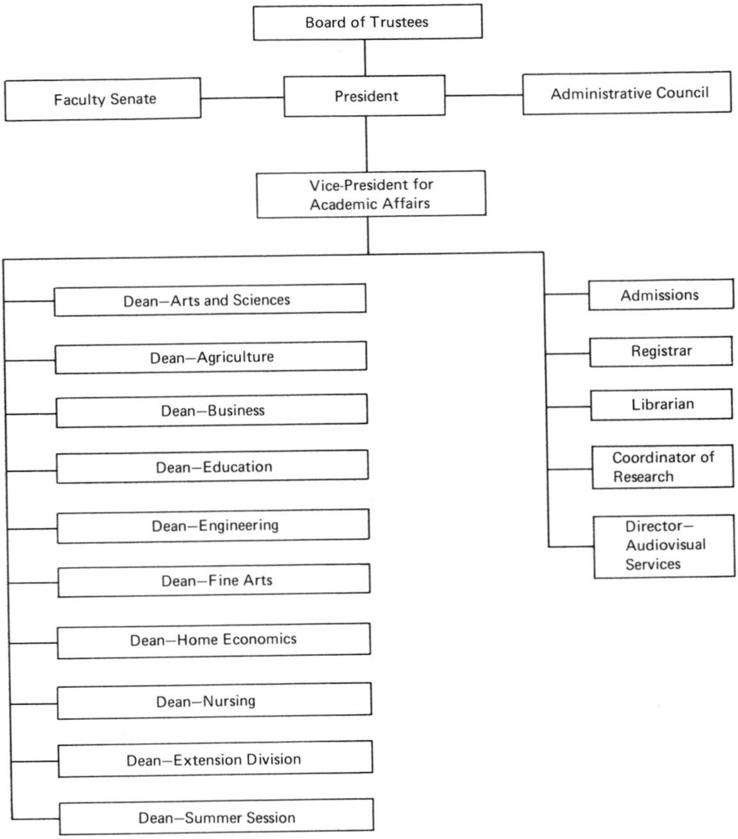

Fig. 3 *University.*

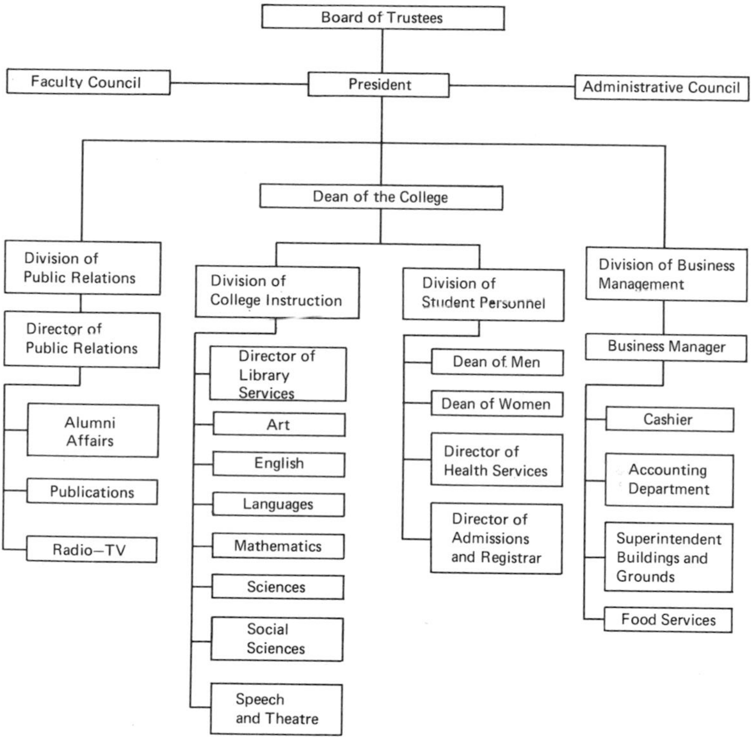

Fig. 4 *Small, single-purpose college.*

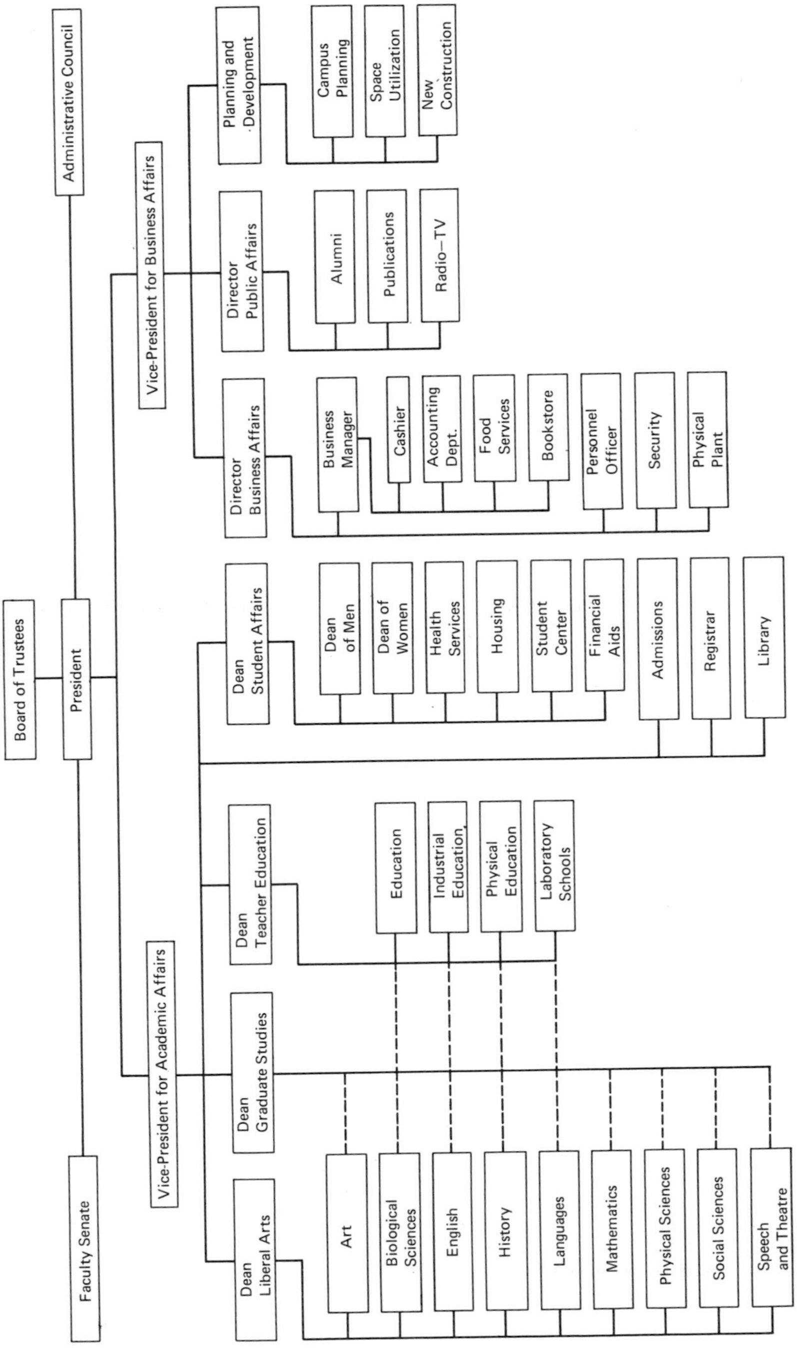

Fig. 5 *Multipurpose college.*

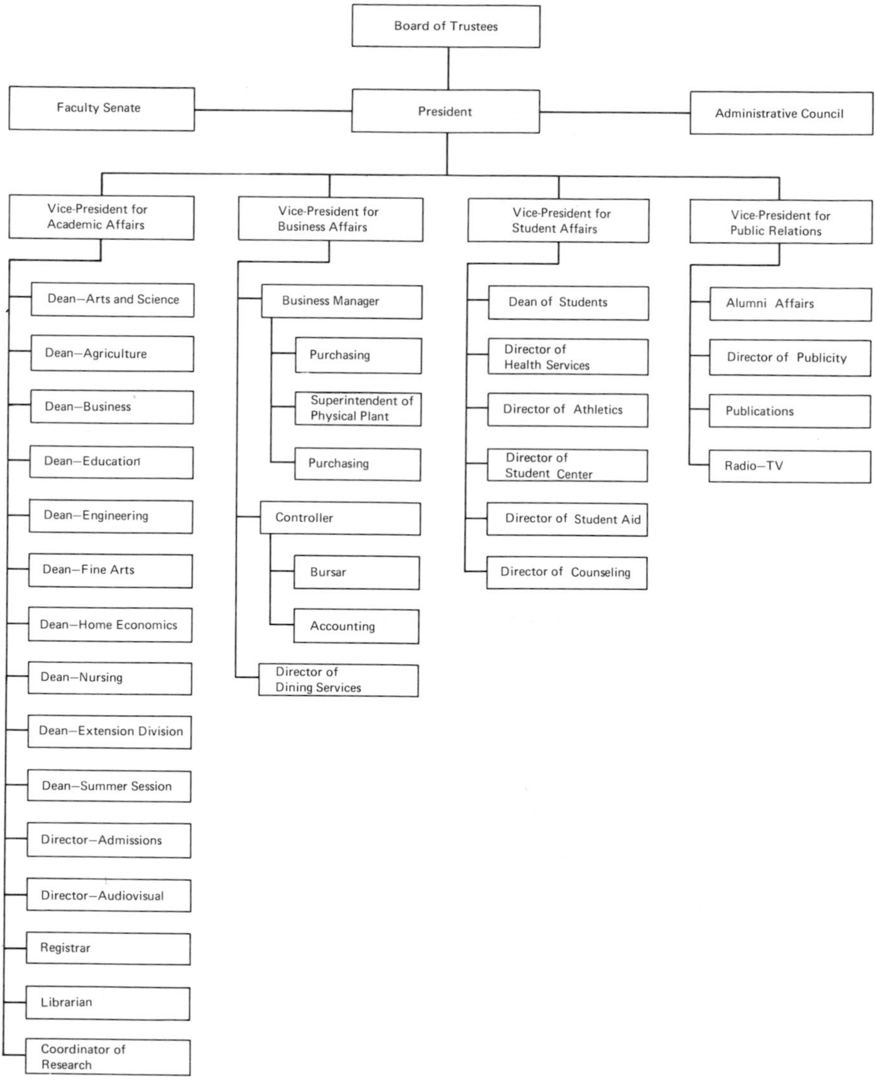

Fig. 6 *University.*

Chapter **2**

Faculty Organization and Administration

F. DON JAMES

President, Central Connecticut State College, New Britain, Connecticut

ORGANIZATION OF GENERAL FACULTY

The ultimate authority of the faculty of any educational institution, even when relegated in part to a representative group such as a senate, council, or to various committees, rests with the general faculty. Though the membership varies according to the constitution and bylaws, in most institutions all full-time faculty members carrying academic rank have voting privileges in the general faculty. With the increasing number of large and complex institutions, there is also an increasing number of institutions where many of the responsibilities of the general faculty are relegated to a representative body in order to expedite the handling of the business matters that require faculty action and approval. Smaller institutions, however, may still carry on their faculty business through general faculty meetings in a most effective manner with no delegation of authority and responsibility to representative groups.

Constitution, Bylaws, Regulations

It is of great importance to the stability of the organization to have spelled out clearly and in some detail the organizational structure and authority of the general faculty. Usually this is accomplished through a constitution and/or bylaws or a set of regulations for the faculty. The essential elements in such a document include sections on (1) membership, (2) officers, (3) meetings, (4) quorum, (5) legislative authority, (6) committees, (7) regulations, and (8) a policy statement on academic freedom and responsibility of faculty. Many other areas are included in such documents in various institutions.

It is the practice of most institutions to have the document containing the constitution, bylaws, and regulations revised and printed annually and distributed to all faculty members. Such a document—usually bearing a title such as *The Handbook, The Blue Book, The Gray Book,* etc.—becomes the "bible" for the institution's faculty.

Officers of the General Faculty

In general, whether elected, appointed, or in office by virtue of position, the officers of the general faculty include:

Chairman The presiding officer of the general faculty is in most institutions the president. He or his designate thus serves as the chairman. Some institutions have an elected chairman for the general faculty with the president of the institution serving in an ex-officio capacity.

Vice-chairman This officer, whose main responsibility is to chair faculty meetings in the absence of the chairman, may be an appointee of the president or an elected member of the faculty. According to the structure of the institution itself, the vice-chairman may be responsible for the committees of the general faculty or the handling of other matters under the jurisdiction of the faculty.

Secretary The office of the secretary of the faculty varies in institutions over the wide range from the responsibility and authority of a clerk who merely serves as the recording officer to a person of great influence and authority within the institution, from involvement merely with the recording and distributing of minutes of faculty meetings to a multiplicity of functions and responsibilities, and from an office filled by an elected faculty member to one that is an academic administrative appointment of high responsibility and authority.

Accordingly, the functions of the secretary of the faculty can include any or all of the following:

1. To keep minutes of faculty meetings
2. To keep records and minutes of special divisions of the faculty
3. To keep records and minutes of faculty committees
4. To prepare faculty handbooks
5. To serve as inventory officer of the institution by maintaining plans of classrooms and laboratories, showing equipment, size of rooms, capacities, chairs. etc.
6. To serve as institutional space officer with control of assignment of offices to faculty and other space to departments
7. To maintain faculty folders and files
8. To maintain master index of faculty addresses and general information
9. To maintain master student index for institution
10. To complete questionnaires on academic matters
11. To maintain and review catalog of materials relative to courses and programs
12. To assist faculty in publishing manuals, notes, papers, etc.
13. To arrange for special meetings of faculty and faculty groups
14. To control employment and assignment of faculty secretarial assistance
15. To control student assistance for faculty

The above list of responsibilities is far from inclusive for some institutions, while for many other institutions it includes responsibilities delegated to other faculty or administrative officers within the institution. Perhaps it can be summarized by indicating that the office of the secretary of the faculty, or whatever he may be called, is as diverse in responsibilities as that of any officer of an institution.

Other Officers Other officers of the general faculty may include a parliamentarian, a marshal, etc.

Executive Committee

In an institution that has not yet moved to the representative system, such as a faculty senate or council for handling the matters of business pertaining to the general faculty, an executive committee which often carries a title such as "educational policy committee," "policy and planning committee" etc., serves as the "working" committee of the general faculty. This committee usually carries only recommending authority with final action and authority resting with the general faculty. Such a committee is charged with responsibility for curriculum, educational policy, rules and regulations for both faculty and students, and in general with all matters that rest within the jurisdiction of the general faculty.

Committees

It has been said half facetiously and half seriously that many institutions have more committees than faculty members, and that faculty members often need to find released time from their committee assignments in order to teach. Though such hyperboles perhaps have more truth in them than might be admitted, it is a fact that much of the deliberation and decision making in an institution must rest within the established committees.

Faculty Organization and Committees The committee structure of an institution is derived from the organization of the faculty itself. Accordingly, there may be general faculty committees, college faculty committees, faculty senate committees, committees of the executive committee of the faculty, committees representing several faculties, committees of special faculty groups, etc. In general, there are committees of all major legislative and authoritative faculty groups within an institution.

Because of the importance of the committee structure in fulfilling the authority and the functions of the faculty, many faculties have established definite regulations governing committee appointments, committee structure, committee jurisdiction, and the general role of committees within the faculty organization. Such regulations are often quite explicit, especially regarding the selection and the makeup of the membership of committees.

Creation of Committees Committees are created either by election, by appointment, or by joint election and appointment by administration and faculty. In general, the committee structure of any institution would include those created by all three methods. Appointed committees stem usually from the president or other academic administrators or from the chairman of the general faculty or faculty senate. Elected committees stem from election by members of the faculty. Many committees are created by both appointment and election, with a fixed ratio between appointed and elected members. The organization of committees follows the same variance, with the chairman or other officers of any committee being chosen either by election or appointment. The origin of the committee almost always determines the agency or person to whom the committee is responsible. Presidentially appointed committees are responsible directly to the president. Committees appointed or elected by the faculty usually are responsible to the chairman of the faculty or to the faculty as a whole. Some committees in some institutions may have joint responsibility, namely, to the faculty and to the president, who represents the administration.

The selection of faculty to serve on committees may have restrictions of rank or tenure, though most committees have no such requirements. Special committees, however, such as an advisory committee on promotions, would carry particular requirements. For example, a committee on promotions probably would consist of only those faculty members who had already attained the rank of full professor.

Committee Types Committees are of several types, namely standing, special, and ad hoc. Standing committees are those which carry ongoing responsibilities and are thus somewhat permanently established committees. Membership may be either elected or appointed and may be for a fixed or indefinite period of time. Rotation of membership on standing committees is important to ensure that the committees' work will maintain vitality and freshness. Special committees are those appointed or elected for special purposes or problems. Special committees terminate at the conclusion of their assigned tasks and the adoption or rejection of their reports. Ad hoc committees are by definition special committees. Membership of special and ad hoc committees endures with the life of the committee itself. Additions or deletions from such committees are not uncommon, but the work of a special or ad hoc committee is best carried on with a continuity of original membership.

Functions of Faculty Committees The functions of committees vary with the specific purposes of the committees. These functions may include handling faculty business, advising the administration, gathering data and making studies, screening matters for consideration by the faculty or administration, formulating policies relative to academic and/or administrative matters, handling grievances, and handling the multitude of various and specific responsibilities within an institution.

Committee Assignments and Teaching Loads It can safely be said that most committee assignments are added to the regular teaching and research responsibilities of faculty members. It is certainly the wise administration, therefore, that watches closely and controls carefully the committee assignments of faculty members. A complete and up-to-date listing of all committee assignments is essential to spread committee responsibilities throughout the faculty and ensure some balance of responsibilities and work loads. Faculty members who carry committee assignments, especially as chairmen of committees, that demand a great deal of time and responsibility are sometimes compensated with a reduced teaching load for the duration of their service on such committees. Another means of compensation for unusually heavy committee responsibilities includes special compensation during the summer months. Certainly, all committee responsibilities of a given faculty member should be carefully weighed, along with his teaching and research capabilities and his productivity, when decisions on salary increments, promotion, and tenure are made.

Student Representation on Committees It is important in educational institutions that the student voice be heard and an opportunity be provided for the expression of student opinions and concepts. One of the excellent means of accomplishing this is to include student representation on particular committees within an institution. Some committees, by virtue of their particular responsibility and charge, should exlude student representation. On the other hand, many committees within the college or university could well profit by involving students in their deliberations. For some time, disciplinary committees, student publications committees, and others have involved student representation. More recently, curricular committees, academic policy committees, and others that previously were considered the concern only of the faculty and administration have begun to involve student participation. It is the experience of many institutions that such student involvement has been of great benefit to the institution. The alert, imaginative, and serious student can bring a perspective to faculty and administrative deliberations that is both important and helpful.

Organization of Committees Once the membership of a committee has been constituted and a chairman and other necessary officers have been chosen, the committee, to be productive, must establish its own organization, whether simple or complex. Frequency of meetings and meeting times must be set. The charge to the committee must be fully understood by all members and the authority to fulfill that charge must be clearly outlined. The means to fulfill that charge must be explored, including possible requirements of a budget and secretarial assistance.

Departmental Committees Though smaller departments usually operate as a committee of the whole, as institutions continue to grow and departments become larger, departmental committees become increasingly important. The larger department often finds it important and necessary to have committees on curricular matters, the advising of graduate students, group handling of basic survey courses, space and equipment inventories and needs, new faculty recruitment, etc. Such committees are appointed by the department chairman or head and report directly to him.

Committee on Committees It is vitally important that an annual review of committee activities throughout an institution be made and that a study of the committee structure be maintained. This is usually handled by a committee on committees whose scope should embrace the following areas:

1. This committee should survey the entire committee structure on an annual basis, determine which committees are no longer active or no longer serving useful functions and recommend that they be abolished, and determine which new committees should be established to perform the necessary tasks of the institution.

2. The committee should review the existing committees, their activities, and their function within the organizational structure of the institution.

3. It should review committee assignments of faculty with the responsibility of seeing that some faculty members are not unduly burdened by committee assignments and that newer and younger faculty members are brought into the committee structure.

Examples of Special Committees

1. New Administrative Appointments (dean, department heads, etc.)
2. New Programs
3. Formulation of Particular Policies
4. Grievance
5. Promotion

6. Salary Review
7. Selection of President

Examples of Standing Committees The following list is not nor could it be exhaustive—it serves only to give examples of standing committees in an institution:

1. Academic Standards
2. Activities
3. Admissions
4. Adult Education
5. Advanced Standing
6. Appeals
7. Appointments
8. Arts Series
9. Athletics
10. Beautification
11. Bookstore
12. Building and Grounds
13. Bylaws
14. Calendar
15. Ceremonials
16. Commencement
17. Constitution
18. Curriculum
19. Development and Planning
20. Discipline
21. Faculty Club
22. Faculty Social
23. Graduate Studies
24. Honors Program
25. Housing
26. International Students
27. Lecture Series
28. Library
29. New Student Week
30. Parking and Traffic
31. Peace Corps
32. Placement Advisory
33. Policies
34. Promotions
35. Publications
36. Religious Organizations
37. Research
38. Resident Status
39. Scholarships and Loans
40. Space Utilization
41. Student Communications
42. Student Health
43. Student Life
44. Student Union
45. Theater
46. Visiting Scholars

Meetings

The number of meetings of the general faculty of an institution held each year varies considerably throughout institutions of higher education. Usually, the frequency of the meetings is determined by the organizational structure of the institution and the amount of business transacted by the faculty as a whole. In those smaller institutions that handle faculty matters through the entire faculty, the meetings are most generally monthly or, at a minimum, bimonthly. In those larger institutions where a representative body handles the business of the general faculty, meetings of the entire faculty are infrequent, perhaps only once a semester. Most institutions have provisions in their constitutions to call special meetings of the general faculty, either by direction of the president or by petition from the faculty.

Rules of Order That some form of parliamentary procedure be followed in meetings of the faculty is considered important. To expedite and to ensure orderly handling of the business before the body, rules of order should be established and followed. Most institutions follow *Robert's Rules of Order*, Alice Fleenor Sturgis's *Standard Code of Parliamentary Procedure*, or others.

Quorum What constitutes a quorum to conduct business of the general faculty varies perhaps as greatly as do institutions themselves. A quorum may consist of a simple majority of the total faculty, a specified number of voting faculty, or a specified fractional portion of the total faculty. The ease with which the quorum is attained at general faculty meetings also varies from institution to institution and is usually directly dependent upon the nature of the general faculty meetings and the items of business that are discussed. It is important for an institution to have a definite statement on quorum, so that all actions taken at faculty meetings will be valid and can stand unchallenged as to their legality.

AUTHORITY OF THE GENERAL FACULTY

All faculty authority within an educational institution resides in the general faculty. Even when some of this authority is relegated to other bodies, such as a faculty senate or a faculty council, the ultimate authority still rests with the general faculty itself. Authority to act without general faculty consultation is often delegated, but the general faculty still retains the power to confirm or overturn such action. The authority of the general faculty may include but is not limited to the following. It may:

1. Control academic affairs, including general academic policies and academic regulations
2. Regulate academic matters affecting more than one college or division
3. Determine requirements for degrees in all programs
4. Approve general education requirements for all degree programs
5. Recommend candidates for degrees in all programs on recommendation of college faculties
6. Approve general admission requirements
7. Approve curricula and program changes affecting more than one school or college faculty
8. Approve interdisciplinary programs involving more than one school or college and recommend to trustees the degrees to be conferred for such programs
9. Establish residence requirements for undergraduate and graduate degrees
10. Establish basic language requirements for admission of foreign students
11. Approve college or university wide grading system and QPA (quality point average) system
12. Enact and enforce academic regulations for students in matters of attendance, examinations, grading, scholastic standing, honors, etc.
13. Recommend regulations governing student discipline, conduct, dismissal, probation, etc.
14. Control policies governing appointments and ranks
15. Control policies governing promotions
16. Recommend tenure regulations and modifications
17. Recommend considerations for economic welfare of faculty
18. Recommend administrative action on policies affecting faculty members as a whole
19. Call meetings of faculty members when needed
20. Determine voting rights
21. Determine what constitutes a quorum
22. Elect faculty officers
23. Establish and elect university wide faculty committees
24. Recommend organization of faculty senate and bylaws for operation
25. Control senate or council, if one exists
26. Elect faculty members-at-large to faculty senate or council
27. Recommend teaching loads for both undergraduate and graduate faculty
28. Approve college or university calendar (unless delegated to the faculty senate)

FACULTY SENATE

Known by various names such as "faculty senate," "faculty council," "executive council," and so on, the representative body for handling the matters under the jurisdiction of the faculty and academic administration has become more and more prevalent in institutions of higher education as the size and complexity of such institutions have increased. In those institutions where such a representative body has become strong, the need for handling matters through the general faculty has diminished. It is not uncommon to find that meetings of the general faculty are almost completely devoid of business matters, all of which are handled through the representative group.

The growth of strong faculty senates or their counterparts is synonymous with the change in the concept of academic governance that has transpired in this country over the past few decades. A strong faculty senate is evidence within an institution of a "shared" concept of academic governance, wherein both the administration, under the leadership of the president, and the faculty, especially through its representative body, are deeply involved in the cooperative leadership of the institution. A recent publication entitled *Faculty Participation in Academic Governance*,[1] which was produced by the American Association for Higher Education Task Force on Faculty Representation and Academic Negotiations of the Campus Governance Program, is an excellent summary of the role of faculty in the governance of institutions of higher education. Such a "shared authority" concept of academic governance has obviously changed the role of both the president and the faculty. This concept, when carried out intelligently and responsibly, can certainly strengthen an institution immeasurably.

Membership

The membership of a faculty senate or council varies widely according to the peculiarities of the institution in which it operates. It may range from a body which has representatives from both the faculty and administration to one which has full membership only from the faculty and ex-officio membership from the administration. In many institutions the size of the membership is based on the representative principle; that is, the number of representatives constitutes a fixed ratio of the total number of the faculty. Many deviations from this pattern, of course, exist, such as having a proportionate number of representatives from each school or college of an institution, having members chosen at large from the entire faculty, or having representatives from each major academic area of the institution. Qualifications for membership in the faculty senate differ from institution to institution. In general, only full-time faculty members with faculty rank of instructor, assistant, associate, or full professor are eligible. Some institutions place further restrictions by allowing only tenured faculty or faculty of specified ranks to be members.

How Members Are Chosen Election and appointment are the two methods used in choosing members for a faculty senate. Many institutions employ a combination of these two methods with a certain percentage of the membership elected and the remaining numbers appointed; others follow the practice of having all members elected or, in rare cases, the reverse, with all members appointed. A not unusual pattern is to have some members elected by and from the general faculty with the remainder appointed by the president. Some members of the faculty senate may hold membership by virtue of their office, namely the president, the academic vice-president, the dean or deans, etc.

Powers and Authority

In general, the powers and authority granted to the faculty senate include all, or almost all, of those granted to the general faculty. For a representative body to be effective, it must have this broad scope of authority which in essence gives it the full authority to speak and act for the whole faculty. In most institutions the general faculty, however, retains the power to override any action by the senate either through a formal meeting of the general faculty or through petition.

[1] AAHE Task Force on Faculty Representation and Academic Negotiations, Campus Governance Program, *Faculty Participation in Academic Governance*, AAHG, Washington, 1967.

An example of the powers of a faculty senate is contained in the following statement from the constitution and bylaws of the faculty senate of the University of Rhode Island:[2]

> The Senate, subject to the provisions of state and federal law, subject to consistency with the general objectives established by the Board of Trustees, and subject to the referendum, however, of the general faculty, has ultimate legislative power on educational policies. It shall, with a concurrence of the President, formulate policy concerning teaching and research, study, exercise, discipline and government: for example, and without excluding others not listed, academic standards, (scholastic standing, admission and dismissal policy, class attendance, grading systems, etc.), the University calendar, University-wide curriculum matters both graduate and undergraduate, and research and patent policy as they may affect the faculty as a whole. Nothing in this article shall be constructed to interfere with the authority or responsibility of the appropriate administrative officers in the carrying out of established policy, or in proposing, through the President, such changes in policy as they deem desirable.
>
> The Senate, with the concurrence of the President, shall formulate such policies regarding student activities as it may deem appropriate to advance the educational purposes of the University and to promote satisfactory discipline and behavior.
>
> The Senate may make recommendations to the Board of Trustees through the President in regard to policies affecting faculty status and welfare, including such subjects as promotion, tenure, rank, leaves of absence, salaries, grants, and contract.
>
> The Senate shall establish such standing and special committees as it deems necessary to carry out its functions: for example, Academic Standards, Curriculum, Faculty Welfare, and Research and Patent Policy.
>
> The Senate shall exercise all authority delegated to the University faculty by law and all authority lawfully delegated to it by the Board of Trustees, except that the General Faculty shall act upon the recommendations made by the various college faculties and by the Graduate Faculty for granting of degrees in course to those recipients who have fulfilled the requirements for the appropriate degrees.
>
> The General Faculty may review decisions made by the Senate. Upon petition to the President of the University signed by ten percent of the members of the General Faculty, and notice to the Chairman of the Senate, any vote of the Senate shall be submitted to the General Faculty at a meeting that shall be called for that purpose within five (5) weeks after the time of the Senate vote. . . .

For a detailed listing of some of the powers and authorities of the faculty senate, see "Authority of the General Faculty," page 6-24.

New University-wide Senate

Columbia University has established a new 101-member university-wide senate composed of 45 tenured and 15 nontenured faculty, 21 students, nine administrators and six staff members, two alumni, and six representatives from affiliated institutions. In light of the disorders which plagued the campus at Columbia, the effectiveness and longevity of this innovation is being closely watched throughout the nation. The success of this senate, which has decision-making powers ranging from educational policy to community relations, could usher in one of the most significant and far-reaching changes ever made in the history of institutional governance.

COLLEGE OR SCHOOL FACULTY

In the complex institution of higher education, it is important that the organizational constitution and/or bylaws include not just a statement of the authority and power of the general faculty and the authority and power delegated to a representative body such as the faculty senate but that the individual school or college be prescribed as a legisla-

[2] *The University Manual,* 8th ed., University of Rhode Island, Fall, 1967, p. 87.

tive entity with particular powers and authority of its own. The parallel of the relationship of the federal government with the state governments is not inappropriate. There are many areas of concern and matters of jurisdiction within a complex institution that must originate and be acted upon through a college or school faculty before being channelled on to the body representing the institution as a whole.

Composition

Normally, all faculty members assigned to a particular college or school within an institution are members of the faculty of that college or school. The requirements for such membership usually would follow the requirements for membership in the general faculty of the entire institution. Membership may include all full-time faculty members with the rank of instructor or above, it may be limited to particular ranks, or it may be inclusive of all persons who hold faculty appointments. In many institutions, some faculty members hold joint appointments with two or more colleges or schools of the university. In such cases, it is the normal practice that such a faculty member will hold membership on the faculty of each of the colleges or schools to which he is appointed.

Organization and Meetings

Ordinarily, the only officers of a college or school faculty would include a chairman, vice-chairman, and secretary. In many instances, the dean of the college serves as the chairman and his associate or assistant dean or a senior member of the college faculty would serve as vice-chairman. The secretary is usually elected from the faculty itself. The committee structure of a college or school is similar to that of the institution as a whole and would include such committees as curriculum, dean's advisory committee, advisory committee on promotion and tenure, academic standards, academic advising, etc.

It is important that the college or school faculty meet regularly to handle its business and to forward its recommendations through the appropriate channels of the institution. These meetings of the college or school faculty should be conducted in the same businesslike manner as the meetings of the general faculty, with specific regulations governing matters of voting privileges, quorum, etc. This will ensure that all actions taken by the college or school faculty and transmitted to the general faculty, faculty senate, or executive council will carry proper and legal status.

Reports of Meetings and Actions

All actions taken at meetings of the college or school faculty should be reported through the appropriate channels, including reports to the institutional curricular committee, the faculty senate, the general faculty, and the academic administration. It is important that an institution establish definite routing procedures for such actions, so that the deliberations and actions of a particular college or school faculty find their appropriate place in the overall institutional policies and procedures. This reporting is especially important in curricular matters which involve the establishing of new courses and the changing of existing courses.

Powers of School or College Faculty in a University Organization

A school or college faculty in a university has numerous powers. It may:

1. Elect officers of faculty
2. Establish and elect and/or approve appointed faculty committees
3. Elect representatives to faculty senate or council
4. Establish admission requirements to various programs (undergraduate and graduate)

The development of faculty personnel policies has been an evolutionary process, expanding in breadth and scope as higher education has grown.

In evolutionary terms, there are some institutions which have not yet "seen the light" and others which are vastly more "enlightened." Many of the fringe benefits which are taken for granted on some campuses are virtually unknown on others. For example, some institutions have highly developed systems of academic leaves and others have practically no leaves at all.

The following pages represent a study of faculty personnel policies on some forty campuses across the country. Public, private, church-related, rural, and urban colleges and universities are represented. It is the editor's hope that these pages will prove to be a valuable reference source for those who may ask, "What do they do about this at other institutions?"

PERSONNEL RECORDS

The keeping of faculty personnel records is a responsibility of every institution. These records become the source of written information about the faculty member, his achievements, his responsibilities, and his progress. Ordinarily, the complete personnel files are kept in the office of the president of the institution or some designated administrative officer such as the academic vice-president. Duplicate files are often kept in the office of the dean of the college and/or the department chairman. Such personnel files are a necessity not only in the annual evaluation of a faculty member's performance but also in the making of recommendations, both inside and outside the institution.

The following items should be contained in the personnel records of each faculty member:

1. *Appointment Form.* See "Faculty Appointments," below. The appointment form should contain all the pertinent information about the faculty member, including letters of recommendation made at the time of his initial appointment. This form should also contain the terms of the contract given to the faculty member and the responsibilities assigned him.

2. *Academic Record.* Records should include the faculty member's academic responsibilities—semester by semester; academic achievements, such as publications, speeches, honors, study, educational travel, etc.; and academic advancement, such as new degrees.

3. *Faculty Record.* Assignments to faculty committees and other special assignments should be a part of the permanent records. Faculty status such as tenure, rank, promotions, and all matters of salary information also should be included.

4. *Correspondence.* All pertinent correspondence with a faculty member that pertains to his status and institutional record should be included in the permanent files.

FACULTY RECRUITMENT POLICIES

Customarily the institution's deans and department heads are responsible for recruiting suitable faculty to fill authorized positions. In recent years, many universities have created faculty committees to assist in this work. These committees may be departmental, interdepartmental, or intercollege in nature. There is a tendency among faculty to want to make their own search for personnel, but the compilation of a list of candidates can be done by others. The director of personnel, therefore, may be asked to give assistance in the recruitment process.

The department head must define the nature of the job (the teaching, research, and administrative responsibilities involved) and then define the qualifications of the person needed to fill it (degrees, amount of experience, sphere of research or specialized knowledge, etc.). Once this has been done, the process of locating potential candidates can be handled by someone such as the director of personnel. There are many ways of locating qualified applicants—through graduate schools, other institutions, advertisements in professional journals and quality newspapers, the Retired Professors Registry, consulting firms, commercial agencies specializing in academic personnel, lists of academic openings maintained by the various professional societies, the American Association of University Professors, and the United States Employment Service.

Once the names of potential candidates have been gathered and their interest in the position has been determined, professional and personal data records can be obtained and reviewed and the interview process may begin. It is preferable that these interviews be conducted at the expense of the institution. Late fall is the best time of year for recruiting in order not to impose undue hardship on the candidate's present employer. This is a matter of professional courtesy. Although it is recognized that emergencies will occur and recruiting may sometimes take place late in the academic year, it is preferable that all such negotiations be concluded by May 1 at the very latest.

The question as to who should pay the moving expenses of a new employee is resolved in a variety of ways. Most institutions make some effort to contribute something. Newly appointed deans, directors, department heads, and full professors are usually

PURDUE UNIVERSITY
Lafayette, Indiana

________________ is hereby appointed to the staff of Purdue University as__________ __________ for the period ______ to ______ at the rate of $______ on an academic-year fiscal-year basis under the following conditions:

1. *a.* Salaries for academic-year employees are paid in ten equal installments on the last working day of September, October, November, January, February, March, April, and May; the first working day following the Christmas vacation; and the first Friday following the spring commencement.
   b. Salaries for fiscal-year employees are paid on the last working day of each month with the exception of December; payment for December will be made on the first working day in January.
   c. If for any reason service ceases before the term of appointment is ended, payment shall be at the above rate for the time of actual service and no allowance shall be made for the uncompleted term of employment.

2. Except where appointment is for a specific limited term, it shall continue from year to year without further notice. Such appointment may be terminated by the University for causes relating to the conduct or the efficiency of the appointee or because of the discontinuance of the department or work to which the appointment is related. It may be terminated by the appointee by resignation, but it is expressly agreed that this appointment will not be resigned after July 1st for the succeeding academic year without permission of and upon conditions approved by the President of the University.

3. The vacation allowance for each classification of employee is described on the reverse side of this page, which description is an official part of this appointment memorandum and is so acknowledged by the undersigned appointee.

4. All members of all staffs of the University are under obligation to become familiar with the general administrative practices and requirements of the University as set forth in the University Code and in Executive Memoranda. It is incumbent upon all members of the University staff engaged in teaching to be familiar with all regulations relating to students, not only those contained in the University Code as now published, but also those adopted from time to time by the Faculty or the Trustees. University policies and regulations relative to political activities of the staff are prescribed in Executive Memorandum No. A-58 and the policies and regulations concerning patent rights and copyrights are prescribed in Executive Memorandum No. A-93.

5. All appointees to the administrative staffs and to the instructional, research, extension, and library staffs of the University holding rank equivalent to instructor or above are required to participate in the group life and group major medical or group hospitalization insurance programs of the University and to make the stipulated payments thereunder as provided by the regulations of the Trustees.

6. All appointees to all staffs of the University eligible for participation in one of the retirement annuity plans in effect at Purdue University shall become parties thereto and shall enter into the regular contract arrangements for such retirement annuity with the Teachers Insurance and Annuity Association of America or with the Public Employees Retirement Fund of Indiana, whichever applies in each individual case.

7. It is understood that the indicated compensation is subject to modification in the event that there is any legislative reduction in the State or Federal appropriations from which such compensation is paid. Salaries derived from other sources will be paid only to the extent of funds available.

8. The undersigned appointee certifies that he/she is not afflicted with any physical disability or chronic illness which may interfere in any way with the satisfactory performance of all the duties belonging to the position here specified.
   a. For academic-year staff, the periods at Christmas and in the spring when classes are not in session will apply as vacation.
   b. For fiscal-year staff in the instructional, research, extension, library, or administrative officer classification, a vacation allowance equivalent to the working days of one calendar month is granted, at the convenience of the University, for each fiscal year of service completed.

Fig. 2 *Certificate of appointment.*

c. For fiscal-year staff in the administrative assistant classification, a vacation allowance equivalent to the working days of two weeks is granted, at the convenience of the University, for the first fiscal year of service completed; equivalent to the working days of three weeks for the second fiscal year of service completed; and equivalent to the working days of one calendar month for the third and following fiscal years of service completed.

d. For all fiscal-year staff, if employment is terminated before the close of the fiscal year, vacation allowance will be granted for that part of the fiscal year for which service was completed. Vacation allowance is not granted for service of fewer than six months from the time of first appointment.

e. Vacation allowance may not be accumulated from year to year.

The undersigned appointee acknowledges receipt of Executive Memorandum No. A-263 and Executive Memorandum No. A-93 and accepts the appointment on the foregoing terms and conditions.

Signed ____________ Signed ____________
(For the President of the University)

Date ____________ Date ____________

Fig. 2 *(Continued)*

indicates in detail the nature of the proposed assignment; the rank, salary, and fringe benefits; the tenure consideration which will apply; any special agreements as to moving expenses; and special research facilities or equipment which are to be a condition of employment. Finally, the letter asks that the candidate send a written acceptance to the president or the vice-president for academic affairs.

Terms of Appointment and Reappointment

Once again it is important to state that there is no clear-cut standard, but the pattern of appointments and reappointments would seem to be as follows:

Position	Initial appointment	Reappointment
Teaching fellows and instructors	1-year term	2- to 3-year term
Assistant professor	3-year term	3-year term
Associate professor	Multiple term* (3–5 years)	Relates to tenure policy
Professor	Multiple term*	Relates to tenure policy

* Many schools grant tenure with an appointment to the rank of associate or full professor.

A notice of reappointment is usually given by March 1 for first-year appointees. Those in their second year of appointment may expect to receive notice six months in advance of the termination of their contract. One year's advance notice is given those employed for three years or more. In the event a faculty member is not to be reappointed, the dean of the faculty should send the individual concerned a written letter indicating the intent not to continue his services, indicate the reason for this action, and offer to discuss the matter with the individual.

Appointment of Visiting Professors and Other Special Appointments

All such appointments are made for one year or one academic year (nine months, beginning one week prior to registration day and ending with commencement). Reappointments are on a year-to-year basis, seldom exceeding a total of three years.

Appointment of Administrative Personnel

Applicants for administrative positions are usually interviewed by the department head and, if favorably received, by the president. Some institutions also require an interview with the vice-president for administration. Unlike faculty appointments, administrative appointments are made with no expressed time limit. Letters of appointment specify the terms of appointment, fringe benefits, salary, title, and vacation allowance.

TERMINATION OF EMPLOYMENT

Faculty Resignations

The American Association of University Professors suggests that a nontenured faculty member should not resign—in order to accept other employment as of the end of the academic year—later than May 15 or 30 days after receiving notification on the terms of his continued employment the following year, whichever date occurs later. Some schools require three to four months' notice, further stating that the administration has the option of not accepting one's resignation after that date. Tenured faculty are expected to give one year's notice of their intention to resign.

On occasion, an institution finds it necessary to terminate a tenured faculty member's appointment. There are four generally accepted reasons for this action: retirement for age, the financial exigency of the institution, the abolition of a program in which the individual is engaged, and termination "for cause."

Retirement Policy

Most schools require retirement of the faculty as of September 1 or the start of the new school year after the occurrence of the 65th birthday. Many, however, call for retirement on the June 30 or July 1 after the 65th birthday. A few specify age 66 or 67. If retirement is not mandatory at some point near age 65, the tendency seems to be to permit the continuation of service until age 70. Many schools which permit their faculty to continue teaching until age 70 do require that all administrative responsibilities be dropped as of age 65. Even among those schools at which retirement is compulsory at 65, faculty often are permitted to continue teaching on a year-by-year appointment basis until age 70. The University of California permits voluntary retirement after age 62, with all the rights and privileges usually granted at the time of compulsory retirement. At the University of Massachusetts, retirement is compulsory at age 70 but optional at age 55 or at the completion of 20 years of service.

Very few schools have a formal policy relative to the rights and privileges accorded retired personnel; however, some do state that office space and other privileges are available to those requesting same.

Retirement insurance plans are discussed in Chapter 7, Section 8, of the companion volume.

Termination for Cause

A tenured faculty member may find his services terminated for cause if he is guilty of any of the following: incompetence in teaching or research, gross personal misconduct, physical or mental disability resulting in below standard performance, immorality, neglect of duty, gross insubordination, criminal acts, or conduct inconsistent with the religious commitment of the school. In some church-related institutions, a tenured faculty member may be dismissed for failure to adhere to the given faith or for any offense committed against church doctrine. Dismissal "for cause" carries with it the right to a hearing in accordance with AAUP standards and procedures.

FACULTY ORIENTATION PROCEDURES

The orientation of new faculty on campus appears to be a badly neglected administrative responsibility. Very few institutions operate formal orientation programs. Even fewer publish orientation handbooks. It is possible for a college or university to inform new faculty of many important items by means of a special handbook instead of a formal orientation program, but failure to provide either one is most unfortunate.

If a formal orientation program is offered, the faculty handbook and the orientation handbook can be used primarily as a reference. If, on the other hand, there is no formal orientation program, these two handbooks need to be presented in far greater detail. Faculty orientation is discussed in Chapter 6 of this section.

POLICIES REGARDING ACADEMIC RANK

To the laymen in the field of education, the definition of the word "faculty" is a simple and concise one, namely, all those who teach. To an academician the word "faculty" requires a far more complex definition since it is inclusive of many persons within the academic community whose responsibilities vary greatly from classroom teaching to research to academic administration, and in many cases they may include a combination of two or more functions. In general, the word "faculty" includes all those whose responsibilities relate directly to the teaching and research functions of the institution.

Very few schools have a formal policy with regard to the qualifications necessary for appointment or promotion to each of the various academic ranks. Therefore, it is possible to sketch only in broad terms the differences in rank. The following represents a compilation of definitions gleaned from large and small, public and private institutions insofar as it was possible to obtain such information:

Graduate teaching assistant	A part-time teaching appointment for one who possesses a bachelor's degree and is enrolled in a graduate school in pursuit of an advanced degree.
Graduate research assistant	A part-time research appointment usually restricted to predoctoral or doctoral candidates.
Assistant	A temporary appointment, often granted on a part-time basis, for which the bachelor's degree is required. The position often is held by graduate students.
Fellow	A pre- or postdoctoral appointment, indicating temporary affiliation with an institution for research or further training.
Research associate	A title given to one engaged in the planning, conduct, and supervision of independent research; a terminal degree in the field is usually expected.
Research assistant	An appointment for nonstudents employed to conduct research under supervision; appointee may be employed on a full- or part-time basis.
Lecturer	A title given one appointed for a yearly contract to give a series of lectures or courses in a given professional field; appointee is not eligible for tenure.

Instructor	To qualify for this title, the Ph.D. or active pursuit of same is usually required and some teaching experience is expected; three years in rank is customary.
Assistant professor	This rank requires a Ph.D in hand or all thesis work completed; yearly contract; time in rank counts toward tenure; promotion usually requires two to three years as an instructor and five years in rank.
Associate professor	The Ph.D. or equivalent is required for this rank; a contract is for three years; eight to ten years' total teaching experience required; person should be in process of establishing a reputation in teaching and scholarly endeavors.
Professor	Bestowal of this rank indicates a foremost scholar of authoritative reputation; Ph.D. or equivalent is required; contract is given for three years if not appointed with or already in possession of tenure; ten or more years of academic experience expected.
Visiting professor	A full-time appointment, usually for no more than one or two years, of one who holds academic rank elsewhere and is presently on leave of absence.
University professor	A special rank reserved for a full professor who has attained a national or international reputation in his field and is preeminent among his own colleagues in an institution.
Adjunct professor	An open-ended appointment, with or without stipend, of one who holds no professorial position elsewhere but is a person of substantial professional caliber; usually appointed for the supervision or instruction of graduate research and studies; position holds no tenure; appointee may or may not be granted professorial fringe benefits.
Research professor	A tenured position of full professorial rank, also may be employed as a courtesy title to one holding a temporary appointment without tenure.
Clinical professor	A title given a competent professional meeting the requirements of professorial rank but serving on a part-time basis.
Professor emeritus	A rank given one who has reached age 65 or retirement after several years' service as a full-time faculty member in the rank of full professor or the position of department chairman.
Endowed professorship or chair	Many institutions have endowed professorships or chairs named in honor of a person who has donated sufficient funds to support the entire salary of an individual or at least a substantial portion of the

appointee's salary. Frequently, the income is sufficient to pay secretarial, library, and other costs incident to the professor's work. Such an appointment is a distinct honor, given only to an outstanding scholar.

Named professorships . . . . Like the endowed chair, a named professorship is given only to one who has achieved high distinction in his field. Such a professorship is named in honor or memory of a person as the result of a gift of funds sufficient to augment the salary that the university would normally pay to a level sufficient to attract a distinguished person to the faculty.

Head (chairman) of department . . . . One of the positions within an academic institution that is regarded as a faculty position and yet carries heavy administrative responsibilities is that of head or chairman of a department. This is a key position inasmuch as the degree of excellence with which this office is administered is vitally important in determining the degree of excellence of the department itself.

The responsibilities of the department head (chairman) involve the overall leadership of the department including management of the day-to-day operations, the long-range planning for departmental development, encouragement of excellence on the part of each member of the department, and the maintenance of a friendly and productive departmental *esprit de corps*. The department head (chairman) is responsible for the preparation of the departmental budget for submission to the dean of the college and the administration of the budget after it has been finally approved by the president and the board of trustees. He must oversee the planning and coordination of course offerings, the assignment of faculty loads, the planning of necessary library and laboratory facilities for the department, and the recruitment and recommendation to the dean of the college of persons to fill vacant and new positions on the department staff.

The qualifications for a department head (chairman) include, above all, the ability to provide leadership for the department and to work well with the majority of the members of the department. In most cases, he should have an earned doctorate or a terminal degree in the appropriate field and a record of effective teaching and scholarly productivity.

Executive officer . . . . The executive officer or vice-chairman, as he is sometimes called, is appointed by the chairman with the approval of the dean of the college and the president. This position is most often created when the chairman has heavy responsibilities as an academic leader or is greatly involved in academic research. The executive officer is responsible for relieving the chairman of such responsibilities as overseeing the business operations, supervising teaching assistants, assigning faculty loads, space assignments, class scheduling, etc.

Use of Special Titles and Ranks

The use of special titles often requires the permission of the president or the dean of faculty. An excellent procedures statement published by the University of Oregon is included herein as an example of the policies involved:

Procedures for Securing Approval for the Use of Special Titles and Ranks

1. Special Titles or Ranks for Staff Members Engaged Primarily in Instructional and Research Activities
   - *a.* The Dean of Faculties has the responsibility for the procedures used in securing approval of the use of special titles or ranks for all staff members to be employed primarily in instructional and research activities. Accordingly, requests for changes or appointments will be submitted to that office.
   - *b.* Normally, unless special policy questions are involved, the Dean of Faculties will have authority to give final approval to all requests for the use of special titles or ranks in this category, except that of graduate teaching and graduate research assistants. This authority is subject to redelegation.
   - *c.* Recommendations for appointments to the rank of Research Associate or Research Assistant must be accompanied by a job description in sufficient detail to determine whether the services to be performed are academic in character and do not involve primarily the performance of clerical, secretarial, administrative or editorial duties.
   - *d.* The Dean of the Graduate School will have approval authority in connection with the employment of graduate assistants of the various types defined above.
2. Special Titles or Ranks for Staff Members Engaged Primarily in Administrative or Service Activities
   - *a.* The President has the responsibility for the procedures used in securing approval of the use of special titles or ranks for all staff members to be employed primarily in administrative or service activities.
   - *b.* Unless otherwise delegated, the President will have final approval authority for all requests in this category.
   - *c.* In requesting approval of the use of any of the special titles or ranks defined above, the recommending officer shall include in the file a statement as to why the proposed position is in accord with the same position definition included herein, and is not otherwise more properly a position for inclusion in the classified Civil Service.

Faculty Status of Graduate Teaching Assistants

The faculty status of a graduate student engaged in university teaching is a point which should be clearly defined at the time of appointment to the staff. This is necessary in order to determine draft status, academic privileges, and the question of sanctions when participation in protests, demonstrations, or endeavors to disrupt the university is involved. The payment of compensation, or granting of tuition and voting rights in departmental or college faculty meetings are among those matters to be considered in determining faculty status.

Academic Rank for Administrators

Those promoted from the teaching ranks to administrative positions such as dean, assistant dean, etc., carry with them their professorial rank and tenured status. Any administrator who teaches also carries academic rank and tenure privileges. Those administrators concerned with the business operations of the university usually are not accorded academic rank or tenure. Frequently, universities require the relinquishment of administrative responsibilities at the age of 65 while permitting teaching to continue until age 70. A dean of many years' standing would therefore retire as dean at age 65 but retain his professorial and tenure options until age 70.

Combination Appointments

With the complexity of college and university organization and the diversification of the responsibility of faculty members, many combination faculty and administrative appointments are used in academic institutions. Positions such as directors of institutes, directors of special programs, directors of divisions of instruction, assistants to academic administrators, coordinators of special programs, coordinators for special areas of research, and others are often filled by persons who carry joint appointments to faculty and administrative positions. Often such a joint appointment is given a faculty member whose primary responsibility is to his teaching function, but his qualifications give him a special competence for a particular function in administration. In the case where administrative areas of responsibility do not require more than part-time commitments, such areas are often handled through combination faculty and administrative appointments.

Faculty Equivalencies

Many institutions, especially the land-grant institutions that have cooperative extension programs, appoint extension specialists and directors with a faculty equivalency rank. These may be called "Extension Professor," "Associate Extension Professor," "Assistant Extension Professor," "Professor Equivalent," "Associate Professor Equivalent," "Assistant Professor Equivalent," etc. These equivalency appointments do not ordinarily entail teaching responsibilities in the classrooms but involve the work of the cooperative extension specialist in working in the community at large and with persons throughout the region or state outside the academic community. Examples of their nonacademic titles would be "Home Demonstration Agent," "County Agent," "4-H Agent," "Urban Agent," etc. The faculty equivalency ranks usually do not carry privileges of promotion or tenure but are compensated on a salary scale equivalent to that for the regular faculty.

Part-time Faculty

Most institutions use, to varying degrees, part-time faculty in order fully to man the teaching responsibilities. Though the use of part-time faculty is perhaps limited in the day colleges, such use is extensive in most evening colleges and in extension teaching. It is safe to state that very few colleges and universities could fulfill their total teaching commitments without the use of part-time faculty.

The titles for such part-time faculty are legion, including such titles as "Lecturer," "Teaching Assistant," "Special Assistant," "Special Instructor," "Assistant Instructor," and the four regular faculty ranks. Often the use of regular faculty rank appointments is avoided since most institutions do not grant to part-time faculty the rights and privileges of full-time faculty as to promotion, salary increments, and tenure. In most institutions, part-time faculty do not enjoy voting privileges, nor are they eligible for assignment on committees or official groups of the faculty.

Responsibilities Most part-time faculty are appointed to handle the teaching responsibilities of one or more courses and are not expected to contribute in any other way to the institution itself. For the most part, they are not given any nonteaching responsibilities such as committee assignments, faculty senate responsibilities, or administrative tasks. Since their appointments are usually on a temporary basis and they are assigned responsibilities for only one semester or one year at a time, little institutional involvement can be expected of them. Unfortunately many, therefore, feel little involvement with a student outside of the class itself. Many institutions, therefore, have had to utilize special counselors or regular full-time faculty to handle the academic advising responsibilities for students attending evening division or extension classes.

Remuneration Ordinarily, remuneration is based on a fixed amount per credit hour taught. Often, said compensation, when prorated to the equivalency of a full-time position, is lower than the pay for full-time faculty. In most institutions, fringe benefits are not accorded to part-time faculty. Therefore, their total salary is also their total compensation. This is justifiable inasmuch as part-time faculty bear no committee, counseling, or other administrative responsibilities as do their full-time counterparts. As institutions begin to require greater responsibilities of part-time faculty, the rate of compensation must rise accordingly.

Qualifications In all institutions, many full-time faculty teach in the part-time program, but it is always necessary to hire additional personnel. Such personnel are usually drawn from business, industry, and the professions. A great deal depends on the location of the institution, but in areas having highly developed research, science, and business communities, it is not difficult to locate excellent people who meet the standard academic qualifications for terminal degrees. Furthermore, most such individuals have a tremendous wealth of experience to draw upon in teaching their particular subject. Wives of faculty and administrative staff also are a valuable source of part-time teaching personnel as many are competent professionals in their own right.

Policies Regarding ROTC Faculty

The policy of bestowing academic rank on military officers assigned to a campus ROTC unit varies among institutions. By contract with the government, the professor of military science (PMS) is given professorial rank. In view of this fact, the government takes care to assign as PMS only those individuals whose qualifications justify this academic appointment. Many institutions grant academic rank at the level of instructor or assistant professor to all commissioned officers in the ROTC. Similar rank may be accorded a noncommissioned officer assigned teaching responsibilities where the individual's academic background justifies such appointment. The above policies are largely influenced by whether or not academic credit is given for ROTC courses.

PROMOTION POLICIES

The criteria for faculty promotion vary from institution to institution and at times from one department to another within a given institution. Much depends on how the institution envisions its purpose. Teaching, research, student rapport, and community service are all important, but some institutions value one more than another. Faculty, in turn, will be promoted to the extent that their personal priorities reflect their institution's sense of educational values.

The 10 most frequently cited criteria for promotion are as follows:

1. Excellence in classroom teaching
2. Productive scholarship and creative activities (research, publishing, authorship)
3. Participation in college activities
4. Community service
5. Guidance and leadership in student activities
6. Active participation in professional societies
7. Personal attributes such as integrity, objectivity, industry, etc.
8. Possession of the doctoral degree
9. Years of prior service and length of time in rank
10. Presence of an institutional quota with regard to number of positions available in each rank

The last point is not always publicly admitted even though it is rigidly enforced. Nevertheless, the fact remains that there are some institutions, both public and private, which operate under strict quotas of full professorships, tenured positions, etc. Where such is the case, it is possible for a man or woman to meet all the various qualifications necessary for promotion and still be denied an elevation in rank.

Many of the above-mentioned criteria also apply to university librarians who are accorded academic rank. Certain modifications and special interpretations are necessary due to the nature of librarianship, and, to this end, the Association of College and Research Libraries has published a preliminary statement of criteria based on the association's study of existing practices.[1] These criteria are as follows:

A. Teaching or instructional effectiveness shall be interpreted to mean the special kind of teaching, either group or individual, direct or indirect, that a librarian does. Such instruction may be judged by:

1. qualified student and faculty opinion;
2. informal opinion of colleagues;
3. effectiveness in the development and use of library resources for undergraduate, graduate, and research programs;
4. efficiency in the performance of library technical operations supporting instructional and research programs.

B. Research or creative work should be rewarded, recognizing the severe limitations on such activities because of the demands on time and energy. This may be judged by:

1. publication of books, articles, reviews, and reports of a scholarly nature;
2. creative achievement involving musical composition, creative writing, original design, skillful production, and superior artistic performance;
3. preparation of high-level administrative studies;
4. mastery of bibliographic resources.

C. Professional competence and activity. This may be judged by:

1. active participation in professional associations;
2. efforts for professional growth through further study;
3. study for advanced degrees;
4. knowledgeability in matters of educational philosophy and administration.

D. Service to university, including committee and administrative activity, is judged by:

1. service and leadership in the internal affairs of the university beyond the duties of the position held on the faculty;
2. supervision of library personnel;
3. demonstrated administrative ability and capacity for administration.

E. Public service includes participation on statewide committees, participation in professional activities in the state and nation, consultation, and community service.

The application of the above criteria for faculty and for librarians to an individual being considered for promotion is not an easy task. An ad hoc committee charged with

[1] Carl Hintz, "Criteria for Appointment to and Promotion in Academic Rank," *College and Research Libraries*, p. 341, September, 1968.

this responsibility will need to consider each criterion in great detail. An excellent guideline to the evaluation of effective teaching, for example, may be found in Brandeis University's Criteria and Guidelines for Promotion:

In judging the effectiveness of the candidate's teaching, departments and committees should consider the candidate's command of his subject; his continuous growth in his field; his ability to organize and present his materials with clarity and force; his capacity to awaken in students an awareness of the relationship of his subject to other fields of knowledge; his grasp of general objectives; the spirit and enthusiasm which vitalize his learning and teaching; his ability to excite intellectual curiosity in beginning students and to stimulate advanced students to original work; his personal attributes as they affect his teaching, his students, and his colleagues; and the extent and skill of his participation in the general guidance and advising of students.

Consideration for Promotion

Two policies appear to be in practice relative to the periodic consideration of those eligible for promotion. These are (1) annual consideration of all eligible faculty and (2) consideration of all eligible faculty at least once every three years. Of these two, the first appears to be the more common.

Procedures for Recommending Promotion

With minor variations, the following procedures are in common practice:

1. A recommendation for promotion originates with the department head after consultation with a faculty committee of all faculty members in the department having a higher rank than the individual being considered.
2. The department head makes his recommendation to the college dean, who then transmits his recommendation to the dean of faculty or vice-president for academic affairs. The dean of faculty then submits the recommendation to the president, who in some instances forwards it to the board of trustees for final approval.
3. Occasionally, recommendations for promotions pass through an academic council prior to being presented to the president.

PRINCIPLES OF ACADEMIC TENURE

Many of the criteria for tenure are similar to those for promotion. There are, however, apt to be more academically stringent criteria where the granting of tenure is involved. To the common requirements of teaching effectiveness, participation in college activities, service to the university, evidence of scholarly teaching and writing, service to the community, and participation in professional activities are added competence in research, a thorough knowledge of a field as well as its related disciplines, promise of future professional development, the ability to direct graduate studies, and the long-range needs of the university for a given individual's services.

Probationary Period

The most common probationary period appears to be seven years. This may be interpreted in one of two ways. At some schools, six years of experience are required with appointment to the seventh year indicating the bestowal of tenure. At other institutions, seven years of service are required with tenure coming in the eighth year of appointment. There also are a few institutions which follow a three-four pattern; i.e., three years of experience with appointment to the fourth year carrying tenure.

Most institutions require three years of service at the institution granting tenure, regardless of the individual's total number of years in academic service. This varies with rank, however. Full professors and often associate professors may be required to serve but one or two years at an institution before being eligible for tenure. This assumes that their previous experience is sufficient to meet the school's overall years-of-experience requirement. Oftentimes, promotion from within or outside appointment to the rank of professor automatically carries tenure.

A detailed discussion of tenure policies may be found in Chapter 4, entitled "Academic Freedom and Tenure."

PROFESSIONAL DEVELOPMENT

Seminars for Improved Teaching

Many institutions periodically offer seminars for faculty interested in improving their methods of instruction. Faculty who are new to the teaching profession may need instruction in some very basic dos and don'ts of academic lecturing. The new Ph.D. may have had limited experience in classroom teaching, particularly in the sciences and engineering where the conduct of research may have had precedence over classroom experience. In addition, individuals who have worked in business and industry may be quite knowledgeable in their fields but less qualified in their ability to communicate this knowledge to those with a limited professional background.

There are those who will argue that a good teacher is born and not made, but even proponents of this philosophy will admit that there are advantages to be derived from teaching technique seminars. Technology constantly is developing new learning devices which can effectively supplement the traditional lecture presentation. The astute faculty member will want to be informed about such matters in order to adapt said devices to his particular needs.

Release of Time

In the interest of professional development, it is sometimes advisable to agree to a reduction in a man's teaching load in order that the time subsequently released may enable a faculty member to undertake research for the wholesale revision of courses or segments of the curricula. It is assumed that most faculty, as a simple matter of course, recognize their responsibility to constantly update their lecture materials without requiring released time to do so. There may be instances, however, when the nature of the restructuring is such that released time is advisable. When such is the case, the college administration should be willing to cooperate.

Exchange Professorships

A system of exchange professorships can provide further opportunity for staff professional development. Such exchanges can give faculty access to new resources for course development, new equipment for research, and a new outlook which can prove of benefit to both the individuals and the institutions involved.

Leave of Absence

A good program of leaves of absence is extremely important to any academic institution, however large or small its faculty and student enrollment. Some might consider these leaves a fringe benefit, but they are more than that. They are an integral part of academic personnel policies, as vital to many faculty members as promotion in rank and academic tenure. Much is said about the growing tendency for faculty to place loyalty to their professions above loyalty to the institutions in which they practice those professions. A good system of leaves of absence can do much to enable a faculty member to merge these two important loyalties. The opportunity to set aside periodically a block of time in which one can devote one's full energies—devoid of teaching and administrative responsibilities—to the active pursuit of one's particular sphere of knowledge is imperative to all but the completely lethargic academician.

The manner in which leaves of absence are administered at various schools is almost so diverse as to defy description. At some institutions a formal process is involved in the requesting, the investigating, and the granting of a leave. An application proceeds from a department head to the dean and on to the president, occasionally by way of a university committee on leaves of absence. At other colleges and universities, the process is so informal that the bulk of the business conducted through the previously mentioned red tape can readily be accomplished in the course of one lengthy luncheon meeting with the right man.

Sabbatical Leave The term "sabbatical leave" is frequently used, but not always with the same definition. In most instances it is difficult to distinguish a sabbatical leave on one campus from a leave with pay on another; therefore, both types of leaves shall be discussed as one. In either event, the purpose for such leave is generally recognized as that of enabling a member of the faculty to undertake such research, writing, study, advanced degree work, or other creative endeavor as he would not be able to do in the course of his full-time university responsibilities. This is, by and large, the advantage to the individual. The advantage to the institution is that of increasing the usefulness, the effectiveness, and the productivity of its faculty. In some institutions, such leaves are viewed as deferred compensation, inasmuch as some form of financial assistance is given during the individual's absence from his college or university duties.

Eligibility. Eligibility for a sabbatical leave appears to be relatively standard. Most schools require six years of service within the institution granting the leave before one is eligible to apply. Approximately one-half of our colleges and universities specify that the applicant must be a tenured member of the faculty. Professors and associate professors are uniformly eligible, but some schools will not grant sabbaticals to those holding the rank of assistant professor or to anyone below that rank. Many schools also specify that an individual, regardless of his rank or years of service within the institution, is not eligible after the age of 60. This is not uniformly true, however, as many schools permit their faculty to teach until the age of 70 if they are mentally and physically capable and do not, therefore, limit the age of sabbatical application.

Finances. The most common of all financial arrangements for those offered a sabbatical is the choice between one-half year (or one semester) at full pay as opposed to one full year at half pay. The amount granted sometimes depends on the purpose of the leave as well as the amount of outside financial support the faculty member can obtain. At some institutions, leaves to conduct research are given greater financial reward than leaves for less significant purposes—from the institution's point of view. By the same token, the university may lessen its contribution to a research-oriented leave if the faculty member has substantial outside funds available to him. Here it is important to note, however, that the faculty on leave generally are not free to engage in full-time employment elsewhere. Most sabbatical grants require that the individual do no teaching and many require the "home" university's permission for all other types of employment. (See also Chapter 6, Section 8, in the companion volume.)

Fringe Benefits while on Leave. Generally, the individual's membership in institutional group life insurance is continued during his leave of absence. Retirement insurance payments tend to follow the faculty member's salary arrangements; i.e., full payment when on leave at full pay and half payment when on leave at half pay.

Tenure. About one-half of our institutions do not count time on leave toward the individual's tenure probationary period. This policy is obviously applicable only in those institutions which agree to grant leaves to nontenured faculty. By and large, the policy of not counting leave time toward tenure is more common in public institutions than in private institutions. Promotion in rank and salary increments need not be delayed by leaves of absence, however.

Duration. Leaves are usually one year in duration. They may be less but are seldom more.

Number on Leave at One Time. There are many factors which affect the number of faculty which can be spared at any given moment. Large universities can better absorb absences than small colleges. Teaching loads, the amount of money available for leaves, supervision of graduate-student research—all are important factors. Some statistics indicate that 5 percent of the faculty on leave for any given term is common, but this would scarcely hold on a nationwide average.

Provision of Substitute while on Leave. The necessity of providing a substitute in a faculty member's absence will depend on the nature of the tasks to be covered. At non-research-oriented colleges where each faculty member bears a relatively large teaching load, it is usually impractical to ask other colleagues to shoulder an additional load. In such instances, a substitute may be brought in as a visiting professor (or he may be given some other mutually agreeable title). Some colleges make use of retired faculty, while others simply hire a young instructor for a one-year contract. If the individual going on sabbatical is involved in research, it is quite unlikely that anyone

APPLICATION AND CONTRACT FOR SABBATICAL LEAVE

OREGON STATE BOARD OF HIGHER EDUCATION

____________, 19__

To the Oregon State Board of Higher Education:

I, ____, hereby apply for sabbatical leave from ______________________, 19__, to ______________________, 19__, for the purpose of

____

____

____

on a salary basis during period of leave of ___ half salary, ___ three-fourths salary, ___ full salary, in accordance with the regulations of the State Board of Higher Education covering such leaves.

My salary is $_____ on the basis of ___ months of service.

I have been a member of the faculty at __________ for ___ years, holding academic ranks as follows for the years indicated: ____

____

____

My previous sabbatical leaves have been as follows:

From _____ 19__ to _____ 19__; salary basis during leave _____

From _____ 19__ to _____ 19__; salary basis during leave _____

From _____ 19__ to _____ 19__; salary basis during leave _____

If granted sabbatical leave, I hereby agree to abide by the terms of the regulations governing sabbatical leave, as fully set forth on the reverse side of this sheet.

I hereby further agree to remain in the service of the Oregon State Board of Higher Education for at least one year after the expiration of the sabbatical leave herein applied for. In case I am responsible for terminating my connection with the Board within the period of one year after the expiration of my sabbatical leave, I agree to refund to the Board within three months the amount paid during this period of sabbatical leave; provided, however, that, in case of my permanent disability or death, due to ill health or accident, neither I nor my heirs shall be obligated to refund any part of the amount paid me as salary while on sabbatical leave.

Approved:

	____________________ Signature of Applicant
____________________ Head of Department	____________________ Present Rank or Title
____________________ Dean	____________________ Department
____________________ President	
____________________ Chancellor	

Date _______

For distribution, after execution, to applicant, Department, Dean, President and Chancellor.

Fig. 3 *Application and contract for sabbatical leave.*

can be found to substitute in the fullest sense of the word. In this case, the supervision of graduate students is usually carried out by correspondence and the gracious assistance of fellow colleagues. The use of a substitute causes some strain on the institution's budget, which it may or may not be capable of withstanding. In essence, two men have to be carried on the payroll, one fully and the other partially in order to perform the same amount of service to the institution. The use of a substitute, therefore, is dependent on many factors, with the result that each case needs to be individually considered.

Obligation to Return. Almost all institutions require a member of the faculty to return for at least one year's service following a sabbatical leave. With some, this is a moral obligation. With others, it is a binding contract by virtue of the faculty member having signed an agreement to this effect before his departure. In some states, it is a state law that the leave recipient must return. Some institutions put this obligation on a "forgiven loan" basis. A faculty member is essentially given a "loan" while on his sabbatical, which is "forgiven" if he returns to the university for an agreeable length of time (one to three years). If he does not return, the "loan" becomes payable upon his departure from the university. The practice of legally requiring faculty to return or holding the threat of a payable loan over their heads is more the exception than the rule, however. Most colleges and universities rely on the integrity and responsibility of the individual faculty member to do what is best for all concerned.

Leave without Pay A faculty member may request a leave without pay for his own professional development if he knows the institution cannot or will not award a leave with pay. Furthermore, there are fewer restrictions on leaves without pay, and virtually all ranks are eligible with no minimum service requirement. The opportunity to continue or complete one's advanced degree studies is a common reason for requesting a leave without pay. Often these leaves are of shorter duration than leaves with pay or sabbaticals. Few are granted for a duration in excess of one year. Some institutions continue the group life insurance benefits for staff on such leaves but discontinue most other compensation benefits.

Sick Leave There are very few institutions which have formal policies on sick leave. Many cover it by granting a leave with pay or leave without pay, depending on the duration of the illness and the length of service of the individual. A few have a sliding scale of *x* number of days per rank and years of service. Most, however, tend to handle each case individually, and provisions are usually quite generous. The University of Michigan policy is here set forth as an example of the sliding scale:

1. Any professor, associate professor, or member of the academic research staff who has been a full-time member of the staff for ten years or more, may apply for sick leave with salary during incapacity, but not exceeding one year of leave at full salary and thereafter one year of leave at one-half salary.

2. All members of the teaching or academic research staff not included in paragraph 1, but who have been full-time members of the staff for two years or more, may apply for sick leave with salary during incapacity, but not exceeding one-half year of leave at full salary and thereafter one-half year of leave at one-half salary. In the event of successive periods of incapacity, a total sick leave of not more than the foregoing maximum will be allowed in any five-year period. For teaching staff, the first three weeks of any period of incapacity because of accident or sickness shall not be included in computing the maximum allowable under the foregoing provisions. Research staff are eligible for sick leave with full salary up to three weeks in any one year. In each instance of incapacity in excess of three weeks, application for sick leave shall be made to the Board of Regents through the appropriate dean.

Military Leave Few schools have a published policy on military leave; however, those that do generally state that leave without pay is granted for those desiring military training or those called into active-duty service. The following policies in effect at Northeastern University may serve as a guideline for those interested in establishing a formal policy.

Military Leave and Military Service Policy

1. Military Leave. Some employees participate in military-reserve programs which require periods of active duty for training. It is the policy of the university that employees should request military authorities to schedule their training periods during the summer months only. The employees are expected to include these military assignments during their normal vacation periods.

Occasionally an exceptional situation arises in which an employee is required to carry out his two weeks of annual military training duty at some period other than during the summer months. In such cases the time will be granted as military leave with pay with the understanding that employees on a 12-months' basis will be expected to reduce their next earned vacation period by two weeks. Members of the teaching faculty on a contract of 40 weeks shall be granted two weeks' leave and shall be paid the difference between their regular salary and the military base pay.

All arrangements for emergency military leaves shall require the approval of the department head and the appropriate executive council member.

2. Military Service. When a full-time employee of the university is called into the Armed Forces, he shall be given a leave of absence the length of which shall be determined by the executive council, and he shall receive the following salary and benefits:

a. The terminal salary will consist of remuneration for the actual number of days of service to the university in the semimonthly period, accrued vacation pay, and one-half a month's salary.

b. The existing group/life-insurance coverage is to be carried by the university on the individual during the leave of absence period and in accordance with the TIAA regulations.

c. If the person is a participant in the university retirement plan, the university will continue to contribute its share of the retirement premium for a six-month period beyond the month of service-to-the-university termination.

d. Major medical expense insurance coverage will end with the month of service-to-the-university termination.

Any TIAA retirement premiums being paid by those on military leave should be sent to the financial office of the university, not directly to TIAA.

Vacation Leave The amount of vacation leave given a 12-month appointee appears to be relatively standard in spite of the phraseology in which the terms are couched. Some schools say 30 days, some say one month, some say 22 working days, and some say 2 working days per month or 24 working days per year. Six months' service appears to be a minimum length of employment before an appointee becomes eligible for any vacation. Some schools require one year, and some have a sliding scale of vacation time in relation to the length of employment beyond six months but under one year. Some schools permit vacation leave to be accumulated for up to two years, others permit no accumulation at all. Those on a nine- or ten-month appointment basis are granted no additional vacation beyond the holidays and vacations occuring during the school year.

Internal Course or Degree Enrollment

In general, officers of instruction employed on a full-time basis are not admitted to full-time degree programs by the institutions where they are employed. They may be permitted, however, to enroll in part-time or evening programs to earn undergraduate and graduate degrees. Frequently, individual courses may be taken for credit to be applied elsewhere. Some schools, such as New York University, exempt administrators below policy-making rank from this ruling.

Professional Societies and Society Meetings

Every college and university encourages the members of its faculty to maintain an active interest in the major professional societies in their academic fields. Some encourage active participation in the management of society affairs. Although few go beyond verbal encouragement, occasionally an institution agrees to subsidize professional society membership dues in an effort to foster faculty involvement. One major university pays 50 percent of the costs of professional society membership beyond the first 15 dollars. This benefit is available to all full-time faculty at the rank of instructor and above. Full society membership is paid if a faculty member is asked by his dean to join a particular society in the interest of the university as a whole.

Expenses for travel, usually to professional meetings, are subsidized in a variety of ways. The most common practice is to pay the round-trip transportation expenses for any member of the faculty who is delivering a paper, serving as a speaker or panel member, or is an officer or important committee member acting in an official capacity at the convention. Round-trip fare usually is based on railroad and pullman fare or air fare on either a coach or first-class basis. For those using a private automobile, mileage is reimbursed at the rate of 8 to 10 cents per mile. The declaration of garage fees, parking fees, and tolls also is permissible so long as the total amount, including mileage, does not exceed the cost of rail fare. Many institutions will not subsidize more than one trip per year per man. Some schools specify that they will pay transportation costs only within a radius of 1,000 miles. Others restrict subsidized travel to the continental United States. Those who subsidize lodging and meals often have an established allowable rate such as 16 to 18 dollars per day, pending the availability of accommodations and services within this range. Where specified, incidentals covered usually include taxi, bus, streetcar, airport limousine, telephone, telegraph, and conference and registration fees. All such travel allowances are offered within the budgetary confines of the individual departments and all requests for travel aid must be approved by the department chairman, the president, and/or the vice-president for academic affairs.

Professional Colloquia

Professional seminars and colloquia are commonplace in institutions offering advanced degree study. Such meetings are vital for the academic stimulation of faculty and graduate students alike. Where more than one institution is located in a given area, it is customary for departments to send a list of colloquia dates and speakers to their colleagues in sister institutions in order that faculty from one institution may have the opportunity to hear visiting speakers at another institution. The latter may be particularly important at undergraduate institutions which may or may not sponsor colloquia of their own. In the interest of good, up-to-date undergraduate instruction, however, it is fully as important for undergraduate institutions to feel the need for colloquia sponsorship as it is for their graduate-study counterparts.

UNIVERSITY-FACULTY RELATIONS

Use of University Property for Private Purposes

Virtually every college or university makes its physical resources available to its faculty when said resources are not needed for the institution's basic educational program (i.e., physical education and recreation facilities, conference rooms, computer centers, etc.). There is one notable exception, however. Many schools restrict the use of school facilities for outside work for which a faculty member may receive compensation. This is especially true if the use of these facilities will give the faculty member an advantage over another competitor. Restrictions also may be placed on the use of institutional property or equipment for noncollege or university functions or purposes.

University printing and mailing services generally are not available to faculty wishing to produce printed material for outside political, religious, or other special interest groups. Some institutions do permit the use of facilities and services on a paying basis, however.

Purchasing through the University for Private Purposes

Three different systems appear to be in operation:

1. Almost all colleges offer discount purchasing on educational materials at a cooperative store or campus bookstore.
2. Some schools support a faculty purchasing association which offers a counseling service for discount buying.
3. At other institutions, the director of purchasing is officially authorized to assist faculty in the purchase of personal items, such as household appliances and furniture, at discount rates.

Regulations Governing Outside Consulting

Faculty are generally permitted to engage in outside consulting as long as said consulting does not detract from their basic commitment to the university. The Massachusetts Institute of Technology, many of whose staff members are involved in consulting activities, grants a full-time member of the staff "the privilege of devoting an average of about one day per week to his outside personal professional activities." To further quote the handbook of M.I.T. policies and procedures:

> The Institute believes that its educational program and effective teaching in all its aspects can flourish only when sustained by continuous, active participation of its staff in research, enriched in many cases by interaction with the realities of our industrial, economic and social life.
>
> This interaction, including outside consulting service to and research for government and industry, is of greatest value when it contributes significantly to the public welfare, offers an opportunity for professional challenge and growth, or otherwise enhances the effectiveness of a staff member's service to the Institute.
>
> However, the magnitude of such outside professional activity and its rate of growth are such that orderly procedures must be followed to ensure the evolution of policy to avoid ethical and legal conflicts of interest and to ensure that such activities do not conflict with the proper discharge of Institute responsibilities. . . .
>
> Situations of unusual complexity or those incapable of satisfactory resolution between a staff member and his department head may be referred to the Faculty Committee on Outside Professional Activities.

In addition to the above, faculty usually are required to obtain prior approval from a designated university official before undertaking consulting work. Income thus derived, however, is considered a private matter. This policy is typical of research-oriented institutions. Although some attempts have been made to establish more specific regulations, particularly in relation to conflict-of-interest situations, most institutions operate under a highly flexible set of guidelines.

Faculty Support of University Functions

One suspects that an institution's requirements of its faculty relative to attendance of major functions is largely dependent on the size of the institution and the availability of space for faculty and students at major university events. All colleges at least "expect, urge, or encourage" their faculty to attend commencement exercises, but many require faculty attendance unless an excuse from the president or the appropriate dean is obtained. Attendance at convocations, special assemblies, etc., is specifically encouraged, though generally not required. Faculty also are urged to participate in academic processions when such are scheduled. Finally, most schools ask their faculty to support student activities and attend student-sponsored events in an effort to strengthen student-faculty relations.

Regulations Governing Smoking and Alcoholic Beverages

Many institutions have a dual standard regarding alcoholic beverages, depending on whether an event is held on or off campus and whether or not students are in attendance. It is not uncommon for religiously oriented or state schools to ban drinking at all university events. Some schools will restrict on-campus drinking, but require only "responsible conduct" at off-campus affairs. Smoking restrictions often are placed on classrooms, gymnasiums, and library study areas, and faculty are expected to observe these regulations.

COMMUNITY-FACULTY RELATIONS

Use of University Name

It is general practice for colleges and universities to specify that the name of the institution cannot be used in any advertising or commercial publicity in such a manner as to indicate institutional endorsement or support of any non-university-associated enterprise. This also is meant to include consulting or other private projects of faculty and staff. In addition, faculty are urged to refrain from permitting their names and university affiliation to be used for commercial purposes. Such restrictions are not meant to apply to a faculty member's scholarly activities in instances where he is presenting a paper or engaging in research or some similar activity as part of his university commitment. In the event of any question, faculty are advised to consult the director of public relations. The above restrictions generally hold true for the use of stationery bearing the institution's letterhead as well. An institution may be caused embarrassment by an individual's use of official stationery for nonuniversity business. Some schools further stipulate that those asked to participate in interviews and surveys conducted by outside agencies qualify their opinions by stating that they speak as private individuals rather than as members of the faculty.

Faculty Political Activities

Most academic institutions do not restrict the political activities of their faculty as long as these activities do not interfere with their work as members of the university staff. On the other hand, almost all state that a faculty member may not run for or be appointed to a public office without the written permission of the university president. At some schools the president then has the option of deciding whether or not a faculty member may continue at the university while campaigning for or serving in public office. In practice, this policy often refers only to full-time positions. Most institutions are willing, if not eager, to have their faculty serve on school boards or in other similar positions through which they might contribute to the betterment of the community. In recognition of growing faculty interest and participation in political activities, the following statement in effect at Purdue University is set forth as a guideline for institutions endeavoring to establish a working policy of their own:

I. Actions of the Board of Trustees
At the meeting of the Board of Trustees of the University on 17 October 1951, the following regulations governing the "political activities" of employees of Purdue University were established.

1. No employee of Purdue University shall use or attempt to use his official authority or position in the University, directly or indirectly
   a. to affect the nomination or election of any candidate for any political office,
   b. to affect the voting or legal political affiliation of any other employee of the University or of any student, or,
   c. to cause any other employee of the University or any student to contribute any time or money (whether as payment, loan, or gift) to the support of any political organization or cause.
2. No employee of the University shall engage in any political activity while on University property, or while on duty for the University, or while traveling on behalf of the University.
   For the purpose of this regulation "political activity" shall be defined as active participation in political management or in political campaigns, or knowingly attempting to use official position or influence for the purpose of promoting the success or defeat of any political party or candidate for office in any election. All employees of Purdue University shall retain the right to vote as they may choose and, except as subject to the limitations of this regulation, to express their opinions on all political subjects and to discuss national and international issues. The above definition of political activity shall not be construed to prohibit activity expressly authorized in II-*A*-2.
3. No employee of the University shall represent that any political party, political candidate, political cause, or partisan activity has the official or unofficial support of Purdue University.

II. Actions of the Administration

A—Administrative Regulations

The following administrative regulations are hereby established and shall remain in effect until superseded by the formal issuance of new regulations.

1. Any employee of the University who wishes to campaign for any political office requiring full-time service over a period exceeding two weeks must ensure that he will be able to campaign and to serve, if elected, by obtaining leave of absence from the University for the appropriate period of service or, alternatively, resigning. Before accepting appointment to any office requiring similar service, he should similarly obtain leave of absence or resign. This leave of absence will be granted only on the explicit condition that during this period the person involved shall neither represent himself nor knowingly allow himself to be represented as an employee of Purdue University.
2. Any employee who wishes to campaign for or hold any political office requiring part-time service or to serve part-time as a registered State or Federal lobbyist will come under the regulations of the University Board of Trustees which apply to any outside activity. In particular, the employee must apply for permission to engage in such activities by submitting President's Office Form 32.

B—Guidelines

While it is not possible to codify all considerations which should govern a faculty member's engaging in political activity, a few examples of what may be considered proper procedure are given below.

1. In general, letters dealing with partisan politics, whether written to private persons, to political figures, or to newspapers, should not be written on University stationery or signed with a University title.
2. Each employee should make clear that any mention of his connection with Purdue University for purposes of identification does not imply University endorsement of the view which he expresses. Such a disclaimer may be necessary when
   a. taking part in a public political meeting or speaking on behalf of a candidate,
   b. writing a letter or signing a statement on behalf of a political candidate or partisan cause or when his name appears on a letterhead supporting a candidate or cause,
   c. supporting his own candidacy for an office.
3. In order to maintain the University's non-partisan position, a faculty member should not take part in polls intended to disclose the opinion of the University

staffs as such on partisan political matters. This, of course, does not imply any restriction on participation in polls conducted among the general public.

III. Faculty Resolution

The following resolution was approved by the University Senate at its stated meeting on 15 November 1965. This resolution is not an addition to the University Code and therefore does not have the force of official regulation. It is an expression of the consensus of the University Senate which should be carefully considered by every member of the University staff.

"The faculty of Purdue University affirms the right of each of its members to engage in political activities, provided that such participation does not unduly divert his interest and attention from University duties.

"Actions of the Board of Trustees and the administrative regulations designed to implement them are intended to ensure that the positions taken by individual faculty members are clearly their own and do not represent the official position of the University. The University does not take an official position either on partisan political questions or on partisan matters of public policy.

"The faculty recognizes that the position of the University as a State-supported but non-political institution necessitates that a faculty member (or any other University employee) assume special responsibility to avoid involving the University in political matters. This responsibility applies equally to elective, appointive, or consultative relationships."

Off-campus Speakers

Academic tradition dictates that a college or university serve as a forum for the free exchange of ideas; therefore, most institutions permit the faculty to invite anyone to speak on campus as long as it is publicly made clear that the individual's appearance does not constitute university endorsement. Variations in this policy may be found in institutions governed by state or clerical law, however. Where restrictions exist, it is usually necessary for the sponsoring body to obtain written permission from the university's speakers committee or other appropriate body before inviting a speaker of prominence to appear.

Faculty-Legislative Relations

State universities, dependent as they are upon state legislatures for the bulk of their operating funds, have a legitimate right to outline who may and who may not address the legislature or individual legislators on the individual's, his department's, or the overall university's behalf. Such restrictions must not interfere with an individual's right to act as a private citizen, however. The following policy statement enforced at the University of Oregon may serve as a guideline for administrators at other state institutions:

LEGISLATIVE RELATIONS

No faculty member, administrative officer, or employed person should appear before the Legislature or its committee or confer with legislators during or between sessions as a representative or agent of the University without written authorization from the Chancellor's office. This does not prevent a faculty member, administrative officer, or employed person from exercising his rights of citizenship in a personal capacity; nor does it prevent him from appearing before a legislative committee upon the request of the committee. Nor does the regulation forbid a member of the faculty from visiting the Legislature with his students in the interests of furthering the effectiveness of organized class work.

Faculty Religious Activities

Religious freedom is in theory, if not in practice, an accepted premise in academic life. It is important to note, however, that some church-related institutions publicly state that failure to support the religious tenets of the sponsoring ecclesiastical body is cause for removal from service. Some institutions will not hire anyone who is not a member of a given faith. If, in subsequent years, an employee, though professionally competent, is found to be disloyal to the church, he may find his appointment terminated. In other instances, staff members may not be required to be members of the faith, but neither are they permitted to perpetrate any offense against church doctrine. The tenacity of such policies currently is being studied by the American Association of University Professors, accreditation agencies, and other similar bodies. No action has as yet been taken, however.

Chapter 4

Academic Freedom and Tenure

HAROLD W. SEE

Vice-president for Research and Planning, University of Bridgeport, Bridgeport, Connecticut

ACADEMIC FREEDOM

Purpose and Benefit to Society

Academic freedom is one of the most universally cherished concepts in American higher education, but more than that, it is a bulwark in the structure of our entire democratic society. A society is as free as its institutions of learning. Where the pursuit of knowledge is inhibited, the progress of society itself is encumbered. The existence of academic freedom creates and maintains protected islands of free discussion and dissent vital to the mental health of the nation. Academic freedom guarantees the right of the faculty, without fear of reprisal, to teach fully and discuss thoroughly what some may consider unpopular views. The absence of such freedom negates the existence of a true university environment.

Academic freedom must be more than a statement of policy. It must be the very spirit of the institution itself. To the administration falls the responsibility of preserving this spirit, and a university functions as a university in direct proportion to the degree of administrative success in this regard. There are, therefore, few topics of greater concern to today's college and university administrators.

Definition

A concise yet comprehensive definition of academic freedom may be thusly stated:

Academic freedom consists in the absence of, or protection from, such restraints or pressures—chiefly in the form of sanctions threatened by State or church authorities, or by the authorities, faculties, or students of colleges and universities, but occasionally by other power groups in society—as a design to create in the minds of academic scholars (teachers, research workers, and students in colleges and universities) fears and anxieties that may inhibit them from freely studying and investigating whatever they are interested in, and from freely discussing, teaching or publishing whatever opinions they have reached.[1]

The most widely used reference for defining academic freedom is the 1940 statement adopted by the American Association of University Professors (AAUP). Many institutions have adopted in principle the entire section on academic freedom promulgated by this association. However, it is common practice for each college or university to develop supplementary statements which reflect its interpretation of academic freedom as it applies to the particular institution. In fact, academic freedom refers not only to

[1] George Louis Joughin (ed.), *Academic Freedom and Tenure*, Handbook of AAUP, The University of Wisconsin Press, Madison, Wis., 1967.

the professional freedom of the faculty member but implies institutional freedom and student freedom, all of which must exist for full realization of a climate of academic freedom in a community of scholars.

Current Policies and Practices

AAUP Statement It will be noted that no specific reference to tenure is made in the academic freedom definition. However, there is no question that it is fully implied in the 1940 statement of principles set forth by the American Association of University Professors on academic freedom and tenure. Since the initial adoption of this 1940 statement, no substantive change in wording has been made, and it has now been endorsed by 62 other associations. This statement in its entirety is given below:

The purpose of this statement is to promote public understanding and support of academic freedom and tenure and agreement upon procedures to assure them in colleges and universities. Institutions of higher education are conducted for the common good and not to further the interest of either the individual teacher or the institution as a whole. The common good depends upon the free search for truth and its free exposition.

Academic freedom is essential to these purposes and applies to both teaching and research. Freedom in research is fundamental to the advancement of truth. Academic freedom in its teaching aspect is fundamental for the protection of the rights of the teacher in teaching and of the student to freedom in learning. It carries with it duties correlative with rights. Tenure is a means to certain ends; specifically: (1) freedom of teaching and research and of extramural activities and (2) a sufficient degree of economic security to make the profession attractive to men and women of ability. Freedom and economic security, hence, tenure, are indispensable to the success of an institution in fulfilling its obligations to its students and to society.

ACADEMIC FREEDOM

a. The teacher is entitled to full freedom in research and in the publication of the results, subject to the adequate performance of his other academic duties; but research for pecuniary return should be based upon an understanding with the authorities of the institution.

b. The teacher is entitled to freedom in the classroom in discussing his subject, but he should be careful not to introduce into his teaching controversial matter which has no relation to his subject. Limitations of academic freedom because of religious or other aims of the institution should be clearly stated in writing at the time of the appointment.

c. The college or university teacher is a citizen, a member of a learned profession, and an officer of an educational institution. When he speaks or writes as a citizen, he should be free from institutional censorship or discipline, but his special position in the community imposes special obligations. As a man of learning and an educational officer, he should remember that the public may judge his profession and his institution by his utterances. Hence he should at all times be accurate, should exercise appropriate restraint, should show respect for the opinion of others, and should make every effort to indicate that he is not an institutional spokesman.[2]

In a large majority of colleges and universities, faculty handbooks and policy manuals indicate that the institution subscribes to the above statement. It is of some importance to note that, with few exceptions, while these institutions recognize the statement by the AAUP, they include supplementary statements that reflect the organization and special interests of the institution. Below, three examples of statements in faculty handbooks are presented. Those statements represent a sectarian institution, an urban university, and a heavily endowed university. It will be noted that the degree of specificity varies widely.

[2] *Ibid.*, p. 34.

Duquesne University

In his research and in his teaching, the scholar in a Catholic institution is or should be the servant and minister of Truth. His work and teaching are not determined for him by the opinion of the majority—even a political majority—still less the opinions of administrators or directors or fellow faculty.

His choice of doctrine must be determined for him by its truth and not by public opinion or political policy, nor by the personal whims of college founders or benefactors, nor by the tyranny of any group.

Every teacher must be free to adapt his methods to the conditions under which he works, to his own personality, and to the talents and character of his pupils.

He can and should present to students newly-discovered facts and laws, new developments or new applications of old knowledge, new theories which may be advanced in explanation of the known data, physical, political, or social.

But he cannot and should not teach as true what he knows to be false, teach as a fact or as a universal law what is yet but hypothesis or theory.

If he wishes to communicate his own opinions, he must label them opinions and not facts.

He can never teach anything that contradicts certain Truth, whether that Truth be known to him from its own evidence, from reliable human authority, or from the Catholic Church speaking within its legitimate scope.[3]

A university is a university is a university . . .

A church-related university is a university is a university . . .

Protection is not our aim. Knowledge is.

To question the foundations of his life and ways demoralizes a child and the child-like mind. It can strengthen a man's conviction.

Universities were not meant for children. Our faculties are not governesses, but comrades a little further along the way.

Duquesne is a community of scholars. . . . They (our faculty) are specialists in many fields. They are native to many countries. They have studied in many universities. They are products of many cultures. They have arrived at many different personal beliefs.

They teach in a Roman Catholic university, but three out of every ten of them are not of the Catholic faith.

They were hired as authorities within their fields of competency. Their judgment within that area as mature, educated and responsible adults is not taken lightly. Their freedom to speak, to advance their own ideas is unchallenged. We want them for those ideas. We hired them for those ideas.

We know that in the intimate relationship of student and teacher, and in the starkly revealing pursuit of Truth, a man's personal convictions will be communicated. This is right and proper, so long as personal convictions are not labeled objective truth. Our faculty of other faiths are men and women whom we are proud to offer our students as guides, confidants, and trusted friends.

They are not free to teach that Roman Catholicism is false. They are not free to teach that there is no God. Why should they be?

Even for "unbelievers" such theories are just theories, not demonstrable objective Truth.

We do not ask that they believe. We merely ask them as men of sincerity, as scholars of integrity to grant our faith the respect accorded matters which should be taken seriously.[4]

Northeastern University

Northeastern University subscribes to the statement on academic freedom adopted by the American Association of University Professors. The essential features of this policy are the following:

[3] *Duquesne Faculty Handbook*, pp. 3–4.

[4] *Report of the President for 1963–64*, Duquesne University.

A. The Board of Trustees of the University will place no restraint upon the extra-mural pursuits of any member of the faculty unless the time devoted thereto unduly interferes with the duties of his primary employment at the University.

B. The Board of Trustees will not impose any limitations upon the freedom of a member of the faculty in the exposition of the subject which he teaches either in the classroom or elsewhere, but it is expected that such faculty member shall exercise appropriate discretion and good judgment.

C. No member of the faculty may claim as his right the privilege of discussing in the classroom controversial matters outside his own particular field of study. Such member shall consider himself morally bound not to take advantage of his position by introducing in the classroom a provocative discussion of matters not within the field of study for which he is employed.

D. The Board of Trustees recognizes that a faculty member in expressing himself at places beyond the confines of the University upon a subject not within the scope of the field in which he teaches is entitled to the same freedom and subject to the same responsibility as attaches to any other American citizen.

If the extra-mural statements of a member of the faculty raise serious doubts as to whether his continuing service to the University is prejudicial to the best interests of the University, the question shall be submitted to the Senate Committee on Faculty Grievances and Appeals for its consideration and recommendation. Recommendation of said Committee shall be submitted to the President of the University in writing and shall in turn be submitted by him with his recommendation to the Board of Trustees. The final authority to pass upon such member's continuance in service of the University shall vest in the Board of Trustees.

E. The Board of Trustees assumes no responsibility for the extra-mural statements of members of the faculty and every such member shall in an appropriate case make it clear that his statements so expressed are personal with him and are not sponsored or approved by the University Faculty or by the Board of Trustees."[5]

Duke University

Duke University has had a long history of responsible academic freedom in which it takes justifiable pride. Academic freedom and academic tenure provide the security within the University to pursue the search for truth and its exposition which are essential to the furthering of human knowledge and to the continued intellectual growth of the faculty and the students. Therefore the President and the Academic Council of Duke University reaffirm the basic principles of academic freedom and recognize specific procedures for achieving and preserving academic tenure.

I. Academic Freedom

A member of the instructional staff is free:

A. To teach and to discuss in his classes any aspect of a topic pertinent to the understanding of the subject matter of the course which he is teaching.

B. To carry on research and publish the results subject to the adequate performance of his other academic duties.

C. To act and to speak in his capacity as a citizen without institutional censorship or discipline.[6]

Special Administrative Considerations

Extramural Utterances There may be instances when an administration may feel that a member of the faculty has spoken out of turn at an off-campus gathering under the guise of academic freedom. The individual as a citizen has a right to freedom of speech. He does not, however, have the right to convey the impression that his opinions are those of a representative of the university. This is a thin line to draw inasmuch as the individual in question may be identified as a member of the faculty and the listening or reading public is not apt to divorce this identification tag from the speaker. A

[5] *Faculty Handbook—Northeastern University*, 1966–67, pp. 56–57.

[6] Duke University, *Faculty Handbook*, 1968, p. 97.

further discussion of the political aspects of this problem may be found in this handbook under "Use of University Name" and "Faculty Political Activities" in Chapter 3 of Section 6 in this volume. Finally, it may be helpful to review the AAUP statement on the matter, which reads as follows:

> The college or university teacher is a citizen, a member of a learned profession, and an officer of an educational institution. When he speaks or writes as a citizen, he should be free from institutional censorship or discipline, but his special position in the community imposes special obligations. As a man of learning and an educational officer, he should remember that the public may judge his profession and his institution by his utterances. Hence he should at all times be accurate, should exercise appropriate restraint, should show respect for the opinions of others, and should make every effort to indicate that he is not an institutional spokesman.[7]

Teaching Subversive Ideas The teaching of ideologies in opposition to a democratic government is perfectly proper if it is done within the framework of an established curriculum, as a part of free inquiry into the subject. It would be most inappropriate, however, for a faculty member to utilize his classroom for the espousal of personal, political philosophies, were this not his field. In recognition of the controversy relative to this topic, it may be helpful to point out that the topic is discussed in detail in the AAUP handbook *Academic Freedom and Tenure,* to which previous reference has been made.

Loyalty Oaths There are many states in which loyalty oaths remain on the statute books, but there is a definite trend toward the repeal of such laws where they still exist. In some instances, loyalty oaths declared constitutional a decade ago are now being declared unconstitutional, the New York Feinberg Law being a case in point. As many other states have based their loyalty oaths on the Feinberg Law, it is reasonable to expect that these too will be declared unconstitutional in the near future. In other instances, such oaths are being declared unconstitutional because the wording is considered too vague, uncertain, and broad.

The AAUP has long opposed such oaths on the grounds that they tend to single out the teaching profession, "thus casting doubt upon the integrity of an honorable and respected segment of the American public."[8] The AAUP further takes the stand that dismissal of a faculty members mut be on the basis of personal misconduct and not by virtue of an individual's personal membership in or affiliation with a given association.

Religious Limitations It can be argued that academic freedom is at stake when a faculty member is prohibited from speaking out on behalf of a policy which is in opposition to the religious principles of the institution in which he is employed. By and large, however, the feeling has been that an individual knows the religious limitations which may be placed upon him when he accepts an academic appointment and in his acceptance thereby agrees to conform to these principles.

Questions of National Security In discussing questions relative to academic freedom and national security, it is again helpful to reference the AAUP statements on academic freedom and tenure. At stake are both questions of freedom to speak and freedom to remain silent, freedom of action and academic responsibility. The AAUP states that ". . . the invocation of the Fifth Amendment by a faculty member under official investigation cannot be in itself a sufficient ground for removing him," but it further states that "The fact that a faculty member has refused to disclose information to his own institution is relevant to the question of fitness to teach, but not decisive." Still further, the AAUP states:

[7] Joughin, *op. cit.*, p.132.
[8] *Ibid.*, p. 117.

We are aware that statements made by a faculty member to his institution are not legally privileged and that his interrogators may be compelled in a later official proceeding to testify that he made them. If such statements tend to incriminate him, he may in effect lose the protection of the Fifth Amendment. But we believe that the institution's right to know facts relevant to fitness to teach should prevail over this consideration.[9]

Reflection of Change Academic freedom and tenure are inextricably entwined in the academic and administrative policies and practices of higher education and cannot be easily isolated as functional concepts. While definitions, for more than fifty years, have remained comparatively static, interpretations and applications have been in a constant state of evolution. To understand fully academic freedom and tenure in contemporary education requires an identification of the stresses and strains that influence and change them.

Internally, academic freedom and tenure have been both self-generated movements and reflections of the changing patterns of administration and academic process in higher education. There is evidence that increased participation by faculty in policy determination has a direct influence on the demand for broader interpretation of academic freedom and tenure. Parenthetically, there appears to be a certain loss of individual freedom of expression as faculty become more deeply ensconced in the democratic process of academia. Externally, the social revolution now taking place in the United States and the world has had a profound impact on the attitudes of and actions taking place on nearly all colleges and university campuses.

Faculty and Student Rights Historically, there has been a major shifting within the academic community of responsibilities for the educational program. Whereas most universities were administration-dominated educational activities, there is now a substantial movement toward an acknowledgement of extensive faculty rights and an encouragement of faculty involvement in policy determination. In many instances, the nature and scope of faculty involvement has not been clearly defined and becomes a matter of expedience which has led to confusion in the application of academic freedom. As faculty members and administration attempt to clarify meanings in this area, the problem is compounded by student demands for "student rights" and a greater social conscience in the academic community. It is not meant to suggest that academic freedom and rights of faculty and students are definable as semantic terms, but it is suggested that the educational community does not make a clear distinction.

All evidence would indicate that higher education may expect a demand for increased academic freedom for students and an acceleration of faculty demands for such things as a broadening of the meaning of academic freedom and the adoption of carefully developed tenure policies.

While limited accommodation and understanding between administration and faculty has taken place, a reconciliation of student interests with those of faculty may not be so readily achieved. The major issue in administration-faculty relationships has been the assignment of the function of each and the separation of academic policy determination from its implementation. The limits of the functions and prerogatives of the student body are not so easily identified, nor do they fit into any traditional structure of higher education. Many student requests, if acceded to, could preempt many of the long-accepted rights and privileges of the faculty; e.g., participation in curriculum planning; selection and evaluation of curriculum; selection, evaluation, and tenure determination for administrative and instructional staff; etc.

Academic freedom has long dictated that the faculty alone have a say on curriculum. The administration is not within its rights if it endeavors to tell a faculty to water down, expand, or limit any phase of the curriculum. Nevertheless, while protecting the rights

[9] *Ibid.*, p. 59.

of the faculty, the administration also has a right to protect the right of the students to make known their opinions on curriculum matters. But the students' right to be heard cannot be superimposed over the faculty's right to determine curriculum structure. A further discussion of this topic may be found in Chapter 2 of Section 2.

Surprisingly, many of the student demands for change and evaluation are consistent with the desires of the administration. Often, the administration has been frustrated under the guise of infringement of academic freedom. It now appears that understanding between students and administration might be more easily achieved than a reconciliation of views and demands by faculty and students. The effort to juxtapose, rather than superimpose, the limits of the responsibilities and privileges of each places the administration in the difficult position of arbiter for these two factions. In addition, there are times when the administration must arbitrate between opposing faculty groups who would seek to usurp the rights of others. For example, it is not uncommon for the faculty of one college to seek to block the actions of the faculty of another college relative to such matters as curriculum change or the granting of new types of degrees.

Impact of External Forces With increasing regularity, college and university administration are also having to protect the institution against various outside interests. Institutions are feeling coercion from state and national politicians and legislators, from municipal bodies, racial minorities, financial agencies, religious organizations, the news media, academic and professional groups, trustees and regents, alumni, and national student associations, all of which are discussed in a separate chapter entitled "External Forces in Higher Education," Chapter 5 of Section 3 in the companion volume.

Recent court rulings, actions by the American Civil Liberties Union and by the many groups actively demanding rights in American society, have effectively penetrated the sheltered academic community and generated a degree of unrest and uncertainty. The pressure from student activists, organized and funded by outside forces, in addition to increased internal unrest, has served to compound the dilemma. It is reasonable to anticipate a major redefinition of academic freedom and tenure in terms of these new conditions. Certainly, we can expect some erosion of traditional faculty rights as students challenge the basic principles on which these rights are founded.

Evidence leads to the conclusion that the next decade will be one of great turbulence and acceleration in change as administration and faculty alike grapple with the student confrontation on issues of greater involvement in the total educational program.

Relationship of Tenure to Academic Freedom

Academic freedom is as much a right of the nontenured as the tenured members of the faculty. The right to speak and act responsibly without fear of reprisal from those who disagree is a right of all members of the academic community. Conceptually, tenure was an initial outgrowth of a need to protect and support academic freedom, but both have been constantly subjected to new interpretations brought about by the external forces of society and by the internal pressures of faculty and students. Tenure has increasingly become an instrument for job security rather than the bulwark protecting academic freedom that it was originally conceived to be. By practice, rather than rational definition, many areas of faculty action and performance have erroneously been included under an ever-broadening application of academic freedom.

The timidity of administrations in developing techniques for evaluating faculty performance has allowed faculty members to think that the classroom is a sanctuary, that supervision or evaluation therein is tantamount to an infringement upon academic freedom. As a result, the administration's abandonment of this responsibility has created a vacuum which students now are attempting to fill.

Academic Freedom, Tenure, and Activism No aspect of higher education has become more sacrosanct than that of academic freedom and tenure. Unfortunately, there has been a growing tendency on the part of some to use both as a shield behind which to shelter irresponsible activity. Faculty activism, or student activism spurred on by faculty supporters, has resulted in disruptive tactics which are in complete violation of the whole purpose of higher education.

There are those who would take advantage of their tenured position to promote extremism, violence, or the threat of same. Those who encourage, either directly or indirectly through students, the promulgation of disorder which tends to deprive members of the academic community of the freedom to carry on their legitimate university functions ought to be subject to censorship by their colleagues or suspension by the institution. Those who hold tenure have responsibilities as well as privileges and ought never to consider themselves above rational criticism.

TENURE

Definition

Tenure, unlike academic freedom, is not defined everywhere in precisely the same terms. As in academic freedom, the most commonly used frame of reference for tenure is the 1940 statement of the American Association of University Professors. In the case of academic freedom, the Association statement is often adopted in its entirety; whereas institutions tend to develop their own standards for tenure. Joughin defines academic tenure as:

. . . the "title" to this (qualified) permanence of the position or as the ground on which the teacher or investigator may confidently expect to hold his position until he is retired for age or permanent disability or separated for adequate cause under due process or because of financial exigencies of the institution. We may distinguish four grounds of such expectations, or four types of tenure:

1. Tenure by law.
2. Tenure by contract.
3. Tenure by moral commitment under a widely accepted academic code.
4. Tenure by courtesy, kindness, timidity, or inertia.

Tenure by law exists for certain state institutions. Tenure by contract exists in a good many institutions where the bylaws contain provisions about the continuity of appointments and where these laws are made an integral part of the contracts with the faculty members. Tenure by moral commitment, or moral code, rests on what the profession has come to regard as "acceptable academic practice," as it is, for example, spelled out in the 1940 *Statement of Principles*. Tenure by courtesy, kindness, timidity, or inertia is merely a de facto status without legal, contractual, or moral commitment.[10]

Current Policies and Practices

AAUP Statement

After the expiration of a probationary period, teachers or investigators should have permanent or continuous tenure, and their service should be terminated only for adequate cause, except in the case of retirement for age, or under extraordinary circumstances because of financial exigencies.

In the interpretation of this principle it is understood that the following represents acceptable academic practice:

1. The precise terms and conditions of every appointment should be stated in writing and be in the possession of both institution and teacher before the appointment is consummated.

2. Beginning with appointment to the rank of full-time instructor or a higher rank, the probationary period should not exceed seven years, including within this period

[10] *Ibid.*, p. 310.

full-time service in all institutions of higher education; but subject to the priviso that when, after a term of probationary service of more than three years in one or more institutions, a teacher is called to another institution, it may be agreed in writing that his new appointment is for a probationary period of not more than four years, even though thereby the person's total probationary period in the academic profession is extended beyond the normal maximum of seven years. Notice should be given at least one year prior to the expiration of that period.

3. During the probationary period a teacher should have the academic freedom that all other members of the faculty have.

4. Termination for cause of a continuous appointment, or the dismissal for cause of a teacher previous to the expiration of a term appointment, should, if possible, be considered by both a faculty committee and the governing board of the institution. In all cases where the facts are in dispute, the accused teacher should be informed before the hearing in writing of the charges against him and should have the opportunity to be heard in his own defense by all bodies that pass judgment upon his case. He should be permitted to have with him an adviser of his own choosing who may act as counsel. There should be a full stenographic record of the hearing available to the parties concerned. In the hearing of charges of incompetence the testimony should include that of teachers and other scholars, either from his own or from other institutions. Teachers on continuous appointment who are dismissed for reasons not involving moral turpitude should receive their salaries for at least a year from the date of notification of dismissal whether or not they are continued in their duties at the institution.

5. Termination of a continuous appointment because of financial exigency should be demonstrably bona fide.[11]

University of Rhode Island

6.4 Tenure

6.4.1 The purpose of any system of tenure is two-fold: (1) to protect the individual; (2) to protect the institution.

The University during a stated number of years has the opportunity to observe and evaluate the capabilities and services of a faculty member. Each time a contract comes up for renewal the administration is charged with the responsibility of judging all the qualifications of every faculty member. This should be an affirmative and not a passive judgment. Upon this judgment must be based a decision not to reappoint those who have failed to adapt themselves to the standards of this situation, or to promote those who have achieved beyond the normal expectation or who have performed satisfactorily over a period of years. No system of tenure will work unless the administration acts with firmness in not renewing contracts of those who are not adapted by training, experience, or temperament to the institution. It goes without saying that lack of success here does not necessarily imply lack of success elsewhere. In most instances, persons whose contracts are not to be renewed should be aided by the administration in securing another position.

After a faculty member has served his apprenticeship for a specified number of years and has been found worthy of retention on the faculty, he should be granted tenure and given the assurance of continuous appointment which cannot be terminated except for cause after the individual has been accorded the rights of due process if he elects to seek them as hereinafter provided.

6.4.2 Definition. Tenure at the University of Rhode Island shall provide for continuing appointment which may not be terminated by the University except for cause and after the individual has been accorded the rights of due process if he elects to seek them as hereinafter provided.

6.4.3 Elibibility for Tenure.

a. Instructors (and those of equivalent rank) shall not be eligible for tenure.

b. Assistant Professors (and persons of equivalent rank) who have been advanced to the rank while in full-time service at the University of Rhode Island and who have

[11]*AAUP Bulletin*, vol. 51, no. 3, pp. 388, 389, Autumn, 1965.

completed seven years of such service including years of service in the rank of instructor (or its equivalent) but excluding any service performed in a rank below that of instructor (or its equivalent) shall be granted permanent tenure with the issuance of contract for their eighth year of full-time service. No credit toward tenure shall be allowed for previous experience in another college or university.

Assistant Professors (and persons of equivalent rank) who begin their service at the University of Rhode Island in that rank and serve on a full-time basis shall be credited with one year toward tenure for each year of previous service in the rank of Assistant Professor or above in standard college work, to a maximum of three years of credit. The amount of credit to be allowed for previous experience, if any, shall be indicated in the first contract to be issued.

c. Associate Professors (and persons of equivalent rank) who have been advanced to that rank while in full-time service at the University of Rhode Island and who have completed a minimum of three years of full-time service at this institution shall be granted permanent tenure with the issuance of contract for their fourth year of full-time service. Associate professors (and persons of equivalent rank) who begin their service at the University of Rhode Island in that rank shall be granted permanent tenure with the issuance of contract for their fourth year of full-time service.

d. Professors (and persons of equivalent rank) who have been advanced to that rank while in full-time service at the University of Rhode Island and who have completed a minimum of three years of full-time service shall be granted permanent tenure with the issuance of contract for their fourth year of full-time service.

Professors (and persons of equivalent rank) who begin their service at the University of Rhode Island in that rank shall be granted permanent tenure with the issuance of contract for their fourth year of full-time service.

e. Time spent on leave of absence shall not be accredited toward tenure.

f. Members of the County Extension staff. Because their employment is not under control of the University alone, members of the county extension staff shall not be eligible for tenure under the system outlined herein.

g. When not recommended for tenure. If after action by the Board of Review it is determined that a faculty member will not be recommended for tenure, he shall be notified in writing by the President of the University at least one academic year before the faculty member would have met the time requirements of eligibility. However, failure to notify a faculty member shall in no way prevent the withholding of tenure and termination of appointment for unanticipated cause that becomes evident after this date.

h. Research Associates and Research Assistants shall not be eligible for tenure; however, should a person who has held either of these titles be employed by the University of Rhode Island in the rank of instructor, or above, on a full-time basis at some later time, he shall be credited with one year toward tenure for each two years of prior employment under these titles, to a maximum of four years of credit.

6.4.4 Appraising Previous Experience at this University. To determine previous experience that cannot be classified as either research, extension, or teaching experience of standard college grade, the dean and the department chairman concerned shall assess the time to be credited for the particular experience under scrutiny, or if the person being considered is a candidate for department chairman, then the dean and the President shall evaluate the experience in terms of years and apply the formula stated in the foregoing paragraph.

6.4.5 Definition of Year of Teaching and Research. Experience for purposes of tenure and promotion of instructors. A year of teaching experience shall consist of two semesters or three quarters, except that three semesters or four quarters taught during one fiscal year (twelve-month period) shall not count for more than one year of credit toward tenure. Teaching in summer sessions shall not be considered. A year of research or extension experience shall consist of a fiscal year minus the authorized vacation period.

6.4.6 Dismissal under Tenure. A member of the teaching, research, or extension (with the exception of the county extension staffs) faculty who has been granted tenure under the conditions provided above in Section 6.4.3 may not be dismissed except as provided in the following statement on tenure formulated by a joint conference of committees from the Association of American Colleges, and the American Association of University Professors:

"Termination for cause of a continuous appointment, or the dismissal for cause of a teacher previous to the expiration of a term appointment, should, if possible, be considered by both a faculty committee and the governing board of the institution. In all cases where the facts are in dispute, the accused teacher should be informed in writing of the charges against him and should have the opportunity to be heard in his own defense by all bodies that pass judgment on his case. He should be permitted to have an adviser of his own choosing who may act as counsel. There should be a full stenographic record of the hearing available to the parties concerned. In the hearing of charges of incompetence the testimony should include that of teachers and other scholars, either from his own or from other institutions. Teachers on continuous appointment who are dismissed for reasons not involving moral turpitude should receive their salaries for at least a year from the date of notification of dismissal whether or not they are continued in their duties at the institution."

The University of Rhode Island accepts this statement as its basic policy governing dismissal under tenure, with the following modification: All provisions of the paragraph shall apply to members of the extension and research faculties who have been granted tenure as well as to teachers on tenure.

6.4.7 Tenure not Automatic. No statement either expressed or implied above in 6.4.1–6 Tenure shall be construed to imply that tenure is automatic. To meet the conditions of eligibility for tenure shall not in itself presume or grant tenure. Only by vote of the Board of Trustees, to issue the contract for the fourth or eighth year, as described in 6.4.3*a–h* shall a faculty member acquire tenure.

6.4.8 Resignation or Retirement under Tenure. Notification of resignation or retirement by a faculty member under tenure shall be made early enough to obviate serious embarrassment to the institution, the length of time necessary varying with the circumstances.

A professor or an associate professor shall be expected to give not less than four months' notice and an assistant professor not less than three months' notice.[12]

Boston University

The services of faculty members may be terminated for adequate cause, extraordinary circumstances because of financial exigencies, and retirement for age. This principle applies to faculty members during term appointments and to those with permanent tenure.

1. "Adequate cause" as used in the preceding paragraph means (1) immorality on the part of the faculty member in the sense of acts that are gross and criminal in nature; (2) gross neglect of duties, defined as gross, continuous, or willful failure to give attention to the tasks and duties specified in the faculty member's letter of appointment and reasonably expected of members of the faculty; or (3) physical or mental incapacity which substantially impairs the ability of the faculty member to perform such duties.

2. "Extraordinary circumstances" mean financial exigencies affecting the University which require termination of service of a number of faculty members. It is understood that the University shall exert every effort to make suitable adjustments in assignments and personnel, with weight being given to seniority of service. The place of any faculty member so released shall not be filled by a replacement within a period of four years, unless the released faculty member has been offered in writing reappointment at the rank he held at the time of termination with comparable remuneration, and he has declined.

3. Once acquired, tenure as a faculty member is retained regardless of promotion to a higher rank or appointment to an administrative position.

4. Tenure is given to a faculty member as a member of the staff of instruction of Boston University, rather than in any particular School or College.

Eligibility and Conditions of Granting Permanent Tenure. Tenure should be

[12] *University Manual* (8th ed.), University of Rhode Island, Fall, 1967, pp. 45–48.

granted on the basis of professional achievement and length of service in the University. The criteria and procedure underlying recommendations for promotions as set forth in Section VII* shall be followed in making recommendations for tenure.

Only full-time faculty members as defined in Section V may be considered for tenure. Of such faculty members only Associate Professors and Professors are eligible for tenure at such stages in their respective careers as are specified in Section VII entitled "Terms of Appointment." Nothing contained herein shall be deemed to derogate from any tenure rights of any full-time faculty member of lower rank who had achieved tenure before these provisions became effective.

The granting of tenure requires that the faculty member be recommended by his Dean and the Vice President for Academic Affairs, and the President and approved by the Trustees.

When a faculty member is given tenure he, his Dean and his Department Chairman shall be notified in writing by the President or his representative.

Term Appointments

When term appointments are not to be renewed, notification shall be given by the appropriate Dean as soon as possible. Such notification should be given in writing by December 15, if possible, and in any event, not later than February 1 of the terminal year, for all one-year appointments; and for all other term appointments, preferably by May 1, but not later than the beginning of the terminal year.[13]

Duke University

Academic Tenure

A. Academic tenure may be achieved for a specific period of time in the case of "term appointments" or indefinitely in the case of "continuous academic tenure appointments." Article XIX, Paragraph 2 of the University bylaws states: "Members of the University Faculty, above the rank of instructors, shall have tenure after seven years of continuous service at the University, or such shorter period as may be determined for individual cases, by the Board of Trustees or the Executive Committee; provided that any such person shall be subject to dismissal by the Board of Trustees or the Executive Committee for misconduct or neglect of duty."

B. Nominations for appointment or promotion to the rank of Associate Professor or Professor on the faculty of Duke University for full-time service, unless the duration of the appointment is stated in writing, normally will include a recommendation that the nominee receive continuous academic tenure.

C. An Assistant Professor with continuous full-time service at Duke University for a total period of seven years in the rank of Assistant Professor or Instructor (Associate in the Medical School) and whose appointment extends beyond the seventh year of full-time service, attains continuous academic tenure at the beginning of his eighth year of service. A full-time Assistant Professor may be granted continuous academic tenure before completing seven years of full-time continuous service at the University by specific action of the Executive Committee of the Board of Trustees. Consideration may be given to the years of service at other institutions of higher learning in awarding continuous academic tenure at Duke University.

D. Persons holding administrative positions achieve academic tenure by reason of their academic instructional rank as provided by paragraphs *B* and *C* above.

E. A faculty member who has been granted continuous academic tenure will not lose his tenure status if, with mutual consent of the periodic review by the University and the faculty member, he transfers to a part-time service.

Mutual Obligations

The principles of academic freedom and academic tenure impose certain obligations both upon Duke University and upon the members of its faculty.

A. The University will give a faculty member at the time of his appointment a precise statement in writing of the conditions of his appointment.

B. The University may terminate the appointment of a full-time academic staff member having a term appointment prior to the expiration of the appointment, or may termi-

* See paragraphs headed "Professional Competence," p. 6-70.

[13] Boston University, *Faculty Manual,* December, 1967, pp. viii–2, viii–3.

nate the appointment of an academic staff member having continuous academic tenure prior to his retirement, for misconduct, or neglect of duty; or because of a change in the academic program, made with the advice of the appropriate body or bodies of the Faculty, as a consequence of a University-wide financial exigency or for any other reason which discontinues or reduces a segment of the University's research or educational program. Whenever an appointment is terminated because of a decision not to continue a segment of the research or educational program, every effort will be made to reassign the academic staff involved to other University programs. If an academic position is terminated it will not be reestablished and filled with new academic staff within a period of two years unless the appointment has been offered to the staff member who was originally displaced and he has declined the appointment.

C. In case of the termination of a term appointment prior to its stated expiration date because of a change in the academic program and in case reassignment to another position is not feasible, the University will pay the incumbent one academic year's salary or will notify him one year prior to the date on which the appointment will be terminated.

D. In case a term appointment of two years or longer is not renewed, the University will notify the incumbent of its intention to renew the appointment in September of the last academic year of the appointment.

E. In case of the termination of a continuous academic tenure appointment, the University will pay the incumbent one academic year's salary or will notify him one year prior to the date on which the appointment will be terminated.

F. The University will not extend the appointment of a full-time teaching Instructor (Associate in the Medical School) for more than seven years except in unusual circumstances which are to the advantage of the Instructor.

G. As a member of a learned profession, a faculty member of Duke University should remember that the public may judge his profession and his institution by his actions. He should also remember that in a deeper sense he cannot separate his freedom as a member of the academic community from his responsibility as a privileged member of society. While the University will always protect his freedom to espouse an unpopular cause, he has a responsibility not to involve the University. Hence, when speaking, writing, or acting in his capacity as a private citizen, he should make every effort to indicate that he is not a spokesman or a representative of the University.

H. A faculty member who resigns voluntarily should give due consideration to the problem that may arise in obtaining a replacement and should fix the effective date of his resignation with this commitment in mind.

I. A faculty member should devote his professional efforts primarily to the promotion of the academic objectives of the University.[14]

Principles of Academic Tenure

As may be seen from the previous statements of policy, the principal criteria for the granting of academic tenure are length of service, academic rank, and professional competence.

Eligibility in Terms of Service and Rank Most institutions have stipulated probationary periods, the most common being seven years. Even in this, the interpretation varies. At some schools six years of experience is required, with appointment to the seventh year indicating the bestowal of tenure. At other schools, seven years are required, with tenure coming in the eighth year of appointment. There are also a number of schools following a three-four year pattern, i.e., three years of experience with appointment to the fourth year carrying tenure.

The rank of instructor as a probationary status is losing some of its meaning since beginning teachers with the doctoral degree are now accorded the rank of assistant professor. The instructor level is more and more looked upon as a temporary appointment with the rank of assistant professor taking on the probationary role.

Although some institutions still grant probationary credit for time spent in rank as an instructor, by and large those serving in said rank are not eligible for tenure. The most

[14] Duke University, *Faculty Handbook*, 1968.

widely practiced policy affords tenure to those in the rank of assistant professor and above. There are many institutions, however, which grant tenure only to associate and full professors. Promotion to or appointment at the rank of full professor often carries automatic tenure. But there are institutions which still require from one to four years of service prior to tenure even for those appointed at the full professor rank.

Administrators, unless in possession of faculty rank, usually are not accorded tenure. Tenure also is withheld from county extension staff inasmuch as their employment is not under the control of the university alone.

Research associates, visiting professors, etc., are generally not eligible for tenure since often their assignment is terminal in nature to respond to a specific need of the university, i.e., in the case of foundation and government grants that are by definition terminal in design. Without guarantee of long-term financing, the institution cannot make such guarantees and assume such obligations.

When a researcher accepts employment at another institution, research time may count toward tenure in those institutions whose policies provide for such previous experience.

Policies regarding credit for prior university experience vary, often in accordance with academic rank. In some instances, policies are worded to the effect that a set maximum number of years of outside previous experience will be credited toward eligibility for tenure, while in other instances, institutions require a set number of "in residence" years of service regardless of previous outside experience. The number of "in residence" years required usually is in reverse proportion to academic rank. If any rule of thumb can be stated, however, it would be that three years of service is required prior to tenure for faculty being employed with prior university experience. Responsibility for determining the amount of credit to be given usually lies with a committee of tenured faculty in the department concerned.

For purposes of determining an individual's length of service, one year is defined as two semesters or three quarters. In selected cases, where schools are on the trisemester plan, it is customary to count any two of three semesters. Credit usually is not given for summer-session employment. There is no general agreement relative to leave-of-absence time counting toward tenure probation. Some institutions count it and some do not. Some count it if the leave does not exceed one year. Similarly, there is no uniform pattern relative to the amount of tenure probationary credit granted for full-time research. Some institutions grant such credit on a full one-year-for-one-year basis, but others give one year's credit for two year's research. Some specify a maximum of three years of research credit toward the total tenure probationary period. Almost all require said research to be of faculty-level status if it is to be considered for probationary experience credit. Finally, assuming a normal academic-year operation, some institutions specify that, in order to be given credit for an academic year's work, an appointment must have been made on or before December 31.

Professional Competence In a review to determine eligibility for tenure, a number of common elements can be identified—teaching effectiveness, participation in college activities, service to the university, evidence of scholarship in written work and in teaching, professional activities, membership and leadership in professional organizations, professional degrees, awards, and achievements.

There are a number of other attributes considered in varying degrees, according to the stated objectives of the institution—service to the community, research, advisory service to students, direction of graduate students, personal qualities, promise of professional growth, and the long-range needs of the university.

Example of Evaluation of Professional Competence

The performance of each faculty member shall be evaluated each year in regard to reappointment, promotion, salary increases, termination (except for those appointed for a stated term or on tenure), or such combination of these possibilities as may be relevant.

Each full-time faculty member, after the year of his initial appointment, shall prepare and forward each year to the Chairman of his Department, otherwise to his Dean, an annual written report that will aid in the evaluation of his performance.

This evaluation shall be made initially by the appropriate Department Chairman where a School is organized departmentally; otherwise it shall be made by the Dean. In each instance the evaluation and recommendation shall be in writing and will be based on the policies and principles stated above. The Department Chairman, otherwise the Dean, shall consider the faculty member's report and other pertinent evidence in his evaluation and his recommendation. He shall consult all members of the department senior to the member under consideration, or with a faculty committee named for the purpose, before submitting his written evaluation.

Reports for faculty members who are not to be recommended for reappointment shall be filed with the Dean by department chairman by December 1, if possible, but, to allow for possible notice of termination, in no case later than January 15. Written evaluation for all other members of the department with recommendations for reappointment and promotion shall be filed by the department chairman by February 15.

The Dean shall review all recommendations. When the faculty member involved has an assignment in other Schools or Colleges, the Dean shall consult with the Dean of those Schools and Colleges.

Recommendations for promotion shall be related to the University's objective of achieving a proper balance in the distribution of faculty members at each rank in order to develop a salary schedule that is effective in the recruitment and retention of a superior Faculty. Recommendations for promotion, when appropriate, will normally be made effective upon completion of a given term appointment.

If any faculty member believes that he has been unjustly treated in any recommendations pertaining to reappointment, promotion, salary increase or tenure he shall have the right to appeal to the Vice President for Academic Affairs or the President. Any Dean consulted from other Schools and Colleges who dissents may state his objectives in writing to the Dean of the faculty member or to the Vice President for Academic Affairs.

The Dean shall transmit on the appropriate forms provided all recommendations for reappointment, promotion or tenure and salary level to the Vice President for Academic Affairs by December 1 of each year. No such recommendation shall become effective until adopted by the President and the Trustees.[13]

Special Administrative Considerations

Procedures for Approval of Tenure Tenure recommendations and decisions are usually handled in one of two ways. Initial recommendations may originate with the tenured members of the department concerned or with special tenure committeees established expressly for the purpose. The procedure then moves as follows:

Department tenured faculty	Department Chairman
to	to
Department Chairman	Faculty Advisory Committee
to	Committee on Tenure
Dean of College	Executive Committee
to	Outside Committee
	to

Vice-president for Academic Affairs
Dean of Faculty
to
President of the University
to
Board of Trustees

[13] *Faculty Manual,* Boston University, December, 1967, pp. vii–4, vii–5.

Use of Outside Committees Some institutions make use of ad hoc committees composed of both internal and external personnel in an effort to gain greater objectivity in tenure decisions. Harvard University is a case in point. At Harvard,

> . . . all recommendations for permanent positions are reviewed by an *ad hoc* committee appointed for the special purpose of considering the merits of the department's choice as well as the qualifications of possible candidates outside of the University. The committee may find that in its opinion someone other than the person named by the department is the best qualified candidate.
>
> These *ad hoc* committees are appointed by the President after consultation with the Dean of the Faculty of Arts and Sciences. As a rule there is only one member from the department concerned; the other members being drawn either from related departments or faculties or from other universities.
>
> Faculty participation is important . . . but in addition there should be in so far as practical, a critical appraisal of the situation by those who have less personal interest and who see the national situation as a whole from the point of view of men of distinction in residence at another seat of learning.[14]

In evaluating the effectiveness of this system, the *Report of the Faculty of Arts and Sciences Committee on the Recruitment and Retention of the Faculty* states:

> Although we can report no deep and general disaffection with the *ad hoc* system, we can report complaints, both open and oblique, about the glacial tempo of naming and assembling these advisory groups, about their preconceptions as to what is or is not good for a department, and about the way their cumbersome machinery sometimes inhibits a chairman's freedom to maneuver in a competitive situation.
>
> . . . On the one hand, they serve not only to protect and even strengthen the recommending power of the departments, but also they help to check the local jealousies, the favoritism, and the inbreeding to which departments are notoriously prone. On the other hand, they enable the administration not only to maintain a sensitive contact with the teaching personnel but also to meet their wants and needs, as channeled through departments, with an objective and informed response.

Limitations of Number on Tenure Some institutions have stated or implied regulations governing the absolute number or percentage of tenured faculty positions. This is done in order to avoid long-range financial commitments which might tend to jeopardize the university's fiscal stability. In some instances, this fixed figure is based on endowment; i.e., the institution's total endowment income for salary purposes is divided by the average salary for tenured faculty in order to determine the total number of tenured positions to be maintained universitywide. This number must then be divided amongst the various academic departments. When such restrictions exist, real interdepartmental battles may develop when a tenured position becomes available.

In some states, the granting of tenure is closely related to promotion in rank. Often there is an established statewide formula for the distribution of the faculty among the various ranks. When tenure is equated with the rank of associate professor and above, this has the effect of regulating the numbers on tenure, despite the lack of any such official tenure regulation.

Tenure and Change of Status in Academic Organization There are three ways in which tenure may be affected by a change of status in academic organization: interinstitutional merger; elimination of college, department, or position; and transferral from an academic to an administrative rank.

A university is free to follow its own policy in regard to interinstitutional mergers. It may elect to bring the faculty of the institution losing its identity in with full credit for service or treat them as new faculty giving maximum credit (usually three years)

[14] *Annual Report of the President,* Harvard University, 1943–44.

for academic experience elsewhere. The AAUP asks only that the tenure rights of all members of the affected faculties be respected.

The elimination of a college, department, or program is sufficient reason for the dismissal of tenured personnel; however, the institution is under the moral obligation to endeavor to place the displaced faculty in new positions within the institution or assist them in locating work elsewhere. A minimum of one year's notice is expected. At some institutions, Yeshiva University, for example, the name of a faculty member separated for reasons beyond his control is placed on a preferred eligibility list and, for a period of two years thereafter, no discontinued tenure position can be filled before the option of filling it at his former rank shall have been offered to the faculty member separated.

Relative to the question of academic to administrative transfers, most institutions follow the policy of honoring the individual's right to maintain his tenure as a member of an academic department even after the conclusion of his service as an administrator. This privilege sometimes is even accorded college presidents. There are some institutions which bestow professorial rank and tenure on their president at the time of his appointment in order that he may revert to a tenured teaching position at the conclusion of his administrative career.

Tenure and Problems of Motivation The continued motivation of tenured members of the faculty is a problem common to all college and university administrators. For all the advantages which tenure may afford individuals and institutions alike, there are instances where tenure can work to the detriment of both. The simple fact is that some professors, once assured of their job security, lose their incentive and tend to deteriorate as teachers and as scholars. Strong leadership on the part of department chairmen and close supervision of a man's teaching, research, and student counseling efforts can help to offset the problem. It also may be helpful to provide refresher training programs and to encourage student-faculty rating systems in an effort to jog those who are inclined to become lackadaisical. Still further, the use of programmed instruction may eliminate the out-of-date classroom presentation by forcing faculty to prepare materials anew.

Terminations of Faculty Not on Tenure Prior to the awarding of tenure, the institution has the right to renew or not renew a contract at will as long as failure to renew is not in violation of a man's academic freedom. Where academic freedom may be involved, the AAUP states:

> Dismissal or other adverse action prior to the expiration of a term appointment requires the same procedures as does the dismissal of a faculty member with tenure; but no opportunity for a hearing is normally required in connection with failure to reappoint. If, however, there are reasonable grounds to believe that a nontenure staff member was denied reappointment for reasons that violate academic freedom, there should be a hearing before a faculty committee. In such a hearing the burden of proof is on the persons who assert that there were improper reasons for the failure to reappoint. If a prima facie case of violation of academic freedom is made, the administration of the institution is then required to come forward with evidence in rebuttal.[15]

Terminations of Faculty on Tenure There are a number of reasons for termination of faculty on tenure. These reasons fall into two categories—those unrelated to a person's actions and reasons that lead to termination "for cause." The university is released from tenure obligations upon a faculty member's reaching retirement age as stated in university policy, financial exigencies of the institution, and abolition of program in which the individual is engaged. In the case of the latter two, the institution must be prepared to document that these conditions actually exist.

[15] Joughin, *op. cit.*, p. 56.

Termination "for cause" is a most serious act and many institutions have an appeal procedure built into their tenure statements. Dismissal "for cause" carries the right to a hearing if the institution subscribes to AAUP "Standards and Procedures."

Termination "for cause" might include incompetence in teaching or research, gross personal misconduct, physical or mental disability, immorality, neglect of duty, gross insubordination, criminal acts, and conduct inconsistent with the religious commitment of the school. Higher education institutions have been struggling with many of these problems for decades and have failed to develop adequate criteria and evaluative techniques to support dismissal for areas of professional incompetence. In matters of immorality, insubordination, and criminal acts, the current interpretations of the courts leave administrations in a most difficult position. Specifically, the courts contend that administrative action that involves a court test severely prejudices the case. Accordingly, administrations have needed to use every technique and method available to adjust to difficult situations rather than make frontal attacks on these matters.

Student Voice in Tenure Decisions In recent years, students have asked that their voice be heard in all tenure decisions. As tenure decisions are traditionally the right of the faculty, it is doubtful that many faculties will welcome students as voting members of tenure committees. Students can be consulted, however, as they alone may be in the best position to comment on teaching effectiveness, absenteeism, organization of material, etc. At some schools, the existence of a faculty rating system can provide information on these same matters in a regular, systematized manner.

Role of the University President The president's role in tenure options can be a difficult one. He has one of two choices. He may concur with the faculty close to the situation, or he may choose to disagree. In the latter instance, he must be prepared to support his objections under the full pressure of an AAUP hearing. If the president opposes the bestowal of tenure on an individual for reasons other than financial, moral, or other "accepted" grounds, there is little he can do short of involving the AAUP, the press, and the reactions of the university's many publics. There may well be times when the president would like to take a stand on tenure matters, but in so doing he may win the battle and lose the war, with his name and that of his institution being publicly smeared. Such has been the case with more than one college president in recent years.

Where there is a difference of opinion among the tenured members of a department and their college dean, for example, the president may be able to play an adjudicatory role. This is quite different from an all-out stand in opposition to a faculty vote.

Role of Faculty Committees and AAUP in Upholding Academic Freedom and Tenure

The AAUP and the various faculty committees or faculty senates have a major responsibility relative to the preservation of academic freedom and just tenure regulations. It is their responsibility to watch that administrative actions do not impede the free status of either. One cannot say in these days of ever-changing values that academic freedom, for instance, is a rigidly defined entity to which there must be strict adherence. Academic freedom, as was said earlier, is the very spirit of the institution itself. Its preservation and growth, therefore, requires the cooperative spirit of all parties concerned. Tenure regulations also are in a state of flux as new situations demand new solutions. There is every reason to believe that the days ahead will place increasing demands upon both faculty and administrations in the determination of academic freedom and tenure matters. It can only be hoped that both parties will seek to operate in the best interests of their institutions.

SELECTED BIBLIOGRAPHY

Bauer, Ronald C.: *Cases in College Administration*, Columbia University Press, New York, 1955.

Biddle, William W.: *Growth toward Freedom*, Harper & Brothers, New York, 1957.

Calkins, Robert D., Edgar N. Johnson, Edward C. Kirkland, Joseph L. Lilienthal, Jr., M.D., J. Robert Oppenheimer, and Eugene V. Rostow: *Freedom and the University*, Cornell University Press, Ithaca, N.Y., 1950.

Educational Policies Commission: *Higher Education in a Decade of Decision*, National Education Association of the U.S. and the American Association of School Administrators, Washington, 1957.

Hullfish, H. Gordon (ed.): *Educational Freedom in an Age of Anxiety*, Harper & Brothers, New York, 1953.

MacIver, Robert M.: *Academic Freedom in Our Time*, Columbia University Press, New York, 1955.

Joughin, Louis (ed.): *Academic Freedom and Tenure*, University of Wisconsin Press, Madison, Wis., 1967.

Wilson, Logan (ed.): *Emerging Patterns in American Higher Education*, American Council on Education, Washington, 1965.

Chapter 5

Faculty Rights and Responsibilities

KENNETH G. RYDER

Vice-president for University Administration, Northeastern University, Boston, Massachusetts

During the past three decades most American colleges and universities have witnessed a substantial change in the status and influence of faculty members. Stimulated by the publications of the American Association of University Professors, activities of professional societies, and revised standards of many accrediting organizations, faculty members at most institutions have moved from a relatively weak position as institutional employees to a rather powerful role as partners in academic administration, with dominant control over academic content and professional standards.

During this period of professional change much has been written stressing the need for expansion of faculty rights. Books and articles have elaborated upon the critical importance of academic freedom in institutions of higher learning; and procedural safeguards, including systems of tenure, have gained wide acceptance in American colleges and universities. While it is not possible to delineate at this time a precise code of faculty rights and privileges that is universally accepted, it is nonetheless true that an increasing number of institutions have accepted certain common principles in dealing with members of the faculty. As a kind of convenient guide to harried administrators, the following checklist is offered embodying those faculty rights which seem to have gained wide professional support:

CHECKLIST OF FACULTY RIGHTS

Conditions of Appointment

1. Right to have a clear statement of terms of appointment, including:

Period of time for which appointed
Expected teaching or research assignments
Overtime load, if any
Special committee or administrative assignments
Special counseling, advisory, or other responsibilities
Daily or weekly schedule of hours when individual is expected to be physically present
Annual salary and how it will be paid
Fringe benefits and any special perquisites which are to be received by the appointee, including conditions governing sabbatical or other leaves of absence which may be granted
Any limits placed on appointee's right to engage in outside employment, such as consulting, part-time teaching at another institution, or operating a private business

2. Right to expect that teaching assignments will be within his area of professional competency and that when new courses are assigned, he will be given reasonable advance notice so that proper preparation may be made.

Evaluation and Promotion

3. Right to periodic evaluation of performance by immediate superior or appropriate faculty committee. Such reviews should allow opportunity to work at overcoming weaknesses and give faculty member a realistic estimate of the likelihood of obtaining a tenured appointment.
4. Right to periodic review of salary, with annual or merit increases in keeping with the established practices of the institution. Such practices, preferably including salary ranges, should be made known at time of employment.
5. Right to have salary increments based upon fair and equal treatment, considering the rank, experience, and a clearly presented evaluation of performance.
6. Right to fair and impartial consideration for promotion in rank based on clearly stated criteria.
7. Right to receive full explanation from an administrative superior or appropriate faculty committee if faculty member does not receive merit raise or promotion in rank when expected.
8. Right to request review of his case by higher administrative authority or appropriate faculty committee if faculty member feels unfairly treated in matters of salary or promotion.

Tenure and Dismissal

9. A clear definition of the policies and conditions under which tenure may be gained, if tenure is not granted at time of initial appointment.
10. Right to receive a written statement at the time of appointment indicating the years of credit towards tenure granted for prior service at another college or university.
11. Right to appropriate advance notice when a decision is made not to grant tenure.
12. Right to be considered for tenure by appropriate academic colleagues and ad-

ministrative authorities, following procedures clearly formulated and publicly announced.

13. Prior to tenure, the right to have reasonable advance notice of dismissal or termination of contract. (The AAUP guidelines recommend from three months to a year's advance notice, depending upon length of prior service.)

14. The right of the faculty member dismissed without adequate notification to have his case reviewed by an impartial faculty committee or higher administrative authority, with full protection of his rights through clearly defined procedures.

15. The right of a tenured faculty member dismissed for any reason to have his case reviewed by a committee of his peers and by higher administrative authorities, including the governing board of the institution. Arrangements for such review should be clearly established with full provision for procedures that will protect the rights of the individual. (See AAUP 1940 *Statement on Principles of Academic Freedom and Tenure.)*

16. Right to have a clear, written statement of conditions which will apply at time of retirement because of age, including compensation, fringe benefits, and whether full- or part-time service may be contracted after official retirement age.

17. Right to clear statement of minimum guarantees which will govern continuance of employment in case of accident or serious prolonged illness.

Academic Freedom

18. Right of the individual faculty member to seek and report truth as he interprets it in his area of academic competence.

19. Right to set forth in the classroom ideas and information in his field of academic competence without fear of interference from the governing authorities of the institution or special student or faculty pressure groups.

20. Right to set forth in public statements, ideas, and information in his field of academic competence without the fear that punitive action will be taken against him if those views happen to be unpopular.

21. Right to involve himself in extramural pursuits and associations as a free American citizen except as such activity may unduly interfere with his college duties or conditions of appointment.

Under this heading, he should be free to:

Join any educational, social, fraternal, or professional organization provided such organization is legal

Espouse any religious or political cause, according to the dictates of his own conscience and convictions

Participate in volunteer community activities or as part-time elective official in local or state government, including enlistment in military reserve organizations and accepting commission in same

Speak out and take public positions on controversial public issues, even those unrelated to his special field of academic competence

22. Right to criticize academic programs, administrative organization, policies, and procedures within the institution and recommend changes.

23. Right to express views relative to appointment of academic administrators (including department chairmen, college deans, etc.). The degree of formal faculty participation in selection of such officials will vary among institutions, but vital faculty interest is apparent and faculty should feel free to express views.

24. Right to communicate through appropriate channels with higher administrative authorities, including the governing board, concerning matters of institutional concern.

25. Right to invoke the Fifth Amendment to avoid self-incrimination when under governmental investigation without thereby jeopardizing his faculty appointment.

RESPONSIBILITIES OF FACULTY MEMBERS

During the recent years when faculty rights and freedoms have been substantially increased, little attention has been given to specifying in precise terms those obligations and responsibilities which should be associated with a faculty appointment. Where faculty members have gained substantial freedom from administrative controls, it seems essential that there be a general agreement as to those obligations which faculty members assume voluntarily as a matter of professional responsibility.

A faculty member in a present-day college or university clearly carries a wide range of specific responsibilities—to students, professional colleagues, and to the institution where he is employed. While the following summary should not be considered as all inclusive, there seem to be substantial reasons for including the following items in any checklist of faculty obligations:

Student-related Responsibilities

1. Responsibility to deal seriously and conscientiously with the teaching assignment, including careful planning of courses, preparation of lectures, regularity in meeting scheduled classes, clearly informing students of course requirements, and fair and impartial grading according to standards established by the institution.

2. Recognition that students deserve respect as individuals and have certain rights that must be protected. This encompasses an active interest in individual academic and personal problems of students, the giving of mature professional advice, courteous treatment of students in class, and keeping in confidence personal information about students which may come to the faculty member's attention in his role as counselor.

3. Recognition that the faculty member serves as a model and exercises a great influence in shaping young minds. This being true, he must try to set a high standard in:

Academic and scholarly excellence
Personal integrity
Professional ethics

4. Recognition that in his influential classroom role he is morally bound not to take advantage of his position by repeatedly introducing into his classes discussions of subject matter outside the scope of the course and not within his field of professional competence.

Professional Responsibilities

5. Special responsibility to keep up to date with developing knowledge in his academic discipline through familiarity with recent publications and journals and participation in local or national professional societies and meetings where appropriate.

6. Responsibility to seek ways of improving his effectiveness as a teacher, exploring new ways of presenting academic subject matter, motivating students, and improving methods of evaluating student performance.

7. Responsibility to advance knowledge in his academic discipline through individual research, creative writing and analysis, and presenting papers at colloquiums or professional meetings.

8. Responsibility to assist faculty colleagues in academic department and college activities including:

Contributing to curriculum studies at both the departmental and college levels

Participating in department, college, and university faculty meetings for the better operation and strengthening of the educational program of the institution

Carrying a fair share of the burden of special faculty committee assignments, including participation in such bodies as curriculum committees and honors program committees as well as sharing in joint faculty responsibilities such as registration counseling and examination proctoring

9. Responsibility to exercise an active role in protecting and enhancing the academic and professional standing of the faculty by:

Assisting with recruitment of competent new faculty members

Giving appropriate recommendations regarding promotion or tenure appointments for able faculty colleagues

Recommending the removal of colleagues who, after fair hearing, have been proved incompetent, guilty of moral turpitude or gross misconduct, or lacking in personal or prefessional integrity

10. Responsibility to demonstrate respect for the right of others in the university community to hold divergent opinions, including other faculty members, students, and administrators.

Institutional Responsibilities

It is reasonable for an employing institution to expect that a faculty member will:

11. Conscientiously fulfill all the contractual obligations for the period of time agreed and that he will give the institution reasonable notice when resigning to accept another position.

12. Make conscientious use of the funds of the institution entrusted to his care, such as those allocated to budgets of academic departments or special research projects.

13. Make every effort to avoid professional and personal actions which may cause economic loss or legal embarassment to his institution.

14. Without specific permission, avoid use of university resources, equipment, or labor for his own personal gain in research or consulting projects in which he may be interested.

15. Give reasonable support to general institutional activities by participating as a faculty representative at meetings such as convocations, commencement exercises, and honors day assemblies.

16. Commit himself to a reasonable amount of service on universitywide committees such as faculty senate committees, committees on student discipline, and library or computer center operations.

17. In making public statement of his views, indicate clearly that he does not speak as a representative of the institution but as an independent scholar and citizen.

Chapter 6

Orientation of New Faculty

ASA S. KNOWLES

Editor in Chief

IMPORTANCE OF ORIENTATION

The beginning of the school year is a busy and often confusing time for all academicians, but it is apt to be particularly chaotic for a newly appointed member of the faculty. When one is new to an institution, new to its policies, new to its students, and perhaps even new to the community, there is a definite need for assistance through some form of organized orientation program. Such a program is the most efficient means of informing new faculty of important university routines and policies in order that they may function with both students and colleagues more smoothly.

Ironically, although every institution faces the problem of acclimating new faculty each year, very few colleges or universities have a well-thought-out orientation program. Far too many expect their faculty to fit into the scheme of things with little or no assistance.

METHODS OF CONDUCTING PROGRAMS

The general responsibility for any faculty orientation program lies with the office of the president. It is customary for the president to meet with the new faculty at the beginning of the school year and, by his comments, define the scope and objectives of the college or university. Following his remarks, the orientation may be carried out by one of two means.

Lecture Series Orientation may be accomplished by a series of lectures in which deans and key department heads speak on their respective operations, i.e., the bookstore, the library, the registrar's office, etc. This is a very effective method as it gives new arrivals an opportunity to meet and ask questions of the individual associated with each operation. Some institutions schedule these orientation lectures throughout freshman orientation week. Others prefer to space them throughout the first academic term. Still others advocate an intense two-day institute prior to the beginning of the new term.

In some universities, individual college deans may assume the orientation responsibilities in lieu of the president. There are both advantages and disadvantages to this system. While the division of the new faculty into small college groups may offer a more personalized approach, it also may result in a duplication of effort and a sense of fragmentation which may be quite contrary to the overall objectives of the university.

Another approach is that of one central program whereby all new faculty are brought together to participate in a common agenda after which college meetings and meetings with department heads serve as a supplement to the basic program.

There is much to be gained by operating a formal orientation program. Such a program is of immense help in making the new arrival feel a part of his new institution and in fostering the development of institutional loyalty.

Orientation Handbook When a lecture series does not seem feasible, it is possible to accomplish many of the same objectives by means of a highly detailed faculty orientation handbook which supplements, but does not duplicate, the regular faculty handbook. Such a handbook can assist a faculty member who is new to the community by offering information on faculty housing, school districts, the location of hotels or motels near the campus, etc. It also may seek to answer questions regarding where to look for an apartment to rent or a house to buy, what highways or public transportation routes offer the fastest access to the campus and whether automobile or real estate taxes and insurance vary from one suburb to another. Although some institutions maintain a faculty housing office to assist new arrivals with these problems, many do not, and it is somehow necessary, therefore, to bridge the gap.

Once the immediate concerns of finding one's quarters and moving into both a home and an office have been cared for, the new arrival needs further orientation to the community and the institution as a whole. In the latter instance, a handbook may be helpful in answering questions relative to university policy on grading, homework, outside reading, field trips, library usage, cheating, disciplinary action, or even the extent of faculty involvement in student activities. The use of a handbook alone, however, is a very cold means of welcoming a new member into the academic family.

Combined Lectures and Handbook The best method of conducting an orientation program would seem to be a combination of a lecture series being supplemented by an orientation handbook which could be mailed out in advance of the staff member's arrival and subsequently serve as a reference book at the start of the new school year.

Regardless of the methods employed, certain key topics need to be covered. The following outline has been prepared as a guideline for those responsible for the preparation of an orientation handbook or the scheduling of orientation lectures.

TOPICS TO BE COVERED IN THE ORIENTATION OF NEW FACULTY

Prearrival Orientation

1. Campus map in relation to city map showing major highways and public transportation routes to the campus
2. List and rates of hotels and motels located near campus
3. Housing information—guidebooks, real estate brokers, rent rates, proximity of residential areas to campus
4. Taxes—community tax rates, auto insurance rates, etc.
5. State regulations governing new residents—automobile registration, driver's license, automobile insurance, voting registration
6. Public and private school system—opening day of classes, colleges and universities in area, adult education opportunities
7. Local churches (particularly important in small towns)
8. Procedures regarding university reimbursement or payment of moving expenses
9. Transfer of books and equipment from previous institution

Campus Orientation

1. Detailed campus map with guide to buildings
2. Faculty parking areas
3. Facilities instructions—keys, parking permits, nameplate, office space, office equipment, etc.
4. Financial instructions—payroll arrangements, enrollment in group benefit plans
5. Health instructions—mandatory physical examinations, chest X rays, etc.
6. Academic instructions—oath of allegiance (where required), patent policy agreement, completion of forms for personnel records, student registration duties
7. Distribution of appropriate literature—history of institution, all faculty, staff, and student handbooks, catalogs, campus fact book, staff directory

Institutional Orientation

1. History of school and basic facts about institution if not covered by printed literature
2. Policies regarding appointments, tenure, academic freedom, political involvement, etc., if not covered during preappointment interviews or included in basic faculty handbook
3. Research policies—role of faculty and administration, rules governing proposals and contracts, specific research funds available, sponsored research
4. Nature of student body—admission requirements and policies, attrition, standards, etc.

Academic Orientation

1. Educational resources
   (*a*) Television
   (*b*) Programmed learning
   (*c*) Library—library resources, divisions and special collections, reference services, catalog, purchasing books through library
   (*d*) University bookstore—textbook adaptations and orders, internal supplies
   (*e*) Computation center
2. Responsibilities as faculty adviser
3. Unique or special programs in operation—cooperative plan if operative, advanced placement, honors programs, part-time study
4. Classroom teaching—credits and class hours, grades and grading practices, quality point averages, reporting of grades, warnings, homework assignments, outside reading, course syllabi, lectures versus discussions, failures, makeup work, conference hours,

cheating and academic discipline, registrar's office, examinations (regulations concerning correcting, preparation and typing, giving of examinations, proctoring and security)

Student Activities Orientation

1. Explanation of scope of program
2. Policies governing organizations and their activities (may refer to student handbook)
3. Activities hours (if applicable)
4. Faculty responsibilities—adviser, chaperone, etc.
5. Faculty tickets to student events

Community Orientation

1. Annual university functions
2. Special community offerings—cultural, recreational
3. Faculty club
4. List of guidebooks to the locale

Chapter 7

Faculty Role in Governance *

C. ADDISON HICKMAN

Vandeveer Professor of Economics, Southern Illinois University, Carbondale, Illinois; President, American Association for Higher Education, 1968–1969

* Acknowledgement is made of the assistance and encouragement of Mr. Edward H. Witkowski in the preparation of this chapter.

A measure of agreement as to rationale and principles of academic governance in our colleges and universities now seems to be emerging.

Having attained more income and status, faculty members now want the involvement and self-determination that usually accompany professional activity. Their roles as citizens of the academic world have been joined to their roles as citizens of the community, state, and nation. They want to be involved in the governing of their institutions.

As the reports of the American Association for Higher Education (AAHE) Task Force note, ". . . professors . . . seek direct participation in the formulation of the policies and roles that govern the performance of their duties.[1]

Faculty members are caught up today in the student protest movement. They want a voice in it. They are concerned with personnel and educational policies and with procedures for faculty representation. They are also interested in their economic welfare. Hopefully this interest goes beyond the purely personal and manifests itself in the nature and quality of the educational services their institutions provide.

In recent years, colleges and universities have been widely hailed as our hope of the future and have been called upon to educate more students, do more research, and perform a multitude of services. Their traditional isolation from the mainstream of society lessening, they are increasingly drawn into the vortex of economic and political life. Colleges and universities are being asked to help solve some of the great social problems of our age.

But there is a widespread feeling at many colleges and universities that communication, consultation, and involvement have broken down or function inadequately.

The phenomenal recent growth of higher boards of education, master plans, and systemwide or statewide coordination and control, as well as the increasing number of multicampus universities, has had clear reverberations in the attitudes of faculty toward their roles in academic governance. Many feel that gains achieved in their growing involvement in campus decision making are now being jeopardized by the change in the locus of power and control.

THE FACULTY ROLE

The position and role of the faculty in the division of labor in academic governance must first be viewed within the total context.

The Division of Labor

In a certain sense everybody wants to be in on everything in a college or university.[2] The trustees have overall responsibility by statute or charter. The administration is interested in the effectiveness of teaching, research, and the curriculum. And the faculty is interested in who becomes dean, in promotion and salary policy, in whether a new building is inhabitable, and whether the thermostats work. Although we do have overlapping interests, there seem to be certain areas for which the various parties can assume a primary responsibility without denying a general share to others.

[1] *Faculty Participation in Academic Governance,* Report of the AAHE Task Force on Faculty Representation and Economic Negotiations, American Association for Higher Education, Washington, 1967, p. 9.

[2] This paragraph and others noted later are substantially taken from an address by the author, not widely available in published form. This address, "Faculty Participation in Academic Governance," is found on pp. 49–69 of *The Faculty and Academic Policy,* Proceedings of the Second Minnesota Intercollegiate Faculty Conference, sponsored by the Minnesota Conference of the American Association of University Professors and the Senate of the University of Minnesota, held at Grand Rapids, Minnesota, 1968.

The Joint Statement This statement,[3] formulated by national associations representing the faculty, administration, and boards of trustees, makes a brief attempt to suggest at least the broad outlines of such a division of labor. It is reproduced in full at the end of this chapter.

The AAHE Task Force Report This report focuses on the administrative-faculty division of labor. Its intensive study of the faculty role was predicated upon the assumption that the administration also has profoundly important functions and responsibilities, complementary and necessary to the faculty role.

The administration is not simply a clerical force; it is part of the heart of the institution. As the report notes,[4] the administration has certain roles it must perform. Many of these are also shared in some measure with faculty and students, but much of the proximate responsibility lies with the administration.

A first and fundamental role is that of overall leadership, combining the interests and efforts of a diverse constituency and achieving a commitment by all the various groups to the general objectives of the institution without stifling individual fulfillment.

A second role is that of coordination. Because top-level administrators are responsible for the operation of the entire institution, they presumably can help to keep the pieces fitted together.

A third role is that of planning and innovation. This is not an exclusive role. It is also not a role exercised through fiat, but rather through helping to provide leadership and by suggesting new programs or changes in working with faculty and students.

A fourth function is to help assure that particular departments or divisions meet the general quality standards of the institution. One of the difficulties in peer-group evaluation and in departmental autonomy is that while good departments can get better this way, weak departments can stay weak. The administration should help identify such departments and mobilize faculty involvement in a program to bring them to quality standards.

A fifth function is to serve as a mediator or buffer among the board of trustees, general public, and the faculty.

The President as Agent of the Faculty Another view of the president's role is expressed by McGeorge Bundy. He begins with a disarmingly casual statement:

> The faculty needs a president because like any large group of people, it needs an agent and a spokesman for much of its business. To assert that the faculty has the final political authority is not to assert that its members wish to spend their lives at this job. They need to have more interest in it than they have shown in recent decades, and one good thing about a time of troubles in any modern university is that the conscience of the faculty is awakened. But day in and day out there is business to be done and decisions to be made which the faculty as a corporate body simply cannot make. It needs an agent, and that agent is the administration.[5]

Bundy goes on to make it clear, however, that that agent is no clerk but rather a zestful, politically skillful, innovative leader. He feels that a first-rate man can thrive in this role, unlike the president who sees himself as either "the unmoved mover" or the agent of his board, and who "is doomed, in this generation, to disappointment and

[3] "Statement on Government of Colleges and Universities," formulated by the American Association of University Professors, the American Council on Education, and the Association of Governing Boards of Universities and Colleges, *AAUP Bulletin,* no. 52, pp. 375–379, Winter, 1966. This is also readily available in reprint form from the American Association of University Professors. Page numbers in subsequent citations are taken from the reprint.

[4] This paraphrase of the AAHE Task Force report is found in the Grand Rapids address.

[5] McGeorge Bundy, "Faculty Power," The Atlantic, no. 222, pp. 44–45, September, 1968.

perhaps also to destruction."[6] The president who accepts his role as agent of the faculty, who shares its basic universe of discourse, and who knows and likes the art of politics, will find it a good life with plenty of opportunities for leadership and for "being where the action is." Bundy does not believe, however, that the president should merely be a nose-counter or a reflector of short-run consensus. He concludes:

> The academic administrator never serves the faculty more faithfully than when he looks past its present desires to its future judgment. Of course this is a hard and dangerous game, but I remain convinced that it is a necessary part of the good government of a great university. To put it on no higher level: a faculty that expects the president to act as its strong and perceptive agent on all the other tough problems had better let him in on some of the fun, too, if it wants a good man on the job. And the professors do want a good man on the job.[7]

The Role of the Faculty

The Joint Statement The Joint Statement has a section on the role of the faculty that is explicit and that gains special interest because of its joint formulation.

The AAHE Task Force Report The report examines the role of the faculty at some length.[8] It notes that although the faculty has a role of its own, it does not preclude the exercise of an effective influence in areas belonging in a proximate sense in the administrative domain. The faculty has a role that rests on the nature of the so-called "product" of institutions of higher education, the role of the faculty as members of a profession, and the nature of higher education in an industrialized society.

Presumably the product of higher education consists of the discovery and dissemination of knowledge, and this can scarcely take place without the primary and overwhelming responsibility of the faculty. The faculty is not alone in its interest in the production and dissemination of ideas. All parties are interested, but the faculty serves as the primary agent.

The role of the faculty also rests upon its own professional status and function. The faculty does differ in some respects from practitioners of law and medicine, particularly in that they are seldom self-employed. The faculty does have the responsibility for maintaining professional standards and levels of competence, which is largely exercised through control of curriculum and a voice in personnel decisions.

The role of the faculty also involves helping to determine not only the mission of the institution but the whole mission of higher education. In a pluralistic society there are many views of what higher education is to do. Two views, not necessarily incompatible but often in conflict, may serve as examples. There is a view that higher education is primarily an investment in human capital, that it is essentially a productive investment. In the grossest form, this view assures the public that if they go to college, they will earn x number of dollars more. In a more refined sense, this view takes the form of estimates that the return on human capital is probably about twice the return on physical capital. This is very difficult to prove, although it may well be correct. Another point of view is that whether higher education is a good investment in human capital or not, we are also trying to produce literate, civilized human beings.

Educational policy often reflects an uneasy mix of these views. Such a resolution of this kind of tension is generally found through immediate decisions on curriculum, personnel, research, etc., not through debate on the great questions of overall mission. When we are visited by accrediting teams we do produce self-studies, but most of the time we are not all that introspective. Yet, day after day we do try to determine our institutional mission.

A Growing Faculty Role McGeorge Bundy has some relevant things to say about the

[6] *Ibid.*, p. 45.

[7] *Ibid.*, p. 46.

[8] This paraphrase of the AAHE Task Force report is found in the Grand Rapids address.

faculty role in governance. He argues that it is the faculty that is the "necessary center of gravity of the politics of the university for teaching, for learning, for internal discipline, and for the educational quality and character of the institution as a whole."[9] The faculty's voice is decisive, he believes, in all fields save one—economics. This is a very big exception.

Bundy believes that the growth of faculty responsibility and power in academic matters has increased markedly in the post-World War II period. The faculty then had great strength and power in only a few places; now that strength is being generalized to the academic profession as a whole by the authority of the market place. Many places exist, of course, where the faculty has no such power, but Bundy believes that what is now still only best practice is spreading rapidly and will be true elsewhere in time.

All of this does not deny, Bundy concedes, that the faculty sometimes abdicates its authority and responsibility. Nor does it deny the powerful role of the president as an innovative, farsighted leader-agent, nor the role of the board, nor the role of students.

Requisite Attitudes

If the faculty role in academic governance is to be effectively performed, certain attitudes must be held or developed by the principal parties. For example, both the faculty and the administration must develop certain necessary supportive attitudes if the division of labor is to be realized and if the faculty role based upon that division of labor is to be played.[10]

This is not the place for an exhaustive catalog of such requisite attitudes, but a few will suffice. At the outset, it is evident that any division of labor and any set of prescribed roles in cooperative decision making rests upon at least minimal mutual trust and confidence. If this is lacking, prospects for joint decision making are not very promising. Mutual trust, like friendship and love in human social relations, can grow if nurtured and given a chance. Sometimes faculty members and administrators enter into collaborative patterns with evident residual mistrusts and reservations, yet they find that they really can work together.

Fashioning a system of joint decision making based upon shared authority and responsibility also requires a certain willingness to gamble. The scheme may not work, and countless man-hours may be wasted. Or, the scheme may work, but in unexpected ways and producing kinds of change not envisioned at the outset. Or, stereotypes that greatly simplify thinking about other people may be weakened by close contact. All these are risks. Yet, the alternatives to collaboration involve risks too.

Any system of joint cooperation involves the willingness of all parties to devote the necessary man-hours, focusing, and endless patience required to make it work. Many have noted that faculty members, absorbed in their teaching and research and often very mobile, are not always willing to spend the actual time required to make something like a faculty or academic senate work. It is equally true that consulting, cooperating, and collaborating is a very time-consuming and often exasperating task for active administrators who have to take a pragmatic, get-the-job-done attitude. It takes much more time to arrive at a decision by agreement, or after consultation, than it does to make it unilaterally. Yet, there is some reason to believe that a decision made the hard way may "stick" better than one made unilaterally and that it may even sometimes be a wiser one.

[9] Bundy, *op. cit.*, p. 42.

[10] For a rather critical study of faculty attitudes toward their role in governance, based upon the interviewing of a sample of faculty members at one large, midwestern university, see Archie R. Dykes, *Faculty Participation in Academic Decison Making*, American Council on Education, Washington, 1968. No comparable study of relevant administrative attitudes toward faculty participation has yet been made, to the author's knowledge.

THE CONCEPT OF SHARED AUTHORITY AND RESPONSIBILITY

Any division of labor is essentially cooperative in character. Each party does what he does best, but the total pattern is one of sharing in the process and the product. The optimal pattern of academic governance is not the creation of a series of watertight decision-making compartments, but the establishment of a pervasive rationale of shared authority and responsibility.

The Nature of the Academic Environment[11]

This rationale rests, ultimately, upon one's conception of the nature of the academic community and of the kinds of interpersonal relationships that should exist within it.

The Academic Community It is legitimate to ask, "How can anyone assert, in the face of so much contrary evidence, that there is or can be an academic community?" It is argued that all is fragmentation, diversity, and conflict. Manifestations are said to include student unrest, faculty frustration, and administrative attrition.

It is claimed that the various parties in academic life may be divided into warring camps: the faculty versus the administration versus the trustees versus the students. We are reminded by David Reisman and others that what he terms "the guilds" (what we might call the disciplines) may frequently look at the world somewhat differently than do institutions. Those whose primary allegiance is to the disciplines may on occasion find themselves differing from those whose loyalty is primarily to the institution.

It is further argued that, even in the professorial community, people really can't talk to each other. Economists and physiologists and philosophers and engineers are said to talk separate languages as esoteric to each other as to the general public, leading many of them, in the words of A. C. Pigou, to hide behind a little "potted calculus." It is further observed that one of the reasons you don't see your colleagues around the campus is that everybody is on a jet plane, on a Fulbright in Washington, or at a conference in northern Minnesota.

It takes a certain amount of temerity to reaffirm the conviction that there is an academic community, parallel perhaps to the community of a neighborhood, a social group, or even a family. In these cases, too, there are different roles, responsibilities, and points of view. In these groups, too, there are varying vantage points and bodies of experience and divergence in language and dialect. In these instances, too, there are tensions, competitions, rivalries, and frustrations.

But in academic life as well as in the family, the group, or the community, there are common goals and loyalties and even a common body of experience. This is especially true if one emphasizes not the differences and the divergences and the dichotomies within the academic community but rather thinks of this community in the context of (and in contrast with) the larger society. For all the vaunted administrative pragmatism and despite the many points of view of the faculty, there is a common concern with ideas per se, with increasing knowledge, and with involvement with young people. Almost everyone in academic life has a perennial green thumb, either toward ideas or toward young people or both. Assuredly academic people should still be able to talk to each other if they try. There is so much traffic now, going both ways between faculties and administration, that there are now a large number of persons who have lived in "both worlds." In any event, call it obvious, moot, or wrong, there does seem to be an academic community.

Collegial versus Adversary Relationships Within that community, should relations be collegial, on a partnership basis, resting on an assumed commonality of interest; or should they be essentially on an adversary basis, resting upon power and accenting

[11] The sections on the academic community and on collegial versus adversary relationship are essentially as found in the Grand Rapids address.

the divergent roles, positions, modes of thought and interests of the different parties? The AAHE Task Force report hinged essentially on its answers to this question. The task force was initially appointed because of growing realization in Washington and elsewhere that collective bargaining is beginning to spread very rapidly in higher education. This task force, composed equally of industrial relations professionals and liberal arts professors, was appointed to study the phenomenon.

As a matter of fact, with several of its members industrial relations professors, mediators, and arbitrators and one a professor of law, it was not at all certain that the task force would end up opting for a collegial basis. It finally did agree, however, that relations should be collegial rather than adversary. This was decided despite the fact that it recognized that in many situations, where no collegial alternative was available and where the only choice was between the adversary relationship or authoritarianism, that collective bargaining would probably come and that it might well be justified.

Why this choice of partnership and collegiality over an adversary relationship? The term "community" strongly implies elements of group action, of collaboration or partnership, among persons of equal human worth although not necessarily equal power, responsibility, or experience.

A second reason is because it is this element of the academic tradition that has drawn many, if not most, into academic life. Many are reluctant to abandon it unless they must, and they see as yet no firm evidence that they must. It is possible to use the word "colleague" with a sardonic twist, but most of the time academic people use it as a sort of a password or accolade, an indication of a whole complex of shared values, ideas, and responsibilities.

Probably the most important reason why the task force opted in this direction is because it believed that academic governance is better served, and a college or university is healthier, on the basis of collegiality than on the basis of an adversary relationship. If adversary dealings are assumed, the whole atmosphere of academic life is changed, introducing new rigidities and dichotomies and putting less emphasis upon individual worth and more emphasis on the we-they relationship.

Some Approaches to the Concept

The Joint Statement The statement pleads the case for joint effort and mutual involvement, and it is given special force by the constituencies represented in its formulation.

The AAHE Task Force Report This report opts decisively for the shared authority—shared responsibility concept of academic governance. The task force felt that the major parties to the governance process could only carry out their roles in a collaborative, sharing context.

The Duff-Berdahl Report This report, entitled *University Government in Canada,* is permeated with the assumption, now explicit, now implicit, that academic governance is a sharing process based on mutual trust. Nowhere in the report, however, is this more eloquently stated than in its concluding section:

> Constitutional reform may improve a system of university government to a point but, in the last analysis, its successful functioning will depend more on the good will and mutual trust of the participants. That is why we have aimed in this report at creating a spirit of governance which is more than the sum total of our separate recommendations. It is fortunate that the achievement of this spirit does not require the elimination of disagreement within a university; for a university is so inherently, and rightly, a battleground of clashing ideas that no structure of government—not even a reformed one—could produce a cozy consensus. Academics, a tribe to which both of us belong, are not the easiest of men. It is their professional duty to think and express their thoughts and they cannot be prevented from thinking outside the range of their own subject matter. They are certain therefore to disagree, not only with each other but

with those in authority, from their faculty dean upwards to the national government. But the academic often has one virtue corresponding to this defect (if it is a defect). His training should have taught him to disagree, even violently, without supposing that his opponent is a bad man. Disagreement within a university can therefore take place without loss of good will if channels of communication, consultation, and participation are open wide to receive the inevitable dissent and carry it to constructive outlets. It is healthier for disagreement to be expressed and argument to take place before decisions are made than for decisions at any level to be made "by authority" for fear lest previous debate would have a disruptive effect. Good will can be quickly restored after even a fierce argument. It is much more permanently eroded and destroyed by a system of authoritarian decisions.

This brings us to the topic of mutual trust. We visited some universities which, based on mutual trust between faculty and president, had a high degree of informal faculty participation in university government. We urge, in such cases, that the informal practices be made formal *now*, because if this action is postponed until a time of crisis, it will be doubly difficult to perform.

On the other hand, once such a reformed structure has been established, it is essential that the responsible officers be trusted and allowed to get on with the enormously complex task of university governance. One faculty association impressed us with its recognition of the need for "creative administration," a concept which implies the existence of sufficient discretion for the exercise of imaginative leadership. University administration, from department chairman up to president, may be only a means, a service to the actual ends of teaching and research; but few other tasks can match it in complexity, particularly in the upper reaches. A university president, for example, is subject to the vocal and insistent pressures of many constituencies: faculty, students, board, alumni, lay public, provincial government, and others. If outstanding men are to be attracted to these positions, the faculty must be willing to extend its trust. On the other hand, the administrators' readiness to share power will be a key factor in the building of that trust by the faculty. If the delicate balance is caught, the spirit of governance that we mentioned will have been achieved.[12]

ALTERNATIVE ORGANIZATIONAL FORMS

A host of organizational forms and devices have been devised in order to facilitate some manner of faculty participation in academic governance. Some of these are widely used, others rarely. Some of these assume shared authority and responsibility, some do not. Some assume a collegial relationship, others are predicated on an adversary stance.

The AAHE Task Force report has established a system of classification for these alternative organizational forms that may be useful.[13] The task force sets forth three major categories of organization for faculty representation: internal organizations, external associations, and bargaining agencies.

Internal Organizations

The internal organization, established as a recognized part of the official governance system, is found in some form at most colleges or universities. Most institutions have a number of such organizations, operating at many decision-making levels. Most studies of academic governance tend to assume, perhaps too readily, effective faculty representation at the departmental and school level, and therefore they focus on the all-college or all-university level.

At that level, a host of devices have been developed, generally involving some

[12] *University Government in Canada,* Report of a Commission sponsored by the Canadian Association of University Teachers and the Association of Universities and Colleges of Canada (Sir James Duff and Professor Robert O. Berdahl, Commissioners), University of Toronto Press, Toronto, 1966, pp. 86–87.

[13] *Faculty Participation in Academic Governance, op. cit.*, pp. 33–39.

combination of the committee system and an integrating or overarching organization often called the "faculty senate" or "academic senate." Interestingly enough, most of the major studies of the faculty role in academic governance have opted for such a senate. This is not to take the place of representational forms closer to the academic grass roots, but rather to provide effective involvement at the institutional level.

The AAHE Task Force Report This report bases its support of an academic senate as the preferred central organ for faculty participation in large part on the belief that it brings the major parties to governance together on a face-to-face basis early enough in the decision-making process for information sharing and reason to have effect.

If we assume an academic community, and if we assume a basically collegial relationship, are we thinking about a relationship exercised at arm's length or about one that is close and face-to-face?[14] This is a real issue, with genuine implications for academic governance. One's answer to this question would decide (with an institution of any size) whether one is to be content with a committee structure alone, and without some kind of unifying face-to-face body that would provide at least an element of federation. On the answer to this question would depend one's position as to whether it is sufficient to have faculty involvement in departments, schools, and colleges again without any overarching body. On the answer to this question also rests one's position about the makeup and nature of an academic senate as well as its size. The question is whether this body is expected to be responsible or to be largely ceremonial.

A further question about the senate is whether it is to be "pure" or "mixed." It has been pointed out to the AAHE Task Force that the fact that seven professors wrote this report may not be unrelated to its use of terms, because what is meant by "pure" is faculty alone. What is meant by "mixed" is that you also have representation on this body from administration and perhaps from the students. After all the semantics are done, the question remains: "Is it more effective to have the representatives of the administration and the faculty in some kind of continuing face-to-face relationships, or should they be organized along parallel lines, exchanging ambassadors from time to time and not operating as a single body?" The task force opted for as close-in and face-to-face a relationship as possible.

The task force also opted in favor of a so-called "mixed senate." Its conviction here is that in a mixed senate there is a continuing flow of information and there are deliberations involving all vantage points, hopefully before decisions are made (rather than ex post facto) and before adversary relationships can harden. The task force also felt that, although it may be messy to make decisions together, decisions will hold up better and require less repairing if they are arrived at jointly.

The task force does make some stipulations on this pure versus mixed senate matter. It feels that if the academic senate is merely an advisory body with no de facto policy-making power, then perhaps it would be better to have the undiluted voice of the faculty. Likewise, in those situations (found on some campuses) where the faculty feels a lack of identity or a sense of insecurity, perhaps separate organizations and a separate voice are necessary. This is something that can be worked out, depending on the situation, on any given campus.

The task force report also goes into considerable detail in describing the nature of an academic senate;[15] outlining the functions a senate can perform, the issues it can legitimately confront, supplementary procedures it can use, and techniques of decision making it can employ;[16] and suggesting the optimal structure or organizational requirements of a senate.[17] Reference to the task force report leaves many procedural and

[14] This discussion of the AAHE Task Force deliberations is essentially found in the Grand Rapids address.

[15] *Faculty Participation in Academic Governance, op. cit.*, pp. 34–35.

[16] *Ibid.*, pp. 57–61.

[17] *Ibid.*, pp. 39–43.

structural problems relating to a senate unresolved, but most of the issues are raised and some suggestions made.

The Duff-Berdahl Report This report makes an intensive examination of the academic senate, and it does so very perceptively. The contexts of academic governance in Canada and the United States may be somewhat different, but not so much as to prevent this from being a highly relevant analysis.

The report describes academic senates as the commissioners found them to exist. Although the authors later reveal great confidence in the capacity of reorganized and revitalized senates, they concluded, "We say with regret that all too few of the universities that we visited in Canada have really effective Senates."[18]

The report then makes recommendations as to the composition and structure of the senate, including size, method of election, eligibility for seats, and committee structure.[19] This section roughly parallels the treatment of these matters found in the AAHE Task Force report, but it goes into somewhat greater detail on some matters and differs slightly in its recommendations.

The report also goes into some detail in recommending a rather sweeping set of functions for the academic senate, acknowledging that some of these may not be needed at a smaller institution and that a senate may not be able to perform them all at the very outset. The report states:

> To avoid all doubt about the Senate's powers, we recommend that they should include specifically the power to make recommendations to the Board on any matter of interest to the university. This power would not in any way diminish the Board's ultimate control. Furthermore, a Senate would be wise to exercise this power with restraint, for a Senate which tries to do everything will end up doing nothing very well. Most definitely, the Senate must concentrate on the "commanding heights" of educational policy and leave the day-to-day administration of the university to the President and his associates.[20]

More specifically, the report indicates that the academic senate should have a meaningful although not always commanding voice in these areas: long-term academic planning; approval of short-term educational policy; review of departmental and faculty affairs, including curriculum, tenure, promotion, and appointments; graduate studies and research; the library; special services; and the university budget.[21] The report suggests with some care the degree of possible faculty involvement and even some of the forms it might take from one of these areas to the next.

External Associations

The AAHE Task Force report finds a useful complementary role for the so-called "external associations."

The report defines these as being outside the framework of formal campus government. "They do not have, nor do they seek, decision-making authority within the formal structure of the institution."[22] The report describes some of these external associations, national, regional, statewide, and local. Their historic preoccupation has been with broad professional standards and practices, academic freedom, salaries, and only in recent years and in very limited fashion with representation or negotiation. The task force report observes:

> . . . the emergence of external associations appears to reflect, in part, the deficiencies in existing internal arrangements for faculty representation. As organizations outside

[18] *University Government in Canada, op. cit.,* p. 9.
[19] *Ibid.,* pp. 28–32.
[20] *Ibid.,* p. 32.
[21] *Ibid.,* pp. 32–41.
[22] *Faculty Participation in Academic Governance, op. cit.,* p. 35.

of the formal structure of campus governance, they seek to bring some version of a faculty point of view to the attention of the administration by creating new lines of communication or sources of pressure.[23]

Even so, the task force believes that external associations will continue to play a valued and necessary role, even if effective academic senates are created.[24] Such associations can provide technical information concerning the organization and operation of a successful senate; they can establish communication channels among the senates at different institutions or in different systems; and they can provide valuable information regarding such substantive issues as salaries, fringe benefits, teaching loads, etc. These associations can also act as mediators or as broker in obtaining third-party intervention. They can also apply sanctions, such as censure.

Bargaining Agencies

One of the spectacular developments in academic governance during the past few years has been the emergence of the bargaining agency and collective bargaining. This aspect is treated in detail in the following chapter.

Supracampus Coordination and Control

It is possible that faculties and administrations will get so absorbed in decision making on the campus that joint participation may be won there and lost at the higher levels where the big decisions may increasingly come to be made.[25] This does not mean that we should cease to concentrate and to focus on the campus. Joint involvement begins at home. It would be difficult to imagine a democratic, sharing superstructure on the state, regional, and local levels resting upon authoritarianism on the campus. It is there that the faculty gets the experience, the sense of identity, and the confidence that it will need at higher and more elusive levels. And, always, many major academic decisions will remain on the campus level. The evidence seems increasingly to indicate that the national trend is for more and more major decision making at levels well above and beyond the local campus and the reach of the local faculty.

These developments relate especially to public institutions, yet private institutions are also involved. This is partly because many of these supracampus influences are not restricted to public education and partly because anything that causes public education to wax or wane or change direction is surely going to impinge upon the private sector as well. Although some may bask in the serene assurance that they will probably never be under a public higher board of education, for example, they can scarcely be disinterested in this possibility or its implications. We see, across the country, multicampus operations involving decisions made on a centralized as well as a campus basis. We see statewide systems of state colleges, junior colleges, and community colleges. We see the development of statewide "systems of systems" under higher boards of education, by whatever name. We see the development of master plans setting forth educational targets, allocating resources, dividing and allocating functions between and among institutions. We see state budgetary controls, often operating through line budgets. We also see interstate compacts, the activity of accrediting agencies, and the impact of federal granting and lending agencies.[26]

Yet, in most states there is little or nothing at the state or regional level comparable to faculty participation machinery on the campus level. I would suggest that one of the challenges to our ingenuity in the years ahead is not that of "rolling back the tides,"

[23] *Ibid.*, p. 38.
[24] *Ibid.*, pp. 61–63.
[25] This brief section is essentially found in the Grand Rapids address.
[26] For additional data and perspectives on this matter, see Paul E. Fenlon, "State-Wide Coordination and College and University Faculties," *AAUP Bulletin*, no. 53, pp. 408–411, Winter, 1967.

but of intelligently extending both the spirit and the machinery of joint involvement in developing new and as yet unknown machinery for getting an effective voice at all levels where it counts. Otherwise, we may find that all our parameters have been set before our machinery ever comes into play.

METHODS OF INFLUENCING DECISION MAKING

In addition to varying forms of organization for faculty representation, a wide variety of methods are employed by these organizations to press their case. These vary from reason and persuasion, the traditional devices of the "community of scholars," through neutral third-party intervention, to sanctions, including the strike.[27]

Information sharing, reason, and persuasion have long been the presumed primary means of influencing decisions. In institutions where shared authority and responsibility prevail and where effective face-to-face contacts are maintained, this device continues to be powerful. On some issues, at some times, on most campuses, this will still be effective.

Yet, the AAHE Task Force concedes, ". . . not all men are always reasonable, and even reasonable men have strong differences of opinion. The parties must then turn to other means to resolve disputes."[28]

One increasingly common method when an impasse threatens is to enlist the help of a neutral third party, through mediation or conciliation. Other forms of third-party intervention, common in the industrial sector, may come into increasing use in higher education. Incidentally, many of the new state laws regarding collective bargaining by public employees have made provision for some sort of neutral third-party intervention.

Rehmus suggests that even if faculties do not adopt collective salary bargaining, there is another feature of the "union model" that might fit higher education.[29] This is a regularized grievance procedure, culminating in neutral arbitration. He feels that this brings major elements of due process into the employment relationship and that this is needed even in higher education.

There are sanctions available to help enforce a point of view or position. They are many and diverse, but the AAHE Task Force has classified them as political, educational, and economic.[30] Political sanctions rely on the use of the political process and often involve lobbying of one sort or another. Educational sanctions may be defined as attempts to constrain the institution by challenging its professional standing or its administration. Threatened or actual censure or loss of accreditation are cases in point. Finally, economic sanctions are measures that aim at an institution's use of its resources, largely its human resources. The strike is the principal sanction at issue in much of the current debate about collective bargaining in higher education and about its supporting devices.[31]

[27] *Faculty Participation in Academic Governance, op. cit.*, pp. 47–50.

[28] *Ibid.*, p. 48.

[29] Charles M. Rehmus, "Collective Bargaining and the Market for Academic Personnel," paper delivered at meeting of Midwest Economics Association, Minneapolis, 1968, pp. 14–15.

[30] *Faculty Participation in Academic Governance, op. cit.*, pp. 48–55.

[31] For discussion of the strike as a sanction in higher education, see *ibid.*, pp. 51–55. For the AAUP position on strikes, see Special Joint Committee on Representation, Bargaining, and Sanctions, AAUP, "Faculty Participation in Strikes," *AAUP Bulletin*, no. 54, pp. 155–159, Summer, 1968. For a thoughtful personal statement by a member of that Special Joint Committee, see Sanford H. Kadish, "The Strike and the Professoriate," *AAUP Bulletin*, no. 54, pp. 160–168, Summer, 1968. For a statement of the current AAUP position on the whole collective bargaining issue, see "Policy on Representation of Economic Interests," *AAUP Bulletin*, no. 54, pp. 152–154, Summer, 1968.

STATEMENT ON GOVERNMENT OF COLLEGES AND UNIVERSITIES PREPARED BY THE AMERICAN ASSOCIATION OF UNIVERSITY PROFESSORS, THE AMERICAN COUNCIL ON EDUCATION, AND THE ASSOCIATION OF GOVERNING BOARDS OF UNIVERSITIES AND COLLEGES [32]

Editorial Note. The Statement which follows is directed to governing board members, administrators, faculty members, students and other persons in the belief that the colleges and universities of the United States have reached a stage calling for appropriately shared responsibility and cooperative action among the components of the academic institution. The Statement is intended to foster constructive joint thought and action, both within the institutional structure and in protection of its integrity against improper intrusions.

It is not intended that the Statement serve as a blueprint for government on a specific campus or as a manual for the regulation of controversy among the components of an academic institution, although it is to be hoped that the principles asserted will lead to the correction of existing weaknesses and assist in the establishment of sound structure and procedures. The Statement does not attempt to cover relations with those outside agencies which increasingly are controlling the resources and influencing the patterns of education in our institutions of higher learning; e.g., the United States Government, the state legislatures, state commissions, interstate associations or compacts and other interinstitutional arrangements. However it is hoped that the Statement will be helpful to these agencies in their consideration of educational matters.

Students are referred to in this Statement as an institutional component coordinate in importance with trustees, administrators and faculty. There is, however, no main section on students. The omission has two causes: (1) the changes now occurring in the status of American students have plainly outdistanced the analysis by the educational community, and an attempt to define the situation without thorough study might prove unfair to student interests,* and (2) students do not in fact presently have a significant voice in the government of colleges and universities; it would be unseemly to obscure, by superficial equality of length of statement, what may be a serious lag entitled to separate and full confrontation. The concern for student status felt by the organizations issuing this Statement is embodied in a note "On Student Status" intended to stimulate the educational community to turn its attention to an important need.

This Statement, in preparation since 1964, is jointly formulated by the American Association of University Professors, the American Council on Education, and the Association of Governing Boards of Universities and Colleges. On October 12, 1966, the Board of Directors of the ACE took action by which the Council "recognizes the Statement as a significant step forward in the clarification of the respective roles of governing boards, faculties, and administrations," and "commends it to the institutions which are members of the Council." On October 29, 1966, the Council of the AAUP approved the Statement, recommended approval by the Fifty-Third Annual Meeting in April, 1967, and recognized that "continuing joint effort is desirable, in view of the areas left open in the jointly formulated Statement, and the dynamic changes occurring in higher education." On November 18, 1966, the Executive Committee of the AGB took action by which that organization also "recognizes the Statement as a significant step forward in the clarification of the respective roles of governing boards, faculties and administrations," and "commends it to the governing boards which are members of the Association."

[32] This joint statement first appeared in the *AAUP Bulletin,* no. 52, pp. 375–379, Winter, 1966.

* Note: 1950, the formulation of the *Student Bill of Rights* by the United States National Student Association; 1956, the first appearance of *Academic Freedom and Civil Liberties of Students,* published by the American Civil Liberties Union; 1961, the decision in *Dixon v. Alabama State Board of Education,* currently the leading case on due process for students; 1965, the publication of a tentative *Statement on the Academic Freedom of Students,* by the American Association of University Professors.

I. INTRODUCTION

This Statement is a call to mutual understanding regarding the government of colleges and universities. Understanding, based on community of interest, and producing joint effort, is essential for at least three reasons. First, the academic institution, public or private, often has become less autonomous; buildings, research, and student tuition are supported by funds over which the college or university exercises a diminishing control. Legislative and executive governmental authority, at all levels, plays a part in the making of important decisions in academic policy. If these voices and forces are to be successfully heard and integrated, the academic institution must be in a position to meet them with its own generally unified view. Second, regard for the welfare of the institution remains important despite the mobility and interchange of scholars. Third, a college or university in which all the components are aware of their interdependence, of the usefulness of communication among themselves, and of the force of joint action will enjoy increased capacity to solve educational problems.

II. THE ACADEMIC INSTITUTION: JOINT EFFORT

A. Preliminary Considerations

The variety and complexity of the tasks performed by institutions of higher education produce an inescapable interdependence among governing board, administration, faculty, students and others. The relationship calls for adequate communication among these components, and full opportunity for appropriate joint planning and effort.

Joint effort in an academic institution will take a variety of forms appropriate to the kinds of situations encountered. In some instances, an initial exploration or recommendation will be made by the president with consideration by the faculty at a later stage; in other instances, a first and essentially definitive recommendation will be made by the faculty, subject to the endorsement of the president and the governing board. In still others, a substantive contribution can be made when student leaders are responsibly involved in the process. Although the variety of such approaches may be wide, at least two general conclusions regarding joint effort seem clearly warranted: (1) important areas of action involve at one time or another the initiating capacity and decision-making participation of all the institutional components, and (2) differences in the weight of each voice, from one point to the next, should be determined by reference to the responsibility of each component for the particular matter at hand, as developed hereinafter.

B. Determination of General Educational Policy

The general educational policy, i.e., the objectives of an institution and the nature, range, and pace of its efforts, is shaped by the institutional charter or by law, by tradition and historical development, by the present needs of the community of the institution, and by the professional aspirations and standards of those directly involved in its work. Every board will wish to go beyond its formal trustee obligation to conserve the accomplishment of the past and to engage seriously with the future; every faculty will seek to conduct an operation worthy of scholarly standards of learning; every administrative officer will strive to meet his charge and to attain the goals of the institution. The interests of all are coordinate and related, and unilateral effort can lead to confusion or conflict. Essential to a solution is a reasonably explicit statement on general educational policy. Operating responsibility and authority, and procedures for continuing review, should be clearly defined in official regulations.

When an educational goal has been established, it becomes the responsibility primarily of the faculty to determine appropriate curriculum and procedures of student instruction.

Special considerations may require particular accommodations: (1) a publicly supported institution may be regulated by statutory provisions, and (2) a church-controlled institution may be limited by its charter or bylaws. When such external requirements influence course content and manner of instruction or research, they impair the educational effectiveness of the institution.

Such matters as major changes in the size or composition of the student body and the relative emphasis to be given to the various elements of the educational and research program should involve participation of governing board, administration and faculty prior to final decision.

C. Internal Operations of the Institution

The framing and execution of long-range plans, one of the most important aspects of institutional responsibility, should be a central and continuing concern in the academic community.

Effective planning demands that the broadest possible exchange of information and opinion should be the rule for communication among the components of a college or university. The channels of communication should be established and maintained by joint endeavor. Distinction should be observed between the institutional system of communication and the system of responsibility for the making of decisions.

A second area calling for joint effort in internal operations is that of decisions regarding existing or prospective physical resources. The board, president and faculty should all seek agreement on basic decisions regarding buildings and other facilities to be used in the educational work of the institution.

A third area is budgeting. The allocation of resources among competing demands is central in the formal responsibility of the governing board, in the administrative authority of the president, and in the educational function of the faculty. Each component should therefore have a voice in the determination of short and long-range priorities, and each should receive appropriate analyses of past budgetary experience, reports on current budgets and expenditures, and short and long-range budgetary projections. The function of each component in budgetary matters should be understood by all; the allocation of authority will determine the flow of information and the scope of participation in decisions.

Joint effort of a most critical kind must be taken when an institution chooses a new president. The selection of a chief administrative officer should follow upon cooperative search by the governing board and the faculty, taking into consideration the opinions of others who are appropriately interested. The president should be equally qualified to serve both as the executive officer of the governing board and as the chief academic officer of the institution and the faculty. His dual role requires that he be able to interpret to board and faculty the educational views and concepts of institutional government of the other. He should have the confidence of the board and the faculty.

The selection of academic deans and other chief academic officers should be the responsibility of the president with the advice of and in consultation with the appropriate faculty.

Determinations of faculty status, normally based on the recommendations of the faculty groups involved, are discussed in Part V of this Statement; but it should here be noted that the building of a strong faculty requires careful joint effort in such actions as staff selection and promotion and the granting of tenure. Joint action should also govern dismissals; the applicable principles and procedures in these matters are well established.*

D. External Relations of the Institution

Anyone—a member of the governing board, the president or other member of the administration, a member of the faculty, or a member of the student body or the alumni—affects the institution when he speaks of it in public. An individual who speaks unofficially should so indicate. An official spokesman for the institution, the board, the administration, the faculty, or the student body should be guided by established policy.

It should be noted that only the board speaks legally for the whole institution, although it may delegate responsibility to an agent.

The right of a board member, an administrative officer, a faculty member, or a student to speak on general educational questions or about the administration and operations of his own institution is a part of his right as a citizen and should not be abridged by the

* See the 1940 *Statement of Principles on Academic Freedom and Tenure* and the 1958 *Statement on Procedural Standards in Faculty Dismissal Proceedings.* These statements have been jointly approved or adopted by the Association of American Colleges and the American Association of University Professors; the 1940 Statement has been endorsed by numerous learned and scientific societies and educational associations.

institution.* There exist, of course, legal bounds relating to defamation of character, and there are questions of propriety.

III. THE ACADEMIC INSTITUTION: THE GOVERNING BOARD

The governing board has a special obligation to assure that the history of the college or university shall serve as a prelude and inspiration to the future. The board helps relate the institution to its chief community: e.g., the community college to serve the educational needs of a defined population area or group, the church-controlled college to be cognizant of the announced position of its denomination, and the comprehensive university to discharge the many duties and to accept the appropriate new challenges which are its concern at the several levels of higher education.

The governing board of an institution of higher education in the United States operates, with few exceptions, as the final institutional authority. Private institutions are established by charters; public institutions are established by constitutional or statutory provisions. In private institutions the board is frequently self-perpetuating; in public colleges and universities the present membership of a board may be asked to suggest candidates for appointment. As a whole and individually when the governing board confronts the problem of succession, serious attention should be given to obtaining properly qualified persons. Where public law calls for election of governing board members, means should be found to insure the nomination of fully suited persons, and the electorate should be informed of the relevant criteria for board membership.

Since the membership of the board may embrace both individual and collective competence of recognized weight, its advice or help may be sought through established channels by other components of the academic community. The governing board of an institution of higher education, while maintaining a general overview, entrusts the conduct of administration to the administrative officers, the president and the deans, and the conduct of teaching and research to the faculty. The board should undertake appropriate self-limitation.

One of the governing board's important tasks is to ensure the publication of codified statements that define the over-all policies and procedures of the institution under its jurisdiction.

The board plays a central role in relating the likely needs of the future to predictable resources; it has the responsibility for husbanding the endowment; it is responsible for obtaining needed capital and operating funds; and in the broadest sense of the term it should pay attention to personnel policy. In order to fulfill these duties, the board should be aided by, and may insist upon, the development of long-range planning by the administration and faculty.

When ignorance or ill-will threatens the institution or any part of it, the governing board must be available for support. In grave crises it will be expected to serve as a champion. Although the action to be taken by it will usually be on behalf of the president, the faculty, or the student body, the board should make clear that the protection it offers to an individual or a group is, in fact, a fundamental defense of the vested interests of society in the educational institution.

IV. THE ACADEMIC INSTITUTION: THE PRESIDENT

The president, as the chief executive officer of an institution of higher education, is measured largely by his capacity for institutional leadership. He shares responsibility for the definition and attainment of goals, for administrative action, and for operating the communications system which links the components of the academic community.

* With respect to faculty members, the 1940 *Statement of Principles on Academic Freedom and Tenure* reads: "The college or university teacher is a citizen, a member of a learned profession, and an officer of an educational institution. When he speaks or writes as a citizen, he should be free from institutional censorship or discipline, but his special position in the community imposes special obligations. As a man of learning and an educational officer, he should remember that the public may judge his profession and his institution by his utterances. Hence he should at all times be accurate, should exercise appropriate restraint, should show respect for the opinion of others, and should make every effort to indicate that he is not an institutional spokesman."

He represents his institution to its many publics. His leadership role is supported by delegated authority from the board and faculty.

As the chief planning officer of an institution, the president has a special obligation to innovate and initiate. The degree to which a president can envision new horizons for his institution, and can persuade others to see them and to work toward them, will often constitute the chief measure of his administration.

The president must at times, with or without support, infuse new life into a department; relatedly, he may at times be required, working within the concept of tenure, to solve problems of obsolescence. The president will necessarily utilize the judgments of the faculty, but in the interest of academic standards he may also seek outside evaluations by scholars of acknowledged competence.

It is the duty of the president to see to it that the standards and procedures in operational use within the college or university conform to the policy established by the governing board and to the standards of sound academic practice. It is also incumbent on the president to insure that faculty views, including dissenting views, are presented to the board in those areas and on those issues where responsibilities are shared. Similarly the faculty should be informed of the views of the board and the administration on like issues.

The president is largely responsible for the maintenance of existing institutional resources and the creation of new resources; he has ultimate managerial responsibility for a large area of nonacademic activities, he is responsible for public understanding, and by the nature of his office is the chief spokesman of his institution. In these and other areas his work is to plan, to organize, to direct, and to represent. The presidential function should receive the general support of board and faculty.

V. THE ACADEMIC INSTITUTION: THE FACULTY

The faculty has primary responsibility for such fundamental areas as curriculum, subject matter and methods of instruction, research, faculty status, and those aspects of student life which relate to the educational process. On these matters the power of review or final decision lodged in the governing board or delegated by it to the president should be exercised adversely only in exceptional circumstances, and for reasons communicated to the faculty. It is desirable that the faculty should, following such communication, have opportunity for further consideration and further transmittal of its views to the president or board. Budgets, manpower limitations, the time element and the policies of other groups, bodies and agencies having jurisdiction over the institution may set limits to realization of faculty advice.

The faculty sets the requirements for the degrees offered in course, determines when the requirements have been met, and authorizes the president and board to grant the degrees thus achieved.

Faculty status and related matters are primarily a faculty responsibility; this area includes appointments, reappointments, decisions not to reappoint, promotions, the granting of tenure, and dismissal. The primary responsibility of the faculty for such matters is based upon the fact that its judgment is central to general educational policy. Furthermore, scholars in a particular field or activity have the chief competence for judging the work of their colleagues; in such competence it is implicit that responsibility exists for both adverse and favorable judgments. Likewise there is the more general competence of experienced faculty personnel committees having a broader charge. Determinations in these matters should first be by faculty action through established procedures, reviewed by the chief academic officers with the concurrence of the board. The governing board and president should, on questions of faculty status, as in other matters where the faculty has primary responsibility, concur with the faculty judgment except in rare instances and for compelling reasons which should be stated in detail.

The faculty should actively participate in the determination of policies and procedures governing salary increases.

The chairman or head of a department, who serves as the chief representative of his department within an institution, should be selected either by departmental election or by appointment following consultation with members of the department and of related departments; appointments should normally be in conformity with department members' judgment. The chairman or department head should not have tenure in his office; his tenure as a faculty member is a matter of separate right. He should serve for a stated term but without prejudice to re-election or to reappointment by procedures which involve appropriate faculty consultation. Board, administration, and faculty should all bear in mind that the department chairman has a special obligation to build a department strong in scholarship and teaching capacity.

Agencies for faculty participation in the government of the college or university should be established at each level where faculty responsibility is present. An agency should exist for the presentation of the views of the whole faculty. The structure and procedures for faculty participation should be designed, approved and established by joint action of the components of the institution. Faculty representatives should be selected by the faculty according to procedures determined by the faculty.

The agencies may consist of meetings of all faculty members of a department, school, college, division or university system, or may take the form of faculty-elected executive committees in departments and schools and a faculty-elected senate or council for larger divisions or the institution as a whole.

Among the means of communication among the faculty, administration, and governing board now in use are: (1) circulation of memoranda and reports by board committees, the administration, and faculty committees, (2) joint *ad hoc* committees, (3) standing liaison committees, (4) membership of faculty members on administrative bodies, and (5) membership of faculty members on governing boards. Whatever the channels of communication, they should be clearly understood and observed.

ON STUDENT STATUS

When students in American colleges and universities desire to participate responsibly in the government of the institution they attend, their wish should be recognized as a claim to opportunity both for educational experience and for involvement in the affairs of their college or university. Ways should be found to permit significant student participation within the limits of attainable effectiveness. The obstacles to such participation are large and should not be minimized: inexperience, untested capacity, a transitory status which means that present action does not carry with it subsequent responsibility, and the inescapable fact that the other components of the institution are in a position of judgment over the students. It is important to recognize that student needs are strongly related to educational experience, both formal and informal. Students expect, and have a right to expect, that the educational process will be structured, that they will be stimulated by it to become independent adults, and that they will have effectively transmitted to them the cultural heritage of the larger society. If institutional support is to have its fullest possible meaning it should incorporate the strength, freshness of view and idealism of the student body.

The respect of students for their college or university can be enhanced if they are given at least these opportunities: (1) to be listened to in the classroom without fear of institutional reprisal for the substance of their views, (2) freedom to discuss questions of institutional policy and operation, (3) the right to academic due process when charged with serious violations of institutional regulations, and (4) the same right to hear speakers of their own choice as is enjoyed by other components of the institution.

OTHER SUGGESTED READINGS*

Bundy, McGeorge: "Faculty Power," *The Atlantic*, no. 222, pp. 41–47, September, 1968.

Dykes, Archie R.: *Faculty Participation in Academic Decision Making*, American Council on Education, Washington, 1968.

Faculty Participation in Academic Governance, Report of the AAHE Task Force on Faculty Representation and Academic Negotiations, American Association for Higher Education, Washington, 1967.

Gross, Edward, and Paul V. Grambsch: *University Goals and Academic Power*, American Council on Education, 1968.

* Note: These readings are restricted to reports, studies, or articles dealing broadly with faculty participation in academic governance. Specialized citations are also found in footnotes within the chapter.

Mouat, Lucia: "Faculty Power—1968: Down from the Ivory Tower," *The Christian Science Monitor,* August 20, 1968.

"Policy on Representation of Economic Issues," *AAUP Bulletin,* no. 54, pp. 152–154, Summer, 1968.

Rehmus, Charles M.: "Collective Bargaining and the Market for Academic Personnel," paper delivered at meeting of the Midwest Economics Association, Minneapolis, 1968.

University Government in Canada, Report of a Commission sponsored by the Canadian Association of University Teachers and the Association of Universities and Colleges of Canada, (Sir James Duff and Professor Robert O. Berdahl, Commissioners), University of Toronto Press, Toronto, 1966.

Chapter **8**

Collective Negotiations

JOHN C. LIVINGSTON

Professor of Government, Sacramento State College, Sacramento, California

FORMS OF COLLECTIVE NEGOTIATION

Collective negotiation encompasses a range of relationships in which representatives of faculty and administration employ the techniques of bargaining in an effort to resolve disagreements. The faculty may have only a recognized right to express and discuss their grievances; they may have the additional right to be consulted before policy decisions are made; or they may have the right to participate in "good faith" bargaining leading to a written agreement binding on both parties. All these varieties of negotiation imply an adversary relationship, decision by compromise, and the potential use of sanctions by each party to coerce the other into the granting of concessions.

Collective negotiations are a recent phenomenon on college campuses. Up to now the process of bargaining has seemed to be incompatible with the values of academic life and with traditional views of the campus as a community of scholars; but times are changing.

Faculty are exhibiting an increasing readiness to support collective action to press their claims against administrators, governing boards, etc. There is a willingness to accept a conflict-oriented model and to approve the use of coercion and threats of coercion in pressing for certain interests and objectives through an exclusive bargaining relationship. There is, however, a serious danger of oversimplification in the interpretation of these changes. A recognition of common goals and values, reliance on information sharing, and appeals to reason may and do occur even within the framework of a bargaining relationship, just as bargaining and compromise occur in what are ostensibly patterns of shared, collegial authority. Even "unionism" is not a single, simple, all-or-nothing package. Adversary relations and the threat of sanctions may coexist in subtle company with collaborative relationships, even as they do in traditional patterns of campus government.

While the form and structure of campus government will help to determine whether an adversary or a collegial climate is dominant, the range of possible forms of collective negotiation is broad. A faculty may be represented in negotiations by an academic senate, an internal voluntary association, an external professional organization (such as a local chapter of the American Association of University Professors or an affiliate of the National Education Association), an American Federation of Teachers local affiliated with the AFL-CIO, or a negotiating council made up on a proportional basis of representatives of several faculty organizations. Different faculty organizations may negotiate on different issues on the same campus or in the same system, or faculty may press for the recognition of an exclusive bargaining agent. An exclusive agent may seek to confine its negotiations to economic issues, leaving educational issues to the jurisdiction of an academic senate. Negotiation may or may not lead to a written and binding agreement.

While all collective negotiation implies the possible use of the entire range of sanctions, including the strike, they may or may not be regarded as legitimate. The willingness to invoke a particular sanction will depend upon the gravity of the situation. It is even conceivable, particularly in public systems, that sanctions may be employed in the absence of negotiation or as a substitute for negotiation. Thus one faculty organization in a large state system proposes to impose sanctions in order to pressure state legislative and executive officials into providing fiscal support for specific faculty goals and policies. In the absence of formal negotiation such sanctions would be withdrawn when and if governmental authorities made an adequate response.

These examples suggest the possible range of practices that might be accommodated within a framework of collective negotiation. They warn against any easy conclusion that the choice is between conventional modes of organizing campus government and industrial-style collective bargaining. While the recent mood of increasing faculty militancy seems to point in the general direction of the latter, the situation on most campuses and even the attitudes of many of the most militant faculty remain open-ended and tentative.

Faculty militancy and the movement toward academic unionism have had their major impact on three types of academic situations: junior and community colleges; emerging institutions undergoing a transition from teachers' colleges to full four-year institutions, especially where these are parts of a large state system; and private institutions confronting crises involving academic freedom and tenure.[1] Academic unionism, of

[1]AAHE Task Force on Faculty Representation and Academic Negotiations, *Faculty Participation in Academic Governance*, American Association for Higher Education, Washington, 1967, pp. 10–11.

course, is not confined to these situations. Its strength varies widely among campuses which appear to be similarly situated and may change rapidly over time on a single campus. On some campuses union locals have grown from a small minority to a majority or a near majority in a single year, often in response to a single dramatic issue.

FACTORS WHICH CONTRIBUTE TO FACULTY MILITANCY

A History of Administrative Authoritarianism The immediate objective of faculty militancy is perhaps most likely to be an inherited pattern of authoritarian or paternalistic administration which has proved resistant to traditional methods of reform. On junior college campuses, where union successes have been greatest, pressures have often been a response to a history of authoritarian administrative practices, to rigid administrative control of curriculum and personnel policies, and to the persistent application of an employer-employee relationship in the development of rules governing professional conduct (a common example is a requirement that faculty spend a fixed number of hours on campus or in their offices). Especially in junior colleges that are shifting from terminal and vocational programs to membership in larger systems of higher education, faculty may see collective bargaining as a means to the traditional status and rights of college professors. The same motivation may operate in four-year institutions.

The Upward Drift of Decision Making Recent trends in the development of statewide systems of coordination in public higher education have had the effect of shifting the locus of decision making upward to higher control or coordinating agencies. As the American Association for Higher Education Task Force put it, "If the faculty members at junior colleges have been aroused by the demand for powers that they never had, the faculty members at many of the four-year institutions have become restive over the loss of control that they once thought was theirs."[2]

Breakdown of the Academic Community The internal collapse of the campus as a community of purpose has been widely recognized in recent years and its causes have been examined. Among the factors that have been described as contributing to this result, and to a consequent sense of alienation and powerlessness on the part of the faculty, are the rise of an impersonal bureaucratic structure within the institution; the limitation of effective, functional faculty organization to the departmental level; increasing specialization and consequent splintering of the curriculum; overemphasis on specialized research to the detriment of teaching; the increasing importance of the disciplines and the decreasing role of the campus as a focus of effort and loyalty; and a tendency for traditional forms of college government to function as a process of accommodating conflicting interests rather than as a means of deliberating on and defining institutional goals.

A Favorable Market and "Rising Expectations" Market conditions in the profession in recent years have provided a favorable climate for pressing the economic demands of faculty. Professional incomes have risen, although the increases have been spotty and relative only to the former status of faculty and not to the rising incomes of other professions. If the history of industrial relations in the private sector furnishes a guide, these are the conditions of increased economic militancy.

One response to these favorable market conditions has been increased mobility. Faculty, however, do not benefit equally from this situation; nor have all those whose mobility is potentially enhanced chosen to exercise this personal leverage. Among those who have benefited least are young faculty who have not yet established their professional credentials and older faculty who have not published or whose achieve-

[2] *Ibid.*, p. 12.

ments lie in teaching. But it would be a mistake to assume that faculty militancy draws its main strength from the less mobile and therefore, putatively, the less able faculty. The AAHE Task Force investigation suggested that the new faculty militancy generally and its thrust in the direction of collective bargaining in particular tend to attract many newer and younger faculty members "with exemplary academic credentials."[3] This conclusion, if it is valid, undercuts the suggestion that unionism is partly or mainly a product of a labor market situation which has forced the employment of inadequately or marginally prepared persons who, in virtue of their inadequate professional preparation, lack commitment to traditional professional values. It suggests that where conditions are otherwise conducive to the growth of collective bargaining it is a mistake to assume that the portion of the faculty whose scholarly and professional qualifications are most distinguished can be expected to put the prestige of their attainments on the scale against collective bargaining or unionism.

The existence of favorable market conditions in recent years has no doubt raised the level of personal economic expectations of members of the profession. Nevertheless, the AAHE Task Force concluded that personal "economic considerations are not of primary importance among the factors giving rise to faculty discontent."[4] This fact has had important implications for academic unions. Potential members of AFT may be unwilling to purchase the substantial economic advantages of affiliation with the AFL-CIO at the price of accepting or supporting national labor's political stance on Vietnam and other public issues. The tensions may even produce a rift between national AFT leadership and local members and leaders as they did in California in 1967 when the national organizer called off the organizing campaign in the state colleges with the complaint that local and statewide efforts centered too much around "social issues such as racial relations and Vietnam, and not enough around 'bread and butter' questions of teacher wages and conditions."[5]

Changes in Political Attitudes In some measure, increased faculty militancy and an increased tendency to see academic government as essentially a power conflict probably reflect broader changes in the American political culture. The politics of "confrontation," the development of group strategies of political coercion by minorities of all sorts, the tendency of political parties to serve as mere brokers in the development of coalitions of the organized and powerful groups, the prevalence of a political "realism" and a philosophical positivism that find no meaning in the concept of a "public interest"—all these testify to a growing acceptance of the concept of democratic process as a pluralistic group struggle held together by countervailing power. Group strategies and tactics that would be regarded as inimical to the effort to define and act on a public or common interest become legitimate when viewed from this perspective. Much of the recent militancy of faculty appears to assume this view of the political process.

STRATEGIES OF FACULTY ORGANIZATIONS

Not surprisingly, in this varied and rapidly changing scene, the positions of the national faculty organizations are increasingly difficult to identify or describe. Moreover, the diversity of local situations, the imperatives of organizational competition, and the necessity of adapting old attitudes to new situations inevitably mean that there will be a wide diversity among the local units of the national organizations.

Nationally, the AAUP has a traditional position which envisions a campus as a community with common interests and goals which override conflicting interests and

[3] *Ibid.*, p. 11.

[4] *Ibid.*, p. 12.

[5] Harry Bernstein, "Teachers' Union Drive Folds at State Colleges," *Los Angeles Times*, December 29, 1967.

permit the development of patterns of shared, collegial authority. Older and prestigious institutions with strong academic senates furnish the traditional model, the main outlines of which are summed up in the joint AAUP, ACE, AGB, *Statement on the Government of Colleges and Universities.*[6] The national leadership and staff have resisted the softening of the organization's opposition to exclusive collective bargaining, even where AAUP local chapters are under AFT pressure and in the face of minority pressures within the organization to authorize collective bargaining or to merge with the AFT.[7] The Association's 1966 statement of policy on the "Representation of Economic Interests" reaffirmed its preference "that all faculty members participate in making decisions and protecting their economic interests through structures of self-government within the institution, with the faculty participating either directly or through faculty-elected councils or senates." The statement opposed the principle of exclusive representation and recommended as an alternative the passage of state legislation which would require public institutions to establish "adequate internal structures of faculty participation in the government of the institution."[8] An interim policy provided that, under certain extraordinary conditions, approval might be granted to a chapter to seek to become the exclusive representative of the faculty and laid down the policies that should guide a chapter functioning in that capacity, including the prohibition of the use of strikes or work stoppages. Further development of AAUP policy on collective negotiations in 1968 reaffirmed the general outlines of this position but with some modifications and amplifications. While continuing to oppose exclusive representation, the association responded to the trend toward statutory authorization of collective bargaining in public institutions by expressing its preference for permissive legislation which would authorize a system of joint representation and which would make faculty-elected councils or senates eligible to serve as bargaining representatives. Provision for the possibility of AAUP chapters to function as bargaining representative where other preferred alternatives are unavailable was reaffirmed, and the policy against strikes was repeated but with exceptions in extraordinary circumstances. A provisional statement on the use of the strike describes it as "inappropriate as a mechanism for the resolution of most conflicts within higher education." The statement then adds:

> But it does not follow from these considerations of self-restraint that professors should be under any legal disability to withhold their services, except when such restrictions are imposed equally on other citizens. Furthermore, situations may arise affecting a college or university which so flagrantly violate academic freedom (of students as well as faculty) or principles of academic government, and which are so resistant to rational methods of discussion, persuasion, and conciliation, that faculty members may feel impelled to express their condemnation by withholding their services, either individually or in concert with others. It should be assumed that faculty members will exercise their right to strike only if they believe that another component of the institution (or a controlling agency of government, such as a legislature or governor) is inflexibly bent on a course which undermines an essential element of the educational process.

Finally, the statement adds the provision that "participation in a strike does not by itself constitute grounds for dismissal or for other sanctions against faculty members."[9]

[6] *AAUP Bulletin,* Winter, 1966, pp. 375–379.

[7] See "Representation of Economic Interests," *AAUP Bulletin,* pp. 229–234, Summer, 1966; "Policy on Representation of Economic Interests," *AAUP Bulletin,* Summer, 1968; Israel Kugler, "The AAUP at the Crossroads," *Changing Education,* pp. 34–43, Spring, 1966; Peggy Heim, "Growing Tensions in Academic Administration," *North Central Association Quarterly,* pp. 244–251, Winter, 1968.

[8] *Op. cit.,* p. 229.

[9] "Statement on Faculty Participation in Strikes," *AAUP Bulletin,* p. 157, Summer, 1968.

Local AAUP chapters adopt positions which display a wide range of activity and of degrees of militancy. Beyond the organization's traditional concern with questions of academic freedom and tenure, these chapters play a vigorous role in other areas of local policy making, making formal proposals to and entering into negotiations with administration on economic and educational issues.

State and local affiliates of the NEA display, in general, a preference for "professional negotiation" as opposed to "collective bargaining." This distinction does not rule out the desirability of written agreements, but it does tend to oppose the development of exclusive bargaining arrangements, primary reliance on economic sanctions, and the use of the strike weapon. NEA affiliates have been the major supporters of negotiating teams based on proportional representation of the several faculty organizations. They have not uniformly opposed all economic sanctions or even in dire circumstances the strike, although where such ultimate weapons are admitted there is a tendency to prefer such strike substitutes, used in the public schools, as mass resignations and "professional holidays" or "meetings." Generally, however, faculty organizations affiliated with the NEA have urged primary reliance on political sanctions, made effective through the power of the state education lobbies, in the belief that legislative action will be the prime determinant of faculty salaries and benefits, especially in public institutions. It is, of course, an open question whether NEA affiliates, under pressure from increasing faculty militancy and from the AFT, will maintain an effective distinction between professional negotiation and collective bargaining. If the public school experience is a reliable precedent, this does not appear likely.

Nationally, the AFT seems not yet to have developed firm policies on the form and details of bargaining relationships in higher education. Locals consequently have had considerable autonomy on policy questions. Moreover, as with other organizations, the positions of the parent body, even where these are clear, are not a sure guide to the attitudes and behavior of local groups. The situation is made even more obscure by the fact that it is often difficult to distinguish a group's tactics from its long-run objectives. The general posture of the AFT, however, is clear. In the language of a local AFT brochure, "it is necessary, we believe, to build upon the strength of organized labor while retaining our professional identity and functional autonomy." This position assumes an adversary relationship and implies acceptance of the general model of industrial bargaining, including the principle of exclusive representation and the use of the strike as an ultimate weapon. These commitments do not imply a literal adherence to all the practices of industrial bargaining, even assuming it to be possible to identify those practices (there is much greater diversity in industrial practice than is ordinarily recognized by those not intimately familiar with it). Within the general framework of the trade union tradition, adaptations to the academic situation generally and to the unique circumstances of particular campuses are both possible and likely. AFT locals, for example, do not always define the adversary relationship as pitting faculty against administration. Especially in public systems AFT locals may take the position that, while agreement on most economic matters among the internal groups can be achieved on a collaborative rather than an adversary basis, similar arrangements are not possible in dealing with such external authority as a super board, the executive, and the legislature. In this view collective bargaining is a necessary device for formalizing a power relationship with external agencies.

In all faculty organizations various stages of organizational growth may dictate tactical departures from long-run goals, and local situations may call forth responses which differ from the group's national posture. Thus it is not unusual for a union local to reflect attitudes and to function in ways that make it distinguishable from other faculty organizations only in its greater militancy. The AAHE Task Force found that, while some AFT locals were characterized by a commitment to traditional trade union objectives and tactics, "most of the local affiliates encountered were similar in outlook and function to the independent faculty organizations or the professional associations."[10] In these circumstances a local tends to operate as a pressure group, dramatizing issues (both economic and professional), serving as a watchdog over an academic senate, and in some cases playing down long-range union goals. Its members very often retain their memberships in other associations and tend to see a militant union as a necessary complement to and source of leverage on the more conservatively led organizations, or as a necessary part of a "mix" of approaches and techniques necessary to effect changes in particularly recalcitrant conditions.

Union locals having these characteristics tend to flourish in situations where neither internal agencies of faculty government nor other professional associations respond adequately to an issue over which there is intense faculty concern and which is capable of being effectively dramatized. The relatively high degree of autonomy of local AFT chapters makes possible the effective exploitation of such situations. As a result, on some campuses AFT membership does not invariably reflect a commitment to the principles and tactics of industrial unionism (the strike, for example) or even, for some members, the principle of exclusive bargaining. It follows, if these observations are accurate, that it would be a mistake to treat every union success as evidence of firm faculty commitment to trade unionism on the industrial model or to regard a movement toward collective bargaining as irreversible.

A successful organizing drive by the AFT may hinge almost entirely on a particular, dramatic, noneconomic issue. Even if it falls short of majority support, it is likely to produce increased militancy as a response in other organizations. It is most likely to be successful where there is no senate, where the senate is ineffective and administration dominated, and when other faculty organizations have failed to develop aggressive and militant leadership.

Where AFT membership and support reaches a point that seems to promise success in a representation election, and where no statutory provisions or ad hoc agreements provide regularized procedures for requesting and conducting an election, AFT locals may seek to have informal faculty polls conducted or to hold "quasi-legal" elections conducted under the supervision of some neutral or outside agency. Other organizations may feel compelled to enter the contest. The results may then be used to pressure the administration for recognition; to request board sponsorship of a subsequent election; or, where statutes preclude exclusive bargaining, to pressure the board and the legislature to move for permissive legislation.

NEGOTIATING OBJECTIVES OF FACULTY ORGANIZATIONS

The change in attitudes toward permissible and legitimate techniques for achieving faculty goals described in the preceding section has been accompanied by changing attitudes toward some traditional professional practices. Particularly with regard to the structure of academic personnel administration (tenure, academic ranks, salary structure, and promotion policy), there is evidence of faculty dissatisfaction. In addition to salary levels, teaching load, and related matters, faculty concern and unrest focus on the traditional salary differential between the lower and the higher ranks and the principles that historically have determined the movement of individual faculty within and between ranks. Faculty disagreement on these issues is often reflected in opposing positions and goals of different faculty organizations.

On the question of tenure the AFT has argued for a reduction in the length of the probationary period—a three-year maximum in contrast to the AAUP's advocacy of a seven-year maximum is a common position. The AFT would accompany the reduced tenure period with greater protection for the nontenured, including the requirement of

[10] AAHE Task Force, *op. cit.*, p. 37.

written reasons for nonreappointment; AAUP policy leaves these matters to the individual institutions, insisting on more general standards of academic due process but granting the right of institutions to decline to reappoint without furnishing reasons.

The structure of academic salaries, especially the differential between lower and higher ranks, has emerged in recent years as a source of faculty unrest. In rapidly growing institutions there has often been a rapid rise in salaries in lower ranks under pressure to improve the institution's recruiting position; in those situations discontent among senior faculty, especially the less mobile, may occur. This situation, moreover, may appear to some faculty as undesirable on grounds that the long-run objective of increasing the general level of faculty salaries is most likely to be promoted by efforts to push up the maximum salaries in the higher ranks in the expectation that increases there will exert a pull on all salaries. This has tended to be the position of the AAUP. The AFT, on the other hand, responding to the rising expectations of the lower ranks, has tended to argue for further narrowing of the spread between the ranks. The issue itself, it should be noted, is not strictly or entirely a matter of self-interest; it involves faculty self-images, and on many campuses senior faculty may count themselves in the ranks of those seeking to narrow traditional differentials.

The movement of individual faculty within and between ranks is another focus of faculty interest and discontent. The issue here goes beyond the question of faculty participation in the making of individual decisions. Even where the determination of individual rank and salary has become a faculty prerogative, administered through faculty committees, faculty discontent may not be allayed. At issue here is not simply the anxiety, frustration, and resentment generated by any process of invidious comparison of individual ability, merit, or worth, but an apparently growing mood among faculty that the making of such comparisons does not effectively serve educational purposes. Here again, the positions of the AAUP and the AFT reflect rival faculty appraisals of this problem. The AAUP seems committed to the desirability of the process of merit evaluation; its efforts are directed to ensuring that criteria are established with faculty consultation in each institution and that individual decisions reflect peer evaluation and review. The AFT is inclined to challenge the process itself by working toward formalized salary structures, automatic annual seniority increments within ranks or, in some cases, the separation of rank from salary determinations. The AFT opposition to merit evaluation, however, is not rigid. It may, for example, be accommodated in some situations to a two-track system after the model of theatrical and television unions. Moreover, it would be a mistake to assume that the AFT position on this issue is mainly or merely an application of the seniority principle so firmly entrenched in collective bargaining practices in the private sector. For their part, many unionists reverse this argument and see the system of academic rewards and punishments itself as an antiprofessional application of the psychology of competitive private enterprise.

On questions of salary levels and working conditions, the goals and demands of AFT locals tend to be more militant than those of other faculty organizations. Nine and six hours are commonly regarded as maximum undergraduate and graduate teaching loads, respectively, while the most recent provisional draft of AAUP policy recommends twelve and nine hours, respectively, as maximum loads.[11] AFT salary demands are likely to be higher than those of other organizations and to draw for support on comparisons with salaries of personnel with comparable "qualifications and responsibility" in private industry and government as well as the other professions.

RECOGNITION OF A BARGAINING AGENT

The question of collective bargaining in higher education is likely to remain a controversial one. Whatever views on this question may be held by board members and ad-

[11] "Statement on Faculty Workload," *AAUP Bulletin,* pp. 256–257, Summer, 1968.

ministrators, however, there are strong grounds in American social precedent and in democratic theory for the conclusion that a clearly expressed desire by a majority of the faculty to be represented by an exclusive bargaining agent should be recognized and respected. Whether faculty opt for a negotiating council or for an exclusive bargaining agent, "like other employees, professional or non-professional, [they] should have the right to select organizations of their own choosing."[12] John W. McConnell, president of the university of New Hampshire, has added to this argument the conclusion that recognition of a faculty's judgment in this matter is the only effective and constructive response:

> Whether faculty members or nonacademic staff join a union is their business. Administrators may have firmly fixed opinion on the issue. Any attempt to prohibit or prevent the organization of a union on the campus, however, will increase the attractiveness of joining and provide further evidence of need. The most constructive approach is to accept the fact of the organization, and face squarely the gripes and grievances the leaders of the organization will bring to the table for discussion.[13]

For the same reasons, boards and administrations should maintain a position of neutrality and noninvolvement as regards the organizations that may be competing for representational status. They should also refrain from making interpretations of the failure of some faculty to cast ballots. Counting those not voting as friendly to one's own side has no basis in legitimate inference. As an old trick of seeking to weight the outcome, it is a readily recognizable tool of administrative coercion which is likely to generate ill will and resentment. For these reasons both the NLRB and the administrators of collective negotiation in the federal service have held that a majority of those voting, rather than of the eligible electorate, is required.

In the absence of majority faculty support for a formalized bargaining relationship, administrators should be willing and ready to engage in discussion with any organizations of their faculty. President McConnell warns that it ought to be recognized that a minority organization may in fact be "representative of the opinion of a larger group of faculty,"[14] a judgment that is borne out by the fact that when elections are held an AFT local typically gets a larger vote from nonmembers than is the case with other faculty organizations.

Where the issue of collective bargaining is squarely joined, disputes may arise over whether an organization which seeks to serve as an exclusive bargaining agency for faculty in fact represents a majority. In the private sector regularized procedures for making these determinations were instituted by the National Labor Relations Act of 1935, which provided the rules for representation elections and for the certification of a union which had won such an election. Since most colleges and universities are not covered by federal labor law, they face potentially the same uncertainties which often had led in the private sector to bitter strikes. Indeed, at least two strikes have occurred on campuses in the last few years over the issue of recognition of a bargaining agent. Statutes recently adopted in several states covering faculty in public institutions generally parallel the provisions of federal law with respect to election and recognition procedures. Where the issue of collective bargaining has been joined and where such provisions are absent, fruitless and bitter strikes are likely to be avoided only if ad hoc recognition rules and procedures can be agreed to by faculty and administration.[15]

[12] AAHE Task Force, *op. cit.*, p. 44.

[13] John W. McConnell, "Autocracy versus Democracy in Top Administration," paper presented at the 22nd National Conference on Higher Education, sponsored by the Association for Higher Education, March 6, 1967.

[14] "How to Negotiate with a Professors' Union," an interview with President John McConnell of the University of New Hampshire, *College Management*, p. 25, January, 1967.

[15] AAHE Task Force, *op. cit.*, p. 45.

In public institutions there may be legal barriers to the designation of a bargaining agency. State legislation in this area is characterized by wide diversity, ranging from silence through provisions requiring public jurisdictions to "meet and confer" with teachers' organizations either separately or through a "negotiating council" (junior colleges in California, for example) to provisions permitting negotiation with an exclusive bargaining agent (New York and Michigan, for example). Legislative provisions may apply differently to junior college districts and four-year state institutions, and their applicability to the latter situation may require adjudication. Moreover, the ambiguity of some state statutes leads to legal disagreement about whether public agencies may, under the terms of the law, bargain with an exclusive agent. Whatever existing statutory arrangements may be, most authorities appear to agree that it would be a mistake to appeal to statutory prohibition or to statutory permissiveness in discussions of the merits of collective bargaining in higher education. The legal and legislative aspects of the issue are put in their proper context when they are addressed after full discussion and decision on the merits of the case.[16] Finally, the establishment of collective bargaining, including the recognition of an exclusive bargaining agent, does not imply compulsory membership in bargaining organizations, and there is general agreement among faculty organizations that compulsory membership is not a legitimate condition of a bargaining relationship. The AFT has consistently supported the principle of free association and disavowed the principles of the "union" or the "closed" shop; for example, a clause in a model contract prepared by the College Council of the California Federation of Teachers, AFL-CIO, provides that "no faculty member shall be required to join or refrain from joining a campus organization as a condition of employment or retention." NEA affiliates and the AAUP have taken the same position.

The compulsory payment of dues or fees to help defray representation and bargaining costs and the costs of grievance machinery including arbitration (which in industrial practice is shared equally by the parties) is a separate issue. It is, of course, a common practice in the industrial sector. The AAUP, in both its 1966 and 1968 statements on "Representation of Economic Interests," has taken the position that where an AAUP chapter acts as exclusive representative of the faculty, "No person shall be required to become a member of *or to make any financial contribution to* the Association as a condition of his enjoying the benefits of representation."

EXCLUSIVITY OF THE BARGAINING AGENT

Should an organization which has established itself as representative of a majority of faculty have the right, as in the private sector governed by federal statute, to serve as the exclusive bargaining agent for that faculty? Exclusivity implies that other organizations are denied the right to participate directly in negotiations leading to binding agreements. Exclusive representation is firmly established in industrial collective bargaining, both as an application of the majority principle and as a practical precondition of a stable and effective bargaining relationship. It can be argued that where a majority of the faculty has chosen a single organization as its representative, the resulting negotiations will depend primarily on power and that, in this situation, industrial experience furnishes a strong case that exclusivity is a condition of stability.[17]

At the same time, industrial practice need not be taken as an infallible model, especially in view of the traditional faculty commitment to individual and minority rights. The AFT seems to be committed to the principle of exclusivity except that in matters which remain in the jurisdiction of an academic senate, other organizations would presumably continue to have access. AAUP policy statements would provide a

[16] Myron Lieberman and Michael H. Moskow, *Collective Negotiations for Teachers,* Rand McNally & Company, Chicago, 1966, pp. 117–119.

[17] AAHE Task Force, *op. cit.,* p. 46.

procedure guaranteeing "full access" for all individuals and groups to present grievances, but they are ambiguous with regard to how this access would affect the bargaining process. The position of some NEA affiliates in favor of negotiating councils furnishes another alternative. A precedent for according rights to minority organizations exists in the federal service where, under Executive Order 10988, any minority organization may achieve "informal recognition" by virtue of which it is entitled to be heard, though not to be consulted, and to represent individuals in grievance and appeal procedures.

At the same time, the dynamics of organizational competition will have much to do with the positions adopted by faculty organizations and will probably exert pressures in the long run in the direction of exclusivity. Thus, a local faculty organization which is in a minority is not likely to push for exclusive recognition, whatever the position of its national body on that issue may be; an organization which has stood for multiple representation is likely to change its position when success in an election to choose an exclusive agent seems assured. It may be expected that college and university experience will duplicate the public school record and that "state and local affiliates of both the NEA and AFT will adopt positions contrary to national policy, or even positions contrary to what these same state and local affiliates have publicly recommended, when such action is deemed necessary to safeguard a vital organizational interest."[18]

The choice of a bargaining agent is not, of course, irrevocable. Private industry under the NIRA, the federal service under Executive Order 10988, and state and local public jurisdictions under some state statutes all provide regularized procedures for testing continued majority support. Here again, in the absence of statutory provisions applicable to higher education, the parties may agree on ad hoc procedures.

UNIT DETERMINATION

Another continuing problem in collective negotiations is the determination of what constitutes an "appropriate unit" of employees. In higher education the problem is likely to take two major and familiar forms: the homogeneity, and the geographic inclusiveness of the unit. In industrial practice, supervisory personnel and those who participate in making management policy are excluded from an employee bargaining unit. These distinctions, at least in institutions whose practices reflect traditional academic values and professional procedures, are more difficult to make in higher education. The AFT's position, for example, seems to be that the recognized unit should include those who hold academic rank and are engaged primarily in instruction and those engaged in "very closely related professional activities" such as professional librarians. Ordinarily, this would probably exclude administrators above the level of department head. But the heads of divisions or schools, like department heads, may be elected or selected with faculty advice and consent, and their supervisory authority may be undertaken through established procedures of faculty consultation. The difficulties thus posed are reflected in the judgment of one trustee of a large state system that, under a collective bargaining arrangement, the trustees "would probably insist that faculty participation in the selection of administrative personnel must cease" since among other potential conflicts of interest, the administration would probably be equally represented at all stages of grievance procedure.[19]

The geographic basis of unit definition is posed in higher education by the existence of multicampus public systems. Where authority to make decisions affecting the conditions of employment is located at the system level, there are obvious reasons for con-

[18] Lieberman and Moskow, *op. cit.*, p. 114.

[19] Louis H. Heilbron, Memorandum to the Members of the Board of Trustees of the California State Colleges, September 20, 1967.

sidering that only a systemwide unit is appropriate. Sometimes, however, the strategy of a faculty organization has been to concentrate efforts on the larger urban campuses in the system and to seek representation rights on those campuses. It is prepared, where it succeeds, to bargain for that campus and, on the model of some industrial practices, to leave it to the systemwide administration to decide whether to apply the negotiated rates and conditions elsewhere. Where state legislation covers public higher education, determinations of an appropriate unit by the state labor board are likely to be required.

WHO NEGOTIATES FOR MANAGEMENT?

The question of who should negotiate for management is open to a wide variety of answers. The choice may fall to administrators, to the governing board or a committee thereof, or to trained negotiators employed on either a full-time or an ad hoc basis. Where adversary roles have been clearly drawn and where faculty are supported in the negotiations by the resources and skills of outside organizations, it is more likely that administration will feel compelled to seek outside assistance. Insofar as negotiation is a continuing process and the situation is characterized by mutual desires to maximize communication and to promote a community of interest wherever possible, the negotiating role will fall to administrators. For these reasons, McConnell has suggested that the leading spokesman should be the person in the administration who has the best rapport with the faculty, although the president should evidence his view of the importance of the matter by his presence.[20]

In public multicampus institutions the problem is more complex, because the ability to make binding fiscal decisions may involve not only the presidents and local boards, but systemwide executives, higher boards and coordinating boards, the fiscal officers in the executive branch of the state government, and the legislature (including the leadership and the fiscal committees of the two houses). In these circumstances even agreements negotiated by the systemwide administration ordinarily would be only tentative and in the nature of recommendations to executive and legislative authorities. The only exception would appear to be a situation in which a governing board has been delegated the power to fix tuition and to negotiate binding agreements, an unlikely situation the constitutionality of which would be in question in most state jurisdictions. "Tentative bargaining," subject to higher review, would put a board or an administrator in a very difficult position.

To meet these difficulties the California AFT College Council has proposed that a faculty agent could bargain with a committee of trustees, augmented by representatives from the fiscal agency in the executive branch of state government and the fiscal committees of the legislature. Such an arrangement, they argue, would provide a practical solution to the problems of "tentative bargaining." The viability of this approach is of course, open to question.

THE SCOPE OF COLLECTIVE NEGOTIATIONS

Collective negotiation, in any of its forms, raises the question of what issues are properly subject to negotiation. In the industrial sector economic issues constitute the typical content of bargaining agreements, including such items as wages, hours, working conditions, vacation rights, holidays, overtime, and pensions. These direct cost items are usually supplemented by agreement on general policy governing personnel administration and the establishment of grievance machinery by which individual employees or similarly situated groups of employees may raise complaints alleging

[20] "How to Negotiate with a Professors' Union," *op. cit.*, p. 26.

that policy had been misinterpreted or misapplied. Matters not covered by written agreement remain in the status of management prerogative.

Examination of these typical industrial practices discloses several important respects in which unique problems are posed for academic institutions. Is it possible in higher education to distinguish between economic issues and issues of professional and educational policy? At issue here is the question whether collective bargaining on economic issues can be reconciled with collegial or shared authority over educational issues. The issue is important because all the leading faculty organizations, including the AFT, profess a desire to maintain the distinction by delegating control over educational and personnel policies to faculty bodies or to processes of shared authority.

In the early stages of formalized bargaining, the scope of negotiation is likely to be limited to the question of recognition, to economic issues (salaries, teaching load, health and pension benefits, and other economic "fringes"), and to grievance machinery. In principle it seems possible to separate these issues from issues of educational policy (admission standards, introduction of new curriculum, degree requirements, and the like). In practice, however, genuine difficulties arise. Admission policies have a direct bearing on teaching load, for example; so, also, the introduction of a new degree program may put new strains on institutional resources available for other uses which are also valued by the faculty. The interconnection of these issues is likely to put strains on any effort to maintain a stable differentiation of function between a bargaining agent and an academic senate. It may be argued that a faculty which has decided to submit the economic bases of its professional task to the coercive and manipulative processes of bargaining has effectively surrendered its claim to exercise a disinterested custodianship of professional standards and conditions. Even if that argument is not compelling, conflicts between these dual roles are likely to develop. A faculty organization functioning as a bargaining agent is likely to have taken positions on educational and personnel policy issues as well as on economic issues. Whether the differentiation of function between a bargaining agent and an academic senate could be maintained if they disagreed on educational policy or if a senate position on educational policy had adverse consequences for a bargaining agent's economic priorities seems doubtful.

Adversary relationships once formalized in exclusive bargaining may tend, for these reasons, to spread to all aspects of institutional decision making, but there is insufficient precedent to permit any final or very firm conclusion in this regard. The development of a bargaining relationship confined to the economic and personnel questions arising from the employee status of the professor may not necessarily preclude the development or continuance of some form of collegial or shared authority on educational issues. It might be speculated that, in the absence of effective faculty participation through a senate on educational issues, the scope of collective bargaining is more likely to expand to include them. The militancy that gives rise to the demand for collective bargaining is not likely to accommodate itself to the claim that these are areas of managerial prerogative.

Thus, there seems to be no compelling reason to assume that changes in the scope of formal bargaining will be unidirectional. The argument that a bargaining relationship, once established, will inevitably expand in the direction of encompassing all issues reflects the assumption that the faculty's overreaching interest is in the wage bargain in the narrow sense of economic self-interest. Experience thus far with the collective bargaining movement seems to suggest, on the contrary, that the chief interest of faculty remains "professional" in the sense of seeking to acquire greater control over the conditions in which their professional tasks are undertaken. Insofar as this is in fact the case, collective bargaining will not be an irreversible process. If it coexists with an academic senate or other agencies of collaborative decision making, an experience of successful decision making through such agencies may result in the shifting to them of issues once subject to bargaining.

Administrative and board attitudes toward the bargaining relationship are also likely to affect the outcome. An intransigent attitude toward a faculty's desire for bargaining, efforts to affect the faculty's choice of a bargaining agent, or evident efforts to obstruct good-faith bargaining are only likely to confirm faculty views that an adversary relationship is unavoidable.

THE NEGOTIATING RELATIONSHIP

Academic negotiations, even under the conditions of exclusive bargaining with a professional union, need not mirror the common or prevailing practices in private industry. There are few hard and fast rules for the conduct of bargaining in higher education, and differences from the industrial situation open up a variety of alternatives. The negotiating process in some academic situations may, indeed, come much closer to the model of rational persuasion than to a bargaining relationship in which false maximum demands and offers are advanced as means to a compromise based on bargaining skill and power. As McConnell has put it, "In dealing with faculty people, who are accustomed to looking at facts and trying to understand situations, this kind of sham, of petty bargaining as I would call it, is likely to produce very harmful results."[21]

McConnell concludes that offers and proposals should be genuine and carefully thought out, and that every effort should be made to avoid agreements which are "package deals" reflecting trade-offs of competing claims. What saves these recommendations from being visionary and unrealistic is the potential community of interest of the parties, rooted in common professional standards and educational goals. Salaries, teaching load, and class size, for example, are substitutes from a fiscal point of view; a change in one has fiscal consequences for the others. The issues have to be settled together, but not in the sense of composing a package deal. Where both parties are willing to conduct discussions on the basis of educational criteria and the educational consequences of various combinations, an alternative to the give and take of power-based bargaining is possible.

From a faculty point of view, teaching load is obviously an important "condition of employment," but contact hours and class size are not so obviously analogous to hours of work and production schedules in private industry. Faculty goals, that is to say, tend to be "professional" in nature, with the result that even salaries to some extent and what might be called "working conditions" to a much greater extent are likely to be put in a negotiating context that recognizes the interdependence of all these issues and their common bearing on the quality of education. Faculty, moreover, are likely to have a direct concern for the effects of agreements on the "pricing" policies of the institution because of their distinctive commitment to students and to educational opportunity. These considerations suggest that, even in formalized collective bargaining, relationships not commonly found in the industrial sector may be possible. Bargaining "in good faith" in the educational context may have a professional referrent and be tested by professional standards not ordinarily available in the private sector.

SANCTIONS AND IMPASSE-RESOLVING PROCEDURES

Notwithstanding the possibilities under favorable conditions of reasoned persuasion, the essence of a negotiating relationship is the existence of conflicts of interest which may be amenable only to a process of compromise in which both parties resort to the use and the threat of use of coercive techniques. Moreover, in the absence of third-party intervention, the actual and potential use of sanctions may fail to produce a settlement, and the resulting impasse may be put to a trial of strength by the invocation of the ultimate sanction of the strike.

[21] *Ibid.*, p. 11.

Neutral third-party intervention as a procedure for resolving impasses has had extensive but limited application in the private industrial sector. It has taken a variety of forms: fact-finding, with or without recommendations; advisory arbitration; and binding arbitration. The use of compulsory and binding arbitration is largely limited to the settlement of disputes over interpretation of an existing contract, and its wider use as an alternative to the strike is generally opposed on the familiar ground that the existence of such machinery will encourage the weaker party to refuse to agree, thus precipitating an arbitration proceeding in which there is some hope of winning what could not be won in negotiation.

In academic situations the range of sanctions potentially available to faculty is broad. It includes the political avenues of lobbying and public relations; professional pressures, including censure; efforts to effect the withdrawal of accreditation; refusal to recruit new faculty and efforts to discourage prospective faculty from accepting employment; and economic sanctions. The last category includes, in addition to the strike, a range of strike substitutes, such as: refusal to teach classes beyond a certain size or to schedule and teach more than a given number of hours; refusal to staff graduate or other programs; refusal to supervise independent study, to advise students, or to turn in grades.

Traditionally, the strike and strike substitutes have generally been regarded as incompatible with "professionalism" in higher education. As the description of the positions and attitudes of faculty organizations in an earlier section of this chapter makes clear, this conclusion is currently under critical review. It is true, of course, that strikes by public employees are generally illegal. The courts have held them to be enjoinable under common law; in some jurisdictions, including the federal service, they have been declared statutorily illegal; no political jurisdiction in the United States has authorized legislatively the right of public employees to strike. But, as George W. Taylor has argued, "a ban on strikes by public employees is not viable in the absence of alternate and effective procedures, other than the strike, to assure equitable treatment of employees."[22] For this reason, and until effective alternate procedures are available, legal proscription is not likely to prevent strikes. Legal penalties, to be sure, might be put high enough effectively to discourage them, but the consequences of their suppression could well be disastrous. One result might be to increase the likelihood of resort to strike substitutes, the results of which might well leave a "legacy of bitterness" more harmful in the long run than a strike.[23]

CONCLUSION

The mood of increasing faculty militancy on American campuses is strikingly apparent. Even this dramatic evidence of faculty militancy is likely to be a deceptive index of the strength and prospects of the collective bargaining movement in higher education. The movement itself is very recent, and the rapidly changing circumstances of higher education provide a favorable climate for its growth. There is, nevertheless, insufficient evidence to support a description of collective bargaining as the wave of the future. Exclusive bargaining, the use of an external bargaining agency, and reliance on the threat or use of sanctions appear to represent for faculty a last resort growing out of feelings of the futility of other arrangements. They are most likely to prevail where the essential conditions of professionalism—collegial or shared authority over and responsibility for the standards and conditions of the professional calling—are not otherwise attainable.

[22] "The Public Interest in Collective Negotiations in Education," *Phi Delta Kappan*, p. 22, Summer, 1966.

[23] AAHE Task Force, *op. cit.*, p. 51.

ADDITIONAL READINGS

AAHE Task Force on Faculty Representation and Academic Negotiations: *Faculty Participation in Academic Governance,* American Association for Higher Education, Washington, 1967.

Day, J. F., and W. H. Fisher: "The Professor and Collective Negotiations," *School and Society,* pp. 226–229, April 1, 1967.

Heim, Peggy: "Growing Tensions in Academic Administration," *North Central Association Quarterly,* pp. 244–251, Winter, 1968.

Howe, Ray A.: "Collective Bargaining for Teachers," *North Central Association Quarterly,* pp. 252–255, Winter, 1968.

Kadish, Sanford H.: "The Strike and the Professoriate," *AAUP Bulletin,* pp. 160–168, June, 1968.

Levine, M. J.: "Higher Education and Collective Action," *Journal of Higher Education,* pp. 263–268, May, 1967.

Livingston, John C.: "Collective Bargaining and Professionalism," *Educational Record,* pp. 79–88, Winter, 1967.

Marmion, Harry A.: "Unions and Higher Education," *Educational Record,* pp. 41–48, Winter, 1968.

McIntosh, Carl W.: "The Unionization of College and University Teachers," *Journal of Higher Education,* pp. 373–378, October, 1965.

Chapter 9

Work Load Assignments

DOROTHY C. GOODWIN

Assistant Provost and Director of Institutional Research, The University of Connecticut, Storrs, Connecticut

INTRODUCTION

At the heart of a college's problem of resource allocation is the disposition of its primary resource—its faculty. In a modern American institution, the typical faculty member engages in a bewildering array of activities that may be considered germane to the mission of the institution and its role in society and which the institution wants to promote. At the same time, there is probably no other major type of employer in the country that finds so difficult the problem of distinguishing between the job assignments and the spare-time avocations of its labor force.

Most institutions seek a happy medium between a too narrow dedication to classroom instruction that may lead to professional deterioration and such a wide scattering of activities that it can result only in the frittering away of energy. On the other hand, it is the rare institution that seeks to find this happy medium through rigid policing. In recognition of the fact that few, if any, of the variables that must underlie a policy of rigid policing are subject to precise definition, most institutions try to maintain considerable flexibility in administering assignments. In fact, a probably growing number of the best complex universities operate with almost complete flexibility under the broadest possible kinds of nonquantitative guidelines.[1]

Even in a highly flexible system, however, the orderly administration of faculty assignments is essential to the welfare of the institution for many reasons. The most conspicuous of these is probably the equitable treatment of faculty. From the point of view of faculty themselves, this is surely the dominant reason.

But the administrator must go beyond this question, important as it is, and relate assignment of faculty to the total mission of the institution. The resource allocation problem involves not only the competing claims of individual faculty or teaching departments but also those of the teaching function and other activities essential to the institution's goals. And all these competing claims must be satisfied in ways that will meet the obligations of the institution to its customers and its sponsors at the highest attainable level of quality. Solutions that focus too narrowly on the question of equity, with inadequate regard for quality or other institutional goals, are not likely to advance the institution's cause.

The problem would be conceptually simpler if the alternate goals of an institution were genuinely antagonistic to each other. But they are not. They are, in fact, both competing and complementary. Teaching and research may compete for a man's time, but he probably does a better job at both if he engages in both, for each reinforces the quality of the other. An institution that focuses on the one to the exclusion of the other must lose something in the process.[2] The case is similar to teaching and student counseling, teaching and the administration of teaching, administration and participation in faculty committee assignments, etc.

Finally, the institution must consider the claims of students as well as those of faculty or competing goals. For with a given student body and a given budget, teaching loads can be lightened or increased by the simple device of increasing or decreasing the size of class. It is in this way that the conflicting nature of teaching and research probably most conspicuously displays itself. Even an institution dedicated single mindedly to the teaching function has access to this device, moreover, as a budget adjustment tool.

[1] The University of Connecticut, in the spring of 1967, made an informal survey of general policy with respect to teaching assignments at 12 major universities in the United States. A summary of returns, prepared by the writer for the use of a faculty committee states: "As a general verbal summary, it seems fair to state that with rare exceptions, institutions with widely diverse programs do not use university-wide norms for determining faculty loads; that some institutions have fairly formal norms for individual programs, but that others decentralize the problem of teaching assignments to deans, department heads, and/or faculty advisors almost entirely, and permit wide discretion and negotiation with respect to individual loads. Most institutions have no 'by-law' on loads, even in cases where in practice they apply fairly rigid standards." (Letter of July 19, 1967.) Following this study the University of Connecticut dropped from its bylaws any reference to a numerical standard, such as "the equivalent of twelve credit hours of teaching," formerly specified.

[2] This is a view widely shared within the profession and widely contradicted by those outside it. Statistical support for the hypothesis is hard to come by, but a recent study by Jack B. Bresler, "Teaching Effectiveness and Government Awards," reported in *Science*, vol. 160, no. 3824, pp. 164–167, April 12, 1968, suggests that it is demonstrably true at least at Tufts University.

We are thus dealing with a complex, multidimensional problem, most of whose dimensions cannot be reduced to simple formulas or even precisely quantified. There is no "best" way to administer faculty assignments, even for closely similar institutions. Solutions will vary with circumstances, personalities, educational philosophies, historical precedent, and outside pressures from coordinating boards and legislatures.

The discussion that follows, therefore, will not outline a unique, recommended system. The procedure will be to review the relevant variables, with special reference to their quantifiability, and to examine their use in relation to rigid as compared to flexible administrative approaches. This discussion will try to relate the whole process of assignment to some of the evolving attempts to engage in program budgeting by formula and by this means to emphasize the relation of assignment to the broad resource-allocation problem.

THE INGREDIENTS OF A WORK LOAD

The Teaching Function

The teaching function is a collection of related activities that combine, supposedly, to promote learning in students. At its boundaries, it is an extraordinarily fuzzy concept, blending by infinitesimal gradations with virtually every other area of faculty activity. Is the recording of grades primarily teaching or administrative? Is the counseling of students an instructional or a student personnel activity? Is the supervision of graduate assistants administrative, or related to the teaching of the undergraduates with whom these assistants work, or part of the instruction received by the graduate assistants themselves? Is research performed by a graduate student under the supervision of his major advisor as an intrinsic part of that student's education to be credited to the advisor as a teaching or a research effort? Is "keeping up with the literature" as a necessary backstop to both teaching and research to be classed as the one or the other, or is the messy distinction to be ducked by calling it "professional activity"?

If one were to fool himself into believing that precise measurement of the teaching function were possible, he would need answers to these questions, for they are relevant to the question of faculty assignments. Since they are fundamentally unanswerable, one is forced to use very imperfect partial measures to approach the problem at all.

Deferring for the moment the problem of fitting other assignments around teaching, assume that faculty members are assigned full-time to teaching duties as that term is generally understood. These duties include "normal" counseling, "normal" departmental duties, and a "normal" amount of self-directed research and work toward professional improvement. Consider such a person to be at once a full-time equivalent employee (FTE) and a full-time teaching equivalent (FTTE). The more complex uses of the concept of a full-time teaching equivalent as it applies to persons having both teaching and nonteaching assignments will be considered later.

The Credit Hour Probably the most common shorthand measure of a faculty member's teaching load is the semester, quarter, or similar credit hour. The real purpose of a credit hour, however, is to measure a *student*'s progress toward a degree. Since it is thus inherently a dummy variable for student output rather than faculty input, its relevance to measurement of the latter is indirect at best. As a measure of faculty input, it probably distinguishes inaccurately between hours of class and hours of laboratory instruction. It does not distinguish at all between differences in levels of instruction, sizes of classes, preparation requirements for independent study versus regular classroom instruction, or between instructional methods used, i.e., team teaching, TV instruction, use of essay examinations and term papers as compared to objective testing, and many other factors. Indeed, it fairly cries aloud for amplification.

Contact Hours A slightly more precise tool with its own set of disadvantages is the contact hour. This concept may be applied to instructional hours, called here teacher-contact hours (TCH) or student-contact hours (SCH). Both TCH and SCH refer to the same real time dimensions. The contact hour is more satisfactory to faculty in the laboratory sciences because it answers their objection to the credit hour, i.e., that a laboratory hour requires at least as much faculty input as a class hour. At the same time, it is subject to all the other criticisms of credit hours, and it is subject to the further objection that contact hours must be simulated for tutorials, private music lessons, clinical instruction, and similar atypical kinds of instruction.

In spite of these difficulties, its use has some major advantages over the credit hour for many statistical purposes. As noted, the credit hour's real operational significance is its use as a bookkeeping device for recording student progress. It does not really lend itself to more general statistical uses.

The contact hour, on the other hand, is an operational concept with a wide range of planning and decision-making applications. It is not the purpose of this chapter to develop these other uses, but some mention of them may be helpful in assessing the desirability of substituting contact for credit hours as a measure of faculty input.

First, the TCH show how many hours of class and laboratory sessions have been staffed and thus, immediately and directly, how many hours of room use must have been associated with it. The SCH show how many hours of student participation have been provided for and thus, simultaneously with TCH, how many seats have been committed in the rooms used.

The most important derivative statistic, however, is SCH/TCH, which is, by definition, class size or average class size. This formulation may be used to describe one class, or aggregated and averaged to describe all classes taught by one instructor, or aggregated for departments by level of instruction, or it may be used to describe the whole institution. It is a concept central to educational policy, budget control, and faculty assignments simultaneously. This general-purpose nature of the contact-hour concept, in addition to its slightly greater precision as a measure of faculty input, recommends its substitution for the credit hour in connection with faculty assignments. It will be used throughout the rest of this chapter, although it is recognized that the choice between credits and contract hours will be one of preference and that much of the manipulation of the contact measure developed below can be applied *mutatis mutandis* to credit hours. In fact, the use of both measures side by side may provide interesting comparisons of faculty loads in laboratory and nonlaboratory fields.

The Weighted Contact Hour If one is willing to accept arbitrary and subjectively derived weights, some of the complexities noted above can be built in to the contact-hour concept to increase its sensitivity to differing circumstances. While weighting can quickly become an unmanageable numbers game, some real progress can be made with two relatively simple devices: the level of instruction and the size of class.

Weighting the Contact Hour by Level of Instruction. A number of institutions now introduce weights at least for program budgeting purposes. This is especially true in state systems of public higher education, where the competing claims of different kinds of institutions for funds must be adjudicated.[3] Two kinds of weighting systems may be used. The simpler one merely states that a contact hour at the upper-division level is worth x times as much in terms of faculty effort as one at the lower-division level, while graduate instruction may merit a weight of $2x$ or $3x$ or kx. Such weights are then simply multiplied by the TCH involved, and the resulting values for different faculty members or departments may then be compared with each other and with some definition of a standard aggregate of weights.

This approach says nothing about *why* one level of instruction is more demanding than another, nor does it of itself embody any internal standards. It simply permits

[3] See Robert L. Williams, *Legal Basis of Coordinating Boards of Higher Education in Thirty-nine States*, The Council of State Governments, Chicago, 1967.

comparison of existing conditions, analyzed with the use of subjectively determined weights, with existing standards.

The Use of Target Weights: Applications to Budgeting. A somewhat more complex method that is more directly useful for program budgeting is to build the weights for the different levels of instruction by examining some of the more easily measurable factors that in some sense entitle the different levels to different weights. Any number of variants on this approach could be constructed. One system that has proved useful was introduced in 1967 into the budgetary processes of the Connecticut Commission for Higher Education for construction of the budgets of constituent institutions.[4] The reader may elaborate on this system as freely as his imagination permits. The idea is not patented.

Connecticut's target standards include number of TCH per faculty member and size of class per TCH, weight these variables by level of instruction, and convert them into lower-division equivalents. These lower-division equivalents are expressed in student-contact hours as SCHLDE (student-contact hour lower-division equivalent). Table 1 is quoted from instructions to constituent members for budget presentations for the 1967–1969 biennium.

In essence the formulation in Table 1 takes as its index of desirable load the definition of normal load for a full-time teaching equivalent (FTTE) at the lower-division level. According to its system of weights, such a load will include 12 TCH, with 25 students per TCH, for a total SCH of 300. The arbitrary unit, 300, then becomes the definition of total load for a single FTTE instructor engaged entirely in lower-division teaching without graduate-assistant or teacher-aide help. How this load is made up may then be varied to fit different teaching situations by varying inversely the number of TCH per instructor and the size of class per TCH. Under the standard, 12 TCH × 25 SCH/TCH = 300 SCH; 10 TCH × 30 SCH/TCH or 5 TCH × 60 SCH/TCH also equal 300.

Similarly, a single instructor teaching entirely at the upper-division level without assistants is expected to cope with 180 SCH (9 TCH × 20 SCH/TCH). For each 300 upper-division SCH, then, 1.667 instructors are needed (300/180), and upper-division SCH can be converted to student-contact hour lower-division equivalents (SCHLDE) by multiplying them by 1.667.[5]

Parallel calculations, using the TCH/FTTE and SCH/TCH postulated in the table, then permit derivation of weighting factors for various categories of graduate work. Additional weights to permit distinction between day and evening teaching, TV teaching, private music lessons, clinical nursing instruction, or other special circumstances can easily be introduced. Tutorial and other atypical forms of instruction are handled by simulations of SCH, which are then converted to SCHLDE by dividing the simulated SCH into 300.

In the Connecticut situation, the primary use of this device is in adjusting the budget requests of the highly diverse constituents of the state's system of higher education. It permits the calculation of future faculty requirements in a manner immediately sensitive to both differences among institutions in enrollment composition and changes in enrollment composition within an institution. Projections over the budget period are made by means of the following steps:

1. Estimate roster enrollments for each level of instruction.
2. Estimate or apply past experience to the estimation of SCH per enrollee for each level of instruction.

[4] This system is basically that developed by Mr. John M. Evans, vice-president for financial affairs of the University of Connecticut, and refined in its applications by the writer and other users.

[5] The writer should apologize for having introduced this etymological horror into the language. The only excuse is its extraordinary usefulness.

TABLE 1 Weighting System Used by Connecticut Commission for Higher Education to Assess Requirements for Teaching Faculty in Constituent Institutions

Level of instruction involved	Students per class (SCH/TCH) (1)	×	Class hours per faculty member (TCH/FTTE) (2)	=	SCH per instructor (SCH/FTTE) (3)	SCHLDE/SCH = instructors (FTTE) per 300 SCH* (4)
Regular courses						
Lower division	25	×	12	=	300	1
Upper division	20	×	9	=	180	1.667
Graduate division master's and professional †	15	×	6	=	90	3.333
Master's and doctorate combined	12.5	×	6	=	75	4
Doctorate only	10	×	6	=	60	5
Independent study (undergraduate and graduate)						
25 enrollments × 3 assumed contact-hour equivalents = 75 (simulated)						4
Thesis and dissertation supervision						
25 enrollments × 3 assumed contact-hour equivalents = 75 (simulated)						4

* Weighting factor for differentiating among levels of instruction. SCHLDE is a student-contact hour lower-division equivalent. It shows the number of instructors required per 300 SCH at each level of instruction.

† Include here all work beyond the baccalaureate where the student has not been formally accepted in a doctoral program.

3. Multiply the results of step 1 by those of step 2 to project future SCH by level of instruction.

4. Convert these SCH aggregates to SCHLDE by multiplying SCH by the appropriate weights in column 4 of Table 1.

5. Divide the total number of SCHLDE derived in step 4 by the target number of SCHLDE per instructor (300 in Connecticut's case).

It will be recognized immediately that 300 SCHLDE per FTTE is an entirely arbitrary standard. By varying any or all of the ingredients of the standard, TCH/FTTE, SCH/TCH, and/or the relationships among levels, alternate standards can immediately be established. Or, if the critical factor, the relationship among levels is considered "about right," then this relationship can be preserved intact while the total is adjusted by simply changing the percent of the standard allowed.

Roster enrollments are used instead of FTE, because the use of ratios of SCH to enrollees automatically adjusts for part-time students without introducing the ambiguities of defining FTE students.

When used for budget purposes, the "instructors" found by the formula to be required are not, of course, real people with real loads. It is obvious that in most teaching situations, more than one level of instruction will be involved. It is also obvious that no single person will ever embrace the range of expertise needed to give real supervision to 25 different dissertation topics at one time. The proposition that during a given semester a single dissertation will command the equivalent of three graduate-student contact hours per week is probably not wholly unreasonable, however.

Target Weights and Individual Faculty Teaching Loads. We turn now to adaptation of target weights to adjustment of individual faculty loads. A sensible reader will dismiss much of the arithmetic developed below as meaningless intellectual gadgetry. Yet there is some value in going through the exercise, if only to show how much less useful a piece of gadgetry is the simplistic, uniformly applied 9- or 12-credit load.

The first step in adapting broad standards to individual loads is to adjust for mixed-level loads, with or without tutorials and thesis advisorships. This may be done by means of weighted averages which produce alternate constraints against which other ingredients of the load may be varied.

Table 2 shows weighted average computations that might be used to provide target standards for mixed-level teaching loads that do not include tutorial-type instructional situations.

This table says that for the situation portrayed in sample 1, the instructor, in an arithmetically perfect world, should have a total of 185 SCH distributed over 9 TCH in average classes of 20.5 students. Alternatively, he might have any combination of TCH and SCH/TCH that would produce 185 SCH. A further and more open-ended possibility is that the number of TCH will be taken as given, with SCH/TCH varied to fit actual classroom demand needs provided the resulting SCH equals 185 ± some predetermined tolerance limit and SCH/TCH is reasonably consistent with institution policy with respect to class size for the teaching situation involved.

When tutorials and thesis-major advisorships form part of the load, the problem becomes more complicated. Under the standard, 25 such advisorships simulated at

TABLE 2 Computation of Sample Standard Teaching Loads for Mixed-level Teaching Assignments Involving No Independent Study Registrations, Using the Formula in Use for Connecticut's System of Public Higher Education

Level of instruction involved	TCH ×	SCH/TCH =	SCH =	No. of FTTE instructors' loads represented
Sample 1 (for an instructor teaching at three levels):				
Lower division	12	25	300	1
Upper division	9	20	180	1
Mixed graduate	6	12.5	75	1
Total for 3 FTTE	27	......	555	3
Derived average		20.5		
Weighted average per FTTE	9	......	185	1
Standard average		20.5		
Sample 2 (for an instructor teaching at one combination of two levels):				
Lower division	12	25	300	1
Mixed graduate	6	12.5	75	1
Total for 2 FTTE	18	......	375	2
Derived average		20.8		
Weighted average per FTTE	9	......	187.5	1
Standard average		20.8		
Sample 3 (for an instructor teaching at an alternate combination of two levels):				
Lower division	12	25	300	1
Upper division	9	20	180	1
Total for 2 FTTE	21	......	480	2
Derived average		22.9		
Weighted average per FTTE	10.5	......	240	1
Standard average		22.9		
Sample 4 (for an instructor teaching at a third alternate combination of two levels):				
Upper division	9	20	180	1
Mixed graduate	6	12.5	75	1
Total for 2 FTTE	15	......	255	2
Derived average		17.0		
Weighted average per FTTE	7.5	......	127.5	1
Standard average		17.0		

3 SCH per advisorship comprise a full-time equivalent load of 75 simulated SCH. Since this is identical with the definition for the mixed graduate load, advisorships can be treated in a first approximation as an additional mixed graduate entry, as illustrated in Table 3, which adjusts sample 4 from Table 2.

If, in an individual case of the type represented in Table 3, there are, say, 5 advisorships, the distribution between advisorships and course work can be computed as:

Total SCH restraint	110 SCH
−5 advisorships × 3 SCH per advisorship	−15 simulated SCH
Course work SCH	95 SCH
Total TCH restraint	7 TCH
−15/75 × 6 TCH to cover advisorships	−1.2 simulated TCH
Course work TCH	5.8 TCH

Average class size for formal upper-division and graduate course work would then be 95/5.8 = 16.4, or if our inconveniently discrete TCH variable is rounded, 95/6 = 15.8.

The literal application of this complicated procedure to every situation is not suggested. For one thing, pedagogical problems vary among fields, and some variation around the literal average standard for a whole institution is certainly desirable. It is seriously suggested that the consideration of variables other than credit hours or even TCH is of vital importance, and that two such variables that any system should consider are level of instruction and average class size. Additional variables can be added at will if one wants to extend the numbers game even further. Weights could be introduced for evening classes, multiple preparations, inexperience, etc. In some sense, such weights are mandatory for any team-teaching situation, including the use of graduate assistants in any part of the teaching process.

An institution may prefer to cope with the need for variations around an institution-wide target by simply permitting them on a subjectively evaluated basis or conceivably by establishing multiple targets. The former may be easier for the faculty to live with. The latter implies either an extraordinary degree of omniscience on the part of administrators or perhaps an inability to operate without the crutch of exact numbers.

Because of the impossibility of controlling precisely the number of sections to be manned and the number of students in each section, the real administrative problem is not the literal achievement of either single- or multiple-target standards but the analysis of differences in deviations from the standards to ensure that they are within the limits of tolerance set by personnel and educational policy.

Target Weights and Team-teaching Arrangements. If a course uses graduate assistants to conduct discussion or laboratory sessions, these TCH with their SCH must be deducted from the main lecturer's load and attributed to the number of FTTE graduate assistants involved. The main instructor's work in supervising the assistants may be subsumed or adjusted for separately. If two lecturers alternate in the handling of a course, its TCH and SCH may be distributed between them in approximate propor-

TABLE 3 Sample 4 from Table 2 Adjusted for Thesis Advisorships

Level of course work	TCH	×	SCH/TCH	=	SCH	=	FTTE
Upper	9		20		180		1
Mixed graduate	6		12.5		75		1
Simulated advisorships	6		12.5		75		1
Total	21 TCH		...		330 SCH		3 FTTE
Derived average			15.7				
Weighted average per FTTE	7 TCH		...		110 SCH		1 FTTE
Standard average			15.7				

tion to the actual distribution of responsibility. When an instructor teaches a very large section without assistants in the classroom but with the help of paper graders, some distribution must be made because the full burden of the course does not fall on the main instructor.

In such cases, the simplest procedure is to attribute assistants' time to the course, add in the balance of the instructor's teaching assignment, and average the load per FTTE. For example, an instructor lecturing three times per week to a class of 600 students in a lower-division course and three times per week to 18 students in an upper-division course would have the following load description before adjustment for graduate assistants:

Lower division	3	TCH × 600	SCH/TCH = 1,800	SCH
Upper division	3	TCH × 18	SCH/TCH = 54	SCH
Total	6	TCH at 309	SCH/TCH = 1,854	SCH

In terms of SCH, this load is 7.7 times as large as the target load of 240 SCH computed in sample 3 of Table 2 for a teaching assignment consisting of one lower- and one upper-division course.

If such an instructor has 7 half-time graduate assistants whose job assignments involve nothing but papergrading, proctoring, and bookkeeping for this course, these 7 assistants can be converted to 3.5 FTTE at 2 assistants per FTTE, and we can now distribute the lower-division course over these additional FTTE as well as the main instructor. If all FTTE involved are treated alike, the computation for the main instructor would be as shown in Table 4.

TABLE 4 Computation of Load for the Main Instructor in a Situation Involving Graduate Assistants

Lower division:	3 TCH × 600 SCH/TCH =	1,800 SCH
Less SCH attributed to 3.5 FTTE graduate assistants at	300 SCH/FTTE =	1,050 SCH
SCH attributed to main instructor:		750
Upper division:	3 TCH × 18 SCH/TCH =	54
Total:	6 TCH	804 SCH,
		with his SCH/TCH simulated at 134

The resulting SCH attributed to the main instructor are now about 3.4 times the target shown for sample 3 in Table 2.

Two judgments must then be made: (1) What comparative weights should be applied to the contributions of the main instructor and his assistants? Is a straight device reasonable, or should unequal weights be used? (2) Does 804 SCH attributed to the main instructor (or whatever value may result from use of alternate weights) represent a serious overload or not? Neither question can be answered categorically.

No attempt has been made here to apply the target-standard approach to special situations such as TV-teaching. Such problems should be dealt with as special cases.

Faculty Assignments Other than Teaching

This chapter has dealt so far with persons assigned full-time to teaching where this term is intended to include "normal" departmental duties, student counseling, and professional self-improvement. The discussion turns now to the infinitely more difficult problems of measuring appropriate teaching assignments for faculty with multiple assignments.

The Part-time Employee Who Has No Nonteaching Duties If the part-time person with no nonteaching duties is expected to engage in "normal" departmental duties, counseling, and professional upgrading, the procedure described above can be applied directly by prorating. It probably should be applied by prorating even in the case of the man who comes in to teach one course, is not available for student counseling, and in whose professional upgrading the institution has no interest, if only because for differences in duties the adjustment is usually made by means of a lower salary. In the discussion that follows a prorating procedure is assumed and no further distinction will be made between part-time and full-time employees.

The FTE Concept and Its Subdivisions It is convenient to develop a construct that will schematize the duties of faculty members.[6] Divide the overall FTE concept into the major assigned duties that make it up. Individual institutions will want to classify duties to fit their own needs. Any classification will present both logical and practical difficulties. These are probably easier to cope with in a general classification, such as one using our broad definition of teaching, than in one that is minutely subdivided. The specific terms to be dealt with include:

FTE Full-time equivalent employee.

FTTE Full-time teaching equivalent, in essence an accumulation of individual teaching assignments described directly or indirectly by the standard developed in the previous section.

FTAE Full-time administrative equivalent, or the sum of percents of time allocated by different individuals to administrative duties.

FTRE Full-time research equivalents, or the sum of percents of time allocated to research by different individuals. This may be subdivided into "sponsored research" (FTSRE) and university-supported research (FTURE), and may or may not make distinction between sponsored research conducted under the aegis of the individual's home department and "organized research" conducted by interdisciplinary research institutes, depending on other uses made of the data.

FTPE Full-time public service equivalents, or the sum of percents of time allocated by different individuals to duties such as cooperative agricultural extension or adult education.

FTOE Full-time "other" equivalents, or the sum of any individual assignments not classifiable under one of the above headings. It would include major committee chairmanships for which formal time allocation has been made.

The sum of FTEs then, becomes the sum of FTTE + FTAE + FTRE + FTPE + FTOE. A logically complete system, used to allocate all faculty resources within an institution among the above headings, might show for each individual how his duties were distributed between his home department and other organizational units, thus accounting specifically for joint appointments. In such a case departmental duties might be shown as DFTTE, DFTAE, etc., while duties in other units would be shown as OFTTE, OFTAE, etc., and organized research would be classed as OFTRE in reporting regular departmental assignments.

In such a system, each organizational unit would show all assignments within it, and the sum of DFTEs for the institution would equal the sum of FTEs for the institution. The sum of any individual's assignments would be given by the sum of DFTEs plus the sum of OFTEs for the individual.

Measuring Nonteaching Assignments This tidy system of initials completely begs the question of how the percentage time allocations referred to are arrived at. Here the

[6] The writer is indebted to Dr. Malcolm Serverance, chairman of the economics department and former director of institutional research at the University of Vermont, for the very useful abbreviations used in this construct, although his system is enlarged here and the actual usage has been modified in important ways. For his usage, see his "Program Budgeting: A Case Study in Its Application," paper delivered at the 1968 Annual Forum of the Association for Institutional Research, San Francisco, May, 1968.

writer takes a position that is at sharp variance with that held by some of the outstanding authorities in the field. The reader is, of course, always free to reject what he reads, but in this case he is specifically invited to discount the writer's bias.

The controversy arises because of the impossibility of measuring what is being allocated. Here it has been called "time," but the faculty person's overall time obligation to his institution is universally undefined. How then does one calculate fractions of 100 percent when 100 percent cannot be calculated?

The Bureau of the Budget, in its original Circular A–21 on federal research grants to educational institutions, tried to wiggle out of this problem by substituting "effort" reporting for "time" reporting in documentation of grant disbursements. But what on earth is a percent of effort? The bureau has finally faced this dilemma itself, and has eliminated time and effort reporting for faculty working on research grants. The only sensible alternative, the allocation of the faculty member's total obligation to his institution in his current written or implied contract with his institution, has been substituted.[7]

This procedure frankly admits the impossibility of measuring the unmeasurable and rejects the use of irrelevant input substitutes for the real variable sought—the quality and quantity of output. For even if "time" or "effort" could be measured, they would not give the value of output.

A secondary benefit of this procedure is that it relieves one of the obligation to pester faculty members to find out what they think they do with their time. For the results of such studies are both meaningless and dangerously unreliable. Faculty members do not know what they do with their time because their duties are so diverse and no two days or weeks are alike. Moreover they cannot be made to take time reporting seriously because they know that it is not concerned with the significant ingredient.

Such reports are dangerous if they are used for significant comparative purposes because definitions cannot be held constant from one faculty member to another. A thousand faculty will use a thousand different definitions of 100 percent of time or effort, and each will also set the logical boundaries between functions in his own way. An impressive-looking statistic that is seriously flawed is surely a worse basis for comparative evaluation than a frankly subjective analysis based on detailed dossiers of faculty accomplishments judged against the terms of the faculty member's contract. (If time reports should not be used for significant purposes, one wonders why so much work should be dedicated to insignificant purposes.)

The Contract Approach. Under this approach, a faculty member will have an understanding with his department head or dean as to the composition of his total obligation to the institution. If he teaches, he will also be assigned a specific set of courses each semester. If his contract says that he is 50 percent teaching and he teaches 6 TCH with a total of 400 SCH, then a full-time teaching load *for him* would be twice this amount. Otherwise his load should be adjusted to match other similar loads or to fit whatever standards the institution sets.

Continuance of other assignments preempting the remainder of his total obligation will depend on evaluations of the worth of his contributions in these other areas. For any academic assignments such evaluations should clearly depend on the opinions of colleagues, senior faculty members, and in some cases outside experts in the field as well as administrators. Evaluation of research contributions presents probably the most difficult area, for research results are not identical assembly-line products produced according to rigid schedules and some of the most valuable contributions may be a long time in the pipeline.

[7] Bureau of the Budget, *Principles for Determining Cost Applicable to Research and Development Under Grants and Contracts with Educational Institutions,* Circular A–21, effective August 16, 1965, revised June 1, 1968. See also Philip M. Boffey, "Effort Reporting: Government Drops Much Criticized Paperwork," *Science,* vol. 150, no. 3834, p. 1332, June 21, 1968.

The Contract Approach and Overloads. A continuing bone of contention between faculty and their administrations in many institutions is treatment of paid assignments within or outside of the institution that are in some sense in excess of a normal full-time job. Additional evening teaching, either in the home institution or in a sister institution, consulting work of various sorts, and a wide range of possible public service activities are the most common sources of difficulty.

The position may be taken that what a faculty member does with his "spare" time is no one's business but his. If he makes a hobby of teaching, as some faculty members surely do, then in this view he should be allowed to take on extra teaching with the same freedom that he is allowed to putter in his garden or spend his evenings reading professional journals. The question of extra pay is considered incidental, for many people enjoy the jobs on which they moonlight or turn a penny on the fruits of hobbies.

The alternate view, that "no member of the professional staff or other employee in the service of the University shall devote to private purposes any portion of the time due the University without the consent of the President,"[8] is, perhaps, more commonly held by institutional administrators, although it may of course be administered with varying degrees of flexibility. In interpreting this type of rule, one confronts again the impossible problem of defining the "time" due the university.

Certain approximate criteria suggest themselves, however. There is, of course, the obvious accounting requirement that an institution has an obligation to make sure that it gets the amount and quality of services it pays for. Beyond this, a prime guideline must be protection of the users of the additional service, particularly the students in evening courses. Maintenance of quality in evening programs is hard enough at best; it is almost impossible when evening courses are taught as an overload, coming at the end of a fully committed day. The rights of evening students, especially in degree credit programs, to equal consideration with daytime students suggest the propriety of counting evening teaching as part of the regular load whenever this is administratively possible. Short courses, noncredit workshops, and the occasional public service lecture cannot be so treated, and extra compensation for such assignments is usually justified.

When teaching at two different institutions is involved, a possible solution in some cases to the problem of protecting teaching quality may be consortium arrangements. An example might be the case where the secondary institution pays the primary institution for the service, which is then counted as part of the faculty member's obligation to the primary institution and is covered by his pay from it.

A second guideline must involve the extent to which the additional assignment enhances the faculty member's professional competence, as it surely does in research assignments, many types of consulting work, and a wide range of possible public service activities. Where services of this type are performed without special compensation, they are seldom questioned unless they cut conspicuously into performance of regularly assigned duties. Where the staff member receives pay, many institutions impose some limitations. Northeastern University, for example, limits consulting work to one day per week out of five and stresses that such work is *in addition* to regular duties.[9]

In institutions that as a matter of policy emphasize research, sponsored research is usually handled by contract agreement releasing the individual from a portion of teaching or other institutional duties. Many research-oriented institutions assume a "normal" amount of unsponsored research by faculty in the setting of standard loads.

In teaching institutions that do not as a matter of policy insist on research activities, sponsored research would have to be handled by contract adjustments, but unsponsored research would normally be part of a voluntary overload, undertaken by the individual on his own initiative, probably without reference to administrative channels.

[8] *Laws and By-Laws of the University of Connecticut,* (9th ed.), June, 1966, p. 42, Art. X.K.6.
[9] *Northeastern University Faculty Handbook,* 1966–1967, p. 51.

The Contract Approach, Target Teaching Weights, and The Allocation of Faculty among Departments One now has the basic tools in hand for allocating any additional faculty positions among departments. Rule out for the moment complications such as the need to hire an additional faculty member to cover a new subarea of a teaching or research field and deal only in numbers.

One can now accumulate for each department a statistical description of its teaching function. Available are total SCH, total TCH, and total FTTE after nonteaching contract assignments have been subtracted. From these values one can compute TCH/FTTE, SCH/FTTE, and SCH/TCH with detailed ratios for subcategories of teaching as appropriate. These data on the teaching function show its magnitude, its distribution among levels of instruction, and precisely how it is handled in each organizational unit. The reader can, if truly enamored of numbers, relate the actual ratios per FTTE to target ratios as described in Table 2 and produce weighted averages of the results for whole departments. It is then possible to examine two things: trends over periods of time within departments and differences among departments.

One may perhaps want to probe into the situation in a department that has been increasing class size over a period of time while reducing TCH/FTTE. Does this mean that the welfare of students is being sacrificed to provide the morale benefits of lowered TCH/FTTE standards? Or does it mean that the undergraduate program is being skimped in favor of the graduate program? If the increase in class size is undesirable, one must then judge whether the institution's goals are served better by increasing staff or increasing TCH/FTTE.

If important differences in teaching loads among departments exist, one has the choice of allowing for them by use of explicit or informal multiple standards or reducing them by the ways in which new positions are allocated. The answer will depend partly on how well the departments appear to be using their resources and partly on differences in pedagogical requirements.

WORK LOADS, FACULTY MORALE, COSTS, AND QUALITY

There is probably no more pervasive status symbol in the modern academic community than the light teaching load conceived in terms of TCH/FTTE. That this is extraordinarily costly unless compensated for by very large classes is a matter of simple arithmetic.

That light teaching loads conceived of both in terms of TCH/FTTE and SCH/TCH have important implications for quality is also generally accepted, as is evidenced, for example, by the concern of accreditation agencies with these variables. The definition of "light" will vary with the mission of the institution, but both internal and external pressures for reducing loads are enormous. These pressures are competitive among individuals, among departments, among institutions. In the current seller's market for academic personnel, they have been all but irresistible.

The administrator's problem is twofold: How much can he resist these pressures in today's setting, and how hard should he try? If dollar cost were the only consideration, the answer would be simpler; for the larger the pound of flesh that is exacted, the cheaper is the operation. But this is, of course, exactly the point: the operation is cheaper in quality as well as in dollars, for we get what we pay for.

It is the administrator's business to make hard choices between imperfectly measured alternatives. No rule of thumb, no formula, no tidy calculation will do this job for him. In last analysis the role of judgment dominates.

This chapter has not attempted to assume the administrator's task by making his judgments for him. Its intent has been to identify the elements in the problem, to examine some of their interrelationships and their bearing on other administrative problems, and to produce a skeleton on which the intellectual processes of one kind of decision making can be hung. In developing in detail one set of administrative techniques, the author has tried to illustrate the wide range of alternate techniques possible, and at the same time has tried to show that techniques are not answers, that rigid rules are not solutions, and that scope for choices is an administrative necessity.

REFERENCE

Kohler, Emmett T.: *A Survey of Faculty Work Load Policies of Selected U.S. Universities,* Mississippi State University, State College, Mississippi, August, 1968 (mimeographed).

Section Seven

Student Personnel Administration

Chapter 1

Organization for Student Personnel Administration

PHILIP A. TRIPP

Vice-president for Student Development, Georgetown University, Washington, D.C.

ORIGINS: THE TORCHBEARERS

Of all the sectors of administration in higher education, student services administration has grown most dramatically in the last quarter century. Mainly responsible are (a) the impact of burgeoning numbers of students, (b) a growing sensitivity to the human factor in the educative process, and (c) an awareness of the increased sophistication required for the effective integration of the personal features of students' lives with substantive educational programs. The shift from a fairly simplistic view that, beyond instruction, institutional responsibility to students was limited mainly to the provision of bed and board and appropriate religious indoctrination, supervised by disciplinarians, to a contemporary view that this aspect of higher education has authentic educational purposes and functions is a main feature of recent higher educational history.

It is true that some form of student personnel work has always been an integral part of the higher educational process. The first American colleges took responsibility not only for their students' intellectual growth but also for their moral, spiritual, and social development. During the nineteenth century, this work consisted mainly of a pervading paternalistic concern for ensuring the religious commitment of the students and for their conformance to acceptable, conventional folkways and mores. The educational corps in this epoch saw as its principal mission the transmission of the cultural heritage and the inculcation of acceptable levels of deportment and piety.

The turn of the present century brought with it the birth of several social sciences, including sociology and psychology, and significant changes in the forms of higher education. New populations of students were enrolling in the new public institutions. The reaction of American philosophy against authoritarian thought provided the seedbed which produced a central concept of this changing social institution. The notion of the whole man as the subject of education was born.

It is somewhat ironical that the French military concept of *personnel* should have been selected as the cognomen around which present theory and practice were to be organized. It is a cold and impersonal word to invoke in the name of the ideas and activities it purports to comprehend. In the period between World War I and World War II, several events combined to produce present history. These included the invention of industrial management, progressive education, the rapid development of psychology and psychometry, and growing political libertarianism.

Present history dates from the conclusion of World War II. Federal support of great masses of students produced dramatic changes. Many logistical problems were faced and solved in the postwar years. But concomitant with them were more important educational and philosophical problems from which present programs of student personnel services derived.

NATURE, PURPOSES, AND MISSIONS

Programs of services for students may be classified under four general headings. The first of these comprises the *welfare functions.* Counseling services of various kinds typify this work. Also included are health services, programs of financial aid, testing, placement work, and, more recently, services for alumni.

The *control functions* have the longest history in student personnel administration. They comprehend admissions, the maintenance of records, discipline functions, and responsibility for living arrangements.

The third category of functions includes the *cocurricular and extracurricular* activities exemplified by student political organizations, social and cultural programs, and various creative activities. More recently this functional area has been broadened to include student involvement in the larger community and has given promise of great educational consequences.

The *teaching functions* are the most recently recognized, although they have long been operative in many colleges and universities. These may be seen in the orientation programs, the special offerings of remedial services, and in the work done with foreign students. The growing area for teaching has been in the residence hall, where increasingly it is demonstrable that significant learning can be accomplished when sufficient talent and energy are invested. The most dramatic frontier presently being developed in student personnel work involves making use of students as teachers in a variety of settings both on and off campus.

STUDENT SERVICES PARTICULARIZED

With the magnification of mission and complexity has come a general augmentation of programs of student services. Some nineteen major categories of administrative functions are generally recognized and included in the basic categories. The problem of definition is difficult, for in many smaller institutions several functions may be served by one professional staff member. However, in a large institution specialists for each service will be found.

The first service is that of *recruitment*. This is closely related to the *admissions* function, which is highly important in the life of both students and institutions. Two varieties of record making are identifiable. These are *academic* and *nonacademic record making*, both of which are critical to a well-functioning program. Counseling accounts for several major services. These include *personal, vocational, educational, financial, religious,* and *placement counseling*. All of these are supported by *testing services* of various kinds. Closely related is specialized work with *foreign students*, which has advisory as well as counseling features.

Residence hall services and programs account for a substantial part of the student services program on many campuses. They are supplemented by specialized *services for married students and for students who commute or reside off campus.*

Of growing importance is the increasingly complex area of *cocurricular and extracurricular programs*. As was noted earlier, they have progressed rapidly from essentially recreational and entertainment purposes to a much broader and richer zone including much that may be described as educational in its thrust. Examples are community action programs and innovative enterprises such as the free university movement.

Many institutions operate elaborate *college-union centers* which constitute still another service. They not only serve as vehicles for the programs alluded to earlier but also may support myriad other special purposes. Frequently, they are in fact what they like to be called, "the living room of the institution."

Food services cannot be ignored. Not only armies travel on their stomachs. An effective food service strongly affects the morale of an institution and it can be argued that this mundane activity can and ought to have an educational impact on those it serves.

Two varieties of athletic programs manned by different specialists may be found on many complex campuses. These are the *intercollegiate athletics programs* and the *intramural athletics programs*.

Finally, colleges and universities have increasingly accepted responsibility for providing *medical* and *nursing services* to students and sometimes to faculty and administrative staff as well. Although the range of service is considerable, extending from first-aid treatment to full hospital services, these programs are in a fast-evolving stage.

These, then, constitute presently identified, major student service functions provided by American colleges and universities.

Table 1 provides a summary of major student service functions.

PROFESSIONAL QUALIFICATIONS

The requirements to do satisfactory professional work in these functional areas are still in the process of study and development. They are obviously a far cry from the

TABLE 1 Major Student Service Functions—Programs of Service

Welfare	Control	Cocurricular–Extracurricular	Teaching
Counseling	Admissions	College unions/centers	Foreign students
Personal	Recruitment	Athletics	Remedial work
Vocational	Record keeping	Intercollegiate	Orientations
Educational	Academic	Intramural	Residence halls
Financial	Nonacademic	Social/cultural activities	Off-campus
Religious	Residence halls	Student government	
Placement	Resident	Community relations	
Testing	Off-campus resident		
Foreign students	Married		
Food services	Commuters		
Health services	Discipline		
Medical			
Nursing			
Alumni services			

fairly elementary and simplistic perceptions of what was involved in the appointments of the first deans of men and women in the late nineteenth century. It is clear that more than administrative talent is required if truly effective educational consequences are to follow. Not only are new, adequately educated specialists required, but more traditional specialists are required to reexamine their purposes, assumptions, and methods. These must be relevant to the facilitation of the growth and development of the American student affectively, socially, and physically as well as intellectually.

Professional staff members are increasingly holders of advanced degrees in the behavioral sciences. Psychology has produced a new field identified as counseling psychology. The specialized field of higher-education student personnel administration has appeared. The clergy and the medical professions have both now developed preparatory programs for college work. In fact, in every pertinent area it is recognized that professional competence is necessary. No longer is it feasible to eke out the work load of persons principally engaged as teachers, counselors, or administrators of other areas with assignments in the student services program.

Although there is no general consensus, there is a developing agreement about what is required professional preparation, and the prospects for strong programs of preparation in the various sectors of student personnel work are increasingly good. There is good reason to assume that, within the next decade, the work of this educational area will generally be staffed by persons whose professional competence is equivalent to that of members of the academic faculties. In leading institutions, this is already the case.

THOSE IN CHARGE

Although student services may be essentially functional in character, the measure of adequacy of such programs may be taken by their dynamic and complementary connection to the formal instructional programs and with the institution's avowed educational missions. This is the responsibility of those in charge. A brief note on their history and status may be of interest.

The title "Dean of Students" has the broadest currency in the higher education community. This title or some variant thereof was reported in about 75 percent of the institutions studied in a U.S. Office of Education national survey published in

1966. With the broadening of responsibility and authority at the policy level and wider recognition of the educational mission of this work has come the designator "Vice-president for Student Affairs," especially in the larger institutions. This is a significant change because, historically, the officers of this area have been, in the main, action-oriented executives who took direction from the president or other academic superiors. The increased complexity and the growing acceptance of the validity and importance of concern for student development as a principal feature of collegiate life may account for this new status.

The title in widest usage in this aspect of administration is "Dean of Men." In the formative days of the profession, it was this officer who was designated to relieve the president of responsibilities involving the personal and social affairs of students. His first concern was student discipline, and, although his function has since expanded many times, he remains a principal institutional representative in this form of work. The changing responsibilities of the dean of men do typify, however, the dramatic change in mission and purpose of student personnel programs. Increasingly, the title is being replaced with that of "Associate Dean of Students." The holder of this title is engaging in the generation and implementation of broader educational programs and purposes to a greater extent than was historically the case. With the decline of authoritarian philosophical premises, the work of this executive is being modified and modernized to focus on the developmental aspects of students' lives.

The most common title for principal women executives in this field of work is "Dean of Women." The first deans of women were employed to care for the special educational, social, and psychological requirements of girls who began to seek higher education in the latter days of the nineteenth century. The present-day deans similarly carry much broader and deeper educational responsibilities than their predecessors and have made significant contributions to the development of the role of women in modern society.

A CHANGE TO FUNCTION

Although the title "Dean of Women" continues to have very broad usage, there is a noticeable trend to substitute "Associate Dean of Students" in the case of reorganization of administrations. This tendency, also noted in the case of "Dean of Men," reflects a fundamental revision in the nature of student personnel work. From a tradition which was based on the peculiar problems and needs of men as men and women as women, there is a growing trend to recast programs of student services on functional lines which minimize the sex differences. Although specialized problems are still recognized and served, the emphasis of these newer programs is on similarities in the developmental patterns of the young adults and on the contributions which may be made by student personnel work to the facilitation of that development.

STUDENT PERSONNEL SPECIALISTS

There is a large and growing number of specific positions filled by people who are indeed assistants to the dean of students, but whose areas of operation are sufficiently distinct to call for the assignment of separate designations. Not all titles are common to every institution, but the following will serve as examples of those which occur most frequently.

Associate Dean of Students for Freshman Affairs. This title is becoming common in large universities. This most critical year in a student's life requires special coordination in the areas of counseling, housing, and orientation. This dean and his assistants, with the aid of the instructional staff as well as specialists from several areas, concentrate on improving the "survival rate" for freshmen. This dean's office will usually handle academic counseling as well, since most freshman problems are involved with scholastic attainment.

Assistant Dean. A key person moving into the student personnel area is the assistant dean for the educationally disadvantaged. He is usually a staff member who relates particularly to minority-group students and coordinates the special efforts necessary in the acclimatizing process. In this connection it should be pointed out that the sensitive areas of student services require people of great empathy and would naturally attract those attuned to the special needs of minority ethnic groups. An increasing number of regular staff members from these groups can be expected in the years ahead.

Director of Student Activities. The staff member holding this title has a well-defined position and—increasingly today—a highly sensitive one. He must supervise a sizeable and diffuse budget, and manage the operation of a program which is of primary importance to the morale of a student body.

The office of student activities requires a growing list of specialists to handle the needs of the hundreds of student extracurricular organizations. Although the faculty members continue to function as advisers to student organizations, the financial operation particularly calls for the treasurer to be a full-time, skilled staff member. The sophistication and scope of organizations related to drama, music, and publications require managerial skills to supplement the student effort. The wide-ranging activities of a large college union require specialists that a few years ago were unknown.

Director of Student Financial Aids. Student financial aid is increasing exponentially as more young people attend college, as the cost of higher education continues to grow, and as the philosophy of deferred payment becomes popular. The number and complexity of government aid programs has in very recent years caused this function to become distinctive and highly specialized. As a result, most institutions have a separate office which oversees all forms of aid including scholarships, grants in aid, loans, and part-time jobs.

The amount of money distributed through all forms of aid causes the operation to take on the aspect of a strictly fiscal function, but the decision-making interviews with students involve personal and confidential information; therefore, staff people with a student personnel orientation are required.

Counseling and Testing. Years ago all functions of this office were performed by the dean of students and his staff. Today the sophistication and the depth of both tests and procedures has brought into being a whole new area of specialists. Their basic discipline has generally been the field of psychology with a specialty in counseling. The American Personnel and Guidance Association (APGA) is a useful and productive source of counseling and testing personnel.

Housing Officer. The dean of men (or women) is usually responsible for formal counseling programs in residence halls and other housing units. However, an office headed by a "Director of Housing" is often in overall charge of the mechanical and housekeeping aspects of residence because of the basic needs and requirements which exist apart from student personnel matters. There is a delicate relationship between the disparate elements here, but each must recognize and emphasize the common goals toward which each is striving. Personnel in the office of the director of housing relate to the business manager's overall operation.

Foreign-student Adviser. If an institution has a significant number of foreign students, common prudence dictates the presence of a foreign-student adviser. The multiplicity and complexity of problems in the areas of housing and diet, finances, immigration laws and procedures, as well as the academic maze, make this a full-time job. A special kind of sympathetic understanding, combined with an up-to-date knowledge of international, federal, and local programs, is essential to a good adviser.

RECRUITMENT OF STAFF

A principal concern of the chief administrator is the recruiting and developing of his supporting staff. The in-service training, upgrading, and search for specialists goes on continuously in any large university. An important source through which talent is located is the placement service of the National Association of Student Personnel Administrators (NASPA). This organization, although staffed by volunteer help, is the one best medium with national coverage. NASPA provides a listing of vacancies among its more than seven hundred member universities and provides the members with lists of those searching for placement opportunities.

As with any professional group, there is much placement by personal contact, particularly in the upper levels. The graduates in master's and doctoral programs usually will have participated in internships in the areas of housing, student activities, union management, counseling, financial aid, and admissions. They can expect to enter into full-time employment as assistants in these areas. Many young people prefer to take positions in smaller four-year or two-year institutions with the opportunities for a variety of administrative experiences. Those joining large institutions will tend to find themselves in more limited and restricted positions simply because size brings more fragmentation of responsibilities.

The entry occupations appear to include positions in the residence hall programs, student activities, financial aid, and admissions. These areas show considerable turnover of young people, many of them moving to more responsible student personnel positions within the university. Because of the tremendous growth of our collegiate population, the opportunities for young administrators to move rapidly up the ladder have been enhanced. The area of student personnel administration is no exception.

As each of the following chapters of this section unfolds, the reader will appreciate more the wide-ranging role that student personnel administration is playing in our colleges. When the details of operation and function of each of the score or more areas are enlarged upon by the authors and when the duties and responsibilities of the chief specialists and their assistants are delineated, the comprehensive nature of the work becomes apparent.

ORGANIZING AND ADMINISTERING

It is a commonplace that administration and the organization for administration are nothing more than instruments employed to assist and provide leadership in an institution in the accomplishment of the purposes of the organization. All administrative officers should perceive their roles in direct relationship to those ends. Continuing and constant analysis of his administrative organization is a chief responsibility of each major executive. This exercise is essential in present-day colleges and universities if they are to be responsible and responsive to a changing social order. The institutions themselves are in a state of high flux which requires great flexibility and sensitive response to the needs of our times.

The search for the perfect model of organization of complex societies such as our higher educational institutions is unending. The variety of examples to be seen in the present community includes procrustean authoritarian models as well as group models where authority and responsibility are broadly shared. It may be affirmed, nonetheless, that a sound administrative organization for student services should provide itself with a line-staff chart indicating the working relationships among the officers and showing or making explicit their several relationships with each other and their subordinates. Such an organization chart for a large and complex university is shown in Figure 1. There should be a clear distinction evident, insofar as possible, between the instruments of policy making and policy administration. A clear statement of the nature of committee functions, either advisory or executive, should be included. The role of the faculty as an organized group should be clearly identified and enunciated. Finally, such a plan should describe the explicit responsibilities and statements of commensurate authority delegated to the various officers and it should give some information about procedures established for the realization of the general program as well as institutional goals.

It is of great importance that the basic plan clearly identify those members of the staff who work with and report to the major administrator. Lines of responsibility and au-

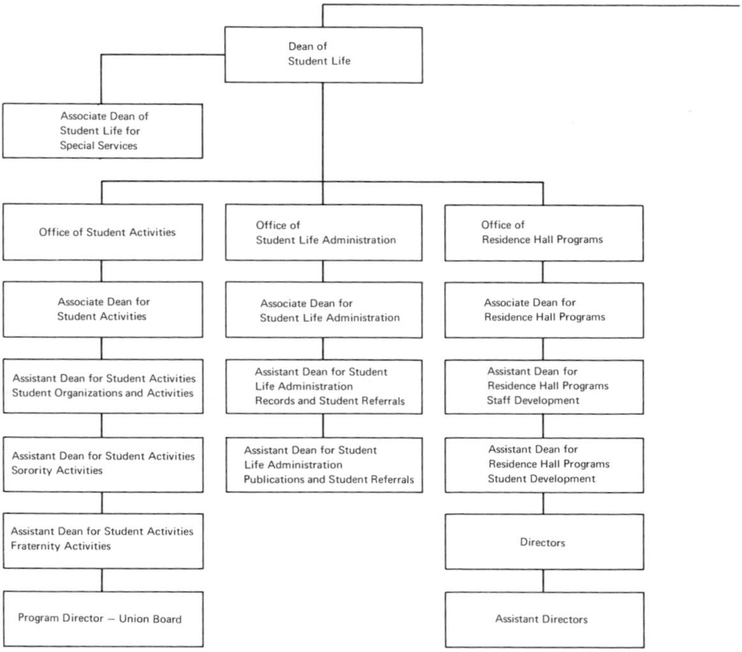

Fig. 1 *An example of administrative organization in a large and complex university. (Courtesy, Indiana State University.)*
Objectives of Student Life
1. To assist students in their growth and development by providing opportunities for them to exercise their sense of responsibility, their leadership potential, and their interpersonal relationship abilities.
2. To operate as a service agency for students, faculty, parents, and other administrative officials.
3. To provide opportunities for one-to-one relationships between administrative officials and students to discuss concerns of the student.
4. To develop a style of relationship among students, faculty, and staff which encourages frequency of interaction and the strengthening of commitments in areas of common interest.
5. To provide opportunities for broad student participation in the governance of the university in areas where students can make valuable contributions.
6. To strive for a high quality of student participation and leadership in the life of the university.

thority for performing particular sets of functions must be clearly articulated. This is true irrespective of the size of institution. Even in small institutions, where part-time assignments are made in more than one area of service, such specificity is required for the effective accomplishment of the missions.

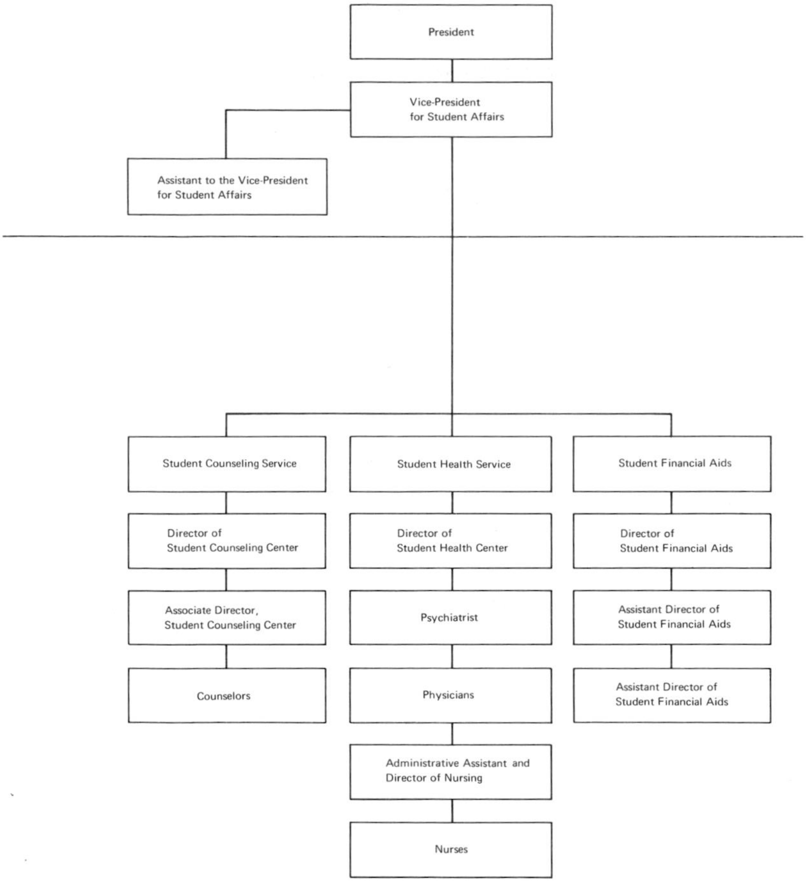

Objectives of Student Affairs

1. To stimulate students to integrate formal and informal learning, encouraging education of the "whole man" by emphasizing the interdependence of the concepts learned in the classroom and the discoveries made through out-of-class experiences.

2. To provide enrichment experiences for all students by developing student programs, encouraging student participation, and providing special services for students who need individual attention.

3. To encourage relationships among professors, administrative officials, and students which will enhance increased communications and provide bases for decision making by all groups.

4. To create a climate in which each student may have equal access to all the educational opportunities of the university.

5. To encourage an atmosphere in which each student may seek self-identification and to create avenues through which he may express his individuality.

6. To establish a climate in which each student can be challenged to higher levels of intellectual development and personal and moral maturity.

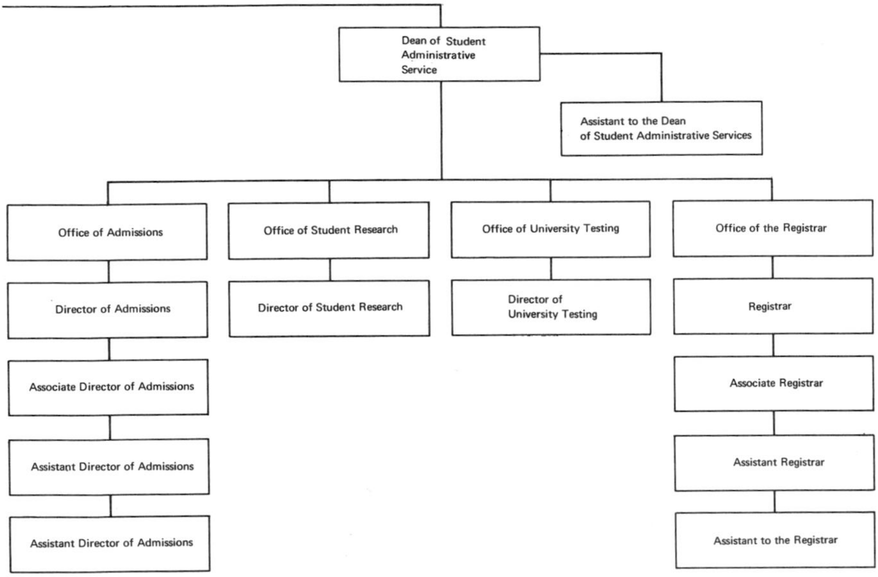

Objectives of Student Administrative Services

1. To provide admission, registration, student research, testing, and related services to students, faculty, and administrative officers.

2. To establish and maintain a Student Information System with common and unique student data readily available for administrative and academic decision making.

3. To provide a special coordinated program between academic offices and student administrative services based upon the comprehensive Student Information System.

4. To conduct student research and provide comprehensive data to the university community for immediate and long-range planning.

5. To coordinate and design information processing, retrieval, and flow for all areas of student affairs.

6. To interpret the educational opportunities of the university to prospective student.

AT THE PRESENT TIME

Student services administration shares in the institutional mission of increased effectiveness and efficiency of operation and thereby contributes to the realization of the major purposes of the institution. Organizational structure should be designed to enable the institution to fulfill most effectively its current purposes. To this end, the chief student services officer is responsible for the centralization, coordination, organization, direction, and staffing of the program comprehended by the area delegated to his control by competent authority.

Although programs of student services may be found universally on college and university campuses, they are not yet organized under one administrative head in all institutions. However, the previously noted survey published by the U.S. Office of Education reported that nearly all institutions indicated the presence of an officer classifiable as the chief student personnel officer. It in general appears that such an administrative responsibility is firmly established in the management of higher education. Only very small and simply organized schools can function with only part-time administrative attention to this area.

THE WORK OF THE CHIEF STUDENT SERVICES OFFICER

The functional areas over which he has control define and prescribe the responsibilities of the chief student personnel officer. A typical example of the responsibilities of a dean of students in a small to medium-sized undergraduate institution is presented in Figure 2. However, this officer shares with the other principal administrators a number of obligations common to them all. These include serving as an alter-ego of the president. Inevitably, his office is an extension of the president's office. He has broad and specific authority for his area of responsibility and he is expected to exercise it with respect to his president's wishes. He has obligations to cooperate and coordinate with others who lead the various divisions of the institution. The chief student personnel officer has an advisory obligation to make recommendations regarding plans, policies, and procedures in his area of responsibility which are consonant with the cardinal objectives of the institution. He has obligations to ensure the provision of adequate staff and equipment to discharge the responsibilities assigned. Integration and coordination of the subdivisions within his span of control and articulation of this work with that of other areas are imperatives. Of growing significance is the necessity for professional leadership in recruiting and staff development in these changing times. Budget preparation and development fall to every administrative officer. And finally, the chief student personnel officer has obligations to respond to the need for information by his president and other qualified persons.

The specialized responsibilities of the chief student service officer focus on the life of the students singly and collectively. He is responsible for the creation and maintenance of an educational environment calculated to serve the total development of each student. Such a task requires the development of a sound philosophical grounding and practical administrative skill. It obviously includes each of the functional areas earlier defined. He has obligations to ensure that recruitment and admissions activities are approached from the perspective of the student and with a view to protecting his interests. It is important that adequate records be developed but that the rights of individuals remain paramount in the handling of the records.

It is the chief student service officer's responsibility to attend to the individual needs for advice and counseling of students by the provision of adequate staff and faculty for those purposes. Such requirements ramify to include the provision of qualified staff members not only in counseling centers but in the residence halls, in the placement office, and in the areas of financial aid and religious affairs. It extends to providing assistance to the student at the time of his departure through the placement counseling program.

Although he shares the obligation for academic advisement with colleagues in other areas of administration, the chief student services officer nonetheless is responsible for ensuring that adequate policies, procedures, and programs are provided to enable students to reach their academic goals, both curricular and cocurricular. This is accomplished by the creation and maintenance of a cultural, social, and spiritual environment calculated to those ends.

The temporal requirements of students fall into the chief student services officer's jurisdiction. These include the provision of housing, food service, and health care commensurate with the needs and interests of the student community.

His teaching responsibilities are multifaceted and include the development of a teaching attitude on the part of his staff members and a teaching base in the specialized programs under his supervision. As was noted, his responsibilities include orientation programs, residence halls, social, cultural, and entertainment programs, and the facilitation of student involvement in institutional life through student government or through other creative extracurricular activities.

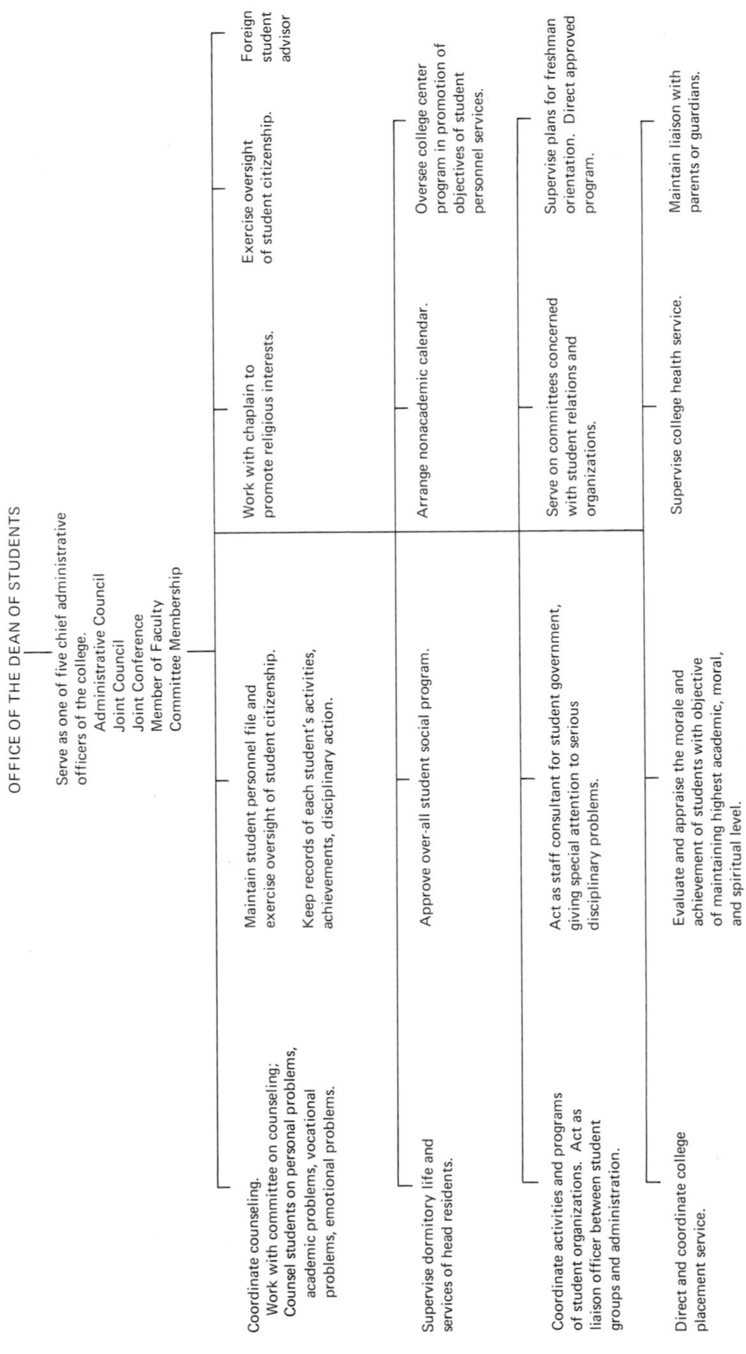

OFFICE OF THE DEAN OF STUDENTS
Serve as one of five chief administrative officers of the college.
Administrative Council
Joint Council
Joint Conference
Member of Faculty
Committee Membership
Coordinate counseling.
Work with committee on counseling;
Counsel students on personal problems, academic problems, vocational problems, emotional problems.
Maintain student personnel file and exercise oversight of student citizenship.
Keep records of each student's activities, achievements, disciplinary action.
Work with chaplain to promote religious interests.
Exercise oversight of student citizenship.
Foreign student advisor
Supervise dormitory life and services of head residents.
Approve over-all student social program.
Arrange nonacademic calendar.
Oversee college center program in promotion of objectives of student personnel services.
Coordinate activities and programs of student organizations. Act as liaison officer between student groups and administration.
Act as staff consultant for student government, giving special attention to serious disciplinary problems.
Serve on committees concerned with student relations and organizations.
Supervise plans for freshman orientation. Direct approved program.
Direct and coordinate college placement service.
Evaluate and appraise the morale and achievement of students with objective of maintaining highest academic, moral, and spiritual level.
Supervise college health service.
Maintain liaison with parents or guardians.

Fig. 2 *A typical example of the responsibilities of a dean of students in a small to medium-size undergraduate institution.*

The chief student services officer has facilitative and integrative responsibilities to the total academic community and to the larger world. The promotion of educationally promising encounters both intra- and extramurally with all members of the community are proper to his interest. The chief student services executive is clearly a person with a broad scope of responsibilities.

WHAT THE FUTURE PORTENDS

The future of student services in higher education is a subject of growing interest both within and outside professional circles. It is increasingly clear that if this work is to be truly effective it must proceed on sound scientific bases. The day when administrative talent, general insights, good intentions, and sympathy were sufficient for the management of student affairs in higher education is past. In the future, high-level professional and scientific background as well as basic research competencies will be required of leading student services educators.

It is now evident that the higher education institution of the future will be substantially different from that of the past. The roles of students are undergoing enormous revision at the present time, and the effect of the changes imposes new requirements on the student services educator and modify his present work significantly.

Increasingly, the students will play larger roles in institutional affairs. The nature of the teaching and learning process itself is concurrently undergoing major revision. The day when individual disciplines could be wholly mastered by individual scholars is gone. Present-day scholarship involves a lifetime of work and an acceptance of the fact that the myriad facets of any field of inquiry are beyond the scope of any one individual. This changes the teaching-learning relationship. The role of the administrator as a philosopher-king is also passé. The administrator of the future will be effective insofar as he can see and communicate relationships among disparate persons and ideas. He will be a catalytic force whose object is to facilitate scientific inquiry, effective teaching, individual development, and social change, both within the campus and beyond it.

STUDENT DEVELOPMENT—A CENTRAL CONCEPT

The specialized work of the student services educator will involve his becoming effectively an expert in student development. Obviously this involves much more than a knowledge of developmental psychology. Inasmuch as he will be charged with the task of fostering student growth and serving students' complex human needs, he will have to develop increasingly sophisticated knowledge and insight into many humanistic and social scientific studies. These include, for example, the arts and sciences related to personal and social growth and interpersonal relations. Among them are social anthropology, political science, and communication science. He will have to acquire research skills not generally found in his present-day counterpart. He will be a student of students and be responsible for translating his findings concerning them into programs and services that facilitate their education individually and collectively. He will have responsibility for developing data useful to students in the accomplishment of their developmental goals and to fellow faculty members facilitative of their professional needs and interests as teachers.

The student development administrator of the future will be competent to describe the students' characteristics upon entering college. He will be knowledgeable about dimensions and characteristics of his institution. He will study the students and institution in the process of interaction. Finally, he will be competent to describe and appraise in a variety of ways student characteristics at the point of departure.

A principal mission of the student services program in the coming years will be to assess educational effects on students and to evaluate the impact of the educational experience provided by institutions in light of a variety of specific criteria. Assessments will be made of the effects of various educational opportunities on individual students exposed to different educational programs. The impact of educational experiences on students and their meaning to them will be subjects of scientific inquiry in this work in the future.

In the area of communication, increased emphasis will be given to assisting all the members of the collegiate community in communicating about educational processes, both personal and collective. It is here that the student personnel educator's catalytic function will focus. Student studies of their own development can help them grow. Development of this kind of information in collaboration with students, faculty, and fellow administrators exemplifies the catalytic function. In fine, the vital function of this work in the future will be to assist all concerned in the understanding of motivations and educational processes and in assessing the effectiveness of various programs of learning.

Generally speaking, the student personnel educator of the future will be that member of the collegiate community most concerned with the developmental and process phenomena involved in the educational experience. His mission will be to make use, in both scientific and artistic terms, of knowledge and experience to the end of facilitating the most effective personal and interpersonal growth that can be devised in the frame of the collegiate experience.

SELECTED REFERENCES

Ayers, Archie R., Philip A. Tripp, and John H. Russel: *Student Services Administration in Higher Education,* U.S. Department of Health, Education, and Welfare, Office of Education, Washington, 1966.

Butts, Porter: *State of the College Union Around the World,* Association of College Unions—International, Cornell University, Ithaca, N.Y., 1967.

Chauncey, Henry, and John E. Dobbin: *Testing: Its Place in Education Today,* Harper & Row, Publishers, Incorporated, New York, 1963.

Erikson, Erik H. (ed.): *The Challenge of Youth,* Doubleday & Company, Inc., Garden City, N.Y., 1963.

Feder, Daniel D. (chairman), et al.: *The Administration of Student Personnel Programs in American Colleges and Universities,* Committee on Student Personnel Work, American Council on Education, Washington, 1958.

Friedenberg, Edgar Z.: *Coming of Age in America,* Random House, Inc., New York, 1965.

Katz, Joseph, et al.: *The College Student,* Jossey-Bass, San Francisco, 1968.

Leonard, Eugenia A.: *Origins of Personnel Services in American Higher Education,* University of Minnesota Press, Minneapolis, 1956.

Lipset, Seymour M. (ed.): *Student Politics,* Basic Books, Inc., Publishers, New York, 1967.

Lloyd-Jones, Esther, and Herman Estrin: *The American Student and His College,* Houghton Mifflin Company, Boston, 1967.

Lloyd-Jones, Esther, and Margaret Ruth Smith: *A Student Personnel Program for Higher Education,* McGraw-Hill Book Company, New York, 1938.

Mueller, Kate Hevner: *Student Personnel Work in Higher Education,* Houghton Mifflin Company, Boston, 1961.

Newcomb, Theodore, and E. Wilson (eds.): *College Peer Groups,* Aldine Publishing Company, Chicago, 1966.

Shaffer, Robert, and William Martinson: *Student Personnel Services in Higher Education,* Center for Applied Research, New York, 1966.

Stroup, Herbert: *Toward a Philosophy of Organized Student Activities,* University of Minnesota Press, Minneapolis, 1964.

Wallace, Walter L.: *Student Culture,* Aldine Publishing Company, Chicago, 1966.

Williamson, E. G.: *Student Personnel Services in Colleges and Universities,* McGraw-Hill Book Company, Inc., New York, 1961.

Yamamoto, Kaoru (ed.): *The College Student and His Culture: An Analysis,* Houghton Mifflin Company, Boston, 1968.

Chapter **2**

Student Personnel Administration Policies *

PETER H. ARMACOST

President, Ottawa University, Ottawa, Kansas

* The author gratefully acknowledges the assistance of Dr. Earle W. Clifford, University Dean for Student Affairs at Rutgers University, in the preparation of this chapter. Dr. Clifford made a particular contribution to the development of the section on Student Participation in Institutional Governance.

College and university policies affecting student life have been a subject of great controversy in recent years as students have pressed for greater freedoms and as educators have gained new insights into the learning process and reconsidered their understanding of the role of the student in higher education and of the relationship between the university and society. Students and faculty alike have challenged the traditional bases for institutional policies affecting student life, and in recent years a number of court decisions have suggested legal principles to be considered in formulating and evaluating such policies. In this context, the present chapter attempts:

To identify basic premises for consideration in establishing institutional policies affecting student life

To outline fundamental principles concerning student freedoms, rights, and responsibilities

To discuss more specifically student participation in institutional governance

To review and report research upon institutional policies on selected topics

Institutional approaches to policies affecting student life differ markedly from campus to campus. Clearly no one set of policies will suffice for all colleges and universities, since such policies should indeed reflect the aims and objectives of the institution, its assumptions about the efficacy of various approaches to teaching, and such other relevant factors as the size and complexity of the institution, the type of control (e.g., public versus private nonsectarian or private church-related), and the proportion of its students who commute rather than live in residence. At the same time, a number of national higher education associations have reached agreement recently on a number of basic student rights and freedoms.

BASIC PREMISES

An institution's approach to policies affecting student life derives from its position on a number of basic issues. For example, is a college or university truly a community of learners, or must the concept of community be realistically replaced by either the view that the institution is merely an extension of the civil community or the view that the college or university is a "nest of adversaries" in which students, faculty, and administrators negotiate and bargain to maximize their own legitimate interests? Is the nature of the relationship between students and the college best characterized in the term *in loco parentis,* which denotes an extension of the family authority and the hierarchical relationships between parent and child to the academic institution which becomes a substitute parent in the student-college relationship, or in terms which denote some form of colleague or apprentice relationship? Where does the most significant learning occur during the college years, and to what extent can and should college authorities legitimately concern themselves with the various nonclassroom settings for learning?

On each of these issues, and others as well, there are a variety of possible responses by any given academic institution, and these will have direct bearing on institutional approach to policies affecting student life. In response to such issues, the following basic premises are advanced as central to our approach to the topic.

The Institution as a Community Institutional approaches to student life policies rest first upon an assumption about the nature of a college or university as a community—a community of persons associated together for the pursuit of learning. In such a community each person participates as a partner in the community according to his experience and abilities, and there should be little difference in point of view between the "senior" colleagues of the faculty and the "junior" colleagues of the student body, for the welfare of the institution as a whole is a concern and responsibility of all. Each person voluntarily joins such an academic community for the pursuit of educational objectives which he holds in common with other members of the community. On the basis of their common cause, both junior and senior colleagues in the academic institution relinquish certain freedoms in order to attain objectives which can only be achieved by membership in the academic community. Institutional approaches to policies affecting student life based on this premise may differ in substance and will certainly differ in the method of their determination from approaches based either on the view that college is merely an extension of the political community or the view that the college consists of three "power blocks"—students, faculty, and administrators—each trying to maximize its own position in the community and to administer its own affairs.

Student-Institution Relationships Within the context of this perception of the learning community, historical definitions of the student-institutional relationship under the *in loco parentis* rubric have little currency. Indeed, the legal phrases "fiduciary" or "contract" have limited applicability as general terms defining the relationship and are, therefore, also of minimum value. Instead, as indicated, the most useful general concept may be that of the relationship among colleagues.

There are a number of important implications of such an approach to student-institutional relationships. The first and most critical of these is that the relationship between a college or university and its students is primarily an educational one. The pursuit of shared educational objectives becomes the basis for association.

Second, the "colleague" approach is undergirded by a sense of mutual respect which is a normal affective stance toward others involved in such a relationship.

Third, real criteria—differences in experience and ability—rather than artificial assumptions of immaturity and irresponsibility become the yardstick for evaluations that credit or discredit the contribution of the individual student as he participates as a colleague in the institution's decision-making process.

Fourth, the "colleague" approach suggests that all matters of policy and *all* issues affecting the community are of proper concern to *all* members of that community, and that there should be a process to involve effectively students in any issue in which they have a stake. At the same time, such a process may take a variety of forms and does not necessarily assume representation of all segments of the community on all committees.

It becomes just as important, for example, for faculty colleagues to participate in decisions about student social life as for students to be involved in curricular matters.

Fifth, if students are in fact to be colleagues, then rules and regulations defining expectations of student conduct need to be reexamined. Consideration might even be given to the establishment of standards applicable to *all* members of the community. Whatever the outcome, however, such reexamination should begin with a clear definition of institutional goals, and the resulting regulations should be required to pass the test of being both reasonable and relevant in terms of those goals.

Areas of Significant Student Learning Policies affecting student life should also be developed within the context of an awareness that significant student learning occurs in a variety of settings—inside and outside the formal classroom and both on campus and off campus—and that the total institutional climate of learning and the conditions for learning in these settings is the proper concern of all segments of the university community. Thus, administrators and faculty members have a legitimate concern for the nonclassroom behavior of students, and they substantially reduce their educational effectiveness if they completely relinquish all responsibility for policies affecting such matters as student social conduct. On the other hand, the educational experience of students is truncated and the student social conduct policies are likely to be less effective if students do not have a major responsibility for policy determination and enforcement in areas directly affecting student life. Furthermore, it is imperative that such policies do not illegally violate constitutionally guaranteed freedoms which the student enjoys as a citizen.

STUDENT RIGHTS, FREEDOMS, AND RESPONSIBILITIES

Within the past three years a *Joint Statement on the Rights and Freedoms of Students* has been developed and approved (with clarifying interpretations in several cases) by five associations—The American Association of University Professors, The Association of American Colleges, The U.S. National Student Association, The National Association of Student Personnel Administrators, and the National Association of Women Deans and Counselors. Campus policies and procedures affecting student life should be developed on the basis of both the Joint Statement and the aims and objectives of the institution. The basic principles embodied in the Joint Statement should be incorporated in institutional policies and procedures affecting student life, and the document itself is deserving of serious study. The Joint Statement includes both statements of principle or policy on the one hand and statements of procedures on the other. In order to emphasize the essential concepts, the following paragraphs attempt to summarize (using the language of that document) the basic principles concerning student rights and freedoms established in the Joint Statement and to indicate the corollary responsibilities relative to each. Most of the suggested responsibilities, however, are not actually incorporated in the Joint Statement itself, but some such statements are frequently found in policy statements adopted by individual colleges and universities.

Freedom to Learn

The primary right of students is to cherish and to exercise the freedom to learn. Fundamental to the freedom to learn are the rights of freedom of inquiry, freedom of expression, freedom to develop integrity of thought and action, and freedom from disciplinary action without due process. The correlative student responsibility is to be aware of one's freedoms and to use them to create educational opportunities for one's self in ways which contribute to the educational purposes of the student and of the academic institution.

Freedom of Inquiry Students should have the right to inquire freely into any subject matter which is of interest to them and to form reasoned beliefs on the basis of such inquiry. In order to present and to consider various points of view outside the classroom, students should be free to hear any speaker of their choosing and, within the limits of the orderly operation of the primary educational program of the institution, to utilize institutional facilities for educational programs of their own design. Students have a responsibility, however, to use freedom of inquiry in the serious pursuits of learning, to develop educational opportunities which enhance the educational mission of the institution, and to learn to the limits of their capacities.

Freedom of Expression Students have a right to the free expression of their opinions and beliefs in a variety of ways. In exercising this freedom, however, students have a responsibility to respect the rights and opinions of others including fellow students, faculty, and the administration and to give preference to means of expression which are appropriate within the academic community. Thus, written articles, forums, debates, or discussion are to be preferred to picketing, demonstrations, chanting, and similar actions which are inappropriate unless other alternatives are unavailable or have been clearly shown to be inadequate as techniques for obtaining a fair hearing of points of view. In all cases, students have a responsibility to refrain from such tactics as prevent the expression of opposing points of view. No member of the academic community has a right to have his point of view adopted by the majority of the members of the community, and each member has a responsibility to refrain from tactics which involve the use of coercion in attempting to force his point of view on others. Furthermore, there is the responsibility to inform the community at large that a student position statement or action does not represent the university—officially or unofficially.

The student rights of free inquiry and free expression include the freedom in the classroom to take reasoned exception to the data or views offered in any course of study and to reserve judgment about matters of opinion. In exercising this freedom the student should be protected through orderly procedures against prejudiced, capricious, or other improper academic evaluation in the classroom and against improper disclosure of student views, beliefs, and political associations either by individual professors or by means of notations on official college records. Students have the corollary responsibility to maintain the standards of academic performance and to learn the content of each course in which they are enrolled.

Freedom of the Student Press. A special case of the right of free expression is freedom of the student press. Except where the student press has the legal and financial status of an independent corporation, the institution, as the publisher of the student publications, must bear the legal responsibility for the contents of the publications and for all editorial freedoms exercised by these publications. In the delegation of editorial responsibility to students, the institution must provide sufficient editorial freedom and financial autonomy, however, for the student publications to maintain their integrity of purpose as vehicles for free inquiry and free expression in an academic community. In all cases editorial freedom involves freedom from censorship and advance approval of copy and freedom for the editors and managers to develop their own editorial policies and news coverage. Likewise, editors and managers of student publications should be protected from arbitrary suspension and removal because of student, faculty, or administrative disapproval of editorial policy or content.

At the same time, the editorial freedom of student editors and managers entails corollary responsibilities to be governed by the canons of responsible journalism such as the avoidance of libel, indecency, undocumented allegations, attacks on personal integrity, and the techniques of harassment and innuendo. Editorial freedom also entails responsibility to recognize that the public sometimes erroneously assumes that the student publications represents the institution and that the welfare of the institution as an academic community may be negatively affected by their content.

Freedom to Develop Integrity of Thought and Action Students have a right to freedom to develop integrity of thought and action. As part of the educational process, students are encouraged to inquire freely into any subject which is of interest to them and they are urged to form opinions and beliefs on the basis of reasoned inquiry. They should not be told that if this inquiry leads to certain beliefs which are in conflict with the value position of the institution they cannot act on the basis of such beliefs. Although such prohibitions confront the student with a situation which is no different than that which a citizen faces when his beliefs would lead to action which is illegal, a college or university must be certain that its prohibitions of student activities on the basis of reasoned belief are indeed relevant to its educational mission, since forcing students not to act on the basis of beliefs may truncate the educational process, hinder student growth, and compromise the integrity of the student.

Freedom of Association. Essential to the freedom to develop integrity of thought and action is the freedom to associate with other persons on campus or off campus, in local groups or national groups, and to support causes by any orderly means which do not disrupt the regular and essential operation of the institution. Likewise, freedom of speech, peaceful assembly, and the right to petition that citizens in the larger community enjoy should also be shared by students in the academic community.

At the same time, students contemplating activities as expressions of their belief have a responsibility to be clear in their objectives and to be fully aware of the legal situation and the possible consequences of their actions to themselves and to the college community. It should be made clear to the academic and the larger community that in their public expressions or demonstrations students or student organizations speak only for themselves.

Disciplinary Standards The student right and responsibility to cherish and exercise the freedom to learn involves, fourthly, freedom from disciplinary action except through due process. Disciplinary action against a student should be taken only for violations of institutional standards of behavior and regulations which are as clearly defined as possible, which are relevant to the objectives of the institution, and which represent a reasonable degree of control over students. The disciplinary processes which guarantee fundamental procedural fairness to an accused student may vary in formality with the degree to which the institutional officials have prior direct acquaintance with student life in general and with the involved students and the circumstances of the case in particular, with the presence or the absence of an honor code, with the gravity of the offense, and with the sanctions which may be applied. In all situations, however, procedural fair play requires that the student have advance knowledge of the standards of student behavior which have been developed within the academic community, that he be informed of the nature of the charges against him, that he be given a fair opportunity to refute them, that the institution not be arbitrary in its actions, and that there be a provision for appeal of a decision. (Specific discussion of procedures for handling disciplinary matters and the legal basis for these procedures are found in other chapters of this handbook.)

Each student as a member of society has a responsibility to conduct himself in accordance with generally accepted standards of conduct as embodied in society's laws and regulations. More specifically, each student has a responsibility as a member of the academic institution to be fully informed as to the institutional standards of student behavior and to comply with the rules governing students at the university.

Participation in Institutional Governance

A second right and responsibility of students is to participate through clearly defined means in the formulation of the institutional policy and especially to participate in the student government, which has been established within the university with authority to administer, legislate, and adjudicate in all areas within its constitutional jurisdiction.

Knowledge and Support of Institutional Goals and Programs

In view of the fact that freedom to learn is not necessarily synonymous with opportunity to learn, and in view of the fact that each college or university has a right and responsibility to define its own institutional purposes and procedures within the context of generally accepted standards, a third statement about student rights and responsibilities is necessary. Students have a right and a responsibility to be informed accurately and in advance of registration as to the educational goals of the institution, the general institutional provisions for policy determination and administration, and the educational opportunities which will be provided. It follows that the student has a right to competent instruction and adequate counseling by able and interested teachers and to adequate facilities commensurate with the educational responsibilities which the institution has taken unto itself.

In turn, the student has the responsibility to cooperate in the achievement of institutional goals. He may advocate change and should have the opportunity to discuss and work to achieve alternative structures, purposes, and educational opportunities, but he may not demand such changes as a right.

Merit Evaluation

There is one final statement of a student right and responsibility. Each student has a right to be considered for admission, advancement, degrees, honors, and all academic and cocurricular activities and benefits on his own merit without regard to ancestry, race, or country of origin and to continuation in his educational program as long as he is not in violation of any scholastic or conduct requirements or as long as his state of health is not harmful to others.

He has the correlative responsibility to be informed of admissions, academic standing, and degree requirements, of the standard for participation in student activities, and of standards for student behavior. He is expected to govern his behavior in accordance with these requirements and standards.

STUDENT PARTICIPATION IN INSTITUTIONAL GOVERNANCE

As constituents of the academic community, students should be free, individually and collectively, to express their views on issues of institutional policy and on matters of general interest to the student body. The student body should have clearly defined means to participate in the formulation and application of institutional policy affecting academic and student affairs. The role of the student government and both its general and specific responsibilities should be made explicit, and the actions of the student government within the areas of its jurisdiction should be reviewed only through orderly and prescribed procedures.

The above section from the *Joint Statement on the Rights and Freedoms of Students* indicates that there are two dimensions to student involvement in institutional governance, for a distinction is made between student government and student participation in university government. Identified first is the right and responsibility of students to be involved through clearly defined means in the formulation of institutional policy. There is provision also for participation in student government established within the university with responsibility and authority to legislate, administer, and adjudicate in all areas within its constitutional jurisdiction.

There are a number of assumptions basic to student involvement in both areas of governance. First, it follows from the view of the academic community mentioned earlier in this chapter that it is essential for each college and university to establish an appropriate pattern for the genuine involvement of students in the formulation of educational policy. Significant student involvement in college policy-making must be based on the belief that students, as colleagues, have an important perspective and can make important substantive contributions which will increase the probability of insightful decisions by college administrators and policy-making committees in most areas of college policy. Such student involvement must *not* be based upon the false assumption that the academic community is a political community in which the citizens are the ultimate source of power and have an inherent right to participate in the governing process, for the academic community exists in the context of a corporate charter through which the state vests full responsibility and control in the lay governing board of the college or university.

Second, student participation in college policy should be based on the belief that all areas of college life are the mutual concern of all colleagues in the academic community, with each participating as a colleague according to his interest, stake, and competence to make a contribution to the necessary decisions. Parenthetically, it should be noted that it is just as important for faculty to be involved in the government of student life as for the students to be involved in the other areas of college policy.

Third, significant student involvement in college policy formation must be based on the clear understanding among all members of the academic community that genuine student involvement in college policy formation can be achieved by providing students with a regular and meaningful opportunity to influence decisions without delegation of sole responsibility for a particular policy area and even without *pro forma* requirements of equal representation and voting rights on faculty committees.

Involving students in college policy formation is a complex problem, as has been pointed out by many writers, and the means of participation may well vary from one policy area to another. The attitudes of college administrators, faculty members, and students about each other and about the student-college relationship and a desire to find a pattern of student involvement suited to each particular academic community are key elements, however, in the genuine student participation in college policy formation which is basic to the achievement of a sense of community.

Models of Student Participation Given the complexity of the institutional governance problem, it is hazardous to attempt any systematic description of the forms of student participation in university governance. There may be some value, however, in an overview of four possible approaches or models.

Model of Denial. The first model is really a pattern of noninvolvement. In effect, students are denied any role in the decision-making process. College policies and programs are developed for the student rather than either by or with him, and decisions are based on the perception by "adults" in the academic community of "what's good" for the student. Although it is clearly unlikely that many institutions today qualify as fitting this model completely, a careful study might very well document that the actual situation on many campuses still matches this pattern of participation better than any of the others described. This is especially the case where delegation of authority and responsibility to student government is more symbolic than substantial, where all decisions by student groups are processed as recommendations, or where the student view of "his" government is that it engages in "Mickey Mouse" activities.

Sphere-of-authority Pattern. The second form of involvement in governance is the so-called "sphere-of-authority" pattern. Here then are five subtypes of participation. First, certain areas are labeled as of primary concern to students, and student government, as a result, has complete jurisdiction. Second, there are areas where there is basic student authority and responsibility, but with limited involvement of faculty or administration. Third, there are "joint committees" with equal representation of all elements in the academic community usually concerned with issues identified as being of concern to all. Fourth, additional areas are set aside as basically within the jurisdiction of the faculty but where students have limited representation on faculty committees. And finally there are areas completely under the jurisdiction of the faculty.

Parallel Government Model. In the third or "parallel government" model, students form what is essentially a "shadow" government by duplicating the faculty committee structure. The parallel committees meet separately unless by mutual agreement a joint meeting is scheduled. Any division of authority and responsibility that may occur on a given campus usually follows academic/nonacademic lines; any primary responsibility for an area of governance falls to students as what is "left over" from faculty government. The chief argument for this form of governance is the opportunity it affords students to initiate proposals independently and free of faculty or administrative "interference" or even primary involvement. The quality of such proposals and the effectiveness of their presentation and promotion become the criteria determining student impact on institutional government.

Community Government Model. Joseph Cole (1968) describes the fourth model, community government, as "the most extreme form of government reorganization." Cole's excellent paper on *Student Involvement in Institutional Governance* was prepared for NASPA's 50th Anniversary Conference, at Minneapolis, in April, 1968. In the paper he writes:

> [Community Government] perceives the college or University as a single unified community and accepts students, faculty, administration and trustees as partners in the establishment of goals, policies and operational practices . . .
>
> The Community Government concept initially is very attractive to students. Acceptance as contributing members in all forms of university governance has considerable appeal. However, sometimes enthusiasm is dulled when students recognize that the new role they acquire in certain coveted areas of University affairs (curriculum, faculty appointments, course evaluation, planning, etc.) is accompanied usually by a similar loss of autonomy in many aspects of student affairs (publications, residence hall policy, common forms of student government, etc.).

Clearly the models described do not exhaust the alternatives. Variations on these themes, combinations of these forms, creative responses daily to the complexity of institutional governance problems continue to add options. The model developed to reflect the life style of a given campus is a function of decisions made in response to issues raised earlier in this chapter. The prevailing perception of students and their role in the particular academic community is perhaps the most basic determinant of the nature of student involvement in institutional governance.

Brown University—A Case Study A case study reflecting the response of one campus to these governance considerations may enhance understanding of the process of policy determination and review in the area affecting student life. Brown University provides such a case and reflects that institution's attempt to:

Provide for the broadest possible participation in the decision-making process

Identify the locus of primary responsibility, authority, and jurisdiction to initiate and review policy

Define the nature of student involvement in the decision-making process

Brown's vehicle for policy determination and review is a University Council on Student Affairs consisting of three faculty members elected by the faculty for staggered three-year terms: the dean of the college or, in his absence, the associate dean; the dean of Pembroke, or, in her absence, the associate dean; the dean of the graduate school, or, in his absence, the associate dean; and three undergraduate men selected in a manner decided by the student government organization of the college; two undergraduate women selected in a manner decided by the Pembroke Student Government

Association; and one graduate student selected in a manner decided by the Graduate Student Council. The University Council on Student Affairs elects its chairman from among its faculty representation.

Jurisdiction of the University Council on Student Affairs extends to "the making of all student conduct rules." Recommendations are made only by majority vote of the council and must be approved by the president of the university. There is a stipulation that the council must meet at least twice each semester.

In addition to legislative functions and responsibility there is provision that the University Council on Student Affairs "shall have authority to sit as a disciplinary committee in all cases involving offenses in which the potential sanction for the violation of a rule is suspension or dismissal." In all such cases the student involved in the violation is offered the option of appearing before the dean or the council.

In the following section of this chapter we turn from the process of policy determination to the policies themselves and principles relevant to their formulation.

POLICIES AFFECTING STUDENT CONDUCT

Standards of Conduct Expected of Students. The institution has an obligation to clarify those standards of behavior which it considers essential to its educational mission and its community life. These general behavioral expectations and the resultant specific regulations should represent a reasonable regulation of student conduct but the student should be as free as possible from imposed limitations that have no direct relevance to his education. Offenses should be as clearly defined as possible and interpreted in a manner consistent with the aforementioned principles of relevancy and reasonableness. Disciplinary proceedings should be instituted only for violations of standards of conduct formulated with significant student participation and published in advance through such means as a student handbook or a generally available body of institutional regulations. [Joint Statement, VI *A*.]

Changing Student Values Existing policies and regulations affecting student life on many campuses reflect a tradition in which the institution stood *in loco parentis* and sought to influence student value development by means of such policies. Although enforced obedience may, at times, be an effective device for influencing student values, it has generally not been a very successful approach. Furthermore, there are other equally effective strategies which may well be more appropriate in higher education. (See Dressel [1] for a thorough discussion of techniques of changing student values and their appropriateness in education.) According to Philip Jacob [2] those colleges with the greatest impact on student values have (1) clearly defined, high-level expectations of students which are widely understood and shared by all members of the community, (2) faculty members who broadly define their role to include serving as examples to students, (3) opportunities for students to have meaningful experiences in the exercise of significant responsibility, and (4) opportunities for "value laden experiences" which confront students with the necessity for examining their values and making decisions among alternative values and behaviors. Thus, student value development seems to be relatively unaffected by specific regulations but is strongly influenced by clearly articulated statements of institutional expectations of students including standards of student behavior.

Standards versus Regulations A desirable first step, then, for colleges concerned with value development is to distinguish between carefully formulated institutional expectations and standards for behavior on the one hand and social conduct regulations on the

[1] Paul Dressel, "Factors Involved in Changing the Values of College Students," *Educational Record,* vol. 46, no. 2, pp. 104–113, Spring, 1965.

[2] Philip E. Jacob, *Education for Social Responsibility,* American Red Cross, Washington.

other. The standards for behavior reflect institutional goals for student development and institutional expectations concerning behaviors such as sex, etc., which are issues for the personal decisions of students; they communicate the ideals of the academic community and help determine the educational climate and program which influences growth toward these ideals. In contrast, social conduct regulations are the bare minimum of specific prohibitions which will be enforced by means of institutional sanctions. This approach seems to reflect a belief that man is neither wholly good nor wholly bad. It establishes the basis for educational and counseling approaches to help man fulfill his potential; it provides minimal rules and sanctions to cope with the worst in man. The present task for most colleges, then, is to develop statements of institutional expectations and standards while reviewing and revising their specific codes of regulations.

Purposes of Student Conduct Policies A college cannot function without at least a minimal set of policies and regulations affecting student conduct which it will enforce by means of institutional sanctions. The chief purposes of such policies are as follows: (1) to maintain order and to control behavior that impinges upon the freedom and privacy of other persons; (2) to maintain a way of student life that is physically and psychologically healthy; (3) to protect the institution from behaviors which threaten its ability to exercise its responsibility and to achieve its educational mission; and (4) to preserve sufficiently satisfactory relations with the larger civil community of which the institution is a part so as to enable the institution to marshal the necessary resources and to devote its attention to its primary educational tasks.

If the objective is a minimal set of social conduct regulations, how many such rules are necessary? One response to this question is suggested by the Committee on the College Student of the Group for the Advancement of Psychiatry:

> [A] sound rules structure will attempt to take into account the student who needs or seeks shelter as well as the more mature student whose development will require some elbow room for experimentation. . . . The student who finds rules useful as a protection or a limit will have some acceptable backing, and the student who feels less need for rules will have avenues open to establish greater independence. Many colleges employ a gradient of rules throughout the college experience that shifts to the student more and more responsibility for his own behavior and supports his expectations of himself as growing toward more autonomy.[3]

A SAMPLE STATEMENT OF POLICIES

In light of the mass demonstrations on a number of campuses in recent years and in accordance with the purposes here suggested for college policies affecting student life, Brown University has thoroughly reviewed its regulations and policies which make students liable to university discipline, within prescribed hearing procedures, for the following behaviors:

1. Those forms of on-campus student protest whose distinctive character is physical force or physical obstruction
2. Forcibly assaulting or restraining public speakers or preventing speakers from being heard
3. Student behavior which is (a) damaging to property or which inflicts physical harm on persons, as for example, assault on a person, an act of stealing, or a defacing of property; (b) disruptive or disturbing to other persons, as for example excessive noise; (c) obscene, as for example indecent exposure or the shouting of obscenities
4. The use of residence units for sexual intercourse
5. The possession, use, or distribution of marijuana, LSD, or other hallucinogens and narcotic drugs

[3] *GAP Report*, no. 60, p. 127, 1965.

With particular reference to the latter two offenses, the emphasis in administering the policies is upon the emotional and physical well-being of the individuals.

INSTITUTIONAL POLICIES ON SELECTED ISSUES

In 1968 the Division of Research and Publications of the National Association of Personnel Administrators published a monograph on *Institutional Policies on Controversial Topics*.[4] Base-line information concerning the nature and extent of institutional policy on 18 selected controversial topics was obtained from 348 different colleges and universities. We report here a portion of the summary of the major findings of that study in order to indicate the issues on which institutions tend to have policies and to suggest the approach to policy on these issues which seems characteristic of institutions of higher education:

Deviant Sexual Behavior. This problem was treated as a health or counseling problem in a relatively small number of institutions. The common pattern was to view the problem in terms of control and discipline. Sixty percent of the institutions had policies but less than one quarter had policies that were formally adopted and systematically communicated. The personnel staff and administrative councils played a prominent role in the development of the policies, which were intended to control student behavior. The personnel dean and his staff most commonly dealt with violations along with conduct committees, and violations most frequently resulted in disciplinary action.

Dress and Appearance. Two-thirds of the institutions had some type of policy on dress and appearance, and 41 percent of these institutions had prescribed dress codes. Three-quarters of the responding institutions had formally adopted policies. Policies on dress and appearance were most often developed by student committees or committees made up of representatives of the academic community. The most commonly stated purposes for the policies were related to order and control and to the development of a desirable campus atmosphere. The personnel staff most frequently processed dress problems, but student participation in the discipline process was mentioned by nearly one-half of the respondents. The penalties when violations occurred were in the lower ranges of severity and did not include dismissal.

Drugs. Although the majority of respondents indicated concern for the handling of this issue, only 41 percent stated that their institution had an established policy regarding this matter, and only 32 percent had formally adopted the policies. The policy stated most often enabled the institution to treat abuse of drugs internally as much as possible through regular disciplinary channels. Most of the institutions recorded that the purpose of their policy was to maintain campus standards, control, or institutional values or to protect students from harm. Usual disciplinary actions were rather severe.

Entertainment of Members of the Opposite Sex in Residence Hall Bedrooms. Most of the institutions had policies on visitation, and nearly one-half of the schools prohibited the activity. Only a small percentage of the sample allowed the activity on a regular basis. The policies were developed by officially established and important decision-making bodies with limited student involvement and were, for the most part, formally adopted and systematically communicated. The two most prominent purposes of the policies were to maintain behavioral standards and to support educational goals and principles. The personnel dean and staff had a major role in processing violations along with conduct committees, which include students. The most common pattern was to treat violations with penalties of less than suspension.

Excessive Use of Alcoholic Beverages. Most institutions had a policy on excessive consumption of alcohol. The policies reflected an effort to restrict the use of alcohol and were intended to control behavior. Generally, the policies were formally adopted and systematically communicated and were established by official decision-making bodies. The personnel dean and staff along with conduct committees most frequently

[4] NASPA Division of Research and Publications, *Institutional Policy on Controversial Topics*, NASPA Monograph no. 1, 1968.

processed infractions. The penalties used were usually less than suspension or the institution acted on the merits of each case.

Financial Irresponsibility. Eighty-three percent of the respondents stated that their institution has an established policy concerning this matter. In most cases, personnel in the dean of students office or the business office handled violations, and the usual response was to bar future registration or to withhold grades, transcripts, or graduation records.

Off-campus Misconduct. Eighty-two percent of the respondents indicated that their institution had a policy with regard to unacceptable off-campus behavior. The largest block of institutions accepted responsibility for student behavior off-campus and used either a general conduct statement or a specific regulation dealing with off-campus behavior as a basis for action. At the same time, a number of schools suggested that the institution should be involved in off-campus affairs only when student behavior was detrimental to the welfare of the institution or when requested by civil authorities to act.

Although a relatively high percentage of respondents recorded policies regarding unacceptable off-campus behavior, there was a surprising lack of specificity in institutional expectations and of clear guidelines for processing violations.

Premarital Pregnancy. Only 50 percent of the institutions had a policy regarding premarital pregnancy, and only 17 of the 194 institutions had formally adopted some policy regarding this matter. Those few institutions which provided some rationale for their policy tended to be most concerned about campus standards and student values and only secondarily about the welfare of individual students. It was common for the problem to be treated outside the normal channels for disciplinary matters and to be handled in a counseling context. Parents often were consulted when the woman student was under 21 years of age. Depending upon the circumstances of the case (i.e., time in semester, parental reaction, and distance from home to school) the girl might be asked to leave the institution. Medical withdrawals were encouraged for advanced stages of pregnancy.

Student Organizations. Nearly all of the institutions had policies regarding student organizations, and most of these institutions had policies requiring the official approval of all student organizations. Although they varied with regard to the specific conditions for approval, most institutions required student organizations to have a faculty adviser and to provide a list of officers and a constitution. Very few schools requested a list of members from prospective organizations. At a limited number of institutions, the student government had the sole responsibility for the recognition of student organizations. Although the most frequent purpose for existing policy was the maintenance of control and orderliness of procedures, many institutions expressed a concern for the educational value of the exercise of both freedom and responsibility by student organizations. In most institutions policies were formally adopted and systematically communicated and were most frequently established by a committee of students, faculty and administrators. Violations of policy, however, were handled by personnel administrators more frequently than by committees. Policy violations seemed to be very little problem. When they occurred the usual consequences entailed some type of sanction or denial of the privileges accorded to recognized organizations.

Women's Hours. All but two institutions that have women students on campus had formulated a policy with regard to women's hours. This reflects the degree of attention given to this tradition-bound issue. The specific hours imposed varied greatly and seemed dependent on such conditions as whether the institution was located in an urban or rural setting. The largest number of institutions had developed specific hours for all women on some graduated basis (i.e., class, age, and academic standing) and as many as 14 percent of the respondents stated that some women students had no hours. The primary reason for women's hours seemed to revolve around a concern for the security of campus buildings and women students. A number of institutions also used women's hours as a means of ordering student and staff hours. The respondents stated some dissatisfaction with their policy, more interest in liberalization than was noted in most other policy matters, and a concern for simplification. Several called for a rethinking of the entire policy by a student-faculty-administrative committee.

Controversial Speakers. Three fourths of the institutions had a policy requiring the approval or clearance of campus speakers. In most cases, however, the policies were not intended to restrict speakers from appearing on the basis of their controversiality or the content of their topics, but rather to insure that invitations came from bona fide student groups or individuals within the institution and that orderly procedures were maintained. In addition to procedural reasons, freedom of expression and the value of exposing students to a variety of viewpoints formed the purposes for the policies at the majority of the institutions. Generally, policies were formulated by administrative officials or committees and were formally adopted and systematically communicated to the campus community. Similarly, violations of policy were most frequently handled administratively. The typical type of action taken was a reprimand or limitation of privileges.

Student Demonstrations. A sizable number of institutions (40 percent) did not have policies on this type of activity. Nearly all of the institutions with policies permitted demonstrations under certain conditions and controls. Nearly 50 percent allowed demonstrations without advance registration. A standard condition was that the activity should not interfere with the orderly conduct of institutional functions. Over one-half of the respondents indicated that their policy was formally adopted and systematically communicated. Decision-making bodies below the trustee level and above the student level, in the highest percentage of cases, formulated the policy. The policies were designed to permit freedom of expression and to maintain objectives and the educational process. Violations were most frequently handled by the personnel dean and his staff, and faculty and student conduct committees played an important role. The most common pattern was not to have set penalties for violations and to use penalties of less than dismissal.

Student Publications. Although over 50 percent of the institutions maintained some type of supervision over student publications by requiring them to be responsible to either an administrative or faculty body, very little control or censorship was exercised. The primary institutional concerns were the prevention of slanderous material and the provision of learning experiences for students through the exercise of freedom and responsibility. There was some student involvement in policy making in this area although it was predominantly an administrative responsibility. Policy violations seemed to be inconsequential.

Faculty-Student Drinking. Well over half of the institutions did not have a policy regarding this matter. Of the institutions that had established policies, a small number prohibited student-faculty drinking per se. The concern in most cases was that faculty not contribute to student violations of civil law or regulations against on-campus drinking, become involved in conduct exhibiting bad taste, or cause embarrassment to the institution. In those institutions that had policies, the policies were formally adopted and systematically communicated. Policies regarding student-faculty drinking were formulated almost exclusively by administrative officials. Violations of policy were usually handled by the personnel staff, and since the faculty member was the primary object of concern, formal action was rarely taken.

Provision of Contraceptives. Only 40 percent of the institutions had given attention to the development of policies regarding the provision of contraceptives. Ten percent of all respondents indicated that their institution would, in certain circumstances, provide contraceptives, while most of the institutions considered this matter to be a private medical concern. The policies tended to be simply a matter of consistent practice.

Student Records. Sixty percent of the institutions had not found it necessary to establish formal policies pertaining to the use of student records. There was, however, a general concern for maintaining certain safeguards to protect the confidentiality of student information. Policy formulation was handled administratively, and virtually no violations of policy were cited.

Use of Students as Research Subjects. The use of students as research subjects has presented few problems in most institutions; consequently, policy formulation on this matter received little attention. There was a general concern, however, that students not be exploited for research purposes.

APPENDIX: JOINT STATEMENT ON RIGHTS AND FREEDOMS OF STUDENTS

In June, 1967, a joint committee, comprised of representatives from the American Association of University Professors, U. S. National Student Association, Association of American Colleges, National Association of Student Personnel Administrators, and National Association of Women Deans and Counselors, met in Washington, D.C., and drafted the Joint Statement on Rights and Freedoms of Students *published below.*

Since its formulation, the Joint Statement has been endorsed by each of its five national sponsors, as well as by a number of other professional bodies.

Preamble

Academic institutions exist for the transmission of knowledge, the pursuit of truth, the development of students, and the general well-being of society. Free inquiry and free expression are indispensable to the attainment of these goals. As members of the academic community, students should be encouraged to develop the capacity for critical judgment and to engage in a sustained and independent search for truth. Institutional procedures for achieving these purposes may vary from campus to campus, but the minimal standards of academic freedom of students outlined below are essential to any community of scholars.

Freedom to teach and freedom to learn are inseparable facets of academic freedom. The freedom to learn depends upon appropriate opportunities and conditions in the classroom, on the campus, and in the larger community. Students should exercise their freedom with responsibility.

The responsibility to secure and to respect general conditions conducive to the freedom to learn is shared by all members of the academic community. Each college and university has a duty to develop policies and procedures which provide and safeguard this freedom. Such policies and procedures should be developed at each institution within the framework of general standards and with the broadest possible participation of the members of the academic community. The purpose of this statement is to enumerate the essential provisions for student freedom to learn.

I. Freedom of Access to Higher Education

The admissions policies of each college and university are a matter of institutional choice provided that each college and university makes clear the characteristics and expectations of students which it considers relevant to success in the institution's program. While church-related institutions may give admission preference to students of their own persuasion, such a preference should be clearly and publicly stated. Under no circumstances should a student be barred from admission to a particular institution on the basis of race. Thus, within the limits of its facilities, each college and university should be open to all students who are qualified according to its admission standards. The facilities and services of a college should be open to all of its enrolled students, and institutions should use their influence to secure equal access for all students to public facilities in the local community.

II. In the Classroom

The professor in the classroom and in conference should encourage free discussion, inquiry, and expression. Student performance should be evaluated solely on an academic basis, not on opinions or conduct in matters unrelated to academic standards.

A. *Protection of Freedom of Expression*

Students should be free to take reasoned exception to the data or views offered in any course of study and to reserve judgment about matters of opinion, but they are responsible for learning the content of any course of study for which they are enrolled.

B. *Protection against Improper Academic Evaluation*

Students should have protection through orderly procedures against prejudiced or capricious academic evaluation. At the same time, they are responsible for maintaining standards of academic performance established for each course in which they are enrolled.

C. Protection against Improper Disclosure

Information about student views, beliefs, and political associations which professors acquire in the course of their work as instructors, advisers, and counselors should be considered confidential. Protection against improper disclosure is a serious professional obligation. Judgments of ability and character may be provided under appropriate circumstances, normally with the knowledge or consent of the student.

III. Student Records

Institutions should have a carefully considered policy as to the information which should be part of a student's permanent educational record and as to the conditions of its disclosure. To minimize the risk of improper disclosure, academic and disciplinary records should be separate, and the conditions of access to each should be set forth in an explicit policy statement. Transcripts of academic records should contain only information about academic status. Information from disciplinary or counseling files should not be available to unauthorized persons on campus, or to any person off campus without the express consent of the student involved except under legal compulsion or in cases where the safety of persons or property is involved. No records should be kept which reflect the political activities or beliefs of students. Provisions should also be made for periodic routine destruction of noncurrent disciplinary records. Administrative staff and faculty members should respect confidential information about students which they acquire in the course of their work.

IV. Student Affairs

In student affairs, certain standards must be maintained if the freedom of students is to be preserved.

A. Freedom of Association

Students bring to the campus a variety of interests previously acquired and develop many new interests as members of the academic community. They should be free to organize and join associations to promote their common interests.

1. The membership, policies, and actions of a student organization usually will be determined by vote of only those persons who hold bona fide membership in the college or university community.

2. Affiliation with an extramural organization should not of itself disqualify a student organization from institutional recognition.

3. If campus advisers are required, each organization should be free to choose its own adviser, and institutional recognition should not be withheld or withdrawn solely because of the inability of a student organization to secure an adviser. Campus advisers may advise organizations in the exercise of responsibility, but they should not have the authority to control the policy of such organizations.

4. Student organizations may be required to submit a statement of purpose, criteria for membership, rules of procedures, and a current list of officers. They should not be required to submit a membership list as a condition of institutional recognition.

5. Campus organizations, including those affiliated with an extramural organization, should be open to all students without respect to race, creed, or national origin, except for religious qualifications which may be required by organizations whose aims are primarily sectarian.

B. Freedom of Inquiry and Expression

1. Students and student organization should be free to examine and discuss all questions of interest to them, and to express opinions publicly and privately. They should always be free to support causes by orderly means which do not disrupt the regular and essential operation of the institution. At the same time, it should be made clear to the academic and the larger community that in their public expressions or demonstrations students or student organizations speak only for themselves.

2. Students should be allowed to invite and to hear any person of their own choosing. Those routine procedures required by an institution before a guest speaker is invited to appear on campus should be designed only to insure that there is orderly scheduling of facilities and adequate preparation for the event, and that the occasion is conducted in a manner appropriate to an academic community. The institutional control of cam-

pus facilities should not be used as a device of censorship. It should be made clear to the academic and large community that sponsorship of guest speakers does not necessarily imply approval or endorsement of the views expressed, either by the sponsoring group or the institution.

C. Student Participation in Institutional Government

As constituents of the academic community, students should be free, individually and collectively, to express their views on issues of institutional policy and on matters of general interest to the student body. The student body should have clearly defined means to participate in the formulation and application of institutional policy affecting academic and student affairs. The role of the student government and both its general and specific responsibilities should be made explicit, and the actions of the student government within the areas of its jurisdiction should be reviewed only through orderly and prescribed procedures.

D. Student Publications

Student publications and the student press are a valuable aid in establishing and maintaining an atmosphere of free and responsible discussion and of intellectual exploration on the campus. They are a means of bringing student concerns to the attention of the faculty and the institutional authorities and of formulating student opinion on various issues on the campus and in the world at large.

Whenever possible the student newspaper should be an independent corporation financially and legally separate from the university. Where financial and legal autonomy is not possible, the institution, as the publisher of student publications, may have to bear the legal responsibility for the contents of the publications. In the delegation of editorial responsibility to students the institution must provide sufficient editorial freedom and financial autonomy for the student publications to maintain their integrity of purpose as vehicles for free inquiry and free expression in an academic community.

Institutional authorities, in consultation with students and faculty, have a responsibility to provide written clarification of the role of the student publications, the standards to be used in their evaluation, and the limitations on external control of their operation. At the same time, the editorial freedom of student editors and managers entails corollary responsibilities to be governed by the canons of responsible journalism, such as the avoidance of libel, indecency, undocumented allegations, attacks on personal integrity, and the techniques of harassment and innuendo. As safeguards for the editorial freedom of student publications the following provisions are necessary.

1. The student press should be free of censorship and advance approval of copy, and its editors and managers should be free to develop their own editorial policies and news coverage.

2. Editors and managers of student publications should be protected from arbitrary suspension and removal because of student, faculty, administrative, or public disapproval of editorial policy or content. Only for proper and stated causes should editors and managers be subject to removal and then by orderly and prescribed procedures. The agency responsible for the appointment of editors and managers should be the agency responsible for their removal.

3. All university published and financed student publications should explicitly state on the editorial page that the opinions there expressed are not necessarily those of the college, university, or student body.

V. Off-Campus Freedom of Students

A. Exercise of Rights of Citizenship

College and university students are both citizens and members of the academic community. As citizens, students should enjoy the same freedom of speech, peaceful assembly, and right of petition that other citizens enjoy and, as members of the academic community, they are subject to the obligations which accrue to them by virtue of this membership. Faculty members and administrative officials should insure that institutional powers are not employed to inhibit such intellectual and personal development of students as is often promoted by their exercise of the rights of citizenship both on and off campus.

B. Institutional Authority and Civil Penalties

Activities of students may upon occasion result in violation of law. In such cases, institutional officials should be prepared to apprise students of sources of legal counsel and may offer other assistance. Students who violate the law may incur penalties prescribed by civil authorities, but institutional authority should never be used merely to duplicate the function of general laws. Only where the institution's interests as an academic community are distinct and clearly involved should the special authority of the institution be asserted. The student who incidentally violates institutional regulations in the course of his off-campus activity, such as those relating to class attendance, should be subject to no greater penalty than would normally be imposed. Institutional action should be independent of community pressure.

VI. Procedural Standards in Disciplinary Proceedings

In developing responsible student conduct, disciplinary proceedings play a role substantially secondary to example, counseling, guidance, and admonition. At the same time, educational institutions have a duty and the corollary disciplinary powers to protect their educational purpose through the setting of standards of scholarship and conduct for the students who attend them and through the regulation of the use of institutional facilities. In the exceptional circumstances when the preferred means fail to resolve problems of student conduct, proper procedural safeguards should be observed to protect the student from the unfair imposition of serious penalties.

The administration of discipline should guarantee procedural fairness to an accused student. Practices in disciplinary cases may vary in formality with the gravity of the offense and the sanctions which may be applied. They should also take into account the presence or absence of an honor code, and the degree to which the institutional officials have direct acquaintance with student life in general and with the involved student and the circumstances of the case in particular. The jurisdictions of faculty or student judicial bodies, the disciplinary responsibilities of institutional officials and the regular disciplinary procedures, including the student's right to appeal a decision, should be clearly formulated and communicated in advance. Minor penalties may be assessed informally under prescribed procedures.

In all situations, procedural fair play requires that the student be informed of the nature of the charges against him, that he be given a fair opportunity to refute them, that the institution not be arbitrary in its actions, and that there be provision for appeal of a decision. The following are recommended as proper safeguards in such proceedings when there are no honor codes offering comparable guarantees.

A. *Standards of Conduct Expected of Students*

The institution has an obligation to clarify those standards of behavior which it considers essential to its educational mission and its community life. These general behavioral expectations and the resultant specific regulations should represent a reasonable regulation of student conduct, but the student should be as free as possible from imposed limitations that have no direct relevance to his education. Offenses should be as clearly defined as possible and interpreted in a manner consistent with the aforementioned principles of relevancy and reasonableness. Disciplinary proceedings should be instituted only for violations of standards of conduct formulated with significant student participation and published in advance through such means as a student handbook or a generally available body of institutional regulations.

B. *Investigation of Student Conduct*

1. Except under extreme emergency circumstances, premises occupied by students and the personal possessions of students should not be searched unless appropriate authorization has been obtained. For premises such as residence halls controlled by the institution, an appropriate and responsible authority should be designated to whom application should be made before a search is conducted. The application should specify the reasons for the search and the objects or information sought. The student should be present, if possible, during the search. For premises not controlled by the institution, the ordinary requirements for lawful search should be followed.

2. Students detected or arrested in the course of serious violations of institutional regulations, or infractions of ordinary law, should be informed of their rights. No form of harassment should be used by institutional representatives to coerce admissions of guilt or information about conduct of other suspected persons.

C. Status of Student Pending Final Action

Pending action on the charges, the status of a student should not be altered, or his right to be present on the campus and to attend classes suspended, except for reasons relating to his physical or emotional safety and well-being, or for reasons relating to the safety and well-being of students, faculty, or university property.

D. Hearing Committee Procedures

When the misconduct may result in serious penalties and if the student questions the fairness of disciplinary action taken against him, he should be granted, on request, the privilege of a hearing before a regularly constituted hearing committee. The following suggested hearing committee procedures satisfy the requirements of procedural due process in situations requiring a high degree of formality.

1. The hearing committee should include faculty members or students, or, if regularly included or requested by the accused, both faculty and student members. No member of the hearing committee who is otherwise interested in the particular case should sit in judgment during the proceeding.
2. The student should be informed, in writing, of the reasons for the proposed disciplinary action with sufficient particularity, and in sufficient time, to insure opportunity to prepare for the hearing.
3. The student appearing before the hearing committee should have the right to be assisted in his defense by an adviser of his choice.
4. The burden of proof should rest upon the officials bringing the charge.
5. The student should be given an opportunity to testify and to present evidence and witnesses. He should have an opportunity to hear and question adverse witnesses. In no case should the committee consider statements against him unless he has been advised of their content and of the names of those who made them and unless he has been given an opportunity to rebut unfavorable inferences which might otherwise be drawn.
6. All matters upon which the decision may be based must be introduced into evidence at the proceeding before the hearing committee. The decision should be based solely upon such matters. Improperly acquired evidence should not be admitted.
7. In the absence of a transcript, there should be both a digest and a verbatim record, such as a tape recording, of the hearing.
8. The decision of the hearing committee should be final, subject only to the student's right of appeal to the president or ultimately to the governing board of the institution.

SUGGESTED READING

Advisory Committee on Student Conduct: *Community and Partnership: Student Conduct at Brown University,* Brown University, 1967.

Committee on the College Student of the Group for the Advancement of Psychiatry: *Sex and the College Student,* Atheneum Publishers, New York, 1966.

Dressel, Paul: "Factors Involved in Changing the Values of College Students," *Educational Record,* vol. 46, no. 2, pp. 104–113, Spring, 1965.

Jacob, Philip E.: *Education for Social Responsibility,* American Red Cross, Washington, D.C., 1962.

"Joint Statement on the Rights and Freedoms of Students," *AAUP Bulletin,* vol. 53, no. 4, pp. 365–368, December, 1967.

Lunn, Harry H., Jr.: *The Student's Role in College Policy Making,* report prepared for the Commission of American Council on Education, Washington, 1956.

NASPA Division of Research and Publications: *Institutional Approaches to the Adjudication of Student Misconduct,* NASPA Monograph no. 2, 1969.

NASPA Division of Research and Publications: *Institutional Policy on Controversial Topics,* NASPA Monograph no. 1, 1968.

Presidential Commission on Student Life: *Report and Recommendations,* Middlebury College, March, 1968.

Stroup, Herbert H.: *Freedom and Responsibility in Higher Education, A Study of the Institutional Limitations on Human Freedom,* United Presbyterian Church, 1964.

Williamson, E. G., and John L. Cowan: *The American Student's Freedom of Expression,* The University of Minnesota Press, Minneapolis, 1966.

Chapter **3**

Disciplinary Administration—Traditional and New

WILLIAM J. BOWERS

Director of Research, The Russell B. Stearns Study, Northeastern University, Boston, Massachusetts

RICHARD G. SALEM

Research Associate, The Russell B. Stearns Study, Northeastern University, Boston, Massachusetts

THE NATURE AND EXTENT OF STUDENT DISCIPLINARY PROBLEMS

Any discussion of student disciplinary problems must first address itself to the question of what the major disciplinary problems are. H. W. Bailey * identifies three types of disciplinary problems, distinguishing between on- and off-campus misconduct and then subdividing the former group into those which occur in the academic area and those which do not.

E. G. Williamson and J. D. Foley prefer a larger number of more specific categories which are empirically derived from an analysis of cases which have come to the office of the dean of students at the University of Minnesota over a six-year period. They distinguish among financial irresponsibility, minor misconduct, disorderly conduct, sex misconduct, theft and burglary, destruction of property, misuse of privileges, and miscellaneous (including dishonesty in examinations). (The authors note that cases of academic dishonesty were handled by a student disciplinary board; presumably, too few fell under the primary jurisdiction of the deans' office to merit a separate category.)

We shall also rely on data about student disciplinary problems as a basis for classification. Our data provide a comparative picture of them at a variety of colleges and universities from national surveys conducted in 1962, 1963, and 1966 and analyzed at the Russell B. Stearns Study during the past several years. The data come from both students and administrators, from those responsible for the problems and from those responsible for controlling them.

Seriousness of the Problems: Deans' Point of View

Data on the views of college administrators toward various disciplinary problems are available from a 1962 survey of deans of students at 626 colleges and universities across the country. They comprise 55 percent of all regionally accredited, four-year, degree-granting colleges and universities in 1962, and they are generally representative of such institutions.[1]

Each was asked what he considered "the most serious problem of student discipline at his college." Table 1 presents the distribution of responses.

Disorderly conduct and drinking-related behavior ranked first and academic dishonesty ranked second in terms of seriousness. Sex misconduct, theft or shoplifting, and destruction or damage to property complete the list. These categories represent what may be regarded as the more traditional forms of student misconduct. Current

* See references at the end of the chapter for full statement of works cited.

[1] See Bowers, 1964, Appendix C, for further information on the sample. Data from student body presidents parallels that of the deans; see Bowers, 1964, Chapter 1.

TABLE 1 Problems of Student Discipline Named Most Serious by Deans

	Percent naming each kind of offense	
Specific kinds of offenses	53	
Drinking, partying, and disorderly conduct *		50
Academic dishonesty		23
Sex misconduct and sex-related social misconduct		12
Theft or shoplifting		10
Destruction of or damage to property		5
		100
General disciplinary problems (not living up to standards of conduct, breaking school rules or regulations, weak morals, poor attitudes, etc.)	24	
No serious problems or no answer	23	
	100	

* Ninety percent of the respondents of this category mentioned drinking, drunkenness, or some form of drinking-related behavior.

problems such as drug use and disorderly student protests did not appear since they are of such recent vintage.

Extent of Student Misconduct: Students' Point of View [2]

The Russell B. Stearns Study, in 1966, surveyed approximately 1,000 seniors from 97 campuses, asking about their attitudes toward and involvement in different forms of conduct (cf. Bowers, 1968b). Students were asked whether they disapproved of and whether they had engaged in each of 28 forms of conduct, most of which violate campus regulations or socially accepted standards. Table 2, adapted from "A Survey of Campus Misconduct" (Bowers, 1968b), shows the percentage of college seniors who admitted engaging in each of these forms of behavior.

The offenses in Table 2 are ordered in terms of the extent of disapproval students personally felt toward them (from most to least disapproved). The *major offenses* are distinguished by the fact that a majority of the college students "strongly disapproved" of them, the *minor offenses* were disapproved to some extent (but not strongly) by a majority; and the *acceptable behavior* includes actions which a majority of students say that they "do not disapprove."

Generally speaking, as we move up the list in terms of disapproval, the actions become less prevalent. There are some notable exceptions—actions which are substantially more or less common than might be expected in light of their level of disapproval.

Some actions are quite a bit less prevalent than might be expected in light of students' feelings about them. Thus, "trying out" marijuana, LSD, and similar drugs is the least prevalent of the major offenses, although it is not the most disapproved. Even more "undercommitted" is engaging in an act of civil disobedience. Although this ranks twelfth in disapproval, it is the least prevalent on the entire list. Protest demonstrating or marching and unconventional appearance are also relatively uncommon. These four items are our best indicators of newly emerging problems. The fact that these forms of behavior were undercommitted in 1966 may mean that they were then on the rise.

[2] Studies of specific forms of misconduct including academic dishonesty (Bowers, 1964), drinking behavior (Strauss and Bacon, 1953), and sexual behavior (Reiss, 1967), have gathered information from students at a variety of schools.

TABLE 2 Involvement in Various Forms of Conduct among a Sample of 690 Seniors from 97 Colleges

	Percent engaging in each action
Major offenses	
Destroying school property	6
Taking articles from school store without paying for them	6
Cheating on an exam or paper	24
Disorderly conduct in local community	9
Trying out marijuana, LSD, or similar drugs or narcotics	5
Actively participating in a student uprising, riot, or mob action	10
Taking books from library without properly checking them out	27
Lying to parents about grades, social activities, or other aspects of college life	21
Underlining or marking library books	20
Showing general lack of respect for academic rules; e.g., failing to show up for exams, consistently getting to class late	14
Becoming friendly with a teacher in hopes of getting a better grade	22
Minor offenses	
Violating the law in an act of deliberate civil disobedience on behalf of a social cause	3
Violating campus regulations about having members of opposite sex in students' rooms	20
Using vulgar and obscene language in talking with friends	61
Drinking alcoholic beverages on campus in violation of campus regulations	51
Getting drunk	54
Masturbating	44
Having sexual intercourse before marriage	39
Gambling on campus	16
Overcutting class	46
Taking tranquilizers or other medication to relieve or reduce tension	22
Using stimulants such as "NoDoz" or benzedrine to facilitate studying and meeting academic deadlines	45
Pulling pranks on other students	70
Acceptable behavior	
Arguing with teachers or trying to prove them wrong	43
Participating in a social protest demonstration or march	20
Wearing a beard or dressing unconventionally	18
Talking a lot more in class discussions than other students	47
Drinking enough to get high or lightheaded	77

Locus of Responsibility for Disciplinary Action

While the dean is apt to be involved in disciplinary administration at all schools, he is not necessarily the sole authority. Faculty or students may play a part or even take primary responsibility for disciplinary cases at some institutions. The honor system typically puts responsibility for dealing with problems in the hands of students.

There may be consistent differences in the ways various forms of misconduct are handled. Academic dishonesty may be handled by the course instructor at most institutions, and drinking-related misconduct may be handled largely by administrators. The way cases are handled may be linked with the institution's success or failure in controlling such conduct and the perceived seriousness of the problem.

In the 1962 survey, deans were asked, "What individual or group on your campus *usually* decides upon disciplinary measures in cases of the following types?" Table 3 shows their responses.

The items concerning alcohol, disorderly conduct, and dormitory rules show the highest levels of student involvement and the highest levels of group decision making, which may reflect administrative concern over the seriousness of these problems.

TABLE 3 Deans' Responses to a Question about Who Handles Various Kinds of Student Disciplinary Cases at Their Colleges *

	An individual from the:			A group composed mostly of:		
Type of conduct	administration	faculty	students	administration	faculty	students
Destruction of property	44	1	1	30	11	13
Sex misconduct	42	1	0	33	16	8
Misconduct in relations between students and members of the local community	40	2	0	31	13	14
Riots or mob action	40	1	1	35	13	10
Theft	36	1	2	27	17	17
Misconduct regarding possession or use of alcoholic beverages	36	0	1	26	16	21
Disorderly conduct or improper social behavior	27	1	2	25	15	30
Breaking rules in the dormitories	23	1	5	13	5	53
Cheating or plagiarism	14	31	2	10	25	18

* Rows total to 100 percent.

Administrators may feel that with the cooperation of student leaders their decision will carry more weight, or that predominantly student groups can win the support of the student body.

Academic dishonesty is the offense over which administrators typically have least control, as it is primarily the faculty who handle discipline.

The fact that some offenses are handled by faculty, others by students, and others by the administration may affect the kinds of penalties.

Penalties Imposed in Various Disciplinary Cases

We might expect those offenses which are most strongly disapproved by members of the campus community (as shown in Table 2) to be the ones most severely sanctioned. Of course, some actions may be overcommitted or regarded as serious disciplinary problems because they are less severely sanctioned than other offenses of comparable disapproval.

In the 1962 survey, the deans were given a list of penalties which are sometimes imposed and were asked which comes *closest* to the one usually imposed. Table 4 shows the penalties imposed for 10 different forms of student misconduct. Academic violations, including cheating and plagiarism, are separated from the rest, since the usual penalties are quite different in such cases.

For each of the five nonacademic offenses, students are either suspended or expelled at most schools. The drunk and disorderly behavior is treated more strictly than is violating campus regulations about the possession or use of alcoholic beverages. The former conduct has greater potential for creating a public disturbance and for causing the university considerable embarrassment. Violating the rules about visitation in students' rooms also has the potential of causing a campus scandal. It may be that judgments of seriousness and severity of sanctions are affected, at least in part, by the chance that a given form of misconduct can create an embarrassing situation for the campus community.

Sanctions for academic dishonesty appear much less severe. Although deans say

TABLE 4 Punishments Imposed in Various Kinds of Disciplinary Cases as Reported by the Deans

Offenses	Punishments or penalties imposed			
Nonacademic disciplinary cases	Reprimands, demerits, warnings	Campusing or restrictions	Suspension	Dismissal
Stealing possessions or money from other students	10	6	46	38
Violating rules about having guests of the opposite sex in dormitory rooms	10	18	40	32
Being drunk or disorderly	16	18	44	22
Stealing books from the library	39	9	36	16
Violating rules regarding the possession and use of alcoholic beverages	17	24	46	13
Academic disciplinary cases	Reprimands, warnings, demerits, and others	Failing paper or exam	Failing course	Dismissal or suspension
Cheating on a final exam	4	20	58	18
Giving answers to another student on a final exam	13	26	43	18
Cheating on a midterm paper	6	43	36	15
Plagiarizing on a term paper	18	45	27	10

this is a serious disciplinary problem and a majority of students strongly disapprove of it, at less than 20 percent of the schools are students suspended or expelled for any of these forms of cheating or plagiarism. This may reflect the fact that these cases are typically handled by those who do not have the authority to suspend or dismiss students. The sanction more readily available to the course instructor is the withholding of credit on academic work, and it appears that this is the one most often used.

This observation needs some qualification. The intermediate penalties, such as failing the paper, exam, or course, are perhaps more harsh than campusing or restriction of privileges (the intermediate penalties for nonacademic violations). The student's overall grade average will suffer and loss of credit may even prevent him from graduating.

We know from a number of studies that the students who cheat are generally less academically oriented, less concerned about their grades, and actually receiving below-average grades. While teachers and administrators may view these as harsh penalties, their judgments may not be shared by those on whom they are usually imposed. As a form of deprivation, these sanctions generally apply to the students upon whom they will have the least effect.

The kinds of conduct for which most students are suspended or expelled are the nonacademic kinds—those which have to do with quite external matters such as sex, misappropriation or destruction of property, and disorderly or inappropriate social behavior. This is especially ironic in light of the fact that academic dishonesty represents a serious disciplinary problem to many deans.

TRADITIONAL FORMS OF STUDENT MISCONDUCT

Rather than trying to touch briefly upon the myriad of specific problems, we shall deal primarily with the areas which have been described as serious problems by college deans.

The tremendous variety of institutional forms in higher education also complicates the picture. Variations in size, sex composition, and type of control are bound to be linked with the kinds of misconduct that emerge and the ways they are handled. The approach of one institution will not necessarily be suitable for another.

Disorderly Conduct and Drinking-related Behavior

Background The most serious disciplinary problem according to deans' reports in 1962 was disorderly conduct and drinking-related behavior. Nine out of ten explicitly referred to the use of alcohol. No doubt, the seriousness of the problem is due partly to the fact that alcohol lies at the root of other problems such as sex misconduct and property destruction. Partying and rowdiness off campus can produce strained relations between students and members of the community, including the local police.

Another reason for the seriousness of the problem would seem to lie in the considerable pressure on the campus for students to become involved. Table 2 showed that such conduct is much more widespread than are other forms of behavior at the same level of disapproval. Such pressures are also evident in a survey of more than 4,000 students from 11 universities (Goldsen, et al., 1960) which indicates that students drink when they are on dates or socializing even though many of them would prefer other activities.

A number of things may explain why many students feel compelled to drink, often to excess. Drinking and drinking-related behavior have long played a central part in campus social life. There are traditional songs and ceremonies which accompany college drinking. Such behavior in college can be traced back to colonial times (Brubacher and Rudy, 1958). Over a long period of time, drinking has become an institutionalized aspect of the college student culture. Recent studies of drinking among college students show that it is quite widespread, that the rates of such conduct increases substantially from freshman to senior year, and that such conduct may be on the rise (cf. Strauss and Bacon, 1953; Bowers, 1968b). The pivotal role of drinking in relation to other forms of misconduct has recently been suggested in a factor analysis of campus deviance (Bowers and Sidel, 1968).

Two studies have shown that there is considerable variation in drinking and drinking-related misconduct by school (Strauss and Bacon, 1953; Bowers, 1968a), suggesting that different types of institutions may have quite different problems in this area, requiring different disciplinary approaches.

Table 5 shows some aspects of disciplinary administration in 12 different institutional contexts.

Further Analysis Table 5 also raises additional questions. Are the lower rates of disorderly and drinking-related misconduct at female schools a result of the greater student control? Are the lower rates at the small coed schools a result of the fact that penalties are generally stricter at these institutions?

Generally speaking, particular disciplinary arrangements have relatively little effect on the rates of disorderly and drinking-related misconduct. Much more important is the type of school. Lowest rates occur at female schools, next are the small coed institutions, and highest rates are found at the male schools. Stronger sanctions are definitely associated with lower rates of misconduct, but the relationship is neither strong nor totally consistent. The locus of disciplinary responsibility seems to make little difference. In no context are lower rates of misconduct associated with student control.

Implications for Control Although there are considerable variations among schools in the rates of disorderly and drinking-related behavior, these differences are due only in

TABLE 5 Disorderly Conduct and Drinking-related Behavior: Disciplinary Responsibility, Disciplinary Action, and Rates of Misconduct in Varying Institutional Contexts*

	Single-sex schools				Coeducational schools							
	Catholic		Other		Catholic	Protestant		Private nondenominational		Public		
	Male	Female	Male	Female	All sizes	Small	Large	Small	Large	Small	Medium	Large
Data from 1962 survey of college deans												
Number of schools	(28)	(48)	(38)	(43)	(29)	(60)	(56)	(106)	(46)	(44)	(111)	(92)
Who handles:												
Disorderly conduct												
Student	11%	44%	34%	87%	9%	36%	28%	33%	35%	18%	21%	19%
Faculty	33	5	12	0	23	13	18	20	10	13	17	22
Administration	56	51	54	13	68	51	55	46	55	69	62	60
Misconduct-alcohol use												
Student	12%	10%	30%	65%	5%	24%	24%	25%	28%	3%	7%	19%
Faculty	44	7	12	0	36	15	14	19	14	13	19	15
Administration	44	83	58	35	59	61	62	57	58	85	74	66
Penalties for:												
Being drunk and disorderly												
Warning	7%	2%	13%	0%	14%	6%	7%	18%	21%	14%	12%	30%
Restriction of privileges	4	2	37	29	11	11	24	29	33	12	23	17
Suspension	59	17	37	50	50	40	56	36	38	45	46	46
Dismissal	30	78	13	21	25	43	13	16	8	29	19	7
Violating alcohol use rules												
Warning	4%	7%	13%	0%	14%	9%	7%	19%	17%	20%	18%	31%
Restriction of privileges	19	12	48	44	11	19	24	32	38	20	25	20
Suspension	56	26	26	38	50	44	59	37	40	43	45	45
Dismissal	22	55	13	18	25	28	11	13	4	18	12	4
Data from 1963 survey of students												
Number of schools	(3)	(9)	(13)	(7)	(2)	(13)	(6)	(8)	(8)	(6)	(11)	(13)
Number of students	(195)	(546)	(774)	(473)	(106)	(699)	(327)	(398)	(394)	(319)	(502)	(689)
Rate of misconduct												
Getting drunk	49%	11%	66%	24%	36%	16%	30%	32%	39%	42%	34%	44%
Violating alcohol use rules	61%	10%	47%	17%	31%	19%	38%	31%	37%	46%	35%	45%
Disorderly conduct in local community	16%	7%	20%	7%	12%	8%	12%	11%	11%	7%	10%	12%

*Among Protestant and private nondenominational institutions, small schools have enrollments of less than 1,000 students, large schools have 1,000 or more. Among the public institutions, small schools again have fewer than 1,000 students, medium-size schools have 1,000 to 2,999 students and large ones have 3,000 or more.

small measure to differences in the way cases are handled. They are more associated with college characteristics, particularly sex composition, and to a lesser degree with the size of the institution.

The extent of pressures toward drinking and associated behavior among students at most colleges suggests that the problem is one of regulating rather than eliminating or drastically reducing such conduct. By implication, excessive regulations concerning the possession and use of alcohol may simply invite a higher rate of misconduct by broadening what is included as a violation. One constructive step may be to provide for controlled drinking. By offering attractive social and recreational facilities on campus and making alcohol available under controlled conditions, the school may be able to encourage a more responsible approach.

Since the disciplinary arrangements we have examined show relatively little effect, it may be that disciplinary counseling should have a prominent place in the control of such conduct. Students do not need to be told that drinking leads to other forms of misconduct, but they may not as clearly sense that they, not the alcohol, are responsible for their behavior, and that they should be held accountable in full for its consequences. Disciplinary counseling also provides an opportunity to identify those cases in which excessive drinking and associated misconduct is symptomatic of underlying personality problems.

Academic Dishonesty

Background Academic dishonesty is considerably more prevalent than might be expected in light of students' attitudes toward it. Here again, there would seem to be intense campus pressures contributing to such conduct.

Grades determine whether a student can stay in school and ultimately graduate; they affect his chances of furthering his education beyond the undergraduate level and eventually entering the occupational structure at a relatively high level with a good opportunity for advancement.

In 1962, the U.S. Office of Education supported a national survey of more than 5,000 students from 99 colleges and universities on student dishonesty. The following quotation is from that survey:

> Our data show that those who have difficulty adjusting to the role of student, as evidenced by poor study habits and low grades, are indeed more likely to cheat than the good students . . . those who value the social aspects of college life are more apt to cheat than those who emphasize intellectual interests and activities, even when we take their academic performance into account. . . .
>
> Students' college peers have a powerful effect on their cheating behavior. Students who perceive that their fellow students strongly disapprove of cheating are not nearly as likely to engage in academic dishonesty as those who believe that their peers are more tolerant of cheating. . . .
>
> Moreover, the data indicate that students' cheating behavior is influenced not only by their close associates, but also by the broader peer group—the student body as a whole. Thus, no matter how strongly their close circle of peers disapproves, students are less apt to cheat as the campus-wide climate of disapproval increases. . . . [Bowers, 1964, pp. 195–197]

The report concluded that some schools are able to create and sustain a normative climate against academic dishonesty which tends to prevent students from becoming involved who might at another school succumb to the temptation. Perhaps this ability stems from the way these schools handle cases of cheating and plagiarism.

Further Analysis The fact that we find severe sanctions and student-centered control at the schools with the lowest rates of cheating suggests that one or both of these factors contribute to more effective control. It could be that certain types of schools tend to

TABLE 6 Academic Dishonesty: Disciplinary Responsibility, Disciplinary Action, and Rates of Misconduct in Varying Institutional Contexts

	Single-sex schools				Coeducational schools							
	Catholic		Other		Catholic	Protestant		Private nondenominational		Public		
	Male	Female	Male	Female	All sizes	Small	Large	Small	Large	Small	Medium	Large
Data from 1962 survey of college deans												
Number of schools	(28)	(48)	(38)	(43)	(29)	(60)	(56)	(106)	(46)	(44)	(111)	(92)
Who handles:												
Cheating or plagiarism:												
Student	4%	17%	48%	67%	4%	21%	31%	12%	14%	3%	6%	10%
Faculty	74	50	24	8	67	60	45	67	61	64	62	64
Administration	22	33	27	26	29	19	24	21	25	33	31	26
Penalties for:												
Plagiarism on term paper:												
Other lesser penalties	27%	34%	6%	19%	20%	28%	11%	21%	13%	19%	18%	9%
Fail paper	42	60	22	29	64	49	52	46	37	55	51	40
Fail course	19	2	36	21	16	15	33	23	39	21	25	39
Dismiss or suspend	12	4	36	31	0	8	4	9	11	5	6	12
Cheating on midterm:												
Other lesser penalties	4%	17%	0%	7%	4%	9%	2%	5%	7%	2%	6%	3%
Fail exam	45	65	8	31	54	46	52	48	35	61	42	35
Fail course	45	11	38	21	42	35	37	29	43	23	46	47
Dismiss or suspend	7	7	54	41	0	10	9	18	15	14	7	15
Cheating on final:												
Other lesser penalties	0%	9%	0%	5%	0%	5%	2%	2%	4%	2%	5%	2%
Fail exam	19	52	5	21	30	26	20	29	9	33	18	13
Fail course	67	32	27	33	70	59	70	52	63	47	69	65
Dismiss or suspend	15	7	68	40	0	10	9	18	24	19	9	20
Data from 1963 survey of students												
Number of schools	(3)	(9)	(13)	(7)	(2)	(13)	(6)	(8)	(8)	(6)	(11)	(13)
Number of students	(195)	(546)	(774)	(473)	(106)	(699)	(327)	(398)	(394)	(319)	(502)	(689)
Rates of misconduct:												
Plagiarizing	44%	26%	23%	21%	45%	27%	28%	20%	32%	29%	36%	29%
Copying on exam	59%	15%	21%	13%	48%	23%	34%	25%	36%	38%	44%	36%

have lower cheating rates inherently, and that the presence of student control and severe sanctions add little to their ability to control cheating. We examined cheating rates by disciplinary authority and penalties imposed within five categories of schools: Catholic single sex, other single sex, Protestant, private, and public.

Implications for Control For academic dishonesty, rates of misconduct appear to be closely related to the mode of disciplinary administration. Where students have a predominant voice in disciplinary decisions and particularly where they impose severe sanctions, cheating is at a minimum. The apparent effectiveness of student control may be in its ability to marshal student support and commitment to standards of integrity. That students feel a strong sense of disapproval is shown in Table 2. Cheating ranks well ahead of drinking-related behavior or sex misconduct in terms of disapproval, suggesting that there is a reservoir of potential support for effective cheating controls. The student dishonesty report found that honor systems, a form of student-centered control, are more effective than other arrangements:

> In all categories of school size and sex composition, schools with honor systems are less apt to have a high level of cheating than those with other arrangements for control. Moreover, the difference that the honor system makes in the level of cheating of the college is greater on the average than the difference due to variations in school size and sex composition. Presumably, in return for the privileges and trust students are accorded uder the honor system, they develop a stronger sense of commitment to norms of academic integrity and, thereby, a strong climate of peer disapproval of cheating emerges on the campus. [Bowers, 1964, p. 198]

Successful administration-centered control depends on the willingness of faculty to pass cases on to the appropriate authority. Faculty members may be reluctant to do so if the student is doing well academically or if the evidence against him is not conclusive. If they have personal contact with the students, and particularly if the offender is a good student, they may feel that they are in a better position to handle the case than is someone from the administration. So there is apt to be a good deal of "slippage" in handling cases under administrative control.

There are also problems under faculty-centered control, especially under a relatively informal system. For example, a student may be caught for cheating in several different courses and in each case be treated as if it were his first offense. An instructor will be unlikely to know that a student has cheated in another course, especially at a large university, unless formal records are kept at a central location. It seems particularly important under such a system to have explicit regulations about how cases should be handled and to keep a complete record of the disposition of cases available for reference.

Sanctions are also limited under faculty control. Faculty members will generally use the sanctions available to them in their courses (e.g., withholding credit for the piece of work on which the cheating occurred). The data indicate that penalties are most lenient under faculty control.

By comparison with other forms of misconduct, cheating is treated leniently, even though campus administrators view it as one of the most serious problems. Considering students' own feelings about cheating (it is among the most disapproved forms of student misconduct with a sizable majority of students *strongly* disapproving), there would seem to be room for a firmer approach to the problem on many campuses.

Sex Misconduct

Background Since the pioneering work of Kinsey and his associates (1948; 1953), there has been a growing body of research on sexual attitudes and behavior, much of it focusing on college students (cf. Ehrmann, 1959) and, more recently, drawing students from several different college campuses (cf. Reiss, 1967). Extensive research is now under way at the Institute for Sex Research established by Kinsey at Indiana University.

These studies have shown that sexual experience develops in a relatively uniform sequence of steps during adolescence.

> The average youngster begins his sexual contact at age 12 or 13 and before marriage at least a third of the adolescent population has reached the stage of sexual intercourse. The process starts slightly earlier for girls and proceeds slightly faster for boys, but before it is over, about half the males and a quarter of the females have experienced premarital intercourse. [Bowers, DeLong, and Furstenberg, 1967]

Clearly, the college years are a period when young people are reaching the advanced stages of sexual contact. For females, in particular, the rate of premarital intercourse increases fourfold over the college years (Bowers, DeLong, and Furstenberg, 1967).

Standards of sexual conduct have become more permissive in recent years (Reiss, 1960), and the group most responsive to this trend is college youth. Presumably, the pressures of the courtship process together with college students' predisposition to question traditional standards lead to a more permissive view of premarital sex. In addition, students perceive their peers as having relatively permissive standards. This may be due in part to a tendency to exaggerate, particularly among boys, in their discussions of sexual exploits.

On the other hand, parents are becoming more restrictive (Reiss, 1967). Perhaps considerations of unwanted pregnancy, forced marriage, or abortion are more salient to them. When the student goes away to college, his parents expect the school to oversee his conduct in this area—to stand *in loco parentis*. This may well account for the fact that responsibility for cases of sex misconduct is very largely in the hands of the administration (Table 3) and for the relatively severe sanctions imposed for violating parietal rules (Table 4).

Further Analysis As may be noted in Table 7, the rates of misconduct are based on a much smaller sample than in the previous two tables. While the number of schools is essentially the same, only about one-fifth as many students were included in the 1966 survey, reducing the reliability of our results.

Implications for Control It would appear that parietal violations, like academic dishonesty, can be controlled through appropriate disciplinary administration. In this case, sanctions are more important than the locus of disciplinary responsibility. Premarital intercourse, on the other hand, varies largely by type of institution, much like disorderly and drinking-related violations.

The fact that girls' schools have lower rates of parietal violations and of premarital sex does not mean that the problem of sex misconduct is less serious there. Quite the contrary, campus authorities more often name sex misconduct as their most serious problem. The reason undoubtedly is that these institutions must deal with the ensuing social and emotional problems.

A recent book entitled *Sex and the College Student*, prepared by the Group for the Advancement of Psychiatry (1965), provides a valuable discussion of some guidelines for the development of an adequate policy on sex-related conduct. They argue that rules should be explicit and firmly enforced, yet open to review in response to student needs and opinion. They point out that firm and explicit regulations protect the right to privacy of roommates and other students in the residence halls. They also note the danger of a punitive policy on sexual conduct. The student may need counseling and should not be afraid to seek it on the campus because of the threat of punishment. The same holds for other forms of sex misconduct such as homosexuality, exhibitionism, etc., which we have not dealt with in this section. Although they occur infrequently, they are problems which require treatment, not just discipline.

TABLE 7 Sex Misconduct: Disciplinary Responsibility, Disciplinary Action, and Rates of Misconduct in Varying Institutional Contexts

	Single-sex schools				Coeducational schools							
	Catholic		Other		Catholic	Protestant		Private nondenominational		Public		
	Male	Female	Male	Female	All sizes	Small	Large	Small	Large	Small	Medium	Large
Data from 1962 survey of college deans												
Number of schools	(28)	(40)	(38)	(43)	(29)	(60)	(56)	(106)	(46)	(44)	(111)	(92)
Who handles:												
Sex misconduct:												
Student	0%	3%	15%	29%	0%	7%	7%	13%	4%	3%	4%	5%
Faculty	46	5	15	2	35	12	12	16	17	11	18	22
Administration	54	92	70	68	65	81	81	71	79	87	78	73
Penalties for:												
Violation of rules regarding opposite sex in dorm rooms:												
Warning	22%	7%	0%	3%	0%	15%	12%	12%	9%	9%	8%	15%
Restriction of privileges	0	0	33	34	4	23	28	32	16	14	12	12
Suspension	28	3	42	25	19	29	42	28	56	43	50	55
Dismissal	50	90	24	38	77	33	19	28	19	31	30	18
Data from 1966 survey of students												
Number of schools	(3)	(9)	(13)	(7)	(2)	(13)	(6)	(8)	(8)	(6)	(11)	(13)
Number of students	(30)	(79)	(108)	(98)	(13)	(138)	(49)	(89)	(63)	(46)	(96)	(92)
Rates of misconduct:												
Having members of opposite sex in students' rooms	36%	4%	46%	8%	0%	15%	22%	20%	42%	18%	16%	21%
Sexual intercourse before marriage	31%	13%	66%	28%	14%	31%	26%	55%	41%	18%	52%	51%

The foremost concern for disciplinary administration in this area is not controlling students' sex lives but identifying and treating students who have problems in this area and protecting the rights to privacy of other students.

Property Offenses

Background Colleges and universities suffer considerable losses from theft and property destruction. Although such offenses can occur almost anywhere on campus, perhaps the locations hit hardest are the school store, the library, and the residence halls. A recent news release reports that a major university bookstore lost more than $90,000 in one academic year to shoplifters (*Boston Globe,* December 5, 1966). College libraries report that as much as 35 percent of their annual budget is devoted to the replacement of missing volumes (Van Every, 1962; Morrison, 1966; Talmadge, 1960). Some residence halls record several thefts a week during the entire school term.

Much less is known about those responsible for these losses. Studies of theft and property destruction are typically concerned with lower-class youth, those not fortunate enough to be in college. For lower-class delinquents, there seems to be a meaning in theft and property destruction which is quite apart from the money they receive for the stolen goods. According to Cohen (1955), the property offenses of delinquent boys also represent a form of "reaction formation" against the value placed upon property in middle-class society. Similarly, students who engage in theft and property destruction on the college campus may also be reacting against "the establishment"—in this case, what they see as the impersonal bureaucratic institution which fails to respond to their needs.

What little analysis has been done on those who commit property offenses tends to indicate that there is a syndrome of associated offenses. Those who shoplift from the school store are also more likely to be the ones who steal books from the school library and the ones who indicate that they have destroyed school property. These actions tend to constitute a distinct set of behaviors which are relatively unrelated to other forms of student misconduct (Bowers and Sidel, 1968).

Some forms of property destruction occur largely as an outgrowth of pranksterism, rowdiness, or the excessive use of alcohol and do not reflect any underlying alienation or antagonism toward the campus community.

Compared to other areas of traditional misconduct, property offenses are among the most disapproved and the least prevalent. Sanctions against such conduct are severe and cases are usually handled by someone from the administration.

Further Analysis Stealing books from the library is the only behavior for which we have data on both rates of misconduct and disciplinary action. Our further analysis is confined to this form of behavior alone, with the following results:

1. There seems to be no relationship between who handles the case and the rates of misconduct. Nor is there any difference in the strictness of the sanctions imposed by the person handling the case.

2. Rates of theft in the library are generally lower where stricter sanctions are imposed except at the large schools. At the large schools there is no relationship between sanctions imposed and rates of theft, regardless of whether faculty, students, or administration handled the case.

3. The higher rates of such violations at Catholic schools seem to be largely a result of the fact that sanctions are less severe.

Implications for Control That the large schools show no correspondence between penalties imposed and rates of theft from the library may stem from the fact that students perceive penalties at such institutions as quite remote. As the institution becomes larger and more bureaucratic, students may not see the sanctions as representative of campus attitudes toward such conduct. Students may also feel somewhat anonymous in the larger student body and not as likely to be caught. It would appear that the best

TABLE 8 Property Offenses: Disciplinary Responsibility, Disciplinary Action, and Rates of Misconduct in Varying Institutional Contexts

	Single-sex schools				Coeducational schools							
	Catholic		Other		Catholic	Protestant		Private nondenominational		Public		
	Male	Female	Male	Female	All sizes	Small	Large	Small	Large	Small	Medium	Large
Data from 1962 survey of college deans												
Number of schools	(28)	(48)	(38)	(43)	(29)	(60)	(56)	(106)	(46)	(44)	(111)	(92)
Who handles:												
Destroying property												
Student	4%	5%	22%	23%	4%	17%	14%	19%	22%	7%	5%	14%
Faculty	15	5	11	0	30	9	16	5	10	5	13	17
Administration	82	90	68	78	67	74	70	76	69	88	82	69
Theft												
Student	4%	7%	34%	46%	4%	24%	14%	18%	16%	5%	8%	20%
Faculty	37	2	19	2	38	14	19	18	20	10	23	21
Administration	59	91	47	51	58	62	68	64	64	85	70	59
Penalties for:												
Stealing possessions												
Warning	8%	28%	3%	3%	0%	8%	7%	11%	10%	8%	8%	8%
Restriction of privileges	13	15	0	6	4	10	11	15	10	3	11	6
Suspension	12	8	30	54	35	39	60	39	56	46	50	63
Dismissal	68	49	68	37	62	44	22	35	23	44	32	23
Stealing books												
Warning	4%	8%	0%	15%	4%	11%	12%	17%	6%	14%	12%	12%
Restriction of privileges	63	78	25	42	52	46	43	56	27	30	30	17
Suspension	13	5	33	30	22	29	36	15	50	38	38	58
Dismissal	21	8	42	12	22	14	10	12	17	19	20	14
Data from 1963 survey of students												
Number of schools	(3)	(9)	(13)	(7)	(2)	(13)	(6)	(8)	(8)	(6)	(11)	(13)
Number of students	(195)	(546)	(774)	(473)	(106)	(699)	(327)	(398)	(394)	(319)	(502)	(689)
Rates of misconduct:												
Reported by students												
Taking books from library	28%	30%	22%	15%	41%	14%	10%	20%	14%	8%	12%	9%
Shoplifting from school store	11%	2%	9%	3%	4%	3%	7%	4%	6%	4%	6%	5%
Destroying school property	7%	2%	16%	7%	3%	7%	6%	6%	5%	3%	3%	5%
Known to dean												
Theft	0.2%	0.3%	0.1%	0.1%	0.1%	0.6%	0.2%	0.4%	0.1%	0.3%	0.2%	0.1%
Destroying property	0.2%	0.2%	0.2%	0.2%	0.1%	0.2%	0.2%	0.2%	0.2%	0.2%	0.2%	0.1%

measures for control available to the large institution are firm and explicit regulations about library use and security in the procedures for checking out books.

Theft and academic dishonesty have several things in common. Both are strongly disapproved by students and both seem to be responsive to the mode of disciplinary administration in all but the large coed institutions. These factors may be associated with the fact that theft, like academic dishonesty, has been incorporated under the honor system at some schools. There is an indication in continuing research on academic dishonesty at the Russell B. Stearns Study that honor systems which incorporate both theft and cheating under the same system are especially effective, presumably because both are strongly disapproved and the system provides a means of bringing this strong disapproval to bear in the social context.

Theft is potentially more difficult than cheating to bring under the control of an honor system. It may be discovered without any indication as to the offender. Theft, particularly of personal property, leaves a victim who symbolizes the failure of the system to control until the offender is caught.

Our analysis of theft from the library should not be generalized to other forms of theft or to property destruction. It serves only as an illustrative case which may suggest some more general principles of control.

RECENT FORMS OF STUDENT MISCONDUCT

Drug use and campus protest are of relatively recent vintage as student disciplinary problems.[3] The 1966 survey indicated that:

> Campus protest and drug usage, while they come to the forefront of public attention as current problems, were comparatively uncommon in 1966. This is not to say that these were insignificant problems; in fact, they were large and perplexing problems at some schools. Yet the impact on higher education in the country at large is to be found in the newness of these forms of behavior and in their threat of becoming more widespread. [Bowers, 1968b]

Drug Use

Background Although the use of drugs (other than alcohol) by college students is a fairly recent occurrence, it has a fairly long history in American society (Polsky, 1967). Marijuana has been widely used throughout the world for centuries and is unquestionably the most commonly used of the drugs by college students, followed by amphetamine and barbiturates (Pearlman, 1967).

While the level of drug use on the college campus may be on the rise, existing evidence indicates that such conduct involves only a small minority of the students. In a recent study done on urban colleges, Pearlman (1967) reports that of the seniors graduating in 1967, 6 percent of those who returned the questionnaires indicated that they had used drugs. Marijuana was most frequently used, while amphetamines and barbiturates ranked second and third respectively.

More recently, a survey of students at 426 colleges was conducted in the latter part of 1967 by Gallup (Dickerson, 1967). Approximately 6 percent of the students responding had at least tried marijuana. When questioned about the use of LSD, 1 percent indicated that they had used the drug at least once.

The 1966 survey of college seniors conducted by the Stearns study showed that 5 per-

[3] In the survey of deans and student body presidents conducted in 1962, no one mentioned either of these areas as serious disciplinary problems. Consequently, no questions about attitudes or behavior in these areas were included in our 1963 student survey. By the time of the follow-up questionnaire in 1966, it seemed clear that these forms of behavior were becoming major disciplinary problems, at least at some schools, and the decision was made to include questions about them.

cent of the students had tried marijuana, LSD, or a similar drug or narcotic. The rates of drug use were by no means uniform by school.

> At the leading institutions . . . the use of marijuana and other drugs approaches four times the rate in the college population as a whole. About one in five students at these schools in 1966 had at least tried marijuana. At the less selective institutions, on the other hand, this sort of drug usage was almost non-existent. Only one percent of the seniors at the "moderately selective" and "not very selective" schools, which, by the way, constitute more than half the schools and more than half the students in our sample, had ever tried such drugs. [Bowers, 1968b]

To the extent that the nation's top ranking institutions in terms of prestige set the standards and styles for students at other schools, the suggestion is that in 1966, the rate of drug use might have been on the rise. This projected increase is also supported by the fact that this form of behavior was "undercommitted" in 1966—the proportion not disapproving was greater than the proportion ever becoming involved.

These findings suggest that variation in drug use might also appear in terms of our breakdown by sex composition, type of control, and size. For purposes of comparison, there are presented below data on the use of "tranquilizers or other medication to relieve or reduce tension" and "using stimulants such as NoDoz or benzedrine to facilitate studying or meeting academic assignments." While these may not be a violation of the law, nor what is typically considered under the rubric of college drug use, they will provide a comparison context for the use of marijuana, LSD, and similar drugs or narcotics.

It should be noted that the figures in Table 9 come from the 1966 survey and, as in the case of Table 7 on sex misconduct, they are less reliable than those drawn from the larger 1963 survey.

Implications for Control Without systematic information by institution on the ways in which cases are handled or penalties imposed, we have no basis for evaluating the effectiveness of a particular system of control.

It would be desirable to include some concrete answers on ways to improve the disciplinary administration. But since these answers are yet to come, we shall conclude with a set of questions offered by Nowlis (1967) as important considerations in the development of an adequate institutional policy on drug use:

> 1. Can the university, while attempting to treat each case in an individual manner, also provide the procedural safeguards which have been established by the courts in the general society? Would they in fact be depriving the individual of the right of privacy, due process, to be considered innocent until proven guilty, legal search and seizure, civil disobedience, and trial by a jury of peers?
> 2. To what extent can or is the university willing to guarantee confidentiality in cases that arise which might be construed to be relevant to civil authorities?
> 3. Should the institution take action in cases which violate civil laws but are no clear hindrance to the educational function?
> 4. Who shall be responsible for the development and implementation of rules which are made, and what part should the students play in the development of university policy?

Campus Protests and Demonstrations

Background The growing interest in social and political issues on the college campus is unquestionably a healthy sign, but today's students are showing an increasing willingness to violate campus and community norms. In a number of cases, the protests are explicitly designed to violate the law or campus regulations as a means of drawing attention more directly and more forcefully to the subject of the demonstration.

According to the 1966 Stearns Study survey, about 20 percent of the country's college

TABLE 9 Drug Use: Disciplinary Responsibility, Disciplinary Action, and Rates of Misconduct in Varying Institutional Contexts

	Single-sex schools				Coeducational schools							
	Catholic		Other		Catholic	Protestant		Private nondenominational		Public		
	Male	Female	Male	Female	All sizes	Small	Large	Small	Large	Small	Medium	Large
Data from 1966 survey of students .												
Number of schools	(3)	(9)	(13)	(7)	(2)	(13)	(6)	(8)	(8)	(6)	(11)	(13)
Number of students	(30)	(79)	(108)	(98)	(13)	(138)	(49)	(89)	(63)	(46)	(96)	(92)
Rates of misconduct:												
Tranquilizers	7%	23%	17%	22%	14%	33%	22%	22%	14%	16%	19%	9%
NoDoz	31%	30%	55%	33%	0%	53%	35%	57%	40%	44%	40%	53%
Marijuana and LSD	15%	0%	10%	2%	0%	0%	3%	15%	6%	0%	2%	4%

seniors had engaged in some form of campus protest or demonstration (see Table 2). A much smaller number of students—3 percent—have actually violated the law in a deliberate act of civil disobedience. Apparently only a small fraction of those involved in student political activism have actually taken it to the point of violating the law. Still, in absolute numbers, this represents enough students to create a serious problem for the university administration.

The current student activism may also be attributed to the changing structure of higher education itself. The tremendous growth of graduate education, the relative shift of emphasis to research, and the use of graduate students to carry the undergraduate teaching load have changed the nature of the educational process at many of the nation's leading institutions. The student, particularly the undergraduate, has become a lesser concern in the overall operation of the institution. This may be why those involved in the student movement are asking for greater "student power." Thus, according to Katz (1967), ". . . in curricular and administrative areas many students call for considerably expanded student *participation* and in many social areas there is a call for student autonomy."

Implications for Control The evidence indicates that the restrictiveness of a school's stand on student protest does not necessarily limit the extent of such protest activity. Catholic schools take a relatively restrictive stand against such behavior, according to Williamson and Cowan, and yet the extent of demonstrations and civil disobedience is relatively high. Small schools take more restrictive stands than large ones, but their rates of such conduct are not consistently lower.

GUIDELINES FOR DISCIPLINARY ADMINISTRATION

Student demonstrations are directly challenging the college or university's authority to develop rules of conduct and to impose sanctions upon students (Singletary, 1968; Shoben, 1968). As a result, administrators at a number of institutions have begun to review and to reconsider disciplinary procedures and regulations (Magrath, 1968; Sindler, 1968; Intercollegiate Press, 1968). This review includes not only a consideration of the respective roles of faculty, administration, and students in the disciplinary process but also a consideration of the place of psychologists, psychiatrists, and disciplinary counselors (Williamson, 1961).

In response to students' demands for more responsibility and a greater opportunity for self-determination in both educational and disciplinary matters, the Association of American Colleges has prepared the *Joint Statement on Rights and Freedoms of Students,* a concise statement of suggested guidelines. This document was prepared in conjunction with national organizations representing both faculty and students and is presently being adopted by a number of colleges and universities as a basis of policy. The Joint Statement provides basic assumptions concerning student-university relations which should be incorporated in the more specific campus disciplinary structures. This is discussed in detail in Chapter 2 "Student Personnel Administration Policies."

We shall next consider a model code for the administration of discipline which specifies misconduct and the sanctions imposed for it. This model is essentially a means of making functional the guidelines and spirit of the *Joint Statement on Rights and Freedoms of Students.* The University of Oregon student conduct program will be used here as a model.

Campus Disciplinary Structure: The University of Oregon Model

Forms of misconduct are described under two headings, individual and group. First, with respect to the individual:

TABLE 10 Campus Protests and Demonstrations: Disciplinary Responsibility, Disciplinary Action, and Rates of Misconduct in Varying Institutional Contexts

	Single-sex schools				Coeducational schools							
	Catholic		Other		Catholic	Protestant		Private nondenominational		Public		
	Male	Female	Male	Female	All sizes	Small	Large	Small	Large	Small	Medium	Large
Data from 1966 survey of students ..												
Number of schools	(3)	(9)	(13)	(7)	(2)	(13)	(6)	(8)	(8)	(6)	(11)	(13)
Number of students	(30)	(79)	(108)	(98)	(13)	(138)	(49)	(89)	(63)	(46)	(96)	(92)
Rates of misconduct:												
Activism												
Protest march	37%	27%	30%	14%	0%	6%	19%	37%	23%	15%	22%	17%
Civil disobedience	4%	2%	5%	0%	0%	0%	0%	7%	0%	0%	10%	0%

Individual Offenses

1. No sanction or other disciplinary action shall be imposed on a student by or in the name of the University except in accordance with this Code.

2. Expulsion or suspension from the University or any lesser sanction may result from the commission of any of the following offenses:

a. Academic cheating or plagiarism.
b. Furnishing false information to the University with intent to deceive.
c. Forging, alteration, or misuse of University documents, records, or identification cards.
d. Physical abuse of another person in the University community.
e. Malicious destruction, damage, or misuse of University property, including library materials, or of private property on the campus.
f. Theft occurring under the conditions of Paragraph 3 below.
g. Vandalism or kidnapping committed on other campuses.
h. Participation in hazing.
i. Lewd or indecent conduct occurring under conditions of Paragraph A–3 [above and not cited here, specified behavior which interferes with the goals of a university or the welfare of the university community].
j. Two or more (or the repetition of) offenses listed in Paragraph 3 below.

3. Disciplinary probation or any lesser sanction may result from the commission of any of the following offenses:

a. Possession, consumption, or furnishing of alcoholic beverages on University owned or controlled property (except in living quarters of married students, in University related housing for single students, or at University sponsored or supervised functions).
b. Disorderly conduct, including disorderly conduct resulting from drunkenness, occurring under the conditions of Paragraph A–3.
c. Raiding of University related living unit.
d. Violation of closing hour restrictions.
e. Violation of visiting hour rules.
f. Violation of any University rule approved by the Student Conduct Committee for the infraction of which sanctions may be imposed under this Code. [*University of Oregon Student Handbook, 1967–1968*]

Next, group offenses are described thusly:

Group Offenses

1. Living organizations, societies, clubs and similar organized groups are responsible for compliance with University regulations. Upon satisfactory proof that the group has encouraged, or did not take reasonable steps, as a group, to prevent violations of University regulations, the group may be subjected to permanent or temporary suspension of charter, social probation, denial of use of University facilities, or other like sanctions.

2. The determination that a group is liable to sanction under the foregoing Section 1, and of the sanction to be imposed, shall be made by the Student Conduct Committee at a hearing held for that purpose. The president or principal officer of the group must be given reasonable notice of the time and place of said hearing and the nature of the charges. He or any other member of the group is entitled to attend and be heard at the hearing.

3. Nothing herein authorizes the imposition of individual sanctions on any person other than in accordance with the Code of Student Conduct. [*University of Oregon Student Handbook, 1967–1968*]

A detailed description of the sanctions which are imposed for the violation of the above rules is presented in the following manner:

Sanctions

1. Sanctions which may be imposed for the commission of University offenses shall include the following:

a. Expulsion from the University.
b. Suspension from the University for a definite or indefinite period of time.
c. Disciplinary probation with or without the loss of designated privileges for a definite period of time. The violation of the terms of disciplinary probation or the infraction of any University rule during the period of disciplinary probation may be grounds for suspension or expulsion from the University. The parents of any student under 21 years of age who is placed on disciplinary probation, suspended, or expelled shall be so notified.
d. Loss of privileges:
(1) Restriction to campus living quarters.
(2) Denial of use of an automobile for a designated time.
(3) Removal from dormitory or other University housing.
(4) Loss of such other privileges as may be consistent with the offense committed and the rehabilitation of the student.
e. Admonition and warning.
f. Such other sanctions as may be approved by the Student Conduct Committee.

2. The sanctions of expulsion or suspension shall not be imposed except upon proper determination by the Student Court of the Student Conduct Committee.

3. The General Policies, Violations, and Sanctions shall be printed and made readily available to all students. The campus newspaper shall be requested by the Student Conduct Committee to publish the same at the beginning of each school year. [*University of Oregon Student Handbook, 1967–1968*]

Here, we see an orderly and concise exposition of both the general modes of behavior which require administrative attention and the types of institutional responses which may result. What links the alleged misconduct to the various responses is, of course, the court or disciplinary counseling structure.

The Student Conduct Committee at the University of Oregon coordinates, develops, and governs all aspects of the student conduct program. It is responsible to the president of the university and also acts as an appellate court when necessary. The committee is described as follows:

Student Conduct Committee

1. The Student Conduct Committee, by faculty legislation and by delegation of the President of the University, is designated as the agency within the University which has primary responsibility for the student conduct program. The Committee shall be responsible to the faculty and to the President of the University for recommending policies relating to student conduct, for formulating and approving rules and enforcement procedures within the framework of existing policies, for disposing of such individual cases as may properly come before it, and for recommending to the President of the University changes in the administration of any aspect of the student conduct program.

2. The Committee shall consist of four faculty members and three student members, each appointed by the President of the University. Each student member shall serve for a period of one year with one member retiring at the end of each academic term (fall, winter, spring). Members of the Committee may be reappointed. The President may appoint temporary members of the Committee to serve during a summer session or such times as is necessary to assure full membership of the Committee.

3. The President of the University shall designate an Associate Dean of Students who shall serve as Secretary of the Committee in the discharge of its responsibilities. He shall coordinate the activities of all officials, committees, student groups, and tribunals responsible for student conduct.

4. All regulations or rules relating to student conduct that are established by any University official, committee or student group, and for which sanctions may be imposed in the name of the University, must be submitted to the Committee for approval. Such written regulations or rules shall be effective fifteen days after filing with the Secretary of the Committee unless disapproved within this period by the Committee. Fraternity, sorority, or co-operative "housekeeping" rules adopted by members for

the internal management of the living unit are not considered University rules for the purpose of this Code.

5. The Committee may delegate jurisdiction to handle infractions of University rules to the Student Court and such other tribunals as may be established. With the consent of the President of the University, the Committee also may delegate such jurisdiction to appropriate University officials. In all instances such jurisdiction shall be defined by the Committee, ordinarily in terms of specified offenses, maximum sanctions, or designated living units. The Committee may, at its discretion, withdraw delegation of jurisdiction in any case and dispose of such case itself.

6. The Committee shall require from University officials and tribunals periodically written reports of the disposition of all student conduct cases handled under their jurisdiction. The gathering of such reports and their submission to the Committee shall be the responsibility of the Associate Dean of Students. The Committee shall examine such reports for consistency with existing policies and, where necessary, review the reports with the appropriate officials or tribunals.

7. The Committee shall submit to the faculty and the President of the University each spring term a written report covering the entire student conduct program including an evaluation of existing rules, policies, and enforcement proceedings. It shall recommend changes in policy to the faculty and the President and changes in the administration of the program to the President. [*University of Oregon Student Handbook, 1967–1968*]

As indicated in the above description of the Student Conduct Committee, the Student Court and lesser tribunals are also the responsibility of the Committee. These tribunals are the primary decision-making bodies of the program. At the Student Court, expulsion and suspension may be used as sanctions, while the lesser courts (e.g., traffic and living unit) may impose lesser sanctions. In addition, such individuals as dorm counselors may, without formal deliberation, impose certain limited sanctions. In describing the Student Court, the Student Conduct Code states:

Student Court

1. The Student Court shall be composed of five students and two faculty members, each appointed by the President of the University. The student members shall be recommended by the President of the Associated Students and shall serve for a term of two years with two members retiring in alternate years. Whenever possible, one member shall be a second- or third-year law student. The court will elect a chairman from its student membership.

2. A quorum of the Court shall consist of three student members and one faculty member. A decision that a student has committed an offense requires an affirmative vote of two-thirds of the members of the court deciding the case. Sanctions of suspension or expulsion may likewise be imposed only by two-thirds of such members. Sanctions of lesser severity than suspension or expulsion shall be made by majority vote.

3. The Court shall prepare its own rules of procedure.

4. The Court shall maintain, with the assistance of the Associate Dean of Students, an adequate record of the history and disposition of each case to come before it. The record shall include a summary of the evidence upon which the Court based its decision.

5. The jurisdiction of the Court shall extend to all violations of the Code.

6. The Court may impose any authorized sanction which is warranted by the circumstances of the case. Pursuant to the authority vested in the Student Conduct Committee by sections 1C1f and 1E5 (see 1f under *Sanctions*, paragraph 5 under *Student Conduct Committee*), the Student Court is hereby authorized by said Committee to impose sanctions involving the rendition of labor or services. Such sanctions should be employed only in cases where principles of restitution or rehabilitation render such type sanctions peculiarly appropriate. This sanction may be in addition to other authorized sanctions.

7. Any student whose case is referred to the Court shall be notified of such referral in writing by the Associate Dean of Students at least three days before the hearing and

shall be apprised in the notice of the charges against him. During the hearing, the student shall have the opportunity (*a*) to appear in person or through counsel, (*b*) to know the evidence against him, and (*c*) to present evidence and argument in his own behalf. A request by a student for a hearing closed to the public will be given due consideration. In the resolution of factual disputes, the Court will request the testimony of witnesses and otherwise seek the best evidence obtainable.

8. The Associate Dean of Students shall appoint, subject to the approval of the Student Conduct Committee, a special assistant to the Student Conduct Program who will serve as prosecutor for the Student Court and who shall be responsible to the Student Conduct Committee. The special assistant will be in charge of all cases which are to be heard by the Student Court. The assistant shall then prepare the case for hearing and may either present it to the Student Court or recommend to the Conduct Committee that it be dropped without a hearing.

9. The Associate Dean of Students shall execute the decisions of the Court. [*University of Oregon Student Handbook, 1967–1968*]

Although the structure developed by the University of Oregon includes other aspects as well, we believe the sections presented here give a reasonable outline of their system of student disciplinary administration. Specific administrative procedures regarding difficult recent problems such as drug use and campus protest are not, however, covered in the above outline. We shall draw on other sources for specific recommendations in these areas.

The New York University School of Law has developed detailed guidelines with respect to protests and demonstrations:

FREEDOM OF PROTEST

The right of peaceful protest within the University community must be preserved. The University retains the right to assure the safety of individuals, the protection of property, and the continuity of the educational process.

Commentary

Times of turbulence and student unrest require special forebearance on the part of University officials in tolerance of demonstrations and protests in opposition to University policy. Even when the subject of the demonstration or protest is not clearly relevant to the educational process or to University functions, the University must be at least as hospitable to this form of expression of opinion as would the outside community where inconvenience and even some interruption of normal activity are accepted as the price paid for freedom of expression.

Picketing and External Access to University Buildings

Orderly picketing and other forms of peaceful protest are protected activities on University premises in the absence of interference with free passage through areas where members of the University community have a right to be.

Commentary

Interference with ingress to and egress from the University, interruption of classes, or damage to property exceeds permissible limits. When a University facility abuts a public street, student activity, although on public property, may unreasonably interfere with ingress to and egress from University buildings. Even though remedies might be available through local enforcement bodies, the University may, in rare instances, choose instead to impose its own disciplinary sanctions.

Control of University Buildings

Peaceful picketing and other orderly demonstrations are permitted in public areas of University buildings, including corridors outside auditoriums and other places set aside for public meetings.

Commentary

Where University space is in use for an authorized University function, whether conduct of a class, a public or private meeting under approved sponsorship, normal administrative functions, or service-related activities (e.g., health services, recreational activities, or personnel placement), respect must be accorded any reasonable regulations imposed by the person in charge. That is, any requirement to desist from specified activities or to leave the premises must be obliged unless manifestly unreasonable or outside the scope of authority of the person issuing the requirement. [*Student Conduct and Disciplinary Proceedings in a University Setting,* N.Y.U., 1968]

The Counseling Role

The discussion thus far has dealt primarily with basic assumptions, specific regulations, and formal procedures in disciplinary administration. We have been concerned largely with the way in which regulations should be developed and the manner in which an individual's guilt or innocence should be determined so that his rights and freedoms are protected. There is, however, another dimension to disciplinary administration—determining the causes of misconduct and helping the individual recognize his responsibility to the campus and also the general community. Williamson (1961) sees this as the counseling function in disciplinary administration:

Discipline as organized student personnel work proceeds in an orderly fashion to help the individual search for an understanding of the causes of his misbehavior and for means of achieving his personality without continual disruptive *and* interfering expressions of his motivations. [Williamson, 1961]

Although recognizing the need for due process and the maintenance of individual integrity, he feels that the disciplinary counselor should be an integral part of disciplinary administration. He provides a sequence of steps to be followed in disciplinary cases, several of which (*f, g, h, i, j,* and *o*) explicitly involve counseling. Although the sequence in which they can be accomplished can vary according to the situation, Williamson presents them in the following order:

a. Identification of alleged disciplinary situations
b. Identification of students allegedly involved
c. Reporting of students allegedly involved
d. Making of charges against students
e. Case investigation
f. Student interviewed for counselling purposes
g. Appraisal of causes of incident behavior
h. Assessment of potentiality for rehabilitation
i. Tentative formulation of needed steps in rehabilitation
j. Comprehensive report to committee or official
k. A review and deliberation by committee or official
l. Consultation and review by committee or official with student in an informal face-to-face situation
m. Action by committee or official
n. Enforcement of committee action
o. Rehabilitation counselling as long as necessary or profitable [Williamson, 1961]

The Student Conduct Program at the University of Oregon provides for a flexible administrative response including counseling:

1. All serious violations of law and of the Code will be immediately reported to the Associate Dean of Students by any person who has knowledge of the commission of any such violation. The reporting practices of those in a position of responsibility for student conduct may be delineated by the Dean of Students.
2. The Associate Dean of Students shall insure that the best interests of any offending student are served, regardless of whether disciplinary action is taken, by making full use of appropriate medical counselling and other professional services.
3. Where sufficient evidence exists that a violation of law has occurred, the Associate

Dean of Students ordinarily shall refer the case and transmit the evidence to the appropriate law enforcement agency.

4. Violations of University rules which are brought to the attention of the Associate Dean of Students, but which in his judgment do not warrant the sanction of expulsion or suspension, may be referred to an appropriate minor judicial tribunal.

5. In those cases of violation of the Code involving psychological abnormality, mental illness, or other unusual circumstances, the Associate Dean of Students, with the consent of the Student Conduct Committee, may take prior action other than the initiation of judicial proceedings.

6. Where the evidence establishes to the satisfaction of the Associate Dean of Students that a University offense has occurred and the case has not been disposed of under Paragraphs 3, 4, or 5 above, the following procedures shall govern:

a. The Associate Dean of Students shall advise the student of the charges and evidence against him.

b. The Associate Dean of Students shall afford thc student an opportunity to state informally or present evidence in support of his side of the case, including mitigating circumstances.

c. The Associate Dean of Students may seek professional assistance and advice, consult with the student's parents or guardian, or take other measures to assume a fair disposition of the case.

d. The Associate Dean of Students shall refer the case to the Student Court for action.

e. The conduct of the hearing before the Student Court shall be governed by the established rules of procedure of the court.

f. A student who pleads guilty may elect not to appear for a hearing. The plea and waiver of hearing shall be in writing. In such instances the Associate Dean of Students shall present the written plea and the facts of the case to the Student Court for disposition.

g. In extraordinary cases where the interests of the student or the University can best be served, the Associate Dean of Students may refer the case directly to the Student Conduct Committee.

7. [Not particularly relevant to this discussion, therefore omitted]

8. In all instances involving a reported alleged violation of the Code where the Associate Dean of Students does not refer the case to the Student Court or an appropriate minor judicial tribunal for action, the Associate Dean of Students shall make a full report of the basic facts and the reasons for the non-referral for judicial proceedings to the Student Conduct Committee. [*University of Oregon Student Handbook, 1967–1968*]

Here, in paragraphs 2, 5, and 6, provisions are made which allow the Associate Dean to take advantage of counseling and other professional services in specified ways without impeding due process. (See also Byse, 1966; Perkins, 1967.) It is important that the relationship between counseling and due process be made explicit; otherwise, one may interfere with the other.

SUMMARY

Essentially this section has attempted to indicate the direction of current thought on the rights and freedom of students. Recently, programs such as those at the University of Oregon, Brown University, and Cornell University (Magrath, 1968; Sindler, 1968), have been developed to give the student a greater role in disciplinary matters. In addition, a specific disciplinary program was presented as a model in an attempt to provide a concrete description of program components and mechanisms.

In the last analysis, successful student disciplinary administration rests upon the acceptance by students of the standards which are supposed to govern their conduct. No expenditure of time and effort in disciplinary administration can compensate for ill-conceived and ill-defined campus regulations. Students' compliance depends on their understanding of and support for campus regulations. If they feel that such regulations are unreasonable or illegitimate, the institution stands a chance of massive disobedience. Such disobedience may even take on a defiant character and spread to other kinds of rules and regulations which were not originally in question. It is, therefore, of the utmost importance that campus rules and regulations be conceived and formulated to ensure maximum student support.

REFERENCES

Bailey, H. W.: "Disciplinary Procedures," in W. S. Monroe (ed.), *Encyclopedia of Educational Research,* The Macmillan Company, New York, 1941.

Bowers, William J.: *Student Dishonesty and Its Control in College,* Bureau of Applied Social Research, Columbia University Press, New York, 1964.

———: "Normative Constraints on Deviant Behavior in the College Context," *Sociometry,* vol. 31, no. 4, 1968a.

———: "A Survey of Campus Misconduct," The Russell B. Stearns Study, Northeastern University, Boston, 1968b.

———, Jane DeLong, and Frank Furstenberg: "Courtship Patterns and Premarital Sexual Relations," The Russell B. Stearns Study, Northeastern University, Boston, 1967.

———, and Andrea Carr: "Sex Roles, Peer Group Solidarity and Deviant Behavior," The Russell B. Stearns Study, Northeastern University, Boston, 1968.

———, and Philip Sidel: "Dimensions of Campus Deviance," The Russell B. Stearns Study, Northeastern University, Boston, 1968.

Brubacher, John S., and Willis Rudy: *Higher Education in Transition,* Harper & Brothers, New York, 1958.

Byse, Clark: "Procedural Due Process and the College Student: Law and Policy," in Lawrence E. Dervis and Joseph F. Kauffman (eds.), *The College and The Student,* American Council on Education, Washington, 1966.

Cohen, Albert K.: *Delinquent Boys,* The Free Press of Glencoe, New York, 1955.

Cuff, Dan: *Boston Globe,* December 5, 1966.

Dickerson, Fred: "Drugs on Campus: A Gallup Poll," *Readers Digest,* August, 1967.

Ehrmann, Winston H.: *Premarital Dating Behavior,* Holt, Rinehart, and Winston, Inc., New York, 1959.

Goldsen, Rose K., et al.: *What College Students Think,* D. Van Nostrand Company, Inc., Princeton, N.J., 1960.

Group for the Advancement of Psychiatry: *Sex and the College Student,* Atheneum Publishers, New York, 1965.

Katz, Joseph: *The Student Activists: Rights, Needs, and Powers of Undergraduates,* U.S. Department of Health, Education, and Welfare, 1967.

Kinsey, Alfred C., Wardell B. Pomeroy, and Clyde E. Martin: *Sexual Behavior in the Human Male,* W. B. Saunders Company, Philadelphia, 1948.

———, and Paul H. Gebhard: *Sexual Behavior in the Human Female,* W. B. Saunders Company, Philadelphia, 1953.

Magrath, Peter C.: "Student Participation: What Happens When We Try It?" in *The Future Academic Community: Continuity and Change,* American Council on Education, Washington, 1968.

Morrison, Perry D.: "Lost Book Campaign at Sacramento," *Wilson Library Bulletin,* no. 40, February, 1966.

Nowlis, Helen H.: *Drugs on the College Campus,* National Association of Student Personnel Administrators, Detroit, 1967.

Pearlman, Samuel: "Drug Use and Experience in an Urban College Population," *American Journal of Orthopsychiatry,* no. 38, April, 1967.

Perkins, James A.: *The University and Due Process,* American Council on Education, Washington, 1967.

Polsky, Ned: *Hustlers, Beats, and Others,* Aldine Press, Chicago, 1967.

Reiss, Ira L.: *Premarital Sexual Standards in America,* The Free Press of Glencoe, New York, 1960.

———: *The Social Context of Premarital Sexual Permissiveness,* Holt, Rinehart, and Winston, Inc., New York, 1967.

Research Seminar on Student Conduct and Discipline: *Student Conduct and Discipline Proceedings in a University Setting,* New York University School of Law, New York, 1968.

Shoben, Edward J.: "Demonstrations, Confrontations, and Academic Business as Usual," American Council on Education, Washington, 1968.

Sindler, Alan P.: "A Case Study in Student-University Relations," in *The Future Academic Community: Continuity and Change,* American Council on Education, Washington, 1968.
Singletary, Otis A.: *Freedom and Order on Campus,* American Council on Education, Washington, 1968.
Strauss, Robert, and Seldon Bacon: *Drinking in College,* Yale University Press, New Haven, Conn., 1953.
Talmadge, Robert: "College and University Library Statistics, 1958, 1959," *College and Research Libraries,* no. 21, January, 1960.
University of Oregon: *University of Oregon Student Handbook, 1967–1968,* University of Oregon, Eugene, Ore., 1967.
"Anonymous," University of Wisconsin, Intercollegiate Press Bulletins, 33, September 9, 1968.
Van Every, Joan: "Is It Worth Doing Anything About Book Losses?" *Library Journal,* no. 87, September 1, 1962.
Williamson, E. G.: *Student Personnel Services in Colleges and Universities,* McGraw-Hill Book Company, New York, 1961.
———, and John Cowan: *The American Student's Freedom of Expression,* University of Minnesota Press, Minneapolis, 1964.
———, and J. D. Foley: *Counseling and Discipline,* McGraw-Hill Book Company, New York, 1948.

Chapter 4

Campus Unrest

ASA S. KNOWLES

Editor in Chief

CHESTER W. STOREY

Assistant to the President, Northeastern University
Boston, Massachusetts

PROBLEM NOT NEW, BUT QUALITATIVELY DIFFERENT

Student unrest is an integral part of the world's educational heritage. Students in medieval times threw garbage at people, read tempestuous poems on church steps, and even threatened their professors. In colonial times they rioted, stole, shot at their presidents, and protested infringement of their privacy. In the nineteenth century they began demanding a voice in institutional governance. They signed the Oxford Peace Pledge in the twentieth century, joined in the Spanish Civil War, and experimented with sex.

Student unrest has always been somewhat connected with the "growing-up" process, but it is qualitatively different in our time. This is a dynamic age, characterized by specialization and an accelerating pace of change brought on by the rapid advance of science and technology. Higher education is now for everyone, as opposed to the time when the select minority prepared for careers in law, medicine, or the church. This causes problems not only in terms of numbers of students but in content of study as well.

This is an age in which college youth are looking within themselves as never before, searching for life's meaning, for their own human values.

Many are dissatisfied with parental mores and with societal hypocrisy, and develop a lack of respect for authority and an unwillingness to abide by any disciplinary code. They search for individual freedom and self-determination, and unfortunately many of them, in particular the militants, feel that any means is allowable to an end.

RESTIVENESS BOTH A CAUSE AND RESULT OF OUR TIMES

S. L. Halleck, Director of Student Health Psychiatry and Professor of Psychology at the University of Wisconsin, sees today's restive student as both a cause and a result of the times in which we live. He cites overpermissiveness on the part of parents during the upbringing period, which results in an inability on the part of the child to react maturely when his demands are not immediately met. Being raised in an affluent society is another factor. It is argued, Professor Halleck says, "that affluence that is unearned, and that is unaccompanied by a tradition of service and commitment, creates a sense of restlessness, boredom, and meaninglessness in our youth."

Other elements affecting youth are the exposure to a disturbed family life and the lack of response to responsibility. In the latter case, youth in what the author refers to as a "psychologized" society tend to act as though they are not to be held accountable for actions which can be totally explained. "It is almost as if they say, 'Because the world is so bad and because it has treated me so badly, I cannot be blamed for my actions. There is no point in holding me accountable for things I cannot help anyway.' "

The troubling behavior of students can also be traced to some degree to modern technology, the growth of new communications media, especially television, and our increasing reliance on scientism. In order for us to make commitments, not only to goals but to other people, it must be possible for us to in some measure predict the future. This is what gives us hope. Due to the massive and continuous growth of technology, however, we find it difficult even to predict what life will be like a few short years from now. So, according to Professor Halleck, hope diminishes and we learn to live for the present.

The effects on youth of our communications media have also been substantial, especially in the case of television, which can expose the hypocrisies of older generations rapidly and readily. The presentation of the cynical facts of life to youth at too early an age creates "a deep skepticism as to validity of authority. Neither the family, the church, the law, nor any institution demands the automatic respect it once did."

Concerning the impact of our increasing reliance on scientism, Professor Halleck cites the fact that today's youth seek answers to life's questions in science rather than religion. Many of today's young people believe in the perfectibility of man, only to become bitterly and sadly disillusioned when encountering the harsh realities of life.

Today's youth look at the world around them. There is the cold war, the war in Vietnam. There is racial injustice. They see a deterioration in American life, as evidenced to them by spiraling crime and divorce rates, by overpopulation, mass-production, and impersonalization. They see political hopelessness and an overly complex society immutable to change.

In this morass of frustration, our youth then lash out in rebellion at the most vulnerable, the most tolerant institutions in our society—the colleges and universities. From the virtually nonviolent Free Speech Movement at Berkeley in 1964, there has unfortunately developed the dissent-to-resistance theme among the more militant campus activists. This culminated in the tragic series of events at Columbia in 1968 and subsequently at other institutions across the nation. Resistance took on the form of disruption and physical violence.

THE EXTREMIST, HARBINGER OF CHAOS

It is vitally important now to recognize and make a clear distinction between the legitimate campus protester and the activist whose only goal is the destruction of the college or university. The latter is the inevitable extremist, the unreasoning student who bars entry to classrooms and buildings, who takes control of facilities by force, who stages unlawful rallies, demonstrations, and sit-ins so that his voice only can be heard. He is the one who publishes the "underground" newspaper, who distributes anti-university posters and documents, who tries to coerce the university into meeting his demands blindly and with no recourse to free and open discussion. Disruption now and destruction later are his only true goals. Although it may feel it has established policies equitable to all individuals and campus groups, no institution is safe from this type of radical.

Extremists are a very small minority on our campuses, but they are still the most dangerous. Although much recent publicity has been centered on Students for a Democratic Society (SDS), there are a number of other "new left" radical organizations whose activities are cause for grave concern, not only in our colleges and universities but in other institutions as well. They run from the Student Nonviolent Coordinating Committee and the Black Panther Party to such Communist-influenced groups as the Revolutionary Action Movement, Youth International Party, Progressive Labor Party, Young Socialist Alliance, and the W. E. B. DuBois Clubs.

SDS, however, has become the chief perpetrator of campus chaos and, according to FBI Director J. Edgar Hoover, "has seized upon every opportunity to foment discord among the youth of this country."

New York University philosophy professor Sidney Hook says: "By their lawless actions, the members of SDS threaten to become the true grave diggers of academic freedom in the United States."

It is SDS's avowed purpose, as part of its overall effort to "restructure" society, to completely overthrow the American educational system. SDS offers no alternatives, of course, and is content to play the disruptive role of negative critic on our campuses. Belying its name, this organization is intent upon doing everything it can to dispense with both democracy and society.

Information on the activities of "new left" organizations, and SDS in particular, should continually be distributed throughout the academic community by the administration. This is information which should be as specific as possible, naming names when they are known, whether they are students at the institution itself or paid organizers from neighboring campuses or elsewhere.

The New University Conference, a newly emerging organization of radical faculty members, is making its discontented voice heard on many of our campuses also. Their goal, they say, is to liberate women from male supremacy, to give male chauvinism equal billing with racism, corporate capitalism, imperialism, etc. They call this the Female Liberation Movement, demanding day care centers for women for their children, increased numbers of female faculty members and students, courses to refute male points of view, and centers for female liberation within the institution itself. In brief, some propaganda programs.

It is particularly interesting to note that this group's national secretary is a co-founder of SDS and that its membership claims that they are professors who work "in and around and in spite of institutions of higher education."

According to a statement issued in May 1969 by the National Council of Scholars, these are the types of faculty members who can best be described as "alienated." They are the professors who "have built themselves a world view of ideas or ideologies that bid them attach themselves to another world . . . either a mythical utopia or an actual totalitarian regime. Through their example and their teaching they propagate alienating ideas among students, with the full weight of their authority."

The reasons for their alienation? Personality problems, a need for identification, mental distress, imagined horror of nuclear devastation and the war in Vietnam? Any of these and possibly others, singly or combined, according to the Council, may have produced the effect of alienation in particular cases.

In summary, the National Council of Scholars states that:

a. The influence of alienated professors is the most sustained source of radicalism on the campus.

b. The alienated activists constitute no more than two percent of the campus population.

c. Alienated activism at the university is never unrelated to revolutionary activism outside, and academic activist groups maintain various kinds of connection with revolutionary parties and foreign totalitarian regimes.

d. The discontented elements on our campuses become either willing or reluctant followers of the alienated activists because of various types of confusion, fear, and/or guilt.

There should be no attempt, the Council's statement continues, to enter into a dialog with the ideologically alienated. They have removed themselves from our world and meanings are not the same to them as to us.

The Council suggests:

a. A carefully reasoned attempt to formulate and implement an academic policy to counteract the use of academic chairs for the propagation of alienating ideas;

b. A dam of positive and constructive ideas to counter the flood of negative and destructive ideas;

c. Acknowledgment and exploration of institutional deficiencies in such a way that it becomes possible to separate legitimate campus discontents from demands belonging to an outside political struggle; and

d. Promotion of a clarification of the nature of Communism and other subversive movements.

REFORMS MUST BE GAINED THROUGH SYSTEM OF DUE PROCESS

Higher education has always welcomed constructive reform and improvement in its procedures. In today's rapidly changing world, many reforms are needed. They must be attained, however, through a system of due process which presents views of the entire academic community and which recognizes the special competences of some of its members. What constitutes due process itself may become a subject of revision. Students have every right, as do all other elements in a free academic community, to legitimately protest. No voice should be excluded, but neither should any voice be permitted to prevail because it chooses to employ threats, disruption, or obstruction.

Because of opposition to the military on the part of many, stemming from the war in Vietnam, much controversy has developed concerning ROTC and institutional policy toward recruitment on campus by military oriented companies. There is need for our institutions to review these aspects of academic life, just as there is need for them to (1) update curricula, (2) reevaluate all roles in institutional decision making, (3) liberalize parietal rules, (4) improve the adequacy of teaching, and (5) strengthen student-faculty relationships through increased personalization.

These are the major issues on our campuses, and our colleges and universities are well aware of them. They also readily acknowledge the usefulness of legitimate and orderly student protest in making them sensitive to shortcomings.

Concerning student dissatisfaction with the relevancy of courses to the times in which we live, a potentially positive development seems to be taking place. It is the establishment of the so-called "free universities," academic utopias where students and teachers can study and discuss whatever is of interest to them. There are no examinations, grades, or degrees.

Usually these "shadow" schools arise on existing campuses and supplement standard academic curricula. Their greatest value seems to lie in their role as educational "laboratories," out of which may come courses and programs worthy of integration into the regular academic curriculum of the institution.

Unlawful and disorderly demonstrations have affected all types of colleges and universities in this nation. No institution has been immune. Intellectual turmoil, traditionally proper and indispensable to a healthy campus, has been to a large degree supplanted by physical turmoil, traditionally repugnant and foreign. Tumult, fear, personal injury, and destruction of property have accompanied physical confrontations, threatening invasions of classrooms, forceful occupations of buildings, harassment of university officers, and even acts of arson and bombing. Faculty members are threatening to leave their institutions. Many have already done so. Angry public reaction to campus disorders threatens the financial stability of many public and private institutions.

There must be a rejection of the notion of the small group of extremists that the university as a place of academic order, reason, and intellectual freedom not exist until they remake it—and the outside world—according to their own vision.

STATE, FEDERAL RESPONSE TO DISORDERS INCREASING

State legislatures are beginning to react strongly to the outrages being perpetrated on our campuses. Colorado has passed a "Campus Disorders Act," apparently the first legislation enacted on the state level to control disruptions. This law provides penalties of up to $500 in fines and/or jail sentences of up to a year for anyone who interferes with the normal functions of a college or university. According to a publication released in March, 1969 by the American Council on Education, some eighteen other state legislatures are considering legislation on student violence and disruption. See page 7-81.

Tennessee has gone so far as to pass a law permitting the state district attorneys general to take over a campus during an illegal demonstration. This idea, of course, is deplorable to a free academic community. Such an action, however, may also become a necessity if hard-line militants continue to display blatant irresponsibility and lack of respect for law and order.

In California it is now a misdemeanor to fail to leave university property when ordered to do so under specified circumstances, to maliciously and willfully disturb the peace of a campus, and to return to the campus without permission for 72 hours if told not to return. Another California law permits interim suspension of students and faculty members who disrupt normal campus activities, and would cut off scholarship aid to students convicted of participating in disturbances.

Reaction has been similar at the federal level. According to United States Attorney General John M. Mitchell, authorization will soon be forthcoming to criminally prosecute those who have been crossing state lines to incite riots on college and university campuses. He has said a great deal of evidence has been amassed on this aspect of the disorders, and that Justice Department investigations are centered on possible violations of antiriot provisions of the 1968 Civil Rights Act.

President Nixon has made his voice heard also. At his request, Vice-president Agnew has been consulting with state governors about "what action, consistent with the traditional independence of American universities, might be taken at the state and federal levels to cope with the growing lawlessness and violence on our campuses."

The President has expressed major concern over the moral and political threat posed by campus radicalism, not over its physical challenge. Force can be contained, he said in a June address. "We have the powers to strike back if need be, and to prevail. The nation has survived other attempts at insurrection. We can survive this. It has not been a lack of civil power, but the reluctance of a free people to employ it, that so often has stayed the hand of authorities faced with confrontation."

President Nixon has also chided the campus insurgents for what he terms their "moral arrogance," which denies the most fundamental of all our values—respect for the rights of others. The greater the victory for the radical, the President stated, the more he will have undermined the security of his own rights.

ROLE OF THE COURTS NOW A MAJOR FACTOR

There has been much evidence that the injunctive powers of the courts have a much more positive effect on students than threats of prosecution for criminal trespass, the usual charge resulting from refusal to leave a campus building. A number of demonstrations have been peacefully ended when the participants were confronted with a restraining order. The university, by removing the onus from itself and placing it in the hands of the courts, thus hurts the student protest movement. If police must be brought in to enforce an order, they are upholding the dignity and power of the courts rather than of the university officials.

Also, it is much more difficult for lawyers to defend students charged with contempt for defying a court order than to defend them for criminal trespass. Defendants in contempt cases usually do not have the right to jury trial and are tried by the very person whose order they ignored.

Restraining orders, of course, will not be successful every time. There are some students who will not obey a law of any kind, regardless of the consequences. If any such distasteful action must be taken by an institution, it would appear that the restraining order is much more palatable, at least as a first step, than calling in the police.

An injunction may be obtained in the following general manner, depending of course on the varying legal requirements of different geographical areas:

In the event of the threat of a riot on campus, the university lawyer should file a bill in equity in court, asking that the named defendants (and their followers) be enjoined from doing something considered illegal by the academic community and asking for a temporary injunction. The judge will consider it and assent to it if he finds it has merit. The court clerk's office will prepare the document, which will be served upon the defendants by the sheriff or his deputies. If they are not available and an emergency situation exists, it may possibly be served by a disinterested person.

If the emergency exists in the middle of the night, the lawyer may prepare both the bill and the injunction order and find a judge (at home in bed, if necessary) to sign it. It may then be served. The remaining formalities may be attended to at the clerk's office the following day.

In summary, the basic grounds for injunctions sought and received by colleges and universities are:

1. The presence of an immediate threat of damage or destruction to property of the institution or violence or the threat of violence in the educational community.
2. A significant interference with the educational mission of the institution.
3. An unlawful trespass or occupation of university facilities.
4. The lack of any other enforceable legal remedy.
5. The immediate threat of irrevocable harm or damage to the institution or community through the disruption of its educational mission.

The advantages of proceeding to secure injunctions in cases of student disorders are:

1. Public declaration by the courts of the unlawful nature of the acts.
2. Favorable public reaction to the declaration.
3. Imposition of restraint upon the disrupting students by a non-university governmental entity.
4. Furnishing of an excuse to cease disruption to students who are looking for an excuse to return to classes.
5. If contempt proceedings are instituted to enforce the injunction: (*a*) the hearing on the contempt citation is generally accelerated on the court's docket which results in a speedier determination than that which could be secured through injunction in the overcrowded criminal docket, and (*b*) except in the federal courts there is no requirement for jury trial on a contempt citation in most states.

The disadvantages are:

1. Injunction is not self-enforcing.
2. Local sheriffs are required to serve copies of the injunction.
3. Enforcement of the injunction is through complicated contempt proceedings which result in the arrest of student offenders by law officers which could have been accomplished by the enforcement of criminal laws rather than via the injunction route.
4. Unless the university is prepared to enforce the injunction through contempt proceedings, the majesty of the law may be actively flouted by students who know the university will be reluctant to proceed by the institution of contempt actions.
5. An improvidently secured injunction can have the effect of polarizing resistance to university discipline.

FEDERAL LAWS RELATING TO VIOLATIONS OF CRIMINAL STATUTES

In any case, the Department of Health, Education, and Welfare has already brought to the attention of colleges and universities the recently enacted federal laws relating to violations by students of criminal statutes. They are as follows:

Student Unrest Provisions

Departments of Labor and Health, Education, and Welfare, Appropriation Act, 1969 (Public Law 90-557):

Sec. 411. No part of the funds appropriated under this Act shall be used to provide a loan, guarantee of a loan, or a grant to any applicant who has been convicted by any court of general jurisdiction of any crime which involves the use of or the assistance to others in the use of force, trespass, or the seizure of property under control of an institution of higher education to prevent officials or students at such an institution from engaging in their duties or pursuing their studies.

Higher Education Amendments of 1968 (Public Law 90-575), Eligibility for Student Assistance:

Sec. 504 (*a*) If an institution of higher education determines, after affording notice and opportunity for hearing to an individual attending, or employed by, such institution, that such individual has been convicted by any court of record of any crime which was committed after the date of enactment of this Act and which involved the use of (or assistance to others in the use of) force, disruption, or the seizure of property under control of any institution of higher education to prevent officials or students in such institution from engaging in their duties or pursuing their studies, and that such crime was of a serious nature and contributed to a substantial disruption of the administration of the institution with respect to which such crime was committed, then the institution which such individual attends, or is employed by, shall deny for a period of two years any further payment to, or for the direct benefit of, such individual under any of the programs specified in subsection (*c*). If an institution denies an individual assistance under the authority of the preceding sentence of this subsection, then any institution which such individual subsequently attends shall deny for the remainder of the two-year period any further payment to, or for the direct benefit of, such individual under any of the programs specified in subsection (*c*).

(*b*) If an institution of higher education determines, after affording notice and opportunity for hearing to an individual attending, or employed by, such institution, that such individual has willfully refused to obey a lawful regulation or order of such institution after the date of enactment of this Act, and that such refusal was of a serious nature and contributed to a substantial disruption of the administration of such institution, then such institution shall deny, for a period of two years, any further payment to, or for the direct benefit of, such individual under any of the programs specified in subsection (*c*).

(*c*) The programs referred to in subsections (*a*) and (*b*) are as follows:

(1) The student loan program under title II of the National Defense Education Act of 1958.

(2) The educational opportunity grant program under part A of title IV of the Higher Education Act of 1965.

(3) The student loan insurance program under part B of title IV of the Higher Education Act of 1965.

(4) The college work-study program under part C of title IV of the Higher Education Act of 1965.

(5) Any fellowship program carried on under title II, III, or V of the Higher Education Act of 1965 or title IV or VI of the National Defense Education Act of 1958.

(*d*) (1) Nothing in this Act, or any Act amended by this Act, shall be construed to prohibit any institution of higher education from refusing to award, continue, or extend any financial assistance under any such Act to any individual because of any misconduct which in its judgment bears adversely on his fitness for such assistance.

(2) Nothing in this section shall be construed as limiting or prejudicing the rights and prerogatives of any institution of higher education to institute and carry out an independent, disciplinary proceeding pursuant to existing authority, practice, and law.

(3) Nothing in this section shall be construed to limit the freedom of any student to verbal expression of individual views or opinions.

COLLEGES AND UNIVERSITIES MUST IMPLEMENT LEGISLATION

It is now the responsibility of our colleges and universities to implement this legislation. It is law. It must be enforced. There is no longer any excuse for institutional authorities to allow rioting, vandalism, or terrorism on the campus. Education is a civil right and must be protected.

Under no circumstances should a college or university stifle reasonable and legitimate protest. Our students' concern with the quality and direction of higher education today can be a monumental gain for our society. It is a concern which should be fostered and followed where reasonable. The absence of intelligent protest in an educational atmosphere would be a major tragedy of our time.

The success of many recent unlawful disruptions on our campuses can be attributed in part to a lack of procedures and procedural rights on the part of the institutions involved. They simply didn't know what to do in the face of confrontations. Confusion reigned. There were contradictions, so-called "back offs," and false promises.

Colleges and universities must establish and enforce rules relating to student protest. They should be drafted and agreed upon by all elements of the academic community. Their enforcement must be positive and immediate. These rules should be carefully defined, as should the institutional authority for any possible disciplinary action. Specific offenses and relating penalties must also be clearly understood. No amnesty should be given to any individual who disobeys established rules.

An intense, coordinated effort should also be made to anticipate and, if possible, solve campus problems which eventually give rise to unlawful demonstrations and militancy. The president or an appointed administrator can play a major role in this by getting to know student leaders on a personal basis, by moving about the campus as frequently as possible, and by attending as many student functions as he can.

MORE EFFECTIVE COMMUNICATIONS VITAL TO OUR CAMPUSES

Another effective vehicle which can be used to discover potential problems is a special committee charged with the responsibility of studying means of developing greater student participation in university affairs and more effective channels of communication among students, faculty, administration, and trustees.

Such a committee, specifically, can study and make recommendations concerning three of the most important relationships in any university community, those of students to administration, students to faculty, and students to students.

Definitive answers to certain basic questions simply must be provided. To what extent should students participate in formulating fiscal priorities and policies governing the operations of bookstores, food services, and dormitories? Should students participate as consultants or as voting members of decision-making committees? To what extent should the administration participate, or the faculty itself, in the judicial phase of student discipline? How can student viewpoints best be represented on administrative committees, including those of the governing board?

There are many others. To what extent should student judgment influence decisions on faculty tenure and promotions? What is the proper role of students in shaping their own curricula? Whether students are consultants or voting members of decision-making curriculum committees, how should they be chosen?

All these are questions demanding intensive study and careful consideration of varying viewpoints. Change, of course, must be initiated in accordance with the best academic traditions, and a group problem-solving committee such as the one suggested here must do justice to campus ideals of scholarship and academic freedom.

At Columbia University, perhaps hit harder by student revolt than any other institution, change has taken the form of a new 101-member universitywide senate. The Student Council and the University Council, a 79-year-old presidential advisory body, have been dissolved.

Membership in the senate—which has the potential to affect all future policies of the university—is composed of 45 tenured and 15 nontenured faculty, 21 students, 9 administrators and 6 staff members, 2 alumni, and 6 representatives from affiliated institutions.

With broadly based decision-making powers ranging from educational policy to community relations, this new senate (or varying but similar concepts of it at other institutions) could well herald one of the most significant and far-reaching reforms ever made in the governance structure of our colleges and universities. The hoped-for success of this innovation could be a major step toward defusing the radicalism of campus discontent and laying the groundwork for a new university spirit of cooperation and understanding throughout the nation.

In the event that a demonstration cannot be averted, the roles of the various administrators of an institution must be clearly defined. So must the roles of the campus police and the local police and firemen. Institutional and neighboring public property must be protected in the interest of good community and press relations. Periodic meetings should be called by the institution to discuss potential problems, how possibly to handle them, and whether public police should be called and under what circumstances.

The following specific steps may also be taken to help alleviate conditions that lead to disorders:

1. Invite students to attend meetings of individual faculties and the faculty senate or similar group.

2. Invite student groups to college faculty meetings to discuss matters of mutual concern.

3. Disseminate information to all elements of the university community on all matters of mutual concern. Unnecessary secrecy traditionally creates an atmosphere of suspicion and distrust.

4. The president should meet regularly with the faculty senate or similar group and appropriate student groups to consider the "state of the campus."

DEFINITION OF THE ACADEMIC COMMUNITY

The university community must clearly define itself to all those who are a part of it and to all those who want to become a part of it. The definition of the academic community should come in the form of a statement from the institution's governing board. As in the case of establishing rules relating to student protest, this statement should be drafted and agreed upon by all elements of the community. The following may be used as a general guideline for such a statement:

> This institution supports as fundamental to the democratic process the rights of all members of the academic community to express their views and to protest actions or opinions with which they disagree. A university is a place where diverse ideas and viewpoints contend for acceptance in an atmosphere free of any recourse to physical force.
>
> This institution offers no sanctuary to any individual or group which condones, advocates, or exercises the taking over of private property or the use of intimidation or physical force. Any person who engages in such activities will be punished promptly and sufficient to the cause, which may include expulsion.
>
> This institution believes in a government of laws and not in a government of men. Any citizen may criticize, protest, and attempt to change the law according to constitutional procedures.
>
> This institution admits students who come here voluntarily and presumably to further their education. Students do not come here to demand, nor to direct. Those who do not like some of the rules and regulations of the campus do not have to enter. Once having entered this institution, however, they are expected to abide by not only the laws of the campus but the laws of this nation as well. Criticisms and suggestions will continue to be welcomed, but threats, disruptions, or force of any kind will not be tolerated.

REGULATIONS FOR THE CONDUCT OF DEMONSTRATIONS

Recognizing protest as an integral part of academic life, the institution must establish campus regulations for the conduct of peaceful and orderly demonstrations. Such regulations may include the following:

The blocking of corridors or entrances to any area or the use of loud noise to disrupt a conference, meeting, or assembly is prohibited.

Demonstrations may not be conducted in faculty or administrative offices, classrooms, libraries, or study areas.

Moving picket lines in corridors are prohibited. Protests may be registered by individuals or groups standing in a single line against a corridor wall, but corridors must be kept open at all times for the free passage of other members of the community.

Such regulations can be followed by a statement similar to the following:

Students, faculty, or other members of the community who violate these regulations will be subject to disciplinary action and jeopardize their right to continue in the university community.

PROCEDURES IN THE EVENT ORDER IS THREATENED

Further clarification of the institution's attitude toward unlawful demonstrations should come in the form of a set of procedures to be followed when the normal and free functioning of the institution is threatened. Following is a general guideline for such procedures:

1. Try to help the demonstrators by suggesting normal procedures and people to see for dealing with the matter.
2. Politely ask the demonstrators to leave so that they do not interfere with the normal conduct and operation of university activities.
3. Inform the demonstrators that they may be subject to formal charges and disciplinary action. Read the student handbook statement to them.
4. If possible, allow a reasonable waiting time, provided the demonstrators are nonviolent.
5. If they appear unwilling to leave, ask the demonstrators to identify themselves; request that all students hand over their ID cards.
6. Again warn the demonstrators.
7. Ask the campus police to remove the demonstrators.
8. If the campus police are unable to do so, call the local police.

If demonstrators barricade themselves inside a building, they should be warned of the consequences and given as much opportunity as possible to vacate peacefully. If they do not, the police should then be instructed to enter the building and place the demonstrators under arrest.

UNIVERSITY-POLICE RELATIONS

If police action is necessary, it should follow plans mutually agreed upon in advance between civil authorities and university officials. A close personal and continuing liaison between these two elements is imperative. Regular meetings should be held to update plans for emergencies, including disciplinary measures, and to review the degrees of force suitable to particular situations.

The police and the university must also keep each other continually aware of any possible threats to campus order or rumors of any kind which might indicate student disruptive action. The police should be fully aware of the procedures the university will follow prior to their being called as well, so that they can better coordinate their efforts with those of the university's own campus forces.

The president of the institution or his appointed designate should be solely responsible for any police contact. This will avoid confusion during times of disorder and make certain that no lesser administrative official, perhaps during a period of overreaction or nervousness, calls in the police at a time when they are not absolutely needed and possibly without the president's knowledge. Such an event could prove disastrous as well as embarrassing.

In some cases it has been necessary for institutions to deal with both local (city) and state police. When this becomes necessary it is in the best interests of good university-community relations for the institution to make initial contacts with local authorities. Even if the university wants to call the state police in for a particular matter, the local police should be notified first.

Policies naturally vary from institution to institution, depending upon a number of circumstances. Whatever those policies are, the institution must be sure of itself and stand determinedly behind them in the face of coercion and intimidation. Institutions must always invite reasonable, noncoercive discussion about how things can be improved. Steps toward this improvement, which is admittedly needed, must not include rebellions which threaten not only our colleges and universities but, because of the consequences, all of society itself.

OVERREACTION TO DEMONSTRATION CAN BE HARMFUL

It must also be borne in mind that many demonstrations are staged to create a spectacle and to provoke officials into punitive action designed to gain sympathy from others. This forces institutions into the position of bargaining under duress, which often leads to concessions which would not be granted under normal circumstances.

Overreaction to a demonstration can be harmful. Forceful actions should be taken on the basis of protecting the rights and freedoms related to the normal operation of a university, the preservation of academic and financial records, the protection of property, etc. Agreements to meet and negotiate after a demonstration are in order, but negotiations during a demonstration are not.

In summary, a university should never be closed down except in the direst emergency. The university must exclude whatever threatens to paralyze its normal operation, i.e., seizures of buildings, disruptions of classes, closings of access routes, etc.

Many states have passed and many others are now considering antigun laws to be applied specifically to colleges and universities. The university community must have its own distinct gun law, however, regardless of municipal legislation.

The university should call police only as a last resort. It should settle its own problems if possible and preserve its traditional autonomy. If forced to extremes, the university should use the court injunction, warn students of the consequences, and leave police action to the courts. The militant minority is then clearly left without an issue.

The university should use suspension and expulsion as its ultimate sanctions. Faced with the prospect of losing one of the most crucial experiences of his life, both from an economic and personal-development viewpoint, only the most fanatical student will dare embrace such a penalty.

The university should never provide amnesty. The traditional rules of university law and university ideals must never be abdicated.

The importance of strict and immediate enforcement of regulations as set down by the academic community cannot be overemphasized. It is a vital step toward reestablishing strength and faith in the American educational system, not only in this nation but throughout the world.

According to historian Arnold J. Toynbee:

> The watchword for higher education in a time of accelerating change is a line written in old age by the Athenian businessman-statesman-poet Solon—"As I grow old, I keep on teaching myself many new things."
>
> Solon was writing from experience; for Solon's country, Attica, had been passing through changes during his lifetime which, in their magnitude and their speed, are comparable to those to which we are having to try to adapt ourselves in our day.

Let men of the twentieth century, also writing from experience, say that higher education during their lifetimes also passed through changes of great magnitude and great speed. Let them say it survived because compassion triumphed over self-centeredness, good taste over vulgarity and obscenity, lawful dissent over violent disruption, reason over emotion, and responsibility over irresponsibility.

A DECLARATION ON CAMPUS UNREST BY THE AMERICAN COUNCIL ON EDUCATION

The unprecedented, comprehensive, and often unpredictable changes that are taking place in this age both disturb and alarm large segments of our society. Most of the changes and attendant alarms affect the operations of our institutions of higher learning. They are also related to the values, concerns, and behavior of our young people. In coming to grips with the compelling issues, all who would think seriously about them must recognize that present-day society—in America and in many foreign lands—is in serious trouble on many fronts. We see around us racial conflict, continued poverty, and malnutrition midst unparalleled prosperity and seemingly unlimited promise. We are confronted by pollution of our environment, decay of our cities, the continuation of wars and the threat of war, and everywhere a vague but widespread discontent with the general quality of life.

These problems affect all of society, not the university alone or the young alone. We must all be concerned to deal intelligently and responsibly with these problems that are neither the exclusive discovery, nor the sole responsibility of the young. Yet the depth of feeling among young people in many countries today about the issues, their general dissatisfaction with the slow-moving ways of society, and the extreme behavior of a small minority of students are evidence of the profound crisis that involves our entire society and, specifically, the university community.

The university itself has often become the immediate target of student discontent, sometimes couched as legitimate complaints about the deficiencies of the universities, sometimes devised as a softening-up exercise for assault on the wider society.

How to deal with campus crises arising from the widespread protests has become a major public issue and the cause of confused and angry debate. That there should be deep anxiety about the course of the conflict and its possible outcome is understandable. No social, racial, or age group that perceives itself and its values to be seriously threatened will fail to strike back. Increasingly there are backlash temptations to enact strong, often ill-considered, and largely futile measures to cope with a youth rebellion that none of us fully comprehends, not even the youth themselves.

Certain balanced judgments are proper to make, however, as we search for understanding and solutions:

1. It is important for the public to understand that, despite the nationwide publicity given to student disorders, the great majority of American campuses have remained peaceful. On campuses where conspicuous disorders have occurred, educational programs generally have gone along their normal ways. Most students and faculty have continued to carry on their regular work. In the main, good teaching and good research, as traditionally defined, have been uninterrupted.

2. On the undisturbed campuses and among the majority of orderly students, how-

ever, there are widely shared discontents which extremists are at times able to manipulate to destructive ends. Moreover, even in the absence of violence, there has developed among some of the young a cult of irrationality and incivility which severely strains attempts to maintain sensible and decent human communication. Within this cult there is a minute group of destroyers who have abandoned hope in today's society, in today's university, and in the processes of orderly discussion and negotiation to secure significant change. Students and faculty are increasingly aware of the true nature of this group and are moving to deal with its destructive tactics. The necessity to deal with extremists, however, is placing an extraordinary burden upon the whole educational enterprise and upon those who man it. Consequently, universities are having to divert their energies and resources from central educational tasks in order to deal with student unrest in its various forms.

3. The spectacular events precipitated by the extremists should not be allowed to obscure the recent accomplishments of those students, faculty, and administrators who have serious interest in constructive changes in society and in the university. They have broadened the curriculum and improved teaching. They have moved toward a more open and participating pattern for university governance. And they have begun to make the work of universities more meaningful in dealing with the problems of society. Those efforts must continue. Reform and self-renewal in higher education are ongoing imperatives.

4. Meanwhile, the speed and scale of social change have imposed many kinds of demands upon educational institutions for which their programs, their capabilities, and their funding are not always adequate. Moreover, universities are increasingly asked to perform functions for society, particularly in reshaping the behavior, values, and life-styles of the young, on which the family and other social institutions have already had major influence—or lack of influence. Some of society's expectations for universities are quite unrealistic. Insofar as these expectations can be dealt with, they involve a sharing of responsibilities among diverse social institutions. Many of society's demands require new resources and fresh approaches to old and new problems.

5. Recognizing the right of and even the necessity for constructive dissent—and allowing for inevitable arguments over what is in fact constructive—certain axioms must be accepted as basic to the operation of any university:

a. Disruption and violence have no place on any campus. The academic community has the responsibility to deal promptly and directly with disruptions. If universities will not govern themselves, they will be governed by others. This elementary reality is increasingly becoming understood by all components of the university community. Student and faculty groups, including the American Association of University Professors and the National Student Association, have recently joined in efforts to improve disciplinary procedures and to formulate clear and realistic codes for dealing with misconduct, and more particularly with violence and disruption. Also, by involving students and faculty effectively in the governance of the university, it can be demonstrated that there are better ways of getting views considered and decisions made than by disruption.

b. The historic concern of the university community with academic freedom needs to be restated, reaffirmed, and vigorously defended against all, within or without the university, who would obstruct the right of scholars to investigate, teachers to teach, or students to learn. This reiteration is not to claim for the university special privileges that put it above the law or that free it from critical public appraisal—rather it affirms that the university must maintain a basic institutional integrity to function as a university.

c. Violations of criminal law must be dealt with through the ordinary processes of the law—and universities must attempt to deal with disruptive situations firmly before they reach the stage of police action. Governmental attempts to deal with these problems through special, punitive legislation will almost certainly be counterproductive. Meanwhile, students and faculty whose consciences demand that they express dissent through law violation must be prepared to accept the due processes and the penalties of the law. They should not be encouraged to expect amnesty from the effects of the law. Such an expectation would be the ultimate use of the *in loco parentis* concept against which many young activists passionately protest. Nor should they expect amnesty from academic discipline, which is the most effective sanction in disruptive incidents.

6. The education community needs to undertake a far more comprehensive effort than ever before attempted to study the underlying bases of youthful discontent and alienation and the broad social problems to which they are related. As social critic, the university must help society understand and solve such problems.

7. All universities should give particular attention to a continuing search for ways, including new social inventions, by which the life of rationality and civility, shared concern, and mutual respect may be supported and strengthened within the university community. The survival of the university and its long-term contribution to society depend upon the ability of the institutions to make their everyday life reflect that spirit and pattern.

STATEMENT BY THE NATIONAL COMMISSION ON THE CAUSES AND PREVENTION OF VIOLENCE

The following are excerpts from the interim statement on campus disorder issued in June 1969 by the National Commission on the Causes and Prevention of Violence:

The members of this commission, along with most Americans, are deeply disturbed by the violence and disorder that have swept the nation's campuses. Our colleges and universities cannot perform their vital functions in an atmosphere that exalts the struggle for power over the search for truth, the rule of passion over the rule of reason, physical confrontation over rational discourse.

We are equally disturbed, however, by the direction of much public reaction to campus unrest. Those who would punish colleges and universities by reducing financial support, by passing restrictive legislation, or by political intervention in the affairs of educational institutions, may unwittingly be helping the very radical minority of students whose objective is to destroy our present institutions of higher education.

So threatening is the situation, so essential is the need for understanding and calm appraisal, that this commission feels compelled to speak now rather than to remain silent until publication of its final report next fall.

During the past year, many of America's universities and colleges have been seriously wounded. These wounds arise from multiple causes. . . .

Students are unwilling to accept the gaps between professed ideals and actual performance. They see afresh the injustices that remain unremedied. They are not impressed by the dangers that previous generations have overcome and the problems they have solved. . . .

To students, these triumphs over serious dangers serve primarily to emphasize other problems we are just beginning to solve.

Today's intelligent, idealistic students see a nation which has achieved the physical ability to provide food, shelter and education for all, but has not yet devised social institutions that do so. . . .

At a time when students are eager to attack these and other key problems, they face the prospect of being compelled to fight in a war most of them believe is unjustified. This traumatic experience has precipitated an unprecedented mass tension and frustration. . . .

We emphasize that most students, despite their view of society's failures, accept as valid the basic structure of our democratic system; their main desire is to improve its ability to live up to its stated values. . . .

A small but determined minority, however, aims not at reform but at the destruction of existing institutions. These are the nihilists. They resort to violent disruptions as the means best suited to achieve their ends.

By dramatic tactics of terror, they have focused widespread public attention upon themselves and have often induced university authorities either to surrender or to meet force with force.

When they have managed on occasion to provoke counterforce to an excessive degree, they have succeeded in enlisting the sympathies of the more moderate campus majority.

They are the agent that converts constructive student concern into mindless mob hysteria. They are the chief danger to the university and its basic values.

There is also a minority of students who are not nihilists, but who feel that violence and disruption may be the only effective way of achieving societal and university reform.

Forcible obstruction and violence are incompatible with the intellectual and personal freedom that lies at the core of campus values. . . .

While violent protest is sometimes followed by the concessions sought, it more often produces a degree of counter-violence and public dismay that may gravely damage the cause for which violence is invoked.

Even when violence succeeds in achieving immediate social gains, it tends frequently to feed on itself, with one power group imposing its will on another until repressive elements succeed in reestablishing order. . . .

The university is the citadel of man's learning and of his hope for further self-improvement, and is the special guardian of this heritage. Those who work and study on the campus should think long before they risk its destruction by resorting to force as the quick way of reaching some immediate goals. . . .

Several attitudes held by members of the university community have often interfered with the application of sensible standards. One is the belief of many that the civil law should not apply to internal campus affairs. . . . Now that students themselves have firmly discarded school authority over their personal lives, they must logically accept the jurisdiction of civil authority. They cannot argue that of all Americans they are uniquely beyond the reach of the law. . . .

Out of many discussions with faculty members, students and administrators, and with full appreciation that no two institutions are the same, we offer the campus community the following specific suggestions:

1. A broad consensus should be achieved among students, faculty and administration concerning the permissible methods of presenting ideas, proposals and grievances and the consequences of going beyond them. . . .

Codes for campus conduct should place primary reliance on the power of the institution to maintain order in its own house, and on its courage to apply its own punishment when deserved. These codes should also recognize the universal duty to obey the civil and criminal laws of the larger society, and the right of the civil authorities to act when laws are violated.

2. Universities should prepare and currently review contingency plans for dealing with campus disorders. Advance plans should be made to determine, insofar as possible the circumstances under which the university will use: I Campus disciplinary procedures. II Court injunctions. III Other court sanctions. IV The civil police. A definite plan, flexibly employed at the moment of crisis, is essential. . . .

Most importantly, university authorities should make known in advance that they will not hesitate to call on civil police when circumstances dictate, and should review in advance with police officials the degrees of force suitable for particular situations. . . .

There is reason to believe that a primary objective of campus revolutionaries is to provoke the calling of police and the kinds of police conduct that will bring the majority over to their side.

3. Procedures for campus governance and constructive reform should be developed to permit more rapid and effective decision-making. There is great misunderstanding and confusion as to where ultimate authority for campus decision-making lies. . . .

Faculty control of education and research is the best guarantee we have of academic freedom. . . . Often some faculty members have mistakenly joined with students in using coercive force against administrative offices when it is the faculty itself that should deal appropriately and effectively with the issues in question.

Most other powers in the university are diffused. For most purposes, shared power is an asset. But to prevent disorders, universities must be able to respond quickly. Campus protests are sometimes escalated to the level of unlawful disorders even after they have been referred to university committees because they were slow to respond.

Faculties therefore have a special obligation to organize themselves more effectively, to create representative groups with power to act, and to maintain constant and systematic lines of communication with students.

Students should . . . serve too, on committees dealing with educational and related questions, exercising their right to be heard on these subjects, so long as the faculty remains paramount.

4. Faculty leaders and administrative officers need to make greater efforts to improve communications both on the campus and with alumni and the general public. Campus difficulties are constantly aggravated by misinformation and misunderstanding.

STATEMENT BY THE AMERICAN ASSOCIATION OF UNIVERSITY PROFESSORS

Adopted at the 55th Annual Meeting, May 3, 1969

The Fifty-fifth Annual Meeting of the American Association of University Professors recognizes that demonstrations and confrontations on campuses across the nation are frequently a manifestation of deep and sometimes profoundly moral discontent arising out of social injustice, public policy, and, in some cases, out of inefficiency, irresponsibility, and unresponsiveness within the institutions themselves. The Annual Meeting therefore calls on all members of the academic community to seek appropriate remedies, encourage necessary change, and discourage disruptive action.

American colleges and universities have long cherished a tradition of institutional autonomy. Disruptive actions of militant students and faculty can profoundly threaten that autonomy because those actions may provoke distrust and hostility and lead to countermeasures on the part of other students, government, and the public. The current crisis can thus only be compounded by vengeful reprisals, such as repressive legislation, punitive reduction of public or private financing of higher education that will penalize all students alike, or the withdrawal, on outside initiative, of grants from students alleged to have taken part in riots. Regular academic procedures, when utilized, can provide sufficient sanctions, and it is both unjust and destructive of institutional autonomy for additional punitive measures to be automatically imposed by outside authority as a consequence of institutional discipline.

Whenever possible, the maintenance of essential academic order should be the responsibility of the institutions themselves; breaches of that order by students should be judged by institutional tribunals, in accordance with the *Joint Statement on Rights and Freedoms of Students*, and breaches of academic order by faculty members should be dealt with in accordance with accepted professional standards. Academic due process, both procedural and substantive, must be guaranteed. Should the maintenance of academic order prove a task beyond the powers of regularly constituted institutional organs, and should it prove unhappily necessary to resort to the civil power, decisions as to its use should be made in the first instance by responsible administrative officers and faculty members in the service of academic criteria and not of political expediency. Thereafter every effort should be made to restore ordinary academic processes as quickly as possible.

LAWS ENACTED IN 1969 TO DEAL WITH CAMPUS DISORDERS AND STUDENT UNREST[1]

Alabama No legislation enacted.

Alaska No legislation enacted.

Arizona No legislation enacted. (A riot control measure passed last year.)

Arkansas H.B. 588—Provides criminal penalties for persons engaging in violent campus disruptions at the state's public and private universities.

California A.B. 534—Any student or employee suspended or dismissed for involvement in a campus disruption and who is advised that he shall not enter the campus is guilty of a misdemeanor if he enters. Also, any person other than a student, officer, or employee directed to leave by the chief campus officer must stay off campus for 72 hours. Restates existing law that anyone who disrupts the quiet of a campus is guilty of a misdemeanor.

A.B. 1286—Requires the chief campus officer to take disciplinary action against any student, faculty member, or employee convicted of or found by a campus disciplinary body to have committed a disruptive act. Allows the chief campus officer to declare a "state of emergency" when a civil disturbance exists. Requires trustees and regents to adopt and distribute rules of conduct and penalties. Permits forfeiture of financial aid for those involved in disorders.

S.B. 496—Provides up to $500 fine or imprisonment up to one year or both for willful obstruction or attempted obstruction of any student or teacher seeking to attend or instruct classes.

S.B. 1382—Provides up to $5000 fine or 5 years imprisonment or both for threatening to inflict an injury upon any officer or employee of any public or private educational institution.

Colorado H.B. 1016—Provides criminal penalties to those willfully impeding staff or faculty in the performance of their duties or students in the lawful pursuit of their educational activities at any college or university in the state. College administrators are empowered to remove or have removed persons disrupting the institution or those threatening or inciting others to disrupt the college. Maximum penalty is a fine of $500 or one year's imprisonment or both.

Connecticut No legislation enacted, but out-of-state tuition was increased as a result of some incidents at the University of Connecticut.

Delaware House substitute for H.B. 218. Makes it a misdemeanor to block entry to or exit from a public building.

Florida S.B. 820—Requires the Board of Regents to adopt rules and regulations to discipline members of the college community who interfere with the orderly functioning of their college campus.

S.B. 821—Provides for fines of up to $500 and imprisonment up to six months for persons disrupting any educational institution.

S.B. 824—Defines lawful aims of universities.

S.B. 989—Provides for suspension following an administrative hearing of students arrested for possession of certain drugs, central nervous system stimulants, and barbiturates. Any student expelled under this act may not be readmitted for two years to a state-supported school.

The Legislature also enacted a bill defining disruptive activities and wrote into the appropriations bill a provision that no state funds can be used for financial aid to students convicted of disrupting universities and junior colleges, and an additional provision that no state funds can be used to pay the salaries of students, faculty, or other employees of the universities who advocate the overthrow of the federal or state governments or state university administration by force or violence, or who advocate with clear intent the disruption of the university.

[1] The authors are indebted to Mr. Joseph E. Gonzalez, Jr., Special Assistant for Legislative Relations, Rutgers, the State University for the material which appears in this appendix. This material was originally prepared for the Office of Institutional Research, National Association of State Universities and Land-Grant Colleges, Washington, D.C. 20036.

Georgia No legislation enacted.

Hawaii No legislation enacted.

Idaho H.B. 296—Makes it unlawful for any person to unlawfully seize or take over any building on any campus of any institution of higher education. Also applies to those who prevent freedom of movement or entry to and exit from the campus.

Illinois H.B. 1894—Requires state-supported colleges and universities to formulate and enforce a policy on campus demonstrations.

S.B. 191—Provides for the immediate revocation of any scholarship funded wholly or in part by the state if the holder of the scholarship participates in an unlawful disturbance. No court conviction is required, but the chief executive officer must make the determination, and machinery for a hearing is provided.

S.B. 331—Establishes crimes of criminal damage, criminal trespass, and unauthorized possession of weapons on state property. Under the trespass section of the law a person must leave the premises after a notice to depart. Makes it a crime to possess, among other things, a firearm, bludgeon, blackjack, sand bag, switchblade knife, or explosive or noxious substances without the permission of the chief security officer.

S.B. 1144—Establishes a new crime of interference with an institution of higher education, which includes interfering with the movement of a person or one's use of facilities and obstruction of duties of an employee at an institution of higher education.

Indiana H.C.R. 22—Instructs the trustees of the four state universities to enact a code of conduct and behavior for students, faculty, and staff.

Two bills also became law. One redefines the powers and duties of the trustees of a university and clarifies their authority. The second (H.B. 1257) makes it a misdemeanor to remain on the property of an educational institution after being asked to leave by an appropriate person.

Iowa An "anti-riot" amendment was added to the State Board of Regents operating appropriations bill providing that no part of the appropriation shall be used for assistance to any student or teacher convicted of riot activity.

Kansas SCR 18—Encourages the students, faculty, and administrative personnel at each of the state colleges and universities to maintain an environment for the orderly expression of protest and dissent. Authorizes and directs the separation of any person expressing their dissenting opinions in a violent or disruptive manner or who disrupts the orderly processes of an academic community.

Kentucky No legislative session in 1969.

Louisiana Act 58—Prohibits interference with normal educational processes at institutions of higher learning and sets penalties for violations.

Act 59—Provides for expelling students who participate in campus disorders.

Act 176—Declares the public policy of the state with respect to riots and other unlawful disorders.

Maine No legislation enacted.

Maryland S771—Provides that persons who are not students, staff, or faculty of state colleges may be denied access to such institutions if they are acting in a disruptive manner.

Massachusetts Two similar laws were enacted in 1969. One prohibits carrying loaded or unloaded firearms on college campuses except by authorized personnel. The other outlaws Molotov cocktails without specifically mentioning college campuses.

Michigan Under a new Michigan statute, students convicted of crimes or violations of city ordinances or university rules in the course of campus violence would become ineligible for state scholarships or tuition grants.

Minnesota A law enacted in 1969 makes it a gross misdemeanor to interfere with access to a public building.

Mississippi No legislative session in 1969.

Missouri No legislation enacted.

Montana No legislation enacted.

Nebraska No legislation enacted, with the exception of a general statute affecting riots and civil disorders.

Nevada S.B. 139—Outlaws the commission of an act in a public area which interferes with the peaceful conduct of activities in the area.

New Hampshire H.C.R. 13—Recommended to faculty and student government officials that they "continue their commendable attitudes" within the framework of the state's legal and constitutional processes and pledged the legislature's support of any appropriate action needed to continue orderly education in New Hampshire.

New Jersey A-705—Prohibits firearms on college campuses.

ACR-86—Directed the legislative education committees to hold public hearings on the "operational programs" of Rutgers University. The resolution was prompted by a building takeover.

New Mexico H. 256—This legislation, which made it a misdemeanor for any person in or around a college, university, or school to interfere by force or violence with any administrator, faculty member, or student in the performance of his normal duties or studies, was declared unconstitutional by a state court.

New York A. 6610-A—Requires all colleges to adopt rules and regulations for the maintenance of public order and an enforcement program.

A. 7148—Bans firearms from college campuses.

The legislature also created a temporary state commission to study the causes of student unrest.

North Carolina H. 321—Omnibus riots-civil disorders bill. Includes a provision under which the head of an institution can seek injunctive relief from the courts in the event of a campus disorder.

H. 802—Prohibits outsiders on campus during university-declared curfews.

S. 832—Authorizes the governor to order public buildings evacuated during emergencies.

H. 134—Increases the punishment for sit-ins in public buildings.

H. 985—Provides for immediate termination of state scholarships or grants to students convicted of a serious crime committed during a campus disorder.

North Dakota H.B. 99—Directs the State Board of Higher Education to establish rules for maintenance of law and order at state colleges and universities, including regulations providing for the expulsion of any student who willfully obstructs normal administration of college. The president of an institution is directed to file criminal complaints against any person who wilfully damages college property.

Ohio No legislation enacted.

Oklahoma Two acts were passed during 1969. A general anti-riot law makes it a felony for four or more persons to engage in disturbances. Those convicted could serve up to ten years. Another act makes it a misdemeanor for any person not a student to refuse to leave a campus during a disturbance.

Oregon H.B. 1880—Gives the governor emergency powers during a disturbance to bar outsiders from a campus.

Pennsylvania Act 116—Increases the maximum amount for student loans, but the state may deny loans to students convicted of serious crimes, students who have been expelled, dismissed or denied enrollment because of refusing to obey a lawful order during a disturbance, or who have been convicted of any offense when they interfered with the orderly conduct of college classes and other activities.

S.R. 14—Provided for the establishment of a Senate committee to investigate conditions giving rise to student militancy.

Rhode Island No legislation enacted.

South Carolina Act 277—Makes entering any private or public school or college for the purpose of destroying records or other property a misdemeanor.

Act 278—Makes carrying or displaying a firearm in any private or public school or college a misdemeanor.

Act 280—Provides that no person shall manufacture or possess any object to cause damage by fire. Those violating the act shall be deemed guilty of a misdemeanor.

South Dakota No legislation enacted.

Tennessee S. 376—Provides that it shall be a misdemeanor for a person who interferes with, or tends to interfere with, the normal conduct of activities to refuse to leave a public college or university if directed to do so by the chief administrative officer. Also makes it a misdemeanor to obstruct the ingress or egress of persons at a public college or university, and a felony to incite others or to participate in a public disturbance which constitutes a breach of peace or results in, or should reasonably be expected to result in, injury to persons or damage to property.

Texas H.B. 57—Replaces disorderly conduct statute that was ruled unconstitutionally vague.

H.B. 141—Prohibits disruption and unlawful assembly on property of public and private schools and colleges.

H.B. 1450—Prohibits as a felony the possession of firearms on a college campus.

Utah S.B. 112—Declares unlawful acts interfering with peaceful conduct of the activities of any state university or college. Failure to leave a campus after being advised by the chief administrator or his designate to cease violating any rule or regulation of the college is prohibited. Destruction of the property of an institution of higher education is classified a misdemeanor. Public colleges or universities are also authorized to call for assistance from local law enforcement agencies. The local authorities shall serve under the control of the institution's chief administrative officer.

S.B. 117—Authorizes police departments at state educational institutions.

Vermont No legislation enacted.

Virginia No regular session of legislature in 1969.

Washington Chapter 7—Any person who occupies a building without being licensed or privileged to do so shall be guilty of criminal trespass, a misdemeanor. The act is general and not limited in its application to colleges and universities.

Another new statute, which is a repeat of a federal statute dealing with NDEA loans, affects state aid to students who disrupt.

West Virginia H.B. 617—Provides criminal penalties for riots and unlawful assemblings.

Wisconsin Chapter 26—Prohibits a person convicted of a crime arising from obstruction at the university, or a person who has been expelled or suspended for such conduct, from reentering that institution without permission from the administrative head of that institution.

Chapter 27—Prohibits the use of sound amplifying equipment on the grounds of the university without permission of the administrative head or chancellor of that campus.

Chapter 89—Authorizes the administrative head or chief security officer of a campus to designate closed periods during which only specifically authorized personnel, in addition to students, faculty, and staff, are allowed to be present.

Wyoming No legislation enacted.

ORGANIZED OPPOSITION TO SDS MOUNTING

As the 1969–1970 college year began, the split in SDS appeared to be widening between the Progressive Labor (PL) and Revolutionary Youth Movement (RYM) factions. As one radical graduate student at Boston University stated, "PL and RYM are the poles of our (SDS) unrest. PL is gearing up for many years of long, hard struggle. RYM takes for its standard the gory black flag of red-eyed chaos. They will bite and tug and gouge . . . . disruption before all."

The Worker-Student Alliance (WSA), which is the major faction within PL, is "economist" in nature and in no particular hurry to realize its overall objective. Its goal is to organize white working class adults to achieve class consciousness and, when it feels the time is right, to join the blacks in revolution.

RYM, on the other hand, feels that revolution cannot wait. Their commando tactics, carried out by a closely knit elite corps of revolutionaries called "Weathermen," are die-hard and flamboyantly spectacular. As reported by the *Boston Sunday Herald Traveler* in September, 1969, "They are domestic guerrilla fighters, and their revolution is hopping with the madcap props of a drive-in movie—closed meetings, karate, guns, bodyguards, and tight-fisted screams of violence."

If SDS succeeds in healing its internal rift, it will have to do so amid increasing echoes of anger and opposition from a right-wing student group called Young Americans for Freedom (YAF). Now with a national membership of 50,000, YAF has held to its views, has sponsored conservative rallies, and has waited patiently in the wings for a chance to play center stage. Its officers now feel that chance has finally come, due in large part, and ironically, to the fact that new stages of militancy entered into by SDS help YAF attract uncommitted students fed up and often frightened by the continuing violence and disruption.

This turbulence, however, is predicted in many quarters to continue both on and off the campus this year and in years ahead. Student unrest appears destined to stay, at least for a while longer, and the issues seem to be shifting away from student power, race, and Vietnam.

Protests are focusing on such areas as open admissions, finances, the tightening job market, protection of the consumer, control of fire-arms, abortion law reform, and pollution and crime control. These latter two issues in particular, according to a recent research report by the American Council on Education, could "unify the entire college community" into protest action. Because of the greater numbers that would thus become involved, the report suggests, future protests may become more passive (obstructionist) than violent.

SUGGESTIONS FOR FURTHER READING

The Campus Crisis: Legal Problems of University Discipline, Administration, and Expansion, Practising Law Institute, New York, 1969.

College Law Bulletin, U.S. National Student Association, 20 East 9th St., New York, N.Y. 10003 (published monthly except July and August).

Eurich, Alvin C. (ed.): *Campus 1980,* Delacorte Press, New York, 1968.

Fortas, Abe: *Concerning Dissent and Civil Disobedience,* The New American Library, Inc., New York, 1968.

The Future Academic Community: Continuity and Change, American Council on Education, Washington, 1968.

Methvin, Eugene H.: "SDS: Engineers of Campus Chaos," *Reader's Digest,* October, 1968.

"Rights in Conflict," The Walker Report, *The New York Times,* New York, 1969.

Shoben, Edward Joseph, Jr., and Philip R. Werdell: "SDS and SNCC: Profiles of Two Student Organizations," *School & Society,* October 26, 1968.

Skolnick, Jerome H., *The Politics of Protest,* Ballantine Books, New York, 1969.

Smith, Kerry G. (ed.): *Stress and Campus Response,* Jossey-Bass, Inc., San Francisco, 1968.

Student Power, Penguin Books (in association with *New Left Review*).

Student Protest and the Law, The Institute of Continuing Legal Education, Michigan, 1969.

Williamson, E. G., and John L. Cowan: *The American Student's Freedom of Expression,* University of Minnesota Press, Minneapolis, 1966.

Chapter **5**

Black Student Affairs*

JOHN F. POTTS

President, Voorhees College, Denmark, South Carolina

JOY WINKIE VIOLA

Editorial Assistant to the President, Northeastern University, Boston, Massachusetts

* The authors wish to acknowledge the assistance of those who contributed their time to lengthy discussions of the many issues discussed in this chapter. A special note of appreciation is due Mrs. Hermione Holloway, Voorhees College class of 1957, currently employed at Northeastern University, Boston, and Mr. Roland E. Lathem, Assistant Dean of Students, Northeastern University.

Social changes currently taking place in our nation are confronting college administrators with problems they have never before experienced. Some of these changes have revolutionary rather than evolutionary characteristics. Among the most serious of these is the growing militancy and in some instances actual rebellion of certain segments of the student body.

Students are vitally concerned with society's ills as they see them and feel a keen sense of responsibility to act upon humanity's wrongdoings. The problems associated with the administration of Black student affairs are the result of the Black students' intense efforts to further the cause of their people. In spite of the civil rights legislation which finally has come to pass, there is an "administrative gap" between the existence of certain statutes and their implementation in daily life. Today's youth, of which Black students are a part, is an "action now" generation. Responsible educational leaders are sincerely trying to implement action in many areas of student concern. Nevertheless, the relationship between Black students and college administrators is, by and large, one of great frustration. Much verbalization but painfully little communication is taking place between the two groups. Trust, mutual respect, and cooperation are generally lacking. And yet, the laws of integration have bound Black and white alike to an "educational marriage" which Congress and the Supreme Court have ordained. The success of this union will depend on the willingness of both parties to speak truthfully and to listen understandingly. At this point, neither is doing either to the best of his ability.

As this discussion is for the benefit of but one of the parties involved—i.e., the college administrator—emphasis will be placed on giving administrators information which may be helpful to them in their effort to meet their responsibilities in this new partnership.

Before discussing present conditions, fluid as they may be, it may be helpful to briefly review the events and circumstances which have brought us to our present situation. Despite one's supposed familiarity with the past, a reflective thought often can prove beneficial.

THE STATUS OF INTEGRATION IN HIGHER EDUCATION SINCE THE CIVIL RIGHTS ACT OF 1964

Francis Keppel, former United States Commissioner of Education, once described the Civil Rights Act of 1964 as "a great watershed dividing the past from the present in our national life." There is no question that this legislation, like the judicial decision of 1954, stands as another great turning point in the history of our country. Even though this decade (1954 to 1964), in terms of the legal status of the Black man, was a period of phenomenal change, to some it appeared to be an era of gradualism, circumvention, and tokenism. The Civil Rights Act of 1964 provided the impetus needed to overcome the foot dragging in complying with judicial decisions. Opponents of desegregation had achieved considerable success with the uninformed by arguing that the 1954 Supreme Court decision was not the "law of the land" because Congress had not legislated it. Few arguments in the history of our nation have had less validity, but it was used quite effectively by the proponents of segregation. By enacting Title IV Congress made it very clear that all three branches of the government, judicial, executive, and legislative, were of the same persuasion on this particular issue.

The Civil Rights Act of 1964 contains 11 titles covering racial discrimination in most of its manifestations. Under Title VI, provision was made for the cutting off of federal funds from programs operated in a discriminatory manner. In addition, colleges were required to issue a statement of compliance with the Civil Rights Act in order to qualify for federal financial assistance.

By 1966, fewer than 3 percent of approximately one million college students in the South were attending institutions which had not yet agreed to comply with the provisions of the Civil Rights Act. While this represents substantial progress in two years, it must be remembered that legal access to institutions of higher learning is one thing and ethnic congeniality is quite another. Hence one very serious administrative problem resulting from integration in higher education has been and continues to be the acceptance of students of a different race, background, and culture. A change of attitude does not necessarily accompany compliance with provisions of the law.

The Acceptance of Black Students on a White Campus

In the early history of desegregation in higher education, the primary goal was to provide Black students access into historically white colleges and universities. Hence the first problem to be considered is the extent of acceptance of Blacks by white students, faculty, staff, administrators, and the community in which the college is located. This process of acceptance has passed through three stages. The first stage was one of hostility which in most cases came about as a result of court-ordered desegregation; incidents at the universities of Mississippi, Alabama, and Georgia providing the best examples. There was very little if any hostility when compliance came voluntarily.

The second stage was one of toleration, during which time Black students were treated with civility and courtesy but were not fully accepted in the total institutional program. Through devious methods they were excluded from fraternities, sororities, and social affairs and generally were not made to feel welcome in the dormitories, student centers, and cafeterias. Still further, the opportunity to participate in the student government association and other extracurricular activities was not provided in some of the predominantly white institutions.

The third stage was one of general acceptance, a state which has yet to be reached by many Southern institutions but one which is gaining in the overall view.

There have been varying degrees of acceptance of Black students by the different segments of the white college community. Studies indicate that white students have shown the least opposition to the admission of qualified Blacks to their colleges. As a matter of fact, in some institutions the white students have even encouraged it. The faculty and administrators of these colleges too have shown very little opposition to the admission of Blacks. Most of the unfavorable reaction has come from the community in which the institution is located, especially if it is in a rural area. Some unfavorable reaction has come from alumni and from the parents of students.

Because of these varying stages of acceptance, the question has arisen as to the progress Black students have made in the white academic environment. A study by the National Scholarship Service and Fund for Negro Students supports the contention that if the students are properly selected on the basis of achievement and scholastic ability and given financial support and personal encouragement, their achievement in the academic and social life of the college community is virtually assured. There is rather conclusive evidence that qualified Black youth can succeed in predominantly white institutions which impose high academic standards.

The Acceptance of White Students on a Black Campus

The acceptance of the white student on the Black campus has not been quite the same for a number of reasons. Most Black colleges are seeking qualified white students in order to stop having to apologize for not being integrated. Some presidents have said that they do not like to justify a student body which is 100 percent Black by saying that charter amendments have provided for the admission of all qualified students. They want their college to be integrated in fact rather than in principle, so as not to be accused of perpetuating segregation. Indeed some denominations are urging their church-affiliated colleges to move in this direction as soon as possible. This does not mean that white colleges are not seeking qualified Black students for the same reason, but their task is not as difficult. Consequently, the climate of acceptance on the Black college campus tends to be more cordial, in spite of the Black Power adherents who have given white students some concern about their acceptance.

In those border-state colleges where the percentage of white student enrollment ranges from 33 to 60 percent, most students commute, are primarily interested in the classroom work, and by choice do not fully identify with the total school program.

A Black student attending a formerly all white college may be somewhat sensitive about white teachers and classmates due to unpleasant past experiences and may tend to interpret certain circumstances and incidents as evidences of nonacceptance. However, the white student enrolled in a predominantly Black college would not be there if he did not have the desire to accept Blacks as equals. Furthermore, the white student's reactions are not tainted by the problem of being placed there as the result of a court order or civil rights legislation. Consequently, the white student would be less inclined to look upon an unpleasant experience as evidence of unacceptability.

The magnitude of the acceptance problem is greater in white institutions because the number of Black students in attendance is so much larger than the number of white students enrolled in Black institutions. Nevertheless, there are and will continue to be some problems stemming from nonacceptance of white students by Blacks which only time and education will improve.

Integration Creates New Problems

The imbalance in the number of Black students attending white colleges as compared with white students attending Black colleges is creating a problem of two dimensions. The white colleges are attracting the academic "cream of the crop" from the Black colleges, and an increasing number of white colleges and universities with high entrance requirements, including some of the strongest Southern institutions, have adopted high-risk quotas for the admission of disadvantaged students. Since financial assistance is provided by the institution, this new policy has substantially increased the number of Blacks enrolled in white colleges and universities. It is difficult, if not impossible, to ascertain the exact number of Black students enrolled in these white college high-risk programs, but informed estimates indicate that 50 percent of all Black students will be enrolled in white colleges and universities by 1988. The present figure is between 20 and 25 percent.

To compound the problem, the Black colleges, except those in the border states, are not attracting white students in any significant numbers and certainly are not enrolling the top-flight white student at all. This puts the Black institution in the unenviable position of losing the best prepared Blacks and the promising high-risk students to the predominantly white colleges without receiving comparable white students in return. For integration to really be effective it must be a two-way street, and yet who can criticize students for seeking the best possible education from the best possible sources? The answer to this perplexing problem lies in substantially strengthening the Black college to the point that it will attract the students it seeks from any ethnic group. The Southern Regional Education Board has recommended special "catch-up funds" for this purpose.

Still another administrative problem which desegregation has created is the reluctance on the part of Blacks and whites, whether students, professors, or administrators, to voluntarily join an institution in which they will be in the minority. While this situation has affected most integrating institutions, it has been and still is a much more serious problem in the predominantly Black college for several reasons. Some Blacks holding the doctorate degree feel that it is a promotion to accept a position at a predominantly white institution, especially if it is one of the prestige institutions; but the reverse is not necessarily true. The white holder of a doctorate coming to the Black college is sometimes viewed with suspicion and his motives are questioned.

The present emphasis on Black awareness, Black power, and the desire on the part of some Black people to create a Black institution has caused some dedicated white teachers to feel that they are unacceptable to the Black community.

Most predominantly Black colleges cannot meet the salary competition of the white colleges and consequently have difficulty in attracting the competent white professor.

The majority of the predominantly Black colleges cannot offer the research opportunities which scholars are seeking. Since promotion in rank and salary and prestige among his peers, as well as the satisfaction of discovering new knowledge, depends upon research and writing, the white scholar for the most part prefers to remain in those institutions where these opportunities are readily available.

A considerable number of Black colleges are in geographical locations which do not provide the cultural and recreational advantages the better qualified faculty member desires.

Some white faculty members are deeply concerned about their acceptance by the community in which the college is located.

Latent or blatant prejudice is not the only reason for the problems which have surrounded integration efforts within higher education. A genuine lack of understanding coupled with a flagrant inability to communicate has spawned many of the Black-white conflicts on today's college campus. The fact that the passage of a legislative act did not prove to be the panacea for the problems of the American Black man have left many Blacks, and particularly Black youth, with a feeling of desperation and contempt which is currently threatening every fiber of American society.

The academic community cannot and should not be expected to solve the entire racial issue, but because so many Black youths are in the forefront of the civil rights battle and because these same Black youths are enrolled on college campuses across the land, it behooves the college administrator to make a concerted effort to understand the Black man's thinking if the campus, let alone the society, is to survive.

THE SEARCH FOR BLACK IDENTITY

Black people, and Black students in particular, are starved for a dignity and understanding they have never been accorded. In an effort to achieve a higher status in society, the Black community has been overorganized into an infinite number of local and national groups with each spending its energies in a different direction. The Black community sees its youth, with its new-found opportunities for education, as the hope for the future. As a result, a maze of organizations and individuals—NAACP, CORE, Black Muslims, Black Panthers, Black Students' Unions, and followers of individual leaders from Eldridge Cleaver to Nathan Hare—are tugging at the coattails of the Black college student in a confusing and conflicting struggle for his support.

The long struggle for integration has only served to verify what the Blacks already knew—black is not white and no amount of legislation will make it so. But if black is not white, then what is black? And herein lies the Black man's vehement search for identity. It is important that college administrators try to understand this all-consuming drive, because many of the "demands" with which they are being and will continue to be confronted are the result of a search for identity.

As has been said, black is not white, but in addition, there are many degrees of blackness. And one's blackness has nothing to do with the pigmentation of one's skin. It is a state of consciousness—a degree of inward (self) as opposed to outward (Black community) interest. There are Blacks who do and those who do not wish to associate with whites. There are Blacks who see the success of their people in terms of their own individual measured accomplishments and there are Blacks who prefer to sub-jugate their own sense of accomplishment to the success of the Black community. Although there is no divine ordinance as to which path is most correct, the followers of both philosophies are convinced as to their own righteousness. Unfortunately, the result is a game of name-calling and idle semantics. Terms such as "Whitey," "Honky," "Uncle Tom," "Negro," "Black," "middle-class white values," "middle-class Black Sambo," "Black Power"—are inclined to be used all too frequently in place of intelligent reasoning. Semantics can provide convenient excuses—a lack of success in a venture being charged off to racism, "Charlie," etc., with little honest thought being given to the issue at hand. This does not mean that there are no legitimate meanings to many of these terms—one need only talk to a reasonable Black militant to realize that—but too often whole dialogues revert to nothing more than the reiteration of these clichés.

A further example of the semantics of the Black movement may be found in the terms "Black," "Negro," and "White Anglo-Saxon Protestant" (WASP). Such terms have come to be less indicative of the color of one's skin or the nature of one's parentage than the state of one's thinking. One can no longer talk, within this reference, in terms of white versus nonwhite. There are nonwhites who are devout WASPs in their thinking. And there are those born of a WASP environment who are closely identified with Black thinking. The WASP philosophy of hard work and clean living as the proper road to success is equally characteristic of the thinking of some Blacks. But many Black brothers feel that regardless of one's good efforts, a Black man will never get his due reward because he is not the master of his own destiny. He is "a victim of the white man's power to hold him down."

Quite clearly, therefore, Blacks do not constitute one true brotherhood. Skin pigmentation alone is insufficient to unite diverse modes of thinking. With whom, therefore, does the young Black identify? Virtually every other racial or ethnic minority finds some dignity in having a culture with which to identify. Even the American Indian, as mistreated as he has been, has at least some romantic tradition with which to associate himself. But there are few real heroes in the Black community, including those who temporarily make the headlines with avowals of Black militancy. Such individuals are held in esteem by some Blacks only because they appear to be functioning effectively at the moment, but their fame is fickle, being completely subject to the continued popularity of their methods and accomplishments.

Relevance—An Aspect of Identity

The concept of relevance is an integral part of the Black man's search for identity. College faculty have felt confused when told that the white man's curriculum holds little relevance for the Black. The Roman Empire is history, Beethoven is music, and Rembrandt is art to all men, are they not? But the answer is that they *are not* as relevant to some young Blacks who find it difficult to identify with a European-based culture. Such things are a part of what the Black terms "white values" which, by and large, are absent from the Black man's way of life. The Black does not mean to say that he thinks Beethoven any less a great composer or Rembrandt any less a painter, they simply fail to "turn him on" for he sees them as no part of his cultural heritage. There is a parallel to this in the white man's reaction to the culture of the Orient. There are some whites who truly delight in Oriental music and art as cultivated tastes, but most Americans, being of European ancestry, do not identify with the traditions of the Orient. So too, some Blacks feel that European cultural traditions are foreign to their African origins.

The Blacks have a unique culture of their own, complete with a language or dialect, an array of food, and a type of music which is basic to the Black community. In the past, Blacks have been made to feel that such expressions of individualism were a poor imitation of the white man's culture. Now, they are finding pride in the differences they once sought to conceal. Nowadays, while many may wish to escape the poverty of the ghetto, these same individuals may wish to preserve the flavor of ghetto life.

In an effort to establish their culture as a long-time heritage, Blacks have reverted to an interest in the traditions of their African ancestors, but these attempts to identify with an African culture have not been without problems. There are evidences that this cultural identification may be a one-way street. For example, African students studying in the United States frequently do not care to associate with American Blacks. Such foreign students often are from upper-class African society and find no bond with the economically disadvantaged American Black. Like water, education and social class seem to seek their own level, and some Blacks appear to have as much class consciousness as their white counterparts. Efforts to introduce African modes of dress have been quite successful, but attempts to introduce the Muslim religion of Africa have met with great resistance.

This effort to establish a Black tradition is the basis of the Black Studies programs currently being sought by militant Black students on college campuses across the land. College administrators need to realize that in many cases, a Black student is a Black first and a student second. For this reason, an administrator must endeavor to understand the person before passing judgment on his actions as a student.

The Black man is not exempt from society's current fixation on the need for higher education, consequently he is eager to become a part of academia—relevant or not at this point. But higher education can be both friend and foe to Blacks, inasmuch as it can make a Black man an outsider among his own people while at the same time failing to make him acceptable among whites. A Black man's education may elevate the Black man, but it may not elevate him above the prejudices of some whites. As a result, a Black youth may attend a university, learn new patterns of speech, assume a different manner of conduct and even a different style of dress only to find himself, by virtue of rental and real-estate discrimination, confined to the ghetto where such "education" is of no relevance. The first-generation Caucasian college student can leave his ethnic community and integrate into a new way of life; i.e., the great American middle class. But such is not the case with the Blacks. The suburbs have not been willing to accept the Blacks, with the result that a well-educated Black who has *mentally* left the ghetto community life must remain *physically* within its confines for lack of any alternative. And herein lies another reason for the Black man's concern over "relevance."

Equality

One need not be a psychologist to understand the pathos of the Black author who wrote, "There is an enduring grief in being made to feel inferior." A person passing through a lifetime of spoken or unspoken "colored" and "whites only" labels in life looks at the college experience and wonders if this is indeed a golden opportunity or merely the opportunity to become exposed to a more sophisticated system of "labels." There is little difference between the hurt one feels over having to use a segregated water fountain and the hurt that comes from finding a suburban dwelling suddenly removed from the market in the face of a Black man's down payment.

The equality of all mankind is a deeply cherished concept to the Black, from whom equality so often has been withheld. Even the most understanding white administrator cannot expect to have a Black student pour out his heart about the hurts and slights he has experienced. Communication breaks down because such hurts are so intimate as to defy discussion. And yet, more often than not, the accumulation of these hurts is the very thing which is barbing the arrow of Black militancy on the college campus. Man always has been quick to recognize a wounded animal as a dangerous foe, and yet he seems surprised at the actions of wounded human beings half mad with the indecencies of mental cruelty. Frustrated college administrators endeavor to hold rational discussions with Black college students in an effort to understand the Black man's thinking. But, to quote one Black spokesman, "You don't deal with a psychotic in rational terms. Black thinking is admittedly irrational at times because it is frustrated by the feeling that Blacks can do only what the whites will allow them to do."

The demands, the sit-ins, the riots, the burnings, the violent militancy of some of today's Black youth—right or wrong—are the result of years of silently endured hurts which are only now beginning to come to the surface. In the heat of dissent, it is difficult for administrators confronted with long, irate lists of demands to look beyond the fury and perceive the simple truth that what the Black is really demanding is the right to self-pride and society's acknowledgment of his value as a human being, created "in the image of God."

THE ROLE OF THE BLACK STUDENT

Ever since the early sit-ins in Mississippi, college students have been in the forefront of the civil rights movement. Initially, the white students were as active in the movement as the Blacks. But as the Blacks grew in strength and organization they made it known to white sympathizers that this was the Blacks' "thing" and they preferred to go it alone. In addition, Black students found white dissenting groups entirely too philosophical and impractical for their own Black purposes. Although both groups object to society as they find it, the Blacks have a slightly clearer idea of the goals and objectives they are pursuing.

The importance of the Black college student in the civil rights movement has been augmented by virtue of the fact that college campuses have provided civil rights organizations with a nationwide network of recruiting grounds. The general growth of student unrest, spurred on by indecisive administrative response to student protest, provided a fertile spawning ground for Black student dissent as well. As a result, many of the "adult" Black militant organizations have come to the campus to seek potential workers for "the cause" from among the ranks of Black student dissenters. Black youth, therefore, has assumed a major role in furthering the Black man's cause. Although many members of the older generation (as well as more conservative members of the younger generation) are not in agreement with the young militants, they hesitate to speak out, for they see the militants' tactics winning ground they have been endeavoring to gain by less violent means for generations. The Black community is proud of its young collegians, seeing in their very admission to college an accomplishment which few of their predecessors have attained. If these cherished students then choose to identify with the Black Power movement, much of the Black community will refrain from questioning the right or wrongness of the act but will instead adopt the "wait and see" attitude they have followed for years.

The Black Power movement on campus presents every Black student with a difficult decision. Should he direct much of his effort toward campus rebellion and risk losing the educational opportunity of the moment? Or should he direct his full energy toward the attainment of a degree (however "irrelevant, white-oriented," etc., etc., it may seem to be) in order to guarantee himself an improved economic status in the future? For some students, this is a very real dilemma. For others, very frankly, the Black Power movement with its many demands and demonstrations is nothing more than a convenient excuse to "cop out" on the hard work necessary for academic scholarship.

The Development of Black Power on Campus

Black consciousness originated with the sit-in movement which began at A & T College in Greensboro, North Carolina in 1960. This tactic proved very successful in desegregating public facilities and in awakening the conscience of America. The impact of this movement was such that Congress passed two civil rights acts to remove the intolerable conditions of segregation. Afterwards, the sit-in movement began to wane because many of the segregation practices which it sought to eliminate were prohibited by law. The civil rights movement then assumed a new dimension as Black student activists from SNCC and CORE began to advocate Black Power and to urge Black students to organize, challenge, and change the institutions of higher learning whose educational programs had no relevance for them.

This Black student movement hit the white campus as early as 1962, when eight undergraduates at Columbia University met to discuss their conditions as Black students in a predominantly white university. Hilton Clark, one of the eight students, described the feelings of these students when he said, "We felt we were lost mentally in a white college. I realize the words 'identity crisis' have become a cliché, but we really didn't know who we were, and we were tired of becoming something we could not be. We had lost all connections with the reality of what we were."

These eight Columbia University students then called a conference of 32 Black students attending various schools in Columbia University in order to organize an Afro-American Society. About the same time an American Black and an African established a similar group at Harvard and Radcliffe—The Association of African and Afro-American Students. These students expressed the same dissatisfactions voiced by the Columbia students; i.e., their feeling of isolation from the mainstream of the university; having to conform to standards and values that had little meaning for Blacks; losing something of value in their own background as they attempted to conform; their desire to improve the Black ghetto while they were still students. One of their most serious criticisms of Blacks who graduated from Ivy League colleges in the past was the fact that these people used diplomas as passports to white middle-class status and subsequently had no concern for the larger Black community.

One of the criticisms of the Black Power movement is that it is segregation in reverse. The "Soul Table" occupied entirely by Black students, the all Black clubs and organizations, excluding white students because they "can't relate," and the Black student unions are separating the Black students from students of other ethnic groups and making desegregation and integration more difficult. The Afro groups admit this is self-segregation, but since it is voluntary rather than compulsory, it is acceptable to them.

The Black revolt has created numerous problems for college administrators, the following being but a few of the more common concerns:

1. The chartering of an organization which has a restrictive clause limiting it to one race. In most instances where this restrictive clause was dropped in order to get a charter, the practice has still been to exclude non-Black students anyway.

2. Disruptive practices which interfere with normal educational and administrative processes and procedures. These practices have ranged all the way from boycotting classes to taking over buildings and switchboards and holding administrators as hostages until demands were met.

3. Violence and the use of force, which sometimes resulted from disruptive student practices.

4. The demands of Black students for a Black Studies curriculum, a Black faculty, and more financial aid for Black students.

5. The growing hostility of Black students to white faculty.

6. The demands of Black students for separate living quarters and all-Black social centers.

7. Black student demands at white colleges for racial quotas and flexible standards in admissions.

The Emergence of a Separatist Philosophy

Many of the demands put forth by Black students would institutionalize the withdrawal of the Blacks into their own community. This development is in direct opposition to the entire concept of integration, a legal battle long fought and only recently won. The reason for this withdrawal is simple. Many Blacks feel that integration has not worked and will not work in the future for a variety of specific reasons. First, the "melting pot" concept of integrated minorities in America has functioned chiefly for members of the white race. Quality education for Blacks is still nonexistent in numerous communities, and there are no miracle solutions to the problem on the horizon. Without improved education, economic and political integration are impossible. All in all, the sit-ins, voter registration efforts, and the marches on Washington have had very little effect on the plight of the average Black man. Disillusionment has given rise to a "we didn't want it anyway" reaction, with the development of Black separatism being the overall result. Many Blacks, impatient with the laborious pace of social progress, feel that the Black man's greatest hope lies in banding together as Blacks for their own economic and political development. "We will work among ourselves," they say, "as the Jewish and Irish communities, for example, have done in order to compete with the white community on an equal footing." This "pull yourself up by your own bootstraps" philosophy is an honored American tradition, but the Blacks' adaptation of this concept threatens to enhance the segregated society so many other Blacks and whites alike have worked diligently to destroy. The result is a major split between ranking Black leaders as to the path the Black community should follow. It is possible that this current interest in separatism is but another phase through which the racial problem will pass, the next step being as yet unknown. Nevertheless, at present, Black militants are touting the separatist doctrine and Black college students are echoing the cry on campus after campus across the land.

HIGHER EDUCATION'S RESPONSE TO BLACK STUDENT NEEDS

The University and the Black Community

A college or university's relationship with the Blacks will be predicated on a number of specific variables; i.e., the number of Black students enrolled, the economic status of these students, and the presence or lack of same of a large number of Blacks residing in the same locale.

Black students enrolled in an isolated campus environment tend to direct their concerns toward a restructuring of the college academic program and organization in accordance with such specific goals as modified admission standards for Black youth, the establishment of Black Studies programs, the hiring of Black faculty, etc.

Black students attending urban institutions tend to combine the above objectives with concerted efforts to involve the university in the overall problems of the ghetto. The latter results in an infinitely more complex relationship than the former.

Questions relating to Black student demands for academic change will be discussed later in the chapter. Our purpose here is to discuss the university's relationship with the off-campus Black community.

Many new government- and privately sponsored programs are now under way to improve the social, educational, and economic structure of the Black ghetto, but many, many more are needed. In the cities, the Black community has turned to the urban university for assistance in organizing and operating community-improvement programs. This is in keeping with a national trend to involve urban institutions in the problems of the urban area. This is a controversial trend however, with many able spokesmen voicing the opinion that such direct involvement on the part of the university is in violation of academia's basic purpose. A more thorough discussion of this subject may be found in the chapter on community relations.

But regardless of the manner in which a university views its community responsibility, the fact remains that the university community does not have the wherewithal to meet many of the problems of the ghetto. Even university involvement in ghetto education is not without its problems. For example, it is generally recognized that the primary and secondary educational systems in many urban areas are of a very poor quality. Spokesmen for the Black community sometimes find it difficult to understand why local colleges cannot bring pressure to bear upon the local school committees to raise academic standards and provide a better education for core-city youngsters. And yet, more often than not, the political strife that tends to exist between tax-exempt urban universities and municipal bodies is such that any attempts in this direction would be bitterly received.

Colleges and universities may feel frustrated by situations such as that which occurred in one Eastern city recently wherein the valedictorian of a core-city high school did poorly on the college board examinations. But they are at a loss to know how to strike at the heart of the problem. Instead, most community-minded institutions have responded by establishing special tutorial or "high-risk" programs designed to help Black youths to overcome their educational deficits to the point where they can cope with a college program.

There have been other attempts by colleges and universities to extend their resources into the ghetto, of which the following are a sample:

Experimental schools for high school dropouts designed to enable young people to earn high school equivalency certificates

Participation in VISTA training programs, graduates of which often are placed in the Black communities in our larger cities

Tutoring programs designed to train adults in the techniques of teaching language skills in order that they may return to their communities to train additional tutors in an attempt to upgrade the literacy level of their neighborhoods

Participation in urban planning aimed at alleviating racial imbalance in urban schools

The sponsorship of training workshops for municipal personnel working in the problem areas of the ghetto

Educational seminars designed to benefit Black businessmen and give further impetus to the development of Black entrepreneurs

The operation of summer camps and other special recreational programs for disadvantaged children

Separatism and the Civil Rights Act of 1964

In some instances, certain of these white-sponsored programs have been thwarted by the recent trend toward separatism within the Black community. Spokesmen for the separatist philosophy voice the position that Blacks working and studying among Blacks can better serve as agents of social change and more quickly bring Blacks into the decision-making process of both the government and the economy. But many other Blacks see this approach as ineffective in eliminating white apathy and breaking down white prejudices. The separatist philosophy is one of Black self-determination; however, at times the implementation of this ideal operates to the exclusion of other races. On the college campus this new pattern of Black activity has taken the form of all-Black dormitories, social centers, clubs, and academic programs which the Department of Health, Education and Welfare has had to declare in violation of the Civil Rights Act of 1964. In March of 1969 it issued a special memorandum directed to this point which reads as follows:

MEMORANDUM TO PRESIDENTS OF INSTITUTIONS OF HIGHER EDUCATION PARTICIPATING IN FEDERAL ASSISTANCE PROGRAMS

SUBJECT: Separate programs for minority group students

It has come to our attention that many colleges and universities are initiating special programs for Negro and other minority group students. These programs range from those that will help the minority student who may have unique problems to those that look to the establishment of a separate school on campus solely for the use of the minority student. We wish to make you aware that, for whatever minority group is sought to be served, certain actions on the part of an institution of higher education constitute a violation of compliance requirements of Title VI of the Civil Rights Act of 1964.

1. Separate Housing for Students Based on Race—All housing which is owned, operated or supported by the institution or a public agency must be available to all students without regard to race, color or national origin and assignment to such housing must be made in a nondiscriminatory manner.

2. Separate Social Activity Space—Where the institution donates or otherwise makes available institution-owned facilities or land for student use or activities or where it provides funds or other financial assistance to acquire or operate facilities for such activities, it must be assured that the activities are to be operated without discrimination based on race, color or national origin.

3. Separate Colleges, Schools or Institutes—Every service and benefit offered by the institution to students must be open and available to all students without regard to race, color or national origin.

The Office for Civil Rights has encouraged, and will continue to support, the institutions' efforts to recruit, enroll and matriculate "high risk" students, minority or otherwise, and to offer such students a well-rounded and relevant social and academic environment on campus. However, we must enforce the congressional intent of prohibiting Federally-assisted institutions from offering services and benefits which result in segregation on the basis of race.

As will be noticed, the above statement makes no reference to the policy of establishing scholarships or special tutorial programs for the benefit of an individual race, the feeling being that such activities are in keeping with the spirit of the Civil Rights Act. Lest there appear to be a conflict here, it may be helpful to quote an earlier memorandum issued by the U.S. Office for Civil Rights in October, 1967. Special attention also is called to section 2 regarding the requesting of college applicants to submit racial information prior to admission.

SUBJECT: *Student assistance* limited to a particular race or nationality; requiring indication of race on college application forms.

The following is in response to your request for an opinion as to whether the above practices are consistent with requirements under Title VI.

1. *Special provision for particular racial or nationality groups.*

Section 601 of Title VI expresses the policy that no person shall, on the ground of race, color, or national origin be excluded from participation in, be denied the benefits of, or be subjected to discrimination under any program receiving Federal financial assistance. Where there are no artificial impediments to participation in a program by members of particular racial or nationality groups, any difference in treatment of persons because of race or national origin would be inconsistent with Title VI requirements.

On the other hand, there are many Federally-assisted programs which have not been fully available to particular races or nationalities. This could be so because of legal or other rules or customs barring participation by certain groups, because general patterns of discrimination have made some programs (including many college programs) appear irrelevant to the needs of certain groups, because general patterns of discrimination have put the programs outside the economic reach of certain groups and have even left these groups unaware of the existence of the programs, or for a variety of additional reasons.

In these instances, a recipient may—and under some circumstances must—give consideration to race or nationality groups not being adequately served by the recipient. Thus a college might make special efforts to recruit minority group students or faculty, including the use of special criteria to determine eligibility and the offering of financial inducements limited to members of minority groups.

This conclusion is in line with the following statements made by the Court of Appeals for the First Circuit in considering a plan to improve educational opportunities by reducing racial imbalance:

"It has been suggested that classification by race is unlawful regardless of the worthiness of the objective. We do not agree. The defendants' proposed action does not concern race except insofar as race correlates with proved deprivation of educational opportunity. This evil satisfies whatever 'heavier burden of justification' there might be. Cf. *McLaughlin v. State of Florida,* 1964, 379, U.S. 184, 194. . . . It would seem no more unconstitutional to take into account plaintiffs' special characteristics and circumstances that have been found to be occasioned by their color than it would be to give special attention to physiological, psychological, or sociological variances from the norm occasioned by other factors. That these differences happen to be associated with a particular race is no reason for ignoring them." *Springfield School Committee v. Barksdale,* 348 F.2d 261, 265 (1st Cir. 1965).

This principle would not extend, under Title VI, to making an entire program available only to members of a particular race or nationality, even though the objective of the program (e.g., a remedial reading program for Negroes) would be to assist in overcoming barriers or the effects of barriers based on race or nationality. This is so because Title VI prohibits discrimination under any *program* receiving Federal financial assistance, and the rationale for allowing special treatment based on race or nationality is that it is necessary to make the program more readily available to all persons. For example, it would not be permissible under Title VI for a college to restrict admission to Negroes only, or for an organization unrelated to a school system to devote its entire resources to providing remedial reading and other special educational activities for Mexican-American children if it excludes other minority group children from participation. On the other hand, a school system might determine that Negroes in the system are restricted in the educational opportunities open to them because of a *de facto* segregation and other racial factors, and choose to alleviate this disadvantage by providing special activities for Negroes only.

Where a recipient accords special treatment to one group not adequately served by its program, it would not necessarily have to make similar provision for all such groups. If the recipient previously excluded Negroes and Chinese it would have to make a special effort to overcome the effects of this discrimination for *both* groups. But if the benefits of the recipient's program have not been adequately available to Negroes and Mexican-Americans for reasons primarily outside of the recipient's control, the recipient could make a special effort to attract Negroes or Mexican-Americans. Thus a school which has not excluded either group, but also does not serve either group adequately, could adopt a special program for one group but not the other.

Finally, each case of special treatment based on race or nationality must be judged individually to determine whether the purpose and effect are consistent with Title VI requirements. In most cases, however, there should be no reason to question the justification given by the recipient.

2. *Requesting college applicants to submit racial or nationality information prior to admission.*

While Title VI bars discrimination, it does not prevent the collection and retention of racial or nationality data *unless* that data is used in a manner that results in discrimination.

In many cases, the collection and retention of racial data may assist recipients in avoiding discrimination in programs and in giving special consideration to race or nationality as discussed in the answer to your first question. If, however, racial data is used in a manner that discriminates, Title VI requires that the recipient eliminate this discrimination either by ceasing to collect racial data or by preventing the use of the data in a manner that results in discrimination.

Recruitment of Black Students

Spurred on by an awakened sense of social responsibility, many colleges and universities actively have begun to recruit Black students for enrollment on predominantly white campuses. But the successful recruitment of Black youth is not an easy accomplishment. The recruitment of outstanding Black athletes is eliminated from this discussion, for they have long been sought by colleges and universities and their circumstances are not typical of the overall problem. What is of concern here are the thousands of Black youths who have the basic potential to handle a college program but lack the motivational and/or financial wherewithal to proceed. Recruitment procedures in the Black community must of necessity be different if they are to overcome certain major obstacles.

First and foremost is the question of motivation. The average Black youth has not been raised in an educationally oriented environment. The so-called "American dream" of a college education for every son and daughter has not been characteristic of most Black parents. Neither has it been characteristic of the teachers and guidance personnel employed in the ghetto school systems.

By and large, high school systems are not geared toward directing Black youth into the college preparatory program. In addition, very few young Blacks are ever encouraged to take the college board examinations during their junior year. With little or no encouragement from either parents or teachers, it is little wonder that the Black high school student does not think in terms of higher education. Still further, many Black youth either know or know of Black college graduates who have been denied employment in spite of their education and this, too, is a deterrent to the average student's motivation. Finally, many Blacks realize that they are obtaining an inferior education in ghetto schools and therefore lack the confidence to try to compete with white student graduates of advanced suburban high school systems. Quite understandably, a lack of motivation is one of the chief obstacles for college recruitment officers to overcome.

A second major obstacle is that of finances. The expense of a college education is beyond the means of most of today's Black families. Scholarships are being made available in ever-increasing numbers, but the supply is minute compared to the demand. The white American tradition of working one's way through college is not possible for most Blacks because discrimination often prevents Black college students from obtaining the jobs offered their white counterparts. This situation is further complicated by the fact that most Black students, if gainfully employed, would be required to donate most of their earnings to the support of their families.

As a result of the above, attempts are being made to educate whole communities to the concept of higher education for Black America. Federal, state, and municipally sponsored community improvement groups are working together with church groups, college representatives, and parent organizations in a concerted effort to stimulate the motivation of youth and increase the availability of financial assistance for potential college enrollees.

Special Postsecondary Preparatory Programs

It is extremely difficult for college administrators to determine the academic potential of many Black youths who have been the unfortunate victims of poor elementary and secondary training. The College Board examinations often are meaningless, for they are geared toward testing students in terms of an experience and environment in which Black youth has not been privileged to participate. A student's high school record also is an unreliable index in view of the low academic standards of many ghetto schools. As a result, most admissions counselors admit to a trial-and-error admissions procedure, with the individual student's success often being predicated on the availability of a strong postsecondary preparatory program. Such programs are becoming popular on many campuses, however diverse their format. At present, there are three basic patterns being followed: (1) special tutoring programs which begin in the early years of high school, (2) summer orientation programs held in advance of the college freshman year, and (3) supportive tutorial and counseling programs conducted in conjunction with the student's full-time college enrollment. Admittedly, these are remedial programs, the core problem being the improvement of elementary and secondary school systems. But, as has been stated, the latter is a long-term program which is basically outside the realm of higher education and, for the moment, remedial programs are necessary in order to help the present Black college generation. One can offer no immediate answer to the question of how effective these programs are, for they are very few in number and very young in age. The most that can be said is that attempts are being made in this direction, and that, at least, is progress.

High-risk Programs for Disadvantaged Youth

It is difficult to structure a discussion of the various special help programs being offered for disadvantaged youth, as each is experimental and therefore in a class by itself. As mentioned above, some of these programs begin while the students are still enrolled in high school. Others involve a totally reorganized college curriculum designed for the student with substandard preparation. Still others are based on a traditional college program undertaken at a slower pace, with up to six years being permitted for completion of bachelor's degree requirements.[1] The only characteristic common to all is a flexibility in admission standards and a somewhat similar flexibility in postadmission standards of performance.

An interesting report entitled *Higher Education for "High Risk" Students,* prepared for the Southern Education Foundation, presents a number of points germane to this discussion. It states:

> The biggest question facing institutions helping high risk students seems to be whether they should be accorded special attention or treated in the same manner as all other students. Some say high risk students have enough problems to overcome without the stigma of identification as a risk, and institutions which subscribe to this point of view make every effort to keep the students' academic and economic handicaps concealed, sometimes even from the students themselves. The opposite argument holds that students who are genuine risks must be given support that is bound to be visible—lighter class loads, special courses, extensive tutoring and the like—or their chances for success will be greatly reduced. The risk students themselves understandably have mixed emotions about the question, expressing at times both resentment and appreciation for either approach.
>
> For most Negro students admitted to college as high risks, the ideas of Black Power and white help are often in conflict. The Negro student on the campus of a predominantly white college today is sometimes forced to choose between absorption into the prevailing middle class culture and withdrawal into a separate black society. That neither choice is fully acceptable—or fully possible—is reflected in the students' own expressions of ambivalence and frustration. For the high risk student, these competing pressures are particularly agonizing; he is in a position of accepting what amounts to special assistance from whites in order to get his college education, while being warned by black militants that he is being seduced into deserting his own people.[2]

In summarizing the results of a survey inquiring into the sponsorship of high-risk programs, the report states the following:

> 215 senior colleges and universities widely considered to be the ones most likely to have formal programs for high risk students were queried, but on the basis of a 75 percent response, almost half of them have no such programs.
>
> A great many things are being tried by a relatively small number of institutions to mine the untapped potential of disadvantaged students, but only a handful of these institutions have marshalled all the resources available to them for this task.

[1] There is some question as to whether or not local draft boards will consider participation in a five- or six-year bachelor's degree program in keeping with the requirement that a student be making normal progress toward a degree. Thus far, however, draft boards have been sympathetic to the arrangement.

[2] John Egerton, *Higher Education for "High Risk" Students,* Southern Education Foundation, Atlanta, Ga., April, 1968, pp. 14–15.

Information on attrition rates is still sketchy, but what there is indicates that even the most prestigious colleges could exercise far more flexibility in choice of students than they now do, without increasing the percent of failures.

Colleges which do in fact try to exercise flexibility do not do it at the expense of their existing academic standards; concessions are made to get "different" students in, but not to let them out.[3]

Obviously, much more needs to be done than is being done, and the failure of college educators to do more is one of the reasons for the Black student's skepticism and often arrogant attitude in his relationship with college administrations.

Communication with the Black Student

A college administrator's effectiveness in communicating with his Black student body will depend largely on the administrator's ability to think and speak within a Black frame of reference. To this end, it may be helpful to note a few basic attitudes and conclusions which appear to be common to many Black students and administrators working with them:

1. The Black student feels that it is the Black counselor's job to get Blacks through school, not to gain special favors in terms of the double standard.
2. Black students are quick to identify so-called "Uncle Toms" among Black faculty and Black administrators, and militant Blacks do not like to deal with such people.
3. In any tutorial program, Blacks feel that other Blacks should tutor Blacks.
4. Blacks are critical of Black counselors who do not meet their demands. When they do not get their way, their attitude is often, "We helped to get you this job here and we will fire you."
5. Blacks want to plan their own programs (cultural and educational) because they feel that white professors are prejudiced in terms of the white man's education and do not understand the needs of the Black man.
6. When consulted in the planning of Black student programs, Black students may expect to be paid for their efforts.
7. Black students often become so involved in the political activities of their community that it reflects in the quality of their academic endeavors.
8. Black students often feel no need to express gratitude for considerations given them, the feeling being that such considerations are due them and, in fact, long overdue.

Some Thoughts on the Subject of Demands

It is unfortunate that college administrations have not been more aggressive in anticipating Black student demands. More often than not, college administrators heave a great sigh of relief after completing negotiations over a list of demands and then complacently sit back and wait for the next onslaught. College administrators should be on the offensive, originating new programs and services with such force as to astonish the most militant of Blacks. Their failure to do so antagonizes the Black who feels he must make boisterous demands and stage demonstrations for every inch of ground he hopes to gain. Until administrators show more initiative, however, demands and demonstrations appear to be here to stay.

In this light, it would at least be helpful if college administrations made known the procedures they deem acceptable in the negotiation of student-administration differences. A number of colleges have done this by having a policy statement concerning protests and demonstrations approved by the board of trustees, after which it is submitted to the administrative staff, the faculty, and the student body for concurrence. Other colleges have formulated joint administrative, faculty, and student policy-making

[3] *Ibid.*, p. 49.

committees in an effort to provide more opportunities for student participation in policy decisions.

Secondly, colleges which have not already done so would be well advised to amend regulations in their student handbooks to conform with the Joint Statement on Rights and Freedoms of Students as issued in June, 1967 by a joint committee of the American Association of University Professors, the United States National Student Association, the Association of American Colleges, the National Association of Student Personnel Administrators, and the National Association of Women Deans and Counselors. (See Section 7, Chapter 2, page 7-31. Since this statement was formulated, it has been endorsed by each of its five national sponsors as well as a number of other professional bodies. This statement protects the rights and freedoms of students and recommends orderly means of bringing about change in place of measures which tend to disrupt the educational and administrative functions of the institution.

Finally, college administrators must realize two salient points: individual demands are not goals in and of themselves, but tactics designed to bring about an overall objective which more often than not has yet to be clearly defined. Secondly, this lack of a clearly defined objective will lead to fluctuations in specific demands with every change in the student body.

Black Studies Programs

To the uninitiated it may appear that academia has been dragging its heels in the implementation of one of the most frequent Black demands—the establishment of Black Studies. And yet, a good Black Studies program is difficult to initiate for several reasons:

1. The Blacks themselves are in disagreement as to how the program should be established, its content, its method of administration, and its means of presentation.
2. This is admittedly a neglected area of scholarly research. As a result, "textbooks" are difficult to come by and those books which are available are often biased in their presentation and therefore not suitable for an objective classroom discussion.
3. Just as there is a lack of appropriate text materials, there is a lack of qualified faculty to teach Black subjects. This problem is further complicated by the fact that the demand often is made that Black Studies be taught by Black faculty only, and Black faculty are extremely hard to come by.
4. Many Blacks insist that only Black students be admitted to the Black Studies program, and in view of current rulings by the Department of Health, Education, and Welfare, this would be in violation of the Civil Rights Act of 1964.
5. Finally, more often than not, the Blacks are insisting that the administration of a Black Studies program be undertaken by the Blacks themselves—which usually means students. This violates faculty rights as protected by the American Association of University Professors and further conflicts with overall university administrative policies which are shaped by accreditation requirements, etc.

Much has been written about the structure of Black Studies programs, and yet while some Blacks question the white man's ability to present the Black story objectively, other Blacks speak of the need for Black Studies to be revolutionary and nationalistic in nature. It is not the purpose of this discussion to outline what should or should not be a part of the Black Studies program—whole volumes may be written on this subject—but rather to urge that colleges and universities vigorously attack this vastly neglected area of academic knowledge. It may be that by virtue of Black student demands for Black Studies programs, a "humanistic sputnik" has been launched which will awaken social scientists to their responsibilities.

The increasing number of demands for Black Studies programs or Afro-Centers is giving rise to discussions relative to the merit of interinstitutional cooperation in the organization of such programs. As has already been pointed out, the shortage of available faculty and texts will be further aggravated by the development of several similar programs. Furthermore, the financing of such programs is extremely difficult in that nondiscrimination laws preclude the use of government funds for the benefit of Blacks only. Private foundations are being besieged by requests for financial aid and, simply stated, there is not enough to go around. The individual college must, therefore, divert funds from its own resources for the establishment of Afro-Centers, which more often than not means an Afro-Center at the expense of rather than in addition to something else.

Interinstitutional cooperation in this matter could be the answer to many acute problems. Fewer faculty would be needed to serve an increased number of students; one strong library could be established in place of several smaller facilities; a uniform system of preparatory, high-risk, and relaxed performance requirements—i.e., six years for the B.A. degree—could be maintained. A more thorough program of research into materials for course development could be enacted. Still further, there would be greater stimulation for students and faculty alike in the formation of one central community of Afro-scholars as opposed to several smaller ones.

The academic merit of research and course development in African and Afro-American culture cannot be denied, but it is vital that one note of caution be voiced in relation to this matter. The tendency for Black students to flock to Black Studies courses is understandable, and yet enrollment in such courses may well be a luxury Black students can ill afford. The study of Swahili may be good for one's ego but disastrous to one's wallet. Revelling in the cultural laurels of its ancestors will not raise the economy of the Black community. Such studies will not elevate urban primary or secondary education, produce Black doctors, engineers, mathematicians, scientists, or lawyers. There is already an overemphasis on the social studies within the Black college-student body and undue emphasis on Black Studies could perpetuate this trend. For what career is a Black student graduating with a degree in Black Studies prepared? America needs the Black man's contribution in all phases of endeavor—in business, in conservation, in government, in science. The Black Studies program could easily become the greatest vehicle of education for limited opportunity yet devised!

Black Faculty

The new trend toward Black emphasis has created many new problems in terms of the hiring of Black faculty. To begin with, the supply is quite inadequate to meet the demand. Black militants have voiced the view that this situation could be rectified, in part, by hiring Black men and women who do not meet the customary requirements for teaching positions. But this suggestion is riddled with difficulties. To what extent should the academic requirements be waived? Can one intelligently suggest that blackness in and of itself makes a good teacher? On what qualifications should a potential Black teacher be judged, assuming a lack of the usual credentials? Is the hiring of personnel who are not professionally trained fair to those Blacks who have taken the time and made the effort to gain proper accreditation? What will be the impact of the hiring of such individuals on other members of the faculty and on the academic rating vis-à-vis accreditations, honor society charters, etc., of the institution as a whole? Finally, is there a sufficient number of these "qualified by virtue of experience" individuals available to meet the needs of the country?

Undoubtedly, there are some outstanding Black leaders who could do justice to a classroom situation, but they are few in terms of the need, and most would not wish to leave their present occupations to become full-time college lecturers. Obviously, it takes time to develop talent, and stopgap measures will have to be employed in the interim. Is it not better to have even Black Studies programs taught by whites until sufficient Black personnel are available than to have no Black Studies programs at all? And is it a fair assumption to say that only the Black man can properly teach in the Black

Studies program when scholars of all races are teaching the history and culture of all races the world over?

Finally, although the custom of one institution raiding the faculty of another has been in practice for years, this procedure poses a serious threat to the existence of the Black colleges and universities in America. Black college presidents are being seriously handicapped by the offers being extended to their faculty by white institutions. The Black college holds a position of unique importance in higher education and should not be jeopardized in the "rob Peter to pay Paul" process. Finally, Black faculty should watch that they do not fall victim to circumstances of the Black militants' making; i.e., the hiring of Blacks because they are Black regardless of individual ability. In the long run, unions born of such motivation will not be happy ones, however appealing the initial offer. The Black man wants to be accorded the dignity due him. The hiring of a Black faculty member because of his Blackness rather than his ability is as much an insult as a failure to hire for the same reason, and it violates the dignity of the individual.

When Black "Rights" Violate the Rights of Others

Changes being sought on the college campus are a reflection of the Black students' desire for a new structure in society. Blacks see in our present university structure a perpetuation of the status quo. For this reason, the university is viewed by some as an enemy of the Black man's cause. Recognizing that higher education molds the thinking of a nation's leadership, Black students are striving to alter the educational mold in order that future generations may view the Black man in a new light.

The desire is understandable and the purpose is reasonable, but in certain respects the drive for so-called Black "rights" threatens to violate the rights of others. Some Blacks will answer this with emotionalism, saying, "So what, our rights have been violated for years." But this is neither an intelligent nor an honest response. The errors of the past do not sanction the errors of the future, and two wrongs do not make a right.

The frequently voiced desire for Black control of Black Studies programs is in violation of faculty rights as long fought for by the American Association of University Professors. Now, the American Federation of Teachers, AFL-CIO, is seeking to gain support for what it believes to be its rights. Student organizations also are seeking control over various administrative and curricular matters, and what they consider their "rights" also would be jeopardized by the Black-control policy. Black men are members of both of these groups and would do better to work within existing frameworks than to seek to fragment the question of control still further.

The so-called "faculty-administration conflict," real or otherwise, which is assumed to be present on every campus is held in rein by a system of academic checks and balances through department heads, college deans, deans of faculty, faculty senates, etc. The desire to circumvent this system would not appear, in the long run, to be in the Black man's best interests. But once again, this question reflects the difference of opinion between integrationists and separatists and is, therefore, a part of the larger problem.

This last phrase provides the key to all that has been discussed in the preceding pages. The individual circumstances confronting college officials are a part of the larger problem. Black identity, Black Power, separatism, special programs, Black student demands—all are effects stemming from a single cause. In the final analysis, the understanding of this cause, the Black man's search for dignity and honor, is the only real solution to the administration of Black student affairs.

THE DISADVANTAGED STUDENT—HOW IT WAS AND HOW IT IS

EDITOR'S NOTE: The following article published in the *AGB Reports*, vol. 12, no. 3, November–December 1969, was deemed so pertinent to the understanding of Black student affairs that it has been included as an appendix to this chapter, with the permission of the author and the Association of Governing Boards of Universities and Colleges.

The Disadvantaged Student— How It Was and How It Is

Ruby G. Martin *

An interpretation of the disadvantaged student from the inside

Some of you may question my credentials and qualifications to be your speaker this evening, for I am neither on the board of trustees of an institution of higher education nor am I connected in any way with the administration of an institution of higher education. If you have qualms, they are not without merit, for I readily admit that I do not comprehend the inner workings of governing boards and administrative bodies of colleges and universities.

However, the agenda item for this conference, Higher Education and the Disadvantaged Student, is of utmost concern to me—not only as an observer but as a participant—because quite frankly, I was educationally disadvantaged as a child, as were most black adults in this country. By existing academic standards, I suppose I am an educationally disadvantaged adult. I was born in a deep south state and my first three grades of formal education were in a segregated, grossly inferior school in a little southern town that my parents were forced, physically and emotionally, to leave when I was only eight or nine years old. They were forced to leave their home, their livelihood, and a section of our Nation, which in terms of physical appearance is probably the most beautiful and picturesque section of America, with its green flat lands and rolling hills, with its ever-blooming trees and delightful climate. But my folks had little time for nature gazing because they were consumed wholly and simply with the urge to survive and to protect their children.

So I was disadvantaged from the moment I was born; and when my family moved to Cleveland, Ohio, I entered a Cleveland public school. I was frightened nearly to death because, although I didn't realize it, I was reading two or three grade levels below my classmates, and my language was a dialect which few people understood. I had never seen a library or a new textbook. Indeed, I had never heard of a microscope or a laboratory. A white teacher and a girl and a white boy in the same classroom with me nearly reduced me to tears. But I didn't cry very long. By the time I reached the sixth grade, the schools that I attended in Cleveland were not too different from the one that I attended for three years in Arkansas—predominantly black, overcrowded on double sessions, with the newest teachers. They were the most inferior schools in the system.

I point to my background, not to gain your sympathy, but in an effort to give some credibility to my remarks. For although I'm not a member of the education establishment, I am a black American. As such, I have been confronted with educational problems in ways that are peculiar to minority groups in general, and to black people in particular. Because of my own experiences I am beginning to understand some of the problems that many young black Americans now enrolled at predominantly white colleges and universities are wrestling with.

Recently, for reasons still unclear to me, I was invited by the law school and faculty to visit a major university in California. They wanted to talk to me about a number of

* Mrs. Martin was in the Department of Health, Education and Welfare for several years, and during 1967–69 was director of the Office of Civil Rights, in the Office of the Secretary. An attorney, Mrs. Martin is now with the Washington Research Project, where she is engaged in research. She presented this address at the dinner session, October 7, 1969 of the AGB conference in Washington.

things, but primarily they said they wanted to discuss their two-year-old special program for educationally disadvantaged students. This particular institution had, during a two-year period, enrolled nearly 100 Black and Chicano youngsters at the undergraduate level and an equal number throughout the graduate and professional schools. They were quite proud of this achievement. The university people were genuinely concerned and perplexed about the attitudes of many of the educationally disadvantaged students toward the program itself and toward the university. These young people were variously described as arrogant, ungrateful, disinterested, unconcerned, and trouble makers. The university people were honestly frustrated by these attitudes, and finally asked me the ultimate question:

"*What do they want?*"

They said, "We have special tuition programs for them, special tutorial programs, special recreation and social areas for them, we have special housing for them since they want to live together, and we even have soul food on the menu:

"*What else do they want?*"

I was disturbed by the question—no—not by the question itself, but by the way it was asked. In my view, the question was not asked in a searching sense, but rather it was asked with a sense of resignation—that we have done all we *can* and we have done all that we are *going* to do.

And, even though I had the feeling that the people who asked the question were not really asking it in an honest sense, I felt obligated to say something; after all they had transported me across the country at their expense. My answer, I am sure, was totally unsatisfactory to them, because in all honesty, it's not entirely satisfactory to me because nobody can really answer the question, *What do they want?* But my answer was that while these young people are disadvantaged—by your standards, by academic standards—there are areas in which they are *not* disadvantaged and they want you to understand that. They want to be accepted for what they are and not to be tolerated because you have placed labels on them—*educationally disadvantaged, special.* They want to be understood and not stared at; and perhaps most of all they want to survive, not just physically (believe me, they know how to do that), but they want to survive emotionally in a hostile environment, indeed in a racist environment. I think you and I would have to accept their feelings that the colleges and universities mirror the bigger society, and that society is hostile and racist.

Please don't misunderstand. I am not talking about individual hostility and individual racism; these black youngsters know how to deal with that. It's the institutional racism—the all-white sororities, fraternities, and social clubs; the all-white cheer leading squad and debating team. To these young black students these institutions are just like the all-white institutions they left behind "in real life"—the all-white labor unions, city governments, banks, and social workers, and the white truant officers that have been harassing them all of their lives.

The thing that college and university administrators must remember is that many of the so-called high-risk students—the educationally disadvantaged and culturally deprived youngsters, particularly if they are black—come to the universities not only from the worst possible schools, academically and socially, with the poorest teachers, overcrowded classrooms, and major discipline problems. They also come to the university right off the streets of the ghetto. These are the young people who have seen the prostitution, the crime, the drug traffic, the police brutality. They know about racial confrontations because they live in the areas that were destroyed and devastated by the race riots two summers ago. These are the young people who have watched their mothers work from sun-up to sun-down in some white family's home and kitchens and still make hardly enough money to survive. It is their fathers who are fighting and demanding that the labor unions and the construction industry open their doors so that they can get a decent job, despite a faulty education. And it's sheer folly for university people to think that simply by changing these youngsters' environment, by bringing them onto a beautiful university campus, simply by putting them into living quarters where they have a room—or indeed—a bed of their very own, by simply serving them three well-balanced meals a day—it is folly to think that this will immediately overcome the years of deprivation, fears, and hostilities that have built up within these youngsters from the day they were born.

It is extremely difficult for some college officials to grasp that these youngsters have been exposed all of their lives to a living situation that some of you can't even imagine. You may have seen it in the newspapers, in magazines, on TV, but it's not the same as seeing for yourself a place where nine or ten people share a one or two-bedroom, rat-infested apartment; where the food is adequate only a few days out of the month, when the mother gets paid, when the welfare checks come in, or when the father is able to pick up a day's work. Some of these young people have had to hustle the streets for a hot dog and play all kinds of games, con games, in order to survive in our society.

University people have got to remember something about the background of these students. You must appreciate their suspicions and distrusts, for they have been tricked and lied to all of their lives. Many of them feel that every helping hand that is extended, including special college programs, is just another illusion or a trap which they must not fall into.

College and university officials must understand that most of these young adults are not impressed by their special programs—some of them call them "white-conscience programs." They are not impressed when they are told that the university violated all of its high entrance requirements, made all kinds of concessions, kept out some qualified students, just so they could enroll them. They are not impressed because they have seen these institutions enroll the dumbest boy on the block, or they have seen 50 colleges trying to recruit the dumbest boy in school, simply because he was an outstanding football or basketball player. If you try to impress upon them that a special concession was made for them, their answer is that those with power, those with the authority to determine who shall be enrolled, always violate their regulations when it's convenient—when they can use people.

University people must realize that these educationally deprived and disadvantaged youngsters are caught between two emotions. On the one hand, they want to escape the environment they grew up in, and they see the university as a tool to make that escape possible. On the other hand, they do not want to "fink" out on their parents and friends whom they left behind in the ghetto; so they want to change the conditions of the environment they grew up in; and they see the university as a tool to make that change possible. One of their greatest fears is that they will be co-opted, that they will sell out or be bought off by the man, the white man and his shining institutions of higher education, and never go back to help their brothers and sisters on the block, who they know are drowning in despair and desperation and hatred.

College and university people must understand the obligation a young black man feels toward his mother and father who struggled and sacrificed to see him graduate from high school, who now finds himself a student on a university campus. He feels an obligation to help out with the family, to get a job to help feed the younger children in the family. Going to college does not permit him to, in a sense, pay the family back. It does not afford him an opportunity to help the younger children as he could if he got a job or joined the military instead of enrolling in college. Some of these black young men have terrible feelings of guilt about being a college student and not being able to help their mothers who may be on welfare with a dozen other children in the home. Some of them ask me, "Why is it that our society will contribute millions of dollars to support big white farmers *not* to farm their land, but at the same time won't even consider contributing a single dime toward the support of our mothers and sisters and brothers who need our financial help while we are in college?"

One of them said, "Why can't this country have a *child depletion allowance* to mothers of college boys like us, like the oil depletion allowances for the big white oil tycoons? Why not a *parent subsidy program* to help our families while we are in college like the agriculture subsidy program to help the rich farmers?"

College and university officials must realize that many disadvantaged youngsters who find themselves on the campus of a predominantly white institution feel that the *institution* is more concerned about its *own* image than it is their needs. I am not talking about "black history" or "black studies" programs; I am talking about their feelings of urgent need for them to do something about the ghetto and about their people and their feelings that the university has a responsibility to use its facilities to help them learn how to deal with these problems. I have heard them say, "The health problems in my neighborhood are unbelievable. Children go without vaccinations; children and adults with broken arms and legs have to wait hours at a racist hospital to get any kind of relief." They say, "It takes nine years to be a doctor; but I don't want to be a doctor, I just want to learn how to give vaccinations and to fix these poor little broken arms and legs—and nothing else. I don't want to perform open-heart surgery or wear a white suit. Why should all these young children have to go unattended because this society won't accept the concept of paramedical services? Why can't this institution, which reached out for me, set up a course of study which will put me back on the streets in less than nine years so that I can just set broken bones?"

This may sound shocking to most administrators of medical schools and certainly the AMA would not dream of such a thing. But this is a real problem. We need to listen to these young people, to think about what they are saying. If we are honestly asking, "What do they want?" we can hear at least some of the answers, if we will only listen.

Some of these students who have seen their parents, relatives, and friends exploited by cunning and ruthless business people are not interested in learning about ancient ethics, nor are they interested in going to school seven years to become a lawyer. They want the colleges and universities to equip them to go back on the streets as soon as possible, not to practice law in the traditional sense, but to be able to teach their people something about their rights as debtors. They don't want to be a Perry Mason or Edward Bennett Williams or even to go into a courtroom, but they do want to counsel the people in the ghetto about fraudulent deals and schemes, about reading the small print. They are impatient and could not care less about tradition. They know what being patient and being traditional has done to their parents and grandparents, and they are not going to accept that fate.

When I was briefed on this Association, it was pointed out that most of you are not college administrators and are not concerned with the day-to-day problems of administration, and I appreciate that. But you are the people who make policy; and you are in the very best possible position to influence the direction your particular institution takes toward meeting these deep feelings of frustration that many black youngsters on college campuses are experiencing these days. They talk in terms of demands. But I urge you to go behind the demands. Try to figure out what they are saying, and most of all try to understand the human product you are dealing with. Then you will begin to grasp why they speak in terms of demands. The human product might be inarticulate—inarticulate because he has been excluded from the dominant society and has been forced to develop his own system of communication and dialect. The human product may have little respect for law and order and justice because he has witnessed legal authorities protect, defend, and sometimes collaborate with the power structure that has kicked, criminally assaulted, and even killed black men, women, and children. And of greatest importance, the human product is most likely to be young and vigorous with a new-found pride in his being—feeling inside as well as outside that "black is beautiful." And the human product has a determination to correct the injustices that his parents have so long endured, and therefore he is prone to have little respect for any institution, including institutions of higher learning, that do not recognize his goals and offer to help him achieve them.

My former boss at the Department of Health, Education, and Welfare, Mr. John Gardner, was fond of saying, "Impossible problems are really unlimited opportunities in disguise." I believe that. I hope you believe it. Our society and our institutions are being challenged from within and without on almost every front. If we consider these challenges as opportunities to be creative and to be innovative, I think we will survive as a strong nation. On the other hand, if our institutions fail to be flexible and if they fail to be "relevant," as the young people say, they are going to be destroyed, not necessarily destroyed physically (although that too is a real possibility), but destroyed as a viable force in our society. They are going to take on a kind of Citgo gas station characteristic—"A nice place to visit on your way somewhere important."

In dealing with the issues of race relations that are certain to confront you as trustees of institutions of higher learning, I simply urge you to be thoughtful before you are critical, to be conscious and aware before you are condemning, and to be understanding and tolerant before you make your final decisions.

Chapter 6

Administrative Concerns of Women Deans

PATRICIA A. THRASH

Associate Dean of Students and Associate Professor of Education, Northwestern University, Evanston, Illinois, and Vice-president of the National Association of Women Deans and Counselors, 1967–1969

The purpose of this chapter is to examine the concerns of women deans in the university administrative structure. Because the role of all student personnel administrators is changing, these changes and their particular effects on women deans will be briefly examined. But the major function of this chapter is to present specific areas of concern which a women dean may have, whether her title is "Dean of Women," "Associate Dean of Students," or "Assistant Dean of Students," or "Director," or "Assistant Director" of some division of student personnel services.

CHANGING ROLE OF STUDENT PERSONNEL ADMINISTRATORS

There are at least three ways in which change on the university campus is affecting the roles of student personnel deans. First, there is the move toward appointing a vice-president for student affairs or student services to do the job once performed by the dean of students. Although placing a student personnel administrator at the top echelons of authority may take some of the pressure off the university president and may make the needs of students more fully known at the major decision-making level of the university, it also may further remove deans of men and deans of women from decision-making levels of authority and thereby redirect their functions.

Second, as institutions become larger and less personal, there is a growing tendency to develop functional student personnel services which provide specialized help to students. Under this structure, deans of men and deans of women are eliminated—their titles are, at least—as directors and assistant directors of various services are appointed. If the division of functions by sex is eliminated, those who were formerly deans of men and deans of women and their staffs may become associate and assistant deans of students or directors and assistant directors of various services.

Third, even if the titles remain the same, the positions are different because of changing responsibilities. Although the major areas of concern to be delineated later remain, there is a shifting of priorities as some student needs disappear and others emerge. As students ask for more autonomy to direct their own lives and become increasingly involved in the world around them, student personnel administrators are confronted by crisis situations and are called upon to work with groups, often angry groups, of students. Individual appointments may be cancelled and individual students with difficulties may be neglected as deans deal with the confrontation of the moment. Although there are fewer records to keep because many personal evaluations of students have been eliminated, there are more meetings with groups of students and with colleagues to consider immediate and long-range solutions to current crises. Letters from parents, concerned citizens, and alumni come more often; and they demand thoughtful answers. With the elimination of many regulations, disciplinary functions of deans are lessened. But the dean's work as a counselor increases as the individual student who is sometimes confused by the rapidity with which freedoms have come calls to ask, "What should I do?"

EFFECT OF CHANGING PATTERNS ON WOMEN DEANS

These three changes have a particular effect on the role of women deans in student personnel administration. Although some disagree with this view, many believe that, with the changes, positions for women deans will remain because women are a part of an administrative subculture.[1] To the writer's knowledge there are no women vice-presidents for student affairs and few women deans of students in coeducational institutions. The position that carries the title "Dean of Women" is disappearing in large universities and many smaller institutions as restructuring of student personnel services occurs; but the person who held the title continues in a supportive role in the restructured student personnel service. Most women seem to prefer performing a supportive role or a specialized function to taking charge of a total program. This may be because they are not offered the opportunity to direct a total program, but it may also be that they have freely and thoughtfully chosen the supportive role. In his introduction to Jessie Bernard's *Academic Women,* David Riesman writes, "Women are trained to be less assertive, to move in narrower orbits, to be (contrary to legend) less exhibitionistic."[2] He classifies women as teaching-oriented and service-oriented. Although some would disagree, it could be generalized from Riesman's comments that women administrators are a part of a supportive subculture not only because society has conditioned them for this role but also because it is the kind of role in which they feel most comfortable and can be most productive.

The most important reason why women will remain significant contributors to student personnel programs, however, is the fact that any program of services to students needs to include both men and women in order to be complete. Anthropologist Paul Bohannan stresses that "Every person in order to be fully himself must react to both men and women. . . . He needs models on which to base and gauge his behavior—and he needs both male and female models."[3]

In summary, women deans are indispensable and significant contributors to student personnel programs because of their competence but also because of the special contribution which they make as women. The effective student personnel service needs both men and women, whatever their titles may be, who can work together to discern the changing needs of students on the university campus and who can respond positively to those changes.

SPECIFIC AREAS OF CONCERN FOR THE WOMAN DEAN

Specific areas of concern for the woman dean will be determined, of course, by the nature of the institution of which she is a part. The woman who is dean of students of a women's college will have the responsibilities of the administrator concerned with a total program of services for students. The dean of women of an urban coeducational institution will concentrate on the special needs of commuting students and their relationship to the city of which they are a part. The dean of women in a small, church-related college; a private college; a college isolated geographically from major urban areas; a burgeoning community college; or a large coeducational public or private university will have particular responsibilities and concerns dictated by the nature of her institution.

[1] Patricia A. Thrash, "This Place in the Ways," *Journal of the National Association of Women Deans and Counselors,* vol. 30, no. 4, pp. 184–186, Summer, 1967.

[2] David Riesman, "Introduction," in Jessie Bernard (ed.), *Academic Women,* The Pennsylvania State University Press, University Park, Pa., 1964, p. xvi.

[3] Paul Bohannan, *Love, Sex and Being Human,* Doubleday & Company, Inc., Garden City, N.Y., 1969.

Because of the complexity of institutions of higher learning, no one job description can fit the work of all women deans. In a smaller college the dean of women may perform all the tasks which in a larger institution are shared with supportive staff members. She may have a more direct disciplinary responsibility for women students; and she may be more deeply involved in planning and attending social events and supporting an intramural sports program for women. Perhaps she has a more direct and continuing role in orienting women students to the institution through an informal or credit course.

It may be helpful, however, to delineate specific responsibilities of the dean of women in one institution, even though the description will not be applicable to the work of all deans. This description of the work of a woman dean in a large, private university of 10,000 men and women students – 7,000 undergraduates, 3,000 of whom are women, and 3,000 graduate students – can serve as a model to be adapted for use by administrators, some of whom are seeking information for the first time and others who are seeking to gain perspective and new ideas. Although institutions are changing rapidly and student personnel services are changing along with them, these are areas of concern with which most women deans might have to deal.

SPECIFIC RESPONSIBILITIES OF THE DEAN OF WOMEN IN A LARGE, PRIVATE, URBAN UNIVERSITY

The dean of women is charged with responsibility for the welfare of all undergraduate women students. To carry out this responsibility requires professional competence, awareness of every phase of student life, a commitment to the goals and purposes of the university as they affect the individual student, an ability to work productively with colleagues in developing a program of services to students and a responsiveness to change.

Working with the dean of women, who has a Ph.D. degree in counseling, are three assistant deans who have M.A. degrees in counseling. In addition to her own staff, the dean of men's staff, the staff of the director of activities, and directors of the various specialized student personnel departments work with the vice-president of student affairs to maintain a program of services to students.

The dean of women has an administrative role. She is responsible for the selection, supervision, and training of her staff. She has advisory responsibilities for student groups. She is responsible for the rushing activities of sororities and is concerned with programs for independent and commuting women students. She is aware of and responsive to emerging student needs, and she is involved in personal counseling. She disseminates information especially relevant to women students. Her office provides a limited amount of financial assistance to students. She has a public-relations responsibility. There are publications, records, reports, and paper work for which she is responsible. She has responsibilities after regular working hours. In addition, she is involved in professional organizations and contributes to the journals of her profession. As a faculty member, she has teaching and advisory responsibilities. Finally, she has the special responsibility for maintenance and growth of herself as a person if she is to make an effective contribution to students, her colleagues, and her institution.

Here is an examination of each area of responsibility.

Administrative Role The dean of women, who is charged with responsibility for the welfare of all undergraduate women students, is directly responsible to the vice-president for student affairs and dean of students. She submits the budget for her program for his approval. Working with him and other administrators as well as with students and faculty, she determines policy which affects all students; but her major responsibility is to work with programs and policies affecting women students. She is a member of the Council on Undergraduate Life, a student-faculty-administrator group concerned with all regulations regarding student life outside the classroom. She is a member of similar groups which determine policies and programs in the area of new-student orientation and student facilities.

At regularly scheduled meetings with the dean of students' staff and with the women's staff, current problems are discussed and programs and policies are articulated. In times of great change or crisis, the vice-president for student affairs may call upon the dean of women and other staff members to help him in the development of a response to be disseminated to students and those outside the university.

Selection, Supervision, and Training of Staff The functions of the dean of women's office are carried out with a staff selected by the dean of women with the approval of the vice-president for student affairs and dean of students. The immediate administrative staff includes three assistant deans and an administrative intern with supportive secretarial staff. Although the dean and the three assistant deans are available to any individual student or student group, each has special areas of responsibility. Other staff members with specific areas of responsibility are the residence hall directors, resident assistants, and sorority housemothers.

Assistant Dean of Women and Director of Women's Housing. This assistant dean, who has a great deal of autonomy and whose office is located in a separate building, is responsible for the housing of all women students, for the supervision and training of residence hall staff, for developing residence hall programs, and for working with administrative committees which determine housing policy and programs. All resident assistant applications are processed and appointments made through her office. As an adviser to Associated Women Students she works with student leaders in developing programs for all women. She is also particularly concerned with the needs of independent and transfer women.

Assistant Dean of Women and Panhellenic Adviser. Although this assistant dean works with many student groups and also counsels individuals, she has a great deal of autonomy in determining Panhellenic policies and programs. She serves as adviser to the Panhellenic Association, working closely with the officers and attending all Panhellenic meetings and workshops. She supervises the rushing program for the 18 sororities and meets with individual officers of the chapters. She meets with Panhellenic committees called to deal with university or sorority infractions during rush. Often she serves as a liaison between affiliated students and their housemothers or alumnae officers. She communicates to national officers who visit the campus the university's concern for the Greek letter groups. She works with the assistant dean of men and Interfraternity Council adviser to develop positive changes in the rushing program and the fraternity system on campus. She supervises the orientation and in-service training program for sorority housemothers and schedules periodic individual conferences with them. Because half the women of the university belong to sororities, she comes to know a great number of students through her contacts with the individual chapters.

Assistant Dean of Women. The third assistant dean of women has the special responsibility of counseling individual students, administering and interpreting educational and vocational tests, and serving as a liaison between the student and the educational counseling laboratory as well as the mental health department of the student health service. In addition, she is concerned with the needs of commuting students, serving as an adviser to commuting women's organizations. She is also involved in programs to meet the emerging needs of black students and disadvantaged students, working with the admission staff to coordinate services to these students.

Administrative Intern. The intern, a doctoral candidate in student personnel administration, observes all phases of the women's program, conducts research, and prepares information for dissemination to the staff. She reads professional journals and alerts staff members to relevant articles. She conducts a continuing evaluation of staff programs.

Secretarial Staff. The assistant dean of women and director of women's housing, located in a separate building, has a secretary and two student assistants. The dean and assistant deans, who are located in one complex of offices, have two secretaries and additional part-time help when help is needed. Both secretaries have bachelor's degrees and an excellent aptitude for working with people, as well as an appreciation of the confidential nature of their work. As the persons who greet those who come to the office, interact on a regular basis with students, and handle telephone inquiries from countless callers within and outside the university in addition to performing routine secretarial tasks, they are essential members of the student personnel staff.

Residence Hall Directors. Selected by the dean of women in consultation with the assistant dean of women and director of women's housing, the directors of the eight residence halls for women are responsible for developing the programs in their living units. In the four large halls, directors who are experienced, full-time staff supervise the resident assistants and work with student officers to develop policies and programs for the residence. In each of the four smaller residences the director, a doctoral candidate, represents the university as she works with students in developing a house program.

All directors meet frequently for individual and group conferences with the assistant dean of women and director of women's housing, to whom they are directly responsible. Monthly work sessions for the directors are scheduled with the dean and all assistant deans.

Resident Assistants. Working closely with the dean of women, the assistant dean of women and director of women's housing coordinates the selection, orientation, and in-service training program for resident assistants, full-time graduate or undergraduate women students who are directly responsible to the directors of their living units. All staff members participate in the orientation and in-service training program and are available for individual conferences or group sessions with the resident assistants and their directors.

Sorority Housemothers. Housemothers, whose salaries are paid by the sorority alumnae boards, are responsible to the boards and to the university. Their appointment is approved by the dean of women, who countersigns their contracts. The assistant dean of women and Panhellenic adviser processes the applications of prospective housemothers, arranges interviews with the sororities, and recommends the appointment of qualified candidates. She supervises the orientation and in-service training program for the 18 sorority housemothers. All staff members participate in the orientation program for the housemothers and are available for individual conferences with them. The assistant dean of women and Panhellenic adviser visits each housemother during the year to see the chapter house and to discuss with the housemother any special concerns which she may have.

Advisory Responsibilities for Student Groups The dean of women serves as an adviser to a number of student groups. This responsibility is shared with the assistant deans of women, each of whom has major responsibility for some student group. This sharing of advisory responsibilities enables each staff member to have some program of student activities as her major area of concern and to know a sizeable number of students. In addition, this sharing frees the dean of women to meet with organized and spontaneous groups of students who wish to have her join them. It also helps to dispel students' perceptions that the dean of women works only with student leaders in traditional activities.

As advisers to student groups, the dean of women and assistant deans serve as consultants, resource persons in the realm of ideas. They acquaint the officers with the responsibilities and traditions of the group, approve the budgetary plans of each group, and are responsible for seeing that the group's plans are in accord with the purposes and regulations of the university.

In their roles as advisers, the dean of women and her staff often entertain group members in their homes. These are usually informal occasions, such as Saturday morning coffees, Friday afternoon teas, or buffet suppers. The dean of women has a limited expense account to cover the cost of entertaining students.

Here are the major groups which the dean of women and her staff advise:

Associated Women Students. Through Associated Women Students (AWS), the dean of women interprets university policy and raises questions of concern to the university. She has a weekly conference with the president of AWS, during which they discuss areas of mutual concern. She attends executive-board sessions and meetings of the AWS House Council, the governing group of all women students. She works closely with officers in charge of workshops and programs of AWS: Standards Training, Scholarship, and Social Programs; Careers Programs; New-student Week Programs; and Student Assistants for Faculty.

While the dean of women has no direct disciplinary function, she serves as an adviser to the AWS Committee of Appeals, which reviews decisions made by residence hall judiciaries; and she counsels with students who may request appointments to discuss disciplinary matters with her.

The assistant dean of women and director of women's housing also serves as an adviser to AWS, and she shares with the dean of women the responsibilities of meeting with the group.

Panhellenic Association. The assistant dean of women and Panhellenic adviser, working closely with the dean of women, has the major responsibility for all matters relating to the Panhellenic Association and the Greek letter organizations for women, as described in her job analysis. The dean of women attends Panhellenic meetings and workshops upon invitation of the group.

New-student Week Programs. The Dean of Women works closely with New-student Week programs, serving as a member of the Orientation Committee, a student-faculty-administrator group which plans and evaluates the New-student Week program each year. With the assistant dean of women and director of women's housing, she advises the AWS New-student Week program and approves the publications and budgets involved in the program. The assistant dean of women and Panhellenic adviser advises a coeducational student group which welcomes new students and gives them individual assistance and encouragement.

Honor Societies. The dean and assistant deans of women share advisory responsibilities for women's honor societies. The dean of women is responsible for approving official reports of Mortar Board, a national women's honor society, and Alpha Lambda Delta, a national freshman women's scholastic honor society; but she or an assistant dean—not both—attends regular meetings of each group. An assistant dean advises a local junior-senior women's activities honorary. Another assistant dean coordinates the activities of the Professional Panhellenic Association, which is made up of speech and music honor societies for women.

Rushing Activities of Sororities Consulting with the dean of women, the assistant dean of women and Panhellenic adviser supervises the rushing program of the 18 sororities. Assisting her are an undergraduate central rushing chairman, a Panhellenic secretary, and the Panhellenic officers. Although the computerized rushing program which takes place immediately after New-student Week in the fall is financed by Panhellenic, the Panhellenic adviser approves the program as well as the Panhellenic *Handbook.* She works closely with rush chairman, Panhellenic officers, and rush counselors. In addition, she counsels with students who have questions about rushing or pledging and interviews each student who depledges or deactivates. She also presents sorority concerns to her fellow staff members and recommends changes to be made in the system of rushing.

The dean of women and assistant dean of women and Panhellenic adviser are often called upon to represent the university's point of view in meetings with sorority alumnae groups. In times of crisis they communicate the university's concern to these groups and invite their members to discuss the situation with them.

Programs for Independent and Commuting Students Although women students have rejected the idea of a special organization for independents, the dean of women and assistant deans work with student groups in the residence halls through Associated Women Students to develop special programs for those who wish them. One of the assistant deans advises commuting women students' organizations. Members of the dean of women's staff contribute most to these two groups of students by working as individuals with individual students. They help, too, by assisting students who wish to organize new groups to meet their needs.

Emerging Student Needs The dean of women and her staff must be responsive to emerging student needs. Each staff member attempts to learn all she can about black students and their desires and about the special problems of disadvantaged students. While it is unlikely that they will be advising these students gathered in groups, they may be called upon to respond to the individual needs of these students, whose numbers are increasing on the campus. One dean of women serves as adviser to one group of black women students who are attempting to have a national sorority on campus because individual students in the group knew of her interest and concern for them and sought her help.

Personal Counseling The dean of women and her staff are involved in personal counseling of students each day. As professionally trained counselors they can help students work out alternatives or refer them to appropriate agencies on campus. The deans see students with personal problems, financial problems, vocational problems, social problems, disciplinary problems, and academic problems. Students are advised at the beginning of the year that counseling is available to them, that appointments are easily made, and that confidentiality is assured. Others are involved in the counseling situation only with the student's permission.

To assure ample time for individual counseling, the dean of women makes appointments from 10 A.M. to 12 P.M. and from 2 to 5 P.M. daily. From 8:30 to 10 A.M. and 1 to 2 P.M. each day, appointments are not scheduled. This leaves the dean of women time to see students with emergencies, to make telephone calls, to receive calls from staff members who are advised that she can be reached during these hours, and to attend to correspondence.

Dissemination of Information Especially Relevant to Women Students The dean of women, because of the nature of her position, has a special responsibility to disseminate information especially relevant to women students. In her office, files are maintained containing information about women's roles, continuing education for women, vocational opportunities for women, graduate resident counseling positions in other colleges and universities, part-time jobs, summer jobs, study abroad, graduate study, as well as information about other institutions of higher learning. Students are advised that these files are open to them. Women students who are considering transferring, part-time employment, study abroad, or graduate study will find the files helpful; and they are encouraged to talk with one of the staff members about their concerns.

Financial Assistance to Students Students can obtain emergency financial assistance through loan funds in the office of the dean of women. The dean and her staff refer to alumnae groups students in need of special help. They serve on scholarship selection committees for various groups which award help to women students. In addition, they work closely with the staff of the financial aid office, informing that office of students with special need who are not receiving university assistance.

Public Relations The dean has a responsibility to represent her philosophy and her programs to those inside and outside the university. She accepts invitations to participate in campuswide discussions and meetings in the living units on campus, and she is available to members of the student press for interviews. In addition, she has an obligation to communicate what is going on in the university to those outside the institution. She speaks to community groups and to alumni groups upon invitation. She gives interviews to the press and participates in radio and television shows with the approval of the public relations office.

Publications, Records, Reports, and Paper Work The dean of women approves publications by student groups which she serves as adviser and prepares handbooks for staff orientation and in-service training programs.

Records are kept of student interviews. In addition, students who wish to do so are invited to fill out personal information forms which contain information to be used in writing recommendations which students request. Because residence-hall staff members no longer provide student evaluations, this is the only information available. All records are confidential to the dean of women and the assistant deans.

Reports are made of women students on academic probation. Other reports are prepared about particular issues as the need arises. Because reports should be prepared only if they have value for those who are to receive them, they should be evaluated carefully and continued only if they have genuine significance.

Paper work includes the vast amount of correspondence which is one of the dean of women's daily tasks. The dean of women writes a letter of sympathy to a student who loses a member of her immediate family. She writes or telephones students who are hospitalized. She writes thank-you notes after being a dinner guest in a campus living unit, and she congratulates students who win honors and awards. After interviewing students, the members of the dean of women's staff write recommendations for them. Applications for staff positions are processed by the dean of women's office.

One of the most important areas of correspondence is with the parents of students. The dean of women acknowledges any letter from parents and attempts to answer in detail any questions which concern parents. She interviews students whose parents write and answers the letter with the students' knowledge.

Another important area of communication is that of confirming memos sent to fellow staff members or to faculty as a preamble to discussion of an issue or as a follow-up to a discussion or telephone conversation. Such memos give the dean of women records of information which she might otherwise remember inaccurately.

All letters to the dean's office are acknowledged. The dean of women answers all letters addressed to her, and she asks an assistant dean to answer letters concerned with her special area of interest.

Responsibilities After Hours Responsibilities after regular working hours include meetings and emergencies. The dean of women and the assistant deans share these responsibilities so that each has some time of her own. In addition to frequent invitations to dinner and regularly scheduled evening meetings, there are events scheduled on campus which staff members may wish to attend because students have a special interest in them. Occasionally there are commitments on the weekend, particularly on Saturday morning or Sunday afternoon.

Emergencies can occur at any time, but they usually occur after office hours. The dean of women receives emergency telephone calls from her staff members and, in turn, relays the information to the dean of students. The dean of women may see an individual student with a serious problem; she may be called to the hospital after an accident; or she may go to the police station if a student is arrested. Whatever the emergency, it is an integral part of the dean of women's responsibilities and often provides an opportunity for counseling.

Professional Organizations, Publications The dean of women is involved in professional organizations at the state and national level. National groups of particular interest are the National Association of Women Deans and Counselors and the American College Personnel Association. In addition, the American Association for Higher Education is a vital source of information about matters which concern college administrators. Working as an officer, a committee member, or a program participant in any of these organizations is an experience which enriches the dean of women, for she gains perspective as she learns how her colleagues elsewhere respond to the same situations which are confronting her.

Whenever possible, the dean of women contributes to the journals of her profession, offering her own ideas and programs for evaluation by her peers.

Dean of Women as Faculty Member The dean of women who also has an academic appointment is fortunate because she knows faculty and is known by them, which can increase mutual understanding. She conscientiously attends all faculty meetings, teaches regularly, and has advisees. Teaching in the student personnel field helps the dean of women in two ways: the teaching provides theory which is excellent background for what she is practicing daily as a dean; and her work as a dean helps her to take realistic and urgent concerns into the classroom.

Dean of Women as Person This final area is included in the job analysis because it is vital to the dean's effectiveness that she be herself. In addition to doing her job enthusiastically and well, responding openly and honestly to students and to the tasks at hand, she must learn to leave the cares of the position at the office whenever possible. She has lively interests which have nothing to do with her work. She takes vacations, confident that everyone on her staff is competent to handle all crises without her as she takes time to read, relax, and gain perspective. This kind of dean is the one whom students will regard as a person and not a position.

These specific responsibilities and concerns are not, of course, applicable to women deans in every situation. There are some who predict that many of the functions just described will cease to be valid areas of attention in the future. For example, on many large campuses a separate women's government no longer exists and therefore there is no opportunity for a woman dean to work with such a program. However, whatever the structure in the institution, the woman dean will continue to have an opportunity and a responsibility to work with women students because of the special needs and concerns of women as they plan a future which is likely to include a number of years of gainful employment in addition to marriage and the raising of a family. Perhaps the most important function of the woman dean, after all, is to serve as an educator in the area of women's roles and the options open to educated women.

ADDITIONAL READINGS AND SOURCES OF INFORMATION

Ayers, Archie R., Philip A. Tripp, and John H. Russel: *Student Service Administration in Higher Education,* U.S. Government Printing Office, Washington, 1966.

Dennis, Lawrence E., and Joseph F. Kauffman (eds.): *The College and the Student,* The American Council on Education, Washington, 1966.

Freedman, Mervin B.: *The College Experience,* Jossey-Bass, Inc., San Francisco, 1967.

Greenleaf, Elizabeth A. (ed.): *Undergraduate Students as Members of the Residence Hall Staff,* National Association of Women Deans and Counselors, Washington, 1967.

Klopf, Gordon (ed.): *College Student Personnel Work in the Years Ahead,* Student Personnel Series N. 7, The American Personnel and Guidance Association, Washington, 1966.

Lloyd-Jones, Esther, and Herman Estrin (eds.): *The American Student and His College,* Houghton Mifflin Company, Boston, 1967.

Mueller, Kate H.: *Student Personnel Work in Higher Education,* Houghton Mifflin Company, Boston, 1961.
Shaffer, Robert H., and William D. Martinson: *Student Personnel Services in Higher Education,* The Center for Applied Research in Education, Inc., New York, 1966.
Siegel, Max (ed.): *The Counseling of College Students: Function, Practice, and Technique,* Collier-Macmillan, Toronto, 1968.
Smith, Margaret Ruth: *Guidance-Personnel Work: Future Tense,* Teachers College Press, Columbia University, New York, 1966.
Williamson, E. G.: *Student Personnel Services in Colleges and Universities,* McGraw-Hill Book Company, New York, 1961.
Woodring, Paul: *The Higher Learning in America: A Reassessment,* McGraw-Hill Book Company, New York, 1968.
Yamamoto, Kaoru (ed.): *The College Student and His Culture: An Analysis,* Houghton Mifflin Company, Boston, 1968.

Periodicals and Professional Journals

Journal of College Student Personnel
Journal of the National Association of Women Deans and Counselors
Journal of the Association of Deans and Administrators of Student Affairs

Chapter **7**

Orientation of New Students

ROBERT H. SHAFFER

Professor of Education, Former Dean of Students, Indiana University, Bloomington, Indiana

INTRODUCTION

The primary purpose of orientation activities is to communicate to the new student the concept of college as a self-directed, intellectually oriented experience. Secondary purposes include informing the student and his parents about the institution and its services, counseling the new student and his parents regarding educational, vocational, and personal problems which have to be met while in college, completing various mechanical procedures needed to enroll the student in his classes, and, in general, getting the new student off to the best possible start in his new career.

Orientation as a needed educational service developed out of the problems caused by the increasing heterogeneity of student populations, the development of complicated educational programs, and the broader range of courses offered by most institutions. In addition, as higher education became more newsworthy and the object of concern of a vastly greater percentage of the total population, it became important for colleges to expend effort in interpreting higher education to their constituencies. In fact, the purpose of the orientation process might well be summarized as that of communicating to the student and all those influencing him what a college, a college education, and a college-educated person are.

Failure to understand and provide for the varied backgrounds of students has led to needless disillusionment, failure, and alienation on the part of many potentially successful students. Many college faculty members and administrators fail to comprehend the importance of orientation activities for students who have had fairly good academic preparation in high school. Such students require a shift from traditional emphases on factual information about college social and academic life to an emphasis on what the college expects of them, the variety of academic programs available for advanced students, and the flexibility which can be provided by most institutions. Competent students particularly need to be challenged to establish high academic and intellectual standards for themselves and to develop concepts of themselves as young adults as contrasted with concepts of themselves as rebellious, bright adolescents. Further, they need encouragement to utilize the full range of resources available in the typical college community. Charges by many bright students that their college experience is irrelevant to their lives and the world about them often arise out of faulty orientation to the college experience in the transition from high school to college.

STEPS IN THE ORIENTATION PROGRAM

The Initial Precollege Contact The logical starting point for orientation is at the initial contact between the college and the student. This usually occurs through visitation by an admissions counselor to a local high school or through correspondence. Failure to realize the importance of this initial contact has caused many institutions to create a low-quality and contradictory image in the eyes of the prospective student, an image which is carried over to campus even if the student follows through and is ultimately enrolled. If the admissions counselor views his duties as those of a salesman in the narrow sense, his attitude and bearing reveal such a concept and, as a result, the image of a customer is created in the mind of the prospective student. Thus, it is important for every institution utilizing admission counselors to be very clear as to the function of these counselors and to analyze their approach to students. From the orientation point of view, it is important that, from the very first contact, the institutional representatives emphasize the nature and significance of the educational programs which the college offers and that they make the distinguishing characteristics and features of these programs clear. If one of these characteristics is service to educationally underdeveloped individuals, then such a statement should be made. However, to urge students who are not properly qualified by virtue of their high school course of studies or achievement to enter a college by assuring them, falsely, that suitable remedial services will be provided is only to court failure, encourage disillusionment, and cheapen the total institution.

Even more care should be taken in the writing and editing of the bulletins and other explanatory materials which are sent out in answer to requests for information about the college. Unfortunately, many mailing pieces are marvels of advertising copywriting, straddling such contradictory issues as high-quality education, service to all types of students, and provision of extensive custodial procedures combined with maximum opportunity for independence, creativity, and individual expression. It is possible to fulfill the functions of an initial mailing piece from an advertising or sales point of view and still represent fairly, consistently, and forcefully the essential and distinguishing characteristics of an educational institution. Correspondence subsequent to the mailing of the general explanatory material should similarly reflect the college expectancies, academic standards, and the general characteristics of the student body. Such correspondence need not be brusque or brutal but should be frank and to the point. If the majority of students entering a particular institution has advanced standing in some courses, for example, and such standing is expected by the faculty, then it is unfair to both entering students and the institution for them to be encouraged to pursue application and enrollment only to be told later that they should have had certain courses in high school. Staff members engaged in correspondence with prospective students should clearly understand their importance in the total communication exchange and their relationship to the process of communicating the nature of the institution and the opportunities afforded by it.

Preregistration – Campus Visit Another step in the orientation process which has also been frequently overlooked by faculty and administrators alike has been the visit to the campus by prospective students. Such visits may be made in connection with some social or athletic event, they may be informal personal visits, or they may take the form of scheduled group visits coming under the auspices of the college admissions office. Many institutions have failed to realize that the essential flavor of the institutional climate has often been conveyed to prospective students through such visits in an impressive and dramatic way. Such visits often outweigh statements by admissions counselors and the words in descriptive brochures. Failure of the institutional orientation committee to coordinate its efforts with the hosts of residence units, directors of special events, and similar individuals has resulted in a lack of coherence in the presentation being given to prospective students by the total institution. If the initial visit is in connection with a weekend or an elaborate social event, the prospective student often gets the impression that such activities are of greater importance and meaning in the college experience than the academic activities which the college has tried to hold out as most important in the total environment. It is obviously impossible to control all informal experiences. However, it is possible to understand the nature of these experiences and to provide for corrective or balancing activities to the overall program. The effectiveness of such corrective action rests upon an understanding of the importance of the communication taking place in such situations.

Group Meetings of Students and Parents in Home Locality Another phase of the total orientation program which has been used to great advantage by many institutions has been the promotion of group meetings of students and parents in the home locality. Such meetings can be held either in a central location under the leadership of a college representative or in the home of an alumnus in the area who serves as the nominal host. These meetings are particularly valuable in laying the foundations of loyalty to the institution, for interpreting expectancies to parents and students alike in an informal atmosphere, and for answering the myriad small questions which trouble many families when they first send a son or daughter to college. The best time for such meetings is when the student has been accepted by the college but is still in high school. At such a time, they provide a logical transition step from the high school to the college and enable the college representative to illustrate the difference between high school and college. At the same time, he can emphasize the continuity of the educational endeavor and the importance of a thorough foundation in the tool school subjects for later academic achievement in college. Further, such meetings give the institution an excellent opportunity to build up alumni loyalty in a geographic area. The use of alumni enables the college to tell its story to the alumni and gain their support, and it also gives them the informational background they need to carry out their job as the institutional representatives in the local area. Perhaps the best example of the use of local alumni has been in the somewhat tainted field of recruiting athletes. The same principles and procedures can be used to recruit outstanding students, students from culturally deprived homes, and students from minority groups. Just as the use of alumni has had to have restraint placed upon it in the athletic field, so is it important to delimit very carefully the function of alumni in the total orientation process.

If there are no local alumni, group meetings can be arranged in an appropriate school by the college representatives themselves. In such cases, it is possible to show a movie, have a panel discussion among faculty and students, and otherwise provide for an informal, audience-participation meeting.

Summer Parent-Student Orientation The step in the orientation process which has received the most publicity in recent years and which is often erroneously thought of by many administrators and faculty as the first step in the orientation program is the summer orientation conference. It is at this time that many institutions bring the parents and the prospective students to the campus for a day or two to test, advise, register, enroll, and learn about the mechanics of college life. Typically the students and parents live in the university residence halls for this period and thus learn at first hand the features of mass living. Such experience gives college officials an opportunity to emphasize to the new student and his parents the responsibilities that go with group living. It is particularly important to be frank and direct in discussing the citizenship obligations that go with crowding scores of energetic young people into relatively small spaces. Those parents who have been ambivalent or vague in interpreting their rules of behavior to their college-bound offspring have the opportunity to reaffirm their own expectancies and support the college at this time. Where parents show reluctance to support the college and its rules and regulations, college representatives have time to go into possible problems in a direct and specific way even to the extent of suggesting that the family refrain from sending their son or daughter to the college until personal matters or expectancies can be clarified. For example, the parent who is determined to provide an automobile to his freshman son, even though the college regulations specifically forbid freshmen to have automobiles, needs to be challenged regarding his expectancies of the college experience and his contribution in supporting the college in its endeavors.

More importantly, however, the summer conference enables the college to get many of the mechanics traditionally associated with the fall registration week out of the way. If the institution does not use, by the end of the high school career, some of the standardized tests which are available, then it is at the summer conference that tests can best be administered. Thus they can be scored and the results can be used at the summer conference session. At least the results can be available by the fall for use in appropriate placement in class sections. If testing must be done at the summer conference, it should be scheduled at the very opening of the conference so that the test bureau can have time to complete scoring and to report results to academic advisers before the students have their individual program-planning sessions. If, however, the institution uses the College Board examinations or other standardized tests, then special placement examinations can be given at the beginning of the schedule. These include examinations in music, foreign languages, mathematics, science, and other types of achievement tests which will assist the college advisers in placing the student in the appropriate class section. Such testing is increasing in significance because of the progress of many high schools in providing advanced classes for competent students.

A typical program consists of an overnight stay on the campus, with parents and prospective college students arriving by 10:30 A.M. for a mass meeting and general welcome. Students then are tested while the parents have question-and-answer sessions with various college authorities. Following lunch in one of the residence halls, the group is divided by fields of interest and meets with representatives of the academic divisions concerned with those special interests. Provision should be made for attendance at at least two such group meetings at this time to prevent the premature forcing of choices and to avoid depriving parents and prospective students of the chance to get all the information they need about a variety of fields.

A very successful feature of such programs is often a sample lecture by a faculty member who gives a typical lecture from his course and asks the students and their parents to take notes. He then distributes notes which he has made of the same lecture to enable students to test their note-taking ability against his outline. Such an experience provides ample material for informal discussion and lays the groundwork for an evening program on study techniques, study schedules, and related matters. Usually a social event concludes the evening.

After a night in the residence halls the students are scheduled to have group meetings with their faculty advisers followed by individual conferences at which the course programs are planned. Following the individual conferences, the students go to a central point where they complete registration, including enrollment in the classes. Often, at this time, book lists are distributed and provision is made for the students to purchase their books for the fall with the hopeful thought that many might start studying before coming to school. By actually enrolling students, having them pay their fees, and disposing of other mechanical matters, the fall orientation program is relieved of mechanical obligations and thus is able to concentrate on orientation to the college environment as its major emphasis.

Large, complex institutions have found some mechanical difficulties in actually enrolling students in class sections during the summer because of the many class changes that may be required by the fall. Some institutions follow the preceding steps up to the point of actual class enrollment, but they have the students hold their materials until the fall and enroll them in classes at that time.

New-student Days What is often thought of as "orientation" is the welcoming period, new-student days, or orientation week at the opening of school in the fall. The parody on the term, "new student daze," is often all too accurate. Many students are not psychologically or mentally equipped to absorb all of the messages that traditionally have been crowded into the typical orientation week. As described above, many institutions have moved the mechanical aspects of orientation to the summer and have reduced the new-student days in the fall to a one- or two-day period with the special purpose of accepting the student into the community, welcoming him into his social group, emphasizing to him the intellectual and scholastic nature of his experience, and starting him in his regular classes as soon as possible. Thus, an institution which utilizes summer orientation typically has a brief program in the fall. It usually consists of the following: a general assembly; division of all new students into small groups led by student leaders; meetings and programs related to study skills; tours of the library; dissemination of information regarding other resources in the community; and a social event, usually held at the campus center, at which the student leaders of the center are able to explain the services and advantages of the center's program.

Despite the summer program, many institutions will be required to take care of certain mechanical details for students who fail to participate in the summer conference and for those who have changed their minds since the programs were planned. In such cases the fall orientation programs must be "double tracked" in order to provide mechanical services for those who need them while at the same time enabling those who do not need such services to avoid retracing the steps they took in the summer. This duplication of effort has been one of the traditional criticisms of the old-fashioned freshman week in the fall.

Opening Class Sessions The opening sessions of classes constitute one of the most important phases of the orientation process and yet one which is typically ignored. It is this period which is so important in establishing relationships between the professor and the student, between the specific courses being taken with the general field of knowledge they represent, and between the college experience and the world of knowledge as a whole. It is tragic indeed when enthusiastic and stimulated freshmen are dumped into class only to have cold water thrown upon their hopes and aspirations by dull, drab, boring sessions which seem totally unrelated to the college experience they have been led to anticipate. More than this, many students never understand that the immediate course they are enrolled in is related to a broader field of knowledge. Instructors should be encouraged to relate the opening days of class with what has gone on in the orientation process and to regard their opening class sessions as a part of this process. It is important that class assignments be made immediately so that students will understand that they are expected to get to work promptly. If at all possible, class assignments should be given out at the time of enrollment or at least at the time of reporting to school, so that students will be impressed with the expectancy that they have an obligation to perform and a standard to live up to from the first hour in class.

As one means of bridging the gap between the busy pace of orientation week and the challenging months ahead in the student's college career, many colleges and universities use one of the several books which discuss problems and issues which the student will face as he pursues his college career. Some of these books are textbooks which may be used in formal orientation courses and others are primarily designed to serve as a basis for discussion sessions concerning such topics as the relationship of the student to his education; the so-called "generation gap" between students and faculty; development of social maturity; problems related to sex, drugs, alcohol, and cheating; developing creativity and individuality; the question of joining fraternities; and the development of religious insights and commitment.

Examples of such books include those edited by Charles W. Havice and by Rivlin and others.* The Havice book dwells particularly on the subject of values and relates a student's maturation and development of standards in various areas of campus life to the problems he faces as a collegian. The Rivlin book tends to emphasize development through the various academic fields. Other books include a strong emphasis on vocational, educational, and personal planning and related topics. The particular book used by any one institution should be chosen carefully on the basis of the objectives and emphasis of that phase of the orientation program.

If nothing else, assignments made at the time of their enrollment keep freshmen busy during the last day or two prior to classes. More than that, however, initial assignments provide a dramatic and impressive link between orientation and the regular school year by illustrating the challenges and tasks facing students. The day when the opening class session was an abbreviated, meaningless exercise during which the name of the text and general repetitive material was given out should be gone. Instead, the opening class session must be regarded as the launching pad for a stimulating and challenging year. To achieve such an impressive opening, faculty members must be

* See bibliography at the end of this chapter.

considered key participants in the planning and conducting of the total orientation program.

Orientation Follow-up Formal orientation classes at many institutions have been discontinued because of staffing and financial problems. However, the concept of carrying orientation throughout the first semester or first year is a viable and significant one. Therefore the orientation program should be construed as continuing throughout the student's transition to the college. Therefore, group meetings conducted by the orientation group leaders can be utilized to great advantage in residence units as well as by other campus groups. Furthermore, a follow-up to orientation by having evaluation sessions approximately six weeks after the beginning of school gives counselors and others an opportunity to disseminate valuable information and to invite students in for individual conferences without seeming to force themselves upon students.

The need for orientation continues through the freshman year, and the wise administrator will see to it that some type of orientation is carried on even though it is impossible and perhaps needless to have formal orientation classes. Utilization of freshman English composition classes or other courses for continued orientation not only gives meaning to the class but provides an excellent mechanism for continuing the general emphasis. Students are more interested in learning about preparing for and taking examinations just prior to their first round of examinations. Discussing preparation for examinations in the summer is not nearly as impressive or effective as it is during the week or two prior to the assignment of examinations in classes.

Thus, the continuing orientation program can be built around student experiences, needs, and anxieties developed from their campus and class experiences. Recognizing and meeting these needs provides an excellent opportunity for the centralized student personnel services and the specialists within the college community to communicate the nature of their services at a time when students are most likely to pay attention to the message.

CONTENT OF THE ORIENTATION PROGRAM

The content of the orientation program must be decided upon by each institution in accordance with the needs of its students and its individual characteristics. Programs which are adopted without change from other institutions invariably create boredom, contain irrelevant material, and reflect lack of creativity and ingenuity on the part of the institution. Depending upon individual circumstances, most institutions will need to include the following general areas of subject matter in one or more aspects of the total orientation program:

Completion of Academic Procedures One of the essential tasks required of any orientation period is the completion of such procedures as academic advising, class sectioning, advanced placement, meeting with academic deans, and the handling of special problems associated with transfer and graduate students. Criticism of most orientation weeks often revolves about the totally inadequate time provided for necessary academic procedures. A brief, meaningless, mechanical conversation with a faculty member under the guise of academic counseling is an all too obvious negation of the institution's emphasis upon academic achievement. Disclaimers saying that specific programs are not rigid or sacred do little to lessen the anxiety of new students who feel that it is of the utmost importance that they take precisely the course which they have read about in a bulletin or been told to take by some alleged authority. Thus, the planning committee in charge of the fall portion of orientation should make certain that adequate time and emphasis is given to academic problems.

Registration and Enrollment Procedures One of the important functions of the orientation program is the smooth and efficient placement of students into classes. Therefore, provision should be made for registering and enrolling the student in class sections following his counseling. However, in making this provision it is important to realize that not all students are involved in registration and enrollment at the same time. Therefore, some other activity should be provided for those individuals not actually engaged in the registration process. This is particularly true of large institutions which may have set aside several days for registration and enrollment. Frequently optional programs can be scheduled at this time, with students attending sessions when they are not scheduled for registration. Also, some registration can take place while other students are being advised, examined by the health service, or otherwise participating in other aspects of the program. Unfortunately the folklore among students is that registration is an annoying, irritating bore. Often, no matter how efficient the registration process is, students will complain. Therefore, it is important to have students related to the planning of this aspect of orientation as well as to others. When students themselves see the problems that the registrar has in making the necessary arrangements and accomplishing the necessary tasks, they will be more understanding of any lines and delays and will be able to interpret the reasons for them to their fellow students.

Orientation to Living Arrangements and Social Activities Residence units are particularly important as the locale for this phase of the orientation program. Parents and new students arriving at a residence hall are pleased to find well-mannered young men and women greeting them, assisting them in checking in, and making them feel expected and welcome. Participation in this orientation program gives residence unit governments a big boost because they realize the importance the activities have for the welfare of the total unit. It is important to have the parents entertained or occupied while the students go through the mechanics of checking in and orienting themselves. Often this can be accomplished by having a coffee hour at which parents can meet the counselors and other staff members of the hall while student leaders are taking the students through the various procedures in the hall. Fraternities and sororities are generally alert to their responsibility in this area; their activities must be coordinated with the entire orientation activity. Frequently institutions have found that the excessive zeal of some housing groups has resulted in keeping new students out of other orientation activities. The number of social functions associated with the orientation period should be limited and directed toward a specific purpose. The idea of "keeping students busy" by throwing numerous so-called "mixers" simply results in boredom, disillusionment at orientation, or the development of competing interests through the various segments of the community. Normally, the campus center can be utilized as the locale for one main mixer or social function and then the president's home or some other location can be utilized for an opportunity to meet the president and chief administrative officers as well as members of the faculty. Some institutions provide for all incoming freshmen to be invited to the homes of all faculty members during the fall orientation period also. They assemble in a given place and are divided into small groups and accompany a student guide or the faculty host himself to his home for a picnic-type supper and general, informal discussion.

Orientation to the Physical Layout of the Campus, Institutional Facilities, and Landmarks One important aspect of the orientation program is to make the new student feel at home in a strange geographic environment. In a few short days most students will know every nook and cranny of even a complicated campus. However, during those first few days even a small campus can seem strange, foreboding, and confusing to an overanxious freshman. Therefore, tours of physical facilities, orientation to the library, introduction to the athletic program and facilities, and tours of the counseling office, health service, and related facilities are an important part of assisting the student to resolve needless concerns and to give his wholehearted attention to significant problems and tasks.

Personal Counseling Another aspect of the orientation program is the provision of educational, vocational, and personal counseling for those individuals needing it. Many students are unduly troubled by all the decisions which have to be made upon entering college and particularly with the detailed information they must give on the various registration forms regarding their vocational and educational plans. The sheer mechanics of many colleges require premature vocational and educational choices. The rush of events during the typical registration and enrollment prevents any real counseling by faculty members while advising students regarding the selection of courses. For this reason it is important to make specific provision for "undecided" students as well as to explain to the student the resources within the community for more extensive personal counseling of various types. Information regarding financial aid and part-time employment should also be disseminated in a specific manner during the orientation. Many new students are reluctant to raise personal questions in large meetings. Therefore it should be easy for them to make application for a job and ask for counseling about financial and other problems. Most of this information should be disseminated prior to the student's arrival on campus. Specific questions can then be handled when the students arrive on campus.

General Information In addition to the above topics, there is a wide variety of general information which must be provided to students during the orientation program. This includes information regarding ROTC, the existence of special dining facilities for students, the rental of lockers in commuting situations, parking and automobile regulations, check cashing facilities, etc. It is in connection with such topics that the student members of the orientation planning committee are particularly valuable. They know the information needed by the new students, information that administrators and faculty members often overlook. Consequently, the special information section of the printed orientation program or panel sessions to give out information during the orientation can be arranged by students with suggestions from the general planning committee.

PLANNING THE ORIENTATION PROGRAM

The Coordinating Committee As with most other activities involving the entire institution, it is important to include all segments of the college community on the committee in charge of developing and conducting the orientation program. All persons who have a contribution to make should be involved in the planning and operation of the program regardless of their office or position. The committee should include student representatives from housing units, all-campus organizations, scholastic honoraries, and representatives from groups having special needs, such as the handicapped, commuting, employed, and married students. In view of the current national concern, it is particularly important to include members from minority groups. In addition to student representatives, staff members representing all segments of the campus must be included. The program is not the property of any one office or division of the university. Most institutions have had the best success with standing orientation committees which are self-perpetuating in some aspects. In this way the committee which is evaluating one orientation program is also observing tradition and gaining experience from year to year.

A timetable for planning orientation must provide for adequate lead time to disseminate the necessary information and to marshal the necessary resources. The fall program must obviously be established before school closes in the spring if adequate student input and involvement are to be provided for. Similarly, the precollege aspect of the orientation program must be decided upon many months before the actual dates so that the necessary materials can be prepared and visitation schedules can be established. The use of alumni groups for the parents' get-together in the home localities likewise makes it imperative that alumni representatives be included in the planning committee. Records are important in building programs from year to year. Therefore, each orientation planning committee should have a secretary whose job it is to maintain the permanent file of records so that subcommittees will have a basis for estimating such things as the numbers of participants in the various events, facilities required, costs, and publication needs.

Role of Students and Student Organizations Members of student organizations justifiably feel resentful when their services have been committed to some aspects of orientation without any provision for their involvement in the details of program planning and operation. It is important that those organizations which have been called on traditionally to render services be involved in a direct way with the orientation planning committee. It is not adequate to have one or two students such as the president of the student body represent all students and student organizations. Rivalry and lack of communication among themselves often causes students to feel resentful and alienated when, in fact, considerable effort has been expended to involve students in a significant manner. Likewise, student leaders must understand the extent of their involvement so that they may be in a position to interpret the entire program to friends in their home town, to alumni, and to fellow students on campus. Students are particularly effective in relating their own experiences to the problems of new students. Their experience and mode of expression are invaluable in making panels and meetings more meaningful. Further, student participation lifts formal occasions out of drab, boring patterns and helps make them more relevant and pertinent to student life. A frequent criticism of utilization of students is their tendency to give information and advice beyond their scope of experience, training, or expertise. Realistically, it is probable that this tendency will never be completely curbed. Therefore, the planning committee must take every step possible to train the students participating and to provide checks on their exuberance, helping them to avoid extending themselves to areas of counseling and guidance for which they are unprepared and unqualified.

Role of Faculty Members in Orientation Orientation is basically the faculty's show. Therefore, it is important to involve representative members of all segments of the faculty in all phases of the orientation program. Where possible, the faculty members should accompany college representatives to off-campus meetings and certainly should be highly visible through their participation in all of the campus programs. Because the campus orientation program often conflicts with departmental duties associated with registration and enrollment, faculty members often feel overworked at this particular period of the academic year. Therefore, faculty participation must be planned carefully to provide suitable recognition and released time for those faculty members who participate in the orientation program. Many academic departments do not consider such participation as significant and therefore tend to pass off duties in this area upon young members or upon a few particularly agreeable individuals. Those who participate should do so willingly and in complete confidence of the importance and significance of the undertaking. Administrators responsible for the program must take specific steps to establish suitable recognition for those faculty members who do participate.

Role of the Administration The official role of the administration is to coordinate the efforts of all those involved in the total orientation program and to keep the show moving. This involves a great deal of routine work, record keeping, and office assistance. Some one administrator usually associated with the dean of students' office should have specific responsibility for the coordination and direction of the orientation program. Despite the fact that policies and procedures must be a committee responsibility, it is important that one individual be assigned the key administrative role. Otherwise the responsibilities fall among too many individuals and offices. The administrator particularly has the responsibility for stimulating the overall planning committee to clearly define the objectives of the orientation program and to establish procedures to meet the objectives once they have been set. As described below, evaluation and constant study are additional significant functions which the administrator in charge must fulfill.

EVALUATING THE ORIENTATION PROGRAM

As in every enterprise, it is important to check the achieved results with the objectives. Usually, orientation programs are evaluated by means of a questionnaire distributed to the participating students soon after the opening of school in the fall. Such a questionnaire lists all the main programs of the orientation period together with rating scales in which the participants are asked to indicate their reactions, ranging from very poor to excellent. The program evaluation should include a rating of the procedural operation as well as a rating of the content and the contribution to the individual. Sometimes a program will receive a high rating because of the obvious work and effort which the sponsoring committee put into it. However, the overall contribution of that activity may be rated low in the light of the objectives of the total orientation program. Similarly, some potentially valuable aspects of the program might be rated poor or of little value because mechanical details have been bungled or because the individuals in charge have failed to make adequate preparations.

Further, any evaluation results must be carefully interpreted in order to ascertain whether the rating actually reflects the activity as such or whether it is related to other aspects such as duplication in the program. Thus a meeting in a home town might be rated poor or insignificant because the content of that meeting duplicated the content of a prior conference with a college representative from the local high school. If the summer orientation conference merely duplicates what has been offered at other times or if a fall orientation program duplicates what has been done in the summer, then obviously the programs might be rated of no value. New developments in some institutions, in keeping with the student involvement trend across the country, have taken the form of one or two student-conducted meetings at which there are no faculty or staff members present. Properly planned, these can be a valuable opportunity to facilitate exchanges among students. Such a program further evidences the institution's concern for student dialogue and prevents later changes that the institution controls the information and the points of view expressed during the orientation process.

By seeing the component parts of the total orientation program, it is possible to plan properly the timing of messages which are being communicated to the students and thus to utilize the resources within the college community to the best advantage. Students will best understand material when they feel a personal need for learning what is being explained to them. Complaints of dead, meaningless meetings often arise from the fact that the orientation program has been heavily loaded with information which is good for the student but which is being presented in too heavy a fashion and without effectively preparing the student to receive the material. The evaluation process should include an effort to evaluate the timing of the material which was given in the total orientation program.

GENERAL CONSIDERATIONS

There are a variety of sociological and psychological theories and principles which underlie concepts related to the orientation of new students. Probably the most valid is that each institution must build its orientation program upon the characteristics and problems of its own incoming student body. Institutions drawing heavily from families and localities which have traditionally not sent many students to college will need to emphasize the nature and characteristics of an institution of higher learning and to base much of the content of the orientation program upon problems and tasks incident to crossing from one cultural and social setting to another. However, those colleges which tend to draw students from families which are already well informed concerning college and which tend to have family environments conducive to verbal and intellectual activities will probably need to deemphasize the information-giving function of orientation and emphasize the challenge of the present-day university experience, the opportunity it provides for individual development, and the need for each student to set standards for himself as a measure of his own achievement. In such cases the institutions may want to place a greater amount of responsibility for the transition process upon the individual student and upon his own motivation in securing the assistance he might need from the appropriate service agencies in the college community. It would seem that the institution should do nothing for the individual which the individual can do for himself and should do nothing which tends to rob the individual of his self-responsibility for making the appropriate adjustment to college. Therefore, great care needs to be taken that students not get the idea that everything is being done for them, that they are being placed in courses rather than being assisted in choosing courses, or that the college is determined to give them an education whether they want it or not. Probably one of the danger signals of overambitious advising is the prevalence of complaints that "the counselor gave me the wrong course," or "I don't know why I'm taking that course. My adviser told me to."

Finally, it is important that all concerned with the orientation program understand that it is essentially a program designed to communicate ideas and concepts concerning the college to a wide variety of individuals new to the community. Communications research therefore reveals valuable lessons for the orientation committee. Among these lessons are the following:

1. Agreement must be reached regarding the essential message or emphasis to be communicated during orientation week specifically and in all other phases of the program. All segments of the college must understand this decision and relate their presentations to the general emphasis. Garbled or foggy messages are received from a varied mixture of activities, value statements, or contradictory programs.

2. The message or emphasis which orientation is intended to convey must be phrased in such a way that the new student will select it for attention from among the many other possible messages and distracting forces affecting the typical college freshman. The wonders of the college world call to a new student with many voices and with a variety of appeals. To be successful, the appeal of the dean for academic purpose must be able to compete with the allure of a beauty queen or the prestige of the BMOC by its use of status appeals, timing, language, and sheer force of expression.

3. An individual responds to new experiences in terms of prior experiences and in relation to his needs and interests as he sees them. Therefore, to be effective, a message must be expressed in approximately the same language used by its recipients and must not conflict too much with their previous experience. A student who has always "gotten by" with minimum effort will not be particularly receptive to warnings that he will have to work harder in college, particularly if he is able to "get by" the first few weeks in the fall with minimum effort.

4. All individuals have certain basic needs. The most effective message will be one which appeals to such needs and arouses a drive within the individual to satisfy his needs by taking action. The fear of failure is one of the most common appeals used in higher education. However, research has demonstrated the much greater effectiveness of appeals to status, self-fulfillment, and personal worth.

5. Individuals respond to most stimuli in a group context and, therefore, group approval and sanction is significant and important to the individual in determining the nature of his response. For this reason the current trend to use student leaders and to divide new students into groups for orientation purposes is sound in many ways. However, the influence of these groups, as well as that of the more permanent and pervasive

groups on the campus, must be examined and carefully considered in designing the orientation program. By careful planning, the positive force of these groups can be utilized and their negative influence neutralized.

6. The follow-up to the formal orientation program is of great importance to the effective transmission of any significant understanding of college. The natural follow-up will be by professors in the opening stages of their classes and by programs in student residences.

The transition from school to college is a confusing and often traumatic experience for many students. Despite the increasing awareness of higher education of all segments of our population, there still exists a lot of misleading folklore. The orientation program should begin with the first contact a college has with a prospective student and extend to his experience in the classroom.

Such a program performs a significant and needed function in all institutions of higher learning, but it should be based on specific institutional characteristics and the needs of particular student bodies. Properly planned and administered, the orientation program will prevent student alienation and failure as well as save the institution many hours of staff time.

RECOMMENDED ADDITIONAL READINGS

Brown, Nicholas C.: *Orientation to College Learning—A Reappraisal,* American Council on Education, Washington, 1961.

Freedman, Mervin B.: *The College Experience,* Jossey-Bass, San Francisco, 1967.

Havice, Charles W. (ed.): *Campus Values—Some Considerations for Collegians,* Charles Scribner's Sons, New York, 1968.

Libaw, Frieda B., and William D. Martinson: *Success in College,* 2d ed., Scott, Foresman and Company, Chicago, 1967.

Mueller, Kate H.: *Student Personnel Work in Higher Education,* Houghton Mifflin Company, Boston, 1961.

Rivlin, Harry N. et al., (eds.): *The First Years in College,* Little, Brown and Company, Boston, 1965.

Shaffer, Robert H., and William D. Martinson: *Student Personnel Services in Higher Education,* The Center for Applied Research in Education, New York, 1966.

Yamamoto, Kaoru (ed.): *The College Student and His Culture: An Analysis,* Houghton Mifflin Company, Boston, 1968.

Chapter **8**

Counseling and Testing

GEORGE W. YOUNG *

Dean of Student Affairs, Broward Junior College, Fort Lauderdale, Florida

* George Young was formerly Director of the University Counseling Center, Florida State University, Tallahassee, Florida.

THE OBJECTIVES OF COUNSELING

The principal objectives of counseling are (*a*) to aid the student in making decisions either about career choice, choice of an educational program, or other important matters; (*b*) to enable the student to be more effective in his relationships with other people; (*c*) to assist him in gaining self-understanding and acceptance; (*d*) to help him improve his skills in academic and social matters; and (*e*) to provide support for the student during an emotional crisis.

SCOPE OF SERVICES

Kinds of Students Served

An adequate counseling agency must provide services for all students. It must be able to deal with all types of students bringing to the campus scene a wide variety of socioeconomic, ethnic, educational, religious, and cultural backgrounds. With ever-increasing numbers of students coming from culturally deprived backgrounds, it is vital that counselors be available who are sensitive to the special problems experienced by such students.

Other Kinds of Clients

Students, of course, constitute the main concern of the counseling staff; but why not provide counseling services to the faculty and staff as well as the community at large? The answer to this question is not easily provided, for an institution (public or private) must decide whether or not it wants to offer services to its own employees and to the general public. If it answers affirmatively, it must then decide whether the costs of such services are to be subsidized either partially or totally by the institution.

Present practice in this area is mixed. Albert, in a study of nearly four hundred senior colleges and universities in the United States, found that slightly more than one-fourth of the institutions sampled reported that their services were not available to nonstudents. Of the remaining three-quarters, whose services *were* available to nonstudents, slightly more than half reported that they charged for all or part of the services to nonstudents.[1]

Of the 83 college counseling centers listed in the 1967–1968 Directory of Approved Counseling Centers, 72 stated that they accepted nonstudents as clients.[2] (It is probable that the agencies who seek accreditation are more likely to take persons outside their institutions as clients.) In many instances, however, these agencies note that their outside work is done on a limited basis or that their students' needs come first.

Some college counseling centers operate on a contract basis with the Veterans Ad-

[1] Gerald Albert, "A Survey of College Counseling Facilities," *Personnel and Guidance Journal*, vol. 46, p. 542, 1968.

[2] American Board on Counseling Services, Inc., *Directory of Approved Counseling Agencies*, American Personnel and Guidance Association, Washington, 1967.

ministration to provide vocational-educational counseling to war orphans and to veterans. The institution is paid a fixed fee per client which is based on the actual cost of providing such service.

Kinds of Counseling Offered

It is also possible to describe the scope of counseling services at any institution in terms of the various kinds of counseling offered. Two of the most frequent areas center around educational-vocational topics and personal adjustment problems. In some institutions there may be a vocational counseling center which deals with the former type of concern and a separate psychological clinic which aids students with adjustment and personality problems. In other universities, one agency may deal with both kinds of problems.

Improvement of reading and of study skills is another area which is a primary concern of some counseling centers, whereas in other institutions it may be dealt with by a separate agency.

Counseling with small groups of students on social, educational, or emotional problems is frequently done. A survey of 95 college counseling centers indicated that two-thirds of them had run one or more such groups during the year 1966–1967.[3]

Another facet of counseling, termed "disciplinary," has also been described.[4] Student offenders against institutional rules are treated not as criminals (and subjected to student-faculty courts and committees) but as erring members of the educational community. Since the institution's reaction to the offender must be essentially educational, he must be treated by a person whose role is primarily rehabilitative and not punitive. This counselor is most often administratively attached to the dean of students' office. In any case, in this writer's opinion, he should not be attached in any formal way to the counseling center. The reason for this is that even though the disciplinary counselor sees himself as a counselor, many students will view him as a quasi dean of men, and running the risk of generalizing this percept to the counseling agency is too great.

No listing would be complete without mentioning religious counseling, which is frequently done by campus ministers, university chaplains, and local pastors of various denominations. The counseling agency can be useful by serving as a clearinghouse and general support agency for pastoral counselors.

Consultation Services

The counseling agency may provide consultation to the faculty, administrators, residence hall counselors, and student groups. This assistance might include such services as a group discussion with freshmen on adjustment to college life, a conference with a dormitory counselor on how to encourage a student to seek professional help with his problems, and a talk with the admissions staff on the validity and reliability of test scores.

Testing Services

Since the information gained from psychological tests can often be a valuable aid in counseling, it is typical to find testing as one of the basic functions of a counseling agency. In some institutions, however, testing may be set up as an administratively separate department.

Nearly all tests fall into one of the four following general areas: tests of ability or aptitude, measures of achievement, interest inventories, and personality (or adjust-

[3] American College Personnel Association Data Bank, 1967.

[4] Ernest Koch, "Disciplinary Counseling," in Max Siegel (ed.), *The Counseling of College Students*, The Free Press of Glencoe, New York, 1968. E. G. Williamson and J. D. Foley, *Counseling and Discipline*, McGraw-Hill Book Company, New York, 1949.

ment) measures. Tests can also be classified as to whether they are "pencil and paper," in which case they can be administered and scored by a person without highly specialized training, or whether they are individually administered tests of intelligence or personality which call for specific graduate training in the use of such measures. In some counseling agencies the psychometrist may be qualified to administer individual intelligence tests as well as the pencil-and-paper tests. In other settings, the individual tests may be administered by the counselor who wishes to use them.

The counseling agency may also have the responsibility for the administration of national testing programs (e.g., The American College Testing Program, The College Entrance Examination Board tests, etc.).

Career and Educational Information

Another important service of a counseling agency is to provide information about other colleges, graduate and professional schools, careers, leadership, mobility, social issues, adolescent behavior, and the like. While it is true that counselors possess much information on these and related problems, it is important to recognize that no one counselor is able to retain anything but a small fraction of available information. For this reason counseling agencies should have developed sources of information accessible to students as well as counselors.

Information on the kinds of available materials can be obtained in several ways. Current occupational literature is listed in the *Vocational Guidance Quarterly*,[5] and these references are compiled periodically in the *NVGA Bibliography of Current Occupational Literature*.[6] The Superintendent of Documents publishes a biweekly listing of selected U.S. government publications, some of which are relevant to a college information center, and it also periodically publishes price lists of available materials on occupations[7] and on education.[8] Two valuable though somewhat dated annotated bibliographies are Klein's *Guide to American Educational Directories*[9] and Forrester's *Occupational Literature*.[10]

Other sources of information on careers are professional associations, state employment services, and private industry.

The most basic reference on occupations is the *Occupational Outlook Handbook*, a compendium and analysis of over 600 occupations, published biennially by the U.S. Department of Labor.[11] Another comprehensive guide is the recent *Encyclopedia of Careers and Vocational Guidance*.[12] Monthly subscription services of current occupational literature are also available.[13]

Caution should be taken that all materials used meet the standards set up by the National Vocational Guidance Association.[14]

[5] National Vocational Guidance Association, *The Vocational Guidance Quarterly*, Washington.

[6] National Vocational Guidance Association, *NVGA Bibliography of Current Occupational Literature, 1966 Edition*, Washington.

[7] *Occupations, Professions and Job Descriptions*, price list 33A, Superintendent of Documents, U.S. Government Printing Office, September, 1967.

[8] *Education*, price list 31, Superintendent of Documents, U.S. Government Printing Office, June, 1968.

[9] Bernard Klein, *Guide to American Educational Directories* (2d ed.), McGraw-Hill Book Company, New York, 1965.

[10] Gertrude Forrester, *Occupational Literature*, The H. W. Wilson Company, New York, 1964.

[11] *Occupational Outlook Handbook*, U.S. Department of Labor.

[12] W. E. Hopke (ed.), *The Encyclopedia of Careers and Vocational Guidance*, Doubleday & Company, Inc., Garden City, N.Y., 1967.

[13] Science Research Associates, Chicago.
Careers, Largo, Fla.
Chronicle Guidance Monographs, Moravia, N.Y.

[14] National Vocational Guidance Association, "Standards for Use in Preparing and Evaluating Occupational Literature."

A counseling service should have a designated area, comfortably furnished, to serve as a repository or browsing library for students interested in securing occupational information. Institutions should make provision for a check-out procedure which enables students to peruse materials in the comfort of their apartments, residence halls, or homes.[15]

Another desirable quality of any informational system is accessibility, which depends upon a definitive topical index to permit students to locate information quickly and efficiently.

There should also be a reference library for counselor use which will contain books, tapes, and other materials to foster their professional development.[16]

The cost of informational systems ranges from a few hundred to several thousand dollars a year depending on the number of students to be served and the comprehensiveness of the system. Cost should be treated as a general expense item equal in importance to the testing program and counselors' salaries.

Research

Counseling agencies vary widely concerning research activities. Some may do very little and devote almost their entire emphasis to service functions. Others may have a very active research program which might include follow-up of clients, validation of psychological tests, and the study of the effectiveness of various counseling procedures, to mention but a few. Individuals involved with research should be given active support through such means as reduced caseloads and clerical services.

Training Functions

One of the important functions of the counseling agency is to serve as a training laboratory for graduate students preparing to enter the counseling profession. At many universities it is common practice for these graduate students to participate in practicum or intern situations supervised by the professional counseling staff.[17] To be sure, a few counseling centers view these arrangements as providing additional work for their staffs which, they feel, should be reflected in their budgets. The more common view about these counseling practicum students is that they actually provide an expanded counseling staff and thereby increase the service to students. This writer holds a third view, closely related to the "expanded counseling staff" idea. It seems that too often institutions, having developed highly effective practicum programs, tend to rely on these programs to the extent of sometimes failing to provide adequate, full-time, professionally competent counselors to work with students. The comment has often been heard from students when asked about their perception of the counseling bureau, "Well . . . I didn't get to see a counselor, just a graduate student." This is not to deny or even question the need for counselor intern and practicum experiences for graduate students who will soon be professional counselors. It simply is intended to serve as a caution to administrators to consider carefully, with the preparation of each budget, the ratio of full-time professional staff to graduate students and to avoid the "graduate-students-are-cheaper" doctrine.

A survey of 40 institutions in 1965 indicated that 80 percent of them used graduate students in their counseling centers.[18] These students provided the equivalent of a 30 percent increase in counseling-staff time. Supervision of the graduate student

[15] Willa Norris, F. R. Zeran, and R. N. Hatch, *The Information Service in Guidance*, Rand McNally & Company, Chicago, 1960.

[16] *Ibid.*, pp. 370–371.

[17] Albert S. Thompson and Donald E. Super (eds.), *The Professional Preparation of Counseling Psychologists*, Teachers College Press, Columbia U., New York, 1964, pp. 140–150.

[18] Stanley B. Escott, "Expanding Counseling Services Through Graduate Student Utilization," *Counselor Education and Supervision*, vol. 7, pp. 36–41, Fall, 1967.

counselors was done in 97 percent of the institutions. In counseling, as in all of higher education, one receives what one is able to pay for.

THE ORGANIZATION AND STRUCTURE OF COUNSELING SERVICES

In one recent study of 700 institutions of higher learning, over 99 percent reported that counseling as a discrete administrative function existed at their institutions.[19] However, another study of 415 institutions revealed that only 71 percent had organized student counseling facilities.[20] As this discrepancy indicates, the form of counseling services in colleges and universities is indeed varied. At many institutions counseling services are centralized in one administrative unit which is under the general direction of the dean of students or his counterpart. At other institutions the counseling service is diffuse and somewhat undefined in terms of administrative structure. Some of these institutions view counseling as part of a fabric intrinsic to the teaching function and therefore inseparable from it. College faculty serve as counselors (as well as academic advisers), and residence halls are staffed with counseling-oriented personnel.

Whether or not the institution has a highly developed counseling center, psychological clinic, or center for student development or whether it has a decentralized system of counseling-oriented faculty and staff seems to be dependent upon several factors. The first factor seems to revolve around enrollment, size of the on-campus student body, and the degree to which the institution is able to obtain funds for each service. In smaller institutions, where operating budgets are relatively small, the decentralized counseling service seems to be the usual arrangement. In larger institutions with infinitely larger educational and general budgets, the centralized counseling service is more likely to be the rule.

Clearly, counseling is viewed as one of the most important functions of the student personnel area of college and university administration. This is not to suggest or imply, however, that counseling is somehow "owned" by the student personnel practitioners on campus, for, quite to the contrary, the faculty should be (and often are) involved in certain kinds of student counseling, particularly as they relate to the educational problems of students. The primary responsibility for the organization, administration, and coordination of counseling should, however, rest with the specialized counseling staff of the student personnel department or division.[21]

The responsibility for counseling is delegated to a director of counseling in about half of the institutions reported in the U.S. Office of Education survey.[22] When enrollment is considered, it is evident that in institutions with enrollments over 2,500, the director of counseling reports to the chief student services officer; while in those institutions whose enrollments are under 2,500 students, the director of counseling most often is directly responsible to the president. It may be that in smaller institutions, the director of counseling serves in a quasi chief-student-services-officer position, reporting to the president. In larger situations the counseling service is considerably more specialized and requires a specialized director of counseling.

The foregoing characteristics of counseling responsibility seem to apply generally regardless of type and size of institution and irrespective of whether control is public or private.[23]

[19] Archie R. Ayers, Phillip A. Tripp, and John H. Russel, *Student Services Administration in Higher Education,* Bulletin no. 16, U.S. Government Printing Office, 1966, p. 112.

[20] Gerald Albert, "A Survey of College Counseling Facilities," *Personnel and Guidance Journal,* vol. 46, p. 540, 1968.

[21] Robert H. Shaffer and William D. Martinson, *Student Personnel Services in Higher Education,* The Center for Applied Research in Education, Inc., New York, 1966, p. 36.

[22] Ayers, Tripp, Russel, *loc. cit.*

[23] *Ibid.*

The Formulation of Counseling Policy

As might be expected, the formulation of policy for counseling services is most likely to be the responsibility of the dean of students or director of counseling, regardless of type of institution, size of enrollment, or control (public or private). These facts strongly suggest that counseling policy is most often considered to be a discrete function of professionally prepared student personnel administrators and counselors. It cannot be overemphasized, however, that counseling should have a close relationship to general academic and educational objectives as well as to the faculty. A counseling service administered and operated without faculty support and, more importantly, faculty participation in the formulation of policy runs the risk of alienation and isolation. Several institutions involve faculty in policy development through ad hoc faculty committees. A counseling center director who sidesteps faculty involvement because it is "too time-consuming" or because faculty frequently have little professional preparation and understanding of counseling is guilty of not capitalizing on valuable resources. Faculty frequently have different and valuable perceptions about the general campus climate as well as new ideas for "reaching" students with problems. In this writer's experience, one of the best ideas for reaching into certain problem groups on a campus (a plan which involved specific types of information placed in the student newspaper) came from an interested faculty member. In addition to faculty participation in policy development, it is important to recognize the significance of the participation of other administrative department heads such as the financial aid director, director of placement, director of admissions, and others concerned about the services for students. With the current press for student involvement in administrative decisions, it may be desirable to seek suggestions from students about both procedural and policy matters.

Line and Staff Organization

The counseling-service staff is generally organized on a line just below the director of counseling or, in some cases, the dean of students. In larger institutions an intermediate level exists between the counselors and the director of counseling. This position, most frequently that of an assistant or associate director, is usually assigned specific areas of responsibility such as in-service training, direction of internship programs, or research. In smaller institutions these functions, if not performed by the director of counseling, are typically assigned to various counselors. Assignments of this nature are most often made so as to be congruent with the counselor's particular type of training, background, and interests.

In those institutions not large enough to justify a director of counseling, the counselor(s) usually report directly to the dean of students or his equivalent.

Job Descriptions of Staff Members

Written job descriptions are becoming a necessity in the administration of all student personnel services. They become increasingly important as institutions grow and administrative and budgetary responsibility is stretched through several offices. Provision should be made each year for each staff member to review and revise his or her job description. The director of counseling or the dean of students should assume the responsibility for the construction and modification of job descriptions and, by paying particular attention to the accuracy of each one, ensure that counseling staff do not leave out such important functions as committee assignments, research, and consultation with other staff and faculty.

Relationships with Other Agencies

The nature of the organization and structure of the counseling service will, in large measure, determine the relationships which exist with other agencies both on and off the campus. For example, in those institutions which place counseling in a student affairs office, cooperative associations with other departmental units in student affairs are administratively facilitated.

For a counseling service to be maximally effective, however, cooperative ties must exist with all on-campus units to or from which students may be referred. This would include the campus health service, the reading improvement center, the speech and hearing clinic, the psychological clinic, the placement office, the financial aid office, the student activities office, etc.

It is also highly desirable that the counseling agency have some existing structure for communication with and for referral to off-campus resources such as local clergy, mental health clinics, private therapists, employment services, and vocational rehabilitation offices.

It is highly desirable to experience face-to-face contact between staff members in different agencies in order to establish both knowledge of and trust in the others' services. Information gathered about the client by the referring agency may be transmitted to the referral agency, provided the written consent of the client is obtained.

GENERAL OPERATING PROCEDURES

To ensure that staff time is effectively utilized, carefully developed operating procedures must be an integral part of the counseling process.

Personalized Attention

Beginning with the client's first association with the counseling service, all procedures should be directed toward making him feel as comfortable as possible. Naturally, intake and referral procedures should therefore be as simple as possible—requiring only those "red tape" procedures that are absolutely essential. Many counseling services recognize the importance of simplicity, particularly during intake or initial visits of counselees, and a friendly secretary offers a cup of coffee in a casual, informal setting in order to ensure the counselee's security in the reception area of the counseling bureau. At the same time certain biographical information can be obtained about the client in the same relaxed manner and atmosphere. Lengthy biographical questionnaires should be, as a rule, avoided during the client's first contact with the counseling service.

Procedures should be geared to secure *essential* information for the counseling staff. The important role of secretaries and other support personnel cannot be overemphasized, and counseling staff should be constantly attuned to the impressions their clients have of the reception-intake staff. A hostile secretary can do serious, irreparable damage to a counseling center's image and overall effectiveness.

Prospective clients contact the counseling agency in various ways ranging from the popular telephone call requesting help to simply walking in unannounced and unexpected. It is therefore most important that intake procedures be simple and flexible as well. It is a simple matter to schedule an appointment by telephone but considerably more difficult to provide a counselor on demand to "walk-ins." However, due to the very impulsive nature of some walk-in clients, it is essential to provide a counselor as soon as possible. The general practice of most counseling agencies is to provide counseling as soon as possible depending upon staff availability and the immediate needs of the client.

In some centers the client's first contact is with the secretary who books an appointment with whichever counselor is available. In other agencies a trained counselor is on duty to conduct a short intake interview with the client when he first appears. The intake counselor then decides how soon the client should have his first regular interview and to which counselor he should be assigned. In some instances the intake counselor may refer the student to another service which will better serve his needs.

The important principle is to treat each counselee in such a way as to facilitate counseling. For most counselees the helpful, confidential, accepting manner of the counselor and counseling staff is most appropriate. Unusual exceptions do occur, such as the young woman who refused to use the front door of the counseling center for fear her sorority sisters would "find her out." After several sessions with her counselor, however, she finally acquiesced to a frontal assault of the front door.

Caseloads

Perhaps one of the most overlooked considerations of counseling procedure is the daily work load or caseload of each counselor. It is not possible to state a specific caseload for counselors, but the caseload per counselor should be flexible in order to permit professional development, record-keeping, staff development, research, and other professional activity associated with the counseling agency or the institution. Naturally, the length of counseling sessions, which normally range from thirty minutes to one hour, should in no case be decreased in order to increase caseload.

Testing

Testing programs of a quality nature naturally require appropriate financing. The acquisition, administration, and scoring of standardized tests ranges from $1 for the less expensive interest inventories, which many students find invaluable in discussing their future careers, to $25 and up for specialized tests of intelligence and achievement and in-depth personality assessments. A counselor, of course, is most often free to select any number of tests for his clients depending upon his ability to understand and utilize the data provided and the general needs of the client.

Counseling agencies vary in their approach to the financing of testing programs. Some, of course, are able to budget the entire cost of the testing program as a necessary part of the counseling program. A few agencies charge their counselees the full cost of all tests, and others charge a nominal amount (usually for scoring which has to be done by outside agencies). The most desirable arrangement seems to be the first, for many students do not have the economic resources to enable them to pay for extensive testing and therefore are reluctant to seek counseling. Another reason for not charging test fees is that such a practice usually involves considerable bookkeeping effort which ties up staff and may actually increase the cost of operating the counseling service.

Several possibilities exist for reducing the cost of testing programs. The most obvious one, particularly to budget officers, would seem to be to limit the number of tests given to students. While this suggestion may seem to infringe upon the professional prerogative of counselors, it has been the experience of this writer that counselors are sometimes guilty of indiscriminate and injudicious use of tests. Counseling administrators must therefore be alert and question any practice which seems arbitrary or philosophically unsound. Particular attention should be given to lengthy batteries of diagnostic tests given to all incoming counselees before they have had initial interviews. (There is also the possibility of making excessive demands on the students' time, which is often at a premium.)

A second possibility exists for reducing the cost of testing programs. It is becoming increasingly attractive to utilize scoring equipment either in conjunction with institutional computing facilities or large firms which specialize in scoring tests. Several of these national scoring organizations offer fast, efficient, and economical services to colleges and universities, thereby permitting support personnel to concentrate their efforts on other services within the counseling agency. A few companies even offer more information than many institutions can obtain locally. For example, one outside agency can score a well-known personality inventory, plot a profile of the client's personality characteristics, and provide a narrative description. The latter has previously been available only to those diligent counselors willing to spend time searching reference material. The computer provides this information in a matter of a few milliseconds and obviously at a reduction in cost.

Counseling agencies may also assist other institutional agencies in testing. For example, they frequently cooperate in the evaluation of prospective secretaries and clerical workers by administering typing and shorthand tests. They may give tests to certain applicants for admission and, in addition, they are frequently called on to work with various academic departments in administering advanced placement examinations. When test-scoring equipment is available, the counseling center may serve as a general institutional test-scoring service.

Many large institutions, having anticipated the rising popularity of machine-scored tests, have established separate agencies whose principal function is to score objective tests for faculty and also to provide them with data for the construction of institutional norms. Counseling agencies are beginning to recognize the desirability of using these newer agencies to assist in the scoring of their own tests.

A last point to be mentioned is that university testing agencies frequently enter into desirable contractual agreements with private agencies similar to, and in some cases including, the contractual counseling services mentioned earlier in the chapter.

Counseling Records

The primary purpose of keeping counseling records is to collect information in a systematic fashion so that the needs of clients will best be served. A secondary but also important function is to provide statistics about the overall volume and scope of the counseling center's operation.

Although each institution has its own specific forms, the contents of the client's folder typically include personal data sheets, interview summaries, test results (including answer sheets and profiles), notations about referrals or other specific action taken, and any correspondence pertaining to the client. One basic guideline to follow concerning individual client records is that they should reflect enough about what has transpired so that a new counselor could pick up the case and continue with a minimum of delay and confusion.

Summary statistics, which are usually compiled annually, vary from one institution to another. Some of the more meaningful data are the total number of clients dealt with, the total number of interviews held, the different types of problems dealt with, the number of referrals made to other agencies, and the number of clients coming to the counseling center as a result of specific referral. If desired, more detailed breakdowns can be made; e.g., number of males and females, number of fee clients, number of residential students seen, numbers of students from the different divisions or colleges within the university. By comparing proportions of clients seen in the counseling center with proportions in the university population, it is possible to see if all segments of the population are being served equally.

No one should have access to counseling information about a student without the student's written consent. Quite apart from possible legal liability in cases of improper disclosure, no counseling relationship can be said to truly exist unless confidentiality is guaranteed by policy and practice. The conditions of legal liability and privileged communication vary from state to state,[24] and it is suggested that counseling administrators, deans of students, and even college and university presidents secure expert legal opinion in this complex matter. The writer would go a step further in suggesting, also as a general practice, that only information essential to the counsel-

[24] Clarence J. Bakken, *The Legal Basis for College Student Personnel Work*, American College Personnel Association, Washington, 1961, pp. 26–30.

ing relationship, such as test scores, biographical data, and the like be kept on file. Other personal information of a potentially embarrassing character should be periodically reviewed and destroyed, particularly if counselors do not enjoy privileged communication in the legal sense.

The importance of adequate security and protection for counseling records cannot be overstressed, for there are many cases on record wherein a student's future was seriously jeopardized by the release—to unauthorized persons and without the student's consent—of records containing information obtained in a confidential counseling setting. Counseling records should be kept apart from all other institutional data and under the custody of the counseling agency head. References on the subjects of confidentiality and student counseling records are included in the list of selected readings.

Hours of Operation

The most prevalent pattern of counseling-agency hours of operation is the typical eight-to-five pattern found in most college and university administrative offices. Although this pattern seems adequate for many students' problems, it does not take into account the crisis nature of some problems which do not respect the eight-to-five pattern. In recognition of this, counseling centers should, if at all possible, provide evening services to those students caught in crises and those whose class schedules or employment commitments make it difficult to secure counseling during the normal eight-hour workday. Several counseling centers, notably at the larger institutions, have developed late-hour and weekend programs by, for example, employing graduate-student counselors. Students at the University of Texas (Austin campus) are now able to secure help with personal and academic problems by telephone. A staff of five counselors provides confidential counseling to increasing numbers of students by telephone, which is but one indication of the need for easily accessible counseling.[25]

PHYSICAL FACILITIES

One of the most important requisites of physical facilities is that they provide privacy, so that the client will feel free to discuss his problems without fear that someone will overhear. This means providing a relatively soundproof office for each counselor. If the counseling agency is closely identified as the place where people with emotional problems go, then it is advisable that it not be located in a prominent spot where many passers-by would see clients entering and leaving.

There needs to be a reception area where students may wait for their appointments. It is desirable for this to be near the reference room, so that the student who may have a considerable wait may spend time looking at information on careers or other useful materials if he so desires. The reference room itself should be comfortable, well-lighted, and set up so that it is conducive to browsing.

The testing room should be spacious enough so that students are not crowded. Here the point is less likely to be avoidance of cheating (since usually the student is motivated to do his own work when taking tests for counseling purposes) as it is to avoid distractions and to prevent students from being self-conscious about their answers on personality inventories.

It is very desirable to have a conference room where staff meetings and group counseling can take place.

Additional offices must be available if the counseling agency is used as a training

[25] "Telephone Counseling at Austin Campus," *American School and University*, vol. 40, p. 68, September, 1967.

center, in order to provide space for practicum and intern students. These quarters should be comparable in quality to those of full-time staff members.

It is essential that locked files be provided for the safekeeping of all client records to prevent data from reaching unauthorized hands.

PERSONNEL POLICIES

Although written policies are a decided advantage, many institutions continue to operate with ill-defined personnel policies which depend in large measure on the management style of the chief administrator. Institutions often have definitive policies for subprofessional or support personnel, but their published policies frequently say little about the recruitment, hiring, promotion, and termination of counselors and counseling directors.

The following sections are offered only as general guidelines, with the understanding that institutions must establish uniquely distinctive personnel policies.

Salary Schedule

The problems intrinsic to an intelligent discussion of personnel policies are amplified to a great extent in attempts to discuss salaries.

As a foundation for the discussion it ought to be clear that counseling staff should be treated equitably in salary matters. Their specialized training has required the same kind of sacrifice and hardship that most teaching faculty have encountered, and it is therefore to be expected that salaries would be roughly comparable. Of course, counseling positions are more likely to be administrative, 12-month positions and hence adjustment must be made for the discrepancy existing between 9- or 10-month teaching faculty and 12-month counseling-staff members.

In actual practice, however, the marketplace is likely to be the final determinant in salary matters—just as it is in faculty recruitment—so a discussion of current salary levels seems to be relevant. In a 1964 study of counseling administrators' salaries, the U.S. Office of Education found that the median salary of counseling directors ranged from a low of $9,000 to $10,000 at institutions with enrollments less than 1,000 to $13,000 to $14,000 at institutions with more than 10,000 students.[26]

The American College Personnel Association 1967 Data Bank previously referred to showed a range of 93 counseling-center directors' salaries from $9,500 to $24,000, with a median in the $14,500 to $14,900 bracket. Directors' salaries in larger institutions had a median of $1,500 greater than those in smaller institutions. The same survey showed that the range of salaries for counselors holding the doctorate and having four years' experience was from $9,500 to $16,900. The median of $12,000 to $12,400 was the same for both the larger and smaller institutions.

As might be expected, salaries vary according to the geographic location of the institution, but not in a strictly predictable fashion.

A number of institutions, particularly those which are publicly supported and coordinated by boards of regents or control, have devised published salary schedules for counselors and counseling administrators which take into account such factors as the extent of graduate preparation and the number of years' experience in counseling-related positions.

Recruitment

The recruitment of counseling personnel is not at all unlike the recruitment of teaching faculty. Once a vacancy occurs, the agency head begins communicating with

[26] E. R. Oetting, *Problems and Issues in the Administration of College and University Counseling Services*, ERIC Report ED 010 553, U.S. Office of Education (undated).

colleagues at other institutions about possible contact with prospective counselors. Of course he may also elect to wait until the annual meetings of the American Personnel and Guidance Association, The American Psychological Association, The National Association of Student Personnel Administrators, or The National Association of Women Deans and Counselors. These associations represent the bulk of counseling personnel in the United States and offer efficient, inexpensive placement services. Any member may notify these placement services of his institution's openings and be assured of making contact with several qualified applicants. Applicants range from young, inexperienced graduate students just about to complete degree requirements to experienced holders of the doctorate with impressive pedigrees. Placement bulletins published by both national and regional professional associations are often used to bring the job seeker and the prospective employer into contact.

The institutional recruiter should possess all relevant information including a description of the position, salary range, qualifications, and general information about the institution as well. It is highly desirable for the recruiter to be the person empowered to fill the open position.

Hiring

Four criteria should be employed in hiring counselors:

1. The applicant should possess at least a master's degree in the behavioral or social sciences with some specialization in counseling.
2. The applicant's training should include a period of supervised counseling during training.
3. The applicant's personality and general attitude should be compatible with those with whom he or she is to be associated.
4. The applicant must demonstrate a sincere interest in students.

Faculty Rank and Tenure

The assignment of faculty rank to counseling staff would seem to be appropriate if the counseling program is seen as an integral part of the academic climate and program. If counselors are to serve as resource personnel to teaching faculty working in a professional manner on problems of mutual concern, then the assignment of faculty rank would tend to facilitate communication and mutual respect.

If the rank is nondepartmental in nature, for example, counselor–assistant professor, no association with a particular academic department is necessary. If, however, the rank is assigned by an academic department, for example, counselor and assistant professor of education, then the expectation exists that the counselor is to be an active member of the department, teaching occasionally, attending departmental meetings, and the like.

Tenure for nonteaching professional personnel is discussed in Chapter 4, Section 6. The question of whether or not to grant tenure to counseling staff is an extremely delicate and complex one. Academic tenure involves academic freedom and other important questions as well. It has been suggested that a new concept of tenure be developed for student personnel workers.[27] This writer is not certain of the validity of tenure for nonteaching professionals, particularly administrators.

Fringe Benefits and Vacation Schedules

An institution of higher learning, because of its special place in society and due to characteristics unique to its operation, is able to offer many fringe benefits to employees. Such benefits are attractive to prospective counseling-staff members and also

[27] J. Martin Klotche and William R. Butler, "Should Student Personnel Administrators be Given Tenure?" *Journal of College Student Personnel*, vol. 8, pp. 225–230, July, 1967.

help to maintain turnover at low levels. Benefits range from participatory retirement plans, group insurance (including health, life, and major medical), credit unions, and tax-deferred annuity plans to special discounts on tickets to athletic and cultural affairs and occasional, unscheduled time off between terms and during holiday periods. All of these and others serve as attractive inducements to teaching faculty and, in most instances, to counseling staff as well. The general effect of these fringe benefits is to boost morale and thereby help ensure the overall effectiveness of the counseling program. (A further discussion of compensation and fringe benefits may be found in Chapters 6 and 7, Section 8, of the companion volume.)

Vacations present a slightly different morale boost for counseling staff. In dealing with several students a day, many of whom may be experiencing some degree of emotional or psychological disturbance, a counselor must concentrate continuously on each student and his particular personality. Counseling involves intense and perceptive intellectual work, and the counselor must do it over a protracted period of time. Counseling also requires a depth of understanding which is not easily obtained. Although experienced counselors do not become subjectively involved in the personal affairs of their clients, nevertheless most counselors experience a kind of total intellectual fatigue after a steady diet of this intense work. Consequently a paid, scheduled vacation of not less than two weeks and preferably four is an absolute necessity for the counselor and, incidentally, his family, which also shares in his fatigue.

Larger institutions have a distinct advantage in scheduling vacations because they have larger counseling staffs. This makes it possible to ensure that the normal operation of the counseling center is not impaired. In smaller colleges, where counseling is done by a small group of individuals (frequently only one), vacations must be scheduled during times of least student demand.

Irrespective of the size of the institution, however, the importance of a vacation cannot be overstressed.

FINANCIAL FACTORS

Financial support for counseling agencies comes essentially from two sources in addition to the contracts discussed earlier in this chapter. The first and major source of funds is the institutional budget. Many colleges have devised budgeting systems based on functions which, when analyzed, yield major areas such as instructional, administrative, maintenance and plant operations, and auxiliary enterprises. Counseling is frequently funded through the administrative area and the student affairs office. Counseling is therefore placed in a position which requires its constant competition with other student personnel functions, thereby ensuring a balance of the functions contained within the student affairs area.

Funds provided in this manner are typically earmarked for salaries, general expenses (including office supplies, telephone, informational materials, and test supplies), travel, and capital equipment (which may or may not include book purchases). A balanced budget does *not* mean that a counseling agency has no deficit at the end of the fiscal year. What it does mean is that each of these budgetary divisions is adequately funded and contributes a fair share to the total expenses of the agency. The budget is seen as a dynamically balanced system which is flexible to the point of permitting modest adjustments throughout the fiscal year as various changing needs arise. A rigid budget not only encourages wasteful spending in areas of surplus funds but it reduces the effectiveness of the overall counseling operation. Of course, the major responsibility for budget preparation and modification should fall principally on the administrator in charge of counseling.

Funds are also derived from fees charged to clients for all or part of the counseling service rendered. Many institutions charge a general activities fee, part of which is used to defray some of the counseling costs. Others charge an additional fee for testing and for counseling in order to ensure responsible use of counseling and also to defray costs. Of the 83 approved counseling centers previously mentioned, 22 either stated or implied that students were assessed fees for services. The range of such fees was from $2 to $50. One writer points out the value of this practice and suggests that counseling agencies follow the practice of family agencies which scale fees to clients based on their ability to pay.[28]

In considering whether a nominal fee interferes with or affects the testing process, Thompson and Handy found that a $5 fee for testing did not significantly affect the process.[29]

The question of whether to charge for counseling and whether accessibility of counseling to economically deprived students would be attenuated has not been definitively or empirically answered. The recommended practice is for colleges and universities to continue to assume full financial obligation for the counseling program.

PUBLICITY

Any counseling agency must have a vehicle for communicating the availability of services to prospective clients. Students themselves serve this function quite well. The student grapevine, as it is sometimes called, is most effective in transmitting information. It must be recognized however, that in such an information system input rarely equals output; i.e., gross distortions of fact occur frequently. Other media must be employed if the counseling agency is to place accurate information about its services in the hands of students. One of the most common and effective means of accomplishing this is the use of attractively designed brochures. A recent, well-controlled study demonstrated the effect of counseling-center brochures. Students receiving counseling-center brochures after eight weeks of campus life responded in significantly larger numbers than those students who received no information.[30]

A word of caution must be expressed at this point about professional versus commercial standards in preparing brochures. The brochure should be dignified, avoiding promises of "results" or offers of low-cost testing. It might well contain descriptions of the types of problems handled by the staff, a statement about the confidentiality of interviews, an outline of procedures for making appointments, and a description of the location of the center—a campus map might be included.

Other types of publicity which have been used effectively are statements in college catalogues, student handbooks, and other appropriate publications about the counseling services. An occasional feature article in the student newspaper is also worthwhile as long as professional standards are respected. Care must be taken that publicity via mass media does not cause such a sudden influx that the agency will be swamped.

STAFF DEVELOPMENT

In-service Training

A well-organized counseling staff is developed in several ways. In-service training for counselors provides a continuous opportunity for sharpening counseling skills and can be one of the most effective techniques for staff development. This technique involves case conferences and seminars, both of which provide opportunities for the

[28] John E. Reinhold, "College Mental Health Service: Fee or Free?" Paper read at American Personnel and Guidance Association, Washington, April, 1966.

[29] A. Thompson and L. C. Handy, "To Charge or Not: An Empirical Question," *Journal of Counseling Psychology*, vol. 14, pp. 358–360, July, 1967.

[30] Gordon S. Bigelow et al., "Impact of Counseling Center Brochures," *Journal of College Student Personnel*, vol. 9, p. 99, 1968.

presentation of new information as well as innovative counseling techniques which can be applied to particularly perplexing types of problems. Most valuable adjuncts to these techniques are observation facilities which permit counselors to be evaluated and constructively criticized by other professionals while they are under actual counseling conditions. Audio and video taping equipment also enables the counselor to become more perceptive of his own behavior and attitudes.

Formal Study

One of the best ways to improve the quality of a counseling agency's staff is by providing opportunities for staff members to participate in further graduate work. If the graduate program is located on the same campus, problems are frequently minimized inasmuch as staff members are able to complete a course or two each term until degree requirements have been met. On those campuses not fortunate enough to have an advanced graduate program in counseling, psychology, or some other appropriate area, the difficulty is far greater. Even though leaves of absence are frequently granted for advanced formal study, they are infrequently granted with full pay privileges. This means that the counselor must secure funds for tuition and living expenses—a process requiring personal savings, loans, assistantships, and fellowships. Many counselors assume large personal debts in securing advanced degrees (in some cases far out of proportion to the salaries they receive from their respective institutions). For this reason it is important that the institution offer assistance, in some form, to counselors returning to school. It is just as important for counselors receiving such assistance to agree to return to their institution for a specified period of time just as teaching faculty, who receive sabbaticals, are expected to return to their institutions for a specified number of years.

Professional Meetings and Conventions

Another source available for counseling-staff development lies in attendance at various regional and national professional meetings. The American Personnel and Guidance Association (APGA), to which all counselors should belong, meets annually during the spring. In addition, many states have branch organizations of APGA which hold meetings at various times of the year. Some counselors belong to the American Psychological Association (APA), particularly its Division of Counseling Psychology. APA meetings are held annually in late summer. There are also meetings of regional groups at various times of the year.

All of these meetings and conventions are planned for counselors by counselors in order to provide new and supplemental information about various aspects of counseling as a profession. Although it may not be financially feasible for all counseling-staff members from a particular institution to attend all such meetings, it is desirable for each counselor to attend one or two meetings a year. The cost for attending meetings and conventions should be anticipated each year as budgets are prepared so as to ensure maximum participation for the entire staff.

EVALUATION OF COUNSELING SERVICES

It has already been mentioned that the evaluation of a counselor's effectiveness is as difficult as evaluating the effectiveness of a teacher. The evaluation of the overall effectiveness of a counseling program is equally complex. The main difficulty lies in the identification of criteria which relate in a valid way to counseling effectiveness. With the understanding that we cannot accurately measure the effectiveness of counseling programs, a selected number of techniques for assessing general program effectiveness will be described.

First, of course, the general reputation of the counseling center among students and faculty provides some basis for assessment. It should be readily apparent that this represents crude measurement and is unlikely to provide valid or reliable information upon which to make judgments about counseling effectiveness.

A second approach to evaluation involves the use of follow-up studies of clients and former clients. Studies of this type trace the development of the student through his college years and into later life. One of the best studies of this nature was done at the University of Minnesota and involved a follow-up of students who were counseled 25 years previously.[31] The results in this study indicated that students who were counseled 25 years ago were slightly better off than noncounseled students. One of the more significant contributions of this study, however, was in the development of criteria with which to evaluate the "success" of the individuals participating in the study, thereby making indirect evaluation of counseling possible. In this writer's opinion counseling agencies must continue to devise such innovative techniques for self-evaluation.

Perhaps the most significant type of evaluation of counseling programs occurs in the form of accreditation. Each of the regional accrediting associations has developed general criteria for gauging the effectiveness of counseling programs. Each counseling director and dean of students should be familiar with the established standards of his particular accrediting association.

A slightly different type of accreditation, generally much more rigorous, occurs when a counseling agency makes application for approval of its services by the American Board on Counseling Services, Inc., established by the American Personnel and Guidance Association. This agency attempts to inform the public about reputable counseling agencies that adhere to high professional standards by publishing a biennial directory which includes not only a descriptive listing of all approved agencies but standards in the form of general criteria as well.[32] The criteria represent a comprehensive set of guidelines for counseling agencies, and all counseling agencies could profit from a thorough study of this reference.

SELECTED READINGS

American Board on Counseling Services, Inc.: *Directory of Approved Counseling Agencies,* American Personnel and Guidance Association, Washington, 1967.

American Personnel and Guidance Association: *Ethical Standards Casebook,* Washington, 1965.

American Psychological Association: *Ethical Standards of Psychologists,* Washington, 1967.

American Psychological Association: *Standards for Educational and Psychological Tests and Manuals,* Washington, 1966.

Arbuckle, D. S.: *Student Personnel Services in Higher Education,* McGraw-Hill Book Company, New York, 1953, chap. VI.

Arbuckle, D. S.: *Counseling: An Introduction,* Allyn and Bacon, Inc., Boston, 1961.

Ayers, A. R., P. A. Tripp, and J. H. Russel: *Student Services Administration in Higher Education,* U.S. Department of Health, Education, and Welfare, Office of Education, 1966.

Bakken, Clarence J.: *The Legal Basis for College Student Personnel Work,* American College Personnel Association, 1961, pp. 26–30.

Barclay, J. R.: *Testing for Higher Education,* The American College Personnel Association, Washington, 1965.

Clark, D. D.: "Characteristics of Counseling Centers in Large Universities," *Personnel and Guidance Journal,* vol. 44, pp. 817–823, 1966.

Cottle, W. C., and N. M. Downis: *Procedures and Preparation for Counseling,* Prentice-Hall, Inc., Englewood Cliffs, N.J., 1960.

Goldman, L.: *Using Tests in Counseling,* Appleton-Century-Crofts, Inc., New York, 1961.

Hardee, M. D.: *The Faculty in College Counseling,* McGraw-Hill Book Company, New York, 1959.

[31] David P. Campbell, *The Results of Counseling: Twenty-Five Years Later,* W. B. Saunders Company, Philadelphia, 1965.

[32] American Board on Counseling Services, Inc., *Directory of Approved Counseling Agencies,* The American Personnel and Guidance Association, Washington, 1967.

Hardee, M. D. (ed.): *Counseling and Guidance in General Education,* World Book Company, Tarrytown-on-Hudson, N.Y., 1955.

Hopke, W. E. (ed.): *The Encyclopedia of Careers and Vocational Guidance,* Doubleday & Company, Inc., Garden City, N.Y., 1967.

Lewis, E. C., and R. E. Warman: "Confidentiality Expectations of College Students," *Journal of College Student Personnel,* vol. 6, no. 1, pp. 7–11, 20, 1964.

National Vocational Guidance Association: "Standards for Use in Preparing and Evaluating Occupational Literature," Washington, 1966.

Norris, Willa, F. R. Zeran, and R. N. Hatch: *The Information Service in Guidance,* Rand McNally & Company, Chicago, 1960, p. 366.

Rogers, C. R.: *Client-centered Therapy,* Houghton-Mifflin Company, Boston, 1951.

Shaffer, R. H., and W. D. Martinson: *Student Personnel Services in Higher Education,* The Center for Applied Research in Education, Inc., New York, 1966, chap. IV.

Siegel, M. (ed.): *The Counseling of College Students,* The Free Press of Glencoe, New York, 1968.

Super, D. E.: *The Psychology of Careers,* Harper and Brothers, New York, 1956.

Williamson, E. G., and J. D. Foley: *Counseling and Discipline,* McGraw-Hill Book Company, New York, 1949.

Chapter 9

Financial Aid

ROBERT J. KATES, JR.

Assistant Director of the Northeastern Regional Office, College Entrance Examination Board, New York, New York

INTRODUCTION

The passage of the National Defense Education Act of 1958 marked the beginning of substantial, long-term, institutionally administered student financial aid support available to students in institutions across the country. The Higher Education Act of 1965 and other acts and amendments have provided the basis for a comprehensive federal program of aid to students in the form of grants, loans, and employment. The concept of aid to students as opposed to general aid to institutions of higher education has received greater support from federal and state legislative bodies in recent years and the trend should continue at least for the foreseeable future.

The major thrust of these new aid programs is to provide access to higher education for those previously unable to afford it. Reliance on institutionally administered student aid programs to achieve equality of educational opportunity, among other legitimate aims, requires that institutions of higher education have a firm commitment to educational opportunity as reflected in admissions policies and procedures, curricula, and especially in financial aid administration. As the numbers of students and dollars involved continues to grow, virtually every institution must provide the professional staff necessary to carry out the many diverse functions of an effective aid office. The investment in staff, facilities, training, and support will return benefits to the institution and its students many times over. Students have a right to expect the administration to make every effort to obtain the maximum possible funds for student support and to distribute them in an equitable and efficient fashion. This is the ultimate objective of any student financial aid program.

COLLEGE FINANCIAL AID PRINCIPLES

In 1961, the institutions participating in the College Scholarship Service adopted a statement of college financial aid principles that not only sets guidelines for these institutions but, in large measure, describes the operation of their programs. The statements are based on the belief that educational opportunities and choice should not be controlled by the financial aid resources of the applicant. The list does not presume to be either exhaustive or entirely appropriate for the individuality of each institution. It does, however, express a basic philosophy that can be subscribed to by a large number of institutions and that has formed a base from which financial aid officers have developed their own statements for their own institutions. [3, pp. 22–23] *

* Bracketed numbers refer to the references at the end of the chapter.

1. The primary purpose of a college's financial aid program should be to provide financial assistance to students who, without such aid, would be unable to attend the college.

2. Financial assistance consists of scholarships, loans, and employment, which may be offered to students singly or in various combinations.

3. The family of a student is expected to make a maximum effort to assist the student with college expenses. Financial assistance from colleges and other sources should be viewed only as supplementary to the efforts of the family.

4. In selecting students with need to receive financial assistance, the college should place primary emphasis upon their academic achievement, character, and future promise.

5. The total amount of financial assistance offered a student by a college and by other sources should not exceed the amount he needs.

6. In determining the extent of a student's financial need, the college should take into account the financial support which may be expected from the income, assets, and other resources of the parents and the student.

7. In estimating the amount that a student's family can provide for college expenses, the college should consider the factors that affect a family's financial strength: current income, assets, number of dependents, other educational expenses, debts, retirement needs. In addition, it should consider such special problems as those confronting widows and families in which both parents work.

8. A student who needs financial aid should provide a reasonable part of the total amount required to meet college costs by accepting employment or a loan, or both. Acceptance of a loan, however, should not be considered by the college as a prerequisite to the award of a scholarship or job.

9. Because the amount of financial assistance awarded usually reflects the financial situation of the student's family a public announcement of the amount by the college is undesirable.

10. Consultation between colleges on the kind and amount of financial assistance to be offered a mutual candidate should be encouraged since this assures relatively equal aid offers to the student, making it possible for him to choose a college on educational rather than financial grounds. This benefits both the student and the college.

11. The college should clearly state the total yearly cost of attendance and should outline for each student seeking assistance an estimate of his financial need.

12. The college should review its financial assistance awards annually and adjust them, if necessary, in type and amount to reflect changes in the financial needs of students and the cost of attending the institution, as well as to carry out the college's clearly stated policies on upper-class renewals.

13. The college itself should make every effort, and should cooperate with schools and other colleges to encourage college attendance by all able students.

14. The college should strive, through its publications and other communications, to provide schools, parents, and students with factual information about its aid opportunities, programs, and practices.

ORGANIZATION OF THE FINANCIAL AID PROGRAMS

The policies under which the programs will operate should be established and reviewed periodically by a committee on student financial aid composed of representatives of the student body, teaching faculty, financial aid and admissions offices, fiscal office, and the dean of students. The committee should be responsible for policy matters and not involved in the review of individual applications unless it is used as an appeals board. When such use is intended, the procedure a student must follow for appeals should be outlined in detail.

Since student representation on this committee would not be substantial, it may be desirable to establish an advisory committee of students broadly representative of the entire student body. Such a committee would include representatives of full-time and part-time students, minority groups, recipients, and nonrecipients. Representatives could be designated by student organizations or the financial aid staff, and from this advisory group could be elected representatives to the committee on student financial aid.

Structure The financial aid office provides not only financial support but also counseling services to the student population and as such should be part of the total student personnel services program. For this reason the financial aid officer should report to the dean of students or the equivalent. As a general rule the business office should not be responsible for the administration of student aid programs. Sound fiscal practice dictates a separation of responsibility for the authorization of awards and the actual disbursement of funds.

Responsibilities The aid office should be responsible for the administration of all institutional student aid programs, scholarships, loans, and employment for graduate and undergraduate students regardless of their program of study. The aid office should assist where possible in the administration of extrainstitutional aid. Centralization of aid activities provides for more efficient administrative operation and easier access for students, assures compliance with federal and other outside agency regulations, and pinpoints responsibility for development of satisfactory aid programs.

In smaller institutions the aid officer may also be responsible for career placement of graduates in addition to part-time job placement.

Budget Where possible, the financial aid office should be established as a separate operating department with its own budget, both for student aid program expenditures and operating expenditures. Presently, reimbursement for administrative expenses under the National Defense Student Loan Program, College Work-Study Program, and Educational Opportunity Grant Program requires that the institution be able to account for and document the cost involved in operating those aid programs. Regulations also require an institution to maintain a three-year average level of expenditure for aid programs which is subject to audit.

Staffing Suggested minimum staffing levels for financial aid offices, based on experience and observations in a number of institutions, would be [9, p. 64]:

1. Up to 750 students—a director and a full-time secretary or administrative assistant
2. Between 750 and 2,500 students—a director, a full-time secretary or administrative assistant, two full-time clerical workers
3. Between 2,500 and 5,000 students—a director, an administrative assistant or assistant director, two secretaries, two clerical workers
4. Over 5,000 students—a director, three assistant directors (one—grants, one—loans, one—employment), one administrative assistant, three secretaries, three clerical workers

The number and types of staff will vary depending on the functions assigned to the aid office, the availability and utilization of electronic data processing facilities or management information services, the size of the aid program, and the size and type of student body that it serves.

Many aid offices can employ students on a part-time basis for routine clerical tasks and, in larger institutions, for semiprofessional assignments, particularly in supervising student employment programs. The possibility of utilizing undergraduate and graduate student assistants should not be rejected without thorough investigation. Although such students will have access to confidential information, judicious hiring and assignment policies and adequate orientation and supervision should minimize or eliminate any problems of disclosure. In addition, such staff provide an excellent source of feedback on the satisfactory or unsatisfactory nature of the operations and are a source of future university administrative personnel.

OPERATIONAL ACTIVITIES

Informational Programs The aid officer must ensure that those who might profit from the programs he administers know about the opportunities available. Intensive efforts to reach the prospective and enrolled students and their families can be made through up-to-date publications, news releases, and group presentations. While the aid officer may not personally visit secondary schools, he should provide the admissions representatives with adequate information for the counseling staffs of these schools. The aid and admissions officer may work directly with community agencies, Talent Search programs, and other groups involved in recruiting disadvantaged students for postsecondary education.

Information summaries should be prepared for present and potential donors and for faculty and staff members. The latter particularly should be aware of the financial resources available to a student and the persons to whom students in difficulty should be referred.

Counseling A primary function of the aid office is financial counseling for students and their families. Because the aid officer already knows of the family's situation and may have prior contacts with the student, he is frequently the first person to whom enrolled students will turn for assistance on personal problems. Staffing levels must be adequate to provide time for personal interviews with applicants and recipients. Students may need advice on handling their resources, which may be adequate to meet their expenses if properly managed. Families may need assistance in understanding the necessity of their fiscal support of a student and the substantial expense involved in attending even a tuition-free institution. The family and the student may need assistance in resolving the conflict between the student's desire for independence and the family's desire for control over his activities and the stresses that develop when funds are used as a weapon.

The aid officer must be able to effectively refer students with problems beyond his scope to appropriate departments or agencies on campus or in the community and to handle referrals from them of students whose problems in whole or part are financial.

An advisory service should be maintained on funds available for further study for graduates of associate or bachelor's degree programs.

Planning and Budgeting The aid officer must be able to forecast and document his needs for funds, personnel, and facilities for several years ahead. This requires that he have access to or develop information on enrollment, costs, new programs of study, residence and commuter patterns, renewal and packaging policies, socioeconomic background of the student population, compensatory programs, and other changes within the institution.

Because of the impact of federal student aid programs, the aid officer must keep informed of new programs and changes in existing federal programs, especially those changes which would make the institution eligible to participate in a given program. Developments in appropriation bills in Congress must be analyzed in light of their effects on institutional requests and needs. Few programs are enacted without prior legislative history. An aid officer who is aware of current legislative developments will consider the effects of proposed legislation on his institution and should formulate general plans of action.

Determination of the total student aid needs is the first step in the planning process. Total student expenses can be estimated by multiplying the number of resident and commuter students by their respective budgets. When married and/or independent students form a significantly large group, they may be factored in separately with an appropriate budget. For an unmarried commuting student, the budget would consist of tuition, fees, room, board, books and supplies, personal expenses, standard commuting costs, and maintenance at home. The latter two items may vary considerably from student to student.

Commuting costs are typically and unrealistically set at $100 to $200 without regard for local conditions. However, if public transportation is not readily available or reasonably priced or if students commute by car because of distance or time required on public transportation, then the expense budget should be adjusted accordingly both for individuals and the institution.

Maintenance at home is an expense allowance that recognizes the cost to a family of feeding, housing, and maintaining the student during the academic year. This allowance may range between $500 and $900 at the discretion of the institution. Additionally, some students, especially those from extremely low-income families, may be required to contribute to the support of the family if they are to continue in college. In determining institutional needs, the institution should be prepared to recognize the full, actual expenses incurred by its student population, especially where commuter costs may be higher than resident costs. In public institutions, especially community colleges, a preoccupation with the benefits of low tuition may cause an administration to ignore the real financial needs of its students.

Total student resources for education are the sum of parental contributions, student savings and earnings, and aid from institutional or other financial aid sources.

Total parental contribution can be estimated by developing a model distribution of family income of the student population and applying standard expectations for various levels of income. The following example illustrates the results for a student body of 2,000, assuming a median income of $8,500, a two-child family, and an average student expense budget of $2,400.

Income level, $	Number of students	Parental contribution, $	Total parental contribution, $
0– 3,999	180	100	18,000
4,000– 5,999	300	300	90,000
6,000– 7,999	420	700	294,000
8,000– 9,999	400	1,150	460,000
10,000–12,499	240	1,600	384,000
12,500–14,999	80	2,050	164,000
15,000–over	150	2,400	360,000
	1,770		1,770,000

The financial aid officer should survey his entire student body to obtain the information necessary for accurate estimates and projections of future needs. Students will cooperate and provide data of sufficient accuracy if they understand the reasons for the request. In addition to providing data on family income and support, such a study can provide data on student savings and earnings as well as support from a variety of noninstitutional sources. Institutional student aid funds can be added to these figures to provide an estimate of total aid resources. The difference between total resources and total expenses represents the deficit in resources presumably being met by a combination of unusually strong support from parents and unreasonably heavy term-time employment or borrowing by the student.

The gross deficit figure is the keystone of the aid officer's request for institutional, state, and federal funds and the development officer's campaign for scholarship support from foundations, alumni, and friends of the institution. The deficit figure provides a yardstick by which to measure institutional progress in meeting student needs. However, the resources and priorities of the institution may make it impossible to achieve substantial gains, even over several years. The depressing thought of a constant chasm between resources and expenses should not prevent an institution from gathering the facts on student aid needs.

Institutional budgets should be prepared separately for aid programs for entering students and for students applying for renewal of awards. The awards made to entering freshmen will shape the aid-budget needs for the following four years. In proposing new or expanded student aid programs, aid officers should provide projections showing the effects of the renewal awards on the institutional budget resulting from these changes. As an example, a program to recruit 25 additional students a year for four years and to provide each with a $1,000 award is not a $100,000 program over four years. Assuming a constant attrition of four students per year from each group and a fixed $1,000 stipend level, the program commits the institution to $304,000 in support over a seven-year period. Also, sufficient staff time must be budgeted to meet the counseling needs of the students.

The aid officer should be consulted on tuition changes and projections, since the increased income may be offset by increased student aid awards, thus reducing the net income to be gained by the increase. It is also to be remembered that a rise in student charges brings about an increase in requests for financial aid from students who have previously not felt the need for assistance.

Selection Procedure Application for all types of aid should be made at one time and with a single form. The application form should request only that information which is necessary for the awards process and not readily available from the admissions application. Avoid requesting duplicate high school transcripts, score reports, or letters of recommendation.

Design the application form with the student population in mind. If the majority of students come from the local area, from low- or moderate-income families with no prior college experience, then phrase the instructions and questions in a simple, direct, nonthreatening manner. The objective is to obtain sufficient information on which to base an award rather than screen out applicants by using a complex form.

Deadlines for filing should be coordinated with admissions application deadlines for the institution.

A sample application form appears in Figure 1.

Need Analysis. Student aid programs are effective only when the contribution expected of each student and his family is determined in a uniform, systematic manner. Such a determination is required in the administration of major state and federal programs, and many institutions consider this approach in the distribution of their own aid resources as well.

An institution may use local procedures or procedures based on income tax information for determining need. Local procedures require that the institution perform the computational work itself. For large programs, the staff time involved is too costly and the hazards of local procedures are too great. A common practice is to utilize one of two national services providing need-analysis reports. These are:

College Scholarship Service
475 Riverside Drive
New York, N.Y. 10027
American College Testing Program
P.O. Box 767
Iowa City, Iowa 52240

In the case of both these services, the basic information document is distributed to the students through secondary school guidance offices. The student and his family complete the document and return it to a processing center. The services then prepare a need-analysis report which is forwarded to the institutions or scholarship programs designated by the student. The College Scholarship Service (CSS) also sends a copy

APPLICATION FOR FINANCIAL AID

For the period September – June

GENERAL INSTRUCTIONS

All students must complete both the Application for Financial Aid and the Confidential Statement Renewal Form. The *Application for Financial Aid* form must be returned to the Financial Aid Office, no later than April 30, 19 The Confidential Statement, accompanied by a check or money order for must be mailed immediately to the College Scholarship Service, P. O. Box 176, Princeton, N. J. 08540.

This application is submitted for the purpose of:

1. Applying for renewal of financial aid ☐
2. Applying for reconsideration for financial aid previously not approved ☐
3. Applying for financial aid for the first time ☐

— Check one of the above —

(Please type or print in ink)

Name .... *Last* .... *First* .... *Middle*

Home Address .... *Street and Number* .... *City or Town* .... *State* .... *Zip*

Student Identification No. .... Telephone No. .... *Area Code*

1. I hereby apply for financial aid in the amount of $........ (complete budget on reverse side before entering this amount) to assist in payment of my educational expenditures while in attendance during the September 19 through June 19 academic year.

2. Check type(s) of aid in which you are interested:

*Academic Scholarship ☐ *Grant-in-Aid ☐ .... *Specify*

NDSL Loan ☐ *Donor Award ☐ .... *Specify*

EOG ☐ Work Study ☐

For details, see Pertinent Information data enclosed.

* If funds are not available, or I do not qualify, I wish to be considered for a NDSL Loan ☐.

3. Where will you reside during the 19 school year?

At home ☐ Residence halls ☐

Off-campus residence (other than home) .... (Specify address)

With relatives .... (Specify address)

4. Date of Birth: Month / Day / Year	**5.(a)** U.S. Citizen ☐ Yes ☐ No **(b)** If no, specify type of visa.	**6.** ☐ Male ☐ Female	**7.** ☐ Single ☐ Married	**8.** Date you entered University

9. Proposed Academic Major	**10.** Vocational Objective	**11.** If you plan to teach, list subject	**12.** Date of graduation

13. Student Status
Check one
Undergraduate: ☐ Full-time ☐ Part-time
Graduate: ☐ Full-time ☐ Part-time

Check one
☐ Day Program ☐ New College
☐ University College

14. If you have ever received a National Defense Education Act Student Loan, complete following for EACH loan.

School in which enrolled at time of loan	Academic periods covered	Amounts awarded
(a)		
(b)		
(c)		

1

Fig. 1 *Application for financial aid.*

of the original document filed by the student. In both cases, the processing fee is paid by the student.

Based on this need-analysis report and any pertinent information from the aid application, interviews, or reports from the secondary school or community agencies, the aid officer determines the amount of the family contribution. While the aid officer will agree with the results of a system such as CSS in a majority of cases, surveys show that aid officers modify the results in as many as one-quarter of the cases. Such an approach is essential to ensure adequate consideration of nonstandard circumstances affecting some families and students. Cases involving business or farm owners, large families, heavy indebtedness, or impending retirement may require special consideration.

Independent students, including married undergraduate or graduate students, must establish their independent status to the satisfaction of the aid officer and meet the basic

15. The following loans or other forms of awards from sources *outside* of University will be a basis of *part* of my financial resources for educational expenses for the academic year covered by this application.

	Have been awarded	*Have applied or will apply for*
State Scholarship Award	.... per yr.	.... per yr.
State Incentive Award	.... per yr.	.... per yr.
Civic, church or corporate award	.... per yr.	.... per yr.
State or personal loan	.... per yr.	.... per yr.
Federal assistance (Do not include NDSL or EOG)	.... per yr.	.... per yr.
Other .... Specify	.... per yr.	.... per yr.
TOTAL:	....	....

Use this space for comments concerning the source, the conditions and the likelihood of renewal of the above outside financial aid.

....

....

....

16. If you were employed last summer, outline type of job, employer, location, duration, earnings (before taxes), and how much was saved for use against expenses for the 19' academic year.

....

....

....

....

17. If you plan to work during the coming summer, outline anticipated type of job, employer, location, duration, earnings (before taxes), and anticipated savings for use against expenses for the 19 academic year.

....

....

....

....

18. If you have a part-time job during the present school year, outline type of job, employer, location, hours of work required each week, and total anticipated earnings (before taxes), and anticipated savings for use against expenses for the 19 academic year.

....

....

....

....

19. If you plan to maintain a part-time job during the academic year covered by this application, and (a) you now know the type of job, employer, location, hours of work required each week, and the total anticipated earnings (before taxes) for the school year, outline details here; or (b) if you are interested in securing campus employment, outline any special skills which you have (such as typing, stenography) and approximate hours per week you can devote to such employment.

(a) ....

....

(b) ....

....

2

Fig. 1 *(continued)*

U.S. Office of Education criteria of having received no financial support from parents (or others *in loco parentis*) for the previous year and not having been claimed as tax exemptions for the previous calendar year for federal income tax purposes. Notations of the basis for judgment and any evidence necessary for the support of the action, such as copies of family income tax returns, must be retained for audit by HEW if federal student aid programs are involved.

20. BUDGET *(Totals must agree)*

Estimated educationally-connected expenses for academic year:		Estimated sources of financial support for academic year:	
Tuition and fees	$	From parents' income	$
Books and supplies		From parents' assets	
*Room		From income of spouse	
*Board		From present student assets (savings)—Re: Items 16 & 18	
*Transportation		From student summer earnings Re: Item 17	
*Personal (itemize) Clothing		From student term-time earnings Re: Item 19	
Laundry		From friends or relatives	
Other		From other sources—Re: Item 15	
		**From *THIS* application	$
TOTAL	$	TOTAL	$

*Married students ONLY may show one total for items starred which should reflect full family expenses.

**Enter this figure in Item 1, Page 1.

21. RESPONSIBILITIES OF FINANCIAL AID RECIPIENT

I am in need of the amount of financial aid indicated in order to pursue my college education.

I will be a full-time student enrolled for a minimum of twelve credit hours each semester, or at least a "half-time student." Half-time is defined as enrollment each semester for eight or more semester hours (six or more for graduate students) but less than 12 semester hours.

I will use the proceeds of the aid awarded me only for tuition, fees, instructional equipment, materials, books, room and board, transportation, and similar expenses.

Any monies received through scholarship aid may be applied only to undergraduate courses taken prior to the date of graduation.

I will inform the Financial Aid Office of any additional assistance I receive that is not reported on this application.

I hereby acknowledge that the information submitted herewith is true and correct, and I fully understand my obligations incurred by the grant of aid.

Date .... *Signature of Applicant* ....

DO NOT WRITE BELOW THIS LINE

Work Sheet

Total .... Net

Federal State University Other Coverage

Date: Approved by: For the Period:

DECISION ....

3

Fig. 1 *(continued)*

Awards Criteria. Once financial need has been established, the applicants can be grouped into priority categories according to a general pattern such as high need–high ability, high need–moderate ability, moderate need–high ability, moderate need–moderate ability. The level of ability can be determined according to a predictive grade-point average or other system which would take into account academic and non-academic factors, among them athletic, musical, or dramatic ability; minority-group representation; alumni relative; or cultural differences.

DO NOT WRITE ON THIS PAGE

Hold Docket For:

Tax Forms	Business Statement	Medical Bills	Student Interview	Dept. Recomm.	Up-to-Date PCS	Donor Award

Special circumstances ....

Financial Aid Information:

GPA	Hours Net	Hours Earned	A.D.G.	Regents Scholarship	Scholar Incentive	Other Outside

Work Sheet

Total .... Net

Federal State University Other Coverage

Date: .... Approved by: .... For the Period: ....

DECISION ....

4

Fig. 1 *(continued)*

In many institutions the final decision about awards can be made by the financial aid officer or his staff according to the policies specified by the financial aid committee. As a general rule, it is cumbersome and unwieldy to involve a committee in the actual selection of recipients.

Packaging. The introduction of federal grant and employment programs along with rising costs and student needs has given impetus to the acceptance of the "packaging" concept. Packaging means that student need is met by an award from a combination of sources, typically scholarship or grant, loan, and employment. While the total award to students of the same need should be the same, the amount of scholarship aid in the package may vary according to the academic ranking of the applicant or other criteria selected by the institution. The balance of the award in this case would be offered in the form of loans or employment. The package may also be built up by awarding loans and/or jobs to those applicants with lower needs and adding scholarship assistance only when need exceeds a predetermined figure. For students of exceptionally high need, the Educational Opportunity Grant would be the first component of the package, since the grant must be matched by awards from appropriate sources.

Recipients should not be required to accept loans as a condition for receiving scholarships or grants. Where funds permit, a student should be allowed to utilize loan programs instead of employment where the latter would seriously interfere with his academic program.

Notification. Applicants must be notified of the action taken on the application as early as possible. An award letter should indicate the student's need, the nature and conditions of the component parts of the award package, the conditions for renewal, and the action necessary by the student to ensure the crediting of the award to his account. A rejection letter should indicate specific reasons, where possible, and suggest alternative sources of assistance such as the Guaranteed Loan Program that may be known to the financial aid office. A rejection letter may also indicate a willingness on the part of the aid officer to counsel the student on financial aid matters.

Notifications should also be sent to the secondary school or community college from which a student is entering. This notice should contain the same information received by the student, with the caution that the amounts and types of assistance are not to be made public. The detailed information is necessary if the counselors in these institutions are to serve their students adequately.

Adjustments of Awards. Since the stipends are based on financial need, the aid officer must make provision for adjustments if a recipient receives awards from outside sources or if his financial circumstances change dramatically. The award letter should contain a general statement to this effect and should explain the student's responsibility to inform the aid office about other awards.

If a student receives an outside scholarship, the aid officer may reduce a loan award by a corresponding amount, reduce a scholarship award by an amount less than the outside scholarship to permit some benefit to accrue to the student, or let the original award stand. The course of action depends on the amount and duration of the outside award, the student's budget, the student's circumstances, and institutional resources. In many cases, no adjustment is made if the additional award is less than $300 and is nonrenewable.

DATA COLLECTION AND REPORTING

Data collection should be approached in a systematic fashion so that all information necessary for management and reporting is readily available in usable form at the appropriate time. Requirements of federal and state agencies, sponsors, foundations, and internal offices should be reviewed periodically and any new items of information added to applications, internal forms, or other basic sources of information.

For small programs, data can be transferred to summary cards which can then be used to compile reports. Such cards can be adapted to contain a cumulative record of aid. For moderate numbers, a system such as McBee Keysort can serve a number of uses in addition to reporting. Representatives of business systems organizations should be willing to assist aid officers in systems and forms design.

For extensive programs, some form of data processing is the only efficient way to collect and manipulate the information necessary to compile meaningful reports. If computer facilities are not available at the institution, then time could be purchased from an outside source. When using EDP, a keypunch machine and operator should be part of the financial aid office staff to ensure that incoming data and changes can be keypunched quickly and accurately without having to rely on a separate office for this service. Both the College Scholarship Service and the American College Testing Program are developing services to aid colleges with this aspect of aid administration. Detailed information can be obtained directly from the organizations.

A requirement that information be provided on the racial origin of recipients of aid from federal programs means that the aid officer must collect this information by some means after the award has been made. A survey card to be included with the award letter and returned by the applicant or inclusion of questions on race and financial aid in a survey of all students taken during registration are possible methods.

Reports on the activities of the aid office should be made at the end of an academic year to the president, members of the faculty and administration, and to those organizations which provide funds. The U.S. Office of Education and other government agencies require detailed operations reports on awards for the previous year. The totals for specific programs such as the National Defense Loan Program should be reconciled with the fiscal office to ensure that both offices agree on data to be reported.

Periodic reports on the status of aid funds, showing commitments and acceptances against budget allocations, should be prepared monthly or even more frequently during peak periods of activity and distributed to the admissions and fiscal offices.

RESPONSIBILITIES FOR SPONSORED SCHOLARSHIP PROGRAMS

Sponsored or funded scholarships are those awarded by the institution from funds provided by outside sources—individuals, professional organizations, business and industry, and foundations. The aid officer must be made aware of all such scholarships received by the institution so that he can ensure that the funds are awarded when available. The institution cannot make a sound case for additional grants if the donor discovers that previous grants have not been awarded. The aid officer should carry out certain steps for all sponsored awards:

1. Ensure that the recipient meets the requirements of the donors. If the donor specifies a particular academic year, grade-point average, major field of study, or geographic area, then the recipient must meet the criteria that the donor has specified. If no recipient can be found who meets the donor's requirements, then the aid officer should inform the donor of this fact and suggest that the requirements be modified.
2. Notify the donor of the selections and provide as much background information on the recipient as seems appropriate or as institutional policy permits.
3. Where appropriate, provide the student with the name and address of the donor or his representative so that the student may acknowledge the receipt of the award.
4. If the program provides for campus visits, ensure that arrangements are made for the sponsors to meet with recipients and members of the faculty or administration as appropriate.
5. Prepare progress reports and renewal applications, consulting with the recipient's academic adviser on his progress. In addition, reports on developments within the institution should be provided to give the sponsors some perspective on the institution's needs and encourage continued and expanded awards.

RESPONSIBILITIES FOR LOAN PROGRAMS

The responsibility for administering loan programs is divided between the financial aid and the fiscal offices. The financial aid office is responsible for awarding the loan, the fiscal office for transferring funds to the students' accounts and collecting the loan when it falls due. Sound awards procedures are essential for the success of the lending operation, particularly in the collection phase. The student borrower must be aware at the time of his application of the nature of the loan, the responsibilities that he incurs, and the need for prompt repayment. First-time borrowers may have no prior experience in negotiating a loan and thus need an orientation to the nature of the obligation they incur before they sign a promissory note. In addition to the normal application and needs-analysis records which are used in other aid programs, the aid officer must be certain that the student properly executes a legal note, the form of which meets the requirements of the federal regulation or institutional needs, depending on the program. The signed note must be adequately protected as a major asset of the loan fund.

Prior to the time a student ceases to be a full-time student, the aid office must conduct an exit interview to review the repayment features and to arrange a repayment schedule. When a student withdraws or completes his program, the aid office should transfer the executed loan note and signed repayment schedule to the bursar so that the bursar may begin the billing cycle.

Loan Collection Upon receipt of the notice that a student borrower has graduated or withdrawn, the fiscal office moves the borrower into the repayment cycle. The key feature of the cycle is a systematic billing process which provides notification of due dates and amounts due, information about provisions for deferment of payment or cancellation of principal, and follow-up on unpaid accounts. Billing may be handled by the institution, by cooperative arrangement with other institutions, or by a responsible outside billing service.

The *National Defense Student Loan Program Collections Manual* is a comprehensive presentation of the requirements for a sound collection program. Because failure to apply extensive and forceful practices consistently and with due diligence could result in the discontinuation of federal loan-program operations at an institution, every effort should be made to define "due diligence" in the light of the institution's established policies. Administrators should not interpret as law those steps which are included as desirable or even mandatory but which in actuality are recommendations or guidelines, such as withholding transcripts or diplomas or resorting to legal action.

The aid officer should assist the fiscal office at any point where detailed information on the background of the borrower is necessary to assist in the collection process, and he should keep the fiscal office informed of changes in regulations affecting borrowers in the repayment cycle.

RESPONSIBILITY FOR STUDENT EMPLOYMENT

The student employment program has a number of benefits which follow from its effective operation. The student can obtain experiences which aid his growth as an individual in areas related to his academic interests. At the same time he can contribute toward the expenses of his own education, carrying out specific responsibilities, working in harmony with colleagues and superiors, managing his own personal budget, and developing individual skills and abilities. Each of these have value to him in later life.

Institutional commitment is essential if the program is to provide a reasonable amount of assistance to a sufficient number of students. Faculty and staff must be willing to hire students on a part-time basis on schedules which do not conflict with the academic program. The institution must provide sufficient placement staff to counsel adequately students seeking employment. The institution should also be receptive to innovations in student employment and make provisions for them in the academic calendar or schedules.

Work loads in job assignments should be in line with a student's academic program and ability. For this reason, an adequate counseling staff is needed to work with the student in this area and also to resolve student-employer conflicts.

The wage rate must be reasonable and provisions should be made for an increasing level of responsibility and compensation for students as they progress through their academic program. Wage rates for given jobs can be set on a sliding scale from prefreshman to senior or graduate student, or a bonus system such as a work scholarship could be employed for the reward of satisfactory performance. Where there are a sufficient number of jobs, a planned system of assignments can assure that upper-class students are placed in the more responsible positions according to their previous work record.

A central task of a student employment program is the development of responsibility. This involves the education of a student to his responsibility as an employee and the evaluation of his performance based on a report from his employer. This report should be evaluated by the placement staff and discussed with the student at least once each year, preferably more often.

The College Work-Study Program funded by the federal government has injected considerable vitality into student employment programs. While an institution must maintain a prescribed level of institutional effort, the College Work-Study Program can be used for expanded on-campus activity, for faculty aides, and for off-campus summer and cooperative education programs. The College Work-Study Program may provide on-campus assignments for undergraduates as tutors or counselors in Upward Bound or other summer programs. Prefreshmen may be employed during the summer even while they attend compensatory programs. Off-campus arrangements can be made with public and private nonprofit agencies at some distance from the campus if satisfactory supervisory arrangements can be made. While the federal program does require a determination of financial need and a limitation on the earnings of a student according to his need, the basic elements of a sound program are the same no matter what the source of funds.

Student agencies have provided a wide range of campus services while producing profits and experience for student managers and employees.

Summer employment opportunities under the control of the institution vary with the location of the institution. In any case, the aid office can provide a clearinghouse for off-campus employment, developing contacts with summer camps for counseling jobs, with business and industry for vacation replacement opportunities, with government agencies for internships and special programs. Such a service may be open to all students whether or not they have financial need.

AID FOR FOREIGN STUDENTS

The basic question an institution must answer is whether or not it desires to provide financial aid to foreign students. The benefits of increased mutual understanding, the significant educational experience for the recipients, and the exchange of ideas and values with the institution's native student body may be offset by the fact that funds to foreign students may be provided at the expense of aid to local students.

If an institution decides to assist foreign students, then it should determine the extent to which this aid will be for undergraduate or graduate study and whether it will be for a period of a year or for the entire period necessary to complete degree requirements.

The principle of financial need should be applied to aid for foreign students in the same way as to others on campus. The responsibility of the student and his family to provide funds for his education to the extent possible according to their earnings is valid, and the aid officer must attempt a need analysis for a foreign student in a similar manner to the method described earlier. The student budget should be realistic, including the cost of travel to and from the student's home and providing allowances for unusual expenses, such as clothing, which may be incurred because of the change of climate.

Assistance from the college would take the conventional forms of scholarship and employment. The conditions of the initial award should be clearly spelled out for the student, as should renewal policies. Renewal should be made reasonably available to the student, particularly if outside agencies are providing part of the student's assistance. Part-time employment may be used to assist foreign students with their expenses, but it is necessary to use discretion in the assignment of jobs and to provide adequate counseling to the student on his responsibilities. Students from some countries may not be receptive to the idea of employment as an acceptable way of meeting their expenses and thus will need assistance in seeing the role of employment in the financial aid programs in this country.

Long-term loans are usually not a major source of financial assistance to foreign students. Because of the repayment problems involved when a student returns to his own country, many institutions do not make such loans to foreign students. However, the point can be made that loans may be repaid if a student remains in this country or does have an income on his return which would enable him to discharge his obligation.

Short-term or emergency loans are a necessary ingredient in foreign-student assistance programs in order to take care of those situations which arise when funds are delayed in transit from parents or sponsoring organizations or to meet unexpected bills which do occur. Repayment would be required before a student completes his academic program or within a nine-month period, whichever is shorter. Outside support is available to foreign students from their own governments, from the United States government, and from various private agencies. A good resource for information and bibliography is the College Entrance Examination Board's publication entitled *Financial Planning for Study in the United States* [4].

AID TO GRADUATE STUDENTS

Those institutionally administered programs of financial assistance for graduate students in which financial need is a factor should be administered by the office of financial aid. For those federal programs available to graduate students which require a determination of need (National Defense, Health Professions, and Nursing Loan Programs; Health Professions Scholarship Program and College Work-Study Program) the aid office can assure the consistent application of need-analysis principles. Graduate students cannot be assumed to be independent of their families even though they have completed their undergraduate studies. The same criteria used for undergraduates must be applied in determining whether a student is, in fact, independent of his family. However, the aid officer must rely heavily on his considered judgment because of the basic differences in individual situations at this level.

Fellowships and assistantships are usually administered by the individual major departments and do not depend upon financial need. However, it is possible for students receiving fellowships or assistantships to still have financial need and thus be eligible for other student assistance programs. The aid officer should coordinate his activities with the departmental chairman so that he has full and complete information on each applicant.

INSTITUTIONAL RESOURCES

Gift Assistance This form of assistance is given without expectation of repayment or services to be rendered. The term "scholarship" is generally used where academic criteria are involved, the term "grant" when nonacademic criteria are used.

Endowed scholarships are those made available from earnings on capital invested by the university. The amounts available annually will vary with the return on investment, and the aid officer must coordinate with the fiscal office to ensure that funds are not overcommitted or undercommitted.

Funded scholarships are those made available from annual gifts by individuals, corporations, or foundations. Typical examples are the General Motors Scholarship Program and Uniroyal Foundation Program, where selection of the recipients is the responsibility of the institution.

Nonfunded scholarships are made available as an operating expense budget item. There is no actual cash transfer but simply a bookkeeping entry which reduces a student's tuition.

Tuition waivers or tuition remission plans are usually used for children of faculty and staff or members of the religious orders in church-related institutions. Usually nonfunded, these awards represent a tuition write-off.

Grants-in-aid are given on the basis of need without regard to academic achievement and may also be used for recognition of proficiency in certain activities or sports. Grants may be made from endowment or from operating expense budgets.

Loan Assistance Long-term loans are made available from earnings on endowment funds, annual gifts, or from operating expense budgets. They are characterized by low interest and repayment over an extended period of time after graduation. In many cases the terms and conditions parallel those of the federal student loan programs. An institution may be able to participate as a lender in the guaranteed student loan program and thus receive an interest subsidy for eligible students while they are enrolled in the institution.

Emergency loans are cash awards to meet temporary emergency needs of enrolled students. The account may be established from gifts or from a direct college appropriation. Little or no interest is charged and the repayment period extends for no more than a year.

Employment Student employment as financial aid would consist of work opportunities where a college assists in the placement of the student or where preferential treatment is provided for students. In addition, the employment program would provide a job listing service available to all students regardless of their financial situation.

MAJOR FEDERAL STUDENT AID PROGRAMS

The following programs are administered by the Division of Student Financial Aid of the U.S. Office of Education. Application is made in the fall of each year by the institution for funds for the succeeding academic year. In addition, the institution may receive an allowance (not to exceed $125,000) for administrative expenses in the amount of 3 percent of the annual expenditures for any program except the U.S. Cuban Loan Program.

National Defense Student Loan Program This is a program of long-term, low-interest loans, 90 percent of the funds for which are provided by the government and the remaining 10 percent by the institution. Students carrying at least one-half the normal academic work load are eligible, based upon their financial need. Repayment to the institution begins nine months after the borrower ceases to carry at least one-half the normal academic work load and must be completed within ten years. However, no interest accrues and repayment may be deferred during periods of eligible study or service in the Armed Forces, Peace Corps, or VISTA programs.

Under certain conditions, all or part of the loan may be cancelled for teaching service. Current provisions can be obtained from the Division of Student Financial Aid.

College Work-Study Program Designed to stimulate part-time employment of needy college students, this program provides 80 percent of the wages from government funds, the remaining 20 percent coming from the institution or other employers. Eligibility is limited to full-time students in need of the earnings from this employment to pursue their studies, and preference must be given to students from low-income families. The program may be used to employ accepted students during the summer prior to their enrollment.

Students may be employed off campus either for the institution or for a public agency or nonprofit organization. The institution retains a responsibility for placing students, dispersing funds, and assuring adequate supervision and satisfactory performance on the part of the students.

Educational Opportunity Grants Qualified high school graduates in exceptional financial need may receive grants under this program to enable them to attend an institution of higher education. The grant is based on need, may range from $200 to $1,000 and may not be more than one-half of the total amount of student financial assistance provided to the individual. Therefore, insofar as the grant program is concerned, the institution must package aid awards.

The criteria for the award include the requirement that the student show evidence of academic or creative promise and the capability of maintaining good standing. This has been interpreted to mean admission to the institution. At the same time the renewal award is based on his continuing to be a full-time student and need not be withdrawn for academic probation.

Institutions participating in this program are required to make vigorous efforts to recruit students of exceptional financial need and to cooperate with Talent Search or Upward Bound programs which would assist them in recruitment. Institutions are also encouraged to make commitments to students before their twelfth year of school. The uncertainty of federal funding, however, has diminished the institutional enthusiasm for this feature.

U.S. Cuban Refugee Loans This program was established to provide Cuban nationals in need of funds with assistance toward continuing their education. The provisions parallel those of the National Defense Student Loan Program. However, no institutional contribution to the loan fund is required, nor is the institution involved in the collection process. The repayment of the loan is made by the student to the U.S. Office of Education.

The following programs are administered by the Public Health Service—Division of Health Manpower Educational Services. No provision for administrative expense allowance is provided at this time. The institution is responsible for loan collection.

Health Professions Scholarship Program Grants are made to public and private nonprofit schools of medicine, osteopathy, dentistry, optometry, podiatry, and pharmacy for use in awarding scholarships to students from low-income families. The amount of the award cannot exceed $2,500 a year. While no formal matching requirement is specified for individual awards, the program assumes the integration of other financial aid programs to assist the student in meeting the expenses of his program.

Health Professions Student Loan Program Designed to assist students who have the capacity to pursue certain careers in health professions and who would not otherwise be able to afford the training, the program provides loans of up to $2,500 for an academic year to full-time students in the fields of medicine, dentistry, osteopathy, optometry, pharmacy, podiatry, and veterinary medicine. Repayment begins three years after the student finishes his program of full-time study and extends over a ten-year period. This loan has a cancellation provision for students engaging in the practice of their profession under certain conditions.

Nursing Student Opportunity Grants This program is patterned after the Educational Opportunity Grant program described earlier. Recipients must have exceptional financial need and may receive awards ranging from $200 to $800 depending on financial need and parental contribution. This program is administered by the Division of Nursing of the Public Health Service.

Nursing Student Loan Program Available to students in all types of professional nursing schools including diploma schools, this loan program also parallels the National Defense Student Loan Program. Cancellation of up to 50 percent of the loan for full-time service as a professional nurse in any public and nonprofit institution or agency is permitted.

Under the Omnibus Crime Central and Safe Streets Act of 1968, loan and grant programs were authorized to enable institutions offering a program related to law enforcement to provide financial assistance to students interested in or pursuing law enforcement careers. The programs are administered by the Office of Academic Assistance of the U.S. Department of Justice.

Law Enforcement Loan Program The loan program, limited to full-time students enrolled in programs leading to degrees in areas directly related to law enforcement, provides a maximum loan of $1,800 per academic year to be repaid over a 10-year period and carrying a 3 percent interest rate. The loan may be cancelled at a rate of 25 percent for each year of full-time employment in an eligible agency.

Law Enforcement Grant Program The grant program, available to full- or part-time students, provides for payments for tuition and fees not exceeding $200 per academic quarter or $300 per semester. Recipients must be full-time employees of a publicly funded law enforcement agency. They must also agree to remain in the service of the employing agency for a period of two years following the completion of any course of study funded by a grant or, failing this commitment, repay the full amount of grant funds awarded.

In both programs, the amount of the awards is based on financial need as well as academic qualifications.

Because of the rapidly changing nature of new programs such as these, institutions should examine any series of amendments to the basic act which would affect the initiation or operation of these programs at the individual school.

NONINSTITUTIONAL RESOURCES

The following programs represent only the major programs or general categories of noninstitutional resources. While some programs, such as social security, are not designed as student financial assistance, the availability of such programs provides funds for a significant number of needy students. Because a student who meets the eligibility criteria is guaranteed to receive benefits, it is important for aid officers to publicize the availability of these benefits, to encourage or assist students to make application, and to act as advocates for students where necessary.

The Veterans Administration The VA administers educational assistance programs for children of deceased or disabled veterans and for veterans themselves. The first program provides assistance to children of veterans who died from injury or disease or who are permanently and totally disabled as a result of military service. Stipends of $130 per month for full-time study, $95 for three-fourths-time study, and $60 for half-time study are paid upon completion of each month for a maximum of 36 months.

The cold war GI Bill provides allowances to honorably discharged veterans who have served on active duty after January 31, 1955. Monthly payments for full-time study would be $130 for a veteran with no dependents, $155 for a veteran with one dependent, and $175 for a veteran with two dependents. Proportionate payments are made for less than full-time study. A veteran would have one month of eligibility for each month of service to a maximum of 36 months of educational training. As of publication proposed revisions of veterans benefits are under consideration by Congress.

Social Security Social security benefits for children aged 18 to 21 are provided to full-time students attending public and private schools. The benefits, ranging between $30 and $120 per month, are paid to children of deceased, retired, or disabled workers. The local social security office can provide further information.

Aid programs for families with dependent children may provide for payments to aid children aged 18 through 20 who are attending a school or college. This provision is at the option of the individual state and further information should be obtained from the local public welfare agency.

State Scholarship Programs These are currently in operation in 17 states and under consideration in 7 states. In general these programs, administered by a central agency, follow common practices of basing the award on financial need with an upper limit of tuition or tuition and fees, renew the award for 4 years, but provide very limited funds for graduate study. State programs assume the availability of other forms of financial aid to supplement the state award. Close cooperation is required between financial aid officers and the directors of state scholarship programs.

Guaranteed Loan Programs Such programs, now operating in all states as a result of the Higher Education Act of 1965, provide low-interest, insured loans and an interest subsidy for students in institutions of higher education including eligible business, trade, technical, or vocational schools. Loan funds are made available from commercial banking sources or other lenders upon application by the student. Financial need is not a factor in the loan at the present time. Because of the widespread variances in lending policies, the aid officer should be aware of the climate for lending under this program in those states from which he draws his students and take every step to ensure that his students are able to secure adequate financing from this program. The institution may lend its own funds under an agreement with the state agency.

Since the subsidy is paid to the lender (i.e., the institution) on behalf of the student, this arrangement is beneficial if the institution has not been charging interest on its loans while the student is in school.

Community Scholarship Programs Programs of this type provide limited amounts of assistance to students going on to higher education. Aid officers should encourage applicants to check on the availability of funds from their own community. The aid officer should encourage the growth of community programs and, where possible, give advice and counsel on their operation. The Citizens Scholarship Foundation in Boston is also a source of information and assistance on the development of coordinated community scholarship programs.

Rehabilitation Programs These programs, operated by the states through directors of vocational rehabilitation, provide assistance for a broad range of handicapped students who wish to further their education. Originally limited to vocational training, the activities of these agencies have generally been extended to include college-level training.

Commercial Loan Programs Although such programs are not usually considered as student aid, they can play a role in the financial aid program of the institution, providing credit to parents to assist them in meeting their obligation and eliminating the necessity for the college to operate a short-term loan program of its own. In general, the loans are made to the parent rather than to the student and provide insurance on the life of the parent which guarantees funds toward the completion of the student's education. The insurance provisions with the plan should be carefully studied, since this benefit may be of great importance if the borrower is unable to obtain additional life insurance in a conventional manner. Two national plans of this type are:

Education Funds Inc.
10 Dorrance Street
Providence, R.I. 02901

Tuition Plan Inc.
535 Madison Avenue
New York, N.Y. 10022

Some programs provide no insurance but involve simply a commercial loan at a more favorable rate. Parents should be advised to investigate all possible sources of loan assistance available to them and to choose that which provides the greatest benefits at the lowest cost. The prepayment features of a plan may mean that the parent is operating largely on his own money and paying a relatively high fee for limited benefits.

The following formula can be used to determine the true annual interest rate for a given loan:

$$R = 2PC/A\ (N + 1)$$

where R = rate
P = payment periods in one year
C = finance charges
A = loan principal
N = number of installments

REFERENCES

1. The American Legion: *Need a Lift? to Educational Opportunities,* The American Legion Education and Scholarship Program, Indianapolis, Ind.
2. Babbidge, Homer D., Jr.: *Student Financial Aid: Manual for Colleges and Universities,* American College Personnel Association, Student Personnel Series, no. 1, Washington, 1960.
3. College Entrance Examination Board: *Financing a College Education: A Guide for Counselors,* College Entrance Examination Board, New York, 1968.
4. College Entrance Examination Board: *Financial Planning for Study in the United States: A Guide for Students from Other Countries,* College Entrance Examination Board, New York, 1967.
5. College Scholarship Service: *Manual for Financial Aid Officers,* College Entrance Examination Board, New York, 1967.
6. College Scholarship Service: *Student Financial Aid and Institutional Purpose,* College Entrance Examination Board, New York, 1963.
7. Hill, W. W., Jr.: *An Analysis of College Student Loan Programs,* United Student Aid Funds, Inc., New York, 1965.
8. Nash, George, with the collaboration of Paul F. Lazarsfeld: *New Administrator on Campus: A Study of the Director of Student Financial Aid,* a study for the College Entrance Examination Board, Columbia University Bureau of Applied Social Research (in press).
9. Taylor, Graham, and Robert J. Kates, Jr.: *New Horizons: A Study of Student Financial Aid in the Commonwealth of Massachusetts,* Massachusetts Board of Higher Education, 1967.
10. U.S. Office of Education: *College Work-Study Program Manual,* U.S. Department of Health, Education and Welfare, 1968.
11. U.S. Office of Education: *Educational Opportunity Grants Program, Manual of Policies and Procedures,* U.S. Department of Health, Education and Welfare, 1967.
12. U.S. Office of Education: *National Defense Student Loan Program, Manual of Policies and Procedures,* U.S. Department of Health, Education and Welfare, 1967.
13. U.S. Public Health Service: *Health Professions Student Loan Program, Manual of Policies, Procedures, and Information,* U.S. Department of Health, Education and Welfare, 1963.
14. U.S. Public Health Service: *Nursing Student Loan Program, Temporary Manual of Information, Policies and Procedures,* U.S. Department of Health, Education and Welfare, 1965.
15. Van Dusen, William D., and John J. O'Hearne: *A Design for a Model College Financial Aid Office,* College Entrance Examination Board, New York, 1968.

Chapter **10**

Student Activities

PAUL A. BLOLAND

Dean of Students and Associate Professor of Education, University of Southern California, Los Angeles, California

THE SCOPE OF THE ACTIVITIES PROGRAM

When we speak of student activities, we most often refer to noncurricular but formally organized programs which are sponsored by students with the approval of the college or university. Actually, however, it would be more accurate to include in this definition the wide range of informal, recreational, or leisure-time activities in which students participate as well as spectator-type activities. This broader definition is important because the ways in which students live outside of their academic work strongly influence the environment or climate of the campus. The terms "extracurricular" or "extra-academic" are often substituted for "student activities" to convey a greater sense of relationship to the academic program.

The "over-30" college or university administrator may still tend to view student activities with some condescension, remembering the activities area as a kind of lightweight campus charade peopled by football players, student politicians, the big dance, and fraternity initiations. At best they represented a harmless means of releasing excess energies, while at their worst they resulted in a police raid on a fraternity beer bust, a friendly riot after the big game, or other unnecessary competition with serious learning—which was what went on only in the classroom, of course.

For an administrator-educator to hold such views today would be to ignore the remarkable potential of the extracurriculum not only for disruption of the ongoing institution but, more importantly, for the development of a total campus climate for learning, a climate which by its very nature embraces both the curriculum and the extracurriculum and is created by both.

In recent years, students, acting through the extracurriculum, have closed down major universities, changed parietal rules, and forced the resignation of college presidents; they have also created "Free University" seminars and classes, evaluated courses and faculty members, tutored slum children, and created campus dialogue on the reform of higher education. Few of these activities were classroom activities born of a departmental curriculum committee; they were extra-academic, and yet each undeniably had a significant impact upon the college community and affected the kind of experience the students had in that community. That these were learning experiences cannot be denied. The only real choice the institution had was between working with the students in helping them to forge an educationally relevant campus experience or resisting student-initiated change.

Less dramatic perhaps but still with educational implications are the thousand and one out-of-class activities, formal and informal, which make up the life style of the campus: coffee in the grill, a rally in the gym, presiding over a meeting of the International Relations Club, attending a YWCA tea, voting in student elections, attending a student piano recital, organizing a new political group, preparing a brief for the student judiciary, singing in a midnight serenade on fraternity-sorority row—it is these things which to a considerable extent determine the personality or character of a particular campus.

The institution has relatively little to say about whether or not there will be a student activities program—there will be one. The question for the administrator would seem to be, "Is the activities program to be peripheral to and uninfluenced by the goals and objectives of the college, or is it to be an integral part of the college's overall program?" If the institution opts for the latter, then it must include the needs of such a program in its planning for facilities, budgeting, staffing, and even curriculum.

While the informal life of the campus will be greatly influenced by the presence or absence of residence halls, a student center, fraternity and sorority houses, acres of grassy lawn, or by the decor and atmosphere of the campus cafeteria, the location of bulletin boards, and the scheduling of classes, for the purposes of this discussion the activities program shall be constituted of the recognized or registered student organizations and the programs, projects, and events which they sponsor.

Subsidiary to or allied with the formal organizations on the typical campus are as many or more ad hoc groups, committees, and subcommittees. These too are an aspect of the formal activity program. Separate chapters have been devoted in this handbook to certain student-operated programs which properly can be considered to be part of the overall student activity program but which deserve extra attention because they are particularly significant segments of that program. Chapters have been written on the orientation of new students, student government, student publications, fraternities and sororities, and the student union or center. In addition, a substantial amount of the administrative attention given to student religious-work programs, international students, student housing, and the student judiciary involved in disciplinary administration involves the guidance and supervision of student activities.

This chapter will be devoted to an overall view of the campus program of student activities and its administration; hopefully, it will serve as an introduction to those chapters dealing with special phases of the extracurriculum.

STUDENT GROUPS

The scope of the student activities program is defined in part by the kinds of student organizational interests which are found in a particular college or university. Many schools have established a simple classification system for their official student organizations, and some have categorized them in terms of the varying requirements which they must meet; e.g., an organization maintaining a residence for its members must adhere to different and often more stringent regulations than a nonresidential group.

Below is a classification system typical of those employed by many colleges and universities:

1. Governing boards and councils
2. Social fraternities and sororities
3. Professional fraternities and sororities
4. Residence hall organizations
5. Cooperatives
6. Honorary organizations and societies (leadership and/or academic achievement)
7. Political action groups
8. Departmental and professional organizations
9. International student organizations
10. Recreational and hobby groups
11. Religious organizations

Recognition In order to define and identify those organizations which are bona fide elements of the college and those which are not, a device called "recognition" may be used.

A group of students may apply or petition for recognition by submitting certain required documents and information such as a constitution and bylaws, a statement of purpose, a list of officers, the name of a faculty adviser, criteria for membership, rules of procedure, any extra-university affiliation, etc. The application or petition is acted upon by the student personnel office, the faculty-student affairs committee, or the student government, and the newly recognized organization is then free to conduct its activities on the campus. Recognized groups usually have certain privileges such as the free use of college facilities, sponsorship of programs on campus, solicitation of funds, etc.

Rather than recognize student groups, a procedure which implies approval, some institutions merely ask new organizations to register, a procedure which they feel neither involves them in making judgments about the group's purposes nor implies college endorsement of its views.

The "Joint Statement on Rights and Freedoms of Students," drafted by the representatives of six national organizations, recommends that student groups "should not be required to submit a membership list as a condition of institutional recognition."[1]

Disestablishment If recognition is the procedure employed to bring new student organizations officially into campus life, a reverse procedure, often termed "disestablishment," is used to clear from the list groups which are no longer active. Procedures to remove a group from official status are initiated when it has not been active for a specified period of time (for example, when it has gone for two years without electing officers or sponsoring an activity), when the organization officers request disestablishment, or, after a hearing, as a penalty for the violation of rules.

In order to maintain a list of currently active groups, some institutions require them to register annually or to submit a list of new officers after each election. Groups which do not do so are presumed inactive and may be disestablished and have their campus privileges withdrawn.

Faculty and Staff Advisers As a condition for recognition, student organizations are often required to have a faculty or staff adviser or sponsor. He is ordinarily invited to serve by the student group and does so because of his interest in the group's program. Often he brings expertise in the field of the group's interest and concern. The Joint Statement recommends that "If campus advisers are required each organization should be free to choose its own adviser, and institutional recognition should not be withheld or withdrawn solely because of the inability of a student organization to

[1] "Joint Statement on Rights and Freedoms of Students," *The Journal of College Student Personnel,* vol. 8, p. 417, November, 1967.

secure an adviser. Campus advisers may advise organizations on the exercise of responsibility, but they should not have the authority to control the policy of such organizations."[2]

Off-campus Affiliation Many student organizations such as fraternities and sororities, political organizations, and professional associations and societies are affiliated as local campus chapters or branches of off-campus organizations the control of which is outside of the purview of the institution. The Joint Statement recommends that "Affiliation with an extramural organization should not of itself disqualify a student organization from institutional recognition."[3] However, problems are created when the purposes and policies of the parent group conflict with those of the college; e.g., discriminatory national membership policies. The college should be informed of such extramural affiliations when they exist and may require the local group to clarify its position vis à vis the policies of the parent organization.

Membership The Joint Statement recommends several practices or policies regarding membership in student organizations which should be considered by every institution. It states, for example, that the control of the membership, policies, and actions of a student organization should remain in the hands of those persons who hold bona fide membership in the institution. It also recommends that "campus organizations, including those affiliated with an extramural organization, should be open to all students without respect to race, creed, or national origin, except for religious qualifications which may be required by organizations whose aims are primarily sectarian."[4] Both the Joint Statement[5] and the American Council on Education[6] recommend that lists of members of student organizations be neither required nor kept by the college.

Policies and Regulations Every college or university needs to establish a viable set of regulations and policies in order to maintain the orderly conduct of campus activities and to make clear the proper channels and delegation of authority. It would seem good institutional practice to keep these to an absolute minimum and to establish procedures whereby such policies and regulations can be quickly reviewed and revised in the light of changing circumstances.

The process whereby policies and rules governing the conduct of campus activities are considered and adopted should receive careful attention. Representative students should participate as full partners in the campus legislative machinery, from the formulation of policies to their enactment and enforcement.

The policy statement may not necessarily be restrictive. It may indeed define the limits of the institution's authority rather than the limits of student organization authority, or it may simply state the general ground rules, restrictive or permissive, so that all concerned are aware of them and may proceed accordingly.

Handbooks In fairness to all involved, the college should publish a handbook for students in which, as a minimum, those formal policies and regulations which they are responsible for observing are published in full. It is helpful to have the name of the body enacting the policy and the date it was enacted published with each policy for future reference and to have those regulations or policies which apply to the personal conduct of individuals separated from those which apply to campus organizations. The handbook should outline the enactment or legislative process and the enforcement procedures, including the channels for appeal from the application or substance of a policy.

Activities Calendar The campus activities director or similar officer should main-

[2] *Ibid.*, p. 417.
[3] *Ibid.*, p. 417.
[4] *Ibid.*, p. 417.
[5] *Ibid.*, p. 417.
[6] American Council on Education, "Statement on Confidentiality of Student Records," July 7, 1967 (mimeographed).

tain a calendar of current or future activities. The calendar is particularly important where a limited number of facilities must be scheduled for maximum use by campus faculty and student groups. Each spring, student organizations should be requested to list those major programs or activities they plan to sponsor during the coming year and the facilities they will require. The procedure should include a campuswide meeting of organization leaders called by the activities office to resolve calendar and facility conflicts. If conflict between faculty groups or departments and student groups over scheduling seem likely, representatives from these groups should also be invited to attend. Once agreement is reached, the decision should be final except as changes are mutually negotiated between principals and placed on the revised calendar.

If feasible, the calendar should be published as a booklet and given wide distribution at the beginning of the next academic year. Campus groups should then be required to register their events, whether on the calendar or not, so that programs which do not eventuate can be cleared and the time and facilities can be released for other programs.

REGULATIONS GOVERNING STUDENT ORGANIZATIONS

Current campus policies and rules regulating the activities of student organizations have, for the most part, evolved over a number of years in response to specific crises, incidents, or problems. A problem occurs, it is resolved, and a new regulation is written to minimize the possibility of its recurrence. Policies have been borrowed from other colleges or universities in anticipation of potential problems, to implement the college's educational philosophy as it pertains to student life, or, more recently, in response to student demands for written, explicit statements of position to replace unwritten, implicit understandings.

Rule Making Many of the current regulations have come under attack by students in recent years as obsolete, unnecessary, or undesirable. While most students will admit that a need exists for defined and orderly procedures and an indication of acceptable limitations on organizational activity, they are raising questions about what rules are necessary and who should make them.

The college should establish clearly delineated procedures by which current policies and regulations may be reviewed periodically and upon request. The same or similar procedures should be established for the formulation and formal adoption of new rules covering current exigencies.

Student representatives should be involved in the decision-making process at all stages, although the formal enactment may be the responsibility of the chief student affairs officer, the president, or the board of trustees or regents. Some institutions have delegated specific areas of authority and decision making to student-faculty committees or representative student governments with no further approval required. However, few institutions can afford to surrender veto power since final accountability cannot be delegated or transferred. Whether this veto power can be exercised in the future in the face of mass student action remains to be seen.

Most policies and regulations which govern student organizations fall into the following areas:

Use of Campus Facilities. Which campus buildings, classrooms, meeting rooms, auditoriums, open-air areas, etc., may be used by campus groups and under what conditions? Organizations may reserve rooms or other facilities at a central office, usually a student activities office or the office which maintains the master calendar. Groups may be required to indicate on a reservation form the facility requested, the date of the event, the time span covered, the nature of the event, and the person responsible for the event.

Posting of Materials. What materials may be posted within the environs of the campus, where, and for what activities? The institution has a responsibility for making adequate bulletin boards available for campus publicity. It would be well to have each item posted bear the name of the sponsoring group and some indication of the date on which the poster is to be removed. Some colleges have found it advisable to maintain one or several uncontrolled bulletin boards for personal notices or for commercial off-campus advertising.

Distribution of Materials. What materials can be distributed on campus, where, and when? Student organizations, particularly political- and social-action groups, require a clear-cut definition of the ground rules governing the distribution of their literature. Distribution may be limited to certain prescribed areas of the campus or to tables placed in a central location. Trash cans should be provided in each such area or unsightly litter will result.

Solicitation of Funds. How may organizations solicit funds from students and faculty members on or off campus? Regulations, if needed, should specify minimum financial controls to ensure that funds thus collected are used for the purpose for which they were collected. The rules should indicate whether groups may solicit for off-campus causes or organizations, and they should establish a time limit.

Approval of Activities. What kinds of activities may be conducted by student organizations? Colleges and universities have long controlled the kinds of activities sponsored by student groups through a process of approval. In part, the approval function was designed to maintain essential controls over the time and place at which events took place as well as the manner in which they were presented. In part, approval also exercised controls over the nature or presumed content of the proposed events.

Approval has been generally required for social activities both on and off campus, the invitation to the campus of off-campus speakers, shows and concerts, rallies and demonstrations, and parades. These are a few of the areas which have been controlled through the approval function. Today, however, many of these approval requirements, once considered essential, are being discarded. For example, the requirement for approval of student social events and the allied requirement that faculty chaperones be present are quietly being dropped by many institutions, particularly the larger ones, as being an unenforceable extension of the *in loco parentis* philosophy. Registration of social events has often been substituted.

While time, place, and manner rules have not particularly been contested, much student and faculty discontent has centered around attempts by university authority to regulate the content of student programming. Specifically, much of the contention has focused on campus policies designed to regulate or control the invitation by students of controversial speakers from outside the campus. The Joint Statement suggests that "students should be allowed to invite and hear any person of their own choosing. Those routine procedures required by an institution before a guest speaker is invited to appear on campus should be designed only to insure that there is orderly scheduling of facilities and adequate preparation for the event, and that the occasion is conducted in a manner appropriate to an academic community."[7]

Colleges and universities should continually review their policies and procedures regulating the conduct of student activities, particularly those relating to political and social action. The resources of the student body, the faculty, and the staff should be utilized so that the resulting policies represent the end product of community consensus, tempered by a recognition of institutional responsibility for the educational process as reflected by the ways in which it permits its facilities and name to be used. The ways in which colleges and universities interpret their responsibilities will, of necessity, differ from campus to campus because of local exigencies; but the message

[7] "Joint Statement," pp. 417–418.

would seem to be clear that rules should be held to a necessary minimum and that a campus is unlikely to err, as far as the students are concerned, if it opts for greater rather than lesser freedoms while requiring the continued exercise of student responsibility in the exercise of those freedoms.

INFORMAL AND SPECTATOR ACTIVITIES

The climate of a campus is formed by more than the organized, student-directed extracurriculum. Of great significance are those activities, whether college- or student-directed, which affect the educational experience of a relatively passive audience. Organized student programs are not only of benefit to those who participate in their planning, organizations, and implementation but also to those for whom they are intended. The students who organize a symposium learn a great deal in its implementation. The actual program itself is of value to those who simply attend, and it will add to the richness of the campus environment through its own merits.

In the consideration and planning of a campus program, the college should not ignore or minimize events or activities which fall outside of the traditional, organized extracurriculum. An active, dynamic campus will offer a full range of events which contributes to the ongoing education of the student body.

Concert and Lecture Series Often the college will offer the best available artists, lecturers, and performances in a concert or lecture series planned and financed by the college through a concert director or a student-faculty committee. Attractions are contracted for through a concert or lecture agency, usually a year in advance, and the series is planned to fulfill the institution's obligation to develop cultural and intellectual interests in its students.

Intramural Activities Physical activity in a largely sedentary campus culture is important to the maintenance of health and bodily tone and to the reduction of tensions. A full program of intramural athletic competition is a necessary aspect of the extracurricular program and is most often provided by the college or university through its athletic department or department of physical education. The institution should provide fields for touch football, intramural track, soccer, softball, and other outdoor activities. Lighted outdoor tennis courts may be provided for both informal activities and intramural competition. A gymnasium should be available for basketball, volleyball, indoor track, wrestling, and other indoor sports, while an indoor swimming pool will make possible intramural competition in swimming, diving, and water polo. Tennis courts can be used for intercollegiate competition, intramural sports, and informal recreation. Bowling alleys, pool tables, and table-tennis facilities add to the variety of the intramural program.

A part-time or full-time staff person is necessary to establish leagues, arrange schedules, and supervise and assign referees. An intramural sports program can be supported in part by a system of entry fees which go to defray the costs of administration and of referees.

Informal Recreational Activities In addition to organized activities, students, particularly those in residence on or near the campus, should have the opportunity for physical activity on an informal basis. The gymnasium facilities can be kept open on weekends for pickup games of basketball or volleyball. Time for free swim periods should be arranged on the pool schedule. Tennis courts and playing fields should have unscheduled blocks of time available for non-team participants. Free play periods should also be maintained for the bowling alleys and pool tables. Space for card playing and other leisure-time activities should be provided and supervised, usually in the student union. Even outdoor and indoor areas used as commuter lunchrooms will enable students to get together for conversation at noon or during free periods. Quiet lounge space in the student union and in the various classroom buildings can provide a place to relax, to meet other students and faculty, and to talk. Facilities for hobbies, photography, and crafts are often an integral part of the services of the student union and provide additional leisure-time recreational opportunities.

Spectator Activities In addition to the regular college program of lectures and concerts, variety is added to the recreational opportunities available to students by programming weekend motion pictures of artistic or cultural interest. The student union or student governing body may program big-name "pop" artists, musical groups, and shows of contemporary interest or plan symposia, lecture series, panel discussions, and the like for the campus.

Of course, intercollegiate sports at most colleges and universities add to the color and life of the campus and provide an opportunity for a variety of related activities such as pep rallies, spirit groups, homecoming celebrations, and similar programs.

The vitality and excitement of a campus as well as much of the cultural and intellectual stimulation which should be a part of the college scene are provided by a well-planned and balanced variety of activities which call for active participation as well as merely passive attendance. Such programming permits the student to expand the range of his experience by exposure to recreational, cultural, social, and intellectual activities which may form the basis of new and lasting interests and tastes.

FINANCING STUDENT ACTIVITIES

Central to any program of student extracurricular life is adequate financial support. Much of the color and personality of a campus derives from the creativity and interests of its students, and the climate thus created affects the faculty and administration as well as the students themselves. If the student program is to exhibit richness and diversity and make a genuine impact upon the total college community, it must have access to sufficient funds.

There are a number of ways to develop financial support for organizational activities, and it may be helpful to consider these under the headings of (1) individual membership groups and (2) broadly representative governing groups.

Individual Membership Groups Most such organizations are supported primarily by a membership fee collected from each member on a regular basis. Additional funds may be raised by group-sponsored programs such as benefits, food sales, button sales, dances, concerts, drama productions, campus solicitation, queen contests, etc. To prevent proliferation and excessive harrassment of the faculty and student body, many colleges and universities have found it necessary to develop ground rules regulating on-campus fund-raising activities.

Individual membership organizations have raised funds by off-campus solicitation, usually in consultation with the university's development or fund-raising office, to avoid unfortunate competition with the institution's own sources of support. Some enterprising groups have even applied for government grants or private foundation support for programs related to the counseling of disadvantaged students.

At institutions where there is a general student body fee, membership organizations may also be eligible for allocations from the fee to supplement their own budgets or, in some few cases, for their total support.

Representative Governing Groups While all of the above sources of financial support may also be employed by governing groups, they are usually financed by one or a combination of the several plans listed below:

Compulsory Student Fees. Each eligible student, usually defined by credit load or graduate-undergraduate status, is assessed a fee which is collected by the institution at the time of registration and payment of tuition and fees. At its inception the fee is usually authorized by vote of the student body, which agrees thereby to assess itself. The fee may be defined as payment for membership in the student government, in which case it may be managed and allocated by the representative governing body.

More commonly, however, the fee is defined as a student activity fee and administered by an independent allocations board or committee. These funds may then be disbursed by the allocations board to a variety of activity groups including not only the student governing body but also the student union, the student newspaper, and major campus projects or programs functioning under independent committees. In some cases the fee is used to support drama, forensics, musical organizations, athletics, a recreational program, and the professional staff advising and supervising them.

Voluntary Student Fees. Rather than having the institution collect a compulsory student fee, some student governing groups have selected to sell voluntary memberships on a campuswide basis. While a certain amount of financial autonomy is obtained in this fashion, the procedure usually results in insufficient financing and the student governing body is forced to direct much of its energy into additional fund-raising activities.

Institutional Appropriations. At some universities and colleges an allotment is made from the institution's own general budget for the support of student activities and/or student government. It may be a fixed allocation each year, or it may be a fixed percentage of tuition income, which is dependent upon enrollment each year. It may then be disbursed by an independent allocation board or committee.

Variations of these plans are found at many colleges and universities. Public institutions in the West, for example, have set up associated student organizations, often quasi-independent corporations. These manage funds developed by mandatory student fees and use them to support a wide variety of programs for which state budget support is not available. Student unions and residence hall governing groups may assess their own independent fees on a compulsory basis and administer them through their representative governing boards.

SAMPLE LIST OF STUDENT ORGANIZATIONS RECEIVING BUDGETARY ALLOCATIONS FROM THE OFFICE OF STUDENT ACTIVITIES

Student Services

Cauldron (yearbook)
Cheerleaders
Distinguished Speakers Series
Dramatics
News (weekly university newspaper)
Spectrum (university literary magazine)
Student Union
Student Council
University Band and Dance Band
WNEU (student radio station)

Minor Sports

Men's Ski Team (fully supported)
Rifle Club (partially supported and dues-collecting)
Women's Intercollegiate Ski Club (fully supported)
Yacht Club (partially supported and dues-collecting)

Clubs (fully supported)

Art Club
Chorus
Debate Council
Folk Dance Society
International Relations Club

Clubs (partially supported and dues-collecting)

Auto Club

Camera Club

Husky Key Society (works to promote school spirit, campus social activities, and special activities at athletic events)

Jazz Society

Omega Sigma (women's society seeking to further particular interests of women students)

New Clubs (initial payment only to help new clubs get started)

Chaperones and Fraternity and Sorority Advisers Chaperones and fraternity and sorority advisers are also funded to partially repay these staff members for their extra assistance and to enhance student-faculty relationships.

Note: Allocations are made by the director of student activities with the advice of the dean of students and on the recommendation of members of the Student Activities Committee, composed of faculty and students. As a long-standing policy, it has been the custom of the university to support completely the service-type organizations on the grounds that these groups are serving basic needs of the student body and are operated almost as departments of the university's total educational program.

There are quite a number of organizations which are partially supported, the rest of the money coming from dues, and others which are given very modest grants to cover their simple requirements.

Financial Control and Responsibility Because of the frequently very large amounts of money generated by student activities and because of the transiency of the student population, good business practice dictates that reasonable safeguards be established to assure that these funds are properly managed and accounted for. Financial supervision may take a variety of forms depending upon the complexity and size of the institution, its philosophy concerning the supervision of student activities, and the source of the funds.

Student Organization Bank. All student groups may be required to bank their funds with the college, which then deposits them in a special account and conducts a deposit and withdrawal system much like that of a commercial bank, including deposit slips, checkbooks, periodic auditing services, centralized bookkeeping, and the like.

Business Office Management. All student organizations may be required to maintain their funds with the institution's business office, which establishes an account for each group and provides bookkeeping and simple auditing services. Deposits and withdrawals are made in the same manner as that required of the various departments, colleges, and agencies of the official institution, using requisitions, vouchers, etc.

Off-campus Banking. Organizational funds may be deposited in an off-campus commercial bank selected by the organization with little or no supervision by the college or university.

Periodic Auditing. Student treasurers may be required to submit their books annually to the college business office or student financial service, which may perform a simple audit on them, checking balances, accounting for cash, and examining the record of deposits and expenditures for irregularities. The institutional auditing function may be required for funds maintained off-campus as well as for those deposited with the college.

Organizational Budgeting. As an important aspect of financial management, particularly when funds are allocated from a compulsory student fee, organizations may be required to submit an annual budget for approval by the allocations committee or by the business office. Budgeted funds may then be spent without additional authorization, while nonbudgeted expenditures may require further organizational authorization or business office approval.

Countersignature. Whether organizations conduct their banking activities off-campus or maintain funds with the college, it would be well to suggest or require that all checks or similar instruments be countersigned by a faculty adviser, a college official, or an officer of the organization in addition to the treasurer.

University Services When student organizations deposit their funds with the business office it becomes a simple matter for these organizations to requisition various services from the institution in the same manner as departments or offices. Student groups may then use other services of the college business office for discounts; requisitioning of audiovisual services, books, mimeograph and poster materials; tax-exempt travel; petty cash funds; ticket sales; and the like. The organization's ability to pay for such services can readily be ascertained at the time the requisition is approved, and the organization itself benefits from the service.

FACILITIES FOR STUDENT ACTIVITIES

If the activities program is to function properly as an integral part of the college's educational program, adequate physical facilities must be provided and an appropriate priority granted to their renovation or construction. Facilities suitable for student activities will include not only buildings and rooms but equipment as well. A well-planned campus program will provide adequate headquarters rooms for departmental and professional groups as well as for organizations which draw their membership from the campus at large.

The Student Center At the heart of the student activities program will be the student center, student union, or university center. The student center is a university building designed specifically as a nucleus for student life or, more broadly, as the campus community center where students, faculty, administration, guests, and alumni can meet and, hopefully, interact. Its facilities will provide for recreational and leisure time activities as well as the more structured extracurricular program. It should have space available for student offices, workrooms, storage space, and organizational lockers. Most student organizations will have their headquarters in the student union, and many of their activities will take place in its environs.

For the student center to serve educational ends most effectively it should not become a student ghetto, a building where student life is segregated from the rest of the ongoing institutional concerns and programs. It is recommended that activities staff offices be intermingled with student headquarters, with the staff advisers playing a role in the day-to-day planning and organization of the programs and events being developed.

Organizational Headquarters Facilities While some large universities have constructed student office buildings, it is likely that most student offices will continue to be housed in a centrally located student union or student center along with a variety of other student-centered services and facilities. Because many student groups are closely identified with particular academic departments, professional schools, colleges, or residence halls, it would be advantageous for them to be housed in or near the office of the department head, director, or dean of the unit from which they draw their membership. At the time academic buildings or residence halls are being planned, some space should be reserved in these buildings for professional associations or academic societies.

The central facilities should be reserved for major organizations which recruit members on a campuswide basis. While not every student organization can be provided with office space in the student center, a system of priorities can be established with some permanent office space assigned, some facilities assigned on a year-to-year basis, and one or more offices rotated among important but temporary projects or programs. For permanent and major organizations, such as the student governing body, space can be designed to serve their specific needs and assigned to them on a permanent basis. Other offices can be of a standard design and size.

Meeting Rooms Rooms for group meetings will always be at a premium, and student organizations should have the opportunity to reserve vacant classrooms and seminar rooms in addition to rooms specifically reserved for student groups. They will need space for business meetings of the organization and many will require larger auditorium or classroom-type facilities for meetings to which the campus community is invited to hear a speaker or join in discussion.

Several conference and committee rooms should be available for student group use, fitted with tables and chairs and provided with blackboards. Because space is usually limited, no group should be given exclusive jurisdiction over a meeting room; but priorities can be established for certain meetings such as sessions of the student governing body, judicial groups, and others which have established a regular schedule of meetings.

The Activities Center If student activities and organizations are to serve as educational experiences for the participating students, provision must be made for the equipment which makes learning more effective. As an integral part of the office of the director of student activities, a workroom should be provided with appropriate equipment and tools. The activities office or center would then not only process the clearances, work orders, approval forms, requisitions, calendar dates, and other procedural requirements but would provide at a central location in the student union the basic office equipment which student organizations might not be able to afford or maintain separately.

The activities center should have at its disposal such items as low-power amplifiers and microphones, movie projectors, screens, mimeograph and ditto machines, a podium, blackboards, folding tables, an adding machine, addressograph equipment, a postage meter, a photocopy machine, typewriters, and materials and paints for poster making. There will be sufficient use of these items to justify having them immediately available for student projects without requiring a trip across campus to another service agency or office to obtain them.

Thus equipped, the student activities office and activities center should serve as the focal point for most student programs and projects. The professional staff is available for consultation and advice as programs develop and can serve as a technical and educational resource. With these various facilitating functions located centrally, much student and staff time can be saved, bureaucratic delay can be reduced, and the staff can be kept informed of current and future programs as they develop.

ADMINISTRATIVE ORGANIZATION

The administrative organization and staffing of the activities program will depend, of course, upon the unique characteristics of each institution: its size, its resources, its commitment to the educational values of the activity program, and the nature of the student body. No single "best" staff structure can be prescribed for all institutions, but a fairly consistent pattern of titles and duties can be discerned.

Organizational Structures It may be helpful to look at the organization of the student activities staff in terms of small and large institutions, since the complexity of the operation will vary with institutional size.

Small Institutions. In colleges and the smaller universities, no specialized director of student activities is usually provided for as such. The chief student personnel officer such as the dean of men/women or director of student personnel supervises the overall activity program as an integral aspect of his responsibilities. The work load may be distributed among members of the faculty and staff who advise individual organizations and committees, but the direction and coordination is assigned to the student personnel officers who in turn report to the president or, in some instances, the academic dean.

Larger Institutions. The complex organization of the larger universities is reflected in their activity offices. A director of student activities may report to a dean of students or a vice-president of student affairs. On the activities staff itself will be program directors and advisers with responsibility for advising and supervising various elements of the activities program. In addition to the director of student activities and his staff, other administrative officers may be assigned student activity responsibilities. The director of residence halls may have responsibility for residence hall student government. The deans of men/women will work closely with fraternities and sororities. The director of the student union will have assistants developing and supervising programs associated with the union facility, while members of the journalism faculty may advise student publications.

Centralization versus Decentralization. With a multitude of activities taking place in even the smallest of colleges, there is an obvious need for coordination so that scheduling conflicts do not develop, college regulations are applied to all, and some sense of direction and purpose will be sustained. In the small institution, coordination is quite simple. One single staff member merely relates one activity to another in his mind, the most efficient central-headquarters control unit. As soon as more than one person becomes involved in the program, problems of organization, coordination, and communication arise and must be resolved.

In larger institutions with many staff members dealing with a great variety of activities and programs, some form of central direction and control is needed. A master scheduling calendar may be maintained in the activities office, the various forms and approvals are processed, university policies and regulations are interpreted and implemented with a greater degree of consistency, and needed programs can be identified and initiated. As a division of the larger, centralized student affairs program, the work of the activities office can be coordinated with the other divisions, many of which may be seeing the same students.

Staffing The size of the activities staff and the scope of its responsibilities will depend in part upon the size of the university and its activity program. Below are listed some of the titles and the duties associated with each of the positions that are often found in complex institutions.

Director of Student Activities. The director is in charge of the activities office and is responsible to the dean of students or vice-president of student affairs. He may also carry the title of associate dean, coordinator, dean of student life education, etc. He is responsible for the coordination of student activities and the interpretation and implementation of policies and regulations pertaining to student organizations and activities. He may supervise a program staff and prepare a budget for his office. He often consults with student organizations on their budgeting problems, recommends policy changes and additions (hopefully policy deletions as well), and advises one or more major student organizations or programs such as the student governing body and its related committees.

Director of the Student Union. While the student union or student center is often administratively separated from the activities offices, there are many advantages to having it function as an integral part of the activities office. In this type of centralized organization the director of the student union will report to the director of student activities. Student union programming then becomes a coordinate part of the overall campus activity program.

The director may have responsibility for programming only, for the advising of the many activities planned around the facility, or he may have responsibility for the entire building, including the food facilities and the business management of all income-producing activities.

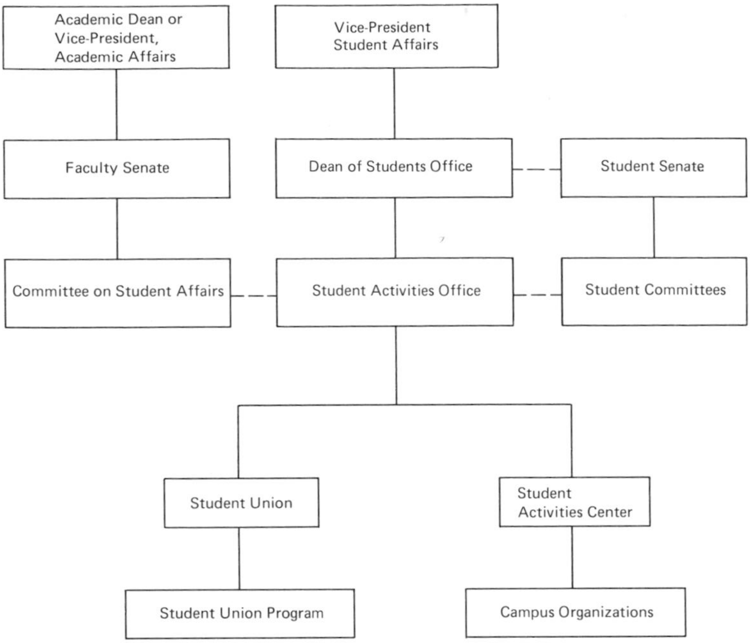

Fig. 1 *Table of organization.*

Program Director. In a large activities office or student union staff office, there may be one or more program directors who will be responsible for supervision and for the giving of counsel and advice to the student boards and committees which plan and carry out programs. The program director may have a staff of program advisers working under his direct supervision, and he usually advises several student groups himself.

Program Adviser. The program adviser is usually a junior staff member, often a recent graduate or a beginning graduate student for whom this is an initial professional staff experience. He will be assigned a number of student organizations and/or committees for which he will be the principal day-to-day adviser, attending their meetings and conferring with the members as they work on the details of their programs.

Financial Director. Because student activities and programs involve a heavy financial commitment, problems of contract negotiation and approval, cash income and expenditure, and an often bewildering variety of accounts, even medium-sized institutions will find it expedient to appoint a staff member to be the business manager for all student enterprises. He may report to the business office or to the director of activities, but he must be fully involved in both the financial and program aspects of the activities program. In one institution, the financial director will simply process the requisitions and other paper work while maintaining the accounts. In another university, all student organization funds will be banked with his office and he will have a staff to handle the accounts and transactions.

Graduate Assistants. If the university provides graduate-level training in student personnel work or related disciplines, an opportunity in the activity office should be available to qualified students for part-time professional-level experience under supervision. The graduate assistant may serve as an administrative assistant to the director of student activities or the program director and/or adviser to several organizations or committees.

Professional Associations While each activities staff member may hold individual membership in any of a number of professional societies or associations depending upon his disciplinary identification, there are several organizations which provide publications, conferences, and workshops concerning student activities and related programs. Institutional or individual membership in these groups is important because it provides an opportunity for the staff members to keep abreast of the latest thinking in the field, to learn of new program ideas, to exchange information or seek experienced assistance, and to recruit staff. Professional membership is one index of the extent to which the staff is attempting to professionalize and upgrade itself.

The American College Personnel Association (ACPA), an individual membership organization, is the college-level division of the American Personnel and Guidance Association and is concerned with the formulation and maintenance of professional standards among college student personnel workers, college teachers, counselors, deans, directors, or research staff. Its Commission IV, "Students, Their Activities, and Their Community" is of particular interest to activities staff members.

The National Association of Student Personnel Administrators (NASPA) is the national organization of deans and administrators of student affairs programs. Membership is largely institutional, but there have been provisions for individual membership since 1964.

The Association of College Unions-International (ACU-I), is an organization of college unions. Its purpose is to provide an opportunity for unions to join in studying and improving their services and to assist in the development of new college unions.

The National Association of Women Deans and Counselors (NAWDC) admits to active membership any woman who holds a master's degree from an accredited institution and who holds a position such as dean, counselor, adviser, administrator, or teacher in the field of student personnel in an educational institution.

Staff Qualifications The members of the activities department will often have training in a variety of disciplines, but graduate-level course work in the various behavioral sciences, student personnel work, higher education, counseling, and field research techniques will be most relevant.

Activities staff members who have had undergraduate leadership experience in student government, student union activities, and other extracurricular programs will find these experiences useful.

WHAT OF THE FUTURE?

The future direction of the student activities program is not at all clear at this time. While much has been written about the extracurriculum as a significant aspect of the overall educational program of the college and university, it has been the source of much concern to the institution. Students simply do not regard college public relations as an important consideration in the planning of their programs, and the general public does not always understand or accept the current interests and mores of the contemporary student culture.

Because of its potentiality for negative public relations, the student activities program has been subject to a variety of rules and regulations designed to limit its negative impact upon the public and upon the ongoing academic program. While regulations have also been designed to maximize the educational values inherent in the extracurriculum, the net result, nevertheless, has been a continuing tension between student desires and institutional concerns.

Whether colleges and universities can continue to regulate student activities as in the past, for whatever reasons, is not certain. The Joint Statement attempts to establish, on a national basis, certain rights and freedoms for students and student organizations which it states are necessary for the freedom to learn. "Freedom to teach and freedom to learn are inseparable facets of academic freedom. The freedom to learn depends upon appropriate opportunities and conditions in the classroom, on the campus, and in the larger community."[8] The statement assumes that freedoms of inquiry and expression are essential to the general well-being of society.

The fact is that these freedoms, if exercised irresponsibly, may well jeopardize the welfare of the parent institution as alumni and community pressures converge upon behavior which is not sanctioned by the greater community.

Irrespective of the concept of political freedom of expression, there is still considerable divergence of opinion about the best ways in which to maximize the educational values inherent in the extracurriculum. Can the extracurriculum be most potent under conditions in which the adult members of the college community, the faculty and the staff, are vigorously excluded from participation in student activities? Can the extracurriculum be educationally potent when it is controlled by the adult members of the campus community and not permitted to move in directions which seem of value to the student participants?

The dilemma, in all probability, will not be solved by the rationally derived balance between the two extremes. The current drive for student freedoms, backed by mass action and protest, may undoubtedly result in a minimum of campus regulation and a maximum of student organization autonomy. Then the college or university which wishes to affect the quality of extracurricular activities as an important aspect of its educational offerings will have to do so through the influence of adult advisors, faculty or staff, who will not have supervisory responsibilities but will, instead, provide experience, expertise, and continuity for student enterprises.

REFERENCES

Bloland, Paul A.: *Student Group Advising in Higher Education,* American Personnel and Guidance Association, Washington, 1967 (34 pp.).

Bloland, Paul A., and Robert L. Hall: "Surveying the Facility Needs of Student Organizations," *The Journal of College Student Personnel,* pp. 188–194, 1963.

"Extracurricular Activities: Students Thrive on Freedom in a Framework," *College Management,* vol. 2, pp. 24–49, September, 1967.

Klopf, Gordon J.: "The Role of the College Faculty Adviser With the Student Group," *The Journal of College Student Personnel,* vol. 2, pp. 38–42, 1961.

Pruitt, Wilton: "College Students, Their Community, and Their Activities," in Klopf (ed.), *College Student Personnel Work in the Years Ahead,* The American Personnel and Guidance Association, Washington, 1966, pp. 10–21.

Stroup, Herbert: *Towards a Philosophy of Organized Student Activities,* University of Minnesota Press, Minneapolis, 1964.

Stroup, Herbert: "The Extra-Activities Curriculum: What Student Needs Must Be Met?" *Liberal Education,* vol. 53, no. 1, pp. 33–40, 1967.

Zissis, Cecelia: "Changes in Activities Programs," *Journal of The National Association of Women Deans and Counselors,* vol. 30, pp. 164–166, Summer, 1967.

[8] "Joint Statement," pp. 416–417.

Chapter **11**

Governing the Student Community

JAMES P. MC INTYRE

Vice-president for Student Affairs, Boston College, Chestnut Hill, Massachusetts

Colleges and universities have a responsibility to prepare a student to make a life as well as to make a living. Part of the student's life will revolve around the fact that he will be a citizen in a democratic society. This status brings with it responsibilities and opportunities both for the individual and for society. These responsibilities cannot be assumed automatically the day after graduation unless the student has had an opportunity to bear the responsibilities of being a citizen while in college. The extent to which an academic institution considers this objective important will inevitably determine the extent to which the institution provides meaningful opportunity to bear citizenship responsibilities within its community. This in turn will determine, in large measure, the extent to which the college has prepared its students to bear their larger civic responsibilities after graduation.

It is well for the future citizen to learn early in his life that democratic processes have limitations; that they may engender frustrations; that, as guarantors of individual liberties, they cannot tolerate personal license; and that a democratic system provides wide opportunity for experimentation with programs, strategies, and objectives.

Properly structured, student government will provide many opportunities for students to blend theory with practice, thought with action. Students need opportunities not only to learn about group dynamics in a psychology class but to feel the dynamics of a group in action. Students should not only be exposed to the science of administration from a textbook but also be able to experience its complexities in action. Although thought must precede action, thought becomes more comprehensive and meaningful when it is tested by practice. Contemporary students will not permit academic institutions to exist merely as citadels of conceptualization. Nor should they. Appropriately structured student-government bodies will serve both as channels and outlets for their energies.

It is not difficult to appreciate how these educational benefits can accrue to those students who are actively involved in student government. Yet to be a viable force on campus, an effective student government should capture the interests of other students by arousing them to activity in the workings of the college community.

HISTORICAL BACKGROUND

The seeds for what is known today as "student government" were evident as early as two centuries ago in some colleges. Even in those institutions in which there was no formal structure of student government, the communication of student needs, interests, and wishes has left an indelible mark on American higher education. Although specific and valuable contributions have been made over the years, more important is the fact that students have effectively altered, broadened, and embellished the very definition of American higher education.

A novelty at William and Mary in the eighteenth century, student government in some form is as common as are students in the twentieth-century American college. Although the initial attempts at formal student government were not always successful, its roots are evident in the early history of the American college. Early traces of student government can be found at institutions such as Oberlin, Union, and Yale, which made many contributions to the blossoming of American higher education. Yet, although college student government existed in the eighteenth century, it did not develop as a viable and integral part of the American college until the middle third of the twentieth century.

An historical perspective suggests that student government has followed an evolutionary pattern beginning with a focus on exclusively social functions and student activities to modern examples of students being involved in every way in the governance of their institutions. In some colleges, this evolutionary process is in the embryonic stage; in others, it is rather advanced.

The factors which have accelerated or retarded the growth of college student governments evolve around differences in student-body abilities, attitudes of faculty and administrators, and the ecology of the different campuses. The result is that the powers, the practices, and the effectiveness of college student government are represented at every point on an extended continuum which runs from nonexistence to a point at which the student government is accepted as a representative of a constituency which is collectively a partner with the faculty and the administration.

Whether student government exists because students first felt a need to institutionalize it or because college administrators first felt that its existence would make educational contributions to the student body is not important. It is essential, however, that we consider why it does exist or what deficiencies would endure in its absence.

Those who argue against student government suggest that it interferes with the primary obligation of the student—to obtain an education. Unmindful of the difficulty of measuring the benefits of student government, its adversaries would allow that its productivity and its results are incommensurate with the time, effort, and commitment that it requires. It is also argued that a strong, viable student-government force becomes destructive of the academic community since it vies for power against its natural foes—the faculty and the administration. It is sometimes alleged that student government has been ineffective and that it has not been successful in dealing with the problems it has had to face, including representing and governing its own constituency. Critics point to student riots, sit-ins, and demonstrations as firm evidence in advocating this point of view.

On the other hand, one might consider the void that would exist if there were no student-government structures. There would be no formal agency for the direction of social and student activities. There would be one less means of a student learning the essence of democracy, the complexities of the communication process, and the importance of understanding interpersonal relationships.

The impact of the loss of student government would vary from college to college. Although the general deficiencies cited above would be felt by all colleges, some might experience even more mortal losses as, for example, the college whose student body had matured to a point of sophisticated and professionalized accomplishment.

In the absence of a productive student-government body through whose mechanism student needs can be perceived, communicated, and, perhaps, filled, there would be no organized means by which the breadth, relevance, and urgency of needs could be expressed. And student opinion will be expressed if not in an organized way, then in a sporadic, ad hoc way.

College administrators and faculty have often viewed student government with a jaundiced eye. In many cases they are willing to concede to students the jurisdiction of proms, parties, and yearbooks, but little else. Administrative and faculty myopia may be symptomatic of a transferral from the classroom situation in which the student is laboring within a superior-inferior relationship.

Many student-government groups have been obstructed in arriving at optimal success due to three factors: (1) their dependence for financial resources on the institution itself, (2) their inflexible organizational structures which have failed to keep pace with the quantitative and qualitative growth of institutions, (3) their inability to attract to service large numbers of the most academically talented student-body members, a failing which can be at least partially attributed to the tendency of many members of the university community to caricature all student-government representatives, regardless of their abilities and achievements.

In the final analysis, student-government groups will only be successful when they are able to overcome these problems which have plagued their existence. Beyond this, the criteria for successful student government can only be set by the individual group, operating within the framework of a particular institution. The success of a student government cannot always be measured by its quantifiable achievements, since the objectives being worked toward may lie outside its jurisdiction. The standard, then, for successful student government may often have to be determined by observing the manner in which a particular issue was handled, the depth of preparation, and the strategy employed in its presentation, rather than in the final outcome of issues.

PHILOSOPHICAL BACKGROUND

In this age of dramatic change and quantitative growth in our colleges, we have, paradoxically, seen students in a less sharp focus than their importance suggests. There are more colleges, more students, more courses, more problems than ever before. Paralleling the quantitative growth of our colleges has been a qualitative change in the colleges' constituencies. The faculties have been burdened with ominous warnings of "publish or perish" and have then been forced into teaching fewer and more esoteric courses in their academic disciplines. Administrators, for the most part, are being recruited from the teaching ranks and are being asked to perform tasks for which they are not specifically and professionally prepared.

These changes in American higher education, complicated by its rapid growth, have changed the relationships of students to their colleges and universities. There is, then, a need for a more precise definition of the role to be played by students within their institutions. Much of the unrest that has erupted on American campuses during the past few years has been aggravated by a breakdown in communication among administration, faculty, and students as to just what the role of the latter is or should be.

One basis of student power is inherent in the students' numbers. Whenever this strength is focused on a particular issue, it can exert an overwhelmingly positive or negative force. An equally important root of student power, especially in the private college, is the financial contribution of the students. Student tuitions and fee payments contribute, generally, from 60 percent to nearly 100 percent of the revenues for the operating budgets of private colleges. On the other hand, a negative aspect of the financial weight of students, which is as important to public as it is to private colleges, is the possibility that indecorous student behavior on campus will have an adverse influence on the potential generosity of donors, foundations, and legislators.

Latent as well as real student power must be recognized and understood. Building a viable student government will be one of the most effective means of recognizing, understanding, and dealing with the power that students wield.

THE PURPOSE OF STUDENT GOVERNMENT

Meaningful student-government bodies have three essential functions to perform: to represent, to provide service, and to communicate. The last of these transcends and unites the first two.

Representation Too often, student representatives rely on their informal contacts with their own peer groups for timely assessments of their constituencies. The unilateral point of view gathered from monolithic groups demonstrates its own inadequacy. To be effective, student-government leaders must be able to assess accurately the interests, the needs, and the points of view of those they are representing. This may be accomplished in the following ways:

1. Student-government people should establish a permanent and visible location for those of their constituency who wish to meet with them.
2. They should be willing to go out and meet with those personality types who are reluctant to visit with them.
3. They should consider the possibility of suggestion boxes or similar devices for

those who feel more comfortable about putting their views in writing than expressing them orally.

4. On the more important issues, student governors ought to consider the possibility of establishing a poll mechanism so that a more scientific sampling and student consensus may be garnered.

Inevitably, the problem for the individual student representative will be to decide for himself when to respect and when to disregard the view of the majority of his constituency, depending on what will be best for his college at the particular time. This internal conflict is the same as the inner turmoil that any elected representative will encounter when he must decide whether he should follow the popular point of view, which may run counter to his own, or whether he must have the courage of his convictions and act in opposition to the opinion of the majority.

Service Services should be supplementary and/or complementary to those offered by other agents or agencies of the institution. The types of services to be provided will depend on the sophistication of the institution and its student-government group. The basic charge to the government will have to be to find needs and to fill them to whatever extent its resources will allow. In the past, services have been principally social, focusing on dances, mixers, and concerts, as well as lecture series. More recently, student-government groups have sponsored special courses, have published literary works such as compendiums of student-authored poems and short stories, and have inaugurated course critiques, student directories, faculty evaluation procedures, etc. The breadth and depth of services that can be provided depend merely on the group's imaginative energies and the degree of cooperation that may be evidenced by a college's faculty and administration. By observing the services sponsored by student groups, an institution's administration can gain a realistic insight into the current needs and interests of students. More specifically, the sponsored noncredit courses may be a valid barometer for college administrators of the adequacy and relevancy of the institution's curriculum.

Communications The mishandling of this responsibility may be one of the root causes of both student-body apathy and a poor understanding of student government by faculty and administrative groups. Adequate communications will exist only if attention is focused on the necessity of its being two-way as well as on the fact that it has both horizontal and vertical dimensions. In a very real sense, the first two responsibilities of student government can only be fulfilled if the prior requirement of adequate communications is met.

It is the obligation of student-government groups to communicate formally with their constituency and to foster, by establishing the appropriate apparatus, the constituency's communication with the governing group. In addition, the student-government body must communicate not only *with* administration and faculty but also *to* the student body from these groups. Student-government communication has been most erratic when it has been attended to informally. Informal communication can be effective and will exist even if one does not desire its existence. Its weakness, however, lies in its exclusive use. Again, it is important to stress the need for establishing the means by which grass-roots sentiments may be filtered to the upper echelon of the student-government apparatus.

Effective communication can be accomplished formally by the systematic use of bulletin boards, the publication of regular student-government newsletters, and the conduct of at least some meetings which are open to the public.

BENEFITS OF STUDENT GOVERNMENT

In this age of rapid quantitative and qualitative growth, American higher education is beset with more problems than ever before. A student governing body of high quality can provide its institution with a fresh pool of talent which, while it may not contribute maturity and experience to the solution of problems, can contribute intelligence, imagination, and creativity. A viable student-government group can assist an institution in broadening the scope of its vision and at the same time assist it in maintaining the proper perspective on its problems. In an age of disintegration and fragmentation in American higher education, it should be remembered that students are the last important means for integration and cohesion in the college. Certainly the institution's academic administration can tell its student body how well-qualified its faculty is, but only the students can tell the administration how effective the teaching is. Although the student-affairs administration can inform the student body about the comprehensiveness of its services, only the student body can tell the administration how relevant these services are. Although a college's administration can *con*ceive the scope and urgency of students' needs, only students can *per*ceive them.

The objectives of a particular student government will vary with the campus and, within the individual frame of reference, particular goals have to be delineated. The absence of a philosophy will inevitably lead to a rather chaotic and ineffective existence for student government. The result will be to leap from effort to effort, to dissipate energies, and, undoubtedly, to make a negative impression on all of the institution's constituencies: the students, the faculty, and the administration.

PURPOSES, POWERS, AND SCOPE

There is probably no more sensitive, complicated, or more flexible aspect of American higher education today than the changing roles of students, faculty, and administration. If a trend has developed in our recent past, it is that college administrators have begun to share their powers with their faculty and, more recently but to a lesser extent, with their students. This evolution has forced college educators to attempt to define in precise terms the powers, the rights, and the freedoms of each of these three segments.

The most recent suggestion of what the rights of students in all colleges should be can be found in the "Joint Statement on Rights and Freedoms of Students," issued by the American Association of University Professors, the American Council on Education, and the National Student Association. This document proposes that "the student body should have clearly defined means to participate in the formulation and application of institutional policy affecting academic and student affairs." There is no explicit defense of this position as a right of the student within the Joint Statement. Its justification lies in the definition of colleges and universities as academic communities in which common goals are shared by the students, faculty, and administration, who are partners in the pursuit of these goals.

Although there are historical precedents for student involvement which can be traced back to the medieval university, an institution's trustees have been regarded as the only group in a position to share its ultimate authority over an institution with other individuals or groups. While it has been pointed out recently that students are not divested of their civil rights when they become members of an academic community, to the best of the author's knowledge there is no provision or precedent for transferring guardianship of all the student's individual civil rights to any body.

Philosophically, it can be argued that students have a right to those things which are necessary to achieve their objectives. The fact of the matter is that beyond respecting individual civil rights and future interpretations of the contractual agreement that may exist between a student and his institution, the individual institution, through its trustees, may do as it pleases. It should be remembered, however, that the way in which it chooses to share or to withold its powers will proclaim publicly the type of institution that it is and dramatize the kind of institution that it is going to be.

AREAS OF INVOLVEMENT

Several criteria should be employed when determining the areas in which students could be involved. It is reasonable to suggest that students should be involved in those areas which affect them directly and to which they can make a contribution. One difficulty that arises is that many of the areas which qualify for student involvement are areas in which the faculty and administration have jurisdiction. Yet there are few areas within an institution which should be the exclusive prerogative of a single constituency.

The extent of involvement of a constituency should reflect the extent of impact that a particular sovereignty will have over an individual constituency. Therefore, students could have a major jurisdiction over their own student activities, social events, and discipline, whereas it would be tenable to have students involved in only a minor way in areas such as admissions, academic affairs, and curriculum matters. Even having criteria available to be employed in determining those areas in which students could be involved does not absolve the individual institution from the necessity of determining the readiness of its campus for such involvement and of the best means of accomplishing such involvement.

Students can be involved in institutionwide affairs in any number of ways. It is possible to assign jurisdiction of a particular area to student government; it is possible to establish a mechanism which will permit student government to propose a point of view for consideration, encouraging student government and the student press to openly discuss all matters which develop within the institution. An increasingly popular method of involving students has been to define the institution as a community in which students are accepted as sharing in the pursuit of its goals.

SCOPE OF INVOLVEMENT

In addition to determining the area in which students may be involved, administrators must decide the scope of involvement. Again, the amount of concern that a particular area has for students could be an appropriate criterion in determining whether students should be involved merely in policy making or whether they should also assume responsibility for the administration of a domain.

There are fewer difficulties with involving students in general policy formulation than in letting them participate in the actual administration of the policy. This can be appreciated when one considers again the general contributions that can be made by students—relevance, intelligence, imagination, and creativity. These qualities can never be in oversupply when the broadest possible implications of policy making are being sought. However, there are practical problems in involving students with the specifics of administering a particular policy.

It should be remembered that the first burden of a student is to meet his prior responsibilities. The application and administration of policy could require specific knowledge of a technical field that it may be impractical to ask the student to master. Although students have the potential to make a substantial contribution to an admissions policy committee, for example, it would not be easy for a student to acquire a sufficient knowledge of standarized tests, to understand the vagaries of feeder schools, or to become attuned to the subtleties of written recommendations to the extent that his membership on a committee that reviewed individual applications would be valuable to the student, the institution, or the process.

It might prove difficult to be respectful of the principle of confidentiality if students were involved in the administration and application of all policies. For example, a policy committee which was discussing the merits of recruiting certain types of teachers could benefit from student contributions. However, student participation in a similar group which was charged with the responsibility of reviewing the personal credentials of a faculty member to determine whether he should be hired or fired could conflict with the faculty member's right to confidentiality.

A final practical limitation would be the student's inability to represent his constituents in each and every individual decision. Since a consensus cannot be reached as to how a particular policy should be applied to an individual person, this may raise the question of practicality in justifying the student's membership on this particular committee.

Historically only the least sensitive areas for adjudication have been bequeathed to student-government groups. However, college officials should realize that responsible people will come forward only when they are given opportunities to assume responsibility. Although an academic community is indeed somewhat unique and different from other communities, there are many areas within it besides student activities, social events, and discipline in which students can be involved meaningfully and at the same time make contributions to the governance of the institution.

As student governments mature and prove themselves to be capable of becoming involved in some of the major decision making of the institution, it is possible that the traditional areas of student jurisdiction will become less attractive. The more traditional areas must be restudied and analyzed to ensure that they permit the students to become involved in continuously meaningful experiences which will provide challenging growth opportunities for them. This will also serve as a reminder that student, faculty, and administrative efforts should be focused on the total good of the academic community. To some extent, the opportunity for involvement with major areas may have to be won after competence has been demonstrated in the more traditional domains of students. The underlying principle here is that the three constituencies of the institution do not each have a right to an equal third of the jurisdiction. The sharing should not be determined merely on quantitative terms but on qualitative considerations; that is, each section should be expected to make that contribution which it can make better than the other two.

FORMS, STRUCTURES, AND PERSONNEL

It is impossible to propose one form of student government as the paragon of efficiency for all campuses. A number of workable structures are available and in operation on American campuses. In addition to considering the abilities of a student body, the attitudes of faculty and administration, and the climate of the campus, it would be well to consider the history of student government, its evolutionary pattern, and its successes and failures in the past at each institution.

The major goals to be achieved in fashioning a student government are to provide for full representation with respect to all student segments and their opinions while, at the same time, providing a governing body which will be manageable and efficient.

Councils There are many types of student government which carry the title of "council." Usually councils are small in relation to the constituency that they represent. When the council is of the common variety and is called a "student council," it is often somewhat unsophisticated. It is usually incipient in the sense that its powers are often limited and sometimes undefined. Its tasks, although not weighty, are too time-consuming for the few students responsible for accomplishing them, and there is insufficient opportunity for the representative members of the council to keep in contact with many elements of the student body.

A council does, however, offer some positive advantages. Its members come to know and understand each other, and its cohesiveness makes it a visible albeit sometimes depersonalized unit. Yet, in contrast, it is not the type of government that can extend the democratic process to large numbers of students.

A modification of the basic council structure is the organizational council, which normally consists of representatives from all student activities and organizations. Unfortunately this type of council does not represent those students who have no activity affiliation, even though it does bring together a good-sized nucleus of active students. It is vulnerable in that its representatives may be more interested in their particular activity than in the total good of the student body or the institution. It is possible, then, for some important student issues to be neglected. Although this structure of student government offers many advantages, it, like the broader type of council, does not maximize the democratic process. In a very real sense, it entrenches an aristocracy of representation. If this form of student government is considered to be desirable in an institution at a particular time, provisions should be made to guard against its becoming faction-oriented and to assist it in representing the broader interests of a student body so that students not affiliated with an activity will not be alienated.

Bicameral Organizations Some more highly advanced student-government groups have formed bicameral organizations because of their built-in safeguards for checks and balances. The federal pattern of two houses of government is not totally appropriate for many campuses. It would have some value for larger universities which are composed of more than one college or campus. In these institutions, one house of representatives may be elected to serve the college's interests while a second house or senate may represent the broader and more general concern of students. A more popular, and probably more practical, bifurcated type of student-government organization consists of two segments, an executive branch and a legislative branch. Examples of polychotomous student governments can also be found.

A two-branch student government would tend to maximize the democratic process. In order to be as representative as possible, its size and sometimes its efficiency must be sacrificed. However, a properly designed executive branch can do much to enhance the efficiency of a leviathan legislative branch.

Since this type of government will provide a system of checks and balances, since it will involve large numbers of students, and since it can be efficient, it is recommended to those schools whose objectives it will meet. Caution should be exercised so that this type of government does not become overly bureaucratic, with an accompanying diminution of benefits.

Student Associations A final major form of student government is that which is loosely categorized under the title of "student associations." These groups vary greatly and may include such features as legal incorporation, mandatory or voluntary membership, and dues-paying members. Although some student associations are highly developed and sophisticated, their basic paradigm is the social or fraternal type of club.

Although a student association which encourages all students to be members may give the semblance of total democracy, it seems to be no more effective in creating student interest or stimulating student activity than are the other major forms of student government. One of its major effects is to solidify a unilateral student viewpoint and, consequently, it does little to lower the barriers which exist between the students and the faculty and administrative sectors of an institution.

Even after a student association has been formed, some types of executive and legislative offices will have to be filled by election. Inevitably, their structure will still have to be patterned after one of the types outlined above.

ELECTIONS

After a structure for student government has been determined, consideration should be given to the matter of obtaining students who will give life to the structure. The most common although not the only method of obtaining personnel for student-government vacancies is through elections, the pragmatic means of achieving a more idealistic goal.

The goals of a student government place restrictions on the types of elective procedures to be employed. Considerations include the size, the membership, and the equality of the constituencies to be represented and served. Several bases for representation are available on all campuses, and the one or several which will produce the most representative government should be chosen.

Class representation is the most popular and appealing method of election since it is a readily available and convenient means of limiting constituencies. It is also attractive from an institution's point of view since it establishes and strengthens a class identity for all students which continues to have organizational value in alumni associations. Negatively, it can be argued that identifying student-government representatives by class introduces an unnecessarily divisive force into the student body. The result is that the representatives overemphasize the fact that they are sophomores or juniors rather than thinking of themselves as undergraduate students who share more similarities than differences. Class representation does have many advantages for many student governments, especially those focusing a great deal of energy on social events.

Another popular method of seeking student-government representation is on the basis of dormitory houses, fraternities, and even the commuting status of students. In a largely residential type of institution, this type of representation can be very effective in terms of communicating directly with one's constituency. If resident or commuting status is the determinant of student-government representation, a danger is that the resident groups tend to be more actively involved than the commuter groups. A second peril is that this type of representation tends to amplify the differences that exist between the two groups. In an institution which has a large number of fraternities, the student-government group faces the same inherent factional problems as the organizational council. As in all other types of representation, the merits of readily available constituencies and an interest in the democratic process must be weighed against their potential limitations, which will vary from one campus to another.

Student-government representation on the basis of sex seems far less necessary than it may have been in previous years. Its relevancy can only be justified to the extent that a particular institution administers its women students' affairs vastly differently than its men students' affairs. In such cases, the feminine needs, interests, and services might require representation by sex.

It is not uncommon to find student-government representatives elected on the basis of enrollment in the different schools or colleges of a university. The merits of this system will depend, in large measure, on the differences that exist among the schools or colleges. If the location, hours, curriculum, or regulations vary widely, this is sufficient reason for having representatives elected on this basis. These types of differences could justify a multi-unit type of student-government structure. On the other hand, since American higher education tends to be evolving toward homogeneity, the necessity for this type of representation may be waning.

It is very uncommon to find students who are elected on the basis of their affiliation with a particular political party within an institution. More sophisticated student bodies which could expend the time and effort necessary for meaningful debate might find this possibility intriguing. It certainly has the advantage of extending the educational benefits of student politics and, at the same time, it offers the real possibility of mollifying student apathy. The current interest of college students in society's political systems may foreshadow the implementation of the party system in college student politics in the future. One would hope that the transference from the larger society could take place without the creation of the political machines and unbridgeable chasms that sometimes attend political battles.

The use of at-large representation as an exclusive basis for student-government membership is unusual. It is an extensive practice as a supplement to some of the other bases that are available. At-large elections as a major method of filling student-government vacancies are most desirable at smaller institutions where the students have an opportunity to know the nominees well. Larger institutions would be well advised to permit some government vacancies to be filled on an at-large basis. The fewer the restrictions that are placed on student government's ability to attract the widest possible pool of qualified students, the more likely is an institution to attract the most qualified candidates for office and to produce more highly competitive campaigns. This approach, in turn, will sow the seeds for a more inspiring and attention-gathering student government once it takes office.

CONSTITUTIONS AND BYLAWS

The best manner of ensuring clarity and consensus as well as defining purposes and objectives is to prepare a student-government constitution. Many of these constitutions are prefaced by preambles which espouse the general philosophy of student governments at given institutions. It is very customary to find these preambles focusing on two major considerations of students—their rights and their responsibilities, cast within the balance which has been agreed upon within an institution.

The actual writing of a constitution is not a difficult task when the question of student government has been studied intensively, debated seriously, and exposed to a broad spectrum of viewpoints. In addition to taking every precaution to write a lucid document which bears the stamp of professionalism, care should also be taken to ensure that the document is flexible. Adaptability is an absolute requirement for a constitution, as is evident when one considers the rapid change that has characterized American higher education during the past two decades—not to mention the personality differences that one might expect in student governors from one year to the next. A major obstacle to student bodies which have been reaching out for more professional status and performance has been presented by inherent structural limitations stemming from overly precise legislation.

ORIENTATION OF NEW STUDENT LEADERSHIP

Each year many members of student government are neophytes. Unless their predecessors have taken measures to keep adequate records and files or unless some provision is made for the orientation of these new student representatives, discontinuity becomes a major and potentially fatal problem. The new representatives must take time to become familiar with their own powers, their institution's power structure, and the key faculty and administrative personnel who can assist them in their work.

Some type of orientation and training session should be planned to give new representatives an overview and perspective of their new duties. It is particularly critical that these sessions be planned as early as possible in the life of a new government to take advantage of the idealism, enthusiasm, and conscientiousness that normally characterize neophyte student-government leaders.

Orientation sessions can be of many types, such as a weekend off campus with the opportunity to meet some major administrative and faculty staff; day-long or part-day sessions over an extended period of time; and, if the campus desires training sessions which are not so specifically issue-oriented, training sessions can be focused in the areas of sensitivity training, interpersonal relationships, group dynamics, or the process of communications.

Summer Work Depending on the time of year when newly elected student representatives assume office, an established program of summer work for some of the key representatives of the student body may be in order. Obviously this advantage must be circumscribed; it would not be practical or perhaps even fair to nongovernment students if a commitment were made to all student representatives. Such a summer program is easily defensible for at least the chief executive officers of the student-government group when it is realized that a great deal of the success or failure of student government in a particular year will depend on the ability and readiness of student-government leaders to lead. Certainly the president must be in a position to guide his government to the achievement of realizable goals, to prevent the government from repeating past mistakes, and to ensure that key administrators and faculty are attuned to understand the government's position. Even in those cases in which the president and his major aides cannot be committed exclusively to student-government work in a summer program, some consideration could be given to employing these students in other areas so that they will at least have the opportunity to be available on their campuses to discuss their objectives among themselves and with others.

RELATIONS WITH OTHER INDIVIDUALS AND GROUPS

As important as it is to create strong structures and attract capable personnel to the student government, it is nearly as crucial that the governing group cultivate positive relationships with individuals and other groups, both on and off the campus. Internally, it is acutely important to cultivate good relationships with key personnel because the amount of jurisdiction and influence which the student governing body will enjoy will depend directly on the esteem in which it is held. On the other hand, the institutional staff should desire to keep in touch with student government so that its educational benefits can be continuously maximized.

Faculty Advice Perhaps one of the best ways of ensuring that the student government operates within a positive and educational pattern is to have a qualified staff person serve as its faculty adviser. One of the foremost functions of the adviser will be to provide a balanced continuity to the organization. The adviser is in an ideal position to provide the student governing body with an historical perspective of the government's evolution at the institution, to inform them of the mistakes of the past, and to advise them regarding the best approach for their objectives within the framework of the institution.

An adviser should also be expected to expand the point of view of the governing body. As a more experienced person he should, for example, see a legal, community, institutional, or alternative perspective and point it out if it has not been perceived by the students.

The role of faculty adviser, taken seriously by a staff person, can be extraordinarily time consuming. The adviser should attend the meetings of the governing body and make himself available to the individual students as needed. He should be willing to help the faculty and administration understand the role and objectives of student government and, as well, help the students to understand the faculty and administrative positions if these are different from their own. In addition to playing the very important roles of adviser, educator, counselor, information officer, and mediator, the adviser will be called on to assist the representatives in working through the bureaucratic entanglements of their institutions.

Since the role of faculty adviser is so crucial, a great deal of thoughtful effort must be directed toward his selection. Whether the student-government group or an institutional administrator has the responsibility of selecting the adviser is not the most critical factor. It is important that the adviser have the respect of the students and the administration. Certainly, an adviser who does not have such an amenable relationship with the students should not be thrust upon the student-government organization. Similarly, a student-government group should not be in a position to select an adviser who will merely leave the students to their own devices and who is not sensitive to the educative role that he and his group must fulfill.

In order to eliminate any confusing conflict that may develop over the role of adviser, it is suggested that a job description be mutually agreed upon prior to the acceptance of an adviser. This clarification will assist the adviser in understanding his responsibility, not only to the student group but also to his institution.

The title "Faculty Adviser" is oftentimes a misnomer since an administrator or other staff person may assume that role. This presents no particular problem, since it tends to emphasize the educational role that all administrators and staff persons are expected to accept. A fairly common practice is for the chief student personnel officer of an institution to assume the duties of faculty adviser to the major student-government group. This practice makes eminently good sense because many of the circumstances which affect student welfare reside within the jurisdiction of this administrator. Moreover, this type of appointment may contribute additional prestige to the group. The dean of students or the vice-president for student affairs, as the case may be, is also in a strategically well-placed position to assist other major administrators in understanding student government and to assist the governing body in assuming more meaningful jurisdictions when it is ready.

Major Staff Student-government representatives should make every effort to assist their institution's principal staff in understanding the objectives, concerns, and problems of student government. Again, to the extent that the key staff of an institution has an opportunity to respect the capabilities of student government, the chances are meliorated that student government will be assigned increasingly impactful responsibilities.

It is particularly critical that the president of the institution hold student government in some esteem since his commendation is not only prestigious but, just as importantly, it is infectious. The esteem of other key officers—vice-presidents, deans, and directors—is no less important. In addition to the anticipated positive attitude of administrators toward student government, more pragmatic results can be achieved by a mutually fiducial relationship. Major staff can and should be prepared to assist student government in growing increasingly toward beneficial objectives. For example, the deans of law, business administration, or journalism schools are experts who can be of immeasurable assistance to a student-government body; and they are usually willing to assist when requested, especially if they have had the impression that the work to be accomplished is consequential and meritorious. These cooperative relationships also assist in ensuring that all groups within the institution concentrate their focus on the overall good of the institution.

Student Groups In addition to the institutional officers with whom student government should strive to develop a positive relationship, there are student groups whose relationship to the government is also important. Perhaps the most sensitive relationship among student groups that the governing body will have is with the student press. This sensitivity stems from the fact that the newspaper can be a natural competitor of the government to the extent that both will be seeking to be the spokesman for the student body. The best interests of both can be served if the barriers between them are lowered so that a peaceful coexistence will ensue. The successful accomplishment of student government's objectives will be contingent in many cases on its press.

In many cases, the student newspaper will rely on student government for its appropriations. In no case should the student government be permitted to use its financial resources to proselytize or to purchase an optimum image. Indisputably, however, there can only be one official representative spokesman for the student body. Definitions of the roles and responsibilities of the student government and press so that each can perform its legitimate function will only be worked out in a cooperative climate which will permit an open discussion of the potential and actual points of conflict.

With respect to other student activities, student governments have had some jurisdiction over these for decades. This jurisdiction may have included the recognition of new activities, their funding, their regulations, their censuring, and their dissolution. It is not entirely inappropriate that student government should have pervasive jurisdiction over student activities. An institution, however, through its appropriate personnel, has an obligation to ensure that student government's actions in this area are conducted in an objective, impartial, and unbiased fashion.

External Relationships On many campuses, student government has been oriented only toward the internal life of the institution. During the past few years, its interests and activities have catapulted to the larger community, the region, and even the nation. Many observers regard this change of focus to be symbolic of the greater maturity and sophistication of the contemporary college student. As this tendency grows, it will inevitably become more popular for institutional student governments to increase their affiliations with national organizations. Although these affiliations can be valuable in assisting student-government bodies in many ways, their utility can only be measured by the needs that they may be able to fill in an individual institution. Since the needs of an institution's student government vary, national affiliations cannot be considered in all cases to be indispensable in aiding a student government to become more effective or more complete. The primary consideration has to be not external affiliation but internal effectiveness. Beyond this consideration, outside affiliations can be helpful in broadening the scope of a particular campus issue and in assisting a local group with the benefit of more universal experience and knowledge.

There are a number of groups with which a student-government body can affiliate, depending on the particular objectives and services that are desired. The most widely known, and in many quarters accepted as the national advocate of interests and opinions of students and their governments, is the National Student Association.

The National Student Association has focused primarily on providing service to its member schools. Aside from its other services, the Association will supply an abundance of useful and informative documents on students, their interests, and their governments; provide access to files of pertinent information from all member schools; and give assistance, in the form of visits and research by association personnel, to member schools involved with various problems and projects.

THE CONCEPT OF COMMUNITY

It is becoming increasingly common for institutions of higher learning in America to define themselves as "academic communities." The implication behind the word "community" is that the members of the community—students, faculty, and administrators—are bound by a common goal: the pursuit of truth. Since all three sectors of the institution are dedicated to this goal, students, faculty, and administrators are considered partners in this quest.

No clear and definitive position has appeared which proclaims that the status of students as partners is a right, a privilege, or even a responsibility. Most of the discussion evolving around the "students as partners" theme focuses on its benefits as suggested by its protagonists or its problems as cited by its antagonists.

Those who argue against involving students in institutional government point to the problem of time as a chief argument, as was noted in an earlier section. In addition, they say, it is a fact that many students cannot be held responsible in a legal sense to accrediting agencies, civil authorities, or boards of trustees for any decisions to which they may have contributed.

Also, the number of students who can be actively involved will represent a small percentage of the student body, and these few students will not be in a position to measure student-body sentiment with regard to the issues that they will deliberate. Finally, it is pointed out that the roles of faculty and administrators are just different from the roles of students, and that no amount of politicizing affability or conviviality will alter the responsibilities of one sector to another. Those who argue against granting students additional responsibilities in the governance of their institutions synthesize their arguments by pointing out that students are whimsical, changeable, immature, impractical, and irresponsible, that involving them in serious decision making would contribute nothing, that their participation would make present decision-making bodies and their procedures less effective, and that it would engage everybody in protracted and obtuse discussions.

Those who would defend the greater involvement of students in the governance of their institutions argue that many of the ills which have accompanied the growth of American colleges and universities might be helped toward solution if students shared in seeking to resolve them. Those who champion this position suggest that the centrum of the college could again become the student; that higher education's progression toward fragmentation and specialization could be replaced with integration; that our breakdown in communications could be solved not only by permitting the constituencies to talk to each other but also by requiring them to listen to each other; that the broadening gaps between sectors of the college could be bridged; that involving students with meaningful responsibilities would convert student power to adult power; that our overemphasis on vocationalism could be replaced by intellectualism; and that the student energies expended on citing the irrelevancy of our programs could be applied to an enduring loyalty to the institution, which they would better understand and to which they could relate more significantly.

It is also pointed out that since students are unique, their point of view will be different; that a student who spends four years at an institution has a far stronger commitment to it than the faculty member who spends an equal amount of time, because the student must defend the unique origin of his baccalaureate degree for a lifetime.

Whether the benefits or the problem cited materialize at a particular institution or not will depend on the campus. Student readiness, faculty and administrative attitudes, and campus climate again will be the chief determinants. There are historical precedents which suggest that student responsibility for participation in institutional governance in some cases has been a burden to bear rather than a right to be enjoyed.

There are some excellent examples of community government presently in existence in American colleges. Although its benefits and results have been impressive, it should be remembered that the most notable examples of community government have come from institutions whose student bodies are somewhat elite.

THE FUTURE

When we look at the history of student government in American higher education retrospectively, it is easy to see that a type of evolutionary continuum has developed. The most advanced student-government organizations have clearly evolved substantially during the past two centuries. Even today, although the student-government continuum has been elongated incalculably during the past few decades, we can see many rudimentary governments still in existence. It should be remembered that readiness is a viable educational concept even in the development of student government. No single student-government structure can be canonized as ideal. No single student-government structure will work everywhere because of the differing climates and needs of individual campuses and the differing attitudes and readiness of their people.

If there is a zenith or capstone of student government for American higher education, it undoubtedly lies in community government. This presents the American college with a paradox. The extent to which student government is augmented is innately destructive of a viable community government, because the fortifying process entrenches unilateral thinking and induces an almost combative spirit among the constituencies for power. The reverse is also unfortunately true, that focusing on a strong community government is inconsistent with a strong student government. Fortunately there are precedents which indicate that the theoretical paradox and incompatability can be resolved. It is likely that an effective community government cannot be achieved until a campus has reached a point of mature acceptance and broad experience with a strong student government.

Everywhere that one looks in American colleges, very evident governmental trends are developing. First, student governments are becoming more relevant and important to their constituencies as they become involved in more meaningful jurisdictions and are bequeathed more significant influence. One of the major powers that is being conceded is financial jurisdiction over many social and student activities. Second, student governments are participating more actively and completely in institutional judicial systems. The horizontal growth in this area can be seen in the fact that students are not merely administering justice but are involved in institutional definitions of justice and in the very formulation of rules of conduct.

Increasingly, student governments are seeing themselves as the proctors and defenders of student rights and freedoms. This fact is dramatized by the increasing number of governments which are publishing students' bills of rights.

In addition to the more active involvement of student-government groups on their own campuses, there is increasing evidence that these groups are interested in the larger problems of society and will seek greater opportunities for uniting with each other in the pursuit of mutually desired goals.

There is ample evidence to attest to the fact that the pace of evolutionary development of student government has been quickened during the past several years. As the government bodies have matured, an interesting effect has been realized—they have been better able to unify their own constituencies.

It seems inevitable that the next step is to unify the entire university through the formation of a community government. Working together toward the solution of the community's problems, the three groups can bring to focus all the talent and dedication that can be found in the university. To be sure, each group has its individual perspective and differing as well as common concerns. These differences will not be smothered or ignored in a successful community government. Rather, they will be recognized and dealt with in an institutionalized process. This prospect is more than a vision; it is already in the rudimentary stages of fulfillment in some American colleges.

Wherever a particular college or university stands in the development of its governmental systems, if the past several years' experience has any predictive value, there will be no regression on the evolutionary continuum as students, student power, and student government become more visibly active elements on American campuses.

BIBLIOGRAPHY

Corson, John J.: *Governance of Colleges and Universities,* McGraw-Hill Book Company, New York, 1960.

Freidson, Eliot (ed.): *Student Government, Student Leaders, and the American College,* United States National Student Association, Philadelphia, 1955.

Klopf, Gordon J.: *College Student Government,* Harper & Row, Publishers, Incorporated, New York, 1960.

Knorr, Owen A., and W. John Minter (eds.): *Order and Freedom on the Campus,* Western Interstate Commission for Higher Education, Boulder, Colo., 1965.

Liebert, Roland: *Problems in Student Rights and Freedoms,* United States National Student Association, Washington, 1964.
Lipset, Seymour M.: *Student Politics,* Basic Books, Inc., Publishers, New York, 1967.
Lunn, Harry H. Jr.: *The Student's Role in College Policy-making,* American Council on Education, Washington, 1957.
Meehan, Mary (ed.): *Role and Structure of Student Government,* United States National Student Association, Washington, 1966.
Rudolph, Frederick: *The American College and University: A History,* Random House, Inc., New York, 1962.
Schwartz, Edward: *The National Student Association on the Campus, 1966–1967,* United States National Student Association, Washington, 1967.
Scott, James H.: *Selected Case Studies and Principles in Student Government,* University Microfilms, Ann Arbor, Mich., 1968.
Terte, Robert H.: *Toward a Democratic Campus,* United States National Student Association, Philadelphia.

Chapter **12**

Student Publications

HARVEY VETSTEIN

Assistant Professor of English and Faculty Adviser to Student Publications, Northeastern University, Boston, Massachusetts

THE COLLEGE PAPER—THEN AND NOW

The student newspaper is one of the most powerful voices in the academic community today. Since its inception at Dartmouth College in 1839, the student paper has grown steadily, so that it today commands a work force of hundreds of faculty advisers, thousands of student reporters and editors, and a budget reaching into the millions of dollars.

At birth, the student newspaper was, in many ways, simply an extension of the public relations office or press bureau of an institution. It printed material describing the bright side of an institution's academic and social life. It congratulated donors for contributions, slapped the backs of deans for jobs well done, discussed the future of the institution in flowery terms, and reported a host of mundane items ranging from regulations about keeping off the lawn in front of a certain dorm to the news that "Joe

Jones and Mary Smith are pinned." It served as a bulletin board, listing sports schedules, prom announcements, dates of club meetings, etc. It angered no one, and, in fact, very few people read it, as very few today read certain papers put out by large corporations. In short, the student paper, from its beginnings until a few years ago, provided a service for the institution but not, in the journalistic sense, the service it should have performed. It had never been the student voice.

Today, however, things have changed considerably in the news offices across the country. Student editors have taken their jobs literally. They insist that students have the last say as to what goes into the paper. They want the paper to be the true student voice; they want to editorialize on various subjects within and without the academic community; they want to write stories geared to a student audience. Many editors have become overzealous; many have alienated members of the faculty, caused administrators much chagrin, embarrassed institutions. Some have been libelous, extremely irresponsible, nihilistic. Yet many have editorialized for social and academic changes constructively. A few Southern student editors were discussing social injustices and social inequities long before it became journalistically fashionable to do so. Many editors were spat upon by their peers or physically assaulted, and some found burning crosses on their fraternity-house lawns and in their own front yards long before the commercial press saturated its pages with similar discussions. These are, therefore, the two differing roles the student newspaper has played during the last 130 years. Of these, the latter has been a far more feasible, far more professional role. A part of the "Tufts Plan for Student Publications" sums up this view quite well:

> A university literary publication exists to provide an experimental ground for the efforts of writers who have yet to achieve the balance of technique and experience. Such writers, moreover, are likely to be moved by powerful emotions. In the history of all literatures the madmen have shared at least equal honors with the calmly reasoned.
>
> It sometimes happens that the disproportions of student writing, as they spring onto the page from the unmanaged or half-managed compulsions of the writer, offend the more literal and less venturesome attitudes of the community. It can follow then that the "image" of the university will suffer in the eyes of the community; particularly so since this difference between the language-intoxicated young seeker and the more stable of the community around him is one that can be readily distorted to sensationalism by rumor and journalism.
>
> The university is a stable and central member of that community. But in its dedication to ideas and to their pursuit for their own sake it must also stand *in loco parentis* to the young man, and even to the young madman who has plunged into the wild sea of language and experience in the hope of floundering toward some vision of life.
>
> Unless we are prepared to defend him at those times when his compulsion toward the honesty of his vision, no matter how mismanaged, brings him into conflict with the more sedate views of the community, we cannot wish him well in his seeking, nor can we fulfill our purpose as a university.[1]

The student newspaper, therefore, exists to report accurately and objectively news of particular concern to its institution. The paper should be free to editorialize on pertinent subjects with no shadow of pressure groups or censorship committees hanging over the editors' heads. The editors should strive toward journalistic excellence and should foster intellectual honesty.

Physically and economically, student papers range from one-page monthlies with annual budgets of a few dollars and press runs of 100 copies or less to mammoth multipage dailies, serving the institutions as well as the local communities, with budgets

[1] "Tufts Plan for Student Publications," Tufts University, Medford, Mass. (adopted Spring, 1965).

upwards of one-quarter of a million dollars and press runs of 25,000 copies per issue. Office space may range from a corner of a secretary's work area to an entire building equipped with its own wire services and telephone switchboards.

The reasons for the phenomenal growth of the student paper are obvious. Along with the basic skills and experiences afforded both the journalism students and students with other majors, the paper is *the* student voice; it is their podium; it offers the students a medium to express themselves; it reports news to them as well as acting as their journal of opinion. In short, because of its audience the student paper today has more power and commands more respect than did its journalistic sisters of yesteryear.

NEWSPAPER POLICIES

Most institutions have guidelines or constitutions governing student publications. Many students react defensively to these various rules, fearing that they represent a latent and/or overt form of censorship. This may be true in certain institutions, but on the whole these guidelines help rather than hinder the publications. Many of them are, in fact, drawn up partly or wholly by the student editorial board. They incorporate an understanding of the canons of good journalistic taste; they provide instructional values for the students; and, most important, they provide the student editors with their own built-in measuring device of responsibility.

The guidelines usually consist of a table of organization, outlining specific editorial duties and responsibilities; definitions of the role of the newspaper in the academic community and the role of the faculty adviser and/or board of publications; a description of the physical makeup of the paper; discussions of printing contracts, and so forth.

Some institutions have a board of publications whose job ranges from advising on newspaper policies to actively participating in the physical running of the paper. The members of these boards are usually drawn from the administration, the faculty, and the student body. Their main function, historically, has been to deliberate issues of a controversial nature which might cause, in some context, damage to the institution. The fact that these boards often control the budgets of the papers provides them, as far as many editors are concerned, with a potential means of halting the press run of any issue not to their liking. From a practical standpoint, however, those boards which have controlled the budgets have made the jobs of editors much easier by taking care of the business end of newspaper production.

Most student papers have faculty advisers. Whether or not the student-adviser relationship will be personally rewarding and creative depends in part upon the method of appointment of the adviser. Unfortunately, many institutions delegate the role of adviser to the lowest-ranking member of an academic department, usually the department of English or Journalism. The student editors react violently to this type of assignment and, in many cases, communication between the adviser and the editors breaks down. The editors feel that the adviser *had* to take the job, that he is merely a member of the academic community whose chief function is to blunt the swords of student warriors.

The adviser should have had some experience working in either the commercial or college press. Perhaps some of the major points in the "Code of Ethics of the National Council of College Publications Advisers" best express the role of an adviser:

> He should be a professional Counselor whose chief responsibility is to give competent advice to student and staff members in the areas to be served—editorial or business.
>
> He should be a teacher whose responsibility is to explain or demonstrate.

He should be a critic who will pass judgment on the work done by the staff and who will commend excellence as well as point out fault.

He must have personal and professional integrity and never condone the publication of falsehood in any form.

He must be firm in his own opinions and convictions while reasonable toward the differing views of others.

He must be sympathetic toward staff members, endeavoring to understand their viewpoints when they are divergent from his own.

He must seek to direct a staff toward editing a responsible publication that presents an unslanted report.

He should direct the staff or individual members whenever direction is needed, but place as few restraints as possible upon them.

He should never be a censor; but when staff members are intent on violating good taste, the laws of libel, or college or university principles, he should be firm in pointing out such errors.

He should make suggestions rather than give orders.

He should be available for consultation at all times.

He should instill in the staff a determination to make the publication as professional as possible by being truthful and recognizing that fidelity to the public interest is vital.

He should lead the staff to recognize that the publication represents the college or university, and that the world beyond the campus will in part judge the college or university by the product.

He should encourage accurate reporting and see that editorial opinions expressed are based on verified facts.[2]

BALANCE OF NEWS COVERAGE

The student paper is usually divided into four main parts: news, features, sports, and editorials. The most important and, in most cases, the most controversial sections are the news and editorial pages.

The news pages cover events on campus, distinguished speakers, cultural and social meetings—in effect, all that is going on of student concern at the institution. One of the major problems facing the editors and institutions today is the question of how much coverage should be allotted to news *outside* of the academic community.

Many would argue that the students are not divorced from the society outside of the institution, thereby justifying this type of coverage. Others argue that the commercial press covers news of a local, national, and international flavor, thereby causing the student coverage to be merely redundant. Both views are valid at least in part. The trend in college newspaper writing today is reflective of the times in which we live. Recognizing this, we see that as long as students participate actively in the political, social, and cultural spheres of our society, their peers, the editors, will cover this participation. We can see, with few exceptions, that the students are quite knowledgeable in the area of public affairs and do quite well reporting this type of news. Some editors, however, feel that their primary purpose is to cover "outside" news, or, as one editor once put it somewhat dramatically, "It is senseless to discuss frat parties and building funds for the institution while the world burns." It is obviously true that war, social injustices, and similar matters far outweigh campus activities in terms of import, but this is not really the point to be argued. The editors have a perfect right to express their views on anything they choose, but, in fairness to the students, they should not do this to the exclusion of campus news. The editors should recognize their responsibilities

[2] Herman A. Estrin and Arthur M. Sanderson, "Code of Ethics of the National Council of College Publications Advisers," in *Freedom and Censorship of the College Press,* Wm. C. Brown Company, Dubuque, Iowa, 1966, pp. 283, 284.

to the students and to their institutions. Many students want to find out about news on campus, and the editors should recognize the prerogatives of others, especially if the paper bears the name of the institution and is funded by that institution and/or the students. If editors want to put out their own political or social newsletters, that's their business. But using the student paper for this purpose without leaving space for campus news is an infringement of the rights of others.

The editorial page usually consists of the paper's stand on a particular issue, a feature column, perhaps an editorial cartoon to complement the editorial, and a "Letters to the Editors" section where any member of the academic community can voice his views.

One of the main functions of an editor in chief is to write the editorial. Allowing the editor in chief to write anything he wants on any subject may cause trouble with many of his editors, however, because of its dictatorial implications. An editorial should be the voice of the majority of the editorial board and not just the editor's. Therefore, many boards get together to decide on the subject of the editorial and to vote on the stand of the paper. Because simple majorities do not really represent a true editorial voice, many boards will not take a stand with less than a two-thirds vote. The editorial roles are discussed more extensively in the next chapter.

The feature pages consist of interviews, critiques of plays and movies, humorous and serious columns, and special-interest stories; the content of the sports pages is obvious.

THE EDITORIAL BOARD AND ITS STAFF

Most editorial boards are comprised of individuals who have worked their way up as staffers. The most common method of choosing editors is by a vote of outgoing editors. Other methods, such as university appointments and student-body voting, are used also, but the former method gives the paper another measure of autonomy. The major editorial positions are editor in chief, managing editor, news editor, feature editor, sports editor, art editor, photo editor, advertising manager, and circulation manager. Other titles such as city, town, and copy editor are used frequently but are not as popular. Then come their rewrite editors and staffers. A full editorial board is usually made up of 12 to 15 members. The editors are responsible for their respective sections of the paper. They make up assignments; proofread materials for their pages; arrange headlines for stories; and, with their rewrite editors, make up their pages. They meet with the managing editor, editor in chief, and adviser frequently and turn in their copy to the major editors. They vote on editorial stands and recruit students for their respective staffs.

The managing editor, usually the number-two man on the paper, is in charge of the financial and distributive aspects of the paper. He takes care of meal money, supervises the work done by the advertising manager and circulation manager, discusses budgetary matters with those in charge of the paper's finances, and acts as editor in chief in the latter's absence.

The editor in chief is one of the most powerful students on campus today. He is elected by his peers, and the final newspaper decisions are his. As stated earlier, this position may have dictatorial implications; and many editors in chief have been expelled, suspended, or in some way blacklisted because of a paper's stand on a particular issue. Ideally, the editor in chief is a mature, responsible student who would not allow his power to affect the prestige of the newspaper. He works well with his fellow editors, is respected by them, and is completely well versed in interpretive journalism. He is one who is not afraid to speak out against inequity, and he recognizes his responsibility to put out a paper that is completely factual and devoid of conjecture. Knowing that he has, in effect, a captive audience, he recognizes his obligations to this audience and strives to report as much information of student concern as his pages will allow.

The paper does not become his personal podium. He strives for accuracy and takes pride in the newspaper. He has worked hard to get to his present position and will not demean the paper for personal aggrandizement. He delegates authority and recognizes and respects the majority rulings of his editorial board.

CENSORSHIP

Using the word "censorship" in regard to college papers is much akin to mentioning the name of Haman to Jews during the Purim holidays. If censorship means the ability of some person or body to prevent publication of something he or they deem dangerous to the welfare of society, then it is easy to assume that this definition conflicts with earlier statements in defense of the students' rights to print "what they want."

Historically, institutions have been reluctant to explicate their views of censorship when surveyed. Libel, sedition, and obscenity (in some contexts) are reasonably clear-cut examples of what a governing board would suppress in a publication. But these three journalistic vices need not be the measuring devices used by institutions to come out against a particular newspaper article. Most administrators and advisers unequivocably state that there is no censorship at their institutions; yet advisers have been fired, students expelled, and newspapers disbanded or at least left budgetless because of stories that didn't even come close to what is generally thought of as censorable material. Therefore, it is safe to assume that most institutions have no censorship until the time that something not to their liking is about to go to print. This makes a good case for adopting a set of rules and procedures for each publication, so that the students know beforehand what they can and cannot write about. Then, on this basis they can decide whether or not they want to remain with the publication; or they can attempt at this time to modify the existing rules. The modification of rules on censorship is done quite frequently in many schools.

Hopefully, the adviser has created, before problems of this type arise, a rapport with his editors, so he can at least talk over controversial stories with them prior to publication. Many advisers have proven that meetings of this type have not necessarily blunted the swords of their editors but rather have allowed the editors to carry their views forward knowing full well all the implications involved in their stories.

BUDGETS

Some student newspapers are sold, while others subsist on advertising revenues. Most, however, are either funded directly by the institution or through the students' activities fees. Many newspapers are attempting to exist autonomously because it is felt that university funding or student-activities funding suggests various forms of control. Many administrators are in favor of having the papers become autonomous. As long as the paper retains the name of the institution and as long as students from that particular institution comprise the staff, however, the institution is susceptible to suits in cases of libel, etc.

The budget for the coming academic year is usually prepared by the concerned group or board in the spring, and it goes into effect on July 1. Most larger institutions break down the budget into various categories; i.e., printed supplies, travel, food, awards, photo supplies, conferences, etc. The group working out the budget must anticipate rising printing costs, more pagination, etc., before submitting the budget to the institution's finance office.

Newspapers funded in any manner by the institution and not dependent upon advertising or other revenues usually set a maximum of 30 percent for advertising coverage. Most of the advertising is of a local variety, but many newspapers have contracts with national advertising firms which place recruitment ads and ads from various large companies. Generally, editors would rather print a host of small ads than a couple of larger ads simply because it affords the student more of a variety of products and services to become aware of. The advertising manager's job is an important one mainly because he must place the ads on the various pages before the editors of the respective sections can work in their copy. Ads are usually *verboten* on the front and back pages and in a centerfold. Otherwise, most pages have a percentage of ads at the bottom.

PRINTING CONTRACTS AND PHOTOGRAPHY

Most institutions do not have their own press facilities for putting out a campus paper. Therefore, the person or group in charge of the publication's finances initially calls in a number of representatives of local presses to find the one best suited to the paper's needs. The major considerations in contracting a press are price, method of printing (the two most popularly used are letterpress and offset), arrangements for pick-up of copy and delivery of papers, and quality of work. Many presses will give a number of editors the opportunity to watch the composition of the newspaper and to help with paste-ups, etc., so that they may gain practical knowledge. This, oftentimes, is the added inducement which sells one press over another.

It is usually wise to choose a press that has had experience working with college publications. Such a press is cognizant of the students' problems, realizes that exams may cause the paper to go over a deadline, and is, in effect, sympathetic to student problems.

In line with selection of a press, the people in charge of the budget must anticipate the number of issues and the number of pages a paper will run that academic year, and they must govern the budget accordingly.

Photography is usually taken care of by students. If photography facilities and/or student photographers are unavailable, the institution will usually hire a photographer who is familiar with the institution, having done work for the institution in another capacity.

STUDENT AWARDS, CONSIDERATIONS, ETC.

Since most student newspapers come under the category of "extracurricular activities," only a small percentage of editors receive any type of remuneration. In some schools the paper is a form of laboratory correlated with the classroom journalism course. Therefore, editors receive a certain amount of academic credit in this situation.

Many of the larger institutions which publish dailies have more than one editorial staff and pay salaries to the editors. The most popular remunerative procedure is the giving of tuition grants and/or scholarships, and these are usually given to the top editors. One of the major reasons editors receive stipends of this nature is that they have to put in long hours to get out the paper, hours which could be spent on part-time jobs. Institutions recognize that they lose some of their best journalistic talent due to the financial needs of students. The remunerations also provide an incentive to reach the top. Morale is usually high on student papers which are able to reward their editors financially. Advertising managers sometimes receive a percentage of the money turned into the institution in ad revenues.

Many schools offer journalism prizes at the end of the academic year in the form of money for editors and/or staffers who have shown unusual professional ability in their journalistic endeavors.

COLLEGE PAPER ORGANIZATIONS AND RATING SERVICES

There are many rating services in the country that the college paper may enter for quality classification. Ratings may range from "All American" to "Fourth Class" and the papers are judged in categories of student population, frequency of issue, etc., so that a junior college two-page paper is not judged alongside a university daily. The institution should make every effort to see that the student paper enters one of these grading services. It affords the newspaper staff the opportunity to see their paper judged with many others. Most grading services return a critique with the paper's classification, thus giving the staff the opportunity to see their strong points and shortcomings as judged by professional journalists.

The newspaper should also join an organization made up of representatives of other college papers such as the Associated Collegiate Press, Intercollegiate Press, etc. This will provide the staff opportunities to meet with other staffs and to go over their respective papers. At the same time, it would be beneficial to the faculty adviser and the newspaper if the adviser joined an organization of his peers such as the National Council of College Publications Advisers (NCCPA) to discover current trends in student journalism and to find out about a host of other subjects that would help him immeasurably in his capacity as adviser.

THE YEARBOOK

The policy and procedural rules for the yearbook or annual are quite similar to those of the campus newspaper. Obviously, there are basic physical and thematic differences.

The yearbook staff is made up mostly of seniors, since, in many institutions, seniors are the only students who receive yearbooks. It is difficult to keep a large staff interested in the production of a yearbook, for, unlike the staff of the paper, they are aiming at the production of one "issue." Since that seems to them a long way off, many tend to leave the staff. Those who remain, however, deserve a large measure of gratitude from the senior class, for in years to come the yearbook becomes their most important memento of their days in college.

Most yearbooks are funded through student activities so that the senior, in effect, receives a free copy upon graduation. There are many institutions, however, that do charge a nominal fee (approximately $5) for each book. The budget for the yearbook, like the newspaper, is usually broken down into categories such as the following: printed supplies, food, travel, awards, photography supplies, memberships, etc.

Yearbooks vary according to their respective institutions and the whims of the student editors, but there are basic inclusions that most yearbooks adhere to. Among these are the president's message to graduates; a dedication; faculty and staff pictures; a history (covering the graduate's years at the institution); a student activities section (if any); and, last and most important, graduate portraits and biographies.

Occasionally yearbook editors undergo the same trials endured by newspaper editors. Sometimes editors will editorialize throughout the history section, include or exclude some dean or faculty member, dedicate the book to a cause found to be unpopular with many who are associated with the yearbook, etc. (One coed editor recently issued the yearbook with 25 or so pictures of herself alone. The book was sent back to press and the pictures were deleted.) These instances are very rare, however, because most editors realize the basic purposes of printing a yearbook and act accordingly.

One of the most difficult decisions editors and advisers have to make with regard to yearbook production lies in the choosing of printers and photographers. Most printing companies service the institution for printing alone or they may be associated with a yearbook cover company. There are some, however, that also maintain photography facilities and an institution may, in effect, buy a package deal. There are still others who deal only in the printing of school yearbooks, and added consideration should be given to these companies since they are specialists in this work.

With the budget uppermost in their minds and the desire to give the seniors the best physical quality available, the editors and advisers meet with the printing representatives. They decide on paper stock, use of color (generally four-process or second color), and layout. They tell the printing representatives how many pages will be needed (generally pages must be bought in forms or eight-page sections or signatures, sixteen-page sections). All of this information is given to the printing representative at the first meeting. At the same time, the representative will show the editors and advisers some of the company work. (It is wise to see if this company is serving other local institutions and to see if they can properly handle a school the size of yours.)

The representative will take the information given him by the editors, etc., and in a short time he will send a bid or a contract. After meeting with a few representatives interested in your institution, comparisons can be made of prices and quality of work before reaching any decision.

Some of the main printing contract inclusions are dates and schedule deadlines, pagination, number of books, size of pages and paper stock, type of composition, presswork and color, number of pictures, type of cover, and date of delivery.

The main photography contract inclusions are prices of sittings and sitting schedule, availability of photographer for candid and group shots as well as portraits, delivery of proofs to students, prices commensurate to student budgets, number of poses per student, and pledge of faithfulness in cooperating with the editorial board of the yearbook. Some photographers also return a commission percentage of sales (approximately 10 percent) to the institution and/or yearbook.

The photographer generally does not profit from services to the institution, so price, of itself, is not the most important feature when choosing a photographer. He makes his profit from the individual pictures bought by the students. One major point to consider, however, is that once a photographer is chosen, the students must buy or not buy from him alone. With this in mind, the editors and advisers must consider the best photographer and the one who will most readily make himself available to the students for portraits. He will charge a small fee for a sitting (usually from $3 to $5), and the student is under no obligation to pay anything beyond this fee. For this sitting fee, the student gets his picture in the yearbook and an 8- by 10-in. black and white print. When sending the students their proofs, the photographer will usually include a brochure listing package arrangements—but these dealings are between the photographer and the students and are of no concern to the yearbook staff.

Once a printer and photographer are chosen, contracts are signed by the appropriate officer of the institution and production schedules and student photo appointments are arranged.

It is important to meet the deadlines of the printer because too many delays may postpone delivery of the yearbooks until after graduation when the students have taken off for the four quarters of the globe. Most institutions give out the yearbooks when caps and gowns are handed out, and the yearbook becomes an integral part of the enjoyment of senior week.

THE LITERARY MAGAZINE

Since the materials of a literary magazine are closely associated with the materials discussed in most English courses, a member of the English department usually serves as faculty adviser. Most magazines have a semiannual distribution; most also have relatively small budgets and editors and advisers are hardpressed in getting out even two quality issues. Budget allocations have not increased as rapidly as has the student interest in literary magazines, yet there are many issued with professional expertise throughout the country. Literary magazines are usually funded by the institution, either directly or through student activities fees. Because the budget of a literary magazine is usually much smaller than that of the newspaper or yearbook, the budget is not usually broken down into various accounts.

Many literary magazines contain short stories, poetry, an occasional play, an editorial (usually oriented toward some literary subject), photography, and line sketches or drawings. Most are issued either annually or semiannually.

As in the case of the yearbook, printing representatives offer their bids based on the specifications of the editors and advisers. Most literary magazines are sold to students or members of the academic community. It has been noted that many of our name writers today got their starts as editors or writers of their college literary magazines.

The printing contract for the literary magazine is quite similar to the yearbook contract.

Editors are afforded writing and makeup experience and experience as critics, for they must choose which contributions of their peers are best suited for inclusion in the magazine. The main problem editors run into concerns the use of certain words that some find objectionable; if the words are contexually correct, however, very little comes of this.

THE FUTURE OF THE COLLEGE PRESS

There are some 2,600 college newspapers in the country today, and with the added growth of suburban colleges and junior and community colleges, it does not look as though the number will diminish. As a matter of fact, there are many institutions today that print more than one student paper.

It is, therefore, reasonable to assume that the college paper is fast leaving the category of "extracurricular activities." There's nothing very extracurricular about printing costs totaling upwards of 60 million dollars.

Dr. Dario Politella, president of the National Council of College Publications Advisers, foresees a revolution in the campus press in the next few years and outlines the reasons that rationalize this revolution. Dr. Politella's nine reasons are commented on below.

1. *The student press is fast losing the monopoly it has enjoyed these many years.*

Because of expanded news coverage, diversity of subject materials, and the large number of special interest groups, the lone campus paper has not been able to afford the space and time necessary to meet the needs of the campus. Many organizations, fraternities, social groups, etc., have, therefore, decided to create campus papers dealing primarily with their respective interests. Although many of these papers grow out of a group's dissatisfaction with the amount of coverage they had been getting in *the* campus newspaper, many of these new papers are not, in any way, in conflict with the established press. In many ways they expand upon stories that are given skeletal treatment because of space limitations. Most of these papers are funded by the respective organizations. They are usually mimeograph papers or dittos or, at any rate, inferior in physical quality to the established press because of their limited budgets.

There is a marked growth of what is now called the "dissident" or "underground" press on campuses today. The thematic format of these papers is reasonably commensurate to the thematic format of the commercial "underground" press in relation to the commercial "established" press. These papers grow out of the dissatisfaction of a number of students with the way in which the campus paper covers news. Many students who join the dissident press feel that the established student paper has too many ties with the administration, that it is, in fact, a "company" paper and, therefore, not free to voice the true student views. There is obviously a closer relationship between the established campus paper and the institution than there is between the institution and the dissident press, but the latter's views of suppression are usually unfounded. Most of the dissident papers emphasize editorial writing rather than news, and a large percentage of the subject matter covered does not pertain directly to the campus. Views of current events, politics, Vietnam, racism, drugs, sexual expression, religion, etc., receive the most coverage in papers of this type. These papers are really journals of opinion rather than newspapers. It would be unfair to take these papers lightly or to condemn them collectively as irresponsible because, in fact, many of these papers have breathed fresh air into stodgy and intolerable situations that have existed on some campuses.

2. *There's a fight brewing for financial independence of the campus press.*

Indeed, there is a growing trend for newspapers to become autonomous from their respective institutions. Most papers have at this time reached a halfway point; i.e., although they exist as financially independent entities, they still retain their physical plants on school grounds. Autonomy, as mentioned earlier, is probably every editor's dream, not simply because it, in effect, takes them from under an administrative wing, although this is an important consideration, but because it gives the editors more leeway in expanding the paper, coming out more frequently, using color, etc. It also frees the editors from worries about budget cuts by the administration or the student groups controlling the budgets, although the newspapers certainly have to have large audiences or good advertising revenues to exist. It would be difficult for administrators to deny that many of the papers that have become autonomous have, indeed, improved in quality and content.

3. *There is increasing agitation among college journalists for greater access to news and the broadening of coverage beyond the campus.*

Administrators are finding that editors, more and more, are arguing for admittance to trustee and corporation meetings, faculty senate conferences, etc., which had been, by and large, previously *verboten.*

Also, more and more papers are picking up various wire services, columns, and cartoons from the commercial press. They are also sending staffers to areas of social and political unrest for first-hand stories, in many ways doing what the commercial press does in these same situations. Some college papers have even sent correspondents to Vietnam, financed usually by contributions from the student bodies. The civil rights marches and sit-ins were extensively covered first-hand by the college press, and there's no reason to believe that activity of this kind will not continue. Editors have actively supported or attacked political candidates and issues to the point of lobbying, sending student staffers to Washington, and running for political office themselves. Quite often legislative battles have erupted, especially in state schools, because of student-press editorials. The community outside of academia had not recognized the power of the college press until recently, and it doesn't expect the power and influence of this press to diminish. More college editors have been invited to political and social news conferences than ever before, so that the college press has, in this context, made its mark.

4. *The confines of the extra-curriculum are being strained by agitation of the journalists for greater independence and reward.*

As stated earlier, the campus paper is fast moving out of the realm of extracurricular activities, mainly for the sake of financial and journalistic independence. Surveys show that more and more editors are receiving remuneration, and the trend seems to be to get as many editors salaried as possible. The printing of a campus newspaper can become quite lucrative for the editors, especially those who need money for schooling. Along with this very practical consideration is the fact that a more earnest desire for professionalism takes form on the editorial board, especially if this journalistic improvement attracts more advertisers for the paper and sells (if it is sold) more copies.

In terms of journalistic independence, the quest for autonomy has been discussed. Equally important is the desire not to be eclectically grouped with such disparate organizations as the student council, the model-railroad club, etc., when budget time rolls around.

The academic community is generally agreed that the newspaper serves a separate and distinct function from other campus groups; it services the community, and many feel that this service should not go unrewarded.

Lastly, with few exceptions, members of the editorial board and staff spend far more hours putting out a paper for the institution than members of other groups spend in their respective functions.

5. *There is growing sophistication being experienced by the student press with the use of modern electronic devices to increase the efficiency of production.*

More and more, modern technology has been able to speed up various services for the commercial press, and the college press has not been blind to the improvements in professional journalism. Some papers have picked up closed-circuit television to directly dispatch stories from news office to press. Wire services are in great demand on many campuses. Editors of various campus papers have pooled their photographic and art resources so that their respective institutions can receive as quickly as possible materials for stories that break. New equipment, of course, requires vast amounts of money, and, generally speaking, most campus budgets cannot cope with drastic increases—one more reason for the desire for financial independence.

6. *In this age of practicality, one foresees increased consultative services being demanded by student journalists who would be trained for a practical craft against the time they are graduated.*

The editor, in his desire to develop professionalism, has, early in his tenure, virtually picked his adviser's brain clean of the latter's store of journalistic knowledge. But no man, certainly no faculty adviser, is journalistically omniscient; therefore experts in various areas of journalism are quite often called in to have their "brains picked," as it were. This same desire for professionalism would also involve field trips to various newspaper plants to view operations from the writing of the story through composing and finally seeing the newspaper hit the streets. In effect, the editors want the practical experience to ready them for journalistic careers after graduation.

Institutions which have the cooperative system of education (briefly, in the co-op system, one-half of the upperclassmen are in school while the other half are employed in occupations appropriate to their respective majors) are perhaps best equipped to give the would-be professional journalist the best practical as well as academic background available. Those editors who are majoring in journalism work on town and city papers while on co-op, thus gaining first-hand training prior to graduation.

7. *The campus journalist is developing a social conscience.*

Perhaps "has developed" would be more correct, because it is doubtful that campus papers have ever before editorialized or reported stories about social inequities as frequently as they do now. Mentioned earlier were the actions of the Southern editors who, in many instances, put their institutions on the proverbial carpets for advocating civil rights and social equality. Others have editorialized about various subjects such as sex on campus, drugs, birth control, Vietnam, draft-card burning, etc. These editorials and stories have embittered some, exhilarated others, and interested just about everyone. Many things have been written intemperately, perhaps irresponsibly; other subjects have been discussed as frankly, as candidly, and as professionally and maturely as they ever have been.

The point of all of this is that editors do not have any compunctions about speaking out on any subject. As a rule their views are closely aligned to the views of the student body and far removed from the views of people outside the academic community. Society, generally speaking, is relatively conservative when it comes to speaking about subjects of a controversial nature. Even the commercial press buckles under to the pressure of its conservative readership. With this in mind, it is easy to see that the college press has a receptive liberal audience to work with. Some editors do go overboard in their zeal to correct the social wrongs they see, but most editors reflect the thinking of the student body at large; i.e., they mirror the views of their readership, as the commercial press does the views of its.

8. *The taboos once attached to advertising subject matter are becoming accepted as a matter of course.*

Advertising, like reporting, has its share of taboos to contend with. Many institutions wouldn't allow (some still don't) ads for alcoholic beverages, bars, cigarettes, theaters featuring "risque" movies, political causes, or companies and bookstores in direct competition with the respective institutions. Many of these taboos have been done away with. For example, not only do campus papers use political ads, they now editorialize for certain candidates, much to the consternation of political rivals. (Some political rivals have been trustees or corporation members of these institutions.) Practically anything can be advertised today, even to the point of running such personal ads as "Male wants female roommate. Call so and so," etc.

Advertising is not something that should be glossed over, especially when it involves selling to a 15-billion-dollar teen-age market. Many national agencies woo editors and many papers remain solvent solely on ads.

9. *The format of student publications is undergoing change to the extent that some media which are moribund are being integrated into completely new formats like the general interest magazine, which, on some campuses, includes the humor magazine, the literary magazine and the yearbook's picture coverage of the campus.*[3]

Because of the increasing costs of publication, etc., few student publications besides the newspaper are remaining solvent. Literary magazines, often regarded as "third sister" publications behind the paper and the yearbook, are fast disappearing or reducing publication to a once-a-year basis. Because of this, many newspapers have incorporated into their pages fiction and poetry sections to pick up the slack. Rising costs have reduced the size of many yearbooks to a point where only graduate photos and brief biographies are now printed. These sections formerly constituted approximately one-fourth of some of these same yearbooks. Newspapers, therefore, attempt to pick up the slack here by running group shots, faculty and administration shots, sports, history, candids, etc.

With all of these changes, Dr. Politella's term "revolution" seems immediately apropos to what is going on in the student press today. One can only hope to keep up with the changes, to, perhaps, anticipate many of them. There is no question, however, that in the future as now and as in the past, tempers will flare, students will "rock the boat" and will sometimes rock themselves out of it, the telephones of advisers and college presidents will jump off the desks on the day of publication, and all one can meekly suggest is compliance to the words of Ralph Waldo Emerson, "Adopt the pace of Nature; her secret is patience."

[3] The nine italicized statements are taken from Dario Politella, "The Campus Press— A Revolution Coming," *The Quill*, pp. 14, 15, September, 1967.

BIBLIOGRAPHY

Duke, John: *The Publications Adviser,* San Joaquin Valley Scholastic Press Association, Fresno, Calif., 1960.

Estrin, Herman A.: "Adviser Talks to His Editor," *School Activities,* pp. 147–148, January, 1959.

———: "The Role of the Faculty Adviser," *College Press Review,* pp. 14–15, February, 1958.

———: "Student Publications in Higher Education," Pi Delta Epsilon, Pittsburgh, Pa., May, 1962.

Estrin, Herman A., and Arthur M. Sanderson: *Freedom and Censorship of the College Press,* Wm. C. Brown Company, Dubuque, Iowa, 1966.

Hand, Harold C.: *Campus Activities,* McGraw-Hill Book Company, Inc., New York, 1938.

"How Free Is College Journalism? A Symposium," *New Republic,* vol. 134, pp. 11–14, April 2, 1956.

Lunn, Harry: *The Student's Role in College Policy Making,* American Council on Education, Washington, 1957.

Musgrave, Arthur B.: "The Excessive-time Problem in College Student Journalism," University of Minnesota, Minneapolis, 1961.

Politella, Dario: "Patterns of Press Freedom in a Selected Group of Colleges and Universities in Indiana, 1964," Syracuse University, Syracuse, N.Y., 1964.

———: "The Campus Press—A Revolution Coming," *The Quill,* pp. 14–17, September, 1967.

Sanderson, Arthur M.: "National Survey of College and University Student-edited Newspapers in the United States," Iowa City, Iowa, 1961. Report I: Daily newspapers; II: Semiweekly newspapers; III: Weekly newspapers; IV: Semimonthly newspapers. (From a survey of 2,000 institutions, some 900 responses analyzed and tabulated for production, format, finances, advertising, circulation, staffs and salaries, control structure and policies, adviser duties and qualifications, and relationship of the newspaper to the curriculum.)

"Tufts University Plan for Student Publications," Tufts University, Medford, Mass. (Adopted Spring, 1965.)

United States Student Press Association: "1964–65 Codification of Policy: Toward a free and responsible student press," Philadelphia, 1964.

Chapter **13**

Fraternities and Sororities

EDWARD C. MC GUIRE

Dean of Students, Rutgers—The State University, Newark, New Jersey

INTRODUCTION

For most college and university administrators, the vexing question regarding the place of fraternities on the campus is resolved. If fraternities are already a part of the campus scene, the attitude is usually, "let's have them be as sound as possible"; if fraternities are not on the campus, the attitude is usually, "let's remain uninvolved by keeping fraternities off the campus."

Regardless of particular administrative attitudes, fraternities are big business. In January, 1967, there were over 4,000 active chapters registered as members of the National Interfraternity Conference and over 2,000 active chapters registered as members of the National Panhellenic Conference. There are over 200,000 undergraduate members of fraternities and almost 100,000 undergraduate members of sororities. The alumni members of fraternities and sororities number about 3,000,000. Fraternities and sororities are found at some 4,000 colleges and universities and own approximately 3,000 chapter houses.

TYPES OF FRATERNITIES

There are essentially six types of fraternities:

Men's Social Fraternities These groups are organized as mutually exclusive, self-perpetuating groups which attempt to organize the social and extra-class life of their members and to assist these members in achieving their educational goals. A men's social fraternity draws its membership from the male undergraduate population of the institution and is the traditional college fraternity.

Women's Social Fraternities More often than not these groups are called "sororities" and are organized as mutually exclusive, self-perpetuating groups. The sororities are generally more organized than the male fraternities. They demonstrate a greater control of the social, educational, and extra-class life of their members. A women's fraternity draws its membership from the female undergraduate population of the institution at which it is located.

Professional Fraternities The professional fraternity is a specialized fraternity which limits its membership to undergraduate students studying within a specific academic discipline. The professional fraternity confines its membership to either male or female undergraduates; never are both included. The professional fraternity is organized to promote various professional objectives that are formulated by the fraternity.

Honor Societies The honor society is composed of college and university students and faculty members whose purposes are to encourage and recognize superior scholarship and leadership in either a single academic discipline or in general academic areas of higher education.

Recognition Societies The recognition society is an organization which confers membership on undergraduates in recognition of a special interest or ability on the part of a student within a given academic discipline or extracurricular activity.

Service Fraternities Service fraternities usually choose their membership from the undergraduate student body. Members of both sexes may participate in the service fraternity and usually all students who show some interest in joining are given membership. They are organized primarily to be of service to the college or university.

ORGANIZATION AND ADMINISTRATION OF FRATERNITIES

Among college and university social fraternities, there are wide variations both in size and mode of operation. There is, however, a common foundation upon which these groups are built. The common factor that binds fraternities together is the fact that each fraternity is organized to operate as a more or less autonomous unit in which the major responsibility for successful operation is carried by the members themselves.

Each fraternity has the usual elected officers, president, vice-president, secretary, treasurer, etc., and other officers peculiar to this type of organization, such as a rush chairman, a pledge chairman, etc. The fraternity officers are most frequently upperclassmen. The fraternity officers are concerned with the day-to-day operation of the fraternity. The undergraduate officers are usually backed up by a group of older men who are alumni of the fraternity. Depending upon the amount of dedication and interest of the alumni members, the students will have either a large or small measure of responsibility for the fraternity. Where the alumni are active, control and responsibility for the fraternity tend to slip out of the hands of the undergraduates and into the hands of the alumni.

The local chapter of a national fraternity and its alumni are directly responsible to the national fraternity for the business and social affairs of the local. The national fraternity usually has one or more full-time, salaried staff members whose responsibility it is to be concerned about the affairs of both the local and the national fraternity. The national fraternity generally establishes overall fraternity policy at an annual meeting of members of the fraternity, including both students and alumni. Because of the voting procedures used, many national meetings of fraternities are controlled by the officers and alumni. It is not often that graduate students exercise enough power at a national convention to get their wishes and needs fulfilled.

The Chapter House The fraternity chapter-house movement, which began just prior to the Civil War, has had a marked effect upon the college fraternity movement. The interest of the fraternity alumni can rarely be so fully roused and maintained by any other feature of fraternity life as by the efforts which must be made to build and maintain a chapter house.

The development of the chapter house has picked up momentum in recent years in spite of the high cost of construction. The number of chapter houses built and owned by fraternities is large, and the combined value of fraternity houses runs into many millions of dollars. Most national fraternities and some colleges and universities will financially assist the local fraternity in one way or another in the building of a local chapter house. Some national fraternities will invest little or nothing in a local chapter house while others will become involved to the extent of a mortgage on the total value of the property. (See Volume 1, Section 8, Chapter 22.)

Living in the fraternity chapter house can have advantages and disadvantages for the student. "Living in" can develop pride of organization, social discipline, and positive habits of business and administration. Further, living in can help promote close and lasting friendship and can offer a small group in which self-identification can be explored. On the other hand, living in can foster social exclusiveness, can create an anti-intellectual haven, and in some cases may increase the expense of college life to the student or his family. When symptoms of the latter situation become apparent, corrective measures should be immediately taken.

FRATERNITY COOPERATIVE ASSOCIATION

Because the day-to-day fiscal management of the fraternity chapter house is usually left to the undergraduate students, some colleges and universities have promoted a cooperative buying and training association which comprises all the fraternities on the campus.

The purposes of the association are usually threefold: (1) to provide the services and the personnel through which the fraternities can purchase commodities in volume in order to effect cash savings; (2) to train and advise the fraternity stewards and treasurers in the use of sound business-management techniques; and (3) to foster, promote, and perpetuate the best interests of the fraternity system at the particular college or university.

To achieve these purposes the fraternity cooperative association usually attempts to purchase food, fuel, furnishings, supplies, and equipment for all the fraternities on the campus. The association also budgets funds for each fraternity; provides data for the pre-costing and analysis of fraternity operational costs; and gives information and advice on the bookkeeping, menu planning, nutrition, and general management of each fraternity.

It is generally necessary for the fraternity cooperative association to conduct training programs in bookkeeping and in food and house management for the students and for the hired help of the fraternities. The association also advises the fraternities on repairs, replacement of equipment, and maintenance of facilities in the chapter houses. As a service to the college or university administration, the association will often collect the room, board, and other fees applicable to the fraternities.

LEGISLATION AFFECTING FRATERNITIES

Taxation There are at least four state-court decisions that have ruled, in effect, that a fraternity-owned chapter house in which the members live and take their meals is not exempt from taxation because a fraternity is not a benevolent, charitable, literary, or scientific society. The extent of these court rulings makes it rather clear that fraternity-owned chapter houses are liable for state and local taxes unless state law specifically indicates that fraternities shall be exempt from such taxation. However, if the college or university owns the buildings and/or property, then the taxation is based on the ratable status of the institution.

The Bureau of Internal Revenue has ruled that contributions made to fraternities are not tax deductible. This ruling has been upheld by the Board of Tax Appeals on the ground that fraternities, per se, are not organized and operated exclusively for charitable, literary, or educational purposes.

Although active fraternity chapters are nonprofit institutions and are not subject to certain forms of taxation such as income tax, fraternity chapters are subject to the provisions of the workmen's compensation statutes of the federal government. Many fraternities have established local educational foundations to which the alumni and others may make tax-deductible gifts. The income from the corporates of these foundations is used to give scholarships and loans or other financial assistance to the undergraduates within a given chapter. In some instances these educational foundations may take over the buildings and property of the individual fraternity and then, because of the tax-exempt status of the educational foundations, the property may no longer have to remain on the state or local rolls.

Status In a legal sense, fraternities are "voluntary associations," and on this definition are based the rights that fraternities possess in respect to their operation and organization on college and university campuses.

Several state courts have ruled that membership in a fraternity is a privilege which may be accorded or withheld and not a right which can be gained independently and then enforced. Some state courts have further indicated that the courts cannot compel the admission of a student into a fraternity and, if the application for admission is refused by the fraternity, the student is without legal redress no matter how unjust his exclusion may be.

The federal courts upheld the right of the State University of New York to bar from the university educational system any social organization which has a direct or indirect affiliation with any national organization. The federal courts have clearly indicated that a state may legally adopt measures outlawing certain social organizations in order to exercise the duty of supervision and control of the educational institutions of the state.

Discriminatory Clauses Both the federal government and various state governments have explicitly and implicitly indicated to fraternities that it is illegal for any state-supported or federally supported institutions to recognize, to grant privileges, or to make facilities available to any organization which restricts membership on the basis of race, color, or creed. Unresolved to date is the question of whether or not colleges or universities that accept federal support either in loans, grants, or contracts are operating outside the law by recognizing fraternities that may be practicing some membership discrimination based upon race, color, or creed. If fraternities are controlled by a college or university or occupy facilities owned by a college or university, under the Civil Rights Act of 1964 the college or university is responsible for assuring that fraternities on its campus do not practice racial or religious discrimination.

INTERFRATERNITY RELATIONS

There are essentially three organizations that devote all their time and activities to the coordination of the affairs of social fraternities: (1) The National Interfraternity Conference, which is an association of men's national social fraternities; (2) The National Panhellenic Conference, which is an association of women's national social fraternities; and (3) The National Panhellenic Council, which is an association of men's and women's social fraternities which have predominantly Negro memberships.

The professional fraternities and the honor societies also have national organizations which devote time and energy to the coordination of the affairs of these organizations.

Local versus National Affiliation Since 1942, the number of colleges and universities having chapters of national fraternities has increased by more than 60 percent. During this period of time, the average membership per chapter has at least doubled. There is good evidence that the growth of national fraternities on college and university campuses will continue at a fairly rapid rate in the years to come.

During the past few years, the number of colleges and universities having only local fraternities has declined by more than 50 percent. The growth of national fraternities and the decline of local fraternities clearly indicate a strong trend in favor of national fraternities.

There are many advantages in having national instead of local fraternities on the campus. The national fraternity attempts to stimulate the undergraduate student to be a better scholar. National fraternities generally place heavy emphasis on scholarship by rewarding good academic achievement, by taking steps to remedy poor academic performance, and by insisting that the local chapters provide study facilities and tutorial programs for their members.

Most national fraternities provide some systematic training in business management for the student members. Most chapters of a national fraternity will do an annual dollar volume of business ranging from $25,000 to $100,000. To manage a fiscal operation of this magnitude is a major responsibility for the student members of the fraternity. The national fraternity provides advice and systematic training in an attempt to help those students charged with the fiscal operation to develop their knowledge and skills in business affairs.

National fraternities have recognized the importance of guiding the student members to positions of leadership. Nationals have attempted to create programs that start preparing men to be leaders early in their fraternity experience. In the chapter house and in annual leadership schools, the influence of the national in attempting to develop leadership abilities is usually felt.

Of great importance to the college or university administrator is the fact that membership in a national fraternity offers the stability and resources of continuity. Local chapters of national fraternities seem to be stronger groups, more consistent, and richer in programs because of their national affiliation. The accumulation of years of experience plus the adult leadership offered by the national office helps to create a sound fraternity.

There is, however, an argument against the national fraternity. Local fraternities appear to generate a greater degree of loyalty to the college or university than do the national fraternities. Local fraternities do not get caught up in the mysticism and the demands of the national fraternities. No matter how they try, national fraternities cannot avoid demanding loyalty and interest from their local chapter members and alumni. All too often, when this struggle of divided loyalty goes on, the college or university takes second place.

Many times, when there are national fraternities on the campus, the administration assumes that the training and supervising of these fraternities will be done at the national level, thereby relieving the college or university of a great deal of tedious administrative work. This is frequently not the case. The national offices are understaffed and generally overworked, and therefore they cannot effectively control or supervise local chapters. This responsibility has to remain with the college or university officials or else the fraternities will soon run into either fiscal or behavioral difficulties.

RELATIONSHIP TO THE INSTITUTION

A fraternity does not have the right to establish itself as an affiliate of a college or university unless it obtains explicit approval from the college or university. The policy statements of the National Interfraternity Conference and the National Panhellenic Conference, as well as recent court decisions, make this perfectly clear. Because the institution becomes a party to the establishment of a fraternity or a fraternity system, it is expected that the institution will assume some responsibility for the fraternity.

At the very least, it is necessary for the college or university to have a well-thought-out, clearly articulated policy concerning fraternities. Nothing is more difficult for fraternities, both national and local, than to be in the dark as to the official posture of the institution regarding fraternities. If the institution is supportive of fraternities, it should clearly indicate this fact; if the institution is merely going to tolerate fraternities, it should also make this clear; if the institution does not approve of fraternities, once again, this should be clearly indicated. On an issue as debatable and debated as fraternities, colleges and universities must have clear and concise policy statements.

REGULATION AND CONTROL

Most policies governing the operation of fraternities on most campuses are determined by an interfraternity council for fraternities and a panhellenic council for sororities. The college usually delegates to these councils the responsibility for devising and maintaining those regulations that are necessary to the good order of the fraternities and sororities.

The interfraternity council and the panhellenic council are composed of undergraduates and have the usual complement of officers: president, vice-president, secretary, treasurer, etc., and one or two member representatives from each fraternity or sorority. The councils legislate and enforce regulations covering rushing activities and the social affairs of the fraternities or sororities. The councils are also responsible for disciplining those fraternities or sororities that break campus rules, civil or criminal laws, or interfraternity or panhellenic regulations. All the actions taken by the councils are generally subject to the approval of the college or university administration.

ADVISORY SYSTEM

One of the most difficult tasks facing a fraternity or sorority is securing a faculty member who will act as an adviser to the group. Most colleges insist, as a matter of regulation, that each fraternity and sorority have a faculty member who will act as a "faculty adviser," otherwise they are refused the right to organize. Because of today's campus climate, it is generally difficult for the fraternity to obtain the services of a faculty member.

The role of faculty adviser to fraternities is often a thankless task requiring the adviser to attend fraternity parties, at which he is often ignored, to sign endless papers authorizing the fraternity to hold affairs and spend money in ways of which he knows little, and to defend the fraternity against administrators and faculty colleagues when the fraternity misbehaves. The fraternity adviser usually receives small personal or professional recognition from the college for his efforts and only token recognition from the fraternity that he advises.

However, for the faculty member who is willing to accept this difficult role, there can be a great deal of personal satisfaction. He or she can help to mold a group of young men or women during the most formative stage of their lives. The faculty adviser can further present a model of what an adult should be for the student to follow and emulate—a most important responsibility for any adult.

Some colleges have found it helpful to pay fraternity advisers for their services. A fraternity adviser who exercises his responsibilities well spends a significant amount of time advising young adults, attempting to bring about a better working relationship between the fraternity and the college, and in general just being available to the members of a fraternity. To pay a faculty adviser for this kind of service to young people and to the institution can make some sense.

SOCIAL FUNCTIONS

The first order of business for fraternities and sororities, regardless of what is currently being said, is to direct time, money, and energy to the social needs of the members of the fraternity. A fraternity or a sorority is a social organization, and therefore all other endeavors take a back seat. There is great concern on the part of fraternities and sororities for their members to succeed academically but not, it appears, purely for the sake of knowledge. Rather, they hope that the successful members of the group will, as alumni, continue to contribute their experience, prestige, and money to the fraternity.

The national officers and some alumni are diligently attempting to get a better balance within the fraternity between social activities and academic activities. The national fraternity has established elaborate procedures for the recognition of good scholarship on the part of the members, but the members of the local fraternity cling tenaciously to the idea that the heart of the chapter is in its social activities.

Because of the heavy accent on social activities by fraternities and sororities, college and university administrators have had to impose, either through the interfraternity council or independently, some regulations controlling the social affairs of fraternities and sororities.

There is beginning to be developed within some fraternity structures a concern with social awareness and the responsibility of a college-educated person in the social sense of mankind. This is a new definition of the word "social" as used by fraternities which should be promoted and, where found, encouraged by the college.

PROCEDURES FOR RECOGNITION OF A NEW FRATERNITY

The usual procedure followed is to have the persons involved in forming the new fraternity approach the dean of students or his campus equivalent with the following information:

Name of fraternity
Date of founding of the fraternity if it is a national fraternity
Names of possible members and tentative officers
Possible committees that will be part of the fraternity
Name of faculty adviser
Copy of constitution and bylaws of the new fraternity

Recognition can be given to the newly formed fraternity after consideration of its intentions, the need for such an organization on the campus, and whether the formation of such an organization will adversely affect the status quo of other, similar organizations.

Often new fraternities are formed by students who have been barred from existing fraternities and who, in their newly forming group, intend to compete with the already existing fraternities. The administration may decide, as a method of satisfying this group, to authorize a new fraternity, or this step may be deemed an unwise move at the time.

In establishing criteria for a new fraternity, the college or university must maintain certain requirements for academic standing. These may simply conform to the already established rules governing academic probation and the like. There is also usually a minimum number established for membership before recognition is granted.

Official recognition of the group is frequently withheld for a period of at least a year, during which the college or university will have opportunities to observe the activities of the new fraternity and to judge its suitability for the campus. Formal recognition, in many cases, must be approved and conferred by the board of trustees of the university.

In the case of a national fraternity, it is often best to have a letter from the national office which acknowledges that the national will be willing to form a new chapter.

As part of the recognition procedure, the college or university should also present to the new fraternity the rules and regulations that govern fraternities. These rules, in addition to the rules governing the use of the university name, should be clearly stated. There can at this time be some assistance in the form of helping to establish sound fiscal policies. Once recognition is established, it becomes the duty of the college or university to assist in every way practicable in order to assure the fraternity of a continuing successful operation.

GAINING RECOGNITION FROM A NATIONAL FRATERNITY

The first step is for the local group to get permission from the college to write directly to the national headquarters of the fraternity which the local group is interested in joining. The national organization, if it is interested in the local group, will then send some representatives to discuss affiliation with the local group.

After this preliminary discussion, if both parties are still interested, the national organization will work with the local group in trying to establish alumni contacts in the area and in building up an organization.

Once the national organization feels that the local group is making progress, the group is usually made a colony of the fraternity. Colony status usually lasts from one to three years. The improvements and status of a colony are evaluated periodically during this time. Once, in the opinion of the national organization, the colony has fulfilled its obligations, the colony is allowed to petition for a chapter.

When the local colony petitions for a chapter and after the national convention has approved the charter, then the local group is "chartered" as a chapter of that fraternity.

SPECIAL FRATERNITY PROBLEMS ON AN URBAN CAMPUS

Fraternities on the urban campus are faced with problems peculiar to the urban world. Housing is often expensive, and many times the houses are old. Large urban universities often have as many commuter students as residents. If many commuters belong to the fraternity, the fraternity can become just a lunchroom facility. The houses are often located several blocks from the campus and thus tend to decentralize the campus. This geographic diversity of the fraternity houses makes central control and coordination by the college or university exceedingly difficult. One of the great advantages of the urban university is the diverse nature of the student body, but this diversity is often reduced within homogeneous fraternity groups.

Fraternities connected with the urban universities do have unique opportunities as well as unique problems. The forms of diversion that urban centers offer are many and varied, ranging from cultural activities to sports events. There are also excellent opportunities to work with the many volunteer programs in the urban centers. As representatives of the university, fraternities can often present a profile to the city that the university itself cannot create, thereby reducing the eternal conflict between town and gown.

FIRE PROTECTION AND SAFETY REGULATIONS

All fraternity houses should be inspected annually by the fire authority. Also, there should be regular self-inspection reports as well as university inspection.

The insurance companies that write the coverage for the fraternities are very useful sources of information regarding fundamental fire and safety procedures and programs.

INSURANCE

The liability relationship of the fraternity and the university should be very clearly and definitively spelled out. This statement should cover all facts of fraternity and university life with no details omitted. Such details are necessary for the protection of both the fraternity and the university.

ADDITIONAL RESOURCES

It is an absolute must that every college or university officer charged with fraternity or sorority responsibility have the latest copy of *Baird's Manual of American College Fraternities*. This is an excellent, up-to-date, and authoritative reference book regarding fraternities and sororities.

The National Interfraternity Conference, The National Panhellenic Conference, and the National Panhellenic Council will all offer sound advice to any college or university interested in fraternities and/or sororities.

APPENDIX 1

Example of Statement of Principles and Policies Relating to Faculty Advisers of Fraternities

The university considers extracurricular activities as a significant part of the total university program of academic and cooperative education. The university requires that all recognized activities be under the guidance of a faculty adviser. Upon the recommendation of the Director of Student Activities, the Dean of Administration appoints faculty members to serve as advisers to organizations.

In the case of fraternity advisers, such recommendations are made by the Dean of Men in consultation with the individual fraternities. The fraternity adviser is given a stipend of $350 per year to help cover the expenses he will incur in this type of work.

The adviser, above all, should be interested in working with the young people in his group. Advisers are expected to attend weekly meetings and many of the major social events that the fraternities sponsor during the year. The adviser must work closely with the brotherhood and be especially close to the officers of the fraternity so that they will seek his advice and guidance on important issues which are faced during the year.

The fraternity adviser should refer to the *Handbook for Faculty Advisers* prepared annually by the Director of Student Activities. This booklet covers all phases of this important work and should answer all questions that advisers might raise.

APPENDIX 2

Example of Fraternity Adviser Expense Account

Fraternity adviser expense form for the three-month period ending ________
Name of adviser ________ Name of fraternity ________

Faculty fraternity advisers must report their expenditures on the form below. It is assumed that stipends paid to advisers are to help cover the out-of-pocket expenses incurred in their work with the fraternities. Please show the three-month expenses for all items listed and submit to the dean of men as soon as possible.

Expenses	*Total for the three-month period*
A. Meals (all foods, meals, and beverages)	
B. Hotel	
C. Baby-sitting expense	
D. Formal attire (including purchase or rental for you or your wife)	
E. Entertaining (includes *all* expenses at your home or at the fraternity)	
F. Special fraternity expense paid by you (tickets to events, dues, etc.)	
G. Travel in your automobile (at 10 cents per mile)	
H. Travel by other means than your automobile	
I. Miscellaneous	
Total for three-month period	________

(For further comments, please use reverse side.)

APPENDIX 3

Sample Procedure for Approval for National Fraternities

General Acceptable national fraternities are those of good reputation whose aims, objectives, and policies are not in conflict with university practices. National fraternities considered unacceptable by the university are those which restrict membership by reason of race, religion, creed, or national origin and those whose reputations would reflect discredit upon the university.

Procedure This procedure is to be followed by a fraternity desiring to affiliate with a national fraternity:

1. When a local and a national fraternity, in the process of their investigations, have reached agreement that they are mutually desirous of affiliation and before the local fraternity files a formal petition to the national fraternity to be accepted as a local chapter, the local fraternity must submit a request for approval to affiliate to the Interfraternity Council.

2. When the Interfraternity Council has approved the fraternity's request for approval, the Dean of Men will submit the request to the Committee on Student Activities for investigation and decision.

3. When the Committee on Student Activities has approved the request, it will be submitted to the President of the university for final action.

APPENDIX 4

Bowdoin College Fraternity House Social Rules (1969) [1]

The Faculty has approved the following hours, principles, and procedures regarding fraternity house guests for the academic year 1967–68 when the College is in session:

1. Women shall be allowed downstairs in the fraternities from 7 A.M. until midnight, Sunday through Friday, and 7 A.M. until 1 A.M. Saturday.

2. Women shall be allowed in the living rooms of the upstairs suites which are approved by the Dean of Students at the following times:

Sunday	Noon–8 P.M.
Friday	Noon–Midnight
Saturday	Noon–1 A.M.

(Note: These hours define maximum limits and may be further limited at the discretion of each fraternity.)

3. When women are staying overnight in the fraternities, chaperones shall be required.

4. A student who serves as a host in a Bowdoin fraternity is responsible for the well-being of his guests and for conduct becoming a gentleman. Other members are likewise expected to conduct themselves responsibly. At a fraternity party at which women are not the guests of individual hosts, the fraternity shall accept all responsibility for dates within the house.

5. A seven member Judiciary Board, comprised of one house advisor and six undergraduate members, appointed jointly by the house advisers and the elected officers of the house, shall serve a one year term of office under a chairman selected from the board in each fraternity.

6. This Judiciary Board shall adjudicate cases of social irresponsibility within the house. The house within which social irresponsibility occurs shall initiate appropriate action. Actions of any one Judiciary Board will be upheld by all other houses. Major violations will be referred to the Student Judiciary Board. Each House Judiciary Board shall file monthly minutes of its meetings with the Student Judiciary Board.

7. Disputed decisions of House Judiciary Boards may be appealed to the Student Judiciary Board.

Office of the Dean of Students

Bowdoin College Fraternity House Social Regulations (1969) [2]

I. Rules Regarding Fraternity House Guests

1. Women shall be allowed downstairs in the fraternities from 7 A.M. until midnight, Sunday through Friday, and 7 A.M. until 1 A.M. Saturday.

[1] Reprinted by permission of Bowdoin College.

[2] Reprinted by permission of Bowdoin College.

2. Women shall be allowed in the living rooms of the upstairs suites which are approved by the Dean of Students at the following times:

Sunday	Noon–8 P.M.
Friday	Noon–Midnight
Saturday	Noon–1 A.M.

II. Rules Pertaining to Social Events

The following rules pertain to specific social events:

Formal Houseparties (Winter and Ivy Houseparties)

1. Formal houseparties shall begin at 2 P.M. Friday and shall end on Saturday night at 3 A.M. There shall be no organized activities on Sunday.

2. The Special Social Hours as defined above shall be in effect.

3. In fraternities housing dates, undergraduates are not allowed above the first floor from midnight Friday until noon Saturday or from 1 A.M. Saturday night until noon Sunday and undergraduates (except the men designated as fire watch) are excluded from these fraternities between 3 A.M. and 7 A.M.

4. In fraternities not housing dates, women are not allowed above the first floor from midnight Friday until noon Saturday or from 1 A.M. Saturday night until noon Sunday and women are excluded from these fraternities between 3 A.M. and 7 A.M.

5. Each fraternity shall have chaperones for the duration of the party if it is housing dates. At least one set of chaperones shall be the parents of a student. Chaperones are in charge at all times and shall be present at social functions of the house. Chaperones shall be approved by the Dean of Students *one week in advance* of the occasion.

6. Each fraternity shall file a *Houseparty Information Sheet* for the approval of the Dean of Students at least two days before the houseparty begins. The Dean shall be notified of any change in this schedule. An accurate list of guests should be filed at the same time. A copy of the *Information Sheet* and list of guests should also be kept by the house president.

7. Each Fraternity President shall make certain that the following matters are taken care of:

a. That adequate precautions are taken to meet any danger; that the chaperones and guests are informed of the fire escape exits;
b. That a responsible man is designated to be on fire watch in the House through the night;
c. That his House is properly protected against theft or intrusion when students and guests are away;
d. That the House and grounds are kept in thoroughly presentable condition and that reasonable consideration is exercised with respect to noise;
e. That students are urgently requested to exercise the greatest care in the use of cars;
f. That students are warned to keep cars locked to avoid theft of any valuables;
g. That students use beaches or other property only when definitely authorized to do so, and leave any places used in an orderly condition.

Homecoming Weekend

1. Houses may remain open to women in downstairs areas until 1 A.M. Friday night and 2 A.M. Saturday night.

2. The Special Social Hours as defined above shall be in effect.

3. The Dean of Students may grant permission for women to remain overnight Saturday in the fraternities, and he will set the conditions under which permission is granted.

Saturday Night Parties

1. A fraternity may apply to the Dean of Students for a special party on a Saturday night. The request should be made *one week in advance*.

2. Fraternity houses may remain open until 2 A.M. and the Special Social Hours as defined above shall be in effect.

3. The Dean of Students may grant permission for women to remain overnight in the fraternities, and he will set the conditions under which permission is granted.

III. Use of Alcoholic Beverages

The College supports the ordinances of the Town of Brunswick and the laws of the State of Maine.* The College expects and urges compliance by its students with local, state, and national laws, and emphasizes to them their obligations both as citizens and as members of the College. Violation of the law by students subjects them to discipline by the College.

The following regulations govern the use of alcohol on campus:

1. Drinking on campus shall be confined to the fraternity houses and dormitories. Public drinking (i.e., drinking on streets, in cars, on the lawns and walks of the Campus, or in College buildings other than dormitories and fraternities) and littering are contrary to State laws and College rules.

2. The house administration shall insure that there is no sale of alcoholic beverages of any kind and that orderly conduct prevails at all times where alcohol is being served.

3. When house sponsored dispensing facilities are used, they must be closed one hour before the closing of the house.

4. All house sponsored cocktail parties must be registered at the Office of the Dean of Students.

5. Whenever an approved cocktail party is being conducted, nonalcoholic beverages must be made available.

IV. General Fraternity Rules

1. No firearms, air rifles or other weapons may be kept in fraternity houses unless registered at the Office of the Dean of Students.

2. Possession or use of firecrackers or other explosives is forbidden by the College and by State Law and will result in separation.

3. Roofs are out of bounds as recreational areas.

Text of Statement Formally Adopted by the Governing Boards of Bowdoin College at Their Meetings in June 1962

It is the policy of Bowdoin College that each fraternity on the campus should be completely free to choose its members from among all the students who have been admitted to the College, without restrictions as to race, creed, or color. It also is the policy of the College to permit early pledging and initiation of freshmen.

It is not consistent with the high ideals of good faith, honesty and straightforwardness, which a fraternity should cherish, for a national fraternity to influence or force its local chapter to evade, flout, or obstruct in any way the policies of the institution where it is located.

The College expects any national fraternity which cannot in complete good faith permit its Bowdoin chapter to abide by these policies to withdraw its affiliation. The College hopes that such withdrawal will be found unnecessary.

* Relevant points in the State of Maine law regarding alcoholic beverages:

1. No fraternity or student may engage directly or indirectly in any commercialization of alcoholic beverages.

2. The use of assessments, contributions, or board receipts from minors (those under 21 years of age) for the purchase or serving of intoxicating beverages (including beer) is in violation of the law of the State.

3. Individual procurement or purchase of intoxicating beverages for or by minors is contrary to the law of the State of Maine.

4. Public drinking is contrary to the law of the State of Maine. This includes drinking on streets, in automobiles, and in such public places as athletic fields, the Gymnasium, the Arena, theaters, and auditoriums.

Chapter 14

International Students

IVAN PUTMAN, JR.

Acting University Dean, International Studies and World Affairs,
State University of New York, Albany, New York

What to call students from other countries who enroll in our colleges and universities troubles many people on campuses. Some feel that "foreign student" is derogatory and seek some euphemism to substitute for it. A common choice is "international student," which unfortunately equates "international" with "foreign" and tends to make Americans feel unwelcome in "international student" activities. "Overseas student" is sometimes used, in spite of the fact that Canadians and Mexicans are foreign students but need to cross no oceans to reach the United States. "Alien student," the term used in immigration laws, has quite unacceptable connotations for common usage.

"Student from another land" and "student from abroad" are acceptable but cumbersome. "Foreign student" remains the most succinct and accurate term yet devised, and is the one in most common use throughout the country. It should always be used as a term denoting respect and distinction, and should therefore be acceptable both to those so designated and to their hosts.

Study abroad has been common for 2,500 years, but since World War II it has become big business and the United States has emerged as one of the major host countries. In 1968–1969 the annual foreign student census in the United States conducted by the Institute of International Education[1] reported a total of 121,300 students from 172 countries and territories of the world studying in 1,846 U.S. colleges and universities. However, 58 percent were enrolled at 72 institutions reporting 400 or more foreign students, and the other 42 percent of foreign students were distributed among the other 1,774 institutions reporting foreign students.

New York University had the largest number of foreign students enrolled, 3,293. Miami-Dade Junior College had the second highest number enrolled with 3,084. Among major institutions Woodbury College reported the highest percentage of foreign student enrollment: 22 percent. Howard University had 16 percent; Massachusetts Institute of Technology had 15.5 percent; Miami-Dade Junior College had 11.7 percent; University of San Francisco had 11 percent; Columbia University had 10.7 percent; and University of California at Berkeley had 10 percent.

Again, the Far East, with just over a third of the total, far outranked the other world areas in numbers of students in the United States. Latin America accounted for 19 percent; Europe, 14 percent; the Near and Middle East, 12 percent; North America, 11 percent; and Africa 6 percent.

Among major fields of study engineering claims 21 percent of the total foreign student population in the United States; the humanities, 20 percent; the physical and life sciences, 16 percent; the social sciences, 14 percent; business administration, 11 percent; education, 6 percent; medical sciences, 4 percent; and agriculture, 3 percent. The remaining 5 percent were either in other fields or failed to designate a major.

OBJECTIVES

The foreign student, his family, his government, the educational institution receiving him, the host country government, and any other sponsor of the student's sojourn abroad all have their reasons for being involved. The effective education of the student is perhaps the only goal upon which they all agree, and beyond that they may have quite different objectives. The student and his family may be primarily concerned with enhancing his prestige and prospects in life. His government wants him to be trained as quickly as possible to return home and help solve the country's development problems. The host institution may be most interested in the foreign student's helping to educate American students internationally, or having him on campus as a visible sign of the institution's own reputation and maturity. The chief interest of the United States government may be to develop favorable attitudes toward the United States among future leaders of other countries.

These and other objectives of the parties vitally interested in the study-abroad experience of the student may all be legitimate, but they are not always compatible. For example, the student may wish to remain in the United States to complete a graduate degree, while his government wants him to return home immediately when he finishes his undergraduate study. Or the student may feel that his best chance for a satisfactory position and for optimum use of his education and talents would be in the United States, while other parties to the arrangement insist upon his return home.

[1] *OPEN DOORS 1969*, Institute of International Education, New York, 1969.

Thus the student may find himself the center of a conflict of interests, and his host institution is inevitably in the position of having to help resolve the conflict.

INSTITUTIONAL OBLIGATIONS

Whether an institution has one, a hundred, a thousand, or more foreign students, it accepts certain obligations when it admits them. It must have been approved by the Immigration and Naturalization Service of the U.S. Department of Justice to accept foreign students, and it has thereby agreed to certain procedures and obligations required by immigration regulations. It has also in effect entered into a contract with its foreign students, as it does with American students as well, to provide quality education appropriate to their needs.

But beyond these basic contractual obligations, American institutions of higher education have recognized the fact that human resources are of paramount importance and those most in need of development everywhere in the world. Therefore, the institutions have generally assumed responsibility for trying to deliver their students to the classrooms in the optimum condition to learn by assisting them in the solution of problems that interfere with their effective academic performance. Some of the needs and problems of foreign students are much the same as those of Americans, but some are quite different because the foreign students come from other cultures and educational systems. It is for this reason that foreign student advisers have been designated by virtually every educational institution that enrolls even one foreign student, and that attention has been given by most colleges and universities to the special problems that foreign students have because they are foreign and to the problems and opportunities created by their presence on the campuses.

MAJOR PROBLEMS WITH FOREIGN STUDENTS

Selection and Admission The better the processes of selection and admission of foreign students, the fewer and less serious will be the problems they have when they come to our campuses. However, the processes of selection and admission are not simple. There are even more unknowns and variables with foreign students than with Americans.

One of the crucial factors in the foreign student admissions process is the kind of admission information sent in response to the letter of inquiry from the prospective student from abroad. Sending the catalog to individual foreign students is not recommended because (1) probably no more than a tenth of the information it contains is relevant to any individual student, and it confuses the foreign applicant more than it helps him understand what he is getting into; (2) the information on student expenses in most college and university catalogs is inadequate; (3) the foreign student is misled by the list of scholarships and other financial aids which he assumes are the answer to his prayers but virtually none of which he would be eligible for; and (4) the catalog is expensive to produce and is usually too large to send by airmail—if it reaches the student at all it is likely to arrive long after he has had to submit his application for admission.

It is therefore becoming increasingly common for institutions to prepare special airmail-weight bulletins of information for foreign students, including more careful explanations of facilities, procedures, requirements, expenses, financial aids, language facility, curricula offered, housing, and any other information important in determining their interest in applying to the institution.

Similarly, most admission application forms designed for Americans do not adapt very well for foreign students. Special forms on airmail-weight paper are therefore an economy in the long run. Special care should be taken to instruct the applicant on providing information about his previous educational experience. It is probably best to ask for his entire educational background from elementary school on, since such terms as "college" and "bachelor's degree" may have quite different meanings abroad than they do here. Knowing the total years of schooling helps avoid embarrassing errors. A good foreign student application will also include either special sections or separate forms on finances and English. If a health examination report is required, the form is best sent with the admission letter rather than with the initial application in order to get more up-to-date information and to enable the student to have it filled in at the same time he takes the physical examination required by immigration authorities before granting him a visa. The Institute of International Education has a very complete set of admission application forms for foreign students which many institutions have adapted for their own use and others purchase for continuing use instead of printing their own.

When the completed application is in hand, the admissions officer is faced with the difficult problem of evaluating it and deciding whether or not to admit the applicant. Only institutions with large enrollments of students from abroad usually can boast staff experts in the very complicated business of keeping up to date on foreign educational systems and evaluating the applications of students from around the world. Whoever does this job should have at hand the excellent publications in the field provided by the U.S. Office of Education, the American Council on Education, the American Association of Collegiate Registrars and Admissions Officers (AACRAO), the National Association for Foreign Student Affairs (NAFSA), the Institute of International Education (IIE), and the College Entrance Examination Board (CEEB). The latter four have jointly sponsored a number of useful reports. The U.S. Office of Education has for many years maintained an evaluation service for academic credentials of foreign applicants. The agency has announced that the service is to be terminated. Institutions desiring such service can profit by becoming Educational Associates of the Institute of International Education. The Institute provides an Application Information Service in some 25 countries and territories. A representative will interview applicants and provide reports on academic and English-language competence, financial status, motivation, health, and personality.

The in-service training of admissions officers handling foreign student applications is a continuing concern of the National Association for Foreign Student Affairs, which includes this problem on the agendas of many of its one-day, drive-in workshops and regional and national conferences. The American Association of Collegiate Registrars and Admissions Officers likewise gives considerable attention to the problem. NAFSA operates a consultant service to enable foreign student admissions experts to visit campuses requesting the service and can also make occasional grants to enable individual admissions officers to visit other institutions in which the work is well organized. Whatever the competence of the admissions officer, valuable assistance can often be given by faculty with experience abroad, the foreign student adviser, and even mature foreign students currently on the campus.

There are three crucial admission criteria for foreign students which must be emphasized in the preadmission information sent to them, in the application forms, and in evaluation of the completed applications. The first is the academic background. Except in very unusual circumstances, no student who has not been a considerably better than average student in his home educational system should be accepted for study in another country. He has so many handicaps to overcome in a foreign environment that he must have superior academic ability to have very much chance of success. Previous academic standing is the best criterion for predicting the success of foreign students and Americans alike. While we may give a chance to a mediocre student from the next town or county or state in this country, the risks are much too great to justify such a course for a foreign student who may be coming halfway around the world with all the hopes and financial resources of his family invested in his educational venture. Neither we nor he can risk his coming if his chances are not considerably better than even. Financial resources and facility in the English language are also major admission criteria which will be discussed at greater length later in this chapter.

When the foreign applicant's admissibility has been determined, it is essential that the terms of admission and of any financial aids offered be set forth in the admission letter and in the accompanying Immigration Form I–20 or the Department of State Form DSP–66 (the latter for those coming under Exchange Visitor programs approved under the provisions of the Fulbright-Hays Act). It is also important to specify the date the student is expected to arrive (without mentioning the dates of registration or of the first classes), the hours within which he should plan to report, the place and person to whom he reports, the means and costs of transportation from usual port-of-entry cities to the campus, what to bring, how to send luggage and mail ahead, housing arrangements, and all the other things a person might want to know about a new place to which he is coming.

Orientation to the American Scene Adjustment to the American environment in general and to the campus in particular is an initial problem of most foreign students. To help them in this process all foreign students, transfers, and graduate students as well as freshmen, need careful orientation. The process of course begins with the reply to the initial inquiry from the prospective student. It continues throughout the admissions process, but it should not end there. There should be a planned orientation program which introduces the new foreign students to the campus and its resources and gives them sufficient instruction in the major aspects of student life so that they know what is expected of them and feel comfortable in their new situation. A few experienced American and foreign students can contribute very significantly to the planning and leadership of orientation programs for new students from abroad.

It is essential that new foreign students be given careful instruction in the facts of academic life on the particular campus. The academic system in a country tends to be one of the cultural constants so taken for granted that it never occurs to either the foreign students or their American hosts that there are other academic practices than their own. Foreign students coming from different systems may have learned study methods and academic procedures that not only are unfamiliar to Americans but may be completely unacceptable. It is therefore necessary to inform new foreign students at all levels concerning academic rules and requirements, approved methods of study, how to write and document term papers, how to cover heavy reading assignments adequately, how to use the library, the academic advisement system, how to take examinations, the grading system, etc.

Nonacademic aspects of student life also need to be covered. These include campus and community resources, traditions, housing rules and customs, student activities, American-foreign student relations, student-faculty relations, arrangements for school vacations, and the like.

Some aspects of orientation may be carried on with foreign and American students together, but much of it should probably be done in separate groups. Foreign students just do not have the same educational or cultural backgrounds nor equal ability to comprehend rapid and often slurred speech, slang, or the unfamiliar American accents they are likely to hear. Furthermore, their comprehension of what is said in an orientation meeting will probably be inversely proportional to the size of the group. Even within the foreign student group there may need to be some further separation of freshmen, transfer students, and graduates for some sessions, particularly those on the academic rules and requirements.

While most institutions concentrate orientation within the first few days of the term and undoubtedly cover too much information too quickly for good comprehension, some continue the process in regularly scheduled meetings and activities during the first term or longer. A few are beginning to recognize that orientation is a continuing process which really involves two streams of emphasis: (1) adjustment to American life—which starts at a high level and diminishes, ending perhaps just before the student finishes his studies—with some attention to interpretation of his experience and what he has learned about the United States; and (2) concern for his home situation, which may be almost completely submerged in the beginning but should gradually increase in emphasis during his sojourn with more and more frequent attention to his country and its problems, the adaptation of what he is learning to the home situation, and the readjustment problems he will face when he returns home. The latter phase may be greatly helped by some flexibility in academic program to focus on home country needs by encouraging the use of home problems for term papers, seminar reports, and the like and by increasing emphasis in advisement sessions on adapting American methods to home country needs.

Academic Advising The academic advisement of foreign students, particularly in their first term of enrollment, is crucial to their ultimate success. Ideally it should be done by faculty who have had experience abroad, understand the differences in educational systems of the United States and other countries, know the institution and its requirements thoroughly, appreciate the adjustment problems that the foreign student has, and have the time and patience to explain the requirements and to help the student understand what he is taking and why. The same advisers should remain with the students over several terms. Continuity is important, but even more important is that only knowledgeable and understanding faculty be chosen to advise foreign students and that they be given whatever training they need to do the job well.

Language Scores on the Test of English as a Foreign Language (TOEFL), administered by the Educational Testing Service, or on the University of Michigan test are being increasingly required by many institutions as part of the admission application. However, no matter how carefully foreign students are tested in English some are bound to have problems with the language. There are two extremes: (1) those who speak and understand the spoken language quite acceptably but cannot read or write it adequately, and (2) those who handle the written language well and perhaps have used English textbooks in their major courses at home but whose speaking and oral comprehension leave much to be desired. Students whose native language is other than English tend to think their English facility is better than it turns out to be. In fact, part of the cultural shock that many of them suffer when they arrive is the discovery that with all their study of English they cannot understand what people say nor make themselves understood.

It is almost essential, therefore, that the institution make some kind of arrangements for supplemental assistance in English as a foreign language for its foreign students. If the selection process has been good, three to five hours a week of instruction should bring them up to an acceptable performance level, and they should be able to carry some additional courses as well. But in a few cases more help may be needed, even to the extent of requiring full-time, intensive English study at one of the many institutions offering such programs. It is no kindness to the student who needs intensive language work to allow him to enroll in a regular program of studies for which he lacks adequate language facility. He runs the danger of failing, thus jeopardizing his whole academic future, whereas if he studies English full time he runs no risks beyond the cost in time and money.

Rarely is it wise to put a foreign student in an English class in competition with Americans unless he is an English major. Learning a foreign language is quite a different problem from improving one's native language. If he must be in a class with Americans, the student from abroad should receive some special help, and assignments should be adjusted in an attempt to fit his needs. For him English is a temporary tool which may be only a social grace when he returns home. While he is here he should be expected to communicate his ideas both orally and in writing sufficiently well to demonstrate his mastery of the material covered in his courses, but it should not be essential that his speaking and writing be absolutely correct in every detail.

If there are enough foreign students to justify an English-as-a-foreign-language class, it should be taught by someone with training in this special field. Such classes require a great deal of individual work and should be kept small, perhaps 10 to 12 students and in no case more than 15. Most institutions recognize credit in such courses as satisfying the freshman English requirement for those whose native language is not English and who have had relatively little experience in English-speaking countries. Transfers and graduate students should be able to take English as a foreign language without credit. Those foreign students writing graduate theses and dissertations in many cases will need help with grammar and idiom to get their product into acceptable form.

In some cases both courses and informal language aid to foreign students have been provided cooperatively by contiguous institutions or have been worked out in cooperation with adult education programs for immigrants offered in the community. Community groups interested in foreign students are sometimes willing to provide informal language assistance.

Finances Money constitutes a major problem for many foreign students in the United States. Education is probably more expensive here than anywhere else in the world, and financing it therefore presents serious problems to those students dependent upon their own resources, as more than half of those in the United States are.

Unhappily the problem is in part caused by the fact that American colleges and universities with few exceptions fail to inform prospective students of the true costs involved in attending the institutions. Published bulletins very carefully list the cost of tuition, fees, board, and room—items for which the institutions themselves collect. In many cases no estimate of total cost is given. This may be just poor public relations with respect to Americans, but with foreign students it may be, and all too often is, disastrous misrepresentation. The foreign student simply must have some idea of the reasonable minimum total cost to expect. This should include the expense of books and supplies, such special fees as laboratory and diploma fees, cost of a winter wardrobe for those from tropical areas, health insurance, research and dissertation costs, local transportation, vacation expense, recreation, other incidental expenses, and the added costs to expect if dependents accompany the student. It is wise to base the estimates on an actual survey of what foreign and American students are spending on each campus. The total is likely to be a surprise to the institution's own officials, and to the person abroad it will probably seem unbelievably high. It is therefore imperative that it be set forth so specifically that there can be no misunderstanding.

It is also very important to indicate the expected schedule of payments. It may be a real shock to the student to find he is expected to pay all of his tuition, board, room, and book cost the first week instead of prorating them on a monthly basis through the term. It is equally upsetting to the business office to find that the process of osmosis, the grapevine, or whatever the means by which American students learn about these things hasn't worked with foreign students, and they are therefore unprepared to meet the payment schedule.

It is equally important that educational institutions carefully specify the limitations of financial aids available to foreign students. The reputation of the United States as the wealthiest and most generous country in the world leads many foreign students to assume that if they can just get to this country they will somehow find the money they need. Hopefully each institution will have some scholarships to help bring foreign students to the campus as part of its international education program. Part-time jobs may be helpful also if they do not take too much time from studies and if the required clearance is obtained from the U.S. Immigration and Naturalization Service. Full-time summer work is also possible for foreign students if suitable jobs can be found.

Foreign students are sometimes successful in the competition for graduate assistantships and fellowships. But few campuses have enough aid to meet the needs of all the foreign students who seek it, and the students simply must be made to understand the financial facts of life in an American college or university.

However, no matter how good the communication on financial needs is and how careful the institution and the student have been in making financial arrangements, it is almost inevitable that a foreign student will occasionally have a serious financial problem. His country may devalue its currency, or the government may change and alter policies on scarce dollar exchange, or the relative financing his education may die, or the student himself may have an accident or a serious illness. It is therefore very desirable to have at least a small emergency loan or grant fund that can be called upon in such circumstances until alternative arrangements can be made.

Housing and Food Foreign students are probably best off in campus residence halls, at least for their first semester or year, when such housing is available. There may be some difficulties at first with group living, particularly with students who have not lived away from home before and may have been used to having others do all their housekeeping for them. There may also be some problems in adjusting to living with roommates. A little special orientation on this subject as well as on the use of common facilities, room care, and the like may be desirable. It is also very helpful to brief American roommates, neighbors, and residence hall staffs on the backgrounds and adjustment problems of foreign students. Very often understanding American hosts can be of great help to new foreign students settling into the new situation in which they find themselves.

It is desirable to have foreign students live with Americans insofar as it can be managed, in spite of their common desire to live with one another. In the long run the purposes of their coming to the United States will be far better served if they do not room with their own countrymen. They will improve their English much more rapidly, make the adjustment to the American academic situation more quickly, gain more from the total experience, and contribute more to the international education of their American counterparts.

Help in finding suitable housing is usually necessary for those foreign students who live off campus by preference, because of lack of on-campus facilities, or because they have dependents with them. They need careful instruction concerning the types of housing available, desirable locations, rents to expect, what the rent does and does not cover, provisions and obligations of the usual lease or rental agreement, use and care of appliances, etc. Some may also need some help on ordinary housekeeping practices, particularly men, who in most countries of the world will have had no experience of this sort.

Many institutions have found it desirable to develop a list of satisfactory rooms and apartments in which it is known that foreign students will be accepted. Unfortunately too many foreign students have had the experience of being referred to an available place only to be told when the landlord sees them that it has already been rented. In fact in many college and university towns community groups provide people to go with new foreign students to look for housing in order to explain to suspicious landlords who the students are. These community hosts can help assure that there is clear understanding of terms between landlord and student and also that there will be no possible suspicion of discrimination. Some institutions also include some discussion of foreign students in their orientation programs for householders and landlords who rent to students to help forestall misunderstandings and problems that sometimes arise.

Foreign students from many parts of the world find American food bland, unsavory, and difficult to adjust to. Some are vegetarians and are distressed by our practice of flavoring vegetables and soups with meat and meat juices. Some observe religious dietary restrictions—for example, orthodox Moslems and Jews do not eat pork, and Hindus do not eat beef or veal. Fowl and fish are usually acceptable in most cultures. Rice of course is a staple food in many countries of the world, and the practice of serving it regularly can go a long way toward solving food problems. It also helps if in the cafeteria service now so commonly used the foods can be clearly labelled so the foreign student will know what he is getting.

The desire to prepare their own national foods is very often the chief reason given by foreign students desiring to live in off-campus apartments with others from their own countries. Sometimes this practice works out reasonably well, but there can be problems. The most difficult one of course is that the practice tends to isolate the foreign students in little national enclaves, thus negating many of the values we hope will accrue from having them here. There are also problems of balanced diets and proper handling and storage of food as well as complaints from neighbors about the unusual cooking odors.

Many institutions help solve the food problem for foreign students and also contribute to the intercultural education of the entire student group by regularly featuring foreign dishes on their menus. Sometimes foreign students are asked to advise the food service as to what to serve from their areas and how to prepare it. It is fairly common also to have periodic "international dinners" which feature full meals from various parts of the world and become the means for foreign students to be hosts and to tell their American friends about their countries and cultures.

Housing and food can be difficult for foreign students, but they can and should be the means for significant interpersonal and intercultural contact and learning and should therefore help achieve the goals of international educational exchange.

Academic Standards Foreign students are in academic competition with their American counterparts and often find the going difficult. They of course are handicapped because they come from different educational and linguistic backgrounds. There is sometimes a tendency on the part of American professors to be overly sympathetic and to grade foreign students on a lower standard than they do the American students. This practice is rationalized on the basis that leniency is necessary in order to make of these students firm friends of the United States, or that most of the foreign students will be working in underdeveloped countries where having a substandard education really won't matter. Neither of these curious notions can be supported. Even though the foreign student may apply all kinds of pressure to secure a better grade than he has earned and may insist that his life is ruined if he does not get it, he can hardly have real respect for those who yield to such pressures. Without respect there can never be real understanding or friendship of the kind the United States would like to have abroad. Neither does it do the individual foreign student, his country, or the relations between his country and ours any good to send him home with a second-class education which has not equipped him to do a first-class job in his field. We in the United States have sufficient trained manpower resources that we can afford some mediocrity, but a developing country simply cannot. The foreign student returning home may be the only person in his country with training in his field, and he must be good.

It is therefore essential that we maintain our academic standards for foreign students. We should help them compensate for the handicaps they have because they are foreign through such devices as giving them extra time on examinations because they are slower in handling the language, giving them essay or oral examinations instead of objective tests to reduce the verbal handicap, arranging for them to check class notes with good American students or with the professor to be sure they are getting the essentials, encouraging them to seek extra help from the professor during his office hours, allowing them to use topics and problems from their own countries for term papers and seminar reports, and the like. But when the end of the term comes, the foreign student, by whatever means he is tested and through whatever communication barrier there may be, must have demonstrated sufficient mastery of the subject matter of a course to justify the grade he is given. American education is not highly regarded abroad—people in authority in government, business, education, and other fields, operating as they do in European-type educational systems in which standards for the entire country are set by a central ministry of education, find it extremely difficult to understand the American system and its diversities. Maintaining good educational standards is essential if our education is to earn the respect it deserves.

Assimilation of Foreign Students Assimilating foreign students into the student body and assuring that they are successful and comfortable in their work in the United States of course begins with the admission and orientation processes. But in large measure it depends upon interpersonal relationships which develop between the foreign students and Americans on the campus and in the community.

There is a strong tendency to assume that the mere presence of students from other countries in and of itself assures that significant relationships with others will automatically develop. Unfortunately it is not quite that simple. The involvement of foreign students in the ongoing life of the campus requires careful planning and continuing attention. Whatever plans are made should be based upon certain fundamental facts:

1. Foreign students are also human and usually gregarious, and they have the same needs to be accepted and respected and to feel a part of their environment.

2. Foreign students are not all alike. They come from widely varying cultural backgrounds, often within the same country, and are as different from one another as they are from Americans. There is no such thing as "*the* foreign student."

3. Students from abroad tend to be older and more mature than their American counterparts, and on most coeducational campuses the men among them outnumber the women by eight or nine to one.

4. Student activities and organizations as we find them on American campuses are not known in some areas of the world and in others tend to be strongly political in nature.

5. Foreign students tend to feel that they are guests in the United States.

In our attempts to be friendly and kind to foreign students we have too often depended upon activities in which we do things for them or expect them to perform in some way for us. All too seldom do Americans and foreign students work together on common interests that are mutually beneficial. They are students with all the rights, privileges, and opportunities of students. However, they are often reticent to claim these rights, and Americans as hosts need to draw them into all aspects of campus life. This may sometimes need to be done by personal invitation—few foreign students will respond to a public notice of an activity when they are not sure of what they would be getting into or whether or not they would be welcome. In some cases failure of a foreign student to participate will not be due to lack of interest or uncertainty about his welcome but will be simply a matter of the time his studies require.

Most campuses have international clubs which are intended to draw both American and foreign students. These may be strictly local groups or may be affiliated with the national organizations of International Relations Clubs, the Collegiate Council for the United Nations, or Collegiate International. They range all the way from those whose sole activity is discussion of international political issues to those that are entirely social. Perhaps a middle course is most often sought by these groups, with opportunity for serious discussion, for learning about cultures and problems of other parts of the world, and for recreation and social life. At their best they are successful in bringing American and foreign students together in common activities. At less than their best they can become too much involved in one kind of activity, often campus politics, or they can be largely taken over by one group to the exclusion of others. A common experience is that they become known as "foreign student clubs" in which Americans are not welcome.

An important factor in the successful involvement of foreign students in campus life is the attitude of the student leadership on the campus. If student government officials and other leaders are concerned with the international dimensions of the campus scene, as leaders should be, significant and successful activity is much more likely to result. Foreign students should be the best from their countries, and our best should be the ones most closely involved with them—not those American students who are maladjusted in their own group and see the foreign students as similar isolates with whom they can make common cause.

It is perhaps most difficult to involve foreign students in campus social life, particularly in those institutions in which virtually all social activities are for couples only. American dating patterns are sometimes shocking and repugnant to foreign students from more conservative cultures. Others take to the American way with enthusiasm, and in fact may read into the easy and unchaperoned relationships between men and women connotations that are neither intended nor accepted. This is perhaps the area of greatest difficulty for foreign students in adjusting to American campus life, and the one from which they are most likely to be excluded.

An area of considerable interest for foreign students, and one often neglected, is that of professional contacts in major academic fields. Contacts of course are achieved to some extent in classes, particularly at the graduate level. But all too rarely is there opportunity for either foreign or American students to relate to working members of their chosen professions. Community groups interested in foreign students often can help meet this need.

Communities also contribute to the assimilation of foreign students in other ways. They of course should provide shopping facilities and personal services as freely to foreign students as to anyone else. Traditionally community groups take the lead in providing opportunities for foreign students to visit in homes—some have excellent host family programs which provide continuing and very valuable relationships with foreign students. Opportunities are also provided to foreign students to visit schools, churches, courts, businesses, community service organizations, local government units, and the like. Every foreign student when he returns home will be considered an expert on the United States, and it is therefore to his advantage and ours to give him as much exposure to the country while he is here as we can.

Returning Home Sometimes the assimilation of the foreign student into American life is so complete that he does not want to return home at the conclusion of his studies. The "brain drain" in fact has become something of an issue in international relations and has prompted careful consideration of the problem by government departments, legislative bodies, and organizations and institutions in this country and abroad. It is a very complex problem which inevitably involves conflicts between the interests of the individuals, governments, and potential employers of graduating foreign students in the United States and their home countries. Inevitably educational institutions find themselves involved in trying to help foreign students work out their future course of action, which may involve more advanced study, temporary employment in the United States for practical training purposes, permanent employment outside their own countries, or return home. The latter is obviously the intended result when study abroad is undertaken; but education inevitably changes people and their horizons, and the situations at home may change drastically also during their years of study abroad. It is therefore not surprising that some change objectives.

Other kinds of problems are posed when a student does return home, particularly if he has been away for some time. He faces the problems of finding employment, re-adjusting to his family and friends and their foods and customs, interpreting his experiences, adapting what he has learned to home-country needs, etc. Some institutions and occasional sponsoring agencies conduct prereturn orientation for foreign students prior to their departure to help them anticipate and cope with these problems more intelligently and effectively.

THE FOREIGN STUDENT ADVISER

All the problems discussed above and others are in some degree problems of Americans as well as foreign students. However, they have a certain uniqueness with foreign students that demands a different approach. The statement sometimes heard that "we don't have foreign students—we just have students" is both naive and misleading in its implications. No American educational institution ever treats all its students alike, and student personnel services in some form are always provided to meet the unique needs of those individuals who need the assistance.

The foreign student adviser provides to foreign students the specialized assistance to meet their unique needs. As is true with other officials in student personnel work, he does not and should not try to handle every foreign student problem personally, particularly in areas in which he lacks professional competence. He is the hub of the wheel that represents services to foreign students. He is the first port of call for foreign students, no matter what their needs. He provides information, refers to other resources, interprets regulations and laws, suggests alternatives, listens, and explains. He provides opportunity for a "trial run" for consideration of any problem, no matter what campus official may ultimately deal with it. He does not assume responsibility for the students' problems, nor does he dictate solutions unless the problems involve institutional regulations or matters of law in which there is no choice. He may frequently interpret the foreign students' backgrounds and points of view to faculty and officials and vice versa.

He may be assigned partial or complete responsibility for foreign student admissions, administration of financial aids for foreign students, academic advising, and other functions, or he may have only concern for them with no direct responsibility. He is often the campus authority on immigration regulations for both foreign students and visiting faculty, and he is commonly responsible for issuing authorization forms for visas and for extensions of stay in this country. He is the coordinator of all matters having to do with foreign students and all resources as they affect foreign students—he functions as the dean of students for the particular group of students who come from other countries.

Effective foreign student advisers have come from many backgrounds. The majority are or were teaching faculty. Many are in some form of educational administration, and it is increasingly common for those with training and experience in student personnel work to be chosen for this function. Whatever their background, it is important that they be people with warmth, patience, understanding, sensitivity to feelings, tact, and integrity. It is also important for them to have sufficient maturity and status to be accepted by foreign students and visitors, many of whom are from prominent families or are themselves persons of distinction at home. He must also merit the respect and cooperation of his own campus colleagues from the top administration down if he is to be effective in his job. Knowledge of a foreign language and significant experience abroad are desirable qualifications, but they are not essential. An interest in working with people, and specifically with people from other cultures, is a far more important requirement.

Continuity in the foreign student adviser's position is extremely important. It should not be considered a committee assignment to be rotated each year. Location and furnishings of the office are also indicators of the status of the position and of the importance that the institution attaches to its foreign student program.

The question often asked is how much staff time should be assigned to the foreign student advising function. This varies greatly in practice, depending upon the duties assigned and the size of the foreign student group. However, as a general rule the National Association for Foreign Student Affairs has long recommended that advisory staff be assigned on the basis of one full-time person for each 150 enrolled students from abroad. Secretarial service in the same ratio is also recommended. When the number of foreign students justifies only a part-time adviser, it is very desirable to have the office set up in such a way that there can be full-time receptionist coverage. There should be someone there who can talk with a foreign student at any time during office hours and reach the adviser if the situation warrants his immediate attention to a problem. Secretaries who deal with foreign students need some of the same warmth, patience, and tact as the adviser.

The administrative location of the foreign student program varies widely from campus to campus. It is perhaps most commonly in the student personnel division administratively responsible to the dean of students or vice-president for student affairs. However, on some campuses the foreign student adviser may report to the president, the academic dean, or some other official. Who his boss is is not really important as long as the foreign student adviser has enough time, secretarial help, budget, support of his program from his superiors, and cooperation from his colleagues that he can carry out his functions satisfactorily.

Increasingly people trained and experienced in working with people from other cultures are available for appointment as foreign student advisers. However, many are still appointed who have no background for the work. Recognizing this fact, the National Association for Foreign Student Affairs since its founding in 1948 has considered its major function to be the in-service training of foreign student advisers, admissions officers, teachers of English as a foreign language, and leaders of community programs for foreign students. This has traditionally been accomplished through national and regional conferences and numerous professional publications. In 1963, through a Department of State grant, the association was able to establish the NAFSA Field Service which has provided four principal services: (1) one-day, drive-in workshops in all parts of the country; (2) a consultation service to send an experienced generalist, admissions expert, teacher of English as a foreign language, or community leader to a campus requesting the service to advise on development of its foreign student program; (3) in-service training grants to enable individual foreign student advisers, admissions officers, and teachers of English as a foreign language to visit other campuses where the work is well developed; and (4) a series of "how-to-do-it" publications called *Guidelines* covering various phases of foreign student work—a set has been sent without charge to every campus in the United States known to have foreign students enrolled.

SUMMARY

The numbers of foreign students coming to the United States for study are continually increasing. Any college or university enrolling foreign students assumes the same kind of obligation for helping them to meet their problems as it assumes for U. S. students. The best way of handling these obligations has proven to be to appoint a qualified foreign student adviser to coordinate services to foreign students and to assure that their unique problems are given proper attention.

The highly select groups of foreign students on our campuses represent an important potential source of top-level manpower for the entire world. They may be likened to a source of nuclear power which, through chain reactions, extends far beyond what might reasonably be expected from so small a source of energy. A high percentage of these students from abroad will be the leaders of their professions in their countries and of their governments. Many of them will be the molders of public opinion, the determiners of relationships between their countries and others. They, along with their American contemporaries, will be high among those who will influence the course of history. It is therefore clearly in the interest of American institutions of higher education to do whatever is possible to assure that the education and the total American experience of foreign students is good.

BIBLIOGRAPHY [2]

Committee on Educational Interchange Policy: *The Goals of Student Exchange,* 1955; *Orientation of Foreign Students—Signposts for the Cultural Maze,* 1956; *The Foreign Student: Exchange or Immigrant?* 1958; Institute of International Education, New York.

Committee on the Foreign Student in American Colleges and Universities: *The College, The University, and the Foreign Student,* Committee on the Foreign Student in American Colleges and Universities, New York, 1963 (26 pp.).

Hall, Edward T.: *The Silent Language,* Doubleday & Company, Inc., Garden City, N.Y., 1959.

Handbook on International Study for Foreign Nationals, Institute of International Education, New York, 1965 (420 pp.).

NAFSA Committee on Ethics: *Statement of Responsibilities and Standards in Work with Foreign Students,* National Association for Foreign Student Affairs, Washington, 1964 (7 pp., 50¢).

NAFSA Field Service: *Guidelines: Selection and Admission of Foreign Students,* March, 1965 (15 pp.); *English Language Proficiency,* November, 1965 (15 pp.); *Initial Orientation of Foreign Students,* September, 1964 (10 pp.); *Academic and Personal Advising,* April, 1966 (16 pp.); *Housing of Foreign Students,* 1967 (15 pp.); *Finances and Employment of Foreign Students,* November, 1966 (20 pp.); *Interpretation of the United States to Foreign Students,* October, 1965 (16 pp.); *American-Foreign Student Relationships,* January, 1967 (11 pp.); National Association for Foreign Student Affairs, Washington (50¢ each).

Open Doors 1969, Institute of International Education, New York, 1967 (81 pp., $3).

Putman, Ivan, Jr.: *The Foreign Student Adviser and His Institution in International Student Exchange,* National Association for Foreign Student Affairs, New York, 1965 (24 pp., $1.25).

[2] The National Association for Foreign Student Affairs; the Institute of International Education; the U.S. Advisory Commission on International Educational Exchange, Education and World Affairs; and UNESCO are some of the additional sources of publications useful to those interested in further reading on foreign student programs.

Chapter 15

Veterans Affairs

ALBERT L. QUINAN

Associate Bursar, Northeastern University, Boston, Massachusetts

CAVEAT:

At this writing, the Congress is considering new legislation which, when enacted, will increase veterans educational benefits and provide new incentives to aid "educationally disadvantaged" veterans. Much concern has been voiced over the low rate of participation in the current veterans education programs. (See note at end of chapter.)

On March 3, 1966, the Congress of the United States enacted Public Law 89-358, termed the "Veterans Readjustment Benefits Act of 1966," and more popularly known as the "GI Bill." This law, together with other existing legislation, now serves to provide financial assistance to veterans and the families of deceased or disabled veterans who may wish to pursue a program of higher education.

The laws which apply to educational benefits under the jurisdiction of the Veterans Administration are published in Title 38, United States Code and are put forth in Chapters 31, 34, and 35.

Chapter 31 deals with Vocational Rehabilitation, which provides benefits for those with service-incurred disabilities.

Chapter 34 deals with Veterans Educational Assistance, which grants funds for veterans and servicemen who have served on active duty on and after February 1, 1955.

Chapter 35 deals with War Orphans and Widows Educational Assistance, which aids sons and daughters, wives, and widows of veterans who have died or have become disabled as a result of service-incurred injuries.

The degree of assistance available under the provisions of Chapter 31 is unique in that V.A. makes payment directly to the educational institution for expenses of tuition, fees, books, supplies and the like. In addition, monthly subsistence allowances of $110, $150, or $175 (determined by dependency status) are paid to the veteran.[1] The period of assistance generally may not exceed four years, and training must be completed within nine years from date of discharge. Scholastic achievement under Vocational Rehabilitation is closely supervised by V.A. Record keeping by the school is greatly facilitated in that only one form is required to be filed at the beginning of each year as the student enters into training. (See Figure 1.)

Educational assistance payable under the terms of Chapters 34 and 35 of the code is designed to help the eligible person defray the cost of tuition, books, and subsistence. The law contains specific prerequisites and limitations to be complied with by both the student and the school. An examination of these requirements especially with respect to how they affect the veteran will enable the veterans' coordinator to answer many of the questions with which he is faced.

Eligibility and Entitlement

Chapter 34	*Chapter 35*
A veteran with less than 18 months of continuous active service and each serviceman with at least two years of active duty is entitled to one and one-half months of educational assistance for each month of active service up to a maximum of 36 months. A veteran with not less than 18 months of active duty is entitled to full-time educational assistance for a period of 36 months.	The son, daughter, wife, or widow of a deceased or disabled veteran may qualify to receive up to 36 months of full-time training depending upon the length of service. Benefits payable to a son or daughter may not continue after his or her twenty-sixth birthday. Entitlement may extend to 48 months for a person eligible for assistance under both Chapters 34 and 35.

[1] Allowances proposed in 1970 are $135, $181, and $210 respectively.

Selection of a Program

Upon choice of a course of study, the veteran may apply to V.A. for approval by filing Form 21E-1990, "Application for Program of Education," along with Form DD-214, "Report of Discharge from the Armed Forces." (Servicemen use Form 21E-1990a.) V.A. offers counseling to aid in choosing an objective if the veteran wishes to avail himself of this service.

At least six months before post-high school training the son or daughter should make application to V.A. (Form 21E–5490) to determine his or her eligibility. The eligible person will be scheduled for educational and vocational counseling to assist in selection of an educational plan. (Counseling is not required for a wife or widow.)

Change of Program

A change of program is a change in the educational, professional, or vocational objective for which the eligible person originally applied. The law permits one change of program. (War orphans must receive counseling when making such a request for change.) A second change of program may be approved if it can be shown that there is a reasonable chance of success in the new field of endeavor. V.A. Form 21E-1995 (or, in the case of war orphans, Form 21E-5495) contains instructions for making these changes.

Change of School

The law allows numerous changes of school for continuing the same course or program provided no loss of credit is involved. Permission must be given by V.A. The student should obtain Form 21E-1995 (or, in the case of war oprhans, Form 21E-5495).

Certificate of Eligibility

Confirmation of eligibility and approval of a course of study is indicated when the student receives Form 21E-1993, "Certificate of Eligibility." It is the student's responsibility to see that this form is forwarded to the certifying official of his school at the time he first enrolls.

Change in Status

If the student modifies his program by reducing or increasing his credit-hour load, by terminating his training, or by changing to another objective, it is his responsibility to promptly notify both V.A. and the veterans' office of his school.

Certification of Attendance

College-level Courses. In the next-to-last month of his enrollment period, the student will receive V.A. card Form 21E-6553, on which he will be asked to certify his rate of attendance for the school year, semester, or term. He will also indicate his plans for reenrollment.

Below College-level Courses. Those students involved in courses not granting credit toward a standard college degree (even when given in an institution of higher learning) will be asked to complete *monthly* certification of attendance cards and to forward them to the school for verification.

Form Approved
Budget Bureau No. 76-R543

FOR VA USE ONLY	VETERANS ADMINISTRATION **VETERAN'S APPLICATION FOR PROGRAM OF EDUCATION** *(Under Chapter 34, Title 38, United States Code)*	1. VA FILE NUMBER *(If known)* C-

NOTICE: If you have a SERVICE CONNECTED disability, you may be entitled to Vocational Rehabilitation Training under Chapter 31, Title 38, USC, which usually provides more favorable benefits. Application for such benefits should be made on VA Form 21E-1900, and not on this form.	IMPORTANT - Before completing this form read the instructions. Answer all questions fully. Type or print answers in ink. Attach reproduced, certified or official carbon copies of ALL Reports of Separation (DD 214) from the Armed Forces since January 31, 1955.

2. FIRST - MIDDLE - LAST NAME OF APPLICANT	3A. MAILING ADDRESS *(Number and street or rural route, city or P.O., and State)*	3B. ZIP CODE

4. SOCIAL SECURITY NUMBER	5. SEX	6. DATE OF BIRTH
	☐ MALE ☐ FEMALE	

7. VA BENEFITS PREVIOUSLY APPLIED FOR

A ☐ NONE
B ☐ HOSPITALIZATION OR MEDICAL CARE
C ☐ WAIVER OF NSLI PREMIUMS
D ☐ DISABILITY COMPENSATION OR PENSION

E. EDUCATION OR TRAINING BASED ON SERVICE IN:
☐ WW II
☐ KOREAN CONFLICT

F. ☐ WAR ORPHAN'S EDUCATIONAL ASSISTANCE
G. ☐ DENTAL OR OUT-PATIENT TREATMENT
H. ☐ OTHER *(Specify)*

7I. VA OFFICE HAVING YOUR RECORDS *(If known)*

8. SERVICE INFORMATION

NOTE: Enter the following information for each period of active duty. Show ALL active duty.

VA USE ONLY	DATE ENTERED ACTIVE DUTY (A)	DATE SEPARATED FROM ACTIVE DUTY (B)	TYPE OF SEPARATION OR DISCHARGE (C)	SERVICE NUMBER *(Prefix and suffix)* (D)	BRANCH OF SERVICE (E)	GRADE OR RANK AT SEPARATION OR DISCHARGE (F)
BR						
ASC						

NOTE: Failure to attach DD Forms 214 and other Separation papers since January 31, 1955, will delay the processing of your application until verification of active duty is obtained from the service departments. To assist in locating your service records, check your present status below.

PRESENT MILITARY, RESERVE OR SEPARATION STATUS *(Complete applicable items)*

9A. IF COMPLETELY SEPARATED GIVE TERMINAL DATE OF RESERVE OBLIGATION	9B. IF MEMBER OF RESERVE GIVE TERMINAL DATE AND COMPLETE ITEM 9D	9C. RETIRED STATUS *(If checked, complete item 9D.)* ☐ PAY STATUS ☐ NON PAY STATUS ☐ MEMBER TEMPORARY DISABILITY RETIRED LIST	9D. BRANCH OF SERVICE OR RESERVE

EDUCATION OR TRAINING RECEIVED WHILE ON ACTIVE DUTY

10. IF YOU ATTENDED ONE OF THE SERVICE ACADEMIES, CHECK APPROPRIATE BOX	11. DATES ATTENDED *(Month, day, year)*	
☐ USMA - WEST POINT ☐ USNA - ANNAPOLIS ☐ USCGA - NEW LONDON ☐ USAFA - COLORADO SPRINGS	FROM	TO

12. LIST THE COURSES TAKEN, IF ANY, IN OTHER SERVICE SCHOOLS WHILE ON ACTIVE DUTY

NAME AND ADDRESS OF SCHOOLS (A)	DATES ATTENDED (B) FROM	DATES ATTENDED (C) TO	DESCRIPTION OF SUBJECTS COVERED (D)	QUALIFICATION OR RATING ATTAINED AT END OF TRAINING (E)

13A. WERE YOU SENT BY A SERVICE DEPARTMENT TO TAKE A COURSE IN A CIVILIAN SCHOOL AS A PART OF YOUR ASSIGNED MILITARY DUTIES WHILE ON ACTIVE DUTY? ☐ YES ☐ NO *(If "Yes," complete Items 13B and 13C)*	13B. NAME AND ADDRESS OF SCHOOL	13C. APPROXIMATE DATES ATTENDED

14. PREVIOUS EDUCATION AND TRAINING UNDER LAWS ADMINISTERED BY THE VETERANS ADMINISTRATION

NOTE: If you checked Item 7E or 7F above, please furnish the following information

DATES ATTENDED (A) FROM	DATES ATTENDED (B) TO	PUBLIC LAW *(If known)* (C)	NAME AND ADDRESS OF SCHOOL OR TRAINING ESTABLISHMENT (D)

FOR VA USE ONLY	STATE		ED LEVEL		DEP.		23-22		COUNS.

VA FORM MAR 1966 **21E-1990**

Fig. 1 *Form 21E-1990, veteran's application for program of education.*

15. CIVILIAN EDUCATION *(Do not include education and training shown in Items 10, 12 and 14.)*

TYPE OF SCHOOL (A)	EDUCATION COMPLETED (B)		DATES ATTENDED (C) FROM	(D) TO	NAME OR DESCRIPTION OF COURSE (E)	NAME AND ADDRESS OF SCHOOL (F)
ELEMENTARY	YEARS					
HIGH SCHOOLS	YEARS					
COLLEGE	NO. OF HOURS					
	SEM.					
	QTR.					
VOCATIONAL OR TRADE SCHOOL	YEARS					
CORRESPONDENCE						
OTHER *(Specify)*						

16. IF YOU DID NOT GRADUATE FROM HIGH SCHOOL, DO YOU HAVE A HIGH SCHOOL EQUIVALENCY DIPLOMA OR CERTIFICATE?

☐ YES ☐ NO

17. WHAT COLLEGE DEGREES HAVE YOU BEEN AWARDED?

18A. HAVE YOU EVER HELD A LICENSE TO PRACTICE A PROFESSION OR JOURNEYMAN RATING TO WORK AT A TRADE? *(Examples: Electrician, Radio Operator, Teacher, Lawyer, CPA, Bricklayer, Carpenter, etc.)*

☐ YES ☐ NO *(If "Yes", complete Items 18B and 18C)*

(DO NOT WRITE IN THIS SPACE)
(VA DATE STAMP)

18B. NAME OF LICENSE OR JOURNEYMAN RATING

18C. STATE IN WHICH HELD

19A. HAVE YOU EVER HAD APPRENTICE TRAINING OR OTHER ON THE JOB TRAINING FOR A TRADE OR OCCUPATION?

☐ YES ☐ NO *(If "Yes", complete Items 19B and 19C)*

19B. NAME OF OCCUPATION OR TRADE

19C. DATES OF TRAINING

EMPLOYMENT EXPERIENCE

20A. PRINCIPAL OCCUPATION BEFORE ENTERING MILITARY SERVICE

20B. NUMBER OF MONTHS EMPLOYED IN THIS OCCUPATION

21A. PRINCIPAL OCCUPATION AFTER SEPARATION FROM MILITARY SERVICE

21B. NUMBER OF MONTHS EMPLOYED IN THIS OCCUPATION

22A. DO YOU EXPECT TO RECEIVE EDUCATIONAL BENEFITS FROM ANY OTHER AGENCY OF THE FEDERAL GOVERNMENT DURING THIS NEW PERIOD OF EDUCATION? *(Do not include Federal Educational Loans)*

☐ YES ☐ NO *(If "Yes", explain in Item 22B)*

22B. NATURE AND EXTENT OF OTHER FEDERAL BENEFITS

PROGRAM OF EDUCATION APPLIED FOR

CAUTION: Read instructions carefully before completing the following.

23. ON WHAT DATE DO YOU PLAN TO START YOUR EDUCATION UNDER THIS LAW?

NOTE: If you have decided on the program of education you want please complete Items 24A through 24D. Counseling from the Veterans Administration is available to help you make such a decision. If you want counseling answer Item 24E below.

24A. WHAT IS THE FINAL EDUCATIONAL, PROFESSIONAL, OR VOCATIONAL GOAL YOU PLAN TO REACH THROUGH THE PROGRAM FOR WHICH YOU ARE APPLYING? *(See paragraph 2C(1) of instructions)*

24B. DESCRIBE THE PROGRAM YOU PLAN TO TAKE *(See paragraph 2C(2) of instructions)*

24C. EDUCATION WILL BE BY

☐ SCHOOL ATTENDANCE ☐ CORRESPONDENCE COURSE

24D. NAME AND ADDRESS OF SCHOOL

24E. IF YOU WANT COUNSELING FROM THE VETERANS ADMINISTRATION CHECK THE APPROPRIATE BOX BELOW

☐ I NEED COUNSELING TO HELP ME DECIDE ON MY EDUCATION PROGRAM

☐ I HAVE INDICATED MY PROGRAM ABOVE BUT I WOULD LIKE COUNSELING FROM THE VETERANS ADMINISTRATION

2

Fig. 1 *(Continued)*

DEPENDENCY INFORMATION

25A. MARITAL STATUS *(Check one)* ☐ NEVER MARRIED *(If so, do not complete Items 25B through 28B)* ☐ MARRIED ☐ WIDOWED ☐ DIVORCED	25B. NUMBER OF TIMES YOU HAVE BEEN MARRIED	25C. NUMBER OF TIMES YOUR PRESENT SPOUSE HAS BEEN MARRIED

26. FURNISH THE FOLLOWING INFORMATION ABOUT EACH OF YOUR MARRIAGES

DATE AND PLACE OF MARRIAGE (A)	TO WHOM MARRIED (B)	HOW MARRIAGE TERMINATED *(Death, divorce)* (C)	DATE AND PLACE TERMINATED (D)

27. FURNISH THE FOLLOWING INFORMATION ABOUT EACH PREVIOUS MARRIAGE OF YOUR PRESENT SPOUSE

DATE AND PLACE OF MARRIAGE (A)	TO WHOM MARRIED (B)	HOW MARRIAGE TERMINATED *(Death, divorce)* (C)	DATE AND PLACE TERMINATED (D)

28A. DO YOU LIVE TOGETHER? ☐ YES ☐ NO *(If "No", complete Item 28B)*	28B. PRESENT ADDRESS OF SPOUSE

29. List each of your living unmarried children who is: (A) under 18 years old, or (B) over 18 and under 23 years and attending school, or (C) child of any age who became permanently incapable of self-support due to physical or mental illness before age 18.

FULL NAME OF CHILD (A)	DATE OF BIRTH *(Mo., day, year)* (B)	PLACE OF BIRTH (C)	NAME AND ADDRESS OF PERSON HAVING CUSTODY OF CHILD (D)

NOTE: Please identify in Item 30A any child named above who is over 18 years old and indicate in Item 30B whether attending school or permanently incapable of self-support.

30A. NAME OF CHILD	30B. STATUS OF CHILD ☐ ATTENDING SCHOOL ☐ PERMANENTLY INCAPABLE OF SELF-SUPPORT
31A. IS YOUR FATHER DEPENDENT UPON YOU FOR SUPPORT? ☐ YES ☐ NO *(If "Yes", complete Item 31B)*	31B. NAME AND ADDRESS OF DEPENDENT FATHER
32A. IS YOUR MOTHER DEPENDENT UPON YOU FOR SUPPORT? ☐ YES ☐ NO *(If "Yes", complete Item 32B)*	32B. NAME AND ADDRESS OF DEPENDENT MOTHER

I HEREBY CERTIFY THAT all statements herein are true and complete to the best of my knowledge and belief, and I herewith apply for a program of education, under Chapter 34, Title 38, United States Code.

33. DATE SIGNED	34. SIGNATURE OF VETERAN *(Do not print)* *SIGN HERE IN INK* ▶

PENALTY - Willful false statements as to a material fact in a claim for education is a punishable offense and may result in the forfeiture of these or other benefits and in criminal penalties.

3

Fig. 1 *(Continued)*

Form Approved
Budget Bureau No. 76-RO327

VETERANS ADMINISTRATION

ENROLLMENT CERTIFICATION

(Under Chapter 34 or 35, Title 38, United States Code)

IMPORTANT - Schools will use this form to certify the student's enrollment or reenrollment in the program of education approved by the VA. TYPE OR PRINT IN INK. If additional space is required, use the reverse side and key answers to item numbers. All schools will complete items 1A thru 4 and 13-15.

1A. LAST NAME - FIRST NAME - MIDDLE INITIAL OF STUDENT	1B. VA FILE NUMBER C-
1C. STUDENT'S CURRENT ADDRESS *(Number and street or rural route, city or P.O., State and ZIP CODE. If serviceman on active duty, furnish complete military address.)*	2. CREDIT ALLOWED FOR PREVIOUS TRAINING - REQUIRED ON FIRST ENROLLMENT *(Show credit hours, extent training shortened, or "NONE." If reenrollment in same course and same school, no entry required.)*

3. NAME OF COURSE OR CURRICULUM IN WHICH STUDENT IS CURRENTLY ENROLLED *(Example: A.B. Liberal Arts; Stenographic; Electronics; etc.)*

4. TYPE OF COURSE *(Check one only and complete selected items as directed for the course checked)*

☐ UNDERGRADUATE STANDARD COLLEGE DEGREE *(Complete items 5-9)*
☐ GRADUATE OR ADVANCED PROFESSIONAL DEGREE *(Complete items 5-10)*
☐ COURSE NOT LEADING TO STANDARD COLLEGE DEGREE *(Complete items 5, 6, 9, and 11)*
☐ COOPERATIVE COURSE *(Complete items 5-8)*
☐ CORRESPONDENCE COURSE *(Complete item 12)*

LEGEND
IHL: INSTITUTION OF HIGHER LEARNING
BCL: BELOW COLLEGE LEVEL

INSTRUCTIONS-Enter applicable information in columns provided below. Make additional entries for separate semester, qtrs., etc., to show scheduled changes during period certified.

5. PERIOD OF INSTRUCTION CERTIFIED	6. EFFECTIVE DATES FOR PERIOD SHOWN IN ITEM 5		7. CREDIT HOUR LOAD		8. SUMMER SESSION, ACCELERATED SEM., TERM, ETC. **OR** ATTENDANCE FOR CO-OP COURSE	9. CHARGES FOR PERIOD OF INSTRUCTION *(Chapter 34 only)*		10. TRAINING TIME FOR GRADUATE OR ADVANCED PROFESSIONAL COURSES
IHL-BCL: Enter school year, fall term, summer or other period as applicable. CO-OP: Enter cycles of training as "classroom" and "on-job".	*IHL: Enter date of registration or date student was required to report in advance of registration and end of period. BCL-CO-OP: Enter first and last date of attendance.*		*Enter number of hours for which credit may be granted.*	*Enter credit hour equivalent of non-credit deficiency courses.*	*IHL: Enter number of standard class sessions per week. CO-OP: Enter clock hours of class attendance or on job training per week.*	*Complete only when: 1. Student is in service,* **OR** *2. Student is enrolled for less than 1/2 time.*		*Enter full time: 3/4 time, or 1/2 time. IF CHAPTER 34, may also be "more than 1/4 but less than 1/2 time" or "1/4 time or less."*
	6A. BEGINNING	6B. ENDING	7A. HOURS	7B. HOURS		9A. TUITION	9B. FEES	

11. ATTENDANCE FOR COURSE NOT LEADING TO A STANDARD COLLEGE DEGREE

A. CLOCK HOURS OF ATTENDANCE PER DAY	B. NUMBER OF DAYS PER WEEK	C. DAYS OF REGULARLY SCHEDULED ATTENDANCE *(Check applicable box(es).)*
HRS	DAYS	☐ 5 DAY WEEK *(Mon. thru Friday)* OR ☐ M ☐ TU ☐ W ☐ TH ☐ F ☐ SAT

12. CORRESPONDENCE COURSE *(Chapter 34 only)*

A. DATE FIRST LESSON SENT TO STUDENT	B. NUMBER OF LESSONS FOR WHICH STUDENT IS ENROLLED	C. CHARGE PER LESSON	D. WERE ANY LESSONS SERVICED PRIOR TO DATE IN ITEM 13?
		$	☐ YES ☐ NO *(If "Yes", list lesson number and date serviced on reverse.)*

IT IS HEREBY CERTIFIED: (1) That the facts stated above are true and correct;

(2) That the enrollment of this student does not exceed any limit established by the State Approving Agency for enrollment in this course at any one time;

(3) That this educational institution agrees to report promptly to the Veterans Administration any enrollment changes made in the student's institutional records which will affect his educational assistance allowance and whether the change was due to unsatisfactory progress and/or conduct; and

(4) **[**FOR ENROLLMENTS UNDER CHAP. 34 IN NONACCREDITED COURSES BELOW THE COLLEGE LEVEL OFFERED BY A PROPRIETARY PROFIT OR PROPRIETARY NONPROFIT EDUCATIONAL INSTITUTION**]** That, on the date indicated in Item 6A not more than 85% of the students enrolled in the course, including this student, are having all or any part of their tuition, fees, or other charges paid to or for them by the educational institution or the Veterans Administration under Chapter 31, 34 or 35, Title 38, United States Code.

13. DATE SIGNED	14. SIGNATURE AND TITLE OF CERTIFYING OFFICIAL	15. NAME AND ADDRESS OF SCHOOL

CAUTION - Willful false statements concerning matters in any document required by this law may subject the person to fine or imprisonment or both.

VA FORM APR 1967 **21E-1999** SUPERSEDES VA FORM 21E-1999, OCT 1966, WHICH WILL NOT BE USED. ☆ GPO : 1967 O - 252-195 (283)

Fig. 2 *Form 21E-1999, enrollment certification.*

Form Approved
Budget Bureau No. 76-R546.1

VETERANS ADMINISTRATION

NOTICE OF CHANGE IN STUDENT STATUS

(Under Chapter 34 or 35, Title 38, U.S.C.)

1. LAST NAME - FIRST NAME - MIDDLE INITIAL OF STUDENT	2. VA FILE NUMBER C-

This form is to be used by the school certifying official to report any change in status which is made during a period for which enrollment is certified.

3. ADJUSTMENT OF CREDIT HOUR LOAD AND TRAINING TIME, IF APPLICABLE

A. DATE ADJUSTMENT IS EFFECTIVE	CREDIT HOUR LOAD		NUMBER OF STANDARD CLASS SESSIONS PER WEEK *(Complete for accelerated semester, term, quarter or summer session only).*	
	B. BEFORE ADJUSTMENT	C. AFTER ADJUSTMENT	D. BEFORE ADJUSTMENT	E. AFTER ADJUSTMENT

F. TRAINING TIME AFTER ADJUSTMENT *(Check ONLY if graduate or advanced professional courses)*

(Chapter 34 only)

☐ FULL TIME ☐ 3/4 ☐ 1/2 ☐ LESS THAN 1/2 ☐ 1/4 OR LESS

NOTE: Complete Item 4, if veteran student's load after adjustment is less than 1/2 time, or for any change in load for an In-service student.

4. CHARGES FOR PERIOD OF ENROLLMENT (Chapter 34)

List customary charges of the ADJUSTED load by term, quarter, semester or summer session for period of enrollment. For example: Fall term - tuition $150, fees $15; Spring term - tuition $85, fees $10, or 1st summer session - tuition $90, fees $10; 2nd summer session - tuition $90, fees $5.	A. PERIOD *(Enter inclusive dates for spring or fall term, etc.)*	B. TUITION	C. FEES

5. CHANGE IN ENDING DATE

A. IS ENDING DATE OF ENROLLMENT PERIOD PREVIOUSLY CERTIFIED STILL IN EFFECT? ☐ YES ☐ NO *(If "No", complete Item 5B)*	B. REVISED ENDING DATE FOR PERIOD OF ENROLLMENT

6. TERMINATION

A. LAST DATE OF ATTENDANCE	B. REASON FOR TERMINATION ☐ END OF TERM ☐ COMPLETED COURSE ☐ VOLUNTARY WITHDRAWAL ☐ DISCIPLINARY DISMISSAL ☐ ACADEMIC DISMISSAL

7. REMARKS

IT IS HEREBY CERTIFIED that the student's status changed on the date indicated and in accordance with the facts shown above.

8. SIGNATURE AND TITLE OF CERTIFYING OFFICIAL	9. DATE SIGNED

10. NAME AND ADDRESS OF SCHOOL

VA FORM FEB 1967 **21E-1999b** EXISTING STOCKS OF VA FORM 21E-1999b, MAY 1966, WILL BE USED. ☆ U. S. GOVERNMENT PRINTING OFFICE : 1967 O - 252-192 (231)

Fig. 3 *Form 21E-1999b, notice of change in student status.*

INSTRUCTIONS TO APPLICANTS

1. RESTRICTIONS ON CHANGES OF PROGRAM - The law places certain restrictions on changes of program. You should not make any actual change until you receive VA approval of that change on VA Form 21E-1993.

2. COUNSELING - The law permits you to make one change of program. You should carefully plan your program so that more than one change is not necessary. The VA will generally approve your request.

a. The VA may approve one additional change of program if appropriate. If you want counseling to help you decide whether to change your program, or to help you select a suitable program, you should check "Yes" in Item 12, and omit entries in Items 13 through 16.

b. In some situations, you are required by law to appear personally for counseling before we can take final action on your request for a change of program. We will notify you if counseling is required.

c. Counseling is not available in foreign countries, except in the Republic of the Philippines.

3. OBJECTIVE AND PROGRAM - If you do not want counseling before you decide on your new program of education or training, complete Items 13 through 15 as explained below:

a. In Item 13 show the final educational, professional, or vocational goal or objective for which you expect to qualify. This means the goal you expect to reach by completing your training program. Your goal or objective may be stated in terms of a profession, trade, or vocation, or in terms of an educational goal such as a high school diploma or college degree. If your goal is educational, you should list as your objective the highest degree you wish to receive.

b. In Item 14 check the method of education you plan to pursue.

c. In Item 15 describe your complete program as follows:

COLLEGE OR UNIVERSITY PROGRAM - State the curriculum or curricula to which you would like to change, such as Bachelor of Science, Bachelor of Arts, Master of Arts, etc. If you do not plan to take a degree or certificate course, list all the specific subjects you wish to take. If more than one degree is required to reach the degree listed in Item 11, name each curriculum required.

EDUCATIONAL PROGRAM IN OTHER SCHOOL (such as high school, business school, vocational or trade school, or any other school) - List the course or courses you plan to take by the exact names as given in the school literature.

4. EXAMPLES OF OBJECTIVE AND PROGRAM DESCRIPTIONS:

a. Objective ACCOUNTANT, GENERAL, in Item 13; Junior Accounting course in Item 15.

b. Objective BACHELOR OF LAWS DEGREE in Item 13; Bachelor of Laws degree in Item 15. NOTE - If you also wish to include a bar review course in your program, you should enter LAWYER as your objective (Item 13), and enter Bachelor of Laws degree and Bar Review course as your program (Item 15).

5. PROGRAMS WHICH MAY NOT BE APPROVED

a. You should not apply for a program leading to an objective for which you are already qualified. The law provides that the VA shall not approve an application for an educational, professional, or vocational objective when the person is already qualified for such objective by reason of previous education and training.

b. The law also prohibits the approval of a program for avocational or recreational purposes. If the course you wish to take is one usually pursued for such purposes, you must submit justification showing the course will be of bona fide use in the pursuit of your present or contemplated business or occupation.

6. DUPLICATION OF BENEFITS - You cannot be paid Educational Assistance Allowance under this law for any period during which you are enrolled in and pursuing a program of education or course paid for by the United States under any provision of other laws where the payment of an allowance would constitute a duplication of benefits paid from the Federal Treasury. However, educational loans from a Federal agency or other assistance under a State or private financial program does not preclude benefits under this law.

7. CHANGE OF ADDRESS - Keep the Veterans Administration informed of your latest address. Whenever you move, notify the VA immediately. You may obtain a Change of Address form (VA Form 572) from the nearest VA office.

ALWAYS FURNISH YOUR COMPLETE NAME AND VA FILE NUMBER

☆ U. S. GOVERNMENT PRINTING OFFICE : 1966 O - 202-196(214)

Fig. 4 *Form 21E-1995, request for change of program or school.*

Form Approved
Budget Bureau No. 76-R332.6

VETERANS ADMINISTRATION

REQUEST FOR CHANGE OF PROGRAM OR SCHOOL

(Under Chapter 34, Title 38, U.S. Code)

1. VA FILE NUMBER
C-

IMPORTANT - Before completing this form read the instructions. Answer all questions fully. Type or print answers in ink.

SECTION A - GENERAL INFORMATION

2. FIRST NAME - MIDDLE NAME - LAST NAME OF APPLICANT

3. MAILING ADDRESS *(Number and street or rural route, city or P.O., State and Zip Code)*

4. LOCATION OF RECORDS *(Address of VA office)*

5A. ARE YOU NOW ON ACTIVE DUTY IN THE ARMED FORCES?
☐ YES ☐ NO *(If "Yes", complete Item 5B)*

5B. DATE COMMENCED ACTIVE DUTY

6A. REASON FOR LEAVING COURSE OR SCHOOL

6B. NAME AND ADDRESS OF PRESENT OR LAST SCHOOL ATTENDED

7. ON WHAT DATE DO YOU PLAN TO RESUME YOUR EDUCATION, IF APPROVED?

8A. DO YOU EXPECT TO RECEIVE EDUCATIONAL BENEFITS FROM ANY OTHER AGENCY OF THE FEDERAL GOVERNMENT DURING THIS NEW PERIOD OF EDUCATION? *(Do not include Federal Educational Loans)*
☐ YES ☐ NO *(If "Yes", complete Item 8B.)*

8B. NATURE AND EXTENT OF OTHER FEDERAL BENEFITS

9A. PRESENT DEPENDENTS *(Check and complete all applicable items.)*
☐ NONE ☐ WIFE ☐ CHILDREN *(Specify number)* ☐ DEPENDENT HUSBAND ☐ PARENTS *(Specify number)*

9B. HAVE YOU HAD ANY PREVIOUS MARRIAGES?
☐ YES ☐ NO

9C. HAS YOUR SPOUSE HAD ANY PREVIOUS MARRIAGES?
☐ YES ☐ NO

SECTION B - REQUEST FOR CHANGE OF SCHOOL *(To continue same program)*

10. NAME AND ADDRESS OF SCHOOL OR TRAINING ESTABLISHMENT WHERE YOU WISH TO CONTINUE YOUR PROGRAM

11. NAME THE COURSE OR CURRICULUM YOU WISH TO TAKE AT THE NEW PLACE OF TRAINING

SECTION C - REQUEST FOR CHANGE OF PROGRAM OF EDUCATION

12. DO YOU WISH TO HAVE EDUCATIONAL OR VOCATIONAL COUNSELING FROM THE VA?
☐ YES ☐ NO *(If "No", complete Items 13 through 16)*

13. WHAT IS YOUR NEW EDUCATIONAL, PROFESSIONAL, OR VOCATIONAL OBJECTIVE?

14. METHOD OF EDUCATION
☐ SCHOOL ATTENDANCE ☐ CORRESPONDENCE COURSE

15. DESCRIBE THE PROGRAM YOU WISH TO TAKE IN REACHING YOUR NEW OBJECTIVE

16. NAME AND ADDRESS OF SCHOOL

I HEREBY CERTIFY THAT all statements herein are true and complete to the best of my knowledge and belief.

17. DATE SIGNED

18. SIGNATURE OF APPLICANT *(Do not print)*
SIGN HERE IN INK ▶

PENALTY - Willful false statements as to a material fact in a claim for education is a punishable offense and may result in the forfeiture of these or other benefits and in criminal penalties.

FOR VA USE ONLY ▶	EFFECTIVE DATE OF COURSE APPROVAL	DATE APPROVAL CHECKED	CERTIFIED BY	R.O. NO.

VA FORM JUN 1966 **21E-1995**

Fig. 4 *(Continued)*

The laws governing veterans' educational assistance clearly dictate the need for a college or university to have, as an integral function of its registration or admissions offices, a well-oriented veterans' affairs department. It is vital that this area be able to maintain a pulsating network of communications between itself, the veteran student population, and all other segments of the academic community.

Following is a procedural outline discussing the school's role of implementing its responsibilities which, in union with the student's cooperation, will bring forth all the benefits which the laws are intended to provide.

Approval of Courses A school wishing to enroll veterans or eligible persons must make application for approval of its courses or programs to its state approving agency. Generally, approval is readily obtainable for any course which is offered by a nonprofit educational institution of college level when the course is recognized for credit toward a standard college degree. The law prohibits approval of courses which are avocational or recreational in character.

Enrollment Certification On the reverse side of each certificate of eligibility which the veteran furnishes to the school is an enrollment certification which is completed by the school and filed with V.A. at the time the student enrolls. To facilitate continuity of payments to the veteran, it is suggested that the student be certified for a full academic year. Certifications for subsequent periods are made on V.A. Form 21E-1999.

Award Letter After the enrollment certification has been acted upon by V.A., the student will be mailed an award letter which will outline:

1. Dates of enrollment
2. Monthly benefit rate
3. Reminders to report promptly changes in enrollment or dependency status.

An initial payment will be mailed shortly after the award letter, and, thereafter, monthly checks will follow over the period of certification.

Change in Status Because the amount of assistance a veteran receives is directly related to the number of semester or quarter hours he is carrying, it is of the utmost importance that changes in the rate of attendance be promptly reported to V.A. The law places the responsibility for notification squarely on the veteran. The school must report all changes or terminations which come to its attention by completing Form 21E-1999b, "Notice of Change in Student Status."

Measurement of Courses *Undergraduate.* Leading to an associate, baccalaureate, or higher degree:

1. Full-time: 14 semester or quarter hours
2. Three-fourths time: 10 to 13 semester or quarter hours
3. One-half time: 7 to 9 semester or quarter hours
4. Less than one-half but more than one quarter time: 4 to 6 semester or quarter hours
5. One-quarter time or less: Less than 4 semester or quarter hours

Graduate. Training will be measured on the same basis as that of the undergraduate level unless the school has established a policy which considers less than 14 semester or quarter hours as full-time enrollment. In such instances, V.A. will accept the certification of the school in determining whether the student is attending full, three-fourths, one-half, less than one-half but more than one-quarter, or one-quarter or less time.

Educational Assistance Allowances

(Figures in parentheses proposed 1970)

Type of program	No dependents	One dependent	Two dependents	Each additional dependent
Institutional				
Full-time	$130(175)	$155(205)	$175(230)	$10(13)
¾ time	95(128)	115(152)	135(177)	7(10)
½ time	60(81)	75(100)	85(119)	5(7)
Cooperative				
Full-time only	105(141)	125(167)	145(192)	7(10)

Less than one-half time but more than one-quarter time: Payment at the rate of tuition and fees but not to exceed $60 monthly (approximately $85 at the 1970 rate).

One-quarter time or less: Payment at the rate of tuition and fees but not to exceed $30 monthly (approximately $45 at the 1970 rate).

In-service Students

One-half time or more: Payment based on the cost of tuition and fees, but not to exceed the single veteran rate.

Less than one-half time: Same rates as those for veterans.

Reporting Fees A reporting fee of $3 a year per beneficiary is paid by V.A. to the institution based on the total number enrolled on October 31 of the year.

Laws pertaining to Veterans Educational Assistance contain a great many reservations. While the foregoing is a general summary of the regulations as they now exist, specific interpretation of certain provisions can best be ascertained by reference to the legislation itself.

Sources of Reference

Veterans Administration regulations.

American Association of Collegiate Registrars and Admissions Officers: *Certification of Students Under Veterans Laws.*

Author's Note While it appears that the new benefit rates will be set by compromise, it seems useful to review briefly that section of the amendments (proposed 1970) which would establish active efforts to recruit the GI who is about to return to civilian life:

1. Payments would be made to educational institutions for remedial tutoring and other aid provided to enrolling veterans.
2. Grants and contracts would be made available to colleges and universities for educational programs.
3. Veterans could complete elementary and high school work without losing entitlement for college benefits.
4. Allowances would be made for veterans to take college preparatory courses at colleges and junior colleges in addition to secondary schools.
5. Payments would be made to educational institutions for educating and training military service personnel prior to their discharge.
6. There would be a reduction from 14 to 12 semester or quarter hours, the load a veteran would have to carry to qualify for full-time benefits, provided that full tuition is charged for less than 14 hours or that all undergraduates carrying less than 14 hours are considered full-time by the school.
7. An expanded "outreach" program would be created under which the V.A. would seek out educationally disadvantaged veterans and offer them a wide range of services and information.

Section Eight

Athletics Administration

Chapter **1**

Intercollegiate Programs

JAMES W. LONG

Director, Division of Physical Education, Oregon State University, Corvallis, Oregon

INTRODUCTION

Clearly defined objectives and policies for intercollegiate athletics and efficient administration are essential to the growing athletic enterprise. The development of intercollegiate athletics has been an unbelievably fascinating phenomenon in the United States. Athletics has come to command the attention and interest of vast numbers of American people. Athletics has become a part of the power structure of our society. Its impact has given it a cultural, social, and economic status of increasing importance. Therefore, athletics has an important role to play in higher education.

SELECTED PROBLEMS FACING INTERCOLLEGIATE ATHLETICS

Varying Philosophies For the last several years there has been a ferment in the administration of intercollegiate athletics. When one includes physical education as a related part of athletics or as a broad field which includes athletics, the complexities seem endless. Philosophies run the gamut from educational progressivism to essentialism. In progressivism, athletics is considered an integral part of physical education and it is therefore held to be properly administered under the same head. In essentialism, athletics and physical education are looked upon as closely related but separate enterprises which require separate administrators. In the latter case, the administration might be placed under one head if the institution were not large enough to justify an economic separation. Without a doubt, the relationships between education, especially physical education, and athletics need to be clarified. The proper organization and administration of either integrated or separate administrations need to be defined. Each individual institution will need to reevaluate its programs in the light of actualities and philosophy.

Student, Staff, and Financial Problems The increasing emphasis upon educational achievement and the pursuit of academic excellence by the student athlete is of prime importance. Standards are evolving that require higher grade-point averages for the awarding and retention of grants in aid. The efforts expended by the athletic personnel, faculty, administrators, and conference officials in upgrading these standards are paying dividends. These are sound practices. However, the law of supply and demand for student athletes with exceptional physical attributes creates recruitment pressures. It may also tend to encourage acceptance of marginal academic risks.

The selection, number, and background of the staff are critical administrative decisions. The specialist in one sport or area does not present too many difficulties. The combination personnel who have coaching responsibilities in two or more sports and/or coaching and teaching responsibilities present more serious problems. Should the instructor/coach meet the same academic requirements demanded of subject-matter fields, or should these requirements be bypassed in deference to the needs of the athletic program? Since the field of physical education is expanding into a full-fledged profession and discipline, how can the waiver of academic standards be justified if the coach is selected with little or no consideration of his teaching or academic background?

Financial pressures are constant. There is no doubt that intercollegiate athletics is a thriving enterprise in many of the larger universities. The "Big" in "Big Business Entertainment" involves literally hundreds of millions of dollars. The 1967 Television Committee Report of the National Collegiate Athletic Association gives figures on advertising, attendance, and financial benefits that are almost unbelievable [1].* Along with this affluence, the aim of winning and the practices that are necessary to maintain the will to win place athletics in the extracurricular and entertainment fields. Emotionalism and the desire for a status symbol sometimes color sanity. Success is measured by the win-loss column; coaches are hired and fired on this basis; and pressures never end. Then there are countless numbers of schools that have not tapped the TV monies and large gate receipts. To these schools, the financial struggles are real and burdensome.

OBJECTIVES AND POLICIES FOR INTERCOLLEGIATE ATHLETICS

One of the greatest concerns of administrators of institutions of higher learning and athletic administrators should be the reemphasis of the broad educational, social, ethical, and physical values inherent in intercollegiate athletics. Objectives for intercollegiate athletics should be carefully delineated by the individual institutions. They may vary from school to school. Policies are generally interpreted according to the basic beliefs of the administration. Obviously, many problems and pressures have developed in highly competitive athletic programs which make it even more essential to establish sound policies. No matter what the stated purposes, athletic programs may have evolved from different purposes. The win-loss status-symbol objectives have become powerful influences. The alumni and the power structure may have become involved in decision making. Profit-loss and big business entertainment pressures are closely related. There is also the realization that educational and concomitant values are not achieved automatically. Constant effort should be generated in the direction of reaching educational goals.

* Bracketed numbers refer to the references at the end of the chapter.

In order that intercollegiate athletics may have definite guidelines, basic objectives should be established. The following are some selected objectives which could serve as possible examples from which each school might develop its own set:

1. To develop an understanding and appreciation of the potent force that intercollegiate athletics is in American society and to develop sane attitudes toward these sports.

2. To educate the student body, faculty, and alumni in the appreciation and enjoyment of intercollegiate athletics for the sportsmanship, respect for others, adherence to rules, ethics of the game, and democracy in action which can be promoted.

3. To provide a focal point for the morale, spirit, and loyalty of the students, alumni, and friends; to offer a common ground where enthusiasm is shared by all and the university may be strengthened and united.

4. To provide opportunities for students to develop their talents through a wide variety of individual and team sports suitable for different body types, interests, and needs; and to do this in keeping with the philosophy of education for the normal youngster.

5. To provide competent guidance by creating a strong faculty committee on athletics which establishes policies and procedures governing the program of intercollegiate athletics.

6. To provide trained and dedicated leadership for the optimal development of physical skills, team play, sportsmanship, healthful practices, and mental, moral, and emotional growth.

7. To encourage the student athlete's wholehearted endeavors in acquiring an education worthy of his best efforts.

8. To provide adequate funds, facilities, and equipment within the college or university's financial capabilities. Such funds should include income from all legitimate sources, so that there will be a minimum of outside pressure or infringement on other departments or programs.

9. To evaluate continually the intercollegiate athletic program in all of its phases to ensure consistent adherence to the stated objectives.

10. To apply the standards accepted by academic departments to all personnel who have administrative or teaching responsibilities in the areas cf health, physical education, or recreation.

INTERCOLLEGIATE ATHLETIC DEPARTMENTAL ORGANIZATION

Importance of President as Chief Administrative Officer Since the chief administrative officer is ultimately responsible for the conduct of athletics, it behooves him to be well informed about athletic policies and practices and to take the necessary steps to assure that the athletics program is making its full contribution to the attainment of its objectives.

Most college and university presidents have experienced pressures of varying types and degrees as a result of problems arising from intercollegiate athletics. Many problems become public affairs that may be fanned into conflagrations by press, radio, and television coverage. The president, therefore, needs to keep in close touch with the faculty athletic committee and the director of athletics. Their responsibilities should be carefully delegated and understood. The president and the board of trustees should also have a meeting of the minds as to the objectives and policies of their athletics program. Another means of handling controversial problems or establishing sound objectives for intercollegiate athletics is a cooperative endeavor with other presidents who are members of regional conferences. Through the concerted action of presidents with similar problems, changes and controls can be established with minimum outside pressure.

Scope and Interrelationships Unfortunately there is no simple answer to the question of departmental organization. Surveys of existing organizations show a variety of patterns. Colleges and universities are complex educational structures with different emphases, traditions, size, personnel, and objectives. Both the progressivist and the essentialist philosophies applied to administration have strong advocates. There are departments of intercollegiate athletics combined with departments of physical education. Required general education courses in physical education, undergraduate and graduate curricula in health, physical education, and recreation, and intramural sports are the more common filial arrangements. There are several common areas which require cooperation in these related fields, such as joint use of facilities, equipment, and personnel. Where facilities, personnel, and finances are minimal, practical exigencies sometimes dictate organization. There seems to be an increasing trend toward the structuring of intercollegiate athletics, wholly or in part, as a separate enterprise. This is especially true in colleges with major sport classifications or for schools striving to attain major status.

A sample organizational chart shows the departments, faculty, and staff needed to organize and administer broad health, physical education, and recreational programs for students majoring in academic fields, intramural sports and recreational programs for all students and faculty, and the intercollegiate athletic program. The lines of authority should be adapted to meet the needs of the individual institution and to be consistent with sound academic and administrative procedures. In smaller institutions, several functions will need to be performed by one individual. (See page 8-8.)

Importance of Establishing Objectives and Philosophy The first step in determining the organizational pattern is to define the philosophy, objectives, and functions to be served and then to design the programs and administrative organization which will most effectively contribute to the attainment of the objectives and functions.

It is when the objectives, functions, and programs are in conflict that the problem of determining the organizational hierarchy becomes critical. In institutions of higher learning, academic standards, maintenance of professional integrity, and other prerequisites for high-quality educational programs should certainly receive the wholehearted support of the top administrators. At the same time, the pursuit of excellence in athletics cannot be neglected.

The rapid growth of institutions, the increased number and enrollments of junior and community colleges, the changing emphasis from lower-division courses to upper-division and graduate work, and the expansion of professional athletic programs should all be watched carefully in the event that they should call for modification of existing programs.

The Developing Professions of Health, Physical Education, and Recreation In the last few years, the professions of health, physical education, and recreation have been coming of age with signs of maturation common to other recognized and reputable professions. Areas of knowledge within these disciplines have been extended immeasurably, and research, advanced study, and creativity are regular parts of them. The administration of these three disciplines with their academic objectives and with their close interrelationships with other academic disciplines should be similar to that of other academic departments. The administrators should also be academically oriented and should meet the same standards demanded of other academicians. Separate departments of health, physical education, and recreation compose the general organizational structure, with more and more departments being organized into divisions or schools. There are also administrative differences between physical educa-

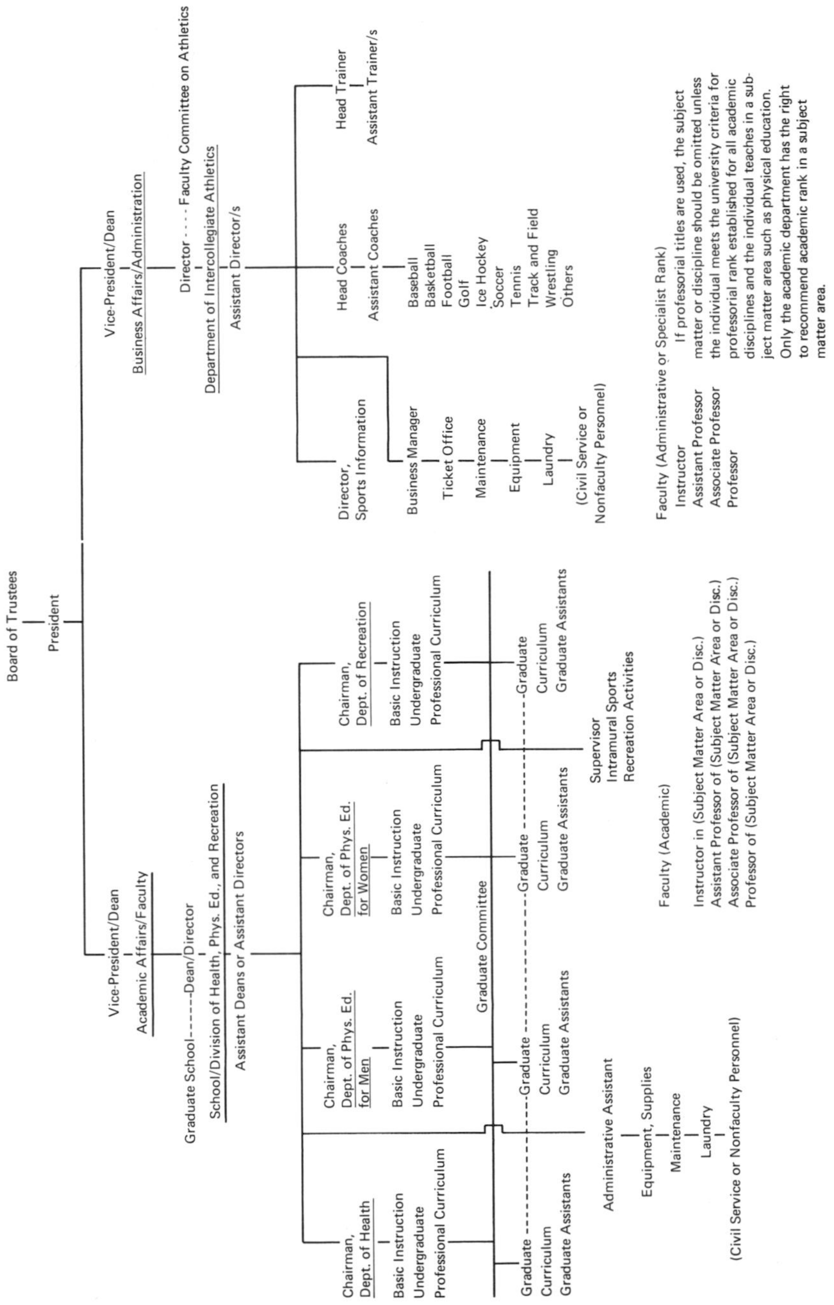
Board of Trustees
President
Vice-President/Dean
Academic Affairs/Faculty
Graduate School------Dean/Director
School/Division of Health, Phys. Ed., and Recreation
Assistant Deans or Assistant Directors
Chairman,
Dept. of Health
Basic Instruction
Undergraduate
Professional Curriculum
Graduate
Curriculum
Graduate Assistants
Chairman,
Dept. of Phys. Ed.
for Men
Basic Instruction
Undergraduate
Professional Curriculum
Graduate
Curriculum
Graduate Assistants
Graduate Committee
Chairman,
Dept. of Phys. Ed.
for Women
Basic Instruction
Undergraduate
Professional Curriculum
Graduate
Curriculum
Graduate Assistants
Chairman,
Dept. of Recreation
Basic Instruction
Undergraduate
Professional Curriculum
Graduate
Curriculum
Graduate Assistants
Administrative Assistant
Equipment, Supplies
Maintenance
Laundry
(Civil Service or Nonfaculty Personnel)
Supervisor
Intramural Sports
Recreation Activities
Faculty (Academic)
Instructor in (Subject Matter Area or Disc.)
Assistant Professor of (Subject Matter Area or Disc.)
Associate Professor of (Subject Matter Area or Disc.)
Professor of (Subject Matter Area or Disc.)
Vice-President/Dean
Business Affairs/Administration
Director - - - - Faculty Committee on Athletics
Department of Intercollegiate Athletics
Assistant Director/s
Director,
Sports Information
Business Manager
Ticket Office
Maintenance
Equipment
Laundry
(Civil Service or
Nonfaculty Personnel)
Head Coaches
Assistant Coaches
Baseball
Basketball
Football
Golf
Ice Hockey
Soccer
Tennis
Track and Field
Wrestling
Others
Head Trainer
Assistant Trainer/s
Faculty (Administrative or Specialist Rank)
Instructor
Assistant Professor
Associate Professor
Professor
If professorial titles are used, the subject matter or discipline should be omitted unless the individual meets the university criteria for professorial rank established for all academic disciplines and the individual teaches in a subject matter area such as physical education. Only the academic department has the right to recommend academic rank in a subject matter area.

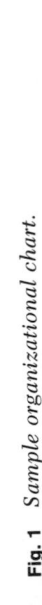

Fig. 1 *Sample organizational chart.*

tion departments for men and those for women. In many institutions these departments are distinct. The question of whether separate facilities, separate personnel, and separate curricula are justified demands careful evaluation of objectives, the source and amount of resources, and the type and size of institution. In most instances, however, the separation of men's and women's programs is not complete or clearly delineated. It is hard to justify a separation in the upper-division courses and graduate courses based on a dichotomy of sex. Since there should be no question that these academic areas should be administered as is any other academic department, the departments of health, physical education, and recreation will not be included with the department of athletics in the discussion that follows unless they are specifically mentioned. This does not imply, however, that these schools need have separate administrations.

ATHLETIC DEPARTMENT ORGANIZATION VARIES

Administrative patterns for the departments of intercollegiate athletics vary widely, but there are many similarities when terminology is standardized and personnel responsibilities and operational procedures are compared with those of similar administrative settings. In the larger institutions with major sports classifications, typical titles and positions are as follows: the director of athletics; assistant and associate directors; business manager; sports publicity director; head coaches and assistant coaches; athletic trainers; equipment, maintenance, and custodial personnel; and the board of athletic control. These people handle specialized responsibilities that vary according to the type of intercollegiate athletic program that is prevalent at the particular institution. A highly competitive program geared primarily to mass entertainment and involving elaborate financing, called "big business entertainment" by the more realistic person, necessitates a business-type organization and calls for sufficient personnel to carry out extensive recruitment, public relations, and promotional campaigns. There are increased pressures for more spectator facilities, more equipment and supplies, and more personnel to produce winning teams to keep the cycle in operation.

In many institutions, philosophy and objectives as well as size and financial status require a staff that must perform a combination of duties, such as teacher, coach, recruiter, administrator, and business manager. From a practical standpoint, the philosophy and objectives of the key administrators will again decide such matters as, in the hiring of athletic personnel, the choice between academically trained individuals with athletic backgrounds or specialists with limited education who then must teach. This choice becomes especially critical when undergraduate or graduate curricula are involved. "Fickle success" in athletics is measured oftentimes by the win-loss column with the other manifestations of status. Academic work, both undergraduate and graduate, is judged by academic standards, so that there cannot always be a happy marriage. Under these circumstances, it is important to the individuals concerned, and to the college or university, that divergent objectives be met while standards of excellence and integrity are maintained.

ATHLETIC DEPARTMENT STAFF

Personnel practices with regard to athletic staff often seem to be heavily influenced by the athletic objectives of the particular college or university. These practices are not always consistent with those that are routinely applied to other members of the faculty, much to the consternation of those involved. There seems to be agreement that athletic department personnel should be members of the faculty and that they should receive the rights and privileges of full-fledged faculty members. There does not always seem to be agreement that they should meet the same standards of academic attainment, experience, and teaching competence as do the other faculty members. If an evaluation of the backgrounds of athletic staff members indicates consistent shortcomings in academic areas, it is likely that a dual standard and undesirable personnel practices are being used. In such instances the educational objectives would seem to have been relegated to a secondary position.

Present Status of Athletic Administrators A survey of directors of intercollegiate athletics would reveal a wide spectrum of unbelievable backgrounds. To mention a few, there are coaches with losing records, coaches with winning records, politicians, lawyers, physicians, FBI men, businessmen, journalists, name athletes, educators, physical educators, and alumni secretaries. Their educational backgrounds range from no degree to the doctoral degree, with majors in practically every field of study. This is not to imply that directors of athletics are not capable, dedicated, and successful men. It does, however, point out the need for the development of standards of preparation for administrators of intercollegiate athletics.

Development of Profession There are elements common to recognized professions. One important element is that a profession is based on an organized body of knowledge with appropriate educational experiences. Theory and practice are interdependent. A professional person should also have the sort of general education that will give him a broad background in the liberal arts. Scientific investigation and research are becoming essential to progress in business administration, educational administration, and related areas such as the behavioral sciences. Administrative theory and the related areas of knowledge pertaining to the improvement of athletic administration as a profession are just as important but have been slow in developing. The Joint Committee from the Division of Men's Athletics of the American Association for Health, Physical Education and Recreation and the National Association for Collegiate Directors of Athletics has defined several broad areas of competence upon which the training curricula for athletic administrators ought to concentrate. The areas of competence or understanding identified as of utmost importance are the following:

1. *The role of athletics in education:* historical, cultural, philosophical, sociological, and ethical aspects; professional role and related professional organizations
2. *Business procedures:* accounting practices, budget and finance, fund raising, purchase, and operational policies
3. *Equipment and supplies:* purchase, care, maintenance, and inventory
4. *Planning, construction, maintenance, and use of facilities:* indoors and outdoors; multiple use
5. *School law and legal liability:* institutional liability, insurance, transportation, personal liability
6. *Administration of athletic events:* contracts, scheduling travel, game management, ticket sales, promotions, tournaments, spectator control
7. *Public relations:* communication media, audiovisual techniques and equipment, individual and group relationships, oral and written communication
8. *Staff relationships:* professional status, staff morale, selection, promotion, salary, tenure, supervision, communication, policies
9. *Health aspects of athletics:* nutrition, safety procedures, medical supervision, first aid, care and prevention of injury, conditioning policies, relationship with health services, insurance
10. *Evaluation and interpretation of research*

The Joint Committee, consisting of representatives from the American Association for Health, Physical Education and Recreation, the National College Physical Education Association for Men, and the National Collegiate Athletic Association, has sponsored three important national conferences for directors of athletics since 1959. One of these conferences resulted in the formation of the National Association for Collegiate Directors of Athletics, which is concentrating on the improvement of the professional status of directors and the improvement of the athletic programs. The National Conference on Graduate Education in Health, Physical Education and Recreation, held in Washington, D.C. in January, 1967, specified administration as a field worthy of further study for graduate work [2].

Emergence of Administrative Theory and Practice The emergence of sound administrative theory and practice will undoubtedly receive increasing attention in institutions of higher education. Scholars and researchers from many disciplines will need to be involved by the departments or schools of physical education to supplement the core or basic theory courses and practices that should form the nucleus for this professional training. It seems logical that colleges and universities of the future will demand professionally trained administrators, with athletic experience, to handle the tremendous investments in student athletes, to administer operational expenditures, to manage capital outlay, and to exploit the public-relations potential.

PROFESSORIAL RANK AND TENURE

Selection of athletic personnel is generally based on three premises: (1) the individual's reputation and ability to coach winning teams; (2) his educational qualifications and ability to assume academic responsibilities; and (3) the way in which these qualifications are combined in a given candidate.

Combination Personnel Where personnel are selected for academic qualifications and responsibilities in the department or school of physical education, professional rank and tenure should follow university policies for all qualified academic ranks. These persons should perform the duties imposed by such rank in the life of the institution. Academic and institutional integrity need to be upheld in the department or school of physical education as much as in other academic departments. This is also true for the combination personnel who teach and coach. There is no justification for ignoring academic integrity because of pressures for winning athletic teams.

Athletic Staff The intercollegiate athletic staff that is selected for its reputation and ability to produce winning teams poses some rather difficult academic problems. Where the intercollegiate athletic department is separate and the academic qualifications of the personnel are secondary, the granting of academic rank and tenure violates the fundamental precept of specific academic qualifications for academic rank. Many institutions give additional compensatory salary in lieu of tenure. However, there are other questions that must be resolved. If tenure is granted, will the athletic department or the university absorb the personnel when coaching responsibilities are discontinued, or will an academic department such as physical education be expected to find a place for the athletic personnel? Where professorial rank is considered necessary for coaches, one solution is to grant professorial rank with no reference to an academic field. In other words, this may be an administrative rank comparable to an academic rank with comparable salary ranges.

Many institutions award regular contracts with tenure ranging from one to several years. Assistant coaches are often responsible to the head coach for their tenure. Contractual arrangements between coaches and the institution should carry a two-way obligation. It was recommended by the athletic directors at the 1959 National Conference that when contracts are terminated by either party prior to the end of said contracts that the party violating the contract should be required to pay damages of a previously designated amount [3]. However, this has up to now generally been a one-way obligation, with the institution seldom or never receiving damages.

There should be no doubt that the athletic staff who work with and coach student athletes should be men of sound educational background with high standards of ethical conduct and good technical skills. The practice of hiring personnel on the basis of win-loss records, popularity, and athletic reputation is fraught with potential trouble. If the intercollegiate athletic program is to be an integral part of the educational life of the institution, coaches and athletic administrators should be trained in and devoted to the primary purposes of higher education.

The National Association of Intercollegiate Athletics has developed a "Code of Ethics" to clarify, promote, and emphasize the many contributions that coaches and athletic administrators can make to their institutions and to student athletes [4]. There are certain obligations and responsibilities that are essential. The "Code of Ethics," which follows, emphasizes the highest standards of conduct that are consistent with broad educational purposes:

I believe in the power of athletics as a program for the training of youth for a strong and efficient democracy.

I believe in athletics for the building of good character and personality.

I believe in athletics as a significant part of a sound educational program.

I believe in athletics as a constructive force in the lives of the millions of sports followers throughout our nation. Therefore, I will hold sportsmanship and fair play high above all other values to be gained through sports participation.

I consider the privilege of guiding youth through participation in sports as a sacred trust and not merely a means of livelihood.

I will always keep the best interest of each boy as my aim and shall never be guilty of enhancing my professional progress by use of his skill to my benefit and his hurt.

I will ever keep before the youth under my direction the high ideals, honesty, sincerity, and integrity which have made our nation great, and will not encourage or even tolerate any form of trickery or evasion of rules in order to gain an advantage over an opponent.

I will do all in my power to instill in those under my direction tolerance for all races and creeds and will stand out against intolerance wherever it may occur.

I will strive to instill in every youth great purposes and aims in living and will use the desire to play not as an end but as a training ground for the highest development of which each youth is capable.

I will strive to instill in every youth a keen desire to win, to excel, to achieve, but always fairly and according to the spirit of the rules.

I will strive to teach each youth to be humble in victory and gracious in defeat, and shall help him to develop inner strength and poise from each; to be above bragging or alibiing.

I will use only fair and honest means in my desire for personal achievement and shall count the good will of my fellows far above any achievement unfairly gained.

I will not sacrifice the values to be gained by youth through a wholesome enjoyment of challenging sports activity to institutional pride or commercial ends.

I will use only fair and honest means of securing talent for athletic teams and never stoop to trickery or insincere promises in influencing youth in the selection of their educational experience.

I will use every means at my command to protect the moral, mental, and physical health of the youth under my guidance, and will never be a party of any use of athletics for the financial, personal, or political gain of any office or group.

I will encourage each youth to avail himself of the best experiences to be gained in a well-rounded education, and to progress normally toward graduation. I will never encourage participation in athletics as an end in itself.

I will help each youth under my guidance toward the development of honest habits of work and pride in work well done, and shall not practice or allow evasion in any obligation surrounding the athletic program.

I will shoulder my total responsibility as a leader of youth through athletics and will not allow that responsibility to be transferred to any person or group outside the educational institution. I will not violate this sacred trust for financial support or political prestige.

REGULATIONS GOVERNING CONDUCT OF INTERCOLLEGIATE ATHLETICS

Faculty Committee on Athletics It is general practice for a faculty committee on athletics (with this or a similar title) to be responsible for determining athletic policies and giving guidance to the intercollegiate athletic program. This committee can perform several other specific functions, such as advising the president on athletic matters; providing a close liaison with faculty, students, and friends; maintaining educational objectives; and serving as a buffer against possible outside pressures.

This group of faculty members may either be appointed, elected, or both. The term "faculty committee" may in some instances be a misnomer since alumni, trustees, and students may also be members. The committee then becomes a reflection of institutional philosophy and general objectives, whether the faculty members give the guidance or whether nonfaculty members provide leadership. In some institutions, the board of athletic control is of composite membership and is not subject to faculty control. If intercollegiate athletics is to operate as a part of the educational institution, the athletic committee or council should be composed of faculty members representing a cross section of the faculty rather than individuals who are handpicked for their prejudices or misguided loyalties. They should be elected, or at least a good proportion should be elected. The policy of heaping "fringe benefits" on faculty athletic-committee members and selected administrative officials also needs study. The giving of special compensations to these committee members is an irregular and inconsistent practice on college campuses and sometimes presents additional problems. The committee cannot become a "rubber stamp" if proper guidance is to be given to intercollegiate athletics. The decision must also be made as to whether the committee is to be policy-making and advisory or whether it is to have implementative or administrative functions. The trend is definitely toward advisory and policy-making duties. The dividing line between policy making and implementation is not always clear cut; therefore, the committee or board may become administrative in nature. This group may establish policies on such matters as budgets, grants in aid, scholarships, schedules, recruitment and retention of student athletes, counseling and guidance of student athletes, eligibility, awards, public relations, and ticket distribution, to mention a few. In the final analysis, however, the president of the institution must represent the basic and final control of intercollegiate athletics. The director of athletics should have direct access to the president in order to interpret and implement policies and programs. The function and makeup of the faculty committee must be clearly defined.

Regional Conference Intercollegiate athletics are governed by the objectives, rules, and regulations of the appropriate regional conference and national athletic associations.

The individual institutions that belong to regional athletic conferences have rules and regulations that have been developed for and by members of their athletic conference. These rules must be followed.

These rules and regulations are generally printed in the form of "operating codes" which are constantly revised as the need arises. The codes will generally include detailed rules concerning recruiting, amateur status, financial aid, academic and athletic eligibility, athletic contests and management, and general rules concerning awards, spectator control, and public relations.

Conference Commissioners In the more affluent regional conferences, the office of the commissioner carries with it important responsibilities in interpretation or application of the rules and regulations, assignment of officials, and overall promotion of the conference.

The faculty representative of the faculty committee on athletics and the director of intercollegiate athletics are generally the representatives to regional conference meetings, with one being appointed as the voting member.

National Collegiate Athletic Association The National Collegiate Athletic Association is a voluntary organization made up of collegiate institutions and affiliated associations. It crosses regional lines in the promotion and administration of intercollegiate athletics. It serves various purposes and provides a variety of services to the institutions in the college and university divisions. In the endeavors of constituent members to improve athletics, encourage the adoption of and compliance with rules and regulations, and maintain athletics on a high plane, the NCAA serves as the overall national discussion, legislative, and administrative body for colleges and universities. Another important aspect of the NCAA is the cooperative enforcement machinery it maintains together with its member institutions. This is best explained by a direct quotation from the NCAA Manual [5]:

> Individuals employed by or associated with member institutions for the administration, the conduct or the coaching of intercollegiate athletics are, in the final analysis, teachers of young people. Their responsibility is an affirmative one and they must do more than avoid improper conduct or questionable acts. Their own moral values must be so certain and positive that those younger and more pliable will be influenced by a fine example. Much more is expected of them than of the less critically placed citizen.
>
> All representatives of educational institutions are expected to cooperate fully with the NCAA Committee on Infractions and Council to further the objectives of the Association and its enforcement program. The enforcement program should be considered as a joint enterprise requiring full and complete disclosure by all institutional representatives of any relevant information requested by the NCAA Committee on Infractions and Council during the course of an inquiry.

National Association of Intercollegiate Athletics The National Association of Intercollegiate Athletics is known as the "small college" organization. In terms of athletics, a small college is defined as one whose administrative policies dictate that it compete with institutions below the major competition level. A stated major function of the NAIA is that of providing a program within which institutions can be recognized for skill and achievement without being subjected to the pressures and educational inconsistencies involved in attempting to live beyond their means. There is a very active faculty athletic representative and a College Presidents' Committee which concentrate on this aim. The emphasis is on having athletics remain an integral part of the total educational program. As a general policy, they favor physical education and athletics under one administrative head.

ADVANTAGES OF CONFERENCE MEMBERSHIP

The advantages of conference memberships can best be judged by the commonly stated purposes and services of the conferences, both regional and national, as given below:

1. To recognize and uphold the principle of institutional control and responsibility for intercollegiate sports in conformity with the constitutions and by-laws of the Associations.
2. To stimulate and promote intercollegiate sports.
3. To aid in scheduling contests and extra-season events.

4. To encourage the adoption and enforcement of uniform rules and regulations dealing with financial aid, recruiting, scheduling, amateur standing, and good sportsmanship.
5. To promote fair, clean, evenly matched competition among institutions which have similar policies regarding the conduct of intercollegiate athletics.
6. To formulate, copyright and publish rules of play governing collegiate sports.
7. To preserve and publish collegiate athletic records.
8. To supervise regional and national athletic contests indirectly or directly under the control of the regional and national association.
9. To legislate through by-laws or resolutions of a conference meeting or convention upon any subjects of concern to the members.
10. To represent the colleges or universities before the Congress of the United States in legislative matters involving collegiate sports or television and other commercial companies bidding for salable rights.
11. To assist in procuring or administering group travel and medical insurance programs for student-athletes.
12. To serve as a clearing house, conduct surveys and studies, and to cooperate in developing solutions to athletic problems.
13. To assist the various coaching and administrative associations in providing better competition and sounder administration.
14. To study possible rules infractions, recommend penalties, and establish an effective enforcement program.

Since a large majority of colleges and universities are allied in regional and national conferences, the advantages of conference membership seem to be clear. There are a few so-called "independent" institutions on the regional level, but practically none on the national level. The question, therefore, seems to be how the member schools can improve the status of intercollegiate athletics through their cooperative efforts.

PRINCIPLES, POLICIES, AND REGULATIONS FOR INTERCOLLEGIATE ATHLETICS

Regional and national conferences have developed principles and regulations concerning interrelated problems such as recruitment, financial aid, academic standards for admission and retention, and amateur status. Regional conferences have developed standards of their own, but these cannot be lower than those of the national conferences. There is a great deal of similarity among like institutions. This, again, is one of the chief advantages of membership in a strong conference.

Even though there is a range of operation from the so-called "simon-pure" athletic program to the highly structured program geared toward major competition, there are several basic principles for the conduct of intercollegiate athletics. The cynics or realists would say that much of the actual operation is relative and that there is a great deal of lip service and empty rhetoric. However, the codes are quite specific for the member schools. With official interpretations and continual study of the codes, there should be no excuse for violation of the rules and regulations. The complete codes will not be reproduced here since the college and university people responsible for intercollegiate athletic programs will have copies and are responsible for seeing that the provisions are carried out. However, it must be made crystal clear from the university or college president on down through channels that the spirit and letter of the rules must be upheld if the persons involved are to continue in intercollegiate athletics.

Principles for Conduct of Intercollegiate Athletics The National Collegiate Athletic Association through its constituent members has developed a set of "Principles for the Conduct of Intercollegiate Athletics" which are extremely helpful in the administration of intercollegiate athletics [5]. These "Principles" appear in the *NCAA Manual.* They are reproduced below, either in part or in toto:

1. *Principle of Amateurism and Student Participation.* An amateur student-athlete is one who engages in athletics for the physical, mental, social and educational benefits he derives therefrom, and to whom athletics is an avocation. One who takes or has taken pay, or has accepted the promise of pay, in any form, for participation in athletics or has directly or indirectly used his athletic skill for pay in any form shall not be eligible for intercollegiate athletics; it being understood that a student-athlete may accept scholarships or educational grants-in-aid from his institution provided such aid is not in conflict with the governing legislation of this Association.

2. *Principle of Sound Academic Standards.* A student-athlete shall not represent his institution in intercollegiate athletic competition unless he has been admitted in accordance with the regular published entrance requirements of that institution; unless he is in good academic standing as determined by the faculty of that institution, and unless he is maintaining satisfactory progress toward a degree as determined by the regulations of that institution.

4. *Principle Governing Financial Aid*

a. Any student-athlete who receives financial assistance other than that administered by his institution shall not be eligible for intercollegiate competition; provided, however, that this principle shall have no application to assistance received from anyone upon whom the student-athlete is naturally or legally dependent, nor shall it have application to any financial assistance awarded on bases having no relationship whatsoever to athletic ability.

b. When unearned financial aid is awarded to a student and athletic ability is taken into consideration in making the award, such aid combined with other aid the student-athlete may receive from employment during semester of term time, other scholarships and grants-in-aid (including governmental grants for educational purposes) and like sources, may not exceed commonly accepted educational expenses. Benefits received by student-athletes under the G.I. Bill of Rights need not be counted in computing the maximum allowable financial aid under this section.

c. In all cases, the institutional agency making the award of aid shall give the recipient a written statement of the amount, duration, conditions and terms thereof.

5. *Principle Governing Recruitment.* The recruitment of student-athletes shall be controlled by by-laws enacted by the Association.

6. *Principle of Ethical Conduct.* It shall be a member institution's responsibility to apply and enforce the following principles:

a. Individuals employed by or associated with a member institution for the administration, the conduct or the coaching of intercollegiate athletics, and students competing in intercollegiate athletics shall deport themselves with honesty and sportsmanship at all times to the end that intercollegiate athletics, as a whole, their institutions and they, as individuals, shall stand for the honor and dignity of fair play, and the generally recognized high standards associated with wholesome competitive sports.

b. Staff members of the athletic department of a member institution shall not accept compensation, directly or indirectly, for the scouting of athletic talent or the negotiating of talent contracts for professional sports organizations.

7. *Principle Governing Competition in Post-season and Non-collegiate-sponsored Contests.* Competition by member institutions in post-season contests and in contests, meets and tournaments which are not sponsored, promoted, managed and controlled by a collegiate entity shall conform to the provisions of this Constitution and to the rules or regulations prescribed by the by-laws of the Association.

8. *Principle Governing Playing and Practice Seasons.* Organized practice and playing seasons in football and basketball shall be controlled by by-laws enacted by the Association.

9. *Principle of Educational Objective of Intercollegiate Athletics.* The competitive athletic programs of the colleges are designed as a vital part of the educational system. A basic purpose of this Association is to maintain intercollegiate athletics as an inte-

gral part of the student body, and, by so doing, retain a clear line of demarcation between college athletics and professional sports.

10. *Principle Governing the Eligibility of Student-Athletes.* An institution shall not permit a student-athlete to represent it in intercollegiate athletic competition unless he meets specified requirements for athletics. These requirements must be known and observed.

Recruitment Two of the most crucial problems facing intercollegiate athletics are the recruitment of athletes and financial aid to athletes. A majority of the disciplinary actions taken by the NCAA involve infractions of recruiting regulations. Because of highly competitive recruitment practices by alumni, school officials, students, and coaches, the student athlete as well as the institution can be placed in some untenable positions.

The following questions regarding potentially dangerous situations were posed at the 1962 Second National Athletic Directors Conference [6]:

1. Are your athletes academic liabilities?
2. Are players given courses designed only to maintain their status as students?
3. Are your players being conditioned to illegality by the recruitment methods being employed?
4. Do the athletes attending your school truly intend to obtain a college education?
5. Are the members of your athletic teams being treated academically the same as other students?
6. How many of your athletes actually stay to graduate after they finish college sports?
7. Have those ball players who do receive a degree actually acquired what is generally understood to be a college education?
8. Does the position of your coach depend upon his win-and-loss record?

The right answers to these questions and strict adherence to other sound principles governing recruiting are necessary for the welfare of the institution, the student athlete, and intercollegiate athletics.

There is some agitation for the discontinuance of recruitment of student athletes solely on the basis of their athletic prowess. There are good arguments for establishing a central admissions office which will recruit all students under the same policies and procedures. This approach would theoretically prevent athletic personnel from soliciting or recruiting student athletes either indirectly or directly. Subsidization would be the same for all students and money would not be made available for visiting and entertaining student athletes. Some schools purport to follow this procedure or to have similar plans in operation.

Until the time, however, that the regional conferences, colleges, and universities will accept and follow uniform recruitment procedures for all students, other guidelines and regulations should be followed closely. Regional and national conferences have adopted specific rules governing recruiting. These regulations generally state that financial aid or equivalent inducements must remain within stated limits. All funds should be deposited and handled by the institutions. Outside organizations, agencies, individuals, or groups should not administer or expend funds for recruiting. Practice sessions or workouts on the campus by the prospective student athlete are not allowed. Travel and expense money may not be provided for the student-athlete's relatives or friends to visit the campus or go elsewhere. Visitation is limited to one trip to the campus and the length of the visit is limited. Procedures for contacting high school students and student athletes at other collegiate institutions are prescribed.

The effectiveness of regulations governing recruitment practices and procedures should be evaluated constantly. The cycle of recruiting the top student athletes to win more games which will bring in more money and prestige to make possible the recruitment of more student athletes who will, in turn, win more games, places a tremendous premium on recruitment, and it will continue to do so as long as this highly competitive system exists.

Financial Aid It is almost impossible to discuss recruiting without including a discussion of financial aid or subsidization of the student athlete. Some general regulations and principles have already been listed.

There are also conflicting philosophies concerning the subsidization of athletes because of the competition for athletic skill and the pressure for athletic victories. As the number of students mounts and more strain is placed on facilities, equipment, curricula, and faculty, the justification for subsidization is increasingly questioned. The amount of aid to the student athlete may become disproportionate and may limit the scholarship funds available to other students. Where profit from the athletic enterprise is used for subsidies, will the evaluation of the financial structure of the athletic department by a certified public accountant show actual net profits or will much of the profit be "paper" or "bookkeeping" profits? Should not institutions award scholarships or grants in aid on the basis of academic ability and/or economic need? It is held that subsidization sometimes promotes an overemphasis on winning and that the donors in "booster clubs" become most unhappy and vociferous when losses occur.

Again, until such time as there is general agreement among institutions that scholarships or grants in aid will be awarded to all students on the same basis, existing regulations should be followed by members of regional and national conferences. There should be no excuses or pampering of violators where the regulations are specific. There seems to be a need for additional study and evaluation of present practices by responsible faculty athletic committees and athletic administrators. The results of any proposed action will need to be comparable and uniform among all like institutions. The "status symbol" is a powerful motive.

RETENTION AND GUIDANCE OF STUDENT ATHLETES

Careful Selection of Student Athletes The retention and guidance of student athletes will certainly be facilitated by selection and admission requirements that are sufficiently high to confirm the candidate's ability to take a degree. The same admission standards should apply for all students. These admission standards should be enforced by the university admissions personnel. The student athlete who is both physically and mentally endowed must somehow be the sole objective of every athletic department. Fortunately, faculties and coaches are enforcing higher standards, and selection of student athletes is much more restrictive than it was in the past.

Careful Selection of Administrator and Coaches One of the primary responsibilities of the administration is to employ competent, well-prepared coaches with integrity who will exert a positive influence on the college student. The director of athletics is the key, since his philosophy and resulting action must be slanted toward this objective. Superior physical performance by the student athlete requires concentration, some innate ability, dedicated practice and training, effective motivation, and superior teaching. Therefore, great care must be exercised in the selection of the coaching staff. The coach must be able to inspire his players to see the importance of an education and encourage them to achieve academic success. Most coaches take great pride in the academic attainments of their players as well as in their athletic prowess.

Faculty Committee on Athletics Provides Supervision The faculty committee or council on athletics should provide academic supervision of the educational aspects of the athletic program. Improper scheduling and too much absenteeism for classes play havoc with the student athlete's academic performance. Most regional conferences have studied this problem and have passed general "guidelines" which limit excessive scheduling. Since some of these guidelines are permissive in nature, the athletic committee or council should assure that absences from classes are held to a minimum. This is especially true in some of the winter and spring sports that require heavy schedules in short spaces of time with postponed games that must be rescheduled and played later. Careful attention to proper counseling and cooperation by the major academic departments are essential. Athletic personnel should not recommend any course or procedure that is not within the policy and sequential program of the appropriate department. Student athletes should be referred to their major advisors and should be encouraged to fulfill their academic obligations.

Counseling Is Important Many of the intercollegiate athletic departments select one or more academic counselors or assign one or more staff members for student athletes. This advisory function should not take precedence over that of the academic department, but it should be coordinated with the faculty. Supervised study periods and tutors are also common. If tutors are used, they should be selected after consultation with the academic departments involved. Approval from the department involved should be secured before assignments are made.

The retention of student athletes is somewhat like preventive medicine. Every appropriate measure should be taken before attrition occurs. Athletic personnel should never be allowed to exert any pressures on members of the faculty or on departments for the purpose of influencing the grades of athletes. The securing of favors for student athletes either directly or indirectly should never be tolerated.

It also should go without saying that student athletes should meet the same conditions that other students must meet in order to retain financial aid and get satisfactory grades.

MANAGEMENT AND CONDUCT OF INTERCOLLEGIATE ATHLETICS

The director of athletics should develop a sequential set of procedures for the efficient staging of athletic events. The 1959 Athletic Directors' National Conference developed the following seven chronological steps [3]: (1) the contract for each event; (2) the selection of officials; (3) the preparation of facilities for the event; (4) arrangement for hosting the visiting team and the officials; (5) arrangement for spectators; (6) services; and (7) details of game closure and final summary. For each of the seven phases of management, certain general principles were listed by the athletic directors in colleges and universities of varying sizes or circumstances. This *Conference Report* and other basic textbooks on administration will give pages of check-list items for the pregame and postgame details. The many problems that may arise need to be anticipated, and arrangements should be made to avoid them.

Scheduling Besides the efficient staging of athletic events, the scheduling of athletic contests with like institutions is a sane and logical approach to good competition. The objectives as well as the procedures of intercollegiate athletics should be similar. Opening dates for practice, off-season practice, the use of freshmen and transfer students, selection of officials, facilities, night or day games, on- or off-campus sites, seating arrangements and spectator relations, concessions, radio, press and television coverage, difficulty of schedule, and gate receipts are some of the other considerations that enter into scheduling policies. The general rule of "what is in the best interests of the students and the institutions" should not be bypassed for the more materialistic objectives of ratings, possible athletic success, and financial rewards. Any emphasis on false values or the fickleness of ratings can become a boomerang and may undermine the basis for good student-faculty-alumni relationships. One has only to remember losing the "big" game or the losing season to realize the meaning of unstableness among sports fans and its many repercussions.

Pregame, Game, and Postgame Details The director of intercollegiate athletics and his delegated assistants are responsible for the myriads of details involved in the management of athletic contests. The check lists should be cumulative and kept up to date. Even with complete check lists, the athletic director should go one step beyond by trying to anticipate problems that might arise and to take precautionary measures to avoid these problems. For example, special emergency personnel should be on a standby basis. The electrical services may be functioning fine before the game, but a short circuit may occur or a fuse may blow with overloading. An electrician can save serious embarrassment. Nurses, physicians, and ambulance service may also prevent fatalities.

The preparation of the physical plant and the readying of equipment and playing facilities require extensive planning. Sometimes, long-range planning for capital improvement, location of the site, traffic patterns, parking areas, and actual construction can alleviate many problems. The reverse may also be costly in good public relations and income.

Planning and handling officials; visiting and host teams; visiting and home officials; press, radio, and TV personnel; and spectators are most important to an efficient and smooth operation. The public-relations impact is most potent.

BUSINESS POLICIES AND PROCEDURES

Financing Intercollegiate Athletics The financing of intercollegiate athletics must be under the control of the college or university. Actual management practices should be channeled through the financial structure of the institution.

There are many ways of financing athletic programs. Policies and procedures generally reflect the objectives and philosophy of the institution. Financial support and procedures are basic to the implementation of the program. The main sources of income for athletics are scholarship or grant-in-aid funds, gate receipts, concessions, general university funds, booster club donations, game programs, alumni funds, student fees, television and radio fees (for a small number of the schools in major competition), and guarantees (generally reciprocal arrangements).

There are also indirect methods of financing athletics, such as the transference of capital improvement, maintenance of facilities, and cost of utilities to other budgets. Other bookkeeping methods may be used to charge salaries of custodians, combination instructor/coaches, and administrators to other budgets. In some instances, rooms for student athletes and tuition charges may be written off and not charged as disbursements against the athletic department.

Methods of direct or indirect financing vary from school to school. Again, they are dependent upon the individual school, which is free to decide its own course of action as long as the rules of the conferences are upheld. Where cooperative working arrangements exist between the physical education department and the intercollegiate athletic department, separate budgets are generally developed for each area to facilitate fiscal procedures. It is rather difficult to apportion equitable costs to each department where there is overlapping use of facilities, equipment, and personnel. Some schools have utilized certified public accountants to study assets and liabilities and to offer analyses of profits, losses, or budget procedures. Such analyses sometimes reveal surprising facts about the quantities of general school or state funds that are being used for intercollegiate athletics and about the size of income in excess of expenses.

Where possible, financing of intercollegiate athletics should come from college or university general funds. This statement implies no slight to the importance of gate receipts, contributions, and other sources of financial support. Budgetary allotments should be authorized and guaranteed in the same manner as for other departments. The preparation and administration of the budget should be guided by a systematic effort to carry out the type of program that is desired by the individual institution of higher learning.

There are several alternative systems for the preparation and administration of the budget. One possible system would employ a *budget code,* as follows:

BUDGET CODE

1000—General Administration	01—Faculty
	02—Staff
1100—Baseball	03—Student help
	04—Graduate assistants
1200—Basketball	05—Public relations
	06—Printing, promotion
1300—Golf	
	11—Freight and express
1400—Hockey	12—Postage
	13—Telephone and telegraph
1500—Lacrosse	14—Dues and subscriptions
1600—Skiing	16—Office supplies
	17—Banquet
1700—Track-Cross Country	18—Awards
1800—Tennis	21—Conference/s
1900—Band	25—Insurance
2000—Intramurals and Recreation	30—Supplies (expendable)
	31—Equipment (lifetime of 5 years or more)
2100—Physical Education for Men	32—Maintenance of supplies
	33—Maintenance of facilities and equipment
2200—Physical Education for Women	34—Laundry
	35—New facilities
2300—Rugby	36—Renovation of facilities
2400—Soccer	40—Intramural sports game expense
	41—Freshman game expense
	42—Varsity game expense
	43—Medical supplies
	44—Medical services
	45—Movies and films
	46—Guarantees and options
	47—Tickets and schedules
	48—Programs
	49—Cheerleaders
	51—Recruitment
	52—Scouting
	53—Staff travel
	54—Conventions
	55—Freshman team travel
	56—Varsity team travel

With this system, each department or activity has a specific code number (left-hand column) with accountability made possible by combining it with the appropriate classification from the right-hand column. For example, the purchase of 100 dozen practice golf balls for the Department of Physical Education for Men would look like this on a ledger page:

2100–30		Supplies	Total–$3,400
7-6-68	P.O. 1723–100 doz range golf balls @ $3.		$3,100

Each department or activity would have a day-to-day cumulative balance with a minimum expenditure of time and effort on the part of the appropriate administrator. Experience over a period of years would give the administrators an evaluative tool as to how the money is being spent by categories and by departments or activities. This budget information would also serve as a reliable basis for estimating future budgetary needs.

Specific items required to operate complete programs in these areas are listed in some of the more recent textbooks on administration. One of the better sources is the book entitled *Equipment and Supplies for Athletics, Physical Education and Recreation* [7].

PLANNING, CONSTRUCTION, AND MAINTENANCE OF ATHLETIC FACILITIES

Need for Planning Physical education and athletic facilities require large investments of money, space, time, and personnel in their planning, construction, and maintenance. There are no shortcuts to proper planning and maintenance. If these special areas, both indoor and outdoor, are to meet the multiple-use needs of ever-expanding numbers of students and faculty, there should be immediate and long-range plans. The personnel involved in these special areas should play a leading role in university-wide planning. They should not only know the needs of the programs involved but should be knowledgeable about planning facilities.

Recognition of Philosophy and Scope of Program One of the first steps in planning is the recognition of the philosophy, nature, and scope of the programs for which the facilities are to be designed and constructed. A carefully delineated and functional plan should be worked out specifying the type of facility that is wanted, the use to which it will be put, and the way in which it will fit into the overall program. Questions such as the following must be resolved: Is the facility to serve for physical education, recreation, and intercollegiate athletics? Is it to be used by men and women? Is it to be used chiefly as an intercollegiate athletic center and entertainment facility? Is the multiple-use factor and planning for it to be controlled by the intercollegiate athletics department or by the physical-education department?

Multi-use Building Since the majority of buildings must be multi-use facilities, facilities should be planned so that each phase of the program receives proper emphasis. Units should be sufficient in kind and number to provide opportunities for peak-load participation. They should be planned to meet the needs for coordinated use by men and women in physical education and recreation. Intercollegiate athletic practice and competition should be planned so that spectator loads may be handled with a minimum of interference with the functional use of the entire plant.

Buildings for Intercollegiate Athletics Buildings for intercollegiate athletics may serve only one purpose or they may be constructed to serve several purposes. These facilities may adjoin the physical education building, they may be connected in a complex, or they may be located at fringe areas where the traffic pattern is advantageous and there is plenty of parking space. There are at least four basic types of buildings that are possible either as separate buildings or in related combinations:

1. *The fieldhouse* was originally designed to provide a dirt surface indoors so that early-season practice could go on despite unfavorable climatic conditions. In recent years, many new synthetic surfaces have been used instead of dirt floors and multi-use, as for indoor basketball, track competition, and other mass meetings, has been common.

2. *The arena* is a structure providing mass seating for spectators around an activity area. An arena can be used for competitive events and also for exhibitions, concerts, commencement exercises, and mass meetings.

3. *Ice-skating arenas,* either indoor or outdoor, are becoming more common. Modern technology is making its impact with the provision of artificial ice which makes it possible to extend the ice season from 5 to 12 months. An enclosed ice arena can also be a practical physical education/athletic facility for use during the ice season for instruction, recreation, and competition. Out of the ice season, it can be used for many purposes, like the arena described earlier.

4. *The stadium* is a permanent seating structure around a sports field for viewing sports events and other activities. The program or sport dictates the structure. Many earlier stadiums included a track around the football field, but there seems to be a trend now to separate the two.

Basic Outline for Planning In all planning, there are general rules and a basic outline that should be followed. Planning functions must be carefully organized. The professional planning group, either on the basis of a retainer fee or as part of an extensive long-range study of the university, should develop a master plan for the university. This should be done in collaboration with the project planning committee, which will furnish an overall view and establish general guidelines. These two groups should work closely together. In some instances, a campus planning committee may be the sole group to establish long-range plans and a master plan. After the responsible planning groups have been selected, adherence to the following brief outline of planning procedures might offer guidance and prevent some mistakes:

A. A planning committee should be selected only after careful consideration of the program specialists and the varied interests of the college or university.
   1. The chairman and the key members should be those who will use the completed facility.
   2. Other faculty members not on committees should be called in on a consultant basis from time to time.
   3. Services of professional consultants should be cleared and financed.
   4. Committee members should have responsibilities delegated to them so that their time and talent may be utilized efficiently.

B. Present and future facility needs should be determined.
   1. Future enrollments and population trends should be studied.
   2. Programs must be clearly defined and the following basic facts should be stated and accepted:
      a. Number and type of student athlete scholarships or grants in aid to be awarded
      b. Number and type of sports to be included
      c. Basic and elective physical education requirements for all students
      d. Intramural sports and recreation programs for students and faculty
      e. Undergraduate and graduate programs to be included
   3. A survey of existing facilities, sites, topography, traffic patterns, and parking space should be made.
   4. A thorough screening of available literature is in order, including such works as the *College and University Facilities Guide* [8].
   5. Personal visits to other existing plants should be made to save money and prevent mistakes.

C. Financial resources should be explained to all parties concerned.
   1. Sources of financing should be explained, including:
      a. Capital funds
      b. Student fees

   c. Federal or state funds
   d. Foundation grants or private donations
   e. Combination of (*c*) and (*d*)
2. If resources are limited or if bid costs exceed resources, alternate plans should be made.

D. An architect who has experience, ability, and a reputation for honesty should be selected. This is of utmost importance.
1. Screening of the architect's work and staff should be careful and complete.
2. The architect should be able to interpret the program into functional and economical use.
3. The campus planning committee or board of trustees should make the final selection.

E. Selection of the building site should be the result of a great deal of study and consideration.
1. The location, size, topography, traffic flow, soil condition and drainage, parking areas, costs, and relationships to other parts of the campus are important and should be considered.
2. Program specialists, engineers, campus planning committees, and architects should be involved.

F. Plans for the number and variety of teaching stations and related areas should be outlined after careful study of needs and proposed programs.
1. An outline of teaching stations and related areas should be given to the architect.
2. A check list of common conveniences and special features for each area should also be made available to the architect and his staff.
3. Discussions should be held with the architect and his staff.
4. Formulas for determining dimensions and square footage are helpful and should be worked out. The *College and University Facilities Guide* has formulas for predicting needs for both indoor and outdoor square footage. Room for growth and individual needs should be taken into consideration, such as the breadth of the intramural program or the seating capacity.
5. Schematic drawings by the architect (preliminary interpretations of the programs) are next in order.
6. A review of these drawings and sketches may involve many meetings, discussions, and revisions.
7. Specifications for materials, finishes, equipment, and special construction features must be developed through further discussion.

G. The official acceptance of the working drawings and specifications should allow plenty of time for the architect and staff to complete the final plans and specifications.
1. Adequate time for writing the specifications should be provided. This will save many change orders and prevent shortcuts or the use of inferior materials.
2. The quality of the specifications also gives confidence to bidders.

H. Arrangements must be made to initiate bidding procedures and the awarding of the contract. This requires finalization of building costs and official confirmation by the appropriate bodies.

I. Construction must be supervised and inspected as a matter of course and a part of good business.

J. Plans should be made for proper maintenance, custodial services, and keying of the building.

K. Plans must also be made for occupancy and utilization of areas, purchasing of equipment not mentioned in the contract, assignment of offices, and the establishment of policies governing use.

L. The acceptance of the building should come only after a careful inspection made after all necessary construction has been completed.
1. There should be an inspection of the building before the guarantee period is over.
2. Ethical contractors carry a reserve for work and adjustments that must be made during the guarantee period.

PUBLIC RELATIONS AND PUBLICITY

Definition and Importance One of the simplest definitions of public relations is "anything that one says or does that results in reactions by the individual and group." Hopefully, the reactions will be beneficial and will engender goodwill and support for intercollegiate athletics. A good public-relations program utilizing the appropriate media should be given top priority by the administrator of intercollegiate athletics. The athletic program is continuously in the limelight and is probably the greatest rallying point for students, faculty, alumni, and friends. The image engendered by good public relations may have other effects such as influencing students to select a specific college or university, encouraging support from persons and organizations, serving as a source of pride to alumni and supporters, and improving relationships with the public. There also seems to be an "emotional irrationality" among some sports fans that needs constant attention. One incident resulting from poor public relations may get a disproportionate amount of adverse publicity or unfavorable reaction. It is, then, the sum total of publicity from all of the media that is important and creates the final image.

Sports Information, Personnel, and Relationships One of the most important means of achieving good public relations is a good sound program and the concerted team effort of all personnel from the director and the sports information director to all personnel and players. A good athletic program is sometimes considered the only public-relations program that is needed. It is true that this is a most effective agent, but it is not as complete as is needed.

A good public-relations program needs careful planning and organization. It should be beneficial to have this plan in writing with all staff members conversant with the overall plan. The public-relations plan should be consistent with the type of institution and its goals. It must be realized, too, that a distortion of the academic program, the institution's image, and the welfare of student athletes may be possible with an oversubsidized publicity program for athletics. This is especially true where the athletic program may be financed well beyond the range of similar academic programs. This may be a relative matter, too, since the overall public-relations program of the college or university may not be supported to the same degree. In other words, all phases of the institution's programs should be carefully planned and carried out.

Public-relations Media Media for public relations are almost unlimited. Many techniques for utilizing these media are available. A listing of some of the more common media may serve as an evaluation tool or as a check list for other possibilities:

1. Publications
   a. Alumni and institutional bulletins and magazines
   b. Brochures, flyers, newsletters, booklets, handbooks, and programs
   c. Yearbooks, catalogs, and special celebration and promotional editions
   d. National magazines, regional and national conference publications
2. News releases
   a. Student, local, state, and national news services and departmental releases
   b. Regional and national conference records and news releases

3. Radio and television
   a. Local, state, regional, and national radio and television programs
   b. Regional and national conference programs
   c. Relationships with television and radio personnel
4. Personal and special services
   a. Student, faculty, alumni, and public relationships
   b. Clinics, demonstrations, conferences, and summer camps for children
   c. Talks, banquets, interest and campus clubs
   d. Recruitment organization and contacts with secondary schools and alumni
5. Audiovisual aids and techniques
   a. Practice and game films
   b. Training and technique films
   c. Bulletin boards, billboards, and varied pictorial displays
   d. Audio tapes, television programs
6. Miscellaneous
   a. Direct mail, telephone, and ticket campaigns
   b. Rallies, parades, and special events
   c. Courteous and fair treatment of students, faculty, and public at contests
   d. Housing and privileges of student athletes on campus
   e. Use of facilities for programs other than intercollegiate athletics
   f. Advertisement through selected media

Continuous Program The success of a well-planned and well-implemented public-relations program must be continuous. The attainment of the specific objectives of intercollegiate athletics and the general objectives of the institution should be in balance. In a sense, good public relations is a way of life. This way of life must be worthy of the dignity and standards of an institution of higher learning.

HEALTH ASPECTS

Safeguarding the student athlete's health, providing for his proper conditioning, and the prevention and care of injuries are essential to any athletic program. Competitive athletics demands the maximum of effort and efficiency and requires concentrated training and maintenance programs. Many sports involve body contact as well as grueling routines, which also increase the possibilities for athletic injuries.

Organization of Athletic Medical Team A good athletic medical team requires coordination and cooperation between health services, athletic trainers, coaches, and the administration. In organizing the medical staff, the selection of highly trained, experienced, and interested personnel is the ideal approach. Medical staffs can be of three basic types: (1) those that provide full coverage, (2) those that provide partial coverage, and (3) those that provide minimal coverage. The medical needs of the student athlete should be met either by the athletic medical team or by means of adequate provision for services from outside the institution. An adequate medical staff should consist of the following:

1. An athletic trainer who has had practical as well as formal training in first aid and physiotherapy. Ideally, he should be a registered physical therapist. Assistant trainers, some of whom may be advanced student trainers, should work under the direction of the senior trainer.
2. A dentist should be available to care for injuries to the teeth and mouth.
3. A team of physicians who have an interest in athletics and the athlete is important. Generally, 90 percent of the medical problems can be handled by an internist and an orthopedist.

Needs for Adequate Health Service Program Some of the things that are needed for an adequate health-service program are:

1. Preseason examinations. These examinations should be thorough. They should uncover any physical impairments which would be aggravated by strenuous activities.

2. Special consultations and follow-ups. These should ensue from the above examinations.

3. Special equipment, such as contact lenses, mouth guards, and braces, for those who require it.

4. Immunizations.

5. Provisions for the care of different types of injuries and illnesses. There will be minor injuries such as simple contusions, abrasions, and sprains. Some injuries, unfortunately, may require the services of a physician, consultations with specialists, and hospitalization.

6. Emergency care at scrimmages and games both at home and on the road. A physician should be present at all scrimmages and games or he should at least be available in case of serious injuries.

7. A trainer who is prepared to recognize and refer injuries to appropriate medical or dental personnel. He should demand strict adherence to the principles of good health, proper conditioning, and treatment prescribed by the physician. He should be skilled in preventive and supportive taping procedures, application of heat, and exercise.

8. A physician whose authority in medical decisions regarding the student athlete is absolute and unquestioned. After a significant injury or illness, the physician should prescribe the treatment and determine when the athlete is ready to return to the scrimmage or game. The recurrence of an injury can be more serious than the original injury.

Health and Safety of the Student Athlete The safety and health of the student athlete should have top priority in intercollegiate athletics. The organization of the medical team and the plans made by it are important steps, but these are not sufficient by themselves. There are other requisites.

The Committee on Injury in Sports of the American Medical Association has developed a "Bill of Rights for the College Athlete" with provisions as follows:

> 1. *Good coaching:* The importance of good coaching in protecting the health and safety of athletes cannot be minimized. Technical instruction leading to a skillful performance is a significant factor in lowering the incidence and decreasing the severity of injuries. Also, good coaching includes the discouragement of tactics, outside either the rules or the spirit of the rules, which may increase the hazard and thus the incidence of injuries.
>
> 2. *Good officiating:* The rules and regulations governing athletic competition are made to protect players as well as to promote enjoyment of the game. To serve these ends effectively, the rules of the game must be thoroughly understood by players as well as coaches and be properly interpreted and enforced by impartial and technically qualified officials.
>
> 3. *Good equipment and facilities:* There can be no question about the protection afforded by proper equipment and right facilities. Good equipment is now available and is being improved continually; the problem lies in the false economy of using cheap, worn out, outmoded, or ill-fitting gear. Provision of proper areas for play and their careful maintenance are equally important. [9]

LEGAL AND LIABILITY RESPONSIBILITIES

Understanding of Laws Necessary The administrator of intercollegiate athletics should understand the legal and liability implications in the various aspects of the athletic program. Since the laws of the various states differ, it is important to become acquainted with the statutes and court decisions of the home state. Rulings may also be obtained from the state legal authorities where the meaning of the statutes is not clear. The administrator and entire staff should take the necessary precautions to prevent any case for liability from occurring. Administrators, coaches, and other personnel are becoming increasingly concerned about legal liabilities. Many cases are being decided in favor of the plaintiffs. The danger of liability for negligence rests heavily upon employees. This is especially true in private colleges and universities. State universities usually enjoy common law immunity, although the immunity law is being modified or waived by legislation.

Negligence Negligence, either through omission or commission, implies that someone has failed to act as a reasonably prudent and careful person. The legal wrong resulting from the possibility of negligence generally involves tort law. Thus, a tort is a legal wrong resulting in direct or indirect injury to another individual or to property. Negligence can be avoided if there is some common knowledge of basic legal principles, if danger is anticipated, if necessary precautions are taken, and if common sense is used. The administrator, coach, and teacher have a moral obligation as substitute parents (*in loco parentis*) to observe safe and recommended practices for all phases of an intercollegiate athletic program, such as medical care, conditioning and coaching techniques, maintenance of proper equipment and safe facilities, travel and insurance. In case of accident or injury, an established and regular procedure for the handling of the case as well as a detailed record of the accident or injury and the handling and treatment of the patient are wise provisions.

INSURANCE

In the college or university of today, it is not a question of whether there should be an insurance plan but of what kind of plan it should be and how it should be managed. Insurance plans that cover intercollegiate athletics are relatively scarce or quite expensive. In many instances, package plans for all students exclude varsity sports in their coverage. The payment of premiums varies from full payment by the student athlete or parent to full payment by the department of intercollegiate athletics. In other instances, the university may elect to cover itself from contingency funds rather than pay heavy premium dues. It is thus hoped that the total cost will be less in the long run. There may also be combinations of payment wherein medical and accident costs are absorbed with the purchase of catastrophe insurance. Insurance coverage is beginning to include hospitalization, X-ray films, and dental and medical fees as well as travel insurance and 24-hour accident coverage.

To meet the need for adequate coverage for the college and university student athlete, the National Collegiate Athletic Association sponsors an athletic medical insurance and death and dismemberment travel insurance. The plan has been most beneficial to colleges and universities.

Administrative, coaching and teaching personnel also need protection against being sued for accidents or injuries to student athletes. Some professional associations have sponsored this type of insurance, too, which has been most beneficial.

PURSUIT OF EXCELLENCE

The field of intercollegiate athletics subscribes as wholeheartedly to the pursuit of excellence as do other fields in higher education. Athletics is a social phenomenon that has limitless potential for developing some of the best qualities in mankind. Athletics is a vital part of the educational process and will undoubtedly remain so in the future. The organization and administration of intercollegiate athletics should be such as to ensure, insofar as possible, balance in the offerings and programs. There is a need to protect the program from its overzealous friends and supporters. There is a need to continually reevaluate objectives, principles, and policies in order that the great potentialities may be attained. The administrator of intercollegiate athletics, with the guidance of the president of the college or university as well as that of key committees and athletic personnel, should strive constantly toward this pursuit of excellence.

SELECTED REFERENCES

1. *Report of the 1967 NCAA Television Committee,* The National Collegiate Athletic Association, Kansas City, Mo.
2. "Graduate Education in Health, Physical Education, Recreation Education, Safety Education and Dance," *Report of a National Conference,* American Association for Health, Physical Education and Recreation, Washington, 1967.
3. *Report of Athletic Directors' National Conference,* American Association for Health, Physical Education, and Recreation, Washington, 1959.
4. *Official Handbook,* The National Association of Intercollegiate Athletics, Kansas City, Mo.
5. *Official NCAA Manual,* The National Collegiate Athletic Association, Kansas City, Mo., 1968.
6. "Athletic Administration in Colleges and Universities," *Report of Second National Athletic Directors' Conference,* American Association for Health, Physical Education, and Recreation, Washington, 1962.
7. *Equipment and Supplies for Athletics, Physical Education, and Recreation,* The Athletic Institute, Chicago, 1960.
8. *College and University Facilities Guide,* American Association for Health, Physical Education, and Recreation, Washington, 1968.
9. Farnsworth, Dana L. (ed.): *College Health Administration,* Appleton-Century-Crofts, Inc., New York, 1964.

Chapter 2

Intramural and Extramural Programs

JAMES W. LONG

Director, Division of Physical Education, Oregon State University, Corvallis, Oregon

MEANING OF INTRAMURALS

Almost everyone knows that "intramural" means "within the walls." However, the terminology and the extent of intramural programs are not understood quite as well. Terms such as intramural athletics, intramural sports, intramurals, and intramural activities are quite commonly used. Now, other terms have been added, such as recreational activities, recreation, co-recreation, sports clubs, extramural sports, and extramural activities. Then, too, the modern intramural sports program has expanded so greatly that it has been difficult to keep up with new objectives, new types of activities, and other interesting developments. Intramural programs of today are generally defined as including all physical recreational sports and activities which are sponsored by the intramural sports and recreation department. The "within the walls" or "on campus" restrictions still hold in the majority of programs sponsored by this department or unit.

PURPOSE OF PROGRAM

The objectives of intramural and recreation programs have broadened as the programs have grown. From a limited number of competitive team sports, the scope of intramurals and recreation has been expanded to include a wide variety of sports and recreational activities. The objectives parallel the objectives of education whether one uses the "seven cardinal principles" or the four well-known objectives of the Educational Policies Commission. Man's most important asset is his health and fitness. Participation in constructive, active physical recreation is essential to maintaining one's physical and mental efficiency. Mental therapy and physical relaxation go with physical conditioning. The importance of good human relations is borne out in many of the activities, which promote social growth and development and which call for group spirit, teamwork, loyalty, democratic participation, leadership, and adherence to principles of fair play and sportsmanship. The development and improvement of skills and interests increase the worthy use of leisure time. It is possible that some of the skills acquired will develop into lifelong leisure pursuits. Directing the abundant energy and enthusiasm of college students into socially approved activities should increase their awareness of civic responsibilities. This channeling of energies toward broad educational objectives through constructive participation in intramural and recreation programs should undoubtedly prevent many needless and questionable outbursts of energies in undesirable directions.

Place in University Life The intramural movement probably was started because of the interest of men who could not qualify for varsity teams but wanted to participate in team sports. There was a void between the required physical education program and the varsity sports program. The needs and interests of the majority of the students were not met, so the students began to form their own teams and to compete against one another. Difficulties soon arose from lack of supervision, equipment, officials, and facilities, so that intramural programs were generally placed under the control of the physical education department. Relationship with physical education departments made intramurals prosper. Instruction preceding intramural sports, competent leadership, and scheduling of contests and facilities by the professional group responsible for most of the facilities, equipment, and instruction was beneficial to the students' intramural activities. Women's physical education departments also adopted intramurals and recreation, but they were organized somewhat differently. As the programs expanded, recreational activities were added, and these have involved an increasing number of participants. The one distinguishing difference between intramurals and recreation is that intramurals are generally organized into mass competition through teams. Recreation is the voluntary participation in nonscheduled recreational activities. Intramurals are formally organized and scheduled for competition, while recreation is the voluntary pursuit of leisure-time activities on an informal basis. Intramurals and recreation have been accepted on college and university campuses as important parts of campus life.

Direction of Program Several interesting directions are developing for programs. Different patterns of administrative organizations have been set up. Professionally trained people have been delegated responsibility for administering the programs. Special buildings and outdoor facilities have been built for these programs. Special recreation fees or other means of financing have been provided. The philosophy of providing for individual differences and interests and a growing concern for a "program for all" have been prevalent. The faculty and staff are being included in the programs. Student leadership is being encouraged. The cooperation of many different groups and individuals has been needed as the programs have expanded. Many recreational facilities around the different housing complexes, both university and private, have been constructed, equipped, and put to use. Voluntary and informal recreational activities are becoming much more common. Co-recreation activities are increasing and fostering an understanding and appreciation of differences in skills between men and women. The interests and skills developed should increase participation in recreational activities which will carry over into adult life. Recreational clubs and sports clubs are making an impact on the intramural and recreational scene today. They are composed of individuals with considerable skill and high interest. Sports clubs are increasing in number. They differ from intramural groups in that they compete with like organizations both on and off campus. With this off-campus competition, many of the problems of intercollegiate athletics arise, such as those involved with equipment, travel funds and hazards, officiating, health and safety, and adequate supervision.

Extent of Program Studies show that intramural sports extend to as many as 80 different activities. The average range of activities is from 12 to 24, with 20 as the average number. These activities may be classified on the basis of team, individual, competitive, noncompetitive, recreational, social, outing, seasonal, and other categories.

The types and number of activities are selected and modified according to many local conditions. Climate and geographical assets are favorable to certain sports, such as winter sports or water sports. Geographical areas and schools within these areas have a nucleus of students with certain traditions and backgrounds that affect the type of program that is set up.

The types and number of facilities and the sort of equipment that is available also have a great deal to do with the selection of activities and the breadth of the program. Oftentimes, the presence of adequate facilities does not assure good programs, nor do inadequate facilities deter successful and comprehensive programs. All other things being equal, facilities that meet the needs of increasing numbers of students and faculty will certainly assure the best programs. The extent of the program is dependent to a large degree on the financial support which is manifested in leadership, supplies, equipment, variety of activities, and other essentials for success.

The National Conference on Intramural Sports for College Men and Women sponsored by the American Association for Health, Physical Education and Recreation, the National Association for Physical Education for College Women, and the College

Physical Education Association have pointed out that intramural activities should provide for the following:

1. The opportunity for offering the activity in such a manner as to provide fun and enjoyment for the participants.
2. The needs, interests, and abilities of the individual and of the group, including the handicapped, the commuter, the married student, and special interest groups.
3. The opportunity for experience in human relationships, such as cooperation, development of friendships, and acceptance of group responsibility.
4. The opportunity for development of desirable personality traits, such as perseverance, self-confidence, self-discipline, self-direction, courage, and ethical conduct.
5. The contribution to the physical development desirable for the optimal functioning of the individual in his environment, such as organic strength and neuro-muscular skills.
6. The inherent possibilities for adjustment of tensions and emotional strains.
7. The health protection and safeguards for individual well-being and safety.
8. The opportunity for men and women to participate together in wholesome play for continuing enjoyment and understanding.
9. The increased emphasis on individual and dual activities for the development of life-long interests in leisure-time activities.
10. The utilization of knowledge and skills which have accrued from the instructional program.
11. The opportunity for creative expression, such as that provided by dance forms, synchronized swimming, carnivals, and festivals.
12. The opportunity to understand and appreciate activities typical of one or both sexes in order to promote intelligent spectator enjoyment and common bonds of interest.
13. The utilization of the opportunities afforded by geographical location, climatic conditions, and community resources.
14. The increased emphasis on the various outing activities leading to understanding and appreciation necessary for optimum use and conservation of our great natural resources.
15. The potentiality for maximum development of student leadership and "followership." . . . Each activity may not fulfill all of the requirements, but no activity should violate any one. It is realized that the practical items of budget, administrative organization, supervisory personnel, adequate time, necessary facilities and equipment, and participant safety will be limiting factors that may temporarily curtail the optimum operation and development of the intramural program. In no way should these factors be considered as permanent deterrents to the necessary growth of this essential program which embodies an increasingly large and important part of college life. It is assumed, therefore, that those individuals responsible for the administrative control and development of the intramural program will utilize nationally accepted standards available in the areas of facilities, equipment, and staff load, and will work constantly toward achieving the optimum conditions possible in their particular situation [1]. *

ORGANIZATION AND ADMINISTRATIVE PLANS

The administration of intramural and recreation programs for men and women generally varies in the different institutions, although there are many similar organizational plans. There are basic administrative principles that are necessary for any sound organization. There must also be the wholehearted cooperation of many, whether they are members of committees, team managers, officials, participants,

* Bracketed numbers refer to the references at the end of the chapter.

or administrative personnel. The university administration, headed by the president, should give consistent and substantial support to administrators and programs.

Qualifications of Administrator The administration of intramurals and recreation demands competent and dedicated leadership. The administrator should be a highly qualified director who is energetic, resourceful, and a good organizer. The administrator must be guided by a knowledge of and a sound philosophy of intramural sports and their relationship to higher education. His duties should be clearly defined and relationships with the other, complementing organizations need careful delineation.

Centralized Administration Practically all of the more successful intramural and recreation programs have a distinct departmental organization with a part- or full-time director. This person is given the responsibility and staff to develop and supervise a broad, well-organized program of intramural sports and recreation. This centralized plan has many advantages. It gives an identity to the department and reassures the students that their interests and needs are being met. This plan also tends to specify staff time, use of facilities, budgetary support, and an operational plan which is not subjugated to other departments. It facilitates the provision of trained leadership, which is essential, as well as the cooperation of all staff members.

Departments of intramural sports and recreation have generally been under the administration of the department or school of physical education as a departmental or administrative unit. This enables the intramural director to (1) maintain a close liaison with the physical education instructional program, (2) coordinate the use of facilities and equipment more effectively, and (3) utilize the efforts and interests of major students, both undergraduate and graduate. This is still the most effective and logical arrangement for the majority of colleges and universities. In many departments or schools, the men and women operate under separate administrators or supervisors and with varying degrees of student control. The women's recreation association is an organization of women students with its own set of officers and advisors from the women's physical education departments. The advisor is a resource person, consultant, and supervisor. She helps the students plan and operate their own program. The recreation program is open to all students, and they meet their needs and interests by planning and developing their own programs.

A few departments of intramural sports and recreation are responsible to the department of athletics. The athletic department in some schools contributes funds to assist in the operation of intramurals. Sometimes coaches are assigned responsibilities for the supervision of intramural sports. However, this has not been a successful arrangement. This method of financing the program is unsound, and the chief interests of the athletic department generally follow the continuous demands of producing winning teams and highly trained athletes.

In some instances, the department of intramural sports and recreation is responsible administratively to the department in charge of recreation education. Such affiliations have not been too successful because they do not allow for sufficient control by the department of intramurals of existing facilities and equipment.

In a few cases, intramurals and recreation are under the control of the dean of students or the director of the student union. This has serious drawbacks, even though in some instances the dean of students may have a leading role to play in the allocation of student fees. Lack of qualifications, lack of control over facilities and equipment, and difficulties in coordinating schedules rule out this arrangement except in the case of social and creative recreational activities.

The administration of and responsibility for sports clubs are especially confusing. Whereas intramural sports and recreation are generally accepted as integral to departments or schools of physical education, sports clubs have not found consistent acceptance or an administrative home. Since sports clubs compete off campus, many of the same problems exist as with intercollegiate athletics except that administration, supervision, health and safety, and travel precautions are much more lax. One possibility, then, is to place these sports clubs under intercollegiate athletics and operate them on a safe and sound basis. As the sports club becomes more highly organized and "adoption pressures" increase, the clubs may be accepted as varsity sports with both freshman and varsity competition. There is also some acceptance of sports clubs as a part of the intramural sports and recreation administration. This concept follows the philosophy that all students should be provided with opportunities to enjoy satisfying recreational experiences which meet their needs and skill levels. It is assumed that sports clubs and intramural sports have mutual objectives and that the director of intramural sports is therefore the logical administrator. Since the department or school of physical education has control of most of the facilities, equipment, and skilled personnel, there is logic in the argument for making sports clubs a division in the department or school of physical education. A staff member would then be assigned the administration of sports clubs and would then have primary responsibility for the sports clubs. Other administrative plans link sports clubs under the dean of students or a representative sports club committee. Sports clubs for women are generally affiliated with the women's recreation association, which is under the direction of the department of physical education for women. No matter which administrative plan is used, sound administrative policies regarding sponsorship, adequate budget, medical supervision, insurance protection, safe facilities and equipment, and competent leadership should be mandatory.

Intramural Council and Women's Recreation Association An intramural council and the women's recreation association are essential to the administration of intramurals and recreation. College departments are consistent in using some form of student council. The councils generally have student representatives from the units of competition such as fraternities or sororities, independent units, and off-campus units. The councils hold regular meetings and help plan the program, establish rules for participation and awards, handle forfeits and protests, and serve as a liaison to the student body. The director or advisor is a member of the council and helps shape and mold the programs. There are a few who believe that the students should have complete control of their programs. The opportunities for developing leadership and responsibility and solving problems are certainly there, but it is not always practical to exploit them. The time involved, complexities of scheduling, officiating, safety and liability problems, and the breadth of the programs make an efficient student administration most difficult. The director should certainly involve the students in every way possible, but he also needs to give appropriate guidance and direction.

Coordinating Committee Where intramural and recreation programs are combined and broad, a coordinating committee can serve a useful purpose. This committee is usually composed of student, faculty, and administrative representatives from the office of the dean of students, the student union, the student government, the intramural council, and the women's recreation association. The department of intramurals and recreation and the main administrative office of the department or school of physical education should have the majority of members, since they will be responsible for most of the physical education courses, active intramurals, and recreation on the campus.

Recommendations from National Conference on College-University Recreation The dedevelopment of guidelines for coordinating recreation activities to ensure maximum use of facilities was the primary purpose of the National Conference on College-University Recreation which was held in Washington, D.C., in January, 1968. Some of its recommendations for the development and coordination of campus recreation programs follow:

1. That there exist in written or printed form a positive statement of recreation philosophy which undergirds program effort and supports a concept of coordination.

2. That a broad administrative structure to operate a total recreational service program on the campus be established at a level that reaches to the highest university authority for campus leisure affairs, preferably at the vice-presidential level, and that the administrator of this structure be charged with the coordination of recreational and cultural opportunities.
3. That the person selected to coordinate campus recreation services be a competent professional with an interest in, and concern for, leisure education.
4. That there be centralization of control of areas, facilities, and equipment most frequently used in recreation programs under the person administratively responsible for campus recreation.
5. That a Council on Cultural and Recreational Affairs be established whose membership is composed of representatives of the disciplines and organizations involved in the promotion of cultural and recreational experiences, and that the function of this Council be to assist in determining priorities and to advise on the programing and promotion of widely diversified and enriching leisure activities.
7. That there be adequate long-range financial support for the campus recreation program.
8. That the development of leadership, as part of total education, be one of the objectives of the campus recreation program.
9. That student representatives be included on all policy-making committees concerned with recreation, and that, wherever possible, student representatives be granted voting rights and privileges.
10. That colleges and universities offering, or planning to offer, programs for the professional preparation of recreation personnel include in such programs the requirement of practical field-work experience. [4]

Staff Assistants The director of intramurals and recreation must rely on the cooperation of other staff members, faculty advisors, and others. The staff members should be qualified for their duties through experience and education. Where part-time staff such as graduate assistants, undergraduates, and nondegree personnel are used, these persons should be properly oriented and supervised. Continuing in-service education to encourage professional growth and improved services to students is a common mark of a good intramural program. Quite often in the development of intramurals and recreation, part-time staff members as well as the directors have donated a great deal of their time and efforts, largely for altruistic reasons. This is not in the best interests of either the faculty member or the student. Intramural duties assigned and accepted should be credited toward each individual's work load on the same basis as class instruction, administrative duties, and other departmental assignments.

The activity supervisor or advisor is one member of the intramural team. The supervisor or advisor is generally a staff member who is responsible for a particular sport or activity to which he or she is assigned. This person carries out the responsibilities assigned by the director of intramurals, working closely with the students and following the general policies established for intramurals in regard to such things as officiating, safety, and administration.

Colleges and universities that have professional preparation curricula in physical education and recreation education have the advantage of career-oriented and partially trained personnel to assist in various capacities. These students, especially graduate assistants, often contribute a great deal to the program. The benefits to the student in training and to the student participating are mutually advantageous. Many departments of intramurals rely heavily on graduate assistants.

The student managerial system is also an important cog in the machine. Student managers represent organizations such as fraternity or dormitory teams. They help to organize the teams, keep up with the schedules and arrangements, and cooperate with the intramural and recreation department in administrative details. The managers are responsible for an important share of the success of the program. They are generally members of the intramural council and serve a very important liaison function.

The details of maintaining records, preparing reports and schedules, preparing materials, answering phones and students' questions take a great deal of time. The services of a full-time secretary should be provided in the larger schools with broad programs. This person can relieve the director of a lot of minutiae and add greatly to the efficiency of the operation. The secretary also plays a most important role in fostering goodwill and good public relations.

MANAGEMENT PROBLEMS

Financial Support Adequate financial support is the basis for the development and continuation of intramurals and recreation in our colleges and universities. Historically, intramural and recreation programs have not always been supported from regular budgetary sources. Gate receipts from the athletic program have been allotted, but this has proved to be an undesirable and inconsistent source of support. Gate receipts fluctuate so much that other means of support have become necessary. All sorts of money-raising plans have been used to provide money for programs, but these, too, have not been successful nor are they consistent with the needs of recreation for all students. General student activity fees have been used as a source of revenue, and this approach has some merit. However, the philosophy of the committee or administrators allotting the fees may not be sympathetic with the needs of recreation. Fortunately, educators have become aware of the great value of a good recreational program for the entire student body and are providing regular funds for these programs. It is an established fact that financial support now comes from the regular college or university budget. Even though this principle has been accepted, financial support has not kept pace with increasing enrollments and the rising cost of materials and services.

One of the more recent means of support and one of the most promising is the establishment of a special intramural and recreation fee. This fee is mandatory for all students and is restricted to use for intramurals and recreation. When one compares the fee with the cost of other forms of entertainment and recreation, it can represent one of the best buys the student will ever make. This fee is a supplementary fee that varies from campus to campus. Students see the value of such an arrangement and are beginning to support special fees of this type. Generally, a special advisory committee is established to develop short- and long-range plans for the use of the funds. This committee has student representation and selected members from allied organizations. The department or school of physical education and the director of intramurals and recreation need such advisory committees to plan and interpret the broad program possible under adequate financing.

Efficient management of funds should ensure maximum returns for each member of the student body who desires constructive and active recreation. In comparison with intercollegiate athletics and other activities, the cost of a successful and broad intramural and recreation program is very low, considering the number of individuals who participate. The planning of a realistic budget which contains a fair, proportionate share for intramurals and recreation and their efficient management certainly becomes one of the keys to a successful program.

Facilities Use and Scheduling Although several colleges and universities have special outdoor and indoor intramural and recreational facilities, the large majority must share them with the physical education department and sometimes with the department of intercollegiate athletics. There is generally an inadequacy of facilities, especially at peak-load hours. Even the colleges and universities that have special intramural and recreational buildings are generally overscheduled, and these buildings do not always meet the demands for recreation. Serious consideration should be given to the establishment of a priority building plan for intramurals and recreation or a combination physical education and recreation building that will meet the needs of the students.

Multiple use of facilities is necessary. Coordinated planning by those responsible for the various programs should assure an equitable use of facilities with respect to time and space. There should also be maximum use of all existing facilities which have been designed and adapted to accommodate a variety of activities. The acceptance of the principle that equitable use of limited facilities should be made would assure good relationships between departments and students. A calendar of events and the establishment of a priority-use list prevent many conflicts and a great deal of confusion.

As a general rule, where a multi-use facility is involved, instructional classes take priority until the peak-load hour, generally starting at 4 P.M. If intercollegiate athletic practice and games must be scheduled in the same facility, intramurals generally fit their schedules around the practice periods and games. Since this is a hardship on the large number of students participating in intramurals, careful consideration should be given to providing adequate facilities for intramurals and recreation. An equitable distribution of time and facilities is "pressure laden," but a fair adjustment should be made. The lack of on-campus facilities need not restrict the program completely. Generally, off-campus recreational facilities are available for use at nominal rates. Public relations and increasing the use potential of commercial companies should encourage the use of facilities such as bowling alleys, golf courses, ski areas, skating rinks, and swimming pools.

A close working relationship with the maintenance department should increase the maximum use of facilities. Cleaning and marking of floors, lining fields, and maintaining auxiliary services are time-consuming tasks. If they are performed by maintenance personnel, the burden of the intramural staff is lightened and opportunities for more activities and proper supervision are increased. If the maintenance department does not have responsibility for these services, provision must be made for adequate maintenance and service personnel responsible to the intramural and recreation director.

Equipment and Supplies Ideally, the intramural and recreation departments should furnish a large portion of the sports equipment and supplies that are essential to the success of the program. The availability of good-quality equipment is related to the degree of success and safety achieved in the program. The amount and kind of equipment vary. In most instances, balls for team games such as football, softball, and basketball are furnished. Protective equipment is generally furnished for catchers in softball, fencers, goalies in ice hockey, and for coeds in field hockey. More and more schools are furnishing uniforms, swimsuits, towels, and laundry service. Personal sports equipment such as golf clubs and balls, tennis racquets and balls, handball gloves, tennis and basketball shoes, and skis is seldom furnished.

Funds for equipment and supplies should come from the general budget. In addition, supplementary finances quite often come from a student fee system which may be assessed by sport, by season, or allotted from general student fees. The colleges and universities that have adopted the special intramural and recreation fee discussed previously are generally in the best financial condition to furnish both team and personal equipment and supplies.

The purchase and care of equipment and supplies requires competent and knowledgeable personnel. Efficient accountability procedures also are essential. The *Report of the National Conference* on "Equipment and Supplies for Athletics, Physical Education, and Recreation" goes into detail concerning these problems [2]. Every director or supervisor should have a copy of this report and follow its directions carefully.

Many intramural departments operate an extensive check-out system for selected equipment such as footballs, basketballs, and handballs. This requires personnel to issue the equipment, check it in, and keep it repaired. In some instances, sports equipment is placed on loan to housing units throughout the campus for use by students during free-play time. In this case, the cooperation of the dormitory manager or dormitory sports manager is necessary so that he may take responsibility for the equipment.

Student Managers As previously stated, the student managerial system is the backbone of an efficient intramural program. Student managers give invaluable assistance to the director and his staff. The selection of the student team manager is the responsibility of the competing organizations. Although most of the organizations demand competent representation from their manager, this does not always occur. The orientation and education of student managers become important tasks for the director of intramurals. In most of the better programs, an apprentice system, which places increasing responsibilities on the managers as they gain experience and competence, is used. Student managers who assist the director and the intramural department instead of serving as unit team managers find this experience helpful, and their services are extremely advantageous to the entire intramural organization. The managers perform a variety of important functions such as interpreting regulations to students, officiating when needed, maintaining sportsmanlike conduct, serving on the intramural council, and seeing that the necessary game equipment is available. The time and effort spent in developing an ongoing managerial system is not wasted. It has become a necessity.

Officials The selection and training of intramural officials has become a serious problem for intramural directors. In many cases, intramural competition is extremely spirited, with insufficient safety guards. A lack of proper conditioning among the contestants increases the incidence of injuries. It develops, then, that intramural sports need the best officiating, but, in too many instances, officiating is mediocre and adds hazards to the participants.

Since inept officiating is a serious detriment to the welfare of the participant and to the program, officials must be trained, given experience, supervised properly, and evaluated. Where more than one official is used, care should be exercised in the assignment of inexperienced with experienced officials. Training programs should include clinics, written examinations, and experience with the usual procedures that are expected of all trained officials. Regular meetings should be held with officials to discuss mechanics, rules interpretation, and actual game situations.

Insistence upon a wholesome and sportsmanlike atmosphere is conducive to good officiating and to enjoyment for the participant. Sportsmanship as a major objective is an extremely valuable asset and should be cultivated throughout the entire program.

The payment of officials for their services is now an accepted practice. Some departments pay officials on a game basis, while others pay by the hour. The simplest and probably the most common method of payment is by the game. The pay per game ranges from one to several dollars. The pay is nominal, but it is generally possible for an official to work two or more games per night, thus adding to his income. As a general rule, it is much more common to have paid officials in men's programs than in women's programs. Departments or schools of physical education with undergraduate and graduate major students in physical education encourage their students to gain valuable experience in participation as well as officiating. In some instances, a course in officiating is included in the curriculum for major students.

The practice of requiring officials to wear officials' uniforms and to carry out the mechanics of good officiating helps to inspire respect for the officials. Rating of the officials by team managers and supervisors also improves officiating.

Protests No matter how good the officiating is, there will always be protests. There are general rules which cover most of the possibilities. Most value judgments on play situations are rendered by the official at the occurrence of the difficulty. Nonvalue judgments, as on whether ineligible players have participated, are generally announced to both teams when the violation is noticed, but the protest should be put in writing within 24 hours. Most intramural councils serve as protest boards, or an executive committee may handle protests. Representatives from the teams involved are invited to the meeting to present their arguments and receive the decision. It should go without saying that an efficient operation, including an up-to-date *Intramural Handbook* and regular managers' meetings, should forestall many difficulties and protests.

Awards The question of awards versus rewards and intrinsic versus extrinsic values comes up for discussion and a policy decision in intramurals. This is an issue that each college or university should settle after careful study and discussion. The majority of schools seem to lean toward awards of no intrinsic value that are merely symbols of recognition of accomplishment. Awards should be used as the means to an end rather than the end itself. Expensive awards may promote false values and give rise to competitive problems that may become quite acute.

There are arguments for and against using an award system. The arguments for awards revolve around the incentive motive, suggesting that awards increase interest and participation and serve to recognize achievement. Arguments against awards point out that they are often monopolized by the highly skilled; that more genuine interest is elicited without them; that the money invested in awards could be used to a better advantage; and that awards are not necessary.

The recognition and establishment of a sound philosophy concerning awards and incentives is essential. After this philosophy has been agreed upon, policies and procedure for an award system are relatively easy to work out. Practically every college and university has an *Intramural Handbook* which explains a wide variety of plans for administering awards. These handbooks are available by request. Many departments have reciprocal agreements for exchanging handbooks.

Public Relations There is no need to emphasize the importance of and need for a broad and continuous public-relations program. Evaluations of intramurals and recreation sometimes show that enough attention has not been given to planning and carrying out an extensive program of public relations. Special attention and effort, therefore, need to be channeled in this direction.

HEALTH AND SAFETY POLICIES

The protection of the health and safety of the participants in intramurals is a necessity. There are several safeguards that should be put to use. The administration and staff have a moral as well as a legal responsibility for the safety and welfare of the students.

Health Examination A thorough medical examination by the family physician or health-service physicians should precede active participation in physical education and intramurals. Where the family physician's examination record is required for admission, the health service should screen all health records carefully and advise the physical education and intramural departments of any individual limitations. This requires a close working relationship with the health-service department. Clearly defined policies and procedures with respect to medical examinations, classification for participation, first aid, accident reports and records, and follow-up procedures should be established and carried out. Computerized medical records aid greatly in previously time-consuming checking and screening for students with physical limitations.

Subsequent examinations should be required as deemed necessary by the health service. Students with serious illnesses, injuries, or postoperative problems should be reinstated for participation in intramurals by medical authority. This again requires continuous communication between the health service and intramural departments. Some intramural departments require a permit card and a clearance slip from the individual before he is permitted to participate. This puts the burden on the student to clear his own name for participation. However, this may throw too much of a burden on the health service. The simplest and most foolproof method of record keeping should be adopted at each institution.

Pre-event Practice and Conditioning Opportunities for practice and conditioning should be made available before the strenuous sport seasons. The relationship between good physical condition and the incidence of injuries is well known. This procedure also increases the potential physical efficiency of participating individuals.

Care of Injuries Procedures and proper routine for handling of accidents and injuries should be carefully worked out and cleared with the health service. The supervisor should be trained in first aid. Transportation should be available. The student health service should be contacted and the prescribed routine followed. These services should be available during all hours of scheduled competition.

Insurance Protection At the Fourth National Conference on Health in Colleges, uniform coverage of all students was recommended, and a number of ways by which stipulated coverage could be provided were suggested [3]:

1. Purchase of commercial insurance
2. Self-insurance
3. Blue Cross or Blue Shield plans, or other plans specifically tailored for college needs by the various state physicians' services
4. Contracts for service, usually associated with group practice and capitation fees
5. Any possible combination of the above four methods

Each institution should take steps to assure appropriate protection of students through its health service or some form of insurance. The director of intramural activities should work cooperatively with others involved to obtain such protection for all purposes.

Miscellaneous Safety Precautions Proper supervision of activities, periodic examination of playing areas and equipment for hazards, and the furnishing of protective equipment are all measures designed to ensure the safety and welfare of the student.

LIABILITY

The problem of lawsuits is increasing in intramurals and recreation. The law varies somewhat in each state, so that it behooves all administrators to determine the law and its interpretation in their home states. The discussion of liability in Chapter 1 of this section holds true for intramurals and recreation.

CRITERIA FOR APPRAISAL OF INTRAMURALS

This check list is designed as a tool for appraisal of the intramural program in a college or university. It is based on the recommendations made by the conference [1].

It is recommended that this instrument be used by administrative and faculty personnel. Each item should be discussed fully and a consensus should be obtained on the degree to which the principle is operative. The values to be obtained are inherent in the discussion and the evaluative process. No overall score or rating is expected.

To what extent are the following general principles operative with respect to your institution's intramural policies and practices?

	(5) Completely	(4) To a great degree	(3) To a moderate degree	(2) Very little	(1) Not at all
1. The educational philosophy of the department has been formulated in writing and is subscribed to wholeheartedly by the intramural staff and is stated in the Departmental Handbook.					
2. The intramural philosophy is in harmony with the over-all educational philosophy of the college or university as stated in the appropriate publications of the institution.					
3. The intramural philosophy is compatible with the principles set forth in the *Report of the President's Commission on Higher Education* as they relate to the education of college men and women.					
4. The major objectives of the intramural program have been formulated in writing, and these specific objectives are compatible with the over-all educational philosophy of the department and the institution.					
5. The major objectives of student intramural participation are directed toward recreational contributions and values to the student.					
6. A concerted effort is made to interpret a broad concept of the intramural program to the students, faculty, administration, and community.					
7. In the development and conduct of the program of intramural activities, the administrator is committed to action through a democratic process which includes both students and faculty.					
8. Campus-wide planning and coordination of all recreational activities is effected through a Campus Recreation Coordinating Committee whose membership is composed of students, faculty, and administrative personnel representing such groups as the dean's office, student union, Department of Physical Education, student government, and other interested student and faculty groups.					
9. Provision is made for a student-faculty intramural council or board and also for intramural committees.					
10. The intramural program provides opportunity for student leadership in the planning, organization, and administration of the program.					

	(5) Completely	(4) To a great degree	(3) To a moderate degree	(2) Very little	(1) Not at all
11. The administrator gives equal consideration to the problems of men and women in regard to policy, budget, use of facilities, equipment, and scheduling of intramural and other campus recreation activities.					
12. The standards in the institution relating to staff qualifications, work load, tenure, retirement, academic rank, and salary apply equally to intramural staff members.					
13. Intramural duties assigned to the intramural staff members are credited toward each individual's total work load on the same basis as class instruction, administrative duties, and departmental assignments.					
14. The source of financial support for the intramural program is the general college budget.					
15. All entering students are given a thorough medical examination as a requisite to participation in the intramural program, and subsequent examinations are given as deemed necessary.					
16. The institution provides appropriate protection for all students participating in the intramural program, either through its health service or through an adequate insurance coverage plan.					
17. Adequate supervision is provided for intramural responsibilities carried by qualified graduate assistants, and other college and off-campus personnel.					
18. The intramural program is considered in the over-all plan for the scheduling of the use of facilities and time in the total college program.					
19. Guidance and counseling of students is an integral part of the intramural program.					
20. When transportation is necessary for intramural and extramural trips, it is provided by the institution either in college cars or busses with bonded drivers, or in bonded public carriers.					
21. The organization of units for participation is such that all students have an opportunity to participate in a variety of activities.					
22. Properly selected and trained officials are used in the intramural program.					
23. All intramural sports are played under approved rules.					

	(5) Completely	(4) To a great degree	(3) To a moderate degree	(2) Very little	(1) Not at all
24. The methods of organizing competition strive to equate the abilities of the participants; and in all cases where facilities permit, attempt to give the competing teams or individuals a chance to play a number of times rather than eliminate them immediately.					
25. The campus recreation program is well rounded, including social and creative activities, intramural sports, and outing activities.					
26. The intramural activities are integrated with other college agencies and services concerned with campus recreation (student union activities, physical education, varsity athletics, and so forth).					
27. Through the participation of the students in the planning of the program, the interests and needs of the participants receive full consideration.					
28. The program is broad in scope and challenges the varying needs, interests, and abilities of all participants.					
29. The program provides opportunities for participation by individuals or groups whose limitations may require particular attention.					
30. The program emphasizes individual and dual activities for the purpose of developing life-long interests in leisure-time activities.					
31. The program offers opportunities for the development of desirable personality traits such as self-confidence, self-direction, courage, and ethical conduct.					
32. Through proper organization and environment, the activities afford pleasurable experiences for the participants.					
33. The program provides for experiences in human relationships, such as cooperation, acceptance of responsibility, and the development of friendships.					
34. The intramural activities utilize the knowledges and skills gained in the instructional program.					
35. The intramural program provides progressive experiences through which each student derives the growth and satisfaction in achievement which is essential for continued participation after college.					
36. The activities offer opportunities for the development and maintenance of the healthful functioning of the body.					

	(5) Completely	(4) To a great degree	(3) To a moderate degree	(2) Very little	(1) Not at all
37. The activities encourage students to develop and to understand the importance of habits of regular relaxation and play.					
38. The program provides opportunities, through co-recreation activities, to develop mutual interests in activities acceptable to both men and women.					
39. The program offers opportunities for understanding and appreciation of the activities ordinarily engaged in only by the opposite sex.					
40. Extramural events, other than intercollegiate athletics, are an outgrowth of the intramural program and they enrich and complement this program.					
41. In co-recreation activities, the selection of activities is with the joint approval of the departments of physical education for men and women.					
42. In intramural activities for women and co-recreation events, the policies and standards of the National Association for Physical Education of College Women and of the National Section for Girls and Women's Sports are followed.					
43. The intramural program provides for orientation of each student with regard to its purposes, policies, and opportunities. This may be accomplished by orientation week programs, handbooks, or other means.					
44. The activities make full use of geographical location, climatic conditions, and community resources.					
45. For each activity offered in the program, prescribed safety and health standards are observed.					
46. Awards are inexpensive, a symbol of achievement rather than the motive for participation.					
47. Facilities and equipment are adequate with respect to quality and quantity.					
48. The facilities provide for a broad program of organized and informal activities for both men and women students, faculty, and families of students and faculty.					
49. Program analysis is used as the basis for development and utilization of facilities and for gaining the support of university officials for expansion.					
50. Facilities for intramurals are readily accessible to all potential users, that is, students, faculty, and families of students and faculty. On a large campus, this means that facilities are decentralized.					

	(5) Completely	(4) To a great degree	(3) To a moderate degree	(2) Very little	(1) Not at all
51. Some facilities are available for free play throughout the day.					
52. Facilities, if adequate, are shared by off-campus groups in consideration for the use of off-campus sites by students.					
53. Campus facilities are used to the maximum and, if inadequate, are supplemented by off-campus facilities.					
54. Facilities for intramurals are controlled by the intramural director, but are scheduled with full consideration of total institutional needs.					
55. Existing facilities have been adapted to maximum use, and a minimum of unused space exists.					
56. Decisions concerning planning, construction, care, and scheduling involve everyone concerned with facilities, that is, participants, administrators, and maintenance personnel.					
57. New scientific techniques and knowledge are used in construction and care of facilities.					
58. The institution has a plan of development of such nature that it insures adequate facilities for increasing numbers of students, faculty, and families of students and faculty.					

SELECTED REFERENCES

1. *Report of National Conference,* "Intramural Sports for College Men and Women," American Association for Health, Physical Education and Recreation, Washington, 1955.
2. *Report of National Conference,* "Equipment and Supplies for Athletics, Physical Education, and Recreation," American Association for Health, Physical Education and Recreation, Washington, 1960.
3. *Report of Fourth National Conference on Health in Colleges,* American College Health Association, New York, 1966.
4. "Report of National Conference on College-University Recreation," *Journal of Health, Physical Education and Recreation,* vol. 34, no. 4, April, 1968, pp. 10–12.

Chapter 3

Extramural Programs for Women

JAMES W. LONG

Director, Division of Physical Education, Oregon State University, Corvallis, Oregon

MEANING OF EXTRAMURALS

The term "extramurals" needs clarification. It has several connotations. Extramurals comprise those sports activities which are conducted beyond the immediate surroundings of the campus with other teams. In a broad sense, extramurals include all athletic competitions conducted outside the school, but generally they have not been limited to players with the highest level of skill. Extramurals generally have arisen as extensions or outcomes of the intramural program, with few or no eligibility requirements, minimal practice periods, and no gate receipts. Sports days, invitational events, telegraphic meets, and informal competition between teams are common forms of competition. Recently, extramurals have included intercollegiate athletics for women, which involves trained teams which compete in a series of scheduled games or tournaments with like teams from other schools, cities, or organizations. The term "intercollegiate athletics for women" will be used henceforth in this discussion so as to specify the subject.

PRESENT STATUS OF INTERCOLLEGIATE ATHLETICS FOR WOMEN

Intercollegiate athletics for women is now in a period of rapid change. The future of competitive sports for girls and women is challenging, somewhat controversial, but promising. The concept of an intercollegiate athletic program for college women is a new concept to many of the professional physical educators, and in some instances it is somewhat foreign to their philosophy. The attitude toward competitive sports for women needs careful evaluation and guided cultivation on the part of the players, the teacher/coaches, and the public. This will take time. The American Medical Association Committee on the Medical Aspects of Sports explains the need for a greater development of sports opportunities for girls and women, pointing out that:

> Whether from culturally imposed restrictions, untenable physiological taboos, or from disproportionate allotment of time, facilities and leadership, many [girls and women] are not receiving the desired experiences from suitable and regular physical exercise. The health benefits of wholesome exercise are now well substantiated, and are just as pertinent to the female as to the male. Programs of sufficient breadth and depth to permit progressive involvement and continuing interests are essential. Basic to the administration of healthful and safe sports programs are proper conditioning, careful coaching, good officiating, right equipment and facilities, and adequate medical care [1].*

At the 1965 Conference on Competition for Girls and Women sponsored by the Division of Girls' and Women's Sports of the American Association for Health, Physical Education and Recreation, three of the major problems which seemed to cause the greatest concern for sports competition were identified:

> 1. Differences in philosophy as to what is appropriate for girls. Women tend to resist competition because of tradition, prejudice, or fear of the unknown.
> 2. Providing adequate facilities and finances (without relying on gate receipts).
> 3. Providing a sufficient number of women leaders or competent coaches and officials. [2]

Statement of Beliefs The Division of Girls' and Women's Sports' statement of beliefs sets forth a total philosophy for the participation of girls and women in sports programs:

> We believe that opportunities for instruction and participation in sports should be included in the educational experiences of every girl. Sports are an integral part of the culture in which we live. Sports skills and sports participation are valuable social and recreational tools which may be used to enrich the lives of women in our society.
>
> We believe that sports opportunities at all levels of skill should be available to girls and women who wish to take advantage of these experiences. Competition and cooperation may be demonstrated in all sports programs although the type and intensity of the competition will vary with the degree or level of skill of the participant. An understanding of the relationship between competition and cooperation and of how to

* Bracketed numbers refer to the references at the end of the chapter.

utilize both within the accepted framework of our society is one of the desirable outcomes of sports participation.

We believe in the importance of physical activity in the maintenance of the general health of the participant.

We believe that participation in sports contributes to the development of self-confidence and to the establishment of desirable interpersonal relations.

For these reasons, we believe that girls and women of all ages should be provided with comprehensive school and community programs of sports and recreation. In addition, they should be strongly and actively encouraged to take part in such programs.

We believe that sports programs for girls and women should be broad, varied, and planned for participants at differing levels of skill. There should be full awareness of the wide span of individual differences so that all types, ages, and skill levels are considered in the planning of sports programs. In conducting the various phases of sports programs, principles must guide action. These principles should be based on the latest and soundest knowledge regarding

1. growth and development factors
2. motor learning
3. social and individual maturation and adjustment
4. the values of sports participation as recognized in our culture.

We believe that college and university instructional programs should go beyond those activities usually included in the high school program. There should be opportunities to explore and develop skills in a variety of activities, with emphasis on individual sports. It is desirable that opportunities for extramural experiences beyond the intramural program be accessible to the highly skilled young women who wish those opportunities. [3]

The development of a program that is unique and of optimal benefit to girls and women is not only possible but most likely. One of the first steps to be taken by the women leaders in physical education and sports is the establishment of a philosophy or set of basic beliefs to guide future developments.

Levels of Competition There are three progressive levels of sports competition for women. These should be based on the level of skill and the interest of the participant. The first level of competition for women with average skill should be on the intramural level. As the interest and skills develop, the women should compete in the sports-day and invitational events. The highly skilled women who are interested in a specific sport or sports should become members of an intercollegiate sports program. The pursuit of excellence is, and should be, an increasing concern for women in sports participation. It is a natural and fundamental urge of people enjoying the American way of life.

ORGANIZATION OF PROGRAM FOR INTERCOLLEGIATE ATHLETICS FOR WOMEN

The development of intercollegiate athletics for women has been quite different from that of men's programs. Intercollegiate athletic competition for women up to this point has been centered largely around the individual sports, such as golf and tennis. Team sports will undoubtedly be developing as the entire sports program expands. The emphasis on intramurals and sports days has overshadowed the rather limited intercollegiate athletic competition.

As intercollegiate athletics for women develops, however, the college and university president will need to be knowledgeable about the differences between the men's and women's programs. As the interest and team competition develop, pressures should be prevented from mounting. Such pressures have arisen in girls' interscholastics and men's intercollegiates in some instances. Emotionalism and other problems can become quite serious if the proper controls that are now being planned are allowed to be diluted.

Role of Division of Girls' and Women's Sports The Division of Girls' and Women's Sports of the American Association for Health, Physical Education and Recreation has evolved through several different organizations. Today, it is the guiding and controlling force in girls' and women's sports. Its services to the profession of physical education and intercollegiate athletics for women are innumerable. Standards and guiding principles for administrators, leaders, officials, and players; official guidebooks and rule books for sports; officiating clinics and ratings; and special projects and conferences are a few of the more important services and accomplishments.

Probably one of the most important new developments is the establishment, in 1966, of the Commission on Intercollegiate Athletics for Women (CIAW) by the Division for Girls' and Women's Sports (DGWS). The functions of the CIAW are:

1. To encourage organizations of colleges and universities and/or organizations of women physical educators to govern intercollegiate competition for women at the local, state, and regional levels.
2. To hold DGWS national tournaments as the need for them becomes apparent.
3. To sanction closed intercollegiate events in which at least five colleges or universities are participating.

The definition of some of the terminology should make the functions more meaningful:

1. *Open athletic events*—Those events for which participants who meet a minimum age limit are eligible. The participant may or may not be affiliated with a high school or college.
2. *Closed intercollegiate or collegiate events*—Those events in which only full-time junior college, college, or university women students may participate.
3. *Sanction*—Approval of plans for an intercollegiate meet, event, or tournament in which there are participants from at least five or more schools. To be granted a sanction the event must meet prescribed conditions.
4. *Athletic grant in aid or athletic scholarship*—Financial aids specifically designated for athletic ability. This practice is not approved by the commission.
5. *National DGWS (name of sport) tournament*—This title may be used only after the commission has approved and designated the sport and the site for the tournament.
6. *District or regional tournaments*—Events, meets, and tournaments which involve participants from three or more adjoining states.

A manual has been developed by the commission to give guidance in the administration of closed intercollegiate events. [4]

CONTROLS FOR COMPETITION

It has already been stated that intercollegiate athletics for women should be built upon sound instructional physical education, intramural, and extramural programs. These are the bases for sound intercollegiate athletic programs. The intercollegiate athletic program should not be attempted until these programs are operating successfully and competent leadership, budget, and facilities are provided. Staff time needed for coaching, supervision, and travel should either be a part of the teaching load or adequate compensation should be made. Furthermore, the athletic program should meet the approved objectives and standards for women's sports, including the appropriate essentials discussed for men's intercollegiate athletics such as proper and safe travel, proper equipment, adequate health and safety measures, and insurance.

It is essential, too, that the intercollegiate athletic program for women be designed for and by the women. This throws the responsibility squarely upon the department of physical education for women for its development, supervision, and operation. The

Women's Extramural Committee of the Athletic Association of Western Universities has developed an excellent set of policies for women in intercollegiate athletics. Their statement maintains that intercollegiate participation for women should develop from the desire and need of the women students, and that it should not be imposed by others upon the highly skilled performer. This is an excellent control measure [5]. The appropriate administrative authorities of the colleges and universities should exercise the prerogative of approval of the program. The administration should also certainly support the program and give the department of physical education for women every encouragement.

Budget The budget, unfortunately, becomes one of the main control factors. At the present, there are limited or no gate receipts, so that intercollegiate athletics for women should be a regular budgetary item that is allocated specifically for this program. This does not mean that funds such as state monies, gate receipts, student fees, or other sources of income should not be used if they are available. The income should not fluctuate from year to year, though, since regularity and adequacy are two essentials for a budget.

Scheduling The number and kinds of contests that are scheduled control competition and the direction in which intercollegiate athletics may go. Equitable and comparable schedules with like teams should be an objective. The amount of travel and time required and the most convenient day of the week must also be considered in scheduling contests. It is quite easy to allow contests to interfere with educational objectives. The scheduled games should in no way infringe on the students' time for study and classwork.

The number of games per season, length of the season, number of contests per week, and formal practice time out of season should be discussed with competing schools and common agreements should be reached.

The planning of tournaments needs careful consideration so that problems such as overemphasis, entertainment, and pressures do not develop. The formation of the Commission on Intercollegiate Athletics for Women and its sanction program is certainly a valuable control.

Eligibility In the past, there have been some women who have participated on or against men's intercollegiate teams or against a man in a scheduled athletic contest. This was not a sound practice and has been prohibited by the Division of Girls' and Women's Sports. The rules now specify that the woman athlete should be a full-time undergraduate student who has an academic average at least comparable to that of students participating in other major activities. Transfer students should be eligible for participation immediately following their enrollment.

A medical examination should be required for athletic participation within a six-month period prior to the start of the sports season each year. If the family physician's usual examination record is used, a cover letter giving permission for participation in the program of activities should be required from the family physician. After a serious illness or injury, clearance for participation should be issued by a physician.

Officiating The DGWS has developed an excellent training program for officials and has written approved rules and guidebooks for the sports. DGWS-rated officials should be used for intercollegiate events. Officiating by competent and trained women adds to the maintenance of standards of conduct and competition for women.

ADMINISTRATION OF PROGRAM

The intercollegiate athletic program for women should be under the direct supervision of the women's physical education department. The director or head as well as the women who teach and coach should meet the background and educational standards required of all physical education personnel. It is important that the director or head of the women's program should have had personal experience in organized extramural competition if at all possible. Integrity and a concern for the welfare of the women participants should be evident in all administrative action.

Guidelines for Intercollegiate Athletic Programs for Women The Division of Girls' and Women's Sports has established guidelines that serve as minimum standards for planning and administering an intercollegiate athletic program for women. The guidelines are not meant to be directives or the final word in the governing of competition [6].

It is hoped that intercollegiate athletic programs for the highly skilled woman athlete will continue to develop and follow the goal of "pursuit of excellence." This pursuit of excellence should not be only for the development of the highly skilled woman athlete, but also for the development and administration of an organizational pattern that will be a "model of excellence" on the American sports scene.

SELECTED REFERENCES

1. American Medical Association Committee on the Medical Aspects of Sports: "AMA Committee Urges Sports for Girls," *The Physical Educator,* vol. 24, no. 3, October, 1967, p. 133.
2. Division of Girls' and Women's Sports: *Guidelines for Intercollegiate Athletic Programs for Women,* American Association for Health, Physical Education and Recreation, Washington, 1965.
3. Division of Girls' and Women's Sports: *We Believe,* American Association for Health, Physical Education and Recreation, Washington, 1965.
4. Division of Girls' and Women's Sports: *Procedures for Women's Intercollegiate Athletic Events,* American Association for Health, Physical Education and Recreation, Washington, 1965.
5. Women's Extramural Committee of the Athletic Association of Western Universities: *Policies for Women in Intercollegiate Competition,* Member Institutions, Pacific 8 Conference, rev. ed., 1967.
6. Division of Girls' and Women's Sports: *Guidelines for Intercollegiate Programs for Women,* American Association for Health, Physical Education and Recreation, Washington, 1965.

Section Nine

Health Programs and the Collegiate Community

Chapter 1

General Aspects

MAURICE M. OSBORNE, JR.

Director of Student Health Services, Tufts School of Medicine
and Dental Medicine, Boston, Massachusetts

RELEVANCE TO HIGHER EDUCATION

Health is indispensable to and indivisible from the goals and administration of higher education. No college or university can afford to ignore its particular health responsibilities.

Prevention of Academic Wastage

Education promotes the development of youth to the best of its capabilities for life and citizenship. To whatever extent academic wastage exists, in the form of dropouts, absenteeism, or underachievement, the educator's purposes are defeated. Insofar as teaching, scholarship, and research depend on faculty, administration, and staff working together, ill health affecting any member may also contribute to academic wastage.

Consideration of Individual Differences

The individual develops and learns best in a program that takes into account his particular capabilities and limitations, which may be in part defined by his health.

Obligations to National Well-being

Higher education is a major force for societal well-being. In the field of health it succeeds only as well as it demonstrates by care, example, and effective health education the relevance of health and means to its preservation.

Expectations for Health Benefits

Americans show a rapidly rising level of expectation for comprehensive and high-quality care as a right, not a privilege, and want available services close to their principal places of living and working.

Students and their parents are much more sophisticated about what constitutes good medical care, will increasingly expect it of colleges, and are increasingly critical of second-rate service.

Faculty and staff, along with salaried workers in every field, have come increasingly to expect health benefits of some sort as a part of their employment. As such expectations increase, institutions become more vulnerable to loss through disability retirement benefits and compensation, a concern giving rise to the beginning of most occupational health programs.

Special Health Concerns

When such parental functions as feeding, housing, and protection of students are taken on by the institution, a concomitant concern for their health is expected.

Living, working, eating, playing, and congregating in large groups is characteristic at most institutions, thus exposing students and others to the hazards of group contagion, mass cookery, rumors, experimentation, etc.

Institutionally sponsored programs, such as intercollegiate and intramural athletics, laboratory study, and research involving use of dangerous chemicals and radiation hazards pose special risks and demand special programs to minimize them. Finally, the very educational nature of the institution presents expectations and opportunities for research, discussion, and education in health-related matters.

CONSIDERATIONS IN PLANNING

Each institution's role in helping to meet its health needs will in part be determined by and vary with the population, risks, and expectations peculiar to it and with the range of resources and services available. But of prime importance is an understanding of health needs in terms of an overall concept of services and programs necessary to the institutional community as a whole. Without this, no rational or appropriate division of responsibilities can be made nor health programs determined.

Comprehensive Community Health Program

For optimum health preservation and care, all the members of any community require protection by and ready access to services and programs that embrace the whole range of their needs. When they are not only available but are effectively reaching and being used by the people, such services and programs together form a comprehensive community health program.

While the health program components may be divided, defined, and ranked differently, the parts are presented here in units and in the rough order by which they are most often specifically included in (or excluded from) institutional and community programs, insurance agreements, etc.

Outline of Components in the Comprehensive Community Health Program

I. Components affecting the general community
  A. General environmental health and safety
    1. Provision of pure water, milk, and food, plus proper sewage and waste disposal, etc.
    2. Reasonable protection from general hazards of fire, traffic, climate, accident, and disaster
  B. First-aid and emergency care for acutely and seriously ill and injured
    1. Prompt on-premises first-aid and emergency short-term care
    2. Routine communications and transportation between institution and more definitive sources of care
    3. Special first aid and support for public functions
  C. Cooperative disaster planning
  D. Community information and education for health

II. Components of personal medical-surgical care
  A. General ambulatory care
    1. Prevention, such as immunizations, screening, etc.
    2. Minor injury and illness first aid, counseling, referral, liaison, and program modification—*the core service*
    3. Usual doctor's office functions in diagnosis and treatment (general ambulatory care)
    4. Support by basic laboratory, X-ray, and testing services
    5. Pharmaceutical, medical supply, and other treatment services
    6. Routine channels for referral
  B. Specialized ambulatory care—emphasis on availability of most needed specialists but potential access to all specialties for:
    1. Consultation to generalist in his management of cases
    2. Actual administration of specialized treatment
    3. Performance of special and uncommon diagnostic procedures
  C. Infirmary-level or family-based bed care for temporarily disabling or contagious but simply managed conditions
  D. General hospital care
    1. Emergency, diagnostic, and intensive care for commonest serious illnesses and injuries
    2. General surgical services
    3. Obstetrical services
    4. Appropriate support (dietary, nursery, etc.)
  E. Special hospital care—plastic surgery, open-heart surgery, etc.

III. Components of mental health
  A. Safe and humane emergency restraint and transfer to care of seriously disturbed individuals
  B. Psychiatric/psychological consultation to responsible doctors, teachers, administrators, etc., in their work with others
  C. Direct psychiatric/psychological services for diagnosis, limited therapy, and referral for selected referred cases—usually those more disturbed
  D. General "open" ambulatory services in psychiatric/psychological counseling and therapy, individual and group

   E. Psychoanalytic and other special or long-term services—ambulatory, electroshock treatment, etc.
   F. Infirmary-level or home-based psychiatric care
   G. Open ward—general psychiatric residential care
   H. "Locked" or high-security psychiatric facilities

IV. Dental health components
   A. Emergency dental care and consultation
   B. Periodic general dental care
      1. Professional cleaning and prophylaxis
      2. Dental-oral diagnosis, including necessary X-ray
      3. General operative dentistry
   C. Special dentistry—prosthetics, oral surgery, etc., with appropriate backup dental laboratory services
   D. Proper fluoridation

V. Components of eye health
   A. M.D. eye specialist (ophthalmologist) for eye emergencies and consultation on any eye problems
   B. Reliable vision testing, prescription, and lens supply

VI. Occupational health for students and others
   A. General preemployment, prematriculation health evaluations and preparation
      1. Fitting the person to the job or the school
      2. Screening of conditions dangerous to individual, job, or public health (TB control, etc.)
   B. Protection of individuals from general risks—immunizations, safety training, etc.
   C. Special-risk situations
      1. Athletic and sports programs
      2. Laboratories, especially those using radioactive machines or isotopes, etc.
      3. Field trips and special-risk activities—scuba, geology trips, etc.
   D. Continuing study and redefinition of hazards and risks

The purpose of the outline is to provide a comprehensive general checklist of potential health needs for reference.

Local Determinants of Institutional Health Responsibilities

In terms of function and of choice about divisions of responsibility, the chief determinants should be those that define each institutional community according to the expectations of and relationships between:

1. The academic population of students, faculty, administrators, staff, and others
2. Closely related groups, such as parents and alumni
3. The setting and institutional program, whether urban or rural, commuter or residential, rich or poor in locally available resources, coeducational or not, supporting athletic programs or not, and so forth

The less able the members of the institution are to recognize their needs or to seek, use, and support necessary services, the more will the institution have to take some active role; and the less available needed services are in the vicinity, the greater will be the institution's need to provide them or make them available.

Thus, the institution will tend to assume increasing shares of health responsibility when:

1. The institutional membership has greater proportions of young people (particularly minor students), single women, and students living away from home, especially if fed and housed on campus

2. Parents and, to some extent, alumni and other related groups expect the institution to act *in loco parentis*

3. Special-risk programs and situations (athletic, laboratory, etc.) increase

4. General programs affecting the community as a whole are considered, such as environmental health and safety, general emergency services, and health education

5. Programs are preventative—such as immunization, tuberculosis control, etc.—rather than in response to personal distress

Sheer size, to some extent, is a determinant in that smaller institutions (under 500 enrollment particularly) have a harder time per capita in supporting a desirable range of quality direct health services.

Institutional Examples

Community College When students usually live with families or other established households within easy commuting distance, institutional health responsibilities might appropriately be limited to:

1. Those affecting overall campus health; i.e., environmental health and safety, emergency and first-aid services; a coordinated disaster plan; and appropriate community health education and information

2. Core student health services, including evaluation, advice, and first-aid treatment and comfort for "minor" student illness and injury—with referral as needed, via families or directly, to needed sources of further medical care; and appropriate liaison with school officials for modification of program and consultation about recognition, handling, and referral of students' health problems (see discussion of core student health service, page 9-24).[1]

3. Group preventive programs, such as tetanus boosters, tuberculin testing, vision and hearing tests, etc., unlikely to be realized through independent medical sources

4. At least part-time mental health consultation

5. Occupational health and special-risk programs—athletic medicine, shop safety, workmen's compensation, etc.—where such risks exist

The other components of health care are presumed and *stated* to be matters of student and/or family responsibility, provided through independent local resources, with whatever referral advice and liaison the core student health service can provide to assist the process. Some community colleges have training programs in nursing, health-aide, and dental assistance and hygiene and may extend appropriate services to students or others for educational and training purposes.

Any other institutions drawing *strictly* local, nonresidential students could follow the same pattern.

The chief weaknesses in "community college" health programs are:

1. Inadequate "core student health" awareness, in which the student's needs for easy access to personal health advice *outside the home* (associated with his tendency in college to reject parental guidance) are unmet—along with his needs for medical backing for needed changes in program

2. Overreliance upon student-family relationships to see that needs for individual health care are met through family physicians and other local health resources. Youth (even if living at home) are not eager to accept parental advice on health

Small, Independent Residential College Generally with an enrollment well under a thousand, consisting mostly of undergraduates (i.e., legal minors) living away from home in college owned or controlled housing, such an institution is usually expected to have considerable direct concern for the personal health, welfare, and conduct of the youth entrusted to it by parents who often are paying tuition partly for such supervision.

[1] See page 9-30 for recommended staffing and support.

Thus, in addition to community protection and first aid, core student health service, preventive immunizations, and special-risk protection for sports as required for the community college, there is a keen expectation for personal health care, including most general and some specialized medical services, diagnostic and therapeutic services, and bed care—mostly infirmary-level care. And when even one or two students are far from home, hospital availability is expected.

Student residences and additional food service pose an obligation for safety and sanitation control beyond that of the day college.

A mature nurse, experienced and trained in community health and backed up by on-call or part-time physicians and by clerical and aide assistance, can adequately manage first aid, core student health, immunization, infirmary bed care, and can even cover the volleyball and field hockey games. She will usually establish good working relationships and communications with the most frequently needed physicians, pharmacies, and hospitals, so that most medical-surgical parameters of health care and treatment are made available by prearrangement with local doctors and services and are followed through as a matter of institutional policy.

The most common weaknesses in such college health programs are:

1. Overemphasis on individual student health to the neglect of community health needs for emergency care and transport, safety and sanitation, and health education

2. Overreliance upon the nurse—to make diagnoses, decisions, and to prescribe treatments for which, even when capable, she is unlicensed; and concomitant failure to appoint a qualified available and licensed physician as the institution's responsible medical officer or chief medical officer

3. Overprotection and medical parochialism, with unnecessary reliance upon "bed rest" and insufficient scope and flexibility in up-to-date ambulatory health care, resulting in academic wastage as students are confined or sent home unnecessarily—students that a more sophisticated health program would usually have returned to class

Regional State College Originally intended for almost entirely local and close regional enrollments, these colleges are often founded on the same premises for health responsibility as the commuter college and are still too often so functioning despite their growth, the building of campus residences for some students (often three to four thousand), and the increasing attendance of students who, while having no access to institutional housing, are still living several hundred or more miles away from family protection.

Health programs for such institutions tend to include general campus needs, particularly emergency and safety services and academic health education, and to include part-time outpatient services for the commonest minor ambulatory health needs of students (core student health with some extension into general doctor's office care) but to exclude most if not all specialized consultations and diagnostic procedures and bed care of the most commonly needed kind at the infirmary level while making hospitalization available through voluntary insurance of a limited kind.

Intercollegiate athletic medical care and programs tend to receive much attention in the fall, diminishing in other seasons, while other athletic and sports risks receive little or no attention and nonathletic risk situations receive virtually none.

Main weaknesses are:

1. Frequent exclusion of students from eligibility for health service benefits when they do not live in college residences, on the grounds that they are therefore commuters. In fact, increasing numbers of such students come from far away, live independently in the community, and are just as much at risk as those in dormitories.

2. Limited scope and hours of health services, leaving many students inadequately diagnosed and treated and poorly cared for during nights, on weekends, on holidays, and in risk situations.

The University The university generally has an enrollment of several thousand students, including a high proportion of graduate students in master's and doctoral programs and high proportions of residential students.

In this setting truly comprehensive health programs are more often practical and desirable and often have student health programs that offer directly or make available with some subsidy the whole spectrum of preventive services and general and specialized ambulatory care, the latter usually via insurance but often within university hospitals. Environmental health and safety programs must often be large and sophisticated because of the proliferation of research laboratories, sources of radiation, and other special risks.

Here, the size, the usually metropolitan but self-contained setting, the residential character, the availability of high-quality medical advice (often through a school of medicine), and the complexity and number of special-risk situations all conspire to produce a fuller program.

The College Consortium (Common Services for Groups of Colleges) In regions where a number of small colleges exist in relatively close proximity, some aspects of service, including those in short supply and hardest to compete for or to support individually, may be well managed by a consortium. Here, by pooling funds, a common service of high quality can be available to students of separate colleges. Some successful examples exist, notably one for psychiatric services in Boston in which over twenty institutions contribute an agreed per capita amount to a centrally located psychiatric clinic for their students' use.

Chapter **2**

Programs Affecting the Health of the Entire Community

MAURICE M. OSBORNE, JR.

Director of Student Health Services, Tufts School of Medicine and Dental Medicine, Boston, Massachusetts

ENVIRONMENTAL HEALTH AND SAFETY

Too often taken for granted until some disaster occurs, such as a typhoid outbreak, a dormitory fire, or a lab accident, this broad program area must be among the very first considered and administratively organized. Two principal areas, sanitation and safety, form the backbone of the program, but there are many overlaps with emergency care and planning and with community health education. Accordingly it should be organized with the support of an advisory committee representing the interests and expertise of those with responsibility for physical plant, planning, food services, security, student housing, health services, and health education, as well as necessary technical consultation.

Even in certain tax-supported institutions with so-called "immunity" from local ordinances, it is potentially dangerous and negligent to ignore them (see page 9-16). Each institution should at least make sure that local and state codes and ordinances are being met, and where the latter are inadequate or missing, should create standards for general sanitation and safety in:

1. Provision and distribution of pure food, water, and milk supplies
2. Proper sewage, waste, and garbage disposal
3. General in-plant safety from accident, fire, etc.

In general, municipal and/or state agencies have primary responsibility for such provision, including inspection and enforcement, but the institution must either make sure that, as it extends intramurally, proper provision and inspection is in fact being satisfactorily provided by official agents or it must provide such functions itself.

At least, a conscious program of accident reporting and analysis should be maintained, with emphasis on correction of local hazards.

Special Sanitation and Safety

Student Residences Student residences, both institutionally owned and any others of which the institution approves, must periodically be inspected for sanitation and safety.

In-plant Food Service Whether in dining halls, cafeterias, student unions, residences, by vending machines, or by temporary concessions, every meal served under institutional auspices or permit is a potential source of food poisoning, for the results of which the institution is liable. Standards[1] for sanitary supply, preparation, and service are available for dining halls and cafeterias. They also exist for vending machines and catering operations.[2] These standards should be followed, and no noncomplying vendor should be allowed on the premises. The program should include:

1. Health examination, instruction, and supervision of food handlers
2. Periodic inspection and cultures in food preparation areas
3. Planning and maintenance of clean facilities and equipment
4. Epidemiologic investigation and follow-through in event of any outbreak possibly connected with food service

Swimming Pools Swimming pools or any other bathing places used by institutionally sponsored groups must be constructed, controlled, and inspected according to existing national standards for safety and sanitation, with proper filtration and circulation, chlorination or bromination as determined by regularly done and recorded professional tests and inspections performed by a qualified person not directly connected with the swimming facility.

Laboratories Laboratories where toxic and/or flammable or infective materials may

[1] *U.S. Public Health Service Ordinance and Code Regulating Eating and Drinking Establishments,* U.S. Public Health Service Publication no. 934.

[2] *Standards for Operation of Vending Machines,* American College Health Association, Evanston, Ill.

be in use, should be planned, constructed, and operated to prevent accident from such hazards as:

1. Fumes, by adequate ventilation, hoods, and storage
2. Mercury spills, by prompt reportage and professional cleanup
3. Chemical contact injury, by emergency showers, eye fountains, proper protection gear, and by constant instruction and supervision in safe laboratory use

Radiologic Hazard Radiologic hazard, whether via X-ray or ionizing radiation from isotopes, is increasing on all campuses having active research programs in the sciences, engineering, etc. While the Atomic Energy Commission, which controls the distribution of radioactive isotopes, has some regulations which must be in effect if the institution is to be licensed, the institution itself must exert full control, through some central and qualified agent, over:

1. Purchase, central registration, calibration, and safe shielding of all X-ray and other radiating machinery (including lasers, nuclear-particle accelerators, etc.)
2. Periodic safety monitoring of all such equipment (X-ray equipment used in engineering and earth science areas for crystal and stress analysis and in art for analysis of paintings is more apt to escape attention and control than are diagnostic X-ray machines, and the operators are less aware of potential hazard.)
3. Central control of all isotopes as to purpose, ordering, receiving, storage, and use, and monitoring of use areas
4. Prompt professional investigation and cleanup of radioactive "spills"
5. Personnel monitoring by film badges and appropriate health examinations
6. Safe disposal of radioactive wastes, including carcasses and excreta of laboratory animals used in work with radioactive isotopes

Industrial and Occupational Safety For a discussion of industrial and occupational safety for shops, garages, storage places, etc., where employees and others work, see below under "Occupational Health," Chapter 5.

Staffing

Whether on the payroll, on retainer, or paid by services performed, each institution should have available to it the services of:

1. A qualified sanitarian, for proper inspection of all food service operations, refuse and waste disposal, swimming pools, and general sanitation and safety inspections of buildings—particularly dormitories and other student residences. For smaller institutions, arrangements can usually be made with sanitarians employed by local municipal or state health departments to consult at fee part time. For full-time positions, the same sources may be tapped or inquiry may be made via military sources for chief medical corpsmen or medical service corps officers who are about to retire from active duty. One full-time sanitarian just barely covers the job for a residential university of 10,000 students.
2. A sanitary engineer, usually as consultant, is desirable when new construction is being planned, and in some very large and complex institutions may be justified on a full-time basis.
3. A health physicist, at least on a part-time basis, is essential whenever radiation hazards are present—for inspection, monitoring, and other control functions. For sanitary engineers and health physicists, inquiry can be made through university schools of public health or through the state and the larger local health departments.

STANDING FIRST-AID AND EMERGENCY SERVICES FOR THE ACUTELY AND SERIOUSLY ILL OR INJURED

Even when no other medical function exists or is provided, there must be formally organized provisions for:

1. Prompt, on-the-spot first-aid and emergency holding care (pending transfer to definitive care).

2. Routine procedures for rapid communication with sources of more definitive medical-surgical care, with necessary transportation to bring the patient to such care or vice-versa.

Failure to have such provisions is both morally and legally indefensible (see Section 1, Chapter 7), and even if primary responsibility must be delegated to a lay person trained in first aid (as may obtain in a very small and isolated institution), some degree of medical responsibility is involved.

For this reason, such services, no matter how simple or seldom used, should be organized under the advice, supervision, and responsibility of a licensed physician who, even if on a part-time or voluntary, basis, is officially appointed by the institution as its chief medical officer or physician in charge.

Organization and Policy Making Considerations

In even the smallest colleges, first-aid and emergency services should be planned and operated by the person immediately in charge (preferably a licensed registered nurse) in close consultation with:

Administrators These include all needed to determine written policies and procedures for:

1. Appropriate notification of college officials, parents, and others responsibly concerned in emergencies of students, staff, and visitors

2. Reporting of accidents for potential liability, Workmen's Compensation and other insurance claims and for review by the safety program for purposes of correcting hazards (see above, under "Environmental Health and Safety," page 9-11).

3. Distribution and updating of emergency information to the campus—to students, faculty, and staff

4. Case disposition and transfer of responsibility for different categories of people, namely minor students, other students, faculty and staff, adult visitors, unaccompanied minors—each of which may require different policies

5. Hours of first-aid station official operation and statement of prearranged alternatives when the station is closed

Fire, Police, Rescue, and Ambulance Units These may be both campus affiliated and municipal, as may be needed to determine responsibility, procedures, and communications channels for:

1. Telephone and radio emergency communications between the aid station, these units, and other sources of help. Some means of emergency contact with security or police units outside of the telephone is essential, whether needed because of telephone failure for any other reason, or if situations involving disturbed or violent persons prevent telephone use or other verbal communication. For the former situation, portable (walkie-talkie) two-way radio communication with police and/or fire units is invaluable and should be a normal part of emergency and health service equipment and operations as it is for other protective and emergency community services. When neither telephone nor radio can be used, a concealed switch or button that can be operated unobtrusively by the nurse or others on duty, connected to an alarm in security or police headquarters, will promptly bring help to the scene.

2. Training and advice in and provision of techniques and equipment for rescue and resuscitation

3. Emergency transportation by trained persons in properly equipped vehicles of the seriously injured or ill to hospitals and necessary but less critical transportation of other patients who should not drive or walk—as by taxi or "Medicab," etc.

4. Safe restraint and transportation of seriously disturbed persons to designated psychiatric hospitals (a separate function often restricted by statute to a specific agency,

such as the county sheriff or the local health officer, which should be located early and with which procedures should be worked out)

5. Legally required reports to designated public agencies concerning certain injuries (e.g., gunshot wounds)

Health Professional and Care Resources These are liaisons which should be made and maintained by the nurse in charge and/or the college's chief medical officer or director.

1. Establishment of a group of physicians willing to be on call, preferably by schedule, for emergency consultation by the aid station, by phone or in person whenever the unit is in operation and for other special functions (see below). Procedures should be periodically established in writing setting forth mutually agreeable terms of compensation by fee, retainer, or other benefits for services.

2. Liaison and agreement with accredited[3] hospitals for responsible transfer of patients for specialized, definitive, and intensive care

3. Establishment of general referral lists of local professional resources for less serious ambulatory cases who request referral for medical, surgical, dental, or other health problems

4. Adoption and periodic revision of all first-aid and emergency medical policies and procedures to be used (e.g., "Handling of Lacerations and Wounds," "Nosebleeds," etc.) as well as selection and use of necessary equipment and supplies, staff appointments and duties, planning for addition or change of service, etc.

All such procedures should be in writing, dated, and approved by the signature of the physician in charge (for both medical and legal reasons, who should also approve the annual program and budget, all staff additions and appointments, and purchase of all medical equipment, supplies, and medications (see below, "Pharmacy, Drugs, and Medical Supply Services," page 9-64).

Location, Space, and Equipment of First-aid Station

The first-aid and emergency station should be centrally located and clearly identified, with as ready access to both foot and vehicular traffic as possible, and with corridors, doors, elevators, and exits capable of receiving and discharging patients by wheelchair, gurney, or stretcher.

Space and facilities should include areas and appropriate furnishings for:

1. Reception, and waiting; closely coupled with
2. Records, clerical support, and communications.
3. General emergency examination and treatment area, with highly accessible storage of immediately needed drugs and supplies.
4. Separate isolation and rest area, with one or more daybeds or cots for transient care and rest for those awaiting transfer, relief from administered treatment, or the passing of temporarily disabling symptoms such as headache, menstrual cramps, etc. (By addition of a small writing shelf or desk and a telephone extension, this area can serve part time as a quiet area in which nurse and/or doctor may conduct confidential interviews, referrals, or examinations.) This area must be adjacent to
5. Toilet and lavatory.
6. General storage of medical and clerical supplies.

As rule of thumb, for each thousand students or major fraction thereof, 2 cots or daybeds and 10 waiting chairs should be provided.

Equipment and supplies, as approved by the physician in charge, must be adequate for anticipated emergencies. Oxygen with portable equipment for its administration should be available. Personnel, including registered nurses, should be trained in resuscitative procedures and in external cardiac massage. For cardiac emergencies

[3] Accredited by Joint Commission of Hospital Accreditation.

and major toxicity or trauma, a respirator or resuscitative unit is essential. The AMBU® respirator is inexpensive and adequate for first-aid purposes if accompaned by a standard double-ended plastic airway.

In addition, simple and inexpensive mechanical assistance[4] for external cardiac massage can make even a 90-pound nurse effective in this lifesaving technique.

At least one fold-up wheelchair and one collapsible stretcher, if not a gurney, should be on hand, for fetching and discharging persons who cannot or should not walk—particularly essential for such operations within a building or building complex.

Medications may be administered or dispensed in the first-aid service only upon a physician's order, and in this limited service should be restricted to those intended for true emergency. A locked kit of emergency medications for use on telephone or direct order and use by a physician should be provided for use in acute situations. The supervising physician is responsible for purchase, security, and administration of all such drugs as well as legally required records of narcotics and dangerous drugs dispensed and on hand.

Records include at minimum an emergency log of the format used in hospital emergency rooms and a folder for each student enrolled and each other person treated filed alphabetically or by registration number, in which are filed usual identifying information and such health data as the institution requires for matriculation (see "Health and Admissions," Chapter 4), plus any medical correspondence, nurses' or doctors' notes, and carbons of reports.

The contents of these folders, including all medical information received from patients, their families, or medical sources in connection with admissions, employment, illness, injury, etc., is legally and ethically confidential and may be read, evaluated, and interpreted only by qualified licensed nurses or physicians and divulged only with the consent of the patient.

Accident report forms for the recording of medical and circumstantial data, including disposition of the patient, should be maintained in duplicate; one copy should be filed in the individual's folder and the other copies sent routinely to a designated administrative officer. In case of serious injury, a copy of the original report should be sent immediately to the appropriate administrator.

Referral follow-up recording mechanisms should be a part of the log or patient folder. For this purpose, a standard form, with automatic carbon, entitled "Request for Consultation or Transfer of Care" is very useful. On this are noted the patient's identifying data, date and hour, reason for request, person to whom referred (i.e., local professional, family, or other helping resource), and whether direct contact was made or not. There should also be space for a brief reply indicating that transfer of care took place and for any pertinent information of use to the institution. Made up in triplicate, in pads, the original plus one copy accompanying patient to referral point (or, if legal adults refuse referral against advice, is signed to that effect and left at aid station) and the third copy being retained as a "tickler" until completed follow-up is obtained. The consultant or person accepting responsibility for transfer of care or consultation is asked to return one copy to the institution, retaining the other if desired for his own records.

Daytime staffing for this station and function *alone* requires at least:

1. One RN (registered nurse) or LPN (licensed practical nurse) for up to 2,500 students, with part-time clerical help.

2. One RN and one clerical-worker aide, both full time, for 2,500 to 5,000 students, and for each increment or major fraction of 2,500.

If staffed at night or during off hours, one nurse and one aide for each 5,000 students is adequate. For smaller institutions with nighttime and off-hours obligations to resi-

[4] Rentsch Cardiac Press Board (available through United States Medical Controls, Inc., E. Hartford, Conn.).

dential students or others, emergency functions may be delegated, with the medical director's approval, to local hospitals, clinics, or practitioners which, by mutual agreement, should send a copy of the patient-visit record to the college.

Emergency Services for Special Events

In addition to expectable day-in, day-out health emergencies, colleges and universities often sponsor and arrange events bringing large numbers together, including the general public—such as football and other athletic events, theatrical and other cultural events, and academic convocations such as commencement.

Such events and convocations require specific plans and assignments of responsibility to assure that, in immediate proximity, are:

1. One or more qualified nurses or doctors in actual and continuous attendance with basic emergency supplies
2. Immediate communications to sources of help (on-call doctors, ambulance, police, hospitals, etc.), best provided by portable two-way radio, but otherwise by telephones on site and student "runners"—least desirably by public address
3. Immediately available ambulance or equivalent transport service, preferably on site
4. Predetermined plans for evacuation to hospital or other appropriate sources of care

For large gathering of several thousand or more, and most particularly in warm weather, screened-off or otherwise protected and shaded areas for cots are necessary for cases of fainting from heat exhaustion. A single nurse, with physician on call close by and rapid communication and transportation at hand, can cover crowds of ten thousand in warm weather and twenty thousand in cool.

Disaster Plans

Coordinated General Disaster Plan The occasional catastrophe should remind us of the need for some plan for mobilizing and directing the community's resources for rescue, communications, evacuation, and emergency care and lodging in the event of major fires, floods, earthquakes, and other disasters.

Such plans should be roughly considered for three general situations in order of priority:

1. Those in which the disaster is confined to the institution, which must then summon outside help for fire control, rescue, evacuation, etc.
2. Those in which the disaster is outside the institution, but for which its helping resources are needed
3. Those in which institution and neighboring communities share in disaster

Plans must clearly be coordinated and developed jointly between institutional authorities; local and state authorities for hire, police, and public health; local medical and hospital societies; the local Red Cross; and with Civil Defense authorities theoretically for defense but more practically for additional sources of assistance. Plans must also be made for a practical, central contact point for coordination plans, as the necessary committee and communications structures are often located there.

"Limited" Disaster Plans Similar categories and priorities of thought should be applied to relatively small but still very dangerous situations on campus such as laboratory explosion, localized fires, etc.

If there is an infirmary with staff, there should be first a plan for evacuation and transfer and getting needed help for fire or disaster within the infirmary; second, a plan for mobilization of health-center resources and personnel to help with disaster elsewhere on campus.

"Epidemic" Disaster Plans Two relatively common epidemics today, while not serious in mortality, can within a period of hours to days temporarily prostrate hundreds of victims requiring bed rest or medical attention of some kind. They are influenza and (broadly speaking) "food poisoning." While one hopes that proper immunization, sanitation, and food preparation will prevent them, the appearance of new influenza strains and the inevitability of occasional lapses in sanitation make it possible for such outbreaks to occur.

The principal administrative problem is that of the simultaneous acute illness of large numbers, numbers too large for accommodation by any infirmary or hospital or to be seen by normal clinic processes.

In largely commuter colleges, the administrative problem is lessened in that the patients expect to look homeward for care and rest. In largely residential colleges it is greater, but the solution lies in the same direction; i.e., in organizing the rest and feeding function around the dormitory and the medical screening and supervision function around roving teams of nurses, with doctor's backup, to visit patients in the residences and to transfer to the infirmary or hospital only the sickest.

Community Health Education and Information

In addition to formal curricular approaches appropriate to general undergraduate education, general teacher education, and special preparation of professional health educators, institutions have other needs and opportunities for the effective presentation of health-related information. They may be categorized as follows:

General Public Information for Emergencies This is information on fire, security, and accident, etc., in the form of prominently posted placards in phone booths, on bulletin boards, etc.; telephone stickers, material for inclusion in student handbooks, orientation sessions, and routine information to new faculty and employees. Such information should include alternative procedures for such times as regular facilities may not be in operation.

Health Care and Service Information A regular provision should be a brochure for students, parents, and others concerned in institutional health services describing briefly but precisely what responsibilites and services the institution will and will not undertake for students; what health insurance coverage is offered and/or required; under what circumstances parental consent or responsibility will be required and sought; and when the institution will normally expect to proceed with care without special permission or notification.

The professional in charge of health services should be expected to draft this information, which should then be approved and distributed by administration to all students, student-personnel staff, and department heads.

Education by Example The manner in which the institution acts in its concern for members' health is important in the formation of attitudes and health behavior. Any number of verbal warnings about the health hazards of smoking, for instance, do not make much impact if cigarette advertising is permitted in college papers and magazines or if cigarette vending machines abound on campus, particularly in the health service or hospital.

Each contact with a health service is potentially one for poor or good impressions: inadequate or inappropriate care given in an offhand and impersonal manner, in a dingy, crowded health facility is negative education as well as bad medicine and cancels the confidence and trust without which the informal but valuable and relevant education that should be a regular part of care is useless.

Information and Communication between Health Professionals and Others Student personnel officers, residence hall directors, etc., deal constantly with students who may present health problems. A deliberate and organized program of regular liaison between professional health resources, through the health service and these others, is an absolute necessity to maintain and improve the abilities of academic officers to recognize and to make effective use of health consultation and referrals for emergency with confidence, flexibility, and skill. The students whose dormitory director does not know what services are available nor how or when to use them are suffering from the inadequate health education of their director. (See Chapter 4.)

Health Program Advisory Committee. A well-constituted health program advisory committee is a useful mechanism. Minutes of its meetings should be kept and distributed to all administrators, department heads, and student groups.

Membership on Other University Committees. Health service professionals should be involved in institutional committees involving health, such as committees on environmental health and safety, radiation hazards, student life and affairs, personnel and faculty improvement, and insurance. They should also, in other appropriate ways, involve themselves actively in institutional affairs.

Assigned Liaison to Institutional Groups. The deliberate assignment of liaison duties to health service personnel is an excellent practice in which, for instance, one staff physician might have responsibility for two or three student residences to which he would act as general adviser, meeting regularly with dormitory staff and student leaders, while another might relate primarily to a foreign student program.

Health Program Subcommittee of Governing Board. The establishment of a health program subcommittee of the board, for periodic and ad hoc review of health problems, budget, and program, is of great help to the institution (see Chapter 6).

Extracurricular Health Education Students, their parents, and others in the institutional community have many predictable and occasionally special concerns relating to health, such as drugs and drug abuse; the changing sexual and moral value system, contraception, etc.; the threat (or more commonly, exaggerated fear) of epidemics raised by the press or by rumor; and recurrent concerns and confusions about such common conditions as infectious mononucleosis, colds, menstrual disorders, acne, and weight problems.

A wide range of extracurricular approaches is both available and desirable, such as:

1. Topic-oriented publications or announcements, including pamphlets, newsletters, brochures, newspaper and radio spots, etc., which are most useful for the publicizing of new or special programs (i.e., immunization program for influenza, etc., addition of psychiatric services, etc.); for giving information about common conditions; or for correcting rumors, etc. Such publications are useful for display in health-service waiting areas, for handing out by nurse or doctor to individual student patients, and to amplify and reinforce verbal explanations and instructions.

2. Informal discussions and seminars with small student groups, most profitably when the invitation comes from them. Sponsorship may be by associated students, deans of students, student union committees, health service directors, local medical societies, etc. While each of these sectors may have important contributions to make, there is still a need for a health educator with community orientation and experience, administratively assigned to work with all community elements, to involve them and guide them in the development of effective and appropriate programs, and to integrate health education with other activities of the health program that reach and influence the community.

Administrative Organization

Coordinator of Extracurricular Health Education Such a coordinator or director of extracurricular health education, whether part or full time, may be found among academic departments of health education or among health educators with public health and community training. Administrative placement should be under the health service if the health service directorship has sufficient breadth of community involvement and understanding, but otherwise under student personnel (as part of extracurricular and residential education programs). Academic appointment should be to whatever school or department for which he is qualified by degrees in education and/or public health. In addition to his community involvement and program coordination, he should be qualified and prepared to serve as an expert resource in the preparation of bulletins, brochures, pamphlets, and articles relating to health and in the proper use of audio-visual and meeting techniques.

Chapter **3**

Student Health

MAURICE M. OSBORNE, JR.

Director of Student Health Services, Tufts School of Medicine and Dental Medicine, Boston, Massachusetts

The nature and purposes of the student health program are largely defined by the needs, vulnerabilities, and risks common to the age group, while the sharing of responsibilities for different aspects of the program among institutions, families, and local health resources will depend on the proportion of students living at home, the availability of local resources, and institutional programs such as athletics.

HEALTH CHARACTERISTICS OF STUDENTS

Although in terms of mortality and serious or handicapping illnesses the student age group is the healthiest, it has a high incidence of infectious disease, particularly respiratory and intestinal, and has not completely outgrown the childhood diseases, such as measles or mumps. Tuberculosis is more frequent in late adolescence and early adulthood than it is until late middle age, and carries, particularly for young women, a fairly serious risk.

Youth is very frequently subject to automotive and other types of injury. Although mostly minor, such injuries do cause the greatest portion of deaths in this age group.

The transition from childhood dependency to adult independence and self-confidence has never been easy, but with today's deep uncertainties, changing values, and awesome array of choices, it can be overwhelming, with manifestations ranging from underachievement and dropping out to antisocial behavior, drug abuse, psychosis, and suicide. Of all health-connected reasons for academic wastage, emotional and personal problems far outrun all others, and while it is infrequent (one to two per 10,000 students per year), suicide is the second leading cause of death among students.

Skin conditions are very frequent (e.g., acne, boils, and fungus infections), and while seldom threatening to general health, their importance to students superbly illustrates the intensity of a young person's reaction and concern about anything that makes him look or feel different and that appears to threaten his acceptability or his potential for success.

Every student-health worker must accept that it is of equal and often greater importance to recognize and manage the student's anxieties about a condition as to provide him an appropriate prescription.

This is also illustrated by youth's tremendous anxiety about still tentative manhood or womanhood, bringing to the student health service a high proportion of genitally oriented symptoms such as menstrual cramps and irregularities and many other symptoms often the result of concern and guilt over sexual fantasy and behavior, ranging from the harmless (e.g., masturbation) up to possibilities both real and fancied of unwanted pregnancy or venereal disease.

A few other conditions affecting this age group are worthy of special mention. Of these, infectious mononucleosis is the foremost, having its very highest incidence in the college-age group. It holds, for perhaps 10 to 15 percent of cases, the possibility of being too ill to work for several weeks; but for the great majority it is, with knowledgeable management, a relatively minor and passing problem which should not result in significant loss of time or credits and does not result in "epidemics."

Spontaneous pneumothorax (lung collapse due to rupture of a lung "blister") is more frequent in this age group than any other, and acute appendicitis occurs as often as in earlier childhood. Both conditions require ready availability of surgical services.

Although numerically rare (one to two cases per 10,000 students per year) some tumors, notably cancer of the testicle and malignancies of lymph and blood tissue, are relatively frequent in college students, and with all other malignant tumors (which in youth tend to be severe) they account for the third leading cause of death.

Chronic diseases are relatively rare, with epilepsy, diabetes, asthma, other allergies, ulcers, and colitis most often seen. Generally these are not incompatible with most programs in higher education provided adequate medical supervision is available.

Two rare conditions deserve specific mention because they may, in an apparently healthy youth, particularly during physical exertion, result in sudden and shocking death.

One is congenital aneurysm (thin-walled bulge) in a brain artery that under stress "blows out" with massive, sudden, and usually fatal results from brain hemorrhage. It is, for practical purposes, undetectable before rupture, occurring in otherwise healthy people.

The other is congenital aortic stenosis, a disease which should *not* escape detection if it is looked for in routine examinations or at least prior to physical education, particularly as it is now surgically curable.

In the student's experiences of personal illness or concern, even a single episode of unsympathetic, careless, or obviously inappropriate treatment often prejudices him strongly against seeking needed care. Conversely, well-organized, dignified, and relevant handling of his health program inspires the student with confidence to seek answers to and help for further health problems.

Health Science, Judgment, and the Human Condition

Good care and management are ideally based on a very sound but oft-ignored principle that the best decisions are reached when the responsible professional understands (1) the person he is attending; (2) the disease he is confronted with; (3) the environment in which the patient lives, works, ails, and seeks relief, and with which the professional must also work; and (4) the operative relationships among each of these.

Students are particular kinds of people. They live in a complex and special environment of people and pressures and have some frequently expectable diseases and injuries to which they react in certain ways. Anyone not familiar with students, their reactions to health problems, and the environmental hazards and opportunities of college living can too often only make a partial diagnosis and will too often prescribe a common chemical when the important prescription has at least to include the human touch.

Youth and the Need for a "Neutral Corner"

In the student's "going to college," he often must put behind him the need for his parents' support, but in transition he sorely needs a substitute source of personal adult acceptance, comfort, and guidance.

The perceptive and open-minded health professional in the student health service should help a great deal in meeting this need. Health professionals, helping and comforting in the institutional setting, are uniquely situated to provide the confidential and nonjudgmental adult contact so needed and wanted by youth, contact in which the concern and attention are directed to the person and not just his performance, where how he feels is as important as how he does, and no marks are given.

THE CORE STUDENT HEALTH SERVICE

In addition to handling true emergencies, the core service must be staffed and prepared to:

1. Receive students and pay personal, confidential attention to them on the basis of their concerns about a wide range of health problems, however "minor"

2. Render appropriate advice, comfort, first aid, and information that students understand and can believe

3. Isolate and give temporary rest to students awaiting transfer, the passing of temporary symptoms, or the effects of medication

4. Provide and use effective communications with, and referral mechanisms to, necessary community sources of definitive health care, involving families as appropriate

5. Arrange, administer, or cooperate with preventive programs

6. Handle the administration of two-way communications and interpretations involving:

a. Bringing about necessary program changes and institutional adaptation for health reasons (such as preferential seating, course-load reduction, exam postponement, modified physical education or medical withdrawal, etc.) through appropriate intervention with administrators, faculty, counselors, etc.

b. Interpretation to students, families, and their private health resources of institutional policy relative to health (such as matriculation requirements, requirements for physical exams, immunizations, etc.: requirements for medical clearance for readmission, for participation in special-risk activities, etc.)

7. Stimulate, and cooperate with, health-educational efforts by learning about and using appropriate health information literature and displays, by locating and contacting local professionals who can act as speakers and group discussion leaders, and by

maintaining close working relations with other institutional officers and personnel with responsibilities for students (see page 9-17 on community health education)

Specific Core Service Administrative Responsibilities and Guidelines

In addition to the record keeping, referral and follow-up, accident reporting, and communication responsibilities of the basic first-aid station,[1] the core student health service will have special responsibilities for:

Records

1. Receiving, storage in lockable files, and interpretation of all medical information bearing on administrative decisions, rematriculation, academic program changes, and withdrawls relative to all health requirements. As a normal part of student folders there are entrance physical reports and immunization records.

2. Providing separate locked storage for personal and/or medical information considered sensitive or prejudicial by either the health professional or the patient. Such information should be in writing solely as a help to the student's care and welfare and should not be treated as part of his official medical record (see "Legal Aspects," page 1-90, on confidentiality).

Program Policy and Information The key person or persons in the core service, or any student health service, has the responsibility to advise and consult with the administration concerning all health-related policies and to draft or approve drafts for administrative adoption of:

1. Statements for students and parents of program intent, coverage, and limitations.
2. Health-insurance policy provisions
3. Admissions, matriculation, and other health requirements

Symptomatic, Short-term Medication and Treatment of Minor Complaints and Injuries In terms of absolute legality, the provision of diagnosis and treatment by other than licensed physicians must be limited to standard first-aid procedures for the control of hemorrhage, shock, the splinting of injuries, comfort and reassurance, and prevention of further injury or damage until care can be assumed by more definitive and legal resources.[2] In general, medications should not be given in the physician's absence, but it is virtually impossible to refuse all medication.

For practical purposes, and with minimal if any likelihood of legal action or other difficulties, some symptomatic, short-term, and simple medications and treatments may be given to students for some of the numerous minor problems they present (such as simple headache, particle in eye, menstrual cramps, uncomplicated colds, etc.) if, but *only* if:

1. There is an officially appointed licensed physician in charge and readily reached.

2. There are direct, specific physician's orders for the particular case, given in person by telephone or on the premises; or there are standing orders, dated and signed by the current physician in charge, which describe and define:

a. Conditions which may or may not be symptomatically treated without further consultation and any limiting criteria (such as fever, rash, abdominal pain, etc.) which would annul the standing order;

b. Specific symptomatic medication and dosage, limited to no more than 24 hours' use; and

c. Instructions to patient for medical follow-up if symptoms persist over 24 hours.

3. Any medications so dispensed are given by a person (physician, pharmacist, registered nurse, or licensed practical nurse) licensed to do so and are stored and accounted for legally under the physician in chief's name. (See discussion of drugs,

[1] See page 9-14

[2] See Chapter 7 of Section 1, on legal aspects of health services.

dispensing, storage and pharmacies, page 9-64; and "Legal Aspects of Health Services," page 1-78.)

4. Specific record of complaint, findings, and medication dispensed or treatment given is made by the nurse and subsequently initialed by the physician.

Basic facilities equipment and location are basically those of the first-aid and emergency station (see page 9-14), but, as the core service is intended to make students welcome and inspire their confidence and trust as well as to allow their being interviewed privately and personally and as an educational and health-promotional function is assumed, the facilities should include conscious attention to provision of comfortable waiting areas in which health-educational and other educational and cultural materials may be displayed and made casually available.

In addition, whenever patient volume and numbers of waiting patients exceeds more than a half dozen, dispersed waiting areas should be provided.

Dispersed waiting areas, for four to five students at the most per area, should relate to the function or person for which the student is waiting; i.e., to see doctor x or y, to see the nurse, to ask about insurance, to have a lab test, etc. Such dispersal lessens enormously the inevitable tensions and disappointments (for both patients and staff) inherent in massed waiting, in which patients watch to see who is taken next, misinterpret the reasons for priority of call, are embarrassed to confront their peers when not at their best, and in which the staff looks out with apprehension to see "so many" waiting.

Personal interview and examination areas for use by nurse or on-call doctor should ideally, in the core service, be more private, dignified, and separate than in a straight emergency service, with standard examination table and equipment and effective soundproofing.

Treatment and preventive service areas, because of the desirability of public-health preventive programs of tuberculin testing, physical examination, and immunizations (if these are to be administered by the institution), should be increased in area and equipment to provide for refrigeration of biologicals; measurement of height, weight, temperature, and blood-pressure; vision screening; and both space and traffic flow for handling large numbers in rapid mass screening and/or inoculation as at registration or in epidemic prevention programs.

Such areas may, in small institutions, be "borrowed" for special programs from other school or local areas; but in institutions with enrollments of over 1,000 they should be built in.

Staffing needs at minimum are roughly twice those needed for basic "industrial" first-aid and emergency stations; i.e., for daytimes:

1. Full-time registered nurse (or properly student-and-community-health trained licensed practical nurse) for 1,000 to 1,500 students, with one full-time clerical worker.

2. One additional full-time registered nurse or licensed practical nurse for each additional 1,500 students or major fractions thereof over 1,000 base, with additional part-time clerical-aide help. An appointed medical director, or physician in charge on call, is even more crucial to the core student health service than to the straight first-aid station as the demands and expectations for symptomatic treatment, for diagnostic and liaison functions to aid for interpretation of medical information and advice, availability, and assumption of ethical and legal responsibility, occur at twice the rate as for first-aid supervision alone.

Limitations of Core Services and Staffing

Where such a core student health service (staffed by nurses and aides, with on-call physician in charge, and organized in conjunction with the campuswide first-aid and emergency service) represents the limit of college facilities, it should be clearly defined and recognized as such, and a statement of the extent of services should be included in brochures or catalogs. (See "Legal Aspects of Health Services," page 1-78.)

The institution should make sure that other aspects of health care are realistically available to all its students, through families and local resources. In general, student health services may wisely and safely be restricted to the core service and staff only when 95 to 100 percent of its students live at home, within a practical half-day's transfer to home, or in other established households which will assume responsibility; or when that percentage are over 21 and independently established and when no general expectation exists for additional services.

Criteria for Provision of Additional Student Health Service

If the case is otherwise and any number of minor and dependent students live (in or out of official residences) more than a half day's practical transfer to family responsibility or other household adult responsibility, the institution must make some provision for availability of additional local medical and health care by prearrangement.

Extension of Core Service Concept

Although the discussion preceding has dealt primarily with the core service in its basic organizational aspects and minimal staffing patterns, the core concepts (with their emphasis on students as people, the flexible use of both health and institutional machinery to get results and reduce academic wastage, and the conscious attempt to instill sound health attitudes and behavior) do not, or must not, cease with the core organization. The same principles and viewpoints should characterize each increment in student health service and be strongly evident throughout even the largest and most sophisticated and comprehensive of institutional health programs.

PREVENTIVE SERVICES—GENERAL

In addition to the general kinds of screening of students that should go with the process of admissions and matriculation that are designed to

1. Exclude those with disabilities incompatible with the school's environment or program
2. Provide sufficient information on accepted matriculants to permit early identification of needs for modified programs and for special and/or continuing health care

Several other preventative health requirements should be applied whenever possible.

Tuberculosis Screening and Control

(See "Health Characteristics of Students," page 9-22.)

To protect the health of the institutional community, a screening program for tuberculosis prior to or just following matriculation is appropriate, particularly in residential institutions and those drawing a substantial portion of students from poor urban and other endemic areas or cultures (e.g., predominantly Negro, American Indian, or Asian groups). It is also of special importance in professional schools such as medicine, dentistry, nursing, and paramedical training in which students are under increased risks of exposure and where tuberculosis screening should be a continuing annual program. (Note: To be truly effective to the public health, such screening should include not just students *but all new employees and faculty members.* See "Occupational Health," page 9-83.)

Immunizations

In the interest of the general health and to some degree as a protection against institutional liability, entrance to college offers an administrative mechanism and opportunity to secure up-to-date immunity for a large population group against the commonly expected and immunizable diseases. For most Americans, these include smallpox, poliomyelitis, diptheria and tetanus. For women students they include rubella (German measles), and, for institutions with certain epidemic risks,[3] typhoid. For health-professional schools, mumps immunization is desirable; for special field trips and overseas study, the requirements for the area as set forth by the U.S. Public Health Service should be followed. (See "Sponsored Field Trips, etc." below.)

Administration of tuberculosis screening and immunization programs will vary with the background of the students and the quality of care available to them.

If most students are not drawn from poverty areas and if the institution can realistically enforce it, it is by far most efficient and practical to require submission of bona fide records of recent negative tuberculin skin test or negative chest X-ray and of recent immunization as a prerequisite to initial registration, with a fine imposed for late filing.

Where this is not possible, the institution should require tuberculosis screening and at least encourage immunizations after matriculation, and it should carry out the program itself. In many localities, public health personnel, materials, and X-ray facilities are available at minimum or no cost through departments of public health and tuberculosis associations. Such agencies often will provide testing and immunizing materials, mobile or other X-ray units, and follow-up of families of positive tuberculin reactors, particularly to smaller and to "community" colleges. With such consultation and assistance, even the core student health services of small colleges and "commuter" and junior colleges can include these services.

Larger colleges and universities with more developed health services and X-ray facilities may organize and provide these services intramurally if such tests are not required prior to arrival.

Special Case-finding Programs

The routine performance of physical examinations on entering students is less and less productive as a tool for the discovery of unrecognized and treatable health conditions. Review of such examinations at Stanford University revealed that, at least since 1960, fewer than 1 percent of all entering students were found by these means to have previously unknown conditions for which treatment was needed. Although some credit is given to the entrance physical as an "educational experience" and introduction to the health service, it must be carried out with great thoroughness and corresponding expense to be a positive experience.

However, when students are drawn in any number from previous environments of special risk and/or from backgrounds of medical deprivation, (e.g., students from underdeveloped and poverty cultures, both foreign and domestic) institutionally sponsored programs for medical examination are both desirable and fruitful.

(For preventive examinations and programs associated with participation in college and university programs of special risk, such as athletics, see "Special Situations," page 9-51, and discussion of other preventive-medicine programs.) "Prevention" is a very broad concept and applies to all health-educational efforts (see community health education), mental health programs, dental programs, environmental health and safety, athletic medicine, and all special-risk programs.

GENERAL AMBULATORY MEDICAL-SURGICAL CARE

Approximately 80 to 85 percent of all needs for medical and surgical care of students can be quite adequately met by the general-purpose physician or clinic with the help of nursing service, the support of relatively simple laboratory and X-ray services, and a readily available source of commonly used drugs and medical supplies. Professionally satisfactory diagnosis, counseling, and treatment of the majority of students is

[3] Particularly those in the Southwest, whence students may travel easily to Mexico.

rendered by the general family internist, pediatrician, or general practitioner in or out of a college health service.

He will function best for any patient if he also has frequent contact with and access to a broad range of specialist colleagues through whom his diagnostic sharpness, his ability to manage more complicated cases, and his knowledge of when and how to refer appropriately are all enhanced.

His value is greatest when he works within and as an integral part of the institution, as an extension of the "core" principle of student health service.

This is yet another vital argument for the appointment of a physician in charge, even part time, to even the smallest or most basic student health service. By his regular contact with the institution and its people, he can amplify the private physician's capabilities in school-related diagnosis and treatment if his communications with his colleagues and with the academic community are tactful and friendly.

For these reasons, a number of "commuter" institutions have found that having such services as part of the institutional health program has paid off in terms of student welfare and attendance, family satisfaction, and health education.

For small residential colleges, at least part-time on campus and full-time local availability of general ambulatory medical-surgical care must be arranged, preferably by prepayment or by fee for service chargeable to parents via the college (which is more expensive in both total outlay and overhead). Larger institutions with any number of residential students will be expected to provide general medical-surgical ambulatory service as part of the core service.

Facilities and Performance

Wherever offered, this general care function should be, as the core service, highly accessible to students in terms of location, hours, and lack of financial or procedural barriers. It should provide a confidential and confidence-inspiring setting for the reception, waiting, interviewing, and examination of students, who should feel that they are receiving personal and dignified attention in a manner equal to that expected in a private physician's office.

Rigid appointment systems do not fit variable student needs and tend to break down, while a total laissez faire or "walk-in" policy leads to predictable log jams and inequities, particularly if strict "first-come-first-served" policies are applied. What is needed is a flexible system, related to differing needs, and controlled by triage (systematic sorting and disposition), by both receptionists and nurses, of students who require:

1. Rapid inspection and/or handling; e.g., minor scrapes, splinters, and other little injuries, follow-up inspection, changes of bandage, report or instructions, injections, etc.
2. Privacy of doctor's office for personal problems, history taking, examination for current problems, etc.
3. Physician's service for review, counseling, examination, or special procedures on routine or follow-up problems

Facilities are thus basically of the core service except that:

1. The personal interview and examination areas (i.e., the "doctors' offices") may need additional equipment as required for particular physicians to utilize their skills, and in general these areas are to be used only by the attending physicians.
2. The nursing service will require its own confidential interviewing and examination area for screening and initial evaluation of sensitive cases, for making referrals—as, for example, to gynecology—best not made in an open treatment room, and for counseling. This area should be located as nearly as possible between or equidistant from the reception area and the general treatment area.
3. The general treatment area will need to include some additional waiting space and an additional treatment space with necessary equipment for doctors and nurses who will use this area for minor, rapidly handled complaints which account for nearly

50 percent of all student visits and who will at the same time be able to conduct preliminary measurement for physicals, preventive programs, and other nursing functions.

Records Records are basically the same as for the core service, except that they should generally involve a thorough past medical and personal health history (which may be part of the prematriculation requirements) for each student in addition to immunization records, doctors' and nurses' notes, etc., and they should provide space for recording or other inclusion of laboratory and X-ray reports.

Staffing (Medical, Nursing, and Clerical)[4] Including the time that can be given to clinical work with students by director or chief medical officer, there should be at least one full-time equivalent M.D. in general clinical work for each 1,500 students or major fraction thereof if more than perfunctory service is to be given. His chief requirement is for understanding and liking people, the skills to perform well the ordinary tasks of general office practice, preferably some minor surgical abilities, and the ability to decide when to refer or call for consultation. He is drawn chiefly from the ranks of general practitioners, internists, and pediatricians. (See Chapter 6 for qualifications, appointments, salaries, etc.)

Daytime nursing services require, in addition to the registered nurse in charge (or head nurse), roughly one registered nurse or licensed practical nurse per full-time physician equivalent. In larger services, this ratio may be diminished somewhat or may be altered by the substitution of aides or nursing clerks when it is found that too many functions—such as ordering, record keeping, telephoning, and appointment making—are being expensively done by registered nurses. The rule of thumb is one full-time equivalent (FTE) in nursing services to each medical FTE, and the same rule applies roughly to clerical workers. Student health demands greater clerical input than an equivalent private doctor's office, particularly if the director is active in academic and/or professional activities.

Hours and Night Coverage Regular clinic hours should be arranged to allow student visits with a minimum of class and activity disruption. It is best to plan and staff for maximum walk-in loads during times of fewest classes and to schedule appointments primarily during class times.

To render general office care during daytime imposes an obligation to provide for some means to follow it up or render it on emergency basis at night, particularly for residential campuses.

For smaller institutions, with only one or two physicians on the staff, it is necessary, as in the core service, to provide by prearrangement, and preferably covered by prepayment or by insurance (1) arrangements for care through local hospital emergency rooms, which have the advantages of being staffed and equipped and the disadvantages of being impersonal and often totally unsympathetic to student needs; or (2) an on-call roster of local practitioners; or (3) an indefatigable health-service physician willing to be on call 24 hours a day.

The night and after-hours alternatives must be clearly designated and appropriate information must be given on emergency placards to residence-hall personnel, switchboards, etc.

For larger institutions, with roughly five or more physicians on the staff, a rotating on-call roster may make it possible for the student to perceive that his daytime student health practitioner is a "real doctor" and will see him at night. Conversely, the health service physician who takes night call will see an entirely different and illuminating side of student life and customs, which will strengthen his understanding and effectiveness.

Alternatives are to hire resident physicians from local hospitals, but this is expensive and generally unsatisfactory.

[4] For support service staffing, see below, page 9-61 on laboratory, X-ray, and pharmacy.

Larger institutions may keep a nurse on duty for after-hours calls and screening, but unless such nurses are on duty for infirmary service already it is an expensive outlay, particularly as it is both unwise and potentially dangerous to have a nurse alone on night duty. The staffing needs to keep a nurse and an attendant on 24-hour duty 7 days a week, amount to 4.2 FTEs for each position over and above daytime base staff, so unless this staffing is also serving inpatients, it is costly service, particularly when the doctor on call must usually be called in any case and may often handle the problem by phone or at any rate without nursing assistance.

SPECIALIZED AMBULATORY MEDICAL-SURGICAL CARE

Approximately 10 to 15 percent of all student ambulatory health care needs are specialized, even though the generalist often may know how to treat the situation quite adequately.

For example the evaluation, including pelvic examination and interpretation of pelvic pneumoradiograms, of an overweight girl with no menstrual periods and excessive facial hair almost certainly requires the specialist's experience and knowledge. Another instance is the treatment of acne, which virtually any physician knows how to perform, but which often demands the dermatologist's services.

For student health purposes, specialized ambulatory services should be considered in two main categories:

1. Those most frequently needed, that is, aside from psychiatric/psychological services (see "Mental Health," page 9-41): the dermatologist, the gynecologist, and, wherever athletics and sports programs exist, the general surgeon and/or orthopedic surgeon
2. All other specialized medical-surgical consultants, treatments, and services such as cardiology, neurology, and plastic surgery.

Employment of Most Frequent Specialists

Anything that affects a student's appearance, his sexuality, and/or his performance is of special concern to the student, and therefore the categorical specialists (skin, gynecology, and musculoskeletal or orthopedic) are those most in demand and most frequently used. Such specialists are best utilized as extension of core and basic ambulatory care services, although it is seldom that any of them will have enough business or variety to warrant full-time employment as a specialist per se.

These "most frequent" medical-surgical specialists are most commonly employed as regular, part-time, salaried staff members who are on call at their regular offices for emergency or special consultations (or telephone consultations) and present at regularly stated hours by appointment only at the health service. It is wise for them to keep one or two appointments open, if possible, until the day or days of their regular clinics, either to accommodate some "emergency" patients or—and more importantly—to give an opportunity for consultations with their general physician colleagues.

Facilities and Equipment The dermatologist generally needs little beyond the use of a segregated space with natural light, but he may require laboratory use (for microscopic examinations for fungi and for making cultures) and "Wood's" light in a darkened space for diagnosis, as well as ultraviolet-light treatment equipment and space.

The gynecologist needs a completely private examining space, at least 10 feet by 6 feet, capable of containing comfortably a special examining table with stirrups, spotlight, and stool, and storage for special examination instruments and laboratory materials, as for "Pap" smears and hanging-drop preparations. It is most desirable that this examination space be privately accessible to a lavatory and toilet or that it have its own.

The orthopedist and/or traumatic surgeon needs an area with excellent surgical illumination, unused for infectious or "dirty" cases, and appropriate instruments and other materials including sutures, local anesthetics, plaster, and other supplies, and he needs an immediately adjacent X-ray viewing frame or box.

Staffing So much depends upon the demand factor. At one large university, a half-time physician who happened to be a qualified gynecologist was employed for general medical duty. After one year's employment, this doctor's entire time (20 hours per week) was booked up to 3 weeks ahead for premarital, prenatal, and gynecologic problems alone. At the same university, 2 hours per week of dermatologic service seemed more than sufficient, in addition to those specialists nearby on call.

All such staffing by specialists within the health service should be aimed primarily at the education of their generalist colleagues. Even for large universities, the pattern should be that of weekly or twice weekly attendance by a qualified specialist whose time is divided almost equally between examination of patients referred by his generalist colleagues and consultation with and training of the latter.

(Dental and eye health consultants and services are frequently needed and demanded; see respective sections below.)

Availability and Arrangements for Other Specialized Services

Other medical-surgical specialists' services, consultations, or diagnostics are so infrequently needed as to make regular campus attendance or predictable retainer fees unnecessary and irrelevant. If their services are to be made available, and they should be if one considers the student convulsing for the first time or the unconscious student following head injury, it is generally best done on an on-call basis, by prearrangement, through insurance, or by fee for service.

Alternatives for Specialized Care Services

See discussion of professional recruitment, appointment, qualifications, salaries, and alternatives in Chapter 6.

INFIRMARY BED CARE AND HOSPITALIZATION

Infirmary or Intermediate Bed Care

The great majority of students needing bed care are those whose conditions temporarily preclude regular activity or who are contagious but do not require full hospital services.

To utilize general hospital beds and services for such common and relatively minor needs is often a needless and expensive use of hospital beds, if infirmary-type or home care can be provided.

Whatever provisions are made, they must fulfill the following criteria:

1. Permit the student-patient to rest undisturbed, if necessary isolated from susceptible contacts, and with separate toilet and lavatory.

2. Provide regular linen and food service with provision for separate disposal and/or cleaning of linen, waste, and utensils.

3. Provide observation and personal attention on call 24 hours, recording of temperature and general conditions, and carrying out physicians' orders (medication, etc.) on both scheduled and on-call basis by licensed nurses and/or doctors or by other responsible adults specifically assigned, trained, and supervised by health professionals.

4. Provide clear written criteria for admission to infirmary versus admission or transfer to general hospital, conditions, symptoms, and signs demanding transfer.

5. Patients must be "ambulatory" (they have to be able to get out of the building unassisted). There can be no restraints, major sedation, anesthesia, major surgery, traction, etc.

Alternatives for Intermediate Bed Care

Dormitory Care While it is possible to take care of many minor bed cases in dormitories, there are several disadvantages to this practice, some of them potentially dangerous:

1. Irregular and inexpert attendance and supervision, particularly in off-campus and unofficial housing, with missed medications, inadequate nourishment, and occasionally dangerous complications developing unrecognized
2. Difficulty in securing isolation for protection of other students
3. Unrestful surroundings in dormitories, making rest and recovery difficult
4. Imposition upon dormitory staff and fellow students
5. Inefficient and wasteful use of professional time and effort in making rounds
6. Overreaction to minor symptoms and "dormitory reverberation," rumor, and group anxieties

If there is no alternative, the criteria should come as close as possible to those listed above, with high priority on the patient's being able easily to summon and obtain prompt adult attendance at any hour.

Epidemics and Dormitory Care The one circumstance in which dormitory bed care is not only necessary but recommended is in the case of widespread epidemics (most commonly influenza) in which the number of concurrently ill students usually is far greater than the bed capacity and "isolation" is meaningless. (See "'Epidemic' Disaster Plans," page 9-16.)

Home Care Whether at the family's or relatives' residence or in the home of friends or local faculty families willing to provide it, home care is often ideal and as a policy is both practical and desirable for institutions such as community colleges.

For very small residential colleges, care by reliable and willing local households of faculty or "friends of the college" is preferable to dormitory care.

The administrative criteria should be positively stated, not left to default, and should be that:

1. Students live nearby, in or within an easy day's transfer to households of their families, adult relatives, or clearly designated family friends
2. Households involved are explicitly willing and able to accept responsibility, an agreement which for each minor and unmarried student should be a routine part of registration procedures and signed by the responsible adult involved

It is a lazy and potentially dangerous "policy" for the institution to assume that any students not living directly in dormitories or in institutional housing are therefore under practical adult home care in case of illness (and the explicit agreement or nearby families or other responsible adults to undertake such care should be obtained and understood).

Special Hospital Arrangements for Intermediate (Infirmary-type) Bed Care In some portions of the country, hospital organization and economics are such that the equivalent of intermediate bed care is feasible, and some established hospitals are already working to set up such care facilities for convalescent and other less acutely ill patients, in which the cost of care may be one-half to one-third that of care in general hospital beds.

Special Institutionally Operated Infirmary Facilities These should be considered:

1. When the institution provides facilities and medical staff for general ambulatory care already
2. When significant numbers (50 to 500) of students are living in institutional residences or are beyond easy transfer to family or other household responsibility
3. When local hospital and other community bed care arrangements are too expensive or inappropriate
4. When dormitory arrangements (see above) are impractical
5. When *in loco parentis* expectations are high, especially in rural residential colleges with 500 or more students

Criteria and Requirements for Operation

Local and state codes and laws relative to bed care of patients must be followed. They control many aspects of construction, fire safety, staffing, records, equipment, and types of cases and treatments permitted, and then vary widely from place to place. (See "Legal Aspects of Health Services," page 1-78.)

If the following criteria are met in addition to those listed above, the operation will be satisfactory:

1. That no student-patient be admitted to bed care who would be incapable of leaving the building unaided in case of emergency. (This excludes giving of any general anesthetic, major surgery, patients in traction, and unconscious or seriously ill patients who should be in a general hospital anyway.)
2. That, if even a single patient is under care, there be a responsible, trained adult awake and on duty 24 hours a day, with a licensed registered nurse or licensed practical nurse on immediate call on the premises if not actually on duty herself.
3. That general nursing supervision and operations be under a licensed head registered nurse, responsible to the medical director or chief medical officer.
4. That designated physicians be on call at all times.
5. That adequate emergency equipment (oxygen, drugs, etc.) be maintained to sustain life in an emergency until transfer to a hospital can be made.
6. That rapid communications with and transportation to general hospitals and security be available.
7. That a written disaster and evacuation plan be prepared, known to all personnel, and periodically rehearsed.
8. That adequate facilities for isolation and sanitary handling of linens, utensils, and leftover foods are present.

Number of Beds Infirmary facilities are ideally located directly in conjunction with the ambulatory services to allow for sharing of staff, equipment, laboratory and X-ray services, drug supplies, utilities and telephone services, purchasing, etc.

While the number of beds will vary, depending on such factors as ratio of men to women students, degree to which institution assumes *in loco parentis* role, athletic involvement, etc., the following figures may be used as a rough guide for planning.

Minimum Capacities. Because different contagious disease patients cannot be bedded down with each other or with noninfectious and susceptible patients, and since coeducational rooming is at most institutions not encouraged, minimum and expectable bed capacities should be thought of in terms of *separate bed spaces* rather than just in terms of total beds.

Thus even for the small schools a minimum of four to five separate bed spaces for noncoeducational institutions and six to eight spaces for coeducational institutions should be provided and will serve for schools with enrollments of up to 1,000. The use of multiple-bed wards is obsolete and a false economy; a single case, say, of virus pneumonia, can deny the use of the other beds to other patients.

For the sake of some companionship for the less ill and for future expansion, it is wise to plan these spaces as two-bed units, each with its own toilet and lavatory.

For additional beds, plans should call for four to six more beds for each 1,000 enrolled over the minimum base.

Food Services Proper food services, particularly if variable diets and special handling of contaminated service and utensils are intended, can be an administrative headache.

Preparation on the premises is, paradoxically, most appropriate for very small, informal infirmaries where the patient census is usually no more than three or four and family-style cooking can be easily done, or for very large facilities where patient census averages fifty or more and utilization by staff and visitors on a cafeteria-style paying basis can support the necessary kitchen and dietary staff. The advantages of in-plant food service lie chiefly in flexibility, convenience, and the ability to have special medical diets that are very difficult to manage in usual dormitory facilities.

Delivery from dining hall kitchens requires special hot and cold sanitary delivery carts which are expensive and in certain terrains are impractical without motorization, special ramps, lifts, and so forth. Moreover, they require labor for thrice-daily delivery and retrieval. There can be very little variety in diet. Also, the food must generally be transported in bulk and served with infirmary-owned service and utensils (as it is not proper sanitary practice to return contaminated dishware and utensils to general dining-hall kitchens) or delivered on individual trays and services which are completely disposable. All-disposable dishware and utensils may sound like a practical solution, but to ill persons with puny appetites, the repeated service of paper plates, cups, and plastic utensils can be most unappetizing.

Catering services, both national and local, should be explored. Some such services are developing new food techniques that permit the rapid delivery, relatively long storage, and rapid preparation of a wide variety of foods in frozen, precooked and refrigerated, and dehydrated forms at increasingly attractive prices. Some will provide salt-free or low-fat items, so that special diets can be put together.

Hospital dietary services are in some areas either utilizing such services or duplicating them, and, if available, contracts with such hospitals may be made for delivery of food.

The necessary facilities at the infirmary for utilization of such services consist of a modified "ward kitchen" which must include

1. Storage for sufficient dishware and utensils
2. Both ordinary (40 to 45°F) and deep-freeze refrigeration
3. Two sinks, one for handwashing only
4. High-capacity, heavy-duty dishwasher, with reliable temperature over 170°F (which may require heat boosting)
5. Garbage disposal
6. Small two- to four-burner range
7. An electronic or so-called "radar" oven for rapid reconstitution of precooked and refrigerated foods

Such electronic ovens will reheat and reconstitute the average entree, precooked and refrigerated on individual service, in anywhere from 30 to 90 seconds. The resulting food is every bit as good as it was when originally prepared.

The advantages of such a system are:

1. No need for special kitchen help. The nursing staff and aides can reheat and serve 30 piping-hot meals in as many minutes, and the automatic dishwasher and disposal do the rest.
2. Meals can be quickly and easily served at any time. The patient admitted late or delayed in X-ray can be fed on the spot.
3. Only as many meals need be prepared as there are actual patients on hand, a great saving of waste and frustration when the census may go from 4 to 20 to 12 in a 24-hour period.
4. With routine stocking of staples and perishables, such as milk, eggs, lettuce, and some frozen items (TV dinners), great dietary variation and flexibility can be achieved and an unexpected influx of patients can be fed.

Costs of food services will obviously vary from place to place and year to year, but they will not vary very much among the three main alternatives: i.e., preparation on the premises, delivery from nearby dining halls, and the catering or "airline" type of service. The food is more expensive for the latter, but the labor is more costly for the former.

A figure including all overhead, transportation, amortization of equipment, etc. of $4 to $5 per bed patient per day is realistic for budget purposes; food services in the institutionally operated infirmary will run about 10 to 12 percent of the total infirmary budget.

Additional Facilities for Infirmary Care In addition to beds and food services, there must be provisions for:

1. Nursing station functions of record keeping, communications, and infirmary reception.

2. Drug and medical supply storage facilities.

3. Annunciator or other patient-aid call system.

4. Linen storage areas and segregated areas for temporary bagged storage of contaminated linens until laundered.

5. Special examination and treatment room for special procedures adjacent to nurses' station, equipped with standard examination table, spotlight, and examination instruments.

6. Bathtubs and/or sitzbaths (rectal conditions and prostatic and local skin infections such as boils are quite common among young college men). Most contemporary dormitory construction provides showers but no place in which to lower the ailing rear end.

7. Specially screened and glassed windows.

If it is intended to house emotionally disturbed students in the infirmary, it must of course be understood that no violent or seriously disturbed students should be cared for there. It must also be understood that all student patients must have free and usual egress from the building without physical restraint. Any restraint applied must be mainly that of the nurse's watchful eye, personal concern, and firm direction. However, for maximum safety and prevention of possible self-injury, such patient rooms, as well as being immediately visible to the nurses' station, should be equipped with special-strength window screens and tempered glass windows to prevent unexpected, unnatural, and possibly fatal egress from windows.

8. Lounge or recreational areas for less ill patients to begin ambulation, to watch television, read, and visit family and guests during convalescence.

Equipment, such as blood pressure manometers, emergency tray and oxygen tank, scales, etc., should be on wheels whenever possible, so as to allow easy movement to bedside.

Beds should be at minimum 7 feet in length with mattresses, plastic covers, and blanketing to fit. They should have at least two adjustments for position and be on lockable casters.

Linen service must be provided at a rate of about five times per student per day over and above that for residence halls. Each newly admitted patient requires clean bed linen, and patients with fever and many other conditions require daily linen changes while in the infirmary. Arrangements must be made with the contracting or institutional laundry service for (1) frequent and flexible delivery and (2) physical and visual segregation and separate sterilization at the laundry of contaminated linens and supplies (usually by separately colored or red-striped laundry bags).

In addition to bed linens, supplies of both pajamas and terry-cloth bathrobes, bath towels, and other bath linens should be arranged for.

Nobody likes the standard hospital "johnnies" (gowns), and all young people positively loathe them.

Records A separate set of inpatient or infirmary record forms should be devised, preferably of a particular color, to permit easy recognition and tabbing in the general health record. These should include:

1. Admission and discharge sheet with student's identification, local and home residence, telephone of parents, guardians, next of kin, etc., religion, admitting complaint, and brief space for summary of admitting illness, physical findings, major

elements of course and treatment, and final diagnosis on discharge, with recommendations for follow-up and dates

2. Temperature, pulse, and observation chart
3. Progress notes by doctors, laboratory and X-ray reports, operative, tissue, and procedure notes if pertinent
4. Nurses' notes
5. Order sheet and indication of completed orders

Upon discharge these should be incorporated into the basic student health record.

Special Record and Report Forms Although provisions for sign-out against medical advice are very infrequently needed, there must be a means of legally recording and notifying student personnel and/or parents when student patients refuse to accept or remain in infirmary care despite and against competent medical advice. Students over 21 may take this upon their own responsibility; for minors, either parents or parent surrogates must assume responsibility. In either case such assumption of responsibility against medical advice must be recorded, signed, appropriately witnessed, and dated, preferably on a prepared standard form.

Daily census and record of admissions and discharges should be recorded with copies to the chief medical officer at least, and (*without diagnoses*) to any other responsible student personnel official upon request.

Notification of Parents and Others Since no seriously ill, unconscious, general surgical, or violently disturbed patients may be admitted (but should go to general and/or psychiatric hospitals), routine notification of parents or others of infirmary admissions by the staff other than by daily census, admissions, and discharge sheets should be both unnecessary and discouraged. For practical, psychological, and educational reasons, the responsibility for notifying parents and residence hall personnel (or for not notifying them) *should be purposefully and clearly placed upon the student,* the staff's role being (1) to so inform him, and (2) to ask if he would like their assistance in so doing. Occasionally good personal and professional judgment directs that parents or others should be notified even when the minor student does not wish it or ducks the responsibility. Every effort should be made first to persuade him of the importance of doing so. Failing that, the student must be told why notification must be made.

Staffing Physicians should not be required over and above those already employed or used for general outpatient care and should, for continuity of care and quality, be expected to cover all their bed patients.

An infirmary operation demands a chief or head nurse who is responsible for all nursing, nursing aides, and ancillary staffing and housekeeping as well as performance of all nursing care. The minimum operation requires at least one nurse on each of three eight-hour shifts whenever patients may be expected, or, during term, seven days a week or 3.4 FTEs. Experienced and mature licensed practical nurses (licensed vocational nurses) may fill some of these positions alone, with prompt and competent physician backup and supervision and selection by a registered nurse.

Day (7 A.M. to 3 P.M.) and evening (3 P.M. to 11 P.M.) shifts are busiest, and one nurse can adequately care for an average census of 10 to 12 patients alone and up to 15 to 16 patients for short stretches if relieved of too many unskilled tasks by aides. These may be relatively untrained but trainable, and by bedmaking, giving back rubs, serving meals, and taking temperatures, they can extend the nurses' case load to the above capacities. Without aides, the lone nurse's case load capacity will drop to 6 to 8 on the average, with short peaks to 10 or 12.

Thus, basic infirmary staffing depends primarily on expectable average and peak census and the types of illness cared for.

The following guidelines may be helpful in planning:

TABLE 1 Suggested Infirmary Staffing Patterns as Related to Census and Enrollment (Depending on Heaviness of Use, Census is the More Important Figure)

Number of students eligible for infirmary care	Expectable census		Staffing							
			Weekdays		Evenings and weekend		Night		FTEs† total	
	Average	Peak	Nurse	Aide	Nurse	Aide	Nurse	Aide	Nurse	Aide
Less than 1,500	2–3	8	1	0	1	1*	1	1*	3.4	2.4
1,500–5,000	3–5	10	1	0	1	1	1	1	3.4	2.4
5,000–7,500	7–10	15	1	1	1	1	1	1	3.4	3.4
7,500–10,000	15–18	30	2	1	2	1	1	1	5.8	3.4
For each additional 5,000 eligible students	Add 7–10	Add 15	Add 1	Add 1	Add 1	Add 1	Add 1	Add 1		

* The "aide" position for evenings, nights, and weekends for small infirmaries is primarily for *protection* of the nurse, who should not be left alone in the building. In small, or even larger services, such aide positions may be filled by students who receive room and board in return for being on hand for these shifts.

† Full-time equivalents.

Costs are primarily those for staff, and as a rough rule of thumb will range from 8 to 12 percent of total personal health service costs, with about 1/10 for food service, 1/10 for utilities, 1/10 for drugs and supplies, 1/10 for linens, and 6/10 for personnel.

In terms of cost per patient day, such infirmary care, depending mostly on local nursing salaries, amortization policies, etc., and upon bed utilization, will amount to $20 to $30 per patient day on the average (1969), as opposed to general hospital costs of twice or three times that amount.

HOSPITALIZATION

Between 2 and 5 percent of the average student population will require admission to a general hospital in the course of a year, most frequently for injuries, surgical problems such as appendicitis, and less often for serious medical problems requiring intensive care.

The responsibility of the institution is to be sure that each student, whether through family auspices, insurance programs, or direct provision, has ready and immediate access to an accredited[5] general hospital with full diagnostic, surgical, and intensive care capabilities.

Choice of Accredited Hospital and Bed Availability

The institution's chief medical officer or director should investigate and/or be able to assure the administration that (1) the hospital or hospitals to be used are currently accredited, and (2) there is both sufficient bed availability and staff willingness to permit ready admission of students at any time necessary.

If possible, assurance should be obtained from the hospital that at least one bed per 1,000 students will be reserved for student priority use and may be released for use by other patients only by express permission of the director or chief medical officer or his delegate, who should be on the staff of the hospital.

While relatively small numbers are involved, the costs, in threat to health and life and in dollars, are great. It is the unusual institution that can afford to subsidize these costs directly, even through a university-owned and operated hospital, and the unusual student or family that can afford them either. The solution must be sought through appropriate and adequate hospitalization insurance. (See Chapter 7.)

[5] By the Joint Commission on Hospital Accreditation, the sole accrediting authority.

Hospital Insurance

Part of the institution's responsibility is to see that such insurance is available to students, either through family-held policies or through special student policies, which are generally much cheaper.

When special policies are written, the admitting and business offices of local hospitals should be made thoroughly acquainted with this coverage, procedures for claims, etc.

For students not under direct or immediate family supervision (whether in institutionally controlled living quarters or not), hospitalization and emergency medical insurance should be universal; and for the following groups it should be mandatory:

1. Foreign students
2. All students living in institutional residences
3. All minor students living more than an easy half-day's journey from direct family supervision
4. All students engaged in institutionally sponsored programs of risk, such as intercollegiate athletics, field trips, overseas study, etc. (For further details on insurance, see Chapter 7.)

Staff Relations to Hospital

Whenever possible, the student's regular college physicians where such are employed or private physicians when these are used should be members of the hospital staff to which students are admitted and should, within their competence, admit and care for them in the hospital. Even when the hospitalization is surgical, the general physician should visit the student and retain contact. In situations where it is not possible for all health-service physicians to belong and admit their student patients to the hospital, it is essential that the chief medical officer or director be on the hospital active or courtesy staff with admitting privileges.

The great importance of this lies:

1. In better continuity of medical care
2. In giving the health-service physician excellent communications with and an equal role with his privately practicing colleagues (thus attracting and holding better doctors)
3. In assisting better the patient's academic needs and allaying his anxieties by assurance of legitimate and official extensions, delays of examinations, arranging for appropriate materials such as readers so that he may work within the capacities of his state of health (good "occupational therapy")
4. In demonstrating not just the hospital's but the *institution's* concern for his welfare

General surgeons and orthopedists, used to a preponderance of older patients, tend to forget the tremendous resiliency of the student and his great anxieties about "lost time." They may also be unaware of the institution's ability to modify the student's program, provide halfway-house and convalescent services (as through an infirmary), and unless tactfully nudged by their health-service colleague, they may tend either to keep students hospitalized longer than necessary and/or to discharge them with insufficient or unrealistic orders for follow-up and transfer of responsibility.

Student Admissions to Teaching Hospital Services

With some exceptions, admission to teaching services usually results in longer admissions, the performance of more laboratory and X-ray examinations, and greater possibility of embarrassing confrontations between students—one the patient and the other the medical student—than when the student is admitted to the personal service of a staff member. The latter procedure is apt to be more efficient and less costly.

Notification and Permission Procedures

Although accredited hospitals will have standard procedures for notification of parents when any legal minor is admitted and for obtaining necessary parental or next-of-kin permission prior to surgery, the institution should establish with the hospital and health-service staff its own mutually agreeable procedures, which should include the following:

1. Whenever possible the student himself should be encouraged or assisted to notify his family, with the college physician, nurse, or personnel worker standing by for support or making the contact himself when the student is unable to. The purpose is to assure parents and next of kin of the institution's concern and involvement and to give parents the reassurance that their own child's voice can often best provide before they receive a routine notice from the hospital "out of the blue."

2. Occasionally there are situations in which, even though the student is a legal minor, the best judgment involves not informing parents or next of kin, particularly when the patient is strongly against it and the situation is not threatening. In such cases the hospital should agree to suspend its routine notification and rest *in loco parentis* responsibility with the institution by prior arrangement.

3. However, in any case of serious or threatening illness, of general anesthesia and/or major surgery, need for intensive care, and in all cases of admission for psychiatric reasons, notification should take place promptly even though the minor patient may object.

4. The hospital admitting office must understand and agree that the institution should be immediately notified through specified channels of any student's admission.

5. Specific permission and informed consent must be obtained from any patient before surgery and, in the case of minors, from their parents or legal guardians. This may be done (*a*) directly, if parents are nearby, or (*b*) by telephone with either parent as long as a third party is both announced to be on the line as a witness and records or tapes the essentials of the conversation between the doctor and the parent or guardian. It is most convenient and effective in this situation for the third party to be an institutional officer.

6. In the event that delay of surgery or other treatment may endanger the student's welfare and life and no responsible parent, guardian, or close kin can be located, the institution must be prepared to take parental responsibilities for authorization of necessary emergency surgery and treatment. This responsibility should be

a. Spelled out in all health informational material sent to matriculants and their families

b. Spelled out to hospitals

c. Include specific authorization by both the chief medical officer and the chief student personnel officials or one each of their designated delegates

d. Include continued efforts to reach responsible kin

Records

The content, format, and all other internal management aspects of hospital records are prescribed in accredited hospitals by the Joint Commission on Hospital Accreditation. However, the institution should arrange with local hospital record librarians for routine transmittal to institutions' chief medical officers of copies of

1. Students' emergency-room visits
2. Daily census of students hospitalized, with names, hospital location, diagnoses, and attending physician of all students admitted, operated upon, remaining, and discharged
3. Copy of doctor's discharge orders
4. Discharge summaries

MENTAL HEALTH

General Considerations

For many the importance and benefits of a well-organized mental health program are difficult to understand and accept. The difficulty lies primarily in common cultural conceptions linking psychiatry or even clinical psychology with mental illness and "craziness." The subject tends to be approached from an oversimplified two-dimensional viewpoint that classifies persons as healthy or sick, normal or abnormal, conforming or deviant, or as balanced or disturbed. To one who conceptualizes mental health versus ill health in this way, there seems little visible evidence of obvious mental disease among students except for the occasional dramatic and frightening case of gross breakdown with suicide, violence, or "crazy" behavior that is usually promptly removed for treatment in a mental hospital. Such cases make the need for prompt psychiatric services quite logical and desirable but do not seem to justify an ongoing program or the employment of full-time mental health professionals.

The greatest proportion by far of academic wastage results not from physical or biologic illness and injury but from psychological and emotional problems. Paradoxically, such problems are if anything more frequent and often more serious among the most intellectually gifted students.

The college student, particularly the bright and idealistic, is in transition from the child's more passive trust and identification with the adult standards of home toward the man's more active trust in himself and in his mutuality as an equal with other adults and their world. Erik Erikson likens this transition to the position in midair of the trapeze artist who, having just let go of the bar of his own familiar swing, wonders for an awful suspended and lonely interval if the catcher will be there, if he will be caught or catch on safely himself, and wishes that he hadn't let go.

Perhaps the easiest and most appropriate way to describe the college's role in mental health is to compare it to the aerial catcher who is in position at the right time, firmly anchored to his perch, and who reaches with encouragement, skill, and strength to secure the youth suspended between past and future and swings him to the further platform. If the college as a whole can succeed in encouraging and securing the personal trust and confidence of the student, it will have admirably served the purposes of education, maturation, and mental health.

The college mental health program is the result of all the points of personal interaction between the student and the human environment—his peers, the opposite sex, his teachers and counselors, coaches and dormitory directors, and, occasionally, his doctors and health-service contacts.

Such administrative matters as the registration process, methods of assignment to residences, quality of social regulations, course requirements, and the overly literal application of tight grading curves all hold potentials for inviting the respect and cooperation or the scorn and resentment of students.

Students of course differ widely in the combinations of strengths, weaknesses, and adaptive powers which they bring with them. The majority have a good deal of resiliency. They appear to get along without much adult help, don't seem to experience much trouble or give it, and usually graduate.

A sizeable proportion, however, often including some of the most gifted, have less strength and adaptability, more complex entanglements with families, and greater vulnerabilities. For these students, the normal stresses of college can often undermine a tentative confidence or arouse a latent resentment which, if mishandled, may result in dysfunctional behavior manifested by excessive anxiety, ritualistic but unproductive "work," apathy and withdrawal, or by the acting out of hostility in antisocial behavior, excessive drinking, or drug abuse.

The accommodation and handling of such distressed and often distressing students in group and residential situations is difficult and trying for those responsible and for other members of the group who are often, perhaps unconsciously, threatened by seeing and sensing a breakdown of control that they feel powerless to prevent but cannot ignore. In such situations both responsible adults and peers have enormous potential for reacting in truly supportive and constructive ways that can accomplish much in the resolution of the student's problem by the restoration of his confidence and the reenlistment of his trust and cooperation. Conversely, there is equal potential and greater likelihood for reactions and attitudes that may intensify problems and render management more difficult.

The manifold ways in which the institution relates to students as people, in its teaching, its living arrangements, and in the quality of its personal interactions, have significant bearings on the attitudes and learning of students in general and the mental health of a fair number of students. It is toward the quality and relevance of these personal interactions and attitudes that the college mental health program is ideally oriented, rather than toward overemphasis on the professional treatment of the casualties.

The Mental Health Professional as Counsel to Staff, Faculty, and Student Leaders—The Primary Objective

The mental health professional plays an important role in direct application of clinical skills in the evaluation and therapy of disturbed individuals and, more importantly, in helping people and groups living and working together to recognize and trust their own abilities to be helpful to disturbed and distressed students by showing constructive and personal concern, to recognize varying degrees of emotional disturbance with increasing discrimination and objectivity, to react to them with less anxiety or hostility, and to approach them person to person with more confidence and skill, whether for simple support and the relief of sharing a problem or for an approach to referral for more professional education or therapy.

No matter what the size of the institution or the size and sophistication of its mental health program, this function remains a central one without which no number of professionals will satisfy the needs and purposes of community mental health. There are not now and probably never will nor should be enough professionals to treat the problem on an individual clinical basis, and it has been both out of this scarcity and out of a realization of the importance of community personal interactions that, mostly in small colleges, a basic model has emerged.

The Core Mental Health Program

This program should aim to provide:

1. Emergency handling of acutely disturbed individuals pending transfer to more definitive care

2. Both regular and ad hoc opportunities for consultation about students among student personnel workers, residence hall personnel, key faculty and others directly concerned with and responsibly in touch with students, and qualified mental health professionals

3. Some provisions for direct interview and evaluations of students who appear to be or feel significantly disturbed

4. Establishment of referral channels for more definitive psychotherapy or other care and education of staff in effective approaches to referral

Emergency handling procedures must be worked out among the chief medical officer or his psychiatric or psychological delegate, local security and police agencies, and the nearest source of secure psychiatric hospitalization, usually but not necessarily a public or state institution. While local and state laws may differ, they will usually provide:

1. For certain designated officials and professionals, often including any licensed M.D., to have legal powers to authorize temporary commitment for the protection of the individual or of others pending further observation, treatment, and review that usually is followed by court action if commitment is to be continued

2. For such temporary commitment to be restricted to specifically designated facilities

3. For designated agencies (sheriff's office) to have legal authority for accepting temporary commitment papers and receiving, protecting, and transporting the individual

The college administrator and his subordinates in student personnel and the health program should be familiar with and have written out locally appropriate policies, procedures, and regulations, so that in emergency the proper sequence of people and agencies may be promptly contacted. Responsibility for initial professional evaluation and control is up to the chief medical officer, and when possible he should have prompt availability of medical-psychiatric consultation, both to reinforce the validity of any possible commitment and to prevent unnecessary commitment. Many cases which may appear extremely dangerous to the layman can quite adequately and preferably be handled without commitment through families, low-security psychiatric facilities in general hospitals, special psychiatric hospitals, and infirmaries.

Needless commitments are not only potentially very traumatic to the patient but may give rise at least to parental and family resentment if not to lawsuit. In the case of foreign students, it may result in deportation.

Referral sources will obviously vary widely from one community to the next, but they may include the following, the local availability of which should be learned and used by even the core student health service and counseling services:

1. Public resources, such as state and city hospital psychiatric clinics or community mental health centers (such as Short-Doyle in California), which are usually federally and state assisted

2. Private or semiprivate resources, such as privately controlled clinics, family service agencies, and private psychologists and psychiatrists

3. Where available, institutionally connected resources such as medical school clinics, training programs of departments of clinical psychology, social casework, etc.

The consortium approach (briefly mentioned in the introductory material) is appropriate for regional groups of small institutions which together underwrite mental health resources for consultation, on-campus conferences, emergency referral, and short-term therapy that no one of them can as well afford or arrange for independently.

Consultation between mental health professionals and college communities, as stressed above, is an essential part of any college mental health program, and for some small colleges it may be the only feasible use of available professional time. In such situations, with regular services of a clinical psychologist, psychiatric social worker, or psychiatrist limited to a few hours a week, it is essential that the bulk (perhaps two-thirds) of that time is spent in indirect counseling with those responsible for and close to students, people living and working with them in personally significant ways, counseling that starts with and deals with their problems and anxieties about students and their responsibilities toward them as they see them.

No attempt is made to encourage amateur psychotherapy, but to foster and encourage more open, more informed, and less anxious exchange between the troubled student and those around him, to help each person be himself and do his own job.

Direct student consultation and evaluation in the situation of limited availability of professional time should be directed at backing up and informing the primary ongoing business of human relationships and, when appropriate, the effective approach to and referral of troubled students, but it should not be allowed to become a substitute for them.

The consultant's job is to help people at all levels to feel less afraid than they plainly do to seek help, to offer it, to tell someone that, whatever the reason, offensive behavior is offensive, but to tolerate reasonable differences in personality and attitude and, when necessary, to make more informed and effective referrals.

Conversely, the consultant's job does not exist to straighten out difficult and troubling students whose behavior is labeled "abnormal."

The consultant can only help those who want his help in being themselves or doing their own jobs better. He cannot and should not lend himself to the purposes of those who want him to change, reform, cure, or dispose of students.

Direct Student Mental Health Service

This is designed to supplement, where possible, the core functions of community mental health described above by providing readily available and appropriate professional therapy over and above evaluation and referral for the 5 to 10 percent of students whose emotional health and development are best assisted by professionals and who would not otherwise receive such help.

Barriers to such help include:

1. Reluctance to turn to parents unless they are helped to do so
2. Reluctance or inability to seek independent help for financial reasons
3. Ignorance of how to receive or seek appropriate help
4. Local scarcity of mental health resources
5. Fears of seeking psychiatric/psychological help because of its connotation of "insanity" and because of the even more painful stigma of such diagnoses being applied by peers or teachers

For all of these reasons, it is desirable whenever possible to facilitate and provide highly accessible, confidential, and trustworthy psychotherapeutic services for students upon their own self-referral or referral by others and to have these services understand both the student and his environment. The ideal arrangement is for prepaid, on-campus services, as a part of health and/or counseling programs, if competent professionals can be secured. If not, it is preferable to make outside arrangements.

Scope and Intended Purposes of Institutionally Directed Psychotherapeutic and Diagnostic Services While the scope and functions of college mental health services in therapy vary widely, some general guidelines may serve to help define the depth and distance to which any institution may go. Mental health preventive and therapeutic efforts should be aimed at the most frequent problems of personal and emotional development as they affect the student's college adjustment and learning and at those problems that can most frequently be helped by relatively short, problem-oriented therapy. The college should devote its chief therapeutic efforts to those cases and those methods that are most likely to help students to stay in school, to learn, and to grow.

Conversely, its obligation to cope therapeutically with the case of such severity as to preclude normal participation in collegiate life is much less clear, as is its obligation to accommodate and/or treat the student whose problems disrupt and adversely affect the group.

The practical problem of defining just what the institutional program will or will not do is difficult. Exceptions are numerous. Most often, such services are defined as being confined to short-term therapy, excluding long-term analytic services.

One approach is to define institutional program responsibility as consisting of reasonable efforts that are compatible with the student's continuing academic and personal progress and growth within the institution without undue disruption of academic, social, or health service capabilities and requirements. If the student seems to himself, to the mental health professional, and the academic and social environment as if he can make it with some help, that help the institution should give. If not, the responsibility probably belongs to the student, the family, or the state.

Residential Care In addition to ambulatory services, the direct services to students in the fulfillment of these ideals should include refuge for short periods in a general hospital or infirmary. Often a crisis can be handled successfully if the student does not simultaneously have to cope with dormitory or other stresses.

Records It is recommended that all personally sensitive and psychiatrically detailed information be segregated, not only from any general student records but from the regular medical record as well, available only to the individual therapist or his delegate, to the chief mental health officer, and, rarely, to the chief medical officer. The contents of such records may be made available to others only with the student's consent and only when that consent is informed and in the student's interest.

Staff No hard-and-fast staffing recommendations can be made to fit all situations, with the exception that the very minimum requirements include availability to the institution of the functions and legal privileges of both the qualified, clinically oriented mental health professional (for indirect counseling, diagnosis, and direct therapy) and the M.D. (for his privileges and ability to prescribe medications, to hospitalize and/or commit, his ready access to other medical collaboration, and the stature his degree confers in advising the institution, parents, and others).

Presently the M.D. psychiatrist is the only person combining both functions, but for any given situation he may neither be available nor appropriate, or he may be too expensive.

The commonest and often most practical combination is that of clinical psychologist (often attached to a counseling service or department of psychology), M.D. director or chief medical officer, and locally available on-call psychiatric consultant with admitting privileges to psychiatric sections of general or psychiatric hospitals. A variation on this would include a psychiatric social worker with available M.D. backup, both general and psychiatric, but the common denominators are:

1. Qualified mental health clinical consultation by psychologists, psychiatric social workers, or psychiatrists to college community and for individual diagnosis and therapy
2. M.D. capabilities for prescription, residential care, and emergency commitment
3. The availability of professionals for recruitment, the ability of the program and/or students to afford the "mix," and the local expectations for professional status as they may bear on program effectiveness and credibility

Desirability of Multiple Access to Help. While it is desirable for the overall mental health program to be under the direction of an M.D. psychiatrist with community orientation, in some cases an experienced psychologist or social worker may make a better coordinator.

No student should be ever "stuck" with a single door through which he must pass for personal help. "Psychiatry" or "testing" labels scare off many students looking for help who would accept a referral to or advice from a teacher, coach, vocational guidance man, doctor, or clergyman. All these "doors" should be recognized and made functionally aware of each other through appropriate regular meetings and readily known channels for interreferral and consultation. Counseling services and psychiatric departments should work cooperatively when both exist on campus.

Numbers and Costs of Staff. The following are guidelines derived from the ways in which some programs have met their staffing needs:

1. Emergency, spot, and "indirect" consultation (core service) only: About 1 FTE mental health consultant for each 5,000 eligible students, plus about 1/10 FTE M.D. backup if mental health clinician is not an M.D.
2. Core service plus direct student therapy: About 1 FTE mental health clinician for each 2,500 students plus 1/10 FTE M.D. backup if mental health clinician is not an M.D.
3. With multiple and highly accessible services, the most highly developed and experienced mental health services estimate that (*a*) between 8 to 10 percent of their

student enrollment will profitably use direct, personal mental health services at a rate of three to four visits each; (*b*) approximately 10 percent of enrolled students (whether seeking care or not) could, as judged by psychological testing, behavior, performance, and utilization, profit by direct professional help.

All these semiactuarial figures come out to the closest rule of thumb that this author can devise, which is about 1.2 FTEs in combined clinical mental health and M.D. service for indirect, direct, and therapeutic services for each 2,500 eligible students.

Cost mixtures will vary according to the proportions of M.D. psychiatrists, clinical psychologists, or social workers employed whose current average salaries (1969) are about as follows, per FTE:

M.D. psychiatrist: starting salary
Just through training: $17,000 to $20,000
With board certification plus experience: $20,000 to $27,000
Clinical psychologist (Ph.D.): $10,000 to $15,000
Psychiatric social work (M.S.W.): $8,000 to $12,000

Use of Trainees Where medical school departments of psychiatry or institutional training programs in clinical psychology or psychiatric social work exist, the program may include at considerably less cost trainees in psychiatry, clinical psychology, and social casework who are near the end of their training and preferably who elect such service out of interest. In no situation should they work unsupervised by qualified and licensed superiors.

DENTAL HEALTH

The Student Population and Expectable Dental Needs

The great majority of Americans can expect their teeth to deteriorate and be lost unless they receive proper diets, continuing dental hygiene, and regular professional care. While it is true that the college years may usher in a period of relative quiescence, there remain a significant number with continuing rates of decay and continuing problems of development despite excellent dental care prior to entering college. And there are many students who have had little or no previous dental care and arrive at college with serious conditions that occasionally require complete extraction and false dentures. For many international students subsisting on very meager budgets, this can represent a very serious problem, as it may for students from poorer backgrounds in the United States. In terms of institutional concern, priority should be directed at foreign students and at domestic students on scholarships and financial aid or students giving other evidence of underprivileged backgrounds.

There are still plenty of unsuspected and significant dental problems that develop in students who believe their dental health to be good, and regular professional examinations should always be urged. There is no student who can be guaranteed not to present some dental emergency, most commonly accidental injury or loss, toothache, and/or periodontal infection.

Program Components in Dental Health and Institutional Responsibilities

Emergency Dental Care and Consultation Even the smallest college and the core Student Health Program must have some prearranged and effective channels for emergency referral to and consultation with local dentists and dental clinics when it is unable to provide its own direct service.

For satisfactory and effective prearrangements, personal contact should be made between local dental leaders or dental association officers and the institution's health representative. Any plans for referral, lists of dentists, etc., should be worked out with their advice and approval. The institution's objective should be to tie in to any existing dental emergency system and service or to establish, with official professional approval and cooperation, its own list of dentists willing to accept emergencies and to be, in fact, on call and available by a mutually agreeable schedule.

In such negotiations, it is very helpful if not essential to specify a mutually agreeable manner and amount of compensation for such services, according to a written schedule of fees for expectable dental emergency procedures and services.

Temporary Medical Relief. When no dentist is immediately available, the health service may provide symptomatic relief of pain and control of dental and periodontal infection by appropriate medication, pending follow-through to definitive professional care.

General and Continuing Dental Care Referrals For any student requesting or needing it, but particularly for those with obvious chronic problems and those from underprivileged backgrounds, the institution should at least have in parallel and often in unison with its dental emergency referral system a system for general dental referral, organized and prearranged to an approved list of cooperating general dentists in the locality.

Beyond organizing and facilitating effective referral, the institution is generally neither called upon nor able to organize and support continuing general dental care for all its students as a part of direct health service, although it may, depending on local availability and as a matter of prevention and education, wish and be able to support or direct a general program in dental hygiene, examination, and education.

Basic Institutional Dental Health Program Where local needs and opportunities allow or encourage the organization of intramural dental programs for students, the emphasis should be on practical dental health education delivered through a service organization that provides for:

1. Dental screening and information in conjunction with whatever routine programs of general health evaluation and advice are offered to students, as at entrance, job application, etc., coupled whenever possible with prophylactic cleanings and topical fluoride application
2. Emergency care and management services for any student
3. Consultation and close association with doctors, nurses, and other health service professionals in order to sharpen their awareness of oral and dental conditions needing care and thus enhance referrals and reinforce students' acceptance of regular dental hygiene and care; and, conversely, to increase recognition and referrals for medical diagnosis of oral-dental conditions that may signify more generalized health problems
4. Liaison and promotion of good professional relations with local and other sources of dental hygiene and care, both general and specialized, including students' regular dentists, in order to maintain effective channels and prearrangements for needed referral of students
5. Early identification, examination, and arrangements for care of dentally underprivileged groups
6. Cooperation with student personnel, health services, and student organizations for provision of dental health information and encouragement of good hygiene and use of dental care resources, promotion of proper flouridation, and athletic dental injury prevention

This type and degree of dental health service may well be compared to and be part of the core student health service in that its emphasis is on understanding and caring for dental problems as students perceive them, relieving efficiently their dental emergencies, and effectively using both professional and institutional resources in their overall management and health education.

Extended Dental Services Including some necessary and uncomplicated extractions and general operative dentistry, such intramural services should be strongly considered when there are considerable numbers of foreign or domestic students from underpriviledged backgrounds who lack independent finances and when other factors such as availability of staff, patient demand, and willingness to underwrite the program favor the development of a general clinic service.

Additional Reasons for Institutionally Based Dental Programs

1. When the institution is actively training health professionals, as in medical, dental, nursing, and other allied schools, the full range of dental services should be available to these students for care and, more importantly, for education through example and involvement.

2. When institutional programs, particularly in contact sports and athletics, place students at special risk, there should be a professionally directed program for injury prevention (through fitted mouth guards and examination and restoration of serious dental conditions prior to contacts) and for both emergency and restorative treatment after injury. (Such postinjury treatment may be at least partly defrayed by general health insurance for most injuries and by special insurance for intercollegiate athletics, as available through the National Collegiate Athletic Association (NCAA). (See section on special risks and athletic medicine, page 9-51.)

Facilities Whenever possible these should be located within and/or immediately adjacent to other health service facilities. In planning, it should be remembered that a dental unit will need utilities over and above those of the average doctor's office: i.e., gas, 110- and 220-volt electric service, as well as hot and cold water. In construction, the maximum foreseeable services should be at least "stubbed-in," even though all services may not be immediately needed.

For core dental services, a minimum of one dental examination area, at least 10 by 10 feet, is needed, with separate but adjacent clerical and waiting space. Preferably the unit should be 12 by 12 feet to allow for adequate equipment storage, X-ray unit, hand-washing facilities, and for expansion to more extensive services, including the bulkier equipment required for the most efficient practice of "four-handed" dentistry.

If X-rays are taken and if any restorative work is done, space must be provided immediately adjacent for a darkroom and small dental laboratory.

If extractions are done or any anesthesia (other than local) is given, the entire unit should be immediately adjacent to the general medical-emergency section of the service.

Equipment Equipment may be somewhat simpler for the core program than if extended service is rendered, but in any case it is the dental director's responsibility to submit specifications for all capital and expendable equipment. X-ray equipment should meet all local regulations for proper shielding and protection of both patient and staff, and should be periodically monitored by the environment health and safety program and given at least annual clearance by the radiation hazards control committee.

Records For even the core service, a dental record allowing (1) prematriculation examination results and advice; (2) in-service examination results; (3) notes of referrals and follow-ups, and (4) notations of treatment should be kept on each student and made a regular part of the total student health folder, although it may be convenient to keep one copy separately in the dental unit.

Staffing Alternatives

For Core Dental Service. The appointment of a qualified and licensed general dentist as dental program director or adviser is essential. If any institutionally based program is to be considered, it is desirable to appoint a dental adviser for liaison and consultation even when no services are provided beyond those of communications and referral.

With the dental director's backup and supervision, most other aspects of the core dental program and service can be handled by a well-trained dental hygienist with experience in patient education and in community dentistry. While there is still all too little experience in this field, preliminary recommendations by college dental health leaders suggest that one hygienist per 3,000 to 5,000 eligible students can, with part-time clerical help, handle the essential or core services of dental examination, prophylaxis, patient education, and coordination of all aspects of students' dental care, not counting on-site X-ray examination, emergency diagnosis, and treatment.

If the core service provides anything beyond simple examination, education, and prophylaxis including the interpretation of dental X-rays, emergency service, and oral consultation and diagnosis, the services of a qualified, licensed general dentist are required, in addition to those of the hygienist, at the rate of approximately 1 FTE dentist to each 5,000 students or major fraction thereof; or without the hygienist, to each 2,500 to 3,000 students.

If general operative and restorative dentistry is to be performed, the services of a dental assistant allow the dentist to increase his service at a cost considerably less than that required for an equal amount of work to be done by dentists alone.

When this is added to core and emergency and consultation services, staffing and facilities should include 1 FTE dentist plus 1 FTE dental assistant, with one dental unit for each 2,500 students or major fraction thereof to be served, and 1 FTE hygienist with separate dental unit for each 5,000 students or major fraction thereof.

Financial Considerations Core service for emergency referral, dental examination and prophylaxis, and patient and community education and record keeping should be prepaid and financed along with all other core student health programs (page 9-103).

Costs per student per year (12 months), including full-time or prorated hygienist's salary and dental director's salary or retainers, should average about $5 to $7.50. If dental X-rays are routinely added, the cost is increased by about $5.

Core plus general operative dental care and selected extractions (less bridgework, inlays, prosthetics, and orthodontia) will cost approximately $40 per student per year for maintenance and should be financed either on a modified fee-for-service basis or by prepayment.

"Start-up" costs, in addition to capital and equipment outlay, include the backlog costs of previously unmet dental needs. These are greatest for students new to the program, and in one freshman class of young women [6] cost on the average $90 for the first year. Freshmen in this program required 2½ to 3 times the expenditure for direct services than that which was required for maintenance thereafter.

Prematriculation requirements for records of up-to-date dental/oral care are increasingly being asked as a routine part of general prematriculation health requirements, both as an educational tool and to reduce backlog expenditures for new students.

Prepayment; Modified Fee for Service; and Institutional Input Essential and core services (costing about $5 to $7 per eligible student per year, or $10 to $12.50 if routine full-mouth dental X-rays are included) should be divided on a 1:2 ratio between general institutional support (for educational, coordinative, and administrative costs) and general student capitation for direct personal service costs. It should be prepaid as a normal part of health service activity, the student prepaying about $4 to $8 per year.

Extended or general dental services can be provided for those students with greatest dental and financial needs either by assessing all students for the support of their neediest fellow students' dental needs, an assessment which should be less than $10 annually, or by instituting a modified, sliding-scale, fee-for-service dental program at "student rates." Such programs, with lesser or even token fees for those most in need,

[6] Personal communication, Walter J. Pelton, D.D.S., M.S.P.H., University of Alabama School of Dentistry, September, 1968.

can be arranged when sufficient local dentists are available and interested by the institution's offer of space, equipment, assistance, and utilities, all of which reduce the dentists' overhead to a point where his fee for service is not only reasonable to those who can pay but may subsidize virtually free care for that minority of students needing it.

EYE HEALTH

Visual problems are very common among students. Those who will require or demand eyeglasses or contact lenses will predictably account for 35 to 40 percent of the student population, while perhaps 50 to 60 percent will seek examination for them. For those with genuine vision problems, the college years are often a time when fairly rapid changes can occur, so that the very high proportion needing vision attention is somewhat comparable to dental health need in its near universality. In addition to locally available optometrists and lens fitters, there should be an available M.D. ophthalmologist for emergency and supervisory consultation on campus.

A very common problem is the acute formation of small ulcers on the cornea in students who wear contact lenses for overly long periods without interruption. When it occurs, it requires immediate medical care; but it can be completely prevented by periodic removal of the lenses to let the eye "breathe."

Core Services

These services are thus responsible for provision of ready referral channels and prearrangements for

1. Emergency referral to qualified M.D. ophthalmologist, via private or clinic sources, for eye injury or disease and other consultation
2. Lists of optometrists and lens fitters approved by chief medical officer and eye M.D.
3. Routine education and information

Extended Services

If general ambulatory care is provided as a part of student health, the availability of an M.D. ophthalmologist should be considered in the same light as any other specialized consultant; i.e., either made available at student expense (with insurance coverage for injury) or included in prepayment. If his office is nearby, there is usually not enough consultation business for him to warrant his setting up regular hours at the health service.

Optometric and lens-fitting functions can seldom be prepaid or included in automatic coverage. The great frequency and the expense either bankrupt the program or raise prepayment fees to unreasonable levels.

If on-campus services are considered, it would seem best and perhaps very helpful to students to offer them on a modified "student-rate" basis. By making an initial investment in space and optometric equipment and supplying some part-time clerical help, the institution could enable a qualified optometrist to operate at a reduced fee-for-service rate while still making a reasonable profit.

Special Eye Hazards For contact sports, the program should make sure that players not only wear contact lenses but have available at all times a set of replacements. And, of course, the wearing of safety goggles and masks in certain shop and laboratory areas and the provision of eye-irrigating fountains is part of both environmental health and safety and of occupational medicine.

HEALTH PROGRAMS FOR SPECIAL SITUATIONS AND NEEDS

College and university life frequently presents situations involving risks and vulnerabilities that require special approaches. Athletics and sports programs expose students to greater risks of injury, and field trips and overseas study programs bring possible exposures to unfamiliar infections and hazards. The existence of two sexes poses its own opportunities and problems; and for some students, such as foreigners and the handicapped, survival and adjustment in collegiate life are challenges that require special assistance.

Athletic and Sports Medicine

Institutionally sponsored athletics and sports, particularly those involving contact, expose both the participant and the institution to extra risks.

Objectives and Goals The basic objective of the athletic medicine program should be the overall health and welfare of participants. As such, it should be an integral part of his total health care system, preferably under the direction of the health service or at least closely coordinated with it. Its component principles should apply to both intercollegiate and intramural sports and athletics and to physical education activities. They are described here without reference to distinct divisions except where significant.

The special objectives of the athletic medicine program are the prevention, care, and rehabilitation of injuries incurred in, or illnesses aggravated by, active participation in sports and physical activities.

Medical Determination of Fitness to Participate The determination of fitness of students to participate in any sponsored sports or physical activity is a medical responsibility and should be ascertained:

1. Prior to initial participation
2. At least annually for strenuous and contact sports and for any physical education participation by students with known chronic conditions (e.g., heart murmurs, diabetes, etc.)
3. After any absence from participation or regular attendance of more than 6 months
4. At the request of the student, his coach, or responsible physician
5. Following illness or injury, causing absence from regular participation

Criteria for such fitness will vary according to the type and stress of the sports or activities involved, but in each case these criteria should be jointly spelled out by the responsible medical and athletic/physical education officers, preferably in writing, with the understanding that the medical officer, with the explicit backing of the institution, has final and binding authority for participation or restriction of individual students.

Restrictions from participation in contact and/or very strenuous sports should routinely be ordered if significant valvular heart abnormalities exist, particularly aortic stenosis, if any residual symptoms or signs persist after injury, particularly to the head, neck, or joints, or if any condition is found that the physician feels to be incompatible with safe participation.

Contact sports should be permitted to students missing one member of a paired organ system (i.e., vision, hearing, kidneys, testes, etc.) only after (1) the student has been thoroughly apprised of the risks of blindness, deafness, sterility, or death should the remaining sole organ be seriously injured, and if still wishing to compete, assumes in writing personal responsibility for so doing; and (2) appropriate special protective gear is secured. (Many institutions prefer to exclude such cases from contact sports without exception.)[7]

[7] In the case of students under 21, parents must concur in the decision.

Water sports participation should be restricted for those with chronic or active conditions of ears, nose, or sinuses, with extra careful evaluation of and education of candidates for scuba diving, where even mild colds, hay fever, or asthma may have serious results.

Intercollegiate Athletic Participation In all institutions belonging to the National Collegiate Athletic Association (NCAA), direct preseason examination of candidates by the institution's physicians is a requirement and should be required of *all* candidates for strenuous and/or contact and water sports, both intercollegiate and intramural.

Intramural athletics, particularly the contact sports, produce as many if not more serious injuries than do intercollegiate athletics due to inadequacies of both medical and athletic control at all levels, including the inadequacy of preparticipation medical screening.

The frequently very large numbers of seasonal participants make it difficult to find time, doctors, and money to examine each candidate individually, and other mechanisms may be necessary to determine fitness and set restrictions.

Classification and Clearance Procedures for Intramural Sports and Physical Education There should be an approved official system of classification and clearance for all physical education and athletic activities on standard and official forms, in addition to those for intercollegiate athletics, by which system no student participates in any sponsored physical activity without official medical clearance. His participation is classified and, when necessary, restricted by his degree of fitness for:

1. Unlimited physical and sports participation
2. Strenuous but noncontact sports and activity
3. Water sports and/or scuba diving
4. Low-stress sports and activities (e.g., bowling, sailing, archery, etc.)
5. Adapted physical education

Any exceptions, special conditions, etc., should be spelled out.

Such classifications, and the data supporting them, should be built into prematriculation health histories and examinations to allow preliminary classification and clearance. For the great majority, on the basis of records review alone, this will safely allow unlimited activity without additional direct examination. For the minority whose entrance medical data suggest some abnormality or the need for possible restriction, clearance will require direct review, examination, and classification.

Review, renewal, and necessary revision of this entrance classification and clearance when required under the conditions described above under "Medical Determination of Fitness to Participate" is well handled by use of a standard reclassification and clearance request form, available at both athletic and health facilities, which specifically describes illness or injury, other reasons for request, and provides for current medical classification and clearance. Such a form must be presented to and approved by the responsible athletic or physical education official before any activity is resumed or changed.

Special Medical Evaluation Problems in Connection with Athletic Scholarships Although serious efforts that will probably succeed in correcting the situation are being made, at present it is not uncommon for an institution to award an athletic scholarship to a promising high school athlete only to find in the required preseason medical examination that he has a previously undisclosed injury or condition that precludes his participation, but that the institution may be required nonetheless to support his attendance. Administrators responsible for signing contracts or making athletic scholarship awards and agreements should be aware of this risk and should support the policy of insisting upon a medical evaluation by the institution before an agreement is made.

Prevention of Injury during Participation In addition to the prevention of injury or damage provided by proper examination, classification, and clearance described above, prevention of sports injury includes:

1. Special conditioning and physical training, as appropriate, prior to full activity. This is spelled out specifically for intercollegiate football and some other intercollegiate sports by the NCAA, but should also be mandatory for such activities as rowing, in which the author has all too often seen preseason conditioning restricted to general fitness.
2. Necessary and sensible dietary regimens, all too often subject to faddist and unscientific practices.
3. Provision of proper protective gear appropriate to the sport involved; necessary supportive strapping (as of ankles, etc.); and fitted dental mouth guards for contact sports.
4. Provision of playing fields, courts, tracks, pools, etc., and equipment that is in good condition.
5. Perhaps most importantly, adequate supervision and control by coaches, officials, etc. over the rules and conduct of the sport. Well-trained and well-coached athletes, playing under officials who firmly impose the rules, have many fewer injuries than poorly trained and supervised athletes.

Prevention of Special Risks Any athletes who risk vigorous contact with dust- and earth-contaminated surfaces with resultant "dirty" abrasions and cuts should receive yearly tetanus immunization prior to participation. Many athletic departments insist on this for all intercollegiate athletes, as well as influenza immunization in the fall.

Athletes in contact sports should, if they require glasses, wear contact lenses; and for intercollegiate teams the management should routinely provide for duplicate sets of lenses to be available at the site of practices or games.

Care of Injuries Procedures for bringing the injured athlete and competent medical care together as rapidly and effectively as possible must be understood and followed by all officials responsible. For contact sports, a physician should be present at all scrimmages and games. At the very least a qualified trainer must be present, with a physician within close call, to prevent aggravation of injury by injudicious moving of the injured player or by unwise resumption of play.

Transport by on-the-spot stretchers for short distances and standby ambulance for intercollegiate contact sports (as well as readily available on-call ambulance service for other events) must be available.

Rehabilitation of Injuries An injured player, unless given specific reconditioning and rehabilitative measures prior to resumption of competition, is more vulnerable to reinjury that he was prior to the original injury. A good athletic medicine program includes such specific and skilled rehabilitation and requires the physician's judgment before play may be resumed.

For handicapped and other special students, a program of adapted physical education is preferable to no physical education.

Treatment of Illnesses The diagnosis and medicinal treatment of illness is legally the sole responsibility of the physician, and athletic officials must be restrained from giving any medications except under the direct order of the physician.

Facilities Whenever possible, special facilities close to athletic areas should be made available for athletic-medical services to *all* participants. Aside from the provision of clean locker rooms, clean equipment, showers, etc., these facilities should include:

1. First-aid facilities and equipment
2. Physician's and trainer's offices and examination areas
3. Space, supplies, and equipment for protective strapping, physical therapy, and

rehabilitation of injuries (such as whirlpool treatment, heat treatment, ice therapy, progressive-resistance exercise equipment, etc.)

Records Forms for recording athletic and sports injuries on the spot, including any action taken on the field, should be provided and used by all trainers, coaches, or supervisors and transmitted daily to the person in charge of athletic medicine to allow follow-up and correction of hazardous conditions, practices, equipment, etc.

A case log of all visits to the athletic-medical quarters should be kept with name, date, time, reason for visit, action, and recommendations.

The physician in charge of the athletic medicine program should review this log and the field-injury reports daily to approve actions taken and secure needed follow-up. He should sign or initial such reports.

Copies of injury reports should be filed both in the field-house training quarters and in the general student health record.

Current classification and clearance forms signed by the responsible physician(s) should be on file and should be required for participation.

Personnel Athletic medical officers (commonly called "team doctors") should be licensed physicians with a special interest in athletes and sports who can appreciate the many ways in which sports and health interact to either the benefit or the detriment of the athlete. Thus, although prevention and initial handling of injuries is a prime responsibility, the job is more general than that function alone and requires sensitivity to psychological and general medical factors that must enter into good judgments concerning an athlete's participation, care, and recovery. And, while basic and periodically updated knowledge of injury management is required, an orthopedic specialist as primary athletic medicine officer is not only unnecessary but is often less effective than a good generalist who knows how and when to use specialized consultants.

Such consultants should include the orthopedist, the general surgeon, the neurosurgeon, the dental or oral surgeon and plastic-reconstructive surgeon, the ophthamologist, and the internist, who should be available through the athletic physician's office and referral.

The physician in charge of athletic and sports medicine should be a member of the basic, general institutional health service, so as to coordinate the care of the special problems of the athlete with the overall health supervision of the student, to avoid duplication of services, and to see that good athletic and general medicine extend to all participants, both intercollegiate and others.

Trainers and other special paramedical athletic personnel should ideally include at least one with full training and credentials in physical therapy, and all trainers should have at least some physiotherapy training, on-call consultation, and should belong to the National Athletic Trainers Association.

Whether paid by athletic departments or health services, all such trainers and physiotherapists must be under the professional control of the responsible physicians and operate under clear written instructions as to which injuries they may handle on their own and to what extent.

Student trainers or athletic-medical aides can be trained in first aid, proper transportation procedures, when to summon trainer's or physician's help, and accident reporting and follow-up. They may with proper supervision perform simple ankle wraps and taping.

Insurance Special insurance (available through the NCAA) must be provided by the institution for all intercollegiate athletics. Such coverage is virtually always excluded from other student health insurance policies.

Participants in "unofficial" or "club" sports that compete with other clubs (as in skiing, horsemanship, sailing, etc.) should be required to have adequate insurance against costs of care for injury, as should all participants in sponsored intramural contact sports.

Sponsored Field Trips and Overseas Study

General Principles Research and study in the field and overseas expose those involved to risks which require specific preventive and protective measures. Needed medical care in other countries may be difficult for travelers to find and may be, aside from portable first-aid measures, unobtainable short of evacuating the patient.

Any institution sponsoring, endorsing, or otherwise underwriting such activities is responsible for seeing that all participants receive adequate protection and that they will have adequate information and means for maintaining health and for getting to sources of care while abroad. The responsibility incurred in sponsorship of these extra-risk activities is such that the institution should allow no person to participate until all appropriate requirements have been met.

Prevention of Infectious Diseases. Any given location or itinerary presents characteristic infectious disease risks requiring measures that may include:

1. Specific immunizations (e.g., against typhus or cholera) prior to departure
2. Protective medicines (prophylactic medication) against such infections as malaria, often started prior to departure, maintained throughout travel, and continued for a period following return
3. Clear and realistic information on avoidance of infection by contaminated water, milk, and foods

Protection against Other Special Risks. Climate, terrain, and special environments may provide such diverse risks as those of extreme cold or heat, altitude, underwater and "high" seas, and for some locations indigenous poison snakes, scorpions, insects, marine life, or poisonous foods. The special risks must be ascertained and specific protection provided through appropriate equipment, clothing, and specific antidotes and antivenins, but above all through careful predeparture instruction and training.

Emergency and General Medical Arrangements. The nearest sources of competent medical consultation and hospital care should be ascertained in advance and definite, mutually satisfactory agreements should be reached between them and the institution for their assumption of responsibility as official medical representatives of the institution.

Health and hospital insurance coverage acceptable and appropriate to the area should be required, for coverage not only at study locations but for necessary hospitalization and emergency care during travel and for costs of necessary evacuation or repatriation.

Written procedures and necessary funds and/or equipment for emergency communication with the institution are necessary.

Prior arrangements should be made for necessary evacuation of ill and injured participants to nearest sources of general medical and hospital care and/or to home.

For field trips and expeditions to remote areas, there must be adequate predeparture training, equipment, and medical supply as well as designation of responsibilities for emergency treatment and first aid, for common illnesses and injuries, and for evacuation procedures.

For overseas or field trips with special physical or medical qualifications, the institution should arrange for necessary predeparture medical evaluation and examination of candidates and set forth criteria for acceptance and/or rejection.

Medical Follow-up on Return. Provision should be made for post-return medical evaluation for any participants who:

1. Have been ill while away, which implies some record of such illness being made in the field or upon return.[8]
2. Have been exposed to high endemic disease risks

For practical purposes, this would include requirement for reporting of field illness

[8] Failure of such a routine mechanism led, at one university, to the introduction of typhoid by two students who were ill while traveling; they recovered, and, not being reported, were allowed to resume work as food handlers in the college.

and/or injury to the institutional health officer and placement of a medical "hold" requiring evaluation and medical clearance before resumption of collegiate pursuits.

Common follow-up procedures should include recheck for tuberculosis and specific examination for most likely diseases such as intestinal infections, parasites, malaria, etc.

Special Administrative Considerations *Infectious Disease Prevention.* For travel outside the continental United States, the "International and Official Record of Immunizations" (International Certificate of Vaccination)[9] as a requirement, must be stamped by an official agent of the U.S. Public Health Service, and is no less necessary than the passport.

Governmental requirements and medical recommendations for immunizations, prophylaxis, and other preventive measures for each country and region are to be found in current editions of *Immunization Information for International Travel*[10] and *The Traveler's Medical Guide for Physicians,*[11] which should be required on health-service shelves.

Lead time for proper immunization often requires a minimum of 6 weeks. All acceptances and information concerning health and other requirements should reach probable participants at least 8 to 10 weeks prior to departure.

Special Risks. Costs and provisions of necessary medical consultation, equipment, training, and supplies should be written into any grants or contracts that support special field study or research trips.

Emergency and General Medical Arrangements. Participants with special needs, such as for contact lenses, insulin, or any regularly required medications, should be advised to take extra supplies with them and arrange for resupply from home prior to departure until overseas availability is known.

Laws and regulations concerning transportation and/or evacuation of contagious cases and of deceased persons from other countries should be learned from the state department and proper procedures made known to institutional officials.

Marital and Premarital Counseling, Examination, and Contraception

The number of married students has steadily increased over the past decades, particularly among graduate students. Among all college and university students 25 to 30 percent are married, with very few among freshmen and the greatest number among seniors.

In addition to curricular and informal educational approaches to marriage, sexuality, and family life, there is both need and opportunity for nurses, physicians, and other clinicians to provide confidential and professional individual counseling, examination, and advice to both men and women.

It should be made known and available to any students desiring it as a part of general preventive and educational service.

Written policies defining the purposes, methods, and limitations of such services should be prepared by the chief medical officer and approved by the institution. They should in general reflect generally accepted practices and attitudes of the community and of the medical profession at large. The absence of overt and accepted written policies can lead to well-meaning but potentially explosive individual action on the part of health-service staff members who may forget that they represent not only their own opinions but the institution as well. With local exceptions, such policies should usually include definition and any qualifications pro and con of program as it concerns:

[9] U.S. Public Health Service Publication 731, rev. ed., September, 1966 (for sale at $5 per 100).

[10] U.S. Public Health Service Publication 384, rev. ed., 1967–1968 (40¢ per copy).

[11] By B. H. Kean, M.D., and Harold A. Tucker, M.D., Charles C Thomas Publishers, Springfield, Ill., 1966.

1. The rights of any student to discuss and receive professional information in confidence

2. Examination of and medically appropriate advice and contraceptive prescription to those requesting it who:

a. Are already married

b. Present bona fide evidence (such as receipt of legally required premarital blood tests and signature of certificates) of intent to marry

3. Provision of legally required premarital blood tests and certificates

4. Examination and contraceptive prescription for those requesting it who are neither married nor about to be but who are seriously involved sexually

5. Any differences in policy between legal minors and individuals over 21

Institutional endorsement of the first three items above, barring religious or other strong counterpositions, will generally reflect acceptable community medical and societal attitudes. Endorsement of the fourth item for all but a few institutions will prove controversial and unsupportable. Responsibility is best placed upon individuals, couples, and families.

Intramural Services and Facilities If provided as an integral part of the health service, as it should be whenever possible, it should be as an appointment service, with predictable seasonal peaks, on half-hour appointments. Adequate space and examination equipment must be supplied for pelvic examinations and appropriate screening tests, such as "Pap" (Papanicolau) smears.

Such examination areas should (1) be 3 to 4 feet longer than general medical examination rooms (to allow for proper lighting and room for examiner and assistant) and (2) ideally have a toilet and lavatory immediately and solely adjacent to the examination area.

Staffing Many mature and experienced general physicians can perform satisfactory examinations and give responsible and wise counsel premaritally, but it is good policy to have them consult with and be approved professionally for such service by a qualified obstetric-gynecological specialist first. Such specialists are often less sensitive to and less skilled in the counseling aspects and in general are best reserved for consultation and technical supervision and for referral when no intramural service is provided.

For peak periods (March to June especially), staff time for premarital counseling should be made available for coed and all-women's institutions approximately on the ratio of 5 hours per week for each 1,000 eligible women students. For male physicians, pelvic examinations should always be chaperoned and attended by a female staff member. Women gynecologists or otherwise qualified women doctors are often excellent choices for appointment as premarital counselors and examiners of female students because they are often more available than men and prefer part-time work; if married and mothers themselves, they can shed special and personal light on a girl's concern; and they do not require additional staff chaperonage.

For nonpeak times and for counseling and examination of men students, no extra staff time need be planned; the regular staff, with proper consultation, indoctrination, and supervision from qualified colleagues, can absorb the need.

Obstetric and Other Medical Services to Students' Dependents Most institutions consider that the student's assumption of responsibility for the welfare of spouse and children by simply being married and/or a parent extends to the dependents' health as well. Fewer than 6 percent of all colleges and universities in America make any direct provision for health care of students' dependents, and less than half offer purposeful information on availability of health insurance plans. The majority of health insurance plans available to and held by student families are primarily hedges against financial loss and serious illness and offer very little provision to meet most common needs.

The student's welfare and success may often be importantly related to that of his spouse and children, and family health problems in fact are a real contribution to academic wastage. While it is true that the institution has for students a very specific set of compact and mutually understood responsibilities that it does not have in the same way with his dependents, the institution at least owes the married student some appropriate information, advice, and assistance.

Referral Services At the minimum level, the health program (even the core program) must be prepared responsibly to advise the student as to available sources of emergency, obstetric, pediatric, dental, preventive, and general medical and psychological care. General information concerning availability of such services to student dependents should be a routine service, in catalog information, special brochures, etc.

Insurance Information and Options For dependents not adequately insured via employment or other means, it is often possible to write policies tailored to their needs as part of the overall institutional health insurance program and make them available, through his choice, to the student's dependents as a voluntary option. Such policies are generally two to three times more expensive than those supplementing the student's direct campus health services but are still often less than either average, unplanned, out-of-pocket expenses or Blue plans. (See page 9-39 and Chapter 7 on insurance.)

Direct Clinical Services Because of the great variability among student families as to composition, expectations, means, and actual medical-dental needs and because of a real lack of actuarial data on expectable utilization and costs, few institutions are in a sound position either to plan for prepaid direct service or to know how much staff, space, and equipment might be needed.

A few institutions are pioneering in this field, and although present plans appear both very expensive and cumbersome, cumulative experience and data should allow sounder planning and more appropriate ranges of program options to be made available to student families in the next few years.

Foreign Students

Students from other lands may bring with them infections and may have suffered also from relative medical and dental neglect. Their previous experience with medical care and their expectations about it are often markedly different than those of native Americans and American physicians. Their reasons for seeking (or not seeking) care, their ways of describing symptoms and problems, and their ability to accept either diagnosis or treatment are largely culturally determined, and, even when they appear to make no sense, these cultural perceptions and expectations must be understood if effective health advice or care are to be rendered. For example, to many Latins, "good" medications come in solid colors, and they instinctively mistrust both the common multicolored American capsule and the service that dispenses it.

Medical certificates, chest X-rays, and insurance coverages provided by some foreign nations, even when "screened" through the U.S. Consular Service, are unfortunately unreliable. Normal chest films can be purchased by tubercular students and certified by consular officials who lack their own physicians or facilities to do otherwise. Some international programs assure students that they will be fully covered for all medical expenses and in fact provide very limited coverage.

Their admission to study programs for which they are not in fact academically or linguistically qualified produces enormous and pathological strains upon some foreign students. Such strains, always aggravated by fears of the special disgrace that attends having to return home a failure, produce numerous psychosomatic, behavioral, and fatigue syndromes requiring much medical and psychological attention.

Academic Admissions Policies Great progress has been made by American higher education in better evaluation of foreign educational credentials and in better and more realistic placement of students in institutions in the United States; but, in order to prevent gross academic and linguistic incompatibilities, each institution should make every effort to know realistically just what preparation and capabilities the student has and provide extra preparatory courses in language and/or prerequisite study.

Health Admissions Requirements Increasing numbers of American institutions are establishing their own requirements and procedures for health, including:

1. Institutionally controlled screening (skin test and/or X-ray) for tuberculosis, intestinal carrier states of typhoid, amebiosis, and other parasites, and general medical evaluation
2. Full insurance for accident, liability, and hospitalization as defined by the institution and supplied by it or written into foreign scholarship agreements, with special provision for wives and children and provision for repatriation when necessary
3. Obligatory enrollment in the institutional health program whenever enrollment is not otherwise required

Special Orientation and Information Foreign student groups should have special opportunities and programs for learning about when, how, and where to turn for medical needs, preferably by an assigned member of the health service team who continues to have special liaison relationships with the foreign student program.

For foreign student families, information should be specially stressed on availability of maternity care, child care, and dentistry.

Services Whether provided through insurance, prepayment, or grant, services preferably in excess of those provided other students should be made available, because foreign students are likely to have less ability to support independent care, to know how to find or use it, and often have greater need.

Mutual Acculturation of Foreign Students and Health Program Staff American nurses, physicians, and other health professionals are more often than not untrained and ineffective in understanding the foreign student's concerns about his health. The chief medical officer and the officer in charge of foreign student education should confer on a scheduled basis and should arrange for informal group discussions between staff members of the health service and representative cultural groups of students at the latter's instigation.

When faculty and/or staff members with special competence in or insight into the particular medical-cultural patterns of any foreign student group are available, they should be involved as consultants and advisers to this program.

Financial Support Basic care, insurance, and repatriation should not be taken for granted, and should whenever possible be written into grants, agreements, health budgets, and insurance policies.

Health and Deportation In some instances the interference with study by illness, particularly if it involves hospitalization in tax-supported hospitals or granting of medical leaves of absence, may involve the risk of deportation or cancellation of visas. The health officer should require that the institutional officer responsible investigate and inform him in writing of those medically related actions and situations which may impose the risk.

Handicapped Students

Every institution should deliberately evaluate its capabilities for accommodating students with various handicaps. If unable to accommodate certain types of handicaps, it should clearly state this in all literature sent to prospective applicants. For pursuit of many courses in general education and in some special fields, the handicapped can and should be accommodated whenever possible by relatively simple modifications of plant and of the student's program.

Physical Arrangements Whenever possible, all general-use buildings should have access by gently graded ramps as well as by stairs and elevator service to upper floors. Generally traffic ways between buildings and different parts of the campus should have gently graded ramps over curbs and other elevations. At least some ground-floor living spaces should be made accessible by ramp and made free of thresholds. Doors should be at least 3 feet wide. Toilets and showers in these special quarters should be equipped with sturdy "grab bars," and showers should also be equipped with benches built into walls. Such living quarters should have telephones for emergencies.

Other Aids Most handicapped students should be prepared to underwrite the necessary costs. For sources of both expert advice and financial help, these students and the institution's health personnel should turn to both state and federal vocational rehabilitation agencies, regional offices of the National Society for the Prevention of Blindness, and other agencies as appropriate.

Cooperation Between Institutional Health Program and Regular Sources of Rehabilitation and Care This is essential for the handicapped student. The institution's health and medical officers must have full records, current recommendations for follow-up, etc. from the student's regular source of medical and rehabilitative care, and it is very desirable that prior to matriculation and periodically as needed there be actual verbal conferences between them and between the student, his parents, and institutional health and student personnel officials.

Physiotherapy

In considering injury rehabilitation, the orthopedic surgeon (or experienced athletic medicine physician) should determine the cases, the criteria, and the methods for chronically handicapped persons. The rehabilitation specialist, often with the orthopedist and neurosurgeon, is necessary. For some kinds of conditions (i.e., arthritis or chronic skin problems), an appropriate specialist (e.g., rheumatologist or dermatologist) should define the program.

With all due deference to the individual preferences in treatment held by most generalist physicians, few of them have had the specific training or experience requisite to intelligent and effective use of this area of therapy. The results are, at least, the often seen overuse of staff-time and space in rendering lots of harmless but questionably effective "therapy." Inexpert therapeutic measures may result in the substitution of a "treatment" for an adequate diagnosis, and (more rarely) may result in a condition actually being made worse.

Simple Treatment Modalities—Suitable for Limited Use by Registered Nurses or Licensed Practical Nurses under Physicians' Orders. The application of moist heat is perhaps the single most useful modality available and often the hardest to obtain for such common conditions as hemorrhoids, pilonidal sinuses, prostatitis, boils, etc., which require sitting in hot water. Most modern residence-hall and other construction omits bathtubs, and some provisions within the health service for sitzbaths (including ordinary bathtubs) is virtually essential.

Whirlpool treatments for ankle sprains, knee sprains, mucsle contusions, etc., only after proper examination and orders by the physician, are safe and helpful.

Infrared heat lamps for treatment of back strains, etc., are safe if closely supervised and timed and if not allowed to continue day after day without reexamination; but electric heating pads and even hot-water bottles can cause burns.

Application of cold to acutely burned or traumatized areas is always permissible as an emergency measure until the physician makes final orders.

Ultraviolet-light treatments for skin conditions, if endorsed by the consulting dermatologist, may be administered by nurses with standard written precautions against burns, particularly protecting the eyes, and under specific orders of the doctor for each case.

More complex modalities (i.e., ultrasound, diathermy, progressive-resistance, etc.) should be performed only by or under the direct personal supervision of a licensed physical therapist upon the orders of the appropriate specialist.

SUPPORTING SERVICES

Technical and Paramedical Support

The health program must be supported by several services, principally laboratory, X-ray, pharmacy and medical supply, etc., and medical records and statistical services.

Laboratory Services The great majority of students' laboratory diagnostic needs are those of ordinary hematology, urinalysis, and simple bacteriology, which, with a few exceptions, can be readily performed on the premises by a qualified person.

Core Laboratory Functions. In some states the only people legally qualified and licensed to perform such laboratory examinations are either physicians or state-licensed medical technologists (e.g., California), but in many no such restrictions exist, and nurses, aides, and reasonably intelligent clerical workers (including medical and nursing students) can be trained to perform such tasks as urinary specific gravity; dipstick urine examination for sugar, albumen, and blood; microhematocrits or photoelectric hemoglobins; and throat cultures for streptococci.

Extended Clinical Laboratory Functions. If ordinary doctor's office functions are in effect, means need to be found to obtain more complex blood examination, including white counts, smears, etc., and more complex bacteriologic, immunologic, and chemical determinations. If any number of sick visits are part of the service, such laboratory support is indispensable and will require competent and properly supervised technologic services and facilities for actual performance of tests and examination.

Collection of Samples. Except where laws or regulations forbid, the collection of samples (blood, urine, sputum, excised skin lesions, cardiographic tracings) should be done by basic health-service personnel. If the patient's specimen can be secured on the premises and forwarded to the proper laboratory, it is preferable to sending the entire patient.

Facilities, Equipment, and Staffing for Ordinary Laboratory Support. Core Service and Specimen Collection. Sterile plastic prepackaged urine collection bottles, test tubes, sterile prepackaged culture swabs and tubes, and preconstituted culture media may be obtained through any local or regional medical/hospital supply house.

Facilities include about 100 to 120 square feet for storage including refrigeration, toilet with immediate pass-through or other private access to laboratory area, cot or armchair for blood sampling (to accommodate fainters), sink, electric and gas supply, and room for lab stools to be used at counter-height level.

Basic equipment should include a miscroscope with appropriate light source, a small 37°F electric incubator, Bunsen burner, small urine centrifuge, and a microhematocrit centrifuge with attached preparation and reading equipment.

A direct writing multilead electrocardiographic recorder, a simple multifrequency audiometer, an Ishihari color chart, and Massachusetts Vision Test or Snellen Chart can produce very adequate records for both staff and consultant interpretation.

Staff need consist of no more than existing health-service personnel for simple on-site urinalysis, hematocrit and throat cultures, and collection of other specimens except where laws demand special technologists. For small services, the physician can legitimize on-site sample determinations without need for special technologists or the referring of all tests out to licensed laboratories.

Special Requirements for Premarital and Other Blood Tests for Syphilis (Wasserman, Hinton, VDRL, Etc.). In most states, laws specifically say that blood tests for syphilis may be legally performed only in laboratores specially licensed and approved, especially for premarital tests. Official state forms, specimen tubes, requisitions, and reports are also frequently specified legally, and the acceptance of one state's report by another is by no means automatic, nor is the minimum legal interval between date of negative blood test and marriage always the same.

Even in core services that merely obtain and forward blood specimens for this purpose, every effort must be made to learn and cooperate with relevant regulations through the state health department.

General "Office Medicine" Laboratory Support. The minute the service assumes general ambulatory-care responsibilities, needs arise for more complex and varied tests requiring special skills and equipment, supervision, and quality control.

Whether such laboratory services are financed on the premises, through local clinics, or through commercial laboratories, the following criteria should be met:

1. The laboratory must be under supervision and responsibility of a qualified clinical pathologist and day-in-day-out management by a qualified and licensed technologist.
2. Regular quality control programs (as provided by the American College of Pathologists or equivalent) must be in effect and recorded.

On-site Laboratory Service. For eligible student enrollments of 3,000 to 5,000, particularly with infirmary services, the on-site services of one FTE laboratory technologist is both practical and economical, with one additional FTE or laboratory assistant for each 5,000 additional students.

Alternatives include sending samples or, less frequently, patients, to local hospital, clinic, or commercial laboratories, which is especially appropriate for smaller (less than 1,500 enrollment) institutions and performance of specialized tests such as blood chemistries, hormone assays, pathology, etc. Agreements should include arrangements in writing for prompt or immediate reporting of abnormal or requested results.

Laboratory Costs. Core start-up costs for microscope, incubator, centrifuges, etc. will come to about $2,000. Start-up costs for general laboratory service will be closer to $10,000.

One qualified FTE in medical technology costs about $8,000 to $10,000 annually.

If full services are purchased, costs will amount to about 2 to 5 percent of total ambulatory care budget.

X-Ray Services It is virtually impossible to provide even basic emergency and preventive services without radiologic service; and, if general office medical care is provided, it becomes even more important. In addition to the screening and diagnostic importance of X-ray examination, there are frequent instances when films are required for medicolegal reasons.

Professional and Safety Control. All X-ray services must be under the official supervision of a certified radiologist. All equipment, installation, and operations must be at least annually monitored by a health physicist and approved by either official local health departments or the institution's radiation board committee, with such written approval submitted via the chief medical officer to the institution's administration.

Types of Service. For emergency use, whether on site, at local hospitals, or in independent radiologists' offices, definite prearrangements for service, payment, and reporting should be made.

For preventive use (primarily chest X-rays for preemployment and tuberculosis screening) similar arrangements may be made, but local public health and tuberculosis association resources should be explored as well. This may be a good deal cheaper and for periodic programs may supply mobile chest-X-ray units on the premises.

General Office Diagnostic Use. Such X-ray services consist mostly of chest films and films of extremities (to rule out fractures, etc.) and other common radiologic examinations.

A general-purpose X-ray unit for chest and extremities with 1 FTE technician, part-time clerical help, darkroom, and a part-time radiologist for program control and both emergency and routine film reading can adequately serve 5,000 to 10,000 students for all but special examinations.

The advantage of such basic on-site service lies in better care and in conservation of student, doctor, and staff time and expense in following up tuberculosis screening programs and ensuring that clinically indicated examinations (such as for sprained ankles, persistent cough, etc.) are actually made and promptly interpreted. Such facilites will also serve the great majority of student health X-ray needs at a cheaper rate. For example (exclusive of initial equipment and facility costs), a chest X-ray, including the cost of film, the technician's time, machine maintenance, and radiologist's reading and report, costs about one-third to one-half of the same procedure in an all-purpose radiologic office.

For institutions of fewer than 5,000 eligible students, it is seldom necessary or wise to provide permanent on-site X-ray facilities and technologists as long as reasonably close extramural facilities are available. The volume of work would not, except at brief peak times, justify the services of a radiologic technician, and although it is one alternative, nurses or other medical workers trained to do partial and part-time radiologic work (chests and extremities) are not as skilled, produce too many unreadable films, and have to be pulled off other tasks for the job. This alternative should be elected only when, for smaller institutions, there is no other reasonably close, reliable X-ray source.

Special Diagnostic Use. All radiologic examinations beyond chest films and extremities should be done by offices with the immediate supervision of a radiologist. Such examinations would include intestinal barium studies, fluoroscopy, skull and facial bone studies, and kidney X-rays.

Whether prepaid, insurance covered, or paid individually by the student, such services should be available through the advice and recommendations of the consulting radiologist.

Radiation Therapy. This is a service virtually confined to the treatment of malignant tumors. It is costly but can be included in most supplemental health insurance policies at a very small premium increase.

Costs and Financial Consideration—Costs of Extramural Services. For preventive programs, chest X-rays obtained through local resources will cost on an average of $2 to $5 each for photofluorograms (miniature chest X-rays) including readings if done by public health or tuberculosis associations. Some health departments make no charge for such films. Miniature films have the disadvantage of significantly greater amounts of radiation exposure per film and significantly greater errors and difficulties in interpretation of films. For these reasons, the chief medical officer and the radiologic consultant may not approve the use of photofluorograms.

Standard (14- by 17-inch) chest films (with lower radiation exposures and greater accuracies) may be obtained through the same sources, but less often. One is usually forced to rely on hospital and/or private radiologists' offices. Costs will vary between $10 to $20, including interpretation, for standard front and lateral views if purchased at individual rates.

(Such costs render the tuberculin skin test at pennies per examination, with X-rays only for positive reactors, the administrative choice for tuberculosis screening for young people, most of whom are negative reactors.)

Films most likely to be required in emergency and accidents in addition to chest films include films of extremities (at costs ranging from $10 to $30) to more complicated examinations such as spine, skull, facial bones, etc., which may cost up to $50. Most properly written insurance policies will cover the cost of necessary emergency radiology and, when this must be obtained extramurally, the administrator should see that the institution's health insurance options specifically include such coverage.

From a budgeting and planning viewpoint in the institution which must use extramural sources of X-ray services, the attempt should be made:

1. To minimize X-ray use in routine preventive programs, and when it is necessary to use X-ray, to explore all public health and health association channels for provision at low cost

2. To cover the costs of accident and emergency radiology and of all in-hospital radiology and of radiation therapy by inclusion in insurance coverage.

3. To cover costs of general and special diagnostic X-ray services for ambulatory

patients by a combination of prepayment (for general services) and insurance (for special services), in which the prepayment acts as a "deductible" feature and helps to reduce the premiums required to insure for less frequent but more expensive X-ray services

If prepayment is intended, the costs will approximate, for routine office diagnostic use without special examinations, $2 to $3 per student per year (about 2 to 3 percent of total budget). For comprehensive coverage (any or all examinations needed), costs will come to almost $6 to $7 per student per year for "outside" services.

Costs of Intramural Services. Initial installation of an X-ray unit will range from $50,000 to $150,000, depending on type and complexity of equipment ordered, construction costs, etc.

Full-time radiology technicians are paid from $6,000 to $10,000 annually. If simpler, less time-consuming examinations are the rule, examinations may be made and films read and interpreted in writing by the radiologist for between $3 to $8 each (not including proportion of technician's time).

Overall, such general, nonspecialized intramural services, including salary of technician and clerical help, machine maintenance, film and supplies, and radiologist's supervision and film reading, will cost about $2 to $4 per student per year.

Pharmacy, Drugs, and Medical Supply Services

The institution's objectives in this area are to combine legal and ethical operations and practices with medically effective and economically practical and accessible sources of needed medicines.

Legal and Ethical Considerations Affecting Programs. While no medical program is complete or effective without the availability of medicines, drugs, and related materials, their purchase, storage, packaging, prescription, dispensing, and accountability are, in every state, specifically limited and regulated by law.

However, most pharmacy and drug codes have some common features, the most important of which are as follows:

1. Storage and ownership of drugs and medicines is in most areas legally confined to licensed physicians,[12] dentists, and licensed pharmacists, and in the case of drugs defined by the state and/or federal government as "dangerous drugs" only by those who are registered with the Bureau of Narcotics. Purchase of narcotics requires such registration and the use of official government order forms, and storage requires special security.
2. Prescription of drugs is the sole privilege of the physician or dentist.
3. Sale of drugs or medicines is the privilege of the pharmacist. It is unethical for physicians and dentists to sell them, and unless directly supervised by a pharmacist, unethical and unwise for the institution to do so.
4. Dispensing of drugs, that is, the actual handling of packaged drugs and medications to a patient for subsequent use together with clear, direct instructions to the patient, is restricted to the physician, dentist, and pharmacist. The pharmacist may dispense certain drugs only with the physician's prescription or order, but may dispense "over-the-counter" items without prescription.
5. Administration of drugs, that is, the actual giving of them on the spot for immediate use, may be performed by licensed physicians and dentists and, upon specific orders from the physician or dentist, may be legally performed by registered nurses and in most states by licensed practical nurses (or licensed vocational nurses).

Practical and Economic Considerations. If sources of needed medication are too remote, too difficult to reach, and/or too costly, they will not be used as intended. The

[12] In this chapter, the term "physician" includes, in addition to M.D.s, licensed osteopaths and doctors with the degree of D.O.

institution should try to make needed medicines as readily, easily, and cheaply available to students as possible.

In usual private-office or hospital practice, the trio of physician, pharmacist, and nurse are employed, with most medications prescribed and later filled at or through the pharmacy.

However, in student practice, if one relies solely upon written prescriptions to be filled at local independent drugstores, only 30 to 40 percent of all prescriptions written ever get filled. Students are not apt to have extra cash and drugs are expensive, so intended treatment too often is not carried out.

Dispensing drugs directly from the health service has the medical advantages of ensuring that the student receives what is intended, but it raises both legal and financial problems.

Alternatives. In small or core services, a common practice is to purchase and dispense "ordinary" medications (aspirin, cough mixtures) and prescribe "expensive" or less ordinary medicines. All too often, such dispensing is (illegally) ascribed to the institution, and important medications may be abused or not obtained at all.

The nurse serving a health service in the doctor's absence should never dispense or administer *any* medication (including aspirin) without specific, written and signed or clear verbal orders from the physician or dentist. In acting upon verbal orders she should:

1. Note the orders, date and time, the doctor's name, and her action on the patient record
2. Request the doctor's endorsement of this note by his initials as soon thereafter as practicable.

(See also page 9-12 on emergency services and page 9-64 on core student health services for additional comments on handling of drugs in small services, including "physicians' standing orders.")

All medications and drugs purchased and stored should be in the name of the chief medical officer, who must be prepared to endorse all purchase orders, signed inventories, etc. and who must have current narcotics registration if narcotics are to be kept.

All storage should be in lockable spaces, and for "dangerous drugs" storage must be in extra secure equipment. A special record should be kept of all withdrawals, specifying patient's name, address, or other identification; drug dispensed; strength, dose, and/or number dispensed; date; and doctor's name.

The doctor on the premises may dispense or administer any drug, but if dispensing packaged drugs for subsequent use, he must do so only with written instructions, specifically including the patient's name and identification, the date, the name of the drug, clear directions for use, and the doctor's clearly written name on the package.

In the absence of an officially supervising pharmacist, it is unethical, sometimes illegal, and usually an administrative nightmare for the institution and its health service to sell drugs and medications. The handling of cash is a nuisance and student billing procedures are inefficient, inaccurate, and may cost more than the amounts collected. For this reason, most small and many large student health services include overall drug costs in their budgets and dispense at no additional costs.

When a wide range of both "common," proprietary, and "legend" drugs are so budgeted and dispensed, the cost per student is approximately $3 to $4 per year.

Accordingly, most services limit their prepaid dispensable inventories to "less expensive" and "common" medications. This approach is unwise unless no nearby drugstores are available for reasonably priced over-the-counter sale of ordinary and common medication.

Such medicines are generally not expensive and may not make therapeutic differences in disease but are more for symptomatic relief. The student can usually afford them, and if he cannot, no major harm is done.

It seems preferable to stock and dispense the more therapeutically active and important drugs (such as antibiotics, steroids, and prescription tranquilizers) that the physician feels are of major importance to treatment. Although more expensive, they are used less frequently, and overall costs are about $1 to $2 per student per year.

Regularly required medication for chronic conditions, such as allergy, diabetes, or seizure controls, should be the student's financial responsibility, although the health service may help him with starting and interval supplies.

Such a policy helps to identify the health service as a professional resource of qualified diagnosis, advice, and treatment rather than a "cut-rate drugstore" where the student feels entitled to free aspirin, Band-Aids, and criticism.

Pharmacist-operated health-service facilities should be considered when (1) registered pharmacists are available to serve at reasonable salaries or fees, particularly when the institution has or is closely adjacent to a college of pharmacy; and (2) there are large (over 10,000) student enrollments and available space and facilities. (Spaces required for pharmacist-operated facilities are usually prescribed by law as to square footage and utilities and usually exceed drug room and storage spaces that seem adequate to nurses and physicians.)

To keep either item purchase prices or prepayment fees at low rates, volume of health-service utilization has to be high and overhead reduced as far as possible by sharing of space and utilities and by keeping drug inventory as free of inessentials and duplication as possible.

With a pharmacist on the premises, a modified fee system may be both practically and ethically used and has great advantages both in maintenance of quality, legal drug service, and in practical education of students about costs of medicines and drugs as well as the difference between a physician's and a pharmacist's functions. Under this system, drugs are sold at wholesale cost rates, with the student having option to pay cash on the spot, within a 10- to 14-day period, or to be billed an overhead charge of $2.50 to $3.

Under this system, the institution pays for facilities, utilities, maintenance, equipment, and salaries while the student pays a minimum cost for drugs actually used, with excellent accountability and the saving of valuable nurse and physician time otherwise spent in ordering, stocking, inventorying, dispensing, and recording functions.

Maintenance Services

Whether or not costs for janitorial, custodial, cleaning, and other maintenance are assigned to health program or other budgets (such as physical plant), these costs are among the highest per square foot of any in the institution.

Where sick people are cared for there is necessity for extra and continuing janitorial and maintenance service, particularly in areas of direct examination and treatment.

Permanently assigned staff janitorial and custodial service should be provided whenever possible to general-purpose health services serving 5,000 or more students, and particularly so if infirmary services are included. The advantages of a custodian who considers himself an integral part of the health service are enormous. The tasks are irregular, unpredictable at times, and lend themselves poorly to routinized or "formula" maintenance but superbly to the staff member who comes to know the people, the special problems, and the importance of his job. His presence also helps to reassure the nurse and her patients and cuts down on minor repair requisitions.

By contrast, custodial care by contract from changing pools is less flexible, less specific, and less thorough as well as exposing tempting sources of drugs or theft of salable equipment to the drifting, changing personnel who tend to fill such jobs.

Costs as a general rule should be budgeted at about 1½ times the going rate for general maintenance and janitorial service; and, if not directly assigned to health program budget, they should be included as health program costs.

Maintenance, safety, and sanitary standards for special areas such as food services and infirmary kitchens, patient rooms, toilets and lavatories, and laboratory and surgical areas should be set up and supervised by the environmental health and safety services.

Administrative Support

Records The necessity, use, and special content of records and forms in the health program are described in more detail under specific program descriptions but are summarized below with additional comments on quality, confidentiality, and administrative uses.

Individual Health Record. Such a record must for legal, medical, and administrative reasons be initiated and kept on all individuals affected by the health program. For practical purposes, this would include all students. If preemployment examinations are required, it would also include employees and any individual with whom the health program has direct professional contact or about whom it receives medical information.

Segregation and Confidentiality of Record. Such individual health and medical records are to be kept separate from all other records, in lockable files, and accessible only to designated and qualified health professionals with legitimate responsibility.

Medical information of a sensitive nature, including psychological and psychiatric information, should be further segregated in locked files to minimize casual handling and "leaks."

It is illegal with rare exceptions to share such information with a third party without the patient's express and informed consent (Chapter 7 of Section 1, on legal aspects of health services) and any suspicion or evidence that such information is being shared without the individual's knowledge or permission, particularly if with disciplinary officials, completely undermines and ruins any trust the student may have in the health service.

Quality of Record. However simple or complex the record, it should allow a professional not previously familiar with the case to know clearly who the patient is, of what sex, age, and residence, and at the very least must inform him of any special health problems, risks, or restrictions that apply as well as giving an account of each direct contact between the individual and the health service.

All such contacts must be dated, and the entry must allow the reader to know why the visit took place, why a given diagnosis, treatment, or disposition was made, and by whom.

Particularly if direct medical care is being rendered, each entry should contain sufficient notation of pertinent history and physical and/or laboratory findings to justify both the written diagnosis and the therapy and disposition ordered.

Storage of Records. The length of time medical records should be kept depends upon their usefulness for medical and/or legal reasons. Some records contain considerable information which may be very useful for providing future medical care. This is especially true in the case of colleges or universities which provide extensive personal services, including hospitalization, and which therefore will have more detailed information concerning treatment of serious and/or chronic health problems. In these cases a decision may be made to microfilm all medical records and store them more or less indefinitely. More limited services will find their records contribute little unique information and are not worth preserving for long periods for medical reasons alone.

Legally, records are important both for the protection of the patient in the case of tort and other civil action and for the protection of the institution and its staff if allegations are made of negligence or malpractice. The time records should be kept depends upon statutes of limitations and varies widely among the states. Each institution must become familiar with pertinent laws of the jurisdiction in which it operates.

Chapter **4**

Relationships with the Community

MAURICE M. OSBORNE, JR.

Director of Student Health Services, Tufts School of Medicine and Dental Medicine, Boston, Massachusetts

HEALTH-SERVICE RELATIONSHIPS—ADMINISTRATIVE FUNCTIONS AND DEPARTMENTS

Admission of Students

Health Considerations in Policies and Procedures for Application and Selection Requirements for detailed health evaluations from applicants provide admissions officers with little information of value in selection, may be needlessly prejudicial, and create a superfluous burden of paperwork. With rare exceptions, criteria are seldom made explicit for the use of health data in accepting or rejecting applicants, and in about 40 to 50 percent of the submitted forms the physician has not actually examined the applicant or has omitted or minimized material which he feels might be prejudicial to his patient's selection.

Questions on application forms relating to previous psychiatric care or illness are useless and needlessly prejudicial: useless because they have not yet proved of any predictive value and in any case are usually answered in the negative; prejudicial because honest reports of brief and helpful contacts between a temporarily troubled adolescent and a school psychiatrist have in fact led to rejection of excellent candidates all too often.

Health considerations in the application and selection process should be limited to structural, environmental, or programmatic limitations within the institution that preclude the accommodation of students with certain kinds of disabilities.

For example, in X College, the lack of ramps or elevators, a hilly campus, the location of many classes on upper stories, and a bitter winter climate obviously makes acceptance of wheelchair-bound students impractical.

Or, in the Oceanographic Institute of Y University, the program requires each student to be physically fit for underwater work, thus precluding applicants with chronic ear, nose, throat, and cardiopulmonary conditions.

Application Procedures Informational material issued to applicants should include:

1. Clear statements of limitations and of conditions that will therefore be disqualifying
2. A clear statement of the kinds and degrees of health responsibilities the institution is and is *not* prepared to undertake
3. A brief statement of what health requirements the institution may have for accepted applicants, both prior and subsequent to initial matriculation

Matriculation and Registration

Basic Health Information and Requirements Health information and requirements asked of matriculants will vary with the scope and intent of the student health program and the interests of the public health and are demanded mainly in the interests of discharging these institutional responsibilities.

In the core health service, the person responsible should require that all matriculants furnish, on a standard form:

1. Name(s), home and office addresses, and telephone numbers of parents, guardians, or others who are to be notified in case of medical emergency
2. Name, address, and telephone number of physician, dentist, and/or hospital to be notified
3. Statement of any restrictions to be placed on the student's full participation or of modifications in his program to be made for medical reasons
4. Statement, signed by physician, of either a negative tuberculin skin test or a negative chest X-ray within the preceding six months
5. Statements of any restrictions upon the school's provision of emergency medical services to the student for bona fide religious reasons and for medical reasons

The matter of inquiring into a prospective student's religious affiliation can be relevant to the student's and his family's religious wishes in receiving medical care and in the event of serious accident or illness, and may be quite safely and tactfully elicited on the emergency health information form if explicitly made optional. Those to whom it is important readily supply the information.

(For other health requirements, see section on preventive services, page 9-27.)

Registration Procedures and the Health Program The registration process provides for the health program the best mechanism for getting current information and providing recurrent access to all students. Once registered for the current term, students become immersed in their own affairs, and attempts to complete records, ascertain coverage, or obtain compliance are tedious, time consuming, and often ineffective in the absence of the registrar's power to deny, delay, or penalize late and/or incomplete registrants.

Health program personnel should make regular provision to have an allotted place and/or time in the registration sequence and to be included in registration "check-off" lists of required procedures so as to ensure regular, enforceable, and recurrent contact as needed with all students for any relevant purposes such as:

1. Updating address, emergency, and personal data
2. Determining current eligibility for health program coverage, or changes in eligibility
3. Determining health insurance status and offering available options, requirements, etc., for selves or dependents
4. Where feasible and applicable, performance of entrance tests and required immunizations, etc.
5. The exercise of waiver privileges from program or insurance requirements
6. Determination of "interval" history and needs for follow-up, by interview or questionnaire, or illness or injury occurring since last contact
7. Placing of "holds" for return after medical leaves, failures to complete health requirements, etc.

The term "holds" here is used to denote those official notices to the registrar that the health service has legitimate business with the student which must be cleared with the service directly before the hold may be released and the current registration sequence completed. Usually appearing in the student's registration material as a special notice or slip directing him to report to the service before he can complete registration, it must be signed for release by a health-service official. Holds may be placed for any legitimate reason such as failure to complete required information, to receive required examinations, immunizations, tests, etc., or information suggesting needs for early medical review, program modification, or medical recheck. Holds should routinely be placed in cases of withdrawal for medical reasons[1] to ensure evaluation of the student's medical readiness to reregister.

Temporary staff assignment of health-service personnel to registration procedures includes not only time spent at registration but preparatory time in coordinating schedules and time and/or space allotments in the sequence and preparing and collating necessary data, forms, insurance information, etc. Depending on complexity of program and length of time for registration, etc., a minimum of one clerk should be assigned to registration for each 5,000 students.

Forms and materials should include:

1. Alphabetical rosters of students for checkoff
2. Health Service checkoff spot on registration completion sheets and on hold cards or sheets
3. Cards or forms for updating addresses, emergency data, changes in marital, family, or eligibility data, etc.
4. Where voluntary, forms for enrollment in health and insurance programs

[1] See below on withdrawals and medical leaves.

5. Official waiver-request forms where indicated
6. All appropriate informational brochures and materials
7. Health-service appointment schedules and reminder slips for follow-up and indicated referrals, completion of requirements, etc.
8. Blank entrance or interval history forms for necessary completions

(For additional information, refer to sections on records, leaves and withdrawals, etc.)

Use of Entrance Health Data for Program Modifications Additional prematriculation health information will be required:

1. As the institution's educational and activities programs become more complex and specialized. For example, in physical education, particularly if required, the responsible administrators should know, preferably before matriculation, whether full participation, some limitations, special ("adaptive") classes, or complete restriction is medically advisable.
2. As the institution assumes increasing responsibility for students' personal health and welfare, particularly if living away from families. In this case, the prematriculation completion and submission of a current (within six months) full health history and examination is important in order to give health officials the necessary background medical information to give good care in continuity and cooperation with students' home health care resources.
3. For early identification and contact with students having need for special and/or continuing health care.
4. For special living or educational programming, etc., and very rarely for identification and special review of students whose more detailed health evaluation suggests that matriculation should best be delayed or denied in their best interest.

Confidentiality of Prematriculation Health Information Aside from basic information about emergency notification and care procedures and simple statements of a student's ability to participate fully or with certain restrictions on activity, or religious and medical restrictions which can be ethically and practically handled and interpreted by any responsible administrator, all other detailed medical information and any evaluations and recommendations arising from it may be received, filed, examined, and used only by qualified health professionals.

Change in Academic Program for Health Reasons

Reasonable changes in "normal" or usual academic schedules and requirements should be made for bona fide health reasons.

Procedures and guidelines for such changes should be established, in writing, between the chief medical officer and those responsible for authorizing academic changes and should include statements and procedures for the following:

Absence from Required Classes, Examinations The responsibility for attendance is the student's, and decisions as to how to explain, to condone, or otherwise to make decisions concerning absence are the business of the student directly with the academic officer involved. For the faculty to require "passes" or "excuses" of college students is not only to treat them with a mistrust which they will promptly return, but in the case of the "medical excuse" invites dishonesty and sham illness. It puts the physician on the spot of making an essentially disciplinary judgment on behalf of the faculty member concerned in a situation in which the physician cannot usually know the relationship between student and instructor. His decisions may therefore in one instance unjustly serve the student and in the next unjustly serve the instructor.

When set as a routine requirement, the "medical excuse" system results in an administrative and clerical load on health personnel that is not only sizable and expensive but tends to become routine, perfunctory, and meaningless.

The policies and procedures should spell out that matters of attendance and absence are strictly between student and instructor, it being up to the student to explain his absence directly to the instructor and for the instructor to make his own decision. If he doubts the student's veracity, he has an obligation to say so or to state his reservations directly. If the student then wishes to authorize the health service to verify bona fide health reasons for absence, he may do so, but no health service should release any information direct to the instructor without that student's voluntary authorization.

Change and Modification of Program Health reasons should never be used as excuses or justifications for waiver of educational standards and requirements of which the student, with proper help, scheduling, and adaptation, is potentially and ultimately capable. Thus while health reasons might well justify the dropping of a course, the reduction of semester or quarter course load, the waiver or modification of extracurricular requirements, or delay, extension and/or modification of required examinations, papers, etc., health reasons should not be used to lower an institution's basic academic requirements for promotion and graduation but only to assist the student to meet them insofar as he can. Here again the basic relationship should be between the student and the administrative and/or academic authorities.

The health-service role is best confined to that of personal adviser to the student, and at his explicit request, as verifier of need and recommender of appropriate modifications.

Ground rules should be established, including deadlines for dropping courses with and without medical cause and later deadlines beyond which courses may not be dropped for medical reasons, but, where such reasons exist, requirements may be postponed or modified (granting of "incompletes," etc.).

The student should petition the appropriate academic or administrative office directly unless he is incapable of doing so, and only if necessary and valid should the petition be endorsed by the health service.

Such endorsements should consist of no more than a simple statement such as "the student's petition for delay of examinations is justfied for reasons of health" or some equivalent, and on no account should they contain any details of illness, injury, diagnosis, or treatment, although they may include some information concerning probable duration of illness or prognosis.

Withdrawals and Leaves of Absence There are frequent instances in which it is wisest for the student to suspend his college attendance while still in good standing rather than to jeopardize his overall career by attempting to proceed under handicaps.

The institution should have written guidelines and procedures for application for, granting of, and termination of leaves of absence, whether by permanent withdrawal or resumption of study. If the withdrawal is for medical and/or psychological reasons, health service endorsement should be required, a medical hold placed, and reregistration permitted only after health-service clearance and release of hold (see section on registration procedures above).

Supervisory and Disciplinary Functions

The health service cannot function as controlling, supervisory, or disciplinary agent, with the sole exceptions of the protection of life and the public health, if it is to meet its primary obligations toward the student.

Supervisory. Absence from a dormitory beyond stated allowable times is between the student and the residence staff, with the health service only serving to explain this when necessary (see sections on infirmary care and hospitalization, page 9-32), but provision to administrators and others of regular lists of students admitted to the infirmary or hospital is to be strongly discouraged. Such lists or routine reports serve no real purpose, require extra clerical time, and in some instances may be needlessly prejudicial to the student. The suspicion on the part of students that any regular "lists" flow between the health service and campus agents of supervision and control seriously undermines their trust in the health service and will prevent those most needing help from seeking it.

Disciplinary. The health service must not allow itself to become an arm of disciplinary functions. Most cases, and the need for disciplinary action, arise out of some unacceptable form of behavior, behavior outside of expected norms, whether in the form of cheating, stealing, violent or abusive behavior, repeated failure to abide by rules, or acting out in sexual ways, through abuse of alcohol or drugs, etc.

While it may be true for any given case that psychological and emotional problems are important contributing factors in such behavior and should be dealt with in their own right, it is not necessarily true that the case is best handled exclusively as a health problem. It is a perversion of both the judicial and the health functions for either one to assume the other's role or to abdicate its own. While the health and psychological function may at times inform and illuminate the judicial decision, it cannot and should not make that decision.

The judicial authority has a prime duty to be explicit in recognizing and making clear to the student that, whatever the underlying reasons and regardless of "fault," the bounds of acceptable behavior have in fact been transgressed and that some corrective action is necessary.

If so empowered, the judiciary function may judge some situations or certain behaviors to be in themselves unacceptable, and on that basis alone may act to correct them.

If either the judiciary body or the student feel that health and/or psychological factors are important in the case, several alternatives are available:

1. Disciplinary action may be deferred pending professional evaluation and recommendations to the judicial authority, providing that the student understands and accepts the nature of the referral and that a report and recommendations are expected. Also that the student understands he has the right either to accept or refuse such referral and/or evaluation, to accept or reject the introduction of medical/psychological recommendations, and that the judicial authority retains final judgment unless it specifically waives it.

2. Disciplinary action may be suspended at the outset or upon professional advice, and with the student's and health service's concurrence, further action may be assigned to a direct relationship between the student and a professional source of help, with the judiciary stepping out after making this specific judgment.

Subsequent recognition and judicial action should then be made upon acts and behaviors that have already been brought to the student's attention as being unacceptable.

Professional medical/psychological help in the disciplinary situation should be seen and clearly explained as serving to illuminate final decisions or actions and/or to help the student toward more constructive and mature decisions and behavior for himself. It must not be used to carry out prejudicial penalties in the name of "health." The health professional's opinion may be requested, but is not necessarily binding upon the judicial authority when clearly requested and understood as a consultative and recommendatory action. Alternatively, the health professional may be requested to assume responsibility for further handling and action in the case, and if both the student and health authority agree to it, the judicial function must suspend its jurisdiction in good faith and allow the student and his professional advisers to work out the case toward more functional behavior according to their best judgments.

Unusually Violent or Threatening Behavior

When professionally qualified judgment is made that an individual's behavior constitutes a clear danger to himself or others and that such behavior is beyond the individual's ability to recognize or control, the health professional making such a judgment has not only the right but the duty to assume direct responsibility for protection of the individual and those about him by whatever measures. ("Mental Health," page 9-41.)

Problems often arise when others in the institution feel that an individual's behavior is dangerous and request the health authority to remove the perceived threat.

When qualified professional judgment and action coincide with what the lay official concerned expects, there is no conflict or difficulty. But when professional judgment sees little or no danger in the situation, the health authority has the duty and right to:

1. Reevaluate the case with both the individual and with the staff person involved, considering the rights, needs, and psychology of both the individual and the institution and being open-minded to institutional limitations and problems as well as to the patient's with the hope of reconciliation when practicable

2. Assume full responsibility if professional reevaluation warrants it and the situation tolerates it

3. Deny responsibility for restrictive action when professional judgment is that no real danger or threat exists, and if the lay official or community member nonetheless persists in perceiving danger and in demanding "action," charge him with preferring legal charges on his own, or the institution's, responsibility, but not as a health function

Student Organizations and Living Groups

The personal identification of the health program representative with the particular activity or living group is enormously helpful in promoting communications, mutual understanding, and therefore better and more appropriate interaction and service.

Student government and other organized student groups should be contacted purposefully by the health program; and student participation in grievance solutions, planning, handling of issues, and policymaking should be honestly accepted.

A majority of students will have rather stereotyped and negative viewpoints toward health services, an attitude entirely expectable given the background and the need to deny dependency common to most college students and the prevailing impressions of many students and their parents that college health services are second rate.

The most vocal criticisms come from the bright and verbal student leaders who have never used the health services but who instinctively detect an air of condescension and failure to recognize the relative importance of problems as the student sees them. They understandably characterize such health services as "just giving you an aspirin no matter what's wrong."

The program ideal is to emphasize and act upon the importance of treating the student's concerns as he sees them, with respect and attention, and administratively to seek and pay real attention to the honest concerns of students. (See also remarks on advisory committees, page 9-77.)

Academic Records and Transcripts

All health-related records and information should be functionally and physically separate from other student and personnel records.

In particular, it is of vital and central importance, if the confidentiality of medical information and relationships is to be maintained, and if the concept is accepted of health functions and services existing to enable and help the student to meet educational standards that official academic records contain no indication of, or information concerning, medical/psychological problems.

The final achievement is the measure, and if the transcript indicates interruptions and hiatuses in chronological sequences of academic fulfillment of requirements, it is by far better for the individual to explain and reconcile these with prospective employers or institutions himself than to invite irrelevant prejudice through the suggestion and overly easy misinterpretation of medical and/or psychological disabilities.

From the health viewpoint, official academic transcripts should record, with appropriate and accurate dates, the individual's academic achievements and failures, and should include medical information only at his request.

INTRAMURAL HEALTH PROFESSIONALS AND HEALTH RESOURCES

While mutually advantageous relationships between health-service programs and institutional schools and training programs should be developed whenever possible, the inherent missions and purposes of each party should be clearly understood, without one's being subordinated to or confused with the other.

The primary mission of the institutional health program is that of service and general community protection and health education, with specialized (i.e., professional or technical) teaching and research as subordinate activities.

By contrast, the primary mission of professional schools and training programs is teaching, training, and research, with service as a necessary but subordinate activity.

When the primary purposes are blurred and confused in the name of "health" or "medicine," neither function is likely to be well served, and apparently common interests are apt to turn into conflicts.

Medical Schools Where institutions include or have nearby affiliated medical schools, the question will arise as to what relationship the medical school should have with the overall institutional health program. And the honest question will arise, and require answers, as to why the school and its hospital should not take over responsibility for the health program.

The answer cannot turn out the same in each case, but the guiding principles should arise out of local answers to the following questions:

1. Is the medical school, including some administrative and logistic capability and commitment, prepared and able to render service at the community's level of expectation and need and with reasonable costs and efficiency; i.e., putting the community ahead of its need to teach and do research?

2. If the medical school attempts this, will its academic and scholarly functions be blunted and diluted?

In most instances today the medical school and the general institutional health program should remain administratively separate, with mutually helpful relationships to be negotiated.

One reason is that the understandable but serious mistake is made of identification of the school's department of internal medicine as the source of most generalized care, and assignment to it of health-service responsibility, in the mistaken belief that the careful and painstaking diagnosis and treatment of illness is equivalent to a comprehensive health program. Top internal-medicine staff is (correctly) preoccupied with teaching and research and has little or no understanding of or time for the "ordinary" problems that constitute the bulk of community health needs. While often assigning subordinates and trainees to such duty, it does so without supervision, encouragement, or conviction in too many instances.

Although many medical school departments of preventive medicine may be genuinely interested in and concerned with the community, there are few that are as yet strong enough to command the interdisciplinary resources and support needed to deliver comprehensive care and simultaneously realize valid teaching and research goals. Such departments too often see themselves as being apart from the patient-care portion of the whole program, particularly the hospital care of patients. They will usually neither reach for nor be granted administrative control, nor should they be unless they have the leadership, authority, and realistic ability to deliver not only what they wish to but also what the institutional community needs and expects.

Much change in social expectations and in health-professional education and response is in process right now. Accordingly, it may be relevant and fruitful at some campuses now and more in the future for medical schools, through well-organized and strong programs and/or departments of community health and medicine, to be administratively and academically responsible for truly comprehensive programs. Such programs would integrate prevention, community health education, environmental health and safety; occupational health, general ambulatory medical, surgical, and mental-health care; some ambulatory specialists' care, special-risk programs, family planning and care, emergency care; home, infirmary, and convalescent care; and hospital care with appropriate professional teaching and research in a service and teaching continuum.

Such comprehensive programs in general colleges and universities where they do exist have developed as administratively independent organizations, responsible and responsive to the institutions' health needs and expectations as a whole through their *general administrations* (rather than through their more specialized and academically responsive sectors in the medical schools). They should continue to function in this manner unless a school is clearly committed to and organizationally capable of meeting both its own and the institutional community's needs.

Most medical schools are geared primarily to teaching and research in the specialized branches of medicine and surgery and to the study and care-in-depth of selected patients, usually those requiring special diagnostic skills and facilities and/or those with needs for intensive care and/or general surgery. For the complex case, they are uniquely and importantly ready and needed; and within the overall health program, arrangements for such special and complex cases are most wisely made with the nearest university/medical-school teaching hospital. When justified by professional qualifications, health program physicians should be on such hospital staff and should hold appropriate medical-school rank.

For the more ordinary hospital cases, and even more for those who could be handled at home or in infirmary-level facilities, admission to university teaching hospitals will result in needless and wasteful expenditures of the patient's time, comfort, and money. Hospital (or clinic) care under "teaching hospital" auspices takes roughly twice the time and costs two to three times as much for management of the same condition as it would under the practitioner's care in a community hospital of excellent quality.

Other Health Professional Schools, Departments, and Training Programs In affiliated paramedical areas, the institutional health program may find valuable and needed care resources at relatively low cost while creating important teaching and experience opportunities for the students and trainees.

Third-year psychiatry residents, with proper supervision, are capable of meeting many mental health program needs, as are clinical psychology and social work trainees. Many special service needs may often be available solely and most economically through training clinics in physiotherapy, audiology, etc.

But the primary considerations for the health programs are (1) is the patient well served, without excessive loss of time, convenience, or money? and (2) can the training function be adequately and fruitfully served without overly encumbering the service function?

Academic Schools and Departments of Health Education The important consideration here is that there be a working liaison between the health program in its clinical and community action aspects and the resources and expertise of academic health education personnel and departments.

Ideally, this would be embodied in a professional health educator, responsible for extracurricular health education, attached administratively to the appropriate teaching department.

The program emphasis should be on health education via service and community action, with the didactic and expert academic backup of the scholarly branch of the field.

Relationship of the Health Program with Counseling, Guidance, and Testing Programs On a great many campuses, programs of counseling and personal guidance were well established and accepted long before health programs had begun to accept their own responsibilities for the problems of mental health care. Many counseling, guidance, and testing programs, although retaining special and important skills in education, vocational, and testing psychology, have long recognized the need for the inclusion of the techniques and practice of clinical psychology in the fulfilment of their role in student guidance. Quite correctly and naturally, the individual psychotherapeutic approach to student problems is expected of and employed by the psychologists who usually staff such services.

Where the more strictly "medical" or "health" program component of the institution has no mental health personnel or division of its own, it must rely on close working and referral relationships with counseling, guidance, and similar departments.

The chief medical officer should arrange with the counseling group of psychologists for definition of criteria and means of interreferral and consultation, with the understanding that the physicians must be called upon where there is: (1) any question or use of medication in psychotherapy; (2) any question of hospitalization or residential care; and (3) any question of psychotic or dangerous mental problems.

The physician's role should also include frequent scheduled meetings with the counseling and guidance group for mutual case review, interreferral, and disposition. Moreover, if he is professionally qualified, the physician should be available and expected to render personal psychological and psychiatric care at the student's request.

Combination of all clinical-psychological functions under a single health program administration and unified locational arrangements has been suggested, with the educational psychometric, and vocational psychology and guidance functions remaining separate.

For several reasons, both unitary and categorical modes of organization are undesirable. Psychological problems are not usually neatly assignable to specialized cubbyholes. Vocational, educational, personal, and clinical problems all merge in the individual case, and the counselor, whether located under the "guidance" or under the "health" banner, should have an awareness of the student's overall problem and how to share it when necessary.

Students are not equally amenable to accepting personal help and guidance in any case and, if forced to seek it through unacceptable or frightening portals, will avoid it. Although they may need psychiatric help, they cannot all at first accept it. They may, however, accept vocational advice, or "plain doctor" advice, or the "true talk" from a coach or teacher.

The student needs many doors through which to approach help, and the helpers behind those doors must work together and know of each other so that entry through any door may lead to the right and necessary kind of help.

Research Projects Involving Students, Other Individuals and Groups, or Health-service Facilities

Any college or university which plans or sponsors any research involving human subjects must have a formally appointed and authoritative review mechanism for the scrutiny of designs in order to prevent risks to and abuse or undue disruption of rights, normal pursuits, and capabilities. A committee on research and human subjects should have a standing membership involving competent representation from the health professional staff, physicians and psychologists, and from student personnel and faculty at large, with ad hoc specialists added in the review of proposals as appropriate to the particular study involved.

The chief medical officer should be a regular member of such committees and in addition must insist on having the right to approve or veto any research proposal involving the use of his staff, facilities, student-health or other health records, or of students within and through the health service.

Pharmaceutical and therapeutic trials and double-blind studies may be carried out when there is little or no likelihood that risk above the ordinary is introduced by the student's receiving or not receiving the treatment or drug evaluated and if the committee has approved.

In addition to its duty to prevent exposure of people to unwarranted risk through research, the committee must be alert to the possibility of misinterpretations and damaging public relations to the institution that may be inherent in even the most innocently intended and careful research proposals. For example, the administration of a "simple questionnaire" to all freshmen that includes questions about parents' use of alcohol, tobacco, etc. may bring the wrath of parents down upon the institution unless it is handled with great tact and confidentiality.

The volunteering of minors for special projects should be avoided whenever possible, as their parents will seldom be enthusiastic.

In the use of health-service facilities for research purposes, the effort should be made and the criterion insisted upon that the service's primary function of personally oriented care is not disrupted and that the student does not feel that he is being "used" without his free consent and understanding. With the latter—i.e., full explanation and openness, clear freedom of choice, and guarantees of anonymity and confidentiality—the great majority of students will willingly and even enthusiastically partitipate in reasonable research projects.

EXTRAMURAL HEALTH PROFESSIONALS AND HEALTH RESOURCES

While many extramural relationships may be straightforward ones, between seekers and providers of desired services (as between patient and physician or patient and pharmacist), the size, makeup, and attitudes of the extramural health-professional community and of the local population it serves are critically important determinants of the institution's decisions and actions in meeting its own health and medical responsibilities, and thus the nature of its relationships with the professional community is crucial.

To the extent that local professional organizations determine the norms of practice and privilege, define the population groups and types of service which they consider to be their responsibility and jurisdiction, and can control key components such as hospitals, referral channels, and professional approval, any individual or institution attempting to work in the local medical, dental, or health fields must have at least a clear understanding of local professional norms, prerogatives, and powers. Good working relationships are desirable in any case to minimize the chances that competition or the threat of it will be perceived where there is none and to convert needless competition into cooperation, but they are absolutely essential when the institution is to any degree dependent on the local health-professional community for services, manpower, hospital and referral access, or for approval.

The institution's chief medical officer and his subordinates should be members of and active within county medical and other appropriate professional societies. In instituting new programs or practices, they should make every attempt to gain the understanding and support of the local professionals by involving them in the planning process, minimizing real or apparent competition, and by using their services and respecting their rules whenever doing so will help the institutional health program.

In some instances in which the institution is very powerful or the local professions are relatively weak, the institution may be able to define and develop its health services with minimal or no regard to the local professionals. In this case, however, it is neglecting an opportunity to help them and thereby improve health in the entire community.

Students' Personal Physicians and Other Extramural Personal Health Resources The health program has the obligations of a two-way relationship with the students' home bases and personal physicians and dentists. The institution may often ask such professionals to provide its own health personnel with appropriate information on accepted students prior to matriculation (see "Matriculation and Registration," above) and with other pertinent information and opinion following medical withdrawal or absence, or it may ask their cooperation in completing prematriculation health requirements for immunizations, etc. Conversely, the students' regular extramural physicians, dentists, etc. may request that, while at college, their patients receive ongoing treatments and care through the health program, such as allergy desensitizations, diabetes supervision, weight control, etc., until returned to original sources of care.

The institutional health program must make very explicit to students, physicians, and other professionals:

1. That information requested, such as "entrance medical records," is for purposes of assisting in the patient's care while at college, not for purposes of screening him for admissions

2. That, while the health service wishes to cooperate as far as it can in carrying out the hometown physician's or dentist's plans and orders for continuing care and treatment while at college, its responsibility to do so must be governed by the skills, personnel, facilities, and equipment available to it and by the willingness and ability of the institution's medical or other health officers to accept professional responsibility for carrying out or supervising any given regimen or method of treatment

3. That, with appropriate student consent, the health service expects to consult with and share pertinent information with the student's hometown or extramural health-care resources, at the latter's request, or upon any occasion when it will assist their professional service

As a matter both of professional courtesy and of obtaining reliable data, requests and forms for routine entrance health data should be as uncomplicated and simple for physicians and other professionals to complete as is consistent with relevant data needs that cannot be supplied by the student himself. Requirements for matriculation (immunizations, dental repair, etc.) should be clearly and simply stated. Physicians in particular are inundated with "routine" but all too often overcomplicated, irrelevant, and obscure "health forms" for admission to schools, colleges, summer camps, jobs, life insurance, etc., which require far more effort and time than they are worth. Seeing no reason for the information and not being rewarded for conscientious completion, the physician gives it only as much attention as he thinks it is worth and tends to think poorly of institutions requiring it.[2]

In acceding to requests for continuing treatment at college ordered by extramural professionals, the institution must insist on absolutely clear and unambiguous written instructions, signed and updated as necessary by the extramural professional, a procedure which often requires the transcription of such instructions and schedules onto standard forms made up by the health service. It must also insist on its right to decline any such request through its chief medical officer when in his opinion it exceeds program capabilities or exceeds in any way his or the institution's ability or willingness to be responsible for it, whether as a matter of professional judgment or of reasonable practicality.

In addition to reasonable requests for medical record summaries, photostats, and other usual informational transfer to students' extramural sources of health care, the health service has a professional obligation to initiate contact and consultation with the home-based physician or other health professional whenever a student's health problems are at all likely to involve his family, as in critical illness, need for general surgery, unusual referrals, hospitalization for psychiatric reasons, or for medical leaves of

[2] The Joint Liaison Committee of the American Medical Association and the American College Health Association have approved a standardized and brief form for college entrance health records, available from either organization and adaptable to both manual and machine sorting.

absence. This enables the health professional to be of more help and support to the family, to supply the institution's health officials with pertinent information, and to resume direct professional responsibility effectively.

Other Collegiate Health Programs

Problems arise in this area chiefly when (1) one institutional health service is requested to complete multiple and complex "entrance medical records" or forms for students applying for graduate study or transfer to other institutions, and (2) when students are participating in instructional or study programs under joint sponsorship of two or more institutions.

The first problem is compounded both in effort and degree of irrelevance when such forms are required of all applicants. For some applicants it is both typical and realistically necessary to apply to several schools or programs, each of which may have a different health form and only one of which at the most will have practical use for the information. Both students and health-service physicians are contemptuous of the great majority of such forms and irrelevant requirements, which paradoxically are probably required more frequently by schools of medicine and by internship programs than by other educational programs.[3]

The same criteria for the use of health information in application, selection, and matriculation at all levels of education should be used, as outlined above under "Matriculation and Registration."

When students study and work under joint programs at two or more institutions, the respective responsibilities of each for the student's health must be spelled out, procedurally and financially, as an integral part of the overall intercollegiate agreement and program and made explicit both to students and health program personnel, with one cooperating institution having designated principal responsibility.

Others Outside the Institution

Potential Employers, Grantors of Funds and Scholarships, Insurability, Clearance for Government Service The relation of collegiate health professionals and services to these functions should be no different from that of any physician or other personal health consultant serving the individual and no different from the relationship of the individual's personal health advisers to the college admissions process. (See above, under "Admission of Students.") The relationship exists for the welfare and protection of the individual. Only very rarely may his health adviser oppose his wishes, and then only with every attempt to explain and bring the patient to accept the professional's advice.

The health professional is under no obligation to share, supply, or divulge any medical information unless his patient clearly wishes him to do so or unless he must do so in order to protect his patient or the public health.

In most instances there is no conflict, and the student or other individual initiates freely a request for the completion of routine health forms for employment, insurance, etc.

But in other situations he is under duress to supply personal and/or medical information in the sense that, if he refuses or fabricates, he may not obtain the job, the grant, or the clearance. If, however, he tells some kinds of relatively unimportant truths, he may not obtain it either.

The health professional appealed to in this situation is also under duress and may jeopardize his patient's chances by refusing to complete health forms, by resorting to fabrications, and/or by being truthful, let alone ruining his ability to be of personal and trustworthy help.

[3] The American College Health Association; the Association of American Medical Colleges; and other concerned organizations are undertaking study towards uniform standards and practices in this area.

Ideally, if employers, insurers, grantors, and government agencies use health criteria in selection and decision, they must be pushed toward stating increasingly explicit health criteria for selection versus rejection and toward use of their own professional services for direct evaluation of applicants in questionable cases.

The governmental investigator (FBI, etc.) seeking personal and health information in connection with any student or other individual under the health service's care or of whom it has knowledge has no right to demand or receive such information, nor do the institution or its health officials have any right or obligation to give it. Claims of "national security" and the display of credentials do not alter this.

As a rule, no medical personal information may be given by any health professional concerning any patient or client without either his free, informed consent or bona fide court order, warrant, or subpoena signed by a judge, regardless of who requests it.[4]

The temptation is hard to resist to report on "negative" or "clean" records to police or other official investigators, which gives the appearance of "cooperation," but the problem arises quickly when in the next case one declines to give out any information or appears to "edit" it.

At the risk of some verbal browbeatings, and the lesser risk of having to yield to legal authority, it is best to respond to all requests by lawyers, employers, insurance and other investigators for "confidential" information by a standard statement and reply that simply denies one's legal obligation or right to give out any privileged and/or confidential information without the individual's personal, direct, private, and informed permission to the health professional to do so or a properly executed and legal court order, which must further be verified by the institution's or the patient's legal adviser.

Press and General Public

For the great bulk of health program activities, there is little that is apt to generate news, and most collegiate health programs feel unfairly ignored and unpublicized. In some situations news is inevitable, as is public reaction, and the administrator must act to prevent or minimize bad relations and to capitalize on"good news."

Adverse press and public relations may be very damaging to the institution and to the health program if health matters are involved and may be set off by individual acts or pronouncements that runs strongly against public opinion or involve controversy. That the individual triggers an uproar unintentionally or professes to be acting or speaking as an individual only is seldom if ever taken into account by the press and/or the public. If he is employed by the institution or acts or speaks from within its structure, his controversial behavior is usually attributed to the institution and the health program as a whole and his individual opinion or action is publicly implied to reflect institutional policy or practice, with greater censure and penalization of the institution itself and the health program than of the individual.

Within the health program, physicians, nurses, and other staff members must be clearly made to understand that while working within the program they at all times represent the institution. And they must understand that while they may sincerely act and speak in the context of the mutually confidential doctor-patient relationship, the patient often regards the transaction as being between himself and "the health service" (rather than between himself and Dr. Jones), and in any case is under no obligation whatsoever to remain silent. Not surprisingly, when something unexpected or controversial takes place under professional auspices, the student is usually eager to share it with others and with the grapevine that exists. The event, usually with considerable distortion, becomes public property with a vengeance. Institutional health services and professionals are much more in a "glass house" than those in private practice. The relationships are more "person to person" in the latter situation, and less "student to authority." The grapevine is less active, and the news media and gen-

[4] See Chapter 7, Section 1.

eral public are considerably less interested in the individual physician than in the institution. Practices that might offend in the private doctor's office are generally "punished" by the patient's switching to another physician and perhaps getting some friends to do likewise. In the institutional physician's office, they are punished by public assaults on the institution.

In addition to understanding and accepting this crucial difference, institutional health services should in general avoid any practice that is controversial unless they have the full understanding and support of the institution and of the profession at large, and they should avoid and prevent misinterpretations whenever possible.

For example, the dispensing or prescribing of contraceptive pills or devices to unmarried minor females is still controversial and unlikely to have the full backing of either the institution or of the profession at large.

The "routine" physical examination of young women students by male doctors without female chaperonage, however professionally and disinterestedly conducted, is highly subject to emotional and vocal criticism and distortion.

In the interests of professional growth and stimulation, health-service professionals must be free to voice or publish any reasonable and professionally respectable opinions or articles, but they should remember that the health service does not exist and should not be abused, for the purposes of intellectual debate but rather that it is there to give impartial service. Academic departments, with teaching and research as primary missions, are the expected and proper arenas for intellectual challenge and response and are appropriately protected in this role by the doctrine of academic freedom. But the expression or testing of controversial ideas and methods that may be quite proper to academic departments are neither expected nor desirable in health services or in their representatives. The potential damage to the service is too great, and those who wish the protection of academic freedom should work and speak from academic departments.

Special health problems and the illness or injury of prominent personalities are very apt to be legitimate topics for reporting by news media, and the institution's administration and its chief medical officer should be prepared to handle such situations by procedures that:

1. Prevent the issuing of conflicting statements
2. Emphasize the positive aspects of the situation and enhance the institution's image
3. Provide truthful information without violating personal confidences or the patient's privacy

Among special health-related problems that would invite public attention would be the occurrence of unusual or potentially epidemic diseases on campus, such as typhoid fever, "spinal" (i.e., meningococcal) meningitis, or influenza. The chief medical officer should be responsible for collecting, updating, and preparing all relevant information and interpreting it, in draft form or verbal form, to the institution's press or public relations officer. Whenever possible, all written releases should be prepared by the latter officer, approved by the medical officer, and no other written releases should be made.

In such situations, or when public attention is drawn primarily because of the person who is ill or injured (such as a star athlete, the son of a prominent public figure, etc.), the medical officer may confirm the patients' names if, as is almost always the case, they are already known to the reporter. He may also confirm the general nature and severity of the condition but should volunteer no more without the patient's permission and should exercise his duty and power to protect the patient's privacy.

All inquiries should be directed to one responsible administrator (the press or public relations officer when available) and/or to the chief medical officer, and all information should be issued by one of these or by others only with their permission. All written releases should be issued from the administration rather than from the health services.

Chapter 5

Occupational Health and Health Options for Faculty and Staff

MAURICE M. OSBORNE, JR.

Director of Student Health Services, Tufts School of Medicine and Dental Medicine, Boston, Massachusetts

GENERAL CONSIDERATIONS

The health and well-being of faculty and staff are indispensable to the purposes of any institution and must not be wholly on a *laissez faire* basis. Although many faculty and staff members are self-supporting and should be expected to assume important responsibilities for their own health care, there are many disease and injury risks that cannot be left up to individuals.

Unrecognized disease or disability may pose threats to the public health or expose the individual to unwarranted occupational risks and the institution to suit or the payment of disability pensions.

The special hazards of a variety of occupations on the campus (such as the use of pesticides, machinery in shops, radiation hazards, etc.) are not by any means well recognized or controlled by faculty or staff employed in them without the purposeful measures for control which it is the institution's moral and legal responsibility to provide.

Some kinds of assistance to faculty and staff in the protection of their own health serve both to prevent needless illness and disability and to enhance the institution's ability to recruit and retain good faculty and staff.

It is not only the institution's moral and legal responsibility to protect its members, but it is to its positive self-interest to do so. The savings in man hours, workmen's compensation premiums, adverse legal judgments, disability pensions, and faculty-staff turnover, as well as the enhancement of morale and loyalty, will far outweigh the expenses of such a program.

PREEMPLOYMENT AND PREPLACEMENT HEALTH EVALUATIONS

The examination, by various means, of faculty and/or staff members prior to employment, to final signing of contracts, or to actual job assignment has as its primary functions:

1. Protection of the public health
2. Protection of the individual and the institution from the assumption of unwarranted job risks

Protection of the Public Health

Tuberculosis, although greatly reduced in the United States, is by no means eradicated; and, chiefly, because of its commonly unrecognized existence, it still gives rise to occasional campus outbreaks. The desirability and need for screening of students for tuberculosis has been well accepted and is widely applied. But the adoption of tuberculosis screening of new faculty and/or staff as standard practice is unfortunately far from universal. Some states require it, and may even require, as in Massachusetts, triennial clearance of all individuals employed by educational institutions at any level. In many others it is neither required nor practiced, and at some institutions it has been considered proper for staff but not for faculty, for whom it was seen as infringing upon academic freedom.

Public health is not a matter of academic or personal freedom, and as a middle-aged teacher is statistically far more likely to pose the risk of tuberculosis to his students than vice versa, there is every reason to insist on tuberculosis screening for all new faculty and staff members and on periodic retesting.

Large institutions may have their own personnel and X-ray equipment on the premises for such use as a part of the health-service program; those lacking such facilities should explore local public-health resources, which often provide skin testing and/or X-ray services through mobile or other units. Routine skin testing of individuals over 40 years of age is inefficient, as increasing numbers of them will already be positive reactors and will thus require X-rays in any case.

Prospective food handlers should also be screened for any history suggestive of typhoid or other intestinal infection and any chronic skin infections. They should be given adequate training and supervision in the hygienic handling of food and cleared before being allowed to work. The use of routine stool and/or rectal-swab cultures in this connection is controversial, some claiming that it gives a false sense of security and others claiming that it both enhances the health education of the food handler in emphasizing the seriousness with which both institution and employee must treat their hygienic responsibility and that the occasional discovery of a true carrier justifies it. The most vital effort in any case consists in the general screening by history and examination, as it serves to introduce the food handler to an ongoing educational and supervisory program aimed at promoting the hygienic and safe handling of food.

Mutual Protection from Unwarranted Assumption of Job Risks

People should not be employed in jobs which by their nature are likely to aggravate or cause injury through an individual's handicaps or weaknesses.

It is unfair and irresponsible to both the individual and to the needs of the job to employ, for example, an individual with chronic or recurrent eczema or dermatitis of the hands as a dishwasher or laboratory equipment washer. The skin condition will almost surely be aggravated. Inevitably the employee will lose time, be less effective, and almost inevitably blame the employer if not collect disability or compensation from him.

Proper preemployment or preplacement evaluation would have at least made the condition a matter of record, so that subsequent claims as to its having been "caused" by the conditions of employment might be mitigated.

In each case, the special requirements of the job must be known and the applicant specifically evaluated for his fitness for the job. Many jobs pose no special requirements or risks, such as general clerical positions and other nonstrenuous jobs in usual environments, and it may be thought that if the applicant is skilled enough for the job that no preplacement evaluation is needed. Many institutions, to save money, often require such evaluations only for high-risk occupations such as work with radiation, campus fire forces, etc.

Even "low-risk" occupations have their stresses for certain individuals, particularly psychological stresses, and whenever possible the institution should evaluate all employees before placement or final signing of contracts to avoid unhappy and unproductive appointments at the least and at worst to avoid the occasional but extremely troublesome person with mild but chronic or recurrent problems who proceeds to blame excessive absenteeism and/or subsequent worsening of the problem upon the conditions of employment. Such persons are often successful in obtaining compensation, particularly where no record exists of the employer's knowledge of the condition or of any attempt to make less stressful placement. Not even careful evaluation will identify all such persons, who may deny ever having had certain symptoms at interviews and whose problems do not reveal themselves to the usual examinations. When they subsequently surface, the institution is in a much better position than when no evaluation has been made at all.

At the very least, the institution should provide health questionnaires for all applicants for "low-risk" jobs, to be completed and signed by the applicant and reviewed by an official of the health program. This review must be done only by a qualified health professional, a registered nurse or physician, and may result in clearance or in the placing of an administrative "hold" pending further evaluation.

For any extra-risk job, including jobs involving physical labor; exposure to physical hazard; exposure to chemicals, radiation, or infection; or high noise levels, the institution must provide for direct professional evaluation and appropriate examination and testing and must make accurate job descriptions and requirements available in writing to both applicants and professional examiners. This important but often overlooked administrative procedure not only enables the examiner to concentrate more effectively on the appropriate areas but makes more sure that the employee cannot easily deny knowledge of the risks involved or claim that he was not informed of them.

JOB PREPARATION, TRAINING, AND SUPERVISION

In addition to preemployment public-health screening and preplacement health evaluation, those newly employed for certain jobs may require specific protection, preparation, and training in order to minimize risks, and the institution must work continuously to maintain safe practices.

Immunizations

These are required for some occupations where extra risks of exposure to specific infections exist. The commonest is exposure to tetanus, to which those doing outside work are especially vulnerable, but others using tools, equipment, or having any occupation in which the chances of being cut or sustaining puncture wounds are inherent are also at extra risk and should be boosted when needed or given basic immunization when any doubt exists as to prior immune status. (The requirement to give dangerous antitoxin to unimmunized workers who have sustained contaminated wounds makes their routine active immunization a far safer and more satisfactory practice.)

For those in animal work, clinical work, or laboratories where specific exposures may take place, immunization should be initiated or brought up to date.

The institution should make appropriate immunizations and instruction available to any faculty or staff participating in academically or institutionally related work in the field or overseas.

Training and Equipment for Job Safety

Unless an employee is able to demonstrate a thorough familiarity with the safe use of the tools and materials of his job and of the hazards involved to himself and others, there must be a deliberate pre-use training program and an objective set of criteria that must be passed or "checked off" before he can graduate from the status of trainee to that of an employee capable of independent and largely unsupervised work.

The element of safety and reduction of risk involves not only the employee himself but, in certain jobs (such as that of food handler, X-ray technician, and in the use of pesticides), potential danger to others. Both elements of safety must be demonstrated to have been satisfactorily learned before final job assignment and responsibility are given.

It may be preferable (particularly when the institution has no one already on its staff prepared to make such judgments) to contract some jobs[1] to licensed and/or recognized experts and to specify in the contract their responsibility for defining both the risks and the means used to avoid them. Alternatively, a specialized ad hoc consultant in the relevant field should be employed to define job and safety requirements, to design appropriate training and safety programs, and to supervise and approve the original employees and subsequent employees as needed.

Local, state, and/or federal agencies often have available consultation and help in such matters as effective and safe use of pesticides, radiation hazards, and food handling and restaurant sanitation and should be contacted before the decision to obtain independent consultation is made.

Administrators should not be content with unsupported statements or wholly independent programs of departmental responsibility for such training and supervision. Departments, unless under some surveillance, are apt naturally to place their categorical missions ahead of other considerations, to be impatient with safety routines, and to read their own enthusiasm and knowledge into any willing and eager source of help with projects, often on thin evidence.

Written programs of safety training, including description of job risks, safety mea-

[1] For example, pest control.

sures, and criteria for approval for active and responsible work should be required of each department or division before payroll approval or contract approval is given, and it should be clear that, with appropriate appeal to competent professional authority, the general institutional administration has final authority for both the adequacy of job training for safety and for the safety of the job itself. If, not the department, bears final responsibility for results.

In addition to the preparation and training of employees to preserve their own and others' safety on the job, there is the obligation to make the job itself as safe as possible through the use of proper protective devices and equipment. Just as the intercollegiate football player is required to wear proper protective gear for play and scrimmage, the welder must be required to wear his mask, the machinest his goggles, and the bacteriologist must be required to use the mechanical pipette.

Just as the athlete has every right to expect fields, tracks, and equipment in good condition, the faculty or staff person working in a laboratory has every right to find safe equipment and to find such equipment maintained, overhauled, and updated as required.

Supervision and Surveillance

Special-risk Jobs In principle this is no more than an extension of job training, preparation, and initial design for safety, but it is separately emphasized here to point up the need not only for initial training, screening, and safety design but also for scheduled continuation of job supervision, surveillance, and risk evaluation of both individuals and work settings. (See also "Environmental Health and Safety," page 9-11.)

A very pertinent example is afforded by any institutional program involving radioactive sources. Here, not only must prospective workers at any level be (1) initially screened for previous exposure and for any possible vulnerability or weakness of bone marrow, skin, gut, or ocular lens, and (2) be checked out and trained for use of the machinery and/or materials for safety to self and others, and (3) original program, equipment, and facilities be designed for maximum safety, but there must be ongoing programs for surveillance of the individual's personal health, personal handling of safety practices, and physical monitoring of radiation sources, including the necessity to know when neutron emitters are in use and to include slit-lamp examinations at preemployment and periodically thereafter.

Both X-ray and radioisotope handling and machinery tend to lapse into less safe patterns with time and familiarity, and once they have been approved they should not be left without routine checks.

Administratively, the most powerful tools for achieving both initial and continuing control are to require central administrative-professional control of licensing (as for AEC), for grant approval for special projects, of contract approval, and an approved policy for withholding institutional paychecks from those at risk or responsible for risk control who do not comply with safety standards.

The same sanctions should be used to reinforce regular and periodic reports of occupational accidents, of current program, and very importantly of any and all changes in program, modification of equipment, and/or change in personnel.

Other Employees Any employees and/or faculty members may be absent from work or present themselves with illnesses or other conditions that hold at least the possibilities of (1) seriously interrupting their service, thus requiring substitute coverage; and (2) their exposing others to infection or other disease or injury risks.

Policies should be established relative to sick leave (see the chapter on Personnel Policies) and to requirements for both exclusion from and readmission to work, depending on job requirements and on specific health problems.

In addition, surveillance of key executives and officers through periodic comprehensive health examinations may be required or offered as a benefit.

HEALTH BENEFITS AND OPTIONS

In addition to the screening, job training and safety provisions, and surveillance functions mentioned above, there are health benefits and options, some of almost required nature (such as workmen's compensation) and others depending on circumstances.

Workmen's Compensation

Nearly every state has laws providing for compensation to employees injured or made ill on the job for time and income lost and the expenses of related medical care. Details of workmen's compensation are taken up in another section of the handbook (see the chapter on personnel policies) and only those aspects directly relative to the health service will be considered here.

Aside from the obligation to provide first-aid and emergency services to any persons injured or acutely ill on the premises, whether employees or not, the health service should, in consultation with the insurance carrier, determine just what its role is to be with regard to workmen's compensation cases.

The chief considerations are the assumption of responsibility for definitive and full care of the case, who is both prepared and capable of undertaking it, and the most effective and rapid resolution of the case at the least cost. The health service should not be involved in any case, beyond immediate first aid and transfer, for which it cannot assume or arrange definitive care satisfactory both to the employee and to the insurance carrier.

In negotiating with the company's agent, the chief medical officer should attempt to establish:

1. A level of care up to which the service can competently assume responsibility by itself
2. A mutually acceptable group of services and specialists to whom referral will be made as needed
3. Whether the health service's care of compensation cases is to be reimbursed at fee for service or by reduction in the premium

If the service is of the "core" variety, with physician on call only, it should not attempt any care beyond first aid and transfer to company-approved resources (see item 2 above). If it is regularly staffed by physicians, it may elect to assume responsibility for relatively minor work-connected injuries and illnesses not likely to need referral, but it should not do so without some reimbursal (see item 3 above). The company would be required to pay for such service if rendered elsewhere and should be required to reimburse the institution for its health service's care.

Unless the service has very extensive facilities and staff, it should not in general attempt to assume definitive care responsibilities for any cases that are likely to be complicated, prolonged, and/or involve probable litigation but should refer such cases early to an approved and relevant consultant accustomed to handling them.

Distinction must be made in accident reporting and statistics between routine accident reports (that should be made on any accident case seen in the health service) and standard reports of treatment of workmen's compensation cases. If the treatment consists only of the physician's examining the patient and giving temporary relief prior to referral, it is still the compensable practice of medicine and should be reported as treatment on the company's standard form just as if the physician had assumed continuing and more extensive responsibility for care, such as suturing a laceration.

Finally, the health service should, if there is even the remote possibility of an employee's injury or illness being work connected, report it through under workmen's compensation; but it should avoid any verbal or written statements to the employee concerning coverage. Only the company and, in disputes, the official review board has the responsibility for deciding that a case is or is not compensable under the law. The health service should stay out of making such judgments if it wishes to avoid serious misunderstandings. The company will decide and, if compensable, the service will be reimbursed for its services as reported.

Health Insurance

Various health insurance plans to assist faculty and staff may be offered through the institution. The advantages of such auspices (as opposed to letting each individual purchase his own on the open market) are that:

1. Group rates are significantly lower than individual rates.
2. Therefore, as a fringe benefit, it costs the institution less than equivalent increases in salary.
3. It achieves more nearly universal coverage.

No single combination of plans can possibly fit all institutions, but in general the principal areas to consider are:

1. Hospital coverage (usually including temporary treatment for accidents and emergency in hospital emergency rooms)
2. "Catastrophe" or so-called "major medical" coverage for the occasional severe case that exceeds ordinary hospital expenses
3. General ambulatory coverage, for expenses incurred in ordinary doctor's office visits, tests, and treatments when not in hospital

This combination amounts to comprehensive health insurance.

General ambulatory coverage is still quite costly, although some companies offer it. Few institutions or their faculty and staff members will feel justified in supporting it and will prefer to absorb necessary expenses for such service as an individual responsibility.

Part of the reason for its cost is that it is generally written to cover individuals and families of any age, including children and elderly people whose actuarial risk and utilization of care is high. If young individuals and couples (ages 20 to 40, for example) alone are included, the risks, utilization, and premiums are less, and since this is the faculty-staff group with fewest resources and lowest salaries, the possibilities of age-restricted plans for them should be considered and explored.

The most usual "package" is a combination of a general hospitalization policy and a major medical rider or policy, the cost of the latter seldom amounting to more than $30 to $40 per annum. Thus many institutions prefer to pay all of the major medical premium for all faculty and staff as an outright benefit.

The general hospital insurance, being somewhat (four to five times) more expensive, is not usually paid for unilaterally by the institution, although it may be and is commonly shared by a combination of institutional and individual input. Although rates are lower if 100 percent enrollment is secured, in reality it is not usually practical or possible to enforce enrollment as long as the employee is required to pay all or part of the premium. A practical compromise is to make the plan "automatic" through payroll deduction, with an option to waive the plan if desired.

The particular mixture for any institution depends upon its faculty and staff needs, desires, and satisfaction with salary levels; in short, on what they are willing to support. For this reason, various options should be discussed with representative faculty and staff committees before plans are finalized. If any group can be said to be left vulnerable by the more common plans excluding ambulatory coverage, it is the younger, low-salaried group, particularly the single female living independently, for whom an age-restricted policy covering general care should be considered.

A group which feels vulnerable and frequently asks about insurance is made up of expectant couples who wish obstetrical insurance or fuller insurance than that commonly included in general hospital policies. However, comprehensive obstetrical coverage even when "spread" over an entire population group is not cheap, and other nonexpectant members of the group are not usually willing to subsidize a minority who they feel should be prepared to undertake the financial as well as the other responsibilities of parenthood.

Informational and Referral Services

In addition to making available health insurance plans at reasonable rates, the institution has an obligation to provide information to its faculty and staff about availability of medical, obstetrical, pediatric, dental, psychiatric, and other health resources in the area. It should also be prepared to make responsible and appropriate referrals upon request through the health service.

More than any single factor except finances, the lack of information about what services are available and how to use them is responsible for faculty and staff dissatisfaction with health care.

In compiling and preparing such information, and particularly in selecting and recommending physicians or dentists, the health service must work closely with local professional societies and groups and should consult local public health officials and voluntary agencies to learn of special and often free or low-priced resources.

In the absence of previous consultation with professional groups, arbitrary recommendations to a few physicians or dentists, particularly in relatively small communities, may arouse the hostility and effective noncooperation of these organizations. (See "Extramural Health Professionals and Health Resources," page 9-78.)

Direct Benefits and/or Prepaid Options

General Considerations Quite often any attempt to bring up the question of direct clinical and medical care services to those outside the student constituency, particularly to faculty, staff, or their families, evokes a reaction in adminstrators which expresses at once the feeling (1) that this wish on the part of the prospective clients is understandable, but (2) that even if the college could afford it, it *should not* subsidize such a program.

Institutions, except if located in splendid isolation, do not in fact "owe" and can seldom afford to offer direct services to adult and compensated faculty and staff who "should be expected to support themselves."

They (the institutions and their faculty and staff) are quite right, and if they will stop for a moment wistfully equating *health service* with *student* and will believe that indeed they should underwrite their personal health care, they might wish and agree to reorganize and redirect their health dollars toward the financial support of health services and care for themselves. Depending on location, available community resources, etc., many faculty-staff groups might find that an on-campus source of general and personal health care was more convenient, more understanding of their particular problems and needs, and cheaper.

That basic principle of good medical care that finds the best diagnosis and therapy in the knowledge not just of disease but of the person and his living habitat is no less applicable to the faculty or staff member just because he is unfortunate enough to have a salary. Not even the affluent should be deprived of personally relevant and good medical care, let alone those on marginal salary.

It is chiefly at the initiative and with the responsible financial and planning support of faculties and staffs that some campus-based health services do exist for them; and without such active support and voluntary financial contribution by a majority of faculty and staff, no institution has any business providing them direct service, much less any obligation to underwrite it unilaterally.

However, the institution may have good and self-interested reasons for stimulating and educating its faculty and staff toward a more effective and satisfactory reorientation of their health-care expenditures if additional money is required only to produce and arrange adequate staffing and facilities and no other significant political, geographic, or professional barriers exist.

Thus, while institutions may find justifiable reasons for making some direct contributions to the health care of their faculties and staffs, they neither can nor should be expected to do so without the active financial and planning support of these groups. Organized and recognized faculty and staff committees are in existence on many campuses and constitute an excellent means for responsible and active involvement of these groups in ongoing review, recommendation, and even significant control of their general welfare in salaries, fringe benefits, insurance options, and direct-service options.

The groups most likely to be threatened are those making up the local professional community, but if the initiating and decision-making groups (instead of the hapless administrator) are composed of a democratically operating patient group, workable relationships and compromises are quite apt to be developed.

Alternatives for Direct Service Benefits *"Executive" and Other Periodic Physical Examination.* Many business firms and some colleges underwrite the costs of thorough annual medical evaluations for their top and most important officers on the theory that by such careful health supervision they may forestall or prevent premature or unnecessary loss of executives through illness, particularly cardiac.

While some physicians and some companies and their executives are enthusiastic about such programs, there is little convincing evidence that much more is gained than a sense of mutual satisfaction and executive loyalty. That such extensive annual medical reviews (costing $200 to $300 per executive) in reality prevent serious illness in more than a handful of men has not been clearly shown, but the personnel satisfaction and loyalty may be worth the price.

Less extensive periodic medical review of all personnel is another direct service alternative, and where such programs have been offered, they have been enthusiastically received by faculties and staffs. Probably the most important contribution such periodic reviews may make to individual and group health is educational. While, to be sure, occasional cases of unsuspected and treatable disease are so discovered, the principal impact is probably upon the person's attitude, which is reinforced toward taking better care of himself. The costs of such reviews, including a basic "package" of the physician's review and discussion of pertinent medical history, general physical examination, hematocrit and urinalysis, and chest X-ray, range between $20 to $30, depending on local availability and costs of physicians' time, X-rays, etc.

For certain age groups and for each sex, special examinations should ideally be added, and their expense over and above the base costs may logically be borne by the faculty or staff members involved. All individuals over 40 should have glaucoma tests as normal parts of the periodic examinations. Women over 40 should have routine "Pap" smears for cervical cancer, and men over 40 should have electrocardiograms. Many other age-, sex-, or risk-specific tests may be added, some of which, such as expiratory spirography (for heavy smokers, or any with chronic bronchitis) can be done very cheaply. The principal additional examinations listed above will add between $5 and $10 to the basic package and are specific tests that, in contrast to a general physical, are effective in early detection of serious but successfully treatable conditions such as glaucoma, cervical cancer, and coronary heart disease.

Use of Institutionally Related Professional Schools and Training Programs. As discussed briefly in Chapter 4 ("Other Health Professional Schools, Departments, and Training Programs"), such schools and programs, through affiliated teaching hospitals' outpatient departments of medicine, surgery, obstetrics, pediatrics, etc. or through psychiatrists and psychologists in training and others, may not only offer care at reduced rates to any patient but may be willing to offer faculty and staff and their dependents care at still lower rates or at no cost. These options should be explored.

Prepaid General Care Options. Where large and sophisticated health services exist or where there are competent local group practices, the opportunity also exists (and has been grasped in some institutions) for negotiating prepaid general health care plans, provided once again that there is sufficient faculty-staff support and willingness to pay.

The scope and costs of such plans may vary enormously, depending on local needs, resources, and degree of comprehensiveness, but in general the costs of ambulatory care are more effectively and more cheaply borne by prepayment than by insurance.

At one institution, the cost per employee of providing general office-type ambulatory care through the health service, with whatever laboratory, X-ray and specialist's use can be provided on the premises and with no limit on number of visits or services within the program, comes to about $60, or $5 per month. This does not include drugs or the costs of laboratory, X-ray or any other service outside the health service proper, but it does meet about 80 percent of the population's health care needs.

At another institution, the same services are provided largely through a local group practice, but in addition the prepayment covers all ambulatory laboratory and X-ray examinations, all available specialists' services both in and out of hospital, and excludes only the cost of drugs and hospital room, board, and service charges. The cost per employee ($17 per month) of this plan is more than three times the previous plan and reflects the greater costs of caring for the more complicated illnesses and problems that make up 15 to 20 percent of the population's health care needs.

When wives and children are added, they will usually require more services per year than males and so costs for their care are not simple multiples of the employee's but 15 to 20 percent more.

No "ideal" plan can be recommended, but in each case it must be worked out among faculty and staff committees, local and institutional health professionals, and the administration.

Chapter 6

Administrative Organization and Management

MAURICE M. OSBORNE, JR.

Director of Student Health Services, Tufts School of Medicine and Dental Medicine, Boston, Massachusetts

GENERAL INSTITUTIONAL RESPONSIBILITY

Services and programs which are sponsored or directly controlled by the institution, including any liability for damages due to the omission of necessary services,[1] are the responsibility of the institution. The college or university should make sure that it understands its responsibilities within the comprehensive health program and that its operating choices of both assumption and denial of responsibility for program components are clearly enunciated and agreed upon in writing. This body of written policies and agreements forms the basis for the institutional health program.

The Institutional Health Program

The official program should include written policies and statements of what responsibilities the institution will assume for health, *and those which it will not.* In so doing, the responsibility should be clearly designated as belonging to parents, to insurance carriers, to local agencies, etc., as appropriate to local needs. Such conscious and written decisions should extend to each phase of the comprehensive program including general campus environmental health and safety; emergency care; personal health services to students, staff, and faculty; special-risk programs; and so forth, through the entire range of expectable health concerns of the institutional community.

Advantages of Written Program and Policies Approved by the Governing Board

The written program attaches the responsibility firmly to the governing board, thus strengthening its necessary support, and serves as a rational guideline to program planning, internal organization, development of facilities, operational policies, delegation of responsibilities, budgeting, and relationships with students, faculty, parents, other agencies, and the general public.

The lack of an orderly set of program policies and the institution's tendency to see the health program as primarily a "medical" program are the chief causes for the presence of weak and inadequate campus health programs. Professional matters within the program must be delegated to appropriately qualified professionals, but the latter cannot stand in ultimate responsibility, nor can they discharge their duties without the understanding and support of the governing board and the chief administrator of the institution.

INSTITUTIONAL CONTROL OF THE HEALTH PROGRAM

Role and Responsibilities of the Governing Board

The governing board should require the preparation and periodic revision of a written set of general health program policies and guidelines and should set this as a prior condition to its subsequent approval of budgets and the approval of key professional appointments.

Health Program Subcommittee Many governing boards have subcommittee structures for review of financial, legislative, construction, academic, student affairs, and other matters, and it is a useful mechanism to designate a group for health related matters as well, either separately or as part of a larger committee of the board.

Role and Responsibilities of Chief Institutional Administrators

The principal administrator of the institution is responsible to the board for the organization, programming, budgeting, staffing, and results of operation of the health

[1] See Chapter 7 of Section 1, on legal aspects of health services.

program. Because the health program is of such multifaceted and often such a technical nature, he must delegate this responsibility to others within the institution.

In carrying out his responsibilities, he needs to:

1. Provide for advice and representation from the principal administrative areas concerned with and affected by health-related matters and programs
2. Secure competent technical and professional advice on any pertinent phase of the health program
3. Provide qualified professional direction and assigned responsibility for the planning and operation of any health program components assumed by the institution
4. Provide for clear-cut and coordinated lines of reporting and responsibility for all aspects of the health program, preferably to one general administrator

It is important for the chief executive to appoint an administrative officer for health and medical affairs. In all but the smaller institutions, the chief administrator rarely has time to have many program and department heads reporting directly to him, and usually he will delegate broad program areas to others. While this is both proper and necessary, it has tended to produce several poor results:

1. Several administrators may have general policy and budget control over separate areas of the program, in almost autonomous ways, with resulting competition for funds. Under these circumstances, coordination, if any, is achieved only at the presidential level.
2. The health program may be too narrowly construed and administratively assigned to the student personnel or student affairs area, which may result in an excellent student health program but in the neglect and poor management of other components. Another inherent danger is associating the disciplinary role of the "dean's office" with the confidential, helping, and technical roles of the health services.

Some health service directors report directly to the president or chief administrative officer, and, in smaller institutions, this practice is both workable and desirable. In larger institutions, however, this practice may lead to infrequent or perfunctory contacts. Therefore, it is advisable to appoint an officer with broad administrative powers who is responsible for the entire health program.

The appointment of a broadly representative general health program advisory committee or panel is advisable and desirable. This committee should serve to:

1. Keep two-way communications flowing between administration and principal areas of concern, such as students themselves and student personnel officials, faculty and staff and their personnel administration, etc.
2. Provide the key administrator with pertinent information about the whole range of institutional health problems and operations and supply him with important community support and understanding for program planning and development
3. Serve as a search committee for key professional personnel
4. Serve as the parent committee for various program areas requiring subcommittees

The panel should be required to examine and comment in writing on annual programs and budgets before their submission to the president and governing board.

Some institutions have found it advantageous to appoint special advisory and technical committees for community involvement and support purposes and for technical advice. Some of the more common and continuing health advisory committees include the following:

1. Radiation hazards control committee
2. General safety committee
3. Faculty-staff health and improvement committee
4. Counseling services' coordinating committee (including psychiatric, psychological, vocational, educational, and spiritual counselors)
5. Community health-education committee

In addition, it can be most helpful for the director to have a medical advisory committee of recognized experts on whom he can call for advice and professional support.

APPOINTMENTS AND ORGANIZATION OF PERSONNEL

Recruiting Procedures for Professional Appointees

The general advisory committee, with medical advice, should assist the administrator in charge in both the development of broad health policies and in determining procedures for recruiting and selecting professional appointees. This assistance may take the form of writing job descriptions and qualifications, helping with search and review procedures, and/or making recommendations for appointment.

The lack of such deliberate mechanisms in many institutions has led to the informal, unilateral, and often unfortunate choice of professional advisers and directors, appointments vastly more difficult to undo than to make in the first place and a practice that would be unacceptable in the selection or appointment of an adviser or departmental official in any academic department.

The fault lies partly in the layman's general acceptance of "the doctor" or "the nurse" as competent and relevant to all of his health needs because he or she is a health professional and in the layman's tendency to think of the health program as a professional responsibility in the narrower sense rather than an institutional responsibility that is to be guided and operated by professionals but by no means left to their exclusive control.

Professional and Technical Advice and Control

No decent program, and in most instances no legal health program, can exist without competent and qualified professional participation appropriate to the scope and complexity of the institutional setting. The evaluation of health needs and problems; the planning and decision making as to general scope and character of program components; and specific program development, budgeting, and staffing should all be informed and illuminated by appropriate technical and professional expertise. The functions agreed upon must then be combined and placed under control of an administratively responsible professional officer, the chief medical officer or health program director.

The Chief Medical Officer

While such an appointed officer may often be qualified to serve as the principal executive administrator for the entire health program, he must at the very least be qualified and prepared to be directly and administratively responsible for the planning and supervision of any medically related program activities, and in even the smallest colleges he should be appointed to do so if only on a part-time basis. (See section on first-aid and emergency services, page 9-12.) Also, he must be qualified and prepared to advise the administration and the advisory groups on any medically related questions and decisions, calling upon other professionals as needed. If, as in the small college, he is serving primarily as the legal director and supervisor of a first-aid and core student health service, his appointment should also specifically include the understanding that it will be both his duty and his right to be consulted in the writing of health insurance policies for any constituent group and in any and all matters of relationships with community health resources, including the writing of disaster plans, agreements and prearrangements with local hospitals, physicians, laboratories, etc.; and that he should sit or be represented on any and all health-related committees.

The chief medical officer should be responsible for the professional planning, operation, and staffing of any medical program components directly supported by the institution—from the core service with a single full-time nurse and some clerical help to the comprehensive program with full preventive, diagnostic, therapeutic, laboratory and X-ray services and specialized services and infirmary facilities. He is principally responsible for preparation of program plans, budgets, and staffing proposals for review by the top administration and the advisory committee and for approval by the governing board. He is responsible for recruiting and dismissal of all subordinate personnel and for the approval or disapproval of any contractual or other agreements with extramural sources of services, such as laboratories, clinics, consultants, etc.

ALTERNATIVES FOR ARRANGEMENT OF HEALTH-SERVICES PROFESSIONAL SUPPORT

General

Aside from the basic core health services with first-aid functions and a chief medical officer in charge and its necessity to be located within and administratively supported by the institution, additional service components may be arranged in a number of ways, depending on local circumstances. Each arrangement has both advantages and disadvantages which should be weighed before definite decisions or agreements are reached, and, in each case, the four main considerations should be as follows:

1. The arrangement must be approved by the chief medical officer for its quality and professional reliability.

2. It must satisfy as closely as possible the needs and guiding principles of the core service; i.e., as serving the student or other patient with personal attention, minimum losses of time, and good communications with the institution.

3. It should be established for specific lengths of time, with assured provisions for renegotiation and review. It should not be open ended nor place the institution under restrictive obligations over lengthy periods.

4. The institution, its students, and others involved will be served best and at lower cost when the service functions and components most commonly required and used can be practically located on campus, as parts of and extensions of the core service. Among those which may be added are the following:

a. General ambulatory medical-surgical office care

b. Preventive programs—immunization, tuberculosis screening, etc.

c. Most commonly used laboratory and X-ray support

d. Selected specialists' services which comprise psychiatry, dermatology, gynecology, and, for schools with sports programs, general surgical and/or orthopedics for traumatic care

e. Basic dental program

f. Commonly used pharmaceuticals and supplies

g. Infirmary-type bed care

The advantages are those of convenience, pooling of personnel and resources, efficiency, and good interrelationships with the institutional community. In addition, it is usually less expensive to provide services through salaried individuals than to purchase them at fee-for-service or hourly rates.

Contractual Services with Extramural Physicians and Other Services

For specialized service backup, this may be the best arrangement, particularly if well-organized local group clinics exist. In several instances, such contracts supply virtually the entire professional and supporting personnel for health services. It is most successful when the program director remains responsible to and paid by the institution and when the core student health function has its own departmental and special organization and identity as being primarily student and college oriented.

Such contracts are usually prepared by the contracting clinic on the basis of utilization at its customary fees. Since the institution can pay on a regular basis, with little or no billing or "bad debt" overhead, it should insist upon a 20 to 25 percent discount from ordinary fee-for-service rates.

Supplementation of Health-service Physicians' and Other Professionals' Salaries by Concurrent Private Practice

Although this practice may allow an institution to hire a physician at a lower salary, it is a problem for the generalist, who will almost always favor his private patient and leave the student patient and the service if a conflict arises.

For the medical-surgical specialist however, student health practice is insufficient in volume and variety to support either his deserved income or to utilize his skills, and, except for the psychiatrist, he is almost obliged to be a "part-timer" in student health.

Generalists' and psychiatrists' services are best retained on full-time or no less than half-time bases. Combined practices and hourly employment is a poor third alternative.

PERSONNEL: QUALIFICATIONS, COMPENSATION, AND APPOINTMENTS

Medical Staff for General Medical-Surgical Ambulatory Services

The chief ingredient in the basic personal health service component is available, willing, and competent physicians to perform general office practice. The chief problem is recruitment. It is most desirable to have this service as part and extension of core services, and several means exist to do it. The character and professional standing of the chief medical officer is of utmost importance, and his selection and appointment should be made with the understanding that he must handle most of the staff recruiting and that the quality of the medical staff will depend very largely on his own caliber.

Full-time or Prorated Salaried Appointments Whenever possible, generalist physicians should have full-time, salaried appointments or, if working a significant, regular, and predictable part time, salaries prorated to full-time equivalence. Although physician availability will not always permit, it is better to have fewer full-time and half-time physicians than more part-time physicians. It is also more desirable to employ part-timers for whom the service is their only medical job—such as women physicians with families or physicians with part-time research or teaching positions—than part-timers with private practices. Such physicians will feel greater loyalty to the institution, identify more strongly with the service and its patients, and will render greater service for the moneys received.

Appointments should be to the health service as "physician" or "consultant," etc., and should be without tenure in themselves, as they are more in the nature of staff than of academic appointments. Additional internal administrative appointments may be made as staff physicians assume added duties within the health program, and recognition may be given accordingly, based on the recommendation of the chief medical officer.

Academic appointments should not be automatic or routine. Some institutions routinely offer academic titles such as "Assistant Professor of Hygiene" or "Instructor in Health," or even "Professor of Medicine" to full-time health-service physicians. These are usually intended as a beneficence and perhaps an inducement. Unless such titles either enhance the appointee's real influence or represent actual appointments by academic departments based on scholarly achievement, they are seldom worthwhile and are often unacceptable to the academic community. Tenured academic appointments may be made to and by an academic department, but that tenure and appointment should not extend to clinical service in the health program, nor should the health program budget support whatever time or service may be rendered in the academic position.

The disadvantages of full-time appointments on salary lie in the difficulty of securing highly qualified physicians at the salaries and fringe benefits most institutions feel they can afford and in the limited programs they offer. The majority of practitioners at the peak of their powers can command far higher incomes in private practice and, until very recently, have felt that only their less able or more tired colleagues go into "student health." It is true that a great many physicians in institutional health services are among the older practitioners, the retired military doctors, and the less aggressive younger physicians. This is not to say that they are unsatisfactory, but only that college health still has a hard time in recruiting the very best for full-time service.

The institution's strongest assets in securing good full-time physicians lie in the caliber and character of the chief physician and in the scope and comprehensiveness of the health-service program. If the chief has recognizable professional status and the staff physician is able to treat his patient to the full extent of his capabilities, very good physicians may be recruited on a full-time basis for reasonable salaries. These assets are increased if there are allowances and opportunities for advancement, for attending professional meetings and belonging to professional societies, and if the institution has prestige and an affiliated medical school.

Fringe Benefits In addition to the salary benefits and "assets" mentioned above, the institution must offer liberal fringe benefits including low-cost housing or building sites, use of an institutionally owned vehicle, TIAA-CREF or other retirement plan, group life and health insurance, liberal paid vacations, free tuition for family, etc.

Full-time Salaries for General Service Physicians Salaries and salary ranges will vary with the locale, the relative abundance of doctors, the importance and value of fringe benefits, the credentials and experience of the physician as he begins employment, and with his seniority, length of service, and administrative position. In 1965–1966, an independent study of 25 universities of 5,000-plus enrollments showed full-time salaries for general staff physicians to range from a low of $11,000 to a high of $20,000. Median salaries were $13,050 for those with 3 or fewer years since receiving M.D. degrees; $13,945 for those with 4 to 10 years' experience; and $15,656 for those with 10 or more years' experience since receiving the M.D. Private institutions tended to pay somewhat more, as did schools in the Northeast and Far West.

However, in 1968–1969, the same figures would probably be 7 to 15 percent higher, and for any given locality they may be meaningless. In one large Southeastern state university, the health service has had to consider starting salaries of $25,000 to $30,000 to relatively inexperienced men in order to compete with salaries offered by local industry and by local hospital emergency rooms.

Establishment of Salary Scales—General Physicians While salary scales of general physicians cannot be uniform and should not be absolutely rigid, it is important to orderly procedure and maintenance of staff morale to establish some clear guidelines for starting salaries and for both length-of-service and promotional increments. Failure to do so can and has resulted in severe staff morale problems as, for example, hiring a staff physician at a salary in excess of the director's.

A Suggested Guideline

1. Base starting salary should be the "low" on the scale and should be for the physician with minimum training and experience; i.e., legal minimum of M.D. and one year internship and less than two years' experience.

2. A training increment of 15 to 20 percent over base should be accorded to physicians who are eligible for or already certified by the following organizations:

a. The American Academy of General Practice, as having completed its prescribed 3-year residency program

b. The American Board of Internal Medicine

c. The American Board of Pediatrics

3. An experience increment of 10 to 15 percent of base and in addition to training increment should be accorded in starting salaries for each 5 years or major fraction

thereof after the first 5 years of active and relevant clinical experience following cessation of formal training or certification.

4. Periodic increments for length of service should be equal to or slightly greater than increments for experience prior to employment. It is demoralizing for a competent staff physician of 20 years' service to receive less than a man of equal training and 20 years in practice who is just joining the staff.

5. Administrative increments of more than token size should be accorded upon a staff physician's promotion to recognized and approved positions such as Assistant Director for Clinical Services, Associate or Deputy Director, etc.

6. Provision should be made for general cost-of-living increments coinciding with those for personnel in general.

Within each bracket, there is still room for some negotiation and bargaining, but the system assures that better qualification and training are recognized and that new staff members of equal training and post training experience do not receive more than established members.

A representative pay scale for full-time or major part-time general physicians in 1969–70 is presented in Table 1.

For initial budgeting purposes, the most likely mixture of available staff men and the number of positions should be used to strike an average salary per FTE (full-time equivalent) and a total cost.

Full-time and Prorated Salaries for Chief Medical Officers, Health Program Directors, Etc. Whether full-time or part-time, the chief medical officer should be on salary, prorated as necessary for time contracted for, based on full-time equivalence, with the following provisions:

1. The same general guidelines must be used for base salary and increments for training, prior experience, and length of service as for general physicians.

2. He must not have a lesser salary than any of his subordinates. The same survey of 25 universities previously mentioned revealed that in 1965–1966, chief medical officers' salaries ranged from a low of $15,000 to a high of $26,000 per annum with a median of $18,768, or $3,000 to $5,000 more than the average staff man, and $2,000 to $4,000 more than subordinate medical administrators. The median in 1969–1970 is probably closer to $21,555, but the salary should realistically and properly be set in relation to the general professional pay scale to be $2,000 or more in excess of that received by his next-highest-paid full-time subordinate.

Full-time and Prorated Salaries for Other Health Professionals *Nurses.* In the past 3 to 5 years, nurses have experienced greater relative pay increases than any other major group of health professionals. Despite these recent gains, they are still underpaid and will, through organization, be able in the near future to command 10 to 15 percent more than at present.

For 1969–1970, representative full-time starting salaries for various nursing positions may be expected to range around the following salaries:

1. Licensed Practical Nurse (LPN) or Licensed Vocational Nurse (LVN)–$5,200 to $6,200, with increments

2. Registered Nurse (RN) without baccalaureate degree and with no experience–$6,500 to $7,500; with some experience–$7,000 to $8,000

3. RN with baccalaureate degree but no experience–$7,000 to $8,000; with some experience–$8,000 to $10,000

4. RN with desirable experience in supervisory or "chief nurse" role–$8,000 to $12,000

Psychiatrists. In general, psychiatrists in private practice or in state mental institutions are able to command slightly higher (about 10 to 15 percent) starting salaries than general physicians. No psychiatrist should be employed who has not fulfilled prescribed training for board eligibility by the American Board of Neuro-Psychiatry.

TABLE 1 Illustration of Possible Incremental Pay Scale for Full-time General Physicians, 1969–1970
(All Figures in Thousands of Dollars per Annum)

Preemployment training and clinical experience	Length of health program service and rank									
	Starting	0–5 yrs.	5–10 years		10–15 years		15–20 years		Over 20 years	
	Staff	Admin. title	Staff	Admin. title	Staff	Admin. title	Staff	Admin. title	Staff	Admin. title
"Minimal" M.D. with one year internship	15.00 ("base")	17.00	16.75	18.75	18.25	20.25	19.75	21.75	21.25	23.75
Plus experience:										
5–10 years	16.50	18.50	18.25	20.25	19.75	21.75	21.25	23.75	22.75	24.75
10–15 years	18.00	20.00	19.75	21.75	21.25	23.25	22.75	24.75	24.25	26.25
15–20 years	19.50	21.50	21.25	23.25	22.75	24.75	24.25	26.25	*	*
Over 20 years	21.00	23.00	22.75	24.75	24.25	26.25	25.75	27.75	*	*
"Board eligible"	17.25	19.25	19.00	21.00	20.50	22.50	22.00	24.00	23.50	25.50
Plus experience:										
5–10 years	18.75	20.75	20.50	22.50	22.00	24.00	23.50	25.50	25.00	27.00
10–15 years	20.25	22.25	22.00	24.00	23.50	25.50	25.00	27.00	26.50	28.50
15–20 years	21.75	23.75	23.50	25.50	25.00	27.00	26.50	28.50	*	*
Over 20 years	23.25	25.25	25.00	27.00	26.50	28.50	28.00	30.00	*	*
"Board certified"	18.00	20.00	19.75	21.75	21.75	23.25	22.75	24.75	24.25	26.25
Plus experience:										
5–10 years	19.50	21.50	21.25	23.25	23.25	24.75	24.25	26.25	25.75	27.75
10–15 years	21.00	23.00	22.75	24.75	24.75	26.25	25.75	27.75	27.25	29.25
15–20 years	22.50	24.50	24.25	26.25	26.25	27.75	27.25	29.25	*	*
Over 20 years	24.00	26.00	25.75	27.75	27.25	29.25	*	*	*	*

*Retirement

Psychiatrists may have to be started at base salary with training and experience increments *plus* a 10- to 15-percent increase above if they cannot be hired for less.

Clinical Psychologists and Psychiatric Social Workers. Persons in these categories must hold Ph.D. degrees in clinical psychology and the M.A. or M.S. in social work (M.S.W.), respectively. At full-time employment, the former's salary will range between $10,000 and $16,000, depending on experience. The range for the psychiatric social worker is $9,000 to $14,000.

Laboratory and X-ray Technologists. Qualifications vary among states. In some states such as California, no unlicensed medical laboratory technologist may be hired to perform laboratory work in connection with patient care, although X-ray technologists do not require such licensure.

The principal criteria are to determine the state's legal requirements for licensure if any, hire only licensed technologists if required, and obtain the endorsement of the lab technologist's qualifications from a qualified, board-certified clinical pathologist who should be in charge of laboratory operations. For X-ray technologists, endorsement from the health program's certified radiologist is also required.

Salaries for technologists range widely from $7,500 to $14,000.

Physical Therapists. Qualifications include licensure in most states and membership in their national organization. In case of doubt, the evaluation and endorsement of a qualified board or certified orthopedist or physiatrist (M.D.) should be obtained. Full-time salaries range from $7,500 to $15,000.

Part-time Physicians' and Nurses' Salaries General physicians can rarely be retained on a part-time or hourly basis for under $15 per hour. For planning purposes, $20 is more realistic.

Specialists, hired as such on an hourly basis, command at least $20 per hour and more often $25.

Nurses hired as replacements or "extras" charge by the shift or 8-hour period or any portion thereof in excess of 3 hours. The normal rate is $38 to $40 per shift.

Part-time Personnel – Benefits Part-time personnel are not generally entitled to fringe benefits, with the exception of physicians or nurses who may receive academic titles such as "Clinical Instructor," "Clinical Associate Professor," etc. without other compensation or fringe benefits.

Chapter 7

Financing the Health Program

MAURICE M. OSBORNE, JR.

Director of Student Health Services, Tufts School of Medicine and Dental Medicine, Boston, Massachusetts

INTRODUCTION

General Problems and Inadequacies: Narrow Concepts and Slender Budgets

The frequently observed problems and inadequacies of so many college and university health programs are widely and vocally attributed to money, or rather the lack of it; and administrators are blamed for being stingy and unsympathetic, or health professionals are charged with being greedy and making unrealistic demands upon the institution in excess of evident needs.

From personal observation it appears that most of the problems stem from the following major factors and a number of related or correlated factors, as follows:

1. Lack of current, generally agreed upon, and officially approved statements of purposes, objectives, and definitions for the institutional health program as a whole and for its components

This lack may be due to administrative belief that the institution already has an adequate program, to administrative trust that the "health professional knows best" and would articulate and press for new programs and resources if he really thought them necessary to the health professional's frequent failures to see overall program needs for change and to articulate them effectively, or to a combination of these factors.

2. Persistence and institutionalization of habits of thought by professionals and administrators alike who tend to equate the entire collegiate health program with its original focus upon "the necessary care of ill and injured students away from home"; who believe this to be a necessary, if burdensome, institutional liability of its role *in loco parentis;* and who tend to regard other health programs and functions as beyond the institution's responsibilities

3. Failure to perceive and to define the many different ways in which health concerns affect the campus community, and that different program areas may and must be planned, operated, budgeted, and supported in different ways, not necessarily all as items from general funds or as institutional liabilities

4. Failure of budgeting practices to reflect and to follow program definition and development; failure to understand the proper significance of a budget and its functional relationship to a program

5. Limited funding concepts and failure to explore the many different available funding mechanisms (ways of spending money to save money) and to relate these functionally to different program areas

Many institutions are limited by existing statutes and by political considerations and legislative attitudes in their freedom, for example, to charge tuition, to set fees, or to use certain appropriated funds for purposes other than building and construction. As long as the health service is seen as an institutionally supported liability, it is also seen as being in conflict and competition with other institutional needs. Many of these limitations could be removed or changed by program definition and reallocation of support.

The current plight and financial anemia of many college and university health programs stems basically from the lack of current, accepted, and officially adopted definitions of program; narrowness of interpretation of the program as student medical care; limitations of understanding of sources and responsibilities for support of different program components; and failure to derive budgets from defined program areas and their appropriate support sources.

All these are interrelated and interdependent but have in common the basic lack of understanding and definition of the collegiate health program for which administrators look to professional guidance but find little beyond the narrowly clinical. It is for this reason that this section has been presented and organized as it is, leaving the financial aspects to the last as the servants, not the masters, of program rationale and content.

Terms, Definitions, and Units in Financial Consideration of Health Services

While it is understandable that financial terminology should vary among institutions, it is dangerous when commonly used terms are interpreted differently within an institution and even more so when the concerned parties are unaware of their differences.

There may be good or, at least, functional reasons for the use of different terms and interpretations in one college as opposed to another. However, by pointing to the more common differences in the interpretation of usual terms, it is hoped that any one institution in attaching financial structure to its health program will agree within its membership on what is meant by such terms as "budget," "prepayment," "fee," and so forth. For example:

"Health service budget" may mean any of the following or any combination of them or none of them:

1. The total of salaries, supplies and expenses, capital equipment and renovation (but excluding maintenance) involved in rendering direct on-campus student health services
2. The above plus maintenance
3. The above with or without maintenance and with or without amortization costs
4. The above including or excluding cost coverage for certain program elements by insurance
5. An amount of money arbitrarily allocated to the service

Commonly, the term includes only expenditures and rarely balances expenditures against income sources.

In general the most common failure is to describe in budgetary terms the true program costs of delivering the agreed-upon amount and quality of services and—by restricting the financial program description to such fixed and identifiable institutional expenditures as salaries, expendable supplies and equipment, and some capital expenditures—to give partial and self-limiting criteria for decisions. For instance, there is a common tendency to exclude from budgetary descriptions those elements covered by insurance or even the premiums for such insurance and maintenance items which, although accounted for under physical plant, nonetheless contribute to the total costs of the health program.

"Prepayment" is often confused in function and semantics with "insurance," the separate functions and meanings of which will be discussed below.

"Fees" may (or may not) mean:

1. Categorical prepaid amounts applicable to the health program and/or to a range of programs
2. Designated portions of tuition allocated to health and/or other special programs
3. Specific charges or cash payments made upon individual receipt of services or goods or combinations of these

"Costs per student" may mean direct budget divided by number of students, or any number of combinations, with stated or unstated variables relative to total versus eligible students, units of time used (such as semester, quarter, calendar or academic year).

It is essential that within any single institution all terms that relate program activity or function to budgetary and financial structure be agreed upon and defined in writing as part of administrative procedures for health services and activities.

PROGRAM BUDGETING VERSUS USUAL BUDGETING PRACTICES

Common Budgeting Practices and Their Problems

Budgeting practices and statements usually tell something about who is directly employed, what they use and where, and what these staff, supply, and facility resources cost in net terms. They are commonly restricted to student health service directly supplied on campus but otherwise reflect very little about what is done, even in that area, and therefore tell very little about what different direct functions and programs cost. Little information is supplied about health education or program areas such as environmental health, occupational health, or even student health, about indirectly supplied functions, overhead costs, or about the probable and appropriate sources and amounts of income.

Program Budgeting

Program budgeting, by contrast, describes a program or parts of it in financial terms of who is required, from where they are drawn, for what units of time, what is required of them, where and when, the things and facilities they need and relates these to costs, overhead, and to income sources for a particular function. It gives the administrator better information about what is being done that is needed and about what the components and totals cost are, and it gives him greater control over results as opposed to line item budgets, especially when these come from several departments.

The administrator should be less interested in the fact that a certain account number covers the expenses of a given number of staff, etc., in a particular department than in the fact that a required function, such as tuberculosis screening, is or is not being performed, what it is costing as presently organized, and whether if reorganized it could be performed more efficiently and/or less expensively. Program budgeting allows him to do this and to have a better idea of whether or not his resources are fulfilling needed functions or just drawing salaries to serve less needed activities. In practice the administrator, with all necessary technical and community advice and support, proceeds as follows:

1. Program budgeting starts from the definition of a need and an activity or function that will meet that need. A program may be defined as a set of needs, appropriate functional responses, and the amounts of staff time, supplies, equipment, facilities, and therefore costs required to fulfill that function or group of functions for a defined situation or population group or special project.

2. The procedure then organizes into service areas, in accordance with local determinants, those elements of the particular function or program that are:

a. To be directly organized as intramural functions, whether through single or interdepartmental participation

b. To be organized by agreement and arrangements with specified extramural resources

c. To be provided independently through miscellaneous sources and services without direct institutional organization or affiliation; i.e., nonaffiliated resources.

3. The methods of cost coverage are determined for services and materials within each service area, by, for example:

a. Preallocation or appropriation of funds, usually including those for specified, relatively fixed or predictable functions and costs which may exist in intramural and affiliated service areas and may include premiums for insured components in any of the main areas, including an unaffiliated service

b. Recovery of costs through claims on appropriate insurance, usually for specific but less predictable, unusual and/or potentially more expensive service needs but rarely for intramural services; often for nonaffiliated services such as hospitalization and ambulance service, and for a variety of unaffiliated services

c. Cash payment or item charging for services and goods as needed and used that are not covered by specific preallocating or insurance, with or without contingency or reserve funds for such "out of pocket" expenses. Most commonly these charges will be found to include the following: intramurally, some drugs, injections (particularly allergy shots), some laboratory and X-ray examinations, routine physical examinations and reports at student third-party requests (e.g., insurance exams, some dental services if any are offered intramurally, and some kinds of psychological testing and therapy); at extramural-affiliated sources, charges for all or some specialists' examinations and treatments, drugs and appliances, special laboratory and X-ray examinations; through unaffiliated resources, charges for virtually all services or material that are not insured.

4. The sources of actual funds and services are determined; i.e., who and/or what will actually contribute the monies required to support different program components and service areas, in what proportions, and by what methods and means (such as from capital or endowment income, direct tax appropriations, prepayment by various forms, purchase of premiums, transfers of already funded services or accounts, etc.) municipally supplied services and materials, use of traineees or otherwise funded personnel, etc.

Division of Program Areas According to Main Responsibilities and Methods of Support

Preliminary Division by Source of Responsibility In addition to frequent lack of program definition and a tendency to think of the health service in terms of an institutional burden, there is seldom evident a clear-cut division of health activities into those which should:

1. Be centrally supported as institutional obligations by various means, as items of general and special expectable overhead or liability

2. Be supported from combined sources as items specially relative to instruction, academic function, research, and extracurricular activities

3. Be supported largely by the potential and actual beneficiaries as relative primarily to personal health services and individual welfare

Although the overall mix of components judged to be relevant according to local determinants will vary widely from one setting to another, the components adopted as institutional programs may be most constructively examined within the above framework for purposes of financial planning and fair use of funds. For example, a student health fee if levied should apply primarily to personal health and welfare services and not to support environmental and safety programs or occupational health programs.

Separation of Capital and Operational Financing While most of the foregoing discussion may seem to imply operational considerations alone, they are equally relevant to capital expenditures for new construction, renovations, and equipment. The purposes of the latter may be related to general institutional need and use, special use for educational purposes, personal services and welfare, or to mixtures of all three, and funding potentials then may be appropriately allocated and sought.

For example, construction of student unions, conceived primarily as serving informal student welfare and extracurricular educational functions, is often financed through a combination of student activity fees, educational grants, and overhead funds that provide campus control of planning, contract design, construction supervision, and subsequent maintenance.

It is very important whenever possible to separate capitalization and amortization funding from operational funding.

While it is entirely appropriate to utilize the student health fee for construction and/or amortization of a student health-service building, this should not be at the expense of adequate operational funds, and the fee should include and designate both functions.

Direct Payment and Support versus Insurance

Some confusion exists, particularly among health professionals and others not knowledgeable about insurance, concerning the purposes of insurance: how it differs from prepayment for services and the criteria that should govern the choice between covering anticipated costs through budgeting and prepayment or through insurance of different kinds. These choices, whether for individuals or institutions, become more critical when it is realized that meeting the costs of health care is some combination of (1) anticipatory savings, (2) purchase of insurance policies, and (3) cash on the line. While some are fortunate enough to require so little service that even a small amount of unplanned extra change will suffice to squeak by and others are so burdened with extraneous funds as to be able with no plans to cover any contingency, the majority of individuals and institutions are in neither position and must plan ahead. For practical purposes this requires that we pay in some anticipatory fashion, either through some method of budgeted savings and prepayments or through insurance premiums, leaving a small margin for out-of-pocket and unanticipated expenses.

What Should Be Budgeted and What Insured In this choice, the general guiding rules are:

1. Save, budget, or prepay for those expenses and services which will be most commonly and most predictably required, which can be most responsibly and reliably provided and controlled directly, which have relatively low and predictable unit costs, and which may reduce the probability of major and serious incidents and costs.

2. Insure for service and costs which are less commonly required, less predictable in both utilization or cost, less capable of being responsibly and efficiently controlled directly, and which, being potentially more costly per unit of service or unit of illness or injury, may exceed budgeted funds.

A very large university may, through its ownership and control of a general hospital and through its very large population base and budget total, be able to budget and pay directly for hospitalization of students in its health program and have the reserves required to absorb a 5-to 10-percent overdraft on its hospital budget occasioned by one or two unexpectedly severe and costly hospitalizations. It may also find that even such an "overdraft," i.e., planned budget *plus* deficits, is *cheaper* to the combined funding sources that the total cost to them of equivalent hospitalization insurance premiums and co-insurance payments.

By contrast, a small institution and the families supporting it, relying on hospital facilities they do not manage and having a small population base and total budget, cannot realistically afford even a *single* costly hospital case with their own resources. Here, the potential budget overdraft can amount to an excess of 50 to 100 percent over budgeted or other available funds—an unrealizable amount—and such institutions must hedge, through insurance, against such direct and catastrophic liabilities.

Or, for a different example, it is wastefully expensive in premiums, administrative time, and salaries to include in health insurance policies the coverage of services such as ordinary X-rays or skin biopsies which are readily and commonly done within the health service when the volume of demand and enrollment can directly support the requisite equipment, supplies, and qualified personnel within the service.

Assignment of Responsibility for Direct Funding and Insuring Components Considerations so far have covered:

1. Broad assignment of responsibility for support of major program areas to the major institutional sectors relating most appropriately to those areas
2. A general division between the kinds of health activities usually best supported by direct funding and service as opposed to those more appropriately supported through insurance

In the first instance, the division is one of general responsibility for support, without reference to *method;* in the second, the issue is one of method, without particular reference to responsibility or *source* of support.

While each major program area will rest upon the base of combined "direct" and "insured" funds appropriate to its functions, there often appears to be a quality of magical thinking in reference to insured program components, as if such components and their costs were somehow in someone else's hands and no longer items of institutional liability or parts of its budget. For example, if 25 to 30 percent of the total costs of services rendered to students are covered by insurance, the administration is apt to point with pride to the "savings" thus afforded the institution, through the students' purchase of the health insurance, even in instances where the students are actually or supporting virtually the *entire* service (both "direct" and "insured" portions) in any case, whether through tuitions, fees, cash, *and* premiums—or a combination of them. In institutions which feel that "they cannot afford to support" more than the skimpiest of student health services, it is often considered proper and "economical" to offer the students the privilege of paying for the bulk of their health services through purchase of expensive insurance policies, or even to require it of them, as a means of relieving the institution of this financial strain and keeping its "health service budget" down.

In some public institutions, legislative and general fund appropriations may be low and restrictions may be placed on these funds and on student fees and tuition with regard to health purposes. It is incumbent on the family unit to plan for underwriting a substantial portion of both the direct on-campus services and supplemental insurance premiums that are appropriate to the setting and that are often more effective and less expensive than either very comprehensive health policies or fee-for-service on the open medical market.

Insurance, then, is not a valid substitute for institutional planning and program responsibility. It merely offers the program, *and those who support it,* a supplemental method of fulfilling program objectives and responsibilities along with directly funded and provided functions. As an excuse for shifting the support of personal health services onto the consumer, it is an illusory avoidance of institutional responsibility as long as the support can and should be mainly borne by the consumers anyway, and can be done so much more effectively, more appropriately, and less expensively by their support through the institution of combined direct services and insurance supplements rather than through insurance alone and a laissez faire approach.

Regardless of source of support, *both direct expenses and premiums should be considered as budget items in themselves,* and the misconceptions should be avoided that equate "direct expenses" with "budget" and "insured expenses" with "somebody else's responsibility."

FINANCIAL PLANNING FOR GENERAL AND SPECIFIC COMPONENTS OF THE HEALTH PROGRAM

Budgeting for Operation of Campuswide Health Program Areas Environmental health and safety, disaster planning, general campus first-aid provision, information, and transportation are items of general institutional liability. Because needs, problems, and resources vary so markedly from one place to another, it is not possible to give "usual" or expected costs for these services, nor has much systematic study been done to define common elements and typical programs and resulting costs. They are usually made available through a wide degree and variety of contributions of time and manpower, equipment, supplies, and facilities from several sources. Local conditions determine the importance of these elements. For example, note the clear differences in effort needed for food service sanitation inspection, food-handler examination, and training between an all-residential college with twenty different kitchens and dining facilities and an all-commuter college where only vending machines are provided. Or note the differences in need and type of emergency services in a small girls' college where no cars or motorcycles are permitted and the large suburban college where no restrictions exist. For each location the requisite services can usually be located from intramural and extramural sources, and the main financial problems are those of determining the method of payment (preallocation, insurance, or item purchase and contribution) and the sources.

General Environmental Health and Safety Funding Methods These should include preallocation for the necessary components of ordinary, expected service, with payment of premiums for insurance against general institutional liability arising from potential failures of program such as serious food poisoning outbreaks, collapse of spectator stands, fire, etc. Some contingency or direct-purchase funds should be set aside, with the advice of competent experts, to handle unanticipated and/or uninsured costs as for the hiring of consultants, the necessity to conform to newly enacted codes requiring the installation of a dumpster system, or emergency power sources for critical areas.

The sources of support for general environmental health and safety will vary in proportion but will generally come from institutional overhead, gathered proportionately from all its sources of income. That is, each community project and sector protected should include a proportion of its income in grants, tuitions, rents, endowments, appropriations, etc., for this general protection. In tax-supported institutions, legislative appropriations and tax support for this function within college and university communities should parallel that of towns and cities. Some municipal and state services may be available at no extra charge, as well as some federally assisted programs; but the organization and exploitation of fund sources is the institution's responsibility.

Special Environmental Health and Safety Costs of dealing with special problems such as food service sanitation, which involves predictable expenses, should be built into cafeteria and "board" fees as items of overhead freely available from local municipal or state sources. For new construction, the safety and sanitary engineering design and construction costs should be built into contracts and fund-raising efforts. X-ray and radiation-hazards control expenses should be included in X-ray fees, research grants, and departmental budgets as well as in insurance policies for incidents and accidents.

General Disaster Planning and Expenses Planning time and expense is shared among health services, security departments, local hospitals, local professionals, police and fire, Red Cross, etc., and may often be federally funded to a large degree including costs of emergency equipment, cots, instruments, etc. for setting up of emergency field hospitals.

Some kinds of disaster expenses are covered by fire insurance and general personal liability insurance, and others are covered through federal, regional, Red Cross, and other voluntary and civic agencies.

Special Disaster Expenses Methods and sources of funding here are largely through special insurance, the premiums for which are built into the financing of the risk area, such as those described above and in the section on funding.

General First-aid and Emergency Service While this is a general institutional liability, the responsibility must be shared as, for example, between health services, security, affiliated ambulance and hospital services, local and county police and sheriff's offices, and informational and student affairs officers.

All intramural contributors should estimate the amount of their departmental time and cost going into this program and receive reimbursement from the institution.

Fund responsibility includes funds for maintenance of standby services, which should come from general funds and local community contributions of service. They also include fund responsibility for emergency services used and reimbursable to the program by workmen's compensation, Blue Cross-Blue Shield holders, an amount proportionate to use from student health budgets, and direct billing at fee for service when appropriate.

Some specific staffing costs have been discussed in Chapter 2 and work out approximately to a figure equal to $15 per student, but as suggested above, these costs should not be entirely charged to student health.

Emergency and Ambulance Transportation It is easy to think of campus and local police and fire units in this connection; and while some indeed have the equipment, manpower, and training to perform emergency transportation of sick or injured persons within or without the campus, they often have other primary duties. In many cases, they are called for medical situations which turn out to be nonemergencies at the same time that real emergencies are happening.

These problems give rise to questions of establishing an on-campus institutional ambulance service. Conferences usually find that the actual rate of need and use is not to justify the purchase and maintenance of equipment, the training and salaries of nine full-time positions required to stand by and man one ambulance (with two men per ambulance) 24 hours a day, 7 days a week.

It is more economical and efficient for the institution located in any town with a private ambulance service and a taxi service to establish contracts or arrangements with them for flat-rate billing per ride, as authorized by an official chit (held by health-service, residence-hall, and other student personnel officials). The average monthly costs for such services at one university of 10,000 enrollment is approximately $75, or less than $1,000 per year, a figure which cannot begin to pay for one full-time standby driver.

Relative Costs of Student Health Care Components

Relative Utilization and Costs in Meeting Needs through Major Program Areas in a Comprehensive System Comprehensive care for students includes a wide range of service potentially needed by this group. Some are commonly needed and used; others much less so. It is also obvious that in different collegiate settings the mixture of available components will vary widely; but for practical planning and financial consideration, the existing components break down into a relatively small number of functional or program categories. These can be identified as common to virtually any student health care system, regardless of where the components are provided, by whom, and how supported or by whom. These major function and program categories represent not only major categories of service need and utilization for the group that are fairly constant and predictable but also correspond to the *organizational groupings* of relevant functions (i.e., as in clinics as opposed to hospitals) and permit some relative costs to be examined.

The four principal categories of service function and program into which virtually any and all components can most practically be subsumed are:

1. General and ordinary ambulatory care
2. Specialized ambulatory consultation and care
3. Intermediate ("home-style" or infirmary) bed care
4. Full or "general hospital" bed care

Their general and approximate relation to meeting health needs and to relative costs may be tabulated as follows (assuming, for the moment without discussion, the technical and administrative support services necessary to each category, and that ready access is available):

TABLE 1 Approximate Percentage by Individuals and by Relative Costs of Students' Health Care Needs Met by Principal Functions in a Comprehensive Program
(Figures in Medians, without Range Specified)

Functions*	General ambulatory care	Special ambulatory care	Ambulatory subtotal	Minor bed care	Hospital- ization	Bed-care subtotal
Approximate percentage of health care needs met..........................	75	15	85	12	3	15
Percentage of total costs, approximate	55	20	75	10	15	25

* Eyeglasses and refraction exams excluded.

As shown, the great majority of needed and used service units (85 percent) are ambulatory, and 75 percent of them are of a kind provided by rather usual and uncomplicated services – general medical, dental, preventive, minor trauma and first aid, with common laboratory and X-ray tests included. Ambulatory services of all kinds account for almost 75 percent of costs, with bed care accounting for 25 percent of total costs and hospitalization alone accounting for 15 percent of costs in the care of 3 percent of students requiring care.

Put another way, the bulk of needed and used service (85 to 90 percent) is provided through rather general and unspecialized service areas ("doctor's office" and infirmary or home bed care – with relatively simple diagnostic and administrative supports) and is met by 65 to 70 percent of total expenditures. Conversely, the less commonly needed and used service (specialists' services, special diagnostics and hospitalization) required in only 10 to 15 percent of cases account for 30 to 35 percent of total expenditures.

Elements within the Principal Program Categories Within each principal category, there are separate components that, through differential inclusion or exclusion, allocations to intramural or other service areas, and sources of payment make up any particular health method of source of payment, it is useful to start from the comprehensive framework and then to proceed to divisions.

Ambulatory Care. If all elements are available, ambulatory care accounts for about 85 percent of use needs and about 75 percent of costs. *Within* this category, the following elements account for percentages of total utilization and costs approximately as follows:

TABLE 2 Approximate Percentage of All Utilization and Relative Costs of General Professional Ambulatory Services for Students in a Comprehensive System, with All Components Available (Except Eyeglasses and Examinations Therefor)

Program components	Preventive service	Emergency services	General office care	Special services	Mental health	Dental health	Miscellaneous*
Approximate percentage of all utilization	15	5	45	10	3.5	15	5
Approximate percentage of all costs	3	15	40	10.5	5	15	1

* Elective, or cosmetic procedure, etc.

The principal *utilization* is in general office care, preventive services, and specialist backup (*including* general dentistry), which together account for approximately 80 to 85 percent of all used service visits, and 65 to 70 percent of all costs. While emergency services seem to account for a small proportion of use, the expense is relatively high because of the need for maintaining standby staff and facilities.

Variations within Ambulatory Care Programs. The greatest variations and differences among collegiate health programs for students occur in direct intramural ambulatory services in terms of what is "provided free" and what is left to insurance and for individual responsibility.

1. Virtually no institutions provide direct coverage of eye refraction examinations (other than screening types, such as Snellen, etc.) or eyeglasses and/or contact lenses. Because 30 to 40 percent of all students wear glasses or lenses at least part time and seek examinations and/or receive new prescriptions about once a year at examination costs of $15 to $25 and spectacle or lens costs of between $15 and $50, the total cost per population is high and would add between $10 and $15 per student per year appled to *all* students if prepaid. (In one program that attempted to include these services in prepayment, the demand for examinations—most of them unnecessary—flooded the eye doctor's offices and bankrupted the program. Coverage was discontinued the next year).

2. The next-to-most common variant is to provide no coverage for dental service other than some insurance coverage for accidental injury to sound teeth, thus "saving its own budget" (although not necessarily the students') about 15 to 20 percent of a potential total.

Other common variants of omission from direct intramural provision are:

3. Omission of some or virtually all preventive components—particularly routine physical examinations, tuberculosis screening, and immunizations (with about 3 percent budget reduction—and a 10 to 15 percent decrease in visits—or shift of visits to general-care purposes when staff is short).

4. Exclusion from direct coverage of "outside," less used consultants' and specialists' services[1] such as neurology, endocrinology, plastic surgery, etc., while providing part-time hours for commonly used specialists, including dermatologists, gynecologists, and orthopedists, with a cost and use saving of 3 to 5 percent.

5. Exclusion from direct coverage of *all* specialists' services[1] with a direct budget saving of 15 to 20 percent.

6. Limitation of mental health services to diagnosis, evaluation, short-term therapy

[1] Psychiatric and mental health services are not included as specialists services in these paragraphs. See below for variants involving them.

(or so-called "crisis intervention"), and referral (that is, omitting long-term therapy for a relatively very few individuals with great individual costs and disproportionate expenditure of staff time).

7. Limitation of all mental health services to indirect counseling and emergency intervention only.

8. Ommission of all professional psychiatric and clinical psychologists or psychiatric social workers' services, with a total direct budget saving of 5 to 8 percent out of a potential comprehensive program.

9. Laboratory and X-ray services, if freely and appropriately used, account for the following approximate percentages of ambulatory care costs, wherever provided:

TABLE 3 Costs of Laboratory and X-ray Services as Approximate Percentage of Total Student Ambulatory Care Costs

Service	Routine and usual	Special and unusual	Total
Laboratory	3	2	5
X-ray	5	2	7
Total	8	4	12

It is fairly common to assign special and/or unusual laboratory and X-ray expenses to insurance or direct student payment, thus again "saving the budget" another 4 to 5 percent of potential expense. However, when *all* laboratory and X-ray tests are assigned to insurance or direct charge, the apparent "savings" tend to cancel out because of the administrative overhead involved in accounting, billing, and claims handling, and important tests or X-rays are not obtained by the student. The same is apt to be true for the following items.

10. Pharmacy, drug, and prescription services, whether purchased directly and dispensed or directly charged, amount to approximately 3 to 5 percent of the total costs, like common laboratory tests, may cost in accounting, billing, and claims overhead as much or more than simply to purchase them by prepayment and dispense directly. Despite this fact, many services "save" by so doing, although the patient is saved little or nothing and will usually fail to obtain the medication at all.

11. Another program variant is to limit directly budgeted intramural services and insured services to certain kinds of cases, commonly excluding (particularly from insured components), coverage for care and expense of elective and primarily cosmetic treatment and of preexisting and/or chronic conditions such as perennial allergies, etc. (In one program that had previously covered all expenses, including reparative surgery, for preexisting defects such as bone-cartilage tears, congenital heart disease, etc., the curtailment of available health service and other funds by the university necessitated a reduction of $50,000 from anticipated and requested funds—a cut that was accomplished almost soley by exclusion of previously covered reparative surgery for chronic defects from coverage. The percentage reduction, in a $1-million budget, was, at 5 percent, not excessive; but a reduction of $50,000 without damage to the rest of the program was a sizable contribution to the university's financial balance).

12. Curtailment or omisson of physical therapy from general ambulatory intramural services is common. This is a service which, if allowed to proliferate without qualified specialists' control, can add significant expense to the program without clear-cut benefits. (See Chapter 3.)

Variations within Bed-care Programs. Necessary bed care accounts for about 15 percent of use need and 25 percent of costs for general student health purposes.

As pointed out in Table 2, the utilization need ratio is about 5:1 for home and/or infirmary type care over hospital care. The cost ratio is reversed to about 1:1.5 for population total costs and 1:3 for individual case costs. Therefore very few institutions (except the largest universities with on-campus university-owned hospitals and large enrollments) budget and pay directly for hospitalization costs. Most institutions and/or individuals cover hospitalization, with varying limits, through insurance, being in the "less frequent but more expensive" category. (Overall, hospitalization for the college-age group meets 2 to 3 percent of case needs at approximately 15 percent of costs in a large system, although, as pointed out, in a small college even one severe case could amount to an extra 10 to 15 percent over total expected costs.)

Most colleges with residential students provide intermediate or infirmary bed care, which serves about 12 percent of the case needs and accounts for about 10 percent of costs.

Some colleges with large "commuter" enrollments, but also some with significant numbers of residential students, omit any organized infirmary-type bed care and rely either on improvisations on dormitory care, use of hospitalization for such cases (charged usually to insurance), or on sending students home. The "direct budget" may, as a result, show a "saving" of approximately 10 percent, but the real costs in overutilization of expensive hospital beds and/or in lost credits and tuition may far outweigh the "savings."

Variations within Special-risk Programs. The presence of such programs as intercollegiate and other athletics, field trips and overseas study programs, programs for the handicapped, etc. mean the addition to or subtraction from the total health program of significant expenses, but these are expenses that should be in principle proportionately assigned to and drawn from the budgets and income sources of the special activities involved and not charged across the board to all students or to general funds.

Relative Costs per Student of General Student Health Programs This most used and abused term of measurement of program costs is so frequently referred to because, when defined, it has very significant functional meaning that ties the program to the number of students involved (and thus hopefully allows functions to respond proportionately to enrollments) and suggests as well the quite logical notion that students or their families and sponsors should have some responsibilities for supporting the costs of health services rendered.

The unit of costs per student is useful as a rough unit of measurement and comparison with other programs within an institution and is potentially useful in comparisons of cost and health programs between different alternatives and different institutions as long as its variables are precisely defined.

1. "*Costs*" means the total student health service direct expenditure budget for general intramural and some extramural services and usually excludes both insurance premiums and the costs reimbursable through insurance and any costs or charges made for individual services.

2. "*Per student*" usually means students other than part-time or special students, i.e., the usual full-time student.

3. *The time period* to which these costs apply is usually the ordinary academic year. However incomplete this definition may be for accurate analysis and true cost comparisons and however crude the term "cost per student," it is a practical starting point for estimation, comparison, and appropriation of the directly budgeted funds that will describe and support the bulk of student health service actually provided by a given institution.

Using this unit of "cost per student per academic year," a rough scale can be constructed relating these figures to the main elements and the combination of elements that make up the range of commonly found student health-service models, from the most elementary to the most complex, *exclusive* of general hospitalization, general dental treatment, long-term psychiatric care, and of special group-risk programs (athletic medicine, etc.). With these exclusions, the cost per student per academic year of a "wide open," very inclusive prepaid program of ambulatory and infirmary-type care approximates (with 1969–1970 salaries and costs) $100. There is some variation in this figure in that it tends to be higher for smaller institutions and somewhat lower for larger institutions, probably because some elements of overhead such as the need for printing or duplicating information, record forms, etc., purchasing functions, and the need for emergency standby staff and facilities cost the small institution almost as much as a larger one even though use volume is smaller. The figure will also vary depending on local salaries, costs, fees, and other factors, but it is a conveniently round figure for discussion and not too far from the truth.

TABLE 4 Approximate Cost per Student for the Usual Academic Year of Individual and Combined Elements in Typical Directly Budgeted Student Health Services (Elementary to Inclusive, from the Top Down)

Components provided (with recommended staff, supplies, equipment, etc.)*	Approximate costs per student per year	
	Per component	Cumulative
"Core" and emergency services	$15	$15
General physicians' services with appropriate nursing and other support	25	40
Common laboratory services	3	43
Common X-ray services	5	48
Ordinary medications and treatments	5	53
Basic preventive services	5	58
Limited specialists' services (dermatology, gynecology, and orthopedics)	8	66
"Crisis" and indirect psychiatric consultation service part time	2	68
Basic diagnostic, short-term therapy and referred psychiatry	5	73
Unlimited specialists' services (all cases covered)	4	77
Unlimited laboratory services	2	79
Unlimited X-ray services	2	81
Unlimited medication and other treatments	9	90
Full infirmary-type bed care	10	100
Totals	$100	$100

* See Chapter 3 for recommended adequate staffing, supplies, etc., for each component relative to student enrollment, etc.

By referring to the right-hand column in Table 4 one can roughly figure that the amount charged per student per school year will include all the components on that line and above it; i.e., $53 per student will buy a basic program of general-practice-type care with most of the needed staff, laboratory, X-ray, and medication/treatment backup to handle the run-of-the-mill student injuries and illnesses, and $10 more will buy usual infirmary services as well, for a total of $63 per student to provide what is probably the most common "package" in student health for residential students. Components can be added, subtracted, or internally altered to fit needs and means.

Relative Costs per Student of Special Student Health Programs and Components Considerably less work has been done and less data is available on costs of special programs outside of those roughly indexed above. The following figures and guidelines are approximate and best used as jumping-off places rather than as actuarial tables.

Dental health costs are beginning to be studied by the small number of pioneer dentists engaged in collegiate health work,[2] and systematic information is available from one or two programs. As stated in Table 3, dental health costs account for approximately 15 percent of all costs for the total health care of the average student population if services are regularly used. However, where studied, at least in sections of the country where precollege dental care has been relatively infrequent, the costs per student for the initial year of regular service are approximately three times as high as in subsequent years due to the extra professional time, procedures, and materials necessary to bring neglected dental-oral conditions up to acceptable levels. Thereafter the cost of maintaining that given level drops markedly. In the particular study alluded to, first-year costs per student were in the $90 range, dropping thereafter to approximately $27.

In the author's present program, the costs for a simple type of dental health program are at the rate of $25 per student per year. This includes prepaid dental examinations, X-rays, prophylactic service, and oral-dental consultation, emergency services, and selected operative chemistry for some students of lesser means. It is exclusive of other dental costs to be paid by direct fee for service.

TABLE 5 Approximate Costs per Student per School Year for Dental Health Services—All Sources

Components	Costs per student per year			
	For students with previous good care		For students with neglected oral health	
	By item	Cumulative	By item	Cumulative
Dental examination and prophylaxis referral	$ 7.50	$ 7.50	$ 7.50	$ 7.50
Dental X-rays	5.00	12.50	5.00	12.50
Emergency treatment plus ordinary operative chemistry and consultation (maintenance level)	12.50	25.00	12.50	25.00
Special "start-up" costs for first year dental rehabilitation and/or other prosthetic or restorative or extra prophylactic work obtained	15.00	40.00	65.00	90.00

Relative Costs of Insured Portions of General Student Health Programs and Their Relation to Budgeted Portions *Relation of Insured to Budgeted Portions.* This is one of the chief determinants, if not the very most important, of how the insured portions of the program will be written. As a general rule, the more comprehensive the directly budgeted services, the less the required insurance coverage. With a broad and direct service, there are fewer areas for potential insurance claims and fewer total claims both in dollars and numbers, so that premiums may be kept within very reasonable limits.

Conversely, the less extensive and less inclusive the budgeted services, the more gaps are left for the insurance or the patient to fill directly. When insurance policies are written to fill a great many such gaps (for example, all laboratory and X-ray tests, drugs, all specialists' consultations, and infirmary-level as well as hospital bed care), the premiums rise sharply because of the greater dollar volume of claims and the greater number of claims, plus the accompanying administrative overhead.

[2] Only 18 or approximately 1 percent of all American College Health Association members are in the dental profession.

Administrative and clerical overhead is very often placed in large part upon the health service or other college staff. This is not illogical, since the health program is often in the best position to verify the claim; and furthermore, the health service is often written into policies as the gatekeeper or "valve" for claims. That is, many policies, in an understandable attempt to hold down unnecessary or self-prescribed medication claims, consultation claims, etc., will cover such items only if ordered or arranged through the health service.

Thus, in a fair number of health programs in which a relatively low budget is supplemented by a relatively extensive health insurance policy, the institution may be "saving money" only to find out that, although direct budget services are kept low, the administrative costs are unusually high. (In one such program, the extra clerical staff and overhead required in handling a very large volume of claims restricted the amount of physician time available, with no overall budget savings and no savings or improvement of service to students.)

In a reasonably comprehensive program in which the insurance portion is intended to cover only the least likely, least controllable, and most expensive contingencies and care away from college and during vacations, the ratio between directly budgeted amounts per student and the insurance premium should be approximately 3:1; i.e. health service budget per student per 9-month year = 3:1. Ratios significantly below this are suggestive of underbudgeted and inadequate direct services, or of overreliance on insurance as a substitute for service, or both.

Costs of Insured Components of the Student Health Program. Because the scope and the premium costs of insured portions of the program may vary principally with the proportion of directly budgeted services, it is not possible to state with any confidence what student health insurance premiums cost or even should cost. In approaching it from the point of view of program cost (i.e., hospitalization), the wide variations in hospital room rates and ancillary charges from one part of the country to another make absolute figures meaningless.

The relative proportions for costs of program components most appropriately assigned to insurance coverage in a comprehensive program can be approximated as shown in Table 2 where hospitalization is shown as requiring approximately 15 percent of all costs in the total program.

Within the ambulatory program, the proportion of less frequent, less directly controllable, but more expensive specialists', laboratory, X-ray, and treatment services is approximately 45 percent of all such specialized services, 4.5 to 5 percent of all ambulatory service costs, and 2.5 to 3 percent of total program or care costs.

The gaps per student per school year most appropriately filled by insurance coverage would be:

1. Hospitalization and its attendant surgical, other professional, laboratory, X-ray, and other ancillary charges

2. Expenses for necessary treatment of unexpected (but not extra-risk) medical or accidental conditions away from institutionally or family provided services

Further inclusions in insurance coverage may be established by their omission (as from Table 4) from directly provided services where this is absolutely necessary and wise, but not to the point of substituting insurance coverage for the more basic, ordinary, and frequent services that the institution can better provide itself.

Commonly justifiable insurance inclusions are:

1. Expenses for rarely needed by expensive ambulatory tests and services, such as radioisotope tests and radiotherapy, rheumatology consultation, and the extra specialists', diagnostic, and therapeutic services listed as items 10 to 13 in Table 5

2. Some protection against very unlikely but catastrophically expensive situations involving prolonged hospitalization, multiple operations, etc., over and above more usual hospital and other costs

While these principal insurance components are not *usually* sold separately (with the exception of the fourth component—usually called "major medical" insurance) their comparative costs in premiums will be approximately as follows:

TABLE 6 Approximate Relative Apportionment of Student Health Insurance Premiums to Program Purpose and Relation to Directly Budgeted Cost per Student*

Premiums for insured components					Budgeted
Hospitalization and incidental costs	Highly special ambulatory service, tests and treatment	Ambulatory emergency care away from program	"Major medical"	Sub-total	Direct ambulatory services
$20.00 21%	$4.50 4.7%	$6.50 6.8%	$7.00 7.3%	$38.00 39.8%	$95.00 100%

* When very complete direct services are provided and the supplemental insurance is not heavily encumbered by exclusions, deductibles, limited fee schedules, etc.

Reasons for Variations in Supplemental Health Insurance Premiums. In addition to the primary reason of its inverse relationship to the inclusiveness of the directly budgeted program, the other main reasons for premium variability are:

1. Size of student body eligible, and proportion of students obtaining the insurance. The greater the student-body size and the higher the proportion buying the insurance, the lower will be the premium for the same policy.

2. Various restrictions on coverage such as deductible features and co-insurance, ceilings on total reimbursable amounts or on fee schedules and room rates or both, exclusion of treatment for chronic or "preexisting" conditions and many other limiting features designed to keep premiums low while still realizing an acceptable "premium/loss ratio."[3]

In general, it is safe to state that a comprehensive student health supplemental health insurance premium at much *over* $40 to $50 indicates an extremely weak or inadequate intramural budgeted program; a premium significantly *under* $20 is probably so encumbered with restrictions and exclusions as to be virtually worthless.

Insurance for Special-risk Programs. Special coverage is necessary for medical, surgical, and hospital expenses for illness or injury incurred in the course of institutionally sponsored activities having any extra or special risk, such as (1) intercollegiate athletics; (2) field trips, overseas campus operations, etc.; (3) special study area risks, such as those involving ionizing radiation and isotopes, dangerous chemicals, microorganisms, etc.; (4) programs for the handicapped and other disadvantaged groups.

In figuring such special program budgets, it is useful and necessary to determine total program costs and to relate these to the number of students participating in that special program. It is not usually helpful or fair to ascribe these costs to the entire student body or to imply that either the general student body or the special participating student group have main and direct financial responsibilities for the extra risks and unusual problems involved. These costs and particularly the costs of premiums for any extra risk insurance involved belong to the program and to the institution as a whole.

Total Student Health Care Costs through Institutional Plans in Contrast to Unplanned or Individually Purchased Care. Costs for very comprehensive ambulatory

[3] Acceptable "premium/loss ratios" should be between 3:2 and 4:3; i.e. the insurance carrier and/or agent should be expected to retain (for his overhead and profit) 25 to 33 percent of total premiums. If retaining significantly less, he is losing money (and will raise subsequent premiums or restrict coverage); if retaining significantly more, he is overpricing (or underservicing) the policy and the program.

health services organized and directly budgeted through the institution have been quoted above (Table 5) as approximately $100 per student per school year.

If the principal, justifiable, and usual insurance components are added to fill the gaps left by these services, as described above, the additional premium costs per student (usually per 12-month year) will range between $20 and $40, very rarely over $50, and, if much under $20, rarely worthwhile.

Finally, if one adds the unbudgeted and uninsured expenses—usually dental, eye glasses, etc. (with no attempt to guess at the miscellaneous more than to add the 1 percent shown in Table 2 to the total)—it can be said that the total average cost per student per 12-month year for comprehensive care, as organized through the institutional health program with appropriate supplemental insurance and some contingency funds, is about $180, of which $135 is planned as shown in Table 7.

TABLE 7 Approximate Expenditures per Student for 12 Months for Fully Comprehensive Health Care

Component	Expectable ranges	Average
Institutionally based and budgeted ambulatory services and infirmary care	$ 80–120	$100
Insured components (premiums)	25–45	35
Unbudgeted and uninsured "miscellaneous"	35–55	45
Totals	$140–$220	$180

By contrast, a person of student age seeking coverage on the open medical market *may* through some plans obtain fairly comprehensive ambulatory care for about $150 per year through prepayment, although such plans are far from common. They may purchase individual health insurance policies costing between $150 and $200, which generally do not cover doctors' office visits, examinations, lab and X-ray costs, preventive services, and other ambulatory services, which are then either not used or are paid out of pocket at fee-for-service rates. Hospitalization costs are usually partially covered, leaving further amounts to be paid. When such policies are procured at group rates, as through places of employment, the premiums are lower but seldom under $120 for the type of hospital-oriented partial coverage described above, are not prorated by age-group risk, and leave the most commonly needed costs uncovered.

The student is unlikely to obtain comprehensive care at all levels for much under $250. He will pay in fees for service, payroll deductions for occupational care, and insurance premiums in excess of that for incomplete and fragmented service.

In summary, very complete services for students can be financed through well-organized college health services for lower total expenses per student than through any other present plans or organizations.

FUNDING SOURCES AND METHODS IN PROGRAMS FOR GENERAL PERSONAL HEALTH

General

There is no such thing as "free" medical or health care, but a generation and more of students, educators, and health professionals have accepted the position that student health service is "free."

If students and their families and administrators, professionals, and boards can be shown the benefits and advantages of a decent institutionally organized student health program, ways can usually be found to obtain the funds, and most students and parents are willing to contribute reasonable amounts if they can see the benefit.

Shifting the principal funding responsibility to the consumer, through a variety of means, tends to remove health programs from the restrictions of being considered "an institutional burden," from the stigma of "free" (or "socialized") medicine, and from unnecessary competition with other program areas.

Methods of Health-service Funding from Consumer Sources

While the original student health services came to be regarded as institutionally supported, history shows that many colleges and universities charged separate "infirmary fees" and that quite a few health services were originally started and funded by voluntary associations of students.[4] Many continue to be built by student fees that also build unions, swimming pools, etc.

Colleges and unversities have moved away from the levying of numerous special fees. They have spread the necessary amounts across tuitions, tax appropriations, or special department grants and income and have expanded the insured portions of their programs.

While many variations and combinations of collection methods may be found across the country, the most common general methods are:

1. Capitation, the periodic collection, usually in advance, of some standard and equal amount from each eligible person for support of directly budgeted services to be then made freely available to any or all eligible for a given period
2. Voluntary prepayment for budgeted services
3. Charges for premiums, for insured portions of the program which are then available to those holding the insurance and
4. Direct sales, fees, or item charges for goods or services

Waivers of Fees and Insurance: Exemptions from the Program

While a solid student health operation depends on a very broad, virtually universal subscription in both the directly budgeted and insured program portions through capitation or "automatic" charging in advance, several issues make a waiver system desirable.

First, there are situations involving special religious beliefs and situations in which, because of some other reasons, it is both desirable and diplomatic to offer a graceful and administratively acceptable way out of required health fees or of participation in the institutional health program.

Second, there are situations in which students are already covered by family.held insurance at least to a degree where adding the student insurance offers no significant medical and/or financial protection.

Formal procedures for such waivers should be developed in the form of "Applications for Waiver of Health Service Fee," etc., and should be made known and available to each student. It should be stated that the student will be automatically charged and responsible for all health fees and premiums unless he actively makes formal application for waiver, through specified channels, on specific forms, and within a certain time limit. Approval of waiver requests should be predicated on the conviction on the part of the health service official or dean having the approval power that the applicant has at least a clear understanding of what his action means and hopefully that he has equivalent or adequate protection outside of the program.

Funding Sources for Special-risk Programs in Student Health

Basically, these special-risk programs are departmentally oriented and usually involve special sets and kinds of risks depending upon the program.

[4] The old "Contagious Hospital" at Stanford University, for example, was completely supported for years by a student organization and called "The Student Guild Hospital."

The various income sources applying to the health aspects of special programs may come from:

1. Allocation from general tuition or educational appropriations for general departmental, educationally connected purposes
2. Specific educational or research grants—as for rehabilitation institutes and training programs
3. Special insurance programs—as for example the NCAA insurance for intercollegiate athletics, usually underwritten by the department
4. Contracts for special research and development—as in nuclear physics, etc.
5. Sales and gate receipts—as in athletic events
6. Special student participation fees—as for overseas study, field trips, athletics, etc.
7. Categorical gifts or endowments and income therefrom
8. Governmental services—such as vocational rehabilitation services for handicapped students
9. Voluntary agencies—such as Family Planning, Society for Prevention of Blindness, etc.

The sources should be combined as appropriate for each special-risk activity and not applied to all sources equally. The other important point is that the activity-specific extra health expenses and risks should be predetermined and apportioned to the funding sources built into contracts and grants as direct items and/or overhead and into athletic and international student scholarships.

The student should not bear the brunt of the extra-risk expense except when he elects some unofficial and unsponsored extra-risk activity on his own, in which case he should provide the extra costs or premiums.

Miscellaneous Sources for Health-service Operational Funds

There are several federal granting sources which may provide traineeships for certain categories of health workers and which should be explored when relevant services can be performed by such trainees.

There is also a federally funded grant usually referred to as a "Basic Improvement Grant"[5] which can be used for matching funds in the support of salaries for key health service personnel, such as director, chief nurse, psychiatrist, etc., if the service can be shown to relate in specific ways to the educational purposes of the institution in applying for funds.

Support of Occupational Health and Safety Programs

The costs of the occupational health and safety program are analogous to insurance and are usually lower than the costs of premiums with no preventive programs and definitely lower than uninsured losses.

For example, the prevention of even one single total disability retirement case can save many thousands of dollars in high premiums and/or direct pension payments with the expenditure of a very few thousands of dollars to run an effective program. Liability and workmen's compensation premiums are considerably higher when policy holders provide no preventive, occupational health measures themselves; indeed, these premiums are often higher than the direct expenses of providing such services.

Planning and Financing of Health-service Facilities

Planning and Budget Preparation Factors Site planning for maximum accessibility to all, whether on foot, bicycle, or by car and/or ambulance and by stretcher and wheelchair is a must, and with modern internal acoustical techniques, central locations take precedence over "quiet, restful, out-of-the-way" locations.

[5] #BE 6–P8 6.

Future vertical and/or horizontal expansion must be included in both site planning and basic structure.

If future addition of infirmary or hospital-type bed care is intended over and above existing or currently planned patient facilities, either the basic structure or adjacent land must be capable of supporting the generally heavier construction required for most inpatient facilities without having to demolish the recently built outpatient structure.

Facilities-project budgets should always start with a statement of goals, purposes, and functions from which specific functions are defined (i.e. "reception, waiting, record, storage, nurses's treatment area, etc."), drafted with the advice of the health-service staff, any experienced consultants, and the health program advisory committee. The planning can then proceed to enumerate staff, numbers, types, and square footages of spaces needed and their relationships, all in writing, before detailed architectural service is sought. From such a written "program," preliminary estimates of gross and usable square footage can be made for construction.

"Final" preliminary estimates on construction should not be quoted or publicized until:

1. All local and state codes and regulations have been studied relative to general construction and to any possible special features relative to patient-care facilities of any type. It is a mistake to assume that outpatient facilities require no special licensing, building code modifications or specifications such as sprinklers, corridor widths, number, lighting, types of egress, and storage of flammables, etc. It is also possible that these specifications may change if any bed-care facilities are added, or that hospital licensure of some type may be required and will potentially affect construction and costs. If inpatient facilities of any kind are planned, it is preferable to insist upon hospital-grade construction at the outset rather than to be unable to convert later.

2. It cannot be too strongly emphasized that many and repeated conferences with local fire departments, state fire marshals, general and state building code officials, and hospital licensing authorities prior to establishment of even the basic preliminary budget for working purposes are essential and may save budget for working purposes. Such conferences may also save budgeting misestimate by as much as 30 to 50 percent.

3. Routine submission of schematics and even full blueprints to building, hospital licensing, and fire officials for their approval is not adequate. They have the power, and will exercise it, to change their minds and enforce change orders during construction even when they have approved the blueprint. The architect should be held responsible for personal and continuing contact and conferences with these officials prior to and during construction.

"Final" estimates and project budgets should include, if at all possible, funds not only for construction but for furnishings, equipment, "start-up" (so-called "activation") costs for moving, and initial stocks and supplies (all of which should amount to between 10 and 12 percent of the total project budget); a 5 percent contingency fund over and above the usual extrapolations for increase in building and materials costs with time, and sufficient funds for landscaping and approaches. An overcautious and timid approach to estimations of final budgets often leads to no saving of money and to an inadequate plant.

Architects should be selected who will work to the institution's program and specifications rather than vice versa. Those with extensive experience in standard hospital architecture are not automatically preferable and may, in fact, tend to overbuild and overcomplicate subhospital types of facilities. The architect's contract should include, in addition to his final preparations of regular detailed construction blueprints:

1. Preparation of schematic drawings, plans, elevations, and color site sketches for board and administrative approval.

2. Preparation of alternative internal decor and color schemes and furniture mock-

ups for approval *before* furnishings are purchased and installed. It should be decided at the beginning whether the architect will himself perform or subcontract the necessary decorating and furnishing functions.

3. Requirements for all clearance with officials before and during construction and construction supervision.

When budgets cannot afford some functions such as air-conditioning, dental services, etc., the potential ductwork, conduits, and utilities should be "stubbed in" rather than omitted entirely, only to be installed later at vastly greater cost.

If both outpatient and bed-care facilities are planned together, construction in two or more stories, with outpatients on the ground floor, is cheaper both to build and to operate than single-level, spread out facilities.

Comparative Costs of Facilities With such tremendous changes in costs from year to year and place to place, reliable predictions cannot be made here; but some experiences can be cited and necessary extrapolations made.

For outpatient student health services, including full preventive, doctors' office, nursing and emergency service, mental health services, laboratory, X-ray, drug room, record room, reception, waiting, and clerical functions—with adequate storage space, a total square footage of 15,000 to 16,000, including hallways, etc., adequately serves an eligible student population of 10,000 and an average of 250 to 300 patient visits a day.

Infirmary-type services for the same population, with 40 beds arranged in 20 two-bed units and supporting nurses' station, kitchen, lounges, storage, and treatment room, requires about 10,000 to 12,000 square feet.

In 1966, such a combined facility, of about 25,500 square feet (in basement, ground-floor clinic, and second-floor infirmary, with full furnishings and equipment, landscaping, and activation costs) was completed at a *total* cost of approximately $47 per square foot. Due to the regulations of the particular state, the highest grade of construction was not required; *had* it been, the total cost would have been closer to $55 per square foot.

Sources of Funds In many colleges and universities, particularly state schools, tax funds from the legislature are restricted to construction for educational buildings, specifically excluding dormitories, unions, and health services. Such institutions may organize various general or special student activity fees to contribute regularly to a "building fund" for single or multiple purposes. In addition to recreation centers and student unions, a number of health services have been built out of such funds, and it is a thoroughly useful and proper way to utilize them.

However, the construction and operations allocations from such fees should be separately determined, maintained, and used. Student fees intended for service should not be used to erode that service through amortization use. Nothing is more useless than a beautiful health center with an inadequate program.

Where state laws and legislatures do not forbid or inhibit it, special appropriations may be sought, to be financed through bond issues or other tax revenues.

Special gifts, from foundations,[6] industry, special donors, alumni, etc., may be sought in the course of general development for categorical health facilities use.

For more isolated institutions, in which the service may intend and need to have a hospital-grade inpatient facility, the possibility of Hill-Burton Act Funds should be explored.

An amendment to the Higher Education Facilities Act passed by the Congress in

[6] The Cowell Foundation of San Francisco has specifically funded (in both state and private universities) at least five health service facilities in northern California, and may finance more; but it will not finance them outside that region, as far as is known.

1969 but not yet funded, is specifically designed to provide matching funds for construction of college and university health-service facilities.

In closing this chapter and this section, it should be remembered that the main ingredients of good health programs in collegiate communities consist first of all in good planning, backed by the institution, and the people and activities to carry them out; and that however important new facilities may be, there are some superlative programs being run out of Quonset huts and hospital basements.

BIBLIOGRAPHY

General References

Dana L. Farnsworth, M.D.: *College Health Services in the United States,* monograph of the American College Personnel Association, 1605 New Hampshire Ave., N.W., Washington, D.C. 20009, 1965 (revision in progress).

Recommended Standards and Practices for College Community Health Programs, monograph of the American College Health Association, revised and adopted April, 1969 (available as reprint from ACHA, 2807 Central Street, Evanston, Ill. 60201). This covers standards for all phases of a health program.

Ethical and Professional Relationships: A Supplement to Recommended Standards and Practices for a College Health Program, American College Health Association, Evanston, Ill., 1969.

Dana L. Farnsworth, M.D. (ed.): *College Health Administration,* Appleton-Century-Crofts, Inc., New York, 1964.

The Journal of the American College Health Association, American College Health Association, 2807 Central St., Evanston, Ill. 60201.

Standards for Hospital Accreditation, Monograph of the Joint Commission on Accreditation of Hospitals, 200 E. Ohio St., Chicago, Ill., 1964.

Special References

Environmental Health and Safety; Disaster Planning

U.S. Public Health Service Ordinance and Code Regulating Eating and Drinking Establishments, U.S. Public Health Service Publication 934.

The following monographs are published by the American College Health Association and are purchasable upon request:
Accidental Injury Reporting
Emergency and Disaster Plans
Fire Emergency Plan
Student Housing Standards
Vending Machine Operations

Health Education

Standards for College Health Education, American College Health Association monograph.

Preventive Services

Douglass S. Thompson, M.D., Gordon Bergy, M.D., and Henry B. Bruyn, M.D.: *Adult Immunization Guide,* American College Health Association monograph, 1967 ($2).

Mental Health

Graham B. Blaine, M.D., and Charles MacArthur, Ph.D.: *Emotional Problems of the College Student,* Doubleday & Company, Inc., Garden City, N.Y. 1966.

Academic Underachievement, American College Health Association monograph, 1968.

"Multiplying the Hands of the Psychiatrist: The Use of Limited Psychiatric Manpower in a Small College Setting," *Journal of the American College Health Association,* vol. 17, p. 76, October, 1968.

Dental Health

Walter J. Pelton, D.D.S., and George E. Mitchell, D.M.D.: "Prepaid Student Dental Care Programs: A Valuable Teaching Aid," *Journal of Dental Education,* vol. 29, p. 297, September, 1965.

Special Programs

Paul C. Trickett, M.D.: *Prevention and Treatment of Athletic Injuries,* Appleton-Century-Crofts, Inc., New York, 1965.

B. H. Kean, M.D., F.A.C.P.: *The Traveler's Medical Guide for Physicians,* Charles C Thomas, Springfield, Ill., 1966.

Arthur E. Gravatt, Ph.D. (ed.): *Proceedings of a Symposium on Sex Education of the College Student,* American College Health Association monograph.

William F. Eastman, Ed.D., and Clifford B. Reifler, M.D.: "Marriage Counseling in the Student Health Service," *Journal of the American College Health Association,* vol. 17, p. 289, April 1969.

Relationships

"Recommended Practices and Relationships for Counseling and Psychiatric Services in the University and College Campus," *Journal of the American College Personnel Association.*

Health Service Construction

Standards for Planning of College Health Service Facilities, American College Health Association monograph (in preparation).

Section Ten

Religion on the Campus

Chapter 1

Religious Organizations and Programs on the Campus

CHARLES W. HAVICE

Professor of Philosophy and Religion and Dean of Chapel, Northeastern University, Boston, Massachusetts

Almost all our early institutions of higher learning were founded either specifically for the purpose of training clergymen or more generally for the purpose of serving the cause of religion. Harvard College is illustrative. Founded in 1636, this college, "dreading to leave an illiterate ministry to the churches when our present Ministers shall lie in the Dust," in its early years graduated three-fourths of its classes into the ministry. Even as late as 1840, most of the presidents of the well-established colleges and universities were clergymen. These and related facts indicate how influential religion has been in the development of American higher education.

RECENT CHANGES AND NEW EMPHASES

With the unprecedented ferment and rapid changes now occurring on our campuses, what is happening to the religious factor once so central? No simple answer can be given. It is clear, however, that the religious life is profoundly involved in the ferment, sometimes as cause and sometimes as consequence. This ferment and flux are to be found in the nature of the religious organizations themselves as well as in their emphases, programs, and goals. The information on the following pages will reflect this involvement. In view of the rapidity of change, long-range trends are at best speculative. Yet it can be pointed out that the current consensus of college chaplains and coordinators of religious affairs points up these observations about religion on the American campus today:

1. The religious institution must become more concerned over human rights, social issues of our time, and the general human situation. Involvement and commitment are central concepts; religion today is equated more with social and political activism than with ecclesiastical structures and organizational demands.
2. Ecumenical and unitive concerns take precedence over denominational loyalties, especially on the larger and more pluralistic campuses. On such campuses many of the denominational organizations are less active; much of their programming is of interfaith character.
3. Experimentation with new forms of worship and religious expression indicates varying degrees of rejection of institutionalism and of some of the inherited, conventional patterns. Liturgies in vernacular arrangements, folk as well as jazz music, coffee houses (nearly a hundred campuses now operate coffee houses), films, dramatic productions, art festivals, and spontaneous "happenings" are some of the directions this experimentation in religious expression takes.
4. Formal and informal courses in religion are flourishing; indeed, they have markedly increased in number and variety. Over half of our state universities and land-grant colleges now provide courses in religion for which full academic credit is given. Such institutions are forbidden by law to use public funds for the advancement of any given religion or set of doctrines, but it is clearly within existing laws to support from such public funds the general study and comparison of religions and thus to encourage religious scholarship and literacy. Professor Milton D. McLean in his recent study [1] shows the extensive growth and popularity of such courses.
5. Small group discussions in depth and more intimate dialogues are regarded as more meaningful than the massive intercollegiate conferences which students formerly attended in large numbers but with little involvement. As an instance of this trend, note the recent assembly of over three thousand religiously motivated students, both Catholic and Protestant, who met during the Christmas holidays in 1968 to form a large number of small "Depth Education Groups" for discussing their basic concerns. Minimal structuring and maximum spontaneity characterized these intimate groupings.
6. Basic theological and doctrinal positions are questioned and challenged with unprecedented forthrightness. Radical theology, including the so-called "No God Movement" and the underground church movement, provides examples of this phenomenon.

[1] Milton D. McLean (ed.), *Religious Studies in Public Universities*, Southern Illinois University, Carbondale, Ill., 1967.

CHAPEL BUILDINGS AND SERVICES

The physical evidence of religious concern at the American college or university has been traditionally a steepled chapel building. Some of these edifices, with their Gothic and cathedralesque proportions, dominate the campus landscape. The chapel at Duke University serves as an example. More common are the chapel buildings of conventional types of ecclesiastical architecture which provide areas for formal religious services and for conferences, and meeting rooms, chaplains' offices, lounge and reading areas, and facilities for limited food service. Brandeis University has three chapels which serve the special ways of worship for Jewish, Catholic, and Protestant students. The chapel at Massachusetts Institute of Technology has no design or symbolism which would identify it with any specific religious expression. These two examples are atypical and therefore afford interesting contrasts to the usual housing for campus religion.

As to the central function of the chapel buildings for the college community, most commonly they provide the setting for religious services on Sundays and at regularly scheduled hours during the week. Daily services are no longer the prevailing pattern nor is compulsory attendance, yet both practices continue at some denominational colleges.

Because the form and content of the chapel service vary markedly from one campus to another, it is impossible to give a generalized account of their nature. To offer one example, here is the format successfully used for a number of years at an urban university where the weekly services are interfaith and voluntary in nature: Sermons are given by carefully selected clergymen, representing a broad spectrum of denominations, and occasionally by the university president, the dean of chapel, a denominational chaplain, a faculty member, or a student. The other participants are student or faculty organists, faculty choir directors, student mixed choirs, student liturgists, and student ushers. The congregation participates in hymns and reading. A brief coffee period precedes the service, providing an informal occasion for students and faculty members to socialize. Various fraternities, clubs, and other campus organizations request to be recognized as sponsors for a service and to have a section of pews reserved for them. A typical order of worship is as follows: organ prelude, call to worship, hymn, responsive reading, prayer, anthem, sermon, hymn, benediction, and organ postlude. Often at special chapel services—at Easter and at Christmas particularly—the director of music arranges for cantatas and other appropriate programs of music.

Occasionally the campus chapel takes on the role of a church which ministers in the fullest sense to the needs of its members. Holy Communion, pastoral counseling, ordinations, baptisms, marriages, and funerals are all part of its ministry. The Church of Christ at Yale University, housed in Battell Chapel, provides such an instance. Much more commonly, however, the college chapel is not intended to serve the student in this pastoral fashion nor to be a church home away from home.

A large percentage of the independent, private, and church-related colleges appoint a chaplain, dean of chapel, campus minister, or college pastor—the titles are in the order of frequency of usage—to take responsibility for the religious life on the campus. An increasing number of such institutions have added one or more assistants in order to serve the student body and faculty more effectively. In some instances Danforth Foundation Campus Ministry appointees assist the chaplain.[2]

As to the basic concepts concerning the role of the chaplain, Dr. Lloyd J. Averill, when he was dean of the chapel at Kalamazoo College, outlined these four points: (1) The primary role of the college chaplain in the church-related college is that of

[2] For information concerning the various Danforth grants and fellowships, write The Danforth Foundation, 607 North Grand Boulevard, St. Louis, Mo. 63103.

a Christian apologist. (2) The college chaplain in the church-related college must always remember that he ministers to an entire academic community. (3) The college chaplain is called upon to be the critic-prophet within the college itself. (4) Even though the college chaplain is thought of primarily in relation to the academic community, his task is not complete until he also becomes a critic-prophet within the church.

Since a following chapter by Dean John P. Eddy (Chapter 3 in this section) deals with various aspects of the chaplaincy, only these several summary items of information will be given here: (1) Full-time chaplains are almost without exception fully ordained, seminary-trained clergymen. Many have earned doctorates or are pursuing doctoral programs of study. (2) Normally the chaplain is accountable to the president, a vice-president, or to the dean of students. (3) His salary is paid by the institution, although in uncommon cases the denomination provides for his support in part or in full. Information concerning salaries is not generally available; at least there is not enough of it to warrant reliable statements. Salaries of chaplains will in general correspond to those paid full professors or college deans. Usually their salaries include payment for teaching a partial load.

RELIGIOUS CENTERS AND COORDINATORS

In place of the easily recognizable chapel found at the church-related college, a multipurpose religious center building is often found at the large state and secular university. Since these buildings usually represent a more recent development in campus religious life, they are not only impressive in size but are more functional and more modern architecturally. An example of one of the earlier structures of this sort is the Anabel Taylor Hall at Cornell University. The more recently constructed religious centers at Pennsylvania State University, the University of Houston, and Wayne State University are further examples of the adequate housing provided for the various religious programs. Religious centers may or may not replace a separate chapel. In almost all cases the large university is also served by a number of denominational houses and churches near the campus. Ohio State University provides an instance where there are many such denominational centers.

The religious center is integrally a part of the state institution and is directly controlled by it. Denominational meetings can be housed in the building but, in the interests of state-church separation, denominational worship services may not be. Instead of a chaplain or dean of chapel, the center with its extensive programming is administered by a coordinator or director (the titles differ but slightly in emphasis) of religious affairs along with his assistants. This staff is employed and compensated by the institution. Salary scales are not divulged, but a well-seasoned judgment is that they range from assistant-professor to full-professor levels.

The coordinator is often an ordained clergyman, but his denominational affiliation is kept in the background and his interfaith role is given primacy. Yet in some instances the coordinator is not an ordained clergyman. He is trained in administration or personnel or in some specialized field of higher education. To cite several examples, one successful coordinator holds a professorship in philosophy, another in sociology, another in psychology, and yet another in accounting. Two have formerly served as college presidents.

Dr. Henry E. Allen, one of the most experienced leaders in this field of directing religious affairs, presents in Chapter 2 of this section a comprehensive account of the profession. But let it be noted in these preliminary observations that even a brief visit to the office of the typical coordinator or director will demonstrate beyond the effectiveness of any verbal description the range of responsibilities he carries: presiding at interfaith councils (comprising from 10 to 36 denominations), working directly with the various denominational chaplains and local ministers to students (supported by the respective denominations), administering regular and special programs, serving on various faculty committees, counseling students, and relating the religious life of his own campus to numerous national organizations and programs. Later in this section some indication will be given of the increasing number of these national relationships in which both chaplains and directors need to participate in order to be of maximum effectiveness.

STUDENT YOUNG MEN'S CHRISTIAN ASSOCIATION AND STUDENT YOUNG WOMEN'S CHRISTIAN ASSOCIATION

The student Young Men's Christian Association and Young Women's Christian Association for well over a century has been a religious movement of profound and pervasive influence. Established first at the University of Virginia in 1857 and shortly afterward at the University of Michigan, the movement spread across the country and soon became the dominant religious force on many campuses. At the beginning of this century it had established over six hundred associations and had enrolled over thirty-two thousand student members. In 1934, the YMCA and YWCA student movements joined efforts more fully and formed the National Student Council of the YMCA and YWCA.

There are currently 225 student YMCAs or YMCA-YWCAs on American campuses; they are active especially at the large state and southern institutions. Each field council has intercollegiate conferences, council meetings, and assemblies through which members share in experiences beyond their own campus.

The stated purpose of their national student council is as follows:

> Student YMCA's, part of a world-wide Christian movement, seek to study and work for rich and full human life and free and just society. They seek to attract and unite in active fellowship and service persons of all Christian confessions, adherents of other faiths and those who affirm no religious belief. They are committed to encouraging individuals in their search for life purpose to confront the power and relevance of the Christian faith.

THE NATIONAL STUDENT CHRISTIAN FEDERATION

In 1959 the National Student Christian Federation was organized. It combined the United Student Christian Council (formed in 1944), the Student Volunteer Movement, and the Interseminary Movement. This Federation then became part of the World Student Christian Federation, embracing over eighty countries.

WORLD UNIVERSITY SERVICE

It is this Federation that sponsors World University Service, the organization of students helping students across the world. In the United States it is given support by all major denominational groups in the National Council of Churches of Christ, the National Student Association, the Catholic community, and the Jewish community.

THE UNITED CAMPUS CHRISTIAN FELLOWSHIP

The United Campus Christian Fellowship, instituted in 1960, originally comprised four denominational student Christian movements: Christian Churches (Disciples of Christ), the Evangelical United Brethren Church, the United Church of Christ, and the United Presbyterian Church, U.S.A. In 1964 the Moravian Church in America, Northern Province, became the fifth denomination to join. At later dates the Church of the Brethren, the Presbyterian Church in the U.S., the United Methodist Church (which now includes the Evangelical United Methodist Church), the Episcopal Church, and the American Baptist Convention were added. Very recently the United Campus Christian Fellowship has completely merged with the United Christian Movement and therefore no longer exists as a separate entity.

UNITED MINISTRIES IN HIGHER EDUCATION

The United Campus Christian Fellowship in 1964 established the inclusive national agency known as United Ministries in Higher Education. The Council for Policy and Strategy considers, develops, and proposes policies for its constituent members. A Committee of Administrators deals with national administrative procedures.

United Ministries in Higher Education exists to provide for united policy planning, administration of resources, staff services, and financial assistance to support the ministry of the church in higher education. The national leadership of United Ministries in Higher Education (UMHE) affirms:

> . . . that we are called to participate in the proper work of the university, and, while not yet fully understood, this concept continues to be more and more significant in providing direction for ministry; that a truly ecumenical ministry is the only faithful expression for our time; and that we must continue to explore and develop new responses and new forms of ministry in the context of the ever-burgeoning dimensions of higher education.

To make real and operative such affirmations, the national UMHE communions have organized themselves, assigning their resources of funds and personnel, for a united strategy which reaches across the country. What follows is a report of what UMHE is doing to fulfill its aims and affirmations.

United Ministries in Higher Education is guided in the development of policy and strategy by a council composed of representatives of the communions including students, faculty members, higher education administrative personnel, campus ministers, and communion officials.

The rationale of this union of campus ministries has been set forth in these two paragraphs:

> The basis for the United Ministries in Higher Education is the faith, attested by the Holy Scriptures and affirmed in the confessions and life of the church, that God incarnate in Jesus Christ and present in the Holy Spirit wills to reconcile men to himself, and that he is acting in history creating, judging and redeeming.
>
> We affirm that in the church of Christ we are members of one body, and we believe that we are called to unite our ministries in higher education as a more adequate expression of our unity in the church, that we may better proclaim the gospel in campus and community life.

United Ministries in Higher Education maintains helpful but not as yet clearly defined connections with the Department of Higher Education, National Council of Churches of Christ in the U.S.A. Several more denominations are now in process of joining the United Ministries.

NATIONAL CATHOLIC STUDENT ORGANIZATIONS

While there are a number of Catholic associations that have maintained national offices and national student officers, the two who have had elaborate representative functions have been the National Newman Apostolate and the National Federation of Catholic College Students.

The Newman Apostolate began in the first decade of this century when Catholic students at the University of Pennsylvania organized a club and secured a chaplain to serve their spiritual needs. It was essentially a protective association intended to preserve what may have seemed to be in danger from the secular campus. The Newman movement expanded with essentially these ideas. It was to offer Catholic students a religious education in an atmosphere of which they were deprived on the secular campus. It was basically a student organization.

In the early decades there was little Episcopal support, and direction was set by the National Student Federation which came to be a representative organization of Newman Clubs. In the late 1950s, the roles of the chaplains emerged in a more significant context and a more sophisticated structure was established. Six national groups comprised the Newman Apostolate: (1) The National Newman Chaplains' Association, (2) the National Newman Student Federation, (3) the National Newman Association of Faculty and Staff, (4) the National Newman Foundation, (5) the John Henry Cardinal Newman Honor Society, and (6) the National Newman Alumni Association.

The presidents and priest-chaplains of these groups then formed the National Newman Coordinating Board, which became the decision-making body together with the Director of the National Newman Apostolate.

At the National Convention in Dallas in 1966, a restructuring program was begun by the appointment of the Catholic Commission on the Church and the American University. This process is now in operation and its directions have become clear. The Newman Apostolate is no longer merely a student movement but rather one of the entire Catholic community. It no longer attempts to be protective but to be of service to students and to the university. Since there are few if any national predicates which apply to all situations, organization is on local and diocesan levels. The American bishops have now become involved; the need of service to this huge academic community has become evident; archdiocesan and diocesan directors have been appointed and in many areas Newman work is considered the major priority.

The National Newman Apostolate is now a department of the National Conference of Catholic Bishops. The National Newman office, located in Washington and headed by a priest-director, fulfills the roles of research, planning, and service to local efforts. The National Newman Chaplains' Association has recently been renamed and reconstituted as the Catholic Campus Ministry Association. It is a professional organization of priests, nuns, and laity who are involved in the campus ministry. They seek to provide guidelines and assistance for recruiting qualified persons to work in the campus ministry; to provide a program for preparation and continuing education of its members; to provide liaison with other individuals and agencies of the Church interested in the campus ministry and the role of the Church in higher education; to listen to and speak to both the Church and the university about these matters; to advance ecumenical understanding; and to provide a supportive community for its members. The National Newman Student Federation no longer exists as a representative student association. The role of the students in the Newman Apostolate is seen more as part of the effort of the whole Church. The National Newman Foundation presently operates as a funding service for chaplains' training programs and for grants and loans to individual Newman operations.

The present state of the apostolate is therefore markedly different from its origin but more in parallel to the real situation in our complex society. It is loosely organized, concentrated on the local and state levels, and more concerned with service and research as related to the institutions as they now exist. The major factors in the change of direction have been the persuasion of the American bishops of the real need and the appointment of diocesan directors.

The National Federation of Catholic College Students, a representative organization of students enrolled in Catholic colleges with elected officers in Washington, is about to close its national office because of lack of support. This indicates that this group will not remain in existence for long.

Suffice it to say at this point that the direction seems to be a much deeper association, on the local level, with the Newman Apostolate. Catholic colleges are now appointing chaplains to students. The needs of students in Catholic and secular colleges are much the same, and the total effort in local areas will tend to be far more unified.

B'NAI B'RITH HILLEL FOUNDATIONS

Beginning with one foundation at the University of Illinois in 1923, B'nai B'rith Hillel now comprises 260 full-time foundations and part-time counselorships at institutions of higher learning in the United States, Canada, Great Britain, Holland, and Israel.

Named for the noted Hillel the Elder, Hillel's function is to give Jewish students a deeper understanding of their moral and spiritual heritage as well as to strengthen their identity with the Jewish life and community.

Other stated purposes are as follows: (1) Counseling students on the basis of personal needs with the emphasis on development through a guidance agency. (2) Preparing students for participation in the adult community, including such programs as working with the United Jewish Student Appeal, social service, interfaith programs, and human relations projects. (3) Educating the academic community in the areas of the ideology, faith, and history of the Jewish people by means of classes, courses, discussions, lectures, and other educational devices through the sponsorship of the Jewish Educational Institution.

ORTHODOX STUDENT MINISTRY

The concern of a religious ministry to Orthodox students on campuses of American colleges and universities is the responsibility of the Orthodox Campus Commission. This Commission, under the sponsorship of the Standing Conference of the Canonical Orthodox Bishops in the Americas, is composed of Orthodox clergymen, theologians, educators, and professional people who have shown special interest in campus religious work and represents the main thrust of Orthodox involvement in student ministry.

The Orthodox Campus Commission was established in 1965 and entrusted with the formulation of its program for the more than seventeen thousand Orthodox students in the Americas. There are currently 125 officially organized Orthodox Student Fellowships. The Commission is a member of Syndesmos, a world organization of Orthodox Student Movements, and also of the University Christian Movement.

THE ASSOCIATION FOR THE COORDINATION OF UNIVERSITY RELIGIOUS AFFAIRS

Founded in 1959, the Association for the Coordination of University Religious Affairs presupposes that our tax-supported college and university campuses enroll students not of one religious persuasion but of many. This pluralistic nature of the student population means that no single program of pastoral care or counseling can serve the needs of all students unless we provide religious resources for, and serve without bias, Christian and Jew and the varieties within Christianity and Judaism, as well as those of religions outside the Judeo-Christian tradition. Recognizing the multiple faith needs on many campuses and refusing to rule out the freedom of religious observance—a freedom supported by our Constitution and way of life—administrators of tax institutions have taken steps to extend a welcome to all responsible representatives of the various faiths and denominations. Faculty and student personnel staff members are increasingly being assigned to assist and facilitate the work of clergy and other religious leaders serving campus groups. Because such policies of acceptance are unprecedented in American higher education, the need has arisen to consult and share experience. Friction caused by unfamiliar situations involving pastors, priests, and rabbis must be minimized and policies examined for their acceptability in the light of church-state relationship traditions. An underlying assumption of ACURA is that religious resources—curricular and cocurricular—can not only be increased but can also be more effective. For these reasons the Association for the Coordination of University Religious Affairs was established.

Annual meetings deal with such topics as the following: Interreligious dialogue and communication in the academic community; problems of student religious work on the secular campus; evaluation of university departments in the student personnel as well as academic fields; consultation on legal problems; reports on studies of pretheological education as well as research in counseling; and seminars on the construction and organization of religious centers, both denominational and multifaith.

Among ACURA's other activities are:

1. Sponsorship of student conferences dealing with interreligious councils and activities. This undertaking has developed to a point where three regional conferences are held each spring.

2. Circulation of the publication *Dialogue on Campus*, which provides information concerning the various aspects of religion at the university.

3. A program of research in the whole area of campus interreligious thought and experience.

4. Continuing communication with organizations in the religious personnel fields such as the National Association of College and University Chaplains (NACUC), denominational and interdenominational chaplaincy groups, the American Personnel Guidance Association, and American College Personnel Association. The Association is a member of the Council of Student Personnel Associations in Higher Education.

Institutional membership in ACURA includes those persons who are employed as university staff members in the field of religious coordination. Each university may designate up to five representatives at any meeting. Individual (associate) membership includes one or more of the following: (1) Full-time workers in the campus ministry; (2) persons authorized by their universities for such membership and coming from universities where there is at present no pattern of administrative responsibility for the coordination of religious affairs but where there is a genuine interest in developing such a pattern; (3) persons working with religious groups which are recognized as student religious organizations by their universities; and (4) regional and national officers of the educational boards of denominations and faiths.

NATIONAL ASSOCIATION OF COLLEGE AND UNIVERSITY CHAPLAINS AND DIRECTORS OF RELIGIOUS LIFE

The National Association of College and University Chaplains and Directors of Religious Life, founded at Yale University in 1948, is the principal organization for chaplains, deans of chapel, directors of religious life, and others related professionally to the religious life on the campus.

Its membership is composed almost exclusively of ordained clergymen who regard the chaplaincy as a special kind of ministry and sacred vocation. Membership in the association is open, however, to all persons who are engaged in the work of religion in higher education. Full membership "shall consist of Chaplains, Deans of Chapel, Directors of Religious Activities, and such other administratively employed and/or designated personnel as are responsible for the total religious program of the college and university community." Affiliate membership "shall consist of such other persons as are engaged or actively interested in the work of religion in higher education who request to be so enrolled and who pay annual Association dues." There is also institutional supporting membership.

National and regional conferences serve the 600 members by dealing with various aspects of the profession. The chief Catholic chaplains at Catholic institutions are also members of this preponderantly Protestant organization. Rabbis and Orthodox priests are often participants in conference programs.

The stated purposes of this association are as follows:

1. To provide means for more responsible and effective participation in religion in higher education by college chaplains and persons with similar functions.
2. To provide a continuing professional fellowship for chaplains and directors of religious life.
3. To provide for expression of convictions relative to the vital religious concerns of students, faculties, and administrations.
4. To share mutual interests and to search for solutions to common problems in the religious life of colleges and universities.
5. To engage in such organizational functions as are necessary to achieve these purposes.
6. To further the spirit of ecumenicity and understanding among all religious groups as they relate to the university environment.

The *Newsletter,* the official publication of the association, is published several times during the year. It prints information concerning programs and meetings as well as articles of special interest to members. The association also is represented on the editorial board of *Humanity,* a journal devoted to religious concerns on the campus.

NATIONAL CAMPUS MINISTRY ASSOCIATION

The National Campus Ministry Association was formally established in 1965. Some months earlier representatives of various campus ministry agencies convened to draw up a preamble and statement of purpose, both duly accepted, which are as follows:

Preamble: Called to oneness in Christ; called to one field of ministry and mission in higher education; convinced of the importance of the service of the church in higher education and of higher education to the church; confident that together we may minister more adequately to those whom we are called to serve; we covenant to establish the National Campus Ministry Association.

Purposes: To foster the educational development of its members; to facilitate approach with other individuals and agencies of the churches to ministry and mission in higher education; to listen to and speak to the church and to the university on these matters; and to provide a supporting fellowship for its members.

This association has experienced remarkable growth in the few years of its existence, now having a membership of over six hundred chaplains and ministers serving in higher education of many denominations. National and regional meetings are held regularly. Strong emphasis is given to the continuing education of its members. Seminars are regarded as important ways of providing new knowledge and insights.

Financial support is given by the United Ministries in Higher Education and several denominational headquarters.

CAMPUS MINISTRY OF THE AMERICAN BIBLE SOCIETY

The formation in 1965 of the Campus Ministry of the American Bible Society was effected to deal with three special concerns: assessment, research, and promotion of distribution and use of Scriptures on the campus.

The American Bible Society, a lay organization of 68 Protestant denominations, developed this latest unit of its work with the special intention of serving higher education.

CHRISTIAN FAITH AND HIGHER EDUCATION INSTITUTE

Established in 1962, the Christian Faith and Higher Education Institute has the task of exploring higher education to the end that resources may be developed for both the church and higher education.

Explorations are conducted into issues and philosophies of higher education and the disciplines of discourse. The methodology is to bring scholars together who by interest and competence are willing to discuss philosophies and clarify issues. When explorations require more depth and time, scholars in the profession or the discipline are given support as they continue the exploration.

Experiments in adult and continuing education are also conducted by the institute. Where possible, the work of the institute is carried on in relation with other institutions.

When printed resources are developed, the institute seeks to place them in existing organs of publication. The institute itself occasionally publishes papers.

In its relations with institutions of higher education, the institute seeks to preserve the integrity of both bodies, such that there is no attempt to make the church the university nor the university the church. In such a relation, the principle of neither is compromised.

The institute conducts three types of programs in developing explorations and resources by (1) experimenting in programs of education and continuing education, (2) exploring philosophies of higher education and the disciplines of discourse, and (3) collaborating or consulting with other institutions.

DIRECTORY OF RELIGIOUS ORGANIZATIONS AND PROGRAMS ON THE CAMPUS

American Baptist Convention
Department of Campus Christian Life
Valley Forge, Pa. 19481

American Bible Society
Campus Ministries Department
1865 Broadway
New York, N.Y. 10023

American Ethical Union
National Ethical Youth Organization
2 West 64 Street
New York, N.Y. 10023

Assemblies of God, Christ's Ambassadors
1445 Boonville Avenue
Springfield, Mo. 65802

Association for the Coordination of University Religious Affairs (ACURA)
Professor Clifford A. Nelson, Secretary-Treasurer
The Pennsylvania State University
105 Helen Eakin Eisenhower Chapel
University Park, Pa. 16802

B'nai B'rith Hillel Foundations
Director of Programs and Resources
1640 Rhode Island Avenue N.W.
Washington, D.C. 20036

Buddhist Churches of America
National Young Buddhist Association
1710 Octavia Street
San Francisco, Calif. 94109

Campus Crusade for Christ International
Arrowhead Springs
San Bernardino, Calif. 92400

Christian Churches: Disciples of Christ
222 South Downey Avenue, Room 418
Indianapolis, Ind. 46219

Christian Faith and Higher Education Institute
1405 South Harrison Road
East Lansing, Mich. 48823

Church of the Brethren General Offices
1451 Dundee Avenue
Elgin, Ill. 60120

Church of Christ
Campus Evangelism Movement
1924 Broadway
Lubbock, Tex. 79401

The First Church of Christ, Scientist
Department of Branches and Practitioners
107 Falmouth Street
Boston, Mass. 02115

Church of God
Board of Christian Education
1303 East Fifth Street
Anderson, Ind. 46010

Church of Jesus Christ of Latter Day Saints (Mormon)
National Secretary, Deseret Clubs
B-346 Smoot Administration and General Services Building
Brigham Young University
Provo, Utah 84601

Church of the Nazarene
Department of Education
6401 The Paseo
Kansas City, Mo. 64100

The Danforth Foundation
607 North Grand Boulevard
St. Louis, Mo. 63103

Episcopal Church Society for College Work
17 Dunster Street
Cambridge, Mass. 02138

Episcopal College and University Division
815 Second Avenue
New York, N.Y. 10017

Fellowship of Christian Athletes
Traders National Bank Building
1125 Grand, Suite 812
Kansas City, Mo. 64106

Free Methodist World Headquarters
Department of Educational Institutions
Winona Lake, Ind. 46590
Friends General Conference
Society of Young Friends
1520 Race Street
Philadelphia, Pa. 19102
International Students, Inc.
P.O. Box 4848
Washington, D.C. 20008
Inter-Varsity Christian Fellowship
130 North Wells Street
Chicago, Ill. 60606
Jehovah's Witnesses
124 Columbia Heights
Brooklyn, N.Y. 11201
American Lutheran Church
Board of Youth Activity
422 South Fifth Street
Minneapolis, Minn. 55415
Lutheran Church in America
Student Association
231 Madison Avenue
New York, N.Y. 10016
National Lutheran Council
Division of College and University Work
130 North Wells Street
Chicago, Ill. 60606
Lutheran Church: Missouri Synod
Commission on College and University Work
77 West Washington Street
Chicago, Ill. 60602
Mennonite Board of Education
1700 South Main Street
Goshen, Ind. 46526
Mennonite Brethren
Student Services
2016 South Boulevard
Edmond, Okla. 73034
General Conference Mennonite Church
Student Services
722 Main Street
Newton, Kans. 67114
Mennonite Student Services
Box 370
Elkhart, Ind. 46514
Moslem Faith
Islamic Center
Washington, D.C. 20013
National Association of Christian Student Foundations
Ed Bernard
The Exchange
R.R. 1
Cynthiana, Ky. 41031
National Association of College and University Chaplains and Directors of Religious Life
Dr. J. Claude Evans
Southern Methodist University
Dallas, Tex. 75222

National Baha'i Headquarters
536 Sheridan Road
Wilmette, Ill. 60091
National Campus Ministry Association
P.O. Box 92
King of Prussia, Pa. 19406
National Council of Churches
Room 754
475 Riverside Drive
New York, N.Y. 10027
United States Catholic Conference
National Newman Apostolate
1312 Massachusetts Avenue N.W.
Washington, D.C. 20005
The Navigators
9096 Grace Avenue
Niles, Ill. 60648
Orthodox Campus Commission
777 United Nations Plaza
New York, N.Y. 10017
Pentecostal Assemblies of the World, Inc.
3040 North Illinois Street
Indianapolis, Ind. 46208
Pentecostal Church of God of America, Inc.
312–316 Joplin Avenue
Joplin, Mo. 64801
Pilgrim Holiness
Youth Department
230 East Ohio Street
Indianapolis, Ind. 46200
Presbyterian Church of the United States
Division of Higher Education
Box 1176
Richmond, Va. 23209
United Presbyterian Church U.S.A.
Division of Campus Christian Life
Witherspoon Building
Walnut and Juniper Streets
Philadelphia, Pa. 19107
The Provincial Elders' Conference
The Moravian Church in America
69 West Church Street
Bethlehem, Pa. 18018
Reformed Church in America
Room 1807
475 Riverside Drive
New York, N.Y. 10027
Reorganized Church of Jesus Christ of Latter Day Saints
Department of College Ministry
The Auditorium
Independence, Mo.
Salvation Army
120 West 14 Street
New York, N.Y. 10011
Seventh-day Adventists
Young Peoples' Department
6840 Eastern Avenue N.W.
Washington, D.C. 20012
Southern Baptist Convention
Student Department: Education Division

127 Ninth Avenue
Nashville, Tenn. 37203
United Church of Christ
Department of Campus Ministry
287 Park Avenue South
New York, N.Y. 10010
United Methodist Church
Department of College and University Religious Life
Box 871
Nashville, Tenn. 37202
United Ministries in Higher Education
P.O. Box 7286
St. Louis, Mo. 63177
(or 475 Riverside Drive, New York, N.Y. 10027)
Unitarian Universalist Association
Liberal Religious Youth
25 Beacon Street
Boston, Mass. 02108
Vedanta Society
34 West 71 Street
New York, N.Y. 10023
Wesleyan Church of America
P.O. Box 2000
Marion, Ind. 46952
World University Service
20 West 40 Street
New York, N.Y. 10018
Young Men's Christian Associations
National Student Council
291 Broadway
New York, N.Y. 10007
Young Women's Christian Associations
National Student Council
600 Lexington Avenue
New York, N.Y. 10022

ADDITIONAL SOURCES OF INFORMATION ABOUT RELIGIOUS ORGANIZATIONS ON CAMPUSES

Allen, Henry Elisha: *Religion in the State University,* Burgess Publishing Company, Minneapolis, 1950.
Ambrose, W. Haydn: *The Church in the University,* The Judson Press, Valley Forge, Pa., 1968.
Cantelon, John E.: *A Protestant Approach to the Campus Ministry,* Westminster Press, Philadelphia, 1964.
Chamberlin, J. Gordon: *Churches and the Campus,* Westminster Press, Philadelphia, 1963.
Earnshaw, George L.: *The Campus Ministry,* The Judson Press, Valley Forge, Pa., 1964.
Eddy, John P.: "A Comparison of the Characteristics and Activities of Religious Personnel Employed in Selected Four-Year State Colleges and Universities in the United States," Southern Illinois University, Carbondale, Ill., 1968 (Ph.D. dissertation).
Hammond, Phillip E.: *The Campus Clergyman,* Basic Books, Inc., Publishers, New York, 1966.
Havice, Charles W.: *Religion on the American Campus: A Bibliography,* Northeastern University, Boston, 1969.
McLean, Milton D. (ed.): *Religious Studies in Public Universities,* Southern Illinois University, Carbondale, Ill., 1967.
Michaelsen, Robert: *The Study of Religion in American Universities,* The Society for Religion in Higher Education, New Haven, 1965.
Minneman, Charles E. (ed.): *Students, Religion, and the Contemporary University,* Eastern Michigan University Press, Ypsilanti, Mich., 1969.
Perry, John D., Jr.: *The Coffee House Ministry,* John Knox Press, Richmond, Va., 1966.
Underwood, Kenneth W.: *The Church, the University, and Social Policy,* vols. I and II, Wesleyan University Press, Middletown, Conn., 1969.
Waking, Edward: *The Catholic Campus,* The Macmillan Company, New York, 1962.

Chapter 2

Religious Activities in State and Independent Colleges and Universities

HENRY E. ALLEN

One-time Professor of Religion and College President, Coordinator of Student Religious Activities, University of Minnesota, Minneapolis, Minnesota

In the whole panorama of higher education there is probably no segment less standardized or more difficult to categorize in systematic fashion than religious activities in institutions not operated by a specific church. Each college or university has its own peculiar pattern of development and relationships with the community, and these will vary according to the geography, the social and political setting, and the volatility of local religious leadership.

Because of the strength and historic predominance of reformed Protestantism in the East and South, the prevailing atmosphere is likely to be congenial to the individualistic pietism and congregational antiauthoritarianism sometimes described as the Protestant establishment. The acceptance of YMCAs and Protestant programs and the infrequency of Catholic, Orthodox, Jewish, and even Lutheran speeches or services illustrates the somewhat monolithic nature of theological presuppositions in these areas.

In the Midwest and Far West, however, where the land-grant tradition has built secularism or religious neutrality into the fabric of publicly supported institutions, administrations may maintain a hands-off policy, maintaining relationships with no religious groups and virtually excluding them from campus precincts. If, however, they do have a policy cordial to religious expressions, they will be more conscious of the pluralism inherent in our diversity of faiths and will accordingly provide equal opportunities for all faiths—not giving special privileges to the Protestant groups which are in a majority position.

The impartial administrator must be careful to distinguish between religious activities and curricular credit courses in religion. As a general principle, it might be stated that wherever instruction is given for academic credit, primary responsibility lies with the faculty. Where the subject is *Religion*, however, complications arise because of the diverse meanings and expectations clustering around the word. There will be found faculty members unfamiliar with recent trends in religious scholarship and research who are suspicious of any effort to deal with religion in the classroom.

The irrelevant issue of church-state separation may be raised both on and off campus by persons who lack acquaintance with the academic dimensions of religion as currently dealt with at our leading universities, both independent and tax supported. There are also churchmen who suspect that analytical and impartial scholarship of the kind expected in other areas of the curriculum will have a harmful effect upon beliefs taken on faith. Controversy may thus be injected into the curricular area despite the United States Supreme Court's position that even in the public school classroom instruction in facts about religion is not only permissible but desirable.

Persons who support the academic presentation of religion would probably argue that funds for salaries and facilities should come from the same sources as those for other scholarly endeavors. However, there are a number of state universities where privately funded schools of religion exist adjacent to the campuses and maintain respectable reputations for research and publication. If the courses they give are to receive transfer or elective credit in the secular university, the responsibility of the accrediting faculty must be emphasized, and no apology should be made for insistence on standards and competence on the same level as applied to other branches of learning.

RATIONALE OF ADMINISTRATIVE RESPONSIBILITY FOR RELIGIOUS LIFE

A college or university which is supported by and takes seriously its obligations to a denomination or faith will encourage the cultivation of religion and quite generally support a chaplain. While it is to be expected that the worship and activities carried on will be those of the supporting body, even here there is increasing sensitivity to religious differences. Seldom does one hear today of insistence that Catholics attend chapel services on a Protestant campus or vice versa. Institutions have many different ways of providing "safe-conduct passes" for students whose faith is not the same as that of the official governing group.

Where there is no church commitment to start with, as in the case of tax-supported and most independent colleges, the administration may well be puzzled regarding its responsibility, if any, in the area of faith and its cultivation. One response, still occasionally found, is that of irresponsibility: religion is a private matter, the administration is impartial; therefore we will leave it alone—with each church operating off-campus on a "catch as catch can" basis. By contrast, there may be an administration which is responsive to the ecumenical trend—either that of like-minded Protestantism or the more inclusive Catholic, Orthodox, Lutheran, and Reformed Protestant consortium exemplified by the University Christian Movement. Pressures are occasionally brought in the name of interdenominational cooperation for special favors and privileges on the ground that a majority viewpoint is represented.

The sophisticated administrator must preserve his equilibrium and remember that, even with much desirable consolidation, he must still reckon with Christian Scientists, Latter Day Saints, Unitarian-Universalists, Pentecostals, and Friends as well as Jews, Buddhists, and Muslims. Even within the Christian majority it may be many years before there is attained a singleness of approach to creed, Scriptures, sacraments, and ecclesiastical polity.

Granting, then, that disagreement—pluralism, if you will—is here to stay, the administrator is faced with this dilemma: on the one hand he or the college cannot be all things to all people in religious matters; on the other hand, he cannot ignore the importance of religion as a factor in the lives of students and staff members.

Fortunately a solution is available in the provision by churches, "Y"s, and evangelical groups of competent pastor-counselors to serve the diverse affiliations of the campus population. The only question then is how properly to incorporate these vital resource people into the pattern of campus life. Here it is important to differentiate between the college campus and the primary or secondary public school. Several Supreme Court decisions have ruled against religious programs, prayer, and Bible reading on public school property. Their intention is to protect children of impressionable age in situations where an insensitive majority population would subject children of minority dissident groups to expressions of faith which more properly belong in a church, meeting house, or synagogue.

The compulsion by law to attend school until age 16 sets up a situation where *public school* machinery can be misused to impose a majority concept, usually Protestant, upon children whose parents believe differently or not at all. The *college student*, on the other hand, is attending school voluntarily. Moreover, he is at an age of intense intellectual activity and curiosity. To cut him off from opportunities to hear protagonists of diverse theological viewpoints, to restrict his exposure to what Dr. Franklin H. Littell has termed "the raging dialogue," is to interfere with the free flow of academic inquiry. It would seem no more appropriate for a tax-supported campus, attended by all varieties of church and synagogue members, to outlaw religious groupings than it would be for a town of similar size to forbid the organization of parishes and congregations within municipal confines. Applying this parallel further, we can easily recommend the policy existing on numerous campuses whereby the appropriate accrediting agency for extra-classroom activities certifies the validity of any configuration of students and staff for the pursuit of religious goals and makes sure that there is no favoritism shown as between large and small membership groups. If, however, approach to the campus is made by neighborhood adult parishes or clergymen, there may be sticky questions raised regarding intrusion by the church on state precincts.

POLICIES AND ADMINISTRATIVE PROCEDURES

Reference has already been made to the distinction between religion as an academic subject-matter area and religion as the cultivation of faith and worship. Religious groups will not expect to relate to the college through the academic faculty, which does not and should not enter into denominational matters except as objects of study and research. It is through the administration that relationships between the campus and religious groups will be negotiated.

The history of private colleges has revealed the traditional pattern of designating a chaplain salaried by the college and charged with responsibility for the manifold expressions of religious life, official and unofficial. Such administratively appointed chaplains have differing definitions of functions in accordance with the traditions of each institution. While the chaplain may have a cognate appointment to teach in an academic department, as chaplain he will probably be responsible directly to the president's office or that of the administrative dean. Many large institutions with well-developed student personnel services may provide a "place in the chart" through the counseling or student-activities area. Here is normally found the official concern for the personal and group interests of students, and one might expect a congeniality of viewpoints between the religious and personnel functionaries. An increasing number of campuses are making designations of staff members—responsible to a dean of students or vice-president for personnel services—to serve in a contact or coordinating role in the area of religious affairs.

FUNCTIONS OF A COORDINATOR–LIAISON OFFICER

Among other possible functions, this appointee might be asked to:

1. Assist religious groups to function. That is, answer inquiries as to approved or appropriate procedures and help identify the constituency of each organization through the processing of religious census cards.
2. Channel communication both ways between the college and religious groups.
3. Maintain a spirit of fair play so as to preserve the rights of minority groups in line with the pluralism safeguarded in the First Amendment of the Constitution. He must clarify the axiom, not always accepted in certain sections of the United States, that in matters of conscience we do not operate on the basis of majority rule.
4. Encourage cooperation wherever possible without forcing any group into embarrassing or distasteful situations but constantly stressing the importance of dialogue for a clearer understanding of positions—perhaps even a sharpening of areas of disagreement in a nonvindictive spirit.
5. Help the success of programs originating in the religious groups. On some campuses where the term "director" is used, the staff person may take considerable responsibility for organizing and implementing religious events, especially those with campuswide implications. Use of the term "coordinator" suggests that this office not be used to originate and set up observances but rather to encourage team play involving the participation of the largest possible number of groups. This may not involve common worship or endorsements, but rather the presentation of a visible expression of religious vitality, whether in unity or in patterns respectful of theological disagreement.
6. Make sure that his office is not perceived as a bottleneck which would limit contacts between religious groups and varied departments of the university. The coordinator should be active in seeking to open doors to appropriate areas of campus life.

STATUS OF RELIGIOUS FUNCTIONARIES

Assuming that campus religious groups will have qualified leadership in the form of specially equipped campus ministers, priests, or rabbis, every effort should be made to involve such staff members in the life of the campus. Even though they are not salaried by the university (which cannot be all things to all people), pastors and "Y" secretaries should be welcomed into faculty activities and be accorded library, social, and sport privileges.

The graduate training expected of today's campus minister qualifies him, as in the case of M.D.s, lawyers, and engineers, to play roles as a lecturer, counselor, and discussion leader. Campus chaplains, as differentiated from typical parish clergy, will be more perceptive of the dynamics of the pursuit of knowledge. The campus which does not welcome and utilize them will miss an important resource which can both upgrade and enrich the total dedication to scholarly responsibility and also stimulate among students, faculty, and administration a qualitative and evaluative scrutiny of what has been taught and what significant values accrue.

Chapter 3

The Chaplaincy at Church-related and Other Colleges

JOHN P. EDDY

Dean of Students, Johnson State College, Johnson, Vermont

Church-related colleges and universities, while having considerable divergence as to their basic purpose and functions, have played a major role in educating American citizens since the founding of Harvard College in 1636. Although enrollment has steadily increased in church-related institutions, their percentage of total enrollment has recently been declining. Student enrollment in 817 of these institutions in the fall of 1966 was only 17.3 percent of the national total.

These 817 church-related colleges and universities, located in 48 of the 50 states, are affiliated with 64 different religious bodies. Approximately 57 percent are affiliated with Protestant groups or smaller Christian denominations (e.g., Mormon), 42 percent are Roman Catholic, and 1 percent are Jewish. According to accrediting agencies, they include both highest- and the lowest-rated institutions.

DESCRIPTION OF CHURCH-RELATED INSTITUTIONS AND PERSONNEL

It is difficult to define a church-related college today. The National Council of the Churches of Christ in the United States of America has said:

Each body or official has made the definition of "church-related." The concept of the college being church-related varies from that of institutions altogether independent of control by the religious body but with some historical connections, to those with widely different contractual arrangements, to actual current control of an educational institution by a church body.

The most recent report (1966) of this National Council claims 465 Protestant church-related institutions of higher learning, and the Roman Catholic Church reported (1966) 314 colleges and universities with an enrollment of 417,115 students. The proportion of America's college students in Roman Catholic colleges and universities is one in every twelve students. One college in every three related to the Roman Catholic Church (1966) ". . . is involved in some form of shared facilities and faculty with one or more other institutions today, and two-thirds of these programs did not exist prior to 1960. Many of the programs involve joint use of facilities or staff with state colleges and universities and other non-Catholic institutions."

The majority of church-related colleges are in the eastern part of the nation, and they constitute more than one-third of the 2,238 total institutions throughout the country. The colleges range in size from fewer than 100 students (with a stress on piety and undergraduate courses in religion) to large universities with over 20,000 students (with a pluralistic emphasis and extensive graduate offerings). The average enrollment is about 1,000 students, with the typical undergraduate curriculum emphasizing the liberal arts and the preprofessional vocations, especially teacher education.

There is no single model or definition of a church-related college in terms of philosophy or quality. A Danforth Foundation study (1966) distinguishes four patterns that describe the principal types of such institutions. They have been characterized as the "defender of the faith college," the "free Christian (or Jewish) college," the "non-affirming college," and the "church-related university."

Various challenges are effecting changes in the church-related colleges. First, the varying needs of society continually transform the curriculum, thus requiring new staff and technological equipment. Second, the religious pluralism of students tends to eliminate required chapel and to have the chaplain relate to all religious groups in an ecumenical or interfaith manner. Third, there is a serious financial crisis involving all areas of the college. Fourth, there are new student pressures upon traditional patterns, such as, for example, the practice of expecting college authorities to serve *in loco parentis.*

The majority of religious personnel (variously called chaplains, deans of chapel, directors of religious affairs, religious coordinators, etc.) have graduate degrees in religion and are fully ordained ministers. They work with committees on religious life that are composed of students, faculty, and administrators. Sometimes they perform the usual pastoral functions. Often they teach credit courses. Working with students in religious activities and counseling students require a large segment of their time. Some chaplains also are expected to do some public relations work as well as to serve as resource persons to the community.

RECENT STUDIES ON CHAPLAINCY

The first study on the chaplain was done in Protestant church-related and private colleges by Seymour A. Smith (1951). Smith's study reveals the college chaplaincy as one of the major religious forces at work at American private colleges and shows that chaplains fulfill four major roles: as teachers, preachers, counselors, and advisors or directors of voluntary religious groups.

James Windsor (1963) reported the second study done on the chaplain in church-related, private, and—for the first time—public colleges. His research provides the following pertinent information: (1) Sixty-four percent of the chaplains are primarily responsible to the president, 14 percent to the dean of students, and 22 percent to other persons. (2) The academic preparation of the chaplains was found to be as follows: all had bachelor's degrees, 23 percent had master's degrees, 23 percent had doctorates, and 49 percent were studying for the doctorate. (3) Forty-eight of the institutions have Sunday or regular weekday chapel where the chaplain has worship responsibilities. (4) Almost all of the chaplains have their counseling integrated into the school counseling center. (5) Fewer than 5 percent of full-time chaplains taught classes in the regular academic curriculum; however, more than 80 percent of the professor-plus-chaplains did teach. (6) The basic changes desired by chaplains were the following: 29 percent desired more counseling, 22 percent more study time, 16 percent less administration, 16 percent fewer outside activities, 11 percent less teaching, and 6 percent felt no need of change. (7) Most full-time chaplains received salaries in the bracket of full professors or deans. (8) Church-related college and university chaplains had much more positive and aggressive goals for their office than did the chaplains associated with institutions that are not church related.

Some of the most significant trends in the chaplaincy are the following, in order of frequency: (1) Improved status of the chaplaincy; (2) increasing professionalization of the chaplaincy; (3) increase of new chapels; (4) development of small-group work and deeply personal emphasis of religious work on campus; (5) better preparation and in-service training opportunities for the chaplaincy; (6) more coordination of academic and religious efforts of both students and faculty; (7) a tendency toward a sense of mission in denominations providing more support for the religious welfare of students; (8) a higher degree of interdenominational coordination and cooperation; (9) a greater amount of experimentation in worship and in service opportunities; (10) a larger concern for presenting all sides of religious questions and allowing the student to choose responsibly his own faith for himself.

In the most recent study of Protestant college chaplains, entitled *The Campus Clergyman* (James Blumyer's study, *The Catholic College Chaplaincy,* remains to be published), Phillip Hammond (1966) makes the following observations on Protestant chaplains: (1) Ninety-nine percent base their operations in an office in a college building; (2) 93 percent are primarily responsible to or dependent upon the college administration for planning their program; (3) 93 percent have a telephone listing in the college directory; (4) 98 percent have a regular channel to the college administration; (5) 50 percent frequently give help or advice on policy matters, disciplinary measures, or similar matters, whereas 35 percent indicated that they were asked occasionally and only 4 percent responded that they were never called in for consultation with the college administration; (6) 76 percent replied that they have more contact with students of other denominations than with their own denominational students, since being chaplain to a total student body alters the nature of student contacts; (7) 21 percent have formal or informal contact with students each week in denominational activities; (8) 16 percent have weekly duties other than those connected with college and university people; (9) 57 percent have differentiated role conceptions; (10) 35 percent show creative and innovative factors in their work.

PLACEMENT AND SALARY CONSIDERATIONS

There are few official placement agencies for religious personnel at present. The American Academy of Religion and the National Association of Student Personnel Administrators list persons in their publications who are seeking positions. The annual meetings of (1) the National Association of College and University Chaplains, (2) the Association for the Coordination of University Religious Affairs, (3) the National Campus Ministry Association, and (4) the American Academy of Religion have limited or no official placement resources, but there is often an informal type of discussion that occurs at these annual conferences through which religious personnel learn of openings and even are interviewed for positions. The National Association of Student Personnel Administrators and the American Personnel and Guidance Association both have placement centers at their national meetings, where an increasing number of religious personnel are placed each year. The theological seminaries, such as Yale Divinity School, Union Theological Seminary, Chicago Theological Seminary, and others have served as placement bureaus through professors of theology who teach in higher education and in similar areas.

Who pays the salary of religious personnel on campus will depend upon the particular appointment terms. The college chaplain or college director of religious life usually has his salary paid from the regular budget provided by the college board of trustees.

However, if there is a college church or chapel which serves as the regular Sunday worship center, part of the salary of the chaplain or his assistants may be provided by the respective local church board. Campus ministers who are assigned to a campus usually have their salaries paid by a denominational agency or a combined number of denominational or ecumenical agencies. The trend is for more campus ministers to receive their salaries from ecumenical agencies.

QUALIFICATIONS OF RELIGIOUS PERSONNEL

The typical qualifications for religious personnel (chaplain, dean of chapel, director of religious life, religious coordinator, or similarly titled persons) include both academic training and professional experience. Minimum academic background consists of at least an undergraduate degree and almost always a bachelor of divinity or master of sacred theology degree. However, either a steadily increasing number of religious personnel are doing additional graduate work and obtaining doctorates in fields such as theology or philosophy or colleges tend to employ those who have the highest academic credentials. With reference to professional experience, the majority of religious personnel have had some prior church work or clinical counseling experience before taking a position at a college. This experience may include serving a local congregation on a campus as an associate minister, serving as campus minister of a religious foundation, or serving in an ecumenical ministry. Training in psychological counseling may be obtained at a variety of centers in institutional settings such as hospitals or community clinics.

Since the religious personnel often teach one or more academic courses in a college curriculum, it is essential that they have a solid background in at least one discipline or area of study. Usually, the teaching position is in religion, philosophy, sociology, or education, since these are the areas in which religious personnel tend to specialize during their own academic preparation. Consequently, religious personnel will often receive and desire faculty ranks such as lecturer, instructor, or assistant professor when being appointed to their first campus post, depending on their educational qualifications and teaching experience. Religious personnel will hold faculty rank from lecturer to full professor.

In the job analysis of chaplains or directors of religious life, teaching will vary from 10 to 90 percent of their work load. Thus a chaplain may teach anywhere from one course a year to four courses each term.

Chapter **4**

Summary of Basic Information for Chief Administrators Concerning the Religious Affairs Programs

CHARLES W. HAVICE

Professor of Philosophy and Religion and Dean of Chapel, Northeastern University, Boston, Massachusetts

DUTIES OF THE CHAPLAIN OR DEAN OF CHAPEL

Since institutions have such marked dissimilarities in their religious organizations and programs, few hard and fast generalizations concerning them can be made—an observation which applies to almost all statements in this summary. With this in mind, a sample profile of the chaplain's duties can be drawn as follows:

1. Arranging and conducting worship services; filling preaching and speaking engagements both on campuses and off-campus.

2. Counseling students and colleagues in many areas of the human situation: religious, moral, philosophical, marital, familial, emotional, and interpersonal; giving guidance in crisis occasions, providing referral information, and assisting in other matters of a confidential nature. The chaplain works closely with academic, medical, and other appropriate colleagues.
3. Participating in the various national professional associations. (These are described in an earlier chapter of this section.)
4. Chairing regular meetings of the faculty committee on religion, the religious council, and similar groups.
5. Teaching one or two courses in his field of specialization.
6. Offering invocations at college occasions—dinners, assemblies, anniversaries, dedications, etc.
7. Relating incoming students to the church of their choice and working closely with local clergymen.
8. Preparing brochures for campus use and writing articles for religious journals.
9. Directing and counseling student religious organizations on campus.
10. Officiating at weddings, baptisms, and funerals.
11. Representing his institution at various religious, educational, and civic meetings.
12. Preparing and administering the budget.
13. Reporting at regular intervals to the president or other assigned superior.
14. Taking responsibility for emphasizing to the campus the spiritual dimensions of such basic issues as human rights.
15. Corresponding with colleagues, clergymen, organizations, alumni, and especially with parents of students. (A chaplain will expect to have a heavy correspondence, including the frequent supplying of character references and recommendations.)

ORGANIZATIONAL STRUCTURE AND CHAPLAINCY

The chaplain at the church-related institution works closely with the ministers of the local churches, although meetings are not often on a regularly scheduled basis. A faculty and administration committee or council on religious affairs, with the chaplain as chairman, is the prevalent pattern. A student committee works with the chaplain in programming.

At the large secular university, the coordinator or director of religious affairs necessarily functions in a less simple fashion. With his one or more assistants, he meets regularly with the council of chaplains and ministers to students. He cooperates with them in relating the incoming student to his preferred denomination, coordinates the many scheduled activities, and directs such inclusive projects as World University Service and ecumenical worship services on special occasions.

TO WHOM CHAPLAINS REPORT

The chaplain of the church-related college usually reports directly to the president. If it is a comparatively large college, he may report to the vice-president or dean of students; yet even in these instances there is a close working relationship between the president and the chaplain.

The coordinator or director of religious affairs at the large university normally reports to the vice-president in charge of student affairs or to the dean of students (sometimes the same person holds both positions).

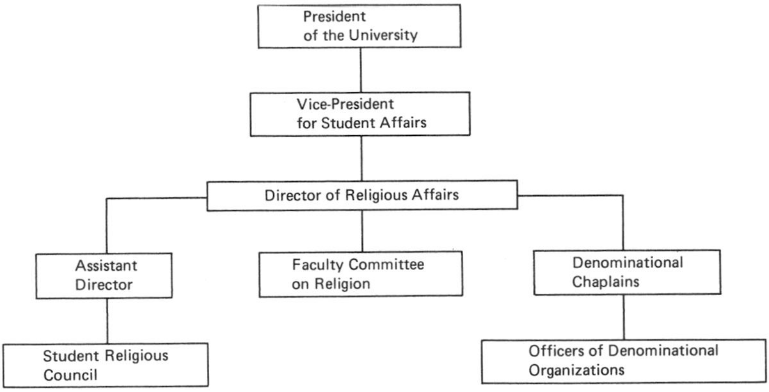

Fig. 1 *Administrative organization.*

ADMINISTRATIVE POLICIES REGARDING CHAPLAINS

The administration should establish these policies as guidelines for the religious personnel and programs:

1. Office space and areas for the chaplain should be provided. Details of such housing have been delineated in Chapter 1 of this section. A central and attractive location is essential.
2. An adequate budget, in keeping with the importance of the religious concern of the institution, should be provided and its amounts reviewed annually.
3. The chaplain should be recognized as a principal staff member and accorded the academic recognition he merits by reason of his degrees, experience, and years of service.
4. One of the chaplain's most important roles is that of counselor and confidant. He is in a unique position to deal in strictest confidence with many intimate and interpersonal situations. The administration should enable the chaplain to fulfill this role and should respect its confidential nature.

FACILITIES NEEDED BY CHAPLAINS

In the church-related college, the chaplain is provided with at least such minimal facilities as the following:

1. Office space so planned as to ensure strict privacy for counseling sessions. Telephone, desk, several chairs, and bookcase constitute the usual equipment. Office space for secretary.
2. Area adequate to seat from 12 to 20 persons for conferences and furnished with a large table and needed number of chairs. The chaplain's area is commonly located in the chapel building, but it may also sometimes be in the nonsectarian student-union building, the student activities building, or the general administration building. At the large university, the coordinator or director of religious affairs will usually require, in addition to space for his own office, areas for his assistants and secretaries. A conference room that can accommodate from 20 to 35 persons will be in frequent demand. At many universities the denominational chaplains have their headquarters and all facilities in their own religious centers. Where such arrangements do not exist, the university will need to provide an area of modest size for each chaplain, which he can use both for office and counseling purposes.

3. An adequate lounging and reading room, well stocked with appropriate books and magazines, is strongly recommended.
4. The coordinator's areas are usually in the student-union building, the student activities building, or the general administration building.

TYPICAL BUDGETS FOR CHAPLAINS

Two typical budgets are given below, one for the smaller institution and the other for the large university.

Typical Annual Budget for 1967–1968 for Religious Program at a Church-related College*

Salaries (chaplain, secretary, and part-time student assistant)	$21,000
Fringe benefits	700
Honoraria (preachers and lecturers)	1,000
Off-campus conferences	800
On-campus conferences and programs	500
Books, journals, and other religious literature	200
Printing, office supplies, and postage	400
Choir expenses (gown replacements, music, awards)	250
Chaplain's discretionary account	200
Miscellaneous	300
Total	$25,350

* NOTE: Space, furniture, maintenance, entertainment of guests, light, and heat are provided by college.

Annual Budget for 1967–1968 for Religious Affairs at a Large University

Gift support (alumni)	$ 30,000
Religious groups (use of building)	14,000
Building service (other groups)	1,200
Endowment	14,000
Sermon fund (endowment income)	8,000
University appropriation	51,484
Total	$118,684

EXPENSES

SALARIES (director; two associate directors; administrative aide; four secretaries; coffee house director)	$ 64,408
HOURLY WAGES	4,306
GENERAL EXPENSE	
Director's discretionary	1,500
Staff travel	1,500
Telephone and telegraph	2,200
Development (fund raising)	1,200
Office supplies and postage	2,300
Publicity	1,200
FRINGE BENEFITS	
T.I.A.A. (retirement)	3,450
Social security	2,490
Workmen's compensation	170
Health insurance	360
Employees' children tuition	1,000
Total	$ 17,370

BUILDING SERVICES	
Salaries	$ 8,300
Furniture and equipment	500 *
Furniture and equipment repair	1,100
Supplies	300
Total	$ 10,200
PROGRAM—SOCIAL RESPONSIBILITY	
Staff discretionary	$ 500
Program development	500
Project administration (national and international)	3,550
Newsletter	150
Student service program (local: tutorial, juvenile work, etc.)	1,700
PROGRAM—UNIVERSITY LIFE	
Student leadership conference	300
Freshman program	600
Coffee house, art, film, drama	600
Student leadership training	200
International students	150
Campus chest (token administration cost)	50
Publication	800
Total	$ 9,100
STUDIES	
Staff discretionary	$ 500
Program development	500
Subscriptions, literature, films	300
Lectureship (annual)	1,000
Fall, winter, spring conferences and lectures	3,000
Total	$ 5,300
Grand total	$118,684 †

* Hereafter, major furniture and equipment requirements will be submitted to the budget office as needed.

† An additional $200,000 is budgeted annually by the 15 denominational groups. The grand total is therefore $318,684.

PROVISIONS FOR MEETING BUDGETS

The chaplain at a church-related college receives his salary directly from the institution. Occasionally, the denominational headquarters may contribute partially to his support, but payment is made through the usual channels at the college in the same manner as it is to any faculty member or administrator. Sabbaticals and fringe benefits are also to be recognized as part of the chaplain's expectations. Student activities funds and alumni gifts are sometimes allocated to the chaplain's programming budget.

At the large secular university the coordinator or director of religious affairs is normally on the payroll of the institution and receives all the fringe benefits accorded his fellow administrators. The denominational chaplains are paid by their respective denominations. Their off-campus religious centers and their program budgets are also provided by their denominations.

Money-raising drives for special projects are often organized on the campus. World University Service is an example.

PRIVILEGES GRANTED CHAPLAINS

The administration usually extends to principal chaplains or to the dean of chapel the usual privileges granted a faculty member, such as the stipulated opportunities for him and members of his family to be exempt in part or in whole from tuition fees for courses and to be provided with health insurance, many free admissions, parking privileges, etc.

In the instance of the denominational chaplains, the university usually does not extend the privilege of tuition-free courses, but it does grant such courtesies as parking privileges, free admission to certain events, and free use of the gymnasium.

RELATION OF SIZE OF INSTITUTIONS TO NEED FOR CHAPLAINS

In view of the rapidly increasing number of chaplains and directors of religion serving the campuses in America, the question may be raised as to how large the student body should be to justify the appointment of a professionally trained person to give leadership to the religious program. No simple answer can be given. Some church-related colleges of only several hundred students are served by a part-time chaplain, who is likely also to be a professor of religion, philosophy, sociology, or some other discipline. From this minimal level the professional leadership increases to that of the complex religious programs of a large university. At least three such institutions have over thirty different denominational organizations actively involved. One university has established the rule that no denominational group can have official recognition unless it has at least ten charter members. This regulation is probably representative. At the maximal end, it is not uncommon to have a denominational organization of several hundred members.

NOTES

The editor of this chapter is indebted to a number of colleagues and national officers for their generous response to requests for information. Because of very recent changes made in the structuring of the campus ministry to Catholic students, a special note of thanks goes to the Reverend Robert W. Bullock, director of the Newman Apostolate of the Archdiocese of Boston, for his clarifying account.

An extensive study of religion on the campus is soon to be published under the sponsorship of the Danforth Foundation. The first volume is scheduled for distribution in 1969. The Foundation established in 1963 a commission and staff to undertake a full description and evaluation of ministries in higher education. Professor Kenneth W. Underwood of Wesleyan University was the director of this extensive project.

Upon request the editor of this chapter will be pleased to send without charge a comprehensive bibliography pertaining to religion on the campus. (For a brief bibliography see page 10-17.)

Section Eleven

Campus Community Facilities and Enterprises

Chapter 1

College Unions— Programs and Services

FRANK NOFFKE

Director, College Union, California State College at Long Beach, California

THE IMPORTANCE OF THE SOCIAL-EDUCATIONAL PROGRAM

Basic Philosophy and Goals

The college union is generally considered to be the college community center, the headquarters of out-of-class life for the college. As such, it provides the social, cultural, recreational, and hospitality programs which complement academic learning and the curriculum.

Recent events of local, national, and international importance point up more than ever the absolute necessity for making the development of proper human behavior and the understanding of one's fellow man a part of education. More than ever, colleges need to accept and discharge their obligation to take advantage of this last chance in formal education for teaching and providing actual experience in the positive development of human relations skills.

College unions have come to be recognized as a training and practice ground in the understanding of human behavior and the settlement of disagreement as well as a service and recreational facility. Now the union must be given its place as a *fully* accepted and respected partner in education, or we shall commit the sin of blundering over one of the greatest means of personal development toward civic and, eventually, international leadership in the United States system of education.

Whatever the union's architectural form, size, or facilities, uppermost in its effect must be a truly educational contribution to the college or university. Relative to this, a statement of the goals of the college union follows:

1. To provide a balanced, coordinated program of educational out-of-class experiences
2. To provide for the student, through this program, personal, social, and cultural development; practice in leadership and management; fullest development of leisure-time activities; and learning experiences in human relations
3. To increase perspective, concern, and sensitivity to the local, national, and international citizenship responsibilities of an educated person
4. To serve as a part of the program of student personnel services
5. To provide facilities for the activities program and recreational and hospitality services for students, staff, faculty, alumni, friends, parents and visitors—all on a financially sound basis
6. To provide, through its programs and services, a major contribution to the college's public relations program as well as to higher education in general

A college union or student activities program may be defined as that series of experiences and events planned *by* students (sometimes with faculty), *for* students (and faculty), individually and collectively, as an aid to their pursuit of their educational goals.

Contribution to Student Development

Graduates who perform well in jobs and civic life often have drawn upon both classroom and out-of-class experiences to achieve this end. If our college union programs intelligently relate academic and out-of-class learning, students will be able to draw upon their college union experiences for concepts, principles, values, skills, and techniques with which to perform effectively. The following three examples show how this has actually come about:

A timid sophomore girl, serving as college union committee chairman, becomes an outstanding, responsible and respected leader before even her senior year.

A group of four students, college union leaders, do a masterful and successful job in presenting needs for substantial financial support for a college union to a foundation.

A union program chairman brings cultural and recreational programs to the student body in new dimensions of educational experiences.

World events and student activist movements give evidence of a new tenor in out-of-class life. While student interests will always change, one doubts that student interest in higher levels of concern is likely to be lost as an integral part of future student-life patterns; e.g., concern over participation in decision making, college problems and government, academic freedom, civil rights, racial and minority equality, concern for the underprivileged, foreign policy, world image, and the actual influence of the United States in the world community. Contrast these concerns with debate over what band to hire.

Currently, the acquisition of new principles and techniques for dealing with deeper student concerns constantly preoccupies advisers, deans, and faculty. Greater faculty participation in discussions and guidance of students who raise questions and see problems and inconsistencies in the college union and society must be stressed—even made an equal concern to classroom teaching.

Great numbers of individual students benefit by the value of worthwhile recreational diversion and relaxing activity in planned recreational, cultural, and social events and in the learning and development that comes from casual, accidental social contact and conversation.

While this is a substantial benefit, the greater and perhaps more important benefit is the development of the smaller number of student leaders who, in discharging their responsibilities as chairmen, members, or officers learn fiscal and personnel management, effective communication skills, and human relations skills including the *resolution of conflicts* among their fellows. Performance is measured in the results obtained rather than in a letter grade.

These relatively few constitute that handful who are likely to have real impact on our society as leaders.[1]

Significance to Faculty, Alumni, and Remainder of College Family

Faculty members who serve as advisers to student groups and as speakers for their events enjoy a close relationship of mutual significance and have the opportunity to know how students act and think in personal, informal, one-to-one relationships. The opportunity to give advice, to shape lives in other than classroom situations, and to test and observe students' thinking in real-life situations is cherished by most faculty members. It is often a fringe benefit which enhances the appeal of the teaching role.

Alumni benefit by taking part in activities and programs and frequently use the services provided by the college union for their own enjoyment and edification. The union should be the chief rallying point on campus for alumni. Alumni in close touch with the college are an indication of its cohesive and unifying effect.

A significant educational program in the union can have much to do with institutional image and reputation as the types of programs and services become known to the community, the city, the state, and often even to the nation; for example—the appearance of respected, renowned speakers, performers, and statesmen at the union may bring the institution into the public eye.

As the goals of the union suggest, not only does the union provide its program for students, faculty, and staff but it also becomes a major public relations agency, a medium for enhancing the college's cultural influence in the community. Its many services and facilities come to be relied upon, first of all by students, but also by alumni, friends, prospective students, conference planners, visitors, speakers, lecturers, and people throughout the area.

[1] Edwin Siggelkow, "The College Union and Leadership Development," in Chester A. Berry (ed.), *College Unions—Year 50*, Association of College Unions–International, Palo Alto, Calif., 1966.

INITIAL PLANNING TO ACHIEVE PROGRAM GOALS

Experience in planning for a college union is summarized in the following: "To solve social problems requires program planning as well as building planning."[2] In fact, program planning must come first and be part of the total development of the union operation. The planning committee, with existing campus program staff and program committees, should discuss and determine solutions to those campus social needs which are most often met by *program* solutions. For example, if there is a lack of easy means for dating on the campus, then the type of event that will permit stag attendance and early and subtle means of mixing is necessary. Determination must be made as to how often such events should take place. A study must be made of the weekend habits of the students who leave the campus. The next step after a survey of campus social problems is the preparation of a typical program of events, meetings, and activities that will help solve these problems.

To illustrate a method that could be adapted to almost any situation and drawing upon the information discussed above, one should develop a chart with column headings reading from left to right as follows:

1. Problem, social, or service need
2. Event or type of program to solve the problem or satisfy the need
3. Specific facility or type of facility required to house the program event
4. Brief description of the facility

Such a line of methodical reasoning should produce a charted program giving an overall view of generally what facilities should be in the college union. This is one of the major points at which professional consulting is indispensable: for guiding such analysis, for sizing, and for final recommendations.

As in proper planning of food services where we start with a menu and work from it to the necessary facilities, equipment, planning, and schedules, to produce this menu, so we must with the college union begin with its program menu, or types and kinds of events that will provide satisfactorily and wholesomely the menu for students' needs and appetites in out-of-class life.[3]

Planning must come initially from the functional, operational, and program points of view. A building that functions well is not incompatible with handsome design. It is the eventual operator's (or consultant's) job to see that the building serves programs well and functions well; and it is the architect's job to see that the functional is made beautiful.

What is the union building? A conception often held is that the union is a utilitarian service building, available for casual campus use. It should be made clear that the building is a physical facility which also houses an informal educational program and which also serves as an important factor in students' personal development and complete education. The building is the means to an end—the program carried on within it; and this basic concept should be understood and agreed upon before planning begins.

To design a building so that its program becomes the expected "all things to all people" would seem to be sufficient reason for the utmost thoroughness in planning. The program of the college union should satisfy the students (and others); that is, it should meet their needs for daily services and recreation as well as for social, cultural, and educational growth. The desired outcome of a building, in order to accomplish these objectives, demands that every step of the planning be examined carefully and that

[2] Frank Noffke, *Planning for a College Union*, 4th ed., Association of College Unions–International, Palo Alto, Calif., 1965.

[3] Frank Noffke, "Subjective Analysis of Need for a College Union," preliminary proposal for a college union for California State College at Long Beach, 1965.

sufficient time be allotted to permit clear-cut, satisfying, simultaneous solutions to the many problems in planning and in program.

THE CORE UNION PROGRAM

Typical areas of programming in which unions are involved, as indicated by representative college union program committees and the 10 core areas of Wolf's study,[4] are:

Dance
Discussion, forum (current issues)
Music
Art
Games
Hospitality-house
Movies
Outings
Crafts
Special projects, experimental or trial programs

These programs are almost always planned and executed by student committees with the help of a faculty or staff adviser. Much resource information on programming is available in the Association of College Unions' "College Unions at Work" series.[5]

What types of programs are worthwhile, significant, and lasting? Extensive surveys of college union program activities made in 1951 by Andrew Wolf[6] and in 1965 by Chester A. Berry,[7] using the same questionnaire instrument, show 20 basic types of activities persisting over the years. A model program developed by Berry in 1965 gave, broadly, a picture of today's student interests.

What are the criteria for judging the worthwhileness of a union program? Wolf gives five:[8]

1. Does the activity broaden social and cultural experiences and develop social competence?
2. Does the activity stimulate creative self-expression and develop new leisure-time skills?
3. Is the activity geared to the leisure-time interests and needs of the campus community? Does it open new possibilities?
4. Does the activity bring into action leadership from within the group?
5. Does the activity provide fun, and equality of opportunity, a balance between passive and active participation? Is it readily accessible?

What do union directors, generally, say are the "must" programs? Berry's survey[9] shows the 41 programs in the order in which, in 1965, these union directors ranked them.

[4] Andrew G. Wolf, *Determining Basic Designs for the College Union Activity Program*, Association of College Unions–International, Palo Alto, Calif., 1965.

[5] "College Unions at Work," series published by the Association of College Unions–International:

Boris Bell, *Administration and Operation of the College Union.*
Norman Moore, *Art in the Union.*
Theodore Crabb, *The College Union Outdoors.*
Frank Noffke, *Planning for a College Union.*
George F. Stevens, *The Union Recreation Games Area.*
Douglas C. Osterheld, *Food Service and the College Union.*

[6] Andrew G. Wolf, *Determining Basic Designs for College Union Activity Program*, Association of College Unions–International, Palo Alto, Calif., 1965.

[7] Chester A. Berry and Tom Reeve, *Proceedings of Association of College Unions Conference*, Association of College Unions–International, Palo Alto, Calif., 1965.

[8] Andrew G. Wolf, *Determining Basic Designs for College Union Activity Program*, Association of College Unions–International, Palo Alto, Calif., 1965.

[9] Berry and Reeve, *op. cit.*

TABLE 1 Student Union Programs as Rated by Union Directors

Rank	Program	Percentage of directors considering the program a "must"
1	Art exhibitions (traveling, etc.)	70
2	Acquaintance party for freshmen	60
3	Exhibitions of student art	58
4	Billiard room	57
5	Lectures by off-campus speakers	55
6	Space for informal card playing	51
7	Space for chess and checkers	50
8	Publication of all-campus calendar	48
10	Special celebration dances	46
10	Popular magazines for leisure	46
15	Table-tennis room	43
15	Open house for all students	42
15	Exhibitions of faculty art	42
15	Orientation for freshmen in union activities	42
15	Regular showing of feature films	42
18	Orientation for freshmen in campus activities	40
18	Special interviewing for union committee applicants	40
18	Public forum by faculty	40
19	Poster making service	38
20	Training for union chairmen	37
23	Contemporary foreign films	36
23	Photography exhibits	36
23	Recognition dinner for union	36
24	Training for union members	33
26	Forums by off-campus speakers	32
26	Informal discussions fostering student-faculty relations	32
28	Major concert artist series	31
28	Bowling lanes	31
30	Newspapers from other cities	30
30	Intramural bowling league	30
30	Parents' day open house	29
35	Regular evening dateless dances	29
35	Student-faculty coffee hours	29
35	Billiard tournament	29
35	Bridge tournament	29
39	Special concerts (symphony orchestra, etc.)	28
39	Public forums led by students	28
39	Concert record library	28
39	Lectures on art	28
40	Merit award for union committee	27
41	Table tennis	26

The complete study[10] and commentary are invaluable in program work.

Programs will vary depending on the location of the institution and the types of students attending it. The college union in an urban area, with a large commuter student population, may need to run programs somewhat different from those needed in a more rural area. In these areas there is usually a greater emphasis on cultural pro-

[10] Berry and Reeve, *op. cit.*

grams which involve visiting artists and dramatic groups, whereas in the urban area art galleries, symphony concerts, and the theater are readily available to students, sometimes on a free basis.

The changes in emphasis since 1951 are related by Berry and Reeve:

If any trends or innovations can be detected they might include:

1. A tendency towards depth or breadth of programs, as in wide-ranging *Arts Festivals* or *Nationality* or *United Nations Weeks*.
2. Jazz and java hours and folk music programs. Is either the wave of the future?
3. Serious programs like *Great Books* seminars and poetry reading hours, as well as diversionary items like ski trips and demonstrations by bowling and billiard experts.
4. Trips overseas. It's obvious also that more unions are emphasizing the contribution of their foreign students.
5. The upsurge in games reflected in shuffleboard and other table games.[11]

Also of aid in general program planning is the listing by Dr. Lois Swanson [12] under the headings:

1. Programs to help students identify with the institution, its departments, and its recognized organizations
2. Programs to create more informal opportunities for learning and for significant discussion, student with student, student with faculty, faculty with faculty
3. Programs to broaden the cultural interest and enrich cultural opportunities
4. Opportunities for personal development
5. A variety of recreational and social programs
6. Programs calculated to develop skills and understanding in organization and leadership

Changes in Emphasis and Future Potential

At present, student interest and involvement in political issues, both national and international, is pronounced and widely recognized. What the future will bring is speculative. However, that students will attempt to take a greater part in the governance affairs of colleges or at least in influencing both them and the formulation of administrative policies is almost certain. The residue of significant current students' interests and issues, while sometimes we might be glad to forget them, are likely to have an effect in formulating the political or role-developing nature of that age group's contribution to society 10 to 15 years later.[13]

Getting used to the radical changes in our society may be the single greatest challenge to the college union program. The psychological impact of vastly increased leisure, the search for more comfort in fewer working hours, increased communications, speedier transportation, automation—all have their focus in values and change, and all have an impact on the individual psyche. Can we help in coping with it? Could there possibly be any dearth of material for college union programs—both in developing current programs and in teaching the worthwhile use of leisure for the future?

The many ways in which programs and services will be changed by the technological development of equipment such as closed-circuit television, the automated locking of buildings, and automated food preparation are cited by Berry.[14]

New programs are limited only by the ingenuity of program planners attuned to

[11] Berry and Reeve, *op. cit.*

[12] Lois Swanson, "Preliminary Proposal for a College Union for California State College at Long Beach," 1965.

[13] Jack Newfield, *A Prophetic Minority*, The New American Library, 1966.

[14] Chester A. Berry (ed.), *College Unions—Year 50*, Association of College Unions–International, Palo Alto, Calif., 1966.

the times. The use of more sophisticated teaching and international games[15] (such as the "Big Board") and the development of student-planned "experimental colleges" are examples. Many sources are in the literature of the Association of College Unions (e.g., "These Are Our Best," by the Association of College Unions).[16]

Berry[17] goes on to say:

> What is the essence of a college union? Is it the building, the program, the staff, the service, the orientation towards its community, the participation of the various segments of the community? Or is the essence a philosophy that says a union is people doing many worthwhile and useful things together in an atmosphere of mutual interest and respect? Is the essence of a union, people? If it is the latter, we can be quite certain that there will be unions in 2014, even though we might not recognize them. The union is part of higher education and higher education is part of society. The union works with people during their leisure. Each of us must form his own opinions concerning the place of the college union in 2014. In my judgment, discovering and implementing the moral equivalent of work is the important job of the union.

David Gray[18] calls our attention to these matters in discussing leisure, its values and its impact on the future in the following paragraphs:

> There has been much confusion in discussion of leisure, largely, it appears, because there has been no general acceptance of a definition of the term. Ott Romney suggested in 1934 that leisure is "Choosing Time" free of attention to the necessities of living and available for use according to one's wish. This definition divides time into three great classes: time for existence--sleeping, eating, sanitation, and the like; time for subsistence—working on one's job; and leisure which was the time left over when at least a minimum level of existence and subsistence had been accomplished. This definition of leisure, though it departed from the classical use of the term, has been widely adopted. . . .
>
> The years between now and 1980 will be years of transition. During these years Americans will be evolving some kind of adjustment to the radically different society automation and other forces are now creating. Presumably in the latter years of this century we will generally have a substantial amount of leisure and hopefully, a value system and enough security to permit us to enjoy it. In the interim, however, the developing time off the job which is being thrust on our people could be a heavy burden. We do not have the traditions or the philosophy or the skills to deal with it. . . . How much work time will be reduced by 1980 will depend on the response to the social and economic pressures wrought by automation. . . .
>
> We are embarking on a society which is apt to be quite different from the one we have now; powerful currents now flowing will float us progressively further from known charts. The quiet times are gone forever, but there is no such thing as an inevitable society. Society is man made. What it is to be we shall help it become.

Also, the Commission on Current and Developing Student Issues of the Council of Student Personnel Associations[19] and the College Student Personnel Institute[20] are developing a coordinating approach to the existing literature as well as deriving a list of emerging issues felt to be significant and identifiable.

[15] David Page, "Games and Leisure Activities in 20 Years," California State College at Long Beach, 1967.

[16] *These Are Our Best,* Association of College Unions—International.

[17] Berry, *op. cit.*

[18] David Gray, "The Changing Pattern of American Society," paper, California State College at Long Beach, 1965.

[19] Commission on Current and Developing Issues of the Council of Student Personnel Associations, 5440 Cass Avenue, Detroit, Mich.

[20] *Student Personnel Digests,* College Personnel Institute, Claremont, Calif.

Prediction studies[21] of the future in scientific, sociological, and logistic areas offer fruitful sources of exploration for staffs interested and deeply concerned with projecting their programs into the future.

HOW IS THE UNION PROGRAM DIFFERENT? WHAT ARE ITS DISTINCTIVE CHARACTERISTICS?

The events and programs which are developed by the college union have traditionally had the unique flavor contributed by groups of students concentrating themselves on the task of developing cultural, social, recreational, and service programs for the student body at large, programs which are distinctively administered, planned, and executed by students; developing, in other words, as Butts has so well put it, "A comprehensive, well-considered plan for the community life of the college."[22]

However, the word "college" means, significantly, that this program is for *all* members of the college community—students, faculty, administration, staff, parents, alumni, and friends.

Thereby a spirit, élan, or esprit de corps is created, a feeling of fellowship which everyone shares; and the means are developed for meeting human needs on campus, needs so often not met in the classroom in the competitive, often stringent pursuit which tends to throw human feelings aside.

Another distinction is the emphasis on *social, recreational,* and *cultural* as contrasted to political action programs, although college union programs have long taken the lead in presenting discussions of current issues.

While expressions such as "living room of the campus" may seem to be clichés worn by time, they are nevertheless honored by time in that they express needs which were never more pressing in our society than they are today.

Program-Organization Relationship

The traditional college union organization is developed under a governing board to which are responsible a series of program committees headed by a program directorate (council). The governing board reports directly to the president and serves as a separate department. The advantages of this form are:

1. The opportunity to concentrate on the "well-considered plan for the community life of the college."

2. Independence from influence by vested-interest groups, including certain academic departments and chiefly student government, with its political volatility, which can change drastically from year to year. Information about the development of this traditional program and its values and benefits is found in the literature of the Association of College Unions and particularly in the writings of its editor, Porter Butts.[23]

At many institutions, a combination or consolidation of other campus activities and the union program is developed which, in essence, combines into a related working organization the various areas which are often autonomous and independent, such as student government, student activities, college union, student clubs, and other organizations, without removing the essential autonomy and the basic function and purpose of each. The value is in eliminating needless duplication and competition between staff, committees, facilities, and services offered. The prototype of this program is developed in a master's thesis by Beryl Roberts.[24]

[21] T. J. Gordon, "The New Determinism," paper, Douglas Corporation, Long Beach, Calif.

[22] Porter Butts, *Planning and Operating College Union Buildings,* Association of College Unions–International, Palo Alto, Calif., 1967.

[23] Publications of the Association of College Unions–International, Office of the Executive Secretary, P.O. Box 7268, Stanford, Calif.

[24] Beryl Roberts, "The Essentials of an Activities-union Program with Emphasis on Its Educational Implications," Master's thesis, University of Minnesota, 1957.

FINANCING THE PROGRAM

In most unions, funds for the program of student committees are budgeted by having the committees submit requests justifying their planned programs and events to the college union board (in some cases, to student government). Boards usually look favorably upon sound (but not too ambitious) student program budgets, since the client is the student who paid his fees.

Programs of other college departments, financed by such departments, often are significant contributions to the union program and the campus; e.g., fine arts exhibits installed or sponsored by the art department; lectures arranged by lectures committees; intramural programs sponsored by the physical education department.

It has been said that one of the greatest sources of students' learning is what they learn from one another. This principle may be extended to the formal program of events planned and executed *by* students *for* students, but in order to apply it there must be stable, reliable sources of financing. Such financing is the key to serving the many with a quality program of educational events (fun included).

The literature of Association of College Unions offers important advice. In a paper at the Association of College Unions–International Conference in 1966, for example, Blackburn[25] states:

> Any beginner in the union field knows that a college union's function can be divided into two general categories—business and educational. This is not an either-or situation, but rather a case of both being essential to the successful fulfillment of the union's purpose. Without the educational function, the heart of the union role is missing; and without the business function, a union cannot long survive. But as any union director will tell you, the trauma and the test of operating philosophies comes in the establishment of the proper *balance* between these two basic functions. What program advisor among you has not been confronted with your union director's budget-time interrogation, "How do you justify the cost of this program?"
>
> A union program's financial structure will be on the right track, both philosophically and economically, if it does all of these:
>
> 1. Helps support its own programs and broadens the scope of programming by having some charged-for activities. One can expect these revenue-producing activities, taken collectively, to show a net earning.
> 2. Presents a wide range of free (no admissions charge) programs, concentrating on those where the cost of presentation is not high.
> 3. Provides one full-time program advisor for each three or four general areas of committee program activity.
>
> What is important is that money is earmarked in advance to present a program, just as it is assured for maintenance and administration. Union committees will move much more effectively if they know where they stand with regard to spending the union's money. If the staff advisor sees to it that they get a budget, and have a voice in its preparation, and authority to then use it, the union program will be well on its way to making most effective use of dollars in this laboratory for learning called a union.

Funds for the Program

What it costs to present a suitable social-cultural program, or *should* cost, is one of the least explored areas of all areas of union operation. The principal guidelines to date are given in "Financing Programs," a paper presented in the 1962 Wisconsin Union Summer Course in College Union Operations,[26] brief highlights of which follow:

[25] Richard Blackburn, "Financing Union Programs," *Proceedings*, Association of College Unions–International, 1966.

[26] Papers on History, Goals, Operations, and Program Administration of College Unions, Wisconsin Union Summer Course in College Union Operations, Madison, Wis., 1962.

The mark of a union that believes in what it says about its purposes is a good social-cultural program for the campus, adequately financed.

What is adequate financing?

Here one has to start by distinguishing between (*a*) the cost of staff to guide the program, (*b*) the costs of custodial and clerical services that support the program, and (*c*) the direct out-of-pocket costs of the program itself.

It is the last item—the direct out-of-pocket costs—that is dealt with here: costs of supplies, printing, postage, lecture and dance band fees, rental of films and art shows, books for the library, records for the music room, refreshments for coffee hours.

The distinction is important. The custodial and office services that make the program possible, the staff time that goes into guidance and supervision, can easily run 10 times the out-of-pocket program costs—not to mention the *indirect* cost of utilities, repairs, and depreciation of building and equipment, and a share of the department charges which could be attributed to programmed use of the building if you could find a sensible way to do it.

A further distinction needs to be made. Out-of-pocket costs means costs not offset in whole or part by income from the program.

With these distinctions firmly in mind, then the best evidence points to the costs of a reasonably adequate program being in the range of 75 cents to $2.25 per student per school year. The range is necessarily wide because obviously—with some costs fairly constant—with an enrollment of, say 2,000, it will be necessary to spend more on program per capita than with an enrollment of 12,000. An orchestra for a free mixer, an art show, or a visiting lecturer costs about the same regardless of how many students are enrolled.

The following is a suggested scale of expenditures per full-time student for the out-of-pocket costs of programs presented without ticket charge:

Enrollment	*Suggested free-programs budget per full-time student* *
Over 8,000	$0.80
3,000 to 8,000	1.50
Under 3,000	2.00

* These per-capita expenditures were suggested in 1962. Because of steadily rising costs of supplies, printing, services, and fees—especially performers' fees—these figures should be increased, to provide equivalent programming in 1969, by 15 to 28 percent.

Hence, if you have 2,000 full-time students, you would be shooting for a $4,000 program budget; if 15,000 students, $12,000. Funds for summer programs, now rapidly expanding, should be provided in addition.

Where does the money come from?

The typical sources are the union fee, direct college appropriation, allocation from a general student activities fee, earnings of building revenue-producing departments, net proceeds of revenue-producing programs, or a combination of the above.

A major means of expanding regular program offerings, and often realizing net earnings that help pay for free activities, is the self-financing program.

Some of the programs that are likely to finance themselves, and possibly produce net earnings, are dances; talent shows; concerts and plays with "name" performers; some lectures; movies; travel lecture-films; outings; rentals of skis, bikes, boats; dance and bridge lessons; darkroom use.

Often the student reaction is: "If it's free, it must not be very worthwhile." In any event, it's fairly clear that students have the money to pay for certain programs and will spend it if it's a good program, and that the program can expand significantly when charges are made.

PROGRAM COORDINATION WITH OTHER AGENCIES

The college union program, while a key area on most campuses, cannot operate or serve as successfully as it might without coordination with, or help and support from, other departments of the institution.

Coordination with Student Personnel Services

Whether within or outside the formal student personnel organization of the college, the union is a department that serves student personnel and as such should work regularly and integrally with other student personnel services, chiefly student government, student activities, residence hall programs, international programs, orientation programs, and counseling.

Coordination with Related Academic Departments

Almost without exception there is in the teaching faculty a specialist in each area in which the college union operates or programs. It follows that the union's efforts to present an effective program will be strengthened by good working relationships with other departments. Most of these departments can contribute if asked, and in turn they may benefit from the services and programs in the college union.

Since some are more closely related than others, it will suffice to name them and search for new ways and means in which the seemingly remote departments can be made integral contributors. For example, a microbiology faculty which might previously have had no interest in the college union program might be willing, if asked, to provide a display of the department's work in a "college in review" program of the union.

Chief among the more directly related academic departments are music, drama, fine arts, physical education and intramurals, recreation, photography and journalism, industrial arts, business administration, hotel-restaurant management and home economics, and radio and television.

Often, in a number of institutions, certain programs of academic pertinence (such as those in the fields of music, drama, fine arts, intramurals, physical education, etc.) receive funds from the student government and union sources. In some cases such funds are channelled through the union program alone, which includes cultural programs developed and presented by the academic department. Thus the relationship in these cases is one beyond that of common interest and cooperation.

Coordination with Student Organizations

Student organizations and clubs on the college campus usually provide programs for their own memberships. However, through the college union's program of services to all clubs and organizations (services which include work-preparational facilities and space) the programs of student clubs and organizations become naturally interrelated with those of the college union, if only by proximity. This close physical relationship has given emphasis to closer program relationship.

One of the services of the college union staff and the committees is to aid clubs and organizations in the use of the facilities and in developing their own programs within the union. Another chief outreach of the college union is to invite clubs and organizations to participate in appropriate programs which are included in the union program; e.g., an all-campus activity "fair" in which all clubs and organizations display their talents and solicit membership. Another is the coordination of a comprehensive activity, such as a creative arts festival, to which appropriate clubs and departments are invited to contribute programs. Still another is the invitation by the program council of the college union to liaison representatives of clubs and organizations to give advice on or to supervise a given event; e.g., tournaments by the physical education department clubs. In some instances, special areas, such as photography and its supervision and development, may be delegated to specialized clubs which then become part of the college union program council or directorate. This approach ensures the availability of services for specialists, yet it prevents special interests from appropriating facilities or programs which are intended for use on an all-college basis.

Appropriate policy boards governing all student organizations also regulate the all-campus aspect of college union programs and activities.

Every college union program should have a special-projects committee which is constantly searching for new programs, new ways and means of making these programs available to everyone on campus, and ways of capitalizing on the talents on campus. In this way new programs such as coffee houses, computerized dating, and "after events" buffets are developed. When a program takes hold on its own merits, it can become a separate new entity within the college union program framework. Then the special-projects committee can move on to develop other new areas.

Master Calendaring

The complexities involved in coordinating time and space for the many events that are sponsored by a college union are a distinct challenge on all campuses and are best handled by using a "master calendar." This system provides for the listing, after necessary approvals have been obtained, of all events scheduled to take place on campus. Typically included among the prerequisites are student organization approval or committee approval, adviser's signature, and check by staff for adherence to college policy. The event is then listed in the appropriate block of space under time and date, and at the same time an examination for conflicts is made; that is, the calendar is checked to make sure that more than one event has not been scheduled at the same time and place, or that two or more major events are not expected to take place at the same time but in different places.

While the above seems elementary, it nevertheless can become complicated and is a prime means of efficient administration of the master calendar. The campus must develop its own policy concerning how many different events can take place at one time (at the same hour on a given day) and this, of course, relates to the size of the campus, the nature of the events, and any priority given by policy.

Although information on scheduling is generally available to those who need it, many large campuses print calendars that list major activities only. These activities would include formalized programs of such agencies as the college union, student government, fraternities, etc., which are processed for approval and then published. On many campuses, no program events can become official until approvals from the designated staff person or board are obtained and the event is listed on the master calendar.

The benefits of master calendaring are many.

First, in planning for the future, a review of what has been previously scheduled by others will induce (force) some degree of self-regulation and judgment to prevent conflict.

The listing may be used to publish a weekly calendar of events which is in turn a prime means of advertising events and allowing the students and campus to get the most for their money, both in terms of the cost of the program and the educational values therein.

The master calendar set up in a visual-aid form with a card for each day of the year takes relatively little space and creates visual interest, interest in the program, and chiefly the awareness of the need for coordination and planning on the part of all who view it. Placed in a prominent place in the college union it speaks for itself and, by example, teaches an essential lesson in planning.

In addition, the master calendar can provide a "one stop service" which enables planners of events and meetings to obtain all of the related information on place, accommodations, basic equipment, food service, and audiovisual equipment without having to contact several offices on campus.[27]

The union is a natural focal point of calendaring and scheduling and in many instances has become the location of the campuswide master calendar by request of other agencies. Sometimes the calendaring includes scheduling of all space, including classrooms, for extracurricular events on the campus.

SPECIAL SERVICES TO THE COMMUNITY

The usual services of the college union are often taken for granted and their value is not realized by some segments of the college community. Among these services is the dissemination of information; the provision of facilities for rest and relaxation, routine food services, recreational facilities, and facilities for special programs involving music, art exhibits, lectures, and other special events. These usual programs become *special ones to those who do not take advantage* of the services of the college union.

Special Services for the Faculty

Faculty clubs and organizations may schedule the rooms and services of the college union in the same way as students do, thus offering a new dimension to faculty life at the institution as well as providing generally a "faculty club" on a broader base than could ever be realized by charging a faculty fee and building a separate club. The dining facilities of the college union are available to faculty members, thus providing easy, convenient access to food services, a good place to bring one's family to have dinner, and a place to entertain guests or visiting colleagues. Faculty members' academic business can be carried out by scheduling rooms in the union for committee meetings as well as for conferences and institutes which may be sponsored by academic departments.

Other typical services to faculty are family nights, bowling leagues, kitchenettes for wives' clubs and social activities, and catering for social functions. Sometimes hotel rooms for guests and charge accounts are also available.

A great deal of work needs to be done to get faculty to reach out to the students and to participate in informal discussions with them on an everyday basis.

The use of the general building services and a good union program are talking points to prospective faculty members and are viewed as a fringe benefit by most faculty members.

Adult Education Conferences

Many if not most college unions are equipped to handle conferences in great variety by virtue of the fact that they have food services, meeting rooms, and assembly areas. Within a policy that provides for the timing of conferences within the union so as not to infringe upon student and faculty use, the college union serves the college and its departments in the provision of usually excellent facilities for conferences. Often, in turn, adult conferences serve the community and state in a manner not possible without a union. The college community is served at the same time, since the college union has the opportunity to increase its volume of business and its revenue through appropriate charges for the use of facilities. For this latter purpose a good conference program can enable the union to remain solvent while it also adds to the prestige and service role of the university. Use of the conference facilities by students for regional

[27] Susan Daniels and Frank Noffke, "Coordinate Your Activities Program with a Master Calendar," *College and University Business*, October, 1952.

student conferences, which involves students in planning, executing, and serving conferences for others, can be an extremely valuable educational experience.

Hospitality for Visitors

The program and services of the college union very often make the difference between an unsatisfactory impression and an excellent one on visitors to the campus. For example, it is important to have a pleasant, helpful student at the information desk who can speak to the visitor about the college intelligently. The teaching of a genuine concern for visitors to the university brings about helpful attitudes which go beyond mere routine.

The general services available at the union for visitors are virtually the same as for all others. They include information services, lounges, food services, places to meet, and special program features such as art exhibits, recreational services, bowling, billiards, movies, and discussion groups.

A number of unions provide overnight guest rooms which answer the convenience and service needs of visitors to the campus. Hospitality should, of course, be extended to the alumni as well, for they are among the very important visitors to the campus. Services to the alumni may include, for example, assistance to the alumni association on special alumni days.

Chief among the visitors are prospective students and their parents. Each college interested in putting its best foot forward for this all-important group should leave no stone unturned to train its personnel to extend a welcome. It should develop its services at the information desk and in the focal lounges of the college. Whenever possible, tours of the building and, on occasion, of the campus should be available.

Use of the Union by the Local Community

The concept that the college union is the college community center implies a building that is only for the use of persons and groups directly related to the college—except on occasions when others (e.g., members of the local community) are especially invited to a college event or, as in some cases, when the union has a membership plan under which a resident of the community may become eligible to use the college union by paying membership dues. Difficulty arises in opening the union to the community when:

1. Teenagers and other younger people attempt to make the union their hangout, arousing student antagonism.

2. The union opens the doors of its revenue-producing facilities to all. Some consider this to be unfair competition because of the tax-exempt status of the institution in comparison to businesses in the community. Relations with town merchants may be seriously impaired, and lawsuits have occurred in some cases.

3. Vandalism by younger groups is likely.

4. The building can be overused by outside groups, to the detriment of student-faculty use of the building.

Yet, the college does not want to build a wall around the campus. Therefore, in the interest of good town-and-gown relationships, the college can rightly allow certain functions sponsored by town organizations to take place in the union, or, on occasion, it may invite the public to a college or union event such as a concert, festival, art exhibition, or open house. It is important that clear-cut policies for the regulation of use of the union be drawn up and publicly announced. A method should also be established for clearing the use of the college union by community groups. This should not be done through the union itself, but through another college agency that can evaluate officially for the college the appropriateness of the request in the context of the college's general town-gown policy.

PROGRAM OUTREACH

The college union program is not necessarily limited to the walls of the college union building. In fact, the very nature of the union's unifying purpose often requires that the union reach outside its physical premises to the total campus community, making use of college facilities in whatever way it can to best serve the college community. There need be no limits on such activities as long as the college union is not usurping or duplicating the programs and services of others and as long as its expenditures remain within its means. A good union program taken to a larger lecture or concert hall than that in the union is entirely appropriate. Some college union special events for the entire campus may take place in the gymnasium, stadium, or large auditorium, or union-sponsored discussions may be held in residence halls or fraternities. In other words, the program can go where it best serves the campus community.

Branch Facilities

Perhaps the best example of program outreach is the establishment of branches or "satellites" of the college union in those parts of very large campuses where students congregate when they do not have time, especially between classes or at lunchtime, to get to the union. The emphasis usually is on such conveniences as food service and lounges, but offerings may also extend to recreation, supplemental art exhibits, and certain program services. In many cases the setting up of a branch is preceded by the establishment of a small snack bar or the development of a noon-hour program where students congregate, particularly when the union is of moderate size. To repeat here what might be done would simply duplicate early portions of this chapter. The preceding material can be drawn upon for ready adaptation to a branch program.

Outdoor Program

In warmer climates, and during warm months of the year in cold climates, many programs can and should be taken out of doors. Such programs may include rallies and festivals, square dancing, the sale of tickets, sidewalk art exhibits and the sale of art works, soap-box discussions, picnics, and sometimes movies and concerts. This again, in other words, is taking the services and programs to the places where students are. With higher education always in the position of having to make more efficient use of its limited funds, innovations are always in order. A little thought can produce many benefits in this direction.

The great caution in program outreach is to avoid contradicting the unifying purpose of the college union by segmenting the campus and isolating groups from the main focal center of student life. This could be an inadvertent result of decentralizing the union's services.

Besides the outdoor areas of the campus itself, the union can go still further afield. In our greatly urbanized society and even in suburban or semirural areas, people tend to ignore, for the most part, the great out-of-doors and the values of "returning to nature." College union outdoor programs have the value of drawing upon untapped and undiscovered areas of educational value by developing the following:

1. A council of clubs, groups, and organizations dedicated to outdoor programs.
2. Programs for the entire college that provide for the use of off-campus facilities (a number of colleges have recreation areas within easy driving distance of the campus) and recreational opportunities such as riding, skiing, rock climbing, biking, swimming, camping, fishing, sailing, surfing, and discovering nature in all its forms.
3. Outdoor physical recreation and games such as volleyball, soccer, horseshoes, chip-putt golf, badminton, and square dancing.
4. Creation of an outdoor sports headquarters as the planning center and assembly point for these activities—including facilities for storing and renting bikes, skis, camping gear, and picnic and game equipment.

These untapped resources are a source of low-cost activity of largely undiscovered value on almost every college campus in the country.

Our current generation's reassessment of values, with its strong indication of the desire to "re-create" in the out-of-doors as indicated by the overcrowding of our national parks and the drive to conserve our natural resources, is also an indication that use of the untapped sources should be begun earlier in the serious planning of union programmers.

A discussion of how to proceed may be found in the excellent monograph by Ted Crabb[28] which spells out in detail the ways and means of developing the outdoor program.

EVALUATING EXISTING PROGRAMS

How does a union decide what programs are worth doing, or still worth doing? Evaluation of college union programs may take place in the following ways:

1. A general image evaluation. What people in general think and feel—the impression they get about the program. While this is general and not reliable enough, it is nevertheless a factor to be dealt with in making evaluations.

2. Committee evaluation of the union's programs through evaluation by questionnaire and through discussion sessions.

3. Participants' and spectators' evaluation by means of questionnaire.

4. Academic evaluation. Through questionnaire and discussion one can learn what academic departments feel about the educational relatedness of programs of the college union.

5. Evaluation by advising and operating staff should take place in almost every meeting throughout the year, but a special year-end evaluation program should be held.

6. Use of the brainstorming discussion and group-dynamics techniques involved in "Subjective Analysis of Needs in Campus Life"[29] by the author.

Content of evaluation instruments and agenda for discussion are readily devised through use of material contained in earlier portions of this chapter ("The Core Program"). An important element of evaluation is establishing the work-load assignment for staff and the time required for these assignments as an integral part of the philosophy of operation and administration. See also the work of Wolf and Berry, cited earlier.

EDUCATION AND TRAINING OF STAFF

The greatest need in all college union programs and operations is the development of qualified, well-trained staff. This should begin at the level where student assistant programs and committee programs are the common meeting ground of those interested in the college union field. Attention should be given to this need along with everyday operation, for college unions and their programs are expanding rapidly and, like other agencies of higher education, they need vastly increased numbers of qualified personnel.

Once students are interested, a bona fide, reliable program of education in the college union profession is required. Reference is made to the *Guidelines for a Master's Degree in Program and College Union Administration*.[30] The many pamphlets and

[28] Theodore Crabb, *The College Union Outdoors*, Association of College Unions–International, Palo Alto, Calif.

[29] Noffke, "Subjective Analysis of Need for a College Union," *op. cit.*

[30] Professional Development Committee, *Guidelines for a Master's Degree Program in Program and College Union Administration*, Association of College Unions–International, Palo Alto, Calif.

training and informational aids developed by the Association of College Unions are available by writing to the Executive Secretary, Association of College Unions–International, Box 7286, Stanford, California. In-depth and in-breadth development of college union professional staff within the general framework of student personnel work can be achieved by way of programs set forth in *Professional Preparation in Student Personnel Work.*[31]

Programs for master's degrees in the college union field at the time of this writing are available at New York University, Oregon State University, and the University of Iowa. Week-long summer courses have been held in recent years at the state universities of Minnesota, Wisconsin, Oklahoma, Florida, and Texas.

Additional programs in student personnel work exist at many universities and colleges throughout the country. For a list of these write to Executive Secretary, Council of Student Personnel Associations, International Inn, Suite 412, 5440 Cass Avenue, Detroit, Michigan 48202.

The many materials in management publications, textbooks, and journals as well as in textbooks on institutional management, counseling, guidance, and student personnel work provide the ready means of establishing workshops and training programs within one's own organization to achieve the purpose of training the incumbent staff.

THE ASSOCIATION OF COLLEGE UNIONS–INTERNATIONAL

Special reference is made to the Association of College Unions[32] here in order that college administrators may recognize that the "place to start" with any problem involving the college union, particularly in its developing ramifications, should be contact with the consultants of the Association of College Unions and reference to its literature. Information about the association and its services can be obtained by writing to the Executive Secretary, Association of College Unions–International, Box 7286, Stanford, California.

PLANNING THE PROGRAM AND COLLEGE UNION FACILITIES

By and large, the end result of the program is shaped considerably by the facilities with which union committees and staff members work. Therefore, the currently available program is made possible through the physical planning which has previously been done, but it is also shaped by the limitations of the physical plant. Plans for a program should, therefore, precede the planning of a college union building. The desired program should, at least, be planned to be flexible and adaptable. Programs can be planned well through the techniques indicated earlier in this chapter ("The Core Program," "Evaluating Existing Programs") and in the chapter called "College Unions—Facilities and Administration," by Porter Butts, in this handbook.

As a broad principle, the actual program of the college union is either begun or enhanced when the representative planning committee is formed. This is the point at which a program really begins, since the primary purpose of the college union is to provide for a program. This is accomplished when a representative group's deliberations on the common problems of the college or university begin seriously.

[31] Professional Development Commission, *Professional Preparation for Student Personnel Work,* Council of Student Personnel Associations, 5440 Cass Avenue, Detroit, Mich.

[32] Ernest Christensen, *Annotated Bibliography of the College Union,* Association of College Unions–International, Palo Alto, Calif., 1967.

THE ROLE OF THE ADVISER

The key to a good college union program is the presence and activity of qualified, professional program advisers. While the program is student-administered, the brief term of office of students requires the continuity of staff in order that proven programs may continue to benefit the entire student body. The role of the professional staff member is one of helping students in the best sense of helping; i.e., helping them to develop and execute their own programs, staying out of the way when this is advisable, but subtly stepping in and providing guidance when it is required. The adviser must give advice that will be received most of the time, yet must do so in such a way that student leaders will continue to accept him. The activities and union adviser is especially valuable in view of the upsurge of students' desires for greater responsibility and participation in our society, since the adviser is on the front line with students every day, where staff influence counts most.

Deans sometimes feel that college union and activities staff are closer to more students than many deans. This feeling is becoming more pronounced because students are asking for a direct voice in all the college's affairs; and they are asking that student activities and college union programs be made more important and relevant, aiding in the creation of desirable changes in the college and society.

BIBLIOGRAPHY

Berry, Chester A.: *Planning a College Union Building,* Association of College Unions–International, Palo Alto, Calif., 1965.

Bulletin of Association of College Unions–International.

Butts, Porter: *Planning College Union Facilities for Multiple Use,* Association of College Unions–International, Palo Alto, 1966.

———: *Standards for Professional Staff Preparation and Compensation in College Union Work,* Association of College Unions–International, Palo Alto, Calif., 1967.

———: *State of the College Union Around the World,* Association of College Unions–International, Palo Alto, Calif., 1967.

Catalog of the Association's 50th anniversary art exhibition, Association of College Unions–International.

Christensen, Ernest: *Annotated Bibliography of the College Union,* Association of College Unions–International, Palo Alto, Calif., 1967.

College and University Business (magazine).

"College Unions at Work," series of monographs published by the Association of College Unions–International, Palo Alto, Calif., including:

Bell, Boris: *Administration and Operation of the College Union.*

Crabb, Theodore: *The College Union Outdoors.*

Moore, Norman: *Art in the Union.*

Noffke, Frank: *Planning for a College Union.*

Osterheld, Douglas C.: *Food Service and the College Union.*

Stevens, George K.: *The Union Recreation Games Area.*

College Unions—Fifty Facts, Association of College Unions–International, Palo Alto, Calif.

Papers from the Wisconsin Union Summer Course in College Union Operations, Madison, Wis., 1962.

Chapter **2**

College Unions — Facilities and Administration

PORTER BUTTS

Director of The Wisconsin Union and Professor of Social Education, University of Wisconsin, Madison, Wisconsin

INTRODUCTION [1]

The development of college and university union buildings, or campus "community centers," has reached the point where almost every institution of higher education has a union or is planning to have one.

Where it once waited on gifts, the union now assumes a high priority in the campus plan. Almost all colleges, small as well as large, recognize that where young people are gathered together away from home, a center and program for their out-of-class life are needed if the college is to fulfill the needs of living along with learning—that the union is as normal and necessary a part of the college equipment as a gymnasium, residence halls, or even a library.

Accepted methods of borrowing have made union construction possible for even the smaller and newer institutions. Borrowing in the commercial financing market, usually by way of revenue bond issues, has been common since World War II, though this has been more characteristic of public than of private institutions, which do not have the benefit of the low interest rates of tax-exempt obligations. Private institutions have had to rely much more upon gifts and general college building funds—and currently upon the federal college housing loan program.

Since the 1955 amendment to the Federal Housing Act, federal loans at low interest rates for terms up to 40 years have given a great impetus to the whole union development. More than four hundred unions, or additions to unions, have been financed in part by funds loaned through the Department of Housing and Urban Development, and there has never been a default on principal or interest.

In recent years state legislatures have played an increasingly prominent part in establishing unions at public institutions—by direct appropriation, by matching grants, by purchasing sites, and by specific legislation facilitating borrowing. In a survey by the U.S. Office of Education, state institutions planning unions for the period 1965 to 1970 reported that they expected 29 percent of the funds to come from state appropriations.

There were, in 1968, approximately nine hundred unions in operation or in the active planning stage. And an estimated eight- to nine-hundred additional institutions, at least, are potential builders of new unions in the near future, not counting the rapidly proliferating two-year colleges.

THE NATURE OF THE UNION

A college union performs a combined educational and service function that is unique. It usually implies, therefore, not only a building but also an organization to govern and operate it, with a series of committees and a professional operating staff which together plan and present extensive services and a social-cultural-recreational program designed to meet the needs of students, faculty, alumni, and college guests in their life together on the campus. From the point of view of many college administrations, the union represents a conscious effort to deal educationally with the broad area of time outside the classroom and to add, thus, a new dimension to education.

The more specific and generally accepted aims of the union, as set forth by the Association of College Unions–International, are to provide a common meeting place for informal association outside the classroom; to furnish the services and conveniences students and faculty need daily; to provide a general cultural, social, and recreational program which enriches the educational experience of students; to serve as a laboratory for training students in social responsibilities and leadership by enlisting students in the planning and direction of community services and programs; and to serve as a unifying force in the life of the college.

[1] Much of the material of this chapter is drawn from the surveys and publications of the Association of College Unions–International. The author is editor of publications for the Association.

The union, as a campus community center serving diverse needs, embraces a wide range of facilities and has multiple functions to perform. The Association of College Unions delineates these facilities and functions in this way:

> It is a lounge, dining room, information center, student club headquarters, reading room, art gallery, workshop, theater, music room, forum, game room, dance and party center, public relations agency, student office building, outing center, ticket bureau, post office, conference headquarters, and book store. It may provide all of these facilities, or part of them, or perhaps still others—but all brought together under one roof so that physical proximity does its part in furthering a sense of community.
>
> Further, it is an active encourager of student management and self-expression; caterer to the campus at large, housing the bulk of its meetings and serving its dinners; advisor to student committees; trouble shooter in certain problems of student personnel; teacher of the arts of leisure and recreation. It concerns itself with the whole area of student life and interests outside the classroom. It is, or can be, the social-cultural heart of the campus.
>
> The days when the union was merely "a place to meet," or an incidental supplement to housing—a kind of service station, filling accidental gaps in the provisions for out-of-class needs—are long since gone. The union has become on many campuses a community center of the first order, with an identity and meaning of its own.

THE PLANNING OF UNION BUILDINGS

General guidelines for the planning of a new union, or an addition to an existing union, are available to the college or university administrator in the association's 1967 reference manual, *Planning and Operating College Union Buildings.* Key considerations especially worth noting are outlined below.

A Suggested Procedure

The planning of a union is now regarded neither as a matter of roofing over a set of miscellaneous, unrelated facilities nor the opposite: erecting a certain kind of physical structure with pre-determined standard elements (as with a dormitory or gymnasium). The planning of a union, in the best sense, means arriving at a comprehensive, well-considered plan for the community life of the college. The most successful unions are those that have developed as general campus community centers.

Under this approach the union becomes, fundamentally, an expression of the needs of the people of the college at leisure. Whatever interests them, whatever is important to them outside their working time becomes interesting and important also at the center of their campus life we call the union.

If a union is to respond effectively to the wide range of needs and interests of a college population at leisure, if it is to become genuinely a community center—the social and cultural heart of the campus—it will draw together in one place those facilities and activities which will give everyone in the college family—students, faculty, staff, alumni, and their guests—reasons for coming to the center.

It will provide first for the things that human beings do in their more elemental daily activity: places and means for meeting friends, for conversation, for lounging, for reading the newspapers, for dining and refreshment. In addition, and for young men and women especially, it will provide for dating and social occasions, and for active games. It will provide rooms and equipment that will incite activity and encourage the congeniality and friendships that come from working together on common projects. And finally, it will offer facilities that will introduce students to the enduring satisfactions of the arts, books, hobbies, and generally the productive use of leisure.

Provisions for personal, for dining, and for social needs will heavily populate the union. The presence and the message of the arts will add grace and purpose to social activity. Coming to the union for one activity, students will be exposed to, and perhaps inspired by, another activity. Cultural interests, community activity, and daily living thus may blend into truly an art of living, one and indivisible.

From this it follows that the known unmet social, dining, and cultural needs of the college population should be arranged for, wherever possible, in a new or expanded union; further, that the college should provide there the means of cultivating new, worthy interests that may not at the moment be in demand locally but which, upon trial, have had strong appeal to other young people and which have inherent recreational or cultural value.

It follows, also, that some realignment of campus facilities and of plans for the future may be necessary so that there will not be missing at the union an element essential to its functioning as a true center of campus life or a facility important as a matter of sheer convenience to the student-faculty body. The college will be richly repaid if with the creation of a new union, or the expansion of an old one, the over-all design for campus living is made right, even though this involves some readjustments and shifts of existing facilities and plans.

Certainly it is a mistake in planning if the union is treated, as it still is on some campuses, merely as a catch-all for just miscellaneous college needs, without regard to their appropriateness in the union or without regard to implanting in the union the core of activity essential to a good campus center.

It is probably correct to say that inadequate or misguided architectural planning has cost colleges collectively, in both construction and operating expense, millions of dollars.

What can be done to get better results?

First of all, the college would do well to start with a careful study of its own needs and a formulation of a guiding philosophy and program of what it wants the union to do for its campus, rather than looking for pat answers in other union plans. A thorough-going survey of the local campus situation and careful sampling of large numbers of students to learn their facility preferences will be useful, almost indispensable.

How many students are housed in organized houses and have a social life—and dining rooms—of their own? What are the distinguishing local student social and recreational customs? What do students want that they haven't already got? What else does the campus or town offer recreationally? What facilities should be logically shifted to the union to make it complete? What objectives in informal student education is the union expected to accomplish?

How will each campus organization make use of the new center and how often? Will townspeople and conference groups use it? How many students live at home or at a distance from the campus? How many commute and need a parking place? Future enrollment prospects? Ratio of men to women? What are the college plans for future dormitories and dining halls? Theater? Conference center? And many other similar factors, which the architects will want to know about and out of all of which the desirable nature of the union will emerge.

There is value, of course, in learning what other unions are like and what facilities and programs are popular and profitable. There is danger in assuming that all relevant and necessary information is present on the campus and in the faculty. Simply assigning the union to the architect or to one college office to plan is even more dangerous. So, to gain perspective and not miss any good bets, it is highly useful to have a planning committee which brings together as much union information as possible, through visits to representative unions and through the aid of the publications of the Association of College Unions—providing such information is intelligently sifted and applied to the local circumstances. And it is important to combine all the findings and recommendations in a detailed and specific "building program"—a comprehensive written statement of purposes, functions, areas, and estimated costs—which ultimately receives the final approval of the college administration and trustees.

Then comes the stage of active architectural planning, not before.[2]

[2] For a further discussion of union planning approaches see *Planning for a College Union* by Frank Noffke. Association of College Unions–International, Palo Alto, Calif., 1965.

Commonly Adopted Facilities

While any union, in the end, should be the outcome of a careful identification of local needs and should be tailor-made for a given campus, it is useful to know what facilities are most commonly adopted. Such a listing provides a kind of core building program that can serve as a reference point.

In the latest nationwide survey conducted by the Association of College Unions (in 1963),[3] the following facilities appeared in more than 50 percent of existing unions at institutions large and small, public and private, liberal arts and professional, urban and nonurban:

Facility	*Percent of existing unions providing facility*
Offices for student organizations	95
Committee rooms	91
Snack bar	89
Information desk	87
Cafeteria	84
Television area	83
General lounge	82
Table tennis	82
Meeting rooms	79
Billiards	79
Ballroom	72
Music listening room	70
Coat room	67
Parking adjacent to union	61
Poster-making room	59
Bookstore	59
Card-playing area	57
Private dining rooms	56
Ticket selling office	52
Art gallery	50

Some Planning Principles

While it is never possible to prescribe solutions closely and wisely without a study of the variant local conditions, a few typical principles and cautions (there are many others) may at least be suggestive of the nature of the union planning problem:

1. In selecting the site and planning the building, start with the assumption of growth. Most unions are not nearly large enough. Many have built two or three additions; some are now two to five times as large as when they first opened.

2. Union building development, more often than not, has been a development in stages—mainly because of initial fund limitations, though sometimes because of doubt concerning the size or need for one or more units until other campus developments take place, or because it is uneconomical to operate and maintain a plant designed for, say, a future 8,000 enrollment during the interim when there are only 5,000 students.

Obviously, when several units of a building can be constructed at one time, there are substantial savings in cost, as compared to building the same units in stages. If the needs are clear and the initial funds sufficient, erecting the entire structure at once is sometimes the wisest course (although such construction savings may be largely offset, or more than offset, by the greater expense of amortizing, operating, and maintaining the larger plant until enrollment expands and the building is more fully utilized and thus more fully supported by the income generated by such increased use).

[3] Boris Bell, *Administration and Operation of College Unions,* Association of College Unions–International, Palo Alto, Calif., 1965.

But by and large construction in stages has seemed the more feasible and practical course.

Even though funds become available for what is presumed to be a complete center, the possibilities of expansion should be considered basic in union planning. No one has the last word on what the college or university may want the union to be and do fifteen or even five years from now.

An important lesson from the universal experience of existing unions is that these centers need to grow to meet unanticipated uses and demands. A building design that is final and cannot readily be added to later is not right.

As every experienced building operator knows, the original building investment has a way of preempting the available fund resources of a union. The amortization of debt is a first lien on all operating receipts. The costs of utilities, housekeeping, repairs, and replacements are inescapable. The larger the physical plant, the larger these costs.

What so often happens is that these necessities rapidly use up the union's financial substance and there isn't much left, at least not enough, for a good program and an adequate staff. The administration is hard put, in the face of the inexorable limits of college budgets and student pocketbooks, to cure the situation by increasing the union's share of the general student fee, cutting back custodial costs, or increasing prices to the student customer. And so the program and the services the building was built for languish. And this applies to the affluent institution which had ample funds for construction as well as to the others.

The most important thing about a union, by far, is not the building but the program within it and the adequacy of the staff, in numbers (and of course calibre), to develop a program of worth and to respond to the needs of the building users.

So any means that can be devised, by way of prudent phasing of construction or feasible contraction of nonvital space, that conserve funds for program and staffing are of the utmost significance. Else the building, no matter how ample, may substantially fail in its purpose.

3. As a major means of saving space and cost, study each facility with a view to its possibilities for multiple uses, and where multiple uses are genuinely feasible, provide the basic design and accessory space and equipment that will make the facility work for the purpose intended. Do not assume, however, that *all* rooms can serve multiple purposes; there are many instances where multiple use does not work.[4]

4. Take into account the fact that peak loads are characteristic of college dining and union social occasions. Arrange and relate facilities so that a given facility can be readily expanded for peak loads or contracted for normal use.

5. Do not overlook the importance of providing adequately for the following:

Parking (a union isolated from auto access and parking suffers critically, both financially and socially, from loss of use).

Snack bar (considered by students the most essential single facility to have in a union; more important as a casual drop-in and lounging center to students than a regular lounge; usually much too small).

Rooms for small parties (there is usually much more demand for these than for a large ballroom).

Facilities for adult conferences and short courses (most unions serve as conference centers).

6. Consider fully that a union is no longer merely a place to eat and meet, but has to do broadly with the constructive employment of student time outside the classroom; that it represents an experience in a way of living. Hence, consider facilities for cultural and creative pursuits (theater or auditorium, music rooms, library, art display

[4] For an extensive treatment of multi-use possibilities see *Planning College Union Facilities for Multiple Use*, by Porter Butts, Association of College Unions–International, Palo Alto, Calif., 1966.

space), for hobbies and crafts, for motion pictures, and for outdoor activity (outing headquarters and program) as well as for social and dining activity.

7. Consider with special care whether or not it is advantageous locally to include these facilities:

Bookstore
Faculty lounges or club quarters
Swimming pool
Offices for college administrative officers (other than union) or for alumni and religious organizations
Staff apartment
Merchandise shops
Hotel unit
Separate lounges for men and women
Beauty shop, barber shop
Chapel
Health clinic
Ballroom for large dances

These are facilities about which there is widely varying opinion. On some campuses separate lounges, nonunion offices, quarters exclusively for faculty, beauty shops, chapel, alumni offices, and staff apartments have been abandoned or have met with doubtful success. Some believe certain facilities in the above list (i.e., chapel, health clinic, merchandise shops, even bookstore) have a doubtful relation to the central purposes of a union. And currently there is a fairly universal downtrend in interest in large all-campus dances. On the other hand, compelling local circumstances sometimes provide special justification for the inclusion of certain of the facilities in question.

8. Observe the natural flow of traffic on the campus; choose a location and include in the building those services and facilities that give students reason to use it almost daily—if you would have a *social* center.

9. Remember that students are rarely interested in just a place to sit down. Plan rooms and lounges in which students can do something—listen to music, read, debate, play games, make things, produce shows, view art works, plan activity.

10. Plan, at least broadly, the nature and number of building staff members and employees before going too far, and then make provisions for offices and employee quarters accordingly. Employ the union director *before* the building is built so that he can assist in the planning, help ensure that operating requirements are met, understand fully himself how the plant is to work, and assemble and train an operating staff before the building opens.[5]

GENERAL ORGANIZATION OF A UNION AND ITS ACTIVITIES

Boards and Committees

The prevalent practice in organizing a union (75 percent of the cases) is to establish, under authority of the college trustees or regents, a general union governing board comprising representatives of the typical college groups which use the union, pay for a large part of its operating cost through membership fees or payments for services, and in some cases subscribe funds to construct the building.

[5] For other planning guides and cautions, see Porter Butts, *Planning and Operating College Union Buildings*, Association of College Unions–International, Palo Alto, Calif., 1967; and Frank Noffke, *op. cit.*

These component groups of the college community are students, faculty, and alumni. Their representatives are chosen variously by the appointment or elective method or by a combination of the two, according to local institutional practice.

Faculty members are usually appointed by the college president; alumni members are appointed by the president or alumni association; and students are either elected by the student body, appointed by the outgoing union governing board on the basis of previous service or special merit, or they may serve ex officio because they are officers of the general student body. In the case of students the selection pattern sometimes combines two or all three of the methods mentioned. Appointment or "selection," based upon the merit of candidates who have served apprenticeship on union committees, is the predominant method (rather than campuswide election). Selection is considered more likely to ensure the presence of students better qualified to carry out the rather specialized administrative responsibilities expected of them; it removes essential social and cultural programming for the campus from the arena of personal popularity contests or irrelevant contests between campus political parties.

The college administration, the union staff, and/or the dean of students' office are often represented on the governing board by certain staff members ex officio.

This general governing board ordinarily has broad *policy-making* functions (i.e., policies regarding building use, space allocation, services to be offered, approval of student committee appointments and program budgets). It is directly responsible for the policies under which the union functions, but it reports to the college administration and trustees, who are ultimately responsible.

Whatever the composition of the policy board, it is essential that its authority be real, reasonably complete, and spelled out, or what one is likely to have is the window dressing of self-government and not the real article.

There is a second board comprised entirely or largely of students which has the functions of *program* planning and *program* administration. These students are usually chosen (87 percent of the cases) on the basis of past union service and special interest and aptitude in one or more areas of union programming. This board made up primarily of students heads up and coordinates a series of student union committees (4 to 25 committees with a total of from 50 to 700 members) which have day-to-day responsibility for planning and presenting social and cultural programs (dance, discussion, music, art, games, hospitality, films, outings, crafts, etc.).

Members of the union staff usually work with such committees and the student program board in an advisory capacity, providing continuity, furnishing useful information, coordinating plans with college policies, counseling students in the performance of their duties, and helping to organize leadership training programs.

The Staffing of a Union

There are—as in the conduct of the college as a whole—two staff functions to be performed in every union large or small, each paralleling and supplementing the other and both under one directing and coordinating head: (1) the *educational function*, which includes the direction of a recreation program for the campus and the counseling (even organized instruction) of students—individuals and groups—in social, educational, and recreational fields; and (2) the *business and administrative function* of operating the building plant and its varied services.

In practice (especially in small buildings), both educational and administrative functions are often discharged by the same personnel. It should be noted that where these dual responsibilities are assumed in large measure by the same person, it is often at the expense of one function or the other. Most unions, regardless of size, have need for two types of personnel, each especially qualified and free (under the coordinating direction of the union director) to concentrate his efforts in either the educational or the management fields respectively.

A clue to the relative sufficiency of the union staff at a given college will be given by an examination of the number of staff members appointed to care for the physical health and physical recreation and sports program of a student body in comparison to the number appointed at the union to care for the social health and social-cultural recreation program of the same students.

One important practical consideration often overlooked in staffing a union is that union buildings normally operate seven days a week, including holidays, from early morning to late evening—in other words, two eight-hour work days each day of the week. The requirements for staff supervision during a sixteen-hour day and a seven-day week appropriately should lead to an increase in the number of supervisory positions in a union over those provided for the normal eight-hour, five- or five-and-a-half-day operation of other college departments. Otherwise injury will either be done to the program or to the staff members who are given supervisory and administrative responsibility during these long hours.

All members of the union staff should have a conception of a community center's place and purpose in the college educational scheme, a sympathetic comprehension of the recreation needs of students, and an interest in making a student's experience within the union of educative and self-developmental value.[6]

Centralization of Management

Emphasis is placed by the Association of College Unions upon the desirability and importance of having a single directing and coordinating head of the union plant and its departmental operations.

In an association survey among 200 unions on this particular subject, two-thirds of the institutions reporting reported single, centralized management of the union, with the most popular chain of command being from trustees to the college president and business manager to a general union governing board to the union director to the various operating departments of the union building. Of the unions reporting divided management (i.e., food service at the union under the management of a separate general campus food department, or social program under the direction of a dean's office), only a few believe in and advocate this separation of authority.

(It should be noted that centralized management does not result merely from the preference of a union director; it has necessarily been the outcome of the combined policy decisions of business officers, presidents, and trustees.)

The bookstore presents a special situation, partly because only about 60 percent of all unions include bookstores—in contrast to food services, social-cultural programs, and housekeeping and building maintenance, which are universally necessary accompaniments of union operation. When the store is in the union, there is widely divided opinion regarding who should manage it. In practice the union is responsible for management in only 29 percent of the cases. Much more commonly the space is leased, either to a private operator (6 percent) or to a store organization which reports to the college business office.

The prevalent view, favoring total and centralized management by a union staff, except for the bookstore, is related by the Association of College Unions' reference manual[7] as follows:

> The various operating departments of a union building need to be on the basis of a "combined operation" every day, with a single unified command. The management and the educational and social functions of a union are interlocked at every point.

[6] For a further discussion of union staffing questions see Porter Butts, *Planning and Operating College Union Buildings* and *Standards for Professional Staff Preparation and Compensation in College Union Work,* Association of College Unions–International, Palo Alto, Calif., 1967.

[7] Porter Butts, *Planning and Operating College Union Buildings, op. cit.*

A single command, in principle, is as necessary here as in an armed forces operation. Otherwise, there is divided responsibility for results, with alibis and buck-passing; less flexible and efficient use of employee manpower and of building facilities; difficulties in scheduling multiple-purpose rooms; a slow-down in making plans and decisions; variant standards in performance and maintenance; inability to take care of complaints effectively; danger of conflicting loyalties among employee groups; dissatisfaction on the part of all the various responsible operating heads.

On the positive side, a single director of over-all operations is able to muster *all* resources and services of a union toward the achievement of a goal, and students and faculty have the opportunity, through their governing board, of affecting all, not just part, of the policies and program of the building.

GENERAL RELATIONSHIPS TO OTHER COLLEGE AGENCIES

It is noteworthy that in its relationships to the college administration, student government, and other campus agencies, the union in the United States, as compared to unions in the rest of the world, is, with few exceptions, unique. It is almost universal in other countries, again with a few exceptions, that unions operate or attempt to operate quite independently of their colleges. Indeed, the student union (often a strictly student organization which controls, among many other things, union building facilities) usually is, primarily (except in the Anglo-American and some Scandinavian countries), a general student government body or other student group which is highly politicized and deeply involved in partisan political or social action on many fronts, often at a national level.[8]

Relation of the Union to the College

But in the United States in only a very few instances is there no official legal or organizational relationship between the union and the college. The few cases in the United States are those unions which were begun by alumni associations or the Associated Students (as on the West Coast) almost independently of any responsibility on the part of their colleges and which operate under alumni corporations or independent student associations; in these instances the title to the union building and land rests with the alumni corporation or the student association and the college has little or no jurisdiction. This situation has been rapidly changing to one of full college jurisdiction as the complications of maintaining tax exemption, legally assessing a compulsory student operating fee, and financing bond issues or loans for construction under non-college ownership have become apparent.

A number of unions operate primarily as business enterprises or service agencies without educational purposes or results, functioning more nearly like hotels or clubs than college unions as now generally conceived. The proportion of unions without educational program goals, however, has decreased sharply in recent years.

For the most part, unions have been established as departments or divisions of the college, coordinate with other student welfare and service departments and report to the president or to his representative (as, for example, to the business manager in business matters).

Though there are some discrepant points of view and some discrepant cases, the trend is toward greater recognition of the educational potentialities of the union and consequently toward closer relationships of the union to the college's educational organization and program.

[8] An extensive discussion of union relationships with the administrative offices and student governments of their institutions, in 60 countries, is given in Porter Butts, *State of the College Union Around the World,* Association of College Unions–International, Palo Alto, Calif., 1967.

Comparatively few colleges have explicit organizational relationships for the professional working together of union officers and other staff members of the college beyond the administrative line responsibility of the union staff to the president or his representative. Most prefer as a general policy, others as an occasional arrangement, interdepartmental planning on a consultative basis without organizational provisions of a prescribed nature.

Relations with Academic Departments

The general educational aims of the union, as previously described, are to prepare students for leisure as well as for work, to make the recreation of students and the campus environment cooperative factors with study in student education, and to assist in achieving the college goal of preparing students for constructive leadership and community responsibilities. These aims have grown out of the widely held view of educators that what the college does educationally in the hours outside the classroom is of major importance.

The programs and services which the union staff supervises and for which it trains student volunteer leadership are related to many departments. Community social and cultural life, the concern of the union, at once touches several other corollary subject-matter fields (group work, recreation leadership, education, journalism, English literature, art, drama, music, etc.) necessitating a complex of cooperative teaching and service arrangements.

In some cases the union cosponsors a program with another department (i.e., a concert with the music department or a creative-writing contest with the English department). In some cases a departmental faculty member serves as adviser to a union student committee (i.e., an art department faculty member may serve as adviser to the union art exhibition committee). In other cases a faculty member is asked to lead or teach a student group in the union (i.e., square dancing or craft class). And in still other cases the union staff member is appointed by another department to conduct the laboratory section of a credit class or to supervise thesis studies (i.e., in such fields as institutional management, group leadership, recreation field work, or student activity counseling).

An eminently useful relationship is one of *joint* enterprise. When the union has a competent staff, teaching departments are often glad to have access to the special talents of such staff and the sometimes unparalleled laboratory facilities of the union building. They may even pay for the union staff service, through the standard device of a joint appointment and shared salary.

Whatever the union does in its arrangements with academic departments, it is well advised to consult closely with those that have a professional and vested interest in music, art, drama, literature, debate, and sports so that the union program in these areas proceeds with the benefit of agreeable working understandings and the guidance these departments can give. And there are rich rewards—for the union in enhancing its acceptance and prestige in the academic community and for the department in obtaining a wider audience—in the joint sponsorship of programs of mutual interest.

Relation to Student Affairs Agencies

Some unions render direct counseling services to other student organizations. Some conduct personnel recruiting, guidance, and referral services for student activity organizations generally. Some serve as the central agency for reservations of all campus building halls for noninstructional purposes and prepare the all-college calendar of events for clearance by a college student affairs committee. On a number of campuses union staff members are participant members of student personnel councils; some are members of the staff of the student personnel division.

The assumption is sometimes made that because the union involves students outside the classroom it is ipso facto part of the student personnel program and belongs in the student personnel organizational structure, and hence that it should therefore be under the direction of the dean of student affairs.

This view tends to overlook the fact that the union also has extensive responsibilities to faculty, alumni, conference groups (83 percent of all unions serve adult education conferences), teaching departments, and many others, not to mention heavy financial responsibilities that belong under the supervision of the business manager. And especially it overlooks the merits of *self*-direction on the part of the student, faculty, and alumni members and users of the union.

There is usually no college office which includes an official concern with *all* the groups and interests with which the union deals except the president's office; hence it is desirable to have a union governing board which represents all interests, with line responsibility to the president's office and on to the trustees, as outlined in the foregoing sections of this chapter.

At the same time there is a trend toward greater coordination with student welfare and personnel services through periodic joint conferences, the adoption of common procedures and policies, reports by the union director to a vice-president or dean in general charge of student affairs, and sometimes interlocking board and committee personnel (for example, appointment of the dean of student affairs to the union governing board, and of the union director to the general student affairs committee or a campus recreation planning council).

Relation to Residence Halls

Both the union and the residence halls are concerned with student living needs—the hall with the student's "home" life, the union with his "neighborhood" life. Together they can form a close working partnership in which each strengthens the other, with union services flowing toward the halls and dormitory traffic flowing toward the union. Some have arranged it so that there is a union representative in each house unit who tells the story of coming union events to the house and tells the union what the house wants. The union at times takes its discussion leaders to the house, loans its pictures and records, or outfits the house for a ski or bike trip. In such ways the partners help each other; student life both at the union and at the halls takes on a much broader dimension.

This approach, in many ways, can also apply to the union's relationship with fraternities, sororities, and church centers—proceeding here also toward the goal of a viable campus unity. In this sense the living units and church centers may be looked upon as the spokes and rim of the student activity wheel, with the union serving as the hub.

Relation to Student Government

There is virtually universal agreement in the United States, except at times on the part of some student governments, that it is best when union boards and student government boards work in close cooperation but are independent of each other in their jurisdictions. Basically the reason for this view is that student government's primary role is, or should be, legislative and the union's administrative, specifically in social and cultural fields. The responsibility of the student government board, within the limits set by the college, runs to the student electorate; while the responsibility of the union board, charged with the management of college property and funds, is—and must be—to the college. And along the way the union has all sorts of responsibilities to faculty, alumni, and college visitors as well as to students which student government does not encompass.

There are also many practical considerations. If student government is to do its legislative job adequately, it hasn't the time to tend as well to the policies and problems of an operation as large and complex as a union. If a union is to do what the student body and the college expect it to do, to realize anything like its full potentiality, it has to be freed from the frustrations and delays of waiting for and working through another board, especially one politically elected and oriented toward other objectives, which may or may not be interested in the union purposes and necessities. In short, the union has to govern itself.

There is every reason, of course, for avoiding friction between the union and student government and, indeed, for giving student government a voice in union affairs. The consensus, shared by the National Student Association (of campus government boards), appears to be that this is best accomplished, first, by defining clearly in their charters the functions and jurisdiction of the union and student government respectively, keeping them from getting in each other's way; and, second, by providing for representation of student government on the union governing board—producing direct and official liaison and coordination. Then the college has the kind of union governing board that almost everyone can understand and respect, and it also has what a union really needs for effective functioning: representation of student body government as the "voice of the people," of the students who do the union work and of the faculty and alumni in due proportion.

Relation to the Business Office

The relation of the union to the business office varies greatly from campus to campus. In some cases the union, even though it is a college department, formulates its own financial policies and keeps its own books independently of the business office, while in others no accounting records are kept by the union.

In some instances (11 percent) the heads of the union are advised in financial matters by the union governing board; in others (30 percent) there is line responsibility to the business manager (otherwise to the president or dean). In only 12 percent of the cases does the business office unilaterally establish general business policy for the union. The most prevalent practice (49 percent) is for the business office and the union to set policy jointly. In general, the union conforms to overall college policy in financial and business matters which also affect the union.

In the case of conflict between the college policy and the desires of the union governing board, the union staff attempts reconciliation through conference and recommendation. If the differences cannot be reconciled, the college policy controls (where the union is a department of the college), but with the governing board having an avenue of appeal to the president or to the college board of trustees. Such appeal is seldom found necessary.

In the main, the union looks to the business office for direction in:

1. Coordination of wage levels (55 percent of the cases) and general employee policies such as sick leave, vacation allowances, holidays, retirement, group and hospital insurance, etc. (62 percent).
2. Accounting and purchasing policies and procedures (76 percent).
3. Establishment of financial policies including food price coordination with other college food departments (40 percent), profit goals (48 percent), and amount of reserves for repairs and replacements (59 percent). In some cases—food service (8 percent), profit goals (16 percent), and reserves (9 percent)—policies are the responsibility of the union governing board.

In addition, the business office often functions as a servicing agency for the union in the following ways:

1. It collects union fees from students at registration time.
2. It serves as depository for all union receipts.

3. It makes audits.
4. It processes requisitions, invoices, and payrolls.
5. It carries reserves as interest-bearing accounts.

Closely allied with the business office on most campuses are the central purchasing department, the personnel department, and the department of buildings and grounds. In general it is necessary for the union to work through these departments. Experience has shown that it may not always be as economical or as satisfactory to have the physical plant department do repairs (because of higher college wage rates and benefits, lack of skilled craftsmen, delays in service, overhead charges on central storeroom, etc.), but there are other factors that often make it desirable or necessary to rely upon the physical plant staff.

Where a union is a department of the college, the college administration ordinarily exercises (in the United States, but rarely elsewhere) such financial control as it deems necessary. How far it goes depends in part on what each office—union and college business office—is prepared to do.

A useful principle in attaining the most effective direction and management of the building is to give the managing organization within the union all the desirable tools of management including budget making, record keeping, and internal controls.

The union typically prepares its own budget for submission to the college administration and governing body (88 percent). (Student committees usually assist only in preparing the budget for social and cultural activities.)

The union should have available at all times detailed records of operation for the information of and utilization by both the union management and the college business office.

The relationship with the business office is likely to work out best (1) if the union recognizes that there are certain overall fiscal and budget policies that apply to *all* college operations and conforms without question; (2) if the college recognizes that the union director is the key party responsible for the total outcome of the union enterprise, including all its financial operations, in the same sense that a dean or director of athletics is in charge of the destiny of the program *he* heads; (3) if the business office gives the union the necessary tools of good management to work with, including record keeping and internal cost controls, so the union knows what's happening and can do something about it promptly; and (4) if the union director and the business manager have taken the trouble to sit down and determine together what the dining profit margin and other financial objectives ought to be.

If the union is given real responsibility for the conduct of its financial affairs—not partial or fictitious responsibility—the union can take quite a burden off the business office. And the business office in its turn can perform extremely helpful services in terms of financial counsel, central purchasing, and, best of all, sympathetic understanding that *students* are playing a part in the union operation and are entitled to some elbow room—including mistakes—in financial practice. It helps immensely also when the business office perceives that the union is usually the showcase of the college, has to earn its own way, and therefore needs a different approach in maintenance and in what it spends money for than, for example, the "science hall."

FINANCIAL POLICIES

Most unions are financially self-sustaining, paying for costs of operation and administration through student membership fees and building earnings (mainly from dining facilities, the bookstore, games, ticket sales, supply sales, and rental of space).

Financing Construction and Operation through Student Fees

A uniform union membership fee for students is the customary chief source of revenue of almost all college unions, not only to provide the coverage, where necessary, for construction debt financing but also for operation. This fee is collected ordinarily by the college at registration time. The amount of the fee is conditioned, of course, by the size of the building plant in relation to enrollment, the amount of the debt, and the extent of free services and programs. The fee may be adjusted from time to time as enrollment or the dollar value changes. In 1967 the median fee was approximately $12 per semester, but it ranged as high as $60 per semester. (At a number of institutions provisions are also made for faculty and alumni to pay an annual or life-membership union fee on an optional basis.)

In only a few cases do *operating* funds come not from student fees but from one or a combination of the following sources: general college funds, endowment, profits from large bookstore or dining operations. In one case the college simply makes up the operating deficit at the end of the year. In another case the college budgets for the union in the same manner as it does for its academic departments.

The uniform student fee (instead of a college appropriation for operation or a voluntary fee) has been widely adopted because:

1. The conception of most unions from the beginning has been that of a center and organization in which a student participates by virtue of being a member and for which membership he pays a moderate sum. Having paid the fee, he has a greater feeling of belonging. He interests himself in the operation and activities of the union. He uses the building more.

2. The union undertakes to give students the widest possible experience in self-government processes and training for citizenship. Part of that training consists in having students feel the responsibility of paying for the benefits which all may enjoy. As future citizens they will find taxes inescapable.

3. In practice, the union fee usually saves a student much more than it costs. The fee makes the union and its services possible. Indirectly this often controls the cost of meals in the entire college district (because of the standards and prices maintained by the union); directly, it reduces greatly the cost of recreation.

4. A large proportion of the union building is non-income producing and must be maintained and serviced. The social and educational program must be provided for. The equipment which students wear out and use up must be paid for and replaced. To try to meet these necessary expenses from the uncertain revenues of the business departments would make the prices of meals and other services prohibitive to students without producing sufficient revenue. To meet such expenses out of college appropriations would mean placing the union requirements in competition with other essential educational enterprises.

The union student fee is often petitioned for or voted by the student body. The fee receipts are earmarked for union use only, and, in accord with self-government practice, the union governing board representing the student "taxpayers" is given extensive jurisdiction over the use of fee receipts, especially for program purposes.

Amortization of Debt

Many unions in completing their buildings have incurred debt averaging up to 60 to 65 percent of the cost of plant construction and up to 100 percent of the cost of furnishings and equipment, of remodeling, and of plant additions. (A few unions have financed up to 100 percent of construction by borrowing—at increased interest rates and, of course, with higher-than-usual student fees.)

Such indebtedness (usually in the form of a federal housing loan or of revenue bonds, sometimes mortgages secured by pledges of revenue) is most often retired out of the combined fee and net operating receipts of the union—over a 20- to 40-year period in the case of the building, and over a 10- to 15-year period in the case of furnishings and portable equipment.

Amortization charges are a first lien on union receipts. Principal reliance of both the Federal Housing Agency and private financing houses is on the compulsory student-union fee and the college trustees' authority to levy and, if necessary, raise the fee. At times the fee is levied before the building is constructed and accumulated to start the fund for construction. In some cases union fees are pledged exclusively to retirement of indebtedness, but this method has many disadvantages of inflexibility in meeting both amortization and other necessary operating costs. Without available fee revenue, the union is hard put to maintain reserves, to provide adequate staff, or to present even a minimum social program. In short, it may be unable to do the job for which the building was erected.

Reserves for Repairs and Replacements

At some colleges no provision is made for equipment repair and replacement reserves, which is a serious detriment to proper maintenance. The recommended practice is to set up an annual cash reserve of about 8 percent of the original cost of equipment and furnishings. If the bond or loan redemption provisions permit (which is desirable), accumulated cash in the reserve can be profitably invested in advance payments on indebtedness with a considerable saving of interest charges.

Building repairs in many cases are made by the college out of general maintenance funds without charge to the union, usually because the college wants to minimize the student fee assessment and/or feels this is an appropriate way of offsetting the union's expenses of serving nonstudents (adult conferences, faculty, departmental meetings, etc.).

Preferred practice, however, is for the union to initiate and pay for building repairs. The appearance of the union vitally affects how much it is used and therefore its income. By paying for its own building repairs, the union provides more complete and more frequent maintenance than the general college maintenance budget can usually afford. Major work is usually done by the college physical plant department, sometimes by private contractors; minor repair work is frequently done by the union's maintenance employees.

A reserve for replacing the building is seldom established, the theory being that current users should not be asked to pay for both the existing building (as in the case of a large indebtedness) and a future building.

Utilities

Practice in payment for utilities (heat, water, gas, light, and power) follows several patterns.

Most colleges pay all or part of the utility charges (in widely varying combinations) out of general college funds as an offset (as in the case of building repairs) to the expenses incurred by the union in serving the college generally—expenses not related to the club services and recreation program for which students pay a union fee. College administrations in the main hold the view that the expenses of servicing conferences of off-campus groups, faculty affairs, and nonstudent offices should not fall directly or indirectly upon the student fee.

Some colleges pay out of college funds the utility costs for just the non-revenue-producing areas of the union. Revenue-producing departments of the union are charged.

Some expect the union to pay its entire utility cost out of union receipts. In such cases the costs of the nonstudent use of the union are sometimes paid for by the college through a book credit to the union.

Profit Objective

Where consideration has been given to stating a building profit objective, the aim commonly is "to make expenses annually and allow for a margin of safety" or "to serve students better than elsewhere in town at the same or slightly less cost, and at least break even."

Most colleges realize that what the union charges for meals and recreation (about one-half of a college student's expenses) substantially governs the level of prices elsewhere in the whole college community and therefore vitally affects the cost of going to college. The result is a conscious policy to hold down student costs, which in turn means slim profit margins. In the case of the main revenue-producing department of a union—the dining service—the profit margin often aimed at as "safe" is 5 percent.

To accomplish its overall objectives it is important that the college so arrange the fundamental financing of the union—through an adequate student fee and other underwriting of non-revenue facilities—that the revenue departments will not be under constant pressure to make a high margin of profit to pay for other building operating costs.

Disposition of Balances

Any surplus which does accumulate from union operations is used typically in one of the following ways:

1. It is carried over to the next year as protection for current price levels when conditions are uncertain.
2. It is carried over and utilized to reduce prices or to add services for students.
3. It is invested in prepayments on indebtedness, to save interest and establish a future margin of safety in operations.
4. It is invested in needed new construction or equipment.
5. It is transferred to a reserve fund for major repairs or a new building addition.

BIBLIOGRAPHY

Bell, Boris C.: *Administration and Operation of the College Union,* Association of College Unions–International, Palo Alto, Calif., 1965.

Berry, Chester A.: *College Unions—Year 50,* Association of College Unions–International, Palo Alto, Calif., 1966.

———: *Planning a College Union Building,* Association of College Unions–International, Palo Alto, Calif., 1960.

Bulletin and *Proceedings* of Association of College Unions–International, P.O. Box 7286, Palo Alto, Calif.

Butts, Porter: *Planning and Operating College Union Buildings,* 7th ed., Association of College Unions–International, Palo Alto, Calif., 1967.

———: *Planning College Union Facilities for Multiple Use,* Association of College Unions–International, Palo Alto, Calif., 1966.

———: *Standards for Professional Staff Preparation and Compensation in College Union Work,* Association of College Unions–International, Palo Alto, Calif., 1967.

———: *State of the College Union Around the World,* Association of College Unions–International, Palo Alto, Calif., 1967.

———: "The College Union Story," *Journal of the American Institute of Architects,* pp. 59–66, March, 1964 (reprints available from Association of College Unions–International, Palo Alto, Calif.).

Christensen, Ernest: *Annotated Bibliography of the College Union,* Association of College Unions–International, Palo Alto, Calif., 1967.

College Union Planning Aids, College and University Facilities Series, U.S. Office of Education Bulletin, August, 1962 (includes extensive bibliography).

Noffke, Frank: *Planning for a College Union,* Association of College Unions–International, Palo Alto, Calif., 1965.

Osterheld, Douglas C.: *Food Service and the College Union,* Association of College Unions–International, Palo Alto, Calif., 1967.

Papers (mimeographed) on History, Goals, Operations, and Program Administration of College Unions, Wisconsin Union Summer Course in College Union Operations, Madison, Wis., 1962.

Chapter 3

Conference and Continuing Education Centers

LLOYD W. SCHRAM

Dean, Continuing Education; University of Washington, Seattle, Washington

RICHARD E. MEYER

Assistant to the Dean, Continuing Education; University of Washington, Seattle, Washington

There are many approaches which could be followed in discussing a topic as complex as centers of continuing education. Rather than attempting to direct our remarks and observations at persons and institutions presently operating continuing education centers, the position was taken that the larger and potentially more significant audience for this chapter would most likely be college and university officials at institutions currently in the process of planning centers or hoping to initiate such planning at some time in the future. Thus, while much of the information contained within the chapter might appear "old hat" to institutions presently operating centers, it is our hope that the main value of the chapter will be in the suggestions and guidelines it offers to those just entering the business.

In attempting to deal with such matters as budget and general regulations, a number of problems presented themselves leading to a decision to omit their consideration in "model" terms. Basically, this involved a realization that the innumerable circumstances governing the operation of any one particular center, no matter how generalized, would make anything even approaching universal application of these principles a practical impossibility. For example, as regards budgetary implications, a wide spectrum of possibilities is presented even when one considers a single factor such as the means by which initial construction is funded and the concomitant debt obligations which the center must fulfill.

Other extremely variable considerations involve the nature and extent of housing and dining accommodations, the type of program most frequently held within the center, and the amount of staff required to operate a given center. Likewise, in the matter of general regulations, widely varying institutional policies and procedures, oftentimes compounded by requirements of state and local legislation, would seem to preclude the possibility of presenting model regulations which would prove useful as guidelines to individual institutions. Rather, such considerations, where appropriate, have been discussed briefly at certain points in the text of the chapter, usually with the suggestion that the individual institution approach these matters in the context of its own particular circumstances.

ON CONTINUING EDUCATION CENTERS IN GENERAL

Within recent years, universities and colleges throughout the United States have been faced with increasing demands for short courses, seminars, workshops, and other forms of instruction designed to provide the latest and most pertinent knowledge and information to persons representing a vast array of professional, occupational, cultural, and social fields. Because of the increasing rapidity of social, technological, scientific, and cultural changes, such programs have become a virtual necessity if the time lag between the discovery of knowledge and its practical application is to be shortened. Today, no profession or occupation is immune to the consequences of inexorable and rapid change. Engineers, educators, physicians, businessmen, and, indeed, members of all contemporary professions and occupations, are striving to keep updated—to them has come the realization that such endeavor is necessary to professional fitness. In increasing numbers they are turning to institutions of higher learning, which have a responsibility for the advancement of knowledge through research and scholarship and which therefore should be equipped to provide them with timely knowledge and information. In recognition of this fact, it is of special relevance to note that continuing education activities in the past several years have received great stimulus through the enactment of several significant federal legislative measures. Some of the most recent examples of this type of legislation are Title I of the Higher Education Act of 1965; the State Technical Services Act of 1965; the Heart Disease, Cancer, and Stroke Amendments, 1965; and the National Sea Grant College and Program Act of 1966. A more detailed discussion of the federal grant programs may be found in Chapter 9 of Section 3 of the companion volume on general administration.

The impressive developments in occupational, professional, and general education made two things painfully clear. The first was that the traditional physical facilities of colleges and universities, which were designed for young people, did not lend themselves effectively to the special circumstances involved in adult learning programs. Secondly, the increasing undergraduate, graduate, and professional enrollments were already placing great strains upon the physical resources of the institutions, and in many cases accommodations of any type were not available to house this latest and fast-growing member of the academic family. Thus it was perhaps inevitable that consideration would ultimately be given by universities and colleges to the construction of facilities specially designed for and exclusively used by adults.

In 1936, a striking symbol of the growing need and an imaginative response to it was provided by the University of Minnesota. This was the dedication of the Center for Continuation Study, the first facility in the United States to be specially designed for exclusive use by adults as a center for residential continuing education. The then president of the University of Minnesota, Lotus Coffman, in describing the facility said:

> The Center is designed primarily for the use of men and women who wish to spend relatively short periods of time in serious and intensive study of problems related to their professional, civic, or cultural interests. In general, the studies pursued will be those which the University is especially qualified to direct.
>
> The purposes of the new department are suggested by its name. It is a *center* in which students live and work together under one roof during their period of residence on the campus. It is a *continuation* school in the sense that it is designed to give opportunities for acquiring further education to those who have already received the usual professional, technical, and general instruction in the regular schools and colleges. It is primarily a place for definite *study* rather than for conventions or social gatherings.[1]

By far the greatest single impetus to the advancement of the concept of the continuing education center, however, was the financially assistive program of the W. K. Kellogg Foundation of Battle Creek, Michigan. From 1951 to 1968, the Kellogg Foundation made a total of over 20 million dollars available as foundation grants to 10 universities in the United States and to Oxford University in England.

The pioneering institution under these grants was Michigan State University, which opened its Kellogg Center for Continuing Education in 1951. The great success of this center led to grants to other universities: Georgia in 1957; Nebraska, 1961; Oklahoma, 1962; Chicago, 1963; Notre Dame, 1965; and Oxford, 1965. The remaining three grants were as follows: in 1965 for a New England Center for Continuing Education located at the University of New Hampshire and serving the universities of the six New England states; in 1966 for an International Center for Continuing Education at Columbia University; and in 1968 for a center to be constructed as "Kellogg West" at California Polytechnic State College, Kellogg-Voorhis Campus at Pomono, California, which will serve the 19 institutions comprising the California state college system.[2]

[1] *NUEA Spectator,* vol. XXVI, no. 4, p. 4, National University Extension Association, April–May, 1961.

[2] For additional information see Harold J. Alford, *Continuing Education in Action,* John Wiley & Sons, Inc., New York, 1968. (Dr. Alford, through this book, has performed an excellent service for institutions considering the construction of continuing education centers. It consists of a study of the planning, operation, and purposes of the 10 centers which were given financial assistance by the W. K. Kellogg Foundation of Battle Creek, Michigan, and for whom Dr. Alford wrote the book. Its reading is a virtual must for those planning centers.) Other valuable sources of information on centers and center programs are *Continuing Education: An Evolving Form of Adult Education,* W. K. Kellogg Foundation, Battle Creek, Mich., *Continuing Education Reports,* nos. 1–16, a series of occasional publications of the Studies and Training Program in Continuing Education at the University of Chicago, and *A Directory of Residential Continuing Education Centers in the United States, Canada, and Abroad,* Studies and Training Program in Continuing Education, University of Chicago, 1968. For additional references, see the section on "Residential Centers for Continuing Education" in George F. Aker (ed.), *Adult Education Procedures, Methods and Techniques: A Classified and Annotated Bibliography,* Syracuse, 1965, pp. 14–24.

As might have been expected, a great many more applications for financial assistance were made by universities to the W. K. Kellogg Foundation than were accepted. Disappointed as they may be, those in university continuing education who received rejection slips are, at the same time, highly conscious of a great debt of gratitude owed to the W. K. Kellogg Foundation for having made its case for the need of continuing education centers so effectively to its own credit and to the benefit of the entire concept and movement of continuing education. One persuasive piece of evidence in this respect is the fact that today there are some eighty facilities, in addition to the Kellogg-assisted centers, at institutions of higher learning which, in varying sizes and capabilities, qualify as residential instructional facilities for continuing education.

Because so many proposals were being received by the foundation (53 were submitted between 1957 and 1961), the trustees asked the staff to prepare a statement which might be used by the trustees as a basis for evaluating requests. The result was the preparation of a document, in 1957, which has become known as the "Fifteen Criteria." These criteria, according to Dr. Harold Alford of the University of Minnesota, "have served as guides for the development of many proposals for continuing education centers in addition to the 10 founded in part by the foundation." Further, they "remain the most useful single guide for educators contemplating the construction of a continuing education center."[3]

No doubt there is some difference of opinion as to what might properly be defined as a continuing education center, owing in large measure to the diverse elements which comprise all centers as well as to the distinctive features which invariably set off one center from another. Indeed, the *NUEA Spectator*, a publication of the National University Extension Association, once devoted an entire issue to the question, "What is a Continuation Center Anyway?"[4] But at the same time there would probably be only minor disagreement on a definition of a center in its total, ideal sense. This would be a specially designed facility wherein adults can participate in institutionally sanctioned short courses, conferences, seminars, and similar programs under circumstances permitting them to study, converse, eat, sleep, and relax all under one roof or within a closely interrelated group of facilities. Perhaps the most thoughtful answer in recent times, both to the question of what a center *is* and what a center *does*, has been provided by Dr. Cyril O. Houle, professor of education at the University of Chicago and long one of the nation's outstanding leaders in the field of continuing education. Professor Houle conceives of a center, in its mature form, as a place wherein three basically important services or functions are performed. These are as follows:

The Educational Function. The continuing education of adults as performed through a variety of methods, both traditional and experimental

The Training Function. A training ground or "laboratory" for the education of faculty and administrators involved in programs of continuing education

The Research Function. A focus or site for research into the nature and methods of continuing education as well as certain allied fields

Although the educational function is and should always remain the foremost goal of any continuing education center, Dr. Houle maintains that it is nonetheless true that a university-operated center worthy of that name should perform all three of these functions.[5]

Why special facilities for continuing education? What are the special characteristics and circumstances of the adult which make such facilities desirable?

As distinguished from the usual undergraduate or graduate student, the adult participating in continuing education programs is not a full-time student devoting most of his time and energies to the pursuit of an education. The average adult has a job, a family

[3] Alford, *op. cit.*, pp. 23–27, *passim.*
[4] *NUEA Spectator, op. cit.*
[5] *Continuing Education Reports, op. cit.*, nos. 7, 8, and 9.

and a great variety of responsibilities and relationships which place many demands upon his time and energies. The point is that the time which an adult can make available for participation in continuing education activities is decidedly limited. He must, therefore, make the most effective use of that time. This characteristic of the average adult makes it highly desirable for a continuing education center to be, insofar as possible, a self-contained or all-inclusive complex which is conducive to carrying out a learning experience in the most time-saving and convenient manner possible. In short, the physical components for instruction, housing, and dining should be under one roof or in close geographical association.

Perhaps the most distinguishing characteristic of the average adult participant is that he comes to the learning situation with a background of education, training, experience, and maturity which usually qualifies him to participate actively in group discussions. This consideration has two significant and direct implications for the design of the physical accommodations. First, the adult would prefer, under most circumstances, not to be just lectured to at length by the instructor but rather to be given an opportunity, by way of accommodations for small group meetings, to participate in discussions not only with the instructor but with his colleagues and associates. Second, his interest in discussions with his peers must be given special consideration in the facility's design by providing opportunities for him to exercise his capabilities not only in the more formal instructional periods but also in the equally valuable conversational and social interludes which take place in the dining room, the corridor, the hallway, the library, and the recreation areas.

In any discussion of continuing education centers, a basic differentiation should be made between two major types of such facilities which are found in many parts of the United States. These are the on-campus center and the off-campus or remote center. Two primary factors tend to distinguish the on-campus facility: its comparatively large size and its location on or very near the campus of the parent institution. The 10 Kellogg-assisted centers generally fall within this category, accommodating from 150 to 450 persons in instructional, dining, and housing facilities. The on-campus centers are designed to accommodate large conferences involving several hundred people or several smaller conferences running concurrently. Furthermore, some of the programs held within the on-campus facility are organized in a fashion which requires irregular participation by many members of the faculty over a period of one or more days. Under such circumstances, the faculty member must accommodate his other responsibilities of teaching and research and therefore cannot take the time to travel very far to participate in the program and return to the campus.

Remote centers, on the other hand, derive their uniqueness in part from their smaller size, generally accommodating from 40 to 100 persons, but more particularly from the fact that they tend to be placed at some distance from the institutional and community setting. Although they may easily be reached by conventional modes of transportation they generally are, insofar as possible, in settings both remote and attractive. The remote center, because of its smaller size, is looked upon usually as a place where preferably only one conference or program is scheduled at one time. Thus, meetings usually scheduled in a remote center are those which benefit from the intimacy and closer association provided by a smaller facility as well as from a greater degree of seclusion with a commensurate reduction of distractions. Existing facilities which qualify as remote centers would include the Adirondack Centers of Syracuse University, Allerton House of the University of Illinois, Lake Arrowhead of the University of California, and Lake Wilderness Lodge of the University of Washington.

The selection of an appropriate site for a remote center is, of course, a prime concern in planning such a facility. It is of interest that a faculty-administration committee at the University of Washington, in establishing the basic criteria for the selection of a remote center site for the university, concluded that the site should provide (1) a sense of remoteness and seclusion, (2) reasonable accessibility by one or more approaches from the university (ideally requiring not more than one hour of traveling time), (3) a preponderance of the aesthetic characteristics of the Pacific Northwest—water, mountains, and evergreens, and (4) sufficient space (at least 10 acres and preferably more) to ensure continued seclusion and to allow for any future expansion of facilities.

PHYSICAL COMPONENTS OF CONTINUING EDUCATION CENTERS

In the following pages, the discussion will focus on the large residential center for continuing education built in the style of the W. K. Kellogg-assisted centers rather than upon the remote residential type. Generally, the basic concepts and types of physical components of the large center are equally appropriate to the remote center, the essential difference being that fewer persons usually are served by the smaller remote center.

In considering the physical make-up of centers, questions arise as to the various types and sizes of the physical components which make up a facility properly called a center. At what point does a facility become a center? There may be differing views on the matter, but it is not necessary to belabor the point. As a bare minimum, a center should include a reasonable number and variety of instructional rooms which are devoted primarily to the continuing education of adults and which are clustered in such a way as to set them apart operationally from the other facilities of the parent institution. Such a facility, however, falls far short of the ideal continuing education center which, as noted earlier, is a self-contained, residential-instructional complex. To the "bare bones" of instructional areas one must add kitchen and dining areas, overnight accommodations, administrative offices, and other associated requirements such as lounges, work and storage spaces, special services areas, and, hopefully, recreation facilities. To the extent that a center provides these areas and facilities, it may be said to approach the ideal of a continuing education center.

Any query as to the appropriate size of a center, obviously, cannot be answered in the abstract. There are many questions which can be effectively answered only by the institution considering construction of a center: Has the institution a demonstrated record of support for continuing education programs? Is the institution located in a highly urbanized area? What types of programs and how many such programs will be presented in the center; that is, what has been the past history of these programs and what might be anticipated as being a reasonable future growth of these activities over the next 5, 10, and 20 years? Will use of the facility be restricted to institutionally sponsored programs, and if not, what additional uses will be involved? Will the center house all or a major portion of the continuing education administrative and service offices, or will the administrative offices be confined to those necessary for the programming and administrative personnel? To what extent should space be provided for research activities, for in-service and internship programs? Would a single building or a cluster of buildings be more suited to the role of the center? Should the construction be staged in order to accommodate future needs more adequately?

The answers to these and other pertinent questions can be provided only at the institutional level after a careful study of all relevant information by those persons responsible for policy determination, for program planning and instruction, for administration, and for the construction process. Nevertheless, a few remarks might be made regarding some of the general considerations governing the physical components as distinguished from specific institutional needs.

At the outset, a paramount consideration is that the facility in its totality, whether it be a single building such as the center at Michigan State University or a cluster of buildings constituting a mini-campus as at Oklahoma, must involve components in type, number, and size which functionally facilitate the total learning process. The design must be a workable design in relation to the purposes and programs of the facility. At the University of Oklahoma, for example, Dean Thurman White envisaged a "community in miniature" with a facility designed to accommodate a plan for a coming together, a withdrawal, and a coming together again. Participants come together for a large meeting involving various presentations, then there is a "withdrawal" to smaller meetings for discussions, then a return to the large meeting for an exchange of ideas resulting from the small group discussions. The design of the Oklahoma center, with a central forum facility and many smaller rooms, functionally reflects this concept of the learning process.

Another highly relevant consideration is that the center facility in the totality of its conception and execution should possess a quality of attractiveness, both architecturally and functionally, which will engender a desire on the part of participants to return to the center on many occasions and for many purposes. Inasmuch as the facility will probably be the primary, if not the only, residential instructional center for adults in the area, many people over the years will have reason to attend a variety of continuing education programs in the center. A center which discourages rather than encourages attendance obviously defeats its purpose.

Although some of the components of a center are strikingly similar in purpose to those of a commercial hotel in that both provide overnight and dining accommodations as well as meeting rooms, the center should not be patterned after the blueprint of a commercial hotel. Rather, the center design should reflect the style and quality of the environment of which it is a part—an academic environment, a place for quiet study, for discussions, for conversations, and for meditation and reflection. As such it should be simple but attractive and quiet, convenient and comfortable.

There is much to be said on behalf of comfort when considering the needs of adults, ranging in age from 25 to 70, who must spend long hours of the day and night participating in discussions, listening to lectures, studying, and in other ways trying to derive maximum educational benefits within a limited time. An uncomfortable chair can be a deterrent to sustained attention and a room which is oppressively warm or filled with smoke, or both, is more conducive to nodding than learning. Comfortable furniture is a must and air conditioning, while it is highly desirable ordinarily, is a virtual necessity in some climates.

As indicated above, the various components of a center must be functionally interrelated to accommodate the purposes and types of programs to be presented in the center. This is particularly true in relation to the types and sizes of the areas which comprise the instructional component.

Instructional Facilities

Although views with respect to the need for an auditorium span all the way from "we don't need one" to "it is the most heavily used instructional area," general experience suggests that an auditorium of fair size is highly desirable, not only for plenary sessions of large conferences but also for certain lectures and demonstrations. Auditoriums ranging in seating capacity from 250 to 1,200 are found in presently operating centers. In most instances they are equipped with sloping floors, theater-type seats, and complete audiovisual facilities.

Lecture rooms varying in seating capacity from 40 to 250 are an important feature of any center. Frequently they can be used for plenary sessions of groups too small to use the auditorium effectively. Generally these rooms feature flat floors, movable seats, and audiovisual capabilities. The larger of these rooms are sometimes divisible by means of movable partitions. However, partitions usually must provide more than visual exclusion, and the greatest care must be exercised to select partitions which are truly soundproof and easily operable. When not being used for other purposes these rooms can often be utilized as exhibit areas. In some instances, when located near the food service areas, they can also be used as auxiliary banquet rooms.

The great majority of continuing education programs rely heavily upon small areas such as seminar rooms to provide opportunities for extensive discussion among the participants. Many short courses, conferences, and seminars have sharply defined purposes and are often action-oriented. The participants must assemble to review and discuss specific problems and issues for the purpose of drawing firm conclusions or arriving at a consensus which may even form the basis for follow-up action. For such purposes, the small seminar rooms with capacities up to 40 persons are particularly appropriate. Depending upon the programs to be presented, a considerable number of these rooms, representing from 20 to 50 percent of the total instructional floor space, should be included in the center. The furnishings should stress both utility and comfort inasmuch as participants often spend many hours in these small, intensive learning sessions.

If a substantial array of instructional activities related to health services—for example, medicine, dentistry, nursing, and other health-allied fields—will be presented in the center, careful attention should be paid to any special needs for laboratory and demonstration areas. It is, however, most unlikely that a full complement of facilities should be provided to meet the total need for each subject-matter area, such as by providing operating rooms, X-ray equipment, dental chairs, and great quantities of additional equipment representing an extensive financial outlay. Accordingly, a careful study should be made by all subject-matter areas to determine the precise character of the programs they will present in order that specific space and equipment requirements for those programs may be established. Decisions must then be made on a cost-use basis. Will the frequency of use justify the costs? Can the design of the space and selection of the equipment permit a flexibility of use which would allow for uses other than those for which the area will be specifically designed? Will the center be located in such proximity to the university's regular professional instructional facilities that those more expensive and extensive facilities might be used in appropriate cases, thus obviating the need for duplication in the center facilities?

Kitchen and Dining Facilities

A satisfactory or helpful discussion of the appropriate kitchen and dining facilities to be included within a center is virtually precluded in a short paper concerned with continuing education centers. However, certain information obtained from surveys and visits to various centers makes it possible to offer a few observations. The character and size of the food services areas, as in the case of the other center components, can be determined only after a careful study has been made of the types, numbers, and sizes of programs which are to be accommodated in the center. Questions must also be answered with respect to peripheral uses. Will the dining facilities be open to the general public as they are at at least one major center? Will faculty, staff, and students not identified with activities within the center be permitted to use the dining facilities? Will the administration of the university wish to conduct small luncheon meetings and other activities for visiting dignitaries, public officials, and others?

Nearly all of the currently operating centers have at least one large dining room for banquet sessions, and one of these can accommodate as many as 885 persons. Contrary to the hopes of many, it appears that the large banquet and the after-dinner speaker are not vanishing from the American scene.

Most centers, in addition, contain one or more smaller rooms accommodating from 50 to 250 persons. A seemingly successful system of folding doors makes it possible for some centers, such as the Georgia center, to provide a measure of flexibility of use by subdividing the main banquet area into smaller rooms.

At least one small, attractively appointed dining room accommodating from 10 to 20 persons frequently is found extremely useful not only for continuing education programs but for other university functions as well, including those of an official character.

A cafeteria style of serving is often found in use in addition to the table service of the banquet rooms in order to provide for more casual and informal meal arrangements. A buffet arrangement seems highly workable at the McGregor Memorial Community Arts Center, located on the campus of Wayne State University in Detroit. Here the participant makes his food selection from an attractive buffet and takes it to a table of his own selection where a place setting is provided.

Two other services should be kept in mind. One is the informal snack bar for off-hour use, which might involve one segment of the cafeteria. The other service involves the seemingly universal coffee break which would require bringing the service to the participants or giving them time to go to a dining area.

The key considerations which should govern the design of kitchen and dining facilities are easily stated but difficult to realize: flexibility in terms of the number of persons to be served and the style of service; an attractive dining environment; convenience for both the servers and the served; food of a high quality; and a price commensurate with these considerations. Again, we should be reminded that the clientele of the center is a voluntary adult group. They do not have to return and sometimes will not do so if the accommodations are below the general standards to which they are accustomed.

Living Accommodations

While overnight accommodations are a necessity in fulfilling the concept of the ideal self-contained center, a decision on the amount of floor space which should be devoted to these accommodations can be made by each institution only on the basis of the character and number of the programs to be presented. The overnight accommodations in centers currently in operation range from a few rooms to space for 425 or more guests. In some instances, outside factors such as the center's proximity to other accommodations in the form of commercial hotels and motels may have some influence on the number and type of accommodations required, particularly in the first of two or more stages of a long-range construction program.

At this juncture it should be said that in some cases where the plans for the construction of a center have been under way, representatives of nearby hotels have expressed concern that the center might take away some of their clientele and reduce their volume of business. Discussions with center directors suggest, however, that although this matter may be an issue in the planning of a center, the concern of the hotel operators may be allayed when it is shown, as it can be on the basis of experience elsewhere, that the existence of the center will increase rather than decrease their business. Their concern is further quieted when they have assurance that only persons participating in the center's programs will be staying there. In Oklahoma, the president of the Oklahoma Hotel Association urged the W. K. Kellogg Foundation to stipulate that the center restrict its use of the bedroom and dining facilities to those participating in the seminars. The foundation thereafter received assurances from University of Oklahoma officials that the facilities would not be available for nonuniversity transients. Programs at the university have brought business to local hotels and the operators seem to be satisfied with arrangements.

A problem for careful study during the planning stages concerns the proportion of effective occupancy of the rooms which would be required to make the housing units financially self-sustaining. Under some circumstances a cautious approach might be indicated: the number of living units would be limited but would provide a relatively consistent level of occupancy, making it possible to meet all costs. Later, as future needs and financing are verified by operating experience, additional accommodations could be added in financially feasible stages.

The question as to what type of living accommodation should be provided also provokes an assortment of answers. From a strictly economic point of view, modified dormitory-type arrangements might be suggested. But the counter argument is that adults may not choose to use them—more than once.

Another issue revolves around the pros and the cons with respect to single rooms as against double rooms. The double-room advocate maintains that he likes to meet new people, and that one can, if necessary, resort to single occupancy of a double room. If the advocate be the business manager, he points to the economic virtues of the double room. The single-room advocate, on the other hand, points up the need for privacy after a long day of personal associations; of the need to study in quiet; of the discontent to be endured if a roommate is a vocal sleeper, or a heavy smoker, or wants to study when the other occupant wants to sleep. It should be of interest that during a visit to West Germany recently, one of the authors observed three adult residential instructional centers, accommodating in their totality approximately 275 overnight guests, all of which contained only single rooms.

The larger centers currently operating in the United States include far more double than single rooms. It is probably safe to assume that financial considerations materially influenced decisions to that end. The fact that continuing education programs are becoming increasingly long in duration should tend to support the case for the single room. A recent report from the University of Chicago covering a survey of continuing education programs conducted within 12 operating centers demonstrates that 36 percent of all programs conducted within the centers lasted for more than three days. Furthermore, 9 percent of all programs were over a week long.[6]

Administrative Areas

In any general discussion of the components to be included within a continuing education center, a key question arises as to which administrative areas should be located within the centers. At Michigan State University, for example, the administrative offices for virtually all the programs conducted under the aegis of continuing education are housed in the center. Dr. Armand Hunter, Director of Continuing Education at Michigan State, supports this type of arrangement but would smilingly acknowledge that the programming and administrative staff of the center would prefer exclusive occupancy. Thus, in some centers one will find offices for credit and noncredit classes, lectures and concerts, radio services, and television programming as well as other offices related to university extension, continuing education, or however else these services are labeled.

Unquestionably, limited resources and space demands not infrequently dictate something short of ideal arrangements, but if a center is to serve the purpose of residential adult instruction and if no compelling circumstances dictate compromise, it would seem that only those offices should be located within a center which are directly related and necessary to the program and operations management of the center. If compelling circumstances require that other facilities be housed in the center, they should be designed within the complex so as to reduce their visibility to a minimum for the benefit of those participating in programs as well as staff personnel involved in program management and operations.

This is especially important if the center is contained within a single structure. Where a group of buildings is involved, however, as at the University of Oklahoma, it would seem feasible to house other functions of continuing education within the complex in such a way as to minimize traffic problems in the administrative areas and permit the instructional activities to take place in relative quiet and isolation.

A special type of administrative space might well be included in the center under the heading of program administration; this would consist of small offices to be made

[6] *Ibid.*, no. 15.

available to representatives of the academic departments involved in arranging particular programs. Assignments of such space would be on the basis of intermittent needs and would facilitate working relationships between academic representatives and the center personnel charged with programming and administration.

Lounge and Recreation Facilities

Adequate lounges are a basic requirement for a well-conceived center. As indicated earlier, a surprising measure of the total learning experience within a center takes place outside the formal instructional areas, where conference participants gather informally to discuss matters of mutual interest. To encourage this process of exchange, the center should contain a suitable number of informal lounge areas which would be in convenient proximity to both the instructional areas and the living accommodations and be of such a nature as to invite repeated use by the conference participants. Space of this type takes on added importance if the living accommodations are too small to permit three or four persons to get together comfortably in one room.

Another area of importance to the instructional program is the library or libraries. Apart from the general reading which may engage the attention of a participant, it is often necessary or desirable to place in the library a number of books or other reading matter related to the subject matter of a particular program. Under some circumstances, two or more small libraries may be more useful and effective than a single larger library.

A center should also incorporate recreational facilities which would permit a reasonable amount of exercise, whether it be swimming, running, walking, games of tennis, badminton, volleyball, or other forms of activity which tend to relieve the physical and mental tensions which can build up during a day of meetings, discussions, and study which commences at 8:30 A.M. and continues until 10 P.M. and beyond. These facilities take on increasing importance in direct ratio to the length of the programs, some of which may be conducted over periods of weeks and perhaps even months.

Special Service Areas

The self-contained character of a center involves the provision of certain special areas and services to facilitate the instructional process as well as to expedite the administration of the center. Day-to-day conference activities require the storage of a surprising amount of materials which are necessary to the programs being presented. In some instances center directors have found it necessary to install extensive duplicating and printing facilities to meet general requirements and also to provide materials on an emergency basis which are necessary to the instructional process.

In addition to requirements for the instructional activities, a careful study must be made to determine the storage and service areas necessary to effective management of the entire center complex. Observations of center directors suggest that no matter how much provision is made for storage and service areas, it won't be enough.

Another matter which confronts center planners concerns the provision of adequate facilities for audiovisual services and computer programming. The problem is complicated by the fact that what is appropriate today may well be obsolete tomorrow. The primary guideline under these circumstances is to design the center in such a way as to permit maximum flexibility, facilitating future adjustments to new and improved types of equipment which might reasonably be expected to become available. In this area, the services of highly qualified consultants should be obtained.

Registration, information, and canteen areas must also be provided for. There are two types of registration that take place in a center: registration for meetings or conferences and registration for housing accommodations. Whether these two types of registration can take place at the same counter would depend upon a variety of factors which need not be discussed here. Center directors do not suggest any final answer, but they do agree that registrations should not take place in a hallway designed only to accommodate a normal flow of pedestrian traffic. Another point which some have made is that in the interests of economy and convenience the information desk and canteen should be combined, and that in a very small operation they might well be placed adjacent to the registration area.

Before leaving the area of physical components, it would be well to reemphasize the point that, while one may generalize as to the types and quantities of components which go to make up a center in its ideal sense, the fact still remains that each center is unique unto itself. Even when considering the larger and better known centers currently operating in this country, one is struck with the diversity of factors related to physical components. To better enable the reader to appreciate the nature and extent of this diversity, a comparative "facilities profile" of three currently operating Kellogg Centers, concentrating upon the major aspects of physical components, is given in Table 1.

PLANNING AND FINANCING

Advanced Planning

There can be no more important period in the history of a continuing education center than that devoted to its planning and design. This period takes on increased significance owing to the fact that centers are for the most part relatively new to the academic landscape with the consequence that their history is lacking in the vast accumulations of planning and operating data which are available in relation to the more traditional physical resources of the university. Further, the problems which are inherent in this lack of data become compounded when it is recognized that although the center's physical components are close relatives to the more traditional university facilities, they do not conform to a common mold but must be designed with a view to performing similar but different services. Thus, the planning program should not be inhibited by any attempt to modify concepts of traditional facilities to accommodate the new needs. The governing concept, rather, should be to plan and design those physical accommodations which will be best suited to the characteristics and circumstances of the programs.

Before any consideration is given to the specifics of planning and design, however, an institution should conduct a rigorous self-analysis with respect to the seriousness of its commitment to the field of continuing education both presently and in the future in order to determine whether in fact its commitment to this field would justify the outlays of money, space, time, and energy which are inescapably involved.[7]

A measurement of the extent of the institutional commitment raises several key questions: What has been the experience to date with regard to the number and character of continuing education activities? What reasonably might be expected with respect to future growth of the activities? Is the faculty in support of these programs and actively involved in their planning and presentation? Are the programs being directed by able leadership at the operational level? Are they given institutional support at the highest administrative and policy levels of the institution? To what extent are funds provided by the institution to continuing education in addition to those which are derived from program income? Thus, at the preplanning stage, the institution must be able to confirm an institutional commitment to the field as represented by present and future programming as well as by tangible and effective support of the faculty, the staff, and the university administration.

[7] The "Fifteen Criteria" prepared by the staff of the W. K. Kellogg Foundation as a guide to the evaluation of grant requests suggest a number of pertinent questions to which an institution might address itself in the preplanning stage. See footnote 3.

TABLE 1 Facilities Profile of Three Operating Kellogg Centers

Location	Began operations	Number of buildings	General configuration	Approximate number of beds	Approximate number of eating spaces	Approximate number of student stations	Number of large meeting rooms *	Number of small meeting rooms *	Seating capacity of auditorium
Michigan State University	1951	1	Rectangular; high rise	430	1,440	1,520	11	3	355 †
University of Oklahoma	1962	15 ‡	Satellite cluster; mainly low rise	270	720	1,540	4	16	525 §
University of Notre Dame	1966	1	Square; low rise	None ¶	350 ¶	1,230	6	15	375

* Large meeting rooms are defined as those with a capacity of 40 or more student stations, exclusive of auditoriums; small meeting rooms are defined as those with a capacity of less than 40 student stations.

† Michigan State also has a lecture room with a seating capacity of 350.

‡ Ten of Oklahoma's fifteen buildings are duplex cottages for overnight accommodation of center guests.

§ Oklahoma also has a lecture room with a seating capacity of 250.

¶ Notre Dame has no overnight guest accommodations within the center itself, although these are available within the Morris Inn which is located immediately adjacent to the center; limited dining arrangements may be provided within the center on a catered basis, but center guests normally take their meals at the Morris Inn.

Having proved its case to itself, and assuming both adequate funding and an appropriate site for a center, the institution should initiate procedures leading to the preparation of a program-planning report which will contain everything the architect will need to know to design the facility at the highest possible degree of accommodation for the various programs, activities, and services which the institution desires to conduct within the facility. The report should deal with all key considerations such as the nature and number of continuing education programs and services to be conducted over a 5-, 10-, and 20-year period; special or additional uses to which the facility will be put; siting requirements; general aesthetic considerations; descriptions of each type of room or other identifiable space contemplated for the center; an estimate of the square footage required for each space; a general description of the appropriate types of furnishings; an estimated construction budget and timetable; a statement of parking requirements; and any other information which the architect will require to design a highly specialized facility reflecting the needs and values of the particular institution.

Any university official or staff member closely associated with the processes of a university's building program is aware of the specific policies and procedures which govern a construction program from conception to execution. Admittedly, the policies and procedures vary among institutions, but there is probably enough similarity between the University of Washington's procedures and those of other institutions that a description, or a brief "case-study," of the specific processes pursued in relation to the university's proposed center might be informative for those having little knowledge of the general subject.

The staff members in continuing education at an early date (1958) began to gather pertinent data concerning the type of facility which would ultimately be constructed. As time passed, a growing awareness of need developed in many quarters of the university, and in October, 1967 the vice-president and chairman of the Capital Construction Board appointed a seven-member Ad Hoc Programming Committee for a Campus Continuing Education Center, which was composed of faculty and staff members with considerable experience in the planning and presentation of continuing education programs. The dean of continuing education served as chairman, and an architect from the staff of the Department of Facilities Planning and Construction was assigned to assist the committee in its deliberations. The committee was charged with the first three steps of the following timetable set forth for the project: (1) the establishment of criteria for siting the project, (2) completion of the programming report, (3) approval of the program by the Capital Construction Board, (4) appointment of the architect and selection of the site by the Board of Regents, and (5) approval of schematic drawings by the Board of Regents.

Because planning for the center is regarded as a process which should involve, in varying degrees of interest, all departments of the university which ultimately would use the facility, the charge specified that prior to final submission of the report:

> The recommendations as to site and program should be made known to each dean who presently conducts continuing education programs so that each may comment on the proposals. These comments in any event should be included with the committee report, and may be the basis for committee reconsideration and possibly for changes in the recommendations. In the final report a statement on consensus should be included in regard to each major recommendation. This facility is to serve the entire University so should involve as much as possible an all-University view in the program recommendations.

The committee was further instructed to consider various sources of possible funding for the first phase of the facility.

As a basis for preparing the programming report, the committee relied upon several means of securing relevant data with respect to present and future needs. Information was obtained from the Office of Short Courses and Conferences in Continuing Education for the period 1960 to 1965 concerning the types of program presented during that period, their number and duration, the number of persons involved, the types of rooms and other facilities utilized, the extent of the use of local housing accommodations, and the parking facilities which were necessary. This information, with the help of staff and faculty specialists, was then projected for the years 1970 and 1975 as one basis for determining the program requirements.

Questionnaires were then sent to all schools, colleges, and departments of the university to ascertain whether they might have any special needs which would not otherwise come to the attention of the committee.

Special guests were invited to meetings of the committee to assist in reviewing the need for specific components and to offer guidance in other matters pertaining to their areas of expertise. Included among those consultants were the university's director of student residences and campus food services, the construction grant coordinator, and other representatives of the university business manager's office.

Discussions were also held with key representatives of the university administration, such as the vice-president for university relations, to determine whether they foresaw any additional uses for the center.

An extensive survey was undertaken by mail, involving the continuing education centers located at 11 selected institutions throughout the country, the purpose of which was to obtain representative information and statistical data on a great many matters which might be helpful in detailing specifications within the report for the proposed University of Washington center.

Finally, the committee, in cooperation with the university's Office of Facilities Planning and Construction, made a detailed analysis of potential sites for the center and incorporated a recommendation for a specific site within the planning report.

After weeks of work and study, the report was completed and submitted to the university's Capital Construction Board. After hearings with the chairman of the committee, the board approved the report including the committee's recommendation concerning the most desirable site, and transmitted the report to the president of the university. The president reviewed the report with the advisory assistance of the university's Architectural Commission and recommended approval to the Board of Regents, who subsequently gave their approval and also appointed an architect for the design process.

The next series of developments involved a careful study by the appointed project architect of the report of the programming committee, several meetings with the committee, as well as numerous discussions with the Architectural Commission and representatives of the university's Office of Facilities Planning and Construction in order that the architect would gain a full understanding of the nature, purpose, and specific program requirements of the facility he had been called upon to design.

At this writing, the project architect is in the process of preparing a number of schematic drawings for the purpose of demonstrating graphically such factors as scale and gross component relationships of the proposed center to its selected site. With the approval of these drawings by the university administration, he will commence the preparation of preliminary design plans. Following approval of these preliminary designs, final plans will be drafted, and it is hoped that construction will begin reasonably soon thereafter.

Funding

The construction of a large, self-contained continuing education center inevitably involves a considerable funding program that most institutions have found difficult to approach. Even some of the Kellogg-assisted centers found the financing problem to be extremely difficult, notwithstanding the generous aid from the foundation.[8] Desirably, of course, a center would be financed to the greatest possible extent by means of the regular capital construction resources of the institution. Unfortunately, however, centers over the years have not generally been successful in competing for traditionally limited resources with other, equally pressing building needs of the institutions.

The center has some advantage, however, in being a facility which produces income from its housing and dining accommodations as well as, to a lesser degree, from the tuition or registration fees which it generates. The situation is also brightened somewhat by the fact that employed adults are usually in a position to pay for services rendered; indeed, some companies pay the total instructional and living costs for the employees whom they select to participate in programs of continuing education. However, special facilities and special services are expensive, and there is a line beyond which charges can become a burden, particularly where the educational program lasts for several days or weeks and where the participant must himself meet all or a large portion of the costs.

Federal sources have been of assistance to some centers. The center at the University of Minnesota, which opened its doors in 1936, was financed in depression times by funds made available through the then Public Works Agency of the federal government. Construction of the University of Chicago center, in addition to the Kellogg Foundation grant, was materially assisted in its financing by a long-term, low-interest loan from the Federal Housing and Home Finance Agency. More recently, a substantial grant was made for instructional facilities to the New England Center for Continuing Education by the U.S. Department of Health, Education and Welfare under Title I of the Higher Educational Facilities Act.[9]

Another form of assistance has come through private gifts of facilities which are easily convertible to use as centers for residential continuing education. The Lake Arrowhead Center of the University of California, the Pinebrook Center of the University of Syracuse, and Allerton House of the University of Illinois may be cited as examples of such gifts.

The question of funding a center cannot be answered in the form of an abstract generality. It requires a careful exploration of potential resources by each institution facing the question. A thorough review should be made of all possible sources such as institutional resources, bonding possibilities, federal or state loans or grants, grants from philanthropic foundations, and gifts from business, industry, alumni, and other private sources. Indeed, it is extremely unlikely that any one of these possible sources will be in a position to provide the total amount of funds necessary to put a center into operation; rather, institutions should be aware of the possibilities of utilizing these and perhaps other sources in some combined form.

ADMINISTRATION AND OPERATION

It would be impossible to treat comprehensively within a few pages the myriad problems and intricacies inherent in the administration and operation of a large, self-contained, residential center for continuing education. The Michigan State Center for good reason serves not only as a continuing education facility but also as a laboratory for teaching university courses in hotel administration. Thus the operation of any large center similar to the one at Michigan State involves not only the scope and complexities of hotel administration but also those operations which constitute the primary purpose of the center, the programming and presentation of educational programs

[8] Alford, *op. cit.*, p. 47.
[9] *Ibid.*, pp. 48, 128.

and related activities. But even these operations, in some cases, do not complete the scene. An additional layer of administrative services is imposed in cases where the center houses all the programs to be found on the organizational chart of continuing education. In this brief discussion, however, a more restricted view is taken and attention is focused exclusively on the center which adds to the usual components of housing, dining, and instructional facilities only those offices and accommodations which are necessary for program planning and operations management. At the same time, however, this is certainly not meant to exclude provision for research, in-service training, or internship programs. The planning and presentation of educational programs, one must remember, is the prime reason for the existence of the center. Although all other activities and services of the center might reach the highest levels of quality, they serve no purpose if the educational enterprise fails in its mission. The facilitating services included under the heading of operations management are important; indeed, poor management can vitiate the effectiveness of the educational effort. But it is important to bear in mind that these facilitating services are not the primary operation—they are ancillary services.

Program planning and presentation involves basically the planning of continuing education and related activities which cover a wide range of subject matter, a great variety of participants in both small and large numbers, an array of faculty members representing many academic departments, and many representatives of the professions, occupations, and civic and cultural groups.

This activity, apart from other aspects of operations management, requires many assistive facilities and offices such as those related to secretarial and clerical services, to the printing of brochures and other information pieces, to mailing operations, and to public information and press relations.

At the same time, operations management, although involving only the physical components of the center, is highly interrelated with program planning and presentation. While the services included within this function vary somewhat among institutions, the basic operations include such facets as budgeting, purchasing and disbursing, collection of conference fees, billing for rooms, space and room assignments, housing and dining, parking, and general maintenance.

If there is any one problem which is central to the effective administration and operation of a center, it is the establishment of an efficient and viable relationship between the two basic functions of program planning and operations management. The problem is in part traceable to the patently essential difference between the two functions; one is educational and the other managerial. Training for one is certainly not qualification for the other. Notwithstanding, the two functions must operate as one in a smooth and complementary fashion. This being a fundamental goal, that form of organizational relationship should be established between them which would be most conducive to an effective working relationship. The prime function of the center, as noted above, is education, and yet because that function is highly dependent upon operations management for its success, complications will arise if the person in charge of operations management does not report to the same supervisor as the person responsible for program planning. In an operation of substantial size, both the operations manager and the supervisor of program planning should report to the dean or director of the total continuing education complex or to an intermediate officer who would be in overall charge of the center. In illustration of this concept, an organizational chart for a large, self-contained center is shown in Figure 1.

No doubt there are instances where the lines of authority are not as clearly drawn. Such would be the case if, for example, the director of residence halls were to be assigned full or partial responsibility for center operations under the officer responsible for business and finance. Such an administrative arrangement might work quite well if the fullest measure of goodwill and cooperation prevailed; but something less

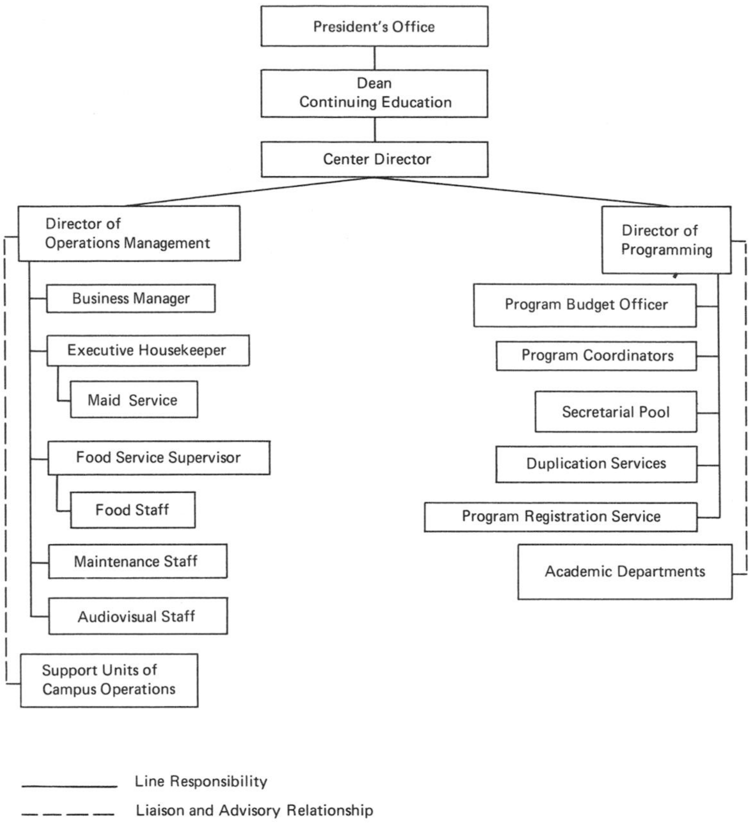

Fig. 1 *Organization chart for continuing education center.*

than that surely would place great strains upon the administrative process and inevitably impair in some measure the success of the instructional program.

A university continuing education center inevitably has a strong attraction to many off-campus organizations and agencies which schedule meetings and conferences in the conduct of their activities. This interest in use of the center poses a very important question: To whom should the center facilities be made available?

In attempting to answer this question, one must again call attention to the influence of local circumstances. For example, the uses of the facilities of a public university are often restricted by state law, whereas private universities are generally in a position to operate more freely; also, a facility not located in a large metropolitan area might find itself virtually committed to accommodating certain needs of local outside organizations which could not otherwise be accommodated. But whatever the case, the parent university should establish a clear policy with respect to the uses of the center by outside organizations. This is important for a number of reasons, one of which has immediate relevance to the first few years after the center opens its doors. A facility must be designed to accommodate the increased volume of activity which is expected to develop 5 or 10 years after its opening. It necessarily follows that during the first years of operation a fair proportion of the accommodations will not be in use. During this period, because of economic pressures, the persons reviewing applications for use might be tempted to approve them on a somewhat indiscriminate basis. Such indulgence faces a day of reckoning when university programs per se find it difficult to obtain accommodations. If the pressures are too great to be opposed, then, at the very least, care should be taken to inform outside users that one use does not constitute a continuing license.

In a discussion of the general problem of use, it is perhaps best to ignore the imponderables posed by local circumstances and to center attention instead on other considerations related to the issue of appropriate use. At the outset, two factors are obvious: one is that the facility's chief purpose is to serve as a residential center for continuing education, and the other is that the center is a university facility. Accordingly, the center should serve its avowed purposes within the university's rules and regulations governing the use of university facilities. Such uses obviously would include university-sponsored programs of continuing education. But this seemingly simple and straightforward statement poses an issue for adjudication. What constitutes sponsorship? This is clearly an issue for the attention and decision of each institution, but it is important to note that the issue usually centers around the uses by outside organizations under the "sponsorship" or "cosponsorship" of a university department which is otherwise qualified to sponsor or cosponsor programs in the center. A clear policy should therefore be enunciated by the institution with respect to what constitutes sponsorship. The reason for having such a policy is twofold: (1) it assists the institution in its use of the center in such a way as to maximize the purpose for which it was established—to advance the mission of the university, and (2) it also protects the academic department head who is placed in the position of being asked to sponsor or cosponsor a program which he may regard as being unrelated to the role of his department or of the university. With the stated policy as a guideline, he is able to make clear the policy which he is obliged to observe.

By way of illustration, the University of Washington has established the following rules with respect to the sponsorship of short courses and conferences, ". . . especially in cases where co-sponsoring off-campus organizations are involved":

1. The sponsoring department must have ultimate control over the subject matter and staffing of the program.
2. The program must involve a level and quality of subject-matter content consistent with the role of the department and the University.
3. The services of academic coordination and instruction must be performed by members of the faculty or by other qualified persons approved by the department.

Inasmuch as a center is a university facility, there are a number of activities which easily qualify for secondary albeit not unimportant uses. These would include meetings of academic societies which are sponsored by one or more departments, meetings of the faculty and of faculty committees, and official functions conducted by members of the faculty or administration.

As a final point under this heading it might be pointed out that, with any statement of policy, provision must be made for its effective interpretation. Operationally, it would seem that interpretations and judgments with respect to appropriate academic uses of a center facility should follow the normal academic-administrative lines of authority within the university.

In cases, however, where the issue relates more to some external concern or relationship of the university, channels leading through the office of university relations or some similar office might be more appropriately utilized. There are often cases where the rules concerning the use of university facilities provide for specific uses by certain outside organizations. The policies of the University of Washington provide that its facilities may be used for the following: "Activities or programs sponsored by educational institutions, by state or federal agencies, by charitable agencies or civic or community organizations whose activities are of widespread public service and of a character appropriate to the University." Under rules such as these, interpretation in relation to a specific request often becomes necessary. To meet this need, the president has appointed a university committee on the use of university facilities.

CONCLUSION

It should be said that the foregoing presentation has discussed only peripherally the inner workings and purposes of that activity of a center for continuing education which constitutes its highest and best purpose, indeed, its sole purpose—the planning and presentation of residential continuing education programs. A discussion relating to the process through which these programs are conceived, designed, and presented involves many considerations which are too extensive for adequate treatment within this brief presentation. However, institutions planning to construct centers should give careful consideration to the establishment of policies and procedures governing this basic process.

If the writers are to be allowed one further observation, it would be to say that although the foregoing discussion clearly implies the educational benefits which flow *from* a continuing education center to the community, one should not be unaware of the many benefits which also flow *to* the institution and its faculty through this reciprocal learning process.

Chapter 4

Theaters

CLYDE W. BLAKELEY

Theatre Arts, University of Maryland, Baltimore, Maryland

PURPOSE AND ADMINISTRATIVE STRUCTURE OF THEATER PROGRAMS

Introduction Although extracurricular dramatic activities date back to the earliest days of American colleges and universities, it has been only recently that theater has been considered a subject worthy of inclusion in serious academic institutions. Eastern universities, patterned after the British style of higher education where theater was considered too frivolous or immoral a profession for young men of university caliber, were slow to introduce formal instruction in any area of the theater except that of dramatic literature. When theater courses were introduced, instruction was usually under the administration of the English department. Midwestern and western state universities evolving from agricultural and mechanical colleges were more accustomed to applied education and hence less reticent about the inclusion of dramatic arts and crafts. Theater instruction included more courses in practice and was usually administered by a department of speech which also included forensics, speech and hearing correction, and, later, radio and television courses.

As smaller liberal arts colleges with a more humanistic approach began to introduce theater instruction, they either followed the eastern pattern with emphasis on dramatic literature or developed theater instruction through the fine arts department along with music, dance, and plastic and graphic arts. Some few conservatory-type colleges have developed independent theater departments, usually for the express purpose of training professional practitioners of the art.

Rarely did the theater departments develop independently of the administration of other long-established departments; most owe their existence to an activist in another department, such as English, who used his position in that department to develop theater instruction. Most older theater departments have strong "personality complexes" reflecting the characteristic philosophy and approach of the founding individual and the department to which he belonged. In some cases the personality complex was strong enough to breed a second generation of disciples who founded departments in other institutions. The personality cult is still relatively strong in theater administration. But departments of drama have now existed long enough for college administrators to view the operation of a theater department with sufficient perspective to make critical judgments, divorced from the bias of the founders, concerning the effectiveness of the theater program.

Purposes of Drama Programs Theater departments are organized for a variety of purposes, some of which are virtually incompatible with one another:

Professional Training. Programs in this category are intended to train professional actors, actresses, designers, technicians (e.g., Carnegie Tech, N.Y.U. School of Drama, Yale Graduate School). This is essentially the conservatory approach.

Teacher Training. Theater departments in state universities are largely oriented toward teachers of theater. They prepare most of their students to teach in other colleges, universities, and secondary schools.

Cultural Training. Some, particularly small liberal arts colleges, have humanistic programs designed to give students broad experience in the performing arts. They are neither professionally nor educationally oriented, but include theater as part of the total liberalizing experience of cultural education. They tend to involve students in an extracurricular or semicurricular program and have no intention of providing training for any professional career in theater.

In addition to formal or classroom instruction, almost all theater departments have a performing arm—a theater where productions are presented to help fulfill the department's educational functions. The emphasis here may be the training of audiences; plays are selected and a company of professional actors is engaged to present high-caliber productions of great plays from all periods. Or others, particularly the conservatory programs, use the performance situation primarily to train actors and other practitioners of the art, choosing their plays with no concern for audience needs. Most theater departments reflect some compromise between the needs of the audience to see good plays well presented on the one hand and the need to provide a training ground for fledgling practitioners on the other. Some schools engage professional actors or actresses to perform with student actors, providing examples for young performers as well as satisfying the audience need for professional-quality productions. This artist-in-residence concept has proved quite successful and is being used increasingly by colleges of all sizes.

Functional Classification of Theater Programs The American Educational Theatre Association began a college curriculum project in 1957 which eventually led to the publication of its findings in the 1960 edition of the *Directory of American College Theatre.* A greatly enlarged and revised second edition under the editorship of Richard G. Ayers was published in 1967. The research by the association reported in the directory was performed pursuant to a contract with the U.S. Department of Health, Education and Welfare, Office of Education, and is a comprehensive report of educational theater in 1,581 regionally accredited United States colleges and universities. It is the principal source for the statistical information in this chapter. The directory created the following five functional categories to best describe the pattern of theater education identified in the various institutions: [1]

1. *Recreational.* Extra-curricular dramatic production is the chief or only activity or program. Few or no theatre courses are offered. The theatre program is carried on through a campus club related to a field of the humanities or sciences. Students are not expected to pursue careers in theatre.

2. *Avocational.* The theatre program consists of extra-curricular dramatic production and a few courses taught in established department of humanities or arts. Theatre is not considered a distinct field of study, but a subject which an educated person should appreciate. Cultural values sought in dramatic literature and criticism. Workshops or symposia in the arts stress creative methods and experimental approaches.

3. *Liberal Arts—Humanistic.* The equivalent of eighteen or more semester hours is offered in theatre courses. The student takes some work in each theatre area, is encouraged to demonstrate scholarly and research abilities as well as practical skills. Two or more faculty assigned to the theatre program. Three or more featured productions are staged annually. The value of a liberal arts education is stressed and students are discouraged from specialization. Many students become teachers of theatre.

4. *Liberal Arts—Vocational.* Extensive curriculum in theatre subjects (more than 40 semester hours) is offered, four or more full-time faculty assigned. Students are expected and encouraged to specialize in one area of theatre while developing competence in several areas. Practical production experience is valued as students will enter one of the theatre's professions, probably educational or community theatre. Liberal arts background considered helpful to a professional career.

5. *Pre-Professional.* An extensive curriculum is provided in each specialty of theatre practice. Students are expected to become theatre professionals. Numerous

[1] Richard G. Ayers (ed.), *Directory of American College Theatre,* 2d ed., American Educational Theatre Association, Inc., Washington, D.C., 1967, pp. 1–2.

faculty with credits in professional theatre. Few non-theatre students participate in frequent play productions.

Out of the 1,581 accredited schools surveyed, 93 percent, or 1,472, supplied classifiable information indicating that over 85 percent have some form of drama program. Those 1,297 schools with programs are classified as follows: 43 percent, or 560, have programs whose purpose falls into the first two categories—recreational or avocational; 558, or 43 percent, were classified as liberal arts—humanistic; while only 135, or 10.5 percent, could be called liberal arts—vocational; and only 44, or 3.5 percent, are preprofessional. Although few of the accredited colleges and universities in the United States have programs professionally or vocationally oriented (less than 12 percent), over one-third of all the colleges offer enough courses in drama to grant an academic major in theater arts.

Administrative Organization It is important that the administration of the theater department be sympathetic with its purposes and functions as outlined above. As previously mentioned, few theater programs have independent status as theater departments or departments of dramatic arts, but most are included in one of the following departments:

1. English or language and literature, or language arts
2. Speech, or speech-drama, or English-speech, or communications
3. Fine arts, or performing arts, or drama and dance
4. Humanities department

A theater intended to be liberal arts, humanistic, or avocational in purpose is best included in fine arts or humanities programs, where the emphasis is more likely to be the broader cultural impact of the performing arts, rather than in English departments, where the emphasis may shift to plays or literature. However, no matter in which department it is included, theater is complete only in the performance situation and a thorough and sympathetic understanding of the production program is essential if the theater department is to be effective.

PRODUCTION PROGRAM

The most complicated and least understood of any aspect of the theater department is the production program. This lack of understanding can lead to an almost untenable situation when an academic department is called upon to run a business operation producing a product for public consumption in addition to its educational function. It could be likened to having a chemistry department produce and market a line of plastics as well as train students in general chemistry. Inevitably, conflicts in the allocation of time, personnel, budget, and physical plant will arise. Public relations and promotional problems affecting the image of the entire college will arise over choice of plays and quality of production. The varsity football team can lose a whole season of games without reflecting on the academic caliber of the institution, but a whole season of bad productions will raise questions about the quality of the education the institution's students are receiving.

Time Schedule. The rhythm of theater production is vastly different from the academic schedule and demands a considerable commitment of time from the students and faculty involved. Not only do the responsibilities make the commitment absolute and take precedence over other academic obligations, but they tend to increase geometrically as opening night approaches. The student playing Hamlet must learn his part and rehearse until the play is ready for performance. The opening has been set and the tickets have been sold. An audience will come expecting to see an acceptable level of production. Hamlet must spend the necessary time to learn all his lines; he cannot delegate half of them to someone else.

The responsibilities of coordinating the production schedule with the academic schedule in order to avoid unnecessary conflict and hardship on student participants must rest with the theater faculty. They are the only ones who can determine the amount of rehearsal and building time a play will demand, when rehearsals should begin, how many hours must be devoted to them each week, and the number of performances the play should receive. The time span from beginning of production to opening is usually shorter than an academic quarter or semester. The rehearsal period in most educational theaters varies from four to eight weeks, with rehearsal occurring from three to five times per week. The total student commitment then will be determined by the preproduction period of tryouts and casting (one to two weeks), the rehearsal period, and the length of the run (one to three weeks). A student playing a major role may be committing himself to 100 hours of rehearsal time, 25 hours of line-learning time, and up to 30 hours of performance time, totaling over 150 hours to be divided over a six- to ten-week span with very high concentration in the last week before opening. A student stage manager or production crew head may also find that he has obligated himself to a similar time commitment.

The trend in American colleges and universities to increase the pressure of academic course work has seriously impaired the operation of recreational-avocational theaters and even some liberal arts—humanistic programs. The average student must spend so much time maintaining his academic standing that he is unable to assume the commitment of time that participation in dramatic activities demands. Academic departments, including the theater, are reluctant to allow academic credit for production work or acting in the drama program, insisting that practical and empirical education does not deserve the same academic recognition as classroom activity. Colleges must somehow reconcile participation in time-consuming creative programs with the academic credit system before such cultural activities are starved for student support. Too often, upgrading academic education has been equated with increasing the quantity of material to be covered in each course, leaving students with little time to develop avocational activities.

Faculty also need relief from their academic schedule if the theater program is to flourish in any meaningful way. Most colleges allow a reduction of three semester hours' teaching load for each major production directed or produced by a faculty member and a like credit for the designer-technical director. This is a reasonably fair allotment inasmuch as the average major production requires from 200 to 300 hours of time from both the director and the technical director. A director spends approximately 100 to 150 hours in rehearsal and performance and a like time in script preparation, casting, and conferences with actors and production personnel. The designer-technical director requires 50 to 100 hours in conference and design time and up to 200 hours to supervise the building and running crews.

Unfortunately, the time required to produce a play is just as great for a college whose program is recreational or avocational as for one whose program is primarily concerned with training professional practitioners of the art. The college that feels that theater is a worthwhile part of a student's cultural education recognizes the function of a drama club organization in students' lives and realizes the public relations value of the town and gown audience experience. Even though such a college may not wish to develop a professional program, it must nevertheless recognize the cost of the program in both time and materials.

Budget. No educational theater today can be a fiscally balanced operation. In addition to providing and maintaining an adequate theater plant and a professional supervisory staff of at least a director and a technical director, most colleges find that they must also subsidize the production budget by sometimes as much as 50 percent of the operating costs. Even though the income from the sale of tickets may be considerable, the expenses of even a modest college production are high. A sample production budget is included here as an illustration of thc usual expenses met by a typical college drama department to produce a single play. The figures are typical but can vary widely depending on the type and elaborateness of the production, the imagination and ingenuity of the production staff, and the size and flexibility of the theater plant. They do serve, however, to indicate the approximate proportion of expense that must be allocated to various items. The budget areas have been annotated to explain more fully the nature of the expenses. This budget assumes a completely equipped theater with all the necessary lighting equipment, draperies, and the typical stock of old scenery from past productions that can be modified to meet the needs of a new production. It does not include the maintenance of the plant or the capital improvements in plant or equipment. The budget is entirely for materials and services and does not include any personnel expenses such as box-office people or backstage technicians. The problems of personnel expenses are discussed later in this section under "Production Personnel and Organization."

Production

Scenery and supplies:
Includes wood, canvas, scene paint, and all necessary materials to build and rig the scenery of the stage.......... $300

Props:
Includes furniture and all small items handled by actors.......... 100

Lights:
Includes maintenance and relamping of spotlights, color media, and materials for special effects.......... 50

Sound:
Includes tapes, sound-effects records, and maintenance of recording equipment.......... 30

Costumes:
Includes all clothing worn by the actor as well as shoes and wigs.......... 400
(Most plays produced by college theaters are from the classics, which usually call for large casts and period costumes. If the department builds its own costumes, the cost must also include cleaning. If costumes are rented, the cost will be slightly higher.)

Makeup:
The professional actor is expected to supply his own makeup, but college theaters generally supply all that is necessary for the production.......... 40

Scripts.......... 25

Royalties:
Many plays performed by college and university theaters are copyright free, but when a contemporary play is done the usual amateur rights prevail.......... 35 to 50 per performance

Subtotal expenses for first performance.......... $1,000

Cost per performance for each additional performance up to maximum of six.......... approximately $75

Front of House

Tickets:
Cost of reserved-seat tickets varies with the size of the house, the number of ticket sets ordered, and changes per set.......... $20

Programs:
Varies with number ordered and degree of elaborateness.......... 20 to 60 per night

(Note: Many additional expenses are incurred in operating a box office, but the way they are handled varies from college to college, making it difficult to arrive at any figure for telephones, office supplies, commissions for sales, etc.)

Subtotal front-of-house expense per performance.. $60

Publicity and Promotion. Expenses in this area vary widely depending on the size of the community in which the organization is located. Whether student tickets are handled through a student activities fee, subscription tickets are sold once a year, or a publicity campaign is mounted to sell individual tickets for each play will also affect promotion costs. The areas of expense are:

Advertising: Includes all paid advertising in newspapers and radio.

Mailing: Includes addressing and postage or flyers, etc.

General Promotion: Cost of printing and distributing flyers, handbills, and posters, materials for window displays, etc. Assuming that the publicity campaign is handled through some sort of seasonal subscription drive with smaller promotional drives for each production, a pattern that is followed by most college theaters, a conservative estimate of the total yearly promotional cost divided by the number of performances would be approximately $50 per performance.

The cost of mounting a typical college production exclusive of labor and maintenance would total $1,100 to $1,200, with expenses of approximately $200 for each additional performance. The above are conservative figures in an area where production facilities and time considerations can cause them to vary widely.

Income. The average college theater seats approximately five hundred people, and the usual run is three performances. If the attendance averages 75 percent of capacity, a common enough figure, then the total attendance would be 1,125. Most college theaters price their tickets at about $1.50, but they discount them to students (usually 75 cents or $1) and to seasonal subscribers (approximately $1.25). The average ticket price, including discounts and considering the ratio of students to general public, would then be somewhere between $1 and $1.25. The average total income would then be approximately $1,300 as against $1,500 to $1,600 in expenses for the three performances.

A 20-percent operating subsidy would be required to make up the $200 to $300 deficit. Although it is not within the scope of this chapter to justify a theater program for any college, this would seem a small enough price for the cultural and educational advantages in having a living theater on the campus.

There is a limited potential audience for classic drama. This is true even in a high-powered academic community, where one could expect a higher ratio of playgoers, because there one will find a greater number of activities which compete for the culture seeker's time. Most theaters increase the number of performances (up to a maximum of six or seven, after which the learning experience for the actor and technician reaches a point where it is not worth additional expenditure of time) until the average attendance per performance drops to about 60 percent. This seems to provide an optimum number of opportunities for potential audience members to see the play without unduly increasing the cost of the operation. As compared to the professional theater, labor cost in college productions is not much of a factor and therefore it costs very little to add performances.

Colleges with professional training programs usually have higher production expenses because the staging is more elaborate. Although they can sometimes command higher ticket prices, these are not likely to completely offset the increasing cost. The increased deficit is justified by providing the student with a laboratory or intern-type training situation.

Production Personnel and Organization Although the producing organization in an educational theater does not necessarily resemble that found in a professional theater, an examination of a typical professional personnel chart will reveal the lines of authority and responsibility that exist in all theaters irrespective of size and purpose. It will provide a clearer understanding of the division of labor in a smaller organization where the professional staff must oversee many student volunteers, training them to the various arts and crafts of the theater while producing an artistic product.

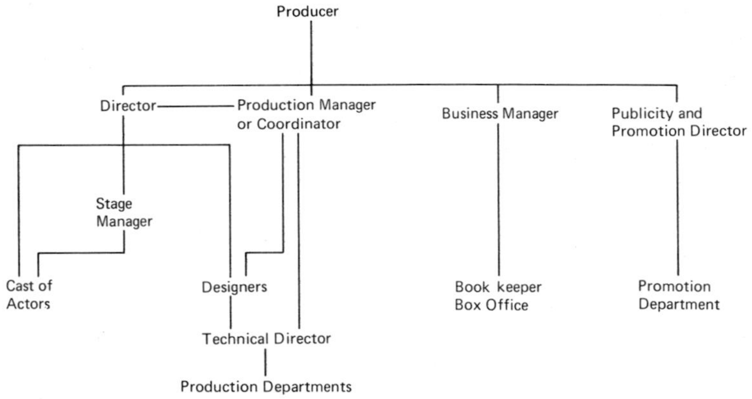

Fig. 1 *Typical production personnel chart.*

Production Personnel. In a typical Broadway production the director may move up the organizational ladder to a position just below that of the producer and exercise considerable influence over promotion and the business office as well as complete artistic authority.

In an educational theater the function of producer is quite naturally assumed by the college through the head of the drama department. The college provides the operating capital as well as the producing facility. The department head chooses which of his staff will fulfill the functions of artistic director, designer-technical director, and production coordinator. The adequate discharge of these responsibilities requires at least two staff members—one to act as artistic director and the other to execute the various production chores. It is imperative that faculty members involved in any production be relieved of academic responsibilities to a degree commensurate with the degree of their involvement. Larger departments will have a greater division of labor, frequently adding student assistants in the production department for responsibilities such as supervisor of costumes and wardrobe, supervisor of scene construction, shop manager, lighting technician, properties master, and stage manager. Unless the faculty is expanded to the proportions of some of the very large conservatories, an extensive production program makes the use of paid assistants a necessity. As these student assistants become more experienced, they are provided with opportunities to act as assistant designers in their particular areas. The remainder of the producing organization will be composed of participating students.

The cast of actors is almost invariably made up of students who compete in tryouts or readings conducted by the director. A mixed cast composed of students, faculty, community, and occasionally professional actors is highly recommended. The enthusiasm of the student is tempered by the maturity and discipline of the older members of the cast and a healthy dialogue across the generation gap ensues. The use of an occasional professional actor provides a marvelous opportunity for students to observe the dedication and the discipline necessary to be a successful actor. Most students develop a healthy respect for the difficulties of the profession and are able to assess more realistically the state of their own development. After working with a professional actor the student is not so likely to leave for New York stage struck and blinded by some dream of glory.

Students participate in production crews for a variety of reasons: some enjoy the avocational relaxation of physical work and handling materials after a day of mental activity; some are frustrated actors who were not cast but wish to be involved in the theater at any cost; some simply enjoy the excitement and romance of backstage activity; some want experience in all phases of theater to deepen their appreciation and make them better actors, directors, teachers, etc.; and some participate because there are not enough people for the backstage labor and they have been assigned backstage "lab time" for a theater course they are taking. Very few are backstage because they wish to pursue careers in technical theater.

Business Management. Because considerable sums of money are involved, the functions of the business manager and box-office operation are frequently assumed by the college business office. College administrators are inclined to view the budgeting efforts of their faculty with a jaundiced eye. Financial headaches created by the theater department are not necessarily due to the inability of the drama faculty to manage money or think practically about budgets. Some are caused by the difficulty of fixing a price tag on a work of art. Spending $100 more than was originally budgeted for materials to construct an elevator to lower Dr. Faustus to hell may mean the difference between a successful production and a failure, but it will not necessarily be reflected in increased income. And if it were (if the device were of great publicity value), it would be impossible to know that until after the money had been committed. However, most conflicts between the college business office and the theater arise from the compression of time in a theatrical venture. What is normal in theater seems to the comptroller a crisis due to bad planning. Theater production frequently requires spending considerable sums of money on short notice, a problem that the bureaucracy of most college purchasing departments finds difficult to understand. Theater is a social art that relies on the cooperative efforts of many artists whose ideas cross-fertilize one another. Only a limited amount of planning can proceed before the entire producing organization is formed. Staging a play is somewhat like having to design and erect a building in eight weeks without necessarily knowing in advance if the construction will be masonry or wood. Many of the materials used cannot be stockpiled or ordered in advance. Costumes, for example, cannot be designed until the play is cast. One does not clothe a 5 ft 6 in. actor the same as one who is 6 ft 3 in. tall, regardless of the role he is playing. Some provision, within the framework of responsible fiscal policy, must be made to allow the production coordinator to purchase materials without the usual business-office delays. Administrators are quite justified in their apprehension over large petty cash funds and can usually meet the needs of the theater by supplying open purchase orders with outside limits to the more common local supply houses. It then becomes the responsibility of the theater department to see that the purchase order is renewed when the amount is nearly exhausted. Colleges and universities with larger theater departments engage a faculty member with theatrical business-management experience to establish a departmental business office. He will manage the box office as well as maintain the control over the operating expenses. Part of the expected operating deficit may be advanced at the beginning of the year as a "producer's account" to allow supplies to be purchased before box-office income from the first production is collected. Audit controls are established for the protection of all parties.

Physical Plant A building completely equipped as a theater can house a variety of other activities—lectures, films, concerts, and readings—fairly successfully, but a lecture or concert hall cannot double as a theater. The main concern in a lecture hall is the audience environment; the lecturer requires only some kind of presentational platform, good acoustics, and sufficient light. In the presentation of plays, the stage and its equipment are of major importance. The stage must be flexible enough to allow the creation of many environments for the performer, ranging from the "topless towers of Ilium" to the interior of a lighthouse. Any college contemplating the construction of an auditorium that will be used as a theater should insist that the architect engage a reputable theater consultant. Many theaters are badly designed because architects and college administrators do not understand the way the stage functions during the actual performance.

Types and Sizes of College Theaters. The distinguishing features of the most common type of theater, the *proscenium arch theater,* are the narrow audience configuration and the picture-frame proscenium that separates the audience from the stage house. For best results with amateur actors, the auditorium should not exceed 600 seats. It is too difficult for the untrained voice to project to the rear of a larger house. The stage should not have an opening more than 35 feet wide—preferably below 30 feet unless musicals and dance programs are to be presented. The excess width of larger stages must be reduced in order to avoid an enormous sense of scale in the scenery, even if some of the side seats are rendered unusable. Lincoln would look ridiculous in a cabin with a 40-foot living room. The height of the proscenium should be in proportion to the auditorium architecture, and in no case should it be less than 15 feet. The dimension of the rest of the stage house should be as follows: wing space (the space from the side of the proscenium to the stage wall), at least half the proscenium width; depth of stage, 30 feet, height to gridiron (the open metal floor located below the roof from which scenery is suspended), at least twice the proscenium height plus 6 feet.

Recently, a style of modified proscenium stage known as the *platform, thrust,* or *open stage* has become popular among smaller colleges and universities. The distinguishing feature of this type of auditorium-stage configuration is the deep apron (the part of the floor that thrusts in front of the proscenium in a conventional stage) surrounded on three sides by seating sections. Sometimes the proscenium is completely eliminated with standing scenery arranged only across the back wall. Some advantages of this system are (1) lower initial cost of the building—expensive stage rigging and scenery facilities are eliminated, (2) less scenery is required to fill the stage, (3) actors are closer to the audience and the audience-actor relationship is more intimate. Such theaters work well for presentational styles of production but are most difficult for illusionistic styles. The audience cannot surround the stage by more than 120 degrees without having difficulty hearing and seeing the action. It is also difficult to arrange stage entrances other than across the back wall, which limits the pattern of stage movement.

The third popular theater configuration is the *arena stage,* where the audience surrounds the playing area on all four sides. Arena theaters are frequently set up in converted classrooms or lecture halls. They have the advantage of great intimacy and are economical to operate. They do not work well with the student actor when their size begins to exceed 250 seats. A good arena stage should be equipped with an extensive and flexible lighting system to help compensate for the limited opportunity to use scenic elements.

Flexible stages where the actor-audience configuration can be modified from proscenium through arena are not recommended. They are more expensive in initial construction and require more maintenance than conventional forms. Flexible stages are always a compromise between various optimum designs, and most users eventually find themselves settling on the configuration that works most satisfactorily and seldom converting to any of the other forms. It is often possible to build two auditoriums that share production facilities for very little more than the cost of one convertible auditorium.

Theater Equipment. Mechanical equipment for the stage should be simple, flexible, and hand-powered so that students can be trained to rig and manipulate all devices.

Electronically controlled grid winches and elaborate hydraulic elevator systems should be avoided. Opportunities for students to learn are eliminated by automation and labor-saving devices that can only be operated by trained experts.

Although electronic dimmer boards are slightly more expensive in their initial installation, ease of maintenance and flexibility are two advantages that virtually eliminate consideration of other forms of lighting control. However, elaborate memory systems and other control embellishments should be avoided. A two- to four-scene preset system is sufficient for all but the most professionally oriented theater department.

Auditorium Sharing. Auditorium sharing between the theater department and other users is possible although not highly desirable. When circumstances make sharing necessary, authority and control over the auditorium should be vested in the theater department, as its needs are the most demanding and time-consuming. The theater department will also have more people, both faculty and students, trained in the operation of the facility so that through their assistance the greatest use may be enjoyed by all.

INSTRUCTIONAL PROGRAM

A.E.T.A. Quantitative Minimum Criteria for Theater Departments—1966 In a theater program, classroom instruction is only part of the influence at work. To recognize the combined elements that constitute an effective instructional program, the American Educational Theatre Association officially adopted the following criteria to quantitatively describe the minimum standards for a department that grants undergraduate degrees in theater: [2]

Senior Colleges: (U.S. Office of Education Class II)

1. Curriculum. Not fewer than thirty semester hours, or equivalent, of theater or drama content courses.
   a. These to be exclusive of dramatic literature, broadcasting and film, public speaking or forensic courses.
   b. Courses to be offered regularly and taught by qualified instructors who are regular members of a theatre or theatre-speech department faculty.
   c. Content and distribution of courses in curriculum, at least three semester hours in each subject.
      (1) Introduction to Theatre
      (2) Introduction to Technical Production
      (3) Theatre Speech
      (4) Theatre and Drama History
      (5) Directing
      (6) Beginning Acting
      (7) Technical Production
      (8) Elective. Advanced theatre or drama courses; e.g., Playwriting, Dance, Costume, History, Dramatic Literature, etc.
2. Library. Adequate reference facilities.
3. Staff.
   a. Training. Drama instructors to have M.A. degree, or equivalent, with no fewer than 45 semester hours of drama content courses, at least 21 of which will be graduate level courses from an accredited college. (Professional training or experience as approved by individual institutions may be substituted for degree requirements.)
   b. Teaching Load. Teaching load not to exceed twelve semester hours of classroom instruction. Drama instructors responsible for production as director or technician to be granted a three semester hour credit on the teaching load.

[2] *Ibid.*, p. 193.

c. Number. A minimum of three full-time faculty members or equivalent in charge of the program, and a student scholarship or work-aid program sufficient to carry on the production schedule recommended below.

4. Physical Plant. Adequate physical plant and production facilities to present open stage, arena, or proscenium productions.

5. Production. Annually four long plays (directed by regular faculty members) and three short plays or one interdepartmental production.

The Extent of Educational Theater in the United States Although the *Directory of American College Theatre* findings indicate that approximately 75 percent of the colleges offer some course work in theater, about half of that number offer less than enough to constitute an academic major (from just a few survey courses to the equivalent of a minor),[3] and

. . . 24.9 per cent at all accredited institutions in higher education schedule enough work to warrant the granting of specific degrees in theater as a field of study. An annual audience of approximately five million witnesses more than 10,000 play productions staged by these campus programs, which teach about 116,000 enrolled students in formal classroom situations and engage over 100,000 different students (some of whom undertake no theatre courses) in the business of putting on plays.

Areas of Instruction Although the number of courses offered, their emphasis, and their content will vary according to the purpose of the instructional program (liberal arts—humanistic, liberal arts—vocational, or preprofessional), the following areas are generally considered part of theater instruction (some professional programs proliferate courses within areas sufficiently that a student must specialize even on the undergraduate level. For example, he may major in acting and take only one or two courses in each of the other areas of the theater):

General Introductory Courses. "Introduction to the Theater" service courses for students other than theater majors should consist of a survey of drama and the art and craft of the theater. Not an applied course—no play production.

Acting. The art and craft of the actor, practice and theory. Related courses in this area include theater dance, actor movement, mime, fencing, and theater speech (which includes breath control, projection, articulation, and phonetics but does not include speech correction or forensics).

Directing. Theory and practice of play production from the standpoint of the artistic director.

Technical Production and Design. "Introduction to Technical Production" includes theory and practice in scenery construction, painting and rigging, scene shifting, properties construction, elements of stage lighting. More advanced technical courses are offered in scene design, stagecraft, lighting design and execution, costumes (including history of dress, costume design, pattern making, and costume construction), and stage makeup.

History of the Theater. Courses in this subject should include the function of theater in each society, its expression in the dramatic literature and the style of presentation in the playhouse. Related courses in the dramatic literature of various periods are frequently taught by faculty of the English department.

Dramatic Theory and Criticism.

Playwriting.

Children's Theater. Theater for children including creative dramatics and play production with children is popular in liberal arts—vocational programs, especially among women.

[3] *Ibid.*, p. 186.

Teaching Theater. Under this heading come methods courses in education colleges.

Special Courses.

1. Religious drama
2. Theater management
3. Theater architecture
4. Advanced and seminar courses in all above areas

Courses in Related Mass Media. In this category belong courses in television, radio, and cinema.

Chapter **5**

Museums

THOMAS H. GARVER

Director, Newport Harbor Art Museum, Balboa, California; formerly Assistant Director, Rose Art Museum, Brandeis University, Waltham, Massachusetts

INTRODUCTION

The years since 1945 have seen an enormous increase in the number of museums and galleries of various sorts on university campuses. Generally speaking, this increase of numbers is in art museums and art galleries, reflecting a new interest in the visual arts that is comparable to the heightened interest in the natural sciences in the nineteenth century. This chapter, therefore, stresses art museum problems and policies, for these museums are usually newer to the campus and face greater controversy than museums of other types.

Frequently today, the new museum is placed within a larger complex, an art center which houses many activities related to one another philosophically but not functionally; and the specific needs of the public and private spaces within the museum portion of the structure are often submerged within the better-understood or more obvious requirements of studios or concert halls, for example.

Frequently, too, the staff requirements and activities of museums and galleries are not clearly understood by university administrators who may expect their art museum to be a "jewel box" or a "temple of repose," but who are shocked to find instead exhibitions which challenge every sensibility. The limits of art are constantly being explored and challenged, as are the limits of science. This is an important point to consider, as administrators may be called upon to defend to some segment of the public the activities or policies of the university's museum. An early realization should be that the best protection for the institution will be competent personnel—hire them, pay them salaries commensurate with their talent, and then support their professional decisions.

POSITION OF A UNIVERSITY MUSEUM WITHIN THE UNIVERSITY STRUCTURE

A university museum, no matter what its direction—art, archaeology, natural history, science—must be regarded as a serious academic undertaking and a valid teaching organization. Therefore, the museum should be given the status of an independent academic department; and its director, having the equivalent status of a department chairman, should report directly to a dean or academic vice-president. (For, unless it is simply an exhibition space operated without any full-time staff, the museum should not be regarded as an adjunct to another academic department.)

University administrators or deans may wish to appoint a committee to assist the director of the museum in establishing policy. Most such committees, in order to be effective, are informal and intrauniversity in nature; their function is chiefly to suggest and advise and to make available to the director men from different academic areas on whom he can sound out his thoughts and ideas. Some universities appoint committees from individuals outside the institution—professional museum people who can offer suggestions from their own experience, and lay people who can broaden the museum's program through assistance in funding, gifts of objects or works of art, or support of the museum within the larger community.

A note of caution: As an academic instrument, the museum should not be placed under a business vice-president or other officer who does not have as his first interest the academic quality of the institution. This is likely to lead to a lack of support for the museum, especially if its programs are at all controversial.

PERSONNEL

Of first importance, of course, is the selection of the director of the museum. In every case, this man's title should be "Director," as he is responsible for the operation of the museum. (Within the museum field, the title "Curator" is not given to an overseeing authority but rather to an individual scholar responsible for specific areas of the museum's collections or exhibitions—e.g., "Curator of Paintings and Sculpture," "Curator of Drawings," "Curator of Oriental Art"—and he is in turn responsible to the director.)

The director will, through his knowledge, taste, and sensibilities, set the tenor of the museum. It is important that this man combine in almost equal measure a sure knowledge of his field and an ability to transmit his knowledge through the vitality of his exhibitions to the museum visitor. An individual should be sought for the position of director who has evinced competence in both areas. Certainly the position should be held by an individual of faculty rank and privilege, although the position itself, like a departmental chairmanship, might be an administrative, nontenure one.

If university regulations require that the director teach in order to maintain faculty status, his teaching load should be minimized and so organized as to free him for at least half of the academic year to organize exhibitions. The organizing of exhibitions frequently requires extensive travel and concentrated periods of research, writing, and installation, and it is difficult to reconcile this cyclic type of time use with the more linear time schedule required for lecture or seminar courses.

Consideration should also be given to having the director work an 11-month year instead of a 9-month academic year, for frequently much organizational work and maintenance of the permanent collection must be done during the summer months when the exhibition or academic schedule is lighter.

The number and qualifications of members of the museum staff will vary with the type and size of the operation, but certain positions and functions are common to all institutions. These are outlined below.

Director. The director's job is to administer the museum, to set the exhibition and acquisition policies, and to oversee proper care of the museum's collection. He is also required to integrate museum activities with university programs and to act as liaison between university and citywide cultural affairs.

Curator/Staff Assistant. The curator/staff assistant carries out policy formulated by the director and assists in the organization of exhibitions. If the position is curatorial, the individual holding it will be expected to suggest items which might be acquired for the permanent collection and to maintain the catalog and scholarly records of the objects in the permanent collection.

Registrar. The registrar is expected to maintain the records of the permanent collection of objects and to know their location and condition at all times, to handle the logistical problems connected with the borrowing or lending of objects for exhibition, and to maintain all insurance records of objects owned by or on loan to the museum.

Museum Superintendent/Preparator. The job of this staff member is to supervise museum facilities, particularly in the matter of security; to handle the construction of packing boxes and exhibition furniture, cases, panels, etc.; to direct the actual installation of exhibitions while working with the director and his assistant or curator; to be responsible for the proper packing and shipping of works of art or other museum objects; and to direct the upkeep of the physical plant.

The staff will also include secretaries, assistants of various sorts, and possibly volunteer help or paid undergraduate and graduate staff. Volunteer and student staff should be carefully selected and their performance monitored to assure their interest and competence.

A further word on the matter of staff: Both the positions of registrar and museum superintendent are critical to the smooth, accident-free operation of the museum, and the persons who are to hold them should be carefully chosen. The registrar should be able to type and handle routine registration chores, have a logical mind and, if at all possible, a museum background. He or she can frequently gain extra professional knowledge through a short, informal apprenticeship with the registrar of any large, cooperative museum.

The museum superintendent's job is a vital one in that he handles the objects on exhibition in the museum and supervises others doing so. He must be knowledgeable in packing and exhibition procedures and must be able to organize himself and the staff under him to work on a deadline basis. Under no circumstances should the registrar's position be regarded as clerical or the superintendent's as custodial; both of these positions are fully professional, and persons filling them should be paid accordingly.

PHYSICAL FACILITIES

Location There is no completely satisfactory answer as to whether a museum should be located in its own building or incorporated in a larger complex. If the gallery is modest, it may be in the same building as the parent department (e.g., a room set aside for geological specimens in the geology department).

Assuming the museum to be of more sizable proportions, it might be well to find a more permanent structure for it. If funds are not available for new museum construction, an older building, which is sound but no longer large enough or whose original function is outmoded, might successfully be remodeled into museum space. If this is to be done, the structure should meet certain necessary criteria outlined below.

Using a portion of the student union building as a gallery is not to be recommended; for, assuming that the museum is a serious academic venture, there is potential conflict between the museum purpose and the union purpose. The union is a place for relaxation, not intellection. Some student unions run their own art programs, but these are usually of an informal nature—rental of reproductions for student rooms, craft courses for students, exhibitions of student work. The museum staff may be of assistance to the union staff in an advisory capacity in planning programs and the museum may plan and organize small exhibitions in the union; but their relationship should not extend beyond mutual assistance.

Division and Allocation of Space The problem of allocation of space within museum buildings or gallery areas is woefully misunderstood. There are two types of museum space, public and private; they are totally different in function, yet the museum cannot successfully and efficiently operate a program within its public galleries without the facilities provided by the private spaces (shops, storerooms, shipping areas, offices, etc.). It is these private spaces, however, that are the first to fall when a museum program is subjected to budget restrictions. Trustees and administrative officers allow the construction of large exhibition spaces but are loath to provide funds to build, for example, secure, weatherproof facilities for the storage of crates, which are essential parts of any traveling exhibition. Well-organized and well-planned museums require a public-space to private-space ratio of about 40 percent public to 60 percent private, so most of the space should be allotted to internal functions rather than to public exhibition. This is a point that cannot be stressed too strongly in planning a new building or remodeling an old one.

Outlined below is a brief review of necessary museum facilities which has been prepared by following the path a work of art or other object takes from the time it arrives at the museum until it is exhibited. The object's path through the museum should be as "linear" as possible. Changes of floor level, low doorways, numerous twisting corridors, too small elevators, and the like must be avoided as each rehandling of the object increases the chance of damage to it and decreases staff efficiency.

Shipping and Receiving Area. The object will enter the museum building almost invariably by truck, and an elevated loading dock, protected from the weather, must be provided to unload trucks as efficiently and safely as possible. Shipping areas must be large enough to accommodate the entire contents of a "high-cube" over-the-road van (its floor area approximately 10 by 40 feet and its roof height 10 feet). Obviously, all building ceilings and doorways must be high enough to accommodate, at the very least, an object that will fit the height of such a truck with room to spare—12 feet is a suggested minimum ceiling height.

A minimum shipping-area space would be 2,400 to 2,500 square feet, which would hold the contents of two vans, or two exhibitions.

Shipping crates and other packing materials are both costly and vital for the protection of the objects shipped, and storage space for this material should be provided adjacent to the shipping room.

Shop Area. The workshop area should be directly adjacent to but not part of the shipping area. The workshop would contain the power tools, saws, and work tables and have the storage areas for lumber, paint, and other materials necessary to carry out large-scale construction. As museum construction is much akin to theater stage-set construction in scale, a museum shop much on the order of a theatrical scene shop should be provided. High ceilings and area for temporary storage of completed constructions are both necessary. The shop area should approach the size of the shipping room.

Storage Areas. Several different types of storage areas should be provided for different classifications of objects. These storage areas should be between the shipping area and the gallery area and, if possible, also convenient to the museum offices.

In these storage areas, one will probably be storing the following: exhibition objects owned by the institution; objects for exhibition only, owned by others and held in storage for a relatively short time before and after exhibition; exhibition pedestals, cases, vitrines, wall panels, and temporary partitions (although because of their size these are best stored immediately adjacent to the gallery space and on the same floor).

These storage spaces for different types of objects might be adjacent to one another, but under no circumstances should they be combined. Because museum objects vary so widely in their storage requirements, the reader is referred to the book *Museum Registration Methods* (noted in the bibliography) for specific data on various objects. Storage of any objects, however, should be subject to three considerations: (1) objects must be provided a safe climate and environment; (2) like objects should be stored together; and (3) objects in storage, like books in a library, should be readily accessible when they are needed. In a university museum, provision should also be made for study storage or a combination small gallery-classroom where objects from the collection may be exhibited in conjunction with classes or student projects.

Recording and Examination Space. This is an area, critical in larger museums and useful in smaller ones, where objects are examined prior to being sent to storage or exhibition areas. Photographs may also be made here.

Corridors and Elevators. These spaces are so "subversive" as to go almost unnoticed in architectural plans, yet they are important to the smooth traffic of exhibition objects and materials through the building. Corridors should be at least as wide as a standard moving van and wider if possible (a 12- to 15-foot minimum is suggested). A 12-foot height minimum, including pipes and doorways, should be observed; and the elevator, if one is necessary, should be of 6,000-pound capacity at least and should be capable of taking any object that can fit into a standard van. A 10-foot height, 12-foot depth, and 15- to 20-foot length would be safe minimum dimensions for the elevator. While elevators are expensive to construct, they are vastly more expensive to reconstruct; and a too small elevator, as too narrow or too low corridors, can be disastrous to an otherwise good building plan.

Public Spaces, Galleries, Auditoriums. The public will enter the museum space from a different point than the object. The public entrance should be equipped with several facilities, the need for which should be self-evident but which are frequently overlooked. Provision, no matter how informal, should be made for coats, hats, and other articles brought into the museum, and this facility must be adjacent to the public entrance to the museum.

Security control of entering traffic should be provided: this may be done by an attendant, standing alone or seated in a guard station, to count admissions and to survey visitors.

Sales desk facilities, if there are to be any, should also be located near the entrance.

If an auditorium or other sizable meeting room is provided within the museum structure, it should be large enough to accommodate outside functions. An auditorium which seats less than 250 will be of limited use for anything other than class lectures.

Projection equipment and room should be provided for both slides and films. Access to the auditorium should be so arranged that it may be opened when the secure gallery spaces are closed, yet it should be so connected with the gallery that both can be made accessible if the occasion warrants.

Exhibition Galleries. Specific requirements of gallery spaces vary according to usage so widely that it is impossible to discuss them all here. (For a more detailed review of particular kinds of galleries, the reader is referred to Michael Brawne, *The New Museum, Architecture and Display,* noted in the bibliography.) Several general points can be made, however, about gallery spaces and their functions:

1. The gallery must be safe for objects on exhibition. Consideration must be given not only to security but also to type and method of lighting, heating, and ventilation. For example, certain types of objects, watercolors and textiles among them, are very susceptible to ultraviolet deterioration from both natural and fluorescent lights. The latter should be banned from the gallery, and natural light, if used, must be under control so that direct sunlight does not strike the objects on exhibition. Too, the placement

of heating and air-conditioning equipment must be so arranged as not to send blasts of heated or cooled air onto walls where objects are placed. The system should also be so flexible that rearranging partitions or exhibition furniture will not hinder its operation.

Outside walls in buildings constructed for severe climates should be well enough insulated so that no inside humidity will condense on them or on works hanging on them.

2. The gallery must be functional for the types of objects it is designed to show. Oddly enough, this is one of the most frequently overlooked points in museum design. A handsome space may prove to be overly difficult to work in because the architects and clients thought only of the appearance of the room, not its use.

Both the structure and quality of works of art and museum exhibition methods have changed dramatically over the past few years, yet museum design has not kept pace with these changes. A museum director has characterized a museum as "a place where things occur." The museum's exhibition galleries must be thought of as a theater for exhibitions. They must be constructed to provide the flexibility of exhibition presentation analogous with the flexibility of dramatic presentation facilities found in most modern theaters. Finally, it should be obvious that a gallery for the exhibition of objects should be architecturally restrained and tasteful, a subdued background for exhibitions of whatever nature. Structures of a blatantly palatial sort, designed for maximum ego effect on the donors, should be rigorously avoided. The objects on exhibition must be protected and subtly enhanced by their surroundings, not overpowered.

Lighting While a great deal of research has been expended on the psychological effects of the color temperature of light on the appearance of objects and of the deteriorating effects of light on various materials, little research seems to have been done on the various ways to light those objects. As a result, lighting for museum spaces is frequently designed with only one sort of exhibition condition in mind. The lights are fixed into the ceiling around the permanent walls, making their adjustment and redirection very difficult, and they are placed with little concern for the illumination of temporary installations such as partitions or objects on display in areas of the room away from the walls. The difference in lighting quality and quantity between permanent and temporary walls must be eliminated, making all spaces more flexible. The Whitney Museum of American Art in New York has developed a system whereby all walls, fixed and movable, are illuminated from movable fixtures which can be placed on 6-inch centers along one axis of the room and 2-foot centers along the other axis.

To increase greatly lighting flexibility, an abundance of electrical circuits should also be provided, as should outlets along the walls and in the floor. Most freestanding cases require internal light sources, and numerous contemporary works of art now use electricity for their operation. Provision for television coaxial cable outlets in all galleries might also be useful for transmission from the galleries.

Heating, Ventilating, Air Conditioning Any building conceived or remodeled for museum purposes should be so designed that atmospheric conditions as well as lighting conditions can be carefully controlled within the structure under extremes of external heat and cold. All too many museums are designed for the comfort of the visitor only, without consideration for the exhibition objects. Humidity levels for works of art and furniture, for example, should be maintained at 50- to 55-percent relative humidity; this is much higher than is common in cold climates where humidity levels in buildings without humidifiers can drop to 10 to 15 percent, resulting in paint cracking and peeling, deterioration of natural specimens, and cracking of furniture. Such requirements as accurate and steady maintenance of temperature and humidity under all climatic conditions should be specified in all architectural designs and engineering contracts.

Walls The ideal museum wall would be good looking, support almost any weight fastened to it, be easy to maintain, and permit easy changes of color. A wall material into which an object or case can be directly fastened is superior to plaster or other hard material that requires that all objects be suspended in front of it.

Wooden walls covered with cloth have long been used as "nailable" surfaces in galleries; but cloth is subject to discoloration and smudging, and the wall color cannot be changed easily. Again, the new Whitney Museum of American Art seems to have solved the problem with large sheets of heavy plywood which are joined with tongue and groove. The hairline seams between panels are unobjectionable; the panels can support enormous weights; and holes can be filled and touched up or a whole wall can be repainted with ease. Other special textures can be nailed or stapled onto this surface and removed again with minimum damage.

Ceilings More and more museums are adopting a "working ceiling"—one that becomes more like the overhead of a theatrical stage—containing electrical fixtures and power lines and capable of supporting temporary wall panels or exhibition objects which are suspended from it. The Whitney Museum (one of the best-designed museums constructed in many years) uses a heavy grid suspended about 6 feet below the ceiling to carry all electrical lighting systems, support temporary panels, and carry suspended objects. The 6-foot clearing permits access to the top of the grid, which is itself 12 feet or 18 feet above the floor (the height varying with gallery size).

Floors The gallery floor must be able to sustain a concentrated weight equivalent to that of a library, yet must be serviceable and pleasant in both appearance and feel. Use of rubber or asphalt tile should be avoided as these are cold in appearance, require too much maintenance, and are marred when heavy weights remain on them. Natural wood also marks, but it is more comfortable underfoot and better looking. An ideal museum floor would be a heavy wooden flooring laid on sleepers above a concrete base and covered with one of the new "miracle fiber" carpeting materials, the carpet being cemented directly to the wood. This, again, follows theatrical practice. Exhibition structures could, if necessary, be fastened to the floor without leaving marks; and any areas of carpeting that are damaged can be cut out and replaced without leaving a mark.

RECORD KEEPING

At the heart of any museum, but out of public view and thus frequently ignored, is the philosophical and physical fact that a museum exists to compile objects and facts about them. Groups of ethnographic objects or natural history specimens may be rendered almost worthless if the data pertaining to them are not at hand. Dates, makers, locations of finds, season of the year—these are only a few of the many questions that must, if possible, be answered. With objects of art, questions of previous ownership, exhibition history, and restorations must be recorded as well. For those who must pursue the matter further, *Museum Registration Methods*, noted in the bibliography here, is the most complete and concise source of information about the records that should be kept and the methods for keeping them. It is well to point out, however, that every museum will need a system of some sort for documenting its own collection and the objects on loan to it.

Not only must museum record-keeping procedures suit the institution but responsibility for the procedures must be placed in the hands of competent personnel. The tasks are extremely time-consuming, and hence the museum secretary cannot be expected to type records and accession data in her spare time. Museum records must be kept up to date and should be reviewed periodically to check the objects for their condition and their insurance value. Also, scholarly research will require that acquisition data be brought up to date on a regular basis. Thus a competent museum registrar, like a competent acquisitions librarian, is essential to the operation of any museum which has a permanent collection or operates an active program of loan exhibitions.

BUDGETING

Operating Expenses While the college or university generally supplies utilities, building services, and plant maintenance, there will be numerous areas where the museum will have to supply budgeted funds.

Office Services. The cost of operation of the office would include the usual costs of stationery, copying machine, office supplies, and the like, although telephone and postage charges are usually substantially higher for university museums than for other university departments due to the far-flung aspect of arranging exhibitions, and heavy mailing of yearly schedules, invitations, and catalogs.

Freight. Funds for shipment of objects other than those for specific exhibitions should be provided. This would cover shipments of goods or objects which are part of the permanent collection.

Conservation. A sum must be provided for the maintenance of objects in the museum's collection. These services are generally provided by an outside professional. If possible, funds for these services should be provided yearly but held in a suspense account so that funds unexpended in one year can be applied against major restoration expenses which occur periodically.

Photography. Photographs of the permanent collection, loan objects, installations, etc., are necessary for recording the collection and documenting the activities of the museum.

Installation and Operating Supplies. A sum should be provided for the purchase of incidental shop supplies and general installation supplies not directly chargeable to exhibitions. This would provide a reserve for the replenishment of small supplies and the purchase of small items (such as wire, hooks, lumber, small light fixtures) as needed.

Capital Equipment. This sum would provide for more substantial purchases, of an almost nonrecurring nature, which pertain directly to the museum's operation. Generally, such items are requested and budgeted at the beginning of the fiscal year.

Travel. This item, which might also fall under the exhibition budget, is an important one because extensive travel is frequently necessary in planning programs and organizing exhibitions.

Printing. This sum would cover the printing of materials not directly connected to exhibition—yearly schedules, registration forms, stationery.

Exhibition Budget This budget should be kept separate from the operating budget so that it is easier to calculate individual exhibition costs and balance the budget. The exhibition budget includes such items as the shipment of objects to the museum for loan exhibitions, loan exhibition insurance, catalog of exhibitions, materials and labor to cover major construction for the installation, guards, additional part-time labor, and any expenses which are directly attributable to mounting and operating exhibitions.

It is difficult to give any dollar figure for the cost of exhibitions, but it would seem that a reasonable minimum might be $2 per year per square foot of gallery space for loan exhibitions and 50 cents to $1 per year per square foot of gallery space for exhibitions of a more permanent nature.

INSURANCE

Insurance as discussed here deals with insurance on objects, not on the physical museum structure. While many universities self-insure their buildings, this is not recommended for objects in the permanent collection as they generally cannot be duplicated exactly if lost or destroyed; but cash insurance settlements can help to cover the cost of some suitable replacement.

Before discussing specific types of insurance, the author again calls attention to the chapter devoted to fine-arts insurance in *Museum Registration Methods* (see bibliography) which is highly detailed in its discussion of insurance and insurance problems.

Permanent Collection Insurance There are two broad types of insurance, described below, used by art museums to insure their permanent collections.

Coverage Based on a Stated Limit of Liability. This type of insurance is frequently used when the museum's collection is of great value, and it limits the amount of loss to a set dollar figure for any one loss. If, for example, the limit of such a policy were $1,000,000, a claim could be entered for no more than this amount for any one incident or damage. This sort of insurance is valuable for an institution with a very valuable collection on which insurance on every piece would be prohibitively expensive; but there is the risk that a major loss might exceed the limits of the policy.

Scheduled Coverage Based on the Value of Individual Objects. This type of policy insures each object according to a list or "schedule" maintained by the institution and the insurance broker. For permanent collections, the policy may be written to cover the objects while they are in the museum only or out of the museum only. But the scope of this type of policy can be greatly expanded by writing it with floater coverage —coverage which will insure the work against "all risks." (Certain losses are almost always excluded from insurance policies, among them: wear and tear; gradual deterioration; inherent vice; repairs or retouching; acts of government leading to war, insurrection, or confiscation; and nuclear reaction.) Such a policy will cover the object at all times and in all locations.

Loan Exhibitions Insurance This is generally all-risk floater coverage, sometimes referred to as "wall-to-wall" insurance because it covers the object from the moment it leaves the owner's wall until it is returned there. This policy covers the object for the amount stated by the owner.

Generally, these policies are written as monthly reporting policies whereby the museum supplies the insurance broker or university staff member in charge of insurance with an itemized list of all objects and their values at risk during the entire month or relevant portion of it, and premiums are based on the total amount.

Insurance Service on Claims While *Museum Registration Methods* documents the methods whereby claims may be made and settled, the author would like to point out that individual brokers and insurance adjustment agencies vary widely on their knowledge of museum insurance problems and in their speed and efficiency in settling claims.

Nothing is more frustrating to the museum or more damaging to its reputation than interminable delays in settling claims or paying for repairs to objects damaged. Private collectors who lend to museums are acutely aware of the conditions of their objects and expect repairs or settlements to be made promptly when a damage has occurred. Undue delays in settling a claim can ruin an institution's goodwill forever with another museum, commercial gallery, or private lender.

SECURITY

Museums are protected by several means, one of them more philosophical than practical, and they are outlined below:

The Appearance of Security. This is a philosophical consideration, but it has been the author's experience to find that if a museum gives the impression of being well run and well cared for, loss or damages are less likely to occur. Such things as open doors leading to nonpublic spaces, crates piled in dimly lighted corridors, and damages to objects and exhibition furniture which remain unrepaired may lead to the visitor's realization that the museum is operated in a slack and unprofessional manner and he may react by attempting theft or vandalism.

On the other hand, good lighting, clean surroundings, and exhibition objects in good order will discourage casual disrespect on the part of the visitor and security will be easier to maintain.

Security as the Presence of Guard Personnel. Obviously, some sort of control must be maintained in museum areas that offer any opportunity for theft or vandalism by visitors, and the most common sort of security control is a man stationed at one main entrance and exit and, in larger museums, men or women patrolling through the galleries watching the objects and the visitors. The best of this sort of guarding is unobtrusive but effective. The viewer knows that he is in a watched area, but he is not made uncomfortable by it. At worst, guard personnel can be surly and overbearing and this sort of attitude should not be tolerated. Having an individual in the gallery who represents the university and who is in authority is essential, both for direct security reasons and to give assistance in any emergency.

The importance of hiring competent guard personnel cannot be stressed sufficiently. University museums are frequently badly protected because of chronic shortages of funds, and too often the "security staff," a secretary or student who is assigned to "watch the gallery," is given other jobs to do while guarding, resulting in an obviously casually guarded space. Use of the university security staff is equally problematic as security personnel are frequently disinterested in the museum and its exhibitions, and they are frequently shifted from job to job so that a guard has no time to familiarize himself with museum exhibitions. The presence of such a uniformed guard, frequently armed, can also be intimidating to the museum goer.

Students, both graduate and undergraduate, are frequently used as guards; but they have a tendency to be too casual about guarding; and their academic schedules conflict with the museum schedules, resulting in acute guard shortages during examination and vacation periods.

Perhaps the best solution is the hiring by the museum of its own guards, and the author suggests the use of retired people who wish to supplement their income. These people are usually steady workers, neat in appearance, and careful in noting attendance, catalog sales, and unusual occurrences. They are usually more polite than younger people and more willing to work in a physically confined area.

Guard staffs, no matter what their composition, must be neat but not militaristic and well-informed but not garrulous. They should not express opinions about the exhibitions they guard and should leave gallery tours up to the curatorial staff.

Security through Electronic Devices. Electronic monitoring devices have now been so perfected that all gallery spaces and secure storage spaces can be protected without watchmen during the hours the museum is closed. Various devices utilizing ultrasonic waves, radar, and infrared light will detect the slightest movement within the building; and this protection, coupled with fire alarms, can signal instantly any change within the building to university security personnel or local police.

If an electronic burglar-detection system is added to an old building or built into a new one, it should be of the "central station" type, where the system is monitored from a central alarm station. This monitor serves as a check on the performance of museum employees in turning on the system at night; should the system not be turned on, the central station will notify university security or museum staff so that it may be set in order.

No amount of sophisticated equipment, however, will replace old-fashioned common sense in protecting a building. Doors should be solid enough to withstand the attack of a "smash and grab" burglar. Large windows opening out into lobby areas or outdoor spaces should be of polished wire glass or laminated plate glass to make entering this way more difficult. Keys to various gallery and other secure areas should be given out sparingly, and not at all to university staff, including top administrators, who have no *need* to enter the building. Locks and master-lock combinations should be changed yearly, especially if any keys are issued to student workers. Key control should be rigorous and continuous.

ACQUISITION POLICIES

Gifts Acquisition policy in university museums is usually erratic at best. If an object offered to the museum is desirable, it is usually accepted by the director or curator on the spot. If it is undesirable, the director will convene an informal "acquisitions committee" which will decline the gift with thanks. It is best, however, if all proposed gifts are submitted to an acquisitions committee comprising the director as chairman and the curatorial staff and possibly art department faculty as committee members.

At times, gifts are offered which are only conditionally acceptable. Such items as objects with excessive repairs or restorations or objects of questionable authenticity or of only peripheral interest to the museum should be accepted, if at all, with the understanding that they may be sold, exchanged, or disposed of as the university sees fit. Then they may be sold, the proceeds going to acquire other suitable objects (which would bear the donors' names); or they may be put in a "study collection" which would be available to interested scholars but which would most probably never be put on public exhibition.

Special limitations should be avoided, if at all possible, when considering gifts. Requirements that a collection be on permanent exhibition, or that objects never be sold or exchanged, or other restrictive requirements should be weighed carefully. The quality of the collection or object should be balanced against the problems that would be caused in the museum by accepting whatever restrictions are demanded. Each case certainly should be weighed on its individual merits.

University administrative personnel can be of great help in the area of acquisition by encouraging donors to give suitable objects or funds for acquisition. This is an area that is particularly rich for development in state universities.

It is always well to remember that the acceptance of objects implies that they will be cared for and be given protection. There is nothing more embarrassing to university administration than a donor returning to see his gift only to find that it has been destroyed through carelessness or lost through neglect. Proper facilities must be extant before objects are accepted.

Purchases If purchase funds are available, their expenditure should be localized rather narrowly to the director in consultation with his professional staff and members of the academic department concerned and with the approval of his superior. The purchasing agent, bursar, and other university staff members should not concern themselves with what is purchased but only with whether the purchase is executed with proper university procedure.

USE OF A MUSEUM FOR ACADEMIC PURPOSES—ITS RELATIONS TO INSTRUCTIONAL PROGRAMS

The very presence of a museum on a university campus implies that it exists there primarily for academic purposes and for the benefit of the university community.

All too frequently, however, either university-based museums do not coordinate their activities with the academic departments to which they are related or they coordinate too closely. In the latter case, the museum shows only exhibitions which favor the department; the museum turns in upon itself and operates centripetally, thus avoiding controversy but losing vitality as well. It is for this reason that the museum, and especially the art museum, should not be under the supervision of the art department.

On a more positive note, there are numerous ways in which the museum can serve as a valuable adjunct to academic departments.

Making the Permanent Collection Available for Students. Like the library's books, the objects in the museum's permanent collection should be made available to students to see, handle, and study provided that security precautions are observed. A problem here is space and manpower. Either the museum's permanent collection must all be accessible to qualified students or else a space must be made available within the secure zone of the museum to which objects may be brought. This of course requires supervisory staff, which may be in short supply at times.

Originating Special Study Exhibitions. This is an effective way of mixing museum collections with objects borrowed from outside sources. Such exhibitions should be organized with departmental and academic needs foremost and might be of only limited interest to the general public. Exhibitions dealing with objects within narrow historical or physical areas and exhibitions demonstrating specific techniques are examples of this sort of show.

Sponsoring Student-organized Exhibitions. The museum can sponsor exhibitions which are organized by students, thus giving them insights into the problems and solutions of museum organization and installation. Such an exhibition might be of the nature outlined above.

Sponsoring Interdisciplinary Exhibitions and Programs. One of the most exciting concepts in theory, although little explored in practice, is the organization of exhibitions and programs which draw on the expertise of many departments. Numerous possibilities suggest themselves. Perhaps the most common example is that of a museum concert, performed by members of the music department playing music written in the period of the works of art on exhibition. Cooperation between the physics, geology, and archaeology departments to demonstrate how archaeological evidence is preserved by geological action and dated by carbon-14 tests would be another simple example. Clearly the possibilities of this sort of cooperation are enormous, but it will be up to the director of the museum to foster such cooperation. It goes without saying that the museum experience is also enriched by other coordinated activities such as lectures, film programs, concerts, plays, and demonstrations that can take place within the museum.

THE MUSEUM AND THE COMMUNITY

The museum is one of the most important and widely used interfaces between the university and the larger community. While the university museum usually organizes exhibitions which are of primary interest to the university, these exhibitions will most probably have communitywide appeal as well; and it is important that this community interest be exploited for the benefit of the university. Regrettably, all too few university museums make use of their community potentials. As in municipal museums, efforts should be made to form special-interest groups within both the academic and lay communities. Such groups might include print societies, a "Friends of the University Museum" organization which would sponsor exhibitions, and an acquisition society (possibly part of the "Friends") which would contribute purchase funds for the museum's collections. A sales desk might also be inaugurated, using volunteer assistance to run it. Using volunteers to give gallery tours or for other special purposes such as running the sales desk, research or organization of special exhibitions, and hosting museum functions can be rewarding, although the museum staff time required for the training and supervision of volunteers is sometimes difficult to provide.

Outside service organizations can also be called upon to undertake museum projects as part of their community service, and such groups can, under proper leadership, both fund and organize exhibitions and programs which the museum could not undertake by itself.

Children's programs are an area in which service organizations or volunteers can be effective, but the university should bear in mind that such programs are really peripheral to the museum's function.

Admission fees should be avoided if at all possible, and certainly admission into the museum should be free, even if under extraordinary circumstances a fee must be charged for certain exhibitions.

SUMMARY

The university museum, no matter what its field, must be regarded as a serious academic endeavor and an important complement to the academic departments of the university. It must be adequately funded and competently staffed with professional personnel.

The building, old or new, must be suitable for its function.

Museum programs are to be structured essentially for the university, but they will have communitywide interest also, and the community should be encouraged to assist the museum in acquisitions, exhibitions, and special programs.

BIBLIOGRAPHY

Note: The two books listed below are regarded by the author as essential to art museum design and operation.

Brawne, Michael: *The New Museum: Architecture and Display,* Frederick A. Praeger, Inc., New York, 1965.

Dudley, Dorothy H., and Irma B. Wilkinson: *Museum Registration Methods,* American Association of Museums and The Smithsonian Institution, Washington, D.C., 1968.

Chapter 6

University Press

GENE R. HAWES

Consultant, Columbia University Press, New York, New York

BASIC FUNCTIONS OF AMERICAN UNIVERSITY PRESSES

The Role of the University Press in American Higher Education and Intellectual Life

Originated with University Research American university presses serve fundamentally as an essential means through which the thought and findings of professional scholars are communicated and used. Although audiences for scholarly works have broadened substantially since university presses began appearing on the scene in the late nineteenth century, publishing costs have multiplied still more. The central function of a university press remains the publishing of works by or for scholars which could not otherwise appear, particularly in book form. University presses today do publish two hundred or more journals, but they are predominantly publishers of books. The work of American scholarship in research and teaching as we know it would be unthinkable without these university press books.

University presses today constitute one of the fastest growing sectors of American book publishing. About 2,500 new book titles were issued by the 70 existing university presses in 1967, representing advances in knowledge of some significance in almost every conceivable direction of human endeavor.

The Role of the University Press in an Individual Institution

Building Faculty Strength The basic need for a university press begins at home, to make available a steady stream of research writings by faculty members. However, scholars move to other institutions (especially at the start of their careers), presses develop publishing and marketing powers in certain disciplines, and scholars at those institutions without presses produce works well worth issuing. For these reasons, at an older and larger press, only about a third of the books issued will typically originate at the home institution (though as much as another third may originate with persons once connected with the institution as graduate students or faculty members). For its own faculty, a press:

1. Provides an outlet for writings, especially those of the younger scholars
2. Encourages faculty writing and research by furnishing nearby publishing capability
3. Trains and develops scholars as authors
4. Helps develop the reputations of scholar-authors

Building Institutional Strength A university press indirectly increases the powers and stature of its university by:

1. Helping to attract and hold distinguished faculty members
2. Helping to attract research grants and financial support
3. Cultivating the reputation of the institution nationally and internationally

The Role of an Individual Press

Every university press performs the following eight basic functions as a book publisher.

1. Planning the Publishing Program A university press publishes according to a general conception of the kinds of books that well represent its university. These books often naturally reflect areas of particular strength in faculty, library, and program at the institution. Planning long-range programs constitutes a prime responsibility for the director of a press, and he is aided by his editorial board and his senior staff members.

2. Search Editing to Cultivate and Evaluate Potential Books The general plans for a press's publishing program are set into motion by what is called "search editing." This consists of all work done by the staff to attract books and authors to the press, to advise authors on writing or rewriting, and to evaluate ideas. It also often includes making the contractual arrangements for accepted manuscripts. In evaluating manuscripts, the director or editors most often rely on the reports of "readers" who are expert in the various fields represented.

Those serving as search editors seldom make the decision to publish. Almost every university press has an editorial board composed of leading faculty members (and leading administrators, in some cases) at the home institution. This board, with the advice of the director and editors, makes the decision to publish.

3. Manuscript Editing This consists of going through the manuscript word by word to ensure that it is correct, consistent, clear, and in conformance with the press's editorial style. The manuscript editor is normally the one who works most closely with the author while his book is being prepared.

4. Design Book designers who are highly skilled and experienced specialists design most university press books. A small press will often rely on free-lance design services, while a large press usually has from one to three full-time designers on its staff.

5. Production The large majority of American university presses commission varieties of outside suppliers to manufacture their books rather than have them produced by an associated printing plant. Managing book production is a complex technical, financial, and scheduling process, one often carried out by specialists at larger presses or by the director or designer at smaller ones.

6. Presses without Printing Plants Only ten university presses have printing plants, while about six more have some of their printing production done in separate plants at their universities. With presses of all ages and sizes flourishing without plants on campus, it is obvious that such a facility is not a necessary part of a university press.

7. Distribution Professional methods of promotion and sale are used to distribute books throughout the country and around the world. Even smaller presses often have full-time sales managers. Larger presses have sales departments that frequently include an advertising manager and a publicity manager. The presses make most of their domestic sales by direct-mail advertising sent to the specialized audiences interested in the various works, though salesmen from the larger presses develop a substantial proportion of volume through sales to various types of bookstores. Foreign sales are made by overseas representatives of the presses.

8. Warehousing and Shipping Like commercial publishers, university presses stock copies of their books in print and fill orders through shipping offices or departments. The presses tend to keep books in print longer than their counterparts out of a sense of responsibility to scholarship. Warehouse facilities of older presses hence need substantial space and are often some distance away from the crowded campus centers where the presses' main offices are. Some two-thirds of the annual sales income of a long-established press typically comes from sales of titles in print for more than two or three years. The warehoused inventory of books represents the largest form of capitalization of the press—a prime capital asset and source of operating funds which has been built by slow accumulation over many years.

9. Accounting and Fiscal Management Presses of any but the smallest size most often have their own accounting offices or departments and follow regular publishing procedures in accounting. Customary university accounting procedures have proved ill-suited to a press's operations. University presses also must often conduct fiscal management of the press's funds independently of the business or financial officers of their home universities. Presses have such independence because their fiscal decisions hinge largely on publishing considerations that involve extensive special knowledge of the publishing business.

UNIVERSITY COMMITMENT REQUIRED TO START A UNIVERSITY PRESS

A Minimal Program for a Press as Defined by the Presses

At Least Five Books or Journals a Year Because universities issue varieties of publications in many ways, the Association of American University Presses has set membership eligibility guidelines that define the minimum program necessary to become a true university press. To apply for membership, a press is expected to have published at least five scholarly books or journals a year for two years. It should also have three or more full-time employees, including a chief executive who reports directly to the university or college president or an appointee thereof. Also required are statements on what scholarly and intellectual results the institution expects to realize from its press and on the funds made available to the press by its parent institution. These and other stipulations, which require a substantial commitment by the institution, appear in full in the Association's annual *Directory*.

Complete and Continuing Support by the President and Board of Trustees

Although presses eventually recover much of their out-of-pocket costs by receipts from sales, they invariably face responsibilities to issue books that have great scholarly significance but cannot return their costs. Presses very often receive substantial annual appropriations from their universities to cover this expense. And regular appropriations for a press will obviously be endangered unless the institution's president and board of trustees remain fully convinced of the press's importance. Full presidential backing is a vital factor in ensuring the necessary support of faculty members.

Large, Permanent Subsidy Financing

Facilities as Well as Funds Are Usually Provided Regular annual appropriations by the parent institution to cover deficit operations commonly range from $25,000 to $50,000 and extend up to $300,000 or beyond. These subsidies must continue permanently if the press is to meet its responsibilities to scholarship. The subsidies are provided in addition to grants from many different sources for particular books or series. Indirect subsidies provided for a press almost always include rent-free quarters, usually with equipment, supplies, and services like maintenance and telephone and sometimes with the salaries of some or all staff members.

Sound Selection of the Press Director

Drive, Ability, and Publishing Experience Are Needed Qualities Unusual energy and basic ability are cited as necessary qualities in the director of a new university press. Most press directors establish unusually good reputations in commercial or scholarly publishing before being named to head presses.

Alternatives to Starting a University Press

Established Presses Publish for Other Colleges and Universities Many colleges and universities that do not assume the heavy responsibility of inaugurating a true university press find various workable alternatives. Some mount casual, intermittent operations issuing scholarly books from time to time, in some cases under a press imprint of the college or university. In another approach, faculty members who have close ties as authors or readers with established presses at other institutions will give scholarly publishing advice and introductions to their own colleagues. A third and quite effective alternative is for an institution to contract with one of the larger presses to have the institution's books published by the press under a joint imprint (such as "Temple University Publications; Distributed by Columbia University Press"). An adapted form of this arrangement can result in valuable advantages to a small, new press in its early years.

UNIVERSITY ORGANIZATION FOR A UNIVERSITY PRESS

Autonomous Departmental Structures

Most Are Integral Parts of Their Universities All but three or four of the country's university presses are integral parts of their institutions. They have been organized essentially as special-purpose departments established in the bylaws and statutes of the institutions themselves. Most successful presses operate with a large measure of autonomy, which they need to meet their unique responsibilities as scholarly publishing houses. Unfortunately, presses at most state universities find their effectiveness reduced through limitations on the use of state funds.

Creative Service and Setting of Standards by the Leading Faculty Members

On the Editorial Board or as Authors, Scouts, and Advisers Faculty members at the home institution play four major roles in the publishing program of a press. Most significantly, editorial boards composed in full or in part of faculty members "control the imprint" (i.e., approve each work for publication) at virtually every press (with some presses having a minority of outside scholars or other authorities sit on their boards). Through their decisions and formulation of publishing policies, they set the press's standards of quality. Professors at the parent institution also serve as authors of works issued by the press. Also important is their work as informal scouts for promising ideas and manuscripts and as informal or formal advisers on what the press could or should be publishing.

Professional Status for Press Staff Members

On the Levels of Deans and Professors Staff members of university presses are normally accorded full professional status. The compensation and authority of a press director customarily compare with those of deans of constituent schools in the campus hierarchy, while heads of the press's departments are usually on a professional par with full professors. Faculty appointments are held by a few directors and senior staff members. Respected status and adequate compensation are essential for a successful press because of currently brisk demand for able scholarly publishing personnel.

Independence in Administrative Procedures for Publishing Purposes

Publishing Needs Often Differ from University Needs Press officers handling business and administrative matters develop press procedures that best fit publishing needs. These procedures invariably differ in certain ways from the institution's established ones, which were designed to fit its own needs. Without such independence in internal administration, a press is handicapped in striving to serve as the publishing arm of the university.

FINANCIAL ADMINISTRATION FOR A UNIVERSITY PRESS

University Press Finances in Broad Outline

Major Cost Categories in Accounting Presidents and other chief university administrators responsible for a press generally delegate complete financial administration to its director. They often exercise supervisory fiscal responsibility by reviewing only at such major checkpoints as audited annual financial statements of the press, annual projections of fiscal operations, and fiscal plans for projects or facilities which would require long-range major commitments. They also review the needs for annual subsidy appropriations to the press and help with arrangements for any major new or different facilities.

Presidents and their fellow chief administrators generally understand what the major categories of costs in book publishers' accounting are and how they apply. These major cost categories are:

1. Overhead, or "general and administrative expense." In essence, all costs that are in any way involved with book publishing but which are not chargeable to specific titles come under this heading. Scholarly publishers most often divide overhead equally among all titles published annually.

2. Production (or "plant costs" and "manufacturing" costs). The costs for the physical making of the finished copies of an individual title. "Plant costs" cover all steps up to the book's printing; manufacturing costs, all steps from that point on.

3. Promotion (including advertising and publicity) and other selling expenses.

4. Shipping and warehouse costs. These are sometimes termed "direct overhead." They are charged against individual titles.

5. Royalties. The percentage of the title's list price payable to the author under the contract for each category of sale. University press royalties commonly match those paid by commercial houses.

The "Break-even Point" for a Book These cost categories apply to a basic concept in publishing, the "break-even point," as shown in Table 1 below (the values given in the example are all hypothetical, but their pattern and size are representative for university press costs in 1967).

TABLE 1 Break-even Point for a University Press Book, $6 List Price, 4,000 Copies Printed *

Production costs	$5,300	
Advertising & publicity costs	1,900	
Total	$7,200	
Publisher's gross income per copy ($6 less 33⅓ percent in discounts and commissions)		$4.00
Additional publisher's costs per copy sold:		
Royalty	$ .60	
Direct overhead	.21	
General overhead	1.49	2.30
Publisher's net income per copy		$1.70

Break-even point = $7,200 divided by $1.70 = 4,235 copies

*Reprinted with permission of American University Press Services, Inc.

Even if the 4,000-copy edition were to sell out completely, the university press would still lose $400 on it (incurring in cost $7,200 less sales income of $6,800, or 4,000 times $1.70). That $400 would have to be made up by a subsidy from the press's funds, a grant from an interested organization, the university's regular subsidy appropriation, or some other source. If anything, a subsidy on the order of $400 for an individual title is low. Subsidies required for the individual titles issued by 21 large presses in 1965 averaged 7 percent of sales income—which here would have amounted to $1,120.

University presses can publish at break-even points substantially lower than those of commercial publishers, in part because the presses qualify for the same tax-exempt status as their parent institutions. Raising the $6 price of the book analyzed above to $9 would reduce the break-even point to 1,675 copies. The presses not infrequently have to publish highly specialized books at break-even points this low or lower.

Standard for Comparison in Financial Performance: The Annual Financial and Operating Ratio Report

Major Cost Categories in Overall Press Operations University presses jointly sponsor and use an important analytical tool for financial management. This confidential annual survey report, available only to participating presses, is called the *Financial and Operating Ratio Report to American University Press Services.* It enables a press to compare its distribution of costs for book publishing operations with the corresponding average (and high and low) figures among a number of other presses. The figures are given as percentages of book-sales income for the year. For example, Table 2 below gives a summary of the report's average figures for 21 large university presses that participated in one recent year.

TABLE 2 Distribution of Costs for Book Publishing Operations in the Average Experience of 21 Presses in One Recent Year*

	Percentage of book sales income
Manufacturing costs and write-offs	43.7
Royalties	9.9
Nonmanufacturing costs	
Editorial department	6.6
Design and production department	2.6
Advertising and promotion department	13.2
Sales department	5.2
Shipping and warehousing	5.3
General, accounting, and administration	20.3
Total cost of commission books sold	4.8
Total cost	111.6
Loss on operations	11.6
Subsidies for individual titles and income from sales of subsidiary rights and of publishing and managerial services	9.2
Overall loss	2.4

* Reprinted with permission of American University Press Services, Inc.

"Commission" books cited in the table are books which the press accepts for publication according to its regular standards but which have their production and possibly other publishing costs underwritten by an outside sponsoring organization. They are books which the press is commissioned to publish on such terms. Among them are those which a larger press publishes for a small new press, as mentioned earlier.

"Write-offs" include the substantial amounts by which the value of books in inventory is written down annually in the press's ledgers. Each title first goes into the warehouse at its cost value, which is entered in the press's accounts. The presses then usually apply some conservative formula to all titles in inventory, most often a formula that results in writing off the title's cost completely within five years after publication. In university press finance, the particular system used for inventory write-down is not so important as consistency in using the same system, because this consistency makes possible comparisons of the press's financial performance on the same basis from year to year.

Virtual Necessity for a Press: Independence in Financial Administration within Basic Requirements

No Successful Press Is Supervised by a University Business Officer Not one of the successful American university presses has a chief business officer at its parent institution supervise its financial administration. The business affairs of a press lie in a special field which differs markedly from the equally intricate and extensive field of college and university business management. Moreover, scholarly publishing is a complex specialty within publishing generally, a specialty in which academic values must often be translated into publishing costs. For such reasons as these, successful presses have found it virtually essential to be independent in financial administration, operating only within basic and general fiscal requirements set by their parent institutions.

UNIVERSITY PROBLEMS AND OPPORTUNITIES IN FUTURE PUBLISHING DEVELOPMENTS

Current Financial Stringency in Higher Education

Basic Service to Scholarship in Jeopardy Perhaps the most fundamental problem faced by university presses is posed by the deepening financial crisis of higher education. College and university administrators already know its key features: climbing costs without climbing income and income prospects to match. The resulting squeeze can lead to questions about the size of the subsidy support given a press by its parent institution.

How often such questions of reducing or withdrawing support can arise was indicated in a *Saturday Review* article of June 1968 by Thomas Lloyd, then executive director of the Association of American University Presses. "For some otherwise 'established' presses this painful reminder has come almost yearly," he stated; "for others it has been less frequent but may well become familiar in the decade to come."

Some presses that have been capably run for a number of years can continue operating with drastically reduced support from their institutions or none at all, he noted. But the kinds of books such presses would thereby be forced to issue, he declared, "would rule them out of serious consideration as scholarly publishers, though they would continue to provide their institutions with a source of prestige." These presses would be forced to default on much or all of their obligation to publish the kinds of books that are of unquestionable scholarly significance but which cannot return their costs—to default on their basic service to the scholarly world.

Prestige among the superficial, however, counts far less for a college or university than reputation among the informed. Institutions that continue to subsidize their presses as the needs of scholarship warrant will find their reputations growing among informed scholars and leaders. And they will also have the satisfactions and rewards that come with truly furthering the work of scholarly research.

Developing Fields of University Publication

New Fields Reflect Scholarly Innovation and Public Interest As in the past, scholarly publishing fields that are developing especially fast today reflect innovative scholarly research, which in itself at times reflects growing public interest. For example, the total university press output of works in international affairs continues to increase with enlarging scholarship in the discipline as well as rising public interest. Scholars and the public similarly have increasing interest in other peoples of the world. University presses have accordingly begun extensive programs to make available English translations of major works in the literatures of other countries. Substantial progress has been made thus far in the literatures of Latin America and the Orient.

Works in the sciences are growing generally on university press lists, particularly in molecular biology (the sector in which study of molecules of DNA and RNA is realizing epochal advances in our understanding of heredity and of the very nature of life). Historical and literary scholars alike have discerned a vital need in recent years for documentary works of definitive authenticity. Such interest has led university presses to introduce ambitious, multivolume series on the papers of significant figures in American history (perhaps most notably Jefferson, Hamilton, Franklin, the Adams family, and Madison). There are also definitive editions of the works of Melville, Twain, Whitman, Emerson, Thoreau, and Poe.

Publishing as well as research needs in five areas were explored in conferences held in 1968 by the Association of American University Presses with the sponsorship of the National Endowment for the Humanities. They are: local history, art and architecture, early exploration in North America, the Negro in American history, and bibliography and reference. Further development in poetry and short fiction was also spurred in 1968 with the joint announcement of a special program by the Association and the National Endowment for the Arts. In the program's first year, up to ten volumes of poetry and five of short fiction that are accepted for publication by university presses will be aided by grants to the authors and partial publication-cost subsidies to the presses.

Electronic and Other New Media

Continued Copyright Protection Crucial Information storage and retrieval through computers and other electronic means promise to become economically feasible in the coming years for at least some academic applications. Some of these applications will very likely supplant certain functions now performed by books and libraries (and even lectures).

Through their association, university presses have considered whether electronic media might eventually replace books altogether. Their finding, voiced in the recent report of a committee on new printing technologies, was essentially that books would not necessarily vanish, nor would publishers. This encouraging answer hinged, however, on how broadly the form now known as a book is defined, and on what precautions the country takes to preserve the interests of authors and publishers through copyright protection.

In essence, the report defined a book as an extended expression of thought (in words and illustrations) by the author that was given a specific graphic form by the publisher. At present, the graphic form has the familiar qualities of a book. In the future, the graphic form could be an electroprint, a photoprint, or just a fluorescent image. Men will need the extended expressions of thought that books essentially represent, the report observed, so long as men think and communicate in writing. However, it warned, books in this sense will not continue to be created if the public does not ensure continued protection to authors and publishers at the central points of whatever systems of copying and transmission may be used.

In this, as in all else, the interests of scholarly publishers are one with the interests of the colleges and universities they serve.

ADDITIONAL SOURCES OF INFORMATION

Books and Booklets

Directory, Association of American University Presses, New York (1 Park Avenue, New York, N.Y. 10016; revised annually).

Grannis, Chandler (ed.): *What Happens in Book Publishing*, 2d ed., Columbia University Press, New York, 1967.

Harman, Eleanor (ed.): *The University as Publisher*, University of Toronto Press, Toronto, Canada, 1961 (out of print).

Hawes, Gene R.: *To Advance Knowledge: A Handbook on American University Press Publishing*, American University Press Services, New York, 1967 (1 Park Avenue, New York, N.Y. 10016).

Kerr, Chester: *A Report on American University Presses*, Association of American University Presses, New York, 1949 (out of print).

———: *American University Publishing, 1955: A Supplement to the "Report on American University Presses,"* Association of American University Presses, New York, 1956 (out of print).

LMP (Literary Market Place): The Business Directory of American Book Publishing, R. R. Bowker Company, New York (revised annually).

Nickerson, Thomas (ed.): *Trans-Pacific Scholarly Publishing: A Symposium*, University of Hawaii Press—East-West Center Press, Honolulu, 1963.

Scholarly Journals Committee, Association of American University Presses (ed.), *A Handbook of Scholarly Journal Publishing*, American University Press Services, New York, 1969.

Smith, Datus C., Jr.: *A Guide to Book Publishing*, R. R. Bowker Company, New York, 1966.

Steckler, Phyllis B. (ed.): *The Bowker Annual of Library and Book Trade Information*, R. R. Bowker Company, New York.

Underwood, Richard G.: *Production and Manufacturing Problems of American University Presses*, Association of American University Presses, New York, 1960 (out of print).

Welter, Rush: *Problems of Scholarly Publication in the Humanities and Social Sciences*, American Council of Learned Societies, New York, 1959.

Periodicals

Publishers' Weekly, R. R. Bowker Company, New York.

Saturday Review, New York (especially the "Annual University Press Issue" published each spring).

Scholarly Books in America, American University Press Services, New York (quarterly, distributed free to scholars, librarians, and educators; gives brief general commentary on American scholarly publishing and capsule descriptions of all new books issued by university presses).

Chapter **7**

Faculty Clubs

WARREN T. GRINNAN

Campus Center Manager and Lecturer, Restaurant and Hotel Management Program, University of Massachusetts, Amherst, Massachusetts

THE PURPOSE, CHARTER, AND BYLAWS OF A FACULTY CLUB

The purpose of a faculty club, as stated in one such club's constitution, is "to promote the unity and effectiveness of the teaching, administrative and professional forces among men and women of the University and to provide opportunity for greater co-operation in their academic work and for formal and informal consideration of the problems of University life and work." Therefore, a faculty club's chief responsibility to its members and to the institution with which it is associated lies in the fulfillment of these goals.

In addition, the club also has responsibilities toward its employees and in encouraging the continued vigor and growth of the club.

The club is, in general, concerned with promoting the academic effectiveness of its members. In particular, the club must fulfill the real needs of the members and their families with regard to dining services on a day-to-day basis. Energetic committees working on social and recreational activities add to a club's overall appeal. Worthy of mention is the fact that the general welfare of a university or college is often enhanced by the contributions of the faculty club's facilities. Such a club can promote its institution's interests as well as its own financial welfare by making its facilities available for conferences, symposiums, recruiting, and—in the case of private institutions—fund-raising activities.

Charter Before elaborating the possibilities of club utilization, the all-important club charter must be mentioned. Generally the club is incorporated as a private, nonbusiness, nonprofit corporation. After the necessary federal and state legal regulations have been met, other technical legal points should be examined. Federal, state, and local taxes as they apply to nonprofit corporations vary widely, especially with regard to sales taxes on purchases for resale. So great has this problem become that the Club Managers Association of America has found it useful to maintain an excellent tax consultant to deal with such matters. Problems connected with such matters as state and federal income tax exemptions, federal excise taxes on initiation fees and dues, withholding taxes on contracted services (such as those of musicians), and withholding taxes on gratuities and bonuses to club employees may become sources of consternation to the unwary club official. With regard to income tax exemption, a club should have its exempt status determined by the Internal Revenue Service before operations are actively undertaken. A faculty club's business with nonmembers must conform to certain standards upheld by the Internal Revenue Service if the club wishes to maintain its tax-exempt status. All these matters should be checked scrupulously and the proper procedures should be clearly understood before a faculty club opens its doors for business.

Bylaws The bylaws of a club are usually those internal regulations that every organization finds it necessary to impose upon its operations. Normally the bylaws consist of rules, issued by the board of directors, governing the club's management and use.

The club's charter may take up some or all of the following:

1. Membership qualifications including eligibility applications, policies, and other recommendations and regulations
2. Membership dues, assessments, initiation fees, and deliquency policies
3. Annual meetings, orders of business, special meetings
4. Board of directors' and committees' makeup and powers
5. Amendments to the charter and bylaws

In short "By-laws instruct the officers, members of the board, committees and members as to their responsibilities and duties and the manner in which they should perform." [1]

[1] Henry Ogden Barbour, *Private Club Administration,* Club Managers Association of America, Washington, 1968, p. 176.

In the case of faculty clubs, it would also be necessary to elaborate in the bylaws the specific special privileges the associated college or university may be granted and who in the university or college has the right to request these services. For example, they are normally restricted to the president and other key officers of the university.

FACULTY CLUB FINANCING AND RESPONSIBILITIES

Financing through Institution Funds The majority of the clubs now in existence were established with financial aid from the institutions with which they are associated. Such support usually comes in the form of physical plant and facilities and continued financial cooperation for expansions and renovations as they are needed. Where the facility exists on the institution's grounds or in one of its buildings, the annual cost of such items as heat, light, power, and grounds maintenance is customarily contributed to the club by the institution. In the case of a small but significant number of clubs, the associated institutions also provide all or part of the payroll, some free personnel, employee benefit costs, and accounting, as well as other benefits and services which are furnished to the club free or at low cost.

Financing by Membership Subscription One-quarter of all faculty clubs now in existence are financed by membership subscription.[2] As to the amount of initial help obtained from the institution, statistics are not available; however, as one might surmise—a well-run subscription drive would be necessary in this day and age to establish a completely independent club. According to Harris, Kerr, Forster and Company's pamphlet entitled *Clubs in Town and Country* (1966–1967), the average city club in 1967 received $202 in dues, $308 in food and beverage revenue, and $120 representing all other sales and income per member and just about broke even. If a faculty club were to attempt to "go it alone," it should refer to sources such as the one mentioned above.

Endowments or Gifts as a Part of Club Financing Any club, either aspiring for establishment or already established, should investigate the use of endowments or gifts as sources of capital for club operations and building. There are a few clubs that have been established in this manner.

Once initial financing is established, it is suggested that the club be organized in such a manner:

1. That the club and its members are engaged in the pursuit of a common purpose as the primary reason for association, which extends not merely to the broad general aims of the group, but to the specific activities or operations in which the group engages to accomplish those purposes.
2. That costs and expenses incurred by The Club are jointly shared; hence there are no operations permissible which contemplate a commercial activity for profit therefrom, nor any operation for the benefit of a minority group of members unless such operations are positively approved by the majority group of members as clearly furthering the common purpose of The Club.
3. That joint sharing as interpreted in the full sense imposes joint sharing in capital expenditures for property and facilities to be acquired and used directly in furtherance of the common purpose objectives of The Club.
4. That whatever assets are acquired through the jointly shared contributions of the members become the jointly owned property of the members.[3]

THE FACULTY CLUB ORGANIZATION

Administrative Organization Not quite half of the 341 institutions that have special social facilities for the faculty are organized as bona fide faculty clubs. However, since

[2] In something over one-quarter of the cases the dues and operating receipts cover operating expenses.

[3] Barbour, *op. cit.*, p. 309.

we are discussing the faculty club in the "bona fide" sense, let us consider its administrative organization.

Normally a club through its charter and bylaws would make provision for a president, vice-president, secretary, and treasurer. It would be good policy to consider the manager as the fifth member of this executive committee. Other administrative committees that are usually established are known as the finance, house, and university or college relations committees, which should all be considered standing committees. Special committees are usually established as needed and should exist only for as long as they serve their intended purpose.

Operational Organization Operationally, the manager usually makes good use of such committees as entertainment, library, and athletic committees. They may be established as either standing or special committees. Since they serve an important function and are an aid to management, their importance should not be overlooked.

THE MEMBERSHIP

Requirements for Own Faculties, Administrators, and Professional Staffs Establishment of membership policies and rules concerning the extent of members' responsibility for liabilities and debts incurred by the club could consume volumes. However, in general terms, faculty clubs usually restrict membership in the club to the full and part-time faculties, the trustees, and the administrative staff (usually those termed "professional," or "executive," or those within certain personnel classifications—depending on the institution and the personnel organization). Rarely is sex a factor, and most clubs designate memberships as family memberships. Restrictions are enforced often, especially at noontime, to control usage by unauthorized persons and minors unaccompanied by a parent. Membership dues can be established by many variations of formulas based on salary, professional rank, title, or geographical proximity to the club (usually used at universities where there are several campuses or unusual physical layouts). In at least one club, none of the above is used since membership is considered a benefit and dues are provided for in exactly the same way as Blue Cross, Blue Shield, retirement, and paid holidays. Individual members' liability for the club debts should be spelled out on the application form. Many different types of forms exist.

Affiliated, Alumni, Associate, Temporary, and Retired Classifications A club may also have other forms of membership including:

Affiliated membership: Given to persons who may be connected with other institutions in the area or who may have a special interest in the college or university. Such membership entitles the holder to temporary use of the club facilities.

Alumni membership: Many of the larger faculty clubs have a limited number of memberships open to alumni. These are usually broken down into resident (within so many miles of the club) and nonresident memberships.

Associate membership: Often granted to "illustrious confederates," employed by industry or nearby research companies who actively engage in communications and cooperation with various departments in the college or university.

Temporary membership: Usually given to visitors who hold academic or administrative rank in other institutions or to special guests whose use is deemed acceptable. (It is not uncommon to extend privileges to persons conducting special campaigns or studies for the institution even though they may not have any official employment connected with the institution.)

Retired membership: Usually made available to those who retire from the institution while members of the club. Sometimes special dues structures are applied.

Honorary or Conferred Memberships These memberships are usually given to distinguished friends of the college or university, selected public officials, and sometimes widows of former members and others whose services to the club deserve special recognition. Many times dues are waived for this classification. Such memberships are limited in number.

PHYSICAL FACILITIES

If a club is just being started or a new site is being chosen, it would be best to choose a central campus location with easy access to parking—preferably controlled parking—where favorable arrangements are available to both guests and members. The student union or campus center should not be overlooked as a potential site, especially since such an arrangement might make possible the sharing of space such as a ballroom or amphitheater which is needed only occasionally by the club and which could probably not be included in a physically independent facility.

In planning the interior of the club, the first consideration will be the facilities for food service, which are the most common. Many informal clubs consist of lounges with coffee and snack counters. As clubs become more elaborate and larger, the dining room usually comes first. The determining factor in laying out the dining area or areas is whether the club will be only a luncheon club or whether it will offer complete dining services at noon and at night.

In the case of luncheon service only, it is wise to depend mainly on cafeteria service and to make tables or private room service available by special arrangement or reservation. Where complete dining service is to be made available and evening dinners are to be served, then a dual service arrangement should be attempted. In either case, efficiency and fast service both at noon and night should be striven for.

Facilities for conferences, banquets, and social functions, in those instances where they can compete with services available elsewhere both on and off campus, can provide a faculty club with a good source of income. In the case of larger institutions, the provision of such facilities can usually be justified if a real need for them is known to exist.

Among the more common additional rooms or areas that a club may provide are the following: club rooms for lounging; dining and meeting rooms that may be reserved by individuals; and game rooms, most commonly equipped for bridge and other card games or for billiards. The library and lounge facilities, as a rule, cannot be reserved for private groups and are always available to the membership at large when the club is open. The library usually contains basic reference texts and periodicals, daily newspapers, and magazines.

Among the more common facilities found in faculty clubs of all sizes are lodging accommodations. These may range all the way from a few rooms for overnight guests to whole wings of thirty to forty rooms, some having efficiency-type kitchen units. The manager of one Midwestern faculty club with efficiency suites was eventually forced to give them up because misuse of the kitchen units had made them difficult to keep clean and had, besides, produced heavy and unpleasant cooking odors. Apparently guests had attempted to cook gourmet meals for entertaining on units meant to serve one or two persons for breakfast and an occasional snack. However, efficiency units may be useful to guests who plan an extended stay—of, perhaps, from two weeks to a month. A small one-burner cooking unit and an efficiency refrigerator should serve the purpose, and proper house rules should be provided and enforced. The kitchen-unit difficulties previously described seemed to arise among visiting faculty living in for a whole term.

The type of room most in demand would be a simple, overnight accommodation suitable for a campus visitor, guest lecturer, or potential candidate for faculty membership, especially during the recruiting season, since a "well developed faculty club is generally believed to make a real contribution to the recruitment and retention of the faculty."[4]

[4] Ingraham, *op. cit.*, p. 103.

As to additional facilities, there are a few isolated clubs that have private beaches, golf courses, or stables. More common, however, would be a bar or lounge (serving alcoholic beverages), bowling alleys, a gymnasium, sauna baths, tennis courts, and swimming pools. A good breakdown is given in Table 1.

TABLE 1 Services Provided by Faculty Club or Social Facility*

	All institutions			Public institutions			Private institutions		
Service or facility	Total	University	College	Total	University	College	Total	University	College
1. Dining room	109	53	56	34	23	11	75	30	45
2. Private dining rooms	123	57	66	44	26	18	79	31	48
3. Cafeteria or lunch counter	106	44	62	40	25	15	66	19	47
4. Coffee break service	250	63	187	78	33	45	172	30	142
5. Bar (alcoholic beverages)	20	15	5	3	3	...	17	12	5
6. Reading room	162	66	96	57	37	20	105	29	76
7. Lounge	284	91	193	92	52	40	192	39	153
8. Separate public rooms for men and women	71	22	49	23	12	11	48	10	38
9. Billiard room	56	37	19	27	23	4	29	14	15
10. Bowling alley	15	6	9	6	3	3	9	3	6
11. Game room	51	36	15	25	21	4	26	15	11
12. Gymnasium	28	9	19	8	4	4	20	5	15
13. Tennis courts	27	9	18	5	3	2	22	6	16
14. Swimming pool	23	7	16	6	3	3	17	4	13
15. Library	51	22	29	12	10	2	39	12	27
16. Conference rooms	122	39	83	36	21	15	86	18	68
17. Total with club or social facility	341	100	241	110	57	53	231	43	188

* Mark H. Ingraham, *The Outer Fringe,* The University of Wisconsin Press, Madison, Wis., 1965, Appendix III, p. 261.

It might be useful to stress here the fact that, when an organization is planning extended facilities, it should set up strong supporting committees holding proper powers through the provisions of the charter and bylaws. So many times facilities are inadequately or improperly used because active committees to supervise them and plan for their use are lacking. Usually what happens is that since the space taken up by the facility is not justified in terms of expense, a survey is taken and that facility is converted into a banquet room or some other revenue-producing enterprise.

HOUSE RULES AND MANAGEMENT POLICIES

House rules are usually composed by a committee or committees and passed by the club directors according to the policies established by the charter and bylaws. They are meant to help management carry out certain necessary policies and to guide it in decision making. A good set of house rules can save management, the committee members, and the board considerable time and effort if the rules effectively help to provide unanimity in decisions and actions. They, in fact, decide many similar types of cases, requests, and denials at one time. The following statement contains some guidelines that might be used in establishing house rules:

Specific House Rules, being controlled by local custom and problems, do vary from club to club. However, an exhaustive review of 322 representative clubs [author's note: representative clubs meaning country and city clubs—not faculty clubs, but these rules are equally applicable to faculty clubs] shows that those with most workable regulations organize them to cover these four general areas:

1. The days and hours the club is open, method of admittance, times at which specific services are available, and the method of paying charges.
2. Rules and restrictions applying to the admittance and conduct of guests.
3. Rules governing the dress and deportment of members and their families. Special clubhouse rules.
4. Regulations governing the treatment of employees and registering of complaints.[5]

In establishing management policies, the key seems to be communication. The charter, bylaws, house rules, and actions of the board of directors give the manager the necessary directives and tools with which to work; however, communications unfortunately are not always perfect. Changes in the membership of the board of directors, the fact that the manager may regard certain directors as outsiders, and the election of directors who either have no real interest in the club or refuse to become intimate with the policies and progress of the club seem to be the most prevalent reasons for communications breakdown. Reasons such as the aforementioned underline the need for a program of acclimation for new directors, for a written manual, and for minutes designed to keep the directors and the manager properly informed.

The authority of various committees to propose, initiate, and enact house or activities rules is governed by the charter and bylaws. It is well to have reasons for rules and changes in some sort of log form so that continuity may be added and, as committees change, past problems and proposals can be referred to. All too often a change of committee means a change of rules without regard to past experience. Many a club has faced financial disaster because of such radical practice.

In the case of faculty clubs, it is well to remember the unique relationship that exists between the club and the college or university. Where special services or facilities are to be made available to that institution, it is well to establish rules and to set up a committee to govern such services. Just as misunderstanding can arise between a club and one or several of its members, problems are bound to crop up concerning the institution's rights and privileges in the club. Along these same lines, definite policy should be established concerning use by other groups. As was stated earlier, tax laws and incorporation charters may rule on the facilities used by outsiders or the public, but the question of policies concerning other groups within the academic community is one for the club's management to handle. Special student groups, combined faculty-student groups, and alumni or reunion groups probably would head the list of potential users of club facilities. Since these groups are often represented by members or groups of members, it is well to establish clear-cut rules, easily interpreted, as to the conditions of accepting or denying these groups some or all of their requests for usage or services.

SERVICE BY THE CLUB

Ideally, service to the individual club member has to head the list as to a club's reason for existence. Admittedly the usual goal—profit—is nonexistent in most clubs. Since service is therefore the key reason for belonging to a club, the members and, in particular, the staff of that club should be made well aware of this fact. Historically it can be said that clubs depend on their management and staff for popularity. Actionwise, it then becomes the primary task of management to provide the best facilities and services available at the price being charged. A well-developed faculty club then becomes a source of pride for its members, a true contributor toward recruiting faculty, and a hospitable meeting place where members may enjoy informal exchanges with their colleagues. It should truly be the congenial center for the social life of the faculty and administration. Again, its policies with regard to its relationship to the institution

[5] Barbour, *op. cit.*, p. 519.

it serves must be clearly evaluated. It is not uncommon to find the faculty club serving the catering needs of the institution's officers and directors. It is generally accepted that this unique relationship, in fact, serves a definite purpose, especially in the area of faculty-administration relations. The club more often than not can cater to such special needs at a fairly competitive price, and thus it may improve its financial status.

SOME MANAGEMENT PROPOSALS FOR FACULTY CLUBS

Financial Since a club by its very purpose is designed to render service, profit motives are always secondary. Therefore, a club's chances of ever attaining financial independence are few. A club that can be an autonomous venture of the faculty and also receive financial aid from the institution in such areas as heat, light, power, insurance, and physical plant seems assured of being the safest financial risk.

Personnel In the area of personnel management, two factors usually apply to faculty clubs. Usually the employee-benefit program of the sponsoring college or university is attractive enough to greatly aid the club in employee recruitment. Secondly, if the few unique job descriptions that apply to club-oriented personnel can be incorporated into the overall job positions and classifications within the institution, then the club personnel can be hired through the university personnel office and will be included in its personnel program.

Purchasing Clubs usually spend more money on food than anything else. They can effect substantial savings by making bulk purchases, of such items as milk, bread, coffee, and other staples, in cooperation with the university. However, because of the nature of its business and variety of its cuisine, a club should go, or be able to go, to outside sources for high-quality produce, meats, fish, poultry, and the necessary specialty items.

In purchasing office supplies and business forms the club will usually do best to cooperate with the institution except where the quantities involved are too small.

Problem Areas:

1. *Liquor Policies.* The statistical analysis that appears in Table 1 reveals that only 15 out of 341 existing facilities have liquor service. There is a trend toward more liberal policies concerning the use of alcoholic beverages on most campuses. The author recommends that, where bar facilities are required, they take the form of a service bar rather than a conventional bar complete with stools, etc. A small lounge area where drinks are served seems to be most adequate. The availability of a cocktail before a meal, wine with a fine dinner, or an occasional beer after the day's final class seems to be what is wanted. Keeping this in mind, it is recommended that the same hours be maintained for beverage service as for food service. The idea of a bar open on campus late into the night just somehow doesn't seem fitting.

2. *Gambling Policies.* The best approach here seems to dictate a no-gambling rule within the club. At least no open transaction involving money. Many clubs absolutely refuse to provide poker chips or to allow poker or other games usually associated with gambling to be played within the club. This seems to be the best policy.

3. *Credit Policies.* Historically, credit is an acceptable privilege connected with clubs. In the case of faculty clubs, a reverse policy seems to be the case—that is, most clubs operate on a cash basis. However, where credit is extended, it is an important factor in attracting membership and a service that has been spoken of as one of the club's "greatest benefits." The bylaws may grant the privilege of credit, but all too often they fail to include provisions for dealing with delinquency. Mr. Eckert has covered the subject exceptionally well in the following:

1. STATEMENT. An itemized statement of due, assessments and current charges shall be mailed monthly to each member, and any member failing to pay his indebted-

ness to The Club within thirty (30) days from the date shall be notified in writing by the treasurer.

2. POSTING. If payment in lawful funds is not received within fifteen (15) working days after such notice, the name of the member together with the amount due The Club shall be posted on the official bulletin boards of The Club and the delinquent member's credit shall be automatically suspended.

3. SUSPENSION. If such indebtedness is not then paid within fifteen (15) working days after posting, the delinquent members may be suspended by the Board of Directors. Suspended members may not be admitted to the club property. Suspended members may be reinstated by the Board of Directors within six (6) months of suspension upon payment of all dues, assessments and charges accrued since the initial time of delinquency plus a sum equal to 1% monthly interest. Unless he shall have been reinstated by the Board of Directors or the members prior to twelve (12) months from the time of suspension, his membership shall be automatically cancelled and his membership and all interest, rights, and privileges shall cease.

4. REPEATED DELINQUENCY. Any member who shall have been suspended for nonpayment of his account with The Club, shall, upon the third such suspension, be subject to expulsion by the Board of Directors without recourse to the twelve month provision. . . .

5. SURETY. The Certificate of Membership [stock] owned by a member shall stand at all times as security for his indebtedness. Before any transfer of membership, The Club may deduct the amount of any outstanding indebtedness. The Board of Directors shall have the power to limit the credit of any member and to take such legal actions for the collection of any indebtedness as it may deem advisable under the circumstances then obtaining.[6]

4. Preemption of Facilities by the Institution Officers. At the risk of too much reiteration, mention is made again of the policy regarding club-institution relationship. This time the subject is taken up in respect to requests from college or university trustees, the president, or other officers for the closing of the club on days when it is normally open to the members. The club's members should be made aware that these isolated interruptions do take place from time to time and that the club must accommodate itself to them (assuming that the club's rules concur). In this way, much comment and consternation on the part of individuals is avoided. Somehow this problem seems magnified in faculty clubs as opposed to comparable situations in city or country clubs.

PERSONNEL PRACTICES—DUTIES AND SALARY RANGES

Club Manager. The job description for the club manager must be general enough to be applicable to various types of operations but specific enough to help the manager define his position within the organization. A sketch of work performed by the club manager follows:

1. The *Club Manager* is given the responsibility for heading the line functions of the operations, such as beverage and food departments, food serving departments, and Club recreational areas.
2. He must cooperate with the governing body of the Club whether it is a board, committees, or an owner. He advises and furthers the goals of the Club as specified in its organizational structure.
3. Establishes policies and operating procedures for the Club.
4. Hires personnel in the Club or reviews hiring selections of various department heads. Coordinates practices with the university personnel office.
5. May write directives, manuals, and work schedules covering policies, rules, and regulations or approves directives written by department heads.

[6] Barbour, *op. cit.*, p. 159.

6. Has ultimate authority over interdepartmental disputes and implements policies concerning employee-employer relations.

7. Is in charge of the financial conditions of the Club. He carries out procedures which result in the financial condition desired by the governing body.

8. As head of all departments within the Club, he must be consulted as to policy and other changes in the implementation of the change.

9. Although he delegates his authority to various department heads, he is still responsible for all operations within the Club and he may make changes within his authority as he deems necessary to the successful operation of the Club.[7]

Office Manager. Supervises the offices of the club. Directs and trains other front-office employees. Responsible for courteous and efficient service to members and guests.

Work performed:

1. Supervises and directs the activities of all office personnel and is responsible for the efficient operation of the offices

2. Works closely with the bookkeeper or may himself be the bookkeeper

3. May supervise the club secretary and aid in clerical matters as they pertain to dues, charges, and accounts payable

4. Supervises other office personnel so that service to members and guests is courteous and efficient

Food Service. In this area usually the cooperation of two persons is needed—the dining room manager and the executive chef.

The dining room manager's job description would include the following:

Job Summary

Directs the formal dining areas of the Club. Supervises employees, orders supplies, helps plan menus, and maintains payroll and bookkeeping records.

Work Performed

1. Is in charge of all formal dining areas of the Club and may also be in charge of informal areas such as grills and cafeterias. Supervises Club food service employees in accordance with operating policies which he may help to set up.

2. Responsible for maintaining records of personnel performance and dining room costs.

3. Inspects food service personnel as to their appearance.

4. Checks special function sheets against room setup and personnel scheduled. Supervises the service of Club dining areas.

5. May schedule periodic food service employee meetings to assure correct interpretation of Club policies; covers proper procedures of food and beverage service in Club areas.

6. Trains *Head Waiters, Captains,* and *Staff* to handle the various types of food service.

7. Handles complaints of members and guests as they relate to his area of responsibility.

8. Executes the general responsibilities necessary to minimize the costs of operating the Club.

9. Assists in the planning of menus with the *Executive Chef* for special parties.

10. May schedule employees for each dining room.

11. Establishes standards of performance such as the amount of linen to be used in dining areas, number of covers to be served per employee, setting of labor cost goals.[8]

The executive chef is a working chef in most cases. A description of his duties would include:

[7] *Job Descriptions for Club Occupations,* Club Managers Association of America, Washington, 1964, pp. i–13 (analysis of the 201 jobs in the private club industry).

[8] *Ibid.,* pp. iv–86 and 87.

Job Summary

Plans menus, supervises and coordinates the work of all kitchen personnel.

Work Performed

1. Plans menus, considering probable number of guests, purchasing conditions, the popularity of dishes and such things as holidays, etc.
2. Cooperates with manager in establishing prices.
3. Full responsibility for purchasing on a day to day basis.
4. Consults with dining room manager in coordinating service of meals, layouts, etc.
5. Supervises, employs and discharges kitchen workers within personnel guidelines.
6. Keeps necessary records such as payroll, food inventory and statistical information on menus and customer count.
7. Usually takes an active part in recipe construction, food preparation, and service.[9]

Beverage Service. If beverages are to be a part of the club's services, then it would be best to place the responsibility for this on the assistant manager or some other person when the manager is not on duty.

The job description of this individual would include the following:

Work Performed

1. Manages the beverage department with full responsibility as to purchasing, serving and maintenance of the beverage area.
2. Is in charge of keeping the bar or lounge in a neat condition.
3. Directs the procedures of bartenders and bar waitresses.
4. Responsible for requisition or purchasing of glassware and other supplies as needed.
5. In cooperation with management, establishes drink recipes and mixes. May actually make up mixes and work as barkeep.
6. In charge of purchasing and maintaining inventories of various beverages.
7. Is responsible for proper accounting for sales to members and the necessary charges and cash requirements.
8. Must have a working knowledge of the mixing of all types of alcoholic beverages, wines and beers.
9. Must be knowledgeable in establishing prices, controlling portions, and maintaining necessary records.[10]

Housekeeping. Depending on the arrangements with the college or university as to major housekeeping, the usual faculty club finds itself in need of a good houseman. Although this is not an executive-type position, it is quite imperative that the person who fills it have certain special qualifications, including the following:

1. He should have knowledge of the care and maintenance of club furnishings.
2. He should have the ability to perceive where and when work should be done without waiting for specific orders.
3. He should be able to supervise and plan the work of other employees under his jurisdiction.
4. He must be able to supervise and be responsible for overall cleanliness, order of furnishings, and room arrangement.

Maintenance. Again major maintenance usually would be carried out by the university. However, the club may find itself in need of an all-around maintenance per-

[9] *Ibid.*
[10] *Ibid.*

son especially in regard to maintaining expensive restaurant and kitchen equipment. An all-around knowledge of the specific equipment involved would be the main requirement for this position.

Special Facilities. In a club containing a special facility—such as a pool, for example—a person knowledgeable in the overall care and management of that facility may be needed. Such needs should be determined in advance, along with the salary scales of specialized personnel, and all necessary expenditures in this connection should be included in the facility's budget.

In the consideration of payroll, emphasis must be put on

1. the prevailing rates within the geographical area of the club,
2. the job classification and payroll structure of the institution,
3. guidelines such as those outlined below based on the need for certain "professionals" or persons with specialized trades.

HOW MUCH IS A JOB WORTH?

This information, gathered at the request of both club officials and managers, is intended to be used only as a guideline to arrive at a proper and fair remuneration for a club executive. Again, our statistical hands are somewhat tied by having to report averages and normal ranges. Special circumstances in a club's membership or physical plant might dictate the need for an exceptionally outstanding executive whose remuneration would be well above normal or average.

In both the 1963 and 1966 studies we found that the relationship between remuneration and club size was most accurately expressed when the TOTAL JOB VALUE (Salary plus bonus plus what it would cost a manager to duplicate his fringe benefits) was compared to ANNUAL GROSS CLUB REVENUES (Dues, Food & Beverage, and other club income). *The average managerial position, both in 1963 and 1966, is worth 3.2% of a club's annual revenues from all sources.* The average annual total job value for a club manager was $16,100 in 1963, but this likewise had increased by 1966 to $17,440.

While 3.2% is a good rule of thumb to use for the average size club, what happens to the manager's remuneration when he works for an exceptionally large, or very small club? Will a club with an annual income of two million dollars pay its chief executive 3.2% of this income, or $64,000, in salary and fringes a year? Can a club with an annual income of $200,000 find a C.M.A.A. member who will work for $6,400 of combined salary and fringes a year? Obviously, there are practical restrictions on both ends of this straight 3.2% scale that bend it into a curve which is more representative of the average remuneration in this field.[11]

CONCLUSION

In conclusion, it must be said that every college or university should provide at least the minimum lounge with coffee-break facilities.

As to the growth of a faculty club from that point, only an analysis of the unique conditions involved—such as size of the university or college, size of the town or city, and nature of nearby services, especially restaurant facilities—can be useful. To build a club because of supposed faculty support or on the basis of administration directive alone does not justify the investment. The "market" conditions must be right in order to make the club successful and appealing both to the members and the institution it serves.

BIBLIOGRAPHY

Books

Kotschevar, Lendal H., and Margaret E. Terrell: *Food Service Planning,* John Wiley & Sons, Inc., New York, 1961.

[11] *Job Descriptions for Club Occupations, ibid.,* p. 5.

Miller, Edmund (ed.): *Profitable Cafeteria Operation,* Ahrens Book Company, Inc., New York, 1966.

Brodner, Joseph, Howard M. Carlson, and Henry T. Maschal: *Profitable Food and Beverage Operation,* Ahrens Publishing Company, Inc., New York, 1955.

Graves, Charles: *Leather Armchairs,* Coward-McCann, Inc., New York, 1963 (Introductions by P. G. Wodehouse).

Barbour, Henry Ogden, C.C.M.: *Private Club Administration,* Club Managers Association of America, Washington, 1968.

Paperback Books

Connor, J. William: *Food and Beverage Merchandising,* Cornell University Press, Ithaca, N.Y., 1958.

Lundberg, Donald E., and James P. Armatas: *The Management of People in Hotels, Restaurants, and Clubs,* Wm. C. Brown Company, Publishers, Dubuque, Iowa, 1956.

Job Descriptions for Club Occupations, Club Managers Association of America, Washington, 1964 (an analysis of the 201 jobs in the private club industry).

Ingraham, Mark H.: *The Outer Fringe,* The University of Wisconsin Press, Madison, Wis., 1965.

Pamphlets

Club Managers Association of America, *Profile of a Club Manager,* Club Managers Association of America, Washington, 1966.

Harris, Kerr, Forster and Company: *Clubs in Town and Country,* Harris, Kerr, Forster and Company, New York, 1966–67.

National Club Association: *What the National Club Association Can Do for You,* National Club Association, Washington, 1966.

Slowinski, Walter A., and Terry Nevel: *Federal Income and Excise Tax Considerations for Social Clubs,* Baker, McKenzie and Hightower, Washington, 1965.

Index